Living Systems

James Grier Miller

Living Systems

McGRAW-HILL BOOK COMPANY

New York St. Louis San Francisco Auckland Bogotá
Düsseldorf Johannesburg London Madrid
Mexico Montreal New Delhi Panama
Paris São Paulo Singapore
Sydney Tokyo Toronto

Library of Congress Cataloging in Publication Data

Miller, James Grier.
  Living systems.

  Includes Bibliographies and indexes.
    1. System theory. 2. Biological systems.
3. Social systems. I. Title.
Q295.M54   574'.01   77-23362
ISBN 0-07-042015-7

  34567890   VHVH   765432109

The editor for this book was Ruth L. Weine, the designer was
Naomi Auerbach, and the production supervisor was Teresa F. Leaden.
It was set in VIP Palatino by University Graphics, Inc.

Printed and bound by Von Hoffman Press, Inc.

.

*The pronouns "he" and "his" have sometimes been used
in a purely generic sense in this book to accommodate the
text to the limitations of the English language and avoid
awkward grammatical constructions.*

TO JESSIE, colleague in every line

Contents

Tables of the Critical Subsystems   *xi*

Color Plates   *xi*

Preface   *xiii*

Outline of Chapters 3, 4, and 6 through 12   *xxiii*

List of Hypotheses   *xxxi*

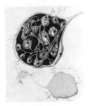

CHAPTER ONE

The Need for a General Theory of Living Systems   1

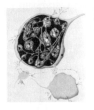

CHAPTER TWO

The Basic Concepts   9

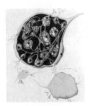

CHAPTER THREE

Structure and Process   51

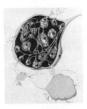

CHAPTER FOUR

Hypotheses Concerning Living Systems   89

CHAPTER FIVE

Information Input Overload   121

CHAPTER SIX

The Cell   203

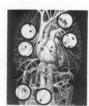

CHAPTER SEVEN

The Organ   315

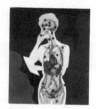

CHAPTER EIGHT

The Organism   361

CHAPTER NINE

The Group   515

CHAPTER TEN

The Organization   595

CHAPTER ELEVEN
The Society   747

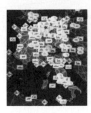

CHAPTER TWELVE
The Supranational System   903

CHAPTER THIRTEEN
Conclusions   1025

Bibliographic Index   1055
Subject Index   1071

Tables of the Critical Subsystems

		Page
TABLE 1-1	The 19 Critical Subsystems of a Living System	3
TABLE 3-1	The 19 Critical Subsystems of a Living System	54
TABLE 6-1	Components of the 19 Critical Subsystems of a Cell	219
TABLE 7-1	Components of the 19 Critical Subsystems of an Organ	323
TABLE 8-1	Components of the 19 Critical Subsystems of an Organism	365
TABLE 9-1	Components of the 19 Critical Subsystems of a Group	520
TABLE 10-2	Components of the 19 Critical Subsystems of an Organization	606
TABLE 11-7	Components of the 19 Critical Subsystems of a Society	776
TABLE 12-2	Components of the 19 Critical Subsystems of a Supranational System	914
TABLE 13-1	Selected Major Components of Each of the 19 Critical Subsystems at Each of the 7 Levels of Living Systems	1028

Color Plates

James J. Van Hare, M.D., *artist*

		Facing Page
Fig. 1-1	A generalized living system interacting and intercommunicating with two others in its environment	2
Fig. 6-9	Human cardiac muscle cell	218
Fig. 7-2	The blood and lymph vascular components of the human distributor organ	322
Fig. 8-1	A woman	364
Fig. 9-1	Communications team of a modern ocean liner	518
Fig. 10-1	A modern ocean liner	604
Fig. 11-2	The Netherlands	764
Fig. 12-1	The European Economic Community (as of 1971)	912

Preface

This book began sometime in its author's prehistory—whenever an inclusive curiosity and a need to order and integrate arose. Hardly viable at first, the seminal ideas germinated during my college and graduate years, under the influence of one man particularly, my teacher, sponsor, and friend: Alfred North Whitehead. A number of these ideas stem directly from his "philosophy of organism." Nowadays other terms are popular and, if he were alive today, he might prefer to call his viewpoint a "philosophy of system." Key concepts later accepted as basic to systems science occur in his writings. Several sentences from his *Science and the Modern World* show how clearly his thought was a precursor of what today is called systems theory:[1]

"Science is taking on a new aspect which is neither purely physical, nor purely biological. It is becoming the study of organisms. Biology is the study of the larger organisms; whereas physics is the study of the smaller organisms. . . . The concept of an organism includes. . . the concept of the interaction of organisms. . . . There are also organisms of organisms. Suppose . . . that electrons and hydrogen nuclei are . . . basic organisms. Then the atoms, and the molecules, are organisms of a higher type, which also represent a compact definite organic unity. But when we come to the larger aggregations of matter, the organic unity fades into the background. . . . When we come to living beings, the definiteness of pattern is recovered, and the organic character again rises into prominence."

Life to Whitehead was made up of systems of systems. Observing that the physical sciences concern themselves with a hierarchy of systems, he extended such concepts to more complex biosocial phenomena. Reality is continuous. Respect for these views motivated my first serious publication, written under his close guidance.[2] Analysis of his concepts of historical change in societies—which he held to be complex and vigorous organisms—showed that he conceived them to have many of the characteristics of life at other levels. It interpreted his search for general principles of the rise, decline, and fall of societies—their historical aspect—which he compared to the stages of existence of their component individuals. Not only was he interested in organismic structure and its long-range historical change, but he also laid stress on the continuous dynamic process which to him was the essence of all reality. "Event," one of his favorite concepts, became in his writings almost a morphological term:[3]

" . . . nature is a structure of evolving processes. The reality is the process. . . . The realities of nature are . . . the events in nature. . . . The word *event* . . . means one of these spatiotemporal unities."

He looked on the event as pulling together assemblages into unities, making systems out of unorganized heaps. It not only dynamically mirrors the impact of its own contemporary and preceding events but also anticipates and to an extent determines future events. The event is the organism or system at the present moment, an interlocked community of connexity which is part of the vast organization of the universe, yet bounded and constrained. So Whitehead understood systems in depth.

L. J. Henderson, biochemist and sociologist, was a close friend of Whitehead, and his view of nature was similar in many ways. He also was one of my mentors while I was in the Harvard Society of Fellows, and I was influenced by his writings, including such statements as:[4] "It is in systems that all forms of activity manifest themselves. Therefore any form of activity may be produced by a suitable system." Since Henderson was deeply immersed in the tradition of Pareto, it was not surprising that he should write in such a fashion. As Schanck pointed out:[5] "Gibbs, Le Châtelier, Bancroft, Cannon, Pareto and others were to attempt to rationalize an entirely new approach to complex systems which cannot be treated mechanically. . . . The new approach was to study systems of developing societies of trends, in which each trend describes the events in a collectivity without predicting a behavior of the individual elements out of which the collectivity is made."

A scientific generation patterns its models upon its dominant metaphors.[6] Scientific figures of speech in the nineteenth century concerned linear effects rather than field forces. The action of electricity, for instance, was compared to the flow of water. The twentieth century characteristically has drawn its metaphors from Einstein's relativistic field theory, which clearly influences the philosophy of organism of Whitehead, the Gestalt psychology of Wertheimer, Köhler, and Koffka, and general systems theory. Field theory, Gestalt theory, and systems theory, in spite of their differences, all recognize that the interrelationships among coacting components of an organized whole are of fundamental importance in understanding the totality. The organic analogy, becoming sophisticated in a new century, is the dominant metaphor of our time in scientific analyses of complexity. Today we think in terms of systems, and our characteristic models and simulations deal with a system or a component of one.[7] My concern with the organismic, organizational approach of systems theory puts me in a main channel of current thought.[8]

Two other outstanding professors and colleagues of my earlier years had significant influence on me. Edwin G. Boring and Henry A. Murray differed in many ways: biotropic psychologist *vs.* sociotropic biochemist; physiologist *vs.* psychologist physician; hard scientist and historian *vs.* imaginative humanist and scientist; deep plunger into restricted subject matter *vs.* soaring creator; laboratory investigator *vs.* clinician. But they had in common exciting minds capable of stimulating others to concern themselves with central issues. The gaps in the sciences of man were clear to both of them, and by different routes they tried to close some of those gaps. Under their joint and often conflicting influence I started as a student to write essays which have led, by a direct line of many generations of drafts, to this book.

The Reverend Canon C. Leslie Glenn, at one time rector of Christ Church, Cambridge, later my colleague at The University of Michigan, and still later subdean of the Washington Cathedral, was my close friend for nearly 40 years. He combined training in religion and in engineering with broad and sensitive comprehension of his fellow human beings. In many ways he aided in the preparation of this statement of my views, highlighting its ultimate humanistic purposes in his own inimitably human ways.

It is impossible to list all the scholars whose ideas and researches have contributed significantly to my theory of living systems. In the period during which the ideas expressed in this book were taking form, systems theories have proliferated in mathematical, physical, biological, and social sciences. They vary greatly, but all emphasize the interrelatedness of the parts in a whole, whether that be a nonliving system, a cell, an organism, or an organized interrelationship among societies. At the same time, developments in information theory, in cybernetics, and in communications science have proved applicable to the analysis of systems. New and increasingly useful mathematical models of systems have been created and new generations of computers, each with greater capability, have enabled scientists to create sophisticated simulations of multivariate systems too complex for precise study by other means. Many scientists in all these disciplines, often striking common notes but unaware of their harmony, have influenced this book.

The spirit and the metaphors of our time account for the fact that many similar intellectual activities have been going on independently, one often quite isolated from another. Each worker or group has known something about a particular field, a chosen island, but frequently has been unaware of related work in other disciplines. Oftentimes the same idea seems to have been discovered over and over again under diverse names in different areas. My efforts at integration have been partly attempts to establish a communication network among the islands.

This book was written in the inspiring companionship of an interdisciplinary group concerned with developing a general theory of behavior. It was conceived of in 1949 when, to describe our joint activities, I coined the term "behavioral science," first used in its current connotation by the Committee on Behavioral Sciences of the University of Chicago. Donald G. Marquis was my close friend and adviser then. He not only helped us at Chicago to formulate our goals but also played an important role in establishing the activities of the Ford Foundation in the behavioral sciences.

Our committee began regular meetings in 1952. We were stimulated to undertake our activities by suggestions from physical scientists, among them

Enrico Fermi and Leo Szilard, who felt a heavy responsibility for the fearsome developments in nuclear weapons, and who thought that, because we understood so little about why men fight and kill, the development of the sciences of man should be accelerated. They pointed out that natural science had advanced speedily after general theories were proposed and suggested that we try a similar strategy. We were at first skeptical of the value of such endeavors, since we were aware of the primitive state of the behavioral sciences, the important disagreements within them, and the lack of common speech and understanding among them. Yet it seemed worthwhile to bring these divergent points of view together and begin to work toward the distant goal of common understanding.

First we tried to determine areas of agreement as precisely as possible, so that we could then specify critical areas needing further investigation. We wanted to find a number of interrelated assumptions on which we could base a set of hypotheses capable of being evaluated empirically. We hoped that such work would yield confirmable microtheories about specific aspects of living and behaving entities which appeared important to all of us, microtheories which could ultimately be combined toward the goal of integrative general theory.

As we talked together, a number of us began to see promise in the general systems theory proposed by Bertalanffy and others, and gradually our point of view was organized into what I call *general living systems theory*. We were not attempting to develop a new school, but rather to do what we could to eliminate schools. We assumed that the sort of theory we were searching for would select, from among different and sometimes opposing viewpoints, fundamental ideas already worked out by others, and fit them into a mosaic, an organized picture of previously unrelated areas.

Our theory group was composed of senior professors in history, anthropology, economics, political science, sociology, social psychology, psychology, psychiatry, medicine, neurophysiology, and mathematical biology. Sometimes representatives of other disciplines such as physics, physiology, and the humanities met with us. As our group got to work, our psychodynamics began to show. At first we were embarrassed that we had not all read each other's works, though how this would have been possible is hard to fathom. Then it became apparent that the constraints of group activity were not congenial to all the members, and some dropped out. There were depressing periods when we appeared to be getting nowhere, and our effort seemed wasted. But finally we developed sufficient consensus to begin to work together on empirical evaluation of some of our theoretical ideas.

Establishment of an Institute of Behavioral Sciences was authorized at the University of Chicago in 1953, and we began to search for financial support for it. In 1955 several of us who were members of the group in different disciplines moved from Chicago to The University of Michigan in Ann Arbor, to establish there the Mental Health Research Institute, which, with stable financing, over the years continued the group's theoretical and empirical work, adding personnel in related fields.

This book—a greatly revised expansion and extension of articles I wrote in 1953 and 1955—is my attempt, as one participant of this group endeavor, to express what I consider to be the most valuable aspects of the work.[9] Each of the others would have points of disagreement, since at times it has seemed that our watchword stemmed from the world of Pogo the Possum: "I disagree with every word you say, and will fight to your death for my right to deny it." Nevertheless, we probably agree more than we disagree, and there appears to be a growing consensus.

At both Chicago and Michigan we had unusual support for research and intercommunication.* We also had relative freedom from teaching and administrative responsibilities, and the continual stimulation of visiting scholars and consultants. Our regular seminars facilitated the exchange and development of our ideas. They also provided means to train graduate, professional, and postdoctoral students to become generalists as well as specialists. Our commitment to joint research by no means excluded individual scholarship and investigation, which continued to be our fundamental way of proceeding. All told it was a climate favorable for discovery. But if sound general theory is ever to exist in the behavioral sciences, the empirical and conceptual work on which it is based cannot be done by one man or by the staff of one institute. The voluntary and enduring cooperation of many individuals and teams, each motivated by the promise of such an approach, will be required.

Several persons had important roles in shaping our efforts at the University of Chicago: Ralph W. Tyler, the administrator to whom the Committee on Behavioral Sciences reported at the beginning, always sympathetically recognized the desirability of integrating the behavioral fields. In subsequent years he contributed imaginatively and with distinction toward this goal in directing the Center for Advanced Study in the Behavioral Sciences at Stanford, California. Ralph W. Gerard, to a degree unique among biologists, was both a creative experimenter in his own field and broadly informed in the social sciences. His achievements in the direction of a biosocial synthesis had deep impact on my own thought. Anatol Rapoport's insights into informational, game theoretical, and other mathematical models of behavior have often enlightened my ignorance. I have particularly appreciated his

*I wish to express my gratitude for contracts and grants to support work involved in producing this book to the Foundations' Fund for Research in Psychiatry; the United States Army (Contracts DA-49-083-OSA-611, DA-49-007-MD-575, and DA-49-007-MD-684); the United States Public Health Service (Grants M-1871 and NIH MH-08607); and to the Carnegie Corporation of New York, which gave specific support to our research on information input overload reported in Chapter 5. Much of the material in Chapters 6 and 7 was printed in *Currents in Modern Biology*; the substance of Chapter 8 was published in *The Quarterly Review of Biology*. The present form of these chapters appears here with permission.

continual, objective criticism of my ideas. John R. Platt, an agile-minded physicist, has in recent years turned to the study of the fascinating self-adaptive systems that are life. In many contexts he has enriched my intellectual experience. Robert I. Crane, historian and observer of the current scene in Southeast Asia, now at Syracuse University, has spent years in communion with biological and physical scientists, contributing to the total activity of our group his grasp of the nature of long-range social change. Richard L. Meier brought the encyclopedic background of a natural scientist to the study of present-day society, and the impact upon it of technological changes such as the new techniques in communication.

The last five named were my associates both in Chicago and in Ann Arbor. There were other members of the former group at Chicago who contributed importantly, merging their scholarship in our cooperative, interdisciplinary endeavor. One was Jacob Marschak, an unusual combination of economist and mathematician, who also saw the need for empirical study of behavioral variables. David Easton, a theorist in the political affairs of man, continues his broad concern with all human process. Roger W. Sperry, a quiet and deeply competent experimentalist, has also written on fundamental philosophic issues of the nature of life and behavior. Donald T. Campbell, a social psychologist, early urged our group to search out the similarities in our thought which were cloaked by the multiform terminology used in different disciplines. At Northwestern University he has written several important theoretical papers on individual and group behavior in the systems theory tradition. Donald W. Fiske, my friend and colleague for many years, a psychologist from the statistical side of the street, sees beyond measurement to the behavioral reality. Henrietta Herbolsheimer participated in a few sessions, contributing insights from internal medicine, as did Edward A. Shils from sociology.

Fowler McCormick, never an official member of the group but often a helpful participant over many years, added the spicy wisdom of a man of the world with a lifetime interest in the study of human experience and behavior to the occasionally dull observations of the professors.

Over the years a number of my students and research assistants have also contributed. I am particularly grateful to E. Roy John, who was especially helpful in some of my first theoretical formulations in Chicago and who became a colleague after being my student, as well as Israel Goldiamond, an enthusiastic contributor and amanuensis in the early days.

At The University of Michigan our endeavor was sympathetically understood, supported, and advanced by Raymond W. Waggoner. Thoroughly comprehending the potential usefulness of integrative theory in the fields of mental health as well as other aspects of behavior, he was more than an administrator, colleague, and friend—he collaborated helpfully in various aspects of our experimental and theoretical work. As mentioned above, Donald G. Marquis had an interest in the work while it still went on at Chicago, and this turned to lively participation in both theoretical and experimental activities during the years we were together at The University of

Michigan and later when he was at M.I.T. Another intimately involved collaborator was Theodore M. Newcomb, whose expertness in social psychology and whose systems-theoretical viewpoint advanced our analyses of interpersonal reactions. E. Lowell Kelly also collaborated in a number of ways, as a friend, helpful critic, and participant in some of our experimental activities. Merrill M. Flood brought to our group a deep understanding of ways to apply basic mathematics to the issues before us. Bernard W. Agranoff, from his broad background in biochemistry, contributed important insights about the relationships between molecular processes in the brain and organismic behavior. Karl W. Deutsch, a wide-ranging generalist, excelled in innovative applications of systems concepts to large-scale national and international processes. J. David Singer was another colleague who investigated the turbulence of international relations with a systems-oriented conceptual approach. Others who were associated with our Institute at Michigan and who participated in the theoretical work or data collection reported in this book included: William J. Horvath, Paul M. Fitts, Kenneth E. Boulding, Irwin Pollack, Manfred Kochen, William R. Uttal, James V. McConnell, Sylvan Kornblum, Caxton C. Foster, H. Merrill Jackson, Leonard M. Uhr, Kent H. Marquis, Stanley M. Moss, John T. Burns, Richard A. Cabot, Frederick C. Fensch, Bertram E. Peretz, and Robert F. House, who cooperated in the writing of pages 169–195 of Chap. 5.

From late 1971 to 1973 I was on the faculty of the Department of Psychiatry and Behavioral Sciences at Johns Hopkins University School of Medicine. During that period my longtime friend, Joel Elkes, was director of the department. I greatly appreciate his sophisticated understanding and personal support of this scholarly work.

I profited from the resources and support generously provided to me by the International Institute for Applied Systems Analysis (IIASA) at Laxenburg, Austria, during parts of 1973 and 1974 when I was in residence as a scientist on the Institute staff. The personal concern of its director, Dr. Howard Raiffa, greatly facilitated the completion of this book.

And most recently of all, I have found a congenial working environment with my associates at the University of Louisville. I appreciate the essential support they have provided.

Throughout most of the time of writing, Carol L. Miller was my assistant in research and administration. Deeply dedicated to the goals of our total effort, which she understood with singular clarity, she always gave priority to facilitating creation of this book, participating in the many activities which led to the synthesis of this work. Full responsibility for preparation of the final manuscript and production of this book were hers. I thank her particularly.

James J. Van Hare combined medical training and unusual artistic talent in making the color plates and certain other illustrations for this book. Catherine M. Bauscher, Gene A. Mulhall, and Barbara Rankin drew most of the black and white figures in this book.

A wide range of support services was constantly available at the Mental Health Research Institute. Helen Sheldon devoted many days to bibliographic and artistic coordination and to the preparation of the manuscript. Renata Tagliazcozzo, Thomas E. Jennett, Joseph R. Weeks, and Loris D. Schoenberger also participated in the bibliographic work. Cecile Penland, Barbara Sper, Janice Hobbs, and Virginia Spinks typed numerous drafts. Marilyn Brock at the University of Louisville contributed many months of devoted and efficient service, assisting in preparation of the final manuscript and collaborating in many aspects of its publication. I am most grateful to them all.

The experience of Ruth Weine of McGraw-Hill, who edited this manuscript, improved the quality of the book in many ways. I thank her for her informed, flexible patience.

At all stages of preparation of this book my wife, Jessie, was centrally important. A broad review of the literature is required for such an undertaking: the reading and analysis of thousands of references. By surveying this material she cast scintillas around each topic as we confronted it, contributing her thoughts and ideas. She participated in organizing the material, in drafting the presentation, and in improving the style. It is absolutely accurate to say that without her years of effort this book could not have been completed.

Like all junior fellows, I subscribed to a declaration of the aims of the Harvard Society of Fellows, when I became a member in 1938. This statement was written by A. Lawrence Lowell, with collaboration of Lawrence J. Henderson, Alfred North Whitehead, James Livingston Lowes, and Charles F. Curtis. It included a paragraph which, years ago, became a directive for this volume:

"You will seek not a near, but a distant, objective, and you will not be satisfied with what you may have done. All that you may achieve or discover you will regard as a fragment of a larger pattern, which from his separate approach every true scholar is striving to descry."

Louisville, Kentucky   JAMES GRIER MILLER

NOTES TO PREFACE

[1]Whitehead, A. N. *Science and the modern world.* New York: Macmillan, 1925, 145, 146, 156.

[2]Miller, J. G. Whitehead: history in the grand manner. *Harvard Guardian.* 1937, **1**(1), 23–29 and **1**(2), 25–30.

[3]Whitehead, A. N. *Op. cit.,* 102.

[4]Henderson, L. J. *The order of nature.* Cambridge: Harvard Univ. Press, 1917, 172.

[5]Schanck, R. L. *The permanent revolution in science.* New York: Philosophical Lib., 1954, xiii.

[6]Meadows, P. Models, systems and science. *Amer. sociol. Rev.,* 1957, **22**, 3–9.

[7]Cf. McLeod, J. Simulation: from art to science of society. *Simulation Today,* June 1974 (20), 77–80.

[8]Zieleniewski, J. Spojrzenie na rzeczywistość jako na "system systemów" a materializm dialektyczny. [Reality seen as a "system of systems" and dialectical materialism.] *Prakseologia,* 1973, **2**(46), 131–142.

[9]Miller, J. G. Introduction. In Members of the Committee on Behavioral Sciences, University of Chicago (Eds.). Symposium: profits and problems of homeostatic models in the behavioral sciences. *Chicago Behavioral Sciences Publications,* 1953, **1**, 1–11.

Also Miller, J. G. Toward a general theory for the behavioral sciences. *Amer. Psychol.,* 1955, **10**, 513–531.

Outline

This book analyzes the structure and process of seven hierarchical levels of living systems in the terms of general living systems theory. In order to demonstrate similarities and differences across these levels the chapters concerned with each level follow the same outline. This outline, with similarly titled and numbered divisions, is used also in Chapter 3, Structure and Process, and in Chapter 4, Hypotheses Concerning Living Systems. This uniformity of presentation makes it possible either to read the book in the usual way, from beginning to end (following the order of the chapters indicated in the Table of Contents, p. vii) or to compare particular aspects of the structure and process of systems at two or more levels. In order to make it easy for the reader to follow the second procedure, the table beginning below gives the page numbers for each of the numbered sections of each of the chapters that follow the same outline. To compare aspects of living systems at each level, the reader may select any row in this table and read in sequence the pages given for each chapter.

Outline of Chapters 3, 4, and 6 through 12	Chapter 3 Structure and Process	Chapter 4 Hypotheses Concerning Living Systems	Chapter 6 The Cell	Chapter 7 The Organ	Chapter 8 The Organism	Chapter 9 The Group	Chapter 10 The Organization	Chapter 11 The Society	Chapter 12 The Supranational System
					Page Numbers				
1. Structure	51	92	207	316	361	516	596	747	904
1.1 System size	51	—	207	319	361	516	597	748	904
1.2 Structural taxonomy of types of systems	51	—	208	319	362	517	597	748	905
2. Process	51	92	216	319	362	517	597	748	905
2.1 System and subsystem indicators	51	—	216	319	363	517	599	750	905

Outline of Chapters 3, 4, and 6 through 12 (Cont'd)	Page Numbers								
	Chapter 3 Structure and Process	Chapter 4 Hypotheses Concerning Living Systems	Chapter 6 The Cell	Chapter 7 The Organ	Chapter 8 The Organism	Chapter 9 The Group	Chapter 10 The Organization	Chapter 11 The Society	Chapter 12 The Supranational System
2.2 Process taxonomy of types of systems	52	—	216	321	363	517	599	754	906
3. Subsystems	52	93	217	321	363	519	605	763	910
3.1 Subsystems which process both matter-energy and information	55	93	223	321	363	519	605	765	915
3.1.1 Reproducer	55	—	223	321	363	519	605	765	915
3.1.1.1 Structure	55	—	223	321	363	519	605	765	915
3.1.1.2 Process	55	—	224	321	363	519	608	769	915
3.1.2 Boundary	56	93	228	321	367	522	609	770	915
3.1.2.1 Structure	56	—	228	321	367	522	609	770	915
3.1.2.2 Process	56	93	229	324	367	523	609	771	916
3.2 Subsystems which process matter-energy	57	93	231	326	368	524	611	773	917
3.2.1 Ingestor	57	—	231	326	368	524	611	773	917
3.2.1.1 Structure	57	—	231	326	368	524	611	773	917
3.2.1.2 Process	57	—	232	326	368	525	611	773	917
3.2.2 Distributor	57	94	234	326	369	525	613	774	918
3.2.2.1 Structure	57	94	234	327	369	525	613	774	918
3.2.2.2 Process	57	94	234	327	369	526	613	774	918
3.2.3 Converter	57	—	236	328	370	526	616	775	919
3.2.3.1 Structure	57	—	236	328	370	526	616	775	919
3.2.3.2 Process	58	—	236	328	370	526	616	775	922
3.2.4 Producer	58	—	238	328	370	527	616	777	923
3.2.4.1 Structure	58	—	238	328	370	527	616	777	923
3.2.4.2 Process	58	—	238	329	370	527	617	777	923

Outline of Chapters 3, 4, and 6 through 12 (Cont'd)	Chapter 3 Structure and Process	Chapter 4 Hypotheses Concerning Living Systems	Chapter 6 The Cell	Chapter 7 The Organ	Chapter 8 The Organism	Chapter 9 The Group	Chapter 10 The Organization	Chapter 11 The Society	Chapter 12 The Supranational System
3.2.5 Matter-energy storage	58	94	241	330	371	527	619	779	923
3.2.5.1 Structure	58	—	241	330	371	527	619	779	923
3.2.5.2 Process	58	94	241	330	371	528	620	779	924
3.2.6 Extruder	59	—	242	331	373	529	621	781	925
3.2.6.1 Structure	59	—	242	331	373	529	621	781	925
3.2.6.2 Process	59	—	242	331	373	529	621	781	926
3.2.7 Motor	59	—	244	332	374	529	622	782	926
3.2.7.1 Structure	59	—	244	332	374	529	622	782	926
3.2.7.2 Process	59	—	244	332	375	530	622	782	927
3.2.8 Supporter	60	—	247	333	376	531	623	783	927
3.2.8.1 Structure	60	—	247	333	376	531	623	783	927
3.2.8.2 Process	60	—	247	333	377	531	623	783	927
3.3 Subsystems which process information	60	94	247	333	377	531	623	783	927
3.3.1 Input transducer	62	94	248	333	377	531	623	783	927
3.3.1.1 Structure	62	—	248	333	377	531	623	783	927
3.3.1.2 Process	62	94	254	335	379	531	624	784	928
3.3.2 Internal transducer	62	—	257	335	389	532	625	785	929
3.3.2.1 Structure	62	—	257	335	389	532	625	785	929
3.3.2.2 Process	63	—	258	336	390	532	625	785	929
3.3.3 Channel and net	63	95	260	336	390	536	627	788	931
3.3.3.1 Structure	63	95	260	336	390	536	627	788	931
3.3.3.2 Process	63	96	260	337	392	537	629	789	931

Outline of Chapters 3, 4, and 6 through 12 (Cont'd)

Page Numbers

	Chapter 3 Structure and Process	Chapter 4 Hypotheses Concerning Living Systems	Chapter 6 The Cell	Chapter 7 The Organ	Chapter 8 The Organism	Chapter 9 The Group	Chapter 10 The Organization	Chapter 11 The Society	Chapter 12 The Supranational System
3.3.4 Decoder	64	97	265	338	394	540	635	792	934
3.3.4.1 Structure	64	—	265	338	394	540	635	792	934
3.3.4.2 Process	64	97	265	338	395	540	635	792	934
3.3.5 Associator	65	99	266	339	407	543	637	794	935
3.3.5.1 Structure	66	—	266	339	407	543	637	794	935
3.3.5.2 Process	66	99	266	339	407	543	637	794	935
3.3.6 Memory	66	99	267	339	413	547	639	796	937
3.3.6.1 Structure	66	—	268	339	413	547	639	796	937
3.3.6.2 Process	66	99	268	339	414	547	639	797	937
3.3.7 Decider	67	100	272	340	422	548	642	799	939
3.3.7.1 Structure	67	—	272	340	422	548	642	799	939
3.3.7.2 Process	68	100	273	341	424	549	644	800	940
3.3.8 Encoder	68	—	276	342	438	554	662	824	942
3.3.8.1 Structure	69	—	276	342	438	554	662	824	942
3.3.8.2 Process	69	—	277	343	439	554	662	824	942
3.3.9 Output transducer	69	—	279	343	442	555	664	826	943
3.3.9.1 Structure	69	—	279	343	442	555	664	826	943
3.3.9.2 Process	69	—	279	343	443	555	665	827	943
4. Relationships among subsystems or components	70	103	281	343	445	556	665	828	944
4.1 Structural relationships	70	103	281	343	445	556	666	828	944
4.1.1 Containment	70	—	281	343	445	556	666	828	944
4.1.2 Number	70	—	281	343	445	556	666	828	944

Page Numbers

Outline of Chapters 3, 4, and 6 through 12 (Cont'd)	Chapter 3 Structure and Process	Chapter 4 Hypotheses Concerning Living Systems	Chapter 6 The Cell	Chapter 7 The Organ	Chapter 8 The Organism	Chapter 9 The Group	Chapter 10 The Organization	Chapter 11 The Society	Chapter 12 The Supranational System
4.1.3 Order	70	—	281	343	445	558	666	828	944
4.1.4 Position	70	103	281	344	445	558	666	828	944
4.1.5 Direction	70	—	281	344	445	560	666	828	944
4.1.6 Size	70	—	281	344	445	560	666	828	944
4.1.7 Pattern	70	—	281	344	445	560	666	828	944
4.1.8 Density	70	103	281	344	445	560	666	828	944
4.2 Process relationships	70	103	281	344	445	560	666	828	944
4.2.1 Temporal relationships	70	—	281	344	445	560	666	828	944
4.2.1.1 Containment in time	70	—	281	344	445	560	666	828	944
4.2.1.2 Number in time	70	—	281	344	445	560	666	828	944
4.2.1.3 Order in time	70	—	281	344	445	560	666	828	944
4.2.1.4 Position in time	70	—	281	344	445	561	666	828	944
4.2.1.5 Direction in time	70	—	281	344	445	561	666	828	944
4.2.1.6 Duration	70	—	281	344	445	561	666	828	944
4.2.1.7 Pattern in time	70	—	281	344	445	561	666	828	944
4.2.2 Spatiotemporal relationships	70	103	281	344	445	561	666	828	944
4.2.2.1 Action	70	—	281	344	445	561	666	828	944
4.2.2.2 Communication	70	—	281	344	445	561	666	828	944
4.2.2.3 Direction of action	70	—	281	344	445	561	666	828	944
4.2.2.4 Pattern of action	70	103	281	344	445	561	666	828	944
4.2.2.5 Entering or leaving containment	70	—	281	344	445	561	666	828	944
4.3 Relationships among subsystems or components which involve meaning	70	—	281	344	445	561	666	828	944

Outline of Chapters 3, 4, and 6 through 12 (Cont'd)	Chapter 3 Structure and Process	Chapter 4 Hypotheses Concerning Living Systems	Chapter 6 The Cell	Chapter 7 The Organ	Chapter 8 The Organism	Chapter 9 The Group	Chapter 10 The Organization	Chapter 11 The Society	Chapter 12 The Supranational System
5. System processes	71	103	281	344	446	561	666	828	944
5.1 Process relationships between inputs and outputs	71	103	281	344	446	561	666	828	944
(a) Matter-energy inputs related to matter-energy outputs	71	—	281	344	446	561	667	829	944
(b) Matter-energy inputs related to information outputs	71	—	282	345	446	561	668	829	945
(c) Information inputs related to matter-energy outputs	71	—	282	345	447	562	668	829	945
(d) Information inputs related to information outputs	71	—	282	345	447	562	669	830	945
5.2 Adjustment processes among subsystems or components, used in maintaining variables in steady states	71	105	284	345	448	562	670	830	945
5.2.1 Matter-energy input processes	71	—	284	345	449	562	670	831	945
5.2.2 Information input processes	72	—	285	346	452	563	671	833	948
5.2.3 Matter-energy internal processes	72	—	285	346	455	564	672	835	949
5.2.4 Information internal processes	73	—	287	347	456	565	673	844	956
5.2.5 Matter-energy output processes	75	—	288	347	461	572	683	850	966
5.2.6 Information output processes	75	—	288	347	462	572	684	851	966
5.2.7 Feedbacks	75	—	288	347	462	572	684	851	966
5.3 Evolution	75	—	289	347	464	574	687	854	967
5.3.1 Emergents	78	—	295	349	468	574	692	861	968
5.4 Growth, cohesiveness, and integration	78	108	295	349	468	575	692	862	968
5.4.1 Growth	78	108	295	349	468	575	692	862	968
5.4.2 Cohesiveness	79	—	298	352	472	575	698	866	969

Page Numbers

Page Numbers

Outline of Chapters 3, 4, and 6 through 12 (Cont'd)	Chapter 3 Structure and Process	Chapter 4 Hypotheses Concerning Living Systems	Chapter 6 The Cell	Chapter 7 The Organ	Chapter 8 The Organism	Chapter 9 The Group	Chapter 10 The Organization	Chapter 11 The Society	Chapter 12 The Supranational System
5.4.3 Integration	80	109	299	353	472	576	699	867	970
5.5 Pathology	81	110	299	353	473	581	702	869	970
(a) Lacks of matter-energy inputs	81	—	299	353	473	581	703	870	970
(b) Excesses of matter-energy inputs	82	—	299	353	474	581	703	870	971
(c) Inputs of inappropriate forms of matter-energy	82	—	300	353	474	581	708	871	971
(d) Lacks of information inputs	82	—	300	354	475	581	708	871	971
(e) Excesses of information inputs	82	—	300	354	476	581	708	871	971
(f) Inputs of maladaptive genetic information in the template	82	—	300	354	476	581	708	871	971
(g) Abnormalities in internal matter-energy processes	82	—	301	354	478	582	708	872	971
(h) Abnormalities in internal information processes	82	—	301	354	479	582	708	872	971
5.6 Decay and termination	82	110	302	354	480	583	711	873	972
6. Models and simulations	83	114	302	354	482	583	712	873	973
(a) Nonliving artifacts	85	—	302	355	482	583	—	—	—
(b) Living, usually human, representations	85	—	—	—	484	—	712	874	974
(c) Models in words, numbers, or other symbols, including computer programs	85	—	303	355	484	583	716	875	980
(d) Living system–computer interactions	85	—	—	—	—	—	737	892	1000
7. Conclusions	85	114	304	357	499	586	737	892	1017

List of Hypotheses

This list includes the chapter and page numbers of each hypothesis presented in this book. It will assist readers interested in making cross-level comparisons of many aspects of living systems. No hypotheses are mentioned in Chaps. 1 and 13.

Hypothesis	Chapter 2 Basic Concepts	Chapter 3 Structure and Process	Chapter 4 Hypotheses Concerning Living Systems	Chapter 5 Information Input Overload	Chapter 6 The Cell	Chapter 7 The Organ	Chapter 8 The Organism	Chapter 9 The Group	Chapter 10 The Organization	Chapter 11 The Society	Chapter 12 The Supranational System
1. Structure											
1–1			92				423		595 642	799	
1–2		81	92 109				423		601		
2. Process											
2–1			92								
2–2			92								
2–3			92			362		519	601	748 893	1017
2–4			92								

List of Hypotheses (Cont'd.) Hypothesis	Chapter 2 Basic Concepts	Chapter 3 Structure and Process	Chapter 4 Hypotheses Concerning Living Systems	Chapter 5 Information Input Overload	Chapter 6 The Cell	Chapter 7 The Organ	Chapter 8 The Organism	Chapter 9 The Group	Chapter 10 The Organization	Chapter 11 The Society	Chapter 12 The Supranational System
3. Subsystems											
3.1 Subsystems which process both matter-energy and information											
3.1.2 Boundary											
3.1.2.2-1			93		230	324	367	523	610		916
3.1.2.2-2			93					523 524 587		772 790	
3.1.2.2-3			93					523 524 587	610	772	916 930
3.1.2.2-4			93							772	
3.2 Subsystems which process matter-energy											
3.2-1			93				461			831	991
3.2.2 Distributor											
3.2.2.1-1			94								
3.2.2.2-1	31		94		235	327	369		615	775 838	919
3.2.2.2-2	31		94 110				369		615	775 838	
3.2.5 Matter-energy storage											
3.2.5.2-1			94 104		241	330	371 372				925
3.3 Subsystems which process information											
3.3-1			94				449			893	927
3.3.1 Input transducer											
3.3.1.2-1			94		256 282 283	335	379				

	Page Numbers										
List of Hypotheses (Cont'd.) Hypothesis	Chapter 2 Basic Concepts	Chapter 3 Structure and Process	Chapter 4 Hypotheses Concerning Living Systems	Chapter 5 Information Input Overload	Chapter 6 The Cell	Chapter 7 The Organ	Chapter 8 The Organism	Chapter 9 The Group	Chapter 10 The Organization	Chapter 11 The Society	Chapter 12 The Supranational System
3.3.1.2-2			95								
3.3.3 Channel and net											
3.3.3.1-1			95			338 355		538 588	630	735	
3.3.3.2-1			96			338					
3.3.3.2-2			94 96 97 109 110		264	338	393 394	537	634 701		933 999
3.3.3.2-3		31	94 96 97 109 110		264	338	394		634 701		
3.3.3.2-4			96		264	338	393 394	537	634 701		933
3.3.3.2-5			96			338			631		1018
3.3.3.2-6			96			338			626		
3.3.3.2-7			96 97 99 109 110			338					933
3.3.3.2-8			96			338			631		932
3.3.3.2-9			96 97 98 112			338		542 588			
3.3.3.2-10		31	96 98 112			338					

List of Hypotheses (Cont'd.) Hypothesis	Chapter 2 Basic Concepts	Chapter 3 Structure and Process	Chapter 4 Hypotheses Concerning Living Systems	Chapter 5 Information Input Overload	Chapter 6 The Cell	Chapter 7 The Organ	Chapter 8 The Organism	Chapter 9 The Group	Chapter 10 The Organization	Chapter 11 The Society	Chapter 12 The Supranational System
3.3.3.2-11			96 97 109 110	124		338			629 634	825	
3.3.3.2-12			97 111			338				893	
3.3.3.2-13			97			338			636		
3.3.3.2-14	31		97			338			636		
3.3.3.2-15	31	81	97 99 109			338			636		
3.3.3.2-16			97 98 100			338			633		934
3.3.3.2-17			97		269	338		539	663 660		932
3.3.3.2-18			97		264	338			630		
3.3.3.2-19			97			338					
3.3.3.2-20			97			338			634		1011
3.3.3.2-21			97			338					
3.3.4 Decoder											
3.3.4.2-1			98		305	339	396 401 404 501	540 542 588			
3.3.4.2-2			98			339	452	542			
3.3.4.2-3			98 100			339	396 401 404	541 542			
3.3.4.2-4			98			339	396 404	542 588			

Page Numbers

List of Hypotheses (Cont'd.) Hypothesis	Chapter 2 Basic Concepts	Chapter 3 Structure and Process	Chapter 4 Hypotheses Concerning Living Systems	Chapter 5 Information Input Overload	Chapter 6 The Cell	Chapter 7 The Organ	Chapter 8 The Organism	Chapter 9 The Group	Chapter 10 The Organization	Chapter 11 The Society	Chapter 12 The Supranational System
3.3.4.2-5			98			339	396 404				
3.3.4.2-6			98			339	467 469	541 542 588			
3.3.4.2-7			96 97 98 111			339	396	542 545 588	629		
3.3.4.2-8			98 100			339		541 542	636		
3.3.4.2-9			99			339	436	542			
3.3.4.2-10			99			339	436	541 542			
3.3.5 Associator											
3.3.5.2-1			99		267	330	408				
3.3.5.2-2			99				408			795	
3.3.5.2-3			99 111				409 464	545	638 686		
3.3.5.2-4			99				409				
3.3.5.2-5			99				410		639 738		
3.3.5.2-6			99					544	638	794	936
3.3.6 Memory											
3.3.6.2-1			99		271		421	547			
3.3.6.2-2			99		271		421				938
3.3.6.2-3			99 113				421				
3.3.6.2-4			100								940 1018

List of Hypotheses (Cont'd.) Hypothesis	Chapter 2 Basic Concepts	Chapter 3 Structure and Process	Chapter 4 Hypotheses Concerning Living Systems	Chapter 5 Information Input Overload	Chapter 6 The Cell	Chapter 7 The Organ	Chapter 8 The Organism	Chapter 9 The Group	Chapter 10 The Organization	Chapter 11 The Society	Chapter 12 The Supranational System
3.3.6.2-5			100								1018
3.3.6.2-6			100			340					1018
3.3.7 Decider											
3.3.7.2-1			100		273	342	429	550	645 651 680	802	940 963
3.3.7.2-2			100						682		
3.3.7.2-3			100		275				682		
3.3.7.2-4	38		100						661		
3.3.7.2-5			100						654	866	
3.3.7.2-6			100	156					631 656	808	977
3.3.7.2-7			100								
3.3.7.2-8			100								
3.3.7.2-9			101						660	808	
3.3.7.2-10			101						660	808	
3.3.7.2-11			101						651 698 738	866	
3.3.7.2-12			101								
3.3.7.2-13			101				437		651	802	
3.3.7.2-14			101 113			342	372 436 479		670	831	
3.3.7.2-15			101			342					
3.3.7.2-16			101			341	436	550	651 657		1018
3.3.7.2-17			101		236 276		436			893	

Page Numbers

List of Hypotheses (Cont'd.)

Hypothesis	Chapter 2 Basic Concepts	Chapter 3 Structure and Process	Chapter 4 Hypotheses Concerning Living Systems	Chapter 5 Information Input Overload	Chapter 6 The Cell	Chapter 7 The Organ	Chapter 8 The Organism	Chapter 9 The Group	Chapter 10 The Organization	Chapter 11 The Society	Chapter 12 The Supranational System
3.3.7.2-18			101		237 287 289	341	455				
3.3.7.2-19			101			342				831	
3.3.7.2-20			102							831	
3.3.7.2-21			102				437	551		894	1018

4. Relationships among subsystems or components

4.1.4-1			103		281						
4.1.8-1			103		281						
4.2.2.4-1			103								

5. System processes

5.1 Process relationships between inputs and outputs

5.1-1			103		122 164 170		447 452				
5.1-2			103		123 170		447 452				
5.1-3			103		124 170		447 452				
5.1-4			103		124 170 192		447			830	1018
5.1-5			103		284		447				
5.1-6			103		284		447				
5.1-7			103				447				
5.1-8			103				447				
5.1-9			103		284		447				
5.1-10			104				447				

List of Hypotheses (Cont'd) Hypothesis	Chapter 2 Basic Concepts	Chapter 3 Structure and Process	Chapter 4 Hypotheses Concerning Living Systems	Chapter 5 Information Input Overload	Chapter 6 The Cell	Chapter 7 The Organ	Chapter 8 The Organism	Chapter 9 The Group	Chapter 10 The Organization	Chapter 11 The Society	Chapter 12 The Supranational System
5.1-11			104		284		447				
5.1-12			104		284		447				
5.1-13			104				447				
5.1-14			104				447				
5.1-15			104				447				
5.1-16			104				447				
5.1-17			104				447				
5.1-18			104				447				
5.1-19			104				447				
5.1-20			104		284		447				
5.1-21			104				447				
5.1-22			104				447				
5.1-23			104				447				
5.1-24			104				447				
5.1-25			104	124 170 192							
5.1-26			104		284						
5.1-27			104		284						
5.1-28			104		284				638 669 738	634	
5.1-29			104		284				669		1018
5.1-30			104		284						1018
5.1-31			104								
5.1-32			104				448				
5.1-33			105				448				

Page Numbers

List of Hypotheses (Cont'd) Hypothesis	Chapter 2 Basic Concepts	Chapter 3 Structure and Process	Chapter 4 Hypotheses Concerning Living Systems	Chapter 5 Information Input Overload	Chapter 6 The Cell	Chapter 7 The Organ	Chapter 8 The Organism	Chapter 9 The Group	Chapter 10 The Organization	Chapter 11 The Society	Chapter 12 The Supranational System
5.1-34			105								
5.1-35			105								
5.1-36			105								
5.1-37			105								
5.1-38			105								
5.1-39			105								
5.1-40			105								
5.1-41			105								
5.1-42			105 109		284 300		452 475	564			
5.2 Adjustment processes among subsystems or components, used in maintaining variables in steady states											
5.2-1			105				447 451				
5.2-2			106			346 347	372 452 459	563 566		831	
5.2-3			106		287			571	671		
5.2-4			106				449 462		670 671 705		
5.2-5			106				450		671 705	832	
5.2-6			106					573			
5.2-7			106				479	572			
5.2-8			106 114								
5.2-9			107							893	

List of Hypotheses (Cont'd.)	Page Numbers										
Hypothesis	Chapter 2 Basic Concepts	Chapter 3 Structure and Process	Chapter 4 Hypotheses Concerning Living Systems	Chapter 5 Information Input Overload	Chapter 6 The Cell	Chapter 7 The Organ	Chapter 8 The Organism	Chapter 9 The Group	Chapter 10 The Organization	Chapter 11 The Society	Chapter 12 The Supranational System
5.2-10			107						705	870	
5.2-11			107								
5.2-12			107							894	1018
5.2-13			107 109					588			999 1018
5.2-14			107		299	346				893	964 1018
5.2-15			107								
5.2-16			107						681		964 1019
5.2-17			108							893	1019
5.2-18			108							893	
5.2-19			108								
5.2-20			108				458				
5.2-21			108								
5.2-22			108								
5.2-23			108								
5.2-24			108				461				
5.2-25			108								
5.2-26			108					566		893	
5.2-27			108								
5.2-28			108								
5.2-29			108								

5.4 Growth, cohesiveness, and integration

  5.4.1   Growth

Page Numbers

List of Hypotheses (Cont'd.) Hypothesis	Chapter 2 Basic Concepts	Chapter 3 Structure and Process	Chapter 4 Hypotheses Concerning Living Systems	Chapter 5 Information Input Overload	Chapter 6 The Cell	Chapter 7 The Organ	Chapter 8 The Organism	Chapter 9 The Group	Chapter 10 The Organization	Chapter 11 The Society	Chapter 12 The Supranational System
5.4.1-1		78	108		296	352	470			863	
5.4.1-2			108			350	468	577		762 865	
5.4.1-3			109						698	866	
5.4.1-4			105 109		300		470 475				
5.4.3 Integration											
5.4.3-1	31		109					568		867	
5.4.3-2			109						643 701	893	
5.4.3-3			109			350			697		
5.4.3-4			109		299		473		701		
5.4.3-5			109				473		701		
5.4.3-6			97 109 110				473		701		
5.4.3-7			107 109					577 588		867	
5.4.3-8			109					579	661		
5.4.3-9			109						701	893	
5.5 Pathology											
5.5-1			110		299	329 353 354	474				
5.5-2		81	110								
5.6 Decay and termination											
5.6-1		83	110		302		481	581	706 711	873	

Living Systems

The Need for a General Theory

of Living Systems

What is a living system and what does it do? Many scientists coming from diverse scientific backgrounds, when engaged in the search for general principles to integrate our understanding of the phenomena of life, have placed major emphasis on the notion of living systems composed of interrelated units. The various "systems theories" differ greatly in their concepts and definitions of basic terms. Their common goal is to organize the findings in some or all of the sciences of life and behavior into a single conceptual structure.

1. One general theory of living systems

The general living systems theory which this book presents is a conceptual system concerned primarily with concrete systems (see page 17) which exist in space-time. Complex structures which carry out living processes I believe can be identified at seven hierarchical levels (see page 25)—cell, organ, organism, group, organization, society, and supranational system. My central thesis is that systems at all these levels are open systems composed of subsystems which process inputs, throughputs, and outputs of various forms of matter, energy, and information. I identify 19 critical subsystems (see page 32 and Table 1-1) whose processes are essential for life, some of which process matter or energy, some of which process information, and some of which process all three. Together they

make up a living system, as shown in Fig. 1-1. In this table the line under the word "Reproducer" separates this subsystem from the others because that subsystem differs from all the others by being critical to the species or type of system even though it is not essential to the individual. Living systems often continue to exist even though they are not able to reproduce. Subsystems in different columns which appear opposite each other have processes with important similarities—for instance, the processes carried out by the ingestor for matter and energy are comparable to those carried out by the input transducer for information. In general the sequence of transmissions in living systems is from inputs at the top of Table 1-1 to outputs at the bottom, but there are exceptions.

Systems at each of the seven levels, I maintain, have the same 19 critical subsystems. The structure and processes of a given subsystem are more complex at a more advanced level than at the less advanced ones. This is explained by what I call the evolutionary principle of "shred-out," a sort of division of labor (see Fig. 1-2). Cells have the 19 critical subsystems. When mutations occurred in the original cells, the mutant could continue to exist only if it could carry out all the essential processes of life of the 19 subsystems; otherwise it would be eliminated by natural selection. The general direction of evolution is toward greater complexity. As more complex cells evolved, they had more

Fig. 1-1 A generalized living system interacting and intercommunicating with two others in its environment.

Subsystems which process both matter-energy and information: Reproducer (Re); Boundary (Bo).

Subsystems which process matter-energy: Ingestor (IN); Distributor (DI); Converter (CO); Producer (PR); Matter-energy storage (MS); Extruder (EX); Motor (MO); Supporter (SU).

Subsystems which process information: Input transducer (it); Internal transducer (in); Channel and net (cn); Decoder (dc); Associator (as); Memory (me); Decider (de); Encoder (en); Output transducer (ot).

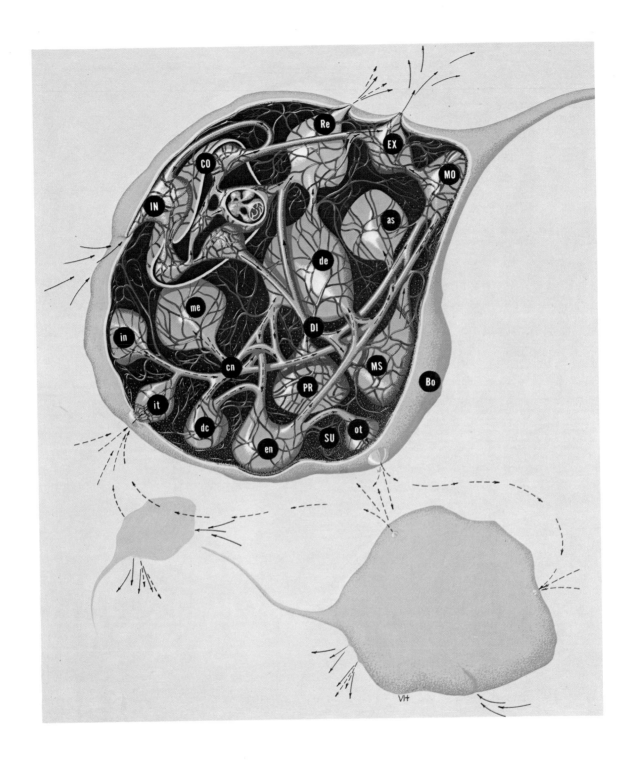

complex subsystems, but still the same 19 basic processes. Similarly as cells evolved into more complex systems at advanced levels—organs, organisms, and so on—their subsystems shredded out into increasingly complicated units carrying out more complicated and often more effective processes. If at any single point in the entire evolutionary sequence any one of the 19 subsystem processes had ceased, the system would not have endured. That explains why the same 19 subsystems are found at each level from cell to suprasystem. And it explains why it is possible to discover,

observe, and measure cross-level formal identities (see page 17).

For each subsystem I identify about a dozen variables representing different aspects of its processes. It would be easy to identify more if one wanted an exhaustive list. Each of these variables can be measured at each of the levels, and the sorts of variation discovered can be compared across the levels. The interactions between two or more variables in a single subsystem or in multiple ones can also be observed, measured, and compared across the levels. This is how cross-level formal identities, basic to a general theory of living systems, can be examined (see page 27).

This book is an effort to integrate all the social, biological, and physical sciences that apply to structure or process at any of the seven levels. Physiology, biochemistry, genetics, pharmacology, medicine, economics, political science, anthropology, sociology, and psychology are all almost entirely relevant. Physical science and engineering also contribute. Logic, mathematics, and statistics yield methods, models, and simulations, including some involving the relatively new approaches of cybernetics and information theory.

2. Problems in presenting a general theory

Presentation of a general theory covering the wide range of living systems from cells to supranational systems creates special problems in exposition, as readers of this book will discover.

First, the conceptual system must be stated in terms which are as nearly applicable as possible to all the levels of living systems; otherwise it would not be general. No words, however, are designed or precisely adapted to describe comparable structures and processes at all these levels. The accepted specialized terms at one level are not exactly appropriate for another level. Consequently any term selected will appear a little inaccurate to specialists at one or more levels. I have tried to use the words which apply most satisfactorily to all levels. Nevertheless the reader will, unfortunately, have to adjust to certain awkwardnesses of language. They seem unavoidable in many sentences if the generality of the conceptual system is to be maintained.

Second, the book must be written for intelligent laypeople rather than for specialists at any level of living systems, because specialists at one level are usually not experts on the content matter of other levels. As a consequence, when specialists read chapters concerning their own fields, they will find that they already know much or all of their contents. Some

LEVEL

Cell

Organ

Organism

Group

Organization

Society

Supranational System

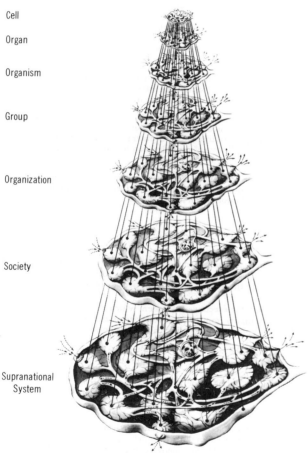

Fig. 1-2 Shred-out. The generalized living system (see Fig. 1-1) is here shown at each level. The diagram indicates that the 19 subsystems at the level of the cell shred out to form the next more advanced level of system, the organ. This still has the same 19 subsystems, each being more complex. A similar shredding-out occurs to form each of the five more advanced levels—organism, group, organization, society, and supranational system.

of the material is basic content in the field which has been taught in beginning courses for decades; other material is advanced and new. In order to keep the book within reasonable limitations of length, I have had to select for discussion only a few studies out of a wealth of alternatives. My selection of studies is almost certainly not exactly what the specialist would have made himself, and many details of the studies I do consider cannot be presented. But that is the nature of such a book as this. I hope that no inaccuracies or inappropriate popularizations appear in my surveys of the research in different fields and that my emphases on different aspects of the research are judicious. Beyond that, I ask the reader's patience in enduring the constraints inherent in the presentation of an embracing general theory.

3. The potential contributions of a general theory

In 1949 when our work in systems science began, an integrative theory of living systems seemed desirable, but barely possible. The outlook is better today. The potential of such general theory is more generally recognized.[1]

Many scientists have expressed the need for a commonly accepted language, systematic theories, and basic laws to organize the huge volume of research findings and bridge the gaps of our knowledge about living systems.[2] George Miller's description of scientific journals as " . . . catalogs of spare parts for a machine they never build"[3] is an eloquent statement of need for an integrative theory. Royce defines the place of theory in psychology:

The big contribution which theory makes is that it brings order out of chaos; it provides meaning where it had previously not existed. Note, however, that this orderliness cannot be provided unless the previously unrelated mass of facts has first been funnelled through the cortex of some thinking scientists. . . . Empiricism without conscious attempts at conceptualizing and showing logical relationships simply does not lead us automatically to theoretical unification. The history of science is replete with instances of all the facts being in, but because of the lack of an interested and insightful theorist, the development of the unifying concept, law, or theory was retarded. Facts remain isolated until some synthesizing mind brings them together.[4]

General theory has other important functions besides clarifying the meaning of established research findings, as Mendeleyev's periodic table of the elements did for chemistry. Like his theory it can also supply a structure into which new discoveries can be fitted. The sheer physical bulk of scientific and technical periodicals in the United States has been doubling approximately every 20 years since 1800.[5] There are in the world at least 75,000 such journals, publishing about 1.2 million articles a year. Further, at least 60,000 books and 100,000 other research reports appear annually.[6] The world list of scientific periodicals, like a colony of rabbits, has grown exponentially, doubling in number about every 15 years, increasing tenfold in 50 years, a thousandfold in a century and a half, and a millionfold in the 300 years since 1665 when the first such journal was published.[7] The numbers of books and scientific abstracts grow at similar rates. Moreover, though most aspects of societies double every 30 to 50 years, science is growing much faster. The number of scientists appears to be doubling in Western Europe every 15 years, in America every 10 years, in Russia every 7 years, and in China perhaps every 5 years. Moreover, more than 90 percent of all the scientists who ever lived are alive today. And they are hard at work. Twenty-five years ago a competent scientist had read most of the significant publications in his field. Today this is not possible even in subfields. Consequently, unless there is an accepted structure into which each new finding can be fitted, the "immortality" of scientists' ideas will vanish. Experimenters sometimes unwittingly repeat research already accomplished by someone else, because the unsystematic arrangement of facts and the unclear relationships of concepts make it hard to retrieve earlier studies which, no matter how excellent, get buried under the avalanche of new researches. An organized theory allows new findings to be added to past knowledge in an orderly manner.

Perhaps the most valuable service of general theory, as Merton has observed, is suggesting how to make new observations or to conduct experiments on a wide range of phenomena in order to extend our grasp of the basic principles underlying them.[8] Without such theory the scientist does not know how to decide which of an overwhelming number of possible observations are worth making.

A general theoretical structure also provides common measurement units that make research at different levels comparable in a way they are not when each field has its own idiosyncratic measures (see pages 16 and 1026 to 1030).

The fact is that, while physical science is approaching the goal of an integrated mathematical theory of the cosmos, the biological sciences today are a congeries of partial theories of varying degrees of sophistication. And if an egg instead of an apple had dropped on Newton's head, physics might now be in the same state as the behavioral sciences. After a new theoretical integration, as the history of natural science repeatedly has shown, basic discovery, experimentation, technological advance, and isolated facts suddenly fit together to make new meaning.

4. Critiques of a general theory

There are various arguments against such a general theory as I shall present. Among these are (*a*) that the sciences of living systems, particularly social systems, are necessarily so vague and inexact that fundamental disagreements cannot be resolved; (*b*) that behavioral phenomena are too numerous and complex for meaningful classification and not available to exact measurement; (*c*) that living systems can be understood by "common sense" and that therefore scientific evidence about them is not necessary; (*d*) that man is unique in the scheme of nature and unpredictable, and that his inviolable subjectivity cannot be quantified; and finally (*e*) an emotional but forceful argument, that understanding means control so that a truly scientific approach to life would restrict rather than advance human freedom.

My answers to these arguments are:

(*a*) The subject matter of the sciences of, life and behavior, even social science, is not so intangible as it may seem. Tangibility is attested by measurable regularities, and living processes are both measurable and regular. There are, for example, regular relations of inputs and outputs from which intervening processes in an organism or social organization are inferred in the same way that the characteristics of a vacuum tube or amplifier are deduced from comparisons of its inputs and outputs. When a physicist reads a flickering needle, he is observing behavior—"motion" in the inanimate world—and drawing conclusions from it. Even the "subjective metrics" of psychometricians eventually reduce to behavioral indices and so are not exceptions to ordinary scientific practice. In the study of society the opinions and activities of people are becoming increasingly better understood as methods of sampling and analysis improve.

(*b*) Man's complexity is great, but in the history of science everything which has not been thoroughly analyzed appears complex. I shall later demonstrate that behavior as purposive as man's—orientation toward future goals—appears in other living and non-living systems. And even subjectivity can, in a sense, be submitted to psychometric measurement.

(*c*) Furthermore, "common sense" does not reign supreme in the sciences of life and behavior any more than it does in the physical sciences, where a pound of feathers is obviously lighter than a pound of lead. The commonsense approach was amusingly challenged by Lazarsfeld, who listed several commonsense, obvious generalizations about attitudes of American soldiers, such as:[9] "Better educated men show more psychoneurotic symptoms than those with less education," or "Men from rural backgrounds were usually in better spirits during their Army life than soldiers from city backgrounds." To those who know the Army these statements seem obviously correct. The only drawback is that an attitude survey among the soldiers has indicated them to be wrong.[10]

(*d*) Man is unique. In fact, each man is unique. All particular things are unique. No two snowflakes and no two paramecia are alike.

Natural scientists attempt to view all phenomena dispassionately, somewhat as the supernatural observers looked down upon the Napoleonic era in Hardy's epic *The Dynasts*.[11] These celestial beings watched the movements of human armies and the vacillation of men's fortunes just as the natural scientist views the stars. Such objective observation of man has not been part of our cultural tradition. A scientific attitude about man first emerged in the first half of the nineteenth century.[12] At that time it became accepted that literary and philosophical discussion, scattered observations about behavior, and subjective experience were not enough. To them must be added sophisticated quantitative empirical method and data analysis, specification and testing of propositions by collection of facts concerning individuals and their social interactions. (I use "empirical" here in the sense I shall use it throughout this book, meaning "originating in or relying or based on factual information, observation, or direct sense experience usually as opposed to theoretical knowledge," and not in its often derogatory other common meaning "relying on experience or observation alone without proper regard for considerations of system, science, and theory.") There is still outcry against such an objective attitude by some social scientists. Adding detail to the contention that science cannot probe man's true nature, they maintain that his acts are not caused in the same way that the motions of nonliving matter are caused. He is unpredictable; he can will to offset influences upon him; and he can produce novel solutions to his dilemmas. His behavior is purposive. He is too complex for analysis, and his subjective privacy cannot be penetrated. There has long appeared to be conflict between the search for general laws and the intensive study of individual cases, the "idiographic" and the "nomothetic" approaches. As Whitehead observed:[13] " . . . all the world over and at all times there have been practical men, absorbed in 'irreducible and stubborn facts': all the world over and at all times there have been men of philosophic temperament who have been absorbed in the weaving of general principles. It is this union of passionate interest in the detailed facts with equal devotion to abstract generalization which forms the novelty in our present society."

There are legitimate scientific approaches to details of individual cases and to the causal history of a single event. One may place the individual event under scrutiny and ask about its complex interactions, as does a psychoanalyst with his analysand or an anthropological field mission with an isolated tribe. One may apply statistics to an individual. Or, on the other hand, one may want to know in general how sense organs operate or how galaxies are formed. Both sorts of endeavor are part of science.

(e) Perhaps harder to deal with is the question of the increased control by one man of another, which greater understanding and predictability may bring. Various warnings have been expressed about the dangers of this. For instance Whyte fears that many modern "organization men" may cease to make the distinction between right and wrong because of their belief that a precise science of man can determine ethics.[14] A world like that of *1984* would make a nightmarish uncivilization of the society of the future.[15] The more powerful and central to the human condition a new scientific discovery is, the more danger there is in its irresponsible misuse. We are acutely aware of the potentialities of expanded control in the field of atomic physics. Prediction, however, need not lead to control. As Harper said, because we can predict the course of the planets, we do not gain the ability to change their motions. He added:

This becomes knowledge to live by, not a tool for interplanetary dictatorship. . . . New scientific knowledge does not really mean the acquiring of an ability to exercise control according to whatever may be the wishes of the controller. It means, instead, learning the self-controlling laws of the universe, thus acquiring a greater ability to adjust ourselves to things as they are—to live in greater harmony with our environment. That, I believe, is the way to greater freedom rather than less, in social science as elsewhere. The biological nature of man will not be eliminated by learning what it is. Development of the science of human affairs is, then, not something that must be feared by the lovers of freedom.[16]

5. Conclusions

Increasing understanding of the physical universe has provided the skills to engineer great monuments and public works, to communicate over vast distances, and to move into space with incredible speed. Atomic research has given us tremendous sources of power. All this has increased our ability to control our environment even though it has not provided freedom from fear, at least as yet. Physical science so far has been used more to help man than to harm him, in spite of some obvious and dangerous misuses of it. The same is true with biological science. Medicine and biology know how to kill in more complicated and effective ways than were possible a hundred years ago, but medical and biological knowledge have been used for the public welfare vastly more often than for harm. While the specters of biological warfare and of starvation in overpopulated regions cannot be over-looked, the advance of these fields has freed man from many sorts of illness and pain and increased his span of life. Unquestionably the science of living systems as it develops may give opportunities for intimate forms of control and drastic threat, but on the other hand, it can also serve to free us from emotional disturbance, problems of interpersonal relations, and ultimately from the international disease of war which has scourged man throughout history. The expansion of such science is not likely to be avoided long by any nation. We can view this eventuality constructively, willingly accepting the challenge of its inherent dangers in order to realize its potentials for expanding the quality of human life.

Somewhere in this suggestion lies the hope that the same method which has harnessed physical forces can give us control over ourselves, a hope that adequate understanding of man and society can ultimately lead to constructive freedom and avert mass destruction. A general theory of living systems—viewed, as in this book, as a particular subset of all systems—implies a unity of science. It contends that the method which has advanced physical science can also advance the science of living systems. As Oppenheimer has put it:[17] "In the whole of our knowledge of the natural world including ourselves as natural objects, this whole area that reaches from the earliest days of history, from the farthest our telescopes and imaginations can see to the most subtle questions of human behavior, there are no signs of any unmanageable inconsistency."

NOTES AND REFERENCES

[1]Cf. Thom, R. *Stabilité structurelle et morphogenèse.* Reading, Mass.: W. A. Benjamin, 1972.
Also Braham, M. A general theory of organization. *Gen. Systems,* 1973, **18,** 13–24.
Also Laszlo, C. A., Levine, M. D., & Milsum, J. H. A general systems framework for social systems. *Behav. Sci.,* 1974, **19,** 79–92.
Also Glassman, R. B. Selection processes in living systems: role in cognitive construction and recovery from brain damage. *Behav. Sci.,* 1974, **19,** 149–165.
[2]Cf. Baker [Baker, W. O. The paradox of choice. In D. L. Wolfle (Ed.). *Symposium on basic research.* Washington, D.C.: AAAS Publication No. 56, 1959, **62,** 58 Copyright 1959 by The American Association for the Advancement of Science. Reprinted by permission.], who writes: "While brilliant hypotheses and shrewd applications of statistics have dramatically advanced our understanding of biological events and effects, there is yet hardly a case where guiding theoretical precept is established. Further, the need is intense, because in the life sciences the fragmented structure of many gifted individuals working independently may be a problem in our present national position in science. . . . Another powerful way to harmonize the freedom of the individual scholar in science with the achievement of useful and desired products is to be sure that everybody speaks the same language. This is a simple convenience which is often overlooked. It means that basic

expressions of scientific concepts ought to contain common units and, hopefully, common meanings."
Cf. also Lewin, K. *Principles of topological psychology.* (Trans. by F. Heider & G. M. Heider.) New York: McGraw-Hill, 1936, 4.
Also Cattell, R. B. Concepts and methods in the measurement of group syntality. *Psychol. Rev.,* 1948, **55,** 48.
Also Cartwright, D. Social psychology and group processes. *Ann. Rev. Psychol.,* 1957, 211.
Also Carmichael, L. Cobb's pyramid. *Contemp. Psychol.,* 1959, **4,** 238.
Also Easton, D. Shifting images of social science and values. *Antioch Rev.,* 1955, **15,** 17–18.
Also Rapoport, A. The systems view of the world. By Ervin Laszlo. (Book review.) *Gen. Systems,* 1973, **18,** 189–190.
[3]Miller, G. A. Psychology's block of marble. *Contemp. Psychol.,* 1956, **1,** 252.
[4]Royce, J. R. Toward the advancement of theoretical psychology. *Psychol. Rep.,* 1957, **3,** 404. Reprinted by permission of author and publisher.
[5]U.S. Library of Congress Reference Department, Scientific Division. *Scientific and Technical Serial Publications,* 1950–53. Washington: U.S. Government Printing Office, 1954.
[6]Killian, J. R. Report on scientific information of the President's Scientific Advisory Committee, 1958. *Nature,* Jan., **17,** 1959, 136.

[7]Price, D. J. de S. *Science since Babylon.* New Haven: Yale Univ. Press, 1961, 100–113.
[8]Merton, R. K. *Social theory and social structure.* (Rev. ed.). Glencoe, Ill.: Free Press, 1957, 88.
[9]Lazarsfeld, P. F. The American soldier—an expository review. *Publ. Opin. Quart.,* 1949, **13,** 378–380.
[10]Stouffer, S. A. The American soldier. In R. K. Merton & P. F. Lazarsfeld (Eds.). *Studies in the scope and method of "The American Soldier."* Glencoe, Ill.: Free Press, 1950.
[11]Hardy, T. *The dynasts.* New York: St. Martins, 1961.
[12]Glazer, N. The rise of social research in Europe. In D. Lerner (Ed.). *The human meaning of the social sciences.* New York: Meridian, 1959, 45–47.
[13]Whitehead, A. N. *Science and the modern world.* New York: Macmillan, 1925, 3–4. Copyright, 1925, by The Macmillan Company. Reprinted by permission of The Macmillan Company and Cambridge University Press.
[14]Whyte, W. H., Jr. *The organization man.* New York: Simon & Schuster, 1956, 28.
[15]Orwell, G. *1984.* New York: New Amer. Lib., 1954.
[16]Harper, F. A. *On the science of social science.* Paper read at the Texaco Research Club, Beacon, New York, February 1956. Reprinted by permission.
[17]Oppenheimer, J. R. Tradition and discovery. *A.C.L.S. Newsletter.* 1959, **10,** 14. Reprinted by permission.
Cf. also Price, D. J. de S. *Op. cit.,* 107.
Also Thom, R. *Op. cit.,* 325.

The Basic Concepts

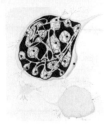

General systems theory is a set of related definitions, assumptions, and propositions which deal with reality as an integrated hierarchy of organizations of matter and energy. General living systems theory is concerned with a special subset of all systems, the living ones.

Even more basic to this presentation than the concept of "system" are the concepts of "space," "time," "matter," "energy," and "information," because the living systems which I shall discuss exist in space and are made of matter and energy organized by information.

1. Space and time

In the most general mathematical sense, a *space* is a set of elements which conform to certain postulates. Euclidean space, for instance, consists of points in three dimensions which are subject to the postulates of Euclid. In a metric space a distance measure is associated with each pair of elements. In a topological space each element has a collection of neighborhoods. The *conceptual spaces* of mathematics may have any number of dimensions.

Physical space is the extension surrounding a point. It may be thought of as either the compass of the entire universe or some region of such a universe. Classically the three-dimensional geometry of Euclid was considered to describe accurately all regions in physical space. The modern general theory of relativity has shown that physical space-time is more accurately described by a Riemannian geometry of four nonuniformly curved dimensions, three of space and one of time.

My presentation of a general theory of living systems will employ two sorts of spaces in which they may exist, *physical* or *geographical space* and *conceptual* or *abstracted spaces*.

1.1 Physical or geographical space This will be considered as Euclidean space, which is adequate for the study of all aspects of living systems as we now know them. Among the characteristics and constraints of physical space are the following: (*a*) The distance from point *A* to point *B* is the same as that from point *B* to point *A*. (*b*) Matter or energy moving on a straight or curved path from point *A* to point *B* must pass through every intervening point on the path. This is true also of markers (see page 12) bearing information. (*c*) In such space there is a maximum speed of movement for matter, energy, and markers bearing information. (*d*) Objects in such space exert gravitational pull on each other. (*e*) Solid objects moving in such space cannot pass through one another. (*f*) Solid objects moving in such space are subject to friction when they contact another object.

The characteristics and constraints of physical space affect the action of all concrete systems, living and nonliving. The following are some examples: (*a*) The number of different nucleotide bases—configurations in space—which a DNA molecule has determines how many bits of information it can store. (*b*) On the average, people interact more with persons who live near to them in a housing project than with persons who live far away in the project. (*c*) The diameter of the fuel supply lines laid down behind General Patton's advancing American Third Army in World War II determined the amount of friction the lines exerted upon the fuel pumped through them, and therefore the rate at which fuel could flow through them to supply Patton's tanks. This was one physical constraint which limited the rate at which the army could advance, because they had to halt when they ran out of fuel. (*d*) The small physical size of Goa in relation to India and its spatial contiguity to India were, in 1961, major determinants in the decision of erstwhile neutralist India to invade and seize it. (*e*) Today information can flow worldwide almost instantly by telegraph, radio, and television. In the seventeenth century it took weeks for messages to cross an ocean. A government could not send messages to its ambassadors so quickly then as it can now because of the constraints on the rate of movement of the marker bearing the information. Consequently ambassadors of that century had much more freedom of decision than they do now.

Physical space is a common space because it is the only space in which all concrete systems, living and nonliving, exist (though some may exist in other spaces simultaneously). Physical space is shared by all scientific observers, and all scientific data must be collected in it. This is equally true for natural science and behavioral science.

Most people learn that physical space exists, which is not true of many spaces I shall mention in the next section. They can give the location of objects in it. A child probably learns of physical space by correlating the spaces presented by at least two sense modalities—such as vision (which may be distorted by such pathologies as astigmatism or aniseikonia), touch, or hearing (which may be distorted by partial or unilateral deafness). Physical space as experienced by an individual is that space which has the greatest commonality with the spaces presented by all his sense modalities.

1.2 Conceptual or abstracted spaces   Scientific observers often view living systems as existing in spaces which they conceptualize or abstract from the phenomena with which they deal. Examples of such spaces are: (*a*) Peck order in birds or other animals. (*b*) Social class space, in which Warner locates six social classes (lower lower, upper lower, lower middle, upper middle, lower upper, and upper upper classes). (*c*) Social distance among ethnic or racial groups. (*d*) Political distance among political parties of the Right and the Left. (*e*) The life space of Lewin, environment as seen by the subject, including the field forces or valences between him and objects in the environment, which can account for his immediately subsequent behavior (see page 434). (*f*) Osgood's semantic space as determined by subjects' ratings of words on the semantic differential test (see page 406). (*g*) Sociometric space, *e.g.*, the rating on a scale of leadership ability of each member of a group by every other member (see pages 537 and 538). (*h*) A space of time costs of various modes of transportation, *e.g.*, travel taking longer on foot than by air, longer upstream than

down. (*i*) A space representing the shortest distances for messages to travel among various points on a telephone network. These may not be the same as the distances among those points in physical space. (*j*) A space of frequency of trade relations among nations. (*k*) A space of frequency of intermarriage among ethnic groups.

These conceptual and abstracted spaces do not have the same characteristics and are not subject to the same constraints as physical space. Each has characteristics and constraints of its own. These spaces may be either conceived of by a human being or learned about from others. Interpreting the meaning of such spaces, observing relations, and measuring distances in them ordinarily require human observers. Consequently the biases of individual human beings color these observations. Perhaps pattern-recognition computer programs can someday be written to make such observations with more objective precision.

Social and some biological scientists find conceptual or abstracted spaces useful because they recognize that physical space is not a major determinant of certain processes in the living systems they study. For example, no matter where they enter the body, most of the iodine atoms in the body accumulate in the thyroid gland. The most frequent interpersonal relations occur among persons of like interests or like attitudes rather than among geographical neighbors. Families frequently come together for holidays no matter how far apart their members are. Allies like England and Australia are often more distant from each other in physical space than they are from their enemies.

Scientists who make observations and measurements in any space other than physical space should attempt to indicate precisely what the transformations are from their space to physical space. Other spaces are definitely useful to science, but physical space is the only common space in which all concrete systems exist. A scientist who makes observations and measurements in another space, which he or someone else has conceptualized, is developing a special theory. At the same time, however, he is fractionating science unless he or someone else makes an effort to indicate the relationship of the space he is working in to physical space or to some other conceptual or abstracted spaces. Any transformation of one space to another is worth carrying out, and science will not be complete and unitary until transformations can be made from any given space to any other.[1] One can, of course, conceive of spaces that cannot be transformed to other spaces, but it seems unlikely that they will apply to systems in physical space.

Not knowing at the moment how to carry out the transformation from the space one is making observations in to another space does not prevent one from conducting profitable studies. Many useful observations about heat were made in the space of degrees of temperature before the transformation from that space to the other spaces of the centimeter-gram-second system were known.

Any scientific observations about a designated space which cannot be transformed to other spaces concern a special theory. A general theory such as I shall develop here, however, requires that observations be made in a common space or in different spaces with known transformations. This is essential because one cannot measure comparable processes at different levels of systems, to confirm or disconfirm cross-level hypotheses, unless one can measure different levels of systems or dimensions in the same spaces or in different spaces with known transformations among them (see Sections 2 and 3 below and page 91). It must be possible, moreover, to make such measurements precisely enough to demonstrate whether or not there is a formal identity (see page 27) across levels.

1.3 Time   This is the fundamental "fourth dimension" of the physical space-time continuum. *Time* is the particular instant at which a structure exists or a process occurs, or the measured or measurable period over which a structure endures or a process continues. For the study of all aspects of living systems as we now know them, for the measurement of durations, speeds, rates, and accelerations, the usual absolute scales of time—seconds, minutes, days, years—are adequate. The modern general theory of relativity, however, makes it clear that, particularly in the very large systems studied in astronomy, time cannot be accurately measured on any absolute scale of succession of events. Its measurement differs with the special reference frame of each particular observer, who has his own particular "clock." A concrete system can move in any direction on the spatial dimensions, but only forward—never backward—on the temporal dimension. The irreversible unidirectionality of time is related to the second law of thermodynamics (see page 13); a system tends to increase in entropy over time. Without new inputs higher in negentropy to the system, this process cannot be reversed in that system, and such inputs always increase the entropy outside the system. This principle has often been referred to as "time's arrow." It points only one way.[2]

2. Matter and energy

Matter is anything which has mass (m) and occupies physical space. *Energy* (E) is defined in physics as the ability to do work. The principle of the conservation of energy states that energy can be neither created nor destroyed in the universe, but it may be converted from one form to another, including the energy equiv-

alent of rest mass. Matter may have (*a*) *kinetic* energy, when it is moving and exerts a force on other matter; (*b*) *potential* energy, because of its position in a gravitational field; or (*c*) *rest mass* energy, which is the energy that would be released if mass were converted into energy. Mass and energy are equivalent. One can be converted into the other in accordance with the relation that rest mass energy is equal to the mass times the square of the velocity of light. Because of the known relationship between matter and energy, throughout this chapter I use the joint term *matter-energy* except where one or the other is specifically intended. Living systems need specific types of matter-energy in adequate amounts. Heat, light, water, minerals, vitamins, foods, fuels, and raw materials of various kinds, for instance, may be required. Energy for the processes of living systems is derived from the breakdown of molecules (and, in a few recent cases in social systems, of atoms as well). Any change of state of matter-energy or its movement over space, from one point to another, I shall call *action*. It is one form of process. (The term "action" is here used as in biology and behavioral science rather than as in physics.)

3. Information

Throughout this presentation *information* (*H*) will be used in the technical sense first suggested by Hartley[3] in 1928, and later developed by Shannon[4] in his mathematical theory of communication. It is not the same thing as meaning or quite the same as information as we usually understand it. *Meaning* is the significance of information to a system which processes it: it constitutes a change in that system's processes elicited by the information, often resulting from associations made to it on previous experience with it. *Information* is a simpler concept: the degrees of freedom that exist in a given situation to choose among signals, symbols, messages, or patterns to be transmitted. The set of all these possible categories (the alphabet) is called the *ensemble* or *repertoire*. The amount of information is measured as the logarithm to the base 2 of the number of alternate patterns, forms, organizations, or messages. (When $m^x = y$, then x is referred to as the logarithm of y to the base m.) The unit is the binary digit, or *bit* of information. It is the amount of information which relieves the uncertainty when the outcome of a situation with two equally likely alternatives is known. Legend says the American Revolution was begun by a signal to Paul Revere from Old North Church steeple. It could have been either one or two lights "one if by land or two if by sea." If the alternatives were equally probable, the signal conveyed only one bit of information, resolving the uncertainty in a binary choice. But it carried a vast amount of meaning, meaning which must be measured by other sorts of units than bits. Signals convey information to the receiving system only if they do not duplicate information already in the receiver. As Gabor says:

Incomplete knowledge of the future, and also of the past of the transmitter from which the future might be constructed, is at the very basis of the concept of information. On the other hand, complete ignorance also precludes communication; a common language is required, that is to say an agreement between the transmitter and the receiver regarding the elements used in the communication process. . . . [The information of a message can] be defined as the 'minimum number of binary decisions which enable the receiver to construct the message, on the basis of the data already available to him.' These data comprise both the convention regarding the symbols and the language used, and the knowledge available at the moment when the message started.[5]

In many ways it is less useful to measure the amount of information than the amount of meaning. In later chapters, however, I reluctantly deal more with measurement of the amount of information than of meaning because as yet meaning cannot be precisely measured. Development of a rigorous and objective method for quantifying meaning would be a major contribution to the science of living systems.

Information is the negative of uncertainty. It is not accidental that the word "form" appears in "information," since information is the amount of formal patterning or complexity in any system.[6] Information theory is a set of concepts, theorems, and measures that were first developed by Shannon for communication engineering and have been extended to other, quite different fields, including theory of organization[7] and theory of music.[8] When all the assumptions about the situation and all its parameters are precisely stated, the amount of information can be rigorously measured in the structure and process of all sorts of living systems greatly different though they are.

The term *marker* was used by von Neumann to refer to those observable bundles, units, or changes of matter-energy whose patterning bears or conveys the informational symbols from the ensemble or repertoire.[9] These might be the stones of Hammurabi's day which bore cuneiform writing, parchments, writing paper, Indians' smoke signals, a door key with notches, punched cards, paper or magnetic tape, a computer's magnetized ferrite core memory, an arrangement of nucleotides in a DNA molecule, the molecular structure of a hormone, pulses on a telegraph wire, or waves emanating from a radio station. If a marker can assume n different states of which only one is present at any given time, it can represent at most $\log_2 n$ bits of information. The marker may be

static, as in a book or in a computer's memory. *Communication* of almost every sort requires that the marker move in space, from the transmitting system to the receiving system, and this movement follows the same physical laws as the movement of any other sort of matter-energy. The advance of communication technology over the years has been in the direction of decreasing the matter-energy costs of storing and transmitting the markers which bear information. The efficiency of information processing can be increased by lessening the mass of the markers, making them smaller so they can be stored more compactly and transmitted more rapidly and cheaply. Over the centuries engineering progress has altered the mode in markers from stones bearing cuneiform to magnetic tape bearing electrons, and clearly some limit is being approached. Cuneiform tablets carried approximately of the order of 10^{-2} bits of information per gram; paper with typewritten messages carries approximately of the order of 10^3 bits of information per gram; electronic magnetic tape storage carries approximately of the order of 10^6 bits of information per gram; and it has been demonstrated that one can write with microbeams, through a demagnifying electron microscope on ultrafine grain films of silver halide in letters so small that they could store the content of more than a million books on a few cubic centimeters of tape, about 10^{12} bits per gram.[10]

The mass of the matter-energy which makes up a system's markers significantly affects its information processing. On the basis of quantum-mechanical considerations, Bremermann has estimated the minimum amount of energy that can serve as a marker.[11] On the basis of this estimate he concluded that no system, living or nonliving, can process information at a rate greater than 2×10^{47} bits per second per gram of its mass. Suppose that the age of the earth is about 10^9 or 10^{10} years and its mass is less than 6×10^{27} g. A system the size of the earth, then, could process no more than 10^{93} bits of information in a period equal to the age of the earth. This is true even if the whole system is devoted to processing information, which never happens. It becomes clear that the minimum possible size of a marker is an important constraint on the capacity of living systems when one considers Minsky's demonstration that the number of all possible sequences of moves in a single chess game is about 10^{120}.[12] Thus no earthly system, living or nonliving, could exhaustively review this many alternatives in playing a game. The human retina certainly can see more than a matrix of 100×100 spots, yet a matrix of this size can form 10^{3000} possible patterns. There are, therefore, important practical matter-energy constraints upon the information processing of all living systems exerted by the nature of the matter-energy which composes their markers.

According to Quastler, information measures can be used to evaluate any kind of organization, since organization is based upon the interrelations among parts.[13] If two parts are interrelated either quantitatively or qualitatively, knowledge of the state of one must yield some information about the state of the other. Information measures can demonstrate when such relationships exist.

The antecedents of the information concepts include the early work related to thermodynamics of Maxwell,[14] Planck,[15] Boltzmann and Nabl,[16] Helmholtz,[17] and Gibbs.[18] Gibbs formulated the law of the degradation of energy, or the second law of thermodynamics. It states that thermodynamic degradation is irrevocable over time: *e.g.*, a burned log cannot be unburned. This law states that "even though there is an equivalence between a certain amount of work and a certain amount of heat, yet in any cyclic process, where a system is restored to its original state, there can never be a net conversion of heat into work, but the reverse is always possible." That is, one cannot convert an amount of heat into its equivalent amount of work, without other changes taking place in the system. These changes, expressed statistically, constitute a passing of the system from ordered arrangement into more chaotic or random distribution. The disorder, disorganization, lack of patterning, or randomness of organization of a system is known as its *entropy (S)*. It is the amount of progress of a system from improbable to probable states. The unit in which it is measured empirically is ergs or joules per degree absolute.

It was noted by Wiener[19] and by Shannon[20] that the statistical measure for the negative of entropy is the same as that for information, which Schrödinger[21] has called "negentropy." Discussing this relationship Rapoport says:

In classical thermodynamics, entropy was expressed in terms of the heat and the temperature of the system. With the advent of the kinetic theory of matter, an entirely new approach to thermodynamics was developed. Temperature and heat are now pictured in terms of the kinetic energy of the molecules comprising the system, and entropy becomes a measure of the *probability* that the velocities of the molecules and other variables of a system are distributed in a certain way. The reason the entropy of a system is greatest when its temperature is constant throughout is because this distribution of temperatures is the *most probable*. Increase of entropy was thus interpreted as the passage of a system from less probable to more probable states.

A similar process occurs when we shuffle a deck of cards. If we start with an orderly arrangement, say the cards of all the suits following each other according to their value, the shuffling will tend to make the arrangement disorderly. But if we start with a disorderly arrangement, it is very unlikely that through shuffling the cards will come into an orderly one.[22]

One evening in Puerto Rico I observed a concrete illustration of how information decreases as entropy progresses. Epiphany was being celebrated according to Spanish custom. On the buffet table of a large hotel stood a marvelous carving of the three kings with their camels, all done in clear ice. As the warm evening went on, they gradually melted, losing their precise patterning or information as entropy increased. By the end of the evening the camels' humps were nearly gone and the wise men were almost beardless.

Since, according to the second law, a system tends to increase in entropy over time, it must tend to decrease in negentropy or information. There is therefore no principle of the conservation of information as there are principles of the conservation of matter and energy. The total information can be decreased in any system without increasing it elsewhere, but it cannot be increased without decreasing it elsewhere. Making one or more copies of a given informational pattern does not increase information overall, though it may increase the information in the system which receives the copied information. Writing an original poem or painting a new picture or composing a new concerto does not create information overall, but simply selects one of many possible patterns available to the medium. Creating or transmitting such patterns can have great influence on the processes in any receiver of the pattern, but this is an impact of the meaning in the pattern not the information itself. Of course the information must be transmitted for the meaning to be transmitted.

3.1 Information and entropy   At least three sorts of evidence suggest that the relationship between information and entropy is more than a formal identity based simply on similar statistical characteristics.

First, Szilard wrote a paper about Maxwell's sorting demon, which constituted a paradox for physicists since 1871.[23] This is a mythical being

. . . whose faculties are so sharpened that he can follow every molecule in its course, such a being whose attributes are still as essentially finite as our own, would be able to do what is at present impossible to us. . . . Now let us suppose that . . . a vessel is divided into two portions, A and B, by a division in which there is a small hole, and that a being, who can see the individual molecules, opens and closes this hole, so as to allow only the swifter molecules to pass from A to B, and only the slower ones to pass from B to A. He will thus, without expenditure of work, raise the temperature of B and lower that of A, in contradiction to the second law of thermodynamics.[24]

Szilard made important progress in resolving Maxwell's paradox by demonstrating that the demon transforms information into negative entropy. Using thermodynamics and quantum mechanics he calculated the minimum amount of energy required to transmit one bit of information, *i.e.*, the minimum marker. Comparable calculations of the smallest possible amount of energy used in observing one bit of information were carried out by Brillouin.[25] His work was based on the assertion that unless there is light the demon cannot "see" the molecules, and if that light is introduced into the system the entropy in it increases. This supports the second law. Like Szilard, Brillouin employed the statistics of thermodynamics and quantum mechanics. It is clear that he believed his work to apply both to microsystems and to macrosystems.[26]

Calculations of the amount of information in various inorganic and organic chemical compounds have been made by Valentinuzzi and Valentinuzzi.[27] They calculated that in order to organize one bit of information in a compound approximately 10^{-12} erg per bit is required. They suggested that such methods could be applied to calculations of the amount of information accumulated by living systems throughout growth.

Other relevant material can be found in a discussion by Foster, Rapoport, and Trucco[28] of work by Prigogine,[29] De Groot,[30] and others on an unresolved problem in thermodynamics of open systems. They turn their attention to the concept of Prigogine that in an open system (that is one in which both matter and energy can be exchanged with the environment) the rate of entropy production within the system, which is always positive, is minimized when the system is in a steady state.[31] This appears to be a straightforward generalization of the second law, but after studying certain electrical circuits they conclude that this theorem does not have complete generality, and that in systems with internal feedbacks (see page 37), internal entropy production is not always minimized when the system is in a stationary state. In other words, feedback couplings between the system parameters may cause marked changes in the rate of development of entropy. Thus it may be concluded that the "information flow" which is essential for this feedback markedly alters energy utilization and the rate of development of entropy, at least in some such special cases which involve feedback control. While the explanation of this is not clear, it suggests an important relationship between information and entropy.

The other evidence is the work of Pierce and Cutler, who calculated the minimum amount of energy used in transmitting one bit of information, the minimum marker, in macrosystems.[32] They arrived at the same value that Szilard[33] and Brillouin[34] independently derived for microsystems. In a communication channel with thermal noise the minimum value was calculated by Pierce and Cutler as 9.56×10^{-24} J per bit per K. At the body temperature of a human being

(37.0°C), for example, this would be 2.96×10^{-21} J per bit. Their approach to this question was to determine how much energy is required to overcome the thermal noise in a channel, which is the unpatterned, random motion of the particles in it. Thermal noise is referred to as "white" noise, that is all frequencies are equally represented in it up to the frequency of W cycles per second, W being its bandwidth. Also it is referred to as Gaussian, which means that if a large number of samples of it are taken, each of the 2W samples per second from it is uncorrelated and independent. Knowing N, the average energy of certain samples, does not help in predicting the energy of others. If $2WT$ (where T is a duration in time) is a large number of samples, however, the total energy of $2WT$ samples will be very close to $2WTN$. Noise has the statistical character of entropy. In auditory transmission this random motion of particles in channels is heard as noise, and in visual transmission, as in television, it is seen as "snow" on the screen.

The amount of this noise times the length of the channel determines the amount of energy required to increase the signal above the noise and transmit the information. Several factors must be taken into consideration:

Take, for example, a satellite which is sending information. First of all, there is the "housekeeping" energy required to hold the molecules of the system together and keep it operating, maintaining the transmissions along the channel. In a satellite this involves the energy in the atoms and that holding together the molecules, as well as the energy stored in the batteries which operate the transmitter, and so forth. Then the level of thermal noise in the channel must be considered. At lower temperatures this is less, so that less energy is required to transmit information over the noise. The energy expended around absolute zero is very much less. Therefore we must calculate the temperature of any channel above absolute zero and compute from this a factor by which to multiply the minimal amount of energy required to transmit information at absolute zero. Furthermore, another factor must be allowed for the lack of efficiency in whatever coding is used, the degree to which the code is less than optimal. By calculations of this sort, Shannon figured the upper and lower bounds of the error probability in decoding optimal codes for a continuous channel with an additive Gaussian noise and subject to an average power limitation at the transmitter.[35] Also transmitting systems ordinarily are not optimally efficient, achieving only a certain percentage of the highest possible efficiency. This means that they will need proportionately more energy to accomplish the transmission.

Of course the amount of energy actually required to transmit the information in the channel is a minute part of the total energy in the system, the "housekeeping energy" being by far the largest part of it. For this reason it seems almost irrelevant to compare the efficiency of various information processing systems by comparing the energies they require to transmit similar amounts of information. This can be done only in situations in which other factors accounting for more of the energy use can be held constant, or in which the parts of the system directly involved with the transmission are considered while all other parts are neglected. That is, such calculations may be important to one studying a single neuron, but when the whole brain or the entire body is considered, so many other "housekeeping" uses of energy appear that the slight changes in energy arising from information transmission may be unrecognizably small.

For such reasons information theorists tend to neglect the calculation of energy costs, so missing an important aspect of systems theory. In recent years systems theorists have been fascinated by the new ways to study and measure information flows, but matter-energy flows are equally important. Systems theory is more than information theory, since it must also deal with energetics—such matters as the muscular movements of people, the flow of raw materials through societies, or the utilization of energy by brain cells.

Only a minute fraction of the energy used by most living systems is employed for information processing. Nevertheless it may well be possible in specific experimental situations to determine rigorously the minimal amount of energy required to transmit one bit of information, and so to determine for such systems a constant relationship among measures of energy, entropy, and information.

I have noted above that the movement of matter-energy over space, *action*, is one form of process (see pages 11 and 70). Another form of process is information processing or *communication*, which is the change of information from one state to another (see pages 12 and 70) or its movement from one point to another over space.

Communications, while being processed, are often shifted from one matter-energy state to another, from one sort of marker to another. If the form or pattern of the signal remains relatively constant during these changes, the information is not lost. For instance, it is now possible to take a chest x-ray, storing the information on photographic film; then a photoscanner can pass over the film line by line, from top to bottom, converting the signals to pulses in an electrical current which represent bits; then those bits can be stored in the core memory of a computer; then those bits can be processed by the computer so that contrasts in the picture pattern can be systematically increased; then the resultant altered patterns can be displayed on a cathode-ray tube and photographed. The pattern of the chest structures, the information, modified for easier interpretation, has remained largely invariant throughout all this processing from one sort of marker to another. Similar transformations go on in living systems.

One basic reason why communication is of fundamental importance is that informational patterns can be processed over space and the local matter-energy at the receiving point can be organized to conform to, or comply with, this information. As I have already said, if the information is conveyed on a relatively small, light, and compact marker, little energy is required for this process. Thus it is a much more efficient way to accomplish the result than to move the entire amount of matter-energy, organized as desired, from the location of the transmitter to that of the receiver. This is the secret of success of the delivery of "flowers by telegraph." It takes much less time and human effort to send a telegram from London to Paris requesting a florist in the latter place to deliver flowers locally, than it would to drive or fly with the flowers from London to Paris.

Shannon was concerned with mathematical statements describing the transmission of information in the form of signals or messages from a sender to a receiver over a channel such as a telephone wire or a radio band.[36] These channels always contain a certain amount of noise. In order to convey a message, signals in channels must be patterned and must stand out recognizably above the background noise.

Matter-energy and information always flow together. Information is always borne on a marker. Conversely there is no regular movement in a system unless there is a difference in potential between two points, which is negative entropy or information. Which aspect of the transmission is most important depends upon how it is handled by the receiver. If the receiver responds primarily to the material or energic aspect, I shall call it, for brevity, a matter-energy transmission; if the response is primarily to the information, I shall call it an information transmission. For example, the banana eaten by a monkey is a nonrandom arrangement of specific molecules, and thus has its informational aspect, but its use to the monkey is chiefly to increase the energy available to him. So it is an energy transmission. The energic character of the signal light that tells him to depress the lever which will give him a banana is less important than the fact that the light is part of a nonrandom, patterned organization which conveys information to him. So it is an information transmission. Moreover, just as living systems must have specific forms of matter-energy, so they must have specific patterns of information. For example, some species of animals do not develop normally unless they have appropriate information inputs in infancy.[37] Monkeys cannot make proper social adjustment unless they interact with other monkeys during a period between the third and sixth months of their lives as Harlow showed.[38]

This treatment of the relationships of information and entropy can be epitomized by Table 2-1. It indi-

TABLE 2-1   Information versus Entropy

H	=	$-S$
Information		Uncertainty[39]
Negentropy		Entropy
Signal		Noise
Accuracy		Error
Form		Chaos
Regularity		Randomness
Pattern or form		Lack of pattern or formlessness
Order[40]		Disorder
Organization		Disorganization
Regular complexity		Irregular simplicity
Heterogeneity		Homogeneity
Improbability (Only one alternative correctly describes the form)		Probability (More than one alternative correctly describes the form)
Predictability (Only one alternative correctly describes the form)		Unpredictability (More than one alternative correctly describes the form)

cates that there are several pairs of antonyms used in this section, one member of which is associated with the concept of information (H) and the other member of which is associated with its negative, entropy (S). Some of these are precise, technical terms. Others are commonsense words which may be more vague. Noting that such terms as regularity, pattern, and order are listed in the column under information, one might ask if there is not less rather than more information in a system with highly redundant pattern, order, or regularity. The answer is that information about a small portion of such an arrangement provides much understanding of the total system, which is not true of an arrangement characterized by randomness, lack of pattern, or disorder.

4. System

The term *system* has a number of meanings. There are systems of numbers and of equations, systems of value and of thought, systems of law, solar systems,

organic systems, management systems, command and control systems, electronic systems, even the Union Pacific Railroad system. The meanings of "system" are often confused.[41] The most general, however, is: A *system* is a set of interacting units with relationships among them.[42] The word "set" implies that the units have some common properties. These common properties are essential if the units are to interact or have relationships. The state of each unit is constrained by, conditioned by, or dependent on the state of other units.[43] The units are coupled. Moreover, there is at least one measure of the sum of its units which is larger than the sum of that measure of its units.[44]

4.1   Conceptual system

4.1.1   Units   *Units* of a *conceptual system* are terms, such as words (commonly nouns, pronouns, and their modifiers), numbers, or other symbols, including those in computer simulations and programs.

4.1.2   Relationships   A *relationship* of a conceptual system is a set of pairs of units, each pair being ordered in a similar way. For example, the set of all pairs consisting of a number and its cube is the cubing relationship. Relationships are expressed by words (commonly verbs and their modifiers), or by logical or mathematical symbols, including those in computer simulations and programs, which represent operations, *e.g.*, inclusion, exclusion, identity, implication, equivalence, addition, subtraction, multiplication, or division. The language, symbols, or computer programs are all concepts and always exist in one or more concrete systems, living or nonliving (see pages 17 and 18). The conceptual systems of science exist in one or more scientific observers, theorists, experimenters, books, articles, and/or computers.

4.1.3   The observer   The *observer*, for his own purposes and on the basis of his own characteristics, selects, from an infinite number of units and relationships, particular sets to study.

4.1.4   Variable   Each member of such a set becomes a *variable* of the observer's conceptual system. He may select variables from the infinite number of units and relationships which exist in any concrete system or set of concrete systems, or on the other hand he may select variables which have no connection with any concrete system.[45] His conceptual system may be loose or precise, simple or elaborate.

4.1.5   Indicator   An *indicator* is an instrument or technique used to measure fluctuations of variables in concrete systems (see page 51).

4.1.6   Function   A *function* is a correspondence between two variables, x and y, such that for each value of x there is a definite value of y, and no two y's have the same x, and this correspondence is determined by some rule (*e.g.*, $x^2 = y$, $xn = y$, $x + 3 = y$). Any function is a simple conceptual system. Conceptual systems also may be very complex, involving many interrelated functions. This sense of "function" is the usual mathematical usage. In a concrete system this word has a different meaning (see page 23).

4.1.7 Parameter An independent variable through functions of which other functions may be expressed.

4.1.8 The state of a conceptual system This state is the set of values on some scale, numerical or otherwise, which its variables have at a given instant. This state may or may not change over time.

4.1.9 Formal identity One system may have one or more variables, each of which varies comparably to a variable in another system. If these comparable variations are so similar that they can be expressed by the same function, a *formal identity* exists between the two systems. If different functions are required to express the variations, there is a formal *disidentity*.

4.1.10 Relationships between conceptual and other sorts of systems A conceptual system may be purely logical or mathematical, or its terms and relationships may be intended to have some sort of formal identity or isomorphism with units and relationships empirically determinable by some operation carried out by an observer, which are selected observable variables in a concrete system or an abstracted system (see pages 19 and 20).[46] The observer selects the variables of his conceptual system. As to the many other variables in the concrete or abstracted system that are not isomorphic with the selected variables in his conceptual system, the observer may either (*a*) observe that they remain constant, or (*b*) operate on the concrete or abstracted system in order to ensure that they remain constant, or (*c*) "randomize them" *i.e.*, assume without proof that they remain constant, or (*d*) simply neglect them.

Science advances as the formal identity or isomorphism increases between a theoretical conceptual system and objective findings about concrete or abstracted systems.

The chief purpose of this book is to state in prose a conceptual system concerning variables—units and relationships—which have important formal identities or isomorphisms to concrete, living systems.

4.2 Concrete system A *concrete, real,* or *veridical system* is a nonrandom accumulation of matter-energy, in a region in physical space-time, which is organized into interacting interrelated subsystems or components.

4.2.1 Units The units (subsystems, components, parts, or members) of these systems are also concrete systems.[47]

4.2.2 Relationships Relationships in concrete systems are of various sorts, including spatial, temporal, spatiotemporal, and causal.

Both units and relationships in concrete systems are empirically determinable by some operation carried out by an observer. In theoretical verbal statements about concrete systems, nouns, pronouns, and their modifiers typically refer to concrete systems, subsystems, or components; verbs and their modifiers usually refer to the relationships among them. There are numerous examples, however, in which this usage is reversed and nouns refer to patterns of relationships or processes, such as "nerve impulse," "reflex," "action," "vote," or "annexation."

4.2.3 The observer of a concrete system The observer, according to Campbell, distinguishes a concrete system from unorganized entities in its environment by the following criteria: (*a*) physical proximity of its units; (*b*) similarity of its units; (*c*) common fate of its units; and (*d*) distinct or recognizable patterning of its units.[48]

He maintains that evolution has provided human observers with remarkable skill in using such criteria for rapidly distinguishing concrete systems. Their boundaries are discovered by empirical operations available to the general scientific community rather than set conceptually by a single observer.

4.2.4 Variable of a concrete system Any property of a unit or relationship within a system which can be recognized by an observer who chooses to attend to it, which can potentially change over time, and whose change can potentially be measured by specific operations, is a variable of a concrete system. Examples are the number of its subsystems or components, its size, its rate of movement in space, its rate of growth, the number of bits of information it can process per second, or the intensity of a sound to which it responds. A variable is intrasystemic, and is not to be confused with intersystemic variations which may be observed among individual systems, types, or levels.

4.2.5 The state of a concrete system The state of a concrete system at a given moment is its structure (see page 22). It is represented by the set of values on some scale which its variables have at that instant. This state always changes over time slowly or rapidly.

4.2.6 Open system Most concrete systems have boundaries which are at least partially permeable, permitting sizable magnitudes of at least certain sorts of matter-energy or information transmissions to cross them. Such a system is an *open system*. In open systems entropy may increase, remain in steady state, or decrease.

4.2.7 Closed system A concrete system with impermeable boundaries through which no matter-energy or information transmissions of any sort can occur is a *closed system*. This is a special case, in which inputs and outputs are zero, of the general case of open systems. No actual concrete system is completely closed, so concrete systems are either relatively open or relatively closed. In closed systems, entropy generally increases, exceptions being when certain reversible processes are carried on which do not increase it. It can never decrease. Whatever matter-energy happens to be within the system is all there is going to be, and it gradually becomes disordered. A body in a hermetically sealed casket, for instance, slowly crumbles and its component molecules become intermingled. Separate layers of liquid or gas in a container move toward random distribution. Gravity may prevent entirely random arrangement.

4.2.8 Nonliving system   Every concrete system which does not have the characteristics of a living system is a *nonliving system*. Nonliving systems constitute the general case of concrete systems, of which living systems are a very special case. Nonliving systems need not have the same critical subsystems (see page 1) as living systems, though they often have some of them.

4.2.9 Living system   The *living systems* are a special subset of the set of all possible concrete systems. They are composed of the monerans, protistans, fungi, plants, animals (see page 362), groups, organizations, societies, and supranational systems. They all have the following characteristics:

(*a*) They are open systems, with significant inputs, throughputs, and outputs of various sorts of matter-energy and information.

(*b*) They maintain a steady state of negentropy even though entropic changes occur in them as they do everywhere else. This they do by taking in inputs of foods or fuels, matter-energy higher in complexity or organization or negentropy, *i.e.*, lower in entropy, than their outputs. The difference permits them to restore their own energy and repair breakdowns in their own organized structure. Schrödinger said that "What an organism feeds upon is negative entropy."[49] In living systems many substances are produced as well as broken down; gradients are set up as well as destroyed; learning as well as forgetting occurs. To do this such systems must be open and have continual inputs of matter-energy and information. Walling off living systems to prevent exchanges across their boundaries results in what Brillouin calls "death by confinement."[50] Since the second law of thermodynamics is an arrow pointing along the one-way road of the inevitable forward movement which we call time (see page 11), entropy will always increase in walled-off living systems. The consequent disorganization

will ultimately result in the termination of the system, but the second law does not state the rate at which dissolution approaches. The rate might even be zero for a time; the second law has no time limit.

(*c*) They have more than a certain minimum degree of complexity (see page 204).

(*d*) They either contain genetic material composed of deoxyribonucleic acid (DNA), presumably descended from some primordial DNA common to all life, or have a charter. One of these is the template—the original "blueprint" or "program"—of their structure and process from the moment of their origin (see page 55).

(*e*) They are largely composed of an aqueous suspension of macromolecules, proteins constructed from about 20 amino acids and other characteristic organic compounds, and may also include nonliving components.

(*f*) They have a decider, the essential critical subsystem which controls the entire system, causing its subsystems and components to interact. Without such interaction under decider control there is no system (see pages 32 and 67).

(*g*) They also have certain other specific critical subsystems or they have symbiotic or parasitic relationships (see page 32) with other living or nonliving systems which carry out the processes of any such subsystem they lack.

(*h*) Their subsystems are integrated together to form actively self-regulating, developing, unitary systems with purposes and goals (see pages 39 to 41).

(*i*) They can exist only in a certain environment. Any change in their environment of such variables as temperature, air pressure, hydration, oxygen content of the atmosphere, or intensity of radiation, outside a relatively narrow range which occurs on the surface of the earth, produces stresses to which they cannot adjust (see page 35). Under such stresses they cannot survive.

4.2.10 Totipotential system   A living system which is capable of carrying out all critical subsystem processes necessary for life is *totipotential*. Some systems are totipotential only during certain periods of their existence. For instance, a chick at hatching cannot lay an egg, even though chickens are a precocious species that can take care of themselves as soon as they hatch. The chick, therefore, should not be called totipotential until it has matured to henhood and its reproducer subsystem is functional.

4.2.11 Partipotential system   A living system which does not itself carry out all critical subsystem processes is *partipotential*. It is a special case of which the totipotential system is the general case. A partipotential system must interact with other systems that can carry out the processes which it does not, or it will not survive. To supply the missing processes, partipotential systems must be parasitic on or symbiotic with other living or nonliving systems.

4.2.12 Fully functioning system A system is *fully functioning* when it is carrying out all the processes of which it is capable.

4.2.13 Partially functioning system A system is *partially functioning* when it is carrying out only some of the processes of which it is capable. If it is not carrying out all the critical subsystem processes, it cannot survive, unless it is parasitic on or symbiotic with some other system which supplies the other processes. Furthermore it must do its own deciding, or it is not a system.

4.3 Abstracted system

4.3.1 Units The units of *abstracted systems* are relationships abstracted or selected by an observer in the light of his interests, theoretical viewpoint, or philosophical bias. Some relationships may be empirically determinable by some operation carried out by the observer, but others are not, being only his concepts.

4.3.2 Relationships The relationships mentioned above are observed to inhere and interact in concrete, usually living, systems. In a sense, then, these concrete systems are the relationships of abstracted systems. The verbal usages of theoretical statements concerning abstracted systems are often the reverse of those concerning concrete systems: the nouns and their modifiers typically refer to relationships and the verbs and their modifiers (including predicates) to the concrete systems in which these relationships inhere and interact. These concrete systems are empirically determinable by some operation carried out by the observer. A theoretical statement oriented to concrete systems typically would say, "Lincoln was President," but one oriented to abstracted systems, concentrating on relationships or roles, would very likely be phrased, "The Presidency was occupied by Lincoln."[51]

An abstracted system differs from an *abstraction*, which is a concept (like those that make up conceptual systems) representing a class of phenomena all of which are considered to have some similar "class characteristic." The members of such a class are not thought to interact or be interrelated, as are the relationships in an abstracted system.

Abstracted systems are much more common in social science theory than in natural science.

Since abstracted systems usually are oriented toward relationships rather than toward the concrete systems which have those relationships, spatial arrangements are not usually emphasized. Consequently their physical limits often do not coincide spatially with the boundaries of any concrete system, although they may. Speaking of system hierarchies, Simon says:

There is one important difference between the physical and biological hierarchies, on the one hand, and social hierarchies, on the other. Most physical and biological hierarchies are described in spatial terms. We detect the organelles in a cell in the way we detect the raisins in the cake—they are 'visibly' differentiated substructures localized spatially in the larger structure. On the other hand, we propose to identify social hierarchies not by observing who lives close to whom but by observing who interacts with whom. These two points of view can be reconciled by defining hierarchy in terms of intensity of interaction, but observing that in most biological and physical systems relatively intense interaction implies relative spatial propinquity. One of the interesting characteristics of nerve cells and telephone wires is that they permit very specific strong interactions at great distances. To the extent that interactions are channeled through specialized communications and transportation systems, spatial propinquity becomes less determinative of structure.[52]

There are other reasons why abstracted systems are sometimes preferred to concrete. Functionalists may resist the use of space-time coordinates because they seem static. But one must have such coordinates in order to observe and measure process. Subjectivists may resist such coordinates because their private experience does not seem to be presented to them in external space-time. But where else do their inputs arise from?

Parsons has attempted to develop general behavior theory using abstracted systems.[53] An interesting colloquy at a conference on unified theory conducted by Grinker spells out ways in which a theory developed around abstracted systems differs from one using concrete systems. Ruesch, Parsons, and Rapoport are speaking:[54]

RUESCH: Previously I defined culture as the cumulative body of knowledge of the past, contained in memories and assumptions of people who express this knowledge in definite ways. The social system is the actual habitual network of communication between people. If you use the analogy of the telephone line, it corresponds to actual calls made. The society is the network—the whole telephone network. Do you agree with these definitions?[55]

PARSONS: No, not quite. In the limiting conception a society is composed of human individuals, organisms; but a social system is not, and for a very important reason, namely, that the unit of a partial social system is a role and not the individual.

RAPOPORT: The monarch is not an individual, but is a site into which different individuals step. Is that your unit of the social system?

PARSONS: Yes. A social system is a behavioral system. It is an organized set of behaviors of persons interacting with each other: a pattern of roles. The roles are the units of a social system. We say, 'John Jones is Mary Jones' husband.' He is the same person who is the mail carrier, but when we are talking about the mail carrier we are abstracting from his marriage relationship. So the mail carrier is not a person, just a role. On the other hand, the society is an aggregate of social subsystems, and as a limiting case it is that social system which comprises all the roles of all the individuals who participate.

What Ruesch calls the social system is something concrete in space-time, observable and presumably measurable by techniques like those of natural science. To Parsons the system is abstracted from this, being the set of relationships which are the form of organization. To him the important units are classes of input–output relationships of subsystems rather than the subsystems themselves.

Grinker accurately described this fundamental, but not irresolvable, divergence when he made the following comment:

Parsons stated that . . . [action] is not concerned with the internal structure of processes of the organism, but is concerned with the organism as a unit in a set of relationships and the other terms of that relationship, which he calls situation. From this point of view the system is a system of relationship in action, it is neither a physical organism nor an object of physical perception. On the other hand, some of us consider that the foci or systems which are identified in a living field must be considered as being derived through evolution, differentiation and growth from earlier and simpler forms and functions and that within these systems there are capacities for specializations and gradients. Sets of relationships among dimensions constitute a high level of generalization that can be more easily understood if the physical properties of its component parts and their origins and ontogenetic properties are known.[56]

4.4 Abstracted versus concrete systems   One fundamental distinction between abstracted and concrete systems is that the boundaries of abstracted systems may at times be conceptually established at regions which cut through the units and relationships in the physical space occupied by concrete systems, but the boundaries of these latter systems are always set at regions which include within them all the units and internal relationships of each system. To some it may appear that another distinction between concrete and abstracted systems is something like the difference between saying "A has the property r" and saying "r is a property of A."[57] This translation is logically trivial. In empirical science, however, there can be an important difference between discovering that A has the property r and finding an A which has the property r.

It is possible to assert connections in abstracted systems among all sorts of entities, like or unlike, near together or far apart, with or without access to each other in space—even Grandpa's moustache, Japanese haiku poetry, and the Brooklyn Bridge—depending upon the particular needs of a given project. How and

why this is done will determine whether the results are trivial, like a sort of intellectual "Rube Goldberg apparatus," or whether they are functional.

A science of abstracted systems certainly is possible and under some conditions may be useful. When Euclid was developing geometry, with its practical applications to the arrangement of Egyptian real estate, it is probable that the solid lines in his figures were originally conceived to represent the borders of land areas or objects. Sometimes, as in Fig. 2-1, he

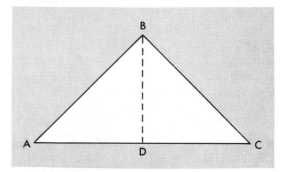

Fig. 2-1 A Euclidean figure.

would use dotted "construction lines" to help conceptualize a geometric proof. The dotted line did not correspond to any actual border in space. Triangle ABD could be shown to be congruent to triangle CBD, and therefore the angle BAD could be proved to equal the angle BCD. After the proof was completed, the dotted line might well be erased, since it did not correspond to anything real and was useful only for the proof. Such construction lines, representing relationships among real lines, were used in the creation of early forms of abstracted systems.

If the diverse fields of science are to be unified, it would help if all disciplines were oriented either to concrete or to abstracted systems. It is of paramount importance for scientists to distinguish clearly between them. To use both kinds of systems in theory leads to unnecessary problems. It would be best if one type of system or the other were generally used in all disciplines. Past tradition is not enough excuse for continuing to use both. Since one can conceive of relationships between any concrete system and any other, one can conceive of many abstracted systems which do not correspond to any reality. The existence of such systems is often asserted in science, and empirical studies frequently show there really are no such systems.

Confusion of abstracted and concrete systems has resulted in the contention that the concept of system is logically empty because one cannot think of anything or any collection of things which could not be regarded as a system.[58] What is *not* a concrete system? Any set of subsystems or components in space-time which do not interact, which do not have relationships in terms of the variables under consideration, is not a concrete system. Physicists call it a *heap*. My heart and your stomach, together, are not a concrete system; the arrangements of cells in your fingernails and in your brown felt hat are not a concrete system; the light streaming through my study window and the music floating out from my stereo are not a concrete system. All the coal miners in Wales were not a concrete system until they were organized into an intercommunicating, interacting trade union. Sherlock Holmes did not assume that red-haired men in general were a concrete system, but when he got evidence that some of them were interacting, he deduced the existence of an organized Red-Headed League.

When abstracted systems are used it is essential that they be distinguished from abstractions. Is "culture" an abstraction, the class of all stored and current items of information which are shared in common by certain individuals who are members of a group, organization, society, or supranational system, as revealed by similarities of those persons' customary behavior or of their artifacts—art objects, language, or writings?[59] Or does the term culture imply interactions among those items of information, so representing an abstracted system? Or, to take another example, is an individual's "personality" merely a class of traits as represented by repeated similar acts, gestures, and language of a person, or does it imply interactions among these traits, which would be an abstracted system? Terms like culture or personality can be useful in behavioral science to refer to commonalities among people or among characteristics of a single person, but they must be used unambiguously as *either* an abstraction *or* an abstracted system.

No scientist, in social science or any field, will change his traditional procedures without reason. There are, however, a number of simple, down-to-earth practical reasons why theorists should focus upon concrete systems rather than abstracted systems, as Etzioni has suggested.[60]

(*a*) In the first place concrete systems theory is easier to understand. Our sense organs reify, distinguishing objects from their environment (see pages 134 to 139). Since childhood concrete objects ("mamma," "cup") have been the nouns of most of our sentences, and words representing relationships or changes in relations ("loves," "runs") have been the verbs. We are used to seeing the world as a collection of concrete objects in space-time, and these objects naturally draw our attention. Relationships are less obvious. Abstracted systems oriented toward relationships are unnecessarily complicated for our ordinary thinking processes. We are used to putting things into the framework of space and time. It helps us orient them accurately to other things. Movies which jump around in time puzzle us. We are confused when the action of a novel or play skips about in space from one place to another. For general theory embracing biological and social aspects of life and behavior, conceptualizations referring to concrete systems in space-time enable us to profit from a lifetime of experience in thinking that way. Abstracted systems are usually at best inconvenient and clumsy conceptual tools. Spatial propinquity or accessibility to information transmitted over physical channels is essential for all social interactions, except those based on mutual agreements remembered from past interactions. Even then, spatial contact in the past is essential. Spatial orientation, therefore, is important, for both biological and social science: (1) It is a significant fact about cellular function that deoxyribonucleic acid (DNA) is found only in a cell's nucleus and some other organelles (see pages 224 and 228). (2) The location of pain sensory tracts near the central canal of the human spinal cord explains why pain sensation is halted, in the bodily regions to which those tracts lead, when the disease process of syringomyelia widens the central canal until it transects the tracts. (3) The wings of the ostrich are of inadequate size to carry its large weight, so it must run rather than fly. (4) That the spatial positions of jury members around the table significantly affected their behaviors (see pages 559 and 560) was shown by Stodtbeck and Hook.[61] (5) The groups which make up organizations interact most frequently and most effectively when they are close together in space. Differences in proximity of houses in two Costa Rican villages were found by Powell to be associated with differences between the two villages in the frequency of visiting among families.[62] In the village in which the houses were close to each other, 53 percent of the visiting occurred daily; in the more open village only 34 percent was daily. (6) It is well recognized by sociologists, economists, and political scientists that many sorts of behaviors differ in rural regions and in urban areas. (7) International relations are often affected by the spatial locations and geographical characteristics of nations and the relationships of their land masses, their bodies of water, and the seas around them. The histories of the Panama Canal or the Suez Canal, of Switzerland or Cyprus attest to such geopolitical factors.

(b) Variations in the units of systems appear to contribute as much more to the total variance in the systems than variations in their relationships, although of course the total system variance arises from both, plus interactions between the two. Any cell in a given location at a given time, any ruler of a given nation in a given period, receives comparable matter-energy and information inputs. But they may act quite differently. If their inputs or relationships vary, of course their actions vary. Process of systems is explained only when we take account of both units and relationships of cells and the internal environment around them, of the leader and the *Zeitgeist*.[63]

(c) Theory which deals with concrete systems avoids two common sorts of confusion. One is the confusion of conceptualizations which seem to assume that information can be transmitted from system to system without markers to bear it. The other is the confusion of some social science theories which appear to assume that actions, roles, or relationships carry on a life of their own, independent of other aspects of the people or other concrete systems whose processes they are. When the head of a brokerage firm, who is also a Sunday school teacher, in his role as chairman of the board connives with the bookkeeper in an embezzlement, the chairman takes the Sunday school teacher right along with him into jail. They are aspects of the process of a concrete system in a suprasystem.

(d) If a surgeon does not cut along planes of cleavage, he may become confused about spatial relations as he gets farther and farther into a region like, for instance, the pelvis. Not only is it harder for him to reconstruct firm muscles when he sews up again, but it is more difficult for him to conceptualize the relationship between different structures. Behavioral scientists, if they deal with abstracted systems and establish their own conceptual boundaries which cut across concrete systems, easily forget the intrasystem relationships in concrete systems which influence processes within and among those systems. Consequently their understanding of the phenomena they study is often incomplete and inaccurate.

(e) If the social sciences were to formulate their problems, whenever possible, in the way which has proved most convenient for the natural sciences over centuries, unification of all the sciences would be accelerated.

4.5 Abstracted versus conceptual systems Because some of the relationships in abstracted systems are selected by scientific observers, theorists, and/or experimentalists, it is possible that they might be confused with conceptual systems, since both units and relationships of conceptual systems are so

selected. The two kinds of systems differ in that some units and/or relationships of every abstracted system are empirically determined and this is not true of any conceptual system.

All three meanings of "system" are useful in science, but confusion results when they are not differentiated. A scientific endeavor may appropriately begin with a conceptual system and evaluate it by collecting data on a concrete or on an abstracted system, or it may equally well first collect the data and then determine what conceptual system they fit. Throughout this book the single word system, for brevity, will always mean "concrete system." The other sorts of systems will always be explicitly distinguished as either "conceptual system" or "abstracted system."

5. Structure

The *structure* of a system is the arrangement of its subsystems and components in three-dimensional space at a given moment of time.[64] This always changes over time. It may remain relatively fixed for a long period or it may change from moment to moment, depending upon the characteristics of the process in the system. This process halted at any given moment, as when motion is frozen by a high-speed photograph, reveals the three-dimensional spatial arrangement of the system's components as of that instant. For example, when anatomists investigate the configuration of the lobules of the liver, they study dead, often fixed, material in which no further activity can be expected to occur. Similarly geographers may study the locations of the populations in the cities of China and its interconnecting routes of travel in the year 1850. These are studies of structure. Time slices at a given moment reveal spatial relations, but they do not indicate other aspects of the system. For instance, they may show the positions of molecules but not their momenta, or the locations of members of a group but not their attractiveness to one another. Measures of these other aspects must be represented on the dimensions of other spaces, just as physicists may represent the locations of particles in three of the six dimensions of "phase space" and their forces or momenta in the other three.

When systems survive, maintaining steady states over prolonged periods, their structures are stable. Consequently the concept of *stability* is often confused with the concept of structure. Structure, of course, is easier to observe if it is stable, but the spatial organization of a system's parts is its structure whether it changes slowly or rapidly. Anyone can define slowly changing process as "structure" and rapidly changing process as "function," but when he does so he is using "structure" in a different sense than its most frequent usage in common speech or in natural science. These two quite separate meanings must not be confused. It is also vital to distinguish my use of the word structure from another scientific usage of the term to mean *generalized patterning*. This definition, which recognizes that information and structure are connected, states that the latter is an entire set of relations, as indicated by a form of nonmetric correlation, among any group of variables.[65] This usage makes it possible to speak of the "structure of French," the "structure of music" or the "structure of a nerve impulse"—conceptual patterns or patterns in time—as well as the "structure of a crystal" or the "structure of the pelvis"—patterns in space. It is a contribution to science to recognize that there is patterning among conceptual or temporal variables which is comparable to patterning among spatial variables. Indeed, spatial variables can be transformed to temporal, or vice versa, as when one plays a piano roll with a configuration of holes on a player piano, or when one records a dance in choreographic notation.

For empirical science, however, the distinctions between spatial and temporal dimensions, between physical space and conceptual spaces, must be maintained, and my definition of structure does so. The word is not used to mean stability, or to mean generalized patterning among *any* set of variables. It refers only to arrangements of components or subsystems in three-dimensional space.

6. Process

All change over time of matter-energy or information in a system is *process*. If the equation describing a process is the same no matter whether the temporal variable is positive or negative, it is a *reversible* process; otherwise it is *irreversible*, or better, less readily reversible. At least three sequential time slices of structure must be compared before reversible and irreversible or less readily reversible processes can be distinguished. Process includes the ongoing *function* of a system, reversible actions succeeding each other from moment to moment. This usage should not be confused with the mathematical usage of function defined earlier (see page 16). Process also includes *history*, less readily reversed changes like mutations, birth, growth, development, aging, and death; changes which commonly follow trauma or disease; and changes resulting from learning which are not later forgotten. Historical processes alter both the structure and the function of the system. I have said "less readily reversed" instead of "irreversible" (although many such changes are in fact irreversible) because structural changes sometimes can be reversed: a com-

ponent which has developed and functioned may atrophy and finally disappear with disuse; a functioning part may be chopped off a hydra and regrow. History, then, is more than the passage of time. It involves also accumulation in the system of residues or effects of past events (structural changes, memories, and learned habits). A living system carries its history with it in the form of altered structure, and consequently of altered function also. So there is a circular relation among the three primary aspects of systems—structure changes momentarily with functioning, but when such change is so great that it is essentially irreversible, a historical process has occurred, giving rise to a new structure.[66]

I have differentiated carefully between structure and process, but often this is not done. Leighton has shown that the meanings of structure and function (or process) are not always clearly distinguished. He contends that what is meant by structure in the study of societies is what is ordinarily called function in the study of bodily organs. He lists components of a sociocultural unit like a town as:[67] "family, including extended families; neighborhoods; associations; friendship groups; occupational associations; institutions such as those concerned with industry, religion, government, recreation, and health; cultural systems; socioeconomic classes; and finally societal roles." In my terminology not all of these are structural components. Some are abstractions about classes of processes, relationships, or abstracted systems.

Leighton says:

Components such as these and their arrangement in relation to each other are often called 'structure' by sociologists and anthropologists. This usage of the term parallels that of psychiatrists and psychologists when they speak of the 'structure' of personality in referring to the relationships of such components as the id, ego, and superego. In both instances the word means process. It stands for patterned events which tend to occur and recur with a certain amount of regularity. Hence, when one says that the structure of a community or a personality has such and such characteristics, he is, in effect, talking about an aspect of function.

It seems to me that 'structure' as a term can be troublesome when one is trying to grasp and analyze the nature of sociocultural and psychological phenomena. This is probably not the case with those authors whose names are associated with the term, but in my experience it does confuse people new to the field, especially those from other disciplines trying to master the concepts and develop an understanding of both personality and sociocultural processes. Hence some impressions on the reasons for these difficulties may be worth recording.

The meaning attributed to 'structure' by sociologists, anthropologists, psychologists, and psychiatrists is one that is limited, denotative, and reasonably clear. Trouble arises from the fact that connotative meanings are carried over from other contexts in which the word has markedly different significance. For example, the usage with reference to personality and society is dynamic, while in anatomy, in architecture, and in many everyday contexts the word refers to the static aspect of things. A structure is not something which keeps coming back in a regular flow of movement like a figure in a dance; it is something which just sits there like a chair.

Another and more important connotation is that of substance. The overwhelming force of the word in everyday usage is of an entity which can be seen and felt. It is—relative to other experiences in living—something directly available to the senses. This common meaning is also found in many sciences, particularly biology. When one speaks of the structure of the heart he is talking about visible-palpable substance, not the rhythmical contractions. The latter are an aspect of its functioning. Yet it is precisely the analogue in behavior of these contractions, this regular functional process, that is meant when one speaks of 'structure' in a society. The brain offers another example. Its 'structure' consists in the arrangements that can be seen with and without the aid of instruments such as the microscope—cerebellum, medulla oblongata, layers of the cortex, and so on. The recurrent electrical events called brain waves are not considered structure, but rather a manifestation of functioning. Again, however, they are the kind of phenomena which in discussions of society are called 'structure.' The closest analogue in the community of the anatomical use of 'structure' is the arrangement of streets, houses, and other buildings.

A further point is this: in common terms, and also in biology, 'structure' is for the most part a *description* of observed nature, whereas in discussions of personality and society it is usually an *inference from* observed nature. No one, for instance, has ever seen a class system in the same sense in which the layers of the body can be seen—skin, fascia, muscles, etc.[68]

The term structure appears so misleading to Leighton that he suggests it should perhaps not be used.[69] He continues by saying that, in a personal communication, Hughes suggested to him that[70] "'Structure' refers to configurations which pre-exist other processes that are the focus of our attention—namely the 'functions.'" Then he quotes Bertalanffy, who said:

The antithesis between *structure* and *function, morphology* and *physiology* is based upon a static conception of the organism. In a machine there is a fixed arrangement that can be set in motion but can also be at rest. In a similar way the pre-established structure of, say, the heart is distinguished from its function, namely rhythmical contraction. Actually this separation between a pre-established structure and processes occurring in the structure does not apply to the living organism. For the organism is the expression of an everlasting orderly process, though, on the other hand, this process is sustained by underlying structures and organized forms. What is described in morphology as organic forms and structures, is in reality a momentary cross-section through a spatio-temporal pattern.

What are called structures are slow processes of long duration, functions are quick processes of short duration. If we say that a function such as a contraction of a muscle is performed by a structure, it means that a quick and short process wave is superimposed on a long-lasting and slowly-running wave.[71]

My terminology avoids this semantic morass. I agree with Leighton that the family, various groups, associations, and institutions are parts of the structure of a town or other such concrete system. The cultural systems, societal roles, and socioeconomic classes

which Leighton refers to are, however, abstractions, relationships, or abstracted systems.[72] Structure is the arrangement of a concrete system's parts at a moment in three-dimensional space. Process is change in the matter-energy or information of that system over time. The two are entirely different and need not be confused.

7. Type

If a number of individual living systems are observed to have similar characteristics, they often are classed together as a *type*. Types are abstractions. Nature presents an apparently endless variety of living things which man, from his earliest days, has observed and classified—first, probably, on the basis of their threat to him, their susceptibility to capture, or their edibility, but eventually according to categories which are scientifically more useful. Classification by species is applied to free-living cells or organisms—monerans, protistans, fungi, plants, or animals—because of their obvious relationships by reproduction. These systems are classified together by taxonomists on the basis of likeness of structure and process, genetic similarity and ability to interbreed, and local interaction—often including, in animals, the ability to respond appropriately to each other's signs. The individual members of a given species are commonly units of widely separated concrete systems. The reason the species is not a concrete system is that, though all its members *can* interbreed and interact, they do so only locally, and there is no overall species organization. Of course at some time in the past their ancestors did, but that may have been long ago. Complete isolation of one local set of members of a species from other local sets, after a time, may lead to the development of a new species because mutations occur in one local interbreeding set which are not spread to others of the species.

There are various types of systems at other levels of the hierarchy of living systems besides the cell and organism levels, each classed according to different structural and process taxonomic differentia which I discuss in later chapters. There are, for instance, primitive societies, agricultural societies, and industrial societies, just as there are epithelial cells, fibroblasts, red blood corpuscles, and white blood cells, as well as free-living cells. Biological interbreeding as a way of transmitting a new system's template, which is a specialized form of information processing (see pages 55 and 217), does not occur at certain levels. At these levels—like the organization or society—it may well be, however, that the template, the "charter" information which originally "programmed" the structure and process of all individual cases of a particular type of system, had a common origin with all other templates of that type.

Types of systems often overlap one another along a given variable. Within one animal species, for instance, there may be individuals which are larger than many members of another species which on the average is much larger. Primitive societies in general have been less populous than agricultural societies, but there have been exceptions. Rank ordering of types is also different depending upon the variable. The rabbit, though larger, seems less intelligent than the rat. He has much larger ears—more like those of a horse in size—but a very much shorter and better upholstered tail.

8. Level

The universe contains a hierarchy of systems, each more advanced or "higher" *level* made of systems of lower levels.[73] *Atoms* are composed of *particles; molecules,* of atoms; *crystals* and *organelles,* of molecules. About at the level of crystallizing *viruses,* like the tobacco mosaic virus, the subset of living systems begins. Viruses are necessarily parasitic on cells, so cells are the lowest level of living systems. *Cells* are composed of atoms, molecules, and multimolecular organelles; *organs* are composed of cells aggregated into *tissues; organisms,* or organs; *groups* (e.g., herds, flocks, families, teams, tribes), of organisms; *organizations,* of groups (and sometimes single individual organisms); *societies,* of organizations, groups, and individuals; and *supranational systems,* of societies and organizations. Higher levels of systems may be of mixed composition, living and nonliving. They include *ecological systems, planets, solar systems, galaxies,* and so forth.[74] It is beyond my competence and the scope of this book to deal with the characteristics—whatever they may be—of systems below and above those levels which include the various forms of life, although others have done so.[75] This book, in presenting general systems behavior theory, is limited to the subset of living systems—cells, organs, organisms, groups, organizations, societies, and supranational systems.

It would be convenient for theorists if the hierarchical levels of living systems fitted neatly into each other like Chinese boxes. The facts are more complicated, as my discussion of subsystems and components indicates (see pages 30 to 34). I have distinguished seven levels of living systems for analysis here, but I do not argue that there are exactly these seven, no more and no less. For example, one might conceivably separate tissue and organ into two separate levels. Or one might, as Anderson and Carter have suggested, separate the organization and the community into two

separate levels—local communities, urban and rural, are composed of multiple organizations, just as societies are composed of multiple local communities, states, or provinces.[76] Or one might maintain that the organ is not a level, since there are no totipotential organs.

What are the criteria for distinguishing any one level from the others? They are derived from a long scientific tradition of empirical observation of the entire gamut of living systems. This extensive experience of the community of scientific observers has led to a consensus that there are certain fundamental forms of organization of living matter-energy. Indeed the classical division of subject matter among the various disciplines of the life or behavior sciences is implicitly or explicitly based upon this consensus. Observers recognize that there are in the world many similar complexly organized accumulations of matter-energy, each identified by the characteristics I have already mentioned above (see page 17): (*a*) Physical proximity of its units. (*b*) Similar size in physical space of its units, significantly different from the size of the units of the next lower or higher levels. (*c*) Similarity of its constituent units. Such organized accumulations of matter-energy have multiple constituent units, ordinarily a preponderance of their components, which are systems of the next lower level, *i.e.,* just as molecules are made up of two or more atoms and atoms are composed of two or more particles, so groups are made up of two or more organisms, and organs are composed of two or more cells. This is the chief way to determine to what level any system belongs. Such nomenclature is comparable to standard procedure in physical science. For example, one does not call a system a crystal unless it is made of molecules composed of atoms. (*d*) Common fate of its units. And (*e*) distinctive structure and process of its units (see pages 22 and 23).[77]

It is important to follow one procedural rule in systems theory, in order to avoid confusion. Every discussion should begin with an identification of the level of reference, and the discourse should not change to another level without a specific statement that this is occurring.[78] Systems at the indicated level are called systems. Those at the level above are *suprasystems,* and those at the next higher level, *suprasuprasystems.* Below the level of reference are *subsystems,* and below them are *subsubsystems.* For example, if one is studying a cell, its organelles are the subsystems, and the tissue or organ is its suprasystem, unless it is a free-living cell whose suprasystem includes other living systems with which it interacts.[79]

8.1 Intersystem generalization   A fundamental procedure in science is to make generalizations from one system to another on the basis of some similarity between the systems which the observer sees and which permits him to class them together. For example, since the nineteenth century, the field of "individual differences" has been expanded, following the tradition of scientists like Galton in anthropometry and Binet in psychometrics. In Fig. 2-2, states of sepa-

$$I_1. \ldots .I_n$$
$$\underbrace{}$$
$$T_1. \ldots .T_n$$
$$\underbrace{}$$
$$L_1. \ldots .L_n$$

Fig. 2-2 Individual, type, level.

rate specific individual systems on a specific structural or process variable are represented by I_1 to I_n. For differences among such individuals to be observed and measured, of course, a variable common to the type—along which there are individual variations—must be recognized (T_1). Physiology depends heavily, for instance, upon the fact that individuals of the type (or species) of living organisms called cats are fundamentally alike, even though minor variations from one individual to the next are well recognized.

Scientists may also generalize from one type to another (T_1 to T_n). An example is cross-species generalization, which has been commonly accepted only since Darwin. It is the justification for the patient labors of the white rat in the cause of man's understanding of himself. Rats and cats, cats and chimpanzees, chimpanzees and human beings are similar in structure, as comparative anatomists know, and in function, as comparative physiologists and psychologists demonstrate.

The amount of variance among species is greater than among individuals within a species. If the learning behavior of cat Felix is compared with that of mouse Mickey, we would expect not only the sort of individual differences which are found between Mickey and Minnie Mouse, but also greater species differences. Cross-species generalizations are common, and many have good scientific acceptability, but in making them, interindividual and interspecies differences must be kept in mind. The learning rate of men is not identical to that of white rats, and no man learns at exactly the same rate as any other.

The third type of scientific generalization indicated in Fig. 2-2 is from one level to another. The basis for such generalization is the assumption that each of the levels of life, from cell to society, is composed of systems of the previous lower level. These cross-level generalizations will, ordinarily, have greater variance than the other sorts of generalizations since they include variance among types and among individuals. But they can be made, and they can have great conceptual significance.

That there are important uniformities, which can be generalized about, across all levels of living systems is not surprising. All are composed of comparable carbon-hydrogen-nitrogen constituents, most importantly a score of amino acids organized into similar proteins, which are produced in nature only in living systems. All are equipped to live in a water-oxygen world rather than, for example, on the methane and ammonia planets so dear to science fiction. Also they are all adapted only to environments in which the physical variables, like temperature, hydration, pressure, and radiation, remain within relatively narrow ranges.[80] Moreover, they all presumably have arisen from the same primordial genes or template (see page 34), diversified by evolutionary change. Perhaps the most convincing argument for the plausibility of cross-level generalization derives from analysis of this evolutionary development of living systems. Although increasingly complex types of living systems have evolved at a given level, followed by higher levels with even greater complexity (see pages 75 to 78), certain basic necessities did not change. All these systems, if they were to survive in their environment, had, by some means or other, to carry out the same vital subsystem processes. While free-living cells, like protozoans, carry these out with relative simplicity, the corresponding processes are more complex in multicellular organisms like mammals, and even more complex at higher levels. A directed graph (somewhat like an organization chart) was drawn by Rashevsky to indicate how these various processes are carried out by, or mapped on, particular structures in simple cells like protozoans.[81] Then, the same processes are "shredded out" to multiple components in a more complex system at a higher level (see Fig. 1-2, page 4). This shredding-out is somewhat like the sort of *division of labor* which Parkinson made famous in his law.[82] Each process is broken down into multiple subprocesses which are mapped upon multiple structures, each of which becomes specialized for carrying out a subprocess. If this allocation of processes is not to be chaotic in the more complex systems which have more components involved in each process, the rationale for their division of labor must be derived from that which prevailed in their simpler progenitor systems. This shred-out or mapping of comparable processes from simpler structures at lower levels to more complex structures at higher levels is a chief reason why I believe that cross-level generalizations will prove fruitful in the study of living systems. Cross-level comparisons among nonliving systems may not be so profitable, for they are not derived by any genetically determined evolutionary shred-out, and there is no clear evidence that to share a given environment, nonliving systems must have comparable structures and processes.

The shred-out principle has implications for scientific method. Every scientist's academic freedom guarantees him the right to select his preferred procedures. We may, however, question the wisdom and responsibility of anyone who originates his own categorization or taxonomy of system processes without regard to the other such classifications developed by his colleagues working at his level. Yet this is often done. It is even commoner for a scientist to originate such a classification independent of those made at other levels of systems. This is more understandable, however, for unless one accepts the emphasis of general living systems theory on cross-level generalizations, recognizing that evolution requires that the processes of systems at higher levels have been shredded out by division of labor from those at lower levels, there is no reason to attempt to classify processes comparably across levels.

A formal identity (see page 17) among concrete systems is demonstrated by a procedure composed of three logically independent steps: (a) recognizing an aspect of two or more systems which has comparable status in those systems, (b) hypothesizing a quantitative identity between them, and (c) empirically demonstrating that identity within a certain range of error by collecting data on a similar aspect of each of the two or more systems being compared. Thus a set of observations at one level of living systems can be associated with findings at another, to support generalizations that are far from trivial. It may be possible to use the same conceptual system to represent two quite different sorts of concrete systems, or to make models of them with the same mathematical constructs. It may even be possible to formulate useful generalizations which apply to all living systems at all levels. A comparison of systems is complete only when statements of their formal identities are associated with specific statements of their interlevel, intertype, and interindividual disidentities. The confirmation of formal identities and disidentities is done by empirical study.

In order to make it easier to recognize similarities that exist in systems of different types and levels, it is helpful to use general systems terms. These words are carefully selected according to the following criteria:

(a) They should be as acceptable as possible when applied at all levels and to all types of living systems. For example, "sense organ" is one word for the subsystem that brings information into the system at the level of organisms, but "input transducer" is also satisfactory, and it is a more acceptable term for that subsystem at the society level (e.g., a diplomat, foreign correspondent, or spy) or in an electronic system. Consequently I use it. I select terms which refer to a commonality of structure or process across systems. Such a usage may irritate some specialists used to the traditional terminology of their fields. After all, one of the techniques we all use to discover whether a person is competently informed in a certain field is to determine through questioning whether he can use its specialized terminology correctly. A language which intentionally uses words that are acceptable in other fields is, of necessity, not the jargon of the specialty. Therefore whoever uses it may be suspected of not being informed about the specialty. The specialist languages, however, limit the horizons of thought to the borders of the discipline. They mask important intertype and interlevel generalities which exist and make general theory as difficult as it is to think about snow in a language that has no word for it. Since no single term can be entirely appropriate to represent a structure or process at every level, readers of general systems literature must be flexible, willing to accept a word to which they are not accustomed, so long as it is precise and accurate, if the term is useful in revealing cross-type and cross-level generalities. I do not wish to create a new vocabulary but to select, from one level, words which are broadly applicable, and to use them in a general sense at all levels. This is done recognizing that these terms have synonyms or near synonyms which are more commonly employed at certain levels. Actually, with the current usages of scientific language, it is impossible always to use general systems words rather than type-specific and level-specific words because the discussion would appear meaningless to experts in the field. In this book I use the general systems words as much as seems practicable.

(b) The terms should be as neutral as possible. Preferably they should not be associated exclusively with any type or level of system, with biological or social science, with any discipline, or with any particular school or theoretical point of view.

What are some examples of the sort of general systems terms I shall use? For a structure, "ingestor." This is the equivalent of a number of different words used at the various levels, for example: cell—aperture in the cell membrane; organ—hilum; organism—mouth; group—the family shopper; organization—the receiving department; society—the dock workers of a country; supranational system—those dock workers of nations in an alliance who are under unified command. For a process, "moving." This is a close equivalent of: cell—contraction; organ—peristalsis;

organism—walking; group—hiking; organization—moving a factory; society—nomadic wandering; supranational system—migration (but it is questionable whether any supranational system has ever done this).

8.2 Intersystem differentiation   All systems at each level have certain common and distinct characteristics which differentiate them from systems at other levels. There are regular differences across levels, from lowest to highest, for several variables of structure and process. Although the ranges of these variations at two or more levels may overlap, the average is ordinarily distinctive for each level. These variables include average size (cells are small, supranational systems large); average duration as a system; amount of mobility of units in physical space; degree of spatial cohesiveness among units over time; density of distribution of units; number of distinguishable processes; complexity of processes; transferability of processes from one component to another; and rate of growth. The striking cross-level differences in mobility of system units are among the chief reasons why many scientists have difficulty in recognizing the fundamental similarity of the living systems studied by biologists and those studied by social scientists. Systems at the organism level, for instance, have components with much less mobility in relation to one another, more fixed spatial relationships, and more readily observable boundaries than groups, whose members often move about rapidly and easily disperse to reunite at a later time. A given process is usually carried out by the same component in organisms; in groups it is often transferred from one member to another.

Within each level, systems display type differences and individual differences. No two specific organisms—two lions or two dandelions—are exactly alike. No two groups—two teams or two families—have exactly identical compositions or interactions.

When interindividual, intertype, and interlevel formal identities among systems are demonstrated, they are of absorbing scientific interest. Very different structures carry out similar processes and also perform them similarly, so that they can be quite precisely described by the same formal model. Conversely, it may perhaps be shown as a general principle that subsystems with comparable structures, but quite different processes, may have quantitative similarities as well.

In Chaps. 4, 5, and elsewhere I shall discuss numerous hypotheses about cross-level formal identities concerned with either structure or process. They are the warp of general living systems theory. The woof comprises the disidentities, differences among the levels. The ultimate task in making predictions about living systems is to learn the quantitative characteristics of the general, cross-level formal identities on the one hand and the interlevel, intertype, and interindividual differences on the other, combining both in a specific prediction. One example of this sort of formal identity which I have studied in detail is the response of systems at five levels to "information input overload." This will be considered in Chap. 5.

8.3 Emergents   I have stated that a measure of the sum of a system's units is larger than the sum of that measure of its units (see page 16 and Note 43). Because of this, the more complex systems at higher levels manifest characteristics, more than the sum of the characteristics of the units, not observed at lower levels. These characteristics have been called *emergents*. Significant aspects of living systems at higher levels will be neglected if they are described only in terms and dimensions used for their lower-level subsystems and components.

It is the view of Braynes, Napalkov, and Svechinskiy that the remarkable capabilities of both the computer and the human brain derive from the complex way in which the elements are combined.[83] Individual nerve cells, and parts of the computer, have less functional scope. I agree that certain original aspects—new patterns of structure and process—are found at higher levels which are not seen at lower ones. For these new qualities new terms and dimensions are needed. But that is no reason for a complete, new conceptual system. Scientific unity and parsimony are advanced if we simply add the necessary new concepts to those used at lower levels. Moreover, it is vital to be precise in describing emergents. Many have discussed them in vague and mystical terms. I oppose any conceptualization of emergents (like that held early, and later rejected, by some Gestalt psychologists) that involves inscrutable characteristics of the whole, greater than the sum of the parts, which are not susceptible to the ordinary methods of scientific analysis.[84]

A clear-cut illustration of emergents can be found in a comparison of three electronic systems. One of these—a wire connecting the poles of a battery—can only conduct electricity, which heats the wire. Add several tubes, condensers, resistors, and controls, and the new system can become a radio, capable of receiving sound messages. Add dozens of other components, including a picture tube and several more controls, and the system becomes a television set, which can receive sound and a picture. And this is not just more of the same. The third system has emergent capabilities the second system did not have, emergent from its special design of much greater complexity, just as the second has capabilities the first lacked. But there is nothing mystical about the colored merry-go-round and racing children on the TV screen—it is the output of a system which can be completely explained by a complicated set of differential equations such as electrical engineers write, including terms representing the characteristics of each of the set's components.

Shred-out—the adoption by living systems at higher levels of newer, more complex ways of carrying out fundamental processes (see page 1)—may explain the evolutionary rise of emergent characteristics. Butler discusses these concepts, giving examples from the level of the atom on up, as follows:

We may be able to break down the organism into its cells, and the cells into the interlocking component cycles of activity, yet the functioning cell is more than the sum of the chemical processes of which it is made up and the organism is more than the sum of the cells of which it is composed.

This can be illustrated by a simple example. If we combine a number of atoms of carbon, hydrogen, nitrogen, and oxygen together in a particular way, we obtain the vivid blue dye, methylene blue. We could not have suspected from what we knew of these atoms that, when combined in this way, they would exhibit this property. Nevertheless, once we have the dye, we may be able to account for its properties in terms of the atoms and their mode of combination. We can, for example, account for the colour as due to the oscillation of electrons in a particular cyclic molecular framework, and this can be 'explained' in terms of the electronic structure of the atoms themselves. If necessary we may and we frequently must add to our description of the atoms in order to enable us to account for methylene blue and other substances in terms of them, but we could hardly have predicted methylene blue (or other dyes) if we were completely ignorant of its existence and behaviour. . . .

In just the same way we see new kinds of behaviour emerging at the different levels of life, which could hardly have been predicted if only the simpler systems which are made use of were known.

The new level of organisation can be analysed into its component mechanisms, and the new organisation is implicit in the components, but nevertheless when it has been achieved, something new has appeared, which is more than the sum of the separate mechanisms of which it is made up.

From this point of view, we see, as Bergson did in his concept of emergent evolution, that in the course of evolution there has not only been an increase of complexity of the parts, but also the emergence of new properties, which although they are *potentially* present in the simpler systems, do not really exist until they are actually produced and when they are achieved are essentially more than the isolated parts.[85]

9. Echelon

This concept may seem superficially similar to the concept of level, but it is distinctly different. Many complex living systems, at various levels, are organized into two or more *echelons*. (I use the term in the military sense of a step in the "chain of command," not in the other military sense of arrangement of troops in rows in physical space.) In living systems with echelons the components of the decider (see pages 18 and 67 to 69), an information processing subsystem, are hierarchically arranged. Certain types of decisions are made by one component of that subsystem and others by another, each component being at a different *echelon*. All echelons are within the boundary of the decider subsystem. Ordinarily each echelon is made up of components of the same level as those which make up every other echelon in that system. Characteristically the decider component at one echelon gets information from a source or sources which process information primarily or exclusively to and from that echelon. At some levels of living systems— *e.g.*, groups—the decider is often not organized in echelon structure.

After a decision is made at one echelon on the basis of the information received, it is transmitted, often through a single subcomponent (which may or may not be the same as the decider) but possibly through more than one subcomponent, upward to the next higher echelon, which goes through a similar process, and so on to the top echelon. Here a final decision is made, and then command information is transmitted downward to lower echelons. Characteristically information is abstracted or made more general as it proceeds upward from echelon to echelon, and it is made more specific or detailed as it proceeds downward (see pages 65, 68, 397 to 400, 629, and 630). If a component does not decide but only passes on information, it is not functioning as an echelon. In some cases of decentralized decision making, certain types of decisions are made at lower echelons and not transmitted to higher echelons in any form, while information relevant to other types of decisions is transmitted upward. If there are multiple parallel deciders, without a hierarchy that has subordinate and superordinate deciders, there is not one system but multiple ones.

10. Suprasystem

10.1 Suprasystem and environment   The *suprasystem* of any living system is the next higher system in which it is a component or subsystem. For example, the suprasystem of a cell or tissue is the organ it is in; the suprasystem of an organism is the group it is in at the time. Presumably every system has a suprasystem except the "universe." The suprasystem is differentiated from the *environment*. The immediate environment is the suprasystem minus the system itself. The entire environment includes this plus the suprasuprasystem and the systems at all higher levels which contain it. In order to survive, the system must interact with and adjust to its environment, the other parts of the suprasystem. These processes alter both the system and its environment. It is not surprising that characteristically living systems adapt to their environment and, in return, mold it. The result is that, after some period of interaction, each in some sense becomes a mirror of the other (see pages 35, 58, and 67). For example, Emerson has shown how a termite nest, an artifact of the termites as well as part of their environment, reveals to inspection by the naturalist, long after the termites have died, much detail about the social structure and function of those insects.[86] Likewise a pueblo yields to the anthropologist facts about the life of the Indians who inhabited it centuries ago. Conversely, living systems are shaped by their environment. Sailors' skins are weathered and cowboys' legs are bowed. As Tolman pointed out, each of us carries with him a "cognitive map" of the organization of his environment, of greater or lesser accuracy—stored information, memories, which are essential for effective life in that environment.[87]

10.2 Territory The region of physical space occupied by a living system, and frequently protected by it from an invader, is its territory.[88] Examples are a bowerbird's stage, a dog's yard, a family's property, a nation's land. The borders of the territory are established conceptually and stored by the occupants as information, a more or less precise cognitive map in the memory, being conveyed by signals to neighboring living systems (sometimes including scientific observers) which also store a similar cognitive map in their memories. Neighboring living systems may not have identical maps stored in their memories, which can lead to conflict among them. The border of the territory must be distinguished from the boundary (see page 770) of the living system occupying it, the boundary being made up of living components and sometimes also artifacts. The boundary may be coextensive with the edges of the territory, but often it covers a smaller region, and it may move over the edges of its system's territory into others surrounding it.

11. Subsystem and component

In every system it is possible to identify one sort of unit, each of which carries out a distinct and separate process, and another sort of unit, each of which is a discrete, separate structure. The totality of all the structures in a system which carry out a particular process is a *subsystem*. A subsystem, thus, is identified by the process it carries out. It exists in one or more identifiable structural units of the system. These specific, local, distinguishable structural units are called *components* or *members* or *parts*. I have referred to these components in my definition of a concrete system as "a nonrandom accumulation of matter-energy, in a region in physical space-time, which is organized into interacting, interrelated subsystems or

components" (see page 17). There is no one-to-one relationship between process and structure. One or more processes may be carried out by two or more components. Every system is a component, but not necessarily a subsystem of its suprasystem. Every component that has its own decider is a system at the next lower level, but many subsystems are not systems at the next lower level, being dispersed to several components.

The concept of component process is related to the concept of *role* used in social science.[89] Organization theory usually emphasizes the functional requirements of the system which the component fulfills, rather than the specific characteristics of the component or components that make up the subsystem. The typical view is that an organization specifies clearly defined roles (or component processes) and human beings "fill them."[90] But it is a mistake not to recognize that characteristics of the component—in this case the person carrying out the role—also influence what occurs. A role is more than simple "social position," a position in some social space which is "occupied." It involves interaction, adjustments between the component and the system. It is a multiple concept, referring to the demands upon the component by the system, to the internal adjustment processes of the component, and to how the component functions in meeting the system's requirements. The adjustments it makes are frequently compromises between the requirements of the component and the requirements of the system.

It is conceivable that some systems might have no subsystems or components, although this would be true only of an ultimate particle.[91] The components of living systems need not be alive. Cells, for example, are composed of nonliving molecules or complexes of molecules. Systems of less than a certain degree of complexity cannot have the characteristics of life (see pages 18 and 204).

Often the distinction between process units and structural units, between subsystems and components, is not clearly recognized by scientists. This results in confusion. For example, when most physiologists use the word "organ" they refer to a process unit, while most anatomists use the term to refer to a structural unit. Yet the same word is used for both.

Sometimes confusion is avoided by giving a unit of a system both a structural name and a title referring to the process or role it carries out. Elizabeth Windsor is a structural name and her process title is Queen.

It is notoriously hard to deduce process from structure, and the reverse is by no means easy. Thomas Wharton, the seventeenth-century anatomist, demonstrated how delightfully wrong one can be in determining a subsystem's process from its structure. After carefully examining the thyroid gland, he concluded that it had four purposes:[92] (*a*) to serve as a transfer point for the superfluous moisture from the nerves through the lymphatic ducts to the veins which run through the gland; (*b*) to keep the neck warm; (*c*) to lubricate the larynx, so making the voice lighter, more melodious, and sweeter; and (*d*) to round out and ornament the curve of the neck, especially in women.

Such confusion about the process carried out by a structure can exist at any level: a lively argument still persists as to whether during President Woodrow Wilson's illness he was the nation's chief executive and decision maker, or whether it was his wife or his physician, Dr. Cary T. Grayson. Everyone who has ever served on a committee knows that Cohen may be the chairman, but Kelly can be the leader, or vice versa.

In defining "system" I indicated that the state of its units is constrained by, conditioned by, or dependent upon the state of other units. That is, the units are coupled (see page 16). Some systems and components are also constrained by their suprasystems and subsystems. The form of allocation of process to structure determines the nature of the constraint or dependency in any given system. Living systems are so organized that each subsystem and component has some autonomy and some subordination or constraint from lower-level systems, other systems at the same level, and higher-level systems. Conflicts among them are resolved by adjustment processes (see page 39).

The way living systems develop does not always result in a neat distribution of exactly one subsystem to each component. The natural arrangement would appear to be for a system to depend on one structure for one process, but such a one-to-one relationship does not always exist. Sometimes the boundaries of a subsystem and a component exactly overlap; they are congruent. Sometimes they are not congruent. Other possibilities include: (*a*) a single subsystem in a single component, (*b*) multiple subsystems in a single component, (*c*) a single subsystem in multiple components, or (*d*) multiple subsystems in multiple components.

Systems differ markedly from level to level, type to type, and perhaps somewhat even from individual to individual, in their *patterns of allocation* of various subsystem processes to different structures. Such process may be (*a*) localized in a single component, (*b*) combined with others in a single component, (*c*) laterally dispersed to other components in the system, (*d*) upwardly dispersed to the suprasystem or above, (*e*) downwardly dispersed to subsystems or below, or (*f*) outwardly dispersed to other systems external to the

hierarchy it is in. Which allocation pattern is employed is a fundamental aspect of any given system. For a specific subsystem function in a specific system one strategy results in more efficient process than another. One can be better than another in maximizing effectiveness and minimizing costs (see page 4). Valuable studies can be made at every level on optimal patterns of allocation of processes to structures. In all probability some general systems principles must be relevant to such matters. Possible examples are: Structures which minimize the distance over which matter-energy must be transported or information transmitted are the most efficient (see Hypotheses 3.2.2.2-1, 3.2.2.2-2, and 3.3.3.2-3, pages 94 and 96). If multiple components carry out a process, the process is more difficult to control and less efficient than if a single component does it (see Hypotheses 3.3.3.2-14, 3.3.3.2-15, and 5.4.3-1, pages 97 and 109). If one or more components which carry out a process are outside the system, the process is more difficult to integrate than if they are all in the system (see Hypotheses 3.3.3.2-14, 3.3.3.2-15, and 5.4.3-1, pages 97 and 109). Or if there are duplicate components capable of performing the same process, the system is less vulnerable to stress and therefore is more likely to survive longer, because if one component is inactivated, the other can carry out the process alone (see Hypothesis 3.3.3.2-10, page 96).

In this book I shall emphasize cross-level and cross-type formal identities among similar subsystems (units which carry out comparable processes) rather than among components (units which may look alike but which carry out unlike processes). The history of the life sciences suggests that it is more profitable to generalize about similar subsystems than about similar components. Generalizing about similar subsystems, therefore, is a central principle of the research strategy outlined in succeeding chapters.

The following sorts of subsystems and other contents exist in living systems or are associated with them:

11.1 Local subsystem   If the boundary of a subsystem is congruent with the boundary of a component, and all its parts are contiguous in space, it is a *local subsystem,* limited to one component. The system in this case is dependent on only one component for the process.

11.2 Combined subsystem   If the boundary of a subsystem is not congruent with the boundary of a component, and the subsystem is located in a smaller region than the component, sharing the region with one or more other subsystems, it is a *combined subsystem.* The system in this case is dependent on part of one component for the process.

11.3   Laterally dispersed subsystem   If the boundary of a subsystem is not congruent with the boundary of a component, and the subsystem is located in a larger region, including more than one component of the system, it is a *laterally dispersed subsystem*. In this case the system is dependent on multiple components for the process. To coordinate these components there must be a sufficient degree of communication among the parts so that they are able to interact.

11.4   Joint subsystem   At times a subsystem may be simultaneously a part of more than one local concrete system—for example, when one person plays the fourth position at two bridge tables or when a yeast cell is budding into two. A *joint subsystem* usually interacts with only one system at a given level at any one moment, though its relationships fluctuate rapidly. In this case the system is dependent for the process on a component it shares with another system.

11.5   Upwardly dispersed subsystem   If the subsystem boundary is not congruent with a component boundary, but the process is carried out by a system at a higher level, it is an *upwardly dispersed subsystem*. In this case the system is dependent on a suprasystem for the process.

11.6   Downwardly dispersed subsystem   If the subsystem is not congruent with any component, but the process is carried out by a subsubsystem at a lower level, it is a *downwardly dispersed subsystem*. In this case the system is dependent on a subsubsystem for the process.

11.7   Outwardly dispersed subsystem   If the boundary of a subsystem is not congruent with the boundary of a component, but the process is carried out by another system, living or not, it is an *outwardly dispersed subsystem*. If the other system performs the process in exchange for nothing or at its own expense, *parasitism* exists (see pages 18 and 79). If it carries out the process in exchange or economic trade-off for some reward or service which constitutes a cost to the first system, *symbiosis* exists (see pages 18 and 79). In either case the system is dependent for the process upon another system, at the same or at another level. By definition we shall not call it parasitism or symbiosis if the dependence is on the system's suprasystem or systems at higher levels which include it, or on a subsubsystem or systems at lower levels included in it. A person may be parasitically or symbiotically dependent on cells of another person (*e.g.*, blood transfusion recipients) or on organs of another (*e.g.*, kidney transplant recipients) or on another organism (*e.g.*, a blind man with a leader dog) or on another group than his own family (*e.g.*, the "Man Who Came to Dinner") or on another organization than his own

(*e.g.*, a visiting professor) or on another nation (*e.g.*, a foreign tourist). Such assistance is required for all partipotential systems and all totipotential ones which are not functioning fully. If they did not have this aid they would not survive.

When a member of a family goes away to college he ceases to be a subsystem of the local concrete family group and becomes parasitic or symbiotic on the college organization. He may keep in sufficient touch through the use of the telephone or by mail to coordinate his plans with the family and play a part in its interactions. The family may spend a large part of its existence in dispersed form, coming together only for reunions. The group can be coordinated by information flows so that all members convene at the same time. If the information flows break down, the group may cease to exist. Foreign secret agents who are dispersed into social systems are sometimes detected because their secret radio messages or other information transmissions are monitored and their participation in another system discovered. The coordination and mutual influence require information flow, and the agent must communicate if he is to follow the directives of his government and also send back intelligence to it.

11.8   Critical subsystem   Certain processes are necessary for life and must be carried out by all living systems that survive or be performed for them by some other system. They are carried out by the following *critical subsystems:* reproducer, boundary, ingestor, distributor, converter, producer, matter-energy storage, extruder, motor, supporter, input transducer, internal transducer, channel and net, decoder, associator, memory, decider, encoder, and output transducer. The processes carried out by these critical subsystems are described in Chap. 3. Of these, only the decider is essential, in the sense that a system cannot be parasitic upon or symbiotic with another system for its deciding (see pages 18 and 67 to 69). A living system does not exist independently if its decider is dispersed upwardly, downwardly, or outwardly.

Since all living systems are genetically related, have similar constituents, live in closely comparable environments, and process matter-energy and information, it is not surprising that they should have comparable subsystems and relationships among them. All systems do not have all possible kinds of subsystems. They differ individually, among types and across levels, as to which subsystems they have and how those subsystems are structured. But all living systems either have a complement of the critical subsystems carrying out the functions essential to life or are intimately associated with and effectively interacting with systems which carry out the missing life functions for them. Fungi and plants may lack a motor and some information processing subsystems.

Often there are structural cues as to which are the critical subsystems. Natural selection has wiped out those species whose critical subsystems were vulnerable to stresses in the environment. Those have survived whose critical subsystems are either duplicated (like the kidney) or especially well protected (like the brain suspended in fluid in a hard skull or the embryo suspended in amniotic fluid in the uterus). So structural characteristics may reveal the secrets of process.

11.9 Inclusion Sometimes a part of the environment is surrounded by a system and totally included within its boundary. Any such thing which is not a part of the system's own living structure is an *inclusion*. Any living system at any level may include living or nonliving components. The amoeba, for example, ingests both inorganic and organic matter and may retain particles of iron or dye in its cytoplasm for many hours. A surgeon may replace an arteriosclerotic aorta with a plastic one and that patient may live comfortably with it for years. To the two-member group of one dog and one cat an important plant component is often added—one tree. An airline firm may have as an integral component a computerized mechanical system for making reservations which extends into all its offices. A nation includes many sorts of vegetables, minerals, buildings, and machines, as well as its land.

The inclusion is a component or subsystem of the system if it carries out or helps in carrying out a critical process of the system; otherwise it is part of the environment. Either way, in order to survive, the system must adjust to its characteristics. If it is harmless or inert it can often be left undisturbed. But if it is potentially harmful—like a pathogenic bacterium in a dog or a Greek in the giant gift horse within the gates of Troy—it must be rendered harmless or walled off or extruded from the system or killed. Because it moves with the system in a way the rest of the environment does not, it constitutes a special problem. Being inside the system, it may be a more serious or more immediate stress than it would be outside the system's protective boundary. But also, the system that surrounds it can control its physical actions and all routes of access to it. For this reason international law has developed the concept of extraterritoriality to provide freedom of action to ambassadors and embassies, nations' inclusions within foreign countries.

An employee, an officer, or a stockholder of a company is certainly a component in that system. But what about a client who enters the company's store in order to buy or a customer who goes into a theater in order to see a movie? If a shopper simply wanders into a store, looks at a television set on display, and then wanders out, he was probably just an inclusion. But if a significant interaction occurs or a contract, implicit or explicit, is agreed to (as when a customer buys a ticket to enter the theater or hires a lawyer to represent him), the customer or client is an inclusion (not a component) and he is at the same time another system in the environment of the organization or firm, interacting with it in the suprasystem (see page 596).

11.10 Artifact An *artifact* is an inclusion in some system, made by animals or man. Spider webs, bird nests, beaver dams, houses, books, machines, music, paintings, and language are artifacts. They may or may not be *prostheses*—inventions which carry out some critical process essential to a living system. An artificial pacemaker for a human heart is an example of an artifact which can replace a pathological process with a healthy one. Insulin and thyroxine are replacement drugs which are human artifacts. Chemical, mechanical, or electronic artifacts have been constructed which carry out some functions of all levels of living systems.

Living systems create and live among their artifacts. Beginning presumably with the hut and the arrowhead, the pot and the vase, the plow and the wheel, mankind has constructed tools and devised machines. The industrial revolution of the nineteenth century, capped by the recent harnessing of atomic energy, represents the extension of man's matter-energy processing ability, his muscles. A new industrial revolution, of even greater potential, is just beginning in the twentieth century, with the development of information and logic processing machines—adjuncts to man's brain. These artifacts are increasingly becoming prostheses, relied on to carry out critical subsystem processes. A chimpanzee may extend his reach with a stick; a man may extend his cognitive skills with a computer. Today's prostheses include input transducers which sense the type of blood cells that pass before them and identify missiles that approach a nation's shores; photographic, mechanical, and electronic memories which can store masses of information over time; computers which can solve problems, carry out logical and mathematical calculations, make decisions, and control other machines; electric typewriters, high-speed printers, cathode-ray tubes, and photographic equipment which can output information. An analysis of many modern systems must take into account the novel problems which arise at man-machine interfaces.

 Music is a special sort of human artifact, an information processing artifact.[93] So are the other arts and cognitive systems which people share. So is language. Whether it be a natural language or the machine language of some computer system, it is essential to information processing. Often stored only in human brains and expressed only by human lips, language can also be recorded on nonliving artifacts like stones, books, and magnetic tapes. It is not of itself a concrete system. It changes only when man changes it. As long as it is used, it is in flux, because it must remain compatible with the ever-changing living systems that use it. But the change emanates from the users, and without their impact the language is inert. The artifactual language used in any information transmission in a system determines many essential aspects of that system's structure and process.[94] Scientists sometimes neglect to distinguish between living systems and their artifacts. Because artifacts are the products of living systems, they often mirror aspects of their producers and thus have systems characteristics of their own. Termites' nests, pots and jewelry of primitive tribes, and modern buildings are all concrete systems which can be studied for themselves alone as well as to understand the living systems that produced them. But they themselves are not living systems. Systems theory can also be applied to the history, dynamics over time, rules of change, and other aspects of languages or music, if they are viewed as abstracted systems independent of the living systems that produced or used them. This may be desirable because their producers or users may be long dead or unavailable for study.

12. Transmissions in concrete systems

All process involves some sort of transmission among subsystems within a system, or among systems. There are *inputs* across the boundary into a system, *internal processes* within it, and *outputs* from it. Each of these sorts of transmissions may consist of either (*a*) some particular form of matter; (*b*) energy, in the form of light, radiant energy, heat, or chemical energy; or (*c*) some particular pattern of information. The terms "input" and "output" seem preferable to "stimulus" and "response," which are used in some of the behavioral sciences, because the former terms make it easy to distinguish whether the transmission is of matter, energy, or information, whereas the latter terms often conceal this distinction.

The *template,* genetic input or charter, of a system is the original information input that is the program for its later structure and process, which can be modified by later matter-energy or information inputs from its environment. This program was called an "instruction" by von Neumann.[95]

13. Steady state

When opposing variables in a system are in balance,

that system is in equilibrium with regard to them. The equilibrium may be static and unchanging or it may be maintained in the midst of dynamic change. Since living systems are open systems, with continually altering fluxes of matter-energy and information, many of their equilibria are dynamic and are often referred to as *flux equilibria* or *steady states.* These may be *unstable,* in which a slight disturbance elicits progressive change from the equilibrium state—like a ball standing on an inverted bowl; or *stable,* in which a slight disturbance is counteracted so as to restore the previous state—like a ball in a cup; or *neutral,* in which a slight disturbance makes a change but without cumulative effects of any sort—like a ball on a flat surface with friction.

All living systems tend to maintain steady states (or homeostasis) of many variables, keeping an orderly balance among subsystems which process matter-energy or information. Not only are subsystems usually kept in equilibrium, but systems also ordinarily maintain steady states with their environments and suprasystems, which have outputs to the systems and inputs from them. This prevents variations in the environment from destroying systems. The variables of living systems are constantly fluctuating, however. A moderate change in one variable may produce greater or lesser alterations in other related ones. These alterations may or may not be reversible (see page 81).

13.1   Stress, strain, and threat   There is a *range of stability* for each of numerous variables in all living systems. It is that range within which the rate of correction of deviations is minimal or zero, and beyond which correction occurs. An input or output of either matter-energy or information which, by lack or excess of some characteristic, forces the variables beyond the range of stability, constitutes *stress* and produces a *strain* (or strains) within the system.[96] Input lack and output excess both produce the same strain—diminished amounts in the system. Input excess and output lack both produce the opposite strain—increased amounts. Strains may or may not be capable of being reduced, depending upon their intensity and the resources of the system. The totality of the strains within a system resulting from its template program and from variations in the inputs from its environment can be referred to as its *values* (see page 39). The relative urgency of reducing each of these specific strains represents its *hierarchy of values.*

Stress may be anticipated. Information that a stress is imminent constitutes a *threat* to the system. A threat can create a strain. Recognition of the meaning of the information of such a threat must be based on previously stored (usually learned) information about such situations. A pattern of input information is a threat when—like the odor of the hunter on the wind, or a change in the acidity of fluids around a cell, or a whirling cloud approaching the city—it is capable of eliciting processes which can counteract the stress it presages. Processes—actions or communications—occur in systems only when a stress or a threat has created a strain which pushes a variable beyond its range of stability. A system is a constantly changing cameo, and its environment is a similarly changing intaglio, and the two at all times fit each other. That is, outside stresses or threats are mirrored by inside strains. Matter-energy storage and memory also mirror the past environment, but with certain alterations (see pages 30, 58, and 67).

13.1.1 Lack stress   Ordinarily there is a standard range of rates at which each sort of input enters a system. If the input rate falls below this range, it constitutes a *lack stress.*

13.1.2 Excess stress   If the input rate goes above this range, it is an *excess stress.*

13.1.3 Matter-energy stress   Systems undergo stress in various ways. One class of stresses is the *matter-energy stresses,* including: (*a*) matter-energy input lack or underload—starvation or inadequate fuel input; (*b*) matter-energy input excess or overload; and (*c*) restraint of the system, binding it physically. (Alternative *c* may be the equivalent of *a* or *b*.)

13.1.4 Information stress   Systems also undergo *information stresses,* including: (*a*) information input lack or underload, resulting from a dearth of information in the environment or from improper function of the external sense organs or input transducers; (*b*) injection of noise into the system, which has an effect of information cutoff, much like the previous stress; and (*c*) information input excess or overload. Informational stresses may involve changes in the rate of information input or in its meaning.

13.1.5 The Le Châtelier principle in closed and open systems   Le Châtelier stated his principle, which applies to nonliving systems and possibly also to living systems, as follows:[97]

"Every system in chemical equilibrium undergoes, upon the variation of one of the factors of the equilibrium, a transformation in such a direction that, if it had produced itself, would have led to a variation of opposite sign to the factor under consideration." A common restatement of this principle is: "A stable system under stress will move in that direction which tends to minimize the stress." That is, a compensatory force will develop which will tend to minimize the effect of stress; it will be exerted opposite to the stress, and it is usually accompanied by changes in other related, subsidiary variables. By this we mean system variables not primarily and directly affected by the applied stress.[98]

This principle or theorem was originally stated after a consideration of the thermodynamics of closed systems, but it has been adapted for open systems by Prigogine.[99] Furthermore, a related theorem has been developed by Prigogine concerning steady states in open systems. He has stated that, for a fairly general class of cases, such steady states approach minimum entropy production.[100] It is possible for entropy not to increase in such systems, and they are able to maintain steady states.

Figure 2-3 represents one possible model for such a system in steady state. If a ping-pong ball is held in a

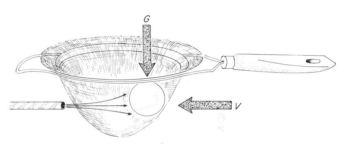

Fig. 2-3 A steady state in an open system. Symbols: *G*, vertical downward gravitational force; *V*, horizontal variable tending to return ball to equilibrium point.

kitchen strainer, it is possible to blow horizontally through a straw at the ball. The faster the stream of air moves, the higher the ball rises in the strainer, until finally it passes a critical point and goes over the edge. Then a change of state results.

Vertical downward forces (*G*) tend to return the ball as close as possible to the equilibrium point. Something is minimized in such systems, and it appears to be the rate of change of entropy production. The single variable (*V*) which, according to Le Châtelier's principle, tends to return the ball as close as possible to the equilibrium point, is equal and opposite in effect to the stream of air coming in. Within the system this variable or equilibratory force tends to operate at the expense of certain other associated variables related to adjustment processes of the system. There are, of course, fluctuations in these variables over time. Systems which maintain stability over long periods of time apparently tend to reduce the costs involved in the activation of these associated variables (see page 41).[101]

13.2 Adjustment processes   Those processes of subsystems which maintain steady states in systems, keeping variables within their ranges of stability despite stresses, are *adjustment processes.* In some systems a single variable may be influenced by multiple adjustment processes. As Ashby has pointed out, a living system's adjustment processes are so coupled that the system is ultrastable.[102] This characteristic can be illustrated by the example of an army cot. It is made of wires, each of which would break under a 120-kg weight, yet it can easily support a sleeper of that weight. The weight is applied to certain wires, and as it becomes greater, first nearby links and then those farther and farther away, take up part of the load. Thus a heavy weight which would break any of the component wires alone can be sustained. In a living system, if one component cannot handle a stress, more and more others are recruited to help. Eventually the entire capacity of the system may be involved in coping with the situation.

13.2.1 Feedback   The term *feedback* means that two channels exist, carrying information, such that channel B loops back from the output to the input of channel A and transmits some portion of the signals emitted by channel A (see Fig. 2-4.)[103] These are tell-

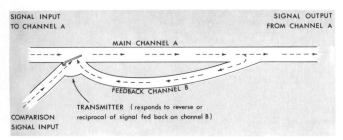

Fig. 2-4 Negative feedback.

tales or monitors of the outputs of channel A. The transmitter on channel A is a device with two inputs, formally represented by a function with two independent variables, one the signal to be transmitted on channel A and the other a previously transmitted signal fed back on channel B. The new signal transmitted on channel A is selected to decrease the strain resulting from any error or deviation in the feedback signal from a criterion or comparison reference signal indicating the state of the output of channel A which the system seeks to maintain steady. This provides control of the output of channel A on the basis of actual rather than expected performance.

The feedback signals have a certain probability of *error*. They differ in the *lag* in time which they require to affect the system. Their lag may be minimal, so that each one is fed back to the input of the latter channel before the next signal is transmitted. Or their lag may be longer and several signals may be transmitted before they arrive to affect the decision about what signal to transmit next. Feedback signals also differ in their *gain* or extent of corrective effect. When the

signals are fed back over the feedback channel in such a manner that they increase the deviation of the output from a steady state, *positive feedback* exists. When the signals are reversed, so that they decrease the deviation of the output from a steady state, it is *negative feedback*. Positive feedback alters variables and destroys their steady states. Thus it can initiate system changes. Unless limited, it can alter variables enough to destroy systems. Negative feedback maintains steady states in systems. It cancels an initial deviation or error in performance. As Ashby says:[104] "the importance of feedback as a necessary method for the correction of error is now accepted everywhere."

Cybernetics, the study of methods of feedback control, is an important part of systems theory. It has led to the recognition of certain formal identities among various sorts of nonliving and living systems.[105] In a complex system, control is achieved by many finely adjusted, interlocking processes involving transmissions of matter-energy and information.[106]

There are many such systems, living and nonliving. An automatic tracking device is one nonliving example. By means of such a device, aircraft-to-aircraft fire-control systems may be set up that keep guns or missiles pointed accurately at a maneuvering target in spite of the motion of the plane in which they are mounted.[107]

Steady states in all living systems are controlled by negative feedbacks. A living system is self-regulating because in it input not only affects output, but output often adjusts input. The result is that the system adapts homeostatically to its environment. Elkinton and Danowski point out how complex these physiological self-regulating servomechanisms of mammalian organisms are. They illustrate this by the example of bodily water balance:

The output of water in excess of electrolyte controlled by the antidiuretic hormone in the kidney, produces a rise in extracellular electrolyte concentration. The rise in this concentration feeds back to the osmoreceptors in the hypothalamus to stimulate the production of antidiuretic hormone (ADH) [vasopressin, see pages 391 and 456] in the supraoptico-hypophyseal system, and so the error in output of water tends to be corrected. At the same time this system is linked to regulation of intake through thirst. Hypertonicity of extra-cellular fluid with resultant cellular dehydration stimulates thirst and increased intake of water as well as the production of ADH. Thus both intake and output are regulated to minimize error in water content of the body.[108]

They go on to describe the further relationships between intake of sodium, appetite, and water balance:

It is tempting to consider the possibility of describing all these linked servomechanisms in the organism in terms of control of energy exchange with the environment. Thus the total body content of solids and fluids is maintained in the healthy adult at a constant level with oscillation about a mean. . . . The dynamics of the body fluids are one aspect of the integrated function of the organism by which a steady state is maintained with the aid of exogenous energy ultimately derived from the sun.

Vickers describes adjustment processes of living systems in terms of feedbacks which correct deviations of systems from desirable states, as follows:

The problem for R [a regulating process] is to choose a way of behaving which will neutralize the disturbance threatening the maintenance of E [a desirable state]. Success means initiating behavior which will reduce the deviation between the actual course of affairs and the course which would be consonant with E; or at least preventing its nearer approach to the limit of the unacceptable or the disastrous.

This decision is a choice between a limited number of alternatives. Men and societies have only a finite number of ways of behaving, perhaps a much smaller number than we realize; and the number actually available and relevant to a given situation is far smaller still. It is thus essential to regard these decisions as the exercise of restricted choice.

These decisions are of four possible kinds. When the usual responses fail, the system may alter itself, for instance by learning new skills or reorganizing itself so as to make new behaviors possible; it may alter the environment; it may withdraw from the environment and seek a more favorable one; or it may alter E. These are possible, if at all, only within limits; and all together may prove insufficient.

It remains to ask how men and societies choose from among these alternatives, when choose they must. In brief, the answer is "by experience."[109]

At every level of living systems numerous variables are kept in a steady state, within a range of stability, by negative feedback controls. When these fail, the structure and process of the system alter markedly—perhaps to the extent that the system does not survive. Feedback control always exhibits some oscillation and always has some lag. When the organism maintains its balance in space, this lag is caused by the slowness of transmissions in the nervous system but is only of the order of hundredths of a second. An organization like a corporation may take hours to correct a breakdown in an assembly line and days or weeks to correct a bad management decision. In a society the lag can sometimes be so great that, in effect, it comes too late. General staffs often plan for the last war rather than the next. Governments receive rather slow official feedbacks from the society at periodic elections. They can, however, get faster feedbacks from the press, other mass media, picketers, or demonstrators. Public opinion surveys can accelerate the social feedback process. The speed and accuracy of feedback have much to do with the effectiveness of the adjustment processes they mobilize.

There are various different types of feedback:

13.2.1.1 Internal feedback   Such a feedback loop never passes outside the boundary of the system. An example is the temperature-control mechanism of mammals.

13.2.1.2 External feedback   Such a loop passes outside the system boundary: for instance, when a patient asks a nurse to bring him an extra blanket for his bed.

13.2.1.3 Loose feedback   Such a loop permits marked deviations from steady state, or error, before initiating corrections. In a democratic country, for instance, an elected official usually remains in office for his entire term even though his constituency disapproves of his actions.

13.2.1.4 Tight feedback   Such a loop rapidly corrects any errors or deviations. An illustration is a tightrope-walker's balance control.

From a study of electronic systems which carry out some sort of adaptive control, Kazda has listed five functional types of feedback.[110] Each of these types, and combinations of them, can be found among the complexly adaptive living systems. They are:

13.2.1.5 Passive adaptation   Achieves adaptation not by changing system variables but by altering environmental variables. Examples: a heater controlled by a thermostat; a snake's temperature control.

13.2.1.6 Input-signal adaptation   Adapts to changes in characteristics of the input signal by altering system variables. Examples: automatic radio volume control; the iris of the eye.

13.2.1.7 Extremum adaptation   Self-adjusts for a maximum or minimum of some variable. Examples: a computer which minimizes passenger waiting time for a battery of elevators; a department store buyer who purchases as cheaply as possible articles which he thinks his store can sell for the best profit.

13.2.1.8 System-variable adaptation   Bases self-adjustment on measurement of system variables. Examples: an automatic train dispatcher; a political system which counts votes to determine policies.

13.2.1.9 System-characteristic adaptation   Self-adjustment based on measurements made on the output of the system. Examples: an autogyro; a student who practices speaking in a foreign language by listening to recordings of his own speech.

13.2.2 Power   In relation to energy processing, *power* is the rate at which work is performed, work being calculated as the product of a force and the distance through which it acts. The term also has another quite different meaning. In relation to information processing, *power* is control, the ability of one system to elicit compliance from another, at the same or a different level. A system transmits a command signal or message to a given address with a signature identifying the transmitter as a legitimate source of command information. The message is often in the imperative mode, specifying an action the receiver is expected to carry out. It elicits compliance at the lower levels because the electrical or chemical form of the signal sets off a specific reaction. At higher levels the receiving system is likely to comply because it has learned that the transmitter is capable of evoking rewards or punishments from the suprasystem, depending on how the receiver responds. Characteristically, in hierarchies of living systems, each level has a degree of autonomy and is also partially controlled by levels above and below it. None can have complete autonomy if the system is to be integrated effectively. A mutual "working agreement" thus is essential.

How is power or control exerted? A system transmits an information output, a command signal or message. Such a message has certain specific characteristics: (a) It has an *address*—it includes information indicating to what specific receiver system or systems it is transmitted, those which are to be influenced. If the channel on which it is transmitted does not branch, simply sending it on that channel gives the address information. If the channel branches, the address indicates the appropriate routing at branching points. (b) It has a *signature*—it includes information indicating which system transmitted it. If it travels on a channel that has only one transmitter, its presence on that channel gives the signature information. Simply having a form that can be uniquely produced by only one system can give the information. Or it may have specific signature symbols added to the content. (c) It contains evidence that the transmitter is a *legitimate* or appropriate source of command information to influence decisions of the receiver. In some systems commands of a certain sort are complied with regardless of the source. For example, thyroid cells respond to thyrotropic hormone regardless of whether it comes from the pituitary gland of that system or is an intravenous injection. Telephone information operators respond to requests for telephone numbers regardless of who makes them. In such systems the form of the command carries its own evidence of legitimacy. In other systems the message must include the title of the transmitter or other evidence of its legitimacy, along with the context of the command. (d) It is often literally in the *imperative mood,* styled as a command, but even when it is not couched in this form, it implies expectation of compliance. (e) The primary content of the message *specifies an action* the receiver is expected to carry out. It reinforces one alternative rather than others in a decision the receiver is constrained to make.

Why can such a message elicit compliance? At lower levels, because the electrical or chemical form of what is transmitted sets off a specific reaction. At higher levels, because the receiving system is part of a suprasystem that can transmit rewarding and punishing inputs to it. The receiver has learned that, because the signature indicates that the message is from a legitimate source capable of influencing some part of the suprasystem to make such inputs, there is a certain significant probability of receiving such rewards or punishments, depending on how it responds (see Hypothesis 3.3.7.2-4, page 100). This is why legitimacy of the source is important; it indicates that the message is from a transmitter which has an established relationship with the suprasystem and can therefore influence the receiver through it. This fact helps to determine values and purposes or goals of the system, motivating it to act in compliance with the command (see page 68). Mrs. Martin, for example, can command Mrs. Wrenn's support in the women's club election because Mrs. Martin is on the committee which selects the girls to be invited to serve at the annual Christmas party, and Mrs. Wrenn has a daughter who wants to serve. Consequently Mrs. Martin has "fate control" over Mrs. Wrenn, being able to influence her actions (see pages 570 and 571). Power among nations frequently depends on the ability to make exchanges with other countries; a nation which can offer favorable trade inducements or foreign aid often gains a measure of control over others.

Measures of power are joint functions of: (a) the percentage of acts of a system which are controlled, *i.e.,* changed from one alternative to another; (b) some measure of how critical the acts controlled are to the system; (c) the number of systems controlled; and (d) the level of systems controlled, since control of one system at a high level may influence many systems at lower levels.

Certain differences among systems influence how power is wielded. As I have noted (see pages 31 and 32), systems can be either *local* or *dispersed.* Transmitting commands throughout dispersed systems requires more energy than in local systems because the components are farther apart, and the markers must be dispatched over longer channels.

Systems, also, may be either *cohesive* or *noncohesive.* They are cohesive if the parts remain close enough together in space, despite any movement of the system, to make possible transmission of coordinating information along their channels. Otherwise they are noncohesive.

Systems, also, may be either *integrated* or *segregated.* If they are integrated, they are centralized, the single decider of the system exercising primary control. If they are segregated, there are multiple deciders, each controlling a subsystem or component. The more integrated a system is, the more feedbacks, commands, and information relevant to making and implementing the central decisions flow among its parts. Therefore the more integrated a system is, the more one part is likely to influence or control another. A system is more likely to be integrated if it is local rather than dispersed. Integration, of course, requires less energy in local than in dispersed systems. The degree of integration of a system is measured by a joint function of: (*a*) the percentage of decisions made by the system's central decider; (*b*) the rate at which the system accurately processes information relevant to the central decisions, without significant lag or restriction of the range of messages; and (*c*) the extent to which conflict among systems and components is minimized.

13.2.3 Conflict   In branching channels or networks, commands may come to a receiver simultaneously from two or more transmitters. If these messages direct the receiver to do two or more acts which it can carry out successfully, simultaneously or successively, there is no problem. If they direct the receiver to carry out two or more actions which are incompatible—because they cannot be done simultaneously or because doing one makes it impossible later to do the other—a special sort of strain, *conflict,* arises. The incompatible commands may arise from two or more systems at the same level or at different levels. For example, two subsystems may demand more energy input, and the system may be unable to meet the demands. (Jean Valjean could not provide the bread to feed his whole family.) Or two systems are in competition for a desired input, but there is not enough for both. (An embryo develops with stunted legs because the blood supply to the lower part of the body is partially blocked.) Or a system makes demands which threaten the existence of its suprasystem. (The great powers demand a veto on all significant actions of the United Nations.) An effective system ordinarily resolves such conflicts by giving greater compliance to the command with higher priority in terms of its values (see below). But it may resolve the conflict by many sorts of adjustment processes.

13.2.4 Purpose and goal   By the information input of its charter or genetic input, or by changes in behavior brought about by rewards and punishments from its suprasystem, a system develops a preferential hierarchy of values that gives rise to decision rules which determine its preference for one internal steady-state value rather than another. This is its *pur-*

pose. It is the comparison value which it matches to information received by negative feedback in order to determine whether the variable is being maintained at the appropriate steady-state value. In this sense it is normative. The system then takes one alternative action rather than another because it appears most likely to maintain the steady state. When disturbed, this state is restored by the system by successive approximations, in order to relieve the strain of the disparity recognized internally between the feedback signal and the comparison signal. Any system may have multiple purposes simultaneously.

A system may also have an external *goal,* such as reaching a target in space, or developing a relationship with any other system in the environment. Or it may have several goals at the same time. Just as there is no question that a guided missile is zeroing in on a target, so there is no question that a rat in a maze is searching for the goal of food at its end or that the Greek people under Alexander the Great were seeking the goal of world conquest. As Ashby notes, natural selection permits only those systems to continue which have goals that enable them to survive in their particular environments.[111] The external goal may change constantly—as when a hunter chases a moving fox, or a man searches for a wife by dating one girl after another—while the internal purpose remains the same.[112]

It is not difficult to distinguish purposes from goals, as I use the terms: an amoeba has the purpose of maintaining adequate energy levels, and therefore it has the goal of ingesting a bacterium; a boy has the purpose of keeping his body temperature in the proper range, and so he has the goal of finding and putting on his sweater; Poland had the purpose in March 1939, of remaining uninvaded and autonomous, and so she sought the goal of a political alliance with Britain and France in order to have assistance in keeping both Germany and Russia from crossing her borders.

A system's hierarchy of values determines its purposes as well as its goals. The question is often asked of the words "goal" and "purpose," as it is of the word "value," whether they are appropriately defined as whatever is *actually* preferred or sought by the system, or as what *should* be preferred or sought. I shall use it in the former sense, unless I indicate that the latter sense is being employed. When the latter meaning is used, I shall not imply that the norm as to what the goal should be is established in any absolute way, but rather that it is set by the system's suprasystem when it originates its template, or by rewards and punishments. Ashby has said that:[113] " . . . there is no property of an organization that is good in any absolute sense; all are relative to some given environment, or to some given set of threats and disturbances, or to some given set of problems." A system is adjusted to its suprasystem only if it has an internal purpose or external goal which is consistent with the norm established by the suprasystem. Since this is not always true, it is important to distinguish the two notions of the actual and the normative.

The reason it is important to a receiver whether a command signal is transmitted from a legitimate source (see page 38) is that, if it is legitimate, it can influence the suprasystem to make reward and punishment inputs to the receiver and so potentially can alter both its purposes and its goals.

It is necessary to distinguish two meanings of the term "purpose." One is function or role (see page 30) of the system in the suprasystem, and the other, independent concept is the internally determined control process of the system which maintains one of its variables at a given steady-state value. In their early paper on cybernetics, Rosenblueth, Wiener, and Bigelow saw rudimentary purposive behavior in some nonliving systems, like a torpedo, which can "home" to a moving target.[114] The concept of purpose has been made suspect to most scientists by teleological formulations which suggest that living systems strive for mystical ends which are not clearly formulated. These formulations are from the viewpoint of the scientific observer. On this topic, Rothstein has written:

One would not introduce the notion of purpose unless the system were only partially specified. With complete specification the 'stimulus' is specified, likewise the action of the regulator and ditto the response of the system. It is only when an ensemble of possible stimuli is considered and *no information is available* to predict *a priori* which of the ensemble will materialize that one is motivated to introduce the concept of purpose.

One can say the initial state causes the final state, or that the final state is the purpose of the initial state. In this form one can object that the concept of purpose has been reduced to an empty play on words. However, consider an experimenter interested in producing some particular situation. In many cases he sets up an initial configuration from which the desired situation will ensue because of the laws the system obeys. The final situation is the goal or purpose of the experimenter, which has determined his choice of initial conditions. In this sense, we can call his purpose the cause of the initial condition. For completely defined physical systems, there is thus no logical distinction between cause and purpose as either determines the other. Meaningful distinctions are only possible in terms of considerations extrinsic to the system. It now follows that physics is as incapable of finding a purpose or goal of the whole universe as it is of finding its origin or cause.[115]

Rothstein believes that the next-to-last sentence is true of systems in general.

But if purpose is defined not in terms of the observer but in terms of specific values of internal variables which systems maintain in steady states by taking corrective actions, then the concept is scientifically useful. Reinterpreting purpose in concepts of modern physics, Sommerhoff maintains that the notion concerns a certain future event, a "focal condition" (in my terms, a goal).[116] This focal condition, he says, is a determinant of a "directive correlation." Such a correlation is characteristically found between processes in living systems and in their environments. Variables in them are so "geared" or interrelated that, within certain ranges, they will at a later time only bring about the focal condition. Such a situation requires that there was some prior state of affairs which gave rise jointly both to the processes in the system and to those in its environment. Feedback is one way such joint causation can be accomplished. Sommerhoff believes that this sort of process explains such phenomena of living systems as adaptation of individuals and species to their environments, coordination and regulation of internal system processes, repair of systems after trauma, and various sorts of behavior including learning, memory, and decision making. For example, one cannot distinguish between products which are put out by a system and wastes which are excreted without knowing the purpose of the system internally and its related goals in the suprasystem. This is graphically demonstrated by the following "Ballad of the Interstellar Merchants":[117]

> Among the wild Reguleans
> we trade in beer and hides
> for sacks of mMomimotl leaves
> and carcasses of brides.
>
> They love 'em and they leave 'em,
> once affection's been displayed,
> to the everloving merchants
> of the Interstellar Trade.
>
> Chorus: Don't throw that bride away, friends
> don't turn that carcass loose.
> What's only junk on Regulus
> is gold on Betelgeuse.

Engineers must know the purposes which a machine is to have, what steady-state values its variables are to have, before they begin to design it. This may or may not be related to some purpose or function in the suprasystem. Occasionally comics have built apparatuses with wheels, cogs, gears, pistons, and cams that merely operate, without any useful function in the suprasystem, or gadgets that function only to turn themselves off. If one is to understand a system, know what it is to optimize, or measure its efficiency (*i.e.,* the ratio between the effectiveness of its performance and the costs involved), one must learn its expected function or purpose in the suprasystem. The charter of a group, organization, society, or supranational system describes this. Biologists, however, have a difficult time defining the functions of a cell, organ, or organism, except in terms of the survival of the system itself, or of the organism of which it is a part, or of its particular type.

Such facts as that a normal sea urchin can develop either from a complete egg or from a half egg led Driesch to embrace vitalism, the doctrine that phenomena of life cannot be explained in natural science terms.[118] This sort of *equifinality*, he contended, could be explained only by some mystical vitalism. Equifinality means that a final state of any living system may be reached from different initial conditions and in different ways.[119] But this is exactly what all cybernetic systems do, living and nonliving.

Bertalanffy has opposed Driesch's views on the basis of an analysis of living systems as open systems.[120] The steady states of open systems depend upon system constants more than environmental conditions, so long as the environment has a surplus of essential inputs. Within a wide range of inputs the composition of living tissue, for example, remains relatively constant. Of course—and Bertalanffy does not always make this clear—inputs outside the "normal" range may destroy the system or affect its structure and functioning. Each separate system, moreover, has its own history, different from others of its kind, and therefore any final state is affected by the various preceding genetic and environmental influences which have impinged upon the system. All organisms do not develop into perfect adulthood, and presumably each single cell may have slightly different characteristics as a result of its history. These limitations upon Bertalanffy's principle do not destroy its importance. The obvious purposive activities of most living systems, which have seemed to many to require a vitalistic or teleological interpretation, can be explained as open-system characteristics by means of this principle. Some open physical systems also have this characteristic.

13.2.5 Costs and efficiency   All adjustment processes have their *costs*, in energy of nonliving or living systems, in material resources, in information (including in social systems a special form of information often conveyed on a marker of metal or paper money), or in time required for an action. Any of these may be scarce. (Time is a scarcity for mortal living systems.) Any of these is valued if it is essential for reducing strains. The costs of adjustment processes differ from

one to another and from time to time. They may be immediate or delayed, short-term or long-term.

How successfully systems accomplish their purposes can be determined if those purposes are known. A system's *efficiency*, then, can be determined as the ratio of the success of its performance to the costs involved. A system constantly makes economic decisions directed toward increasing its efficiency by improving performance and decreasing costs. Economic analyses of *cost effectiveness* are equally important in biological and social science but much more common and more sophisticated in social than in biological sciences. In social systems such analyses are frequently aided by *program budgeting*. This involves keeping accounts separately for each subsystem or component that carries out a distinct program. The matter-energy, information, money, and time costs of the program in such analyses are compared with various measures of the efficiency of performance of the program. How efficiently a system adjusts to its environment is determined by what strategies it employs in selecting adjustment processes and whether they satisfactorily reduce strains without being too costly. This decision process can be analyzed by a mathematical approach to economic decisions, or game theory. This is a general theory concerning the best strategies for weighing "plays" against "payoffs," for selecting actions which will increase profits while decreasing losses, increase rewards while decreasing punishments, improve adjustments of variables to appropriate steady-state values, or attain goals while diminishing costs. Relevant information available to the decider can improve such decisions. Consequently such information is valuable. But there are costs to obtaining such information. A mathematical theory on how to calculate the value of relevant information in such decisions was developed by Hurley.[121] This depends on such considerations as whether it is tactical (about a specific act) or strategic (about a policy for action), whether it is reliable or unreliable, overtly or secretly obtained, accurate, distorted, or erroneous.

14. Conclusions

The most general form of systems theory is a set of logical or mathematical statements about all conceptual systems.[122] A subset of this concerns all concrete systems. A subset concerns the very special and very important living systems, *i.e.*, general living systems theory.

My analysis of living systems uses concepts of thermodynamics, information theory, cybernetics, and systems engineering, as well as the classical concepts appropriate to each level. The purpose is to produce a description of living structure and process in terms of input and output, flows through systems, steady states, and feedbacks, which will clarify and unify the facts of life.

In such fundamental considerations it would be surprising if many new concepts appear, for countless good minds have worked long on these matters over many years. Indeed, new original ideas should at first be suspect, though if they withstand examination they should be welcomed. My intent is not to create a new school or art form but to discern the pattern of a mosaic which lies hidden in the cluttered, colored marble chips of today's empirical facts. I may assert, along with Pascal,

Let no man say that I have said nothing new—the arrangement of the material is new. In playing tennis, we both use the same ball, but one of us places it better. I would just as soon be told that I have used old terms. Just as the same thoughts differently arranged form a different discourse, so the same words differently arranged form different thoughts.

The last thing one does in writing a book is to know what to put first.[123]

NOTES AND REFERENCES

[1]NOTE: Deutsch and Isard have addressed themselves to this problem. Cf. Deutsch, K. W. & Isard, W. A note on a generalized concept of effective distance. *Behav. Sci.*, 1961, **6**, 308–311.

[2]Franklin, W. S. On entropy. *Physical Rev.*, 1910, **30**, 766–775.

[3]Hartley, R. V. L. Transmission of information. *Bell Sys. tech. J.*, 1928, **7**, 535.

[4]Shannon, C. E. A mathematical theory of communication. *Bell Sys. tech. J.*, 1948, **27**, 379–423 and 623–656.

[5]Gabor, D. A summary of communication theory. In W. Jackson (Ed.). *Communication theory*. London: Butterworths, 1953, 2. Reprinted by permission.

[6]NOTE: In de Beauregard, O. C. Sur l'equivalence entre information et entropie. *Sciences*, 1961, 54, we read that "cybernetics is led to define *'negentropy'* and *'information'* with a sort of subjective doubling, and to admit the possibility of a transition in two senses.

negentropy ⇄ *information*

"Let us note that the meaning of the word 'information' is not the same in the two senses: in the direct transition *negentropy* → *information*, 'information' signifies acquisition of knowledge; it is the current modern sense, and the corresponding transition appears to be like the elementary process of *observation*. In the reciprocal transition *information* → *negentropy*, 'information' signifies *power of organization;* it is the ancient Aristotelian sense, and the corresponding transition appears to be like the elementary process of *action. To admit, as cybernetics does, reciprocity of the transition negentropy ⇄ information, is to admit ipso facto the equivalence of the two meanings, modern and Aristotelian, of the word 'information.'"* (My translation.)

And Zeman (Zeman, J. Le sens philosophique du terme "l'information." *La Documentation en France,* 1962, **3**, 20–21) writes:

"The Latin word 'informare,' from which is derived the word 'information,' signifies to put in form, to give a form or an aspect, to form, to create, but also to represent, present, create an idea or emotion. It is possible to understand information in general as whatever is put in form or in order. Information signifies the formation of several elements or parties—either material or nonmaterial—into some form, into some classed system—that represents classification of something. Under this general form information is also the classification of symbols and of their relations in a nexus like the organization of the organs and of the functions of a living being or the organization of any social system or any other community in general. Information expresses the organization of a system, which is capable of mathematical description. It does not concern itself with the matter of that system but with the form, which can be the same for very different kinds of matter (black marks of characters on paper, neurons in the brain, ants in an ant nest, etc.).

"If mass is the measure of the effects of gravitation, and of the force of inertia, and energy the measure of movement, information is in the quantitative sense the measure of the organization of the material object. It is evident that the characteristics of organization are linked not only to matter but also to the characteristics of matter: space, time, and movement. Matter, space, time, movement, and organization are in mutual connection." (My translation.)

[7]Simon, H. A. *The new science of management.* New York: Harper, 1960.

[8]Cohen, J. E. Information theory and music. *Behav. Sci.*, 1962, **7**, 137–163.

[9]von Neumann, J. *The computer and the brain.* New Haven: Yale Univ. Press, 1958, 6–7.
NOTE: Christie, Luce, and Macy (Christie, L. S., Luce, R. D., & Macy, J., Jr. *Communication and learning in task-oriented groups.* Cambridge, Mass.: Research Lab. of Electronics, MIT, Tech. Rep. No. 231, May 13, 1952) call the physical form which the communication takes the "symbol design" and the information itself the "symbol contents."

[10]Fernandez-Moran, H. Potential application of electron-optical methods to storage of information in direct retrieval. In C. S. Pittendrigh (Ed.). *Biology and the exploration of Mars.* Washington: National Academy of Sciences, 1966, 503–506.

[11]Bremermann, H. J. Optimization through evolution and recombination. In M. C. Yovits, G. T. Jacobi, & G. D. Goldstein (Eds.). *Self-organizing systems.* Washington: Spartan Books, 1962, 93–106.

[12]Minsky, M. Steps toward artificial intelligence. *IRE Proc.*, 1961, **49**, 3–30.

[13]Quastler, H. Information theory terms and their psychological correlates. In H. Quastler (Ed.). *Information theory in psychology: problems and methods.* Glencoe, Ill.: Free Press, 1955, 159–160.

[14]Maxwell, J. C. *Theory of heat.* London: Longmans, Green, 1871.

[15]Planck, M. *Treatise on thermodynamics.* New York: Dover, 1945.

[16]Boltzmann, L. & Nabl, J. Kinetische Theorie der Materie. *Encyklopädie der Mathematischen Wissenschäften.* Vol. 5, Part I. Leipzig: B. G. Teubner, 1903.

[17]Helmholtz, H. L. F. v. *Abendlungen zür Thermodynamik.* Leipzig: Engelmann, 1902.

[18]Gibbs, J. W. *Elementary principles of statistical mechanics.* New Haven: Yale Univ. Press, 1902. Reprinted by permission.

[19]Wiener, N. *Cybernetics.* Cambridge, Mass.: Technology Press, 1948, 76.

[20]NOTE: The basic Shannon statistical measure of information is $H = \Sigma p_i$. Cf. Shannon, C. E. *Op. cit.*, 392–394.

[21]Schrödinger, E. *What is life?* New York: Macmillan, 1945, 72.

[22]Rapoport, A. What is information? *Synthese*, 1953, **9**, 169. Reprinted by permission.

[23]Szilard, L. Über die Entropieverminderung in einem thermodynamischen System bei Eingriffen intelligenter Wesen. *Zeitschr. f. Phys.*, 1929, **53**, 840–856. (Trans. by A. Rapoport and M. Knoller as: On the increase of entropy in a thermodynamic system by the intervention of intelligent beings. *Behav. Sci.*, 1964, **9**, 301–310.)

[24]Maxwell, J. C. *Op. cit.*, 308–309.

NOTE: C. A. Muses (in his Foreword to J. Rothstein. *Communication, organization, and science.* Indian Hills, Colo. Falcon's Wing Press, 1958, xcii–xciii) points out the amusing fact that all three laws of thermodynamics can be expressed in demoniacal terms: "The first law excludes the existence of a demon who creates energy from nothing [Rothstein calls it Aladdin's demon in Rothstein, J. Physical demonology. *Methodos*, 1959, **11**, 99–121.], the second does the same for Maxwell's demon, while the third disposes of Laplace's demon."

[25]Brillouin, L. Maxwell's demon cannot operate: information and entropy, I and II. *J. appl. Phys.*, 1951, **22**, 334–343.

[26]NOTE: Brillouin's application of his concepts to large-scale systems is seen in the following passage. He is discussing gas in a container: (*Ibid.*, 342–343. Reprinted by permission.)

"Assume plane parallel walls and an initial situation where a plane wave is moving from one wall to the opposite one; the wave will go on propagating from left to right, be reflected, then come back from right to left, be reflected on the first wall, and so on for a certain time, until viscosity effects finally destroy the wave and change its energy into heat motion. The information contained in the wave persists for a practical length of time before it eventually disappears. The system can be used for storage of information (replace the gas by mercury and you have the mercury delay line memory system) or for communication. The case of electromagnetic waves propagating along a cable is very similar. The wave may be picked up by a receiver at the end of the cable, or it may be reflected and propagate back and forth until it finally dies out by ohmic resistance. At any rate, when information disappears, the whole system goes back to its maximum entropy value.

"Transmission or storage of information is associated with the temporary existence of the system in a state of lower entropy. The decrease in entropy can be taken as a measure of the amount of information."

There has been much discussion pro and con as to whether microscopic physical entropy is the same as the entropy of functionally interdependent macrosystems like living systems. Perhaps at each level of system the principle is the same in that the entropy depends on the number of possible arrangements of the units and the particular arrangement which exists at a given moment, but the relevant units are larger and more complex at each higher level. Among the articles concerning this difficult problem are several in H. Quastler (Ed.). *Information theory in biology.* Urbana: Univ. of Illinois Press, 1953: Linschitz, H. Information and physical entropy, 14–15; Augenstine, L. Information and thermodynamic entropy, 16–20; Baer, R. M. Some general remarks on information theory and entropy, 21–24; Branson, H. R. A definition of information from the thermodynamics of irreversible processes, 25–40; and Linschitz, H. The information content of a bacterial cell, 251–262. Cf. also, Morowitz, H. J. Some order-disorder considerations in living systems. *Bull. math. Biophys.*, 1955, **17**, 81–86.

[27]Valentinuzzi, M. & Valentinuzzi, M. E. Information content of chemical structures and some possible biological applications. *Bull. math. Biophys.*, 1962, **24**, 11–27.

[28]Foster, C., Rapoport, A., & Trucco, E. Some unsolved problems in the theory of non-isolated systems. *Gen. Systems*, 1957, **2**, 9–29.

[29]Prigogine, I. *Introduction to thermodynamics of irreversible processes.* Springfield, Ill.: Charles C Thomas, 1955.

[30]De Groot, S. R. *Thermodynamics of irreversible processes.* New York: Interscience, 1952.

[31]Prigogine, I. *Op. cit.*, 84.

[32]Pierce, J. R. & Cutler, C. C. Interplanetary communications. In F. I. Ordway, III (Ed.). *Advances in space science.* Vol. 1. New York: Academic Press, 1959, 68–69.

[33]Szilard, L. *Op. cit.*, 309.

[34]Brillouin, L. *Op. cit.*, 334.

[35]Shannon, C. E. Probability of error for optimal codes in a Gaussian channel. *Bell Sys. tech. J.*, 1959, **38**, 611–656.

[36]Shannon, C. E. A mathematical theory of communication. *Op. cit.*, 380–382.

[37]Beach, F. A. & Jaynes, J. Effects of early experience upon the behavior of animals. *Psychol. Bull.*, 1954, **51**, 239–263.

[38]Harlow, H. F. & Harlow, M. K. Social deprivation in monkeys. *Sci. Amer.*, 1962, **207(5)**, 137–146.

[39]NOTE: As information increases about some thing or event outside the system that receives a communication, uncertainty or ignorance about it decreases. How large the maximum uncertainty or ignorance can be is determined by how many possible outcomes there are or how many states the thing or event under consideration can take. If there is no correlation, or a random relationship, between the actual outcomes or states and the internal view or concept, within the receiving system, of these outcomes or states, the receiving system has maximum uncertainty or ignorance and is capable of receiving maximum information. As the correlation increases, the amount of uncertainty or ignorance decreases, as does the amount of information it is capable of receiving. When uncertainty or ignorance about it is 0, no further information can be received. So information is the negative of uncertainty or ignorance. Cf. Pask, G. *An approach to cybernetics.* London: Hutchinson, 1961, 26–27. Cf. also Garner, W. R. *Uncertainty and structure as psychological concepts.* New York: Wiley, 1962, especially 2–7.

Cf. also Quastler, H. (*Op. cit.*, 41. Copyright 1955 by the Free Press, a Corporation. Reprinted by permission.) who says that information "is relating to such diverse activities as arranging, constraining, designing, determining, differentiating, messaging, ordering, organizing, planning, restricting, selecting, specializing, specifying, and systematizing; it can be used in connection with all operations which aim at decreasing such quantities as disorder, entropy, generality, ignorance, indistinctness, noise, randomness, uncertainty, variability, and at increasing the amount or degree of certainty, design differentiation, distinctiveness, individualization, information, lawfulness, orderliness, particularity, regularity, specificity, uniqueness."

[40]NOTE: Burgers (Burgers, J. M. On the emergence of patterns of order. *Bull. Amer. Math. Soc.*, 1963, **69**, 1–25) points out that any arrangement represents some form of order or

pattern of regularity when viewed mathematically. And no form is more important or meaningful than any other. He holds that the distinction between order and disorder is made by the living observer and is not inherent in the physical world as viewed by physicists.

And Schafroth [Schafroth, M. R. The concept of temperature. In K. Messel (Ed.). *Selected lectures in modern physics.* London: Macmillan, 1960, 268. Reprinted by permission of Macmillan London and Basingstoke.] observes:

"It is, in fact, not such a trivial matter to define 'disorder.' Scientists exist who have the habit of piling up papers and books in a seemingly random fashion on their desks, yet know all the time how to find a given thing. If someone brings apparent 'order' to this desk, the poor owner may be unable to find anything. In this case, it is obvious that the apparent 'disorder' is, in fact, order, and vice versa. You will see easily that in this sense the order on the desk can be measured by the information the owner has about its state. This example illustrates that, by trying to define 'disorder' more precisely, we return to the previous definition in terms of 'lack of information.'"

[41]Cf. Sadovsky, V. N. General systems theory: its tasks and methods of construction. *Gen. Systems,* 1972, **17,** 171–179.

[42]Bertalanffy, L. v. General systems theory. *Gen. Systems,* 1956, **1,** 3.

NOTE: He suggests that systems can be defined much as I define them, as "sets of elements standing in interaction." And he says that this definition is not so vague and general as to be valueless. He believes that systems can be specified by families of differential equations.

[43]NOTE: Rothstein (Rothstein, J. *Communication organization, and science.* Indian Hills, Colo.: Falcon's Wing Press, 1958, 34–36. Reprinted by permission.) deals with the constraints among units of organized systems in terms of entropy and communication as information processing:

"What do we mean by an organization? First of all an organization presupposes the existence of parts, which, considered in their totality, constitute the organization. The parts must interact. Were there no communication between them, there would be no organization, for we would merely have a collection of individual elements isolated from each other. Each element must be associated with its own set of alternatives. Were there no freedom to choose from a set of alternatives, the corresponding element would be a static, passive cog rather than an active unit. We suggest the following general characterization of organization. Consider a set of elements, each associated with its own set of alternatives. We now define a complexion as a particular set of selections, such that one selection is made from each set of alternatives. There are, of course, as many complexions as there are ways of selecting a representative from each set of alternatives. The set of complexions then has an entropy which is merely the sum of the entropies of the individual sets of alternatives so long as the elements do not interact. Complexion entropy is a maximum for independent elements. Maximal entropy, *i.e.,* zero coupling, will be said to constitute the condition of zero organization."

Ashby [Ashby, W. R. Principles of the self-organizing system. In H. Von Foerster & G. W. Zopf (Eds.). *Principles of self-organization.* New York: Pergamon Press, 1962, 255–257. Reprinted by permission.] also deals with this. Speaking of what "organization" means as applied to systems, he says, "The hard core of the concept is, in my opinion, that of 'conditionality.' As soon as the relation between two entities A and B becomes conditional on C's value or state

then a necessary component of 'organization' is present. Thus *the theory of organization is partly co-extensive with the theory of functions of more than one variable.*"

He goes on to ask when a system is not a system or is not organized: "The converse of 'conditional on,' is 'not conditional on,' so the converse of 'organization' must therefore be, as the mathematical theory shows as clearly, the concept of 'reducibility.' (It is also called 'separability.') This occurs, in mathematical forms, when what looks like a function of several variables (perhaps very many) proves on closer examination to have parts whose actions are *not* conditional on the values of the other parts. It occurs in mechanical forms, in hardware, when what looks like one machine proves to be composed of two (or more) sub-machines, each of which is acting independently of the others. . . .

"The treatment of 'conditionality' (whether by functions of many variables, by correlation analysis, by uncertainty analysis, or by other ways) makes us realize that the essential idea is that there is first a product space—that of the possibilities—within which some sub-set of points indicates the actualities. This way of looking at 'conditionality' makes us realize that it is related to that of 'communication;' and it is, of course, quite plausible that we should define parts as being 'organized' when 'communication' (in some generalized sense) occurs between them. (Again the natural converse is that of independence, which represents non-communication.)"

"Now 'communication' from A to B necessarily implies some constraint, some correlation between what happens at A and what at B. If, for a given event at A, all possible events may occur at B, then there is no communication from A to B and no constraint over the possible (A, B) couples that can occur. Thus the presence of 'organization' between variables is equivalent to the existence of a constraint in product-space of the possibilities."

[44]NOTE: Von Foerster (Von Foerster, H. Communication amongst automata. *Amer. J. Psychiat.,* 1962, 118, 866–867) points out that, in systems, components or subsystems join in coalitions in which the interacting elements follow a superadditive composition rule: a measure of the sum of its units is larger than the sum of that measure of its units—$\phi(x + y) > \phi x + \phi y$. E.g., if ϕ is the square, then $(x + y)^2 > x^2 + y^2$, for $x^2 + y^2 + 2xy$ is greater than $x^2 + y^2$, by $2xy$. A man with his head is something much more than a man's body plus his separate head.

This is a recent formulation of the classical view that a system must be viewed as a Gestalt, or total configuration. For example, Köhler (Köhler, W. *Die physischen Gestalten in Ruhe und im stationären Zustand.* Braunschweig: Vieweg, 1921) pointed out many years ago that the pattern of electrical charges on a conductor is a resultant of its particular overall form and that it is practically impossible to synthesize such a whole from its parts. If some of the charge is withdrawn locally, the entire pattern of distribution of charges over the whole system is altered. Gestalt theory has had an important influence on current systems theory (cf. Bertalanffy, L. v. *Problems of life: an evaluation of modern biological and scientific thought.* London: Watts, 1952, 147–151, 189–194), just as physical field theory influenced Gestalt theory. Weiss (Weiss, P. Animal behavior as system reaction. *Gen. Systems,* 1959, **4,** 1–44, trans. and rev. from Tierisches Verhalten als "Systemreaktion," *Biologia generalis,* 1925, **1,** 167–248) recognized in an early and classic publication that the behavior of animal organisms is integral system reaction and "not simply the product of a string of component reactions." Recent research on the theory of automata (cf. Hartmanis, J. Symbolic analysis of a decomposition of information processing machines. *Inform. & Control*, 1960, **3**, 154–178) has investigated the necessary and sufficient conditions for decomposing a system into several simpler ones which, when operating in parallel, can produce the same output as the original system.

[45]Cf. Ashby, W. R. *Design for a brain*. (2nd ed. rev.) New York: Wiley, 1960, 16.

Also, Pask, G. *An approach to cybernetics*. London: Hutchinson, 1962.

[46]Pask, G. *Ibid*.

[47]Cf. Hall, A. D. & Fagan, R. E. Definition of system. *Gen. Systems*, 1956, **1**, 18.

[48]Campbell, D. T. Common fate, similarity, and other indices of the status of aggregates of persons as social entities. *Behav. Sci.*, 1958, **3**, 14–25.

[49]Schrödinger, E. *Op. cit*.

[50]Brillouin, L. Life, thermodynamics, and cybernetics. *Amer. Sci.*, 1949, **37**, 558.

[51]NOTE: In Cervinka, V. A dimensional theory of groups. *Sociometry*, 1948, **11**, 100–107, the author very precisely distinguishes, at the group level, between a concrete system, which he calls a "socius," that is a single person in a group together with all his relationships, and a "groupoid," an abstracted system, which is a pattern of attachments of a single kind of relation selected by an observer, which interrelates a set of people.

[52]Simon, H. A. The architecture of complexity. *Proc. Amer. Phil. Soc.*, 1962, **106**, 469.

[53]Parsons, T. & Shils, E. A. (Eds.). *Toward a general theory of action*. Cambridge, Mass.: Harvard Univ. Press, 1951.

[54]Grinker, R. (Ed.). From *Toward a unified theory of human behavior: an introduction to general systems theory*, edited by Roy R. Grinker, Sr., with the assistance of Helen MacGill Hughes, second edition, © 1956, 1967 by Basic Books, Inc., Publishers, New York, p. 328.

[55]NOTE: Ruesch appears to confuse structure and process here.

[56]Grinker, R. *Op. cit.*, 371.

[57]NOTE: Levy (Levy, M. J. *The structure of society*. Princeton: Princeton Univ. Press, 1952, 88–90) makes a very similar distinction between what he calls "concrete structure" and "analytic structure."

[58]Buck, R. C. On the logic of general behavior systems theory. In H. Feigl & M. Scriven (Eds.). *Minnesota studies in the philosophy of science*. Vol. 1. *The foundations of science and the concepts of psychology and psychoanalysis*. Minneapolis: Univ. of Minnesota Press, 1956, 224–226.

[59]Cf. Kroeber, A. L. & Kluckhohn, C. Culture: a critical review of concepts and definitions. *Papers Peabody Museum*, 1952, **47**, 157.

[60]Etzioni, A. *The active society*. New York: Free Press, 1968, 123–125.

[61]Strodtbeck, F. L. & Hook, L. H. The social dimensions of a twelve-man jury table. *Sociometry*, 1961, **24**, 397–414.

[62]Powell, R. M. Sociometric analysis of informal groups—their structure and function in two contrasting communities. *Sociometry*, 1952, **15**, 367–399.

[63]NOTE: I cannot accept Kaplan's overemphasis on relationships when he writes (Kaplan, M. A. *System and process in international politics*. New York: Wiley, 1957, 9. Reprinted by permission.), "The inclusion of the set of essential rules in the state description of political or social action systems reflects the belief that the most important descriptive aspects of these systems are represented in those general relationships which are independent of the specific role occupants. No matter how important labeling was to the Tarquins, sociological and political analysis of the Roman

Kingdom must be directed to the social and political relationships between rulers and led rather than to the fact that a particular family, the Tarquins, was incumbent in that role. Political theory aspires to discover why such a system arose, how it operated, and why it declined. Political theory assumes that had any other family the same attributes and opportunities, the same kind of system would have arisen. Essential rules permit the investigation of types rather than of particulars."

In a later paragraph Kaplan (*Ibid.*, 11) appears to modify his view, admitting that: "An actor may fail to do something he has the capability to do if he is unaware of his capabilities. He may attempt something he is unable to do if he overestimates his capabilities." He may also not be motivated to do it, not think of it, have religious taboos against it, or act in an unexpected fashion for many other personal reasons related to his particular situation as an individual system. In 1960 many Protestants did not want a Catholic president of the United States because they thought in some decisions his personal biases might prevail. And these biases may indeed have affected his decision not to support federal aid for parochial schools, though in a way the electorate did not expect: Kennedy may have "leaned over backward" away from the view of most of the Catholic hierarchy.

[64]NOTE: This definition is consistent with the usage of Weiss [Weiss, P. A. In R. W. Gerard (Ed.). Concepts of biology. *Behav. Sci.*, 1958, **3**, 140]. Murray [Murray, H. A. Preparations for a scaffold of a comprehensive system. In S. Koch (Ed.). *Psychology: a study of a science*. Vol. 3, New York: McGraw-Hill, 1959, 24] prefers the word "configuration" for an instantaneous spatial arrangement of subsystems or components of a system (or "entity," in his terms) and "structure" for an enduring arrangement. He distinguishes these clearly from an "integration" of recurrent temporal relations of component processes, a patterning of temporal variables.

[65]Cf. Garner, W. R. *Uncertainty and structure as psychological concepts*. New York: Wiley, 1962, 140–145 and 339–343.

[66]NOTE: Gerard [Gerard, R. W. Becoming: the residue of change. In S. Tax (Ed.). *Evolution after Darwin*. Vol. 2. *The evolution of man*. Chicago: Univ. of Chicago Press, 1960, 255] uses for structure, function, and history, the terms "being," "behaving," and "becoming."

Life is fundamentally process, exquisitely controlled change over time. Merton [Merton, R. K. *Social theory and social structure*. (Rev. Ed.) Glencoe, Ill.: Free Press, 1957, 46–47) notes the recent increase in emphasis on function at all levels of systems, and indeed in this book I have included much more on process than on structure, for there is much more in the literature. Science is increasingly concerned with dynamics, which I certainly emphasize in this book. But all systems have both structure and process, and all general theories must deal with both.

Murray [Murray, H. A. Preparation for a scaffold of a comprehensive system. In S. Koch (Ed.). *Psychology: a study of a science*. Vol. 3. New York: McGraw-Hill, 1959, 22] conceives a range or hierarchy of events or processes from very brief submicro events of atomic particles to prolonged macro events. This concept fits well with the concept of a hierarchy of levels of system structures.

[67]Leighton, A. H. *My name is legion: foundations for a theory of man in relation to culture*. Vol. 1. The Stirling County study of psychiatric disorder & sociocultural environment. © 1959 by Basic Books, Inc., Publishers. New York: Basic Books, 1959, 204.

[68]*Ibid.*, 221–222. Reprinted by permission.

[69]NOTE: But Turner, the historian, has distinguished structure and process quite distinctly. (Turner, R. Personal communication.)

"As the scientific understanding of phenomena has developed, they have come more and more to be dealt with in terms of two general concepts: (1) 'structure' and (2) 'process.'

"The concept 'structure' predicates that a phenomenon consists of identifiable parts organized in functional relations; *i.e.*, the parts work together as a whole. . . . In each instance the part is a whole, and the whole is a part. Where this relation appears not to exist may be taken as indicating a limit of man's knowledge rather than as an end of the relation. Therefore, it may be held that within the boundaries of observation, all phenomena enter into a structure of one kind or another.

"The concept 'process' predicates that a structure under the play of external forces and through its own energy undergoes action or acts so that change affects it. By processes, therefore, structures are broken down and built up, and all structures may be conceived as having existence in terms of some process.

"Together the concepts 'structure' and 'process' may be seen as exhibiting the static and dynamic aspects of phenomena. In some phenomena the static aspect may appear more significant, while in others the dynamic aspect may seem decisive; actually they should be viewed together, each as a manifestation of the other. Structure, however enduring, exists in terms of process, and process, no matter how slowly or rapidly it operates, always moves through structure. Structure and process are correlative, not opposing, aspects of phenomena.

"To study human affairs in terms of the concepts 'structure' and 'process' would seem, therefore, to be the scientific way to an understanding of them."

[70]Hughes, C. C. Personal communication to A. H. Leighton. In A. H. Leighton, *Op. cit.*, 223.

[71]Bertalanffy, L. v. *Problems of life: an evaluation of modern biological and scientific thought*. London: Watts, 1952, 134. Reprinted by permission.

[72]NOTE: Hearn (Hearn G. *Theory building in social work.* Toronto: Univ. of Toronto Press, 1958) makes an interesting effort to apply general living systems theory to the field of social work, but in places (cf. pages 59–62) he confuses structure and function.

[73]NOTE: This concept is not a product of our times. It developed long ago. For instance, in the middle of the nineteenth century, Virchow (Virchow, R. Atome und Individuen. *Vier Reden über Leben und Krankheit.* Berlin, 1862. Trans. by L. J. Rather as: Atoms and individuals. In *Disease, life, and man, selected essays by Rudolph Virchow.* Stanford: Stanford Univ. Press, 1958, 120–141) wrote that the scope of the life sciences must include the cellular, tissue, organism, and social levels of living organization. In modern times the concept of hierarchical levels of systems is, of course, basic to the thought of Bertalanffy and other general systems theorists (cf. Bertalanffy, L. v. General systems theory. *Op. cit.,* 7). Even some scientists not explicitly of such persuasion, who have perhaps been skeptical in the past (cf. Simon, H. A. The architecture of complexity. *Op. cit.,* 467), recognize value in such an approach. For example, Simon (*Ibid.,* 467–468. Reprinted by permission.) writes: "A number of proposals have been advanced in recent years for the development of 'general systems theory' which, abstracting from properties peculiar to physical, biological, or social systems, would be applicable to all of them. We might well feel that, while the goal is laudable, systems of such

diverse kinds could hardly be expected to have any nontrivial properties in common. Metaphor and analogy can be helpful, or they can be misleading. All depends on whether the similarities the metaphor captures are significant or superficial.

"It may not be entirely vain, however, to search for common properties among diverse kinds of complex systems. The ideas that go by the name of cybernetics constitute, if not a theory, at least a point of view that has been proving fruitful over a wide range of applications. It has been useful to look at the behavior of adaptive systems in terms of the concepts of feedback and homeostasis, and to analyze adaptiveness in terms of the theory of selective information. The ideas of feedback and information provide a frame of reference for viewing a wide range of situations, just as do the ideas of evolution, of relativism, of axiomatic method, and of operationalism."

He goes on to assert that "hierarchic systems have some common properties that are independent of their specific content. . . .

"By a hierarchic system, or hierarchy, I mean a system that is composed of interrelated subsystems, each of the latter being, in turn, hierarchic in structure until we reach some lowest level of elementary subsystem. In most systems in nature, it is somewhat arbitrary as to where we leave off the partitioning, and what subsystems we take as elementary. Physics makes much use of the concept of 'elementary particle' although particles have a disconcerting tendency not to remain elementary very long. Only a couple of generations ago, the atoms themselves were elementary particles; today, to the nuclear physicist they are complex systems. For certain purposes of astronomy, whole stars, or even galaxies, can be regarded as elementary subsystems. In one kind of biological research, a cell may be treated as an elementary subsystem; in another, a protein molecule; in still another, an amino acid residue.

"Just why a scientist has a right to treat as elementary a subsystem that is in fact exceedingly complex is one of the questions we shall take up. For the moment, we shall accept the fact that scientists do this all the time, and that if they are careful scientists they usually get away with it."

Leake sees value in the concept of levels for contemporary theory about biological organization (cf. Leake, C. D. The scientific status of pharmacology. *Science,* 29 Dec. 1961, **134,** 2076. Copyright 1961 by the American Association for the Advancement of Science. Reprinted by permission.). He writes:

"Life begins with complex macromolecules such as genes and viruses, and here the principles of physics and chemistry directly apply. Macromolecules may be organized and integrated with many other chemical materials to form cells, which at Virchow's time were thought to be the basic units of life. Cells, however, may be organized into tissues or organs, with specific integrations serving their specific functions. These tissues and organs may further be integrated into organisms, constituting individuals such as human beings. Human beings, and indeed many other organisms, are capable of further integration and organization into societies. These societies in turn may be integrated with a more or less limited ecological environment."

The view is also well stated by Teilhard de Chardin (de Chardin, P. Teilhard. *The phenomenon of man.* New York: Harper, 1959, 43–44. Reprinted by permission.):

"The existence of 'system' in the world is at once obvious to every observer of nature, no matter whom.

"The arrangement of the parts of the universe has always been a source of amazement to men. But this disposition proves itself more and more astonishing as, every day, our science is able to make a more precise and penetrating study of the facts. The farther and more deeply we penetrate into matter, by means of increasingly powerful methods, the more we are confounded by the interdependence of its parts. Each element of the cosmos is positively woven from all the others; from beneath itself by the mysterious phenomenon of 'composition,' which makes it subsistent throughout the apex of an organized whole; and from above through the influence of unities of a higher order which incorporate and dominate it for their own ends.

"It is impossible to cut into this network, to isolate a portion without it becoming frayed and unravelled at all its edges.

"All around us, as far as the eye can see, the universe holds together, and only one way of considering it is really possible, that is, to take it as a whole, in one piece."

Kaplan (Kaplan, M. A. *Op. cit.*, 12. Reprinted by permission.) has applied the concept of a hierarchy of systems to international relations:

"The same variables will be used at different system levels. The international system is the most inclusive system treated by this book. National and supranational systems are subsystems of the international system. They may, however, be treated separately as systems, in which case inputs from the international system would function as parameters. This holds also for subsystems of nation states and even for personality systems."

The Panel on Basic Research and Graduate Education of the President's Science Advisory Committee of the United States in 1960 appeared also to recognize value in a general systems approach [cf. Seaborg, G. T. (Chairman), Panel on Basic Research and Graduate Education of the President's Science Advisory Committee. Scientific progress and the federal government. *Science,* 16 Dec. 1960, **132,** 1810. Copyright 1960 by the American Association for the Advancement of Science. Reprinted by permission.]. They wrote: " . . . we suggest that there is great promise in such an emerging subject as a general study of complex systems in action, within which such very large questions as the communication sciences, cognition, and large parts of biology itself might conceivably be treated as special cases."

A textbook of psychology has been written which embodies a conceptualization of a hierarchy of living systems like that which I advance in the present book (cf. Coleman, J. C. *Personality dynamics and effective behavior.* Chicago: Scott, Foresman, 1960 and also Coleman, J. C. & Hammen, C. L. *Contemporary psychology and effective behavior.* Glenview, Ill.: Scott, Foresman, 1974).

A presidential address delivered to the Association of American Medical Colleges included a passage emphasizing the desirability of synthesizing the medical curriculum around the concept of the relations among levels of living systems. Hubbard (Hubbard, W. N., Jr. Janus revisited. *J. med. Educ.*, 1967, **42,** 1079. Reprinted by permission.) wrote: "For the medical student . . . the significance of descriptions at the molecular and submolecular level must be presented in the context of their relationship to the more complex organizations of these same living systems at the level of the organ, the individual, and the family group."

A presentation by Mesarović and his colleagues of a general theory of systems has emphasized a hierarchy of levels (Mesarović, M.D., Macko, D., & Takahara, Y. *Theory of multi-level hierarchical systems.* N.Y.: Academic Press, 1970). And so has a recent article by Zieleniewski [Zieleniewski, J. Reality seen as a "system of systems" and dialectical materialism. *Prakseologia,* 1974, **2**(46)].

And there is widespread scientific and popular implicit recognition of hierarchical levels of living systems. As one instance out of many, six banners in one of the halls of the United Nations Palais des Nations in Geneva depict six levels of social organization. They say: Family, Village, Clan, Medieval State, Nation, and Federation.

[74]Concerning ecological systems. Cf. Watt, K. E. *Principles of environmental science.* New York: McGraw-Hill, 1973. Also Emlen, J. M. *Ecology: an evolutionary approach.* Reading, Mass.: Addison, Wesley, 1973.

[75]Neyman, J. & Scott, E. L. On a mathematical theory of populations conceived as conglomerations of clusters. *Gen. Systems,* 1958, **3,** 180–192.

Also Newman, J., Scott, E. L., & Shane, C. D. Statistics of images of galaxies with particular reference to clustering. *Gen. Systems,* 1958, **3,** 193–219.

[76]Anderson, R. E. & Carter, I. E. *Human behavior in the social environment.* Chicago: Aldine, 1974, 45–73.

[77]Mesarović, M. D., Macko, D., & Takahara, Y. *Op. cit.,* 30–31.

[78]Cf. Herbst, P. G. Situation dynamics and the theory of behavior systems. *Behav. Sci.,* 1957, **2,** 28. Herbst makes it clear that one should make the level of reference explicit. He says that often, in writing on group research, for instance, an author will change his level of reference from the leader (organism) to the group and back to a group member (organism) again without explicitly referring to the change. This produces confusing conceptual ambiguity.

[79]NOTE: Illustrative of the similarities between the approach outlined here and relevant thinking about electronic system design is the following statement by Goode (Goode, H. H. Intracompany systems management. *IRE Trans. engng. Mgmt.*, EM-7, 1960, 15. Reprinted by permission.) concerning the need to identify the level of reference:

"Confusion . . . arises from consideration of the level of design. System design may be done:

"1) At the *set* level: that is, a radar, an ignition system, a navigation set. Any of these may be designed on a system engineering basis, given a need and the necessary analysis of requirements.

"2) At the *set of sets* level: thus an airplane, a telephone exchange, a missile system, each is itself a set of sets and is subject to system design.

"3) At the *set of sets of sets* level: thus an over-all weapon system, a telephone system, an air traffic system, represent such sets of sets of sets."

In a similar analysis Malcolm [Malcolm, D. G. Reliability maturity index (RM)—an extension of PERT into reliability management. *J. industr. Engng.,* 1963, **14,** 4–5] distinguishes eight hierarchical levels in a large weapon system: system, subsystem, component, assembly, subassembly, unit, unit component, and part.

[80]Henderson, L. J. *The fitness of the environment: an inquiry into the biological significance of the properties of matter.* Boston: Beacon, 1958.

[81]NOTE: Rashevsky (Rashevsky, N. Topology and life: in search of general mathematical principles in biology and sociology. *Gen. Systems,* 1956, **1,** 123–138. Reprinted by permission.) expounded his ideas about topological transformations as follows:

"Unfortunately, we do not know enough even about the simplest protozoa to describe their graphs in any detail. From the knowledge we have we can, however, make some plausible surmises. Let us see what the graph of a relatively simple organism may look like.

"It should be very strongly emphasized that neither the proposed graph shown [in Fig. 2-1N] nor the transformation to be discussed presently is to be considered as hypotheses proposed for a development of a theory. As such hypotheses they are definitely not good. They are introduced here only as illustrations of the basic idea. Even when later on in this paper we discuss some biological implications of the suggested transformation, we do so only to show what kind of biological implications may follow from a future properly selected transformation. It is more than likely that an abstract study of different types of trans-

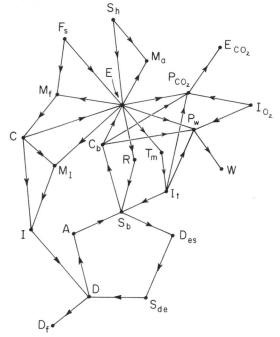

Fig. 2-1N   Graph of a protozoan.

formations hitherto not studied in topology will have to precede any further development of a biologically applicable theory.

"The feeding mechanism begins with the contact of the organism with food, which we represent by the point C [in Fig. 2-1N]. This is followed by the ingestion of food, usually into the food vacuole, which process is represented by the point I, the arrow C → I indicating that I follows C. The ingested food is digested, digestion D following I. This is followed by the adsorption A of the digested food into the protoplasm of the cell, as well as by the rejection of indigestible waste, or defecation D_f. The adsorbed food is transported to various parts of the cell where a synthesis S_b of the body of cell follows. These general synthetic processes result among other things in the synthesis D_{es} of digestive enzymes. This is followed by the secretion S_{de} of the digestive enzymes into the digestive vacuole, where they come into contact with the ingested food, and digestion D results. The directed path $IDAS_bD_{es}S_{de}D$, which contains the cycle $DAS_bD_{es}S_{de}D$, expresses a very fundamental property of every organism: in order that food may be assimilated and the body of the organism synthesized, the organism must be already present. The convergence of the arrows I → D and S_{de} → D upon the point D expresses that

digestion cannot take place without previous ingestion of food, nor can it take place without digestive enzymes, which presuppose the existence of the organism producing them. Similarly, the synthesis S_b needs both a previous adsorption A, and a transport of the absorbed substance through the protoplasm of the cell. This inner transport I_t in a protozoan usually takes place by diffusion. However, protoplasmic streamings or other mechanisms may conceivably be possible. The above is expressed by the convergence on S_b of the arrows $I_t → S_b$ and A → S_b. The process S_b is also followed by catabolic processes C_b. At this state the intake I_{O_2} of oxygen (for aerobic organisms) combines with C_b to produce on one hand a release of energy E, on the other production P_{CO_2} of carbon dioxide, which is followed by the elimination E_{CO_2} of carbon dioxide, as well as the production P and the elimination W of other catabolic waste products. Some of the released energy is necessary to maintain the inner transport I_t. If the latter involves any special movements, like protoplasmic streamings, then E affects first that movement T_m, and the latter results in I_t, as indicated by the arrows. In the light of present biochemical knowledge . . . we should not regard the liberation of energy as directly connected with oxygen consumption, and therefore, we do not connect I_{O_2} with E on the graph. This in some cases may be a debatable question, which is, however, not essential for our purposes. The graph [in Fig. 2-1N] is rather tentative anyway, and used largely as an illustration.

"A stimulus of some kind coming from the food results in the process of stimulation F_s. How this process acts in a protozoan is little known. In some ways it affects the energy liberation E, and through this it produces certain movements M_f (cilia, flagella, protrusion of pseudopods), which bring the organism in contact C with food. This contact with food again acts as a stimulus, which in a similar way produces some movements M_I which result in food ingestion. A harmful stimulus S_h results in a similar manner in a motion M_a, the avoiding movement. It is very likely that M_f and M_a are in some way connected through a mechanism which produces a reciprocal inhibition of the two functions. We shall not, however, go into this detail.

"Last but not least the body synthesis S_b, as well as the release E of energy, result eventually in the more or less complicated processes R of reproduction.

"Thus constructed, the graph [in Figure 2-1N] strikes us with its complexity. Yet the true graph of a protozoan is undoubtedly more complex. We have not one digestive enzyme but many, produced through different processes, which should be represented by separate points. There is sensitivity for stimuli of different modalities which again complicates the graph. The synthesis S_b is not a single process, but a series of separate processes.

"The determination of the graph of a unicellular organism is ultimately a matter of experimental study. . . .

"We may now state somewhat more precisely the principle of biotopological mapping: There exists one, or very few, primordial organisms, characterized by their graphs; the graphs of *all* other organisms are obtained from this primordial graph or graphs by a transformation, which contains one or more parameters. Different organisms correspond to the different values of those parameters. . . .

"The growth of organisms in complexity proceeds through differentiation of tissues and through their specialization. A biological function f_i; which originally is possessed by all cells, is lost by some of them and retained by others. (To avoid confusion we shall use the word 'function' when referring to a mathematical function. 'Biological function' will be used in the sense adopted in biology.) These other cells are said to have specialized in the performance of the function f_i. At the same time, as a rule, those cells which lost the biological function f_i specialize in another biological function f_k, which in its turn becomes lost in those cells which specialize in f_i. A 'division of biological functions' is thus established, and instead of n identical cells, represented by the original graph, we now have two classes of cells, the cells of one class differing from those of the other. The problem is to derive the graph of this organism from the graph of the original homogeneous colony.''

Rashevsky (*Ibid.*, 134) also supported the concept of cross-level formal identities and suggested extending this method not only from cells to individuals but also to societies.

[82]Parkinson, C. N. *Parkinson's law.* Boston: Houghton Mifflin, 1957, 2–13.

[83]Брэйнс, С.Н., Напалков, А.В., Свечипский, В.В. Учсные записки (проблемы нейроксбернетики). [Braynes, S. N., Napalkov, A. V., & Svechinskiy, V. B. *Scientific notes (on the problem of neurocybernetics).*] Moscow: Publishing House of the Academy of Medical Sciences USSR, 1959.

[84]Köhler, W. *Gestalt psychology.* New York: Liveright, 1929, 187–223.

[85]Butler, J. A. V. *Inside the living cell.* New York: Basic Books, 1959, 159–160. © George Allen and Unwin Ltd., 1959. Basic Books, Inc., Publishers, New York. Reprinted by permission.

[86]Emerson, A. E. The organization of insect societies. In W. C. Allee, A. E. Emerson, O. Park, T. Park, & K. P. Schmidt. *Principles of animal ecology.* Philadelphia: W. B. Saunders, 1949, 419–435.

[87]Tolman, E. C. Cognitive maps in rats and men. *Psychol. Rev.*, 1948, **55**, 189–208.

[88]Cf. Ardrey, R. *The territorial imperative.* New York: Atheneum, 1966.

[89]Cf. Levinson, D. J. Role, personality, and social structure in the organizational setting. *J. abnorm. soc. Psychol.*, 1959, **58**, 170–180.

[90]Weber, M. *The theory of social and economic organization.* (Trans. by A. M. Henderson and T. Parsons.) New York: Oxford Univ. Press, 1947.

[91]NOTE: The criticism has been made that it is impossible to prove or disprove the statement that every system has subsystems. (Buck, R. C. *Op. cit.*, 226.) This is not really a problem in relation to concrete systems. If one found a system, however small, in which the distribution of matter-energy was entirely homogeneous and without parts, one could say that it did not have subsystems.

[92]NOTE: Wharton, T. *Adenographia: sive glandularum totius corporis descriptio.* Amstelaedami. Sumptibus Ravesteinii, 1659, Cap. XVIII, 110–111: "Usus harum glandularum primus ac praecipuo videtur, superfluas nervi recurrentis humidates excipere, et in venosum genus denuo deducere per lymphaeductus susos;

"2. Cartilagenes, alioquin frigidiores, quibus affigitur, calore suo fovere. Est enim copiosis arteriis perfusa et sanguine abundat, unde commode vicinis partibus calorem impertit;

"3. Laryngis lubricationi suis halitibus conducere adeoque vocem laeviorem, canoram, suavioremque reddere;

"4. Ad colli rotunditatem et ornatum multum contribuere, implent enim vacua spacia circa laryingem, partesque eius protuberantes fere in laevorem ac planitiem

deducunt; praesertim in foeminis, quibus ab hanc causam majores obtigerunt, eorumque colla aequaliora ac venustiora reddunt."

Translation:

"It seems that the first and most important use of these glands is to extract the superfluous moisture from the recurrent nerve, and, through their lymphatic ducts, to lead it again into the venous system;

"2. To warm the colder cartilages to which (the thyroid) is attached. In fact it has numerous arteries and is richly supplied with blood, and therefore it can properly distribute warmth to the adjacent regions;

"3. To lubricate the larynx and thus to make the voice lighter, melodious, and sweeter;

"4. To contribute to the roundness and embellishment of the neck, filling the empty space around the larynx, and smoothing its protuberant parts; especially in women, who for this reason were endowed with larger (thyroid glands), the neck is made smoother and more beautiful."

[93]Cf. Meyer, L. B. Meaning in music and information theory. *J. Aesthet. art. Crit.*, 1957, **15**, 412–424.

Also Cohen, J. E. *Op. cit.*

[94]Cf. Whorf, B. L. *Language, thought, and reality.* Cambridge: Technology Press, 1956.

[95]von Neumann, J. The general and logical theory of automata. In L. A. Jeffress (Ed.). *Cerebral mechanisms in behavior.* New York: Wiley, 1951, 1–41.

[96]NOTE: The most extensive work applying the concept of stress to living systems, at the organism level exclusively, has been done by Selye. Cf. Selye, H. *The stress of life.* New York: McGraw-Hill, 1956.

[97]Le Châtelier, H. Recherches experimentales et théoriques sur les équilibres chimiques. *Annales des Mines*, Huitième série, Mémories, XIII, Paris: Dunod, 1888, 200.

[98]NOTE: Students of living systems at all levels have maintained that some principle like that of Le Châtelier operates to maintain variables in them in steady states. For instance, Pareto (Pareto, V. *The mind and society.* Vol. 4. New York: Harcourt, Brace, 1935, 1435) described what happens to a social system if its state is artificially modified. He said: "At once a reaction will take place, tending to restore the changing form to its original state as modified by normal change."

In his early article on organisms as systems, Weiss (Weiss, P. Animal behavior as system reaction. *Gen. Systems*, 1959, **4**, 8, trans. and rev. from Tierisches Verhalten als "Systemreaktion," *Biologia generalis*, 1925, **1**, 167–248. Reprinted by permission.) wrote that "A *system* may therefore be defined as any complex which tends to retain its constancy as a whole relative to the outer world during and notwithstanding the changes taking place in its parts. . . . This tendency to retain constancy denotes that the systemic state represents the stable, *i.e.*, unequivocal condition of the complex in the total field of external conditions. . . . The maintenance of constancy by the system as a whole despite alternatives of some of its parts can only be achieved by reactive changes of opposite sign in the remaining parts. . . ."

Writing about the concept he named homeostasis, Cannon (Cannon, W. B. *Wisdom of the body.* New York: Norton, 1939, 293. Reprinted by permission.) stated the proposition: " . . . that a certain degree of constancy in a complex system is itself evidence that agencies are acting or are ready to act to maintain that constancy. . . . When a system remains steady it does so because any tendency toward change is met by increased effectiveness of the factor or factors which resist the change." And he went on to propose a cross-level generality: (*Ibid.*, 287) "Are there no general principles of stabilization? May not the devices developed in the animal organism for preserving steady states illustrate methods which are used, or which could be used, elsewhere? Would not a comparative study of stabilizing processes be suggestive? Might it not be useful to examine other forms of organization—industrial, domestic, social—in the light of organization of the body?" Buck (Buck, R. C. *Op. cit.*, 235) has wondered whether a "nonhomeostatic" system might exist. My answer is that no such concrete system could exist. Every one must maintain at least one variable in steady state. Locating a concrete system which is not homeostatic would create serious doubts about my whole conceptual approach.

Schumpeter (Schumpeter, J. A. *Business cycles.* New York: McGraw-Hill, 1939) has used equilibrium theory extensively in economics. Ashby (Ashby, W. R. *Design for a brain.* New York: Wiley, 1954) has applied similar steady-state theory to living systems generally, including brains. Easton (Easton, D. Limits of the equilibrium model in social research. *Behav. Sci.*, 1956, **1**, 86–104) has considered its applicability to social systems generally. Kaplan (Kaplan, M. A. *Op. cit.*, 6–8) has applied it to political systems.

Kempf (Kempf, E. J. Basic biodynamics. *Ann. N. Y. Acad. Sci.*, 1958, **73**, 894–895) notes that every level of organization (atomic, molecular, crystalline, enzymatic, protoplasmic, cellular, organismic, and social, among others) has components which interact in space and time, which function to maintain internal and external equilibria in the presence of stresses capable of disturbing them. If they did not, they would not continue to exist.

Gifford (Gifford, J. V. *The nature of the city as a system.* Unpublished paper. San Francisco: Dept. of City Planning, City of San Francisco, 1962) has applied steady-state theory to cities as systems.

[99]Prigogine, I. *Op. cit.*, 82.

[100]*Ibid.*

[101]NOTE: This may be a general statement of the much misunderstood and often mystically used principle of least effort of Zipf. Cf. Zipf, G. K. *Human behavior and the principle of least effort.* Cambridge: Addison-Wesley, 1949.

[102]Ashby, W. R. *Design for a brain. Op. cit.*, 153–158, 210–211.

[103]Rosenblueth, A., Wiener, N., & Bigelow, J. Behavior, purpose and teleology. *Philos. Sci.*, 1943, **10**, 19.

[104]Ashby, W. R. Cybernetics. In G. W. T. H. Fleming & A. Walk (Eds.). *Recent progr. Psychiat.*, Vol. 3, 1959, 94 (Suppl. to *Brit. J. Psychiat.*, 1958).

[105]NOTE: These formal identities have been repeatedly pointed out by the pioneers of cybernetics, Wiener (Wiener, N. *Op. cit.*) and Ashby (Ashby, W. R. *An introduction to cybernetics.* London: Chapman, 1961). That they are also recognized in the Soviet Union is indicated by the following statement of Veltistov (Veltistov, Y. E. *USSR improves computers. Ogo-*

nec, 1962, **36**, 14–16): "The basic principle of cybernetics permits a new science to compare machines, organisms, and society, for if we consider a student solving a problem, an automatic device controlling a complicated production process, or a commander guiding a course in battle, there is a common pattern in all these cases: living or artificial systems receive or process certain information or make an expedient selection aimed at an effective result."

[106]Cf. Elkinton, J. R. & Danowski, T. S. *The body fluids: basic physiology and practical therapeutics.* Baltimore: Williams & Wilkins, 1955, 24.

[107]Truxal, J. G. *Automatic feedback control system synthesis.* New York: McGraw-Hill, 1955, 2.

[108]Elkinton, J. R. & Danowski, T. S. *Op. cit.*, 26. © The Williams and Wilkins Co., Baltimore. Reprinted by permission.

[109]Vickers, G. Is adaptability enough? *Behav. Sci.*, 1959, **4**, 223. Reprinted by permission.

[110]Kazda, Louis F. Personal communication.

[111]Ashby, W. R. *Cybernetics today and its future contribution to the engineering-sciences.* New York: Foundation for Instrumentation, Engineering and Research, 1961, 6–7.

[112]Cf. Deutsch, K. W. *The nerves of government.* New York: Free Press of Glencoe, 1963, 186–187.

[113]Ashby, W. R. Principles of the self-organizing system. In H. Von Foerster & G. W. Zopf (Eds.). *Principles of self-organization.* New York: Pergamon Press, 1962, 266.

[114]Rosenblueth, A., Wiener, N., & Bigelow, J. *Op. cit.*, 18–24.

[115]Rothstein, J. Thermodynamics and some undecidable physical questions. *Philos. Sci.*, 1964, **31**, 40–48. Reprinted by permission.

[116]Sommerhoff, G. *Analytical biology.* London: Oxford Univ. Press, 1950.

[117]Eberhart, S. S. The ballad of the interstellar merchants. *Galaxy*, 1964, **23(2)**, 92–93. Reprinted by permission.

[118]Driesch, H. A. *The science and philosophy of the organism.* London: Adam & Charles Black, 1908.

[119]NOTE: A closely related concept, *finalism*, was described by Rignano (Rignano, E. The concept of purpose in biology. *Mind*, 1931, **40**, 335–340).

[120]Bertalanffy, L. v. Der Organismus als physikalisches System betrachtet. *Die Naturwissenschaften*, 1940, **28**, 521–523. Also Bertalanffy, L. v. General systems theory. *Op. cit.*, 3–4.

[121]Hurley, W. V. *A mathematical theory of the value of information.* Report 63-3. New York: Port of New York Authority, Engineering Department, Research and Development Division, May, 1963.

[122]Садовский, В. Н. Основания общей теории систем. (Sadovsky, V. N. *Fundamentals of a general theory of systems.*) Moscow: Publishing House Science, 1974.

[123]Pascal, B. *Pascal's pensées.* (Orig. ed., 1670. Adapted from the translation by H. F. Stewart.) New York: Pantheon, 1950, 358. Reprinted by permission of Pantheon Books, a Division of Random House, Inc.

Structure and Process

(The outline of this chapter, with similarly numbered sections dealing with related topics, is repeated in Chap. 4 and Chaps. 6 through 12. Chapter 4 contains cross-level hypotheses, and each of Chaps. 6 through 12 concerns a different level of living systems. Comparison of similar topics in all these chapters is facilitated by this numbering procedure. Certain sections are skipped in Chap. 4 because no material relevant to their topics was found.)

1. Structure

The term "structure" has already been defined (see page 22). It is generally used to refer to the arrangement of a system in three-dimensional space at a given moment at the levels which are the chief concern of the biological sciences. But at the levels dealt with primarily by the social sciences, there is less agreement; and here structure often refers to configurations that are stable over time or to patterns in process.[1] I shall use the term at all levels only in the defined sense in order to achieve a comparable approach to them.

1.1 System size There are differences in size among various individual systems of a certain type, among types of systems, and among levels of systems. That is, they vary in extent of distance, area of surface, and volume of space occupied. The median size of systems at each higher level seems to be larger than at the next lower level, but there is great variation in size at each level.

1.2 Structural taxonomy of types of systems Classifications according to structure exist at all levels. These depend upon distinctions of shape, patterning of subsystems and components in space, size, color, constituent materials, and other aspects of systems. The same differentia are not applied at all levels. Form and color are the chief bases of biological classifica-

tion. A difference in shape, for instance, distinguishes Jack from Jill, a difference in facial pattern distinguishes him from Ivan, and a difference in hair color distinguishes him from Hans. Social systems may be classified according to their numbers of components and their forms or organization, but at the group level and above, process taxonomies are more frequently used to distinguish types of systems.

2. Process

I have already defined process (see page 23) as all change over time of matter-energy or information in a system. More empirical and theoretical effort has been devoted to the study of process at all levels than to the study of structure, although studies of structure often precede studies of process.[2]

2.1 System and subsystem indicators Many subsystem and systemwide variables fluctuate constantly in every living system. Throughout this book I mention many such variables. If the changing values of conceptual variables are to be measured in a concrete system in space-time, an observer or scientist must use some measuring instrument or technique, that is, an indicator, to do so. There are many kinds of such indicators. Those used in studies at one level of system may be very different from those used at another level.

2.2 Process taxonomy of types of systems Process classifications are used at all levels. Common modes of process classification are in terms of what variables the system maintains in steady state (*e.g.,* a homotherm keeps its body temperature constant) or what adjustment processes it can mobilize to maintain those stabilities (*e.g.,* through gills fish take in the oxygen dissolved in the water in which they swim). Or classification may be by the function of the system in its suprasystem. A cell, for example, may secrete an enzyme or a hormone, or it may transmit impulses. An organ may excrete wastes: several diverse structures, including the kidneys, the colon, and the skin, may be classified together as excretory organs in the same way that the hormone-producing endocrine glands are grouped. Animals may be sled dogs or beasts of burden; men may be tailors or lawyers. Groups can exist for recreation, for psychotherapy, or to accomplish a mission—like a construction crew. Organizations may be banks, churches, factories, or military units. Societies may be chiefly producers and exporters of agricultural or of industrial goods. Supranational systems may exist for economic cooperation, mutual military defense, or the regulation of international transportation.

Process taxonomy may also be in terms of a system's irreversible changes or history as well as its reversible changes or function. Is it in a period of growth or is it in decline? Is it retarded or advanced in development as compared with other systems of its kind? The Freudian classification of personality types according to the stage at which psychosexual development is "fixated" is such a taxonomy. So is the common grouping of nations into "underdeveloped" or "developing" and "advanced."

3. Subsystems

[*This chapter and Chaps. 4 and 6 through 12, which follow the same outline, all have a section on the structure and process of the system's subsystems and of the system as a whole but none on its suprasystem. This is not because a system's relations to its subsystems are more important than its relations to its suprasystem—they are equally important. However, if Chaps. 6 through 12 (each of which, in order of increasing complexity, examines a higher level of living system) had both sections, the section on the suprasystem in one chapter would of necessity cover the same material as the chapter at the next higher level. This would be useless duplication.*]

Each subsystem, as I have said (see page 30), carries out a particular process for its system and keeps one or more specific variables in steady state. All of a given subsystem may be in a single component, or it may be in several. Those components may not be spatially contiguous, although an actual channel in space-time always exists to convey the messages among them which coordinate their processes. On the other hand, one component may take part in the processes of a number of different subsystems (see page 30). Simple animals with relatively few cells, such as coelenterates for instance, use the same opening for taking in food and extruding wastes. Larger animals, like mammals, have a number of separate structures for extrusion of wastes alone. If groups with few members—like a family on a camping trip—are to carry out all their essential processes, some or all of the members must participate in more than one, since there are at least 19 such processes (see Table 3-1, page 54).

Unless the parts of a system have relationships and interact, by definition it is no system. To accomplish this coordination, its subsystems must be so arranged that the system is continuous in space-time. This is necessary if the essential flows of energy and information are to occur and if the controlling feedbacks are to operate. At the levels of cell, organ, and organism the continuity is apparent. That a group, organization, society, or supranational system is continuous is sometimes less easy to demonstrate. Consider the fictional flotilla of which the mutinous *Caine* was a part.[3] The ships were distributed within an area of ocean. The men in them were exchanging information by means of blinker and radar, thus maintaining themselves as a social organization interacting under the orders of a single commander. Certainly this organization of men was a living system made up of components in each ship. The channel through which the blinker and radar waves were propagated provided the necessary space-time continuity. Then the flotilla was hit by a typhoon, and its communications were disrupted. It ceased to function as a system. The component ships were unable to act in a coordinated manner, and there was danger that they would collide. Social systems have been disrupted by communication blocks throughout history—when fog blanketed Indian smoke signals, or winds blew down television antennae, or electrical storms blanked out radio signals. Coordinating or command signals must be conveyed through channels connecting components if they are to interact. If the transmitter or the receiver is not operating, if noise in the channel is too great, if power is inadequate to convey the messages over the requisite distance, if messages are not properly coded or decoded, or if commands are not obeyed, then frequently the coordinated actions among the components will cease, and the system boundaries will disappear.

Systems differ in their degrees and types of independence or isolation from the systems which surround them. Functional characteristics of their boundaries—which inputs are processed and which are rejected—to a large extent determine how independent or dependent they are. The amount of spatial connection of one system with another is an unreliable indicator of how dependent they are on each other.[4] Two adjacent pieces of electronic equipment may be firmly attached to each other by an insulator and yet function entirely independently. On the other hand, a satellite may be separated from its controls by hundreds of thousands of miles and yet interact intricately and precisely. As Ashby asserts, we learn about the degree of independence of a subsystem, not from its connections in space, but from its processes. One subsystem is independent of another if all variables in the first alter in ways uncorrelated to the alteration of any variables in the second. The amount of correlation is a measure of the degree of dependence.

Up to now I have considered in detail only continuity of boundaries in three-dimensional space, but my definition also mentions their continuity in time. If at some time in the past the components have been in contact so that information could flow between them, and if they can store information over time in some sort of memory, then in the future they can interact as a system even though their boundaries no longer are spatially continuous. Thus fighter pilots on an air raid can rendezvous at a given spot, even though they observe radio silence and so cannot communicate for hours, because they store in their memories their orders as to place and time of rendezvous. Thus the ships of the *Caine's* flotilla could interact to prevent collision when hit by a typhoon if they had a previous agreement to head northeast when the storm struck. In such situations preprogrammed stored information substitutes for currently transmitted information; but without such memories, disruption of communication means the dissolution of a system.

Some living systems have unusual shapes which depart greatly from the rounded, globular appearance of many cells and other systems. At times the systems are dispersed to several components, so that the system must transmit information, and perhaps also matter-energy, from one component to another across space in the environment or suprasystem outside its own boundary (*e.g.*, external feedbacks). It is essential that some sort of control be exerted by the suprasystem over this space to prevent interference with these external transmissions. To remain a dispersed system, the Mafia depends on free travel and unobstructed use of national and international telephone, telegraph, cable, and mails. Similarly, to remain an empire, England in the sixteenth century depended on freedom of the seas and could not put up with pirates or

the Spanish Armada. Such common external routes and channels, outside system boundaries, must be kept clear of interference if the systems dependent on them are to survive. Since they are outside, this is often hard to do; and use of such channels may be perilous—as repeated crises over West Berlin since World War II have shown. The control of such extra-system space may begin with cooperative endeavor among systems (*e.g.*, international law) and ultimately may lead to the development of a suprasystem (*e.g.*, a potent world union of nations).

Table 3-1 lists the critical subsystems whose processes every living system must have if it is to survive.[5] These subsystems can be classified into those involved in the metabolism of matter-energy (the left column), those involved in the metabolism of information (the right column), and those involved in both metabolisms (crossing both columns). The reproducer subsystem is separated by a line from the others because it is critical in a different sense from the others. It is essential if the species is to continue to another generation, though it is not needed for the survival of the system in which it exists. For example, castrated animals can continue to live. The processes of all the other subsystems appear to be critical to the survival of living systems at all levels.

The order in which the subsystems are listed is meaningful, indicating the commonest sequence followed by the processes that make up the metabolism of matter-energy or of information. This is suggested in the diagramed flows which appear in Fig. 1-1 (facing page 2), a vastly simplified conceptualization of a generalized living system. It resembles an organism, organ, or perhaps cell more than the higher levels because it is impossible to represent in a single picture a system with a continuous and a discontinuous boundary, or with localized and dispersed subsystems. Typically, the higher-level systems differ from the lower-level ones in such characteristics. If the boundary is envisioned as discontinuous, and the subsystems as highly mobile in relation to each other, however, many of the components represented in this figure will be seen to exist at the group level and above. It is a graphic representation of the basic concepts in this chapter. Being an open system, part of its boundary is permeable to matter-energy and information flows, which are seen as inputs to it, internal processes, and outputs from it, its subsystems, and subsubsystems. There are also feedbacks of information both within and outside the system, in its environment or suprasystem. An untold variety of such transmissions, following many paths and controlling a multitude of variables, are needed for even the simplest living cell.

Because matter-energy markers must be conveyed over some channel if information is to be transmitted, and because in living systems both matter-energy and information flow at finite rates through distributors or channels of limited capacity, and for other reasons, there are in such systems interesting formal identities between matter-energy and information flows. When a hypothesis has been confirmed for one sort of flow in a system, therefore, it is worthwhile to find out whether it applies to the other sort as well. This can extend the usefulness of the finding. So, as I shall demonstrate later, queuing theory mathematics—originally applied to transportation problems and other matter-energy flows—can also be applied to information flows (see pages 94, 104, and 105). Further, network theory applies to both. For instance, Elias, Feinstein, and Shannon have proved theorems which they believe are relevant to flows in two-terminal networks with branches of limited capacity, whether they be communication channels transmitting information or matter-energy distributors like a railroad system, a power feeding system, or a network of pipes conveying matter or energy.[6]

When there is a degree of similarity in the processes of a matter-energy processing subsystem and an information processing subsystem, they are placed on the same line opposite one another in Table 3-1. Thus the ingestor admits matter-energy from its environment to a living system, and the input transducer admits information from its environment. The parallel is more tenuous between the converter and the decoder.

Nevertheless they cope with a common problem—that "public" input from the environment often is not in a form in which it can be used internally within the system. The converter makes matter-energy suitable for "private" uses of the system, and the decoder changes information to a "private" code of the system. The producer synthesizes raw materials or matter-energy from the converter into more complex matter-energy forms, and the associator combines separate bits of information into information complexes we call knowledge or wisdom, by some sort of "association bonds," so that bit A elicits bit B in the future with a probability greater than 0. The matter-energy storage retains matter or energy over time, and somewhat similarly the memory stores information. No other subsystem has processes like those of the reproducer and the boundary. The supporter's processes are unlike any information processes, and the decider and encoder have no parallels in matter-energy processes. Consequently in Table 3-1 all these subsystems appear on lines alone, opposite no other subsystem. The output transducer puts out information as the extruder puts out matter-energy and indeed uses the extruder or motor to transmit the necessary markers beyond the boundary.

Under each subsystem I list a representative set of subsystem variables. These, plus other systemwide variables, are the sorts of variables which appear in systems simulations at each level (see pages 83 to 85). In each chapter on a level of systems, i.e., Chaps. 6 to 12, I present an example for each subsystem

TABLE 3-1   The 19 Critical Subsystems of a Living System*

3.1. SUBSYSTEMS WHICH PROCESS BOTH MATTER-ENERGY AND INFORMATION

3.1.1 Reproducer

3.1.2 Boundary

3.2. SUBSYSTEMS WHICH PROCESS MATTER-ENERGY	3.3. SUBSYSTEMS WHICH PROCESS INFORMATION
3.2.1 Ingestor	3.3.1 Input transducer
	3.3.2 Internal transducer
3.2.2 Distributor	3.3.3 Channel and net
3.2.3 Converter	3.3.4 Decoder
3.2.4 Producer	3.3.5 Associator
3.2.5 Matter-energy storage	3.3.6 Memory
	3.3.7 Decider
	3.3.8 Encoder
3.2.6 Extruder ⎫	
	3.3.9 Output transducer
3.2.7 Motor ⎬	
3.2.8 Supporter ⎭	

*The subsystem structures are listed in this table. The number before each subsystem is the number of the section in which that subsystem is discussed in this chapter as well as in Chaps. 6 through 12. The names of the subsystem processes carried out by the above 19 structures are formed regularly (e.g., Reproducer—reproducing; Ingestor—ingesting) except for the following: Boundary—boundary processing; Matter-Energy Storage—matter-energy storing; Motor—moving; Channel and Net—channel and net processing; Memory—remembering.

variable, for that particular level of systems. These examples illustrate the kinds of indicators that can be employed to measure changes in these variables.

Some living systems possess noncritical subsystems or components which are not essential for survival. The human vermiform appendix is such a component, so are many aged citizens of any nation. One reason organisms with noncritical subsystems survive evolutionary natural selection is that a noncritical subsystem may be produced by the same genes which also produce a critical subsystem. But since there are costs to maintaining nonessential subsystems, in general they are few; for although evolution wastes many species which die out, its natural selection rewards parsimony when it occurs.

3.1 Subsystems which process both matter-energy and information   The reproducer and the boundary process both matter-energy and information.

3.1.1 Reproducer,   the subsystem which is capable of giving rise to other systems similar to the one it is in.

This process fundamentally involves transmission of information, the template of the new system.[7] The matter-energy which is organized to compose the new system, however, must also be processed. The care of the next generation of systems until they become independent and self-supporting is also a function of this subsystem. In all systems the reproducer operates by many complex, reversible functions, but the ultimate effect is to bring about an irreversible, historical change—the creation of the new systems of a new generation.

3.1.1.1 Structure   The basic structures which carry out this process are in cells, particularly in eggs and sperm. The nuclei, containing chromosomes and genes made of DNA, are the most important, but certain other organelles are also involved. Systems cannot reproduce themselves if they have less than a certain minimum of complexity, as von Neumann showed.[8] Reproduction is dispersed downward from organs to cells. Reproductive organs in organisms make reproduction possible, and in sexual species, mating dyads—with differing structures according to sex—are necessary. At the group, organization, society, and supranational levels there can be subsystems—founders, committees to draft a constitution, or charter conventions—which create and implement explicit or implicit templates which program the reproduction of the entire system.

3.1.1.2 Process   Every system is originated by one or more parents or founding systems which make it by combining its components in relationships. The parent system or systems originate the new system from a template created by one of two fundamental processes: (a) by some form of biological reproduction in which it produces both the components and their relationships or (b) at the group level and above, by creation and implementation of an implicit or explicit charter establishing the relationships among components made by biological reproduction by a system at a lower level. Process b is emergent at the group level, dependent on the use of symbolic language, which is emergent at the organism level (see page 468).

A cell is originated by biological reproduction, which is either (a) asexual fission from a single parent cell or (b) sexual reproduction which requires the combining of genetic material from a union of two parent cells, egg and sperm. Organs are not originated by systems at their own level but by the reproductive activity of (a) the cells which are their subsystems, (b) the organisms which are their suprasystems, and (c) the mating dyads which are their suprasuprasystems. Organisms are originated by (a) cells which are their subsubsystems and (b) in some species (e.g., hydra) by single parent organisms or in others by a mating dyad. Groups may be originated by the process of chartering, which is carried out by systems at any level from organisms on up. An individual parent organism or several (who may or may not be members of the group themselves) program a set of structural and process relationships—the template or charter—and then implement this program with individual organisms as components. This programming may not be planned; in friendship and social groups it often just arises out of the customs of the society common to all the members. The living tissue of these organisms, with all its structural and process characteristics, is produced by the processes of reproduction described above. Organizations, societies, and supranational systems are chartered like groups, by parent or founding systems at any level from the organism on up, and these charters are implemented by living systems whose tissue has arisen by the reproductive processes described above. For example, a mother "gives" her son to their country.

DNA can now be synthesized in the laboratory using a DNA template.[9] It is conceivable that, in the future, groups or systems at higher levels may jointly create, in a "laboratory" or "factory," living organisms like those which compose them. Aldous Huxley predicted this in his novel *Brave New World*.[10] But we are far from that now, and until it happens systems at the group level and above will be symbiotic or parasitic on (a) cells, (b) organisms, and (c) mating dyads, to produce the new organisms which compose them. This dependency explains the special protections and prerogatives given to reproducing cells, organisms, and dyads by higher-level systems.

Representative *variables* of the process of reproducing are: Sorts of matter-energy used in reproducing.

Meaning of information used in reproducing. Sorts of information used in reproducing. Changes in reproducing over time. Changes in reproducing with different circumstances. Rate of reproducing. Frequency of reproducing. Lag in reproducing. Costs of reproducing.

3.1.2 Boundary, the subsystem at the perimeter of a system that holds together the components which make up the system, protects them from environmental stresses, and excludes or permits entry to various sorts of matter-energy and information.

3.1.2.1 Structure The boundary ordinarily is structured to resist penetration from the environment. It may be a region of increased density or it may present a barrier to matter-energy or information transmissions (*e.g.,* an empty zone or territory which supports little life, a fence, wall, desert, jungle, body of water, chain of mountains, fortifications, or guards for matter-energy transmissions; walls, censors, or electronic jammers for information transmissions). Living systems differ from many nonliving systems by having such specialized structures at their perimeters. The latter ordinarily are not denser or provided with barriers at their perimeters, unless they are artifacts designed to carry out some boundary function, *e.g.,* a box, a bottle, a case, an automobile, or a ship. The boundary may be made up of living components and/or artifacts which are fixed in space or which move freely about the edges of the territory.

System boundaries at the various levels are quite different. Cells have membranes or walls; organs have covering membranes or capsules; organisms have skin, fur, scales, feathers, hair, exoskeletons, and other structures. All these have many gaps in them, through which matter-energy and/or information can pass. Components of groups and systems above that level ordinarily are not arranged in space to make direct contact. Consequently they often have no common matter-energy boundary at all beyond those of the individual members, *e.g.,* the backs of football players in a huddle or children dancing around a maypole. They always have a common information boundary in space-time, however, consisting of the limits of the channels over which they communicate. A system's components may share a single artifact to perform a boundary function for them. Artifacts often serve living systems well as boundaries because many nonliving substances can resist stresses more effectively than living tissues. In a sense the thick cell walls of the higher plants are nonliving artifacts, for they are made of cellulose which does not exchange matter-energy as do other cellular components. The outer cells of animals' skins as well as hair, fur, scales, and exoskeletons are all nonliving artifacts of living cells. Human beings wear clothes and armor; families pro-

tect themselves from intruders with houses, caves, or fences; medieval cities were walled; nations have often fortified their frontiers.

The boundary does its filtering more at some regions of the boundary than at others. Living systems, being open systems, must at places admit matter-energy and information, but matter-energy is taken in only at those parts of the boundary where the ingestor is. Information is admitted only at the regions where the input transducer is. In different sorts of systems these subsystems are quite differently distributed over the boundary.

3.1.2.2 Process Boundaries carry out three separate but related processes: (*a*) They constitute a barrier to flows of matter-energy and information in and out of the system. Transmissions across this barrier require more work than transmissions inside or outside it. (*b*) They filter certain sorts of matter-energy and information, selectively permitting some to pass in or out but not others. The degree of filtering for each sort of transmission varies from time to time, dependent upon the states of the system and its environment. (*c*) They maintain a steady-state differential between the interior of the system and its environment, making it more likely, within a specific range of probability, that a given sort of matter-energy or information will be on one side of the boundary than on the other.

When functioning normally, boundaries selectively admit inputs lacking to the system and block out excessive or dangerous matter-energy and information inputs. To do so, they may be closed over the ingestor subsystem (see page 157): snails, when attacked, draw into their shells; families move to tornado cellars when the winds are high. They also may shut out the markers bearing impinging information: eyelids close for sleep; censors block delivery of mail revealing military secrets. Openings in the boundary may be increased in size or number in order to facilitate inputs. Moreover, boundaries are selective in what they filter out, keeping from the system matter of inappropriate size, shape, or chemical structure, energy of too great intensity, or markers with inappropriate informational patterns (*e.g.,* bitter substances, or persons who say *sibboleth* rather than *shibboleth*).[11]

The boundaries of concrete systems can be located by empirical operations available to scientists generally, rather than being set conceptually by a single observer. Ordinarily, where a step function or sudden change in rate of flow of matter-energy or information is found, there is a boundary.[12] This is true because the boundary usually has a barrier or impediment to the transmission of matter-energy or information that is not present in the environment or the center of the system. Since more work is usually required to cross a boundary than to approach it, transmission often is slowed. The region where the step-function change occurs for one sort of matter-energy or information input may be somewhat differently located in space than that for another sort of input, but usually they overlap quite precisely. Operations which indicate the location of a living system's boundary and which commonly occur at or close to the same region in space may include a sharp change: in temperature, registered by a thermocouple or thermometer; in resistance to motion of a solid body, measured by a pressure gauge; in density, measured by a densitometer or by counting the number of components in a given volume; in illumination, measured by a photometer; or in rate of information flow, measured by an observer or a machine that can count messages or bits transmitted per time unit.

Representative *variables* of boundary process include: Sorts of matter-energy crossing the boundary. Meaning of information crossing the boundary. Sorts of information crossing the boundary. Degree of permeability of the boundary to matter-energy or information. Percentage of matter-energy or information arriving at the boundary which enters the system. Changes in matter-energy or information processing at the boundary over time. Changes in matter-energy or information processing at the boundary with different circumstances. Rate of matter-energy or information processing at the boundary. Frequency of matter-energy or information processing at the boundary. Lag in matter-energy or information processing at the boundary. Costs of matter-energy or information processing at the boundary.

3.2 Subsystems which process matter-energy   Inputs, internal processes, and outputs of different kinds of matter-energy constitute the matter-energy metabolism necessary to all systems. This metabolism is accomplished in such a way that living systems at all levels counteract entropic changes and maintain over time steady states of many sorts of matter-energy.

3.2.1 Ingestor,   the subsystem which brings matter-energy across the system boundary from the environment.

3.2.1.1 Structure   The gaps in cell walls, input arteries to organs, and the mouths, noses, lungs, and gills of organisms are all ingestors. Groups may disperse this process down to individual members or assign a single one to bring necessary matter-energy to the entire group. Many organizations have ingestor groups, and higher-level systems commonly have organizations that specialize in ingesting, such as the workers of mines and ports. Often they are aided by artifacts.

3.2.1.2 Process   Ingesting processes are as varied as diffusion through a cell membrane, eating, and importing.

Representative *variables* of the process of ingesting include: Sorts of matter-energy ingested. Degree of openness of the ingestor. Changes in ingesting over time. Changes in ingesting with different circumstances. Rate of ingesting. Frequency of ingesting. Lag in ingesting. Costs of ingesting.

3.2.2 Distributor,   the subsystem which carries inputs from outside the system or outputs from its subsystems around the system to each component.

3.2.2.1 Structure   Various substances diffuse through the intermolecular spaces which constitute the distributor of a cell. A sponge has its components so arranged that they form canals into and out of which sea water can pass freely. This is its distributor. Vascular systems are the comparable structures in more advanced organisms. Groups often designate one member to serve food or issue supplies. There are in higher-level social systems specific groups and organizations which—with the help of artifacts like roads, trucks, railroads, and planes—constitute this subsystem. In a supranational system, like an alliance, supply may be by convoy or air lift. At various levels the distributor subsystem has a hierarchical structure with a geometrical progression from the size of the region served by an average unit of its lowest echelon of the distributor to the size of the region served by an average unit of its highest echelon.[13]

3.2.2.2 Process   Without inputs of matter-energy and removal of wastes, living components of systems cannot maintain their steady states and so cannot survive. When the blood supply of an organism is blocked and cannot reach a finger, leg, or region of the brain, for instance, that part dies. And the rate of flow to each part must be controlled so that it is within tolerable limits. Similarly if cities or nations cannot maintain adequate distribution to all essential components, their organization collapses.

Representative *variables* of the distributing process are: Sorts of matter-energy distributed to various parts of the system. Changes in distributing over time. Changes in distributing with different circumstances. Rate of distributing. Frequency of distributing. Lag in distributing. Costs of distributing.

3.2.3 Converter,   the subsystem which changes certain inputs to the system into forms more useful for the special processes of that particular system.

3.2.3.1 Structure   The structure of the converter necessarily differs greatly from level to level because the levels process widely different sorts of matter-energy. Enzymes in food vacuoles, mitochondria, and other organelles change inputs to cells into other compounds essential to cellular metabolism. Organisms carry out similar functions using cutting, breaking, or grinding structures as well as chemical secretions in their guts. The cooks of family groups and the shop workers of manufacturing firms convert many substances to more useful forms. So do the factories of nations. Organisms and higher-level systems often use artifacts such as tools.

3.2.3.2 Process   Some matter-energy inputs at all levels can be used without being converted. This is true, for instance, of part of the water input to all levels. Homemakers buy prepared foods. Societies import finished goods and harvest crops which need only distribution for use. Most inputs to organisms must be broken down both mechanically, by crushing or dissolving, and chemically, by dividing into smaller molecules or otherwise altering them. Societies may use elaborate artifacts, such as factories operated by large organizations, to prepare substances for general use. Petroleum cracking plants are an example. Elaborate processes in many of the subsystems control the rate and quality of their outputs.

Representative *variables* of the converting process are: Sorts of matter-energy converted. Percentage of matter-energy converted. Changes in converting over time. Changes in converting with different circumstances. Rate of converting. Frequency of converting. Lag in converting. Costs of converting.

3.2.4 Producer,   the subsystem which forms stable associations that endure for significant periods among matter-energy inputs to the system or outputs from its converter, the materials synthesized being for growth, damage repair, or replacement of components of the system, or for providing energy for moving or constituting the system's outputs of products or information markers to its suprasystem.

These associations are maintained either by the interatomic bonds of the chemical molecules which are synthesized or by physical bonds—such as nails, bolts, welding, cement, or stitches—which hold together various sorts of artifacts.

3.2.4.1 Structure   Mitochondria, ribosomes, and other organelles contain the enzymes which carry out the chemical syntheses in cells. Different organ structures, such as the liver, bone marrow, gonads, and endocrine glands, in organisms are specialized for various specific syntheses. Work groups may divide the labor of manufacturing a complex product. Organizations and societies often have comparable allocation of production tasks to different specialized units or industries.

3.2.4.2 Process   Substances may be combined chemically, as in cellular syntheses like those involved in the growing of a new tail by a salamander. Or the combining may be mechanical, as when boards are nailed together to make a house. Complex controls at all levels guarantee that the particular forms of matter-energy needed by the system are produced in the amounts and quality required.

Among the *variables* in the producing process are: Sorts of matter-energy produced. Quality of matter-energy produced. Percentage of matter-energy used in producing. Changes in producing over time. Changes in producing with different circumstances. Rate of producing. Frequency of producing. Lag in producing. Costs of producing.

3.2.5 Matter-energy   storage,   the   subsystem which retains in the system, for different periods of time, deposits of various sorts of matter-energy.

3.2.5.1 Structure   All cells store energy in rapidly available form as high-energy phosphate molecules, and in less rapidly available form as glucose or glycogen. Specialized cells store matter-energy as fats or lipids. Certain bodily structures, like the capsule of the kidney, the subcutaneous tissues, and the omentum may store large amounts of fat. Such deposits act as storage for the entire organism. A single individual may use an artifact for storage, as when a skin diver takes an oxygen tank with him into the sea. Families and stores, as well as other groups, have storage places in the buildings they occupy for food, clothing, and other supplies. Organizations commonly have specialized storage groups. Entire trades and industries are devoted to such functions in larger social systems, often using huge containers, artifacts like giant electric batteries, oil tanks, and warehouses.

3.2.5.2 Process   The process of storing matter-energy at all levels involves three separate stages: (*a*) putting into storage, (*b*) maintaining in storage over time, and (*c*) retrieving from storage. Separate components of the subsystem may be involved in each stage. Efficient retrieval requires a regular rationale for placing certain sorts of matter-energy in specific regions. The subsystems must have some sort of overall control of rates of input to and output from it. What can be obtained from storage to some degree mirrors or samples the system's environment, since many stored contents came from that environment (see pages 30, 67, and 411). But this is only roughly so, because the system samples its environment selectively, filtering out much of it; the system also may move from one place in the environment to another quite different one; it alters the inputs in various ways before they are stored; and it retrieves them selectively.

Among the *variables* in the process of storing matter-energy are: Sorts of matter-energy stored. Total storage capacity. Percentage of matter-energy stored. Place of storage. Changes in storing over time.

Changes in storing with different circumstances. Rate of storing. Lag in storing. Costs of storing. Rate of breakdown of organization of matter-energy in storage. Sorts of matter-energy retrieved. Percentage of matter-energy retrieved. Order of retrieval. Rate of retrieval. Lag in retrieval. Costs of retrieval.

3.2.6 Extruder, the subsystem which transmits matter-energy out of the system in the forms of products or wastes.

If the system has a purpose or goal of transmitting beyond its boundary a certain form of matter-energy which its suprasystem lacks, that particular sort of matter-energy is its product. Its wastes are sorts of matter-energy which are excess to the system and thus not useful in achieving its purposes or goals, or which hamper the accomplishment of these purposes or goals. What are wastes to a system, however, may be useful inputs lacked by its suprasystem. Plants are symbiotic with animals in their environments because the wastes of each are useful to the other.

3.2.6.1 Structure An aperture in a cell wall through which matter-energy can diffuse or be expelled by internal contractile activity; an output vein in a liver, a ureter from a kidney, or a nipple in a breast; a common cloaca or the sweat glands; a sergeant issuing guns or a scavenger; a packaging and mailing office or a firm which hauls junk and garbage to sea; the organization which carries out sewage removal; cities which export, including their associated artifacts such as cranes and shovels, trucks and barges, constitute the extruder subsystem, depending upon the system level. One or more components of a system may serve at one time as part of the extruder and at another as part of the output transducer (see page 69).

3.2.6.2 Process Extrusion of wastes and products may be continuous or episodic. It may occur whenever a message signals that the excess of wastes or products has reached a certain amount or whenever a message from the suprasystem signals a need for a product: The adrenal gland secretes when it receives a signal; a mother cooks dinner when her children say they are hungry; a factory manufactures cars when purchasers demand them. Extrusion of wastes is frequently a rhythmic process, such as expiration. It can follow a period during which wastes accumulate, like the weekly garbage and trash collection at many homes. A suitable destination in the environment and an appropriate time for extrusion must be arranged to prevent other systems from being contaminated by the wastes extruded, which may elicit reprisals or other harmful responses. For instance, a city may have to store its wastes internally during a period when the river is too low to carry them away.

The *variables* of the process of extruding include: Sorts of products and wastes extruded. Percentage of products and wastes extruded. Changes in extruding over time. Changes in extruding with different circumstances. Rate of extruding. Frequency of extruding. Lag in extruding. Costs of extruding.

3.2.7 Motor, the subsystem which moves the system or parts of it in relation to part or all of its environment or moves components of its environment in relation to each other.

Some living systems are sessile. These may—like many plants—live in an environment in which gases or liquids or animals circulate about them, bringing them inputs and bearing off outputs. Or they may, even though attached at one point, sway about, using their own energy to do so. In groups and higher-level systems the motor subsystem may be dispersed downward, so that subsystems or components have their own subsystem or subcomponent motors and move independently in space. This does not make the overall system any the less a system, if it uses channels whose length need not be constant, so that its ability to transmit information among its subsystems or components in four-dimensional space-time is not interrupted (see page 52).

One or more components of the motor may at times act as the output transducer, sending markers bearing information beyond the system boundary (see page 69).

3.2.7.1 Structure In lower levels of systems, outputs—whether of products, wastes, movements, or markers—may be made by the same components. At higher levels it is more common for a different structure to carry out each of these processes. Free-living cells move their walls by protoplasmic flow. Organs and organisms move primarily by the specialized flow of the components of their muscle cells, which in vertebrates are attached to bones. Groups and higher levels of systems disperse their movements down to their component organisms, or they use artifacts, usually powered by engines.

3.2.7.2 Process At all levels, if the total system moves, the motor's decider subsubsystem must exercise centralized control over all components of the subsystem, determining the direction, rate, and other aspects of their motion. But at all levels there are also independent, decentralized movements. In general, the higher the system, the larger it is and the more likely it is that components, rather than the whole system, will do the moving. Too much energy is required to move the total mass. Societies with small populations have on occasion been nomadic, moving in established order. Societies with many members characteristically send some of them out to import needed inputs; the entire society does not migrate to the part of their environment where those inputs are.

Representative *variables* of the moving process are: Sorts of movements made. Changes in moving over time. Changes in moving with different circumstances. Rate of moving. Rate of output of work. Frequency of moving. Duration of moving. Lag in moving. Costs of moving.

3.2.8 Supporter, the subsystem which maintains the proper spatial relationships among components of the system, so that they can interact without weighting each other down or crowding each other.

3.2.8.1 Structure The cell wall and perhaps other structures keep a cell's components in an organized spatial arrangement, with the nucleus and the nucleolus near the center. The structure of the mitochondria arranges enzymes spatially in the exact order they are needed to carry out the essential sequences of intracellular syntheses. In many organs the stroma supports the functioning parenchymal cells. In small, multicellular organisms a framework of cell walls, particularly noticeable in plants, maintains the spatial arrangements of all the parts. In higher animals either an exoskeleton or an endoskeleton, held up by the ground, water, or the air, along with cartilage, fascia, and the capsules of organs, does this. Commonly the supporting artifacts of larger systems are partially or wholly dead.[14] Groups are supported in their particular arrangements by the ground, water, or the air. Small groups occasionally get support by uniting the skeletons of several members (*e.g.,* a "flying wedge" of football players, children in ring games, or circus acrobats in human pyramids). From the group level on up, the individual components move freely on their medium of support, since they communicate through the air and by other means which do not require channels of constant length among them. Also artifacts are often built to support groups (*e.g.,* committee tables, sofas, platforms, houses, and vehicles). The supporters of organizations are much like those of groups. The buildings which house them, however, more frequently rise upward in stories, for organizations commonly include more people than groups. Complex specialized structures like factories, pueblos, battleships, and ocean liners are used to support specific organizations. Societies cannot exist without big and complex supporting artifacts, such as city walls, roads, sewers, telephone poles, aqueducts, overpasses, skyscrapers, subways, and ports. Supranational systems are supported by conference buildings, border fortifications, planes and ships on international routes. Their supporting structures are mainly artifacts, like those of societies, but they cover wider areas of the earth's surface.

3.2.8.2 Process Each supporting structure carries out the task of holding system components in positions where they can interact, often repairing themselves or replacing their artifacts if they are damaged or wear out.

Representative *variables* in the supporting process include: Strength of the supporter. Costs of supporting.

3.3 Subsystems which process information Inputs, internal processes, and outputs of various information signals represent the information metabolism of such living systems. In all such systems information flows through several subsystems, each one being a transmitter to the next one in the sequence, which acts as a receiver. Then, after processing the information in its own specialized way, the second subsystem acts as a transmitter, sending the information on to a third. Because information patterns always are borne on matter-energy markers, because the system privately needs information in different forms from that in which it is usually available publicly (which is also true of matter-energy), and for other reasons, the information flows in living systems are, as I have noted above (see page 54), similar in important ways to their matter-energy flows.

All matter-energy and information subsystems are coordinated by information transmissions. Living systems also maintain their relationships with their environments or suprasystems by inputs and outputs of information. Protoplasm is irritable, and single free-living cells receive signals about the temperature, light, chemical constitution of their surroundings, and mechanical stimuli like touch and gravity, transmit the signals internally, and respond. So do organs and organisms. Social systems all have individuals, groups, or organizations which process information for the whole system. These, like the matter-energy processing subsystems of the same systems, sometimes make use of artifacts to carry out these processes and often to make them more efficient.

A number of technical terms are required for precise discourse about any systems that process information. Their definitions follow:

Input ensemble—The ensemble or repertoire used in information inputs to the system.

Output ensemble—The ensemble or repertoire used in information outputs from the system.

Input–output transfer function—A mathematical statement of the regular differences between the input to a given system and the output from it which is "mapped" upon it.

Input–output compatibility—A measure of the similarity between the input ensemble in which information is displayed to a system and the output ensemble "mapped" upon it, used by that system in responding to it. (It is equally possible for an observer to "predict" the input from the output or to predict the output from the input.)

Transmitted information—The amount of information that flows in a channel. It is the same as the input information if there is perfect input–output compatibility. It decreases from that value as the input–output compatibility diminishes.

Channel—A route in physical space by which markers bearing information can be sent from a transmitter to a receiver (see page 63). A formal mathematical description of a channel has been made by Shannon in terms of its input–output transition probabilities or transfer function.[15] This formal description, of course, gives no clue to the process whereby input changes to output in the concrete system.

Bandwidth—The number of different frequencies, measured in hertz (Hz), which can be employed in a channel. The precision with which the transmitter and receiver can distinguish these frequencies determines the maximum ensemble of symbols that can be used on that channel.

Channel capacity—The maximum amount of information a channel can transmit in a period of time, usually measured in bits per second. The more noise in a channel, the lower is its capacity.

Threshold—The least intensity of information input which on the average is just capable of eliciting a process in the receiving system.

Processing time—The time required to transmit information from input to output.

Lag—The time elapsing between the input of information to a system and the output elicited by it.

Code—A language or convention used by a system, whereby one ensemble of signals is represented by, coupled with, or "mapped" upon another ensemble according to some regular rules. Transmitter and receiver must speak the same language, have established a prior convention, or be coded alike, in advance, or the transmission will convey no meaning to the receiver. Such coding is of two major types, either (*a*) *analog*, in which some physical aspect of the signal varies as a function of some variable it represents, or (*b*) *digital*, in which the variable represented is broken into discrete units which are counted by some numerical scheme, and the signals transmitted represent these numbers in some way.[16]

Distortion—Systematic alteration (as opposed to noise, which is random alteration) in the input–output function of information passing through a system. It is alteration such as occurs to a geometric figure drawn on a rubber sheet which then is stretched in different directions. It is the sum total of the processes (except the addition of noise) which occur to the information as it goes through systems that act upon it as it passes, in the process of reducing their strains.

Redundancy—The existence of signals in a message which do not add to information already transmitted by previous signals in the same message and which therefore, in a noise-free or error-free system, are excess to the receiver in the process of determining what message was transmitted.

Equivocation—The uncertainty as to what signals the transmitter put into the channel which the receiver still has after it has received a message from the channel.

Range—The number of parallel channels.

Input overlap—The presentation of two or more signals simultaneously.

Input priority—The probability that a given message will be preferentially transmitted before other messages waiting for transmission.

Confusional state—The state of a system when it can no longer cope with the rush of information input flooding it.

Omission adjustment process—Failing to transmit certain randomly distributed signals in a message.

Error adjustment process—Incorrectly transmitting certain signals in a message.

Queuing adjustment process—Delaying transmission of certain signals in a message, the sequence being temporarily stored until transmission.

Filtering adjustment process—Giving priority in processing to certain classes of messages.

Abstracting adjustment process—Processing a message with less than complete detail.

Multiple channels adjustment process—Simultaneously transmitting messages over two or more parallel channels.

Escape adjustment process—Acting to cut off information input.

Chunking adjustment process—Transmitting meaningful information in organized "chunks" of symbols rather than symbol by symbol.[17] This enlarges the system's output ensemble, since instead of dealing with written English with an alphabet of 26 letters and a space, it deals with it in units of many words or brief phrases of two or more letters each. In a given sort of writing, some of these words or phrases are much more probable than others. They can be transmitted as units despite the fact that they have a much higher information content than a single letter. Since the units can be read nearly as fast as a letter, information can be processed at a higher overall rate.

Concepts that relate to information processing have spread into other fields than communications engineering, being applied to any situation where patterning is transmitted from one system to another. Baker discusses this:

The realization is growing that in so complex a system as living matter there must be some special communication and control facility. Also, a further sort of recognition that Professor von Neumann's teleological research is particularly appropriate in this field has led to exciting and stimulating connections between information theory and the structure and reproducing capacity of living matter. Claude Shannon's dramatic formulation of the information content of events and the related concepts of the control of events by Professor Norbert Wiener provided general theories going far beyond the ingenious but specific treatments of signal theory and coding produced earlier. Perhaps once more it was this very quality of a unifying theory which attracted many scholars remote from communications science. As diverse but individualistic interests as represented by an astro-physicist (Gamow) and other mathematical and physical scientists have begun to show how subtle sequences of amino acids, which apparently endow protein with their high individualities and specialized functions, could be arranged by synthesis contraposed to ribonucleic acid chains. It is now believed that three or more nucleotide residues can fix by an understandable coding scheme the position of each particular amino acid selected for the sequence desired [see pages 217 and 221]. The protein then produced from such sequential combinations would presumably be the characteristic protein for the special function, which on a higher level, of course, might also be the special function of reproduction of the whole organism itself.

Thus smoothly and quickly have some of the deepest theories of this present time moved from telephony and communications interest to genetics and familial interests.[18]

The following sections describe the subsystems which process information in living systems.[19]

3.3.1 Input transducer, the sensory subsystem which brings markers bearing information into the system, changing them to other matter-energy forms suitable for transmission within it.

The input markers are formed by significant alterations in the environment. Each one is of a particular spatial structure, wavelength, bandwidth, or intensity. The transducer changes them to other matter-energy forms suitable for further transmission within that specific system. An input transducer brings markers bearing information into a system in a manner somewhat similar to the way ingestors bring in matter-energy (see page 57).

3.3.1.1 Structure Organelles, cells, or organs specialized to respond to a given energy form of markers bearing information from the environment—like light or sound or pressure—are input transducer subsystems at lower levels of systems. Groups may delegate specific members to observe the environment, like military scouts; or this process may be carried out by all members. Organizations often have specific units to bring in information to the system—research staffs, reporters, intelligence groups, for example. Higher-level systems have comparable components. At the organism level and above, systems may use artifacts as input transducers, like photoelectric cells or radar sets.

3.3.1.2 Process The biochemical processes by which input transducers or sense organs change input energies to make them appropriate for transmission into the system are now being analyzed with great quantitative precision at the levels of the cell, organ, and organism. At the level of the group and higher, input transducing is either dispersed downward to specific organisms or, in modern times, carried on by artifacts, usually electronic sensors. In recent years these sensors have been developed to operate in a sophisticated manner for many frequency bands of energy transmission, some of which can be sensed by human beings or other living systems and others of which cannot.

Included among representative *variables* of the input transducing process are: Meaning of information input which is transduced. Sorts of information input which are transduced. Percentage of the information input which is transduced. Threshold of the input transducer. Changes in input transducing over time. Changes in input transducing with different circumstances. Channel capacity of the input transducer. Number of channels in use in the input transducer. Distortion of the input transducer. Signal-to-noise ratio of the input transducer. Rate of input transducing. Lag in input transducing. Costs of input transducing.

3.3.2 Internal transducer, the sensory subsystem which receives, from subsystems or components within the system, markers bearing information about significant alterations in those subsystems or components, changing them to other matter-energy forms of a sort which can be transmitted within it.

3.3.2.1 Structure Repressor molecules within cells react to the presence of molecules which are products of chemical reactions within those cells, an internal transducing activity. Some organs have specialized sorts of muscle tissue which carry out internal transducing. Others possibly have sensory neurons which transduce internal information as a part of wholly local reflex arcs. Certain neurons in an organism's central nervous system transduce signals about the states of its organ components which they sense directly or receive from neurons that have sensors of pressure, pain, stretch, chemical, and other sorts of information, transmitting it over neural channels. Groups learn about their internal states by reports from members specially designated to be internal transducers, sensing changes in the group, or perhaps from all members directly, each reporting changes in himself. An organization's component groups often send representatives to make such reports to the organization at conferences or at legislative sessions. Similar delegations report on the states of subsystems or components of higher-level systems.

3.3.2.2 Process The output transducers of subsystems and components send information about their internal states to the system of which they are parts. They also send information to other subsystems and components at their own level. For example, the foreman of one production gang may report his group's progress to another gang without informing the production supervisor. They may also send information to higher echelons of their subsystem without transmitting it to the next higher level of system.

A living system can remain a system only if its subsystems and components report their current states and their needs, so that feedback signals can coordinate their processes with those of the total system. Pressure within an organ, for example, is transduced to a pattern of neural pulses just as external sense organs transduce their inputs. An organ denervated of its fibers to the organism's internal transducer may carry on some of its processes independently, but it can no longer be coordinated well with the rest of the organism. It also cannot report pain, so that the processes which usually protect it cannot operate.

Representative *variables* of the internal transducing process include: Meaning of internal information which is transduced. Sorts of internal information which are transduced. Percentage of the internal information which is transduced. Threshold of the internal transducer. Changes in internal transducing over time. Changes in internal transducing with different circumstances. Channel capacity of the internal transducer. Number of channels in use in the internal transducer. Distortion of the internal transducer. Signal-to-noise ratio of the internal transducer. Rate of internal transducing. Lag in internal transducing. Costs of internal transducing.

3.3.3 Channel and net, the subsystem composed of a single route in physical space, or multiple interconnected routes, by which markers bearing information are transmitted to all parts of the system.

Channels may intersect at points called *nodes* and may thus be interconnected to form a *net*. This net is similar to the distributor in that the former conveys markers bearing information, and the latter conveys matter-energy to all parts of the system (see page 57).

Sometimes the term "channel" is used to refer to an entire system. For instance, the information input–output transfer function of a human experimental subject is studied, and the maximum rate at which he can process information—his channel capacity—is determined. This is an overall system input–output process including several subsystems of the subject and is not just his channel and net subsystem. (Of course the instructions of the experiment direct the subject to be nothing but a channel in the group system composed of the subject, the experimenter, and his artifact equipment.) Although I shall call the system's peak rate of information processing its channel capacity, I shall never call an entire system a channel, but only the channel and net information processing subsystem of that system. Of course that channel and net subsystem may have components which are made up of a complete set of matter-energy and information processing subsystems. For instance, each of the signal corps personnel, who jointly constitute the channel and net of a military outfit, has a complete set of subsystems.

3.3.3.1 Structure Pulses pass down the membranes of neurons, muscle cells, and other sorts of cells, and various kinds of currents flow in the dendrites and cell-body cytoplasm of neurons, as well as in the cytoplasm of free-living cells. The "transverse system" of membranes conveys currents in muscle cells. These regions are the channels and nets of cells. Organs may convey messages through intrinsic neurons or through cytoplasm of adjacent parenchymal cells (as in mammalian guts or hearts). Nervous systems of varying degrees of complexity are the chief channels and nets of organisms. The distributors of various organisms also act as information channels, carrying molecules bearing chemical information, hormones, from one part of the system to others. As they often do for several of their other subsystems, groups and higher systems may use channels composed of nonliving parts of their environments or of artifacts. The channels connecting a group may be in the air between them through which light, sound, and molecules bearing smells are propagated for varying distances. They may be in the ether of outer space. Or they may be artifacts like telephone wires. The living components of the subsystem operate and maintain the artifactual part, and in higher-level systems—organizations, societies, and supranational systems—the number of persons involved in postal and telephonic services, radio, television, journalism, and other mass communication activities can be very large.

3.3.3.2 Process In order to be propagated through channels and nets, signals must be of more than a minimum strength, differing with the particular channels used. Propagation through nets of all sorts of systems is almost never wholly random, on the one hand, or wholly uniform, on the other. Instead, constraints exist, different at the various levels, which make certain pathways more probable than others. If at a junction information is passed on unchanged, that junction is a node; if it is reduced in amount or altered by such adjustment processes as omission, error, filtering, abstracting, or choice among alternatives, the junction is a decider (see page 67).[20] Some channels—as in face-to-face groups—convey information in both directions, but most convey it only in one direction, which may be in or out of a system or among comparable subsystems or components of the same system, as well as upward (often in the form of requests) to higher echelons, or downward (often as commands) to lower. In general, messages to higher echelons have been more abstracted and are more general, while those to lower echelons are more detailed and specific, but therefore they are usually applicable only locally rather than generally.[21] Whenever messages are traveling in an interconnected net, they must have addresses to be sure they are processed in the correct direction at every node they pass, and they must have signatures to identify the sender to the receiver (see page 38).

Since there is a cost in entropy or dissipation of useful energy for every bit of information transmitted (see pages 13 to 16), and since noise increases as the temperature of the channel rises above absolute zero and also as transmission rates rise, Bremermann has concluded that there is an upper limit at which any channel can transmit information.[22] At ordinary room temperature, he calculates that this is of the order of 4×10^{13} bits per second. This is an upper theoretical bound which no living system comes near to reaching, but the technology of data processing artifacts is approaching the point where lower temperatures must be used or multiple parallel channels must be used, if information processing speeds are to be increased. In the noisy channels of living systems these theoretical limitations may be minor considerations, but these calculations at least indicate that there are limits to the channel capacities of living as well as electronic systems. Another important limitation of the capacity of any single channel made of multiple components is that it can never be greater than that of the component with the smallest capacity (see page 124).

Many *variables* of channel and net processing can be measured. Some representative ones are: Meaning of information channeled to various parts of the system. Sorts of information channeled to various parts of the system. Percentage of information arriving at the appropriate receiver in the channel and net. Threshold of the channel and net. Changes in channel and net processing over time. Changes in channel and net processing with different circumstances. Information capacity of the channel and net. Distortion of the channel and net. Signal-to-noise ratio in the channel and net. Rate of processing of information over the channel and net. Lag in channel and net processing. Costs of channel and net processing.

3.3.4 Decoder,   the subsystem which alters the code of information input to it through the input transducer or internal transducer into a "private" code that can be used internally by the system.

This may involve consulting an ensemble of signals (or thesaurus) stored in the memory, determining for a public input the private equivalent, and transmitting the latter. If the public form in which the information enters the system is the same as the private form, this subsystem process need not be carried out. The process is like that of converting in that it changes information, coming from the environment or suprasystem, from its public form to one that can be used privately or internally, and converting does the same thing for matter-energy inputs (see page 57). But the ways the decoder and the converter carry out their processes are not alike. The input transducer and the internal transducer perform quite different processes from the decoder: the transducer subsystems alter the matter-energy form of the marker; the decoder alters the code in which the information appears.

3.3.4.1 Structure   Codes differ in various parts of the nervous system, so there must be decoders in it. One component of a neuron's decoder is on its subsynaptic membrane, where it changes information from the chemical code of the neurohumoral transmitter which crosses the synapse to the bioelectric code of the membrane. At the organ level they may be at the places where neurons from other subsystems synapse. Often they are in the same sensory component as the input transducer, although decoding and input transducing are different processes. At the organism level decoding is performed by sense organs, but that sort of decoding, comparing signals from the input transducer with genetically stored or learned information, which is called "perception" or "pattern recognition," is also carried out by a hierarchy of echelons in the central nervous system. At the group level and above, components which interpret intelligence, translate languages, decode radio signals, and decrypt secret messages are the decoders. These processes are usually dispersed downward to individual organisms. Recently, artifacts, such as electronic data processing systems, are beginning to be programmed to perform such decoding processes as translating foreign languages and recognizing radar patterns, handwritten script, and printed letters.

3.3.4.2 Process   It is useful to distinguish three sorts of codes, increasing in complexity, which are used in decoding and encoding—alpha, beta, and gamma codes. An *alpha code* is one in which the ensemble of markers is composed of different spatial patterns of structural arrangement of physical artifacts, like door keys or chemical molecules. The interatomic forces in macromolecules, studied by Pauling and others, determine their arrangements in space.[23] Such arrangements represent the coded "message" or "signal" in a hormone or in such molecules as DNA and RNA. The fitting of a key into a lock to turn it, the impressing of specific patterns by the genes upon the developing organisms, and the transmission of a hormonal signal from the pituitary gland, which activates the thyroid gland—these are all transmissions of information. The structure of the key is what the lock responds to, rather than the matter-energy in it or whether it is made of wood or metal. The specific pattern of structural complexity of the molecules is what elicits the response. A *beta code* is one based on variations in process, such as different temporal patterns of signals or different patterns of intensity of signals. Such codes are used by living systems which have decoders and encoders with stable programming whereby they can change an input code into a different output code. Neurons do this. A *gamma code* is a symbolic language used by systems which have decoder and encoder subsystems that alter the code on the input markers to a different one on the output markers by comparing the input to a stored thesaurus of information and selecting the output from it. The relations between the symbols on the input and output markers in such codes are entirely arbitrary. This sort of symbolic information transmission is ordinarily dealt with when communication is discussed in the social sciences. A similar distinction was made by Pavlov between the messages conveyed in the more primitive brain centers (the primary signal system conveying "signals of reality") and those in the higher centers—perhaps the frontal lobes, apparently of the human nervous system only—concerned with language and thought (the secondary signal system, conveying "signals of signals").[24]

All decoding or encoding processes as Shannon pointed out, involve a probability of error, so that the input to the subsystem cannot be perfectly determined from the output message.[25] As the signal-to-noise ratio decreases, the probability of error increases, so noise and error are positively related to each other (see page 14). The output code may have a larger or a smaller ensemble than the input code, so each output signal may convey more or less information than each input signal. If it is more, it is a kind of particularizing; if less, a kind of abstracting. Moreover, the codes may differ in their logical categorization of signals, and one may be more efficient than the other in the sense that it includes more aspects of variables relevant to the structure and process of the system.

In cells and higher levels of systems which have more than one echelon, each one may do its own decoding, referring to different thesauruses. For instance, in the organism a set of signals may be seen at the first echelon as several dots, at a higher one as a man, at a higher one as John, and at a higher one as John the scholarly mathematician. In an organization at one echelon a clerk may perceive a letter as incoming mail, her boss may perceive it as a threat of legal action by a competitor, and top management may interpret it, in terms of their private knowledge, as a signal that the competitor is near collapse because of inadequate financial backing.

Included among the *variables* of the process of decoding are: Meaning of information which is decoded. Sorts of information which are decoded. Percentage of the information input which is decoded. Threshold of the decoder. Changes in decoding over time. Changes in decoding with different circumstances. Channel capacity of the decoder. Distortion of the decoder. Signal-to-noise ratio of the decoder. Rate of decoding. Percentage of omissions in decoding. Percentage of errors in decoding. Code employed. Redundancy of the code employed. Lag in decoding. Costs of decoding.

3.3.5 Associator, the subsystem which carries out the first stage of the learning process, forming enduring associations among items of information in the system.

It synthesizes a set of bonds or interrelationships among them so that, at some future time, inputting item A into the system will elicit items $B \ldots N$, as outputs, each with its own probability, which will be greater than 0 and less than or equal to 1. The synthesis formed is at least somewhat different for each individual system, in the items involved and the sorts of relationships among them. Consequently it constitutes a private organization of knowledge or wisdom—as opposed to raw items of information—organized especially for the internal needs of that particular system. In this it carries out a process perhaps somewhat like that of the producer, which subsystem synthesizes out of items of matter-energy complex materials of the particular sort needed privately by the system for repair or replacement of components or for its products (see page 58).

The items of information combined by the associator may come from either the suprasystem through the input transducer, the system through the internal transducer, or the memory (see page 66). There is no association between items of information in a system if an input of item A elicits an output of item B, and a later input of item P elicits an output of item Q, and the input of item A in no way affects the probability that item P will elicit item Q.[26] If it *does* affect the probability, association exists. This, of course, is a purely formal description of association and gives no clue as to how the process occurs in the concrete system. Evidence that the stochastic process of associating is occurring is obtained when the probability increases that one item of information input will elicit another item.

3.3.5.1 Structure   There is no solid evidence that any plants can associate. Free-living cells like paramecia, however, quite possibly can, although there is no evidence what structure constitutes their associator subsystem. Certainly the behavior of quite primitive multicellular animals is modified by their past experience. Such associating must occur in their neural cells, ganglia, or nets. The associative learning of fish, birds, and mammals has been subjected to extensive experimental study, and it seems likely that the structures involved include the cortex of the brain (which is probably not essential), as well as the limbic and reticular regions. There are probably in human beings and some lower animals two bilaterally symmetrical associators, one on each side of the brain, connected across the midline. Groups and higher-level systems can learn as total systems. They do so by modifying their structures and procedures with experience. They find that certain structures or actions are associated with rewards more often than others. The process may be very slow. A great basketball team or restaurant, over years, may learn the procedures which most often are associated with success over competitors. A nation may, after finding which actions succeed and which do not, amend its constitution to improve its government. A supranational system, over decades, may discover what to do to keep more variables in a steady state. In general this sort of learning arises from consensus of a majority of the components. It is dispersed. Computers are beginning to be programmed as learning artifacts by systems at the organism level and above.

3.3.5.2 Process   The conditions of reward, punishment, and feedback under which association of items of information occurs have been investigated in free-living cells, the brain, and several organisms. Sometimes such associative learning is reversible. Sometimes, as in imprinting, it may not be. The process is poorly understood at the group level and above.

Representative *variables* of the process of associating include: Meaning of information which is associated. Sorts of information which are associated. Percentage of the information input which is associated to other information. Changes in associating over time. Changes in associating with different circumstances. Channel capacity of the associator. Rate of associating. Lag in associating. Costs of associating.

3.3.6 Memory,   the subsystem which carries out the second stage of the learning process, storing var-

ious sorts of information in the system for different periods of time.

Until it eventually loses sharpness of patterning by entropic changes, is replaced by other information, or becomes misplaced or unavailable for other reasons, this information is retained in the memory and can be retrieved from it upon demand. In storing information until a lack of it initiates retrieval of it, the process of remembering is similar to that of matter-energy storage (see page 58). Traditionally memory and recall or retrieval have been considered stages which can occur after associating in the learning process. It is true that associating can be demonstrated only through memory and recall, but they seem to be independent processes.

3.3.6.1 Structure   There is a marker on which information in cells is stored over time, certainly in neurons and possibly in free-living protozoans as well. This may be some short-term bioelectric process or reverberatory circuit in one or more cells, or it may be a particular patterning of atoms in macromolecules. In recent years, since the genetic code of the DNA molecule has been discovered, some scientists have suggested that the similar RNA molecule may be the marker that bears the patterns of long-term memories (see page 271). Some neural organs store memories, perhaps briefly in intercellular reverberatory circuits and perhaps dispersed to component individual cells. In some primitive organisms memories appear to be widely dispersed among neural cells. In higher organisms they may be stored in more localized regions. The temporal lobe and other parts of the brain have been suggested as possible sites of memory storage, but what structures are involved is not yet certain. Groups and higher-level systems may disperse remembering to all individual persons in them, or they may delegate this responsibility to a single one, like a secretary. Organizations have specialized groups like filing clerks and librarians for such functions. Societies and supranational systems have whole professions—historians, archivists, librarians, recorders—for storing information about the past. Systems at the organism level and above in literate societies are aided in such processes by a wide range of artifacts, including monuments, letters, minutes, books, journals, files, libraries, pictures, recordings, and electronic memories, which can store information for periods of time up to millenia.

3.3.6.2 Process   The process of storing information involves three stages: (*a*) putting into storage markers bearing the information, (*b*) maintaining them in storage over time, and (*c*) retrieving from storage the information on the same markers or read out onto others. These are the same three stages as for storing matter-energy (see page 58), as would be expected since the markers are forms of matter-energy. Because some stored information comes from the environment or suprasystem, the memory is to a degree a mirror or map of the environment, a cognitive map which is constantly being altered by new inputs of information (see pages 30, 35, 58, and 411). But this is not the only source of input to the memory; some inputs come from inside the system. Inputs from outside are not a complete replica of the environment or suprasystem; they are a biased sample. Memories also are distorted and corrupted by noise over time. Some systems store memories under categories which reduce redundancy but sacrifice part of the information. There are distortions in transmissions and over time. Loss of information through entropic changes occurs in storage, too. Also the system rarely if ever receives a representative sample of its environment or suprasystem. Furthermore, groups and higher-level systems which rely upon the memories of individual organisms suffer loss and distortion when one member leaves and another replaces him, and information must be transmitted from one brain to another.[27] Consequently, culture changes as items of information, such as oral traditions or ceremonials, alter or over time entirely lose their significance.[28] For most levels of living systems little is known about the rationales of storage, search, and retrieval—whether, for instance, items of information stored must have associated to them other information identifying their storage addresses or whether information as to location of storage is "wired into" the system, that is, determined by the template.

Based on the conjecture of Bremermann that no system can process more than 2×10^{47} bits per second per gram of its mass (see page 12), Bledsoe has shown that there is an absolute minimum time limit for retrieving any memory.[29] In the smallest system that processes information, he calculates that this absolute lower bound is 10^{-21} s. No existing systems, living or nonliving, can retrieve a bit of information from memory in anything like so brief a time. Data collected at various levels of living systems confirm this.

Representative *variables* of the process of remembering include: Meaning of information stored in memory. Sorts of information stored in memory. Total memory capacity. Percentage of information input stored. Changes in remembering over time. Changes in remembering with different circumstances. Rate of reading into memory. Lag in reading into memory. Costs of reading into memory. Rate of distortion of information during storage. Time information is in storage before being forgotten. Sorts of information retrieved. Percentage of stored information retrieved from memory. Order of retrieval from memory. Rate of retrieval from memory. Lag in retrieval from memory. Costs of retrieval from memory.

3.3.7 Decider, the executive subsystem which receives information inputs from all other subsystems and transmits to them information outputs that control the entire system.

A hierarchical living system according to Simon, is "a complex system in which each of the subsystems is subordinated by an authority relation to the system to which it belongs. More exactly, in a hierarchical formal organization, each system consists of a 'boss' and a set of subordinate subsystems. Each of the subsystems has a 'boss,' the immediate subordinate of the 'boss' in the system."[30] (This is also true of echelons in the same system—see pages 29 and 68.) The decider is the only essential critical subsystem, and it cannot be parasitically or symbiotically dispersed to any other system. The reason for this is that, if another system carried out the deciding functions, everything it controlled would, by definition, be a subsystem or component of it. As the sign on President Harry Truman's desk said, "The buck stops here."

When I use the term "decider" I do not necessarily imply any assumption of voluntarism and free will. The processes of a decider may be wholly determined in exactly the same circumstances always making the same decision. A decider differs from a node in a channel or net in the following way: The number of alternatives or degrees of freedom in the information output of a decider is smaller than in its information input, but the number is the same in the information output as in the information input of a node (see page 63). This principle from electronic amplifier theory was derived by Platt.[31] Amplifiers increase the volume of a specific output, but along with amplification there is always selection or discrimination. A phonograph, for instance, amplifies only certain vibrations of the needle in the record's groove, not the motion of the pickup arm, the light in the room, the temperature, the air pressure, the line voltage input, or many other variable inputs to the amplifier from its environment. Consequently the amplifier's output has fewer variables than its input, and indeed vast or infinite power would be required to amplify them all. This is also probably true of any living system which makes decisions among options.

3.3.7.1 Structure The nucleus of the cell probably carries out some deciding functions (see pages 272 to 275). Perhaps the decision of some neurons to fire is made in the axon hillock, where the axon connects to the cell body. Movements of an amoeba's pseudopod may be determined by local conditions in the cell's environment and its membrane at that point. Organs like the heart and the gut have neural centers which determine when they contract, even though the nervous supply to the rest of the organism is severed. In lower animals the decider is in the endocrine system and/or in their neural nets or ganglia, but exactly where is not yet known. In higher animals, including man, no single decision-making structure is clearly identified. Higher animals have several endocrine and neural echelons in their deciders, of which the cerebral cortex is the highest in man. A group's decider often is its leader—a committee's chairman, a squad's commander, a family's father—but the process also may be dispersed to all members, who decide jointly. Organizations commonly have multiple echelons with recognized chiefs. Societies have such a hierarchy also—the echelons of governmental officials and agencies. Supranational systems, too, have executive organizations, but so far in history they have usually been relatively impotent, and consequently there have been few full-fledged supranational systems.

3.3.7.2 Process The decider receives information inputs about the environment from the input transducer decoded by the decoder, about all other matter-energy and information subsystems from the internal transducer, and about the past from the memory. All this is transmitted over the channel and net. The decider reviews all these inputs and selects, from among various alternatives, what appears to be the optimal solution for the problem before it, thus cutting down the degrees of freedom, reducing the information. It then transmits command signals to the other subsystems to coordinate their processes, including those of the motor and output transducer, which put out matter, energy, or information beyond the boundary.[32]

The deciding process has four distinguishable stages: (*a*) *Establishing purposes or goals* (see pages 39 to 41)—in this stage is determined the internal steady state (purpose), or external target or relationship (goal) which the system should attempt to attain; this becomes the comparison signal for the system's feedback adjustment processes (see page 75), like the temperature for which a thermostat is set. (*b*) *Analysis*—in this stage, information is obtained about relevant aspects of the situation outside and inside the system, including how far the actual state of the system deviates from the comparison signal, what adjustment processes are available for decreasing this deviation, and what alternative resolutions there are. (*c*) *Synthesis*—in this stage, processes—usually logical in nature—are carried out to diminish available alternatives to a lesser number characterized by the ability of decreasing to a satisfactory degree the deviation of the state of the system from the comparison signal. This makes possible survival of the system while keeping costs of the necessary adjustment processes reasonably small. (*d*) *Implementing*—in this stage command signals are put out by the decider, directed to other

subsystems to carry out the processes selected in the stage of synthesis.[33] Unless there are other, interacting subsystems from which its commands can elicit compliance, the decider's processes are to no avail and, indeed, no system exists. When coups d'états topple governments, nations at times approach such anarchy. Systems also may make decisions that their own resources for adjustment are inadequate to correct the error or deviation from the steady state that exists and that therefore some action from a higher echelon of the system's decider is required. This is often referred to as *motivation*—which I define as a message from a lower echelon or subsystem that a higher echelon or system at a higher level should carry out an action to restore some steady state or maintain one that is threatened. For example, the signal may report that some tissue is so dehydrated that the total organism should drink. Or the governor of a colony may find his people so near to rebellion that the parent nation should send in troops. At the organism level and above, at least, emotion or affect are often associated with the strains which elicit such appeals.

As signals in hierarchical systems pass upward from echelon to echelon, decision after decision is made based upon these messages, and the signals are then transmitted in altered fashion. For example, decisions are made at the level of the retinal cell, when it either does or does not respond to the light rays that bombard it; at the level of the organ, when the optic pathways either do or do not transmit an image; at the level of the organism, when the sentry decides whether friend or foe is approaching; at the level of the group, when the sergeant decides whether to report an attack to headquarters; at the level of the organization, when army headquarters decides whether to inform the government of a provocation; at the level of the society, when the cabinet determines whether to condemn the aggressor; and at the supranational level, when the entire issue is voted on in the United Nations Security Council [if the United Nations truly constitutes a supranational system (see page 903)].

Representative *variables* of the process of deciding include: Meaning of information employed in deciding. Sorts of information employed in deciding. Amount of information employed in deciding. Changes in deciding over time. Changes in deciding with different circumstances. Number of alternatives in input before decision and in output afterward. Rewards and punishments attached to alternatives reviewed in deciding. Rate of deciding. Lag in deciding. Costs of deciding.

3.3.8 Encoder, the subsystem which alters the code of information input to it from other information processing subsystems, from a "private" code used internally by the system into a "public" code which can be interpreted by other systems in its environment.

If the private and public codes or languages happen to be the same, this subsystem need not be used. Encoding is not comparable to the process carried out by any matter-energy processing subsystem because information must be transmitted out of the system in a code which can be understood by other receiving systems, or they cannot interact. But matter-energy as such, put out by the system, is not an instrument of such interaction with other systems, so it need not be put into any special form. (A possible exception is that certain products must satisfactorily meet particular specifications or other systems will not accept them. Complying with such standards is a process which at some levels is carried out by the producer.)

3.3.8.1 Structure   Cells—particularly specialized information processing cells like neurons and cells of endocrine glands—encode in the organelles (perhaps RNA-bearing ribosomes) that produce the neurohumoral transmitter substances which they output across the synapses. Organs encode in their output neurons, which are afferent autonomic neurons. Organisms code alpha-coded signals in the exocrine glands, beta-coded signals probably in the motor cortex, and gamma-coded signals in the frontal, parietal, and temporal areas of the cortex. Groups, organizations, societies, and supranational systems encode through speech writers and translators, but often they disperse much encoding to individual members— *e.g.,* ballet dancers, sales representatives, tourists.

3.3.8.2 Process   In most ways encoding is like decoding, except that it transforms information from a private to a public code rather than the reverse. The encoding process ordinarily does not pass through many echelons, except perhaps in large organizations and nations, in which multiple units check official statements before they are made. Encoding differs in this way from decoding. Often, even in high-level systems, once the decider has acted, the decider or some other single person encodes the message about the decision to the outside world. Since there are few if any echelons in such a subsystem, its noise and the associated error are less than if there were more.

Some of the most important *variables* of the encoding process are: Meaning of information which is encoded. Sorts of information which are encoded. Percentage of the information input which is encoded. Threshold of the encoder. Changes in encoding over time. Changes in encoding with different circumstances. Channel capacity of the encoder. Distortion of the encoder. Signal-to-noise ratio of the encoder. Rate of encoding. Percentage of omissions in encoding. Percentage of errors in encoding. Code employed. Redundancy of the code employed. Lag in encoding. Costs of encoding.

3.3.9 Output transducer,   the subsystem which puts out markers bearing information from the system, changing markers within the system into other matter-energy forms which can be transmitted over channels in the system's environment.

It uses some components, also employed at times by the extruder or motor, that are specialized for putting out markers bearing information (see page 59).

3.3.9.1 Structure   Presynaptic components of neurons and similar components in endocrine and other cells diffuse through the cell membrane special molecules, markers patterned by the encoder subsystem of the cell into a form capable of conveying information out of that system. At the organ level, output transducing is accomplished by neurons which transmit signals to other organs as well as to the internal transducer of the next higher level, the organism. Organisms' output transducers are specialized parts of the extruder (*e.g.,* glands which emit a scent that attracts the opposite sex) or of the motor (*e.g.,* the laryngeal, facial, arm, hand, and other muscles which are responsible for vocalizing, signaling, gesturing, grimacing, tail wagging in dogs, and all the other actions by which organisms transmit information). Families have fathers who traditionally speak for them; committee chairmen have similar output transducing functions. Organizations often have representatives who address official statements to other systems. Nations and supranational systems also have such representatives and news-releasing agencies. At the level of the group or above this process is usually downwardly dispersed to one or more individuals. (Musical, dramatic, and religious groups may do their output transducing in unison. In marching bands which make formations spelling out words, the entire group is the output transducer.) Frequently the encoder and output transducer in social systems are the same, but they need not be. The Queen may address a speech to Parliament which was encoded by others. Artifacts like books, loudspeakers, cinema, radio, or television may be used for output transducing by organisms and higher-level systems.

3.3.9.2 Process   Information output is transferred to markers of spatial structure, wavelength, bandwidth, or intensity suitable for the channels and receivers to which it is transmitted.

Representative *variables* of the output transducing process are: Meaning of information output which is transduced. Sorts of information output which are transduced. Threshold of the output transducer. Changes in output transducing over time. Changes in output transducing with different circumstances. Channel capacity of the output transducer. Number of channels in use in the output transducer. Distortion of the output transducer. Rate of output transducing. Lag in output transducing. Intensity of information output. Costs of output transducing.

4. Relationships among subsystems or components

All descriptions of relationships in a concrete system are either statements about the structure of its organization or about its function or history—reversible or irreversible process. All these relationships can be measured in centimeters, grams, seconds, bits of information, or mathematical derivatives of these, with the exception of the meaning of the information patterns to those who receive them, for which there is as yet no adequate quantification (see page 1030). Examples of such relationships appear in the section below.

4.1 Structural relationships   The structural relationships among subsystems or components of concrete systems are all spatial in character.

4.1.1 Containment   Whether or not a given subsystem or component is within the boundaries of another subsystem or component.

4.1.2 Number   The number of subsystems or components in a system. The interrelationships among subsystems or components increase as a direct function of this number.

4.1.3 Order   The arrangement of subsystems or components relative to each other along a spatial dimension.

4.1.4 Position   The location of components on an absolute, cardinal scale of spatial coordinates.

4.1.5 Direction   The relationship of a subsystem or component to a reference point along at least one spatial coordinate.

4.1.6 Size   The extent of distance, area of surface, or volume of space occupied by a subsystem or component.

4.1.7 Pattern   The form of organization, configuration, or arrangement of subsystems or components within the space occupied by a system.

4.1.8 Density   How closely packed subsystems or components are within a system.

4.2 Process relationships   All functional or historical relationships have a temporal aspect. They may either be purely temporal, or they may involve a spatial change over time.

4.2.1 Temporal relationships

4.2.1.1 Containment in time   Whether or not a given process among subsystems or components occurs within a specified period of time.

4.2.1.2 Number in time   The number of different processes (or frequency of repeated processes) going on between two or more subsystems or components during a given time.

4.2.1.3 Order in time   The relative sequence of processes among subsystems or components along a temporal dimension.

4.2.1.4 Position in time   The location of a process among subsystems or components on an absolute, cardinal temporal scale.

4.2.1.5 Direction in time   The relationship in time of two processes, whether one comes before or after another along a temporal dimension.

4.2.1.6 Duration   Length of time over which a process among two or more subsystems continues.

4.2.1.7 Pattern in time   The arrangement in time of the occurrence of processes among subsystems and components; *e.g.*, evenly spaced or grouped in bursts.

4.2.2 Spatiotemporal relationships

4.2.2.1 Action   A subsystem or component, by transmission of matter-energy, brings about an action on the part of another subsystem or component (see page 11).

4.2.2.2 Communication   A transmission of information from a subsystem or component causes a change in process in another subsystem or component (see page 12). Because all communications require transmission of a marker, which is matter-energy, there are important similarities between action and communication (see pages 54 and 60).

4.2.2.3 Direction of action   The movement of subsystems or components along spatial coordinates over time with relationship to others.

4.2.2.4 Pattern of action   The form of a change in organization or action among subsystems or components over time.

4.2.2.5 Entering or leaving containment   The movement of one or more subsystems or components from or into containment by another.

4.3 Relationships among subsystems or components which involve meaning   Many significant relationships in living systems do not appear above, such as *A* loves *B*, *A* is an ally of *B*, *A* disapproves of *B*, *A* has more prestige than *B*, *A* is richer than *B*, and so forth. All such relationships involve observation of a pattern in space and/or time and then an interpretation by the observer of the meaning of that pattern. Often observers arrive at high agreement as to the meaning, but sometimes they do not. Until a more satisfactory method is developed for quantifying such patterns and their meanings (see page 1030), we have to depend upon relatively inadequate methods of quantifying these relationships such as the use of human raters.

5. System processes

The previous sections of this chapter have dealt with single units of systems—subsystems and components—and relationships among them. This one concerns multiple-subsystem units or total systems. Inputs and outputs of the entire system or major parts of it are analyzed. This section discusses intralevel rather than interlevel phenomena, such as the interactions of systems and their subsystems. Because every system is a component, but not necessarily a subsystem, of its suprasystem, intralevel system processes must be described at each level. This is because they are not the same as processes of subsystems of the next higher level—they are processes of components of the next higher level. Therefore they often differ from the processes of subsystems which can be described for the next higher level.

5.1   Process relationships between inputs and outputs   Input a suprathreshold electric charge to a resting neuron, and a pulse will pass down its axon. Increase the water content of blood input into a renal artery, and that kidney will increase the rate of its output of urine. Yell "attention" to a West Point cadet, and his spine will stiffen. Call the right signal to a football team, and it will run. Send a request for a catalog to a corporation, and it will mail one to you. Order your army to cross another nation's borders, and that country will try to repel your army.

Such input–output generalizations are true with a probability usually less than certainty. But sciences and applied technologies can be based on such regularities if they are more probable than chance, even though the internal processes which bring them about within the system are not understood. Many intralevel hypotheses about such relationships have been confirmed by experiments or repeated observations at each level of living system. The probability of a given input being followed by a specific output is commonly stated by a coefficient of correlation between them.

The process relationships between inputs and outputs fall into four categories: (a) Matter-energy inputs related to matter-energy outputs. (b) Matter-energy inputs related to information outputs. (c) Information inputs related to matter-energy outputs. (d) Information inputs related to information outputs.

5.2 Adjustment processes among subsystems or components, used in maintaining variables in steady states   All processes of subsystems which maintain steady states are adjustment processes (see pages 36 and 37). Many of these are limited to one subsystem, and these are discussed under the relevant subsystem. Only adjustment processes involving multiple subsystems or the entire system are considered in this section.

There are three general purposes for a system to employ adjustment processes: (a) the governing or control of relationships among its subsystems; (b) the governing or control of the system as a whole; and (c) the governing or control of relationships between the system and its suprasystem. Each adjustment process serves to keep one or more variables in a steady state within a normal range of stability. There may be several ways to accomplish this for any given variable. For instance, a dog may maintain his blood sugar within a normal range by chewing and swallowing meat; a baby gorilla may do it by sucking its mother's breast; a child, by eating cereal with a spoon; a patient, by receiving an intravenous injection of glucose.

System variables fall into six classes: matter-energy input, internal, and output variables and information input, internal, and output variables. A change in any variable maintained in steady state in a living system may evoke adjustment processes belonging to any of the same six categories or to all of them, depending upon the grievousness of the threat or stress experienced. For example, a stress altering an information input variable may elicit a matter-energy output adjustment process. Throughout this book I classify each adjustment process according to the class of variable it serves to maintain in steady state and not according to its *own* character, if the latter should fall into a different category.

5.2.1   Matter-energy input processes   When a system lacks adequate rates of inputs of certain essential sorts of matter-energy, it may allocate more components or more effort of the same components to input processing. It may dispatch components to fetch required inputs from regions in the environment where they exist: the roots of plants grow toward water; families send their children to pick berries; cities lay conduits to lakes; nations build and dispatch merchant marines to import needed raw materials and finished products from other lands. In some cases the entire system moves to the location of the desired inputs.

Some types of living systems have limited ability to control either the sorts or the rates and timing of their inputs. Consequently, unless they have stored the inputs they need, they can survive only in particular environments which contain the inputs they require in appropriate concentrations and which do not contain harmful ones. This is particularly true of plant organisms, which often take in through their roots excesses of materials and soluble poisons, as well as needed soluble materials, as inputs from the soil (see page 449).

Sometimes, when there are excesses of matter-energy inputs, the best or only adjustment is to move the entire system to an environment where the inputs are less intense. An amoeba moves out of a strongly acid medium; a soldier gets out of the line of snipers' fire; a home or factory is moved from an earthquake zone; a city is relocated from the route of flow of lava from a volcano. Or systems may send components into the suprasystem or environment to remove the source of excess inputs: killing wild animals, removing heavy snow from the roof, or repelling an attacking enemy nation. Systems may also allocate more components or more effort of present components to the processing of matter-energy input overloads. Or they may do a less adequate job, omitting the processing of some of it and handling some of it erroneously. They may store the excess or retain it in any subsystem or component, consume it more rapidly, or distribute it more widely than before.

5.2.2 Information input processes   Adjustments to both lacks and excesses of information input are often made by the boundary of a system or by various other of its subsystems. Lacks of information may be adjusted to in numerous ways: Several subsystem boundaries may be opened. Subsystem thresholds may be lowered. The noise in signals may be decreased, by focusing or simultaneously using multiple channels. Two ears may be used to hear or two eyes to see. Several pageboys may carry the same messages. Many foreign agents may gather intelligence. Various components of the system may be moved to engender signals from internal transducers—a judge, for instance, may cross his legs and swing one leg fast when he is bored by monotonous testimony in court, thus increasing his internal joint sensations. Systems may move toward an information source or send out components to receive signals from it. A committee may send its secretary to the reference library. The general of an army may order observers up in balloons. A nation may dispatch diplomats to foreign lands. Lack of money input may be adjusted for by decreasing actions which use money in order to keep out of debt or by sending out components to search for more money in the environment or suprasystem.

Excessively intense signals may be blocked by the boundary of a system or by various of its other subsystems. Several subsystem boundaries may be closed or their thresholds raised. Too high rates of information inputs may be adjusted to by omitting some inputs, especially during times when there is high input overlap; by processing some inputs erroneously without correcting the errors; by queuing; by using a wider range in the channel or multiple channels; by filtering in some signals on the basis of input priority and

filtering out others; by abstracting; by escaping from the input entirely; or by chunking (see pages 123 and 147). A king may turn a deaf ear to a beggar. A jury may be locked in so that no one can influence it. A government may block entrance of enemy propaganda by transmitting noise to jam enemy radio broadcast channels.

The meaning of information may determine whether or not it is allowed to enter a system. A person may not listen to a gossipy neighbor; a customs officer may seize pornography; a radio warning of a threatened air raid may quickly be passed on to a theater audience.

5.2.3 Matter-energy internal processes   These adjustment processes reduce strains in systems by moving their components, allocating material and energic rewards and punishments, rearranging which components carry out which processes. Thus they maintain variables in steady state, with satisfactory efficiency and inexpensiveness. Rates of flow of different sorts of matter-energy from one subsystem or component to another may be controlled by decreasing or increasing the rate of output from any subsystem or component. A dog's leg-muscle movements may be slowed by decreasing the rate of blood flow to the leg; a punch-press crew's work may be at least temporarily elevated by increasing the rate of input of metal to it. Adjustments of transmission rates between the distributor subsystem, which conveys matter-energy to all parts of the system, and other subsystems are particularly important. Such adjustments arrange for flows to reach one region of the system faster or in greater amounts than another: the resistance of arterioles is decreased or increased, affecting the blood flow; the vascular tree in muscles opens up when they exercise; a hive of bees always feeds its queen first and most; extra traffic lanes are commonly made available to motorists driving toward a city during morning rush hours.

Other adjustment processes may change the number of components in subsystems or alter the density of such components. They may be shifted to make up for lack, replacing components which have died, or moved, or for other reasons are not carrying out their functions: when cells in the skin are destroyed in a wound, other cells migrate in or proliferate to replace them; an intern operates in an emergency when the senior surgeon is absent; when a regiment is captured, the commanding general of the army orders replacements into the gap in the line. Within certain limits living systems can substitute one sort of matter-energy for another. Some substitutes are better than others. Occasionally there is no substitute: for example, human blood cannot clot unless calcium ions are present. Inputs may be processed more completely to obtain a higher percentage of useful yield: water is resorbed from kidney tubules when the body is dehydrated; metal refineries may attempt a second refining of the dross. Or adjustment processes may make up for an emergency lack of some sort of matter-energy by allocating an unusual number of components to provide it: the number of red cells carrying oxygen in the blood becomes abnormally large when an animal or man lives in an atmosphere of reduced oxygen content; more porters are recruited for a king's safari than for a commoner's; more ships are assembled for a seaborne invasion than for a routine patrol. The rate of output of needed products from subsystems like the converter and the producer may be increased in order to decrease the average costs of a single item produced. This adjustment process is the strategy of mass production, which has been important in elevating quantity and quality of the products of human organisms and higher-level systems.

Among other matter-energy internal adjustments are: Distributing desired sorts of matter-energy or removing wastes, as rewards; *e.g.*, a boss gives the best secretaries a raise. Distributing harmful excesses of matter-energy or causing damaging lacks, as punishments; *e.g.*, a parent spanks his child to prevent repetition of actions he dislikes. Organizing subsystems to be more nearly totipotential when overall system organization breaks down; *e.g.*, nations arm themselves when alliances collapse; survivors in life boats catch fish and collect rain water independently when an ocean liner sinks. Maintaining gradients necessary for proper system functioning; *e.g.*, polarizing neural membranes by an "ion pump," so they can carry pulses; keeping arterial blood pressure above venous pressure; directing traffic to ensure that it travels faster than a minimum rate. Maintaining subsystem and component boundaries inviolate; *e.g.*, fascia, omentum, and other tissues separate organs in the body; the United Nations moves in to prevent armed clashes during border disputes. Localizing a subsystem function to fewer components, or dispersing it to more, to increase efficiency or decrease fatigue; *e.g.*, Switzerland centralizes military command when nearby nations are at war; as a steel factory grows, tasks are broken down into subtasks to keep employees from being overworked. Establishing an order for performing subsystem processes, so that the most critical are carried out first; *e.g.*, the organism restores blood acidity to its normal range of stability before it restores the acidity of other bodily tissues; women and children are removed from battle zones before male civilians are.

5.2.4 Information internal processes   These processes reduce strains and maintain variables in steady states by transferring information from one subsystem or component to another, often modifying the associations between one item of information and another and also changing the relationships among information subsystems and components. Rates of flow of various sorts of messages from one subsystem or component to another may be controlled in the communication networks of living systems by a switching process which facilitates the transmission of certain messages and blocks others which might compete for the same channels. Every component has access to channels a certain part of the time, but this access is not homogeneous. Some get to transmit and/or receive more information and to do it faster than others. In general such adjustments cannot significantly alter the maximum rate at which information travels in the network. This is determined by the channel capacity, related to the bandwidth and the sort of marker employed. They can, however, switch channels among transmitters and receivers, on the basis of priorities established by the system's value hierarchy, purposes, and goals, so that effective and efficient communication occurs; *e.g.*, the reticular activating system in higher animals appears to shift attention from one source of input to another, keeping higher echelons of the nervous system from being overloaded by too much information; a good secretary speeds some messages through to her employer but blocks others; the chairman of a meeting gives the floor to one speaker after another and keeps order, so that several do not speak at once and interfere with each other; a monitoring engineer at the central controls of a national television network carries out a comparable function, switching a complex variety of signals among transmitting and receiving stations all over the country or perhaps around the world. All these adjustments are made in terms of priorities based on a systemwide hierarchy of values.

The number of components in channels and nets, as well as other information processing subsystems, can often be altered, at least in systems at the group level and above—fewer personnel can be allocated to any aspect of information processing which requires less effort and more to those which require greater effort. If there is a lack of adequate information, new components may be added to replace those which have died, or moved, or are not functioning; *e.g.*, in animal and human brains a number of neurons normally die every day—more under pathological conditions—and they cannot be replaced, but others already there assume their functions; in battle one courier is shot, and another replaces him; a government regional office may be closed, but its functions can be carried out by an area office; if a king believes he does not know enough about his people's mood, he may station informers as his personal internal transducers throughout the countryside. The altering of connections among components in a communication network is an important adjustment process; *e.g.*, neural messages can be rerouted over other brain pathways after a stroke; the communication structure of a group can be altered in group experiments; a company's formal table of organization can be revised; ham radio operators can partially replace a city's telephone system after a disaster.

Lacks of information can be adjusted for in various ways. Under some conditions one sort of information can be substituted for a similar sort which may be lacking, by a process of generalization or extrapolation; *e.g.*, the visual centers of the nervous system occasionally, but rarely, make errors by assuming that the pattern of inputs on the blind spot of the retina is continuous with that which can be perceived on its edges; the commuter does not often get into trouble by assuming, without checking, that the train that leaves from Gate 4 at 5:19 P.M. today will stop at Stamford as it has for the past eight years; military strategists have usually been right in making the generalization that, if war breaks out throughout Europe, one Swiss canton will act like another in remaining neutral and resisting territorial aggression.

Excesses in the amount of information anywhere in a living system's information processing subsystems can be at least partially handled by the adjustment processes of decreasing the equivocation of the message; making omissions; making errors; queuing; filtering or making selections on the basis of priorities determined by the value hierarchies, purposes, and goals of the system; abstracting; using multiple channels or a wider range or a wider bandwidth; or escaping from or cutting off the input (see pages 61, 104, 123, and 164). Too abundant flows of information can also be decreased by raising the threshold of any component, by lowering the signal-to-noise ratio, or by decreasing the intensity of the input signal; *e.g.*, a cat's reticular activating system may raise the threshold of its auditory input pathways so that it will not "attend" to sounds, if large amounts of priority smell and visual information are being received by it at the same time; a person may turn down the volume of a radio broadcasting commercial announcement so that it can barely be heard over the sounds of the conversation in the room; the audiences at L'Abbaye night club in Paris may snap their fingers in applause rather than clap so that the neighbors can sleep.

Excesses of undesirable sorts of meaning may be dealt with by various adjustment processes, including distortion; *e.g.*, a merchant passes on to a business associate a rumor he has heard that several stores in his town are in danger of going bankrupt. He names all of them except the one in which he holds stock. Anna Freud has listed several comparable adjustment processes ("mechanisms of defense") which are used at least at the organism level (see pages 458 and 459).[34] Examples include repression (being unable to retrieve from memory anxiety-linked, painful, shameful, or otherwise unacceptable memories) and suppression (not expressing such memories through the encoder and output transducer).

Other information internal processes include: Distributing verbal or monetary rewards and punishments; *e.g.*, the Crown bestows the royal colors on a regiment which has distinguished itself in battle; the World Court orders a nation to pay reparations for damage caused by one of the nation's airplanes. Altering task demands to components; *e.g.*, the Marseilles factory is required to increase its production 20 percent while the Paris factory is allowed a 10 percent decrease. Increasing or decreasing the permeability of subsystem boundaries to information; *e.g.*, the government decides to make all legislative hearings public; the company decides that branch managers may not have access to companywide budgeting figures.

Still other information internal processes include: Localizing an information processing subsystem function in one or a few components or dispersing it to more; *e.g.*, a committee chairman makes the decisions, or the entire group votes on each one; important international decisions are made by two opposing blocs of countries, or the nations organize themselves into many coalitions. Redistributing power among components in order to achieve balance of power or a more stable decision-making structure; *e.g.*, the corporation adds new members to its executive committee to represent minority stockholders; the President consults with leaders of Congress before making a decision to send troops abroad. Changing the sort of commands or other messages transmitted among subsystems or components; *e.g.*, the cerebellum signals a muscle to relax and its opposing muscle to contract; friendship for a person alters to dislike because he supports an opposing political candidate. Responding emotionally to stress; *e.g.*, strong feeling may motivate a football player to fight harder, but it may also confuse his cognitive processes; threat may cause a colony of termites to rush about and make noise by hitting their heads on the ground, which may or may not be adaptive. Altering the costs of information processing; *e.g.*, neural tissue may learn to apply chunking to messages or develop more efficient codes which cut transmission costs; societies may develop more efficient electronic information processing techniques.

5.2.5 Matter-energy output processes   Control of rates of outputs of various sorts of matter-energy—products, wastes, or actions—is exerted by many types of living systems at all levels. It may be accelerated; *e.g.*, the government's mints work extra shifts in order to increase the output of coins when demand goes up; nations increase their exports when their balance of trade becomes unfavorable. Or it may be slowed down until the environment is favorable to receive the outputs; *e.g.*, spores hibernate until their surroundings are proper for their growth; opossums "play dead" in the presence of a stranger enemy; a working group may slow its production in order to forestall management from increasing its work quota (see page 578); countries do not invade other nations until they think they can defeat them.

A system's ability to control outputs, however, may be restricted; *e.g.*, trees cannot completely prevent loss of water, and on a hot day their leaves may wilt; Egypt has lost antiquities, South Africa has lost diamonds, and Iraq has lost oil to more powerful nations.

Lacks of matter-energy can often be avoided by retention of outputs; *e.g.*, animals excrete less water in their urine in hot weather; some farm families eat that part of their produce they need and sell only the surplus; armies rarely discharge healthy soldiers during a war.

5.2.6 Information output processes   Among the information adjustments are alterations in the rates of outputs; *e.g.*, a neuron transmits pulses more rapidly; a radio announcer who has lagged behind schedule rushes to finish reading an announcement before his alloted time runs out. The sort of output may be altered to be appropriate to the receiver at that moment; *e.g.*, a mother speaks about dollies to her daughter and dollars to her husband; a nation may say one thing to its allies and quite another to its enemies. The code of the output information may be changed to suit the receiver, *e.g.*, a translator may shift the language in which he is speaking; a country may make a public proclamation after failing in private negotiations. The intensity, signal-to-noise ratio, distortion, percentage of omissions, errors, amount of filtering or of abstracting of information outputs may be adjusted to a normal range of stability; *e.g.*, a panel uses a microphone so it can be heard in a large room; a chairperson calls for silence so that a singer can be heard; an advertising company's various departments carefully check the completeness, accuracy, and format

of an advertisement; a captain, following orders, decreases the length of the briefing planned for a general.

A system may also transmit a message out to the environment or suprasystem which may elicit aid from other systems. Such aid may be either needed matter-energy inputs on which the system becomes parasitic or symbiotic, like a kidney transplant, a Red Cross team, the National Guard, or a United Nations peacekeeping mission, or essential information such as weather reports or advice on how to build a radio station. Verbal attacks on an external system—a neighboring family, a competing company, an enemy nation—may increase the internal cohesiveness of components of the attacking system. Blocking information output—secrecy—may protect components of a system; *e.g.*, a safecracker may refuse to give evidence against his buddy; members of an alliance may preserve military secrets.

5.2.7 Feedbacks   At all levels many adjustment processes which maintain variables of living systems within ranges of stability involve negative feedbacks (see pages 36 and 37). These may be external, from the system to the environment, via the output transducer and back through the input transducer, or they may be wholly internal, among several subsystems and components.

5.3 Evolution   How have the various levels and types of living systems come to exist? Over time, systems with novel structures and processes appear at all levels as the result of cumulative evolutionary changes. These are historical processes, which are difficult to reverse or essentially irreversible. The doctrine of organic evolution, applied by Darwin to the levels of the cell and of the organism, holds that all the approximately 2 million species of animals and plants now in existence developed from earlier forms. This occurred over a period of perhaps 3 billion years, beginning during the youth of the earth when its atmospheric composition and temperature were favorable to the synthesis of complex organic molecules such as proteins and nucleic acids. Under present conditions on earth these are synthesized outside of living cells only in laboratory experiments. The first living system probably consisted only of nucleoproteins and other essential molecules enclosed within a membrane. It is possible that the next step in evolution was the differentiation of the nucleus of the cell so that the genetic material was separated from the cytoplasm by a membrane (see page 294).[35] The earliest living systems may have left no fossil record, although fossils of ancient single cells have been found. Aquatic plant fossils can be dated as far back as 1.5 billion years. By the Cambrian period, 500 million years ago, representatives of almost every major animal phylum were already in existence.

By processes of genetic change and differentiation, multicellular organisms developed. Alterations of form were accompanied by changes in interactions among subsystems and components and also by changes in relationships between the system and its environment. Major examples of this are: (a) The evolutionary rise of land animals that carry with them inside their boundaries the water medium necessary to all cells. (b) The replacement of genetically determined behavior patterns by more flexible learned behavior in higher organisms. Groups and higher-level social systems of great diversity developed. It seems reasonable to hypothesize that evolutionary processes are cross-level principles, applying to systems at all levels, even though their modes of reproduction differ (see pages 857 and 858). The evolutionary development of social systems may be seen in the fact that some species (of termites, for instance) do not have social organization while closely related species have it in a form that involves clear-cut allocation of functions to different individuals. And there are other species with intermediate degrees of social organization (see page 574).

The general direction of evolution has been to produce systems with more information or greater complexity of organization. In general the higher levels of living systems developed later than the lower levels, and more complex types at a given level later than less complex types. This may well be explained as follows: Any new type of system that arises, by a change in template, either gene or chapter (see page 55), must be (a) equally complex, (b) more complex, or (c) less complex than its predecessor. Its complexity is likely to be correlated positively with its ability to adjust to its environment. If it is more complex, it is in general likely to have more adjustment processes. Thus, on the average, it is more likely to adjust to the stresses in its environment and so to survive. Conversely, a less complex system is, in general, less likely to survive. If the complexity is the same, the probability of survival is similar. As time passes, therefore, the types of systems which survive will, on the average, tend to be increasingly complex. This explains the process of shred-out from level to level (see page 29).

Criteria of progress in evolution of living systems which go beyond mere complexity have been formulated by Sommerhoff, including:

. . . increased adaptability, control over environment, success, independence from environment, self-regulation, social integration, etc.[36]

Some biologists, he adds, maintain that

. . . although isolated strands of evolutionary development have often shown a partial decline of any or all of these attributes, it is, nevertheless, an overriding and undeniable fact, that the broad stream of evolution has been accompanied by a progressive and a very marked increase in the degree to which these attributes can be found among the living forms of any given epoch. . . .

What, in fact, distinguishes the higher organisms from lower forms is their increased power to maintain their existence, and safeguard their future, in the face of contingent and often adverse environmental fluctuations by means of adaptive, regulative, coordinated, and integrated activities.

He refers to the use of negative feedbacks by systems to achieve their purposes and goals (see pages 39 to 41).

Recognizing cross-level applicability of evolutionary principles, he also holds that evolution leads to increasing social integration: "Now from an objective point of view the growth of social harmony and peaceful relationships in an integrated society *ceteris paribus* implies the growth of mutual adjustment and adaptation between the members of the society, between their activities and attitudes toward one another."[37] Hence evolutionary progress leads to increase in the range and degrees of integration, by feedback control toward a common purpose, among components of societies.

Despite the overall trend, evolution does not in every particular case progress in the direction of greater complexity, adaptability, self-regulation, and social integration. Nor does it occur at the same rate for all types of systems. Some fishes like the coelacanths are "living fossils," unchanged since the Devonian period, 345 million years in the past. *Lingula* holds the record. A brachiopod or lamp shell, a small, tongue-shaped, bottom-dwelling marine bivalve, it has persisted with little change since the Ordovician period. It is not much different from an earlier form, *Lingulella,* which existed in the Lower Cambrian, about 500 million years ago.[38]

Others, like *Drosophila,* the fruit fly which has become the geneticist's friend, show frequent mutation. Some species have evolved "backward" to lesser complexity, losing structures and adjustment processes which other, closely related, species have. Parasitic worms, which may lack several subsystems, are examples. Also some animals—seals, for instance—after emerging from the water, losing their gills, and developing limbs for locomotion on land, went back into the water and readapted partially to that environment.

The basic event which explains evolution in systems that maintain many steady states, is *mutation*. It is an historical process which ordinarily is irreversible, a change in the information of a template, whether it be genetic material or a charter. Mutations in DNA molecules in nuclei of cells are believed to occur at random at slow rates differing in various species. Such mutations may be created artificially by radiation or toxic substances. Modifications of its template may affect the capacity of a system to adjust to its environment or suprasystem. Rarely, the mutant can adapt better than the parent stock and so gain an edge in the struggle to survive. More usually, the changes are not of value or are harmful. New ideas or inventions—creative new information patterns—are the mutations in templates of systems above the organism level (see pages 857 to 859).

Some types of systems cannot make the necessary adjustments to survive environmental stresses, so they become extinct as a result of *natural selection*. The suprasystem, therefore, has an important influence on evolution. Natural selection results in survival of the fittest, best-adjusted, or most stable systems. This is true of groups, which can disband; organizations, which go bankrupt; nations or supranational systems, which can be destroyed; just as it is true of organisms and lower-level living systems.

Among sexual species, choice of mates determines which of the genes in the species' genetic pool will be perpetuated. Sexual selection is, thus, an important aspect of the natural selection of generations to come.

The old environment-heredity or nature-nurture controversy now seems to be a pseudoissue, since the processes whereby heredity and environment influence living systems are becoming clear. Biological templates—the DNA in genes—can be altered only by mutations. Lamarck appears to have been wrong in suggesting that the ordinary experience of the system can alter heredity.[39] Information inputs from the environment, however, can affect such processes in a system as learning and the storage of memories, perhaps in RNA (see pages 271 and 420). Charters, the templates which establish systems at the group level and above, can—and so far as we now know this is not true of the genetic material at the organism level and below—be altered by the information acquired from the environment: procedures of a group or organization change with experience; national and supranational constitutions are amended.

Isolation is another significant factor in evolution. The physical characteristics of the environment may limit a given type of system to one niche in it, so individuals of that type cannot breed with or be influenced by other types. Thus Australian species of animals differ greatly from those in Eurasia; thus the

social organization of Japan during the years it was a closed country veered away from that of other nations. Temporal isolation also occurs, as when the reproductive season of one species is different from that of another, thus preventing interbreeding even though the animals may have physical contact with each other.

Adaptive radiation also influences evolution since systems may spread out, searching for space, food, raw materials, or new experience, and encounter other systems or environments they had not experienced before, to which they must make adjustments. A previously insignificant difference in the coloring or structure of a part may in the new environment acquire survival value and be perpetuated. Groups of organisms isolated from others of their species may thus become so different structurally that they cannot interbreed and must be classified as a different species.

Random genetic drift is also important. This results from changes which occur as a result of random fluctuations among the various factors mentioned above or of variance in sampling the genes of the ancestral population.

Evolution is like learning as Pringle has suggested.[40] Both involve feedback with reward or punishment for "correct" or "incorrect" responses. In the case of the development of a species, these are mutations either capable of surviving or not. Taking a somewhat similar view, Jacobson has described evolution in the following general way:[41] The information which specifies the organization of an organism constitutes a *message* which is transmitted around a *feedback loop* (the life cycle). From time to time *noise* (mutations) arises in the message, which diminishes the *gain* of the message around this loop (mutations decrease the fertility of the species). Those messages which pass through the *filter* (environment) with a gain equal to or greater than one, produce *positive feedback* (self-sustaining reproduction of the species). Noisy messages, or unfavorable mutations, which cannot pass through the filter, are bred out of the species after passing over the feedback loop a number of times. Eventually the character of the messages is determined primarily by the filter. The gain is maximized, and the messages which accomplish this may be vastly more complex than the original message (the contribution of natural adaptation to evolution). The filter of environment thus "rewards" and "punishes" the species and results in something very like learning.

Evolution can occur more rapidly Simon asserts if it proceeds from one stable intermediate component form to another, made up of such components, and then to a third composed of the latter and so on, than if there are no such intervening systems.[42] The time required for evolutionary processes to produce a given system, Jacobson says, increases exponentially with the amount of information or complexity in the system.[43] On this basis he calculated that evolution of man from an environment like the earth as we now know it is most improbable in any length of time over which our planet is thought to have existed. He thought it likely, therefore, that the environment might have contained some complex building blocks necessary for constructing living systems. Simon developed this notion, suggesting that if evolution produced stable intermediate forms which become subassemblies or building blocks of more complex systems, the time required to produce complex living systems would be significantly reduced. By such a procedure it would take no longer to evolve multicellular organisms from single cells than to evolve cells from their component molecules. Simon also suggested that this principle applies at higher levels. It is easier to build empires or supranational systems in times and places at which organized nations already exist: Philip united his Macedonian empire and gave it to his son, which made it much simpler for Alexander to combine it with the conquered Persian empire into a larger system.

If evolution proceeds in this way, it explains why living systems exist in hierarchical levels. Perhaps such hierarchies are the only sort of complex systems which have had time to evolve.

The development of artifacts to carry out important subsystem processes is an important part of evolution. Insects and birds build nests; beavers build dams. Some species may use artifacts for purposes which are served by living components in others: the bowerbird appears to make use of elaborate structures and brightly colored objects to attract the female instead of having the brightly colored mating plumage of closely related species. Man has far outdistanced other species in his use of machines and a vast array of other artifacts.

5.3.1 Emergents   At several or perhaps all levels new sorts of structures or processes occur which are not seen at lower levels of systems. These are *emergents* (see page 28). They are made possible by the greater complexity of the higher levels. Because they exist only at a given level and above, any statement of cross-level formal identities about them must be limited to that given level and above. At each level at which emergents occur, they can be listed and described: *e.g.*, life and self-reproduction seem to emerge at the cell level; language at the organism level; and reproduction by a charter template at the group level.

5.4 Growth, cohesiveness, and integration

5.4.1 Growth is a progressive, developmental matter-energy process which occurs at all levels of systems, involves (*a*) increase in size—length, width, depth, volume—of the system; and commonly also (*b*) rise in the number of components in the system; (*c*) increase in its complexity; (*d*) reorganization of relationships among its structures—subsystems and components—and their processes, including differentiation of specialized structures and patterns of action (see "cohesiveness" and "integration," below); and (*e*) increase in the amounts of matter-energy and information it processes.[44] Growth in size need not always be accompanied by the other changes mentioned. For instance, an organism can get fatter without adding to the number of its organs; a nation may expand its territory without enlarging the number of its citizens, so decreasing its population density. To some it seems difficult to explain growth in systems characterized by the maintenance of many variables in steady states. It is accomplished by repeated development of strains, usually initiated by information programmed in the template—genes or charter—which alters the steady states of variables in subsystems and components, producing progressive, often irreversible changes characteristic of the system's level and type.

Curves representing the rate of growth of systems at various levels often show that it is slow at first, rises to a maximum, and then declines toward zero[45] (see Hypothesis 5.4.1-1, page 108). This is a sigmoid (S-shaped) or logistic curve (see Fig. 3-1). There are other forms of growth curves, however. A number of factors accelerate or inhibit growth and hence alter the shape of the curve.[46] The template programs the rate and ultimate amount of growth. Consequently, systems

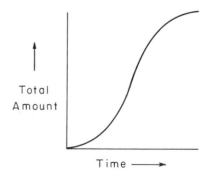

Fig. 3-1   A sigmoid or logistic growth curve.

commonly grow much as their ancestors did, in size, number, complexity, organization, and amounts of matter-energy and information processed. Enzymes in cells, auxins in plants, somatotropic hormones in animals, and abnormally large rates of food or fuel inputs all accelerate growth rates. Predators or competitors for food or other necessities, inadequate space, improper climate, and disease inhibit growth rates. Inadequate rates of food or fuel input also inhibit growth rates. Thus, environmental inputs alter the template's program.

If the number of components in a system grows, some of them must enter the system or be created within it. Others may terminate their membership in it or their existence. This means that the components have been in the system for differing lengths of time. Under some circumstances the rate of increase in the number of components of one system may depend upon the number of components in another system in the same suprasystem. This is a common ecological situation. The populations may be mutually competitive (prey and predator, for example) or they may have a cooperative relationship, parasitic or symbiotic. The growth curves of the two populations under such circumstances are complex functions of each other, their numbers sometimes oscillating about steady-state values.

Growth in size, number, and complexity of components often compels a system to reorganize relationships among its parts. One reason for this is that, as its linear dimensions increase, its volume goes up approximately as the cube of such distances and its surface as the square.[47] In very small systems the surface area may be too great for the volume, resulting in too rapid heat loss. On the other hand, as systems at various levels grow large, such cubic functions as volume, weight, cellular respiration, or tissue combustion become disproportionately great for aspects of systems which grow as the square, such as boundary area, bone strength, muscle strength, plant-stem strength, surface gas exchange, food absorption at the boundary, and heat loss. Growth can finally alter the ratio so drastically that the system cannot survive as it is. Consumption of oxygen by cells and some organisms, for instance, increases as the cube of the diameter of the system, but the rate at which it can diffuse through a boundary membrane increases only as the square of the diameter. A similar circumstance applies to the growth of organizations. Every architect knows that, as the employees in a large office increase in number, the elevators become crowded first, because the floor space available for personnel is roughly the cube of the elevator space. Cities grow in area as the square of the main highways, which are fundamentally linear. Growth therefore eventually overloads them unless additional ones are built. The commonest solution for such overloads is to decentralize the formerly integrated system into multiple, relatively autonomous, segregated components.

Reorganization with growth often results in some subsystems being local (in a single component), some being laterally dispersed (in more than one component), and some being joint (in two or more systems). At every level these arrangements differ from type to type and sometimes individual to individual. Table 3-2 gives examples of components and the subsystems which correspond to them at various levels. There clearly is no one-to-one correspondence. The rationale, costs, and efficiencies of the various arrangements in various types and levels of systems constitute a fascinating study, barely begun as yet at any level.

One of the most intricate sorts of reorganization which occurs as living systems grow is the emergence of new levels or echelons. Examples are the rise of the first organism, the change of the fertilized ovum from the unicellular to the multicellular stage, the transformation of a face-to-face group into an organization with echelons. In all these events the new level or echelon developing on top of the old system must remain viable during the transition period, which may be of considerable duration. A change, usually gradual, occurs over this time. At the beginning of it, all the critical subsystem processes for the new level or echelon are performed by the original system. They are downwardly dispersed. At the end of the change, if it is a new echelon, it is doing its own decision making within the limits of the hierarchy of which it is a part. If it is a new level, it is receiving information from input and internal transducers and from the memory, making its own decisions, and controlling a significant proportion of its critical subsystem processes—although for some of these processes it may be parasitic upon or symbiotic with the system from which it arose or other systems. The new echelon or level exists when it has its own functioning decider, the essential critical subsystem. Can the organism move without a given nucleus selecting a single output from the several inputs to it? If so, the nucleus is not a separate echelon. Can the regiment march without the approval of this particular officer? If it can, he does not represent a separate echelon. As decision making shifts to the newly developing system from the old one, conflicts between the two systems for control and for allocation of scarcities frequently arise.

5.4.2 Cohesiveness is the tendency of systems to maintain sufficient closeness in space-time among

TABLE 3-2   Examples of Correspondences Between Components and Subsystems at Each Level

Level	Component	Some subsystems wholly or partly in component
Cell	Organelle, e.g.:	
	a. Cell membrane	a. Boundary; ingestor; extruder
	b. Nucleus	b. Reproducer; producer; decider
	c. Mitochondrion	c. Converter
Organ	Cell or tissue, e.g.:	
	a. Vascular tissue in bone	a. Distributor; producer
	b. Neural tissue in gut	b. Internal transducer; channel and net; decoder
	c. Muscular tissue in bladder	c. Motor
Organism	Organ, e.g.:	
	a. Skin	a. Boundary; extruder
	b. Eye	b. Input transducer
	c. Central nervous system	c. Channel and net; decoder; associator; memory; decider; encoder
Group	Member organism, e.g.:	
	a. Leader	a. Internal transducer; decider; output transducer; often others
	b. Sentry	b. Input transducer; decoder
	c. Voting member	c. Channel and net; memory; decider
Organization	Group, e.g.:	
	a. Executive group of corporation	a. Channel and net; decoder; decider; encoder
	b. Guards at door of museum	b. Boundary; ingestor; input transducer
	c. Kitchen staff of restaurant	c. Converter; producer; distributor
Society	Organization, e.g.:	
	a. Courts	a. Decider
	b. Steel mills	b. Converter; producer
	c. Army	c. Boundary; motor
Supranational system	Society (or nation), e.g.:	
	a. Ethiopia in 1968	a. All subsystems, but since it is a developing nation, producer is joint with other nations
	b. United States in 1968	b. All subsystems
	c. Philippines in 1910	c. All subsystems except those whose processes were carried out by the United States: the Army and Navy parts of the boundary and motor; input and output transducer for diplomatic information; decider

subsystems and components—or between them and the channels in physical space which convey information among them—to enable them to interact, resisting forces that would disrupt such relationships. At the various levels cohesion is achieved in different ways.

Cells, organs, and organisms are held together by internal mechanical forces and by forces exerted by the cell membrane, organ capsule, or organism skin or exoskeleton. The spatial lengths of the channels over which their subsystems and components communicate are relatively fixed.

The units of groups, organizations, societies, and supranational systems move more freely in space, so they communicate over channels which vary in length. They must, however, keep close enough

together to ensure the effective operation of the channels in physical space among them; these channels are essential in the transmission of information required for them to interact as a system. These channels need not be maintained if the units have in the past stored memories which program them to act in coordination (see page 523). Living systems at the group level and above maintain their cohesion by such memories; by messages signaling the interlocking relationships among their units; by common purposes and goals; by common rewards, payoffs, or gratifications; or by common punishments by boundary-maintaining processes for actions leading to the dissolution of the system.

5.4.3   Integration   When multiple, simultaneous, separate processes of a system work under control of centralized decision making, toward a common purpose or goal, integration or coordination exists.[48] Information flows over a channel or network are necessary to integrate a system, unless all components were preprogrammed by information stored in them at an earlier time. Components ordinarily are only partially independent in decision making. Examples of such integration are the joint and opposing movements of an animal's sets of voluntary muscles and their antagonist muscles; the play of a football team; division of labor in a factory; and the advance of an army.

The molecular markers that carry the information that integrates cellular processes, like messenger RNA (see pages 239 and 240), are chemically quite different from those markers—like hormones and neurohumoral transmitters—which cross membranes between cells to integrate the functions of organs and organisms. These, in turn, differ from the chemical substances which pass from individual to individual among the social insects to integrate their social system by the process of *trophallaxis* (see page 576). In this case the organisms have no protoplasmic proximity. The markers must be ingested and absorbed before they can convey information to the receiver. In spatially discontinuous systems integrative messages are conveyed on other sorts of markers. The "language" of the bees and of higher social animals transmits integrative information through the air by gesture, act, or sound. Human beings accomplish social integration by talking, writing, and gesturing.

Integration of self-regulating and self-adapting living systems at the organism level and above appears to be greater in higher species of animals. Human organisms are more integrated than earthworms, for example, and human groups more than flocks of sheep or nests of insects.

"Progressive systematization" or integration and "progressive segregation" of systems are distinguished by Hall and Fagan.[49] Progressive integration increases centralized control by the system's decider and strengthens preexisting relationships among the units so that a change in one is likely to influence process in many or all others. As the size, number of units, and complexity of a system grow, it reorganizes. Boundaries form where none existed before and semiautonomous, decentralized decision-making subsystems, components, and echelons arise, acting on at least partly segregated information (see Hypotheses 1-2, 3.3.3.2-15, and 5.5-2, pages 92, 97, and 110). This "division of labor" is progressive segregation, and it may ultimately proceed, in some cases, until subsystems or components are a "heap," no longer a system but a set of independent units, as when a child is weaned and no longer "tied to his mother's apron strings," or when a colony becomes a separate nation. If the components are highly heterogeneous (see page 867), Etzioni suggests that a large degree of segregation may be necessary for them to interact as a system at all.[50] Segregation or dispersion of subsystems into duplicate or multiple, "redundant" components may make the system less vulnerable to trauma. Possibly this principle explains why a given memory may be dispersed to several parts of the brain, why many organisms have duplicate organs bilaterally arranged, and why nations elect vice presidents as well as presidents.

A unicellular organism is independent, but cells in a multicellular animal are interdependent. Primitive men were much more independent than men in modern society. Cannon commented that such integrations of parts into larger systems "all involve social organization, social control, and a lessening of the independence of the individual members. . . . The social organism, like the bodily organism, cannot be vigorous and efficient unless its elements are assured the essential minimal conditions for healthful life and activity."[51]

5.5 Pathology   Any state of a system is pathological in which one or more variables remain for a significant period beyond their ranges of stability, or in which the costs of adjustment processes required to keep them within their ranges of stability are significantly increased. Steady states may be disturbed by malfunctioning of subsystems or components or by unfavorable conditions in the environment or suprasystem. If such disturbances are prolonged, they may exhaust the adjustment processes which the system has available to cope with them. Some pathological states are corrected with little permanent damage to the system, by processes of repair or replacement of parts, or other adjustments. Others bring about a new, and often but not always, a less desirable, steady state. This is commonly irreversible, historical change, a process which produces a new structure. The concept of pathology is applicable to all levels of living systems.[52]

There are eight major categories of causes of pathological states in living systems:

(*a*) *Lacks of matter-energy inputs.* Inadequate input rates of oxygen to a neuron of the brain can permanently alter that cell's enzymatic processes; a soldier of the French Foreign Legion lost in the Sahara can die of thirst; a besieged city can be forced to surrender because food supplies have been cut off by the enemy; and a nation's government can collapse because it does not maintain a minimal rate of imports of necessary raw materials like coal and steel.

(*b*) *Excesses of matter-energy inputs.* Hypertonic solutions, containing a higher concentration of salt than is normal for body fluids, can shrivel red blood corpuscles floating in them; too much pressure with a surgical probe can rupture a liver; a soldier wounded in the leg may limp permanently; a factory invaded by a group of strikers who sabotage it may have to shut down production; and a typhoon can crush many of the people, crops, and houses of a Pacific island.

(*c*) *Inputs of inappropriate forms of matter-energy.* A cell may be infected with viruses which alter its normal metabolism; kidneys may be poisoned and irreversibly damaged by mercury; the growth of an embryo may be stunted by thalidomide; a whole dormitory of girls may be kept from classes by the flu; and an army may be put to disorganized rout by poison gas.

(*d*) *Lacks of information inputs.* Whether excessively low rates of information input can cause structural pathology at some levels of living systems is debatable (see pages 833, 834 and 971). Without continuous inputs from a neuron, a gland cell may not secrete; congenital cataracts prevent information about visual patterns from reaching the brain, and unless the cataracts are removed when the child is very young, the neural organs may never be able to process such information correctly; a prisoner may become psychotic after prolonged solitary confinement in the dark; a general may make tragically wrong decisions as to action by his forces if he is not continually supplied with adequate and accurate information about the enemy's order of battle; and a nation cut off from contact with the rest of the world, as Afghanistan was for years, may not progress as its neighbors do.

(*e*) *Excesses of information inputs.* It is uncertain whether excessively high rates of information input can cause permanent structural pathology or whether the effects are always reversible (see pages 164 to 169). It is true, however, that a neuron may stop transmitting its usual signals if information is input to it too rapidly; a court docket may be so overloaded with cases that a defendant may have to wait three years to come to trial; a termite nest, when disturbed by loud sounds, may resound with the noise of many individual insects knocking their heads on it in nonadaptive panic, confusion, or what seems like emotional behavior; and news that a battle has been lost can trigger a revolt that rocks a country. Furthermore, signals conveying inappropriate or threatening *meaning* can have pathological effects even though the *rate* of their transmission may not constitute an overload. For example, word that a son has been killed in battle can precipitate a coronary occlusion in his father.

(*f*) *Inputs of maladaptive genetic information in the template.* Bacteriophage on entering a healthy cell alters

its metabolism (see page 274); in the fetus the structures which form the lips and mouth may not join properly at the midline so that a harelip and cleft palate are formed; a partnership may be established in which each of the two partners has 50 percent of the stock, and since no decision can be made when they disagree, the relationship cannot endure; and the League of Nations, incapable of compelling participation and compliance with its rulings by all the world's powers, may be unable to maintain peace.

(*g*) *Abnormalities in internal matter-energy processes.* These include at some levels tumors and cancer, and at all levels they include the pathology of maturation and aging. It may be that, when these processes are understood better, they will be reclassified into one of the previous classes of causes of pathology. Also included under this rubric are abnormalities in the formation or processing of the matter-energy in information-bearing markers. A cell may become neoplastic; the skin may develop a lipoma, a nonmalignant fatty tumor; an old man may gradually acquire arteriosclerosis, hardening of the arteries; and in France of the eighteenth century cake may be distributed only to royalty and the aristocracy, leaving only bread, and little of that, to the people.

(*h*) *Abnormalities in internal information processes.* This includes pathology in signal transmission, coding, associating, deciding, and the other activities of information processing subsystems. A pain neuron, irritated by a bone spur, may transmit pulses spasmodically; information may be poorly stored in the memory of an elderly woman who has suffered a stroke, and such information is forgotten almost immediately; representatives of management and a union in negotiations over a new contract may be unable to agree upon the meanings of the terms they use; a supervisor may route raw materials incorrectly in a factory, halting production; a merit system which retains superannuated civil servants with seniority may bog down busy junior governmental employees with extra work to make up for what their seniors do not accomplish; and a representative of the Secretary General of the United Nations may indiscreetly hint what is to be announced officially the next day.

5.6 Decay and termination   Many aspects of systems' historical processes depend upon the balance at any period between anabolism and catabolism, growth and decay. In youth anabolism is dominant, in maturity the processes are in balance, and in later years catabolism usually predominates, producing senescence and decay. The seven ages of man have been recognized for centuries, and a commonly employed cross-level analogy between organism and society has often likened them to the rise, decline, and fall of nations. These processes are ordinarily irreversible.

Not all living systems deteriorate with age. Free-living cells, for example, by dividing, attain a sort of immortality. They can be killed, but they do not grow old and die. A noncritical organ, when surgically removed from its organism, dies, perhaps long before the organism does. But a critical organ and its organism die together, unless a prosthesis is found to carry out the organ's critical subsystem functions. Aging and eventual death are normal aspects of the lives of men and lower animals, although some of them live more than a century. Some bristlecone pine trees *(Pinus aristata)* have endured more than 4,600 years. They are the oldest of all present-day living systems with normal life cycles, although seeds of arctic lupine, whose life cycles were interrupted by freezing for 10,000 years, recently germinated and grew normally.[53] There is disagreement as to whether nests of social insects become senescent and die out or whether their processes can be carried on indefinitely, generation after generation. The same question has been asked also of human societies. Do they decline through senescence to their ultimate termination, as Gibbon declared? Perhaps a few have, and all their citizens have died out. Much more often, however, just as a new management reorganizes the employees of a bankrupt firm into a new company, with the fall of a nation or government, one or more new regimes employ an old or new template or charter to reorganize the components of the last society into a new system—or perhaps more than one.

When a system has exhausted all its adjustment processes and is unable to maintain one or more of its critical variables within the proper range of stability, when its control is lost because its information transmissions and feedbacks stop or are so full of noise or so slow as to be useless, when it cannot keep its subsystems and components adjusted to one another and the total system in steady state with its environment, it cannot survive (see pages 481 and 583). Then, after a more-or-less rapid decline, its existence is terminated. For cells, organs, and organisms this is called death. If an organism dies, so do its organs and cells; if an organ dies, so do its cells. The system's organization at all levels undergoes entropic changes. Terminations of human groups and systems of the higher levels are different. They break down to the next lower level, but many or all the components at that level can survive as living systems. Supranational systems disintegrate to their component societies; societies, to the organizations, groups, and individual organisms that compose them; organizations, to the groups and individuals in them; groups, to their members. The supra-

system of the terminated system then assumes control of the remaining parts of the system (see Hypothesis 5.6-1, page 110). As I pointed out above in the case of nations, these components afterward often combine with other systems at their level, under an old or new template or charter, to make up one or more other systems at the level of the former system. Thus life can go on.

Yet one way or another, sooner or later, all living systems appear finally to terminate. For cells, as for societies, time's arrow points ultimately to the dust of entropy.

6. Models and simulations

A powerful technique for the quantitative study of living systems involves the development and manipulation of a model or simulation to analyze its structure and process and, in some cases, to predict the nature of change in it over time and under various circumstances. Models and simulations may also be used as prosthetic devices to replace part of a living system, as an artificial kidney does, and to carry on that component's functions (see page 355). They also may be employed as instructional aids, as business games are (see pages 713 to 715).

A model is one sort of formal identity or analogy (see pages 27 and 91). A simulation is another. Either one transfers concepts about one sort of phenomena to another conceptual realm in the hope that deductions can be made from the second which will hold for the first. The words "model" and "simulation" are rarely defined precisely in writings concerned with living systems. Both, for example, may be used quite loosely to mean "theory." I shall call a formal identity between two conceptual systems, an *isomorphism,* call a formal identity between two concrete systems, a *homology,* and reserve the word *model* for a formal identity between a conceptual system and a concrete (or an abstracted) system. *Simulations* I regard as a special class of models. They exhibit processes in some way like the referent system, as they change from state *A* to state *B,* often between two points in real time. Experimenters can, and often do, change the values of parameters and/or variables between one simulation run and another.

Models and simulations may be expressed in words, numbers, or other symbols. In addition some take the form of mechanical constructions or are carried out by living systems at the same or different levels as the simulated system, *e.g.,* when a group simulates a subsystem of a society (see pages 974 to 979). These mechanical or living systems represent some conceptualization of the simulated system or of one or more of its component structures or processes.

A mathematical model or simulation is a sort of analogy, but it is a good deal more than that. It has, as Rapoport says, a similar quality of "as-if-ness."[54] But it has in addition the characteristic of leading to specific predictions on the basis of specific relations among specific variables—predictions which, in principle at least, can be proved or disproved by experiment or observation. Models can range from loose verbal analogies—like the equating of an explosion and a revolution—to the rigorous mathematical structures of theoretical physics which correspond with great exactness to empirical events and may be approximated but not fully described in any short prose statement.

It is not always easy to distinguish a model from a simulation. A model may exist in the general case and not until precise quantities are stated for its units and relationships does it become a model of a particular system, subsystem, or component. A simulation is a particular sort of model which has a number of variables interacting as they do in a living system. Many simulations are programmed for computers. A model programmed for a computer can be far more complex and draw many more deductions much more rapidly than a person can unaided. Moreover, a computer program, in order to run, must be completely and precisely stated. This means it must be clearer and more consistent than are many models of living systems.

A model or simulation may be deductive or inductive. In the former case, it displays known relationships and characteristics of some living system or set of them. In the latter, it may be predictive of findings on the living system which are not available from observation. It can, for example, extrapolate states or processes of a society into the future and make inductions about the system's processes under changed circumstances. Such a model may be usefully predictive of future actions where actual experimentation is impossible.

Scientists have used simulations at all levels of living systems. If comparable or identical models are used in simulations at different levels, a cross-level formal identity may be revealed. Use of the same computer program to analyze aspects of living systems at different levels is more than an analogical metaphor. It is a cross-level formal identity.

A verbal theory which not only describes observations accurately but also presents an explicit account of how a system is believed to work can be accepted as a conceptual system isomorphic to a given concrete system. If all the consequences of such a model were immediately apparent, there would be no purpose in putting it into mathematical form or making calculations from it on a computer. Since this is not the case, scientists must develop and evaluate models in order to determine how accurate they are.

Models can never represent living systems with perfect completeness or precision. They are simplified approximations for a number of reasons: (a) It is not possible to understand any such system perfectly. (b) A model accurately representing all variables in a living system would be so complex that it could not be handled by present mathematical methods. (c) Collecting and analyzing data on all relevant variables would be too expensive in time and money, the inclusion of additional variables not improving the model enough to justify the costs which would be involved.

Representations of living systems are designed to serve a number of different purposes. They can be separated into two major groupings, although the division is not sharp: (1) Systems whose inputs and outputs are like those of certain living systems and which accomplish some of the same ends, but whose internal processes are formally different. And (2) systems whose inputs and outputs are like those of certain living systems and which accomplish some of the same ends but whose internal processes are planned to be formally as isomorphic as possible to those of the living system. The distinction between classes 1 and 2 is like the distinction between a walking machine and a machine that walks like a man.

In class 1 fall many sorts of machines, tools, prostheses, and working models, as well as some symbolic models. If biologists were actually to succeed in inventing an artificial cow capable of producing milk from grass and water, it would almost certainly be a class 1 representation of a cow. When a mechanical heart is perfected it will be another, at the level of the organ. Models in the burgeoning field of "artificial intelligence" fall partly into class 1 and partly into class 2 (see page 485). Conceptual systems such as theoretical network models or computer programs may display learning and other kinds of information processing found in living systems, but they resemble the actual processes of no living system. Electronic information storage and retrieval systems, for example, are usually planned to be useful and efficient rather than to operate in "manlike" or "organization-like" fashion. On the other hand a successful class 2 representation is no more and no less efficient than the system it models. If it represents a man, for example, it should process information at the same rate he does, make the same sort and frequency of errors, and attain a similar proficiency, no more and no less. Studies occur in both classes which have been called simulations, but a rigorous definition of simulation includes only class 2.

Models or simulations may also be classified along a different dimension into the following four classes, although examples of each do not exist at every level:

(*a*) Nonliving artifacts

(*b*) Living, usually human, representations

(*c*) Models in words, numbers, or other symbols, including computer programs

(*d*) Living system–computer interactions

I shall use this four-way classification in Chaps. 6 through 12. Each of these four classes includes examples of both class 1 and class 2 described above.

We can evaluate the validity of simulations. Different sorts of simulations need not meet identical standards for validity. The requirement that a specific living system (*e.g.*, a reference system) be represented accurately must be more stringently met in some sorts of simulations than in others. How valid a simulation is must be assessed in terms of the purpose for which it is intended.[55] A simulation used for teaching, for example, can be valuable even if it does not closely correspond to the reference system, as long as it provides the intended teaching experiences and as long as students understand its limitations. A model to be used in theory building may fit poorly with the observable universe and yet retain some usefulness if it generates reasonable hypotheses for further tests.

Five types of validity are identified by Hermann:[56]

Internal validity or reliability.   If a simulation is run repeatedly with the initial values of its parameters identical variations in outcomes must be accounted for by identifiable relationships within the simulation. If repeated runs have very different outcomes that depend upon factors external to the simulation, such as characteristics of the participants in a simulation game, internal validity is poor.

Face validity.   This is the impression of realism the simulation makes upon the experimenters or participants. A simulation may have value if the description it gives seems relevant to observers. Sometimes, though, they do not know enough about the range of behavior of the reference system to be able to make such a judgment meaningfully.

Variable-parameter validity.   If the simulation's variables and parameters correspond to their assumed counterparts in the reference system, it has such validity. Sensitivity testing of a simulation throws light on whether it has such validity. This is done by carrying out repeated runs of the simulation with systematic changes of values of variables and setting of parameters. Such testing indicates what difference a given variable makes to the outcomes. Establishing operational definitions for counterparts in a concrete system of the variables and parameters of a model may be difficult, however, when a variable combines a number of features of the reference system.

Event validity.   Since a simulation is intended to represent one or more situations in the real world, events in the simulation can be compared with events in the reference system. The simulation has event validity if the two correspond. A predictive simulation can be compared with actual later outcomes in the reference system. Such comparisons may be useful for checking the total simulation but less useful for determining what aspects of it explain discrepancies between it and its reference system. Before a determination is made as to whether a simulation has event validity, scientists working on the problem must agree as to whether general correspondence to events or close correspondence is to be expected. They must also agree on the dimensions upon which the two systems are to be compared.

Hypothesis validity.   In a simulation a given variable is related to another one in the same way as in its reference system. Some hypotheses have high generality and may be valid in a variety of living systems. The fewer the systems in which a hypothesis is likely to be verified, the more exactly can it be expected to fit findings from these systems. The hypothesis validity of a simulation increases as its particularity increases and as the processes it represents diverge from those of systems which it is not intended to represent. General hypotheses with low hypothesis validity, however, may be more powerful scientifically because they relate to a large number of different systems.

7. Conclusions

Each level of living system has been studied by its specialists. Commonly they are not deeply concerned with phenomena at other levels, and consequently they rarely make cross-level comparisons or search for general systems principles. Indeed, it is unusual for scientists to keep informed about all the types of systems at their own level or even about the whole range of structures and processes in the particular systems on which they concentrate.

There are undoubtedly many similarities and possibly many cross-level formal identities in the phenomena of life. There are also significant differences among the various levels, types, and individuals in the gamut of living systems, as well as in the ways different scientific disciplines investigate them. Before us lies a search for pattern in individuality, for unity in diversity.

NOTES AND REFERENCES

[1]Cf. Ackoff, R. L. & Emery, F. E. *On purposeful systems.* Chicago: Aldine-Atherton, 1972, 16–26.
[2]Cf. *Ibid.*, 26–31.
[3]Wouk, H. *The Caine mutiny.* Garden City, N.Y.: Doubleday, 1951.

[4]Ashby, W. R. *Design for a brain.* New York: Wiley, 1954, 153–158, 210–211.

[5]NOTE: This list is similar to a classification made by Rashevsky. (Cf. Rashevsky, N. Topology and life: in search of general mathematical principles in biology and sociology. *Gen. Systems,* 1956, **1**, 123–139.) Providing such a list of the critical subsystems and describing their structures and processes is a step toward making a detailed description of living systems. This sort of effort was appropriately demanded of general living systems theory by Hearn (Hearn, G. *Theory building in social work.* Toronto: Univ. of Toronto Press, 1958, 54–55).

[6]Elias, P., Feinstein, A., & Shannon, C. E. A note on the maximum flow through a network. *IRE Trans. Inform. Theory,* 1956, IT-2, No. 4, 117.

[7]NOTE: Pattee [Pattee, H. H. The recognition of hereditary order in primitive chemical systems. In S. W. Fox (Ed.). *The origins of prebiological systems and of their molecular matrices.* New York: Academic Press, 1965, 388–389] uses the phrase "hereditary process," which he considers "fundamental at all levels and for all types of organization." By this term he means "any process by which information is transmitted from one structure (the parent) to another structure (the heir) so as to result in a net increase in the physical order of the total system." He recognizes the relation of this sort of order to information. He also states that he considers reproduction (or replication) and evolution both to be hereditary processes, the latter involving the propagation of species with gradual increase in information in the course of time.

[8]von Neumann, J. The general and logical theory of automata. In L. A. Jeffress (Ed.). *Cerebral mechanisms in behavior: the Hixon symposium.* New York: Wiley, 1951, 1–31.
Cf. also Elsasser, W. M. *The physical foundations of biology.* New York: Pergamon Press, 1958, and Wigner, E. P. The probability of the existence of a self-reproducing unit. In *The logic of personal knowledge. Essays presented to Michael Polanyi on his 70th birthday, 11 March 1961.* Glencoe, Ill.: The Free Press, 1961, 231–238.
Cf. also Bernstein, J. When the computer procreates. *N.Y. Times Mag.,* Feb. 15, 1976, 9, 34–38.

[9]Kornberg, A. Biologic synthesis of deoxyribonucleic acid. *Science,* 1960, **131**, 1503–1508.
Also Lehninger, A. L. *Biochemistry.* New York: Worth, 1972, 684.

[10]Huxley, A. *Brave new world.* New York: Harper, 1932.

[11]Judges 12:6.

[12]Ashby, W. R. *Op. cit.,* 87, 232–235.

[13]Waldenberg, M. J. A structural taxonomy of spatial hierarchies. In M. Chisholm, A. Frey, & P. Haggett (Eds.). *Regional forecasting: Colston papers,* 22. London: Butterworths, 1971, 147–175.
Also Waldenberg, M. J. The average hexagon in spatial hierarchies. In R. J. Charley (Ed.). *Spatial analyses in geomorphology.* London: Methuen, 1972, 323–352.

[14]Gerard, R. W. Higher levels of integration. *Science,* 1942, **95**, 309–313.

[15]Shannon, C. E. A mathematical theory of communication. *Bell Sys. tech. J.,* 1948, **27**, 379–423 and 623–656.
Cf. also Pierce, J. R. *Symbols, signals and noise.* New York: Harper, 1961, 145–165.
Also Gallager, R. G. *Information theory and reliable communication.* New York: Wiley, 1968, 73–76.

[16]NOTE: Sebeok (Sebeok, T. A. Coding in the evolution of signaling behavior. *Behav. Sci.,* 1962, **7**, 430–442) discusses analog and digital coding in living systems.

[17]Miller, G. A. The magical number seven, plus or minus two: some limits on our capacity for processing information. *Psychol. Rev.,* 1956, **63**, 92–95.

[18]Baker, W. O. The paradox of choice. In D. Wolfle (Ed.). *Symposium on basic research.* Washington, D.C.: AAAS Publication No. 56, 1959, 63. Reprinted by permission.

[19]NOTE: March and Simon (March, J. G. & Simon, H. A. *Organizations.* New York: Wiley, 1959, 167) have observed that organizations have various information processing subsystems. They list the following sorts of subsystems: (*a*) channel and net; (*b*) that which stores memories; (*c*) input transducer; (*d*) that which searches memories and prepares information on which decisions are based; (*e*) that which carries out other decision-making functions; and (*f*) that which maintains memories. McLachlan (McLachlan, D., Jr. Communication networks and monitoring. *Pub. Opin. Quart.,* 1961, **25**, 194–195) also has noted that social systems have several information processing subsystems. He lists the following: (*a*) input transducer; (*b*) channel and net; (*c*) decider; (*d*) motor or output transducer. Neither March and Simon nor McLachlan list all the information processing subsystems that I list, but each of these sources splits at least one of my subsystems into parts.

[20]Cf. the discussion of "uncertainty absorption," which is similar to the "abstracting adjustment process," as I use the phrase, in March, J. G. & Simon, H. A. *Op. cit.,* 164–166.

[21]For a discussion of principles of channel and net process, derived primarily from a consideration of organizations, but relevant to living systems more generally, cf. March, J. G. & Simon, H. A. *Ibid.,* 166–169.

[22]Bremermann, H. J. Optimization through evolution and recombination. In M. C. Yovits, G. T. Jacobi, & G. D. Goldstein (Eds.). *Self-organizing systems.* Washington, D.C.: Spartan Books, 1962, 97–99.

[23]Pauling, L. *The nature of the chemical bond.* New York: Cornell Univ. Press, 1939.

[24]Pavlov, I. P. Physiology of the higher nervous activity. (Paper read before the XIV International Physiological Congress, Rome, Sept. 2, 1932.) In: *Conditioned reflexes and psychiatry.* Vol. II. (Trans. & edited by W. H. Gantt.) New York: International Publishers, 1941, 93.

[25]Shannon, C. E. Certain results in coding theory for noisy channels. *Inform. & Control,* 1957, **1**, 6–7.

[26]Shannon, C. E. The zero error capacity of a noisy channel. *IRE Trans. Inform. Theory,* 1956, IT-2, No. 3, 8.

[27]Cf. Gerard, R. W., Kluckhohn, C., & Rapoport, A. Biological and cultural evolution: some analogies and explorations. *Behav. Sci.,* 1956, **1**, 6–34.

[28]Cf. Lord, A. B. *The singer of tales.* Cambridge: Harvard Univ. Press, 1960.

[29]Bledsoe, W. W. A basic limitation on the speed of digital computers. *IRE Trans. Electron. Comp.,* 1961, EC-10, 530.

[30]Simon, H. A. The architecture of complexity. *Proc. Amer. Phil. Soc.,* 1962, **106**, 468. Reprinted by permission.

[31]Platt, J. R. Amplification aspects of biological response and mental activity. *Amer. Sci.,* 1956, **44**, 180–197.

[32]NOTE: A similar formulation is suggested by various authors. A particularly comparable statement appears in A. Perez and L. Tandl. Aspects du problème de réduction en science du point de vue de l'information. *La documentation en France,* 1962, (mai-juin), No. 3, 38–46.

[33]NOTE: For a brief overview of current approaches to the process of deciding cf. Handy, R. & Kurtz, P. *A current appraisal of the behavioral sciences.* Great Barrington, Mass.: Behavioral Research Council, 1964, 126–127.

[34]Freud, A. *The ego and the mechanisms of defense.* (Trans. by C. Baines.) London: Hogarth Press, 1937.

[35]Willmer, E. N. *Cytology and evolution.* New York: Academic Press, 1960, 396.

[36]Sommerhoff, G. *Analytical biology.* London: Oxford Univ. Press, 1950, 138–185. Reprinted by permission.

[37]*Ibid.*, 186. Reprinted by permission.

[38]Herrick, C. F. Organic evolution. *Encyclopaedia Britannica.* Vol. 8. Chicago: Encyclopaedia Britannica, 1958, 921.

[39]Lamarck, J. B. *Zoological philosophy.* (Trans. by H. Elliot.) London: MacMillan, 1914.

[40]Pringle, J. W. S. On the parallel between learning and evolution. *Gen. Systems,* 1956, **1**, 90–110.

[41]Jacobson, H. Information, reproduction, and the origin of life. *Amer. Sci.*, 1955, **43**, 119–127.

[42]Simon, H. A. *Op. cit.*, 470–473.

[43]Jacobson, H. *Op. cit.*, 122–125.

[44]NOTE: Boulding's (Boulding, K. E. Toward a general theory of growth. *Canad. J. econ. pol. Sci.*, 1953, **19**, 326–340. Reprinted by permission.) sketch of a cross-level theory of growth has influenced my presentation here. He remarks that (page 340) "The sort of general theory which I have in mind, however, is a generalization from aspects of experience which include more than mere abstract quantity and which are common to many or even to all of the 'universes of discourse' which constitute the various sciences. Growth is one such aspect; organization is another; interaction is another. When, and if, such a general theory comes to be written it will be surprising if the general theory of growth does not comprise an important chapter."

[45]Cf. Pearl, R. & Reed, L. J. On the rate of growth of the population of the United States since 1790 and its mathematical representation. *Proc. Nat. Acad. Sci.*, 1920, **6**, 272–288.

[46]Meadows, D. H., Meadows, D. L., Randers, J., & Behrens, W. W., III. *The limits to growth.* New York: Universe Books, 1972.

[47]Thompson, D'A. W. *Growth and form.* New York: Macmillan, 1942.
Cf. also Bonner, J. T. *Morphogenesis: an essay on development.* Princeton: Princeton Univ. Press, 1952, 11–24.

[48]Sommerhoff, G. *Op. cit.*, 23–25.

[49]Hall, A. D. & Fagan, R. E. Definition of a system. *Gen. Systems,* 1956, **1**, 22.

[50]Etzioni, A. The dialectics of supranational unification. *Amer. pol. Sci. Rev.*, 1962, **56**, 927–935.

[51]Cannon, W. B. *Wisdom of the body.* New York: Norton, 1932, 304. Reprinted by permission.

[52]Cf. Levinson, H. *Organizational diagnosis.* Cambridge, Mass.: Harvard Univ. Press, 1972, 3–9.

[53]Porsild, A. E., Harington, C. R., & Mulligan, G. A. *Lupinus arcticus Wats.* grown from seeds of Pleistocene age. *Science,* 1967, **158**, 113–114.

[54]Rapoport, A. Uses and limitations of mathematical models in social science. In L. Gross (Ed.). *Symposium on sociological theory.* Evanston, Ill., White Plains, N.Y.: Row, Peterson & Co., 1959, 354.

[55]Hermann, C. F. Validation problems in games and simulations with special reference to models of international politics. *Behav. Sci.*, 1967, **12**, 219.

[56]*Ibid.*, 221–224.

Hypotheses Concerning

Living Systems

How can this vast mass of fact be reduced to order as a first step toward interpreting it and generalizing from it? Although it is some centuries since astronomers have thought of the matter in this way, they too were once faced with the same dilemma. They had voluminous data on the locations of the heavenly bodies at many points in time. The first step was to describe these in terms of geometrical paths—the cycles of the Ptolemaic system. A little later these paths were simplified to the circles of Copernicus and the ellipses of Kepler. But the great simplification came, of course, with Newton, who showed that the scheme of the heavens could be represented far more parsimoniously by replacing the time paths of planets with the differential equations that generated those paths.[1]

So Simon spoke of only a small part of the sciences of life, recommending the use of formulations like those of Newton which, in the form of computerized simulations, can generate precise statements explanatory of various aspects of living systems. How much more important—though more difficult—it is to make general formulations applicable to the structure and process of all living systems.

Recognition of the need for propositions in the sciences of behavior is by no means new. John Stuart Mill urged that general propositions be sought, "empirical laws" expressing concisely the commonalities in large classes of findings.[2] Homans has criticized his own field of sociology for not formulating such

general propositions.[3] From the findings of many observers in the psychological and social sciences Berelson and Steiner made a useful compilation of 1,045 such propositions of moderate generality.[4] They stated many of the principles of organismic, group, organizational, and social process known today. Unfortunately they did not deal with biological findings, or the levels of cell and organ. Although they recognized that there are levels of organization, their conceptual framework was not explicitly systems-oriented, and they only rarely devoted attention to cross-level formal identities or analogies. I have freely used their valuable compilation as well as the work of many other scientists in the preparation of this chapter. Almost never do they put forward their propositions, as I do, as possibly having relevance across levels of living systems. At times I have somewhat altered the intent of hypotheses suggested by them and others, and often I have altered terminology to make it consistent with that in the rest of this book.

The general hypotheses or propositions which are part of any general theory must of necessity at the same time involve extensive simplification. A need for a mathematical theory of how best to simplify has been pointed out by Ashby.[5] This would provide guidelines for conducting a process now dependent wholly on intuition and native wit. He suggests that the mathematician's work on homomorphisms might be relevant.

The value of such hypotheses was well stated by Snyder, Bruck, and Sapin:[6] "A conceptual scheme is not a research design or a substitute for one. Nor can we remain intellectually honest without at some point stating some hypotheses and laying down some of the conditions under which low-level predictions are possible." (They use the term "low-level" in two senses at once, implying both a wide margin of error and limited generality.)

The term "hypothesis" I here use in the restricted sense of a proposition which can be demonstrated empirically rather than in the more general sense of any expression which is capable of being believed, doubted, or denied.[7] As employed in this chapter "hypothesis" and "proposition" are essentially synonymous.

At each level numerous hypotheses can be stated concerning the structure and process of living systems. The preceding chapters contain many examples of research studies which have been conducted to prove or disprove propositions about systems at a given level, or about specific species or individual examples of such systems. Moreover, a large number of other possible investigations in the framework of systems theory have been suggested. At each level the structural characteristics of the various subsystems or components can be analyzed. The performance variables of each subsystem can be measured, including their equilibratory ranges, variances, rates of transmission, lags, error rates, omission rates, matter-energy costs, efficiencies, and so forth. The input-output relationships, adjustment processes, feedback characteristics, growth and decay characteristics, degree of cohesiveness, and degree of integration, under many environmental conditions, can be studied.

In this chapter I focus attention on hypotheses which apply to two or more levels of systems, because of their powerful generality. These are more than propositions of systems theory: they are *general* systems theoretical hypotheses. Several of the assertions I have made in my fundamental statement of general living systems theory in the preceding two chapters are, of course, cross-level hypotheses or propositions of this sort. Such, for instance, is the assertion that all living systems which survive have all the critical subsystems, or are parasitic upon or symbiotic with systems which do (see page 32).

A number of observations can be made about characteristics of any good cross-level general proposition (see pages 25 to 28):

(*a*) Such a hypothesis should concern some aspect of structure or process in concrete systems which has been observed at one level at least and which is seriously suspected to have a formal identity with others at other levels. It should be more than a mere definition, declaration of faith, or metaphysical statement.

(*b*) It must be possible to specify practical operations, at two levels at least, whereby the hypothesis can be either confirmed or disconfirmed. It is quite conceivable that some hypotheses may apply to many cases and yet that certain exceptions will be found. The reasons for the exceptions would then need to be sought out, and the hypothesis would then need to be restated so as to account for both the exceptions and the cases which confirmed it. A large number of exceptions would disconfirm it. If it were a proposition central to general living systems theory—such as that all surviving systems possess all the critical subsystems, or are parasitic upon or symbiotic with systems that carry out for them the processes they lack—its disproof would raise considerable doubt about the whole theoretical framework. If it proved true for most, but not all, critical subsystems or for most, but not all, living systems, the theoretical framework would have to be altered but it would not need to be entirely discarded.

Of the hypotheses stated below, some are probably true for all levels, some only for certain levels, some only if modified, and others are probably false. For some the question is: Is it true or false? For others the question is: Does it apply at a given level?

Certain readers may object that some of these hypotheses are logical tautologies following from the assumptions of the symbolic models in which they occur. To this view two replies can be made: First, it is appropriate to collect evidence as to whether this particular tautology is relevant in the sense that it shows that a given model is applicable to a given class of structures or processes in physical space to some interesting degree of approximation. Second, if the tautology is usable and relevant in this sense, its dissemination may result in a saving in time and effort to future researchers collecting or analyzing data at the same or other levels.

The hypotheses presented in this chapter are only a few out of many that could be stated. Because some structures and processes are emergent at a given level, all cross-level hypotheses do not apply at all levels. When I think a hypothesis is restricted in its application to specific levels, I indicate which levels I think they are. I am not sure which of them are true or false and which are relevant or irrelevant to a given level of living system. I have included these particular hypotheses because they interest me and because they appear to me more likely than not to be true and relevant to two or more levels. Some of these hypotheses may appear interesting and important to one reader, while others may appear so to another.

(c) The hypothesis must be of a medium degree of abstractness, neither so abstract that it is vague, obvious, trivial, or incapable of confirmation, nor so specific that it does not have wide relevance.[8] Of course, the more levels that a hypothesis applies to and the more types of systems and specific individuals with all their variations that are included under it, the greater in general must be the restriction upon it. These are not hypotheses of cosmic scope. I am not competent to evaluate hypotheses which range from particles to galaxies. It is much harder to state useful hypotheses relevant to both living and nonliving concrete systems than hypotheses relevant across levels of living systems. The latter are a very special and delimited set of all concrete systems (see page 17). Cross-level similarities usually arise from the fact that higher levels of living systems have structures and processes which are shredded out from lower levels (see page 26).

(d) It must be stated in terms chosen to be, as much as possible, equally applicable at various levels and to represent the general case indicating the commonality across levels rather than a specific case characteristic of a single level.

(e) It must be capable of ultimately being represented by a mathematical statement of the formal identity across levels, in which some variables show regular changes with levels (representing interlevel differences or disanalogies), others change with types (representing intertype differences), and others change with individuals (representing interindividual differences). For an integrative, general theory these differences, as I have said (see page 28), are equally as important as the cross-level identities. I present cross-level hypotheses here, however, because they are fundamental and because they are a new concept in the life sciences, while cross-individual and cross-type hypotheses are not. Few cross-level hypotheses have ever been even seriously proposed.[9] Empirical evaluation of such hypotheses will demonstrate, not just such facts as that all living systems have a boundary or matter-energy storage, but what precisely is common and what is different (and to what extent) in the structure and process of the boundaries and matter-energy storages of *all* systems. Or how structural variations among systems and their subsystems make their processes different in speed, costs, or efficiency. Or exactly what is the formal identity, if any, between matter-energy processing and information processing in particular sorts of subsystems which may appear to have comparable functions.

(f) It must be stated so that the observations and/or measurements carried out at each level for the purpose of confirming or disconfirming it can be precisely compared. This means the analogous measurements at each level must be on the same dimensions of the same space or on dimensions of one or more other spaces which have known transformations to the same dimension of the same space (see pages 9 and 1026). The degree of precision with which each hypothesis is stated is determined by my estimate of the degree of empirical precision which can reasonably be expected with present methods of observation or measurement at one of the levels covered by the hypothesis. Whenever possible, my estimate has taken into account the precision of evidence relevant to it which some worker has collected at that level. Because structures and processes shred out from one level of living system to another (see pages 1 and 4), I assume as a rough rule of thumb that the precision of data collected concerning the phenomenon dealt with by a hypothesis could ordinarily be comparable at other levels to the level at which the original observations were made. It is, after all, the same structure or process, shredded out in the evolution of higher levels from the form it had at lower levels.

(g) It must be stated so that a structure or process common to each level can be identified by one specified operation, and then the characteristic it is hypothesized to have can be measured by another, *independent* one. Simply locating variables in systems at different levels which have formal identities or can be described by similar mathematical models is not enough.

The hypotheses below are not presented as detailed research designs, though possible procedures for cross-level experiments have been sketched out for a few at the end of this chapter (see pages 110 to 114). As I shall demonstrate in our information input overload study in Chap. 5, much work is involved in the steps required to conceptualize one of these general propositions carefully, conceive of comparable empirical situations and dimensions applicable to two or more levels of living systems by which it can be tested, devise the experimental apparatuses, procedures, and control techniques required to make the study rigorous, and then finally carry out these procedures. As the conceptualization of any hypothesis proceeds and the empirical evaluation of it is undertaken, one's idea of it inevitably changes. The simplified, general hypothesis may be seen to be a compound of several more detailed hypotheses. Not all of the latter can be evaluated at once, but ultimately they should be. No specialist is satisfied until they are. General theory is never enough for him, and it should not be. (But special theories are not enough either—they require integration.) When several of the hypotheses have been subjected to careful logical and empirical evaluation, it will probably be seen that the various aspects of living systems they deal with intersect or overlap. In this chapter I point out repeatedly that certain of the hypotheses are logically interrelated. From overlapping hypotheses a hypothetico-deductive system can be developed, the derived theorems, of course, also requiring empirical evaluation. And level, type, and individual differences need to be taken into account. All this involves an ever deepening interaction of theory and experiment. Thus a network of general theory can be woven concerning life's complex phenomena.

The following hypotheses are organized and numbered by the same procedure, distinguishing the various subsystems processing matter-energy and information and separating structure and process, which I employ in Chap. 3 and Chaps. 6 through 12. The origin of all the hypotheses which I did not develop is indicated in the text or notes. They are stated in general form because they appear to be generally true of systems at two or more levels. It must be remembered, however, that when they are applied to a specific system, allowance must be made for the disanalogies among systems. The variables involved show regular changes with level and type of system, and from one individual system of the same level and type to another.

The hypotheses

(A good many representative cross-level hypotheses are presented briefly below. Each is worth consideration for its own sake. My personal confidence that a given proposition could be shown to be true and relevant to two or more levels is indicated by a letter in parentheses after each hypotheses, as follows: (H) means it is high; (M) means medium; and (L) means low. Casual readers, stunned by the large number, may wish to read a few to sample their flavor and then pass on to the last section of the chapter, beginning on page 110, where outlines for cross-level research designs are sketched in more detail for five selected hypotheses. They can then go on to Chap. 5, which analyzes in detail research on a cluster of five interrelated hypotheses.)

1. Structure

HYPOTHESIS 1-1: *In general, the more components a system has, the more echelons it has.* (M)

This principle was suggested by Berelson and Steiner, who consider it to be true of organizations like universities, armies, or corporations.[10] All levels of living systems do not have echelons; for instance, groups do not, by definition. (If groups grow large enough they develop multiple echelons and that makes them organizations.)

HYPOTHESIS 1-2: *In general, the more structurally different types of members or components a system has, the more segregation of functions there is.* (M)

A similar, but not identical, proposition about societies is stated by Berelson and Steiner.[11] I suggest that it may apply to all levels.

2. Process

HYPOTHESIS 2-1: *System components incapable of associating, or lacking experience which has formed such associations, must function according to rigid programming or highly standardized operating rules. It follows that as turnover of components rises above the rate at which the components can develop the associations necessary for operation, rigidity of programming increases.* (H)

This hypothesis, stated by Mishler after a study of a mental hospital, may well apply at all levels.[12] Certainly armies, youth hostels, and conferences, which have rapid turnover of personnel, tend to have rigid operating rules.

HYPOTHESIS 2-2: *The more rapid reassignment of function from one component to another a long-surviving system has, the more likely are the components to be totipotential rather than partipotential.* (M)

The United States Army, like other military organizations, must face the risks in combat of rapid personnel turnover and reassignment of functions. As a result, training and selection for the army emphasize general competence rather than specific skills, so that soldiers will be totipotential, able to take over any task, if need be, as Levy has found.[13] In any system with rapid turnover this is likely to be so.

HYPOTHESIS 2-3: *The more isolated a system is, the more totipotential it must be.* (H)

Isolated cells must be totipotential or they will not survive; only cells in organisms, where they are close to other cells, can be partipotential. Organs are never totipotential, and they are never isolated for long, though some mesozoans which are like organs live independently (see page 436). An isolated group (like astronauts in a space vehicle) or an isolated organization (like the base camp at the South Pole) must be totipotential to survive. This principle seems applicable at all levels.

HYPOTHESIS 2-4: *A system's processes are affected more by its suprasystem than by its suprasuprasystem or above, and by its subsystems than by its subsubsystems or below.* (L)

More aspects of a man's behavior are influenced by his family than by the neighbors in his apartment house or the other citizens of his city. The healthiness of a person's life depends upon the liver as a whole more than it does upon any single liver cell. Comparable examples can be found for systems at other levels besides that of the organism.

3. Subsystems

3.1 Subsystems which process both matter-energy and information
3.1.2 Boundary
3.1.2.2 Process

Matter-energy boundary. HYPOTHESIS 3.1.2.2-1: *When the boundary (except those portions containing the openings for the ingestor or the extruder) of one living system, A, is crossed by another, smaller living or nonliving system, B, of significant size, i.e., no smaller than the subsystems or subcomponents of A, more work must be expended than when B is transmitted over the same distance in space immediately inside or outside the boundary of A.* (L)

An important function of boundary processes is fending off matter-energy excess stresses. These are potentially harmful to a system only if they are of a certain size—the size of subsystems or subsubsystems. If they are smaller than that, they are often allowed to pass freely through boundaries. More work is required to rupture a cell membrane with a wire than to move that instrument in the surrounding tissue fluid or in the cell's cytoplasm. Similarly, more work is needed to rip the capsule of a spleen or a liver with a probe than to pass it through the areas surrounding them or through their internal portions. The same can be said of a knife entering the skin, hide, or exoskeleton of an organism as compared to moving through the outside air or the subcutaneous tissues. Most groups appear to have few regions of their boundaries which are not potential ingestors or extruders, except perhaps the actual bodies of the members at the periphery. Many groups, however, especially totipotential ones, protect themselves from external stresses by making a continuous protective boundary of their bodies or of artifacts, *e.g.*, the "carapace" of a phalanx, the tent or house of a family. This proposition obviously applies to such groups. Organizations are much like groups in the ways they reject potentially harmful inputs at their boundaries. It takes work for an enemy patrol to cross an army's perimeter. A similar situation prevails for true supranational systems. The Iron Curtain was hard to cross by force.

This hypothesis is in some ways comparable to the information processing Hypothesis 3.1.2.2-2 below.

Information boundary. HYPOTHESIS 3.1.2.2-2: *More work must be expended in moving the marker bearing an information transmission over the boundary of a system at the input transducer than in making such a transmission over the same distance in the suprasystem immediately outside the boundary or in the system immediately inside it.* (L)

This hypothesis has some similarities to Hypothesis 3.1.2.2-1 above, because in transmitting information across a boundary, the marker bearing it—which is a unit of matter-energy—must be transmitted. Neurons have thresholds and do not receive information inputs that have less than a certain energy intensity. The same is true of organ and organism input transducers. Since groups and larger social systems must receive information from one or more organisms, the proposition clearly applies to them also.

HYPOTHESIS 3.1.2.2-3: *The amount of information transmitted between points within a system is significantly larger than the amount transmitted across its boundary.* (M)

If we assume that domestic and foreign letters on the average contain a similar number of bits of information, there is evidence relevant to this hypothesis at the level of the society. The ratio of domestic to foreign letters for the United States, according to Deutsch, varied from a low of 21.7 in 1913 to a high of 86.39 in 1938.[14] In modern times, for all countries, it has varied between about 3 and 87, always significantly more than 1. For American cities in 1949 and 1952 Deutsch discovered that the situation was much different. The ratio of local to national mail for the largest 20 cities in the country varied between 0.49 and 1.44. These data would not at first view appear to support the hypothesis, but second thought makes it obvious that the majority of local communication is by word of mouth, face-to-face, or on the telephone. Thus only a small fraction of local communication is carried on by mail, while the opposite is true for the bulk of national communication.

It is reasonable to expect that empirical researchers at other levels of systems would confirm this hypothesis.

HYPOTHESIS 3.1.2.2-4: *The larger a system is and the more components it has, the larger is the ratio of the amount of information transmitted between points within the system to the amount of information transmitted across its boundary.* (M)

At the society level, the above ratio, in units of domestic and foreign letters mailed, increases as the geographical area and the population of nations grow.[15] Probably the hypothesis holds for other levels of living systems as well.

3.2 Subsystems which process matter-energy

HYPOTHESIS 3.2-1: *An optimal mean temperature at which process is most efficient is maintained by a living system.*[16] (L)

For human beings this temperature is the well-known 98.6°F or 37°C, maintained by negative feedback controls. For societies it is an average outdoor temperature of 10° to 16°C, as Huntington concluded.[17] The need for achievement revealed in folktales of various preliterate cultures was measured by McClelland, who found scores of 0.04 for societies living at average temperatures below 4°C, rising to a high of 0.17 at 10°C, falling to 0.06 at about 21°C and to a low of 0.02 at 27°C.[18] The adjustment processes used by societies to maintain temperature stability differ from those used by organisms. They may migrate to avoid extremes of temperature or take various remedial actions to moderate the climates of their environments. This hypothesis applies to at least some types of cells, organs, groups, and organizations.

3.2.2 Distributor

3.2.2.1 Structure   HYPOTHESIS 3.2.2.1-1: *The hierarchical structure of the distributor is arranged so that there is a geometrical progression from the size of the region of the total system served by an average unit of its lowest echelon to the size of the region served by an average unit of its highest echelon.* (M)

This proposition has been studied in reference to river basins, lung and liver vasculature, and market regions surrounding towns by Waldenberg and others.[19]

3.2.2.2 Process   HYPOTHESIS 3.2.2.2-1: *The farther a specific matter-energy transmission passes along a distributor from the point of its input to it and toward the final point of its output from it, the more it is altered by lowering the concentration of the kinds of matter-energy it contains which are used by the system's subsystems and by increasing the concentration of the products or wastes produced by it and output by those subsystems.* (H)

In cells, glucose, among other substances, enters the distributor and lactic acid leaves it. In organisms, food, vitamins, minerals, and water enter the distributor, and excretions leave it. In societies, food, live animals, persons, raw materials, and energy enter the distributor; and wastes, the dead, and lesser amounts of energy leave it. Other levels show similar phenomena. Of course the rates of alteration of some sorts of matter-energy are much faster than others. This matter-energy processing hypothesis is to some extent comparable to information processing Hypothesis 3.3.3.2-2 (see page 96).

HYPOTHESIS 3.2.2.2-2: *In general, total entropy per unit cubic contents increases progressively along a distributor between the points of input and output.* (L)

The rates of increase in entropy differ among various sorts of matter-energy. This matter-energy processing hypothesis is in some ways comparable to information processing Hypothesis 3.3.3.2-3 (see pages 96 and 110).

3.2.5 Matter-energy storage

3.2.5.2 Process   HYPOTHESIS 3.2.5.2-1: *If process A applied to any form of matter-energy always precedes process B (as, for example, converting precedes producing), variations imposed on the rate of process B by variations in the rate of process A can be decreased by storing a supply (or "buffer inventory") of the outputs from process A between the components which carry out the two processes.* (H)

March and Simon maintain this statement to be true of organizations like firms.[20] It appears to me likely to be applicable in general to all system levels. Queuing theory mathematics (see pages 620 and 621) can be applied to such situations in order to determine the size of an adequate buffer inventory for any set of variations in process A and in process B.

3.3   Subsystems which process information

HYPOTHESIS 3.3-1: *Up to a maximum higher than yet obtained in any living system but less than 100 percent, the larger the percentage of all matter-energy input that it consumes in information processing controlling its various system processes, as opposed to matter-energy processing, the more likely the system is to survive.* (M)

Whether more complex species (*i.e.*, those higher in the evolutionary scale) devote a higher percentage of their total cell mass to information processing than do lower species (*e.g.*, the brains of foraging predators are larger than those of sedentary animals in comparison with the rest of their bodies) has been debated by Best and Marschak.[21] No one yet has discovered a species which failed to survive because too large a percentage of its body was neural tissue. It seems likely to me that this hypothesis is generally true at all levels. Certainly advanced societies are devoting a continually higher percentage of their matter-energy to the various communications media and other forms of information processing—vastly more than primitive societies do. This is also true of most organizations in advanced societies.

3.3.1 Input transducer

3.3.1.2 Process   HYPOTHESIS 3.3.1.2-1: *The intensity output signal of an input transducer varies as a power function of the intensity of its input, the form of the power function being* $\Psi = k(\Phi - \Phi_0)^n$, *where* Ψ *is the intensity of the output signal,* Φ *is the physical magnitude of the input energies,* Φ_0 *is a constant, the physical magnitude of the minimum detectable or threshold input energies, k depends on the choice of measurement units, and the exponent n varies with different modalities of the transducer.* (M)

In an explicit effort to find whether this hypothesis, known as the Weber function, applies to a certain class of receptor cells, Mountcastle carried out a neurophysiological experiment (see page 283).[22] He investigated the "touch-spot" input transducers in the hairy skin of cats and monkeys. He created inputs to them with an apparatus which precisely controlled their timing as well as the amount of indentation of these domelike elevations of the skin. They contain unmyelinated afferent fibers which are exquisitely sensitive to mechanical forces. He compared the pulses that resulted from such inputs on single nerve fibers coming from these receptors which were isolated by dissections of the saphenous nerve in both cats and monkeys. These pulses quickly reach a remarkably steady state of regular periodic discharge. He found that the input–output relationship is accurately described by a power function like that stated in the above hypothesis, a function quite similar in form and constants to that which has been obtained in recent years from psychophysical experiments at the organism level by Stevens and others.[23] In touch as well as in other modalities of information input, this power function has been experimentally confirmed with different constants for different modalities (see pages 283, 381, 383, 384, 385, and 387). Mountcastle interprets his findings to suggest that the input–output transfer function of the input transducer neural cell for intensity may well determine the comparable transfer function of the total organism.[24] This means that the sum of the transformations of the signal from the neural cell as it passes through successive higher echelons does not significantly alter that signal.

The above hypothesis may well apply to informational input–output relationships at other levels of living systems besides the cell and the organism.

HYPOTHESIS 3.3.1.2-2: *Living systems divide the intensities of information inputs into about seven categories, plus or minus two.*

By his precise measurements of the extent of indentations of "touch spots" on the skins of cats and monkeys and concomitant readings of the rates of resultant pulse discharges on individual fibers in the saphenous nerve leading from these individual input transducers, Mountcastle found that the maximum information which can be transmitted in such a cell for each information input is about 2.5 bits, the amount of information that results from distinguishing seven or eight categories in the information input (see page 127).[25] This finding at the cellular level is similar to "the magical number 7," which George Miller contended is about the maximum number of categories into which the intensity of a single information input can be divided by a human subject.[26] This latter view is supported by the findings of a number of investigators doing psychophysical research at the organism level in several different sensory modalities. Further experimentation might indicate that this hypothesis applies to levels of living systems other than the cell and the organism.

3.3.3 Channel and net

3.3.3.1 Structure   HYPOTHESIS 3.3.3.1-1: *The structures of the communication networks of living systems at various levels are so comparable that they can be described by similar mathematical models of nonrandom nets.* (L)

One example of such a model is the following, proposed by Rapoport:[27]

$$P_{t+1} = (1 - x) \left[1 - \exp \left| - ap_t \left[1 - \frac{\pi' + \sigma'}{a(1 - x)} \right] \right| \right]$$

$$\pi' = \pi[1 + (a - 1)(p_t + p_{t-1})]$$

$$\sigma' = \sigma[1 + (a^2 - a - 1)x]$$

where

P_t = the number of components in the net contacted through the net by an arbitrary number of new components selected as starting points (P_o) on the tth remove

p_t = the fraction of the total population of components in the net represented by P_t

π = the probability of complete reciprocity, that is, the probability that if a given component contacts another, the second will also contact the first

σ = the probability of partial reciprocity, that is, the probability that if a given component contacts two others, one of those latter two components will contact the other

a = the average number of components contacted by each prior component in the net

At first Rapoport interested himself in making mathematical models taking into account the sorts of biases which lead neural nets, like those in the brain, to depart from random nets. These include a "geographical distance bias," the influence of their relative positions in physical space upon the probability that one component will contact another; a reciprocity bias, the probability that if one component contacts another, the other will also contact the first; and a popularity or "field force" bias, the probability that one component will be more "attractive" than another and consequently be contacted more frequently.

Together with Horvath, Foster, and Orwant, Rapoport applied such probability equations to predict with reasonable accuracy certain aspects of the sociogram representing the friendship network in organizations (elementary and junior high schools).[28] Comparable empirical studies of diffusions of information in larger social units, specifically towns, were made by Dodd.[29] He never applied a mathematical model like the one above to his data, though it clearly would be applicable. Though Rapoport first began his work in this area by considering the structure of the neural network, relevant data have never been collected at the organ level. Impulses passing along the neural nets of sea pansies, which are discoid coelenterates, produce a luminescent glow. Consequently it might be feasible to test this hypothesis at the organism level by tracing the passage of signals through sea-pansy neural nets by sensitive, high-speed motion picture photography.

It has also been suggested that similar models can describe the structure of the distribution network in societies through which the matter-energy passes that produces the spread of epidemics.

3.3.3.2 Process   HYPOTHESIS 3.3.3.2-1: *In all channels* $c = w \log_2 (1 + P/N)$. *That is, the maximum capacity (in bits per s) of a channel is equal to its bandwidth times the logarithm of (1 plus the ratio of the power of the signal to the power of the white Gaussian noise in the channel).* (L)

This theorem is one of the mathematical statements about communication which were set forth and proved by Shannon.[30] He applied the theorem to information transmission in nonliving channels. I find it interesting to speculate that experiments may show that it holds also for channels at all levels of living systems, that when data are collected, their channel capacities will be found to be as the theorem indicates. I hypothesize that the mathematical meaning of "channel" and the meaning of "channel" in concrete living systems are isomorphic, so that the above proposition applies to the channels of living systems.

HYPOTHESIS 3.3.3.2-2: *There is always a constant systematic distortion between input and output of information in a channel.* (H)

HYPOTHESIS 3.3.3.2-3: *In a channel there is always a progressive degradation of information and decrease in negative entropy or increase in noise or entropy. The output information per unit time is always less than it was at the input.* (H)

A sketch for a possible cross-level research on this hypothesis appears later in this chapter (see page 110).

HYPOTHESIS 3.3.3.2-4: *A system never completely compensates for the distortion in information flow in its channels.* (L)

Berelson and Steiner assert as an established proposition that "People typically do not appreciate how prejudiced they in fact are."[31] They support this observation with findings that people who are by objective test more prejudiced than the average tend to believe they are only average or less than average in prejudice.[32] Those who are objectively less prejudiced overwhelmingly (perhaps too much so) believe they lack prejudice. This principle is stated in the hypothesis above, in a way that can apply to all levels of systems. It is likely to have cross-level validity.

HYPOTHESIS 3.3.3.2-5: *Strains, errors, and distortions increase in a system as the number of channels over which information transmission is blocked increases.* (M)

HYPOTHESIS 3.3.3.2-6: *A system tends to distort information in a direction to make it more likely to elicit rewards or less likely to elicit punishments to itself.* (L)

This hypothesis was suggested by Berelson and Steiner's discussion of rumor spread.[33] It may apply at several or all levels.

HYPOTHESIS 3.3.3.2-7: *The farther away along channels a component is from a process, or the more components there are between them, the more error there is in its information about that process.* (L)

This hypothesis was suggested by Berelson and Steiner.[34] It may apply at all levels (see page 111).

See also related Hypotheses 3.3.3.2-2, 3.3.3.2-3, 3.3.3.2-11, and 5.4.3-6 (this page and pages 97 and 109).

HYPOTHESIS 3.3.3.2-8: *In general the farther components of a system are from one another and the longer the channels between them are, the less is the rate of information flow among them.* (M)

In housing projects neighbors talk to each other more than they do to people living farther away.[35] This hypothesis, Berelson and Steiner said, is a general principle for groups.[36] I suggest that it may be true at the group level of living systems and above. One constraint on the principle is that there is often much essential information flow among components of a dispersed subsystem even though they are far apart. Their common function must be coordinated by communication.

HYPOTHESIS 3.3.3.2-9: *Use of multiple parallel channels to carry identical information, which farther along in the net can be compared for accuracy, is commoner in more essential components of a system than in less essential ones.* (L)

This hypothesis is related to von Neumann's principle of how reliable circuits can be made from unreliable components (see Hypothesis 3.3.4.2-7, page 98). Parallel channels carrying identical information are required. Living systems may well afford the cost of such duplication when it is vital that the communication be accurate.

The following two hypotheses come from disaster research (see pages 704 to 708). They seem to be supported by observations or data at the society level and may also apply across levels of living systems.

HYPOTHESIS 3.3.3.2-10: *The probability of breakdown of adjustment processes among subsystems of a system decreases as the number of parallel information channels serving it increases.* (M)

For example, in a disaster the ordinary processes of community integration are more likely to continue if there are many functioning channels (*e.g.,* police, fire, ambulance, taxi, ham radio communication systems) capable of transmitting official messages than if there are few. This hypothesis is closely related to Hypothesis 3.3.3.2-9 above and to Hypothesis 3.3.4.2-7 (see page 98).

HYPOTHESIS 3.3.3.2-11: *The probability of error in or overload of an information channel is a monotonic increasing function of the number of components in it.* (H)

Work groups which arranged their members so that there were a minimum number of channels between them performed their tasks best, Roby and Lanzetta found.[37] Our research on information overload suggests this is a general cross-level principle (see pages 169 to 195 and also related Hypotheses 3.3.3.2-2, 3.3.3.2-3, 3.3.3.2-7, and 5.4.3-6 on pages 96 and 109).

HYPOTHESIS 3.3.3.2-12: *Two-way channels which permit feedback improve performance by facilitating processes that reduce error.*[38] (M)

A design for a cross-level research on this hypothesis is outlined later in this chapter (see page 111).

Numerous propositions based on observations of organizations, particularly industrial organizations, have been stated by March and Simon.[39] Some of these propositions, it seems to me, could reasonably also apply to systems at other levels. Five of these propositions, suggested by March and Simon, are listed below:

HYPOTHESIS 3.3.3.2-13: *The greater the channeling of information processing, limiting the number of components to which a given item of information goes, the more do components of a system differ in how they decode and decide.*[40] (L)

HYPOTHESIS 3.3.3.2-14: *If components of a system are closely connected spatially, have similar functions, or are made up of similar units, they are more alike in decoding and deciding than if they are remote or unlike. That is because interaction among units (for whatever reasons) tends to increase sharing of information.*[41] (L)

It follows that the components of a highly decentralized system will differ more in decoding and deciding than the components of a more centralized one.

HYPOTHESIS 3.3.3.2-15: *The functional segregation of components means that each one receives some information which the others do not. The greater this segregation of information, the more do the components differ in decoding and deciding.*[42] (L)

Salesmen live in an environment of customers; company treasurers, in an environment of bankers—each sees a quite distinct part of the world.[43]

HYPOTHESIS 3.3.3.2-16: *The less decoding and encoding a channel requires, the more it is used.* (L)

As March and Simon say: "The possession by two persons, or two organization units, of a common, efficient language facilitates communication. Thus, links between members of a common profession tend to be used in the communication system. Similarly, other determinants of language compatibility—ethnic

background, education, age, experience—will affect what channels are used in the organization."[44] Comparable phenomena seem probable at other levels. It is particularly obvious at the supranational level.[45]

HYPOTHESIS 3.3.3.2-17: *When a channel has conveyed one signal or message, its use to convey others is more probable.*[46] (L)

Channel usage, that is, is self-reinforcing.

HYPOTHESIS 3.3.3.2-18: *Some information inputs of energic intensity above the threshold of an input transducer can affect behavior mediated by lower echelons of the system without affecting higher echelons.* (M)

There is convincing evidence that people may have subliminal perception.[47] I suggest that phenomena like those described in the above hypothesis could occur at all levels.

HYPOTHESIS 3.3.3.2-19: *The information input with the greatest intensity or greatest signal-to-noise ratio is given priority processing, i.e., attention.*[48] (L)

HYPOTHESIS 3.3.3.2-20: *A system gives priority processing to information which will relieve a strain (i.e., which it "needs"), neglecting neutral information. It positively rejects information which will increase a strain.*[49] (M)

On the basis of extensive evidence, Berelson and Steiner conclude that each of us sees or perceives things that he wants or enjoys and neglects inputs that he dislikes or that he gets gratifications from not seeing.[50] Indeed, the pupil of the eye seems to dilate when a person is looking at pleasant or interesting things as compared to neutral ones.[51] Certainly some nonliving systems do not show such biases, but several or all levels of living systems may.

HYPOTHESIS 3.3.3.2-21: *In periods of stress and/or change in a system, the amount of information processing relevant to both task performance and adjustments among subsystems increases.*[52] (M)

3.3.4 Decoder

3.3.4.2 Process   In recent years much work has been devoted by Shannon and many others to mathematical proofs of theorems relating to the processes of decoding and encoding.[53] These theorems deal with such aspects of these processes as the following: How closely different sorts of codes approach the maximal possible number of bits per symbol, so that the information actually transmitted need fall only a little short of the channel capacity. What methods of coding are efficient. Or how one can reduce or correct errors of transmission in noisy channels. Such theorems, as Ashby has noted, can be applied very generally to any control process correcting any deviation from a goal.[54] They put upper limits on what such control processes can accomplish. I speculate that the next seven hypotheses, suggested by this body of work, may apply generally to all decoding processes in living systems.

HYPOTHESIS 3.3.4.2-1: *As a system matures, it uses increasingly efficient codes, e.g., codes which require fewer binary digits or equivalent signals per input signal. These codes approach but never actually reach the theoretical minimum number of symbols required to transmit the information. Efficient codes also have the following characteristics:*

(a) Simple symbols are used for the most frequent messages and more complex ones for the less frequent ones.

(b) The symbols are selected to minimize confusion among them.

(c) The symbols are chunked in long rather than short blocks.

(d) Limitations on the transmitter of the signal are taken into account. For example, if it transmits highly redundant signals, each one is not coded, but some of the redundancy is removed.

(e) Limitations on the receiver are taken into account. For example, distinctions to which the receiver cannot react are neglected. (L)

These principles have been worked out for nonliving systems by Shannon,[55] Fano,[56] Huffman,[57] Pierce,[58] and others. I find it interesting to speculate that they probably apply to decoding carried out by living systems.

HYPOTHESIS 3.3.4.2-2: *If a transmitter of information is putting out information coded to have H bits per symbol, and a noiseless channel has a capacity (bits per s) of C, then the channel cannot transmit at a rate faster than C/H symbols per s, though it is possible to encode the message so as to transmit at a rate of $C/H - \epsilon$ symbols per s, where ϵ is a positive fraction less than one and usually small, of C.* (L)

This hypothesis is suggested by one of Shannon's basic theorems.[59] It may well apply approximately to all relatively noiseless channels in living systems. In Hypotheses 3.3.4.2-3 and 3.3.4.2-5 I indicate that maturation and association in living systems may decrease the size of ϵ.

HYPOTHESIS 3.3.4.2-3: *The quantity ϵ (see Hypothesis 3.3.4.2-2) decreases as a system matures and associates, gaining practice in coding information.* (L)

That is, the efficiency of coding increases as a system matures and associates, learns, or gains practice. This may be true only of the more complex or higher-level systems.

HYPOTHESIS 3.3.4.2-4: *If a transmitter with an information transmission rate (in bits per s) of R is transmitting over a noisy channel—and all living channels are noisy—with a capacity (in bits per s) of C, and if R is less than C, there is a code which can make the transmission almost free of errors; and as the system matures and associates, gaining practice, it gradually approaches such transmission.* (L)

Another of Shannon's basic theorems suggests this hypothesis.[60] I speculate that research might show that it applies at all levels of living systems.

HYPOTHESIS 3.3.4.2-5: *If a transmitter with an information transmission rate (in bits per s) of R is transmitting over a noisy channel with a capacity (in bits per s) of C, and if R is greater than C, there is no way to encode the message so that the equivocation is less than R − C, but there is a way to encode it so that the equivocation is R − C + ϵ, where ϵ is a positive fraction, less than one and usually small, of C. Moreover, as a system matures and gains practice, it encodes in ways so as to decrease the size of ϵ.* (L)

Another part of Shannon's theorem mentioned under the previous hypothesis suggests this.[61] I speculate that this hypothesis applies to all living systems.

HYPOTHESIS 3.3.4.2-6: *As the noise in a channel increases, a system encodes with increasing redundancy in order to reduce error in the transmission.*[62] (M)

The inverse is also probably true—that as noise decreases redundancy decreases.[63]

HYPOTHESIS 3.3.4.2-7: *If messages are so coded that they are transmitted twice, errors can be detected by comparing every part of the first message with every part of the second, but which of the two alternative transmissions is correct cannot be determined. If they are transmitted three times, they can be both detected and corrected, by accepting the alternative on which two of the three transmissions agree.* (M)

This hypothesis, suggested by Pierce, is a special case of how redundancy can be used to adjust to error (see Hypothesis 3.3.4.2-6).[64] The principle involved is essentially von Neumann's principle of how to make reliable circuits from unreliable components (see Hypotheses 3.3.3.2-9 and 3.3.3.2-10, page 96), except that von Neumann dealt with simultaneous transmissions on multiple parallel channels rather than multiple transmissions sequentially on one. In the latter case errors characteristic of the channel commonly recur.

An outline of a possible cross-level research on this hypothesis appears later in this chapter (see pages 111 and 112).

HYPOTHESIS 3.3.4.2-8: *Over time a system tends to decrease the amount of recoding necessary within it, by developing more and more common systemwide codes.*[65] (L)

Hypothesis 3.3.3.2-16 (see page 97) points out that the less decoding and encoding a channel requires, the more it is used. This probably explains why living systems seem to act as described above. For instance, societies tend to move away from local languages and money and in the direction of a common language and use of a single form of legal tender. Functional segregation of subsystems, as it increases, operates in the opposite direction from this principle and might counteract it (see Hypothesis 3.3.3.2-15, page 97).

HYPOTHESIS 3.3.4.2-9: *As the amount of information in an input decreases (i.e., as it becomes more ambiguous), the input will more and more tend to be interpreted (or decoded) as required to reduce strains within the system.* (L)

HYPOTHESIS 3.3.4.2-10: *As the strength of a strain increases, information inputs will more and more be interpreted (or decoded) as required to reduce the strain.* (L)

The above two hypotheses, suggested by Berelson and Steiner, are supported by numerous researches at the organism level on selective perception and "perceptual defense"—people interpret their experience of the world in ways which satisfy their needs or reflect their biases.[66] For example, hungry subjects see in vague pictures more food objects than do those who have eaten recently.[67] Similar phenomena may well occur at other system levels, particularly those above the organism.

3.3.5 Associator

3.3.5.2 Process   HYPOTHESIS 3.3.5.2-1: *When a new information input B is associated, usually more than once, with a familiar one A that elicits a certain output, B sooner or later becomes capable of eliciting the same output as A.*[68] (L)

At the organism level this is Pavlov's classical conditioning or classical associative learning. Does a similar process occur at other levels? Perhaps cells associate in this way. The evidence for organs is slim. Groups, organizations, societies, and supranational systems sometimes alter their procedures in a comparable way, often very slowly.

HYPOTHESIS 3.3.5.2-2: *A system associates a given strain within it with actions which relieve it, so that such a strain comes to elicit the motor acts.* (L)

This is instrumental or operant, as opposed to classical, conditioning or association (see pages 407 and 408). It occurs in organisms.[69] Does it occur at other levels? If so, in what ways is it like and unlike comparable organismic processes?

HYPOTHESIS 3.3.5.2-3: *A system does not form associations without (a) feedback as to whether the new output relieves strains or solves problems and (b) reinforcement, i.e., strain reduction by the output.* (L)

HYPOTHESIS 3.3.5.2-4: *Associations established early in the life of a system are more permanent than those established later.*[70] (L)

Freudian doctrine holds that infantile experiences are of paramount influence, significantly greater than later experiences. Early imprinting of some birds and other animals is dominant over later experiences. Certainly the procedures and established behaviors adopted by groups early in their history are dispro-

portionately influential. Tradition and custom are extraordinarily difficult to alter in societies.

Whether this principle applies to other levels is unclear.

HYPOTHESIS 3.3.5.2-5: *In associating, there is an optimal ratio of correct trials to error trials, depending on the probability that specific signals will regularly coincide in the system's environment. In most experimental environments and all natural environments this probability is less than 1, and if association were to occur with too few error trials, a system could not properly allow for probable future variations in the appearance of signals. Since the probability of the signals regularly coinciding also is nearly always greater than 0, if association occurs with too many error trials, the system cannot profit soon enough from past inputs.* (L)

The optimum learning rate for a system, then, is somewhere between no learning and one-trial learning, the exact rate being a function of the average probability of association of any two environmental signals.

HYPOTHESIS 3.3.5.2-6: *In general, association is slower the higher the level of the system.* (M)

One reason for this may be that the feedback required for associating (see Hypothesis 3.3.5.2-3, above) is slower at the higher levels because the feedback channels are longer and more subject to error (see Hypothesis 3.3.3.2-7, page 96).

3.3.6 Memory

3.3.6.2 Process   HYPOTHESIS 3.3.6.2-1: *The longer information is stored in memory, the harder it is to recall, and the less likely it is to be correct; but the rate of loss is not regular over time.*[71] (M)

HYPOTHESIS 3.3.6.2-2: *Information stored in the memory of a living system increasingly over time undergoes regular changes—e.g., omissions, errors, or additions of noise, and distortions—resulting from processes of selection, reorganization with other stored information, interpretation, and entropic decay of organization.*[72] (M)

In individual human subjects research has shown that, over time, details, especially if meaningless and incongruous, tend to be eliminated from the stored information in memory, or they may come to be recalled erroneously. If a subject is told to expect a certain sort of information input, his later memory of it will be distorted by that expectation. Attitudes and social stereotypes of the subjects also bias memories. Omission and error adjustment processes and distortion have been defined previously (see page 61).

Evidence at other levels is scanty or lacking, but it is conceivable that similar alterations in memory occur.

HYPOTHESIS 3.3.6.2-3: *The removal from a system of information representing experience stored in the memory (as distinguished from the information constituting its template, whose removal is often fundamentally damaging or lethal) predictably alters stochastic measures of the system's subsequent behavior, and the degree of these changes increases as the amount removed is increased.* (M)

A cross-level research design to evaluate this hypothesis is outlined in this chapter (see pages 112 and 113).

HYPOTHESIS 3.3.6.2-4: *The higher the level of a system, the less are its decider's activities determined by the information of the system's template and the more are they determined by the information of experience stored in its memory.*[73] (L)

This appears to be a regular cross-level difference.

HYPOTHESIS 3.3.6.2-5: *The higher the echelon of a multiechelon system, the less are its activities determined by the information of the system's template and the more are they determined by the information of experience stored in its memory.*[74] (L)

This appears to be true of the organism, organization, society, and supranational levels at least, and perhaps of others.

HYPOTHESIS 3.3.6.2-6: *The higher the level of a system, in general the more complex are its memory storage and search rules, but also the more efficient they are in terms of energy costs per bit of information.* (L)

3.3.7 Decider

3.3.7.2 Process   HYPOTHESIS 3.3.7.2-1: *Every adaptive decision is made in four stages: (a) establishing the purpose or goal whose achievement is to be advanced by the decision, (b) analyzing the information relevant to the decision, (c) synthesizing a solution selecting the alternative action or actions most likely to lead to the purpose or goal, and (d) implementing the decision by issuing a command signal to carry out the action or actions.* (L)

This seems more likely to be true at the organism level and above than at the cell and organ levels.

HYPOTHESIS 3.3.7.2-2: *In systems which survive, the component with the most relevant information available to its decider is the one most likely to exercise power over or elicit compliance from other components in the system.*[75] (M)

For instance, some researches have shown that, in small groups, the member who receives the most information is most likely to be chosen leader (see page 535).[76]

This hypothesis relates closely to Hypotheses 5.4.3-5 and 5.4.3-6 (see page 109).

HYPOTHESIS 3.3.7.2-3: *The fewer the transmitters of information relevant to a decision, the greater is the probability that each will affect the decision.* (H)

According to Snyder and Paige, who suggested this hypothesis, it may be true of major national decisions.[77] It seems also to be generally applicable across levels.

HYPOTHESIS 3.3.7.2-4: *The signature identifying the transmitter of any message is an important determinant of the probability of the receiver complying with it.* (M)

In the rare neurological disturbance, anisognosia, the patient has a paralyzed limb, but when he tries to move it, a message which tells him that it *is* moving passes through his brain; and this message is more convincing to him than visual messages from his eyes and proprioceptive messages from his limb that tell him it is *not* moving. So he decides and insists that he is moving it, even though his senses tell him otherwise. The signature related to the internal message makes it more convincing than the sensory messages. This may well be an illustration of the above hypothesis at the organism level. The hypothesis also describes a well-recognized interpersonal and social phenomenon.[78]

HYPOTHESIS 3.3.7.2-5: *The longer the time during which a system has made decisions of a certain sort, the less time each decision takes, up to a limit.*[79] (L)

Decision times decrease with training. Experienced executives usually make decisions faster than neophytes. In a number of nations the average duration of strikes to decide labor—management disputes has diminished markedly over the years.[80] The principle may well apply at other levels. It may be closely related to those stated in Hypotheses 3.3.3.2-16, 3.3.4.2-3, and 3.3.4.2-8 (see pages 97 and 98).

HYPOTHESIS 3.3.7.2-6: *The shorter the decision period, the less thorough in general is the search within the information processing network for relevant facts and alternative solutions.* (M)

This hypothesis was suggested by Snyder and Paige, who maintain that it may be true of major national decisions, like President Truman's decision to take military action in Korea.[81] It also appears reasonable at all levels of systems. It follows from this hypothesis that after brief searches it is less likely that the best solution will be found than after longer ones, and also that the more readily available information in the network is more likely to influence the decision than that which is less available.

HYPOTHESIS 3.3.7.2-7: *A subsystem or component which makes decisions taking into consideration new information on the average gets it from transmitters in closer contact with the origin of the new information than a subsystem or component which uses such new information later.*[82] (M)

An example of this principle is seen in the adoption of inventions, fashions, and other innovations in society. Are there examples at other levels?

HYPOTHESIS 3.3.7.2-8: *The more bits of information there are in a new message of input information, the more slowly it affects the decisions of subsystems or components.*[83] (L)

HYPOTHESIS 3.3.7.2-9: *A system which decides to take novel action soon after the state of its environment reaches the point at which such action is possible, does so on a smaller scale than does one which decides later.*[84] (L)

HYPOTHESIS 3.3.7.2-10: *Initial decisions are more likely than later ones to favor a course of action that does not rule out subsequent alternatives.* (M)

This hypothesis, suggested by Snyder and Paige as a general proposition relative to national decisions, is probably applicable to decisions at all levels of systems.[85]

HYPOTHESIS 3.3.7.2-11: *The longer a decider exists, the more likely it is to resist change.*[86] (L)

HYPOTHESIS 3.3.7.2-12: *A decision about an information input is not made absolutely but with respect to some other information which constitutes a frame of reference with which it can be compared.*[87] (H)

Neural response to a new input is based on how much it is a change from the previous input. A person judges weights by comparison with previously lifted weights. Groups judge the personal characteristics of members of other groups by the norms of their own groups.

HYPOTHESIS 3.3.7.2-13: *Decisions overtly altering major values of a system are finalized only at the highest echelon.*[88] (L)

HYPOTHESIS 3.3.7.2-14: *A system which survives generally decides to employ the least costly adjustment to a threat or a strain produced by a stress first and increasingly more costly ones later.* (M)

An outline for a research design on this hypothesis is presented later in this chapter (see pages 113 and 114).

HYPOTHESIS 3.3.7.2-15: *A system that survives generally decides to use first the adjustment processes which can be most immediately applied to relieve a threat or a strain produced by a stress and later those which are less quickly available.* (L)

The white cells nearest to bacteria tend to be the ones which move to ingest them. They can do it more quickly than can the cells which are farther away. A person usually strikes back against attack with the nearest part of his body. The soldier nearest the enemy in an infantry squad ordinarily begins the fight. In an army, the units closest to the attack are the first to fight, as, for example, at Pearl Harbor.

HYPOTHESIS 3.3.7.2-16: *The deciders of a system's subsystems and components satisfice (i.e., make a sufficiently good approximation to accomplishment in order to survive in its particular environment) shorter-term goals than does the decider of the total system.*[89] (M)

Units of a business are usually judged by higher management in terms of this short-run effectiveness, for example. Therefore these units tend to satisfice short-run profits.[90] Higher management, however, often alters these unit goals in order to satisfice long-run profits. Similar phenomena probably occur at other levels.

HYPOTHESIS 3.3.7.2-17: *A system cannot survive unless it makes decisions that maintain the functions of all its subsystems at a sufficiently high efficiency and their costs at a sufficiently low level that there are more than enough resources to keep it operating satisfactorily.* (H)

Dinosaurs became extinct when they grew too large to function in their environments. Their moving was probably too slow for them to survive in the presence of faster antagonists and their skeletons may have been too weak to support their bulk. The medieval knight's armor ultimately became so heavy that an unarmored footman with bow and arrow could destroy him even though he had the advantage of a horse and armor; the boundary artifact protected him but at the cost of too greatly slowing his ability to maneuver. Some heavy World War II army tanks similarly exchanged mobility for thicker armor and consequently were more vulnerable than more maneuverable, lighter tanks. The cost to the French nation to support the royalty and aristocracy at the time of Louis XVI became greater than appeared tolerable to the revolutionaries who overthrew them.[91]

HYPOTHESIS 3.3.7.2-18: *Systems which survive make decisions enabling them to perform at an optimum efficiency for maximum physical power output, which is always less than maximum efficiency.* (M)

This principle was applied by Odum and Pinkerton to living and nonliving systems at several levels—weights on a pulley (Atwood's machine); water wheels that run grindstones; electric batteries that charge other batteries; metabolism; capture of food by animals; photosynthesis; a plant climax community; and a civilization.[92] This principle questions the traditional view that the most efficient system survives, maintaining that this is true only if it can, when needed, also put out maximum physical power. They assume it is possible to broaden natural selection theory to apply it to all living and nonliving systems under stress in a changing suprasystem. Unless in a battle an animal can, by an "emergency reaction," temporarily cut down blood flow in the gut in order to increase it in the extremities, he will fight less well, and blood in a cut will clot less well.[93] This adjustment relates directly to survival. Comparably, if the cooks in an army under attack, as in the Battle of the Bulge, are not allowed to leave their camp stoves and pick up guns to participate in a maximum effort, the army may not survive.

HYPOTHESIS 3.3.7.2-19: *Ordinarily if two adjustment processes are of equal cost, a system decides to use the one which most rapidly or efficiently returns a variable to a steady state.* (L)

HYPOTHESIS 3.3.7.2-20: *Ordinarily when (a) two or more variables in a system are displaced from a steady state, and (b) they cannot be returned simultaneously, and (c) the costs of the adjustment process to return each variable to a steady state are identical, the system decides to use first the adjustment process which returns to a steady state the most displaced variable, and then those which return lesser displacements in order.* (L)

HYPOTHESIS 3.3.7.2-21: *The higher the level of a system the more correct or adaptive its decisions are.* (L)

I propose, as a regular cross-level difference, that the decisions of each higher level are ordinarily more correct or adaptive than those at lower levels. Cross-level comparisons of decision making have been made between only two levels—organisms and groups—but many cross-level experimental researches on this topic have been reported. A number of studies with varying research designs have showed that majority or pooled judgments are more correct than the average individual judgments and equal to the superior individual working alone.[94] In a recent comparison of individual, majority, and group discussion decisions on a test of recognition of valid conclusions in syllogisms, Barnlund found that decisions made by majority vote without discussion were not better than those made by individuals, but after discussion the group decisions were far superior.[95]

Various hypotheses have been suggested to explain why group systems are more effective in deciding than organisms. Among these are: the few ablest members of the group determine the results;[96] the more confident members tend to be right more often than they are wrong and exert social influence to get their decisions adopted;[97] individual errors are diluted in pooled decisions;[98] groups produce a higher level of interest and therefore better performance;[99] the need for explaining a conclusion leads to more self-criticism and avoidance of errors;[100] members benefit from each other's criticism;[101] groups are more objective.[102]

One experiment on decision making in the game of "Twenty Questions" (see pages 557 and 558) indicated that two- and four-person groups did not differ in important ways, but they were superior to individuals.[103] The experimenters concluded that the most likely reason for this superiority of groups in decision making, as compared with their components, is that groups have available a broader range of relevant information and also have a more flexible approach to deciding because the members differ in their problem-solving styles.

It has been argued that committees tend to be overly cautious and conservative and that therefore a single person rather than a group should make decisions about problems where daring may be desirable. On the contrary Stoner, working with Marquis, found that groups are more willing to take risks than individuals.[104] He presented problems to groups of graduate students. They were asked to advise a person who was faced with a choice among alternatives differing in both attractiveness and riskiness. Twelve out of thirteen groups accepted greater risks for attractive potential outcomes than the average member of those groups had been willing to accept in prior decisions made individually. Twenty-three control individuals, each of whom made a decision twice on the same problem, several weeks apart, did not shift significantly between trials as group members did. When the original and final private responses were compared, a shift in the risky direction occurred 39 percent of the time and in the cautious direction 16 percent, leaving 45 percent who did not shift.

Marquis investigated this issue further, studying decisions made by groups of executives. Examples of the problems he worked on are: "A man of moderate means may invest some money he recently inherited in secure 'blue-chip' low-return securities or in more risky securities that offer the possibility of large gains." Or "A college senior planning graduate work in chemistry may enter university X where, because of rigorous standards, only a fraction of the graduate students manage to receive the Ph.D. or may enter university Y which has a poorer reputation but where almost every graduate student receives the Ph.D." Group members made individual decisions before group discussion began and again, privately, after the group decision had been made. This work confirmed Stoner's finding that groups make riskier decisions than individuals and showed that the group's increased willingness to accept risk is not because each member shifts responsibility to the others.

As Marquis pointed out, research has not yet explained these results. Group decision itself is not the important factor, since group discussion alone without decision has been shown in other experimentation to make the leader shift to a riskier position. Group pressures toward conformity would explain decreased variability and increased agreement, but not the risky shift. Perhaps the more cautious members are more subject to influence by the more daring. Perhaps the latter talk more, are more respected, more persistent, or more argumentative.

Researches comparing the excellence of decisions across other levels besides the organism and the group certainly could be designed. Would they indicate that higher-level systems in general decide more accurately or adaptively than those at lower levels?

4. Relationships among subsystems or components

4.1 Structural relationships
4.1.4 Position

HYPOTHESIS 4.1.4-1: *The position of components in a system is an arrangement which satisfices a joint function of: (a) the optimal location of nodes in distributors and nets, (b) the location of requisite inputs for particular subsystem functions, and (c) the arrangement which will make for optimal spatial distribution of functions serving all subsystems.* (L)

There is much unsystematic evidence at the level of the society that such determinants affect the locations of cities, and sometimes factories and houses are designed with such considerations in mind.[105] Of course the structures which are formed first may not be optimal for the system as it develops later, and of course they influence later developments, often in a way that is not optimal. Do organisms, organs, or cells follow such principles?

4.1.8 Density

HYPOTHESIS 4.1.8-1: *In general, the greatest density of components in a system is at its center, then along the margins of its distributor, decreasing near the peripheral parts of the system.* (L)

This is characteristic of many cities, although there are variations with size, type, and terrain.[106] The floor of the House of Commons and the Big Board on Wall Street are crowded. It is also true for many cells, though there are exceptions. Possibly there is a more general principle which also explains the other patterns of density.

4.2 Process relationships
4.2.2 Spatiotemporal relationships
4.2.2.4 Pattern of action

HYPOTHESIS 4.2.2.4-1: *The more two or more systems interact, the more they become alike in storing and processing common information.* (L)

This is obviously true of marital partners and business partners, as well as of contiguous organizations and nations. It perhaps applies also to other levels.

5. System processes

5.1 Process relationships between inputs and outputs
The following hypotheses (5.1-1 through 5.1-33) have been suggested by our input-overload research (see Chap. 5). All except 5.1-4 and 5.1-25 through 5.1-31 deal with cross-level formal identities. A number of terms used in them are defined on pages 60 and 61.

HYPOTHESIS 5.1-1: *As the information input to a single channel of a living system—measured in bits per s—increases, the information output—measured similarly—increases almost identically at first but gradually falls behind as it approaches a certain output rate, the channel capacity, which cannot be exceeded in the channel. The output then levels off at that rate, and finally, as the information input rate continues to go up, the output decreases gradually toward zero as breakdown or the confusional state occurs under overload.* (H)

This hypothesis is discussed on pages 122 and 123.

HYPOTHESIS 5.1-2: *Channels in living systems have adjustment processes which enable them to maintain stable, within a range, the similarity of the information output from them to the information input to them. The magnitude of these adjustment processes rises as information input rates increase up to and somewhat beyond the channel capacity. These adjustments enable the output rate to remain at or near channel capacity and then to decline gradually, rather than to fall precipitously to zero immediately whenever the information input rate exceeds the channel capacity.* (H)

This hypothesis is discussed on page 124.

HYPOTHESIS 5.1-3: *Among the limited number of adjustment processes which channels in living systems employ as information input rates increase are: omission, error, queuing, filtering, abstracting, multiple channels, escape, and chunking. Each of these processes applies to random and nonrandom information inputs except chunking, which applies only to nonrandom inputs with repetitive patterning to a system that can associate (or learn). Each of these processes occurs at multiple levels of living systems. Each of these processes has a cost in some sort of decreased efficiency of information processing.* (H)

This hypothesis is discussed on page 124.

HYPOTHESIS 5.1-4: *Higher-level living systems in general have the emergent characteristics (see page 28) of more kinds and more complex combinations of adjustment processes than living systems at lower levels.* (H)

This hypothesis is discussed on page 124.

HYPOTHESIS 5.1-5: *As average information input rate increases, variation in output intensity increases.* (M)

HYPOTHESIS 5.1-6: *As average information input rate increases, the average processing time increases.* (M)

HYPOTHESIS 5.1-7: *As average information input rate increases, variation in processing time increases.* (H)

HYPOTHESIS 5.1-8: *As average information input rate increases, the percentage of internal channel capacity used in nontask communication increases.* (L)

HYPOTHESIS 5.1-9: *As average intensity of input increases, up to a point average processing time decreases.* (L)

HYPOTHESIS 5.1-10: *As average input intensity increases, use of the omission adjustment process decreases.* (M)

HYPOTHESIS 5.1-11: *As input priority increases, average output rate increases.* (L)

HYPOTHESIS 5.1-12: *As input priority increases, average processing time decreases.* (L)

HYPOTHESIS 5.1-13: *As the size of the input ensemble increases, the average processing time increases.* (M)

HYPOTHESIS 5.1-14: *As the size of the input ensemble increases, the use of all adjustment processes increases.* (L)

HYPOTHESIS 5.1-15: *As the size of the output ensemble increases, the channel capacity increases.* (L)

HYPOTHESIS 5.1-16: *As the size of the output ensemble increases, the total processing time increases.* (L)

This is because total decision time (processing time in the decider subsystem) increases.

HYPOTHESIS 5.1-17: *As the size of the output ensemble increases, the processing time per symbol decreases.* (M)

This is because decision time per symbol decreases. This hypothesis and the two previous ones could explain why the adjustment process of chunking is effective.[107] As chunks get larger, decision time increases, but not so fast as the information in the message.

HYPOTHESIS 5.1-18: *As average information input rate increases, the costs measured in energy (ergs per bit); utiles (e.g., cents per bit); time (s per bit); or duration of the state of the system (s before the state changes) remain more or less constant for a period of time and then finally increase rapidly, near the point where the performance curve begins to decrease from the maximum because the system is overloaded.* (L)

HYPOTHESIS 5.1-19: *As the percentage of total resources to meet costs (as defined in Hypothesis 5.1-18) runs out, average output rate decreases.* (L)

HYPOTHESIS 5.1-20: *As the percentage of total resources to meet costs runs out, average output intensity decreases.* (L)

HYPOTHESIS 5.1-21: *As the percentage of resources to meet costs runs out, the size of the ensemble decreases.* (L)

HYPOTHESIS 5.1-22: *As the percentage of resources to meet costs runs out, output range decreases.* (L)

HYPOTHESIS 5.1-23: *As the percentage of resources to meet costs runs out, average processing time increases.* (M)

HYPOTHESIS 5.1-24: *As the percentage of resources to meet costs runs out, use of omission, error, queuing, filtering, abstracting, multiple channels, and escape adjustment processes increases.* (L)

The following seven hypotheses concern regular cross-level differences rather than cross-level formal identities.

HYPOTHESIS 5.1-25: *Channels in living systems at higher levels in general have lower capacities than those in living systems at lower levels.* (H)

This hypothesis is discussed on page 124.

HYPOTHESIS 5.1-26: *Higher-level systems in general have more variation in output intensity because they have more components which are capable of varying.* (M)

HYPOTHESIS 5.1-27: *The higher the level of a system, the greater in general is its output range.* (M)

HYPOTHESIS 5.1-28: *The higher the level of a system, the longer is its average processing time.* (H)

HYPOTHESIS 5.1-29: *The higher the level of a system, the more variation in general is there in its processing time, because there are more components as possible sources for this variation.* (H)

HYPOTHESIS 5.1-30: *The higher the level of a system, the higher is the cost per correct information unit processed.* (L)

If this is confirmed by findings, it would explain why it is efficient to disperse certain information processing functions downward to lower levels.

HYPOTHESIS 5.1-31: *The higher the level of a system, the lower in general is the percentage cost per correct information unit processed.* (L)

HYPOTHESIS 5.1-32: *The queuing adjustment process is employed more frequently the higher the peaks of information input overlap until such time as the length of the queue is greater than the local, short-term memory capacity of the system, and then the use of this adjustment falls off rapidly in a confusional state.* (M)

I have referred to the use of queuing theory in relation to Hypothesis 3.2.5.2-1 above (see page 94). Many aspects of information input overload can also be analyzed in terms of the formal models of queuing theory. These problems, which have been studied at least since 1908, in recent years have been analyzed with a certain mathematical rigor. In general, they have dealt with such questions as traffic flow, toll-gate servicing, telephone switching problems, and machine breakdown and feeding problems. They have been shown to be applicable to situations in which there are units to be processed, a gate or service point, an input process, a situation in which the elements arriving are queued until serviced, and a service process. Questions of interest have concerned the waiting time of the elements before servicing, the number of elements in the queue, and the ratio of waiting time to service time.[108]

Markers bearing information travel in channels, and so queuing theory is applicable. For instance, one measure of the queuing adjustment process is the average increase in processing time, which is a function of the waiting time; the number of bits of information being queued at any moment can also easily be measured; the average processing time is the same as the service time; and the variance in processing time is the same as the variance in service time.

HYPOTHESIS 5.1-33: *As a corollary of the above, the effectiveness of the queuing adjustment process is positively correlated with the amount of local, short-term memory capacity.* (M)

HYPOTHESIS 5.1-34: *When the error adjustment process is studied as an independent variable, other adjustment processes are employed in order to minimize a positive power greater than 1 of the error and not a linear function of it.* (L)

In an investigation of tracking behavior Elkind found that his subjects, without any instruction to do so, moved four times as rapidly to correct an error of two units as they did to correct an error of one unit.[109] Is this learned, or is it innate? Do systems at other levels behave this way? Research could answer these questions.

HYPOTHESIS 5.1-35: *If previously learned or practiced information is processed, channel capacity is higher for the following reasons:*

(a) Chunking is possible.

(b) Only essential information is attended to and the rest is neglected.

(c) The need to attend only to the essential information permits rapid alternation of attention from a channel in which nonessential information is appearing to one in which essential information is appearing.

(d) More efficient codes are used. (L)

Simon has clearly illustrated by an everyday example how chunking can dramatically raise channel capacity.[110]

HYPOTHESIS 5.1-36: *As the average information input rate approaches the average processing rate, the waiting time of elements being queued rapidly approaches infinity.* (H)

When the number of items queued is large, and the waiting time to process them is long, a confusional state develops in the system, and its responses to the input information become essentially random.

HYPOTHESIS 5.1-37: *Queues and waiting times lengthen rapidly toward infinity if the mean waiting time is greater than the mean processing time.* (H)

HYPOTHESIS 5.1-38: *As the percentage of total resources to meet costs runs out, variation in output intensity increases.* (M)

HYPOTHESIS 5.1-39: *If the ratio between the mean waiting time and the mean processing time is less than one and fixed, then the processing is best when the variation in input rate is smallest.* (L)

HYPOTHESIS 5.1-40: *A system is more likely to process information which reduces strain and thus is favorable to its hierarchy of values, rather than information which is neutral or unfavorable.* (L)

HYPOTHESIS 5.1-41: *When a given information input is qualitatively identical with one which a system has learned to process, it provides further practice with it and improves the system's ability to process it. If it is slightly different, however, it interferes with this processing ability. The less the similarity is, the less it interferes until finally it neither improves nor interferes with processing ability.* (L)

There is evidence to suggest that molecules structurally similar but not identical to normal inputs into cells are more toxic than more dissimilar inputs, perhaps because they "throw monkey wrenches" into metabolic processes. At the organism level it has been repeatedly shown that processing an information input identical with a previous one improves memory of it, but processing a slightly different input causes retroactive inhibition, worsening memory of the first item learned. The less the similarity, the less is the effect. Proactive inhibition also occurs, in which previous learning interferes with memory of material learned later.

The following hypothesis derives from information input underload or sensory deprivation research.

HYPOTHESIS 5.1-42: *A minimum rate of information input to a system must be maintained for it to function normally.* (M)

Depriving subjects of normal rates of input can cause them to have subjective experiences which resemble hallucinations. They can also impair their thinking and reasoning processes, and make them more susceptible to propaganda.[111] Animals and human beings, when deprived of information input, strive for it. For instance, monkeys after a time in the dark will press a switch repeatedly in order to turn on a light for a brief moment with each press.[112] Children and adults will pay more attention to inputs with high information content than those with less information.[113] Infant monkeys search for the information input of physical contact even from inanimate "mothers," preferring terry-cloth "mothers" to wire ones.[114] There is good reason to conclude that systems at other levels also need information input and act to increase it if the rate of input falls too low.

Hypothesis 5.4.1-4 is related to this one (see page 114).

5.2 Adjustment processes among subsystems or components, used in maintaining variables in steady states

HYPOTHESIS 5.2-1: *As stress increases, it first improves system output performance above ordinary levels and then worsens it. What is extreme stress for one subsystem may be only moderate stress for the total system.* (L)

For instance, the stress of a very loud noise causes subjects' performances to improve in a pencil-and-paper test requiring them to cross out C's randomly distributed in a field of O's.[115] The noise, however, also causes microtrembling of the subjects' fingers, the same fingers used in crossing out C's. While finger-muscle performance worsens, compensatory adjustment processes come into play so that the total operation of crossing out C's improves. This is an illustration of how, though certain subsystems may develop strain under stress, the total system compensates for it.

HYPOTHESIS 5.2-2: *The greater a threat or stress upon a system, the more components of it are involved in adjusting to it. When no further components with new adjustment processes are available, the system function collapses.*[116] (M)

Our information input overload research findings are one example of this general principle (see Chap. 5).

HYPOTHESIS 5.2-3: *When variables in a system return to a steady state after stress, the rate of return and the strength of the restorative forces are functions—with increasing first derivatives greater than 1—of the amount of displacement from the range of stability.* (M)

To test this statement one could set up a number of experimental conditions in which the range of stability of a variable in a living system at each level could be determined. This system could then be disturbed a specified amount away from the range of stability. The rate at which it returned to a steady state and the strength of the forces restoring it could be measured and compared with similar measurements when there were greater or lesser degrees of disturbance from the steady state. The characteristics of the curves for different sorts of behaving systems could be compared quantitatively.

For example, the rate of motion and the amount of energy expended by an amoeba moving out of cold or hot fluids into fluids of comfortable temperature might be measured. Or similar studies might be made of amoebas moving out of fluids which are too acid or alkaline and into fluids in an optimal range.

At the level of the human individual, the rate of return of a tightrope walker to a position of upright bodily balance and the amount of energy he expended in returning to it after various amounts of displacement, could be measured.

This hypothesis is closely related to the observation by March and Simon that, in industrial firms, search for alternative new programs decreases as satisfaction with the present programs increases.[117]

HYPOTHESIS 5.2-4: *The range of stability of a system for a specific variable under lack strain is a monotonically increasing function of the amount of storage of the input, and under excess strain, it is a monotonically increasing function of the rate of output.* (L)

HYPOTHESIS 5.2-5: *There is an inertia to the matter-energy and information processing variables which a system maintains in steady state, so that change in their ranges of stability is much less disruptive of system controls if it is undertaken gradually.*[118] (L)

In surgery a viscus with smooth muscle walls, like the bladder or uterus, can be pried open by a probe only slowly unless it is completely ruptured. Social change is less likely to produce violence if it is slow, which may be why the Supreme Court of the United States in 1954 ordered that the racial desegregation of schools be carried out resolutely but slowly, or in lawyers' idiom "with all deliberate speed."

HYPOTHESIS 5.2-6: *Positive feedback may produce continuous increments of outputs which give rise to "spiral effects" destroying one or more equilibria of a system.* (H)

The following examples of demonstrated "spiral effects" of this sort at more than one system level are given by Berelson and Steiner:

> Deprived children tend to become poor parents, whose own children then tend to be deprived; the unpopular child, feeling rejected, withdraws, becomes more ingrown and, as a result, more unpopular; a deteriorating area of the city attracts social delinquency, as a result of which it deteriorates further; the official leadership of a formal organization, when opposed by the informal channels of personal relations within it, will tend to tighten up bureaucratic controls, and as a result the informal channels become more cohesive still; a deprived group such as Negroes in the United States are restricted in such social opportunities as education, as a result of which they are thought to be less educable and hence deprived further.[119]

HYPOTHESIS 5.2-7: *When a barrier stands between a system under strain and a goal which can relieve that strain, the system ordinarily uses the adjustment processes of removing the barrier, circumventing it, or otherwise mastering it. If these efforts fail, less adaptive adjustments may be tried, including: (a) attacking the barrier by energic or informational transmissions; (b) displacing aggression to another innocent but more vulnerable nearby system; (c) reverting to primitive, nonadaptive behavior; (d) adopting rigid, nonadaptive behavior; and (e) escaping from the situation.* (L)

On the basis of research on frustration, Berelson and Steiner put forward such a proposition at the organism level.[120] Could it not also apply at least to the group, organization, society, and supranational levels? At the society level, Feierabend suggests, at least part of this hypothesis applies.[121]

HYPOTHESIS 5.2-8: *A system usually associates with other systems which have arisen from similar templates rather than with those derived from dissimilar templates.*[122] (H)

I outline a cross-level research on this hypothesis later in this chapter (see page 114).

HYPOTHESIS 5.2-9: *When there are heterogeneous components in a system, they adjust to each other best if they group together into two or more partially autonomous components on the basis of similarity of their templates, functions, or values.* (L)

This may be the rationale whereby living systems at all levels form differentiated subsystems (see pages 26 and 78). Etzioni (see pages 967 and 968) has indicated how a supranational system may evolve by reintegrating differentiated societies into blocs and subblocs, each with some autonomy, each representing a specific set of common interests.

HYPOTHESIS 5.2-10: *Under equal stress, functions developed later in the phylogenetic history of a given type of system break down before more primitive functions do.* (L)

For example, cortical functions break down before medullary functions under the effects of anoxia and many drugs. When national governments break down, local governments and families continue to function. Is this hypothesis true at other levels?

HYPOTHESIS 5.2-11: *After stress, disturbances of subsystem steady states are ordinarily corrected and returned to normal ranges before systemwide steady-state disturbances are.* (M)

HYPOTHESIS 5.2-12: *More complex systems, which contain more different components, each of which can adjust against one or more specific environmental stresses and maintain in steady state one or more specific variables not maintained by any other component, if they adequately coordinate the processes in their components, survive longer on the average than less complex systems.* (M)

The next 17 hypotheses relate to the adjustment of conflicts.

HYPOTHESIS 5.2-13: *Under threat or stress, a system that survives, in the common good of total system survival, temporarily subordinates conflicts among subsystems or components until the threat or stress is relieved, when internal conflicts recur.*[123] (L)

If a man and wife are arguing between themselves and a neighbor chances by and tries to enter in, the combating dyad is likely to turn on him in complete unanimity and tell him to keep out. Then they return to the battle. If an organization is essential to a society—like a hospital, defense plan, or fire department—public opinion is less likely to permit its employees to strike than the employees of less critical organizations. During extreme danger or disaster economic and social differences in a nation are often disregarded and social solidarity increases greatly.[124] This principle may not apply at the organism level and below, but it quite possibly does at higher levels.

This hypothesis relates to Hypothesis 5.4.3-7, page 109.

HYPOTHESIS 5.2-14: *Segregation increases conflict among subsystems or components of a system, and a higher proportion of adjustment processes must therefore be devoted to resolving such conflicts, which means they cannot be devoted to advancing goals of the system as a whole.* (M)

Delegation of authority to departments in firms, according to March and Simon, increases the disparity in their interests and leads therefore to increased conflict among them.[125] Labor–management disputes, Kerr and Siegel maintain, are more likely when workers constitute an isolated mass, segregated away from employers or other members of the public.[126] Does this principle apply at other levels?

HYPOTHESIS 5.2-15: *The larger the number of subsystems or components in conflict, the more difficult will be resolution of the conflict.* (M)

This hypothesis, Mack and Snyder suggested, applies to international relations.[127] Almost the opposite hypothesis has been asserted by Brody[128] and by Deutsch and Singer,[129] also with reference to international relations. Brody conducted a simulation of a situation in which the number of nations with nuclear capability shifted from two to several and found that, when there were more nuclear powers, the situation was more stable because the strains among blocs were not so great. (Although, of course, there were more powers who might initiate a worldwide holocaust.) Deutsch and Singer take a similar position, arguing that stability of international systems increases as the number of independent blocs or components goes up, because the number of relationships among them goes up much faster and the amount of attention any component can devote to any other goes down equally fast. Therefore, in a system with many components, conflicts between any two components are less likely than in a system with few. (But, of course, there are more pairs of components between whom conflicts could occur.) A study of the relations of alliances to the onset of war in the nineteenth and twentieth centuries has been made by Singer and Small, who found that as the number of blocs increased in the nineteenth century the amount of military conflict increased, but the reverse was true in the twentieth century.[130] Further empirical research will be required to explain this difference between the situations in the two periods, and also to determine whether the hypothesis stated above can be confirmed at other levels of living systems.

HYPOTHESIS 5.2-16: *A system tends to reduce multiple-component conflicts to conflicts among a lesser number of blocs of components.* (L)

This hypothesis has been independently proposed by Mack and Snyder[131] and by Burns[132] as applying to international relations. Does it apply at other levels, such as groups or organizations?

HYPOTHESIS 5.2-17: *The greater the mutual dependence of two or more subsystems or components on a single limited input or store of matter-energy or information, the more probable is conflict among them.*[133] (M)

HYPOTHESIS 5.2-18: *The greater the necessary interdependence in timing of processes of two or more subsystems or components, the more probable is conflict among them.*[134] (M)

HYPOTHESIS 5.2-19: *The greater the resources available to a system, the less likely is conflict among its subsystems or components.* (H)

This proposition was stated by Mack and Snyder in noting that prosperity lessens the intensity of conflicts between ethnic and racial majorities and minorities.[135] A similar proposition was suggested by March and Simon to apply to organizations like firms.[136] This hypothesis may well apply to the organism level of systems and above.

HYPOTHESIS 5.2-20: *The decider of a system must resolve conflicts among other subsystems, which signal their demands for autonomy, and the suprasystem, which signals commands for compliance.*[137] (H)

Conflicts in the nervous system may occur between individual cellular responses and signals from higher centers. Freud's superego–id conflict had much of this character. In organizations such conflict is faced by, among others, middle managers, foremen, and noncommissioned officers.

HYPOTHESIS 5.2-21: *When a system is receiving conflicting command signals from several suprasystems, it intermittently being a component of all of them, it tends to comply with the signals of the suprasystem most important to it. The greater the divergence between its current function and the signals from that group, the more likely it is to comply.*[138] (L)

HYPOTHESIS 5.2-22: *When a system is receiving conflicting command signals from several suprasystems, it intermittently being a component of all of them, the more different the signals are, the slower is its decision making.*[139] (M)

HYPOTHESIS 5.2-23: *When a system is receiving conflicting command signals from several suprasystems, it intermittently being a component of all of them, the more different they are, the more likely it is to change its decisions.*[140] (L)

HYPOTHESIS 5.2-24: *Conflicts among various sorts of alternatives are resolved by a system in different ways:*

(a) Between two mutually exclusive positive goals, resolution is difficult if they appear to be of equal value, but choice is usually made quickly without much vacillation.

(b) With goals that are positive and negative at the same time, approach occurs until the system is near, then avoidance or movement from the goal occurs, and the system tends to vacillate for a time fairly near but not at the goal.

(c) Between two mutually exclusive negative goals, the system vacillates from one to the other but tends not to make a decision.[141] (L)

Numerous researches document these facts well at the organism level.[142] It appears quite likely that the hypothesis may apply at other levels as well.

HYPOTHESIS 5.2-25: *Lack of clarity of purposes or goals in a system's decisions will produce conflict between it and other components of the suprasystem.* (M)

At the cell and organ levels this may not apply because such systems' purposes and goals are unambiguous, being probably simply to maximize duration of survival. The hypothesis applies at higher levels, however. In a study of conflicts between the Indian Bureau and other parts of the United States government, Freeman illustrates this principle.[143]

HYPOTHESIS 5.2-26: *If a system has multiple purposes and goals, and they are not placed in clear priority and commonly known by all components or subsystems, conflict among them will ensue.*[144] (H)

HYPOTHESIS 5.2-27: *The vigor of the search for resolutions of conflict increases as the available time for finding a solution decreases.*[145] (M)

HYPOTHESIS 5.2-28: *The search for resolutions of conflict will be more vigorous if no alternative is available which reduces all strains.*[146] (L)

HYPOTHESIS 5.2-29: *If a conflict arises from incomparability of signals, the time to resolution will be shorter than if it arises from unacceptability of them.*[147] (L)

5.4 Growth, cohesiveness, and integration
5.4.1 Growth

HYPOTHESIS 5.4.1-1: *The rate of increase in the number of components of a young system rises exponentially until it reaches a maximum, but this growth rate may be altered by environmental or other factors.* (L)

There have been many studies of growth rates of various populations, from bacterial cells to Malthus's societies.[148] At least at the levels of cell, tissue or organ, and organism, explicit claims have been made of cross-level formal identities in growth rates.[149] Availability of food supply, changing weight of the system, predators, space for expansion, genetic determinants, effects of toxic excreta upon new generations, and, in humans, economic status are factors which alter these rates.[150]

HYPOTHESIS 5.4.1-2: *Growing systems develop in the direction of: (a) more differentiation of subsystems, (b) more decentralization of decision making, (c) more interdependence of subsystems, (d) more elaborate adjustment* processes, (e) sharper subsystem boundaries, (f) increased differential sensitivity to inputs, and (g) more elaborate and patterned outputs. (M)

HYPOTHESIS 5.4.1-3: *Increase in the number of components in a system requires a disproportionately larger increase in the number of information processing and deciding components.* (L)

This hypothesis was suggested by Passer, who investigated the number of employees in rayon factories.[151] He concluded that the numbers of administrative and staff personnel grow at a faster rate than the total number of employees does. On the basis of studies of growth in a number of organizations, Haire came to a similar conclusion.[152] Evidence tending to disconfirm, or limit the generality of, such a conclusion is also available (see pages 692 and 693).

HYPOTHESIS 5.4.1-4: *If the rate of information input into a system falls below a specific lower limit, normal growth of the system is impossible.*[153] (M)

This hypothesis is related to Hypothesis 5.1-42, page 105.

5.4.3 Integration

HYPOTHESIS 5.4.3-1: *For the same level of system output, more transmission of information is necessary to coordinate segregated systems than integrated systems.* (M)

One reason why this hypothesis may be true is that each part of a segregated or a decentralized system must receive a constant flow of information to keep it informed of systemwide conditions and decision rules. This means much information must be sent over distances, and many components must be involved in doing this. Consequently decentralization increases the number of information processing components in the system as a whole and hence the cost of information processing. For instance, decentralization of a firm will necessarily increase the total number of its staff employees, for the same level of system output.[154] Similar phenomena seem plausible at all levels of living systems. It may be possible to develop a general calculus of decentralization indicating the optimum amount of decentralization for a system with a given number of components and a given rate of information flow.

HYPOTHESIS 5.4.3-2: *As a system grows and adds more components, the components in general become increasingly independent in decision making. This is probably because the system cannot meet the increasing costs of processing the information to the system's decider, as required for centralized deciding.* (M)

See also Hypotheses 1-2 and 5.4.1-3 (pages 92 and 108).

HYPOTHESIS 5.4.3-3: *As a system's components become more numerous, they become more specialized, with*

resulting increased interdependence for critical processes among them. (H)

This can best be seen in comparing primitive and advanced types of systems at a given level, as well as systems from lower and higher levels.

HYPOTHESIS 5.4.3-4: *Decentralization of decision making in general increases the speed and accuracy of decisions which reduce local strains.* (H)

This hypothesis, suggested by Hund, who was concerned only with the organization level, appears equally relevant to all levels.[155]

HYPOTHESIS 5.4.3-5: *As decentralization increases, echelons or components of the system's decider increasingly make decisions without the benefit of relevant information existing elsewhere in the system.* (H)

This hypothesis was proposed by Garfinkel with reference to organizations, but it is reasonable to apply it to all levels of living systems.[156]

HYPOTHESIS 5.4.3-6: *The more decentralized a system's deciding is, the more likely is there to be discordant information in various echelons or components of its decider.*[157] (H)

This hypothesis is closely related logically to Hypotheses 3.3.3.2-2, 3.3.3.2-3, 3.3.3.2-7, 3.3.3.2-11, 3.3.3.2-15, and 3.3.7.2-2 (see pages 96, 97, and 100).

HYPOTHESIS 5.4.3-7: *Up to a certain amount of stress, systems do more centralized deciding when under stress than when not under stress. Beyond that amount, deciding becomes increasingly decentralized until the system terminates or the stress abates.*[158] (L)

This proposition is closely related to Hypothesis 5.2-13, page 107.

HYPOTHESIS 5.4.3-8: *A component will comply with a system's purposes and goals to the extent that those functions of the component directed toward the goal are rewarded and those directed away from it are punished.*[159] (M)

HYPOTHESIS 5.4.3-9: *As long as all relevant information flows among all echelons or components of the decider to keep them all informed of states of the system, the more decentralized the decider of a system is, the better will be the interaction of its echelons or components.*[160] (L)

Persons and units in social interaction are happier when they have a high degree of autonomy, and they cooperate better as a result. Communication nets which make difficult the flow of necessary information in a group, in which each member is doing decentralized deciding, are less efficient and less satisfying to the members of the group than nets which permit all the members of the group to interact with all others as Shaw found.[161] He also found that groups with centralized communication nets (which probably make for centralized deciding as well) were less efficient than decentralized groups.

The above hypothesis may be true as stated only at the group level and above. It is interesting to consider the implications of it in association with Hypothesis 5.4.3-7 above. If both are true, stress—up to a certain intensity—would worsen the interaction of a system's subsystems and components. At greater intensities it is unclear whether it would improve or worsen it.

5.5 Pathology   Most of the hypotheses in this chapter concern adapted, normal, or healthy living systems. In many cases deviations from the principle involved represent maladaptation or pathology. Also some hypotheses can be made about pathological processes themselves; for example:

HYPOTHESIS 5.5-1: *The farther away a component is from the point of trauma to a system, the less pathological is its function, and particularly the less is its relation to the system's hierarchical organization destroyed.* (L)

After a tornado, social dissociation in the immediate contact area goes down to the level of the individual person (see page 708). Some distance from the impact area, the family, school class, or office unit structure remains, but not the community organization. Farther away still, social organization remains and is able to send aid to the impact point. The situation is similar when a foreign body enters a tissue. It causes local damage to individual tissue cells, but less and less at points farther and farther away. At some distance the wound is walled off and white cells and macrophages invade the area of damage from all directions to begin the process of repair. Are there similar situations at other levels?

HYPOTHESIS 5.5-2: *Abnormal or "neurotic" outputs can be elicited by rewarding one information input, not rewarding (or punishing) a similar information input, and then altering one or both until they are indistinguishable.* (L)

Pavlov produced "neurotic" behavior in dogs by feeding them after presenting a circle to them but never after presenting an ellipse, and then making the circles more and more alike until the dogs could not distinguish them. Others have produced similar behavior in cats, using comparable techniques.

It is hard to see how cells or organs could show such processes, but systems at levels higher than organisms might.

5.6 Decay and termination

HYPOTHESIS 5.6-1: *If a system's negative feedback discontinues and is not restored by that system or by another on which it becomes parasitic or symbiotic, it decomposes into multiple components and its suprasystem assumes control of them.* (H)

If too much water enters a red cell, for example, it swells up, the internal osmotic equilibrium is destroyed, and the cell membrane ruptures. Separate molecules of the cells then become small subsystems in the much larger subsystem of the circulating blood. A similar sequence occurs in organismic death, after which the organism's environment takes control, *e.g.,* the body assumes the temperature of its surroundings. A comparable process is seen when a committee dealing with a practical problem dissolves in disagreement. The members disperse while the higher organizational unit, which originally established the committee, takes over the responsibility for settling the issue. Whenever a political body at any level cannot control its territory and breaks down into warring factions, the next larger system takes over control. In recent years this has frequently been true even at the international level, when a supranational body has entered in—as in Cyprus from 1964 until the present—to control a nation which has become embroiled in civil war.

Suggested approaches to cross-level researches on selected hypotheses

HYPOTHESIS 3.3.3.2-3: *In a channel there is always a progressive degradation of information and decrease in negative entropy or increase in noise or entropy. The output information per unit time is always less than it was at the input.* (H)

This information processing hypothesis is in some ways like matter-energy processing Hypothesis 3.2.2.2-2 (see page 94). It is also related to Hypotheses 3.3.3.2-2, 3.3.3.2-7, 3.3.3.2-11, and 5.4.3-6 (see pages 96, 97, and 109). It is explained, fundamentally, by the second law of thermodynamics.

Cell. Neural signals are progressively altered by random noise as they cross synapses and go through neurons. Increasing noise in such transmissions can be demonstrated in electrical recordings of input and output neural pulse sequences.

Organ. Sound frequencies pass through the cochlea of the ear and go through several neurons before reaching the auditory cortex. Electrical recordings at each echelon in the pathway can demonstrate the increasing amount of noise in the signal.

Organism. A subject carrying out a repetitive task, such as typing from copy, makes errors. These are more frequent if the task is carried out at a forced pace or if the subject is tired.

Group. The old parlor game sometimes called "telephone" illustrates how noise can enter into interpersonal communications. In this game one person whispers a story to his neighbor on the right, and he to his neighbor on the right, and so on around a circle. The message is progressively altered, and when the message gets back to the originator, it may be unrecognizable.[162]

Organization. Noise may affect the accuracy of messages as they pass from one group to another. When an employee brings a verbal report from a field office in a corporation to the home office, and it is then relayed from one executive unit to another, errors in the transmission increase progressively.

Society. In ancient times messages coming to the king of a large country from the provinces were notoriously full of error, making governing difficult and often hazardous. Historical research could show whether the messages from the most distant provinces were the least accurate.

Supranational system. In general the channels in supranational systems are longer than in nations. A great deal of noise or error has always been present in supranational communications because of linguistic and cultural differences among component countries. Studies could indicate whether the amount of this noise in general is greater in long than in short supranational channels.

HYPOTHESIS 3.3.3.2-12: *Two-way channels which permit feedback improve performance by facilitating processes that reduce error.* (M)

Cell. If some cells learn, as Gelber contends paramecia do (see pages 266 and 267), feedback may well be essential to the process (see Hypothesis 3.3.5.2-3, page 99).

Organ. At the organ level, cutting neurons which provide feedback decreases the stability or increases the variation of the variables they maintain in steady states.

Organism. Organisms behave less precisely when feedback is disturbed or destroyed. For example, writing done while observing the pencil and paper in a mirror is poor. Or again, even though you may not be thinking about the full coffee cup you are holding on a bouncing airplane, it usually does not spill until you take your eyes off it. Then it easily may. Even though you may be talking to the passenger in the seat next to you and not be aware of balancing the cup, you do so by a feedback loop involving your visual system, your brain, and the muscles of the arm and hand holding the cup. Balancing performance is worse when one of the channels in the loop does not function.

Group. In groups conveying messages with "semantic noise," correction of error by use of redundancy depends on the existence of a feedback channel (see pages 541 and 542). Error correction is superior in groups with the communication networks which are so structured that one or more members can receive information from multiple sources and so check it (see pages 545 and 573). Unrestricted, general feed-

back also is an aid to accuracy in groups. Others in a group recognize the errors of a member and are able to tell him about them (see page 573).

Organization, society, supranational system. It seems probable that organizations, societies, and supranational systems also operate better and have less error in communications if they permit the two-way communication in channels which makes feedback possible. For instance, it is widely held that students and employees of firms perform better if they receive periodic evaluations from teachers or supervisors.

HYPOTHESIS 3.3.4.2-7: *If messages are so coded that they are transmitted twice, errors can be detected by comparing every part of the first message with every part of the second, but which of the two alternative transmissions is correct cannot be determined. If they are transmitted three times, they can be both detected and corrected, by accepting the alternative on which two of the three transmissions agree.* (M)

For centuries kings and military commanders who wanted to transmit an important message would send it by multiple couriers if they wished to be certain that an accurate version of it reached the intended receiver.

Beginning about 1940 Skinner and some associates undertook a set of remarkable experiments on the control by pigeons of the homing in on a target of a wing-steered glider missile called a Pelican.[163] Early in this work a pigeon riding in a mockup of such a missile was trained by food rewards to peck a selected portion of a transparent plastic plate on which a lens threw an image of the target. As the target moved in relation to the missile, the image on the plate moved, and therefore the pigeon pecked on a different part of the plate. The guiding signal was picked up from the point of contact of the beak on the screen. Other similar pigeon–missile interfaces were also used.

Scientists in the United States government questioned whether a single pigeon was a sufficiently reliable system to be trusted to control the homing of a missile full of high explosives on an enemy target. Therefore Skinner decided to use three pigeons. He writes:

By this time we had begun to realize that a pigeon was more easily controlled than a physical scientist serving on a committee. It was very difficult to convince the latter that the former was an orderly system. We therefore multiplied the probability of success by designing a multiple bird unit. There was adequate space in the nose of the Pelican for three pigeons each with its own lens and plate. A net signal could easily be generated. The majority vote of three pigeons offered an excellent guarantee against momentary pauses and aberrations. (We later worked out a system in which the majority took on more characteristically democratic function. When a missile is falling toward *two* ships at sea, for example, there is no guarantee that all three pigeons will steer toward the same ship. But at least two must agree, and the third can then be punished for his minority opinion. Under proper contingencies of reinforcement a punished bird will shift immediately to the majority view. When all three are working on one ship, any defection is immediately punished and corrected.)[164]

Thus Skinner discovered a way to correct the errors of one pigeon by information from two others, applying it to a specific problem. One servomechanism expert said the performance of the team of three pigeons was better than radar. Skinner adds:[165] "Although in simulated tests a single pigeon occasionally loses a target, its tracking characteristics are surprisingly good. A three- or seven-bird unit with the same individual consistency should yield a signal with a reliability which is at least of the order of magnitude shown by other phases of guided missiles in their present stage of development."

In 1952 von Neumann, presumably ignorant of the pigeons in a Pelican, undertook an analysis in terms of probabilistic logic of the problem of how to make reliable information processing systems from unreliable components (see Hypotheses 3.3.3.2-9 and 3.3.3.2-10, page 96).[166] He found a solution in what he labeled "the multiple line trick," which is essentially the same principle that was employed by the kings and military commanders of old and by Skinner in World War II. How to build a reliable system or automaton out of unreliable components is described in the general case by von Neumann as follows:

The trick consists in carrying all the messages simultaneously on a bundle of N lines (N is a large integer) instead of just a single . . . strand. An automaton would then be represented by a black box with several bundles of inputs and outputs . . . [see Fig. 4-1]. Instead of requiring that all or none of the lines

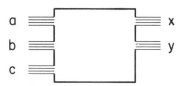

Fig. 4-1 Black box with several bundles of inputs and outputs. Each group ≡ represents a bundle of N lines.

of the bundle be stimulated, a certain critical (or fiduciary) level Δ is set: $0 < \Delta < \frac{1}{2}$. The stimulation of $\geq (1 - \Delta)$ N lines of a bundle is interpreted as a positive state of the bundle. The stimulation of $\leq \Delta$ N lines is considered as a negative state. All levels of stimulation between these values are intermediate or undecided. . . . By suitably constructing the automaton, the number of lines deviating from the "correctly functioning" majorities of their bundles can be kept at or below the critical level Δ N (with arbitrarily high probability).[167]

If multiple channels do not agree that the binary signal is "yes" or that it is "no," the message is not accepted as correct; that is how any desired degree of reliability of information processing can be achieved from the unreliable components in living channels.

Just as Skinner applied this principle at the level of the group—a team of pigeons, McCulloch recognized its potential applicability at the organ level—to networks in the nervous system.[168] He has written about various aspects of such channels and nets, demonstrating by logical analysis how they can function in a stable and reliable fashion even though the neurons in them have variable thresholds and sometimes operate erroneously.

All this background of practical and theoretical expeience with this principle suggests a design for a cross-level study of this hypothesis, at least at certain levels. Fundamentally the studies would determine whether von Neumann's formulation applies at each level of living system:

Cell. Since reproduction of a cell type or species usually occurs with amazing accuracy, there may be redundancy in the genetic template. Further biochemical research on DNA may indicate whether any of the genetic message is repeated multiple times. It may not be repeated, because the template of an organism must be very complex, and there may not be enough atoms in the genetic molecules to permit much or any redundancy.

Organ. McCulloch's theoretical speculations about neural nets could be confirmed by neurophysiological experiments to see if multiple parallel neurons are used to achieve accuracy.

Organism. Researches could be conducted to show increase in accuracy of performance when there is intermodality confirmation of sensory signals, *e.g.*, balancing on a tightrope blindfolded and with normal vision, or receiving a message in spoken form with and without simultaneous written presentation of the same message.

Group. Skinner's research was done with a team of pigeons. It could be repeated with groups of human beings or other animal species, comparing group and individual accuracies.

Organization. Multiple squads could be sent to headquarters with messages by the commander of a military unit to see if this decreased the percentage of erroneous transmissions.

Society. Similar studies to that suggested for the organization level might be devised. Does one nation communicate more accurately with another if several media—diplomats, radio, television, publications— carry the same message at the same time?

Supranational system.   Perhaps a comparable study to that suggested for the society level could be conducted.

HYPOTHESIS 3.3.6.2-3: *The removal from a system of information representing experience stored in the memory (as distinguished from the information constituting its template, whose removal is often fundamentally damaging or lethal) predictably alters stochastic measures of the system's subsequent behavior, and the degree of these changes increases as the amount removed is increased.* (M)

A general outline for a set of cross-level studies to evaluate this hypothesis is as follows: At each level various amounts of information stored in the memory of an experimental group of systems can be removed. Their subsequent behavior can be compared with that of a control group of systems. This can be done by making stochastic analyses of each group, employing methods like those used in stochastic learning research.[169] By such means one could determine how removal of each amount of information affects later behavior; whether the behavior alters at all; if so, whether it returns to what would have been expected prior to removal; and if not, what the new pattern of behavior is.

Possible procedures for removing the information stored in memory at each level are:

Cell.   Nongenetic information in cells may possibly be stored in specific enzymes, in nucleoproteins like RNA, in antibodies, or in other structures.[170] Each of these might be destroyed in quantitatively controllable amounts by an appropriate chemical. For instance ribonuclease destroys or inactivates RNA,[171] and one report indicates that this alters learned behavior in flatworms.[172] Or 8-azaguanine is a protein and nucleic acid antimetabolite, slowing or halting the production of nucleoproteins like RNA. The performance measured to show the effects of this chemical might be the learning of paramecia.

Organ.   Damage to the amygdala, mammillary bodies, or fornix of animal brains has been observed to eliminate recent memory.[173] Such operations might be used quantitatively in order to remove memory in animals. Localized electroshock or strychnine, altering synaptic transmissions in memory storage areas, might have comparable results. The performance measured to show the effects might be conditioning of electroencephalographic rhythms to flickering light inputs, until they assimilate, as they will, the frequencies of the flickering light inputs.[174]

Organism.   Information, such as memories of a maze, can be made unavailable or removed from storage in animals by extinction of training, by cerebral electroshock, by rapid cooling of the brain with liquid air,[175] or by drugs.[176] Any of these methods might be used. The performance employed to measure the effects of removing this information might be maze running.

Group.   One or more members with less training could be substituted in a problem-solving group for others with more, or one or more of the members could be given scopolamine ("twilight sleep" used in obstetrics) to remove his memories temporarily. Or the same groups could solve problems with and without dictionaries or charts containing relevant information. Any quantifiable group problem-solving process could be the performance used to evaluate the effects of removing information from the group.

Organization.   Experienced companies, battalions, or regiments might be removed from brigades and replaced by novices. The effects of such loss of information could be evaluated by objective measures of the efficiency of the performance of the brigade, such as the number of bits of information per hour transmitted by it in official communications, or the number of shells per hour arriving on target.

Society.   Important information can be lost to a society by the sudden death of a king, president, or other ruler, or by the arrest or emigration of leaders or elites. Major disasters or wars can destroy socially valuable information. The performance of such a society could be measured by determining from political documents the nature of policy decisions, made in foreign or internal affairs, during the six months immediately before and a similar period immediately after an important loss of social information.

HYPOTHESIS 3.3.7.2-14: *A system which survives generally decides to employ the least costly adjustment to a threat or a strain produced by a stress first and increasingly more costly ones later.* (M)

This hypothesis is one manifestation of the principle of least effort (see page 436). Systems tend to maximize gains and minimize costs. This principle has often been stated vaguely, in ways that are difficult to confirm or disconfirm quantitatively. This can be done, however, if separate operations define each of the adjustment processes under consideration, if their costs are measured by other, independent operations, and if it is clear whether short-range or long-range costs or both are to be considered.

Cell.   A hungry amoeba, for example, will eat food that is nearby first and later swim to more distant food.

Organism, matter-energy processing.   If a continuously increasing amount of acid is injected into a dog's veins, a number of adjustment processes will protect the stability of the blood acidity from this stress. The first adjustment to reach its maximal effectiveness will probably be overbreathing, which produces alkalosis to compensate for the acidosis. Excretion of more chloride in the urine than usual (as ammonium chloride) and the "chloride shift" in tissue fluids are other adjustments which aid in counteracting the stress; these adjustments probably achieve their maximal effects later than overbreathing does. Those organisms which can survive longest under such stress may well be the ones which first employ the adjustments that use the most easily replaceable inputs (*e.g.,* the nitrogen in ammonium chloride).

Organism, information processing. A normal person's adjustment processes against informational stresses, like his physiological adjustment processes, may ordinarily be mobilized in order of their costs, just as a good chess player sacrifices pawns before bishops and bishops before the queen. When people are unable to solve a problem or achieve a goal, for example, they may lower their levels of aspiration and try something simpler. This is relatively inexpensive. If this does not make them content, they may rationalize their behavior saying, "I could have done it if I had had more time." This is a little more costly since it places them in tactically difficult positions. Someone might say, "All right, take all the time you need," and it would then become obvious that they were unable to do it. Repression, said by many psychiatrists to be a yet more costly adjustment, may be the next way of handling the stress if they are forced to continue working toward the goal. That is, their "attention may wander to other things," but the unresolved strain would still remain within them, which some have said can cause costly psychosomatic symptoms. Finally, to avoid the frustration of having an unresolved problem constantly obtrude on them, they may reject or refuse to attend to the entire information input and a psychotic state may result, which would cut them off from close human contact and in other ways be extremely costly to them.

Organization. An army, in order to repel an attack, may first sacrifice a squad, then companies or regiments, and if still unsuccessful, finally throw into battle large mobile reserves like divisions.

HYPOTHESIS 5.2-8: *A system usually associates with other systems which have arisen from similar templates rather than with those derived from dissimilar templates.* (H)

Cell. When different types of embryonic cells are mixed, they sort themselves out and grow together only with other cells of the same type (see page 351).

Organ. Organ transplants from other individuals tend to be rejected by the receiving organism.

Organism. Family members commonly associate and keep nonmembers out of private relationships.

Group. Irish families that move to America in general choose to live near other Irish families, and Greek families near other Greek families.

Organization. Companies in similar fields meet in conventions more often than they meet with other types of companies.

Society. Nations of comparable origin typically vote together in the United Nations.

In all this there seems to be a principle which serves to maintain homogeneity of systems, perhaps at all levels. It is possible that learning may change this principle at higher levels—all the world's chief nations today are significantly nonhomogeneous genetically. This hypothesis probably has wide applicability at all levels except the highest.

6. Models and simulations

Hypotheses of the sort presented in this chapter deal with living systems, not simulations of them, so there are no hypotheses to present in this section.

7. Conclusions

In this chapter 173 cross-level hypotheses have been stated. Without question many more could be formulated. Some apply to only two or three levels, some to all levels of living systems. As I have said, some can probably be confirmed. Undoubtedly others are entirely wrong or subject to various qualifications and restrictions, since perhaps more contradicting than sustaining instances can be found. The proof of general systems hypotheses is in their empirical evaluation. And many such studies together must constitute the primary basis for determining the usefulness of general living systems theory. The only full-fledged cross-level study of five levels completed so far is the information input overload research reported in Chap. 5. Other investigations covering two or three levels have been carried out.

Multilevel researches are not easy. They demand the most careful and rigorous conceptualization and research design. They require the skills of several disciplines. But their findings are important, crucial in the development of general theory about living systems.[177] Such investigations can best be conducted in interdisciplinary research institutes, centers, and groups.

NOTES AND REFERENCES

[1]Simon, H. A. New developments in the theory of the firm. *Amer. econ. Rev,* 1962, **52,** 1-15. Reprinted by permission.
[2]NOTE: Mill [Mill, J. S. *System of logic.* Vol. 2. Book VI. London: Longman's Green, 1865 (6th ed.), 498–499] states:

"This preparatory treatment consists in finding general propositions which express concisely what is common to large classes of observed facts: and these are called the empirical laws of the phenomena. We have, therefore, to inquire, whether any similar preparatory process can be performed on the facts of the social science: whether there are any empirical laws in history or statistics. . . . To collect, therefore, such empirical laws (which are never more than approximate generalizations) from direct observations, is an important part of the process of sociological inquiry."

[3]NOTE: Homans (Homans, G. C. *Social behavior: its elementary forms.* New York: Harcourt, 1961, 10–11. Reprinted by permission.) writes:

"Much modern sociological theory seems to me to possess every virtue except that of explaining anything. Part of the trouble is that much of it consists of systems of categories, or pigeonholes, into which the theorist fits different aspects of social behavior. No science can proceed without its system of categories, or conceptual scheme, but this in itself is not enough to give it explanatory power. A conceptual scheme is not a theory. The science also needs a set of general propositions about the relations between the categories, for without such propositions explanation is impossible. No explanation without propositions! But much modern sociological theory seems quite satisfied with itself when it has set up its conceptual scheme. The theorist shoves different aspects of behavior into his pigeonholes, cries, 'Ah-ha!' and stops. He has written the dictionary of a language that has no sentences. He would have done better to start with the sentences."

[4]Berelson, B. & Steiner, G. A. *Human behavior: an inventory of scientific findings.* New York: Harcourt, 1964.

[5]Ashby, W. R. *Cybernetics today and its future contribution to the engineering-sciences.* New York: Foundation for Instrumentation, Education, and Research, 1961, 15–16.

[6]Snyder, R. C., Bruck, H. W., & Sapin, B. Decision-making as an approach to the study of international politics. In R. C. Snyder, H. W. Bruck, & B. Sapin (Eds.). *Foreign policy decision-making. An approach to the study of international politics.* New York: Free Press of Glencoe, 1962, 35. Copyright © 1962 by the Free Press of Glencoe, A Division of the Macmillan Company. Reprinted by permission.

[7]NOTE: As Berelson and Steiner (Berelson, B. & Steiner, G. A. *Op. cit.,* 5) say, these are important statements of proper generality for which there is [or could be] some good amount of scientific evidence.

[8]NOTE: As Berelson and Steiner (*Ibid.,* 5. Reprinted by permission.) put it in reference to their propositions: "By *proper generality* we mean a middle ground. Highly specific or topical facts, on the one hand, and highly abstract statements, on the other, are both excluded in favor of findings that apply to a substantial range of human behavior and that make explicit the human content with which they deal."

[9]NOTE: One notable exception is the following statement by Guetzkow (Guetzkow, H. Isolation and collaboration: a partial theory of inter-nation relations. *J. Conflict Resolution,* 1957, **1**, 62*). He recognizes cross-level similarities while not denying obvious cross-level differences. He sometimes

*This excerpt from Isolation and collaboration: a partial theory of inter-nation relations by Harold Guetzkow is reprinted from the *Journal of Conflict Resolution,* Vol. 1, No. 1 (March 1957), 62 by permission of the Publisher, Sage Publications, Inc.

uses the word "group" in a narrow sense and sometimes in a general sense very like "social system:"

"There will be those who question the validity of my interchanging the terms 'group' and 'nation' and of applying concepts developed in the study of groups to nation-states. It has sometimes been argued that the sovereignty of nation-states is a unique characteristic, not possessed by other groups. . . . Such assertions seem to me to be overstatements, resulting from careless conceptualization and the extravagant nurturing of the original sovereignty concept by eighteenth- and nineteenth-century nationalisms. The facts of international life indicate that states, like other groups, are circumscribed in their behavior by political, social, cultural, and economic realities both within themselves and in their external environment. The leaders of nations, just like the leaders of other groups, are dependent for their very positions upon a complex structure of power within the group. . . .

"In this sense, nations share common features with less comprehensive and less powerful groups. . . . My model endeavors to help cross . . . artificial academic barriers by developing a general theory of intergroup relations applicable to nations. Even as the model applies concepts about groups to nations, it, in turn, should be applicable not only to nations but to all groups. It should thus be useful in explaining and predicting the behavior of social and community groups, political parties, cities, states, and both regional and international organizations. By identifying a basic similarity among all these units, it may help to refocus thinking and research in them all."

Other such cross-level propositions can be found in Berelson, B. & Steiner, G. A. *Op. cit.,* 623, 660–661; in Odum, H. T. & Pinkerton, R. C. Time's speed regulator: the optimum efficiency for maximum power output in physical and biological systems. *Amer. Sci.,* 1955, **43**, 331–343; and in Mountcastle's research discussed under Hypotheses 3.3.1.2-1 and 3.3.1.2-2 in this chapter.

[10]Berelson, B. & Steiner, G. A. *Op. cit.,* 368–369.

[11]*Ibid.,* 461.

[12]Mishler, E. G. *The social structure of a mental institution.* Unpublished paper.

[13]Levy, M. J., Jr. *Explorations for a structural analysis of the United States Army.* Unpublished paper.

[14]Deutsch, K. W. International communication: the media and flows. *Publ. Opin. Quart.,* 1956, **20**, 143–195.

[15]Deutsch, K. W., Bliss, C. I., & Eckstein, A. Population, sovereignty, and share of foreign trade. *Econ. Devel. and cultural Change,* 1962, **10**, 353–366.

[16]Suggested by Berelson, B. & Steiner, G. A. *Op. cit.,* 612–613.

[17]Huntington, E. *Civilization and climate.* New Haven: Yale Univ. Press, 1915.

[18]McClelland, D. C. *The achieving society.* Princeton, N.J.: Van Nostrand, 1961.

[19]Waldenberg, M. J. A structural taxonomy of spatial hierarchies. In M. Chisholm, A. Frey, & P. Haggett (Eds.). *Regional forecasting: Colston papers,* 22. London: Butterworths, 1971, 147–175.

Also Waldenberg, M. J. The average hexagon in spatial hierarchies. In R. J. Chorley (Ed.). *Spatial analysis in geomorphology.* London: Methuen, 1972, 323–352.

[20]March, J. G. & Simon, H. A. *Organizations.* New York: Wiley, 1958, 146–148, 160.

[21]Participants in a formal models seminar—the cost of decision making. Round table discussions on behavior theory. *Behav. Sci.,* 1956, **1**, 69–78.

[22]Mountcastle, V. B. The neural replication of sensory events in the somatic afferent system. In J. C. Eccles (Ed.). *Brain and conscious experience.* New York: Springer-Verlag, 1966, 85–115.

[23]Stevens, S. S. The psychophysics of sensory function. In W. A. Rosenblith (Ed.). *Sensory communication.* New York: Wiley, 1961, 1–33.

[24]Mountcastle, V. B. *Op. cit.,* 96, 102, 109.

[25]*Ibid.,* 104–108.

[26]Miller, G. A. The magical number seven, plus or minus two: some limits on our capacity for processing information. *Psychol. Rev.,* 1956, **63,** 81–97.

[27]Foster, C. C., Rapoport, A., & Orwant, C. J. A study of a large sociogram: II. Elimination of free parameters. *Behav. Sci.,* 1963, **8,** 56–65.

Cf. also Rapoport, A. Cycle distribution in random nets. *Bull. math. Biophys.,* 1948, **10,** 145–157.

Cf. also Rapoport, A. Nets with distance bias. *Bull. math. Biophys.,* 1951, **13,** 85–91.

Rapoport, A. The probability distribution of distinct hits on closely packed targets. *Bull. math. Biophys.,* 1951, **13,** 133–137.

Rapoport, A. Contribution to the theory of random and biased nets. *Bull. math. Biophys.,* 1957, **19,** 257–278.

Rapoport, A. Nets with reciprocity bias. *Bull. math. Biophys.,* 1958, **20,** 191–201.

[28]Rapoport, A. & Horvath, W. J. A study of a large sociogram. *Behav. Sci.,* 1961, **6,** 279–291.

Cf. also Foster, C. C., Rapoport, A., & Orwant, C. J. *Op. cit.*

Rapoport, A. Spread of information through a population with socio-structural bias: I. Assumption of transitivity. *Bull. math. Biophys.,* 1953, **15,** 523–533.

Rapoport, A. Spread of information through a population with socio-structural bias: II. Various models with partial transitivity. *Bull. math. Biophys.,* 1953, **15,** 535–543.

[29]Dodd, S. C. The counteractance model. *Amer. J. Sociol.,* 1957, **63,** 273–283.

Cf. also Dodd, S. C. A power of town size predicts an interval interacting. *Soc. Forces,* 1957, **36,** 132–137.

Dodd, S. C. A test of message diffusion of chain tags. *Amer. J. Sociol.,* 1956, **61,** 425–432.

[30]Shannon, C. E. & Weaver, W. *The mathematical theory of communication.* Urbana: Univ. of Illinois Press, 1949, 67–68.

Cf. also Pierce, J. R. *Symbols, signals and noise: the nature and process of communication.* New York: Harper, 1961, 175.

[31]Berelson, B. & Steiner, G. A. *Op. cit.,* 501.

[32]Allport, G. W. & Kramer, B. M. Some roots of prejudice. *J. Psychol.,* 1946, **22,** 9–39.

[33]Berelson, B. & Steiner, G. A. *Op. cit.,* 531.

[34]*Ibid.,* 624.

[35]Wilner, D. M., Walkley, R. P., & Cook, S. W. Residential proximity and intergroup relations in public housing projects. *J. soc. Issues,* 1952, **8,** 45–69.

[36]Berelson, B. & Steiner, G. A. *Op. cit.,* 349.

[37]Roby, T. B. & Lanzetta, J. T. Work group structure, communication, and group performance. *Sociometry,* 1956, **19,** 105–113.

[38]Suggested by Berelson, B. & Steiner, G. A. *Op. cit.,* 356–358.

[39]March, J. G. & Simon, H. A. *Organizations.* New York: Wiley, 1958.

[40]*Ibid.,* 128.

[41]*Ibid.,* 128–129.

[42]*Ibid.,* 153.

[43]*Ibid.*

[44]*Ibid.,* 167.

[45]Cf. Deutsch, K. W. *Nationalism and social communication.* Cambridge, Mass.: Technology Press, 1953.

[46]*Ibid.*

[47]McConnell, J. V. *Understanding human behavior.* (2d ed.) New York: Holt, Rinehart, and Winston, 1977, 217–234.

Also Miller, J. G. Discrimination without awareness. *Amer. J. Psychol.,* 1938, **52,** 562–578.

Also Berelson, B. & Steiner, G. A. *Op. cit.,* 93–95.

[48]Suggested by Berelson, B. & Steiner, G. A. *Op. cit.,* 100.

[49]*Ibid.,* 101–104.

[50]*Ibid.,* 101–104, 529–537.

[51]Hess, E. H. & Polt, J. M. Pupil size as related to interest value of visual stimuli. *Science,* 1960, **132,** 349–350.

[52]Suggested by Berelson, B. & Steiner, G. A. *Op. cit.,* 370.

[53]Among the articles on coding theorems are:

Abramson, N. M. Error-correcting codes from linear sequential circuits. In C. Cherry (Ed.). *Fourth London symposium on information theory.* New York: Academic Press, 1961, 26–40.

Andrew, A. M. A self-optimizing system of coding. In C. Cherry (ed.). *Fourth London symposium on information theory.* New York: Academic Press, 1961, 68–82.

Barnard, G. A. Simple proof of simple cases of the coding theorem. In C. Cherry (Ed.). *Third London symposium on information theory.* New York: Academic Press, 1956, 96–102.

Breiman, L. Finite-state channels. In J. Kozesnik (Ed.). *Transactions of the second Prague conference on information theory, statistical decision functions, random processes.* New York: Academic Press, 1960, 49–60.

Driml, M. A linear method of construction of error-correcting codes. In C. Cherry (Ed.). *Fourth London symposium on information theory.* New York: Academic Press, 1961, 1–10.

Elias, P. Coding for noisy channels. *IRE National Convention Record,* 1955, part 4, 37–44.

Elias, P. Coding for two noisy channels. In C. Cherry (Ed.). *Third London symposium on information theory.* New York: Academic Press, 1956, 61–76.

Goblick, T. J., Jr. Sequential encoding of a binary source with a distortion measure. *MIT quart. Progr. Rep.,* 1962, July, **66,** 231–239.

Jelinek, F. Code construction for two-way channels. *MIT quart. Progr. Rep.,* 1962, October, **67,** 141–155.

Hamming, R. W. Error detecting and error correcting codes. *Bell Sys. tech. J.,* 1950, 147–160.

Khinchin, A. I. On the fundamental theorems of information theory. In A. I. Khinchin (Ed.). *Mathematical foundations of information theory.* New York: Dover, 1957, 30–120.

Laemmel, A. E. A general class of codes and their physical realization. In C. Cherry (Ed.). *Third London symposium on information theory.* New York: Academic Press, 1956, 55–60.

Nedoma, J. On non-ergodic channels. In J. Kozesnik (Ed.). *Transactions of the second Prague conference on information theory, statistical decision functions, random processes.* New York: Academic Press, 1960, 363–396.

Peterson, W. W. *Error correcting codes.* Cambridge, Mass.: MIT Press, 1961.

Peterson, W. W. & Fontaine, A. B. Group code equivalence and optimum codes. *IRE Trans. Inform. Theory,* IT-5, 1959, May, 60–70.

Shannon, C. E. A mathematical theory of communication. *Bell Sys. tech. J.,* 1948, **27,** 623.

Shannon, C. E. Communication in the presence of noise. *Proc. IRE,* 1949, **37,** 10–21.

Shannon, C. E. The zero error capacity of a noisy channel. *IRE Trans. Inform. Theory,* IT-2, 1956, September, 8–19.

Shannon, C. E. A note on partial ordering for communications channels. *Inform. and Control*, 1958, **1**, 390–397.

Shannon, C. E. Certain results in coding theory for noisy channels. *Inform. and Control*, 1957, **1**, 6–25.

Shannon, C. E. Two-way communication channels. In J. Neyman (Ed.). *Proceedings of the fourth Berkeley symposium on mathematical statistics and probability*, 1961, **1**, 611–644.

Thomasian, A. J. Error bounds for continuous channels. In C. Cherry (Ed.). *Fourth London symposium on information theory*. New York: Academic Press, 1961, 46–60.

Winkelbauer, K. Communication channels with finite past history. In J. Kozesnik (Ed.). *Transactions of the second Prague conference on information theory, statistical decision functions, random processes*. New York: Academic Press, 1960, 685–832.

Wolfowitz, J. Strong converse of the coding theorem for semi-continuous channels. *Illinois J. Math.*, 1959, **3**, 477–489.

Wozencraft, J. M. & Reiffen, B. *Sequential decoding*. Cambridge, Mass.: MIT Press, 1961.

Wozencraft, J. M. & Horstein, M. Coding for two way channels. In C. Cherry (Ed.). *Fourth London symposium on information theory*. New York: Academic Press, 1961, 11–25.

Zetterberg, L. A comparative study of delta and pulse code modulation. In C. Cherry (Ed.) *Third London symposium on information theory*. New York: Academic Press, 1956, 103–110.

Ziv, J. New systematic decoding for memoryless channels. *MIT quart. Progr. Rep.*, April 1961, **61**, 135–144.

[54]Ashby, W. R. *Op. cit.*, 7.

[55]Shannon, C. E. A mathematical theory of communication. *Bell Sys. tech. J.*, 1948, **27**, 623.
Cf. also Shannon, C. E. Two-way communication channels. *Op. cit.*

[56]Fano, R. M. *Transmission of information: a statistical theory of communications*. Cambridge, Mass.: MIT Press, 1961.

[57]Huffman, D. A. The synthesis of linear sequential coding networks. In C. Cherry (Ed.). *Third London symposium on information theory*. New York: Academic Press, 1956, 77–95. Cf. also Huffman, D. A. The linear circuit viewpoint on error-correcting codes. *IRE Trans. Inform. Theory*, IT-2, 1956, September.

[58]Pierce, J. R. *Op. cit.*, 94–97, 104, 142.

[59]Shannon, C. E. & Weaver, W. *The mathematical theory of communication. Op. cit.*, 28–31.
Cf. also Pierce, J. R. *Op. cit.*, 98.

[60]Shannon, C. E. & Weaver, W. *The mathematical theory of communication. Op. cit.*, 39–42.
Cf. also Pierce, J. R. *Op. cit.*, 156.

[61]*Ibid.*

[62]Suggested by Pierce, J. R. *Ibid.*, 162–163.

[63]Cf. Ackoff, R. L. & Emery, F. E. *On purposeful systems*. Chicago: Aldine-Atherton, 1972, 183–187.

[64]Pierce, J. R. *Op. cit.*, 149–150.

[65]Suggested by Berelson, B. & Steiner, G. A. *Op. cit.*, 606.

[66]Berelson, B. & Steiner, G. A. *Op. cit.*, 114–116.

[67]McClelland, D. C. & Atkinson, J. W. The projective expression of needs: I. The effect of different intensities of the hunger drive on perception. *J. Psychol.*, 1948, **25**, 205–222.

[68]Suggested by Berelson, B. & Steiner, G. A. *Op. cit.*, 136–137.

[69]Skinner, B. F. A case history in scientific method. In S. Koch (Ed.). *Psychology: a study of a science*. Vol. 2. New York: McGraw-Hill, 1959, 359–379.

[70]Suggested in a personal communication from Stanley J. Wollmans.

[71]Suggested by Berelson, B. & Steiner, G. A. *Op. cit.*, 178–179.

[72]*Ibid.*, 183–187.

[73]Suggested by March, J. G. & Simon, H. A. *Op. cit.*, 63.

[74]*Ibid.*

[75]Suggested by Turner, G. B. The effectiveness of British colonial organization in the seventeenth and eighteenth centuries. Unpublished paper.

[76]Shaw, M. E. Some effects of unequal distribution of information upon group performance in various communication nets. *J. abnorm. soc. Psychol.*, 1954, **49**, 547–553.
Also Gilchrist, J. C., Shaw, M. E., & Walker, L. C. Some effects of unequal distribution of information in a wheel group structure. *J. abnorm. soc. Psychol.*, 1954, **49**, 554–556.

[77]Snyder, R. C. & Paige, G. D. The United States decision to resist aggression in Korea: the application of an analytic scheme. *Admin. Sci. Quart.*, 1958, **3**, 362.

[78]Suggested by Berelson, B. & Steiner, G. A. *Op. cit.*, 537–538.

[79]Suggested by Berelson, B. & Steiner, G. A. *Ibid.*, 414–415.

[80]Sayles, L. R. *Behavior of industrial work groups: prediction and control*. New York: Wiley, 1958, 24.

[81]Snyder, R. C. & Paige, G. D. *Op. cit.*

[82]Suggested by Rogers, E. M. *Diffusion of innovations*. New York: Free Press of Glencoe, 1962, 313.

[83]*Ibid.*, 312.

[84]*Ibid.*

[85]Snyder, R. C. & Paige, G. D. *Op. cit.*

[86]Bruck, H. W. Formal factors and the process of decision: a case study of the 1938 trade agreement between Canada and the United States. Unpublished paper.

[87]Suggested by Berelson, B. & Steiner, G. A. *Op. cit.*, 661–662.

[88]Suggested by Royce, J. R. & Buss, A. R. *The role of general systems and information theory in multi-factor individuality theory. Canadian psychol. Rev.*, 1976, **17**, 1–21.

[89]Suggested by Edwards, E. O. The role of profits as a motive and guide for the operation of business enterprise. Unpublished paper.
Cf. also Passer, H. C. Development of large-scale organizations: electrical manufacturing around 1900. *J. econ. History*, 1952, **12**, 378–395.

[90]Simon, H. A. *Models of man*. New York: Wiley, 1957, 241–260.

[91]Cf. Loomis, S. *The fatal friendship*. Garden City, N.Y.: Doubleday & Co., 1972, 62–64.

[92]Odum, H. T. & Pinkerton, R. C. Time's speed regulator: the optimum efficiency for maximum power output in physical and biological systems. *Amer. Sci.*, 1955, **43**, 331–343.

[93]Cannon, W. B. *Bodily changes in pain, hunger, fear, and rage.* (2d ed.) New York: Appleton, 1929.

[94]Gordon, K. H. Group judgments in the field of lifted weights. *J. exper. Psychol.*, 1924, **3**, 398–400.
Cf. also Watson, G. B. Do groups think more efficiently than individuals? *J. abnorm. Psychol.*, 1928–1929, **23**, 328–336.
Stroop, J. R. Is the judgment of the group better than that of the average member of the group? *J. exper. Psychol.*, 1932, **15**, 550–562.
Gurnee, H. Maze learning in the collective situation. *J. Psychol.*, 1937, **3**, 437–443.

[95]Barnlund, D. C. Comparative study of individual, majority, and group judgment. *J. abnorm. soc. Psychol.*, 1959, **58**, 55–60.

[96]Watson, G. B. *Op. cit.*

[97]Gurnee, H. A comparison of collective and individual judgments of fact. *J. exper. Psychol.*, 1937, **21**, 106–112.

Cf. also Thorndike, R. L. The effect of discussion upon the correctness of group decisions, when the factor of majority influence is allowed for. *J. soc. Psychol.*, 1938, **9**, 343–362.

[98]Gurnee, H. A comparison of collective and individual judgments of fact. *Op. cit.*

[99]Barnlund, D. C. *Op. cit.*

[100]*Ibid.*

[101]*Ibid.*

[102]*Ibid.*

[103]Taylor, D. W. & Faust, W. L. Twenty questions: efficiency in problem solving as a function of size of group. *J. exper. Psychol.*, 1952, **44**, 360–368.

[104]Cf. Marquis, D. G. Individual responsibility and group decisions involving risk. *Indust. Management Rev.*, 1962, 3, 8–23. Reprinted by permission.

[105]Harris, D. D. & Ullman, E. L. The nature of cities. *Ann. Amer. Acad. polit. soc. Sci.*, 1945, **242**, 7–17.

Cf. also Duncan, O. D. Human ecology and population studies. In P. M. Houser & O. D. Duncan (Eds.). *The study of population: an inventory and appraisal.* Chicago: Univ. of Chicago Press, 1959, 689.

[106]Gist, N. P. & Halbert, L. A. *Urban society.* (4th ed.) New York: Crowell, 1956, 119, 121–123.

[107]Suggested in a personal communication from Harold R. Lindman.

[108]Churchman, C. W., Ackoff, R. L., Arnoff, E. L. *Introduction to operations research.* New York: Wiley, 1957.

[109]Elkind, J. I. *Characteristics of simple manual control systems.* Technical Report No. 111. Cambridge, Mass.: MIT-Lincoln Laboratory, 1956.

[110]Simon, H. A. How big is a chunk? *Science*, 1974, **183**, 482–487.

[111]Heron, W. Cognitive and physiological effects of perceptual isolation. In P. Solomon, P. E. Kubzansky, P. H. Liederman, J. H. Mendelson, R. Trumbull, & D. Wexler (Eds.). *Sensory deprivation.* Cambridge, Mass.: Harvard Univ. Press, 1961, 6–33.

Cf. also Hebb, D. O. The motivating effects of exteroceptive stimulation. *Amer. Psychol.*, 1958, **13**, 109.

[112]Fox, S. S. Self-maintained sensory input and sensory deprivation in monkeys: a behavioral and neuropharmacological study. *J. comp. physiol. Psychol.*, 1962, **55**, 438–444.

[113]Berlyne, D. E. The influence of complexity and novelty in visual figures on orienting responses. *J. exper. Psychol.*, 1958, **55**, 289–296.

Cf. also Berlyne, D. E. The influence of the albedo and complexity of stimuli on visual fixation in the human infant. *Brit. J. Psychol.*, 1958, **49**, 315–318.

[114]Harlow, H. F. & Zimmermann, R. R. Affectional responses in the infant monkey. *Science*, 1959, **130**, 421–432.

[115]Miller, J. G. The development of experimental stress-sensitive tests for predicting performance. *Psychol. Res. Assoc., Rep. 53–10*, 1953.

[116]Suggested by Berelson, B. & Steiner, G. A. *Op. cit.*, 619–620.

Cf. also Ashby, W. R. *Design for a brain.* (2d ed.) New York: Wiley, 1954.

[117]March, J. G. & Simon, H. A. *Op. cit.*, 173–174.

[118]Suggested by Berelson, B. & Steiner, G. A. *Op. cit.*, 615.

[119]Berelson, B. & Steiner, G. A. *Ibid.*, 661. Reprinted by permission.

[120]*Ibid.*, 267–271.

[121]Feierabend, I. K. Cross-national analysis of political violence. In D. E. Knight & L. J. Fogel. (Eds.). *Cybernetics, simulations, and conflict resolution.* New York: Spartan Books, 1971, 97–117, 106.

[122]Suggested by Berelson, B. & Steiner, G. A. *op. cit.*, 500–501.

[123]Berelson, B. & Steiner, G. A. *Ibid.*, 622.

[124]National Research Council. A brief review of salient specific findings on morale and human behavior under disaster conditions. Unpublished memorandum, April 18, 1958.

[125]March, J. G. & Simon, H. A. *Op. cit.*, 41–42.

[126]Kerr, C. & Siegel, A. The interindustry propensity to strike—an international comparison. In A. W. Kornhauser, R. Dubin, & A. M. Ross (Eds.). *Industrial conflict.* New York: McGraw-Hill, 1954, 191–195.

[127]Mack, R. W. & Snyder, R. C. The analysis of social conflict—toward an overview and synthesis. *J. Conflict Resolution*, 1957, **1**, 231.

[128]Brody, R. A. Some systematic effects of the spread of nuclear weapons technology. *J. Conflict Resolution*, 1963, **7**, 663–753.

[129]Deutsch, K. W. & Singer, J. D. Multipolar power systems and international stability. *World Politics*, 1964, **16**, 390–406.

[130]Singer, J. D. & Small, M. Alliance aggregation and the onset of war, 1815–1945. In J. D. Singer (Ed.). *Quantitative international politics: insights and evidence.* New York: Free Press of Glencoe, 1968, 247–286.

[131]Mack, R. W. & Snyder, R. C. *Op. cit.*

[132]Burns, A. L. From balance to deterrence: a theoretical analysis. *World Politics*, 1957, **9**, 508.

[133]Suggested by March, J. G. & Simon, H. A. *Op. cit.*, 122.

[134]*Ibid.*

[135]Mack, R. W. & Snyder, R. C. *Op. cit.*, 237.

[136]March, J. G. & Simon, H. A. *Op. cit.*, 126.

[137]Berelson, B. & Steiner, G. A. *Op. cit.*, 372.

[138]*Ibid.*, 583.

[139]*Ibid.*, 584.

[140]*Ibid.*, 580–584.

[141]Suggested by Berelson, B. & Steiner, G. A. *Ibid.*, 271–276.

[142]For example, Barker, R. G. An experimental study of the resolution of conflict by children. In Q. McNemar & M. A. Merrill (Eds.). *Studies in personality.* New York: McGraw-Hill, 1942, 13–34.

Cf. also Brown, J. S. Gradients of approach and avoidance responses and their relation to level of motivation. *J. comp. physiol. Psychol.*, 1948, **41**, 450–465.

Miller, N. E. Experimental studies of conflict. In J. McV. Hunt (Ed.). *Personality and the behavior disorders.* Vol. 1. New York: Ronald, 1944, 431–465.

[143]Freeman, J. L. The new deal for Indians: a study of bureau-committee relations in American government. Unpublished doctoral thesis. Princeton Univ., 1952.

[144]Turner, G. B. *Op. cit.*

[145]Suggested by March, J. G. & Simon, H. A. *Op. cit.*, 116.

[146]*Ibid.*

[147]*Ibid.*

[148]Morgan, H. E. Hormonal control of growth and protein metabolism. In J. R. Brobeck (Ed.). *Best and Taylor's physiological basis of medical practice.* (9th ed.) Baltimore: Williams & Wilkins, 1973, 7-143–7-164.

Also Malthus, T. R. *An essay on the principle of population.* London: T. Bensley, 1803.

Also Starr, C. & Rudman, R. Parameters of technological growth. *Science*, 1973, **182**, 358–364.

[149]Roston, S. On biological growth. *Bull. Math. Biophysics*, 1962, **4**, 369–373.

[150]Meadows, D. H., Meadows, D. L., Randers, J., & Behrens, W. W., III. *The limits to growth.* New York: Universe Books, 1972, 45–87.

[151]Passer, H. C. Determinants of plant size in the rayon industry. Unpublished paper.

[152]Haire, M. Biological models and empirical histories of the growth of organizations. In M. Haire (Ed.). *Modern organization theory.* New York: Wiley, 1959, 272.

[153]Suggested by Berelson, B. & Steiner, G. A. *Op. cit.,* 64–66.

[154]Hund, J. M. A proposed study of managerial decentralization. Unpublished paper.

[155]*Ibid.*

[156]Garfinkel, H. Notes toward a sociological theory of information. Unpublished paper.

[157]Suggested by Berelson, B. & Steiner, G. A. *Op. cit.,* 369.

[158]*Ibid.,* 370.

[159]Suggested by Mishler, E. G. The problem of an individual's commitment to organizational goals. Unpublished paper.

[160]Suggested by Berelson, B. & Steiner, G. A. *Op. cit.,* 369.

[161]Shaw, M. E. Some effects of irrelevant information upon problem-solving by small groups. *J. soc. Psychol.,* 1958, **47,** 33–37.

[162]NOTE: Allport, G. W. & Postman, L. J. The basic psychology of rumor. *Trans. N.Y. Acad. Sci.,* Series II, 1945, 61–81 is a report of a study using the procedure of this parlor game to study how errors slip into rumors.

[163]Skinner, B. F. Pigeons in a pelican. *Amer. Psychol.,* 1960, **15,** 28–37.

[164]*Ibid.,* 31. Reprinted by permission.

[165]*Ibid.,* 36. Reprinted by permission.

[166]von Neumann, J. Probabilistic logics and the synthesis of reliable organisms from unreliable components. In C. E. Shannon & J. McCarthy (Eds.). Automata studies. *Ann. Math. Studies,* No. 34, Princeton, N.J.: Princeton Univ. Press, 1956, 43–98.

[167]*Ibid.,* 63–64. Copyright © 1956 by Princeton University Press. Reprinted by permission of Princeton University Press.

[168]McCulloch, W. S. Agatha tyche: of nervous nets—the lucky reckoners. In *Mechanisation of thought processes. National Physical Laboratory Symposium No. 10.* Vol. 2. London: Her Majesty's Stationery Office, 1959, 611–633.
Cf. also McCulloch, W. S. *Embodiments of mind.* Cambridge, Mass.: MIT Press, 1965, 11–13.

[169]Cf. Flood, M. M. Stochastic learning in rats with hypothalamic implants. *Ann. N.Y. Acad. Sci.,* 1961, **89,** 795–822.
Cf. also Flood, M. M. Stochastic learning theory applied to choice experiments with rats, dogs, and men. *Behav. Sci.,* 1962, **7,** 289–314.

[170]Hydén, H. Biochemical changes in glial cells and nerve cells at varying activity. In F. Brüike (Ed.). *Biochemistry of the central nervous system.* Vol. 3. New York: Pergamon, 1959, 64–89.
Cf. also Gerard, R. W. Fixation of experience. In J. F. Delafresnaye (Ed.). *Brain mechanisms and learning.* Springfield, Ill.: Charles C Thomas, 1961, 21–35.
Schmitt, F. O. *Macromolecular specificity and biological memory.* Cambridge, Mass.: MIT Press, 1962.

[171]Colter, J. S., Bird, H. W., Moyer, A. W. & Brown, R. A. Infectivity of ribonucleic acid isolated from virus-infected tissues. *Virology,* 1957, **4,** 522–532.
Cf. also Wecker, E. The extraction of infectious virus nucleic acid with hot phenol. *Virology,* 1959, **7,** 241.

[172]Corning, W. C. & John, E. R. Effect of ribonuclease on retention of conditioned response in regenerated planarians. *Science,* 1961, **134,** 1363.

[173]Russell, W. R. *Brain, memory, learning.* Oxford: Clarendon Press, 1959.
Cf. also Sweet W. H., Talland, G. A., & Ervin, J. R. Loss of recent memory following section of the fornix. *Trans. Amer. Neurol. Assoc.,* 1959, **84,** 76–82.

[174]Livanov, M. N. & Polyakov, K. L. Electrical processes in the cerebral cortex of rabbits during the formation of the defensive conditioned reflex to rhythmic stimulation. *Bull. Acad. Sci. USSR.,* 1945, **3,** 286–307. As reported in V. S. Rusinov & M. Y. Rabinovich. Electroencephalographic researches in the laboratories and clinics of the Soviet Union. *EEG clin. Neurophysiol.,* 1958, suppl. 8.
Cf. also John, E. R. & Killam, K. F. Electrophysiological correlates of avoidance conditioning in the cat. *J. pharm. exp. Therapeutics,* 1959, **125,** 252–274.

[175]Ransmeier, R. E. & Gerard, R. W. Effects of temperature, convulsion, and metabolic factors on rodent memory and EEG. *Amer. J. Physiol.,* 1954, **179,** 663–664.

[176]Rabe, A. & Gerard, R. W. The influence of drugs on memory fixation time. *Amer. Psychol.,* 1959, **14,** 423.

[177]NOTE: As Berelson and Steiner (*Op. cit.,* 660–661. Reprinted by permission.) said of the 1,045 findings they list in their book:
"Taken together, just as they are, the findings provide an impressive range of prediction, itself a test of theory in science. Beyond that, there is raw material here in which synthesizing minds may see higher-order principles. . . .
"And, illustratively, working with such convergences may be one way to build a more summary, economic, coherent architecture of findings than is offered here—that is, to build better theories in the behavioral sciences."

Information Input Overload

CHAPTER FIVE

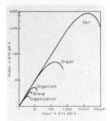

1. Introduction

Without confirmation, general living systems theory is only a philosophical position which emphasizes the value of recognizing regularities and differences among levels of living systems. In this chapter I shall present a literature survey and a quantitative research on similarities and orderly differences in a specific information processing function across five levels of living systems.

In recent years increasing attention has been devoted by physical, biological, and social scientists to the effects of alteration of rates of information input into systems, independent of changes in matter-energy flows.

In Chap. 8 I shall discuss investigations by others on information input underload in the organism, more commonly called "sensory deprivation." Our research group elected to study the opposite situation—information input overload, in which a living system at a given level is presented with more information than it can readily process. This chapter describes this cross-level research. We hear much today about the information explosion. Gluts of information produce information input overloads in receiving systems at various levels. Changes in different aspects of information inputs, including intensity and meaning, may create overloads, but this chapter concentrates upon the effects of increasing the rate of information inputs. As the amounts of information per unit time, often measured in bits per second, that are input to living systems at different levels increase, we have found they respond in comparable ways. As information inputs impinge more and more rapidly on a system, they eventually overload its capacity to transmit information. Ultimately breakdown of efficient information processing occurs, just as children playing "musical chairs" finally end up in confusion as the music plays faster and faster.

2. Statement of the problem

Continuous, accurate information processing is essential for many adjustment processes of any living system. Constant, vigilant visual observation, for example, enables a fish to know at every moment the locations of dangerous bigger fishes about it. When a school of large fish rushes toward it and surrounds it, presenting more and more threatening images, if it cannot process all the information it receives and as a result becomes confused, its survival as a living system is threatened.

The processing of incoming information is carried on by the information processing subsystems, from input transducer to output transducer. This chapter concerns systemwide activities, such as the input–output transfer function or channel capacity of a total system, rather than processes of a single subsystem, *e.g.*, the input–output transfer function or channel capacity of the system's channel and net subsystem. The researches which I report below almost without exception involve observations made at system boundaries rather than at subsystem boundaries, so no evidence is provided as to the channel capacities of the different subsystems. It may be, indeed, that one subsystem has a lower channel capacity than the others and thus is the bottleneck for the whole system, but except for two researches (see pages 138 and 139 and 139 and 140), the studies here reported throw no light on whether that is so. Because these systems have maximal capacities for information processing which they cannot exceed, they can be overloaded. A system's input–output transfer function under such circumstances can be measured, as can the adjustment processes which the system employs to cope with the excess stress resulting from the fact that the rate of information input to it is greater than the maximal processing rate of its information processing subsystems.

2.1   Effects of increase of information input rate on information output rate   The following five related cross-level hypotheses together constitute the topic of this chapter:

Cross-level formal identity in output processes to increases of information input rates.   The primary aspect of the information input overload phenomenon in living systems can be stated as follows:

HYPOTHESIS 5.1-1: *As the information input to a single channel of a living system—measured in bits per second—increases, the information output—measured similarly—increases almost identically at first but gradually falls behind as it approaches a certain output rate, the channel capacity, which cannot be exceeded in the channel. The output then levels off at that rate, and finally, as the information input rate continues to go up, the output decreases gradually toward zero as breakdown or the confusional state occurs under overload.*

The explanation for this phenomenon appears to be as follows: The maximum number of markers a channel can process per second and the maximum number of bits each marker can convey jointly determine the channel capacity, measured in bits per second. After one marker has been transmitted, there is in each channel a refractory period or "dead time" δ before another marker can be processed. In neurons δ can be as brief as 1 millisecond (ms). In systems at higher levels it is usually longer, often much longer. The refractory period limits the number of markers the channel can transmit per unit time.

The marker may be coded in one of three sorts of ways: (a) A code in which the information is conveyed by *when* a signal occurs, *e.g.*, a frequency-modulation or pulse-interval-modulation code in which a number of alternate interpulse or intersignal temporal intervals must be distinguished by the receiver at the end of the channel. (b) A code in which the information is conveyed by *whether* a signal of a given pattern occurs, *e.g.*, an amplitude- or pulse-modulation code in which each marker or pulse may have one or more

different patterns. The simplest such code is a binary one based on the presence or absence of a signal during a given time period. Or (c) a combination of (a) and (b).

There is also a minimum discriminable time interval σ that can be distinguished by the receiver at the end of the channel. Noise or distortion in a channel may alter the temporal interval between any two consecutive output pulses or signals, lengthening or shortening it as compared with the interval between the two corresponding input pulses or signals. The greater this variance or "jitter" in the input–output function, the larger must be the average difference between interpulse or intersignal temporal intervals, if they are to be distinguished reliably by the receiver. As a result, the number of such alternative temporal intervals which can be distinguished is less. Thus noise or distortion diminish the capacity of a channel using codes of type (a) or (c). They can also lower the capacity of a channel using codes of type (b) or (c) by masking the differences between one pattern of marker and another.

Let us assume that time is quantized into σ units and information is conveyed both by whether or not a signal appears in a given σ interval and also by how many σ intervals elapse between one signal and the next. Then calculations of channel capacity can be made by discrete information theory using these σ units. In this way MacKay and McCulloch in 1952 calculated 1,000 to 3,000 bits per second (s) to be the range of maximum rates of information transmission possible over a synapse between one neuron and another.[1] They demonstrated that this maximum rate is probably higher with pulse-interval or frequency modulation than with binary all-or-none amplitude modulation. Channel capacity can also be calculated by continuous information theory, taking into account that noise makes it impossible to determine exactly when a signal occurs. This was done by Rapoport and Horvath, my colleagues during the time we were carrying out our research on information input overload.[2] They assumed that intervals between input signals to a neuron had a Poisson distribution, that the neuron's refractory period $(\delta) = 1$ ms, and that the noise in the neuron had a Gaussian distribution with a standard deviation of σ. Under these circumstances, for various values of σ, they calculated the family of curves shown in Fig. 5-1. As this figure indicates, the maximum channel capacity of a neuron in which $\sigma = 5$ microseconds (μs)—which experiments have shown to be close to the range of values in real neurons (see pages 171 to 173)—is slightly more than 4,000 bits per s.

If similar measurements were made across levels of

living systems—not only cells but also organs, organisms, groups, organizations, and so on—different values for δ and σ would almost certainly be found. Using experimentally determined values for these variables it would be possible to graph families of curves somewhat like those in Fig. 5-1. Instead of showing formal identities in the way channels can be overloaded with information inputs which exist between one type of neuron and another, however, such families of curves would indicate whether there were formal identities representing a similar sort of information overload of channels between one level of living system and another. This chapter examines whether such formal identities exist.

The decrease of information output rates as information input rates exceed channel capacities is not the result of destruction of the systems by overloads of the matter-energy in the markers which convey the information because: (*a*) The process is almost instantly reversible. Decrease of the input rate to one which causes the cell to transmit at its maximum, but does not overload it, immediately raises the output rate back to channel capacity. And (*b*) final irreversible change of channels in living systems does occur, but only when the energy input is orders of magnitude greater than that involved in the various sorts of information overload discussed in this chapter.

It is interesting that some nonliving systems, particularly various sorts of counters, display comparable information input overload phenomena. For instance, as the rate of ionizing radiations entering a Geiger counter increases, the counter reaches its channel capacity and then begins to drop pulses. It is overloaded. The faster the input rate, the more pulses it drops. This results from the fact that, after one input of ionizing radiation, the counter has a dead time because positive ions formed by that input insulate it so it cannot respond to another input until they disperse.

2.2   Adjustment processes to information input overload   In our researches we discovered that several adjustment processes are used by living systems at various levels against the stresses of information input overload. Not all living systems employ all these adjustments. Systems at the lowest level, like the neuron, appear to use fewer of them than systems at higher levels, like the society, which employs not only all of them but also probably numerous complicated variations of them. The following appear to be the chief adjustment processes (see pages 36 and 61). *Omission*—failing to transmit certain randomly distributed signals in a message. *Error*—incorrectly transmitting certain signals in a message. *Queuing*—delaying transmission of certain signals in a message,

the sequence being temporarily stored until transmission. *Filtering*—giving priority in processing to certain classes of messages. *Abstracting*—processing a message with less than complete detail. *Multiple channels*—simultaneously transmitting messages over two

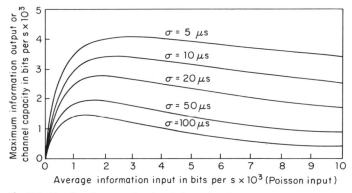

Fig. 5-1   Family of curves showing information input overload in channels. This is a set of theoretical curves calculated by Rapoport and Horvath using continuous information theory. They represent the channel capacities, over a range of rates of information input signals separated by a Poisson distribution of intervals, of different neurons with a refractory period (δ) of 1 ms and a Gaussian noise distribution with different standard deviations (σ). (From A. Rapoport & W. J. Horvath. The theoretical channel capacity of a single neuron as determined by various coding systems. *Inform. & Control*, 1960, **3**, 349.)

or more parallel channels. *Escape*—acting to cut off information input. *Chunking*—transmitting meaningful information in organized "chunks" of symbols rather than symbol by symbol. This last adjustment process, unlike the others, cannot be used with signals which do not convey meaning to the receiving system based on previous learning by it.

Each of these methods of adjustment has its costs, measured in time, matter, or energy consumed, in loss of reward, or in other units. Normally a system will first use the least costly adjustment. It is pathological to do otherwise.

Various sorts of formal identities related to the above adjustment processes and to the channel capacities of system channels may exist at several levels of living systems. A few such possible identities are stated in the following hypotheses:

Cross-level formal identities in adjustment processes to increases of information input rates

HYPOTHESIS 5.1-2: *Channels in living systems have adjustment processes which enable them to maintain stable, within a range, the similarity of the information output from them to the information input to them. The magnitude of these adjustment processes rises as information input rates increase up to and somewhat beyond the channel capacity. These adjustments enable the output rate to remain at or near channel capacity and then to decline gradually, rather than to fall precipitously to zero immediately whenever the information input rate exceeds the channel capacity.*

HYPOTHESIS 5.1-3: *Among the limited number of adjustment processes which channels in living systems employ as information input rates increase are: omission, error, queuing, filtering, abstracting, multiple channels, escape, and chunking. Each of these processes applies to random and nonrandom information inputs except chunking, which applies only to nonrandom inputs with repetitious patterning to a system that can associate (or learn). Each of these processes occurs at multiple levels of living systems. Each of these processes has a cost in some sort of decreased efficiency of information processing.*

Cross-level differences in adjustment processes to increases of information input rates

HYPOTHESIS 5.1-4: *Higher-level living systems in general have the emergent characteristics of more kinds and more complex combinations of adjustment processes than living systems at lower levels.*

Cross-level differences in channel capacities

HYPOTHESIS 5.1-25: *Channels in living systems at higher levels in general have lower capacities than those in living systems at lower levels.*

Hypotheses 5.1-2 and 5.1-3 above concern cross-level formal identities, while 5.1-4 and 5.1-25 deal with cross-level hierarchical disidentities or differences. The cross-level difference mentioned in Hypothesis 5.1-25 probably results from the fact that the more components there are in an information processing system, the lower is its channel capacity. There are several joint causes for this, two of the most obvious being that: (*a*) Recoding of information is usually necessary at the boundary between each component and the next, and since such recoding is never perfect, it always involves some error and loss of information. (*b*) Some components have lower channel capacities than others, and if there are *n* components in any system, the statistical probability of one of them being such a component with a lower channel capacity is always greater as *n* increases. Such a component constitutes a bottleneck, since no channel can transmit information faster than that component which has the lowest channel capacity. The above two reasons explain why in living systems the principle stated by Hypothesis 3.3.3.2-11 (see page 97) seems to apply, that the probability of error in or overload of an information chan-

nel is a monotonic increasing function of the number of components in it.

Now I shall review the evidence in the literature as to formal identities and disidentities among living systems at five levels—cell, organ, organism, group, and organization—in the way they react to information input overloads, giving special attention to (*a*) the input–output transfer function of a system in terms of its information processing rate, accuracy, and other characteristics, and (*b*) the associated adjustment processes used to relieve stress on its information processing subsystems and thus to maintain its output functions.

Later in the chapter I shall discuss our own experiments on the information input–output transfer function and related adjustment processes at the above-mentioned five levels of living systems.

3. Survey of related researches

In reviewing several hundred possibly related researches at the five levels under consideration I uncovered only two explicit mentions of cross-level similarities in information transmission (see pages 132 and 150). Moreover, I found not a single article about a system at one level which contained even one bibliographical reference to related problems of information input overload at any other level. This insularity results from the traditional separation of the academic disciplines. It is not usual—in fact some scientists may even consider it intellectually undisciplined—to refer to formal identities across levels in system input–output transfer functions or adjustment processes. As a result, quantitatively similar phenomena have repeatedly been discovered independently at different levels of living systems. If cross-level generalizing were more pervasive in science, a discovery at one level should immediately suggest that a comparable situation may be found at others. The following report on the literature is not exhaustive, but it attempts to present a few illustrative examples of researches at each of five levels relevant to the topic of this chapter.

3.1   Information input overload at the level of the cell   Information carried in molecules of chemical transmitter substances or on energic markers like pressure, stretch, or light provoke outputs from excitable cells of organisms. Neurons, including those with specialized receptor endings, respond to inputs with propagated action potentials that bring about output of transmitter substances from their endings. The action potentials of muscle fibers cause the fibers to twitch (see page 246). One reasonable way to investigate information processing in neurons is to study the changing frequencies of pulses inside a given neuron's boundary. Such an analysis can be made regardless of how the pulses were initiated in the external environment. The number of pulses or signals transmitted per second in a message on a channel need not, of course, be the same as the number of bits per second. It depends upon the code (see pages 265, 278, and 397). In a code based on an ensemble of alternate patterns of the marker, the maximum number of bits per pulse or signal is the logarithm to the base 2 of the number of those alternate patterns (see page 11). In a code based on an ensemble of a number of alternate interpulse or intersignal temporal intervals, the maximum number of bits per interval between two pulses or signals is the logarithm to the base 2 of the number of distinguishable intervals. If the exact size of the ensemble is not known (as in those studies discussed below in which input and/or output rates are measured in some other units than bits per second, like pulses or signals), the data are not sufficient to calculate the number of bits. We can only assume—perhaps incorrectly—that the rate in bits per second is proportional to that in pulses or signals per second and that therefore the input–output transfer-function curves in bits per second have similar shapes to those in pulses or signals per second. More research on the precise codes used by living systems is required to clear up present ignorance about such matters.

Several neurophysiological studies show that when a neuron—particularly if it is tonic, *i.e.*, has slow signal termination (see page 256)—receives inputs at an increasing rate of pulses per second its refractory period determines that the rate of output of pulses per second at first increases, then levels off at a maximum, and finally, at least in some cases, diminishes.

Making pulse inputs and recording outputs through microelectrodes placed at various locations inside cat motor neurons, Brock, Coombs, and Eccles studied the effects of antidromic pulses—*i.e.*, pulses passing up the axon in the opposite direction from the way they usually go (see page 262)—initiated by inputs of electrical pulses at various frequencies.[3] In one neuron they found that an output somadendritic spike—a high-amplitude electrical pulse in the cell body and in dendrites that accompanies the propagated action potential (see page 263)—was regularly elicited by every input pulse at the lowest frequencies, 13, 20, and 28 per second. Only every second input pulse elicited it at 42 input pulses per s, every third at 61, every fourth at 91, and every seventh at 140. At higher frequencies even more inputs were required to elicit each output. The relation which they found between input antidromic pulse rates and output somadendritic pulse rates is shown in Fig. 5-2. It appears that, as the input frequency increased, the output frequency rose to a maximum of about 25 pulses per s and then gradually declined to about 15 pulses per s when the input reached the highest input rate employed, 630 pulses per s. There is no evidence as to whether the output rate would fall further at even faster input rates.

Also employing intracellular microelectrodes, Eyzaguirre and Kuffler investigated the impulses passing

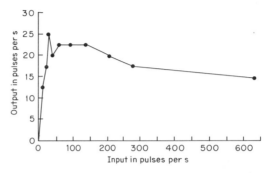

Fig. 5-2 Somadendritic pulses per second output by a motor neuron of a cat to various rates of inputs of antidromic pulses. (Calculated from data in L. G. Brock, J. S. Coombs, & J. C. Eccles. Intracellular recording from antidromically activated motoneurones. *J. Physiol.*, 1953, **122**, 446–447.)

through sensory neurons leading from the stretch receptors in crustaceans.[4] As the muscle fibers were stretched, pulses were transmitted through the dendrites of the sensory neuron and into the cell body, where the experimenters placed their microelectrodes. The pulses came closer together as the stretch became greater, and vice versa.

There are in such crustaceans two kinds of receptor cells, phasic (with rapid signal termination) and tonic (with slow termination) (see page 256). In one experiment as progressively more intense stretch was gradually applied, the pulse output frequency from a tonic receptor cell increased progressively (accompanied by decrease in pulse intensity).[5] Finally, a state of what the experimenters called "overstretch" occurred, and the high-frequency pulse outputs suddenly stopped. When the stretch was relaxed somewhat, the pulse outputs began again, returning slowly back essentially to normal as the stretch was decreased. Comparable results were obtained by these investigators in another experiment on a phasic receptor cell, although it did not always recommence pulse outputs as the stretch was slowly relaxed. Another study on the same preparation indicated that progressive depolarization of a receptor cell caused by increasing stretch in similar fashion reduced the rate of, and finally blocked, antidromic pulses.[6]

Through microelectrodes Granit and Phillips

recorded the outputs from Purkinje cells of the cerebellum that were elicited by antidromic input pulses passing up their axons.[7] They studied the probability that a neuron would output a pulse after the second of two successive electrical pulses. They found that when a second input pulse followed the first at an interval of 3 ms, occasionally each second input pulse elicited an output pulse, but ordinarily it appeared only about 40 percent of the time. If the interval between the first and second input was less than 2.2 ms, the second input elicited only a minute response. The second input had a high probability of producing an output only when the interval was between 3 and 4 ms or even considerably greater than that. These experimenters also found that at brief intervals the output pulses decreased in size and that most cells could not produce outputs which kept up to the inputs if the rates were 200 per second, and very few cells could follow faster rates than that. As an example of their findings, they stated that one cell (cell 9)" . . . when stimulated with shocks somewhat above threshold strength at a range of 180/sec, followed this rate well for some time . . . , but responded with its own rhythm [about 143/s] to 280 shocks/sec. At 0.5 V, near threshold, it fired at a rhythm of its own [about 128/s] to 500 shocks/sec."[8]

The findings from such cells, plotted for the present purposes from the scanty data presented, probably resembled the curves of Fig. 5-3, although insufficient data are available to know the exact shapes of the curves.

Part of a research by Wall, Lettvin, McCulloch, and Pitts concerned the information processing capacity of an afferent nerve, a fiber of the sciatic nerve of the cat.[9] They input suprathreshold electrical impulses to this neuron at frequencies from 10 to 500 per s, mak-

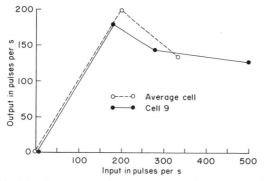

Fig. 5-3 Output rates of an average cerebellar Purkinje cell and of one particular cell (cell 9) under increasingly rapid input rates. (Calculated from data in R. Granit & C. G. Phillips. Excitatory and inhibitory processes acting upon individual Purkinje cells of the cerebellum in cats. *J. Physiol.*, 1956, **133**, 534, 535.)

ing recordings from some distance away on the same cell. They found, as in the other studies reported above, that at high frequencies the intensity of the individual action potential decreased, because a new input came while the neuron was still in a relatively refractory state from preceding inputs. Also at high frequencies the fiber did not respond vigorously to every input, but began to alternate strong and weak pulses.

In 1957 Grüsser and Creutzfeldt reported on the effects of inputs of flickering light on single cells in the retina.[10] They found that as the flicker frequency was increased, the number of pulses produced in the cell per second went up to a maximum and then fell again, the maximum being at a flicker rate of 8 to 20 pulses per s.

The relationships between inputs and outputs of a single afferent neuron to the spinal cord—such as a fiber of the medial gastrocnemius nerve—can be investigated by making intracellular recordings of the excitatory postsynaptic potentials (EPSPs, see page 262) of a motor neuron with which the afferent neuron synapses.[11] One may assume that the size of the EPSP is approximately proportional to the amount of transmitter substance output by the afferent neuron at the synapse with the motor neuron.[12] Confirming the general conclusions of the above researches on input overload, Eccles found that after a few pulses are input to the motor neuron it attains a steady state for a given input frequency which is maintained for hundreds of responses. At input frequencies from 0.4 to 10 per second he found that the magnitude of the EPSPs, and therefore of the rate of output of neurohumoral transmitter substance, decreased. Thereafter the rate of output increased as the input frequency went up to approximately 300 pulses per s, after which it leveled off. It is not known whether some higher rate of input would overload the neuron so that its output rate would decrease.

In recent years Mountcastle, a neurophysiologist, has explicitly applied information theoretical measures to the analysis of data from his experiments on signal transmission in individual neurons.[13] He made mechanical inputs of different intensities to a touch corpuscle (see page 255) lying in the skin of the inner side of the leg of a monkey. This he did with a probe which indented the skin various distances. It was capable of depressing the skin any one of 30 distances, beginning at 20 micrometers (μm) and increasing by 20-μm steps to a maximum of 600 μm. It was accurate to ± 2 μm. These inputs of different intensities elicited pulses which passed up the saphenous nerve and were recorded as outputs from a single fiber of that nerve dissected out higher in the leg. The more intense the input signal was, the higher was the frequency of the pulses it evoked in the neuron. After such a sequence of pulses began, they rapidly developed a metronomelike regularity which continued until the input ended.

A total of 644 inputs of 500-ms duration were made one after another, 3 s apart. All 30 intensities were administered, in random order. The number of pulses elicited on the fiber by each input was recorded. Using standard information measures, the amount of information transmitted by the neuron was calculated. The output perfectly reflected the input if the continuum of input intensities was divided into 2, 3, or 4 categories, *i.e.,* up to 2 bits per input. As the number of such categories was increased, however, the information transmitted leveled out at something less than 3 bits per input averaging around 2.5 bits.

The above data apply to single inputs, not to repetitive input sequences. Consequently they give no measure of neural transmission rates. Approximate calculations of rates can be made, however, if the pulses transmitted in various periods of time are compared with the input. If, for example, the pulses transmitted in only the first 20 ms after each input are considered, the information transmission would be comparable to what would occur if there were 1 input every 20 ms (*i.e.,* 50 inputs per s). If there were 1 every 100 ms, that would be the same as 10 inputs per s. One every 400 ms would be the same as 2.5 inputs per s; and 1 every 500 ms would be the same as 2 inputs per s.

Figure 5-4 shows what transmission curves would look like if inputs varied both in frequency and in amount of information per input. If 1 input were received every 500 ms (*i.e.,* 2 per second), the transmission rates plotted would be 2, 4, 6, or 8 bits per s, depending on the amount of information per input. These rates of input do not produce overload, as the top curve shows. If 1 input were received every 400 ms, the transmission rates plotted would be 2.5, 5, 7.5, or 10 bits per s. These input rates do not overload the neuron either, as the second curve from the top shows. If 1 input were received every 100 ms, the transmission rates plotted would be 10, 20, 30, and 40 bits per s. These rates do not produce overload either, as the third curve demonstrates. If inputs were received every 20 ms, the transmission rates plotted would be 50, 100, 150, and 200 bits per s. The bottom curve in Fig. 5-4 suggests that such inputs may begin to produce overload, since it appears that the output rate may have turned down at the two highest input rates.

3.1.1 Summary of findings at the cell level

(*a*) Research on several kinds of transmission in individual neurons in various species indicates that as the rate of input pulses rises, the rate of output pulses rises for a time to a maximum and then falls. Sometimes it diminishes toward no output at all, and sometimes it levels out at lower rates. Why this difference exists is not clear.

(*b*) Neurons seem to have maximum output rates of about 300 to 500 pulses per s. For some the maximum

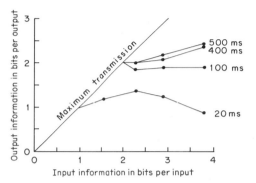

Fig. 5-4 Information transmission in a somatic afferent neuron. [From V. B. Mountcastle. The neural replication of sensory events in the somatic afferent system. In J. C. Eccles (Ed.). *Brain and conscious experience.* New York: Springer-Verlag, 1966, 108. *Reprinted by permission.*]

is much lower. What information channel capacities these pulse rates represent depend on the codes used; but if one pulse represents one bit, maximum channel capacities would be 500 bits per s or more. They might be very much more with some codes. In one study a potential channel capacity near 200 bits per s was calculated to be possible.

(*c*) This survey also shows that at least two of the adjustment processes listed on page 123 occur in neurons: *omission,* when pulses are dropped at high frequencies, and *error,* when some of the impulses transmitted are feebler than normal, quite possibly being too weak to convey a signal to the postsynaptic neuron.

3.2 Information input overload at the level of the organ

Neurons were the cells on which the above experiments were conducted because they are the chief cells specialized to process information. Few studies have been made of information transmission in other cell types (see pages 247 to 254). Similarly, the various parts of the nervous system are the organs or organ components in which information processing is most commonly investigated, even though some other organ components, like the endocrine glands and the muscles, also transmit information. What researches have been done to investigate the overloading of organs with information inputs?

Various studies of multicellular units, in which

information was transmitted from a neuron to a single muscle fiber or between two neurons, yielded similar results as well as some indications as to why transmission broke down at high rates of input. At pulse input frequencies above 50 per s, muscle fibers appear to be unable to contract repeatedly for more than a few minutes at a time, although they can do so for a prolonged period at about 10 per s.[14] In another neuron–muscle-fiber preparation, as input rates increased, the output rates of the muscle fibers fell off much more rapidly than the output rates of the end plates of neurons. Figure 5-5 shows the data on which these findings are based, recalculated and plotted to a format comparable to the findings from other studies in this chapter.

Failure of end plate pulses to release acetylcholine, the substance that elicits pulses in muscle fibers (see page 254), is one explanation of decreased output

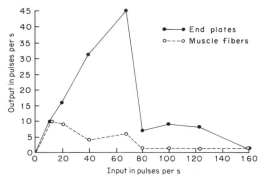

Fig. 5-5 Average rates of responses of muscle fibers and end plates in phrenic nerve-diaphragm preparation after 5 minutes of continuous inputs to nerve at rates indicated. (Calculated from data in K. Krnjević & R. Miledi. Failure of neuromuscular propagation in rats. *J. Physiol.*, 1958, **140**, 446–447.)

rates. Another factor is that, with fatigue, the amplitude of the end plate pulses diminished, and the threshold of the muscle fibers to inputs of acetylcholine increased.

Single cells in the somatosensory area of the cortex of a cat receiving inputs over a multicellular channel from the ulnar nerve acted similarly.[15] As units fatigued, they "dropped" responses during otherwise perfect following of the inputs by the outputs, an example of the *omission* adjustment process to input overload.

Inputs of both constant and flickering light to a cat's eyes evoked complex reactions recorded by microelectrodes from cells in the optical cortex.[16] These neurons output pulses both when inputs begin and when they end. Output rates increased from about 22 pulses per s when the input was 4 light flashes per s to a maximum of about 25 pulses per s when the input was 7 flashes

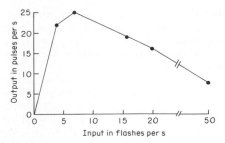

Fig. 5-6 Overloading of a neuron in the optical cortex of a cat by increasing flash frequency. (Calculated from data in R. Jung & G. Baumgartner. Hemmungsmechanismen und bremsende Stabilisierung an einzelnen Neuronen des optischen Cortex. *Pflüg. Arch. ges. Physiol.*, 1955, **261**, 443.)

per s. Further increases in input rates up to 50 pulses per s resulted in diminished output rates (see Fig. 5-6). This was true even though the intensity on the retina was 12½ times as great at 50 pulses per s as at 4.

Increasing rates of flicker of a light in another study on a multicellular, polysynaptic portion of the visual tract of the cat brought about changes in the response of single cells in the lateral geniculate nucleus.[17] Very low frequency of flickering light on the retina elicited first a fast burst of output pulses and then a low-frequency later response. The total number of pulses per second was low. With increase in flicker frequency, only the rapid burst was recorded, with a higher number of pulses per second. Further increase in rate produced only a portion of the initial rapid burst to each flash, and the number of pulses fell. A still faster flicker brought the cell to the fusion point, at which it no longer makes an output to each flash. Human subjects report experiencing a steady light at this rate and above it. Figure 5-7 plots the data from this research.

Recorded output pulse rates rose and fell in single

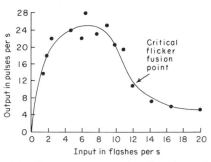

Fig. 5-7 Rate of output from a single cell in the cat lateral geniculate upon input to eye of light flashes at various frequencies. (From R. DeValois. Discussion. In S. H. Bartley. Some facts and concepts regarding the neurophysiology of the optic pathway. *A.M.A. Arch. Ophthalmol.*, 1958, **60**, 784–785. Copyright 1958 by the American Medical Association. *Reprinted by permission.*)

cells in the cochlear nucleus of guinea pigs when tone pips or pure tones were delivered to their ears.[18] When intensity was held constant, for instance, a cell with spontaneous output of about 210 pulses per s responded to increase in input tone frequency with increase of output pulse rate up to an input rate of 4 kilohertz (kHz) (see Fig. 5-8). Frequencies above that elicited decreasing output rates. A change in intensity of the inputs from 50 to 60 decibels (dB) affected the output rates but not the essential form of the curve, as Fig. 5-8 indicates.

In these studies it was found that, as the frequency of the input tones increased, the cells emitted outputs up to a given cutoff point, but above that there was a sudden drop in response rate. For the cell charted in Fig. 5-8 this sudden drop occurred at an input rate

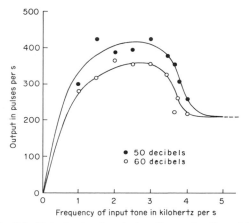

Fig. 5-8 Output rate of a single cell as a function of the frequency and intensity of inputs of pure tones. [Calculated from data in I. Tasaki & H. Davis. Electric responses of individual nerve elements in the cochlear nucleus to sound stimulation (guinea pig). *J. Neurophysiol.*, 1955, **18**, 156.]

somewhat less than 4 kHz. The output rates of another cell increased from 500 hertz (Hz) up to 8 kHz but dropped at about 8.5 kHz.

Similar activity in neurons in the dorsal columns of the thoracic spinal cord of the cat receiving inputs through a multicellular channel from the sciatic nerve was explained in a study by Wall, Lettvin, McCulloch, and Pitts—which I discussed earlier in this chapter (see page 126)—by the fact that new pulses arrived while the channel was still relatively refractory.

In all the above researches, at both cell and organ levels, the inputs and outputs are measured in terms of the characteristics of the marker, in matter-energy units of pulses per second rather than the information carried by the marker in bits per second. As the rates of inputs of markers increase, the data from the various studies all show the sort of rise to a channel

capacity and then fall in performance with increasing input rates which I hypothesize to occur across levels. But my proposition concerns bits of information. Would the data plot into the same sort of curve if the units were bits per second instead of pulses? That depends on how the information is coded in the cell or organ. If the code is a simple binary pulse code, based on either the presence or the absence of a pulse, then the maximum number of bits per second that can be transmitted under any condition is the same as the maximum number of pulses per second which the system can output.

There is no certainty, however, that such is the code. On the contrary, in some components of the nervous system other codes seem definitely to be used (see pages 395 to 397). For instance, Mountcastle and his co-workers recorded from single neurons in the somatic sensory areas of the cat's thalamus and cerebral cortex. In one research Rose and Mountcastle found that a solitary, brief electrical pulse input applied to a specific skin area produced, over the multicellular, polysynaptic somatic sensory tract, either a single output pulse or, most commonly, a repetitive sequence of pulses in a particular neuron in the somatic sensory region of the thalamus, that part of the ventrobasal nuclear area which is activated by touching the skin.[19] Furthermore, the average number of pulses in the sequence as a rule, but not always, increased as the intensity of the input went up. Also, increases in input intensity generally cut down the time before the first pulse appeared. The voltages of a sequence of pulses from the same neuron elicited by a given input to the skin were almost identical. In such sequences the first pulse usually had the greatest voltage, the second was lower, and the others were progressively greater. The average interpulse interval was essentially constant for pulse sequences of a given number of pulses. There was a regular variation within a given set, however, such that each succeeding pulse in it occurred at a slightly longer time after the preceding pulse than it had after its predecessor. The number of pulses per sequence in a given thalamic cell varied between 1 and 7. The fluctuation for a given intensity of input and point of application did not exceed plus or minus 1 pulse over 90 percent of the cases. This suggests that input intensity may be coded in seven discrete steps, at least in the somatic sensory channels to the thalamus investigated in this study. The sequence of pulses was the marker, and since there were seven alternatives, there were 2.81 bits of information per marker.

Individual neurons in the somatic sensory area of the cerebral cortex, according to Mountcastle, Davies, and Berman, responded similarly to a brief input to a specific point on the skin.[20] This finding indicated that a similar code was used as the information was relayed up from the thalamus to higher neural echelons. The chief difference was that the highest number of cortical pulses for a single input relayed over the skin-to-cortex tract, composed of more cells and syn-

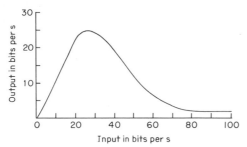

Fig. 5-9 Information processing performance of somatic sensory system of the cat. In this experiment, input is to the skin and output is from the cortex. (Curve from a personal communication from W. J. Horvath, about 1965.)

apses than the skin-to-thalamus tract, was about 5. Apparently, therefore, no more than about 5 different intensities can be distinguished by the cortex, representing a mean information capacity of about 2.6 bits per signal. Perhaps it is more than a coincidence that George Miller, in summarizing recent psychophysical studies on human information processing, concluded that absolute judgments in a number of different single modalities are made in about seven discrete steps,

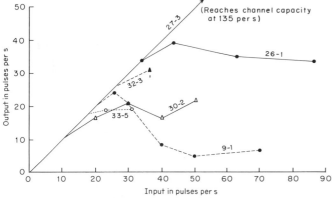

Fig. 5-10 Output rates of individual cortical neurons to various rates of repetitive electrical pulse inputs to peripheral neurons of the somatic sensory system of the cat. Curves are plotted for 6 separate cortical neurons: 9-1, 33-5, 30-2, 32-3, 26-1, and 27-3. (From V. B. Mountcastle, P. W. Davies, & A. L. Berman. Response properties of neurons of cat's somatic sensory cortex to peripheral stimuli. *J. Neurophysiol.*, 1957, **20**, 397. *Reprinted by permission.*)

varying from about five to nine and representing an average information capacity per signal of 2.81 bits (see pages 136 and 137).

Once we know the information content of a single peripheral input pulse that carries a signal centrally to the cerebral cortex, we can calculate the capacity of the entire information processing component for transmitting repetitive inputs from data on how long it takes that component to become responsive again after it has transmitted a pulse to a particular cortical neuron. By varying the intervals between pairs of strong inputs delivered peripherally and by determining the average number of pulses evoked in that cortical neuron by the second input of each pair as a percentage of the average number evoked by the first, Mountcastle, Davies, and Berman demonstrated that such a given multicellular, polysynaptic component in a cat under moderately deep sodium pentobarbital anesthesia was completely unresponsive for 20 to 30 ms and then gradually recovered to be fully responsive again in about 100 ms. The unresponsive period for the entire polysynaptic component, with multiple neurons and junctions, was much longer than for a single cortical cell. The cat's anesthetized neural channels probably recovered more slowly than they would in a normal state. Multiplying the average number of output pulses elicited by the second of a pair of input pulses by 2.6 bits of information (*i.e.,* five equally probable alternatives in the input ensemble, as indicated above) times the number of inputs per second gives the output rate of this component at the cortex, in bits per second.[21] The curve obtained from these calculations appears in Fig. 5-9.

These experimenters also carried out studies of the responses of single cortical cells to sequences of pulses input peripherally at different rates. The performance of the individual polysynaptic components varied, but in general their outputs were at the same rates as the inputs up to about 20 to 30 pulses per s. Then as the input rates increased, the output rates fell behind the input rates, leveled out at a channel capacity, and at last commonly decreased below that maximum (see Fig. 5-10). The modal maximum output rates of the components plotted in Fig. 5-10 are about 28 pulses per s. Assuming that each pulse conveys about 2.6 bits of information, the modal channel capacity would be about 72 bits per s.

In their studies of the reactions of the pupil of the human eye to sequences of light and dark visual input pulses of different durations, Hakerem and Lidsky found that the latency of pupillary contraction decreased as the duration of the preceding dark period increased.[22] The contraction latency was 0.45 s or above when the preceding dark period was less than

0.1 s, but about 0.3 s when the preceding dark period was about 0.7 s or greater.

The pupillary constriction to light is controlled by a polysynaptic neural organ component, a feedback loop. It includes fibers of the optic nerve which synapse in the pretectal nucleus, then go to the Edinger-Westphal nucleus, from which parasympathetic fibers lead to the ciliary ganglion and then on to the iris sphincter muscle which contracts the pupil of the eye (see page 488). The time lag of this entire feedback loop between the original light input and the constriction is so great that other intervening light pulses may enter the eye in the meantime. When this occurs, these intervening pulses, in their turn, also constrict the pupil in a normal fashion, and no information seems to be lost from the signal. The latency of the pupillary constriction appears to the experimenters to be greater than the total of the transmission times of the channels involved plus the lag time of the iris muscle. The experimenters therefore suggest that the signal may be stored temporarily, perhaps in the pretectal nucleus. They believe this may be an example of the *queuing* adjustment process that I have referred to as one way of handling information input overload.[23]

By now a number of studies have been carried out which apply information theory to measurement of processes in the central nervous system. This is not at present a common way to analyze neural process, however. Only certain neurophysiologists have conceived of neurons as information processing channels. As a result, none of the researches referred to so far in this section on the organ level, and only one in the previous section on the cell level (see pages 126 and 127)—though they are sophisticated neurophysiologically—view the performance of channels in terms of information input and output, measuring it in bits per second. Furthermore, in only one of these studies is a reference made explicitly to the fact that performance curves of neurons have comparable characteristics to performance curves of larger neural systems.[24]

The accepted tradition of neurophysiologists is to measure the refractory period of neural systems and the interval between one pulse and the next rather than the rate of transmissions per unit time. Usually they do not analyze their data in terms of the amount of information processed or design experiments which increase the rate of information input until the channel capacity is reached or the system is overloaded. Consequently in this chapter I have repeatedly had to recalculate and replot experimental data to show their relevance to the topic.

3.2.1 Summary of findings at the organ level The following conclusions arise from the studies on information input overload at the level of the organ:

(*a*) In those researches on neural organs or organ components in which rate of inputs can be plotted against rate of outputs, the curves show similar shape and characteristics to those derived for individual cells.

(*b*) Multicellular, multisynaptic neural components whose channel capacities have been measured may have maximum information processing rates of 200 bits per s or above. The channel capacities of these larger neural units may be somewhat lower than those of individual neural cells in general, although the multicellular, polysynaptic component of the auditory tract studied by Tasaki and Davis, whose performance is plotted in Fig. 5-8, appears to be an exception. It apparently has a channel capacity as high as some cells and higher than most other organ components. With a maximum output rate of 400 pulses per s it could transmit 400 bits per s or more, depending on the code.

(*c*) At higher rates of input, outputs of smaller and more variable intensity are invoked by inputs of standard intensity. This may be one reason for the generally lower channel capacity of larger systems with several synapses. At rapid input rates some of the outputs of a preceding neuron may not be sufficiently intense to elicit a response in the subsequent neuron with which it synapses.

(*d*) *Omission* and *error*, or inadequate processing (decreased output intensity) are adjustment processes of organs to information overload. I have not found experiments which indicate that other adjustments are employed at this level, unless threshold processes which permit certain pulses to pass and block others represent a kind of *filtering*.

3.3 Information input overload at the level of the organism The notion that a person can be overloaded or overwhelmed by inputs of matter-energy is not new. It is a theme of folk stories and music. There was the mill that, on command, ground out herrings and pottage until the whole countryside was covered, and then when sunk in the sea, unceasingly ground out so much salt that it made the whole sea salty.[25] Recall also Dukas' *Sorcerer's Apprentice*.[26] The magician's helper learned some of his master's magical phrases and ordered a broom to do the chore he was supposed to do: carry water from the brook to the house. But the apprentice forgot the word that would stop the broom's frantic activity and soon the kitchen floor was flooded. Catastrophe was prevented when the sorcerer returned, uttered the necessary magical word, and halted the broom. It is a modern discovery, however, that an organism can also be overwhelmed by a glut of information inputs.

Experiments relevant to the effects of information

input overload on individual human organisms have been concerned with various aspects of a person's information processing capacities and have used numerous different experimental situations. Among these are: (*a*) Choice reaction time studies, which require a subject to make a rapid selection among several alternate input signals. (*b*) Experiments with visual flash displays, which determine the maximum amount of information that a person can respond to in an exposure of a few milliseconds. And (*c*) researches on signal sequences which investigate the channel capacities of human subjects for information on different sorts of markers and for different output transducer components. Experiments of these various sorts are described below.

When individual animals or persons process information, a set of serial binary decisions—conscious and reportable, or not—appear to be involved. Their channel capacities, therefore, must in some way be related to their choice reaction times, that is, the time it takes for them to make a binary choice or decision. This fact connects two fields of experimentation at the organism level: (*a*) work with "the span of absolute judgment," which is fundamentally concerned with the question of the maximum number of bits of information that can be processed simultaneously or in a brief moment (see pages 136 and 137) and (*b*) research on the channel capacity, which is concerned with the maximum rate of serial transmission of bits of information (see pages 137 to 143).

In 1931 Telford proposed a cross-level analogy to processes in excitable cells like neurons and cardiac muscle fibers.[27] He believed that he demonstrated that a refractory period—such as is found after an information input to these cells (see page 263)—also occurs after "voluntary" responses, judgments, and associative processes of human organisms. He found that the second of two sequential reaction times to an auditory signal was increased over the usual time when the interval between two successive information inputs was 0.5 s or less. This organismic refractory period is much longer than the refractory period of cells, which ranges between 0.4 and 20 ms.

Since a human being's information processing is carried out by a network of neurons with refractory periods, connected at synapses which have their own delays, these must contribute to the delay of reaction time. Whether or not a person expects a certain class of inputs also affects the delay.[28] If the subject is presented with an input from a class which he has learned is small, and if he is expected to give an output from a restricted class, that output will be rapid. But if the input or the mode of response are unusual—members of a much larger ensemble of alternatives—the output will be slow. Both refractoriness and the size of the input and output ensembles affect reaction time.

3.3.1   Choice reaction time research   As early as 1885 data were collected which appeared to indicate that an organism's choice reaction time (or output lag) increases as the number of alternatives goes up.[29] The logarithmic relationship between the two was noted first in 1934.[30] By plotting the reaction times in the original data against the number of equally probable alternatives in the ensemble of the display, George Miller demonstrated that in this experiment reaction time increased linearly with the amount of information in the input.[31] This conclusion has been supported by a number of other researches.[32]

Most of the data in these studies can be fitted by a curve derived from an equation of the form

$$R = a + bH$$

where the average reaction time R is a linear function of the information H in the input, and a and b are constants.[33] The intercept a in the above equation has a value of 0.175 to 0.179 s, which is approximately the value of the simple reaction time. One can interpret b as the time required to make one binary decision and the reciprocal of b as T, the rate of information transmission or output. The values obtained for $1/b$ of the three experiments cited are all close to 6 bits per s. This is considerably less than the 50 bits per s found in some sequential-processing tasks (see page 151). Reaction time can evidently be affected not only by the amount of input information, but also by its discriminability, by the difficulty of motor output, and by the input–output compatibility. Reaction time and errors decrease and information transmission rates decrease also as input signals become more dissimilar.[34] Reaction time also decreases as signals become less complex and as the signal-to-noise ratio increases.[35]

A card-sorting experiment disclosed a number of other determinants of choice reaction time:[36]

(*a*) As redundancy increases, diminishing the amount of information processed per card, the rate of card sorting goes up. This is true whether or not the subject understands the statistical distribution of the cards in the pack and whether or not he feels free to risk making mistakes.

(*b*) The rate of sorting is affected by whether or not the subject understands the statistical arrangement of the pack. Understanding makes him better able to anticipate what the next card will be.

(*c*) The subject sorts faster on the basis of probabilities than on the basis of a statistical prediction of the next card.

(*d*) The more willing the subject is to risk making

mistakes, the better use he makes of his understanding of the redundancy in the arrangement of the pack.

(*e*) The higher the intelligence of the subject, the better is his performance.

In another disjunctive reaction-time experiment relating to a highly overlearned task, typing, the value of 1/*b* or *T* was found to be 16 bits per s, considerably higher than that in the other studies. The experimenters believed that even slightly higher values could be achieved by manipulating the input probabilities.[37]

Studies of the effect of practice on choice reaction time showed that the linear relationship between the amount of information in an input signal and the reaction time does not hold for well-practiced, "overlearned" tasks.[38] In a situation where a single subject has to push buttons when either one of two, or one of four, lights appeared, although the four-choice reaction time had been longer than the two-choice at first, after 45,000 reaction-time determinations spread over 5 months this difference had been reduced to zero. Furthermore, after all this practice, the average reaction time was still decreasing. When subjects were made aware of the number of alternatives or size of the ensemble from which the experimenters were to choose a number to be displayed in each trial, the average reaction time was the same no matter whether the ensemble was 2, 4, 6, 8, or 10. In this work, the reaction time was constant for an overlearned response, regardless of the size of the ensemble.[39] When the same subjects had to respond to inputs randomly arranged in time so that they did not know when to expect them, their reaction times again went up as the size of the ensemble increased. These and other findings led Mowbray to abandon the generalization regarding the increase of choice reaction times as a function of the number of alternative responses. He wrote: "Apparently it arose originally as a reflection of the unpractised state of the responders and has been perpetuated in more recent times because it fitted the hypothesis of man as an information processing machine."[40]

This critique, however, misses two important points: (*a*) The real ensemble of numerals in the experiments. And (*b*) the probable nature of the processes going on during practice. I shall consider each of these points in turn:

(*a*) The proper distinction between the explicit and the implicit ensemble is not made by Mowbray and others, including some whom he criticizes for applying information concepts to reaction-time problems. The explicit ensemble is that which the experimenter tells the subject will be used. For instance, the experimenter says there will be two numerals, or four, or ten. The assumption is that the ensemble can be

changed by instructions, but in all probability it cannot, especially in a highly practiced task like numeral naming. The subject has been naming numbers all her or his life, and for the subject the ensemble—the implicit ensemble—is ten (or 100 or 1,000 or infinity, depending on how he or she conceives of the domain of numbers). Mere instructions in a psychological experiment are unlikely to change this highly practiced implicit ensemble. Only a great many trials to overcome the training of a lifetime might alter it, and such retraining was not done in Mowbray's experiments. So the ensemble of numbers must be assumed to be the same for all his groups of subjects, no matter what instructions he gave them as to how many numbers they would see. From the point of view of information theory, therefore, one would expect that the average reaction times in all conditions of the first number-naming experiment would be the same. It would probably have been the same in the second such experiment also, were it not for the vigilance factors he suggests, which seem to be reasonable explanations for his findings. Certainly there is nothing in the number-naming experiments inconsistent with the view that man processes information in reaction-time experiments. A recognition of the subject's real ensemble makes the findings predictable.

(*b*) There is also the question of practice. According to Mowbray and Rhoades, choice reaction times lengthen with an increased number of alternatives as a result of insufficient practice.[41] They showed that with sufficient practice the difference in average reaction times to two-alternative and four-alternative situations disappears in a task involving the pushing of buttons when the corresponding lights appear. In the past, various experimenters who were proponents of the information theory approach have contended, almost certainly incorrectly, that disjunctive reaction times do not improve with practice. Having shown—as have others—that they do improve with practice, Mowbray and Rhoades comment that Bricker's statement that reaction time is a function of the information transmitted is not very useful if practice makes changes in the direction of uniform reaction times for inputs with ensembles of various sizes of alternatives.[42] In this they are correct, but their implication that the subjects of the other experimenters had not practiced enough, while theirs had, misses the interesting significance of the changes brought about by practice.

The actual situation may well be as follows: The subject enters a new experiment untrained in the sense that she or he considers all alternatives in the input ensemble to be equally probable. This is adaptive, since the subject has no basis for assuming anything else. At this point, information measures based on the number of alternatives fit the data, because the unpracticed subject operates in a way to take all the alternatives into account. Then practice with the situation begins. Certain alternatives are experienced more frequently than others, and come to be viewed as more probable. It may be that only a few alternatives ever occur. In such cases the subject focuses on them and ultimately reduces the ensemble of possible alternatives, and as a consequence reaction times speed up. This is a recoding process, often called improvement with practice. If there are only a few alternatives, like two or four lights to which the subject reacts by pushing their corresponding buttons, I hypothesize that the subject develops some sort of direct neural connection or programming specialized for carrying out each of those particular tasks. Thus the subject can do them with equal speed regardless of their number, so long as that number is not too great. In a later chapter (see pages 412 to 413) I shall discuss experimental evidence which may support my view—evidence showing that with repeated learning trials concomitant brain-wave changes which were diffuse become more and more localized, apparently adapted in an increasingly efficient way for that particular task.

When training has gone on for a long time, then, reaction time is no longer, as it once was, a linear function of the number of alternatives. The highly adaptive nervous system had adjusted to create special connections or programs for making a few of the most frequently required outputs as rapidly as possible. As Mowbray and Rhoades say: "It is even conceivable that with enough practice there is no such thing as a *choice* reaction time, but . . . choice reactions are reducible to the basic reaction time regardless of the number of alternatives provided."[43] But that does not mean information analysis is inapplicable to relatively unpracticed tasks or that it cannot yield important insights about disjunctive reactions.

One might suppose that the subject divides an information input made up of n distinguishable signals into two approximately equally likely sets, decides in which set the signal event is to be located is, then divides that in half, and goes on in this manner until that signal finally is isolated. This would require $\log_2 n$ halving operations or decisions. If this were indeed the case, and if each binary decision took the same amount of time, then except for the relatively minor effect of the simple reaction time (represented by a in the equation on page 132) the reaction time R would increase as a linear function of n and the information transmission rate T would be the same for any value of n.

However, Christie and Luce argue that anyone who has tried to carry out such a procedure when n is a large number, say 100, recognizes how impractical it is.[44] Perhaps a person begins this way in a complex problem like a large grid, but then after successfully isolating the desired component in one quarter (or similar sector) of the grid, she or he counts from the corner to the row and then to the column in which the point actually occurs within that sector. In such a large display, if the sector is a quarter, the person would thus on the average have to make $2 + \frac{1}{2}\sqrt{n}$ decisions (see the experiment on flash displays of dots, page 137). Selecting a sector like this is a case of the *abstracting* adjustment process (see page 123).

Are these decisions made sequentially or simultaneously? For either procedure one can estimate the rate of information transmission T as a function of the amount of input information H. If the average simple reaction time a is equal to the average time for making one binary decision b, then up to a point at which very large inputs may raise special transmission or decision problems, $T = H/(n + 1)$. Figure 5-11 shows this computation when the scale has been normalized so that $T = 1$ when $H = 1$.

The similarity of the sequential decision curve to other information input overload curves is noteworthy.

If some decisions are made simultaneously rather than sequentially, the rate of information processing T would not be the reciprocal of the reaction time $1/b$. Channel capacity does vary with the mode of presentation of the information input. This could be either because the mode of presentation changes b, the time required to make one binary decision, or more likely

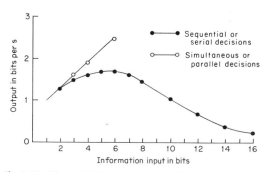

Fig. 5-11 Theoretical information capacity based on Christie and Luce's calculations. The scale is normalized so that the rate of transmitted or output information = 1 when the rate of input information = 1. (From L. S. Christie & R. D. Luce. Suggestions for the analysis of reaction times and simple choice behavior. *Technical Report R-53.* Urbana: Control Systems Laboratory, Univ. of Illinois, 1954, 34a/39. *Reprinted by permission.*)

because the mode of problem solving differs for various presentations, certain ones perhaps involving some simultaneous decision making. For example, in stimulus cards whose backgrounds may be either red or green, which have either one or two spots, whose spots may be either triangles or circles which may be colored either black or white, there are four bits of information per card, transmitted along four dimensions simultaneously. One can believe that decisions concerning such dimensions could be made simultaneously.

The above model of Christie and Luce is one of many which can be devised to interpret data about the information processing performances of subjects collected in the form of time latencies between information inputs and response outputs of sequences of signals. An evaluation of the different classes of such models has been made by McGill.[45] Input–output times vary significantly. Analysis of the distributions of a number of these latencies can potentially indicate how the signals are transmitted through the intricate channels and nets and other information processing subsystems of the organism. Simple reflexes pass through quickly, and their input–output times are quite uniform. Complicated responses take longer and show much variability, suggesting that they are processed by complex and noisy subsystems.

The models include the following classes: (a) Those with random latencies, in which the probability of a response is constant at any instant, e.g., the distribution of interresponse times of a rat undergoing operant conditioning. (b) Those with series latencies, including subclasses of sequences of random delays all with the same time constant, e.g., the distribution of times of a rat running an alley in a maze, and with variable time constants, e.g., several experimental studies (see page 132) in which the choice reaction time is the sum of both a brief reaction time or neural transmission time and a longer decision time. (c) Those with series responses that fluctuate in rate, e.g., the interresponse times of a rat in an operant conditioning situation in which it is differentially rewarded for pressing a bar at slow rates. (d) Those with series responses whose constraints change regularly from response to response, e.g., extinction of conditioned responses. And (e) those with series responses whose constraints fluctuate in time.

The above paragraphs make it clear that the generalization that choice reaction time increases linearly with the amount of information input must be limited by a number of qualifications. One of the most important of these is the probability of repetition of one signal by the next.[46] As the ensemble increases in size, this probability decreases. When there are more repe-

titions, the average reaction time is faster. Apparently the organism is so "set" by responding to one symbol that it can respond faster to another identical symbol next in a sequence than to a different one. Obviously this fact should influence interpretation of any data showing a linear relation between information input and reaction time from those many experiments in which the average amount of information per signal is confounded with the probability of nonrepetition of that signal. In almost all such experiments the amount of information per signal is increased by either (a) making the ensemble larger, which in a random sequence also obviously increases the probability that the next signal will not repeat the last, or (b) altering the probabilities with which the alternatives occur. A change from a higher probability of some signals being input toward a more equal probability for all signals also increases the probability of nonrepetitive signals.

It is possible to present input signal sequences in which the amount of information per signal and the probability of nonrepetition are not confounded, and Kornblum has done this.[47] He used sequences of inputs in which for each symbol in the ensemble the probability of repetitions was identical, the same being true for nonrepetitions. He carried out experiments with such sequences both in discrete presentations (with varying intervals of about 2 or 3 s between each) and in serial presentations (with 140 ms between one response and the next signal). The results of both his discrete and his serial experiments showed that all but one average reaction time increased as the amount of information in the signal went up, but this increase was much more marked for repetitions than nonrepetitions. Reaction times to repetitions were significantly faster than to nonrepetitions. The reaction times to repetitions decreased linearly as they became more probable, and the same was true for nonrepetitions.

Another set of serial choice reaction time experiments carried out in the same laboratory showed that the more frequently a given signal appeared in a sequence, the faster was the nonrepetition reaction time to it, and the fewer errors to nonrepetitions it elicited.[48] The repetition reaction time and the ratio of errors to repetitions were not affected by the signal probability, however.

These findings provide an explanation for certain relationships between information inputs and outputs, suggesting that the organism remains "set" to transmit a signal like the one it has just processed more readily than other signals. In this it is like an elevator that remains at the floor at which it was last used rather than returning to the main floor, thus responding faster at the floor where it was last used than at any other. These findings may require re-analysis of data from many information processing experiments at the organism level as well as at other levels, to see if they need reinterpretation. They do not necessarily, however, change the shapes of information input–output curves like those derived in choice reaction time or input-overload experiments.

3.3.2 Research on span of absolute judgment What is a person's momentary channel capacity, or maximum ability to make decisions or process information precisely in a single brief moment, of duration usually not precisely defined ("the span of absolute judgment")? Unless the time is precisely measured, of course, a rate or channel capacity cannot be accurately calculated. A thoughtful analysis of research on this question has been made by George Miller, and some of his observations are as follows:[49]

(a) Concerning absolute judgments of information inputs differing in only one variable, Pollack experimented with tones varying in frequency from 100 to 8,000 Hz in equal logarithmic steps.[50] Each of a number of listeners had to identify the pitches by giving assigned identifying numerals. When they had to select among only two or three possible tones, they never made mistakes. With four, confusions were rare. But with five or more, errors became increasingly common. When the alternatives numbered 14 there were many errors. The maximum transmission of pitch information was about 2.3 bits per moment. When the tones varied in loudness only, the maximum was about 2.0 bits per moment. Another research investigated responses to tones spaced over the intensity range from 15 to 110 dB, using 4, 5, 6, 7, 10, and 20 different intensities.[51] The data produced a curve much like Pollack's curve for pitch in which, as input information per moment increased, information output per moment plotted against it leveled out at about 2.5 bits. Still another study, on absolute judgments of the concentration of salt solutions—using 3, 5, 9, and 17 different concentrations—produced data which plotted into a similar curve that seemed to peak at about 1.8 bits per moment, falling after that.[52] All these findings probably indicated that a confusional state began when about 3 bits per moment had to be output, increasing progressively above that.

Experiments involving the visual interpolation of a dot between two scale markers on a line indicated that about 3.25 bits per moment were transmitted.[53] In a similar study Coonan and Klemmer found that the length of exposure affected the amount transmitted.[54] It was 3.9 bits for a 0.04-s exposure; 4.3 bits for a 0.16-s exposure; and at least 5.03 bits for a 0.64-s exposure. This last is the largest momentary transmission that

has been measured for any variable differing in one characteristic only.

A person judging the sizes of squares transmits about 2.2 bits per moment.[55] In a separate experiment Eriksen found the transmission was 2.8 bits per moment for size, 3.1 bits per moment for hue, and 2.3 bits per moment for brightness.[56] A research measuring several aspects of visual displays found for spatial area an amount of transmission of 2.6 to 2.7 bits per moment; for length of line, 2.6 to 3.0; for direction or angle of inclination, 2.8 to 3.3; and for curvature, 1.6 to 2.2.[57] The value of 1.6 is the lowest that has been found.

(b) The following findings have been reported concerning absolute judgments of inputs that differ from one another in two variables: For absolute judgment of the position of a dot in a square (i.e., in two dimensions, vertical and horizontal) output information in one experiment increased with input information until it leveled off at a transmission rate of about 4.4 bits per moment.[58] This compares with 3.25 bits per moment for identifying a dot in a line (see above). When subjects in another study were asked to identify both the saltiness and the sweetness of solutions, they found that 2.3 bits were transmitted per moment, as compared with 1.8 bits for saltiness alone (see above).[59] When listeners judged both loudness and pitch of pure tones in Pollack's experiment mentioned above, 3.1 bits were transmitted per moment, as compared with 2.3 for pitch alone and 2.0 for loudness alone.[60] Data in an investigation of confusions among colors of equal luminance can be analyzed to suggest a transmission of about 3.6 bits per moment for colors which varied in two dimensions—hue and saturation.[61] If a somewhat questionable comparison is made between these data and Eriksen's findings mentioned above of a transmission of 3.1 bits per moment for hue, we see that (as in other cases) variation of stimuli in two characteristics, rather than one, increases but does not double the transmission.

In another experiment pressures were applied to the skin that differed in three characteristics—intensity of input, duration of input, and location of input on the body.[62] Good observers could simultaneously distinguish among about four intensities, five durations, and seven locations, making possible a maximum transmission of $2 \times 2.32 \times 2.80 \approx 13$ bits per moment. And one experiment has been done on absolute judgment of tones which differed in six different variables: frequency, intensity, rate of interruption, on-time fraction, total duration, and spatial location. This study indicated that when listeners made a separate rating for each of these six dimensions, the channel capacity was 7.2 bits per moment.[63]

When size, brightness, and hue all vary together in perfect correlation, transmission increases from 2.7 bits per moment, for each of these attributes varying alone to 4.1 bits per moment.[64] (Compare this with the research of Broadbent discussed on pages 144 to 146.)

From all these findings George Miller concluded that as more independently varying attributes are added to information inputs, channel capacity increases, but the rate of this increase is less the more attributes there are.[65] Some neurophysiological research at the organ level may explain this.[66] In this work both "inhibitory" and "occlusive" effects were found of interactions between volleys from two different peripheral sources. Inhibition is the failure of a neuron to fire in response to a previously effective test volley of inputs because of the action of a conditioning volley which does not usually fire the same neuron. If the conditioning volley usually fires the same neuron, that is occlusion. In an anesthetized monkey stimulated from two peripheral sources (the median nerve and the palmar branch of the ulnar nerve), both inhibition and occlusion were observed at test intervals of less than 4 or 5 ms. These observations may explain why, when simultaneous inputs are made through two channels, somewhat less than twice as much information is processed as through one channel.

The three most important adjustment processes recognized by George Miller for extending the limited span and increasing the accuracy of absolute judgments are: (a) Making relative rather than absolute judgments (the *abstracting* adjustment process). (b) Increasing the number of variables in which stimuli can differ simultaneously (the *multiple channels* adjustment process). There is probably a maximum number of variables in information inputs to which a person can react simultaneously. Miller hazarded an unsupported guess that this is in the neighborhood of ten. That may limit use of this process. And (c) making several absolute judgments sequentially (the *queuing* adjustment process). This involves memory and is limited by the short-term memory capacity.

Even though the span of absolute judgment is about seven categories, the span of attention is about six or seven objects, and the span of immediate memory is about seven items, these are not all aspects of a single underlying process.[67] The amount of information transmitted in a single presentation which is recalled immediately is not constant but increases almost linearly as the amount of information per item in the input is increased. In other words, absolute judgment is limited by the amount of information, but immediate memory within wide ranges, by the number of items. Referring to the item as a "chunk" of information (see pages 61 and 123), Miller states that the number of bits of information is relatively constant for absolute judgment while the number of chunks is constant for immediate memory.[68] Moreover, present research indicates that the span of immediate memory is nearly independent of the number of bits per chunk.

It follows that the amount of information in the memory span can be increased by recoding the input from a code with many chunks, each with a few bits per chunk to another code with fewer chunks, each with more bits per chunk. An experiment was carried out to measure the memory span of each of 20 subjects for binary and for octal digits.[69] The span was nine binary and seven octal digits. The experimenter taught the subjects how to recode into larger chunks. Doing this increased their span for binary digits in every case, but not as much as he had expected on the basis of their span for octal digits. He then gave himself a great deal of practice in recoding in chunks with two-to-one, three-to-one, four-to-one, and five-to-one ratios of information. After much drilling he found that his own span with the various forms of coding were what would be predicted from his personal span for octal digits.

3.3.3 Experiments with flash displays Experiments of this sort test subjects on their ability to report visual information presented to them for only a fraction of a second. Does channel capacity for these brief exposures differ from average channel capacity measured over seconds or minutes? Some of the results of such experiments are similar to those reported above for displays of longer duration. An experiment in which information inputs differed in three variables showed that judgments of a particular variable were more accurate if subjects were told in advance which variable to attend to.[70] An experiment in which subjects were asked to report on the number of dots varying from 1 to 200 in flash displays disclosed that above seven they began to estimate rather than count, and errors increased.[71] There was a clear discontinuity in the data at seven dots, similar to results on other displays reported above. Both span of absolute judgment and complexity of the presentation were found to determine the number of bits of information transmitted per glance in an experiment that used dots and squares, dial displays, and scales.[72]

Flash presentations have also been used by various experimenters to determine maximum rates at which people can process information. Different experimental designs have yielded estimates of hundreds of bits per s, 55 bits per s, and—with control for the effect of retinal retention—30 to 50 bits per s.[73]

3.3.4 Research with information input sequences Tasks in experiments of this sort include piano playing, typewriting, reading, comprehending speech, tapping in response to dots, and responding to sequences of numbers, letters, or other symbols. Maximum channel capacities, beyond which input overload occurs, and other aspects of information processing by subjects have been investigated in studies using such tasks. In one research by Quastler and Wulff random music, constructed from a table of random numbers, involving a series of one note at a time produced by one hand or identically by both hands at a constant rhythm, was played by three young pianists who were excellent sight readers.[74] After practice with this sort of music, the subjects estimated the highest rate at which music could be played at sight. This rate was set on an electric metronome, and the first test piece presented. Successive pieces were then played at gradually increasing speeds, up to a rate which was obviously well beyond their capabilities. All performances were recorded on tape and timed with a stopwatch. The errors in the different performances were scored by listening to the tapes. From these errors, plus knowledge of the amount of music played in a given time, rates of information transmission were calculated.

The results were as follows: subjects made few errors up to a speed of about 5.2 keys per s. Thereafter as speed increased, precision was sacrificed, and the error rate increased, so that both the transmission rate per second and the number of correct keys per second remained approximately constant. Then the trade-off of speed for precision went on until a second critical point was reached, which was the highest useful speed, about 10 keys per s. Beyond this rate, the quality of performance deteriorated rapidly as a result of a confusional state. The channel capacity was between 10 and 14 bits per s when 3 to 5 keys of the piano were used; 16 bits per s for 9 keys; 19 bits per s for 15 keys; 23 bits per s for 25 keys; and 22 bits per s for 37 keys. When the range was extended to 65 keys, a few errors occurred even at low speeds, and the channel capacity was only about 17 bits per s. This was because frequent jumps had to be made between distant keys. A wider range would probably limit performance even more. When a subject was allowed to select his own speed of piano playing, his channel capacity was only a few percent below the maximum achieved when input rates were set.

There were individual differences in the adjustment processes to information input overload employed by the subjects. One sacrificed speed but minimized errors; another kept closer to the established speed than the others, though with more errors. There was no obvious evidence of learning during the tests.

Copying a text on a typewriter is a sequential task that often occurs at a high rate of information trans-

mission. Seven good professional typists were presented by Quastler and Wulff with random sequences of equally probable symbols. Each sequence was made up of one of four different alphabets, containing either 4, 8, 16, or 32 symbols. In each trial a subject would copy a sequence of about 100 symbols as fast as he could. Subsequently each subject in each trial was paced by metronome, at either 2, 3, 4, or 6 beats per s. The total time for each trial was measured with a stopwatch.

The channel capacity was calculated by multiplying the speed of pressing keys times the information transmitted per letter typed, allowing for errors. The results were as follows (see Fig. 5-12): Using 4 to 16 keys, all the typists made few errors up to a certain

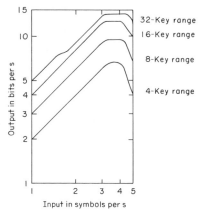

Fig. 5-12 Typing performance curves. (From H. Quastler & V. J. Wulff. Human performance in information. II. *Technical Report R-62*. Urbana, Ill.: Control Systems Laboratory, Univ. of Illinois, 1955, 62–47. *Reprinted by permission.*)

speed. This speed was about 3.2 keys per s with 8 and 16 keys (9.6 and 12.8 bits per s). It was a little higher with 4 keys, in one such case getting up to a rate of 5 key presses per s (10 bits per s). If driven beyond this speed, their precision decreased proportionately to the increase in speed, so that the channel capacity remained constant. Driven to even faster rates, their quality of performance decreased rapidly. With the 32-key range, the highest effective speed was about 2.9 keys per s, or about 14.5 bits per s, which was similar to the transmission rate obtained with 16 keys. The highest transmission rate achieved by any subject was about 16 bits per s. There was evidence of learning with practice in the typing tests, which was not true with the piano test—possibly because the typing task was more unlike ordinary typing than playing random music was unlike ordinary playing.

Further work expanded on these results and linked

serial performance with reaction and decision time.[75] Typing a single, unknown, randomly selected letter required about 0.28 s, plus an extra reaction time of 0.24 s which was added to the time required for the first letter. These quantities altered little whether the number of letters typed was 1, 2, 4, or 192. The typists wrote letters at a more or less constant speed after a brief prolongation of response occurred, which affected only the first letter. That is, the transition from a single choice reaction to serial activity is completed with the transition from one to two letters. It is not gradual. In a practiced task such as typing, habit determines the rate of performance. It does not clearly reflect the information content of the signals. Practice of other tasks may mask the role of information content in determining the output rate.

The channel capacities of subjects reading and doing mental arithmetic were about 24 bits per s. The channel capacities for piano playing, reading aloud, and mental arithmetic (22, 24, and 24 bits per s respectively) agree within the limits of experimental error. It is likely that this transmission rate can be reached only under favorable circumstances. Seven typists could not get beyond 17 bits per s. This value is within the range of experimental variation of the 30 to 50 bits per s found in the last of the flash-display researches mentioned above. The channel capacity for human information processing in any single activity is probably of this order of magnitude. An experiment by Licklider successfully combined two activities, word reading at 25 bits per s and target pointing at 15 bits per s, for a combined output of 35 bits per s, somewhat less than the additive rate.[76]

According to Quastler and Wulff:

> There seems to exist a highest useful speed, a highest useful range, and highest useful transmission rate; if any one of these values is exceeded, the performance drops rapidly. . . . information transmission is limited by effective speed, effective range, channel capacity, or confusion, whichever imposes the lowest limit. . . . The trading of speed for range, speed for precision, range for precision, can be simply described in terms of information units.[77]

They added this important observation:

> It is fairly certain that the limitations of information-processing are associated with the central part of the information-processing mechanism. None of the limitations observed could be ascribed to peripheral input mechanisms. The capacity of the optic nerve is many orders of magnitude higher than 20 or 40 bits per sec [see page 381]; a much wider range of symbols could be accommodated with the resolving power of the retina [see page 397]. As to speed limitations, it is known that about 3 symbols are grouped in the act of reading, and that about 4 such groups can be assimilated in a second; this gives 12 symbols/sec, considerably more than the highest useful speed in typing or piano playing. On the output side, it is easy to see that the limitations of the actual speed, both

alone and in combination with precision, cannot be attributed to mechanical difficulties. In all tests, observed speeds could have been much improved by rehearsing.[78]

Linking serial and momentary information processing capacities of this "control mechanism," Quastler summarized the work of his group as follows:

> . . . in sequential activities, the performance is limited by speed alone, range alone, or by their product, the channel capacity, whichever imposes the lowest limit; in single-glance displays, the factors are orders of complexity, range, or channel capacity. In both cases, over-supply of input information can result in reduction of the performance (confusion effect). . . .
> We find that people *can* make up to 5–6 successful associations per second, *can* transmit about 25 bits per second, *can* operate efficiently over a range of about 30 possible values, and *can* assimilate some 15 bits at a glance. We do not expect that they *will* reach such performance levels with every kind of activity; in fact, we know that usually they do not.[79]

Research on a sequential information processing task specially designed to control several experimental variables indicated that the subjects' output rates were similar to those in the lifelike tasks of piano playing and typing.[80]

Information inputs were presented to groups of 8 to 12 Royal Air Force plane crew members on a band of white-paper tape which passed in front of them, in the following ways: (*a*) horizontal successions of various numbers of dots separated by spaces, requiring for response to each dot a tap of a telegraph key; (*b*) groups of varying numbers of dots presented in clumps arranged vertically, at right angles to the movement of the tape, requiring the same response; (*c*) the numerals one to six, each requiring for response the corresponding number of taps; and (*d*) unevenly spaced groups of varying numbers of dots. Each subject responded by a tap to each dot.

In one experiment dots, each representing one bit of information, were input to the subjects, spaced for runs at various equal intervals: 1.0, 0.5, 0.3, 0.25, 0.17, 0.14, or 0.1 s. At random intervals one dot would be omitted, leaving a gap which also constituted one bit of information. On the average there was one gap for approximately every 2.6 dots. It was found that almost 100 percent of the dots and gaps were responded to correctly at the first two input rates but that the correctness fell rapidly almost to zero at 0.1 s, even though the total number of outputs per second continued to rise. The data are plotted in Fig. 5-13.

A subject's upper "physiological limit" or fastest possible tapping speed obviously could put a constraint on his channel capacity in this experiment. This limit was found to be between 5.3 and 8.2 taps per s. The maximum response rate to grouped inputs was found to be about 6.93 bits per s, close to the physiological maximum.

At high rates of presentation, new sets of input signals overlapped the subjects' responses to the previous set, producing a "block," i.e., a confusional

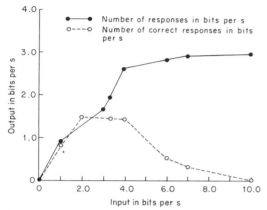

Fig. 5-13 Relationships between rate of information input in bits per second and rate of output in total bits and correct bits per second. Either a dot or a gap represents a bit in the input. For each 2.6 dots in the input, there is one gap. A tap in response to an input dot or the absence of a tap in response to an input gap represents a bit in the output. (Adapted from M. A. Vince. Rapid response sequences and the psychological refractory period. *Brit. J. Psychol.*, 1949, **40**, 28, 35. *Reprinted by permission of Cambridge University Press.*)

state in which subjects failed to produce correctly one or more of the symbols in a group. The average amount of overlap causing a block was 0.64 s, while the average amount of overlap present when one correct set of response groups was followed by another correct set was only 0.096 s.

When the information input was increased to a rate much higher than the physiological output maximum, the response rate actually decreased instead of remaining at that maximum. This was interpreted to mean that blocking in the central nervous system, in addition to the physiological maximum, influenced the output rate. It was assumed that, if the limiting factor were only the physiological maximum, as the input rate increased, the rate of responses would approach a limit and remain constant thereafter. Output rates increased markedly when the inputs could be perceived as a unitary group (i.e., be *chunked*). These results were interpreted by the experimenter to indicate that there is a "psychological refractory period" of 0.5 s during which period the output to a subsequent signal is delayed or blocked (see page 132).

Studies of the relationship between reaction times and sequential processing rates have also produced findings relevant to information input overload.[81] One

of these used an apparatus which periodically flashed from 1 to 5 lights arranged in an arc, and each subject responded by pressing corresponding keys arranged in an arc under the fingers of the subject's preferred hand.[82] Before each run the subject was told what the ensemble would be, i.e., how many lights would be used. The ensemble varied from 1 to 5. Each possible pattern of lights was presented 100 times in a random order, at input rates of 2, 3, 4, and 5 patterns per s. The input light sequences were programmed by a teletype transmitter, and each subject's outputs were also recorded on teletype tape so that his accuracy and reaction times could be determined. The chief findings were:

(a) As the input rate increased, the information output rate went up until the subject began making a few errors. Beyond that point there were marked decreases in information transmission. A characteristic performance curve appears in Fig. 5-14.

(b) Increasing the range from 1 to 5 lights more than tripled the maximum correct information output rate.

(c) At the various input rates used in this investigation, reaction time was not a function of the input rate.

(d) Reaction time lengthened as the ensemble increased, but was not a linear function of the information in the ensemble, as measured in this experiment.

(e) The rate of input of light flashes which gave the maximum correct information output rate in any trial was close to the reciprocal of the reaction time for that test. For example, Table 5-1 shows the input rate of

TABLE 5-1 Comparison of Rates of Input of Light Flashes at Maximum Correct Information Output Rates and the Reciprocals of the Reaction Times

	Number of lights in ensemble				
	1	2	3	4	5
Rate of input of light flashes at maximum correct information output rate	3.7	2.4	2.4	2.4	2.4
Reciprocal of the reaction time	3.8	2.6	2.6	2.4	2.4

SOURCE: From E. T. Klemmer & P. F. Muller, Jr. The rate of handling information: key pressing responses to light patterns. *HFORL Memo Report No. 34.* USAF, ARDC. March 1953, 7.

light flashes at which the maximum correct information output occurred with ensembles ranging from 1 to 5 lights, compared with the reciprocal of the reaction time.

(f) The subjects were capable of pressing keys to output information, whether correct or incorrect, at twice the rate they were able to transmit information correctly from flashing lights, confirming the observation of others that the restriction on information processing is central (probably in the decider) and not in the peripheral output transducer (see pages 139 and 444).

(g) Self-pacing tests were also carried out, and under such conditions correct information output was at rates as high as the maximum forced-pace performance.

Is the rate of information transmission in a forced-pace serial task a function of (a) the rate of input of signals, (b) the amount of information per signal as determined by the size of the ensemble, or (c) a joint function of these two factors? In an effort to answer this question Alluisi, Muller, and Fitts presented Arabic numerals visually to 10 subjects, who responded to them with verbal outputs in one part of the experiment and motor outputs (key presses) in another.[83] In some trials random sequences of two numerals, 4 and 7, were presented, each number therefore representing 1 bit of information. In other trials random sequences of four numerals—3, 4, 7, and 8—were presented, each number representing 2 bits. In still other trials random sequences of eight numerals—1, 2, 3, 4, 7, 8, 9, and 0—were presented, each number representing 3 bits. Each sequence was presented at three different forced-pace input rates—1, 2, and 3 signals per s.

The experimenters found that, as the rate of signal inputs increased, the percentage of the total information input which was output by the subjects decreased. Such a decrease did not occur, however, when the size of the ensemble was increased and the rate of signal input remained the same. They concluded that the rate of information output is not a simple function of the rate of information input. It seemed to them to be more directly influenced by the rate of signal input, a finding that might bring into question some information input–output relationships discovered in the other researches reviewed in this chapter. But the experimenters' interpretation of their own findings might not have been correct. They assumed that when they presented only numerals 4 and 7 in a trial, or only numerals 3, 4, 7, and 8, these explicit ensembles were the real ensembles being used. But they might have been confusing the explicit and implicit ensembles. After years of practice the subjects' ensemble of Arabic numbers could probably not be altered simply by experimenters' instructions, so that the implicit ensemble remained the whole set of Arabic numbers. The findings, therefore, did not, as the experimenters thought, prove that it was the rate of signal input rather than of information input which determined the rate of information output. The experiment did demonstrate as other studies have, however, that verbal responses are more compatible with the sorts of information inputs used in this

experiment than motor responses are. The channel capacity or maximum output rate obtained with verbal responses was 7.9 bits per s. For motor responses it was 2.8 bits per s.

The effects of alternative codings on information output rates and channel capacity were investigated in another research from the same laboratory, using

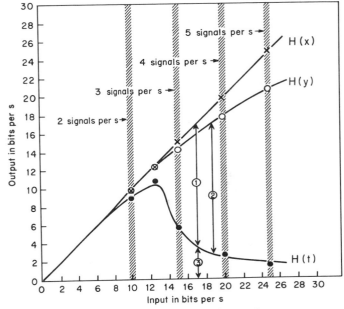

Fig. 5-14 Averages for four subjects in five-light test, showing total informational output and transmitted information as functions of the input rate. H(x) represents information input; H(y) represents subjects' total information output; H(t) represents subjects' correct information transmitted. ① indicates information lost (presented but not transmitted); ② indicates noise or information in output not correlated with input; and ③ indicates transmitted information. (Adapted from E. T. Klemmer & P. F. Muller, Jr. The rate of handling information: key pressing responses to light patterns. *HFORL Memo Report No. 34.* USAF, ARDC. March 1953, 9.)

seven different visual codes, each with an ensemble of 10.[84] These were: the usual Arabic numerals; symbolic Arabic numerals, all of whose edges were square, none being round; simple inclination, in which a circle appeared like a clock face and the position of a single hand corresponded to the numerals one to ten; clock inclination, in which there were two hands, a long one and a short one, the long one pointing directly upward and the short one taking the position of clock hands from one to ten; binary inclination, in which 2 or 3 hands had different angular positions one to the other, representing 10 combinations; ellipse-axis ratio, in which a horizontal line represented one, then gradually wider and wider horizontal ellipses represented the next numbers, then vertical ellipses, and finally a vertical line; and last, a set of 10 different colors.

In one experiment each subject gave motor outputs, pressing 1 of 10 finger keys for each of the signals when it appeared; in the other, each subject orally called out the number assigned to each signal. The performance of the 10 subjects was measured under both self-paced and forced-paced conditions. It was found that the two numerical codes permitted faster information output than the three inclination codes, and that these were all faster than the color and the ellipse-axis ratio codes. The average forced-paced channel capacities ranged from 1.71 bits per s for motor outputs to the ellipse-axis ratio code, to 5.93 bits per s for verbal responses to conventional Arabic numerals. Average self-paced channel capacities ranged from 2.56 bits per s for verbal responses to the ellipse-axis ratio code, to 4.38 bits per s for verbal responses to conventional Arabic numerals (see page 447). The rates of oral information outputs increased as the rates of forced-pace information inputs went up. At the input rates used in this experiment no overloading occurred when the responses were oral. With motor responses, however, outputs to Arabic numeral codes appeared to be leveling out at a channel capacity of about 6 bits per s. No signals were presented at rates above 6 bits per s, though, so it was not determined at what input rate they would have produced overload. The information processing capacity of all subjects in trials with motor outputs to the other codes, however, appeared to be definitely overloaded at levels above 3 bits per s. As the rate of information presentation increased above that, output rates decreased. Above 2 bits per s input rate, under all conditions, output omissions and errors increased as the input rates went up.

The differential effects of variations in information input rate and range on a person's information processing have also been investigated experimentally.[85] There were 10 subjects, students at Ohio State University. Each one called out the number of times any symbol (selected from an explicit ensemble of four alternatives) appeared twice in displays, each made up of four "words" of symbols. Each word had either no duplicate symbols or one set of them, and one only. In some trials there were 2 symbols per word, in some 3, and in some 4. The displays were presented to the subjects at different rates. Jeantheau, the experimenter, found that error percentages increased as either input rate or range increased. (There were a few *omissions* or failures to respond during trials, but none during the experimental trials—only *errors* or correct responses.)

There were only five possible answers as to the

number of duplicate symbols in each display (0, 1, 2, 3, or 4). Since each of these five combinations occurred equally often, there were about 2.32 bits of information per response. The rate of information output of each subject was calculated in terms of these five alternatives.

This output rate, however, was not ordinarily the same as his internal information processing rate. Unless the subject made a correct answer by chance, he had to process and compare 8 symbols, said by the experimenter to carry 2 bits of information each, in each 2-symbol word message; twelve 2-bit symbols in each 3-symbol word message; and sixteen 2-bit symbols in each 4-symbol word message. The symbols used came from the four alphabets shown in Fig. 5-15. In all probability the symbols of alphabets S and C conveyed 2 bits of information each, since the total

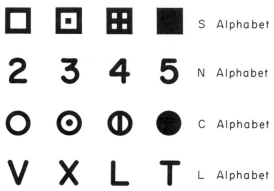

Fig. 5-15 Alphabets used in constructing "words" in Jeantheau's experiment. (From G. Jeantheau. The differential effects of speed and load stress on task performance. *WADC Tech. Report 59-7.* Aero Medical Laboratory. Wright-Patterson Air Force Base, Ohio. July 1959, 3.)

ensemble in each case was four. It was assumed by the experimenter that the symbols of alphabets N and L also conveyed 2 bits of information each, since their explicit ensembles were also 4 each, but actually the implicit ensembles of 10 numbers and 26 letters were probably the real ensembles for these subjects educated to use English letters and Arabic numbers (see page 133). Consequently the symbols in alphabet L most likely conveyed 4.7 bits each and those in alphabet N, 3.32 bits. As a result the amount of internal information processed was greater than the experimenter realized. It seems likely that this rather extensive internal processing was what restricted a subject's information output rate in this particular experimental procedure rather than the output itself, which had less information and a smaller ensemble and which could not occur until the more complex internal processing was finished.

In Fig. 5-16, derived from the reported average findings for the 10 subjects, the information input rate is plotted against the "internal" information which must

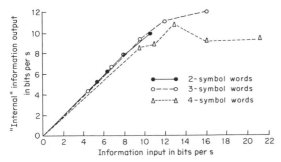

Fig. 5-16 Amount of information processed correctly internally at various rates of information input, for messages of 2-symbol words, 3-symbol words, and 4-symbol words. (Calculated from data in G. Jeantheau. The differential effects of speed and load stress on task performance. *WADC Tech. Report 59-7.* Aero Medical Laboratory. Wright-Patterson Air Force Base, Ohio. July 1959, 6–12.)

have been processed correctly before correct information outputs could be made. This figure shows that the system was not significantly overloaded at input rates up to about 12 bits per s, but processing rates appear to begin to decline above that input rate. Especially the curve for the displays made up of 4-symbol "words" seems to decline under the overload at high information input rates.

3.3.5 Adjustment processes Many of the researches reported above have included findings relevant to the several adjustment processes to information input overload already identified (see page 123). All researches that used high rates of input reported more *errors* as subjects approached their maximal processing rates. Several reported that *chunking* the input increased the subjects' information processing capacity (see pages 137 and 140). Some researches on various aspects of information processing that are especially relevant to adjustment processes to information input underload are described below (see pages 169 to 195).

A research of Jackson's, concerned with the behavior of subjects required to operate several continuously varying control systems at the same time, investigated the effects of increasing range (equivalent to an increase in ensemble size) on performance.[86] The task required the subject to work at one to five tracking tasks simultaneously, keeping dial pointers at the zero point. The dials were out of phase, so at any given

time their pointers moved differently. He found that the character of performance changed markedly as range increased. Not only did the amount of *error* steadily increase, but subjects attempted to avoid overloading by moving more rapidly from one control knob to another, turning the knobs faster, and anticipating coming events. These adjustment processes were used more as the range (number of tasks) increased, but apparently no more than was necessary for any specific situation.

In a research by Mackworth and Mackworth, subjects were required to report on the number of common symbols on a set of cards that moved past windows in a display apparatus, as compared with a card that remained fixed.[87] This study was concerned with the effect on the subject of overlap of information on the various cards. It is relevant to *error, omission,* and *queuing* adjustment processes. Symbols included letters of the alphabet, arrows, crosses, dotted and unbroken lines. Each card bore six symbols, which on different cards were differently arranged. Figure 5-17 illustrates the experimental material. In the experimental situation, the rate of presentation and the number of windows that showed cards to be compared with the fixed card were varied. No overload was imposed in this experiment since the maximum rates and ranges used presented information at well below the number of bits per second (calculated from the experimenters' description of their research) that have been found in other experiments to overload

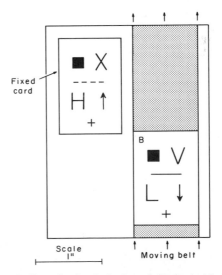

Fig. 5-17 Example of a single-channel display in Mackworth and Mackworth experiment. (From J. S. Mackworth & N. H. Mackworth. The overlapping of signals for decisions. *Amer. J. Psychol.,* 1956, **69,** 32.)

subjects. Nevertheless, a statistically significant rise in errors occurred as the information input rate increased. At the highest speeds there was a large rise in errors for both when many cards were to be compared and when few were.

In order to isolate the effects of overlap, the presentation was made with the rate held constant at 6 s per comparison. Each run lasted 5 minutes (min) and included about 50 comparisons distributed among 4, 6, 8, 10, or 12 windows. Overlap was calculated as the total number of seconds a card was displayed in one window simultaneously with one or more others. Peaks, when information had to be processed rapidly, and lulls, when there was little to report, occurred. Signals appearing early in a time of peak overlap were processed more satisfactorily than later signals. A rise in *omissions* and *errors* lagged behind a rise in input overlap because of the *queuing* adjustment process, becoming worse after prolongation of peak overlaps. On the average, *omissions* were up to nine times as frequent as *errors* during peaks of overlap.

These experimenters had difficulty in understanding why multiwindowed displays diminished the effectiveness of performance, but research which I have reported above suggests that this is primarily because of increase in range or size of ensemble (see page 138). The experimenters suggest that the number of irrelevant inputs increases with the number of windows, that difficulty in deciding the order of comparison might occur under peak overlap, that with more channels overlap peaks lasted longer so that *queuing* benefits did not continue throughout each peak, and finally that extra eye movements required by a large number of channels might decrease the rate at which decisions could be made. Further investigation would be required to determine whether any of these factors influence performance.

Several adjustment processes were employed by subjects in tests that used an apparatus known as a Complex Behavior Simulator.[88] This involves 29 subtasks that must be carried out when corresponding input signals appear—tasks like turning wheels, flipping switches, adjusting knobs, and plugging jacks into sockets. Operating at base rates of 100 to 2,000 such signals per hour (h), the subject was suddenly exposed for 30 s to bursts at the rate of 4,000 signals per h. Major breakdowns in performance occurred, differing significantly from one individual to another. The rate of a subject's motor outputs during the overload bursts seemed not be be affected by the base work rates existing before and after the bursts. Input speed stress effects in this experiment appeared to be related only to the current input rate or information overlap. In this research the subjects employed the

omission, error, queuing, and *multiple channels* (two hands) adjustment processes—the last mainly at moderate input rates. They did not use the *filtering* adjustment process, probably because the instructions implied that they should not do so.

Researches on choice reaction times (see pages 132 to 136) advance our understanding of the *error* adjustment process and of what produces errors in a continuous performance. On the average the reaction time for an erroneous choice reaction is shorter than for a correct one. Input signals which differ from their immediate predecessors produce more errors than repetitive signals. Also the more likely an input is to occur, whether or not it is repetitive, the less likely the response is to be erroneous. In other words, the more variety (or information) there is in the input, the more error or noise there is likely to be in the output.

States of neural activity vary, producing variations in the degree of arousal of the total organism (see pages 426 to 428). Both neural activity and arousal change from moment to moment with the rate of information flow in the organism's nervous system.[89] There appears to be an optimal state of arousal for the performance of a given task. A good deal of evidence supports the conclusion that, up to a point, performance improves as arousal increases and thereafter decreases. If arousal varies with rates of information flow, this is the same as saying that, up to a certain point, output increases as information input does; but thereafter, as information increases further, output decreases.

If at the slower rates of input, however, all or almost all input signals are processed, obviously low performance is not necessarily evidence of lessened arousal. Essentially all the signals are responded to, and there are no others to process. That is the situation in most or all of the researches I have discussed in this section. On the other hand, decrease of output rate as the rate of inputs increases above the channel capacity in every case probably results from overload—inability of the individual to process rapidly enough. Such overload may well diminish arousal, just as it can cause a confusional state, possibly associated with anxiety or strong emotion (see pages 166 and 167). Inattentiveness or lack of arousal is associated with a *filtering* adjustment process. Other adjustments such as *omission, error,* and *queuing* also often occur at the same time.[90]

Constructive insights into the detailed characteristics of the confusional state which may accompany information input overload in the human being have been provided by research of Broadbent.[91] He investigated various situations like simultaneous binaural stimulation, when inputs enter through two channels at once, one being responded to before the other, a phenomenon known in classical experimental psychology as "prior entry."[92] He explained this by asserting that those neural structures responsible for perception (probably corresponding to the decoder in my terminology and possibly also the input transducer and the channel and net subsystems) have limited information processing capacity, but some excess information can be temporarily *queued* by them and processed later. He explicitly notes the role of *queuing* in dealing with two-source information overload in the auditory (as well as the visual) sensory system, when he states that " . . . a temporary peak in the rate of arrival of information can be dealt with by storing some of the incoming sounds and processing them later."[93] But the stored material fades quite quickly, and "The limit on the total amount of information from two channels which can be dealt with in this way appears to be about the same as the amount reproducible from immediate memory on one channel."[94]

According to Broadbent, other adjustment processes besides *queuing* are also employed, an important one being *filtering*. In one of his numerous experiments he examined the time relationships in binaural input interference.[95] Twenty-four Royal Navy sailors wearing earphones heard lists of digits read to them from a tape recording. Sometimes the same digits were heard at the same time in both ears, as in conventional transmission. At other times, different digits were heard simultaneously in each of the two ears. The rate of presentation of the digits was varied. The subject's task was to write down the digits as he heard them. It was found at rapid rates that all digits read to one ear were written down before any to the other, but as the rate of presentation was slowed down, the lists were recalled in the actual order in which they were input. Failures in recording the actual order of input of digits were very high when they appeared at the rate of 0.5 or 1 s apart, but there was considerable improvement between the 1-s and the 2-s rates, suggesting that some interval between 1 and 2 s was the time required to shift from one channel to another and back.

In another research Broadbent's subjects were required to answer a rapid series of questions, and during this series a buzzer was sometimes sounded.[96] The subjects were to respond to this buzzer. This task produced an interference with the speech activity, as compared with the control group, both at the instant of the buzz and also between buzzes. The between-buzz interference was reduced by previous practice in the buzzer reaction, but the interference at the instant of the buzz was not. If the buzzer represented one of two possible signals for a two-choice reaction, the interference at the instant of the buzz was greater.

This suggests that the situation can most easily be understood in terms of information theory: the information in the signal is determined not by the intrinsic character of the signal but by the number of alternative signals which might have occurred but did not. And the greater the information input the more the interference.

Other researches confirm these findings. For instance, auditory thresholds obtained with simultaneous tone and light inputs were higher when subjects reported both inputs than when only the tone was reported. This indicates that the amount of information input determines the amount of interference.[97] Interference between two tasks is reduced with practice (automatization) when the inputs for one of them arrive in predictable sequence (or redundantly) but not when they arrive irregularly and thus continue to carry information.[98]

In Broadbent's view evidence accumulated from studies like those cited in the above paragraphs indicates that the brain has built-in *filtering*. When information is input at a higher rate than the capacity of the neural channel or net, a filter appears to eliminate certain aspects of the input and so cuts down information flow to a more modest rate.[99] Various control centers for this adjustment have been suggested including the reticular formation, lateral lemniscus, inferior colliculus, and medial geniculate (see pages 428 and 429). Broadbent writes:

This . . . seems to justify us in looking at multichannel situations from the point of view of the information passed through the man rather than that of the sounds presented to him. The practical importance of this is obvious, because in designing communication and control systems it is only too easy to consider only the number of signals which may simultaneously reach a man, without considering the size of the ensemble from which each is chosen. Systems designed on such considerations may make too heavy a demand on their listeners in some cases, and too little demand in others. . . . Similarly several experiments have shown that increasing the number of completely irrelevant messages does impair performance. The use of the filter must itself make some demands on the available neural mechanisms, though less than the demands which would arise in its absence.[100]

In order to organize many data, especially all the above findings concerning the confusional state caused by the overloading of a person's information processing channels from multiple input sources, Broadbent developed a conceptual integration, illustrating it by a physical model, which he advances only as an expository device and a mnemonic aid.[101]

He pictures information inputs as being like balls which can be dropped into the arms of a Y-shaped tube with a hinged end flap at the junction of the stem and the arms (see Fig. 5-18). He diagrams only two arms of the tube, but in reality there are as many arms as there are different modalities and separate components of the input transducer subsystem. If two balls are dropped simultaneously, one into each arm, they will strike the flap at both sides and jam at the junc-

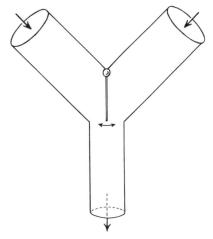

Fig. 5-18 Broadbent information processing model. (From D. E. Broadbent. A mechanical model for human attention and immediate memory. *Psychol. Rev.* 1957, **64,** 206. Copyright by the American Psychological Association. *Reprinted by permission.*)

tion, an input overlap causing overload. This may be similar to what occurs in the confusional state. If the flap is pulled over to one side so that only one arm is "attended to," however, then a ball going down one arm will be blocked or *filtered,* but one entering the other will emerge at the bottom of the stem. If one ball arrives slightly before the other, it will pass through into the stem, but it will delay the other. This can result in *omission.* If several balls are to be put through the tube, it is best to put the majority into one arm, for then jamming is less likely. If the balls go into one arm at random intervals, an increase in rate is less likely to cause jamming than adding the same number of extra balls through the other arm. This may explain why, when each of two input channels simultaneously receives a given rate of information input (use of *multiple channels*), the output is at less than twice the rate as when one channel receives that given rate of input. Doubling the range does not double the output rate.

Since the stem of the Y is narrow, it delays the emergence of each ball by a time representing the reaction time. If balls are inserted faster than they come out, the processing lag results in the development of *queuing.* The queue cannot be longer than the capacity of the tubes. A longer queue will cause some input information to be lost (or "forgotten") in a confusional state. Also a ball inserted at a very short interval after another (during the "psychological refractory period") will remain in the tube longer than normal—a prolonged reaction time. With this model Broadbent is thus able to explain both the confusion which results from central jamming of overlapping information and also some of the adjustment processes, such as *omission, queuing, filtering,* and, of course, use of *multiple channels.*

A special aspect of the *filtering* adjustment process has been noted by Weick, who calls it the "twigging" of information overload.[102] He defines this as an adjustment process whereby a person responds to excessive information input by balancing his need for knowledge with his capacity to absorb it. One result of this is that he restricts his interests, reading and communicating ordinarily on a limited range of topics. This is the basis for the continuing fractionation of technical fields. As knowledge expands, more and more such subfields develop even though, in each one, the size of the readership of the technical documents remains about the same. The trees are much larger, with more branches, but the length of the twigs remains the same—being limited by one man's capacity to process information.

Failure to cope with the stress of information excess, Weick points out, results in emotional responses such as frustration, anger, and anxiety (see pages 430 and 431). These may be followed by a period of apathy or surrender, giving up the battle.[103] These reactions appear to motivate, or be associated with, efforts to adjust by *omitting, filtering* out, or *escaping* from some of the input in order to reduce its flow to a rate the individual can process adequately.

The speed and accuracy of numerical error checking have been studied experimentally.[104] Thirty naive and four trained subjects compared two sets of lists of numbers in which most of the numerals were the same, although an occasional random one was different. On various pages the digits were grouped in *chunks* of different sizes, from 1 to 10. Each subject worked as fast as possible, checking every number and marking every *error,* every digit which was not identical in the two lists. There were three probabilities of such errors in the pages read by the subjects: some pages had .1 error probability (1 digit out of 10 on one page was different from that in the corresponding position on the comparison sheet); some pages had .01 (one digit in 100 was different); and some had .001 (one in 1,000). The time taken for each subject to finish each pair of pages was recorded. Figure 5-19 shows some of the findings. They indicate that in such tasks practiced subjects can reach a channel capacity of 12 bits per s, an improvement of about 4 bits per s over naive subjects. Moreover, persons with ordinary training in numbers can learn to organize random digits into "words" (perhaps based on previous learning about number combinations) and use the *chunking* adjustment process to achieve a high channel capacity, 3 or 4 digits being the optimal size chunk.

With an *error* probability of .1, naive subjects missed (*error* adjustment process) 4 percent, while practiced subjects missed only 2 percent; for an *error* probability of .01 these figures were 13 and 13; and for an *error* probability of .001 they were 24 and 17.

An experiment on immediate memory clearly indicated how *chunking* can adjust to information input overload.[105] The researchers tachistoscopically exposed strings of letters of various lengths for 3 s each. Immediately after each exposure the subject was asked to write in order the letters he remembered. The strings were of four classes: I. Only consonants, in random order. II. Only consonants, but in a regular order. III. Both consonants and vowels, in random order. And IV. consonants and vowels, in a regular order. Classes I and II did not resemble English words. Class III included some sequences that looked like short units found in English. And class IV could readily be decomposed into such units. The short strings contained 6 to 8 letters; the long ones 10 to 12.

In an average trial, subjects recognized 4.9 letters in class I strings; 5.1 in class II strings; 5.7 in class III strings; and 7.5 in class IV strings. The memory of the subjects was less accurate for the long- than for the short-input strings in classes II and III because,

according to the experimenters, subjects who were expected to memorize them in a 3-s presentation were faced with an overload of information input. More letters from long strings in class IV were remembered correctly than from short strings because in class IV strings *chunking* was easy. *Chunking* enabled a subject to adjust to the information input overload of the long strings.

3.3.6 Forms of information input overload on modern man In ancient times and until well after the Renaissance there was a shortage of books everywhere. In many places today there still is a shortage. But acute forms of information input overload have become increasingly common in Western civilization, particularly in urban environments, since the end of World War I. Various futurists predict that the information "explosion" and the development of technology attempting to cope with it will continue unabated.[106] As early as 1921 H. G. Wells was thinking about how to organize the large mass of knowledge that was being collected by civilized man.[107] And in 1937 he wrote prophetically about an automated form of storage of all the world's knowledge. In 1936 the Spanish philosopher Ortega y Gasset recognized that the rapid acceleration of publishing posed a problem of overload upon literate individuals.[108] He concluded that "man must tame the book." Librarians, he thought, should have the major role in controlling overload, preventing unnecessary books from being published, facilitating the printing of useful ones, and developing a "new strictly automatic technique of bibliography." A few years later, in 1945, the mass of books was much larger, and the overload was becoming an overwhelmingly serious problem (see page 5). Vannevar Bush, who had a major part in the construction of the first modern computer and had coordinated America's scientific effort in World War II, became concerned that traditional methods of transmitting and reviewing the growing mass of research information were inadequate.[109] He wrote:

> The difficulty seems to be, not so much that we publish unduly in view of the extent and variety of present-day interest, but rather that publication has been extended far beyond our present ability to make real use of the record. The summation of human experience is being expanded at a prodigious rate, and the means we use for threading through the consequent maze to the momentarily important item is the same as was used in the days of square-rigged ships.[110]

To improve matters, he recommended use of new information processing technology. Specifically he suggested a possible design for a mechanized, private file, library, and memory for an individual, which he named a "memex." He conceived of it as a desk at which a person could get rapid and flexible access to a

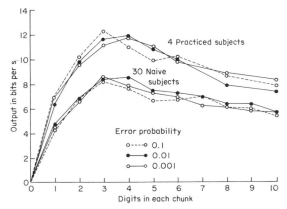

Fig. 5-19 Rate of information handling in numerical error checking as a function of size of chunk and error probability. (From E. T. Klemmer. Numerical error checking. *J. appl. Psychol.*, 1959, **43**, 319 Copyright 1959 by the American Psychological Association. *Reprinted by permission.*)

massive store of indexed microfilmed information. Much of this information would be provided by commercial microfilm publishers. Some of it he would write himself. As he read through materials he would develop for future use his own personal indexing of related ideas. All this is entirely feasible today, and indeed more sophisticated systems than Bush wrote of now exist.[111] These employ modern electronic and computerized methods of information transmission, storage, and retrieval.

At least since Aristotle no one has been able to process all recorded information. A major problem of any student today is to adjust adaptively to the huge amount of knowledge that is available about men and women, society, and the universe. Typically a college student, for instance, must select among many alternative courses to take in the brief time available. More than four courses a semester are ordinarily considered to exceed normal channel capacity. The student can employ the various adjustment processes to information input overload. Some are rewarded by the environment, and others are punished.

For example, in grading true-false tests, a professor often subtracts one point for an *omission* and two for an *error*. There are certain statistical reasons for this, but many also actually think errors are twice as bad as omissions. Why they are not half as bad or four times as bad is not quite clear.

Queuing is coming in late with assignments. The student hands in a thesis a week late. This adjustment process is punished more severely. If a paper deserves a grade of B, the student is given a C. Delaying is bad.

Filtering is favored. Ever since colleges and universities offered elective courses, a college student elects courses totaling about 120 credit hours and emerges an educated and cultured person. Whether these courses in some semester include tap dancing, thirteenth century Chinese art, Old Icelandic, analytic topology—or whatever—makes no difference. The student obtains 120 miscellaneous credits and can say about any other subject, "I didn't learn that." Almost everyone accepts that attitude. She or he graduates and is officially declared educated. *Filtering* is fine!

Abstracting is "bulling" on essay questions and answering imprecisely when a student has not had time to process all the required information in detail. The student may get away with it nicely if the teacher is not on the lookout when grading the examination. If the teacher is alert, on the other hand, the student may be penalized.

A student uses *multiple channels* when someone else writes a thesis for her or him. This is known as plagiarism, and the "clear-cut, obvious penalty" is expulsion.

Escape, going to Tahiti in midsemester, elicits merely suspension. The student will usually be allowed to come back the next year.

And *chunking,* of course, is fine. President Kennedy used this adjustment, and it made him a very fast reader.

Somehow academics seem to agree generally about the right and wrong strategies for handling information overload.

The costs of these various adjustments differ from situation to situation. A random *omission* is serious, but ordinarily it is much more acceptable in our society than a random *error*. Generally in our culture we do not expect a person to have more than 1 or 2 percent errors, even when he is operating rapidly. We are highly critical of a person who makes 4 or 5 percent *errors*. On the other hand, a certain amount of error in some circumstances is desirable, because more rapid information processing is possible if constant error checks are not required.

There is a marked contrast between the freedom of the university and the greater constriction of government service, where taxpayers breathe down the civil servant's neck, where accountants constantly check, and where five years in jail and $10,000 in penalties threaten for any serious deviation. Government builds in motivation to cut down one's error rate, but one is usually allowed to procrastinate, often to build up a queue weeks or months long, as is true of many of our court dockets. Allowing a little more error and keeping up to date would often be better strategy. Perhaps the best way to train students would be for a group of liberally educated professors conversing together to demonstrate to their students the appropriate strategies, least costly in our culture, for using these different adjustment processes as each occasion demands.

Critical situations in space flight may overload an astronaut or cosmonaut, forcing a simultaneous response to information from multiple dial readings, signal lights, auditory messages, and other sensory inputs. As a result of this overload, the astronaut may be unable to process information adequately, and a serious breakdown in performance can result. These points of overload should be considered in designing the equipment and communication facilities for space flight. Also the optimal strategies for using the different adjustment processes to information input overload available in the situation should be investigated quantitatively.

In everyday life we see similar phenomena. For example, voters in West Virginia are faced with information overload every time they vote. It is not exactly an overload from an excessive information input rate because the voter is not forced to read the ballot at a given number of words or bits per minute. But it is an overload in the total number of names which must be processed and in the decisions which must be made within the limited period of time a voter is in the voting booth. Social pressures silently exerted by other voters waiting in line to vote permit her or him to remain there only a brief time. West Virginia voting machines do not give party designations for candidates, but simply long lists of names for each of the many offices. This overload frustrates reasonable decision making, since a voter can at best remember only a few names for the different offices. Consequently, voters frequently leave the rest to the election officials, colloquially called "Lever Brothers," who are appointed to assist voters in operating the machines, but who frequently are also paid by the candidates for helping them get extra votes.

The small print on insurance contracts, seldom read for want of time or motivation, presents a similar situation.

Such overloads are not new to our times, but many others are.[112] Indeed, in parts of our society, excesses of communications exist today of magnitudes much greater than any culture has experienced before. In addition to books we have a glut of newspapers, magazines, letters, and advertisements which come by mail; we must also deal with telephone calls, radio and television broadcasts, phonograph music, conversations, discussions, lectures, conferences, and conventions—all of them situations which feed information to individuals.

These communications media in many nations have expanded their activities explosively in recent decades—many much more rapidly than the population growth; they are impinging on modern humanity with greater intensity than ever before. In the decade of the 1960s in the United States the number of local phone calls increased 57 percent; long-distance calls went up 105 percent; and overseas calls went up 425 percent.[113] Plane travel, an ever more important source of new information inputs, in the decade from 1959 through 1968 rose 255 percent.[114] The expanding use of phonograph records, tape recordings, computers, long-line data transmissions, and communications satellites promises to accelerate communications activities even more.

This extensive information flow presents a person today with many more realistic alternatives for action among which to decide than in the past. As a result of all this, offices are more and more becoming places of frenetic activity where top managers and administrators, particularly, are subjected to continuous sensory bombardment and plagued by mounting demands for rapid and complex decisions with which they cannot cope.[115] Incoming mail mounts up and cannot be answered or is shunted to others for answering. Phones jangle demanding to be answered, but if they are, other urgent business is brought to a halt. A secretary or an automatic answering device may handle the call instead. Letters and memoranda go unread. Magazines and newspapers are thrown away unopened. Computers take over some technical and professional functions such as analyzing management information, providing stock and bond quotations, diagnosing from electrocardiograms, routing phone calls to prevent central-office overloads, and planning menus.

Growth of communications also generates growth of other activities. This may or may not be considered desirable. Making stock market information available to the public sells more stock. Television commercials create a demand for more products. But communication explosions can break down systems as completely as physical explosions can. They may render management unable to make decisions so that an institution does not form policy or does not comply with established regulations. They may overload critical persons in an organization's communication channels so that such channels do not function normally and consequently are bypassed, decreasing the integration of the system.

The home, as well as the office, more and more shows the effects of overload. Homemakers have traditionally been harried by crying babies, yelling children, and noisy adolescents addicted to playing loud popular music. To them are added in ever-increasing amounts influxes of "junk" mail, telephone calls, and radio and television broadcasts.

According to Toffler, information input overload—as conceived of in our experiments (see pages 169 to 195)—is the primary cause of major alterations of lifestyle going on among citizens of present-day technological societies.[116] There is much more change and novelty, more unfamiliar and unpredictable relationships and events, in individual experience in any metropolitan area today than in cultures of the past or in the rural and agrarian nontechnological cultures still existent. The result of this excess stress, which seems to go beyond the adjustment resources of most of us in the technological society of today, is labeled "future shock" by Toffler (see page 166). The first signs of this are fatigue, followed by a confusional state, subjective distortion of reality, and disorientation, followed by apathy and lassitude.[117] Comparable behavior has been seen in a Chindit soldier on a battlefield pinned down under a murderous fusillade of fire who simply went to sleep, or tornado victims who stepped through a broken storefront to purchase an article from an almost wholly destroyed store or who simply stood and stared blankly at the devastation.

Others attempt to cope and find satisfactory ways to make necessary decisions using various adjustment processes, all related to those previously discussed in this chapter.[118] These, according to Toffler, include: (a) Blocking out or escaping from sensory input, denial of evidence that rapid change is occurring in the world around one. (b) Specialism, processing information inputs about one's chief interests—such as homemaking or medicine or merchandising—but filtering out inputs about other aspects of the world—such as social, political, or economic change. (c) Obsessive reversion to methods of processing information which were formerly adequate—such as imitation of life patterns of past pretechnical cultures or unquestioning acceptance of outmoded and maladaptive social standards. And (d) oversimplification, unquestioning adherence to intellectual fads and beliefs that promise unitary solutions to complex problems—such as an extremist political or religious doctrine, drugs, uncontrolled sexual promiscuity, or militant violence.

The most intensive and continuous information input overloads probably exist in the large cities of modern technological societies, such as New York, London, or Tokyo.[119] A chief reason for this is the population density. In midtown Manhattan, for instance, one can meet 220,000 other persons within a 10-min walking radius.

City dwellers develop adjustment processes to help them cope with their informational stresses. As Milgram observes:

One adaptive response to overload . . . is the allocation of less time to each input. A second adaptive mechanism is disregard of low-priority inputs. Principles of selectivity are formulated such that investment of time and energy are reserved for carefully defined inputs (the urbanite disregards the drunk sick on the street as he purposefully navigates through the crowd). Third, boundaries are redrawn in certain social transactions so that the overloaded system can shift the burden to the other party in the exchange; thus, harried New York bus drivers once made change for customers, but now this responsibility has been shifted to the client, who must have the exact fare ready. Fourth, reception is blocked off prior to entrance into a system; city dwellers increasingly use unlisted telephone numbers to prevent individuals from calling them, and a small but growing number resort to keeping the telephone off the hook to prevent incoming calls. More subtly, a city dweller blocks inputs by assuming an unfriendly countenance, which discourages others from initiating contact. Additionally, social screening devices are interposed between the individual and environmental inputs (in a town of 5000 anyone can drop in to chat with the mayor, but in the metropolis organizational screening devices deflect inputs to other destinations). Fifth, the intensity of inputs is diminished by filtering devices, so that only weak and relatively superficial forms of involvement with others are allowed. Sixth, special-

ized institutions are created to absorb inputs that would otherwise swamp the individual (welfare departments handle the financial needs of a million individuals in New York City, who would otherwise create an army of mendicants continuously importuning the pedestrian). The interposition of institutions between the individual and the social world, a characteristic of all modern society, and most notably of the large metropolis, has its negative side. It deprives the individual of a sense of direct contact and spontaneous integration in the life around him. It simultaneously protects and estranges the individual from his social environment.[120]

Such adjustments, Milgram notes, can be applied across levels, being used also by social organizations as well as individual persons. They have distinct social implications, restricting the moral and social involvement of persons with one another. A modern city dweller rarely considers himself his brother's keeper. Good Samaritans are rare. Strangers in need are commonly passed by, and no help is offered or given them. Since so many individuals are in need in big cities, people fear that their personal resources would be exceeded if they were to give aid to all the needy people they encounter. All these circumstances together produce the anomaly of the lonely crowd—thousands or millions of persons crowded together and essentially anonymous to one another.

The concept of information input overload, Milgram states,

. . . helps to explain a wide variety of contrasts between city behavior and town behavior: (i) the differences in role enactment (the tendency of urban dwellers to deal with one another in highly segmented, functional terms, and of urban sales personnel to devote limited time and attention to their customers); (ii) the evolution of urban norms quite different from traditional town values (such as the acceptance of noninvolvement, impersonality, and aloofness in urban life); (iii) the adaptation of the urban dweller's cognitive processes (his inability to identify most of the people he sees daily, his screening of sensory stimuli, his development of blasé attitudes toward deviant or bizarre behavior, and his selectivity in responding to human demands); and (iv) the competition for scarce facilities in the city (the subway rush; the fight for taxis; traffic jams; standing in line to await services). I suggest that contrasts between city and rural behavior probably reflect the responses of similar people to very different situations, rather than intrinsic differences in the personalities of rural and city dwellers. The city is a situation to which individuals respond adaptively.[121]

There are interesting similarities and differences between the adjustments to information input overload described by Toffler and Milgram and those I have identified.

3.3.7 Summary of findings at the organism level The following conclusions concerning information input overload can be made from the literature I have surveyed at the level of the organism:[122]

(a) It has been found repeatedly that as the information input rate increases so does the output rate, until a certain channel capacity is reached. Then the output levels off at that rate. Finally as the information input rate continues to rise, there is a marked decrease in output rate accompanied by a confusional state.

(b) A human being's sequential channel capacity (unless restricted by input–output incompatibility, complex codes, requirements for extensive cognitive processing of input data, limited output ensembles, or other factors) varies between 3 and 12 bits per s for random sequences when the input and output ensembles include up to about 12 alternatives. With larger ensembles total information output rates increase, up to an extreme maximum around 50 bits per s, but symbol transmission rates decrease. Analyzing studies using relatively small ensembles, Hick speculated that processing rates fall into three generally distinct classes:[123] (a) high rates of 10 to 15 bits per s, (b) moderate rates of 5 to 6 bits per s, and (c) low rates of 1 to 2 bits per s. High rates, he believed, come only through use of highly practiced "imitative codes" of the sort we learn in childhood. Moderate rates are typical of specially learned arbitrary codes in which each signal has a high content of information. Low rates result from arbitrary codes with low information content per signal and a high rate of input.

Most of the experimenters who have investigated information input overload at the organism level have been psychologists. A physicist, Breuer, has approached the topic differently from anyone else and has concluded that the channel capacity of the total human organism, and of its decider subsystem, is between 150 and 330 bits per s—several times as high as the values mentioned above.[124] He was puzzled that other investigators and I had published articles indicating that there is a great discrepancy between the channel capacity of a single neural cell, which can transmit hundreds or perhaps even thousands of bits per s (see pages 122 to 123), and that of a human organism, which has a much lower channel capacity.

He stated that experimental tasks like key pressing, typewriting, contour following, or tracking are not sufficiently complex and do not involve high enough rates of information flow to determine the maximum information processing capacity of a total organism. He believes that games like table tennis are more appropriate tasks for such researches, since they require very high rates of information processing.

How can one calculate with reasonable accuracy the information processing rates of a table tennis player? It is possible to study the trajectories and bounces of table tennis balls in typical games and make estimates of the amount of information one must process to play the game adequately. Doing this requires that

assumptions be made as to how data are processed in the human brain. The calculations made by Breuer are somewhat speculative, and not everyone would accept them or agree with the assumptions on which they are based. Nevertheless his argument deserves attention. The total human organism may have a higher total channel capacity than most scientists in this field now believe.

(c) Expanding the input range diminishes the output rate in bits per second. The reason for this appears to be that increasing the range requires more frequent shifting of the eyes or switching of signals from one channel to another within the neural net. Each such shift takes a brief time during which information processing is slowed or halted. At rapid input rates such shifts slow down output.

(d) The original reaction time involved in a single absolute judgment or in the first judgment of a series of serial reactions and the choice reaction time for each new decision in a serial activity seem to be important determinants of channel capacity in unpracticed information processing.

(e) The central decision process appears to be the bottleneck in many experiments on information processing of organisms, rather than either input or output processes. This is indicated by the fact that it is possible to take in information (silent reading of letters or music) at a rate that is faster than the channel capacity for a task involving a motor response. Furthermore, once learned, random music can be played or a set of letters can be typed faster than when they are being seen for the first time, which indicates that the rate limitation is not in the output process.

(f) There are important individual differences in channel capacity.

(g) Habit affects the rate of carrying out learned sequential tasks. Tasks which have been practiced, like typing, are frequently conducted at a learned rate rather than at the original channel capacity. Practice can also speed performance by permitting the subject to group or *chunk* the information inputs and respond to them in larger units. Practice can automatize certain frequent activities.

(h) The way information is coded and the amount of practice the subject has had with the code also affect the rate at which he can process it. So does the type of motor output required and the compatibility between input and output.

(i) The breaking point at which information output begins to decline as information input increases, the beginning of the confusional state, occurs when the time available for processing the average bit of input information becomes less than the average choice reaction time required for processing it. Moreover, increasing the amount of input overlap occurring in multichannel situations results in confusion.

(*j*) Adjustment processes may delay the onset of the breaking point or the confusional state.

(*k*) The following adjustment processes are employed in making single absolute judgments: *omission, error, queuing, abstracting,* and use of *multiple channels.* Exactly the same adjustment processes have been reported in other experiments on sequential information processing. *Filtering, escape,* and *chunking* have also been mentioned.

(*l*) In modern technological society many forms of information overloads upon persons occur. In general they are becoming increasingly common and stressful. Persons differ in how they adapt the above adjustments to their particular situations. Whatever modes of adjustment they select exert important influences on the norms of social behavior in their cultures.

3.4   Information input overload at the level of the group   Research related to information input overload in groups is as sparse as such research on organisms is abundant. An experiment was conducted by Lanzetta and Roby with groups of three subjects seated in separate booths, communicating by an interphone circuit through which, by depressing a hand switch, any subject could speak simultaneously with both other subjects.[125] In each of the three booths were two switches, each with one "off" and three "on" positions. There were also printed operating instructions in the booth. A slide projector threw pictures of two simulated aircraft instruments on the front wall of each booth. The subjects were required to relay information presented to them by instrument readings to the proper booths and to execute control actions with their switches based on relayed or directly available instrument readings. The settings of the instruments were automatically recorded.

Two conditions were employed: (*a*) The "low-autonomy structure," in which all the subjects had two controls but could make none of the four relevant instrument readings in their own booths. The information required by each member in the low-autonomy structure was distributed, some being available in the booth of each other group member. And (*b*) the "high-autonomy structure," in which all the subjects had two controls and could make all but one of the requisite instrument readings in their own booths.

Two aspects of the input were varied by the experimenters. The first was the rate of presentation of the slides, new ones being projected at either 15- or 10-s intervals. The second was the predictability of the change sequence, which was either random or "predictable." In the latter case the order of change was always booth 1, then booth 2, then booth 3. The subjects were not told of these differences but were permitted to discover them.

The output measure used was the total number of errors, *i.e.,* the number of times each control was incorrectly adjusted.

Information processing was least accurate in the low-autonomy situation, in which the largest proportion of information had to be relayed from several different sources.[126] When information input in bits per second was plotted against average group *error,* both low- and high-autonomy groups increased their errors by negatively accelerated curves from low rates of information input to high rates. But the errors for the high-autonomy group were always less than for the low-autonomy group. There were four types of linkage in the group's communication net. The magnitude of the errors for the four linkage types was in the following order, from least to greatest: (*a*) information from a sole source, going directly to the ultimate receiver; (*b*) information from dispersed sources, being partially relayed; (*c*) information from a sole source, being relayed; and (*d*) information from dispersed sources, being relayed.

Errors were frequent even at the lowest rates of information transmission (about 0.2 bit per s). This suggests that the channel capacities of such groups are much lower than the capacities of the persons who compose them. This low capacity appeared to the experimenters to result from the inability of the groups to set up an efficient system for detecting and communicating changes in signals. Group channel capacity could possibly be improved if this communication system were bettered.

The same experimenters also conducted another study in a similar situation, using groups of Air Force trainees.[127] Each group had nine trials. A trial consisted of 18 changes of readings on each of six instruments, these alterations occurring randomly except that each instrument had three. The changes occurred at three different regular rates: one every 6 s, one every 10 s, and one every 15 s.

Operating procedures were also varied. According to one of these the subjects received directions leading them to volunteer whenever there were changes in the information available to them from the dials. According to the other procedure they got instructions leading them to solicit information from the others when needed. Several practice trials trained the subjects in the appropriate way to proceed.

The findings were as follows: *Errors* increased as the rate of change of information increased. They were greater for groups having the low-autonomy structure.

The difference between volunteering and soliciting procedures was not significant, but volunteering appeared to be more effective than soliciting for tasks of intermediate difficulty.

The number of messages went up as the rate of change of information decreased, probably because there were more checking activities during "free" time, which meant that the overall communication redundancy increased. The low-autonomy structure resulted in more communication because more information needed to be conveyed, but relative to the volume of information transmitted, there was much more communication in the high-autonomy structure than in the low. The rate of information exchange increased with practice, which meant that groups learned to pack more communication into a given period of time. There was also some evidence that the more effective groups used the *abstracting* adjustment process, condensing their communications more than the less effective groups. The average message was longer for the low-autonomy structure and shorter for the better performing groups. It decreased with practice. Surprisingly, length of message did not diminish as the rate of information to be transmitted increased. Total talking time went up as the rate of exchange of information went down. It was greater for the low-autonomy structure than for the high-, and it was less for the volunteering than for the soliciting procedure.

The structure and method of communication in groups seems, therefore, to affect their channel capacity. Furthermore, as the rate of transmission of information increases, the number of *errors* increases. With practice, it seems, groups could learn to better their performances. The rate of information processing in this research did not appear to reach an overload.

From such work Roby and Lanzetta have hypothesized that those groups which communicate through the fewest links have the best performance, especially if they adhere to their pattern of communication once it is set up.[128] This is consistent with other studies of channel and net processes in groups (see page 539). It is important to note, however, that if one member of a group becomes the central communicator, processing a high percentage of the group's messages, he is particularly likely to suffer from information input overload. This stress on him can quickly disturb the functioning of the entire group (see pages 549 and 550).

Tracking of an electronically produced moving blip on an oscilloscope by a group of two persons established the group channel capacity.[129] One group member acted as an input transducer who viewed the stimulus and the other as a decider and output transducer who, on the first person's directions, made the appropriate corrective response with a control stick. Such a group was overloaded beyond its channel capacity at an input rate of about 1.4 bits per s and at higher rates developed a confusional state.

A series of related experiments analyzed a number of effects of varying rates of information input upon performance of groups.[130] They studied these groups in experimental simulation environments designed to maximize differences among groups in information processing characteristics. The situation they used most was called a Tactical War Game. Any small number of subjects can play this game, even a single person. Commonly they used four-person groups. They would seat themselves around a relief map of a volcanic island in a room with small chutes through which they could exchange written messages with the experimenters. The experimenters could observe the subjects without being seen, either by one-way vision screens or by closed-circuit television.

The subjects were told they were equal-rank commanders free to organize their decision-making process any way they desired. Their joint task was to capture the island mapped before them. The enemy was supposedly represented by another team in another room, although actually there was no other such team. The subjects were provided with a 24-h weather report and details about the strength and armament of their own forces—ships, planes, infantry, and artillery—but no information at all about the enemy's forces. They were expected to record the positions of their own forces as well as whatever they learned about the enemy's resources and location.

The game was played in ½-h periods, each of which was supposed to represent 12-h periods in real time. During rest times between playing periods the subjects were asked to fill out rating scales and other forms. During the play the group made decisions about the deployment and actions of their forces and then sent written orders to them through a message chute to the experimenters. They were told their messages would all be evaluated by experienced persons in terms of their own and the enemy's positions and that as rapidly as possible they would receive information about the outcomes of their actions as well as about any contact with the enemy or any enemy move for which the group had provided observation capacity. From time to time the experimenters sent messages to the group. The opposing team was said to operate by the same rules.

These experimenters conceived environmental complexity as some summative function of three experimental variables—information input rate, rate of receipt of messages conveying the meaning that the group's efforts are failing ("noxity"), and rate of receipt of messages indicating that the group's efforts are succeeding ("eucity"). In dealing with any group the experimenters could vary each of these independently from playing period to period. They could send group messages at different rates, and the proportion of failure or success content of these messages could also be controlled.

The experimental data were plotted along the time axis of the entire game, period by period. The number and types of decisions made in different periods were recorded, and the proportion of integrative decisions connecting multiple factors into a single strategy as well as the perseverance of the group in maintaining such strategies was measured. Other objective measures of performance and perception of the group were developed. Various tests of individual personality variables were also administered to the subjects. Even though some of the measures were obtained by testing individual members during rest periods, the orders output by the group resulted from decisions of the group as a whole. Therefore these data relate to systems at the group level rather than the organism level.

The data from several of these studies indicated that, though other variables like the meaning (noxity or eucity) of information affect performance, increasing the speed of information input up to a certain rate improves the information processing of a group, but at higher rates the effect is opposite. These researchers did not measure information inputs in bits per second (or other unit of time) but rather less precisely in messages transmitted by them to the group per ½-h playing period.

In one study each subject was tested to determine his "integration index."[131] A low index indicated that his thinking was concrete—categorical, black–white, and inflexible thinking which minimized conflict and was anchored to external conditions. A high index, on the other hand, indicated the opposite—abstract thinking. The subjects were then put into 20 groups of equal intelligence, 10 with members with low (concrete) integration indexes and 10 with members with high (abstract) integration. Figure 5-20 presents the results. The number of messages reporting integrative decisions output by the group went up as the rate of information inputs increased up to about 10 messages per ½-h playing period and then, at higher input rates, fell. The much larger number of integrations in the groups made up of "abstract" subjects as compared to "concrete" subjects is apparent. Another of this series of studies concerned the effects of variations in information input rates on the complexity of perception of group members.[132] In this study 7 four-

person groups of abstract subjects and 7 four-person groups of concrete subjects played the Tactical War Game. During the rest period after every playing period each member of the group answered a questionnaire about her or his views of the relationships between the strategies of the group and of the enemy. These responses of course were not the subjects' exact thoughts during the actual play, but probably were fairly representative of them. The responses to the questionnaire were then scored for perceptual complexity or simplicity. The complex responses were concerned with longer term strategies, with taking into consideration the viewpoint of the enemy, and with a

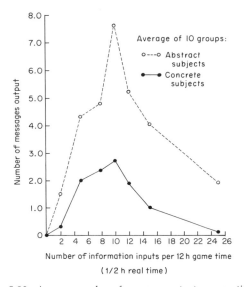

Fig. 5-20   Average number of messages output representing integrative decisions made by groups of "abstract" and "concrete" subjects at various information input rates. (From H. M. Schroder, M. J. Driver, & S. Streufert. *Human information processing: individuals and groups functioning in complex social situations.* New York: Holt, Rinehart and Winston, 1967, 151. Copyright © 1967 by Holt, Rinehart and Winston, Inc. *Reprinted by permission of Holt, Rinehart and Winston.*)

broader range of information. Figure 5-21 presents the results of this study. The curves are like those from the previous experiment. As the rate of information inputs increases, the total number of complex responses output by the groups rises and falls much as the total number of messages representing integrative decisions did. The curves peak at about the same input rate as in the other study, 10 messages per ½ h. The curves of the groups with abstract and with concrete subjects have comparable differences. One adjustment of groups to information input overloads apparently is to decrease the complexity of their per-

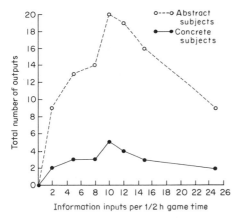

Fig. 5-21   Total number of complex perceptual outputs made by all 28 "abstract" and by all 28 "concrete" subjects after playing periods at various information input rates. (From H. M. Schroder, M. J. Driver, & S. Streufert. *Human information processing: individuals and groups functioning in complex social situations.* New York: Holt, Rinehart and Winston, 1967, 156. Copyright © 1967 by Holt, Rinehart and Winston, Inc. *Reprinted by permission of Holt, Rinehart and Winston.*)

ceptions or analyses of the information they process in making decisions, probably a form of *filtering.*

A third study, carried out by Streufert, one of the members of this group of experimenters, measured characteristics of the decisions of 22 two-person groups playing a Tactical and Negotiations Game, somewhat like the Tactical War Game (see pages 976 to 978).[133] In this experiment the rate of input of

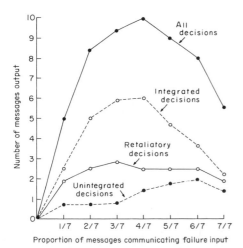

Fig. 5-22   Average number of decision messages of various sorts output by 22 groups at various rates of input of messages communicating failure. (From S. Streufert. Increasing failure and response rate in complex decision making. *J. exper. soc. Psychol.,* 1969, **5**, 318. *Reprinted by permission.*)

messages was the same in each ½-h playing period. But the noxity of the messages, *i.e.,* the proportion of messages indicating failure of the group's strategy as compared to the proportion of neutral messages, varied from 1/7 to 7/7. The decision messages output by the groups in each playing period were counted, and each was rated as to whether it was integrated, unintegated, or retaliatory, *i.e.,* responsive to an action of the enemy but not related to any overall strategy. The average findings for the 22 groups are presented in Fig. 5-22. As the proportion of messages commu-

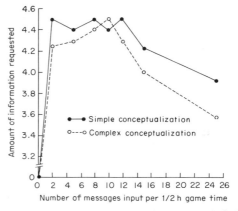

Fig. 5-23   Average amount of information requested of others under various input rates by subjects of simple and complex conceptual structure. (From S. Streufert, P. Suedfeld, & M. J. Driver. Conceptual structure, information search, and information utilization. *J. Personality soc. Psychol.,* 1965, **2**, 738. Copyright 1965 by the American Psychological Association. *Reprinted by permission.*)

nicating failure increased, the decision-making rate first of all rose, up to about four failure messages out of seven, and then fell. The rate of making integrated decisions varied similarly. The rate of making retaliatory decisions did not change, but the rate of making unintegrated decisions rose as noxity rose. Reports of increasing failure clearly were stressful, ultimately diminishing the effectiveness of the decision process.

A fourth study in this series was carried out on 20 four-man teams playing the Tactical War Game.[134] In 10 of the groups, tests showed that the subjects used simple conceptualization. In the other 10 groups they used complex conceptualization. During the game the number of messages input to each group was varied from playing period to period. During each rest time the subjects were asked if they would have preferred to have more or less information input provided to them by others. Figure 5-23 shows what their responses were. As the input rate increased above about 10 messages per ½-h period during the game, the groups asked for others to provide them with less and less additional information, but they still wanted some more. During the game the groups could also initiate efforts to obtain further information by sending messages ordering their forces to carry out information searches or reconnaissance missions. The number of such messages in each playing period was counted. The results appear in Fig. 5-24. As information is input faster and faster, leaving less time for each decision, the amount of self-initiated information search decreases. This finding appears to support Hypothesis 3.3.7.2-6 (see page 100). In these groups it seems that the shorter the decision period, the less thorough in general is the search within the information processing network for relevant facts and alternative solutions.

The number of decisions in each playing period which were influenced by information gained through self-initiated search were counted. The total was considered a measure of integrative use of previously sought information. The findings for all the groups appear in Fig. 5-25. The effects of varied rates of information input are quite similar to the data on integration plotted in Fig. 5-20.

3.4.1   Summary of findings at the group level

(*a*) Information inputs can overload groups.

(*b*) Their channel capacities appear to be slower than those of human organisms, of the order of 0.2 to 1.5 bits per s in the researches I have surveyed above.

(*c*) As in other behaving systems, the *error* and *filtering* adjustment processes seem to be used increasingly as information input rates increase. There is no evidence concerning other adjustment processes.

(*d*) More attention appears to have been devoted at this level to intrasystem variables than at the lower levels, possibly because it has been technically easier

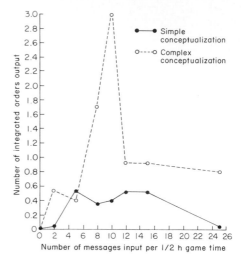

Fig. 5-25   Average number of orders involving integrative utilization of previously sought information output under various input rates by groups of subjects of simple and complex conceptual structure. (Adapted from S. Streufert, P. Suedfeld, & M. J. Driver. Conceptual structure, information search, and information utilization. *J. Personality soc. Psychol.*, 1965, **2**, 739. Copyright 1965 by the American Psychological Association. *Reprinted by permission.*)

to observe these at this level. Special emphasis has been put on communication nets, and in general it appears that information transmission is more effective the fewer the number of links there are in such channels, the more directly members of the group can receive information and ask questions of others, and perhaps the more they volunteer information rather than solicit it. Interestingly, there is evidence that communication in groups does not diminish at slower information input rates, but rather that free time is devoted to communication which increases redundancy but diminishes errors. With practice, groups can increase the rate of their internal communication, although the length of the messages they send does not decrease.

(*e*) Information overload decreases the number of messages representing integrative decisions sent by a group as well as the number of its complex responses. A high input rate of messages indicating failure decreases a group's rate of decision making. Information overload also decreases the amount of searching a

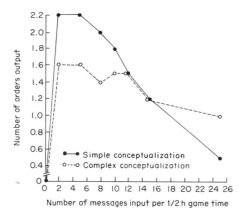

Fig. 5-24   Average number of self-initiated information search orders output under various input rates by groups of subjects of simple and complex conceptual structure. (From S. Streufert, P. Suedfeld, & M. J. Driver. Conceptual structure, information utilization. *J. Personality soc. Psychol.*, 1965, **2**, *soc. Psychol.*, 1965, **2**, 739. Copyright 1965 by the American Psychological Association. *Reprinted by permission.*)

group does for new information of potential value in making decisions.

3.5 Information input overload at the level of the organization   Experimental data relevant to information input overload are sparse at the level of the group, and they are not plentiful at the level of the organization.

Air defense direction center. Some of the earliest organization research was reported by Chapman and Kennedy, who worked with organizations of 30 to 40 men in a simulated air defense direction center. Four air-defense experiments were conducted with these crews of officers, noncommissioned officers, and airmen, each running for about 200 h, the equivalent of nearly 6 weeks of normal life in the real direction center. Their task was to defend an area of roughly 260,000 km², over which in each experiment about 100,000 flights of private, commercial, and friendly military airplanes, as well as hostile airplanes, occurred. Information concerning these flights came to the crew at the average rate of about 300 symbols per minute (min). Recognizing that the organization had useful adjustment processes, Chapman and Kennedy stated:

The outstanding result of these experiments with information was [the indication of] the degree to which an air defense crew can learn to use its resources more effectively. . . . What was startling was the extent to which performance could be improved by exploiting these unused resources. Although the task load was increased gradually so that it was more than three times as great at the end of the experiment as it had been in the beginning, each of the four crews kept up a highly effective defense of the area against enemy air attack.[135]

When enemy attack increased rapidly rather than gradually, without opportunity for learning, the organization eventually suffered an information processing breakdown or confusional state.[136]

With gradually increasing inputs, however, there was only a slight rise in the rate of information flow within the organization, and during the last hour of the experiment when the input rate was more than three times as heavy, the crew used about the same amount of information as during the first hour. Successful processing under this high input rate was possible because the organization used the adjustment process of *filtering*, concentrating on symbols concerning potentially hostile traffic and spending increasingly less time on other symbols. At the beginning it paid attention to all symbols, but in the end it was filtering out 60 percent of them and working with only 40 percent. These changes are explained by the experimenters in terms of organizational learning by the total system under stress with adequate feedback concerning success and failure (see pages 409 and 638).

Air traffic control systems.   One related organizational experiment dealt with communication among only two persons at a time, but they were acting as component members of an organization.[137] In this investigation, transcriptions were made of conversations between pilots and tower controllers during landings at an Air Force training base. The repertoire of words used was found to be relatively limited, and the messages were broken down into "information elements," categories which, rather than words or phrases, became the basis for measuring the information flows. Dependent probabilities for these elements were computed by the authors' original methods.

In this situation the upper limit of information transfer observed was about 9 bits per s, including redundant information. For experienced communicators who frequently could predict parts of the highly redundant conversations from preceding parts, the rate actually turned out to represent about 2 bits per s if the redundancy was eliminated. Since these communications were carried on between two experienced individuals rather than through intermediaries, these conversations occurred at a faster rate than talk within a group usually does. Also they were self-paced, but under conditions which rewarded brevity. The total amount of information processed per landing, for either jet- or propeller-driven aircraft, was about 51 bits. The redundancy was about 80 percent. There was no difference in information transfer rate or total information per landing between periods of high and low traffic density, but pilots frequently made their first report to the tower later in the landing process during periods of high traffic density, presumably because the single communication channel available was in heavy use. This finding supports the observation of Chapman and Kennedy that when rapid information processing is necessary, groups tend to use the *filtering* adjustment process, *i.e.*, limit themselves to essential communications only.[138]

An experiment with an electronic air traffic control simulator was performed to determine human capacities for various control functions, which essentially deal with complex processing of much information beginning with the first input announcing a pilot's arrival in an area and ending with his clearance for landing, the output.[139] The problem studied was that of two controllers moving a group of 32 jet bombers and fighters through the terminal zone which extended for a radius of about 80 km from the ground-control approach gate near the airport. Three primary variables were studied: presence versus absence of direct, face-to-face communication between controllers; presence versus absence of emergencies; and differences in traffic load of randomly arriving aircraft with average separations of 45, 60, and 90 s.

The criteria of efficiency which were employed in the study of this system included the average fuel consumption of the planes, the average time they spent within the control zone before they were permitted to approach for landing, both of which were measures of *queuing;* and the proportion of aircraft not achieving the minimum safe 15-s separation in their approaches to the airport, which was a measure of *error.* As the traffic input rate went up, system efficiency in terms of these criteria dropped significantly. For example, control time increased from about 10 to about 12.5 min, and aircraft which came in without sufficient separation increased from about 3.7 to about 10.7 percent. It was apparent that the increased input rates of traffic accelerated information processing to such a point of overload that the necessary information to ensure optimal landings could not be transmitted. This state of affairs arose not only from the statistical nature of queues but also from information overload on the controllers. Performance of the controllers was slackening because, at the higher input rate, new demands were made on them by messages arriving while they were still processing earlier inputs or because they were still in a refractory state after such processing. The report stated:

The traffic control system did not break down in any sudden or abrupt way as input rate was increased up to one aircraft every 45 sec. However, the . . . fuel consumed by both types of aircraft increased about 25% as the input rate of aircraft to be handled per hour was doubled. As the traffic load increased, the traffic pattern became more fluid. This is interpreted as resulting from an attempt by the controllers to maintain efficiency as well as safety. For example, aircraft were not committed to a fixed sequence or to a rigid landing priority until they neared the GCA gate. Stereotyped traffic lines were not formed but instead a fluid pattern was used . . . which appears to be associated with efficiency. The time each aircraft spent in the control zone increased under high-load conditions with a consequent increase in fuel consumption, and controllers more often failed to achieve safe separation in the terminal area. Also, at the higher loads aircraft were turned over to GCA with less satisfactory lateral spacing—the average deviation to one side of the glide path was greater.[140]

This shows that with a random output, *queuing* could be profitable, a fluid arrangement whereby temporary input overloads or overlaps could be spread out into lulls. At slow input rates there was less input overload and consequently less *queuing* delay. An indication of how fluidity of control handled temporary input overload or overlap is the measure of coherence between input and output sequences. It was shown that input–output coherence, as measured by Fisher's z', gave correlations of .969 for average input

rates of 45 s, .990 for 60 s, and .998 for 90 s. These correlations would be 1.000 if the planes were landed in exactly the same order as they came in, any change in order serving to lower the coefficients.

The variable of intrasystem communication among the different controllers in the simulator was also studied. It was found that whether they were separated and could not communicate except over an intercom arrangement or whether they were face to face had no significant effect on the various measures of efficiency of the system. When they were face to face, however, communication and collaboration increased. The system appeared to be better integrated when the components of its decider interacted frequently.

A case history—not an experiment—concerned similar problems of information overload on the departures controller at the London airport.[141] In 1956, when the study was made, this official carried out certain major functions of the decider as well as some other subsystems of airport organization. Every aircraft being serviced preparatory to departure was visited periodically by an observer (a component of the internal transducer), who reported to the departures controller what activities had been completed and estimated on the basis of his own experience what others might cause delay. The controller was supposed to decide what rearrangement of servicing activities was necessary if a delay in one activity appeared inevitable. He had channels to 22 different sections involved in the servicing, and he had to inform them of rearrangements in servicing activities and tell them the possible extent of delay.

The system came under information input and internal processing stresses during busy periods. Sections had to wait a long time before they could make contact with the departures controller to obtain or impart information. The observers and personnel responsible for arranging to board passengers had to refer all data and problems for decision to the controller but had difficulty getting decisions from him. And the controller garbled and forgot some information, occasionally transmitting faulty instructions. It was clear that the controller was the trouble center. Since he was only one person, information could be processed to him by only one communication channel. His long-term information storage was in the form of data written on a chart, while short-term storage was in his memory, held until it was required for making a decision or answering queries on outgoing calls. The rate of information input to the controller was measured, and it was found that he was handling phone calls 65 percent of his time for an average of 0.23 min per call. Though there was a tacit but complex set of priorities, calls were in effect dealt with at random.

Incoming calls were delayed on the average more than ½ min, and at least 6 percent of the calls were delayed more than 2.5 min (the *queuing* adjustment process). These delays held up operations and unnecessarily consumed the time of personnel in waiting to talk to the controller, so such *queuing* was not an adaptive form of adjustment.

It was decided that these overload effects could be dealt with by either eliminating certain sorts of phone calls involving the controller (the *filtering* adjustment process) or splitting the controller's job between two or more persons (the *multiple channels* adjustment process). Analysis of the phone calls between the observers and the controller showed that 43 percent were queries about the completion of a task which was going along on schedule. Moreover 52 percent of the calls between departures and the airport tower concerned embarcation of passengers when there were no holdups. Instead of having reports come to the controller every time a task was started and when it was finished, therefore, a schedule was established, and all employees were informed as to when these tasks should begin and end. They were then directed to report to the controller only when the schedule was not being followed. This *filtering* at the source cut down calls to the controller by nearly 30 percent, reducing the incidence of the long waiting times and the difficulty of getting decisions.

The garbled or forgotten facts (*errors* in processing) were studied, and it was shown that errors were more frequent during high input rates, when the controller's short-term memory was overloaded. It was decided arbitrarily that a tolerable error level would be 1 percent, and it was calculated that this corresponded to an input of 2 items per min to the memory or short-term store of the controller. It appeared that the effective capacity of the controller's memory was about 6 topics at a time over long periods, though occasionally it rose as high as 10 or 11 for brief periods. It became clear that, given the rates of departing flights to be expected by the summer of 1960, the input to the controller would be so great that he could not satisfy the criterion of less than 1 percent error. It was therefore decided to use two controllers with a carefully planned division of functions, so that little common information had to be stored in short-term memory by both of them. Short-term information of mutual concern to both was stored on a display which could be seen by both of them. So the *multiple channels* adjustment process, a common one in organizations, was used to decrease use of another adjustment process, *error*.

Information input overloads like those experienced by air controllers often impinge also on other executives and leaders. Consequently, as Bennis has observed, we should educate our leaders " . . . to cope efficiently, imaginatively, and perceptively with information overload [since] . . . power is based on control of relevant information."[142] Such overloads also constitute one reason why Dubin concluded that the more input channels there are transmitting information into specific units of an organization, the less stable the organization is.[143] If the number of persons reporting to a decision maker is too great and they all interact with him continuously, perhaps at times providing conflicting data, he may not be able to process all the incoming information. As a result he may make confused decisions or in other ways operate inefficiently.

How do organizations prepare their leaders and decision makers to cope effectively with the inevitable information input overload? Some strategies are suggested by Meier:*

Eventually the specialists in work study and systems analysis will have identified the positions that are the most susceptible to overload and the occasions during which channels are most likely to be flooded. Such posts would be provided assistance, at least during the critical periods. A large share of this aid would take the form of various buffers in the immediate environment of the critical positions—the number and variety of which might be ten or twenty times greater than today. Some of the queuing and priority-setting might be handled through the telephone and postal services by renting special equipment. Auto-abstracts might be compiled for the scanning of large quantities of printed matter. Face-to-face contacts could be filtered and scheduled by receptionists and secretaries. The result would be an accumulation of service personnel and facilities to insulate the hot spots. Since many of the peaks in the desire to communicate are simultaneous for all such positions, the collective reaction time is slowed down; average costs for these vulnerable functions are raised because all this apparatus, mechanical and human, must be kept ready. Most of the extraordinary economies of scale inherent in communications will have been exploited at the stage where overload may be anticipated.

Another interesting consequence of threatened information overload results from the management of the overall decision process. One property that is built into the human filters is a narrowing of the range of relevant messages pertinent to the decisions being made [*filtering*]. Computation under standard assumptions is resorted to instead of judgment which takes into account a wide range of extraneous factors, and a vote or veto is recorded instead of the opening of overtures leading to bargaining.[144]

In their theoretical analysis of organizational behavior, Katz and Kahn accept the view that the persons and groups that make up organizations have limited channel capacity.[145] Consequently from time to time they are subject to information input overloads—

*Reprinted from *A communications theory of urban growth* by R. L. Meier by permission of the M.I.T. Press, Cambridge, Massachusetts. Copyright © 1962 by the Joint Center for Urban Studies of the Massachusetts Institute of Technology and Harvard University.

particularly if they have several roles or receive inputs from many sources. They agree that the various adjustment processes to such overloads which we have described are used by organizations. Also they acknowledge that each adjustment has its costs, which may be reasonable or so great that the adjustment is maladaptive. For example, once a busy official of a large railroad neglected to act on an employee's grievance for so long that the employee went to court. The result of this use of the *omission* adjustment process was that the court set a legal precedent that permitted many other employees also to file suit against the railroad. *Queuing* can be adaptive if it is followed by a lull during which backlogs can be elminated, but if this adjustment process is used by telephone operators merely because they want to work at less than a reasonable rate, the efficiency of a telephone company decreases. Also Katz and Kahn point out that decentralization, which is one sort of use of *multiple channels* in organizations, usually is not a spontaneous and reversible functional change occurring only during periods of overload, but is a planned, often irreversible, structural change. They also note that internal information adjustments in organizations are sometimes used to decrease information overloads on internal channels. A company may, for instance, require that all memoranda written by its employees be no longer than a page, or may provide periods of privacy for executives or reduce the number of roles that place demands on the time of key members of organizations so that they can better accomplish their few most important tasks. Or a university administration may reduce the number of hours a professor spends weekly in classroom teaching so that he can have time to counsel more students individually.

Communications systems. In a paper written in 1953 Norbert Wiener presented an early description of information input overload, one that occurred during World War II on a man–machine organization—a telephone switching system in New York City. Such a central telephone exchange is so constructed that an uncompleted call temporarily reduces the ability of the exchange to complete other incoming calls appropriately. In one part of New York where several war agencies were located the number of telephone calls mushroomed to the extent that at various times the exchange broke down, and it was impossible for a caller to get a dial tone. As Wiener wrote:

In the design of the central, no such increase in active telephone users had been contemplated. The result was that throughout the War, traffic jams occurred during which no message could get through for considerable periods. The company naturally suspected the defective functioning of some parts, and the station was repeatedly examined by experts who repeatedly found nothing wrong. The trouble continued until after the demobilization when the traffic load of that part of the city went down to normal again.[146]

For years after that no difficulty was observed, but in recent years the increase in the number of telephone users has made such overloads a common problem in midtown New York.

A study by Rand Corporation of the New York City fire department in 1970 indicated that its communications system was coming close to a somewhat comparable breakdown from information overload.[147] Tests showed that the delay between the receipt of a message and the dispatch of fire equipment could be as much as 11 minutes, which seemed to the investigators to be "clearly intolerable." To speed the communications a new telephone answering system was devised.

Governmental systems. The nearer the top an organization is in the administrative hierarchy of a country, the more likely it is to suffer from information overload. In the United States the President, the White House staff, the Cabinet, and the Congress are obviously overloaded. So, apparently, is the Supreme Court.[148] Although it is not widely recognized, the docket of that court, which includes several thousand cases annually, has grown to the point that they have resorted to extensive use of the *multiple channels* adjustment process. They have expanded the number of channels beyond the nine justices. The clerk of the court and law clerks in the justices' offices first screen petitions or motions to the court. Any of those which appear to them not to be worthy of serious consideration by the court are put on a "special list" by the chief clerk. These cases are digested by the court staff—a use of the *abstracting* adjustment process. Copies of the digests along with the full petitions or motions are sent to each justice. Such petitions and motions are automatically rejected without debate unless a justice requests a discussion by the full court.

The costs of *queuing* in organizations under some circumstances can be very great. For example, in early December, 1941, the United States Army Signal Corps office that decoded and translated radio messages from Japan was so overloaded that it had big backlogs. Consequently, when two messages were intercepted, they were not processed until middle or late December. One, from Tokyo to Honolulu, said:[149] "In view of the present situation, the presence in port of warships, airplane carriers and cruisers is of utmost importance. Hereafter, to the utmost of your ability, let me know day by day. Wire me in each case whether or not there are any observation balloons above Pearl Harbor or if there are any indications that they will be sent up. Also advise me whether or not the warships are provided with anti-mine nets."

The other message, transmitted by radio from Honolulu and by coded advertisements in the Honolulu newspapers, concerned light signals to be flashed from a house on Lanakai Beach in order to reveal movements and anchorages of the United States Pacific fleet. By the time these two messages, which clearly revealed their plans, were decoded and translated, the Japanese had attacked Pearl Harbor.

Libraries are another type of organization which experience information overloads. For instance, as my former colleague Meier and his associates showed, they occur in the undergraduate library of the University of Michigan during periods of peak use.[150] The inflow of students and faculty into this library, each with his special needs, is not an overload of energy or matter, for the library is never actually physically unable to hold them. Their demands for service by members of the library staff, however, can constitute what is essentially an information overload.

Participant observation and other operations research procedures were used to find how much the library was used at top load periods and what changes occurred in library functions at such times. No significant difference in average time of getting a book was found between periods of light and of heavy use, suggesting that the library may not have been at any time under true performance overload. Rough efforts were made to calculate the number of bits of information flowing through the library. It was determined that the average book title in the card catalog contains about 135 bits of information, and that the average reader processes information at a rate of between 14 and 25 bits per s of reading.[151] The total rate of information processing of the entire organization at any one time is obviously a function of the number of users at that time.

Perhaps the most significant finding by Meier and his associates was that a series of adjustment processes occurred or could occur in the library to cope with the overload. He recognized the similarity of his list to the one that I presented earlier in this chapter. But he found more complex forms of these adjustment processes, or "policies" as he calls them, in this complicated organization with its many components carrying out numerous activities. His list follows: *Queuing;* priorities in queues and backlogs; destruction of low priority inputs *(filtering); omission;* reduction of processing standards *(abstracting);* decentralization (a special case of use of *multiple channels);* formation of independent organizations near the periphery *(multiple channels);* mobile reserve *(multiple channels);* rethinking procedures; redefining bounda-

ries of the system; *escape;* retreat to formal, ritualistic behavior; and dissolution of the system with salvage of its assets. Whether there are new adjustment processes here, or simply special cases of those which I have listed and put in *italics* is a question for debate. But the fact that such policies are used to adjust to overloads cannot be questioned.

Stock exchanges in recent years have been notoriously susceptible to information input overloads. "Buy" and "sell" messages are input to the stock exchange floor by telephone or teletype, often bunching up to create peak loads when there is a wave of investor activity.[152] The exchange cannot control the input rate and must do the best it can to process orders rapidly—in minutes—because if the delays are any longer the prices may change.

In 1959 the procedure of the New York Stock Exchange was as follows: When the order arrived on the floor it was written on a slip of paper and taken by a broker's agent to one of several booths, the one where the particular stock involved was traded. There the specialist in that stock arranged a trade. Then a reporter was given a record of the transaction on a slip of paper. On the average such a slip would carry about 100 bits of information—60 to identify the seller and buyer and 40 to describe the stock, the number of shares, and the trading price. Only the latter 40 bits became public, each report of a transaction on the ticker ordinarily requiring that much information. Anywhere from 6 to 8 reporters were present at each booth, depending on how much business was being transacted there. In the exchange, activity fluctuated over time and space. At a given moment many transactions might be going on at a particular place on the floor near the specialist for a particular stock while the rest of the trading was dull. Shifting around reporters to communicate information about these trades was a constant problem. Whenever a transaction was complete, one reporter received the slip recording it and sent it by pneumatic tube to the two output transducing departments that gave out price quotations and prepared the ticker tape.

More than 150 girls at telephones in the quote department gave out bid and ask prices and the list of closing prices. Peak loads were about 150,000 quotes (approximately 2 million bits per 6-h day, or 93 bits per s), and 25,000 quotes (about 350,000 bits) in the first half hour of a trading session, or 194 bits per s. Every 5 s quote reports were placed on a board before the telephone girls. Several groups of girls divided the task of giving out the information, each group having responsibility for the data on a different part of the board.

The ticker department also received reports on all

individual trades through pneumatic tubes. They were typed out by three teams of three girls each. One girl in each team picked up the slip of paper from the pile of transaction reports that formed at the output of a pneumatic tube, the second typed the message, and the third verified the resultant tape. The tapes from the three teams were then combined and put on the ticker. The maximum speed of the tape was 500 characters or 100 words per min. In a 2.5-million share day the ticker would carry about 10 million bits of information in 6 h, or an average rate of about 48 bits per s.

There was a lag of 1.5 to 2 min in getting reports from the floor to the ticker department and the lag in making the tape was 10 to 40 s. The total channel capacity of the stock exchange would be the sum of the capacities of the quote and ticker departments (plus whatever other components did output transducing).

The adjustments used to prevent overloading of the ticker were as follows: The supervisor estimated the average tape delay at the three stations from the size of the piles of untyped transaction reports. If he decided the tape was 1 min late, they used a *filtering* adjustment, cutting one figure out of the price (*e.g.*, the price of IBM stock was reported as 65 rather than 365), but the number of shares was given in full. If the tape was 2 min late, they *filtered* from the tape stocks traded in small share lots. If the tape was 3 min late, they *filtered* the last two ciphers in the number of shares (*e.g.*, reported the number as 3 rather than 300). If the tape was 5 min late, they *omitted* enough transactions in the queue to keep current. They also bunched sales together if they were made at the same price (the *abstracting* adjustment). During a 2.5-million share day, they averaged 10 to 11 *errors* per day. All errors were automatically totaled each day for each typist, and on the basis of this record each one was rated C, B, A, or Exceptional. The B typists wrote at least 250 characters per minute with 1 error or less. The A and Exceptional typists did better. Errors made on the floor were estimated to be 3 or 4 times as frequent as typing errors. The percentage of both increased with the trading rate.

In 1959 demand for stock skyrocketed and overloaded this system, as Meier reported:*

About the middle of January 1959 a speculative fever caught hold of the stock markets that soon proved itself to be the strongest since 1929. Speculators concentrated upon the American Stock Exchange because it registered a larger rela-

tive price variation. Their demands caused the American Stock Exchange, always a poor second in trading rate to the New York Stock Exchange and recording only about a third of the volume of the latter, to quadruple its transaction rate and come abreast the senior exchange. "Furor on the Amex" headlined the *Forbes Magazine* (Feb. 1, 1959) shortly after the splurge began.

The first sign of trouble arose in the internal operations. The "clearing" of the trades had previously been accomplished within four days but during February this period stretched out to two weeks. Extra clerks and accountants had to be hired, but the supply was far from adequate, and inadequately trained persons were added in desperation. On March 17 the clearing system broke down altogether. A week later 80,000–100,000 pieces of paper worth many millions of dollars were in the backlog waiting to be processed. Priorities had been established, apparently, so that accounts with non-member brokers were straightened out, but the remainder were left in such a complete snarl that the Exchange had to call for outside assistance. ("Big Board Gives Helping Hand" noted *The New York Times* on March 26.) The New York Stock Exchange Clearing Corporation was asked to take over all the routine operations of its neighbor on Broad Street. Authorities asserted that "things would be back to normal by the end of the week."

The Government tried to help out and took action that would otherwise have been resisted by members of the American Stock Exchange. "Securities Exchange Commission Opens War on Manipulators" is the way *Business Week* summed it up. *The Wall Street Journal* had until this time underplayed the story, noting the official statements under small leads, but it apparently had dug into the background and put a finger upon a crucial feature of the episode, "Errors Mount as Stock Sales Flood Brokers, Exchanges." It pointed out that brokers on the trading floor occasionally made a slip, so that records of the seller and buyer did not jibe. The slips were then marked DK ("don't know") and sent back to the brokers to be threshed out. In the previous few weeks the DK's had been piling up, thus explaining the subhead on the story, "Securities Firms Spur Hirings."

When institutions fail to meet well-established standards and contractual guaranties, morale drops, turmoil mounts, and investigations are made to discover how to prevent such a catastrophe from recurring. *Business Week* reviewed the situation a month after the breakdown, "Paperwork Troubles Bog Down American Stock Exchange; Harassed Brokers Turn to Computers." They reported that the American Stock Exchange Clearing Corporation was still trying to get back into operation and gossip was going the rounds that it would never again open up completely. "Corps of accountants and extra help were trying to untangle the mess." The largest brokerage houses had ordered large computers, while the smaller houses were setting up a joint installation, but it would take years to put these systems into full operation. A feeling of guilt resulting from failure to perform according to public expectations was associated with the affair. It was evidenced by the careful exclusion of the press, followed by terse "explanations" which tried to minimize the breakdown, but of course all this did little more than excite curiosity.

Trading activity resumed a more normal state and the American Stock Exchange still does business at the old address and in much the same manner as before. Morale was restored in part by an unusual Christmas bonus. The consequences of a thoroughgoing systems and procedures review appeared in the form of announcements of reorganization. A new ticker network was readied and later a method of reduc-

*Reprinted from *A communications theory of urban growth* by R. L. Meier by permission of the M.I.T. Press, Cambridge, Massachusetts. Copyright © 1962 by the Joint Center for Urban Studies of the Massachusetts Institute of Technology and Harvard University.

ing the DK's generated during hectic moments was devised at the same time that the quality of service was improved; the *Times* headlined "American Board Orders High Speed Quote System," and explained in the story that followed, "this would contrast to the present procedure which does not have the flexibility to allow the history of the activity of a stock action to be incorporated or the ability to speed up during peak periods when the demand for information increases."[153]

After this embarrassing breakdown, the stock exchanges adopted more advanced information processing procedures which enabled them to process and report their transactions much more rapidly. In a few years, however, business activity increased so much that the organization's channel capacities were again exceeded and a very similar overload situation occurred, though at a higher overall rate of information transmission, as reported in the *Washington Post* in 1970:

In 1968, volume climbed to a record 2.9 billion shares, or nearly 13 million a day. [This represents an average rate of about 250 bits per s.]
    Never eager to embrace the costs of modernization and historically sales-oriented, the industry was caught with its pencils and eyeshades down. Little attention had ever been paid to the "back office" paperwork function although a study made for the exchange had shown that completion of each transaction, no matter what the size, involved at least 30 hand processes. (With the inevitable errors, the total can climb above 60.)
    To accommodate the rush of business as stock prices zoomed during a long bull market, the brokers opened more and more offices across the country. In 1967, exchange members added 438 offices, a 12 percent increase. In 1968, another 148 offices were opened. The number of registered representatives, or salesmen, climbed from 38,514 in 1967 to 52,466 at the end of 1969.
    The increase in the number of salesmen and their offices poured business into understaffed and antiquated brokerage headquarters. As far back as the SEC's [Security Exchange Commission's] special study of securities markets in 1963, the industry had been warned that it had to modernize and computerize its back offices. But the advice was ignored. Mammoth branch office networks were built, backed up by processing systems that depended on clerks with pencil and paper rather than automated machinery.
    As volume climbed to record levels and held there, the back offices were swamped in paperwork and the street was headed inexorably toward upheaval.
    First, brokers swamped by paperwork were unable to deliver securities within the required four-day period (since lengthened to five) [*queuing*]. When securities were not delivered, the selling broker could not collect the sales price, although he was often obligated to make payment to his customers. In April, 1968, when the NYSE made its first tabulation of these "fails," it found an undelivered backlog of $2.67 billion. With the tieup in deliveries, the payment of dividends was equally fouled up [*errors*] heaping more costs on the brokers.
    To cope with the avalanche of paper, the exchange in June, 1968, ordered trading halted one day a week, and maintained

that schedule until the end of the year. Brokers began a frantic search for help, hiring almost any applicant [use of *multiple channels*]. Often, bounties were offered to employees who brought in new recruits. The record trading pace, which was maintained well into 1969, drove home to the brokers the need to modernize their back offices. "Crash" computer installations were ordered.
    Under such conditions, mistakes were inevitable. Ill-fated Goodbody & Co. developed an "autocage" computerizing the cashier's department which handled securities and cash. But the firm made no adjustments to handle the inflow and output of the autocage. Although industry sources familiar with the system laud it, the development turned into a $5 million fiasco for the firm.
    John L. Loeb, senior partner of Loeb, Rhoades & Co., says, "I don't think some of these firms knew where they were. Some of them used bad judgment, but for most of them it was just bad housekeeping."
    Irving Pollack, director of the SEC's division of trading and markets, observes, "In this business, when you lose control of your books and records, you're dead."
    As the brokers added computers and other equipment, their break-even point in terms of overall trading volume, increased rapidly. In the mid-1960's, a NYSE volume of 5 or 6 million shares was enough in most cases, to cover costs. By 1969, the break-even had risen to 12 million shares a day. In that year, NYSE volume fell to 2.85 billion shares from 2.93 billion and daily volume slipped to 11.14 million shares, below the level needed by the brokers to balance their costs. This year, volume will run close to the '69 level and the brokers have been forced to make sharp cuts in personnel and overhead to reduce losses.[154]

From 1959 to 1969 the stock exchanges had increased their channel capacities several times, and they would have to increase them even more in the future. But they apparently had not yet come to understand fully the nature of information input overloads and how to adjust to them.

3.5.1 Summary of findings at the organization level   Few quantitative experiments on organizational information input overload have yet been carried out. Those which have been conducted, however, when analyzed along with several obvious cases of such overloads on various types of organizations, lead to the following conclusions:

(*a*) Undoubtedly as the rate of information input to an information processing organization goes up its output rate also increases to a point and then clear indications of overload appear. No evidence exists, except in the cases of telephone central exchanges, that such overloads actually reduce information output rates below the organization's channel capacity, although it seems entirely reasonable that they could.

Information units have rarely been used in measuring the effects of information overloads on organizations. Rather they have usually been evaluated indirectly, by measuring changes in functions of other subsystems or components than those under stress— like the rate of landing of planes at an airport or the delays of airport personnel in carrying out standard procedures.

(*b*) The air traffic study mentioned above (see page 157) set the rate of self-paced information processing of *one channel* in an air traffic control system larger than a face-to-face group at somewhere between about 9 and 2 bits per s. The rate was affected by the amount of redundancy in the message, which, in turn, depended on how experienced a given controller was. This, however, was not a calculation of maximum channel capacity, and there was no overload in this study. Moreover, one can challenge these experimenters' procedures for calculating "information elements." It is even questionable whether an organization was involved, because the communication really was between two persons, the controller in the airport tower and the pilot, rather than between two groups.

No studies are reported which measure the capacity of an organizational channel involving more than one link between one person and another, so there is no evidence of what the capacity of a multicomponent organizational channel is.

Some of those organizations investigated in the studies I have discussed above were highly centralized, and the rate of information processing in them was usually particularly influenced by the processing rate of one person or one group. Examples are the air traffic controllers and the justices of the Supreme Court. In such systems many or all subsystems are indirectly affected if the decider or channel and net is overloaded. In organizations, as in systems at other levels, the decider subsystem seems to be most frequently affected by overload.

(*c*) *Total* channel capacities of organizations can be very large. They appear to go up as the number of component persons and groups in them increases, although the total capacity may rise more slowly than the number of components. It is characteristic of organizations to use the *multiple channels* adjustment process to increase their capacities, *e.g.*, in the stock market quote department or ticker department, or a self-service organization like a library. Total channel capacity for a library was calculated at 14 to 25 bits per s times the number of readers. For a stock exchange it was calculated as the sum of the outputs of the quote department (up to 194 bits per s), the ticker department (in 1959, 48 bits per s, but in 1969 up to 250 or more bits per s), plus the other components of the organization that do output transducing.

(*d*) Organizations employ numerous adjustments to information input overload, including *omission, error, queuing, filtering, abstracting, multiple channels,* and *escape*. In addition certain other complex adjustments (see page 161) also emerge at this level which are not seen at lower levels. They may be special varieties or combinations of the fundamental adjustment processes employed at the lower levels.

3.6 Summary of related literature I have now completed surveying the literature on information input overload. Table 5-2 summarizes the variables investigated in the researches at the five levels with which I have dealt, organizing them as input variables, output variables, system variables, and adjustment processes. In this table many more cells are empty than are filled. This is partly because my review of the literature has been incomplete but partly also because no one has seriously considered measuring some of these variables at some or all levels.

With present methods it appears impossible to measure some of the variables at certain levels (those cells marked $-$). In some cases I may be wrong in concluding this. If I am not, however, more of these variables are now measurable at levels above the cell and organ than at those two lowest levels. This may be because certain processes are emergent at the higher levels which are not present at lower levels (see page 78). Variables 1, 11, 19, and 23 are the only four reported as being measured at all levels.

The general shape of the input–output curve in these studies shows the output (in bits per s) rising as a more or less linear function of input until channel capacity is reached, then leveling off, and finally decreasing in the confusional state, as is consistent with Hypothesis 5.1-1 (see pages 103 and 122). This cross-level generality appears rather convincingly in an overall review of the relevant empirical work of a number of scientists, even though it was not explicitly recognized as being true at more than one level by any of them. It is also possible to glean from these researches suggestions as to hierarchical differences across the levels. The overall impression of the numerous studies mentioned in this chapter is that channel capacity decreases from cells to organs, to organisms, to groups, and to organizations. Certainly there are exceptions to this generality in the literature that has been analyzed, but it has enough support to be interesting. Similar adjustment processes to information input overload appear to be comparable at different levels, *omission*, for example, being found at four levels and *error* at five. More adjustments have been identified at the higher levels than at the lower ones. Conceivably all these processes can be carried out at several if not at all levels.

4. Pathological effects of information input overload

When the adjustment processes to information input overload are adequate to maintain the receiving sys-

TABLE 5-2   Published Researches on Variables Related to Information Input Overload at Five Levels of Living Systems

| | Level | | | | |
Variable	Cell	Organ	Organism	Group	Organization
Input Variables					
1 Average input rate	+	+	+	+	+
2 Variance in input rate (redundancy of temporal patterning of input)			+	+	
3 Average input intensity	+	+	+		
4 Variance in input intensity					
5 Input priority (capacity to alter processing time)					+
6 Size of ensemble			+		
7 Redundancy of ensemble					+
8 Amount of input noise					
9 Input range (number of channels)		+	+		
10 Input overlap		+	+		
Output Variables					
11 Average output rate	+	+	+	+	+
12 Variance in output rate (redundancy of temporal patterning of output)					
13 Average output intensity	+	+			
14 Variance in output intensity		+			
15 Size of ensemble					
16 Redundancy of output ensemble					+
17 Output range (number of channels)	−		+		
18 Output overlap	−				
System Variables					
19 Input–output ratio	+	+	+	+	+
20 Average processing time	+		+		+
21 Variance in processing time			+		+
Adjustment Processes					
22 Omission adjustment process	+	+	+		+
23 Error adjustment process	+	+	+	+	+
24 Queuing adjustment process			+		+
25 Filtering adjustment process			+	+	+
26 Abstracting adjustment process			+		+
27 Use of multiple channels adjustment process	−		+		+
28 Escape adjustment process	−	−	+		+

NOTE: + means a study exists and is mentioned in this chapter; − means a study appears impossible with present methods; an empty cell means no study has been located.

tem's variables within steady-state ranges, no pathology results. Most commonly this stress does not produce any irreversible pathological process. An increasing body of evidence at various levels suggests, however, that sometimes it does.

4.1 Pathology at the level of the cell Excess inputs of hormonal molecules bearing information to cells can have effects opposite to their usual ones. For example, thyroid hormones input at ordinary rates to vertebrate cells convey signals which promote the growth of those cells by increasing the rates of certain enzymatic processes (see page 300). Abnormally high rates of hormonal inputs, on the other hand, retard growth and produce other abnormal biochemical effects in cells. There is no evidence that high rates of information inputs to normal neurons produce any irreversible fatigue or other damage. They appear to have effective cutoff processes which prevent this.

4.2 Pathology at the level of the organ Abnormally high rates of adrenal cortical hormone to many organs over a period of time can damage them (see page 354). In thyrotoxicosis excessive rates of thyroid hormone inputs to the structures surrounding the eyes may cause them to bulge. Such inputs predispose the heart to coronary occlusion. No one has yet found any pathological effects produced by information overloads to neural organs.

4.3 Pathology at the level of the organism A striking indication that an excess of information inputs can produce major pathology in organisms—at least in rats—is found in the researches of Calhoun.[155] Over several years he conducted a number of controlled observations of different rat communities in specifically built enclosures. These observation periods would last for 24 months or more. At the beginning of the experiment the populations numbered from 16 males and 16 females to 28 males and 28 females all just past the age of weaning. They were placed in rooms divided into four interconnecting pens in which were an abundance of food and adequate places to live. The growth of the populations, and the rats' behavior in relation to one another and their specially designed environment were observed continuously. These communities became organized into characteristic structures. For example, a preponderance of the population concentrated in two central pens. Only a very few rats stayed in the two outer pens. These end pens characteristically housed one or two dominant males, each of which established control over a territory in which he kept a harem of several females. In the end pens, where the population density was lowest, the harem females made good mothers, nursing their young, building them nests, and protecting them from harm. The mortality rate among infants and females was low, and in general these rats seemed to be healthy. In the central pens, however, where the rats crowded together and encountered other individuals much more frequently, the overpopulation apparently produced various sorts of pathology, different from one animal to another. Although the pregnancy rates of the females in the middle pens were similar to those in the outer pens, the pregnancies of the former ended in a lower percentage of live births. Of the infants born in the middle pens, 80 percent or more died before they were weaned. Their mothers often failed to feed them, did not build them nests, and often would forget to care for them when they were in danger. The adult males in overcrowded pens also showed a variety of pathological behaviors: Some indulged frequently in homosexual or pansexual contacts; some withdrew passively from other rats, ignoring even females in estrus; others, called probers by Calhoun, were hyperactive, hypersexual, and homosexual, insistently and abnormally pursuing females in estrus, and sometimes indulging in cannibalism of the young.

These various sorts of pathology in individual rats in the crowded pens apparently were not caused by matter-energy stresses of any sort. Rather, as Spitz concluded from Calhoun's work, they arose from the fact that each animal was subjected to an excessive rate of information inputs.[156] These elicited various abnormal internal cognitive and affective processes and overt behaviors, particularly frenetic activity and pathological withdrawal (see pages 167 and 168). He believes that repeated interruptions before completion of normal input–output sequences by new inputs produces this pathology. In his view infants are particularly susceptible to this sort of pathogenic processes.

Such states of information input overload are like those Toffler calls "future shock" (see page 149). In severe or irreversible form this condition has been explicitly identified by Lipowski as a form of pathology.[157] He explains its origins as follows: Our affluent, technical society is characterized by an excess of attractive information inputs. The many communications media increase this surfeit, as do the ease of spread of information in a society that advocates free and often discordant expression, as well as the increasing density of population. Social influences pressure the individual to choose among these attractive inputs, creating in him conflicts as to which of several desirable behaviors he should carry out. Anxiety is associated with these conflicts. The individual attempts to cope with them by such adjustment processes as *filtering, escape,* repeated approaches to many different goals or sources of information inputs, aggressive or violent behavior, and passive surrender. The young appear to be more vulnerable to excesses of information inputs because they have not learned how to choose among attractive alternatives and to strive in a sustained manner for selected goals. Lipowski is developing a theory explaining input-overload phenomena.[158]

Various practitioners have called to my attention case histories which suggest that information input overload can give rise to psychopathology in individual human beings. For example, Ullmann reports the case of a supervisor in a government agency who voluntarily withdrew from a civil service internship training program intended to prepare him for a position with a higher rating, which would have given him more status and salary, because he believed that the training program was jeopardizing his health.[159] He complained of nervousness, insomnia, and elevated blood pressure which persisted in spite of medical care. He had received counseling and guidance concerning his worries that his progress in the training program was steadily deteriorating. His training and writing skills were more limited than those of other interns in the training program, and he felt that he was falling behind in his writing on a required project while the scope of the project constantly mushroomed. His educational background was well below the average of the group, and his general intelligence and information were also low for the group. He was poor in self-insight as measured by an adjective checklist and other procedures. He was unwilling to accept help in his work (to use the *multiple channels* adjustment process), even though others in the program were willing to do so. Moreover, he seemed unable to escape from the confines imposed by the necessity he felt to process information in minute detail. (He could not generalize or use the *abstracting* adjustment process.) He had a reasonably strong need to achieve but also a strong need to defer to the opinions of others and marked inferiority feelings. He contended that his performance was poor because his preparation was inadequate and that he overworked in order to compensate for this. When he felt that he was not meeting his own high goals of performance and that he would be unable to do so, he withdrew from the program, a victim of information overload.

The speedy aging of presidents of the United States, apparently from the rush of their lives and the continual weight of decisions they bear, has frequently been noted. The pressure on generals in wartime often has comparable effects.

It is common for executives in industry, government, and elsewhere to feel strains from a sort of stress French and Kahn have called "role overload" (see pages 159 and 160). They explicitly regard this as a sort of information input overload.[160] They find that, in general, the more important the executive position, the greater is the stress. Increasing numbers of demands are pressed upon executives by various colleagues and by the total mission of the organization. They do not find time in their busy lives to cope adequately with these demands. They use various adjustment processes to this overload in order to handle it the best they can, but they still have constant feelings of guilt that they are not meeting expectations. Many nights they may carry home briefcases full of work which they are too exhausted to complete.

Information overloads on airplane pilots seem to be capable of causing potentially dangerous panic. In one case an experienced, mature, and stable B-47 pilot was flying a plane whose landing wheels had just malfunctioned.[161] He had also received an erroneous message from a ground controller and had been concentrating intensely on his instrument panel on which red collision lights were flashing. He froze at the plane's controls and almost crashed it into some mountains. A later review of the situation indicated that when the pilot froze at the controls he was apparently overwhelmed by "sensory overload."

There is also suggestive clinical and experimental evidence that overloads of information may have some relation to schizophrenic behavior. In schizophrenia it may be that a genetically determined metabolic fault which increases neural noise lowers the capacities of certain, as yet unidentified, channels involved in cognitive information processing. As I shall indicate below, various studies suggest that input channels are particularly affected. In the last century and the first three decades of this century, especially in Europe, attention was paid to the possibility of ameliorating or curing schizophrenia by malaria or other fever therapies. This interest increased greatly after discovery of the favorable long-range effects of malaria on paresis. After the fever receded, many beneficial effects were reported in schizophrenia in the 1920s and 1930s. There appeared to be little consensus as to the immediate effects of the fever and of toxic conditions themselves.[162] While noting that influenza may precipitate or aggravate all known types of mental disease (including schizophrenia, deliria, mania, and melancholia), however, Menninger adds:[163] "It is also known that schizophrenia, for example, may be provoked into external expression by many agents including any and all infectious diseases." (He includes influenza, typhoid, and trauma.) Brain damage, drugs which affect the central nervous system, oxygen deprivation, distraction, fatigue, interruption of ongoing activity, environmental changes, and emotional excitement may also have such an effect. Perhaps these conditions, under some circumstances, diminish channel capacity biochemically and exacerbate schizophrenic symptoms which were themselves caused by some prior, undetermined lowering of channel capacity.

On the basis of our work on information overload, Luby, Gottlieb, Cohen, Rosenbaum, and Domino have suggested that schizophrenic withdrawal, manifested in its most extreme form as catatonia, may be an attempt by the patient to use the *escape* adjustment process to reduce the rate at which information impinges on him, in order to prevent overload and keep the rate within a range he can handle.[164] This may be why a psychotic beachcomber or vagrant or hippie shuns much human contact.[165] Also a catatonic schizophrenic may be unable to respond to information inputs because they overload him and create confusion. Schizophrenic withdrawal may be like the behavior Jaffe has observed in psychotherapeutic sessions.[166] He studied the communication between individuals, as between doctor and patient. He measured a ratio of the number of *different* words (types) to the *total* number of words (tokens) in a sample of

language. This TTR ratio is an index of verbal diversification, or conversely, of redundancy. He showed
how, by signaling that he does not understand, one
person may force another with whom he is talking to
decrease the TTR or increase the redundancy in his
speech. Assuming that the rate of words per minute
spoken remains the same, he thus succeeded in
decreasing the rate per minute at which information
comes to him. Also, his interruptions in themselves
slow down the rate. The doctor does this in the following exchange:

PATIENT: . . . and my doctor took my privileges away because
of it, and what can I do about it? Here I am, it's not very
pleasant.
DOCTOR: Took your privileges away, because of what?
PATIENT: Because—oh—I shouldn't take it to—so to heart—I
shouldn't take anything to heart, that's all.
DOCTOR: Take what to heart?

Jaffe gives another sample in which *A* is explaining
a technical matter at a very high TTR, but his explanation goes over the head of *B*:

B: The—the cell is a tube and it's on or off?
A: Well, it's not a tube, it's a part of a tube really.
B: Mm-hm.

B's interruption slows down *A* and also helps him
achieve an understanding. His second statement indicates that *A*'s clarification reassures him that he is
understanding *A*. Speakers ordinarily slow down
speech and use simple words in a comparable way to
prevent overloads on the restricted channel capacities
of children and foreigners who are not experienced
with the language being used.

Another case history, of a 20-year-old schizophrenic
woman, has been provided by Weiner. He maintains
that her behavior in the following quoted psychotherapeutic session results from information input
overload.

PATIENT: It is like a glass house closing in. You can hear the
confusion on the outside. Everything gets tighter and
tighter, and you get all confused. You can't breathe.
THERAPIST: Tell me about the glass house. . . .
PATIENT: Oh yes. Sometimes it closes when people want to
find out something from me and I don't think I know. It
doesn't always happen.
THERAPIST: Has it ever happened here with me?
PATIENT: I don't think so. It happens when somebody goes on
and on and won't shut up. It happened once when I was
talking with Dr. O. I told him to go away. It seemed as if it
lasted for a long time. It also seems to happen when people
just keep on talking. It doesn't even register. It's just a lot of
noise. They don't even seem to be talking to me after a
while.[167]

According to Weiner, this patient had a low general
capacity for messages with emotional meaning com-

ing either from outside through input transducers or
from inside through internal transducers. He also said
that she *filtered* out many of these messages in order to
keep down the rate at which she must decode them.
He considered this process roughly similar to the
defense mechanism of denial (see page 458) when
applied to external messages, and somewhat like
repression (see page 422) when applied to internal
messages. He thought her to be incapable of using the
abstracting adjustment process or generalizing, capable only of processing specific information about concrete events. This limitation made her behavior stereotyped and often inappropriate.

Such case histories, together with a large mass of
other observations and experiments on schizophrenics, make it apparent that they have difficulty in ordering and organizing the large fluxes of information
inputs which impinge on their input channels.[168]
Among the many formulations of the basic pathology
in schizophrenia are the following: (*a*) "a defect in
central nervous system organization," (*b*) an abnormality of a "cortical regulatory system," (*c*) a defect in
the reticular activating or limbic system, (*d*) a biochemical fault, and (*e*) a metabolic disorder of nervous
tissue (see page 478).[169] Regardless of whether one or
more of these pathologies, or some other one, is the
neural basis of schizophrenia, the fundamental defect
has been said to be an inability to process input
information accurately.[170] They showed that schizophrenics did as well as normals on tasks not involving
distraction, but were worse when selective attention
was involved, particularly when information was
input simultaneously on competing sensory channels.
Schizophrenics, they contend, are unable to *filter* out
irrelevant information input.[171] Consequently their
short-term memory is overloaded. One indication of
this is that schizophrenics are as good as normals in
repeating sentences of low redundancy, but they do
not improve as much as normals when repeating sentences of higher redundancy. In normal speech,
actually, redundant words are distractors for a schizophrenic.[172] His channel capacity is lowered.[173] He
takes longer than a normal person to perceive single
and multiple units of inputs.[174] And his use of the
filtering adjustment process is abnormal.[175]

The responses of normal subjects reacting at their
own rates and of normals reacting under forced pace
on a word-association test were compared in one
research with the responses of schizophrenics.[176] Normal subjects under time pressure made responses
more like those of schizophrenics than did normals
under no time pressure. A related study appears to
lend support to the general viewpoint being presented

here (see page 480). It found that increased rates of information input evoked schizophrenic-like associative errors in normal subjects. In still another experiment schizophrenics, nonschizophrenic psychiatric patients, and normal subjects performed a paced sorting test under time stress and distraction stress—simultaneously responding to a binary choice task.[177] Normal subjects and nonschizophrenic patients under this stress performed like schizophrenics under normal conditions. These findings appear to support the hypothesis that schizophrenics are more readily overloaded with information than normals. Possibly the key variable in these experiments is not the information load as such, but the time stress accompanying paced tasks.[178]

These research findings, as well as other data, suggest, as I wrote in 1964, that the differences in speech between schizophrenics and normals arise from overloading some information processing component or components which in schizophrenia have abnormally low channel capacity.[179] Consequently schizophrenics cannot process signals as fast and correctly as normal persons can. At usual rates of information input schizophrenics make *omissions* and *errors,* and otherwise behave as normal people do under forced-pace inputs. It may be that schizophrenia, by some process as yet unknown (see pages 167 and 478) which increases neural noise or distortion, lowers channel capacity. Infections, trauma, or other events which can precipitate schizophrenia may perhaps further lower channel capacity biochemically, so exacerbating abnormal states which were themselves caused by some prior lowering of channel capacity of uncertain origin.

This view is in basic agreement with that of Yates, who wrote in 1966:

. . . it is possible to elucidate the McGhie-Chapman theory further along the following lines. Broadbent's filter theory [see page 145] postulates that there is a limit to the amount of information which can be processed per unit of time. While the primary processing channel is thus occupied, other information must be held in the short-term memory system. In terms of this formulation, it is here argued that the basic defect in schizophrenia is as follows: first, the rate at which information is processed by schizophrenics is abnormally slow. But, if this is so, an inevitable corollary follows. Since the short-term memory system, by definition, can hold information for only a short time, the amount of stored information lost per unit time will be much greater than in normals. Hence, only a fragmentary part of the relevant stimulation will be successfully processed. From this it follows inevitably that, over long periods of time, bizarrenesses of behavior must appear.[180]

In summary, it appears that schizophrenic behavior may arise from information inputs which overload

persons with pathologically diminished channel capacities.

4.4 Pathology at the level of the group   Certain arrangements of the channel and net subsystems of groups centralize communications in one or a few members, and they consequently tend to suffer from information input overloads (see page 549). Frequently one member of a group—like the chairman of a committee, the quarterback of a football team, or the ranking officer in a command post—takes on an undue proportion of the total information processing being carried out by his group. Under such circumstances pathological group processes can easily arise. There appear to be no experimental studies of such pathology, however.

4.5 Pathology at the level of the organization   It is well known that persons in the primary communication nodes of large organizations, particularly the executives, are often overloaded by information inputs. Such overloads fatigue those who suffer from them. They also delay communications and decisions, make them erratic or wrong, and may result in their not being made or being made by persons not properly equipped to do so. All these effects probably can produce pathological consequences in organizations, but these have not so far been investigated experimentally.

5. Our experiments

In 1957 a group of my associates and I began to plan a coordinated set of cross-level researches to investigate information input overload at five levels of living systems.[181] This work was carried out over several years with a number of colleagues.*

The phenomena of information input overload seemed an appropriate subject for our first intensive

---

*The other members of the earliest group were Donald G. Marquis, Richard L. Meier, William J. Horvath, Caxton C. Foster, Arnold E. Horowitz, Donald M. Maynard, H. Merrill Jackson, Leonard Uhr, and O. Thomas Law. Later Kent Marquis, Lillian Kelly, Paul Halick, Bertram Peretz, Richard V. Evans, and Joanne Denko joined us.

The coexperimenters with me in the investigations at the cell and organ levels were Paul Halick, William J. Horvath, and Bertram Peretz. In the work at the organism, group, and organization levels the primary coexperimenter was Robert F. House. William J. Horvath, Stanley Moss, and Richard Cabot also were major participants. Others involved were John T. Burns, Conrad Juchartz, Tom Mahs, Fred Fensch, and Irwin Pollack. Edith Jay and Robert McCornack, of System Development Corporation in Santa Monica, California, conducted some cooperative research at the organization level. Robert F. House cooperated in the writing of this section of this chapter.[182]

cross-level research because: (*a*) Experimental conditions could be arranged for each of several system levels so that changes in system output as a function of input could be observed and recorded in the same units. (*b*) More information could be input to each of the systems at each level than they could output, *i.e.*, it was feasible for the experimenter to impose an overload which could be quantitatively controlled. And (*c*) information overload was of interest and importance in the real world of many healthy persons as well as many patients with mental illnesses.

Systems at the cell, organ, organism, group, and organization levels were selected for this study. The object of the research was to determine whether there were cross-level formal identities in the performance of systems at these five different levels under conditions in which the information input rates ranged from a slow rate to rates which clearly overloaded the channel capacity of the system. Of primary interest was the regularity across levels of the function relating input in bits per s to output in bits per s, *i.e.*, the input–output transfer function. The expectation based on the review of the literature reported above and our own preliminary research was that a general function would adequately describe performance at all five levels (see Hypothesis 5.1-1, pages 103, 122, and 123). Cross-level differences, it was assumed, would be reflected in variations of some coefficient in that function (see Hypothesis 5.1-25, pages 104 and 124).

A second focal area of interest concerned similarities across system levels in the adjustment processes employed to maintain system output under input overload conditions (see Hypotheses 5.1-2 and 5.1-3, pages 103, 123, and 124). The indication from preliminary work was that the kinds of adjustment processes used might be similar across the system levels but that the percentage utilization would not be constant across these levels. Also, we thought it likely that some sorts of adjustments might not be employed at the lowest levels but might be emergents at the higher ones (see Hypothesis 5.1-4, pages 103 and 124). In our researches we attempted neither to bias nor to constrain the experimental system in a way that would elicit or favor any particular adjustment process. This procedure was followed in order to facilitate the discovery of any new ones that might be used.

The overall strategy was to present information to the various experimental systems over a broad range of input rates, keeping the task information constant and examining the outputs for systematic regularities across system levels and types. Thirteen experiments were conducted, one at the cell level, one at the organ, three at the organism, four at the group, and four at the organization.

We built apparatuses and designed procedures which we hoped would provide stable conditions for collecting performance data from the systems we selected for study, attempting to hold constant as many of the variables not under investigation as possible. We were not concerned primarily with obtaining the maximum possible transmission rates from our systems. Rather we attempted to create stable situations in which we could measure the system's information input–output transfer functions and be sure we knew when overload occurred. Future studies could investigate as independent variables those functions which change a given system's maximum channel capacity.

Since information bits per second had been used as a measuring unit by others in researches at all five levels, we believed it to be a suitable unit for measuring input–output flows in ours. We realized that at each level we would encounter statistical problems if we used limited sequences of inputs. Difficulties also arose, as expected, in calculating bits, particularly in knowing what code was employed at the cell and organ levels and in knowing the exact size of the implicit ensemble at all levels.

5.1 Research at the level of the cell

Pulse-interval coded inputs. A code which conveys information by alterations in the time intervals between pulses or signals rather than by alterations in the signals themselves is called a pulse-interval code. Probably such a code is commonly employed in neural cells and organs (see page 278). In order to study inputs with such codes, an apparatus was constructed which could administer electrical pulses to a neuron at various average rates and at different intensities at each rate. By microdissection we isolated a single fiber in the sciatic nerve of the frog, *Rana pipiens*, and administered inputs at the rates of 100, 200, 400, 600, 800, and 1,000 pulses per s, using four different voltage intensities (1.5, 2.0, 2.5, and 3.0 times the threshold value). Simultaneously we recorded the outputs of the fiber from a microelectrode in the axon of the same cell and also in another cell with which it synapsed.

As the input rate was increased, the fiber eventually ceased to follow every input and started missing some. Among the fibers which we studied, three different types of responses were observed. Some fibers, when they reached the point at which they could no longer follow every pulse, started skipping every other pulse. As the rate was further increased they responded only to every third or fourth pulse, but in a regular fashion. Other fibers skipped randomly, at a given input rate the number of consecutive pulses skipped having a Poisson distribution. Still other fibers transmitted several consecutive pulses and then failed to output any pulses at all for a time, after which they again fired repeatedly. Occasionally all three types of functions were found in the same fiber at various times and at different input rates.

Two other phenomena were also noted. As the input rate was increased, the amplitude of the responses fell, and the lag between the input and the output decreased. The fall in amplitude is probably related to the energetics of recovery of the membrane potential (see page 262). If the recovery time is diminished, the potential generated is less. The decrease in latency must have a similar explanation. It enables the fiber to adjust to a greater input rate, permitting it to follow at much higher rates than would otherwise be possible. Our findings are in harmony with those of others who have worked in this field.

The skipping of pulses which occurred at the higher input rates was, of course, the *omission* adjustment process. The lower output intensities represented the *error* adjustment process if they were below the threshold of the postsynaptic neuron. We found no evidence for other neuronal adjustment processes to information overload.

In order to measure the maximum information transmission capacity of a neuron which employs pulse-interval coding, one must input to it trains of two or more pulses at different interpulse intervals (see pages 122 and 123). By measuring the intervals between any outputs elicited, one can determine the neuron's refractory period or "dead time" (δ). Also one can determine the minimum interpulse interval (σ) which can be discriminated by the neuron system receiving the signal by measuring the variance of the latent period in a fiber, also called its "jitter." The larger the jitter, the larger is the minimum discriminable interpulse interval.

We made such measurements on the peroneal nerve of the frog.[183] The nerve trunk was dissected out and single neural fibers were teased apart by the method described by Stämpfli.[184] Electrical inputs could then be applied to the entire nerve trunk at one end while the recordings were obtained from the axon on a single neuron at the other end. During the experiment, the preparation, except for the parts in contact with the electrodes, rested on a glass slide wetted with a thin film of the modified Ringer's solution used by Stämpfli. Silver–silver chloride recording electrodes were used, and the distance between these and the stimulating electrode was about 2 to 3 cm, depending on the size of the preparation. The experiments were carried out at room temperature. Under these conditions a preparation remained relatively normal for many hours.

We administered the electrical inputs with a Grass Model S4C stimulator. The threshold voltage for such inputs was determined at the start of the experiment, and data about the outputs were taken with the input voltage set at specified values ranging from 25 to 100 percent above this threshold. (The threshold potential is the point at which the probability that an output will occur is 0.5. Outputs occur 100 percent of the time at voltages only a few percent greater than that value.) The voltages of our inputs were well above threshold. Altering the value of the inputs within the range indicated above, therefore, had no measurable effect on the results of our experiments. The action potential was amplified by two Tektronix Type 122 low-level preamplifiers wired in series. Measurements were made of the time interval between the initiation of the input and a fixed point on the negative slope of the action potential by means of a Hewlett Packard Model 523 DR electronic counter. All such time intervals were of the order of 2 to 3 ms. They were recorded to the nearest microsecond. A check on the accuracy of the equipment was obtained by measuring the elapsed time for an electrical pulse to travel down a thread wet by Ringer's solution. The measures were accurate to ± 0.6 μs, the expected accuracy for the electronic equipment for such small elapsed times.

In measuring the jitter or variance in latency of a particular nerve-fiber preparation, readings were taken at the rate of approximately one input per second until a total of 500 or more inputs had been recorded. In the course of such a long series of readings, there usually was a slow drift in the latency in addition to the expected random fluctuations. This drift could be detected easily when groups of ten successive readings were averaged together and the trend of these averages was examined. An example is shown in Fig. 5-26, in which successive average latencies for a particular fiber are plotted for a total of 5 min.

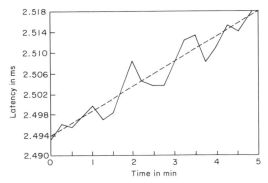

Fig. 5-26 Drift in averages of the latencies of ten consecutive responses of a particular fiber of the peroneal nerve of a frog over a 5-min period.

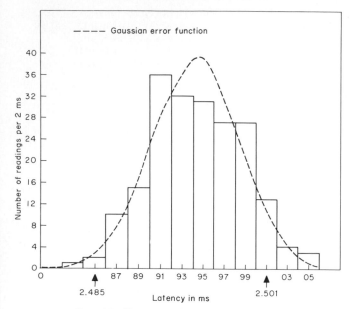

Fig. 5-27 Histogram of latencies corrected for drift of 200 consecutive responses of a particular fiber of the peroneal nerve of a frog. A Gaussian error function, also shown, fits the data reasonably well.

Readings were being taken at the rate of 40 per minute, so that 210 readings are represented in the 21 points plotted. Over this period of time, the average value of the latency increased by slightly less than 1 percent. The increase in this case was approximately linear, amounting to about 4.8 μs per min. Obviously these small drifts would go unnoticed without the accurate measurement techniques employed in this experiment. In most fibers the drift was toward increasing latencies, but in some cases it decreased. In a few cases the drift first increased and then decreased. The amount of drift did not seem to be influenced by the rate of input. A trend line, an example of which is shown dotted on Fig. 5-26, was fitted to each large block of consecutive data so that the mean drift could be subtracted from the individual readings when estimates of the fluctuation were made. In the fiber shown in Fig. 5-26, this procedure meant sub-

tracting an additional microsecond from each consecutive block of 8 readings. Doing this enabled us to take sufficiently large blocks of readings to make an accurate estimate of the jitter or variance in the latency. Otherwise, if small blocks of consecutive readings were used, only approximate values of the latencies could be obtained. On the other hand, if the experiment could have been instrumented to obtain readings at the rate of the normal firing frequency of the nerve, between about 10 to 100 pulses per second, the drift over the period required to record 200 to 500 pulses could have been ignored. Thus even if this drift were a true physiological manifestation, rather than an artifact of the experiment, the messages in the nervous system would be transmitted in a period of time so short that, under the assumed system of coding, drifts in latency of the amount detected in these experiments would not affect the message.

After applying the corrections described above, the data for blocks of consecutive readings were tabulated and graphed. We verified that the data could be fit by the Gaussian error function and determined the value of the standard deviation σ. All the runs on six different fibers gave good fits.

The data for 200 consecutive readings on the fiber shown in Fig. 5-26, corrected for drift, are shown plotted as a histogram in Fig. 5-27. A Gaussian error function estimated from the normal probability plot has been fitted to the data. The fit is reasonably good, giving a χ^2 of 9.57 or a probability of approximately .04 that the observed deviations were due to chance. The standard deviation for this distribution, σ, is about 4.0 μs. The highest value of σ found in these experiments was 9.0 μs, and most of the measured values were clustered at around 5 or 6 μs.

Since these experiments were carried out with an input rate of approximately 1 pulse per s, a very low rate for most neurons, a separate set of experiments was undertaken to determine if a closer spacing of stimulus pulses would affect either the latency or the jitter. Accordingly, two Grass stimulators were arranged to give either 2 or 3 pulses in rapid sequence, and the latency together with its variance were measured for the last pulse. The results of one such experiment, in which the standard deviation σ was calculated for blocks of 25 consecutive readings taken at the rate of one every 2 s, are shown in Table 5-3 below.

TABLE 5-3   Effects of Double Pulsing on the Variance of the Second Response of a Particular Fiber of the Peroneal Nerve of a Frog

Interval between inputs (in μs)	2,000	100	50	20	10	5
Standard deviation (σ)	9.3	9.3	9.5	9.0	8.4	9.1

The first set of readings was taken with an interpulse interval of 2,000 μs. The other readings were obtained at shorter intervals gradually decreasing down to 5 μs, which was near the shortest limit obtainable under our experimental conditions.

The standard deviation of the latency was quite stable, the small fluctuations being well within such statistical limits that they could be attributed to chance. This indicates that the variances were independent of pulse separation. The results of other runs using double and triple pulsing were in accord with this finding, leading us to believe that the values of the jitter of single fibers found in these experiments would also apply at moderately high firing rates.

Using the mathematical model developed by Rapoport and Horvath (see page 122), we were able to calculate the curve of average information outputs of several such neurons at various input rates. We found that the output rate increased, as a function of the input rate up to a maximum of about 4,000 bits per s, at an input rate of about 20,000 bits per s—assuming optimal pulse-interval coding. To the unsophisticated, and even to some of the sophisticated, this seems an astonishingly high channel capacity for such a minute system. As the input rate continued to go up, the output rate leveled off and then decreased. This performance curve is shown in Fig. 5-28.

5.2 Research at the level of the organ

Pulse-interval coded inputs. We used the same apparatus as we used in the above experiment at the level of the cell to input electrical pulses to the optic nerve of several white rats, recording as outputs the resultant evoked potentials from a macroelectrode on the optic cortex. Calculations similar to those carried out in the cellular experiment, when applied to the average data from this experiment, produced a curve of comparable shape (see Fig. 5-29). The channel capacity, however, was much lower, about 55 bits per s at an input rate of about 175 bits per s.

The *omission* and *error* adjustment processes were also employed at the organ level, as at the cell level, and in addition the *multiple channels* adjustment process was used.

5.3 Research at the level of the organism

(*a*) *Pulse-interval coded inputs.* Each of 10 human subjects was presented with light flashed at varying intervals. The subject was directed to press a lever as fast as possible each time he saw a flash. Calculations similar to those carried out in the above two experiments, applied to the measured average output intervals for various input intervals, produced a curve of comparable shape (see Fig. 5-30). The maximum output rate was lower than for either the cell or the organ, about 5.75 bits per s at an input rate of about 10 bits per s.

(*b*) *IOTA experiments.* The two other experiments at the organism level, O-1 and O-2 ("O" stands for organism), concerned the responses of individual

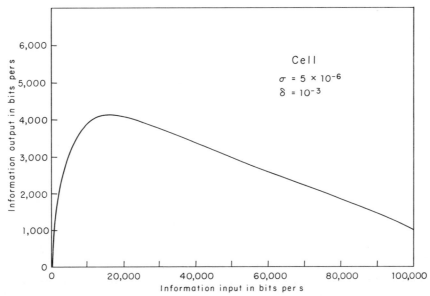

Fig. 5-28 Theoretical curve based on average performance data of cells under various rates of pulse-interval coded information input. σ represents minimum discriminable time interval of the channel; δ represents refractory period of the channel.

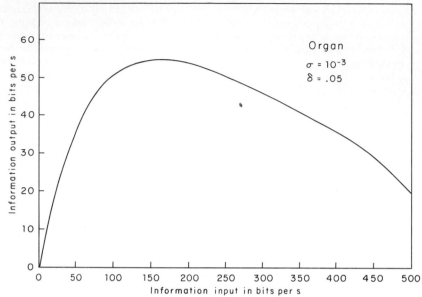

Fig. 5-29 Theoretical curve based on average performance data of organs under various rates of pulse-interval coded information input. σ represents minimum discriminable time interval of the channel; δ represents refractory period of the channel.

human subjects (diagramed in the top row of Fig. 5-31) to the IOTA (*Information Overload Testing Aid*) apparatus. The *O*-1 experiment was designed to provide data for cross-level comparison. The *O*-2 experiment was to demonstrate, by comparison with *O*-1 data, that the relative percent of use of the various adjustment processes could be changed by altering experimental constraints, specifically the instructions to the subject, the payoffs to him, and the instrumentation. The equipment was arranged to make it easier to use the adjustment process of *abstracting* in the *O*-2 experiment.

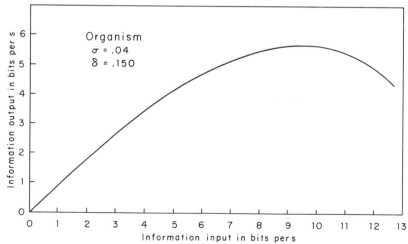

Fig. 5-30 Theoretical curve based on average performance data of organisms (human subjects) under various rates of pulse-interval coded information input. σ represents minimum discriminable time interval of the channel; δ represents refractory period of the channel.

Subjects. The subjects were paid, volunteer, male university students whose ages ranged from 18 to 25 years. They numbered 24 for the O-1 experiment and 12 for the O-2.

Apparatus. The basic apparatus consisted of the IOTA control equipment in a room next to the input–output (I–O) panel (see Fig. 5-32). The IOTA is a special-purpose machine, designed and constructed in our laboratory, which controls the input to and records both the input and the output from one or two I–O panels. The basic components of the IOTA are 2 nine-line brush paper-tape readers, a 60 character per s paper-tape punch, and a switch which determines the rate of signal presentation. The series of signals to be presented are coded on the input tape for processing through the readers, each reader having an independent input tape. Both readers are controlled by the same rate switch. By means of flip-flops, the 60-Hz-line alternating-current frequency is fractionated, making the following rates available: 0.12, 0.24, 0.47, 0.94, 1.25, 1.88, 2.50, 3.75, and 5.00 signals per s. The signal and the output corresponding to it in time are punched out together on the raw-data tape. The output punched out with a particular signal on the data tape is not necessarily the output elicited by the signal. The IOTA cannot match an output to the input which elicited it.

Adjacent to the control room containing the IOTA was a room for subjects, dimly illuminated by indirect light from two 50-W bulbs. On a table in it was an I–O panel (see Fig. 5-32) containing 15 colored pushbutton switches. Each button contained an incandescent bulb. Its lighting, controlled by the IOTA, was a signal to depress that button. The force of a 0.34 km weight was required to depress a button. The signal duration was fixed at about 80 ms, regardless of the signal input rate.

The basic task of the experiment was to push any button that lit up in the top row of eight blue button-lights, the primary row. Each time this was done, a choice was made from eight alternatives, constituting a 3-bit task. There was also a second row made up of four green buttons, constituting a 2-bit task. The third row consisted of two yellow buttons, constituting a 1-bit task. The fourth row was a single red button. As the numbers on the buttons in Fig. 5-33 indicate, the fourth-row button corresponded to all the top row buttons. Each of the two third-row buttons corresponded to half the top-row buttons. And each of the four second-row buttons corresponded to two of the top-row buttons. Thus the alternatives decreased, and the responses became less precise from the higher to the lower rows in the tree of buttons. A subject could respond to the lighting of a blue button by pushing

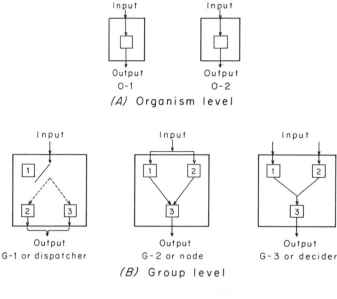

(A) Organism level

(B) Group level

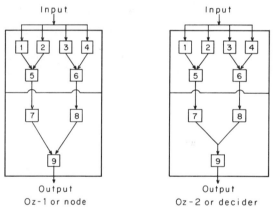

(C) Organization level

Fig. 5-31 Diagrams of structures of systems in our experiments at the (A) organism, (B) group, and (C) organization levels.

any button in any row. He transmitted 3 bits if he pushed a correct blue button, 2 if he pushed a correct green button, and 1 if he pushed a correct yellow one. Pushing the red button was a 0-bit response. Pushing a green or yellow button, because it was a less precise response than pushing a blue button, constituted use of the *abstracting* adjustment process. In the O-1 experiment only the top row of blue buttons lighted up. In the O-2 experiment, each time a blue button lit, the corresponding buttons in the lower three lit at the

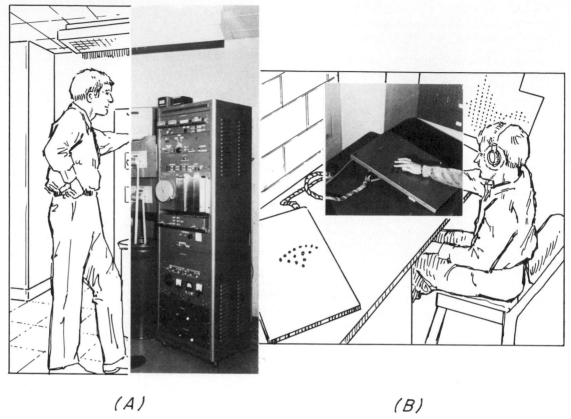

(A)   (B)

Fig. 5-32 Experimenter (A) standing at IOTA control equipment and subject (B) seated in adjacent experimental room at the input–output (I–O) panel used in experiments O-1 and O-2.

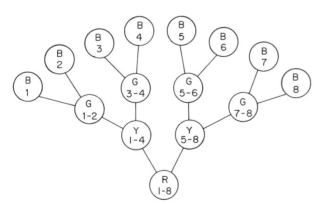

Fig. 5-33 Arrangement of the button-lights on the I–O panel. From top to bottom, the four rows of button-lights were, respectively, blue (B), green (G), yellow (Y), and red (R).

same time. This clearly indicated to the subjects how they could use the *abstracting* adjustment if they chose to do so.

During trials white noise was administered to the subject through earphones to mask any possible auditory cues.

Procedure. At the beginning of the first experimental session, each subject was read detailed instructions. These emphasized that he should be as fast and accurate as possible, attempting to respond always in the exact order in which the buttons lit up. He was not to wait to correct any errors he made. He was to use only one and the same finger to push the buttons throughout the experiment. The relationships among the buttons on the different rows, the relative amount of information processed by a button press on each row, and the forced-pace nature of the task were carefully explained. An effort was made to avoid creating a bias toward use of any particular adjustment process.

TABLE 5-4   Input Rates in Signals per Second in Orders of Presentation Determined by Experimental Design

Order of rates	Tape number (identical with trial number)					
	1	2	3	4	5	6
1	1.25	1.88	0.94	5.00	3.75	2.50
2	0.94	1.25	3.75	1.88	2.50	5.00
3	5.00	2.50	1.88	3.75	1.25	0.94
4	3.75	0.94	2.50	1.25	5.00	1.88
5	1.88	5.00	1.25	2.50	0.94	3.75
6	2.50	3.75	5.00	0.94	1.88	1.25

The range of input rates extended from a rate at which all systems could process the input to a rate at which all systems were clearly overloaded.

Each subject received one trial of each of the six input rates (see Table 5-4) during each daily session. The O-1 and O-2 experiments lasted 5 days each. Just before each trial began, the subject was informed at what rate signals would be input during that trial and then presented with a sample of input at the appropriate rate for a few seconds. Subjects were permitted to rest for approximately 5 min between each trial and the next. No feedback concerning the quality of his performance was given to the subject at any time.

Six different input tapes, each with 256 separate consecutive signals, were generated such that the same signal never occurred twice in sequence, and the eight signals occurred almost equally often. No short repetitive series of signals were discovered on any input tape.

The experimental design which was followed is presented in Table 5-4. Each subject received six trials per day, input tapes 1 to 6 always being presented on the trial with the corresponding number. The input rate was different for each trial, the six rates, 0.94, 1.25, 1.88, 2.50, 3.75, and 5.00 per second, being employed. At 3 bits per signal, the six information input rates therefore were 2.81; 3.75, 5.62, 7.50, 11.25, and 15.00 bits per s, respectively. Each subject was randomly assigned to a given order of input rates and received the same order each day.

Scoring procedure. The scoring of a forced-pace serial-choice response task like that involved in these experiments raised difficult technical issues. The basic problem was how to determine with which input a particular output was associated. As long as the system responds with few errors to nearly all the inputs, the matching of input to output is straightforward. But when several inputs intervene between two outputs, such matches are less than certain. Thus the focal problem in scoring is to determine whether a void time interval reflects the use of the *omission* or of the *queuing* adjustment process. For example, a small sample of raw data might yield for the series of inputs . . . 3, 4, 5, 4, 6 . . ., a series of outputs . . . 2, 0, 0, 0, 4. . . . (The 0's in the output series indicate void time intervals, *i.e.*, no output during an interval between two signals.) Is the 4 in the output series queued three time intervals, being a response to the first 4 in the input series or only one time interval, being a response to the second 4? Or is it an erroneous output to the 5 or 6? Naturally, knowledge of the subsequent input–output series would help to resolve the question, *e.g.*, if the next three inputs were . . . 8, 7, 1 . . . , and the next three outputs were . . . 6, 8, 0, . . . , one would probably score the output 4 as elicited by the second input 4, assuming the subject to be working at a lag of one time unit. The difficulty of fixing the relationship between the serial stimuli and responses increased directly with input rate because subjects tended to omit more and respond more erratically as the input rate increased.

In addition to speed of input, another factor which compounded the scoring problem was use of the lower rows of buttons which make the *abstracting* adjustment process possible. Consider the same input series, . . . 3, 4, 5, 4, 6, 8, 7, 1 . . . , and the same output series using the buttons in the third row, . . . 1–4 (*e.g.*, the button corresponding to buttons 1 to 4 in the top row), 0, 0, 0, 1–4, 5–8, 5–8, 0. . . . Now the original question would be rephrased, should the 1–4 response be matched to the 3, the first 4, or the second 4 as a correct response or to the 5 as an error? The mapping of one output upon several possible inputs when an *abstracting* adjustment was used made the scoring more complex.

Hand scoring of performance at the two slow input rates presented few or no problems, and subjects' outputs were regular and complete enough at medium input rates for scoring to be quite reliable. At the fastest rates, the scoring was less dependable but still sufficient to provide useful data.

In order to save the many man-hours involved in hand scoring and to make the process entirely objective, we wrote a computer program to do the scoring. It matched output to input and determined whether the response was correct. The program also had, as a discretionary check, an "optimizing" subroutine activated by an arbitrary number k of consecutive errors. At the point of the first error, this subroutine rescored an arbitrary number n of outputs, matching them to inputs, and then returned to the usual scoring process.

The scoring rules applied to such data must be able to handle strings of time periods with no outputs, simultaneous outputs, and changes of lag time. Our scoring program was able to handle such data well up to an input rate of 2.50 signals per second and somewhat less adequately at 3.75 and 5.00 signals per second. At the latter two rates, the troublesome responses categories were more frequent, the optimizing subroutine was used more, and the scoring program produced results which were more divergent from those resulting from constant-lag scoring.

Scores of performance and adjustment processes. The data for each subject for each input rate were recorded in an 8 × 16 matrix (see Fig. 5-34). Each signal was recorded in one of the 8 rows (depending upon which of the blue input lights, 1 to 8, was lit) and in one of the 16 columns (depending upon which of the 16 possible responses it elicited). *Omissions* (no response) were recorded in column 0; the 8 top-row or blue-button responses in columns 1 to 8; the 4 second-row green-button responses in columns 9 to 12; the 2 third-row yellow-button responses in columns 13 and 14; and a fourth-row red-button response in column 15. From this matrix of data, several measures were computed.

Information transmitted. Using the Shannon formula (see page 13) a measure of information output was computed from the matrices for each input rate yielding six scores for each system.[185] Each such score was reduced by the Miller-Madow correction and then converted to a score representing the rate of information transmission by multiplying it by the appropriate input rate in signals per s.[186]

The subjects in this experiment could probably have learned to increase their maximum rates of information output somewhat if they had received feedback about their performances. The relatively high input–output compatibility (see page 132) brought about by the spatial contiguity of display and console probably served to raise this maximum rate. The use of one finger of one hand rather than eight, and the need to exert 0.34 km of pressure rather than a lesser amount, on the contrary, probably lowered it somewhat.

Adjustment processes. The adjustments scored in these experiments were measured as follows:

(a) *Omission adjustment process.* In the data matrix of this study (see Fig. 5-34) the distribution of omissions was indicated in column 0, in which they were mapped against input categories 1 to 8. The percentage of omissions for each subject at each input rate was computed as $(n_o \times 100)/N$, where n_o is the number of omissions, and N is the number of scored signals.

This measure was assumed to reflect the strength of the subject's *omission* adjustment process.

(b) *Error adjustment process.* The measure of this process was the percentage of errors at each input rate out of the total number of input signals. In the data matrix, any entry in an off-diagonal cell, excluding omissions, represented an error. For each subject at each input rate the percentage of errors was computed as $(n_e \times 100)/N$, where n_e is the number of errors, and N is the number of scored signals.

(c) *Queuing adjustment process.* Each input signal in these experiments occurred during a fixed time interval. Each such signal elicited either a response or an omission. The response, if any, occurred either during the same time interval as the input or during a later one. Whenever it appeared in a later interval, queuing occurred. The measure of the *queuing* adjustment process was the percentage of inputs that elicited responses in a later time period.

(d) *Filtering adjustment process.* Two sorts of filtering adjustments were scored: (i) *Omission filtering,* in which certain sorts of inputs seemed to be processed

Inputs	Response categories																Total
	0	1	2	3	4	5	6	7	8	1-2	3-4	5-6	7-8	1-4	5-8	1-8	
1	0	30	1	1													32
2	1		30										1				32
3	2		1	27	2												32
4	3			1	27		1										32
5	1			1	1	26	2					1					32
6	1						30	1									32
7	2						2	27	1								32
8	3				1			1	27								32
Total	13	30	32	30	31	26	35	29	28	0	1	1	0	0	0	0	256

Fig. 5-34   Typical data matrix for one trial of one subject in *O*-1 experiment processing 256 signals at an input rate of 5.62 bits per s. (Darkened boxes indicate correct responses in columns 1 to 8 and correct uses of the abstracting adjustment process in columns 1-2 to 1-8.)

preferentially, being omitted less often than other sorts of inputs. And (ii) *error filtering*, in which certain sorts of outputs seemed to be used preferentially, occurring more frequently than the others. This was because the subject responded by pushing a specific button over and over rather than risk missing a response to a signal by taking the time required to move his finger to the correct button.

(i) *Omission filtering* was measured by computing a χ^2 score involving 7 degrees of freedom on the distribution of omissions in the eight cells in column 0 of each data matrix. If the average or expected frequency of omission (column sum divided by eight) for the eight cells was 1 or greater, a χ^2 was computed. This was done to determine whether or not the actual cell frequencies of omissions departed from the essentially equal distribution of frequencies which would be expected if they were determined by chance. The greater the departure from equal cell frequencies, the greater the χ^2. Unequal cell frequencies were taken to mean that the subject had assigned differential priorities to the various sorts of inputs, filtering out some sorts. When the expected cell frequencies were less than one, *i.e.*, the system had seven or less omissions, no score could be computed.

(ii) A second χ^2 score was computed as a measure of *error filtering*. The original 8 × 16 data matrix for each run was separated into three matrices. These were an 8 × 8 matrix for blue-button responses, an 8 × 4 matrix for green-button responses, and an 8 × 2 matrix for yellow-button responses. Red-button responses were neglected. For each matrix a maximum likelihood estimate was made of the proportion of correct outputs made by chance to each sort of information input. These estimates of the number of outputs which were correct by chance were recorded in the diagonal cells, replacing the actual number of correct responses in the original matrices. This operation yielded matrices containing only outputs correct by chance and errors. The data concerning omissions were neglected. If a subject's output did not deviate significantly from chance, the column sums within each of the three corrected matrices should be comparable to such sums within each of the original matrices. The distribution of actual column sums was compared, using the χ^2, to the distribution expected by chance in order to determine how much *error filtering* occurred. If in any matrix, one or more row sums were 0 or the cells within more than one row had an expected frequency of less than 0.75, no χ^2 was calculated. A subject's error-filtering score was the sum of the χ^2's from each of the three matrices divided by the sum of the degrees of freedom of the χ^2's. This score increased as the amount of *error filtering* increased.

In some cases no χ^2 was calculated for a given subject for a particular input rate, for one of the reasons mentioned immediately above. It should be noted that a particular score might reflect error filtering with blue-, green-, or yellow-button responses only, or any combination of them together. The χ^2 score would not detect *filtering* if a subject assigned priorities on any basis other than favoring input signals from one source over those from another, *e.g.*, if he filtered out every third signal, or if he favored inputs from one source for part of a trial and then changed for the rest of the trial, accurately responding to inputs on the left but not to those on the right on the first half of a trial and then accurately responding to inputs on the right but not to those on the left for the remainder. *Filtering* strategies of these sorts may have been used occasionally, but they were probably rare.

(e) *Abstracting adjustment process.* As I have already mentioned (see page 175), the I–O panel was designed to permit abstracting. A subject abstracted if he pushed a correct green or yellow button, or the red one rather than a blue one. The frequencies of such responses, the last seven columns of the data matrix, were summed and converted to a score indicating the percentage of correct abstractions. For each subject at each input rate this percentage was computed as $(n_a \times 100)/N$, where n_a is the number of correct abstractions, and N is the number of scored signals. The percentage scores for correct blue-button responses, *omissions, errors,* and correct *abstractions* summed to 100 percent.

Results. The chief difference between the two experiments conducted at the organism level, O-1 and O-2, was that only the blue buttons lit up in the O-1 experiment, while in the O-2 experiment the corresponding green, yellow, and red buttons lit simultaneously with each blue button (see Fig. 5-33). That is, the IOTA apparatus controls helped the subject use the *abstracting* adjustment in the O-2 experiment, but in the O-1 experiment the subject was given rules for *abstracting* which he had to implement without any such assistance. The subject's task was the same in both experiments. The purpose of the change in functioning of the apparatus in the O-2 experiment was to find out whether the use of an adjustment process, in this case the *abstraction* adjustment, can be altered by external controls. Because the change in functioning of the apparatus made *abstracting* easier under O-2 conditions, the O-2 subjects were expected to use the *abstracting* adjustment more frequently, on the average, than the O-1 subjects.

Information transmitted. The medium input–output curves of subjects in both the O-1 and O-2 experiments indicated that at high input rates overload occurred (see Fig. 5-35).[187] The median curves were representative of each of the individual curves, with the exception of the curve of one subject in each experiment. An analysis of variance indicated that the various input rates elicited significantly different output rates within each experiment. Also both the increase and the subsequent decrease in rates of information output as input rates increased were found to be significant. Both median curves peaked at the 5.62 bits per s input rate, but the fastest single output rates,

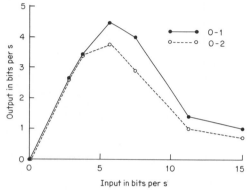

Fig. 5-35 Median information output rate as a function of input rate for the subjects in the O-1 and O-2 experiments.

6.85 for the O-1 experiment and 6.20 for the O-2, occurred at the input rate of 7.50. We demonstrated no significant difference among the six orders of input rates used. By the statistical measure we selected to compare the shapes of the median curves from the two experiments, the curves were similar.[188]

Adjustment processes.   In adjusting to the information input overload, the following five adjustment processes were employed. We measured the extent of the use of each.

(*a*) *Omission adjustment process.*   The median percent *omission* of subjects in both the O-1 and O-2 experiments increased as the input rate went up, being particularly high at the three fastest input rates (see Fig. 5-36). The various input rates evoked significantly different percentages of *omission* in both experiments. The successive rises in input rates, from 3.75 bits per s on, had statistically significant effects except for the rise from 11.25 to 15.00 in experiment O-2. The largest individual scores were 97 percent in experiment O-1 and 75 percent in experiment O-2, both scores occurring at the fastest input rate, 15.00 bits per s. The median percent *omission* curves for the two experiments were much alike.[189]

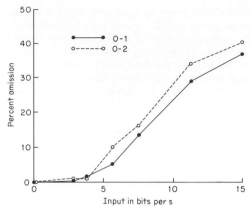

Fig. 5-36 Median percent omission as a function of input rate for the subjects in the O-1 and O-2 experiments.

(*b*) *Error adjustment process.*   The median percent *error* was an increasing function of input rate for both experiments, O-1 and O-2 (see Fig. 5-37). This rise was statistically significant for the successive increases from the input rate of 3.75 bits per s to the input rate of 11.25. The largest use of the *error* adjustment by individual subjects was 51 percent in experiment O-1 and 52 percent in experiment O-2, both at the input rate of 11.25 bits per s. The relationships between input rate and percent *error* were similar for the median scores for the two experiments, O-1 and O-2.[190]

(*c*) *Queuing adjustment process.*   The median percent *queuing, i.e.,* the percent of responses which exceed a lag of zero time interval, has been graphed for both experiments, O-1 and O-2, in Fig. 5-38. The curves are highly similar.[191] During both experiments the subjects generally maintained a zero lag at the

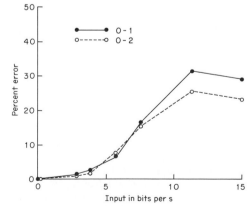

Fig. 5-37 Median percent error as a function of input rate for the subjects in the O-1 and O-2 experiments.

slowest two input rates, followed by successive significant increases at each of the next two rates. At the three fastest input rates virtually all the responses of each subject exceeded a zero lag.

(*d*) *Filtering adjustment process.*

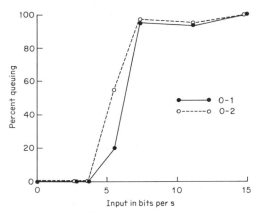

Fig. 5-38 Median percent queuing as a function of input rate for the subjects in the *O*-1 and *O*-2 experiments.

(*i*) To detect *omission filtering*, the distribution of each subject's *omissions* for each of the six input rates was scored as indicated above (see page 178). No score was calculated unless the average or expected frequency of *omissions* for each of the eight blue buttons was one or more. Out of the 144 possible scores for the 24 subjects at six input rates in experiment *O*-1, only 85, or 59 percent, could be calculated. And out of the 72 possible scores for the 12 subjects at six input rates in experiment *O*-2, only 43, or 60 percent, could be calculated. In experiment *O*-1, of those scores calculated, 10, or 12 percent, showed significant *omission filtering*. Only 2, or 5 percent, in experiment *O*-2 showed such *filtering*. With the exception of one subject in experiment *O*-1 who showed significant *omission filtering* for each of the four fastest input rates, no subject showed it for more than one input rate.

In the *O*-1 experiment, significantly more *filtering* occurred at input rates of 5.62 and 7.50 bits per s than at either 11.25 or 15.00 bits per s. The data indicate that, during low input rates, 2.81 and 3.75 bits per s, which did not constitute overload, subjects in general did not use the *omission* or *omission-filtering* adjustments. During the moderate input rates, 5.62 and 7.50, *omissions* increased significantly, and *omission-filtering* behavior peaked. During rapid input rates, 11.25 and 15.00, which constituted overloads, *omissions* again increased significantly but *omission filtering* diminished significantly. In the *O*-2 experiment, the only

between-rate comparison that was significant involved only half the subjects. The six subjects who had scores at the input rate of 5.62 bits per s did less *omission filtering* at 7.50, a small statistically significant average difference. Other statistical calculations concerning use of this adjustment by subjects in this experiment were inconclusive.

(*ii*) The measure of *error filtering* could be calculated for only 32 of the 144 *O*-1 experimental runs, or 22 percent, and for only 15 of the 72 *O*-2 runs, or 21 percent. Analysis of the data did not reveal any unequivocal evidence about the use of this adjustment process.

(*e*) *Abstracting adjustment process.* The percents of green-, yellow-, and red-button presses summed together yielded the percent *abstracting* measure. This measure differed significantly from one input rate to another in both experiments. The percent *abstracting* medians to the three slowest input rates in experiment *O*-1 were close to 0, followed by a moderate increase at the input rate of 7.50 bits per s, a significant increase at the input rate of 11.25, and no great difference at 15.00 (see Fig. 5-39). The *O*-2 medians increased more and sooner, being near 0 for the two slowest

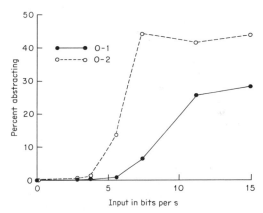

Fig. 5-39 Median percent abstracting as a function of input rate for the subjects in the *O*-1 and *O*-2 experiments.

input rates, after which there was a rise of more than 10 percent at the input rate of 5.62 bits per s followed by a significant step function of about 30 percent at the input rate of 7.50 bits per s, with no statistically reliable differences among the last three input rates.[192]

The outstanding difference between the two experiments resulted from the different way the buttons lit up in the two. As expected, helping the subjects to use the *abstracting* adjustment by lighting the appropriate green, yellow, and red buttons for each blue button led the subjects in the O-2 experiment to do significantly more *abstracting*.[193] This supports the view that use of adjustment processes, like many other sorts of behavior is subject to control by external influences.

Summary of O-1 and O-2 findings. On the whole, the subjects' performances in both experiments were highly similar. Thirty-four out of the combined total of thirty-six subjects increased their transmission rates with input rate up to a point and then decreased, so that at the input rate of 15.00 bits per s they were transmitting information more slowly than at an input rate of 2.81 bits per s. This in spite of the fact that, overall, about three times as many responses were made per s at input rate 15.00 than at input rate 2.81.

Although the shapes of the median input–output transfer functions were alike for experiments O-1 and O-2, the O-1 median output rates were somewhat faster at input rate 7.50 and above (see Fig. 5-35). These small differences accumulated to produce statistical significance.

Measures of the adjustment processes of *omission, error, queuing,* and *abstracting* all significantly increased with input rate for both experiments, and the shape of the functions relating each to input rate were so similar that the correlation coefficients between O-1 and O-2 medians on each measure were large and statistically signficant.

How does the typical subject attempt to prevent decrease in his information output rate as input rate increases? Only the O-1 data will be used to answer this, since it is probably more representative because of the larger number of subjects in that experiment. As input rates increased, first the subject responded faster. Median responses per s were 0.93, 1.24, 1.78, 2.16, 2.66, and 3.13 to input rates in signals per second of 0.94, 1.25, 1.88, 2.50, 3.75, and 5.00, respectively. Clearly, the subjects did not respond fast enough to transmit perfectly at the faster input rates. The next adjustment to be used was *queuing*. It was 20 percent at the input rate of 5.62, and from rate 7.50 on, subjects fell behind in essentially all their responses, responding to one input while perceiving, and perhaps temporarily storing, subsequent ones. The *omission* and *error* adjustments each represented as much as 10 percent of the responses at input rate 7.50, then both showed a sharp rise to about 30 percent at rate 11.25. At rate 15.00, *omissions* increased moderately but significantly, while *errors* diminished slightly. *Omission filtering* was appreciable at rates 5.62 and 7.50, decreasing at the fastest two rates. *Abstracting* occurred most at the fastest two rates.

Under conditions fairly free of overload, rates 2.81 and 3.75, any sort of *filtering* behavior was rare. Under moderate overload, however, rates 5.62 and 7.50, *omission filtering* became pronounced while *error filtering* was still infrequent. Under the greatest overload conditions, rates 11.25 and 15.00, subjects became confused, *omission filtering* significantly diminished (though *omissions* increased significantly), and *error filtering* increased as many more *errors* were made.

5.4   Research at the level of the group

(a) *Pulse-interval coded inputs.* Three groups of three members each were tested on a task which required that each of the first two members respond to a separate light by pressing a lever. These outputs caused lights to flash before the third subject, who responded to each flash by pushing his own lever, creating the system output signals. The curve of the average group, calculated in the same way as the curves in Figs. 5-28, 5-29, and 5-30, was comparable in shape to the cell, organ, and organism level curves (see Fig. 5-40). The maximum output rate was about 3.75 bits per s at an input rate of about 5.5 bits per s, lower than for the cell, organ, or organism.

(b) *IOTA experiments.* Three IOTA experiments were conducted at the group level. In each experiment, the sample was comprised of the identical set of 6 three-man face-to-face groups, but the group structure and instrumentation were changed from experiment to experiment, as diagramed in the middle row of Fig. 5-31. The channel and net subsystem of each group had both living and nonliving (electronic) components. Over these, information flowed in only one direction. The groups in each experiment had a different constraint on their information transmissions. The first group experiment, G-1 (G stands for group), involved a *dispatcher* structure. In these groups the task of Member 1 was not primarily to transduce the input information, but rather to dispatch it or divide it between Member 2 and Member 3 so that they could respond to it most effectively and output it. The combined outputs of Member 2 and Member 3 made up the group output. The dotted lines in the G-1 or dispatcher diagram in Fig. 5-31 indicate that the information flow was from Member 1 either to Member 2 or to Member 3, but not to both simultaneously. In the G-2 experiment, the groups had a *node* structure (see page 63). Members 1 and 2 each transduced half the input and transmitted it to Member 3. The latter acted as a node, outputting the information input to him in unaltered form. The groups in the G-3 experiment had a *decider* structure. Members 1 and 2 simultaneously received identical information inputs. Their task was to transduce the input and transmit it to Member 3. On the basis of these signals, often not simultaneous or identical, he had to decide the correct output for the

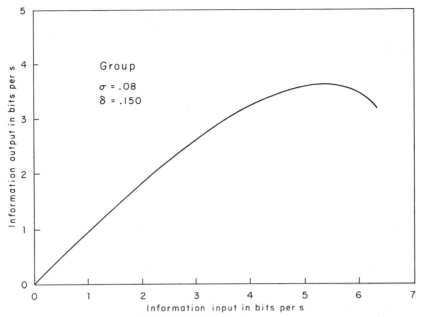

Fig. 5-40 Theoretical curve based on average performance data of groups under various rates of pulse-interval coded information input. σ represents minimum discriminable time interval of the channel; δ represents refractory period of the channel.

group and then make it, using either blue, green, yellow, or red buttons as he chose.

The amount of information presented to each group was the same for corresponding runs. In the G-1 experiment Member 1 did not transduce any information input but he dispatched it to the others in his group. In the G-2 experiment both Member 1 and Member 2 transduced and transmitted such inputs, but only half as fast as Member 1 and Member 2 in a comparable run in the G-3 experiment. Each group output transduced information at the same rate, given optimal performance. In the G-1 experiment, however, Members 2 and 3, who did the output transducing received half as many signals on the average as the output transducer, Member 3, in the G-2 experiment. He in turn received half as many signals as the output transducer, Member 3, in the G-3 experiment.

The different group structures caused the *multiple channels* adjustment to be used most in experiment G-1, less in G-2, and least in G-3. Consequently one could predict how their processes would differ. Because the two members who constituted the output transducer of the dispatcher group in experiment G-1 received signals, on the average, at half the rate of the output transducer of the node group in experiment G-2 (which received signals at half the rate of the output transducer in the decider group in experiment G-3), the average rates of information transmission should de-

crease, at the faster input rates, from experiment G-1, to G-2, to G-3. Because input overloads should occur at relatively slower rates in experiment G-3 than in G-2, and in G-2 than in G-1, the use of adjustment processes should begin at slower rates in G-3 than in G-2, and in G-2 than in G-1. The amount of use of the adjustments should follow the same order. And since any discrepancy between the inputs to the G-3 output transducer could be resolved by the use of *abstracting* responses, one would expect that G-3 would use the *abstracting* adjustment more frequently than G-1 or G-2.

Subjects. In the group experiments the subjects had participated in either experiment O-1 or O-2, but not both. The number of groups was six each in the G-1, G-2, and G-3 experiments. The subjects were assigned to the G-1 groups at random except that the personal time schedules of some prevented them from joining certain groups. This initial assignment to a particular group was maintained throughout the other two group experiments. The assignments of tasks within a group was random for the G-1 experiment. It was also random for the G-2 experiment, except that Member 1 in the G-1 experiment had to serve as a component of the input transducer in G-2. Member 1 in G-1 and Member 3 in G-2 served as components of the input transducer in G-3.

Apparatus. The I–O panels used in the G-1 experiment were described above (see page 175 and Fig.

5-33). A switch was inserted in the electrical circuitry between the IOTA control equipment and the I–O panels. The position of this switch, controlled by Member 1, determined whether Member 2 or Member 3 received the inputs at any given moment.

In the G-2 experiment the two components of the input transducer, Members 1 and 2, used I–O panels that had only blue buttons. That is, they could not use the *abstracting* adjustment process. Member 3, the output transducer, used the I–O panel employed in the G-1 experiment and could use the *abstracting* adjustment if he wished. The circuitry from the IOTA control equipment was so modified that the signals to blue buttons 1, 3, 5, and 7 went to the input panel of Member 1, and the signals to blue buttons 2, 4, 6, and 8 went to the input panel of Member 2. Each response of Member 1 or Member 2 initiated a pulse which activated the corresponding blue button on the I–O panel of Member 3. The responses from the latter panel constituted the output of the group.

The instrumentation of the I–O panels for the G-3

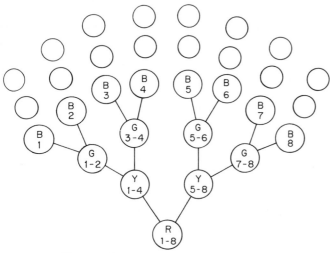

Fig. 5-41 Arrangement of the signal lamps and button-lights on the I–O panel of Member 3 of the G-3 decider group and Member 9 of the Oz-2 decider organization. The top two rows were signal lamps. From top to bottom, the next four rows of button-lights were, respectively, blue (B), green (G), yellow (Y), and red (R).

experiment was the same as for the G-2 experiment except that, for input to the panel of Member 3, two rows of eight signal lamps were added just above the blue-button level (see Fig. 5-41). Outputs from Member 1 lit the top row of these lamps, and outputs from Member 2 lit the lower row. The circuitry from the IOTA control equipment to the input panels of Mem-

bers 1 and 2 was such that each panel received the same complete input series of signals at the same rate.

Procedure. The instructions about the basic task for experiments G-1, G-2, and G-3 were essentially the same as for O-1 and O-2. In addition they stressed that total group performance would be evaluated, not the performances of the individual members. The different structural arrangements and procedures of the dispatcher group, the node group, and the decider group were explained for the G-1, G-2, and G-3 experiments, respectively. Each of these experiments lasted

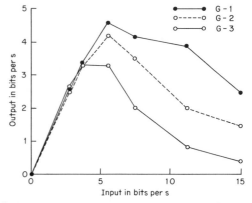

Fig. 5-42 Median information output rate as a function of input rate for the groups in the G-1, G-2, and G-3 experiments.

3 days. Only the blue buttons on the I–O panels were lighted as input signals.

The range of input rates was the same as in the O-1 and O-2 experiments, and the same sequences of trials at the different rates were used (see Table 5-4).

Results

Information transmitted. The median input–output curves of the groups in experiments G-1, G-2, and G-3 indicated that overload occurred (see Fig. 5-42). The three curves were almost identical for the two slowest input rates, but from rate 5.62 bits per s on up, they separated. The decline in median output rate was faster and began earlier for G-3 than for G-2, and for G-2 than for G-1. Analyses of variance indicated that the various input rates in each of the three experiments elicited significantly different output rates. Both increases and decreases in median output rates were significant. The highest single scores for individual groups in experiments G-1 and G-2 occurred at the input rate of 7.50 bits per s and were, respectively, 6.19 and 5.42 bits per s, and for G-3, 5.02 bits per s at rate 5.62. The same G-1 group had output rates of 6.12

and 4.85 bits per s at input rates of 11.25 and 15.00, respectively. Considering all input rates, the G-1 output rates were significantly faster than those in the G-2 and G-3 experiments. Those in the G-2 experiment were higher than in the G-3, but not significantly so.[194] Although the groups differed in the magnitudes of their output rates, the shapes of the median curves were statistically similar.

Adjustment processes. Examples of all the adjustment processes except escape occurred in each of the three group experiments.

(*a*) *Omission adjustment process.* At the input rates of 2.81 and 3.75 bits per s the percentages of *omissions* were very small in all three group experiments, but at all faster rates, the percentages were higher (see Fig. 5-43). Analyses of variance indicated that the percentages of *omissions* differed significantly as the input rates increased in each of the three experiments. There were no differences between output rates for any successive pair of input rates in G-1, but each output rate

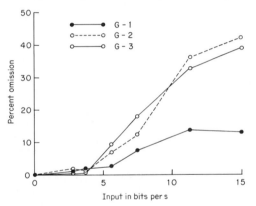

Fig. 5-43 Median percent omission as a function of input rate for the groups in the G-1, G-2, and G-3 experiments.

for the last three input rates was reliably faster than for the first.[195] The 25 percent increase from input rate 7.50 to 11.25 was significant in the G-2 experiment. All successive increments from rate 3.75 to 11.25 were significant in the G-3 experiment. The single largest scores for an individual group were 27 percent at input rate 11.25 in the G-1 experiment, 61 percent at input rate 15.00 in the G-2 experiment, and 52 percent at input rate 11.25 in the G-3 experiment. There were significantly lower percents of *omissions* in the G-1 experiment than in G-2 or G-3, but no significant difference between the latter two. The shapes of the curves, however, were somewhat similar.

(*b*) *Error adjustment process.* In all the group experiments the median percent *error* was almost 0 for the first two input rates and then began to rise (see Fig.

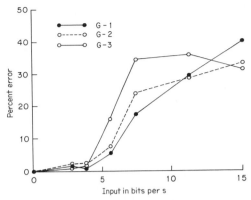

Fig. 5-44 Median percent error as a function of input rate for the groups in the G-1, G-2, and G-3 experiments.

5-44). In G-1 and G-2 it rose at the 5.62 bits per s input and each higher rate. In G-3 it rose rapidly at the 5.62 and 7.50 input rates, but only slightly beyond that at the 11.25 rate and decreased somewhat at the 15.00 rate.

Analyses of variance revealed that variations in input rates elicited significantly different median percent *error* in each of the three experiments. The only significant increases in *percent error* between successive input rates were from 7.50 to 11.25 for G-1, from 5.62 to 7.50 for G-2, and from 3.75 to 5.62 and 5.62 to 7.50 for G-3.[196] The maximum scores of individual groups recorded were 55 percent at rate 15.00 in G-1, 71 percent at rate 7.50 in G-2, and 52 percent at rate 11.25 in G-3. The G-1 and G-2 median curves were much more similar to each other than to G-3. Even so, the shapes of all three curves were significantly similar.

(*c*) *Queuing adjustment process.* In G-1 median percent *queuing* increased with successive significant increments from the input rate of 3.75 bits per s to 5.62 and from 5.62 to 7.50 (see Fig. 5-45).[197] At that rate and above essentially all signals were *queued*. The G-3 median was significantly greater at 3.75 and 5.62 than at 2.81, but then each of the six groups decreased their *queuing* behavior at rate 7.50 and uniformly increased it at rate 11.25, both increase and decrease being statistically significant. Three of the six G-2 groups also showed a decrease at rate 7.50 followed by an increase at rate 11.25. There was a significantly lower percent of *queuing* in G-1 than in G-2 or G-3, the dispatcher structure apparently serving to diminish the use of this adjustment. The shapes of the three curves on inspection appear similar, but this similarity is not statistically significant. Analyses of variance showed that changes in input rate produced significant effects in experiments G-1 and G-3 but not G-2.

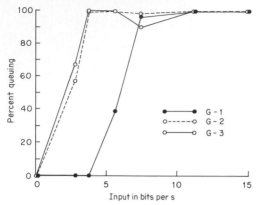

Fig. 5-45 Median percent queuing as a function of input rate for the groups in the *G*-1, *G*-2, and *G*-3 experiments.

(d) *Filtering adjustment process*

(i) The *omission filtering* score could not be computed for any individual group at input rates at which the group made less than eight *omissions* (see page 179). Because there were many such experimental runs, no analysis of variance was computed on the *G*-1 data, though specific individual groups had χ^2 scores indicating significant amounts of *omission filtering* at input rates of 5.62, 7.50, 11.25, and 15.00 bits per s. The scores of one group were significant at each of these rates. For *G*-2 and *G*-3 analyses of variance could be carried out for only the highest three input rates. Changes of input rate affected the amount of *omission filtering* significantly in *G*-2 but not *G*-3. The percent of such *filtering* in *G*-2 was highest at input rates 7.50 and 11.25.[198] There were no other important findings about this sort of *filtering* in the group experiments.

(ii) The data on the second measure of *filtering*, *error filtering*, were so scanty that no important conclusions could be drawn. There was little or no use of this adjustment at the three slowest input rates in any of the experiments. The data suggest that it was used somewhat at the three fastest rates.

(e) *Abstracting adjustment process.* The median percent *abstracting* was 0 or near 0 at all input rates in experiment *G*-2. It was also 0 or near 0 for the first three input rates in experiment *G*-1, after which the percent rose to 26 at input rate 7.50, fell to 18 at rate 11.25, and rose again to 33 at rate 15.00. In experiment *G*-3 it was also 0 or near 0 at the three slowest input rates, rising to 6 percent at the 7.50 rate, 34 percent at 11.25, and 40 percent at 15.00 (see Fig. 5-46). There were no other important findings about the abstracting adjustment in these experiments.

Summary of *G*-1, *G*-2, and *G*-3 findings. In all three experiments the rate of information transmission in bits per second at first increased as the input rate went up and then decreased. Also the adjustment process measures generally increased with the input rate. On those measures for which it was meaningful to compare the shapes of the curves from experiments *G*-1, *G*-2, and *G*-3—percent *omission,* percent *error,* and percent *queuing*—they were shown to be definitely similar.

Consideration of the group structures before the experiments began (see page 183) led to the prediction that the relatively slow rate of inputs to the two members in the output transducer of the dispatcher groups in experiment *G*-1 would result in such groups having higher output rates than the *G*-2 or *G*-3 groups. It was expected also to slow the decrease in output rates as input rates increased to the overload point. The added complexity of the decisions made by Member 3, the decider and output transducer in *G*-3 decider groups, was predicted to reduce their performances relative to the *G*-2 node groups. The results bore out these expectations well. The median dispatcher groups in *G*-1 output significantly more information per second than the node and decider groups, and the median output curves of the *G*-1 dispatcher groups remained at higher rates than the comparable two median curves. The median curve of the *G*-2 node groups peaked at a faster rate than the curve of the *G*-3 decider groups and remained at faster rates at the higher input rates, but the overall difference between the node and decider groups was not statistically significant.

Because the *G*-1 dispatcher groups were able to handle the increases in input rate more easily, they

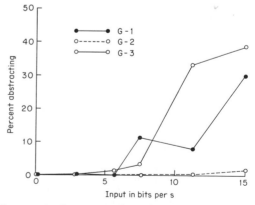

Fig. 5-46 Median percent abstracting as a function of input rate for the groups in the *G*-1, *G*-2, and *G*-3 experiments.

would be expected first to employ the adjustment processes at faster input rates than the other two sorts of groups. This is generally what occurred.

The predictions were supported by the percent *omission* scores. The dispatcher groups *omitted* significantly less frequently than the other sorts of groups. The increase in percent *omission* over the slower rates was greater for the decider groups than the node groups. The node groups increased their percent *omission* more rapidly than the dispatcher groups over the fastest two rates.

The G-1, G-2, and G-3 groups ranked themselves on the percent *error* measure essentially as expected, though the difference between G-2 and G-3 was not statistically significant. The *error* adjustment was used more at slower input rates by the decider groups, averaging between 30 and 40 percent over the fastest three rates. The dispatcher and node groups attained this level of error response only at the fastest rate.

At the input rate of 3.75 bits per s almost all responses from the node and decider groups were *queued*, with lags greater than 0, but the dispatcher group was not stressed to this extent until input rate 7.50. The differences in percent *queuing* between the dispatcher and the other two sorts of groups were statistically significant. The two latter groups had more members in their channels, which added to their lags.

Because of the scanty data it was impossible to make comparisons among the G-1, G-2, and G-3 groups as to how they employed either the *omission filtering* or the *error filtering* adjustments.

The G-3 decider groups used the *abstracting* adjustment more than the G-1 or G-2 groups, as expected.

5.5   Research at the level of the organization

(*a*) *Pulse-interval coded inputs.* In this experiment we set up a small organization in the laboratory. The organization's input transducer consisted of two groups of two members each in one room. One group of two subjects formed the decider in a second room. And a single subject in a third room was the output transducer.

Each subject in the first group of the input transducer responded to the first of two flashes by pushing a lever before him. Each subject in the second group responded similarly to the second flash. These actions flashed lights before the members of the decider. They responded to the flashes, each subject responding only after seeing two flashes.

The first member of the decider responded to the two flashes produced by the two members of the first input transducer group. The second member of the decider responded to the two flashes produced by the two members of the second input transducer group. Waiting in this fashion for two flashes enabled each member of the decider to correct for pushes made in *error* by one member of the input transducer group from which he received signals. But it did not enable him to correct for *omissions*.

The single subject in the output transducer responded by pressing his lever to all flashes in his room, which were the outputs of the two members of the decider group. The signals produced when he pressed his lever were the organization's output.

The curve of this organization, calculated in the same way as the curves in Figs. 5-28, 5-29, 5-30, and 5-40, was comparable in shape to the cell, organ, organism, and group curves (see Fig. 5-47). The maximum output rate was about 2.5 bits per s at an input rate of about 4.0 bits per s, lower than for any of the other levels of systems we studied.

(*b*) *IOTA experiments.* Two IOTA experiments were conducted at the organization level. The structures of the two systems used, Oz-1 (Oz stands for organization), which had a *node* structure, and Oz-2, which had a *decider* structure, are diagrammed in the bottom row of Fig. 5-31. Each organization was composed of 3 three-man groups. Two groups were located in separate parts of one room, and the third group was in another room. The two structures used at this level were analogous to those in the G-2 and G-3 group experiments. Oz-1 and Oz-2 were, therefore, designated as node and decider organizations, respectively.

As may be seen in Fig. 5-31C, members 1 to 4 of Oz-1 each received one-fourth of the organization's input. The tasks of Members 1 and 2 were to transmit signals to Member 5. Members 3 and 4 were to transmit signals to Member 6. Then Member 5 was told to send signals from his group to Member 7 in the next room while Member 6 similarly was told to send signals to Member 8. In turn Members 7 and 8 were both expected to transmit the information they received to Member 9, the organization's output transducer. Much as in G-3, the decider group, Oz-2 received two simultaneous and identical sets of signals. One set was presented, as diagrammed, to the two components of the first input transducer group, Members 1 and 2 each receiving half of the signals. They were to transmit these to Member 5. At the same time Members 3 and 4 received identical signals which they were to transmit to Member 6. Member 5 was asked to relay the signals he received to Member 7 in the next room just as Member 6 was supposed to do to Member 8. Then both Member 7 and Member 8 were expected to

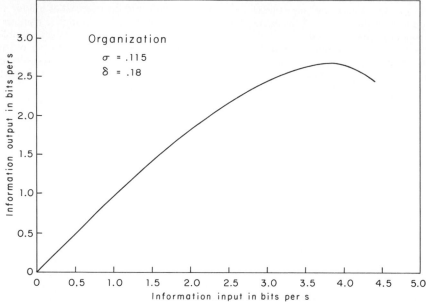

Fig. 5-47   Theoretical curve based on average performance data of organizations under various rates of pulse-interval coded information input. σ represents minimum discriminable time interval of the channel; δ represents refractory period of the channel.

send on the information they received to Member 9, who decided on the appropriate response to be transduced as system output. Although in comparable trials the rate of total information input was the same for both organizations, members 1 through 8 of Oz-1 had to process signals at only half the rate as the corresponding members in Oz-2. The rate was identical, however, for the output transducer, Member 9, in both organizations.

Although the task information was the same for both Oz-1 and Oz-2, twice as many signals were input in any run in the Oz-2 experiment as in the Oz-1. This required Member 9 in Oz-2 continuously to compare two input signals before deciding what signal to output. Member 9 in Oz-1 did not need to make such decisions. We predicted that the output rates of Oz-2 decider organizations would, in general, therefore, be slower than those at comparable input rates of Oz-1 node organizations. More specifically, the Oz-2 organization's output rate should peak at slower input rates, and Oz-2 organizations should begin using adjustment processes at slower rates and use them more frequently. Two organizations were set up, each comprised of nine subjects experienced in previous IOTA tests. Each organization carried out the Oz-1 experiment first and then the Oz-2 experiment. Because practice effects were not controlled, both organizations were more experienced in the Oz-2 than in the Oz-1 experiment. This may have improved

their Oz-2 performances somewhat relative to their Oz-1 performances.

Subjects.   In the organization experiments the subjects had had prior experience in either the O-1 or O-2 experiments, but not both, and also in G-1, G-2, and G-3. The 6 three-man groups in these latter experiments were assigned randomly to one of two organizations, with the exception of three subjects with personal schedule conflicts. The two sets of subjects in the Oz-1 experiment were assigned to their specific positions in accordance with their assignments in G-2. Their positions in experiment Oz-2 were determined by the ones they held in Oz-1.

Apparatus.   Nine I–O panels were used in the Oz-1 experiment. Six small panels were constructed for Members 1 through 6, each of which had only one arched row of eight button-lights. The I–O panels for Members 7 through 9 were the same as those used in G-2 (see page 184). The circuitry was constructed to divide the information input from the IOTA control equipment into four sets of two signals each, namely, signals 1 and 3, 5 and 7, 2 and 4, and 6 and 8, which were presented to Members 1 through 4, respectively. Only Member 9's outputs were recorded.

The I–O panels used in Oz-2 were the same as in Oz-1 except that Member 9, the output transducer, had 16 signal lamps added to his I–O panel (see Fig. 5-41).

Procedure.   The instructions for experiments Oz-1 and Oz-2 were essentially the same as for the organism and group experiments. The fifth order of rates in Table 5-4 was selected at random and used for all the organization level experiments.

Results

Information transmitted. The median input–output curves of both Oz-1 and Oz-2 experiments were similar in shape, showing that information overload occurred at high input rates (see Fig. 5-48). These curves were approximately the same for the first two rates and then separated, with the Oz-1 output increasing to the input rate of 5.62 bits per s followed by a decrease over the last three rates while the decrease for Oz-2 began after input rate 3.75. The two curves were not significantly different.[199]

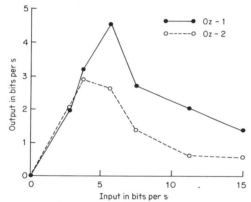

Fig. 5-48 Median information output rate as a function of input rate for the organizations in the Oz-1 and Oz-2 experiments.

Adjustment processes. All adjustment processes except *escape* were used by the organization in these experiments.

(a) Omission adjustment process. The median percent *omission* curves for both types of organization increased with input rate (see Fig. 5-49). The Oz-2 curve was somewhat higher at the input rate of 7.50 bits per s but tended to level out over the fastest two rates in contrast to the Oz-1 curve, which rose at each of the two fastest rates. The shapes of the two curves were significantly similar.[200]

(b) Error adjustment process. The median percent *error* curves appear in Fig. 5-50 for both Oz-1 and Oz-2 experiments. The Oz-1 curve fell between input rates 2.81 and 3.75 and then increased to rate 7.50, after which its rate of rise slowed markedly. The Oz-2 curve increased rapidly to rate 7.50 and then fell somewhat. The two curves were not significantly similar.[201]

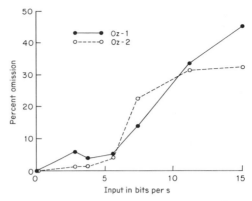

Fig. 5-49 Median percent omission as a function of input rate for the organizations in the Oz-1 and the Oz-2 experiments.

(c) Queuing adjustment process. With all signals passing through four persons, lags in responding to them were almost guaranteed. The data, in fact, showed the *percent queuing* in Oz-1 and Oz-2 to be so nearly 100 percent at all input rates that there is no purpose even presenting the median curves in a figure.

(d) Filtering adjustment process.

(i) The median *omission-filtering* scores based on scanty data from Oz-1 appeared to increase at the slower input rates and then decrease at the fastest two rates. In Oz-2 such filtering seemed to begin at a faster rate and be greater at the fastest two rates.

(ii) The *error-filtering* data were even more fragmentary than the *omission-filtering* data. One Oz-1 organization showed such filtering at input rate 15.00, and each of the Oz-2 organizations showed it at rate 7.50.

(e) Abstracting adjustment process. The percent *abstracting* scores were 0 at all rates for both Oz-1 and Oz-2 with the exception of input rates 7.50, 11.25, and

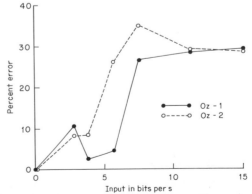

Fig. 5-50 Median percent error as a function of input rate for the organizations in the Oz-1 and Oz-2 experiments.

15.00 for one *Oz*-2 organization. It employed *abstracting* on 80 to 90 percent of the responses at the fastest two input rates.

Summary of *Oz*-1 and *Oz*-2 findings. Because the *Oz*-2 organizations received twice as many inputs as the *Oz*-1 systems on comparable experimental trials and because of the decisions made in the *Oz*-2 experiment that were not required in the *Oz*-1 experiment, the *Oz*-2 systems were expected, on the average, to transmit less information per second and to begin to use adjustment processes at slower input rates (see page 188). For the most part, this expectation was confirmed. The *Oz*-2 or decider organizations transmitted less information per second at each input rate faster than 3.75 bits per s, and their output curves leveled off

between input rates of 3.75 and 5.62 in contrast to an increase of almost 1.5 bits per s in the *Oz*-1 experiment. The sharp drop in output rate in the *Oz*-1 curve at input rate 7.5 bits per s was associated with a large increase in percents of *omission* and *error*. Additional decreases in output rate at the fastest two input rates were associated with increased *omissions* for *Oz*-1 but, for *Oz*-2, the decrease from input rate 7.50 to 11.25 and 15.00, was a function of use of the *abstracting* adjustment in one *Oz*-2 system and increased *omissions* in the other. The lack of an increase for *Oz*-2 between rates 3.75 and 5.62 resulted chiefly from a sharp rise in *errors* since the other adjustments remained relatively unchanged over these rates. The percent of *errors* remained fairly constant over the last

AZ	BZ	CZ	DZ	EZ	FZ	GZ	HZ	JZ	KZ	LZ	MZ	NZ	PZ	QZ	RZ	SZ	TZ	UZ	VZ	ZZ
AV	BV	CV	DV	EV	FV	GV	HV	JV	KV	LV	MV	NV	PV	QV	RV	SV	TV	UV	VV	ZV
AU	BU	CU	DU	EU	FU	GU	HU	JU	KU	LU	MU	NU	PU	QU	RU	SU	TU	UU	VU	ZU
AT	BT	CT	DT	ET	FT	GT	HT	JT	KT	LT	MT	NT	PT	QT	RT	ST	TT	UT	VT	ZT
AS	BS	CS	DS	ES	FS	GS	HS	JS	KS	LS	MS	NS	PS	QS	RS	SS	TS	US	VS	ZS
AR	BR	CR	DR	ER	FR	GR	HR	JR	KR	LR	MR	NR	PR	QR	RR	SR	TR	UR	VR	ZR
AQ	BQ	CQ	DQ	EQ	FQ	GQ	HQ	JQ	KQ	LQ	MQ	NQ	PQ	QQ	RQ	SQ	TQ	UQ	VQ	ZQ
AP	BP	CP	DP	EP	FP	GP	HP	JP	KP	LP	MP	NP	PP	QP	RP	SP	TP	UP	VP	ZP
AN	BN	CN	DN	EN	FN	GN	HN	JN	KN	LN	MN	NN	PN	QN	RN	SN	TN	UN	VN	ZN
AM	BM	CM	DM	EM	FM	GM	HM	JM	KM	LM	MM	NM	PM	QM	RM	SM	TM	UM	VM	ZM
AL	BL	CL	DL	EL	FL	GL	HL	JL	KL	LL	ML	NL	PL	QL	RL	SL	TL	UL	VL	ZL
AK	BK	CK	DK	EK	FK	GK	HK	JK	KK	LK	MK	NK	PK	QK	RK	SK	TK	UK	VK	ZK
AJ	BJ	CJ	DJ	EJ	FJ	GJ	HJ	JJ	KJ	LJ	MJ	NJ	PJ	QJ	RJ	SJ	TJ	UJ	VJ	ZJ
AH	BH	CH	DH	EH	FH	GH	HH	JK	KH	LH	MH	NH	PH	QH	RH	SH	TH	UH	VH	ZH
AG	BG	CG	DG	EG	FG	GG	HG	JG	KG	LG	MG	NG	PG	QG	RG	SG	TG	UG	VG	ZG
AF	BF	CF	DF	EF	FF	GF	HF	JF	KF	LF	MF	NF	PF	QF	RF	SF	TF	UF	VF	ZF
AE	BE	CE	DE	EE	FE	GE	HE	JE	KE	LE	ME	NE	PE	QE	RE	SE	TE	UE	VE	ZE
AD	BD	CD	DD	ED	FD	GD	HD	JD	KD	LD	MD	ND	PD	QD	RD	SD	TD	UD	VD	ZD
AC	BC	CC	DC	EC	FC	GC	HC	JC	KC	LC	MC	NC	PC	QC	RC	SC	TC	UC	VC	ZC
AB	BB	CB	DB	EB	FB	GB	HB	JB	KB	LB	MB	NB	PB	QB	RB	SB	TB	UB	VB	ZB
AA	BA	CA	DA	EA	FA	GA	HA	JA	KA	LA	MA	NA	PA	QA	RA	SA	TA	UA	VA	ZA

Fig. 5-51   Display board for air-raid warning simulator.

three input rates for both organizations. In these large systems essentially all responses of both types of organizations showed *queuing*. The effects on output rate of both sorts of *filtering* are obscure.

(c) Air-raid warning simulator experiment.   In another research, much of which was carried out by Jay and McCornack, we used a mock-up of part of the air-raid warning system of the United States and Canada.[202] The simulator, at System Development Corporation in Santa Monica, California which cooperated in the study, consisted of three groups of three men, each group in a separate room. Because these three groups were included, this was an organization by my definition, albeit a small and atypical one. The first room simulated a radar station in the continental air-raid warning network; the second simulated the room at headquarters in which messages from the local station were received; and the third simulated a plotting screen on which the location of planes was indicated at headquarters. Dots, supposed to represent airplanes in geographical sectors, appeared randomly on a 21 × 21 display (see Fig. 5-51). These dots, each with an associated message member, were thrown on a screen by a movie projector. Each of three readers in the first room was responsible for one-third of the total board. When a dot and its number appeared in his sector, the reader for Team 1 wrote down on a card the coordinates of the cell in which the dot appeared and also the number of the dot. He then presented the card to his corresponding teller in the next room by passing it through a slot. The teller in turn read the card by telephone to the corresponding plotter in the third room, who wrote the message number in the proper cell on the plotting board. This board was photographed automatically at 6-s intervals, so that a continuous record of the appearance of numbers on the plotting board could be obtained. Thus there were three essentially separate channels in this system with little interaction among them, since Reader A always gave his information only to Teller A, who passed the message on only to Plotter A, and so on for Team 2 and Team 3. When input in bits per second was plotted against output in bits per second, the average curve for these three teams had a similar shape to those obtained in our *O*-1, *O*-2, *G*-1, *G*-2, *G*-3, *Oz*-1, and *Oz*-2 experiments. No overload occurred, however, up to an input rate of 10 bits per s. The maximum channel capacity for the average team was about 4 bits per s, approximately in the range of the *G*-1, *G*-2, and *G*-3 groups, probably because information passed through about as many persons as in those groups rather than through more, as would be the case in a larger organization (see Fig. 5-52). Since the teams had only minimal interactions in this experiment, one

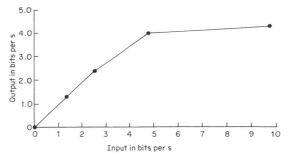

Fig. 5-52 Average performance curves for the three teams in air-raid warning simulator experiment.

might argue that the subjects all together did not constitute an organization but rather three essentially independent groups working simultaneously in parallel. These subjects had much more practice than those in our *G*-1, *G*-2, and *G*-3 experiments. Their transmission rates were markedly faster than in their earlier trials. This may be the reason why an input of 10 bits per s did not produce overload in this experiment as it did in the *G*-1, *G*-2, and *G*-3 experiments.

Four adjustment processes were used by the teams in these studies—*omission, error, queuing,* and *omission filtering.* There was no possibility of using *multiple channels* within a given team, but the three teams, of course, constituted multiple parallel channels. The experimental instructions prevented use of *abstracting.* Use of the first three adjustment processes was measured in percentages. Use of *queuing* was measured in average number of seconds of delay (see Fig. 5-53). The measures of all adjustments increased with

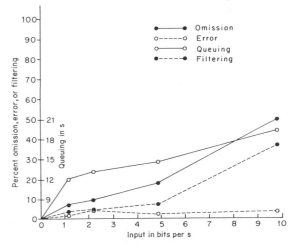

Fig. 5-53 Average use of each of four adjustment processes by the three teams in air-raid warning simulator experiment.

the input rate except the *error* percent which remained below 5 percent throughout.

5.6   Cross-level comparisons

(*a*) *Pulse-interval coded inputs.*   Our findings in the experiments involving pulse-interval coded inputs supported Hypothesis 5.1-25 (see pages 104 and 124), which states that channels in living systems at higher levels in general have lower capacities than those in living systems at lower levels. See Fig. 5-54, which combines the curves of researches on the cell (see Fig. 5-28), the organ (see Fig. 5-29), the organism (see Fig. 5-30), the group (see Fig. 5-40), and the organization (see Fig. 5-47). The data did not reveal any evidence one way or another relevant to Hypothesis 5.1-4 (see pages 103 and 124) which asserts that there are more kinds and more complex combinations of adjustment processes at higher levels of living systems than at lower levels.

(*b*) *IOTA experiments.*   The primary aim of the IOTA studies was to compare three levels of living systems as to how they process various rates of information inputs. Three studies constituted the heart of the research: the first organism-level experiment, *O*-1; the group node experiment, *G*-2; and the organization node experiment, *Oz*-1. The experimental procedure was essentially the same at all levels. Each system was presented the same number of signals at the same rates. A basic difference among levels, however, was system size, or more specifically the number of components in the system through which information was transmitted. The number of persons through which signals passed was 1 for the organism, 2 for the group, and 4 for the organization.

Human beings process information imperfectly, with variations in rate, *omissions, errors,* lags, and distortions. Therefore signals output by a system made up of human beings should be less regular in rate, less complete, and less accurate the more persons there are in the system's channels. Expectations based on such considerations were that the maximum rate of information processing would decrease from experiment *O*-1 to *G*-2 to *Oz*-1, and the average percents of *omissions, errors,* and *queuing* would increase in the same order. It was unclear what would happen to the *filtering* and *abstracting* scores.

Results

Information transmitted.   The differences among levels in output rates at various input rates, when evaluated by analysis of variance, did not approach statistical significance (see Fig. 5-55). The shapes of the three curves were very similar, however.[203] For all system levels, output increased to input rate 5.62 bits per s,

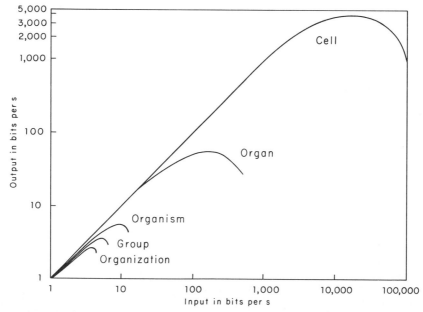

Fig. 5-54   Theoretical curve on logarithmic coordinates based on average performance data of five levels of living systems (cell, organ, organism, group, and organization) under various rates of pulse-interval coded information input. This figure combines the curves of Figs. 5-28, 5-29, 5-30, 5-40, and 5-47.

but with further increases in input rate, output rate decreased—presumably because of input overload.

In O-1, G-2, and Oz-1 all subjects acted as nodes, passing on signals as they received them. They did not have to compare inputs before making a decision on the proper output. To investigate whether such decisions slow the rate of information output, we carried out a subsidiary cross-level comparison at the two levels that had both node and decider, analyzing data from the node group G-2, the decider group G-3, the node organization Oz-1, and the decider organization Oz-2. We predicted that the maximum rate of information output would be faster for the median of both groups as compared to the median of both organizations, as well as for the median of both node structures as compared to the median of both decider structures. As in the preceding cross-level comparison, the differ-

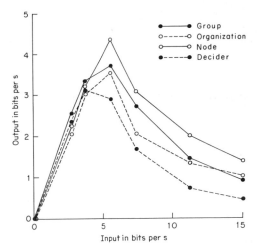

Fig. 5-56 Median information output as a function of input rate for the group and organization levels and the node and decider structures.

Oz-1 systems tending to level out at the fastest rates (see Fig. 5-58).

The percent *queuing* scores, neglecting input rates, were a function of system size. All twenty-four O-1 systems, over all input rates, had lower scores than the six G-2 systems and five of the six G-2 systems scored lower than the Oz-1 systems (see Fig. 5-59). The differences among levels was statistically significant. All levels got close to 100 percent *queuing* by the 7.50 bits per s input rate.

Though there was evidence of some *omission* and *error filtering* at each of the levels, the data were insufficient to make useful cross-level comparisons possible.

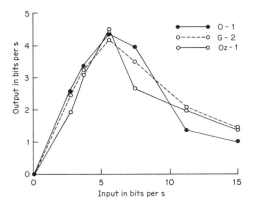

Fig. 5-55 Median information output as a function of input rate for the O-1, G-2, and Oz-1 experiments.

ence in the median curves for the group and the organization levels was not statistically significant (see Fig. 5-56). The maximum output rates of the node structure were significantly faster than those of the decider structure.[204] All the curves had similar shapes, peaking at an input rate of 5.62 bits per s (except for the decider curve which peaked at 3.75) and showing indications of overload at faster rates.

Adjustment processes. Omission, error, queuing, filtering, and *abstracting* adjustments were used at each of the three levels.

The percent *omission* of all three levels increased with input rate (see Fig. 5-57). Analysis of variance indicated that the median curves for the three levels were quite similar.[205]

Analysis of variance indicated that the three levels had quite similar percent *error* scores.[206] Percent *error* generally increased with input rate, the O-1 and

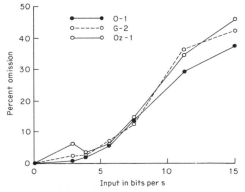

Fig. 5-57 Median percent omission as a function of input rate for the O-1, G-2, and Oz-1 experiments.

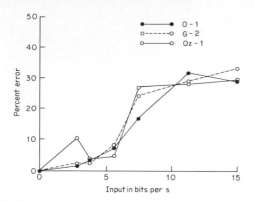

Fig. 5-58   Median percent error as a function of input rate for the *O*-1, *G*-2, and *Oz*-1 experiments.

The percent *abstracting* results indicated that in these experiments lower-level systems tended to use the *abstracting* adjustment more than those at higher levels. Considering the sums of the percent *abstracting* scores over all six input rates, fourteen of twenty-four *O*-1 systems, one of six *G*-2 systems, and none of two *Oz*-1 systems had sums exceeding 1 percent.

Summary of results. From the results it is clear that the three levels of systems were strikingly similar in their functions. The analyses of our measures of system output rates as related to input rates and of the adjustment processes of *omission* and *error* showed this.

The measure of *queuing* increased with input rate, and the overall use of this adjustment was greater the more persons there were in the system channels. The *abstracting* scores suggested that the *O*-1 systems abstracted more than the upper-level systems.

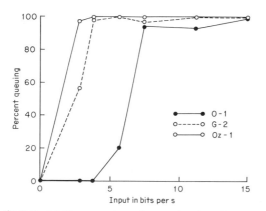

Fig. 5-59   Median percent queuing as a function of input rate for the *O*-1, *G*-2, and *Oz*-1 experiments.

The *filtering* data were so scanty that cross-level comparisons could not be made.

The theoretical curves derived from the data of our pulse-interval studies seemed to show that the maximum output rates of lower-level systems are faster than those of higher levels (see Fig. 5-54). We naturally expected that the organism-level systems would have higher maximum output rates than the groups, and the groups than the organizations (see page 192). This expectation was not supported by the results of our IOTA experiments. On the contrary, the output curves of all the levels were quite similar. A major question, then, requires an answer: How can group and organization channels composed of several successive human components, through which signals must pass, transmit information as fast as a single person?

Two explanations, not necessarily independent, suggest themselves.

(*a*) In our research the subjects were more experienced when they were in the group experiments than when in the organism experiments. They were even more highly experienced in the organization experiments. Transfer of training from one experiment to another should have been primarily positive, tending to speed outputs at the higher levels and so reduce differences among the levels.

Each *O*-1 system had four training sessions prior to the test session. Each member of a *G*-2 system had five sessions at the organism level, three under *G*-1 conditions, in addition to the two training and one test session under *G*-2 conditions. Each member of an *Oz*-1 system had five sessions at the organism level and nine sessions at the group level, in addition to one training and one test session under *Oz*-1 conditions. We discussed this training differential fully at our research planning meetings, and all present agreed that such training differences could not come close to equalizing the output rates from the three system levels. We could have been wrong. Some of our data suggest that the training differences may have been important. Further experiments designed to use comparably experienced systems at all levels could determine if we were.

(*b*) A second explanation goes as follows: If the capabilities of the human elements are roughly comparable, whatever information can be transmitted by one person in a channel in a given time should pose no great problem for the next person in it. For example, at an input rate of 5 signals (15 bits) per s, the *O*-1 output medians were 34 percent *omissions,* 29 percent *errors,* and 32 percent correct. At this input rate each of the input transducers for a *G*-2 group would receive 2.50 signals (7.50 bits) per s and would output 10 percent *omissions,* 13 percent *errors,* and 77 percent correct (the *O-1* median figures for the input rate of 7.50 bits per s). Because 10 percent of the signals have already been *omitted,* the output transducer receives about 4.5 signals (13.5 bits) per s. This still overloads the human organism, which preserves, roughly, the 13 percent *errors* of the input transducer and, at this input rate adds 32 percent more *omissions* as well as 20 percent more *errors,* totaling 42 percent *omissions,* 33 percent *errors,* and 25 percent correct (*G-2* median figures). (A similar example could be presented for the organization level.) Unless large numbers of experimental trials were run, the differences between organism and group outputs at any given input rate might appear not to be statistically significant, to be capable of resulting from chance. This is true of the data in our cross-level comparisons. Repetition of our experiments with many more trials might reveal reliable cross-level differences.

Summary of all our experiments. A few conclusions arise from all our experiments on information input overload:

In all the living systems we studied as the information input rate went up, the output rate increased to a maximum and thereafter decreased, showing signs of overload.

The approximate median maximum transmission rates for the cell were 4,000 bits per s; for the organ, 55; for the organism, 4.75 to 5.75; for the group, 3.44 to 4.60; and for the organization, 2.89 to 4.55. The range for each higher level is lower than the previous level, but there is much overlap among the three highest levels. More extensive data collection is required to determine whether there are significant differences among them.

In general the use of adjustment processes increased as the input rate went up, although the data are insufficient to make it clear whether this was true of either *omission filtering* or *error filtering.* The *multiple channel* adjustment was employed in those systems whose structure permitted it.

Maximum median percentages of use of the adjustment processes were as follows: *omission,* 33 to 46 percent (except in experiment *G-1,* in which it was only 12 percent); error, 23 to 40 percent; *queuing,* 100 percent in all cases; and *abstracting,* 9 to 51 percent.

6. Conclusions

The vast variety of living systems which process information and the ever greater number of information overloads which arise in all aspects of life in themselves are enough to justify attention to the topic of this chapter. We originally decided to study it, how-

ever, purely because it seemed a likely area for a first attempt at cross-level research. Our experiments repeat a common story in the history of science. Begin a basic research, and your subject matter ramifies in many directions. A large number of new questions arise. Begin with basic research and ultimately practical applications commonly appear. By such extension from one or a few related hypotheses eventually perhaps a broad theory of interdigitating propositions can be evaluated.

This chapter has shown how complex are the problems in evaluating even a single cross-level hypothesis. Yet it shows that, with effort, empirical facts and measurements relevant to one such hypothesis can be obtained. Many others deserve investigation.

NOTES AND REFERENCES

[1]MacKay, D. M. & McCulloch, W. S. The limiting information capacity of a neuronal link, *Bull. math. Biophys.,* 1952, **14,** 127–135.
NOTE: Grüsser (Grüsser, O. Die Informations Kapazität einzelner Nervenzellen für die Signalüber mittling in Zentralnerven System. *Kybernetik,* 1962, **1,** 209–211) has proposed a mathematical model for calculating the channel capacity of a single cell in which the information is coded in the number of pulses which are received in a fixed time interval t_i, the neuronal integration time. In this model, if the maximum pulse rate of a nerve fiber is F_{max}, then the maximum number of pulses recorded in one integration interval is $F_{max} \cdot t_i$, and the information content during that interval is $\log_2 (F_{max} \cdot t_i)$ bits. The channel capacity for this mode of coding will be expressed by the equation:
$$I = (1/t_i) \log_2 (F_{max} \cdot t_i) \qquad bits/s$$
The optimum integration interval for a given F_{max} may be obtained by maximizing the function I. Plots of this function are given in the article. F_{max} for synaptic transmission varies from 100 to 400 pulses per s. With integration time constants of 15 to 70 ms, this leads to information channel capacities for single nerve cells of from 20 to 120 bits per s.
[2]Rapoport, A. & Horvath, W. J. The theoretical channel capacity of a single neuron as determined by various coding systems. *Inform. & Control,* 1960, **3,** 335–350.
[3]Brock, L. J., Coombs, J. S., & Eccles, J. C. Intracellular recording from antidromically activated motoneurones. *J. Physiol.,* 1953, **122,** 429–461.
[4]Eyzaguirre, C. & Kuffler, S. W. Processes of excitation in the dendrites and in the soma of single isolated sensory nerve cells of the lobster and crayfish. *J. gen. Physiol.,* 1955, **39,** 87–119.
[5]*Ibid.,* 104–107.
[6]Eyzaguirre, C. & Kuffler, S. W. Further study of soma, dendrite, and axon excitation in single neurons. *J. gen. Physiol.,* 1955, **39,** 121–153.
[7]Granit, R. & Phillips, C. G. Excitatory and inhibitory processes acting upon individual Purkinje cells of the cerebellum in cats. *J. Physiol.,* 1956, **133,** 520–547.
[8]*Ibid.,* 535.
[9]Wall, P. D., Lettvin, J. Y., McCulloch, W. S., & Pitts, W. H. Factors limiting the maximum impulse transmitting ability

of an afferent system of nerve fibers. In C. Cherry (Ed.). *Information theory. Third London symposium*. New York: Academic Press, 1956, 329–344.

[10]Grüsser, O. J. & Creutzfeldt, O. Eine neurophysiologische Grundlage des Brücke-Bartley Effektes: Maxima der Impuls Frequenz retinaler und corticaler Neurone bei flimmerlicht mittlerer Frequenzen. *Pflüg. Arch. ges. Physiol.*, 1957, **263**, 668–681.

[11]Eccles, J. C. *The physiology of synapses*. New York: Academic Press, 1964, 40–42.

[12]*Ibid.*, 83–85.

[13]Mountcastle, V. B. The neural replication of sensory events in the somatic afferent system. In J. C. Eccles (Ed.). *Brain and conscious experience*. New York: Springer-Verlag, 1966, 85–115.

[14]Krnjević, K. & Miledi, R. Failure of neuromuscular propagation in rats. *J. Physiol.*, 1958, **140**, 440–461.

[15]Amassian, V. E. Evoked single cortical unit activity in the somatic sensory areas. *Electroencephalog. & clin. Neurophysiol.*, 1953, **5**, 430–431.

[16]Jung, R. & Baumgartner, G. Hemmungsmechanismen und bremsende Stabilisierung an einzelnen Neuronen des optischen Cortex. *Plfüg. Arch. ges. Physiol.*, 1955, **261**, 434–456.

[17]DeValois, R. Discussion. In S. H. Bartley. Some facts and concepts regarding the neurophysiology of the optic pathway. *A.M.A. Arch. Opthalmol.*, 1958, **60**, 784–785.

[18]Tasaki, I. & Davis, H. Electric responses of individual nerve elements in the cochlear nucleus to sound stimulation (guinea pig). *J. Neurophysiol.*, 1955, **18**, 151–158.

[19]Rose, J. E. & Mountcastle, V. B. Activity of single neurons in the tactile thalamic region of the cat in response to a transient peripheral stimulus. *Johns Hopkins Hosp. Bull.*, 1954, **94**, 238–282.

[20]Mountcastle, V. B., Davies, P. W., & Berman, A. L. Response properties of neurons of cat's somatic sensory cortex to peripheral stimuli. *J. Neurophysiol.*, 1957, **20**, 374–407.

[21]Horvath, W. J. Personal communication.

[22]Hakerem, G. & Lidsky, A. Pupillary reactions to sequences of light and variable dark pulses. *Ann. N.Y. Acad. Sci.*, 1969, **156**, 951–956.

[23]*Ibid.*, 957.

[24]Cf. Wall, P. D., Lettvin, J. Y., McCulloch, W. S., & Pitts, W. H. *Op. cit.*

[25]Lang, A. (Ed.). *Blue fairy book*. London: Longman's, 1948, 148–153.

[26]Cf. Kinscella, H. G. *Music and romance*. Camden, N.J.: RCA Manufacturing Co., Inc., 1941, 278–279.

[27]Telford, C. W. The refractory phase of voluntary and associative responses. *J. exper. Psychol.*, 1931, **14**, 1–36.

[28]Mowrer, O. H., Rayman, N. N., & Bliss, E. L. Preparatory set (expectancy)—an experimental demonstration of its 'central' locus. *J. exper. Psychol.*, 1940, **26**, 357–372.

[29]Merkel, J. Die zeitlichen Verhaltnisse der Willensthatigkeit. *Philos. Studien (Wundt)*. 1885, **2**, 73–127.
Also Woodworth, R. S. *Experimental psychology*. New York: Holt, 1938, 332–333.

[30]Blank, G. Brauchbarkeit optischer Reaktionsmessung. *Indust. Psytechnik*, 1934, **11**, 140–150.

[31]Miller, G. A. *Language and communication*. New York: McGraw-Hill, 1951, 205–207.

[32]Cf. Hick, E. E. On the rate of gain of information. *Quart. J. exper. Psychol.*, 1952, **4**, 11–26.
Also Hyman, R. Stimulus information as a determinant of reaction time. *J. exper. Psychol.*, 1953, **45**, 188–196.

Also Crossman, E. R. F. W. Entropy and choice time: the effect of frequency unbalance on choice response. *Quart. J. exper. Psychol.*, 1953, **5**, 41–51.
Also Crossman, E. R. F. W. The information capacity of the human operator in symbolic and non-symbolic control processes. In J. Draker (Ed.). *The application of information theory to human operator problems. Proceedings of a special technical meeting*. London: Ministry of Supply, Great Britain, 1955.
Also Johnson, E. M. *A bibliography on the use of information theory in psychology (1948–1966)*. Medford, Mass.: Tufts Univ., December 1967.

[33]Bricker, P. D. Information measurement and reaction time: a review. In H. Quastler (Ed.). *Information theory in psychology*. Glencoe: Free Press, 1955, 352.

[34]von Kries, J. & Auerbach, F. Die Zeitdauer einfachster psychischer Vorgänge. *Arch. für Anat. und Physiol. Physiol. Abteilung.*, 1877, 297–378.
Also Henmon, V. A. C. The time of perception as a measure of differences in sensations. *Arch. Philos., Psychol., sci. Meth.*, 1906, No. 8, 1–75.
Also Thurmond, J. B. & Alluisi, E. A. *Choice time in reacting to stimulus pairs at various levels of dissimilarity*. Marietta, Georgia: Human Factors Research Department, Lockheed-Georgia Co., April 1962.

[35]Baker, E. J. & Alluisi, E. A. *Effects of complexity, noise, and sampling rules on visual and auditory form perception*. Marietta, Georgia: Human Factors Research Department, Lockheed-Georgia Co., September 1962.

[36]Ekel, J. Zalezność szybkości podejmowania decyzji od redundancji sygnatow. (Decision-making speed as a function of signal redundancy). *Studia psychologiczne*, 1960, **5**, 104–131.

[37]Quastler, H. & Brabb, B. Human performance in information transmission. *Technical Report R-70*. Urbana: Control Systems Laboratory, Univ. of Illinois, 1956.
Also Quastler, H. Studies of human channel capacity. In C. Cherry (Ed.). *Information theory. Third London symposium*. New York: Academic Press, 1956, 361–371.
Cf. also Kornblum, S. *Reaction time to sequential stimulus presentation*. Unpublished doctoral dissertation. Ann Arbor: Univ. of Michigan, 1959.

[38]Mowbray, G. H. & Rhoades, M. V. On the reduction of choice reaction times with practice. *Quart. J. exper. Psychol.*, 1959, **11**, 16.

[39]Mowbray, G. H. Choice reaction times for skilled responses. *Quart. J. exper. Psychol.*, 1960, **12**, 193–202.

[40]*Ibid.*, 200.

[41]Mowbray, G. H. & Rhoades, M. V. *Op. cit.*, 16.

[42]*Ibid.*

[43]*Ibid.*, 17.

[44]Christie, L. S. & Luce, R. D. Suggestions for the analysis of reaction times and simple choice behavior. *Technical Report R-53*. Urbana: Control Systems Laboratory, Univ. of Illinois, 1954.
Also Christie, L. S. & Luce, R. D. Decision structure and time relations in simple choice behavior. *Bull. math. Biophysics*, 1956, **18**, 89–112.

[45]McGill, W. J. Stochastic latency mechanisms. In R. D. Luce, R. R. Bush, & E. Galanter (Eds.). *Handbook of mathematical psychology*. Vol. 1. New York: Wiley, 1963, 309–360.

[46]Bertelson, P. Sequential redundancy and speed in a serial two-choice responding task. *Quart. J. exper. Psychol.*, 1961, **12**, 90–102.

[47]Kornblum, S. Choice reaction time for repetitions and nonrepetitions. *Acta psychol.*, 1967, **27**, 178–187.

Also Kornblum, S. Serial-choice reaction time: inadequacies of the information hypothesis. *Science*, 1968, **159**, 432–434.

Also Kornblum, S. Sequential determinants of information processing in serial and discrete choice reaction time. *Psychol. Rev.*, 1969, **76**, 113–131.

48Kornblum, S., Burgess, J., & Siguel, E. Sequential dependencies in two-choice reaction time. *M.H.R.I. Communication 216*. Ann Arbor: Mental Health Research Institute, Univ. of Michigan, September 1967.

49Miller, G. A. The magical number seven, plus or minus two: some limits on our capacity for processing information. *Psychol. Rev.*, 1956, **63**, 81–97.

50Pollack, I. The information of elementary auditory displays. *J. Acoust. Soc. Amer.*, 1952, **24**, 745–749.

Also Pollack, I. The information of elementary auditory displays. II. *J. Acoust. Soc. Amer.*, 1953, **25**, 765–769.

51Garner, W. R. An informational analysis of absolute judgments of loudness. *J. exper. Psychol.*, 1953, **46**, 373–380.

52Beebe-Center, J. G., Rogers, M. S., & O'Connell, D. N. Transmission of information about sucrose and saline solutions through the sense of taste. *J. Psychol.*, 1955, **39**, 157–160.

53Hake, H. W. & Garner, W. R. The effect of presenting various numbers of discrete steps on scale reading accuracy. *J. exper. Psychol.*, 1952, **43**, 179–186.

54Coonan, T. J. & Klemmer, E. T. Interpolation and reference marks in reading a linear scale at brief exposures. *AFCRC-TR-55-3*. Operational Applications Laboratory, Bolling AFB, Washington, D.C., 1955.

55Eriksen, C. W. & Hake, H. W. Absolute judgments as a function of the stimulus range and the number of stimulus and response categories. *J. exper. Psychol.*, 1955, **49**, 323–332.

56Eriksen, C. W. Multidimensional stimulus differences and accuracy of discrimination. Wright Air Development Center, *WADC Technical Report 54-165*, 1954.

57Cf. Miller, G. A. The magical number seven, plus or minus two: some limits on our capacity for processing information. *Op. cit.*, 86.

58Klemmer, E. T. & Frick, F. C. Assimilation of information from dot and matrix patterns. *J. exper. Psychol.*, 1953, **45**, 15–19.

59Beebe-Center, J. G., Rogers, M. S., & O'Connell, D. N. *Op. cit.*

60Pollack, I. The information of elementary auditory displays. *Op. cit.*, 745–746.

Also Pollack, I. The information of elementary auditory displays. II. *Op. cit.*, 767–768.

Cf. also Miller, G. A. The magical number seven, plus or minus two: some limits on our capacity for processing information. *Op. cit.*, 87.

61Halsey, R. M. & Chapanis, A. Chromaticity-confusion contours in a complex viewing situation. *J. Opt. Soc. Amer.*, 1954, **44**, 442–454.

62Geldard, F. A. Some neglected possibilities of communication. *Science*, 1960, **131**, 1583–1588.

63Pollack, I. & Ficks, L. Information of elementary multidimensional auditory displays. *J. Acoust. Soc. Amer.*, 1954, **26**, 155–158.

64Eriksen, C. W. *Op. cit.*

65Miller, G. A. The magical number seven, plus or minus two: some limits on our capacity for processing information. *Op. cit.*, 88.

66Amassian, V. E. *Op. cit.*, 431.

67Hayes, J. R. M. Memory span for several vocabularies as a function of vocabulary size. In *Quart. Prog. Rep. Acoustics Laboratory*. Cambridge, Mass.: M.I.T. January–June 1952.

Also Pollack, I. The assimilation of sequentially encoded information. *Amer. J. Psychol.*, 1953, **66**, 421–435.

68Miller, G. A. The magical number seven, plus or minus two: some limits on our capacity for processing information. *Op. cit.*, 92, 93.

69Smith, S. Report before the Eastern Psychological Association, 1954.

Cf. Miller, G. A. The magical number seven, plus or minus two: some limits on our capacity for processing information. *Op. cit.*, 93–95.

70Chapman, D. W. Relative effects of determinate and indeterminate Aufgaben. *Amer. J. Psychol.*, 1932, **44**, 163–174.

71Kaufman, E. L., Lord, M. W., Reese, T. W., & Volkman, J. The discrimination of visual numbers. *Amer. J. Psychol.*, 1949, **62**, 498–525.

72Osborne, J. W., Quastler, H., Tweedell, K. S., & Wilson, K. C. Human performance in information transmission. III. *Technical Report R-68*. Urbana, Illinois: Control Systems Laboratory, Univ. of Illinois, 1955, 1–70.

73Staff Bio-Systems Group. Human performance in information transmission. IV. *Technical Report R-69*. Urbana, Illinois: Control Systems Laboratory, Univ. of Illinois, 1956.

Also Glezer, V. D., Tsukkerman, I. I., & Psykunova, T. M. On the channel capacity of vision. *Moving Picture and Television Technique*, 1961, **2**, 27–32.

Also Sziklai, G. C. Some studies on the speed of visual perception. *IRE Trans. Inform. Theory*, 1956, IT-2(3), 125.

74Quastler, H. & Wulff, V. J. Human performance in information transmission. I. *Technical Report R-62*. Urbana, Illinois: Control Systems Laboratory, Univ. of Illinois, 1955.

Also Quastler, H. & Wulff, V. J. Human performance in information transmission. II. *Technical Report R-62*. Urbana, Illinois: Control Systems Laboratory, Univ. of Illinois, 1955.

75Quastler, H. & Brabb, B. *Op. cit.*

76Cf. Quastler, H. Studies of human channel capacity. *Op. cit.*, 362.

77Quastler, H. & Wulff, V. J. *Op. cit.*, II, 62–59 and 62–60. Reprinted by permission.

78*Ibid.*, II, 62–61. Reprinted by permission.

79Quastler, H. & Wulff, V. J. *Op. cit.*, I, 62–14. Reprinted by permission.

80Vince, M. A. Rapid response sequences and the psychological refractory period. *Brit. J. Psychol.*, 1949, **40**, 23–40.

81Wagner, R. C., Fitts, P. M., & Noble, M. E. Preliminary investigations of speed and load as dimensions of psychomotor tasks. *AFPTRC Research Report No. 54-45*. AF Personnel and Training Research Center, Lackland AFB, Texas, 1954.

82Klemmer, E. T. & Muller, P. F., Jr. The rate of handling information: key pressing responses to light patterns. *J. motor Behav.*, 1969, **1**, 135–147.

Cf. also Klemmer, E. T. & Muller, P. F., Jr. The rate of handling information: key pressing responses to light patterns. *HFORL Memo Report No. 34*. USAF, ARDC. March 1953.

83Alluisi, E. A., Muller, P. F., Jr., & Fitts, P. M. An information analysis of verbal and motor responses in a forced-pace serial task. *J. exper. Psychol.*, 1957, **53**, 153–158.

84Alluisi, E. A. & Muller, P. F., Jr. Rate of information transfer with seven symbolic visual codes: motor and verbal responses. *WADC Technical Report 56-226*. Wright Air Development Center, Ohio, 1956.

Also Alluisi, E. A. & Muller, P. F., Jr. Verbal motor responses to seven symbolic visual codes: a study in S-R compatibility. *J. exper. Psychol.*, 1958, **55**, 247–254.

[85]Jeantheau, G. The differential effects of speed and load stress on task performance. *WADC Technical Report 59-7.* Aero Medical Laboratory. Wright-Patterson Air Force Base, Ohio, July 1959.

[86]Jackson, K. F. Behavior in controlling a combination of systems. *Ergonomics*, 1958, **2**, 52–62.

[87]Mackworth, J. S. & Mackworth, N. H. The overlapping of signals for decisions. *Amer. J. Psychol.*, 1956, **69**, 26–47.

[88]Hartman, B. O. Time and load factors in astronaut proficiency. In B. Flaherty (Ed.). *Psychophysiological aspects of space flight.* New York: Columbia Univ. Press, 1961, 278–308.

Also Hartman, B. O. & McKenzie, R. E. Systems operator proficiency. *Report 61–40.* U.S. School of Aerospace Med., 1961.

[89]Fiske, D. W. & Maddi, S. R. *Functions of varied experience.* Homewood, Illinois: Dorsey Press, 1961, 11–68.

NOTE: When individuals with high cortical reactivity receive inputs which produce high arousal, heart rate slows. This is more common during periods of information overload.

Cf. Silverman, J. Variations in cognitive control and psychophysiological defense in the schizophrenias. *Psychosom. Med.*, 1967, **29**, 243.

Also Lacey, J. I. Somatic response patterning and stress: some revisions of activation theory. In M. H. Appley & R. Trumbull (Eds.). *Psychological stress: issues in research.* New York: Appleton-Century-Crofts, 1966, 14–37.

[90]Cf. Meldman, M. J. PRR study No. 8: the signs and symptoms of hyperattentionism. *Diseases of nervous Sys.*, 1965, **26**, 800.

[91]Broadbent, D. E. The role of auditory localization in attention and memory span. *J. exper. Psychol.*, 1954, **47**, 191–196.

[92]Stone, S. A. Prior entry in the auditory-tactual complication. *Amer. J. Psychol.*, 1926, **37**, 284–291.

Also Welford, N. T. Estimation of the position of a tactile stimulus in a repeated auditory pattern. *Quart. J. exper. Psychol.*, 1943, **1**, 180–192.

Cf. also Adams, J. A. & Chambers, R. W. Response to simultaneous stimulation of two sense modalities. *J. exper. Psychol.*, 1962, **63**, 198–206.

[93]Broadbent, D. E. Growing points in multichannel communication. *J. Acoust. Soc. Amer.*, 1956, **28**, 535.

[94]Broadbent, D. E. Attention and memory in listening to speech. *Report No. 207.* Med. Res. Council, Appl. Psychol. Unit, Cambridge, England, 1954, 4.

[95]Broadbent, D. E. The role of auditory localization in attention and memory span. *Op. cit.*, 191–196.

[96]Broadbent, D. E. Listening between and during practised auditory distractions. *Brit. J. Psychol.*, 1956, **47**, 51–60.

[97]Gregg, L. W. & Brogden, W. J. The effect of simultaneous visual stimulation on absolute auditory sensitivity. *J. exper. Psychol.*, 1952, **43**, 179–186.

[98]Bahrick, H. P., Noble, M., & Fitts, P. M. Extra-task performance as a measure of learning a primary task. *J. exper. Psychol.*, 1954, **48**, 298–302.

[99]Broadbent, D. E. Growing points in multichannel communication. *Op. cit.*, 533–535.

NOTE: Wilcox (Wilcox, R. H. A measure of coherence for human information filters. *Psychometrika*, 1957, **22**, 269–274) has developed a measure of the effectiveness of the *filtering* adjustment process to information input overload. He meant it to be applied to organisms—human beings—but it apparently could also be applied to other levels of living systems. When systems receive inputs of information at rates greater than they can handle, some items are processed immediately and precisely, and others are *filtered* out, to be either rejected or processed later. If its decision rules for such *filtering* are unambiguous, the system can be said to be operating coherently. But if it makes some selections by chance or alternates between several sets of rules by chance, it is operating at least partly on a random basis. A schematic representation of a human information *filter* is presented, in which the task is to divide the total set of information inputs into two subsets according to unambiguous rules, so that the subset that is selected and responded to in a given way is made up of items, each of which has a higher priority than the subset that is rejected by some other response characteristic. This is complete coherence. If errors in *filtering* are made, however, some of the inputs from the lower priority subset may be accepted and some from the higher priority subset rejected. If L is the normalized overload and A is the normalized number of correct selections, Wilcox's measure of filtering coherence C is the normalized difference between the total number of correct selections and that portion of the correct selections which was obtained by guessing. This measure is applicable in any situation where several methods exist for determining priorities among items of input information. Then, if coherence is plotted against the input overload rate, the method of allocating priorities which produces the least variance in the system will become apparent. Individual differences in coherence from one system to another can also be revealed by this measure.

[100]Broadbent, D. E. Growing points in multichannel communication. *Op. cit.*, 534. Reprinted by permission.

[101]Broadbent, D. E. A mechanical model for human attention and immediate memory. *Psychol. Rev.*, 1957, **64**, 205–215.

[102]Weick, K. E. The twigging of overload. In H. B. Pepinsky (Ed.). *People and information.* New York: Pergamon Press, 1970, 67–129.

[103]Mierke, K. *Wille und Leistung.* Göttingen: Verlag f. Psychologie, Dr. C. J. Hogrefe, 1955, 179–184.

[104]Klemmer, E. T. Numerical error checking. *J. appl. Psychol.*, 1959, **43**, 316–320.

[105]Krulee, G. K., Gapp, A., Landi, D. M., & Manelski, D. M. Organizing factors and immediate memory span. *Percept. & motor Skills*, 1964, **18**, 535–548.

[106]McHale, J. The changing information environment: a selected topography. *Ekistics*, 1973, **35**, 321–328.

Also Henry, N. Future as information. *Futures*, 1973, **5**, 392–400.

Also Swedish Working Party. *To choose a future.* Stockholm: Kungl. Batryckeriet, 1974, 99.

[107]Wells, H. G. *The salvaging of civilization.* New York: Macmillan, 1921, 141–166.

Also Wells, H. G. *The shape of things to come.* New York: Macmillan, 1933, 420.

Also Wells, H. G. World encyclopaedia. In *World brain.* Garden City, New York: Doubleday, Doran, 1938, especially 3–35 and 83–88.

Cf. also Kochen, M. (Ed.). *The growth of knowledge.* New York: Wiley, 1967.

[108]Ortega y Gassett, J. Man must tame the book. *Wilson Bull.*, 1936, **10**, 305–307.

[109]Bush, V. As we may think. *Atlantic Monthly*, 1945, **176**, 101–108.

[110]*Ibid.*, 102. Copyright © 1945, by The Atlantic Monthly Company, Boston, Mass. Reprinted by permission.

[111]Cf. Licklider, J. C. R. *Libraries of the future.* Cambridge, Mass.: M.I.T. Press, 1965.

Also Brown, G. W., Miller, J. G., & Keenan, T. A. *EDUNET: report of the summer study on information networks conducted by the Interuniversity Communications Council (EDUCOM).* New York: Wiley, 1967.

Also Lundstet, S. Information retrieval and psychological research. *J. Psychol.*, 1965, **61**, 81–86.

Also *MEDLARS: 1963–67. Pub. Health Serv. Pub. No. 1823.* Bethesda, Maryland: Nat. Lib. Med., 1968.

Also Overhage, C. F. J. & Harman, R. J. (Eds.). *INTREX: report of a planning conference on information transfer experiments.* Cambridge: M.I.T. Press, 1965, 1.

[112]Cf. Pierce, J. R. Communication. *Sci. Amer.*, 1972, **227**(3), 31–41.

[113]Communication from the American Telephone and Telegraph Company.

[114]Lerner, W. (Ed.). *Statistical abstract of the United States.* (91st ed.) Wash., D.C.: U.S. Dept. of Commerce, 1970, 535.

[115]Bird, C. *The communications explosion in the president's office. PA Special Study No. 40.* New York: Presidents Association, 1969.

[116]Toffler, A. *Future shock.* New York: Random House, 1970, 139–141, 305–325.

[117]*Ibid.*, 306–307.

[118]*Ibid.*, 319–322.

[119]Cf. Milgram, S. The experience of living in cities. *Science*, 1970, **167**, 1461.

[120]*Ibid.*, 1462. Copyright 1970 by the American Association for the Advancement of Science. Reprinted by permission.

[121]*Ibid.*, 1465. Copyright 1970 by the American Association for the Advancement of Science. Reprinted by permission.

[122]Cf. Muller, P. F., Jr., Sidorsky, R. C., Slivinske, A. J., Alluisi, E. A., & Fitts, P. M. The symbolic coding of information on cathode ray tubes and similar displays. *WADC Technical Report 55–375.* Wright Air Development Center. Columbus, Ohio: Ohio State Univ. Research Foundation, 1955.

[123]Hick, W. E. Why the human operator? *Trans. Soc. Instrument Technol.*, 1952, **4**, 67–77.

[124]Breuer, H. Evaluation of the information throughput flux. *Acta psychol.*, 1969, **31**, 145–157.

[125]Lanzetta, J. T. & Roby, T. B. Effects of work-group structure and certain task variables on group performance. *J. abnorm. soc. Psychol.*, 1956, **53**, 307–314.

[126]Cf. Roby, T. B. & Lanzetta, J. T. An investigation of task performance as a function of certain aspects of work-group structure. *Report IN-56-74.* Air Force Personnel and Training Research Center, 1956.

[127]Lanzetta, J. T. & Roby, T. B. Group learning and communication as a function of task and structure "demands." *J. abnorm. soc. Psychol.*, 1957, **55**, 121–131.

[128]Roby, T. B. & Lanzetta, J. T. Work-group structure, communication, and group performance. *Sociometry*, 1956, **19**, 105–113.

[129]Elkind, J. I. Characteristics of simple manual control systems. *Technical Report 111.* Cambridge, Mass.: M.I.T. Lincoln Labs., 1956, 108.

[130]Schroder, H. M., Driver, M. J., & Streufert, S. *Human information processing: individuals and groups functioning in complex social situations.* New York: Holt, Rinehart, & Winston, 1967.

[131]*Ibid.*, 15–28; 149–154.

[132]*Ibid.*, 154–157.

[133]Streufert, S. Increasing failure and response rate in complex decision making. *J. exper. soc. Psychol.*, 1969, **5**, 310–323.

[134]Streufert, S., Suedfeld, P., & Driver, M. J. Conceptual structure, information search, and information utilization. *J. Personality soc. Psychol.*, 1965, **2**, 736–740.

[135]Chapman, R. L. & Kennedy, J. L. The background and implications of the Systems Research Laboratory studies. Air Force human engineering, personnel, and training research. *Technical Report 56-8.* Air Research and Development Command. 1956, 72.

[136]Kennedy, J. L. Personal communication.

[137]Fritz, E. L. & Grier, G. W., Jr. Empirical entropy: a study of information flow in air traffic control. *Technical Report R-54.* Urbana, Illinois: Control Systems Laboratory, Univ. of Illinois, 1954, 1–21.

[138]Chapman, R. L. & Kennedy, J. L. *Op. cit.*

[139]Versace, J. The effect of emergencies and communications availability with differing entry rates. *WADC Technical Report 56-70.* Dayton: Wright Air Development Center, 1956.

[140]*Ibid.*, 8.

[141]Lee, A. M. Some aspects of a control and communication system. *Oper. Res. Quart.*, 1959, **10**, 206–216.

[142]Bennis, W. G. A funny thing happened on the way to the future. *Amer. Psychol.*, 1970, **25**, 607.

[143]Dubin, R. *The world of work: industrial society and human relations.* Englewood Cliffs, N.J.: Prentice-Hall, 1958, 228–229.

[144]Meier, R. L. *A communications theory of urban growth.* Cambridge: M.I.T. Press, 1962, 135.

[145]Katz, D. & Kahn, R. L. *The social psychology of organizations.* New York: Wiley, 1966, 231–235.

[146]Wiener, N. Problems of organization. *Bull. Menninger Clinic*, 1953, **17**, 134. Reprinted by permission.

[147]*Los Angeles Times*, January 8, 1971, 1, 26, 27.

[148]*Washington Post*, December 12, 1970, 43.

[149]Hoehling, A. A. *The week before Pearl Harbor.* New York: Norton, 1963, 92–93. Copyright © 1963 A. A. Hoehling. Reprinted by permission of the author's agent, Lurton Blassingame.

[150]Meier, R. L. Information input overload in social organizations, IV: the measurement and analysis of behavior in a modern library. *M.H.R.I. Report 9.* Ann Arbor: Mental Health Research Institute, Univ. of Michigan, 1960.

Also Meier, R. L. Social change in communications-oriented institutions. *M.H.R.I. Report 10.* Ann Arbor: Mental Health Research Institute, Univ. of Michigan, 1960.

Also Meier, R. L. *A communications theory of urban growth. Op. cit.*, 74–83.

Also Meier, R. L. Information input overload: features of growth in communications-oriented institutions. In F. Massarik & P. Ratoosh (Eds.). *Mathematical explorations in behavioral science.* Homewood, Illinois: R. D. Irwin & Dorsey Press, 1965, 233–273.

[151]NOTE: Meier calculated the number of bits in an average library catalog card and book or other document by using the method described by Shannon (Shannon, C. E. Prediction and entropy of printed English. *Bell Sys. tech. J.*, 1951, **30**, 50–64) for determining the information content of English prose.

[152]Based on a personal communication from W. J. Horvath.

[153]Meier, R. L. *A communications theory of urban growth. Op. cit.*, 73–74. Reprinted from *A communications theory of urban growth* by R. L. Meier by permission of The M.I.T. Press, Cambridge, Massachusetts.

[154]Greer, P. *Washington Post*, December 20, 1970, A14. Reprinted by permission.

[155]Calhoun, J. B. Determinants of social organization exemplified in a single population of domesticated rats. *N.Y. Acad. Sci. Trans.*, 1961, **25**, 437–442.

Also Calhoun, J. B. Population density and social pathology. *Sci. Amer.*, 1962, **206**(2), 139–147.

Also Alsop, S. Dr. Calhoun's horrible mousery. *Newsweek,* Aug. 17, 1970, 96.

[156]Spitz, R. A. The derailment of dialogue: stimulus overload, action cycles, and the completion gradient. *J. Amer. Psychoanal. Assn.,* 1964, **12,** 752–775.

[157]Lipowski, Z. J. The conflict of Buridan's ass or some dilemmas of affluence: the theory of attractive stimulus overload. *Amer. J. Psychiat.,* 1970, **127,** 273–279.

Also Lipowski, Z. J. Surfeit of attractive information inputs: a hallmark of our environment. *Behav. Sci.,* 1971, **16,** 467–471.

[158]Lipowski, Z. J. Sensory and information inputs overload: behavioral effects. *Comp. Psychiat.,* 1975, **16,** 199–221.

[159]Ullmann, C. A. Private communication.

[160]French, J. R. P., Jr. & Kahn, R. L. A programmatic approach to studying the industrial environment and mental health. *J. soc. Issues,* 1962, **18,** 3, 22.

[161]Flinn, D. E. Functional states of altered awareness during flight. *Aerospace Med.,* 1965, **36,** 540–541.

[162]Galant, J. S. Die Fiebergehandlung der Dementia praecox. *Monatsschr. Psychiat. Neurol.,* 1930, **76,** 86–101.

[163]Menninger, K. A. The amelioration of mental disease by influenza. *J. Amer. Med. Assn.,* 1930, **94,** 631.

[164]Luby, E. D., Gottlieb, J. S., Cohen, B. D., Rosenbaum, G., & Domino, E. F. Model psychoses and schizophrenia. *Amer. J. Psychiat.,* 1962, **119,** 61–67.

Cf. also Yates, A. J. Psychological deficit. *Ann. Rev. Psychol.* 1966, **17,** 129.

[165]Stevens, J. D. Membrane permeability in schizophrenia. *Diseases nervous System,* 1964, **25,** 21–28.

[166]Jaffe, J. Language of the dyad, a method of interaction analysis in psychiatric interviews. *Psychiatry,* 1958, **21,** 249–258. Reprinted by permission.

[167]Weiner, M. F. Private communication. Reprinted by permission.

[168]Yates, A. J. *Op. cit.,* 111–144.

[169](a) Belmont, I., Birch, H. G., Klein, D. F., & Pollack, M. Perceptual evidence of CNS dysfunction in schizophrenia. *Arch. gen. Psychiat.,* 1964, **10,** 395–408.

(b) Venables, P. H. Changes due to noise in the threshold of fusion of paired light flashes in schizophrenics and normals. *Brit. J. Soc. Clin. Psychol.,* 1963, **2,** 94–99.

Also Venables, P. H. The relation between level of skin potential and fusion of paired light flashes in schizophrenic and normal subjects. *J. psychiat. Research,* 1963, **1,** 279–287.

(c) Snyder, S., Rosenthal, D., & Taylor, I. A. Perceptual closure in schizophrenia. *J. abnorm. soc. Psychol.,* 1961, **63,** 131–136.

(d) Robertson, J. P. S. Perceptual-motor disorders in chronic schizophrenia. *Brit. J. Soc. Clin. Psychol.,* 1962, **1,** 1–6.

(e) Weckowicz, T. E. Shape constancy in schizophrenic patients. *J. abnorm. soc. Psychol.,* 1964, **68,** 177–183.

[170]Chapman, J. & McGhie, A. A comparative study of disordered attention in schizophrenia. *J. ment. Sci.,* 1962, **108,** 487–500.

Also McGhie, A., Chapman, J., & Lawson, J. S. Disturbances in selective attention in schizophrenia. *Proc. Roy. Soc. Med.,* 1964, **57,** 419–422.

[171]Chapman, J. & McGhie, A. Echopraxia in schizophrenia. *Brit. J. Psychiat.,* 1964, **110,** 365–374.

[172]Lawson, J. S., McGhie, A., & Chapman, J. Perception of speech in schizophrenia. *Brit. J. Psychiat.,* 1964, **110,** 375–380.

Also Nidorf, L. J. The role of meaningfulness in the serial learning of schizophrenics. *J. clin. Psychol.,* 1964, **20,** 92.

[173]Pishkin, V., Smith, T. E., & Liebowitz, H. W. The influence of symbolic stimulus value on perceived size in chronic schizophrenia. *J. consult. Psychol.,* 1962, **26,** 323–330.

[174]Harwood, E. & Naylor, G. F. K. Nature and extent of basic cognitive deterioration in a sample of institutionalized mental patients. *Australian J. Psychol.,* 1963, **15,** 29–36.

[175]Payne, R. W., Ancevich, S. S., & Laverty, S. G. Overinclusive thinking in symptom-free schizophrenics. *Can. Psychiat. Assoc. J.,* 1963, **8,** 225–234.

[176]Flavell, J. H., Draguns, J., Feinberg, L. D., & Budin, W. A microgenetic approach to word association. *J. abnorm. soc. Psychol.,* 1958, **57,** 1–8.

[177]Grimes, C. & McGhie, A. Stimulus overload in schizophrenia. *Canad. J. Behav. Sci.,* 1973, **5,** 101–110.

[178]Danev, S. G., Dewinter, C. R., & Wartna, G. F. Information processing and psychophysiological functions in a task with and without time stress. *Activ. nerv. super. (Praha),* 1972, **14,** 8–12.

[179]Miller, J. G. Psychological aspects of communication overloads. In R. W. Waggoner & D. J. Carek (Eds.). *International psychiatry clinics: communication in clinical practice.* Boston: Little, Brown & Co., 1964, 218–223.

[180]Yates, A. J. *Op. cit.,* 128. Reprinted by permission.

[181]Cf. Miller, J. G. Information input overload and psychopathology. *Amer. J. Psychiat.,* 1960, **116,** 695–704.

Also Miller, J. G. Sensory overloading. In B. E. Flaherty (Ed.) *Psychophysiological aspects of space flight.* New York: Columbia Univ. Press, 1961, 215–224.

Also Miller, J. G. Information input overload. In M. C. Yovits, G. T. Jacobi, & G. D. Goldstein (Eds.). *Self-organizing systems.* Washington, D. C.: Spartan Books, 1962, 61–78.

Also Miller, J. G. The individual as an information processing system. In W. S. Fields & W. Abbott (Eds.). *Information storage and neural control.* Springfield, Ill.: Charles C Thomas, 1963, 1–28.

Also Miller, J. G. Adjusting to overloads of information. In D. McK. Rioch & E. A. Weinstein (Eds.). *Disorders of communication.* Baltimore: Williams & Wilkins, 1964, 87–100.

Also Miller, J. G. Psychological aspects of communication overloads. In R. W. Waggoner & D. J. Carek (Eds.). *International psychiatry clinics: communication in clinical practice. Op. cit.,* 201–224.

Also Miller, J. G. Coping with administrators' information overload. *J. med. Ed.,* 1964, **29**(11, Part 2) 47–54 and 182–189.

Also Miller, J. G. The dynamics of informational adjustment processes. In J. Masserman (Ed.). *Science and psychoanalysis, VIII: communication and community.* New York: Grune and Stratton, 1965, 38–48.

[182]NOTE: These researches were supported by Department of the Army contracts DA-49-007-MD-575, DA-49-007-MD-684, and Project MICHIGAN (DA-36-039-sc-78801; USPHS grants MY-1871 and MH 08607; and a grant from the Carnegie Corporation of New York.

[183]NOTE: The report of this experiment is adopted from Horvath, W. J., Halick, P., Peretz, B., & Miller, J. G. Precision measurements of latency in single nerve fibers. *M.H.R.I. Preprint* 115. Ann Arbor: Mental Health Research Institute, Univ. of Michigan, 1963.

Cf. also Horvath, W. J., Halick, P., Peretz, B., & Miller, J. G. Precision measurements of latency in single nerve fibers. *Proc. 4th Internat. Conf. Medical Electronics.* New York: IRE, 1961, 79.

[184]Stämpfli, R. Untersuchungen an der einzelnen, lebenden Nervenfaser des Frosches. Die Preparation der einzelnen

Nervenfaser. *Helvetica physiologica et pharmacologica Acta,* 1946, **4,** 411.

[185]McGill, W. & Quastler, H. Standardized nomenclature: an attempt. In H. Quastler (Ed.). *Information theory in psychology.* Glencoe, Ill.: Free Press, 1955, 83–92.

[186]Miller, G. A. & Madow, W. G. On the maximum likelihood estimate of the Shannon-Wiener measure of information. In R. D. Luce, R. R. Bush, & E. Galanter (Eds.). *Readings in mathematical psychology. I.* New York: Wiley, 1963, 448–469.

NOTE: An experiment designed somewhat like ours, but employing a different mode of data analysis, was carried out to test a theory of psychological development in stages between the ages of 7 and 23.

Cf. Isaac, D. J. & O'Connor, B. M. Use of loss of skill under stress to test a theory of psychological development. *Human Relations,* 1973, **26,** 487–496.

[187]NOTE: In order to show the overload phenomenon to best advantage, we decided to include input rates which could be processed by human organisms, groups, and organizations, at least to the extent that the initial portion of the curve of information output plotted as a function of the input rate would show a positive slope. This experimental strategy produced highly skewed distributions of the measure of information transmitted or output for the first two input rates and contributed to the heterogeneity of variance. As a result it was appropriate to use distribution-free methods of statistical analysis.

The use of input rates well within the processing capability of the system produced distributions in the measures of various adjustment processes which were difficult to treat statistically. Further, the freedom of a system to employ any of the possible adjustments provided for much variation from one experimental run to another in which adjustments were used. For example, seven *O*-1 subjects never used the *abstraction* adjustment, and at all the input rates slower than 7.50 bits per s the average *abstracting* score of the twenty-four *O*-1 subjects was always less than 1 percent. Thus, for this adjustment, the distribution of scores at each of the slowest three input rates consisted essentially of one point, 0, yielding both a mean and a variance of 0. And for each of the three fastest rates, there were at least seven scores of 0. These data gave rise to large variances and skewed or bimodal distributions. Consequently, distribution-free statistics were also appropriate to analyze the measures of adjustment processes. For the above reasons we employed distribution-free statistical techniques in analyzing the data from all the experiments at the organism, group, and organization levels.

There may be some question whether the data from each of the experiments at the organism, group, and organization levels can legitimately be treated as independent sets of data because the upper-level systems consisted of subsets of systems from the organism level studies (see pages 183 and 188). Assuming that they were essentially independent, however, a variable measured at three levels—organism, group, and organization (*e.g.,* system levels)—can be investigated by the Kruskall-Wallis one-way analysis of variance by ranks *H.* We used this statistic to evaluate the null hypothesis that no difference existed in a variable among the levels. The Mann-Whitney *U* test was used to evaluate differences between two independent systems (*e.g.,* organism *vs.* group, or organism *vs.* organization). Differences among three or more measures known to be correlated (*i.e.,* repeated scores of performance of the same system at the same or different input rates) were tested by the Friedman two-way analysis of variance by

ranks χ^2. Comparisons involving two sets of correlated measures were evaluated by the Wilcoxon matched-pairs signed-ranks test *T* or the sign test. Interactions between the correlated and independent dimensions (*e.g.,* input rate by levels of systems) were evaluated by a χ^2 test, a *U* test on difference scores, or a *U* test on appropriate combined cells from the matrix. For correlational analyses, Kendall's rank correlation coefficient τ and his coefficient of concordance *W* were used. Finally, the probabilities reported are one-tailed unless specified otherwise. The one-tailed figures may be converted to two-tailed probabilities by doubling them. For example, a reported one-tailed $p = .05$ converts to a two-tailed $p = .10$, a change from significance to nonsignificance or low significance.

[188]NOTE: That the median curves for the two experiments were statistically similar was shown by a significant τ of +0.87 between them. The variances yielded a τ of +1.00 between findings from the experiments, with small individual differences at the two slowest input rates, large individual differences at the next two input rates, and substantially smaller individual differences at the two fastest rates. The differences in median output rates were small at each input rate, but the overall *U* test, neglecting input rate, approached significance ($p = .0505$). This indicated that, overall, the output rate in experiment *O*-1 was higher than in experiment *O*-2. This probably resulted from the differential drop in output rates at the highest three input rates.

[189]NOTE: The similarity between the median percent *omission* curves for the *O*-1 and *O*-2 experiments was indicated by the significant τ of +0.97 between them. The *U* test between experiments on the data, neglecting input rate, was not significant even though the median was higher for *O*-2 on each of the six input rates. The difference between the averages of the six medians, however, was only 2.42 percent.

[190]NOTE: The similarity between the median percent *error* curves for the *O*-1 and *O*-2 experiments was attested by the significant τ of +0.87 between them. Even though the *O*-2 medians were consistently smaller from input rate 5.62 bits per s to input rate 15.00, this did not produce a significant difference by the *U* test between the two experiments. This is reasonable in the light of the small difference of 3 percent between the averages of the six medians.

[191]NOTE: The similarity between the median percent *queuing* curves for the *O*-1 and *O*-2 experiments was indicated by the significant τ of +1.00 between them. The *U* test comparing experiments *O*-1 and *O*-2 was not significant and neither was the comparison by the *U* test of the output rates in the two experiments at an input rate of 5.62 bits per s, where the difference between the median output rates was largest, 34 percent. The variances were large for the moderately fast input rates, but they and the output rates at 15 bits per s input rate showed strikingly reduced variability among individual subjects.

[192]NOTE: The similarity between the median percent *abstracting* curves for the *O*-1 and *O*-2 experiments was indicated by the significant τ of +0.87 between them.

[193]NOTE: This significance was indicated by the *U* test.

[194]NOTE: The *U* test was used to determine whether there was a statistically significant difference in output rates between the various group types in the *G*-1, *G*-2, and *G*-3 experiments, neglecting input rate. The similarity in the shapes of the three median curves was indicated by a significant coefficient of concordance *W* among the three sets, for the three experiments, of the six median output rates.

[195]NOTE: The *T* test indicated which increases in input rates in the three group experiments elicited significant differences

in median *omission* curves. The *U* test was used to indicate whether the differences in the percents *omission* in these experiments were significant. The significant coefficient of concordance *W* showed that the shapes of the three curves were similar.

[196]NOTE: The *T* test indicated which increases in input rates in the three group experiments elicited significant differences in the median *error* curves. The degree of similarity of the curves for *G*-1 and *G*-2, as compared to *G*-3, was measured by τ, and the similarity of shapes of all three was indicated by a significant coefficient of concordance *W*.

[197]NOTE: The *T* test indicated which increases in input rates in the three group experiments elicited significant differences in the median *queuing* curves. The *U* test indicated that the percent of *queuing* in *G*-1 was significantly different from *G*-2 and *G*-3, but that the latter two were not significantly different from each other.

[198]NOTE: As indicated by significant *T* tests.

[199]NOTE: As indicated by the τ test.

[200]NOTE: As indicated by the τ test.

[201]NOTE: As indicated by the τ test.

[202]Jay, E. S. & McCornack, R. L. Information processing under overload conditions. *Amer. Psychol.*, 1960, **15,** 496.

[203]NOTE: As indicated by a significant coefficient of concordance *W*.

[204]NOTE: The *U* test was used to determine whether there was a statistically significant difference in output rates between the node and decider structures. Significant coefficients of concordance *W* indicated the similarity of the shapes of the curves.

[205]NOTE: As indicated by a significant coefficient of concordance *W*.

[206]NOTE: As indicated by a significant coefficient of concordance *W*.

The Cell

A cell is a minute, unitary mass of intricately organized protoplasm. All living systems either are free-
living cells or have cells as their least complex living
components. This is as true of Monaco as it is of a
French restaurant, as true of a covey of pheasants as it
is of a worm, as true of a goose liver as it is of a truffle.
Free-living cells are ordinarily totipotential, while
cells that are aggregated into the tissues of organs,
organisms, or higher levels of systems are usually
specialized for certain processes, partipotential, and
therefore dependent upon other systems for some critical processes.

Free-living cells are often referred to as "microorganisms," and all multicellular organisms have evolved
from primitive free-living single cells. In the light of
this historical continuity and the fact that free-living
cells carry out their critical processes independently,
such cells are considered by some to be organisms.
And indeed they interact with the same environment
and adapt in many of the same ways as multicellular
organisms. But free-living cells are no more organisms
than are the white cells in a mammal's blood. Their
subsystems and components are not organs or tissues
composed of cells, but are similar to the subsystems of
the cells which are aggregated into the tissues and
organs of organisms. In general living systems theory
a system is considered to be one level higher than the
preponderance of its subsystems and components
(see page 25). Adhering to such a classification maintains the progression from the molecular constituents of living cells through the tissue and organ
levels to the organism. Consequently I define the level

of cells to include free-living cells and discuss both
them and aggregated cells in this chapter.

Slime molds, such as *Myxomycetes* or *Myxamoebae*,
complicate the definition of the cell level by spending
part of their life cycles as free-living cells, called plasmodia (see Fig. 6-3x), which are like amoebas and part
as aggregates with some differentiation of function
(see page 361).[1] Under stresses—like lack of food—
and at other times, these cells clump into a multicellular mass which moves as a unit. It has a dominant
apex—with a "receptive" center and a "directive"
center, possibly identical—that obviously constitutes
the decider for the whole multicellular body. The mass
becomes plantlike, forming a stem with branches,
bearing fruiting bodies at their ends. The signal that
brings them together has been shown to be a chemical
which flows from one cell to another. It has been
named acrasin, for a seductive witch in Spenser's
Faerie Queen who attracted lovers from afar by her
sorcery.[2] Although there is some specialization of processes or division of labor among the cells during the
phase of aggregation, they do not appear different
from one another when in the free state. My nomenclature requires that the aggregate be considered an
organism, just as a sponge, which has little differentiation among its component cells, is an organism.

Viruses occupy a classification near the shadowy
border between living and nonliving systems. The
present consensus of experts is that they are not alive.
In their general structure and chemical properties they
resemble large, inert chemical molecules. Some can be
crystallized, dissolved, and recrystallized. Once

assembled they do not ingest, convert, or produce matter-energy inputs, nor do they grow or locomote. Butler notes that they lack some critical subsystems:

It seems that a certain degree of complexity is needed before an organism [Butler would have been more precise if he had said "living system"] can maintain itself as an independent living thing with the ability to live on its environment and grow and multiply. . . . This ability involves a most complicated apparatus of reactions which will extract raw materials and energy sources from the food and use them not only to maintain life but to make all the enzymes and proteins required. The virus particles do not have this ability, but they can make use of the apparatus which is provided by their host cells.[3]

Like living systems, however, viruses have genes which can undergo mutation and, by making use of the producer of a living cell, they can organize reproduction of themselves. They do not have a complete decider, just the DNA (in some, RNA) but not the cytoplasmic components (see pages 272 and 273).

Not having all essential critical subsystems complete, they are necessarily parasitic upon the cells which contain them (see page 274).

The Rickettsiae are a family of microorganisms falling between viruses and bacteria. Like viruses they are parasitic, but they can convert and/or produce some of their own food.[4] As Stanley and Valens show, there appears to be "a single continuous sequence of gradually increasing complexity" which goes from the atom to man.[5] But there is a vast difference between the structure and process of the simplest and of the most complex living system. The metabolism of a bacterium like *Escherichia coli* is quite dissimilar from that of a human cell, although both types of cells carry out the same critical processes. It is a matter of definition as to which point in the evolutionary sequence represents the lowest of the systems to be called living.[6] I shall call cells living systems, considering *Rickettsias*, viruses, and less complex systems nonliving, since they do not have all the characteristics of living systems.

Thousands of incredibly intricate parts are packed into a cell's minute volume. Persons who have not studied cells often cannot conceive that their degree of complexity justifies comparison of their system characteristics with those of higher-level systems. The minimum complexity (negentropy) in structural organization (*i.e.*, both units and their relationships) of a bacterial cell, *Bacillus pycnoticus,* was computed by Linschitz.[7] His calculations were based on measurements of the growth of this bacillus. He found the informational complexity of this type of cell to be of the order of 10^{13} bits per cell. This value falls within the range of values calculated for the complexity of a cell by Dancoff and Quastler using an entirely different procedure based on the genetic characteristics of cells.

In order to understand the structure and process of cells, the lowest level of living systems, it is necessary to know what are the structures at the two nonliving levels below: the molecules, which are subsubsystems or subcomponents of cells, and the organelles, which are subsystems or components of cells (see page 25). I shall now briefly describe these constituent molecules and organelles.

Molecules, the subsubsystems or subcomponents of cells. On the average, cells are about 75 to 85 percent water, 10 to 20 percent protein, 2 to 3 percent lipids, 1 percent nucleic acids (DNA and RNA), 1 percent carbohydrate, and 1 percent salt. They contain small amounts of various metals and other substances as well. The composition varies with the type of cell. Of the major categories of molecules, nucleic acids with molecular weights between 400,000 and 1 million are least numerous, followed by proteins, with an average molecular weight of 36,000. The other molecules are much smaller. In typical cells there is only one protein molecule to every 18,000 molecules of water, which has a molecular weight of 18. There are 10 molecules of lipids, 6 of other organic materials, and 100 of inorganic materials to every protein molecule.[8]

Proteins are primary determiners of the structural characteristics of protoplasm. They are composed of carbon, hydrogen, oxygen, nitrogen, usually sulfur, and sometimes phosphorus. At times they are found in complexes with metallic elements. These elements, in various combinations, form 20 different common organic acids with (NH_2) groups, which are called *amino acids*. These amino acids are: lysine, asparagine, arginine, serine, threonine, isoleucine, methionine, glutamic acid, aspartic acid, glycine, alanine, valine, glutamine, histidine, proline, leucine, tyrosine, tryptophane, cysteine, and phenylalanine. Each sort of protein is composed of many amino acids— from about 100 to as many as 10,000—selected from these 20 types and organized in its own unique arrangement. A protein molecule is a chain in which amino acids are united by linking the amino (NH_2) group of one with the organic acid or carboxyl (COOH) group of the next. When each such linkage is formed, one molecule of water separates from it (see Fig. 6-1). This linkage is known as a *peptide bond*. Protein molecules can be decomposed by a reverse process called hydrolysis (see pages 236 and 237). This involves restoring the water molecule at each peptide bond.

Proteins are multimolecular chains combined by such peptide bonds and are therefore also called *polypeptides*. Other sorts of linkages may also occur among such chains, producing exceedingly complicated molecules. The spatial arrangements of protein molecules may be either fibrous (*i.e.*, long strands) or globular. Some fibrous molecules can both stretch and contract (see page 245). Other forms contract but do not stretch. Muscle, epidermis, connective tissues, hair, fibrinogen (essential for blood clotting), and other compo-

Remainder of first   Remainder of second
amino acid molecule   amino acid molecule

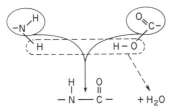

Fig. 6-1 Peptide bond between two amino acids.

nents of the tissues of organisms derive their special characteristics from their particular protein structures.[9]

Enzymes and many other substances produced by cells are also proteins. The names of enzymes usually end in "ase." A few enzymes follow an older nomenclature and end in "in," *e.g.*, rennin, ptyalin, and pepsin. Enzymes are biocatalysts—molecules, some of which use feedback to control the rate of a specific intracellular process, keeping it in a steady state, within an equilibrium range. As the quantity of substances produced by enzymes which are parts of feedback circuits increases, the enzymes decrease the rate of their production and as the quantity decreases, they increase the rate (see pages 258, 275, 286, and 288).

The possible information content of several protein molecules has been calculated by Branson.[10] He made various assumptions to do this. One assumption was that information has a known relation to physical entropy (see pages 13 to 16). He also assumed that the information in a protein molecule has to do with the arrangement of its amino acid residues, that the arrangement of each of these in the chain is independent of the others, and that there are a number of different states (or "complexions") which each amino acid residue can assume at a given place in its molecule. For the insulin molecule, as an example, he calculated that there are 3.55 bits of information per amino acid residue, or since there are 103 such residues in insulin, a total of 365.65 bits per molecule. After making similar computations about a number of kinds of proteins found in cells, Branson concluded that such proteins are usually constructed with remarkably high information, none of the ones he studied having less than 70 percent of the theoretical

maximum for it, and many approaching their respective maximums. This indicates that the design of the protein molecules actually found in living cells is highly efficient from the point of view of information processing.

Water is essential to any cell which is carrying on life processes actively. All the chemical reactions of the matter-energy processing activities important to life take place in watery solutions.

Salts are necessary to the life of cells, both internally and in the fluids surrounding them. A cell placed in distilled water free of salts generally cannot survive. It swells up and bursts. Within cells, salts of potassium are found in highest concentration, and salts of magnesium, sodium, and calcium in lesser concentration. Salts of iron, manganese, copper, vanadium, zinc, nickel, molybdenum, tin, and other metals may be present in small amounts. Certain enzymes essential to the cell's chemical activities must be activated by specific salts.

Lipids are a group of substances which include fats, waxes, phospholipids, and sterols. Lipids are food reserves in some cells (see page 241) and constituents of components of all cells, *e.g.*, lecithin, a phospholipid (see Fig. 6-21).

Carbohydrates, including sugars and starches, are found in cells as food and stored matter-energy, and as component structural materials, importantly in the nucleic acids (see page 217 and Fig. 6-21).

Besides molecules of these major groups, minute amounts of other materials are found in cells. These include *vitamins*, which are frequently parts of enzymes. They are a diverse group of substances, some oil soluble and some water soluble.

Organelles, the subsystems or components of cells. *Protoplasm,* the traditional name for the heterogeneous substance of which all cells are composed (see page 18), gains many of its properties from its complex physical state. *Cytoplasm* is the protoplasm which forms the cell body, exclusive of the nucleus. The cytoplasm consists of the *ground substance* and a number of *organelles,* small "organlike" components of the cell (see Fig. 6-2). The ground cytoplasm of cells contains a framework of several sorts of protein molecules in watery solution, some fibrous, long molecular chains (called *microtubules, microfilaments,* or sometimes *micelles*) and some globular. These form a three-dimensional network, the molecules attracting one another at the points where they intersect.[11] Organelles are complexes of molecules of various kinds with differing structures and processes. Some of these are present in all cells. Others are found only in certain types of cells. They include a *cell membrane* and sometimes other coatings or coverings. *Cilia* or *flagella* may

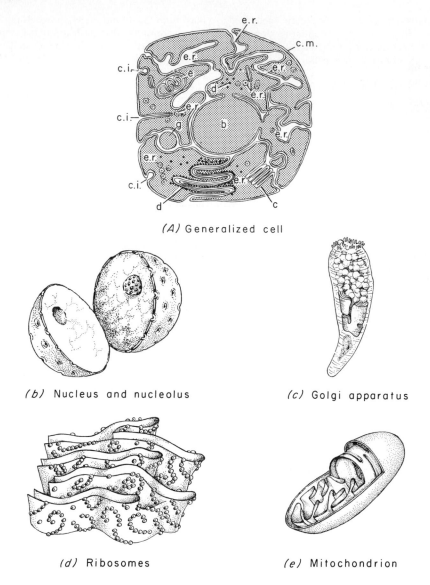

(A) Generalized cell

(b) Nucleus and nucleolus

(c) Golgi apparatus

(d) Ribosomes

(e) Mitochondrion

Fig. 6-2 Generalized cell and chief organelles. (A) Diagram of a hypothetical cell illustrating relationships of the cell membrane to various cell organelles. The cell membrane (c.m.) is shown as a pair of dense lines separated by a light interzone. The invaginations of the cell surface known as *caveolae intracellularis* (c.i.) are indicated in several areas. Some of these extend for a considerable distance into the cell and they may connect with the endoplasmic reticulum (e.r.). The nuclear membrane is composed of flattened sacs of the endoplasmic reticulum, and through the nuclear pores the nucleus (b) is continuous with the cytoplasm. The Golgi apparatus (c) is shown as a modified component of the endoplasmic reticulum. Secretion granules (g) are shown as dense aggregates contained within membranes of the endoplasmic reticulum. Ribosomes (d) are shown scattered through the cytoplasm and in some regions attached to the cytoplasmic surfaces of membranes of the endoplasmic reticulum. In some regions the endoplasmic reticulum is shown as tubules, in either longitudinal section or cross section. One mitochondrion (e) is shown with its cristae formed by invagination of its inner membrane. (From J. D. Robertson. The ultrastructure of cell membranes and their derivatives. *London Biochem. Soc. Symposia,* 1959, **16,** 33.) (b) Nucleus and nucleolus; (c) Golgi apparatus; (d) ribosomes; and (e) mitochondrion. [(c) from M. Neutra & C. P. Leblond. The Golgi apparatus. *Sci. Amer.,* 1969, **220**(2), 102. Copyright © 1969 by Scientific American, Inc. All rights reserved. *Reprinted by permission of Scientific American.*]

extend outward from the membrane, and *kinetosomes,* which activate them, lie just below the membrane at their bases. There may be openings or other specialized areas in this membrane. An arrangement of internal membranes of various degrees of development and diverse structure is found in almost all cells. Some of these membranes have been shown to be continuous with the cell membrane and the nuclear membrane. Some, but not all of these membranes, appear to connect with canaliculi and sacs within the cell. The latter include the *endoplasmic reticulum,* the *sarcoplasmic reticulum* in muscle cells and its *transverse system,* and membranes surrounding the mitochondria, chloroplasts, and perhaps lysosomes. *Golgi apparatuses* or Golgi bodies are present in all cells but are especially prominent in neurons and secretory cells such as glandular and mucus-producing cells. Each one consists of one or more stacks of saccules which are successively more distended from bottom to top with the large carbohydrates which are produced in them. When they are filled, the sacs separate, to be output by the cell.[12] Near or attached to the membranes of cells are *ribosomes,* that are not surrounded by a membrane but that contain a large part of the cellular RNA, on which proteins are produced; *mitochondria,* that are surrounded by membranes and which are the sites where enzymes regulate energy release and conversion; *lysosomes,* that may have membranes and that store enzymes which break complex substances into simpler ones; *chloroplasts,* that have membranes and carry on photosynthesis in some monerans, protistans, and plants (see pages 238 and 239); *secretory granules,* containing the products of some specialized cells; storage or digestive *vacuoles; lipochondria,* that store lipid droplets within protein membranes during the reproductive interphase when cells capable of dividing are not doing so; one or more *centrioles,* that can give rise to part of the reproductive mitotic apparatus; in dividing cells, the mitotic apparatus of *centrosomes,* a *spindle,* and *asters; fat droplets;* and other aggregations of *stored materials.* Nonliving inclusions which do not participate in cell processes may also be found within cells.

All aggregated cells and free-living cells above the monerans contain at least one nucleus or similar organelle. In monerans the genetic material is dispersed in the cytoplasm. A nucleus is a spheroid body within a cell which usually is denser and stains darker than the cytoplasm. Some cells have multiple nuclei. The nucleus, during the cell's reproductive interphase, is almost always separated from other cellular components by a double *nuclear membrane.* Within the nucleus are the *nuclear sap;* a fine network of *chromatin* which carries the genetic DNA, containing all but a small fraction of the cell's DNA; and *nucleoli,* visible under a microscope as spherical bodies which may have amoeboid movement and which produce part of the cell's RNA. During cell division the nuclear membrane disappears, and the genetic material reorganizes so that *chromosomes* can be seen. The mature red blood corpuscles of many animal species are not true cells because they have lost the nucleus which they had earlier in their development.

1. Structure

1.1 System size   Cells are ordinarily measured in such units as the micrometer (μm) (10^{-6} m), the nanometer (nm) (10^{-9} m), and the Ångstrom (Å) (10^{-10} m). The smallest free-living cells so far discovered are the mycoplasms *(Mycoplasmatales).*[13] They can be as small as 2000 Å or 200 nm in diameter, perhaps even smaller. Their diameter is less than that of some viruses. Known viruses have diameters ranging from 16 to 300 nm.[14] The tobacco mosaic virus, a simple virus, is a single nucleoprotein molecule, nucleic acid bonded to a protein which forms a protective coat around it.[15] It is like deoxyribonucleic acid (DNA), a nucleoprotein in the chromatin of cells, except that it consists of ribonucleic acid (RNA), as do the poliomyelitis, influenza, and other viruses. All the known viruses that attack bacteria (bacteriophages) contain DNA. The tobacco mosaic virus is the largest crystalline chemical molecule so far described.[16] Larger viruses may have accessory structures made of other molecules. A virus of 18-nm diameter is close to the minimum size permitting the degree of complexity and number of constituent atoms which are required for any molecule or living system to reproduce itself, according to Stanley and Valens.[17] I have already mentioned (see page 18) that living systems must have a certain minimum degree of complexity and von Neumann has shown that systems require a certain minimum complexity to reproduce themselves (see page 55).

The smallest free living cells are one-tenth the diameter (one-thousandth the mass) of the average bacterium, one-hundredth the diameter (one-millionth the mass) of a mammalian tissue cell, and one-thousandth the diameter (one-billionth the mass) of a protozoan such as an amoeba.[18] The largest cells are visible to the naked eye. The smallest cells are only one-thousandth the diameter of a hydrogen atom, which measures 1 Å. Viruses and the smallest cells are smaller than the wavelengths of visible light. Most viruses fall between one-fortieth and one-half a wavelength of violet light, the visible light with the shortest wavelength. They cannot, therefore, be seen by a light microscope. The electron microscope uses a beam of electrons whose wavelength is much shorter than the dimensions of a virus, so this instrument is suitable for studying them. Virus preparations can also be placed in an x-ray beam to study their diffraction patterns. In this way even the fine structure of these minute systems can be observed.[19]

The most massive cell of any surviving species is the ostrich egg. It is about 20 centimeters (cm) long, 1 million times the length of the smallest cell. It constitutes a special case, however, since almost its entire mass is food included in the cell, the germinal material being minute by comparison. Upper and lower limits to the size at which cells can live are set by physical factors. The upper bound results from the fact that the respiratory rate of cells varies with the ratio of their surface to volume.[20] The surface-to-volume ratio decreases as cell diameter increases. This is because when a cell gets bigger its surface area increases as a square function of its diameter while its volume grows as a cubic function of its diameter. Since the maximum rate of oxygen input is a direct function of the area of cellular surface, as the diameter increases there is a decrease in oxygen input per unit volume. As a result, the increase in the respiratory rate of the largest amoeba, *Chaos chaos,* over that of the much smaller *Amoeba proteus* is only about half the increase in bulk. If an amoeba were to grow much larger than *Chaos chaos* it would probably have too low a rate of respiration to maintain life. The smallest possible cell diameter is probably about 400 to 500 Å.[21] This is the smallest size at which a cell can contain the minimum essential molecular machinery within a membrane (usually about 100 Å thick). A minute cell like this would be continuously threatened with disruptive strains from the random thermal motion of its constituent molecules. Such a threat is another determiner of the lower limit of cellular size. The mycoplasms are about five times larger than this lower limit. They contain less than 20,000 large molecules plus many more small ones.[22]

The median cell diameter is probably about 10^{-6} m or 1 μm.

1.2 Structural taxonomy of types of systems Among free-living forms, the taxonomic classification of types of cells is based on their different shapes, different sorts of constituent organelles, and different processes (see Fig. 6-3). Aggregated cells in plants differ from those in animals, and within an organism cells differ according to the process which they are specialized to carry out and the tissue or organ of which they are components.

Traditional taxonomy has classified all living systems as members of one or the other of two great kingdoms, animals or plants. Protozoans were classified as animals; algae, fungi, bacteria, and slime molds as plants. Some free-living cells, however, do not fit easily into either of these classifications. Some algae, for instance, carry out photosynthesis (see pages 238 and 239) like plants, but propel themselves from place to place by flagella, like protozoans. A recent solution to the issues raised by such facts has been to change the time-honored taxonomic scheme and recognize four or five kingdoms instead of two (see page 362). One such taxonomic scheme—not yet universally accepted—distinguishes five kingdoms, monerans, protistans, fungi, plants, and animals. Of these, only one—the animals—does not include any free-living cells.

(*a*) *Monerans* are those free-living cells whose organelles are only slightly differentiated. They lack nuclear membranes, *i.e.,* they are *prokaryotes.* They also lack plastids, mitochondria, chloroplasts, and advanced flagella. They include bacteria and blue-green algae. (*i*) *Bacteria* are found almost everywhere. Not only do they cause certain diseases in man and other organisms, but they also perform useful functions within some living systems. In addition bacteria present in the soil help to make it fertile and accomplish the release from it of nitrogen, necessary for organisms. Bacteria have a plantlike cell wall, but few of them have chlorophyll. Some have flagella and move rapidly about. Bacteria have three sorts of shapes, which are used in classifying them: (*ia*) spherical (*coccus*), (*ib*) rod-shaped (*bacillus*), and (*ic*) spirally twisted (*spirillum*). Most of them reproduce by fission, but some reproduce by forming buds or other specialized structures. They may have different "sexes" or mating types. Some form spores when stresses increase in the environment. These spores can withstand extremes of temperature and lack of water which would kill the bacteria if they were not in the form of spores. They can sometimes survive for many years under conditions unfavorable for bacterial life. (*ii*) *Blue-green algae* cells often mass together. They may be joined so that they look like strings of beads. Such tissues apparently have no differentiation among their cells and apparently there is no central decider. Such a mass is obviously on the borderline between a colony of cells and an organism. Each such mass I shall call a colony of cells rather than a colonial organism, since it has no single decider. Blue-green algae are able to perform photosynthesis. The pigments which carry out this producing process are distributed in the cytoplasm. Reproduction of such algae is primarily asexual, by fission. If they move, they do so by gliding.

(*b*) *Protistans* have true nuclei, similar to those of the cells of higher organisms, *i.e.,* they are *eukaryotes.*

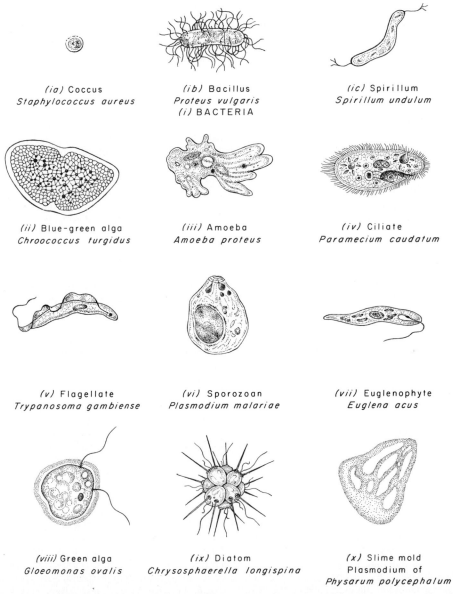

(ia) Coccus
Staphylococcus aureus

(ib) Bacillus
Proteus vulgaris
(i) BACTERIA

(ic) Spirillum
Spirillum undulum

(ii) Blue-green alga
Chroococcus turgidus

(iii) Amoeba
Amoeba proteus

(iv) Ciliate
Paramecium caudatum

(v) Flagellate
Trypanosoma gambiense

(vi) Sporozoan
Plasmodium malariae

(vii) Euglenophyte
Euglena acus

(viii) Green alga
Gloeomonas ovalis

(ix) Diatom
Chrysosphaerella longispina

(x) Slime mold
Plasmodium of
Physarum polycephalum

Fig. 6-3   Types of free-living cells. [(*ii*) from E. Acton. Observations on the cytology of the *Chroococcus turgidus. Ann. Bot.*, 1914, **28**, Plate 33, Fig. 4; (*vi*) from M. Aikawa. The fine structure of the erythrocytic stages of three avian malarial parasites, *Plasmodium fallax, P. lophurae,* and *P. cathemerium. Amer. J. trop. Med. & Hyg.*, 1966, **15**, 467; (*x*) from R. F. Scagel, R. J. Bandoni, G. E. Rouse, W. B. Schofield, J. R. Stein, & T. M. C. Taylor. *An evolutionary survey of the plant kingdom.* Belmont, Cal.: Wadsworth, 1965, 21. *Reprinted by permission.*]

They contain differentiated organelles such as mitochondria, chloroplasts, and other typical cell structures. Some are highly differentiated, with specialized organelles for subsystem processes such as ingesting. Some have chloroplasts and are capable of photosynthesis. Many have motor organelles. Reproduction may be asexual, by division, or sexual. This kingdom includes the protozoans, the euglenophytes, and a number of other algae. Protozoans are classified according to the form of their motor organelles—*e.g.*, those which move by flowing and putting out pseudopodia, like (*iii*) *amoebas;* ciliates, like (*iv*) *paramecia;* and flagellates, like (*v*) *trypanosomes.* Or they may be classified on other structural bases, such as the formation of spores at some stage of the life cycle by (*vi*) *Sporozoa.* (*vii*) Euglenophytes have chloroplasts and flagella. Also classified as protistans with differentiated chloroplasts, nuclei, and other structures lacking in those classified as monerans are (*viii*) *green algae* and (*ix*) *diatoms.*

(*c*) *Fungi* include (*x*) the *slime molds,* the cells of which—as I have already noted—live separately during part of their life cycle and are aggregated during part of it. Fungi lack chloroplasts or other structures for photosynthesis.

(*d*) *Plants* include some unicellular forms which are similar to the cells of multicellular plant organisms, *e.g.*, some of the (*viii*) green algae.

Cells of organisms. Aggregated into tissues, these are classified according to their special structural differentiations which make them distinguishable under the microscope. Shape, colors when stained, number of nuclei, types of organelles or inclusions, characteristics of walls or membranes, and many other structural differences indicate to which tissue a cell belongs.

A common structural characteristic of the cells which form plant tissues is their possession of a rigid cell wall usually strongly cemented to the walls of other cells and thus fixed in position. The wall acts as a part of the organism's supporter. Multicellular plants have differentiation of cell types but in general less than in animals.

The aggregated cells of complex, multicellular animal organisms, like mammals, including human beings, fall into major types which are structurally distinct. The cellular components of various sorts of tissues include the following:

(*a*) In *epithelial tissues,* which are the coverings of the mucous membrane and the skin such as the epidermis, the characteristic epithelial cells—when looked at from the surface—appear polygonal. The nucleus of an epithelial cell as seen from the surface is generally single and oval in shape, although such cells in some organs have double nuclei. Epithelial cells may be (*i*) thin and flat, (*ii*) cuboidal, or (*iii*) columnar (see Fig. 6-4), depending upon number of layers in the epithelium and other factors (see pages 316 and 317). The thickness of the nucleus increases with the thickness of the cell. Some epithelial cells are provided with cilia or other projections from the cell membrane. Mitochondria are abundant in these cells. They may contain granules of the pigment melanin. Glandular cells are epithelial cells specialized to produce and extrude products or wastes as diverse as milk, sweat, and tears. These cells have secretion granules when they are active.

An epithelial cell is polarized, the side of the cell attached to the underlying tissues having fewer organelles than the side directed toward the free surface. The former receives nutritive matter-energy inputs from the surrounding intercellular fluids, while the side toward the free surface is the place where secretory outputs occur. The latter side contains the stored secretory inclusions, as well as structures to carry out processes for which the cell is specialized, such as a brush border, cilia, the enamel layer of a tooth cell, mitochondria, and the Golgi apparatus.

(*b*) *Connective tissues* include *vascular tissues* like blood and lymph, as well as the endothelium which composes capillary walls and lines the other blood and lymph vessels; connective tissue proper; cartilage; and bone. The solid constituents of blood include *red blood corpuscles (erythrocytes), white blood cells (leukocytes)* of different kinds, and *blood platelets* (see Fig. 6-5). (*i*) The red blood corpuscles of mammals are nonmotile. They float passively in the bloodstream. Such a corpuscle starts out as a complete cell, but as it matures it loses its nucleus, Golgi apparatus, mitochondria, and cytoplasmic reproductive apparatus. In some vertebrates, however, mature erythrocytes are nucleated. Red blood corpuscles derive their color from the iron-containing pigment hemoglobin. A single such corpuscle is greenish yellow, its red color appearing only when it is densely packed with many similar corpuscles.

White blood cells are complete cells, capable of amoeboid motion. There are a number of different sorts. They include three kinds of *polymorphonuclear cells,* which develop nuclei with several lobules. These three types contain granules that stain differently—(*ii*) *neutrophils,* (*iii*) *eosinophils,* and (*iv*) *basophils.* They also include round cells with roundish nuclei (*v*) *lymphocytes* and larger (*vi*) *monocytes,* which are found in the blood and lymphatic circulation. White blood cells can wander in and out of the bloodstream, and often all the types are found in connective or other tissues.

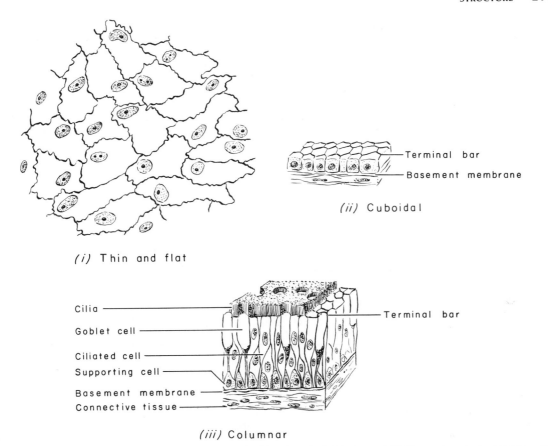

Fig. 6-4 Types of cells in mammalian epithelial tissues. [Modified from A. A. Maximow & W. Bloom. *A textbook of histology* (3d ed.). Philadelphia: Saunders, 1938, 22, 23. *Reprinted by permission.*]

(*vii*) *Platelets,* which are also found in the bloodstream, are not true cells but are round or oval unnucleated biconvex disks, fragments produced by specialized cells in the tissues which form blood.

Endothelium is composed of flattened, tapering cells with elongated or oval, flattened nuclei, not unlike the fibroblasts of connective tissue proper.

Connective tissue proper is composed of several different sorts of cells (see Fig. 6-6). (*i*) *Fibroblasts,* the most common, are elongated or star-shaped, sending out multiple long processes ending in points. Such a cell has a large oval nucleus with one or more nucleoli and chromatin particles, mitochondria, a Golgi apparatus, and other organelles. Fibrils known as *tonofibrils* run along the surface of the cell. (*ii*) *Macrophages* have smaller nuclei than fibroblasts, with irregular shape, and no large nucleoli. During inflammation they show active amoeboid motion. They often have inclusions which they have ingested. (*iii*) *Plasma cells,*

somewhat like lymphocytes in appearance but with a different arrangement of nuclear material, are rare, but appear in connective tissue. They are more common in lymph glands. There are (*iv*) *pigment cells* and also specialized fat-storing cells which, when accumulated in large numbers, crowd out the other cells and form the adipose tissue. These (*v*) *fat cells,* which can develop rapidly at any time in the life of an organism when the inputs of matter-energy to it exceed outputs, are large spherical bodies with flattened nuclei. Every mature fat cell contains only one large drop of neutral fat. The cytoplasm is reduced to a thin membrane surrounding the drop. When the needs of the organism require withdrawal of the fat from storage, the droplet disappears, and the cell becomes small, sending out tapering extensions or processes so that it looks like a fibroblast.

The other connective tissues, (*vi*) *cartilage* and (*vii*) *bone,* have cells similar to fibroblasts with long,

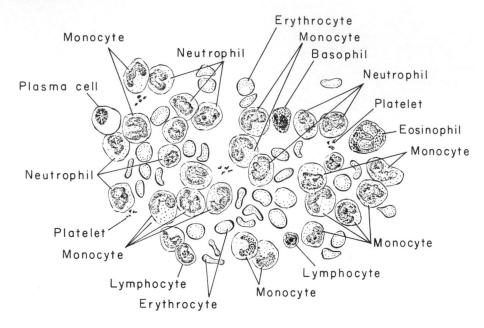

(A) Solid constituents of blood

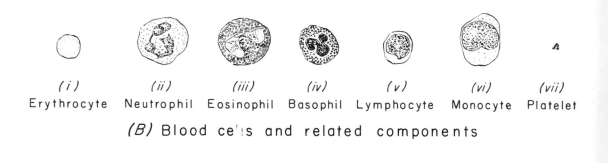

(i)	(ii)	(iii)	(iv)	(v)	(vi)	(vii)
Erythrocyte	Neutrophil	Eosinophil	Basophil	Lymphocyte	Monocyte	Platelet

(B) Blood cells and related components

(C) Endothelial cells in capillary

Fig. 6-5   Types of cells in mammalian vascular tissues. [(A) and (C) modified from A. A. Maximow & W. Bloom. *A textbook of histology* (3d ed.). Philadelphia: Saunders, 1938, 37, 231; (B) modified from W. Bloom & D. W. Fawcett. *A textbook of histology* (10th ed.). Philadelphia: Saunders, 1975, 146. *Reprinted by permission.*]

(i) Fibroblast   *(ii)* Macrophage   *(iii)* Plasma cell   *(iv)* Pigment cell

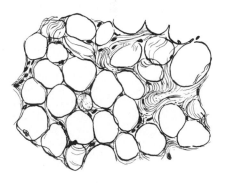

(v) Cluster of fat cells

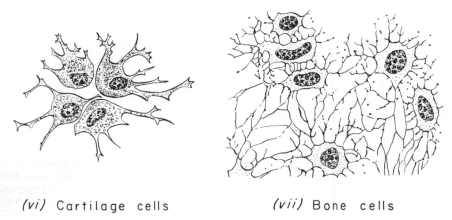

(vi) Cartilage cells   *(vii)* Bone cells

Fig. 6-6 Types of cells in mammalian connective tissue proper. [Modified from A. A. Maximow & W. Bloom. *A textbook of histology* (3d ed.). Philadelphia: Saunders, 1938, 52, 52, 37, 10, 67, 113, 121. *Reprinted by permission.*]

branching processes surrounded by extensive calcium deposits which harden around them and adapt them for their supporting functions.

(c) *Muscular tissue* is made up of cells specialized for a particular kind of motor activity, contraction. There are three types of muscle in the higher animal organisms, including man—visceral, skeletal, and cardiac (see Fig. 6-7). Muscular tissue may be composed of single cells, as in the case of visceral muscle. Or it may

be made up of composite, multinucleated cells called muscle fibers, consisting of many parallel fibrils. Skeletal muscle fibers contain bundles of a few such fibrils, while cardiac muscle is an interlacing network of many fibers.[23]

(i) *Visceral muscle cells* are small, elongated, and spindle-shaped, each with a single nucleus. Bridges interconnect them. Minute longitudinal fibrils are found in such cells.

(ii) *Skeletal muscle fibers* are also composed of many parallel fibrils. In cephalopod mollusks, insects, and vertebrates they are much elongated and have bands of differently defracting substances which are similarly located on all the fibrils, so that each fiber appears to have stripes running at right angles to the fibrils.

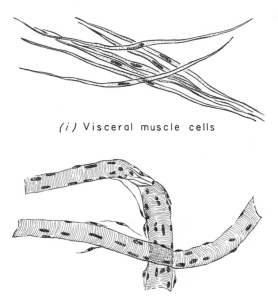

(i) Visceral muscle cells

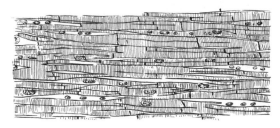

(ii) Two skeletal muscle fibers, upper one crushed in the middle, showing sarcolemma

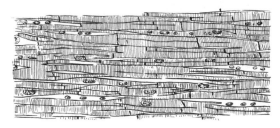

(iii) Cardiac muscle cells

Fig. 6-7   Types of cells in mammalian muscle tissues. [(i) and (iii) modified from W. Bloom & D. W. Fawcett. *A textbook of histology* (10th ed.). Philadelphia: Saunders, 1975, 289, 316; (ii) modified from A. A. Maximow & W. Bloom. *A textbook of histology* (3d ed.). Philadelphia: Saunders, 1938, 151. *Reprinted by permission.*]

This composite cell's cytoplasm surrounding the fibers contains multiple spindle-shaped nuclei. The cell also has many mitochondria, a highly developed sarcoplasmic reticulum, and a transverse system of membranes.

(iii) *Cardiac muscle cells* have multiple nuclei and typical stripes which are less regular and less highly developed than those in skeletal muscle. Thin membranes, called intercalated disks, separate the cells making up the cardiac muscle network. The adjacent cells are in intimate contact at each intercalated disk. These cells function in many ways like skeletal muscle fibers.

(d) *Nervous tissue* is composed of several kinds of cells, of which the chief ones are neurons, the supporting glia, and Schwann cells, which form sheaths for peripheral neurons (see Fig. 6-8).

(i) *Neurons* differ greatly in structure depending upon the species of animal and also upon their locations in the nervous system. Vertebrate neurons all have a cell body and one or more protoplasmic extensions from it. The cell body contains a large vesicular nucleus with a conspicuous nucleolus and a cytoplasm crowded with organelles, including many mitochondria, oriented in a roughly circular fashion around the nucleus. There is also an elaborate endoplasmic reticulum of interconnected *tubules* and *cisternae*. At places in it ribosomes cluster together into polysomes. In a light microscope several of these may appear together as large, dark-staining bodies named *Nissl bodies*. The Golgi apparatus is prominent. The cytoplasm of some neurons also contains pigment.[24]

The diameter of neuron cell bodies varies with the type of neuron from 4 to 150 μm. The shape depends primarily upon the number of protoplasmic extensions from it and upon the mechanical pressures from the surrounding tissues.

Protoplasmic extensions from the neural cell body are of two types, *dendrites* and *axons.* Rarely, a cell has only one process, a single axon. *Bipolar cells,* which are found in the human retina among other places, have a single dendrite and a single axon. By far the majority of neurons have several dendrites. A single axon is the rule, although there are rare exceptions. Axons may give off collaterals.

Dendrites, like the cell body, never have myelin sheaths, but at the ends they branch out like trees. A large dendrite has numerous mitochondria, continuations of the cell body's endoplasmic reticulum extending along its entire length, and ribosomes near the points where they branch. A few fine filaments and minute, parallel canals run the length of the dendrite.

Axons contain *axoplasm,* their particular ground substance. This contains fine neurofilaments, neurotubules, and neurofibrils, usually arranged parallel to the long axis of the cell. Axons are tubular in shape. The tube's center is clear, and the part of the cell membrane which constitutes its external surface is dense. Continuations of the cell body's endoplasmic reticulum, as well as other organelles, are found in

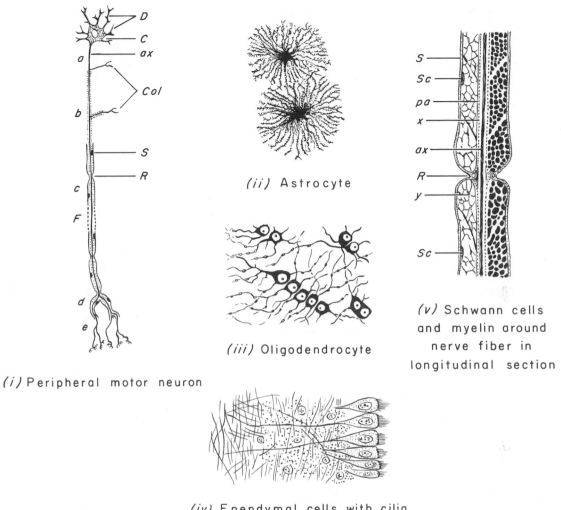

(i) Peripheral motor neuron

(ii) Astrocyte

(iii) Oligodendrocyte

(iv) Ependymal cells with cilia

(v) Schwann cells and myelin around nerve fiber in longitudinal section

Fig. 6-8 Types of cells in mammalian nervous tissues. Symbols in (*i*): *D*, dendrites; *C*, the cell body with its nucleus; *ax*, axon; *Col*, collaterals; *S*, Schwann's sheath; *R*, node of Ranvier; *a*, area of the naked axon; *b*, area of the axon covered only with myelin; *c*, area covered with both myelin and Schwann's sheath; *F*, broken lines indicating drawing does not show entire extent of the fiber; *d*, area in which the axis cylinder is covered only with Schwann's sheath and its nuclei; *e*, area of the naked axis cylinder ending in an arborization (teledendron). Symbols in (*v*): (Myelin dissolved at left and shown at right.) *S*, Schwann's sheath; *Sc*, Schwann cell; *pa*, periaxial space; *x*, coagulated covering layer over axon; *ax*, axon; *R*, node of Ranvier; *y*, protoplasmic net formed by Schwann cell extensions. [(*i*), (*ii*), (*iv*), and (*v*) modified from A. A. Maximow & W. Bloom. *A textbook of histology* (3d ed.). Philadelphia: Saunders, 1938, 169, 205, 202, 184; (*iii*) modified from W. Bloom & D. W. Fawcett. *A textbook of histology* (10th ed.). Philadelphia: Saunders, 1975, 368. *Reprinted by permission.*]

each axon, which joins the cell body at a small conical elevation called the *axon hillock*. The end of the axon, which in some motor nerves of human beings may be more than a meter from the cell body, branches into terminal structures of various shapes which connect with the next neuron or neurons in the nervous system. This junction is the *synapse*. Within the terminals are numerous mitochondria and clusters of small vesicles 150 to 600 Å in diameter. These accumulate against those surfaces of the terminals which make contact with the synaptic cleft, which is the region between the axon of the presynaptic neuron and the dendrite of the postsynaptic neuron with which it connects.

The cell membrane of a neuron is continuous over the entire cell, from the tips of the dendrites to the end of the axon. This membrane differs in thickness from point to point. It is thicker at the tips of dendrites where other neurons synapse, on the cell body at any points where other neurons synapse, and on the axon near the synaptic cleft.

Glia. In the central nervous system glia outnumber neurons 10 or 15 to 1. There are a number of different types, distinguished by shape, including (*ii*) *astrocytes* with many branching processes and (*iii*) *oligodendrocytes* with few. They surround the neurons of the central nervous system and form a sort of meshwork through which the neurons take their course. In addition to neurons, peripheral neural ganglia have *satellite cells* which may be similar to glia since they have similar embryonic origin. Glial cells provide the sheath which all neurons have.[25]

Ependymal cells. The ciliated epithelial cells which line ventricular cavities in the brain and the spinal cord canal are (*iv*) *ependymal cells.*

Schwann cells. The fatty, insulating *myelin sheaths* of peripheral neurons are produced by (*v*) *Schwann cells.* These sheaths are interrupted at intervals by *nodes of Ranvier,* points where the neural cell membrane is not covered by the sheath, as it ordinarily is, and so contacts the surrounding intercellular tissue fluid.

2. Process

2.1 System and subsystem indicators Even though cells are very small, scientists that study them have a wide range of instruments and techniques which can reliably measure changes in numerous cellular variables. These include the light microscope, the ultraviolet microscope, and the electron microscope as well as phase-contrast and interference microscopic techniques. With them it is possible to make precise observations of changes in the sizes and shapes of cells and their organelles, which are indicators of changes in process variables, *e.g.,* mitosis (see Fig. 6-12) or meiosis (see Fig. 6-13), which are changes in reproducing; movement of an RNA helix from the nucleus to the cytoplasm (see Fig. 6-20), which is an information transmission in the cell's channel and net; development of an abnormal nuclear shape, which is a sign of cancer; or alterations in sizes, colors, and shapes of red blood corpuscles, which may indicate that they are maturing or that anemia is developing. Microscopic observation of cells together with accurate time measurement provide indicators of rates of movement of cells, rates of growth, rates of change of size and color of organelles, and rates of input and output of observable substances. A wide range of cytochemical methods, such as use of cellular stains,

make it possible to see and measure otherwise invisible cellular components, and to determine the presence and concentrations of various molecules or classes of molecules to which the stains have chemical affinity. Changes in the colors of certain stains can indicate changes in the acidity of a cell or in the concentrations of various enzymes in it. Rates of change in the concentration of oxygen or carbon dioxide or various substrate substances in the environment of cells can indicate rates of input or output of various sorts of matter-energy by cells. "Labeled" radioactive tracer atoms that can be located on photographic film by autoradiography can be used to measure the flows of particular substances through cells. Remarkable techniques of micromanipulation, microdissection, and microsurgery on cellular components can alter cells' structures and processes and so enable experimenters to measure effects of one cellular variable on another. They can separate nuclear and cytoplasmic components of cells and combine such components taken from different cells.[26] They can even join together DNA molecules from diverse sources.[27] Quantitative histochemical techniques—like microtitrimetry, microcalorimetry, microspectrophotometry, and microfluorometry—can inject into a cell as little as 0.2 microliter (μl) of fluid or remove as small a quantity as 1 μl.[28] High-speed centrifuging of cells can determine their densities and the densities of their various components.

Changes in chemical markers bearing information can be measured by similar techniques. Variations in electrical signals bearing information in neurons and other cells can be observed and measured by microelectrodes placed in or near those cells. With these and various electrical instruments one can measure the timing, voltage, amperage, and waveforms of information transmissions in various types of cells.

2.2 Process taxonomy of types of systems Though the most carefully developed taxonomy of systems at this level is structural, the processes carried out by cells may be taxonomically important as well. The distinction between an aerobic and an anaerobic cell, for instance, depends upon what sort of converting processes it carries out, whether these processes can occur in the concentration of oxygen present in air or only in lesser concentration. The degree and type of pathogenicity of a bacterium toward the cells and organisms upon which it is parasitic is another process distinction which is taxonomically useful. Others include: (*a*) the sorts of materials which a cell ingests and uses as food; (*b*) the sorts of products in its matter-energy outputs, like the secretions of a glandular cell; (*c*) the specialized processes it carries out as an aggregated cell which is a component of an organ and organism, such as the information processing of neu-rons or the ingesting of epithelial cells of the lung; and (*d*) the stage in its life history which an individual cell has reached at a given time, *e.g.,* immature (nucleated) or mature (unnucleated) red blood corpus-cles. Whether or not a cell is parasitic is another pro-cess distinction. Among protozoans, some are classi-fied as parasites because they cannot survive unless they have a dependent relationship with a host cell or organism at some part of their life cycle.

3. Subsystems

The subsystems and components of cells are organ-elles and sets of organelles, each composed of a num-ber of molecules. Within recent years impressive advances have been made in understanding the fine structure and processes of cells. Still, the processes carried out by some cellular structures are not known, and some critical processes cannot yet be assigned to specific structures. In some cases, because the struc-tures being studied are single molecules or little larger, questions arise as to whether what is observed is an actual cellular component or an artifact of the staining or other experimental procedures. Only when such observations have been checked by different techniques can a confident decision be made.

Figure 6-9 is a detailed representation of a cell, showing its subsystems and its relationships to sur-rounding cells. In this particular case the cell pictured is a human cardiac muscle cell surrounded by other cardiac muscle cells, neurons, Schwann sheath cells, a capillary endothelial cell cut in two, and red blood cor-puscles. Most of the critical subsystems of a cell appear in this figure.

In Table 6-1 all the critical subsystems of a cell are listed, and the components which constitute these sub-systems are identified if they are known.

The research of many scientists in the last 20 years or so has revealed a set of facts about DNA and RNA which deepen our fundamental understanding of cel-lular structure and process. These discoveries concern the reproducer, producer, channel and net, associator, memory, decider, and other subsystems of cells, pos-sibly all of them. Because of the general relevance of these findings, I discuss them here rather than under specific subsystems.

DNA and RNA are the two nucleic acids found in all cells.[29] The nuclear chromatin contains most of the DNA in the cell, but some cytoplasmic structures also contain small amounts (see page 228). In the nucleus, DNA occurs as a sort of nucleoprotein called nucleohis-tone, in which the nucleic acid is bonded to a specific kind of protein called histone. The histones of the various types of species of animals and plants differ in

the amino acids which they contain. RNA is found both in the nucleus and in the cytoplasm, particularly in the ribosomes.

Both DNA and RNA are polynucleotides: that is, they are formed from a number of nucleotides, each of which has a pentose (a sugar with five carbon atoms), a phosphate, a nitrogenous base or nucleoside, either a purine or a pyrimidine. The pentose of DNA is deoxyribose, and that of RNA is ribose. The most common purines are adenine (A) and guanine (G), and the most common pyrimidines are cytosine (C), thymine (T), and uracil (U). DNA and RNA differ not only in their pentoses but also in their bases, since only DNA contains thymine and only RNA contains uracil. The proportions of the various bases in DNA differ among types or species of cells and are identical in all cells of a given type. Also, RNAs of different molecular weights carry out different processes within a single cell.

Nucleic acid molecules are extremely large. Molecu-lar weights of DNAs are usually several million.[30] The fundamental DNA unit, as Watson and Crick discov-ered, appears to be a long, fibrous molecule made up of two helically intertwined chains (spirals coiled around a common axis) held together in a specific way by hydrogen bonds (see Fig. 6-10).[31] The nucleotide bases are arranged so that A in one spiral is always connected to T in DNA and to U in RNA. G is always connected to C in both DNA and RNA. The sequence of the nucleotide bases in one chain, whatever it may be, therefore precisely determines the sequence in the other chain. This structure is important in the pro-cesses of reproducing and producing.

Information in the nucleic acid molecules is expressed in the specific order of their long sequences of regularly spaced nucleotide bases. The order differs in the various DNAs and RNAs. The ensemble of *symbols* or *characters* of the nucleic acid code, for each sort of molecule consists of a basic group of four nucleotide bases plus a few others. There are, there-fore, of the order of about 2+ bits of information per symbol or character. The present consensus of the specialists working in this area is that the basic mes-sage units, code words, or *codons* of the nucleic acid code are not single nucleotide bases taken one at a time but three adjacent bases, triplets for RNA such as ATA, ATG, TTT, or CTG for DNA or AUA, AUG, GUA, UUU, or CUG for RNA (see Table 6-2).[32] There would be at least $4 \times 4 \times 4$ or 64 combinations of symbols or characters possible in codons, and more, if more than 4 nucleotides are used. Thus each triplet codon could contain 6 or more bits of information. Redundancy in the message or noise resulting from disarrangement of the structure of the molecule would

Fig. 6-9 Human cardiac muscle cell with surrounding cardiac muscle cells, neurons, Schwann sheath cells, capillary endothelial cell, and red blood corpuscles. Longitudinal sections of one orangish Y-shaped cardiac muscle cell, with large bluish-gray nucleus, and parts of two other such cells in lower half of picture. The Y-shaped muscle cell extends in from edge of picture at about 7 o'clock position. Several reddish-brown intact muscle cells in upper half of picture. A ropelike large neuron extends from edge of picture at about 8 o'clock position to 11 o'clock position, covered by lacy sheath of Schwann with two Schwann cells, each with a bluish-gray nucleus. A whitish smaller neuron, which conducts input pulses to muscle cells, extends across picture between muscle fibers from 12 o'clock to 8 o'clock positions. Near 8 o'clock position, tip of this neuron contacts muscle cell in neuromyal junction. Capillary endothelial cell with bluish-gray nucleus shown severed, open end of one part to left of center with one red blood corpuscle inside and open end of other part between two arms of Y-shaped muscle cell in about 3 o'clock position with one red blood corpuscle inside. A few orangish collagenous connective tissue fibers extend across the picture from 8, 9, and 10 o'clock positions to 12 and 1 o'clock positions. Subsystem components of the Y-shaped cardiac muscle cell are identified.

Subsystems which process both matter-energy and information: Reproducer (Re), nucleus; Boundary (Bo), cell membrane.

Subsystems which process matter-energy: Ingestor (IN), cell membrane; Distributor (DI), endoplasmic reticulum; Converter (CO), enzymes in mitochondria; Producer (PR), nucleic acids of ribosomes; Matter-Energy Storage (MS), glycogen granules; Extruder (EX), cell membrane; Motor (MO), myofibrils; Supporter (SU), myofibrils.

Subsystems which process information: Input Transducer (it), subsynaptic region of neuromyal junction; Internal Transducer (in), enzymes and repressors; Channel and Net (cn), cell membrane, sarcoplasmic reticulum, and transverse reticulum; Decoder (dc), subsynaptic region of neuromyal junction; Decider (de), genes in nucleus. (Since muscle cell has no encoder or output transducer, these subsystems of the smaller neuron are indicated instead.) Encoder of neuron (en), component producing transmitter substance; Output Transducer of neuron (ot), prejunctional region.

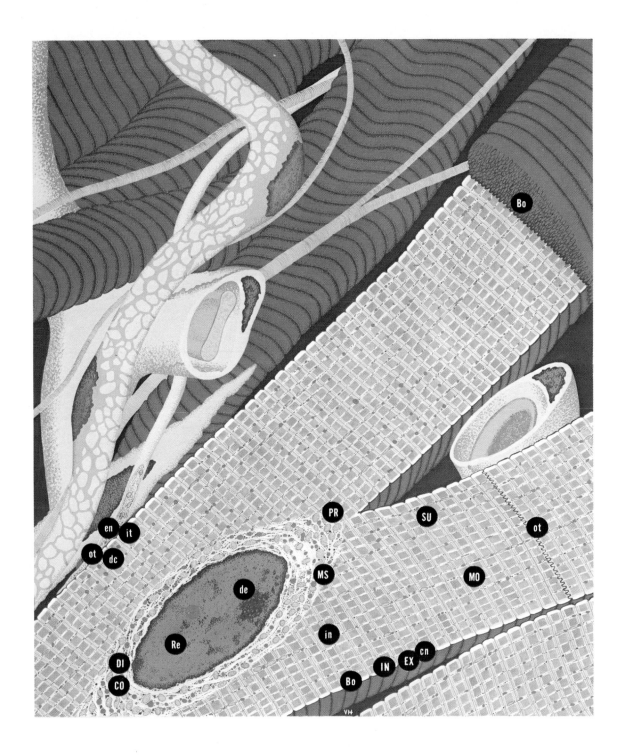

TABLE 6-1   Components of the 19 Critical Subsystems of a Cell*

3.1 SUBSYSTEMS WHICH PROCESS BOTH MATTER-ENERGY AND INFORMATION

3.1.1 *Reproducer*
Chromosomes and chromatin in nucleus; ribosome, mitochondrion, kinetosome, chloroplast; centrosome, aster, centriole, and spindle in cytoplasm

3.1.2 *Boundary*
For matter-energy, cell membrane plus cell wall or other protective structures; for information, cell membrane including specialized areas at synapse and neuromyal junction

3.2 SUBSYSTEMS WHICH PROCESS MATTER-ENERGY	3.3 SUBSYSTEMS WHICH PROCESS INFORMATION
3.2.1 *Ingestor* Cell membrane as a whole or specialized regions such as peristome, cytostome, gullet; tentacles to hold food and cilia to sweep it in	3.3.1 *Input Transducer* Cell membrane; particularly specialized receptor sites of cell membrane, including subsynaptic region of neurons, muscle fibers, glandular cells; light-sensitive pigments, cilia, other specialized parts of receptor cells
	3.3.2 *Internal Transducer* Enzymes and repressor molecules
3.2.2 *Distributor* Endoplasmic reticulum, sarcoplasmic reticulum of muscle cells; ground substance, including axoplasm of neurons; microtubules, microfilaments	3.3.3 *Channel and Net* Endoplasmic reticulum, sarcoplasmic reticulum of muscle cells; ground substance, including axoplasm of neurons; microtubules, microfilaments; cell membrane, transverse system of muscle cells, nuclear membrane
3.2.3 *Converter* Enzymes such as those in mitochondrion, cell membrane, chloroplast, nucleus, or lysosome; vacuoles which carry out phagocytosis or pinocytosis	3.3.4 *Decoder* Molecular binding sites, such as the operator, a ribosomal molecule, or subsynaptic membrane; parts of cell membrane, such as postsynaptic membrane or membrane of initial segment of axon
3.2.4 *Producer* Chlorophyll, chloroplast; enzymes such as those in mitochondrion; Golgi apparatus; nucleic acids of nucleus and ribosome	3.3.5 *Associator* Unknown
3.2.5 *Matter-Energy Storage* Phosphorylated organic compounds (*e.g.,* ATP, creatine phosphate, and argenine phosphate of muscle cells); starch or glycogen granule; glucose, fructose, sucrose, lactose; lipochondrion; lipid, including fat droplet; some protein; secretory granule	3.3.6 *Memory* Unknown
	3.3.7 *Decider* Regulator genes and operon, including structural genes, and perhaps architectural and temporal genes in nucleus; possibly operator, promotor, activator RNA, repressor sites, replicon, initiator, replicator, effector or modifier or modulator components; cytoplasmic DNA; parts of cell membrane, as of axon hillock, initial segment of axon, first node of Ranvier, other specialized cell membrane sites of neurons; other components
	3.3.8 *Encoder* Components producing alpha-coded antigenic proteins, hormones, and other molecules output as signals by cells; component producing transmitter substance output by neurons, perhaps mitochondrion or synaptic vesicle; part of electroplaque cell that produces electric pulses; part of cell membrane that determines axon pulses, perhaps near initial segment of axon
3.2.6 *Extruder* Region of cell membrane capable of matter-energy transport out of cell, including anal pore or cytoproct and vacuole of protozoan; excretory canal of some glandular cells; possibly sarcoplasmic reticulum 3.2.7 *Motor* Cytoplasm, the microtubules and microfilaments of which enable it to move, as in a pseudopodium; cilium; flagellum; myofibril	3.3.9 *Output Transducer* Cell membrane; presynaptic membrane and neuromyal junction; prejunctional region of neuron; synaptic vesicle
3.2.8 *Supporter* Microtubules, microfilaments; myofibrils of muscle cells; cell walls of plant cells; cell membrane; wall of cysts	

*Specific drugs, which are artifacts, may serve as prostheses for a particular pathological cellular subsystem.

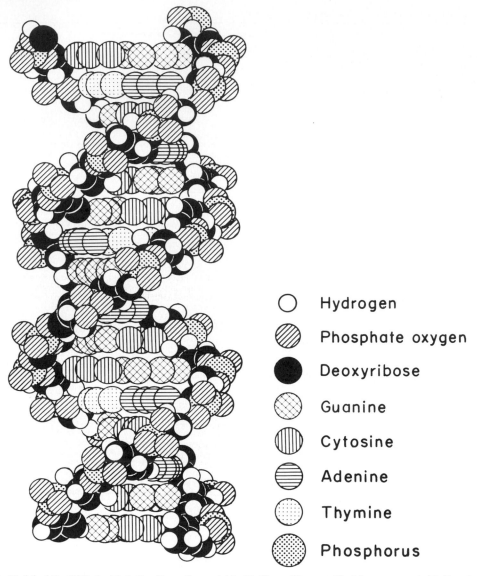

○ Hydrogen

⊘ Phosphate oxygen

● Deoxyribose

⊛ Guanine

⊞ Cytosine

⊟ Adenine

⊙ Thymine

⊛ Phosphorus

Fig. 6-10 Model of the DNA double helix. (From the model in M. Eigen. Wasserstoffbrückensysteme als Medien chemischen Strofftransports. *Naturwissenschaften*, 1963, **50**, 429, and the earlier models in M. Feughelman, R. Langridge, W. E. Seeds, A. R. Stokes, H. R. Wilson, C. W. Hooper, M. H. F. Wilkins, R. K. Barclay, & L. D. Hamilton. Molecular structure of deoxyribose nucleic acid and nucleoprotein. *Nature*, 1955, **175**, 834; and A. Rich. Molecular structure of the nucleic acids. *Rev. modern Phys.*, 1959, **31**, 193. *Reprinted by permission.*)

TABLE 6-2 Possible Code-Letter Combinations as a Function of the Length of the Code Word

Singlet code (4 words)	Doublet code (16 words)				Triplet code (64 words)			
A	AA	AG	AC	AU	AAA	AAG	AAC	AAU
G	GA	GG	GC	GU	AGA	AGG	AGC	AGU
C	CA	CG	CC	CU	ACA	ACG	ACC	ACU
U	UA	UG	UC	UU	AUA	AUG	AUC	AUU
					GAA	GAG	GAC	GAU
					GGA	GGG	GGC	GGU
					GCA	GCG	GCC	GCU
					GUA	GUG	GUC	GUU
					CAA	CAG	CAC	CAU
					CGA	CGG	CGC	CGU
					CCA	CCG	CCC	CCU
					CUA	CUG	CUC	CUU
					UAA	UAG	UAC	UAU
					UGA	UGG	UGC	UGU
					UCA	UCG	UCC	UCU
					UUA	UUG	UUC	UUU

NOTE: Since a minimum of 20 code words is required to specify the 20 common amino acids, a minimum code length would be a triplet, provided all code words are of equal length.

SOURCE: M. W. Nirenberg. The genetic code: II. *Sci. Amer.*, March 1963, **208**(3) 90.

lessen the amount of information. The molecule's message written in nucleic acid code often represents a *structural gene,* which is a template, blueprint, or set of instructions. It controls *how* molecules of specific amino acids are combined to form a particular protein, programming the pattern of spatial organization of that protein, which is usually or always an enzyme. Other molecular messages in nucleic acid code represent *regulatory* genes. These program the pattern of temporal organization, determining *when* syntheses of protein molecules shall occur by controlling rates of synthetic processes. The regulatory process involves *operators,* which on receiving appropriate signals can stop or initiate sequences of chemical reactions necessary to produce enzymes and other proteins for the cell. It also involves *replicators* which, on receiving appropriate signals, can stop or initiate sequences of chemical reactions necessary to reproduce the cell.

The message which contains the template or instructions for an entire enzyme or other protein molecule or polypeptide is a *cistron.* A gene, as Sonneborn defines it, is the same thing, but others do not agree with this terminology.[33] This message, which is the template for a protein containing, say, 200 amino acid units, must contain at least 200 codons, representing at least 600 nucleotide base symbols or characters.[34] Each chromosome contains several genes. The information in the messages in the entire set of chromosomes in the cell is called the *genome.* In the nuclei of the cells of any species there are at least as many

DNA molecules as there are chromosomes. The number of chromosomes differs from one species to another, the less complex species having fewer, presumably because less information is required for the template which bears their spatiotemporal programming. The number of chromosomes in man is 46; in white rats, 42; in pea plants, 14; and in fruit flies, 4. On the other hand, some members of the protozoan phylum *Rhizopoda,* which includes amoebas, have more than 1,500 chromosomes. Presumably these are a different sort of chromosome, each of which bears only a small amount of information.

When a gene or cistron is instrumental in forming an enzyme, it is part of the decider because it indirectly determines, or "decides," how that enzyme operates to catalyze or control the rate of one of the hundreds of chemical reactions which go on simultaneously in the cell.[35] In viruses, molds, and bacteria the site in the genome of a gene or cistron which directs the production of a given enzyme can often be located by eliminating the gene by a mutation and discovering what enzymatic process the cell then cannot carry out.

The message in a gene probably begins at one end of it (conventionally written as the left end) and is read three nucleotides at a time.[36] Certain "nonsense" triplet nucleotide sequences, which are incapable of directing an amino acid into a protein molecule, may serve as "punctuation" indicating the beginning or end of a message.[37] Without such punctuation the message would be hopelessly unintelligible and no protein molecule would be formed. There are relatively few triplet sequences which could serve thus as punctuation.

Scientists have in recent years decrypted the complete code required to specify all the amino acids from which proteins are constructed. It is presented in Table 6-3.

The complete nucleotide sequence of an alanine transfer RNA molecule, isolated from yeast, has been determined experimentally.[38] It is shown in Fig. 6-11. This was the first nucleic acid to have its structure specified. The class of RNAs to which this molecule belongs includes the smallest biologically active nucleic acids known. Nevertheless, they are large and complicated molecules. By determining this molecular structure, these workers have also revealed by inference the complete primary structure of a gene, that gene which directed the formation of the alanine transfer RNA molecule. The complete nucleotide sequence of the DNA genome of the small bacteriophage

ΦX174 was first reported in 1977. In it DNA information is stored so economically that two pairs of genes are coded by the same DNA region.[39]

There are 5 billion nucleotide bases in the nuclear chromatin of a human cell, according to Beadle, who says:[40]

If you were to take all the molecules containing the five billion units and string them end to end, they would form a chain about five feet long. |Wiseman says six.[41] But the molecules are so small in diameter that you would be unable to see the chain with the highest powered light microscope possible. The molecules can just barely be resolved with the most modern electron microscope.

How much information is contained in these five feet of DNA—in five billion units?

He figured that there would be 1,700,000,000 codons, which could convey more than 300,000,000 words of written prose, if one arbitrarily assumes that there are five codons in an average word, each codon representing a letter and the average word having five letters. This would make 600,000 pages, if each page had 500 words. And he continues:

If we say there are six hundred pages per average volume, we will have a thousand volumes. . . . That is a set of genetic specifications for making one of us out of an egg cell, given a proper environment, proper raw materials, and so on.

Let's express the size of this five foot thread in another way. If it were wound back and forth, one layer thick, on the head of a pin, it would cover only about one-half of one percent of the head of the pin. That means you could get a thousand volumes of information on half of one percent of the head of the pin. If you covered the whole head of the pin, you would have the equivalent of two hundred thousand volumes in a monolayer so thin that you could not detect it by anything less than an electron microscope. That's pretty good miniaturization. Let's go one step further. If we took all the DNA code out of all the eggs that gave rise to all the people on earth today—say three billion people—and wound it back and forth like cordwood, how large a stack would it make? It would make a cube an eighth of an inch on a side! Since each person requires a thousand volumes to specify him genetically, this little cube an eighth of an inch on a side is the equivalent of three trillion volumes of library work. In all history since the invention of the printing press, there have been printed only about 50 million different books. In this small cube we can put the equivalent of three trillion volumes—that's 60,000 times as much as is contained in all the books ever published.

The amount of matter-energy in the marker bearing the genetic message is much larger than the theoretical minimum (see page 12), but it is vastly smaller than any marker which man has yet made.

So much for the structure of the information-bearing nucleic acids and proteins which are the "key molecules of living systems."[42] The reproducing of new cells, repairing of old ones, and carrying out of their other functions involves the synthesis of proteins. Since protein is a fundamental component of protoplasm, in living systems production or synthesis of protein is a critical cellular process (see page 18).

TABLE 6-3   The DNA Code

Code triplets	Amino acid	Code triplets	Amino acid
AAA	lysine	CAA	glutamine
AAG	lysine	CAG	glutamine
AAC	asparagine	CAC	histidine
AAU	asparagine	CAU	histidine
AGA	arginine	CGA	arginine
AGG	arginine	CGG	arginine
AGC	serine	CGC	arginine
AGU	serine	CGU	arginine
ACA	threonine	CCA	proline
ACG	threonine	CCG	proline
ACC	threonine	CCC	proline
ACU	threonine	CCU	proline
AUA	isoleucine	CUA	leucine
AUG	methionine	CUG	leucine
AUC	isoleucine	CUC	leucine
AUU	isoleucine	CUU	leucine
GAA	glutamic acid	UAA	gap (comma)
GAG	glutamic acid	UAG	gap (comma)
GAC	aspartic acid	UAC	tyrosine
GAU	aspartic acid	UAU	tyrosine
GGA	glycine	UGA	tryptophane
GGG	glycine	UGG	tryptophane
GGC	glycine	UGC	cysteine
GGU	glycine	UGU	cysteine
GCA	alanine	UCA	serine
GCG	alanine	UCG	serine
GCC	alanine	UCC	serine
GCU	alanine	UCU	serine
GUA	valine	UUA	leucine
GUG	valine	UUG	leucine
GUC	valine	UUC	phenylalanine
GUU	valine	UUU	phenylalanine

SOURCE: Adapted from table prepared by T. H. Jukes and published in W. Braun. *Bacterial genetics.* (2d ed.) Philadelphia: Saunders, 1965, 341. *Reprinted by permission.*

$$
\begin{array}{ccc}
\text{Di} & \text{Di} & \text{Di} \\
| & | & | \\
\text{Me} & \text{H} \quad\quad \text{H} & \text{Me}
\end{array}
$$

Me   Di   Di   Di
| | | |
Me   H   H   Me
| | | |
pG-G-G-C-G-U-G-U-G-G-C-G-C-G-U-A-G-U-C-G-G-U-A-G-C-G-C-G-C-U-C-C-C-U-U-I-G-C-

Me
|
I-Ψ-G-G-G-A-G-A-G-U*-C-U-C-C-G-G-T-Ψ-C-G-A-U-U-C-C-G-G-A-C-U-C-G-U-C-C-A-C-C-A-OH

- = phosphate residue
p = 5'-phosphate (the "left end" of the molecule)
OH = 3'-hydroxyl (the "right end" of the molecule)
A- = adenosine 3'-phosphate
C- = cytidine 3'-phosphate
G- = guanosine 3'-phosphate
I- = inosine 3'-phosphate
T- = ribothymidine 3'-phosphate
U- = uridine 3'-phosphate
Di-H-U- = 5,6 dihydrouridine 3'-phosphate
Di-Me-G- = N''-dimethylguanosine 3'-phosphate
Me-G- = 1-methylguanosine 3'-phosphate
Me-I- = 1-methylinosine 3'-phosphate
U*- = a mixture of U- and Di-H-U-
Ψ- = pseudouridine 3'-phosphate

Fig. 6-11 Structure of an alanine transfer RNA molecule. (From R. W. Holley, J. Apgar, G. A. Everett, J. T. Madison, M. Marquisee, S. H. Merrill, J. R. Penswick, & A. Zamir. Structure of a ribonucleic acid. *Science*, 1965, **147**, 1462–1465.)

The genetic information of the DNA controls such activity. The genetic DNA, however, is within the nucleus while the ribosomes, where proteins are produced under RNA control, are in the cytoplasm. The synthesis of proteins involves integration of nuclear and cytoplasmic processes. The central tenet of the chemistry of genetics is that DNA makes RNA makes protein.[43] The main steps in the process are as follows:

When a cell reproduces itself, the helixes of the nuclear DNA molecules unwind and separate into two separate chains, each of which serves as a template against which molecules present in the nucleus can fit themselves in the right order, forming the hydrogen bonds between the complementary nucleotides. Thus the DNA is copied and forms two identical descendant chains (see pages 224 and 225). This process is called *replication*. In a somewhat similar way the producing of protein begins with the formation of one sort of RNA from the template of the nuclear DNA. This process is called *transcription*. The RNA passes through the nuclear membrane and into the cytoplasm. In the cytoplasm five kinds of RNA are found— three sorts of insoluble ribosomal RNA, each of a different molecular weight, transfer RNA, and messenger RNA. At the ribosome, enzymes assist in attaching amino acids, formed from the decomposing of input proteins, to the template of a transfer RNA molecule specific for making a particular sort of

enzyme or other protein molecule. This process is called *translation*. The ribosomal RNAs act as attachment sites for this synthesis but are not themselves templates for any particular kind of molecule. (For further details see pages 239 and 240.)

It is possible that RNA also participates in the processes of cellular associating and remembering (see pages 266 to 271).

A major scientific advance was made when, about 1958, Kornberg used a small amount of DNA as a template and an enzyme to catalyze the biological synthesis in the laboratory of 20 or more times as much biologically inactive DNA.[44] Previously DNA had always been made in living cells. The newly produced DNA had the same ratio of nucleotide bases as the DNA used for its template. Other important achievements were Haruna and Spiegelman's autocatalytic synthesis of biologically active infectious viral RNA in the laboratory in 1965 and Goulian, Kornberg, and Sinsheimer's synthesis of biologically active DNA in the laboratory in 1967.[45]

3.1   Subsystems which process both matter-energy and information

3.1.1   Reproducer, the subsystem which is capable of giving rise to other cells similar to the one it is in.

3.1.1.1   Structure   Both nucleus and cytoplasm of cells which have a reproducer contain components of this subsystem. Bacteria and other monerans, in which the genetic material, a simple chromosome, is not contained within a nuclear membrane, differ from eukaryotic cells (those with typical nuclei) in both structure and process of the reproducer. The fine network of chromatin is the site of the genes during the interphase, the period when the cell is not reproducing by division. It is probable that the various chromosomes retain their individuality during this time, but they cannot be distinguished by present methods. During cell division the number of separate chromosomes characteristic of the species differentiate out of the chromatin. Chemical analysis of chromatin reveals that it is composed of DNA combined with histone to form nucleohistone, a smaller amount of RNA, a number of different proteins, and some other compounds.[46]

It appears likely that in chromatin each chromosome is a single DNA molecule.[47] The nuclear membrane is present during the interphase but disappears during mitosis. This membrane has been studied under the electron microscope in several kinds of cells.[48] It is made up of two layers. Pores exist in the nuclear membrane (see pages 206 and 207).

The ribosomes, mitochondria, kinetosomes, and chloroplasts may represent components of the reproducer in the cytoplasm, for there is evidence that, either alone or in interaction with nuclear material, they generate their own kind of organelle in the next cellular generation. The centriole also is a cytoplasmic component of the reproducer during the interphase. It is a spherical body which is often double. Some cells have multiple centrioles. During mitosis centrioles disappear, being replaced by the centrosomes, asters, and spindle which develop in the cytoplasm.

3.1.1.2 Process   The crucial event in cellular reproduction is transmission of information, the blueprints or templates for the new generation. The amount of matter-energy transferred in the process of such reproduction is minute. Cellular reproduction can be either asexual or sexual. The latter sort involves two modes of nuclear DNA division, mitosis and meiosis. These are under control of replicons in the nuclear DNA. After these processes occur, cell division takes place. There is also cytoplasmic genetic material which is capable of reproducing certain cytoplasmic structures.

Asexual reproduction.   Some bacteria, protozoans, and fungi reproduce by budding, a process in which the parent cell retains its identity, its DNA is duplicated, and a smaller, less differentiated descendant cell is formed and breaks away. Or they may sporulate, the nucleus dividing a number of times and as many cells forming as there are nuclei. This is a rapid type of reproduction common among parasites such as *Sporozoa.*

Sexual reproduction.   This process occurs in free-living cells, often alternating in cycles with asexual reproduction.

In order to exchange genetic material, the membranes of two cells must be in close contact or adhere to each other. This is believed to be brought about by forces similar to those which bind cells together into tissues (see pages 352 and 353). Studies of different mating types in yeasts suggest that specific substances may be present in the outer membranes of each which neutralize each other, making adherence possible.[49]

In organisms the fertilized egg divides repeatedly by mitosis as the tissues grow and differentiate. Cells of some tissues retain the capacity to divide as long as the organism of which they are parts survives. They can replace themselves and repair damage to the tissue of which they are components. Others, like neurons, lose this capacity.

The process of reproducing new individuals is carried out by cells for the organ and organism levels (see page 55).

Replication.   Research with bacteria indicates that replicons—components of the decider which are parts of the nuclear DNA—start and control the cell's primary reproductive processes. A specific structural gene under control of a regulatory gene forms an *initiator* molecule. It receives a signal, perhaps from the cell membrane, which makes it act on a nucleotide sequence in a narrow region in the nuclear DNA, the *replicator*. This sets into action chromosomal replication. Hormones can also initiate and influence the rate of various aspects of cellular reproduction. Such functions appear to initiate and regulate, in many sorts of cells, the two major processes of cellular reproduction, mitosis and meiosis.

Mitosis is the process whereby the nucleus divides. In many but not all cell types, all parts of the cell are duplicated, and division into two descendant cells takes place. Mitosis occurs in both free-living and aggregated cells. The stages in the processes of mitosis and cell division pictured in Fig. 6-12 are: first, the diffuse chromatin in the nucleus organizes into threads bearing the separate chromosomes (*A, B*). Then the nuclear membrane disappears (*C*). At the same time the centriole—a particle just outside the nucleus—divides into two; and the parts—centrosomes—move to opposite ends of the cell (*A, B, C*). Asters, so named because they look like stars with radiations, form at these two ends. Slender threads connect the asters with the chromosomes (*D*). The threads, arranged in a configuration called the mitotic

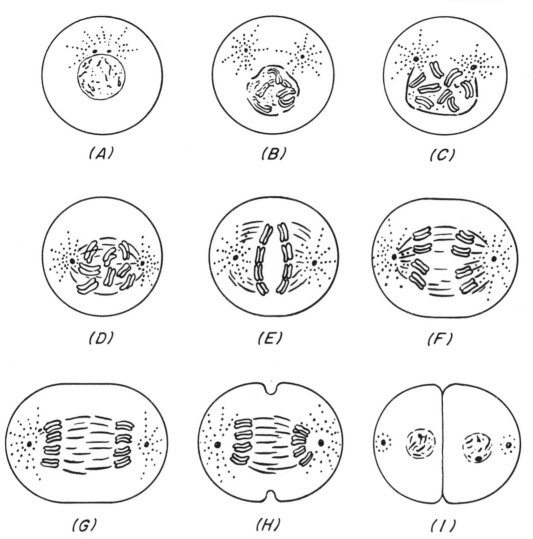

(A)   (B)   (C)

(D)   (E)   (F)

(G)   (H)   (I)

Fig. 6-12   Mitosis and cell division.

spindle, appear to pull the chromosomes apart so that each aster gets half of each chromosome (E, F, G, H). After this the cytoplasm divides, the two descendant cells separate, and each develops a nucleus from the chromatin in it (H, I).

Meiosis. This special form of mitosis provides the cell with only half of the usual number of chromosomes. It occurs during the maturation of a cell in preparation for one of two sorts of sexual reproduction, either (a) the union in organisms of an egg and sperm cell to form a fertilized egg or (b) the conjuga-

tion of protozoans. As any cell in a sexual species begins meiosis (see Fig. 6-13), each chromosome derived from its male ancestor forms a "homologous pair" with the corresponding one from its female ancestor (A, B). Then each chromosome in this pair divides into two chromatids, making a total of four chromatids (C, D). These come to lie parallel to each other. Under some circumstances one chromatid from the male chromosome may exchange parts with one chromatid from the female chromosome, a process called "crossing over" (E). The resultant cell then divides once

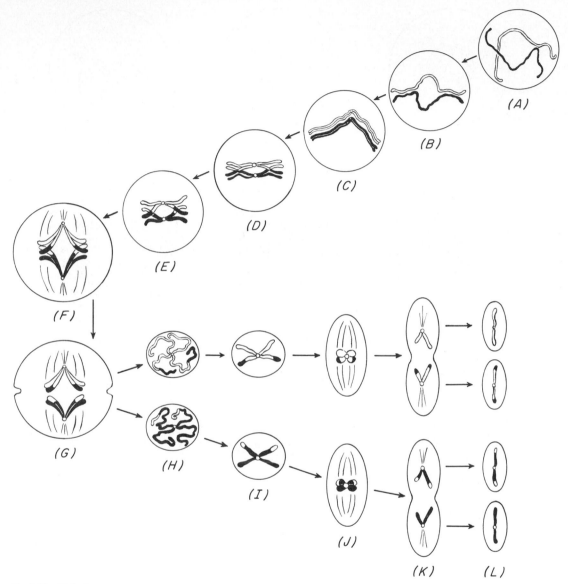

Fig. 6-13 Meiosis.

(F, G, H) and each of the resultant cells divides again (I, J, K, L). None of these divisions involves duplication of chromosomes. One chromatid goes to each new cell produced in the second division and forms a chromosome in it (L). These new cells are egg or sperm cells, and each has only half the usual number of chromosomes for that type or species of cell. "Crossing over" can occur in many patterns, so that some egg or sperm cells of one individual organism may carry different combinations of genes from others. The eventual union of egg and sperm cells gives the fertilized egg the full complement of chromosomes characteristic of the type or species, half from one parent and half from the other. An organism arises from repeated mitoses and divisions of such a fertilized egg, each new somatic cell having the total number of chromosomes. The process is similar in the conjugation of protozoans which have several different mating types.

Cell division. All cell types do not divide during or immediately following mitosis. Some multinucleated cells and some which form syncytial tissues of organisms do not follow this plan.[50] The process of division of the cytoplasm is also different in such cells. In many free-living and aggregated cells, however, division takes place during the final stage in mitosis. In these cells, mitosis and division are the ultimate event in the parent and the initial event in the offspring in life cycles that include several stages.

During the period when the cell is not dividing, the DNA replicates, and the cell grows to the size typical of its species. The signal that starts the division process is not known, but the whole process of reproduction, like the other stages in the life cycle of the cell, is under the direction of genes.

When a cell is dividing, its biosynthetic activities decline, inputs of water through its cell membrane are interrupted, and the cytoplasm outside the mitotic apparatus becomes less viscous.[51] Cells, like amoebas, that are normally irregular in shape, round out into spheres. Amoebas cannot cling to surfaces in their usual manner. Some ciliates become sluggish and sink to the bottom of a culture. The protoplasm of some plant cells stops streaming.

This profound reorganization of the cytoplasm that occurs during cell division must be reversed before new cells are produced, each surrounded by membranes, with genetic material enclosed in a nuclear membrane, and with a full complement of organelles. As the final stage in mitosis begins, a furrow appears in the cytoplasm, exactly in the plane that divides the spindles (see Fig. 6-12H).[52] If for any reason the mitotic apparatus is not centrally located, the new cells will be of unequal size. The process varies from one cell type to another. Some build a wall around or between the nuclei. Others constrict the cell surface between the nuclei. Still others extrude part of the cell, with one nucleus, and pinch off the extruded part.[53] When amoebas divide, the two newly formed cells literally crawl away from each other.

Replication of organelles. The various cellular components replicate in three different ways: (a) self-assembly, (b) under control of cytoplasmic DNA, and (c) under control of nuclear DNA.

(a) *Self-assembly.* Some aggregates of molecules can probably polymerize from monomers in the cytoplasm. Such self-assembly has occurred in experiments in cellular parts as complex as cilia and in whole viruses which, while not complex enough to be living systems, do have both nucleic acids and proteins.[54] The endoplasmic reticulum, and probably the nuclear membrane as well, which is believed ordinarily to connect directly to the reticulum, apparently lose their

continuity and break down into spherical vesicles in the periphery of the cytoplasm.[55] At least the phospholipid parts of these membranes seem to assemble without any nuclear control.

Replication of some organelles cannot take place unless there is a preexisting template in the cytoplasm.[56] These do not depend on the nuclear genes.

The ciliate, *Tetrahymena*, has a highly structured boundary with hundreds or even thousands of cilia arranged in regular rows.[57] At the base of each cilium is a kinetosome (see pages 207 and 244). On the surface of each of these free-living protozoans are one or two mouths; openings of one or more contractile vacuoles; a cytoproct, which is an extruder component; and various numbers of rows of cilia. Individual cells differ in the number and arrangement of these components.

When two cells mate and each divides, the number and arrangement of boundary components of each are preserved unchanged in its offspring, unaffected by the exchange of genetic material that has taken place.

Studies have been made of another protozoan, *Difflugia corona*, which constructs a shell of sand, containing a mouth surrounded by a symmetrical array of teeth, through which pass all matter-energy and information inputs from and outputs to its environment. The mouth components are independent from nuclear control. They constitute a template for their own replication. The number of teeth is a hereditary characteristic. When these creatures divide, one of the new cells is extruded through the mouth and starts to construct its sandy shell while still in contact with the other, beginning with the mouth. The new mouth is therefore constructed in direct contact with the old mouth, which serves as a template. When the number of teeth is decreased by breaking some of them out with a needle, the new cell has the new number of teeth. After a few generations, the teeth rearrange to become symmetrical, eliminating the gap where the teeth were broken out. The new arrangement then becomes a stable form regularly reproduced from generation to generation.

In one experiment, various cytoplasmic structures were cut out and rearranged in paramecia.[58] The altered structures were carried on to future generations, even though the nuclear DNA was unchanged. Cells provided with two or more mouths and gullets by surgery not only lived but transmitted these structures to their progeny generation after generation, even by sexual reproduction. Cells with inverted surface structures transmitted them, too, perpetuating these changes for over a year, through more than 700 cell generations of descendants.

(b) *Replication under control of cytoplasmic DNA.* Some organelles have DNA, which probably carries the template for at least part of their structure. This is true of centrioles, mitochondria, chloroplasts, and kinetosomes.[59] Some of these components can replicate both during cell division and when it is not dividing. Mitochondria also have ribosomes and the RNA necessary for protein synthesis.[60] The DNA in some of these organelles has been shown to differ in structure from nuclear DNA. Mitochondrial DNA appears to specify only some of the proteins that make up mitochondria. The rest of them are specified by nuclear DNA. When a cell divides, apparently each descendant cell receives half the parent mitochondria which, after cell division, divide to restore the number characteristic of that type of cell.[61] The mitochondria then grow to the size of their predecessors.

An experimental demonstration of the transfer of genetic information in mitochondria made use of a mutant of *Neurospora,* a bacterium whose mitochondria respire slowly.[62] When mitochondria from mutants were injected into nonmutated *Neurospora,* a transformation of the recipient cells to a form that respired slowly, like the original mutants, took place after a few generations. This indicated that the injected mitochondria carried the information for generation of slowly respiring mitochondria unlike those in the recipient cells. Other experiments using yeast suggest that not only nuclear but also mitochondrial DNA can be exchanged between mating cells.[63]

(*c*) *Replication under control of nuclear DNA.* The above processes of replication go on in a decentralized manner, but overall nuclear control is still essential to ensure that the descendant cells are organized systems. It may be that *architectural* genes (see page 272) determine the arrangement of components. Other genes control the cellular processes which are essential for their formation and continuing activities.

Representative *variables* of the process of reproducing are: *Sorts of matter-energy used in reproducing.* Example: The mutant bacterial cells failed to proliferate because of lack of substrate. *Meaning of information used in reproducing.* Example: The chromosome pattern of its cells indicated that the fetal organism was female. *Sorts of information used in reproducing.* Example: Both nuclear and cytoplasmic DNA were necessary for replication of a complete *Neurospora. Changes in reproducing over time.* Example: The cortical neurons in the rat's brain lost the capacity to reproduce after the cortex was completely formed. *Changes in reproducing with different circumstances.* Example: The paramecium first reproduced by sexual conjugation and then by asexual fission.[64] *Rate of reproducing.* Example: The cells in culture reproduced twice as fast when the temperature of the culture was raised 20 degrees.

Frequency of reproducing. Example: When the nutrients in the culture were increased to an adequate level, the amoebas in it reproduced more rapidly, on an average once every 24 h. *Lag in reproducing.* Example: The fertilized eggs did not divide until several minutes after fertilization, and similar eggs in a colder environment did not divide for several hours. *Costs of reproducing.* Example: Synthesizing the DNA molecule presumably cost the producing cell slightly more chemical energy, obtained from ATP, than it cost it to synthesize a different kind of DNA molecule with fewer amino acids. [This statement is derived from theory and does not rest on any experiments yet carried out. Biological research has put much less emphasis on costs, efficiencies, and cost-effectiveness trade-offs (see page 41) than has social science research, even though such concepts should be applicable to all levels of living systems. In many situations one does not know whether or not a cell is in an environment with a shortage of necessary inputs, so cost and efficiency may seem less meaningful notions than in the analysis of a social system with such shortages. Nevertheless efficiencies, costs, and effectivenesses are relevant to any system analysis and worth measuring.]

3.1.2   Boundary, the subsystem at the perimeter of a cell that holds together the components which make up the cell, protects them from environmental stresses, and excludes or permits entry to various sorts of matter-energy and information.

3.1.2.1   Structure

Matter-energy boundary.   In cells this is the cell membrane. It may have structures such as cilia or flagella extending from it. Outside the cell membrane of the cells of many plants are cell walls, secretion products of the cytoplasm which contain cellulose as the most important constituent. They also have lignin, pectin, minerals, and waxes. These walls have three layers, each with its fibrils differently arranged.[65]

Bacteria sometimes have tough capsules composed in part of large sugar molecules, polysaccharides. The rod-shaped bacillus which causes tuberculosis, for example, has such a capsule. Without external coatings of this sort to maintain their shape, individual cells suspended in fluid round out into spheres. Aggregated cells are shaped by the constricting physical forces exerted on them by the surrounding cells. If they do not have stiff walls, they, too, become spherical when separated from the cells around them and placed in an appropriate medium.

Although protozoans and cells of animal tissues do not have cell walls, they may have special protective structures. In organisms, either tissue fluid or, in bone and cartilage, a matrix containing calcium surrounds the cells. In bone and cartilage this surrounding substance is a semisolid or solid matrix containing calcium. Nervous tissue consists not only of neurons but also of various sorts of supporting glial cells. It also includes Schwann cells, each of which forms a sheath around a neuron. Schwann cells also lay down the waxy, insulating myelin which surrounds peripheral neurons.

The cell membrane is not visible with the usual light microscope. Electron and polarizing microscopes, however, show its fine structure. As I have already noted (see pages 205 to 207), it connects with other membranes in the cell such as the endoplasmic reticulum, the sarcoplasmic reticulum and its transverse system, and membranes surrounding the mitochondria, chloroplasts, and perhaps lysosomes. The cell membrane varies in width but is typically about 75 Å across.[66] These variations may result partially from different methods of preparing tissues for microscopic study. Most portions of all cellular membranes are double layers of lipids, each layer chemically distinct, in which proteins synthesized in the cytoplasm are embedded. Probably the nonpolar portions of these lipids, chiefly made up of chains of fatty acids, are oriented inward toward each other at the center of the membrane, perpendicular to the plane of the membrane.[67] The electrically charged polar parts of the phospholipids have been thought to be oriented outward, half the molecules toward the outside surface and half toward the inside surface of the membrane. Between them are intercalated protein molecules, including probably some enzymes, forming a fluid mosaic.

In some cells some proteins are joined with carbohydrate, forming mucoproteins and glycoproteins. Cholesterol and small amounts of other neutral lipids may also be present. Myelin, which surrounds axons of peripheral nerves, is shown by x-ray diffraction and electron microscopy to be a multilayered structure, apparently a proliferation of the cell membrane of the Schwann cell which surrounds axons of both myelinated and unmyelinated nerves.[68] Electron micrographs of the Schwann membrane resemble those of other membranes, so it has been concluded that they have similar structure. But myelin, an inert electrical insulator, is chemically, biologically, and functionally unlike all other membranes, so it is risky to generalize from it. Actually membranes have a great range of composition, from myelin, which is low in protein and high in phospholipids and fatty acids, to bacterial membranes which are the reverse. Alternative theories view the membrane as consisting of a protein framework containing lipids, a tubular arrangement

in which proteins surround a core of lipids, or a mixed protein-lipid aggregate.[69]

Information boundary. Much of the information which reaches cells, both free-living and aggregated, comes in the form of chemical molecules, so that the information boundary is the same as the matter-energy boundary for these substances. The boundaries of some cells have specialized information input areas, however, such as regions of the subsynaptic membrane of neurons and the neuromyal junction of muscle cells, both of which respond selectively to molecules of neurohumoral transmitter substances, and the eyespots of some protozoans which are sensitive to light. These are regions of the boundary where there are components of the input transducer. The presynaptic membrane of neurons is a specialized information output area, a component of the output transducer.

3.1.2.2   Process   In such minute systems as cells it is not surprising that a single structure parsimoniously carries out processes of several subsystems. The cell membrane is the chief structure of the boundary subsystem, but it is also involved in processes of several other subsystems, including the ingestor, converter, producer, extruder, motor, supporter, input transducer, internal transducer, channel and net, decoder, decider, and output transducer.[70] In order to understand how the cell membrane can participate in so many varied activities, we must understand some of the basic facts about how it carries out its processes. The cell membrane, as I shall show in this section, physically surrounds and constrains the cellular components and by biophysical and biochemical processes filters matter, energy, and information-bearing markers entering or leaving the cell, permitting some to pass and preventing others from doing so. Ingestion and extrusion go on through the cell membrane. Motions of components of the membrane may help move the cell, and certain sorts of deciding about such movements occur at the cell membrane.

The outside of the membrane of a resting cell is electrically positive in relation to the inside. This potential difference, called the resting potential, varies in different types of cells. Ordinarily it is between 10 and 100 millivolts (mV), although it is greater in some cells, *e.g.*, those of the fresh water alga, *Nitella*, in which it is 100 to 200 mV. The potential results from a difference in ion concentration between the inside of the cell and the medium which surrounds the cell. Inside *Nitella*, for instance, the concentration of potassium is 54.3 millimoles per liter (mmol per l), while it is 0.05 mmol per l in pond water. The potential difference on the membrane is involved in several different subsystem processes. Brief local changes in it convey information, so enabling the cell to have a channel and net. Certain regions of the cell membrane are specialized to serve as input transducer, decoder, encoder, and output transducer.

How does the cell membrane carry out the boundary processes?

Matter-energy boundary.   The cell membrane is denser and tougher than the cytoplasm within it or the usual components of its immediate environment, and so is strong enough to hold together the components which make up the cell and protect them from environmental stresses. Being flexible it can move about, within limits, to maintain its integrity while adjusting to physical stresses outside the cell and strains within it. Indeed the components making it up are in constant, fluid lateral motion along it.[71] It also filters matter-energy which approaches it from outside or from inside the cell. The membranes of living cells are selectively permeable, permitting particular forms of matter-energy to enter the cell and excluding others entirely. Chemical differences in various regions of the membrane determine what substances can cross the boundary at any point.[72] Boundaries are also permeable to substances from within the cell which must be discharged into the environment. These include the cell products and excretions.

Different types of cells are permeable to various molecules, each in different quantities. For example, the membrane of the human red blood corpuscle is 100 times more permeable to water than that of the amoeba. This is clearly adaptive, since the amoeba requires much different boundary-maintaining functions than a red blood corpuscle. An amoeba lives in fresh water and must therefore cope with a large osmotic gradient between the inside and outside of the cell, so that it must let water in only very slowly, while a red blood corpuscle is normally surrounded by plasma which is essentially in an osmotic steady state with the interior of the corpuscle. If such a corpuscle is placed in water, it will swell and burst with the inrush of water which it cannot output.[73]

The permeability of cell membranes is altered markedly by environmental conditions. Changes in temperature affect intake of materials from solution. Permeability to particular materials may be affected by the composition of the medium in which they are placed. For example, amoebas in a medium containing glucose will take in the glucose only if the medium also contains protein.[74] The salt composition of the medium is also important. For example, a red blood corpuscle placed in water with little or no salt swells and bursts. In fluid with too much salt it loses water and shrinks. Large molecules have more difficulty crossing cell membranes than small molecules do, although molecular size is secondary to other factors.[75] Some very large molecules, including ribonuclease, an enzyme and therefore a protein, penetrate some sorts of cells. Ribonuclease can enter amphibian eggs, onion root tips, ascites tumor cells, flagellates, amoebas, and bacteria, but not ciliates, molds, or yeasts.[76] Other proteins have also been proved to enter some cells. Certainly it would seem that Hypothesis 3.1.2.2-1 (see page 93) may apply to cell boundaries, for significant work must be expended in order for large molecules of various sorts to cross them.

The state of ionization of a molecule also affects its entry into cells. Weakly ionized solutions enter more rapidly than strongly ionized ones. By varying the acidity of a solution, a pharmacologist can control the rate of entry of a drug into the cells of an organism. Uncharged particles pass into a cell more readily than ions do. Various drugs affect cell membrane permeability. The boundary of an active muscle or nerve cell is more permeable than that of an inactive one, an adjustment process which reduces lack strains in the cell. (Active muscle cells are permeable to amino acids, glucose, and other materials, while resting muscle is not.)[77] In many instances one form of matter-energy penetrates a cell, but a closely related substance, similar in size and electrical properties, is filtered out by the boundary.

Like nonliving membranes, the membrane of a living cell is permeable to water and other molecules in a passive manner. In addition the cell can call upon its energy sources to carry on active transport across the membrane. A cell of a higher animal lives in a medium containing a high concentration of sodium ions while it maintains a high concentration of potassium ions within its boundary. The cell membrane is passively permeable to both ions and, without an active filtering process, a steady state would develop with the same concentrations of each inside and outside the cell. Blood plasma contains 20 times more sodium than potassium, while the corpuscles contain 20 times more potassium than sodium. To maintain this difference the cell must, by an active "pumping" process that requires energy expenditure, constantly extrude sodium at the same time that it ingests potassium against an aggregate 50-fold gradient.[78] The difference in ionization produced by the "ionic pump" establishes the electrical potential gradient between the inside and the outside of the cell membrane.

An adjustment process involving change in boundaries is used by those free-living cells which are capable of encystment (see page 285).

Information boundary.   Information processing at the cell membrane is affected by membrane permeability, active transport, and the consequent gradients between substances inside and outside the cell in the same way that matter-energy boundary processes are when the marker is an alpha-coded chemical molecule. Cells are also responsive to a range of energy inputs such as light, heat, and touch which bear signals from their environments. The boundary can filter such energic information-bearing markers or material markers, just as it filters other sorts of matter-energy. Thermodynamically, gradients between substances inside and outside of cells represent negative entropy or information. In this sense at least, flows of sodium or potassium ions across a cell boundary which change such gradients are information transmissions.

Representative *variables* of boundary process include: *Sorts of matter-energy crossing the boundary.* Example: Glucose passed out of the watery medium surrounding the amoeba and into the cell only when there was protein in the medium. *Meaning of information crossing the boundary.* Example: The nucleotide arrangement in the RNA of the tobacco mosaic virus that crossed the cell wall represented the template of that virus. *Sorts of information crossing the boundary.* Example: The ciliate received information from changes of temperature, intensity of light, electrical potential, and chemical concentrations, but its boundary filtered out RNA molecules. *Degree of permeability of the boundary to matter-energy.* Example: Almost no matter crossed the boundary of the cell while it was a cyst, but it began to cross the boundary in significant amounts as soon as it was no longer encysted. *Degree of permeability of the boundary to information.* Example: The cell became less permeable to the entrance of information as the electrical potential between the inside and outside of the cell membrane decreased. *Percentage of matter-energy arriving at the boundary which enters the system.* Example: More than 80 percent of the potassium ions which contacted its membrane entered the cell, but only 10 percent of the sodium ions entered. *Percentage of information arriving at the boundary which enters the system.* Example: Since the neuron was anesthetized, only one out of 100 pulses delivered through a microelectrode could be demonstrated to have any effect on it. *Changes in matter-energy processing at the boundary over time.* Example: As the cell overcame its dehydration, the rate at which water inputs crossed its membrane slowed down. *Changes in information processing at the boundary over time.* Example: As the anesthetic wore off, each electrical pulse applied to the membrane of the cell began again to alter the resting membrane potential. *Changes in matter-energy processing at the boundary with different circumstances.* Example: The amoeba took in more matter-energy at 22°C than at 6°C. *Changes in information processing at the boundary with different circumstances.* Example: When the ciliate had encysted in the dry soil, it was no longer affected by any form of signals to it as it had been in its former, active state. *Rate of matter-energy processing at the boundary.* Example: Sodium ion inputs crossed the neuron's cell membrane much more rapidly after a pulse had passed down the membrane than when the membrane potential had been restored. *Rate of information processing at the boundary.* Example: As the concentration of auxin increased outside the plant cell, molecules of it crossed the cell wall at a more rapid rate. *Frequency of matter-energy processing at the boundary.* Example: Light entered the cell continuously for the daylight hours and then stopped for the night hours, beginning again the next morning and so on day after day. *Frequency of information processing at the boundary.* Example: The concentration of acetylcholine at the postsynaptic region of the neural membrane rose and fell 20 times each second. *Lag in matter-energy processing at the boundary.* Example: Large molecules of fat crossed the membrane of the liver cell much slower than hydrogen ions. *Lag in information processing at the boundary.* Example: The thyroxine took less than 1 μs to enter the cell, although it sometimes took longer. *Costs of matter-energy processing at the boundary.* Example: ATP was expended whenever substances were filtered out by the cell membrane, expenditure varying with the amount of substance filtered. *Costs of information processing at the boundary.* Example: Energy was consumed whenever alpha-coded molecules of acetylcholine, markers bearing information, were transported across the cell membrane of the neuron at the synapse, the amount consumed increasing as the number of molecules transported increased.

3.2   Subsystems which process matter-energy

3.2.1   Ingestor, the subsystem which brings matter-energy across the cell boundary from the environment.

3.2.1.1 Structure   Certain   potential   matter-energy inputs, like water and ions, are dispersed throughout the fluid medium which surrounds cells on all sides. Hormones and drugs may also be in this fluid. Ordinarily a cell can ingest all of these through any point on its cell membrane. Cells of certain types—*e.g.,* an amoeba or white blood cell—can also ingest solid matter through any point on their cell membranes. Other types of cells use localized organelles for ingesting food stores or other material inputs. Among free-living cells a great variety of ingestor structures has developed. A cell of some flagellate groups can admit matter-energy only through a region near the base of its whiplike flagella. Many ciliates have a *peristome,* or depression in the surface, into which opens a *cytostome* which leads to a *gullet* leading into the cytoplasm. These structures are differently placed in various species. Some ciliates have specially adapted cilia, and others have undulating *membranelles* located near the peristome. Some, like *Didinium,* which feeds on paramecia, are adapted to seize a particular sort of prey and not others. Every cell of the genus *Suctoria,* which have no cilia as adults, has a tentacle and apparently a poisonous secretion.

3.2.1.2 Process Free-living cells pursue prey, which may be bacteria, protozoans, or other materials. When a particle of solid food or other similar substance approaches or comes in contact with the outer membrane of an amoeba (see Fig. 6-14), the amoeba reaches out toward its goal of the food, surrounding it with pseudopodia, extensions of the cell membrane and cytoplasm. It then forms a vacuole which detaches itself from the cell surface and migrates toward the

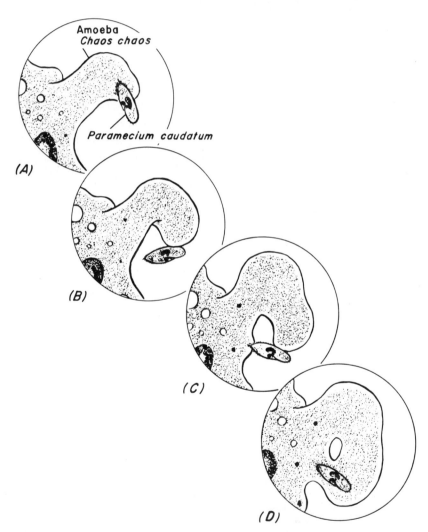

Fig. 6-14 Amoeba engulfing a paramecium. Drawings labeled in chronological sequence. (After a set of photomicrographs taken a few seconds apart by E. Gravé. In N. Tinbergen and the Editors of *Life. Animal behavior.* New York: Time, Inc., 1965, 74–75. *Reprinted by permission.*)

interior. This is known as *phagocytosis*. Within this vacuole chemical conversion takes place. The resultant molecular products pass through the membrane of the vacuole to become involved in other processes in the cell's matter-energy metabolism. Those protozoans which have special structures for ingesting also deliver the ingested matter-energy to membranous vacuoles which separate and float free within the cell. Paramecia have a specialized opening into a gullet. Cilia line this and, by waving, send food substances and some of the environmental water into the gullet, at the end of which a vacuole forms and moves into the cytoplasm.

Materials in solution enter many cells by pinocytosis, a "drinking" process somewhat like phagocytosis. The cell membrane surrounds part of the fluid medium, closes into a "pinosome," and migrates toward the interior of the cell. Cells may take in many sorts of molecules dissolved in the fluid, including glucose and amino acids. In both phagocytosis and pinocytosis, cells ingest food as well as materials which are not suitable for food. Oxygen, which most cells require for respiration, is dissolved in the surrounding medium and diffuses through the cell wall or enters with materials taken in by phagocytosis or pinocytosis. Water, which cells require for their internal processes, passes in and out through the cell membrane at all times.

I have already mentioned passive and active transport across the cell membrane. One process of passive transport is *osmosis*, movement of molecules across the membrane when there is a gradient in concentrations of dissolved substances between one side and the other. A solvent, but not the solute dissolved in it, diffuses across a membrane to achieve a steady state on the two sides of the membrane. Permeability to water is variable among some types of cells, but osmosis occurs in all cells.

Movement across the membrane in response to a concentration gradient occurs with many substances other than water. Oxygen and carbon dioxide freely pass into the cell. Other molecules diffuse into the cell with more difficulty or not at all, depending upon the differential permeability of the cell membrane.[79] The rate of penetration of solutes varies with the *ratio of their solubility in oil to their solubility in water*. Solutes with the highest ratio enter more freely regardless of molecular size, although with some exceptions very large molecules enter cells with difficulty or not at all. Another form of gradient which operates in passive transport is the *electrical potential gradient*. As I have noted above, molecules in the environment that are dissociated into ions move through the cell membrane, which maintains a difference in electrical potential between its inside and outside. The more

strongly a substance is ionized the more slowly it enters.[80] A third force, *solvent drag,* is relatively unimportant unless the movement in a given direction across the membrane is considerable, when particles moving in the direction of flow move more rapidly.[81]

In active transport the cell does work. It calls upon its available energy to assist molecules across the boundary, sometimes against a concentration gradient. It has been suggested that this transport is achieved through the agency of "carrier molecules"—compounds on the surface of cells with binding sites at which, in the presence of certain enzymes, they combine with the molecule to be carried into the cell. When this new compound forms, it passes through the cell membrane, perhaps going through a pore or hole that opens up for it. The size of the opening may limit the size of the molecule that can enter the cell. When it reaches the inner surface of the cell membrane, another enzyme splits it up, and the input conveyed across the membrane is released inside the cell.[82] Possible carrier molecules for a number of different substances have been found. It may be, for instance, that substances soluble in lipids penetrate the cell membrane by being dissolved in lipids on one side and released on the other.

In bacteria like *Escherichia coli,* in some yeasts, and perhaps in other types of cells, a process involving permease enzymes participates in the transport of sugars like lactose and perhaps other substances across the cell membrane and is an important part of the ingestor subsystem.[83] Separate enzymes or sets of enzymes are involved in the ingestion and in the later metabolism of lactose. A *permease* is a type of enzyme that is "inducible," *i.e.,* it is not always present but develops when there is in the medium a substance on which it can work. This results in a lag between the time the substance contacts the cell and the time the cell begins to use it. A number of experiments with different strains of bacteria have shown that a permease is specialized to ingest or transport molecules across the cell membrane and to do nothing else. A single cell may have 30 to 60 different permeases, each one specific for aiding active transport of a particular sort of molecule which the cell ingests across the cell membrane.

Representative *variables* of the process of ingesting include: *Sorts of matter-energy ingested.* Example: Sometimes the muscle cell took in hydrogen, oxygen, and potassium ions, and sometimes it did not because it contained adequate supplies. *Degree of openness of the ingestor.* Example: The rate of ingesting of amino acids by the bacterium increased as the concentration of amino acids went up in the fluid around it, but it leveled off when it reached a critical point at which the transport processes in the bacterial cell membrane were saturated.[84] *Changes in ingesting over time.* Example: As the plant cell grew to the full size possible within its rigid cell wall, its intake of amino acids declined greatly. *Changes in ingesting with different circumstances.* Example: When the temperature of the fluid surrounding the *Nitella* cell increased from 10 to 20°C, the rate of input of potassium ions to that cell doubled.[85] *Rate of ingesting.* Example: As a lower acidity decreased the ionization of the carbon dioxide in the solution around the *Euglena,* the rate at which that cell ingested the carbon dioxide increased.[86] *Frequency of ingesting.* Example: The amoeba formed 4 pinosomes in ½ h. *Lag in ingesting.* Example: The paramecium did not begin to consume the bacteria injected into the fluid around it for more than 5 min. *Costs of ingesting.* Example: Energy was consumed in the work involved in active transport of the dye across a concentration gradient at the cell membrane; the work involved was proportional to a constant times the natural logarithm of the ratio of its concentrations inside and outside the cell.[87]

3.2.2 Distributor, the subsystem which carries inputs from outside the cell or outputs from its subsystems around the cell to each component.

3.2.2.1 Structure   The endoplasmic and sarcoplasmic reticula; the ground cytoplasm, including axoplasm of neurons; and some minute fibrous organelles—the microtubules and microfilaments—are believed to be distributor components. Vacuoles and other membrane-limited particles containing matter-energy such as enzymes and markers for transmitter substances are also distributor components.

The endoplasmic reticulum, a membrane-bounded network of tubules and vesicles, which extends throughout the cytoplasm, varies greatly in different sorts of cells but seems to exist in all of them. Its membranes appear to connect with the cell membrane.[88] It is not present in mature red blood corpuscles, which are not complete cells.[89] In muscle cells there is the sarcoplasmic reticulum, made up of an equivalent of the endoplasmic reticulum and the transverse system, which is a lacework of tubules and vesicles within the sarcoplasm.[90] These tubules and vesicles have been isolated and are believed to be elastic. They vary in size from 50 to 100 nm and are limited by simple membranes about 5 nm thick with no discernible internal structure or content.[91] Either the transverse system alone, or it and the equivalent of the endoplasmic reticulum, connects with the cell membrane.[92]

The microtubules and smaller microfilaments are components of free-living cells as well as the cells of multicellular organisms. These organelles are submicroscopic, appearing in the clear cytoplasm in electron micrographs.[93]

The protein structure of microfilaments has been studied. They are composed of globular protein subunits organized into subunit strands (protofilaments) wound helically around each other to form a rigid structure. Microtubules have not yet been isolated in purified form, and it is not known how the protein compositions of the two types of structures differ. It is known, however, that these proteins are similar, but not identical, with actin, which is one of the fibrous proteins of muscle cells and of motor organelles of free-living cells. Microtubules and microfilaments may also constitute components of the motor, the supporter, the input transducer, and the channel and net.

3.2.2.2 Process   A great deal of movement goes on within cells. Various sorts of matter are transported into and out of the cell and from place to place within it, some of them in vacuoles. Cell components, such as mitochondria and chromosomes, move about as they carry out their processes in subsystems. Exactly how the various components of the distributor accomplish all this transport is not yet completely understood. A number of distribution processes which may be interrelated have been discussed, however, including (*a*) by the endoplasmic reticulum, (*b*) by the sarcoplasmic reticulum, (*c*) by the moving ground cytoplasm, and (*d*) by the microtubules and microfilaments.

(*a*) The *endoplasmic reticulum* has been supposed to convey products of cell metabolism from the ground cytoplasm to all parts of the cell.[94]

(*b*) The *sarcoplasmic reticulum* in muscle cells appears to convey substances needed in their contraction—calcium and ATP—to their contractile units, with which it is intimately related (see pages 244 and 245).

(*c*) *Ground cytoplasm.* In many sorts of cells a "streaming" of the cytoplasm can be observed. It may circulate in one direction, like the continual *cyclosis* of the endoplasm in plant cells, or in two opposite directions at once, like the endoplasm in cells of *Nitella.* Contraction of cytoplasm also takes place. A number of theories have been advanced to account for this motion, which is also an important motor process.

When an axon of a neuron is constricted, either experimentally or by pressure from surrounding structures, the portion proximal to the bottleneck becomes widened and that distal to it thins out. The fibers within the proximal portion become convoluted and distorted. They conform to the folds and twists of the axon itself. Vesicles and mitochondria accumulate near the bottleneck.[95] This, according to Weiss, indicates that axoplasmic flow involves movement of the axon as a whole rather than fluid transport within a static axon.[96] This flow provides for transport of materials of many sorts from their production sites, usually in the cell body, to their destinations. Materials transported down the axon include substances necessary for growth and repair of the axon itself and substances destined for output at the nerve endings, such as markers for information transmissions and the trophic substances upon which muscle cells that synapse with the axon are believed to depend for growth and proper maintenance. These flow downward at the rate of 1 millimeter (mm) per day.[97] This suggests continuous production of replacement parts, including mitochondria, internal fibers, and axoplasm, the axonal ground cytoplasm, and transport of these toward the neural ending. Analysis of the dynamics of this flow indicates that static pressure from the expansion of the cell body cannot account for it. There is evidence that suggests peristaltic waves may develop.[98]

(d) *Microtubules and microfilaments.* The slow movement of the ground cytoplasm cannot be the only means of intracellular distribution. Much faster rates, up to several hundred millimeters per day, of transport of some materials are revealed by radioactive labeling of proteins in neurons.[99] A rate close to 400 ± 35 mm per day has been demonstrated in cat sciatic nerve fibers and similar rates in other mammalian nerve fibers. Glutamate, thought to be a neuromuscular transmitter in snails, is conveyed to their nerve endings at the rate of 720 mm per day when the neuron is electrically stimulated, the fastest intracellular distribution rate yet discovered. Granules containing catecholamines also move rapidly toward neural endings. Both fast and slow rates of protein transport from the eye of the goldfish to the tectum of its brain have also been demonstrated. The faster rates of flow must be achieved by more rapid streaming within the slowly moving cytoplasmic mass, possibly through fluid spaces within or between the neurotubules and neurofilaments. Two-way transport in neurons also occurs.[100]

Microtubules are conspicuous components of the tentacles of the protozoan *Tokophyra* in which two-way transport occurs during ingestion.[101] Forty-nine microtubules arranged in clusters of seven divide the thin cylindrical tentacles into outer and inner tubes. Although these tentacles average only 0.5 nm in diameter and about 50 nm in length, they are remarkably stiff and straight. Knobs on them attach to and immobilize free-swimming ciliates. Particles containing enzymes are concentrated near the tip of each tentacle, presumably toxic to the prey. Additional particles, probably digestive enzymes, flow through the outer tube, and the cytoplasm of the prey moves through the inner tube.

It has long been realized that vacuoles, formed when protozoans take in solid and liquid matter-energy, do not move through the cell at random but appear to follow definite pathways through the cell as their contents are absorbed.[102] Vacuoles containing substances of no food value follow a shorter course to extrusion, a cost-saving adjustment process. Waste matter from cell processes also moves through the cell in vacuoles to the point of extrusion over the boundary, which in some free-living cells is a differentiated structure. Such functioning seems to tend to optimize a process described in Hypothesis 3.2.2.2-1 (see page 94) that the farther a specific matter-energy transmission passes along a distributor, the lower is the concentration of the kinds of matter-energy used by the system, and the higher is the concentration of the system's products or wastes. Why vacuoles move as they do through the cytoplasm has not been explained.

Microtubules are thought to provide a means for moving some particles and organelles within cells. They contain a protein like actin, which occurs in muscle cells. No second protein like myosin, the other molecule essential for motion in muscle cells, has been discovered in microtubules. Until such a protein is found or another way is discovered for microtubules to move their contents, the various explanations which have been proposed to account for such movements will remain only speculations.[103]

The mitotic spindle which brings about the rearrangement of chromosomes in mitosis is thought to form through microtubules.[104]

Particles of pigment or melanin move into and out of the armlike extensions of melanocytes, the pigment cells of animal organisms, in response to neural, humoral, or chemical inputs. These arms have many microtubules arranged to constitute "tracks" along which the granules move.[105] They do not proceed smoothly but, like many other particles and organelles, in a "saltatory" fashion, that is, in a series of rapid jerks or jumps.

The movements of mitochondria may also be saltatory.[106] Except during cell division these organelles move about actively. Occasionally they flow toward the nuclear membrane and attach themselves to it. Perhaps at these times some sort of matter-energy is transported from the mitochondria to the nucleus, possibly the energy-rich compound ATP, which stores much of the energy of cells.[107]

Representative *variables* of the distributing process are: *Sorts of matter-energy distributed to various parts of the system.* Example: Chromatin was transmitted through the epithelial cell's cytoplasm during cell division but not at any other time. *Changes in distributing over time.* Example: More ATP molecules were transmitted from the mitochondria to other organelles when the bacterium was in an active state than when it was a spore. *Changes in distributing with different circumstances.* Example: Between 0° and 50°C, the rate of diffusion of sugar in the cell increased by 37 percent for each 10°C rise in temperature.[108] *Rate of distributing.* Example: The rate of protein transport in the axon differed from time to time, but averaged less than 1 mm per day. *Frequency of distributing.* Example: The cells divided every 14 h approximately, so centrioles passed through their cytoplasms to their reproductive position that often. *Lag in distributing.* Example: As the red blood corpuscle swelled to abnormal volume in the cold, watery solution, diffusion of materials within the cell nearly stopped. *Costs of distributing.* Example: The flow of the axoplasm continuously consumed a small amount of cellular energy.

3.2.3 Converter, the subsystem which changes certain inputs to the cell into forms more useful for the special processes of that particular cell.

3.2.3.1 Structure   Certain enzymes do the chemical converting in cells. In protistan, animal, and plant cells most such enzymes are in mitochondria. Converting hydrolytic enzymes are also present in the cell membrane. Chlorophyll-containing monerans, protistans, and plants have some converting enzymes in their chloroplasts, which also carry out some enzymatic producing processes.[109] Spheroidal, discoidal, or ovoidal, and usually about 4 to 6 μm in diameter, these chloroplasts are of lamellar structure and some contain chlorophyll in granules called *grana*, about 0.3 to 1.7 μm in diameter.[110] The grana are made up of stacked lamellae composed of protein and lipid membranes. Membranes interconnect the stacks throughout the cell.[111] There is also evidence that converting enzymes are present in the nuclei of cells, although the major activity is in the mitochondria.[112] In yeast cells there may be only one single, giant, branched mitochondrion per cell.[113]

The structure of mitochondria has been studied by electron microscopy (see Fig. 6-2e). They are most often rod-shaped, although variations in shape occur in different sorts of cells. They are surrounded by a double membrane. Each membrane has a thickness of from 60 to 70 Å. They are divided by a space of about 60 Å. The inner membrane layer folds inward to form cristae which divide the mitochondrion into a number of compartments that interconnect, since the infoldings extend only part way across the cavity.[114] Within the mitochondrion, enzymes are arranged in particular patterns in physical space as a sort of molecular assembly line. They are arrayed in the order in which the chemical reactions which they control must occur. Those which convert other substances to energy-rich

ATP, an intermediate compound which powers further cellular processes including syntheses of other essential molecules, are on the inner mitochondrial membrane. Those which carry out the oxidation reactions and which catalyze synthetic reactions powered by ATP are located on the outer membrane.[115] A cell may have from 6 to 5,000 mitochondria, placed within the cell at points where energy is particularly needed. In muscle cells, for example, the mitochondria are situated where they can best aid contraction. Placing mitochondria so that their outputs move only a short distance before being used is an example at the cell level of how a living system maintains the functions of its subsystems at a high enough efficiency and their costs low enough that it can continue to carry out its processes (see Hypothesis 3.3.7.2-17, page 101).

Lysosomes are another sort of cytoplasmic organelle which carry out conversion functions. They are about 0.25 to 0.8 μm in diameter, filled with granules about 55 to 80 Å in diameter, containing primarily hydrolytic enzymes.[116]

The vacuoles formed during phagocytosis and pinocytosis are also part of the cell's converter subsystem, since enzymes are secreted into them which catalyze conversion of some of their contents into molecules which can pass through their membranes into the cytoplasm.

3.2.3.2 Process   In cells the conversion of input substances to simpler chemical "building blocks" frequently must precede synthesis of the often complex molecules required by that particular system. For example, in cells with chlorophyll the first stage in the very basic production process of photosynthesis is the decomposition of water molecules into hydrogen and oxygen.

Much of the energy of chlorophyll-containing cells comes directly from sunlight. Plants do, however, derive some energy from respiration, a converting process which, as in protistan and animal cells, is carried on in the mitochondria (see below). Cells without chlorophyll must have a supply of energy. This comes from some input which ultimately derives from chlorophyll-bearing cells. All the energy of living cells and other living systems is, therefore, fundamentally derived from the sun through the synthetic activities of cells with chlorophyll.

Energy for cellular processes is extracted from matter-energy inputs by breaking down the complicated molecules of protein, fat, and carbohydrate into their constituents. Many molecules are too large to pass through the cell membrane and must be split before they can enter the cell. This is accomplished by hydrolysis, a converting process whereby a molecule is divided into two by the addition of water. Cells of many or all types make use of hydrolytic enzymes which accelerate such action. Amino acids are produced by hydrolysis of polypeptide linkages of proteins; polysaccharides are hydrolyzed to glucose; fats to fatty acids, glycerol, and sometimes also phosphoric acid and nitrogenous base. These hydrolytic enzymes make it possible for cells to carry out their chemical reactions at low temperatures. To accomplish the same result without the enzyme, very high temperatures, far above any at which a cell could survive, would be required. To hydrolyze cane sugar by acid, for instance, requires an activation energy of 25,600 calories per mole (cal per mol), while in the presence of invertase it requires an activation energy of only 9,800 cal per mol. In this process the free energy does not change. In the further breakdown of such molecules much greater amounts of energy are liberated. Hydrolytic converting processes characteristically occur in such a stepwise fashion, each reaction being catalyzed by a specific enzyme. This sequence of chemical reactions involving small energy exchanges is nearly 50 percent efficient in converting glucose into ATP. Costs are minimized. Such efficiency which cuts costs, however, may not be best for survival of a living system. It may be more important to be able to mobilize a maximum power output when needed (see Hypothesis 3.3.7.2-18, page 101).

Mitochondria are the organelles of respiration in cells. They are the sites where energy is extracted from input materials and made available for cellular processes. Respiration is the oxidation of nutrients in the cell with the help of atmospheric oxygen, which reaches the cell in solution. The rate at which oxygen is used by cells varies with the cell's ratio of surface to volume.[117] Small cells, which have a large surface-to-volume ratio and therefore a relatively large surface over which oxygen can enter the cell, have a higher respiratory rate than large cells.

Oxidation is one process of the cellular converter. "Oxidation," when used technically, refers to any reaction in which electrons are given by one molecule to another rather than only to reactions in which oxygen is added to an atom or molecule. Glucose is oxidized in cells in two sequences of converting reactions, the first of which can occur in the absence of oxygen. Some types of cells are anaerobic and have only this sequence, known as fermentation in bacteria and yeasts and as glycolysis in other cells. In this sequence of several steps, with the aid of about a dozen specific enzymes, glucose is split into two molecules of pyruvic acid and high-energy phosphate compounds are formed, adenosine triphosphate (ATP) and creatine phosphate.

The high-energy phosphate bonds, found in such phosphorylated organic compounds, liberate about 8,000 to 12,000 cal per mol. These calories are available for the chemical reactions within the cell, such as the production of protein. Inorganic phosphate remains when all the energy is removed. ATP is a nucleotide composed of a pentose sugar, three phosphoric acids, and the nitrogenous base, adenine.[118] The bond between the pentose and the first phosphoric acid is an ordinary low-energy bond, but the two bonds between the phosphoric acids are high-energy bonds. These easily transfer their energy to other organic compounds in the presence of an enzyme. With one phosphate removed ATP becomes ADP, adenosine diphosphate, with only one high-energy bond. These two compounds always occur together in the living cell. The ADP must be recharged with another phosphate to become again a good energy source for cell reactions, much as when a battery is recharged. This is done in the mitochondria and chloroplasts. In muscle cells the sarcoplasmic reticulum, as well as the mitochondria, is thought to synthesize ATP anaerobically and recharge it after it becomes ADP.[119]

To quote from Lehninger:

This conversion of the energy liberated by the combustion of fuel into the third phosphate bond of ATP proceeds with extraordinary efficiency. For each molecule of glucose completely oxidized to water and carbon dioxide in a tissue preparation, approximately 38 molecules of ADP combine to form 38 molecules of ATP. In other words the oxidation of each mole of glucose produces 38 moles of ATP. It has been shown that the formation of one mole of ATP from ADP in this reaction as it occurs in the cell requires about 12,000 calories. The formation of 38 moles of ATP therefore requires the input of at least 38 times 12,000 calories, or about 456,000 calories. Since the oxidation of one mole of glucose yields a maximum of 690,000 calories, the recovery of 38 moles of ATP represents a conversion of 66 percent of the energy. As a comparison, a modern steam-generating plant converts about 30 percent of its energy input to useful work.[120]

The second sequence of reactions in the converting of glucose occurs only in the presence of oxygen. This stage is called the "Krebs cycle," "citric acid cycle," or "tricarboxylic acid cycle." In it, pyruvic acid is broken down to carbon dioxide and water with the release of much more energy as high-energy phosphate bonds. Anaerobic cells, which have only the first sequence, are therefore much less efficient than those which make use of oxygen. The Krebs-cycle reactions also deal with excess organic compounds beyond the needs of the producer subsystem, which result from the conversion of input proteins, fats, and carbohydrates. Instead of being treated as wastes and extruded from the cell, they are oxidized to form high-energy phosphate bonds.[121]

Representative *variables* of the converting process are: *Sorts of matter-energy converted.* Example:

Depending upon what input it received, the cell at one time converted chiefly fat and at another chiefly protein to provide the necessary constituents for producing the proteins it required. *Percentage of matter-energy converted.* Example: The fibroblast in tissue culture on the average converted only 50 percent as much glucose in an hour under anaerobic conditions as under aerobic. *Changes in converting over time.* Example: As the *Nitella* cell grew, it consumed less oxygen per microgram per second.[122] *Changes in converting with different circumstances.* Example: When the potassium cyanide input into the tumor cell rose above 0.001 molar, its converting processes slowed to a stop.[123] *Rate of converting.* Example: As the amount of oxygen in the atmosphere fell to 0.25 percent of normal, the bacterium's rate of converting substances by oxidation fell to 50 percent of normal.[124] *Frequency of converting.* Example: On the average the yeast cell converted one molecule of glucose into glycogen every 1 μs. *Lag in converting.* Example: Since the neuron was anesthetized with urethane, its converting processes started up much more slowly than they usually did after the surrounding medium was saturated with oxygen. *Costs of converting.* Example: The sequence of reactions in the metabolic cycle of the amoeba converted glucose to ATP with 50 percent efficiency.[125]

3.2.4 Producer, the subsystem which forms stable associations that endure for significant periods among matter-energy inputs to the cell or outputs from its converter, the materials synthesized being for growth, damage repair, or replacement of components of the cell, or for providing energy for moving or constituting the cell's outputs of products or information markers to its suprasystem.

3.2.4.1 Structure The primitive chlorophyll arrangements of algae, the chloroplasts of green plants, enzymes such as those in the mitochondria, the Golgi apparatuses, and the nucleic acids in the nuclei and ribosomes of all other cells, including free-living and aggregated cells, are the principal cellular producer structures (see Fig. 6-2).

The cells of algae carry out photosynthesis with chlorophyll arranged in the cytoplasm, but the cells of green plants have it localized in specialized organelles, the chloroplasts, which therefore are the structures in which photosynthetic producing is carried out.

When cells are spun for a short time in an ultracentrifuge, the heavier parts—such as nuclei and mitochondria—are separated from the lighter parts and watery fluids. When centrifuging is carried on further, the ribosomes separate out. When disrupted bacterial cells are centrifuged at 40,000 revolutions per minute (rpm) for 2 or 3 h, three sorts of RNAs of different molecular weights are separated out in the resultant sediment with the fluid on top.[126] The fluid contains soluble transfer RNA with a molecular weight of about 25,000 and a rate of sedimentation (S), which is a direct function of molecular weight and shape, of 4S. It constitutes about 2 percent of the cell's total RNA. The sediment contains ribosomal RNA with molecular weights of about 600,000 and 1.2 million, and sedimentation rates of 16S and 23S. This represents about 80 percent of the cell's total RNA. After lowering the magnesium ion concentration, one can separate from the ribosomal RNA in the sediment another sort, messenger RNA. This has a molecular weight of about 500,000 and sedimentation rates of 8S to 30S. It represents about 20 percent of the cell's total RNA.

Under the electron microscope ribosomes appear to be between 100 and 150 Å in diameter.[127] Sometimes two or more ribosomes are held together by messenger RNA, forming larger units, polyribosomes or polysomes.[128] These can be seen in photomicrographs. Each ribosome has two parts, one large and the other small. Both contain RNA and protein. These are present in equal amounts, protein apparently being the supporting structure. In muscle cells they are not attached to the sarcoplasmic reticulum, but apparently in other cells they are associated with the endoplasmic reticulum.[129]

All the components which carry out the cell's producing activities have by no means been identified, although various hypotheses have been propounded as to what the sites may be. We do know with certainty the sites of synthesis of many of the nonprotein products of cells—like the acetylcholine which is made by nerve cells or the lipids which are regularly produced for repair and replacement of membranes.

3.2.4.2 Process Every cell is continuously making products which it needs for growth, repair of damage to its components, replacements of its components, or other cellular processes. Those with chlorophyll produce glucose. All cells synthesize proteins, a most complex process, as well as carbohydrates, energy-rich phosphates, fats, lipids, and other substances. All this production is mediated by enzymes which are subject to complicated controls. Many details of the producing processes of various components of ribosomes and other organelles are now known.[130]

What cells must have as inputs in order to produce varies from one sort of cell to another. Cells which contain chlorophyll are able to produce substances for their own nutrition. Cells without chlorophyll cannot do this. Protozoa and cells of animal tissues which have no chlorophyll must have these nutritive substances in their inputs. Most cells also require, for their producing processes, inputs of molecular oxygen in solution to carry on respiration, but others, including the anaerobic bacteria, can perform their life processes without such inputs. Cells in an organism's muscular tissue can function anaerobically for a time but must eventually have oxygen to repair the effects of fatigue and carry on their metabolism. Some bacteria are able to use inorganic inputs, including nitrogen from the air. Others can use organic inputs only. Some bacteria can get their carbon from carbon monoxide or even marsh gas, but most must have inputs of sugar or alcohols. Frequently particular vitamins which the cell cannot manufacture must be present in small quantities in their inputs.

A vast number of different compounds is produced by cells. Substances for reproduction of the cell itself are made by any cell capable of reproducing. Substances for its growth and repair are also synthesized. Defects in DNA molecules damaged by radiation or produced in some other way can be repaired by an enzyme known as DNA polymerase. First the enzyme endonuclease locates the defect. Then the DNA polymerase cuts out the damaged part of the DNA and assembles the molecules needed to repair it. After the repair a third enzyme, ligase, reunites the repaired parts.

Many compounds synthesized in cells are proteins, but they include lipids and other molecules as well. In aggregated tissues and organs, specialized secretions are synthesized, such as acetylcholine by nerve cells, digestive juices by pancreatic cells, and hormones by cells of endocrine glands. Mammalian plasma cells produce a great variety of antibodies for fighting bacterial infection, possibly millions of different proteins specific against particular kinds of invaders.[131] A good deal is now known about how cells manufacture certain substances.

Photosynthesis. This, the most fundamental process of cellular producing, is carried out by those monerans, protistans, and plants which contain chlorophyll. It is basic because upon the ability to harness the energy of the sun and produce glucose depends the existence not only of the cells that can do this but also of all cells that do not contain chlorophyll. The latter cannot use the sun's energy themselves, so they must get inputs of glucose or other nutritive substances from cells that can. Photosynthesis is accomplished in two major sets of reactions:

(a) First, light absorbed by chlorophyll sets electrons in motion in it. In a test tube, such chlorophyll glows, immediately losing the energy it has taken in. The structure of the cell that contains chlorophyll, however, ensures that the electrons which are excited whenever light hits it enter into a chain of reactions in which their energy is used to produce carbohydrate. The first set of reactions makes ATP from ADP and inorganic phosphate and also reduces triphosphopyridine nucleotide and produces free oxygen, which plant cells extrude.

(b) The second set of reactions can occur in the dark and in the absence of oxygen. In them the energy in the ATP and triphosphopyridine nucleotide formed in the first series of reactions enables carbon dioxide and water to combine into carbohydrate, oxygen also being given off.[132]

All these processes are complex, involving "electron carriers" believed to be compounds called cytochromes, which are proteins containing iron atoms surrounded by porphyrin groups. These can carry energy to synthesize ATP.[133] The subsequent synthesis of the primary cellular carbohydrate, glucose, also involves intricate reactions and the participation of carrier molecules.[134] A molecule of cellular glucose stores a considerable number of calories derived originally from solar energy. All cells can extract this chemical energy and store it in ATP as a quick source of energy for their processes, even though they have no chlorophyll and thus cannot use the sun's energy to synthesize carbohydrates themselves.

Protein synthesis. Protein is produced in the ribosomes, outside the nuclear membrane in the cytoplasm. The information is transferred from the nucleus to the cytoplasm by RNA. In the nucleus there are three separate RNAs of different molecular weights.[135] DNA is the template for the synthesis of these three sorts of nuclear RNA transcribed from the DNA. Experiments have indicated that in cellfree extracts which contain no DNA, the addition of DNA results in RNA synthesis and in increased use of the amino acids which compose it.

In the cytoplasm there are three sorts of ribosomal RNAs—each of a different molecular weight, transfer RNAs, and messenger RNAs. The ribosomal RNA, which composes ribosomes, does not act as a template and is not specific for any particular protein, but has attachment sites, being a sort of working table in an assembly line where different steps in protein synthesis are carried out.[136] There are numerous kinds of *transfer* or *soluble* RNAs, at least one distinct such molecule for each of the about 20 different amino acids employed in protein synthesis. The nucleotide bases of transfer RNAs are complementary to those of the DNA which patterned them. It is, therefore, possible to deduce from which cistron or gene each molecule of transfer RNA was derived, if the sequence of nucleotide bases of the cistron and the corresponding sequence of the RNA molecule can be determined (see Fig. 6-11).

Transfer RNAs transport amino acids, which are in the cell as a result of the converting of input proteins, to the proper position on the ribosomal template. A special activating enzyme attaches each amino acid to its transfer RNA. Each cell has more than one sort of transfer RNA, each one specialized for acting on a given amino acid.[137] When the amino acids reach the proper position on the developing molecule, as a result of the intervention of still other enzymes, they are united by peptide linkages. A molecule of messenger RNA, perhaps 1500 Å long, passes along the ribosome or polysome acting as a template for assembling amino acids. It serves to translate or recode the message from the nucleic acid code to the protein code. The RNA codons, one at a time, attach amino acids somewhat as a zipper is closed. (A molecule of messenger RNA may serve as a template to produce multiple protein molecules.) This complicated process can synthesize a finished protein molecule of about 150 amino acids in about 1.5 min.[138]

Energy-rich phosphate synthesis. The Krebs cycle described above (see page 237) represents the sequence of processes whereby certain input carbohydrates, fats, and lipids are converted into simpler compounds that can be used by the cell. At the same time new energy-rich phosphate compounds, such as ATP, are produced. Each step of these processes is controlled by an enzyme.

Carbohydrate synthesis. A variety of cellular carbohydrates, although not all of them, are synthesized by the Golgi apparatuses.[139] In many sorts of cells—pancreatic cells, for example—newly produced enzymes migrate to the Golgi apparatuses where they are combined with carbohydrates into glycoproteins and emerge neatly packaged into globules which are excreted from the cell. The pectin in some plant cell walls is synthesized by these apparatuses. They produce more than one sort of granule in some cells.

Repair processes. The many experiments that successfully make use of nuclear transplants indicate that cells are capable of reestablishing their normal processes after their cell membranes and cytoplasm are damaged. An amoeba can survive amputations of its cytoplasm and return to normal function after a period of growth.[140] The nucleus, however, must remain intact. It contains the chief components of the essential decider. If the nucleus of *Amoeba proteus* is removed, the cell immediately stops moving.[141] The pseudopodia no longer form, and the damaged cell becomes spherical. The cell is no longer able to feed on living prey. The fragment will, however, survive as long as a starving nucleated half of an amoeba. If a nucleus is supplied to such an amoeba within a few days, before irreversible changes occur, pseudopod formation again occurs.

Experiments have been carried out on reassembly of living amoebas from dissociated components.[142] Nuclei are removed from some amoebas, cytoplasm from others, and cell membranes from others. It has been found that these can be rearranged in any desired combination of the three sorts of components to produce living cells.

The protozoan *Blepharisma* can survive removal of a large part of its cell mass, leaving only micronuclei and macronuclear fragments. It then regenerates a miniature edition of itself which, after feeding, returns to its original size, an example of the principle of equifinality (see page 41).[143]

Some repair processes in aggregated cells have been studied. Peripheral neurons, for example, can repair themselves if their cell bodies are intact.[144] Both cell body and axon fiber are repaired after a motor neuron is cut. If the cell does not die, growth outward begins from the end of the central stump. At the tip of the new growth are end disks containing vesicles and mitochondria. In the meanwhile, a sheath of Schwann is growing from the other side of the cut, toward the neuron's cell body from the periphery. The fiber of the neuron grows toward this newly developing sheath. It may even enter an old sheath of a degenerated fiber and grow in a peripheral direction in it. Evidently a fiber's peripheral relationships are established by accident, and if an incorrect relationship is made, the cell does not survive. If, however, the fiber of the neuron contacts a muscle fiber, a functioning synapse can be reestablished with complete regeneration of the terminations. The regenerated relationships are not identical with those that existed before the injury. Neurons tend to branch more as they regrow and innervate a larger group of muscle fibers than they did previously. Consequently control of the muscle by the organism is less precise, and its action is less effective. Similar repair processes are found in sensory neurons. Even complex terminations like receptor endings in muscles and tendons regenerate. After a sensory cell is cut, the central fiber degenerates, rather than the peripheral, which is the case in motor neurons. Central neurons do not regenerate. Little growth occurs after damage, never enough in most vertebrates for normal function to return.

When a bacteriophage DNA molecule is exposed to heat, extremes of acidity, or other stresses, the two parts of its double helix separate into two chains.[145] If the stress disappears, DNA molecules so divided may reform into duplex molecules again. The repaired bacteriophage DNA then regains its ability to control the syntheses of bacterial cells into which it penetrates. Early in the normal process of genetic recombination some sort of denaturation, or breakdown of the DNA into its components, occurs. Later continuity of the new, combined DNA must be established. This process must be catalyzed by an enzyme. DNA repair is probably a related process. Bacterial DNA is also capable of repair when it has been damaged.[146] For example, when DNA is damaged by radiation, two bases often fuse. Three enzymes, one of which is DNA polymerase, catalyze the processes of locating defects, repairing them, and recombining the molecule.

Among the *variables* in the producing process are: *Sorts of matter-energy produced.* Example: The epidermal cell synthesized proteins and lipids to repair its boundary whenever it was damaged by stressful mechanical forces applied to the skin. *Quality of matter-energy produced.* Example: In the absence of inputs of vitamin B$_{12}$, the normoblasts in the bone marrow, precursors of red blood corpuscles, produced abnormal hemoglobin. *Percentage of matter-energy used in producing.* Example: About 65 percent of the energy in the glucose inputs to the amoeba was used in synthesizing new substances required in its growth, repair of damaged components, or other metabolic processes. *Changes in producing over time.* Example: During mitosis the liver cell produced only materials needed for reproducing, but afterward it recommenced to synthesize all essential compounds. *Changes in producing with different circumstances.* Example: Plant cells containing chlorophyll synthesized ATP from phosphate and adenylic acid when it was light, but they stopped producing it after dark. *Rate of producing.* Example: The cell synthesized a protein molecule of about 150 amino acids in about 1.5 min, but this time varied. *Frequency of producing.* Example: From the tenth to the thirtieth minute after the T2 bacteriophage infected the *Escherichia coli*, the cell made new viruses at the rate of about 10 per minute, but then the rate slowed rapidly until the cell membrane burst.[147] *Lag in producing.* Example: Five seconds after the glucose was input into the cell, it began to be used to produce molecules of ATP.[148] *Costs of producing.* Example: At different times the cell consumed varying amounts of glucose—ranging between 0.0001 and 0.0003 mol—in producing enough energy for 1 joule (J) of work.

3.2.5 Matter-energy storage, the subsystem which retains in the cell, for different periods of time, deposits of various sorts of matter-energy.

3.2.5.1 Structure   Phosphorylated organic compounds; starch or glycogen granules; glucose, fructose, sucrose, or lactose; lipochondria; lipids, including fat droplets; some proteins; and secretory granules, as of zymogen, acetylcholine, epinephrine, or norepinephrine, are all parts of the matter-energy storage subsystem in cells. Both animal and plant cells, free-living and aggregated, store energy and materials. Cells which form tissues of organisms may be highly specialized to perform a storage function for the organism, *e.g.*, fat cells. A large amount of the total volume of these cells is taken up by storage structures [see Fig. 6-6(v)].

3.2.5.2 Process   Cells store energy, nutritive materials, and other substances. Some specialized cells store secretions which they produce for organisms.

Energy is stored in three forms in cells—one providing rapid access, one providing moderately fast access, and one providing slow access. (*a*) The most immediately available form of energy storage is in phosphorylated organic compounds such as ATP, creatine phosphate in muscles of vertebrates, and arginine phosphate in muscles of invertebrates. These compounds are formed by converting other sorts of matter-energy inputs or, in plants, also by producing ATP from inorganic phosphates and adenosine monophosphate in the presence of light. (*b*) A less rapidly available sort of energy storage is in starch and sugars in plants, and in glycogen in animals. Starch is an insoluble carbohydrate into which glucose is polymerized. This stored food is retrieved for cellular consumption by enzymes that digest it and convert it back to glucose. Some plant cells, as in grapes, store glucose, which can be used directly in some cellular reactions. Others store fruit sugar (fructose) or the sugar used in ordinary cooking, cane or beet sugar (sucrose). Milk sugar (lactose) is found in mammary gland cells. Glycogen, animal starch, is sometimes stored in glycogen granules. (*c*) The least rapidly available sort of energy storage is in lipids and occasionally in proteins. These storages all constitute "buffer inventories" (see Hypothesis 3.2.5.2-1, page 94). Their existence enables the rates of converting energy to usable forms in the cell to vary within wide ranges without limiting the rates of the producing process, which uses outputs from the converting process.

Lipids may be found in the cytoplasm in the form of droplets. When surrounded by a protein membrane they are lipochondria. Specialized food storage cells in plants occur in bulbs, tubers, roots, seeds, and fruit. These can be starches, sugars, fats, or proteins. In man, cells of the liver and muscles store glycogen. Fat is stored in cells of fatty tissues like those below the skin and in the omenta, membranes running between the stomach and the intestines.

All storage in cells is not food reserves. Many secretory cells produce their substances on demand and do not store them within the cell. (Storage in an organ or organism may be provided in a hollow structure.) There is also intracellular storage in secretion granules. These granules, however, are not the production sites of cellular secretions.[149] The zymogen granules of the pancreas are examples of secretory granules. *Zymogens* are inactive proteolytic enzymes capable, when activated, of decomposing protein molecules. They are stored in the pancreas and secreted into the small intestine where an enzyme activates them by making small but essential changes in their molecular structures.

Epinephrine and norepinephrine, which are chemically related and of relatively low molecular weight, act as markers in endocrine and neural intercellular information transmissions. They are stored in granules of varying sizes in adrenergic sympathetic nerve cells and chromaffin cells of such organs as the adrenal medulla. Such granules constitute examples of stored material in a cell. When transmitted out of a cell, they become markers capable of transmitting a signal to another cell.

Among the *variables* in the process of storing matter-energy are: *Sorts of matter-energy stored.* Example: At times the amoeba stored ATP or glucose; at other times it stored undigested bacteria also, in vacuoles. *Total storage capacity.* Example: The pancreatic cell could store nearly twice as many zymogen granules when it had gained full size as it could when it had just been formed. *Percentage of matter-energy stored.* Example: When the muscle cell was inactive it stored up to 50 percent of the glucose input to it, but at its maximum rate of activity it stored none. *Place of storage.* Example: After ingesting bacteria, the paramecium stored them for a while in a vacuole near its gullet, but later the vacuole migrated to other parts of its cytoplasm. *Changes in storing over time.* Example: As the cell grew older, it stored more fat. *Changes in storing with different circumstances.* Example: The protozoan stored much more water in its endoplasm in its dormant period as a cyst during the cold winter than when it was active in the summer. *Rate of storing.* Example: One new chromaffin granule formed in the cell of the adrenal medulla every minute, but this rate slowed as the number of granules increased to more than 100. *Lag in storing.* Example: The food particles did not enter the vacuole of the paramecium until 10 min after they were ingested into its gullet. *Costs of storing.* Example: Only 60 percent of the energy in the glucose input to the cell was available in the glycogen molecules formed from it; the rest was lost in the process of forming the glycogen for storage. *Rate of*

breakdown of organization of matter-energy in storage. Example: As the fast-growing cancer cells put pressure on the fat cell, its stored fat became necrotic and broke down into fatty acids and bases much more rapidly than it would have otherwise. *Sorts of matter-energy retrieved.* Example: The paramecium digested the food particles in its vacuoles and used the resultant glucose for energy when it had recently ingested food, but when it had not, it used up the ATP and glucose in its endoplasm. *Percentage of matter-energy retrieved.* Example: By the time the ground squirrel finished hibernating, about 99 percent of the fat stored in the cell of the omentum of the ground squirrel was withdrawn from storage by the cell and used for its metabolism during the squirrel's hibernation. *Order of retrieval.* Example: The muscle cell first retrieved ATP from storage, then glucose, and finally, as it continued to contract vigorously, glycogen; only occasionally did it retrieve the small amount of fat stored in it. *Rate of retrieval.* Example: The glycogen stored in the rapidly contracting muscle cell was all used in a half-hour—much more rapidly than it had ever been consumed before. *Lag in retrieval.* Example: The fat was in the liver cell more than 10 years before it was used, but previously the cell had used fat within 24 h after it was stored. *Costs of retrieval.* Example: Once the amoeba had used up the glycogen in its endoplasm, it continued to move for only a few minutes and never moved again.

3.2.6 Extruder, the subsystem which transmits matter-energy out of the cell in the forms of products or wastes.

3.2.6.1 Structure   Cells differ widely from one type to another as to what sorts of components make up their extruder subsystems. In some monerans and protistans, and in aggregated cells, apparently any part of the membrane may be crossed by matter-energy outputs. Some protozoans have specialized extruders, anal pores or cytoprocts, as well as contractile vacuoles, food vacuoles from which usable materials have been removed. Some glandular cells have excretory canals (*e.g.,* glandular cells of the pancreas).[150] Possibly the sarcoplasmic reticulum is a structural part of this subsystem.[151]

3.2.6.2 Process   Electroplaque cells of electric fish are modified muscle cells that develop large electric charges. They can output electric energy with peak voltages of 50 to 150 mV.[152] A number of them interconnected in series in an electric organ can produce electric shocks of several hundred volts. Volta's original electric cell was modeled upon electroplaques.

The traffic of various sorts of matter across the cell membrane is two-way. Water, for example, attains equilibrium by passing both ways through the membrane. It diffuses through the cell membrane in response to the concentration gradient between the two sides. The extruding function is the converse of ingesting. Often the two processes are coupled one-to-one. For example, a potassium ion cannot enter a cell unless a sodium ion is extruded at the same time. The bucket that brings the input in, as it were, cannot go back empty. Some electrolytes and other substances such as carbon dioxide and oxygen dissolved in the water pass through the cell membrane in both directions along with the water.[153] Materials dissolved in water decrease the permeability of the membrane. The effects of molecular size are similar in whatever direction the traffic goes (see page 230).

Active transport across the cell membrane also goes in both directions. When a cell receives various sorts of matter-energy inputs which may convey information of different sensory modalities, potassium leaks out, and sodium moves in. To return to its former state, the cell subsequently must extrude sodium and ingest potassium. Sodium is extruded from cells, and potassium is accumulated within them by the active transport of the "ionic pump."[154]

I considered the hypothesis that there are carrier molecules when discussing the ingestor. If it is correct, the carrier molecules can be assumed to move in both directions across the cell membrane. One model for the movement of sodium and potassium ions across a cell membrane pictures the process as involving two lipid-soluble carrier molecules (X and Y) that are specific for the two ions.[155] These form compounds, potassium-X and sodium-Y. These compounds can move across the membrane by diffusion, while the free carriers cannot. At the outside surface of the membrane, sodium carriers are converted into potassium carriers, losing energy; and the opposite occurs on the inside surface of the membrane, with energy furnished by potassium-rich compounds. Such transport could involve allosteric molecules (see page 258). Permeases may also be involved.

Paramecia are highly differentiated free-living forms with well-developed structural subsystems. Food which is input through the gullet of a paramecium enters food vacuoles at the bottom of the gullet. These food vacuoles are components of at least four laterally dispersed combined subsystems, carrying out functions of the distributor, converter, matter-energy storage, and extruder. A feeding paramecium becomes filled with food vacuoles which follow a definite course as they distribute the products of the converting of the food about the cytoplasm. These travel to the anal pore which is located just posterior to the base of the gullet. This is obviously the long way around, but the full circuit of the endoplasm may well

make for efficiency of distribution of the vacuoles' contents. Finally the wastes which remain are extruded.

Paramecia, and some other protozoans, have two or more structures known as contractile vacuoles which are in fixed position near the membrane. From them, canals radiate through the cytoplasm. They collect water which is extruded through a small pore in the membrane as the vacuole contracts.[156] Fresh-water species take in water in response to the concentration gradient, since the water surrounding them contains less salt than the inside of the cell. They must extrude it against the gradient, which is the function of the vacuole. Every 15 or 20 min a paramecium empties, through a contractile vacuole, a quantity of water equal to its entire volume.[157] If its respiration is suspended by poisoning with potassium cyanide, its vacuoles cannot contract, and it will finally burst with unextruded water. The contractile vacuole of another species of protozoan, which inhabits brackish water, is quite inactive unless the water is diluted by more water, as in a heavy rain.

The suggestion that the sarcoplasmic reticulum may serve as "plumbing," along with its other functions, was made by Porter and Franzini-Armstrong.[158] They pointed out that the branching, interconnected tubules and sacs which constitute the sarcoplasmic reticulum are arranged in the cell around and among the myofibrils in such a way that they could distribute calcium, ATP, and creatine phosphate to them and carry off the waste products of contraction, like lactic acid, to the surface of the cell, where they could be extruded.[159]

The cnidoblast of coelenterates contains a cap which is an extruder component. Upon proper stimulation it explodes, ejecting spines and a thread. With these it can harm its enemy or its prey.

Glandular cells and neurons extrude their secretory products across the cell membrane in various ways. When these products are markers bearing information—*e.g.*, hormones or vesicles of transmitter substance at a synapse, the component of the extruder involved is also part of the output transducer subsystem.

The *variables* of the process of extruding are: *Sorts of products and wastes extruded.* Example: The protozoan extruded wastes from the bacteria it consumed every 20 min or so, but it extruded sizable amounts of water only when rain had diluted the salt in the pond. *Percentage of products and wastes extruded.* Example: In the 10 min after the meal passed into the intestine the acinous glandular cell of the pancreas secreted at least 50 percent of its zymogen granules; it also extruded about 20 percent of the carbon dioxide in it in the form of bicarbonate ions. *Changes in extruding over time.* Example: As the embryonic cell in the mucous membrane developed, it secreted more mucin with each day that passed. *Changes in extruding with different circumstances.* Example: After the paramecium ingested the potassium cyanide it no longer could extrude water. *Rate of extruding.* Example: The paramecium extruded its weight in water every 18 min. *Frequency of extruding.* Example: The glandular cell of the dog's stomach secreted its enzyme twice a day—within minutes after the dog ate each morning and each night. *Lag in extruding.* Example: The minute metal particles remained in the endoplasm of the macrophage for over 24 h before they were extruded. *Costs of extruding.* Example: Energy in high-energy phosphate bonds in ATP molecules, which were reduced to ADP moledules, was used up in work every time the cell's contractile vacuole constricted to extrude the wastes which had accumulated in it.

3.2.7 Motor, the subsystem which moves the cell or parts of it in relation to part or all of its environment or moves components of its environment in relation to each other.

3.2.7.1 Structure   The basic components of the motors of cells appear to be made up of one of two different sorts of fibrous protein molecule subcomponents. One is the proteins, not yet completely analyzed, which form the microtubules and microfilaments described above (see page 234). The other is a combination of two proteins, actin and myosin. This actomyosin is found in muscle fibers and some other types of cells, including slime molds. It is probable that the two types of proteins are closely related and that the microtubules and microfibrils are phylogenetically older.[160] Fibrous proteins are present in all cells but differ in their organization from one cell type to another.

Other motor components include a variety of structures.[161] No visible motor organelles are found in some free-living cells which are capable of locomotion. In others, and in some cell components of organisms, pseudopodia—"false feet"—of varying forms are observed. These are deformations of the cytoplasm. In amoebas a single, large, more or less cylindrical pseudopod forms. In other cells they may be sheets or long filaments.

Flagella and *cilia* are similar hairlike components that extend outward from the cell membrane. Flagella are longer, and a cell ordinarily has only one or two. The "tails" of sperm are flagella. Cilia are usually present in great numbers either all around the cell boundary or, in the case of some aggregated cells, concentrated along one side. The substructure of cilia and flagella is the same. They appear always to contain eleven straight fibers of which nine are double fibers surrounding two central fibers.[162] These fibers are microtubules.[163] At the bases of the cilia and flagella are *kinetosomes*. Each is a hollow cylinder 150 nm wide and 300 to 500 nm long with walls containing nine parallel tubules.[164]

Muscle cells are specialized as motor components of organisms.[165] They differ in various species and in the three types of muscular tissues of mammals and other vertebrates (see Fig. 6-7). In general, muscle cells are elongated, spindle-shaped structures. The contractile units of actomyosin, the myofibrils, are oriented along the length of the cell. The skeletal muscle fibers of vertebrates, which have been extensively studied, are very elongated with many myofibrils. These are composite cells. The multiple nuclei and other organelles such as mitochondria lie in the cytoplasm (called sarcoplasm in muscle) which surrounds the myofibrils. The tubules of the sarcoplasmic reticulum run parallel to the myofibrils along the fiber and also transversely around the fibrils.[166] At places some of the tubules fuse and form a sac that girdles each fibril and gives rise to the transverse system which connects across the whole fiber. This transverse part may be continuous with the cell membrane, or sarcolemma, that surrounds the entire fiber. The transverse and parallel systems appear to be distinct.

Electron microscopic and x-ray diffraction studies of the structure of striated-muscle myofibrils have shown that they consist of overlapping arrays of filaments containing actin and myosin, the overlap giving the striated appearance visible with the light microscope. These are made up of repeating units, the sarcomeres (see Fig. 6-15).[167]

3.2.7.2 Process   Contraction is a fundamental process of protoplasm. It is a highly developed function of some specialized cells like muscle fibers and unimportant or entirely absent in other cells. Some monerans, many protistans, and some single-celled fungi such as slime molds are free-living cells with the capacity of locomotion. Single-celled plants, such as those algae which are classified in the plant kingdom, are incapable of locomotion. Every protozoan can locomote in at least one phase of its life cycle.

Research has progressively clarified our understanding of both (*a*) the functioning of molecular subcomponents like microfilaments and microtubules in the movements of muscle fibers and other cells and (*b*) the major types of motion of cellular components such as pseudopodia (in amoeboid movement), cilia, and flagella.

Processes of cellular subcomponents involved in moving.   Any sort of motion in cells requires that chemical energy, present in the cell in molecules of high-energy substances such as ATP, be converted into mechanical

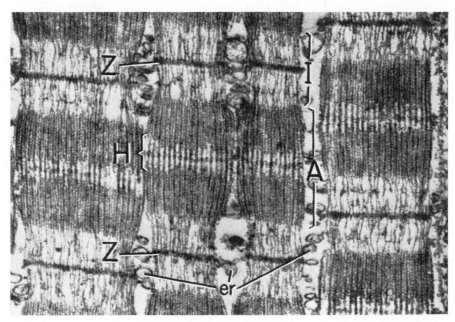

Fig. 6-15 Electron micrograph of four myofibrils, showing the alternating sarcomeres with A-, I-, and H-bands and Z-lines magnified × 60,000. Dense A-band (A) consists of overlapping thick and thin filaments. Lighter I-band (I) consists of thin filaments alone. H-band (H) consists of thick filaments alone. Halfway along their length, the thin filaments pass through a narrow zone of dense material, the Z-line (Z). The sarcoplasmic reticulum (er) is also shown. [From A. C. Giese. *Cell physiology.* (3d ed.) Philadelphia: Saunders, 1968, 573. *Photograph courtesy of H. Huxley. Reprinted by permission.*]

energy. A detailed theoretical explanation by Huxley of the process of contraction has received wide acceptance.[168] The "sliding filament" theory assumes that a myofibril contracts when its actin and myosin filaments slide past each other. This is believed to be brought about by combination of actin molecules with the cross-bridges of myosin molecules in the presence of ATP, molecules of which are split in the reaction. Calcium ions must be present in the sarcoplasm. A regulatory substance, troponin, which is part of the actin filaments, prevents activation when calcium is absent.[169] Huxley suggests that:

. . . the contraction of striated muscle is brought about by some mechanism which generates a relative sliding force between the partly overlapping arrays of actin and myosin filaments. There is very strong evidence that cross-bridges projecting out from the myosin filaments, and carrying the adenosine triphosphatase and actin binding sites, are involved in the generation of this force in some cyclical process. However, it appears that the mechanism must satisfy two conflicting requirements: (i) that the force be produced as a result of a precisely determined set of structural changes in a protein complex consisting of actin, myosin, and other components, and be associated with the splitting of a molecule of adenosine triphosphate; (ii) that the force-generating mechanism can work equally well over a considerable range of side spacings between the actin and myosin filaments. Recent

evidence suggests that these requirements may be satisfied in the following way: the actual force-generating structure is attached to the backbone of the myosin filaments by a linkage, 400 Ångstroms long, which has flexible couplings at either end; the force-generating structure can therefore attach itself to the actin filament, in a constant configuration, and undergo exactly the same structural changes and produce the same longitudinal force over a wide range of interfilament separations. The muscle structure is arranged so that the linkage is under tension, not compression, when a contractile force is being generated, so the force can be transmitted without difficulty. It is suggested that the characteristic feature of the contraction mechanism may be a rigid attachment of the globular head of the myosin molecule to the actin filament and an active change in the angle of attachment associated with the splitting of adenosine triphosphate.[170]

Possibly this model applies also to cell movements involving proteins other than actin and myosin.[171] Studies by Allen of a type of free-living cell which forms pseudopodia have shown that the pseudopodia consist of a network of numerous "moving fibrils" which contain mitochondria and smaller filaments.[172] The fact that microtubules are always conspicuous components of cilia and flagella suggests that they play a role in the motility of these structures, but they have not yet been shown to be contractile or to have the requisite enzymatic activity.[173] Microtubule protein, which resembles actin, might function like actin.[174] The cross-bridges frequently seen between microtubules and the side arms on microfilaments might have processes similar to those which join actin and myosin in muscle cell contraction. The side arms of microtubules contain an ATPase. So far no molecule corresponding to myosin has been discovered in the motor components that have these types of protein molecules—e.g., pseudopodia, cilia, and flagella—and no explanation has been proposed as to how a single component protein structure might convert chemical to mechanical energy within itself.

Processes of cellular components involved in moving.

(a) *Muscle-fiber contraction.* After the neural impulse which is the signal for contraction of a muscle fiber crosses the neuromyal junction, it is propagated along the cell membrane.[175] Then it is thought to be conducted inward from the electrically polarized sarcolemma along the transverse system. Calcium ions are released from the sarcoplasmic reticulum and bound by troponin, allowing the reaction between the actin and myosin to take place. At the end of the contraction the calcium is again bound by the sarcoplasmic reticulum. It has been suggested by Porter that the reticular structures may be the sites of synthesis of the ATP needed for contraction.[176] Because muscle cells use so much energy, perhaps these structures, closely intertwined as they are with the fibers, are needed to provide enough ATP. The more remote mitochondria may be insufficient. Such decentralization of ATP synthesis to locations near where its energy is needed may well increase efficiency and reduce costs to the system. It may be an illustration of the principle of least effort (see note 101 on page 50 and page 436).

Muscle cells are able to maintain their contraction for a period in the absence of oxygen inputs. Under such circumstances they carry out anaerobic decomposition of glucose, producing lactic acid. When oxygen is again available, the remainder of the Krebs cycle (see page 237) is carried out with carbon dioxide and water resulting as waste materials. Heat is produced during contraction.

(b) *Amoeboid movement.* During embryonic development of organisms, cells which will later be fixed in place go to their positions in the tissues by amoeboid movement.[177] In the course of differentiation cell types which will be fixed in tissues lose the capacity for locomotion. When embryonic neurons are released from their cohesion and cultured separately, they are still able to migrate, probably by extending and shortening their fibers, a sort of amoeboid movement.[178] Neurons taken from the nervous systems of older organisms do not do this. Some cells of organisms—white blood cells and plasma cells—retain their motility throughout the life of the organism. The white blood cells, which are phagocytes, seek out and engulf bacteria and other foreign particles in the same way an amoeba captures its prey (see page 232 and Fig. 6-14).

As an amoeba moves, its endoplasm flows forward in the direction the cell is moving. At the front end leading the motion it flows around the sides of the cell and changes from a sol to a gel. At the rear end the opposite transformation occurs. The gel is transformed into a sol which flows forward. As this is occurring, the amoeba changes its shape, putting forth pseudopodia in the direction it is moving. Endoplasm flows passively.

The whole large mass of the aggregated slime mold *Plasmodium,* which has a complex sort of streaming because the mass of protoplasm is large with no cell walls but many nuclei, moves by amoeboid motion. The flow is the same whether it is natural or enforced with applied pressure under experimental conditions. The motion, Kamiya believes, is caused by local changes in pressure.[179] The pressure differential appears to be about 140 grams per square centimeter (g per cm^2), considerable for a small cell. He thinks the changes in pressure are caused by either contraction of the cortical gel on one side or a shearing action that propels the endoplasm sideways across the surface of the cortical gel layer. Students of the question disagree as to whether cortical gel contracting in the rear of an amoeba pushes its endoplasm forward or a contraction in its forward end pulls the endoplasmic material forward.[180] Streaming is explained by Bingley and Thompson, not by pressures and contractility, but by electrical voltage gradients within the cell.[181] When they applied potentials to *Amoeba proteus,* positive potentials caused the particles in the cytoplasm to stop or to reverse their direction of streaming. Negative potentials either increased the rate of streaming in a normal forward direction or had no effect. There was a permanent electrical gradient in the cell with the tail region most negative.

(c) *Movement of cilia and flagella.* Many different sorts of epithelial cells move liquids over the surface of the organ components which they line by beating their cilia. Epithelial cells of the respiratory tract of man and other species, for instance, beat rhythmically and in order, the second after the first, the third after the second, ensuring a flow of water and mucus over the epithelial surface.[182]

The motion of cilia involves two strokes—an effective stroke and a recovery stroke. In the first, the cilium sweeps rapidly, bending near its base. In the second the bending starts near the base and proceeds as a wave toward the tip. Five of the outer filaments on one side of a cilium may contract to produce the effective stroke, and the other four contract to produce the recovery.[183]

The zoospores and gametes of some plants and the sperm of animals propel themselves by whipping their flagella or the very similar sperm tails, as do free-living flagellates. Flagella have an even more complicated movement than cilia since they can be as much as 50 times longer. Waves of bending begin at the attached end of the flagellum and progress toward its tip, exerting pressure on the medium and driving the cell forward. Sometimes this causes the cell to rotate as it moves.

Representative *variables* of the moving process are: *Sorts of movements made.* Example: The protozoan swam rapidly about in the droplet, whipping its flagellum. *Changes in moving over time.* Example: Certain cells of the developing human embryo had amoeboid movement during the early weeks of gestation, but became fixed in place in relation to the other cells as the fetus developed. *Changes in moving with different circumstances.* Example: When the cell became a cyst, it absorbed its motor organelles and remained immobile until it was no longer encysted. *Rate of moving.* Example: The single flagellum of the *Euglena* drove it at the rate of 0.5 mm per s before it had eaten, but it moved no more than one-tenth that fast afterward. *Rate of output of work.* Example: It was estimated that the single fiber of involuntary muscle in the bladder did work which expended of the order of 10^{-5} cal per contraction. *Frequency of moving.* Example: The cardiac muscle cell contracted 80 times per minute. *Duration of moving.* Example: The entire movement of the amoeba toward the particle of food, from the time the food fell into the water until the amoeba contacted it, lasted 17 s. *Lag in moving.* Example: The paramecium's cilia did not begin the vigorous beating which moved the cell away from its location until 5 s after the drop of strong acid had been pipetted into the water next to it, much slower than usual. *Costs of moving.* Example: Whenever the striated muscle cell contracted, it used ATP produced by dephosphorylation from creatine phosphate, which was replaced by the cell through a sequence of syntheses drawing energy from the cell's stored glycogen.

3.2.8 Supporter, the subsystem which maintains the proper spatial relationships among components of the cell, so that they can interact without weighting each other down or crowding each other.

3.2.8.1 Structure   The ground substance of cells is a network of protein molecules in aqueous solution, held together by chemical bonds. This structure is the fundamental supporter component.[184] The organelles are suspended in this network.

Studies of cell process seem to indicate that some sort of "cytoskeleton" exists. The microtubules and microfilaments—which, as I have indicated, are also parts of the distributor and motor—are the components that most closely represent a cytoskeleton.[185] In muscle cells the myofibrils are supporter components. The cell wall of plant cells, the cell membrane of all cells, and the wall of cysts probably also do some supporting. Fluids surrounding cells, though not parts of the system, also are supportive.

3.2.8.2 Process   The electromagnetic forces which attract and repel molecules hold the protein network of the ground substance in its spatial relationships. The viscosity of the resulting substance varies under differing physiological and environmental conditions. The forms and positions of the organelles are also determined by such forces.

When cells are centrifuged, the rotational forces do not cause the particles within them to move smoothly but rather in a series of zigzag jumps, as if they were tearing through a meshwork. This fact has been interpreted as evidence that cells contain some sort of supporting network.[186]

Cross sections of the structures known as "axipods," many of which extend radially outward from the body of the heliozoan *Actinosphaerium*, reveal that a filament, consisting of a double-coiled array of microtubules, extends along the central axis of each one.[187] When such cells were exposed to low temperatures or high pressures, these microtubules disappeared, and the axipods collapsed and withdrew into the cell. When the cells were returned to room temperature or normal pressure, the axipods reformed, complete with microtubules, suggesting that the stresses may have caused the constituent proteins of the microtubules to break down into their component monomers. The return to normal temperature permitted them to aggregate again. The shapes of white blood cells and neurons appear also to be determined by such structures, which are found in a marginal band in the white blood cells and in axons and dendrites.

Representative *variables* in the supporting process include: *Strength of the supporter.* Example: The wall of the plant cell could be indented by a pressure of 1 dyne per square centimeter (dyn per cm²) when it was a few days old, but after six months it rigidly resisted a pressure of 10 dyn per cm². *Costs of supporting.* Example: Because the temperature vacillated widely, the protozoan in the glass dish encysted several times, consuming different amounts of energy each time it formed the cyst wall.

3.3 Subsystems which process information   A fundamental aspect of the activities of every living cell is information processing. Certain excitable cells, however, such as free-living cells, receptor cells, neurons, muscle fibers, and some glandular cells, are particularly specialized for information processing. For this reason these specialized cells will receive particular attention in the following sections on the information processing subsystems.

3.3.1   Input transducer, the sensory subsystem which brings markers bearing information into the cell, changing them to other matter-energy forms suitable for transmission within it.

3.3.1.1   Structure   All specialized receptor regions of the cell membrane are input transducer components. These include the molecular receptor sites for chemical markers, which are assumed on theoretical grounds to be located on the cell membrane, although they have not been directly observed, and a variety of other differentiated transducer and accessory structures. I shall consider free-living cells first and then the cells of organisms, including neurons, muscle cells, receptor cells, and others.

Free-living cells.   Most free-living cells have no discernible differentiation of their membranes for any input modality. A few have specialized structures for one particular marker. The flagellates *Euglena* and *Chlamydomonas,* for instance, have receptors which contain light-sensitive pigments like those in the receptor cells of organisms' eyes.[188]

Cells of organisms.   A variety of structural adaptations at their boundaries fit these differentiated cells to receive specific markers bearing information inputs. The subsynaptic regions of neurons and muscle fibers, specialized regions of receptor cells, and subsynaptic regions of glandular cells are examples.

(*a*) *Neurons.*   The input transducers of neurons of the mammalian nervous system are located on the subsynaptic membranes. Synapses are junctions between neurons where the ending of the neuron which outputs a signal, the presynaptic neuron, is separated by a narrow synaptic cleft from another one which receives that signal, the postsynaptic neuron (see Fig. 6-16 and pages 214 to 216). Presynaptic neurons may synapse with a postsynaptic dendrite, in some neurons with *dendritic spines* extending outward from the dendrite; on the postsynaptic cell body; or, rarely, on a postsynaptic axon.[189] The *subsynaptic membrane,* that part of the postsynaptic cell's membrane which directly fronts the synaptic cleft, is thicker than the rest of the cell membrane. Molecular receptor sites are believed to be distributed upon it as well as pores which are opened up by molecules of chemical markers when they are transmitted from the presynaptic neuron. When these pores are open, ions can cross the cell membrane through them.[190] Typically, a neuron synapses with many other neurons. Commonly 10,000 or more presynaptic neurons synapse with the crowded dendrites and cell body of a single large pyramidal cell of the pyramidal tract leading down from the cortex of the brain (see pages 425 and 426).[191]

Neurons of mammalian nervous systems differ considerably in structure. Much of what is known about the input transducer and other information processing subsystems of neurons has been gained from stud-

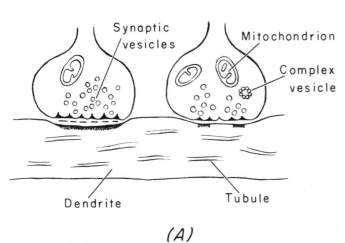

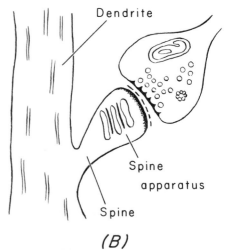

(A)   *(B)*

Fig. 6-16   Two sorts of synapses. (*A*) Synapses on a dendrite. (*B*) Synapse on a dendritic spine. (From V. P. Whittaker & E. G. Gray. The synapse: biology and morphology. *Brit. med. Bull.,* 1962, **18,** 224. *Reprinted by permission of the Medical Department, The British Council.*)

ies of the motor neurons in the spinal cords of cats.[192] These are big cells, ten times larger than the largest pyramidal tract neurons of the cerebral cortex of the brain. They are so large that it is relatively easy to insert intracellular electrodes into them. Their location in the spinal cord makes them quite easily accessible, and their connections with other organism components are well understood (see page 262). From the cell body of these motor neurons extend a number of long, fine dendrites (5 to 6 nm in diameter and up to 1 mm in length) which have branching terminals. They have a single long axon. More than 2,000 synapses may be distributed over their dendrites and cell bodies.[193]

Most synapses in nonmammalian animal species are similar to the mammalian although there are some exceptions, mainly between certain types of invertebrate neurons, which are specialized in various ways for electrical rather than chemical markers (see pages 254 and 337).[194]

(b) *Muscle fibers.* Skeletal muscle fibers differ from visceral and cardiac muscle cells in their input transducers as well as in other details of their structures. Motor neurons synapse with them at a highly differentiated neuromyal junction, the muscle fiber's component of which is the *motor end plate.* Here terminal branches of the neuron are embedded in shallow troughs on the surface of the muscle-fiber membrane, thickened at this point with mitochondria and nuclei beneath it (see Fig. 6-17). The membranes of the two cells are separated by a cleft of about 500 Å.[195]

Less is known about the junctions of neurons with the visceral and cardiac muscle cells which they innervate.[196] True synapses may exist. Electron micrographs of visceral muscle have shown a plexus of axons running in a dense network in such a way that every muscle cell appears to be in contact with it, possibly at many points. The Schwann cell coating of the axons is interrupted at each point of contact.

Junctions have been observed between neurons and cardiac muscle cells.

Both visceral and cardiac muscle cells must have transducers for information on markers carried by the organism's vascular channels as well as those for neural information. Two different kinds of receptor sites are postulated for excitatory and inhibitory chemical molecules.[197]

(c) *Receptor cells.* These cells are specialized to function as components of the input transducer and internal transducer of organisms. Certain sorts, such as the Pacinian corpuscles, are found in both (see Fig. 6-18, page 253, and pages 254 and 255). Some, including Pacinian corpuscles, are neurons with structurally differentiated endings. Others, like the rods and cones of eyes, are separate cells. Table 6-4 lists the various

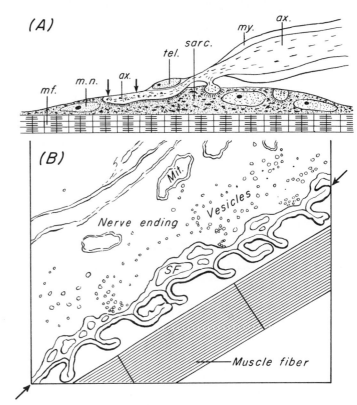

Fig. 6-17 Neuromyal junction. The line of the synaptic cleft between the nerve ending and the muscle is indicated by the arrows in (A) and (B). (A) Schematic drawing of a motor end plate: *ax.,* axoplasm with its mitochondria; *my.,* myelin sheath; *sarc.,* sarcoplasm with its mitochondria; *tel.,* teloglia (terminal Schwann cells); *m.n.,* muscle nuclei; *mf.,* myofibrils. The terminal nerve branches lie in "synaptic gutters" or "troughs." Immediately under the interface axoplasm-sarcoplasm, the ribbon-shaped subneural lamellae, transversely cut, may be seen as rodlets. [From R. Couteaux. Morphological and cytochemical observations on the postsynaptic membrane at motor end-plates and ganglionic synapses. *Exp. cell. Res., (Suppl.),* 1958,**5,** 296.] (B) Tracing of a longitudinal section of a frog neuromyal junction magnified × 19,000. Note the junctional folds of the synaptic cleft extending into the muscle. Four mitochondria (*Mit.*) are shown surrounded by double lines. *SF* denotes one of the "Schwann finger" extensions of the Schwann cell (see above the nerve ending) into the synaptic cleft. [From R. Birks, H. E. Huxley, and B. Katz. The fine structure of the neuromuscular junction of the frog. *J. Physiol.* (London), 1960, **150,** 137. *Reprinted by permission.*]

types of receptor cells in the human organism. Other species of animals have other types, *e.g.,* the mormyromast in skin pores of mormyroid fish such as *Gymnarchus niloticus,* which can sense electrical pulses in the water around it, or the cnidoblast of some coelenterates, which senses simultaneous inputs of food chemicals and pressure and explodes, whipping out a thread

TABLE 6-4   Input Transducer Receptor End Organs in Neural Cells and Cells in Endocrine Target Organs in Organisms

	Type of cell	Location in organisms	Function
I. Cells in an organ that output to the organ or its organism information on changes of variables	A. Pacinian corpuscle	Many internal organs	Reacts to brief, abrupt mechanical forces
	B. Free nerve ending	Many internal organs	Reacts to pain
	C. Muscle spindle	Muscle fibers	Reacts to stretch
	D. Golgi organ (not the same as Golgi apparatus or body)	Ligaments and tendons	Reacts to stretch
II. Cells in an organ that receive from its organism's distributor or channel and net information on changes in the organism which affect control of that organ's processes	A. Baroreceptor (not yet identified)	Left atrium of heart, aortic arch, carotid sinus, perhaps walls of other arteries and veins	Reacts to blood-pressure change
	B. Chemoreceptor	Aortic and carotid bodies and lung	Reacts to changes in blood-oxygen tension, carbon dioxide tension, acidity, and perhaps other variables
	C. Hormone receptor cell	All parts of body	Reacts to presence of hormone, *e.g.*, thyroxine, in all cells; cholecystokinin in cells of gallbladder and its ducts; secretion in acinous glandular cells of pancreas, which secrete pancreatic juice
III. Cells in an organism's input transducer that react to changes in the environment or in the organism produced by changes in its environment	A. Rod	Retina of eye	Reacts to light quanta
	B. Cone	Retina of eye	Reacts differentially to colored light of wavelengths between 390 and 760 nm
	C. Semicircular canal or vestibular hair cell	Epithelia of semicircular canals, utricle, and saccule in vestibule of labyrinth	Reacts to motion of otoliths which move as body moves in endolymph fluid and so respond to changes in the head's orientation in space
	D. Auditory hair cell	Organ of Corti in cochlea	Reacts to sound waves in endolymph fluid
	E. Olfactory cell	Olfactory epithelium in nose	Reacts to smells
	F. Gustatory cell	Tongue	Reacts to taste
	G. Hair follicle nerve ending	Skin	Reacts to movement of hairs
	H. Free nerve ending	Mucous membrane of nose, conjunctiva, mouth, vagina, anus	Reacts to chemical irritants

TABLE 6-4   Input Transducer Receptor End Organs in Neural Cells and Cells in Endocrine Target Organs in Organisms (*Continued*)

	Type of cell	Location in organisms	Function
	I. Pacinian corpuscle	Beneath skin and membranes	Reacts to brief, abrupt, mechanical forces and vibration
	J. Meissner corpuscle	Skin and membranes	Reacts to touch
	K. Merkel disk	Skin and membranes	Reacts to steady touch
	L. Pinkus-Iggo domes	Skin and membranes of furry animals	Reacts to steady touch
	M. Free nerve ending	Skin and membranes	Reacts to pain, probably temperature, possibly itch, tickle, crude touch
	N. Nerve ending	Skin and membranes	Warm
	O. Nerve ending	Skin and membranes	Cold
IV. Cells in an organism's internal transducer that receive from the organism's distributor or channel and net information on changes of variables in the organism's subsystems or components	A. Hormone receptor cell (not yet identified)	Pituitary gland and hypothalamus	Reacts to presence of hormone, *e.g.*, estrogen, by changing some cellular process
	B. Blood temperature receptor neuron (not yet identified)	Supraoptic and preoptic regions of hypothalamus	Reacts to changes in blood temperature
	C. Drug receptor neuron (not yet identified)	Hypothalamus	Reacts to concentrations of narcotics and other drugs
	D. Osmoreceptor neuron (not yet identified)	Rostrodorsomedial hypothalamus	Reacts to water content of blood
	E. Glucostatic receptor neuron (not yet identified)	Hypothalamus	Reacts to glucose content of blood
	F. Chemoreceptor neuron (not yet identified)	Area postrema of dorsal medulla	Reacts to chemical changes in blood by transmitting vomiting signal
	G. Chemoreceptor neuron (not yet identified)	Medulla	Reacts to changes in arterial carbon dioxide tension or in acidity

SOURCES: Various including J. Field (Ed.). *Handbook of physiology. Section I: Neurophysiology.* Vol. 1. Washington, D.C.: Amer. Physiol. Soc., 1959; W. R. Uttal. *The psychobiology of sensory coding.* N.Y.: Harper & Row, 1973; and G. Somjen. *Sensory coding in the mammalian nervous system.* N.Y.: Appleton-Century-Crofts, 1972.

that can penetrate potential prey outside. Each of these types of receptor cells is appropriately differentiated to respond to the sort of energy inputs it transduces. The light-sensitive pigments in receptors of visible light rays, the cilia of some mechanoreceptors, and the naked endings of neurons that mediate pain all illustrate this. The structures of several types of receptor cells are pictured in Fig. 6-18.

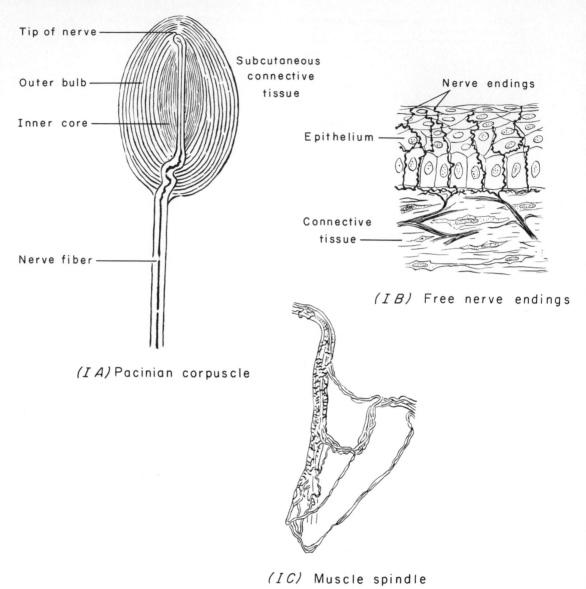

Tip of nerve

Outer bulb

Inner core

Nerve fiber

Subcutaneous
connective
tissue

(I A) Pacinian corpuscle

Nerve endings

Epithelium

Connective
tissue

(I B) Free nerve endings

(I C) Muscle spindle

Fig. 6-18 Some types of receptor cells. Each cell type has same number in this figure as in Table 6-4. All cells are human, except (*I B*) free nerve endings, from the corneal epithelium of a rabbit; (*III C*) vestibular hair cells, from a guinea pig; (*III D*) auditory hair cells, from a guinea pig; and (*III F*) taste bud of a rabbit. [(*I A*) modified from S. W. Ranson. *The anatomy of the nervous system.* Philadelphia: Saunders, 1935, 69; (*I B*) and (*III K*) modified from A. A. Maximow & W. Bloom. *A textbook of histology* (3d ed.). Philadelphia: Saunders, 1938, 196; (*I C*) and (*III J*) modified from W. Bloom & D. W. Fawcett. *A textbook of histology* (10th ed.). Philadelphia: Saunders, 1975, 362, 366; (*III A*) and (*III B*) modified from G. L. Walls. *The vertebrate eye and its adaptive radiation.* Bloomfield Hills, Mich.: Cranbrook Press, 1942, 54–55; (*III C*) modified from J. Wersäll. Studies on the structure and innervation of the sensory epithelium of the *cristae ampullares* in the guinea pig. *J. Acta Oto-laryng.*, 1956, Suppl. **126**:1, 37. (*III D*) modified from H. Davis. Acoustic trauma in the guinea pig. *J. Acoust. Soc. Amer.*, 1953, **25**, 1182; (*III E*) from G. Bloom & H. Engström. The structure of epithelial surface in the olfactory region. *Exp. cell res.*, 1952, **3**,700; (*III F*) modified from W. J. Crozier. Chemoreception. In C. Murchison (Ed.). *A handbook of general experimental psychology.* Worcester, Mass.: Clark Univ. Press, 1934, 1006. *Reprinted by permission.*]

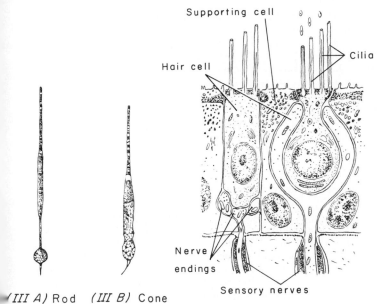

(III A) Rod   *(III B)* Cone

(III C) Vestibular hair cells

(III D) Auditory hair cells

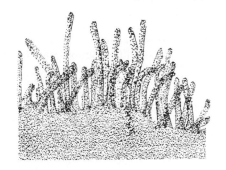

(III E) Olfactory cell
Magnified 23,430 times

(III F) Gustatory cells

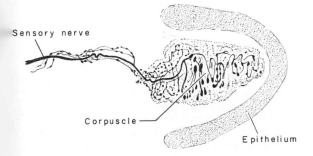

(III J) Meissner corpuscle

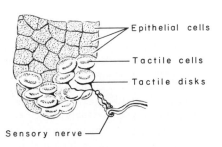

(III K) Merkel disks

The minute subcomponents of some receptor cells have been studied. Microtubules and rings of microtubules are found in some cellular input transducers of olfactory and pressure information.[198] For instance, the olfactory sense hairs in the cuticle of carrion beetles' antennas have "pore tubules" extending inward from the cuticular pores, penetrating the cuticle, and ending inside close to the dendrites of the sensory neuron.

(d) *Other organism cells.* Some glandular cells, like the chromaffin cells of the adrenal medulla, have thickened subsynaptic membranes like those of neurons at the region of synapse with nerve terminals.[199] An autonomic plexus like those observed in visceral muscle has been reported to exist also in glands.[200] Since some glands have no innervation, the input transducers of their cells must be molecular receptor sites upon their membranes, not localized at synapses.

The cells so far described are specialized for particular input–output relationships within organs or organisms. Other organ and organism cells, such as those which are aggregated into skin, subcutaneous tissues, or supporting structures of various kinds also have input transducers, although no specially differentiated subsystem is observable in most of them. These presumably have receptor sites on their cell membranes for the markers they transduce.

3.3.1.2 Process   Input transducing processes in free-living cells and in the cells of organisms—neurons, muscle cells, receptor cells, and others—are discussed separately below.

Free-living cells.   These living systems transduce a range of modalities.[201] Protozoans, for instance, transduce inputs of light, heat, cold, gravity, extremes of alkalinity or acidity, and pressure, although all do not respond to each of these modalities. Paramecia, for example, are probably insensitive to light. In some cases the transduction process can be carried out even by a cell that is not wholly intact. Cut pieces of paramecium react to heat, cold, gravity, and extremes of acidity or alkalinity just as the complete cell does. Those cells with components specialized for transducing a given modality of information inputs may also respond to modalities of inputs for which they have no specialized structures. Differentiated cells may also retain an unspecialized mode of input transducing along with a specially differentiated one. This is true of *Chlamydomonas,* which probably transduces light quanta with the light-sensitive pigment in its eyespot. Mutants lacking an eyespot react to light without it.[202]

Cells of organisms.   Both plant and animal cells transduce information inputs. Information arrives at their boundaries borne on markers similar to those which are transduced by free-living cells, including chemical molecules, radiant energy, deformations of their boundaries, fluxes of temperature, changes of pressure, and others.

(a) *Neurons.*   Neurons ordinarily transduce inputs of chemical transmitter substance into a bioelectric generating potential. The process is different in those primitive synapses in which transmission is electrical.[203] These receive the signal by electrotonic spread from presynaptic neurons, either through a very small synaptic cleft or over some form of bridge or other connecting structure. The signal is then transduced into bioelectric activity similar to that in neurons which receive chemical signals.

The transmitter substances in chemical synapses fall into two classes, one excitatory and the other inhibitory. All these substances are believed to be ions, as are both acetylcholine, a transmitter in some excitatory synapses, and norepinephrine, known to act at some inhibitory synapses. It is possible that excitatory substances are anions and inhibitory are cations.[204] When molecules of one of these substances are released into the synaptic cleft by presynaptic nerve terminals, they interact with receptor sites upon the subsynaptic membrane. These sites are sparsely distributed over the membrane.[205] The transmitter acts very quickly. Then it diffuses away from the receptor sites and is neutralized by enzyme action, by acetylcholinesterase in the case of acetylcholine. Both types of transmitter increase the permeability of the membrane.[206] How they do this is not known.

When the membrane permeability is increased, the ions move along their concentration gradients, so that sodium flows in and potassium flows out. Chloride, which also enters the cell, appears to have little effect.[207] This flow short-circuits the subsynaptic membrane and the resting potential, which is maintained in resting neurons by the "ionic pump," falls to zero (see page 230). This causes an intense current to flow inward in the subsynaptic membrane for about 2 ms. The energy for it is derived from the cell potential. This is the generating current which sets in process further bioelectric events in the postsynaptic membrane.

In inhibitory synapses potassium and chloride ions appear to move in or out of the cell in response to their concentration gradients, but sodium ions in the cell's environment, which are larger, remain excluded from the cell.[208] Potassium flows out of the cell, and chloride flows in.[209] In inhibitory synapses the flow of chloride appears to be important. When they receive transmitter substance inputs, a current flows outward from the subsynaptic membrane. This also is a generating current for bioelectric events in the postsynaptic membrane. Figure 6-19 shows how the excitatory and inhibitory postsynaptic potentials and generating currents flow in a postsynaptic motor neuron.

(b) *Receptor cells.* These cells are specialized to have a low threshold for one form of energy and to react not at all or only to very strong signals carried on other sorts of markers. It is not understood for any type of receptor cell just how it carries out input transducing. If the receptor is not part of a neuron, it is said to transduce the input energy into *receptor potentials*. These are similar to the *generator potentials* of those receptors which are parts of neurons. A Pacinian corpuscle is a receptor which detects brief, abrupt, mechanical forces.[210] It acts in some ways like other types of receptors. Its capsule is made up of specialized, laminated layers arranged as in an onion. Pressure or release of pressure on these layers appears to transmit forces to the nerve ending which they surround. These bring about changes in the cell's ionic permeability which give rise to its receptor potential.[211] Such potentials have been directly recorded within receptor cells of a number of modalities including Pacinian corpuscles responding to mechanical deformation, muscle spindles responding to muscle stretch, photoreceptors responding to light, and auditory hair cells of the cochlea responding to sound.[212]

A theoretical explanation for the input transduction process in the eye of *Limulus*, the horseshoe crab, has been proposed by Lipetz.[213] He considers that his explanation may apply to other sorts of visual receptor cells and, with appropriate changes, to transducer cells of other modalities. The transducer cell of the *Limulus* eye is the *retinula cell*. Within it the initial photochemical response occurs in a part called the *rhabdomere*.[214] These cells somewhat resemble the rods and cones of the vertebrate eye. Like them, the retinula cell is not the ending of a neuron but must transmit information to another cell, called the *eccentric cell*.

According to Lipetz the following sequence of processes may occur in the transduction:

1. Photons are absorbed in a photopigment in the *rhabdomere*. Each absorbed photon causes a rearrangement of the structure of the chromophore of the photopigment molecule. This is the primary photochemical process.
2. The rearranged photopigment molecule now has exposed sites capable of reacting with one or more molecules of another kind. . . . These sites then react with the neighboring molecules to free some particle, A.
3. The freed A particles then catalyze a further reaction which releases large numbers of some particle, B.

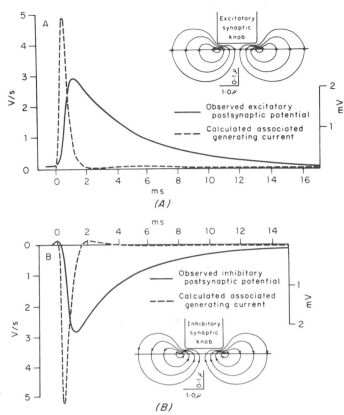

Fig. 6-19 Excitatory and inhibitory postsynaptic potentials and generating currents in a postsynaptic motor neuron. (*A*) The observed excitatory postsynaptic potential and calculated associated generating current in a neuron with a resting potential of −66 mV and a membrane time constant of 3.6 ms. The inset shows the directions of current flow during excitation. (*B*) The observed inhibitory postsynaptic potential and the calculated associated generating current in the same neuron. The inset shows the directions of current flow during inhibition. (From D. R. Curtis and J. C. Eccles. The time courses of excitatory and inhibitory synaptic actions. *J. Physiol.*, 1959, **145**, 532. *Reprinted by permission.*)

4. The B particles diffuse to the surface of the *rhabdomere*.
5. There the B particles affect the membrane of the retinula cell.[215]

What happens after that, including how activity is transferred to the next cell in the channel, the eccentric cell, is not understood (see page 280). It appears, however, that the Weber function (see Hypothesis 3.3.1.2-1, pages 94, 95, and 282) may describe this input transduction. A logarithmic change in input intensity produces a linear change in output.[216]

Perhaps the microtubules and similar components in such transducers as the olfactory-sense hairs of the carrion beetle are the means for conveying odorous molecules to the olfactory receptor cell.[217] The number of pore tubules corresponds to the calculated number of receptor sites on that cell. Microtubules are also present in the hair plate mechanoreceptor of the honeybee. At the end of the sensory neuron there is a cilium composed of microtubules and farther out is a larger ring of many more microtubules. Compression of this ring may give rise to the input signal to the receptor cell.

(c) *Muscle fibers.* Transducing processes at motor end plates are similar to the processes at excitatory synapses of neurons. The potential falls to below zero rather than to zero, and the membrane permeability is somewhat different, but the flows of sodium and potassium are responsible for the activity here as well as in the neural synapses.[218] Like the membrane of the neuron, that of the muscle fiber is electrically excitable, maintaining a resting potential difference between its inside and outside. The transmitter substance interacts with receptor sites on the motor end plate to set up a current on the motor end plate, the end-plate current which, like the generating current in neurons, is an inward flow in the part of the end plate directly under the synapse. Like the current in the neural subsynaptic membrane, this is intense and brief, lasting about 2 ms.[219] It triggers further activity of the muscle cell membrane.

Cardiac and visceral muscle cells receive hormonal information inputs from the organism's vascular channels as well as transmissions from neurons of the autonomic nervous system. These hormones and autonomic transmitter substances are closely related chemically. Each class of substances produces both excitatory and inhibitory effects in the visceral muscle cells of various organs and in the cardiac muscle cells of vertebrate hearts, indicating that such muscle fibers have two sorts of receptor sites.[220] These types of muscle cells undergo autonomous, myogenic, rhythmic contractions. They "beat" when isolated from the organ and organism of which they are components (see page 341), whether or not they receive information inputs. Such inputs, however, speed up or slow down the rate of these contractions. Input transductions in smooth muscle are much slower than in skeletal muscle.

(d) *Other organism cells.* Some glandular cells that have differentiated synaptic structures transduce inputs from chemical molecules into changes in membrane polarization, as neurons and muscle fibers do, although subsequent subsystem processes differ in the various types of cells. Other cells which do not synapse but which have molecular receptor sites for neural transmitter substances or closely related compounds probably also transduce those chemical signals into changes in membrane depolarization.

The active transport processes which bring matter-energy inputs into cells also convey information. Some molecules that are used in the cell's matter-energy metabolism also function as information markers, since they bring into the cell information about the constitution of the substrate outside and may signal its decider to start or stop chemical reactions involving it as it crosses the cell membrane. The transduction is the change of the substrate molecule to whatever new molecule is produced from it during the active transport processes.

Functions of the input transducer. One subsystem can vary from another in various functional characteristics. This is true of the input transducers of cells. Among such variable aspects are the following:

(a) *Input–output transfer functions.* The greater the amount of transmitter substance applied to the subsynaptic membrane at a single time, the greater is the change in electrical potential on the cell membrane. The amount of transmitter substance which reaches the subsynaptic membrane from a single pulse of the presynaptic neuron is probably constant.[221] Under these circumstances the generating current is probably also essentially constant. There is a large amplification factor, the energy in the small amount of transmitter substance being minute compared with the electrotonic potential it elicits. When a neuron or muscle fiber is at rest, with no regular transmissions input to it from presynaptic neurons, its electrical activity may still show miniature changes caused by random output "leakage" of synaptic vesicles from the presynaptic neuron.[222] Some cellular input transductions show the Weber input–output relationship.[223] That is, output intensity varies as a power function of input intensity.

(b) *Mode of adaptation.* Cells may be either *tonic,* with slow signal termination, or *phasic,* with rapid signal termination. After information is input into a tonic cell, its information output rate slowly declines to a steady value characteristic of that intensity of input. On the other hand, after information is input into a phasic cell, its information output rate declines rapidly to zero, or it makes only a single output until there is a change in input. There is no evidence that the input transducer is the subsystem involved when neurons make tonic or phasic adaptations.[224] The adaptation of the retinula cell of the *Limulus* eye, however, appears to be made by its input transducer, being determined by one of the thermal, chemical, or photochemical processes which precede the production of the generator potential.[225]

(c) *Channel capacity.* Since the input transducer of a neuron is the totality of its many cell membrane receptor sites plus any other information input receptors it may have, and since each molecule or other quantum of matter-energy input apparently conveys one bit of information—i.e., it is either present or not present—the channel capacity of the input transducer in bits per second is the number of molecules of transmitter substance or other matter-energy quanta for which the neuron has receptor sites, multiplied by the number of times each site can respond to separate inputs per second. It has been calculated that there can be no more than 4×10^6 receptor sites at the end plate of a muscle fiber.[226]

(d) *Threshold.* Absorption of a single photon can activate the visual pigment of a cell that transduces visible light.[227] The amount of transmitter substance required to produce a single miniature muscle end-plate potential is about 3,000 molecules, thought to be the amount contained in a single synaptic vesicle.[228] The amount of acetylcholine received at the subsynaptic membrane after a single neural pulse is about 1.5×10^{-15} g. This amount causes significant depolarization.[229]

(e) *Lag.* Synaptic delay at mammalian neuromuscular synapses and central synapses is about 0.22 ms. An appreciable part of this time is required to attach the transmitter substance to the subsynaptic membrane and render the membrane permeable to ions.[230]

(f) *Accessory functions.* Certain accessory structures alter input transducer processes. In some sorts of neurons there is a barrier to diffusion of transmitter substance away from the synaptic cleft.[231] The form of the synapse varies. In the synapses of the retina the postsynaptic cell is invaginated into the presynaptic cell. This ensures that the transmitter substance will act over a longer period of time than it does in most synapses.[232]

Included among representative *variables* of the input transducing process are: *Meaning of information input which is transduced.* Example: The arrival of acetylcholine at the subsynaptic membrane signaled excitation to the muscle fiber. *Sorts of information input which are transduced.* Example: Both excitatory and inhibitory signals produced depolarization in the motor neuron. *Percentage of the information input which is transduced.* Example: The postsynaptic neuron responded to no more than 90 percent of the presynaptic neuron's pulses. *Threshold of the input transducer.* Example: The 3,000 molecules of transmitter in the

vesicle that leaked across the resting synapse were just sufficient to produce a miniature response of the muscle fiber end plate. *Changes in input transducing over time.* Example: The entire length of the fetal muscle fiber was uniformly responsive to acetylcholine, but as the fiber matured the neuromyal junction developed, and the responsiveness was restricted to the end plate (see page 249). *Changes in input transducing with different circumstances.* Example: All the neuromyal junctions between the warrior's neurons and his skeletal muscle fibers were blocked by curare from the arrow which struck him (see page 300). *Channel capacity of the input transducer.* Example: The muscle fiber end plate had no more than 4×10^6 receptor sites, each of which was capable of transmitting a signal approximately 3 times per s, for a channel capacity of 1.2×10^7 bits per s or less. *Number of channels in use in the input transducer.* Example: There were 2,000 synapses on the motor neuron. *Distortion of the input transducer.* Example: When the neuron was lightly anesthetized, signals were transmitted only irregularly by its subsynaptic membrane. *Signal-to-noise ratio of the input transducer.* Example: The potential on the neural membrane varied between about 5 and 15 microvolts (μV) and could not be detected above the noise level. *Rate of input transducing.* Example: The generating current in the cat's motor neuron rose in 2 ms. *Lag in input transducing.* Example: Input transducing took almost 10 ms at the autonomic synapse of the guinea pig. *Costs of input transducing.* Example: A significant proportion of the neuron's energy was expended in generating current.

3.3.2 Internal transducer, the sensory subsystem which receives, from subsystems or components within the cell, markers bearing information about significant alterations in those subsystems or components, changing them to other matter-energy forms of a sort which can be transmitted within it.

3.3.2.1 Structure This subsystem is laterally dispersed to many components. Every cellular enzyme is a joint component of this as well as of other subsystems (see pages 273 to 275). Every cellular *repressor* molecule, whose synthesis is controlled by a *regulatory gene,* is also such a joint component. Other internal transducer components must exist, but they have not been identified. They include the region in neurons where electrotonic potentials on the postsynaptic membrane change to action potentials. Another component, in cells which divide, is the initiator molecule that receives a signal which makes it act on the replicator to set chromosomal replication into action.

Study of cellular processes indicates that repressor

substances, like enzymes, are proteins. The only repressor substance so far isolated, the *lactose repressor* of the bacterium *Escherichia coli*, is a protein of about 150,000 to 200,000 molecular weight.[233] A cell probably contains only about 10 repressor molecules for each gene which provides a template for such molecules.

Some complex proteins, including certain enzymes and probably all repressor molecules, are *allosteric, i.e.*, they have "other sites." Such a molecule can bind (*i.e.*, combine by chemical bonds with) multiple molecules of the same or different sorts, having a separate site for each. An allosteric molecule changes from one spatial configuration to another depending upon what molecule or molecules attach to it.

3.3.2.2 Process   The ability of protein molecules to fold in space increases their effectiveness as information transducers. Such folding of these large molecules brings two or more of their amino acid sequences (which are separated by a number of other such sequences and hence would be distant from each other if the molecule were stretched out) close to each other in space. Thus a substrate molecule can easily contact two or more sequences and be "recognized" by the appropriate one.[234] The flexibility of parts of the molecule also allows amino acid groups in a protein molecule to make some adjustment to the substrate, which aids recognition at particular binding sites. Protein molecules transduce information by changing from one spatial configuration to another when they bind some other molecule.

I shall consider in turn below internal transducing by (*a*) enzymes, (*b*) repressor substances, and (*c*) other components.

(*a*) *Internal transducing by enzymes.* An enzyme "recognizes" its appropriate substrate, distinguishing its spatial configuration from that of other substances by reacting specifically with it. Thus it transduces information as a necessary preliminary to its functions in cellular control processes. The information is carried on the substrate molecule, acting as a marker, and is transduced to the marker of the energy involved in the enzyme's catalytic activity.

(*b*) *Internal transducing by repressors.* It is necessary first to understand certain cellular control or deciding processes before one can comprehend how repressors act as internal transducers.

Bacteria have been known for a long time to be able to adjust their production of some enzymes so that they synthesize the particular ones that can metabolize substances that happen to be present in their environment. In the absence of a particular substrate, the enzyme capable of acting on it is not made.[235] *Escherichia coli* bacteria, for example, metabolize lactose, a beta-galactoside, by the action of beta-galactosidase, an enzyme. If *Escherichia coli* cells are grown in the absence of a galactoside, they contain only an average of 0.5 to 5 active molecules of galactosidase per milligram of dry weight, or 1 to 10 units. If they are grown in the presence of a galactoside, they contain 10,000 units. The substrate is said to have "induced" this much greater production.

An enzyme is either subject to regulation as to rate of activity—*i.e.*, inducible or repressible—or it is constitutive. A minority of enzymes are subject to regulation. *Inducible* enzymes are synthesized only in the presence of their substrate. Induction of enzyme formation, a fundamental cellular control process, as analyzed by Jacob and Monod, involves inactivation of a repressor substance that previously has been blocking the synthesis of the enzyme.[236] Repressors probably act by interfering with transcription of the genetic message from DNA to RNA (or possibly with its translation from RNA to protein), so that the cell at any time produces only some of the substances it is capable of synthesizing.[237] The site which binds the repressor is known as the *operator. Repressible* enzymes also exist. Repression of enzyme formation is an opposite process from induction.

Some enzymatic processes are repressible, often those which are involved in synthesizing essential metabolites, like amino acids or nucleotides, rather than in breaking down input substances.[238] Such processes are turned on unless they are repressed. Usually this is done by products of the sequence itself, a process called *end-product repression*. An example is the repression of synthesis of the enzyme tryptophan-synthetase when tryptophan or a related substance is added to the cell's environment. This is economical, cutting costs in materials consumed, because the cell need not carry out the synthesis when enough of the substance is available. Most enzymes are *constitutive*, formed at a more or less constant rate whether their substrate is present or not.

The operator controls the production of the enzyme. When the repressor binds the operator at one site, this synthesis stops. An *inducer*, however, which is usually a small molecule, often the enzyme substrate, can simultaneously bind the repressor, an allosteric protein, at another site. The combined inducer and repressor constitute a configuration which has less affinity for the operator than does the repressor alone. When the inducer is bound by the repressor, therefore, it stops binding the operator. This repression of the operator allows the synthesis of the enzyme to begin. Repressors in general block not a single enzyme but a sequence of them active in successive metabolic steps.

In recognizing and binding the inducer, the repressor transduces information because the inducer acts as a signal rather than as a necessary substance in the chemical reaction (though when the inducer is also the substrate, it is both signal and essential substance).[239] Its use as a metabolite involves the enzyme produced in response to the previous signal or information exchange, and this use is not part of the signaling process.

Although the pioneering studies on inducers, repressors, and the induction process were carried out with bacteria, the essential findings apparently apply to other types of free-living and aggregated cells.[240]

(c) *Internal transducing by other components.* There are regions in neurons where the signals being transmitted through them are transferred from one sort of energy marker to another. Such a place is the region on the postsynaptic membrane where the electrotonic flows, which are the markers and which pass along the membrane as electricity flows along a cable, are changed into action currents, which use stored energy for active propagation (see page 262). Another such place is the initiator hypothesized by Jacob, Brenner, and Cuzin to exist in *Escherichia coli* bacteria.[241] They suggest that contact between cell membranes during conjugation between two bacteria of different mating types may elicit an antigenic reaction which sends a signal to the initiator. Here it is transduced to another form of marker and transmitted to the replicator, which sets chromosomal replication into operation (see page 224). The change from one form of marker to another is internal transducing.

Functions of the internal transducer

(a) *Input–output transfer functions.* Allosteric activators like fructose-1, 6-diphosphate can increase the affinity of an enzyme like pyruvate kinase to its substrate, phosphoenolpyruvate. The interaction of the activator and the allosteric enzyme changes the spatial configuration of the latter so that, at certain temperatures and acidities, the small amount of input energy in the activator can increase the rate of output from the enzyme's activity up to 1,500 times—a large amplification.[242]

(b) *Mode of adaptation.* Cellular internal transduction is phasic in the sense that it terminates completely within a brief period.

(c) *Channel capacity.* This cannot now even be estimated. It is directly related to the number of different enzyme and repressor processes per second going on in a cell, and this number is vast. In general only the substrate of an enzyme, or substances very similar structurally, can act as inducers of that enzyme. Some inducers, however, are not appropriate substrates. For instance, in addition to lactose, its proper substrate,

beta-galactosidase is induced by isopropylthiogalactoside and methylthiogalactoside.[243] If one can assume that biologically the inducer constitutes an alpha-coded signal of its own presence as substrate, then the appearance in the channels of these nonsubstrate inducers constitutes noise. If other variables of the channel functions remain the same, such noise would lower the capacity of any channel in which nonsubstrate inducers appear (see page 14 and Hypothesis 3.3.3.2-1, page 96). It can interfere with, or even block out entirely, adaptive signals in the channels relevant to use of the substrate in cellular metabolism.

(d) *Threshold.* For a single binding site on an enzyme, probably a single inducer molecule is all that is required.

(e) *Lag.* It takes about 10^{-6} to 10^{-8} s for an enzyme to recognize and bind a substrate molecule.[244]

(f) *Accessory functions.* None is known.

Representative *variables* of the internal transducing process include: *Meaning of internal information which is transduced.* Example: The inducer signaled its own presence as substrate in the cell. *Sorts of internal information which are transduced.* Example: Lactose in the medium acted as an alpha-coded signal for synthesis of galactosidase while tryptophane signaled that formation of tryptophane-synthetase should be inhibited. *Percentage of the internal information which is transduced.* Example: The percentage of repressor molecules that the cell synthesized which actually reached the operator site varied from moment to moment. *Threshold of the internal transducer.* Example: The threshold concentration of molecules of threonine substrate required to signal activation of the enzyme threoninedeaminase was greater when the oxygen tension was low. *Changes in internal transducing over time.* Example: At a certain point in the cell's growth, the signal to the DNA to replicate itself was transmitted to the nucleus. *Changes in internal transducing with different circumstances.* Example: When the *Escherichia coli* bacterium was infected with T4 virus, its internal transducing changed within 1 min to involve viral enzymes. *Channel capacity of the internal transducer.* Example: At a maximum each enzyme and repressor molecule in the cell could transduce a bit of information several times a second, but at any given point in time the number of molecular sites actually transducing was always significantly less than this maximum. *Number of channels in use in the internal transducer.* Example: Competition for the acetylcoenzyme A substrate by various cellular components limited its use as a signal to carry out production to only the enzymes involved in the citric acid cycle (see page 237). *Distortion of the internal transducer.* Example: The i^s mutant of *Escherichia coli* could not synthesize galactosidase because it produced a repressor that could not bind lactose, the inducer. *Signal-to-noise ratio of the internal transducer.* Example: Whenever isopropylthiogalactoside, a molecule similar to lactose, entered the cell, it created an important amount of noise in the internal transducing process, because its presence signaled activation of the beta-galactosidase enzyme even though lactose, the substrate, was not present in adequate quantities to induce such activation. *Rate of internal transducing.* Example: The rate of synthesis of the enzyme increased and decreased as a direct function of the concentration of inducer present, thus being an index of changes in the rate of internal transducing. *Lag in internal transducing.* Example: The repressor recognized and reacted with the inducer in 10^{-6} s. *Costs of internal transducing.* Example: The chemical reactions which produced repressor molecules in the *Escherichia coli* were carried on at a cost of a small amount of the cell's stored energy.

3.3.3   Channel and net, the subsystem composed of a single route in physical space, or multiple interconnected routes, by which markers bearing information are transmitted to all parts of the cell.

3.3.3.1   Structure   Some or all of the distributor channels are components of the channel and net of all cells, free-living and aggregated. Among them are the endoplasmic, and in muscle cells, sarcoplasmic reticula; the ground substance, including the axoplasm of neurons; the microtubules and the microfilaments. In addition to this structure that transmits molecular markers, excitable cells have membranes structurally suited for electrical transmission of information. In possessing an information net with channels for two quite different sorts of markers, such cells are similar to animal organisms. A neuron is more highly specialized for electrical transmission of signals than other cells, its elongated cablelike form and the structural modifications of different parts of its cell membrane adapting it for its particular functions in organism information channels. Some neural axons are thick and others are thin; some are myelinated and others are not. These characteristics affect their functioning importantly. Other excitable cells include the cells of *Nitella,* an alga; the receptor cells that mediate the responses of sensitive plants; receptor cells of animal organisms; muscle fibers of all kinds; glandular cells; electroplaques of electric fishes; and cells of the oviduct during ovulation.[245] Their channel membranes are specifically differentiated for the various processes for which they are specialized.

The internal membranes of cells, including endoplasmic and sarcoplasmic reticula and the transverse system of muscle cells as well as the nuclear membrane, are also considered to be structural components of this subsystem. Electron microscopic studies of the nuclear membrane have shown that the nuclear surface is bordered by two unit membranes that enclose a perinuclear space or cisterna.[246] These join at intervals, where circular pores 300 to 500 Å in diameter interrupt the continuity of the membrane. It has been observed frequently that the perinuclear space is continuous with the cavities of the endoplasmic reticulum at these points. The structural arrangements vary from one sort of cell to another. These include small cylinders which project a short distance in both directions from the nuclear membrane in some invertebrate cells. Other cells develop blebs or blisters on their nuclear membranes. *Amoeba proteus* and some other cells have a sort of honeycomb layer consisting of closely packed hexagonal prisms, each of which terminates at a pore in the nuclear membrane (see Fig. 6-20).

3.3.3.2   Process   Alpha-coded information is carried among cellular components over cytoplasmic channels on chemical molecule markers, by the same sorts of processes that distribute other matter-energy (see pages 234 and 235). In excitable cells of various types, bioelectric currents along membranes also conduct beta-coded information. I discuss these two sorts of channel and net processes separately below.

Molecular transmission of information.   A well-organized chemical information network joins components throughout the cell. RNA molecules carry signals to cytoplasmic organelles; inducers and energizers move to the sites where they act in the control of metabolic processes; hormones destined for output from glandular cells move from the location of their synthesis to a region of output or of intracellular storage; and transmitter substances, which can be used for markers to carry signals across synapses, move down axons to cell terminals. Many of these molecules move in precise spatial relationships to each other while carrying out their subsystem processes. Since many substances used in the matter-energy metabolism of cells function also as information markers, the number of such markers transported in a single cell is very great. I have reviewed above the processes which transport matter-energy, including information markers, within a cell. They include movements of the cytoplasm and possibly movements produced by neurotubules and neurofilaments. Over very small distances, such as those within a mitochondrion, the attractive forces between molecules—which are inversely proportional to the distance between them—can move them.

The pores and other structures of the nuclear membrane appear to act as channels between the nucleus and cytoplasm of the cell.[247] Two sorts of channels exist here, indirect and direct. The direct channels

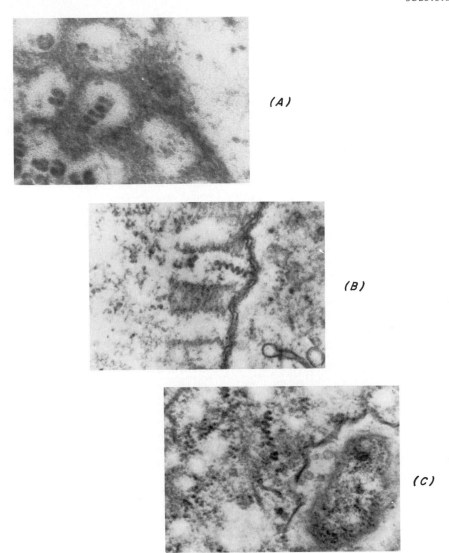

Fig. 6-20   Electron micrographs of RNA helixes passing through nuclear membrane of *Amoeba proteus*. (*A*) Helix in nucleus in one of the openings of honeycomb layer of nuclear membrane; magnified about × 71,600. (*B*) Helix in nucleus touching nuclear membrane precisely in the region of a nuclear pore leading to cytoplasm; magnified about × 110,000. (*C*) Helix in cytoplasm; magnified about × 102,000. [From A. R. Stevens. Machinery for exchange across the nuclear envelope. In L. Goldstein (Ed.). *The control of nuclear activity*. Englewood Cliffs, N.J.: Prentice-Hall, 1967, 225, 227, 229. *Reprinted by permission.*]

connect the perinuclear cisterna and the cisternae (spaces between membranes) of the endoplasmic reticulum. Through them inorganic ions and small molecules can pass. Larger molecules can take the direct route through the nuclear pores, which are large enough to accommodate any molecules that might be involved. Studying the salivary glands of fruit flies

with the electron microscope, Gay clarified how RNA may be transferred from nucleus to cytoplasm.[248] She demonstrated that blebs or blisters, possibly containing RNA, first appeared in the nuclear membrane and then extended into the cytoplasm. Remarkable electron microscopic photographs of *Amoeba proteus* were made by Stevens.[249] These show the above-mentioned honeycomb layer of hexagonal prisms just inside the nuclear membrane, each opening into the nucleus in one direction and terminating in a pore in the membrane in the other. Clusters of helixes up to 7000 Å long and 300 to 800 Å wide were photographed in the nucleus (see Fig. 6-20). Such helixes were photographed at different stages in cell division. They appeared to move progressively from the nucleus through the honeycomb layer and the nuclear pores into the cytoplasm. Experiments showed that the helixes contained either messenger or ribosomal RNA. Other types of cells probably convey nuclear RNA to the cytoplasm comparably.

Other proteins in *Amoeba proteus* have also been observed migrating constantly back and forth between nucleus and cytoplasm. Some move rapidly and others slowly. Certain of these activities may well be matter-energy transfers of structural materials. Others appear to convey signals from the cytoplasm which influence genetic transcription. Thus they are information transfers.[250]

Electrical transmission of information. As I have indicated above (see page 259), electrical signals flow through some cells either (*a*) *electrotonically*, as electricity flows along a cable, or (*b*) as an *action current* actively propagated by the use of stored energy. The first sort of transmission is decremental, decaying as a function of the distance it travels. The second maintains its full strength over distances as long as several meters.

The various types of cells have differing electrical properties. Cells can be ranked with respect to specialization of their membranes for producing action potentials.[251] Fat cells and red blood corpuscles apparently produce none. Glandular cells, such as liver, kidney, and salivary gland cells, respond to an input with a slow action current. Protozoa respond with a stronger action current, the more intense the input. Cells of the alga *Nitella* do the same in response to inputs near the threshold but respond with maximal intensity when they receive stronger inputs. I shall discuss below the electrical information transmission processes in the channel and net subsystem of (*a*) neurons, (*b*) receptor cells, (*c*) muscle fibers, and (*d*) electroplaques.

(*a*) *Neurons.* These cells are in some ways like electrical cables. Their properties as electrical conductors have been described quantitatively employing standard electronic variables.[252] They are not efficient cables because they "leak" excessively and must rely upon stored energy to amplify the signal when they conduct a current for more than a short distance. They have a conducting core of cytoplasm, a membrane with high resistance and a capacitance which produces a time lag in developing the voltage on the membrane. They are bathed in a conducting medium, the intercellular fluid of the nervous system. These electrical characteristics differ from one membrane area of the neuron to another. Also different types of neurons vary in their average time constants for development and decay of voltage across their membranes. Most of the findings discussed in this section come from studies of the motor neurons of cats, which are commonly used in experiments on neural processes for reasons I have stated above (see page 249). Conduction in other types of neurons is somewhat different, although findings on motor neurons have much generality.

The membranes of the subsynaptic area, dendrites, cell body, axon hillock where the axon arises from the cell body, and the initial segment of the axon of vertebrate motor neurons have different electrical characteristics. The receptor sites on the subsynaptic membrane appear to be electrically inexcitable. The others differ in such characteristics as threshold for excitation and mode of conduction of currents.

The inward flow of current produced in the subsynaptic area upon contact of the transmitter substance (see page 254) brings about an outward flow of current on the adjacent postsynaptic membrane, which is called the *excitatory postsynaptic potential*. This spreads electrotonically along the dendrite or cell body toward the axon hillock and initial segment of the axon. Electrotonic conduction is the usual sort of current flow in dendrites, but there is evidence that certain long dendrites in the mammalian central nervous system develop action currents.[253] Certainly some neurons that have dendrites ending with receptor components do.

The excitatory postsynaptic potential decays in a few milliseconds and may die out without producing further activity in the neuron, particularly if it is on a long dendrite, far from the site of impulse initiation. Normally, however, many of a neuron's synapses, which may number in the thousands, are activated simultaneously or in close succession. Some of these may be inhibitory, producing *inhibitory postsynaptic potentials*, which are spreading hyperpolarizations of the membrane that increase the strength of the current needed to propagate a signal. Others are excitatory. The potential that is ordinarily recorded from an electrode on a neuron represents the algebraic sum of all the inputs at that moment, the excitatory potentials minus the inhibitory ones. If this sum is positive and sufficiently large, a spike, or sharp rise in current, develops in the initial segment of the axon, which has a low threshold for excitation. At this point, the flow in the channel is "backward" away from the end of the axon. Such a backward (antidromic) current can be propagated inside a neuron, but it cannot cross a synapse. This current raises the charge on and depolarizes the membrane of the cell body or soma, which has a threshold twice as high as that of the initial segment. Then a second spike, the "somadendritic" spike, occurs. In some types of neurons these two components of the response cannot be separated. This spike is propagated as an action potential along the axon to its end. This transmission does not lose its intensity as it progresses. There is little distortion. It is an "all-or-none" pulse because it is not proportional to the input energies, as the excitatory postsynaptic potential is, but always has the same intensity in a given neuron under normal conditions. Even in very long axons of large animals like giraffes and elephants, the strength of the impulse at the end of its journey is the same as it was at the beginning. Low temperature or pressure on the neuron or an anesthetic drug can alter the intensity of the signal. If a partial mechanical or chemical block decreases the intensity of the pulse, it returns to its original intensity when the block is passed.

In an action potential, local currents are set up, flowing from a region with a positively charged resting potential to the adjacent depolarized region, which is negative with respect to it. This depolarizes the next section of the membrane. As each new section becomes depolarized, current flows toward it. Thus a wave of depolarization moves along the cell. After it passes, the membrane is permeable. Its impermeability and resting potential are then gradually restored by action of the "ionic pump" (see page 230). During the period required for this restoration, the cell is at first completely inexcitable, in an absolute *refractory period* that lasts from 0.4 to 3 ms in different types of neurons. Then it becomes relatively refractory for 10 to 20 ms or more, requiring for the production of a pulse an input which is much more intense than normal. The refractory period makes it practically impossible to fatigue a neuron by repeated inputs. After one pulse the neuron reacts again only when it has returned nearly to its steady state.

(b) *Receptor cells.* Those receptor cells which are modified neurons propagate action currents down their fibers, some of which have the relationship of dendrites to the cell bodies although they conduct like axons. This is true of the receptor cells in the skins and muscles of organisms, whose cell bodies are in the spinal cord (see page 379). The channel processes of receptor cells which are not complete neurons are not well understood.

(c) *Muscle fibers.* The time courses of the end plate potentials and inhibitory postsynaptic potentials of vertebrate smooth muscle cells are much slower than the end plate potentials of vertebrate skeletal muscle (which receive no inhibitory inputs). They take 100 ms to rise to a peak and 150 ms afterward to decrease to half intensity. This cycle is several hundred times slower than the corresponding cycle in skeletal muscle.[254] The hyperpolarization in vertebrate cardiac-muscle inhibitory postsynaptic potentials also shows an extremely long time course.

The electrical processes in vertebrate skeletal muscle are similar to the excitatory processes of neurons, only slower and subject to fatigue.

We do not understand the channel processes by which the excitation on the membrane of a muscle cell is conducted in to the contractile elements deep within the cell. Since smooth muscle cells contract slowly, the signal might be conveyed by diffusion of ions released from the cell membrane during excitation, such diffusion occurring quite slowly. This cannot be how the signal is transmitted in skeletal muscle fibers.[255] The distance from the outside to the center of a rapidly contracting skeletal muscle cell is about 50 μm, too far for diffusion to convey an excitatory substance from the surface to the deepest fibrils in time to produce anything like simultaneous contraction. A suggested channel is the transverse system, which is believed to convey electrical impulses from the cell membrane, of which it is an inward extension, to the contractile elements, setting in motion the chemical processes which produce the contraction.

(d) *Electroplaques.* In some, but not all electric fish, the excitatory postsynaptic potential gives rise to the electric discharge which is the cell's output. An intervening action potential does not develop.[256]

Functions of the channel and net. The functional relationships of the cytoplasmic channel and net have not been studied so nothing can be said about them. They have been studied for neural cell membranes, however.

(a) *Input–output transfer functions.* The excitatory postsynaptic potential varies in amplitude with the intensity of the input since it is the sum of excitations from a number of synapses. It must reach a threshold value sufficient to depolarize the initial segment of the axon before it can trigger an action current. Not only simultaneous currents from a number of synapses, but successive below threshold excitatory postsynaptic potentials may sum with one another if the time interval between them is shorter than the time required for the current on the cell membrane to disappear. The action current along the axon does not vary with the intensity of the input.

The thickest myelinated axons in man transmit at about 100 meters per second (m per s).[257] Conduction is rarely faster than this. Three sorts of axons have been distinguished in vertebrate nerves: large-diameter myelinated A fibers (four types, ranging in diameter from 20 to 2 μm: alpha—large, beta—medium, gamma—small, and delta—smaller); small myelinated B fibers, 3 to 5 μm in diameter; and small, unmyelinated C fibers, 2 μm or less in diameter.[258] In the peroneal nerve of the bullfrog at room temperature, the alpha A fibers typically conduct at 41 m per s; the B fibers at 4 m per s; and the C fibers at 0.7 m per s.

(b) *Mode of adaptation.* Some motor neurons are tonic, with slow signal termination in their channels and others are phasic, with rapid signal termination. The reason for this difference is not understood.[259]

(c) *Channel capacity.* Some neural axons can transmit as many as 1,000 pulses per s, and we have calculated that, if pulse-interval modulation is used, they may be able to transmit up to about 4,000 bits per s, with optimal codes (see page 173).

(d) *Threshold.* The average threshold for the initial axonal segment of motor neurons is about 10 mV.[260] For the somadendritic membrane it is about 25 mV.

(e) *Lag.* Excitatory postsynaptic potentials in various types of neurons take from 1 to 20 ms to rise and from 1 to 120 ms to disappear.[261]

(f) *Accessory functions.* None is known.

Some cross-level hypotheses concerning channel and net processes apply at the level of the cell, and others may be found to do so. Among those that clearly can be confirmed are:

Hypothesis 3.3.3.2-2 (see page 96), which states that there is always a constant systematic distortion between input and output of information in a channel, unquestionably applies at this level in spite of the fact that axonal transmissions have quite high fidelity. Distortion occurs when a neuron's refractory period prevents it from making accurate outputs of input signals above a certain rate.

The same considerations make Hypothesis 3.3.3.2-3 (see page 96) reasonable at this level. That is, as a signal passes along a channel, there is a progressive degradation of information and decrease of negative entropy or increase in noise or entropy. Certainly less information per unit time is output by a neuron than enters it by its subsynaptic membranes.

Hypothesis 3.3.3.2-4 (see page 96) also seems to apply at the cellular level. Its assertion that the system never completely compensates for the distortion in information flow in its channels is probably true of neurons and of other excitable cells as well.

Hypothesis 3.3.3.2-18 (see page 97) is upheld by research on neurons and muscle cells. That is, some information inputs of energic intensity above the threshold of an input transducer can affect behavior

mediated by lower echelons of the system without affecting higher echelons. If the different sections of cell membrane are viewed as different echelons, the buildup of current in the postsynaptic membrane over time until it reaches the threshold intensity for producing an action current confirms this hypothesis.

Many *variables* of channel and net processing can be measured. Some representative ones are: *Meaning of information channeled to various parts of the system.* Example: After the cell received x-ray radiation, the order of nucleotide bases that carried the message of the messenger RNA moving from the nucleus to the ribosomes was changed so that one of the types of enzymes formerly made in the cell could no longer be synthesized. *Sorts of information channeled to various parts of the system.* Example: Excitatory signals were channeled frequently to the cell body over dendrites leading from synapses on the neuron's dendrites, while at other times inhibitory signals came into the cell body over channels leading in from the membrane covering it. *Percentage of information arriving at the appropriate receiver in the channel and net.* Example: Obviously the cell manufactured an excess of messenger RNA molecules, and all of them did not get through the nuclear membrane and reach ribosomes. *Threshold of the channel and net.* Example: The threshold of the axon was much higher during the relative refractory period. *Changes in channel and net processing over time.* Example: When the neuron was developing during its first embryonic days, pulses passed down its axon only occasionally, but they gradually increased in frequency. *Changes in channel and net processing with different circumstances.* Example: When local anesthesia was applied to part of the axon, the pulses passing through that region were of lesser intensity until the anesthesia wore off. *Information capacity of the channel and net.* Example: The axon could transmit 4,000 bits per s at normal body temperature, but the maximum rate decreased at lower temperatures. *Distortion of the channel and net.* Example: Less than one messenger RNA molecule in 1,000 showed any alteration in the order of its nucleotides, so the distortion in their signals was insignificant. *Signal-to-noise ratio in the channel and net.* Example: As the concentration of the drug LSD increased in the neuron in the visual pathway of the cat, the number of random pulses generated in the neuron went up markedly. *Rate of processing of information over the channel and net.* Example: As the rate of inputs to the excitatory synapses of the neuron increased so also did the rate of transmission of pulses over its axon. *Lag in channel and net processing.* Example: The time required for a set of inputs to a neuron to generate a pulse in its axon decreased whenever the number of excitatory synapses receiving inputs or the average intensity of those inputs increased. *Costs of channel and net processing.* Example: The energy costs per minute involved in restoring the resting potential on the cell membrane, sarcoplasmic reticulum, and transverse system of the skeletal muscle cell increased as the rate of the cell's contraction increased.

3.3.4 Decoder, the subsystem which alters the code of information input to it through the input transducer or internal transducer into a "private" code that can be used internally by the cell.

3.3.4.1 Structure This subsystem is dispersed among many components. Some of these are located at molecular binding sites which accept information-bearing molecules (*e.g.,* a subsynaptic membrane, an operator, a replicator, an enzyme, a repressor, a hormone binding site, a receptor site on a chemoreceptor, or an RNA molecule). Parts of the cell membrane where changes in electrical processing occur are also components (*e.g.,* the postsynaptic membrane or the membrane of the initial segment of the axon). Except for an increased thickness of the subsynaptic membrane as compared to the rest of the cell membrane, these regions appear under the microscope to be similar structurally to all other parts of the membrane.

3.3.4.2 Process A cell may receive information in either an alpha code, based on how one molecule differs from another in its pattern of spatial configuration, or a beta code, based on temporal variations in patterning or intensity of signals, or both. The cell transmits the information through its subsystems either in the input code or in a different, "private" code that can be used internally by the cell (see page 278). It may be recoded one or more times inside the cell, finally being encoded into a "public" or external code if it is output.

Alpha-coded information is input to the cell on chemical markers, such as input molecules of a substrate, transmitter substances, hormones, or chemical molecules appropriate to excite chemoreceptors. Some arrive at and are bound by the subsynaptic membrane. Others, after entering the cell, are transmitted by the distributor subsystem to molecular binding sites throughout it. These are molecules capable of "recognizing" the spatial pattern of an input molecule and binding it at least briefly, *e.g.,* an operator, a replicator, an enzyme, a repressor, a hormone binding site, a chemoreceptor, or an RNA molecule. These sites use several different codes including: (*a*) the electrotonic potentials elicited by a transmitter substance which contacts the subsynaptic membrane; (*b*) codes of chemical reactions to other molecules, such as a repressor which is bound by an operator, an initiator which is bound by a replicator, a substrate molecule

which is bound by an enzyme, a substrate molecule which is bound by a repressor, a hormone which is bound by its receptor site, or a molecule which is bound by a chemoreceptor; (*c*) the depolarization or hyperpolarization produced on cell membranes by epinephrine or norepinephrine; (*d*) the extensively studied RNA code of nucleotide bases complementary to the DNA nucleotide-base code (see page 217); and (*e*) the protein code of amino acids, each identified by a triplet of nucleotide bases in RNA (see page 221).

An example of repeated chemical recoding within a cell occurs when DNA is recoded (*i.e.,* transcribed) onto another marker, RNA, which bears a coded message describing the design of an enzyme or other protein needed in cellular processes. Production of such a protein molecule involves another recoding (*i.e.,* translation).

Beta-coded information is input as patterns of energies like light, temperature flux, sound waves, pressures, or direct electrical transmissions such as those input to the mormyromast receptor cells of mormyroid fishes like *Gymnarchus niloticus* (see page 249) or those which occur at some special sorts of synapses or ephapses. Such information inputs chiefly affect excitable cells.

An example of repeated recoding of beta-coded signals within a cell occurs when electrotonic potentials on a subsynaptic neural membrane are recoded into excitatory potentials on the postsynaptic membrane and are then recoded into action potentials on the axon.

Each successive recoding in a system increases the error in the signal and leads to loss of information, no matter whether it is alpha- or beta-coded. Much of the input information, however, is of course preserved in the transmission. The intensity of the input at a synapse is directly reflected in the amplitude of the excitatory postsynaptic potential. When this information is encoded for transmission on the axon and final output from the neuron, information about the intensity of the input may or may not be lost. This depends upon the code used for encoding the information for the all-or-none, digital transmission which occurs on the axon. Codes used by some axons convey this intensity information, but it is lost with the codes used by others (see page 278).

Functional characteristics of channels or other subsystem components limit the codes that can be used in a neuron. In tonic motor neurons with slow signal termination, for instance, the rate of pulse output increases linearly as the intensity of current input through an intracellular electrode increases.[262] Finally, however, they reach a plateau of rate of pulse output, and information is lost about higher input current intensities. Most cat and rat motor neurons are phasic with rapid signal termination. They respond to such an input current with only a few pulses and then stop making outputs. Consequently their output cannot reveal information about the intensity of any prolonged current as can the output of tonic motor neurons. The frequencies of signal outputs from mechanoreceptor cells in the skin of a cat convey information about the intensity of the inputs, as in the tonic motor neurons.[263] This is also true of electroplaque cells of electric fish.[264]

The refractory periods of a neuron eliminate some information in the neuron's coded transmissions. Signals arriving at the cell membrane when it is refractory do not elicit action currents or at least have less effect than they would otherwise have. Consequently information is lost.

Included among the *variables* of the process of decoding are: *Meaning of information which is decoded.* Example: Acetylcholine on the subsynaptic membrane receptor sites acted as an excitatory signal; norepinephrine was inhibitory. *Sorts of information which are decoded.* Example: The cardiac cell received both neural and humoral signals. *Percentage of the information input which is decoded.* Example: When the cell fired, further excitatory input was not decoded. *Threshold of the decoder.* Example: A single miniature end plate potential was insufficient to affect the membrane, but several summated to produce depolarization. *Changes in decoding over time.* Example: The embryonic muscle fiber responded to acetylcholine over its entire membrane, but a few weeks later only the components under the subsynaptic membrane could decode that signal. *Changes in decoding with different circumstances.* Example: After the axon had produced its all-or-none pulse, further inputs to the dendrites and cell body were not decoded until the absolute refractory period ended. *Channel capacity of the decoder.* Example: Inputs above a certain rate could not be decoded by the cell, which at such rates produced no pulses along the axon. *Distortion of the decoder.* Example: Inputs far out on a dendrite did not affect the algebraic sum of excitatory and inhibitory signals which elicited the cellular response. *Signal-to-noise ratio of the decoder.* Example: The antibiotic was similar to the transmitter, but the cell could not decode it and therefore was inactivated. *Rate of decoding.* Example: As the frequency of inputs increased, the phasic motor neuron was unable to decode them, so its responses fell to a low frequency not related to the frequency of the inputs. *Percentage of omissions in decoding.* Example: The postsynaptic neuron responded only to every third pulse from the presynaptic neuron. *Percentage of errors in decoding.* Example: Occasionally the translating of the messenger RNA into protein resulted in a molecule with the bases transposed, but this sort of error occurred much less than 0.01 percent of the time. *Code employed.* Example: The dendrites transmitted electrotonically, while the axon produced a sustained series of pulses at a rate of 64 per s. *Redundancy of the code employed.* Example: The hormone had several repeating groups of molecules any of which could fit a cell membrane's binding site. *Lag in decoding.* Example: After the depolarization of the membrane of the initial segment of the axon, the action current followed in 0.05 ms. *Costs of decoding.* Example: All electrical processes of the neuron, including the decoding of inputs, were carried on at a cost of energy which had been stored in the membrane by the cellular metabolic processes.

3.3.5   Associator, the subsystem which carries out the first stage of the learning process, forming enduring associations among items of information in the cell.

3.3.5.1   Structure   Essentially this is unknown. Some as yet unidentified molecular components of certain sorts of cells, *e.g.,* yeasts, bacteria, and plasma cells, can be regarded as components of this subsystem. Macromolecules like RNA or proteins may be involved. Further components in those and other cells, if any, are unknown.

3.3.5.2   Process   Adaptive enzyme formation in some yeasts and bacteria, the antibody-antigen responses of organisms, and possibly the cellular processes underlying association and memory in organisms depend upon association of input information with information encoded in the structure of molecular components of the cell. This determines which of the possible outputs of the cell will be expressed. These are long-term changes relevant to storage of information at this level.

Experimental evidence has been sought for modification of the behavior of free-living cells by associative learning such as is found in organisms. Relevant experimental data, with some early and inconclusive exceptions, derive entirely from study of paramecia.

Free-living cells meet the same sort of environmental conditions that organisms do, reacting to inputs of matter-energy and information with appropriate adjustments in output. Certainly associative learning could aid them to survive the stresses which they encounter, but it has turned out to be difficult to design experiments which demonstrate whether or not they have this capacity. So far, controls upon variables related to subsystems other than the one under study, the associator, have not satisfied critics, and results have been open to alternative interpretations. Experiments with these minute protistan subjects have also been hard to replicate.[265]

Paramecia are ciliates of relatively large size (0.2 mm) which are sensitive to small changes in input and can be grown easily in culture. A long-term research program, that of Gelber, took advantage of the fact that they swim about actively and will congregate where a supply of food (bacteria) is concentrated.[266] They will also cling to surfaces in the area where food is to be found. Cultures used in her experiments consisted of from 128 to 512 of these microscopic protistans, each culture derived from one cell by repeated fissions. The original cell and a supply of bacteria were placed in 0.3 milliliter (ml) of water (6 to 8 drops) on a microscope slide with a 2-cm hemispherical depression and kept under conditions favorable to growth until the paramecia had increased to the desired number and the supply of bacteria was almost used up. At this time the paramecia were thin and active and suitable for experimental use. They could be kept from dividing further by restricting food.

The experimental procedure followed by Gelber was similar to that used in conditioning experiments at the organism level (see page 408). First, a clean and sterile platinum wire was placed in the culture for 3 min, after which the number of paramecia clinging to it was counted. The wire was then smeared with bacteria and put into the culture for a training trial. A second training trial followed an interval during which the wire was removed. Training consisted of 15 reinforced trials. In different experimental conditions the length of time the wire remained in the culture, and the interval between training trials were varied. Control cultures received no training. At varying intervals, after training, the wire, cleaned and sterilized, was again put into the culture for 6 to 12 min, and the paramecia clinging to it were counted. The number of paramecia clinging to the wire in the experimental cultures was significantly greater than in the control cultures, which had received no training trials. Although the cultures were stirred by rotating them before placing them on the microscope stage, causing all the subjects to swim about actively, Gelber noted that when the wire was lowered they came to it, some immediately and some taking a minute or more. The response observed was a slow and direct swoop toward the wire.

These results were interpreted by the experimenter as showing that the paramecia had acquired an approach reaction to the wire as a result of the food reinforcement.

An alternative explanation which involves pseudo-learning rather than learning has been advanced by Jensen.[267] He found that addition of bacteria to an untrained culture increased the attachment tendencies in paramecia which had had no previous training of any sort. His explanation is that carbon dioxide extruded by the bacteria dissolves in the water and produces weak carbonic acid. This substance is known to increase the attachment tendencies of paramecia.

In evaluating Gelber's work, we must remember that several scientists who have studied paramecia maintain that they are capable only of avoidance and not of approach responses. Replication of this work and further experimentation on free-living cells may possibly lead to a definitive conclusion that such systems have associative capacity, *i.e.*, can show classical conditioned responses (see Hypothesis 3.3.5.2-1, page 99). If, on the other hand, it should be established that explanations other than learning account for the behavior of paramecia in these experiments, the conclusion may be that associative learning is emergent at the level of the organism since it has not been found to occur at the level of the organ (see page 339).

Representative *variables* of the process of associating include: *Meaning of information which is associated.* Example: The paramecium associated a wire with food inputs. *Sorts of information which are associated.* Example: The paramecium made associations to signals indicating the presence of food and other objects in its environment. *Percentage of the information input which is associated to other information.* Example: The concentration of inducer was too low to affect the cell's synthetic processes at all, so no association occurred (see page 258). *Changes in associating over time.* Example: As the concentration of substrate increased, the repressors' binding sites were all filled so no further increase in synthesis occurred (see page 258). *Changes in associating with different circumstances.* Example: When spaced trials were given a culture, the paramecia performed better. *Channel capacity of the associator.* Example: A single item of information was all the protistan could associate. *Rate of associating.* Example: In 15 reinforced trials, the paramecia gave evidence of having associated food with the wire. *Lag in associating.* Example: The recognition time of the repressor–inducer interaction was 10^{-6} s (see page 258). *Costs of associating.* Example: Energy for the chemical interactions in molecular recognition processes came from the cell's metabolism (see page 258).

3.3.6 Memory, the subsystem which carries out the second stage of the learning process, storing various sorts of information in the cell for different periods of time.

3.3.6.1 Structure   The DNA of the nuclei and cytoplasm of cells is known to store information. RNA stores the information which is essential for synthesis of particular proteins. It is uncertain what other cellular components, if any, are involved in this subsystem.

3.3.6.2 Process   Whether free-living cells can remember is still unclear, though they definitely have various memory-like processes, as do cells of organisms. Cells are in some way responsible for the memory of organisms. Several cellular processes which may underlie such memory have been suggested. It may be that all of them can be explained either by changes in synaptic relationships or by information storage in macromolecules like RNA or proteins.

Genetic information is stored, in free-living cells and in cells aggregated into organisms, in DNA molecules. This information is ordinarily modifiable only by evolutionary processes or by invading viruses, but not by experiences of the individual cell or organism. Conceivably DNA may be involved in all cell and organism processes which involve storage and retrieval of information. This includes storage and retrieval of nongenetic information inputs made to an individual cell or organism that are not transmissible to its progeny.[268]

Memory in free-living cells. Paramecia which increased their wire-clinging behavior after training trials with reinforcement in the form of food (see pages 266 and 267) showed statistically significant retention of the response as compared to unreinforced controls after 3 h with spaced, but not with massed, training. The difference between cultures trained on the two types of schedule did not attain significance.[269] Untrained descendant cultures from trained *paramecia,* interestingly, also retained the response.[270] Final tests with a clean wire, designed as extinction trials (see page 421) did not bring about extinction of the response. Whether the nucleus of the paramecium was intact or fragmented, as it is during a stage of the reproductive cycle known as "autogamy," made no difference in the results, leading the experimenter to speculate that the (unspecified) sites for "behavioral plasticity" in these protistans may be in the cytoplasm.

Memory-like processes in free-living cells and in the cells of organisms. Various cellular processes share with memory the characteristic that experience with an information input produces lasting modification of system responses. These include enzyme induction, antibody formation, and circadian rhythm. All these processes in one way or another involve macromolecules, *i.e.,* RNA or proteins.

(*a*) *Enzyme induction.*   The induction of enzymes in bacteria by specific substrates is a case in point. In this process bacteria which lack an enzyme needed to carry out a process, *e.g.,* breaking down lactose, begin to produce the enzyme and cause fermentation in a lactose solution after a period of several hours in a substrate containing lactose. The enzyme molecules are completely different from any present before the exposure to lactose and are not modified from other proteins already present in the cell.[271] This change in the output of the bacteria in response to an environmental signal is possible because the instructions for constructing a very large number of enzymes, including this one, are present in the genetic material of this moneran species. Presence of the substrate "induces" control processes which direct the production of the needed enzyme. This is not done until there is a demand for it, a remarkable case of cost reduction illustrating the principle of least effort (see page 246).

(*b*) *Antibody formation.*   A similar memory-like process, carried out by specially differentiated cells in organisms, is involved in the production of antibodies specific to particular antigens. Antigens are proteins, not produced by the organism, which are different from those synthesized by the organism itself. Antibodies are proteins of the blood serum, made by the organism and known collectively as immunoglobulins.[272] These are large molecules with a number of polypeptide chains. They are capable of neutralizing foreign proteins by combining with them. A part of these complex molecules is identical in all individuals and in all antibodies of a given species of organism. Part is variable from individual to individual. The constant portions are controlled by different genes from the variable ones. Although the number of specific antibodies which can be produced by variations in the structure of immunoglobulin molecules is enormous—possibly as much as 1 million—the number of genes required to determine them is much smaller—possibly 2,000.

The cells responsible for production of antibodies are the plasma cells (see Fig. 6-5A). These are cells with heavily staining chromatin in eccentric round nuclei which develop from stem cells produced in the bone marrow. They are found primarily in lymph nodes, first appearing in immature form as *plasmablasts.*[273] The presence of antigen causes them to proliferate for a time and then to stop dividing and begin to produce antibodies. The presence of antigen also brings about the creation in the organism's lymph nodes of *germinal centers,* nests of rapidly dividing blast cells which probably include plasmablasts specific to the particular antigen that provoked the reaction.

These remain in the body as "memory cells" ready to combat the antigen by proliferating when it is encountered again.

(c) *Circadian rhythm.* Another memory-like phenomenon in cells of an organism is shown by certain neurons of the parietovisceral abdominal ganglion of the sea hare, *Aplysia*.[274] This invertebrate is active during the day but inactive at night. It is said to exhibit a diurnal circadian (around the day) rhythm (see pages 287 and 288). Not only the whole animal, which receives inputs from its environment, but its isolated ganglion and single neurons of that ganglion have this rhythmic activity. The neurons of individual animals which have previously been exposed to a certain light–dark rhythm show increased output of impulses at dawn or, in about 10 percent of cells, at dusk. After the animals have spent 1 to 2 weeks in constant light, the neurons of their isolated ganglia show a change in circadian rhythmic activity. In form and timing it is quite different from activity in animals subjected to a normal light–dark cycle. When such an animal had again experienced 1 normal light–dark cycle, the peak of pulse activity of its ganglion neuron was late, 30 min after the time when dawn would have occurred. When another such animal had again experienced seven such cycles, its ganglion neuron's cycle was timed much more accurately. Apparently information concerning the nature and time of past external events had been stored in single neurons.

The processes underlying circadian rhythms of cells are not understood. The neuron cannot be counting bursts or impulses because the rhythm continues when its capacity to respond to inputs is suppressed by hyperpolarizing its membrane.

Circadian rhythms may result from changes in the cell's synthetic activities. The cell may synthesize a protein or polypeptide that either directly or indirectly initiates excitation or inhibition at the membrane of the neuron cell body by altering its permeability or by activating or inactivating ion pumps in the cell membrane. A coupling, in the sense that the first reaction is dependent on the state of the second reaction (see page 16), probably exists between a process of the subsynaptic membrane and a process in the nucleus. Thus the nucleus can control the phasing of the circadian rhythm. This coupling, Strumwasser suggests, may occur at transcription of RNA or translation of it into protein.

Actinomycin D, which inhibits RNA synthesis, also alters the circadian rhythms of certain free-living cells indicating that the rhythm is dependent upon the unimpaired ability of these cells to synthesize RNA and, consequently, protein.[275]

Memory processes in the cells of organisms. A number of lines of research are presently converging to provide some indication of what the cellular processes are which underlie memory. Among those being considered are: (a) effects of information inputs; (b) posttetanic potentiation; (c) habituation; (d) inhibition; and (e) conditioning.

(a) *Effects of information inputs.* A cell which transmits information to an adjacent cell may have other effects upon it in addition to initiating an impulse in it. To function normally neurons need the "trophic" effect of inputs from other neurons preceding them in the channel.[276] Repeated use of a channel, as Hypothesis 3.3.3.2-17 (see page 97) suggests, makes it more likely to be used in the future—which can be considered a sort of memory. Disuse ultimately may make it inoperative—the equivalent of forgetting.

(b) *Posttetanic potentiation.* Another way in which inputs may alter the function of a neuron is by transmitting a rapid sequence of pulses over a synapse. When this is done, the electrotonic potentials on the subsynaptic membrane elicited by the later pulses are often significantly larger than those elicited by the first pulse. This potentiation may affect the postsynaptic membrane for $1\frac{1}{2}$ to 2 h after prolonged sequences of pulses have been input to it.[277]

(c) *Habituation.* In habituation, a system's outputs to continued similar inputs gradually decrease. If the inputs cease for a while and then begin again, the outputs are restored to their condition when inputs began originally.

Such habituation of the excitatory postsynaptic potential of neurons to repeated inputs has been demonstrated by the use of intracellular electrodes in the abdominal ganglion of *Aplysia*.[278] It was like the habituation of organisms, in that a large increase in intensity of the input restored the potential to its previous value. As in the organism, also, it recovered spontaneously when the inputs stopped.

(d) *Inhibition.* Prolonged slowing of the rate of outputs from a neuron of the abdominal ganglion of *Aplysia* may also result from increased frequency of inhibitory inputs.[279] This slowing may last from several minutes to over an hour and can be regarded as a kind of cellular memory.

(e) *Conditioning.* In conditioned responses a system acquires a new input–output relationship as a result of experience. Cellular analogs of classical conditioning in organisms (see page 408) have been achieved by pairing inputs to a cell from two different afferent nerves, one of which produced a small excitatory postsynaptic potential which alone was inadequate to cause the cell to fire and the other of which then produced a burst of spikes.[280] The one which produced the smaller initial response was the "test" stimulus, possibly an analog of the conditioned stimulus and the other, the "priming" stimulus, conceivably an analog of the unconditioned stimulus. In conditioning experiments with organisms, the unconditioned stimulus elicits an unlearned response from the organism, such as withdrawal of a paw to shock. The conditioned stimulus is one, like a bell, which, when paired with the unconditioned stimulus, can elicit the same response so that the animal begins to lift its paw when the bell is heard. When the test and priming stimuli were paired in cells once every 10 s for one to several minutes, with the test preceding the priming by about 300 ms, some cells showed augmentation of response to the test stimulus, a facilitation which declined only slowly during the 10 to 40 min following the procedure. During this time the previously ineffective test stimulus became effective in triggering an action potential in the cell. This study may have demonstrated a form of memory in a single cell, the postsynaptic neuron. Or it may have dealt with changes in processes of the presynaptic neurons.[281]

Microelectrode studies of single neurons in the visual cortex of cats have shown changes in output patterns after pairing of different inputs both of which elicited an output from the cell but one of which was initially "preferred" (see page 283).[282] For example, a cell which gave an output to either light or sound (a click) by different patterned discharges, responded to a pairing of the two inputs by developing a completely different response pattern. Subsequently, for a time, the light alone elicited a complex patterned discharge similar to that elicited by the combined stimuli. This sort of modification was found in only a small proportion of the cells studied, and these tended to be grouped together.[283] This led to the suggestion that "plasticity" is a characteristic of only certain cells which have the genetic endowment for short-term maintenance of change.[284]

Analogs of conditioned avoidance or operant conditioning have also been suggested. In one research an intracellular electrode was placed in a motor neuron in the leg of a decapitated locust.[285] The cell chosen for study had spontaneous activity in the absence of external inputs. When the leg was shocked each time the average frequency in the neuron fell below a standard set arbitrarily by the experimenter, the frequency was maintained at the elevated rate, in some cells for hours. Another such analog was developed with "pacemaker" cells of the abdominal ganglion of *Aplysia*.[286] These cells have an endogenous rhythm with alternating bursts of spikes and quiet periods. It was

found possible to reinforce either the burst or the quiet period and, with appropriate timing of the input, to produce opposite effects with the same input. The change in process appeared to be in the postsynaptic cell.

The cellular basis of organism memory. The speculations about how neurons may provide for the sort of information storage that is known to occur in organisms have focused on two classes of hypotheses, either (a) that information inputs produce some sort of change in synaptic relationships among neurons or (b) that they cause information to be coded into macromolecules of RNA or proteins and stored within the cell. Research findings exist that support both sorts of hypotheses.

(a) *Changes in synaptic relationships.* Synaptic relationships in the higher echelons of the brains of vertebrates differ functionally from those in lower echelons such as the spinal cord.[287] They have, for example, a greater capacity for frequency potentiation. That is, rapid repetitive bursts of inputs bring about increased excitatory postsynaptic potentials in them more rapidly than in spinal cord neurons. This potentiation does not result from lowering the threshold in the postsynaptic neuron but from raising the output of transmitter substance by the presynaptic neuron.[288]

A second characteristic of neurons in the higher echelons of the brain is that they have more inhibitory synapses. They exert more inhibition and are more prolonged in their activity than neurons in the spinal cord.[289]

A third characteristic of the neurons in the higher echelons of the brain is that their dendrites are more numerous and better developed. Although it is difficult to prove, Eccles believes that these dendrites look, in microscope slides, as if they had been growing rather than maintaining fixed structures.[290] If this is true, and the number of spines and synapses increases with experience, as he suggests, their growing connections could store new long-term memories. Studies which indicate that brain weight increases with experience may support this view (see page 417).

Taking the above and other studies into account, Kandel has listed several changes in neurons which may occur in memory processes of organisms.[291] These include elevations in synaptic efficiency related to increased activity of the presynaptic neuron; synaptic modulation of the endogenous rhythm of pacemaker cells, a postsynaptic change; trophic changes in the properties of the postsynaptic cell, which might include alteration in the spatial extent of the chemosensitive area or other functional properties; and modifications in the spike-generating capacity of a neuron as a result of changes in trigger zones or the extent of excitable dendritic membranes. Under the conditions of these experiments and probably during normal neural function as well, some of these effects are of very short duration. Such processes may be concomitants of the initial stages of information storage, accounting for short-term memory (see page 419) but not the more permanent sort.[292] Others, for example, the trophic changes and changes in extent of excitable dendritic membranes, might result in lasting alterations in channel and net structure, serving long-term memory.[293]

(b) *Information storage in macromolecules.* Since the genetic message has been decoded (see page 217), what have been called "the speculative delights of the nervous system"[294] are now extended to the speculative delights of macromolecules. The evidence that information storage in organisms in some way is concerned with RNA has been gained from studies at the level of the organism (see pages 418 to 420). These experimental results have led many to assume that learned information is stored in the structure of macromolecules within neurons. The form of this storage, if it takes place, is uncertain. A number of the scientists most closely associated with research on the biochemistry of memory support essentially the following point of view, each with his own idiosyncratic modifications: Reading of associated or learned information into storage is similar to the memory-like processes I have described above. Parts of the genome are assumed to contain templates for production of particular neural proteins. An initial association of information induces the synthesis of a particular RNA derived from the genetic template.

Research by Hydén shows that, when brain cells receive physiological stimulation (*e.g.*, when cells of Deiters' nucleus in the brainstem, which is involved in vestibular balance sensation, receive inputs as a result of repeated passive rotation of the body of the animal), the RNA content of the neurons increases and that of the related glia decreases.[295] The RNA formed in the neurons in such a situation has nucleotide base ratios characteristic of ribosomal RNA. During memory storage, on the other hand, the content of RNA increases in both neurons and glia. The RNA formed has a different ratio of nucleotide bases, the chromosomal type. An interesting and unresolved question, as Schmitt points out, is how neurons and glia distinguish between physiological and chemical stimulation on the one hand and memory storage on the other.[296]

The RNA whose synthesis is induced by the associative process is thought to direct production of specific proteins which act at synapses, possibly entering into molecular recognition processes that specify the functional characteristics of the transmission at the synapse. This protein, according to Hydén's speculations, leads to increased differentiation—modulation of the protein pattern in the cell—which would determine responses of the neuron.[297] He points out that conformational changes in macromolecules are speedy enough to satisfy the requirements of a memory storage system since they occur at about 10^{-6} to 10^{-8} s.[298] (These events occur, incidentally, in the same order of magnitude of time as the nanoseconds required for storage of information in core memory or retrieval of it in modern third-generation computers.)

The effects of inhibitors of protein synthesis upon memory (see pages 418 and 419) have been explained in terms of the following process. The initial input of information to be stored triggers synthesis of messenger RNA. This alters the rate of synthesis of the proteins which modify the characteristics of synapses to facilitate passage of impulses.[299] The proteins, in turn, act as inducers of their related RNA, which maintains over the time the concentration of those proteins. Loss of the proteins would lead to loss of memory (see page 418) and inhibition of their continued synthesis might cause their concentration to fall too low for expression of memory. This would be a temporary state, and if production of the proteins commenced again, memory would return (see page 419). This theory is obviously quite compatible with Hypothesis 3.3.6.2-1 (see page 99), which postulates that the longer information is stored in memory, the harder it is to recall, and the less likely it is to be correct; but the rate of loss is not regular over time. Also it could easily fit with Hypothesis 3.3.6.2-2 (see page 99), which proposes that information stored in memory over time undergoes changes such as omissions, errors, additions of noise, and distortions.

A theory of cellular memory must account for the processes of reading into storage, maintenance of storage, loss from storage (forgetting), and retrieval from storage in a way that is in accordance with the observed processes of the system. The suggestion that macromolecules are involved in memory provides for reading into storage. No facts are available that give a clue as to what variations in the protein may constitute the alphabet or ensemble in which the information is stored. The suggested process, however, does have the requisite stability for long-term information storage of the type which is found in higher organisms. The storage capacity of a neuron is not known. The forgetting process has not been specified, although doing so would not seem to be a serious problem for this sort of theory. The suggested process may also provide for retrieval and readout, since inputs similar to the one which brought about the storage in the first place could possibly reactivate it.

Representative *variables* of the process of remembering include: *Meaning of information stored in memory.* Example: The viral antigen was "recognized" as a foreign protein by the dog's cell although the dog had not encountered that antigen since it was a puppy. *Sorts of information stored in memory.* Example: The genetic material of the cells of the horse contained templates for synthesizing antibodies specific to many of the antigens which had been encountered in the evolution of the species. *Total memory capacity.* Example: In the organism's immunoglobulin molecules were more than 10^6 different antibodies. *Percentage of information input stored.* Example: The paramecium was able to store only a few simple memories out of the many information inputs that it constantly received. *Changes in remembering over time.* Example: The cells of the organism gradually lost the capacity to make an influenza antibody, and the immunity disappeared. *Changes in remembering with different circumstances.* Example: The paramecium showed significant retention with spaced but not with massed trials. *Rate of reading into memory.* Example: The paramecium began to store memories only after more than 50 trials. *Lag in reading into memory.* Example: No change in response of the paramecium was observed until after about 3 h. *Costs of reading into memory.* Example: The neuron used energy in the process of synthesizing its macromolecules. *Rate of distortion of information during storage.* Example: As the rate of protein synthesis in the cell decreased, the rate of distortion of stored memories increased. *Time information is in storage before being forgotten.* Example: After 3 h, the paramecium began to lose its trained response. *Sorts of information retrieved.* Example: The measles antibody was available when needed throughout the remainder of the organism's life. *Percentage of stored information retrieved from memory.* Example: The man kept all his childhood immunities into old age except to the common cold and influenza. *Order of retrieval from memory.* Example: The *Euglena* responded to light changes repeatedly, and its actions always followed the same sequence. *Rate of retrieval from memory.* Example: It appeared that memory retrieval in the cell occurred about as fast as storage—in 10^{-6} to 10^{-8} s. *Lag in retrieval from memory.* Example: The stored information in the cell permitted production of new antibodies in about an hour, and this occurred before the bacteria in its environment could multiply. *Costs of retrieval from memory.* Example: Many hundreds of amino acids were used by the cell in synthesizing each new antibody.

3.3.7 Decider, the executive subsystem which receives information inputs from all other subsystems and transmits to them information outputs that control the entire cell.

3.3.7.1 Structure   Components in both nucleus and cytoplasm which are involved in control of cellular processes constitute a cell's decider. The subsystem appears to have at least two echelons. These are described by Eigen as "legislative" nucleic acids (the higher echelon) and "executive" proteins, like enzymes (the lower echelon).[300]

The higher echelon.   The nucleus contains the genetic material. In this DNA are coded programs by which cell processes are governed. The complex genome appears to include *regulatory* genes, each of which is associated with a group of *structural* genes known as an *operon.* *Architectural* genes which specify where in a cell a protein will go and *temporal* genes which specify when the three primary gene classes are activated may also exist.[301] There are also some DNA molecules in the cytoplasm.

The lac operon, which controls the synthesis of beta-galactosidase in *Escherichia coli,* is believed to contain a gene *z,* the structural gene which is the template that specifies the arrangement of that particular enzyme; a linked gene *y,* the template for the enzyme galactoside-permease, necessary for bringing lactose across the cell membrane; an *i* gene (the regulator gene), the template for the repressor for *y* and *z;* and a gene *o* for the *operator,* the site which is bound by the repressor and possibly the place where transcription begins.[302] It may be that the genetic locus *o* is not itself the operator but rather the template for the operator.[303] A *promotor* region, according to another view, is where transcription may begin.[304] The lac operon has been isolated.[305] It is a section of DNA about 1.4 nm long, most of which is said to represent the *z* gene. Other sequences of the DNA contain the genes necessary for enzymes of other biosynthetic pathways and their control structures.

Since bacteria have little differentiation of organelles, the double strand of DNA in bacteria like *Escherichia coli* lies naked in the cytoplasm. Possibly controls in eukaryotic cells with differentiated nuclei, especially in those of higher organisms, may involve additional components such as further special types of genes, *activator* RNA, or additional *repressor sites* in the cytoplasm.[306] A hypothetical set of components for control of DNA synthesis in bacteria has been proposed.[307] Bacterial chromosomes seem to be closed rings. These and some specialized bacterial reproducer structures known as *episomes* may possibly constitute units of replication, or *replicons.* As I indicated earlier in the chapter (see page 224), an *initiator* molecule and an operator of replication or *replicator* are also included in this conceptual system.

The lower echelon.   Enzyme control involves positive or negative *effectors,* also called *modifiers* or *modulators.* Regulator enzymes are believed to be allosteric proteins. Some specialized components in differentiated cells such as the regulatory protein of the actomyosin complex, troponin, are also probably parts of the lower echelon of the cellular decider.

The places at which new sorts of signals originate on the membranes of neurons, muscle cells, and other excitable cells are also components of the decider subsystem. These membrane regions include the area of the axon hillock or the initial segment of axon in some neurons and the first node of Ranvier in the fibers of afferent neurons of the organism's peripheral nervous system (see page 262).

3.3.7.2 Process Decider processes of cells, like those of living systems at other levels, can perhaps be divided into four stages (see Hypothesis 3.3.7.2-1, page 100):

(a) *Establishing purposes or goals.* Maintenance of countless processes in steady states within their equilibratory ranges can reasonably be considered the purpose of a cell. All aspects of this purpose are set genetically and, as far as is known, can be changed only by mutations. They can be achieved by reaching certain goals. For instance, a paramecium achieves the purpose of being fed adequately by contacting bacteria and engulfing them.

(b) *Analysis.* The computation by cells of the relative strengths of signals constitutes analysis. Neurons, for example, compute an algebraic sum of excitatory and inhibitory membrane polarization changes (see page 262). The strengths of signals, such as hormones input into organism cells or various kinds of substrates for enzyme processes, are also analyzed by parts of the cellular decider.

(c) *Synthesis.* The result of these analytic computations is an integration or "command signal" which determines succeeding cell processes.

(d) *Implementing.* Cells implement their decisions by modifying various of their subsystem processes or, alternatively, continuing as in the past. Synthesis of an enzyme may start or stop. The cell may or may not pass from one stage to another of its life cycle. If the cell has the capacity for locomotion, a signal to move may or may not be transmitted to its motor subsystem. An action current may or may not be transmitted down an axon.

An experiment was conducted on decision making in *Escherichia coli*. These motile bacteria were placed in a fluid medium with a gradient of an attractant chemical to the right and a repellant to the left.[308] In this conflict situation each bacterium appeared to carry out decision making in the above four stages. With genetically determined opposing goals of moving toward the attractant and away from the repellant, it compared the opposing signals from its chemoreceptors, one for moving toward the attractant and the

other for moving away from the repellant. It summed the opposing signals and then transmitted a command signal to the flagella that determined the direction of the cell's motion.

A cell carries out its processes by a series of reactions among chemical compounds. The activities of living cells are complex because they include a great number of such separate reactions under a variety of controls which have emerged with cellular evolution. Such controls exist in cells but in no nonliving system. Many regulatory substances participate in controlling the rate and order of chemical reactions within cells. Of course cellular chemical reactions abide by the fundamental chemical law of mass action, that the rate, duration, and reversibility of a reaction between two or more compounds is determined by the quantities of each of them, their degrees of ionization and volatility, the pressure, and the temperature. But, because of its complex control processes, the cell is a very special sort of system; as Monod, Changeux, and Jacob point out:

> . . . while it [mass action] inevitably intervenes, a living system is constantly fighting against, rather than relying upon, thermodynamic equilibration. The thermodynamic significance of specific cellular control systems precisely is that they successfully circumvent thermodynamic equilibrium (until the organism dies, at least). An illustration of this statement is given by certain metabolic pathways which are both thermodynamically and physiologically reversible, such as the synthesis of glycogen from glucose-1-phosphate. It is now established that the cells do not use the same pathways for synthesis and degradation of glycogen, and that each of these pathways is submitted to different specific controls, involving hormones and other metabolites, none of which participate directly in the reactions themselves . . . all this evidently because the physiological requirements could not be satisfied otherwise, certainly not by simply obeying mass action.[309]

In the following discussion of cellular deciding I shall consider first higher echelon (DNA-related) processes, which occur chiefly in the nucleus, and then lower echelon processes, which usually occur in the cytoplasm. Some lower echelon controls probably regulate what protein synthesis goes on in the nucleus, however, and some higher echelon controls operate in the cytoplasm.

Higher echelon control processes. The nucleus carries out two fundamental processes (a) replication of the genetic material and (b) transcription of the DNA into RNA.

(a) Biologists are beginning to understand how the replication process is controlled.[310] In the laboratory an enzyme, DNA-polymerase, isolated from *Escherichia coli*, can catalyze the assembly of DNA from precursors in the presence of magnesium ions and with single-stranded DNA as "primer."[311] The newly synthesized DNA has a base composition identical with the primer. In the cell, also, the single strand of DNA, unwound from the helix and separated from the other strand, is believed to organize the essential compounds, derived from the cell's matter-energy metabolism, into a new strand identical to itself. The process within a cell must be more complicated than that in a test tube, since the enzyme used in the laboratory controls only part of the process. Yet the enzymatic process in the cell is believed not to be too different.

The suggested model for replication of bacterial DNA is a system of *positive regulation,* different from the *negative regulation* believed to take place in protein synthesis.[312] An *initiator* molecule, possibly a specific DNA polymerase or another enzyme which may be able to open DNA to convert it into a primer for DNA polymerase, is synthesized by a structural gene. This is thought to act upon the operator of replication, the *replicator,* thereby allowing the replication. At a certain point in the division cycle of the bacterium, the initiator starts replication, which moves along the circular chromosome until the whole structure is copied and again closes into a ring. This is said to account for the known facts of bacterial reproduction.

While this process is not proposed as a model for the replication of DNA in other cells than bacteria, the reception of a signal by a particular regulatory part of the genome is considered the probable stimulus to replication in all cells that divide. The nature and source of the signal is the central mystery of the process. In bacteria, the chromosome may be connected with the bacterial surface, to which the initiator is also attached.[313] Interaction between the two could begin the replication. When the process is complete, perhaps each of the newly formed rings could attach to the surface, triggering the next stage of division.

Studies with other types of cells indicate that the signal for replication must come from outside the nucleus. An example is research with *Amoeba proteus.* The nuclei of these cells can be transplanted from one individual cell to another by pushing them with microinstruments. As long as the nucleus is always surrounded by cytoplasm of one cell or the other, it can survive. Nuclei of one stage of the division cycle can be put into enucleated cytoplasm of a cell in a different stage, without killing either the nucleus or the cytoplasm. Results of such studies show that, when a nucleus which is not in a stage in which it would normally begin DNA synthesis is transplanted into cytoplasm of an amoeba which is in the stage at which replication is initiated, DNA synthesis begins in the nucleus.[314] A good deal is now known about how "phase-control switches" can trigger DNA synthesis.[315] For replication to be initiated, the cytoplasm evidently must have undergone mitosis recently, but this is not necessary for the nucleus. When the opposite transplantation occurs, and a nucleus ready to divide is put into a cytoplasm not ready to support division, replication does not then occur, possibly because the nucleus is deprived of specific initiators. Given a chance to grow, such a cell will eventually complete normal division.

Signals which elicit replication in aggregated cells may come from outside the cell itself. In insects the hormone *ecdysone* controls the periodic growth characteristic of immature insects (see page 470). It is a product of the prothoracic glands. It appears to act as a signal to begin DNA synthesis in the cells of almost all tissues.[316] Not only does the DNA molecule as a whole replicate in response to such signals from outside the cell, but during differentiation of tissues hormonal signals of this sort cause some chromosomes or regions of chromosomes to grow more than others.[317] This differential replication and accumulation of specific genes results in "puffing" of some insect chromosomes while the rest of the genome does not change.

(*b*) The second major function of the nucleus, in addition to DNA replication, is transcription of the genetic message onto RNA molecules which will be translated, in the cytoplasm, into the various proteins that the cell is capable of making. Some of these are structural proteins; others are enzymes or other regulatory molecules. Each section of the genome is believed to have a *promotor* region, which binds the enzyme RNA polymerase to start transcription of the operon into RNA. I have already described the production of protein by cells and how the genetic code is believed to be transcribed and translated (see pages 217 and 220 to 223).

Research on T_4 bacteriophage, which infects *Escherichia coli,* has clarified the activities of various genes.[318] Less than 1 min after this virus enters the cell, production of viral proteins begins. First made are the enzymes necessary for viral DNA replication, which commences 5 min after infection. Three minutes later production begins of structural proteins that will form head, tail, and tail fibers of the virus. The first virus is completed 13 min after infection. Certain mutations of these viruses produce the viral parts but cannot assemble them into a completed virus. Apparently production proceeds by completing the various parts and then combining them into whole viruses under the direction of genes specialized to do this (see page 293). Over 40 of the more than 100 genes of this virus are of this sort.

Structural genes are normally in a state of repression. When a single one is fully induced (or derepressed), it may control the production of as much as 5 percent of the total cell protein.[319] Since the human being may have 10^4 to 10^7 genes, the large store of alternatives unused at any one time provides the cell with a vast armamentarium of rapidly available preprogrammed adjustments to environmental changes.[320]

In response to information transduced by repressor molecules, cells of higher organisms seem to adjust their protein production differently from the way bacteria do, which I have described above (see page 258). They have larger genomes, which is probably because they require greater complexity of control and decision making. The actual number of metabolic pathways cannot explain the larger genome of higher cells, since it is about the same as in bacteria.

While differentiated cells of organisms synthesize only a limited number of types of protein at one time, they appear to be uneconomical in their production of RNA, continuously transcribing large amounts of it into the nucleus where it is apparently destroyed without translation.[321] It is rare for cells to be wastefully inefficient in this way, so this excess production may have an adaptive function which is not yet understood. Control of protein production in these cells may involve two types of repression. One of these *prevents transcription* of DNA to RNA before the time it is needed in the sequential program of cellular development. It also prevents transcription during most of the lifetime of the cell when all but a limited number of its potential processes whose templates are stored in the DNA are permanently inactivated.[322] The other type of repression represents a sort of control of a cell in an organism by a signal from an echelon of the decider of the organism higher than the decider of the cell. This process occurs when the cell is capable of being induced by a certain hormone, such as adrenocorticosteroid. It acts in the cytoplasm *after transcription*. The inducer molecules which receive the hormones are believed to be allosteric. Other theories have been proposed to explain the same effects in differentiated cells.[323] These conceptual systems hypothesize several other sorts of genes besides those which I have already mentioned in this chapter.

DNA in the cytoplasm also has some deciding functions. Mitochondria have DNA molecules associated with their membranes. These molecules are different in size and base composition from nuclear DNA.[324] Apparently this genetic information controls the mitochondria in a sort of autonomous synthesis of proteins. It is not a wholly independent process, however, since some chromosomal genes also control mitochondrial processes.[325] Cytoplasmic mutations seem to occur in mitochondria of yeasts, but the process is not understood.

Molecular signals act in two ways to control the production of proteins, by induction and by repression. In the latter case, if a molecule which constitutes the signal to repress the gene that controls synthesis of the enzyme is a product of that enzyme, the process is *end-product repression*. Both of these deciding processes involve the higher echelon of cellular control processes. I have already described them (see page 258).

Lower echelon control processes. Other sorts of controls of enzyme processes in the cytoplasm are also achieved without interfering with higher echelon processes which determine the formation of a protein.[326] They operate by lower echelon modification of the function of the enzyme itself, employing negative feedback, so I shall discuss them further when I consider feedbacks. They depend upon inhibition or repression of an allosteric enzyme. This occurs when it binds a regulatory metabolite to its regulatory site.[327] Whenever the metabolite is the end product of a reaction controlled by the enzyme, the process is called end-product repression. (This is a more direct process than the higher echelon end-product repression described above.) The binding alters the affinity of the enzyme for the substrate. The regulatory metabolite is termed an *effector, modifier,* or *modulator.* The action may be either positive or negative, speeding or slowing the rate of enzymatic activity, depending upon whether it increases or decreases the affinity of the enzyme for the substrate.[328] This form of control can interact with repression of synthesis of the enzyme involved and of other enzymes in the same metabolic pathway.

In muscle cells an allosteric protein, troponin, apparently controls contraction.[329] This substance appears to function to keep the muscle fiber from contracting except at the proper time. It prevents the adenosine-triphosphatase of myosin from splitting ATP when calcium, the signal for contraction, is absent. When calcium is output from the sarcoplasmic reticulum and is bound by the troponin, the fiber contracts.

Deciding in excitable cells. How membrane processes are controlled in neurons and other excitable cells is not yet fully understood. Multiple signals transmitted simultaneously are combined or modified, rather than passed on unaltered, at as many as four or five different regions of neurons.[330] Decisions, therefore, are made at these spots (see page 273). Because so many dendrites and regions of the cell membrane carry information relevant to the decision made, no single one has a high probability of affecting a decision, as Hypothesis 3.3.7.2-3 implies (see page 100). The differently excitable components of the membrane have quite diverse individual functional characteristics although for the most part they cannot be distinguished morphologically.[331]

The outputs of neurons depend upon such internally controlled processes as spatial and temporal summation.[332] *Spatial summation* is the process whereby a neuron responds to the algebraic sum of excitatory and inhibitory potentials which arise at more or less the same time at two or more synapses. *Temporal summation* is a similar integration of two or more potentials arising sequentially at a single synapse. Both sorts of summations occur in some neurons. Synapses far out on dendrites are often said to affect production of the axonal action potential relatively less than those closer to the initial segment of the axon, where the axonal potential originates. This assertion is based on an assumption that electrotonic spread is the only activity in dendrites. Some neurons, however, seem to have partial action potentials on dendrites that boost otherwise ineffectual signals.[333] The major determinants of neural outputs, however, are the nature and distribution of the postsynaptic potentials rather than the geometry of the dendrites.

Particularly in neurons that innervate tissues which contract rhythmically (such as heart muscle) slow, spontaneous, more or less regular cyclic variations occur in membrane potentials.[334] These are called *pacemaker potentials*. They may well arise from one or more regions in a neuron which are separate from either the synapses or the membrane of the initial segment of the axon. They may combine with other potentials to produce an action potential at the initial segment of the axon.

The various magnitudes of potentials in neurons, after being summed and integrated, may or may not produce an axonal action current, depending partly upon the strength of the input signals, partly upon preceding activities in the neuron, which may have sensitized it or left it refractory, and partly upon the labile threshold of the initial segment of the axon.[335] These positive and negative aftereffects of a pulse on a neuron are of varying durations, from a few milliseconds to several hours.

Hypothesis 3.3.7.2-17 (see page 101), which states that a system cannot survive unless it makes decisions that maintain the functions of all its subsystems at a sufficiently high efficiency and their costs at a sufficiently low level that there are more than enough resources to keep it operating satisfactorily, probably applies to all cells which survive phylogenetically.

Representative *variables* of the process of deciding include: *Meaning of information employed in deciding.* Example: The presence of tryptophan in the medium meant that the cell should not produce more tryptophan-synthetase, which would make more trypto-

phan. *Sorts of information employed in deciding.* Example: In controlling its internal processes, the liver cell used information from the organism's hormonal channels as well as from its own internal processes. *Amount of information employed in deciding.* Example: A single molecule of inducer in the cell at times could affect the binding of substrate, but sometimes more than one molecule was required. *Changes in deciding over time.* Example: Tyrosine-amino-transferase was induced by adrenal steroids only during part of the period between mitosis and DNA synthesis, after which the cell did not respond to the presence of the adrenal steroids' signal.[336] *Changes in deciding with different circumstances.* Example: When the nucleus from a cell not ready for DNA synthesis was transplanted into cytoplasm ready to support such synthesis, production of DNA began in it. *Number of alternatives in input before decision and in output afterward.* Example: When the presence of lactose presented the cell with a binary choice—either to synthesize beta-galactosidase or not—it began producing the enzyme. *Rewards and punishments attached to alternatives reviewed in deciding.* Example: The cell's metabolic processes were blocked, and it died because it bound a molecule similar to its proper substrate which it could not metabolize. *Rate of deciding.* Example: The entire time for allosteric control of each enzyme-substrate interaction was well under a second.[337] *Lag in deciding.* Example: The cell began making viral proteins less than a minute after the virus entered it. *Costs of deciding.* Example: The cell wasted a majority of its messenger RNA molecules because translation from it to protein was repressed.

3.3.8 Encoder, the subsystem which alters the code of information input to it from other information processing subsystems, from a "private" code used internally by the cell into a "public" code which can be interpreted by other cells in its environment.

3.3.8.1 Structure   There is little or no evidence that most cells, except for neurons, encode information into a "public" code that they can use to communicate with other cells. Other cells, however, encode signals for output in alpha-coded molecules. One paramecium, for instance, can signal others by transmitting antigenic proteins to them.[338] The parts of the transmitting cell which produce the molecules of antigenic protein constitute the encoder components. As I have described above (see page 203), some free-living slime-mold plasmodia produce and output a chemical, acrasin, which signals other free-living plasmodia. Whatever parts of those cells synthesize it are components of their encoder subsystem.

Cells of the endocrine glands of organisms also apparently have encoders. The parts of them that synthesize hormone molecules are also components of the encoder subsystem, because the molecules bear an alpha code which can be decoded by the cells in the target tissues to which they go.

Certain aggregated cells output beta-coded electrical pulses that can be interpreted by cells of other organisms receiving the pulses.[339] The parts of the electroplaque cells that produce the electrical pulses in mormyroid electric fish such as *Gymnarchus niloticus* are examples of such encoder components.

What cellular parts make up this subsystem in receptor cells that are not components of neurons, like visual pigment cells and auditory sensory cells, is unknown.

The cellular encoding which has been most studied and is best understood is carried out by neurons, which do both alpha and beta coding. Alpha coding is also carried out by specialized neurons called neurosecretory cells. These cells run from the hypothalamus to the posterior lobe of the pituitary gland and are found also in other neural tissues of vertebrates and lower animals. They have the structural characteristics of neurons except that they contain large secretory vesicles, and their axons end blindly without typical synapses or neuromyal end plates. In both neurons and neurosecretory cells those parts of the producer that synthesize the transmitter substances constitute the encoder for alpha-coded signals. The encoder component for the neuron's beta coding is a region of the cell membrane, probably near the initial segment of the axon, which determines the frequency and timing of axonal pulses. This is true for neurons which output signals by chemical transmitter substances as well as those which have electrically transmitting synapses.

3.3.8.2 Process Most nonneural cells that encode use alpha codes, the only exception being electroplaque cells, some of which encode in beta codes. Among neurons, the specialized neurosecretory cells do alpha coding. Most or all other neurons do beta coding as well as alpha coding.

Encoding in nonneural cells. Two examples can be given of encoding in free-living cells: (a) By outputting alpha-coded protein molecules, individual paramecia can influence other paramecia to produce a particular sort of surface protein, rather than another sort which the recipients would synthesize if they did not receive such a signal. The transmitting cell synthesizes antigenic proteins and then extrudes them into the fluid which is its environment. These proteins diffuse through this medium to other individual cells of the same species. They are copied by the recipients in synthesizing their surface proteins, since the recipients are capable of decoding the signal in the transmit-

ted protein molecules. (b) The acrasin output by one free-living slime-mold plasmodium signals other plasmodia to clump together into a multicellular mass (see page 203). The chemical structure of acrasin and where in the cell it is produced are unknown, but it is obvious that its "public" alpha code can be decoded by the cells that receive it, for they move toward the transmitter.

Among aggregated nonneural cells two examples of encoding can be given: (a) Cells of the endocrine glands encode molecules of alpha-coded hormonal signals, *e.g.*, epinephrine or thyroxine, for transmission to tissues throughout organisms. (b) The electroplaque cells in the electric organ near the tip of the tail of such electric fish as *Gymnarchus niloticus* encode beta-coded signals which can be decoded by other cells. These are transmitted through the water around the transmitting fish. They are received and decoded by cells in that fish as well as in other individuals of the same species which happen to be swimming within its electrical field.

Encoding in neurons with chemically transmitting synapses. Most neurons encode information in chemical molecules of transmitter substances, an alpha-coding process, and also in the number and temporal spacing of bursts of such substances at synapses, a beta-coding process.

(a) *Alpha coding.* The information in alpha-coded molecules is digital. That is, they are so coded that they bind on to receptors of other cells and either initiate or repress processes in them.

Some neurons which are like glandular cells, called neurosecretory cells, release their alpha-coded molecules of such hormones as oxytocin and vasopressin directly into the organism's bloodstream.[340] It is not certain whether they also transmit beta-coded signals.

A few neural transmitter substances encoded and output by neurons are known. Other substances are under study as possible transmitters. In order to qualify as a transmitter, a substance must:[341] (a) Be present in the synapses of neurons whose action it is believed to transmit. (b) Possess enzymatic processes for synthesizing the substance. (c) Be capable of being inactivated. (d) On experimental application to subsynaptic membranes, mimic the action of normal neural inputs to the neuron. (e) Be detectable in the extracellular fluid in the region of the activated synapses. And (f) be interfered with by those drugs which interfere with transmitter substances of the neuron, the interference occurring in the same way it does in the neuron. Acetylcholine, norepinephrine, and gamma-aminobutyric acid (GABA) satisfy the above criteria and are considered transmitter substances in nervous systems of various species.

Acetylcholine is a transmitter in both vertebrate and invertebrate species. It acts at a variety of mammalian peripheral synapses, including the neuromuscular junction and synapses in sympathetic and parasympathetic ganglia. Acetylcholine is the transmitter in one type of central synapse and perhaps others.[342] Synapses activated by acetylcholine are known as *cholinergic*.

Norepinephrine (noradrenalin) is the primary transmitter of the sympathetic nervous system (see pages 336 and 337).[343] Synapses in which it is employed are called *adrenergic*. Synapses between neurons of the spinal cord and the cells of origin of the sympathetic preganglionic fibers also appear to make use of this substance.[344]

GABA is probably a transmitter in the nervous systems of crustaceans. It is present in mammalian central nervous systems, in the cerebral cortex and cerebellum; but here the evidence that it is a transmitter is suggestive rather than conclusive.[345]

Each neuron produces only one transmitter substance. It always acts to open the same ionic gates in the postsynaptic neuron.[346] Even acetylcholine, which is known to be capable of producing opposite effects in different sorts of channels (excitatory at the neuromuscular end plate, inhibitory in molluscs), never has more than one effect at a synapse of the same neuron. Neurons are, therefore, capable of encoding an excitatory or an inhibitory signal, but never both. One known exception is a mollusc, *Helix,* in which the same transmitter, acetylcholine, excites when a neuron synapses with one sort of cell but inhibits when it synapses with another.

(*b*) *Beta coding.*   If encoding a signal into excitatory or inhibitory transmitter substance were the whole story of neural encoding, interneuronal communication would make use of a digital code. This is not the case. Neurons use digital codes, but in their trains of essentially digital output pulses they also transmit analog signals which can reflect a number of dimensions of the input information.[347] Since large populations of neurons frequently function together, the signals encoded by a single neuron are often symbols in a complex code which can be employed only by many neurons operating jointly (see pages 396 and 397).

Intervals between axonal pulses are not quantized but are continuous variables. The number and timing of these action currents down axons are quite accurately reflected by emissions from the presynaptic endings of quanta of transmitter substance. These are then rapidly inactivated in the synaptic cleft by the action of enzymes such as cholinesterase, so that the discreteness of each all-or-none pulse from the presynaptic neuron is preserved. The length of time the transmitter remains active in the synaptic cleft varies from one type of neuron to another, which is one explanation why the types function differently.

Of the observed variations in activity of neurons, not all are known to constitute codes. In order to establish that any such activity is a coded signal, one must show that a postsynaptic neuron can decode it.[348] Among the codes that are known to be used by some neurons in axonal transmissions are: (*a*) A simple presence or absence signal, a discrete input signaled by a discrete output—like a doorbell.[349] (*b*) The rate of recurrence of rapidly repeated inputs (as to a Pacinian corpuscle) indicated by the same rate of repeated output pulses—frequency encoding frequency.[350] (*c*) Increased intensity of input indicated by a rise in average frequency of output—frequency encoding intensity. (*d*) Intensity of an input represented by the number of output pulses it elicits. (*e*) A latency or phase code, the intensity of regular inputs indicated by the time between some invariant output signaling that they occurred and a delayed second output signal whose frequency is constant. (*f*) Frequency modulation, a rhythmic variation of interpulse intervals found in some neurons of the input and internal transducer subsystems of organisms. (*g*) Variations in length of the modal or dominant interpulse period in a sequence of pulses.

Some other variables of pulse characteristics which could also be used as coded signals are: (*a*) Degree of variance of interpulse intervals about the mean. (*b*) Shape of the statistical distribution of pulses about the mean. (*c*) Presence (and sign) or absence of autocorrelation of successive interpulse intervals.[351]

The types of brain cells which respond to more than one modality of sensory input over the organism's afferent channels encode signals differently for each modality of input and for the combined modalities.[352]

Encoding in neurons with electrically transmitting synapses.   The electrically transmitting synapses of certain invertebrates make use of a pulse code like that in chemically transmitting synapses. The output transducer is different, however, emitting electrical pulses rather than chemical transmitter substances.

Some of the most important *variables* of the encoding process are: *Meaning of information which is encoded.* Example: The neuron encoded only inhibitory signals. *Sorts of information which are encoded.* Example: The receptor cell encoded a signal when the red light went on. *Percentage of the information input which is encoded.* Example: The individual neurons of a particular channel in the organism could signal the rate of inputs but not their intensity. *Threshold of the encoder.* Example: The presynaptic neuron stopped encoding the axonal signal into synaptic vesicles only when an axonal pulse was so weak it did not reach the end of the axon. *Changes in encoding over time.* Example: The neuron could encode only up to a certain rate of inputs, after which its encoding and output rates declined. *Changes in encoding with different circumstances.* Example: An inhibitory input from cutaneous input transducers kept the motor neuron from continuing to encode action potentials. *Channel capacity of the encoder.* Example: The axon transmitted one binary signal per millisecond. *Distortion of the encoder.* Example: Some signals which arrived during the refractory period were not encoded by the neuron. *Signal-to-noise ratio of the encoder.* Example: The physiologist could not determine the code because he did not know what was signal and what was spontaneous noise in the neural activity. *Rate of encoding.* Example: The motor neuron of the cat produced a discharge frequency linearly related to the input current strength at frequencies of 10 to 37 per s. *Percentage of omissions in encoding.* Example: The neuron failed to encode every third input because it was refractory when those inputs occurred. *Percentage of errors in encoding.* Example: A minute percentage of the molecules produced by the glandular cell lacked an amino acid sequence and consequently did not carry information to the target tissues. *Code employed.* Example: The receptor cell output pulsed at a faster rate as the intensity of its inputs increased. *Redundancy of the code employed.* Example: Because the number of vesicles in different bursts across the synapse (which elicited subsynaptic potentials) varied significantly, it seemed that at least the largest bursts—and perhaps all of them—were coded redundantly. *Lag in encoding.* Example: There was a minute, but measurable, lag between the rise of the excitatory postsynaptic potential and the beginning of the action current. *Costs of encoding.* Example: A small part of the energy used in transmission of each pulse was required for the process of encoding it.

3.3.9 Output transducer, the subsystem which puts out markers bearing information from the cell, changing markers within the cell into other matter-energy forms which can be transmitted over channels in the cell's environment.

3.3.9.1 Structure   In many types of cells, components of the extruder subsystem in the cell membranes are also components of the output transducer, since they output alpha-coded information borne on chemical molecule markers. This may be accomplished passively through tubular apparatuses or other parts of the membrane, or actively with the aid of carrier molecules, permeases, or other such subcomponents.

Free-living cells which put out alpha-coded signals that can be decoded by other free-living cells, including paramecia and plasmodia of slime molds, use one or another component of the cell membrane to do so.

Cells of the endocrine glands of organisms use similar components of their cell membranes to output their alpha-coded molecules of hormones, commonly into or near capillaries.

Beta-coded electrical pulses are output through the cell membranes of electroplaque cells located, in mormyroid electric fish like *Gymnarchus niloticus,* below the skin of the afterbody in tubular structures extending forward from the tip of the tail.

It is not known what the output transducer is in receptor cells which are not components of neurons.

In neurons and neurosecretory cells this subsystem includes specialized regions of the presynaptic membranes and prejunctional regions of neuromyal junctions. Certain essential structural uniformities are present in the presynaptic regions of chemically transmitting neurons.[353] The sheath provided by glial cells disappears near the end of the neuron. The membrane fronting the synaptic cleft is denser than the rest of the cell membrane. Near it are a number of mitochondria. Synaptic vesicles, from 200 to 600 Å in diameter, are also concentrated just inside this specialized membrane. Electron micrographs which show these bodies have been interpreted to indicate that each one is spherical and surrounded by a membrane, but some more recent evidence suggests that they may be parts of a continuous tubular apparatus extending from the synaptic region through the membrane at the tip of the neuron into the extracellular space.[354]

The form of ending varies from one type of neuron to another. Motor neurons branch and embed themselves into folds of the muscle fiber end plate, making a number of separate contacts (see Fig. 6-17). In the mammalian central nervous system, neurons end with synaptic knobs, smaller than the endings of the motor neurons, a good arrangement where thousands of synapses must be accommodated by each postsynaptic cell.[355]

The junctions between neurons with electrically transmitting synapses do not show major anatomical differences from chemically transmitting synapses, although in some cases there may be actual contact between the two cells.

3.3.9.2 Process

Output transducing in nonneural cells.   All output transducing so far discovered in free-living cells involves extruding of alpha-coded molecular markers across the cell membrane. This is true of all output transducing of aggregated cells in organisms also, except for electroplaque cells, neurosecretory cells, and neurons with both chemically and electrically transmitting synapses.

Among aggregated cells of organisms, the cells of

the endocrine glands apparently output alpha-coded hormonal chemical markers in similar fashion.

The electroplaque cells of each mormyroid electric fish, arranged in batteries of many such cells in its electric organ, transmit a series of strong pulses into the water surrounding the fish with an oscillating electric field. The fish can alter the temporal patterning of these pulses and these beta-coded altered patterns can be decoded by cells of other mormyroid fishes.

Possibly the transduction in receptor cells which are not components of neurons is into an electric signal, although a chemical transmission process is more likely.[356] The alternatives are these: (a) Illumination of a receptor cell, such as the retinula cell of *Limulus,* changes the permeability of its cell membrane in such a way that a current is conducted passively along the dendrite (distal process) of the receiving neuron (called the "eccentric cell" in the *Limulus*) and out through the membrane covering the latter cell's body and initial segment. Or (b) during illumination a chemical is released from the receptor cell which diffuses to the receiving neuron, depolarizing it and bringing about a propagated action current.[357]

Output transducing in neurons with chemically transmitting synapses. Transduction at the ends of chemically transmitting neurons is from a beta-coded all-or-none pulse into a burst of alpha-coded transmitter-substance molecules that preserves the essential temporal characteristics of the electrical signals.

The transduction process in chemically transmitting neurons is still not completely understood. It is generally believed that the synaptic vesicles are separate bodies. The synaptic vesicles have been observed to move with the axoplasm down the axon toward the presynaptic region. Upon depolarization of the presynaptic membrane, attachment sites on its inner surface increase in number.[358] The synaptic vesicles attach to them and extrude their contents into the synaptic cleft. Transmitter substance is output after an axonal pulse. The pulse itself may not elicit the output, but rather some other event brought about by it. It seems probable that the pulse changes to a weaker electrotonic potential at the nerve ending.[359]

Both acetylcholine and norepinephrine are released into their respective synapses in quanta, presumably from the synaptic vesicles in which they are stored. The amount of transmitter released by a single pulse varies in different neurons.[360] In some, one pulse may release more than enough to provoke a spike in the postsynaptic cell; in others repetitive stimulation is necessary.[361] At the presynaptic axonal terminal of certain neurons, other axons synapse. These latter axons transmit depolarizing pulses and thus produce presynaptic inhibition of the neurons with which they synapse. They depress, perhaps completely, the output of transmitter substance by the latter cells. From time to time a few synaptic vesicles may leak their contents into the synaptic cleft even when there is no action current. This produces miniature postsynaptic or end plate potentials.

Output transducing in neurons with electrically transmitting synapses. Transduction at electrically transmitting junctions is from an all-or-none, beta-coded action current on the cell membrane of the presynaptic neuron to a beta-coded, electrotonically spreading potential.[362]

Representative *variables* of the output transducing process are: *Meaning of information output which is transduced.* Example: The frequency of outputs from the neuron signaled the intensity of its inputs. *Sorts of information output which are transduced.* Example: The receptor cell output signals about changes in pressure on it. *Threshold of the output transducer.* Example: Several successive miniature end plate potentials were required to bring about a contraction in the muscle fiber. *Changes in output transducing over time.* Example: After many minutes of repeated rapid inputs over the neuromyal junction the muscle fiber became fatigued and failed to contract on signal. *Changes in output transducing with different circumstances.* Example: Discrete inputs to the motor neuron, which had slow signal termination, elicited discrete outputs at a rate corresponding to the rate of inputs, but when the inputs became continuous, the neuron adapted to output steadily repeated pulses reflecting the intensity of the inputs. *Channel capacity of the output transducer.* Example: Each molecule of hormone output by the glandular cell was a marker for one bit of information, and it could output 100 molecules per s. *Number of channels in use in the output transducer.* Example: As many as six vesicles could pass simultaneously through the membrane of each synaptic knob. *Distortion of the output transducer.* Example: Whenever synaptic vesicles leaked into the synaptic cleft the postsynaptic neuron's response was distorted. *Rate of output transducing.* Example: The neuron output the contents of about 60 vesicles per second. *Lag in output transducing.* Example: The increase in rate of output of molecules of acetylcholine from the neuron occurred after a fraction of a millisecond. *Intensity of information output.* Example: Sometimes an axonal pulse would cause an unusually large number of vesicles to extrude their transmitter substance into the synaptic cleft. *Costs of output transducing.* Example: The neuron consumed matter-energy whenever it synthesized acetylcholine to make up for molecules which had been output, the rate of this consumption going up as the number of vesicles outputting the transmitter substance from the cell increased.

4. Relationships among subsystems or components

So far this chapter has dealt largely with structures and processes in cellular subsystems and components. Equally important are the observable and measurable relationships these have to one another. These relationships are listed below, with an example of how each occurs in cells.

4.1 Structural relationships

4.1.1 Containment   Example: Most DNA molecules are contained in the nuclei of cells.

4.1.2 Number   Example: Some epithelial cells have more than one nucleus.

4.1.3 Order   Example: The code of the RNA which synthesizes alanine transferase is read in the order indicated in Fig. 6-11.

4.1.4 Position   Example: The sarcoplasmic reticulum is located very close to all parts of the skeletal muscle fibers, a nearly ideal arrangement for distributing the calcium which is essential for contraction of the fibers. This arrangement indicates how components of a cell's distributor tend to be located in optimal positions for carrying out its functions, as stated in Hypothesis 4.1.4-1 (see page 103).

4.1.5 Direction   Example: The flagellum in a *Euglena* is located at its tail end.

4.1.6 Size   Example: The fat deposits in certain subcutaneous cells may occupy several times the volume of all the other components.

4.1.7 Pattern   Example: The nuclei of mature neutrophil white blood cells usually have two or three lobules connected by strands of nuclear material while immature neutrophils are not lobulated.

4.1.8 Density   Example: The nuclei of cells are in general more dense and less transparent than cytoplasm. This fact supports the part of Hypothesis 4.1.8-1 (see page 103) which states that the greatest density of components of a system tends to be at its center.

4.2 Process relationships

4.2.1 Temporal relationships

4.2.1.1 Containment in time   Example: Chromosomes divide during mitosis.

4.2.1.2 Number in time   Example: In the human being there are 46 chromosomes before meiosis and 23 afterward.

4.2.1.3 Order in time   Example: In mitosis disappearance of the nuclear membrane precedes division of the cell into two descendant cells.

4.2.1.4 Position in time   Example: In the human being the gastrula phase of the ovum occurs 48 h after the fertilization.

4.2.1.5 Direction in time   Example: The red blood corpuscles in normal human beings almost always lose their nuclei before entering the blood stream.

4.2.1.6 Duration   Example: Many neurons in the central nervous system of mammals continue to function throughout the entire life of the organism.

4.2.1.7 Pattern in time   Example: Membranes of neural axons are depolarized and repolarized as sequences of pulses pass down them.

4.2.2 Spatiotemporal relationships

4.2.2.1 Action   Example: The ATP molecules convey the energy used in producing many new organic molecules in the cell.

4.2.2.2 Communication   Example: Messenger DNA conveys the information for producing enzymes from the DNA of the nucleus across the nuclear membrane to the cytoplasm.

4.2.2.3 Direction of action   Example: Amino acids move toward the ribosomes where they are synthesized into proteins.

4.2.2.4 Pattern of action   Example: During mitosis the asters move to opposite poles of the cell.

4.2.2.5 Entering or leaving containment   Example: As soon as the sperm cross the boundary subsystem of the ovum, the electrical charges of the cell are altered.

4.3 Relationships among subsystems or components which involve meaning   Example: One molecule represents a signal to the initiator to begin the process of DNA replication while another molecule signals the cell not to produce more tryptophan.

5. System processes

5.1 Process relationships between inputs and outputs   If cells are observed as a whole, rather than subsystem by subsystem, orderly relationships between their inputs and outputs of both matter-energy and information are evident and the interdependence of the two sorts of flows can be seen.

Variations in matter-energy flows affect not only the nature and amounts of a cell's products and wastes but its capacity to output information, whether alpha- or beta-coded. Similarly, but less obviously, input of information necessarily affects the matter-energy as well as the information output from cells. A number of examples follow:

(a) *Matter-energy inputs related to matter-energy outputs.* Parietal cells of the stomach, components of the organism converter, require a continuous supply of carbon dioxide to synthesize their output of hydrochloric acid. At low rates of hydrochloric acid production they make enough carbon dioxide to satisfy their requirements. At high rates they cannot synthesize carbon dioxide fast enough and so must receive inputs of it from the organism's intracellular fluids and bloodstream, so decreasing the carbon dioxide content of the blood.

Muscle cells require continuous inputs of glucose to produce their energic outputs of work. They convert the chemical energy of ATP, produced from the glucose, into the mechanical energy of contraction, with an additional output of heat. This conversion is about 20 percent efficient. This efficiency is somewhat less than that of a steam engine (see page 398).[363] At low rates of contraction and with sufficient oxygen, the aerobic breakdown of glucose proceeds through the Krebs cycle (see page 237). Carbon dioxide and water are output as wastes. With more rapid contraction, the reaction is anaerobic, producing an output of lactic acid as a waste.

(b) *Matter-energy inputs related to information outputs.* Cells of the thyroid glands of organisms cannot output thyroxine, an alpha-coded hormone, without inputs of iodine.[364] Neurons depend upon inputs of oxygen for producing their beta-coded information outputs, since they cannot function anaerobically for much more than a minute.[365] Although there is normally little variation of inputs of matter-energy, under experimental conditions neurons vary in their time course of propagation of inpulses with changes in temperature and in composition of surrounding fluids.[366]

(c) *Information inputs related to matter-energy outputs.* Glandular cells, such as those that output saliva, mucus, and sweat, do so in response to information inputs from the neurons that innervate them.

(d) *Information inputs related to information outputs.* Total cells can be regarded as single channels for information transmission. The outputs from the cell reflect the successive activities of all the information processing subsystems, although for any given output some particular subsystem process may be the primary determinant: Considering all of a cell's information processing subsystems as a unit, their overall input–output information transfer functions can be studied. Some of the facts which have been learned about such transfer functions are presented below:

Mode of adaptation. A neuron or receptor cell may respond to continuous inputs by maintaining outputs at a rate determined by the intensity of the inputs. Such a cell is described as *tonic, i.e.,* having *slow signal termination.* Or it may respond to continuous inputs by one or a series of outputs, then fall silent or decline to a low output frequency without establishing any particular level of adaptation. This is a *phasic* cell, with *rapid signal termination.* The tonic behavior of muscle fibers in organisms is a result of the slow signal

termination of the motor neurons which innervate the fibers and keep them in contraction for varying lengths of time.

An example of a tonic receptor is the muscle spindle, a specialized stretch receptor of the frog. When such a receptor is stretched, there is at first a large initial change to a potential of about 0.7 mV, followed by a decrease in about 10 ms to an amplitude of approximately 0.2 millivolt which is continued sometimes for hours.[367] The faster the stretch occurs, the higher is the initial amplitude. The maintained potential goes up in amplitude as the intensity of the stretch increases. When the stretch is released, there is a reversed-potential pulse which is slower than the onset pulse.

When the intensity of the input rises, a tonic receptor or neuron, with slow signal termination, will increase the frequency of its output pulses beyond that appropriate to the new input, after which the output rate will decline to the correct frequency for the new situation.[368] A decrease in the input, for example, in the force applied to a pressure receptor, will cause the output pulse frequency to fall to an intensity below that expected for the new input and then increase. A similar output pattern can also be seen in temperature-sensitive cells and a number of others.

Phasic receptors and neurons, with rapid signal termination, output one or a few impulses to an appropriate input. These include receptor cells in eyes, which make outputs to changes in intensity of light either above or below the steady level.[369] Some cells are "on," some "off," and some "on-off." Similar on and off cells occur in other sense organs as well (see pages 383, 384, and 397).

In organisms slow and rapid signal termination cells function quite differently. Those with slow signal termination ordinarily signal the change of properties of a steady state if they are receptors, or contribute to the steady contractions of muscles required for posture if they are neurons. Rapid signal termination permits a cell to communicate a change or produce a contraction in a muscle fiber and then be ready almost immediately to do the same thing again.

The relationships between input intensity and output pulse frequency in some cells have been found to conform closely to the Weber function. That is, as Hypothesis 3.3.1.2-1 suggests (see pages 94 and 95), the frequency of the output signal of a receptor varies as a particular power function of the intensity of its input. At the organism level, experiments have shown that, as intensity of the input goes up, there is an orderly increase of this sort in the human observer's report of his sensations (see pages 379 and 380; and 383, 384, and 385). The exponent which is the quantitative measure of the relationship between the input intensity and the subjective report differs somewhat among the various modalities of sensation. The cell's intensity-frequency input–output relationships, as Mountcastle found, closely conform to the input–output relationships of the whole organism, for those sensory modalities which have been studied.[370] If a given exponent describes the curve of increase of subjective report of intensity of a certain sort of sensory input, it also describes a similar curve for the neuron. In certain transducers of mechanical energy of the skin of the hand, for example, the subjective report of increasing pressure appears to have a linear relationship with the increase in intensity of the inputs. The same relationship occurs in single neurons receiving inputs from that area in the monkey hand, which is essentially the same as the human. Fibers arising from the touch receptors of the hairy skin, however, do not have such a linear input–output relationship. Instead, the curve progressively accelerates negatively, being a power function with an exponent of about 0.5 to 0.6. That is, as the input intensity goes up, the output intensity also goes up, but always more and more slowly. These findings of Mountcastle led him to conclude that the peripheral receptor cells are the determining components in the organism's input channels and that higher components in these complex channels transmit the receptors' output signals in a linear fashion. Similar observations have been made upon the human subjective report of light intensity and the response of the retinal receptor cells to light, since for both the exponent is about 0.3.

Channel capacity. The channel capacity of a neuron or receptor cell seems fundamentally to be the channel capacity of the axon, which appears to transmit significantly less information than is input to the cell. As our experiments with neurons have shown, this capacity may sometimes be as high as 4,000 bits per s, although often it is surely much less (see page 173).

Threshold. As I have indicated above, a receptor cell is specialized in such a way that it has a low threshold for a particular form of energy input and high thresholds for all others. Cones of the human eye, for example, transduce wavelengths between 390 nm (violet) and 760 nm (red). Probably different sorts of photoreceptors are particularly sensitive to particular bands within this spectrum. Auditory fibers respond to different input frequency ranges, from 420 to 25,000 Hz.[371] The most sensitive Pacinian corpuscles of a cat's paw can be fired by mechanical displacements as small as 0.0015 mm.[372]

The threshold for a muscle spindle of the soleus muscle in the leg of a cat varies with the diameter of its afferent fiber and the velocity at which it transmits.[373]

Muscle spindles with large afferent fibers, of diameters of 12 μm and larger and of velocities above 7.2 m per s, output signals only to stretches with a pull of 3.3 g or more. On the other hand, the minimum above-threshold intensity of pull is 19 g for small afferent fibers of diameters of 4 to 12 μm and of velocities between 24 and 72 m per s.

Some neurons of the visual cortex of cats output signals in response to more than one sort of input to the animal's receptors (see page 270). Often these inputs are complex, including visual presentations such as edges, bars, or lines of different lengths and orientations. Such cells may also respond to a clicking sound or to a weak electric shock delivered to the hind limb.[374] For all such cells there is a preferred input modality which reliably produces a distinctive pattern of outputs. They are either unresponsive or have a higher threshold to other sorts of inputs. Some receptor cells also have a high threshold to any form of energy, outputting signals only when input reaches a level which threatens damage. These cellular signals are associated with defensive reflexes and other overt signs of pain in higher organisms.[375]

Lag. The lag, or latency, of a cell represents the sum of the times required for all the processes intervening between input and output. When inputs are of such low intensity that two or more of them must summate over time to produce an output, the latency increases as the intensity of the inputs diminishes. In neurons that respond to more than one input, the latency to the "preferred" signal differs from that to the other inputs to which such cells output signals.[376] For neurons, muscle cells, and receptor cells, the weaker an experimentally administered electrical input current is, the longer it must be applied to produce an output. Latency is longer than normal just after a cell has output a signal. Cells differ in the rate at which they return to normal latency after the output.[377]

Accessory functions. Some components of excitable cells have accessory functions. A signal may be initiated in the hair plate mechanoreceptors of honey bees by compression of a tubular body.[378] The hairs of the auditory hair cells (see Fig. 6-18, III-D) are accessory components whose bending initiates the cells' output signals.[379] And the concentric layers of Pacinian corpuscles (see Fig. 6-18, I-A) produce the mechanical movement that initiates the signal in that cell.[380] Their shape and mechanical characteristics affect the nature of the output signal.

Hypotheses. In addition to Hypothesis 3.3.1.2-1 stating the Weber function, which I discussed on page 282, a number of other cross-level hypotheses concerning the relationships between information inputs and outputs of living systems can be applied at the level of the cell. They are particularly relevant to receptor cells, neurons, and muscle fibers, excitable cells specialized for information processing.

Included among them are: Hypothesis 5.1-5 (see page 103) proposes that, as average information input rate goes up, variation in output intensity increases. Experiments show that, as frequency of repetitive pulses goes up, motor neurons vary more and more in the amounts of transmitter substance they liberate.[381] This finding appears to support this hypothesis. Also Hypothesis 5.1-20 (see page 104), which is related, proposes that the intensity of outputs will decrease as the percentage of resources to meet the costs are exhausted. This clearly happens at neuromyal junctions.[382] Very high rates of inputs to presynaptic neurons at neuromyal junctions produce rapid sequences of outputs. These decrease the amounts of acetylcholine available for transmission from the presynaptic neuron, which progressively lessens the quantity of transmitter substance in each output pulse and hence its intensity.

Hypothesis 5.1-6 (see page 103) suggests that as average information input rate increases, the average processing time goes up. This is not generally true of neurons. In fact, at increased input rates, the processing time of some neurons decreases, since impulse generation occurs earlier as the level of the intensities of the excitatory postsynaptic potentials rise, which can happen when successive potentials of this sort summate.[383] With the onset of fatigue, experimentally induced by continued rapidly repeated inputs, neurons do conduct more slowly, and their refractory periods become longer. This cannot occur during normal functioning of the nervous system, since neurons are guarded against fatigue by a number of adjustment processes. Some motor neurons of amphibians react to a rise in frequency of input pulses by a decrease in the rate of output pulses. This results, at least in part, from an increased threshold for initiation of impulses.[384]

Hypothesis 5.1-9 (see page 103)—which proposes that, as average input intensity increases, up to a point average processing time decreases—has been confirmed for those neurons which use a frequency code to transmit information concerning input intensity (see page 278).

Hypotheses 5.1-11 and 5.1-12 (see page 104), which state that output rate increases and processing time decreases with increasing priority of input, may be said to apply to neurons. Synaptic inputs close to the site of impulse initiation, if intense enough, probably have priority in eliciting outputs. If they are not sufficiently intense, they still have priority in influencing summations of potentials which result in outputs (see page 262).

Hypothesis 5.1-42 (see page 105), which states that a minimum rate of information input to a system must be maintained for it to function normally, may apply to neurons and muscle cells. These cells cannot function normally when their innervation is lost and they do not receive their usual trophic inputs. Muscle cells, for instance, contract more and more slowly and finally disintegrate. The "trophic substance" may be matter-energy inputs from a presynaptic neuron or it may be information-bearing molecules of transmitter substance emitted spontaneously by a presynaptic neuron.[385] If the latter explanation is correct, a lack stress of the transmitter substance would constitute the failure of maintenance of the minimum rate of information input which Hypothesis 5.1-42 suggests is necessary for normal function.

Several cross-level differences described in various hypotheses seem to exist between cells and higher levels of living systems, for instance: Cells have less variation of output intensity (see Hypothesis 5.1-26, page 104), a lesser output range (see Hypothesis 5.1-27, page 104), shorter processing times (see Hypothesis 5.1-28, page 104), less variation in processing times (see Hypothesis 5.1-29, page 104), and probably less cost in energy expenditure per correct unit of information processed (see Hypothesis 5.1-30, page 104) than higher levels of systems.

5.2   Adjustment processes among subsystems or components, used in maintaining variables in steady states

5.2.1   Matter-energy input processes   The capacity for locomotion of some free-living cells makes it possible for them, as a result of increased activity within their environments, to avoid matter-energy excess stresses such as noxious substances or harmful energies like excessive heat, cold, or radiation. Locomotion, or the passive motion brought about by movement of waters in which cells float, also increases the probability that they will get to regions of plentiful food supply. Some free-living cells are capable of active pursuit of prey.

Starvation, a matter-energy input lack stress, causes free-living slime-mold plasmodia to output the chemical marker, acrasin, which signals other plasmodia to come together and aggregate. Aggregation permits reproduction by sporulation rather than by cell division of the separate free-living plasmodia, which is their mode of reproduction in a favorable environment. The aggregated organism uses stored energy for its processes and dies after reproducing. The resulting spores have extra thick boundaries and little internal moisture. They can survive until conditions favor their existence as free-living cells, and then they develop into plasmodia.

Bacterial spores, formed by reproduction of the parent cells, can withstand dryness and great extremes of temperature, sufficient to kill bacterial cells.[386] Dry heats of up to 170°C may be necessary to kill some bacterial spores. Boiling, which restores water to them, often only causes them to germinate.

A similar protection against unfavorable environments is encystment, an adjustment process of some bacteria and protozoans, including many ciliates and *Sporozoa*.[387] This is induced by extremes of heat, cold, dryness, or lack of food. When a protozoan encysts, it becomes a small, dormant sphere. It secretes a cyst wall, often with an inner membrane and a hard outer layer, with characteristic structure which may include spines, and which is relatively impermeable to most matter-energy and information inputs. The internal structure is simplified by absorption of organelles not necessary to life, such as cilia or flagella, and by excretion of inert material, food, or water. The respiratory rate falls so low that use of oxygen cannot be measured. Individual *Colpoda* ciliates have lived as long as 38 years in dry soil in encysted form, and small amoebas and flagellates have survived such conditions for 49 years. When the cyst is placed in water, or when temperature or other environmental conditions again become favorable, the cyst wall is dissolved by enzyme action, and the organelles reform to return the cell to its active form.

Aggregated cells, except for a few types that are capable of amoeboid motion, cannot move about in their environments and lack the sorts of adjustment processes used by free-living cells. They must depend upon the higher-level systems whose tissues they form for adjustments to matter-energy inputs.

To certain sorts of such inputs, cells appear to lack adjustment processes. Passive transport of some substances, including water, will proceed to the detriment of cells in the presence of concentration gradients favoring their input. Ultimately the cells may burst and die.

The costs of cellular adjustment processes of all sorts are paid by the high-energy phosphate bonds that power cell processes, as in the ATP molecule. When their energy is released, and the molecules are changed to ADP, the latter must be "recharged." This requires matter-energy inputs and activity by the cell's matter-energy processing subsystems.

5.2.2 Information input processes Because of the use of alpha codes by cells, many of the adjustment processes to information input involve the same sorts of changes in synthetic processes as are used in adjusting to changes in matter-energy inputs. A hormonal information input from the pituitary gland, for example, results in increased synthesis and output of a hormonal information output from cells of the organism's adrenal gland. Hormonal molecules bearing information are ingested by target cells in many tissues.[388] Then they are bound to the genome, so releasing new forms of RNA, some of which are transported to the cytoplasm where they produce new sorts of proteins that alter cellular processes.

Neurons, which respond to beta-coded inputs as well as to the fundamental alpha codes, have adjustment processes to changes in rates and patterning of input information, which I have already discussed. The adjustments of certain types of neurons to information input overload have also already been discussed (see page 171).

5.2.3 Matter-energy internal processes Steady states are maintained among innumerable matter-energy processes within cells. Several thousand simultaneous chemical reactions are kept separate from one another, their order in time and rates controlled, and their interrelationships specified. The adjustments responsible for all this regulated behavior can be described under four headings: (*a*) Those which specify the order of enzyme-catalyzed processes. (*b*) Those which alter the rates of chemical reactions within cells. (*c*) Those which distribute matter-energy among competing components. And (*d*) those which determine the nature of particular steady states. Some adjustments may fall into more than one of these classes.

(*a*) *Adjustment processes which specify the order of enzyme-catalyzed processes.* Cellular synthetic processes take place in a series of steps, each catalyzed by a particular enzyme. The direction of a given process is determined by the law of mass action. That is, its outcome is the same as it would be if the reaction had occurred in a test tube. Glucose, for example, is degraded into carbon dioxide and water with liberation of energy, just as it can be outside of cells. By enzyme-catalyzed processes, the cell achieves control over the pathways which the reaction will take and lowers the "energy of activation," the amount of energy required for a molecule to react in a particular way (see pages 205 and 237). Processes which, if carried on outside the cell, would require temperatures higher than a cell could tolerate, can go on at the lower temperatures compatible with life, as I have already noted (see page 237).

Structural relationships within a cell help to specify and maintain the order of its internal processes. Enzymes are precisely arranged in components which hold those with related activities together in orderly fashion, like stages in an assembly line, according to the sequence of the processes which they control.[389] Enzymes are either organized into multienzyme assemblages or bound to membranes, not randomly distributed in the cytoplasm as was once believed. Both arrangements permit the catalyzed reactions to succeed each other efficiently. Efficiency rises as the probability increases that most or all the products of one reaction will be available for the succeeding one.

An example of a multienzyme assemblage is the complex of enzymes responsible for synthesis of certain fatty acids. They are called "fatty acid synthetases." One such organized unit, which catalyzes a coordinated sequence of seven distinguishable chemical reactions, has been isolated from yeast and found to have a molecular weight of 2.3 million, indicating that a number of different enzymes compose it. The 15 or more enzymes that make up the respiratory chain in mitochondria constitute a different sort of arrangement. They are arrayed on the mitochondrial membranes, possibly attached to a network of structural proteins and phospholipids.[390] Tens of thousands of these enzyme assemblages may occur in a single mitochondrion.[391]

Of course the fact that the product of a reaction is required for a succeeding reaction determines the temporal sequence of the reactions. But the latter reaction does not always occur immediately upon the synthesis of the required compound by the first reaction, even in the presence of the necessary substrate. If an inhibitor is present, the compound can accumulate in the cell without being used. An example of this occurs in the differentiation of an aggregated slime mold. An enzyme, 5'-nucleotidase, and the substance which inhibits it increase in amount in its cells simultaneously, so that the maximum activity of the enzyme is concentrated in the middle of each cell's differentiation process.[392] At the end, when the enzyme's actual concentration is greater, there is relatively even more inhibitor, so that the enzymatic activity is less. In many processes, however, such as the oxidation of glucose in the mitochondria, the successive reactions follow each other rapidly, chemical activity progressing along from one of the enzymes to the next.

(b) *Adjustment processes which alter the rates of chemical reactions within cells.* Enzymes catalyze different sorts of reactions in cells, accelerating some and retarding others.[393] Some facilitate addition of a part of one molecule to another; others split a part from a molecule or add or remove water. Still others transfer electrons or hydrogen ions in reactions of oxidation (giving up electrons to another element) or reduction (accepting electrons from another). Hydrolytic enzymes speed up splitting of food molecules by water molecules into fragments small enough to be used in intracellular processes. Ordinarily this is done outside a cell, but in some free-living forms it is done in food vacuoles within the cell boundary.

The rate of an enzyme-catalyzed reaction ordinarily increases proportionately to the concentration of the enzyme, as long as there is an excess of substrate. Low amounts of either substrate or enzyme can limit the rates of cellular processes. The rates depend also upon temperature and acidity of the medium. These straightforward relationships are altered when regulatory enzymes are involved in any series of metabolic steps. At low concentrations of substrate the rate of the reaction increases faster and faster as the substrate concentration goes up, but at high concentrations it slows down again. In a sequence of several enzyme-controlled reactions, if an effector molecule acts on an enzyme early in the pathway to decrease its affinity for substrate, thus lowering the rate of the reaction it catalyzes, the rates of subsequent processes in the pathway are lowered because the amount of substrate for them is diminished.

In a series of enzyme-catalyzed reactions in a cellular metabolic pathway, several successive reversible reactions with rates determined by enzyme–substrate concentrations are followed by a rate-controlling reaction which is not reversible under the physical conditions found within a cell.[394] These latter sorts of reactions are catalyzed by regulatory enzymes. Usually they occur at points in a metabolic sequence where distribution of products into multiple metabolic pathways takes place.

A different sort of internal matter-energy adjustment process is seen in mitochondria. They evidently adjust their rates of respiration and ATP formation to the available supplies of substrate, ADP, and phosphate.[395] While these quantities ultimately are resultants of the amounts of various kinds of matter-energy inputs to the cell, the adjustment is an internal process since the inputs to the mitochondria come from the cytoplasm. When the ratio of ADP to ATP becomes low, so that there is little more ADP to phosphorylate, a reorganization of the inner membrane, and a small amount of swelling of the organelle occurs in mitochondria. Renewing the supply of ADP reverses this process. Larger variations in size to between 3 and 5 times normal volume occur in mitochondria of liver and kidney cells of organisms as their necessary ADP becomes exhausted. The permeability of their membranes increases. This larger response is also reversed when the needed inputs are made. Similar changes in membrane conformation or volume are seen in chloroplasts, kinetosomes, and bacterial protoplasts.

One higher-echelon control process of the decider subsystem based on signals from the internal transducer is end-product repression (see pages 258, 275, and 288). This process, whereby synthesis of further molecules of an enzyme is halted whenever many of them have been synthesized, is an important adjustment. Consequently cells can adjust rapidly to a lack strain for some compound by accelerating synthesis of the enzyme that then produces the needed substance. In one experiment it was shown in *Escherichia coli* that synthesis of an enzyme which made the amino acid arginine could be repressed by adding to the cell an excess of the enzyme's end product, arginine.[396] When absolutely no arginine was present in the cell, however, the cell explosively produced the enzyme, at a rate 25 times the normal steady-state rate. Is this a confirmation of Hypothesis 5.2-3 (see page 106) which states that, when variables return to a steady state after stress, the rate of return and strength of the restorative forces are functions—with increasing first derivatives greater than 1—of the amount of displacement from the range of stability? One can speculate that the explosive increase in enzyme production, while adaptive and essential, was less efficient than synthesis at the steady-state rate, because more enzyme than needed could rapidly be made. If so, the findings of this study confirm Hypothesis 3.3.7.2-18 (see page 101) that systems which survive make decisions enabling them to perform at an optimum efficiency for maximum physical power output, which is always less than maximum efficiency.

(c) *Adjustment processes which distribute matter-energy among competing components.* How enzymes are arranged in space, in complexes or attached to membranes, is one factor controlling distribution of substances in particular metabolic pathways, since an enzyme that is spatially close to the point of production of a substance is more likely to interact with it than are more distant enzymes.

The regulatory substances that modify the affinities of enzymes for substrates also direct matter-energy transmissions in different ways appropriate to the particular form of the internal steady state of the cell at a given time. One such adjustment, an example of many that take place within cells, concerns distribution of metabolites either into the main energy-producing pathways of the cell or into production of fat for storage, depending upon the supply of ATP. I describe it more fully below (see page 289).

(d) *Adjustment processes which determine the nature of particular steady states.* Steady states within cells involve continual adjustments of matter-energy flows among subsystems and components. Because the rates of processes controlled by various enzymes and the responses to control substances and feedbacks differ, these matter-energy transmissions exhibit a variety of temporal patterns.[397] Along with linear functions these include cyclic, oscillating, and rhythmic alternations which may form the bases for the pacemaker and clocklike changes in steady states that occur in some cells. In addition to their primary catalytic function, enzymes act as gates and switches for matter-energy transmissions. They may also count some substances they process. Some of these adjustments are elicited

by information flows and are discussed below. They all, of course, depend upon information exchanges among cellular components.

One sort of temporal adjustment maintains a steady state between glycolysis and respiration. This is a cyclic process in which glycolysis operates first at a rapid rate and then, after about 40 s, switches to a slower rate. Simultaneously respiration does the reverse. The higher of the two rates is between 5 and 20 times as fast as the second, differing from one type of cell to another. Cytochrome b, an electron carrier essential to the process of cellular respiration, is first oxidized, then reduced, and then becomes steady. The period of this cycle is in a fixed ratio to the times at which the rates of glucose and oxygen uptake switch from fast to slow.

5.2.4 Information internal processes   A number of different types of cells, both free-living and aggregated, have rhythmic or cyclical processes. In the consideration of the memory subsystem above I have already mentioned the endogenous and circadian rhythms of some neurons (see page 269). Although the circadian rhythms of neurons of the abdominal ganglion of the sea hare, *Aplysia,* are related to inputs of light to the organism of which they are components, and their form and timing can be modified by changes in the organism, the rhythmic activity persists when the ganglion in which the neuron occurs is removed from the organism and kept alive in a suitable fluid medium. This indicates that the activity is not simply a response to inputs bringing information about light changes in the organism's environment over organism neural channels but a property of the neural cell itself. It is Strumwasser's contention that oscillations in states of key neurons explain cyclical behaviors in organisms (see pages 451 and 454) rather than changes in inputs to the organism determining the operational characteristics of neurons.[398]

Another sort of rhythm has been disclosed in neurons of the reticular formation of the vertebrate brainstem (see page 347).[399] These cells, over periods of from 10 to 12 h each, alternate from being responsive to information inputs from channels for information from the organism's input transducer (*i.e.,* mild shocks to the sciatic nerve, simulating inputs to a leg) to being responsive to information from the organism's internal transducers (*i.e.,* inputs following the organism's breathing cycle, internal transducers from the respiratory center in the organism's brainstem). The cycle of alternation lasted from ½ to 3 h, the characteristic period differing from cell to cell. During each part of the cycle, each cell was completely unresponsive to the other sort of input. Possibly there was a periodic change in the cell's subsynaptic membranes, making the synapses of neurons from the input transducer capable of activation during one part of the cycle and those from the internal transducer at another. These cycles did not seem to be related to the sleep–wakefulness cycle or any other general physiological changes in the organism. Conceivably they might be evidences of an organism adjustment process which preserves the capacity of cells of the reticular formation to communicate with multiple different neural centers by periodically releasing them from whatever relationship they have developed with one center so that they can be free to communicate with another.

A different rhythm of cells in the reticular formation, unlike the one just mentioned, does conform to the organism's sleep–wakefulness cycle.[400] Rabbits were taught to have regular sleep rhythms. Then some were killed when asleep and others when awake. The rates of activity of the enzyme succinoxidase in neurons and glia of the caudal region of the reticular formation differed when the rabbits were awake and asleep. When they were awake, the enzyme activity was low in the neurons and high in the glia. The situation was reversed during sleep. In the oral part of the reticular formation nearby, only the neurons showed such rhythmic changes. They did not appear during barbiturate-induced sleep. Apparently the succinoxidase enzymatic activities, which are processes of either the converter or the producer subsystem of these cells, operate according to the biological clock responsible for the organism's sleep rhythm.

5.2.5 Matter-energy output processes   When a cell extrudes matter-energy into its environment, as when an organism's gland cells secrete mucus, tears, or other substances which are not information-bearing markers for the organism, the resultant lack strain increases activity of the cell's synthetic machinery as well as demands upon its environment for inputs to satisfy the increased matter-energy needs. The synthetic capacity of such cells can under unusual conditions be strained by continued demands for the products they output. They can be entirely depleted of such products. Ordinarily such lack strains do not occur, since cells can usually accelerate their synthetic processes enough to meet the demands for their products.

5.2.6 Information output processes   As with matter-energy, increased demands for alpha-coded or beta-coded information outputs speed up a cell's producing processes, since matter-energy markers are required. Neurons which output alpha-coded signals greatly increase their production of acetylcholine or some other transmitter substance when they are output transducing at a high rate. Synthesis may accelerate to seven times the resting rate.[401]

Adjustments in the production of norepinephrine with increased and decreased output of it also occur in

the cells in which it is the transmitter. Just how this occurs, however is not well understood.[402]

After a beta-coded pulse has been output by an excitable cell like a neuron with an electric synapse or an electroplaque cell, an adjustment occurs so that, after a refractory period, the potential is provided for the marker of the subsequent pulse. This adjustment involves, as already noted, energy release in the cell and the "ionic pump" at the cell membrane.

5.2.7 Feedbacks   Negative feedback is used in all cells. By it a cell achieves fine control of its internal processing of both matter-energy and information, coordinating a great number of different chemical reactions to make an integrated system. Sometimes cellular biologists invoke feedbacks imprecisely to explain observed phenomena. All parts of the circuit must be specified before a feedback can be dependably identified.

Internal feedbacks.   A number of feedbacks carried out entirely inside cells have been precisely identified. The examples given below are all feedbacks in cellular metabolic pathways. Control of such processes by regulatory enzymes that respond to effector concentrations by increase or decrease in their reaction rates involves feedbacks which vary continuously rather than in discrete steps.[403]

(a) *End-product repression.*   The earliest recognition of cellular feedback control was the discovery of end-product repression (see pages 258, 275, and 286). This is the sort of feedback that adjusts to changes in a system variable (see page 37), the variable in this case being the concentration of a particular sort of molecule. Such inhibition is common in bacterial metabolism and has been identified also in the cells of higher organisms. An example is the inhibition, in *Escherichia coli,* of the synthesis of L-isoleucine by blocking the first enzyme in its synthetic pathway, L-threonine dehydrase.[404]

(b) *Effector activation.*   Activation of an enzyme by an effector is a form of feedback of opposite effect to end-product inhibition. In effector activation a concentration of a metabolite leads to an increase in production of some other substance related to it in the cell's processes.[405] This occurs, for example, when the supply of ATP, and therefore of available energy decreases, as shown by accumulation in the cell of AMP (adenosine monophosphate). This latter compound is formed when ATP is split to release energy for cellular processes. AMP activates the enzyme, glycogen phosphorylase, which then splits stored glycogen, releasing energy for regeneration of ATP. Like the previous example, this feedback adjusts to changes in a system variable. In this example the

variable is the concentration of AMP, which is inverse
to that of ATP.

(c) *Switching feedback.* Another feedback which
also involves ATP and AMP has been analyzed in cells
with aerobic matter-energy metabolism. It determines
whether acetylcoenzyme A will, at any given time,
participate in the production of fat for storage or in the
Krebs cycle (see pages 237 and 240).[406] In this feedback, the changing ratios of ATP to AMP continuously
modulate the relative percentages of acetylcoenzyme
A entering one alternative pathway or the other. In the
production of fat for storage, when AMP is low and
ATP is high, the concentrations of isocitrate and citrate rise. Citrate is an effector which accelerates the
activity of the enzyme catalyzing the first reaction in
the conversion of acetylcoenzyme A to fat. Thus it
facilitates the production of fat. This effect is enhanced
by the negative effector action of ATP which slows the
enzyme that catalyzes the entry of acetylcoenzyme A
into the citric acid cycle. The opposite process, when
AMP is high and ATP is low, speeds the formation of
alpha-ketoglutarate. This favors the distribution of
acetylcoenzyme A into the citric acid cycle, leading to
the regeneration of ATP. This reaction occurs when
the cell uses energy and consequently lowers the ratio
of ATP to AMP. This example of feedback, like the
previous one, adjusts to changes of two system variables, ATP and AMP concentrations.

A cell has a great many feedback controls of its
metabolic processes similar to this one. Some are far
more complicated than this.[407]

These lower-echelon feedback controls, all of which
are negative feedbacks, interact with the higher-echelon controls of enzyme synthesis discussed above (see
pages 274 and 275), which are not feedbacks. Together
they achieve rapid restoration when variables depart
from steady states. They enable concentrations of metabolites within the cell to remain within a range of
stability whatever may be the rates of the internal processes. How such joint control may be effected is
outlined by Atkinson. He suggests that feedback
repression of the activity of a single enzyme in a
pathway and that repression of synthesis of all new
molecules of enzymes for the pathway by binding the
appropriate repressor to the operator controlling the
synthesis act together in "coordinate repression."
Increase in concentration of an end product feeds back
to inhibit the first enzyme in the sequence of the
pathway. This decreases the steady-state concentration of all intermediate products, since a lower rate of
each reaction is now being catalyzed by the same
amount of enzyme. Repression of synthesis of all the
enzymes leads to increase of intermediate substances
back to the original higher steady-state levels, since a
smaller amount of each enzyme is now available to

catalyze each intermediate substance. Increased
demand for the end product cuts down its concentration; this diminishes the feedback repression and permits increases in concentrations of the intermediate
products. Synthesis of new enzyme molecules is then
depressed, increasing the activity of the molecules and
restoring the metabolites to their original levels.

Feedback regulation acts in the same direction as
mass action, as other cellular controls also do. If the
cell had to depend upon mass action, however, it
could not adjust to emergencies by using stored
reserves when extra energy is needed. Such a system,
which would have the lowest concentration of metabolites when it needed them most, would not have
much chance in the struggle for survival, if Hypothesis 3.3.7.2-18 (see page 101) is accurate in asserting
that systems which survive must be able to make
decisions enabling them when necessary to output
maximum physical power and do so as efficiently as
possible, which is always less than maximum efficiency.

A further advantage to a cell in having lower-echelon feedback controls, as well as higher-echelon controls of enzyme synthesis, is that the lower-echelon
controls are tight feedbacks (see page 37) which rapidly and sensitively correct for deviations from the
steady state.[408] The processes controlling enzyme formation proceed at slower rates than those involved in
the synthesis of small molecules. Moreover, if repression of enzyme formation is released for even a minute
or so, a tenfold excess of enzymes might be produced.
Even though repression operated after that, the
enzyme already formed would function at an excessive
rate for more than three bacterial generations, until
cellular growth diluted it to the normal concentration.
End-product inhibition feedbacks can prevent such an
occurrence.

External feedbacks (see page 37) exist in those free-
living cells which can move about in their environments. They respond to changes in input signals
resulting from their own movements (see page 254).
Most aggregated cells, according to Weiss's principle
of "contact guidance," need support of solid surfaces—perhaps other cells—to grow along, as plants
grow on a trellis.[409] Their growth processes are determined by signals from their environment, and their
own growth modifies these signals. Such feedbacks
which guide both moving free-living cells and growing aggregated cells employ input-signal adaptation
(see page 37).

5.3 Evolution   When the environment of our
planet gradually over billions of years became propi-
tious for life, the first cells formed. Researches on the
origins of life indicate the possible nature of the
"chemical evolution" that produced the chief components of cells. Later primitive single cells evolved into

more complex types and then cells in organisms evolved further.

The first cells and their environment. Fossil remains of organic material that must have come from cells have been discovered by electron microscopic study of rocks of the Precambrian period (see Table 6-5).[410] If these are indeed fossil traces of cells, they must have inhabited the waters of Earth more than 3 billion years ago during the time those rocks were forming.

The most widely accepted scientific theory of the origin of life is that of Oparin, who in 1924 suggested that a series of nonbiological steps formed organic compounds of greater and greater complexity until self-replication was achieved, and finally living systems developed.[411] As they proliferated, the scientific dogma continues, conditions that had favored chemical evolution gave way to an environment favorable to biological evolution, so that Virchow's doctrine "*omnis cellula e cellula*" (all cells from cells) had no further exceptions.

Earth's atmosphere for more than the first billion years was like the present atmospheres of Jupiter, Saturn, Uranus, and Neptune.[412] Around those planets are poisonous clouds of methane, ammonia, water vapor, and hydrogen. Chemically this was a reducing atmosphere, since in its early eras Earth had little gaseous oxygen. Both carbon monoxide and carbon dioxide gases, however, became plentiful during the period of chemical evolution (see Table 6-6). More ultraviolet radiations from the sun and cosmic radiations from space reached the surface than can penetrate the present atmosphere. Lightning flashed as static electricity built up and discharged. Claps of thunder and crashing meteorites caused shock waves. Gradually Earth cooled, and the electrical activity decreased. Later, cells capable of photosynthesis added oxygen to the atmosphere. By the early Paleozoic period the atmosphere was much as it is now, and water had condensed into seas. Earth was a much more favorable environment for cellular life than it had been in the Archeozoic.

Chemical evolution. The basic molecules of which cells are constructed and which they use in their processes are all compounds of carbon (or carbon monoxide or dioxide), in different combinations with hydrogen, oxygen, and nitrogen (see examples of major classes of these molecules in Fig. 6-21). Since these elements which compose them were abundantly present in the primitive atmosphere, along with awesome amounts of energy, the conditions of early Earth perhaps favored organic syntheses that rarely occur in nature outside cells under present-day conditions. In pioneering experiments Miller tried to produce organic syntheses in an environment like that of early Earth. He discovered that electric sparks discharged into a mixture of methane, ammonia (a source of nitrogen), water, and hydrogen produced some amino acids.[413] Ultraviolet radiation, x-rays, gamma rays, and thermal energy can achieve the same results as electricity.[414] Since his studies a number of other investigators have attempted to demonstrate in the laboratory how cells and parts of cells might have originated on this planet. The rules of the researches on the origin of life provide that all syntheses use compounds and be carried out under conditions that might have existed on Earth in those times.

Small organic molecules can be synthesized in a reducing atmosphere like that of Earth in early eras. If such organic compounds, in watery solutions supposed to be like the early seas, are subjected to energy fluxes like heating and cooling, however, the very large molecules upon which life depends—proteins, lipids, polysaccharides, and nucleic acids—do not form. To forge the bonds that link the many units of such molecules together, like the peptide bonds of protein, requires "dehydration condensation." In this process a molecule of water is removed, and a bond is formed between chemical groupings at the ends of

TABLE 6-5   The Geologic Eras and Periods

Time to present (in millions of years)	Geologic era	Geologic period	Events
	Pleistocene Paleolithic	Quaternary	Apelike progenitors and man
		Tertiary	
	Cenozoic	Cretaceous	Mammals
		Jurassic	
200		Triassic	
		Permian	
	Mesozoic	Pennsylvanian	Reptiles
		Mississippian	
		Devonian	Forests; fish
400		Silurian	
		Ordovician	
	Paleozoic	Cambrian	
600			Earliest invertebrates
Change of time scale	Proterozoic		
1,000		Precambrian	
2,000			
	Archeozoic		
3,000			Cells?
4,000			Chemical evolution

TABLE 6-6 Energy Conversion Processes During Various Evolutionary Eras

Form of evolution	Era	Environment	Energy source	Structure and process outcomes
Chemical	I	Anaerobic; methane, ammonia, hydrogen	Ultraviolet light; heat	Acetate, glycine, uracil, adenine, other organic molecules in aqueous medium
		Loss of most free hydrogen		
	II	Anaerobic; traces of gaseous oxygen	Ultraviolet light; heat; visible light	Polyphosphates, peptides, porphyrins; porphyrin catalysis of photoreduction and oxidation
		Loss of most ultraviolet light		
	III	Anaerobic; traces of gaseous oxygen and carbon dioxide	Visible light	Replicating organic molecules Photochemical reactions
		Loss of many free organic molecules		
Biological	IV	Anaerobic; gaseous carbon dioxide and traces of gaseous oxygen	Photoreduction; fermentation	Organelles Cells Two-step light-energy conversion process
		Loss of most anaerobic environmental regions		
	V	Aerobic; anaerobic pockets	Photosynthesis; respiration	Free-living cells; organs and organisms

SOURCE: Adapted from H. Gaffron. The role of light in evolution: the transition from a one quantum to a two quanta mechanism. In S. W. Fox (Ed.). *The origins of prebiological systems and of their molecular matrices.* New York: Academic Press, 1965, 450. *Reprinted by permission.*

two molecules.[415] Other compounds, such as dicyanimide, an energy-rich molecule formed by the reaction of one molecule of ammonia with two of hydrogen cyanide, must be added to the solution to do this. In this way the chief constituents of the major large molecules in cells can be formed, although complete syntheses of the entire molecules have not yet been achieved by these procedures.

Other experiments related to the origin of cellular life have produced, under conditions like those on primitive Earth, components of RNA and DNA (see page 217) including the sugars, ribose and deoxyribose; the purines, adenine and guanine; a pyrimidine, uracil; nucleosides; separate nucleotides; and long chains of nucleotides.[416] Also the nucleotides adenosine monophosphate (AMP), diphosphate (ADP), triphosphate (ATP), and tetraphosphate (A4P) have been synthesized.

Although complete proteins have not been synthe-sized under primitive Earth conditions, some remarkable protein-like compounds, proteinoids, have resulted from heating amino acids in a dry atmosphere.[417] These have peptide bonds, but not the helical arrangement characteristic of proteins. When they are dissolved in water and cooled, they form microspheres which have interesting similarities to cells and may connect in algae-like chains. On the early Earth, the dry heat needed to forge the peptide bonds might have been provided by hot lava from the active volcanos that were a common feature of the landscape at that time. Since such great heat would destroy the compounds immediately, it is necessary also to assume that, as they formed, rain washed them into the sea.

Other interesting organic substances, coacervate drops, separate out of solutions containing polypeptide polymers in which nucleotide chains are being formed from adenosine diphosphate with a bacterial

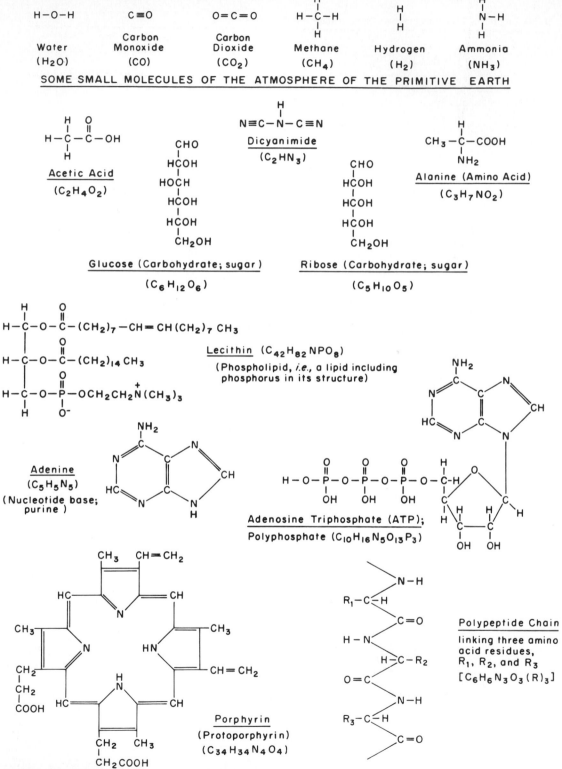

Fig. 6-21 Examples of major classes of molecules possibly involved in chemical evolution.

enzyme catalyst, polynucleotide phosphorylase.[418] These drops are opaque, have internal components such as smaller drops, and are definitely delimited from the surrounding medium. They are open systems, receiving inputs and storing diverse substances from their environment. Chemical reactions take place within them, depending upon the substances in them; and they can enlarge or diminish, depending upon what is input to or output from them.

Even some of the large components of cells can organize themselves into their proper forms. The particular proteins which compose them seem to control this process. This can be demonstrated by breaking them into pieces and observing how they reconstitute themselves. One can assume that if parts of a component assemble themselves in such an experiment they could also have done so in the evolutionary process. When collagen fibers, products of cells of organisms, or bacterial flagella are broken into large fragments, they can reassemble into their typical structures.[419] Certain complex types of enzymes, alpha-keto acid oxidases, when fragmented, can also reconstitute themselves properly into molecules with the correct ratio of three different proteins to each other and with their specific catalytic activities unimpaired. In some viruses nucleic acids as well as proteins can reaggregate. Under the proper conditions, the tobacco mosaic virus, which has a single strand of RNA containing five or six genes and several thousand identical protein subunits forming a shell, can be dissociated and reassociated. When the genetic RNA is removed, the protein can reaggregate, but into random lengths. If both RNA and protein reaggregate together, a more precise reconstitution results.

An even more complicated virus, T4, which infects *Escherichia coli* (see page 274), reconstitutes itself when its components, a head containing tightly coiled DNA, a tail, and several tail fibers, are separated from each other, each part remaining intact.[420] In this situation the parts reassemble under control of the DNA.

Evolutionary increase in cellular complexity. The above experimental reconstructions may be relevant to the evolutionary processes by which cells have increased in complexity. The origin of cellular organelles is obscure. Some may have been incorporated into cells as separate, self-replicating units. The theory that mitochondria originated as bacteria that entered larger cells as infective agents and remained as symbiotes and finally components, sounds like the scientific mind at play and may well not be true. Yet the idea gains interest when one remembers that active DNA is present in these organelles.[421] Perhaps this is the evolutionary remnant of bacterial DNA. The inner and outer membranes of mitochondria may correspond to the bacterial cell membrane and cell wall. The lipids of the inner mitochondrial membrane and bacterial membranes are similar. Some mitochondria (in brain neurons and glia of organisms) carry out protein synthesis. Perhaps this is a residual of the general matter-energy metabolism of their ancestors. A similar origin from chlorophyll-containing bacteria has been suggested for chloroplasts.

A cell is more than an aggregation of components. It has integrated interactions among its components. We do not know what components organized first. Since the system could not carry out any activity without energy, perhaps some sort of energy-conversion process was the initial step toward life.[422] There has been speculation about how present cellular energy conversion processes evolved. According to Gaffron these activities probably changed as Earth's environment and energy sources altered.[423] He hypothesizes that there were three eras of chemical evolution followed by two of biological evolution (see Table 6-6). In Eras I to IV the environment was chiefly anaerobic, with increasing amounts of gaseous oxygen and carbon dioxide. In Era V it was primarily aerobic. First most of the free hydrogen left the atmosphere. Then, as clouds of water and oxygen appeared in the atmosphere, most of the ultraviolet light was filtered out. In Eras I and II it had, along with heat, been the chief energy source. Later the concentration of free organic molecules in Earth's waters decreased because many of them were incorporated into cells. Finally the environment became extensively oxygenated.

These changes required alterations in methods of energy conversion. During the chemical evolution of Eras I and II, ultraviolet light and heat brought about synthesis of organic molecules in Earth's aqueous fluids. Then more complex organic compounds were synthesized by ultraviolet and visible light energy, the latter 20 to 30 times as great as ultraviolet. Among these were the porphyrins which can catalyze photoreduction and oxidation reactions. In Era III new, more complex organic molecules, like the nucleic acids which can replicate themselves, were synthesized with energy from visible light by photochemical reactions. Then Era IV saw cells employing a photoreduction or fermentation process which could go on in an anaerobic environment. And finally in Era V, aerobic photosynthesis energy conversion evolved.

The cellular system had to have a decider subsystem very early in its evolution to coordinate its subsystems. Without a decider it would not be a living system (see page 18). In some way this decider, the genetic nucleic acid, became programmed and an apparatus for reading, transcribing, and translating the code came into being. The pairing of complementary nucleotide bases of the DNA and RNA nucleic acids depends upon small differences of stability of some pairs over others.[424] The duration of all such pairings is short, as is necessary if transcription is to be quick and efficient. Reduction of errors in transcription could possibly have been accomplished by evolutionary processes that further increased the stability of the pairs, but the cost would have been a slowed response. The evolutionary solution was to employ enzymes matching both molecules of the complementary pair to fit them together.

Primitive cells were perhaps something like cocci, the spheroidal bacteria. Cocci have DNA, RNA, and many ribosomes, but lack other organelles, such as mitochondria. Like primitive cells they have more synthetic pathways than more advanced cells, since they manufacture all the complex organic compounds they need. Advanced cells which ingest other cells can get some of these in such inputs, but cocci do not and, of course, primitive cells could not, since at first there were no other species to serve as food. Cocci have aerobic metabolism. In that they are probably unlike the earliest cells since it appears that anaerobic metabolism antedated aerobic. Many quite primitive cells, however, including those that left the earliest fossil remains, had aerobic metabolism.

As cellular complexity increased, evolutionary shred-out (see pages 1 and 4) allocated subsystem processes carried out in bacteria by the relatively undifferentiated cytoplasm, to specialized organelles, often under largely decentralized control. Nuclei and mitochondria, for example, which bacteria do not have, appeared. The mitochondria probably carried out energy conversion, for which they are particularly adapted, more efficiently than it was done in bacteria. Also more advanced cells developed larger genomes even though they had fewer synthetic pathways. These probably permitted more complex higher-echelon controls of the cell's diverse, decentralized components.

From a relatively simple, undifferentiated, primitive type of cell all the variety of free-living and aggregated cells developed and, of course, all the systems at higher levels as well. The evolutionary processes of mutation, natural selection, isolation, adaptive radiation, and random genetic drift (see pages 76 and 77), acting over the period of more than three billion years, produced all the living systems that, literally, cover the Earth. Bacteria, and presumably the primitive cells that preceded them, mutate readily. In fact, mutants capable of surviving in radically altered environments appear so swiftly and are so adaptive that bacteriology was the "last stronghold of Lamarckism," the doctrine of the inheritance of acquired characteristics.[425] Studies of development of drug resistance in strains of bacteria have proved that drug-resistant mutants arise spontaneously and fortuitously several generations *before* exposure to the drug. When the drug is added to the culture, the descendants of the mutants survive to take over the culture. The others die. All would have died if there had been no mutants. Natural selection of cells that can adjust to the environment is seen here and in the adaptation of bacteria to life at high temperatures, such as in hot springs.

The development of regulatory and other enzymes, as well as other regulatory proteins, must have come about by mutation and selection.[426] Cellular controls are exerted by chemical compounds, but their actions appear arbitrary because they cannot be predicted from the chemistry of the substances involved. They are markers carrying coded information. For instance, the effectors that cause the allosteric transition in enzymes are usually totally unrelated to the substrates, coenzymes, or products of the reactions they promote.[427] The regulatory protein can therefore allow an indirect interaction to take place between metabolites that could not otherwise react chemically with one another. If the proper allosteric proteins were employed, control circuits could connect any synthetic pathway with any other. Coding, in the sense that it is employed by these molecules, probably underlies control of cellular phenomena generally, notable examples being the expression of genetic information, intracellular metabolic regulation, and hormonal action.

Evolution of aggregated cells. As the evolution of multicellular organisms proceeded, their cells also continued to evolve. Now, however, the process was influenced by the stresses upon organisms of natural selection and by mutations in the organisms' genetic material rather than in those of the individual differentiated cells. Such mutations have produced progressive divergences generation after generation in the cellular constituents of descendants of a common ancestor in which the mutation is deduced to have taken place. One such evolutionary sequence begins with a protein molecule that was the remote ancestor of both myoglobin, an oxygen carrier in muscle, and hemoglobin, the oxygen transport molecule in blood.[428] Its configuration probably was intermediate between the two present-day molecules. It was a single peptide chain, the gene for which was duplicated and became two genes, each of which specified a somewhat different chain. One of these, that which led to myoglobin, underwent no further duplication but changed by mutations in the millions of years during which phyla separated and families, genera, and species of free-living cells and organisms developed. The gene for hemoglobin duplicated further until there were four genes specifying four peptide chains with different base sequences in each cell. Each species has its own set of hemoglobin genes in which the base sequences are somewhat different from those of any other.

A comparable evolutionary series has been identified in the amino acid sequences of the cytochrome C proteins. These electron transport molecules are similar all the way from yeast through the vertebrates to man, probably because a considerable number of the genes cannot mutate without destroying the essential function of these cytochromes. If 60 of their amino acids can be varied without destroying their necessary functions, there are 180 nucleotide bases for coding them in the triplet code. Of these, 57 are different in vertebrates and yeasts.[429] The lines of descent between these very different living systems seem to have diverged about 540 million years ago.

Phylogenetic relationships among enzymes can be traced in the same way.[430] In a long evolutionary sequence, an ancestral enzyme may have undergone repeated duplication as the genome became larger so that several enzymes that catalyze quite different processes may be traced, by study of their chemical behavior, to the same ancestral gene. In higher animals, for instance, proteases, which are enzymes for digesting protein, clotting blood, breaking down blood clots, and sensing pain, all come from the same ancestral gene.

5.3.1 Emergents Emergents at the level of the cell include the fundamental characteristics by which living systems differ from nonliving. Life itself, and death, emerge at this level, although all cells do not terminate by dying.

Conceivably the capacity to receive, respond to, and output coded information emerged at the level below cells as a necessary step to life. The protein and nucleic acid molecules that can do this, however, are not now found in nature except as components of living systems. Other naturally occurring nonliving systems do not appear to use information adaptively in this way. Nor do nonliving systems use negative feedback control processes as they do.

Cells as systems also differ from nonliving physical and chemical systems in having enzyme catalysts and allosteric proteins to coordinate and control the great number of interdependent chemical reactions that take place within them. The controlled metabolism by which cells regulate their inputs and outputs to maintain a steady state of negative entropy, seemingly disregarding the second law of thermodynamics, is unknown in systems below the cell (see page 18).

Replication of components of the system or reproduction of the entire system under the direction of the genetic material also are not found in nonliving systems.

As cells evolved, reproduction by exchange of genetic material between two cells, as during conjugation, emerged. This is a sort of primitive sexuality which provides for many new genetic patterns as a result of shuffling or recombination of genes. This makes possible entirely new evolutionary processes, giving rise to a wide variety of types of cells.

5.4 Growth, cohesiveness, and integration

5.4.1 Growth The following changes in structure and process characterize the progress of cells through their individual life cycles: (a) stages of development, similar in all cell types; (b) increase in mass; and (c) differentiation of aggregated cells. I shall consider each in turn.

(a) *Stages of development.* All cells that divide have life cycles of four periods.[431] The first, G_1, extends from the time the new cell is organized following mitosis to the onset of DNA replication. During this time the cell must synthesize the RNA and the proteins that will be required in the succeeding stage. The second stage, S, is the period of DNA replication during which the cell synthesizes the DNA and histone necessary for the complete nucleoprotein molecule. G_2, which follows, occupies the time between DNA replication and the beginning of mitosis and appears to be at least partly a period of growth and maturation. In the final period, M (or D), mitosis takes place. The protein synthesis of each of these periods is necessary to the succeeding period. Substances that bind to the genome and prevent synthesis block the further progress of the cell toward mitosis. These may operate to prevent DNA replication or they may operate after replication has occurred. It is possible that blocks also occur during transcription of necessary enzymes in the G_1 or later stages.

Cells of a given type are remarkably uniform in the duration of each of these periods and of the life cycle as a whole. Generation time (time between divisions) is dependent on temperature, which affects the duration of all stages. Most of the variation among cell types is in the G_1 period. In some rapidly multiplying cell types this stage is absent or extremely short, the synthesis of DNA commencing before the final events of cell division are completed.[432] Bacteria, for example, have no measurable G_1 unless they are grown in a medium lacking adequate matter-energy. In an environment with insufficient carbon, the generation time lengthens, and a G_1 period—varying in length with the amount of lack stress—occurs.[433] In cells of a mouse's ileum and colon, G_1 occupies 12 h.

The *S* period is of short duration. It occupies only 3 to 6 h of a 36-h life cycle at 23°C in *Amoeba proteus*.[434] G_2 may also be very short. It cannot be measured in bacteria but occupies 30 to 33 h in *Amoeba proteus*.

The nature of the processes that move the cell from one stage in its life cycle to the next are not yet known but have received a great deal of research attention. The progress through the life cycle is known to be under genetic control. The transcription of the genes is a sequential process that follows a program specific to the cell type. The periods of synthesis of metabolic structures, synthesis of DNA, and synthesis of the division structures do not overlap and appear to be separated by some timing function.[435] In bacteria, recognition factors known as *sigma factors* must be synthesized to bind polymerase to DNA. These small protein molecules detach when transcription has begun. Sigma has not been identified in eukaryotic cells but transcription may be directed sequentially by similar recognition factors. Cells ordinarily grow to approximately the initial volume of the parent cell before dividing.[436] Whatever triggers division will not act until this growth is accomplished. If an amoeba is shaken before it divides, it can be made to produce one large and one small daughter. Each will grow to the size of the parent cell before it divides. An amoeba can be kept from dividing for many months by continually cutting off parts of its cytoplasm. When it is permitted to reach its preprogrammed mass, division follows in approximately 4 h. Apparently some inhibitory substance acts until growth is complete. If cytoplasm is amputated just before division, when the inhibition has evidently been removed, division will take place even though the mass is now less than that originally required. There are, however, experimentally demonstrated exceptions to this.[437]

(*b*) *Increase in mass.* After mitosis, each of the two descendant cells usually starts its life cycle with half the cytoplasm of the cell that divided to produce it and attains the size typical of mature cells of the species after a period of growth. Cells do not grow during division. Rates are different from one cell type to another. Often the rate of growth is linear or decelerating, but in *Paramecium aurelia* it is exponential.[438] Hypothesis 5.4.1-1 (see page 108) states the proposition that the rate of increase in the number of components of young systems rises exponentially to a maximum, although several factors may alter this growth rate. If the hypothesis is true of cells, there obviously are such factors which change the rate.

For cells to grow, the temperature must be favorable for cellular processes, the optimal temperature varying widely among cell types. Growth in mass depends also upon adequate inputs of matter-energy. With limited inputs, cells sometimes divide at less than normal size. Yeasts grown in a medium complete except for nitrogen did not increase in mass normally between division but did divide once or twice, producing abnormally small cells.[439] Research on bacteria indicates that the regulatory processes affecting the distribution of substrates at each step of intermediary metabolism constitute a complex set of controls which keeps cells from growing larger than their environment can support at that particular time.[440]

(*c*) *Differentiation of aggregated cells.* A single cell, the fertilized egg, gives rise by successive divisions to all the different types of cells in the tissues of organisms. The morphological and functional differences that suit each type for its specialized role in the suprasystem develop as the tissues become organized.

The separation between ectodermal, mesodermal, and endodermal cells (see page 316) that occurs very early in embryonic organisms is followed by progressive development of typical cellular components of the various tissues. The embryonic ectoderm, for example, gives rise to two lines of differentiation. One line eventually leads to cells of the skin and its glands, the lens and cornea of the eye, and other components of the organism. The other, the neural ectoderm, produces all the different sorts of neurons and glia as well as the cells of the retina.

Neurons begin as *neuroblasts,* undifferentiated embryonic cells. They reach their final form and position in the tissues during the organism's early developmental period. They are incapable of dividing again after they become differentiated, and no provision is made for replacement if they should die. Skeletal muscle fibers and many other highly differentiated types of cells in organisms have similar life cycles.

Cells of some other tissues are arrested in relatively undifferentiated form and retain their capacity for division. These divide and become differentiated when they are needed for tissue repair and maintenance. Cells of coverings and linings of organism components continuously move from deeper to more superficial layers of the tissue, becoming differentiated to replace cells that are cast off.

Red blood corpuscles originate as *erythroblasts,* complete cells, capable of division. These are rarely found in the circulating blood but are formed and stored in the organism's bone marrow and spleen. They differentiate and enter the circulation as they are needed. In their mature, differentiated form they lack nuclei and retain only those components required to carry out their function as oxygen transporters in the organism's distributor.

As insects undergo metamorphosis from the pupal to the adult stage of their life cycles, changes in form and function of their cells occur.[441] They take place over several cell generations. Some epidermal cells of silk moths, which secrete pupal cuticle, become specialized to produce cocoonase, the enzyme that softens cocoons and permits the moths to emerge. Initially these are typical epidermal cells, each with a flat nucleus and sparse cytoplasm. They are arranged in a single layer. As adult development of the organism proceeds, they enlarge and become cuboidal. DNA synthesis and mitosis occur. By the seventh day, as the cells continue to proliferate, the tissue becomes thicker and forms layers. Three different cell types can be seen: ordinary epidermal cells, synthesizing adult cuticle; duct cells that elaborate tubules extending inward from the surface; and the *zymogen* cells that will produce the cocoonase. These have enlarged nuclei and evidently have a high RNA content.

By the eleventh day they are even more enlarged and are still synthesizing DNA. They now have up to 100 times the usual number of chromosomes and the nucleus of each cell has as many as 100 large nucleoli. A high concentration of ribosomes is bound to the membranes of the endoplasmic reticulum. Abruptly on the eleventh day the production of the cocoonase begins. As it is produced, it is stored in a vacuole which has suddenly appeared. Production of the enzyme is so rapid that the cell doubles in height every two days as the vacuole expands. The cell enlarges to as much as 350 nm in height by the sixteenth day, as compared to the 5 to 10 nm height of the unspecialized epidermal cells. The vacuole accounts for 250 nm. On days eighteen and nineteen, cocoonase is secreted through the duct made by the duct cells onto the surface of the organism.

Cells of the mammalian pancreas progress through three stages of differentiation.[442] In each stage the content of enzymes differs, the alterations being correlated with the appearance of different components involved in their synthesis, storage, and secretion. Differentiation involves changes in a cell's biochemical repertoire. The differentiated cells produce proteins required for their particular structures and for their specialized outputs, if any.

Although parts of the genome are possibly lost as differentiation proceeds in some highly specialized cells, the whole genome is present, possibly "masked" so that parts of it are not available for transcription, in other types of cells.[443] Experimental transplantation of nuclei of differentiated cells of embryonic tissues into enucleated egg cells have shown that they have templates for the development of complete organisms. Also differentiated cells that rarely or never divide in tissues do divide in culture. The differentiated characteristics or components can be inherited unchanged over many generations.[444] In some types of cells, parts of DNA molecules may replicate without replication of the whole molecule.

Differentiation of cells often depends upon effectors produced by neighboring cells (see pages 468 and 469).[445] The nature of these substances and the sites of their actions are not known.

How hormones influence growth and development of the tissues of organisms by directing the synthesis of specific proteins by their cells is better understood.[446] In the first place, a single hormone may have varying effects depending upon the tissue upon which it acts. In amphibian metamorphosis, for example, the same hormone initiates resorption of the tail and promotes growth of limbs. The cells of a tissue may, moreover, respond to several hormones, each of which controls the amounts of different proteins or structural components. Hormones may have either synergistic or antagonistic effects when administered simultaneously. In some cases, multiple hormones may act upon successive generations of cells. Hormones do not all act upon the same cell processes. Some appear to affect transcription by promoting DNA synthesis. Others operate in the translational process or at some subsequent stage.

The process of differentiation has been studied in several different cell types. Differentiated cells arrive at their final form by successive alteration of structure and process over several generations. Only muscle cells synthesize myosin and only red blood cells synthesize hemoglobin. The cells from which they develop do not secrete these substances. Mature muscle fibers are multinucleated, formed by fusion of precursor cells. Holtzer, Weintraub, and Biehl say:

By the time a myoblast synthesizes its first molecule of myosin or an erythroblast synthesizes its first molecule of hemoglobin the major genetic decisions determining what kinds of molecules these cells would synthesize have long since been made. These decisions were made in part in the mother cell, in part in the grandmother cell and in part in even earlier ancestral cells. This point of view generates the following questions: How many sequential decisions have to be made between the zygote and the first cell to synthesize myosin or hemoglobin? How does a succession of such decisions preclude the possibility that cells in the myogenic lineage synthesize hemoglobin and that cells in the erythrogenic lineage synthesize myosin? Lastly, what is the role of the cell cycle in initiating these genetic decisions that change one generation of precursor cells into a later more mature generation within an evolving lineage?

The presumptive myoblast is the mother cell of the myoblast. The presumptive myoblast, unlike the myoblast, does not synthesize myosin, tropomyosin, myoglobin, or any other terminal luxury molecule associated with mature muscle: yet by any criterion the presumptive myoblast is a committed, covertly differentiated myogenic cell. . . . The hematocytoblast is the mother cell of the erythroblast that will initiate the synthesis of hemoglobin. The hematocytoblast does not synthesize hemoglobin, yet is a covertly differentiated hematogenic cell. . . . One cell cycle or cell generation separates the presumptive myoblast or hematocytoblast from the myoblast or erythroblast.[447]

Two types of cell cycles are identified in this work: "quantal" cycles, in which cells move from one compartment to the next within a cell cycle, and "proliferative" cycles, in which the number of cells within a compartment increases. It is possible to culture presumptive myoblasts in a substance (BrUdR) that suppresses the development of myoblasts, which are postmitotic, mononucleated cells that synthesize myosin, actin, and tropomyosin and can fuse with other myogenic cells in cell culture to form multinucleated myotubes. The presumptive myoblasts in the culture undergo division without giving rise to myoblasts. When these daughters are placed in a normal medium for several rounds of divisions, some of the fourth and fifth generation cells develop into normal myoblasts. This same substance also prevents differentiation of retinal precursor cells and the precursors of hematocytes. They undergo only proliferative cell cycles in a medium containing it.

A research on the capacity of myogenic cells to fuse into myotubes in culture suggests that the change in the cell surface that makes fusion possible is correlated with phases of the mitotic cycle and that fusion can take place only with cells in G_1.[448]

5.4.2 Cohesiveness   The cell membrane separates the system from its environment and is important in maintaining cohesion among its parts. The contents of a cell are not, however, contained within the membrane like articles in a sack. For instance, the cytoplasm of amoebas deprived of their cell membranes continues to stream in regular currents regardless of whether the naked cytoplasm is in contact with an environment of distilled water, culture medium, or oil. Sometimes the rate of streaming is initially doubled. Within a few minutes, however, the original pattern breaks up into smaller patterns, and the cell loses its cohesiveness, separating into U-shaped cylindrical bodies of cytoplasm which cannot come together again.[449]

The cell as a whole, its ground substance and membranes, and the formed organelles, large molecules, and other components within it cohere because of electromagnetic forces that act among all aggregations of atoms and molecules, causing them to attract and repel each other and to interact or establish chemical bonds.

These bonds and interactions are of different sorts, varying in strength and in the amount of energy required to break them. They include: (a) *Van der Waals interactions*.   These low-energy interactions between any two atoms or molecules result from relative motions of their nuclei and electrons.[450] Attraction and repulsion occur under different circumstances. To a first approximation, the attractive forces are proportional to the sixth power of the distance separating the molecules, whereas the repulsive forces are inversely proportional to the twelfth power of the intermolecular separation. Although the attractive forces are weak compared to ordinary chemical bonds, they are entirely responsible for liquefaction of gases and are important in making cells cohere. (b) *Hydrophobic interactions*.   These are especially interesting forms of Van der Waals interactions. Since the molecular aggregates within cells are surrounded by an aqueous medium of different molecular characteristics, the tendency of some molecules to form closer Van der Waals bonds with the molecules rather than with water molecules results in a weak interaction that gives greater cohesiveness in space to some cellular constituents. (c) *Hydrogen bonds*.   These form when a hydrogen atom bonded to an electronegative atom such as oxygen or nitrogen is electrostatically attracted to a similar electronegative atom in another molecule. The strength of hydrogen bonds is inversely proportional to the square of the distance separating the interacting atoms. (d) *Chemical valence bonds*.   These are strong bonds that require considerable energy to be disrupted. They are stable chemical bonds which result from a delocalization and sharing of electrons among atoms, linking them into molecules. Some of these can also constitute molecular "bridges" between parts of large molecules. When two electrons are shared between two atoms, the bond is called a single bond. Double and triple bonds are also common. The high-energy phosphate bonds from which the cell derives its working supply of energy are strong valence bonds. (e) *Ionic bonds*.   These very strong bonds result from the electrostatic interaction between unit positive and negative charges in electrically conducting compounds such as salts and bases. As is also true for the much weaker hydrogen bonds, the force of interaction of ionic bonds is inversely proportional to the distance of separation of the charges.

Protein molecules illustrate how these various cohesive forces interact to structure some of the largest units in cells. The primary structure of these big molecules depends upon chemical valence bonds.[451] These include various single and double linkages within the amino acids that make it up as well as the peptide bonds that form them into chains. The helical configuration (see page 217) arises from hydrogen bonds between parts of the chain which attract one another and twist the molecule. Folding, which is particularly characteristic of globular proteins, depends upon Van der Waals interactions between hydrophobic groups of the molecule as well as upon hydrogen bonds. The configurational changes in allosteric enzymes (see page 258) involve breaking a small number of weak interactions of this sort and making others.[452]

The various sorts of connections within and between molecules are differently susceptible to environmental conditions like heat, acidity, oxidation or reduction agents, and the amount of water in the cell. For example, studies of the viscosity of an amoeba over a range of temperatures show that one type of bond is changed at one temperature and another type at a different temperature. There is no simple relationship between heat and viscosity.[453] Viscosity is high at low temperatures. With a rise from about 12.5° to 19°C, the viscosity falls. It increases again above that, but again falls to a low value at 30°C. After this, it rises rapidly as the cell is injured by the heat stress. Cooked cells become stiff.

5.4.3 Integration Centralized genetic controls of cellular processes are effective, and consequently cells are well-integrated systems. Mutual interactions between nucleus and cytoplasm keep both major compartments of cells highly tuned to each other, as the experiments with nuclear transplants in eggs and free-living cells indicate. As Hypothesis 5.2-14 (see page 107) indicates, segregation increases conflict among subsystems or components, and much such conflict is avoided by centralized nuclear control in cells.

The presence of DNA in cytoplasmic organelles and evidence that part of the template for replication of these structures is in this DNA indicate that cellular control is not completely centralized in the nuclear component of the decider. Some enzymes, those which catalyze in a constitutive way, also operate free of nuclear control after they are synthesized from a template transmitted from the DNA in the nucleus. These constitutive enzymes are controlled by substrate levels and other chemical and physical cytoplasmic variables. As Hypothesis 5.4.3-4 (see page 109) states, this decentralization of decision making increases the speed and accuracy of decisions which reduce local strains.

5.5 Pathology Cells, like systems at other levels, sustain structural damage or disturbance of the steady states of matter-energy and information processes as a result of: (a) Lacks of matter-energy inputs. (b) Excesses of matter-energy inputs. (c) Inputs of inappropriate forms of matter-energy. (d) Lacks of information inputs. (e) Excesses of information inputs. (f) Inputs of maladaptive genetic information in the template. (g) Abnormalities in internal matter-energy processes. And (h) abnormalities in internal information processes.

(a) *Lacks of matter-energy inputs.* Cells deprived of the matter-energy necessary for their metabolic processes are damaged in various ways. Light, for photo-synthetic cells, food, oxygen, and special substances required for particular cells must all be available. Rods and cones of the vertebrate retina, for example, require vitamin A in order to synthesize the pigments necessary for their processes. Deterioration of the cells follows continued lack stresses.[454]

Starvation disrupts the orderly progression of amoebas through their life cycles.[455] Several days of lack stresses of food inputs arrest them in G_2, after they have synthesized their DNA. Nevertheless they immediately synthesize DNA when refed, presumably undergoing two rounds of DNA synthesis between the pre- and poststarvation divisions. If the cell has entered mitosis, however, deprivation of matter-energy does not arrest its progress, since the matter-energy costs of division have by then already been met.[456]

Because of the temperature-dependency of the chemical processes of cells, cold—an energy lack stress—causes cells to become inactive. Freezing damages cells because ice crystals form within them, particularly if they are stored for a long time.[457] In order to keep cells alive over long periods of storage, special techniques such as slow freezing in glycerin can protect them against this sort of damage.

(b) *Excesses of matter-energy inputs.* Cells can be damaged by trauma, such as crushing and tearing. Consistent with Hypothesis 5.5-1 (see page 110), the farther away a component of the cell is from the point of trauma, the less pathological is its function. Heat, energy excess stress, disrupts a cell's processes by altering the chemical bonds and interactions within the cell. Radiation of various sorts also damages cells. The transformation of aggregated cells into cancer cells sometimes follows excess matter-energy inputs of this sort.

Cells in culture can be made to divide synchronously by a series of temperature shocks. Starvation, cold, and heat, or combinations of these stresses, produce this effect, but heat is the most effective.[458] If a population of *Tetrahymena* is subjected to a series of shifts from 28° to 34°C, each shift lasting 30 min, cell division is blocked. Growth continues, however, and the cells become oversized. When the cells are brought back to room temperature, the next one, two, or more divisions will be synchronized, after which the cells return to their normal growth and division cycles and do not remain synchronized. Heat shock apparently sets the cell back in "biological time" to an earlier phase of its cycle, and it must make up this loss before it can divide again. Heat stress applied after a critical point is reached does not disturb division.

Radiation of various sorts damages cells. This is particularly true of mammalian cells. Bacteria and yeasts are far less sensitive to radiation damage.[459]

The principal damage brought about by x-radiation is breakage of the chromosomes and reproductive death, but damage to other cell components also occurs. Smaller doses inhibit mitosis. This effect is reversible. It is thought to be caused by breaks in chromosomes which later are repaired.

Ultraviolet light is bactericidal.[460] It can also damage or kill the superficial cells of plants or animals, increase the rate of mutations of free-living cells, and retard cell division.

(c) *Inputs of inappropriate forms of matter-energy.* If a cell's environment becomes too acid or too alkaline, damage or death can result. A small change in the chemical composition of the extracellular fluids surrounding aggregated cells can result in disturbances of the cells' inputs and outputs of matter-energy so that they cannot carry out their processes normally. For instance, alterations in the concentration of sodium chloride in the surrounding fluids affect the cells' exchange of water so that they may either swell and burst or shrink and become dehydrated.

Toxins of various sorts can enter cells, sometimes because they are molecules similar to inputs normally employed in the cell's metabolism. For instance, some antibiotics can be transported across the cell membrane of plant cells because they are molecules similar to plant hormones, but once inside the cell they overstimulate growth. Another instance is a molecule similar to a transmitter substance that binds to the subsynaptic membrane but does not depolarize cells.[461] Curare acts in this way at the neuromyal junction of skeletal muscle fibers. Its presence there blocks the normal transmitter substance from attaching to the receptor site or at least diminishes its ability to attach. Other poisons block or alter cellular enzymatic or other processes, so producing damage which often leads to death.

Intracellular parasites are one class of matter-energy that enter both free-living and aggregated cells, creating damaging strains in them.[462] They are members of a number of different phyla of free-living cells, including bacteria, protozoans, rickettsias, and fungi. They are specialized to live inside a host cell at its expense. The parasites are partipotential, without independent metabolic activities, although each one is similar to a type of totipotential cell that exists as a complete free-living form. Both partipotential and totipotential cells are probably derived from a common free-living ancestor. Parasites get into cells in various ways, sometimes by phagocytosis, when the host cell engulfs them as prey. Once inside, they are able to resist digestion, even by cells that can digest other cells. Sometimes, like viruses, they multiply within the host cell, destroy it, and escape from it to invade others. Sometimes they leave a living host cell, which may or may not have been seriously damaged, a few at a time.

The effects of feeding inappropriate matter-energy to some cells have been tested experimentally.[463] Certain ciliates, such as *Blepharisma,* which ordinarily feed on bacteria, will devour other protozoans under experimental circumstances. If successively larger protozoans, finally including other *Blepharisma,* are fed to them, they become many times the size of normal cells. The enlargement is proportionate, with such organelles as membranes, cilia, macronuclei, and mouths all bigger than normal. When these overfed individuals are returned to a normal diet, the time between their cell divisions shortens until their descendants are again of normal size.

(d) *Lacks of information inputs.* There is no clear evidence that this sort of stress produces pathology at this level. Possibly the trophic effect of inputs from presynaptic neurons upon the postsynaptic neurons and muscle fibers with which they synapse is at least partly a phenomenon of information input, but it is equally or more likely that a matter-energy transmission of some unknown sort takes place. Neurons or muscle fibers deprived of such inputs do not grow normally and, whether or not they are fully grown, they degenerate. If these inputs are information, such are the results which are predicted by Hypotheses 5.1-42 (see page 105) and 5.4.1-4 (see page 109).

(e) *Excesses of information inputs.* Only minute quantities of hormones, which are information transmissions to aggregated cells from components of the organism's decider are required for them to exercise their effects on target cells. Excess inputs may produce opposite effects.[464] Thyroid hormones of vertebrates are signals that promote growth of the cells. These hormones act by increasing the rates of enzymatic processes in cellular respiration and phosphorylation. When excess amounts of such molecules are input to cells, they retard growth and may also provoke abnormal biochemical effects elsewhere in the cell than their usual molecular sites of action. Infection of a cell by a virus is primarily an excess of inappropriate information input because it produces its effect by changing the decider subsystem processes of the cell.

(f) *Inputs of maladaptive genetic information in the template.* Among free-living cells, bacteria are particularly subject to mutation, a characteristic which gives them their great adaptability to environmental change (see page 294). The resultant variations are transmitted to their progeny. Many mutant strains die out or survive only briefly in natural surroundings. A type of cell which dies unless it is in a very special environment is a strain of the bacterium *Thermobacterium acidophilus*. It must constantly receive inputs of DNA or its nucleosides.[465] When these are withheld, the cells cannot divide, but growth of the cytoplasm continues, and they become very elongated—30 to 40 times normal size. When DNA is added, they are once more able to divide, and their descendants again become of normal size. Some *Escherichia coli* mutants must have thymine in their medium to synthesize DNA and, of course, to divide. If they are grown on a medium without thymine, they literally grow themselves to death by increasing in length and diameter and doubling their protein but increasing DNA only slightly.

In aggregated cells, mutations which influence succeeding generations occur only in the sex cells. The resultant variations are then transmitted to the somatic cells (see page 468).

(g) *Abnormalities in internal matter-energy processes.* Malfunctions of this sort can often be attributed to one or more of the preceding classes of pathology. Sometimes, however, the causes cannot be identified, either because scientists do not yet know enough about cellular processes or because the abnormalities arise within the cell—by DNA transcription or RNA translation errors, for instance.

Transformation of a cell from a normal component of a tissue into a cancer cell involves profound changes in its internal matter-energy activities as well as other processes.[466] The transformation often follows known damage to the cell by radiation or trauma or invasion by a virus or known exposure to one of the chemicals that can cause cancer or one of the irritating substances that can produce tumors experimentally in laboratory animals.[467] But no single causative agent appears to exist.

There are 273 distinguishable human neoplasms.[468] Many of these originate in cells of different types but since there are fewer than 273 cell types in the human organism, more than one sort of change can occur in a given cell type. It is difficult to generalize about the nature of the changes because a normal process in one cell type can be pathological in another.

Knowing the usual appearance of a given type of cell, a pathologist can usually identify cancerous changes, although the variation is great from one type of cell to another and in different sorts of cancers.[469] The nucleus of a cancer cell is usually abnormal, often increased in volume, sometimes lobulated or with fissures running so deeply into it in some cases that cytoplasmic organelles appear to be inclusions within it. The amount of chromatin is ordinarily increased, and often it has an unusual appearance. The chromosomes are abnormal in various ways, frequently increased in number. Both the form and the consis-

tency of the chromosomes are changed. They may be sticky so they do not separate during division, giving rise to multinucleated cells in tissues that normally do not have them. Changes in the cytoplasmic organelles are often seen. Differentiated cells often become less specialized and more like primitive cells. An important change in aggregated cells is the loss of the normal relationships of cells within a tissue (see page 354). Cells separate from tissues and are carried in the organism's bloodstream to other tissues to which they adhere. The changes in membranes of individual cells that produce this adhesion are not fully understood.[470]

Respiration and glycolysis are abnormal in cancer cells.[471] Anaerobic rather than aerobic processes are characteristic of them. And, of course, they replicate much more often than normal cells do. Some cells that usually would never divide do so if they become cancerous. Others will not divide under any circumstances. Some pathologists question whether cells that have lost the power of division—as neurons have, for instance—ever regain it.[472] Tumors in the nervous systems of organisms are believed to arise from undifferentiated, primitive neuroblasts left in the tissue from the embryonic period, or from glial cells.

(h) *Abnormalities in internal information processes.* Mutations which arise in cells, sometimes apparently spontaneously, alter the cell's structure or the processes in its metabolic pathways. Some cancers of animals are known to be brought about by infection with viruses.[473] And sometimes such changes can be ascribed to the action of certain drugs or to radiation damage. From whatever causes, there is a fairly steady mutation rate, varying from one type of cell to another and among the cells of different types of organisms (see page 476).

Increasing evidence indicates that abnormalities of processes of the cellular decider subsystem invariably accompany cancerous changes in cells. For instance, a variety of cells of different kinds of human cancer have an excess of a particular chromosome, E16, which apparently plays an important role in normal replication.[474] A cell must synthesize DNA and divide once in the presence of a cancer-producing virus to "fix" the cancerous state.[475] It then produces cancerous descendants in subsequent cell divisions. Full expression of all the pathological changes may take several cell generations, however. Once a virus has induced such a change in a cell, its descendants need not contain either the virus or the viral genome. Three types of plant tumors initiated by three different agents—a virus, a bacterium, and a genetic crossing between two related species, all showed two phases of the development of cancer: (a) transformation to tumor cells and (b) continued proliferation after the alteration is accomplished.[476] The first phase requires induction by the cancer-producing agent. The second phase appears to depend upon two growth factors which are normally controlled but which act as signals eliciting unregulated growth in cancer cells.

5.6   Decay and termination   Ordinarily a free-living cell terminates its individual existence at division, but its substance lives on indefinitely in its progeny. Such cells which divide periodically can thus enjoy a sort of immortality, unless they are killed by any of the pathological processes listed above. Cell division seems to prevent the resultant new cells from aging. If cells are prevented from dividing, however, they do die, evidently of cumulative and irreversible changes as a result of aging.[477] Furthermore, if amoebas do not divide, and their cytoplasm is repeatedly amputated as they grow, they regenerate cytoplasm and do not age, at least for many months.

Aggregated cells of organisms, except for the sex cells, do not have this continuity beyond the life of the organism of which they are components. They die either before, or inevitably at, the death of the organism. The death of some cells is programmed into the developmental cycles of some organisms.[478] Ecdysone, the growth hormone of insects, signals the death of cells which are no longer needed. For instance, when the pupa becomes a moth, it accomplishes this by a final message to components of the cells' decider subsystems. Earlier in the life cycle this lethal effect is prevented by a juvenile hormone (see page 470). If this latter substance is injected into pupas, they molt again and form another pupa with all the cells that would otherwise have died as the insect became a moth. Similar loss of some cells is seen as pollywogs lose their tails and in the regression of the thymus gland in human children.

Differentiated mammalian cells grown in culture die unless they undergo a transformation something like that of cancer cells.[479] One can speculate that they can continue to live out of the organism only if they become less differentiated and more totipotential. Most human cells are hard to grow in culture, and those that do grow show aging and can be maintained in culture for a maximum of 60 cell generations.

As an organism ages, those cells that—like neurons—do not divide often show the effects of aging. Their metabolic processes change, and their composition alters. Within neurons the quantities of lipids, cholesterol, and lipofuscin, a yellow pigment which is found also in aging liver and heart cells, increase.[480] The DNA may decrease in molecular size.[481] Some neurons become shrunken. Others accumulate sufficient pigment or other substances to increase in size.[482] The nucleus grows irregular in shape or even

disappears. The distinction between nucleus and cytoplasm becomes less clear. The Nissl substance decreases. The neurofibrils become massed, losing their regular appearance. The membranes of the endoplasmic reticulum degenerate into clumps. Dendrites often thicken. These structural alterations are accompanied by deterioration or loss of functions. Many neurons die before the death of the organism of which they are components (see page 296). Under these circumstances they decompose into multiple components which come under the control of the suprasystem organ, as Hypothesis 5.6-1 says (see page 110). They are either removed from the site by phagocytosis or other means or replaced by other cells.

6. Models and simulations

Two of the four possible classes of models and simulations (see page 85) have been employed at the cellular level. They are: (a) *nonliving artifacts* and (c) *models in words, numbers, or other symbols, including computer programs.* The other two classes, (b) *living, usually human, representations* and (d) *living system—computer interactions* apparently do not exist at this level.

(a) *Nonliving artifacts.*   Electronic models of neurons can be made to display a number of the characteristic activities of real neurons. They can be connected into networks of varying degrees of complexity to model nerve nets or nervous systems (see page 355).[483] Aside from its interest as an exercise in ingenuity, an electronic system that imitates the processes of a living neuron with reasonable faithfulness can be used as an analog computer to examine functions of the neuron that would be difficult or impossible to study directly.

A "neuromime" that can be studied as a single cell or put together with other neuromimes to simulate organism information channels was developed by Harmon.[484] This simulation embodied more of the characteristics of neurons than some of the earlier attempts to build gadgets of this sort. It consisted of five transistors arranged suitably with resistors, capacitors, and diodes. Five excitatory inputs and one inhibitory input could be activated. The wiring diagram was based upon findings from electrode studies on living neurons. The firing frequency of the neuromime could be varied from 0 to 600 pulses per s.

Among the properties that made the neuromime similar to the living system were: (*i*) Graded "dendritic" function with decremental conduction that built up gradually to the threshold for an all-or-none pulse. (*ii*) Absolute and relative refractory periods and recovery to a resting threshold. (*iii*) A threshold that varied according to the recent firing history of the unit. (*iv*) Different input—output relationships, including one-to-one, in which a single input elicited a single all-or-none output; one-to-many, in which a step function or steady potential elicited a single spike; and temporal summation. (*v*) An input of low intensity takes longer to elicit an output than a more intense input. Some properties of these simulated cells were not modeled, including antidromic currents, facilitation, and variable or slow conduction velocities.

Another artificial neuron simulated inner and outer membrane potentials by an amplifier network for each which combined to produce the potential across the membrane in a third amplifier. This simulation showed—besides some properties like those of the neuromime—accommodation, adaptation, and failure to output signals when repetitive inputs were received (similar to that in some phasic neurons with rapid signal termination). By varying the time constants, this apparatus could simulate neurons of different species of organisms.

(*c*) *Models in words, numbers, or other symbols, including computer programs.* The conceptual systems of Watson and Crick and of Jacob and Monod, both of which are discussed above (see pages 217 and 258), are powerful models of cell structures and processes upon which much subsequent research on cell processes has been based.

Many computer models of internal processes of cells are available. An analog computer has been used to model the uptake of iodine by cells of the thyroid gland.[485] Another analog program modeled the inhibition of oxidation within cells by antimycin A.[486] This produced results consistent with the hypothesis that a lag before onset of the inhibition is caused by alteration of the chemical structure of the antibiotic, in order to allow it to act as an inhibitor.

Digital computers have proved useful in modeling the many interacting constituents of cells. One such model represents a hypothetical and greatly simplified cell.[487] Its processes are embodied in "strings" (lists) of symbols which can be separated and recombined under the control of other strings. This models enzyme-catalyzed synthetic processes, controlled by a "gene" string which embodies the signals transmitted by the DNA to the enzymes. This hypothetical cell can form polymers and reproduce itself. Two programs that are based upon biochemical research and include some of the many variables involved in cell internal processes are the long-term study of cell metabolism carried out by Chance and his colleagues and the model of differentiation in cells of the slime mold, by Wright.

The first of these two simulations of cellular metabolic processes, by Chance and his associates, is part of an intensive study of the ascites tumor cell.[488] The program can represent 40 chemical reactions of various sorts among 49 chemical components in differential equations describing more than 100 different enzymatic steps.[489] The computer is programmed with the relevant chemical reactions, the initial and maximal concentrations of the reagents, and the rates of the reactions. Those reactions that are reversible are represented as such. The known enzyme systems and some characteristic responses, such as the interaction related to ATP and AMP levels (see page 289), are also a part of the original data given the computer. Prediction of experimental results is possible by appropriate manipulation of the variables. A check of the validity of the program by comparing its output with experimental results showed the computed values of concentrations to be accurate to about 0.1 percent.[490]

As slime mold cells differentiate they construct cell walls around spores (see page 284).[491] The process is so complex that computer simulation is a useful technique for evaluating the relative importance of different enzyme-catalyzed functions in accumulating the necessary end products in the differentiating cell and in predicting the rates of change of processes and amounts of substances that occur during the differentiation.[492] The simulation of these slime-mold cellular processes by Wright is carried out in a series of partial models intended to be integrated into a description of the complete system. To model the process of differentiation one must understand the processes in the relevant metabolic pathways. The steady-state concentrations of starting materials, intermediates, and end products, and the important changes in these in the living cell during the critical reactions must be represented. Such a model can test the relevance of data collected *in vitro* to the processes that go on in an intact living cell. One interesting outcome of Wright's simulation was the discovery that had the model been created and used sooner, it would have rendered some experiments that had already been conducted unnecessary because the hypothesis upon which they were based was shown to be invalid.

A computer simulation of the process whereby a single, free-living, flagellated alga cell, *Euglena,* moves to and remains in an illuminated region has been developed by Diehn.[493] Experiments testing the behavior of *Euglena* under various light intensities showed that the simulation could predict such actions moderately well.

Much experimental work on bacteria is done with cells in culture rather than single cells. A digital computer has been used to simulate the growth of such a culture.[494] The growth curves of simulated cultures composed of several variants of a given cell type and of different mutations of it, by adjustment of a few parameters, could be brought close to growth curves of real cellular cultures. Also a mathematical model has been developed and programmed for a computer that simulates the genetic recombinations in a bacterial population.[495]

7. Conclusions

In the last two decades new scientific techniques have revealed many remarkable facts about the world of the cell, the simplest, but still amazingly complicated, level of living systems. Perhaps the single, most important, new technique has been electron microscopy. The light microscope reveals only the largest components of cells. The electron microscope, which can magnify as much as 100,000 times, shows the structure and process of subsubsystems, subcomponents, and even single macromolecules. X-ray diffraction also has revealed aspects of cells never seen before. Biochemical methods, too, have advanced with great speed, making possible laboratory syntheses, with enzymes and primers, of large organic molecules including proteins, which are of major significance in cellular processes. Quantitative histochemistry, microdissection of cells, reassembling of live cells from separate components, and new ways to study the forces which hold together cellular components have all contributed.

These methods have revealed a highly variegated set of concrete, living systems, free-living and aggregated, totipotential and partipotential. They range in size from the smallest mycoplasms, which are about 200 nm in diameter—2,000 times the diameter of a hydrogen atom—to the largest ostrich eggs, about 1 million times as long. They vary tremendously in shape and specialized characteristics, including protozoans with toothlike structures; plant gametes with flagella; red blood corpuscles that have lost both nucleus and reticular structures; and cnidoblasts which, on receipt of proper inputs, whip out threadlike components which had been coiled within them.

Even more fundamental, a series of basic discoveries, like Watson and Crick's description of the DNA double helix and Jacob and Monod's explication of inducible and repressible genetic systems, have explained some of the most important of the multitude of cellular processes. Until the new techniques brought these vital discoveries, scientists' concepts of cells were concerned chiefly with large structures revealed by the light microscope, organelles like the nucleus and the cell membrane or wall, with the cytoplasm between. The stability of these static parts masked the bustling activity of smaller and less easily visible components of the cell—ribosomes, mitochon-

dria, microfibrils, DNA and RNA molecules, enzymes, hormones, ions, and the rest. Many of these compounds move about more or less randomly under the influence of various physical and chemical forces within the multiple regions of the cell partitioned off by the reticular components. Other molecules appear to travel in what seems like goal-directed fashion. For instance, various sorts of molecules are ushered across cell membranes by permeases. Sodium ions are pumped out of cells across the cell membrane, while potassium molecules remain inside. Messenger RNA molecules in the nucleus travel to pores in the nuclear membrane and cross out into the cytoplasm, while DNA molecules remain inside. Enzymes are synthesized in one place and then move to mitochondria, ribosomes, or other specific locations to function. Single transfer RNA molecules seem to search through the endoplasm for a specific kind of amino acid and then transport it back to a ribosome to be incorporated into a protein molecule. Many different synthetic processes, each involving multiple steps in metabolic pathways, go on continually in the mixture of many sorts of moving and stationary substances that make up the cell. Somehow they avoid interfering with one another in the complex traffic flows of the cellular distributor.

All this represents incredible microminiaturization in space and time of a very large number of very rapid processes. Externally the cell is continually interacting with its environment through inputs and outputs of matter-energy and information, adjusting to lack and excess stresses and strains. Internally it is a factory with many molecular assembly lines forever processing a diversity of products and wastes. For their size, cellular components probably move among the fixed components of their system equally or more actively than human beings move in the various regions of higher-level systems.

Cells are even more complex than this rather complicated chapter indicates. I have often simplified the facts for clarity and brevity, as the specialists will recognize. Often I have mentioned only single examples of classes of phenomena, like metabolic pathways, which have many examples. Numerous processes are omitted entirely, and indeed many are certainly still undiscovered. The rapid advance in knowledge of cells has shown that cells are comparable to higher levels in the number of subsystems and the variety of components. Only in recent years have specialists on cellular processes learned about many of their details. To them the cell's incredible intricacy is abundantly clear. This intricacy is not, however, apparent to many experts who investigate higher levels of systems, particularly at the group level and above. Consequently they often assume that their complicated subject matter is utterly unlike that of the cellular experts. This is one reason cross-level formal identities have not appeared relevant to more scientists.

Cellular biologists generally agree that several concepts of systems theory are applicable to cells. They have subsystems and components (organelles) and subsubsystems and subcomponents (molecules). They maintain steady states over time of numerous variables by negative feedbacks and other control processes. They are regulated and organized into a unitary system by various sorts of information flows. An efficient balance is maintained by decentralized segregation of some processes and centralized integration of others. Some are under rapid, local, lower-echelon controls, and others are under slower, more indirect, higher-echelon controls. Both free-living and aggregated cells have evolved from primitive forms to more advanced forms that employ greater specialization of functions and differentiation. Often these shredded-out functions are under largely decentralized control, which permits greater efficiency and speed of action, but at the same time requires more complex higher-echelon decision making to prevent conflicts among the diverse, decentralized activities (see page 275).

Hypothesis 3.3.4.2-1 (see page 98) specifies that, as systems mature, they develop more efficient codes. This may be true of cells. It seems likely also that as new and more advanced species have evolved they have come to use more efficient codes. Although primitive cells, like some amoebas, have over 1,500 chromosomes while fruit flies have 4 and man has 46 (see page 221), each of the chromosomes of the amoeba presumably carries much less information than the more complex chromosomes of the more advanced species. The greater efficiency of coding of the more advanced species is made possible in some way by the greater complexity of their chromosomes.

Biologists in general make less of the distinction between free-living and aggregated cells than I do. In my view this is a distinction between levels and consequently significant. It is also a difference between, in free-living cells, totipotential systems and, in aggregated cells, partipotential, differentiated systems under hierarchical controls from higher levels—particularly the organ and the organism. The structure and process of the two sorts of cells are similar in many—perhaps most—ways, but not in all. Aggregated cells, after specialization, often are unable to carry out some subsystem functions, e.g., some somatic cells cannot reproduce. Free-living cells have all their essential processes. Aggregated cells age; free-living cells usually do not. Aggregated cells respond to signals

input to them from higher levels, e.g., initiator molecules, hormone molecules, transmitter substance molecules at chemical synapses, or electrical pulses at electrical synapses. Except for slime mold plasmodia which respond to acrasin, the aggregation signal (see page 203), constituting an intermediate case between free-living and aggregated cells, there is no evidence that a free-living cell reacts to signals from any higher level, although such a cell does respond to signals from its environment which, together with it, make up its suprasystem.

Investigation at this level of living systems has characteristic emphases and omissions. Rarely are the matter-energy and information metabolisms of the cell explicitly distinguished. With rare exceptions like Mountcastle's research on receptor cell thresholds (see page 283), cross-level analogies or formal identities are neglected. Information and control processes have been studied only in recent years and still are much less adequately understood than matter-energy processes. Little is known about how cells carry out associative learning and memory. Yet they must in some way be involved in such processes, because organisms, which are made up of cells, learn and remember. These important processes have been studied in free-living cells by only a few researchers, and they seem unable to agree. Many have investigated and speculated about these processes in aggregated cells, but most of the questions asked about them remain unanswered.

Many challenging and interesting questions about cells require further study. The following are a few examples:

Are memories stored at synapses or in macromolecules inside the cell (see pages 270 and 271)?

Are memories stored in RNA, in protein, or in other molecules (see page 271)?

In what code are memories stored?

Are the various cellular codes the most efficient possible for their particular functions (see pages 277 and 278)?

What, precisely, are the cross-level differences between cells and higher levels? For example, is it true that, in processing information, cells have less variation of output intensity, a lesser output range, shorter processing times, less variation in processing times, and less cost in energy expenditure per unit of information processed than higher levels of systems (see page 284)?

Exactly how does the information in the genetic template describe the cell's structure and processes? How is its blueprint implemented in a new cell?

How is overall cellular system integration achieved? How do transfer RNA molecules locate in the cytoplasm the particular amino acids needed to synthesize a protein?

How do molecules in the many metabolic pathways keep from interfering with one another in the vigorous traffic of the cell's endoplasm?

How efficient is the cell's strategy of dividing its matter-energy storage into rapid, medium, and slow access (see page 241)?

What is the efficiency of having both higher- and lower-echelon control processes in cells (see pages 273 to 275)?

Why are cellular organelles and components centralized in some cases and dispersed in others?

What steps can scientists take to form living cells in the laboratory wholly from nonliving components (see page 223)?

What makes cells cancerous?

Why and how do cells age?

Several Nobel prizes have been awarded for significant advances in the recent explosion of scientific theory and experimentation in cellular biology. These and other studies have brought us closer to comprehending the nature of life. As our understanding of cells progresses, the manner in which cellular systems processes are carried out becomes increasingly clear. With precision, intricacy, and reliability unequalled by any nonliving system, cells are the ultimate constituents of all living systems. Succeeding chapters indicate how cells enable higher levels of systems to arise as well as how they put constraints upon them.

NOTES AND REFERENCES

[1]Edey, M. A. (Ed.). *A guide to the natural world and index to the LIFE Nature Library.* New York: Time, Inc., 1965, 29.

[2]Bonner, J. T. *Cells and societies.* Princeton, N.J.: Princeton Univ. Press, 1955, 106–107.
Cf. also Blair, D. H. Jr., Princeton's poetic biologists. *Princeton Alumni Weekly,* September 26, 1957, 7.

[3]Butler, J. A. V. *Inside the living cell.* New York: Basic Books, 1959, **69,** 70. © George Allen and Unwin Ltd. 1959, Basic Books, Inc., Publishers, New York. Reprinted by permission.

[4]Stanley, W. M. & Valens, E. G. *Viruses and the nature of life.* New York: Dutton, 1961, 37.

[5]*Ibid.*

[6]Cf. *Ibid.*

[7]Linschitz, H. The information content of a bacterial cell. In H. Quastler (Ed.). *Information theory in biology.* Urbana: Univ. of Illinois Press, 1953, 251–256.
Also Dancoff, S. M. & Quastler, H. The information content and error rate of living things. In H. Quastler (Ed.). *Information theory in biology.* Urbana: Univ. of Illinois Press, 1953, 263–273.

[8]Giese, A. C. *Cell physiology.* Philadelphia: Saunders, 1962, 35.

[9]*Ibid.,* 37–49.

[10]Branson, H. R. Information theory and the structure of proteins. In H. Quastler (Ed.). *Information theory in biology.* Urbana: Univ. of Illinois Press, 1953, 84–104.

[11]Giese, A. C. *Op. cit.,* 73–76.

[12]Neutra, M. & Leblond, C. P. The Golgi apparatus. *Sci. Amer.,* 1969, **220**(2), 100–107.

[13]Morowitz, H. J. & Tourtellotte, M. E. The smallest living cells. *Sci. Amer.,* 1962, **206**(3), 117–126.

[14]Stanley, W. M. & Valens, E. G. *Op. cit.,* 23.

[15]*Ibid.,* 26.

[16]*Ibid.,* 23.

[17]*Ibid.*

[18]Morowitz, H. J. & Tourtellotte, M. E. *Op. cit.,* 119.

[19]Horne, R. W. The structure of viruses. *Sci. Amer.,* 1963, **208**(1), 48–56.

[20]Giese, A. C. *Op cit.,* 372–373.

[21]Morowitz, H. J. & Tourtellotte, M. E. *Op. cit.,* 122.

[22]*Ibid.,* 126.

[23]Giese, A. C. *Op. cit.,* 485.

[24]Palay, S. L. The structural basis for neural action. In M. A. B. Brazier (Ed.). *Brain function, RNA and brain function.* Vol. 2. *Memory and learning.* Berkeley: Univ. of California Press, 1964, 77.

[25]Schmitt, F. O. & Geschwind, N. The axon surface. *Prog. in Biophysics,* 1957, **8,** 207.

[26]Cf. Singer, M. & Soll, D. Letter to the editor. *Science,* 1973, **181,** 1114.

[27]Veomett, G., Prescott, D. M., Shay, J., & Porter, K. R. Reconstruction of mammalian cells from nuclear and cytoplasmic components separated by treatment with cytochalasin B. *Proc. Nat. Acad. Sci. USA,* 1974, **71,** 1999–2002.

[28]Brachet, J. *Biochemical cytology.* New York: Academic Press, 1957, 5–30.

[29]Stanley, W. M. & Valens, E. G. *Op. cit.,* 27.

[30]Brachet, J. *Op. cit.,* 82.

[31]Watson, J. D. & Crick, F. H. C. Molecular structure of nucleic acids. *Nature,* 1953, **171,** 737–738.
Cf. also Nirenberg, M. W. The genetic code: II. *Sci. Amer.,* 1963, **208**(3), 80.

[32]Nirenberg, M. W. *Op. cit.,* 80–94.

[33]Sonneborn, T. M. Nucleotide sequence of a gene: first complete specification. *Science,* 1965, **148,** 1410.
NOTE: Benzer [Benzer, S. The fine structure of the gene. *Sci. Amer.,* 1962, **206**(1), 70–84] prefers to define the gene by a genetic experiment. Rather than define it as that segment of the DNA molecule which contains the template for an enzyme or other protein molecule or polypeptide (*e.g.,* in terms of its synthetic capability), Benzer defines it as that segment which can be distinguished from the rest of the molecule by genetic mutation and recombination.

[34]Nirenberg, M. W. *Op. cit.,* 80.

[35]*Ibid.*

[36]Braun, W. *Bacterial genetics.* Philadelphia: Saunders, 1965, 337–343.

[37]Nirenberg, M. W. *Op. cit.,* 89.

[38]Holley, R. W., Apgar, J., Everett, G. A., Madison, J. T., Marquisee, M., Merrill, H., Penswick, J. R., & Zamir, A. Structure of a ribonucleic acid. *Science,* 1965, **147,** 1462–1465.
Cf. also Sonneborn, T. M. *Op. cit.,* 1410.

[39]Sanger, F., Air, G. M., Barrell, B. G., Brown, N. L., Coulson, A. R., Fiddes, J. C., Hutchison, C. A., III, Slocombe, P. M., & Smith, M. Nucleotide sequence of bacteriophage ΦX174 DNA. *Nature,* Feb. 24, 1977, **265,** 687–695.
Cf. also Szekely, M. ΦX174 sequence. *Nature,* 24 Feb. 1977, **265,** 685.

[40]Beadle, G. The new biology and the nature of man. The

Dewey F. Fagerburg memorial lecture, 1963. *Phoenix*. Ann Arbor, Mich.: Univ. of Michigan, Michigan Memorial-Phoenix Project, 1963, **2**(1), 3–4. Reprinted by permission.

[41]Wiseman, D. R. Personal communication, 1972.

[42]Crick, F. H. C. Macromolecules and natural selection. In M. X. Zarrow (Ed.). *Growth in living systems*. New York: Basic Books, 1961, 3.

[43]Mazia, D. The plan of cellular reproduction. In M. X. Zarrow (Ed.). *Growth in living systems*. New York: Basic Books, 1961, 174.

[44]Kornberg, A. Biologic synthesis of deoxyribonucleic acid. *Science*, 1960, **131**, 1503–1508.

[45]Haruna, I. & Spiegelman, S. Autocatalytic synthesis of a viral RNA *in vitro*. *Science*, 1965, **150**, 884–886.
Cf. also Singer, M. F. *In vitro* synthesis of DNA: a perspective on research. *Science*, 1967, **158**, 1550–1551.

[46]Brachet, J. *Op. cit.*, 80–82, 117.

[47]Swift, H. The organization of genetic material in eukaryotes: progress and prospects. *Cold Spring Harbor symp. on quant. biol. Chromosome structure and function*. Cold Spring Harbor, N.Y.: Cold Spring Harbor Laboratory, 1974, 963–979.
Cf. also Kornberg, R. D. Chromatin structure: a repeating unit of histones and DNA. *Science*, 1974, **184**, 868–871.

[48]Brachet, J. *Op. cit.*, 105.

[49]Crandall, M. A. & Brock, T. D. Molecular aspects of specific cell contact. *Science*, 1968, **161**, 473–475.

[50]Mazia, D. Mitosis and the physiology of cell division. In J. Brachet & A. E. Mirsky (Eds.). *The cell*. Vol. 3. New York: Academic Press, 1961, 311–316.

[51]*Ibid.*, 359–360.

[52]*Ibid.*, 314.

[53]*Ibid.*, 331.

[54]Calvin, M. Chemical evolution of life and sensibility. In G. C. Quarton, T. Melnechuk, & F. O. Schmitt (Eds.). *The neurosciences*. New York: Rockefeller Univ. Press, 1967, 787–789.

[55]Mazia, D. Mitosis and the physiology of cell division. *Op. cit.*, 358–359.
Cf. also Lehninger, A. L. Molecular biology: the theme of conformation. In G. C. Quarton, T. Melnechuk, & F. O. Schmitt (Eds.). *The neurosciences*. New York: Rockefeller Univ. Press, 1967, 41.

[56]Lehninger, A. L. Cell organelles: the mitochondrion. In G. C. Quarton, T. Melnechuk, & F. O. Schmitt (Eds.). *The neurosciences*. New York: Rockefeller Univ. Press, 1967, 91.

[57]Nanney, D. L. Control patterns in cellular morphogenesis. *Science*, 1968, **160**, 496–502.

[58]Sonneborn, T. M. The differentiation of cells. *Proc. Nat. Acad. Sci. USA* 1964, **51**, 915–929.

[59]Mazia, D. The plan of cellular reproduction. *Op. cit.*, 162.
Also Swift, H. *Op. cit.*, 969–970.

[60]Nass, M. M. K. Mitochondrial DNA: advances, problems, and goals. *Science*, 1969, **165**, 33–34.
Cf. also Sager, R. Genes outside the chromosomes. *Sci. Amer.*, 1965, **212**(1), 70–79.

[61]Lehninger, A. L. Cell organelles: the mitochondrion. *Op. cit.*, 92–93, 99–100.

[62]*Ibid.*, 100.

[63]Nass, M. M. K. *Op. cit.*, 33.

[64]Johnson, W. H. Paramecium. *Encyclopaedia Britannica*. Vol. 17. Chicago: Encyclopaedia Britannica, 1958, 265.

[65]Muhlethaler, K. Plant cell walls. In J. Brachet & A. E. Mirsky (Eds.). *The cell*. Vol. 2. New York: Academic Press, 1961, 85–134.

[66]Robertson, J. D. The membrane of the living cell. *Sci. Amer.*, 1962, **206**(4), 67–68.

[67]Korn, E. D. Structure of biological membranes. *Science*, 1966, **153**, 1491–1498.
Also Bretscher, M. S. Membrane structure: some general principles. *Science*, 1973, **181**, 622–627.
Also Marx, J. L. Biochemistry of cancer cells: focus on the cell surface. *Science*, 1974, **183**, 1279–1282.
Also Nicolson, G. L. & Yanagimachi, R. Mobility and the restriction of mobility of plasma membrane lectin-binding components. *Science*, 1974, **184**, 1294–1296.
Also Danielli, J. F. The bilayer hypothesis of membrane structure. In G. Weissmann & R. Claiborne (Eds.). *Cell membranes: biochemistry, cell biology & pathology*. New York: HP Pub. Co., 1975, 3–11.
Also de Robertis, E. D. P., Saez, F. A., & de Robertis, E. M. F., Jr. *Cell biology*. (6th ed.) Philadelphia: Saunders, 1975, 156–157.

[68]Robertson, J. D. *Op. cit.*, 65–72.

[69]Weiss, L. & Mayhew, E. The cell periphery. *N. E. J. Med.*, 1967, **276**, 1356.

[70]Cf. Korn, E. D. *Op. cit.*, 1497.
Also deTerra, N. Cortical control of cell division. *Science*, 1974, **184**, 530–537.

[71]Marx, J. L. *Op. cit.*
Also Nicolson, G. L. & Yanagimachi, R. *Op. cit.*
Also Capaldi, R. A. A dynamic model of cell membranes. *Sci. Amer.*, 1974, **230**(3), 26–33.

[72]Holter, H. How things get into cells. *Sci. Amer.*, 1961, **205**(3), 171.

[73]*Ibid.*, 169.

[74]Rustad, R. C. Pinocytosis. *Sci. Amer.*, 1961, **204**(4), 122.

[75]Giese, A. C. *Op. cit.*, 223–242.

[76]Brachet, J. *Op. cit.*, 35.

[77]Giese, A. C. *Op. cit.*, 240.

[78]Holter, H. *Op. cit.*, 172.

[79]Giese, A. C. *Op. cit.*, 227–230.

[80]*Ibid.*, 231–234.

[81]Holter, H. *Op. cit.*, 169.

[82]Giese, A. C. *Op. cit.*, 255.

[83]*Ibid.*, 252–253.

[84]*Ibid.*, 252.

[85]*Ibid.*, 254.

[86]*Ibid.*, 231–233.

[87]*Ibid.*, 245.

[88]Robertson, J. D. *Op. cit.*, 72.

[89]Porter, K. R. & Palade, G. E. Studies on the endoplasmic reticulum. III. Its form and distribution in striated muscle cells. *J. biophys. biochem. Cytol.*, 1957, **3**, 269.

[90]Porter, K. R. & Franzini-Armstrong, C. The sarcoplasmic reticulum. *Sci. Amer.*, 1965, **212**(3), 74.

[91]Porter, K. R. The sarcoplasmic reticulum. In K. R. Porter (Ed.). The sarcoplasmic reticulum. *J. biophys. biochem. Cytol.*, 1961, **10**(4, suppl.), 220.

[92]*Ibid.*, 221–222.

[93]Porter, K. R. (Discussion leader). General morphology of microtubules. *Neurosci. Res. Prog. Bull.*, 1968, **6**, 145.

[94]Porter, K. R. & Franzini-Armstrong, C. *Op. cit.*, 74.

[95]Weiss, P. Neuronal dynamics. *Neurosci. Res. Prog. Bull.*, 1967, **5**, 375–379.

[96]*Ibid.*, 383.

[97]*Ibid.*, 390.

[98]*Ibid.*, 395.

[99]Lasek, R. J. Slow and rapid transport of proteins. *Neurosci. Res. Prog. Bull.*, 1967, **5**, 314–317.
Cf. also Ochs, S. Fast axoplasmic transport of materials in mammalian nerve and its integrative role. *Ann. N. Y. Acad. Sci.*, 1972, **193**, 43–58.

[100]Weiss, P. *Op. cit.*, 397–399.

[101]Porter, K. R. (Discussion leader). Functional patterns of microtubules. *Neurosci. Res. Prog. Bull.,* 1968, **6,** 154–155.

[102]Woodruff, L. L. Protozoa. *Encyclopaedia Britannica.* Vol. 18.
Chicago: Encyclopaedia Britannica, 1958, 629.

[103]Cf. Schmitt, F. O. The molecular biology of neuronal fibrous proteins. *Neurosci. Res. Prog. Bull.,* 1968, **6,** 138–141.

[104]Stephens, R. E. (Discussion leader). Protein subunits of microtubules. *Neurosci. Res. Prog. Bull.,* 1968, **6,** 157.

[105]Porter, K. R. (Discussion leader). Functional patterns of microtubules. *Op cit.,* 155.

[106]Allen, R. D. Diversity and characteristics of cytoplasmic movement. *Neurosci. Res. Prog. Bull.,* 1967, **5,** 330.

[107]Brachet, J. *Op. cit.,* 313.

[108]Giese, A. C. *Op. cit.,* 200.

[109]Brachet, J. *Op. cit.,* 69.

[110]Giese, A. C. *Op. cit.,* 96–97.

[111]*Ibid.,* 99.

[112]Brachet, J. *Op. cit.,* 340.

[113]Hoffman, H.-P. & Avers, C. J. Mitochondrion of yeast: ultrastructural evidence for one giant, branched organelle per cell. *Science,* 1973, **181,** 749–751.

[114]*Ibid.,* 51.

[115]Green, D. E. The mitochondrion. *Sci. Amer.,* 1964, **210**(1), 66.
Cf. also Lehninger, A. L. Supramolecular organization of enzyme and membrane systems. *Neurosci. Res. Prog. Bull.,* 1965, **3,** 37–46.

[116]Giese, A. C. *Op. cit.,* 95–96.

[117]*Ibid.,* 372–373.

[118]*Ibid.,* 328–330.

[119]Porter, K. R. & Franzini-Armstrong, C. *Op. cit.,* 80.

[120]Lehninger, A. L. Energy transformation in the cell. *Sci. Amer.,* 1960, **202**(5), 105–106. Reprinted by permission of Scientific American.

[121]Giese, A. C. *Op. cit.,* 328–330.

[122]Cf. *Ibid.,* 373.

[123]Cf. *Ibid.,* 377.

[124]Cf. *Ibid.,* 376–377.

[125]Cf. *Ibid.,* 328.

[126]Braun, W. *Op. cit.,* 324.

[127]Giese, A. C. *Op. cit.,* 88.

[128]Braun, W. *Op. cit.,* 322, 334–335.

[129]Porter, K. R. & Palade, G. E. *Op. cit.,* 294.

[130]Cf. Nomura, M. Assembly of bacterial ribosomes. *Science,* 1973, **179,** 864–873.
Also Darnell, J. E., Jelinek, W. R., & Molloy, G. R. Biogenesis of mRNA: genetic regulation in mammalian cells. *Science,* 1973, **181,** 1215–1221.

[131]Nossal, G. J. V. How cells make antibodies. *Sci. Amer.,* 1964, **211**(6), 106.

[132]Giese, A. C. *Op. cit.,* 399–407.

[133]*Ibid.,* 401.

[134]Lehninger, A. L. Energy transformation in the cell. *Op. cit.,* 69.

[135]Warner, J. R. The species of RNA in the HeLa cell. In L. Goldstein (Ed.). *The control of nuclear activity.* Englewood Cliffs, N.J.: Prentice-Hall, 1967, 79–99.

[136]Platt, J. R. Chemical aspects of genetics. *Ann. Rev. phys. Chem.,* 1965, **16,** 506.

[137]*Ibid.*

[138]Giese, A. C. *Op. cit.,* 532.

[139]Neutra, M. & Leblond, C. P. *Op. cit.*

[140]Goldstein, L. & Prescott, D. M. Nucleocytoplasmic interactions in the control of nuclear reproduction and other cell cycle stages. In L. Goldstein (Ed.). *The control of nuclear activity.* Englewood Cliffs, N.J.: Prentice-Hall, 1967, 5.

[141]Brachet, J. *Op cit.,* 299–300.

[142]Jeon, K. W., Lorch, I. J., & Danielli, J. F. Reassembly of living cells from dissociated components. *Science,* 1970, **167,** 1626–1627.

[143]Giese, A. C. *Op. cit.,* 522.

[144]Crosby, E. C., Humphrey, T., & Lauer, E. W. *Correlative anatomy of the nervous system.* New York: Macmillan, 1962, 44–47.

[145]Thomas, C. A., Jr. The recombination of DNA molecules. In G. C. Quarton, T. Melnechuk, & F. O. Schmitt (Eds.). *The neurosciences.* New York: Rockefeller Univ. Press, 1967, 162–182.

[146]Cf. article on speech by A. Kornberg on DNA polymerase in *Cleveland Press,* Saturday, October 18, 1969, Section B, 8.

[147]Cf. Stanley, W. M. & Valens, E. G. *Op. cit.,* 76–77.

[148]Bernhardt, W., Panten, K., & Holzer, H. Gedämpftes Oscillieren der Synthesegeschwindigkeit von DPN-abhängiger Glutamatdehydrogenase in Hefezellen. *Biochem. biophys. Acta,* 1965, **99,** 531–539.

[149]Gabe, M. & Arvy, L. Gland cells. In J. Brachet & A. E. Mirsky (Eds.). *The cell.* Vol. 5. New York: Academic Press, 1961, 72–75.

[150]Brachet, J. *Op. cit.,* 63.

[151]Porter, K. R. & Franzini-Armstrong, C. *Op. cit.,* 80.

[152]Giese, A. C. *Op. cit.,* 446.

[153]*Ibid.,* 223.

[154]*Ibid.,* 248.

[155]Holter, H. *Op. cit.,* 172.

[156]Johnson, W. H. *Op. cit.,* 265–266.

[157]Giese, A. C. *Op. cit.,* 249.

[158]Porter, K. R. & Franzini-Armstrong, C. *Op. cit.,* 77.

[159]*Ibid.,* 80.

[160]Schmitt, F. O. *Op. cit.,* 140.
Cf. also Taylor, E. W. (Discussion leader). Protein chemistry of microtubules. *Neurosci. Res. Prog. Bull.,* 1968, **6,** 156–157.

[161]Allen, R. D. *Op. cit.*

[162]Brachet, J. *Op. cit.,* 65.

[163]Porter, K. R. (Discussion leader). Functional patterns of microtubules. *Op. cit.,* 150.

[164]Brachet, J. *Op. cit.,* 63–65.

[165]Giese, A. C. *Op. cit.,* 499–502.

[166]Porter, K. R. & Franzini-Armstrong, C. *Op. cit.,* 74.

[167]Huxley, H. E. The mechanism of muscular contraction. *Science,* 20 June 1969, **164,** 1356–1366.

[168]*Ibid.,* 1365–1366.

[169]*Ibid.,* 1359.

[170]*Ibid.,* 1365. Copyright 1969 by the American Association for the Advancement of Science. Reprinted by permission.

[171]Reedy, M. (Discussion leader). Mechanochemical coupling in muscle. *Neurosci. Res. Prog. Bull.,* 1968, **6,** 183.

[172]Allen, R. D. *Op. cit.,* 329.

[173]Porter, K. R. (Discussion leader). Functional patterns of microtubules. *Op. cit.,* 150.

[174]Reedy, M. *Op. cit.,* 183.
Cf. also Porter, K. R. (Discussion leader). General morphology of microtubules. *Op. cit.,* 151.

[175]Giese, A. C. *Op. cit.,* 511–513.
Cf. also Huxley, H. E. *Op. cit.,* 1359.

[176]Porter, K. R. The sarcoplasmic reticulum. *Op. cit.,* 224.
Cf. also Porter, K. R. & Franzini-Armstrong, C. *Op. cit.,* 78–80.

[177]Giese, A. C. *Op. cit.,* 476.

[178]Nakai, J. The movement of neurons in tissue culture. In R.

D. Allen & N. Kamiya (Eds.). *Primitive motile systems in cell biology*. New York: Academic Press, 1964, 377–378.

[179]Cf. Hayashi, T. How cells move. *Sci. Amer.*, 1961, **205**(3), 184.

[180]Allen, R. D. Ameboid movement. *Sci. Amer.*, 1962, **206**(2), 112–126.

[181]Bingley, M. S. & Thompson, C. M. Bioelectric potentials in relation to movement in amoebae. *J. theoret. Biol.*, 1962, **2**, 16–32.

[182]Kilburn, K. H. & Salzano, J. V. Respiratory cilia. *Science*, 1965, **148**, 1618–1619.

[183]Hayashi, T. *Op. cit.*, 190.

[184]Giese, A. C. *Op. cit.*, 73–76.

[185]Schmitt, F. O. & Samson, F. E., Jr. Neuronal fibrous proteins. *Neurosci. Res. Prog. Bull.*, 1968, **6**, 117.

[186]Giese, A. C. *Op. cit.*, 74–75.

[187]Porter, K. R. (Discussion leader). Functional patterns of microtubules. *Op. cit.*, 148–149.

[188]Diehn, B. Phototaxis and sensory transduction in Euglena. *Science*, 1973, **181**, 1009–1015.

[189]Eccles, J. C. *The physiology of synapses*. New York: Academic Press, 1964, 15–21.

[190]McLennan, H. *Synaptic transmission*. Philadelphia: Saunders, 1963, 21.

[191]Eccles, J. C. Possible ways in which synaptic mechanisms participate in learning, remembering, and forgetting. In D. P. Kimble (Ed.). *The anatomy of memory*. Palo Alto, Calif.: Science & Behavior Books, 1965, 17–18.

[192]McLennan, H. *Op. cit.*, 26–27.

[193]*Ibid.*, 3.

[194]Eccles, J. C. *The physiology of synapses. Op. cit.*, 138–151.

[195]*Ibid.*, 11–13.

[196]McLennan, H. *Op. cit.*, 10–11.

[197]Wurtman, R. J. Catecholamines (concluded). *N. E. J. Med.*, 1965, **273**, 746.

[198]Schmitt, F. O. & Samson, F. E., Jr. *Op. cit.*, 188–190.

[199]Eccles, J. C. *The physiology of synapses. Op. cit.*, 25.

[200]McLennan, H. *Op. cit.*, 10.

[201]Autrum, H. Nonphotic receptors in lower forms. In J. Field (Ed.). *Handbook of physiology. Section I: Neurophysiology.* Vol. 1. Washington, D.C.: Amer. Physiol. Soc., 1959, 369.

[202]*Ibid.*, 370.

[203]Eccles, J. C. *The physiology of synapses. Op. cit.*, 147–150.

[204]McLennan, H. *Op. cit.*, 21.

[205]Eccles, J. C. *The physiology of synapses. Op. cit.*, 66.

[206]McLennan, H. *Op. cit.*, 21.
Cf. also Eccles, J. C. *The physiology of synapses. Op. cit.*, 177.

[207]McLennan, H. *Op. cit.*, 34–35.
Cf. also Eccles, J. C. *The physiology of synapses. Op. cit.*, 51.

[208]McLennan, H. *Op. cit.*, 44.

[209]Eccles, J. C. *The physiology of synapses. Op. cit.*, 174–183.

[210]Somjen, G. *Sensory coding in the mammalian nervous system.* N.Y.: Appleton-Century-Crofts, 1972, 57–62.

[211]Gray, J. A. B. Initiation of impulses at receptors. In J. Field (Ed.). *Handbook of physiology. Section I: Neurophysiology.* Vol. 1. Washington, D.C.: Amer. Physiol. Soc., 1959, 129–132.

[212]Lipetz, L. E. The *Limulus* eye as an information converter. In C. A. Tobias & J. H. Lawrence (Eds.). *Advances in biological and medical physics*. Vol. 7. New York: Academic Press, 1960, 134.

[213]*Ibid.*, 134–136.

[214]*Ibid.*, 137–139.

[215]*Ibid.*, 143. Reprinted by permission.
Cf. also Somjen, G. *Op. cit.*, 127–133.

[216]Thorson, J. & Biederman-Thorson, M. Distributed relaxation processes in sensory adaptation. *Science*, 1974, **183**, 161–172.
Cf. also Somjen, G. *Op. cit.*, 39–42, 148.

[217]Schmitt, F. O. & Samson, F. E., Jr. *Op. cit.*

[218]McLennan, H. *Op. cit.*, 52.

[219]Eccles, J. C. *The physiology of synapses. Op. cit.*, 47.

[220]Wurtman, R. J. *Op. cit.*

[221]McLennan, H. *Op. cit.*, 32.

[222]Eccles, J. C. *The physiology of synapses. Op. cit.*, 29–36.

[223]Thorson, J. & Biederman-Thorson, M. *Op. cit.*

[224]*Ibid.*, 113–116.

[225]Lipetz, L. E. *Op. cit.*, 159.

[226]Eccles, J. C. *The physiology of synapses. Op. cit.*, 66.

[227]Lipetz, L. E. *Op. cit.*, 135.

[228]McLennan, H. *Op. cit.*, 55.

[229]Eccles, J. C. *The physiology of synapses. Op. cit.*, 62–64.

[230]*Ibid.*, 82.

[231]McLennan, H. *Op. cit.*, 80.

[232]*Ibid.*, 23.

[233]Gilbert, W. & Müller-Hill, B. Isolation of the lac repressor. *Proc. Nat. Acad. Sci. USA*, 1966, **56**, 1891–1898.

[234]Eigen, M. Dynamic aspects of information transfer and reaction control in biomolecular systems. In G. C. Quarton, T. Melnechuk, & F. O. Schmitt (Eds.). *The neurosciences.* New York: Rockefeller Univ. Press, 1967, 138.

[235]Jacob, F. & Monod, J. Genetic regulatory mechanisms in the synthesis of protein. *J. molec. Biol.*, 1961, **3**, 319–322.

[236]*Ibid.*, 318–325.

[237]Braun, W. *Op. cit.*, 354–356.
Cf. also Sadler, J. R. "Model" genetic controls in bacteria. In L. Goldstein (Ed.). *The control of nuclear activity*. Englewood Cliffs, N.J.: Prentice-Hall, 1967, 438.

[238]Jacob, F. & Monod, J. *Op. cit.*, 325–328.

[239]Monod, J., Changeux, J.-P., & Jacob, F. Allosteric proteins and cellular control systems. *J. molec. Biol.*, 1963, **6**, 306–307.

[240]Tomkins, G. N., Gelehrter, T. D., Granner, D., Martin, D., Jr., Samuels, H. H., & Thompson, E. B. Control of specific gene expression in higher organisms. *Science*, 1969, **166**, 1474.

[241]Jacob, F., Brenner, S., & Cuzin, F. On the regulation of DNA replication in bacteria. *Cold Spring Harbor Symposia on Quant. Biol.*, 1963, **28**, 329–348.

[242]Hess, B. Biochemical regulations. In M. D. Mesarović (Ed.). *Systems theory and biology*. New York: Springer-Verlag, 1968, **95**, 109–110.

[243]Jacob, F. & Monod, J. *Op. cit.*, 323–325.

[244]Hess, B. *Op. cit.*, 111.

[245]Giese, A. C. *Op. cit.*, 444–448.

[246]Stevens, A. R. Machinery for exchange across the nuclear envelope. In L. Goldstein (Ed.). *The control of nuclear activity.* Englewood Cliffs, N.J.: Prentice-Hall, 1967, 191–192.

[247]*Ibid.*, 192–207.

[248]Gay, H. Nucleocytoplasmic relations in *Drosophila. Cold Spring Harbor Symposia on Quant. Biol.*, 1956, **21**, 262–265.

[249]Stevens, A. R. *Op. cit.*, 189–271.

[250]Goldstein, L. & Prescott, D. M. Protein interactions between nucleus and cytoplasm. In L. Goldstein (Ed.). *The control of nuclear activity.* Englewood Cliffs, N.J.: Prentice-Hall, 1967, 273–298.

[251]Bishop. G. H. Natural history of the nerve impulse. *Physiol. Rev.*, 1956, **36**, 379.

[252]McLennan, H. *Op. cit.*, 29–31.

[253]*Ibid.*, 102–104.

[254]Eccles, J. C. *The physiology of synapses. Op. cit.*, 47.

[255]Porter, K. R. The sarcoplasmic reticulum. *Op. cit.*, 223.

[256]Eccles, J. C. *The physiology of synapses. Op. cit.*, 101.

[257]Katz, B. How cells communicate. *Sci. Amer.*, 1961, **205**(3), 212.

[258]Erlanger, J. & Gasser, H. S. *Electrical signs of nervous activity.* Philadelphia: Univ. of Pennsylvania Press, 1937.

[259]Eccles, J. C. *The physiology of synapses. Op. cit.*, 116.

[260]*Ibid.*, 104.

[261]*Ibid.*, 40.

[262]*Ibid.*, 115.

[263]Mountcastle, V. B. The neural replication of sensory events in the somatic afferent system. In J. C. Eccles (Ed.). *Brain and conscious experience.* New York: Springer-Verlag, 1966, 92.

[264]Bullock, T. H. & Horridge, G. A. *Structure and function in the nervous system of invertebrates.* San Francisco: Freeman, 1965, 233–234.

[265]McConnell, J. V. Comparative physiology: learning in invertebrates. *Ann. Rev. Physiol.*, 1966, **28**, 111–113.

[266]Gelber, B. Studies of the behaviour of *Paramecium aurelia. Anim. Behav.*, 1965, **13**(Suppl.), 21–29.
Cf. also Gelber, B. Retention in *Paramecium aurelia. J. comp. physiol. Psychol.*, 1958, **51**, 110–115.

[267]Jensen, D. D. Paramecia, planaria, and pseudo-learning. *Anim. Behav.*, 1965, **13**(Suppl.), 9–20.
Cf. also Jensen, D. D. Experiments on "learning" in paramecia. *Science*, 1957, **125**, 191–192.

[268]Magoun, H. W. Introduction. In M. A. B. Brazier (Ed.). *Brain function.* Berkeley: Univ. of California Press, 1964, 1–2.

[269]Gelber, B. Retention in *Paramecium aurelia. J. comp. physiol. Psychol.*, 1958, **51**, 112–113.

[270]Gelber, B. Studies of the behaviour of *Paramecium aurelia. Op. cit.*, 25.

[271]Jacob, F. & Monod, J. *Op. cit.*, 319–322.

[272]Edelman, G. M. Antibody structure and diversity: implications for theories of antibody synthesis. In G. C. Quarton, T. Melnechuk, & F. O. Schmitt (Eds.). *The neurosciences.* New York: Rockefeller Univ. Press, 1967, 188–200.

[273]Nossal, G. J. V. The biology of the immune response. In G. C. Quarton, T. Melnechuk, & F. O. Schmitt (Eds.). *The neurosciences.* New York: Rockefeller Univ. Press, 1967, 183–186.
Cf. also Nossal, G. J. V. How cells make antibodies. *Op. cit.*

[274]Strumwasser, F. Neurophysiological aspects of rhythms. In G. C. Quarton, T. Melnechuk, & F. O. Schmitt (Eds.). *The neurosciences.* New York: Rockefeller Univ. Press, 1967, 523–528.

[275]*Ibid.*, 525.

[276]Kandel, E. R. Cellular studies of learning. In G. C. Quarton, T. Melnechuk, & F. O. Schmitt (Eds.). *The neurosciences.* New York: Rockefeller Univ. Press, 1967, 681–684.

[277]Spencer, W. A. & Wigdor, R. Ultra-late PTP of monosynaptic reflex responses in cat. *Physiologist*, 1965, **8**, 278. (Abstract)
Cf. also Beswick, F. B. & Conroy, R. T. W. L. Optimal tetanic conditioning of heteronymous monosynaptic reflexes. *J. Physiol.*, 1965, **180**, 134–146.

[278]Kandel, E. R. *Op. cit.*, 670–672.

[279]*Ibid.*, 673.

[280]*Ibid.*, 675.

[281]*Ibid.*, 677.

[282]Morell, F. Electrical signs of sensory coding. In G. C. Quarton, T. Melnechuk, & F. O. Schmitt (Eds.). *The neurosciences.* New York: Rockefeller Univ. Press, 1967, 461–463.

[283]*Ibid.*, 467–468.

[284]*Ibid.*, 468.

[285]Kandel, E. R. *Op. cit.*, 679.

[286]*Ibid.*, 680–681.

[287]Eccles, J. C. Possible ways in which synaptic mechanisms participate in learning, remembering, and forgetting. *Op. cit.*, 12–18.

[288]Eccles, J. C. *The physiology of synapses. Op. cit.*, 83–85.

[289]Eccles, J. C. Possible ways in which synaptic mechanisms participate in learning, remembering, and forgetting. *Op. cit.*, 12–18.

[290]*Ibid.*, 13.

[291]Kandel, E. R. *Op. cit.*, 689.

[292]*Ibid.*, 681.

[293]*Ibid.*, 688.

[294]Attributed to C. S. Sherrington.

[295]Hydén, H. RNA in brain cells. In G. C. Quarton, T. Melnechuk, & F. O. Schmitt (Eds.). *The neurosciences.* New York: Rockefeller Univ. Press, 1967, 248–266.
Cf. also Hydén, H. Biochemical changes accompanying learning. In G. C. Quarton, T. Melnechuk, & F. O. Schmitt (Eds.). *The neurosciences.* Press, 1967, 765–771.

[296]Schmitt, F. O. Molecular neurobiology in the context of the neurosciences. In G. C. Quarton, T. Melnechuk, & F. O. Schmitt (Eds.). *The neurosciences.* New York: Rockefeller Univ. Press, 1967, 218.

[297]Hydén, H. Biochemical changes accompanying learning. In G. C. Quarton, T. Melnechuk, & F. O. Schmitt (Eds.). *The neurosciences.* New York: Rockefeller Univ. Press, 1967, 770.

[298]*Ibid.*, 765.

[299]Flexner, L. B., Flexner, J. B., & Roberts, R. B. Memory in mice analyzed with antibiotics. *Science*, 1967, **155**, 1377–1383.

[300]Eigen, M. *Op. cit.*, 138.

[301]Ebert, J. D. (Chairman). Gene expression. *Neurosci. Res. Prog. Bull.*, 1967, **5**(3), 251–258.

[302]Braun, W. *Op. cit.*, 349–352.

[303]Sadler, J. R. *Op. cit.*, 436–439.

[304]Wick, G. L. Molecular biology: moving toward an understanding of genetic control. *Science*, 1970, **167**, 157–159.

[305]*Ibid*

[306]Britten, R. J. & Davidson, E. H. Gene regulation for higher cells: a theory. *Science*, 1969, **165**, 349–357.
Cf. also Tomkins, G. N., Gelehrter, T. D., Granner, D., Martin, D. Jr., Samuels, H. H., & Thompson, E. B. *Op. cit.*, 1474–1480.

[307]Jacob, F., Brenner, S., & Cuzin, F. *Op. cit.*, 329–348.

[308]Adler, J. & Tso, W.-W. "Decision"-making in bacteria: chemotactic response of *Escherichia coli* to conflicting stimuli. *Science*, 1974, **184**, 1292–1294.

[309]Monod, J., Changeux, J.-P., & Jacob, F. *Op. cit.*, 324. Reprinted by permission.

[310]Darnell, J. E., Jelinek, W. R., & Molloy, G. R. Biogenesis of mRNA: genetic regulation in mammalian cells. *Op. cit.*

[311]Braun, W. *Op. cit.*, 55–58.

[312]Jacob, F., Brenner, S., & Cuzin, F. *Op. cit.*

[313]*Ibid.*, 343–344.

[314]Goldstein, L. & Prescott, D. M. Nucleocytoplasmic interactions in the control of nuclear reproduction and other cell cycle stages. *Op. cit.*, 5–9.

[315]Mazia, D. The cell cycle. *Sci. Amer.*, 1974, **230**(1), 55–64.

[316]Schneiderman, H. A. & Gilbert, L. Control of growth and development in insects. *Science*, 1964, **143**, 325.

[317]Ebert, J. D. *Op. cit.*, 232.
Cf. also Swift, H. *Op. cit.*

[318]Wood, W. B. & Edgar, R. S. Building a bacterial virus. *Sci. Amer.*, 1967, **217**(1), 60–74.

Cf. also Maugh, T. H. RNA viruses: the age of innocence ends. *Science*, 1974, **183**, 1181–1185.

[319]Davis, B. D. Metabolic regulation and information storage in bacteria. In G. C. Quarton, T. Melnechuk, & F. O. Schmitt (Eds.). *The neurosciences*. New York: Rockefeller Univ. Press, 1967, 114–115.

[320]Mazia, D. Mitosis and the physiology of cell division. *Op. cit.*, 85.

[321]Tomkins, G. N., Gelehrter, T. D., Granner, D., Martin, D. Jr., Samuels, H. H., & Thompson, E. B. *Op. cit.*, 1475.

[322]*Ibid.*, 1479.

[323]Britten, R. J. & Davidson, E. H. *Op. cit.*, 349–357.

[324]Fernández-Morán, H. Membrane ultrastructure in nerve cells. In G. C. Quarton, T. Melnechuk, & F. O. Schmitt (Eds.). *The neurosciences*. New York: Rockefeller Univ. Press, 1967, 297.

[325]Mounolou, J. C., Jakob, H., & Slonimski, P. P. Molecular nature of hereditary cytoplasmic factors affecting gene expression in mitochondria. In L. Goldstein (Ed.). *The control of nuclear activity*. Englewood Cliffs, N.J.: Prentice-Hall, 1967, 413–431.

[326]Cf. Goldberger, R. F. Autogenous regulation of gene expression. *Science*, 1974, **183**, 810–816.

[327]Braun, W. *Op. cit.*, 356.

[328]Atkinson, D. E. Biological feedback control at the molecular level. *Science*, 1965, **150**, 851–852.

[329]Huxley, H. E. *Op. cit.*, 1359.

[330]Bullock, T. H. Neuron doctrine and electrophysiology. *Science*, 1959, **129**, 998.

[331]Grundfest, H. Synaptic and ephaptic transmission. In G. C. Quarton, T. Melnechuk, & F. O. Schmitt (Eds.). *The neurosciences* New York: Rockefeller Univ. Press, 1967, 356.

[332]Eccles, J. C. Neuron physiology—introduction. In J. Field (Ed.). *Handbook of physiology. Section I: Neurophysiology*. Vol. 1. Washington, D.C.: Amer. Physiol. Soc., 1959, 65–66. Cf. also Bullock, T. H. Signals and neuronal coding. In G. C. Quarton, T. Melnechuk, & F. O. Schmitt (Eds.). *The neurosciences*. New York: Rockefeller Univ. Press, 1967, 347–352.

[333]Purpura, D. P. Comparative physiology of dendrites. In G. C. Quarton, T. Melnechuk, & F. O. Schmitt (Eds.). *The neurosciences*. New York: Rockefeller Univ. Press, 1967, 383–385.

[334]*Ibid.*, 392. Cf. also Bullock, T. H. Parameters of integrative action of the nervous system at the neuronal level. *Exper. cell. Res.*, 1958 (Suppl. 5), 330–333. Cf. also McLennan, H. *Op. cit.*, 61–62.

[335]Bullock, T. H. Parameters of integrative action of the nervous system at the neuronal level. *Exper. cell. Res.*, 1958 (Suppl. 5), 323–337.

[336]Tomkins, G. N., Gelehrter, T. D., Granner, D. Martin, D. Jr., Samuels, H. H., & Thompson, E. B. *Op. cit.*, 1476.

[337]Hess, B. *Op. cit.*, 111.

[338]Finger, I. The control of antigenic type in paramecium. In L. Goldstein (Ed.). *The control of nuclear activity*. Englewood Cliffs, N.J.: Prentice-Hall, 1967, 377–411.

[339]Marshall, N. B. *The life of fishes*. Cleveland: World, 1966, 153–159.

[340]Ortmann, R. Neurosecretion. In J. Field (Ed.). *Handbook of physiology. Section I: Neurophysiology*. Vol. 2. Washington, D. C.: Amer. Physiol. Soc., 1960, 1039–1065. Cf. also Palay, S. L. Principles of cellular organization in the nervous system. In G. C. Quarton, T. Melnechuk, & F. O. Schmitt (Eds.). *The neurosciences*. New York: Rockefeller Univ. Press, 1967, 28, 30.

[341]McLennan, H. *Op. cit.*, 23.

[342]Eccles, J. C. *The physiology of synapses. Op. cit.*, 66–70.

[343]Kopin, I. J. The adrenergic synapse. In G. C. Quarton, T. Melnechuk, & F. O. Schmitt (Eds.). *The neurosciences*. New York: Rockefeller Univ. Press, 1967, 427–429.

[344]Eccles, J. C. *The physiology of synapses. Op. cit.*, 61.

[345]Kravitz, E. A. Acetylcholine, γ-aminobutyric acid, and glutamic acid: physiological and chemical studies related to their roles as neurotransmitter agents. In G. C. Quarton, T. Melnechuk, & F. O. Schmitt (Eds.). *The neurosciences*. New York: Rockefeller Univ. Press, 1967, 440–443.

[346]Eccles, J. C. Postsynaptic inhibition in the central nervous system. In G. C. Quarton, T. Melnechuk, & F. O. Schmitt (Eds.). *The neurosciences*. New York: Rockefeller Univ. Press, 1967, 425–427.

[347]Bullock, T. H. Signals and neuronal coding. In G. C. Quarton, T. Melnechuk, & F. O. Schmitt (Eds.). *The neurosciences*. New York: Rockefeller Univ. Press, 1967, 351.

[348]*Ibid.*

[349]*Ibid.*

[350]Mountcastle, V. B. The problem of sensing and the neural coding of sensory events. In G. C. Quarton, T. Melnechuk, & F. O. Schmitt (Eds.). *The neurosciences*. New York: Rockefeller Univ. Press, 1967, 393–408.

[351]Bullock, T. H. Signals and neuronal coding. *Op. cit.*, 351.

[352]Morrell, F. *Op. cit.*, 462–467.

[353]Eccles, J. C. *The physiology of synapses. Op. cit.*, 11–25.

[354]McLennan, H. *Op. cit.*, 4.

[355]Eccles, J. C. *The physiology of synapses. Op. cit.*, 13–16.

[356]Lipetz, L. E. *Op. cit.*, 143–145.

[357]Cf. *ibid.*, 170.

[358]Eccles, J. C. *The physiology of synapses. Op cit.*, 77.

[359]Bullock, T. H. Signals and neuronal coding. *Op. cit.*, 349.

[360]Grundfest, H. *Op. cit.*, 365.

[361]McLennan, H. *Op. cit.*, 40.

[362]Eccles, J. C. *The physiology of synapses. Op. cit.*, 138–145.

[363]Giese, A. C. *Op. cit.*, 494.

[364]Harris, G. W. & Donovan, B. T. The thyroid gland. In C. H. Best & N. B. Taylor (Eds.). *The physiological basis of medical practice*. (7th ed.) Baltimore: Williams & Wilkins, 1961, 1005–1009.

[365]Chang, H.-T. The evoked potentials. In J. Field (Ed.). *Handbook of physiology. Section I: Neurophysiology*. Vol. 1. Washington, D.C.: Amer. Physiol. Soc., 1959, 302.

[366]*Ibid.*

[367]Katz, B. Depolarization of sensory terminals and the initiation of impulses in the muscle spindle. *J. Physiol.*, 1950, **111**, 261–282.

[368]Gray, J. A. B. *Op. cit.*, 126–127.

[369]*Ibid.*, 129.

[370]Mountcastle, V. B. The problem of sensing and the neural coding of sensory events. *Op. cit.*, 397–401.

[371]Galambos, R. & Davis, H. The response of single auditory-nerve fibers to acoustic stimulation. *J. Neurophysiol.*, 1943, **6**, 39–57.

[372]Gray, J. A. B. Coding in systems of primary receptor neurons. In *Symposia of the Society for Experimental Biology*. Vol. 16. *Biological receptor mechanisms*. New York: Academic Press, 1962, 349.

[373]Hunt, C. C. Relation of function to diameter in afferent fibers of muscle nerves. *J. gen. Physiol.*, 1954, **338**, 117–131.

[374]Morrell, F. *Op. cit.*, 461–467.

[375]Gray, J. A. B. Initiation of impulses at receptors. *Op. cit.*, 124.

[376]Morrell, F. *Op. cit.*, 461–462.

[377]Fain, G. L. & Dowling, J. E. Intracellular recordings from single rods and cones in the mudpuppy retina. *Science*, 1973, **180**, 1178–1181.

[378]Schmitt, F. O. & Samson, F. E., Jr. *Op. cit.*, 188.

[379]Davis, H. Excitation of auditory receptors. In J. Field (Ed.). *Handbook of physiology. Section I: Neurophysiology.* Vol. 1. Washington, D.C.: Amer. Physiol. Soc. 1959, 571–573.

[380]Gray, J. A. B. Initiation of impulses at receptors. *Op. cit.*, 138–139.

[381]Eccles, J. C. *The physiology of synapses. Op. cit.*, 85–87. NOTE: In this reference Figure 32 indicates increasing variance, as input rates go up, among sets of superimposed traces of excitatory postsynaptic potentials resulting from repeated outputs of transmitter substance. Presumably this indicates that the outputs varied similarly.

[382]*Ibid.*

[383]McLennan, H. *Op. cit.*, 36.

[384]Eccles, J. C. *The physiology of synapses. Op. cit.*, 119.

[385]*Ibid.*, 246.

[386]Giese, A. C. *Op. cit.*, 197–199.

[387]Woodruff, L. L. *Op. cit.*

[388]O'Malley, B. W. & Means, A. R. Female steroid hormones and target cell nuclei. *Science*, 1974, **183**, 610–620.

[389]Reed, L. J. Enzyme complexes. In G. C. Quarton, T. Melnechuk, & F. O. Schmitt (Eds.). *The neurosciences.* New York: Rockefeller Univ. Press, 1967, 79–83.

[390]*Ibid.*, 87–88.

[391]Lehninger, A. L. Cell organelles: the mitochondrion. *Op. cit.*, 94.

[392]Wright, B. E. Differentiation in the cellular slime mold. In M. D. Mesarović (Ed.). *Systems theory and biology.* New York: Springer-Verlag, 1968, 95, 118.

[393]Giese, A. C. *Op. cit.*, 303–314.

[394]Hess, B. *Op. cit.*, 90–91.

[395]Lehninger, A. L. Cell organelles: the mitochondrion. *Op. cit.*, 96.

[396]Gorini, L. & Maas, W. K. The potential for the formation of a biosynthetic enzyme in *Escherichia coli. Biochim. Biophys. Acta*, 1957, **25**, 208–209.

[397]Hess, B. *Op. cit.*, 92–111.

[398]Strumwasser, F. *Op. cit.*, 516.

[399]Scheibel, M. E. & Scheibel, A. B. Anatomical basis of attention mechanisms in vertebrate brains. In G. C. Quarton, T. Melnechuk, & F. O. Schmitt (Eds.). *The neurosciences.* New York: Rockefeller Univ. Press, 1967, 585–586.

[400]Hydén, H. RNA in brain cells. *Op. cit.*, 261.

[401]Eccles, J. C. *The physiology of synapses. Op. cit.*, 57–58.

[402]Kopin, I. J. *Op. cit.*, 428–429.

[403]Atkinson, D. E. *Op. cit.*, 852; cf. also note 8, page 857.

[404]*Ibid.*, 851.

[405]Changeux, J.-P. The control of biochemical reactions. *Sci. Amer.*, 1965, **212**(4), 40–41.

[406]Atkinson, D. E. Conformational change and modulation of enzyme activity. In G. C. Quarton, T. Melnechuk, & F. O. Schmitt (Eds.). *The neurosciences.* New York: Rockefeller Univ. Press, 1967, 128–129.

[407]Atkinson, D. E. Biological feedback control at the molecular level. *Op. cit.*, 854–856.

[408]*Ibid.*, 855. Cf. also Pardee, A. B. The role of enzyme regulation in metabolism. In M. X. Zarrow (Ed.). *Growth in living systems.* New York: Basic Books, 1961, 83–84.

[409]Weiss, P. Nervous system (neurogenesis). In B. H. Willier, P. A. Weiss, & V. Hamburger (Eds.). *Analysis of development.* Philadelphia: Saunders, 1955, 346–401. Cf. also Weiss, P. One plus one does not equal two. In G. C. Quarton, T. Melnechuk, & F. O. Schmitt (Eds.). *The neurosciences.* New York: Rockefeller Univ. Press, 1967, 812–814. Also M. V. Edds, Jr. Neuronal specificity in neurogenesis. In G. C. Quarton, T. Melnechuk, & F. O. Schmitt (Eds.). *The neurosciences.* New York: Rockefeller Univ. Press, 1967, 232.

[410]Schopf, J. W. & Barghoorn, E. X. Alga-like fossils from the Early Precambrian of South Africa. *Science*, 1967, **156**, 508–511.

[411]Oparin, A. I. History of the subject matter of the conference. In S. W. Fox (Ed.). *The origin of prebiological systems.* New York: Academic Press, 1965, 97. Also Mills, D. R., Kramer, F. R., & Spiegelman, S. Complete nucleotide sequence of a replicating RNA molecule. *Science*, 1973, **180**, 916–927. NOTE: A chemical examination has been made of a portion of the Murchison meteorite, a carbonaceous chondrite which fell near Murchison, Victoria, Australia on September 28, 1969. Meticulous techniques were used to prevent contamination by molecules from Earth which are found in biological systems. Convincing evidence was obtained that the meteorite contained significant amounts of several amino acids and hydrocarbons. There was some indication that the molecules found were of types not formed in terrestrial biological systems. These findings are reported in K. Kvenvolden, J. Lawless, K. Pering, E. Peterson, J. Flores, C. Ponnamperuma, I. R. Kaplan, & C. Moore. Evidence for extraterrestrial amino-acids and hydrocarbons in the Murchison meteorite. *Nature*, 1970, **228**, 923–926.

[412]Sagan, C. Primordial ultraviolet synthesis of nucleoside phosphates. In S. W. Fox (Ed.). *The origin of prebiological systems.* New York: Academic Press, 1965, 207–210.

[413]Miller, S. L. A production of amino acids under possible primitive earth conditions. *Science*, 1953, **117**, 528–529.

[414]Harada, K. & Fox, S. W. The thermal synthesis of amino acids from a hypothetically primitive terrestrial atmosphere. In S. W. Fox (Ed.). *The origin of prebiological systems.* New York: Academic Press, 1965, 187–193.

[415]Calvin, M. *Op. cit.*, 782.

[416]Ponnamperuma, C. & Mack, R. Nucleotide synthesis under possible primitive earth conditions. *Science*, 1965, **148**, 1221. Cf. also Schramm, G. Synthesis of nucleosides and polynucleotides with metaphosphate esters. In S. W. Fox (Ed.). *The origin of prebiological systems.* New York: Academic Press, 1965, 299–309.

[417]Fox, S. W. Simulated natural experiments in spontaneous organization of morphological units from proteinoid. In S. W. Fox (Ed.). *The origin of prebiological systems.* New York: Academic Press, 1965, 361–373.

[418]Oparin, A. I. The pathways of the primary development of metabolism and artificial modeling of this development in coacervate drops. In S. W. Fox (Ed.). *The origin of prebiological systems.* New York: Academic Press, 1965, 331–341.

[419]Calvin, M. *Op. cit.*, 789. Cf. also Bernal, J. D. Molecular matrices for living systems. In S. W. Fox (Ed.). *The origin of prebiological systems.* New York: Academic Press, 1965, 76–82.

[420]Wood, W. B. & Edgar, R. S. *Op. cit.*, 61.

[421]Lehninger, A. L. Cell organelles: the mitochondrion. *Op. cit.*, 100.

[422]Lipmann, F. Projecting backward from the present stage of evolution of biosynthesis. In S. W. Fox (Ed.). *The origin of prebiological systems.* New York: Academic Press, 1965, 261–265.

[423]Gaffron, H. The role of light in evolution. In S. W. Fox (Ed.). *The origin of prebiological systems.* New York: Academic Press, 1965, 437–455.

[424]Eigen, M. *Op. cit.*, 132.

[425]Davis, B. D. *Op. cit.*, 119.

[426]Atkinson, D. E. Conformational change and modulation of enzyme activity. *Op. cit.*, 129.

[427]Monod, J., Changeux, J.-P., & Jacob, F. *Op. cit.*, 324–325.

[428]Jukes, T. H. Coding triplets in evolution. In S. W. Fox (Ed.).

The origin of prebiological systems. New York: Academic Press, 1965, 407–436.

[429]*Ibid.*, 426–433.

[430]Neurath, H., Walsh, K. A., & Winter, W. P. Evolution of structure and function of proteases. *Science,* 1967, **158,** 1643.

[431]Yost, H. T. *Cellular physiology.* Englewood Cliffs, N.J.: Prentice-Hall, 1972, 869–870.

[432]Goldstein, L. & Prescott, D. M. Nucleocytoplasmic interactions in the control of nuclear reproduction and other cell cycle stages. *Op. cit.,* 5–6.

[433]Ebert, J. D. (Chairman). *Op. cit.,* 287.

[434]Goldstein, L. & Prescott, D. M. Nucleocytoplasmic interactions in the control of nuclear reproduction and other cell cycle stages. *Op. cit.,* 5–6.

[435]Yost, H. T. *Op. cit.,* 863.

[436]*Ibid.,* 879.

[437]Mazia, D. Mitosis and the physiology of cell division. *Op. cit.,* 98–103.

[438]*Ibid.,* 369.

[439]*Ibid.,* 101.

[440]Nierlich, D. P. Regulation of bacterial growth. *Science,* 1974, **184,** 1043–1050.

[441]Kafotos, F. C. & Feder, N. Cytodifferentiation during insect metamorphosis: the galea of silkmoths. *Science,* 1968, **161,** 470–472.

[442]Wessells, N. K. & Rutter, W. J. Phases in cell differentiation. *Sci. Amer.,* 1969, **220**(3), 36–44.

[443]Ebert, J. D. Molecular and cellular interactions in development. In G. C. Quarton, T. Melnechuk, & F. O. Schmitt (Eds.). *The neurosciences.* New York: Rockefeller Univ. Press, 1967, 243–244.

[444]Cahn, R. D. & Cahn, M. B. Heritability of cellular differentiation: clonal growth and expression of differentiation in retinal pigment cells *in vitro. Proc. Nat. Acad. Sci. USA,* 1966, **55,** 106–114.
Also Coon, H. Clonal stability and phenotypic expression of chick cartilage cells *in vitro. Proc. Nat. Acad. Sci. USA,* 1966, **55,** 66–73.

[445]Ebert, J. D. Molecular and cellular interactions in development. *Op. cit.,* 244.

[446]Ebert, J. D. (Chairman). Gene expression. *Op. cit.,* 279–285.

[447]Holtzer, H., Weintraub, H., & Biehl, J. Cell cycle-dependent events during myogenesis, neurogenesis, and erythrogenesis. In A. Monroy and R. Tsanev (Eds.). *Biochemistry of cell differentiation.* New York: Academic Press, 1973, 41–42.

[448]Holtzer, H. The cell cycle and myogenesis. In R. Harris, P. Allin, & D. Viza. *Cell differentiation.* Copenhagen: Munksgaard, 1972, 331–333.

[449]Allen, R. D. Ameboid movement. In J. Brachet & A. E. Mirsky (Eds.). *The cell.* Vol. 2. New York: Academic Press, 1961, 185–186.

[450]Lehninger, A. L. Molecular biology: the theme of conformation. *Op. cit.,* 37.
Also Davidson, N. Weak interactions and the structure of biological macromolecules. In G. C. Quarton, T. Melnechuk, & F. O. Schmitt (Eds.). *The neurosciences.* New York: Rockefeller Univ. Press, 1967, 47.

[451]Giese, A. C. *Op. cit.,* 46.

[452]Lehninger, A. L. Molecular biology: the theme of conformation. *Op. cit.,* 42–44.

[453]Giese, A. C. *Op. cit.,* 77–78.

[454]Wald, G. The photoreceptor process in vision. In J. Field (Ed.). *Handbook of physiology. Section I: Neurophysiology.* Vol. 1. Washington, D.C.: Amer. Physiol. Soc., 1959, 688–691.

[455]Goldstein, L. & Prescott, D. M. Nucleocytoplasmic interactions in the control of nuclear reproduction and other cell cycle stages. *Op. cit.,* 6.

[456]Mazia, D. Mitosis and the physiology of cell division. *Op. cit.,* 147.

[457]Giese, A. C. *Op. cit.,* 195–197.

[458]Zeuthen, E. Synchronized growth in Tetrahymena cells. In M. X. Zarrow (Ed.). *Growth in living systems.* New York: Basic Books, 1961, 154.

[459]Puck, T. T. Mammalian cell growth in tissue culture. In M. X. Zarrow (Ed.). *Growth in living systems.* New York: Basic Books, 1961, 187–188.

[460]Giese, A. C. *Op. cit.,* 177–179.

[461]Kravitz, E. A. *Op. cit.,* 438.

[462]Trager, W. Intracellular parasitism and symbiosis. In J. Brachet & A. E. Mirsky (Eds.). *The cell.* Vol. 4. New York: Academic Press, 1960, 153.

[463]Giese, A. C. *Op. cit.,* 523.

[464]Ebert, J. D. (Chairman). Gene expression. *Op. cit.,* 279–285.

[465]Mazia, D. Mitosis and the physiology of cell division. *Op. cit.,* 103.

[466]Marx, J. L. *Op. cit.*

[467]Maugh, T. H. RNA viruses: the age of innocence ends. *Science,* 1974, **183,** 1181–1185.

[468]Weiss, L. & Mayhew, E. *Op. cit.,* 1357.

[469]Oberling, C. & Bernhard, W. The morphology of the cancer cells. In J. Brachet & A. E. Mirsky (Eds.). *The cell.* Vol. 5. New York: Academic Press, 1961, **407,** 482–484.

[470]Weiss, L. & Mayhew, E. *Op. cit.,* 1358–1360.
Also Marx, J. L. *Op. cit.*

[471]Le Breton, E. & Moulé, Y. Biochemistry and physiology of the cancer cell. In J. Brachet & A. E. Mirsky (Eds.). *The cell.* Vol. 5. New York: Academic Press, 1961, 523.

[472]Ebert, J. D. Molecular and cellular interactions in development. *Op. cit.,* 242–243.

[473]Ebert, J. D. (Chairman). Gene expression. *Op. cit.,* 263–266. Cf. also Rubin, H. Overgrowth stimulating factor released from Rous sarcoma cells. *Science,* 1970, **167,** 1271–1272.

[474]Anon. Chromosome imbalance may lead to cancers. *Chem. & Engin. News,* 1968, **46**(23), 46–48.

[475]Ebert, J. D. Molecular and cellular interactions in development. *Op. cit.,* 243.

[476]Braun, A. C. The origin of the plant tumor cell. In M. X. Zarrow (Ed.). *Growth in living systems.* New York: Basic Books, 1961, 605–619.

[477]Mazia, D. Mitosis and physiology of cell division. *Op. cit.,* 82–83.

[478]Williams, C. M. Insect metamorphosis: an approach to the study of growth. In M. X. Zarrow (Ed.). *Growth in living systems.* New York: Basic Books, 1961, 318.

[479]Ebert, J. D. (Chairman). Gene expression. *Op. cit.,* 268.

[480]Hydén, H. The neuron. In J. Brachet & A. E. Mirsky (Eds.). *The cell.* Vol. 4. New York: Academic Press, 1960, 299–302.

[481]Wheeler, K. T. & Lett, J. T. On the possibility that DNA repair is related to age in non-dividing cells. *Proc. Nat. Acad. Sci. USA,* 1974, **71,** 1862–1865.

[482]Crosby, E. C., Humphrey, T., & Lauer, E. W. *Op. cit.,* 34–37.

[483]McAlister, A. J. Analog study of a single neuron in a volume conductor. *Naval Med. Res. Inst. Report, N. M. 010500.01.01.* 1958, **16,** 1011–1022.

[484]Harmon, L. D. Studies with artificial neurons I. *Kybernetik,* 1963, **1,** 89–101.

[485]Fukuda, N. & Sugita, M. Mathematical analysis of metabolism using an analogue computer: I. Isotope kinetics of iodine metabolism in the thyroid gland. *J. theoret. Biol.,* 1961, **1,** 440–459.

[486]Estabrook, R. W. Observations on the antimycin A inhibi-

tion of biological oxidations. II. Electronic analog computer studies. *Biochim. Biophys. Acta,* 1962, **60,** 249–258.

[487]Stahl, W. R., Coffin, R. W., & Goheen, H. E. Simulation of biological cells by systems composed of string-processing finite automata. *Amer. Fed. Information Processing Soc. Conference Proc., Spring Joint Computer Conference,* 1964, **25,** 89–102.

Also Stark, L. & Dickson, J. F., III. Mathematical concepts of central nervous system function. *Neurosci. Res. Prog. Bull.* 1965, **3,** 30–31.

[488]Chance, B. Analog and digital representation of enzyme kinetics. *J. biol. Chem.,* 1960, **235,** 2426–2439.

[489]Hess, B. *Op. cit.,* 110.

[490]Garfinkel, D., Rutledge, H. D., & Higgins, J. J. Simulation and analysis of biochemical systems. I. Representation of chemical kinetics. *Comm. Assoc. Comp. Mach.,* 1961, **4,** 559–562.

[491]Wright, B. E. The use of kinetic models to analyze differentiation. *Behav. Sci.,* 1970, **15,** 37–45.

[492]*Ibid.,* 40–45.

[493]Diehn, B. *Op. cit.,* 1013–1014.

[494]Ware, G. C. The simulation of bacterial cultures on a digital computer. *J. theoret. Biol.,* 1967, **17,** 91–107.

[495]Fraser, A. & Burnell, D. Simulation of genetic systems. XII. Models of inversion polymorphism. *Genetics,* 1967, **57,** 267–282.

The Organ

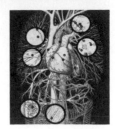

Organs, the level of systems discussed in this chapter, are the subsystems of organisms, animal and plant, although in some species the degree of differentiation is not great. I use the term "organ" to mean "all the components which carry out the processes of a given subsystem of an organism"—subsystem being defined as I use it throughout this book (see page 30). This is like one common meaning of "organ," "a part of the body having a special function,"[1] and different from another current usage, "a more or less independent portion of the body, having a tissue framework, and a special blood, lymph, and nerve supply in addition to its characteristic essential cells."[2] The first two definitions, of course, emphasize process; the third emphasizes structure. The independence referred to in the third definition is structural separateness, not totipotentiality of process.

The organs of an organism are formed from tissues. A tissue is a collection of adjacent cells of like origin and structure which carry out similar, specialized processes. Tissues do not constitute a level of living system because they do not have the essential subsystem— a decider—to coordinate all tissue of a particular kind throughout the organism.

No organ is able to survive by itself, although some tissues can be kept alive for varying lengths of time outside the organism if the temperature and chemical environment are like their usual surroundings.

Two sets of species of minute, wormlike parasites, ranging from less than a millimeter to a few millimeters in length, are classified as *mesozoans*.[3] They infest organisms such as squid and octopuses, and depend on them to carry out some critical subsystem processes. They constitute links between single free-liv-

ing cells and multicellular organisms (see Fig. 7-1). In dicyemid mesozoans there are no discrete subsystems. All their processes are downwardly dispersed to the cellular level, but dicyemids are too complex to be colonial protozoans. In each species of mesozoan the number and arrangement of cells are relatively constant from individual to individual. These partipotential aggregations of cells appear to come as close as any system now living does to being free-living organs.

One can make a case for not considering organs to be a level of living system at all (see page 25). As the structure and process of the subsystems of organs are described below, however, it will become clear that most of the critical subsystems characteristic of living systems exist in at least some organs, enough to justify conceiving of organs as a level. Using "organ" as I define it does not depart too far from the Oxford dictionary definition: "A part or member of an animal or plant body adapted by its structure for a particular vital function." I shall use the words "component" or "part" for one of those unitary, localized structures which some others call an "organ." This will keep clear a distinction between structure and process which many biologists neglect. At some places I use terms that are traditional in biology and medicine, *e.g., nervous system* and *vascular system*, because using my terminology instead would confuse many readers. In my terms the nervous system is an organism component which includes several organs or subsystems. The vascular system is a component of the organism's distributor organ or subsystem.

The term "organ" is sometimes applied quite loosely to refer to both the entire nervous system and also parts of it, like the brain. According to my usage,

315

neither is accurate. The nervous system comprises all the nervous tissue in the body. It has important divisions within it. It includes the structural components of nearly all the information processing subsystems of the organism, though these cannot all be definitely

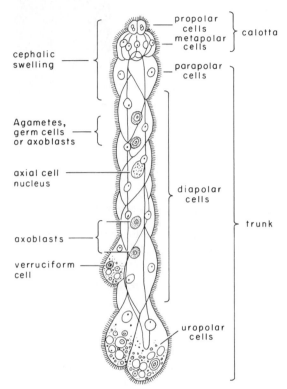

cephalic swelling

propolar cells
metapolar cells
} calotta

parapolar cells

Agametes, germ cells or axoblasts

axial cell nucleus

diapolar cells

} trunk

axoblasts

verruciform cell

uropolar cells

Fig. 7-1 Mesozoan (a dicyemid). [From B. H. McConnoughey. *Mesozoa.* In P. Gray (Ed.). *The encyclopedia of the biological sciences* (2d ed.). New York: Van Nostrand Reinhold, 1970, 547. *Reprinted by permission.*]

ascribed to a given region or subdivision of the nervous system. Another implication of this definition is that an organ defined structurally is often not the same thing as an organ defined, as I do, in terms of the process it carries out. Consider the pancreas, for instance. Glands throughout the organism are of two types: exocrine (secreting into body cavities that lead to the outside) and endocrine (secreting internally into tissue space and bodily distributor subsystems). The pancreas is a single component that includes both types—exocrine gland cells, that carry out some processes of the matter-energy processing converter, and endocrine gland cells that carry out some, but not all, control functions of the information processing decider. Both, however, are enclosed in one capsule, the

endocrine islets of Langerhans being dispersed throughout the pancreatic substance. The pancreas is one of several components that contain parts of more than one subsystem. Especially in lower phyla of organisms, a single component may carry out processes of several combined subsystems. Sponges have tissues that are somewhat specialized to perform various specific subsystem processes, but they have no component sufficiently differentiated to be a local subsystem (see page 31). Coelenterates, like *Hydra* and *Medusa*, have a single opening into the body, a "mouth" which serves for both ingesting and extruding. Occasionally highly evolved organisms have one or more single components each of which carries out a single subsystem process. Frequently one component is involved in multiple processes. The liver, for example, carries out at least 13 different processes after birth, plus others which occur only in the embryo.[4] These are processes of a number of different matter-energy and information processing subsystems. Some of an organism's subsystems may be laterally dispersed into a number of different, and sometimes widely separated, components. The extruder in man, for example, includes the skin, the lungs, the kidneys, the rectum, and the anus. Extruders of some other organisms have added components: the venom glands of the rattlesnake or the special glands of the skunk that deliver its odorous product. These extruder components are linked by control processes and are often related embryologically.

1. Structure

All the tissues in animal organs are differentiated from the three layers of the embryo, the outer covering or *ectoderm,* a middle layer or *mesoderm,* and an inner layer or *endoderm.* In man and other vertebrates, the continuing differentiation and organization of the cells of these layers produces the four primary tissues out of which the organs and components of the organism are formed. As organs form, further adaptation of the basic cell types occurs so that cells of a given organ component are readily distinguishable from cells derived from the same embryonic layer but found in other components. Organs ordinarily include all four of the primary tissues. The four basic tissues are: epithelium, connective tissue, muscular tissue, and nervous tissue. Tissues derived from one of these primary tissues may be as different as blood and bone, but the cells which come from any of the primary tissues and their manner of aggregating have common characteristics. I have already described the cells of these fundamental tissues (see pages 210 to 216).

Epithelium is a sheet of epithelial cells arranged in one or more layers. These cells lie close together, with little cementing substance between them. Their shape in the layer is determined by the pressure exerted on them by other cells and by the movements of the organ they are in, which may stretch or flatten them. The epithelia which are coverings have connective tissue under them, and between these two tissues a basement membrane is ordinarily found which is formed from the intercellular substances of the connective tissue at the point of contact with the epithelial tissue.

Epithelium derived from the embryonic ectoderm forms the outer layer of the skin and its associated structures. It lines internal cavities and organ components and forms most glands as well as parts of the sense organs, including the cornea and lens of the eye. Epithelia derived from the other embryonic layers also form linings and glands. Epithelium derived from endoderm furnishes the lining and glands of the intestinal and respiratory systems. That of mesodermal origin is found in urinary and genital components and lines the blood and lymph vessels.

Glandular epithelium consists of epithelial cells that are specialized for secretion. They may occur singly, like those that secrete mucus, or in multicellular glands.

Connective tissues are derived from the embryonic mesoderm. This is an extremely varied group of tissues including blood and lymphatic tissues, connective tissue proper, cartilage, and bone. While these appear completely different, they do have attributes in common. All the tissues of this group are characterized by abundant intercellular substance, varying from the liquid in which the red corpuscles and white blood cells are suspended through jellylike or rubbery texture to the hard, lime-impregnated fibers of bone. Fibers are usually in this intercellular substance, although in blood they are not evident until it clots, when a dispersed protein, known as fibrinogen, aggregates into threads that form an interlacing meshwork. Lymph, which is related to blood, also clots.

Human blood is composed of red corpuscles, white cells, and platelets circulating in a fluid plasma about 91 percent water. Forty-six percent of the blood volume is made up of red corpuscles, white cells, and platelets, and 54 percent is plasma, in which are found proteins, antibodies, hormones, enzymes, and other organic and inorganic compounds. Some oxygen and carbon dioxide are carried in simple solution in the plasma, but this amounts to only about 1 percent of the total oxygen and a small percentage of the carbon dioxide. The bulk of these gases is carried in chemical combination, the oxygen in the hemoglobin of the red corpuscles, the carbon dioxide in the form of bicarbonate in both red corpuscles and plasma.

Other connective tissues are: (1) Loose connective tissue, a whitish, sticky mass which is largely intercellular substance with long fibers running through it. A number of different types of cells, some of which I have already described (see pages 210 to 213)—including wandering white blood cells, fibroblasts, macrophages, plasma cells, pigment cells, and fat cells among others—are found scattered within this mass. This tissue surrounds and penetrates between the elements of other tissues.

(2) Dense connective tissue, which is found underlying the skin and in some other parts of the body, has elements similar to the loose tissue, but the fibers here are in thick bundles which are woven into a compact feltwork, with elastic networks. Cells are hard to find in all this surrounding intercellular substance.

(3) Regular connective tissue includes tendons, ligaments and other structures, such as the fibrous membranes surrounding organs. The components of these tissues are arranged to comply with the mechanical requirements of the particular tissue so that, for example, tendons form a flexible tissue, offering great resistance to a pulling force. The fibrous membranes of organs may be arranged in sheets.

There are also special connective tissues, such as the reticular tissues which form networks supporting the spleen and many glands. These tissues also have fibers that form networks surrounding and supporting cells or multicellular structures in their meshes. Adipose tissue is a loose connective tissue in which fat cells have displaced most of the other elements (see page 211). Tissues which form or destroy blood, such as the bone marrow, also belong to this group.

Cartilage is a connective tissue which has its intercellular substance in a solid mass with its cells lying in special cavities. The cells of bone also have the cells in "lacunae" widely separated in the dense, calcified intercellular substance.

The three classes of *muscular tissue,* striated or voluntary (skeletal), cardiac, and smooth (involuntary), are all differentiated from the mesoderm. The only exceptions are the muscles of the sweat glands and iris, which are ectodermal in origin, like the skin in which the sweat glands are found and the nervous tissue with which the iris is associated in development.

Smooth muscle is found in the blood vessels and viscera, in the capsules of some glands, scattered in the connective tissue which underlies the skin, connected to the hair follicles, and in some other organs and components of the organism.

Smooth-muscle fibers may occur singly or in small groups, as they do in the skin, where they are welded to the collagenous bundles of connective-tissue fibers. Sometimes they join together into a small muscle, as in those which are connected to the hair follicles. In other places, as in the walls of vessels and hollow viscera, they may be arranged in layers. Sometimes several layers are present, and when this is the case, all the fibers of each layer are oriented in the same direction. The various layers may have different directions, as in the intestine where the internal layer is arranged circularly and the external longitudinally. Connective-tissue fibers from outside the muscle cells continue into the spaces between and bind them into bundles. Between the bundles is loose connective tissue, with fibroblasts, wandering cells, and collagenous and elastic fibers. It is true here, and in other tissues as well, that extensions of the organism's vascular and nervous components penetrate throughout (see page 317 and below). Most smooth muscle is supplied by the autonomic division of the nervous system, but in a few places the skeletal nervous system provides part or all of the innervation. There are also reticular fibers forming a kind of sheath around each muscle cell, acting as a support.

The much larger, multinucleated cells of striated (skeletal) muscles have already been described (see pages 213 and 214). Skeletal muscles are formed of parallel bundles of muscle fibers, held together by connective tissue. Primary bundles are bound into secondary bundles, and these into tertiary bundles. A man's thigh muscle or any other such large muscle consists of many such bundles. Each muscle has its origin and insertion where the ends are attached to bones, cartilage, ligaments, or fascia (connective-tissue layers under the skin), either directly or by a tendon. In small muscles, the muscle fibers may continue for the length of the muscle. In larger ones, one end may be attached to a tendon while the other lies within the muscle, or both ends may be free in the muscle. Muscles are rich in blood vessels. Capillaries form a network throughout. The main nerve supply of striated muscle is from the cerebrospinal division of the nervous system (see pages 374 and 375). The rule is that each fiber is supplied by a terminal from a neuron with which it makes contact at the motor end plate of the neuromyal junction (see page 249 and Fig. 6-17).

The cardiac muscle of vertebrates is composed of a type of muscle which is unique to the heart. It resembles skeletal muscle in being striated, but like smooth muscle it is involuntary (see page 214). It receives its nerve supply from the autonomic division of the nervous system (see pages 336 and 337).

Nervous tissue includes the entire nervous system of the organism. It is all interconnected but is divided into the central nervous system—the brain and spinal cord—and the peripheral nervous system, which has cerebrospinal and autonomic divisions (see page 392). There are differences among these components in both structure and process. Such differences include size of cells, number and length of processes, number of other cells contacted by each synapse, diameter of fiber, and number of neurons in the chain.

Nervous tissue includes both the neurons and their associated glia, all bathed in intercellular fluid, which is capable of conducting electrical currents (see page 262). The entire nervous system except for the microglia, is ectodermal in origin. There are, however, connective-tissue layers protecting nervous structures. As the central nervous tissue is organized, glia outnumber neurons about ten to one.[5] Neurons are surrounded by glia. Capillaries from the organism's vascular system contact glia rather than neurons.[6]

I have already described neurons (see pages 214 to 216) and glia (see page 216). The point of contact between neurons is the synapse if the marker transmitted is chemical; the point of contact is the ephapse if the marker is electrical (see pages 248, 249, 254, and 255, Fig. 6-16, and page 337). Nervous tissue in the central nervous system is densely packed with neural and glial cells.[7] In the peripheral nervous system, neurons and their associated Schwann cells or other sheath cells form bundles—the nerves. The nerves may be parts of even larger bundles in which the component nerves come from different areas of the body, different input transducers, different areas of the central nervous system, or different divisions of the nervous system. Many nerves are surrounded by connective-tissue sheaths (see page 216).

The four fundamental tissues just described are represented in different proportions in the various organs and components of the organism. Some components, for example, may be highly vascular, others much less so. The essential cellular components peculiar to any part, *e.g.*, the glandular cells of the liver or the glomerular and tubular cells of the kidney, are known as the *parenchyma*. The accessory, supporting tissues are called the *stroma*. Differentiation among tissues of similar origin may be great, in the type of cell, its arrangement in the tissue, its color, its texture, its type of product, or the process carried out by the tissue as a whole.

As an example of how the various tissues are intermingled in specific organ components, I shall describe the stomach, which is a part of the converter subsystem of the organism. Less detailed structural descriptions of other organs and components will be given under the relevant subsystems.

The stomach as a component has tissues derived from all the fundamental tissues. The epithelium lining it and its glands are of endodermal origin. The muscles and connective tissue of the walls, including the blood vessels, are mesodermal in origin, and the nerve cells and nerve fibers within the walls are ectodermal. There are marked variations in the structure of the stomach among different species of organisms. The human stomach is a single pouch, lined with a mucous membrane which is covered by a single layer of cells forming an epithelium. The surface of this is furrowed and pitted. At the bottom of these pits are the openings of the multitude of glands which lie within the mucosa. There are three areas which contain different kinds of glands. The first is at the top, or cardia, of the stomach. The second occupies about two-thirds of the remaining area and contains the gastric glands proper. The third is the pyloric region which continues into the pylorus, the opening into the intestinal tract. In the human organism these grade into one another, but some other organisms have separate chambers in the stomach. Between the glands, the mucous membrane consists of a connective-tissue framework containing lymphoid tissue. Below this is a thin layer of smooth-muscle fiber. The submucous coat is of loose connective tissue. Outside it are three layers of smooth muscle, an outer longitudinal, middle circular, and inner oblique layer. Then there is a connective-tissue coat with elastic nets. The outermost layer is a covering of peritoneal epithelium.

1.1 System size   In microscopic plants and animals the smallest organs are only a few cells in size, being of the order of about 10^{-5} meter (m) in diameter. The largest organs are probably the boundaries of the largest sequoia trees (at times more than 300 m in height and 9 m in trunk diameter). The largest animal organs are either the boundaries of whales (at times more than 32 m in length) or the converters of some large animals. A single component of the converter, the small intestine, in the elephant can be more than 60 m long. Considering the fact that there are more small plant and animal species than large and that the small species have many more members than the large, the median diameter of organs is perhaps about 10^{-3} m.

1.2 Structural taxonomy of types of systems Organs are ordinarily not classified according to structure. Sometimes, however, the distinction between hollow and solid organ components is made.

2. Process

Each of the fundamental tissues which were described above is differentiated so that it is particularly suited to carry out certain processes. Within each wider group, other modifications occur which further increase the capacity of a given tissue for the process which it carries out. Some of these alterations are determined by the genetic template. Others are responses to local conditions in the tissue (see pages 351, 468, and 469).

How the primitive progenitor cells have become differentiated and specialized for various processes in different tissues is truly impressive. All matter-energy inputs to and outputs from the body pass through epithelium.[8] Within the connective-tissue group, for instance, the difference in consistency of the intercel-

lular substance makes loose connective tissue a soft sort of packing between components of the organism and makes bone the sturdy supporter that it is. Some connective tissue is elastic for stretchability. The close relationship among the cells of cardiac muscle favors conduction of impulses across the whole component. Smooth-muscle cells in the walls of organs that contract are surrounded by reticular fibers and exert their pull first on the fiber, permitting the force of contraction of an entire layer around a component to be uniform. Cardiac- and smooth-muscle cells are "myogenic," which means that they "beat" or contract regularly without need of a nerve supply. Denervated hearts continue to beat, even while being transplanted from one body to another. Hearts of embryos beat before they are innervated. Skeletal muscle, more highly specialized for holding the body in place and moving it about, has lost this characteristic. Nervous tissue varies in rates of conduction along fibers and in many other ways (see pages 214 to 216, 248 to 254, 262 and 263, 336 and 337).

Within each organ, special modifications fit its tissues to their specific task in the economy of the whole. The human converter, for example, is so arranged that each succeeding tissue carries on a new step in the converting of matter-energy input. Crushing by teeth, bone, and muscle, and chemical action by the enzyme ptyalin in the saliva begin the process in the mouth. The muscular layers of the stomach provide the kneading, churning motion which brings all parts of the mass of food into contact with the digestive juices so that chemical reactions can take place. When the process is complete, the pylorus opens and peristaltic waves move the resultant "chyle" a small amount at a time into the intestine, where further converting occurs. Finally, the product of the organ is absorbed by cells of its wall and passed through its boundary into the organism's distributor while waste is extruded into the organ's environment.

2.1 System and subsystem indicators   A large number of indicators are used to measure variables of various organs, either in or out of the organism of which they are parts. The normal ranges for each of these variables differ from species to species. These indicators include: size; shape; appearance; texture; consistency; microscopic appearance; position in the organism; appearance on x-ray; rate of movement (*e.g.*, breathing, beating); regularity of movement; rate of input or of output of various sorts of matter or energy (*e.g.*, lymph, blood, urine, bile, potassium, chloride, bicarbonate, oxygen, carbon dioxide, calories); acidity of various substances; concentration of various substances in the blood, lymph, urine, stool, tissues (*e.g.*, sodium, calcium, glucose, enzymes); or voltage, amperage, or waveforms of electrical activity in various tissues (*e.g.,* neural tissue, heart, muscle, brain).

Some system indicators of input–output relationships of organs require interference with structure and process of the organism, but other such measures can be obtained from intact organisms. Numerous mechanical devices have been used to secure information about the mean arterial flow rate in an organ.[9] These often require anesthesia, injection of an anticoagulant, and insertion between the cut ends of the vessel in which the flow is being measured. Moment-to-moment changes may be measured by such devices. One measures the differential pressure between two points in the flow. Sonar and electromagnetic devices are also used. Blood flow can also be measured by observing it directly by microscopy or indirectly by high-speed photography, in small components of the distributor, *e.g.,* in capillaries of such thin tissues as rabbit ears, frog skin, and bat wing. It can be measured in the hearts of intact human and animal organisms by x-ray motion-picture photography following injection of a contrast substance into the coronary arteries.

Another method is to collect and measure outflow from a vein that drains a particular organ or organ component. The rate of flow can be read from a graduate or determined by the change in weight of a container. For low rates of flow, drop recorders—in which each drop shorts electrical contacts or interrupts the beam of a photocell—may be employed. Some of the chief ways indicators are used to measure variables of organ processes are the following:

(*a*) Differences at a given moment between the composition of blood in an artery (or, in the liver, the portal vein) entering an organ or organ component and a vein leaving it show how much of any substance is added to or removed from the blood that flows through its vessels.[10] Similarly one can measure the amount of a substance injected into the bloodstream that is removed as it flows through the organ or component. The amount input to the organ from the blood, or output from the organ into it, is equal to the difference between the amount in a standard quantity of the input blood and the amount in a similar quantity of the output blood. Such a calculation can be used to determine the rate at which the heart puts out blood. One way of doing this requires one first to determine the difference between the oxygen content of a standard amount of venous blood going into the lungs (obtained through a heart catheter) and the same amount of arterial blood taken at the same moment. Then one can divide this difference in oxygen content into a measure of the total oxygen consumption of the body in a unit of time (say a minute). The quotient represents the rate of output of blood by the heart per minute.

The discovery that sugar is stored in the liver was made by such a procedure. In the nineteenth century Bernard compared the glucose concentrations in the blood of the portal vein and the hepatic vein—the input and output of the liver.[11] During a meal, there is a higher concentration of glucose in the portal than in the hepatic vein. After a fast, this relationship is reversed as the glucose is removed from storage and output into the general bodily blood circulation.

(*b*) Injections of different substances into the bloodstream and determination of their concentration at a later time can also be used as indicators measuring organ variables. This procedure depends upon knowledge of functions of organs during health. For instance, certain compounds which are known not to be stored, but which are excreted entirely by the liver through the common bile duct into the intestine, can be injected into the blood. Then their rate of disappearance from the serum is determined. Less than 5 percent of one of these, Bromsulphalein is normally retained after 45 minutes (min). Filtration of substances from the kidney into the urine can be studied in much the same way. Such filtration occurs both in the glomeruli and in the tubules of the kidney. A compound which, after filtration through the glomeruli, is neither reabsorbed into the blood nor secreted in the tubules (*e.g.,* inulin, a starchlike polymer of the sugar fructose, obtained from dahlia tubers) can be injected into the bloodstream. The rate of glomerular filtration can then be calculated by the rate at which this injected substance is excreted in the urine. Under normal conditions glucose does not appear in the urine. After being filtered through the kidney glomeruli it is absorbed by the kidney tubules back into the blood. The rate of reabsorption of glucose by the kidney back into the bloodstream can be determined by overloading the blood plasma with glucose. With an overload, an amount appears in the urine proportional to the amount added to the blood.

(*c*) Another method indirectly studies organs which are difficult to investigate directly, by making determinations upon other easily available bodily components which are known to have specific process relationships with that organ. The sugar-storing function of a liver, for example, can be evaluated clinically by giving a fasting organism the sugar levulose, after first determining the blood sugar level, and then testing the blood at regular intervals for 2 hours (h). Only the liver converts levulose to a form appropriate for storing —glycogen—and then stores it. If, therefore, there is no liver disease, the blood sugar will rise only a little. If the liver is functioning poorly, there will be a marked increase.

(*d*) Another related method is to inject a substance which is "labeled" by radioactivity. Its distribution in organs and its excretion can then be traced by x-ray or fluoroscopy. A common diagnostic technique involves ingestion of a radioactive dye into a patient's bloodstream and observation of its filtration by the kidney on a fluoroscope screen.

(*e*) Chemical analysis of an entire bodily component can be made to measure some variables. For example, the total quantities of the enzymes trypsin and lipase in the pancreas and the relative concentration of various enzymes have been compared with the dietary input of protein.[12] It appears that the sort of protein in the diet of animals, particularly its amino acid composition, importantly affects the amounts and concentrations of the animals' pancreatic enzymes.

(*f*) Studies of tissues living in culture outside the body can also provide indicators that measure organ variables. Of course tissues function differently outside the body than they normally do.[13] Slices of mouse and pigeon pancreas have been incubated in bicarbonated saline solution, glucose, pyruvate, casein, and tryptophan, in order to study the synthesis of the enzyme amylase by the pancreas.[14] Synthesis accelerated in slices from both unfed and fed pigeons, and from unfed but not from fed mice, when amino acids were added to the solution in which the organs were incubated.

2.2 Process taxonomy of types of systems   A process taxonomy is the usual sort of classification of organs. "Sensory," "digestive," "excretory," and "reproductive" organs are examples of such classes.

3. Subsystems

The subsystems of organs are described below. The examples considered are all human organs unless otherwise indicated. Figure 7-2 is a detailed representation of a major part of an organ in a human organism. The blood and lymph vascular components of the distributor subsystem or organ are pictured, including the heart, arteries, arterioles, capillaries, venules, veins, and lymphatics. Cells in the heart of this distributor were pictured in Fig. 6-9. Table 7-1 identifies the components which make up the critical subsystems of an organ.

3.1 Subsystems which process both matter-energy and information

3.1.1 Reproducer, the subsystem which is capable of giving rise to other organs similar to the one it is in.

3.1.1.1 Structure   No such structure exists at this level. This subsystem is upwardly dispersed to the organism level.

3.1.1.2 Process   A new generation of organs arises from the reproduction of the organism of which they are subsystems. In the course of embryonic development, each organ produced is a faithful copy of those characteristic of the type or species, according to the template provided by the DNA in the fertilized egg.

Organs can repair some sorts of damage to them, but this is producing, not reproducing (see pages 329 and 330).

Because there is no reproducer at this level, there can be no variables of the reproducing process.

3.1.2 Boundary, the subsystem at the perimeter of an organ that holds together the components which make up the organ, protects them from environmental stresses, and excludes or permits entry to various sorts of matter-energy and information.

3.1.2.1 Structure

Matter-energy boundary. Matter-energy boundaries of organs may be either dispersed or continuous, depending upon whether or not the components of the organ are separated spatially within the organism. The boundary is pierced at points where blood or lymph vessels and nerves pass through it.

The human skin, which is the boundary of the organism, itself has a boundary, a horny layer of epithelial tissue, the stratum corneum, under which lie other epidermal, epithelial layers as well as layers from other tissues. This boundary is continuous, being broken at specific points, such as those where sweat glands open to the surface.

The boundary of the human organism's ingestor—which has two components, mouth and nose—is continuous, consisting of the superficial epithelial layer of the lining mucous membrane of the lips, the mouth, and the nasal passages.

The boundary of the distributor is essentially continuous, since all parts of the vascular components are connected in a closed-loop network of vessels throughout the organism. Any serious breach in this boundary at any point immediately affects the distributing process to an important degree unless it is repaired. The boundary consists of the outer layers of the walls of the heart, the arteries, arterioles, capillaries, sinusoids, venules, and veins of the blood vascular component, and the cisterna chyli, vessels, and capillaries of the lymphatic component. There are three layers in the walls of arteries. The external one, the adventitia, forming the outer boundary, is composed of elastic and connective tissue. There are, in addition, a muscular medial layer and an endothelial connective-tissue inner layer. The arterioles also have three similar layers, but each is much smaller, and as they merge into the capillaries, the inner endothelium is uninterrupted, but the outer layers gradually become thinner and disappear. The veins are like arteries with weak medial layers. Capillary walls are entirely composed of mesenchymal endothelium similar to the fibroblasts of

Fig. 7-2 The blood and lymph vascular components of the human distributor organ are identified. Six microscopic sections from particular locations are included.

  Subsystems which processes both matter-energy and information: Boundary (Bo), outer layer of wall of blood vessel and synaptic membrane of output neuron from the heart.

  Subsystems which process matter-energy: Ingestor (IN), lymphatic capillaries in the walls of the intestine and other parts of the gastrointestinal tract, and alveolar capillaries of the lung; Distributor (DI), coronary artery and vein of the heart, examples of vessels supplying major components of the distributor organ (also intercellular fluids, not shown); Producer (PR), bone-marrow cells forming white cells, red corpuscles, and platelets for the blood; Matter-Energy Storage (MS), bone marrow storing blood; Extruder (EX), capillaries in the renal glomeruli and in the alveoli of the lungs; Motor (MO), the heart; Supporter (SU), stroma, walls, supporting attachments, and connective tissues.

  Subsystems which process information: Input Transducer (it), postsynaptic region of autonomic postganglionic neuron leading to blood vascular component; Internal transducer (in), cells in cardiac muscle which convey signals that enable denervated organs to contract in coordinated fashion; Channel and Net (cn), autonomic nerve plexus of heart and large blood vessels and cardiac muscle which conducts impulses that elicit contractions; Decoder (dc), postsynaptic region of autonomic postganglionic neuron leading to blood vascular component; Decider (de), sympathetic fibers of sinoatrial node, atrioventricular bundle, bundle branches, and Purkinje fibers; Encoder (en), presynaptic region of output neuron from the heart; Output Transducer (ot), presynaptic region of output neuron from the heart.

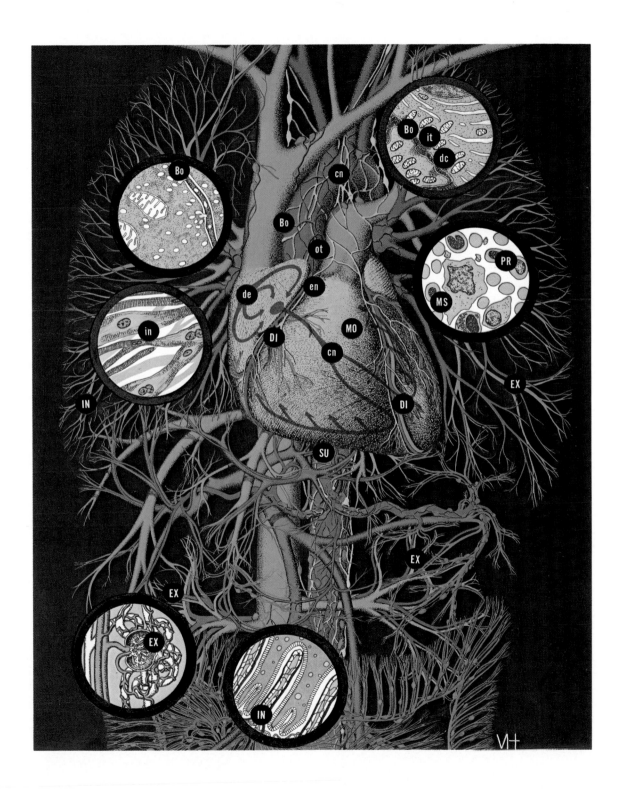

TABLE 7-1   Components of the 19 Critical Subsystems of an Organ *

3.1 SUBSYSTEMS WHICH PROCESS BOTH MATTER-ENERGY AND INFORMATION

3.1.1 *Reproducer*
None known at this level

3.1.2 *Boundary*
Outer layers of coverings of organs, *e.g.*, stratum corneum of skin, mucous membrane of mouth and nose, walls of blood and lymphatic vessels, meninges of brain and spinal cord; synaptic membranes of input neurons to and output neurons from viscera

3.2 SUBSYSTEMS WHICH PROCESS MATTER-ENERGY	3.3 SUBSYSTEMS WHICH PROCESS INFORMATION
3.2.1 *Ingestor* Input artery or lymphatic vessel of organ and portal vein of liver; nose and mouth and alveolar capillaries in the lung of ingestor organ; lacteal lymphatic capillaries in the walls of the intestine and other parts of the gastrointestinal tract of the distributor organ; artifacts such as intravenous injection equipment	3.3.1 *Input Transducer* Receptor cells of various components of organism's input transducer and internal transducer; receptor cells which respond to hormones and other chemical compounds entering organs; autonomic postganglionic and other neurons leading into organs; artifacts (as prostheses for pathological eye or ear) such as corrective lens, hearing aid; (as prostheses for normal eye) such as magnifying glass, microscope, telescope
	3.3.2 *Internal Transducer* May include cells of juxtaglomerular apparatuses of kidney glomeruli specialized muscle cells of sinoatrial and atrioventricular nodes of heart, reflex arcs in enteric plexus of intestine or intramural plexus of bladder
3.2.2 *Distributor* Blood vessels, lymphatics, intercellular fluids, and ducts of organ; artifacts (as prostheses for pathological artery or vein) such as plastic artery or human umbilical cord vein	3.3.3 *Channel and Net* Intrinsic nerves of organs; vascular channels and intercellular fluids of organs; chains of interconnected epithelial cells; smooth muscle; cardiac muscle; synapses, ephapses
3.2.3 *Converter* Some or all cells of organ, particularly parenchymal cells, which can change one form of matter-energy to another for use by the organ as a whole	3.3.4 *Decoder* Receptor cells or second-echelon cells in neural components of organism's input transducer and internal transducer; cells which react to hormonal inputs; autonomic postganglionic input neurons and other input neurons to organs
3.2.4 *Producer* Some or all cells of organ, particularly parenchymal cells which can synthesize new substances for the organ as a whole	3.3.5 *Associator* None known at this level
3.2.5 *Matter-Energy Storage* Intercellular fluids, hollow cavities of some organ components	3.3.6 *Memory* None known at this level
	3.3.7 *Decider* In heart, sympathetic fibers of sinoatrial node, atrioventricular node and bundle, bundle branches, Purkinje fibers; enteric plexuses of intestinal tract; artifacts (as prostheses for pathological heart) such as electrical pacemaker
	3.3.8 *Encoder* Presynaptic regions and perhaps some parts of cell bodies of output neurons from a visceral organ to a neural organ or from one neural organ to another; cells that synthesize hormones
3.2.6 *Extruder* Venous and lymphatic output vessels, glandular drainage, ducts and other openings; artifacts (as prostheses for pathological kidney) such as renal dialysis machine	
3.2.7 *Motor* Smooth-, striated-, or cardiac-muscle tissue of organ; artifacts (as prostheses for pathological limb or joint) such as artificial limb or joint	3.3.9 *Output Transducer* Presynaptic regions of output neurons from a visceral to a neural organ or from one neural organ to another; cells that synthesize and output hormones, and venous and lymphatic output vessels that carry them out of the organ
3.2.8 *Supporter* Stroma, walls, supporting attachments, connective tissues of organ components; artifacts (as prostheses for pathological bony supporting structure, like spinal column), such as brace	

*No artifacts are now used for some subsystems of organs. Many systems are upwardly or downwardly dispersed.

connective tissue. They do not have the impermeable boundaries found in arteries, arterioles, veins, and venules. A capillary wall is composed of a single layer of endothelial cells and is "about the most tenuous structure conceivable."[15] It is no thicker than half a micron. The cells of this structure are joined by an "intercellular cement." Large pores in this cement are mostly plugged by proteins on the inner surface of the capillary wall. This frail tube, of a diameter just large enough for a single blood cell to pass through, is surrounded and supported by a sheath or membrane of connective-tissue origin, with a jellied tissue fluid between them.

The boundary of the converter is also continuous, since its components are the parts and associated glands of the digestive tube between the mouth (which has both ingestor and converter functions) and the beginning of the large intestine. In the mouth and esophagus the wall is surrounded by a dense connective-tissue layer, attached to neighboring structures. The remainder of the converter has an outer serous membrane.

Boundaries of producer, matter-energy storage, extruder, and motor subsystems are dispersed, since all of these subsystems have components in different regions of the organism.

The brain and spinal cord are surrounded by three layers of membranes or meninges, the outermost of the three being the firm, dense dura mater, the middle being the arachnoid, made up of delicate connective tissue, and the innermost being the pia mater, composed of fine, vascular connective tissue. Bone surrounds these meninges, covering both the brain and the spinal cord.

The neural tracts and the great bundles of nerves are covered by three layers, connective-tissue sheaths, epineurium, and perineurium. The information processing subsystems are located in the nervous tissue and sense organs, but in most cases their separate subsystem boundaries cannot yet be located precisely.

Information boundary. The structure of the information boundary in organs is usually the same as that of the matter-energy boundary, with the exception that if the postganglionic fibers, over which information inputs arrive at organs, are considered part of the internal structure of the organ (see page 333), the boundary is located at the point where these fibers synapse with fibers from the central nervous system of the organism. Sympathetic fibers synapse at some distance from an organ's matter-energy boundary, while parasympathetic fibers have their synapses within the walls of the viscus.

Nerves and blood vessels in which hormones flow, which are components of the channel and net subsystem of the organism, enter most organs at a region known as the hilum. In the lungs, for example, sympathetic and parasympathetic fibers of the autonomic nervous system together form the pulmonary plexus outside the lung and send branches into both lungs through their hila. The digestive tube, because of its length, receives sympathetic fibers whose preganglionic connections arise from almost every ganglion of the sympathetic trunk. These form plexuses associated with the various components, which enter the organ through several branches of the arteries. The digestive tract's parasympathetic nerve supply, except for the lowest section, derives from the vagus nerves.

3.1.2.2 Process

Matter-energy boundary. The relatively tough outer coverings of organs and their components can be penetrated only with effort. This is consistent with Hypothesis 3.1.2.2-1 (see page 93) which states that more work must be expended when a small living or nonliving object crosses the boundary of a living system than when it is transmitted over the same distance in space immediately inside or outside the boundary. Consequently they serve a protective function at the same time as they delimit the organs from their surroundings. They filter substances which approach, letting some by and stopping others. They prevent the spread of infection from adjacent structures. The capsules of the kidneys and the outer thin membranes of the gastrointestinal tube, which exude a lubricating watery fluid, protect the inner structures from physical blows. These outer coverings are sometimes elastic, allowing for distention and contraction.

The epidermis, the scaly outer boundary of the skin, can shed damaged cellular components and replace them from the layers which lie directly underneath. The delicate nervous and vascular elements in the lower layers of the skin become covered by extremely thick epidermis where the wear and tear are heaviest. For instance, the soles of the feet of shoeless camel drivers and workers on coral reefs are thick and insensitive.

The heart contact surface between the sac of the pericardium, which also covers the roots of the great vessels leading to and from it, and the epicardium inside, which is the immediate covering of the heart and great vessels, is moistened by watery fluid that lubricates and protects the membranes during the heart's unceasing motion.

Blood plasma, which carries nutrients into the tissue fluids, and wastes and various products from them, goes through the endothelial walls of capillaries, which are permeable to it. The white cells in blood, which move like amoebas, push aside the processes of the endothelial cells of arterial capillaries, going between them, or pass through the substance of the cells. They form temporary openings that close immediately after they have passed. Venous and lymphatic capillary walls can be traversed in the other direction from the tissue fluids into the vascular system.

Cerebrospinal fluid bathes all parts of the external and internal surfaces of the central nervous system. It is in the ventricles within the brain and in the subarachnoid space around it. It is also in the canal running down the center of the spinal cord. These fluids are secreted by the choroid plexus in the lateral ventricles of the brain.

An important boundary in the central nervous system is known as the "blood-brain barrier."[16] Similar barriers exist between the blood and the aqueous humor of the eye and between the blood and the cerebrospinal fluid. These barriers act as filters, allowing some sorts of substances to pass but not others. An important determinant of the rate of flow of substances through the boundary is their solubility in lipid, since cell membranes have a high lipid content (see page 229). The selectivity of the cell membranes of the brain as to what substances pass through them is greater than that of some other cells. They can thus exclude some inputs which are potentially harmful to nervous tissue or which it cannot metabolize. Sucrose, inulin, sodium, inorganic ions, highly dissociated compounds, amino acids, and penicillin pass very slowly from plasma into brain tissue. Oxygen, carbon dioxide, alcohol, barbiturates, glucose, and lipophilic substances, on the other hand, pass quickly from blood to brain.[17]

Information boundary. Information crosses organ boundaries at the points of entrance and exit of nerves or blood vessels, or at specialized sensory regions of input or output (see pages 333 and 335). Other parts of the boundary ordinarily are not permeable to information. An exception is the myenteric reflex of the gut. Pressure which stretches any point on the gut's boundary causes it to contract above the point of contact and to relax below it.

Representative *variables* of boundary process include: *Sorts of matter-energy crossing the boundary.* Example: As the concentration of urea in the arteries entering the renal component of the extruder increased, the rate of glomerular filtration in the kidneys increased. *Meaning of information crossing the boundary.* Example: The alpha-coded hormonal inputs from the pituitary changed, and the ovaries in response progressed from the estrogen to the progesterone phase. *Sorts of information crossing the boundary.* Example: The blood entering the ovary contained gonadotropic hormone which conveyed a message

from the pituitary. *Degree of permeability of the boundary to matter-energy.* Example: As the man's skin gradually tanned in the sun over several weeks, the rate at which ultraviolet rays penetrated the skin decreased. *Degree of permeability of the boundary to information.* Example: Local anesthesia of the autonomic nerves supplying the kidney and lower gastrointestinal tract prevented those components of the extruder from receiving any neural input signals. *Percentage of matter-energy arriving at the boundary which enters the system.* Example: The stratified epithelium on the surface of the skin of the girl's face absorbed about 40 percent of the cold cream within an hour. *Percentage of information arriving at the boundary which enters the system.* Example: Less than 10 percent of the images hitting the retina were accurately conveyed up to higher neural levels. *Changes in matter-energy processing at the boundary over time.* Example: As the animal aged, the rate at which oxygen passed into his various information processing organs decreased. *Changes in information processing at the boundary over time.* Example: At puberty the concentration of androgenic hormones entering all organs of the male rat increased significantly. *Changes in matter-energy processing at the boundary with different circumstances.* Example: The epithelium of the reproductive tract became less resistant to bacterial invasion as the concentration of estrogen in it decreased. *Changes in information processing at the boundary with different circumstances.* Example: During one-half of the menstrual cycle the rate at which luteinizing hormone from the pituitary entered the ovary was high; then it fell, and the rate at which follicle-stimulating hormone entered the ovary rose and remained high for the other half of the cycle. *Rate of matter-energy processing at the boundary.* Example: The dog began to run on the treadmill and immediately blood entered the leg muscle components of its motor organ at a higher rate than when it was resting. *Rate of information processing at the boundary.* Example: More than 100,000 bits per second (s) entered the visual component of the cat's input transducer. *Frequency of matter-energy processing at the boundary.* Example: Blood entered and left the transplanted heart about 80 times per min. *Frequency of information processing at the boundary.* Example: A tone sounded once every second in the experimental cage sending a signal to both of the cat's ears. *Lag in matter-energy processing at the boundary.* Example: The meat was delayed for a fraction of a second in entering the esophagus component of the lion's distributor because at that moment the animal breathed. *Lag in information processing at the boundary.* Example: The chemical reactions of rhodopsin in the retina occurred slowly, delaying the colored signal for 1 microsecond (μs). *Costs of matter-energy processing at the boundary.* Example: The heart beat so fast that it reduced the oxygen in the cardiac muscle to an abnormally low level; this ischemia caused the patient to feel pain. *Costs of information processing at the boundary.* Example: There was some consumption of oxygen and glucose by the autonomic nerves passing in and out of the kidney, but it was only minute.

3.2   Subsystems which process matter-energy

3.2.1   Ingestor, the subsystem which brings matter-energy across the organ boundary from the environment.

3.2.1.1   Structure   Organs are supplied with matter-energy by the circulating blood and lymph of the organism. One or more arteries as well as input lymphatic vessels cross the boundary of every organ. The liver, unlike any other organ, also receives matter-energy through a vein, the portal vein. The organism's ingestor organ also receives matter-energy through the nose (air) and through the mouth (fluids and solids). The distributor organ of complex organisms receives air inputs from alveolar capillaries in the lung and chyle, a milky fluid containing digested food, from lacteal lymphatic capillaries in the walls of the intestine and other parts of the gastrointestinal tract.

Artifacts such as intravenous injection equipment may provide for ingestion into tissues or organs.

3.2.1.2   Process   In ingesting through vessels, most organs cannot select what kinds of matter-energy to take in, since whatever is in the bloodstream flows into the organ through its arterial supply. This is not true, however, of the brain and other components with protective barriers. How organs can select out specific forms of matter-energy from their inputs, however, will be discussed below (see pages 327 and 328). The organism can select what forms of matter-energy to take into the lungs and mouth, but those organ components have no autonomous control of such inputs.

The rate of matter-energy input varies greatly among different organ components. Some tissues, like muscles, are highly vascular with a large blood volume flowing into them. Others, like tendons, have little blood supply. The need for specific substances also differs from organ to organ. Iron is necessary to the bone marrow which forms red blood cells; iodine is an essential raw material for synthesizing thyroxine, the hormone made in the thyroid; bones require vitamins A and D and calcium; muscles require large amounts of glucose to perform their work; nervous tissue needs inputs of oxygen, glucose, and other fuels.

As the organism goes about its daily life, waking and sleeping, moving and resting, experiencing hunger and satiety, heat, cold, and other stresses, the flow of matter-energy into organs and tissues varies. Resting-forearm skeletal-muscle blood-flow rates are estimated to be 1.8 to 9.6 milliliters (ml) per 100 grams (g) of muscle per min.[18] Skeletal-muscle blood flow fluctuates widely with the amount of work done and with other factors, some poorly understood.

The sorts and amounts of matter-energy taken in through the lungs vary significantly from situation to situation. The primary inputs are oxygen, carbon dioxide, nitrogen, and water, with traces of other substances, particularly in polluted air. These substances come into contact with the blood in different concentrations in the organism's distributor organ through the thin walls of the alveoli of the lung. A number of factors affect these concentrations, *e.g.,* the several concentrations in the environmental air, the air pressure, the rate of breathing, and the depth of breathing. These input substances interact with many substances in the blood of the alveolar capillaries, including oxygen, carbon dioxide, nitrogen, hydrogen ion, hydroxyl ion, chloride ion, sodium ion, potassium ion, hemoglobin in red corpuscles, protein in red corpuscles, and protein in the blood plasma. The many complex interrelations of all these variables in the input air, the blood plasma and red corpuscles, and the output air have been studied by mathematical models and computer simulations (see pages 356 and 357).

The kinds of fluids and solids input into the mouth also, of course, vary widely.

Representative *variables* of the process of ingesting include: *Sorts of matter-energy ingested.* Example: The decoder in the cat's brain ingested chiefly oxygen and glucose. *Degree of openness of the ingestor.* Example: The renal artery was permanently dilated after the sympathectomy. *Changes in ingesting over time.* Example: As the brain developed arteriosclerosis with age, the rate at which all the information processing organs in it ingested oxygen decreased markedly. *Changes in ingesting with different circumstances.* Example: The rate of blood flow through the coronary artery decreased as the heart rate slowed down. *Rate of ingesting.* Example: The kidney received 110 cubic centimeters (cm^3) of blood per min. *Frequency of ingesting.* Example: The duodenum took in bile after every meal entered it. *Lag in ingesting.* Example: The blood could enter the uterine muscle only between contractions, so it backed up for a few seconds at the uterine boundary during each contraction. *Costs of ingesting.* Example: When friction from the constant flow of blood constituents sloughed off endothelial cells on the walls of the input hepatic artery of the liver, they were replaced, and the costs of such repairs in matter-energy expended were minimal.

3.2.2   Distributor, the subsystem which carries

inputs from outside the organ or outputs from its subsystems around the organ to each component.

3.2.2.1 Structure The input vessels to organs branch into a distributor network of smaller arteries, arterioles, capillaries, venules, veins, and lymphatics which extend through the organ. At the point where an arteriole branches into a capillary there is a sphincter, a circular smooth muscle which has an important function in the distributor process. The blood and lymph vessels and the intercellular fluids around all cells are components of the distributor of each organ. Where the components of the organ are separated in space, of course the organ distributor is not continuous. The distributor of the suprasystem, the organism, may convey matter-energy from one component to another. The density of the capillary bed varies in different organs and components. Within the pia mater of the spinal cord, for example, is a dense network of arterial tracts that send branches throughout the substance of the nervous tissue with capillary nets meshed throughout. The pia mater of the brain also has vessels running through it, sending branches into the brain substance. As in the spinal cord, there is a dense capillary network reaching all parts of the brain. Within both brain and spinal cord there are variations in vascularity. Sensory nuclei are more vascular than motor nuclei, and the parietal area of the cerebrum more vascular than other areas. The peripheral parts of the nervous system are also well supplied with blood from vessels which are embedded in the various coverings of fibers and tracts.

Various openings, ducts, and tubes distribute matter-energy from one part of an organ to another. For example, several ducts convey digestive juices into the duodenum. The hepatic duct from the liver and the cystic duct from the gallbladder merge to become the common bile duct. This duct, in turn, is joined near its termination by the pancreatic duct, to form the ampulla of Vater which opens into the duodenum just below the pylorus of the stomach. This latter structure opens to convey the chyle (partially decomposed matter in the stomach) into the next component of the organism's converter, the intestinal tract, where it can be conveniently worked upon by the digestive juices entering from the ampulla of Vater. All these structures are components of the converter subsystem of the organism.

The ducts of exocrine glands may open into other components of the same organ, *e.g.*, the salivary glands which pour saliva into the mouth. Or they may open to the outside of the body, *e.g.*, the sweat glands and mammary glands (see page 331).

Artifacts, such as plastic arteries or prostheses made from human umbilical cord veins, may be used to replace diseased blood vessels.[19]

3.2.2.2 Process Distribution of matter-energy to all parts of the organ, in amounts related to current needs of the tissue, is controlled by the dilatation or contraction of the precapillary sphincters. These changes occur when the tissues receive nervous and hormonal signals. Sphincters may be completely closed in resting tissue. They open in a tissue which requires much input, like muscle in action, and this results in a great increase in blood flow to that tissue.

Different sorts of matter-energy cross a capillary wall in different ways. Ions and small molecules diffuse across the wall rapidly—at least 100 percent exchange in 1 min.[20] The penetration of capillary walls by water and dissolved substances seems to require no expenditure of energy by the capillary endothelial cells and is believed to occur through numerous openings or pores about 30 angstroms (Å) wide which pierce the intercellular cement. This cement is continually being washed away and replaced. Lipid soluble molecules, on the other hand, are transported through the membranes of endothelial cells, penetrating them rapidly. Finally, the red corpuscles, white cells, large protein molecules, or other large molecules go out through the intercellular portion of the wall.

Capillaries of different organs and components are not equally permeable, which is one reason why they function differently. Those in skeletal muscle are 100 times less permeable to water than are the glomerular capillaries of the kidney, where filtration of fluids is, of course, the prime function.

The distribution of oxygen is an example of how the distributor of an organ functions. Oxygen is delivered to the distributor by the ingestor of the organ in chemical combination with iron-containing hemoglobin in the arterial blood of the organ. Each molecule of hemoglobin unites with four atoms of oxygen. Carbon dioxide from the tissue fluid is excreted in similar combination with hemoglobin. The small amount of oxygen in simple solution in blood would not begin to meet the oxygen requirements of tissues. Diffusion of oxygen into the blood occurs wherever the capillaries are surrounded by a high oxygen concentration. Since the air in the lungs always has more oxygen than arterial blood, such diffusion occurs there. The lower oxygen concentration in the tissues reduces the affinity of hemoglobin for oxygen. Acidic carbon dioxide and lactic acid, wastes or products of tissue function, diffuse into the blood and, by making it more acid, further decrease the ability of the hemoglobin to hold oxygen. Oxygen is therefore released into the tissue fluid and can be taken up by the cells. As the blood flows from the lungs through the distributor, it loses more and more of its oxygen and takes on more and more of the wastes or products of tissue function. All this is consistent with Hypothesis 3.2.2.2-1 (see page

94), which states that the farther a specific matter-energy transmission passes along a distributor from the point of its input to it and toward the final point of its output from it, the more it is altered by lowering the concentration of the kinds of matter-energy it contains which are used by the system's subsystems and increasing the concentration of the products or wastes produced by it and output by those subsystems.

Thus a muscular organ which is using up its nutrients and putting out work, forming carbon dioxide and lactic acid in the process, is able to get an increased supply of oxygen from its distributor subsystem. In human beings the rate of oxygen used by the muscles during exercise rises. A person who, at rest, has a total oxygen consumption of 0.25 liter (1) per min will use approximately 4.0 l per min during maximum athletic effort.[21] Both the total blood flow and the utilization of oxygen from the blood are increased, the first by the opening of more capillaries, the second by the increase in the percentage of blood oxygen extracted. Other tissues besides muscle, of course, also react to increased activity by increased oxygen consumption. In some pathological states like cerebral arteriosclerosis, oxygen and fuel input rates to the brain diminish.[22]

Representative *variables* of the distributing process are: *Sorts of matter-energy distributed to various parts of the system.* Example: The dog was so ill that bile was passing through its distributor system to parts of its channel and net system, slowing neural conduction. *Changes in distributing over time.* Example: As the horse aged the blood flow gradually slowed in the extremities of its motor organ even though it moved at about the same rate through the heart and lungs. *Changes in distributing with different circumstances.* Example: The blood flow through the brain was only 70 percent of normal 30 min after the cat ate. *Rate of distributing.* Example: Lymph passed into the cisterna chyli at the rate of 1,200 cm^3 per h. *Frequency of distributing.* Example: A spurt of blood passed from the heart to the aorta 92 times a minute. *Lag in distributing.* Example: Because the heart valves were regurgitating, the heart lagged briefly in pumping returning blood into the arterial system and this backed up blood in the vessels of the lungs, constituting congestive failure which resulted in the shortness of breath characteristic of cardiac asthma. *Costs of distributing.* Example: As the heart beat, its muscular contractions required an energy input that produced more than 2 calories (cal) per h.

3.2.3   Converter, the subsystem which changes certain inputs to the organ into forms more useful for the special processes of that particular organ.

3.2.3.1   Structure   This subsystem of the organ consists of some or all of its cells, particularly paren-

chymal cells, which can change one form of matter-energy to another for use by the organ as a whole, extruding the new form as a product available to the entire organ. (In cases in which each cell in an organ produces for itself alone, the subsystem is dispersed downward to the cell level.)

3.2.3.2   Process   Matter-energy which reaches organs has already been extensively broken down by the organism's converter. I have already discussed some of the specific cellular reactions involved in converting (see pages 236 and 237).

Representative *variables* of the converting process are: *Sorts of matter-energy converted.* Example: The enzymes in the lumen of the baby's stomach hydrolyzed many sorts of proteins. *Percentage of matter-energy converted.* Example: The dog's kidney converted, for its own metabolism, only a small percentage of the matter-energy inputs to it, outputting wastes through its glomeruli and tubules; the rest of the unused inputs were extruded through the output renal vein back to the dog's bloodstream. *Changes in converting over time.* Example: Fewer fats in the input to the liver were converted to other compounds as the rat aged. *Changes in converting with different circumstances.* Example: More fats in the input to the liver were converted when the goose was starved than when it was glutted. *Rate of converting.* Example: The reticuloendothelial components of the extruder destroyed 10^{10} *Staphylococcus aureus* bacteria per h. *Frequency of converting.* Example: Chemical conversion processes in the stomach accelerated to a peak a few minutes after the dog was fed twice a day. *Lag in converting.* Example: Two weeks after methylene blue was injected intravenously into the horse, some of the blue dye still was not completely changed to other compounds in the reticuloendothelial components of the extruder. *Costs of converting.* Example: Several molecules of ATP were consumed when each molecule of protein in the liver was broken down into amino acids.

3.2.4   Producer, the subsystem which forms stable associations that endure for significant periods among matter-energy inputs to the organ or outputs from its converter, the materials synthesized being for growth, damage repair, or replacement of components of the organ, or for providing energy for moving or constituting the organ's outputs of products or information markers to its suprasystem.

3.2.4.1   Structure   The producer of new forms of matter-energy within organs is composed of some or all parenchymal cells of the organ. These can synthesize new substances for the organ as a whole, extruding them as products available to the entire organ. They include fibroblasts that make the cells of fibrous tissue; osteoblasts and osteoplasts that make bone; bone-marrow cells that make white cells, red corpuscles, and platelets; lymphocytes that make blood serum and antibodies; glandular cells that secrete digestive enzymes, hormones, and other chemicals; and many others. (In cases in which each cell in an organ produces for itself alone, the subsystem is dispersed downward to the cell level.) The number, arrangement, and sorts of differentiations of the cellular components within an organ which take part in this process differ significantly from organ to organ.

3.2.4.2 Process   The chief process of some organs is producing one or more substances for use elsewhere in the organism. For example, the liver and pancreas produce and secrete digestive juices which are used in the gastrointestinal tract. Organs also produce substances for use in their own processes. Substances produced by an organ may be the work of more than one kind of cell—as is the gastric juice of the stomach, which contains water, hydrochloric acid, enzymes, and various types of mucus. Lack of any of these ingredients causes digestive difficulties. The formation of bile by the liver is also the work of two types of cells: reticuloendothelial cells called Kupffer cells, and the liver glandular cells. Producing cells within organs may release their products continuously or only at the times they are needed.

Other important products of organs are materials needed to repair damage to their cells, sometimes to regenerate organ parts which have been removed surgically or by trauma. For example, if only about 30 percent of the liver of a rat remains after surgery, the organ will return to normal size and structure in four or five weeks. Six or eight weeks after such surgery in dogs, a microscopic section from the regenerated part cannot be distinguished from a section of the normal gland. Lobules produce new lobules, increasing the number of cells by mitosis, as required.[23]

The process of repair or regeneration carried out by organ producer subsystems differs from one type of tissue to another.[24] Epithelium is continually renewing itself as it is damaged by wear and tear. Repair takes place in a membrane type of epithelium by mitotic division of less differentiated cells in lower layers of the epithelial sheet which migrate toward the damaged cells. After trauma a similar process repairs small wounds, but large damage, such as a surgical wound, results in replacement of the epithelium by scar tissue, a connective tissue.

When there is a clean cut through skin and subcutaneous tissues with no loss of substance, and the cut surfaces are brought together and held by stitching, connective and vascular cells at the edges of the wound begin to divide actively. Those farther away from the wound are progressively less affected by the trauma (see Hypothesis 5.5-1, page 110). The nearby connective-tissue cells, fibroblasts which before had had only narrow nuclei and thin cytoplasms, suddenly develop large nuclei and form more cytoplasm. These fibroblasts grow toward each other through the coagulated plasma that collects between the two edges of the wound. They lay down collagenous fibers, formed from their peripheral layers of cytoplasm. These fibers produce scar tissue which firmly attaches the two sides of the wound. Meanwhile vascular cells have proliferated, forming a branching network of new capillaries which supply the nutrients for this rapid growth and which cause a new scar to be red. The capillaries disappear when healing is complete, and the scar loses its redness. The epithelium from the sides of the cut then grows over the top, being at first a thin bluish-white layer but finally thickening. Specialized structures, like hair follicles, are not replaced.

If the trauma has removed tissue from the wound, the repair process is more extensive. The gap must first be filled with a mixture of coagulated blood, fibrin, and inflammatory exudate through which the fibroblasts and the vascular endothelium build granulation tissue, which in time organizes into a fibrous tissue and becomes covered with epithelium. During granulation-tissue formation, many wandering cells appear to fight infection. For this reason a granulating wound's surface is a powerful barrier against infection.

Blood and lymph cells are continually being destroyed and replaced. Free stem cells, which may be the same for all blood elements, proliferate and differentiate. This process also replaces blood lost as a result of trauma.

Cartilage which has been damaged does not regenerate independently. Damaged cells become necrotic and atrophic. The defect is filled by new connective tissue that grows in from the perichondrium or the nearest fascia, both connective-tissue structures. The fibroblasts of this *granulation tissue* become round, produce capsules around themselves, and may become transformed into new cartilage cells. The fibrillar, interstitial substance of the scar tissue becomes homogeneous and produces new interstitial substance in the same way this is produced in the embryo.

In spite of its rigid character, bone is in continual flux, with both growth and absorption continuing throughout life. Repair of bone takes place in two stages. Like other tissues, it reacts to severe injury such as a fracture with hemorrhage and organization of a blood clot by granulation tissue. This tissue becomes dense connective tissue and cartilage develops within it, filling the gap between the bone fragments. The new bone forms at some distance from the line of fracture and invades the callus formed by the preceding process, which forms a framework for the developing bone, calcifying as it is laid down. After the fragments join, reorganization and resorption of excess bone take place and finally the gap is bridged by bone.

In the process of bone regeneration, undifferentiated connective-tissue cells are shown to be capable of transformation into cells characteristic of bone. They also have been observed to return to the undifferentiated state. Such cells normally develop into bone only when connected to the skeleton.

The types of muscular tissue differ in their regenerative abilities. Cardiac muscle shows insignificant regeneration. Skeletal muscle can repair minor damage to some extent. Mitosis has been observed in smooth-muscle cells in the vicinity of injury, but their capacity for regeneration is small. Healing in muscular tissue must ordinarily take place by scarring.

Mammalian nerve cells lose the power of multiplication at an early stage of differentiation. Any cell bodies that are destroyed are never replaced. If the axon is destroyed, neurons of the brain probably always degenerate and die. In other parts of the nervous system, if the axon is not destroyed completely and some function remains, complete recovery may occur. When a nerve is cut, the distal part degenerates. The cells of the surrounding sheath of Schwann proliferate and act as phagocytes, consuming the myelin of the medullary sheath which has been broken. These proliferated Schwann cells on both sides of the cut arrange themselves in the form of a tube through which new neural fibers grow out toward the periphery. A few days after the trauma they grow out as a bulbous projection toward the distal portion of the nerve. If scar tissue intervenes, or if the gap is more than an inch wide, the two parts will not rejoin, although a surgical "bridge" of transplanted nerve can be used in some circumstances. When the bulbous projection grows to the distal part of the nerve, it sends fine fibrils—growing at about 3 millimeters (mm) per day—down the sheath formed by the Schwann cells. Later it becomes medullated again. The entire process takes months.

Among the *variables* in the producing process are: *Sorts of matter-energy produced.* Example: Before the baby was born her liver made red blood corpuscles, but not after birth, although it continued to synthesize bile throughout life. *Quality of matter-energy produced.* Example: When there was a lack stress of iron input, the bone-marrow component of the patient's producer organ made red blood corpuscles of poor quality with insufficient hemoglobin, corpuscles characteristic of an iron-lack anemia. *Percentage of matter-energy used*

in producing. Example: About 60 percent of the amino acids input to the liver were used in synthesizing new protein molecules. *Changes in producing over time.* Example: At the beginning of digestion of a meal, the cat's stomach produced hydrochloric acid rapidly, but the production rate decreased as digestion continued. *Changes in producing with different circumstances.* Example: During the 10 days the guru fasted, his stomach produced an average of 95 cm^3 of gastric juice per day. *Rate of producing.* Example: The rate of secretion of bicarbonate in the dog's pancreatic juice varied directly as a function of the rate of production of the juice.[25] *Frequency of producing.* Example: Secretion of pancreatic juice increased rapidly after every meal the man ate. *Lag in producing.* Example: The rate of production of new epinephrine in the animal's adrenal cortex did not begin to diminish for several minutes after that component stopped secretion. *Costs of producing.* Example: Each molecule of protein produced in the rat's liver used up hundreds or thousands of amino acids.

3.2.5   Matter-energy storage, the subsystem which retains in the organ, for different periods of time, deposits of various sorts of matter-energy.

3.2.5.1   Structure   Matter-energy storage in organs may be within their cells, like glycogen in muscle cells or iron and copper in liver cells. In these cases it is a downwardly dispersed subsystem. Or it may be in intercellular fluids or hollow cavities of some organ components, *e.g.,* the gallbladder (a storage component of the organism's converter) or the urinary bladder (a storage component of the organism's extruder). Some glands, such as the thyroid, have their cells arranged around a central lumen, in which secretions are stored.

3.2.5.2   Process   Organs store matter-energy for later use in their own system, as in "buffer inventories" of intermediate products between various steps in converting and producing. [See Hypothesis 3.2.5.2-1 (page 94), which states that variations imposed on the rate of a succeeding process by variations in the rate of a preceding process can be decreased by storing a supply (or "buffer inventory") of the outputs from the preceding process between the components which carry out the two processes.]

Organs often also store matter-energy for later release to their suprasystem, the organism as a whole. They differ in the manner and timing of release of substances from storage. The gallbladder discharges its bile into the duodenum on receiving a hormone, cholecystokinin, which is released by the duodenal mucosa when fatty food enters the duodenum. Bile carries out an important function in the digestion of fats. The thyroid, likewise, secretes stored thyroxine and triiodothyronine into the blood on receiving a signal in the form of thyrotrophic hormone from the pituitary. Some other organs or organ components, *e.g.*, the sebaceous glands, secrete continually without any storage.

Some organ components are almost incapable of storage, which makes them easily vulnerable to lack stresses. This is true of the brain, which stores little matter-energy beyond the small amounts of oxygen and glucose present in its blood, fluids, neural cells, and glia. Components of the converter and extruder store matter-energy during processing and while awaiting extrusion. Storage in intercellular fluids is greatest during periods after eating or drinking, when there is increased exchange between the vascular or lymphatic vessels and cells.

Among the *variables* in the process of storing matter-energy are: *Sorts of matter-energy stored.* Example: The composition of the fat stored in and around the dog's kidneys varied depending upon the sort of fats and fatty acids in its diet. *Total storage capacity.* Example: The stomach of the fat man who ate four large meals a day had twice the cubic capacity that it had before he developed his neurotic habit of overeating. *Percentage of matter-energy stored.* Example: The gallbladder of the monkey could not store all the bile manufactured; some went directly through the common bile duct into the intestine. *Place of storage.* Example: The autopsy indicated that iron was stored in the bone marrow, liver, and spleen, but also in slight amounts in the brain. *Changes in storing over time.* Example: In the infant child the pituitary stored only minute amounts of gonadotropic hormones, but the quantity increased over time, particularly at puberty, decreasing past middle life. *Changes in storing with different circumstances.* Example: Immediately after the cow had eaten, the hay was stored in the stomach cavity, but 6 h later it was gone. *Rate of storing.* Example: The rate of storing vitamin A in the liver was of the order of several micrograms a month, increasing or decreasing as a direct function of the input rate to the organ. *Lag in storing.* Example: Urine was not stored in the bladder until several seconds after it was excreted by the kidney. *Costs of storing.* Example: After years of storing bile, the gallbladder developed an infection and gallstones formed, these forms of pathology being consequences of such storage, which are costly because they interfere with normal functioning. *Rate of breakdown of organization of matter-energy in storage.* Example: Five months after conception, the ovary of the fetus contained 6.8 million germ cells, but only about 480 ovulated in 40 years, the others undergoing progressive atresia over that time. *Sorts of matter-energy retrieved.* Example: The liver

retrieved at least three forms of matter-energy—glucose, glycogen, and fat. *Percentage of matter-energy retrieved.* Example: Almost 100 percent of the fat which the bear stored in its omentum during its summer feeding was used up during its winter hibernation. *Order of retrieval.* Example: During the sailor's month of starvation, nearly all the fat in the adipose tissues surrounding his kidney was removed from storage, but the intracellular fat in the renal parenchymal cells was not used. *Rate of retrieval.* Example: The dog's liver retrieved energy from glycogen much faster when the animal was awake and active than when it was asleep. *Lag in retrieval.* Example: Energy was obtained by the muscle almost instantly when stored in ATP; retrieval was much slower when it was stored in fat. *Costs of retrieval.* Example: Since the chemical reactions involved in obtaining ATP from fat require more energy than those which obtain ATP from glucose, it cost the cat's liver more to retrieve energy-rich phosphate, for its cellular reactions, from fat than from glucose.

3.2.6 Extruder, the subsystem which transmits matter-energy out of the organ in the forms of products or wastes.

3.2.6.1 Structure   The venous and lymphatic output vessels which drain organs and convey wastes or products from them, together with glandular ducts and openings of other sorts, form the extruders of organs or organ components. Among these extruder ducts and openings are the nipples of the breasts and the openings of the male and female reproductive tracts, which are extruders of the reproducer subsystem at the organism level; the capillaries, alveoli in the lungs, and glomeruli in the kidneys, which extrude matter-energy from the organism's distributor subsystem; the ileocecal junction, between the small bowel, which is part of the organism's converter organ, and its large bowel, which is part of its extruder organ; and the sweat glands, mouth, nose, urethra, and anus, which are components of the extruder subsystem of the organism's extruder organ.

An artifact which can be used as a prosthesis for a pathological kidney is a renal dialysis machine.

3.2.6.2 Process   The intercellular fluids of tissues and the cerebrospinal fluid, which surrounds the entire central nervous system, receive waste products of tissue metabolism such as carbon dioxide, water, and breakdown products of cellular biochemical processes as well as dead cells, bacteria, and foreign particles which may have entered into cells as a result of phagocytic activity. These are taken up into the venous or lymphatic capillaries and flow out of the organ through its output vessels and into the organism's distributor (see pages 324, 325, and 369).

The extrusion of matter from several organs is controlled by a ring-shaped sphincter or other mechanism capable of closing down or opening up to permit passage of products or wastes, upon an appropriate signal. The signal may be external pressure, like an infant's sucking on the breast, or internal neural signals, like those which control the urinary bladder. Or the organ's output passage may be forced open by the pressure of matter which is stored inside the organ.

The endocrine glands, which have no ducts, release their hormonal secretions into the gland's intercellular fluid from whence they pass into the circulation of the organism through sinusoids in those glands. (These are connections between arteries and veins, like capillaries, but more tenuous.) The hormones secreted are markers carrying information, so when they are secreted, the extruder components serve as the output transducer.

The *variables* of the process of extruding include: *Sorts of products and wastes extruded.* Example: The liver component of the dog's converter organ extruded through the intestinal tract varying amounts of products important in digestion (such as bile salts) and wastes (such as bile pigments which are breakdown products of blood hemoglobin). *Percentage of products and wastes extruded.* Example: The lung removed 70 percent of the carbon dioxide carried in the blood which passed through it. *Changes in extruding over time.* Example: As the horse aged, his kidney gradually excreted a higher and higher proportion of the albumin in the blood flowing through it. *Changes in extruding with different circumstances.* Example: The mother's breast did not extrude milk until her baby began to suck. *Rate of extruding.* Example: After the patient took the diuretic, his left kidney increased its rate of excretion from 10 to 22 drops per min. *Frequency of extruding.* Example: The denervated bladder emptied automatically at least once every hour. *Lag in extruding.* Example: The cow's udder began to give a small amount of milk on milking three days after the lactogenic hormone was injected intravenously. *Costs of extruding.* Example: As the contents of the dog's small bowel entered its large bowel, the contraction of the musculature of the ileocecal junction consumed a very small amount of energy.

3.2.7   Motor, the subsystem which moves the organ or parts of it in relation to part or all of its environment or moves components of its environment in relation to each other.

3.2.7.1   Structure   In those organs which have their own motors, they are composed of smooth, striated, or cardiac muscle. The motor processes of all other organs are dispersed upwardly to the organism level. These organs move only when external forces are applied by other organs or organ components, when the motor of the total organism operates, or when forces are applied from outside the organism.

Artifacts, which may be used to replace pathological arms, legs, or joints, include artificial limbs and artificial joints.

3.2.7.2   Process   Organs remain fixed in place by attachments to other structures within the organism. Their motions are relative to their surroundings as the motor of the organism changes the position of the entire organism or parts of it, or are contractions or expansions made possible by elastic and muscular components. The distributor organ of the organism, which includes the blood and lymph vascular components (see pages 369 and 370), has a pump (the heart) which acts as a motor to circulate the blood. Lymph flow in man depends upon mechanical forces exerted on the lymphatic vessels by movement of the organism. This is also an important factor in flow through the venous circulation. Some animal species have a "lymph heart" as well. Cardiac muscle beats regularly. The beat may be endogenous. The nature of input and output neural connections with cardiac muscle cells is not fully understood (see page 249). Embryonic hearts beat before any cardiac innervation could develop.

Layers of smooth-muscle fiber in or on the walls of some components, *e.g.*, the urinary bladder, permit them to distend and contract. Such organ components usually contain elastic connective tissue.

The complex, rhythmic motions of peristalsis depend upon smooth-muscle layers in the walls of components of the converter and extruder. In this sort of motion a rhythmic wave of dilatation followed by constriction travels along the components involved. Muscle layers in the walls of blood vessels, which are subcomponents of the distributor subsystem, permit adjustment of the blood supply in different organs by contracting or relaxing to change the interior diameter of the vessels. Sphincter muscles contract or relax to hold or release products or wastes. The pylorus is such a sphincter, and tiny sphincter muscles are present in arterioles, which I have already mentioned (see page 327).

Motors of some organs or organ components, such as the larynx, may at times output markers bearing information, such as sound waves. At such times they are acting as the output transducer of that organ or organ component.

Representative *variables* of the moving process are: *Sorts of movements made.* Example: The dancer's arm moved up, down, back and forth, to the side, and circularly. *Changes in moving over time.* Example: Because his muscular tissue wasted with age, the old man's legs gradually became more and more feeble. *Changes in moving with different circumstances.* Example: The entire stomach contracted when it was empty, but it moved in peristaltic waves when it was full. *Rate of moving.* Example: The peristaltic waves of the colon of the dog moved at about 1 cm per s. *Rate of output of work.* Example: The patient's right hand exerted a maximum energy of 10^4 ergs each time it contracted, when it was contracting at its maximum speed, which was 88 times per min. *Frequency of moving.* Example: The chest and lungs expanded and contracted 20 times per min. *Duration of moving.* Example: The peristaltic movements of the stomach lasted 40 min for a small meal but over 1 h for a large one. *Lag in moving.* Example: The stomach ordinarily began contractions within 10 s of the time food reached it, but the delay varied between 2 and 20 s. *Costs of moving.* Example: The rapid beating of the heart almost completely exhausted the cardiac muscle of oxygen and produced ventricular fibrillation.

3.2.8 Supporter, the subsystem which maintains the proper spatial relationships among components of the organ, so that they can interact without weighting each other down or crowding each other.

3.2.8.1 Structure The stroma of components, their firm walls, external supporting attachments, or connective tissues constitute parts of the supporters of organs.

An artifact such as a brace may be used as a prosthesis to reinforce a bony supporter structure like the spinal column.

3.2.8.2 Process Parts of organs are held in proper relation to each other and to other organs and organ components by the various parts of the supporter. Thus the strong muscular abdominal wall keeps the viscera in place. Weakness of this wall permits components of the organism's converter and extruder subsystems to fall downward from their proper places and the flow of matter-energy and hormonal information through the organs is affected. Loose connective tissue, including adipose tissue, acts as "packing" around organs and components. The cerebrospinal fluid surrounding the central nervous tissue supports and cushions it, as well as having other functions.

The stroma extends throughout the substance of organs and components, making a meshwork for the cells. The stroma of the spleen, for instance, is composed of a network of reticular fibers and a system of dense connective tissue which extends from the capsule throughout the spleen and forms the framework in which blood vessels, lymphatic tissues, and the parenchyma of the spleen itself are arranged. The glia of the central nervous system have a supportive function. They also participate in other processes.

The firm capsules or other outer coverings of components also act as support. When the walls of arteries weaken, the blood may be forced out into an aneurysm, a sort of sac which may rupture and allow the blood to escape.

Representative *variables* in the supporting process include: *Strength of the supporter.* Example: The boy's broken tibia, once repaired, was stronger at the point of fracture than anywhere else. *Costs of supporting.* Example: The vitamins A and D and the calcium inputs which were consumed were among the costs of maintaining the bones of the spinal column.

3.3 Subsystems which process information The partipotentiality of organs is perhaps best demonstrated in the deficiency of their information processing subsystems. Organ subsystem processes are both downwardly and upwardly dispersed, to both cell and organism levels. In intact organisms, particularly those with highly developed nervous systems, control of subsystem activities is highly centralized. The nervous and vascular tissues of organ components connect with the channel and net and distributor subsystems of the organism. Some subsystems seem to be entirely dispersed. There is, however, some deciding at the organ level. Since I conceive the decider to be the essential critical subsystem (see pages 18 and 32), this is a major justification for identifying the organ as a level.

3.3.1 Input transducer, the sensory subsystem which brings markers bearing information into the organ, changing them to other matter-energy forms suitable for transmission within it.

3.3.1.1 Structure The input transducer of an organ includes four categories of structures. They are:

(*a*) *Receptor cells* of at least some of the various neural components of the organism's input transducer and of its internal transducer (see pages 377 to 389, Table 6-4, Fig. 6-18, and pages 389 and 390).

(*b*) *Receptor cells* in the organ which react to hormonal information in the blood entering through the organ's input artery from a gland for which the receiving organ is a "target organ" (see Table 6-4) and passing from the bloodstream into the organ's intercellular fluid. Such cells also serve as components of the organ's decoder (see page 338).

(*c*) The *autonomic postganglionic neurons,* both sympathetic and parasympathetic (see pages 336 to 338), which bring information from the organism's central nervous system to the organ, *e.g.,* the heart or the urinary bladder (see Fig. 7-3). These cells also are parts of the decoder (see page 338). The postganglionic neurons may be regarded as part of the organ even though some of them extend some distance beyond the main body of the organ. (I view the preganglionic neurons

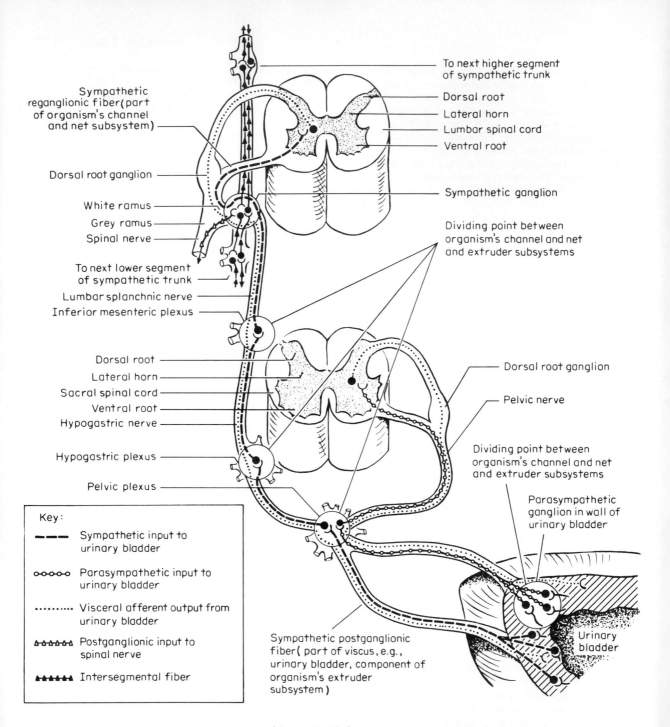

Fig. 7-3 Input and output innervation of the human urinary bladder.

Key:
- – – – Sympathetic input to urinary bladder
- ○○○○○ Parasympathetic input to urinary bladder
- ········· Visceral afferent output from urinary bladder
- ▵▵▵▵▵▵ Postganglionic input to spinal nerve
- ▲▲▲▲▲▲ Intersegmental fiber

(Sympathetic input nerves shown to left of spinal cord and parasympathetic to right for diagrammatic clarity)

as parts of the channel and net subsystem of the organ's suprasystem, the organism.) Autonomic postganglionic neurons also serve as parts of the channel and net subsystem of matter-energy processing visceral organs, branching out within the substance of such an organ to go to all parts of it (see pages 336 and 337).

(d) *Other neurons leading into organs,* including those leading into one information processing organ in the organism's central nervous system from another such organ. We do not know enough yet about the routing of messages in the nervous system to be sure whether all messages input to information processing organs serve organismwide functions. Some may be limited to local organ functions. Neurons bringing the latter sort of messages into the organ are parts of that organ's input transducer. If such a neuron employs a different code from its presynaptic neuron, it is also a component of the organ's decoder (see page 338).

Artifacts may be used as prostheses to improve the function of pathological components of an eye or ear; these artifacts might be a corrective lens or a hearing aid. Some prostheses improve the function of normal eyes such as a magnifying glass, a microscope, or a telescope.

3.3.1.2 Process The matter-energy which is the marker bearing the input information to the receptor cell brings about in it a change in electrical potential which initiates the neural impulse (see pages 254 and 255 and Fig. 6-19). At the synapse between pre- and postganglionic fibers, the chemical information output by the preganglionic fiber in the neurohumoral transmitter is transduced into a neural impulse which is propagated into the organ. A similar transduction occurs at the synapses of all fibers leading in from the central nervous system. The thresholds of individual fibers which receive impulses, the number of the fibers, and the nature of the impulses—whether they are excitatory or inhibitory or both—determine the response of the organ to such neural information inputs (see pages 262 and 263). It is possible that the Weber function applies to organ thresholds (see Hypothesis 3.3.1.2-1, page 94, which postulates that the Weber function applies to an input transducer, its intensity output signal varying as a power function of the intensity of its input). When hormonal information enters a target organ, it activates processes in many individual cells, but exactly how is not yet known.

Included among representative *variables* of the input transducing process are: *Meaning of information input which is transduced.* Example: Both epinephrine and norepinephrine conveyed alpha-coded signals to the coronary arteries to dilate, but only the former substance signaled an increase in the cardiac output and a consequent rise in the blood pressure. *Sorts of information input which are transduced.* Example: Afferent neurons in the sow's teats transduced information representing contacts on those organ components as the little shoats began to suck on them. *Percentage of the information input which is transduced.* Example: The basilar membrane of the auditory component of the input transducer was damaged, so that it transduced only about half of the ordinarily audible frequencies, only from 20 to 8,000 Hz. *Threshold of the input transducer.* Example: The threshold of the eye fluctuated with the input of vitamin A to the organism; with high input of this vitamin the dark-adapted eye could see illumination of an intensity of 0.01 lumen (lm); but with low input, it could not. *Changes in input transducing over time.* Example: The eye gradually transduced a more and more blurred image as the cataract in its lens became more dense. *Changes in input transducing with different circumstances.* Example: For several minutes after it received a strong whiff of ammonia, the toad's olfactory bulb was less responsive to other smells. *Channel capacity of the input transducer.* Example: The eye could transduce up to about 10^4 bits per s. *Number of channels in use in the input transducer.* Example: Thousands of cones and even more rods were present in the eye. *Distortion of the input transducer.* Example: The patient had a partial nerve deafness in his left ear which worsened during the days he was toxic with the influenza. *Signal-to-noise ratio of the input transducer.* Example: The ringing in the subject's ear was higher, and the signal-to-noise ratio less, after he had received 1 g of aspirin every 4 h for 6 doses. *Rate of input transducing.* Example: The ear could distinguish separate beats from tuning forks between 1 and 24 beats per s, but not at higher rates. *Lag in input transducing.* Example: The rhodopsin in the eye had changed color, and a signal had been transmitted within 10 μs of the time the red light hit the eye, but the lag altered somewhat with other frequencies of light input. *Costs of input transducing.* Example: The rate of energy consumption of the autonomic postganglionic fibers to the spleen varied only slightly from day to day.

3.3.2 Internal transducer, the sensory subsystem which receives, from subsystems or components within the organ, markers bearing information about significant alterations in those subsystems or components, changing them to other matter-energy forms of a sort which can be transmitted within it.

3.3.2.1 Structure The internal transducer of most organs and organ components is upwardly dispersed to the level of the organism or downwardly dispersed to the component cells. It is possible that specialized cells of some organs belong to this subsystem. The juxtaglomerular apparatuses of the kidney glomeruli, for instance, may be components of it (see page 346). Specialized muscle cells in the sinoatrial and atrioventricular nodes of the heart may also be included in this subsystem (see pages 340 and 341).

Possibly in some organ components an internal transducer afferent neuron synapses, within the organ or outside in the visceral ganglia, with an efferent neuron to form a complete reflex arc. The myenteric plexus of the intestinal tract and the intramural plexus of the urinary bladder walls may contain such internal transducer cells and reflex arcs, although their existence has not been definitely proved (see page 341).

3.3.2.2 Process   Because decider processes are limited in most organs, much of the information necessary for their control and adjustment processes is transduced by components which transmit information to the decider of the organism rather than to the organs' own deciders (see Table 6-4). On the other hand, some autonomous control is found at this level. Certain organs or components carry out their basic processes after their innervation has been cut and even, in some cases, after being removed from the organism, although in intact organisms the autonomic nervous system controls rates and other variables of their activities.

If the information which initiates such autonomous activity is transduced by each of the component cells individually, as it is in myogenic contraction of the walls of capillaries (see page 347), the internal transducing process is downwardly dispersed. The mechanical characteristics and force of the response are determined by the amount of stretch to which the smooth-muscle fibers are subjected, the population of cells stimulated, and the arrangement of the cells in the structure of the tissue.

Specialized tissues within organs, which transduce information to be used for control of processes in the organ itself, are internal transducers at the level of the organ. Coordination of individual cells into a timed heartbeat and regulation of some kidney functions depend upon such components (see above). If local reflex arcs are involved in control of the gut and bladder (see above), transduction of information for these reflexes is carried out by the afferent neuron which must have a receptor ending similar to those which transduce input and internal information for transmission over organism channels (see pages 248 and 249, Table 6-4, Fig. 6-18, and pages 254 to 256).

I have not been able to discover examples at this level for all the *variables* of the internal transducing process mentioned at other levels of living systems, but a few representative ones include: *Meaning of internal information which is transduced.* Example: The signals indicated that the bladder was nearly full, so the bladder wall contracted. *Sorts of internal information which are transduced.* Example: The internal transducer signaled when the gut contracted and when it relaxed. *Percentage of the internal information which is transduced.* Example: After a large input of sodium pentobarbital, the denervated heart beat only about one-tenth as frequently, showing possibly that the internal transducer was processing only one-tenth of the information, or possibly that some other subsystem was processing less. *Threshold of the internal transducer.* Example: The threshold of the internal transducer of the automatic bladder was such that the bladder was always emptied before it contained 500 cm³. *Changes in internal transducing over time.* Example: After several hours the denervated heart beats became irregular in pace and the contractions of the fibers were not coordinated, resulting in fibrillation. *Changes in internal transducing with different circumstances.* Example: When the cat was under a deep general anesthetic, peristalsis occurred in the intestine only when a bolus of food was present in it large enough to distend it greatly. *Signal-to-noise ratio of the internal transducer.* Example: When the dog was toxic with a high fever, the beat of its denervated heart was irregular, the electromyogram showing random transient pulses. *Rate of internal transducing.* Example: The muscle of the denervated heart would contract to each input from an electrode up to about 1 per s. *Lag in internal transducing.* Example: The animal's gut responded sluggishly to an internal pressure applied by an instrument, often after a delay of seconds.

3.3.3   Channel and net, the subsystem composed of a single route in physical space, or multiple interconnected routes, by which markers bearing information are transmitted to all parts of the organ.

3.3.3.1 Structure   The sorts of routes employed for transmitting information throughout organs are remarkably diverse. Components of the channel and net subsystem of organs include:

(*a*) *The intrinsic nerve nets of organs.* The autonomic nervous system, a part of the channel and net subsystem of the organism (see page 455), supplies visceral organs with their innervation. In autonomic pathways leading to such organs from the central nervous system, there are two peripheral neurons, unlike the skeletal nervous system which has only one (see Fig. 7-3). Autonomic neurons in the spinal cord synapse with preganglionic neurons which synapse with postganglionic neurons. Cell bodies of these postganglionic neurons lie in ganglia either at some distance from the organs which are innervated, as in the sympathetic division of the autonomic nervous system, or actually within the walls of the innervated organ as in the parasympathetic.

Preganglionic neurons of the sympathetic division often synapse with postganglionic neurons in the sympathetic ganglia which lie to both sides of the spinal cord (see Fig. 7-3). Sometimes, however, they pass through them and synapse in more distal ganglia or plexuses, such as the celiac, aortic, superior or inferior mesenteric, hypogastric, or pelvic plexuses. The postganglionic neurons, with long, unmyelinated axons, often pass through other outlying ganglia or plexuses, sometimes without synapsing further, and enter the organ in a nerve composed of sympathetic, parasympathetic, and (sometimes) nonautonomic neurons. Postganglionic neurons may branch soon after leaving the ganglia and again as they pass through the tissues of the organ, helping to form an intricate autonomic plexus which innervates the cells.[26]

Parasympathetic preganglionic neurons (except for those of the cranial division which, like sympathetic neurons, synapse outside organs) are long and synapse with postganglionic neurons either close to the organ or within its walls. The postganglionic neurons are short, branching within the organ to participate in forming the autonomic plexus from which neural fibers branch out to the cells. Some autonomic neurons go with the spinal nerves to the skin of the organism, where they innervate sweat glands and other structures.

In information processing organs of the central nervous system there may well also be intrinsic channels or networks, as in the visceral organs. Certainly their neurons have extremely complex interconnections. Not enough is yet known about the patterns of these interconnections to say with any certainty whether there are separate channel and net subsystems for the different information processing organs that can be distinguished from the overall channel and net subsystem of the organism.

(b) *The vascular channels and intercellular fluids of organs.* Blood and lymphatic vessels convey hormonal markers bearing information throughout the tissues of organs. They pass from them into the intercellular fluids and thence to receptor cells. Usually these hormones are secreted in one organ and responded to in another, but in some cases both secreting and receiving cells may be in the same organ.

(c) *Chains of interconnected epithelial cells in organs.* The epithelial tissues of certain sense organs, the urinary bladder, and perhaps other organs contain chains or groups of interconnected cells.[27] The cell membranes between these cells are much more permeable to ions, and perhaps metabolic products, hormones, and other markers, than are the membranes on the exterior surfaces of the cells. Consequently such matter-energy may move much more freely from cell to cell than from cell interior to exterior. This communication can enable the cells to interact and, at least in the sense-organ epithelium, it may coordinate the interconnected cells so that they act in synchrony.

(d) *Smooth muscle.* Postganglionic neurons end on the cells of smooth muscle and glands. Each fiber of striated muscle is contacted by at least one neuron. In smooth muscle, however, though the neurons end among the muscle fibers, there is no clear relationship of a specific neuron to each muscle cell. Pulses bearing information may well be conveyed through the substance of the smooth-muscle fibers themselves.[28]

(e) *Cardiac muscle.* Although heart muscle is like smooth muscle in some ways, it is more like striated muscle in its channel and net structure. It is not, as was once believed, a syncytium.[29] Electron microscopic studies show that each cell has a complete, although extremely fine, sarcolemma. Minute axons penetrate among the muscle fibers. Synaptic vesicles can be identified, but no real synapses have been found. The vesicles are probably sites of chemical transmission of nerve impulses.

Synapses. The channel and net subsystems of at least some organs contain synapses (see pages 248, 249, 254, and 255). It is uncertain whether the plexuses derived from postganglionic sympathetic and parasympathetic fibers synapse in all visceral organs. In the two elaborate, interconnected myenteric plexuses of the intestinal wall, however, there are synapses.[30] These are believed to be between input neurons from the sympathetic ganglia on both sides of the spinal cord and output neurons with cell bodies in the intestinal wall. These synapses make possible myenteric reflexes (see page 341).

Ephapses. Organ channel and net subsystems in some species, including crayfish and annelids, have some neural junctions with ephapses which employ electrical transmission, rather than synapses which employ chemical transmission (see page 249).

3.3.3.2 Process In an intact organism, control signals from the organism's decider in its central nervous system flow along the input channels to organs to facilitate or inhibit the organs' processes. These processes, however, are only partially dependent upon input innervation (see pages 346 and 347). Information passing only through an organ's channel and net can in many cases maintain its processes. Denervated smooth muscles do not atrophy as do denervated skeletal muscles.[31] Some glands do atrophy when cut off from their nerve supplies, but by no means all of them. The denervated liver carries on many of its processes and the functions of the denervated adrenal medulla are quite normal. The denervated "automatic" urinary bladder continues to empty periodically, whenever it fills up to a critical volume.

An important channel in some organs which have smooth-muscle layers is cell-to-cell conduction of information in the layer. Such muscle gives rise to myogenic pulses and contracts actively when stretched. Typical peristalsis can be carried on by sections of intestinal tract completely cut off from the organism.

Certain experimental findings suggest that the biochemical control processes involved in cell-to-cell conduction of information by hormones, by synaptic transmitters, and by autonomic neurotransmitters may be similar.[32]

Even though several forms of channel and net subsystems have been studied in organs, those studies have rarely been quantitative. As a result there is little precise information to indicate whether any of the hypotheses in Chap. 4 (see Hypotheses 3.3.3.1-1 through 3.3.3.2-21, pages 95 to 97) apply to the channel and net subsystems of organs.

Many *variables* of channel and net processing can be measured. Some representative ones are: *Meaning of information channeled to various parts of the system.* Example: Beta-coded pulses were transmitted periodically through the smooth-muscle layers of the intestine signaling it to contract. *Sorts of information channeled to various parts of the system.* Example: Information on the rate, frequency, and intensity of inputs of tones was channeled through the left and the right auditory components of the cat's input transducer, *i.e.*, the basilar membrane. *Percentage of information arriving at the appropriate receiver in the channel and net.* Example: The network among the cells in the cat's retina channeled the information to the appropriate receiver cells almost without error or omission. *Threshold of the channel and net.* Example: The neural autoregulatory feedback circuits controlling systemic arterial circulation did not convey signals until the arterial pressure reached a specific minimum.[33] *Changes in channel and net processing over time.* Example: As the cerebellum aged, its usual patterns of neural transmission changed. *Changes in channel and net processing with different circumstances.* Example: After his heart attack, the man developed bundle branch block, and the bundle of His no longer transmitted neural signals from the auricle to the ventricle. *Information capacity of the channel and net.* Example: The human eye transmitted thousands of bits per s

through its optic nerve; since this information passed through the channel and net subsystem of the organism's input transducer, the net's total channel capacity must have been at least that great. *Distortion of the channel and net.* Example: Below 26°C the signals which caused the dog's heart muscle to contract became irregular, and the strength of its contraction diminished. *Signal-to-noise ratio in the channel and net.* Example: The ruptured intervertebral disc pressed against the spinal nerve and from time to time gave rise to irregular volleys of pulses on it which had never occurred before the disc ruptured. *Rate of processing of information over the channel and net.* Example: Autoregulatory responses within individual organs occur in 1 to 3 min after a signal is input, while external regulations, as by baroreceptor reflexes, take less than 1 min.[34] *Lag in channel and net processing.* Example: In experiments on dogs in which the central nervous system has been eliminated surgically, the blood vascular component develops autoregulation after lags of 20 to 90 min.[35] *Costs of channel and net processing.* Example: Operation of the intrinsic channels of the organ depended on a continual supply of energy-rich molecules from the organism's bloodstream.

3.3.4 Decoder, the subsystem which alters the code of information input to it through the input transducer or the internal transducer into a "private" code that can be used internally by the organ.

3.3.4.1 Structure   Much like the input and internal transducers, this subsystem is dispersed to (*a*) the receptor cells or second-echelon cells in the various neural components, like the eyes and ears, of the organism's input transducer subsystem, and perhaps the components, like the pain or pressure receptors, of the organism's internal transducer subsystem (see pages 249, 255, Table 6-4, Fig. 6-18, and pages 377 to 390); (*b*) individual target or receptor cells in the organ which react to hormonal inputs and decode their chemical messages; (*c*) the autonomic postganglionic neurons, both sympathetic and parasympathetic, which bring information to the organ from the organism's central nervous system (see pages 336 and 337); and (*d*) other neurons leading into organs, like input neurons to one organ in the central nervous system from another, if they use different codes.

3.3.4.2 Process   The first step in visual decoding for the organism takes place in and behind the retina of the eye (see pages 397 to 401). Signals from separate light receptors are carried on multiple neurons to an intricate nervous center behind the retina. Here they are organized to emphasize certain sorts of input information about edges and boundaries, light, darkness, and color.[36] Comparable integrations take place in the basilar membrane of the Organ of Corti of the ear and in other components of the organism's input transducer (see pages 378, 401, and 402). Neurons entering organs convey various patterns of pulses which are decoded to signal excitation or inhibition of various processes in the organ. The shape of hormonal molecules conveys a coded signal to block or to activate enzymatic processes in the receptor cells.

Few precise observations or measurements of organ-level coding have been made; as a result evidence as to whether any of the hypotheses on decoding (see Hypotheses 3.3.4.2-1 through 3.3.4.2-10, pages 98 and 99) apply to organs is lacking.

I have been unable to discover examples at the organ level for all the *variables* of the process of decoding mentioned at the other levels. I have, however, found the following ones: *Meaning of information which is decoded.* Example: Some neural pulses from the retina were beta-coded signals of the presence of light on it, but occasional pulses had no such meaning, representing neural noise. *Sorts of information which are decoded.* Example: The basilar membrane of the pig turned pitch and intensity differences of sounds into a neural code involving patterns of pulses on multiple parallel fibers in the acoustic nerve, and it also transmitted a sound signal as output whenever it received an electric shock. *Percentage of the information input which is decoded.* Example: The normal eye transmitted a high percentage of the information that reached the retina, but this percentage was greatly decreased after the retina was detached. *Changes in decoding with different circumstances.* Example: The progesterone receptors in the uterus decoded hormonal input signals more actively in the presence of estrogen.[37] *Channel capacity of the decoder.* Example: The man's optic nerve transmitted thousands of bits per s, thus his eye's decoder must have had a channel capacity at least that great. *Percentage of omissions in decoding.* Example: The eidetic child, who had photographic memory of scenes he had viewed, reported precisely detailed visual images, indicating that the visual decoders of his eyes made only a low percentage of omissions. *Code employed.* Example: Quantitative analyses of the patterns of pulses on the ulnar nerve of the arms of human subjects, elicited by various temporal patterns of shocks to the arms, enabled Uttal to discover regular relationships between the two sorts of patterns, *i.e.*, a stable code.[38] *Costs of decoding.* Example: In the prostate the decoding of testosterone into dihydrotestosterone, a molecule capable of being bound to chromatin and conveying a signal to it, involved only a minute expenditure of energy.[39]

3.3.5 Associator, the subsystem which carries out the first stage of the learning process, forming enduring associations among items of information in the organ.

3.3.5.1 Structure   No associator subsystem has been discovered in any organ. This subsystem is upwardly dispersed from the organ level to the organism level. The central nervous system is the site of the associator in organisms.

3.3.5.2 Process   When the neural pathways to and from the central nervous system are cut, organs make no associations. This indicates that this process is upwardly dispersed to the organism level. Reflex or automatic responses remain in some organs, but they do not become conditioned. Therefore no variables of associating processes at the organ level can be described.

3.3.6 Memory, the subsystem which carries out the second stage of the learning process, storing various sorts of information in the organ for different periods of time.

3.3.6.1 Structure   There has been no evidence for such a subsystem in any organ. This subsystem appears to be upwardly dispersed to the level of the organism in all cases, although under certain circumstances an organ's past experiences may alter postsynaptic potentials and perhaps protein synthesis in its neurons.

3.3.6.2 Process   Information storage and retrieval—such as motor habits or conditioned secretory activity—are lost to organs, at least those of higher animals, when their neural connections to the central nervous system are cut. This suggests that memory of organs is upwardly dispersed to the organism level, but certain researches raise the question whether this is always true. I shall mention three groups of such studies.

First are the investigations on posttetanic potentiation.[40] This phenomenon is seen in synapses between neurons and in neuromyal junctions of several organs, including the channel and net and the motor. It is observed in several types of animals, several species—including amphibians, cephalopods, and mammals. Ordinarily multiple signals in sequence pass over a synapse. If one pulse is rapidly followed by one or more—say in less than 100 ms—the electrotonic potentials on the subsynaptic membrane elicited by the later pulses are often significantly larger than those elicited by the first pulse. Long-continued inputs to the postsynaptic neuron resulting from stimulation of the presynaptic neuron with an electrode for 15 to 30 min at 100 to 500 pulses per s produce such potentiation in the postsynaptic neuron which lasts for 1 to

2 h. Thereafter the latter neuron returns to normal. Intermittent, patterned inputs are more effective in producing potentiation than continuous ones. Even after the postsynaptic neuron returns to normal, for at least another 1½ h, it is susceptible to a second set of potentiating pulse inputs. This potentiation occurs because during later pulses increased amounts of transmitter substance are present in the synapse, having been released from the presynaptic neuron by previous pulses. These markers produced by past processes alter future processes in the postsynaptic neuron. Some may question whether posttetanic potentiation is a form of memory, but it is certainly a process whereby the character of past information signals alters the character of later signals. In a primitive sense this is memory, the storage of information in a tissue or organ over a period of time.

Second, several experiments have been conducted on the isolated third thoracic ganglion of the cockroach, from which neurons go to its third leg. This ganglion contains neurons of the motor and perhaps the channel and net subsystems, with many complex synaptic connections. Electrical pulses are transmitted by an electrode to an input neuron to the ganglion, and recordings are made from an electrode on an output neuron to the leg muscle. Several sorts of outputs from the ganglion have been observed by Luco.[41] (a) One sort he calls the labile response. When the ganglion in an intact cockroach with body—but not legs—immobilized was stimulated at the rate of 5 pulses per s, the amplitude of the output pulses progressively decreased until they essentially disappeared. This was not fatigue because a sudden shift to an input rate of 50 pulses per s evoked outputs immediately. After a time this latter response showed fatigue. This may be a rudimentary sort of memory, an effect of past information input—a gradual habituation to 5 pulses per s—is suddenly dishabituated when the input rate changes rapidly. (b) In an entirely isolated ganglion, which had shown no spontaneous activity for a long period, 1-s bursts of 50 pulses per s—the bursts being 9 s apart—produced spontaneous pulse activity between bursts which at times lasted several minutes. In this situation past information input modified the activity between bursts—perhaps a primitive sort of memory.

Third, experiments have been conducted on fixation of experience in the spinal cords of rats.[42] Lesions were made in rats' cerebellums, and this produced postural asymmetry of their hindlimbs. Later the spinal cord was cut, through which neurons of the channel and net subsystem course from the cerebellum to the muscles. If the asymmetry had existed about 45 min or more before the cord was cut, the postural asymmetry persisted. If it had existed a shorter time, the asymmetry disappeared. Furthermore, 8-azaguanine, which slows formation of RNA, increased the fixation time of the asymmetry—a sort of "memory"—from about 45 to about 70 min. One might argue that this finding indicated nothing about memory. It might simply demonstrate that the drug added more damage to the effects of surgery on the cerebellum. But another drug, U-9189, which speeds RNA formation in neurons, cut the fixation time to about 25 min. These findings suggest that the channel and net organ (although conceivably the neurons below the cut in the cord were motor neurons of the motor organ) has its own memory. They also suggest that, at least in this organ, RNA plays an important part in storing memory.

These three sorts of memory, if such they are, are all primitive and extremely simple compared with the sorts of memory seen at higher levels of living systems, which appears to give some support to that part of Hypothesis 3.3.6.2-6 (see page 100), which states that the higher the level of a system, in general the more complex are its memory storage and search rules. It is so questionable whether any organ truly has memory that it is not worthwhile to list variables for this subsystem.

3.3.7 Decider, the executive subsystem which receives information inputs from all other subsystems and transmits to them information outputs that control the entire organ.

3.3.7.1 Structure Organs differ in the structure of their decider subsystems. For some the decider is upwardly dispersed to the central decider of the organism. Interruption of the channels to and from it causes atrophy and complete loss of function in such an organ. Some visceral organs, innervated by the autonomic nervous system, have great autonomy, which suggests the presence of an organ-level decider.

The heart, a component of the distributor organ, has a sort of autonomy of deciding. Three types of muscle are found in it: specialized nodal tissue, Purkinje fibers, and ordinary cross-striated cardiac muscle. The specialized tissue consists of the sinoatrial node, the atrioventricular node, the atrioventricular bundle, its bundle branches, and the network of Purkinje fibers. These structures represent a gradual transition from highly specialized cells into ordinary heart muscle. The sympathetic fibers which are found in these regions are believed to be concerned with regulation of the autonomous activity.

I have discussed the myenteric plexuses of the intestinal tract above (see page 337). These may include components of the organ decider.

Organs with dispersed components must depend

upon the channels of the organism for their coordination, although single components may have a decider with more or less autonomy.

Information processing organs in the central nervous system possibly have their own decider subsystems. We are not sure. Certainly different categories of information are processed and decided on at different echelons in the nervous system.

An artifact which may be used as a prosthesis to improve the pathological functioning of some specialized cells of the heart is an electrical pacemaker which can correct irregular heartbeat rhythms.

3.3.7.2 Process   Clearly some organs have that essential critical subsystem, a decider. Krieg says:[43]

First of all, let it be clear that the viscera in general perform their intrinsic functions without nervous control. Experimental animals have lived long periods in the laboratory and even reproduced, after their autonomic nervous connections have been severed. A constant neural tippling by the viscera is not necessary. Such animals, however, could not survive in nature, because their organs cannot adjust their response to rigors of the environment, pursuit, feasting and famine.

Krieg goes on to indicate how the decider of the organism controls the decider of the organ through the sympathetic and parasympathetic branches of the autonomic nervous system.

The sympathetic system adjusts the organism to all forms of excitement or stress—fear, rage, combat, flight, pursuit. The parasympathetic system functions in quiet, vegetative states. Nearly all organs have a double innervation, and one of these exerts a stimulating effect, the other an inhibitory effect. The sign or nature of the effect can be divined for any organ by asking oneself whether that organ's activity should be exalted or diminished during excitement.

The heart has its own pacemaker. A denervated heart continues to beat. A heart removed from an organism will keep beating for a time. The beat of the heart is controlled by changes in the potential difference between the outside and the inside of individual myocardial fibers (see page 256). The structures described above are responsible for different activities. The specialized nodal tissue and the Purkinje fibers are concerned with initiation and conduction of pulses through the myocardium, the plain cardiac muscle with muscle contraction. The sinoatrial node is believed to be the focus in the mammalian heart from which each heartbeat starts. This is a specialized node embedded in the wall of the right atrial chamber of the heart near the entrance of a major vein, the superior vena cava. If this is inactivated, the atrioventricular node can begin to initiate beats. If both are inactivated, the muscle of the ventricle of the heart can take over, although under such circumstances all components of the heart will not beat in such well-coordinated fashion. This lack of coordination seems to

support Hypothesis 3.3.7.2-16, page 101, which states that subsystems and components satisfice shorter-term goals than does the decider of the total system. Thus the decider of this organ component is organized in echelons. It sets a pace which is efficient when a normal heart output is adequate but which greatly increases when a larger output is required. This supports Hypothesis 3.3.7.2-18, page 101, which states that systems which survive make decisions enabling them to perform at an optimum efficiency for maximum physical power output, which is always less than maximum efficiency.

In other components of the organism's distributor subsystem, the small vessels in the peripheral vascular bed of the heart, kidney, liver, intestine, muscle, and other tissues, vessel diameter is altered by local decision-making processes.[44] They control even when all nerves of the central and autonomic nervous system are severed. This autoregulation changes blood flows in these tissues to minimize the effects of arterial pressure changes and maintain the flows relatively constant (see pages 346 and 347). Also, as the need of these tissues for oxygen inputs increases or decreases, the blood flow to them changes appropriately.

Under normal conditions the gut's activities are regulated by the organism's central nervous system. After all nerves to it have been severed, however, the gastrointestinal tract is still capable of carrying on its major processes. Part of this activity, the essentially rhythmic functions like gastric peristalsis and the segmental contractions of the small and large intestine, are dependent upon the ability of the smooth muscle to initiate contractions. The presence of food in the gut is adequate to initiate peristalsis, even in an isolated intestine. This *myenteric reflex* may be controlled by the myenteric plexus acting as decider for the organ component.

The properties of smooth muscle account for some of the autonomy of visceral organs. This muscle responds to stretch by contraction without needing signals from the nervous system. The primary determinant of activity of the stomach, for instance, is the presence of food, although it is only one of many, including such things as whether the organism sees or smells food.

The ureter, a tube connecting each kidney to the bladder, is composed of smooth-muscle cells linked by intercellular bridges which form a syncytium capable of conducting an action potential without any other neural channels.[45] Even when autonomic nerves present in the ureter are cut, the regular ureteral contractions that propel the urine from the kidney to the bladder continue autonomously in response to signals transmitted over the intercellular bridges.

In an intact organism, emptying the bladder is under voluntary control. Spinal reflexes as well as autonomic are involved. (This is true also of anal control, a socially useful arrangement.) An "automatic," denervated urinary bladder, however, responds to filling by partial emptying. The coordination of the detrusor and internal sphincter muscles in a denervated bladder shows that local reflex arcs through ganglion cells in the bladder wall exist.[46] Such a bladder empties automatically when it fills to a certain point.

Deciding about some other organ processes is downwardly dispersed to the cellular level. Storage of carbohydrate, metabolism of protein, and secretion of bile all are done by liver cells independent of neural control by the organ. Of these three, it is carbohydrate storage that is most affected by denervation.

Denervated organs remain connected to the distributor of the organism, so both matter-energy and chemical information reach them through the blood and lymphatic vessels. The signal for emptying the gallbladder is believed to come over the vascular channel. As a result the continued functioning of a denervated gallbladder is partially dependent upon this and probably also upon the smooth muscle in its structure. How the gallbladder empties is not well understood, however (see page 330).

Selective activities of tissues in intact organisms, such as the selective filtration by the kidney and the filtering by the barriers between the blood and the brain, the blood and the spinal fluid, or the brain and the aqueous humor of the eye, are decider processes. They are carried out at the cellular level.

I know of no evidence whether or not decisions at the organ level are made in the four stages mentioned in Hypothesis 3.3.7.2-1 (see page 100), i.e., (a) establishing purposes or goals, (b) analysis, (c) synthesis, and (d) implementing. It may well be that organ deciders employ less costly adjustments before more costly ones (see Hypothesis 3.3.7.2-14, page 101) and rapidly available ones before those which are less readily available (see Hypothesis 3.3.7.2-15, page 101). Of two equally costly adjustments, they may well select the one which most rapidly or efficiently returns a variable to a steady state (see Hypothesis 3.3.7.2-19, page 101 and 102). But there is little or no evidence relevant to these issues because research on organs traditionally has not dealt with such matters.

I have not found examples for all the *variables* of the process of deciding discussed at the other levels of living systems, but I have discovered the following ones: *Meaning of information employed in deciding.* Example: The beta-coded signals arriving at the atrio-ventricular node indicated whether the sinoatrial node had transmitted a pulse or whether it had arisen elsewhere in the heart. *Sorts of information employed in deciding.* Example: One decision by the denervated heart to beat would be determined by a recent information input such as touch by a probe and the next by the intrinsic rhythm of the tissue and the time since the last beat. *Amount of information employed in deciding.* Example: The only input necessary to cause contraction of the ureter was stretching of the muscle fibers.[47] *Changes in deciding over time.* Example: As the time passed, the denervated heart responded less and less to input information. *Changes in deciding with different circumstances.* Example: Under deep sedation the periodic filling and emptying of the automatic bladder ceased, and it emptied as soon as urine flowed into it. *Number of alternatives in input before decision and in output afterward.* Example: After the strong electric shock, the heart could either beat or fibrillate; it beat. *Rate of deciding.* Example: The automatic bladder emptied about every 90 min. *Lag in deciding.* Example: When the dog was under deep ether anesthesia, the movements of peristaltic waves down the gut were slowed because the enteric plexuses were slower in transmitting the signals to contract. *Costs of deciding.* Example: The oxygen in the heart-lung machine was used up, and the isolated heart stopped beating.

3.3.8   Encoder, the subsystem which alters the code of information input to it from other information processing subsystems, from a "private" code used internally by the organ into a "public" code which can be interpreted by other organs in its environment.

3.3.8.1   Structure   Encoding of neural pulses and information bearing secretions from organs is downwardly dispersed, being carried out by many single cells in each organ; but in addition to the information from each cell, the pattern from all the cells—which elements are active, their number, and their locations— also can convey information to the organism.

The two sorts of downwardly dispersed components of organ encoders are:

(a) Presynaptic regions and perhaps also certain structures in the cell bodies (see pages 277 and 278) of output neurons from a visceral organ to a neural organ, or from one neural organ to another. The dendrites of all such neurons have specialized receptor endings which transmit signals about changes in different variables in the tissues of the organ (see pages 248 and 249, Table 6-4, and Fig. 6-18). These signals are output by visceral components of organs along the vagus, pelvic, splanchnic, and other visceral afferent nerves, which pass through autonomic ganglia without synapsing (see Fig. 7-3). Their cell bodies are in the dorsal root ganglion of the organism's spinal cord, and they synapse in the lateral horn of the cord. Each neuron's presynaptic region is the most likely location for the encoding process by which their neural processes are converted into a chemical neurohumoral transmitter code used at the organism level.

(*b*) Cells that secrete hormones in endocrine glands are also encoders for the organs in which they occur.

3.3.8.2 Process   Most of the information encoded by the components of this subsystem does not reach the higher centers of the organism's central nervous system whose functions are associated with consciousness. It is used in the automatic control of such variables as pulse rate, blood pressure, and breathing rate. Other messages include signals about such vital matters as chemical states; abnormal tissue states which produce pain, irritation, or itching; fullness or emptiness of the stomach; or strains which can be reduced by extruding wastes. Visceral pain differs from pain in surface organs in that, while distention of a visceral organ component is extremely painful, cutting it is painless. Hormonal signals encoded in one organ component serve to coordinate its processes with those in other components or organs.

Representative *variables* of the encoding process could probably be measured much as for the decoding process, but this has not yet been done, and thus at present only speculation about them is possible.

3.3.9   Output transducer, the subsystem which puts out markers bearing information from the organ, changing markers within the organ into other matter-energy forms which can be transmitted over channels in the organ's environment.

3.3.9.1 Structure   The two sorts of laterally dispersed components of the organ's output transducer are:

(*a*) Presynaptic regions of neurons that output signals from a visceral organ to a neural organ or from one neural organ to another, the same neurons that also include encoder structures. At the organ level the processes of putting the marker into the "public" code that is used outside the organ and changing it into a matter-energy form that can be transmitted outside are closely related or identical.

It would be possible to define the neural components of the encoder and the output transducer from any of the viscera as consisting only of the end organs, classing the remainder of each of these cells as parts of the organism's channel and net subsystem, but that would mean that one cell was in three subsystems—encoder, output transducer, and channel and net. To avoid such complication, I consider the neural encoder and output transducer subsystems of the organ to include the entire cell of each output neu-

ron, even though it extends far beyond the main body of the organ into the central nervous system. Either mode of delimiting the subsystems is defensible.

(*b*) Cells of endocrine glands that synthesize and output hormones, as well as the venous and lymphatic vessels that conduct the blood containing those hormones out of the organ. These vessels are combined components, serving at the same time as parts of the output transducer and of the extruder.

3.3.9.2 Process   A diverse array of signals about many internal variables is transmitted from organs to other organs and upward to the organs' suprasystem. Posture of the body, tension of muscles, pressure from direct contact with environmental objects, fullness of hollow viscera, chemical states of the blood and other internal fluids, cellular damage of abnormal states severe enough to cause pain, the presence of potentially or actually harmful substances, and internal body temperatures all can initiate specific chemical or bioelectrical processes which send signals centrally. The channel which carries such a signal is often the first arm of a negative feedback which keeps a vital bodily variable within a range of stability. These signals coordinate the organs to make an integrated organism.

It would be possible to measure for any organ such *variables* as the meaning and sorts of information output which are transduced, its output transducer threshold, how the process changes with time and under various circumstances, the number of channels used and their capacities, the distortion, signal-to-noise ratio, rate, lag, and intensity, and the costs of the process. But no such experiments have been done because organs have not ordinarily been thought of by experimenters as distinct systems in which such variables can be measured.

4. Relationships among subsystems or components

In order to understand organs as systems, we must know not only what structures constitute the organs and organ components and what processes they carry out, but also what observable and measurable relationships they have to one another. These relationships are as important an aspect of the science of systems as are the systems themselves. Illustrative examples of relationships at the organ level follow.

4.1   Structural relationships

4.1.1   Containment   Example: The man's islets of Langerhans were found to be normally placed, in the pancreas.

4.1.2   Number   Example: There were four chambers in the infant's heart.

4.1.3   Order   Example: The order of the dog's cerebral nerves, from front to back, was shown to be as follows: olfactory, optic, oculomotor, trigeminal, trochlear, abducent, facial, auditory, glossopharyngeal, vagus, accessory, and hypoglossal.

4.1.4 Position   Example: One of the lungs was outside the chest wall.

4.1.5 Direction   Example: The man's diaphragm was above his liver.

4.1.6 Size   Example: The malformed left kidney was smaller than the adrenal gland near it.

4.1.7 Pattern   Example: The major arteries of the cat's brain joined properly to form a circle, the circle of Willis.

4.1.8 Density   Example: The concentration of glomeruli was greater in the cortex of the kidney and the concentration of tubules greater in the body of the kidney.

4.2 Process relationships

4.2.1 Temporal relationships   Example: The pylorus usually opened to dump a fatty meal into the duodenum before the gallbladder emptied itself of bile.

4.2.1.1 Containment in time   Example: The time between every contraction of the heart included two periods, systole and diastole.

4.2.1.2 Number in time   Example: The postganglionic fiber transmitted 20 pulses per min.

4.2.1.3 Order in time   Example: The light always entered the pupil of the eye before it contracted.

4.2.1.4 Position in time   Example: Three minutes and ten seconds after the Bromsulphalein was injected intravenously, the kidneys began to excrete the dye.

4.2.1.5 Direction in time   Example: The lemur's glottis closed after he began to swallow but before the water passed into his esophagus.

4.2.1.6 Duration   Example: The knee jerk lasted 0.8 s.

4.2.1.7 Pattern in time   Example: The electrocardiogram showed a typical normal pattern.

4.2.2 Spatiotemporal relationships

4.2.2.1 Action   Example: The tubules of the kidney absorbed most of the water.

4.2.2.2 Communication   Example: The motor area of the brain transmitted to the gastrocnemius muscle of the left leg a signal to contract.

4.2.2.3 Direction of action   Example: The blood passed rapidly into the sinuses as they dilated.

4.2.2.4 Pattern of action   Example: As the kangaroo was deprived of food day after day, the fat disappeared from the regions where it usually was stored.

4.2.2.5 Entering or leaving containment   Example: The spleen contracted, and its blood flowed into the vascular system.

4.3 Relationships among subsystems or components which involve meaning   Examples: The ending of the neural impulse from the retina through various inter-mediate centers to the complex cells of the visual projection area of the cortex signaled to the decider subsystem of the cat's decoder organ that the light had gone off (see pages 397 to 401). The arrival of the thyrotropic hormone, secreted by the pituitary gland, at the secretory cells of the thyroid gland signaled it to increase its rate of production of thyroxine.

5. System processes

5.1 Process relationships between inputs and outputs   Because of the partipotentiality and specialization of all organs, their characteristic outputs, both matter-energy and information, are greatly different depending upon what subsystem process they carry out in the organism. These differing outputs are produced in some cases from similar inputs. Both nervous and muscular tissue receive inputs of glucose and oxygen. The output of the one is markers bearing information, and of the other, work energy. Certain organs require, in addition to glucose and oxygen, special inputs without which they cannot produce their characteristic outputs. Bone marrow, for example, must input iron, which it incorporates into its output of new red blood cells.

Organs have four different types of input–output relationships:

(a) *Matter-energy inputs related to matter-energy outputs.*   Each organ component takes from the bloodstream those substances required for its growth, repair, replacement of parts, and characteristic outputs, and extrudes others that it cannot use. The brains of humans and other primates are highly selective and have protective boundary processes to exclude inappropriate inputs (see pages 428 and 429). It is not hard to compare concentrations of substances in arterial blood with their concentrations in venous blood coming from the brain through the jugular vein. This vein is near the surface and is thus readily accessible, and it drains no other significant area except the brain. Any available artery can provide the arterial blood. Anesthesia is not required to make such a study.

Calculations based on concentrations of nitrous oxide in the blood after it is inhaled by volunteer subjects show that the functioning human nervous system requires a high input of oxygen and glucose which is secured by a rapid rate of blood flow. Blood flows through the brain of a resting normal young man at a rate of about 54 ml per 100 g of brain tissue per min.[48] Function is impaired when it is reduced to 30 ml per 100 g of tissue per min. This compares to the blood flow in resting-forearm skeletal muscle of from 1.8 to 9.6 ml per 100 g of muscle per min (see page 326). The brain oxygen consumption of 3.5 ml per 100 g per min represents nearly 20 percent of the total oxygen use in the entire body of a resting adult who has not eaten. The comparable figure for a 5-year-old child is approximately 50 percent (see page 350.)[49] Although in lower animals oxygen use increases during abnormal states like convulsions and decreases below resting levels after they are over, it is not clear that it alters greatly from one normal functional state to another. Prolonged oxygen lack stress to the brain produces irreversible intracellular metabolic changes in illnesses like anemias and probably cerebral arteriosclerosis. Oxygen excess stress, at least up to the levels produced by breathing oxygen at 3.5 atmospheres (atm), which is near the level of oxygen toxicity, produces no changes in the rate of use of oxygen by the brain and no known behavioral effects. If the internal body temperature is significantly lowered, a decrease in the rate of use of oxygen by the brain also results. It is uncertain whether the reverse is true when the body temperature rises.

The skin of organisms requires inputs of cystine, an amino acid which contains sulfur. Cystine is an essential constituent of keratin, a protein in hair, feathers, nails, horns, and similar bodily parts.[50] These are nonliving artifacts produced and extruded by cells of the skin, to which they remain attached for varying lengths of time. Other amino acids without sulfur cannot be substituted for cystine in their synthesis, although the cells can make cystine from the other sulfur-containing amino acid, methionine, which is an essential input to the organism.

Besides large amounts of iron, which is incorporated into new red blood cells, the bone marrow must input copper, cobalt, and manganese. These are essential inputs in the syntheses which produce red blood corpuscles. Probably some or all of these act as catalysts in some stage of the process.[51]

(b) *Matter-energy inputs related to information outputs.* A hormone bearing alpha-coded chemical information output from endocrine glands may (see pages 390 to 392), as in the case of the thyroid hormones thyroxine and triiodothyronine, have a molecular structure that includes some special chemical substance not required for the output of other tissues or organs. Without iodine the thyroid gland cannot output its hormones which are necessary for normal growth and tissue development in infants and for maintenance of the normal level of metabolism of animals of all ages.[52]

(c) *Information inputs related to matter-energy outputs.* Hormones act as signals for various sorts of activities in organs and tissues of the organism (see pages 391 and 392). An example of an alteration of output from an organ component in response to such an alpha-coded input signal is the decreased rate of

output and consequent increased rate of storage of glucose in the liver produced by the pancreatic hormone, insulin. After a meal, when the amount of sugar in the blood rises, secretion of this hormone reduces the blood sugar by holding carbohydrates in the liver. Increased storage in muscular tissue is also stimulated.

Information inputs also evoke matter-energy outputs when estrogens and progestins, ovarian hormones, act upon the female reproductive organs.[53] Estrogens, among other things, stimulate growth of both the myometrium and the endometrium; maintain a thick vaginal mucosa and indirectly keep the vaginal acidity in a steady state; stimulate cervical glands to secrete copious quantities of viscous mucus; stimulate breast growth and development; elicit deposition of characteristic feminine subcutaneous fat; sensitize the ovaries to gonadotropins; and retard linear body growth while facilitating closure of the epiphyses. Progesterone and related hormones antagonize the growth-promoting effects of estrogen on the endometrium of the uterus and its ability to nourish an ovum, convert the cervical mucus from a viscous to a nonviscous fluid, stimulate mammary gland growth and development, and inhibit uterine motility.

(d) *Information inputs related to information outputs.* Several examples of such input–output relationships in animal organs are readily identified because various pituitary hormones input to other endocrine glands initiate processes which cause the latter glands to output their hormones (see pages 391, 392, and 463). The thyrotropic hormone of the pituitary, for instance, activates an enzyme in the thyroid gland which releases thyroxine from the thyroglobulin in which it is stored, after which it is output into the bloodstream of the organism. The posterior pituitary hormone, oxytocin, released at coitus, appears to signal the uterus to increase the contractions elicited in it by estrogen.

Another sort of information input, a low level of calcium in the circulating blood, signals the parathyroid gland to release parathyroid hormone, which acts upon the kidneys and bones to restore the amount of calcium in the blood, which is vital to the health of the organism.[54]

5.2 Adjustment processes among subsystems or components, used in maintaining variables in steady states

5.2.1 Matter-energy input processes   Some organ components are able to adjust to variations in flows of essential inputs. For example, input of oxygen to the human brain is kept in steady state even when the organism's blood pressure falls to as low as 30 mm of mercury (Hg). This is achieved by increasing the proportion of the body's blood flowing to the brain, thus decreasing the amounts going to other components. Such an adjustment seems to illustrate Hypothesis 5.2-2 (see page 106), which states that when a stress upon a system becomes greater, more components of it are involved in adjusting to the stress. A cost of this adjustment process may be in diminished function of other organs than the brain. I have discussed the uptake of oxygen by tissues earlier (see pages 327 and 328).

Excess stresses of matter-energy are often not important because an organ usually extrudes whatever matter-energy is input beyond its needs. This is not true of excesses of some toxic substances, *e.g.*, oxygen at high tensions, cyanide, strychnine, barbiturates, and various heavy metals input to the brain. Various detoxifying metabolic processes in organs adjust to such excesses within certain concentration limits. These processes have costs—the consumption of substances which have other metabolic uses to the organ.

5.2.2 Information input processes Increases in rates and amounts of information inputs to the neurons of organs can be adjusted to by increased frequency of outputs by individual neurons, a cellular adaptation. There is probably a minute cost, insignificant in magnitude to the organ, in increased energy consumption involved in this more rapid information output.

Adaptations to the stress of inadequate information input caused by cutting the nerve supply to certain organ components can be met by autonomous carrying on of processes, usually at the cost of a lowered degree of efficiency. (See Hypothesis 5.2-14, page 107, which states that segregation increases conflict among subsystems or components of a system.) The heart and the urinary bladder can operate autonomously in this way. The decider subsystem of the organism can make decisions as to how to act in the environment—often erroneously—even when either blindness or deafness deprives it of normal information about the environment. Most other organs and components have no adjustment process to handle a lack stress of information.

Some components of the input transducer of organisms can act to screen out excess inputs of information from the environment. This is true of the eyes, which have adjustable pupils and lids that will close. These muscular movements occur at the cost of small amounts of energy. Within the eye, the retina adapts to the level of illumination. Variations in the concentrations of the visual pigment, rhodopsin, are responsible.[55]

In autonomic ganglia several preganglionic neurons may converge on one postganglionic neuron. These ganglia regulate these inputs in several ways Two or more preganglionic neurons, for example, must fire simultaneously or must fire repeatedly before a postganglionic cell discharges.[56]

5.2.3 Matter-energy internal processes Autoregulation of blood flow is carried out by various organs (see page 341), *e.g.*, the brain, the kidney, and muscle. Cerebral blood flow is determined by the arterial input pressure and the resistance of the cerebral venous output. Cerebral blood flow remains constant over a wide range of arterial pressures. When the blood pressure falls below 60 mm Hg, there is a reduction of blood flow, and below 30 mm Hg, damage results. At these low levels, raising the blood pressure increases the blood flow until the normal steady-state range is reached again. This constancy is produced by changes in vascular resistance within the brain. This cerebral vascular resistance is varied by changes in the diameter of the cerebral blood vessels. The cost of this adjustment process is the very slight energy expenditure by the cells in the vessel walls required to alter their diameter. The sympathetic nerves which supply the cerebral vessels do not control this process, since blocking them bilaterally has no effect on it.[57] The marked sensitivity of the cerebral vasculature to changes in arterial concentration of carbon dioxide and oxygen suggests that local carbon dioxide concentrations alter the diameter of cerebral vessels, perhaps through axon reflexes. Carbon dioxide is the most powerful cerebral vasodilator known. It also causes vasoconstriction in the peripheral circulation.[58]

A similar autoregulation of blood flow goes on in the kidney. In most organs the blood flow is directly proportional to the differences in pressure between the artery and the vein. When this gradient increases, blood flow accelerates faster than the pressure gradient does. The kidney, however, behaves this way only up to a blood pressure of 90 mm Hg. Above this level, vascular resistance increases, and the blood flow remains nearly constant. Under the high pressure of 250 mm Hg and above, the blood flow again becomes directly dependent upon the arterial pressure. This autoregulation goes on when the renal nerves are severed, and is also found in isolated kidneys through which blood is pumped.[59] There are several theories as to what kind of feedback accomplishes the autoregulation.[60] It has been maintained that this feedback is a myogenic response in which distention of smooth muscle, especially in the preglomerular vessels, causes them to shorten. There is evidence that the autoregulation is a function of the muscle cells of the preglomerular vessels. Experimental evidence analyzed by Guyton, Langston, and Navar suggests that osmotic feedback is the most likely explanation.[61] They have developed a mathematical model of kidney internal processes which supports their view (see page 357).

In organs throughout the entire organism, the smallest capillaries of the distributor maintain local control of the degree of contraction of the smooth-muscle fibers in their walls. This contraction can be altered by neural impulses, local electrical stimulation, or physical or chemical changes in the blood and surrounding tissue fluids; but, independent of those, it is also locally controlled. Presumably chemical compounds produced in the vessels themselves accomplish this, but how is not known. This control of contraction persists even after the nerve fibers to the vessels have been cut and after blood-borne neurohumoral substances have been eliminated. Local control seems to be greater in vessels where the organ-level or organism-level control which coexists is neural than where it is neurohumoral.

The costs involved in the various sorts of autoregulation of blood flow are the minor energy expenditures in the constriction of vascular smooth muscle and in the transmission of control signals through the feedback loops.

5.2.4 Information internal processes   Information transmitted through the channel and net subsystem of the human being and other higher organisms flows into and out of the central nervous system. Important adjustment processes take place in the brainstem reticular formation. This is a "nonspecific" area, as contrasted with the specific tracts carrying motor and sensory information. It is located in the brainstem core and is characterized by many interconnections among tracts (see pages 426 to 429). These processes damp down excessive input to the brain, repress activity on some channels, and facilitate it on others. In other words, processes in the ascending and descending tracts of the reticular formation grade activities in most other parts of the brain.[62] These adjustment processes within the channel and net and decider subsystems of the organism importantly influence such aspects of organism behavior as sleep and wakefulness, alertness and attention.

An important adjustment process available to the heart is the ability of other heart regions besides the sinoatrial node to initiate the depolarization which is responsible for the heartbeat. If the sinoatrial node is inactivated, the atrioventricular node can start the depolarization. If both are inactivated, the muscle of the ventricle can keep an inefficient beat going. This appears to illustrate Hypothesis 5.2-2, page 106, which states that when a stress upon a system becomes greater, more components of it are involved in adjusting to the stress. This adjustment, involving three echelons of control, the second and third backstopping the first in case of emergency, is crucial to the maintenance of function of a damaged organ component whose continued activity is essential for life of the organism. One cost of the adjustment is the cost of maintaining three echelons throughout the life of the organ when one would suffice except in rare emergencies. Another cost is the inefficiency of the ventricular beat when the control nodes are inactivated.

5.2.5 Matter-energy output processes   It is important for the organism and its environment that the outputs from the gallbladder, stomach, bladder, and rectum be controlled. This control is arranged by sphincter muscles which resist distention pressures within these organs until they become extreme or until a neural input command signal from the organism's decider relaxes the sphincter. The rate of outflow from the kidney is increased by dilation of the vessels in the glomeruli or by decreasing reabsorbtion of fluid by the renal tubules. The sphincterlike muscles in the cervix of the uterus serve to hold in the embryo until it has grown to viable size. Holding muscles contracted, dilating vessels, and altering fluid reabsorbtion rates—all involve energy costs.

5.2.6 Information output processes   Little is known about such adjustment processes. It is possible that there is neural control of the rate of information output in the organism's output transducer, designed to keep the words from "piling up" on each other or to prevent the intensity or tone of speech from fluctuating inappropriately as it does in the congenitally deaf. More likely these aspects of speech are controlled by feedbacks at the organism level. Whatever information processing is involved has some minute cost, almost unmeasurable by present methods and certainly unmeasured at present.

5.2.7 Feedbacks   Feedbacks controlling blood flow in the brain, kidney, muscle, and other tissues (see pages 341 and 346 and above), as well as other forms of autonomous controls like those of the "automatic" bladder (see page 338) operate at the organism level.

5.3 Evolution   The closest sort of system to an independent, totipotential organ appeared when *Mesozoa* evolved. They are made up of only a few cells and of course are not specialized like organs in organisms. One can speculate that they evolved in a period not long before organisms composed of organ subsystems appeared, perhaps 1 billion years ago. There is no evidence from paleontology that, except for *Mesozoa*, organs ever existed independent of organisms.

In organisms high on the evolutionary scale, organs are usually more differentiated and have more components than in lower species. Within a given phylum we can often arrange structures which perform the same subsystem function in order of ascending complexity. This ordering frequently parallels to a degree the embryonic development of the most highly evolved species in the phylum. The human heart—the motor of the vascular component of the distributor subsystem—for example, goes through several stages of embryonic development which are the final forms of the hearts of organisms lower in the phylum *Chordata,* to which all animals with a central neural cord, all chordates, belong. They include, among the higher species, man and all other vertebrates.

The human heart, like that of other mammals and of birds, has four chambers. The right and left hearts are completely separated by a septum so that there is, except in certain developmental anomalies, no flow of blood between them. Within the vertebrates, there is an orderly series of forms of hearts. This continues the series found in the lower chordates. The first form of a heart in this series is a muscular tube, without valves, which, by contracting, forces the blood toward the head of the organism. The heart of a fish is little more than such a straight muscular tube in which the blood is carried from the aorta to the gills, for aeration, and then circulated through the blood vessels without first going back through the heart. It returns to the heart only after passing through the body. Since blood does not go directly from the heart to supply the organs but passes first through the capillaries of the gills, there is little pressure in the bodily circulation.

Amphibians have a more complicated circulatory system. In these species the ventricle has a single chamber that pumps blood into a vessel which divides into two. One section leads to the lungs, where the blood is aerated. The other goes to the peripheral circulation. Aerated blood from the lungs mixes with unaerated venous blood, which does not make for efficiency, since much blood is recirculated which cannot transport oxygen.

Reptiles have a primitive two-chambered ventricle, but mixture of aerated and unaerated blood still occurs. Mammals and birds have a complete division of the heart into two sides, each of which has an atrium and a ventricle. There is no mixing of aerated and unaerated blood, the right side circulating unaerated and the left side aerated. The bodily and pulmonary circuits are distinct and separate, with blood from the veins going through the pulmonary circulation, entering the left side of the heart and being then pumped to the body. Mammalian circulation has obvious advantages over more primitive vascular systems. In it fully aerated blood flows through the body under higher pressures than in lower species.

There has also been an interesting evolution of the part of the ingestor that admits the oxygen which all tissues require. A single cell provides adequately for input of oxygen, which occurs by diffusion through its membrane. A large mass of cells, with some removed from direct contact with the environment, must make some other provision. Cancer cells, which multiply wildly, fail to organize into orderly tissues; as a consequence, the cells in the midst of a tumor are often dead, because they have not received necessary inputs. Insects have a series of openings along their sides which lead to tubes that go to all parts of their bodies. Contraction and expansion of abdominal muscles circulate air through these tubes. Earthworms and other annelids have blood vessels close to the surface of their bodies into which oxygen passes by diffusion. It is then carried by the bloodstream, as in higher animals. Like them, the worms remove carbon dioxide by a process that is the reverse of oxygen uptake. Amphibians such as frogs manage some exchange of gases through their slimy skins, and as adults they have lungs as well. The young tadpoles have gills. Both fish and land vertebrates absorb oxygen into their blood. The fish have gills in which fine capillaries bring the circulating blood into contact with the water which contains dissolved oxygen. To function, all these ingestors of oxygen—skin, gills, or lungs—require a thin, moist epithelium with blood on one side and either water or air on the other.

Most of the enduring evolutionary changes in organs quite clearly give the organism which embodies them an advantage over its ancestors in the struggle for survival in the environment. The mammalian blood and lymph distributor subsystem, for instance, supplies more oxygen, more efficiently to all organs. The mammalian channel and net subsystem conveys pulses more rapidly, permitting the organism to react more quickly to environmental changes.

In the evolution of organs from organelles of cells and in further evolution up the scale from lower to higher plant and animal phyla, many examples of the principle of shred-out or division of labor appear (see pages 26 and 27). Distributor processes in single cells, for instance, are carried out chiefly by diffusion. In the larger multicellular organisms of the more primitive phyla, open canals lined by many cells develop. I have outlined above the further stages of development of the distributor. At first the heart has a single chamber, and then aspects of its functions are shredded out, so that two, three, and finally four chambers evolve, each type of pump more efficient than the last and each chamber carrying out a specialized aspect of function.

Comparable shred-out is seen in the ingestor subsystem. From a gap or specialized region in a cell membrane this subsystem evolves over the phylogenetic scale of organisms until the ingestor of primates includes large numbers of cells arranged in tissues constituting nostrils and nasal passages for ingesting air, a mouth for fluids and solids, and the skin for heat and light energy and certain sorts of material substances. This is an allocation of different ingesting subprocesses to various components.

The information processing organs also demonstrate evolutionary shred-out. Consider the input transducer, for instance. In cells there is little indication of specialization of organelles to respond to specific types of energy input, except perhaps the light-sensitive region of some protozoans. In higher animals there is more and more shred-out until there is a sense organ for each of several types of sensation. For example the common chemical sense of the lowest animals is differentiated in human beings into smell, taste, and a residual chemical sense.

The shred-out principle is quite general, new emergent components and subprocesses arising as living systems increase in complexity, advance in efficiency, and evolve from level to higher level.

Evolution of multiple specialized components, each carrying out a subprocess, raises the issue of whether their arrangement in relation to each other in physical space is optimal. It would be most efficient to locate the components which interact the most so that they are near to one other. Components that carry out processes involving all parts of the organ should be dispersed. Those which interact with only one or a few parts should be localized near them. Probably the organ satifices rather than optimizes efficiency of spatial arrangement.

The secretions of the cortex and the medulla of the adrenal gland interact in their effects on tissues under stress. Has natural selection resulted in these two components of quite different origins being near each other in the adrenal gland because such propinquity improves the efficiency of their interactions (see Fig. 8-2)? Are the structurally diverse acinar glandular tissue and the islet cells of the pancreas located in close conjunction for a similar reason, since both the external and the internal pancreatic secretions affect breakdown of carbohydrates (see page 316)? Is it for a comparable reason that the anterior, epithelial and the posterior, neural portions of the pituitary gland are so close together, sharing a very short portal vascular system? Such questions, oriented to the organ or the organism as a total system, are rarely asked by biologists. They are raised here as speculations. At present we have no answers. The advantages of specialization in the organs of higher types or species are won at a price, however, since such specialized tissues have much less capacity for regeneration than do tissues of many lower forms. No doubt a species of man which could replace a lost leg or a broken-down heart would have a great selective advantage in the age of automobiles and destructive weapons. It now appears that technology may do what evolution has omitted, and gradually provide replacement parts for the human machine.

5.3.1 Emergents   The evolution of multicellular organs produced certain emergents that are not seen at the level of single cells. Some of them are as follows: (a) *Longer duration of life.* Organs in general live longer than cells. They can survive in an environment that kills a few or even many of their constituent cells. (b) *The ability to adjust to more and severer stresses by pooling resources.* This is a major explanation for organ longevity. Cells in the periphery of organs, for instance, act as a protective boundary against excess stresses of heat or light. The outer cells may even die, but they maintain an internal state in the organ in which other cells may continue to live. Pooling of storage capacity and preferential supply of stored matter-energy to certain parts of the organ may enable those parts to live in the presence of matter-energy lack stresses severe enough to kill any solitary cell. (c) *The ability to conduct various processes throughout a larger region of physical space.* Its markedly greater size not only prevents a total organ from being damaged by a very local stress that would kill a cell but also enables it to have access to a more diverse range of matter-energy and information inputs. For instance, if it is big enough to have two eyes some distance apart, it can develop three-dimensional vision. (d) *Larger amounts of matter-energy or information outputs.* These may enable it, at least for a limited time, to cope with an emergency to which a cell could not adjust. For instance, a single cell cannot generate enough electrical power to stun or kill another cell, but an entire electric organ can generate enough to kill a whole animal. (e) *Increased efficiency.* When certain processes are shredded out they may be carried out better. The four-chamber heart is more efficient than the one-chamber heart, for example. The greater complexity of an organ enables it to profit from such efficiencies in a way that a simpler cell cannot. (f) *Increased genetic variety.* Organs in multicellular organisms have more genes than free-living single cells. This provides them more genetic variety. One can speculate that this may increase the ability of their type or species to adjust to the environment by natural selection.

5.4 Growth, cohesiveness, and integration

5.4.1 Growth   The size range of organs and organ components is great. The distributor organ of the blue whale, the largest living animal, is certainly over 30 m long. Indeed the intestinal component alone must be at least that long. Many other matter-energy processing organs of the giant prehistoric reptiles and the present big animals like elephants are greatly enlarged over the corresponding human organs. The human brain is the largest of any animal species, but the peripheral nervous channels of the larger animals are larger. Some organs of some minute water animals, like *Daphnia,* on the other hand are very small—consisting perhaps of only a few cells.

Organs develop as the consequence of unequal growth of the embryonic layers: ectoderm, mesoderm, and endoderm (see Fig. 7-4). As a result of this unequal growth, folds occur, and these may grow outward as evaginations into the embryonic connective tissue, the mesenchyma, or inward as invaginations into the mesenchyma. The open part of the fold may then fuse and separate from the layer from which it developed.

The nervous system derives from the ectoderm, arising as the medullary groove early in embryonic life. Later this groove becomes a tube, closing first at the anterior end of the embryo and then gradually back to the caudal end. It becomes completely detached from the epidermal layer. Anteriorly there are expansions which develop into the brain and a pair of lateral swellings, the optic vesicles from which arise the retinas of the two eyes. Posteriorly the tube is long and slender and becomes the spinal cord. The peripheral parts of the nervous system arise from detached ectodermal cells in the dorsal region of the medullary groove, with fibers going throughout the body.

The digestive tube begins as two outgrowths of the yolk sac, the foregut and hindgut. These elongate and develop into the stomach and the other structures of the tube, separating from the yolk sac. The liver develops from a pouch of the foregut which projects into the mesoderm at a point near the yolk sac. The foregut produces the pharynx, esophagus, stomach, and most of the small intestine, while the hindgut forms the remainder of the structures. At its anterior end the endoderm encounters the ectoderm, and they fuse to make the oral plate, from the anterior side of which the anterior portion of the pituitary gland grows back to meet a similar growth outward from the brain. These lose their connections with the oral cavity and in the adult are attached to the brain. The ectoderm at the front of the oral plate forms the epithelium of the lips and the peripheral part of the mouth, the enamel organs of the teeth, and the salivary glands.

Organs and components do not all grow at the same rate, and they attain their greatest size and maximal degrees of function at different times in the life of the organism. Sexual organs have their chief growth at puberty, when they begin full function. All the cells of the nervous system are present at birth, and growth from then on involves only increase in the size of cells and the length of processes. For instance, normal cerebral metabolic rate is high in childhood, the presumed time of primary growth and development of the brain. At 5 years of age the brain consumes approximately 50 percent of the oxygen used by the entire body (see page 345).[63] It decreases rapidly until midadolescence and falls more slowly from then until early adulthood, when it is about 20 percent. Then it remains relatively constant into old age. In the next chapter I shall discuss how endocrine information controls growth rates in different organs (see page 470).

Structures which have formed from the embryonic layers continue to differentiate as development of various tissues gives the organ or component its characteristic adult form. As it grows, its parts become more numerous, more differentiated, more specialized and more interdependent. Such changes are the essence of what is postulated by Hypotheses 5.4.1-2 and 5.4.3-3 (see pages 108 and 109). The liver, for example, very early becomes divided into two parts after beginning as a diverticulum of the ventral wall of the foregut near the junction of the yolk sac. These two parts are so different in appearance that they have been thought to proceed from different germ layers, but they do not. The embryonic endoderm forms both. The first of these is a somewhat rounded diverticulum proper lined with columnar cells with pale cytoplasm and a network of cords, or trabeculae, of a substance of quite different appearance. These later become the specialized liver tubules.[64] The veins within the structure ramify and form the typical sinusoids of the liver,

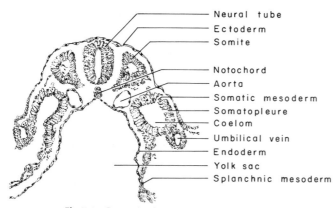

Neural tube
Ectoderm
Somite

Notochord
Aorta
Somatic mesoderm
Somatopleure
Coelom
Umbilical vein
Endoderm
Yolk sac
Splanchnic mesoderm

Fig. 7-4 Organs in a human embryo developing from ectoderm, mesoderm, and endoderm. [From H. Gray. *Anatomy of the human body.* (29th ed.) Philadelphia: Lea & Febiger, 1973, 25.]

and the part of the vein below the liver becomes modified into the portal vein. These processes of segregation and integration continue until the liver has the form characteristic of the adult of that species.

Organ growth proceeds in orderly fashion, with each group of cells organizing itself into the common structure. I have previously described the processes of cellular differentiation (see pages 296 to 298). Further processes appear to be carried on by communication among cells. In a growing epithelial sheet, for instance, when cells touch each other "contact inhibition" occurs to stop further division of the cells. In the last chapter I indicated that sometimes this does not occur in cancer cells (see page 301).

One of the methods of studying these processes is to dissolve the cementing substances between cells and study their reaggregation and development. Reaggregation of dissociated cells from vertebrate embryos was investigated by Moscona.[65] He rotated the separated cells in a flask at about 70 rpm. They all flowed together in the central vortex where, if they were capable of aggregating, they could. Under these conditions cells from different tissues varied consistently in their manner of aggregation. The number, size, distribution, shape, and internal structure of the resultant masses differed. Dissociated liver-forming cells from 7-day chick embryos coalesced into a single spherical or oblong aggregate; neural cells from the retina of the same embryo formed a number of aggregates of characteristic shape. Mesonephron cells produced cell clusters of diverse size while cartilage-forming cells aggregated into numerous regular spheroids. Cell concentration made little difference. Liver cells formed a single aggregate of size depending upon the number of cells, but the typical shape remained the same. Retinal cell aggregates formed with the same average diameter, but the number of aggregates varied. Cells of the same sort of tissue from different species did not vary greatly in their aggregation patterns. Moscona concluded that the patterns established by aggregating cells represent resultants of critical steady states of multiple variables within cells, of group properties, and of environmental effects. As older and older embryos were used as sources for the cells, there was a progressive decline in the size of the aggregates. Cells dissociated near the end of the embryonic period did not cohere, perhaps because mature cells are highly differentiated and will adhere only to exactly similar cells. There were differences among various types of tissues, but the relationship between age of the embryo and cohesiveness was found in all (see page 353).

Cultured cells from two different embryonic regions, one from which cartilage would ordinarily form and the other from which kidney would form, were also intermingled by Moscona. After being stirred together, the cells sorted themselves out and formed aggregates with their own kinds of cells. The cells of such freshly formed masses, although closely packed, moved about like bees in a swarm. Early aggregates were randomly arranged and did not cohere. Then the cartilage cells clumped in the center, while the kidney cells formed renal epithelium around them. An intermediate zone of connective tissue, presumably originating from both the cartilage and kidney cells, formed between them.

By 7 days after fertilization the neural retina of the chick embryo has already differentiated into several functional layers. The cells in each layer already differ in structure. When these cells are separated and intermingled, they reform into aggregates arranged in concentric layers with cells specialized into sensory elements and ganglion cells with axons. Later they become masses of neuroretinal tissue, essentially forming a miniature neural retina. The template which determines this arrangement is evidently carried in chemical substances put out by the cells.

Both the information of the genetic template and that which enters the tissue or organ from its environment and is processed by its associator and memory can influence the structure and process of neural organs or components. The genetic information may have more effect than that input from the environment. According to Sperry much research by himself and others indicates that inherited patterns of neural processes derive from the genetically determined size, number, connections, and excitatory properties of the neurons.[66] At many stages in the embryonic growth of an individual information processing organ it has opportunities to develop its own distinctive pattern of these processes. During such growth, Sperry holds, terminals of central neurons synapse with particular peripheral neurons leading from, say, the skin, for which they have specific chemical affinities. This provides an orderly patterning of interconnection so that the various areas of the skin have conformal representation in the brain. Such genetically determined neural structures mediate action patterns which are capable of being modified by association or learning processes elicited by information inputs.

In many animal species the predetermination of developmental processes producing differentiated organs—brain, intestine, muscles, or future germ cells—is easily recognizable before cell division even begins in the egg. In some species this is evident before the egg is fertilized.[67]

In one study of differentiation in the eggs of animal organisms, cells from a leg muscle of the 12-day-old chick embryo were freed from their bonds to each other by controlled digestion with an enzyme.[68] These cells retained the power to multiply, and as the single cells expanded into a continuous sheet, they differentiated into typical, multinucleated, long, contractile, striated-muscle cells, in association with the connective-tissue components of muscle. Differentiation also occurred when single cells were cultured at distances that precluded influence of the fibroblasts upon the myoblasts. When the nutrient medium in which cells had been cultured was reused, it increased the rate at which differentiation took place, supporting a luxuriant growth of colonies. In their cultures the muscle cell colonies could readily be differentiated from the fibroblast colonies with the unaided eye. Apparently some of the substances required for cell growth can be synthesized by the cells themselves. Even when cells are transplanted into different organisms, the environment exerts important influences upon their development, as I shall indicate in the next chapter (see page 469).

Human tissue cells grown in culture multiply into colonies.[69] Daily count of the number of cells reveals that the rate of growth is similar to that of bacterial colonies. After a lag of about 20 h while the first cell is adapting itself to start growing in a new environment, an exponential acceleration of growth occurs at approximately human body temperatures, doubling about every 18 to 22 h. Such growth conforms to Hypothesis 5.4.1-1, page 108, which states that the rate of increase in the number of components of a young system rises exponentially until it reaches a maximum, but this growth rate may be altered by environmental or other factors. The growth rate of human tissue cells will be maintained for a long time unless necessary nutrients are lacking, toxins form, or some or all of the cells are physically crowded.

5.4.2 Cohesiveness The cells of different tissues cohere with varying strength. In the description of tissues given above (see pages 316 to 318), I have mentioned that some connective tissues are loosely aggregated and include wandering white blood cells or, in blood and lymph, cells suspended freely in fluid surroundings. Some epithelia, on the other hand, cohere so firmly that relatively strong mechanical forces are necessary to separate them. The epithelia of the oral cavity and intestinal tract, for instance, normally withstand the passing of hard substances over them and the vigorous movements of the organs of which they are a part.

The various researches on the regrouping of disaggregated cells, some of which I have already mentioned (see page 351), provide some understanding of the factors involved in the cohesion of cells into tissues and organs.[70] When a simple animal like a sponge, or the embryo of a more complex one, like a toad or a chick, is squeezed through a fine net or placed in a solution free of calcium or magnesium, the cells in the specimen lose their cohesiveness and separate. They then settle to the bottom of the medium in the dish, and no further action occurs until calcium and magnesium are added to the fluid. After these elements are added, however, the cells begin to crawl around and reaggregate, with the following results: (a) If cells of different species of animals are present in the same medium, they often separate and group together by species. For instance, the cells of two species of sponges or two species of newts separate out, but mixed mouse and chick cells do not. (b) Within a given species similar types of cells group together. Ectodermal, mesodermal, and endodermal cells or muscle, cartilage, and kidney cells each clump together. And (c) the various types move into roughly the right position in relation to one another. Sixteen hours after reaggregation of toad embryo cells begins, for example, they sort into a roughly concentric arrangement with ectoderm (precursor of skin and nerves) on the periphery, muscle and notochord mesoderm (precursor of the spine) inside that, and endoderm (precursor of the gut) in the center.[71] Time-lapse photography of these cells during reaggregation shows that they do not move in any direct and definite path to their correct position, as do slime molds which in aggregating migrate in a line toward higher and higher concentrations of the signaling chemical, acrasin, given out by other slime-mold cells (see page 203). Rather, these reaggregating cells move about randomly until they adhere to other cells, usually of like type. This adhesion may be explained as the resultant of two opposite sorts of forces, (a) negative charges resulting from ionization on the surface of every cell, which repel other similarly charged cells and (b) the Van der Waals forces of intermolecular attraction, which attract other cells. In red corpuscles, which do not adhere to each other, a is much higher than in liver cells, which stick tightly to each other. Speculation suggests that the differences in adhesion derive from the fact that in red corpuscles a is higher than b, while in liver cells the reverse is true. Before reaggregation starts, the cells are neither motile nor adhesive; then they become motile and moderately adhesive, sticking particularly to their own type of cell; and finally they become nonmotile and very adhesive. In reaggregation the change to the motile and moderately adhesive state occurs at the same time for all types of cells, but the final change in which the cells stop moving and become very adhesive occurs first in ectodermal cells, when they reach the surface of the cell mass (see Fig.

7-5). This outer layer then traps other cells inside, layer by layer. After all the ectodermal cells are trapped, mesodermal cells become adhesive and are immobilized inside, and finally the endodermal cells become adhesive and are trapped in the center.

The temporal sequence of reaggregation of separated sponge cells rotated in artificial sea water was observed in one experiment.[72] After about 1 h in the aggregation situation, all cells capable of aggregating have been incorporated into cell masses. The masses took from 3 to 6 h to attain their final size. At 12 h the aggregates were similar histologically to the 3-h aggregates except that a layer of flattened cells had appeared on the surface, making them round and smooth. They did not change after that for many hours. After 10 to 14 days, translucent, canal-like areas could be seen in some aggregates. Histologically on the nineteenth day some of these showed canal-like structures, newly formed spicules, and spongin, all characteristics of normal sponges.

A number of variables related to the reaggregation process have been studied. These include: (a) Amount of calcium and magnesium. Reaggregation will not occur if they are entirely absent, for they seem to be essential in the formation of the chemical bonds which hold cells together.[73] They are also required for cell movement.[74] (b) Concentration of cells. The higher the concentration, the larger the final aggregates. (c) Amount of such a cellular product as serum protein or tissue extract. Such a substance is essential at least for the reaggregation of dissociated embryonic cells. (d) Amount of glucose. This also must be present, at least for embryonic cells. (e) Rate of rotation of the fluid containing the cells. The faster the rotation the less readily the cells reaggregate. (f) Temperature. About 38°C is optimal for reaggregation of neural-retinal cells from 7-day-old chick embryos. The optimal temperature differs with the type of cells and the stage of their development. As temperatures lower, reaggregation is increasingly inhibited, and at 15°C it stops entirely. And (g) age of the cell. For example, the older the embryo is from which the cells are taken, the less likely they are to adhere (see page 351).

5.4.3 Integration After cells cohere firmly they can begin to integrate their actions, transmitting coordinating signals along channels which develop among them (see pages 337 and 338). The role of such signals in the coordination of the cells that make up slime molds illustrates this (see page 203). Little is known about how organs in higher animals are integrated.

5.5 Pathology Pathology in organs can result from a wide range of causes, including the following:

(a) *Lacks of matter-energy inputs.* If the blood supply to an organ, *e.g.*, the brain, is sharply reduced, say by massive bleeding from an organism's distributor, its tissues may die, and important functions which it normally carries out in the brain may stop.

(b) *Excesses of matter-energy inputs.* Crushing, tearing, or other mechanical damage may result in

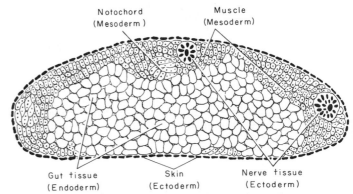

Fig. 7-5 Artist's conception of a typical section through a toad reaggregate some 16 h after reaggregation started. Cells have sorted out to give a roughly concentric arrangement of ectoderm (heavy black) which is skin and nerve, mesoderm (dots) which comprises muscle and notochord (the precursor of the spine), and endoderm (cells without markings) which gives rise to the gut tissue, etc. Note similarities to Fig. 7-4, page 350. (From A. S. G. Curtis. The regrouping of separated cells. *Discovery*, 1961, **22**, 200. *Reprinted by permission.*)

permanent alterations of structure which lead to diminished or abnormal function of organ components like the skin, muscles, lungs, or liver. Large amounts of scar tissue resulting from such damage may cause muscular components to contract weakly or move inefficiently. Since most organ components of higher vertebrates cannot regenerate completely, loss of part of a component may decrease the number of active cells below the number needed for adequate function, although some components—the lungs for instance—have more capacity than is ordinarily needed and can carry out their processes after a portion of them has been removed. In general the farther away a part of an organ is from the point of trauma to the organ, the less likely is it to develop pathology, as Hypothesis 5.5-1 (see page 110) suggests.

(c) *Inputs of inappropriate forms of matter-energy.* Viruses, Rickettsiae, and bacteria which cause infections, and chemical poisons are examples of such inputs to organs. Microorganisms entering organs may cause inflammations and abscesses in them which diminish functions and lead to scarring after the lesion has healed. Arsenic or mercury can permanently damage kidneys or livers. Such inputs usually travel through the organ's distributor, and in general the farther away a part is from that distributor, the less likely it is to be affected by the harmful input, in conformity with Hypothesis 5.5-1, page 110.

(*d*) *Lacks of information inputs.* Congenital cataracts, milky opacities in the lenses of the eyes, will prevent a young animal from receiving patterned inputs of visual information, and its visual pathways may become permanently incapable of processing such information.

(*e*) *Excesses of information inputs.* Increased rates of inputs of hormones to organs can accelerate their metabolism and over a period of time damage them. In the general adaptation syndrome, excessive adrenal cortical hormone can have such effects on many organs (see pages 451 and 452). Excessive thyroxine produced in thyrotoxicosis can also do this; it can, for example, cause the eyes to bulge and increase the likelihood of coronary occlusion.

(*f*) *Inputs of maladaptive genetic information in the template.* These inputs can produce gross abnormalities in an organ which can affect its processes. Absence of important parts of an organ such as ducts or specific tissues are examples of these. Congenital absence of one or both of the kidneys occurs. An organism cannot continue to live with no kidneys unless it is parasitic upon an artificial kidney. One kidney can, however, function well enough so that there is no evidence that the other is missing. Congenital failure of one type of tissue to develop normally is common. For example, if a lip or palate does not join properly at the midline in the developing embryo, a harelip or a cleft palate can be produced. Duplication of all or part of the organ components also occurs. Instances are supernumerary kidneys, usually fused to those normally present, and reduplicated parts of the intestinal tract. Some drugs and ionizing radiation input to a pregnant female can damage genes and result in malformation of her fetus.

(*g*) *Abnormalities in internal matter-energy processes.* Cancer and other tumors are diseases of cells (see page 301), but they affect the organ level as well. They may interfere with an organ's blood supply, by either pressure or invasion, and cause necrosis. They may block lymphatic channels or glandular ducts or cause other mechanical interference. Cancer cells, which multiply wildly, fail to organize into orderly tissues. Although blood vessels grow within tumors, they are usually not continuously connected and thus cannot convey the necessary inputs to cells and remove their waste outputs. As a consequence the cells in the midst of a tumor are often dead or necrotic. A cancer may arise in a component, in which case the cells are similar to those normally present in the tissue but less differentiated. On the other hand, the cancer may have come from elsewhere in the organism, carried by the organism's distributor. Such cancers retain the characteristics of the tissues from which they originated, no matter what tissues they grow upon. Other nongenetic errors in matter-energy processing include diseases of maturation, *e.g.*, eunuchism; and diseases of aging, for example, the development of premature senile changes in various organs.

(*h*) *Abnormalities in internal information processes.* After damage to the brain from bullets or hemorrhages such errors occur. Aphasia in a soldier hit by shrapnel in the left temporal lobe of the brain is an example. He can understand speech but has great trouble speaking because damage to part of his encoder or perhaps part of his output transducer makes it hard for him to form words.

5.6 Decay and termination Except for the reproducer, the life of any whole organ, any critical subsystem, normally must be coextensive with that of the organism. The reproducer completes its development when the organism matures, may become largely nonfunctional as the organism ages, and may have its most important components removed or inactivated without serious threat to the organism's existence. Components, however, may normally function in the embryonic period, childhood, adulthood, and middle age, and then atrophy. The thymus gland, for example, is relatively large in size in infants and changes little until puberty, when it begins to regress or involute. On occasion components may "die" and be removed while the organism lives on. A gangrenous leg, for instance, may be amputated to save a patient's life.

The effects of aging of organisms are widespread and will be discussed later (see pages 481 and 482). Some components, however, appear to be more affected than others by aging processes. In one study, rats were maintained under optimal conditions until they lived out their life spans and became moribund, at which time they were killed and autopsied.[75] Two disease entities approached 100 percent in these animals: diseases of the kidney, chronic nephrosis and glomerulonephritis; and muscular degeneration. Periarteritis, a disease of arteries, degeneration of the heart muscle, and a tumor, adenoma of the pituitary, were also common. Curves of development of these differed. The kidney disease curve starts to rise at birth while no muscular degeneration is found until rats are over 500 days old.

6. Models and simulations

Simulations of organs or components are done for a number of different reasons. Prostheses take the place of missing or damaged parts; working physical models are built for teaching purposes or research; mathematical or computer models aid research either into practical problems of physiology or medicine or into the theory of organ processes. At this level I have found no models or simulations of classes (*b*) *living, usually human, representations* or (*d*) *living system–computer interactions* (see page 85). There are, however, examples of the two other possible classes:

(*a*) *Nonliving artifacts.* This class includes prosthetic appliances such as the heart-lung machine which simulates the process of aeration and pumping of blood so exactly that it can replace these functions in a patient undergoing surgery.[76] An artificial kidney can take over the renal filtering process more or less indefinitely.[77] Such an artificial kidney can keep patients with failure of both kidneys alive until kidney transplants can be done. An artificial larynx is now being used by many patients who have had laryngectomies, often as a result of cancer.[78] Research on an artificial heart which can be implanted into the bodies of victims of heart disease and carry out some functions of their own hearts has progressed to the point that animals have lived for short periods with such replacement hearts.[79] And, of course, people have lived for several years with human heart transplants as well. A machine has been designed which simulates the heartbeat so exactly that it can produce electrocardiographic tracings and be used to demonstrate electrocardiographs.[80] Also an artificial mastoid bone has been built which can be used to study how this bone conducts sound.[81]

The artificial neurons or neuromimes which I discussed in the last chapter (see pages 302 and 303) can be used in combinations that simulate organ functions such as synapses, both inhibitory and excitatory, and organism behavior such as learning. Neuromimes can be used to study the functions of small networks and the process of encoding as well as neural functions of the cochlea of the ear and retina of the eye.[82] As many as 19 neuromimes were used to stimulate the cochlea, and experiments with them suggested that the spinal innervation of the cochlea extends the dynamic range of the ear because of the refractory and summing properties of neurons.[83] The dynamic range appeared to be related to innervation density. The neuromimes were employed in combination with other components to study retinal processes.[84] A simple model was described which indicated a relationship between physiological and psychological data on visual flicker fusion (see page 381). The model suggests that such fusion occurs in the retina rather than at higher neural centers. The simulation fitted the data of various psychophysiological and neurophysiological experiments fairly well but by no means perfectly.

(*c*) *Models in words, numbers, or other symbols, including computer programs.* The interconnections of elements within the nervous systems of organisms have also lent themselves to logical and mathematical simulation. McCulloch and Pitts made use of the notation of mathematical logic.[85] Properties of many of these models, including that of McCulloch and Pitts concern complex organism behavior. I therefore consider them in the next chapter (see pages 485 and 486). The mathematics of net theory has been used by Rapoport to analyze or simulate neurons connected into structures similar to those in nervous systems.[86] In such a procedure Rapoport used:

. . . a "random net," formally defined as a collection of nodes (neurons) among which the synaptic connections are all equiprobable. Statistical computations, then, give the gross connectivity characteristics of such a net, for example, the expected number of paths between an arbitrary pair of neurons, the expected number of neurons so many synaptic connections removed from a given neuron, etc. Given such average gross structural features and certain assumed laws of synaptic transmission, the activity of such a net resulting from some initial input can also be calculated. For example, given the average number of axons per neuron and the average threshold of the neuron, the "critical input" can be established, that is, one which if exceeded results in the spread of excitation through the net and if not exceeded results in a dying out of the initial excitation. [See Hypothesis 3.3.3.1-1, page 95, which states that the structures of the communication networks of living systems are so comparable that they can be described by similar mathematical models of nonrandom nets.][87]

It is possible to go on from the random net model to models in which the nets are "biased." Of these Rapoport says:

Here the connections are no more equiprobable. The probability of connection becomes dependent on any number of parameters, characteristic either of neuron populations themselves (say, biochemical parameters) or of distances between the neurons.[88]

Rapoport points out that these net structures can be important in the study of nervous systems. He says:

Obviously, if the entire structure of a net is given, every one of the parameters characterizing it is determined. . . . The possible importance of such parameters from the neurophysiological or from the behavioral point of view may be demonstrated if it is shown that they are the determinants of precisely those intermediate aspects of neural events which lie between the synaptic and the effector level. For example, they may (perhaps) be shown to be significant measures of such vaguely quantitative concepts as "degrees of organization" or "degree of integration" of the events on the effector level, and so serve as the connective concepts between structure and function.

Another way in which the net parameters may be biologically important is by providing hypotheses concerning the evolutionary or developmental aspects of nervous systems. If the vaguely perceived ontogenetic or phylogenetic increase of complexity or of "organization" of a nervous system can be described by an increase in certain numerical indices, one would naturally look for the genetic determinants of these indices. The question of how changes occur in the structural information locked in the genes is a very difficult one to deal with. On the other hand, genetic changes associated with simply ''more'' or ''less'' of certain quantities are easy to imagine. The singling out of parameters, having demonstrable importance for the ''organization'' of a net, suggests that mutation and selection pressures may be operating on these parameters instead of on the minute details of synaptic connections.[89]

He concluded that the utility of the probabilistic theory of nets depends on how well the concepts which emerge can serve as the building blocks of a theory connecting the genesis, structure, and function of nervous systems.

A coelenterate nerve net has been simulated by a computer.[90] Such nerve nets seem to be randomly organized, but they are capable of some integrative activity. There is also apparently interconnection among the nets of those coelenterates, such as corals, which live in colonies. Spread in such large nets is a function of the strength of the information input. This is a simulation of one part of a net of a single animal. The actual topological relationships in the animal would be difficult to simulate even on a modern computer, so a simplified model was used, but the major features of the net were kept. It was modeled as a square grid of horizontal and vertical lines, missing some segments. Activity in one neuron could induce activity in one with which it intersected. Conduction was all or none, without decrement, and in both directions over the nerves in this model, although sometimes unidirectional conduction occurs in the animals. Some junctions were ordinarily unable to transmit signals, except when they were subjected to facilitation. Some findings of this study appeared to be pertinent to understanding spread in some sorts of living nets. For example, increasing the input strength which raised the number of elements stimulated, would seem at first only to increase the distance of the spread. But it turned out that, as more elements were stimulated, possible pathways were more and more frequently blocked by other transmissions, which reduced the amount of the spread.

The visual receptor network in the retina of the horseshoe crab, *Limulus,* has been simulated on an analog simulator. I shall discuss this work in the next chapter (see pages 488 and 489).

A mathematical model of the human external respiratory system has been developed.[91] It is an input–output model. Input variables, in the air breathed in or in the venous blood, include oxygen, carbon dioxide, nitrogen, hydrogen, hydroxide ion, chloride ion, sodium ion, potassium ion, hemoglobin, plasma protein, and red corpuscle protein. Output variables include similar contents of the air breathed out, the arterial plasma, or the arterial blood corpuscles. The model is concerned with the many steady states of these variables and their chemically and thermodynamically determined interrelationships. Fundamentally a linear programming model, it has been programmed for solution on a digital computer and simulation on an analog computer. Solution of the model yields values which describe the major phenomena of the respiratory exchange in the lungs. It has been compared with an alternate model also.

A comparable mathematical model of the human respiratory control system attempts to explain an abnormality known as Cheyne-Stokes respiration.[92] In this condition the patient overbreathes for a few breaths, and this then damps down or temporarily stops breathing, so that instead of regular breathing continual oscillations of rapid breathing and no breathing occur. The model checks closely with experimental findings about such breathing.

The control processes in the vascular circulation have been analyzed by Warner using computer simulation.[93] He employed two approaches in this work. In the first, he simulated the carotid sinus and its related neural connections which have important functions in controlling arterial pressure. It is known that the frequencies with which action potentials move along the nerve leading from the carotid sinus to the brain are direct functions of the pressure in the artery, as long as it is above a minimum value. They are also directly related to the rate of change of arterial pressure. It is thus possible to write the following equation: $n/(p - p_0) = k_1 s + k_2$ where n is the frequency of impulses on the carotid sinus nerve, p is the blood pressure in the carotid artery, p_0 is the minimum static pressure capable of eliciting impulses on the carotid sinus nerve, s is the Laplace operator, and k_1 and k_2 are constants.

This equation was programmed on an analog computer, which was then attached to a mechanical pressure transducer on a dog's carotid artery. It was substituted for the dog's own blood control mechanism, and its function was analyzed. Variations in blood pressure were produced by altering blood-flow rates, which in turn were controlled by stimulating one of the dog's vagus nerves. It was possible thus to demonstrate details of operation of the dog's own regulating mechanism and to show that the carotid sinus can anticipate blood pressure changes.

Another use of the analog computer in studying the regulation of the circulation is given in the same article. Warner represented several aspects of circulatory function by separate equations on the computer. He wrote as follows in describing the simulation:

The left atrium and pulmonary veins are treated as a single reservoir, the left ventricle is described as a system with two states, systole (contraction and emptying) and diastole (relaxation and filling), and the arterial bed is treated as a transmission line. The system is symmetrical, the equations of the two sides differing only in their coefficients. . . . The first equation expresses the volume of the pulmonary vein-left arterial system as the sum of the initial volume and the integral of inflow minus outflow. . . . This summation and integration is [sic] carried out in the computer by feeding the voltages representing flow 1 and minus flow 2 into an integrating amplifier. The output voltage then represents v_1. Initial condition voltage on the amplifier is set to correspond to the initial volume.[94]

A recording on magnetic tape of the experimental animal's ventricular pressure pulse provides a signal to the computer. By this tape the same transient phenomena can be reproduced over and over again at will. Each of the circulatory system's parameters can be studied systematically on the computer by changing certain coefficients or equations. With these equations we can predict the response of the whole system to a transient disturbance. Since the system is a closed loop, such a prediction involves solving all the equations of the system simultaneously. The equations correctly predict a rapid return of the system to equilibrium following several types of disturbance.

Explaining how they construct a model simulating circulatory functions, Baker, Ellis, Franklin, and Rushmer say:

Analog computers are a powerful tool in the derivation of new concepts of the heart as a pump. Data representing the fundamental parameters or dimensions, pressure and flow, have been reduced to provide such information as heart rate, pressure-volume loops, and functions of power, work, and accumulated flow. . . . An indication of the effective power generated by the heart walls is derived by multiplying the left ventricular pressure by the rate of change of the left ventricular diameter or circumference. If the diameter or circumference can be considered continuously proportional to the volume we then have an uncalibrated record of the power output of the heart. Work is then the integral of power. These functions are recorded as continuous information along with the primary parameters. The output of blood per stroke and accumulated flow per unit time (i.e., two seconds) can be derived from the instantaneous flow information by integration.[95]

The transfer of an injected chemical, Bromsulphalein, from the blood through the liver into the bile also has been simulated on a computer.[96] Equations were set up to describe the process at a given time and replaced by difference equations for the next time step. The flow from one cell to another over time was calculated. One version of this model simulating 24 cells ran on the computer a little more than 3 times as fast as real time.

Mathematical simulations of such metabolic processes as an enzyme synthesis by the producer subsystem have also been formulated.[97]

Earlier in this chapter I referred to the mathematical model developed by Guyton, Langston, and Navar based on evidence that osmotic feedback at the juxtaglomerular apparatus in the kidney controls renal autoregulation (see pages 346 and 347). Their model dealt with such variables as rate of renal blood flow, osmolality of the fluid in the renal tubules, filtration rate in the renal glomeruli, and the rates of change of osmolality of sodium and related anions; urea; creatinine and related anions; and water. They developed an analog computer simulation of the osmotic feedback they hypothesized and checked the solutions of equations it provided against experimental data on dogs, obtaining reasonably good fits with the model.

7. Conclusions

Much of the scientific work on organs is expressed in terminology consistent with that of systems theory. It is clear to all investigators that these systems have inputs and outputs and that they keep a set of variables within ranges of stability by processes involving negative feedbacks, many of which are understood in detail.

This level of living systems is dramatically different from several other levels in its degree of specialization of function or division of labor. Except perhaps in primitive animals, organs are extremely partipotential. No organ in the higher animals is totipotential. Many subsystem processes are downwardly dispersed to cells; some are upwardly dispersed to the suprasystem organism. The degree of interdependence of one organ upon another in the organism is equaled in the entire range of living systems perhaps only by the degree of interdependence of subsystems in modern technological societies. Why there are so many combined subsystems at the organ level, and why many subsystems at this level are laterally dispersed are fascinating and as yet unanswered questions worthy of research. We have barely begun to delve into the principles involved in the arrangements of subsystems of organs and the effects of these structural arrangements on the costs and efficiencies with which subsystem processes are carried out.

Most organs have most of the matter-energy processing critical subsystems, although some of those functions are downwardly dispersed to the cellular level. Almost all organs, including the neural components, however, lack some of the essential information processing subsystems, such as the associator and the memory. Associative learning and memory, like much decision making, are upwardly dispersed to the organism level, and this of course makes organs highly dependent upon their total organism for many control processes. Reproducing is done by total organisms in nonsexual species and by mating dyads in sexual ones. Some organs can regenerate after extensive damage, but none in higher animals can reproduce independently. The distributors and channels and nets of organs are inextricably continuous with those of the organism of which the organs are subsystems. It is certainly legitimate to ask, in the light of all these facts, whether organs truly constitute a level of living systems.

On the other hand, physiological research in recent years has demonstrated local decision making or autoregulation in isolated and denervated organs during the brief periods they remain functional in experiments. When central signaling stops, some organs can still carry on their basic functions with remarkable effectiveness. The decider is the essential critical subsystem, and apparently some organs have a decider. There certainly is an organ level, therefore, even though the deciders of several organs in higher vertebrates, including man, are upwardly or downwardly dispersed. It is also clear that organs are very concrete entities in space-time and that they are part of a structural hierarchy, being all composed of cells or tissues. Many process variables of these systems have been identified and hundreds of experiments have measured the ranges of stability of these variables, demonstrating how they are maintained in steady states and how they interrelate, as system variables characteristically do.

Compared with higher levels, organs appear to have fewer regular outputs representing meaningful responses to specific patterns of information inputs. They are by no means lacking, however. The thyrotrophic hormone of the pituitary gland conveys a message which is decoded and responded to only by the thyroid gland, just as its adrenotrophic hormone is decoded and responded to only by the adrenal gland. It is clear that certain patterns of neural pulses can elicit responses only from specific parts of the nervous system. In recent years in increasing numbers, neurophysiologists are attempting to learn what are the natural ensembles of message patterns transmitted in various parts of the nervous system. Such efforts may enable them to discover much more than we now know about meaningful responses of organs to patterned information inputs. Traditional neurophysiology, however, has concentrated rather on matterenergy transmission aspects of neural functioning, studying such matters as thresholds, chronaxies, and refractory periods of nerves. Until we know the entire ensembles of messages in various neural organs, we cannot begin to apply information theory measures of channel capacity or coding theorems to these functions. Until we can construct matrices showing what

patterns of information these organs output to each pattern of input, we cannot learn the codes of these organs and understand fully the meaningful communications going on in them.

In this chapter examples of subsystem process variables are sometimes omitted, or if they are given, they are not precisely formulated or are not based on reliable data. These omissions are necessary because few researches on the subsystems of organs as yet have been done based on an information processing conceptual framework. A product of the systems approach is the suggestion that there are such variables, but they have not yet been investigated experimentally. Already, though, we know enough of organs as systems to appreciate how complex are their functions, how quantitatively exact is their precision, and how normally harmonious are their interrelationships.

NOTES AND REFERENCES

[1]Dorland, W. A. N. *Dorland's illustrated medical dictionary.* (24th ed.) Philadelphia: Saunders, 1965, 1058.

[2]Bremer, J. L. *A textbook of histology.* (5th ed.) Philadelphia: Blakiston, 1936, 52–53.

[3]McConnaughey, B. H. Mesozoa. *Encyclopaedia Britannica.* Vol. 11. Chicago: Encyclopaedia Britannica, 1974, 1013. Also Kozloff, E. N. Morphology of the Orthonectid RHOPALURA OPHIOCOMAE. *J. Parasitol.,* 1969, **55,** 171–195.

[4]Thomas, J. E. Pancreas, liver and biliary system. In C. H. Best & N. B. Taylor (Eds.). *The physiological basis of medical practice.* (7th ed.) Baltimore: Williams & Wilkins, 1961, 652.

[5]Hydén, H. The neuron. In J. Brachet & A. E. Mirsky (Eds.). *The cell: biochemistry, physiology, morphology.* Vol. 4. New York: Academic Press, 1960, 287.

[6]*Ibid.,* 289.

[7]Palay, S. L. The structural basis for neural action. In M. A. B. Brazier (Ed.). *Brain function.* Vol. 2. *RNA and brain function: memory and learning.* UCLA Forum in Medical Sciences No. 2. Berkeley: Univ. of California Press, 1964, 69–108.

[8]Maximow, A. A. & Bloom, W. *A textbook of histology.* Philadelphia: Saunders, 1957, 34.

[9]Detweiler, D. K. (Ed.). Measurement of blood pressure and flow. In J. R. Brobeck (Ed.). *Best and Taylor's physiological basis of medical practice.* (9th ed.) Baltimore: Williams & Wilkins, 1973, 3-152–3-156.

[10]*Ibid.,* 3-148–3-163.

[11]Cf. Carlson, A. J., Johnson, V., & Cavert, H. M. *The machinery of the body.* (5th ed.) Chicago: Univ. of Chicago Press, 1961, 358.

[12]Magee, D. F. & Anderson, E. G. Changes in pancreatic enzymes brought about by alteration in the nature of the dietary protein. *Amer. J. Physiol.,* 1955, **181,** 79–82.

[13]Cf. Sokoloff, L. Metabolism of the central nervous system *in vivo.* In J. Field (Ed.). *Handbook of physiology. Section I: Neurophysiology.* Vol. 3. Washington, D.C.: Amer. Physiol. Soc., 1960, 1843–1853.

[14]Hokin, M. R. The formation of amylase by mouse pancreas *in vitro. J. biol. Chem.,* 1956, **219,** 77–83.

[15]Detweiler, D. K. (Ed.). The cardiovascular system. In J. R. Brobeck (Ed.). *Best and Taylor's physiological basis of medical practice.* (9th ed.) Baltimore: Williams & Wilkins, 1973, 3-15.

[16]Tschirgi, R. D. Chemical environment of the central nervous system. In J. Field (Ed.). *Handbook of physiology. Section I. Neurophysiology.* Vol. 3. Washington, D.C.: Amer. Physiol. Soc., 1960, 1865–1890.

Also Davson, H. Intracranial and intraocular fluids. In J. Field (Ed.). *Handbook of physiology. Section I: Neurophysiology.* Vol. 3. Washington, D.C., Amer. Physiol. Soc., 1960, 1761–1788.

[17]Bell, G. H., Davidson, J. N., & Emslie-Smith, D. *Textbook of physiology.* (8th ed.) Baltimore: Williams & Wilkins, 1972, 688.

[18]Detweiler, D. K. (Ed.). Circulation through brain, skin, and skeletal muscle. In J. R. Brobeck (Ed.). *Best and Taylor's physiological basis of medical practice.* (9th ed.) Baltimore: Williams & Wilkins, 1973, 3-217.

[19]Dardik, H., Ibrahim, I. M., Baier, R., Sprayregen, S., Levy, M., & Dardik, I. I. Human umbilical cord: a new source for vascular prosthesis. *JAMA,* 1976, **236,** 2859–2862.

[20]Detweiler, D. K. (Ed.). The cardiovascular system. *Op. cit.,* 3-16.

[21]Bell, G. H., Davidson, J. N., & Emslie-Smith, D. *Op. cit.,* 848.

[22]Sokoloff, L. *Op. cit.*

[23]Maximow, A. A. & Bloom, W. *Op. cit.,* 410.

[24]*Ibid.,* 46, 122, 148–149, 177, 218–220.

[25]Hightower, N. C. & Janowitz, H. D. Pancreatic secretion. In J. R. Brobeck (Ed.). *Best and Taylor's physiological basis of medical practice.* (9th ed.) Baltimore: Williams & Wilkins, 1973, 2-50.

[26]Hillarp, N. A. Peripheral autonomic mechanisms. In J. Field (Ed.). *Handbook of physiology. Section I: Neurophysiology.* Vol. 3. Washington, D.C.: Amer. Physiol. Soc., 1960, 979–1006.

[27]Loewenstein, W. R., Socolar, S. J., Higashino, S., Kanno, Y., & Davidson, N. Intercellular communication, renal, urinary bladder, sensory and salivary gland cells. *Science,* 1965, **149,** 295–298.

[28]Hillarp, N. A. *Op. cit.,* 998.

[29]Fawcett, D. W. & Selby, C. C. Observations on the fine structure of the turtle atrium. *J. biophys. biochem. Cytol.,* 1958, **4,** 63–72.

[30]Crosby, E. C., Humphrey, T., & Lauer, E. W. *Correlative anatomy of the nervous system.* New York: Macmillan, 1962, 534–535.

[31]Hillarp, N. A. *Op. cit.,* 992.

[32]Rasmussen, H. Cell communication, calcium ion, and cyclic adenosine monophosphate. *Science,* 1970, **170,** 404–412.

[33]Cf. Detweiler, D. K. (Ed.). The cardiovascular system. *Op. cit.,* 3-8.

[34]Cf. *Ibid.,* 3-6.

[35]Cf. *Ibid.,* 3-7.

[36]Granit, R. Neural activity in the retina. In J. Field (Ed.). *Handbook of physiology. Section I: Neurophysiology.* Vol. 1. Washington, D.C.: Amer. Physiol. Soc., 1959, 704–706.

[37]Cf. Bardin, C. W. Hormonal control of gonadal function. In J. R. Brobeck (Ed). *Best and Taylor's physiological basis of medical practice.* (9th ed.) Baltimore: Williams & Wilkins, 1973, 7-107.

[38]Uttal, W. R. Oscillations in the amplitude of human peripheral nerve action potentials during repetitive stimulation. *Kybernetik,* 1966, **3,** 25–27.

Cf. also Uttal, W. R. & Krissoff, M. Effect of stimulus pattern on temporal activity in the somatosensory system. *J. exper. Psychol.,* 1966, **71,** 878–883.

[39]Cf. Bardin, C. W. *Op. cit.,* 7–99.

[40]Eccles, J. C. *The physiology of synapses.* New York: Academic Press, 1964, 82–100.

[41]Luco, J. V. Plasticity of neural function in learning and retention. In M. A. B. Brazier (Ed.). *Brain function.* Vol. 2. *RNA and brain function: memory and learning.* UCLA Forum in Medical Sciences No. 2. Berkeley: Univ. of California Press, 1964, 135–159.

[42]Chamberlain, T. J., Halick, P., & Gerard, R. W. Fixation of experience in the rat spinal cord. *J. Neurophysiol.,* 1963, **26,** 662–673.

Cf. also Brobeck, J. R. (Ed.). Analysis of neural control systems. In J. R. Brobeck (Ed.). *Best and Taylor's physiological basis of medical practice.* (9th ed.) Baltimore: Williams & Wilkins, 1973, 9-18–9-19.

[43]Krieg, W. J. S. *Brain mechanisms in diachrome* (2d ed.) Evanston, Ill.: Brain Books, 1955, 140. Reprinted by permission.

[44]Detweiler, D. K. (Ed.). The cardiovascular system. *Op. cit.,* 3-5–3-8.

[45]Stratton, R. A. Pathological physiology of the kidney. Micturition. In J. R. Brobeck (Ed.). *Best and Taylor's physiological basis of medical practice.* (9th ed.) Baltimore: Williams & Wilkins, 1973, 5-48.

[46]*Ibid.,* 5-50–5-57.

[47]Cf. *Ibid.,* 5-50.

[48]Kety, S. S. & Schmidt, C. F. The nitrous oxide method for the quantitative determination of cerebral blood flow in man: theory, procedure and normal values. *J. clin. Invest.,* 1948, **27,** 476–483.

[49]Sokoloff, L. *Op. cit.,* 1847–1856.

[50]Salter, J. M. Protein metabolism (cont.). In C. H. Best & N. B. Taylor (Eds.). *The physiological basis of medical practice.* (7th ed.) Baltimore: Williams & Wilkins, 1961, 794.

[51]Haist, R. E. (Reviser). The spleen; the life of the red cell; the regeneration of blood; iron metabolism. In C. H. Best & N. B. Taylor (Eds.). *The physiological basis of medical practice.* (7th ed.) Baltimore: Williams & Wilkins, 1961, 75.

[52]Mortimore, G. E. Control of thyroid function. In J. R. Brobeck (Ed.). *Best and Taylor's physiological basis of medical practice.* (9th ed.) Baltimore: Williams & Wilkins, 1973, 7-29.

[53]Bardin, C. W. *Op. cit.,* 7-102–7-103.

[54]Whitfield, C. F. Control of calcium homeostasis by parathyroid hormone, calcitonin, and vitamin D. In J. R. Brobeck (Ed.). *Best and Taylor's physiological basis of medical practice.* (9th ed.) Baltimore: Williams & Wilkins, 1973, 7-44.

[55]Somjen, G. *Sensory coding.* New York: Meredith, 1972, 128–129.

[56]Hillarp, N. A. *Op. cit.,* 988.

[57]Detweiler, D. K. (Ed.). Circulation through brain, skin, and skeletal muscle. *Op. cit.,* 3-211–3-212.

[58]*Ibid.,* 3-212.

[59]Detweiler, D. K. (Ed.). Splanchnic, renal, and fetal circulations. In J. R. Brobeck (Ed.). *Best and Taylor's physological basis of medical practice.* (9th ed.) Baltimore: Williams & Wilkins, 1973, 3-231–3-233.

[60]*Ibid.,* 3-231–3-235.

[61]Guyton, A. C., Langston, J. B., & Navar, G. Theory for renal autoregulation by feedback at the juxtoglomerular apparatus. *Circulation Res.,* 1964, Suppl. Vols. 14 & 15, I-187–I-197.

[62]Magoun, H. W. *The waking brain.* (2nd ed.) Springfield, Ill.: C. C Thomas, 1963, 187.

[63]Sokoloff, L. *Op. cit.,* 1847–1848.

[64]Bremer, J. L. *Op. cit.,* 299.

[65]Moscona, A. A. Tissue reconstruction from dissociated cells. In M. X. Zarrow (Ed.). *Growth in living systems.* New York: Basic Books, 1961, 197–220.

[66]Sperry, R. W. Developmental basis of behavior. In A. Roe &

G. G. Simpson (Eds.). *Behavior and evolution*. New Haven: Yale Univ. Press, 1958, 128–139.

[67]Fischberg, M. & Blackler, A. W. How cells specialize. *Sci. Amer.*, 1961, **205**(3), 124–140.

[68]Konigsberg, I. R. The embryological origin of muscle. *Sci. Amer.*, 1964, **211**(2), 61–66.

[69]Puck, T. T., Marcus, P. I., & Cieciura, S. J. Clonal growth of mammalian cells *in vitro*. *J. exper. Med.*, 1956, **103**, 273–284.

[70]Moscona, A. A. *Op. cit.*

[71]Curtis, A. S. G. The regrouping of separated cells. *Discovery*, 1961, **22**, 199–203.

[72]Humphreys, T. Chemical dissolution and *in vitro* reconstruction of sponge cell adhesions. I. Isolation and functional demonstration of the components involved. *Develop. Biol.*, 1963, **8**, 27–47.

[73]*Ibid.*

[74]Galtsoff, P. S. Regeneration after dissociation (an experimental study on sponges). I. Behavior of dissociated cells of *Microciona prolifera* under normal and altered conditions. *J. exper. Zool.*, 1925, **42**, 183–221.

[75]Simms, H. Changes in structure and performance of cells and tissues with age. Nutrition, pathologic change and longevity. In A. M. Brues & G. A. Sacher (Eds.). *Aging and levels of biological organization*. Chicago: Univ. of Chicago Press, 1965, 87–122.

[76]Kolobow, T. & Bowman, R. L. Construction and evaluation of an alveolar membrane artificial heart-lung. *Trans. Amer. Soc. Artificial Internal Organs*, 1963, **9**, 238–243.

[77]McCurdy, D. K. & Bluemle, L. W., Jr. The current status of hemodialysis. *Med. clin. North Amer.*, 1963, **47**, 1043–1056.

[78]Gardner, W. H. & Harris, H. E. Aids and devices for laryngectomies. *Arch. Otolaryngol.*, 1961, **73**, 145–152.

[79]Kolff, W. J. An artificial heart inside the body. *Sci. Amer.*, 1965, **213**(5), 38–46.

[80]Roy, O. Z. An electronic heartbeat simulator and a cardiac tachometer. *I.R.E. Trans. on med. Electronics*, 1958, P.G.M.E. **11**, 48.

[81]Weiss, E. An air-damped artificial mastoid. *I.R.E.Trans. on biomed. Electronics*, 1961, B.M.E. **8**(2), 122–127.

[82]Harmon, L. D. Studies with artificial neurons, I: properties and functions of an artificial neuron. *Kybernetik*, 1961, **1**, 89–101.

[83]van Bergeijk, W. A. Studies with artificial neurons, II: analog of the external spiral innervation of the cochlea. *Kybernetik*, 1961, **1**, 102–107.

[84]Levinson, J. & Harmon, L. D. Studies with artificial neurons, III: mechanisms of flicker-fusion. *Kybernetik*, 1961, **1**, 107–117.

[85]McCulloch, W. S. & Pitts, W. A logical calculus of the ideas immanent in nervous activity. *Bull. math. Biophys.*, 1943, **5**, 115.

[86]Rapoport, A. Mathematics and cybernetics. In S. Arieti (Ed.). *American handbook of psychiatry*. Vol. 2. New York: Basic Books, 1959, 1743–1759.

[87]*Ibid.*, 1751–1752. Reprinted by permission.

[88]*Ibid.*, 1752.

[89]Rapoport, A. Net theory as a tool in the study of gross properties of nervous systems. *Perspectives in Biol. and Med.*, Autumn 1965, 146–147. Reprinted by permission.

[90]Josephson, R. K., Reiss, R. F., & Worthy, R. M. A simulation study of a diffuse conducting system based on coelenterate nerve nets. *J. theoret. Biol.*, 1961, **1**, 460–487.

[91]Dantzig, G. B., Dehaven, J. C., Cooper, I., Deland, E. C., Johnson, S. M., Kanter, H. E., & Sams, C. F. *A mathematical model of the human external respiratory system*. Rand report RM:2519, Sept. 28, 1959.

[92]Milborn, H. T., Jr. & Guyton, A. C. An analog computer analysis of Cheyne-Stokes breathing. *J. appl. Physiol.*, 1965, **20**, 328–333.
Cf. also Milborn, H. T., Jr., Benton, R., Ross, R., & Guyton, A. C. A mathematical model of the human respiratory control system. *Biophys. J.*, 1965, **5**, 27–46.

[93]Warner, H. R. The use of an analog computer for analysis of control mechanisms in the circulation. *I.R.E. Proceed.*, 1959, **47**, 1913–1916.

[94]*Ibid.*, 1914–1915. Reprinted by permission.

[95]Baker, D., Ellis, R. M., Franklin, D. L., & Rushmer, R. F. Some engineering aspects of modern cardiac research. *I.R.E. Proceed.*, 1959, **47**, 1917–1924. Reprinted by permission.

[96]Watt, J. M. & Young, A. An attempt to simulate the liver on a computer. *Comput. J.*, 1962, **5**, 221–227.

[97]Heinmets, F. & Herschman, A. Quantitative analysis of metabolic processes III. A model-system for enzyme synthesis by sequential induction and mathematical formulation of the process. *Bull. math. Biophys.*, 1961, **23**, 69–89.

The Organism

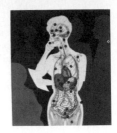

The term "organism" is employed here in its usual biological sense except that free-living cells, which have been discussed in Chap. 6 (see page 203), are excluded. Colonial forms like the coelenterate hydroids are included among the organisms. Slime molds whose cell components, originally free-living, join to form an organized multicellular structure, are regarded as organisms when they are in the aggregated state (see pages 203, 284, and 303). Some colonial algae, whose cells clump together but do not share a single differentiated decider or other subsystems, are considered to be colonies of cells rather than organisms.

1. Structure

1.1 System size The size of systems at this level ranges from microscopic plants and animals to the giant trees like *Sequoiadendron giganteum* that attain a height of more than 83 meters (m) and trunk diameters of more than 9 m.[1] Among extant animals, the blue whale is the largest. Adults have grown to a length of 32 m, more than 50 million times larger in cubic size than the smallest shrews.[2] The real giants are extinct. *Brachiosaurus,* the largest animal known to have existed, must have weighed as much as 45 metric tons. It had a massive 25-m body, short tail, and a neck that would have permitted a well-grown specimen to peer over a three-story building, if any had existed at the time.[3] This animal probably had to live with most of its body in water. Another monster was *Tyrannosaurus rex,* an active carnivore weighing 7 metric tons, 6.5 m tall, and 15 m long. It had a skull more than 1 m long and its teeth were 15 centimeters (cm) long. Also in existence was the slender *Diplodocus,* which was more than 27 m long, and weighed a trim 23 metric tons.

Upper and lower limits are placed upon the size of organisms by physical and environmental conditions. In animals metabolic activities such as heat production and rate of oxygen consumption are limited by body cross-sectional area.[4] When rate of heat production is plotted against body weight on a logarithmic scale, the points fall close to a straight line over a size range from mice to elephants, and a "weight" range from about 10^{-2} to 10^3 kilograms (kg).

Both plants and animals must be able to stand under their own weight unless, like whales, they live supported by water. Trees must become thicker as they grow in height in order to withstand buckling forces.[5] Tree limbs also must be proportioned to endure bending from their own weight. The lengths of both trunk and branches are proportional to the ⅔ power of their diameter. In order to bear their own weight, animals, too, must become thicker as their height increases. Their shapes adjust as they grow. Small animals are, in general, relatively slenderer than large animals. The same relationship between length and diameter is found in animals as in trees. In the size range from rats to human beings, surface area increases as the 0.65 power of body weight.

If a vertebrate is to fly, it cannot weigh more than 15 to 19 kg.[6] The power needed for flight increases more rapidly than the cubic size of the body. Beyond a certain mass, even if the entire body were muscle, it could not supply the necessary motive power.

The information in the genetic template sets the upper and lower limits of size of each species. Variations beyond these limits are pathological (see page 477). A number of influences are known to affect the ultimate size of an individual species member.[7] When large and small breeds of horses are cross-bred, the genetics of the sire set the upper limit of the foal of a large-breed mother, but the size of the placenta sets the upper limit for a small-breed mother. The weight of the placenta and foal of a large-breed mother can be 3 times that of a small-breed mother.

At least 1 million animal species are known, and estimates range from 2 million to 10 million. Plants are less numerous, with somewhat over 250,000 known species.[8] Of the 1 million types of animals, 900,000 are insects. The species with small members tend to be more populous. Estimates of the median size of animals, therefore, fall at the low end of the scale of size. In spite of the great size of the largest plants, the situation is probably similar for them. My estimate of the median diameter of an organism, therefore, is of the order of 10^{-2} m.

1.2 Structural taxonomy of types of systems
Structural similarity (including similarity in structures of component molecules) forms the logical basis for the modern science of taxonomy, which deals with biological classification of living beings. Traditionally, the first and most basic division has distinguished between the two kingdoms of plants and animals. This obvious dichotomy, however, turns out to be no more satisfactory at the level of the organism than at the level of the cell (see page 208). Fungi, which resemble plants in many ways but lack chlorophyll and are unlike either plants or animals in organization of their tissues, do not fit well into either kingdom. Moreover their evolutionary development has been separate from that of either plants or animals.

A number of alternative schemes of classification have been proposed, none of which has as yet received complete acceptance. These increase the number of kingdoms to four or five, making somewhat different divisions of phyla among them.[9] In this book I follow one such proposed taxonomic system, which includes five kingdoms (see page 208).[10]

(a) *Monerans.* All these are cells and have been discussed in Chap. 6. Most are single, but some blue-green alga cells, which are included in this kingdom, mass into clumps or string together into filaments. There is no differentiation of tissues among these, and ordinarily they reproduce by division of cells and breaking up of the colonies. While such colonies are made up of several or many cells, they lack the subsystem differentiation and central decider which would place them among multicellular organisms. Blue-green algae carry out photosynthesis, but many bacteria do

not. The photosynthetic bacteria are distinguished by possession of protochlorophyll or other photosynthetic pigments in place of chlorophyll.

(b) *Protistans.* Most members of this kingdom are single cells, but some colonial forms occur which are considered to be organisms. The cells of some of the golden algae, for instance, attach to each other in filaments. Some species of protistans carry out photosynthesis, but others do not.

(c) *Fungi.* Members of this kingdom often have tissues in which many nuclei are dispersed in a walled mycelial syncytium. Exceptions are the slime molds, which are structured differently at various stages in their life cycles. Fungi do not carry out photosynthesis. They usually live embedded in a food supply and, except for slime molds, they lack the power of locomotion.

(d) *Plants.* These are primarily multicellular organisms, although the kingdom includes some unicellular forms. They usually have differentiated tissues and organs. The green plants carry out photosynthesis. They live anchored to a substrate. A number of algae are included in this kingdom along with all the other organisms ordinarily recognized as plants.

(e) *Animals.* These are multicellular organisms which cannot perform photosynthesis and which can carry out locomotion or at least have motile parts. They include some simple forms with differentiated cells but no true tissue differentiation, such as the sponges. They are, however, ordinarily highly differentiated, much more than the other kingdoms, with complex sensory and motor components and nervous networks.

Within kingdoms, each phylum includes quite divergent species which, nevertheless, are believed to have evolved from the same common ancestor.

2. Process

Many statements about specific processes of single subsystems or components are made later in this chapter. Little can be said about organisms as a whole. One cross-level principle, however, seems clearly to apply at this level: the more isolated a system is, the more totipotential it must be (see Hypothesis 2-3, page 92). A human infant cannot survive alone because it is far from totipotential, and many civilized adults are not totipotential either because they cannot carry out all necessary subsystem functions, such as foraging for food or cooking. Animals domesticated for some months may be similarly handicapped. But primitive men, woodsmen, and adult wild animals have no such problem. The young of many precocious animal species are also totipotential.

2.1 System and subsystem indicators   Indicators are abundant at this level, especially for human organisms. The reliability of different sorts of indicators, however, varies. The findings of physical and neurological examinations; physiological and biochemical laboratory studies, including x-rays; psychological and behavioral tests; and sociological and economic evaluations are among these. Indicators exist for measuring processes of all the subsystems of human organisms, although some subsystems have fewer generally accepted indicators than others.

These include measurements or observations of aspects of external appearance and behavior, like size, posture, color, and deformity; speech and motor behavior; physiological conditions like internal body temperature, temperature of extremities, pulse, blood pressure, rate of breathing, brain electrical activity, excretory processes, sensory functioning, and reflexes; appearance of bodily parts under x-ray or fluoroscope; and appearance of cells or tissues under a microscope.

Psychological indicators include intelligence tests, performance tests, projective tests, situation tests, and clinical interviews. They are often less reliable and valid than the above tests. Many of them, nonetheless, are useful for basic research, school placement, clinical evaluation, vocational guidance, and other purposes.

Measures like amount of income, social status, sociometric status, or attitude and preference scales are also useful.

Probably the most precise and reliable indicators are the biochemical tests. Normal limits and extreme ranges of hundreds of biochemical variables have been determined, methods of measurement specified, instruments perfected, and the meaning of changes in values established. Such standardization has been achieved also for some other indicators and is being attempted for still others.

2.2 Process taxonomy of types of systems   Although taxonomy relies primarily on structural criteria (including the structures of component molecules) in classifying organisms, some distinctions on the basis of process, including overt behavior, are made in assigning names to categories. In the class of mammals, for instance, are the orders *Carnivora* (meat eaters) and *Insectivora* (insect eaters). There is no order *Herbivora,* although animals of several species which ingest only vegetation are described as herbivores.

Distinctions as to process are important also when the structure of an organism does not provide sufficient evidence to classify it. Some animals and fungi, for example, look so remarkably like plants that their processes must be carefully studied to place them properly. Others have parts which look deceptively like components of another species, although the parts in the first species carry out processes quite unlike the components which they resemble in the second species. Such components must be observed in action to be sure what they really are.

In classification of organisms for other than taxonomic purposes, terms describing the individual's processes in its suprasystem may be used: "weed" for certain plants; "beast of burden," "hunting dog," "race horse" for nonhuman animals; "mayor," "plumber," "doctor," "sculptor" for human beings.

3. Subsystems

The subsystems of organisms are organs, which have been defined and discussed in Chap. 7. Figure 8-1 is a detailed representation of an organism, showing its subsystems. In this particular case the organism pictured is a woman, surrounded by dim figures of other people near her, in her suprasystem. The vascular components of her distributor subsystem were pictured in Fig. 7-2. Cells in the heart of this distributor subsystem were pictured in Fig. 6-9.

In Table 8-1 are listed some components which constitute the critical subsystems of an organism. Some species of plants and animals lack certain critical subsystems and must of necessity be parasites or symbiotes of other organisms. Parasitic worms, for example, often lack digestive apparatuses and depend upon predigested matter-energy from their hosts' gastrointestinal tracts. Unless otherwise noted, the organisms referred to throughout this chapter are human beings.

3.1 Subsystems which process both matter-energy and information

3.1.1 Reproducer, the subsystem which is capable of giving rise to other organisms similar to the one it is in.

3.1.1.1 Structure   The spore-bearing organs of fungi, the stamens and pistils that carry the sex cells of plants, as well as spores, seeds, and accessory structures such as fruits and seed pods, are examples of this subsystem.

Among animals the following components all together constitute the structure of the reproducer: the male and/or female genitalia and sex organs, with the eggs and sperm which they contain and their accessory structures; the endocrine, neural, and motor components associated with these; and a variety of other structures, differing from species to species, such as lacteal glands, breasts, nipples, marsupial pouches, and other sex-specific structures, like antlers, colored feathers, and wattles.

An artifact of this subsystem is an incubator.

3.1.1.2 Process   Courtship, mating, nesting, and care of the young are included in the reproducing

Fig. 8-1 A woman. Subsystems of the woman, or major components of them, are identified.

Subsystems which process both matter-energy and information: Reproducer (Re), genitalia; Boundary (Bo), skin.

Subsystems which process matter-energy: Ingestor (IN), mouth, lung; Distributor (DI), heart and connecting vessels of vascular system; Converter (CO), stomach, intestine; Matter-energy storage (MS), liver; Extruder (EX), lungs, kidney, rectum, ureter, and anus; Motor (MO), muscles; Supporter (SU), skeleton.

Subsystems which process information: Input transducer (it), eyes; Internal transducer (in), postsynaptic regions of neurons with which afferent neurons from organs synapse; Channel and net (cn), network of neurons interconnecting centers of the central nervous system; Decoder (dc), cortical sensory projection and association areas for each sensory modality, *e.g.*, occipital visual cortex, temporal auditory cortex, temporoparietal area of dominant hemisphere of brain; Decider (de), nuclei of "nonspecific" and limbic areas and their cortical representation areas; Encoder (en), temporoparietal area of dominant hemisphere of brain; Output transducer (ot), larynx.

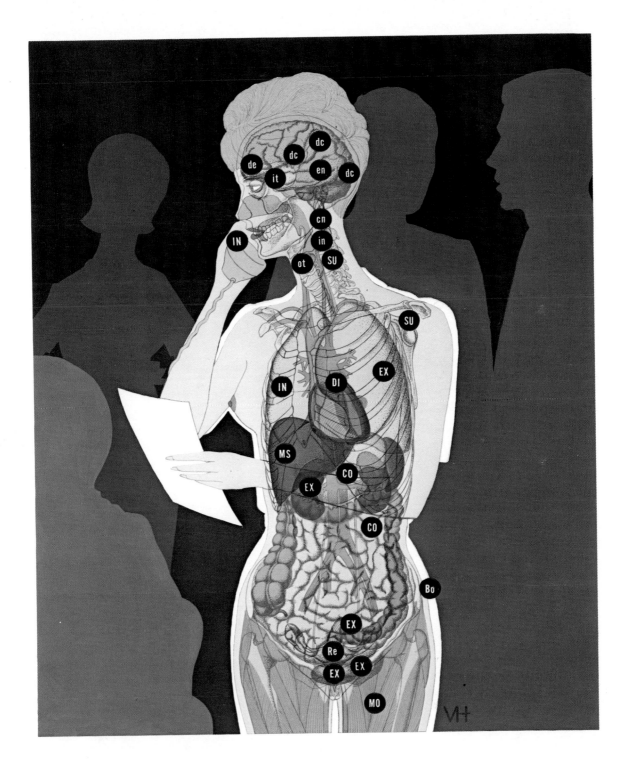

TABLE 8-1. Components of the 19 Critical Subsystems of an Organism*

3.1 SUBSYSTEMS WHICH PROCESS BOTH MATTER-ENERGY AND INFORMATION

3.1.1 *Reproducer.* In fungi, spore-bearing organs; in plants, stamens, pistils, seeds, and their accessory structures, such as fruits and seed pods; in animals, eggs, sperm; the sex glands in which they develop, genitalia, and accessory structures; artifacts such as incubator

3.1.2 *Boundary.* Integument, like epidermis or bark of plants, membranes, skin, external skeleton, fur, hair, feathers, scales, or corneas of animals; artifacts such as hat, cap, coat, suit, diver's suit, astronaut's suit

3.2 SUBSYSTEMS WHICH PROCESS MATTER-ENERGY

3.2.1. *Ingestor.* In fungi, filaments; in plants, root tips, stomata, epithelial cells, and some accessory structures like tentacles and traps; in animals, openings into digestive spaces, such as central cavity of coelenterates or canal entrances of sponges, mouth, nostrils, gills, skin, and accessory structures such as cilia, tentacles, and jaws; artifacts, such as stomach tube, syringe

3.2.2 *Distributor.* In plants, the vascular system, including tracheids and the veins of leaves; in animals, the central cavities of coelenterates, canals of sponges, and blood and lymph vascular systems of higher species

3.2.3 *Converter.* In plants, none known at this level; in animals, the mouth, teeth, tongue, associated musculature, salivary glands, stomach, liver, gallbladder, pancreas, and small intestine

3.2.4 *Producer.* None known at this level.

3.2.5 *Matter-Energy Storage.* In plants, leaves, stems, roots, seeds, tubers, fruit; in animals, fatty tissues, liver, gallbladder, bone marrow, muscles, bones, spleen, urinary bladder, lower bowel

3.2.6 *Extruder.* In plants, membranes and stomata of leaves; in animals, opening of the central cavity of coelenterates, opening of the canals of sponges, kidneys, ureters, urethra, rectum, anus, lungs, breathing passages, sweat glands, birth canal, breasts, mouth, poison glands, musk glands; artifacts such as enema or douche equipment

3.2.7 *Motor.* In fungi, endoplasm of slime molds; in plants, liquid-filled bulbs in sensitive plants; in animals, muscles, fascia, bones and joints of specialized components such as legs, wings; artifacts such as cane, rocking chair, wheelchair, cart, automobile, sleigh, rowboat, broom, hammer, sewing machine, machine tool

3.2.8 *Supporter.* In plants, cell walls, sclerenchyma; in animals, skeleton, tendons, ligaments, joint capsules, muscles, fascia; artifacts such as chair, bed, platform

3.3 SUBSYSTEMS WHICH PROCESS INFORMATION

3.3.1 *Input Transducer.* The totality of the components of all the sensory modalities including, in the human being, the eyes, the vestibular and auditory parts of the ears, chemoreceptors in the nose and tongue, nerve endings and receptors in the skin; specialized receptors in the skin; specialized receptors in other species, such as, in pigeons, for magnetic fields, and in torpedo fish, for electrical fields; artifacts such as radio receiver, television receiver, telephone receiver, public address system speaker

3.3.2 *Internal Transducer.* Postsynaptic regions of neurons with which afferent neurons from organs synapse; receptor cells within the central nervous system that receive and transduce signals about chemical and physical states of the bloodstream;

3.3.3 *Channel and Net.* In plants, the vascular system, including tracheids and the veins of leaves, which convey hormones; in animals, the central cavities of coelenterates, canals of sponges, and blood and lymph vascular systems of higher species which convey hormones; the network of neurons which interconnects all centers of the central nervous system, as well as the peripheral neural network

3.3.4 *Decoder.* Certain cells in sense organs, like retinal bipolar and ganglion cells and cochlear bipolar cells; ganglia, nuclei, and other centers where afferent neurons synapse; cortical sensory projection and association areas for each sensory modality; for gamma-coded linguistic information processing, temporoparietal area of dominant hemisphere of human brain; artifacts such as coding machine, pattern recognition device

3.3.5 *Associator.* In fungi and plants, probably none exists at this level; in animals, specific components not known

3.3.6 *Memory.* In fungi and plants, probably none exists at this level; in animals, specific components not known

3.3.7 *Decider.* In plants, hormone-producing tissues; in animals, certain neurons; pituitary and other endocrine glands; ventral horn nuclei of spinal cords, motor nuclei of all parts of the brain, cortical motor areas; nuclei of preganglionic autonomic pathways and parts of cerebral cortex which send neurons into them; all or many nuclei of "nonspecific" and limbic areas and their cortical representation areas; nuclei and cortical areas of cerebellum; artifacts such as calculator, computer

3.3.8 *Encoder.* None known in fungi and plants; in animals, exocrine glands which output alpha-coded pheromones; for beta-coded information processing, specific components not known; for gamma-coded symbolic information processing, temporoparietal area of dominant hemisphere of human brain

3.3.9 *Output Transducer.* Exocrine glands which produce and parts of extruder which excrete alpha-coded pheromones; for beta- and gamma-coded information processing, components of motor including lips, tongue, soft palate, larynx, lungs, hands, feet, muscles of chest and abdomen, tail muscles of dog, small muscles which raise the hair of a cat, wattles of a turkey, organs that color Siamese fighting fish; areas 44 and 45 and nearby regions of inferior frontal cortex of dominant hemisphere of human brain; artifacts such as pencil, pen, typewriter, microphone, radio transmitter, television transmitter

*No artifacts are now used for some subsystems of organisms.

process. The fundamental cellular reproductive event is the combining of genetic information (see pages 224 to 226) from the parents, leading to the development of the fertilized egg into a new individual.

This subsystem processes information when it transmits the template carried in the genetic material from the parental generation to the offspring. It also processes matter-energy, supplied from stored materials in seed or egg or from the mother's body.

Various aspects of reproduction—mating, nesting, development of embryos, birth, and maternal and paternal behavior—are controlled by hormonal and neural signals, differing among species. These signals may be elicited or modified by information from the internal transducer and the input transducer. For instance, signals flow from the uterus in which a fetus is developing to the pituitary, and back to the uterus from the pituitary—an internal feedback loop.

Physiological and behavioral processes are also turned off and on by signals from other animals and from the environment. The same variations in temperature, and of the length of day and night, that bring flowers to a plant, set off profound changes in animals. The "biological clocks" of organisms, which time the adjustments of the reproducer as well as other subsystems, are precisely regulated (see pages 450 and 451). Signals from other animals may be highly specific, acting as "releasers" for particular processes (see pages 409, 439, and 465).

These fundamental reproductive processes, in nature, require an essentially intact animal that does not vary greatly from species standards. In the laboratory one can study parts of the process by ablation or by severing the neural connections to specific components. Not unexpectedly, species and sex differences are considerable. For example, absence of the neocortex does not eliminate estrous behavior in female laboratory mammals. Female rats with the neocortex removed can still mate and produce young.[11] They do not, however, build nests or care for their young. Male rats, on the other hand, do not mate if more than 60 percent of the neocortex is removed, although the sensory and motor behavior involved in copulation by a male can be carried out without the cortex. Decorticate male cats may attempt to mount females, but are unable to copulate.

Evidently the relatively more passive sexual actions of the female can be controlled by lower neural echelons. If, besides the neocortex, the rhinencephalon and a large part of the striatum and the thalamus are destroyed, estrous behavior continues in the female cat. Female rabbits and rats also mate when even lower structures are included in the ablation.

The hypothalamus is necessary for sexual behavior in both sexes. The pituitary hormones which regulate the ovaries and testes are controlled by hypothalamic centers (see pages 391 and 392). Hypothalamic lesions in females result in permanent loss of estrus, which cannot be regained with estrogens.[12] Other hypothalamic centers are involved in integration of mating performance and sexual excitability, and apparently are essential for recognition of appropriate mates and territorial mating behavior.[13]

Median lesions in the limbic system disrupt the maternal behavior of a rat, apparently by preventing her from organizing her behavior. If the young are scattered, a normal mother rat gathers them all into the nest. A lesioned rat, on the other hand, picks up a baby and returns it to the nest, only to remove it on the next trip. In the end the young are strewn about and left to die.[14]

Genital reflexes can be controlled by spinal centers without involvement of higher neural echelons. A male animal with an intact brain but transected spinal cord can develop penile erection and ejaculate. Similarly, such a female can be impregnated and deliver normal litters.[15] Spinal transection, of course, does not stop the flow of chemical information through the blood vessels, so the hormonal regulation of these reproductive processes continues.

Finally, if inputs from genital components of the input transducer are eliminated by cutting the genital sensory neurons, sexual behavior is almost unimpaired in lower mammals, apparently controlled by information inputs from the other components of the input transducer.

Species differ in the degree to which their reproductive behavior depends upon prior experience.

Representative *variables* of the process of reproducing are: *Sorts of matter-energy used in reproducing.* Example: Iron ingested by the mother reached the fetus and entered into its metabolism. *Meaning of information used in reproducing.* Example: The genetic information carried a pathological gene which produced mental retardation and other signs of phenylketonuria in the child. *Sorts of information used in reproducing.* Example: The cat had three litters, each one by a different father. *Changes in reproducing over time.* Example: As the dog grew old, the number of pups in her litters were reduced from a maximum of 12 to 1. *Changes in reproducing with different circumstances.* Example: The sheep imported from the Southern Hemisphere changed its breeding habits to conform to local seasonal conditions. *Rate of reproducing.* Example: Growth of the flea population accelerated during the soap shortage. *Frequency of reproducing.* Example: For the first 10 years of their marriage, the Smiths had a child each year. *Lag in reproducing.* Example: After 8 years of marriage, Sarah finally found herself pregnant. *Costs of reproducing.* Example: Because her teeth became decalcified during pregnancy, the woman lost two teeth after the birth of her first child and another after her second child was born.

3.1.2 Boundary, the subsystem at the perimeter of an organism that holds together the components which make up the organism, protects them from environmental stresses, and excludes or permits entry to various sorts of matter-energy and information.

3.1.2.1 Structure

Matter-energy boundary. The matter-energy boundary of all organisms is some sort of integument. Plants have an epidermal covering over leaves, stems, and roots. This may be a single layer of cells or a complex tissue with several layers, the outermost of which, in woody plants and trees, is a nonliving bark.

Animals have membranes or skins which have fur, hair, feathers, scales, or other accessory structures. External skeletons form part of the boundaries of molluscs and arthropods.

The skin of human beings and higher animals is continuous with the epithelial mucous membrane lining the digestive tube from mouth to anus and with the linings of lungs or gills so that, strictly speaking, these organisms have the form of a torus (any solid which rings a hole as a doughnut does). The "inside" of the gastrointestinal and respiratory tracts is, in some sense, "outside" the body, though it is universally regarded as "inside" for most ordinary as well as scientific purposes.

Openings of various sorts, such as stomata ("little mouths") of plant leaves and sweat-gland orifices in some animals, pierce the boundary at various points where components of the ingestor, extruder, and perhaps other subsystems open to the surface.

Information boundary. The skin or other outer covering of organisms also is the boundary to information. This covering may be transparent or open at points where input and output transducers are located at the surface or deformable where the structures, such as touch or pressure receptors, lie within it. The outermost layer of the epithelium of leaves is transparent, for example, and so is the cornea of the eye.

Artifacts of this subsystem include hats, caps, coats, dresses, suits, divers' suits, and astronauts' suits.

3.1.2.2 Process

Matter-energy boundary. The physical properties of an organism's boundaries make it able to filter matter-energy inputs and protect internal tissues. The toughness, relative impermeability, and coloring of this integument enable it to fend off excess inputs. A significant amount of work is required for a large object to cross an organism's boundary, usually more than

when it is transmitted over the same distance in space immediately inside or outside the boundary. This is consistent with Hypothesis 3.1.2.2-1 (see page 93). The heavy bark of a tree, like the cornified epithelium of human skin, has ceased to be alive. It no longer processes matter-energy across its boundaries and is largely impermeable to inputs and outputs. Consequently it prevents excessive loss of water and dehydration of underlying structures. When the outer layer of animal skin is damaged and worn off, cells from lower layers are pushed upward to take their place, "dying" in the process.

The skin of warm-blooded animals protects against excessive inputs or outputs of heat by changes in the rate of output of sweat glands, speeding or slowing the cooling caused by evaporation of moisture; by variations in the amount of blood in its vascular layers; and by the insulation of hair, fur, or feathers. Many organisms can fluff out insulating fur or feathers and erect hairs by means of minute muscles in the skin. This increases the amount of warm air trapped close to the bodily surface. Some animals have subcutaneous layers of fat, a poor heat conductor, which thicken when winter comes. The tanning of light-colored human skin is a protective process which increases the pigment near the surface and filters out some of the rays of sunlight which can damage tissues. Skin is a component of other subsystems besides the boundary.

Information boundary. The organism's boundary also can filter out information. When the eyelids are closed they shut out most visual inputs. Other input transducers are less protected at the boundary, although some animals can shut out some sound signals by changing the position of their ears, flattening them against their heads.

Representative *variables* of boundary process include: *Sorts of matter-energy crossing the boundary.* Example: The great whale filtered out everything larger than plankton with its baleen. *Meaning of information crossing the boundary.* Example: The chemical substances excreted by the skunk entered the dog's nose and warned him to stop. *Sorts of information crossing the boundary.* Example: Mrs. Kelly would listen to all jokes except Irish ones. *Degree of permeability of the boundary to matter-energy.* Example: Fat decreased the man's skin heat transfer. *Degree of permeability of the boundary to information.* Example: The dog pricked up its ears when it heard the robbers' footsteps on the roadway outside the house. *Percentage of matter-energy arriving at the boundary which enters the system.* Example: Only a small amount of the medication penetrated the patient's skin. *Percentage of information arriving at the boundary which enters the system.*

Example: Isabelle paid no attention to 90 percent of the gossip she heard. *Changes in matter-energy processing at the boundary over time.* Example: After about 2 minutes (min) water entered the drowning man's lungs. *Changes in information processing at the boundary over time.* Example: The old man became increasingly deaf. *Changes in matter-energy processing at the boundary with different circumstances.* Example: The robin fluffed up its feathers when the wind blew cold. *Changes in information processing at the boundary with different circumstances.* Example: In the absence of reliable news about the fate of his troops, the king would listen to even the wildest rumors. *Rate of matter-energy processing at the boundary.* Example: The young man injected the narcotic into his arm very slowly. *Rate of information processing at the boundary.* Example: The banker read rapidly when he was not tired and usually could finish three newspapers in an evening. *Frequency of matter-energy processing at the boundary.* Example: Each time the boy had a basket full of berries he sorted them and ate the desirable ones. *Frequency of information processing at the boundary.* Example: The judge would receive petitions only on Monday mornings. *Lag in matter-energy processing at the boundary.* Example: The snake lay next to the stunned mouse for several minutes before beginning to envelop it. *Lag in information processing at the boundary.* Example: The snail had withdrawn into its shell and only slowly realized that the bird had flown away. *Costs of matter-energy processing at the boundary.* Example: It took several hours of hard work to skin and clean the deer and prepare its meat for eating. *Costs of information processing at the boundary.* Example: The medical student paid $300 each year for his books.

3.2 Subsystems which process matter-energy

3.2.1 Ingestor, the subsystem which brings matter-energy across the organism's boundary from the environment.

3.2.1.1 Structure   The filaments of some fungi belong to this subsystem. Root tips, stomata in leaves and green stems, and the epithelial cells of green leaves form the ingestor of plants. Some plants also have accessory structures like the sticky tentacles of sundew plants. Venus's-flytrap, called by Linnaeus a "miracle of nature" and by Darwin the "most wonderful" plant in the world, has leaf blades with two lobes each which together make up a trap.[16] The lobes stand separated by 40 to 50 degrees. Their upper surfaces have digestive glandular components which contain red sap. The outer edge of each lobe bears about 13 strong, minute, fingerlike projections and three bristlelike hairs with nectar glands between them. Pitcher plants have another sort of trap.

Openings into the digestive spaces of animals, such as a mouth, the canal entrances of sponges, or the opening into the central cavity of coelenterates are components of this subsystem in animals. Nostrils, lungs, and gills are others. The skin is an ingestor component in some species, but this route for matter-energy input is relatively unimportant in human beings. A great variety of ingeniously adapted accessory structures are also ingestor components, including cilia, tentacles, and muscular jaws.

Artifacts of this subsystem include stomach tubes and syringes.

3.2.1.2 Process   The different phyla of organisms vary greatly in the sorts of materials they can metabolize and in how they are adapted to ingest what they need. Fungi take in matter-energy by absorption, securing food and water by sending their filaments into decaying wood, rotten meat, or the bodies of living plants or animals. Some of them snare their prey with a loop and penetrate the bodies of their captives with their filaments. Sundew plants catch tiny bugs with their sticky tentacles, just as flypaper traps flies. Insect-eating plants, like Venus's-flytrap, can snap shut like a clam. If a fly walks into one of its traps to feed on the nectar and touches one of its hairs twice or two hairs at least once (a single touch is not enough), the trap closes on the fly in 0.25 second(s). Digestive enzymes then disintegrate the fly within 10 days, after which the trap opens again.

Green plants, which are able to carry out photosynthesis (see page 239), need only oxygen and carbon dioxide from the air, water and dissolved minerals from the soil, and sunlight to carry out all their processes.

Animals and fungi cannot carry out the extremely fundamental syntheses which plants can, so they must find inputs containing the products of such syntheses. Animals must ingest carbon, oxygen, hydrogen, nitrogen, calcium, magnesium, sodium, potassium, phosphorus, sulfur, and chlorine, as principal requirements, and small amounts of iron, copper, manganese, molybdenum, zinc, cobalt, iodine, fluorine, and possibly other elements. Animals cannot eat most of these in pure form. They ingest them as proteins, carbohydrates, and fats, when they eat plants or other animals. Water is necessary to all animals, although some drink little and obtain what they need from ingested foods. Air is ingested for its oxygen content. Like plants, animals cannot take nitrogen from the air but must ingest nitrogenous proteins. The need for these substances varies in different species, at different ages, and in different metabolic states.

Simple animals, such as sponges and coelenterates,

are adapted so that the water in which they live can circulate through them, meeting all their matter-energy needs. Muscular action forces ambient air through the lungs or water through the gills of higher animals, supplying oxygen. Specialized components of the ingestor in some species locate, seize, break off, immobilize, or kill potential matter-energy inputs.

Representative *variables* of the process of ingesting include: *Sorts of matter-energy ingested.* Example: The fox preferred young chickens. *Degree of openness of the ingestor.* Example: During the heat wave the stomata of the oak tree closed as much as possible. *Changes in ingesting over time.* Example: Grandfather wanted only soft food and no longer chose steaks. *Changes in ingesting with different circumstances.* Example: During her pregnancy the woman craved dill pickles. *Rate of ingesting.* Example: The pigeon pecked steadily, about once every 2 s, until it was completely satiated. *Frequency of ingesting.* Example: The lion gorged itself about twice a week. *Lag in ingesting.* Example: The wolf stalked its prey for several hours before catching and eating it. *Costs of ingesting.* Example: Margie spent most of her allowance on candy.

3.2.2 Distributor, the subsystem which carries inputs from outside the organism or outputs from its subsystems around the organism to each component.

3.2.2.1 Structure The entire vascular system, including spindle-shaped cells known as *tracheids* and the branching veins of leaves, forms the distributor of plants. Among animals, the central cavity of coelenterates, the canal systems of sponges, and the highly developed vascular systems which are in contact with all cells of higher animals are examples of this subsystem.

The blood vascular system of man and other highly evolved animal organisms consists of a continuous network of vessels—arteries, arterioles, capillaries, venules, and veins—penetrating to all components of the organism. The heart is the central motor of this distributor subsystem.

Another component of this subsystem in higher animals is the lymph vascular system which does not convey fluids to tissues but only away from them into the venous stream. In some vertebrates there is a "lymph heart" which consists of a pulsating enlargement of lymph vessels. Mammals lack this component. Lymph nodes are found at intervals along the course of the lymph vessels and in masses in certain parts of the body such as the neck, the underarm, the groin, and the space under the diaphragm.

3.2.2.2 Process Plants move water and nutrients from the roots to the leaves and other distant structures, and send products synthesized in various structures to all parts of the plant. A giant redwood tree may lift water about 122 m from the root tips to the highest leaves. This is done without a pump.

After matter-energy enters the distributor of mammals by absorption through the walls of the gastrointestinal tract and lungs, it moves in a fluid medium, chiefly the blood. The heart contracts to pump blood through the arteries. When the body's muscles move they force the blood through veins in and near them. This causes venous blood to move toward the heart. Valves in the veins prevent it from going in the other direction. Rates of blood flow through the animal distributor and blood pressure vary from part to part and from moment to moment, being under continuous feedback control.

As the blood circulates throughout the organism it receives secretions and excretions from many structures, synthesized products from various tissues, and oxygen from the lungs, as well as carbon dioxide and other metabolic wastes. Each organ or component ingests substances from the blood and extrudes others into it. Foods or fuels in the arterial blood decrease as it passes through the bodily tissues, and wastes increase. The entropy of the contents of blood per cubic centimeter also increases. These changes are postulated by Hypotheses 3.2.2.2-1 and 3.2.2.2-2 (see page 94).

Lymphatic circulation is achieved by the contractions of muscles throughout the body and by breathing movements. Fluid in lymphatics, as in veins, is forced toward the heart along the vessels, which are provided with valves to prevent back flow. The lymph vascular system carries foreign matter, dead cells, and bacteria to the lymph nodes. Special scavenger cells in the lymph nodes destroy bacteria. Some particulate matter remains in the nodes, which often become dark from soot carried from the lungs. Other substances enter the bloodstream on the venous side. Large molecules of fat output from the intestine enter the lymphatic circulation and later go into the blood vascular system to be input to the liver through the hepatic artery. The lymphatic system also carries wastes from organ components to be extruded from the organism.

Representative *variables* of the distributing process are: *Sorts of matter-energy distributed to various parts of the system.* Example: Glycogen was withdrawn from the liver and sent to the workman's muscles during his energetic physical work. *Changes in distributing over time.* Example: The old man's arteries hardened so that his leg did not get enough circulating blood. *Changes in distributing with different circumstances.* Example: During stress, epinephrine was carried to target organs throughout the cat's body. *Rate of distributing.*

Example: As the horse neared the finish line, its heart pumped faster and faster. *Frequency of distributing*. Example: Increased amounts of nutrients were carried in the woman's bloodstream 3 times per day after meals. *Lag in distributing*. Example: A sudden spasm of the arterioles caused a brief anoxia, and the patient fainted. *Costs of distributing*. Example: At increased activity, more calories per second were consumed by the athlete's rapidly beating heart.

3.2.3   Converter, the subsystem which changes certain inputs to the organism into forms more useful for the special processes of that particular organism.

3.2.3.1   Structure   The converter in plants is downwardly dispersed to the level of the cell (see page 236). In vertebrate animals it consists of the mouth, teeth, tongue, associated musculature, salivary glands, stomach, liver, gallbladder, pancreas, and small intestine.

3.2.3.2   Process   When organisms convert material inputs, the valence bonds of the complex molecules are broken, and other bonds are formed. Energy is released, and some of the simpler compounds can be used in bodily processes. While the reagents used by higher animal organisms in converting are cellular products, many of these processes do not take place within cells but within the organ converter. Cells secrete into acini and ducts which open into the gastrointestinal tract, and successive chemical reactions occur as materials move through this tube until the original substances are reduced to smaller molecules which can pass through the intestinal walls and into the distributor.

Converting in mammals involves three successive sorts of operations: mechanical breaking and grinding up of ingested food; softening and dissolving of it in various fluids; and chemical dissociation of the component molecules' valence bonds.

The first, a mechanical operation, is begun in the mouth by the teeth, tongue, and jaws. Then the churning action of the stomach promotes the separation of food into particles. The second process begins with the saliva and continues with water and hydrochloric acid in the stomach and water in the rest of the gastrointestinal tract. The third is carried on by various enzymes in different components, specialized to break down fats, carbohydrates, or proteins.

Converting carbohydrates begins in the mouth, accomplished by the salivary enzyme, ptyalin. Its action continues until the acid in the stomach destroys it. Ptyalin breaks some starches into double sugars (like ordinary table sugar, sucrose) which are simpler but still too large and complex to be absorbed into the distributor. Some starch gets through this process

intact or is imperfectly broken down. The pancreas secretes amylopsin into the intestine. This is another enzyme which converts starch into double sugars. These sugars are changed into simple sugars which can be absorbed, by several enzymes in the small intestine.

Fats are also converted in the small intestine by bile, which breaks the large droplets into small ones, and by lipase, an enzyme which produces fatty acids and glycerol—compounds that can pass into the distributor.

Representative *variables* of the converting process are: *Sorts of matter-energy converted*. Example: The termite was able to digest wood. *Percentage of matter-energy converted*. Example: The bones and the beak which the dog ate proved to be indigestible. *Changes in converting over time*. Example: After the infant cut several teeth, he began to be able to chew pieces of meat. *Changes in converting with different circumstances*. Example: The banquet speaker was so nervous that his gastric juices did not flow, leaving the food unchanged in his stomach. *Rate of converting*. Example: The insect was able to destroy a rose leaf in a day. *Frequency of converting*. Example: The geranium could carry on photosynthesis only during the hours of sunshine. *Lag in converting*. Example: The child held the pill in his mouth several minutes before chewing it. *Costs of converting*. Example: After eating the rabbit, the snake was torpid, unable to use much energy for anything but digestion.

3.2.4   Producer, the subsystem which forms stable associations that endure for significant periods among matter-energy inputs to the organism or outputs from its converter, the materials synthesized being for growth, damage repair, or replacement of components of the organism, or for providing energy for moving or constituting the organism's outputs of products or information markers to its suprasystem.

3.2.4.1   Structure   This subsystem is dispersed downwardly to the level of the cell (see pages 238 to 241).

3.2.4.2   Process   Matter-energy products of organisms include components of the organism itself as it grows and is maintained and repaired, including regenerated parts in those species which can regenerate. Many organisms also produce secretions which they output into the environment. These include the pheromones which coordinate social behavior of various species of animals including many insects, fishes, and mammals (see pages 404 and 439), the ink of squids, and many others.

Species differ in capacity to produce new components for damage repair and replacement of lost parts.

Planarians are famous for their ability to regenerate complete worms from as little as one-fiftieth of a cut-up individual (see page 418). More complex organisms do not have this capacity. Lizards and salamanders, however, can replace their tails after they are cut or torn, a process which requires the coordinated regeneration of bone, muscle, vascular, and nervous tissue, as well as the various connective and epithelial tissues that make up a complete and functional tail.[17] Tail replacement has adaptive significance for a gecko, which is a type of lizard. This animal is remarkable because the regenerated tail may be bigger than the original. A gecko responds to a predator, such as a snake, by lifting its tail high above its body and waving it back and forth. The snake often strikes at the tail and removes part of it.

In more highly evolved animals, such as humans, repair is much more effective in some sorts of tissues than in others. Bones repair themselves slowly, by a complicated multistage process, but when the process is complete, they are often stronger than they were before. Liver and blood vessels regenerate readily. On the other hand, some tissues, such as the central nervous system and cardiac muscle, the cells of which cannot divide, have little capacity for regeneration.

Among the *variables* in the producing process are: *Sorts of matter-energy produced.* Example: One wounded salamander produced a new tail, and the other repaired a cut in its side after the crow attacked it with its beak. *Quality of matter-energy produced.* Example: The salamander's new tail was shorter and more fragile than the old one had been. *Percentage of matter-energy used in producing.* Example: Only about 40 percent of the materials in the grass were used by the cow in making milk. *Changes in producing over time.* Example: The adolescent began to produce sex hormones. *Changes in producing with different circumstances.* Example: When the time for metamorphosis arrived, the caterpillar began to make silk for a cocoon. *Rate of producing.* Example: During the battle the soldier's adrenal glands synthesized epinephrine at a greatly increased rate. *Frequency of producing.* Example: The vine produced grapes only once a year. *Lag in producing.* Example: There was a measurable moment before the bear's pituitary and adrenal glands reacted to the threat of the approaching hunter. *Costs of producing.* Example: The athlete became tired, since his body could no longer meet his energy requirements.

3.2.5 Matter-energy storage, the subsystem which retains in the organism, for different periods of time, deposits of various sorts of matter-energy.

3.2.5.1 Structure   Both plants and animals produce more of many substances than they immediately require. Storage tissues and organs hold these materials for future needs.

The green leaves and stems of plants, as well as some of their parts which are not green, such as seeds, tubers, and fruit, act as storage tissues for starches, fats, proteins, and other substances. In plants water is stored throughout all tissues; but succulents—like cactuses—which live in arid climates, have specialized storage areas in thickened leaves (like the century plant), in swollen stems (like the saguaro cactuses), or in underground containers in the roots (like the night-blooming cereus). A saguaro may weigh as much as 9 metric tons, 80 percent of this being the weight of liters of water in the stems. Vertebrate fatty tissues (below the skin, in interstitial tissue around most organs except the brain and cornea, and in the omentum, mesenteries, and peritoneum of the abdomen), the liver, the gallbladder, bone marrow, muscles, and others store energy-rich compounds like fats, glycogen, and glucose. The bones are a calcium store. Bone marrow and the spleen store blood cells in lower animals like dogs, cats, and a number of other mammals, but they are not of great significance in man. The urinary bladder and lower bowel store excretions; the gallbladder stores bile.

3.2.5.2 Process   Organisms generally store supplies of matter-energy for the frequent situations when outputs temporarily occur faster than inputs. Variations in output rates impose less strain upon the system if such matter-energy storage exists. This is consistent with Hypothesis 3.2.5.2-1 (see page 94), which states that variations imposed on the rate of a succeeding process by variations in the rate of a preceding process can be decreased by storing a supply (or "buffer inventory") of the outputs from the preceding process between the components which carry out the two processes.

Plants, which require light for photosynthesis, produce starch in their green leaves during the hours of daylight faster than they consume it. This is transported during hours of darkness to all parts of the plant, where it can be broken down and used in metabolism. Materials required for growth of new shoots on branches in the spring are transported upward from older stems. The absolute dependence of plants upon water dictates that they must store at least some of it. An extreme case is the barrel cactus, with a large water storage capacity, which can live for more than a year on its stored water.

Protoplasm, blood, and tissue fluids are chiefly water, so that animals can go from several hours to several days without drinking. Instead they gradually dehydrate their tissues. Desert animals like camels do not resemble desert plants in storing large amounts of water, but they are especially efficient in conserving their bodily water supplies and surviving the effects of water deprivation.

Organisms continually need respiratory gases. Oxygen stored in the blood, tissue fluids, and lungs of animals will last at most a few minutes before metabolic functions exhaust it and loss of awareness and later death from anoxia occur.

Human storage of substances needed for metabolism may be widely dispersed or may be confined to particular tissues. There is no specific storage depot for protein, but the liver, thymus, prostate, pancreas, spleen, and kidneys contain labile protein which they lose rapidly in case protein input rates decrease significantly below normal. The amino acids derived from proteins are used in synthesizing other bodily proteins and, during starvation, in synthesizing carbohydrates to supply energy. With no protein inputs, the store of labile protein is exhausted in a few days, and in severe and prolonged starvation more permanent proteins of muscle and other structures are used up.

Carbohydrate is stored in the form of muscle and liver glycogen ("animal starch") which can be rapidly converted to the sugar, glucose. The liver glycogen constitutes an emergency supply; about a 5-hour (h) store is available in the liver if its synthesis in the body should be blocked. The liver glycogen constitutes a "buffer inventory" which smooths out the rate of glycogen output to the rest of the body when there are variations in input rates (see Hypothesis 3.2.5.2-1, referred to earlier in this section).

If sugar is not supplied from the digestive tract, glucose can be made in the liver and kidneys from noncarbohydrate sources or liberated by the breakdown of glycogen. Glycogen is also stored in the muscles, but muscular glycogen is generally used for the energy of contraction, and supplies glucose to the rest of the body only after the liver glycogen is depleted. When glucose is absorbed from the gut or injected intravenously, the amount of it stored in the soft tissues also increases. Some glucose input is used in the synthesis of fats and proteins, and energy from it is, consequently, stored in these forms.

Animal or vegetable fat inputs are broken down and resynthesized into animal fats typical of the particular species of organism. Fats may also be synthesized from ingested carbohydrates or proteins. Fatty tissues are the chief storage depots of the body, and they contain much energy. Well-nourished animals and human beings can live for many days on this stored fat, with no inputs but water. Though not so immediately available as liver glycogen, matter-energy stored in this form lasts much longer. Fat produces more energy per gram than carbohydrate or protein.

When a matter-energy lack stress exists, first glycogen is withdrawn from storage, then the labile protein and fat reserves, and finally permanent tissue proteins. The substances which are most easily replaced appear to be used first, then those harder to replace. The loss is selectively distributed throughout the body. In the first few days of a fast the subcutaneous and other fat deposits disappear rapidly. Later muscular tissue wastes away. Even in prolonged starvation the neural tissues lose very little weight. This sequence of processes seems to support Hypothesis 5.2-2 (see page 106), which states that the greater the stress upon a system, the more components of it are involved in adjusting to it. Also it appears to support Hypothesis 3.3.7.2-14 (see page 101), which asserts that a system which survives generally decides to employ the least costly adjustment to a strain produced by a stress first and increasingly more costly ones later.

In case of specific deficiencies in input, bodily storage depots which respond to particular stresses release into the bloodstream some of their contents. For instance, when there are insufficient calcium inputs to meet demands, calcium is resorbed from the bones and teeth into the blood.

Excretions are stored, until an appropriate moment, in the bladder and lower bowel. While most glands do not store secretions, the gallbladder does fill with bile which is continuously produced by the liver, secreting only on receiving a signal initiated when food enters the small intestine from the stomach.

Among the *variables* in the process of storing matter-energy are: *Sorts of matter-energy stored.* Example: Mr. Smith put on 4.5 kg of fat during his vacation. *Total storage capacity.* Example: The tick was fully engorged after sucking 0.01 milliliter (ml) of blood from the farmer. *Percentage of matter-energy stored.* Example: About one-quarter of the calories the guinea pig consumed were in excess of its immediate needs and were stored in the form of fat. *Place of storage.* Example: The endomorphic woman became wide in the hips as she gained weight. *Changes in storing over time.* Example: The old woman's bones became thinner and thinner as the rate at which they stored calcium declined, and finally she broke her hip. *Changes in storing with different circumstances.* Example: As soon as the athlete retired, he found he tended to become fat on the same amount of food he had eaten before. *Rate of storing.* Example: The hogs fattened at the rate of several pounds a week after their growth was complete. *Lag in storing.* Example: Glucose circulated in the patient's blood for more than an hour after dinner before being stored in the liver in the form of glycogen. *Costs of storing*. Example: After a heavy meal the dog was inactive because his brain had a small blood flow, most of his blood being employed in converting and storing glucose and other inputs. *Rate of breakdown of organization of matter-energy in storage*. Example: Biopsy indicated that the sheep's fat-bearing tissues were relatively inert, with slow replacement of old cells by new. *Sorts of matter-energy retrieved*. Example: As her pregnancy advanced, calcium was withdrawn from the mother's bones for use by the fetus. *Percentage of matter-energy retrieved*. Example: As his penitential starvation continued, the monk lost more than 90 percent of his body fat. *Order of retrieval*. Example: During the famine, people first became thin, then their tissues lost much of their carbohydrate content, and finally the protein structure of their bodies began to waste. *Rate of retrieval*. Example: Red corpuscles stored in the runner's spleen began to enter his blood within ten seconds after he got on the treadmill. *Lag in retrieval*. Example: The first week on her low-calorie diet was disappointing since Alice did not lose a kilogram. *Costs of retrieval*. Example: The sudden violent activity left the man's energy reserves exhausted.

3.2.6 Extruder, the subsystem which transmits matter-energy out of the organism in the forms of products or wastes.

3.2.6.1 Structure   Specialized openings through the organism boundary, with their associated tubes or ducts, and the neural and muscular components associated with them, form the extruder of organisms. These vary greatly in different phyla. Membranes and stomata of leaves constitute the extruder of plants. The opening of the central cavity of coelenterates which serves also as ingestor, the openings of the canals of sponges, and, in mammals including man, the kidneys, ureters, urethra, rectum, anus, lungs, breathing passages, sweat glands, birth canal, breasts, and, in vomiting and regurgitation, the mouth make up this subsystem. In some species poison or musk glands are also components. Some components of the extruder, like the human chest muscles which compress and expand the lungs, are also components of the motor. They may at the same time force air out through the larynx, making speech and other vocalizations possible. Under such circumstance they are also parts of the output transducer.

Artifacts of this subsystem include enema or douche equipment.

3.2.6.2 Process   Large amounts of water leave plants through their open stomata. The rate of this loss is to some extent controlled when the stomata close, but there is always some loss. During photosynthesis plants release oxygen. They also oxidize some sugar, in the process extruding some carbon dioxide.

The venous blood of animals, which has a high content of carbon dioxide absorbed from tissues throughout the body, carries about 5 percent in simple solution, 2 to 10 percent combined with hemoglobin as carbhemoglobin, and the remainder as bicarbonate.[18] When this blood reaches the lungs, it loses about 10 percent of its total carbon dioxide. This loss occurs because, when it has access to oxygen, hemoglobin becomes less able to hold carbon dioxide. The carbon dioxide is transferred through the lung tissue and expired as the breathing movements of the lungs force it out. Water vapor is also contained in expired air. Sweat, which is important in temperature control of the body, contains, besides water, some dissolved waste substances—sodium chloride, urea, potassium, and lactic acid.

While some water is extruded through the lungs and skin, by far the largest amount passes out through the kidneys. These act as filters, removing from the blood—which enters them through the renal artery—waste products of bodily metabolism, such as ammonia, urea, uric acid, creatine, creatinine, and various salts. The kidney returns to the blood some of the water, glucose, salt, and amino acids it filters. The remainder of the wastes, dissolved in water, form urine and go to the urinary bladder for storage and ultimate excretion.

Ingested materials which are not absorbed into the distributor pass into the lower bowel, colon, and rectum, to be discharged through the anus. Included are many bacteria which have entered in food, water wastes from the chemical processes of decomposing bile, and other digestive agents.

Extrusion of eggs and young takes place through passages which may be specialized for this purpose, as in mammals and birds, or which may be a common passage with other components of the extruder, as in frogs. Contractions of the walls of these passages and of component abdominal muscles of the organism's motor force the products through such extruder canals.

Poison or musk glands open to the environment and extrude either passively, as in the bite of a rattlesnake, or by contraction of the glands, as in the skunk.

The *variables* of the process of extruding include: *Sorts of products and wastes extruded*. Example: The patient had albumin in his urine. *Percentage of products and wastes extruded*. Example: The kidneys removed 95 percent of the injected red test dye from the dog's bloodstream within an hour. *Changes in extruding over time.* Example: The woman's first labor was difficult, but her later ones were quite easy. *Changes in extruding with different circumstances.* Example: The female insect emitted pheromones when she was mature enough to mate. *Rate of extruding.* Example: The pups in the collie's litter were born about every 10 min. *Frequency of extruding.* Example: The old man got up several times a night to urinate. *Lag in extruding.* Example: The doctor diagnosed the woman's difficulty as constipation. *Costs of extruding.* Example: The long labor left the mare exhausted.

3.2.7 Motor, the subsystem which moves the organism or parts of it in relation to part or all of its environment or moves components of its environment in relation to one another.

3.2.7.1 Structure   The endoplasm of slime molds is a component of the motor as well as of other subsystems.

The cells which form the structure of stems and leaves are plant motor components. Some plant species, such as sensitive plants, also have liquid-filled bulbs at the bases of leaf-stalks, branches, or other structures as motor components.

Motor components differ in their gross configurations among types of animals—among phyla and species within phyla. Some coelenterates have differentiated muscle fibers connected by fine fibrils of their neural net directly to input transducer cells. Others move with complex epithelial cells, each of which has a contractile "muscle tail."[19] Obvious structural differences exist among the motors of insects, those with few or many limbs, and invertebrates which swim, fly, wriggle along without limbs, hop, or walk. The fine structure of muscular tissue (see page 318) differs among other animal species also. The organization of the membranous structures within the fibers of wing muscles of certain flying insects, for example, differs from that of other sorts of muscle cells.[20]

Striated skeletal muscles are the principal components of the motor of vertebrates. They account for approximately 40 percent of the weight of the adult human body (see these muscles, labeled MO, in Fig. 8-1). Each separate muscle is surrounded and covered by fascia, a tough connective tissue which forms a layer over most of the body. This fascia is also an essential component of the motor, along with the bones and joints. The striated-muscle motor component includes most muscle in the body, this tissue being interconnected throughout much of the organism. Certain striated muscles are primarily components of other subsystems, such as the diaphragm, which helps to ingest air into the lungs and extrude it from them; the pharynx, which by swallowing aids in distributing; the larynx, which participates in output transducing by speech; and some others which are components of other subsystems, such as the input transducer and boundary. The smooth muscle of viscera and the cardiac muscle of the heart, which are innervated by the autonomic nervous system, are components of motor subsystems of organs (which in turn are subsystems of the organism), rather than components of the whole organism (see page 332).

A muscle consists not only of contractile muscle tissue but also of tendons and other connective tissues which are properly regarded as part of the muscle. These are continuous with the contractile tissue and form junctions with bones, fascia, or skin at the points of origin and insertion of the muscle. The *origin* is the end which is nearer the center of the body and more fixed; the *insertion* is the end which is more distant from the center of the body and more freely movable.

Muscles vary in size, shape, and the manner of their attachment to other structures. The stapedius, a tiny muscle of the middle ear, is only 2 to 3 millimeters (mm) long and weighs 0.1 gram (g) in man. The human gastrocnemius, the bulky muscle in the calf of the leg, can be nearly 60 cm long and correspondingly heavy.[21] Muscles may be elongated, like the gastrocnemius, and like it attached at the two ends by flat tendons, or they may be attached by tendons which run the whole length of the muscle. Some are circular, surrounding bodily openings, like the sphincter which closes the mouth. Some muscles are shaped like flat sheets, such as those which support the abdomen.

Muscles are arranged in structural groups which are also functional groups. Most skeletal muscles occur in opposing pairs with opposite actions (see page 375). Such pairs are known as *antagonists.* A single motor neuron connects with one or more muscle fibers, usually several. The number per neuron is much greater in some muscles than in others. A single motor neuron and the muscle fibers it supplies are known as a *motor unit* (see page 376). This unit includes components of the organism's motor subsystem (the muscle fibers) and its channel and net subsystem (the neuron). The innervation of groups of muscles which act together at the same joints binds them together into a *myotatic unit* (see page 376).[22]

Skeletal muscles of two sorts occur in vertebrates. These differ in their fine structures and in their gross colors. *Flexors* are deep red. *Extensors* are lighter in color. The difference is marked in birds, as evidenced in the roast turkey's dark and light meats. They differ in function: flexors bend joints and extensors stretch them out. Bones are fundamental components of the motor as well as the supporter (see page 377).

The motor, like other subsystems of the organism,

contains cells which are output transducers of the organ (see page 343), including Pacinian corpuscles, free nerve endings, muscle spindles, and Golgi organs. Their fibers enter the central nervous system to communicate directly with the primary motor neurons of the spinal cord as well as with higher echelons in the spinal cord and brain (see pages 424 to 426). Pacinian corpuscles, which are pressure receptors, are found in tendons, joints, the covering of bone, the fascias covering the muscles, and the subcutaneous tissue which overlies all these structures. Free nerve endings, which are pain receptors, are found between the muscle fibers, in tendons, in fascias, and in joints. Muscle spindles transduce stretch in muscles. Golgi organs do the same in ligaments and tendons.

Within the muscle also are branches of the axons of the motor neurons which transmit signals to it, each branch terminating at a specialized region of the muscle fiber known as the motor end plate (see page 249). The number of muscle fibers supplied by each nerve fiber varies in different muscles.[23]

Artifacts of this subsystem include canes, rocking chairs, wheelchairs, carts, automobiles, sleighs, rowboats, brooms, hammers, sewing machines, and machine tools.

3.2.7.2 Process   Much is known about how plant and animal motors act, and I can summarize here only a few of the most salient facts. Plant movement is downwardly dispersed to cells. Invertebrate movement may also be downwardly dispersed in similar fashion or may be carried out in a variety of other ways, dependent on the species. Vertebrates move by striated muscles, bones, and accessory structures which act as levers or pulleys.

Plant movement.   Perhaps Birnam Wood can never come to Dunsinane, perhaps no one can "bid the tree Unfix his earth-bound root,"[24] but rooted plants are capable of moving their parts in relationship with one another and to the environment. There are two sorts of plant motion, both downwardly dispersed to the cellular level: one activated by the growth hormone auxin (see page 470) and the other produced by changes in permeability of cellular structures at the bases of leaves and branches. Auxin controls the responses of plants to light and gravity. It accelerates the growth of shoots and slows the growth of roots. Light destroys auxin, so that the light side of a plant has less auxin than the dark side. When a house plant is placed on a window sill, its leaves soon turn toward the light. The cells of the shaded side elongate more rapidly, producing the bend toward the light. Roots, which have an opposite response to auxin, bend away from the light, into the dark ground. Auxin makes shoots grow

against gravity, and roots grow in the direction of gravitational forces. If a potted plant is placed on its side, the shoots will turn and grow upward while the roots move downward. This sort of motion is very slow.

Sensitive plants, such as the mimosa, move much more rapidly. They collapse their leaves if they are disturbed. A wave of reaction moves down a branch if its tip is pinched, traveling at a speed of 1 to 15 mm per s. Each leaf in order droops when a liquid-filled bulb at its bottom loses fluid, as if it were a balloon that had been pricked.[25] This action is triggered by a hormone which moves down the branch. The process of refilling the bulb is slow. The snapping shut of Venus's-flytrap and the movements by which some other predatory plants catch their prey are caused by changes of permeability of similar structures.

Movement of invertebrate animals.   Some animals are little better off than plants as far as motion is concerned. Sponges have no differentiated muscular or nervous tissue and move only the cilia of the cells which line their canals. The only motion of which they are capable is therefore downwardly dispersed to the level of the cell. Oysters and certain other molluscs are sessile and, like the sponges, must depend upon their environments to move to them the matter-energy inputs that they need. Among the coelenterates are creatures which lack the ability to move themselves from place to place but float about in their environmental waters. Such partipotential animals usually have motor components, used in moving parts of their bodies. Some species are free-swimming as larvae, only to become sessile as adults. Higher invertebrates crawl with a fleshy foot like molluscs; wriggle on their bellies like worms; swim, fly, or walk with legs like flies; or hop like crickets. Each of these methods of locomotion enables the animal to travel in its environment with its characteristic speed, efficiency, and costs of movement. Although contractility is a basic characteristic of protoplasm, most animal motion comes about through the contracting or lengthening of specialized muscle fibers, so arranged into muscular tissue that their change of length exerts force against the structures to which they are attached.

Movement of vertebrate animals.   Vertebrate movements are produced by coordinated groups of muscles. For example, the biceps muscle of the arm, a flexor, and the triceps, an extensor, constitute a group of antagonists at the elbow. A mammalian motor subsystem component does not depend upon gravity, after a part is flexed, to return it to its normal position. Rather the extensors contract to pull it back. Opposed muscles of the face, attached to subcutaneous tissues, enable many sorts of animals to use their mouths to manipulate their environments and also produce all the subtleties of facial expression. The *prime mover,* or *agonist,* is the muscle whose contraction is chiefly responsible for a particular movement. This is actively, but less vigorously, opposed by the *antagonist. Fixation muscles* hold a given part of the body in position by contracting and causing fixation of neighboring joints. The *synergists* assist the prime mover and reduce the need for it to move. These all act as a unit to make a particular movement smooth and steady. In other movements, the function of each muscle may be different. As the frequency of inputs from a motor neuron to a muscle fiber increases up to a point, the fiber's tension increases (see page 246). As more and more neurons activate more fibers, the tension of the muscle they compose increases. And similarly, as the inputs increase even further, more and more muscles are called into play. When the fingers are closed gently, only the extensors of the wrist act as fixation muscles, avoiding undesired flexion of that joint, but when they are forcibly clenched, muscles of the elbow or even the shoulder contract to hold those joints in position.

Bones, muscles, and accessory structures act as levers and pulleys to move parts of the body in relationship to each other and against the pull of gravity. They also enable the organism to exert force against components of the environment. Like automobile motors, the organism's motor subsystem must burn fuel to perform its work (see page 282).

The different sorts of joints provide for various degrees of motion in many planes. The structure of the bones and joints of the spine permits the back to bend forward, backward, and to both sides. Between any two vertebras the amount of motion is limited by the ligaments, bony parts, and muscles, but when motion involves the whole length of the spinal column, the amount of movement is considerable. Hinge joints allow movement in only one plane. Pivot joints permit rotation. Condyloid and saddle joints allow bending up and down and from side to side but no rotation. A ball-and-socket joint allows for the sort of free motion that is found in the hip and shoulder.

The most fundamental muscular reflex, the stretch or myotatic reflex, is the contraction of muscle in response to stretch. Within limits the contraction is proportional to stretch. All normal muscular reactions and reflexes are superimposed upon it, since signals of other sorts arriving at the motor neurons find them in a condition appropriate to the mechanical load being borne by the muscles. Like some other basic reflexes including withdrawal of a part from painful stimulation, the stretch reflex is a flexor reflex. Extensor

reflexes also exist. The stretch reflex depends upon the connection through one synapse from muscle spindles to spinal motor neurons. If stretch is increased, a point is reached at which the muscle "lets go." Instead of contracting further, it lengthens. This protects it from damage. Since muscle spindles are the slowest adapting of vertebrate receptor cells, muscles can maintain contraction for a long time if stretch is continued. When a brief stretch is applied, the myotatic reflex produces a "jerk," like the knee jerk which is elicited by tapping the tendon just below the knee cap. When a muscle contracts in the stretch reflex, inhibitory connections, each involving one synapse, cause its antagonist to relax. The stretch reflex is inhibited by pain signals or by signals from stretched antagonistic muscles.

Some reflexes involve many muscles and much more complicated innervation. The scratch reflex, by which a dog responds to low-intensity inputs from touch receptors in the skin, is one example. Its hind limb is raised to scratch near where the inputs occur. Reflexes may involve both sides of the body. Examples are the crossed extensor reflex, in which flexion of one limb leads to extension of the limb on the opposite side of the body, and the stepping reflex, which involves alternation of motion on the two sides of the body.

Representative *variables* of the moving process are: *Sorts of movements made.* Example: The lion lashed his tail. *Changes in moving over time.* Example: As the dog grew older, he was less able to catch squirrels. *Changes in moving with different circumstances.* Example: The arthritic old man was barely able to walk. *Rate of moving.* Example: The athlete ran the mile in 3 min, 56 s. *Rate of output of work.* Example: The carpenter made more than 100 hammer strokes per min. *Frequency of moving.* Example: The sloth hung upside down without moving for several hours. *Duration of moving.* Example: The wolf followed the flock all night. *Lag in moving.* Example: The deer stood transfixed for a moment and then bounded away. *Costs of moving.* Example: After the marathon race each runner drank a quart of wine and ate a large steak in order to adjust to the matter-energy lacks developed during the long hours of extremely rapid movement.

3.2.8 Supporter, the subsystem which maintains the proper spatial relationships among components of the organism, so that they can interact without weighting each other down or crowding each other.

3.2.8.1 Structure   The hard cell walls, as well as specific supportive tissues known as *schlerenchyma,* form the supporter structures of plants. Schlerenchyma includes specialized supporting tissues, *schler-*

eids, which have thick, lignified walls and fibers throughout the substance of the plant.

Skeletons, either the exoskeletons of such animals as crabs, lobsters, and insects, or the endoskeletons of higher vertebrates, are components of this subsystem. The human skeleton consists of 206 bones supplemented by some cartilage. Tendons, ligaments, capsules of joints, and other connective tissues are also supporter components. Animals which lack skeletons have firm tissues of other sorts. An exoskeleton is part of both boundary and supporter subsystems. Man and other vertebrates also have muscles and layers of fascia which are components both of the supporter and of the motor.

Artifacts of this subsystem include chairs, beds, and platforms.

3.2.8.2 Process   Much of the supporting structure of living systems, as Gerard has pointed out, is made up of materials which no longer are, or which never were, living tissue.[26] This is true of a large part of bone, cartilage, and the exoskeletons of many animals.

Two engineering facts explain many of the differences in supporting processes of animals: *(a)* Animals which live in the sea need lighter skeletons than land animals because they derive some of their support from the water, whereas the bodies of land animals must bear the full pull of gravity unaided. And *(b)* when the supporter is an internal skeleton, it is more flexible and also relatively lighter in weight than when it is an external covering.

The layers of fascia which lie beneath the skin and over muscles and other bodily parts hold these components in the correct relationship with each other. The layer of muscles over the abdomen not only moves the abdominal wall but also contracts firmly to prevent displacement of abdominal organs. The skeleton is connected at the joints by the capsules and by connective ligaments. Ligaments also support the viscera.

The tonic activity of the slow-signal-termination motor units of postural muscles (see page 282) is an important support process, constantly required to maintain the muscular tension necessary to keep an organism from collapsing limply as a man does when he sleeps.

Representative *variables* in the supporting process include: *Strength of the supporter.* Example: The old woman broke her hip when she stepped off the curb because the bone was fragile. *Costs of supporting.* Example: The clerk became tired after standing all day.

3.3   Subsystems which process information

3.3.1   Input transducer, the sensory subsystem which brings markers bearing information into the organism, changing them to other matter-energy forms suitable for transmission within it.

3.3.1.1   Structure   The input transducer in any organism is the totality of its sensory apparatus for receiving signals from the environment. Most plants disperse this subsystem downwardly to the individual cells, but certain sensitive plants have structures, such as the liquid-filled bulbs at the base of leaves, which are specialized components of the input transducer as well as the motor (see page 374).

Among animal organisms, the fundamental components of this subsystem are highly specialized receptor cells, but in all except the simplest of organisms these cells are aggregated into sense organs of various sorts in which the axons from groups of such cells synapse in complicated ways. In an earlier chapter I have described the structure of receptor cells (see page 249 to 254).

The human input transducer, like that of other higher animals, is formed of many components for different sensory modalities, each with sensory cells and associated accessory structures. Furthermore, cells specialized for receiving signals from different aspects of the environment may be found in the same sense organ, *e.g.,* the rods and cones of the eye.

The two eyes, the vestibular and auditory components of the ears, the chemoreceptors in the nose and tongue, and a diverse group of differently adapted nerve endings and receptors in the skin form this subsystem in human organisms. Other species have different sorts of input transducers, such as those specialized for magnetic fields in the pigeon and for electrical fields in the torpedo fish.

Visual component.   Light-sensitive cells occur in the skin of some organisms but are restricted to the retinas of the eyes in others. The hagfish, a primitive fish shaped like a snake, has rudimentary eyes but in addition has light-sensitive cells in other parts of its head and around its cloaca. Many species of worms also have such receptors on parts of the body other than the eyes. Two eyes are the general rule, usually, but not always, placed on the two sides of the head.

Eyes take many forms in different phyla, and there are marked species variations within phyla. Among mammals, there are differences in the proportions of the various types of light-sensitive cells and in the placement of the two eyes in the head. Primates have their eyes close together in the front of the head, unlike rodents, some of whose eyes are as far apart as human ears.

The visual receptor tissue is the retina at the back of the eyeball, a globe surrounded by tough membranes and filled with liquid. The retina of a human eye has both rods and cones, but eyes lacking cones are found in some species.[27]

Retinas of higher animals consist of several layers of cells of different types. The primary sensory cells, at the surface of the retina, synapse with bipolar cells lying behind them. These, in turn, synapse with retinal ganglion cells at the back of the eyeball. The bipolar and ganglion cells are probably decoder components (see page 397 and Fig. 8-4). The ganglion cells give rise to the fibers of the optic nerve. This is the second of the 12 human cranial nerves. Thus I shall refer to it as the optic (II) cranial nerve and shall give the name and number of other cranial nerves in similar form when I mention them below.

Vestibular component.   This component of the input transducer, in human and other higher vertebrates, on both the left and right sides of the head shares the inner ear with an auditory component. Its fibers form a portion of the acoustic (VIII) cranial nerve.

The inner ear, or labyrinth, consists of a series of connecting cavities tunneled in the temporal bones. Within the bony labyrinth is the similarly shaped membranous labyrinth. This is surrounded by one fluid, the perilymph, and filled with another fluid, the endolymph. The organ of spatial steady state and orientation consists of three semicircular canals and two membranous sacs in the vestibule to which they connect, the utricle and saccule.

Auditory component.   The receptors for this component in the human organism and other species above the amphibia are located in the cochlea, which shares the labyrinth with the vestibular apparatus to which it is joined by a duct. The cochlea is a fluid-filled canal, coiled like a snail's shell, within which is the cochlear duct. This duct contains the transducer proper, the organ of Corti, and its accessory structure, the tectorial membrane.

Other structures, beginning with the external ear, are the external auditory canal, an air-filled passage which ends at the tympanic membrane, a cone-shaped, stiff, but flexible structure. The ossicles, a chain of three small bones, lie within the air-filled middle ear and attach to this membrane and to the oval window which separates the middle ear from the inner ear. The round window lies at the other end of the inner ear.

The organ of Corti consists of supporting cells and "hair" cells, the outer ends of which are embedded in the tectorial membrane. Fluid fills the space between. Bipolar cells, with their bodies in a ganglion parallel to the organ of Corti, synapse in the organ of Corti with the hair cells. Their axons go into the auditory portion of the acoustic (VIII) cranial nerve. Many hair cells synapse with each bipolar cell and each hair cell sends fibers to more than one bipolar cell. These bipolar cells are probably decoder components (see Table 6-4, Fig. 6-18, and page 401).

Olfactory component.   Single layers of sensory cells in the olfactory epithelium, one in the dorsal and posterior part of each nostril, are the fundamental parts of this component.

Taste component.   The taste buds, located in the mouth in land-living vertebrates, are chemoreceptors like the transducers of smell and the "common chemical sense" by which the mucous membranes signal high concentrations of chemicals in the mouth and nose. Related chemoreceptors in other species are distributed over the body—like the taste buds of fish—or are in other sorts of specialized organs.

In mammals, taste buds are found on the tongue and other components within the mouth such as the gullet, soft palate, and pharynx. This is true also in human children, but in human adults they are restricted to the tongue.

Components of the input transducer in the skin.   The integument of an organism, in addition to being part of the boundary and of other matter-energy processing subsystems, is a component of the input transducer. The sorts of transducer cells present in the coverings of organisms vary from species to species. Some invertebrates, such as the sea anemone, for example, appear to lack temperature receptor structures.[28] They usually have chemoreceptors and mechanoreceptors. Some fish have lateral line receptors which transduce pressure and low-frequency vibrations. In some animal species, as I have already noted (see page 377), the visual component consists of single cells on the skin rather than specialized organs such as the eyes of higher species.

Among vertebrates a dense subcutaneous network of nerve fibers sends branches into the dermis and epidermis. The great majority of these end in fine, naked (unmyelinated) filaments not surrounded by other sorts of specialized receptor components. They interweave and terminate among the cells of the skin.

Each cutaneous nerve fiber branches to innervate input fields of varying size. The fields of mechanoreceptors, for instance, range from a small point to a diameter of several centimeters. Their extent varies with the part of the body, the trunk having fields 2 to 3 cm² and the ends of the limbs fields only a few millimeters square. The smaller, more slowly adapting fibers have the larger fields.[29]

There is multiple innervation of each sensitive spot on the skin from branches of different cutaneous fibers. Points which respond to more than one sensory modality have been shown to be innervated by different sorts of fibers. Others have a large variety of specialized endings or capsules. Distribution of these is different in various parts of the skin. These include the Pacinian corpuscles, as well as many others including free nerve endings, Meissner corpuscles, Merkel disks, Ruffini endings, and Krause end bulbs (see Table 6-4, Fig. 6-18 and page 255). Unlike other input transducer components, such as those for vision and audition, the neuron which carries out the actual transducing is the same one which carries information to the central nervous system. The endings in the skin are parts of neurons which have their cell bodies in the spinal cord and send their fibers with the afferent, posterior (dorsal) roots of spinal nerves at segments of the cord corresponding to the position of the part of the body from which they transmit information. Those which carry information from the head travel in the cranial nerves.

Other input transducer components. When a librarian gives a book to a user who takes it in his hand, or when a departing diner slips a dollar bill into the headwaiter's palm, technically the receiving hand is an input transducer, taking to the organism a marker bearing information. Other muscled parts of the body may, rarely, serve in such a manner as components of the input transducer.

Artifacts of this subsystem include radio receivers, telephone receivers, and public address system speakers.

3.3.1.2 Process The experimental research on organisms' input transducing processes is extensive. Each of the components of the input transducer concerned with one of the sensory modalities has been studied in various species. I shall now summarize some of the highlights of this work, particularly that on higher mammals with emphasis on man. The same sorts of functions can be investigated and measured for each modality.

The grouping of cells within a transducer component such as an eye or a special area of skin not only increases the amount of information transduced, but provides for interactions among the cells. Such interactions allow for detailed reporting of environmental states (see pages 402 and 403). Where transducer components are separated, as in the two eyes, the two ears, and the distribution of sensitive points in the skin, further information about depth, dimension, location, and other aspects of the environment can be reported. The various specialized components of the input transducer send information about different aspects of the environment. These several information inputs interact at higher centers so that to some degree the processes of the entire input transducer are inte-

grated. For instance, the sight, sound, taste, and smell of an object are associated in a unitary sensory presentation. There are also important interactions among the components, so that a single experience—*e.g.,* taste—may result from interaction of several sorts of receptors. This, of course, involves central decoding processes (see pages 384 and 385).

Generalized functions of input transducers. In every input transducer an information input produces at the receptor site an excitatory state which causes an electrical change that is propagated through the neural tissue, followed by rapid disappearance of the excitation at the receptor site and speedy restoration of the condition of sensitivity which existed before the input occurred.[30] A description of such transducer processes includes the properties of the specific input, the internal subsystem processes, and the nature and destination of the output.

(*a*) *Input–output transfer functions* (see page 60). Input transducers of organisms transform signals in predictable fashion as they transmit them. Amplification is characteristic of the sensory cells which carry out the transducing process, so that the energy output from them is not directly related to the input energy, and may be larger (see page 256).

Some distortion (see page 61) is present in all input transducers of organisms. Systematic alterations of signals occur near the limits of sensitivity of a transducer, *e.g.,* the changes in visual sensitivity during retinal dark-adaptation (see page 381) or in the response of the cochlea to low frequencies of sound (see page 383).

For certain input–output characteristics of organisms, those which are concerned with intensity rather than quality, an orderly relationship exists between physical magnitude and psychological magnitude. The classical statement of the relationship between input energies and reported subjective sensation is the Weber function (see Hypothesis 3.3.1.2-1, pages 94 and 95, and pages 282 and 283). For loudness, brightness, and subjective strength of electrical current, the presently accepted statement of this relationship is expressed by the formula: $\Psi = k(\Phi - \Phi_0)^n$, where Ψ is the intensity of the output signal of the input transducer; Φ is the physical magnitude of the input energies; Φ_0 is a constant, the physical magnitude of the minimum detectable or threshold input energies; k depends on the choice of measurement units; and the exponent n varies among different components of the input transducer.[31] The range of this exponent is from 0.33 for brightness of white light to 1.45 for heaviness of lifted weights, 1.6 for warmth, and 3.5 for electric shock to the fingers. This range of exponents suggests that the sensory modalities which supply information about types of energy capable of injuring the organism may be "expanders," *i.e.*, the strength of their output warning signal which can elicit corrective feedback accelerates more rapidly than the intensity of the input as it approaches potentially damaging levels. Natural selection may well continue the survival of species with such transducers. When the exponent is less than 1, the transducer is a "compressor," *i.e.*, the subjective experience increases more slowly than the intensity of the input.[32] These variations in exponent appear to result chiefly from different processes in the input transducer, but they are probably influenced also by processes in other subsystems.[33]

(*b*) *Mode of adaptation.* The sorts of adaptation shown by the component cells are important aspects of the function of an input transducer component. Eyes with tonic cells having slow signal termination and with phasic cells having rapid signal termination (see pages 256, 257, and 282) can be found among animal species. The more developed eyes of higher species contain phasic receptor cells, allowing a greater amount of information to be transduced, since the cell is almost immediately ready for another response. Such receptors, however, depend upon a highly developed nervous system for storage and correlation of information.

(*c*) *Channel capacity* (see page 61). The total channel capacity of all components of the human input transducer, according to Barlow's highly speculative estimates, is somewhere between 3 billion and 10 million bits of information per second.[34]

(*d*) *Threshold* (see page 61). Thresholds have been determined for input transducer components of some modalities. The theoretical lower limits of sensitivity of transducer components, however, are probably never reflected in organism behavior because such minimal signals are lost in passing through successive subsystems and because the information capacity of the decider subsystem is probably lower than that of transducer components (see pages 139, 140, and 447).

(*e*) *Lag* (see page 61). A measurable time intervenes between the input to an input transducer and the output from it. This varies from one component to another and from one species and individual to another.

(*f*) *Accessory functions.* The accessory structures to input transducers protect, conduct, concentrate, analyze, sensitize, amplify, diminish, filter, or distort the signal, or add noise to it. They alter either the marker or the information or both.

Full details about each of the above aspects of input transducing are not available for each sensory modal-

ity, but I shall now review data concerning several of these aspects for some of the modalities.

Vision.   A single eye receives various cues as to how far away from the organism objects are. Among these are: (*a*) *Interposition.* One object that partially covers another is seen as closer. (*b*) *Relative size.* The larger of two objects seems nearer. (*c*) *Relative height.* The higher of two objects seems nearer. (*d*) *Relative clarity.* The clearer of two objects appears nearer. (*e*) *Perspective.* The more sharply lines of perspective converge the farther away images of distant objects seem. (*f*) *Shadows.* Objects in the shadow of other objects seem farther away than brightly lighted objects. (*g*) *Accommodation of the eye.* Internal transducers in eye muscles signal whether the eye muscles are flattening the lens to focus on distant objects or allowing it to thicken to focus on close objects, thus providing depth cues. (*h*) *Relative movement.* When the head moves to the left, near objects appear to move to the right in relation to more distant ones, and vice versa.

There are also binocular depth cues including: (*a*) *Convergence.* Signals from transducers in the muscles that move the eyeballs indicate whether the two eyes are parallel—therefore looking at a distant object—or converging more or less sharply—therefore looking at an object which is very close or fairly close. (*b*) *Retinal disparity.* The two eyes transmit different images which, unless they are too disparate, are fused by components of the central nervous system to give perception of depth. The amount of overlap of the visual fields of the two eyes varies in different species and so does the amount of the field covered at any one time. Rabbits, with their eyes on the sides of their heads, have little overlap forward. They can, however, see almost all 360 degrees of the environment around them, except for a narrow segment directly behind them. Human eyes point straight ahead and their fields have about 120 degrees of overlap, but a person can see only about 180 degrees from side to side. Often the various monocular and binocular depth cues are in conflict and then the decider of the input transducer component weighs the conflicting input signals to determine a resultant perception of depth.

(*a*) *Input–output transfer functions.*   One can study the various, complex input–output characteristics of eyes in a number of ways. Electroretinography is one of these. A record of the electrical activity of the retina in response to changes in illumination is made by placing electrodes on the cornea and on another point in the body of an intact organism. In excised eyes, one lead is placed on the cornea and the other behind the eyeball. The variations over time are recorded on a kymograph. Such electroretinograms are used clinically to diagnose retinal pathology. It is possible to place microelectrodes at various points in the optic pathways of experimental animals and record changes in electrical potential. Verbal reports of subjects' visual experiences are also used, although it is difficult or impossible to exclude influences on them by other subsystems than the input transducer.

Selective amplification of significant features of the input pattern at the expense of exact fidelity of reproduction is a transfer function of eyes of some species—perhaps all species. For instance, boundaries of figures are often transmitted as being relatively sharper than is actually the case (see pages 397 and 401).

The exponent in the equation relating physical intensity and psychological brightness of white light (see pages 379 and 380) has been found to be about 0.33, indicating that the visual component of the input transducer acts as a compressor.[35]

Many different sorts of distortions have been found in the vision of man and higher animals, resulting from the particular structures and physiological processes of their eyes. Their lenses are ordinarily not perfect, so that some degree of astigmatism is the rule. An eye varies in its sensitivity to different wavelengths. In the human eye, for instance, the yellow lens and some other components filter out most ultraviolet light.[36] An eye from which the lens has been removed, for a cataract or other cause, is more sensitive than a normal eye to the ultraviolet range of the spectrum. The vertebrate retina must adapt to a change from light to dark or the reverse by altering its level of sensitivity. This is achieved by a change in concentration of visual pigments of which rhodopsin is one. Complete dark-adaptation takes about 30 min. Adaptation from dark to light is much more rapid. Over the time-course of these changes the signals from the eye are systematically altered.

When short flashes, rather than continuous light, are delivered to the eye, as the flashing accelerates, the impulse frequency in the optic nerve increases up to a point at which the effects of individual flashes can no longer be discerned. This phenomenon, known as flicker fusion, is an important transfer function of the eye. At a certain point, different from species to species, the organism senses a steady light rather than a flashing or flickering one. The organism experiences fusion at a lower rate of flicker than that required to produce it in the isolated retina.[37] In general, rods fuse flicker at a lower frequency than cones.[38]

(b) *Mode of adaptation.* Eyes of some lower animal species, such as *Limulus*, a crab, exhibit very slow signal termination, emitting a constant frequency of impulses from each of a group of visual cells, the *ommatidia*. A change in intensity of illumination produces a change in frequency of the outputs, there being a constant relationship between the two.

In higher animals and man the cells which transduce visual inputs are phasic, *i.e.*, have rapid signal termination. The retina has three types of cells, each of which emits a different sort of signal: (*a*) a maintained output which consists of a series of impulses continuing as long as the retina is exposed to light; (*b*) an on–off discharge occurring when a light input begins and also when it ends; and (*c*) an off discharge, occurring when the input ends (see page 397).[39] Many cells of each type exist, firing in different temporal patterns. In consequence of the rapid signal termination of retinal cells in higher species, adjustments are necessary to provide the organism with continuous subjective awareness of the visual field. Not all of these are in the input transducer. Some are in the central nervous system.

One way the eyes provide continuous visual experience is by using accessory structures—the ocular muscles. The mammalian eye makes constant movements. If these are prevented, the image fades.[40] If an image is projected continuously on the same area of the retina with no fluctuations resulting from eye movements, the subjective sensation of the image disappears in a few seconds. "When I cast my gaze upon the unchanging hills," Rushton says, "they do not fade away as they would if the receptors fell silent at their immobility. But, though the hills do not change, their image upon the retina does. The incessant dart and tremor of the eye keeps the image dancing upon the retinal receptors, and movement which would ruin the precision of a photograph is found to be essential for seeing."[41]

(*c*) *Channel capacity.* Ignoring color and stereoscopic vision, Jacobsen made a crude and probably inaccurate estimate of the channel capacity for one human eye as about 4.3 million bits per s.[42] This represents a total organism response to visual inputs to one eye and not just the response of a component of the input transducer.

(*d*) *Threshold.* Research on dark-adapted rats, whose receptor cells are almost all rods, has indicated that a light flash lasting 1.5 milliseconds (ms), which illuminates the entire retina with an evenly distributed *a priori* probability of delivering an average of only 1 quantum of light (the smallest possible amount) randomly distributed over each 100 rods, nevertheless can have a distinguishable effect on the rat's electroretinogram; 6 quanta per 100 rods have a marked effect.[43] I have discussed thresholds of single visual receptor cells in Chap. 6 (see page 257).

(*e*) *Lag.* After a 1.5-ms flash of light, the latency in response of the electroretinogram in rats ranges from about 135 ms for the slowest responses to very faint light (1 quantum per 100 rods) to about 4 ms for the fastest responses to strong light (10,000 quanta per rod). Conduction of impulses across the retina is relatively slow, so there are lags, which can be as much as 4 to 6 ms for impulses from the periphery as compared to those from that part of the retina nearest to where the output fibers leave.[44]

(*f*) *Accessory functions.* A number of activities of accessory components in the human eye are important to the processing of visual information inputs. The eyelids close to screen light and blink to keep the cornea clean. The pupil adjusts through neural feedbacks as light intensities change, thus controlling the size of the shaft of rays admitted (see pages 131 and 488). The ciliary muscle changes the thickness of the lens to bring the rays to a focus on the retina. Rapid movements of the muscles which move the eyeball prevent the phasic cells of the retina from stopping the transmitting of signals carrying the image to higher centers. Protection is afforded by the eye's internal humors, the surrounding bone structure, and to some extent the eyebrows.

Maintenance of spatial steady state and orientation in space. The vestibular components of the organism's input transducer are mechanoreceptors which respond to forces of acceleration, retardation, and gravitation. Output signals from these components are integrated with information from other input transducer and internal transducer components to maintain the organism's equilibrium and orientation in the environment.

The utricle transduces changes of the position of the head in space. It is the source of responses to gravity, centrifugal force, and linear acceleration. It is important in postural reflexes, including the distribution of muscle tone in different parts of the body to adjust to position in space. The otoliths move by gravity, differentially stimulating the sensory cells of the macula by bending the hairs. The function of the saccule is less well understood. It is probably closely associated with the cochlea but, in higher vertebrates, almost certainly has no part in the hearing process. It is thought to be responsible for transduction of vibration. In some species, including lower vertebrates, fish, and amphibians, in which the cochlea is absent, the saccule appears to be an auditory transducer.[45]

(*a*) *Input–output transfer functions.* The spatial arrangement of the three semicircular canals enables them to transduce the effects of movement in three dimensions. Their receptor units, the cristae ampullares, respond to a change of rate of rotatory move-

ments. They appear not to be influenced by linear acceleration. When the velocity of rotation changes, the endolymph moves, and the position of the cupulae changes, transmitting information to the hair cells. Motions of the components in the two vestibules are opposite during rotation so that, as with the eye, different signals are transmitted from the two sides of the head. Whenever motion stops, there is backflow of endolymph. When the rotation has been brisk and the stop quite sudden, the organism experiences a sensation of rotation in the opposite direction, which results from distortion in the transfer functions of the transducer components. If the speed of movement becomes constant, no signal is sent from these transducer components, since the endolymph no longer stimulates the receptors.

Two types of gravity receptors appear to be present in the utricle, one of which fires when the head is tilted out of the level position, the other when it is returned to level.

(*b*) *Mode of adaptation.* The mode of adaptation of the receptor cells in the vestibular component is not completely understood. There is evidence that they are both tonic, with slow signal termination, and phasic, with more rapid adaptation.[46] The transducer component as a whole, however, adapts to maintained rates of rotation by the process discussed above.[47]

(*c*) *Channel capacity.* I know of no evidence concerning this.

(*d*) *Threshold.* Studies have been made on the whole organism, using a rotating chair or torsion swing. The product of the time and the acceleration needed to reach the threshold of rotation sensation is constant. The shorter the time of its action, the greater is the required acceleration. Human thresholds have been found as low as 2 to 5 degrees of rotation per second.[48] As in other transducer components, the intensity of input—in this case the rate of rotation— required to pass the threshold of the component transducer itself is probably lower.

(*e*) *Lag.* Lags in transducing resulting from the inertia of the endolymph undoubtedly occur, although I have not seen this question discussed.

(*f*) *Accessory functions.* The supporting cells of the sensory epithelium and the other labyrinthine structures such as the supporting and protecting bony labyrinth; the protective perilymph and the endolymph; the otoliths and the cupula which move to transmit information, carry out the accessory functions in this transducer component.

Hearing. Vibrations propagated through air or water as sound waves constitute the adequate sort of marker to carry information inputs to the ears.[49] Transducer cells within the organ of Corti are specialized mechanoreceptors which respond to varying pressures caused by these waves. The human ear can receive information on sound waves over a spectrum of frequencies roughly between 20 and 20,000 cycles per second or hertz (Hz) and over a wide range of intensities from close to that of the physical background noise of thermal energy (Brownian movement), about −80 decibels (dB) relative to 1 dyne (dyn) per cm², on up to limits set by acoustic damage to the input transducer component, around 100 dB relative to 1 dyn per cm².

(a) Input−output transfer functions. The ear does not simply transduce the input signal. It changes it in various ways. Amplification takes place in the cochlea before the signal is transmitted to the nerve fiber. An electrical response known as *summating potential* persists as long as the tectorial membrane is displaced. Energy for this is derived not from the acoustic input but from the metabolism of the tissues. The acoustic input acts to release this energy, somewhat like a valve. The resulting amplification contributes to the ear's ability to transduce faint signals.[50]

Loudness, measured in subjective units of sones, increases much more slowly than intensity of the signal, measured in decibels relative to 1 dyn per cm², except at the top of the intensity range.[51] The exponent in the equation relating physical and psychological magnitudes of auditory processes (see pages 379 and 380) is less than 1, indicating that the ear acts as a compressor.[52] This characteristic allows it to respond to an enormous range of sound pressures.

The auditory component varies in sensitivity to different frequencies. This is a distortion caused by the resonance frequencies of the external ear canal and the middle ear. The overall acoustic response of the ear is at its maximum between 800 and 6,000 Hz and falls off above and below.[53]

Another distortion, this time produced by the cochlea, is harmonic distortion, known as "peak limiting" at low frequencies. That is, the waveform of the input is altered. At high frequencies, this does not occur.[54]

(b) Mode of adaptation. No evidence of an all-or-none response or a refractory period has been found in the sensory cells of the cochlea. It appears therefore that these cells must be tonic, characterized by slow signal termination. The cochlear microphonic and the summating potentials are continuously graded responses. These show little fatigue or adaptation.[55]

(c) Channel capacity. The channel capacity of a human ear was roughly, and probably incorrectly, estimated by Jacobsen at about 8,000 bits of information per s.[56] No other estimates or measurements of this functional characteristic have been made.

(d) Threshold. The intensity threshold of the human ear varies from frequency to frequency. At

1,000 Hz it is about −77 dB relative to 1 dyn per cm² at the eardrum, and approximately −80 dB relative to 1 dyn per cm² at 2,000 and 5,000 Hz.[57] This is barely enough energy to convey a signal on the background of the noise of thermal energy in the auditory structures.

(e) Lag. After the basilar membrane moves in response to an impulse, a wave of disturbance travels to the apex of the cochlea in 1.5 to 2.0 ms. During this time it is gradually dying out but still producing the initiation of neural impulses. The lag between the beginning of the cochlear microphonic potential and the beginning of the first neural impulse on an auditory neural fiber varies between 0.55 and 2.0 ms, as measured at the round window. As the intensity of the input sound increases, this lag decreases.

(f) Accessory functions. The actual transduction of the energies carried on sound waves into an energy form that can pass along the auditory nerve goes on in the cochlea. The rest of the intricate mechanism of the ear performs accessory functions. The temporal bone offers protection and support; the outer ear in animals may move to focus sound waves; the middle ear matches the impedance of air to the impedance of the fluid of the inner ear; and so forth.

Smell. *(a) Input−output transfer functions.* Many questions about the olfactory process are still unanswered. The sensitive cells of the olfactory epithelium are chemoreceptors. Information reaches them borne on markers of volatile substances either in the environment or within the mouth of the organism. Molecules of these substances dissolve in the liquid on the surfaces of the mucous membranes. The hairs of the olfactory receptor cells possibly beat. If such motion occurs, it probably distributes the input molecules across the epithelium more rapidly than they would pass by diffusion. How the dissolved molecules initiate depolarization in the olfactory cells is unknown, although a number of competing theories exist.[58]

Organisms are sensitive to odors from a great range of substances of widely differing chemical structures. The processes are unknown by which transducer cells signal what odoriferous compound happens to be impinging on them. Different spike responses have been found in the receptor cells in the olfactory bulb, each of which has a special relation to a particular sort of information input. Units which show specificity to one of each of four groups of substances have been demonstrated by microelectrode studies.[59]

Single cells which signal "on," "off," and "on−off" have also been found in the olfactory epithelium by use of microelectrodes. The on cells discharge only at the beginning of an input and then stop; the off discharge only at the end; while the on–off cells signal throughout the duration of an input.[60]

Information outputs from the olfactory epithelium elicited by amyl acetate (which smells like bananas), amyl alcohol, and butyl alcohol have been studied with macro- and microelectrodes.[61] Electrical potentials of various waveforms and magnitudes were found at different points on the epithelium. These appeared when the concentration of the vapor was above a certain value, varying in intensity from several hundred microvolts (μV) to more than 5 millivolts (mV), and in duration from about 0.2 to 4 s. Their magnitude increased as a direct function of intensity and of velocity of flow of the vapor over the olfactory epithelium. Adaptation limited this increase, however. The output signals were superimposed upon an on or off slow potential at the onset or cessation of olfactory input. They were not related to the action potentials of the olfactory cells.

Various odoriferous substances elicit different sorts of output signals. Amyl acetate, for instance, induces an output of large magnitude from the olfactory epithelium, and phenylethyl alcohol one of small intensity. But no relationship has been discovered between waveforms of the potentials and of the kinds of odors in the inputs.[62] Although no interconnections among the receptor cells on the olfactory epithelium have been found, it has been suggested that there may be electrotonic or chemical interaction among these closely contiguous components.[63]

Psychophysical studies of perception of intensity of odors have indicated that the exponent in the equation relating physical and psychological magnitudes of olfactory processes (see pages 379 and 380) varies with different sorts of odors but is in the range of 0.5 to 0.6.[64] This indicates that the transducer as a whole acts as a compressor. The range of intensities (concentrations of odorous substances) to which it can respond is restricted compared to the range of intensities responded to by other transducers, such as the eye and the ear.[65] This may account for the relatively limited number of subjective discriminations of odor intensity that a person can make.

Increases in rates of signals from the organism's sympathetic nervous system to the olfactory component of the organism's input transducer, elicited by such inputs as loud noises, flashes of light, or pinching of a toe, raise the magnitude of the output signals to odors. Whether this is a direct effect upon the transducer cells themselves or upon accessory structures is not known.[66]

When the concentration of odorous substances flowing over the receptor cells is either increased or decreased, a temporary distortion occurs because the input transducer component overshoots in seeking a new steady state, and its output intensity sinks lower or rises higher than the actual amount of change. This probably tends to increase the ability of the organism to discriminate for changes in intensity of the input.

(b) *Mode of adaptation.* It is possible that receptor cells of the olfactory epithelium vary in their rates of signal termination. It is even possible that a single cell may have different rates of adaptation to different odors.[67] This sort of variability occurs in the transducer cells of taste (see pages 385 and 386). The fact that not only on and off cells were found in the olfactory component but also some which signal throughout the duration of an input (see page 381) appears also to indicate variability in signal termination among these cells.

The olfactory component as a whole shows adaptation.[68] Successive inspirations of the same odor produce a decrease in intensity of its outputs to a lower steady state. At high concentrations the output intensity may fall to zero. Adaptation occurs at a lower concentration when the flow of the input is continuous than when it is rhythmically inhaled and exhaled. There are also differences in degree of adaptation among various odors.

(c) *Channel capacity.* This has not been measured.

(d) *Threshold.* Sensitivity of olfactory transducers varies greatly among species of organisms. The performance of a skilled hunting dog, for instance, is far above human capacity.[69] The olfactory cells of a dog have been found to react to a single molecule of certain fatty acids. A human olfactory receptor cell has a threshold of at most 8 molecules. At least 40 molecules, however, are required to produce a subjective report of a sensation.

(e) *Lag.* Information outputs from the olfactory epithelium increase rapidly with the beginning of a respiration and decline at its end, with little persistence between one inspiration and the next under appropriately controlled conditions. Amyl acetate elicits outputs with a shorter latency and more abrupt rise and fall than pentane. The more volatile and soluble in water a substance is, the shorter is the latency before outputs begin. Increasing the concentration of a substance does not affect the temporal pattern of the output.[70]

(f) *Accessory functions.* Mammals are able to sniff air into their nostrils and thus increase the flow of odorous substances over their olfactory mucous membranes. Many mammals dilate their nostrils to increase the amount of input. Turning the head in the direction of the source of the smell is another accessory function.

Taste. (a) *Input—output transfer functions.* When a person enjoys a delicious bite of food, the "taste" which he experiences is a blending of information inputs from the smell, temperature, touch, and taste components of the input transducer. A bad cold, which puts the sense of smell out of operation, therefore also reduces discrimination of flavors. The taste buds themselves mediate only four sorts of inputs: sweet, salty, sour, and bitter. A given sapid input may, of course, fall into more than one of these groups of flavors.

Taste buds appear alike histologically but vary in sensitivity from quite sluggish to highly sensitive.[71] They also vary in the sorts of inputs to which they respond. The central part of the upper surface of the tongue is unresponsive to any tastes. The tip of the tongue is more sensitive to sweet, the back to bitter, and the sides to sour. Sensitivity to salt is distributed quite evenly over all of the tongue except the midportion of the upper surface. It is somewhat greater at the tip than elsewhere.

It does not appear, however, that four types of cells correspond to these four processes. Instead, a single cell may respond to one, two, three, or all four of these basic tastes. Studies of rats have shown that some cells are excited by one combination, like sweet-salty-sour, and some by another, like salty-sour. Some cells respond to water. Probably the magnitude of the response of the taste internal transducer cells is a function of the concentration in the mouth of the molecules that are tasted.[72]

Experimental data lend credence to a theory that information is delivered to taste receptor cells, not by entry of any substances into the cells, but by binding of molecules to particular sites upon the receptor-cell boundary.[73] This process may be similar to the way carrier molecules bind other molecules at the cell membrane (see page 233). Characteristics of the binding process account for a number of the transfer functions of the taste component of the organism's input transducer, such as the different magnitudes of outputs from the receptor with changing concentrations of inputs and differences among types of receptor cells in sensitivity and specificity of response to various tasty substances. Also species differences and individual differences can be explained, such as the genetic character of "taste blindness" to a particular substance but not to others of very similar molecular structure.

The exponent in the equation relating physical and psychological magnitudes of taste intensities (see pages 379 and 380) has been determined experimentally to be 0.8 for saccharine, 1.3 for sucrose, and 1.3 for salt.[74] Since these exponents are all close to 1, taste sensation is neither a strong expander nor a strong compressor function.

(b) *Mode of adaptation.* Outputs from taste cells decline in magnitude during the first 2 s of continual input and then maintain a steady state of electrical output. Cells that maintain such a state must be tonic, displaying slow signal termination. The response characteristics of these cells, including the rate of their adaptation and the level of their steady state of output depend upon the nature and concentration of the particular input they are transducing.[75] It may be that there is a decrease in cell-membrane permeability only for the particular substance to which the receptor cell is adapted, leaving it still excitable by other sorts of inputs.[76]

The fact that subjective taste intensity and taste transducer output processes do not parallel each other suggests that processes in the central nervous system are involved in taste adaptation. This may explain why, though taste cells continue a steady state of output during sodium chloride input, human subjective sensation disappears for all but the strongest concentrations. Adaptation to quinine enhances sensitivity to sour and salt. Distilled water tastes sweet after a weak acid. Adaptation to sucrose or sodium chloride also enhances sensitivity to other inputs. These effects have not been explained and may result from central participation in transducer action. This must also be the reason why sensitivity to salt on one side of the tongue is enhanced when weak sugar solutions are placed on the other side.

(c) *Channel capacity.* This is unknown.

(d) *Threshold.* Thresholds of individual taste cells vary widely depending upon the inputs. There are also marked species differences in what sorts of substances elicit maximum outputs on the chorda tympani nerve which carries taste signal outputs from the tongue.[77] Cats respond little to sugar, rats much more. On the other hand, cats respond more than rats to quinine. When concentrations of a sapid substance on the tongue are increased, the output frequency of each active sensory cell in the tongue goes up and so does the number of cells that are active. In studies with human subjects who give verbal reports, threshold measurements vary with the taste task imposed. The thresholds are usually lower if the subject is asked to say when a difference from water can be detected than when the quality must be recognized.[78] Saliva also acts as a buffer to some substances, so a test in which the saliva is continually rinsed away yields a lower taste threshold for them.

Threshold to taste is importantly affected by temperature. The tongue is nearly insensitive at the extremes of 0 and 50°C. As temperature rises from 17 to 42°C sugar sensitivity increases, salt and quinine sensitivity decrease, and acid is unaffected.[79]

Thresholds are higher when the input is limited to a single drop on one area than when the whole mouth receives the fluid. If an input is intense enough to be tasted, it seems stronger if applied to the whole mouth rather than to one area of the tongue.

Also as the duration of an input increases, the threshold decreases, and the apparent intensity of taste of a substance that can be tasted increases.

(e) *Lag.* The taste input transducer component responds within 50 ms after the input flows over the surface of the tongue.[80] Reaction time (which includes the time required for processing through other information processing subsystems) varies with different taste qualities and with various substances that have the same quality. It is longest at the threshold and shortest at high intensities. It decreases with increase in the area to which the input is applied and with pressure of the substance against the tongue.[81]

(f) *Accessory functions.* Upon input of foods and other tasty materials into the mouth, actions by the teeth and muscles of the tongue distribute them around the tongue and release any flavorful substances enclosed within component cells of the input. Enzymatic action may occur during mastication which releases a flavor from a precursor substance.[82] Saliva dissolves some sorts of inputs and softens others so that they act as taste inputs to the receptor cells.

Somesthetic senses. The skins of vertebrates, including human beings, transduce information inputs which are decoded by higher centers as sensations of warm, cold, touch, pressure, pain, vibration, and a variety of less readily described sensations such as tickle, itch, and the response to electric shock.

Theories of the past that four sorts of transducers with different endings, corresponding to sensations of pain, touch, cold, and warmth, together produce the entire variety of input information transduced by the skin have not been borne out by research. Instead, present-day findings are so complex that some current theories deny that any receptors specific for a single modality transduce cutaneous inputs.[83] Such theories ascribe the differences in the sensations produced to coding of the outputs from receptor cells or to activities of centers higher in the nervous system. While the numerous different sorts of encapsulated nerve endings evidently do not each transduce a different sort of energy, the capsules may be accessory structures. Whatever the structure of the receptor, the actual transducing is quite probably done by naked endings of neurons, as is true for unencapsulated fibers. This does not mean that such nerve endings may not respond selectively to specific energy forms. Similar-appearing endings may carry out different processes.[84] The receptor cells of the skin are ordinarily activated in patterns of different input energies which are transduced simultaneously, so that complex sensations like "hard, rough, cold, metal cube" or "warm, damp, limp rag" are decoded and experienced subjectively by the organism.

(a) *Input—output transfer functions.* Pacinian corpuscles, present in the skin as well as in internal transducer components, are mechanoreceptors which transduce touch and are highly insensitive to any other form of energic marker. The transfer processes of these structures as single cells have been studied, and there is direct evidence for the specificity of at least this one sort of receptor cell in the skin (see page 255).

Indirect evidence of various sorts exists for specificity of some other kinds of receptor cells. These include transducers of pain, pressure, cold, and warmth, none of which has been definitively related to a specific form of receptor. Nor has any ending been identified as the sole transducer of a specific type of energy. Nonspecific transducers, sensitive to all cutaneous inputs, are probably present along with the specific ones.[85]

Pain. At least one specific transducer is known to be sensitive not only to the energy which is its adequate stimulus but to high intensities of another form of energy. If a fine needle is applied to different parts of the skin, at some points it elicits a sensation of pain. Closely adjacent points can be stuck without producing such a sensation. The distributions of these two sorts of points on various parts of the body are different, some parts being exquisitely sensitive, others relatively insensitive. At the points where pain is sensed, the skin is believed to contain fine unmyelinated endings of cutaneous nerve fibers (see pages 378 and 379). At one time these were thought to transduce pain alone, but it seems clear from reports of human subjects that a pressure of the needle insufficient to cause pain elicits a sense of touch. Moreover, the spots on the skin where pain is not felt transduce touch. Jointly these facts lead to the conclusion that the unmyelinated endings of most or even all of these cutaneous nerve fibers are sensitive to touch and some, when more energy is applied, transduce pain.[86] Possibly some also transduce cold and warmth. A single fiber may signal response to a light touch by a short discharge and to a painful prick by a prolonged discharge. Such variations in length of discharge have been recorded in cutaneous nerve fibers.[87] Perhaps no ending is specifically sensitive to pain. Rather, increases in the intensity of inputs sufficient to cause damage may be adequate to elicit a pain signal output from any sort of receptor cell.

Electrode studies of nerve-fiber activity show that certain sorts of inputs are related to outputs along particular classes of fibers. Pain is signaled in *A* fibers and *C* fibers (see page 264). Some observers have described a double pain sensation to a single input, a distortion which could be caused by one signal being transmitted over an *A* fiber and another separately over a *C* fiber, the two beginning simultaneously but being conducted at different rates. The two sensations elicited by these signals may have different qualities. *C* fibers appear to be nonspecific, capable of responding to all sorts of cutaneous inputs.[88]

Touch and pressure. Displacement of the hairs of the skin or deformation of the skin which is insufficient to cause pain can produce sensations of either touch or pressure. Touch activates the thickest cutaneous nerve fibers, whereas pressure is transduced by the next thickest, which is further evidence suggesting that there are specific mechanoreceptors in the skin. Distribution of these receptors in the skin is not uniform. This is shown by the fact that the distance which must separate two points that simultaneously touch the skin, in order for them to be discriminated as two and not one, differs from one area of the body to another. Evidently transfer functions vary from one part of the skin to another.

If a single point on the skin receives a mild electric shock, touch or pressure receptors rather than pain receptors presumably are activated. If two such shocks, each 500 microseconds (μs) long, are applied to the same point 4 ms apart, they are sensed as one sustained temporal event.[89] This effect continues well beyond the recovery period of the receptor cells involved and is probably a central process. Both central and peripheral processes in the receptor cell may contribute to the effect when the two shocks come closer together than 4 ms.

Temperature. "Cold spots" and "warm spots" can be demonstrated on human skin by applying a fine stimulating point, appropriately cooled or warmed, to skin which is adapted to the surrounding temperature. These spots are separate and differently distributed in various parts of the body. They are densest on parts of the face, particularly the eyelids and lips. The forehead is much more sensitive to cold than to warmth. Cold spots, in general, are more numerous than warm spots. For example, the dorsal surface of the fingers, an area highly sensitive both to cold and heat, has 7 to 9 cold spots and about 1.7 warm spots per square centimeter.[90] Attempts to relate these spots to specific forms of receptor cells so far have failed, but it is known that the two sorts of receptors are located at different depths in the skin.[91] The thinnest myeli-

nated cutaneous nerve fibers have been shown to respond to cold, while those which respond to warmth are somewhat thicker. Clearly the whole range of temperature is not transduced by a single type of receptor cell.

The usual thermal input is, of course, not at a tiny point. It involves the whole body or at least large parts of it. Three factors govern termperature sensations: the temperature in the skin, the rate of change of temperature, and the area of the field that receives inputs. Cold fibers, moreover, not only respond to cold, but when the temperature is elevated into the range usually mediated by warm fibers (the lower limit being about 35°C), they start to emit signals again. Warm fibers cease delivering signals at temperatures above 47°C, so the sensation "hot" is not mediated by them. Between 35 and 50°C there is a transient output by warm fibers, followed by a steady output by cold fibers, and at constant temperatures above 47°C pain fibers begin to deliver signals. Constant inputs at higher temperatures will destroy the fibers.

Besides the cold and warm fibers, a group of mechanoreceptive fibers that respond also to severe cooling produce large spike outputs which disappear in a few moments with constant low temperature. This process may explain "Weber's deception," a well-documented illusion in which cold weights seem heavier than warm ones and cooling of the skin elicits a sense of pressure. Cold fibers are also excited by the direct action on receptor cells of certain chemicals such as menthol. Inputs of menthol elicit strong, steady outputs of signals by cold transducer cells when the skin is warm and these receptors would otherwise not be functioning. Thermal receptors are apparently not activated directly by input thermal energy but by processes, probably chemical, which are governed by temperature without exchange of energy in the skin.[92]

The exponent in the equation relating physical and psychological magnitudes of cutaneous input transducing (see pages 379 and 380) has been determined for some of the transducer components in the skin. The exponent for cold is 1.1 and for warmth, 1.6. Cold transducers have little bias, but warmth transducers are expanders. Warmth sensation evidently is an accelerating function of the input intensity. Pressure on the palm of the hand has an exponent of 1.1. For vibration on the finger at 60 Hz, the exponent is 0.95 and at 250 Hz it is 0.6. It is 3.5 for an electric shock of 60 Hz through the fingers, the highest exponent obtained, indicating that great expansion takes place in this component of the input transducer.

(b) *Mode of adaptation.*   Receptor cells of the various cutaneous modalities have different adaptation characteristics.

Pain.   Most pain fibers are tonic, with slow signal termination, transmitting pulses as long as noxious inputs continue.[93] Adaptation characteristics may differ in various parts of the receptive field of the same neuron. One fiber, for instance, which fanned out over about one-fourth of a cat's cornea, showed slow signal termination in the central region of this field and more rapid termination in its periphery.

Touch and pressure.   The skin's mechanoreceptors are both phasic and tonic, with both fast and slow signal termination. Pacinian corpuscles adapt rapidly. Receptors for pressure include types of cells with both fast and slow signal termination. It seems generally true that receptors activated by hairs are fast and those driven by light mechanical stimulation of the skin surface are slow, but there are exceptions. The adaptation characteristics of Pacinian corpuscles are properties of the receptor itself. It has been suggested, however, that the mechanical arrangement of the ending is important in the rate of signal termination. When a frog's skin is stretched, altering the shape of the receptors, those cells which normally have rapid signal termination may develop slow termination, putting out pulses for a long time.[94]

Temperature.   Cold receptors are tonic, displaying slow signal termination and reaching a final steady state of output rate which goes on as long as cold inputs continue at a given temperature.[95] Individual cold fibers vary as to what range of temperature produces such steady outputs from them, but the temperature which elicits the maximum output frequency lies between 20 and 34°C. The total frequency of cold impulses on a nerve, which is the sum of discharges from all its component single fibers, reaches its maximum between 15 and 20°C. Cold fibers do not emit pulses above 41 or below 8°C.

Warm fibers also display slow signal termination, reaching steady output rates between 20 and 47°C. The maximum output rate usually occurs between 37.5 and 40°C. Warm fibers do not emit pulses below 20 or above 47°C.

When the environmental temperature changes, the output rate from receptor cells is a function of both the temperature and the rate of change in it.[96] When the environmental temperature is rapidly lowered, cold receptors begin to deliver impulses at a temperature several degrees above that at which such cells maintain a steady output rate. Warm receptors function in the reverse manner. They begin to emit pulses, when the temperature rises rapidly, several degrees below

the level at which such cells maintain a steady state. Both sorts of fibers adjust to a new steady output frequency when the temperature again attains a steady state.

(c) *Channel capacity.*   No facts are available on how much information the entire skin can transmit in a given period. Obviously, if all modalities are taken together, the channel capacity of this component of the input transducer is enormous. A study of the capacity of the skin to receive coded inputs in the form of vibrations produced a measure of channel capacity for this unusual mode of information transmission.[97] An alphabet of 45 distinguishable signals was worked out using 5 vibrators, 3 intensities, and 3 durations. After 65 h of training, a subject could receive with 90 percent accuracy 38 five-letter words per min. The highest rate achieved was 67 words per min (about 5.6 bits per s).

(d) *Threshold.*   **Pain.**   Studies of thresholds for pain in individual fibers are complicated by the response of these fibers to touch inputs which are not forceful enough to elicit a report of pain from a human subject. Studies of single-fiber pulses in animals, therefore, cannot distinguish certainly between touch and pain. The sorts of energies which are used as the markers for pain inputs are also difficult to quantify. One study on a human surgical patient used electrical inputs to an exposed cutaneous nerve of the leg.[98] When its frequency reached 12 pulses per 5 s, the patient reported unequivocal pain. This coincided with elevation of the action potential of *A* fibers usually associated with pain. The threshold of C fibers in this subject was 5 times higher. Studies of pain thresholds are also complicated by our lack of understanding of both peripheral and the central events that produce the sensation and by the individual variability among human subjects in the intensity at which an input evokes report of pain rather than of touch or some other cutaneous sensation.

Touch and pressure.   The only receptor cell for which a threshold value has been found is the Pacinian corpuscle. If a probe is moved about 0.5 micrometer (μm) in 100 μs it can cause a Pacinian corpuscle in the toe to produce an output signal.[99] Such an output from a single receptor cell, however, would probably be insufficient to elicit a report of a touch from a human subject.

Temperature.   The threshold point for warmth and cold is the same, a point where sensation is neutral.[100] When aluminum stimulators are applied on the inside of the forearm of a human subject, the threshold for reported warm sensation is about 32.7°C.[101] Temperature sensitivity of various parts of the body differs depending upon the distribution of the cold and warm spots on the skin. The eyelids and lips have a low threshold for thermal stimulation. The hairy parts of the head are quite insensitive to warmth.

The adaptive characteristics of the temperature receptors affect their thresholds. As the rate of environmental temperature change slows down, the threshold for warmth moves up to a higher range of temperatures while that for cold moves down to a lower range. The prevalent temperature and its rate of change, therefore, both affect the thresholds for warmth and cold. When the whole human body is in an environment between 32 and 35°C, it feels neither warm nor cold. The threshold decreases markedly as the area of input increases.

(e) *Lag.* **Pain.** Reaction times to pain decrease as the intensity of the input increases. Rate of conduction possibly varies to produce this change in lag, but this is not necessarily so because a number of other subsystem processes are involved.[102]

Touch and pressure. The reaction time to touch has the same relation to intensity as that of pain. Lag decreases as input intensity increases. It also varies with the cross-sectional area of the input, with the location of the input on the skin, and from time to time in the same individual.[103]

The receptor potential in Pacinian corpuscles arises in less than 0.2 ms. Many of these and receptors of other types, of course, ordinarily receive inputs at the same time. A single mechanical pressure on one point on a cat's paw, of course, constitutes an input to many such cells as well as receptors of other sorts. It gives rise to a traveling wave moving at about 12 m per s across the paw, so that the more distant receptors are excited later than the closer ones.[104]

Temperature. The reaction time for warmth is consistently longer than that for cold; this is at least partly because the warmth receptors are located at an average depth of 0.3 mm in the skin and the cold receptors at less than 0.17.[105] Like the lags of touch and pressure senses, the lag in temperature sense varies with the cross-sectional area of the input, with the location of the input on the skin, and from time to time in the same individual.

(f) *Accessory functions.* The capsules of some cutaneous receptor cells may be chiefly protective. Also the skin itself is protective of the receptors within it. Its outer layer contains no endings. It is composed of dead cells in the process of being cast off. The skin varies in thickness, allowing greater exposure of the nerve endings at some points, for example, on the lips.

Included among representative *variables* of the input transducing process are: *Meaning of information input which is transduced.* Example: The subject's auditory threshold for meaningful sentences was lower than for nonsense sentences. *Sorts of information input which are transduced.* Example: The bat guided itself by hearing its own cries bouncing off surrounding objects. *Percentage of the information input which is transduced.* Example: The new court stenographer managed to hear only about half the words that were spoken. *Threshold of the input transducer.* Example: The insect could detect a single molecule of pheromone at a distance of several hundred meters. *Changes in input transducing over time.* Example: As the dog grew older, he became deaf. *Changes in input transducing with different circumstances.* Example: John was normally a light sleeper, but it took a loud alarm clock to awaken him after a hard day on the football field. *Channel capacity of the input transducer.* Example: The cat did not hear the dog approaching because it could not listen for sounds and watch the bird intently at the same time. *Number of channels in use in the input transducer.* Example: Even though he was blind, the man was able to repair electronic equipment using touch and hearing alone. *Distortion of the input transducer.* Example: At low concentrations, the saline solution tasted sweet to the subject in the experiment. *Signal-to-noise ratio of the input transducer.* Example: The trained lookout was able to see the enemy ship in spite of its camouflage. *Rate of input transducing.* Example: When its eye was light-adapted, the frog saw discrete flashes up to 20 per s. *Lag in input transducing.* Example: It took several minutes to get used to the dim light, and then the spelunker could see quite well in the cave. *Costs of input transducing.* Example: After monitoring the radar for a few hours, the operator became tired.

3.3.2 Internal transducer, the sensory subsystem which receives, from subsystems or components within the organism, markers bearing information about significant alterations in those subsystems or components, changing them to other matter-energy forms of a sort which can be transmitted within it.

3.3.2.1 Structure The neurons which deliver information from organs to the organism have already been described (see page 343). Their receptor components, similar or identical in structure to those of the organism's input transducer, lie within muscle spindles or other parts of organs and transduce pain, pressure, stretch, temperature, or perhaps other modalities. The primary components of the organism's internal transducer are: (a) The "postsynaptic regions" (i.e., the regions closest to the synapses) of neurons that synapse with the presynaptic neurons mentioned above. They are located either in the dorsal horn nuclei of the spinal cord or higher up in the central nervous system, where the sensory cranial nerves synapse first. It must be at these points that the information from the organ is first transmitted into the organism's channel and net subsystem, since secondary neurons proceed from these synapses to send their processes into many different tracts and neural centers which are clearly components of the various echelons that make up the organism's decider (see pages 423 and 424). (b) Receptor cells in the central nervous system itself, some of which I have listed in Chap. 6 (see Table 6-4). These cells transduce signals about chemical or physical states of the bloodstream that reflect states of organs. They include cells in the hypothalamic centers for control of eating and drinking (see pages 432, 455, and 456) and for regulation of internal body temperature (see pages 461 and 462) and the osmotic pressure of the blood. They also include cells in the medullary centers for control of carbon dioxide tension and acidity of the blood. Apparently certain receptor cells in the brain also react to opiate molecules.[106] (c) Certain receptor cells in target tissues react to hormones synthesized in the endocrine glands.

3.3.2.2 Process   The postsynaptic regions of the postsynaptic neurons which are components of the internal transducer presumably operate like similar regions in other neural structures (see pages 254 to 257). Undoubtedly higher neural centers in the organism respond not only to individual neural fibers but also to patterns of impulses transmitted on multiple fibers. Those patterns convey additional information, as is true also in input transducing.

The input–output transfer functions, modes of adaptation, channel capacities, thresholds, lags, and accessory functions of internal transducer components have not been studied. When the specific receptor cells involved are clearly identified, investigations of this sort will be possible.

Representative *variables* of the internal transducing process include: *Meaning of internal information which is transduced.* Example: The osmoreceptor's output signaled excess water in the invalid's blood, and this information inhibited the output of antidiuretic hormone from the pituitary gland—an adjustment process that increased the activity of the kidneys, which excreted water faster until the content of water in the blood returned to its range of stability. *Sorts of internal information which are transduced.* Example: Information about the distention of the full stomach was transmitted over visceral afferent pathways, signaling the dog to stop eating. *Percentage of the internal information which is transduced.* Example: Only major changes in blood glucose were transduced by the rat's hypothalamic eating control center, less than one such fluctuation in ten. *Threshold of the internal transducer.*

Example: The small black kitten vomited more easily than any of the others in its litter. *Changes in internal transducing over time.* Example: After the soldier had stood at attention for half an hour, his leg muscles began to hurt. *Changes in internal transducing with different circumstances.* Example: After the stroke had damaged his brain, the man became less aware of pain in his leg. *Channel capacity of the internal transducer.* Example: The cat's target tissue responded to 8 molecules of thyroxin per min but could not respond faster than that. *Number of channels in use in the internal transducer.* Example: Signals about both the amount of water in his blood and the distention of his stomach—the first received by a few osmoreceptors, the second by numerous stretch receptors—affected the boy's decision to stop drinking water. *Distortion of the internal transducer.* Example: After the cut nerve began to regenerate, the man felt a constant raw pain inside his chest for about 5 weeks. *Signal-to-noise ratio of the internal transducer.* Example: The rat's opiate receptors responded to opiates and also to some isomers of opiates with less analgesic activity.[107] *Rate of internal transducing.* Example: The man's gut did not react painfully to the several blows that followed the first one, because its transducers were in a refractory phase. *Lag in internal transducing.* Example: The soldier's visceral pain did not increase to its full strength for more than 50 s after he was shot in the abdomen. *Costs of internal transducing.* Example: The energy consumed by the dog's hypothalamic thirst center amounted to only a fraction of a calorie per hour.

3.3.3   Channel and net, the subsystem composed of a single route in physical space, or multiple interconnected routes, by which markers bearing information are transmitted to all parts of the organism.

3.3.3.1 Structure   The channel and net subsystem in the higher plants is made up of the same components as the distributor, including tracheids and the branching veins of leaves (see page 369). Messages are in the form of hormones, which are alpha-coded chemical signals. Each of these hormones is produced in a specialized tissue. Leaves and the growing tips of stems are known to be sources of hormones. The destination of each hormone is a specific receptor or target tissue. Roots, leaves, stems, and other structures contain target tissues.[108]

The channel and net subsystem of animals consists of (a) the distributor components conveying endocrine secretions, including the central cavities of coelenterates, the canals of sponges, and the blood and lymph vascular systems of higher species which convey hormones, and (b) the network of neurons which interconnects all centers of the central nervous system, as well as the peripheral neural network.

The endocrine net.   As in plants, the sources of hormones transmitted by the distributor are the cells of specialized tissues. In animals these are the endocrine glands. Each gland encodes a hormone or hormones which can be decoded by a particular receptor or target tissue. Including these hormones, more than 60 kinds of chemical molecules carry signals in the human distributor vessel channels. Hormonal and neural flows related to the human endocrine network are diagrammed in Fig. 8-2. Animal species closely related phylogenetically have similar hormones, so that glandular extracts from one species can be used to treat the diseases of another.

The anterior pituitary gland is highly important

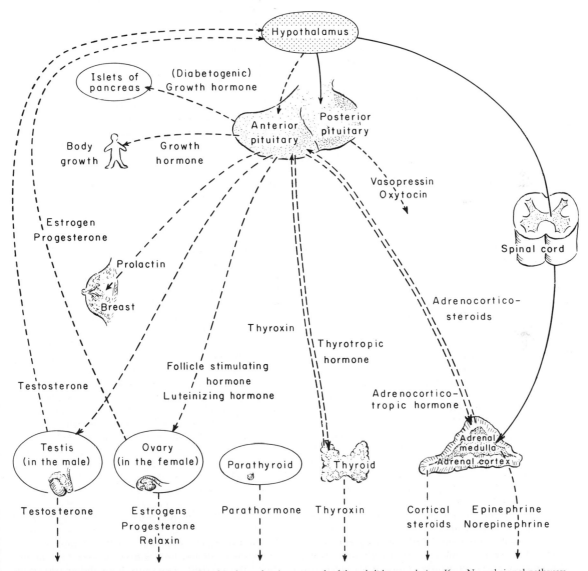

Fig. 8-2   Some hormonal and neural flows related to the endocrine network of the adult human being. Key: Neural signal pathway, →; endocrine signal pathway ⇢; negative feedback loop ⇄. [Modified from H. E. Morgan. Introduction to endocrine control systems. In J. R. Brobeck (Ed.). *Best & Taylor's physiological basis of medical practice.* (9th ed.). Baltimore: Williams & Wilkins, 1973, 7-2. © 1973 The Williams & Wilkins Co. *Reprinted by permission.*]

because it has as target structures other endocrine glands, such as the thyroid, adrenal cortex, ovary, and testis, as well as other tissues throughout the body. Part of this complex gland, the posterior lobe, develops from the embryonic brain and is connected, throughout the life of the organism, to the brain by a direct neural tract. The remainder of the structure, the anterior lobe, is ectodermal in origin, and its secretory cells probably have no innervation. Each adrenal gland also has two parts—a neural component, the medulla, which is innervated by the sympathetic branch of the autonomic nervous system, and the cortex, which receives and transmits through endocrine channels alone.

Endocrine-neural   interconnections.   Of   increasing importance in the ascending evolutionary scale of animals are channels consisting of neurons, which transmit bioelectric signals (see page 262). The phylogenetically older endocrine components and the nervous system, in higher animals and man, are joined into a single net by several pathways.[109] These include: (a) the tract from the hypothalamus to the posterior pituitary, (b) the neural tracts which descend through the brainstem and spinal cord and connect over autonomic nerves to the two adrenal medullas, and (c) the portal blood vessels which probably carry chemical signals from the hypothalamus to the posterior pituitary and from there to the anterior pituitary (see page 424).[110] Neural components within the brain are receptor or target tissues for hormones conveyed to them by the distributor.[111] There is a negative feedback loop from the target glands back to the pituitary (see page 463).

The neural net.   The human nervous system is the most complicated living structure in a single component. There are, of course, more complex structures at higher levels of living systems, groups and above. They are more complex if the arrangement of all the components, subcomponents, subsubcomponents, and so forth, of the higher-level systems are considered. But for complexity of a single component nothing exceeds the human nervous system. Probably no electronic or mechanical artifact has yet been built which comes close to being as intricate as it is. Space restrictions make it impossible to present here a detailed description of the hundreds of components that make up the complicated network of the peripheral and central nervous systems.

The neural components of the channel and net are hard to specify with any certainty, largely because the structures of some other information processing subsystems (i.e., the decoder, associator, memory, decider, and encoder), which are also components of the

central nervous system, have not been accurately identified. In general, the nerves, tracts, fasciculi, and lemnisci which connect brain centers and nuclei with each other and with peripheral neural components belong to the channel and net subsystem. Although the processes carried out by all information processing components are not completely understood, it appears that ganglia, nuclei, and cortical gray matter, where synaptic connections occur among neurons transmitting signals from different sites and where these signals are integrated, are components of other information processing subsystems, while the long processes of neurons or, in some cases, chains of neurons, make up the organism's neural channels or network.

The above description of the intricate structure of the human channel and net subsystem is quite sketchy from the viewpoint of a neuroanatomist. The discussion below will attempt to picture the processes going on in this, the most complex organ produced by biological evolution on earth.

3.3.3.2   Process   There are important functional differences in the organism's endocrine and neural nets, but the two networks are integrated.

Information transmissions in the endocrine net are "broadcast" all over the system, although only the target tissues can decode them.[112] This is a wasteful and therefore costly process. Neurons, on the other hand, deliver an alpha-coded chemical message, the transmitter substance, quickly and over a considerable distance to a precise address.

The structure of the synapse, or of the junction between a neuron and a gland or muscle fiber, ensures that a few molecules of transmitter substance will be delivered exactly where they can be effective. The endocrine net is much less efficient, particularly in a large organism which must react speedily to changes in its environment. But it has the advantage of being able to transmit information widely throughout the organism without the necessity of building a special neural channel to each component, which the neural net requires. The growth hormone of the pituitary gland acts upon many cells in numerous widely separated tissues at the same time. The emergency reaction of the adrenal glands starts and stops a multitude of processes, preparing the organism to react adaptively to external events (see pages 430, 431, and 455). Thyroxin and the sex hormones also have widespread actions.

The two main components of the channel and net subsystem—neural and endocrine—act in conjunction. The information inputs from the environment are carried over peripheral nerve channels to the central nervous system. There they elicit neural reflexes that relay signals to the pituitary by way of the hypo-thalamus. The pituitary releases hormonal signals which control the organism's internal adjustments to such environmental events as the presence of an enemy or a possible mate, or the change in the length of the days as the seasons advance.

The channel and net subsystem processes have the following characteristics:

(a) *Input–output transfer functions.* The nerves through which information flows from transducer components to the chief centers in the net preserve peripheral spatial relationships by the arrangements of individual fibers within them so that the patterns projected upon nuclei and eventually upon the cerebral cortex are present also in the nerves. Just as there are important alterations in signals in the input transducer (see page 379) so there are alterations between inputs to the net and outputs from it. This is consistent with Hypotheses 3.3.3.2-2 and 3.3.3.2-4 (see page 96). The first of these states that there is always a constant systematic distortion between input and output of information in a channel. And the second states that a system never completely compensates for the distortion in information flow in its channels.

The way inputs are "mapped" upon outputs varies among the channels of different sensory modalities as well as among motor and other pathways. The alterations in the ascending tracts between some particular components of the transducer, like the retina, and the sensory cortex are fairly well understood. So are the alterations in the descending tracts between the motor cortex and the muscles that carry out actions.

(b) *Channel capacity.* The channel capacity of the neural channels is certainly much greater than that of the endocrine vascular channels. For the human arterial bloodstream the latter has been calculated as being at most 180 to 210 bits of information per s.[113] In making this calculation, carbon dioxide was selected as representative of an ensemble of about 60 marker substances, including hormones, which control metabolic processes and are carried by the blood. Characteristics of the chemoreceptors involved in the control of the carbon dioxide level and constraints imposed by the beating heart were taken into account. The channel capacity of a resting man's arterial bloodstream for carbon dioxide was found to be 3.5 to 4.7 bits per s. Channel capacities for the other marker substances were assumed to be similar. Possible interactions among them were neglected in the calculation. Estimates of channel capacities for the optic and auditory channels alone, without considering all the other information processing going on at the same time in the organism's channels, are many times as

great as for vascular channels (see pages 381 and 383). The ensemble of possible patterns of neural pulses also is, of course, vastly larger than the 60 or so carried by the blood.

(c) *Threshold.* The threshold of the channel and net subsystem has not been measured, but may be higher than that of some or all components of the input transducer (see page 380).

(d) *Lag.* The lag in the endocrine net, or elapsed time between the input of hormonal information into an organism's vascular system and the output elicited by it, is determined by the rate of flow of the bloodstream. In the human being this ranges from 40 cm per s in the aorta, where it moves fastest, to 0.07 cm per s in the capillaries.[114] Circulation time is 8 to 17 s, measured as the time it takes for a sweet or bitter substance injected into a vein of an arm to reach the tongue so that it is tasted.[115] The normal arm-to-lung time, using injected ether and measuring the time until the subject smells ether, is between 4 and 8 s. This lag is experienced subjectively after an unexpected frightening experience, such as an automobile crash. It is several seconds before the state of fear or excitement is felt which is dependent upon epinephrine released by the adrenal medulla. Neural transmission rates vary with the diameter of the neuron (see page 264) from less than 1 to about 100 m per s. Phenomena such as the reaction time and the "double take" indicate that neural transmission is much slower than electronic conduction, but the lag dependent on it is still much less than the lag based on hormonal transmission in the vascular channels.

Not only do neural nets of relatively simple organisms have fewer components than those of animals higher in the evolutionary scale, but the characteristics of the nets are different. Though primitive neural nets like those found in coelenterates usually have some specialized routes for particular responses, an excitation most frequently spreads through the entire net. Since impulses can travel both ways on a channel in such a net, two signals from opposite directions can meet and cancel each other out. Although under experimental conditions axons of vertebrate neurons can be made to conduct "backward," such antidromic or "backward" conduction does not normally occur in vertebrate neurons. Describing how communication has improved as neural channels have developed phylogenetically, Gerard wrote:

Evolution exhibits striking directional changes in the transmissive capacities of organisms. In speed, for example. The egg membrane rise [the beginning of embryonic organization after fertilization] crawls at the rate of a centimeter an hour; in the adult sponge a message goes that distance in a minute.

With the appearance and improvement of a nervous system rates jump precipitously—to 10 cm a second in the net-like nervous system of the jellyfish bell, to a meter a second in the longitudinally directed nervous system of the worm, and to ten and a hundred times this speed in the nerve fibers of arthropods and finally of vertebrates. Or in distance. Excitation in the sponge dies out in a centimeter or two, but neural transmission is unlimited since the impulse retains full intensity as it travels. In pattern. Transmission is diffuse in the egg or sponge and essentially so along the interlacing nerve cells of the jellyfish. But in the worm, with nerve cells grouped at each segment, most stimuli elicit local reflexes, and behavior is largely segmental and highly stereotyped in terms of fixed nerve connections.[116]

In the channel and net subsystem of organisms, as at all levels (see page 63), information flows through nodes, at which the information is transmitted without alteration, and through decision points, at which operations upon the information distort [as suggested by Hypotheses 3.3.3.2-2 and 3.3.3.2-4 (see page 96) which propose that all channels in systems have some distortion which cannot be compensated for], eliminate, expand, give emphasis, or otherwise edit it. Some of these decisions may be within the channel and net; others are made by other organism subsystems, such as the decoder or the decider. The sheaths which surround neural fibers apparently ensure that little noise is introduced into the channel as a result of activity on adjoining channels, although the signals transmitted in certain sensory nerves can be modified by electrical induction fields from adjacent channels. As Hypothesis 3.3.3.2-3 (see page 96) states, there always is in the organism's channel and net a decrease in negative entropy or an increase in noise or entropy. The output information per unit time is always less than it was at the input.

Interaction of information from many sources is ensured by the great number of connections, particularly high in the nervous system, which form the bases for the complicated reflexes involved in skilled motor activities, and undoubtedly also for higher mental processes such as planning and artistic creation. Elaborate feedback loops exist in this mass of interconnections (see page 429).

Many *variables* of channel and net processing can be measured. Some representative ones are: *Meaning of information channeled to various parts of the system.* Example: The information that a cat was stalking was channeled to hypothalamic and optic projection areas in the mouse's brain. *Sorts of information channeled to various parts of the system.* Example: Collaterals of optic-nerve neurons carried brightness information to the dog's superior colliculus. *Percentage of information arriving at the appropriate receiver in the channel and net.* Example: The axons of the tiger's olfactory neurons propagated the information with negligible

decrement and distortion to the olfactory nuclei. *Threshold of the channel and net.* Example: The thresholds of the secondary neurons of the somatic tracts of the cat were lower than those of the primary neurons. *Changes in channel and net processing over time.* Example: As the baby grew older, the neurons of his corticospinal tract became myelinated, allowing him to manipulate his toys more skillfully. *Changes in channel and net processing with different circumstances.* Example: Tom did not notice the roughness of the water until it became difficult to stand, and his postural adjustments could no longer be mediated entirely by his brainstem and spinal cord. *Information capacity of the channel and net.* Example: The graduate of the reading class could read a 300-page book in an hour. *Distortion of the channel and net.* Example: The low-frequency tones in the message came through at such low intensity that, although the sounds were registered by the sailor's cochlea, they were not strong enough to be propagated through the acoustic (VIII) cranial nerve. *Signal-to-noise ratio in the channel and net.* Example: Some of the signals were so weak that they were near the intensity of the neural noise in the patient's auditory channel. *Rate of processing of information over the channel and net.* Example: The dinosaur's brain received the news that a mammal was biting its tail too late to avoid injury, so slow was transmission over its long neural channels. *Lag in channel and net processing.* Example: The more complicated reflex took the monkey longer because more neurons were involved, each with its own latency. *Costs of channel and net processing.* Example: Less than 2 percent of the dog's matter-energy inputs were used by his neural tissue, and his channel and net expended only a fraction of that.

3.3.4 Decoder, the subsystem which alters the code of information input to it through the input transducer or internal transducer into a "private" code that can be used internally by the organism.

3.3.4.1 Structure   The decoder in animal organisms with highly developed nervous systems is a dispersed subsystem. Some components are in sense organs at the periphery of the organism, such as the retinal bipolar and ganglion cells and the auditory bipolar cells. Decoder components are also found in many ganglia, nuclei, and other centers where neurons synapse throughout the autonomic and central nervous system. These components, like those of the decider subsystem (see pages 423 and 424), are organized into echelons. The lowest echelon (actually the lowest echelon of the decider subsubsystem of the decoder subsystem) involves spinal reflex arcs. The highest is in the cerebral cortex. Nuclei which decode input signals and emit them in another code occur in the spinal gray matter and in such components of the central nervous system as the medulla, midbrain, and cerebellum. Nuclei in the channels leading from peripheral transducer components to nuclei of the central nervous system may also decode. These include the retinal and cochlear ganglia, for instance. Studies of the lateral geniculates reveal that they also are decoder components in the optic channels.

The cortical sensory projection and association areas for each modality are also parts of the decoder subsystem. These receive their primary information inputs from the tracts leading from particular transducer components, but inputs also come from nonspecific tracts and from components concerned with other modalities. The visual cortex, for example, receives inputs from the labyrinth as well as the eyes.[117] In man, the temporoparietal cortex of the dominant hemisphere (*i.e.,* the left hemisphere in right-handed persons or the right hemisphere in left-handed persons) is particularly important to this subsystem, as well as to the encoder (see page 439). Gamma-coded language is decoded and encoded there. The locations of language areas are shown in Fig. 8-3. While speech sounds are decoded in the dominant hemisphere, nonspeech sounds like melodies and sonar signals appear to be decoded in the opposite hemisphere.[118]

Artifacts of this subsystem include coding machines and pattern recognition devices (see pages 488 to 491).

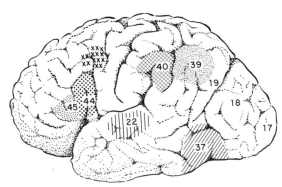

Fig. 8-3 Left lateral surface of the human brain showing the location of some of the areas related to language. Area 22, auditory-association cortex related to auditory aphasia or word deafness; area 37, visual-auditory association area; area 39, angular gyrus; area 40, supramarginal gyrus; XXX, area related to writing. Area 44 and the adjacent part of area 45 constitute approximately Broca's motor speech area.

Primary visual area or striate cortex, area 17, and visual-association areas, areas 18 and 19, mentioned on page 400, in Fig. 8-4, and in Table 8-2, are also shown. These are involved in vision but not in language. (From E. C. Crosby, T. Humphrey, & E. W. Lauer. *Correlative anatomy of the nervous system.* New York: Macmillan, 1962, 515. © The Macmillan Company, 1962. *Reprinted by permission.*)

3.3.4.2 Process   Above, I have summarized the large body of research about organism input transducing relevant to each of the separate modalities. There is a similar, if smaller, body of experimentation on decoding. Before discussing the work relevant to the various modalities, I shall state a number of principles which have been discovered about the decoding process in general. These should be set forth before the various modalities are discussed individually, because they indicate how extraordinarily complicated decoding processes are and how signals of the separate modalities interact. Without this background, a survey of any single sense would be simplistic.

Multivariable coding.   Each component of the input transducer emits information about a number of variable aspects of the environment in a neural code which can be decoded by other parts of the central nervous system. Although the sensitivity of the different components varies in a given type of animal and among types, transducer components in higher animals ordinarily transmit information not only about the presence or absence of an input such as a light or sound, but about its intensity, duration, quality (such as color, pitch, or sweetness), and spatial or temporal patterning. Human eyes, for instance, encode the visual field so as to differentiate objects from background, in three dimensions, in motion, and in color. Internal transducer components ordinarily have less complex structures and encode less complicated signals, in many cases addressed and transmitted to the lower echelons of the nervous system rather than the cortex. The organism remains subjectively unaware of all but a small part of this internal information. Even when it reaches the cortex, as visceral pain does, it is poorly localized and, in man, often difficult to describe. Besides decoding signals about physical variables in the environment, human beings decode further in terms of meaning, including the meaning of symbolic inputs such as language. They often recode experiences into language for processing inside the system. If other animals also do this, we have no evidence of it.

Multiparameter coding.   The decoding of signals on ascending channels by higher centers is quite accurate even though many internal codes are used in numerous different endocrine and neural components and even though these codes vary from one to another along several parameters. Among these are the following: (1) Rate of transmission of the signal from the periphery or from lower centers (*e.g.,* two signals originating at the periphery at the same instant but coming by different channels do not necessarily arrive simultaneously at the cortex); (2) size of sensory field represented by a signal (*e.g.*, the area of skin surface represented by a touch signal from the side of the leg is greater than that represented by a touch signal from the tip of the finger); (3) fineness of change in input represented by a signal (*e.g.*, a spot of light must move much farther in the periphery of the eye than at the fovea before it elicits a signal); (4) unilateral or bilateral signals (*e.g.*, some visual channels carry signals from only one eye, while others carry signals from both. This dual signal improves sight in various ways, one of which is to make possible detection of errors of information transmission by comparing the signals in the left and right visual fields, as described in Hypothesis 3.3.4.2-7 (see page 98); (5) sensory modality specificity of a signal (*e.g.*, a pulse from a single cell in the caudate nucleus may represent either a visual, an auditory, or a somesthetic input, but all signals from the optic nerve are visual); and (6) conceptual generality of a signal (*e.g.*, one signal may indicate that a single retinal rod received a light input, while another at a higher echelon indicates that a large object moved quickly across hundreds of retinal rods and cones). Codes possibly vary also along several parameters of efficiency, those used in the phylogenetically later higher neural centers generally being more efficient than those used in lower centers, in the senses of efficiency referred to in Hypotheses 3.3.4.2-1, 3.3.4.2-3, 3.3.4.2-4, and 3.3.4.2-5 (see page 98).

Multiechelon coding. Information from a single source is channeled to various components at different echelons of the decoder subsystem's decider subsubsystem. At each echelon, information is decoded and used in processes mediated at that echelon. An example of this is the channeling of some fibers of the optic tract directly to the pretectal nucleus and to the superior colliculus, bypassing the lateral geniculate. Light reflexes (the contraction of pupils of the eyes to light) are controlled through the pretectal nucleus. The control of some other simple visual reflexes is through the superior colliculus. (Other, more complicated visual reflexes are controlled through these nuclei in response to signals conveyed by fibers passing downward from the cerebral cortex.) A monkey deprived of its visual occipital cortex retains the response of the pupil to light and can respond to differences in the intensities of light from two sources. But differences of color or brightness (as opposed to the total amount of light reflected) no longer elicit responses.[119]

Signals relating to bodily balance which arise in the labyrinths and pass to the vestibular nuclei in the pons are channeled to virtually all major parts of the central nervous system from the spinal cord to the cerebral cortex, including the reticular areas and the cerebellum. At each echelon they are decoded to par-ticipate in various kinds of reflexes or voluntary behavior involving adjustments of the organism to its orientation in space and to its motion.

Decoding at the highest echelons brings together all information signals from input and internal transducer components, integrating them into a unitary subjective experience.

Multichannel coding. Except for the internal information which is chemically encoded for transmission through vascular channels and subsequent decoding by cells of target tissues, all sights, sounds, smells, tastes, aches, pains, tickles, and feelings of various sorts must pass over neural channels coded in such ways that they can be decoded in the various nuclei and cortical areas to provide a representation of the system itself and its environment on which the organism can base its behavior. The structures of the transducer components and the channels are important in this decoding, since spatial arrangements of the populations of cells in the transducer component are more or less faithfully preserved through the channels and nuclei in the pathways and in the specific cortical areas. The transducer cells in the peripheral sense organs are of different types, each type responding to different aspects of the input signals. This is true also of the cells with which they synapse in successive nuclei. Decoding is built in because a particular type of cell makes outputs to only a given aspect of the input. Others at higher echelons with which a particular sort of cell synapses receive inputs of only that same sort. Specific channels are therefore available for each sort of coded information.

Sorts of codes. Codes transmitted through centers and channels make use of variations in the processes of the individual cells which are elements of those components and of differences in response of populations of cells acting together.[120] Variations in all the following characteristics, and perhaps others, are employed in one or more codes in the human organism:

(*a*) which hormonal molecule is the marker

(*b*) which specific channel carries the signal

(*c*) frequency of transmission of the signals

(*d*) duration of the signals

(*e*) temporal pattern of the signals

(*f*) lag in output of the receptor cell

(*g*) number of parallel cells or channels conveying the signals

(*h*) differences in time of arrival of simultaneously initiated signals in different channels

(*i*) differences in time of arrival of signals from opposite sides in paired transducer components such as eyes and ears

(*j*) differences in intensity of signals from opposite sides in paired transducer components

Modes of adaptation. How components adapt determines the kinds of codes they can employ. A frequency code is unsuitable to a phasic cell with rapid signal termination, for such a cell characteristically emits only a single pulse in response to an input of short duration. But a frequency code can be used by a tonic cell with slow signal termination, the values of some variable in the input being indicated by variations in the rate of its sustained activity. For instance, the cells in the ommatidia, which are segments of the compound eye of the horseshoe crab *Limulus*, are tonic, having slow signal termination. They respond to a given light intensity by a certain frequency of firing. Frequency changes signal changes in intensity.[121]

An example of a code used by phasic cells with fast signal termination is that in the Pacinian corpuscles which signal touch in the cat's foot.[122] Greater intensity of input at one point is signaled by an increase in the number of receptor cells activated. If the place at which the input is applied is moved, the point of earliest activation moves and so does the center of the activated cells. The pattern of cell activity transmits to higher centers information not only regarding the intensity of the applied force but regarding its size and position as well.

With these general principles about decoding in mind, we may proceed to consider special characteristics of the process for individual sensory modalities.

Vision. Coding of visual information has been studied in a number of different species. Formerly it was believed that the optic pathways transmitted information to the brain in the form of mosaics of signals geometrically similar to the patterns of light that strike the two retinas. It is becoming clear, however, that decoding and systematic distortion of the input occur peripherally, in the retinal ganglion. Interactions among adjacent cells serve to emphasize certain characteristics of the input and this "edited" information is transmitted to central decoder components. Studies of the frog's eye, for example, indicate that its function is not only to report light and dark areas of the environment but also to detect insects and let the frog's brain know about their presence. It is constructed to do this by emphasizing those aspects of the image which produce the appearance of shape and motion characteristic of a fly.

The frog's retina has five functional types of ganglion cells with recognizably different structures, according to Lettvin, Maturana, McCulloch, and Pitts.[123] The cell bodies of these five types are distributed in the sixth, or inner granular, layer of the retina. Their axons make up the optic nerve and extend to the colliculi, where the endings of each type of cell cluster together in four distinct layers and synapse with other cells. The functions of the five types of cells, in the order in which their layers occur in the colliculi—except for type *e*—are as follows: (*a*) boundary detection, (*b*) moving dark convex boundary detection, (*c*) moving or changing contrast detection, (*d*) dimming detection, and (*e*) dark detection. Cells of type *e* are rarer than the other types and are distributed through the layer made up of type *c*. In every part of the retina these types have the same relative frequencies. The frog's retina, therefore, performs highly analytical operations on the visual image and transmits a selected and transformed representation to the brain. The decoding alters an image originally formed on the retina as a mosaic of luminous points into signals which are routed on to the colliculi where they are in specialized arrangements. In this process a large amount of information is thrown away, but it is not information that is relevant to the frog's business of catching insects and avoiding predators. When a fly's image enters the visual field, it occupies a small area of the retina in which are all the types of receptors. If the fly is stationary, types *a*, *b*, and *d* become active. If the fly moves, type *c* also fires. Types *a*, *b*, and *c* function in bursts, reflecting the jerky way a fly walks. If the fly stops again, types *a* and *b* fire steadily. Numerous signals of various sorts are transmitted from the limited retinal area receiving the fly's image, while few signals come from other areas. In the colliculi these signals are combined and interpreted to indicate the presence of a single object.

In a related study on anesthetized cats, Hubel and Wiesel placed microelectrodes in single cells at different echelons of the visual components (see Fig. 8-4 and Table 8-2).[124] Their animals faced a wide screen on which different patterns of light were shown in various positions. The investigators found that in certain ways the ganglion cells of the lateral geniculates (echelon IV) are like retinal ganglion cells (echelon III), fibers from many of which converge on each lateral geniculate cell. Each responds to a circumscribed retinal region, its receptive field. Some of them are "on" cells, each one firing when a spot of light hits the center of that cell's receptive field. Others are "off" cells, the firing of each being suppressed except when there is no light at the center of that cell's receptive field. Each type of cell has a concentric ring around it which gives a response opposite to the central response. That is, the on cell has a small circular central on region surrounded by a peripheral off zone, and the off cell the opposite. The lateral geniculate cells, however, differ in other ways from the retinal ganglion cells. The field of the former is large, involving more retinal receptor cells. The higher echelon is more generalized, in the sense that it receives mes-

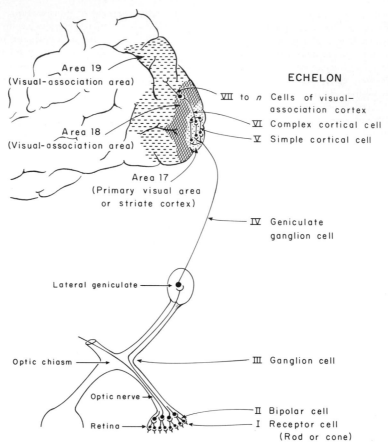

Fig. 8-4 Echelons of the decider subcomponent of the visual component of the human decoder subsystem.

sages from more transmitters. The lateral geniculate cells recode differently also. Signals from the periphery of the receptive field are more able in such cells than in retinal ganglion cells to cancel the effects of information from the center of the receptive field. They are more specialized than the retinal ganglion cells in putting out signals in response to an abstract relationship—spatial *difference* in illumination—rather than to light itself. There is increased disparity between their responses to a small centered spot and to diffused light.

These experimenters also placed their microelectrodes in cells at higher echelons of the visual channels, echelons V and VI of the visual projection cortex, area 17. Unlike cells in the lateral geniculates and the retina, the cortical cells do not respond to inputs to a circumscribed, circular retinal field. There are, instead, different types of cells, each sending output signals to a distinct kind of field.

The *"simple"* *cells* of echelon V constitute one type. They seem to receive their input signals from lateral geniculate cells. They are highly specialized to respond to such specific visual inputs as slits, dark bars, and edges. In this, they are like boundary detectors in the frog's eye. The exact direction of orientation of these inputs—vertical, horizontal, or oblique—determines which cell, out of many simple cells, emits a signal. Like the retinal ganglion and lateral geniculate cells of lower echelons, there are both on- and off-type cortical cells. The receptive field of a simple cell characteristically consists of a long and narrow on area with larger off areas on each side. The magnitude of the on response depends upon how much of either sort of area is covered by light. A long narrow slit that just fills the elongated on region produces the most powerful response. With the slit in a different orientation, the effect is weaker because all of the on region is not illuminated, and some of the off is. A slit at right angles will not stimulate such a cell. Diffuse light apparently balances the on and off effects almost perfectly, so little or no response results. Other kinds of cells respond to other specific types of on and off receptive areas. They have in common the fact that the border or borders separating on and off regions are straight and parallel rather than circular. Quite possibly the input to a simple cell is from many lateral geniculate cells whose on centers are arrayed along a straight line.

The visual projection cortex also contains "*complex*" *cells* of echelon VI spatially mixed with the simple ones, from which they apparently receive their input signals. Like the simple cells, some complex cells are specialized to put out signals to a given spatial orientation of the light input to their retinal fields, but instead of having on and off regions, the on and off outputs depend upon whether the light is on the left or the right of its receptive field. Complex cells respond with sustained outputs to a light moving through their receptive fields. In this, they are like moving or changing contrast detectors in the frog's eye. Their outputs continue as the light moves over a substantial retinal area, while the simple cell responds only as the light crosses a narrow boundary separating on and off regions. These complex cells appear to receive their inputs from a large number of simple cells in the same region with the same kind of orientation. Their output code is generalized in that they produce outputs to inputs from a large retinal area; but their code is very specialized in that they produce outputs in response to an abstract spatiotemporal relationship—motion in space. The information processed by each individual neural unit at the higher echelons of the visual pathways, as compared to lower units, is more general in that it concerns a larger

TABLE 8-2   Structural and Functional Characteristics of Echelons of the Decider Subcomponent of the Visual Component of the Human Decoder Subsystem

Echelon number	Component of visual pathway	Type of cell	Function
VII to n	Areas 18 and 19 (Visual-association area)	Cells of visual-association cortex	Respond to signals from complex cells of area 17 and correlate them with signals from other sensory and nonspecific areas, outputting signals to motor and other areas
VI	Area 17 (Primary visual area or striate cortex)	Complex cortical cells	Responds to linear form of one spatial orientation even when moved within its receptive field
V	Area 17 (Primary visual area or striate cortex)	Simple cortical cells	Responds to linear form in one position and spatial orientation
IV	Lateral geniculate body	Geniculate ganglion cell	Responds more differentially than retinal ganglion cells to spatial differences in retinal illumination as opposed to diffuse illumination
III	Retina	Ganglion cell	Responds to "on" signals or to "off" signals in center of its receptive field
II	Retina	Bipolar cell	Responds to light on larger region of retina than receptor cell, when one or more of the receptor cells converging on it responds
I	Retina	Receptor cell (rod or cone)	Responds to light on a small point of the retina

portion of the inputs from the total visual field. But it is at the same time more specific in that it deals with only a single aspect of those inputs.[125]

The cortex seems to be organized into tiny columns which extend from the surface gray matter down into the white matter. These columns are functional and are not distinguishable structures under a microscope, but the thousands of cells in each all have the same receptive field orientation. Some are simple, others complex. Some respond to slits, while others respond to dark bars and edges. Presumably, input fibers to the simple cells come from the lateral geniculates, and output fibers from them go to the complex cells. Hubel writes:

It is possible to get an inkling of the part these different cell types play in vision by considering what must be happening in the brain when one looks at a form, such as, to take a relatively simple example, a black square on a white background. Suppose the eyes fix on some arbitrary point to the left of the square. On the reasonably safe assumption that the human visual cortex works something like the cat's and the monkey's, it can be predicted that the near edge of the square will activate a particular group of simple cells, namely cells that prefer edges with light to the left and dark to the right and whose fields are oriented vertically and are so placed on the retina that the boundary between "on" and "off" regions falls exactly along the image of the near edge of the square. Other populations of cells will obviously be called into action by the other three edges of the square. All the cell populations will change if the eye strays from the point fixed on, or if the square is moved while the eye remains stationary, or if the square is rotated.

In the same way each edge will activate a population of complex cells, again cells that prefer edges in a specific orientation. But a given complex cell, unlike a simple cell, will continue to be activated when the eye moves or when the form moves, if the movement is not so large that the edge passes entirely outside the receptive field of the cell, and if there is no rotation. This means that the populations of complex cells affected by the whole square will be to some extent independent of the exact positions of the image of the square on the retina.

Each of the cortical columns contains thousands of cells, some with simple fields and some with complex. Evidently the visual cortex analyzes an enormous amount of information, with each small region of visual field represented over and over again in column after column, first for one receptive-field orientation and then for another.

In sum, the visual cortex appears to have a rich assortment of functions. It rearranges the input from the lateral geniculate body in a way that makes lines and contours the most important stimuli. What appears to be a first step in perceptual generalization results from the response of cortical cells to the orientation of a stimulus, apart from its exact retinal position. Movement is also an important stimulus factor; its rate and direction must be specified if a cell is to be effectively driven.[126]

Above the primary visual area, echelons V and VI (area 17 in Figs. 8-3 and 8-4 and Table 8-2), is the visual-association area, echelons VII to n (areas 18 and 19 in

Figs. 8-3 and 8-4 and Table 8-2), which correlate signals from area 17 with other sensory and nonspecific areas, outputting signals to motor and other areas.

There is further evidence that various echelons in the visual component code information differently. Neurons, both when the retina is illuminated and when it is not, put out more pulses per second in the optic nerve (echelon III) than in the lateral geniculate above it (echelon IV), and in the latter than in the visual cortex above it (echelon V or higher).[127] The pulse patterns also differ from echelon to echelon. The time intervals between neural pulses in fibers of the optic nerve (echelon III) cluster around a mode of 8 to 15 ms. Bimodal and trimodal interval distributions are found in lateral geniculate cells (echelon IV), with peaks around 2 to 5, around 10, and between 80 and 200 ms. In cells of the visual cortex (echelon V or higher) the intervals are brief, peaking at 2 to 5 ms, although these are also larger intervals. In darkness, cells of the lateral geniculates transmit random series of excitatory postsynaptic potentials, or rhythmical sequences of large hyperpolarizing potentials alternating with depolarizing potentials that produce groups of strong output pulses. Visual cortical cells, on the other hand, transmit both excitatory and inhibitory postsynaptic potentials.

Only about 10 percent of the neurons in the visual cortex decode binocular information; the others decode inputs from only one eye. It may be that a complete image for each eye independently is formed in the cortex, and that convergence for stereoscopic vision and binocular rivalry occurs secondarily in the cells which are activated by both eyes.[128]

Color, as well as intensity and patterning, affects the decoding of visual signals.[129] In one experiment red and blue lights were periodically input to isolated eyes of frogs, nerve impulses from a single retinal ganglion cell of which were led off to electrodes. On, off, and on–off effects upon the ganglion cell were found, as in other studies. Red light gave rise to different rhythms of pulses from the rhythms elicited by blue light. In volleys arising from inputs of red light the intervals between groups of pulses either increased or remained constant. In response to blue light these intervals periodically diminished or increased. Thus a single nerve fiber can transmit multidimensional information.

In many ways, decoding is similar from one animal species to another, even though there are also important species differences. Many species have on and off retinal cells, but these cells vary from species to species in their precise ways of functioning. The visual decoding of cats differs from that of frogs in that the complexity of coding in the third echelon of neurons in frogs is equaled only by that in the sixth echelon of cats. Frogs' vision appears to be much less flexible, being specialized to perceive only a limited number of stereotyped patterns. In the ommatidia of the horseshoe crab, *Limulus,* decoding and recoding go on in the neural plexus interconnecting the fibers from the receptor cells.[130] This activity integrates information and by contrast systematically distorts signals to accentuate outlines of figures in the visual field. So species differ in the number of echelons at which decoding goes on. In general, the larger the number of echelons, the greater the flexibility of the coding. Coding efficiency may also be greater in higher species as compared to lower, just as I hypothesize it is in mature systems as compared to young ones (see Hypotheses 3.3.4.2-1 and 3.3.4.2-3, page 98).

Maintenance of spatial steady state and orientation in space. There have been no studies of coding of vestibular information.

Hearing. As in visual information processing, the successive echelons of the auditory component not only relay the pattern of events at the periphery but also decode and recode them, systematically distorting or emphasizing certain aspects of the inputs. The midbrain and cortex, for instance, are more "sharply tuned" than the neurons of the auditory nerve, because inhibitory processes in them suppress the effects of a sound wave except in particular channels.[131]

The auditory component uses complicated codes. The position of the excitation on the organ of Corti is an important aspect of these codes, since a comparable spatial relationship is maintained throughout all the auditory channels and components. This assignment to a specific channel encodes tones with frequencies above 20 Hz. Lower tones also make use of this "built-in" code, but in addition they are transmitted in a frequency code. Volleys of impulses are propagated along the auditory nerve at the frequency of the input. In the high-frequency range also, the excitation of successive waves summates, so that information is carried in the "envelopes" of the bioelectrical potential. (An envelope is a line connecting either all the maximum or all the minimum amplitudes of the waves.) For middle and low frequencies, sensing of vibration supplements the sensing of tonal frequencies, improving the ability of the organism to decode such tones.[132] Auditory intensity codes involve both the number of fibers active and variations in thresholds of the fibers. Direction of sound is encoded by differences of intensity of the signals from the two ears as they arrive in central auditory components and by

the duration of the brief interval between the times of their arrival. Also, the side of the head away from the source of the sound receives a slightly different signal than the one toward the source.

Like the visual components, auditory centers carry out progressively more specialized processes at the higher echelons. Channels from the two ears come together at a low echelon, so that information which reaches the inferior colliculus is binaural. The medial superior olivary nucleus carries out coding necessary to the localization of sound in space. If it is destroyed in an otherwise intact animal, this ability is lost. Removal of the auditory cortex, which receives the auditory signals from lower echelons, also abolishes such localization.

When all areas of the cerebral cortex which receive inputs over channels from the medial geniculates are removed, cats can still respond to the onset of a sound and to changes in its frequency and intensity. These are all coding processes which distinguish a change when new neural units receive inputs. However, they no longer respond differentially to alterations in pattern and duration and to localization in space—all coding processes which depend upon changes in inputs to the same cells. The cortex evidently performs a short-term memory storage function as part of its decoding process, comparing a single cell's activities at various moments in time.[133] Without short-term memory adequate for this, that sort of decoding cannot be carried out.

Smell. Decoding and encoding of information in other sensory modalities make use of similar codes and involve several echelons, just as the visual and auditory modalities do. Also the codes are similar. The amount and nature of the systematic distortion vary from tract to tract.

Little is known about how odors transduced by the olfactory epithelium are decoded into the wide variety of scents experienced by human beings. The olfactory sense of many lower animals is, of course, much more discriminating than man's. Probably the olfactory bulb carries out decoding. Oscillations in electrical potential similar to those found on the olfactory epithelium (see page 384) have been recorded from the olfactory nerve and olfactory bulb. These differ in frequency, magnitude, waveform, and time of appearance from oscillations of the peripheral component, and thus indicate that coding of the signals is changed at higher echelons.[134]

Taste. Central decoding of gustatory inputs has also been investigated.[135] In the fibers of the medulla which are channels for taste sensation, response patterns to chemical substances on the tongue are similar but not identical to those on the chorda tympani nerve leading from the tongue. Cells are found there which decode a single sort of gustatory input (see page 385), and others which decode two or more.[136] Some cells that decode chemical inputs as tastes also decode temperature or touch inputs.

Somesthetic senses. Somatic and proprioceptive information is decoded first in the spinal cord. There, input neurons make direct synaptic connections with output motor neurons, forming spinal reflex arcs. These input signals are again recoded in the nuclei of the medulla. A tract from the nucleus cuneatus to the cerebellum transmits information from the upper part of the body to the cerebellum, where it is decoded into a code relevant to the maintenance of bodily balance and other motor coordinating functions of the cerebellum. Tactile and proprioceptive information is decoded also in the cerebellum, being transmitted from other nuclei and from the reticular formation, to which ascending tracts contribute fibers. Also in the thalamus, information flows together from all the modalities of somatic input transducers and internal transducers. These signals are decoded for transmission upward to higher echelons. Thalamic nuclei decode even when the ascending channels are interrupted, so that a monkey or man with one cerebral hemisphere removed can respond to tactile and pain sensations, although some types of discrimination are lost, such as the ability to tell whether one or two points on the body are being touched.[137] The successive recodings distort the projections upon the nuclei in the ascending channels, so that representations of some parts of the body at higher echelons, differing from one species to another, are exaggerated in keeping with their functional importance to that species.[138] In thalamic nuclei the hands and feet of monkeys and the face and jaw of rabbits are emphasized.

Pain. In the ascending spinothalamicocortical channels, through which pain signals travel, the cells at the echelon of the thalamic nuclei have large receptive fields.[139] They may include more than one limb, even both sides of the body. Pain is not coded so that it can be precisely localized in the thalamus. Indeed, it is not clearly known at present what echelons or regions of the central nervous system carry out the various sorts of coding involved in the perception of pain.[140]

Touch. Signals reaching the cortical receptive fields for tactile information, unlike those for pain, are decoded to provide exact localization, even though the cortical fields are from 15 to 100 times larger than those of the receptor cells.[141] The nature of the coding is as follows. A single peripheral touch receptor cell can transmit signals to several cortical cells located near to each other and, conversely, several receptor cells can send signals to a given cortical cell. To a transient light touch, for instance, cells in a zone of the cerebral cortex put out information, but their outputs are not all identical. The center of the zone puts out most actively and with the shortest latency. From the center to the edge, there is a gradual change, with cells at the edge less likely to emit signals. Just outside this zone, cells receive only subthreshold synaptic excitations. The intensity of the peripheral inputs and the number of receptor cells activated are reflected exactly in the pattern of response in the cortex. The information is so coded that the part of the body stimulated determines which cells will put out signals, and the intensity of the input determines the spatial and temporal patterns of their activity.

Decoding multiple modalities of inputs. In higher neural echelons some cells can decode several modalities of input, putting out signals that represent integrations based on them. Integration of information from multiple input and internal sources before it reaches the cerebral cortex can occur through fibers from different tracts which go to nuclei in the midbrain and to the cerebellum. The superior colliculus, for example, receives ascending visual, pain, tactile, temperature, and possibly auditory information.[142]

In the cat, thalamic and cortical neurons which respond to information from differently flavored solutions placed upon the tongue, to touch, pressure, warming, and cooling have been studied by the use of microelectrodes. Ninety-four percent of the thalamic and 75 percent of the cortical neurons emit signals specifically to only one modality of information input. In the thalamus only four cells were found which responded to two modalities (touch and cooling in all four cases). In the cortex more complex combinations of effective inputs were present. Cells that emit signals to touch on the tongue, for instance, also respond to pinching of the nose or ear and to electrical stimulation of the reticular formation.

The cortical projection areas are not the "end of the line" for information concerning sensory events. Rather, tracts which connect the various areas of the cortex provide not only for relay of inputs to motor areas but also for complex recodings and integrations of information through a vast and complex network of interconnections, not only with adjacent association areas but with regions related to other modalities—the prefrontal cortex and the opposite side of the brain.

Perception of the environment. How the nervous system makes use of many inputs to provide the internal representation of the environment upon which organisms rely in their behavior is not known, nor is the process by which meaningful signals, including gamma-coded information, are decoded. Certain inputs may convey innately determined meanings, at least in some species (see page 409). Presumably most objects and symbols usually acquire their meanings to an organism from the different past experiences that organism has had with them—pleasant or unpleasant concomitants or consequences of them.

According to Mandler, whether information inputs are perceived as identical or as different depends not upon what information is input to receptors, but upon whether the organism makes a "differentiating response." Diverse information inputs are perceived as identical if there is no such response (see page 411).[143] People, and apparently most or all animals, selectively organize their world into "things" and background, divide sequences of experiences into significant units, and respond to relations such as "larger" and "heavier."[144] Input signal patterns toward which animals act equivalently appear similar to man.[145] Camouflage influences lower vertebrates as strongly as it does man. The insect that is colored and shaped like a dead leaf hides equally well both from other insects and from man. Higher invertebrates, such as octopods, which have image-forming eyes, organize their visual fields much as human beings do. There are, however, some species differences. Rats have trouble distinguishing figures which are rotated. Apes and human children find that such rotation makes it hard to discriminate them, but they do better than rats.

Theories of perception have dealt with how signals from discrete elements of the peripheral transducers to cells of central regions produce subjective experiences. There is a wide gamut of such experiences, from the basic perception of shapes, like square and round, to the complicated recognition that an image on the retina is distorted. Psychologists have long been divided between those who favor explanations of such perceptual processes involving configurations of discrete elements firing together and those who prefer to look upon the brain as a bioelectric field, isomorphic to the environment. The theory of "cell assemblies" is a conceptual system of the first sort (see pages 411, 413, 484, and 485). The Gestalt theories are among those of the second sort.[146] More recently, the emphasis has been upon logical or mathematical relationships. Mathematical statements can describe a neural network capable of decoding and recognizing common characteristics in patterns of sensory inputs (see pages 485 and 486).[147]

Studies of animals with ablations of brain tissue and with implanted electrodes and of human operative patients have indicated which brain regions are essential for decoding. Perceptual discrimination, except for recognition of the presence or absence of a signal or of major changes in its intensity, requires the projection areas of the cerebral cortex related to the particular sensory modality involved, such as vision. No deficit is found in other modalities when the area for one of them is ablated. The more complex discriminations required for solution of a problem requiring two or more responses to indicate differences among inputs have been shown experimentally to require also the association areas related to the specific modality being tested.[148] A process of "partitioning of the input," Pribram speculates, may be carried out by the "posterior intrinsic sector" of the brain (association areas and related thalamic nuclei), making use of efferent channels.[149] Signals on these efferents "partition" the afferent signals to the "extrinsic sectors" (projection areas and related thalamic nuclei). This process determines the range of possibilities to which an element or set of elements can be assigned. Patterns of information are produced. The activities of the "posterior intrinsic sector" are conceived to provide referents and units while the extrinsic areas provide the inputs. These patterns increase in complexity and permit more and more precise specification of elements in the events occurring in the extrinsic sector. Continued activity of this sort permits any given input to convey more and more information, and differentiation becomes more absolute.

Some interesting research studies relate waveforms of the potentials evoked in the brain and recorded by electrodes on the scalps of human subjects during experimental sessions to the content of the information which they process.[150] Clicks or flashes of light were the input signals to each subject. Potentials elicited by inputs whose occurrence resolved uncertainty were of larger amplitude and different in other ways from the potentials elicited when the subject knew in advance what to expect. Evidently the meaning of the inputs affected the electrical activity of the brain, as measured through the scalp. When a subject was asked to guess what form of inputs he would receive (*e.g.*, loud or soft clicks, or single or double ones), the brain activity changed at the moment when his uncertainty was resolved (on the first click if the question was loudness, on the second if it was doubleness). This change appears to represent decoding of meaning. Variations in waveform of brain potentials also have been seen in response to differences in geometric forms being represented visually to subjects.[151] The evoked brain potential is different for a blank visual field than for one containing a geometric form. It differs from one geometric form to another, even when the areas are equal, and between two printed words of equal letter area. It is similar for two geometric forms of the same shape but unequal areas. In this study, too, the content or meaning of the input was the variable which was responsible for the differences in waveform among the brain potentials.

Alpha decoding. Cells and organs decode alpha-coded information (see pages 265 and 338). The lowest species of animal organisms are equipped to decode only alpha-coded information, conveyed in the patterned chemical structure of molecules known as "pheromones" (see pages 438 and 439). These are molecules produced by exocrine glands of one individual animal which are transmitted over space, usually through the air, carrying odors which are received and decoded by other individuals of the same species. They enter these organisms by the input transducers of the common chemical sense, smell or taste.

Beta decoding. All higher animals can decode alpha-coded signals, but they can also decode beta-coded information, *i.e.*, nonsymbolic signals transmitted by patterns of inputs from systems in the external or internal environments to input transducer or internal transducer components of various sensory modalities. Alpha and beta coding do not drop out when gamma coding appears. They persist all the way up the animal evolutionary scale to man.

Gamma decoding. Man is the only organism known certainly to process gamma-coded information (see page 440), although some other species, such as dolphins, possibly communicate at times with gamma codes, and chimpanzees have been taught to use symbolic hand sign language and plastic chips of various shapes and colors to symbolize words (see page 441). Though they cannot speak, domestic animals and primates certainly can make discriminative responses to human speech. These are probably responses to signs rather than symbols in gamma-coded speech. A series of evolutionary changes, relatively recent compared with most such alterations (see pages 467 and 468), appears to have produced an emergent reorganization of neural interconnections and speech organ components, enabling human beings to do advanced symbolic thinking and to use language. These skills make man significantly different from other species.

Language is so much more complex and efficient than all other kinds of information processing in cells, organs, and organisms as to be qualitatively dissimilar from them. Communication codes become much more efficient when the human species is reached in phylogenetic development and also as the individual human being matures ontogenetically. These facts appear to support the propositions that coding improves as systems mature and practice use of the codes, as is postulated in Hypotheses 3.3.4.2-1, 3.3.4.2-3, 3.3.4.2-4, and 3.3.4.2-5 (see page 98).

Researches with visible displays of spoken speech which are capable of being converted to audible transmissions have provided important insights into the complexity of coding in human speech.[152] A sound spectrogram is a visible recording on a film of words spoken into a microphone as the film moves through the spectrograph. Marks representing sounds at the lowest frequencies appear at the bottom of the film, the highest frequencies appearing at the top. Spectrograms representative of speech sounds can also be painted on film by hand. Figure 8-5 shows a sound spectrogram of a phrase in human speech and below it a hand-painted version of the same phrase. Both of these can be converted into sound by running the film through an instrument called a pattern playback. The playback of sound spectrograms is 95 percent intelligible. The hand-painted spectrograms can be recognized on playback with 85 percent accuracy. By modifying one or another part of the hand-painted spectrogram and then playing it back, one can discover which sound patterns convey various speech sounds.

Researches have clearly shown that there cannot be a separate sound for each of the *phonemes,* the basic sounds of speech. Speech can be understood when spoken as fast as 400 words per minute (about 30 phonemes per second). Yet the ear cannot distinguish discrete sounds as fast as 30 per second. Furthermore, not enough different brief sounds are identifiable so that there is one for each phoneme. (In English there are about 40 phonemes.) An efficient sound alphabet, therefore, is hard to devise, and most phonemes cannot be perceived by a straightforward comparison of the input signal with a set of stored memories of phonemes.

For these and other reasons speech cannot be coded simply with one sound representing each phoneme. Studies of automatically recorded and hand-painted sound spectrograms indicate that the sound patterns for two similar phonemes, *e.g.,* "di" and "du," have common characteristics. The aspects in which they differ turn out to be quite unpredictable. The transition which distinguishes "di," when isolated from the entire pattern, sounds like a rapidly rising whistle or glissando on high pitches. That which distinguishes "du" is a rapidly falling whistle on low pitches. A person listening to ordinary continuous speech does not discern this to be true. Neither the "di" nor the "du" pattern can be cut at any point in time in such a way as to produce a pattern that sounds like "d" alone. At every instant the pattern conveys informa-

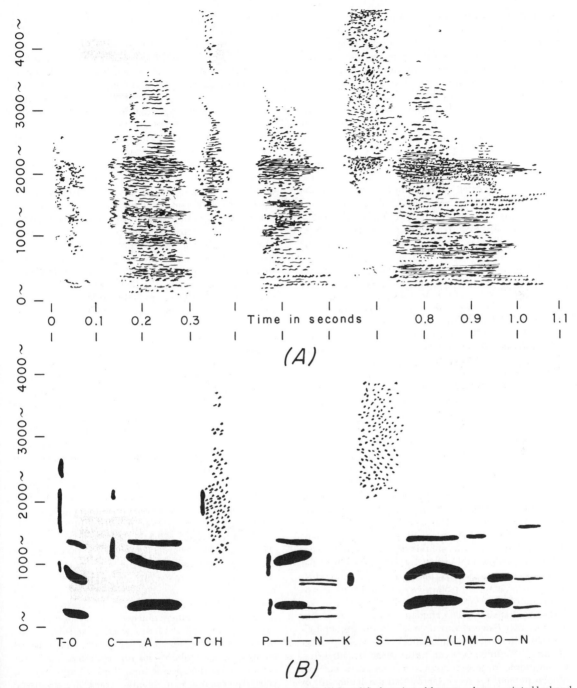

Fig. 8-5 Speech spectrograms. (*A*) Sound spectrogram of human speech. (*B*) Simplified version of the same phrase, painted by hand. Both of these spectrographic patterns are intelligible after conversion into sound by means of a pattern playback. (From A.M. Liberman, P. C. Delattre, & F. S. Cooper. The role of selected stimulus variables in the perception of unvoiced-stop consonants. *Amer. J. Psychol.*, 1952, **65**, 498. *Reprinted by permission.*)

tion about two phonemes—"d" and either "i" or "u." With some exceptions such as vowels which endure for relatively long periods, the coding of speech is generally as complex as the above specific example. Individual phonemes are drastically restructured and are often spoken simultaneously, being overlapped or "shingled" one onto another.

Six communication functions have been described by Sebeok:[153] emotive; phatic (the mere exchange establishing, prolonging, or breaking off of communication, or checking the openness of the channel); cognitive; conative (like calls to others, spoken and written commands, as well as nonlinguistic actions such as the clustering of small birds in a noisy mob, or behavior which points out a predator for all to see); poetic; and metalingual (rewording or translating one code into an alternative one). The first two occur in subhuman animal species. The second two probably do. The last two are exclusively human.

Ordinarily communication is a group process (see pages 537 to 539), although sometimes, as noted above, one organism may communicate to itself. Not only do people talk to themselves, but a single animal may mark his own territory and later recognize it because it has his scent. This is similar to writing a note to jog your own memory.[154] Visual, tactile, auditory, chemical, and possibly electrical signals among individual organisms can be decoded by various types of animals.

The use of language by human beings must be learned (see pages 420, 421, 440, and 441). Like perception of the environment, comprehending language is a complex information-processing function in which certain patterns of input signals are transformed to other patterns that represent them in the ensemble of an internal code of the nervous system. Each person uses his own set of meanings or semantic space, even for common words, which differs somewhat from the meanings of others.[155] This means one person cannot perfectly decode the speech of another. Studies of patients suffering from aphasia indicate that damage to the temporoparietal lobe of the dominant side of the brain (see pages 441 and 442 and Fig. 8-3) can render the patient unable to comprehend symbolic inputs and to carry out other linguistic functions.

Communication bands. Human beings and higher animals can receive and decode information which comes to them—often simultaneously—over different "bands."[156] On each band, information is coded in a way suitable for transmission over that particular sort of channel and for reception by that particular sort of transducer. Each band has its characteristic variables. Since multiple bands may be used simultaneously, supplementary and even contradictory messages can be received from the same source. When a watchdog growls and wags its tail at the same time, the interpretation is difficult.

Verbally coded messages travel on the auditory band, and so do expressive tones and sounds such as cries and whimpers and the sound communications of animals. Human speech also carries messages encoded in other ways than in words. When a contentless flow of recorded low-frequency (100- to 550-Hz) vowel tones is played, produced by filtering out the high-frequency sounds of consonants, which carry most of the cognitive information in speech, there is reasonably good agreement among judges on the speaker's emotional state.[157] With verbally coded meaning included or with it filtered out, voice samples can be reliably judged to convey either "aggressive" or "pleasant" feelings.[158] Singing, with or without words, also carries emotional content.

By postures, gestures, and other behavior, animals of many species transmit to other animals signals about their own internal states. The intention to communicate does not have to be present. Others of their own and often different species are able to decode such behavior. The "dances" of bees are an example of this (see page 440). The field of kinesics studies human communication, including decoding of messages conveyed by postures, gestures, and movements. In such analyses *kines* and *kinemes* are the units in place of the phones and phonemes of linguistics. Apparently the usual accuracy of decoding these expressions out of context and under controlled conditions is low.[159]

Another communication band, used by the blind and some others who read Braille, is touch. Persons have received Morse code by electrical stimulation of the skin at rates up to 50 characters per minute.[160]

Since perceptual classification is a first step in decoding of meaningful signals—they enter the central nervous system on one or another channel like any other input—the projection and association regions of the brain are obviously involved. In what sense are such signals meaningful? For one thing, they effect the control of various organismic activities. Chemical input signals and many such signals carried on other markers (*e.g.,* the visual channel for courtship displays and for particular mating colors and patterns of plumage) regulate fundamental activities of animal life—reproduction in all its phases, feeding, self-defense by flight or fighting, territorial behavior, and seasonal changes. They probably do this by influencing processes in the nonspecific and "limbic" systems and related endocrine components. These are discussed below (see pages 428 to 432).

Included among the *variables* of the process of decoding are: *Meaning of information which is decoded.*

Example: The cryptographer decoded the message and found that its contents were not really secret. *Sorts of information which are decoded.* Example: The naturalist suddenly realized the significance of the tracks in the woods. *Percentage of the information input which is decoded.* Example: John could identify half the objects. *Threshold of the decoder.* Example: Only a few molecules of the pheromone were lingering in the air, but the little bug knew a mate was nearby. *Changes in decoding over time.* Example: The old man no longer recognized his friend. *Changes in decoding with different circumstances.* Example: The reporter interpreted the governor's words much differently when he was speaking publicly than when he was chatting off the record. *Channel capacity of the decoder.* Example: The court stenographer could not take over 200 words per min. *Distortion of the decoder.* Example: The frightened child thought the rope was a snake. *Signal-to-noise ratio of the decoder.* Example: Because the spots on the leaf were about the same size and color as the fly, the frog almost missed a tasty morsel. *Rate of decoding.* Example: The simultaneous translator kept up with the speaker even at 250 words per min. *Percentage of omissions in decoding.* Example: Four of the ten words in the first sentence of the student's essay were illegible. *Percentage of errors in decoding.* Example: The ship's lookout failed to recognize two of the eight signal flags. *Code employed.* Example: The purchasing agent received written confirmation of the phoned agreement. *Redundancy of the code employed.* Example: The archeologist ascertained that the message on the stone was in three languages. *Lag in decoding.* Example: After 10 min the scout was able to identify the enemy tank, hidden as it was by the camouflage. *Costs of decoding.* Example: It took the signal officer 6 h to decode the message from the spy.

3.3.5 Associator, the subsystem which carries out the first stage of the learning process, forming enduring associations among items of information in the organism.

3.3.5.1 Structure Though associating at this level has been investigated by thousands of researchers, it is a remarkable fact that as of now the structure of the associator is not known for any organism. Both naturalistic observations and laboratory experiments indicate that fungi and plants lack the subsystem entirely.[161] Among animals even the quite simple nervous system of planarians appears to include this subsystem, though just what components are involved in it has not yet been discovered (see page 418). The greater the development of the cerebral cortex among vertebrates, the more important and presumably more extensive is this subsystem.

Not only wide areas of the cerebral cortex but sub-cortical and spinal components appear to be parts of the associator. The temporal and frontal lobes of the cerebral cortex, the hippocampus, and nuclei of the thalamus are possibly involved. The subsystem's components must be widely dispersed in the central nervous tissue since removal of no single center stops associating. Larger ablations of brain tissue have been found more damaging to associative learning than smaller ones.[162] It has been suggested than any network of sufficient complexity can exhibit adaptive behavior.[163] The peripheral parts of the vertebrate nervous system probably are not components of this subsystem.

3.3.5.2 Process To understand what is currently known about the associating process in animals and man requires review of a number of topics including the different sorts of learning and related phenomena; the conditions under which associating takes place and some of the important variables in the process; the various theories of learning; evidence for the locus of the process within the neural tissue; and theories of the physiological nature of associating.

The learning process in organisms includes associating and reading information into memory. The chief variables in the associating process concern the number and sort of repetitions of the information inputs, and the effects of these repetitions upon the ability of such inputs to elicit a new output. They may also concern the extinction of an output formerly elicited by such inputs. The primary variables of memory, on the other hand, relate to the conditions of storage and how they change over time, influencing retention, forgetting, and extinction. Forgetting is usually considered to involve gradual disappearance of stored information in the course of time, as opposed to extinction, which is more rapid active elimination of stored information by new information inputs that impinge on it.

Learning has been studied much more extensively than any other psychological process. Besides human subjects, individuals of a number of other species are used as subjects in experimental situations of various sorts. Planarians, earthworms, octopods, fish, pigeons, mice, rats, cats, dogs, and monkeys have been investigated in controlled researches, as well as many other species.

Sorts of learning. Several kinds of associative learning have been identified. These are differentiated by the design of the particular experiment and the nature of the information inputs (traditionally called stimuli) and outputs (traditionally called responses). Organisms are generally thought to be motivated to associate by receiving rewards, inputs to the organism of matter-energy or information that decrease strains (in other words, that reduce drives or satisfy needs, see pages 34 and 431); by avoiding punishments, which are stressful inputs of matter-energy or information that increase strains; or both.

(a) *Classical (type I) conditioning.* Classical conditioning, believed by some to be the paradigm for all learning (see Hypothesis 3.3.5.2-1, page 99), involves presenting an organism with an information input (the unconditioned stimulus or US) which elicits a definite, unlearned response (the unconditioned response or UR). The US is then paired with another information input (the conditioning stimulus or CS) which does not evoke this response. In Pavlov's pioneering studies in this field, the US was the sight and smell of food, presented to a hungry dog; the CS was the sound of a bell; the UR was the dog's salivation. In the course of a number of trials the sound of the bell came to evoke salivation in the absence of the sight and smell of food. Such salivation was the conditioned response (CR).

(b) *Instrumental (type II) conditioning.* In such learning the organism's behavior is instrumental in obtaining a reward or avoiding punishment (see Hypothesis 3.3.5.2-2, page 99). In this sort of experiment the CS, a light or other information input, is followed quickly with a reward, such as food, which the organism can obtain by some action, or a punishment, such as an electric shock, which it can avoid by making a specified movement, such as lifting a foot or paw. After one or more trials the input comes to elicit the reward-obtaining or punishment-avoiding action as a CR.

(c) *Operant conditioning.* This is a variation of type II conditioning in which there is no CS, and the response which becomes conditioned is not normally a UR to the US. For instance, a hungry subject may learn to press a bar to receive a pellet of food (the US) or to avoid a painful shock (another sort of US). Bar pressing is not a natural response (UR) to hunger or pain. It is one of many responses that occurs when an organism is placed in a restricted environment that includes a bar. This particular response becomes conditioned when the subject discovers that it, out of all possible responses, is the way to get food or avoid shock.

(d) *Trial-and-error learning.* This sort of learning is similar or identical to instrumental (type II) conditioning and involves repeated attempts to solve a problem. Many different sorts of apparatus can be used to establish such learning, including mazes; problem boxes from which the animal can escape to avoid punishment by learning how to carry out the necessary manipulations; divided areas in which one part is arranged to provide punishment, and the other is safe;

and discrimination apparatuses in which animals can obtain a reward or escape punishment by making a suitable response, such as jumping against one of two closed doors behind which is the reward.

(e) *Perceptual learning.* This takes place as the organism learns to decode aspects of its environment. There need not be an overt response, except to serve as a sign to the experimenter that the learning has taken place. Two inputs, such as a light and a bell, are associated with each other. This is an indispensable part of decoding, since organisms do not ordinarily depend upon a single input modality for classification of objects. The taste, color, smell, weight, and other characteristics are all interrelated. According to some theories the early learning of organisms must include developing perceptual associations and building up an internal "model" of the world.[164] It is said that this learning is acquired slowly but, once acquired, is markedly resistant to change later in life.

"Insight" learning is a kind of perceptual learning in which a subject's view of relationships among environmental elements changes quite suddenly, when a resolution of a previously difficult situation dawns upon him (see page 434).[165]

(f) *Verbal learning.* Many experimenters have investigated how subjects learn to associate words to other words or memorize lists of words, nonsense syllables, or meaningful material. The course of acquiring new symbolic concepts or other linguistic learning is also studied. This sort of learning chiefly concerns signals that pass through the decoder and encoder subsystems.

(g) *Learning of motor skills.* This sort of learning experiment focuses upon the motor subsystem as the organism acquires skills such as typing or controlling a specific sort of machine or apparatus (see pages 463 and 464). Because of its relevance to industrial and military activities, this is an active applied field as well as an academic discipline.

(h) *Autonomic conditioning.* Muscle tension, glandular secretion, change in size of the pupils of the eyes, blood pressure, pattern of heartbeat, rate of heartbeat, rectal sphincter control, and functions of other viscera under control of the autonomic nervous system can be conditioned by classical, instrumental, or operant methods. Some of these use "biofeedback," indicators of the current states of such autonomically controlled variables.[166] Emotional responses such as fear can also be conditioned.[167]

(i) *Conditioning of brain waves.* Operant conditioning of brain waves has been achieved in cats and people.[168] Human subjects can learn to control the appearance and disappearance, as well as the increase and decrease in frequency, of brain-wave alpha rhythms (see page 426). When instrumental conditioning techniques are used, human beings can also learn to change the amplitude of their brain-wave potentials which are evoked by brief tonal auditory inputs. In the experiments which demonstrated this, the subjects were rewarded with money for an increase in the amplitude of these potentials. Some subjects learn to produce such changes by imagining particular sights, sounds, or events. Evidently a subject can be conditioned by external feedbacks so that a high echelon of his decider influences a process which otherwise he could not control.

(j) *Learning to learn.* In experiments on this phenomenon the effects of earlier learning upon later learning of related problems are investigated. In one such research, monkeys were given a hundred comparable problems. They had difficulty with the earlier problems, but the later ones were learned rapidly or immediately.[169] Other experiments first provide subjects with practice on easier problems and then study their mastery of harder ones administered later.

One can take the view that only two of the above sorts of learning, *(a)* and *(b),* are fundamental. Certain scientists add *(c).* All other kinds of learning *(d), (e), (f), (g), (h), (i),* and *(j)* are special cases of the first two or three.

(k) *Imprinting.* This process is not considered by all theorists to be learning, but if not it is certainly a related sort of associating. It occurs particularly among birds and fish, but it is also seen in other species which have behavior patterns that are either present at birth or appear without learning as the individual matures. In imprinting, a brief exposure to a particular sort of information input at a critical period in the animal's life "releases" an appropriate behavior pattern and from then on that input always does so. Newly hatched chicks and ducks, for instance, have an innate response of following. This serves to keep them close to their mothers. If, however, another object is encountered instead of a mother bird during the critical period after hatching, the infants follow that instead, ignoring their mother. The association is permanent, an example of the principle stated in Hypothesis 3.3.5.2-4 (see page 99) that associations formed early in the life of a system are more permanent than those formed later. (This principle is also a basic tenet of the psychoanalytic conceptual system of Freud, who emphasized the permanent influence of infantile learning on later behavior.)

(l) *Related phenomena.* Association appears to take place also in the phenomena of habituation and sensitization (see pages 268 and 269). In the first, an organism responds to the onset of an information input, but as the input is continued, the response may weaken and disappear. In the second, an organism makes a greater response to an input because a previous input has been experienced. Habituation occurs in some simple creatures such as *Hydra,* a coelenterate.[170] Animals higher in the evolutionary series exhibit both sorts of association.

Conditions and variables of associating. According to most theories of learning, an animal will not learn unless it is *motivated* to do so (see pages 429 and 430). The list of motivating internal strains, and of the inputs which increase or decrease them, is long. Lacks of food or water are the kinds of stresses perhaps most frequently used to produce strains of this sort, subjectively experienced as hunger and thirst. Inputs of signals representing human approval, lack stresses of information inputs, and inputs of electrical signals to particular brain regions are also effective (see pages 431 and 432).

An important assumption of many learning theorists is that associations take place over time and build up as an organism experiences repeated instances in which the information input and response output are temporally connected. On any single trial, the feedback of a strain reduction (a reward) experienced or a strain increase (a punishment) avoided acts as a *reinforcement,* helping to strengthen the association bonds which are being formed, as Hypothesis 3.3.5.2-3 (see page 99) indicates. Learning theories of other sorts also ordinarily include reinforcement, although they differ in their explanations of how reinforcement facilitates learning. Changes in characteristics of the reinforcement, such as the magnitude, frequency, temporal distribution, and delay between the response output and the reinforcement, alter the rate, permanence, and other aspects of the association process.

Some theorists contend that learning can go on without reinforcement. Their view is that, in its usual environment, an organism continually carries on the associating process and stores an unspecifiable amount—some, perhaps all—of the associated information. Not all of it can be retrieved. It is difficult to identify the reinforcement in much of this process. In a laboratory situation, however, the necessity for reinforcement of the output responses which the experimenter wishes to establish seems to be beyond doubt. Ordinarily formation of associations requires not only such reinforcement but also feedback as to whether the newly learned output relieves strains or solves problems (see Hypothesis 3.3.5.2-3, page 99).

Many other sorts of variables affect the time-course and the distribution of errors in learning. Among these are various factors having to do with attention (see pages 426 to 428). The difficulty of the problem in relation to the organism's capacity, the suitability of the experimental apparatus to the organism's bodily structure, the form in which the input information is delivered, and the condition of the organism itself are all important. The overwhelming importance of meaning variables in learning of verbal material, even when the inputs are carefully designed to be nonsense, is evident in much recent experimental work.[171] How the inputs are decoded powerfully affects rates of learning. No generalization on error rates and time required for learning can be made across the various kinds of learning and the various species of organisms unless all the relevant variables are weighed. Single-trial learning certainly occurs in some situations, and in others an individual may have great difficulty or never succeed in learning some specific thing. As Hypothesis 3.3.5.2-5 (see page 99) postulates, the optimal ratio of correct trials to error trials depends on the probability that specific signals will regularly coincide in the system's environment. In all likelihood the optimal ratio increases as the probability of signals coinciding increases.

In a given situation, what items of information become associated? There is considerable disagreement, but probably in a single trial of a learning experiment signals from anything close in space or time to the reinforcement are associated with it. In further trials, however, the association narrows down to the "correct" signal that is unvaryingly related to the reinforcement. If an irrelevant or adventitious input is frequently present in the situation, it too may endure as a part of the association.[172] Associating can occur within the associator subsystem without any output, although output is of course required if the organism is to communicate to other organisms evidence that the association has occurred.

Associations occur between a number of different sorts of information items. For example, two kinds of inputs from a single object arriving over the separate channels of two different sensory modalities, *e.g.,* vision and smell, must be associated before they can become essentially equivalent in eliciting behavior. Or, in verbal learning, a name or word may be attached to a previously unnamed object or pattern of input signals. Or two words may become associated so that input of one brings about output of the other. Or stored information concerning previous experience with the same or similar inputs may be associated with an input, creating a pattern of associations which can be quite complex.

The various theories of learning. Learning theorists have long been divided between "associationists," including followers of Hull, Neal Miller, and Spence, and "structuralists," a group of scientists embracing a number of quite disparate theories, and including followers of Tolman, the Gestalt theorists, and Hebb.

A *stimulus,* as defined by Hull, is an event in the environment which activates a receptor. A *response,* to him, is a pattern of motor or glandular behavior. As I noted in Chap. 2 (see page 34), "matter-energy input," "information input," "matter-energy output," and "information output" are preferable terms because they state explicitly what sorts of transmissions are involved. At times psychologists do not make it clear whether a stimulus or a response is a matter-energy or an information transmission.

The simplest theoretical interpretation made by Hull as to how learning occurs is that synaptic connections are made, establishing a channel from the input neuron through an intervening central neuron to a neuron running to the effector muscle fiber or gland. Although this is admittedly oversimplified, it has been diagramed on many a blackboard to explain conditioned responses based upon spinal reflex arcs.

The conditioned response, however, is always different in many ways from the unconditioned response. The conditioned response, in an intact organism at least, always requires a more complex pathway than a spinal reflex arc. It is an integrated and apparently voluntary act involving both spinal and higher neural centers. A paw, for example, is lifted just enough to avoid an electric shock, rather than jerked in a reflex movement. What is more, in at least certain situations no movement is necessary during the learning period. Rats can learn an avoidance response by being moved in a transparent cage so that they can see the route to follow to avoid a punishment, even without running it themselves. Thus, learning occurs without repeated transmission of signals over the neural channel, which some theories assume to be necessary to establish the requisite synaptic connections. After a rat has learned to run a maze, it will use quite different motor components than were used during the learning trials, even crawling or rolling to the goal if for any reason it is incapable of running.[173] The same output neural channels cannot possibly be involved. Perceptual learning is another sort of associating that does not fit any simple stimulus–response paradigm, because such learning can take place without an overt response.

Learning theories vary in their assumptions about what processes (or intervening variables) relate inputs to outputs. Beginning with Hull, elaborate, precisely formulated theories have been developed which specify what precise positive relationships exist among the amounts of *reinforcement,* strengths of *habits,* and increments in the *stimulus–response bond* (see page 491).

The theories have been elaborated to explain complex behavior, including human symbolic, verbal, and social responses. The intervening variables are not assumed to correspond directly to any known neural process or structural change.

Instead of emphasizing the stimulus–response bond as the associationists do, structuralists conceptualize *cognitive maps, schemata, Gestalten, hypotheses,* or *reverberating circuits* as being developed in the organism as a result of repetitions of a given input pattern. These configurations connect inputs from environmental events with outputs providing appropriate behavior patterns but not necessarily a specific motor response. It was asserted by Hebb that some neurons in a network receiving repeated similar information inputs will develop "reverberating circuits" which form permanent "cell assemblies" (see pages 413, 419, 484, and 485).[174] Except for theories which rely on reverberating circuits and the Gestalt theories which depend on changing electrical fields in the brain, the structuralists do not specify the neural bases of the processes they discuss. Some structural theories have had difficulty explaining how the "cognitive structures" or configurations they hypothesize are translated into behavior. It is said of Tolman's theory, for instance, that it left his rats "lost in thought."

The theoretical work of Mandler helps to unite the associationist and structuralist positions by describing a hypothetical process by means of which stimulus–response associations could contribute to the formation of "cognitive structures."[175] According to his theory, the initial response to an information input is a *differentiating response* which may be verbal, motor, or symbolic. Without such a response, one input cannot be distinguished from any other. If two inputs were to evoke the same differentiating response, they would be perceived as identical whatever their effects upon the input transducer of the organism. If the input is a complex pattern, each of its aspects evokes a separate differentiating response. Organisms come to an experimental situation with a repertoire of separate responses which become integrated into a response pattern suitable for the new situation. Previous learning, therefore, facilitates acquisition of a response to the novel situation. In the course of this integration, trial-and-error behavior may occur, and inappropriate responses may be eliminated. After the behavior responsive to the new situation is built up, the discrete aspects of it meld into a single functional unit which is elicited as its component responses were in the past. At the same time a *central analogic structure* develops which can function independently of the overt response. This is then available for potential application to future new situations. If a number of such central analogic structures are available and relevant to a new input, they can be tested one after another by covert trial and error without actual performance of the associated responses. They function like the hypotheses or schemata which some believe constitute steps or "subroutines" in the solutions of problems. Learning of new concepts, under which future inputs can be classified, may also be explained as involving such central analogic structures.

Neural locus of associating. Although many current learning theories focus upon the input–output transfer processes of an organism in a learning situation and make no explicit hypotheses about the concomitant neural events, some facts are known about these processes in the nervous systems of organisms.

The capacity for higher mental activity, including the more advanced sorts of learning, is greater in the species with the more complex nervous systems. The relatively simple planarians are capable of making the associations required for classical conditioning, for learning the correct pathways in mazes with as many as six choice-points, and possibly for conditioned avoidance of a bright light.

Octopods, which are cephalopod molluscs with well-developed image-forming eyes, actively pursue their prey. They readily associate reward (food) or punishment (electric shock) with objects, among which they can discriminate on the basis of shape, size, and other tactile or visual characteristics. These creatures make both conditioned approach and conditioned avoidance responses, and they can also apply experience gained in solving an easy problem to more difficult ones, a capacity which is unusual in invertebrates.[176]

Vertebrates, with their more elaborate neural structures, can learn more complicated relationships. In learning to solve comparable single concrete problems, however, they do not greatly outshine invertebrates. Higher mammals do not form associations any more speedily than their humbler relatives.[177] In situations requiring an application of prior knowledge to new problems, however, there is an evolutionary progression. Primitive marmosets and squirrel monkeys are much slower in such learning than the advanced rhesus monkeys. Young animals are less adept than adults. Rhesus monkeys do not develop their full capacity to do such learning until the second or third year of life.[178]

Vertebrates such as frogs, kittens, and puppies can apparently be conditioned even when all their neural centers higher than the spinal cord are rendered inactive.[179] Possibly maturation in these species eliminates this capacity, since conditioning has not been found in older animals with only the spinal cord functioning. Nor does spinal conditioning appear in human patients who live for many years after a spinal transection.

Simple conditioning and conditioned avoidance responses definitely can occur in decorticate laboratory animals, but trial-and-error learning requires the cortex.[180] In higher primates, including man, fine motor control depends upon the cerebral cortex (see page 426). Verbal learning is also dependent upon intactness of the higher telencephalic centers, both motor and sensory, and is readily disturbed by brain injuries or disease. For any sensory modality, disturbance of either the input channels carrying information into cortical centers or the motor channels required for execution of the response will interfere with a learned behavior without necessarily destroying any learning "center." Destruction of decoding centers of any sensory modality also makes learned discriminations based upon the sense affected difficult or impossible, depending upon the site or extent of the damage (see page 403).

Cutting the corpus callosum and other cerebral commissures connecting the left and right sides of the brain interrupts learning by preventing transfer of information from one side to the other.[181] The functioning of such "split brains" has been studied in various animal species, including man (see page 414). In experiments using visual inputs, it is necessary to cut not only the corpus callosum but the optic chiasma as well. (Both these structures convey signals between the left and right sides of the brain.) When this is done, information inputs to one eye are not transmitted to both sides of the brain. For example, when one eye is masked, only the hemisphere on the side that receives the information inputs sets up the association necessary for discriminating a square from a circle. When opposing associations exist on opposite sides of the brain, the animal appears to experience no conflict. When the sides are trained at different times, the side trained second gains no benefit from the earlier experience. Simple brightness discriminations are accomplished over channels that cross at the collicular commissure below the corpus callosum; thus they are not affected by the operation mentioned above.

Neither normal afferent inputs nor a functioning motor subsystem are required for a conditioned motor response. A conditioned leg flexion can be set up by stimulating sensory and motor areas of the brain with the peripheral motor tracts temporarily inactivated.[182]

Activity of the cat's brain during acquisition of a conditioned avoidance response to a light flickering 10 times per second has been investigated by John and Killam. These researchers studied recordings of brain waves in electroencephalograms (EEGs) made with electrodes implanted in various regions of the brain.[183] When the cat was being familiarized with the light, high-voltage "frequency-specific" waves occurred in the visual cortex, the auditory cortex, the lateral geniculate, the superior colliculus, and the hippocampus. The frequencies of these waves were at the same 10-per-second rate as the input light, or at multiples or submultiples of that rate. These rates made it possible to trace signals related to the light input against the other background activity of the brain. Occasionally such potentials occurred also in the tegmentum, the septum, and the amygdala. After 19 to 21 days the flickering light no longer evoked such potentials. As conditioning of shock to the light began, the general electrical activity of the brain increased and high-voltage, frequency-specific waves were recorded from all the above parts of it, except the amygdala and the hippocampus. Before any avoidance responses were made, during the period when the cats were showing "conditioned emotional responses" such as growling, cringing, and defecating, the generalized activity of the brain diminished and was replaced by intense and persistent frequency-specific waves in the visual cortex, the reticular formation, and the hippocampus. They were absent in the superior colliculus and auditory cortex and diminished in the lateral geniculate. During early conditioned avoidance responses, the change was not great, but the response of the reticular formation became less discrete and regular. By the time there was a well-established conditioned avoidance response, the responses became stable. There were high-voltage frequency-specific responses in the lateral geniculate body and high-voltage slow activity in the superior colliculus. The visual cortex responded at a multiple of the flicker frequency. There were sporadic frequency-specific waves in the auditory cortex. Activity in the reticular formation decreased. The fornix showed some frequency-specific response. Somewhat higher amplitude activity was seen in the amygdala, and frequency-specific responses no longer appeared in the tracings from the hippocampus, although the amplitude was higher. By the time the flickering light elicited conditioned avoidance responses every time it appeared, it always also instigated bursts of 40-per-second waves in the amygdala. The anterior ventral nucleus of the thalamus for the first time acquired marked frequency-specific responses to the light. Electrical patterns in the visual cortex were only slightly altered. Frequency-specific responses showed increased amplitude in the lateral geniculate body, and slow waves from the superior colliculus were also enhanced. Responses at the frequency of the flickering light were further decreased in the reticular formation and were no longer recorded from the auditory cortex, the fornix, the septum, and the hippocampus.

These findings are important in indicating what brain structures are involved in the learning of a conditioned avoidance response to light inputs. They also give us some understanding of what patterns of processes occur in these centers as the conditioning is going on. But we still understand little about the structural basis for the associating process in any species of organisms.

Physiological nature of associating. What structural alterations take place during the associating process? There is ample provision in the central nervous system for information from all neural structures to be brought together in nuclei and cortical areas and for integrated information composed of items from many pathways and subject to many influences to interact. Current theories frequently assume that association alters certain synapses or other components within nuclei and other centers that receive information from multiple channels, making them more likely to conduct particular signals rather than other ones. If this is so, then associating may be widely dispersed throughout the nervous system. One such theory, which I have already mentioned, concerns reverberating circuits of neurons that form permanent cell assemblies (see pages 411, 419, 484, and 485). Many Soviet scientists maintain that signals pass out over all the channels leading from centers which receive information inputs. They take a course between the region of the unconditioned stimulus and that of the conditioned. Then two-way connections are formed which build up neuron chains. They consider verbal and symbolic learning to depend upon "reflexes" in higher brain centers and upon the "second signal system," speech, which is conditioned to these reflexes.[184] It is hypothesized by John, whose work with Killam was described above (see page 412), that a dominant focus or aggregate of neurons which repeatedly are active at the same time, organizes so that it tends to discharge as a unit. When different dominant foci are active simultaneously, they similarly become interlocked into a set of foci.[185]

I discuss elsewhere (see pages 270, 271, 417, and 418) whether the passage of information over synapses produces discoverable changes in them. This question is particularly relevant to problems of information storage.

Representative *variables* of the process of associating include: *Meaning of information which is associated.* Example: The poodle had learned that the opening of the refrigerator door signified that he was about to be fed, so when he heard it open, he ran to his dish. *Sorts of information which are associated.* Example: The dog associated the input of auditory information to the information from internal transducer components in its raised paw. *Percentage of the information input which is associated to other information.* Example: When the rat completed learning the task, it jumped only at the door marked with a red square. *Changes in associating over time.* Example: As the association became established, the sheep raised its hoof only enough to avoid the shock. *Changes in associating with different circumstances.* Example: The cat pressed the bar with its head when its paws were immobilized. *Channel capacity of the associator.* Example: The girl could learn a maximum of 15 nonsense syllable pairs to a criterion of two correct repetitions every 15 min, and her channel capacity for associating must have been at least as fast and possibly faster than this. *Rate of associating.* Example: The sound of a bell was associated with the presentation of food once every 30 s, and the dog began to salivate to the ringing of the bell on the ninth trial, so associating must have occurred at least within 270 s. *Lag in associating.* Example: It took 20 experimental periods before the planarian began to associate information inputs from the correct arm of the T maze to the feedback information from the reinforcement of the reward. *Costs of associating.* Example: The dog expended a great deal of energy during each training session.

3.3.6 Memory, the subsystem which carries out the second stage of the learning process, storing various sorts of information in the organism for different periods of time.

3.3.6.1 Structure   There is no evidence that fungi and plants have this subsystem, but even quite lowly animals do. The structural basis for the memory of animal organisms is being investigated vigorously, but exactly what it is has not yet been demonstrated. A number of theories are current, each of which has some experimental support. In Chap. 6 (see page 271) I have considered those which concern structural change at the cell level. There is also evidence that structural changes at synapses or in interneuronal patterns in various centers, brought about by information previously input to the organism, are involved in memory storage (see pages 270 and 271).

Although it is still unknown in exactly what structural form memories are stored, the regions of the body essential to the process have been identified in many species. In animals with highly developed nervous systems these are components of the central nervous system. Planarians, however, evidently do not need their head ganglia or central nerve cords for memory storage, since all parts of their bodies retain information after they are cut and allowed to regenerate (see page 418).

Four pairs of lobes of the brains of octopods are concerned with memory, two pairs for visual information inputs and two pairs for tactile.[186] Neural channels pass to these from the input transducers of the modality which they serve and from transducers of taste and perhaps pain. There are also channels to motor centers. These two components of the memory are so distinct that one can be removed without disturbing the other.

Some regions of the mammalian brain are important to the general process of memory, as distinguished from specialized types of memory, e.g., for language. These are probably not storage regions for the accumulation of a lifetime's memories, and indeed no component which stores all of an organism's memories has been identified. The particular regions probably related to memory in mammals include the hippocampus; the fornix (the main tract carrying information downward to the thalamus and the hypothalamus as well as nonspecific fibers upward to the hippocampus); the mammillary bodies (hypothalamic nuclei); some nuclei of the medial thalamus (dorsal medial and pulvinar); the floor and sides of the third ventricle, a fluid-filled cavity in the brain (see page 415) which is bounded by the fornix, the hypothalamus, and the thalamus; and the temporal lobes of the cerebral cortex. Some other areas, such as the amygdala, the hippocampal gyrus, and parts of the frontal lobes may also be important for memory. Many other brain centers and tracts, including the corpus callosum and regions serving particular input modalities, belong to other subsystems but can affect memories of certain sorts. Specialized memory for language is related to the temporal lobe of the dominant hemisphere. The involvement of the dominant hemisphere has been confirmed in "split-brain" human patients.[187]

3.3.6.2 Process Reading into storage (recording or memorizing), maintenance in storage including loss from storage (retention and its opposite, forgetting), and retrieval of information from storage (remembering or recognizing) in organisms have been extensively studied in a number of species. Theoretical positions, experimental findings, and behavioral observations will be considered for each of these in turn.

In order to carry out the information storage processes known to exist in organisms, a component must meet several demanding criteria, among which are the following. Some percentage of the information which is processed by an organism, after a period of reading

into storage, fixation, consolidation, or circulating in a limited capacity channel, must be retrievable after considerable periods of storage. This storage, since it may be retained for many years—in some persons as much as a century—must enjoy impressive invulnerability to the shocks and trauma which can beset a nervous system. The storage is not "dead," since subsequent events can interact with it. Yet under some circumstances the original record may become available. The storage and retrieval processes cannot always be accomplished over exactly the same neural channels, since even the most practiced performance of verbal recall or motor action sometimes shows variation. Retrieval from the store must be rapid, for use in the information processing of both input and internal information. This is a big order, but the information storage of organisms does this and more.

(a) *Reading into storage.* The hippocampus is a region that is essential for the recording of memories.[188] If it is removed bilaterally from a human patient, an operation which has been done occasionally as a last resort in certain cases of uncontrollable psychomotor epilepsy, the patient is permanently unable to record any new information. A less radical operation, leaving more hippocampal tissue, produces a lesser deficit. The relationship of the hippocampus to other brain components is such that it receives information from cortical areas and has a major input from the nonspecific areas of the brainstem and diencephalon. The channels over which inputs of the various sensory modalities, except olfaction, reach the hippocampus after processing in the cortical projection and association areas are largely unknown. Tracts carrying olfactory information have been demonstrated to pass to the hippocampus, which was classically regarded as a center for smell. In man, its removal does not affect the discrimination of olfactory information.

The temporal lobes of the cerebral cortex are also important structures for memory. Unilateral loss of this component usually does not cause permanent generalized memory disturbance, but bilateral ablation has produced a patient who lived for a number of years with no recording of experience.[189] Sectioning the fornix also has permanently affected recording in some patients, although others have had no ill effects from such an operation. A patient in whom the fornix was congenitally absent had no defect of memory.[190]

As the total amount of information input into a brain goes up, both the brain weight and the depth of the cortex increase. As compared to control rats kept in isolation, significant increases of this sort occurred in rats which had opportunities to explore an interesting environment, to sense the sights and sounds of a busy laboratory, and to train in mazes, discrimination boxes, and exploratory boxes.[191] This change has been attributed to an increase in the number of glia and dendritic processes of neurons or of microneurons, which are small neurons that send their axial processes to other neighboring neurons rather than entering tracts leading to other brain regions. Another variable of information input, the extent to which rats are handled during infancy, was also found to influence brain growth. Such growth occurs in the cerebellar cortex, the dentate gyrus of the hippocampus, and the neocortex.

Korsakoff's syndrome is a set of pathological changes which occurs in chronic alcoholics and some other patients, probably as a result of a vitamin deficiency. It produces a disturbance of reading into memory as well as other severe symptoms.[192] A typical patient is almost totally unable to retain new information. Isolated facts in incorrect chronological order are usually the most he can remember. Autopsy discloses lesions of the medial thalamic nuclei (dorsal medial and medial pulvinar) in all such cases. Other lesions are found in the mammillary bodies and in some other hypothalamic and midbrain sites. Both the mammillary bodies and the hypothalamic nuclei in question receive significant inputs from the hippocampus. In one group of patients studied the hippocampi were not affected in Korsakoff's syndrome, but some other cases have been reported in which there was bilateral destruction of the hippocampus.[193] A patient whose mammillary bodies were destroyed by hemorrhage lived seven years without recording a single memory.[194]

Tumors in the floor and sides of the third ventricle have also produced defects in reading into storage.

Neurosurgeons sometimes make electrical inputs by electrodes to the brains of patients who are awake and unanesthetized. Local anesthesia is used on the scalp and skull in approaching the brain, and no pain is felt from the inputs, because the brain does not signal pain. The process of recording memories is arrested if the electrodes touch the hippocampus and some surrounding structures, such as the amygdala and hippocampal gyrus—both of which are closely related by connecting tracts with the hippocampus. A patient receiving such electrical inputs has no recall for the period during which the inputs continue.[195] Electrical activity in the hippocampus during learning was discussed above (see page 412).

Some drugs, including scopolamine or hyoscine, used to produce "twilight sleep" during childbirth, have a similar effect. Under the influence of this drug, the patient appears to be awake and to feel pain but later has no memory of the experience. Reading information into storage can be arrested by many other agents, all of which decrease the electrical activity of the central nervous system. These include trauma, electroshock, severe cold, rapid induction of ether or barbiturate anesthesia, acute anoxia, and focal epileptogenic lesions.[196] Most epileptic patients have no memory for events during a seizure.

The length of time it takes for information to be read into storage can be altered by several drugs. These include protein synthesis inhibitors, like puromycin and acetoxycycloheximide, an RNA synthesis inhibitor, actinomycin D (see pages 418 to 420), strychnine in doses too low to produce convulsions, picrotoxin, amphetamine, 1757 L.S., thyroxin nicotine, caffeine, potassium, and physostigmine. Adrenocorticotropic hormone has also been found to bring the performance of slow-learning rats up to that of more rapid learners. All these substances increase neural excitability. Doses of barbiturates too low to put an animal to sleep, calcium, nonanesthetic concentrations of ether, carbon dioxide, lowered concentrations of oxygen (hypoxia as contrasted with anoxia), and "spreading depression" in the brain inhibit neural excitability and reduce the rate of learning.[197]

Studies of human verbal learning (including reading into storage) disclose that, when a small amount of material (digits, nonsense syllables, or words) is presented so briefly that the subject does not have time to rehearse and memorize it, the subject can usually recall it if asked for a report immediately. A number of variables affect this ability. If, between the time the subject is shown the information and the time she or he is asked to repeat it, other information inputs enter the channel, the original information may be partially or completely lost. If new information does not intervene, the original can be retained for some time without loss.

This recording of briefly presented material is affected by a number of other variables. The number of items which can be apprehended in a single brief exposure is limited. It is variable with the sort of material used and, of course, from subject to subject. The rate of reading or of recognition and naming are important variables.[198] When "chunking" occurs (see page 61), the number of items that can be stored is greatly increased because the subject can organize the field immediately into, for example, 7 groups of 3 items each; whereas without this arrangement the 21 separate items would be beyond the maximum that can be apprehended in a single brief exposure. In storing verbal inputs, their meaning is important since meaningful material is more readily stored than nonsense syllables.

Storage is also dependent upon a number of organismic variables which were discussed above (see pages 409 and 410), upon organismic states such as alertness, and upon relevance of the material to the organism's needs. The attention-commanding characteristics of the inputs are also important (see pages 426 and 427).

Recent evidence suggests that recording of memory takes place over a period of time. The input information is not read into storage during the activity generated by exposure to it in the training situation. Rather it occurs after a lag during which the animal returns to a resting state or at least enters a different situation. Studies on memory in goldfish support this (see pages 418 to 420). If electric shock or protein synthesis inhibitors—such as puromycin or acetoxycycloheximide—are administered after a training session, they disrupt the recording process. By keeping a goldfish in the training tank, one can delay this disruption to a much later time than it would occur under the ordinary procedure of returning the fish to rest in its home tank immediately after the training session.[199] In these animals apparently something about remaining in the situation inhibits the development of firm memory traces. I shall consider the implications of some of these findings below (see pages 419 and 420).

(b) *Maintaining information in storage.* At present there is no unequivocal evidence that there is any region of the central nervous system which is specialized as a "library" or information store. The ablation of no single part can eliminate memory. Different habits, including verbal and symbolic ones, are disrupted by various sorts of damage to the nervous system.

The spinal cord of some animals evidently can store some sorts of information, as I indicated in Chap. 7 (see page 340).

The role of the hippocampus in the recording of memory has already been discussed (see page 414). Bilateral resection of the hippocampus also affects established memories retroactively, sometimes back over several years. Nevertheless, and remarkably, really distant memories are retained, as they are in the aged with arteriosclerosis of the brain.[200] Bilateral temporal lobe ablations also have produced loss of established memories. Since the hippocampus appears not to be the repository of memories, its role in information storage must be accounted for in some other way. Its relationship to both input sensory and limbic components suggests that its function may be adding "significance" to or "stamping in" or amplifying the signal.[201]

Studies of the typical electrical rhythm of the hippocampus, the 4- to 7-Hz "theta rhythm" (see pages 412 and 426), which shows characteristic variations during the learning process, indicate that these discharges

may be involved in the induction of biochemical modifications in neurons.[202] As learning progresses, the widely distributed, irregular theta frequencies become restricted, and the amplitude and frequency of the theta rhythm become regular. During the stage of reading into storage of a learned response, theta waves in the hippocampus lead those in the adjacent temporal lobe. In the well-trained animal, when the conditional signal can be assumed to evoke recall, the temporal relationship is the opposite, a fact suggesting that information flows in the reverse direction, from the temporal lobe to the hippocampus. This communication may be a phase comparator, carrier wave, or comparison generator against which information-bearing signals arriving over different channels can be matched.

Electrode studies carried out by John on animals during the course of acquiring a conditioned response have revealed activity in various parts of the brain (see pages 412 and 413). When the input is an intermittent signal with a characteristic rate of repetition, activity at this rate is taken as evidence that processes of the component are influenced by the presentation of the input.

During conditioning such activity appears between presentations of the stimulus in parts of the brain not specific to any input modality. What is more, during an experiment, when the animal mistook a flicker of the wrong rate (6 Hz) for the correct one (10 Hz), the recorded electrical activity in the visual cortex, reticular formation, and hippocampus corresponded to the 10-Hz signal—even though such a signal was not present. When the reward did not appear, the response in these areas came into correspondence with the signal which was actually being experienced. The 10-Hz waves were attributed to "stored temporal patterns of response established during the conditioning procedure."[203] The inappropriate electrical rhythms appeared to be released from the stored information in the memory of the animal. The experimenter suggested that a coincidence-detection process achieved recognition of the sensory input by comparing the input and internal signal patterns. Spontaneous performance of conditioned responses is often preceded by strong neural rhythms at the frequency of the absent conditioned stimulus.

Investigations have been made of what brain regions are affected by protein synthesis inhibitors which block information storage. Recently acquired information was permanently lost, Flexner, Flexner, and Stellar found, when one day after the memory had been stored, puromycin was injected into both temporal lobes of mice.[204] The distribution of a dye which was injected with the puromycin made it clear that the hippocampus and entorhinal cortex were affected. In order to erase memory after 11 to 60 days, it was necessary to inject those areas plus much of the rest of the neocortex, including the ventricular area and the frontal cortex.

Studies on human epileptic patients during operations have indicated that the temporal cortex between the primary visual and auditory areas was the only part of the brain where the remembered experience which they reported could be elicited (see page 421).[205] This is not the storage area for this information, however. Damage to the temporal lobe results in aphasia, *viz*, disturbance of the ability to use language, but not loss of memory. Damage to the frontal cortex in primates disturbs memory. This results from effects upon processes of other components besides the memory subsystem, however (see page 437).

Except in storage of verbal and certain other kinds of materials, what is stored on one side of the brain is evidently communicated to the other side. It is uncertain whether the information stored on the opposite side of the brain is as complete a record as that on the side on which it was originally presented. When an epileptogenic lesion is artificially produced in rabbits, with no damage to the opposite hemisphere, a similar focus develops on the uninjured hemisphere after a period of a few days to three weeks. This second focus is dependent at first upon the primary one, but in time it becomes independent, so that removal of the primary focus does not eliminate the abnormal discharge on the second side.[206]

In what form do organisms store information? What do they store? Where do they store it? Current theories include those which consider the form of storage to be (a) some alteration of the neural net or (b) coding in macromolecules. Some theories combine these, considering the early stages of memory to be pulses in neural nets whereas long-term storage is in macromolecules. All these theories have experimental and clinical support. All present difficulties.

Nerve nets as storage devices. I have already discussed the possible changes in neurons which would alter a nerve net's connectivity after the basic pathways were laid down genetically (see pages 270 and 271). Also I have reviewed some of the evidence for electrical activity in particular parts of the brain during recording (see pages 412 and 413). Storage of information for extended periods certainly does not depend upon continuous neural activity, because the stored material is not erased when all bioelectric activity is stopped by cooling or when all brain circuits are made refractory simultaneously by intense electroconvulsive shock.[207] Any theory which postulates that the bioe-

lectric activity of the brain is the storage process, therefore, must include other processes as well, specifically some which involve structural change at some level—organism, organ, cell, or nonliving organelle or molecule.

Theories of neural-net alteration in information storage include (a) those which emphasize primarily electrical field effects in the tissue and (b) those which concentrate upon the synaptic connections among neurons.[208]

Changes in brain-wave patterns in different parts of the brain, particularly in the hippocampus, during learning (see pages 412 and 413) and the effects of various agents which alter the electrical activity of the brain have been discussed. In order to serve as storage, such alterations would have to be based on some structure in such a way that they could be reconstituted after disruption, or else the stored information would be erased.

Alterations in the nerve net of an organism, assumed to take place in information storage, are often said to consist of new connections among previously unrelated channels (see page 413). Another sort of change which must occur at the same time involves inhibiting pathways other than the one chosen for reinforcement. At first an animal in a new situation makes a great many motions of various sorts, all of which are in its repertoire of genetically programmed or previously learned movement patterns. As the new learning takes place, the required movement, which may be the output of a verbal symbol, is refined, so that it is made more precisely and economically. Irrelevant or ineffective movements drop out, inhibited by control circuits within the nervous system. Much learning is of this sort.[209] One kind of alteration of a neural net which could provide storage is the development of association or interconnection of masses of neurons which then could be activated simultaneously. No single neuron is irreplaceable in such a scheme, since many others act when it does and will continue to act whether it does or not.

Simulations of neural networks have been published (see pages 485 and 486), and their properties include many processes which are found in nervous systems, including storage of information.

The fastest postnatal growth of the brains of mammals comes when young animals are storing memories rapidly (see page 470). Studies in a number of different species have shown that growth in size and weight of the brain is brought about by increase in dendritic processes of neurons, addition of new glial cells, and development of undifferentiated cells into microneurons.[210] The larger neurons which carry out most of the information processing of the nervous system do not divide after the brain is formed. The short-axoned neurons, which may act as regulatory or associative interneurons, are the last components of the nervous system to develop.[211] They are most prominent in phylogenetically higher organisms and are being studied as possible information storage components.

Evidence for macromolecular storage of information in organisms. The first experimental linking of RNA with storage of information was the work of Hydén, who discovered that rats which had learned a difficult route to a food cup, one which involved balancing on a wire and climbing upward, had an increased amount of RNA in the large Deiters' neurons of the lateral vestibular nucleus, as compared with normal controls which had remained quietly in their home cages and had not learned this skill.[212] Littermates which had received an increased vestibular input by being passively rotated but had been given no special training had an equivalent increase in RNA, which apparently reflected the activity of neurons. These functional control animals, however, had no change in the proportions of the nucleotide bases in the RNA (see page 217), although the experimental animals did. The neurons of the rats that had the learned balancing and climbing skill had a different composition of RNA nucleotide bases than either group of controls. Changes in the quantity, but not the proportions, of the nucleotide bases in glial RNA were also found.

Researches on learning in planarians have also pointed to RNA as related to the process of storing memories. These animals can regenerate as many as 50 complete worms from tiny morsels of a single individual.[213] When a trained animal is cut into several pieces, regenerates from the pieces retain the learning of the original animal to a significant extent. Furthermore, worms which have eaten trained worms, according to McConnell, also acquire some of their training, as measured by the number of training trials they require to reach criterion in the same tasks.[214] If, however, the regeneration takes place in a weak solution of RNase, an enzyme which breaks down RNA, the transfer of learning does not occur.[215] Furthermore, when RNA is extracted from trained animals and injected into untrained ones, the latter worms are superior to uninjected controls.[216]

The possibility that injection studies using higher animals would produce a similar result occurred to a number of experimenters. McConnell, who with Thompson did the original work on learning and memory in planarians, extended his researches to rats and has reported significant results, as do some others.[217]

It thus appears that RNA has something to do with storage of information in organisms. These experi-

ments do not, however, prove that it is the storage molecule. Certain researches on organism retention of information indicate that protein must be produced if storage is to occur. The production of protein, of course, involves RNA.[218] A number of substances which are known to block protein production have significant effects upon the course of memory storage in organisms, particularly in its early stages (see pages 271, 415, and 419). The antibiotics puromycin and acetoxycyloheximide, when injected intracranially into goldfish, according to Agranoff and his associates, block such storage if injected immediately after the fish is trained to swim out of a small pool in order to avoid electric shock. They do not block it if injected an hour or more later. Some environmental variables significantly alter this time. If these chemical compounds are injected prior to training, the fish can learn the required shock-avoidance behavior but will later be found not to have read this information into long-term storage. The antibiotic actinomycin D, an inhibitor of RNA synthesis, also impairs memory in goldfish, but its mode of action is not yet known.[219]

A similar set of experiments with mice also showed effects upon recording of memory.[220] Puromycin injected into brain tissue of the mice blocked the recording of memories. Unlike the fish, the rats showed symptoms of toxicity and decreased alertness, so that testing for memory had to be delayed until they recovered. After recovery they were again trainable, a state indicating that the effects were not caused by permanent brain damage inflicted by the procedure—although lesions were left in the brain. Acetoxycyloheximide injected into mouse brains inhibited protein synthesis in a way different from that of puromycin, but it did not affect recording or retrieval of memories.[221]

Acetoxycyloheximide injected subcutaneously into mice in large doses blocked retention 6 h after training but affected neither the original learning nor the retention in the first 3 h.[222] This large dose made the mice sick, but the onset of symptoms was delayed long enough for training to be carried out, and the survivors recovered within two or three days and could then be tested. The advantage of this experimental method is that it avoids localized brain damage and increased intracerebral pressures.

That substances which block protein synthesis affect memory storage appears to be established. A number of research reports have been interpreted to indicate that puromycin exerts its effect by altering the electrical activity of the hippocampus, known to hamper memory recording, rather than by inhibiting protein storage.[223] The possibility that puromycin's effects upon recording result from its producing abnormal brain waves, such as occur in epilepsy without overt seizures, was tested by combining it with an anticonvulsant.[224] This diminished the memory loss. That resulting from acetoxycycloheximide, however, was not affected by use of an anticonvulsant. One puzzling finding that raises questions about the significance of the above studies is that simply inserting a needle into the hippocampus in mice and injecting nothing can produce a loss of memory.[225] Also injection of physiological saline up to two months after the injection of puromycin restores the memory.[226] The fact that subcutaneous injections of puromycin block memory storage answers the objection that its effects result from local mechanical changes in the brain. But if puromycin produces abnormal brain waves, that effect could cause the observed memory loss, rather than its chemical effect in blocking protein synthesis.

Stages in memory.   Newly stored information is easily disrupted by other information inputs or by alteration of neural processes. Information which has been in storage for some time is much more stable. These facts suggest that *short-term* and *long-term* memories are stored by different processes. Briefer sorts of information storage, such as *very short-term* memory or the *visual image,* which exist for only a second or so, have also been described.[227] Short-term memory stores information until it is read into the long-term storage. It is often conceived to be a continuation of the neural activity which took place as the information was originally processed—"reverberation" of the neural pathways or circulation through some sort of circuit. Short-term memory cannot definitely be said to be lost permanently after electroconvulsive shock to the brain until many hours have passed, since it has been reported that memories of training "lost" after 25 h reappeared in 48 to 72 h.[228] Evidently noise introduced into the channels finally disappeared. Apparently, short-term memory is a limited-capacity channel which holds information only until new information enters to displace it.[229] The durations considered as "short-term" in psychological experiments are much shorter than those in the physiologically oriented work in which electrical and chemical activities of the brain are disrupted after learning. The psychological experiments deal with seconds or minutes; the physiological are concerned with hours and days.

Long-term memory is ordinarily considered to involve one of the structural changes discussed above. The change is considered to be induced by the bioelectric processes of the brain involved in processing the information to be stored and in holding it in short-term storage. An alternative view is that short- and long-term memory are two manifestations of the same process. The greater vulnerability of short-term memory can be explained by the greater fragility of new traces as compared with older ones. It may be that they need more time to be recorded, *i.e.,* more fixation or consolidation time.[230] Perhaps the vulnerability results from interference by later inputs.[231]

Three stages of memory, in addition to the bioelectrical activity which accompanies the learning, have been identified in an ongoing research program of Flexner and his associates (see page 416).[232] (*a*) The initial stage consists of bioelectrical activity which maintains memory even though protein synthesis is inhibited. Such memory can be disrupted by electroconvulsive shock. During this period, Flexner and his associates suggest, memory is based on changes in the concentrations of ions or small molecules or the location of preexisting macromolecules. When puromycin is given before training, memory is not durably read into storage. With acetoxycycloheximide, however, there is an initial period of variable length (up to 14 h in mice trained immediately before receiving the antibiotic, 3 to 5 h in mice trained after receiving it) in which memory is durably recorded in spite of severe inhibition of protein synthesis. (*b*) The second stage is one of temporary loss of memory, although capacity for performance is not impaired and relearning is possible. During this period memory perhaps exists in a form which cannot be given overt expression without protein synthesis. (*c*) The third stage takes place at least 20 h after protein synthesis again becomes normal, 58 to 96 h after training. By then memory is durably recorded. It can be read out and overtly demonstrated by performance of actions which the animal was trained to carry out.

Stages in the development of memory in goldfish have also been identified in Agranoff's ongoing research program. He and Davis found that short-term memory and maintenance of formed long-term memory do not appear to depend on processes blocked by puromycin, that is, upon protein synthesis. When puromycin was injected 1 min after training ended, the loss of memory was not immediate but developed more than 6 h later and was complete in 18 to 72 h.[233] A period of reading into storage, which begins shortly after and not during the 40-min training session, is inferred from these findings. The process of reading into storage is inhibited by puromycin. In goldfish acetoxycycloheximide also has this effect. Actinomycin D, which does not interfere with protein synthesis but does block RNA synthesis, also keeps memories from being read into long-term storage. Agranoff and Davis speculate that the chemical processes in long-term memory are similar to the growth processes which occur in cellular reproduction and differentiation.[234] They also point out that short-term and long-term memory stores may be similar, even though the processes by which they are formed differ. Recording may represent the establishment of a cellular metabolic process which preserves memory as it is formed during training.[235]

In what form are memories stored? Speculation of Hydén, whose work I have already discussed (see pages 271 and 418), explains and integrates much experimental evidence concerning information storage.[236] He divides the storage and retrieval of learning into three sorts.

(*i*) The first is the expression of genetically controlled, complex behavior patterns, such as the behavior of a capricorn beetle larva which bores a chamber twice as big as itself in which to undergo metamorphosis, so that it will not be crowded as an adult, and which also lies with its head toward the entrance because otherwise, as an adult, it would not have room to turn around in order to emerge. Hydén suggests that such information storage may be accomplished by neuron-glia units containing specific proteins and differing from other units in RNA composition.

(*ii*) The second sort involves processes like those by which an animal learns what to do in a new situation. Learned information of this sort, Hydén suggests, may be stored in parts of the genome which are not involved in genetic information processing, being activated by some process similar to that operating in target cells that hormones can activate. This could be initiated by the bioelectrical activity of the brain. The DNA affected would produce specific RNA, which would be the template for producing specific proteins. Such a process would be activated by bioelectric input signals like those which had originally initiated the synthesis of the specific proteins. The proteins may be stored in cell membranes, Hydén suggests.

(*iii*) For the third sort of storage and retrieval we have no experimental evidence. This includes insight learning, problem solving of a complex sort, and such higher mental processes. It might involve a "permanent change of information-rich macromolecules during the life cycle."[237]

Some early speculations about memory assumed that brain cells might store one bit of information each, reading it out on an appropriate signal by either emitting a pulse or not. Such a view leads one to compare the number of brain cells with the number of bits of information which a man is likely to acquire during a lifetime. The brain does not contain enough neurons for each one to store only one bit.[238] But the storage capacity of the nucleic acids in cells is very great, quite sufficient to account for any known memory requirement (see page 222).

In analyzing the significance of the delay in memory fixation of the goldfish, Agranoff and Davis have speculated about the form of memories. They say:

Let us take the view that has been provided by evolution, that only those attributes which lead to survival have meaning and therefore reflect information storage. The only information which a brain possesses consists of those responses that have survival value and those insufficiently lethal to be selected against. Memory function is then the evocation of responses which arose during phylogenesis. DNA very likely stores the blueprints for expression of memory as is believed to be the case for the evocation of immunological and developmental potentialities. When an experimenter attempts to train an animal, he is attempting to evoke a preprogrammed response which arose in the natural environment during that animal's evolutionary development. When investigator, subject, and apparatus coincide successfully, the scientist observes that his subject is "smart" and the experiment is "working."

During acquisition, or learning, the organism rapidly selects a response which has been coupled to a motivational input. This connection decays unless it is conserved as long-term memory. The physical nature of the new neural patterns is unknown. It is commonly described in terms of new synaptic connections which first reverberate and then become fixed. The possibility that short-term memory "reverberates" for two days in the goldfish demands reconsideration of present concepts of the nature of short-term memory.

The environmental effect described above may shed light on relevant physiological factors in the development of long-term memory. What might be the significance of this observation in terms of survival? We can imagine that the fish has several physiological states of activity such as rest, flight, food searching, etc. It is obvious that the fish has preprogrammed or instinctual templates of predators, the presentation of which generates increased response. Perhaps there is a built-in program in the fish which says "when you receive the visual pattern of a predator, become agitated." Agitation or excitement serves to provide possible escape responses in the natural environment and thus leads to survival. The program also says "If the predator pattern, and, therefore, anxiety disappear, fix those most recent sensory-motor patterns and use them first the next time the same visual input occurs." Thus memory for the individual can lead to survival under the special conditions of that individual's environment.[239]

Storage of language in people must require a far more elaborate program than storage of an avoidance response, although there is no reason to suppose that the process is different physiologically. What is known about how language is encoded (see pages 438 to 442) gives some light on storage also. Some linguists conceptualize storage of verbal associations in the same stimulus–response terms in which conditioned responses are classically described.[240] Verbal associations, in this view, constitute habits and clusters of associations known in learning theory as "habit family hierarchies," just as other sorts of learned behavior do. Storage and retrieval of these involve the same variables as do storage and retrieval of other information.

In verbal learning, content and order information are stored either separately or differently. If a human subject is given a list of words to be learned, each one paired with a word from another list, he will learn to respond to each word with the one it is paired with but will usually not be able to recite the pairs in order.[241] Instructions to remember the order will result in that being stored also.

Some clues to the sort of classification procedure by which experience is stored in human beings can be gained from studies made on conscious epileptic patients during brain surgery.[242] After studying many such patients, Penfield suggested that an information input can be related by cortical conditioning to an output in such a way that similar inputs in the future will elicit the same output. He described a patient whose attacks were precipitated by episodes of "grabbing." The first attack followed an incident when he snatched a stick from the mouth of a dog and threw it. A "ganglionic record" corresponding to a "classified file for grabbing," Penfield speculated, was being kept, and each new similar input was being recorded. He maintained that a man recognizes a friend because he has stored a neural record of many different past experiences with the friend. The memory is a generalization of these.[243] This neurological formulation by Penfield is similar to the structuralist learning theories. His neural record is much like the cognitive maps and schemata of the structuralists (see page 411).

(c) *Loss and alteration during storage.* Even if, as some speculate, every input leaves a permanent trace in the nervous system, much of what goes in cannot later be retrieved and is in effect lost. When a conditioned information input is presented repeatedly to an animal but the usual reward does not follow, the appropriate output becomes less and less likely to occur. Finally the output is no longer elicited. This result is referred to as extinction. After this, however, retraining ordinarily takes less time. Well-practiced conditioned responses evidently are represented in the nervous system by lasting traces which can be reactivated. Extinction is unlike the loss of conditioning produced by administration of antibiotics such as puromycin and acetoxycycloheximide, which presumably prevents traces from ever being permanently recorded in the nervous system.

In 1885 the orderly curve over time of forgetting of nonsense syllables was reported by Ebbinghaus.[244] The major amount of loss occurs in the first few hours, and subsequently the rate of loss is progressively slower, a general relation which Hypothesis 3.3.6.2-1 (see page 99) proposes to be a cross-level principle. Psychologists attribute this loss to interference from new information inputs rather than to decay with the passage of time. One evidence of this is that less is lost if the subject sleeps during the time between the original learning and the recall. Interference is variably effective, depending upon the nature of the intervening information inputs. Many variables of the forgetting process, particularly in human verbal learning, have been investigated and their parameters defined.

Information is altered in various ways while in storage—*e.g.,* omissions, errors or additions of noise, and distortions—resulting from processes of selection, reorganization with other stored information, interpretation, and entropic decay of organization, all of which conforms to Hypothesis 3.3.6.2-2 (see page 99). Traces appear to be modifiable by subsequent inputs, so that new significance can be attached to previous experiences, and progressive changes in recall occur. The distortions that produce disagreements in testimonies of eyewitnesses to accidents have been attributed to the way in which the input information was coded for storage.[245] Such variability, which depends upon the whole previous experience of the witnesses, arises from distortions when information is read into storage and does not arise from anything that happens in storage. But a person's memories do change over time to reduce internal strains. This can be demonstrated by comparing what one person recalls with the memories of others or with objective evidence as to what actually occurred in the past. We commonly remember selectively events that put us in a favorable light and we forget (or repress, in psychoanalytic terminology) those that shame us or are painful to us.

Other changes seem to involve a sort of decay or simplification of the information during storage. When subjects were asked to reproduce material at intervals after it was read, heard, or seen, in general the form and style of the most immediate reproduction persisted in succeeding reproductions, but there was a progressive tendency to simplify, to omit details, and to transform the patterns into a more convenient form.[246] Since the nature of traces is still unknown, the precise sort of changes which they can undergo cannot be understood at present, nor can their activation in retrieval be comprehended. It is clear, however, that the absence of memory, as in an elderly patient, predictably alters his later behavior, the effects increasing as the amount of memory loss goes up (see Hypothesis 3.3.6.2-3, page 99).

(d) *Retrieval from storage.* Activation of neural traces by inputs similar to those which originally formed them is usually assumed to be the "readout" process in theories ascribing memory to change in the neural net. How readout could be accomplished from molecular storage is still unclear (see page 271).

The output transducing of stored information is the only indication now available to observers that it has been stored. This output may be a motor or other effector response, a display of the physical indications of emotion, a verbalization, or a symbolization of the information in some other way. The conditions of retrieval of many different sorts of information have been extensively studied. A large number of variables both in the organism and in the situation have been shown to be important in the process, including the degree of motivation of the subject, the relevance of the material to the organism in a particular situation, the position of items in a list of retrieved memories, associations among the items in such a list, the meaning or lack of meaning in the material retrieved, and grammatical and semantic relationships.

At times, what appears to be forgetting is merely a temporary unavailability of information for retrieval under particular circumstances. Further search may make the stored information available.[247] Relationships among items of stored information affect its retrieval. Recall of stored material is facilitated in experimental situations when words to be remembered at any one time all fall into the same cognitive category—*e.g.,* trees, cities, sports, or birds.[248] On the other hand, interference results if words from different categories must be recalled at the same time. Cues as to which category information is stored under, perceptual or logical, facilitate retrieval.

The context (*i.e.,* the time, place, and stated task) in which an association is made is important in recall, since a record of it apparently is stored along with the content of the association.[249] Subjects who have been trained to associate a list of words ordinarily restrict their responses during recall to items from within that list, even though words in the list are strongly associated with other words outside it.

Once a person has begun scanning his memory store for a name or other word, the process can continue for hours or days outside his awareness. Often the desired item is finally located. At times the discovery occurs long after the search has been called off, frequently in response to some accidental cue.

Hypnosis, free association as used in psychiatry, and such drugs as sodium amytal (so-called "truth serum") are known to facilitate retrieval. How they do this is unclear. The psychoanalytic concept of *repression* assumes that an active inhibitory process keeps particular sorts of stored information out of consciousness except when such special aids to retrieval are used. Inhibitory processes that interfere with retrieval have also been suggested as responsible for extinction of a conditioned response after a series of unreinforced trials.[250]

Representative *variables* of the process of remembering include: *Meaning of information stored in memory.* Example: The man remembered that the curve in the path meant he was halfway home. *Sorts of information stored in memory.* Example: The old ewe knew where the best feeding grounds were. *Total memory capacity.* Example: The worm was able to learn a six-choice maze but no maze more complicated than that. *Percentage of information input stored.* Example: The subject could remember only 6 of the 12 items presented in the tachistoscopic exposure. *Changes in remembering over time.* Example: The old man could not recall whether he had eaten lunch, but he remembered many details of his youth. *Changes in remembering with different circumstances.* Example: When the boy was speaking German, he put the verbs last. *Rate of reading into memory.* Example: The actress memorized on the average about six pages of script per hour. *Lag in reading into memory.* Example: The information gained in the training session was not recorded until the goldfish reached its home tank. *Costs of reading into memory.* Example: It took the student more than a dozen hours to memorize the muscles of the back. *Rate of distortion of information during storage.* Example: The witness' story of the accident changed the most during the first few hours. *Time information is in storage before being forgotten.* Example: The elephant never forgot. *Sorts of information retrieved.* Example: The woman could not remember his name, but his face was familiar. *Percentage of stored information retrieved from memory.* Example: John got halfway through the poem and then could not remember the rest. *Order of retrieval from memory.* Example: The child reported the events exactly as they had occurred on the night of the murder. *Rate of retrieval from memory.* Example: It took the subject about 2 s to recall each of the 10 word pairs. *Lag in retrieval from memory.* Example: Robert had to think for several minutes before he could begin to tell the plot of the opera. *Costs of retrieval from memory.* Example: The effort of remembering all the details of the horse race left the old tout exhausted.

3.3.7 Decider, the executive subsystem which receives information inputs from all other subsystems and transmits to them information inputs that control the entire organism.

3.3.7.1 Structure   In plants this subsystem consists of differentiated tissues which produce hormones (see page 470). This more primitive sort of control structure is present in even the most highly evolved organisms. In the ascending phylogenetic scale of animals, more and more neural components are superimposed on those previously in existence.

Components of the decider are evidently widely dispersed in the endocrine and central neural tissue of higher organisms. Much is still unknown about the structure of this most crucial of organism subsystems. Deciders of higher mammals include as components some axons (probably components of the organ decider subsystem); the pituitary gland and other endocrines; ventral-horn nuclei of the spinal cord, motor nuclei of all parts of the brain, and cortical motor areas; nuclei of preganglionic autonomic pathways and those parts of the cerebral cortex which send axons into them; all or many nuclei of "nonspecific" and limbic areas, of both ascending and descending tracts

as well as their cortical representation areas; and nuclei and cortical areas of the cerebellum (see Fig. 8-6). These endocrine and neural components are organized into echelons which can be conceived as corresponding roughly to the commonly recognized divisions of the central nervous system. Each echelon influences decisions over most or all segments of the body, from head to tail.

Hypothesis 1-1 (see page 92), which states the general proposition that living systems with more components tend also to have more echelons, appears to be true of organisms. It is in general true, both if organisms are compared to living systems at lower levels and also if simpler organisms are compared to higher organisms. Hypothesis 1-2 (see page 92), the proposition that the more different types of components a system has, the more segregation of functions there is, seems also to be true in general.

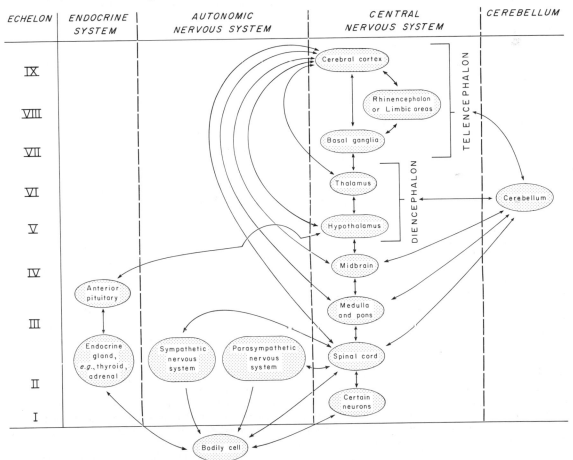

Fig. 8-6 Echelons of the decider subsystem of higher mammals.

In the course of phylogenetic development of animals, the components making up each higher echelon appeared as evolutionary novelties in a species which previously had been complete and capable of surviving without them (see pages 466 to 468). As these new components were added, neural tracts developed to connect them with lower echelons of the nervous system, forming new special pathways for particular sorts of information. The highest echelon, the cortex, has direct connections with almost all the echelons. The close relationships of each group of thalamic nuclei with particular parts of the cerebral cortex are examples of this, and so is the close relationship between the hypothalamus and the prefrontal cerebral cortex.

The distinctions among the echelons of the organism's decider cannot be made precisely, and in rare cases a lower echelon seems to wield some superordinate control over a higher one. The activities regulated by higher echelons seem to be more finely adjusted and more complicated, as well as less localized to a single subsystem, than those governed by lower echelons, but these generalizations have obvious exceptions. Nine echelons of the mammalian decider subsystem are listed below (see Fig. 8-6).

I. Certain neurons. These are neural cells, found in plexuses in the wall of the gut (see page 336) and perhaps associated with blood vessels, in which axon reflexes occur. For instance, the presence of food in the gut is sufficient to initiate a signal to such a neuron in the myenteric plexus in the wall of the gastrointestinal tract. Cells like this, or others with which they synapse, elicit contraction of the smooth-muscle cells of the gut at that point by axonal reflexes. This peristalsis can be carried out even when all input and output nerves to the gut are cut.

II. Endocrine glands (e.g., the thyroid or adrenal gland, but not the anterior pituitary), sympathetic and parasympathetic cells, and spinal cord neurons. These all send signals directly to bodily cells and in some cases also receive signals from them. These signals control processes in these cells. A well-known example is the spinal reflex arc. A drop of acid placed on the leg of a frog will cause that leg to contract even though the spinal cord is separated from the frog's brain.

III. Medulla, pons, and anterior pituitary gland. Breathing and many other reflexes are ordinarily regulated by this echelon. Such processes can continue even when the brain above is inactivated. The anterior pituitary is the "master gland."

IV. Midbrain. Reflexes fundamental to many bodily functions are controlled by midbrain components. For instance, the pretectal nucleus in the midbrain receives input signals from the optic tract and outputs command signals controlling accommodation of the eyes and light reflexes.

V. Hypothalamus. Eating in response to hunger and drinking in response to thirst are examples of processes controlled at this echelon (see pages 432 and 456).

VI. Thalamus (including epithalamus). A wide range of emotional and affective responses are controlled by this echelon. So are reflexes involving salivation, secretion of gastric juice, and peristalsis.

VII. Basal ganglia. This echelon carries out major functions in the control and maintenance of proper tone of the skeletal musculature generally.

VIII. Rhinencephalon or limbic areas. Responses elicited by olfactory inputs, among others, are regulated by this echelon.

IX. Cerebral cortex. Actions and cognitions which appear voluntary, and which human beings report they are aware of and are carrying out voluntarily, are controlled at this echelon.

Intermediate between the other endocrine glands (Echelon II) and the hypothalamus (Echelon V) is another echelon, the *anterior pituitary* (see Fig. 8-2). This gland appears to exercise control over all the others, often by two-way negative feedback loops, *e.g.,* between it and the ovary.

The cerebellum controls bodily movements and some autonomic processes by interacting over direct tracts to other neural components of all echelons from II through IX.

Artifacts of this subsystem include calculators and computers.

3.3.7.2 Process This section describes the organism's processes, reviewing first the functions going on at each of the several echelons of the organism's decider. It then deals with the control of the various degrees of alertness of the organism, ranging from concentrated attention to sleep, and the neural correlates of these states. Then it reviews what is known about the four stages of decision making in organisms, particularly human beings: (*a*) Establishing purposes or goals and the emotions involved in this, (*b*) analysis, (*c*) synthesis, and (*d*) implementing the decisions.

Of these processes, the best understood are those that direct automatic subsystem adjustments, such as those which maintain posture or control components like the heart. The opposing actions of the sympathetic and parasympathetic branches of the autonomic nervous system in control of the viscera and other components which they innervate are discussed below (see page 455). Least understood are those exclusively human activities such as artistic creativity or long-range planning. These latter have up to now been most effectively investigated in psychological studies, since the neural components that carry them out are still unknown.

Information from a number of different sources flows together in nuclei and other neural centers. The outputs from these components are the results of logical processes or computations carried out by the interactions of inhibitory and facilitatory impulses at the synapses within them (see page 262). Alpha motor neurons in the ventral-horn motor nuclei of the spinal cord, for example, receive information inputs from internal transducers in the muscles which they innervate (see pages 375 and 376), from tendons and joints, from the skin of both sides of the body, and from transducers in other muscles with which the innervated muscle is associated in movement patterns. Signals are also received from internal transducers in visceral organs. The motor signals which cause skeletal muscles to contract result from integrations of input and internal information, stored genetic behavior patterns, and stored experiential information which are made higher in the nervous system.

Deciding processes at the various neural echelons. As higher animal species have evolved, they have layered one echelon of control after another on top of the decider components of lower species. This characteristic of phylogenetic development is called encephalization. As a result, in human beings higher brain echelons, such as the neocortex, can on occasion take over control of processes usually regulated by lower echelons, *e.g.,* heartbeat and brain waves (see pages 408 and 409). Transection at any point releases lower components from the influences of those above and produces characteristic alterations in the motor outputs. The decider components which control the motor subsystem in human beings are arranged in several such layered echelons. As indicated below, a transection of the spinal cord at one segment affects a person's or an animal's ability to move in quite a different way than transection at another segment.

All the central nervous system decider components for the spinal reflexes required for posture, locomotion, and certain defensive actions are present in the ventral-horn nuclei and the local circuits within the spinal cord.[251] The organization of the cord itself is similar in all vertebrates, but with the increasing importance of the higher centers in the more advanced species, motor functions become more and more dependent upon them. With good nursing care a human being can regain some reflex activity below a spinal transection, but little useful motor function can be salvaged. Studies of functions of the isolated spinal cord are therefore done on laboratory carnivores, which recover to a greater extent from a spinal transection, after an initial stage of shock.

A dog whose spinal cord is separated from other components of the central nervous system can stand when placed upon its feet and can rise from sitting to standing. It tends to collapse, however, and it can neither make motor adjustments which depend on balance sensation nor right itself when it tumbles over. Such a dog can withdraw a part of its body from a painful input. It retains simple reflexes and some complex ones, like raising a hind foot to scratch near a stimulated spot.

At each successive higher echelon of the nervous system, more information from inside and outside the organism is brought to bear on decisions. When the medulla is present and functioning, a greater degree of coordination of the spinal reflexes occurs than in the spinal cord alone. When the central nervous system is transected above the pons, information from the labyrinths and the pontine reticular formation is able to affect reflex motor activity. The connections from the fastigial nuclei of the cerebellum to the reticular formation bring in proprioceptive information which has been processed in the cerebellum. Animals with high transections of this sort exhibit "decerebrate rigidity." Their spinal reflexes are facilitated.

With the midbrain intact, visual information can influence reflexes, and proprioceptive, cutaneous, and subcutaneous information can be correlated with it. Inputs from the cerebellum to the red nucleus have important effects at this echelon. Righting reactions occur. They are dependably present when the subthalamic nucleus is preserved. Animals with central nervous systems transected immediately above the midbrain have decerebrate rigidity.

An animal with its diencephalon intact but with higher neural centers not functioning makes active clawing, jumping, and running movements. Information from hypothalamic centers adds emotional aspects to its behavior, such as lashing of its tail and raising of its hairs. Violent "sham-rage" reactions occur (the term "sham" is used because, lacking the cortex, the animal is assumed not to feel rage). They differ significantly from the patterns of rage behavior in intact animals.

Motor centers in the telencephalon include those in the basal ganglia and cerebral cortex. The basal ganglia in human beings function differently from those of animals which lack the pyramidal system. These nuclei, in human beings, are part of the extrapyramidal system for motor control. Lesions in them produce a variety of disorders of movement, including tremors and overactivity. Functions of the basal ganglia can be deduced from the effects of disease or damage, but there is little direct evidence about them from experimental studies because they are not present in many lower species, and research on them in human beings is rarely justifiable. All pyramidal and most extrapyramidal motor tracts originate in the cerebral cortex,

The primary motor cortex sends many, but not all, of its fibers through the pyramidal tract. Secondary cortical motor areas also contribute to it. Interruption of the pyramidal tract causes more severe deficits in primates than in lower mammals and more in such advanced primates as chimpanzees than in monkeys. Some skilled movements are lost: the fine motor activity of the fingers, for example. A monkey with its pyramidal tract transected can climb and hang on the wires of its cage but may have trouble in letting go.

Bilateral removal of the area around the precentral gyrus of the cortex in the monkey produces an animal which moves stiffly and is no longer able to use its hands and feet in the delicate tactile adjustments typical of the species. Instead, there is a reflex grasp on heavy contact with the palm or sole.[252] The cerebral cortex must be functioning in higher animals if they are to make movements which appear voluntary or carry out complex cognitive decision making. The entire nervous system is, of course, necessary for the smooth and integrated performance of all parts of the motor subsystem.

Control of other sorts of processes in organisms, those regulated by the autonomic nervous system, for example, is exercised by multiechelon structures. The highest control centers for some of these processes are below the cerebral cortex. When the connections are cut between the peripheral portions of the autonomic nervous system and the central nervous system, the organ components innervated by the autonomic nervous system can still function fairly well. But the autonomic system is not truly independent in its functions, for signals from the central nervous system alter its processes, integrating them with those of the total organism.

Regulation of states of neural activity. On one occasion, an input to a component of the input transducer or the internal transducer will elicit an output, while on another it will not. This difference in response results from the fact that operating characteristics of neural channels alter from one time to another. These variations are brought about by activities of decider components in the organism's own central nervous system.

A continuum of states, from deep sleep at one end to strong, excited emotion at the other, is responsible for observable differences in the input–output relationships of organisms, the full range of states occurring only in higher vertebrates (see Table 8-3). It takes a more intense or otherwise more compelling input to provoke an output from a man when he is in deep sleep than when he is awake. Sometimes the provocative input can be an almost imperceptible sound, if it is inappropriate to its setting, like someone moving

about in what should be a silent house. Activity of the motor subsystem is markedly different in sleeping, relaxed but awake, alert, and excited people. Internal information processing also varies from dreams, during sleep, to daydreams, to logical connected thought, to the disorganized confusion characteristic of extreme excitement. The electrical activity of the brain as revealed in the "brain waves," is quite similar in species from frogs to human beings, varying from one state of alertness to another.

At any time during the life of an organism an electrical potential exists between two electrodes placed at any two different parts of the scalp.[253] The potential between the two electrodes oscillates rhythmically, the recording of these oscillations being the electroencephalogram (EEG). The dominant rhythm is the *alpha rhythm,* at frequencies between 8 and 13 Hz in adult organisms. The alpha rhythm of human beings appears during relaxed wakefulness when the eyes are shut. This becomes faster and more irregular when the subject looks at something. Specific excitation of input transducers or increase in alertness or vigilance makes similar changes in the rhythm. In general, with some exceptions such as the activity during deep sleep, decreased levels of vigilance are associated with more regular, slower rhythms that are *synchronized.* The electrical activity recorded in the EEG arises from the synaptic potentials of the cortical cells. If the intensities of these potentials increase in unison in a region of cortex around an electrode, they are synchronized. They become desynchronized when vigilance increases.

Besides the dominant alpha rhythm, particular regions of the brain have characteristic rates of activity. In man, the motor cortex has a spontaneous resting rhythm of 18 to 24 Hz, the range known as *beta rhythm.* A *theta rhythm,* which is at 4 to 7 Hz, is normally found in the hippocampus. It is more prominent in rabbits and cats than in monkeys and men.

Attention. The gradations between deep sleep and excited activity are all variations in general responsiveness of the nervous system. Another sort of nervous system regulation is attention, which favors one category of inputs over another in an organism that may be in any state from sleep to excited activity. An organism *attends* to information flows over one particular channel or from one source rather than others. We all know what is meant by "attention" when a student says "I wasn't paying attention and so I didn't hear." Yet neither an unequivocal description of the behavior involved in attention nor a satisfactory account of what goes on in the nervous system is available. The essential aspect of attention is its *selectivity.* The particular information commanding attention is transmit-

TABLE 8-3   States of Awareness and Electroencephalographic, Subjective, and Behavioral Correlates

State of awareness	Electroencephalogram	Subjective characteristics	Behavioral efficiency
Strong, excited emotion; fear, rage, anxiety	Desynchronized: low to moderate amplitude; fast mixed frequencies	Restricted awareness; divided attention; diffuse, hazy; "confusion"	Poor: lack of control, freezing up, disorganized
Alert attentiveness	Partially synchronized: mainly fast low-amplitude waves	Selective attention, but may vary or shift; "concentration"; anticipation; "set"	Good: efficient, selective, quick reactions; organized for serial responses
Relaxed wakefulness	Synchronized: optimal alpha rhythm	Attention wanders—not forced; favors free association	Good: routine reactions and creative thought
Drowsiness	Reduced alpha and occasional low-amplitude slow waves	Borderline partial awareness; imagery and reverie; "dreamlike" states	Poor: uncoordinated, sporadic, lacking sequential timing
Light sleep	Spindle bursts and slow waves (larger); loss of alphas	Markedly reduced consciousness (loss of consciousness); dream state	Absent
Deep sleep	Large and very slow waves (synchrony but on slow time base); random irregular pattern	Complete loss of awareness (no memory for stimulation or for dreams)	Absent

SOURCE: D. B. Lindsley. Psychological phenomena and the electroencephalogram. *Electroencephalog. & clin. Neurophysiol.*, 1952, **4**, 445. Reprinted by permission.

ted clearly and in detail. The organism is unaware or less completely aware of other inputs or other internal information, although much of it may be available for later recall. A woman who is concentrating on internal information, such as a poem she is writing or a pain in her stomach, is often unaware of other persons talking nearby. A student who is immersed in reading ignores internal information like a full bladder or an empty stomach until the signals become urgent. A message transmitted to one ear can be selectively attended to in spite of competition of other information flowing into the other ear, and it is even possible to sort out separate messages on the same channel, attending to one and not the other. Experimental study of these selective responses to input has clarified some of the variables important in the process (see page 448).

When something occurs in the environment which is of interest to an animal, it becomes alert, its postural muscles tighten, and the accessory components of its input transducers are directed toward the source of inputs. Ears prick up, eyes open widely, and gaze is fixed. The nose twitches as the animal sniffs. This behavior was described by Pavlov as the "orienting" or "investigatory" reflex.[254] It has its parallels in human behavior, although the pricked-up ears and twitching nose are not typical human responses. The EEG change is similar in all species. The "activation" pattern involves desynchronization of the electrical activity, either diffusely in all regions of both cerebral hemispheres or localized to specific regions of the cerebral cortex related to the inputs.[255] The response is either tonic, *i.e.*, slow signal termination maintaining wakefulness over long periods of time; or phasic, *i.e.*, rapid signal termination producing sudden brief shifts of attention in response to changes in inputs.

Information inputs are more effective in bringing about arousal (and commanding attention) if they are, among other things, intense; spatially extensive; moving; changing; novel; heterogeneous; repeated a few times; contrasting in color, pattern, or in other ways; or complex, *i.e.*, high in information content.[256] Decreased rates of information input lower the degrees of arousal and attention. Monotonous inputs repeated many times have the same effect. This has been tested experimentally. Waves characteristic of arousal appeared in a cat's EEG when a brief tone was presented. When it recurred, the duration of the sign of arousal became shorter until it was limited to the period of the tonal input. By the thirty-seventh trial it disappeared.[257] Tones of different pitch—new information—evoked it full-blown again. Throughout the entire experiment, EEG potentials in the auditory cortex indicated that the auditory inputs were being processed by the cortex. Some research with human subjects suggests that electrical potentials in the brain change as attention changes.[258]

Sleep. When an animal's brain receives neither any signals representing compelling internal strains or drives nor any exciting or interesting inputs from the environment, it often becomes drowsy and falls asleep. Sleep is also a normal part of the diurnal activity cycle (see page 454). Sleep is a positive process, not simply absence of waking activity in the brain. There appear to be at least two different depths of sleep, light and deep. The EEG patterns and behavior of the sleep are different in each. Light sleep may be related to the phenomenon called "internal inhibition" by Pavlov.[259] This is learned inhibition of response which, when it is established in experimental animals, appears to radiate and become generalized in the brain so that the animal actually drops off to sleep in the experimental situation.

In deep sleep, the muscles relax, heart rate slows, and blood pressure falls. The organism is hard to arouse. Paradoxically the brain-wave frequencies are faster than in light sleep, in some ways similar to those in the waking state. These rapid frequencies may indicate that dreaming goes on in deep sleep.

Neural structures in which processes change as states of arousal alter. The components and processes responsible for regulation of alertness are not completely understood. Although the EEG records the electrical activity of cortical neurons, the rate and synchronization of their rhythms are controlled by the ascending component of the mesencephalic reticular formation and the nonspecific nuclei of the dorsal thalamus.[260] The impulses are transmitted to the cortex over the thalamic projections, either directly or by relay through basal ganglia or limbic components. EEG arousal and wakefulness can be achieved either by electrical inputs to the channels carrying signals from input transducers or by direct inputs to the reticular formation of the medulla, pons, and mesencephalon.

Arousal also results from direct stimulation of thalamic and hypothalamic nuclei. The multisynaptic, multisensory connections in the reticular formation provide the pathways for inputs which elicit arousal and produce responses, such as the motor aspects of the orienting reflex. Also signals flowing down from "limbic" components of the cerebral cortex can bring about EEG desynchronization and arousal.[261] Epinephrine circulating in the bloodstream also can affect these centers.

EEG synchronizing components which have effects opposite to those that activate the cortex are also present in the reticular formation and nonspecific thalamic nuclei.[262] Electrical inputs over electrodes to these centers induce sleep. As in arousal, components higher in the nervous system can also bring about sleep. Sleep induced by electrical inputs to the hypothalamus is evidently related to the inactivity and sleepiness which follow satisfaction of drives such as hunger and sex. Endocrine effects also activate the EEG synchronizing component.[263] Controls for light and deep sleep have been demonstrated to be separately situated; light sleep is controlled in the thalamic component and deep sleep in the pons and medulla.[264]

The neural components which make the decisions involved in selecting and focusing on certain items or flows of information in the process of attention have proved harder to identify. In some way, at some part of the pathway from input transducer to cortex, flows of a particular sort of information are facilitated, and other sorts are inhibited.[265] Electrical stimulation of the reticular formation has been found to improve visual discrimination and to facilitate pulses in the visual, auditory, and somatic areas of the cortex.[266] Inhibitory effects also occur.

Some scientists have contended that information in sensory pathways is filtered at or even before the first synapse in the sensory pathways.[267] A number of researches have been conducted which were designed to discover whether such peripheral control exists. Cats with electrodes permanently implanted in the cochlear nucleus received auditory inputs consisting of clicks which evoked activity that could be recorded from the nucleus in the form of evoked potentials. When shown some mice in a jar, the cats became so attentive to this fascinating visual spectacle that the potentials on their auditory fibers became much smaller, only to return to their former magnitude when the mice were removed.[268] A similar effect was discovered in tactile pathways.[269]

Electrodes placed in the optic radiations of patients undergoing operative brain examinations recorded that potentials evoked by flashes of light were reduced while the patients concentrated on arithmetic problems.[270] The intensities of the responses returned to normal when a patient solved a problem. The more difficult the problem, the more the potentials were reduced. Touch-evoked brain potentials, which were recorded from electrodes placed on the scalps of normal subjects, were also found to be reduced when the subjects were conversing. The pathway suggested for such control processes which make decisions about sensory inputs is a neural feedback loop from the internal-transducer component to the reticular formation, returning to the input transducer. The fact that electrical inputs to the reticular formation inhibit activities in sensory nuclei indicates that such controls may exist.[271]

When the above experiments on the effects of attention to other information inputs upon the activities in the cochlear nucleus were replicated with such variables controlled as head position, binaural hearing, spatial position in relation to the sound source, and movement of muscles of the ear, the previous findings were not confirmed.[272]

A tract descending from the cortex to the cochlea, which runs along the afferent tract, has been demonstrated anatomically.[273] Other efferent fibers descend to the cochlea by several different routes, some of which have not been traced. Efferents end also on the end organs of the vestibule.[274] Electrical inputs to the auditory efferents entering the cochleas of both cats and pigeons were shown to reduce the auditory signal transmitted over the acoustic (VIII) cranial nerve to the cerebral cortex. Possibly the whole length of the tract acts in some way to control the afferent signal.

In the brainstem, electrical inputs through electrodes to sites near but not in the afferent tracts carrying auditory information suppressed the auditory signals.[275] These sites were the ventral nucleus of the lateral lemniscus, the ventral and anterior aspects of the inferior colliculus, and the medial aspect of the medial geniculate. Electrical inputs by electrode to the reticular system did not suppress auditory signals. Efferent signals from the afferent olivocochlear nucleus have also been shown to inhibit auditory signals, acting at the synapse between the auditory hair cells and the auditory neurons.

The different sorts of decisions made by organisms are made and implemented in the four stages of the decision process which seem to occur at the cell level and may occur at the organ level (see pages 273 and 342 and Hypothesis 3.3.7.2-1, page 100). I shall consider each of these phases in turn.

(a) *Establishing purposes or goals.* Strains within the organism or inputs from the environment provide the motivation or impetus to behavior. This is as true for plants, which have limited capability for response, as for human beings. Even apparently random or playful behavior is, therefore, invariably directed to some end: to change tension in muscles, scratch an itch, twitch a fly off the skin, relieve a cramp, stop hunger contractions, increase information inputs, bring internal water content into the optimal range and allay the discomforts of thirst, get the riper fruit at the top of the tree, attract the more desirable mate, keep predators from the young, win the game, become patrol leader, earn a doctoral degree, or accumulate a million dollars.

Goals for governance of matter-energy processing subsystems are usually set genetically, although in some cases they are modifiable by experience. The optimal value of a physiological variable, such as heart rate, varies with states of the organism, such as the amount of muscular effort being exerted, and with external conditions, such as the temperature of the environment.

Genetically set goals may be changed as a result of natural selection. This occurred, for example, when some organisms developed the ability to maintain their body temperatures constant during changes in environmental temperature. A human being's "thermostat" is set for about 37°C (98.6°F), while a dog's is set somewhat higher.

Toward which objects in the environment behavior is directed may also be determined genetically. Learning can modify such preferences, particularly in members of higher species. A dog's desire to eat meat cooked rather than freshly killed and its practice of sitting in front of the refrigerator instead of going hunting in response to hunger are examples of this.

Motivation. This is a message or messages from a lower echelon or subsystem that a higher echelon or system at a higher level should carry out an action to restore some steady state or maintain one that is threatened (see page 68). A large list of motivating conditions and situations has been demonstrated in human beings and animals. These include the primary physiological needs or drives, related to strains within the organism, *e.g.,* hunger, thirst, or sexual tension (see page 409). These are strong determiners of an organism's goals at any time. Intense matter-energy or information inputs from the environment, especially those that elicit pain, create internal strains that function similarly in moving an organism to action. Such a strain has been called a *motive,* defined as "an inner state that energizes, activates, or moves . . . and that directs or channels behavior toward goals."[276] Secondary psychological needs or drives are derived from primary drives by associative learning or conditioning. Social motivations and the need to explore or satisfy curiosity have been shown to function much like the primary drives. A matrix algebra model based on general living systems theory has been developed which analyzes the motivation of organisms in terms of interactions of system variables.[277] Since most species of animals are active when they are receiving signals that a strain or absence of steady state exists in them, or when they are receiving painful inputs from the environment, one can question whether all these motivations are derived from primary drives.[278] Monkeys will work as long as 10 h without a reward, to learn to take apart a puzzle.[279] They will also press a bar almost insatiably after a period in darkness in order to obtain a second of light for each bar press (see page 453).[280] Human subjects placed in a darkened room, and wearing earplugs to block auditory inputs, were able to obtain visual inputs in the form of flashes of light on the ceiling by repeatedly pushing a button. The frequency of this response increased with the amount of information contained in the patterning of the lights.[281] Fear, ordinarily considered a disruptive emotion, can also function like a drive in motivating learning in rats (see page 409).[282]

Drive can be measured by the amount of work done to reach a goal, the amount of general activity the drive engenders, the amount of inputs ingested to reduce it, or the frequency, speed, or magnitude of a response elicited by it.[283] Relative strengths of different drives can be compared experimentally. The strength of a tendency to overcome an obstacle to reach a goal, the amount of consummatory behavior related to the amount of deprivation, and the decision as to which drive is to be satisfied first in the presence of competing drives can all be studied.

Goals of human behavior are determined by (i) disturbances in one or more of an individual's subsystems, i.e., his physiological steady states; (ii) the individual's concept of what constitutes the optimal welfare for his total organism; and (iii) his suprasystem's standards, as represented to him by authority figures, of what is an optimal state for him (see pages 39 and 40). These determinants of behavior are comparable, in Freud's psychoanalytic terms, to control (i) by the id, (ii) by the ego, and (iii) by the superego.[284]

For a certain task or problem a person's "level of aspiration" represents the value on a scale of achievement which he makes his goal. This, of course, may be affected by all sorts of internal and external circumstances. Individual differences among people in setting these levels involve their whole personalities and past histories, as well as the strains in the immediate situation. The level of aspiration also varies with preceding success or failure in the same sort of task or problem. Success raises the level; failure lowers it.

An individual's personal achievement scale has been conceptualized in terms of economic utility (see page 496).[285] A person's subjective utility function for a certain object or outcome is often an indication of his level of aspiration with regard to it. Since an individual can list a number of things on a scale of their utility to him (see page 436), levels of aspiration have been found experimentally also to fit subjective scales. In a study of such individual scales, 20 college students agreed to gamble with instructors for their midterm grades. They expected that these grades would be assigned randomly, but actually the grading process was rigged so that each student "won" a C. Dissatisfied students were told they could have an interview to arrange a possible way to raise the grade. It was implied that this could be done by extra work. Students were asked to wait 5 min for the interview, but actually the waiting time was, by a ruse, extended to 1 h. As hypothesized, four students whose levels of aspiration were so low that they considered a C grade acceptable left the room before the hour elapsed. They were sufficiently content with their C's, and they did not bother to wait. The others, with higher levels of aspiration, stayed the whole hour in the hope of improving their grades.

Emotion. Goal setting is strongly affected by emotion. In anger a man will strive toward a goal he would otherwise reject or will abandon one which has been important to him. Emotional states may drive the level of aspiration for an activity or object either up or down. Emotion is a poorly conceptualized psychological concept. Classification of emotions is inexact, involving subtleties better suited to art and literature than to science. Yet the ageless traditional categories of emotion still are widely used and have not been generally replaced by a more accurate classification. A careful description and analysis of the actions of chimpanzees was carried on for over two years.[286] Meaningful understanding of their behavior could not be obtained from describing each action unless concepts of emotion and attitude were employed. Experiments have shown that, using such concepts, there is a high amount of agreement among observers upon the emotion being expressed on a human face.

The totality of physiological processes related to emotion includes activities of endocrine, autonomic, hypothalamic, thalamic, cortical, motor, and other centers. How the body prepares for emergency action and sustains such behavior are discussed below (see page 455). Excretion of epinephrine by the adrenal medulla, and other alterations in endocrine and autonomic functions, produce subsystem adjustments which prepare the organism to deal with dangerous or threatening environmental situations. Accompanying these changes are the subjective experiences which are reported as fear, rage, terror, anger, or other less readily identified feelings.

Emotion is a joint function of several variables, including the degree of physiological arousal of the sympathetic nervous system and the sorts of expectations that are elicited by information inputs from the environment. The importance of such cognitive factors has been recognized by physicians for centuries since they discovered the capacity of placebos, *i.e.*, of biologically inert or nearly inert medications, to bring about therapeutic changes in behavior. Administration of such an agent to a patient is always accompanied by information inputs which convey the suggestion or implication that it has some helpful physiological properties. The suggestion involved in placebos had an average effectiveness of 32.2 percent in 1,082 patients with physical and psychiatric illnesses studied in one research.[287] It ranged from 4 to 52 percent of the psychiatric cases investigated in another.[288] The placebo constitutes a signal which can significantly affect the emotions of the patients who receive it. These clinical findings conform with those of Schachter and Singer, who injected epinephrine into a group of subjects, some of whom were informed correctly of the nature of the drug, some of whom were ignorant of it, and some of whom were misinformed.[289] In addition some subjects received saline solution administered as a placebo. All the subjects were then exposed to conditions designed to produce either euphoria or anger. The experimenters concluded that in a state of autonomic arousal produced by epinephrine, for which an individual has no immediate explanation, he will describe his emotions in terms of any cues available to him. The same state of physiological arousal would be labeled "joy" or "fury" or "jealousy," or by several other terms, depending upon the information inputs the subject receives. When the individual has a completely adequate explanation for the arousal, he will use it and will not label his emotions in alternative terms. In the same cognitive circumstances he will react emotionally or say he has emotions only to the extent that he experiences autonomic arousal.

In a related experiment, Schachter and Wheeler added a set of subjects injected with chlorpromazine, which depresses sympathetic function, to the subjects who received epinephrine and saline solution.[290] All the subjects were shown a slapstick movie. It was found that laughter increased with sympathetic arousal elicited by epinephrine and decreased with sympathetic depression elicited by chlorpromazine. So once again the evidence has demonstrated that emotion is a joint function of, among other variables,

expectations aroused by information inputs (in this case the movie) and degree of arousal of the sympathetic nervous system.

Studies have shown that active, aggressive emotional behavior is associated with increased urinary excretion of norepinephrine; however, tense, anxious, but passive emotional displays result in increased excretion of epinephrine. When fierce, aggressive species such as lions are compared with timid creatures such as rabbits and guinea pigs, it is found that the former have large amounts of norepinephrine in their adrenal medullas and the latter have large amounts of epinephrine.[291]

The James-Lange theory of emotion, which was the dominant one for years, holds that the subjective experiences known as emotions result when some information input excites changes in bodily organs which are sensed by internal transducers and reported to higher levels of the nervous system.[292] That is, a man is frightened *because* his heart beats faster, his blood vessels contract, his breathing accelerates, and his muscles tense.

The current view, proposed by Cannon and by Dana on the basis of experiments, maintains that emotions and the associated bodily reactions result from interactions among the cerebral cortex, the hypothalamus, and the anterior nucleus of the thalamus, elicited by some information input. In this view, visceral and somatic responses are secondary to diencephalic processes which produce feelings like rage, delight, and grief, rather than being the causes of those feelings. Clinical evidence supports this theory. For instance, outbursts of uncontrollable laughter or crying can be produced by lesions in the diencephalon.

Both telencephalic and diencephalic processes are involved in emotions. Lesions in the human frontal cortex or in the dorsomedial nucleus of the thalamus which sends signals to the frontal cortex may produce a destructive, disagreeable patient who becomes quite docile when the prefrontal cortex is removed or the pathway to the thalamic nucleus is cut.[293] Stimulation of the amygdala in experimental animals produces fear and rage. Lesions here may also lead to docility.[294] Little is known about the gentler emotions, although the docility observed after such lesions must have some similarities to them.

Strains (needs or drives). The diencephalon and related midbrain and forebrain components have been shown to be important in what I call strains, which are often called needs or drives, as well as in positive or negative reinforcement. Consequently they are involved in motivation and goal setting. Diencephalic structures as well as cortical and subcortical components are important also in emotion. These may be some of the same parts of the brain that are active in the formation of conditioned emotional responses (see page 408).

Inputs by electrodes chronically implanted in the brains of animals and human patients to centers in the midbrain, hypothalamus, and forebrain elicit such powerfully rewarding output signals that rats trained to press a bar to produce pulse inputs over such electrodes have reached the enormous rate of 7,500 presses per h.[295] Such inputs are more effective than a food reward in motivating these animals to perform other tasks or to cross a painful grid. The human patients, who were under treatment for epilepsy and narcolepsy, reported that the pleasure was sexual in nature.

An input to certain centers in an adjacent area elicits experiences which apparently are unpleasant enough to make an animal unwilling ever to press the bar again. A cat will learn to press a lever to prevent a pulse input to this area.[296] Centers in which pulses from electrodes produce unpleasant experience have also been found in human brains.

Olfactory and visceral information inputs are channeled to the hypothalamus. Outputs related to feeding go to preganglionic parasympathetic centers for salivation, secretion of gastric juice, and peristalsis, and to motor nuclei, for chewing, swallowing, and perhaps sniffing. Other diencephalic areas important in feeding are the habenular nuclei, which receive olfactory inpulses and project them to the superior colliculus where the sight (visual information processed by the cortex), sound, and texture of an object can be related to the odor.[297] The connections of the superior colliculi permit such correlated information to enter motor nuclei at various echelons of the nervous system. Lesions in the hypothalamus can lead to excessive obesity or to refusal to eat. Stimulation of appropriate hypothalamic centers can produce excessive food intake. Similar controls for drinking also exist.[298] The amygdala and the temporal and frontal cortices bring higher-echelon controls to the feeding process. Lesions in these areas also cause intake to vary. Appetite which arises from other causes than a need for food, such as emotional factors, may be mediated through these channels.[299] The amygdala probably can alter the excitability of the lower centers, a process perhaps like changing the criterion comparison or reference signal in a negative feedback loop, for example, resetting a thermostat (see page 36).[300]

Hypothalamic control of the pituitary gland (and therefore of the whole endocrine apparatus) regulates reproductive drives. As in feeding behavior, input signals from both input and internal transducers elicit output signals to autonomic and motor centers which produce reflex sexual behavior. The amygdala and cortex exert higher echelon controls on these functions also.[301]

(b) *Analysis.* Any discrepancy between the present state of a variable in an organism and the comparison signal indicating the appropriate steady-state value for that variable constitutes a problem requiring decision making, or problem solving. Information about physiological variables maintained in steady states is continually obtained and checked for deviation from comparison signals by a feedback loop, the adjustment processes available to correct any deviation are determined, and necessary changes are carried out in the maintenance of homeostasis and in the execution of reflex or habitual activities. For many such processes there is a range of values which a variable may take; for others there is a set of discrete alternatives. Some of them are simply on–off binary choices.

Decisions among alternatives are made (*i*) in decoding of sensory inputs under uncertainty, (*ii*) in judgments of quality, quantity, or meaning of inputs, (*iii*) in economic choices or choices of moves in a game, (*iv*) in choice of a path to follow in physical space or some conceptual space, (*v*) in social or moral choices, and (*vi*) in selections among alternative forms of creative expression. Different specialty fields are concerned with these various sorts of choices, some using specialized mathematical approaches, *e.g.*, psychophysics, game theory (see page 496), or random walk. Some situations present a binary choice. In others, the available alternatives may be numerous. Even a relatively simple card game like "goofspiel," in which each of two players starts with a suit of 13 cards and a third suit of 13 shuffled cards placed face down between them, can start in as many as 13^{13} ways.[302] On the second move the alternatives increase to $12^{2,028}$. The possibilities in chess, which is vastly more complicated, average about 1 million, if a position is analyzed two moves ahead for each player, and 1 billion, if it is analyzed three moves ahead.[303]

Economic choices, such as those involved in buying or selling goods or in accepting or refusing work, may involve known alternatives. Or, as more recent economic theory has stressed, they may require the choice to be made among a limited number of alternatives in ignorance of others which will arise later.[304] In the first case, the assumptions of classical economics are satisfied. For decisions which must be made under uncertainty, other mathematical formulations have been developed. It is hard to identify precisely what are the alternatives from which choices are made in any given situation. This makes it difficult to formulate a theory of choice which embraces all the many different sorts of decisions faced by organisms.[305]

The analytic stage of the decision process may be carried out in, or at least involve, the sensory association areas (posterior intrinsic sector).[306] Monkeys with these components of their brains ablated were put into an experimental situation in which they had to solve the problem of finding a peanut under 1 of 12 objects. The first requirement of this solution is, on successive trials, to move each of the objects until the nut is found. These monkeys find this hard to do. They have no difficulty discriminating among things they see. Rather they have trouble "sampling" the environment and drawing conclusions from what they observe. Ablation of the posterior intrinsic sector of the brain evidently disrupts a monkey's ability to accumulate, from a sequence of input signals, increasing amounts of information which constitute cues leading to the correct solution of a problem.[307]

(c) *Synthesis.* At all echelons of the organism's decider, logical computations characterize the synthesis stage of decision making. At lower echelons these evidently determine the algebraic sum of inhibitory and excitatory signals or measure the magnitudes of inputs from various sources. Spinal motor nuclei, for example, transmit to muscles a signal integrated from the great number of impulses for which they form the "final common path."[308] This information includes signals concerning the state of a number of variables of the muscles to which they send signals, such as the amount of stretch, pain, or discomfort. A single spinal motor nucleus receives and synthesizes information from each joint affected by a muscle it innervates concerning its position, and from the body surface concerning cutaneous inputs. Visceral organs lying beneath a muscle also signal any pain or discomfort that is present. Internal transducers in other muscles which are associated in movement patterns with a given muscle send facilitatory or inhibitory signals. A synergist muscle in a given movement sends facilitatory signals. An antagonist muscle sends inhibitory signals. Direct neural connections ensure that the various muscles surrounding a single joint cannot act independently. They are coordinated through their innervations. Signals from centers higher in the nervous system flow down, carrying commands for both voluntary and involuntary motor behavior, combining input, internal, and stored information, including genetically stored as well as learned behavior patterns. By such synthesis of signals from many sources, the goals, drives, plans, and values of an organism affect its motor outputs.

Centers in the medulla, pons, midbrain, diencephalon, and cortex, which control matter-energy processing variables—such as respiratory rates and temperature—integrate sympathetic and parasympathetic signals with input and internal information to keep steady states of such organismic variables in harmony with environmental conditions (see pages 449 and 450).

At higher echelons the decider also employs computation or logical processes to reduce the number of alternatives to a single choice, except when the situation is beyond the analytic capacity of the organism or when cues are lacking. Then, random choices may be made. Much of the research on decision making has been done with human subjects.

Decisions made in a single trial in a psychophysical experiment are probably the simplest form of organismic decision which can be studied. These present the minimum required for a decision situation: two alternative possible states of the environment, information concerning them input to the organism, and a choice between them, output by the organism.[309] The problem may well be to decide whether a signal is present or not, in a situation in which the signal-to-noise ratio is low. The subject is given a brief period to examine the display and then must respond, often with one word or another, either "present" or "absent." If choice is forced and "don't know" is not accepted as an answer, there may be a range in which behavior is random or in which the subject cannot verbalize the reason for his choice. At slightly higher intensities of the input signal, one answer appears to the subject more correct than the alternatives.

More complicated decision situations have the same elements as these simpler ones, but they differ in a number of ways. Decisions are often sequential, so that a prior choice affects succeeding ones. Experiments have been carried out, some with special apparatus designed to analyze the problem-solving process, which observe and measure every step of such decisions.[310] Increased numbers of alternatives, differences in expected outcomes, changes in probability of success or correctness, all complicate the computations which lead to the decisions.

Plans, strategies, or algorithms. A common and important aspect of synthesis is the existence of an overall program which determines what alternative to select in each single choice of a sequence. For instance, in working on a mathematical problem, an algorithm, which is a rule for solving all problems of a certain kind, may be available. This need only be applied to produce the correct answer. In playing a game, a player may choose a strategy which was developed before the game began and which suggests a play for each situation that arises during the game.[311]

The play of grandmasters of chess has been analyzed to see how they eliminate some alternatives and direct their strategies.[312] Skilled players sometimes work out mating combinations as many as eight moves ahead for each player, involving something like 10^{24} choices. Ideally a player should examine all legal alternatives open to his opponent and to himself. Obviously in the limited time allowed for a game, this sort of detailed computation is impossible. Masters of chess restrict their consideration to moves which are "forceful" and seem promising. Possible pathways to checkmate might be evaluated according to a program embodying the following criteria: Highest priority goes to double checks or discovered checks. Checks with a stronger piece, such as a queen, are preferred to those with a less powerful piece. Those checks are preferred which leave the opponent with the fewest possible replies. A check which adds a new attacker to the list of active pieces is given priority, and so is one which forces the opponent's king farthest from its base. Such powerful selective rules, rather than prodigious memory, rapid information processing, or flashes of insight, appear to enable chess grandmasters to discover mating combinations many moves ahead.

In ordinary life decisions and in creative thinking, the sort of complete specification of procedures for selecting among alternatives that is possible in some mathematical solutions gives way to more general strategies which can be modified to take into consideration changes in available information. Personality (see pages 457 to 461) is important in the sort of plans which a person will consider. In a concept attainment test, for instance, some subjects worked out plans of action, usually heuristic, which were less systematic than algorithms, while others sampled alternatives at random, using little of the information they collected.[313] Some plans involved appeals to others for help, guessing, cleverness, and imagination. When plans of this sort achieve their purposes, they are quick and easy, but frequently they do not succeed. The more systematic plans, such as taking each alternative in order and testing it, are frequently dull and inefficient, but they often lead to success.

Solutions to problems or other decisions also sometimes arise by "insight," when the organism sees a new meaning in one of the elements of the situation or suddenly finds a new alternative or sees previously unperceived advantages in one of the existing alternatives.[314] In an experiment with apes, an insightful solution occurred when an ape fitted two sticks together to pull a banana into its cage (see page 408).

Planning has been conceived of as constructing a list of tests to perform and then comparing the results with an "image" of the desired outcome. If the two are congruous, no further decision is needed.[315] If they are not, further behavior must be undertaken to remove the incongruity.

A similar theoretical formulation holds that new situations are compared with "schemata" stored in the memory.[316] These are either determined genetically or gained through past experience, instructions, communications, reading, or reflections of the individual. They include stored information on the past behavior of the organism in similar situations and its outcomes. If the present situation resembles two schemata which point to opposite decisions, some aspect of the present situation may be disregarded or suppressed to bring it into accord with one or the other. If this cannot be done, no decision is possible. When applicable schemata for some reason cannot be compared, incompatible or random choices may be made.

A number of other decision theories focus upon the internal steady state of the deciding organism. Many of these derive from the work of Lewin.[317] In his form of Gestalt theory, each person or object in the "psychological space" of an organism (the environment as perceived by it) was believed to have its own particular degree of positive or negative valence which derived from the organism itself. Lewin did not conceive valences to be aspects of matter-energy processing but rather related to processing of meaningful information. He did not clearly specify how this function is carried out. His brilliant insights made it clear that decisions arise from the interaction of complex variables, but he wrongly referred to these variables as if they were energic forces. These "forces" determined the organism's behavior. Decisions, in this theory, could only be made when the resultant of the driving "forces" toward one alternative had greater magnitude than the restraining "forces." As the "forces" approached equality, decision time was lengthened, and when they were equal, no decision was possible. Experimental studies have been carried out in which people were found to behave in accordance with Lewin's theory. Resolution of such "forces" is accompanied by adjustment processes designed to reduce "dissonance" or conflict, either during the decision period or in the time immediately following (see pages 460 and 461).

Artistic or scientific creativity is a poorly understood capability of some people, lacking in others. This involves not only discovering alternatives missed by others but also choosing those which result in a work that is considered novel or beautiful or otherwise exceptional by others. Why is the grace note inserted where it is? Why is the bottle cap nailed slightly off center in the museum's latest acquisition?

What made Sherlock Holmes able to see the explanation of the puzzling evidence before him? How did Watson and Crick determine that the DNA molecule is a double helix (see page 217)? Creative people do not just put things together at random. They analyze those alternatives among the many which they find that seem fruitful and interesting. And they use discernment in selecting among them. Others are usually unable to understand how they arrived at their unique results, even when they try to explain.

Some factors are known which lead to a choice of one alternative over others in many sorts of decisions. If a decision must be made when there is uncertainty about the results or when risk of loss or punishment must be considered, *probability of correctness* or of a satisfactory result is important. Also *costs and utilities* (in the economic sense) as well as *personal and social values, attitudes, and behaviors* all enter into the stage of synthesis to help in determining which of the perceived alternatives will be chosen. These factors are far from independent. Economic decision theory, game theory, and statistical decision theory deal with the interactions of such factors in decision making (see pages 496 and 497).

Probability of correctness. Mathematical probabilities of the outcome of bets with known odds, or of drawing to an inside straight, or of rain falling on tomorrow's picnic can be calculated and used to guide behavior. In most human decision making, however, a subjective rather than a mathematical likelihood estimate is used. Most relevant considerations cannot be quantified, and not many people could apply the appropriate mathematics even if they wanted to. In the few situations in which probabilities are known, like poker games, they commonly are ignored in favor of a "hunch." In dealing with probabilities, an individual may feel that nature is a friend or an adversary, or even a passive or random force. Gamblers often risk their winnings on a long shot because they "feel lucky." People differ also in their willingness to take risks. One may typically "go for broke," whereas another has as his motto, "Better safe than sorry." People do not like to lose. A group of experimental subjects consistently preferred low probabilities of losing large amounts of money to high probabilities of losing small amounts.[318] The lesser of two evils was chosen regardless of odds, and the surer of two prizes regardless of their magnitudes, at least for prizes ranging from 0 to 13 cents.[319]

A man's usual standards are important, too. For instance, experimental psychologists are used to research with confidence limits in the area of $p = .01$ (*i.e.*, 1 chance in 100 that the result could just happen).

Clinical psychologists, who deal with many and subtle variables, of necessity become accustomed to $p = .05$. A number of psychologists volunteered to act as subjects in an experiment. Each was led to believe that a pea would be under one of three walnut shells in a situation which duplicated the old "shell game" of the county fair.[320] Actually there was no pea under any shell. Each subject was allowed up to 50 trials in order to discover this and to make qualified or unqualified hypotheses that there was really no pea at all. It was found that the clinicians arrived at their decisions more rapidly than the experimentalists. Subjects of each subspecialty were satisfied with evidence approximating the level of confidence to which they were accustomed. Apparently a human being's standards for accepting probabilities are personal, based, at least to some extent, upon past experience.

In psychophysical experiments, whether the experimenter instructs the subject to report only when he is certain or, on the other hand, directs him to guess when he is unsure about the nature of the input, can affect his report about it. I have demonstrated that, when required to guess about the nature of an input, a subject may turn out to be correct in a significant proportion of trials in which an accurate subjective report would be "I do not know."[321] Punishment of mistakes has the opposite effect. A subject anticipating an electric shock for every error tries to be sure before he reports. In both these opposite situations, a subject's estimate of the probabilities affects his decision about the input.

Utilities, values, costs, and economic behavior. Given a free choice of the world's good things, people select for themselves some rather than others. Since everything costs something in energy expended to obtain and keep it, in time, in money, or in loss of unchosen alternatives, economic behavior, broadly defined, is inevitable. That is, people trade what they have to spend for what they want to possess. They make the best bargain they can. If they possess all the relevant facts — what they want, what the market affords, how much they have to spend, what the various available goods or services cost, and how pleasing or serviceable each would be to them should they secure it, they are in a position to do a rational job of what economists call "maximizing their utilities." The utility of a unit of goods or services to people determines whether they will try to get it and what priority they will give it in their choices. Succeeding units of the same sort have less utility, until a final one is reached which is "marginal." Beyond that, people want no more such units. With less than complete information people can "optimize," *i.e.*, make the best possible choice they can, using the information at hand. Or they may "satisfice," i.e., make a decision adequate for their purposes or for survival in their particular environments even though it may not be the best possible one (see Hypothesis 3.3.7.2-16, page 101).

Economic behavior is dependent upon people's ability to rank order all sorts of things according to their relative worth to them. That is, if their values are the totality of the strains within them (see page 34), they must be able to determine the relative urgency of reducing each specific strain, which is their hierarchy of values.

According to Stevens, subjective values or utilities can be scaled psychometrically in the same way that subjective brightness or loudness can (see pages 379, 380, 381, and 383).[322] Classically, economists have proposed a law of diminishing utility, which states that subjective value increases as a negatively accelerated function of the number of units of goods or services. More recently it has been recognized that dollars have a similar function, i.e., each additional dollar added to a person's wealth has less subjective value than the one preceding it. Traditionally, many have conceived this curve to flatten out as the amount of money increases, i.e., to be concave downward, a negatively accelerated logarithmic curve. But Stevens suggests that, like the subjective intensity of various modalities of sensation, it is, rather, a power function of the amount of money with its exponent less than 1. It flattens out as the amount of money increases and is concave downward, but it is a fractional power function rather than a logarithmic one. Ratio scaling, like that employed in sensory psychophysics, has been used to measure the subjective value of money. Subjects were asked how much money would make them "twice as happy" or "half as happy" as a given sum. Results showed that most typical subjects did not say that double the sum would make them twice as happy or that half the sum would make them half as happy. Instead, the median sum required to double happiness was 3.5 to 5 times as large. The sum had to be cut to about 20 percent for them to be half as happy. These findings confirm Steven's view that subjective values for money approximate a power function. The data show its exponent to be about 0.4 to 0.5 (see pages 379 and 380).

The idiosyncratic preferences expressed in choice behavior have also proved susceptible to mathematical treatment and scaling, including the subjective values of such disparate things as a color television set, a radio, a trip abroad, or a mink coat.[323] Preferences of one or more individuals, which influence how they decide, can be ranked quantitatively by Coombs's "unfolding technique."

The number of theories of organism behavior, most notably that of Zipf, have identified what may be a general principle of work done by organisms, the principle of least effort.[324] This states that systems tend to reduce the costs, in energy expenditure or other units, of their actions (see page 35 and Note 101, page 50; Hypothesis 3.3.7.2-14, page 101, which states that systems use least costly adjustments first and more costly ones later; and Hypothesis 3.3.7.2-17, page 101, which says that systems conserve resources by maintaining their subsystem functions efficient and by keeping down costs). One consequence of this principle is that, in any goal-oriented behavior, an organism tends to move from one position in space to another over the shortest possible path. The route which will be chosen will theoretically be the most economical one possible at that time and in that situation. In the economic sense this is optimization of the organism's behavior.

Influences of other persons. Information inputs about the beliefs and behaviors of others in a person's suprasystem exert potent influences on subsequent decisions. For instance, one study investigated the use of legally required turn signals by car drivers.[325] Among 4,229 drivers observed at four different street intersections over a total of 61 h, there was a significant positive correlation between the use of the signal by one driver and the use of it by the following driver.

The effects of group pressures upon individual judgments have been extensively studied by many people (see pages 570 to 572). In general, the prestige of a group; its size (larger groups are more effective); its familiarity to the subject; how unanimous it is (if only 1 out of 20 disagrees, the subject may side with her or him); how much the subject likes or trusts the group; how much she or he feels liked or disliked by them; how public the decision is; how close to unanimous the group decision must be (it is hard to be the lone holdout on a jury); and how much conformity or deviation is rewarded, are all important influences on decisions made by individual persons in a group. These facts confirm Hypothesis 3.3.4.2-10, page 99, which asserts that as the strength of a strain increases, information inputs will more and more be interpreted as required to reduce the strain. The less certain an individual is about the situation, the greater the influence. If the task is difficult, or if he must depend upon his memory, or if the stimulus is ambiguous or the instructions vague, the decision will more readily be brought into conformity with the group. This is consistent with Hypothesis 3.3.4.2-9, page 99, which states that as the amount of information in an input decreases, it will more and more tend to be interpreted as required to reduce strains within the system.

Group discussion may improve the group's decisions over those of single persons (see Hypothesis 3.3.7.2-21, page 102, which states that the higher the level of a system the more correct or adaptive its decisions are). Group influence tends to make the judgments of its members less conservative. They are, among other things, apparently more willing to take risks, more altruistic, and more likely to support the civil liberties of others.[326] Such group influences even affect judgments of the comparative length of lines. In one experiment all members of a group were in league with the experimenter except a single subject.[327] These others all declared that the longer of two lines presented to the group was shorter. Subjects were loathe to oppose the overwhelming judgment of the other group members, although only one actually claimed to *see* the lines as the group said they saw them. In interviews following the experiment, the subjects admitted to having changed their judgment to be in agreement with the others in the group. This experiment works better when the lines are in fact quite close in length. If the discrepancy is great, subjects get suspicious. Individual subjects differ in their readiness to yield to such group influences.

Brain processes in synthesis. The frontal cortex must function whenever choices are made among alternatives. Following operations which deprived patients of Penfield and Rasmussen of the whole anterior frontal area of one hemisphere, their ability to plan and take initiative was impaired.[328] Possibly this finding supports Hypothesis 3.3.7.2-13, page 98, that decisions overtly altering major values of a system are finalized only at the highest echelon.

Monkeys with the posterior intrinsic cortex removed bilaterally make decisions differently from monkeys with bilateral ablations of the frontal intrinsic cortex (see page 433).[329] The former have trouble in developing strategies by which to search for solutions of problems. The latter experience difficulty in applying previously successful strategies to future problems. Also the latter are unable to make optimal selections among alternatives. These monkeys with frontal ablations also are deficient in estimating the effects of an action, comparing its outcome to other possible outcomes.[330] This was shown in a situation in which each monkey was required to press a lever for food. Rewards were spaced 2 min apart, no matter how the animal pressed the lever. Normal monkeys increased their rate of lever pressing as the interval progressed toward 2 min. Frontally operated monkeys did not. Monkeys with posterior ablations behaved in this situation like the normals.

Some of the deficiencies of monkeys with frontal ablations have been ascribed to memory loss, but it appears that this is not the primary disturbance. Instead, seemingly a fundamental process performed upon information inputs, particularly visual inputs, is affected. If the stream of information inputs to which the animals were required to respond was separated into discrete inputs, their performances improved. It seems that proper "chunking" of inputs is one of the processes carried out by this component. This is related to decoding as well as deciding.[331]

(*d*) *Implementing.* This stage of the deciding process in higher vertebrates involves integration of command signals passing along the extrapyramidal and pyramidal tracts to control the movements of all skeletal muscles, as well as such signals transmitted over the sympathetic and parasympathetic branches of the autonomic nervous system to various viscera and those flowing over vascular channels to endocrine components. While some organs have a considerable degree of self-regulation (see pages 340 to 342), they cannot be coordinated with the rest of the organism without such command signals from various echelons of the organism's decider, particularly the diencephalon and cortex.

How plans and intentions are translated into behavior and what neural structures are involved in this process—among the most interesting aspects of decision implementation—are poorly understood. Some motor behavior is "voluntary," being preceded by an intention to act and accompanied by a different subjective state than that associated with reflex or automatic adjustments. The terms "voluntary" and "willed" as applied to behavior are not popular with some psychologists and physiologists because they seem to imply a mind–body dichotomy and a denial of determinism. This is not a necessary implication of these terms which, like the word "emotion," are difficult to eliminate from the scientific vocabulary because they describe valid physiological and psychological phenomena. The distinction between "voluntary" and "involuntary" motor behavior is necessary in analyzing some illnesses, such as hemiplegia. A patient's muscles on one side may comply with commands carried from the primary motor cortex over the pyramidal fibers, while the other side does not move because a blood clot is blocking conduction along the tract as it passes through the internal capsule. The muscles on the paralyzed side may still show some reflex responses which are mediated at lower centers.

The motor cortex is not the site of either the initiation or the arrest of motor activity.[332] The information inputs which elicit motor behavior (see pages 375 and 376) include highly integrated signals that have already been processed by other cortical regions and by centers elsewhere in the central nervous system. An example of this is information concerning sensory inputs which is carried over tracts from the nucleus cuneatus to the cerebellum and from there to the many centers to which the cerebellum connects, including the reticular formation and the nonspecific thalamo-cortical projections.

The sources of the "willed" impulses which result in voluntary behavior have not yet been identified. It has been suggested that they are nonspecific centers of the midbrain and diencephalon. Because of the effects on movement of lesions of the basal ganglia, such as tremors, changes in muscle tone, underactivity, and overactivity, and because of the importance of the striatum as the highest integrating center in lower species, some investigators have suggested that the striatum has retained control of voluntary functions in organisms in which the cortex is prominent, including human beings.[333]

Damage to the limbic components of the brain produces many changes in behavior related to the basic activities of feeding, fleeing, fighting, and sex. I have mentioned above how some of these limbic components are involved in memory (see page 416). They also are related to deciding, and damage to them can have bizarre effects upon this process. Organisms with such lesions can initiate some actions only with difficulty, and they may, on the other hand, continue some activities beyond the point of satiation. In these organisms, also, animals of the same sex or of different species may elicit sexual responses. Both human and animal organisms with limbic damage have difficulty in carrying out planned or instinctive sequential behavior. A human patient may require a written list as a guide. I mentioned above that a mother rat with a limbic lesion cannot rescue her young when they are scattered out of the nest (see page 366). The basic defect in such cases, according to Pribram, lies in the ability to organize sequences of action to implement the goals, intentions, or plans of the organism.[334] He further suggests that the prefrontal cortex (frontal intrinsic sector) is the association area for the limbic components of primates. Damage here affects both the synthesis and the implementation stages of deciding, because unless instructions or cues are present and can be perceived in the environment, the animal cannot integrate its behavior or carry out its intentions.

Representative *variables* of the process of deciding include: *Meaning of information employed in deciding.* Example: After killing the chicken, the soothsayer read the omens in its entrails and decided they indi-

cated that the time was right for the army to attack. *Sorts of information employed in deciding.* Example: Mr. Smith checked the prices of other houses in the neighborhood before making an offer to buy the one he wanted. *Amount of information employed in deciding.* Example: The junior executive made a snap decision before all the facts were in. *Changes in deciding over time.* Example: The old woman became very indecisive toward the end of her life. *Changes in deciding with different circumstances.* Example: The broker speculated more when her own money was involved. *Number of alternatives in input before decision and in output afterward.* Example: The first rough screening narrowed the field from 20 candidates to 3. *Rewards and punishments attached to alternatives reviewed in deciding.* Example: The gambler could win 1,000 francs on the long shot but risked losing 5,000. *Rate of deciding.* Example: The president settled at least a dozen crucial issues every day. *Lag in deciding.* Example: Priscilla spent a week trying to make up her mind whether to marry John or not. *Costs of deciding.* Example: The duke's refusal to recant cost him his head.

3.3.8   Encoder, the subsystem which alters the code of information input to it from other information processing subsystems, from a "private" code used internally by the organism into a "public" code which can be interpreted by other organisms in its environment.

3.3.8.1   Structure   Whether any fungi or plants have this subsystem is a matter of definition. The colors of plants' petals as well as the odors and perfumes produced by cells in their flowers and fruits transmit signals that attract animals. This might be called communication, but they do not communicate with other plants, even those of their own species. And animals do not communicate back to plants. The subsystem is present in most, if not all, animal organisms. Different structures carry out alpha, beta, and gamma encoding.

Alpha-coded information is conveyed in some species by markers called *pheromones* (see page 404).

Beta-coded information is emitted by a great number of bodily components, which vary from species to species and which can be moved in some way to produce signals. Encoder components are closely related to or are identical with those neural components which control the initiation and arrest of movement of muscles. In higher organisms they are also related to the diencephalic structures which mediate drives and emotions (see pages 430 and 431). The decider and encoder components may well be identical for affective encoding, but little is known about either.

Gamma-coded information processing of such information has been studied almost exclusively in human beings, since this capacity is highly developed in man. The temporoparietal region of the dominant hemisphere of the human cerebral cortex, the left hemisphere in the large majority of people, contains centers essential to encoding as well as decoding of gamma-coded information (see page 395).

The components responsible for vocalization in primates other than human beings are different from those in human beings. Electrical inputs over electrodes to the cortical regions that subserve speech in human beings elicit sounds of vocalization. This is not true in monkeys. Moreover, neither vocalization nor handedness is lateralized in the brains of any primates except human beings.[335] Vocal responses in monkeys are controlled by limbic components and are apparently associated with emotional interactions.

In human beings, damage to any of the brain areas related to language (see Fig. 8-3) immediately results in disturbances of speech, or the comprehension of language, or both.[336] The language process is somewhat localized to different parts of this region, but the structures for the interdependent processes of encoding and decoding do not appear to be separate. A lesion in Broca's area (areas 44 and 45) interferes with the articulation of speech.[337] Near the auditory area (area 22), damage affects understanding of speech and disturbs the speech of the patient who does not understand what she or he has said. A lesion in the angular gyrus of the parietal region (area 39) produces an inability to recognize symbols visually, and so affects reading and writing. A profound inability to use symbolic language results from lesions of the supramarginal gyrus, or area 40, and the white matter underlying it. All the areas concerned with language are closely connected with one another and with relevant motor areas. Some symbolic processes other than verbal, such as emotional speech, singing, or rhythmic speech, may have bilateral cortical representation (see page 441).

3.3.8.2 Process All the elements required for interorganismic communication (see page 12) are usually present when the sender and the receiver are of the same species, and if they are human beings, when they speak the same language. Interspecies communication, particularly of beta-coded information, takes place also. An organism can also encode information for its own later use (see page 406). Ordinarily, higher organisms do not encode signals in the absence of a potential receiver or receivers.[338] Encoding of alpha-, beta-, and gamma-coded information is carried out by different processes. Each process will be discussed in turn.

Alpha encoding. Pheromones include glandular excretions of social insects, which are smelled or tasted by recipient individuals of the same species, as well as odorous substances like those in urine, with which animals of various species mark out their territories. They are classified as olfactory or oral, depending upon the site of their reception.[339]

They act on the nervous system of the receivers as "releasers" of patterns of bodily behavior (see pages 366 and 409) or as "primers," altering endocrine and reproductive physiological processes.

Such chemical signals are most important in the lives of social insects since communications of this sort between one individual organism and another organize and coordinate the activities of their hives or nests. In at least one species of social insects, pheromones convey information required for each of the following functions: distinguishing nest mates from strangers; spreading alarm about intruders into the nest and mobilizing defenses against them; determining an individual's caste; attracting individuals to each other; stimulating grooming behavior, such as assistance in molting; and recruiting individuals for group activities, such as food gathering, maintaining the nest, caring for the young, swarming, and migration. As in nonsocial insects and many other types of organisms, pheromones affect sexual behavior.[340] Among social insects pheromones can start or stop growth and differentiation of individual organism components of the group, much as hormones influence cell growth and differentiation. They can determine an individual's caste, under some circumstances even changing it as an adjustment to alterations in the relative numbers of the various castes in the insect group. Special foods are the markers for information which signals selected larvae to become queens. Different pheromones, distributed by the queen, inhibit other larvae from developing into queens. In some social insects, the queen controls her group's activities by alpha-coded signals.

Beta encoding. Beta-coded signals are encoded in sounds, movements, or changes in some physiological variable like skin color or conformation of an external organ component. Usually the codes are genetically determined, although learning may play a part. Neither intention to communicate nor voluntary motor behavior is essential to beta-coded communication, but both may be present. The cooing of an infant, the roar of a hunting lion, the spring plumage of a male oriole, the bared teeth of a snarling dog, the elaborate rituals of courting male pheasants, the alarm cries of birds, and the slap on the back of a politician are all examples of beta-coded information and are understandable to many of the organisms that perceive them. (Wigwag signal alphabets, the hand alphabet of the deaf, Indian sign language, and certain other human symbolic gestures, however, are gamma-coded rather than beta-coded.)

Some beta-coded communications convey information so precisely that they constitute "languages." The "dance" of bees, which is performed when a member of society returns to the hive after finding a food source, enables other bees to fly to the right place.[341]

Birds communicate with others of their species by calls. These are closer to symbolic expressions than other beta-coded signals, since their development involves learning by each individual bird, and they vary in a single species from one geographical region to another. Crows have four or more distinct sounds which can be decoded by other members of the flock.[342] One of these is an assembly call. Another signals the others to disperse.

Gamma encoding. Expression of gamma-coded signals makes use of stored information, just as expression of beta-coded information does. A large part of the information used in gamma coding is learned. A sizable body of evidence suggests that there are probably two stages in the encoding of an idea into symbolic language.

The first stage of encoding presumably is the conversion of an idea stored in the brain, probably in the cerebral cortex, into a grammatical sentence (see Table 8-4). The idea is transformed into a sentence by a set of syntactic rules, and all three—idea, syntactic rules, and sentence—are stored either as electrical potentials, as synaptic connections in neural networks of the organism's brain, or in macromolecules in its neurons (see pages 417 to 420). All three, and certainly the last

two—syntactic rules and sentence—are probably stored in the temporoparietal region of the dominant hemisphere of the cortex, the center for language processing. Sentences composed of *morphemes,* the smallest possible meaningful syntactic units, are produced according to syntactic rules. Their various parts of speech are arranged in proper order, the verbs in correct moods and tenses, and, in an inflected language, the articles and adjectives in number and gender appropriate to the nouns or pronouns they modify.[343]

The second stage of encoding is probably the conversion of the morphemes of sentences into instructions for producing an orderly sequence of *phonemes,* the basic sounds in which morphemes are expressed in speech (see Table 8-4). This process is carried out according to morphophonemic rules, also probably stored in the temporoparietal region of the dominant hemisphere of the cortex.[344] The phoneme code employs an ensemble of speech sounds of such a sort that messages can be conveyed by several articulatory organ components acting in parallel, independently and simultaneously. This makes it possible for relatively slow acting components to produce speech as fast as 10 to 15 phonemes per second. Such a rapid rate would be impossible if each phoneme had to be articulated separately and in its own distinct time period.

Spoken language is, of course, based upon the babbling sounds which human infants innately produce.[345] Newborn infants of all races and cultures produce the same sounds, but by the time they reach the "babbling" stage, differences begin to appear, in accordance with the language they hear. Before children understand or speak, they learn the significance of objects. These become attached to sounds and even-

TABLE 8-4 Schematic Representation of Assumed Stages in Encoding of Language

Structure	Conversion process	Marker which bears information
Probably cerebral cortex	Idea ↓ ┌─────────────┐ │ Syntactic rules │ └─────────────┘ ↓	
Probably temporoparietal region of dominant hemisphere	Sentence ↓ ┌──────────────────┐ │ Morphophonemic rules │ └──────────────────┘ ↓ Instructions for producing a sequence of phonemes	Electrical potentials or synaptic connections in organism neural networks, or macromolecules in organism neurons

SOURCE: Modified from A. M. Liberman, F. S. Cooper, D. P. Shankweiler, & M. Studdert-Kennedy. Perception of the speech code. *Psychol. Rev.,* 1967, **74,** 445. Copyright by the American Psychological Association. Reprinted by permission.

tually the child learns to encode these sounds, usually as a result of direct teaching and rewards from adults.

The primary use of symbolic language is by human organisms. It may not, however, be entirely restricted to human beings. For instance, the variety of patterned sounds produced by bottle-nosed dolphins suggests to some students of their behavior that they also communicate in this way. Chimpanzees are so intelligent and imitative that prospects for teaching them to talk have seemed good, but their vocal apparatus and typical vocal behavior are unlike the human equivalents. Earnest and prolonged efforts by human teachers have yielded little. The most successful experiment of this sort resulted in a chimpanzee learning four "words" in six years.[346] A chimpanzee uses its hands much more skillfully than its larynx, and chimpanzees that associate with human beings develop communicative gestures spontaneously. Baboons, a species comparable in their communication behavior, transmit most of their information among one another by gestures.

It appeared to Gardner and Gardner that a symbolic code which uses gestures is more likely to be used successfully by nonhuman primates than a verbal code, for which they are evidently unsuited.[347] They secured Washoe, a wild-born female chimpanzee believed to be between 8 and 14 months of age, which is infancy for this species, and brought her up in an environment in which all communication among human beings and between her and her human keepers was nonverbal. A hand-sign code which was developed for deaf humans was chosen as appropriate. The gestures did not spell words, but rather each one represented an idea. Washoe rapidly learned to decode a large vocabulary of such signs. She also learned in the first 22 months of the project, by which time she was at most three years old, to encode more than 30 signs; and after that she rapidly acquired more, at an accelerated rate. The first of these were taught by conditioning, a method appropriate to most animal species. Later, signs could be taught by guiding her hands to the correct position. She spontaneously extended the use of a sign learned in one situation to other appropriate situations. The sign for "more," first used to request more tickling, was extended to ask for more of other pleasant experiences like swinging and feeding. She also transferred the sign for "dog" from a picture of a dog to the barking of an unseen dog. Also she was able to employ combinations of signs, such as were used by her human keepers. Washoe, furthermore, originated her own combinations. These included "go out," "go in," "please open hurry," and "gimme (a single sign) drink please." After she learned the pronouns "I," "me,"

and "you," she produced short "sentences." Another chimpanzee, Sarah, has learned to read and write using plastic chips of various sizes and shapes, each representing a word. Sarah has a vocabulary of about 130 terms, and she uses class concepts and sentence structure.

Millions of human beings have learned and stored in their memories more than one verbal language in addition to gestures and other coded symbols. Verbal and written languages require the storing of separate, entirely arbitrary, codes. A person may also memorize further codes, such as Morse or the wigwag alphabet, which express the same spoken language.

Once the code is chosen, if it has been well learned, the flow of symbols is ordinarily smooth. This automatic adjustment of time, number, gender, and mood is like a subroutine which programs a computer to carry out a repetitive operation, such as adding two zeros to every number ending in 5. A similar routine can be imagined which keeps a bilingual or multilingual speaker encoding in the right language and locks out other codes. After language skill has been acquired, speakers rarely slip from one code into another.

Neural locus of gamma encoding. Much of what is known about neural processes in encoding has been learned from study of pathological conditions, such as the various forms of aphasia. Since the use of symbols depends upon the cerebral cortex, anything which affects cortical function quickly impairs thought and its symbolic expression. Extreme fatigue, anoxia (see page 450), drugs or toxins of various sorts, and generalized damage such as cerebral arteriosclerosis can diminish a person's ability to use words or other symbols. Other cortical processes, such as information storage, are affected at the same time.

Although the dominant hemisphere of the cerebral cortex is essential for any linguistic activity, some symbolic functions appear to involve both sides of the brain.[348] After his left temporal lobe was completely removed, one patient could no longer understand the significance of written and printed symbols. His comprehension of spoken language was also markedly impaired. But he retained his ability to read and write music and to sing. His ability to recognize mathematical symbols and to calculate was much better preserved than his verbal ability, although it too was impaired. In many patients emotional speech, such as swearing, to some extent also survives damage to the dominant hemisphere.

Localized damage to the temporoparietal region of the dominant hemisphere of the human cerebral cortex (see Fig. 8-3) affects a patient's ability to use language without influencing his capacity to process information in the sensory modality in which the signal is encoded. Electrical pulses input to parts of this region can elicit vocalization which the patient, although awake, cannot inhibit; and, conversely, they can bring about speech arrest which involves disturbance of word finding and speech controls.[349]

The classification of aphasias focuses upon the most evident symptoms, but aphasic patients rarely have impairment in just a single aspect of these processes.[350] Both reception (decoding) and expression (encoding and output transducing) of gamma-coded information can be affected by damage to any part of this area. The more abstract and complicated the ideas, the more sensitive they are to such injury.

One reason encoding and decoding are interdependent is that these processes are regulated by feedbacks. Control of the speed, tempo, and rhythm of speech requires that both auditory and motor processes be integrated with symbolic processes.[351] If a speaker cannot decode his own written or vocal production, his ability to continue speaking or writing is impaired.[352]

Some of the most important *variables* of the encoding process are: *Meaning of information which is encoded.* Example: The ship's radio operator stopped routine transmission and sent a distress signal. *Sorts of information which are encoded.* Example: The housewife wrote a note to the milkman and then spoke to her neighbor about the charity drive. *Percentage of the information input which is encoded.* Example: Mrs. Smith told her neighbor only half of the story she had heard, but she related it all to her husband. *Changes in encoding over time.* Example: After he had been in the United States a few years, the Yugoslav immigrant began to speak English rather than Serbo-Croatian, even at home. *Changes in encoding with different circumstances.* Example: Since his audience was not mathematically sophisticated, the scientist presented his theory in verbal rather than mathematical form. *Channel capacity of the encoder.* Example: Occasionally, as the newspaper's deadline approached, the managing editor dictated one article to a secretary while he revised another by hand. *Distortion of the encoder.* Example: The mystic found that mere words rarely gave an adequate picture of his marvelous insights. *Signal-to-noise ratio of the encoder.* Example: About one out of every three words in the boy's speech was mispronounced, although he wrote English perfectly. *Rate of encoding.* Example: The American tourist spoke French more rapidly after he drank some Gevrey Chambertin. *Percentage of omissions in encoding.* Example: When he was 16 years old, 5 of the words out of the list of 100 embarrassed the subject, so he refused to say them aloud; but when he

was given the list again 10 years later, he read them all readily. *Percentage of errors in encoding.* Example: The typist was tired and misspelled 4 words in a letter which was only 80 words long. *Code employed.* Example: The Secret Service agent used a different code every day. *Redundancy of the code employed.* Example: The Tonganese girl spoke for several seconds in her native language in order to say "yes." *Lag in encoding.* Example: At the United Nations Assembly the Russian-speaking official translated the Japanese speaker with only a few seconds lag. *Costs of encoding.* Example: It was more tiring to the girl guide to speak a foreign language than to speak her native French patois.

3.3.9   Output transducer, the subsystem which puts out markers bearing information from the organism, changing markers within the organism into other matter-energy forms which can be transmitted over channels in the organism's environment.

3.3.9.1   Structure

Alpha-coded information.   The exocrine glands which produce pheromones and those parts of the extruder which excrete them into the environment are output transducer components for alpha-coded information.

Beta-coded information.   Any organ component which is used in signaling, like the hand of a man, the tail of a dog, or the minute muscles which raise the hairs of a cat, is an output transducer component if it emits beta-coded information. Many such components are also parts of the motor subsystem. A variety of other structures also transduce information outputs. The erectile wattles which hang from the throat of a turkey and the organ components which produce color changes in fish are both examples. The vocal apparatus described below, as well as other parts of the body, may also produce beta-coded cries and other sounds.

Gamma-coded information.   The specialized human organ components which are necessary for gamma-coded information outputs include the articulatory components (lips, tongue, soft palate, larynx, lungs, and other components necessary for breathing); the hands, each with 30 muscles, one of which, unique to human beings, permits flexion of the thumb; and sometimes other parts, such as the feet.[353] The parts of the motor, such as muscles of the chest and abdominal walls, which move these components, are also output transducer components. Most of these are used also for beta-coded information outputs as well as in processes of other subsystems.

As I have said above (see page 439), areas 44 and 45 in the inferior frontal cortex of the dominant hemisphere of the human brain (see Fig. 8-3) together constitute approximately the region commonly known as Broca's area. This region has long been considered a control center for the motor aspects of speech. A nearby region (see Fig. 8-3) is related to writing. In human beings, these are also components of the output transducer for gamma-coded information outputs.

Artifacts of this subsystem include pencils, pens, typewriters, microphones, radio transmitters, and television transmitters.

3.3.9.2 Process To be emitted across an organism's boundary and to travel in its environment, information must be transduced onto markers appropriate for transmission over suprasystem channels. This transmission can be by direct contact between organisms, as when one insect excretes a pheromone which another ingests, or over channels of earth for underground animals, water for aquatic animals, or air for the others.

Alpha-coded information outputs. Chemical signals from endocrine components are transduced by single cells or exocrine glands which excrete into the organism's environment pheromones that can be transmitted over the channels of its suprasystem. Neural codes can also be transduced into pheromones, since some glands which excrete them do so in response to neurohumoral transmitters released by neurons.

Beta-coded information outputs. These include electrical impulses such as those emitted by electric fish; visible displays, such as Priscilla Alden's blush; courting movements of birds; the contented purring of a well-fed cat; a man's grimace of pain; and a child's scream of fear. Signals which differ in amplitude, color, and pattern constitute the ensemble in which the output information is coded.

Gamma-coded information outputs. Speech is the original and still the primary form of symbolic language, or gamma-coded information output. The inputs that initiate the process of output transducing of speech are probably the instructions for producing the sequences of phonemes which are the final outputs of the encoding process (see bottom of Table 8-4 and top of Table 8-5). Each of these phonemic instructions, numbering about forty in the English language, is made up of subinstructions to particular articulatory organ components to carry out various combinations of a smaller number of subphonemic processes.[354] These latter produce simultaneous sequences of the unit sounds at different frequencies, momentary combinations of which are perceived as phonemes. Each of these subphonemic processes is registered as a separate mark in a sound spectrogram (see Fig. 8-5 and Table 8-5).

The instructions for subphonemic processes may first go through a series of conversions according to neuromotor rules which coordinate the various articulatory organ parts and perhaps make some amplitude adjustments. This probably occurs in Broca's area. The resultant neural motor command signals are then perhaps further converted, according to myomotor rules which determine exactly which articulatory muscles will contract. This also may take place in Broca's area. After that the signals may be converted according to articulatory rules which determine exactly how the muscles related to speech will contract and consequently what shapes the several parts of the vocal apparatus will take while a given sound is being made. Finally, the signals are converted according to acoustic rules, which are now well understood by students of speech processes. These rules determine how at any instant breathing and vibration of the vocal cords will be coordinated with the muscular movements that shape the parts of the vocal apparatus in order to produce a particular speech sound.

Writing, gesture languages (but not genetically programmed gestures), and other uses of the motor subsystem to convey symbolic meanings are alternatives, and very frequently substitutes, for gamma-coded speech. In many, but not all, written languages the characters represent speech sounds. An armless man can learn to write by holding his pen in his foot or mouth. Gamma-coded language can frequently be interchangeably transmitted by various components of the output transducer, *e.g.*, articulatory muscles, hands, feet, or mouth. This is rare for beta-coded information and probably impossible for alpha-coded signals.

Human beings are adapted to produce their characteristic forms of communication not only by their unique neural speech centers, but also by special structural and functional characteristics of their vocal apparatus, face, and hands. In fact, some scholars have suggested that the inability of the other primates to use even simple speech is basically a consequence of their particular laryngeal anatomies rather than the lack of speech centers in their central nervous systems.[355] The development of erect posture freed the hands of human beings for prehension and, eventually, for delicate, skillful manipulations. The human mouth and jaws were also enabled to develop into suitable form to produce speech. The mutation or mutations which produced, in man alone, the muscle that flexes the thumb joint, significantly improved his ability to hold a writing instrument. The human nervous system differs from that of any other species in ways that facilitate the different output transducing processes of which human beings are capable. The human pyramidal tract is better developed. Areas in which hands and face are represented are larger in the human motor cortex.

TABLE 8-5   Schematic Representation of Assumed Stages in Output Transducing of Language

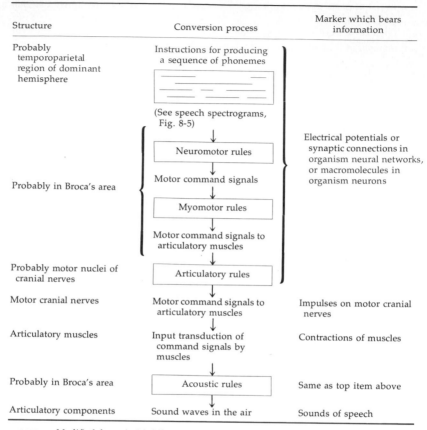

Structure	Conversion process	Marker which bears information
Probably temporoparietal region of dominant hemisphere	Instructions for producing a sequence of phonemes	
	(See speech spectrograms, Fig. 8-5)	
	Neuromotor rules	Electrical potentials or synaptic connections in organism neural networks, or macromolecules in organism neurons
Probably in Broca's area	Motor command signals	
	Myomotor rules	
	Motor command signals to articulatory muscles	
Probably motor nuclei of cranial nerves	Articulatory rules	
Motor cranial nerves	Motor command signals to articulatory muscles	Impulses on motor cranial nerves
Articulatory muscles	Input transduction of command signals by muscles	Contractions of muscles
Probably in Broca's area	Acoustic rules	Same as top item above
Articulatory components	Sound waves in the air	Sounds of speech

SOURCE: Modified from A. M. Liberman, F. S. Cooper, D. P. Shankweiler, & M. Studdert-Kennedy. Perception of the speech code. *Psychol. Rev.*, 1967, **74**, 445. Copyright by the American Psychological Association. Reprinted by permission.

Damage to Broca's area disturbs the expression of speech without producing either paralysis of the articulatory muscles or loss of the ability to think in symbols (encode) or to understand speech (decode).[356] Such damage appears specifically to hamper transduction of spoken gamma-coded information outputs.

Diencephalic components may affect the rate and emotional quality of speech.[357] Stuttering and related speech defects have multiple causes, including perhaps conflicts in the controls on speech exerted by the dominant and the nondominant cerebral hemispheres, since disturbed speech outputs are more common in left-handed people.[358] Other causes may be emotional interference with speech outputs and disturbance of the normal auditory feedbacks (see page 464).

Output transducing is characteristically slower than encoding and the channel capacity of the output transducer is less than that of the decoder. A person can to some extent compensate for this discrepancy by holding encoded ideas in short-term memory and releasing them later, when the channel becomes available. A good typist, for example, will often type at full speed while storing in memory as much as a whole sentence ahead. One reason executives dictate letters is to save time, which is possible because speech is faster than typing or writing. Just as speech is accelerated by emitting phonemes on several frequency bands simultaneously, so human communicators often speed their transmissions by using several output transducer components at once. For example, a new question can be answered by a gesture like a nod of the head while a previous idea is still being expressed in speech.

Representative *variables* of the output transducing process are: *Meaning of information output which is transduced.* Example: The deaf patient made the signal which meant "under." *Sorts of information output which are transduced.* Example: The child said "no" and then began to sob. *Threshold of the output transducer.* Example: After his stroke the aphasic patient was able only to swear. *Changes in output transducing over time.* Example: The old man spoke more slowly than he had but with the same characteristic emphasis. *Changes in output transducing with different circumstances.* Example: The alcoholic's speech became slurred after his fifth whiskey. *Channel capacity of the output transducer.* Example: The speaker's ideas came so fast that he began to stammer. *Number of channels in use in the output transducer.* Example: The executive gestured to her secretary to come in as she continued to talk on the telephone. *Distortion of the output transducer.* Example: The senator's speech was slurred because he was so tired, although he could think clearly. *Rate of output transducing.* Example: The applicant typed at the rate of about 80 words per min. *Lag in output transducing.* Example: The suitor knew exactly what he wanted to say, but he spoke hesitantly because he was embarrassed. *Intensity of information output.* Example: When the woman saw the burglar, she screamed so loudly that a policeman two blocks away came on the run. *Costs of output transducing.* Example: The singer suffered from laryngitis after the opera.

4. Relationships among subsystems or components

Up to this point in this chapter each sort of subsystem and component has been discussed separately. The relationships among them are also important. For example: It is essential to proper physiological function that capillaries, which are components of the distributor, be contained within lungs and gills, which are components of the ingestor. Or it is basic that blood flows more rapidly in the aorta leading from the heart than it flows through any vein. Or it could explain how one word elicits another during free-association experiments if future research should indicate that words of similar meaning are stored in components of the memory which are near one another.

The following sorts of relationships exist in organisms:

4.1 Structural relationships
4.1.1 Containment   Example: The lungs are in the chest.
4.1.2 Number   Example: Coelenterates have a single body cavity.
4.1.3 Order   Example: Food travels through the

ingestor and into the converter. It then passes through components of the converter arranged in space in the following order: first, components that break down large chunks of food into smaller ones and then components that break down large molecules of food into smaller ones.
4.1.4 Position   Example: Input transducers are located near the organism's boundary.
4.1.5 Direction   Example: The spinal cord lies in a caudal direction from the brain.
4.1.6 Size   Example: Rats have a large olfactory cortex but little frontal cortex.
4.1.7 Pattern   Example: Radial symmetry is a pattern characteristic of echinoderms.
4.1.8 Density   Example: The average density of all the components of birds is low as compared to mammals, which makes them light enough to fly.
4.2 Process relationships
4.2.1 Temporal relationships
4.2.1.1 Containment in time   Example: Transmission of the largest quantities of epinephrine from the adrenals to other components occurs during periods of stress.
4.2.1.2 Number in time   Example: Gallbladders ordinarily release bile into the intestine after every meal, or about 3 times in 24 h.
4.2.1.3 Order in time   Example: In many species of animals, transmission of hormones follows input transduction of information that a receptive member of the opposite sex is present.
4.2.1.4 Position in time   Example: Dye injected into the distributor of an organism at 12 noon is usually fully excreted by 2:45 P.M.
4.2.1.5 Direction in time   Example: Increased ingestion of oxygen follows increased use of the motor subsystem in animals.
4.2.1.6 Duration   Example: A high fever causes the heart to beat faster for several days.
4.2.1.7 Pattern in time   Example: During exercise, motor neurons input volleys of synchronized impulses to muscle fibers.
4.2.2 Spatiotemporal relationships
4.2.2.1 Action   Example: The bile normally passes out of the gallbladder and into the intestine.
4.2.2.2 Communication   Example: The movement of a light across the retina is signaled through several echelons up to the visual projection cortex.
4.2.2.3 Direction of action   Example: In the fetus the optic nerve grows outward to meet the developing cornea, lens, and other external structures of the eye.
4.2.2.4 Pattern of action   Example: During metamorphosis, the components of a moth's body reform into a quite different spatial configuration.
4.2.2.5 Entering or leaving containment   Example. An acute strangulation can occur if an automobile

accident causes a driver's stomach to herniate through his diaphragm.

4.3 Relationships among subsystems or components which involve meaning   Example: When a signalman stands with one signal flag held over his head and one at his feet he is transmitting the letter "D."

5. System processes

5.1 Process relationships between inputs and outputs   Important findings can be made about an organism without crossing its boundaries to make internal observations or measurements of its subsystems. When an organism is viewed in order-analytic terms or, in engineering terms, as a "black box," orderly relationships can be observed among its inputs and outputs of matter-energy and of information without paying attention to internal processes of the system. Intralevel, as contrasted with interlevel, hypotheses about these relationships can be made and tested. These alter systematically as inputs are varied by experimenters. A number of leading psychological theorists, including Watson and Skinner, have asserted that this order-analytic approach to the study of behavior is the only useful or valid one. One reason they give for this is that the anatomy and physiology of the bodily components which carry out the processes most interesting to psychologists are so poorly understood that referring to them throws little light on those processes. Another is that a large measure of control over outputs can be achieved experimentally by simply varying inputs without entering the organism at all.[359]

Norms for animal species or types, as well as for individual organisms, have been established for a large number of input–output relationships of both matter-energy and information. Those discussed below are a small sample of the many such relationships for which norms have been determined in experiments using human subjects.

Species norms.   Normal behavior or adjustment for a given species or type of organism can be defined as the maintenance of a set of variable input–output relationships within steady-state ranges characteristic of the species. The degree of responsiveness to inputs of various sorts, rates of processing information from input to output, typical manners of responding to changes in a wide range of environmental variables, and many other observable and measurable relationships between inputs and outputs fit together into a pattern that is characteristic of organisms of each species.

(a) *Matter-energy inputs related to matter-energy outputs.*   Chronic lack stress of oxygen, such as mountain climbers experience at high altitudes, greatly accelerates breathing. In human beings, sudden brief, severe anoxia produced by decompression in a pressure chamber, causes an instant arrest of all motor outputs.[360] The subject is motionless, his eyes stare, and his face freezes. His posture is maintained.

Lack stresses of food inputs over a continued period of 24 weeks in one experiment changed the outputs of a group of healthy young men.[361] On a diet averaging 1500 calories (cal) a day, all lost weight, a change indicating that this amount of input was below the usual intake for each man. Their hand and arm movements were slower. Their coordinated movements were less precise. Their muscular strength was less. The average time they could run on a treadmill before being exhausted decreased from 242 to 50 s. And their general activity diminished.

(b) *Matter-energy inputs related to information outputs.*   Chronic lack stress of oxygen produces progressively more marked behavioral effects. Under anoxia, a person begins to act foolishly and irrationally, even though he has a subjective feeling of confidence and well-being. Impairment of judgment, memory, emotional stability, and function of the input transducers follows. Vision shows the effects of oxygen lack early.[362] Effects are found upon the visual threshold, dark-adaptation, acuity, extent of visual fields, and other functions. Motor tremors also appear early. Hearing remains undisturbed until late. Tests made on climbers who were also members of a scientific expedition showed significant impairment on tests of word recognition, flexibility of decision making, and memory. Complex mathematical computations that were part of the subjects' work, however, were carried out without error.[363]

Often, organisms must carry out a number of tasks simultaneously while they surmount a number of stresses. Astronauts and cosmonauts, for instance, must be able to survive and perform in such situations. An experimental study of stresses that might affect pilots of experimental aircraft combined the matter-energy lack stress of a low-oxygen atmosphere like that at 3650 m above sea level with two matter-energy excess stresses, 110 dB of white noise and an ambient temperature of 41°C.[364] In separate 22-min sessions, each subject was exposed to each of the stresses singly and in all possible combinations. During each session the subject carried out a primary tracking task simultaneously with secondary tasks—monitoring radar warnings and meter readings. The noise stress shortened response times on the meter monitoring task and the low oxygen stress improved tracking performance, although it increased meter-monitoring errors. All three stresses together combined to impair the primary tracking task, but this total effect was less than additive, and actually less than the effect of noise alone. On the secondary task of monitoring radar warnings, the effect of the combined stresses was more than additive. That is, the total effect was greater than would have been predicted from summing the separate effects of the three stresses. Practically, these results warn that, even if the separate effects of a number of stresses are within safe bounds, one cannot assume that a situation which combines them is equally safe. The findings also suggest that attention to the primary task may mean that it is less affected by stresses, but at the cost of poor performance on the associated tasks (see page 35). These results seem consistent with Hypothesis 5.2.1 (see pages 105 and 106), which states that a stress may initially increase output performance above ordinary levels before causing it to deteriorate.

Inputs of normal or excess dosages of drugs that affect the nervous system influence behavior. Catnip produces frolicsomeness in cats, tigers, and other felines, but not in human beings. The behavior of the human species, however, is influenced by a wide range of drugs including sedatives, tranquilizers, antidepressants, energizers like benzedrine and methedrine, stimulants like strychnine and picrotoxin, anesthetics, analgesics, psychotomimetic drugs like LSD and psilocybin, narcotics like morphine, opium, heroin, hashish, marihuana, and many others.

(c) *Information inputs related to matter-energy outputs.* In human beings the information input of a tap on the tendon below the kneecap on the average takes 0.03 s to produce the matter-energy output of a knee jerk.[365] If the information input is a touch on the eye, the resultant wink comes more slowly, in 0.05 s. The times for other species of these same input–output relationships are somewhat different.

Human subjects instructed to start a race or begin boxing or press a key or a pedal as quickly as they can after a signal, respond more slowly to a visual input than to a sound or touch. This may be one reason why pistols are shot to start races. The minimal time for such a simple reaction, a matter-energy output to an information input, regardless of the sensory modality of the signal, is in human beings about 0.1 s.[366]

(d) *Information inputs related to information outputs.* If the organism's inputs and outputs are both information, the total organism can be viewed as a channel, and measurements of variables commonly made on other channels—such as channel capacity, bandwidth, threshold, lag, processing time, and output range—can be applied to it (see Hypotheses 5.1-1 through 5.1-24, pages 103 and 104, which deal with such variables). When a given response of an organism must be preceded by a deci-

sion among alternative reactions, its output is not merely matter-energy. Rather the matter-energy output is a marker which conveys information. The choice reaction time, or decision time, of such a response is longer than a simple reaction time. Other aspects of the input being identical, the more alternatives reviewed, the longer it is (see pages 132 to 136). If, in addition, the response requires other sorts of information processing, such as searching the memory for words or numbers before the output, the response time is even longer.

When a person must control machinery or monitor and report upon instrument readings, the efficiency of his or her responses to changing inputs differs with the sensory modality and the code in which the inputs are presented and with the nature of the outputs required. If inputs and outputs are highly compatible, as they are when Arabic numerals are presented visually and an English-speaking college student is required to name them verbally, both speed and accuracy of responses and rate of information transmission are greater than they are when the inputs to such a subject are less familiar symbolic codes for numerals, such as various sets of lines, colors, or ellipses.[367] When subjects respond to the input signals by pressing keys with their fingers, their reactions are more rapid but less accurate than their verbal outputs. In one experiment of this sort the fastest rate of information transmission, with Arabic numeral inputs and verbal outputs, was 4.38 bits per second. The slowest, with ellipse inputs and verbal outputs, was 2.56 bits per second (see page 142). In general, input–output compatibility increases with practice and is greater if the modes of input and output are similar, *e.g.*, if the input numerals are displayed in ascending sequence from left to right and the keys pressed in making the output are arranged similarly.

Many other input variables affect outputs. Such dimensions as size, weight, color, and position interact with one another so that when a judgment is made about the size of an object, its other characteristics enter unbidden into the calculation. In one experiment, for instance, two gray disks of the same size but of different weight, and a larger black disk which weighed the same as the less heavy of the gray ones, were judged as to size. They were so presented that when the subject held them up, their images on his retina were all of the same size. The experimental data showed that the size of the heavier gray disk was overestimated more often, and that of the black disk less often, than the size of the lighter gray one.[368] Tilting the gray disks in various ways also affected the judgments of size.[369] The value of objects to an individual also influences his estimates of their size, particularly as remembered after an intervening time interval.[370]

Surrounding noise alters outputs to different degrees depending on the task. Under some circumstances it can improve performance, but usually it impairs it. It is hard to ignore novel, intense, or high-pitched noises, so usually they interfere with ongoing activities. Any task of such a character that a person performing it must have continuous vision is easily disturbed by noise, which accelerates the rate at which her or his eyes blink.[371]

When inputs arrive at the same time over different channels—for instance, the visual and auditory communication bands—or when different messages arrive at the two eyes or ears simultaneously, a number of factors influence a person's ability to respond appropriately to them (see pages 145 and 146).[372] If the messages from the two sources are identical, the task is made easier since they facilitate each other. If the two messages compete, the rate of transmission and the amount of information in the signals become important. The slower a message is transmitted and the more redundant it is, the easier it is to receive and respond to. For example, a high school student can study and listen to the radio at the same time if the rate of information transmission in each of the competing inputs is slow enough to allow her or him to alternate attention between them. Another effective adjustment is holding part of the incoming information in short-term memory and responding first to one source and then to the other, as Hypotheses 5.1-32 and 5.1-33 (see pages 104 and 105) suggest. Selectivity or filtering is the rule in everyday life (see pages 61 and 426 to 428). People do not respond to all the flood of information inputs that constantly surrounds them. Filtering is easier if the meaning of some of the information is irrelevant and if the irrelevant material comes from a different source than the relevant, or if the two can be readily distinguished by differences in loudness or pitch.

Individual variations. Some individuals are stronger, larger, healthier, more talented, better educated, or more disposed toward a certain activity than others. Individual genetic constitutions and past histories vary. Consequently, within the range of species norms for different processes, individual organisms differ in their characteristic input–output relationships.

(a) *Matter-energy inputs related to matter-energy outputs.* Clinical medicine uses a large number of measures of matter-energy inputs and outputs as aids in determining whether a patient deviates pathologically from the normal steady-state ranges of a set of physiological variables. Determinations of excretion rates of injected dyes or radioactive materials are examples of such tests.

(b) *Matter-energy inputs related to information outputs.* Individual human beings respond idiosyncratically to a range of drugs which act on the nervous system and affect behavior.[373] For example, some persons develop tolerance to strychnine, alcohol, or opiates. Nembutal, a barbiturate, sometimes acts as an excitant, and LSD effects are notoriously different from one user to another. Food and other allergenic inputs can affect the behavior of recipients by creating a state of anaphylactic shock in which they may vomit, be unable to speak rationally, or lose consciousness. Such reactions also are highly idiosyncratic.

(c) *Information inputs related to matter-energy outputs.* It is common knowledge that individuals differ greatly in physical abilities, in the way they make certain matter-energy outputs that are elicited by information signals. These include athletic skills such as racing, archery, marksmanship, hockey, or baseball, as well as artistic abilities such as ballroom or acrobatic dancing. Tests of mechanical aptitude, manual dexterity, and muscular strength quantify these individual differences.

(d) *Information inputs related to information outputs.* Human judgments of the intelligence and personality characteristics of other persons depend to a great extent upon observation of their personal constancies in response to inputs of various sorts and upon a comparison of these with others' responses. Some of these individual characteristics remain remarkably stable over long periods of time. In early childhood, human beings begin to become expert in sizing up one another. In any particular case, irrelevant variables such as the appearance or social position of the person they are judging can bias their observations and evaluations. People also learn early, with more or less success, to conceal their undesirable attributes from others who are observing them.

Since such observations, even when made by trained observers, are subject to error, standardized tests and situations have been developed for estimating a person's general intelligence, special capabilities, attitudes (see pages 459 and 460), and status in relation to others on literally hundreds of other variables.

5.2 Adjustment processes among subsystems or components, used in maintaining variables in steady states. Each type of organism, from protistans to primates, has adjustment processes to meet the ordinary changes in flows of matter-energy and information which it encounters in the course of its daily life. Each also has some more or less costly emergency adjustments upon which it can call under particularly stressful conditions. The adjustment processes of protistans, fungi, and plants are restricted in number and effectiveness. Organisms at the higher end of the evolutionary scale are sensitive to a greater range of environmental and suprasystem changes and have more resources for maintaining steady states both within and outside the system. Human beings, with their abilities to use gamma-coded language and to employ tools and materials to change their environment, have the greatest capacity of any type of organism both to restore and maintain steady states and to disturb them. In general, the more advanced a species is in evolutionary development, the longer it lives and the more important are its adjustment processes which involve information flows. This generality is consistent with Hypothesis 3.3-1 (see page 94), which states that up to a maximum less than 100 percent, the larger the percentage of its matter-energy input a system consumes in information processing, the more likely it is to survive.

Adjustment processes ordinarily return the organism to approximately the steady state which existed before the input or stress began. Extreme stresses, or those which continue over a long time, call upon costly emergency processes or find the organism with no really effective adjustments available. After such a stress, the steady state which is achieved may be different from that which existed before. Interactions among subsystems may be different, and environmental relationships may also be changed. This alteration can be essentially irreversible, in my terminology a historical rather than a functional process (see page 23). Sometimes the new steady state improves the organism's chances for survival and well-being. A new home, built after a hurricane, may be much better than the old one; a new emotional adjustment after an argument, more stable. On the other hand, an accident or illness may leave the organism permanently crippled.

5.2.1 Matter-energy input processes Plants have few adjustment processes beyond their ordinary subsystem functions to combat either lack or excess stresses of matter-energy. Some, like desert plants and legumes, have unusually large storage tissues to tide them over periods of lack. Others can die back to the ground, preserving a spark of life in roots or bulbs, until conditions are again favorable. Against lacks or excesses of minerals, water, or carbon dioxide, they appear to have no adjustments. On the whole, plants depend upon a beneficent environment to provide the needed inputs in the proper quantities.

Animals, except for primitive sessile forms, are both more mobile and more adaptable than plants. They are able to range beyond their normal territories to avoid excess inputs of any sort or to seek needed inputs which they lack.

Adjustment processes to excesses of matter-energy inputs. If a land animal falls into a lake, it tries to swim out to evade the excess stress of water in which it might drown. If it is in sunlight that is too hot, it moves into the shade, though in some cases this may be so costly in time and energy expenditure that unnecessary thermoregulation is not carried out.[374] If it is pressed down by a rockfall or shocked with electricity or attacked by a larger animal, it tries to escape from that territory. In each case the animal uses its motor subsystem to move out of a spatial region and so avoid the excess stress which exists there.

Once the excess of matter or energy has crossed the organism's boundary, the effective adjustments are different. A foreign body like a splinter, a thorn, or a bullet can be removed by the fingers, extruded with the draining pus of an abscess which forms around it, or sequestered in a pocket of fibrous tissue. Excess inputs of food and water in general are excreted, and probably—as Hypothesis 5.2-4 (see page 106) suggests—an organism's range of stability for the variable measure of the bodily concentration of the input is a monotonically increasing function of the rate of its output.

Ingestion of large amounts of water, or certain other substances, increases the filtration rate of fluids through the glomeruli of the kidneys and consequently the rate of urine formation. Ingestion of large excesses of sodium chloride causes edema fluid to accumulate in tissue spaces between cells throughout the body.[375] Smaller excesses result in slight rises in the rates of glomerular filtration and renal plasma flow, but large increases in sodium and chloride in the urine. This increase in excretion occurs because a significantly smaller portion of the fluid filtered through the kidney glomeruli is resorbed by the renal tubules.

Adjustment processes to lacks of matter-energy inputs. One way in which animals make up for lack of available food is to forage through the environment until they find some. Another is to substitute some less desirable food for the accustomed diet. A third is to use up stored matter-energy. Probably, as Hypothesis 5.2-4 (see page 106) states, in an organism suffering from a lack strain produced by diminished input of a given sort of matter-energy, the range of stability of the variable which serves as a measure of the bodily concentration of that specific sort of matter-energy is a monotonically increasing function of the amount of storage of the input. For some species, however, genetic determination of what foods constitute acceptable inputs is so inflexible that they rarely or never use this adjustment. The decider subsystem may also signal other subsystems to make internal adjustments. When deprivation of food is serious, for instance, motor outputs are reduced because muscle is low in the order of priority for receiving distributions of the scarce supplies available to the system.[376] Studies on farm animals show that the central nervous system has first priority. Bone is next, then muscle, then fat. Fat is a storage tissue, and consequently during starvation it is used up first. It is restored last after food is eaten again.

A diet very low in sodium chloride over three days or more slightly decreases the rates of filtration of the kidney glomeruli and of renal plasma flow, but extrusion of sodium chloride is reduced almost to zero.[377] This is primarily because of a significant rise in resorption of it by the kidney tubules after glomerular filtration.

A decreased rate of oxygen input quickly elicits a number of adjustment processes, since the body does not store significant amounts of oxygen.[378] When the oxygen content of the blood falls or the carbon dioxide content increases, there is a decrease in rate of signals transmitted from the carotid sinus over the glossopharyngeal (IX) cranial nerve to the respiratory center in the reticular formation. Then the inspiratory portion of the respiratory center signals the respiratory muscles to increase pulmonary ventilation by more rapid breathing. The alveoli of the lungs dilate, making more efficient use of what input there is. A faster heart rate, elevated blood pressure, and greater cardiac output improve distribution throughout the body of blood bearing oxygen. The amount of hemoglobin in the blood increases, red blood cells being transferred into the bloodstream from storage. An excess stress of oxygen input has opposite effects, since it depresses the respiratory center.

A number of variables govern an individual's adjustments to high altitude, including the altitude he attains, the duration of his exposure to decreased oxygen input, his rate of ascent, the amount of physical exertion involved, his age, and his physical condition. A person experiencing the stress of high altitude may have headache, lethargy, and other subjective indications of altered physiology. If the change in altitude occurs gradually as it does when a man climbs a mountain on foot instead of taking the train, acclimatization can take place.[379] This is consistent with Hypothesis 5.2-5 (see page 106), which states that there is an inertia to the matter-energy and information processing variables which a system maintains in steady state, so that change in their ranges of stability is much less disruptive of system controls if it is undertaken gradually. Acclimatization occurs more readily in some people than in others. Men living permanently in the Andes at an altitude of 4,400 m did not show a classic response to stress, the increased excretion of adrenal steroids (see page 452), which was found in the urine of new arrivals.[380] The reason for this is not clear. Permanent residents did have altera-

tions in iron metabolism and blood formation, with more red cells in their blood and increased ability to transport oxygen.[381] Guinea pigs kept at a high altitude had a significantly greater number of capillaries per square millimeter of muscle tissue and a higher ratio of capillaries to muscle fibers in the same parts of their bodies than guinea pigs which were kept in Lima, Peru at sea level.[382] So internal adjustments in both human beings and guinea pigs made more effective use of available materials to alleviate the harmful effects of diminished rates of oxygen inputs.

Cognitive functions of members of a scientific expedition to the Andes were impaired at high altitudes. Even at 5,350 m, however, an increased expenditure of energy, more rest periods, and greater concentration of attention enabled the scientists to adjust and carry out complex mathematical calculations without mistakes. They also made only slightly more errors on the Thorndike Mental Test and spent only a slightly longer time completing it.[383]

Adjustments to the seasons. Seasonal changes often stress organisms. Frequently they create lack stresses. The short days of winter deprive plants of the radiant energy they require for photosynthesis, while the frozen ground yields little water. Insects, birds, reptiles, and many species of herbivorous mammals, as well as bears which are partly carnivorous, cannot secure their usual food. Similarly, in hot, dry climates, needed water may be lacking.

Organisms have a variety of different adjustments to such stresses. During the winter, trees and many other plants become dormant, drop their leaves and suspend respiration and photosynthesis. Some mobile animals, especially birds, migrate to more hospitable environments. Others, like squirrels, depend upon stored food to carry them through periods when their usual provender is scarce. Still others, including a large number of vertebrate and invertebrate species, hibernate in winter or aestivate in summer, as the case may be. These include many species of reptiles, insects, amphibians, and mammals. Birds, fish, and carnivorous mammals usually do not have this adjustment process. Birds and fish can move to more comfortable locations. Carnivores can continue to hunt their prey.

Preparation for hibernation or aestivation includes matter-energy storage within the organism, location or preparation of a den, burrow, or other protected spot, and changes in rates of input, internal, and output matter-energy and information processes. Ground squirrels, notable hibernators, increase their feeding with the approach of winter and store the extra inputs until they are decidedly obese, perhaps even doubling their usual weight. Then they retreat to a snug burrow and roll themselves into furry balls. As the cold winter deepens, their body temperature falls to within a few degrees of freezing, a temperature which would be fatal to a nonhibernator. This is resetting of the criterion or comparison reference signal of the "thermostat" (see page 36) rather than suspension of control by the decider, since their body temperature consistently was found to be higher than their environment while their brain temperature was even higher.[384] Their hearts continue to beat but at a rate as slow as 1 per min, as contrasted with waking rates of 200 to 400 beats per min. The respiration rate, normally about 200 in these tiny mammals, drops to 4 per min. In spring they emerge thin and hungry but otherwise unharmed by what may well seem to them no more than a brief nap.

These annual cycles of dormancy found in organisms of widely divergent types are not yet fully understood. Changes in the hypothalamic nuclei responsible for control of body temperature, water conservation, and feeding have been suggested as the fundamental processes underlying mammalian hibernation.[385] The function of the hypothalamus of mediating between the external world and internal organismic controls, including those exerted by the endocrines, makes this suggestion appear reasonable (see pages 392 and 393). Alterations in the relative lengths of day and night are known to be crucial in plant dormancy, as in other plant processes, and may well be involved in triggering annual periodicities in animals.[386] The relationship of light–dark cycles to animal circadian rhythms has been established (see page 454). It has been suggested that the hypothalamus responds to signals from light input transducers.[387] In insects, light effects release of the hormone that produces dormancy (diapause) as well as other changes.

The general adaptation syndrome. Matter-energy input stresses, as well as other sorts, elicit a *general adaptation syndrome* (GAS) in human beings and in physiologically similar animals.[388] Among these stresses are inputs of anesthetics, other drugs, toxins, excessive food, large dosages of x-rays, and excessive sunlight. Each sort of stress, of course, acts primarily upon particular organism components, and often the stress can be eliminated or otherwise handled by local subsystem adjustments. When these are inadequate, however, the organismwide adjustments which constitute the GAS are called upon. This is what would be expected if, as Hypothesis 5.2-1 (see page 105) indicates, what is extreme stress for one subsystem may be only moderate stress for the total system. According to Selye, who first identified this syndrome and has studied it experimentally, it has three stages.[389]

The *alarm reaction* is the first stage. A typical matter-energy input stress is the invasion of tissue by bacteria which are able to survive and reproduce despite the local destructive phagocytic action of macrophages in the tissue and white cells in the blood and tissue. The bacteria multiply and damage the tissue. Information about the location and extent of this damage enters vascular and neural channels, each affected cell sending its signal to constitute part of the total message. One effect of these signals is to cause the adrenal cortex to secrete aldosterone and desoxycorticosterone. These start an inflammatory process in the tissue under stress, a bodily defense against bacterial invaders. Signals are also transmitted to the posterior and medial regions of the hypothalamus, regions which control various endocrine and neural responses. From there signals go to the pituitary gland, which secretes adrenocorticotrophic hormone (ACTH) into the bloodstream. This hormone, in turn, signals the adrenal cortex to secrete the adrenocortical hormones, cortisone and hydrocortisone. These counteract the adrenocortical hormones, such as aldosterone and desoxycorticosterone, which start the inflammatory process. Ultimately, after the bacterial stress is ended, cortisone and hydrocortisone facilitate the return of the involved tissue to a healthy state.

At the same time, the stress can act to increase activity of the sympathetic nervous system and cause acetylcholine to be released at synapses and epinephrine and norepinephrine to be secreted by the adrenal medulla into vascular channels. These substances have opposing effects on the inflammatory process. Acetylcholine dilates capillaries locally in the tissue involved, and so accelerates the inflammatory process. Epinephrine and norepinephrine have the opposite effect.

If the stress continues for hours or days, a second stage of the GAS develops, the stage of *resistance*. Within minutes or hours after the state of shock begins, its signs and symptoms commence to disappear. The organism becomes adjusted to the stress, usually limiting it to the smallest component capable of coping with it. The particular adjustment processes necessary to deal with the specific stress are mobilized, *e.g.,* the inflammatory process and immune reactions ordinarily halt the reproduction of the invading bacteria and kill them. The adrenal cortex becomes enlarged during the alarm-reaction stage in which its rate of secretion is increased, but this rate now lessens because the demand for adrenocortical hormones diminishes. Many or all deviations from normal steady states which occurred in the alarm reaction are corrected.

A final stage of the GAS is *exhaustion*. It occurs

only if the adjustment processes available to the system for keeping critical variables within their steady-state ranges are unable to cope with the stress. More and more resources are called upon to deal with both specific local stress and nonspecific stress affecting the entire organism. Many of the characteristics of the alarm reaction reappear, and if a steady state is not then reestablished, resources for adjustment are finally used up, and the organism dies. This sequence of events conforms to Hypothesis 5.2-2 (see page 106), which states that the greater a stress upon a system, the more components of it are involved in adjusting to it, and when no further components with new adjustment processes are available, the system function collapses.

Whether stress is eliciting the GAS can be determined by counting the subject's white blood cells to see if their number is elevated above normal, finding whether the proportion of eosinophils is lowered, measuring the quantities of excreted adrenocortical hormones or breakdown products from them such as 17-ketosteroids in the subject's urine, and carrying out other tests. Such measurements are frequently made to show that some situation to which an organism has been exposed was in fact stressful. Urinary 17-ketosteroid excretion, for example, was found to increase in climbers at high altitudes. This increase meant that their adrenal cortexes were more active than normal. The 17-ketosteroids form portions of the molecules of adrenocortical hormones and also of the male sex hormones. Also, they are breakdown products of their metabolism. They are found in the urine of both men and women, in greater amounts in the former. Other measures besides known correlates of the GAS indicate whether the organism is under stress. Electrical resistance of the skin recorded from electrodes, for instance, is altered by minute changes of output of sweat under both matter-energy and information input stresses. This is the "psychogalvanic skin response." Muscular tension also increases under stress.

Individual differences exist among organisms of the same species in sensitivity to particular stresses and to stress in general. Hereditary factors determine some individual differences, for instance, a tendency to allergic reactions. Also previous stresses on the organism may have weakened it or rendered it particularly susceptible.

Costs. Matter-energy input adjustment processes vary in cost depending upon the extent to which they preempt resources of the organism and interrupt its normal activities. All physiological processes use energy. Those adjustment processes which involve increased rates of muscular activity, like breathing or heartbeat, temporarily withdraw energy from functions of other components. Far more serious costs, in the form of permanently diminished function, may occur. Since it is not clear that the central nervous system has a high priority for available oxygen when there is a lack stress of oxygen, the body may be kept alive at the expense of permanent damage to the central nervous system. Cortical tissue does not recover its function if it is deprived of oxygen for more than 5 to 8 min.[390]

The cost of the GAS may ultimately be a permanently diminished ability to resist stress. Increased resistance to one stress lessens resistance to others, which is one reason patients who are ill with other diseases frequently die from pneumonia. What is more, the GAS stage of resistance cannot continue indefinitely, since prolonged stress causes breakdown of essential body proteins.

5.2.2 Information input processes   Organisms adjust frequently to both excesses and lacks in amounts of information inputs. They also make physiological and psychological adjustments to long-term alterations in rates of information flows from the environment. The meaning of the information is important in determining what adjustment processes it elicits.

Adjustment processes to excesses of information inputs.   We have conducted experiments on human subjects which confirm Hypothesis 5.1-1 (see page 103) for the total organism viewed as a channel. As information input rates increase, the output rates also go up until they reach a channel capacity, then level off, and finally decrease toward zero (see also Hypothesis 3.3.4.2-2, page 98). In adjusting to such information input overload or excess stress, our research showed that an organism may make omissions or errors or use queuing, filtering, abstracting, parallel processing in multiple channels, escape, or chunking. The input–output curves and adjustment processes of organisms in our studies were comparable to those of cells, organs, groups, and organizations (see Hypotheses 5.1-2 and 5.1-3, page 103), although there were also systematic cross-level differences.

Adjustment processes to lacks of information inputs. Information input underload is a lack stress. Under normal conditions most people are able to adjust information flows to a comfortable level by seeking or avoiding others, changing the direction of attention, increasing physical activity, or making adjustments in the environment, such as putting up shades or turning on lights. Sensory deprivation, which has been investigated extensively in recent years, can be either an information lack or both an information and an energy lack. Hypothesis 5.1-42 (see page 105) states that a minimum rate of information input to a system must be maintained for it to function normally. This has been observed to have validity in experimental as well as naturally occurring situations in which sensory deprivation occurs. For instance, I have referred above (see page 430) to research which shows that, after light deprivation of several hours, monkeys will press a bar almost insatiably to obtain a brief moment of light for each bar press.[391] In one experiment the rate of bar presses, which provide 0.5 s of light each, increased from about 800 per h after no period of deprivation to about 3,800 per h after 8 h of deprivation. The adjustment process of bar pressing was available to these monkeys as a means for maintaining a minimum rate of light and visual information input. They put out a significant amount of energy to keep up the input rate—the longer the deprivation, the greater the energy expenditure. Human subjects, given the opportunity to relieve the underload conditions by pressing buttons for flashes of light, pressed more frequently for series of light containing more information than for those with relatively little.[392]

The effects of social isolation and lack of variability in information inputs upon people, such as truck drivers, who must spend long hours driving alone, prisoners in solitary confinement, patients in respirators, and explorers alone on the sea or in the wilderness, have been described as an "isolation syndrome."[393] Rather extreme subjective experiences like hallucinations have been reported with even relatively mild sensory deprivation such as is experienced in a long drive alone at night.[394] Experimental subjects have also experienced similar symptoms.

The isolation syndrome has a number of stages, commonly including the following. At first the person is able to pass time thinking, but he finally becomes sleepy and may fall asleep. As time goes on, he is unable to direct his thoughts or to think clearly. He becomes irritable, restless, and hostile. Then he may make an explicit attempt to use fantasy material as an adjustment process to supply his need for information inputs. Later he becomes childlike in his emotional variability and behavior. A stage of vivid visual, auditory, or kinesthetic hallucinations follows, succeeded by a final stage in which there is a sensation of "otherness." He "sees" his subjective experience as a bright area in darkness.

Termination of the information input lack stress does not return the person immediately to normal. He readjusts slowly to society. Hallucinations and "blank periods" may continue to bother him. He often finds it difficult to concentrate attention, and he must take care to keep his fantasies out of his speech.

A variety of experimental situations have been designed to cut information input to subjects to a minimum. In the pioneer work on sensory deprivation at McGill University, the subject lay on a bed in a small room where the temperature was controlled.[395] Any incidental sounds were masked by a fan. Sound inputs were cut down by having the subject wear earphones and put his head on a rubber pillow. The room was continuously lighted, but the subject was prevented from receiving patterned visual inputs by wearing translucent eye shields. He also wore loose-fitting cotton gloves inside cardboard cuffs which reached to his elbow.

In another experiment the subject lay on his back in a tank-type respirator so that he could see no part of his body.[396] His arms and legs were placed in comfortable but rigid cylinders. The respirator motor made a dull, repetitive sound. A small constant amount of artificial light was in the room.

Probably the most extreme experimental form of sensory deprivation was experienced by only two subjects, one of whom was the experimenter himself.[397] Each subject was suspended in a tank of slowly flowing water kept at about body temperature. He wore only a blacked-out head mask through which he breathed and which eliminated visual inputs. Auditory inputs were limited to faint noises from the water pipes and the subject's own breathing sounds. Pressures from the harness and mask were kept constant.

While subjects differed markedly in their abilities to withstand such stresses, the severity of the deprivation imposed also differed. In the small isolation room, subjects were able to remain from two to six days.[398] In the respirator, 6 subjects out of 17, paid by the hour to remain in the machine, managed to stay the full time agreed upon—36 h for 5 of them and 12 h for 1 other. The others, however, voluntarily terminated the experiment in shorter times—from 1.6 to 29.7 h. Four subjects terminated it because of anxiety and panic, and seven because of somatic complaints.[399] Extreme symptoms developed in 2½ to 3 h in the water tank.[400]

Comparable real-life events which have been studied also showed individual variations in responses as well as effects attributable to the severity of the situation. These situations included many stressful aspects such as fear, hunger, and the impotence of anyone to end the stress at will. In many of these perilous adventures, some did not live to give their reports.

An organism experiencing information input lack stresses can increase its activity in the environment in order to speed the rate of information inputs to it. Blind rats moved more than seeing rats when put in an activity wheel which turned whenever they walked.[401]

Blind rats also consumed more saccharin when they were free to do so. This increased their matter-energy and also their information inputs. Furthermore blind rats were more active in operating a clicker device which provided information inputs. Human beings and animals can also move their joints and so send signals from their internal transducer through the nervous system. The subjects in the tank did this and reported that the resultant information flow was so pleasant that it was almost erotic. With this exception, however, the adjustments that subjects in such experiments can use concern internal information processing. For instance, one can sleep. In sleep, time passes quickly while the sleeper dreams and is unaware of the lack of information inputs. Organized thought, possible during early deprivation, also maintains a flow of information which is fairly comfortable for the subject. A prisoner in solitary confinement in a prison in Red China made up for his information input underload by spending hours daily searching through the information stored in his memory—"recycling" poems, historical facts, and mathematical principles he had once learned.[402] When such organized thought breaks down, fantasies and hallucinations, sometimes frightening and sometimes not, take over.

The bulk of the research evidence is that drastic curtailment of information inputs has an important influence on behavior. There are individual differences in the optimal rate of information input for a person to maintain arousal, think well, act effectively, and feel good. In an overview of our present knowledge about sensory deprivation, Goldberger says that

. . . one would no longer claim "hallucinations" (or its current operational variant, "reported visual sensations") as effects due directly to sensory reduction; the current view would require more qualification and would speak of them as being facilitated by or occurring with greater frequency in sensory reduction as compared with a number of other conditions, depending on arousal level, set, personality, and so on. Certainly today's researcher would be most cautious about linking these phenomena to psychosis. Similarly, the current position on cognitive impairment would specify that it is more likely to occur on tasks requiring complex, self-directed efforts; and so on down the line with each behavioral index. Nevertheless, the overall conclusion of the early McGill studies remains: namely, that sensory stimulation is an important ingredient in the maintenance of effective functioning. In fact Zuckerman . . . offers the reader a stronger version of the old aphorism when he suggests that variety (in stimulation) [i.e., information input] is the *bread,* not simply the spice, of life.[403]

Circadian rhythms. In addition to adjusting to underloads and overloads of information at any given moment, animals also adapt to long-term alterations which they have learned to expect in the amounts of information inputs from others of their species and from other sources in their environment.

Most animals, nocturnal, diurnal, and crepuscular (*i.e.,* appearing at twilight), have circadian rhythms. Just as they have seasonal rhythms, so they also have alternate periods of activity and inactivity related to the daily cycle of the sun (see pages 269, 287, and 288). Underlying these overt manifestations are many changes in physiological and biochemical processes. Human beings, who ordinarily follow a cycle in which they are more active during the day, apparently exhibit rhythmicity in all subsystem processes.[404] One that can be readily measured is the fluctuation in internal bodily temperature, which is at its lowest point in the early morning and at its highest in the late afternoon.

While the timing of these rhythms is influenced by movements of the sun and by variations in the amount of light in the environment, it appears that it is not the information in such energy inputs to which the system primarily responds. The rhythms originate primarily within the organism.[405] People whose work or inclinations lead them to be more active at night than during the day adapt to the changed circumstances by bringing their internal rhythms more or less into accord with their actual activities. This takes time.

When organisms are put into an artificial environment from which the variations of day and night are excluded, cyclic activity continues. Experiments with birds have shown that the amount of light affects the length of these cycles.[406] When the light intensity in its environment is 1.8 lux, the bird starts to be active at about 5 A.M., and it has a 24-h period. At 120 lux, it awakens two hours earlier each day than on the preceding day, and has a period of 22 h. A rhythm of sleep and activity persists in people who remain in caves or experimental situations designed to eliminate inputs that would act as time cues to set the cycle of activity. In one experiment the cycle was about 25 h. After 18 days the subject had lost one and one-half 24-h days.[407] Two men who stayed five months in a deep cave in France adjusted to a schedule of 36 h awake and 12 h asleep, believing that to be a 24-h period.[408] In mid-January they estimated the date to be November 15.

Meaning. Adjustments to the meanings of alpha-coded, beta-coded, and gamma-coded information inputs include a wide range of organismic behaviors, some determined wholly by the genetic template and others influenced also by associative learning elicited by information inputs from the environment. For instance, a lion smells the scents of a jungle trail and, having "read" the record of the animals which have recently traversed it, strikes out after them as prey. Many pheasant, chicken, and turkey chicks show innate, protective crouching behavior when anything, even a falling leaf, passes overhead; as they mature, however, they become habituated to common objects likes leaves and flying ducks and no longer cringe to them, and show such protective behavior only to objects which they rarely see overhead, such as predatory hawks.[409]

An input signal that carries a threat of a possibly impending stress can elicit in the receiving organism widespread emergency adjustments (see pages 392, 430, and 431) required for pursuit, flight, or self-defense.[410] Such adjustment processes are largely controlled by the sympathetic division of the autonomic nervous system, together with the adrenal medulla which it innervates. The cells of the adrenal medulla are closely related embryologically to the sympathetic ganglion cells. It secretes epinephrine and norepinephrine, the latter identical to a transmitter substance secreted at the synapses of sympathetic neurons (see page 278). The parasympathetic division of the autonomic nervous system functions to maintain steady states of visceral organ components, including those which, under normal conditions, store matter-energy reserves. Among its activities are control of functions of the gastrointestinal tract and constriction of the pupil of the eye to light.

Under sympathetic and adrenal control, normal activities of some bodily components are increased and others are inhibited. The following effects occur: the heart beats more rapidly; the blood vessels of the abdominal and pelvic viscera constrict; contraction of the smooth muscle of the stomach, intestine, and some other viscera is inhibited; the sweat glands excrete faster; breakdown of glycogen by the liver accelerates; breathing is faster; red blood cells stored in the spleen are released to the bloodstream and provide more oxygen transport capacity; and coagulation time of the blood is decreased. As a result, the blood pressure rises: the heart pumps blood at a more rapid rate; the rate of blood flow to the skeletal muscles and brain increases and carries more oxygen and glucose to them; and fatigue is inhibited. At the same time, digestion and other processes not required for the business at hand are stopped or diminished. Providing more oxygen to the muscles at the cost of temporarily decreasing other essential physiological functions enables the animal to flee, pursue, or fight better. Accelerating the clotting of the blood helps protect the animal if it is wounded. These adjustments prolong its survival and are consistent with Hypothesis 3.3.7.2-18 (see page 101), which states that systems which survive make decisions enabling them to perform at an optimum efficiency for maximum physical power output, which is always less than maximum efficiency. All these activities are accompanied by various signs of rage and fear, such as snarling, grimaces, and raised hair. Human beings report such concomitant subjective feelings as rage, fear, terror, and anger.

Information inputs which indicate that a potential sexual partner is present also may bring about profound changes in virtually every subsystem. Information input stresses, like other sorts of stresses, are capable of evoking the physiological responses of the GAS and the psychogalvanic skin response (see page 452). Psychological stresses (in my terms, information stresses) produce less increase in the rates of excretion of steroids than do such matter-energy stresses as tissue damage.[411]

Within the limits of characteristic species behavior, individuals vary in their sensitivity to stressful information inputs and in the availability and nature of the adjustment processes they employ in response to them. Some rabbits are far more aggressive than others, and there are bulls like Ferdinand, who would rather smell flowers than fight.

Costs. Information input adjustment processes involve costs, such as an expenditure of energy to carry out acts necessary to respond to signals, get attention, or interact with other individuals; delay or loss of efficiency in performing necessary tasks (in the case of emergency adjustments); tissue damage caused by some stresses; and possible long-continued or permanent changes in information processing and social adjustment if stress has been extreme, as when a prisoner is kept in solitary confinement too long.

5.2.3 Matter-energy internal processes Matter-energy is in continual flux within organisms as components grow, involute, increase or decrease their rates of activity, undergo stress, are damaged, or are repaired. Special lack strains in one subsystem, such as the motor subsystem during heavy exercise, or the emergency reaction, or the converter during digestion, may be met by a decrease in flows to other subsystems. Such internal matter-energy adjustments preserve a wide range of internal steady states.

Among the innumerable adjustments of this sort carried on within organisms is that which preserves "water balance," the steady state of the water content of the tissues. Body water is taken in or replenished from three sources: (a) liquids drunk; (b) solid foods ingested, which contain a significant proportion of water (some species of rodents get most or all of their water from foods); and (c) water formed in the biochemical processes of metabolism. Also, each day a vertebrate must extrude approximately the amount of water it ingests, in order to keep from either waterlogging or drying out its tissues. All the regular waste-removal components of the extruder carry off water (see page 373), the primary route being through the kidneys and urinary tract.

While an animal or human being is suffering a lack stress of water, rates of extruding through the kidneys and urinary components are also altered. Depletion of body water increases the electrolyte concentration in extracellular tissues, a change which signals the osmo-receptors in the hypothalamus to send messages to the posterior pituitary to secrete vasopressin, an antidi-uretic hormone that acts directly upon the kidney. Vasopressin increases the resorption of water by the kidney tubules into the bloodstream and thus decreases the volume of urine, by retaining water in the body. Damage to the posterior pituitary can cause diabetes insipidus, a condition in which large quan-tities of urine are extruded. The resultant lack strain of water forces the organism to keep drinking to replace the loss. Experimental lesions in the posterior pitui-tary in cats increased the rate of urinary excretion to 3 to 5 times normal. Hormone replacement therapy cor-rects this condition. An antidiuretic effect can also be produced by stresses such as continued loud noise, exercise, pain, or emotional excitement.[412]

Lacks of various sorts of matter-energy necessary to maintain healthy steady states bring about adjust-ments to correct them. Selection of food by animals or by children is controlled partly by the particular bio-chemical needs of the individual organism. For instance, if rats are fed a diet deficient in vitamin D for about 40 days, they prefer to eat food pellets which contain the needed vitamin and will hoard these in preference to otherwise identical pellets deficient in this necessary input.[413] Normal rats in a rat "cafeteria" providing carbohydrates, fats, proteins, minerals, and vitamins in pure form make selections which keep them healthy. If they are deprived of certain endocrine glands which regulate metabolism, they will select substances which compensate for loss of the hormones secreted by those glands. When the adrenal glands in rats are removed, they lose sodium. After such an operation, they choose to eat increased quantities of this element.[414] Rats under stress of forced exercise also adjust their diets appropriately.[415]

Costs.   Internal matter-energy adjustment processes have costs which are paid in the same coin as the costs of matter-energy input processes (see page 452).

5.2.4 Information internal processes   One set of adjustment processes deals with variations in the quantity and the meaning of information processed in central information processing components. These activities include a large portion of a person's subjec-tive experience—the complex flux of ideas and feel-ings, fantasies and dreams so important to all human beings and obviously so far more advanced in human beings than in any other species.

Yet little is understood about structure and process in the highest parts of the central nervous system

which can be related to these processes. It is known that damage to the central nervous system is perma-nent. Once it is destroyed by trauma or disease, little or no repair to such tissue takes place. What slight repair may occur is rarely enough in itself to restore function. Nonetheless, some sort of switching of sig-nals to alternative channels, which is not yet under-stood, can partially restore normal function, days, weeks, or months after damage has occurred. Evi-dently adjustments take place among components so that remaining parts are able to compensate to some extent for even large losses in some areas, including area 4 of the cortex, the primary motor area. Many losses of function are permanent, as in the bilateral hippocampus and temporal-lobe extirpations already discussed (see page 414). The younger the organism, the better is its recovery of function.[416]

Stress.   Internal processing of emotionally charged information which arouses fear or expectation of undesirable outcomes increases pituitary and adrenal activity and elicits other physiological responses simi-lar to the GAS brought about by information input stresses, disease, or tissue damage (see pages 451 and 452). Subjects in various experiments have showed such responses when placed in situations which appeared extremely dangerous to them and which consequently aroused their fears.[417]

Anxiety.   This unpleasant emotional experience, like pain, may be viewed as a signal that a steady state has been disturbed to a threatening degree. In the presence of a threat or stress, the intensity of the anxiety probably signals the relative strengths of the threat or stress, on the one hand, and the adjustment processes available to counter it, on the other. Either an increase in the threat or stress or a decrease in the adjustment processes, as perceived by the organism, can produce this signal. While anxiety can be patho-logical in some people (see page 476), it is often like pain, a useful signal in normal people that a steady state does not exist because available adjustment pro-cesses appear inadequate to cope with a potential or actual stress.[418] When a person experiences anxiety, GAS physiological measures often indicate that he is under stress (see pages 451 and 452). The anxiety signal is transmitted through the frontal lobes of the brain, and it is eliminated by operative techniques that separate the prefrontal areas from their related thalamic nuclei. This destructive procedure is fol-lowed by profound personality changes. It is some-times carried out to relieve the anxiety of patients suffering intractable pain from terminal cancer.[419] With their dread of future agony ended, such patients are sometimes more able to bear the current pain.

Although anxiety evokes GAS physiological responses indicative of stress, stress and anxiety are not synonymous and do not always coexist. A factor-analytic study of over 3,000 subjects, using 325 different variables, was carried out by Cattell and Scheier.[420] The signs and symptoms usually present in a person with anxiety were not confined to a single variable; but one factor conformed closely, in tension, emotionality, and self-ratings of symptoms, to the usual definition of anxiety. This trait was found in both children and adults. Factor analysis of psychiatric interview protocols secured from 86 students by two psychiatrists showed the same factor.[421] Stress effects, as defined by Selye (see pages 451 and 452), were reflected in a different factor.[422]

Personality. Concepts of personality are based upon inferences from an organism's overt behavior, including speech and subjective report. Personality theories are conceptual systems which usually are concerned with abstracted systems of interaction among a set of *traits*—traits being relationships of similarity which some observer recognizes in repeated comparable acts, gestures, or language of some organism (see pages 16 and 20). These theories differ from those order-analytic theories of behavior, such as the viewpoints of Watson and Skinner, that I have mentioned above (see page 446). The latter theories deal only with inputs to and outputs from organisms rather than processes inside them. Personality theories are ordinarily causal analytic, relating inputs to and outputs from an organism to its internal processes. For instance, Murray contends that such formulations should be concerned not only with overt behaviors and interpersonal communications but also with "covert intraverted mental activities" such as interpretation of memories, self-evaluation, clarification of concepts, artistic creation of all sorts, resolution of intrapersonal conflicts, and development of plans for future actions.[423]

A mass of commonsense generalizations about human nature, clinical observations, and case histories, as well as some experimental findings, constitute the raw materials out of which hundreds of personality theories, past and current, have been manufactured. Many of these are more artistic productions than scientific statements. Only a few can claim any degree of precision, because methods for accurately observing the internal information processes of organisms and quantifying their important variables, including the meanings of the messages, have not yet been developed. Nevertheless, we cannot entirely neglect functions which are such central aspects of human experience. Three theories of personality—those of Murray, Sigmund and Anna Freud, and Menninger—which involve concepts that are obviously similar to aspects of the general living systems theory presented in this book are discussed briefly below.

(*a*) From a background of medicine, biochemistry, psychoanalysis, and psychology, Murray has developed a personality theory that in recent years has included a number of concepts of systems theory. Fundamentally, he deals with abstracted systems and emphasizes their processes, although he recognizes that they also have structures. He writes:

. . . for me, system applies to a more or less uniform integration of *reciprocating* and/or *cooperating* functional activities, each of which, under favorable conditions, contributes to the continuation of the entire cycle of activities which constitute the system. As a rule, such a system is boundary-maintaining. According to this view, each entity (form of matter) involved in a cooperating system may be called an organ, relative to that system, each organ being defined in terms of process and its contributing effect, or since organ processes are not always capable of achieving a contributing effect, in terms of their direction, *endeavor,* or intended effort. Thus, each unified, boundary-maintaining system may be partially defined by representing the integration of successive processes and effects which are required to keep it growing and/or to keep it going as a unique and vital whole.[424]

The importance of negative feedbacks in maintaining variables in homeostatic steady states is explicitly recognized by Murray.[425] Basic concepts of his conceptual system include:[426] (*i*) *Need,* a term essentially synonymous with *drive,* which I call an internal strain resulting from disturbance of a steady state (see page 34). He has listed a set of *viscerogenic* (*i.e.,* somagenic or matter-energy) needs or drives such as those for sex, food, or cold avoidance, and another set of informational or *psychogenic* (*i.e.,* informational) needs, such as those for autonomy, nurturance, achievement, aggression, or affiliation (see pages 429 and 430). (*ii*) *Cathexis,* a term originated by Freud to represent the value placed on a loved person. Murray extends this to any valued entity or activity. (*iii*) *Dyadic system,* two interacting persons, the human group with the fewest members possible (see page 516). (*iv*) *Press,* the need-generated response of an interacting member of a dyadic system. And (*v*) *thema,* a need-press combination, the adjustments of both members of a dyad to each other, consisting of a need-generated action by one member of the dyad and the need-generated overt or covert response it elicits in the other one. Examples of themas are: "*A* tells a joke, but *B* is not amused," "*A* commands, and *B* defies the command," "*A* proposes marriage to *B*, who rejects the proposal," or "*A* injures *B*, who forgives *A*."

Micro themas (single, brief such events) and macro themas (overall, much longer such events) are distinguished by Murray. He is also concerned with serial repetitions of themas, perhaps over months or years. He believes psychologists commonly neglect major overall personality adjustment processes in concentrating almost exlusively on studying brief reactions which take seconds or minutes at most, almost always being completed within the time limits of an experimental session which lasts perhaps an hour.

Throughout his writings Murray repeatedly emphasizes the internal information processing which is the basis of creativity. The so-called "higher mental processes," he notes, are often equated with cognition, the processes whereby people obtain objective knowledge about their environment and analyze information inputs from it. He wants more investigation of how a person learns what experiences are satisfying or dissatisfying, beneficial or harmful; how to cope with environmental changes; how to plan future action, imagine, fantasy, and predict future events. He searches for a way to include in personality theory not only concepts about homeostatic steady states which enable the organism to survive in its environment but also about mutations which enable it to create emergent new patterns.

(b) The classical concept of defense mechanisms presented by Freud and developed further by his daughter Anna is similar in some ways to my concept of adjustment processes.[427] I prefer the latter phrase for two reasons. First, the word "mechanism" ordinarily refers to a structure, whereas what is being discussed is a process. It is important to distinguish structure and process clearly. Second, "defense" refers to the psychoanalytic concept of defensiveness, which in Freudian theory carries the connotation of pathological adaptation, but actually most adjustment processes are healthy and normal. Furthermore, "defense mechanism," being a psychoanalytic term, has overwhelmingly been applied to psychological or informational processes, while "adjustment process" is equally applicable to matter-energy and information processing, as is essential in my conceptual system because of the many parallels between the two sorts of processes.

Internal information adjustment processes are hard to study because they go on in central subsystems and components whose activities are harder to observe than those in peripheral subsystems like the input transducer or the output transducer.

In espousing what he called the "constancy principle," Freud recognized that certain adjustment processes produce a "striving for equilibrium."[428] This idea is similar to what Cannon later termed homeostasis (see Note 98, pages 49 and 50). Three times in his life Freud developed a new theory of human behavior, and if he had lived long enough he might well have created still another.[429] Ernest Jones, Freud's biographer, who understood his mind perhaps as well as anyone, suggested that Freud's hopelessness about comprehending brain function might have been partially dispelled if he had known of recent cybernetic approaches to neurophysiology and psychology. Jones added:[430] "It would be interesting to attempt a correlation between Freud's early attempt and the modern outlook." No one can claim that Freud foresaw systems theory, but a few aspects of his work presaged some of its fundamental concepts.

Basic to the Freudian theory of defense mechanisms is the assumption that certain sorts of internal information processing go on which are unconscious and cannot be verbally reported, and that these are often independent of other information processes which are conscious and verbalizable. Processes of the id are typically unconscious, whereas those of the superego are conscious. Conflicts between these separate sorts of information processes can be disruptive to a person's adjustment and integration, according to Freudian theory, unless defense mechanisms of the ego can cope with the conflicts. This view is consistent with Hypothesis 5.2-20 (see page 108) which states that a system's decider (in this case, the ego) must resolve conflicts among other subsystems (in this case, the id), which signal their demands for autonomy, and the suprasystem (in this case, the superego), which signals commands for compliance. Defense mechanisms serve particularly to make adjustments which prevent or allay anxiety aroused by the conflicts. This anxiety derives from threats to self-esteem and feelings of guilt associated with thoughts which are unacceptable to the superego and which might elicit punishment.

In her book on defense mechanisms Anna Freud listed the following ten types: regression, repression, reaction formation, isolation, undoing, projection, introjection, turning against the self, reversal, and sublimation.[431] Numerous other defense mechanisms have been postulated, including denial, rationalization, identification, suppression, and fantasy. All these adjustments involve internal information processes exclusively. Others involve matter-energy processes as well. Included in these are symptom formation, development of psychosomatic symptoms as an outlet for unresolved emotional conflicts. Hysterical paralyses and blindnesses, peptic ulcer, ulcerative colitis, asthma, neurodermatitis, and various other illnesses are often said to represent such adjustments. Neural processes, particularly in the autonomic nervous system, probably are involved in the causation of each of these illnesses. Neural processes are also involved in alcoholism and drug abuse or addiction, in which inputs of certain chemicals into the body alter the mood and block or relieve anxiety signals temporarily. These last defense mechanisms often are pathological, though moderate use of alcohol and some drugs may be normal.

All defense mechanisms have their costs. Temporarily they may resolve a conflict, but later they can get an individual who uses them into trouble. Many clinicians believe that strong emotions, repressed long enough, will produce some sort of symptoms. Walter Mitty can fantasy that he conquers all before him today, but he must return to his humdrum life tomorrow. Isolation of two logically contradictory thought processes may avoid anxiety now, but some day the moment of truth will come. If the costs of a defense mechanism exceed the benefits from it, its use is pathological.

Clearly the evidence which indicates that each of the above defense mechanisms operates as hypothesized is not so precise and controlled as is the evidence for many other statements in this chapter. A few experiments have been done which are relevant to some of the defense mechanisms, but no overwhelming body of scientific data about any of them exists. Support for these concepts comes mainly from the observations of clinicians on many different patients which seem to show that these are "games people play." They concern the most intimate and important human affairs. They are processes carried on by components of the brain which are as yet largely inaccessible to operational, quantitative, public observation. For these reasons, it is reasonable to give serious consideration to the defense mechanisms as constructs, until research tells us more than we know now about internal information adjustment processes.

(c) Another personality theory has been proposed by Menninger.[432] It relates classical psychoanalytic concepts to present-day systems theory. A central feature of it is a detailed analysis of internal information adjustment processes that he calls coping devices, which are much like Freudian defense mechanisms. His theory deals with four major issues: adjustment, or individual–environmental interaction; systems, or the organization of living systems; psychological regulation and control, otherwise known as "ego theory" in psychoanalysis; and motivation, which in psychoanalysis is often called "instinct theory." Like other systems theorists, Menninger makes a salient point of the principle of homeostasis. He considers the maintenance of steady states to be basic to both psychological and physical processes. Also he contends, as Murray does (see pages 457 and 458), that certain forces cause living systems to search for new and unsettled states. He agrees with Ali Ibn Hazm, who lived from 994 to 1064, that all people are constantly attempting to escape anxiety, the primary principle of human motivation being that " . . . no one is moved to act, or

resolves to speak a single word, who does not hope by means of this action or word to release anxiety from his spirit."[433] Also Menninger believes that negative feedbacks maintain the steady states in living systems, which he calls their vital balance. He recognizes that all living systems are open systems and that they are hierarchies composed of subsystems and subsubsystems. He interprets Freudian personality theory in terms of this systems approach. The ego, he says, is the central executive or decider of the organism. The instincts of the id are dual drives which alter adjustment in either one of two opposite directions. The one drive, sex, tends toward positive relationships with other organisms, human and nonhuman. The other drive, aggression, tends toward disruption of such relationships.

Pointing out that all coping devices have costs in the energy expenditures they entail, Menninger lists the following normal processes commonly used to adjust to the emergencies of everyday life: reassurances by touch, rhythm, sound, speech; food and food substitutes—smoking, chewing gum; alcoholic beverages and other self-medications; self-discipline; laughing, crying, and cursing; boasting; sleep; talking issues and feelings out; thinking through stressful problems; rationalization; working off aggression by physical exercise; acting to alter situations to reduce strains; pointless overactivity to reduce strains, such as finger tapping or floor walking; fantasy formation and day-dreaming; dreaming; slips of the pen and tongue, and other minor errors; symbolic acts; reaction formation; seeking out dangerous situations to relieve anxiety that one is cowardly; and physical and physiological processes, such as sneezing, coughing, itching, scratching, yawning, or blushing.[434]

Noting that stresses on organisms and strains within them are of different orders of magnitude, Menninger asserts the validity for the organism of what is essentially the principle stated in Hypothesis 5.2-2 (see page 106), that the greater a threat or stress upon a system is, the more of the system's components are involved in adjusting to it, and when no further components with new adjustment processes are available, the function of the system collapses (see pages 36 and 83).

Three other concepts of major importance in personality theory—each relating to information internal processes—are attitudes, "structural balance," and cognitive dissonance.

Attitudes are ordinarily defined as intervening variables whose existence can be induced from the expressions of opinions and the likes and dislikes of the person who holds them. Sometimes, however, the term is used for the observable responses themselves, with no reference to any intervening variable.[435] A person's attitudes determine how specific sorts of information are decoded and processed internally. They also shape behavior with respect to relevant objects, people, or ideas. Attitudes are subject to change as a result of persuasion, new information inputs which contradict previously held ideas, imitation of others, or internal adjustment processes which bring information within the organism into a state of balance. Many researches have been carried out about attitude change, and much has been learned about the variables which are relevant to it.[436]

Cognitive consistency theory. Adjustment processes to situations in which a person simultaneously entertains two contradictory ideas, opinions, attitudes, or sentiments have been described and conceptualized in at least six different theories, all of which have been subsumed under the label "cognitive consistency theories."[437] These conceptualizations concern the strains, tensions, or discomforts people experience when they hold apparently inconsistent views; they also concern the different sorts of cognitive or behavioral adjustments they may use to reduce those strains. Among these theories the ones which deal with *cognitive balance, cognitive dissonance,* and *conflict* have led to extensive experimental and theoretical activities.

The cognitive balance theory of Heider focused upon the person in her or his relationships with other people and with things in the environment. It provided a notation in which such relationships can be represented.[438] According to this theory, people organize the contents of the environments or "life spaces" in which they perceive themselves to exist, into units which appear to belong together. Examples of such units are the members of a family, or a person and her or his deed. In Heider's notation such a unit is symbolized by p U x, with p representing a specific person, U a relation which combines entities into units, such as causation, ownership, or similarity; and x an impersonal entity, such as a situation, an idea, an event, or a thing. People also experience *sentiments* such as liking, admiring, and valuing toward cognitive entities. The sentiment relationship is symbolized by p L o, which signifies that p likes, admires, or values another person o, or by p L x, which means that p likes, admires, or values the nonpersonal entity x.

Both unit relationships and sentiments may be negative as well as positive. The symbol for "not" is $\sim$, so that $p \sim$ U x indicates that p is segregated from x, and $p \sim$ L o means that p dislikes, does not admire, or does not value o. Unit and sentiment relationships are often interdependent.

When the relations among entities fit together harmoniously, a *balanced state* exists. In the absence of balance, strains which produce forces toward change arise. A dyad consisting of two relationships is in balance when the signs of both are the same, for example, when p both likes and admires o (p L o, p L o). It is unbalanced when one is positive and the other negative, as when p is dissatisfied with x ($p \sim$ L x), x being a lecture that he himself has just given (p U x).

Also Heider analyzed balance in p-o-x triads, in which three relationships are involved—between p and o, p and x, and o and x. A triad is balanced when all three of the relations are positive or when two are negative and one is positive. Imbalance occurs when two of the relations are positive and one is negative. The three-negative case Heider held to be ambiguous although subsequent work by others has determined balance on the basis of the algebraic product. If the product is negative, imbalance exists. If it is positive, balance exists. For example, if p feels neighborly to o (p L o) and o reminds p of an acquaintance whom we can call x (o U x), and if p is fond of the acquaintance (p L x), these three positive relations result in balance.

One research on cognitive balance has subjects predict the most probable outcome in situations such as one in which Bob discovers that Jim, whom he dislikes, wrote some poems that he liked.[439] This is an unbalanced triad. Of 101 subjects, 46 percent said Bob's evaluation of Jim would change from disliking to liking; 29 percent said Bob's evaluation of the poetry would change from positive to negative. Others said Bob would challenge the unit relationship itself, deciding that he would question that Jim was the author of the poetry. Others said he would decide that Jim had some positive traits and other negative ones. A few predicted that Bob would be confused and would not be sure what to do. Subsequent work based upon this theory has concentrated on L relations and paid little attention to U relations, even though both are important in Heider's complete theory.[440]

Newcomb has interested himself in a special set of Heider's triads in which a person, P, simultaneously experiences cognitions about X (an entity such as an object, person, or idea) and about O (some other person) whose cognitions about X are of interest to P.[441] While Heider ordinarily included two sentiment relations and one unit relation in a triad, Newcomb substituted a third attitude for the single-unit relation, making the assumption that if a subject is confronted with a set of cognitive elements, she or he is forced, at least for the moment, to assume some sort of belonging relation among them. Further, he increased the two states which Heider said a person can experience to three: *balance, imbalance* and *nonbalance*. The last is when the person is not under too much strain to accept a set of cognitive elements as they are, believes they can be modified, or is indifferent about such acceptance or modification. This formulation requires revision of Heider's criteria for balance. Also Newcomb uses the concept of *engagement,* the opposite of indifference, uncertainty, or ambivalence.[442] Lack of engagement does not necessarily mean noninvolvement in a $P - O - X$ relationship, but does imply a state of little or no preference for balance or imbalance. It may occur if a person learning about an imbalanced situation is indifferent to or has little confidence in a person who describes it to her or him.

Cognitive dissonance theory, first developed by Festinger, and conflict theory, derived from Freudian and Pavlovian roots, both deal with strains induced when items of information which are inconsistent with each other are processed simultaneously by a person. These, like the two cognitive balance theories I have just discussed, have resulted in large amounts of research and theoretical controversy and in efforts to specify the conditions under which conflict or dissonance are experienced.[443] They attempt to explain the behavior of individuals before and after they make decisions.[444] Conflicts during the period leading to choice are viewed as creating strains between conflicting informational variables. These strains increase as the average magnitude of the opposing variables grows. They are greatest when the opposing variables are strongest and equal. Such conflict is resolved when the choice is made between the opposites. Processes of this sort appear to be consistent with Hypothesis 5.2-24 (see page 108) which says that resolution of conflicts between two mutually exclusive positive goals is difficult if they appear to be of equal value, but choice is usually made quickly.

Cognitive dissonance theory focuses upon any dissonance which follows a decision (see page 434). If a choice has been made which leaves the person with items of information which are still dissonant, these must be resolved in some way. If, for instance, a person has bought a new car, any information which suggests that another make is better or that her or his own car is less than perfect will be dissonant with the reason for having purchased the automobile.[445] The human need to trust one's own decisions was referred to by Pope in his *Essay on Criticism* when he wrote:[446] " 'Tis with our judgments as our watches, none Go just alike, yet each believes his own." A number of adjustments may reduce such cognitive dissonance. People can avoid reading advertisements for other brands of cars and concentrate upon those for their own make. They can forget or repress the fact that they ever

considered any other kind, thus avoiding thoughts that they might have made the wrong decision. They can get so emotionally disturbed that they sell the car soon afterward and buy another. This last maneuver removes the dissonance concerning the original purchase but opens the way for dissonance concerning the replacement.

Proponents of cognitive consistency theories have been aware of the general criticism that, while there is little doubt that the various behaviors they describe do occur, certainly their opposites also occur. All people do not always prefer consistency and avoid conflict. Some actively seek inconsistency and conflict.[447] Probably both behaviors can occur in the same person. Cognitive consistency theories have also been criticized as imprecise, and lacking in specific predictive power.

Costs. One cost of internal information adjustment processes can be in the energy expenditures involved in the GAS, no matter how it is provoked (see page 452). Another cost may be in diminished effectiveness of other sorts of information processing. Perceptual efficiency, for instance, may be diminished.[448] Learning rates also can be affected under some conditions.[449] It is uncertain whether these perceptual and learning effects are costs of the strain in information variables or the adjustments which reduce it.

5.2.5 Matter-energy output processes A cold environment evokes energy outputs or heat losses from an organism over the thermodynamic gradient between it and that environment.[450] In various plant and animal species a fascinating variety of matter-energy and information processes adjust to this loss. All plants and most animals are cold-blooded, taking on the temperature of their environment (see pages 450 and 451). Warm-bloodedness, shared by all birds and mammals, is the ability of an animal to maintain an internal climate or temperature steady state of roughly about 38°C—differing somewhat from species to species—despite large fluctuations in environmental temperature. Bodily temperature is controlled by a neural "thermostat" in the hypothalamus of some animals and of human beings (see pages 390, 429, and 451). It responds to fluctuations in the temperature of the blood flowing through that part of the nervous system by negative feedbacks which in higher mammals elicit shivering that generates heat in the muscles, erection of the hairs which insulates the animal ("goose pimples" is the equivalent in human beings), and constriction of the peripheral blood vessels which minimizes heat loss. Hypothesis 3.2-1 (see page 93), stating that an optimal mean temperature at which process is most efficient is maintained by a living system, seems to apply to plants as well as both cold-blooded and warm-blooded animals, since all must remain above a minimal temperature, or their cells will cease to function. The warm-blooded animals, however, keep their temperatures within an extremely narrow, high steady-state range as compared with the cold-blooded ones.

When there are increased demands for matter-energy outputs from an organism, in some cases the amount of matter-energy available for output rises. This adjustment can be achieved by increased inputs, by stepped-up activity of the producer subsystem, and sometimes by withdrawal of matter-energy from certain internal subsystem processes. All these functional changes occur as the growing young of a lactating female mammal increase their demands for milk. The mother eats and drinks more; necessary proteins, other nutrients, and water are preempted from other subsystem processes; and more milk is produced.

When motor output accelerates, similar processes occur. Breathing rates go up to increase the supply of oxygen, necessary for muscular activity. Glucose is drawn from storage tissues and distributed preferentially to the muscles. Prolonged muscular activity usually increases eating, as weight-watchers can prove. The total mass of muscle grows if the high rate of motor activity continues. Muscular tissue has an adjustment process unavailable to other sorts of tissue since it can function anaerobically for a brief period, going into debt for oxygen and making it up during a rest period which follows (see page 246).

Blocking of matter-energy outputs can be counteracted, up to a point, by a subsystem adjustment process within the extruder. For example, if perspiration is blocked by covering one part of the body, it increases on other parts. If the sweat glands all over the body are blocked at the same time, no such adjustment is possible, and the organism ultimately dies of uremic toxicity. This has been known to occur in about 2 h on a hot sunny day when a child on a float in a parade was covered over his whole body with metal foil. In general, Hypothesis 5.2-4 (see page 106) seems to apply to matter-energy output adjustments of organisms, that the system's range of stability for a specific variable under lack strain is a monotonically increasing function of the amount of storage of the input, and under excess strain, is a monotonically increasing function of the rate of output.

Costs of these matter-energy output adjustment processes are assessed in the amounts of matter and energy which they expend, *e.g.*, to maintain the temperature of a warm-blooded animal, or in lack strains which they create in other components or subsystems.

5.2.6 Information output processes   People adjust their rates of interaction with others, including their outputs of information, to the amount of social interaction to which they are accustomed (see page 566). The suprasystem may demand increased rates of information output, as by requesting someone to transmit a message rapidly or write an article to meet a deadline. The first request can sometimes be met by using multiple channels of the output transducer or by accelerating encoding and output transducing up to the individual's maximum rate. The second request may oblige the person to increase not only the information output rates but also the information input rates, as by reading or studying.

Limitation of information output may be regulated by feedbacks from persons with whom one is communicating. One slows the rate of speech or simplifies the vocabulary used in talking to young children, feeble-minded adults, and persons who speak the language poorly. When the suprasystem influences people to remain silent against their own desires and inclinations, they often adjust by accelerating their motor activity. Enjoined from expressing their thoughts, such people may discharge tension by restless movements. Being required to keep a secret creates a strain in people not accustomed to blocking any outputs from memory, especially if it is a secret they believe would interest or excite others.

Costs of such adjustment processes are sometimes those of the GAS (see page 452) or of depletion of the energy the organism has available for other activities.

5.2.7 Feedbacks   Countless internal and external negative feedbacks coordinate and integrate organisms, adjust rates of activity of subsystems and components, and flows of matter-energy and information among them, and govern the activities and relationships of the organism in its environment and suprasystem.

(a) *Internal feedbacks.*   Out of many examples of internal feedbacks that are known only a very few will be listed:

Matter-energy feedback controls.   Adjustment of the filtration rate of the kidney, in which effects of the kidney's activity upon blood composition act to adjust that activity. Adjustment of the architecture of bones when lines of force of the body's weight on them change direction.

Information feedback controls of matter-energy processes.   More complicated negative feedback loops, involving both vascular and neural transmissions, regulate the circulation and adjust the rate of respiration to the amounts of oxygen and carbon dioxide in the blood.[451] Other negative feedbacks regulate the body's water balance, energy balance, and temperature.

Control of the motor, a decider process dispersed

among numerous components (see pages 425 and 426), makes use of many internal and external feedback loops. Components at all echelons of the nervous system are involved. In one such circuit, impulses from the motor cortex go to centers in the pons, then to the anterior lobe of the cerebellum, where signals from the pyramidal or corticospinal tract are integrated with signals from muscle and tendon receptor components of the internal transducer and probably also from input transducer components. The signal resulting from this coordination is transmitted through the nucleus dentatus of the cerebellum to the red nucleus and back to the motor cortex where it influences ongoing motor signals.

Control of stretch and tension in muscles also is accomplished over feedback loops. The basic response of skeletal muscles to inputs from stretch receptors depends upon monosynaptic connections between muscle-spindle transducers and spinal alpha motor neurons. This synaptic relationship enables muscles to respond directly to the load placed upon them, an input-signal adaptation (see page 37). In an intact organism, however, much more complicated circuits exert their influences to produce the fine adjustments, tight feedbacks (see page 37), which suit motor activity so delicately to the conditions of the environment and the plans of the organism. Information from the muscle spindles is transmitted on ascending pathways and enters into a great number of integrations such as that just described. The signals resulting from such integrations at high levels of the nervous system are then channeled downward through the spinal cord. They pass to both the alpha motor neurons, which transmit the signals that control movements of the muscles, and the gamma motor neurons, which carry the signals that control sensitivity of the muscle spindles (see pages 375 and 376). In this way feedbacks about the condition of the muscle itself affect the signal which controls it, a system-variable adaptation (see page 37). The abundant interconnections among parts of the nervous system described above create innumerable such feedback loops.[452]

Information feedback controls. Many adjustments of flows of information wholly within the endocrine and neural networks are negative feedbacks. Negative feedbacks between the anterior pituitary, on the one hand, and the thyroid and the adrenal cortex, on the other, maintain in steady states the flows of thyroxin and adrenocortical steroids from these glands (see Fig. 8-2, Fig. 8-6, and page 392). Indirectly, they influence the tissue variables the thyroxin and adrenocortical steroids control. A double feedback between the anterior pituitary and the ovary regulates the menstrual cycle in women: the follicle-stimulating hormone from the anterior pituitary evokes estrogens from the ovary, which then signal the anterior pituitary to decrease production of the follicle-stimulating hormone and also to increase secretion of the luteinizing hormone. The latter signals to the ovary to increase production of progesterone. Estrogens first elicit two weeks of tissue repair and proliferation of the uterine lining, and then progesterone activates the changes of the last two weeks, the premenstrual phase of the menstrual cycle. This is followed by menstruation.

The feedbacks which concentrate attention upon signals of one sensory modality rather than another appear to be examples of neural information feedback controls which are wholly within the nervous system (see page 429).

(b) *External feedbacks.* How human beings use external feedbacks has been studied with "tracking" tasks. In these experiments subjects are instructed to keep some variable as constant as possible, *e.g.,* the position of a continually moving spot of light on an oscilloscope. They are to accomplish this by operating a lever which controls that position so as to adjust to changes in feedback information inputs from the environment. This feedback may be the spot on the oscilloscope itself, a fluctuating sound correlated with it, or some other signal. In such a task the mass, viscosity, elasticity, and friction of the machinery attached to the lever determine the characteristics of information inputs to transducers, such as the Pacinian corpuscles and muscle spindles of the subject's hand holding the lever.[453] These inputs provide cues which, in addition to the visual, auditory, or other signals, subjects can use to guide the position of their hands and determine the rates and accelerations of their movements. Various physical characteristics of the machine determine the nature of the signals to their hands. Decreasing the lever's elasticity, for example, improves the subjects' ability to control that position, but it adversely affects their ability to control other variables. It may, for instance, raise the number of times subjects overshoot the mark in correcting a deviation of the spot from its position.

Another experiment about the influence of feedbacks on control of human motions was conducted using equipment which enabled the subject to keep a movable bar-shaped spot of light on an oscilloscope superimposed on a similar stationary spot by holding his finger at a fixed point in space.[454] By looking at the spots on the oscilloscope he received a feedback error signal. Changes in the character of this error signal affected his performance. Amplification of the movable spots' motions, increasing them to 4, 10, 20, and 40 times the distance his finger actually moved, improved his performance. The amplification also altered his patterns of finger movements. Low-amplification error signals resulted in high-amplitude, low-frequency movements, which usually deviated markedly from the reference position. Increasing the amplification raised the frequency of the movements, reduced their amplitude, and diminished their deviation from the reference position. Also auditory error signals were substituted for the visual ones. The intensity of a high tone represented the amount of displacement of the finger from the reference position in one direction and the intensity of a low tone represented the amount in the other direction. Amplification of these tones had the same effects on the finger movements as amplification of the visual signals.

Movement of the eyes in maintaining fixation of a target which travels horizontally back and forth also depends upon feedback.[455] In following such a target, the eye makes two types of movements: a smooth pursuit function which is a velocity tracker and a rapid saccadic (jumping) movement which follows the position. Tracking behavior in this situation is markedly different when the course of the target is predictable than when it is not. When it is predictable, if the eye gets off course, the subject is able to jump it ahead to the correct position.

If feedback is disturbed, performance is disrupted. Ordinarily speech depends upon feedbacks received by hearing one's own voice. This feedback can be artificially delayed for any length of time desired. This is accomplished by having a subject speak into a microphone, recording the signal on a tape with a delay loop, and then playing it back into earphones worn by the subject.[456] Such alteration in feedback increases vocal intensity, slows the rate of speaking, increases repetition of speech sounds, and increases the number of errors. These disturbances are maximal when the delay is about 0.25 s. Similar changes occurred when the task was tapping keys in temporal patterns, and the feedback was provided by the sound of the keys, the delay being introduced in the same way.[457] Greater intensity of tapping, slower tapping, and more errors, such as four taps in one burst instead of three, resulted. Disturbances in visual and tactile feedbacks also caused deteriorations in performance. Complex tasks were more liable to disturbance than simple ones like regular tapping.

In a problem which required subjects to identify the concept under which geometrical patterns were to be categorized, delayed feedback concerning correctness degraded performance as a positively accelerated function of the length of the delay interval.[458] Completeness and probability of feedback also affect performance.[459] In one experiment the subject received either "complete" feedback, being informed after each problem-solving trial which of four possible responses was correct, or "incomplete" feedback, being informed only whether the response was right or wrong. In another experiment the probability of feedback was varied by providing feedback in 100, 90, 80, or 70 percent of the trials. Problem solving was better with "complete" feedback than with "incomplete." It worsened as the probability of feedback decreased from 100 to 70 percent.

Performance in a task in which the subject was required to learn to displace a lever to a position arbitrarily fixed by the experimenter but unknown to the subject depended upon knowledge of results.[460] The subject was told the direction and amount of his error. There was no improvement without knowledge of results, progressive improvement with knowledge of results, and deterioration of performance after withdrawal of feedback. Hypothesis 3.3.5.2-3 (see page 99) is relevant here. It states that a system does not form associations without (a) feedback as to whether the new output relieves strains or solves problems and (b) reinforcement, i.e., strain reduction by the output.

The concepts of feedback and reinforcement are related (see page 409). All reinforcements involve feedback to an organism of the results of its behavior, but not all feedbacks are necessarily reinforcing. For instance, feedbacks about tasks which the subject has learned thoroughly or has overlearned, or about things in which she or he has no interest, or to which he or she does not attend, or about experiences which are neutral—neither rewarding nor unrewarding—may have little or no reinforcing effect. Learning theorists who employ the concept of reinforcement usually make certain assumptions about intervening variables. Feedback theories, which concentrate upon input–output relationships, do not. Magnitude, frequency, rates, and sorts of reinforcement may be minutely specified. Reinforcers are usually assumed to act in an additive way, so that a given amount of reinforcement produces a certain amount of increase in habit strength (see page 491). Reinforcers are also assumed to have drive-reducing (strain-reducing) characteristics which are separate from their feedback effects (see pages 409 and 410, 429 and 430 to 432).

A person's behavior in her or his suprasystem also makes use of feedbacks, specifically, perception of the effects of her or his behavior upon others. This may be received in the form of direct comment, as occurs in a teaching situation, or in more subtle ways.

5.3 Evolution When the conditions of primitive Earth had made chemical evolution and the development of cells possible, the stage was set for the genesis of the first organisms (see pages 289 to 295). Cells aggregated first perhaps into totipotential organs and then they evolved into multicellular organisms with differentiated tissues and organ subsystems. More and more complex organisms evolved. By the beginning of the Cambrian period (see Table 6-5) 600 million years ago, a variety of water-dwelling invertebrate animals—anthropods, molluscs, echinoderms, and others—were living, dying, and leaving fossil records in the rocks.

By the early Devonian period, 380 million years ago, great forests were established on the ground, and a host of fishes inhabited the seas. During the Mesozoic period reptiles spread over the earth on land and sea. Dinosaurs, flying reptiles, and marine forms, now known only by their skeletal remains and their reptilian descendants, were the dominant forms of life. They held this position until they were supplanted by the mammals at the close of the Cretaceous period.

In the succeeding 70 million years of the Cenozoic era, the age of mammals, the warm-blooded, active mammals, with their well-developed brains and consequent good learning capacity, have produced all the diverse species that inhabit the varying environments of the earth and have come to dominate other types of organisms.[461] The genealogy of man has been traced from his earliest ancestors, believed to have been like tadpoles of tunicates of the Paleozoic era, through the vertebrate, mammalian, and primate lines to apelike progenitors, such as *Australopithecus*. *Homo sapiens* has existed in essentially his present form since the end of the Pleistocene ice age, and perhaps considerably longer.[462]

Genetic basis of evolution of organisms. Much of the evolutionary story must be inferred from study of the rocks, bones, and artifacts, which are all that have survived the lengthy past of organisms. Since the forces that are believed to have produced present-day organisms are continuing, however, more immediate evidence of the process of evolution is available.

Genetic recombination (see pages 225 and 226) results from sexual reproduction. By selection of sexual partners, variation among the individuals of a species is ensured in a breeding population, along with the possibility of increasing or decreasing the percentage of organisms in the population with a given trait. Applying genetic principles, human beings have bred domestic animals to shape them to human needs and wishes. The probability that a genetic trait will appear in a given individual can be determined mathematically if the genetic characteristics of its ancestors are known. Genetic mutations (see pages 77 and 476) are less predictable. When they occur, they rarely produce more efficient or adaptable individuals. Yet some-

times they do, and such mutations have been the basis of the evolution of organisms through natural selection (see page 77).

The evolutionary process of "shred-out" (see pages 1, 4, 26, and 27) provides that more components participate in subsystem processes in higher than in lower organisms. The sole extruder component of coelenterates, for instance, is the opening of the body cavity into which the cells eject their metabolic products or wastes. In vertebrates, the subsystem includes lungs, urinary and anal structures, and, in some species, the skin.

The development of different species from a common ancestor is brought about by an interaction of environmental conditions, genetic mutations, sexual selection, and natural selection, in populations which are sufficiently isolated from others of their kind.[463] As time goes on, such populations become different enough from one another (as well as from their common ancestor) that interbreeding no longer takes place and ultimately is no longer possible.

Isolation can be brought about not only by geographical separation, such as that between groups at the opposite extremes of a large territory or on different inaccessible islands, but by any other circumstance which effectively prevents members of diverse groups within a species from interbreeding, for example, differing reproductive seasons (see page 77). When populations are so separated, for any reason, they are said to be in different ecological niches (see pages 469 and 564). If two closely related species compete for the same food supply in the same territory, one will usually be driven out or eventually will fail to survive. The rule seems to be one species to a niche. Groups within a species may become isolated in many other ways. One of these is by having different life cycles, so that one group is dormant while another is active.

Patterns of behavior, particularly the ceremonies among birds and fish which are elicited by releasers (see pages 366, 409, and 439), undergo evolutionary modification. The form and the meaning of the signal conveyed by a particular pattern of behavior may change independently. A behavior pattern which originally was an expression of inferiority in cichlid fishes, for example, has come to have an exactly opposite meaning, that of a threatening gesture, in the dwarf cichlids.[464]

Environmental adaptation. According to the theory of evolution, all the variation and specialization of structure and process of present-day species can be explained by the impact of such factors as natural selection, isolation, and adaptive radiation over the ages since life appeared on Earth. By comparison of the structures of living and fossil organisms, it is possible to identify evolutionary series in which progressive changes of various components can be seen to transform one sort of animal, such as a primitive fish, into another sort, such as a mammal. Series in which the ancestry of living organisms is traced back to a common ancestor have been worked out for each phylum. It is not necessary to rely entirely upon gross anatomy in such series. Variations in chemical constituents of living organisms also give clues to their phyletic relationships (see pages 294 and 295). Comparison of the polypeptide chains in the myoglobin and hemoglobin of various species indicates that the common ancestral molecule of the proteins in horse, pig, cattle, rabbit, and man was found in the bloodstreams of the first amphibians in the Devonian period 380 million years ago.[465]

A number of questions have proved difficult to answer at the level of the organism when the discussion is limited to using the concepts of evolution outlined above. One of these concerns the rise of organisms which are destined to inhabit an environment very different from that in which the ancestral strain has lived. Assume, for example, that land vertebrates originated from primitive amphibians which in turn originated from fish. The long and complex preparation for land living, involving reorganization of many subsystems, seems to have little adaptive value to a fish. Without such adaptation, however, no species could survive on dry land. Romer has discussed this issue and formulated a possible answer:

There are many structural and functional changes necessary to turn a typical fish into an amphibian and, eventually into a reptile; let us merely take two of the most obvious "improvements" needed—lungs and land limbs. To a fish under normal climatic conditions, gills suffice for breathing purposes. But under drought conditions, with stagnation of waters and low oxygen content, it would be highly advantageous for a fish to be able to come to the surface and avail itself of atmospheric oxygen. Today only five genera of fish have retained true lungs (they live in seasonal drought areas), but our evidence suggests that in the late Paleozoic the great majority of freshwater forms possessed lungs.

But legs? Why should a water dweller have these structures, so essential for land life? The answer seems to be that legs did not evolve as a mystical 'pre-adaptation' for a future life on land, but (seemingly a paradox) as structures which would aid a water-dweller, under drought conditions, to continue his life in his own proper element. In early stages of a severe drought, a fish with lungs would survive stagnant water conditions without trouble. But suppose the drought worsened and the water in a pond dried up completely? An ordinary fish would be literally stuck in the mud and would soon perish unless the rains soon returned. But a form in whch there had been some trend of enlargement of fins toward the tetrapod limb condition might be able to crawl up or down a river channel, find a pond with water still present, happily splash in, and resume his normal mode of life. Most fossil amphibians had legs developed to at least a moderate degree. But as far

as we can tell, most of them had no yen for life on land; legs were, for the time being, simply an adaptation for bettering the animal's chances for surviving in his proper environment.[466]

If the descendants of one type of organism are to be transformed into a quite different species, each intervening type must be a complete system with all its critical subsystems able to function properly. Each stage of phyletic development must be a success, or the genetic line will be eliminated and have no part in the future. For instance, a transitional form that was deprived of adequate oxygen inputs by the changeover from water-breathing gills to air-breathing lungs would become extinct. Stable transitional forms for many organs have been discovered (see pages 347 to 349). Furthermore, it is impossible for novel components to be appended to an organism or for established components to be radically altered in structure or function unless relationships among the existing components are revised. Consequently, several or all subsystems are involved in each major evolutionary change.

The rise of forelimbs which are capable of holding and manipulating objects is closely related to development of an erect sitting posture which leaves those limbs free.[467] Usually animals with this adaptation are not so fleet as related species which lack the specialized forelimbs. Beavers, for example, are less speedy than rabbits.

Neural evolution.   It is possible to trace an evolutionary series of increasing complexity of nerve nets and nervous systems of organisms. The simple neural nets of coelenterates appear not to have any single, centralized decider (see page 393). Fibrils from the sensory cells connect with the muscle fibers through primitive synapses. Impulses travel in all directions in this net, but special tracts also develop to channel specific responses. Somewhat higher animals with well-differentiated muscular tissue have nerves connecting sensory structures with muscles. The next major step upward involves chains of ganglia between the organism's input and output neurons. Amphioxus, a tiny marine creature neither worm nor fish but somewhere in between, has a nerve cord which corresponds to the spinal cord of vertebrates, with alternating pairs of sensory and motor nerves. It has no brain, however, only a jawless mouth where its head should be.

As neural complexity increases, a hierarchy of several echelons of centers develops which control increasingly complicated matter-energy and information processes. In the visual pathways of the frog there are only three echelons, and consequently the frog can decode and distinguish only a limited number of stereotyped patterns.[468] The cat's visual decoder, on the other hand, is shredded out by evolutionary development into six echelons, and as a result the cat can make much more precise and versatile perceptual discriminations. Also, as noted earlier (see pages 411 and 412), as species evolve more complex nervous systems, they are capable of more advanced sorts of learning. Planarians are capable of simple classical conditioning; vertebrates can learn more complicated relationships; primates can apply prior knowledge to new problems. Ultimately, in the highest animal species the use of symbols and speech develop. In the most advanced organisms the process of encephalization has brought virtually all processes of the organism under the controlling or coordinating influence of the cerebral cortex (see page 425).

The fossil record for *Homo sapiens* is far less complete than for some other species, but it is full enough to make clear that, like other organisms, human beings evolved by a sequence of adaptive radiations and finally emerged in the Pleistocene era almost hairless, erect, aggressive, carnivorous, and tool-making—adapted from some animal such as *Australopithecus*.[469] Woman differs from other female primates in that she has no sharply defined estrous period. She is usually sexually receptive. This makes it more likely that the male will limit his sexual activity to a monogamous relationship, or at least to a single polygamous family. There are other biological reasons why families of some sort exist in all human societies. Human beings have a longer period of growth. The brain of the human infant continues to grow at the fetal rate for the first 18 months after birth, and in the first months the infant is quite helpless. Apes can be independent immediately after weaning, but human children must become acculturated, learning speech and many other things about their suprasystem, from their parents or parent surrogates, before they can live without them.

The average size of the adult human brain is larger than that of any ape. The human cranial capacity is about 1,000 cm³ greater than that of *Australopithecus*. This increase in size has been held to be the reason why human beings are capable of a wider and different range of behaviors than any other animal. But this is probably only part of the story. The profound reorganization of cranial nervous tissue is probably more important. According to Holloway, the superiority of human beings does not arise simply from the greater number of neurons, since a variation of 1,000 cm³ in capacity is found among normal human crania with no correlation with intelligence.[470] Nor does human superiority come from the greater size of the frontal lobe relative to the rest of the human brain, as compared with apes, since this ratio is the same in human

beings and in apes. Rather, the decreased neural density in the human cerebral cortex, allowing for increased space between neurons, more glia, and greater ramification of dendrites, may be the important difference. There is experimental evidence that dendrites branch more as experience increases in young rats (see pages 414 and 415). Also, administration of growth hormone to pregnant rats diminished neural density, increased dendritic branching, and resulted in greater adaptive behavior mediated by the cortex in their young.[471]

Human beings differ also from other primates in having a much larger cortex, a larger amygdala, and a larger hypothalamic portion of the fornix. The apparatus for controlling motor activity is also different (see pages 412, 425, and 426). Holloway writes:

. . . from the Australopithecines on, the major changes in the brain would have involved increasing degrees of complexity . . . through the increase in connectivity. This increase in connectivity would allow for greater degrees of discrimination of both the social and physical environments, prediction, and memory *control*, as well as capacity. That is, it would mean increasing adaptability or plasticity along essentially continuous lines. It would mean essentially changes in degree rather than kind. Furthermore, and most importantly, such a process in terms of evolution would be a deviation-amplification process, one of positive feedback in the cybernetical sense. One of the delicate problems of the intellectual heritage resulting from the numerous discussions throughout the literature of environment vs. nature has been the limited definition of environment. In a very real sense, the early hominids must have been their *own* environment, and their actions within the more passive context of environment must have in fact *become* an integral part of their environment in the total sense. Concretely, for example, the making of a stone tool, the witnessing of another hominid making one, or its use would then be part of the environment, as much as the social behavior of a fellow hominid would be a part of environment. With a cultural niche (in the ecological sense) there is the capacity and the probability of generating ever-increasing degrees of improbability, or relatedness. It is important to realize that within the niche, the environment is expanding precipitously. Thus the selection pressures for better 'hardware' to handle the ever-increasing complexity of the total environment is built into the process to a much increased degree in comparison to nonhuman environments. Information-processing thus becomes critical. One aspect of handling information is to have either a perfect means of accurately registering signal inputs. or [to rely] on redundancy of the message so that "noise" does not mask the information of the signal completely. The first method has never been attained in any mammalian sensory apparatus, as far as we know. One way of looking at such a mass of neural elements in the cortex would be as a hardware stratagem for handling redundancy and blocking "noise." [See Hypothesis 3.3.4.2-6 (page 98), which states that as the noise in a channel increases, a system encodes with increasing redundancy in order to reduce error in the transmission.] It would be quite interesting to know whether behavior becomes more redundant as it becomes more complicated. If so, there are a number of neural information models from neurophysiology to correlate fairly closely the microstructure with redundancy and noise-masking operations. This interpretation, although incomplete, fits well our present models of natural selection as well as the increasing brain size of latter hominids and the increasing degrees of complexity of their material and socio-cultural environments.[472]

And what of the future? The evolutionary process continues. The human race is still evolving. Genetic variation and adaptation to changing environmental conditions still occur. Dobzhansky saw an optimistic future for the human race despite some unfavorable genetic characteristics, if eugenic principles are applied to human breeding.[473] He pointed out that equality of social opportunity could lead to greater assortative mating. This might increase the likelihood of desirable genetic combinations occurring which could improve the quality of human life.

5.3.1   Emergents   It is uncertain whether associative learning occurs at the level of the cell (see pages 266 and 267). Until that question has been solved definitely, no one can say whether this process emerges first at the organism level. We know it does not occur at the organ level (see page 339). If it is an organism-level emergent, it probably is not present in plants but appears first in some relatively simple phylum such as the flatworms (see page 411).

There can be no question that motivation operates at the level of the cell. Free-living cells, for instance, clearly carry out actions in their environments that adjust them to stresses and strains. On the other hand, there is no evidence that cells or organs experience emotions, and of course we have no way to communicate with them about their affect. Even at the organism level, we must rely on communication for any degree of certainty about subjective emotion. Nevertheless, empathy suggests that rage or fear may be felt by army ants and other social insects, male Siamese fighting fish, fighting cocks, wolves, dogs, elephants, and lions when they attack enemies. Facial and other forms of expression of emotion seemed to Darwin clearly comparable in human beings and lower animals.[474] Talking parrots and birds of related species often demonstrate by chattering that they are jealous of other birds to which human beings show affection. They can obviously show affection by cooing and rubbing themselves against people and other birds. No one who ever has kept a pet cat, dog, horse, porpoise, or, indeed, baby lion can question that it displays emotions.

Perhaps the most profoundly significant emergent at the organism level, which is fundamental to the development of groups and higher levels of systems, is the ability to use gamma-coded language. It is not seen below the primates.

5.4   Growth, cohesiveness, and integration

5.4.1   Growth   An organism begins to grow when the fertilized egg commences to divide, ordinarily soon after fertilization.

(a) *Stages of development.*   Cell division of the fertilized egg is essentially similar in its early stages for all metazoans. The first cleavage, in which two cells are produced, occurs in sea urchins about 1 h and 10 min after fertilization and is complete in about ½ h.[475] The two descendant cells then divide simultaneously into four, without separating; these four divide into eight; and so on until there is a mass of cells. These arrange themselves into a layer, one cell thick, around a cavity. This is a *blastula* or *blastocyst*.

In the next step, a *gastrula* is formed, consisting of an endoderm and an ectoderm surrounding a primitive food cavity. The gastrula proceeds to develop somewhat differently in various types of eggs, but the resulting gastrula is always much like the structure of an adult coelenterate. In all higher phyla a third cell layer, the mesoderm, develops between the ectoderm and endoderm. These three layers form all the specialized tissues of the species to which the egg belongs, following the template laid down in the nuclear DNA of the cells (see page 224) and making use of inputs of energy from the egg or the maternal circulation, depending upon the species.

(b) *Differentiation of tissues.*   In the early stages of cell division, descendant cells are identical. Consequently if newt embryos are cut in half before they reach the stage of the gastrula, a whole embryo develops from each half.[476] Later, only certain parts of the information carried in the genetic material are expressed in the cells of each tissue, although the complete genetic information is still present in each cell. As these somatic cells divide, they form the differentiated cells typical of the tissue to which they belong. This is consistent with Hypothesis 5.4.1-2(a) (see page 108), which says that growing systems develop in the direction of more differentiation of subsystems.

Differentiation of tissues and organs within a developing embryo depends importantly upon the surrounding tissues. If a bit of tissue in the region which would normally form the notochord is taken from a salamander embryo and transplanted to the area which would have developed belly tissue, the notochord develops in the new position. It organizes surrounding cells into tissues of the back such as usually surround the notochord.[477] Also in the region where the notochord is removed from such an embryo, the surrounding cells form another one. In another experiment, belly tissue from a frog, transplanted to the mouth region of a salamander embryo, became a mouth but a frog's mouth, not a salamander's. Possibly some form of chemical feedback occurs among developing tissues, so that when the notochord has begun to develop, surrounding cells are signaled to form back tissue rather than notochord. If the notochord has not been formed, such a message is not sent, and they form the notochord.

Fertilized frog eggs grown in cultures from different frog tissues such as heart, brain, or blood in one experiment developed to the stage at which components like those in which they were cultured should have appeared. But these specialized tissues failed to form. Those eggs cultured with brain, for instance, formed no brain cells.[478] The explanation for this is probably that a chemical signal from the cytoplasm of the surrounding brain cells to the developing egg indicated that the given tissue was already present. This inhibited formation of it. In Chap. 6 I discussed another chemical effect of a cell's cytoplasm. Not only can it inhibit a certain sort of gene expression, it can also signal the cell's nucleus to initiate expression of genetic information (see page 262). For instance, nuclei of brain or blood cells of adult frogs, which no longer divide and consequently no longer synthesize DNA, began such synthesis within 1 h after being transplanted into enucleated frog's eggs.

Chemical cues probably also guide the development of the nervous system in the embryo. The entire nervous system arises from an ectodermal groove which appears on the surface of the embryo early in its development. The groove closes to make a tube, the essential form of the central nervous system throughout its history. Meninges and bony structures develop around it. The order of development does not follow the phylogenetic pattern, in which the brain developed later than the nerve net. Instead, the components of the brain arise first, and the spinal cord grows downward from the brain. The peripheral neural components grow outward from this central region to enter the bodily parts which they will innervate. Those from motor and sensory centers in the central nervous system follow different routes through the tissues to find their way to muscles and sensory components, respectively.[479] This has led to the assumption that chemical cues in the tissues indicate pathways. When they reach the body surface, motor fibers are accepted for synapse only by muscle cells and the sensory fibers only by sensory epithelia and end organs. The cells which are to form synaptic junctions are complementary, prematched by the genetic template. The specification of muscular structure beyond this must be determined in the musculature rather than by the genetic program, because any motor neuron will join with any uninnervated muscle at which it happens to arrive.

The growth of specific neural pathways between peripheral and central components has been studied by observing the process of regeneration of disrupted nerves. Optic fibers arising from different sectors of the retina regenerate in such a way that they terminate in the correct, matching part of the midbrain tectum, selecting the proper central pathways.[480] The specificity of muscular connections has been investigated by grafting limbs onto amphibia in such a way that the grafted limb is made to share in the innervation of a normally placed limb, or by reversing the limbs, so that a right limb is placed on the left side and made to share the left-sided innervation.[481] In both these situations information flowing from the central nervous system activates both limbs in the same fashion. Since, however, the left and right limbs are mirror images in their muscular structure, their motions in this situation are opposite to each other and counteract each other. If normal limbs are replaced by limbs from the opposite side, the animal permanently moves in the opposite direction from the appropriate one.

(c) *Growth patterns.* After an initial period in which the growth of animal organisms follows a similar course regardless of species, patterns of growth differ in various types of organisms. Some, including certain fishes and reptiles, are born or hatched as tiny replicas of their parents and grow slowly, sometimes for their entire lives.[482] At the opposite extreme are some organisms, including insects and some amphibians, which begin life as one sort of creature and undergo metamorphosis to become quite another. The young of some of these organisms often live in water (like tadpoles) and the adults on land (like frogs). Or the young crawl about (like caterpillars), and the adults fly (like butterflies). Quite different ecological niches are occupied by the animal as a juvenile and as an adult.

(d) *Growth curves.* Three types of growth curves, depending upon differing metabolism of the animals concerned, have been identified by Bertalanffy.[483] The first, which includes some fish, mammals, and others, shows a decreasing growth rate as size increases up to the point at which growth ends. The second, which includes insect larvae and some others, follows an exponential curve with the upper limit set only by metamorphosis or seasonal cycles. The third, in which pond snails are found, is s-shaped. Confirmation of these various rates of growth would indicate that

Hypothesis 5.4.1-1 (see page 108), which states that the number of components of young systems grows exponentially until it reaches a maximum, though this curve can be altered by several factors, is probably true only of certain animal species.

Various components of an organism may have different growth patterns, attaining their greatest size and activity at different times in the organism's life cycle. Postnatal growth of tissues of human children shows four different patterns.[484] The first is a rapid growth in infancy with gradually increasing velocity to the fourth year, then relatively constant growth until the spurt at puberty, followed by a slowing until growth ceases. This pattern is characteristic of bones, respiratory and digestive organs, kidneys, the musculature as a whole, major components of the vascular system, some other organs, and the body as a whole except the head and neck. The second pattern, rapid postnatal growth slowing in infancy and coming to a stop before puberty, is exhibited by the central nervous system, components of the eye, and dimensions of the head. The third pattern is seen in lymphoid tissues, which develop rapidly throughout childhood, stop growing at puberty, and then partially atrophy. The fourth pattern is that of the genitalia, which grow little in infancy but develop rapidly at puberty.

Curves of improvement of different information processing skills, *e.g.*, those measured by various intelligence tests, have shapes comparable to those which represent physical growth.[485]

(*e*) *Hormonal control of growth.* Specialized tissues of both plant and animal organisms produce hormones which convey signals that control growth and development. They act as chemical messengers to start and stop synthetic processes (see page 392). The course of growth of field crops such as wheat and rice depends upon the interplay of a number of hormones.[486] When a seed is planted in moist soil, it absorbs water and produces a small amount of the hormone *gibberellin*. This hormone signals a layer of cells surrounding the food storage in the seed to begin synthesizing enzymes which disintegrate and liquefy the cells. One of these enzymes, *amylase*, hydrolyzes stored starch into sugar. Others break the cells down into their component nucleic acids and proteins. The splitting of the nucleic acids generates other hormones, *cytokinins*, and the breakdown of the proteins gives rise to *auxins* (see page 375). The cytokinins make the embryo cells divide, and the auxins facilitate enlargement of the cells by weakening the cell walls and permitting them to take up water by osmosis. Once growth is under way the auxins migrate to the lower side of the seedling and cause it to grow more rapidly so that the plant receives its proper orientation

to gravity. The roots grow downward, and the shoots push upward. It then breaks through the soil and begins photosynthesis. Another sort of plant hormone, *dormin*, acts as a growth inhibitor which prepares trees for their winter dormancy by inhibiting the synthesis of nucleic acids. The beginning of growth in the spring may result when growth-promoting hormones, such as gibberellin and auxin, overcome the effects of the dormin.

Hormones similarly control the maturation and growth of insects.[487] Two hormones, *"brain hormone"* and *ecdysone* (see page 274) bring about the repeated molts which characterize the development of young insects. The first signals the prothoracic glands to release the second, which promotes growth of cells, including the epidermal cells. Even a fragment of isolated insect abdomen will molt if ecdysone is injected into it. Another hormone, the *juvenile hormone* (see page 302), secreted by the corpora allata, which are endocrine glands near the brain, acts to control maturation so that the cuticle which is secreted is larval and not pupal or adult. The same cells secrete these different sorts of cuticle under influence of different amounts of this hormone. Quantitative control of rate of release of this hormone permits the insect to mature through its typical life cycle.

Brain hormone acts upon the prothoracic glands by initiating intense RNA synthesis in the nuclei of their cells, followed by the appearance of cytoplasmic RNA (see page 228) and protein synthesis.[488] These proteins probably are the enzymes necessary for production of ecdysone. Ecdysone appears to act directly upon the DNA, causing puffing of chromosomes, an alteration visible by microscope, associated with increased RNA and protein synthesis. The relations suggest that the changing activity of insect cells during growth may be caused by activation or suppression of different genes.[489]

A similar interplay of hormones occurs in the growth and development of mammals. Under the control of the pituitary gland, the growth hormone, thyroxine, and the various hormones of sex initiate and inhibit processes to produce the typical growth and maturation patterns of each species after birth.

(*f*) *Effects of early experience on growth.* Experiments indicate that permanent effects upon growth and development involving both matter-energy and information processing result from certain sorts of information inputs to the organism during the critical period of infancy (see pages 475 and 476). As Hypothesis 5.4.1-4 (see page 109) indicates, if the rate of such information inputs into the system falls below a specific lower limit, normal growth of the system is impossible. Laboratory rats which were handled for 10 min a day for the 21 days following weaning weighed more, dared to venture closer to the brilliantly lighted center of a field, and showed fewer stress-related physiological responses than rats which were not handled.[490] Handling also has beneficial effects upon food assimilation, growth, thyroid metabolism, curiosity, and emotional reactivity.[491]

These findings have been explained in a number of ways depending upon what aspect of the animal's responses the experimenter studied. Among the explanations proposed for observed performance decrements in animals which were isolated, or not handled, in infancy are: (i) hormonal influences on the central nervous system; (ii) deprivation of information necessary for perceptual development so that the animal fails to learn how to decode its perceptual inputs during the important early period (see pages 402 and 403); (iii) deterioration of patterns of response through disuse; and (iv) failure to become habituated to complex inputs so that emergence from isolation produces an information input overload stress (see Chap. 5).[492]

The varying emotional and physiological responses of animals which have had different amounts of handling, of isolation, or of information input may be determined by the rates of secretion of adrenal steroids and other hormones involved in the general adaptation syndrome (GAS) (see pages 451 and 452, and 452 to 454). Handling an infant animal appears to cause the concentrations of adrenal corticosteroids in its blood to vary more than they do in the blood of animals not subjected to this stress.[493] It has been suggested that the blood concentrations of these steroids are maintained in a steady-state range by a negative feedback process of a "hormonostat" in the central nervous system. Furthermore, it has been postulated that information inputs early in life "set" the hormonostat so that the feedback is loose (see page 37), increasing the range of blood corticosteriod concentrations which can occur without triggering a corrective adjustment. With its neural functions modified in this way the animal responds to relatively nonthreatening inputs, such as an open field into which he is free to venture from surrounding protective cover, by a moderate increase in adrenal corticosteroids. But it responds to severe stress, such as a shock, with a large and rapid increase in blood steroid concentration. A nonhandled rat has a smaller range of concentrations of blood corticosteroids and responds in about the same way to any of a wide variety of inputs. It is hypothesized by Bovard that early handling signals the anterolateral hypothalamus to accelerate the growth processes which it controls.[494] At the same time early

handling reduces posteromedial hypothalamic processes and consequently the pituitary-adrenocortical and sympathetic adrenomedullary stress responses controlled by the posteromedial hypothalamus. These processes, he says, can be modified by activities of the amygdala and the hippocampus.

Human children are also profoundly affected by information lack stresses during infancy and early childhood (see page 475).

(g) *Development of information processing abilities, including intelligence and personality.* Little is known about the extent to which a person's genetically endowed traits can be modified by experience.

Several researches on development of the nervous system generally have tipped the balance toward the relatively greater importance of inherited neural organization and assign relatively less importance to learning. Sperry maintains that the genetically determined aspects of neural processes even in so-called "learned" behavior, may be much more complex than those aspects superimposed by experiential information inputs.[495] In his view, no vertebrate pattern of behavior, except some human activities like language, is too complicated to be programmed in the genetic template. For instance, monkeys were reared in isolation, receiving visual inputs only from colored slides of monkeys in various activities and of other scenes with no monkeys in them.[496] Between 2½ and 4 months of age these monkey subjects reacted strongly to pictures of monkeys in threatening postures, and rarely touched a lever that turned on such pictures. These apparently inborn fear reactions seemed to be responses to signals between monkeys which are innately decodable.

The human ability to acquire and use language also follows a typical maturation pattern, although the particular language which a child uses must be learned, and a child who has no opportunity to hear others speak will not learn to talk or understand language. Six indications suggesting that language has genetically determined foundations were listed by Lenneberg:

(i) It is a form of behavior present in all cultures of the world. (ii) In all cultures its onset is age correlated. (iii) There is only one acquisition strategy—it is the same for all babies everywhere in the world. (iv) It is based intrinsically upon the same formal operating characteristics whatever its outward form. (v) Throughout man's recorded history these operating characteristics have been constant. (vi) It is a form of behavior that may be impaired specifically by circumscribed brain lesions which may leave other mental and motor skills relatively unaffected.[497]

He pointed out that language development is closely correlated with motor development in general and with maturation of the brain.

Children follow typical patterns of development of cognitive functions, as Piaget's classic studies show.[498] Their understanding of physical laws and phenomena, as well as logical and conceptual relationships, expands with advancing age. For example, young children, at least in the culture Piaget studied, often impute life to inanimate objects, whereas older children do not. When cultural and environmental factors are held as constant as possible, individual differences in children's intellects are still apparent. Some are bright and others are dull. It is clear that surroundings which do not provide adequate information inputs can prevent the genetic intellectual potential from being fully realized. Monozygotic twins reared apart correlate highly in their scores on intelligence tests even when they correlate poorly in their separate attainments.[499]

A "general intelligence" factor was included among a set of primary personality factors the hereditary and environmental bases of which were studied by Cattell.[500] Tests of various sorts, among them his culture-free intelligence test, were given to over 800 children including monozygotic twins raised together, fraternal twins raised together, siblings raised together and apart, unrelated children raised together from infancy on, and children from the general population. The data were analyzed by means of multiple variance analysis. Cattell found that heredity affected general intelligence test performance about 12 times as much between families, and twice or more within families, as environment. Specific abilities are also influenced by both. Another study of twins showed that heredity accounts for roughly 70 percent of the variance in general ability but roughly only 15 percent of the variance in specific abilities.[501]

One assumption of much early research on intelligence has been that, like physiological functions, intellectual capacities reach a peak at about adolescence, after which they develop little further. It is now apparent that this is not true. When a group of gifted children were retested as adults twice, 12 years apart, there was a highly significant increase from the first to the second retest.[502] They averaged close to 30 years of age at the first retest, and 41.5 at the second. Working with data from this and other studies, Bayley plotted a curve of intellectual growth between ages 0 and 50 years, which shows a sharp upward trend until the age of about 20 and a modest but continuous increase subsequently.[503]

Development of emotional maturity and adult personality accompany physical and intellectual growth. Freud and his followers have described a succession of stages of *psychosexual development,* each depending upon the asserted predominance during that particular age of signals from a given part of the body.[504] The successive stages, each with its own problems requiring solution, are oral, anal, and genital.

Though culture clearly shapes some of an individual person's personality traits (see page 749), heredity also affects many emotional and social traits, just as it influences cognitive abilities. Of the personality factors which Cattell analyzed, only intelligence and one other, which he calls *commention,* were clearly determined mainly by heredity.[505] (A person is high in the trait of commention if he readily accepts correction of his errors by others.) Additional researches using Cattell's terminology and methods indicate that other personality factors, *e.g.,* social introversion, cyclothymic versus schizothymic characteristics, and general excitability, seem also to show hereditary influence.[506]

5.4.2 Cohesiveness   Organisms are highly cohesive systems, their parts in general moving together and remaining in very close spatial proximity to each other. Those with little tissue differentiation cohere largely as a result of intercellular forces (see page 298). In higher animals, including human beings, bands or sheets of connective tissue (see page 317) bind components together. Many of these are also supporter components.

Although these connective-tissue bonds holding the organism together are strong, they are not so powerful as the forces that bind cells into tissues. Forces sufficient to pull an organism apart ordinarily do so by separating different kinds of tissue from one another, often removing parts extending out from the body, like legs or feelers. Tissues are separated in common sprains and dislocations of joints. Some lizards are apparently able to escape from predators by breaking off their tails and leaving them behind to wriggle and distract the attacker while the rest of the animal scampers away. Such lack of cohesion forms a useful adjustment process to an organism capable of growing a new, if shorter, tail.[507]

5.4.3 Integration   Types of organisms differ in the degree of centralization of control of their deciders. In general, systems at this level are more integrated than cells, in which many subsystem processes are downwardly dispersed to the molecular level (see page 217). Most organisms are very much more integrated than organs, in which most subsystem processes are downwardly dispersed to the cell or upwardly to the organism. Few, if any, systems at the levels of the group and above achieve as much integration as most organisms do, largely because the components or subcomponents of the higher levels are more mobile than those of the organism.

When types of organisms are compared, it appears

that the sponges are the least integrated, inasmuch as they supply the least evidence of any control by a centralized decider.[508] Occupying a borderline between colonies of cells and true metazoans, sponges exhibit some differentiation of tissues. They have no neural tissue. Some coordination among different types of cells nevertheless occurs during reproduction. They also efficiently pump water through their canals. This distributor activity is carried out by the independent motions of a great many flagellated cells aggregated into the tissue lining the canals. Possibly in these least integrated organisms Hypothesis 5.4.3-6 (see page 109) is confirmable. That is, since the system's deciding is decentralized, it is likely that the information is discordant in the various echelons or components of its decider.

Tissue arrangement achieves integration by locating the structures that carry out some processes so that they are made interdependent. For instance, normally the stomach can output matter-energy only into the intestine, which can output matter-energy only into the colon, unless peristalsis is reversed. Certain cellular processes are integrated in comparable fashion (see page 236).

All animals higher than sponges have differentiated tissues with specialized functions, including hormones and neural tissues for transmission of integrating signals. The physiological processes and behavior of such animals follow programs, genetic or learned, that specify how components are coordinated. These are generally stored in the central nervous system. Coelenterates, with endocrine and primitive neural channels and nets that lack special coordinating centers, nevertheless have a number of well-coordinated responses involving many components, including capturing and ingesting prey and withdrawing from noxious inputs.

Higher animals, as I have noted (see pages 423 to 426), have multiple decider echelons, each of which controls particular processes and has regulatory influence over the echelons below. Processes like breathing and feeding, and tendon reflexes like the knee jerk, are controlled by particular centers. Such decentralized control increases the speed and accuracy of decisions which reduce local strains, in accordance with Hypothesis 5.4.3-4 (see page 109). A hand can be withdrawn from the metal handle of a hot teakettle, for example, by a quick jerk controlled by a low echelon in the spinal cord without reference to decision-making processes at higher echelons. This decentralized decision may be made without benefit of relevant information existing elsewhere in the system, as Hypothesis 5.4.3-5 (see page 109) suggests. Under some circumstances it might be better for the cortex to override the

spinal cord and signal the hand to hold the handle of the teakettle even though it is burned. A mother, for instance, would hold on to keep her baby from being scalded by boiling water in the kettle. Rates and other variables of lower echelon processes can be modified by information flowing down from above. Signals from the cortex, for instance, can speed or slow breathing.

5.5 Pathology   Diseases of organisms, like pathologies of systems at other levels, can be caused by lacks or excesses of either matter-energy or information inputs which are too great for the available adjustment processes to handle; inputs of inappropriate forms of matter-energy; inputs of maladaptive genetic information in the template; and abnormalities in either matter-energy or information internal processes. These causes are mutually interdependent, partly because matter-energy and information flows interrelate in all living systems and partly because the integration of an organism's components produces responses from more and more of these components as the stresses or strains on any one of them grow. Each example of pathology in the following sections is classified according to the source of pathology which appears to be predominant in its etiology.

(a) *Lacks of matter-energy inputs.*   Optimum nutrition in any species requires a balance of water and basic food substances and the necessary vitamins and minerals appropriate to the species. If any sort of necessary substance is ingested in inadequate amounts for a period of time, some kind of pathology results.

Man's optimal diet includes inputs of proteins, fats, carbohydrates, certain minerals, and vitamins (see pages 204 and 205). The proteins must include all the essential amino acids, since these cannot be synthesized in the required amounts. Up to a point, any of the three chief categories of food substances—proteins, fats, and carbohydrates—can be used to produce any sort of tissue (see pages 316 to 319). In the long run, however, a human being must ingest some of each of them. The disease kwashiorkor, which afflicts children in areas of the world that chronically suffer severe deprivation of good-quality food, results from protein deficiency. Children with this disease have general underdevelopment, wasted muscles, and grotesquely swollen abdomens. Protein deficiency is not compatible with normal growth or adequate tissue maintenance and repair. Increase of protein inputs of either plant or animal origin in the diet eliminates kwashiorkor.

Dietary deficiency of carbohydrate or fat is less frequent, since the impoverished areas of the world ordinarily maintain their populations on some basic carbohydrate, such as wheat, rice, potatoes, or corn, and usually some oil is available, such as olive or peanut oil.

Vitamins are substances which the particular organism requires in small quantities and either cannot produce in the needed amounts or cannot produce at all. Human beings, for example, can synthesize vitamin D if their skin is receiving light inputs, but in most environments the light is inadequate for them to synthesize all the vitamin D they need. Consequently they must also ingest some vitamin D.

Severe and chronic diet deficiency can also retard intellectual development.[509] The priority whereby the nervous system receives nutrients in preference to other parts of the body can protect its neural tissue from damage by a short period of severe starvation. When the deprivation is chronic, however, this adjustment is exhausted, and neural tissues are also damaged. Under these circumstances, a child's genetic potential in both physical and mental growth is stunted. Commonly, children who experience this sort of deprivation are often subjected to other sorts as well, including poor social and cultural surroundings. Consequently what nutritional deprivation contributes to the sorry whole has often been overlooked or improperly ascribed to a defective genetic constitution of economically disadvantaged families.

Organisms cannot survive complete oxygen lack for more than a few minutes. Oxygen input lack stress or interference with the flow of adequately oxygenated blood to the central nervous system causes signs and symptoms of malfunction, beginning at the top of the nervous system and progressing downward.

Light deprivation is an energy lack which has been shown capable of causing permanent pathology in experimental animals (see pages 475 and 476). Retinal degeneration can occur in animals that have been reared in complete darkness in infancy.[510] Structural and functional changes in brain components have also been found in dark-reared animals, among them reduced diameters of cells in the visual cortex and lateral geniculates, decreased thickness of the visual cortex, possibly fewer dendritic branches of neurons in the visual cortex, reduced vascularity of the cortex, and continued immaturity of the form of cortical evoked potentials.[511]

(b) *Excesses of matter-energy inputs.* Ordinarily, excessive inputs of food or water are either stored or excreted. Pathological obesity can be produced in human beings and some other organisms by inputs of food beyond what is needed. Also more water than the system can use can be ingested, overloading the extruder and upsetting the water balance (see pages 455 and 456). Both excessive buildup of fatty tissue and excessive water in the tissues put extra loads upon distributor components, particularly in the heart, and may produce cardiac disease.

Excessive inputs of specific nutritional elements, such as vitamins and minerals, may be excreted harmlessly, or in some cases may be toxic. Vitamins A and D in great excess produce pathology. Excessive inputs of iron can irritate the gastrointestinal tract.

Oxygen excess stress is rare. One form of tissue pathology from excessive oxygen is known, however. That is the blindness from retrolental fibroplasia brought about in premature infants by excessive oxygen tension in their incubators.

Traumatic damage, such as is caused by a blow or cut or explosion, produces pathology in accordance with the location of the damage, its severity, and the availability of processes of repair or adjustment to counteract it. Hypothesis 5.5-1 (see page 110) applies here: The farther away a component is from the point of trauma to a system, the less pathological is its function, and particularly the less is its relation to the system's hierarchical organization destroyed. Birth trauma can produce permanent damage to neural and other structures. Trauma to tissues may be the precipitating cause of the cellular changes which produce certain cancers (see page 301).

Excessive inputs of radiation, including ultraviolet light, x-rays, or the products of nuclear fission, all damage tissues and may cause cancer.

(c) *Inputs of inappropriate forms of matter-energy.* Toxic drugs, poisons, ingested foreign bodies, allergens, and pathogenic bacteria and viruses are all inappropriate inputs to organisms. There are individual differences in tolerance, but in general, inputs which are poisonous to one member of a species are poisonous to all. Some harm all living cells and are therefore inimical to any sort of organism. There are also species differences in tolerances to inputs of drugs and other substances.

Interesting functional effects of drugs which alter processes of the mammalian central nervous system have been discovered in various species of spiders.[512] Such drugs influence the web-spinning behavior of spiders so that the web artifact constructed under the influence of each is characteristically divergent from normal webs in size, regularity, and shape. All three of these aspects of the web structure vary with dosage.

Allergens are foreign proteins which are innocuous to the majority of organisms in a species but which, when applied to a given individual of that genus, elicit an idiosyncratic response.

Bacteria, viruses, and *Rickettsias,* when introduced into an organism, can cause local and generalized infections of various sorts, some of which can be fatal. Each illness has its characteristic signs and symptoms, usually including fever, weakness, and malaise.

Some cancers are caused by toxic inputs or viral infection (see page 301). These abnormal tissues invade multiple subsystems of an organism, either by direct spread or by dissemination through the distributor, and set up metastatic cancers at points far from the original site. Toxins resulting from tissue destruction, and disruption of both matter-energy and information processing by the malignancy's expansion and invasion, characteristically produce emaciation, weakness, disability, and pain as the disease advances.

(d) *Lacks of information inputs.*   Hypothesis 5.1-42 (see page 105) states that a minimum rate of information input to a system must be maintained for it to function normally. And Hypothesis 5.4.1-4 (see page 109) asserts that, if the rate of information input into a system falls below a specific lower limit, normal growth of the system is impossible. Both these propositions suggest that lacks of information inputs can cause pathology, and this appears to be true at the organism level. Information input underload beyond the power of available adjustment processes to compensate for it, as already noted (see pages 452 to 454), can elicit a variety of subjective experiences similar to hallucinations, as well as changes in behavior. These disappear when the inputs are again normal. They can, however, tip the balance away from survival for a person who is in an exposed or dangerous situation. For instance, near the end of the nineteenth century, Christianne Ritter spent a winter in the arctic with her husband.[513] While there, she experienced "rar," a strange feeling which sometimes overcomes people in the arctic night. She felt that she herself was moonlight. She would have wandered out to probable death by freezing in the frigid polar night had others not prevented her from doing so.

Lacks of certain sorts of information inputs in infancy produce pathology immediately as well as in later life (see pages 470 and 471). In early months the central nervous system is particularly vulnerable to such stresses. For instance, cats reared during the first five months of life in environments that contain contours of a single plane in later life showed decreased ability to perceive contours at 90 degrees to that plane.[514] These perceptual deficits resulted from changes in organization of the visual cortex induced by early visual inputs. An extensive series of studies on how deprivation of maternal care and social relationships affects young monkeys has been conducted by Harlow and his associates.[515] Monkeys raised in social isolation, some with "surrogate mothers" of cloth or wire, did not develop into socially adequate members of their species nor did they develop normal mating behavior.

Human children can also be harmed by social isolation, and by lack of handling and mothering. Serious retardation of general development, including motor, social, and adaptive behavior and use of language, has repeatedly been observed in children who spend long periods in institutions.[516] Such children frequently grow up with a diminished capacity for friendly relationships with others and with lessened emotional responsiveness.[517] In one study, orphanage children used fewer phonemes and a more restricted variety of speech sounds than children from more favorable environments. They showed marked language deficiency after spending their first three years in an institution.[518]

Two sets of children, an experimental group which was thought to be mentally retarded and a control group which was initially considered brighter, were studied 21 years after they were originally investigated.[519] The "retarded" children had been placed as "guests" in an institution for the mentally retarded, where they were given loving attention and stimulation. They were subsequently taken by adoptive parents. Over the next several years they made an average gain of 28.5 points in intelligence quotient. The supposedly brighter group, which remained in the orphanage, lost an average of 26.2 points in the same period. The differences continued into adulthood. The experimental group was self-supporting, some in professions or business. The control group remained in the institution, or if they left it they were unemployed or worked in the least skilled occupations.

Development of normal vision depends upon presence not only of light energy (see page 474) but also of patterned information inputs. In cases of squint, one eye turns in or out and so is less used than the other. If a squint develops in infants or children, the abnormal eye is neglected and, after transient double vision, becomes amblyopic, *i.e.*, has impaired vision. Or the eyes may alternate in use, each fixating in turn on objects in the visual field. If the squint develops in adulthood, it usually produces permanent double vision. Researches with microelectrodes in the neurons of channels involved in binocular vision show that the neurons develop even in the absence of visual experience. When squint is produced by cutting an eye muscle in young cats, however, the resulting lack of correct binocular information inputs prevents these channels from developing and functioning in a normally cooperative fashion.[520]

Light and information lack stresses seem to have

permanent effects on cats only between the fourth and sixth weeks after birth. The effects of various sorts of cataracts on human vision support these findings. A cataract prevents images from entering the eye. After surgical removal of a congenital cataract from an adult, amblyopia persists permanently in an otherwise normal eye. When cataracts which develop in adults are removed, however, the information input lack stress is found to have produced no permanent damage.

On the basis of the research outlined above, Hubel speculates as follows:

Experimental psychologists and psychiatrists both emphasize the importance of early experience on subsequent behavior patterns—could it be that deprivation of social contacts or the existence of other abnormal emotional situations early in life may lead to a deterioration or a distortion of connections in some yet unexplored parts of the brain? If so, one may hope that someday even the concepts of Freud may be explained in neurophysiological terms.[521]

(e) *Excesses of information inputs.* No pathological states are known with certainty to be caused directly by excessive rates of information inputs. Information input overload, however, probably plays a part in breakdowns of executives and related psychological disturbances (see page 167).

Excessive quantities of information inputs can be stressful, but also the meaning of the inputs can be threatening or stressful, independent of how fast the message is transmitted. Terrifying or unpleasant experiences, such as the sight of a physical attack, murder, battle, or disaster can produce permanent changes in the viewer's behavior. These may be based upon one-trial emotional conditioning such that a previously neutral input becomes charged with special meaning or elicits anxiety (see page 456). Such traumatic inputs to a child, psychoanalysts assert, may cause his later behavior to be atypical or pathological. Abnormal matter-energy processing characteristic of psychosomatic illnesses may arise from such information inputs (see page 458).

(f) *Inputs of maladaptive genetic information in the template.* Maladaptive genetic information can be transmitted as either a dominant, a partially dominant, or a recessive genetic trait; or it may be multifactorial. It can arise either from a mutation or during faulty division of the genetic material during mitosis. Disorders of growth or development can occur in almost any part of the organism, although some components are more commonly affected than others. Some deformities are known to be familial because of their occurrence in certain families in numbers which indicate dominant or recessive patterns of inheritance. Others involve damage to parental or fetal chromo-somes by radiation, drugs, or toxins. Often when components are congenitally deformed, missing, or unable to function normally, the causes are unknown.

Species differ in their mutation rates, but the rate for each species is more or less constant unless it is altered by environmental changes such as increases in radiation. Unless a mutation is so harmful that it is lethal in embryo or in infancy for the organism in which it first occurs, several generations must usually pass before it is eliminated by natural selection. All populations of organisms therefore include a "genetic load" of damaged individuals. Some genes are more subject to mutation than others, so that certain sorts of mutations occur repeatedly in a population and propagate the same defect through more than one breeding line.

Of the 46 human chromosomes, one pair is made up of the sex chromosomes, XX in females and XY in males. The other 22 pairs of nonsex chromosomes, or *autosomes,* are collected into 7 sets, A through G. Various disease syndromes result from alterations in the number or structure of these chromosomes.

One of these is *mongolism* or *Down's syndrome.* It consists of mental retardation, eyes somewhat like those of Mongolians, multiple physical deformities, and reduced vitality usually leading to early death. It can arise in three ways. The first, *autosomal trisomy,* results when both chromosomes of a particular autosomal pair (number 21 in set G) go to the same pole during meiosis (see pages 225 and 226). One gamete is, therefore, formed with an extra chromosome, while the other gamete lacks one.[522] The latter sort of gamete never develops into a viable organism. The trisomic gamete, with 47 chromosomes, produces the familiar syndrome, more or less severe. The incidence of such autosomal trisomy increases markedly with maternal age. Another cause of Down's syndrome is autosomal *translocation,* involving an exchange of segments between two chromosomes which are not members of the same pair. The resultant individual has the usual number of chromosomes, but two of them are abnormal. A virus may cause autosomal translocation.[523] Down's syndrome also occurs, less frequently and less severely, in *mosaicism* (when more than one chromosome combination is present in a single organism, some cells having one combination and others having one or more different ones).[524]

In the sex chromosomes one can find monosomy (only X present but not Y), trisomy (XXX or XXY or XYY present instead of a normal pair), polysomy of greater degree (*e.g.,* XXXXYY), or various sorts of mosaicism. Viable organisms with varying degrees of malformation in their reproducer subsystems result from many of these genetic abnormalities, although some of them appear to have little or no effect.[525] Certain genetic diseases, such as *hemophilia, red-green color blindness,* and one form of *muscular dystrophy* are sex-linked. Of such afflictions, some are dominant, others recessive. The genes which determine them are usually on the X chromosome (the Y has few genes). In the case of recessives, they are transmitted from the mother, who does not exhibit the trait but is a carrier to half of her sons. The affected sons pass the gene on to all of their daughters but not to their sons. Genetic traits on the Y chromosome are transmitted solely from father to son.

Chromosomal variations are also found in the normal population. Between 1 in 100 and 1 in 300 live-born children has some chromosomal aberration, according to one estimate, many with no evident pathology.[526] A study of 361 subjects randomly selected from the general population, ranging in age from 15 to more than 85, discovered among them 12 people with abnormal or unusually variant chromosomes.[527] With the possible exception of one man, none had any obvious pathological signs or symptoms.

Out of all the infants born alive in one hospital during one year, satisfactory chromosomal smears could be obtained from 2,081. Of these 10, or 0.48 percent, had some chromosome aberrations.[528] The abnormalities included four XYY's, one XXY, two autosomal trisomies of pair 21, and three other autosomal defects. Of the babies with genetic aberrations, two with autosomal defects were so seriously deformed that they died shortly after birth; two others had mongolism; one had minor developmental anomalies not usually associated with the observed chromosomal defect (XYY); one boy had the Klinefelter syndrome (XXY), a common cause of permanent infertility in men; and the others appeared normal. Only two of the five babies with autosomal effects were known to have a parent with an abnormality similar to that of the baby. Chromosomal abnormalities not inherited from a parent, and therefore presumably arising *de novo,* occurred in 0.38 percent of the total population of 2,081 infants.

Genes exercise their influence by controlling the synthesis of enzymes and structural proteins. The enzymes in turn control the production of other substances required by cells (see pages 238 to 241). A defect in a gene, therefore, affects the synthesis of some specific substance or substances required by the system for normal growth, repair, or function. This constitutes an inborn error of metabolism. The defect may be in metabolism of carbohydrates, proteins, lipids, nucleic acids, porphyrins, or pigments. For instance, the enzyme galactose-1-phosphate uridyl

transferase is necessary for an important step in the conversion of galactose, a sugar in foods, into glucose (see page 241). In the disease, *galactosemia,* a gene mutation prevents this enzyme from being synthesized. This defect is inherited as an autosomal recessive trait. In later years, it may be evident only by minor discomfort after ingesting milk, which contains lactose (which is glucose plus galactose) and an abnormal response to a galactose tolerance test.[529] An infant in whom the trait is fully expressed, however, may appear normal at birth but develops a grave feeding problem, suffering vomiting, diarrhea, and failure to thrive. The liver, where normally the conversion from galactose to glucose takes place, becomes enlarged, and consequently the abdomen swells. The baby may be jaundiced and may accumulate fluid in tissues and body cavities. Cirrhosis of the liver is a possibility. Cataracts develop in more than half the severely affected children, and mental retardation is common among them. As the child matures, some of these symptoms may improve, but much of the damage is irreversible. The effect of this hereditary defect can be avoided entirely if a correct diagnosis is made and a diet free of milk and all other foods containing lactose or galactose is adhered to throughout the first three years of life. In the early stages of the disease, correction of the diet leads to improvement, but later it does not.

Some failures of hormone-controlled processes in human beings may be genetically determined. Dwarfism can occur from an autosomal recessive defect causing a deficiency in growth hormone.[530] Individuals who are affected are of normal size at birth and grow normally during early infancy. By two years of age they are smaller than normal. The full adult heights of a small number of such dwarfs who were studied ranged from 123 to 139.5 cm. Their weights ranged from 30.6 to 42 kg. Aside from being small, they were not deformed. They attained normal sexual development, although sexual maturation was delayed in all of them. All the women had normal pregnancies and lactation, although their small pelves made Caesarean section necessary when they gave birth. Such dwarfism was clearly shown to be genetically determined. Marriages between persons of close blood relationship who had dwarfism in the family produced a high incidence of affected children. Also, in one particular marriage of two dwarfs, two affected children were born. Growth hormone was deficient in the dwarfs studied.

Certain psychoses may be genetically determined. Studies of schizophrenic patients and their relatives have been interpreted as showing this, but the exact nature of the genetic defect, the gene or genes involved, and the probability that the disease will appear in a relative of a schizophrenic patient can be calculated empirically though not theoretically.[531]

(g) *Abnormalities in internal matter-energy processes.* In most diseases some abnormality of internal matter-energy processing exists. Some of these ailments can be ascribed to toxic or infectious inputs, genetic defects, or others of the previously discussed categories of pathology. Still others result from aging and the effects of repeated stresses of life as bodily components become weakened and break down. Cancers also represent an abnormal processing of matter-energy, inasmuch as masses of neoplastic cells grow at the expense of other tissues, some of them producing excessive amounts of hormones or other cellular products.

Defective functioning of any matter-energy processing subsystem may change outputs from it. Other components of the organism which are dependent upon these outputs may, as a consequence, suffer lack or excess stresses. Toxic substances produced by abnormal metabolism in one subsystem may damage functions in others if the toxins are carried through the organism by its distributor subsystem.

The abnormal matter-energy processing involved in many infections, toxic states, and metabolic diseases produce disordered thought, speech, or behavior, or combinations of these. Patients with phenylketonuria, for instance, may have symptoms of both mental deficiency and psychosis.[532] The reasons for the mental disturbance are thought to be toxic effects on neurons of the central nervous system of abnormal amines and amino acids, as well as a number of other abnormal chemical states, including deficiencies in catechol amines such as norepinephrine and dopamine which are normally present in neural tissue (see page 278).[533]

The resemblance of some patients with phenylketonuria or other metabolic diseases to schizophrenic patients suggests that some metabolic abnormality may underlie schizophrenia, and possibly manic-depressive and other psychoses as well. Certain tranquilizing drugs, such as reserpine, which produce behavioral changes in human beings and animals and can counteract the signs and symptoms of schizophrenia in some patients, contain an indole nucleus. Thus they are chemically related to serotonin and other substances found in the brain and elsewhere in nature. Reserpine is believed to act directly on nerve endings.[534] Some indoles such as LSD, psilocybin, and bufotenin can cause psychotic states. Urinary excretion of indole derivatives has been shown to increase as a function of the degree of psychotic symptoms in schizophrenic patients.[535] All these data suggest that indole metabolism may be abnormal in at least some psychotic patients.

Schizophrenia is a term applied to several sorts of psychoses, the various forms of which may represent different defects.[536] These various pathologies respond quite differently to psychoactive drugs or other treatments. In recent years intensive efforts have been made to discover some abnormal substance in the blood, urine, or tissues of schizophrenic patients. Several interesting ones have been identified, but none has been clearly demonstrated to be related to the disease.[537]

One of the problems in asserting that schizophrenia is caused by metabolic error is that stressful childhood experiences or environmental events often seem to precipitate the onset of symptoms, either initially or in subsequent attacks. Some hypotheses have been proposed to suggest how genetic and environmental information inputs might interact to cause schizophrenia.

One hypothesis proposes that the genetic defect is not in the structural gene which determines what enzyme will be synthesized but in a regulatory gene.[538] Pathology determined by structural genes is either present or absent, *e.g.,* a patient either has phenylketonuria or does not. But pathology in the regulatory components of the cell could manifest a range of different expressions at different times, dependent perhaps upon information transmissions internally in the nervous system or to the organism from the environment.

Another hypothesis proposes that some factor found in the schizophrenic's blood serum interferes with the energy production of intracellular glucose metabolism (see page 237), and thus impairs the ability of the schizophrenic to adjust to a range of stresses. The research of Gottlieb, Frohman, and Beckett suggests that such a serum factor impairs schizophrenic patients' ability to adjust to stresses.[539] Experimentally produced disturbance in the intracellular energy transport system increased antisocial, destructive, aggressive, and sexual behavior in these patients. Furthermore, monkeys raised without their mothers, besides showing the behavioral disturbances described above (see page 475), were found to differ from normal monkeys in this serum factor.[540] A normal mother-child relationship during infancy and childhood may, therefore, be essential for the maturation of adjustment processes to stresses. Possibly, then, a disturbance in this fundamental relationship can predispose some people to schizophrenia.

Another confirmation of the importance of a blood serum factor in schizophrenia comes in research in which serum from one class of schizophrenic patients was injected into the third ventricle of a cat's brain and produced changes in the electrical activity of the brain.[541]

(*h*) *Abnormalities in internal information processes.* Endocrine and neural information processing components are subject to the effects of trauma, infection, genetic defects, and other sources of pathology. These may or may not cause illnesses. A few examples of diseases affecting these components are as follows: (*i*) diabetes insipidus, in which damage to the posterior pituitary prevents it from secreting vasopressin, so that it cannot signal the kidney tubules to resorb water, and consequently abnormally large amounts of urine are extruded (see page 456); (*ii*) the neuritis and psychotic manifestations of severe pellagra, a disease produced by nicotinic acid (vitamin B_6) deficiency; (*iii*) the distinctive electroencephalographic patterns, convulsions, and other abnormal behavior seen in epilepsy, an illness which arises after brain trauma, or from brain tumor or other cause; (*iv*) stuttering and related speech defects (see page 444); and (*v*) the progressive muscular weakness of myasthenia gravis, which arises from abnormalities in acetylcholine metabolism.

According to Menninger normal adjustments to ordinary stresses and the resultant strains include such information processes as general irritability, feelings of tension, overtalkativeness, often repeated laughter, frequent losses of temper, restlessness, sleepless worrying at night, and fantasies about solutions to various real problems (see page 459).[542] Beyond these, in response to stresses and strains of greater magnitude, more costly and more pathological adjustments are resorted to. They are pathological if more expensive adjustment processes are employed when less costly ones would suffice. Two hypotheses seem consistent with the view just stated: Hypothesis 3.3.7.2-14 (see page 101), which states that a system which survives generally decides to use first the least costly adjustment to a threat or strain produced by a stress and increasingly more costly ones later; also Hypothesis 5.2-7 (see page 106), which states that when a barrier stands between a system under strain and a goal which can relieve that strain, the system ordinarily uses the adjustment processes of removing the barrier, circumventing it, or otherwise mastering it. If these efforts fail, less adaptive adjustments may be tried, including: (*a*) attacking the barrier by energic or informational transmissions; (*b*) displacing aggression to another innocent but more vulnerable nearby system; (*c*) reverting to primitive, nonadaptive behavior; (*d*) adopting rigid, nonadaptive behavior; and (*e*) escaping from the situation.

Beyond the normal adjustment processes, Menninger identifies the following five degrees of internal information processing pathology: (*i*) "Nervousness," a slight impairment of smooth adaptive control. (*ii*) Neurotic hysterical, obsessional, or anxiety symptoms, including character disorders. (*iii*) Directed aggression and violence, including some forms of "self-defense" or warfare which are condoned in many social contexts as well as chronic repetitions of mild aggressions and explosive outbursts of serious violent and socially unacceptable aggressions, such as murder, associated with pathological lack of self-control. (*iv*) Psychotic states of extreme disorganization, regression, and repudiation of the reality of inputs from the environment. And (*v*) extreme disorganization of control with malignant anxiety and depression, often resulting in death, frequently by suicide.[543] Using this general systems approach, Menninger analyzes the diagnosis, treatment, and cure of cognitive and affective disorders, and pathologies of social adjustment.

The effect of information flows in altering normal matter-energy processing in human organisms is recognized in psychiatry. A great variety of symptoms, including pain, paralyses, and anesthesias of parts of the body, are seen in patients with neurotic conflicts. They often have only a superficial resemblance to symptoms resulting from damage to neural or muscular components. Anesthesias, for example, may not conform to the anatomical distribution of pain nerves. Many psychiatric clinicians hypothesize that such symptoms arise in the central nervous system rather than peripherally, being used by the patient to alleviate guilt or anxiety related to events in the past, usually in childhood. The patient may no longer be aware of the events, having forgotten or repressed them. The evidence for such views is largely clinical and still inconclusive. Structural damage may follow neurotic disability, as when atrophy of disuse of an arm or leg occurs after prolonged hysterical paralysis of that limb.

The importance of information stresses in producing diverse clinical symptoms is recognized in clinical medicine. Their relationship to the GAS and to the emotions was discussed above (see page 456). Some kinds of hypertension, rheumatic diseases, arthritis, kidney diseases, vascular diseases including possibly atherosclerosis, and a number of other illnesses were classified by Selye as "diseases of adaptation," brought about by that excess of anterior pituitary and adrenocortical hormones which characterizes the body's responses to stress.[544] Overdosage with such hormones can cause the formation and eventual perforation of a peptic ulcer.[545] These hormones are assumed to increase the flow of the gastric juices as a result of increased secretion of acetylcholine and consequent increased vagal activity. Experimental results support some of these conclusions. For example, rats placed in a dark box and shocked on a random schedule developed more peptic ulcers than similar rats which were shocked at regular intervals.[546] Presumably this was because rats on the random schedule experienced more stress by having to fear shock at every moment, without letup. Unpredictability of a painful input also affected monkeys during conditioned emotional disturbances.[547] Norepinephrine and 17-hydroxycorticosteroid concentrations in the blood plasma rose in a number of experimental situations involving such disturbances. If they involved uncertainty about when a painful input would occur, however, the concentration of epinephrine rose as well.

The psychoses are among the most extreme sorts of pathology of internal information processing. In the two immediately preceding sections I have discussed possible genetic and matter-energy processing pathologies which underlie schizophrenia. The most obvious aspects of the illness, however, are the difficulties which the patient experiences in information processing.[548] Because of the great range of abnormal behaviors which occur in the various forms of this disease, no general description fits all patients well. Many paranoid schizophrenics have little difficulty with speech, for instance, but they do decode information inputs in a highly personal and idiosyncratic way, forcing signals which they receive from their environment into a pattern to confirm their delusions.[549] On the other hand, some hebephrenic schizophrenics speak in unintelligible "word salads."[550] Such disordered speech has been ascribed to an inability to process incoming information effectively because of chronic information input overload (see pages 168 and 169).[551]

Perhaps sheer information overload is not the only explanation for abnormal information processing by schizophrenics. They may selectively screen out signals with certain patterns or meanings, as in the defense mechanism of denial.[552]

Often it has been assumed that the language disorder in this illness necessarily implies that there is also a thought disorder. This need not be so.[553] Speech can be abnormal in aphasia when thought is normal, and the same can be true in schizophrenia. It is important to find out which information processing subsystem or subsystems are affected by schizophrenia. There is evidence that it is not primarily the input transducer, internal transducer, associator, memory, decider, output transducer, or motor. Schizophrenics and normals do not appear to differ importantly in sensory func-

tions, associative processes, associative learning, long-term memory, syllogistic reasoning, concept formation (at least when the meaning of the content is not threatening to the patient), or perhaps even in the capacity for normal verbal response (although schizophrenics manifest many linguistic peculiarities, possibly because some other subsystem than the output transducer is processing information pathologically).[554] On the other hand, a body of evidence suggests that the decoder of schizophrenics, under the stress of information input overload, functions abnormally.[555] The performance of schizophrenics is worse than that of normals when they must distinguish between signals on competing sensory channels, even though they do just as well in perceptual tasks not involving distraction. Schizophrenics' temporal integration of inputs, particularly speech, is faulty. They also find it hard to screen out irrelevant input signals, which seems to diminish their effective channel capacity. Schizophrenics who manifest withdrawal may be using the adjustment process of escape from information input overload (see page 167).[556]

5.6 Decay and termination   A sequoia tree lives and continues to grow for as long as 4,000 years. Aphids of one species grow to maturity, reproduce, and die in as few as 10 days. Each species fulfills the life span allotted to it.

Every species appears to have a "mean time to failure" programmed into its genetic template.[557] For the cold-blooded animals which continue to grow throughout their lives, this time is often long. Among warm-blooded creatures, size is frequently correlated with length of life, the larger species having the longer life spans. Elephants, among mammals, as compared with small species like rabbits and mice, live a long time. The larger species take longer to grow to their full size and mature later sexually. Slow maturation is apparently a major factor in longevity.[558] Perhaps aging begins when growth ends. Also, possibly, the larger number of cells in big animals enables them to survive longer after some of their cells are lost or damaged. Birds, which ordinarily live only a few seasons in the wild before death from predators or accidents eliminates them, are long-lived exceptions in the animal kingdom.[559] In spite of rapid growth to maturity and a high rate of metabolism, they live long when caged. Chaffinches in captivity have lived to be 29 years old. Finches have survived 30 years and parrots much longer.

From the point of view of a species as a whole, there are advantages in a programmed termination of individual organisms. Evolution depends upon a continual supply of new individuals. Evolutionary changes take place most rapidly if the time from one generation to the next is as short as possible, given the usual period of maturation and reproduction of an individual.[560] The nature of the process of senescence has probably been modified by natural selection.[561] Genes which are expressed in some change in structure or process that occurs late in life, even in a long-lived species, have less chance to affect natural selection than earlier acting ones. Therefore a gene with selective advantage tends, as generations pass, to be expressed earlier and earlier. Conversely, an unfavorable gene tends to be expressed later and later.

The upper limit of human life today, as in Biblical times, is about 70 years, the mean duration being over 70. A small number survive much longer—to a century or beyond. A few years ago a Russian couple lived to celebrate their one-hundredth wedding anniversary. Both were about 120 years of age. On the average, women live a few years longer than men. With the advantages of an advanced culture and modern medical care, more and more people reach the upper limit. The average life expectancy in Western nations in recent centuries has increased without much change in this upper limit. Even if the major causes of death in old age were eliminated by medical improvements, the life expectancy at birth would probably increase by only about 10 years, to an average of 80 years.[562] Early Iron and Bronze Age men could expect to live only 20 to 30 years, on the average.[563] Roman men of the first century A.D. became eligible for the Senate at the age of 40 and could reasonably look forward to a few years of public responsibility after that.

For reasons that are not known, after the age of 30 years, the probability of death doubles about every 8 years.[564] Perhaps the reason is progressive deterioration of enzymes involved in the transcription of proteins so that the capacity for repair diminishes.[565] Perhaps the supply of adaptive energy is exhausted by accumulated wear and tear.[566] Return to chemical steady states after stress takes longer in the old than in the young.[567] Recovery of the blood to normal acidity after a certain degree of experimental alteration of it takes a young subject 6 to 8 h whereas a 70-year-old person requires 36 to 48 h. This recovery may become slower and slower with age until finally the controlling negative feedbacks do not restore the acidity into its steady-state range, and death then follows. This is consistent with Hypothesis 5.6-1 (see page 110), which states that if a system's negative feedback discontinues and is not restored by that system or by another on which it becomes parasitic or symbiotic, it decomposes into multiple components, and its suprasystem assumes control of them. Internal steady states generally remain constant and normal in old people at rest, but even the ordinary stresses of daily living are met with a reduced adjustment capacity.

The fundamental changes of old age are at the cellular level, but different tissues age at different rates. The efficiency of many processes begins to decrease soon after maturity. Those activities requiring coordination among components of different organs are most affected by this decline. Nerve impulses are transmitted at about the same rate at any age, but rates of both cardiac output and flow of air through the lungs decline, so sustained physical exercise is gradually impaired.[568] Individuals differ in the rates at which the various components of their bodies deteriorate with age.[569] These differences are often genetically determined. Renal, cardiac, and vascular degenerations follow such familial patterns. Age of onset of deterioration differs from person to person also. The sexes differ in their susceptibility to aging of various tissues.

Neural processes are altered by aging in different ways, many of which are similar to the effects of toxins, brain damage, or other disease processes.[570] Diffuse damage may lead to psychoses. Or there may be local damage resulting in Parkinsonism, loss of vibratory sensation, or tremor. Diminished cardiac efficiency or vascular accidents also directly affect the central nervous system—the first by diminishing the blood supply, the second by the trauma of bleeding into neural tissues or later local anoxia.

Elderly people lose weight overall, and individual organs also become lighter. The number of cells in a tissue diminishes. The senile brain, for example, is small, reduced in weight, with a wrinkled, shrunken appearance caused by alterations in the cortex.[571] The basal ganglia are shrunken. The nerve cells themselves are also altered, and many have disappeared entirely.

Both matter-energy processing and information processing are affected by these changes in tissues. At 70 years of age, a man's capacity to do work has declined by 30 percent from his capacity at 30 years. On a physical test involving turning a crank, the loss between ages 35 and 80 is almost 60 percent.[572] Among the other matter-energy process variables which decrease with age are rate of blood flow to the brain, rate of cardiac output, maximum rate of oxygen uptake during exercise, total amount of oxygen that can be taken into the lungs in one breath, basal metabolic rate, rate of gonadal activity, and strength of hand grip.

The transmission of information through the nervous system is affected by the loss of brain weight, and the decline in the number of nerve trunk fibers.[573] The number of taste buds decreases. Since conduction velocity in neurons slows only slightly, simple spinal reflexes remain virtually unimpaired and neuromuscular connections are little affected.

Information processing declines in many ways with age.[574] The EEG records of the old look more like those of young people suffering a moderate oxygen lack stress than like those of normal young people. Thresholds of input transducer components for taste, hearing, and pain become higher, and a number of age-related impoverishments in vision appear. Learning ability declines near the end of life. Older subjects are harder to condition and easier to extinguish. Simple reaction times increase and so do choice reaction times, in complicated ways. If meaning of symbols is involved, the more complex information inputs are, the more difficult it becomes for the old to respond to them. Memory for recent events is commonly poor among the old. Short-term memory storage may also be diminished. In general, average intelligence scores are lower in older people than in middle-aged adults. In one study, however, in which the same people were tested in their first year of college in 1919 and then again in 1950 and 1961, their scores increased at the 1950 retest.[575] In 1961, by which time the subjects were past 60 years old, their test performance was still no worse than in 1950.

Like the physiological changes, information processing decrements generally begin in early maturity and proceed slowly for the rest of life. Between the twenties and the forties, for instance, significant decrements were measured in certain tasks deemed to be relevant to air-crew performance.[576] These included tests on comprehension of instruments, learning codes, finding relationships, and orientation to new equipment. No relationship was discovered between age and performance in mathematical reasoning, numerical approximation, numerical operations, reading comprehension, and reoriented reading of words. Another research disclosed a small but systematic impairment, between the middle teens and late fifties, of the ability to judge collision courses of objects moving in space.[577]

Older people are generally considered more rigid, cautious, and dogmatic, and less sociable and adaptable, than younger ones. Research results do not give strong support to such judgments.[578] Many studies which compare the performances or personalities of the old with the young do not control adequately for differences in cultural background, basic intelligence, and other variables. To make valid statements about age-related changes, more longitudinal studies are required in which people are followed for long periods so that changes in their abilities, personalities, and social adjustments can be observed.[579] Little may be left to attribute merely to the passage of time after such researches separate out the effects of brain damage in a significant proportion of the population studied; individual differences in basic personality, intelligence, and lifetime patterns of adjustment to stress; the impacts on the subjects, over the years, of losses of loved and important people, jobs, income, and self-esteem; and the inconveniences created by decline in physical and mental capacities.

The common fate of all men is described by the ancient poet in the medical metaphors of his day: "Or ever the silver cord be loosed, or the golden bowl be broken, or the pitcher be broken at the fountain, or the wheel broken at the cistern. Then shall the dust return to the earth as it was: and the spirit shall return unto God who gave it."[580]

6. Models and simulations

Three of the four possible classes of models or simulations (see page 85) are found at the level of the organism. There appear to be none in class (d) *living system—computer interactions.*

(a) *Nonliving artifacts.* The idea of building an automaton which successfully simulates a human being has a continuing fascination in literature and folklore. Rabbi Loew of fifteenth century Prague is said to have formed an artificial man, a golem, from clay and used cabalistic formulas to animate it.[581] This legendary robot was named Joseph Golem and acted as a temple servant. Lacking the power of speech, it could, nevertheless, understand orders and carry them out so literally that when it was told to fetch water it produced a flood, bringing pail after pail until it occurred to someone to tell it to stop. In this it was like the fabled sorcerer's apprentice, or certain poorly programmed computers, or, indeed, stupid workers of all the centuries. The golem was, nonetheless, capable of independent action and of reasoning. It aided the great rabbi in protecting the people of the ghetto from those who wished to destroy them, but eventually it became dangerous and had to be destroyed.

Rostand discusses an automaton imagined by Villiers de L'Isle-Adam:

Those who have read his marvelous story will remember the seductive "Androïde" which the magician Edison substituted for a woman of flesh and blood in order to save a highly romantic young English Lord from suicide. Villiers' Future Eve was not yet electronic, but she contained golden phonographs stocked—although long-playing records were not yet invented—with hours of fine speech (are not a hundred phrases enough to meet any situation of the heart?)—and wax cylinders inscribed with seventy movements, expressions and attitudes (which is far in excess of the variety necessary to a well brought up woman, for twenty-seven or twenty-eight are already the sign of an exceptional personality). The Count of Villiers raised, with the cruel irony of a great poet, the whole problem of the relations between the natural and artificial, between the living and the mechanical. This problem has now become singularly acute, since intelligent people are wondering very seriously whether the robots of cybernetics do not present us with a valid image of life and thought.[582]

Endowed with "positronic brains" and lifelike appearance but with little or no sense of humor, androids find their places in science fiction as well. One imaginative creator of these robots, Asimov, deemed it wise to formulate "laws of robotics" which are built into their "nervous systems" so that these intelligent and powerful machines could not under any circumstances injure a human being.[583]

The "turtles" which Walter built and named Elma and Elsie might be looked upon as precursors of such artificial men.[584] They crawl about in response to the varying strengths of the light in different regions of their environment, attract and repel each other, respond to punishment by correcting their behavior, and return to their hutches when "tired" in order to recharge their batteries. These machines simulate the gross behavior of animals, although no claim is made that their mechanisms are similar to those which activate the living beast.

A chess-playing automaton, activated by a concealed midget chess expert, fooled Napoleon. Other automata have been built which could play music or draw. One, a "steam man" invented by a Canadian in the 1890s, could pull a light load as it walked along.[585]

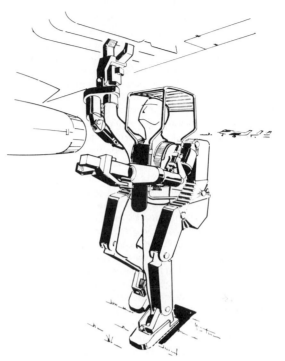

Fig. 8-8 Concept of man in powered exoskeleton. (From E. G. Johnsen & W. R. Corliss. *Teleoperators and human augmentation*. Washington: NASA Report SP-5047, 1967, 178. Courtesy of General Electric Co. *Reprinted by permission.*)

A class of cybernetic machines which make use of negative feedback has been developed to augment and "amplify" human beings. These are general-purpose machines rather than tools developed for a single purpose.[586] Unlike the robots envisaged by Čapek in his play *R.U.R.* or Asimov's intelligent androids, which behaved independently, these are always parts of man–machine systems. They simulate humans only as far as necessary for their design to be efficient.

These teleoperators are useful for replacing human beings in hazardous environments, such as the airless moon or the depths of the sea, to make it possible to lift and carry loads far beyond human strength, to reach into radioactive or germfree fields, act as prostheses for the handicapped, and do other jobs for which a human being's unaided body is inadequate. Teleoperators include: manipulators which extend human dexterity inside nuclear reactors; a "walking truck" which strides over rough and roadless terrain (see Fig. 8-7); and an "exoskeleton" (like a space suit) which protects the vulnerable human body and augments human strength where extreme heat, cold, or deep-sea pressure threaten (see Fig. 8-8).

Fig. 8-7 Walking truck. (From W. R. Corliss & E. G. Johnsen. *Teleoperator controls*. Washington: NASA Report SP-5070, 1968, 95. Courtesy of General Electric Co. *Reprinted by permission.*)

Teleoperators have sensors which gather information about relevant aspects of the machine's environment and transmit them to the human controller. Such sensors are not confined within the limitations of human input transducers. Some can, for example, "see" wavelengths in the part of the spectrum invisible to the human eye. Information is processed by a computer, and the person in the loop can adjust control signals accordingly. Some of them have programs stored for a part of their activities. Means of control differ in the various sorts of teleoperators. In many of them the person moves a part of her or his body to activate the corresponding part of the machine. By moving her or his own fingers, a person may guide corresponding components of a manipulator. Other teleoperators are controlled by buttons or similar conventional equipment. In some, there is a direct mechanical connection between the person and the machine; in others, control signals are transmitted over distances. Probably these would be interplanetary distances, although all teleoperators make use of feedback, and the delay of feedback signals covering millions of miles could become a serious problem to the human component of the system (see page 464).[587] Teleoperators differ from existing devices used in planetary exploration. The latter are largely preprogrammed. Teleoperators would in a sense "project" the human controller to the planet. The person would see with the machine's eyes and feel with its pressure receptors, so that she or he could behave adaptively, using teleoperator components instead of her or his own body.

Most of the adaptively intelligent behavior of teleoperators is brought about by the person in the system, who acts chiefly as the central decider. When a machine is operating on a stored program, however, some analogs of intelligent behavior may occur. One existing manipulator can have in its memory the location and configuration of obstacles which it may encounter, so that it can choose a position which avoids these. It may explore several paths around the obstacle, select the quickest, and move along it.[588] Future computer-controlled machines may be nearly autonomous, learning to improve performance as a result of experience.[589] I discuss machine intelligence below (see pages 485 to 491).

(b) *Living, usually human, representations.* A recently conceived and unusual situation in which one organism simulates another is when specially trained actresses and actors play the parts of patients with various diseases, simulating their speech and behavior and making appropriate answers to questions, as teaching aids for medical students.[590] The actors are more able to present "classic" symptoms than are actual patients, whose diseases often fail to conform to textbook descriptions. This technique also saves ill patients from the added stress of being presented to groups of strangers as is often done in clinical teaching. Examination can be repeated by a number of different students on the same "patient" for comparison of their performances. A patient who is always available when needed for classroom use, never dying and never improving, has obvious practical advantages for instruction. The "patient" also reports upon the student's techniques and manner. This sort of simulation, furthermore, has been used in clinical instruction of physicians in places distant from the medical center, where it would ordinarily be impractical to take real patients.

(c) *Models in words, numbers, or other symbols, including computer programs.* The number of relevant publications at this level is so enormous that only a few representative models can be discussed. Some of these are stated verbally, some in other symbolic form. Verbal models which provide plausible explanations or are useful in research design may later be put into mathematical or other form. In some cases, of course, the translation from one symbolism to another is simply that, and the new form of the model is interesting mainly as an exercise. In others, the implications of the theory may be more completely explored by a mathematical model, or a program may have inductive power which extends the theory. The theory of cell assemblies developed by Hebb (see pages 411, 413, and 419) is a verbal model from which mathematical and computer models have been developed. He asserted that a postulated network of neural elements with characteristics modeled from those of central nervous system neurons will adjust to repeated similar information inputs by developing reverberating circuits which form permanent groups of cells that fire in pattern, "cell assemblies." This sequence of events was programmed for a computer.[591] The expected cell relationships did not develop when the computer program was run. Instead, the spread through the network was such as to prevent reinforcement of a detailed pattern of firing. By adding inhibitory connections to the cell assembly theory (a suggestion of Milner's made reasonable by more recent neurophysiological studies), by greatly increasing the number of neurons in the net from 69 to 512 cells, and by changing the nature of the connections, a model was produced which did organize cells into assemblies.

The conceptual systems to be presented below are arranged in several sets, the members of which, while usually quite disparate, have certain general features in common. The first models represent either nervous systems or total organisms. Then models which concentrate on particular organism processes are arranged under the matter-energy processing or information processing subsystems to which they apply, such as the decoder or the associator. A program which recognizes patterns, for example, is placed under the decoder. Like organisms, computers rarely carry out one subsystem process without involving some others; thus a pattern-recognition program usually must also learn, store information, and make decisions.

An important set of these conceptual systems, most of them computer programs, is relevant at this level only because the processes represented in it have occurred, at least until recently, only in living organisms, and often only in human beings. These "artificial intelligence" studies do not design systems to perform tasks in the same way that a human brain would do them. That is, they are not deliberate simulations. Their goal is to program computers to exhibit actions that we call "intelligent behavior" when it is observed in human beings.[592] These programs make use of heuristics and make inductive rather than deductive inferences, since all intelligent behavior appears to be carried out in this way.

Machines cannot be regarded as living systems, but living systems can be, and often are, considered to belong to a class of machines—automata—which are capable of "self-organizing" or "adaptive" behavior (see page 486). The mathematical theory of automata can be applied to nervous systems as well as to electronic computers.[593]

The realization of machine intelligence depends upon large, usually digital, computers which rapidly perform the enormous number of operations required for intelligent activities. Computer programs play games like checkers and chess, form and apply concepts, recognize visual and auditory patterns, prove logical propositions, and solve mathematical problems. They also carry out the logical processes essential to a vast number of practical tasks like mixing bologna, forecasting the weather, and tutoring students.

Anxiety often attends the suspicion by human organisms that human predominance in the fields of intelligent behavior might be threatened by other sorts of systems. And yet, unless "intelligence" is defined to include *only* living behavior, properly programmed computers can display it.[594]

The list of functions of which an artifact may be capable, according to MacKay, includes (italics his):[595]

(a) *Receiving, selecting, storing, and sending information.*
(b) *Reacting to changes in its "universe,"* including *messages* and *data on its own state.*

(c) *Reasoning* deductively from premises which can include the results of previous deductions and data on the relative success of different courses.
(d) Observing and controlling its own activity, whether symbolic or otherwise, so as to further some *goal.* This may be only a very general objective, such as the maximisation of efficiency in some defined sense, or the attainment of equilibrium, leaving a wide scope for the development of subsidiary "purposes" *ad hoc* by the artifact as the result of its experience.
(e) *Changing* its own pattern of behavior as a result of experience so as to develop quite complex and superficially unpredictable characteristics capable of rational description in purposive terms.

These capabilities, says MacKay, are the consequences of the generally accepted principle that

. . . any pattern of observable behaviour which can be specified in terms of unique and precisely-definable reactions to precisely-definable situations can in principle be imitated mechanically.

Network models of nervous systems.   The structures of organisms' nervous systems have inspired speculation about the form of nets required to produce behavior of various sorts. As indicated above, cell assemblies were postulated by Hebb to develop in a relatively unstructured network of neurons as a result of repeated activity. This was one attempt to describe a net capable of brainlike activities. Starting from facts or reasonable assumptions about the structures and processes of neurons, such forms of behavior as learning, decoding, and memory can derive from operations which can be performed upon these theoretical nets. The great complexity of nervous systems even in the lower animal phyla means that simplifying assumptions must be made if mathematical or symbolic models are to be manageable. In producing such models, mathematicians tend to look for the most elegant and parsimonious theoretical statements which also have the greatest deductive power. We do not know whether the principle of parsimony guides the development of organisms' nervous systems. Even simple network models are, nevertheless, of interest to those who wish to understand how a brain might work.

The work of Pitts and McCulloch is a basic contribution to network theory and automata theory. They showed that processes of neurons characterized by all-or-none discharges, and indeed all the processes of neural networks, could be described by operations using the basic logical relations of implication, negation, conjunction, and disjunction. Their assumptions viewed the nervous system as a digital automaton and ignored possible analog activity in it. Inputs to a neuron are digital. Its output signals transmitted along its axon are also digital. Since that is so, any intermediary processes in its synapses, dendrites, and cell body by which the signal is initiated need not, they contended, be explicitly a part of the theory. An intralevel or "black-box" analysis of the neuron can reasonably view it as wholly digital. They also assumed that a fixed number of synapses must receive inputs to cause a neuron to emit a signal at any time; that this number is independent of previous activity; that all significant delays are synaptic; that activity of an inhibitory synapse absolutely prevents excitation of a neuron at the time; and that the structure of the net does not change with time.[596] Furthermore, they assumed that propagation time through axons of various sizes can be considered essentially uniform because the conduction rate is faster in the longer, thick axons than in the shorter, thin ones. Nets with series of neurons such that the last synapsed back on the first were held to represent reverberating circuits of neurons.

The importance of this work is that even complex patterns of behavior can be reproduced by automata constructed of such elements and relationships. Theoretically, no behavior is too complex to be so reproduced. Since the theory of automata deals with all conceptual systems which are isomorphic to all possible concrete "adaptive" or "self-organizing" systems, living or nonliving, the theory of the behavior of living systems is regarded by many as the theory of a particular subset of automata.[597]

Network models have been criticized for not simulating nervous systems closely enough. The specificity of connection and indispensability of simple elements are unlike nervous systems. Actual living neurons are enormously more complex than these formalized elements. Even if all the neurons in an organism's nervous system could be represented, which is impossible by present methods, the requirement could not be met that the state of each at any moment must be specified. Also, any specific instance of organism behavior involves more widespread activity and many more neurons than this model includes. Representing acts of an organism in this notation would require more than can now be accomplished: identifying a specific pattern of synaptic transmission for each act.

After the paper he wrote with Pitts appeared, McCulloch and his associates altered their network formulations in various ways with the intention of simulating actual neural processes more exactly.[598] Many alternative network models have been proposed by others, using the "McCulloch-Pitts neuron" or related symbolic systems.

Another group of models focuses not upon the activities of single neurons but upon the processes of a large population of interconnected neurons which simulate neural nets. The state of individual cells is not known but the statistical probabilities are calcu-

lated that a proportion of the cells will fire or not fire. In one such model, that of Beurle, the spread of pulses from excited cells to others with which they synapse causes waves of activity to be propagated through the mass.[599] As the peak activity passes, cells become temporarily refractory, as live neurons do, and others in the direction of propagation become active. Thus the wave advances. When cells recover their sensitivity after the period of latency, another wave may follow. When the proper conditions are established the cells simulate various organism subsystem processes, such as learning, memory, or deciding. For instance, inputs to the mass from cells outside it may be varied; thresholds of the cells composing it may be altered; or new connections among the cells may be formed. It would be profitable, as Beurle suggests, to investigate the properties of more complex cell masses, with differentiated cell masses within them.

Neuron networks may be modeled either by special machines built to embody certain characteristics of nervous systems or by computer programs. I shall describe some special network machines below.

A computer program intended to simulate a neural net, which exhibits analogs of electrophysiological activities of natural brains, has been developed by Farley.[600] A system of neuron-like "cells" with specified connections and interactions makes up the net. Each of the cells has a threshold at which it is activated and below which it does nothing. The thresholds of the elements usually are arranged to have a normal distribution. The absolute and relative refractory periods of neurons are simulated by a period of "infinite" threshold which falls exponentially back to its resting value. A signal output from an active element is transmitted to all elements to which it is connected. The receiving elements sum this input with others they receive and emit a signal if their thresholds are exceeded. This relation produces both spatial and temporal summation and simulates some decision processes of dendrites (see page 276). Connection patterns can be varied by the experimenter.

An important technique in the study of nerve nets is Monte Carlo computer simulation. By programming the computer to provide random data of frequencies which reflect different hypothesized biases of a given net, the processes in that net can be simulated. This procedure allows "nervous systems" of various types to be constructed and studied. It may produce hypotheses that can be tested on living systems.[601]

Cybernetic models. These models conceptualize organisms as special classes of machines, systems which operate on engineering principles, particularly control by negative feedbacks (see pages 36 and 37). Use of such models was accelerated by the development of advanced cybernetic steering devices during World War II, although the conception of animals as automata has a much longer philosophical history.[602] Elements of such models often represent input–output relationships between the organism and its environment rather than details of neural events underlying behavior, although some form of representation of the nervous system may be included, such as a flow diagram.

Two early papers, the first by Ashby, [603] emanating from England, and the second by Rosenblueth, Wiener, and Bigelow, [604] emanating from America, stated the fundamental ideas of cybernetics. Although Ashby's early paper did not use the term "feedback," his phrase "functional circuit" is essentially synonymous. He illustrated it by a typical negative feedback instrument, a temperature control for an incubator. He emphasized the importance of maintaining a stable equilibrium for adaptive behavior in animals, holding that this is critical for their continued existence. In the Rosenblueth, Wiener, and Bigelow paper the concept of negative feedback was introduced explicitly, and its importance to purposeful behavior in organisms was stated. (The concept was standard in engineering usage, going back to Clerk Maxwell in 1868.[605]) Oscillations resulting from positive feedback were also described. Later, Wiener developed these ideas further and introduced other such notations as entropy, information, and stable state into the study of organisms.[606] Also he drew parallels between the nervous systems of organisms and computers.

A few years after that a detailed model was developed by Ashby in both verbal and mathematical forms. It was designed to apply to systems, both living and nonliving, with certain characteristics which he specified. He applied it to the behavior of organisms. The two basic principles upon which the model depends are control by feedback and stability. The latter is a sort of steady state which Ashby defined as follows: "Given an absolute system and a region within its field, *a line of behavior from a point within the region is stable if it never leaves the region.*"[607] If such a system is displaced and released, it will return to its original state. Systems with this property can be said to be "goal-seeking" and to have adaptive behavior or adjustment processes.

A further principle, that of "ultrastability," applies when variables in such a system are subject to "step functions," that is, to abrupt changes in values. Ultrastable systems are able to reorganize themselves to adjust to the net values of variables and parameters arrived at by the step-function change. "Multistability" characterizes systems which are made up of many ultrastable systems, that is, of subsystems or compo-

nents. Within each of these, alterations in values of step functions depend only upon changes in the subsystem or component's own main variables. They do not immediately affect other subsystems or components. Such systems can acquire new adjustments while retaining those which are already made, so long as no interaction betweeen them occurs.

In applying this system of concepts to an organism's behavior, the organism and its environment are regarded as two parts of a single system.[608] Each affects the other. In order to survive, the animal must use adjustment processes that keep its essential variables within physiological limits. Such adjustments include learning. The animal is able to do this because it is an ultrastable system. An organism's nervous system is viewed as a multistable system which interacts with a complicated, multivariate environment. Such a nervous system acts selectively and improves the organism's adjustment to its environment. According to Ashby, certain evidence suggests that his model is compatible with others' experimental findings and hypotheses on learning and memory storage.[609] It can be used to explain evolutionary changes in a species. A cybernetic electromechanical device, the *homeostat*, was built by Ashby to illustrate an ultrastable system.[610]

A matter-energy processing model. So far in this section all the models have dealt with information processing. Now I shall discuss a simulation of an organismwide matter-energy adjustment process, dealing with fluid balance and distribution of ions throughout the human body.[611] The conceptual system is necessarily less complex than the concrete system it models, but the model includes many important chemical and electrochemical relationships. The chemical reactions are expressed in differential equations, and the computer is programmed to solve them. The computer makes it possible to experiment with the model and to test hypotheses, specifically some concerning the response of the body to chemical stresses.

For the purposes of this simulation, the body is divided conceptually into five "compartments" which are distinct in chemical content but which communicate across membranes or abstracted boundaries. These compartments are: (*i*) the gaseous components of venous plasma; (*ii*) the interiors, but not the membranes, of all the red cells taken together; (*iii*) the plasma; (*iv*) the interstitial fluid; and (*v*) the intracellular fluid of the entire body cell mass taken together, not including the red cells. The chemical contents and amounts of fluid in the other tissues outside these five "compartments" are taken to be constant, and the effects of kidney function are neglected in the model.

The model concerns a resting young man of 70 kg,

capable of maintaining a steady state of the relevant variables. A variety of biochemical stress conditions, studied in laboratory experiments on dogs with kidneys removed, have been imposed upon the model. The chemical similarity between dogs and human beings makes this feasible, although fine details of differences between the species limit the applicability of such studies. Input excess stresses of sodium chloride, hypertonic sodium chloride, and sodium bicarbonate have been investigated. Computations using the simulation were found to give qualitatively correct responses. They were also reasonable quantitatively. These computations yielded data with many details. Available laboratory findings were not sufficiently extensive to indicate whether or not all the data corresponded to what actually occurs when such organisms are subjected to such stresses. Consequently they suggested further experiments.

Information processing subsystem models.

Input transducer.   An analysis by Stark of the reflex response of the pupil of the eye to light, which describes its control by negative feedback, has yielded a number of different mathematical models of this accessory function of the visual input transducer.[612] His models are based upon experimental studies of human and animal subjects.[613] The components involved in this pupillary response are structures of the eye, including the retina; the neural channels; and the nuclei in which synapses are made. The pathway for constriction of the pupil includes certain fibers of the optic nerve which go directly to synapses in the pretectal nucleus of the brainstem (see page 131), with neurons which send fibers to the Edinger-Westphal nucleus in the midbrain tegmentum from which parasympathetic fibers pass to the ciliary ganglion. Fibers from there pass to the iris. Dilation of the pupil is achieved by a pathway beginning with the optic nerve, synapsing in the midbrain, and following the tectotegmentospinal tract to the thoracic spinal cord. Here it synapses with preganglionic sympathetic neurons which send their processes upward to the superior cervical ganglion. From this ganglion, postganglionic fibers innervate the pupil.

Under normal conditions, the pupil dilates and contracts in response to fluctuations in intensity of light reaching the retina. This is a stable negative feedback system. Its behavior under altered conditions produced by treatment with drugs or by use of an experimental technique which provides that small movements of the iris result in large changes in light intensity at the retina was consistent with predictions based upon servomechanism theory. The drugs used produce a changed pupil, excessive lag making it an unstable system. Both alterations of the system caused positive feedback which resulted in oscillations. A model describing the system as a linear transfer function resulted in a good approximation to the actual input–output relationships of the living system. Oscillation rates of the unstable system were predicted. The use of this linear model required a simplification in the conceptual system, since the actual input–output relations of the eye are not linear. A later, mathematically much more complex model describes the nonlinear behavior of the system.[614]

Decoder.   Models of decoding processes are classified as *pattern recognition* models. Pattern recognition has been defined as "the extraction of the significant features from a background of irrelevant detail."[615] This process is important to intelligent information processing by both organisms and machines. Without classification of inputs each separate occurrence of a pattern such as a printed symbol or a spoken word would have to be handled as a special case.

Pattern recognition is modeled in mathematical networks, special machines, and programs for digital computers. Since the neural processes underlying decoding by organisms are only beginning to be understood, models of this process have not yet been developed upon the basis of detailed anatomical and physiological studies, as were the input transducer models just described. The chief sources of specification of a model of pattern recognition, according to Uhr, are intuition and introspection.[616] Many of the models are not intended to have any reference to organism processes but are strictly artificial intelligence studies, some of them directed toward development of practical machines for such jobs as translating from one language to another or automating library work. Nevertheless, they can shed light on the decoding process in living systems.

Inhibitory interactions within the network of neurons in the eye of *Limulus*, which enable this crab to decode contours and shapes (see page 401) are described in one model by a set of equations.[617] An analog simulator of such a network, designed to process information for a visual pattern-recognition machine as well as to study functions of an eye of this kind, has been built and used experimentally.[618] With it the *Limulus* eye itself, and variations upon it, were studied experimentally. This was done by varying the value of the function that describes the inhibitory effect of one ommatidium upon another and changing parameters like the size of the receptive field of an ommatidium, its threshold, and the arrangement of the ommatidia.

Black and white disks and wedges were used as inputs to the simulator. For all values of the inhibitory function and of the parameters, with any input, activity is greatest in those parts of the net where a spatial change in the illumination impinges upon the receptors. Different experimental conditions produced variations in the activity. Given a particular illumination pattern and the function describing the inhibition in a certain situation, the model can make predictions of the shape of the activity curves. An algorithm for pattern recognition by computer has been derived from this network.

Machines can recognize patterns in several ways.[619] The first, template matching, requires storage in the machine of all patterns or templates that will be used, *e.g.*, all letters, numbers, or geometric shapes, pictures, or fingerprints. Storage is ordinarily coded in binary digits. These indicate whether or not a part of the pattern is found in each cell of a matrix of lines and columns into which the area containing the pattern can be subdivided. These cells may be made as large or as small as the person using the procedure may wish. This analysis of the pattern into cells is much like what the rods and cones do in the retina, or indeed the individual sensory units in any sense organ. Input patterns are then compared with the stored templates, and the decision is made to identify each pattern with that template which it most closely matches. This method can fail even when the template and the input pattern are identical, if there is any change in position, orientation, or size. Some improvement occurs if another operation is introduced before the matching takes place, one that shifts, rotates, or changes the size of the pattern in order to put it into a standard form. This also is not satisfactory, however, because variations in the input pattern which would be insignificant to a human observer may make a pattern fit the wrong template more closely than the right one. A letter "R" might fit the "A" template more closely than other samples of "A."

A quite different approach is to start with a random net which "learns" by practice to generate the features by which it recognizes each pattern and also to develop processing and decision procedures. A large number of on–off computer elements are connected randomly so that each receives inputs from several others. Thresholds are adjustable by the experimenter on the basis of performance so that the machine learns to recognize a pattern by reinforcement. If a set of features characterizing each pattern to be used is programmed into the machine, the net of course becomes less random, but performance can be improved. A description of the letter "A," for example, might contain as features "two upright strokes widely separated at the bottom and close together at the top" and "a more or less horizontal crossbar." Such machines have not as yet succeeded in generating sophisticated features or recognizing very complicated patterns, but activity toward improving them continues.

Perceptrons are a class of random net machines for which detailed mathematical models exist.[620] Theorems concerning their operation can be stated, and proved or disproved. A simple perceptron network has at least three layers, one of sensory units, which transduce the input signals; one of association units, which are decision points where transmissions through the network are regulated; and one of response units, which emit signals. Variables describe characteristics of connections in the network. Perceptrons may be made more complex by adding further layers of units. Such networks have been studied in both pattern-recognition and discrimination experiments. In visual pattern recognition the sensory units form a "retina" on which input may be placed in different positions and in different parts of the retina. For pattern-recognition experiments inputs can be presented in all possible positions. In generalization experiments, the machine is trained on one set of patterns and then tested on another set which sends signals to few or no common sensory elements. Perceptrons are intended to simulate neural processes. The similarity of organization of the units of a visual pattern-recognition perceptron to the cells of the retina is evident.

A simple perceptron is a random network. Performance can be bettered by addition of constraints of various sorts. A system of connections which improves generalization over similar patterned inputs is one such constraint which can give an appreciable gain in performance.[621] Another possible constraint is a set of property-detection configurations such as edge detectors, corner detectors, and line detectors which can be combined to discriminate complex patterns. Too many constraints of this sort make the perceptron less efficient. Comparison of perceptron models with the visual input transducer of a cat shows that the best model of the cat's visual processes is a compromise between a four-layer simple perceptron and one with several property-detection configurations. Cat's eyes have some detectors (about five-sixths of the cells) which respond to lines or edges in a fixed position or orientation and some (one-sixth of the cells) which respond to whole families of lines or edges in any parallel position over a large field (see pages 398 and 399).[622] A "cat" perceptron has been programmed for a digital computer.[623] This has been compared for efficiency with the simple perceptron. The five-layer "cat" model achieves near perfection in discrimination of horizontal from vertical lines one retinal unit in thickness after 60 practice trials, while the simple perceptron has not learned after 500.

After a comparison of six perceptron models with different constraints, including both the simple, random model and the "cat" model, it seemed clear that with increasing resolution of the retina (*i.e.,* with greater numbers of sensory units), the random-connection models must be replaced by models with constrained units designed to detect particular characteristics.[624] Constrained systems operate better than random systems in a complex environment where the amount of information needed for discrimination becomes larger. Constrained systems also learn faster. In order to minimize use of the network, generalization should take place at the most elementary level possible, on parts of figures rather than the whole. It is also possible to use constraints in the first layers and random connections in the deeper layers without loss in efficiency. The "cat" model operates better only in a highly organized environment in which all information inputs consist of straight-line patterns, and classifications are limited to those in which very similar patterns are always classified as being identical.

Pandemonium is a network that makes use of parallel information processing.[625] In such processing, features of all possible patterns or templates are simultaneously applied to an input pattern. Different combinations of features identify each specific template pattern. Its units, whimsically named "demons," are quasi-independent modules, arranged in levels. Like perceptrons, pandemonium models can be simple or complex, according to the number of levels in them. Such network programs are interesting both as attempts to simulate neural processes and as examples of machine intelligence. At the task of decoding inputs in the manner of organisms, their success is not particularly impressive. Of course many people find it remarkable that a machine can learn to recognize patterns at all.

Another approach to pattern recognition by machine is the program for digital computer developed by Uhr and Vossler.[626] This program has proved capable of learning to recognize all letters of the alphabet when hand-printed by different people; line drawings of cartoon faces and simple objects like shoes and pliers, copied from different sources; segmented lower-case handwriting (Arabic letters) by different people; and spoken numbers. The poorest performance was 60 percent success on known and 55 percent success on unknown handwritten Arabic letters. It achieved 95 percent success on known and 70 percent on unknown pictures; and it achieved 100 percent success on both known and unknown spoken numbers. When compared to human performance on "meaningless" patterns, it outperformed the human subjects.

This is a considerable expansion of machine intelligence beyond earlier models. It is achieved by a complicated series of operations.[627] Input is presented to the computer as a 20×20 matrix of zeros and ones. The program composes its own operators, which are small matrices of zeros and ones. The program is written to move these operators across and down a part of the pattern, recording the places where they match the pattern. The operators are generated by one of several random methods. By this means the pattern is transformed into a list of characteristics which can then be compared with lists of previously processed patterns stored in the computer's memory. The name of the previously processed pattern to which it most closely corresponds is given to the unknown pattern. The program checks the operators to find out how useful they have been and then turns amplifiers for the successful ones up and those for the unsuccessful ones down. Eventually those which do not contribute to success are discarded, and new ones are generated to take their place. The program is able to start with no operators at all and generate a set, or the programmer may specify operators.

This program can be regarded as an analog of a neural net, and its originators believe that the assumptions required are plausible and "natural-looking." A retina, with excitatory and inhibitory connections, is suggested. The various specialized retinal cells which detect particular aspects of the input such as edges are considered the equivalent of operators, repeated over the area of the retina. There appear to be many fewer of these in the retina than the program requires, but it may be possible to adjust the program in this respect to bring it closer to the situation in the retina. The program functions comparably to organisms in other ways as well.[628]

Despite the difficulties of adequately simulating speech perception, some advances have been made. One program for a digital computer has been written which can recognize a sequence of spoken words.[629] There are several major constraints, however. Speakers must limit themselves to a specific set of 50 to 100 words—words that do not sound very similar. They must in advance have recorded their own particular pronunciation of each of the words. And they must halt for a brief instant of silence between each word spoken and the next. The lowest error rate under such procedures has been somewhat less than 4 percent. The fundamental strategy of this program is like that of the visual pattern-recognition programs described above—comparing the patterned array of each input word with the stored templates of the entire vocabulary of words.

A number of computer programs designed to

understand natural languages are in process of development. A really good translating machine, for instance, would fill a demand. Publishers wishing to make books available internationally, for example, or government officials interested in the newspapers and magazines of other countries would find it useful. So far, no such machine has been perfected. Another group of programs is being prepared with the goal of answering English questions by computer.[630] Many thorny problems must be solved before a machine which understands what is said to it and answers appropriately is a reality. The practical usefulness of such a machine for routine dissemination of information, for example over a telephone system, is apparent. In spite of the recent expansion of the sciences of language, it is still not possible to analyze speech as fully as would be desirable. The problems of meaning, of syntactic and semantic ambiguity, and of inference are among those which require better solutions.[631]

Channel and net.   Network models of nervous systems, such as those discussed in describing simulations of other organismic subsystems (see pages 488 to 490 and below), necessarily include the channel and net subsystem, which connects components of the other subsystems. In such models, as in nervous systems, the most interesting activities take place at neural centers and decision points. These are generally components of other subsystems. Other aspects of the net, such as differences in conduction in various diameters of fibers, are removed by the simplifications required for making the model manageable. Even the most ambitious present statistical models do not approach the complexity of the least elaborate living neural net.

Associator.   Most of the models applicable to this subsystem deal, not with associating alone, but with the whole learning process, including association of items of information, storage, and retrieval of these associated items. Some of the models discussed under other subsystems include learning as a part of the total process. Although experimental data on learning are not scarce—this being the most thoroughly studied of the psychological processes in many animal species— the design of critical experiments to resolve theoretical disagreements in the field has proved difficult. Controversies have swirled around many such efforts. Learning models reflect the theoretical bias of the modeler as well as the actions of the concrete system modeled.

In network mathematics, associative learning is explained by either reverberating circuits of neurons or changes in the thresholds of neurons as a result of use. One example of the first class is Rashevsky's description of a network in which conditioned responses can be developed, which was first published in 1938 and later expanded to cover other sorts of learning as well.[632] Another is McCulloch's and Pitts's net with circuits.[633] One of many examples of the second class of models is the formation of conditioned responses in the "ganglion brain" modeled by Shimbel in probabilistic mathematics.[634] The ganglion is assumed to have completely random connections among all afferent neurons and other internal neurons, as well as among internal neurons and efferent neurons which leave the ganglion and innervate muscles. The only exceptions are those cells which are channels that transmit the signals for unconditioned responses. Shimbel assumes that the threshold of any neuron in the ganglion will be lowered if a suprathreshold pulse and a subthreshold pulse are delivered to it at about the same time. He demonstrates that learning can occur in such a ganglion. The model includes measures of the learning potential of the ganglion— how many responses can be learned and how much the learned responses are likely to interfere with one another.

Some network machines or computer programs discussed above (see pages 485 to 490) also exhibit learning.

An important group of learning models includes the various forms of mathematical learning theory. The conceptual system of Hull, which influenced generations of behavior theorists (see page 410), was stated in deterministic mathematics. This was the first major attempt at a mathematical statement of any learning theory. His model assumed a process of growth and decay of habit strength under the opposing influences of reinforcement and inhibition brought about by performance of the response. Each reinforcement was considered to produce a definite, predictable increment in habit strength which summed to an exponential growth curve over a series of trials. Each evocation of the response produced a predictable increment in inhibition that decayed as an exponential function of the time following the response.[635] This model becomes hard to manage when applied to complex behavior although it fits instrumental or operant conditioning quite well (see page 408).

Difficulties encountered in use of the deterministic model were avoided by development of probabilistic mathematical or statistical models which reflect the increased likelihood of appearance of a response with no assumptions about the underlying events within the organism.[636]

Estes' *statistical model* was among the earliest of these formulations.[637] In it, the occurrence of members of a class of responses R, each of which is considered an unrepeatable behavioral event, is a function of the presence of a sample from a population S of "small independent environmental events," the information inputs, which create a set of stimulus events in the organism's input transducer subsystem. The sample of these events varies from trial to trial, *i.e.*, there is variation of inputs. Thus, $R = f(S)$. The probability of response is defined as the average frequency of an R class, relative to the maximum possible frequency under the specified experimental conditions, held constant over time. This expresses the likelihood that a response will occur at a given time. As the probability of one R class increases, probabilities of occurrence of members of other R classes decline. All elements of the effective stimulus become conditioned to the member of R present at a given moment. Reinforcement is defined as an experimental condition which ensures that the occurrences of a sample of R will follow a sample from some specified S. The experimentally observed courses of simple conditioning and instrumental conditioning and their extinction can be represented by equations expressing relationships between these terms. In its further development, this statistical model proved capable of distinguishing a number of phenomena which occur in learning experiments as effects of input variations from those which are not affected by such variations.[638]

In a *stochastic model* such as that of Bush and Mosteller, the change in probabilities of occurrence of a response from trial to trial of a learning experiment is represented by use of an operator which indicates a linear transformation on the probability, either positive or negative, of the occurrence.[639] They assume that the amount of change with each correct trial is a constant proportion of the maximum possible increment, and that, conversely, the amount of change with each incorrect trial is a constant proportion of the maximum possible decrement. Parameters a and b represent factors which increase or decrease the probability. If a reward is given, a has a positive value; if not, it is 0. Either punishment or the costs in expenditure of work required to carry out the response, are associated with positive values of b. In extinction trials a is equal to 0. The time required for responses is expressed by an equation which suggests that the average lag time depends on the amount of reward and the amount of work, each response adding an increment to the time. Rate of responding, an important measure particularly in operant conditioning experiments, is derived from this. "Activity level" is defined as the maximum rate of responding when it is certain that the response will be made.

This model can be used to represent responses of organisms to different reinforcement schedules, such as fixed ratio (reward given not on every response but on every nth response, such as 2nd, 3rd, 6th, etc.); random ratio; periodic; or irregular. For each of these, the rates of responding and number of cumulative responses to achieve a previously established criterion of learning differ. Extinction likewise differs according to the reward schedule used in learning. If continual reinforcement has been used, for example, extinction is accomplished more readily.

Mathematical models for learning may represent either the general case, to which the responses of any individual organism may be a poor fit, or the particular responses of an individual animal. Some years ago a new species of conceptual animals was born, the "stat rats" (statistical rats). They are idealized rats, conceived to learn in the same way that real rats do. Some models permit the behavior of these artificial creatures to be compared with that of "real" laboratory rats. One such stochastic learning model, Flood's *symmetry model*, was used to predict the behavior of specific laboratory rats in an experiment which allowed the rats a choice of three bar-pressing responses, each reinforced on a different schedule.[640] The reinforcement was provided by input pulses administered through electrodes chronically implanted in the hypothalamic "pleasure center" (see pages 431 and 432). In such an experiment, the probability of each of the three responses occurring on a given trial is different. Instead of the two parameters of the Bush and Mosteller model of operant conditioning, this three-response model has six parameters. The considerable problem of estimating likelihood ratios for a model with this number of factors was met by special statistical techniques, using search methods carried out by computer.[641] Parameters for individual rats in the experimental situation can be determined.

The living and conceptual systems supplement each other. In conceptual runs of stat rats, parameters can be set and effects of changes in their values observed. Changes in the experimental situation can also be modeled in this way. With parameter values set from data on real rats, stat rats can be used to test alternative research designs to find the most effective approach to testing a given hypothesis. Since these experiments require thousands of runs, this use of simulation saves both time and money.

This model of Flood's has also been tested in an experiment in which dogs learned to jump a barrier to avoid an intense electric shock, in an avoidance learning experiment with rats, and in a binary choice experiment with human subjects. Its goodness of fit to the data compared acceptably with the Bush and Mosteller and the Luce models. In such comparisons, the predictions of each model are checked against various measures of the actual performance of animals. For instance, in a learning experiment in which animals acted to avoid shock, the measures considered might include the mean and standard deviations of number of trials before the first avoidance, the total number of shocks given, the number of trials before the last shock, and the number of trials before the first run of four consecutive avoidances.

Computer learning models. Stat rats which learn to run a simulated T maze have been programmed by Marzocco and Bartram for digital computer.[642] The model they used is Estes' statistical learning theory, discussed above. Information transduced from the environment or from the rat's internal processes and internal and external outputs available to the organism are represented in the computer by patterns of 0's and 1's which can be varied to represent different patterns of signals from the environment and from within the organism. In one situation it happened that 1,152 such elements which a rat could sense when in the stem of the T maze and at the choice-point were represented. All were equally likely to be sampled. Each of these elements is so programmed that it is associated at one time to one and only one output. This is achieved by means of a matrix in which columns correspond to input elements and rows to outputs. When the input represented by the column is connected to the output for the row, a 1 is entered in the appropriate cell. The output produced by an input pattern is that one which is connected to the greatest number of input elements. The system learns by changing association matrix connections. All elements present and sensed by the organism become connected with an output if it is reinforced. The stat rats were assumed to have no relevant prior experience. They were permitted three responses. If they entered the right arm of the T maze, they received reinforcement. If they entered the left arm or did any of the other things a rat might conceivably do, they were not reinforced. They performed until a criterion of nine successive error-free trials was met. Compared with data from maze-learning experiments, the proportion of entries into each of the maze arms fell close to the mean.

An interesting aspect of this simulation is inclusion into the statistics of outputs which are usually considered irrelevant in experimental studies. Also the simulation makes it possible to obtain data about a process which cannot be observed in a real situation but which is of theoretical interest—the change in the association matrix as the stat rats learned. The proportion of elements connected at the beginning and end of every run to each of the three possible outputs was

calculated. The authors suggest that when all the responses available to an organism are considered, the absolute probability of any one is quite small and that this might help to explain both the variability and the plasticity of behavior.

A computer simulation, the Elementary Perceiver and Memorizer (EPAM), has been proposed as an interpretation of verbal learning in human organisms, an alternative to other verbal learning theories. This model describes information processing activities with no reference to underlying neurology. Other information processing subsystems besides the associator are involved in it. Indeed the model includes several subroutines, and these carry out processes which are closely comparable to several of the information processing subsystem activities of my conceptual approach. What goes on when a nonsense syllable is presented to the organism is described as follows:

A *perceptual system* receives the raw external information and codes it into *internal symbols.* These internal symbols contain descriptive information about features of external stimuli. For unfamiliar 3-letter nonsense symbols, it is assumed that the coding is done in terms of (the configurations of) the individual letters (as they might be dealt with in a pattern-recognition program like the Perceptron or Pandemonium), for these letters are familiar and are well-learned units for the adult subject. The end result of the perception process is an internal representation of the nonsense syllable—a list of internal symbols (*i.e.,* a list of lists of bits) containing descriptive information about the letters of the nonsense syllable. . . .

Given a sequence of such inputs, the essence of the learner's problem is twofold: first, to discriminate each code from the others already learned, so that differential response can be made; second, to *associate* information about a "response" syllable with the information about a "stimulus" syllable so that the response can be retrieved if the stimulus is presented.[643]

EPAM is programmed to simulate the transmission of inputs through a branching network. As each such unit of information flows through this discrimination net—sometimes called a "decision tree" (see page 497)—it is tested by a stored program, at some branching or decision point, which determines whether it will flow into one branch or the other at that point. This process is repeated at other decision points until finally an "image" or symbolic representation of the input, in an internal code or private language, is stored at the end of one channel of the network. When an input image is associated with an image of the appropriate output or response, a cue to the latter is stored with the input image. EPAM also grows or develops its own net as more and more inputs enter it. Many of the most interesting aspects of this program are relevant to an organism's storage and retrieval of information rather than its learning, and these aspects of it will be discussed in the section on memory below.

Cybernetic learning models.   One cybernetic behavior theory, developed by Deutsch, postulates a process by which learning might occur in organisms which involves five units:[644] (*i*) an analyzer (a sensory or input transducer subsystem); (*ii*) a link (or channel); (*iii*) a motor; (*iv*) an environment; and (*v*) an internal medium. Thus the model involves four parts of systems, three somewhat like my input transducer, channel and net, and motor subsystems, and one nonspecific "internal medium." These four parts have three kinds of relationships among each other and with the environment: (*i*) activating; (*ii*) switching off; and (*iii*) causing to vary.

An activity begins when a particular link or channel is activated by some strain in the "internal medium." (Another kind of link can be activated by neighboring links only.) This activation causes the motor to act. This action brings about changes in the environment which may eventually activate one of the system's analyzers or input transducer components—a feedback process. This feedback switches off the link.

A behavior sequence takes place whenever links in a connected set activate each other in turn. When a link is active, it partially inhibits outputs from the other links. When the first in the chain is activated by an internal strain in the organism, it remains active even though each of the others in turn terminates its activity. This permits the system to pursue one purpose after another in a predetermined sequence. When it achieves its final purpose, which is the termination of activity in the first link, it ceases to be active.

In the system so far described associative learning is not possible, since the relationships among elements are fixed. If the system is changed to include a number of free links to which no analyzers are attached, however, and if these are available for the attachment of analyzers, learning does become possible—associator and memory subsystems are included in the model. Then learning involves a network in which, when a row of links is switched on by its first member link, unattached analyzers emit signals. The analyzers which make outputs nearest in time to an analyzer already attached to a row of links will be fastened to the free links closest to it. Consequently, analyzers which put out signals simultaneously, or nearly so, become attached near to each other on the row of links. The next time the row is switched on, this link will be the first to vary its output. This process continues until an unattached analyzer develops a permanent connection. This constitutes learning.

Deutsch suggests how his model conforms to the findings of a number of experiments on animal and human behavior. He indicates that it is capable of producing quantitative predictions about behavior, applying not only to learned and unlearned acts and sequences of acts which reduce strains but also to conflict and choice situations.

Memory.   A few models have been especially designed to simulate memory in organisms. A set of probabilistic mathematical models of storage and retrieval of verbal material, for example, is intended to simulate verbal associative learning in a way that will fit experimental data.[645] This group of related models assumes that inputs are channeled to a "memory buffer," or short-term store, and then either to a "lost or forgotten" category or to a long-term store.[646] Information represented in the long-term store remains also in the short-term store, since it is transferred by a process of copying, and it is possible for an item to be in both "lost or forgotten" and long-term categories. The buffer is of limited capacity and is of "pushdown" type, *i.e.,* items of information in it are displaced by items which enter it at a later time, moving successively through a number of slots and finally being eliminated. Once the buffer is filled it always remains full. Items in this store are perfectly represented and perfectly recalled.

Various forms of this model differ in specific features. For example, in one version there may be one or more representations of a given item in long-term store. In another version, partial copies are possible. Retrieval in the various versions is achieved by search processes of differing designs. The drop in recall probability which occurs as the length of the memorized list increases is brought about either by disruption as a result of the search itself or by stopping before an item is found.

While no specific modeling of interference among items in the store is included, the interference theory of forgetting is represented by the push-down loss from the buffer, by destructive search, and by imperfect retrieval. The view that memories decay over time, an hypothesis for which some evidence exists, is not represented in the model, but such decay could be introduced into the buffer by appropriate mathematical changes.

This group of models has been found to produce curves which closely fit data from a number of experiments.[647]

EPAM, the computer program whose learning processes were described above in the section on computer learning models (see page 493), also simulates a number of aspects of organism information storage and retrieval which do not appear in other models. It is capable of receiving inputs encoded to simulate inputs from different sensory modalities, including aural phonemes and visually presented letters and objects. It responds in the appropriate output mode to each sort of input.[648]

In learning to discriminate nonsense syllables, EPAM stores both input images and output images. Input images need be only sufficiently complete for recognition (which in some cases requires only the first of three letters of a nonsense syllable). Output images, on the other hand, must be stored completely if the program is to produce the output correctly. When a previously unknown syllable is presented, it is matched with stored images, the difference found, and a test for the difference created. This test is then stored at a decision point in the net. Since in the nonsense syllable inputs processed by EPAM each syllable has three letters, a noticing order for letter scanning is included in the program. This, too, is adaptive. Originally it considers the first letter, the end letter, and the middle letter in that order, as most subjects have been observed to do in experimental situations. But letter positions rich in differences come to be scanned first.

Internal associations between inputs and outputs are built by storing cues sufficient to enable an input to retrieve its appropriate output. As a learning sequence continues, a cue which has been sufficient for retrieval may no longer be so because it is interfered with by other associations. The response is "mislaid" in the growing network. If the fact that the response is inaccessible can be detected by feedback, the situation may be corrected by adding further information to the cue. Otherwise the information may be permanently lost. Selecting and encoding a response are conceptualized as separate processes.

EPAM has been programmed for a digital computer. One thing it can do is act as subject for another computer program, "Experimenter," which includes a simulated memory-drum apparatus commonly used in learning experiments; timing procedures; stimulus materials of various kinds; error checking and recording procedures; and so on.[649] Experiments have been carried out with EPAM and Experimenter together which simulate: serial learning of nonsense syllables; learning to associate one nonsense syllable of a pair to another; serial learning of nonsense syllables of two lists with a retest of the first list following the learning of the second list; learning of two lists of associated nonsense-syllable pairs; learning of a list of associated nonsense-syllable pairs with the inputs in one sensory modality and the outputs in another; and learning to associate a visual object with its spoken name and that spoken name with its written name, followed by a test of whether, without further learning, such a visual object can be identified from its written name.

Results of these experiments showed that EPAM can carry out a number of organism-like behaviors. (*i*) It makes both *input* and *output generalization* errors. An input generalization error occurs when an output is elicited by an input similar to but not identical with the one which was originally associated to it. An output generalization error occurs when an output similar to but not identical with the one originally associated is elicited by an input. Such errors occur most frequently in early trials when either EPAM or a human subject is learning a second list which contains some similar items to those already stored from a first list, before information to discriminate the similar items is stored. (*ii*) Like human subjects, EPAM produces an irregular pattern of success and failure on items during the learning process. This is known as *oscillation*. A success is commonly followed by a failure; then come more successes; then perhaps a number of failures; and so forth. Interference of later learned items with earlier learned items and associations as the net grows produces this effect. (*iii*) Lists of highly similar items are much harder for both human subjects and EPAM than those which are markedly different. (*iv*) The program simulates *retroactive inhibition*, partial or complete blocking of recall of a list learned first after a second list has been learned. This is a short-lived loss in human beings, for they relearn the first list with little practice. In the EPAM program such forgetting may be temporary if feedback is given that an incorrect response was made, accompanied by presentation of the correct response so that more cue information may be stored. Retroactive inhibition is related to oscillation in this model since both are produced by interference of items, the first by those from within a list, the second by items from another list.

EPAM is unlike its human counterparts in being unable to learn a serial list of items in which the same item appears twice. Human subjects find this task difficult, but they can carry it out. EPAM cannot distinguish between different occurrences of an item. It therefore oscillates between the associations relevant to one occurrence and those relevant to the other.

EPAM does not have a separate forgetting process. Its forgetting is a consequence of its association memory structure and its basic discrimination processes. *Proactive inhibition*, the type of forgetting in which items learned earlier interfere with those learned later, does not occur in EPAM although it does in organisms. Possibly this is an aspect of the organism's long-term memory processes, and these are not modeled by EPAM.

Decider. An abundance of models and simulations have been made of several different classes of organism decisions. None of the programs that instruct computers to write poetry or to compose music is described here, although to the extent that their outputs are accepted as poetry or music, they are models of these creative human decision-making activities. The models considered here deal with decisions about matter-energy processing: economic and other decisions using game theory or statistical decision theory; and logical problem solving and strategic thinking (the latter usually game playing).

Major aspects of the decision making concerning mammalian matter-energy processing are carried out by components of two echelons of the organism's decider, the anterior pituitary and thyroid glands (see pages 391 and 392, 423 and 424). They control the organism's oxygen and nitrogen metabolism. Thyrotropin (thyrotropic hormone) secreted by the pituitary signals the thyroid to secrete thyroxin. This, in turn, is a signal which inhibits secretion of thyrotropin by the pituitary. A mathematical model of these relationships has been developed.[650] It consists of two first-order, nonlinear differential equations. The major terms in them are the concentrations of thyroxin and thyrotropin at any given time, the rate of production of thyrotropin if thyroid production is not inhibited, and various constants. The equations state that the rate of change of either hormone concentration is equal to the difference in the rate of production and the rate of loss of the hormone. The model indicates how the two hormones and the metabolic processes they control can either remain in steady states or escape from such equilibria and fluctuate randomly. When the hormonal feedbacks malfunction, medication with thyroxine can return the organism to a steady state which is different from that in normal organisms, since the concentration of thyrotropin in the blood and other tissues is zero and that of thyroxine is higher than normal. The authors believe this model may explain the signs and symptoms as well as provide a rationale for treatment of an illness known as *periodic relapsing catatonia*. This disease is characterized by fairly regular fluctuations in the patient's behavior, in and out of catatonic states, which are associated with simultaneous fluctuations of the basic metabolic rate and rate of nitrogen metabolism.

A part of economic theory is a set of axioms and differential equations which represent the behavior of a person who must choose from among available goods and services those which most satisfactorily reduce strains or needs, that is, those of the greatest personal value (see page 39) or utility (see page 430). The theory assumes that the person has perfect information concerning the available alternatives and the utility of each. Certain other assumptions are made about the nature of preferences and of utility.[651] The

person is shown to maximize utility, acquiring units of a commodity until a point of marginal utility is reached at which addition of another unit will not increase his satisfaction. This "rational behavior" appears psychologically plausible under the restrictions imposed. The algebraic model is capable of representing how utilities can be maximized when a large number of variables is involved. When two or more participants are involved, however, each with a personal set of variables, the model becomes mathematically difficult, and no entirely satisfactory solution has been found. Since choices among alternatives as they occur in the experience of a person living in a complex social environment are not adequately represented by such theory, searches have been made for more satisfactory models. Among the results are the theory of games and statistical decision theory (see page 432).

As von Neumann and Morgenstern analyzed the economic process, each person must interact with others, all of whom are separately attempting to maximize utilities in the same way she or he is. The behavior of one person cannot, however, be taken as the model for all, since that approach ignores the interactions among variables which in fact occur. A person in a societal economy must exchange goods and services with others, and in many cases opposed interests are involved. A game-theoretical model elucidates these opposed interests. The intention of the inventors of game theory was "to find the mathematically complete principles which define 'rational behavior' for the participants in a social economy, and to derive from them the general characteristics of that behavior."[652] A satisfactory solution consists of a set of rules for each participant that tell him how to behave in any situation which could conceivably arise, including that in which others behave irrationally.

For some games such solutions have been discovered. An example is a game with two opposed interests in which gain for one is balanced by loss for the other, that is, a two-person zero-sum game. Because participants tend to form coalitions, games with larger numbers of participants may collapse into two-person games. For games with a greater number of opposed interests, such as 3, and for games with non-zero-sum payoffs, calculations become extremely difficult, and complete specifications for each player are not available. In the next chapter I discuss some experiments on cooperation and competition using game-theory models (see pages 579 and 580). Experiments in which the Prisoner's Dilemma was made into a set of games have been represented by a number of mathematical models developed by Rapoport and Chammah.[653]

There is an apparent lawfulness of behavior of

organisms in the many different sorts of decision situations with which they are faced. This has led Luce to make a theoretical analysis and develop a set of probabilistic models based upon a *choice axiom* which enables one to determine the probability that a particular one out of a number of related alternative actions will be selected in a given situation.[654] Essentially, the operations in this model describe a process of decision between the first two of three possible choices, followed by decision between the one chosen and the third alternative. In this way the number of alternatives is reduced to one. The axiom is not considered applicable to complex decision situations which must be carried out in stages. This axiom has been applied in the fields of psychophysics, utility theory, and learning (Luce's beta model). It gave results which conformed to traditional ideas in these fields and, in some cases, led to results of empirical interest. Its originator believes that it gives promise of being a general law of choice behavior.

The most interesting computer programs that apply to deciding are heuristic programs which simulate behavior such as the solving of problems or the playing of games like chess and checkers for which the optimal strategy cannot be specified. A fundamental characteristic of human deciding modeled by such programs is that the solutions, strategies, or reasoning processes are carried out in steps, each depending upon the results of the one before.

This multistage information processing is represented by list-processing programs which have "decision trees," described above in my discussion of certain pattern-recognition, learning, and memory programs (see pages 488 to 495). The computer is instructed to perform an operation and, depending upon its outcome, to carry out one or another operation subsequently, and so on until the solution is found or the game is completed. The memory of the program initially contains information which represents the structure of the conceptual system, and as computing continues, information developed by the program itself is stored. A search process selects items from the stored lists according to specified rules or criteria, and performs operations upon them, storing the results in new lists from which later searches may build still further lists.

The Logic Theory Machine (LT) of Newell, Shaw, and Simon was among the first programs of this sort to be developed. It solves problems in elementary symbolic logic.[655] Algorithms can be generated which will produce these proofs, and in fact a computer program has been developed which rather successfully proves all the theorems in Whitehead and Russell's *Principia Mathematica*, using algorithms.[656] Algorithmic methods are certain to find a solution if one exists, since they explore all possibilities. They can in some cases, however, take so long as to be impractical. On the other hand heuristic programs, which may solve problems but are not guaranteed to do so, go about their proofs in a more human way and provide better simulations of human cognitive processes.

LT is initially provided with the necessary symbols and is programmed with the five basic axioms, the definitions, and the rules of inference used in *Principia Mathematica*.[657] From these the theorems are derived. The program also contains the *methods* by which proofs of the theorems are to be discovered. These all depend upon search and matching procedures. They include: (*i*) *The substitution method.* This seeks a proof for the problem expression by finding an axiom or previously proved theorem that can be transformed into the problem expression by substituting for variables and replacing connectives. (*ii*) *The detachment method.* This method uses the rule of detachment which substitutes for the problem expression a new subproblem expression. That is, if B is the problem expression and an axiom can be found which says A implies B, then A is proved, proving B. (*iii*) *The chaining methods.* These also create subproblems, by making use of the transitivity of the relation of implication (that is, if A implies B, then B implies A). Thus, if the problem expression is a implies c, and an axiom or theorem can be found which says that a implies b, then b implies c can become a subproblem. The same is true if a theorem b implies c is found, since a implies b can be the subproblem to be proved. The methods are organized according to algorithms such as that all subproblems are considered in the order in which they are generated. The flow diagram of the executive routine by which the methods are organized appears in Fig. 8-9.

As the process of matching the problem expression with an axiom or previously proved theorem proceeds, LT obtains feedback at each step of the results of a substitution or replacement that can be used to guide the next step. This keeps the search on the correct branch of the tree of possible expressions. In the proofs of 38 out of the first 52 problems in chap. 2 of *Principia Mathematica*, 17 were solved in one application of substitution. Nineteen were proved in two steps, 12 by detachment followed by substitution, and 7 by chaining forward followed by substitution. Two others were proved in three steps. Of the others, most that could not be solved required more time and memory than was available.

In proving theorem 2.17 of *Principia Mathematica* when all the preceding theorems were available, the machine made use of chaining, in three steps: a for-

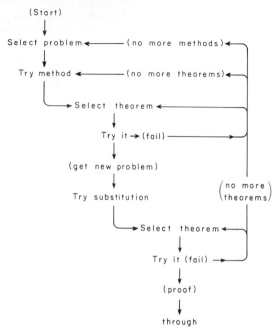

(Start)

Select problem ◄────── (no more methods) ◄──

Try method ◄────── (no more theorems) ◄──

└──► Select theorem ◄──

Try it → (fail) ─────────

(get new problem)

Try substitution   (no more
                        theorems)

└──► Select theorem ◄──

Try it (fail) →

(proof)

through

Fig. 8-9 General flow diagram of LT. [From A. Newell, J. C. Shaw, & H. A. Simon. Empirical explorations with the logic theory machine: a case study in heuristics. In E. A. Feigenbaum & J. Feldman (Eds.). *Computers and thought*. New York: McGraw-Hill, 1963, 119. *Reprinted by permission.*]

ward chaining, a detachment, and a substitution.[658] The theorem to be proved was (not-q implies not-p) implies (p implies q). The proof:

1. A implies not-not-A (theorem 2.12)
2. p implies not-not-p (substitute p for A in 1)
3. (A implies B) implies [(B implies C) implies (A implies C)] (theorem 2.06)
4. (p implies not-not-p) implies [(not-not-p implies q) implies (p implies q)] (substitute p for A, not-not-p for B, q for C in 3)
5. (not-not-p implies q) implies (p implies q) (detach 4 from 3)
6. (not-A implies B) implies (not-B implies A) (theorem 2.15)
7. (not-q implies not-p) implies (not-not-p implies q) (substitute q for A, not-p for B)
8. (not-q implies not-p) implies (p implies q) (Chain 7 and 5; Q.E.D.)

A later, more general program of a comparable sort, but much more complex and sophisticated, the General Problem Solver (GPS), was found to simulate closely the performance of subjects on similar tasks.[659] It was developed by Newell and Simon.

If a digital computer is to play chess or checkers against an opponent, it must store in memory, as a part of its original information, a representation of the board. This must be stored in the computer's digital code of 0's and 1's. It must have a means of receiving information about the opponent's move. It must also have stored information about the sort of moves it should choose to make under the rules of the game. And it also must know these rules. A program of Samuel's learned to play checkers so well that it beat a checker champion.[660] One constraint was that the champion avoided plays available to him which would have resulted in a draw. No algorithm is known which will guarantee a win or draw in checkers, and it is impossible to explore every possible path since that would involve 10^{40} choices and take, at 3 choices per millimicrosecond, 10^{21} centuries to consider. The "tree" of alternatives which the program must consider in choosing its moves is much more complicated than the one described just above for LT. After each play the program evaluates its performance, using a scoring procedure expressed in a numerical function. It then adjusts the coefficients and replaces terms which do not help the game. One variation of this program simulated two players and played against itself.

The many attempts at programming computers to play chess have produced interesting results.[661] Efforts to improve chess-playing computer programs are flourishing, and periodically tournaments are held, with machines in various locations playing against one another. In international tournaments the computer programs of the Soviet Union and the United States have proved to be particularly competent. None is yet a chess grand master.

Encoder and output transducer. Although computer programs always encode for output, no programs were found that modeled or simulated these subsystem processes as they occur in living organisms.

Computer models of personality. The few models in this category are far less detailed and interesting than those which simulate subsystem processes. An example of a program intended to simulate personality is "Aldous," developed by Loehlin and named for Huxley because his was a brave new world.[662] Aldous has several subsystem functions: recognition, emotional reaction, and action preparation. He also has immediate and permanent memory with an associator subsystem which modifies the permanent memory. He is able to print out answers to questions about his "feelings" about a given situation. His inputs come in the form of numbers which represent the environment in both its discriminable characteristics and its potential for affecting him. These vary in power, since some situations can affect him only if he approaches, while others can reward or punish him even if he tries to get away. Two types of environments have been programmed. One is benign and the other hostile. Aldous develops a set of attitudes toward his world which are tested on a personality questionnaire from time to time. In the benign world he becomes ever more optimistic about his future. Several versions of his basic personality have been introduced by varying the amounts of his emotionality, his reliance on past experience, and his tendency to deal with events in terms of general categories rather than individual events. These include "Abstract Aldous," "Decisive Aldous," "Hesitant Aldous," and "Radical Aldous." These changes affected the program's characteristic behavior. Adjustment of a particular type of Aldous to his world depended on the nature of the environment. For example, Hesitant Aldous was the most successful of all in the hostile world but did rather poorly in the benign world. Even large changes of constants in the system did not make it impossible for these models to adjust.

The foregoing list of organism models and simulations is long, but it is only a sample from a large and interesting population. In general those processes which are best understood, such as learning, are most effectively simulated, and models of them fit best the data from experiments with organisms.

7. Conclusions

General living systems theory applies well to organisms. They are real, visible, concrete. My classification of the subsystems seems to fit organisms perhaps better than any other level of living systems.

The various academic fields which study organisms approach their tasks quite differently. None has a complete picture, and communication among the disciplines is often poor. Gross anatomy concerns structure; general physiology primarily deals with matter-energy processing; and endocrine physiology, neurophysiology, genetics, and psychology chiefly concern information processing. General living systems theory brings all these aspects together, both structure and process, both matter-energy and information. Such systems concepts are not novel but are rather well accepted in anatomy and physiology. They are receiving increasing acceptance in psychology and psychiatry as well. The concept of steady state, for instance, serves as a bridge between the notion of homeostasis in matter-energy processing and the notion of adjustment in psychodynamics. It makes clear how homeostasis and adjustment are comparable, and

thus aids the rapprochement of biology and social science. That negative feedbacks maintain these steady states within appropriate ranges and coordinate the various components of the organism is accepted generally in physiology and somewhat less in psychology, although this view is also gaining popularity among psychologists.

At this level the distinction between matter-energy and information is of major theoretical and practical importance. The common terms stimulus and response are ambiguous, for they do not make clear whether, in any particular situation, the matter-energy or the informational aspect of the transmission, or both, are influencing the receiver. The usual systems theory usage which divides "stimulus" into matter-energy and information inputs and "response" into matter-energy and information outputs can resolve such ambiguity and advance the science of organisms. Both biological and social science deal with matter-energy processing and information processing. Yet scholars' traditional insularity so separates their disciplines that there is a wide breach between biological and social science at this level. An organism is a unity and should be studied as such. It is hoped that by analyzing organisms quite differently than the traditional disciplines do, general living systems theory can make it easier to view man as a whole.

Electronic technical advances have led to sophisticated and flexible methods for studying inputs, transmissions, and outputs to organisms. Until recently it has been difficult to make precise quantitative studies at this level of separate internal subsystems such as the decoder, associator, memory, decider, and encoder. It still is. But electronic instruments such as microelectrodes and brain-wave equipment, drugs, and similar research tools in recent years have simplified the techniques for observing phenomena going on inside organisms, and for isolating and measuring subsystem processes. The information processing subsystems are less like the engineers' "black box" than they were a few years ago. We are no longer restricted to input–output analyses but increasingly can examine internal processes as well.

Numerous studies reviewed in this chapter, some dependent upon applications of recent developments in information-theory mathematics, make it apparent that information science is setting new directions in various aspects of psychology and neurophysiology. For instance, quantitative studies have made it abundantly clear that those characteristics shared in common by information processing subsystems, such as input–output transfer functions, channel capacity, threshold, and lag, can be accurately measured at this level. Another basic notion of information science, coding, has led me to distinguish alpha, beta, and gamma coding. These distinctions are particularly important in the study of organisms, for they constitute the first level at which all three types of coding appear. Only in human beings and perhaps a few other species does gamma coding occur. This is made particularly evident by the genetic mutations which enable human beings to transmit and receive speech. Another fundamental concept, the flow of information through multiple echelons of the decider, is well illustrated at this level. The human nervous system is a particularly beautiful example of allocation of decision-making functions. Such concepts about information processing in organisms have facilitated the production of the many models and computer simulations which flourish at this level. These are giving more precision to theories about organisms and therefore are making them more testable. Indeed, there has been a rich cross-fertilization between research on the nervous system and behavior, on the one hand, and the improvement of computer technology, on the other.

Scholarly work at the organism level of living systems has resulted in a huge research literature, good and bad. Experimentation at this level is not especially difficult, but as compared with the lower levels of living systems, it is often limited by important ethical questions as to how human beings should be used as subjects. Out of the totality of research on organisms, I have been able to mention in this long chapter only a small sample that is intended to be representative of the best work. My conceptual system has undoubtedly imposed a bias on my selection of studies to discuss.

Our present detailed knowledge about the human nervous system reveals its fantastic and baffling complexity of structure and process. Composed of billions of subcomponents, it is the most intricate hierarchy produced by biological evolution to date. If the view which I share with others is accurate that complexity in general is greater at each higher level of living systems, study at this level gives some insight into the greater complexity to be found at levels above the organism when comparable bodies of rigorous and precise research on such systems are provided by scientists studying them. If the channel and net subsystem of a human organism is complicated, that of a society or supranational system is orders of magnitude more so. Consider the complexity of the world telephone network and the organizations that operate it. Yet it is only one component of the total channel and net of the earth's supranational system.

The literature on organisms has shortcomings. The neurophysiological investigations are overwhelm-ingly concerned with the energetics of communication and only moderately, and in recent years, with the information in the signals themselves, their codes and meanings. The organism is the lowest level which has had simple and reliable methods for investigating the associator and the memory subsystems. The first of these techniques became available in the 1880s, and many others have been contrived since. Psychologists for years put more effort into studying these subsystems than any other ones, markedly neglecting others, like the decider and encoder. Work on both structure and process of all subsystems, however, has increased in recent years. Much less research than the importance of the subject justifies has been devoted to the interactions among information processing and matter-energy processing subsystems.

One fault of the research on organisms is that studies of affect, emotion, anxiety, motivation, and personality variables have been poorly controlled and usually unquantitative. General living systems theory has not handled these phenomena too well either. They are difficult to analyze and investigate. Nevertheless it *has dealt* with them, and certainly it has put them in a new framework, which to some may appear too cognitive, neglecting feelings. But personality theory and the understanding of psychopathologies like anxiety neurosis or schizophrenia have been advanced by systems-theoretical ideas such as the following: the finding that one band of speech frequencies (the lower, vowel tones) conveys feeling information and another (the higher, consonant frequencies) conveys cognitive information (see page 406); the view of anxiety as a signal comparable to pain (see pages 456 and 457); the possibility that information input underload (see pages 452 to 454, and 475 and 476) or overload (see pages 165 to 169) can cause psychopathology; the discovery that abnormal information inputs in the genetic template can cause psychiatric illness (see pages 476 to 478); the probability that threats, stresses, and the strains they set up also have a part in such etiology; and the recognition that normal and abnormal adjustment processes can cope with these threats, stresses, and strains (see pages 459, 479, and 480).

There are other weaknesses in my conceptualizations of organisms and interpretations of research findings about them. Until we can quantify meaning, the study of information processing at this level will be primitive and unsatisfying. To some it will seem, also, that the objectivity of this approach slights the intangible, evanescent realities of subjective experience. The objective–subjective dichotomy does not exist in computer science. There is hardware, the material entity, and there are the programs and information inputs which are processed by the hardware. The distinction between matter-energy and information goes far to resolve the ancient philosophical dilemma of what in an organism is matter and what is mind.

One final aspect of the state of science at this level is that every responsible investigator wants to be humane in her or his work. Ethical values become involved in research with human and other organisms. The desire of clinicians and counselors to help those who are suffering or in need often limits their scientific objectivity. At lower levels of living systems such humanitarianism rarely if ever biases observations. Not so at the organism level. The investigations on the most important topics are usually those most influenced by such motivations in the investigators. A number of studies reported in this chapter must be analyzed with this caveat in mind.

Most aspects of organisms have been investigated for the organism level alone, without any consideration as to whether the results are also relevant to lower or higher levels of systems. In the future, investigators might profitably delve into whether their findings can be generalized to other levels. In addition, numerous important and challenging questions suggested by considerations discussed in this chapter still require an answer, for example: Are the characteristic psychometric functions of the organism's input transducer determined by all components of that subsystem acting together in an integrated way, or are they really functions of individual sensory cells which are the gates of information into the organism? What are the behavioral implications of each interconnection in the maze of the organism's channel and net? Which centers and nuclei in the nervous system are simply nodes, and which ones represent dispersed components of the decider subsystem? Do the private codes for internal information transmission in organisms improve as a system matures, as Hypothesis 3.3.4.2-1 (see page 98) suggests? Exactly what are the neurological components which make up the associator subsystem? Exactly what are the neural components of the memory? What is the nature of the changes in structure and process of memory traces over time? Exactly what is the neural structure of the decider? How is the deciding process allocated to its echelons? What are the neural concomitants of subjective arousal and attention, and in what structures are they located? What, if any, are the relationships between reaction time and the amount and sort of information in the input? When an organism's channels and nets are overloaded by information, does the output finally drop to zero, or does it level out at some lower rate which it maintains? What can be done to improve the quantification of meaning, particularly in human communication? How can more precise scientific analyses be made of variables related to affect, emotion, anxiety, motivation, and personality? Is the human race the only species that employs true gamma coding in communication, or do chimpanzees and perhaps other species do so as well? In the causation of schizophrenia, what are the different influences of pathologies of (*i*) genetic information inputs in the template, (*ii*) information inputs from the environment, and (*iii*) metabolic processes of the organism?

In the writings of numerous authors the word "organism" has been used to refer to other levels of living systems, such as the cell, the group, the organization, and the society, almost exactly as I use the phrase "concrete living system." This seems undesirable since it confuses the levels. But at least this common usage indicates that many thoughtful people consider that organisms have characteristics common to living systems. Nothing that has appeared in the literature seems to me a basis for denying this. Many findings confirm it.

There is perhaps a greater variety of types of organisms than of living systems at any other level. From minute colonial protistans to huge sequoia trees, from sponges to human beings, the range is vast. Organisms in general are much more independent and totipotential than systems at most other levels—say organs, organizations, or supranational systems. Most of them are clearly individuals, even though at the same time they are "dividuals" composed of moderately autonomous subsystems and components, often intricately integrated. In many ways they are more cohesive and mobile than higher levels of systems, and thus even at the highest levels the organisms that make up the system are clearly distinguishable. The larger systems are characterized by the ceaseless motion and other activities of these organisms, often very large numbers of them. Everything being considered, the scientific evidence makes it certain that organisms truly are concrete living systems.

NOTES AND REFERENCES

[1]Wiggins, I. L. Conifer. *Encyclopaedia Britannica*. Vol. 5. Chicago: Encyclopaedia Britannica, 1974, 1.

[2]Medawar, P. B. *The uniqueness of the individual*. New York: Basic Books, 1961, 110.

[3]Størmer, L. Fossil record. *Encyclopaedia Britannica*. Vol. 7. Chicago: Encyclopaedia Britannica, 1974, 569–571.

[4]McMahon, T. Size and shape in biology. *Science*, 1973, **179**, 1201–1204.

[5]*Ibid*.

[6]Medawar, P. B. *Op. cit.*, 112–113.

[7]Hammond, J. Growth in size and body proportions in farm animals. In M. X. Zarrow (Ed.). *Growth in living systems.* New York: Basic Books, 1961, 321–334.

[8]Moore, R. & The Editors of *Life. Evolution.* New York: Time, Inc., 1962, 89.

[9]Whittaker, R. H. New concepts of kingdoms of organisms. *Science.* 1969, **163**, 150–160.

[10]*Ibid.*, 154–155.

[11]Sawyer, C. H. Reproductive behavior. In J. Field (Ed.). *Handbook of physiology. Section I: Neurophysiology.* Vol. 2. Washington, D.C.: Amer. Physiol. Soc., 1960, 1225–1240.

[12]Magoun, H. W. *The waking brain.* Springfield, Ill. C. C Thomas, 1963, 59.

[13]Sawyer, C. H. *Op. cit.*, 1230.

[14]Pribram, K. H. A review of theory in physiological psychology. *Ann. Rev. Psychol.*, 1960, **11**, 1–40.

[15]Sawyer, C. H. *Op. cit.*, 1229.

[16]Shetler, S. G. Nepenthales. *Encyclopaedia Britannica.* Vol. 12. Chicago: Encyclopaedia Britannica, 1974, 958–962.

[17]Congdon, J. D., Vitt, L. J., & King, W. W. Geckos: adaptive significance and energetics of tail autonomy. *Science,* 1974, **184**, 1379–1380.

[18]Ferguson, J. K. W. The carriage of carbon dioxide by the blood. In C. H. Best & N. B. Taylor (Eds.). *The physiological basis of medical practice.* (7th ed.) Baltimore: Williams & Wilkins, 1961, 459–465.

[19]Stephenson, T. A. Cnidaria. *Encyclopaedia Britannica.* Vol. 4. Chicago: Encyclopaedia Britannica, 1974, 770.

[20]Smith, D. S. The structure of insect fibrillar flight muscle. In K. R. Porter (Ed.). The sarcoplasmic reticulum. *J. cell. Biol.,* 1961, **10** (4,suppl.), 123–158.

[21]Gray, H. *Anatomy of the human body.* (28th ed.) C. M. Goss (Ed.). Philadelphia: Lea & Febiger, 1966, 375.

[22]Lloyd, D. P. C. Spinal mechanisms involved in somatic activities. In J. Field (Ed.). *Handbook of physiology. Section I: Neurophysiology.* Vol. 2. Washington, D.C.: Amer. Physiol. Soc., 1960, 929–949.

[23]Crosby, E. C., Humphrey, T., & Lauer, E. W. *Correlative anatomy of the nervous system.* New York: Macmillan, 1962, 28.

[24]Shakespeare, W. *The tragedy of Macbeth.* IV, i, 91–99; V, v, 44–46; V, vii, 59.

[25]Bonner, J. T. *Cells and societies.* Princeton, N.J.: Princeton Univ. Press, 1955, 144.

[26]Gerard, R. W. Higher levels of integration. *Science,* 27 March 1942, **95**, 309–313.

[27]Granit, R. Neural activity in the retina. In J. Field (Ed.). *Handbook of physiology. Section I: Neurophysiology.* Vol. 1. Washington, D.C.: Amer. Physiol. Soc., 1959, 693–712.

[28]Autrum, H. Nonphotic receptors in lower forms. In J. Field (Ed.). *Handbook of physiology. Section I: Neurophysiology.* Vol. 1. Washington, D.C.: Amer. Physiol. Soc., 1959, 369–385.

[29]Rose, J. E. & Mountcastle, V. B. Touch and kinesthesis. In J. Field (Ed.). *Handbook of physiology. Section I: Neurophysiology.* Vol. 1. Washington, D.C.: Amer. Physiol. Soc., 1959, 387–429.

[30]Cf. Wald, G. The photoreceptor process in vision. In J. Field (Ed.). *Handbook of physiology. Section I: Neurophysiology.* Vol. 1. Washington, D.C.: Amer. Physiol. Soc., 1959, 571–692.

[31]Stevens, S. S. Psychophysics of sensory function. In W. A. Rosenblith (Ed.). *Sensory communication.* New York: Wiley, 1961, 10–12, 27–29, 31.

[32]*Ibid.*, 28.

[33]Uttal, W. R. *The psychobiology of sensory coding.* New York: Harper & Row, 1973, 335–336.

[34]Barlow, H. B. Sensory mechanisms, the reduction of redundancy and intelligence. *Mechanisation of thought processes. Vol. 2. National Physical Laboratory Symposium No. 10.* London: Her Majesty's Stationery Office, 1959, 539–543.

[35]Stevens, S. S. *Op. cit.*, 13.

[36]Wald, G. *Op. cit.*, 682.
Cf. also Fry, G. A. The image forming mechanism of the eye. In J. Field (Ed.). *Handbook of physiology. Section I: Neurophysiology.* Vol. 1. Washington, D.C.: Amer. Physiol. Soc., 1959, 647–670.

[37]Bartley, S. H. Central mechanisms of vision. In J. Field (Ed.). *Handbook of physiology. Section I: Neurophysiology.* Vol. 1. Washington, D.C.: Amer. Physiol. Soc., 1959, 713–740.

[38]Granit, R. *Op. cit.*, 708.

[39]Bartley, S. H. *Op. cit.*, 714.

[40]Ditchburn, R. W. & Ginsborg, B. L. Vision with a stabilized retinal image. *Nature,* 1952, **170**, 36–37.
Cf. also Riggs, L., Ratliff, F., Cornsweet, J. C., & Cornsweet, T. N. The disappearance of steadily fixated visual test objects. *J. Opt. Soc. Amer.*, 1953, **43**, 495–501.

[41]Rushton, W. A. H. The retinal organization of vision in vertebrates. In Society for Experimental Biology. Symposia No. 16. J. W. L. Beament (Ed.). *Biological receptor mechanisms.* New York: Academic Press, 1962, 12–31. Reprinted by permission.

[42]Cf. Barlow, H. B. *Op. cit.*, 540–541.

[43]Cone, R. A. The rat electroretinogram. I. Contrasting effects of adaptation on the amplitude and latency of the b-wave. *J. gen. Physiol.*, 1964, **47**, 1089–1105.

[44]Granit, R. *Op. cit.*, 696.

[45]Gernandt, B. E. Vestibular mechanisms. In J. Field (Ed.). *Handbook of Physiology. Section I: Neurophysiology.* Vol. 1. Washington, D.C.: Amer. Physiol. Soc., 1959, 549–564.

[46]*Ibid.*, 555.

[47]*Ibid.*, 554–555.

[48]*Ibid.*, 554.

[49]Davis, H. Excitation of auditory receptors. In J. Field (Ed.). *Handbook of Physiology. Section I: Neurophysiology.* Vol. 1. Washington, D.C.: Amer. Physiol. Soc., 1959, 565–584.
Cf. also Licklider, J. C. R. Basic correlates of the auditory stimulus. In S. S. Stevens (Ed.). *Handbook of experimental psychology.* New York: Wiley, 1951, 994–998.

[50]Davis, H. *Op. cit.*, 582.

[51]Licklider, J. C. R. Basic correlates of the auditory stimulus. In S. S. Stevens (Ed.). *Handbook of experimental psychology.* New York: Wiley, 1951, 985–1039.

[52]Stevens, S. S. *Op. cit.*, 28.

[53]Davis, H. *Op. cit.*, 569.

[54]*Ibid.*, 577.

[55]*Ibid.*

[56]Barlow, H. B. *Op. cit.*, 540–541.

[57]Licklider, J. C. R. *Op. cit.*, 996.

[58]Adey, W. R. The sense of smell. In J. Field (Ed.). *Handbook of physiology. Section I: Neurophysiology.* Vol. 1. Washington, D.C.: Amer. Physiol. Soc., 1959, 538–539.

[59]*Ibid.*, 542.

[60]Takagi, S. F. & Omura, K. Responses of the olfactory receptor cells to odours. *Jap. Acad. Proc.*, 1963, **39**, 253–255.

[61]Takagi, S. F. & Shibuya, T. Studies on the potential oscillation appearing in the olfactory epithelium of the toad. *Jap. J. Physiol.*, 1961, **11**, 23–37.

[62]*Ibid.*, 28.

[63]Takagi, S. F. & Shibuya, T. The potential oscillations observed in the olfactory epithelium, nerve and bulb of the toad and frog. *Jap. J. Physiol.*, 1960, **10**, 499–508.

[64]Stevens, S. S. *Op. cit.*, 30.

[65]Adey, W. R. *Op. cit.*, 543.

[66]Beidler, L. M. Mechanisms of gustatory and olfactory receptor stimulation. In W. A. Rosenblith (Ed.). *Sensory communication.* New York: Wiley, 1961, 155–157.

[67]*Ibid.*, 155.

[68]*Ibid.*, 154–155.

[69]De Vries, H. & Stuiver, M. The absolute sensitivity of the human sense of smell. In W. A. Rosenblith (Ed.). *Sensory communication.* New York: Wiley, 1961, 159–167.

[70]Adey, W. R. *Op. cit.*, 543.

[71]Beidler, L. M. *Op. cit.*, 144–151.

[72]Somjen, G. *Sensory coding.* New York: Appleton-Century-Crofts, 1972, 86–87.

[73]Beidler, L. M. *Op. cit.*, 147–149.
Also Pfaffmann, C. The sense of taste. In J. Field (Ed.). *Handbook of physiology. Section I: Neurophysiology.* Vol. 1. Washington, D.C.: Amer. Physiol. Soc., 1959, 513–516.

[74]Stevens, S. S. *Op. cit.*, 13.

[75]Beidler, L. M. *Op. cit.*, 146–147.

[76]Pfaffmann, C. The sense of taste. In J. Field (Ed.). *Handbook of physiology. Section I: Neurophysiology.* Vol. 1. Washington, D.C.: Amer. Physiol. Soc., 1959, 525.

[77]*Ibid.*, 511.

[78]*Ibid.*, 514.

[79]*Ibid.*, 523.

[80]Beidler, L. M. *Op. cit.*, 143.

[81]Pfaffmann, C. *Op. cit.*, 524.

[82]Beidler, L. M. *Op. cit.*, 143.

[83]Rose, J. E. & Mountcastle, V. B. *Op. cit.*, 390.

[84]Zotterman, Y. Thermal sensations. In J. Field (Ed.). *Handbook of physiology. Section I: Neurophysiology.* Vol.1. Washington, D.C.: Amer. Physiol. Soc., 1959, 431–458.

[85]*Ibid.*, 425.

[86]Sweet, W. H. Pain. In J. Field (Ed.). *Handbook of physiology. Section I: Neurophysiology.* Vol. 1. Washington, D.C.: Amer. Physiol. Soc., 1959, 459–506.

[87]*Ibid.*, 468.

[88]Rose, J. E. & Mountcastle, V. B. *Op. cit.*, 394.

[89]Rosner, B. S. Neural factors limiting cutaneous spatiotemporal discriminations. In W. A. Rosenblith (Ed.). *Sensory communication.* New York: Wiley, 1961, 725–737.

[90]Zotterman, Y. *Op. cit.*, 431–432.

[91]*Ibid.*, 432.

[92]*Ibid.*, 456.

[93]Sweet, W. H. *Op. cit.*, 468.

[94]Rose, J. E. & Mountcastle, V. B. *Op. cit.*, 392.

[95]Zotterman, Y. *Op. cit.*, 446–449.

[96]*Ibid.*, 449–452.

[97]Geldard, F. A. Cutaneous channels of communication. In W. A. Rosenblith (Ed.). *Sensory communication.* New York: Wiley, 1961, 73–87.

[98]Sweet, W. H. *Op. cit.*, 469.

[99]Rose, J. E. & Mountcastle, V. B. *Op. cit.*, 392.

[100]Stevens, S. S. *Op. cit.*, 29–30.

[101]*Ibid.*, 24.

[102]Sweet, W. H. *Op. cit.*, 472.

[103]*Ibid.*, 473.

[104]Gray, J. A. B. Coding in systems of primary receptor neurons. In Society for Experimental Biology. Symposia No. 16. J. W. L. Beament (Ed.). *Biological receptor mechanisms.* New York: Academic Press, 1962, 345–354.

[105]Zotterman, Y. *Op. cit.*, 432.

[106]Pert, C. B. & Snyder, S. H. Opiate receptor: demonstration in nervous tissue. *Science,* 1973, **179,** 1011–1014.

[107]*Ibid.*

[108]Bonner, J. T. The biology of plant growth. In M. X. Zarrow (Ed.). *Growth in living systems.* New York: Basic Books, 1961, 439–452.

[109]Cf. Wurtman, R. J. Neuroendocrine transducer cells in mammals. In F. O. Schmitt (Ed.). *The neurosciences.* New York: Rockefeller Univ. Press, 1970, 535, 538.

[110]Harris, G. W. Central control of pituitary secretion. In J. Field (Ed.). *Handbook of physiology. Section I: Neurophysiology.* Vol. 2. Washington, D.C.: Amer. Physiol. Soc., 1960, 1007–1038.

[111]*Ibid.*, 1015.
Cf. also Brobeck, J. R. Control systems that establish regulations. In J. R. Brobeck (Ed.). *Best & Taylor's physiological basis of medical practice.* (9th ed.) Baltimore: Williams & Wilkins, 1973, 9-121, 9-124.

[112]Cf. Wurtman, R. J. *Op. cit.*

[113]Yamamoto, W. S. The arterial bloodstream as a communication channel. (Abstract.) *Internat. Conf. Med. Electron.,* 1961, 36.

[114]Gregg, D. E. Functional characteristics of the systemic and pulmonary circulation. In C. H. Best & N. B. Taylor (Eds.). *The physiological basis of medical practice.* (7th ed.) Baltimore: Williams & Wilkins, 1961, 151–168.

[115]Detweiler, D. K. Measurement of blood pressure and flow. In J. R. Brobeck (Ed.). *Best & Taylor's physiological basis of medical practice.* (9th ed.) Baltimore: Williams & Wilkins, 1973, 3-163.

[116]Gerard, R. W. *Op. cit.*, 309.

[117]Jung, R. Neuronal integration in the visual cortex and its significance for visual information. In W. A. Rosenblith (Ed.). *Sensory communication.* New York: Wiley, 1961, 627–674.
Cf. also Crosby, E. C., Humphrey, T., & Lauer, E. W. *Op. cit.*, 500.

[118]Liberman, A. M., Cooper, F. S., Shankweiler, D. P., & Studdert-Kennedy, M. Perception of the speech code. *Psychol. Rev.,* 1967, **74,** 431–461.

[119]Bartley, S. H. *Op. cit.*, 728.

[120]Uttal, W. R. *Op. cit.*, 214–223.

[121]Gray, J. A. B. *Op. cit.*, 347.

[122]*Ibid.*, 348–349.

[123]Lettvin, J. Y., Maturana, H. R., McCulloch, W. S., & Pitts, W. H. What the frog's eye tells the frog's brain. In W. S. McCulloch (Ed.). *Embodiments of mind.* Cambridge, Mass.: M.I.T. Press, 1965, 230–255.
Also Lettvin, J. Y., Maturana, H. R., McCulloch, W. S., & Pitts, W. H. Two remarks on the visual system of the frog. In W. A. Rosenblith (Ed.). *Sensory communication.* New York: Wiley, 1961, 757–776.

[124]Hubel, D. H. The visual cortex of the brain. *Sci. Amer.,* Nov. 1963, **209**(5), 54–62.
Cf. also Hubel, D. H. Integrative processes in central visual pathways of the cat. *J. Optical Soc. Amer.,* 1963, **53,** 58–66.

[125]Somjen, G. *Op. cit.*, 37–38.

[126]Hubel, D. H. The visual cortex of the brain. *Op. cit.*, 62. Reprinted by permission of *Scientific American.*

[127]Creutzfeldt, O., Fuster, J. M., Herz, A., & Straschill, M. Some problems of information transmission in the visual system. In J. C. Eccles (Ed.). *Brain and conscious experience.* New York: Springer-Verlag, 1966, 138–164.

[128]Jung, R. *Op. cit.*, 640.

[129]Liberman, E. A. The nature of the information arriving at the brain by one nerve fiber from two retinal receptors in the frog. *Biophys.,* 1957, **2,** 424–428.

[130]Hartline, H. K., Wagner, H. G., & Ratliff, F. Inhibition in the eye of *Limulus. J. gen. Physiol.,* 1956, **39,** 651–673.

[131]Davis, H. *Op. cit.*, 124.

[132]Ibid., 128.

[133]Neff, W. D. Neural mechanisms of auditory discrimination. In W. A. Rosenblith (Ed.). *Sensory communication.* New York: Wiley, 1961, 257–278.

[134]Takagi, S. F. & Shibuya, T. The potential oscillations observed in the olfactory epithelium, nerve and bulb of the toad and frog. *Op. cit.,* 499–508.

[135]Landgren, S. The response of thalamic and cortical neurons to electrical and physiological stimulation of the cat's tongue. In W. A. Rosenblith (Ed.). *Sensory communication.* New York: Wiley, 1961, 437–453.

[136]Pfaffman, C., Erickson, R. P., Frommer, G. P., & Halpern, B. P. Gustatory discharges in the rat medulla and thalamus. In W. A. Rosenblith (Ed.). *Sensory communication.* New York: Wiley, 1961, 455–473.

[137]Crosby, E. C., Humphrey, T., & Lauer, E. W. *Op. cit.,* 288.

[138]Rose, J. E. & Mountcastle, V. B. *Op. cit.,* 401.

[139]Mountcastle, V. B. Some functional properties of the somatic afferent system. In W. A. Rosenblith (Ed.). *Sensory communication.* New York: Wiley, 1961, 403–436.

[140]Sweet, W. H. *Op. cit.,* 496–498.

[141]Mountcastle, V. B. *Op. cit.,* 403–436.

[142]Crosby, E. C., Humphrey, T., & Lauer, E. W. *Op. cit.,* 230.

[143]Mandler, G. Response factors in human learning. *Psychol. Rev.,* 1954, **61,** 235–244.

[144]Teuber, H.-L. Perception. In J. Field (Ed.). *Handbook of physiology. Section I: Neurophysiology.* Vol. 3. Washington, D.C.: Amer. Physiol. Soc., 1960, 1595–1668.

[145]Ibid., 1610–1614.

[146]Allport, F. H. *Theories of perception and the concept of structure.* New York: Wiley, 1955, 112–147.

[147]Pitts, W. & McCulloch, W. S. How we know universals: the perception of auditory and visual forms. *Bull. math. Biophys.,* 1947, **9,** 127–147.

[148]Pribram, K. H. On the neurology of thinking. *Behav. Sci.,* 1959, **4,** 265–287.

[149]Ibid., 274.

[150]Sutton, S., Tueting, P., & Zubin, J. Information delivery and the sensory evoked potential. *Science,* 1967, **155,** 1436–1439.

[151]John, E. R., Herrington, R. N., & Sutton, S. Effects of visual form on the evoked response. *Science,* 1967, **155,** 1439–1442.

[152]Cooper, F. S., Liberman, A. M., & Borst, J. M. The interconversion of audible and visible patterns as a basis for research in the perception of speech. *Proc. Nat. Acad. Sci. USA,* 1951, **37,** 318–325.
Also Liberman, A. M., Cooper, F. S., Shankweiler, D. P., & Studdert-Kennedy, M. *Op. cit.,* 431–461.

[153]Sebeok, T. A. Coding in the evolution of signalling behavior. *Behav. Sci.,* 1962, **7,** 430–432.

[154]Sebeok, T. A. Animal communication. *Science,* 1965, **147,** 1006–1014.

[155]Osgood, C. E., Suci, G. J., & Tannenbaum, P. H. *The measurement of meaning.* Urbana: Univ. of Illinois Press, 1957.

[156]Osgood, C. E. & Sebeok, T. A. (Eds.). Psycholinguistics: a survey of theory and research problems. *J. abnorm. soc. Psychol.,* 1954, **49**(Suppl.), 1–203.

[157]Soskin, W. F. & Kauffman, P. E. Judgment of emotion in word-free voice samples. *J. Commun.,* 1961, **11,** 80.

[158]Starkweather, J. A. Content-free speech as a source of information about the speakers. *J. abnorm. soc. Psychol.,* 1956, **52,** 394–402.
Cf. also Starkweather, J. A. Vocal communication of personality and human feelings. *J. Commun.,* 1961, **11,** 63–72.

[159]Birdwhistell, R. L. Background to kinesics. *Etc.,* 1955, **13,** 10–18.
Cf. also Osgood, C. E. & Sebeok, T. A. *Op. cit.,* 84–87.

[160]Foulke, E. & Brodbeck, A. A., Jr. Transmission of Morse code by electrocutaneous stimulation. *Psychol. record,* 1968, **18,** 617–622.

[161]Holmes, E. & Gruenberg, G. Learning in plants. *Worm Runner's Digest,* 1965, **7,** 9–10.

[162]Lashley, K. S. In search of the engram. In F. A. Beach, D. O. Hebb, C. T. Morgan, & H. W. Nissen (Eds.). *The neuropsychology of Lashley.* New York: McGraw-Hill, 1960, 492.

[163]Cf. Beurle, R. L. Properties of a mass of cells capable of regenerating pulses. *Philos. Trans. Royal Soc. London, Series B, Biol. Sci.,* 1956, **240,** 55-94.

[164]Hebb, D. O. *The organization of behavior.* New York: Wiley, 1949, 125.

[165]McConnell, J. V. *Understanding human behavior.* (2d ed.) New York: Holt, Rinehart, & Winston, 1977, 337–339.

[166]Cf. Birk, L. (Ed.) *Biofeedback: behavioral medicine.* New York: Grune & Stratton, 1973.
Also Razran, G. The observable unconscious and the inferable unconscious in current Soviet psychophysiology; interoceptive conditioning, semantic conditioning and the orienting reflex. *Psychol. Rev.,* 1961, **68,** 81–147.
Also Miller, N. E. & DiCara, L. Instrumental learning of heart rate changes in curarized rats: shaping and specificity to discriminative stimulus. *J. comp. physiol. Psychol.,* 1967, **63,** 12–19.
Also Harris, A. H., Gilliam, W. J., Findley, J. D., & Brady, J. V. Instrumental conditioning of large-magnitude, daily, 12-hour blood pressure elevations in the baboon. *Science,* 1973, **182,** 175–177.
Also Engel, B. T., Nikoomanesh, P., & Schuster, M. M. Operant conditioning of rectosphincteric responses in the treatment of fecal incontinence. *N.E.J. Med.,* 1974, **290,** 646–649.

[167]Hunt, H. F. Some effects of drugs on classical (Type S) conditioning. *Ann. N.Y. Acad. Sci.,* 1956, **65,** 258–267.

[168]Birk, L. *Op. cit.*
Also Rosenfeld, J. P., Rudell, A. P., & Fox, S. S. Operant control of neural events in humans. *Science,* 1969, **165,** 821–823.
Also Kamiya, J. Operant control of the EEG alpha rhythm and some of its reported effects on consciousness. In C. T. Tart (Ed.). *Altered states of consciousness.* New York: Wiley, 1969, 507–517.

[169]Harlow, H. F. Learning set and error factor theory. In S. Koch (Ed.). *Psychology: a study of a science.* Vol. 2. New York: McGraw-Hill, 1959, 492–537.

[170]McConnell, J. V. Comparative physiology: learning in invertebrates. *Ann Rev. Physiol.,* 1966, **28,** 107–136.

[171]Siegel, W. & Siegel, J. A. *Memory effects in absolute judgment.* Communication No. 234. Ann Arbor: Mental Health Research Institute, Univ. of Mich., 1968.

[172]Kendler, H. H. Learning. *Ann. Rev. Psychol.,* 1959, **10,** 43–88.

[173]Watson, A. J. Some questions concerning the explanation of learning in animals. In *Mechanisation of thought processes.* Vol. 2. *National Physical Laboratory Symposium No. 10.* London: Her Majesty's Stationery Office, 1959, 693–728.

[174]Hebb, D. O. *Op. cit.*

[175]Mandler, G. From association to structure. *Psychol. Rev.,* 1962, **69,** 415–426.
Cf. also Mandler, G. Response factors in human learning. *Op. cit.,* 238.

[176]McConnell, J. V. Comparative physiology: learning in invertebrates. *Op. cit.*, 127.

[177]Harlow, H. F. *Op. cit.*, 508.

[178]*Ibid.*, 505.

[179]Dykman, R. A. & Shurrager, P. S. Successive and maintained conditioning in spinal carnivores. *J. comp. physiol. Psychol.*, 1956, **49**, 27–35.

[180]Galambos, R. & Morgan, C. T. The neural basis of learning. In J. Field (Ed.). *Handbook of physiology. Section I: Neurophysiology*. Vol. 3. Washington, D.C.: Amer. Physiol. Soc., 1960, 1471–1499.

[181]Sperry, R. W. The great cerebral commissure. *Sci. Amer.*, 1964, **210**(1), 42–53.

[182]Galambos, R. & Morgan, C. T. *Op. cit.*, 1485–1486.

[183]John, E. R. & Killam, K. F. Electrophysiological correlates of avoidance conditioning in the cat. *J. Pharmacol. & exper. Therapeut.*, 1959, **125**, 252–272.

[184]Cf. Razran, G. *Op. cit.*

[185]John, E. R. Some speculations on the psychophysiology of mind. In J. M. Scher (Ed.). *Theories of the mind*. New York: Free Press, 1962, 80–121.

[186]Young, J. Z. Is there an addressed memory in the nervous system? In J. Wortis (Ed.). *Recent advances in biological psychiatry*. New York: Plenum Press, 1968, 179–193.

[187]Sperry, R. W. Split-brain approach to learning problems. In G. C. Quarton, T. Melnechuk, & F. O. Schmitt (Eds.). *The neurosciences*. New York: Rockefeller Univ. Press, 1967, 714–722.

[188]Ojemann, R. G. Correlations between specific human brain lesions and memory changes. *Bull. Neurosci. Res. Prog.*, 1966, **4** (Suppl., July 15), 1–70.

[189]*Ibid.*, 19.

[190]*Ibid.*, 32–35.

[191]Krech, D. Discussion of L. Kruger. Morphological alterations of the cerebral cortex and their possible role in the loss and acquisition of information. In D. P. Kimble (Ed.). *The anatomy of memory*. Vol. 1. Palo Alto: Science & Behavior Books, 1965, 88–139.
Cf. also Altman, J. Postnatal growth and differentiation of the mammalian brain, with implications for a morphological theory of memory. In G. C. Quarton, T. Melnechuk, & F. O. Schmitt (Eds.). *The neurosciences*. New York: Rockefeller Univ. Press, 1967, 723–743.

[192]Ojemann, R. G. *Op. cit.*, 37–38.

[193]Magoun, H. W. Neural plasticity and the memory process. In M. Rinkel (Ed.). *Biological treatment of mental illness*. New York: Page, 1968, 154–193.

[194]Ojemann, R. G. *Op. cit.*, 38.

[195]Feindel, W. & Penfield, W. Localization of discharge in temporal lobe automatism. *AMA Archives Neurol. & Psychiat.*, 1954, **72**, 605–630.

[196]Morrell, F. Information storage in nerve cells. In W. S. Fields & W. Abbott (Eds.). *Information storage and neural control*. Springfield, Ill.: C. C Thomas, 1963, 189–229.

[197]Roberts, E. Summation. In D. P. Kimble (Ed.). *The anatomy of memory*. Vol. 1. Palo Alto: Science & Behavior Books, 1965, 292–317.

[198]Mackworth, J. F. The relation between the visual image and postperceptual immediate memory. *J. verb. Learn. & verb. Behav.*, 1963, **2**, 75–85.

[199]Agranoff, B. W. & Davis, R. E. Evidence for stages in the development of memory. In F. D. Carlson (Ed.). *Physiological and biochemical aspects of nervous integration*. Englewood Cliffs, N.J.: Prentice-Hall, 1968, 310–325.

[200]Ojemann, R. G. *Op. cit.*, 11.

[201]*Ibid.*, 64–65.

[202]Magoun, H. W. Neural plasticity and the memory process. *Op. cit.*, 168–169.

[203]John, E. R. Electrophysiological studies of conditioning. In G. C. Quarton, T. Melnechuk, & F. O. Schmitt (Eds.). *The neurosciences*. New York: Rockefeller Univ. Press, 1967, 690–704.

[204]Flexner, J. B., Flexner, L. B., & Stellar, E. Memory in mice as affected by intracerebral puromycin. *Science*, 1963, **141**, 57–59.

[205]Penfield, W. & Perot, P. The brain's record of auditory and visual experience. *Brain*, 1963, **86**, 595–696.

[206]Morrell, F. Modification of RNA as a result of neural activity. In M. A. B. Brazier (Ed.). *Brain function*. Berkeley: Univ. of California Press, 1964, 183–202.

[207]Gerard, R. W. The material basis of memory. *J. verb. Learn. & verb. Behav.*, 1963, **2**, 22–33.

[208]Nelson, P. G. Brain mechanisms and memory. In G. C. Quarton, T. Melnechuk, & F. O. Schmitt (Eds.). *The neurosciences*. New York: Rockefeller Univ. Press, 1967, 772–775.

[209]Eccles, J. C. Possible ways in which synaptic mechanisms participate in learning, remembering, and forgetting. In D. P. Kimble (Ed.). *The anatomy of memory*. Vol. 1. Palo Alto: Science and Behavior Books, 1965, 12–87.

[210]Altman, J. Postnatal growth and differentiation of the mammalian brain, with implications for a morphological theory of memory. In G. C. Quarton, T. Melnechuk, & F. O. Schmitt (Eds.). *The neurosciences*. New York: Rockefeller Univ. Press, 1967, 723–743.

[211]*Ibid.*, 743.

[212]Hydén, H. RNA—a functional characteristic of the neuron and its glia. In M. A. B. Brazier (Ed.). *Brain function*. Berkeley: Univ. of California Press, 1964, 29–68.

[213]McConnell, J. V. Memory transfer through cannibalism in planarians. *J. Neuropsychiat.*, 1962, **3** (Suppl. 1), S43–S48.

[214]*Ibid.*, S46–S47.

[215]Cf. McConnell, J. V. The biochemistry of memory. *Medizinisches Prisma*. Ingleheim am Rhein: C. H. Boehringer Sohn, 1968, 12.

[216]*Ibid.*

[217]*Ibid.*, 12–19.

[218]Agranoff, B. W., Davis, R. E., Casola, L., & Lim, R. Actinomycin D blocks memory formation of shock-avoidance in goldfish. *Science*, 1967, **158**, 1600–1601.
Cf. also Agranoff, B. W. & Klinger, P. D. Puromycin effect on memory fixation in the goldfish. *Science*, 1964, **146**, 952–953.

[219]Agranoff, B. W., Davis, R. E., Casola, L., & Lim, R. *Op. cit.*

[220]Flexner, L. B., Flexner, J. B., & Roberts, R. B. Memory in mice analyzed with antibiotics. *Science*, 1967, **155**, 1377–1383.

[221]Flexner, L. B., Flexner, J. B., & Roberts, R. B. Stages of memory in mice treated with acetoxycycloheximide before or immediately after learning. *Proc. Nat. Acad. Sci. USA*, 1966, **56**, 730–735.

[222]Barondes, S. H. & Cohen, H. D. Memory impairment after subcutaneous injection of acetoxycycloheximide. *Science*, 1968, **160**, 556–557.

[223]Avis, H. H. & Carlton, P. L. Retrograde amnesia produced by hippocampal spreading depression. *Science*, 1968, **161**, 73–75.

[224]Cohen, H. D. & Barondes, S. H. Puromycin effect on memory may be due to occult seizures. *Science*, 1967, **157**, 333–334.

[225]Bohdanecky, M., Bohdanecky, Z., & Jarvik, M. E. Amnesic effects of small bilateral brain puncture in the mouse. *Science*, 1967, **157**, 334–336.

226Flexner, J. B. & Flexner, L. B. Restoration of expression of memory lost after treatment with puromycin. *Proc. Nat. Acad. Sci. USA*, 1967, **57**, 1651–1654.

227Broadbent, D. E. Flow of information within the organism. *J. verb. Learn. & verb. Behav.*, 1963, **2**, 34–39.
Cf. also Mackworth, J. F. *Op. cit.*, 84.

228Zinkin, S. & Miller, A. J. Recovery of memory after amnesia induced by electroconvulsive shock. *Science*, 1967, **155**, 102–104.

229Broadbent, D. E. *Op. cit.*, 35.

230Gerard, R. W. The material basis of memory. *Op. cit.*

231Melton, A. W. Implications of short-term memory for a general theory of memory. *J. verb. Learn. & verb. Behav.*, 1963, **2**, 1–21.

232Flexner, L. B., Flexner, J. B., & Roberts, R. B. Memory in mice analyzed with antibiotics. *Op. cit.*, 1382.

233Agranoff, B. W. & Davis, R. E. *Op. cit.*, 316.

234*Ibid.*, 323.

235*Ibid.*, 311.

236Hydén, H. Biochemical changes accompanying learning. In G. C. Quarton, T. Melnechuk, & F. O. Schmitt (Eds.). *The neurosciences*. New York: Rockefeller Univ. Press, 1967, 765–771.

237*Ibid.*, 771.

238Gerard, R. W. What is memory? *Sci. Amer.*, 1953, **189**(3), 118.

239Agranoff, B. W. & Davis, R. E. *Op. cit.*, 323–325. Reprinted by permission.

240Osgood, C. E. & Sebeok, T. A. *Op. cit.*, 95–96.

241Brown, J. Information, redundancy and decay of the memory trace. In *Mechanisation of thought processes*. Vol. 2. *National Physical Laboratory Symposium No. 10.* London: Her Majesty's Stationery Office, 1959, 729–752.

242Penfield, W. & Perot, P. *Op. cit.*, 684.

243Penfield, W. Studies of the cerebral cortex of man. In E. D. Adrian, F. Bremer, H. H. Jaspers, & J. F. Delafresnaye (Eds.). *Brain mechanisms and consciousness. Council for International Organizations of Medical Science.* Oxford: Blackwell, 1954, 284–309.

244Ebbinghaus, H. *Über das Gedächtnis: Üntersuchen zur experimentellen Psychologie.* Leipzig: Duncker & Humblot, 1885. (Trans. as *Memory: a contribution to experimental psychology.* by H. A. Ruger & C. E. Bussenius. Columbia Univ. Coll. Educ. Reports No. 3. New York: Teachers College, Columbia Univ., 1913.)

245Miller, G. A. The magical number seven, plus or minus two. *Psychol. Rev.*, 1956, **63**, 81–97.

246Bartlett, F. C. *Remembering*. Cambridge: Cambridge Univ. Press, 1932, 63–94.

247Buschke, H. Spontaneous remembering after recall failure. *Science*, 1974, **184**, 579–581.

248Reid, L. S., Brackett, H. R., & Johnson, R. B. The influence of items to be recalled upon short-term retention. *J. verb. Learn. & verb. Behav.*, 1963, **2**, 86–92.

249Postman, L. Does interference theory predict too much forgetting? *J. verb. Learn. & verb. Behav.*, 1963, **2**, 40–48.

250Szilard, L. On memory and recall. *Proc. Nat. Acad. Sci. USA*, 1964, **51**, 1092–1099.

251Lloyd, D. P. C. *Op. cit.*, 929.

252Denny-Brown, D. Motor mechanisms—introduction: the general principles of motor integration. In J. Field (Ed.). *Handbook of physiology. Section I: Neurophysiology.* Vol. 2. Washington, D.C.: Amer. Physiol. Soc., 1960, 781–796.

253Morrell, F. Electrical signs of sensory coding. In G. C. Quarton, T. Melnechuk, & F. O. Schmitt (Eds.). *The neurosciences.* New York: Rockefeller Univ. Press, 1967, 452–469.

254Magoun, H. W. *The waking brain. Op. cit.*, 109.

255Morrell, F. Electrical signs of sensory coding. *Op. cit.*, 452–453.

256Berelson, B. & Steiner, G. A. *Human behavior: an inventory of scientific findings.* New York: Harcourt, Brace, 1964, 245–246.

257Magoun, H. W. *The waking brain. Op. cit.*, 106–107.

258Hillyard, S. A., Hink, R. F., Schwent, V. L., & Picton, T. W. Electrical signs of selective attention in the human brain. *Science*, 1973, **182**, 177–179.

259Magoun, H. W. *The waking brain. Op. cit.*, 158–159.

260Morrell, F. Electrical signs of sensory coding. *Op. cit.*, 453.

261Kaada, B. R. Cingulate, posterior orbital, anterior insular and temporal pole cortex. In J. Field (Ed.). *Handbook of physiology. Section I: Neurophysiology.* Vol. 2. Washington, D.C.: Amer. Physiol. Soc., 1960, 1363–1364.

262Magoun, H. W. *The waking brain. Op. cit.*, 159–162.

263*Ibid.*, 162–170.

264*Ibid.*, 178–182.

265Somjen, G. *Op. cit.*, 218–220.

266Lindsley, D. B. Attention, consciousness, sleep and wakefulness. In J. Field (Ed.). *Handbook of Physiology. Section I: Neurophysiology.* Vol. 3. Washington, D.C.: Amer. Physiol. Soc., 1960, 1553–1593.
Also Magoun, H. W. *The waking brain. Op. cit.*, 87–93.

267Hernández-Peón, R. Reticular mechanisms of sensory control. In W. A. Rosenblith (Ed.). *Sensory communication.* New York: Wiley, 1961, 497–520.

268Hernández-Peón, R., Scherrer, H., & Jouvet, M. Modification of electric activity in cochlear nucleus during "attention" in unanesthetized cats. *Science*, 1956, **123**, 331–332.

269Hernández-Peón, R. Psychiatric implications of neurophysiological research. *Bull. Menninger Clin.*, 1964, **28**, 165, 185.

270*Ibid.*, 174–175.

271Hernández-Peón, R. Reticular mechanisms of sensory control. *Op. cit.*, 515.

272Worden, F. G. Attention and auditory electrophysiology. In E. Stellar & J. M. Sprague (Eds.). *Progress in physiological psychology.* Vol. 1. New York: Academic Press, 1966, 74–83.

273Rasmussen, G. L. Efferent fibers of the cochlear nerve and cochlear nucleus. In G. L. Rasmussen & W. F. Windle (Eds.). *Neural mechanisms of auditory and vestibular systems.* Springfield, Ill.: C. C Thomas, 1960, 105–115.

274Ireland, P. E. & Farkashidy, J. Studies on the efferent innervation of the vestibular end organs. *Trans. Amer. Otological Soc.*, 1961, **49**, 20–34.

275Worden, F. G. *Op. cit.*, 84–90.

276Berelson, B. & Steiner, G. A. *Op. cit.*, 240.

277Golant, S. M. Adjustment process in a system: a behavioral model of human movement. *Geographical Analysis*, 1971, **2**, 120–134.

278Hunt, J. McV. Experience and the development of motivation: some reinterpretations. *Child Develop.*, 1960, **31**, 489–504.

279Harlow, H. F. Learning and satiation of response in intrinsically motivated complex puzzle performance by monkeys. *J. comp. physiol. Psychol.*, 1950, **43**, 289–294.

280Fox, S. S. Self-maintained sensory input and sensory deprivation in monkeys: a behavioral and neuropharmacological study. *J. comp. physiol. Psychol.*, 1962, **55**, 438–444.
Also Wendt, R. H., Lindsley, D. F., Adey, W. R., & Fox, S. S. Self-maintained visual stimulation in monkeys after long-term visual deprivation. *Science*, 1963, **139**, 336–338.

281Jones, A., Wilkinson, H. J., & Braden, I. Information deprivation as a motivational variable. *J. exper. Psychol.*, 1961, **62**, 126–137.

[282]Miller, N. E. Liberalization of basic S-R concepts: extensions to conflict behavior, motivation, and social learning. In S. Koch (Ed.). *Psychology: a study of a science.* Vol. 2. New York: McGraw-Hill, 1959, 196–292.

[283]Stellar, E. Drive and motivation. In J. Field (Ed.). *Handbook of physiology. Section I: Neurophysiology.* Vol. 3. Washington, D.C.: Amer. Physiol. Soc., 1960, 1501–1529.

[284]Freud, S. New introductory lectures on psychoanalysis. In J. Strachey (Tr.). *The complete psychological works of Sigmund Freud.* Vol. 22. London: Hogarth Press, 1964, 72.

[285]Siegel, S. Level of aspiration and decision-making. *Psychol. Rev.,* 1957, **64,** 253–263.

[286]Plutchik, R. *The emotions: facts, theories, and a new model.* New York: Random House, 1962, 38.

[287]Beecher, H. K. The powerful placebo. *J. Amer. Med. Assn.,* 1955, **159,** 1602–1606.

[288]Kurland, A. A. The drug placebo—its psychodynamic and conditional reflex action. *Behav. Sci.,* 1957, **2,** 101–110.

[289]Schachter, S. & Singer, J. E. Cognitive, social, and physiological determinants of emotional state. *Psychol. Rev.,* 1962, **69,** 379–399.

[290]Schachter, S. & Wheeler, L. Epinephrine, chlorpromazine, and amusement. *J. abnorm. soc. Psychol.,* 1962, **65,** 121–128.

[291]Harris, G. W. & Donovan, B. T. The adrenal (suprarenal) glands. In C. H. Best & N. B. Taylor (Eds.). *The physiological basis of medical practice.* (7th ed.) Baltimore: Williams & Wilkins, 1961, 1022–1047.

[292]Bucy, P. C. The basal ganglia. The thalamus and hypothalamus. In C. H. Best & N. B. Taylor (Eds.). *The physiological basis of medical practice.* (7th ed.) Baltimore: Williams & Wilkins, 1961, 1215–1232.
Cf. also Lindsley, D. B. Emotion. In S. S. Stevens (Ed.). *Handbook of experimental psychology.* New York: Wiley, 1951, 437–516.

[293]Crosby, E. C., Humphrey, T., & Lauer, E. W. *Op. cit.,* 338.

[294]Magoun, H. W. *The waking brain. Op. cit.,* 66.

[295]NOTE: The research on animals can be found in: Olds, J. & Milner, P. Positive reinforcement produced by electrical stimulation of septal area and other regions of rat brain. In T. K. Landauer (Ed.) *Readings in physiological psychology: the bodily basis of behavior.* New York: McGraw-Hill, 1967, 246–258.
The research on human subjects can be found in: Heath, R. G. Electrical self-stimulation of the brain in man. *Amer. J. Psychiat.,* 1963, **120,** 571–577.

[296]Magoun, H. W. *The waking brain. Op. cit.,* 62–63.

[297]Crosby, E. C., Humphrey, T., & Lauer, E. W. *Op. cit.,* 427.

[298]*Ibid.,* 331–332.

[299]*Ibid.*

[300]Cf. Magoun, H. W. *The waking brain. Op. cit.,* 66.

[301]*Ibid.*

[302]Brown, G. W. Computation in decision making. In R. E. Machol (Ed.). *Information and decision processes.* New York: McGraw-Hill, 1960, 1–14.

[303]Simon, H. A. & Simon, P. A. Trial and error search in solving difficult problems: evidence from the game of chess. *Behav. Sci.,* 1962, **7,** 425–429.

[304]Simon, H. A. *Models of man.* New York: Wiley, 1957, 246.

[305]Luce, R. D. *Individual choice behavior.* New York: Wiley, 1959, 3–4.

[306]Pribram, K. H. On the neurology of thinking. *Op. cit.,* 268–272.

[307]*Ibid.,* 274.

[308]Sherrington, C. S. *The integrative action of the nervous system.* New Haven: Yale Univ. Press, 1906, 54.

[309]Green, D. M. & Swets, J. A. *Signal detection theory and psychophysics.* New York: Wiley, 1966, 11.

[310]John, E. R. Contributions to the study of the problem-solving process. *Psychol. Monog.,* 1957, **71**(18), 1–39.
Also John, E. R. & Miller, J. G. The acquisition and application of information in the problem-solving process. *Behav. Sci.,* 1957, **2,** 291–300.
And Gyr, J. W. An investigation into, and speculations about, the formal nature of a problem-solving process. *Behav. Sci.,* 1960, **5,** 39–59.
And Gyr, J., Thatcher, J., & Allen, G. Computer simulation of a model of cognitive organization. *Behav. Sci.,* 1962, **7,** 111–116.

[311]Brown, G. W. *Op. cit.*

[312]Simon, H. A. & Simon, P. A. *Op. cit.*

[313]Miller, G. A., Galanter, E., & Pribram, K. H. *Plans and the structure of behavior.* New York: Henry Holt, 1960, 165.

[314]Köhler, W. *The mentality of apes.* (Trans. E. Winter) New York: Harcourt, Brace, 1925.
Cf. also Maier, N. R. F. Reasoning in humans. I. On direction. *J. comp. Psychol.,* 1930, **10,** 115–143.

[315]Miller, G. A., Galanter, E., & Pribram, K. H. *Op. cit.,* 1–19.

[316]Restle, F. *Psychology of judgment and choice: a theoretical essay.* New York: Wiley, 1961, 30–37.

[317]Lewin, K. *Principles of topological psychology.* New York: McGraw-Hill, 1936.
Cf. also Allport, F. H., *Op. cit.,* 148–163.

[318]Edwards, W. The theory of decision making. *Psychol. Bull.,* 1954, **51,** 380–417.

[319]Vail, S. Alternative calculi of subjective probabilities. In R. M. Thrall, C. H. Coombs, & R. L. Davis (Eds.). *Decision processes.* New York: Wiley, 1954, 87–98.

[320]Billodeau, E. A. Statistical versus intuitive confidence. *Amer. J. Psychol.,* 1939, **52,** 562–578.

[321]Miller, J. G. Discrimination without awareness. *Amer. J. Psychol.,* 1939, **52,** 562–578.

[322]Stevens, S. S. Measurement, psychophysics, and utility. In C. W. Churchman & P. Ratoosh (Eds.). *Measurement: definitions and theories.* New York: Wiley, 1959, 18–63.

[323]Coombs, C. H. *A theory of data.* New York: Wiley, 1964, 15.

[324]Zipf, G. K. *Human behavior and the principle of least effort.* Cambridge, Mass.: Addison-Wesley, 1949.

[325]Barch, A. M., Nangle, J., & Trumbo, D. Situational characteristics and turn-signalling behavior. In Highway Research Board, *Driver characteristic and behavior studies.* (H.R.B. Bull. 172, NAS-NRC Publ. 532) Washington: National Academy of Sciences-National Research Council, 1958, 95–103.

[326]Schroeder, H. E. The risky shift as a general choice shift. *J. Person. & soc. Psychol.,* 1973, **27,** 297–300.
Also Walker, T. G. & Main, E. C. Choice shifts in political decision making: federal judges and civil liberties cases. *J. appl. soc. Psychol.,* 1973, **3,** 39–48.

[327]Asch, S. E. *Social psychology.* New York: Prentice-Hall, 1952, 487–492.

[328]Penfield, W. & Rasmussen, T. *The cerebral cortex of man.* New York: Macmillan, 1950, 222–228.

[329]Pribram, K. H. On the neurology of thinking. *Op. cit.,* 275.

[330]*Ibid.,* 277.

[331]Pribram, K. H. & Tubbs, W. E. Short-term memory, parsing, and the primate frontal cortex. *Science,* 1967, **156,** 1765–1767.

[332]Terzuolo, C. A. & Adey, W. R. Sensorimotor cortical activities. In J. Field (Ed.). *Handbook of physiology. Section I: Neurophysiology.* Vol. 2. Washington, D.C.: Amer. Physiol. Soc., 1960, 797–835.

[333]*Ibid.,* 825.

[334]Pribram, K. H. A review of theory in physiological psychology. *Op. cit.,* 19.

[335]Ploog, D. & Melnechuk, T. Primate communication. *Neurosci. Res. Prog. Bull.*, 1969, **7**, 419–510.

[336]Grinker, R. R. & Sahs, A. L. *Neurology*. (6th ed.) Springfield, Ill.: C. C Thomas, 1966, 732.

[337]Crosby, E. C., Humphrey, T., & Lauer, E. W. *Op. cit.*, 514–515.

[338]Sebeok, T. A. Animal communication. *Op. cit.*, 1010.

[339]Wilson, E. O. Chemical communication in the social insects. *Science*, 1965, **149**, 1064–1071.

[340]Barth, R. H., Jr. Insect mating behavior: endocrine control of a chemical communication system. *Science*, 1965, **149**, 882–883.

[341]Dethier, V. G. Communication by insects: physiology of dancing. *Science*, 1957, **125**, 331–336.

[342]Frings, H., Frings, M., Jumber, J., Busnel, R. G., Gibian, J., & Gromet, P. Reactions of American and French species of *Corvus* and *Larus* to recorded communication signals tested reciprocally. *Ecology*, 1958, **39**, 126–131.

[343]Osgood, C. E. & Sebeok, T. A. *Op. cit.*, 132–133.

[344]Liberman, A. M., Cooper, F. S., Shankweiler, D. P., & Studdert-Kennedy, M. *Op. cit.*, 445.

[345]Osgood, C. E. & Sebeok, T. A. *Op. cit.*, 126–139.

[346]Gardner, R. A. & Gardner, B. T. Teaching sign language to a chimpanzee. *Science*, 1969, **165**, 664–672.
Cf. also Ploog, D. & Melnechuk, T. *Op. cit.*, 460.

[347]Gardner, R. A. & Gardner, B. T. *Op. cit.*, 664–672.

[348]Grinker, R. R. & Sahs, A. L. *Op. cit.*, 733–734.

[349]Zangwill, O. L. Speech. In J. Field (Ed.). *Handbook of physiology. Section I: Neurophysiology.* Vol. 3. Washington, D.C.: Amer. Physiol. Soc., 1960, 1709–1722.

[350]Brobeck, J. R. Higher neural functions. In J. R. Brobeck (Ed.). *Best & Taylor's physiological basis of medical practice.* (9th ed.) Baltimore: Williams & Wilkins, 1973, 9-148–9-150.

[351]Crosby, E. C., Humphrey, T., & Lauer, E. W. *Op. cit.*, 515.

[352]Zangwill, O. L. *Op. cit.*, 1720.

[353]Paillard, J. The patterning of skilled movements. In J. Field (Ed.). *Handbook of physiology. Section I: Neurophysiology.* Vol. 3. Washington, D.C.: Amer. Physiol. Soc., 1960, 1679–1708.

[354]Liberman, A. M., Cooper, F. S., Shankweiler, D. P., & Studdert-Kennedy, M. *Op. cit.*, 445–448.

[355]Zangwill, O. L. *Op. cit.*, 1709.

[356]Crosby, E. C., Humphrey, T., & Lauer, E. W. *Op. cit.*, 514.
Cf. also Grinker, R. R. & Sahs, A. L. *Op. cit.*, 735.

[357]Zangwill, O. L. *Op. cit.*, 1716.

[358]*Ibid.*, 1719–1720.

[359]Skinner, B. F. A case history in scientific method. In S. Koch (Ed.). *Psychology: a study of a science.* Vol. 2. New York: McGraw-Hill, 1959, 359–379.

[360]Luft, U. C. & Noell, W. K. *The manifestations of sudden brief anoxia in man.* Air University, School of Aviation Medicine, USAF, Randolph AFB, Texas, Jan., 1956.

[361]Brozek, J. Semi-starvation. In Group for the Advancement of Psychiatry Symposium No. 3. *Factors used to increase the susceptibility of individuals to forceful indoctrination: observations and experiments.* New York: Group for the Advancement of Psychiatry, 1956, 116–122.

[362]McFarland, R. A., Evans, J. N., & Halperin, M. H. Opthalmic aspects of acute oxygen deficiency. *Arch. Opthal.*, 1941, **26**, 886–913.

[363]McFarland, R. A. Psycho-physiological studies at high altitude in the Andes. III. Mental and psychosomatic responses during gradual adaptation. *J. comp. Psychol.*, 1937, **24**, 147–188.

[364]Dean, R. D. & McGlothlen, C. L. *The effect of environmental stress interactions on performance.* Seattle, Wash.: The Boeing Co., Aerospace Division, 1962.

[365]Woodworth, R. S. & Marquis, D. G. *Psychology.* (5th ed.) New York: Henry Holt, 1953, 243.

[366]*Ibid.*, 216.

[367]Alluisi, E. A., Muller, P. F., & Fitts, P. M. An information analysis of verbal and motor responses in a forced-pace serial task. *J. exper. Psychol.*, 1957, **53**, 153–158.
Also Alluisi, E. A. & Martin, H. B. An information analysis of verbal and motor responses to symbolic and conventional Arabic numerals. *J. appl. Psychol.*, 1958, **42**, 79–84.
Also Alluisi, E. A. & Muller, P. F., Jr. Verbal and motor responses to seven symbolic visual codes: a study in S–R compatibility. *J. exper. Psychol.*, 1958, **55**, 247–254.

[368]Holzmann, P. S. & Klein, G. S. Intersensory and visual field forces in size estimation. *Perceptual and motor skills*, 1956, **6**, 37–41.

[369]Gardiner, R. W., Holzman, P. S., & Siegel, R. S. Some variables affecting size judgments. *Perceptual and motor skills*, 1956, **6**, 285–290.

[370]Bruner, J. S. & Goodman, C. C. Value and need as organizing factors in perception. *J. abnorm. soc. Psychol.*, 1947, **42**, 33–44.
Cf. also Allport, F. H. *Op. cit.*, 312–315.

[371]Broadbent, D. E. *Perception and communication.* London: Pergamon Press, 1958, 96–98.

[372]*Ibid.*, 11–35.

[373]Miller, J. G. The individual response to drugs. In S. M. Farber & R. H. L. Wilson (Eds.). *Man and civilization: control of the mind.* New York: McGraw-Hill, 1961, 92–109.

[374]Cf. Huey, R. B. Behavioral thermoregulation in lizards: importance of associated costs. *Science*, 1974, **184**, 1001–1003.

[375]Wiggins, W. S., Manry, C. H., Lyons, R. H., & Pitts, R. F. The effect of salt loading and salt depletion on renal function and electrolyte excretion in man. *Circulation*, 1951, **3**, 275–281.

[376]Hammond, J. Growth in size and body proportions in farm animals. In M. X. Zarrow (Ed.). *Growth in living systems.* New York: Basic Books, 1961, 321–334.

[377]Wiggins, W. S., Manry, C. H., Lyons, R. H., & Pitts, R. F. *Op cit.*

[378]McFarland, R. A., Evans, J. N., & Halperin, M. H. *Op. cit.*, 887–888.

[379]McFarland, R. A. Psycho-physiological studies at high altitude in the Andes. II. Sensory and motor responses during acclimatization. *J. comp. Psychol.*, 1937, **23**, 229–258.

[380]San Martin, M., Prato, Y., & Fernandez, L. *Mechanisms of natural acclimatization. Excretion of urinary steroids at sea level and high altitudes.* Report 55-100. Air University, School of Aviation Medicine, USAF, Randolph AFB, Texas, 1956.

[381]Reynafarje, C. & Lozano, R. *Mechanisms of natural acclimatization. Observations on the iron metabolism and the free protoporphyrins of the erythrocytes in the polycythemia of high altitudes.* Report 55-99. Air University, School of Aviation Medicine, USAF, Randolph AFB, Texas, 1956.

[382]Valdivia, E. *Mechanisms of natural acclimatization. Capillary studies at high altitudes.* Report 55-101. Air University, School of Aviation Medicine, USAF, Randolph AFB, Texas, 1956.

[383]McFarland, R. A. Psycho-physiological studies at high altitude in the Andes. III. Mental and psychosomatic responses during gradual adaptation. *Op. cit.*

[384]Mrosovsky, N. The adjustable brain of hibernators. *Sci. Amer.*, 1968, **218**(3), 110–118.

[385]*Ibid.*, 113–118.

[386]Hendricks, S. B. How light interacts with living matter. *Sci. Amer.*, 1968, **219**(9), 175–186.

[387]*Ibid.*

[388]Selye, H. *The stress of life.* New York: McGraw-Hill, 1956, 25–43.

[389]*Ibid.,* 113–117.
Also Selye, H. Stress and disease. *Science,* 1955, **122,** 625–631.

[390]McFarland, R. A., Evans, J. N., & Halperin, M. H. *Op. cit.,* 886.

[391]Fox, S. S. *Op. cit.*
Also Wendt, R. H., Lindsley, D. F., Adey, W. R., & Fox, S. S. *Op. cit.*

[392]Jones, A., Wilkinson, H. J., & Braden, I. *Op. cit.,* 126–137.

[393]Wheaton, J. L. Fact and fancy in sensory deprivation studies. *Aeromedical Reviews,* 5–59, Air University, School of Aviation Medicine, USAF, Brooks AFB, Texas, August 1959.

[394]*Ibid.,* 10.

[395]Heron, W., Doane, B. K., & Scott, T. H. Visual disturbances after prolonged perceptual isolation. *Canad. J. Psychol.,* 1956, **10,** 13–18.

[396]Solomon, P., Leiderman, P. H., Mendelson, J., & Wexler, D. Sensory deprivation. A review. *Amer. J. Psychiat.,* 1957, **114,** 357–363.
Cf. also Mendelson, J. H., Kubzansky, P. E., Leiderman, P. H., Wexler, D., & Solomon, P. Physiological and psychological aspects of sensory deprivation—a case analysis. In P. Solomon, P. E. Kubzansky, P. H. Leiderman, J. H. Mendelson, R. Trumbull, & D. Wexler (Eds.). *Sensory deprivation.* Cambridge, Mass.: Harvard Univ. Press, 1961, 91–113.

[397]Lilly, J. In Group for the Advancement of Psychiatry Symposium No. 2. *Illustrative strategies for research on psychopathology in mental health.* New York: Group for the Advancement of Psychiatry, 1956, 13–20.
Also Solomon, P., Leiderman, P. H., Mendelson, J., & Wexler, D. *Op. cit.,* 360–361.

[398]Wheaton, J. L. *Op. cit.,* 29.

[399]Wexler, D., Mendelson, J., Leiderman, P. H., & Solomon, P. Sensory deprivation. *Archives Neurol. & Psychiat.,* 1958, **79,** 225–233.

[400]Wheaton, J. L. *Op. cit.,* 21, 22, 29.

[401]Rhodes, J. M. & Wyers, E. J. Effect of blindness on saccharine intake and manipulatory activity in rats. (Abstract) *Amer. Psychol.,* 1956, **11,** 445.

[402]Personal communication.

[403]Goldberger, L. In the absence of stimuli. *Science,* 1970, **168,** 709–711. Copyright 1970 by the American Association for the Advancement of Science. Reprinted by permission.
Cf. also Zubek, J. P. (Ed.). *Sensory deprivation: fifteen years of research.* New York: Appleton-Century-Crofts, 1969.

[404]Schreuder, O. B. Medical aspects of aircraft pilot fatigue with special reference to the commercial jet pilot. *Aerospace Medicine,* 1966, (Suppl. 23), 1–44.

[405]Aschoff, J. Circadian rhythms in man. *Science,* 1965, **148,** 1427–1432.

[406]*Ibid.,* 1427.

[407]*Ibid.,* 1429.

[408]*New York Times,* November 10, 1969, 11.

[409]Tinbergen, N. & the Editors of *Life. Animal behavior.* New York: Time, Inc., 1965, 130–131.

[410]Cannon, W. B. *Bodily changes in pain, hunger, fear, and rage.* (2nd ed.) New York: Appleton, 1929.

[411]Fox, H. M., Gifford, S., Murawski, B. J., Rizzo, N. D., & Kudarauskas, E. N. Some methods of observing humans under stress. In Members of the Committee on Research, Jacques S. Gottlieb, Chairman (Eds.). *Psychiatric Research Reports (7) of the American Psychiatric Association,* 1955–56, 14–26.

[412]Harris, G. W. & Donovan, B. T. The pituitary gland or hypophysis cerebri. In C. H. Best & N. B. Taylor (Eds.). *The physiological basis of medical practice.* (7th ed.) Baltimore: Williams & Wilkins, 1961, 957–996.

[413]Gross, N. B., Fisher, A. H., & Cohn, V. H., Jr. The effect of a rachitogenic diet on the hoarding behavior of rats. *J. comp. physiol. Psychol.,* 1955, **48,** 451–455.

[414]Richter, C. P. Sodium chloride and dextrose appetite of untreated and treated adrenalectomized rats. *Endocrinology,* 1941, **29,** 115–125.

[415]Griffiths, W. J. Diet selections of rats subjected to stress. *Ann. N.Y. Acad. Sci.,* 1956, **67,** Art. I., 1–10.

[416]Terzuolo, C. A. & Adey, W. R. *Op. cit.,* 808.

[417]Berkun, M. M., Bialek, H. M., Kern, R. P., & Yagi, K. Experimental studies of psychological stress in man. *Psychol. Monog.: general and applied,* 1962, **76,** No. 15(534).

[418]Freud, S. Inhibitions, symptoms and anxiety. In J. Strachey (Tr.). *The complete psychological works of Sigmund Freud.* Vol. 20. London: Hogarth Press, 1959, 87–175.

[419]Grinker, R. R. & Sahs, A. L. *Op. cit.,* 725.
Cf. also Crosby, E. C., Humphrey, T., & Lauer, E. W. *Op. cit.,* 496–497.

[420]Cattell, R. B. & Scheier, I. H. The nature of anxiety. *Psychol. Rep.,* 1958, **4,** 351–388.

[421]Cattell, R. B. & Scheier, I. H. Clinical validities by analyzing the psychiatrist exemplified in relation to anxiety diagnoses. *Amer. J. Orthopsychiat.,* 1958, **28,** 699–713.

[422]Cattell, R. B. The chief invariant psychological and psychophysical functional unities found by P-technique. *J. clin. Psychol.,* 1955, **11,** 319–343.

[423]Murray, H. A. Preparations for the scaffold of a comprehensive system. In S. Koch (Ed.). *Psychology: a study of a science.* Vol. 3. New York: McGraw-Hill, 1959, 7–54.

[424]*Ibid.,* 21–22, 51. Reprinted by permission.

[425]*Ibid.,* 17–18.

[426]*Ibid.,* 19–21, 29–34.
Cf. also Murray, H. A. *et al. Explorations in personality.* New York: Oxford Univ. Press, 1938.

[427]Freud, S. Inhibitions, symptoms and anxiety. *Op. cit.,* 111–118, 163–164.
Also Freud, A. *The ego and the mechanisms of defence.* (Trans. by C. Baines.) New York: International Universities Press, 1946, 73–99.

[428]Cf. Jones, E. *The life and work of Sigmund Freud.* Vol. 1. New York: Basic Books, 1953.

[429]*Ibid.,* 365–404.

[430]*Ibid.,* 370.
Cf. also Kubie, L. S. Psychoanalysis and scientific method. *J. nerv. ment. Dis.,* 1960, **131,** 495–512.

[431]Freud, A. *Op. cit.,* 47.
NOTE: Masserman believes that, when ordinary defense mechanisms are not effective against what appear to be overwhelming threats or stresses, men fall back on three classes of ultimate (Ur) defenses—those that deny reality, such as drunkenness and dissipation; those that involve opportunistic human alliances against fellow men, such as crime and war; and those that rely on magical powers of supernatural beings, such as demonology, mysticism, and religion. Cf. Masserman, J. H. Anxiety: protean source of communication. In J. H. Masserman (Ed.). *Communication and community.* Vol. 8 *Science and psychoanalysis.* New York: Grune & Stratton, 1965, 2–3.

[432]Menninger, K. *The vital balance.* New York: Viking Press, 1963.

[433]*Ibid.,* 83–84.

[434]*Ibid.,* 133–146.

[435]McGuire, W. J. Attitudes and opinions. *Ann. Rev. Psychol.,* **17,** 475–514.

436*Ibid.*, 481–504.

437*Cf. Abelson, R. P., Aronson, E., McGuire, W. J., Newcomb, T. M., Rosenberg, M. J., & Tannenbaum, P. H. (Eds.). *Theories of cognitive consistency: a sourcebook.* Chicago: Rand McNally, 1968.

438Heider, F. *The psychology of interpersonal relations.* New York: Wiley, 1958, 107–112.

439*Ibid.*, 176.

440Jordan, N. Cognitive balance as an aspect of Heider's cognitive psychology. In R. P. Abelson, E. Aronson, W. J. McGuire, T. M. Newcomb, M. J. Rosenberg, & P. H. Tannenbaum (Eds.). *Theories of cognitive consistency: a sourcebook.* Chicago: Rand McNally, 1968, 174.

441Newcomb, T. M. Interpersonal balance. In R. P. Abelson, E. Aronson, W. J. McGuire, T. M. Newcomb, M. J. Rosenberg, & P. H. Tannenbaum (Eds.). *Theories of cognitive consistency: a sourcebook.* Chicago: Rand McNally, 1968, 28–34.

442*Ibid.*, 32–33.

443Aronson, E. Dissonance theory: progress and problems. In R. P. Abelson, E. Aronson, W. J. McGuire, T. M. Newcomb, M. J. Rosenberg, & P. H. Tannenbaum (Eds.). *Theories of cognitive consistency: a sourcebook.* Chicago: Rand McNally, 1968, 5–27.

444Brehm, J. W. & Cohen, A. R. *Explorations in cognitive dissonance.* New York: Wiley, 1962, 236–243.
Also Miller, N. E. Experimental studies of conflict. In J. McV. Hunt (Ed.). *Personality and the behavior disorders.* Vol. 1. New York: Ronald, 1944, 431–465.
Brown, J. S. Principles of intrapersonal conflict. *J. Conflict Resolution*, 1957, **1**, 135–154.
Berlyne, D. E. *Conflict, arousal, and curiosity.* New York: McGraw-Hill, 1960.
Festinger, L. *A theory of cognitive dissonance.* Evanston, Ill.: Row, Peterson, 1957.

445Festinger, L. *Op. cit.*, 50–54.

446Pope, A. Essay on criticism. In H. F. Lowry & W. Thorp (Eds.). *An Oxford anthology of English poetry.* New York: Oxford Univ. Press, 1937, 413, lines 9–10.

447McGuire, W. J. Resume and response from the consistency theory viewpoint. In R. P. Abelson, E. Aronson, W. J. McGuire, T. M. Newcomb, M. J. Rosenberg, & P. H. Tannenbaum (Eds.). *Theories of cognitive consistency: a sourcebook.* Chicago: Rand McNally, 1968, 292–297.

448Korchin, S. J. & Basowitz, H. Perceptual adequacy in a life stress. *J. Psychol.*, 1954, **38**, 495–502.

449Korchin, S. J. & Levine, S. Anxiety and verbal learning. *J. abnorm. soc. Psychol.*, 1957, **54**, 234–240.

450Ley, W. & the Editors of *Life. The poles.* New York: Time, Inc., 1962, 73–77.

451Brobeck, J. R. Neural control systems. In J. R. Brobeck (Ed.). *Best & Taylor's physiological basis of medical practice.* (9th ed.) Baltimore: Williams & Wilkins, 1973, 9-121–9-136.

452Jung, R. & Hassler, R. The extrapyramidal motor system. In J. Field (Ed.). *Handbook of physiology. Section I: Neurophysiology.* Vol. 2. Washington, D.C.: Amer. Physiol. Soc., 1960, 863–927.

453Bahrick, H. P. An analysis of stimulus variables influencing the proprioceptive control of movements. *Psychol. Rev.*, 1957, **64**, 324–328.

454Chase, R. A., Cullen, J. K., Jr., Openshaw, J. W., & Sullivan, S. A. Studies on sensory feedback: III. The effects of display gain on tracking performance. *Quart. J. exper. Psychol.*, 1965, **17**, 193–208.

455Young, L. R. & Stark, L. A discrete model for eye tracking movements. *I.E.E.E. Transactions on Military Electronics,* April–July, 1963, MIL-7(2 & 3), 113–115.

456Chase, R. A., Harvey, S., Standfast, S., Rapin, I., & Sutton, S. Studies on sensory feedback. I. Effect of delayed auditory feedback on speech and keytapping. *Quart. J. exper. Psychol.*, 1961, **13**, 141–152.

457Chase, R. A., Rapin, I., Gilden, L., Sutton, S., & Guilfoyle, G. Studies on sensory feedback. II. Sensory feedback influences on keytapping motor tasks. *Quart. J. exper. Psychol.*, 1961, **13**, 153–167.

458Bourne, L. E., Jr. Effects of delay of information feedback and task complexity on the identification of concepts. *J. exper. Psychol.*, 1957, **54**, 201–207.

459Bourne, L. E., Jr. & Pendleton, R. B. Concept identification as a function of completeness and probability of information feedback. *J. exper. Psychol.*, 1958, **56**, 413–420.

460Billodeau, E. A., Billodeau, I. McD., & Schumsky, D. A. Some effects of introducing and withdrawing knowledge of results early and late in practice. *J. exper. Psychol.*, 1959, **58**, 142–144.

461Romer, A. S. Major steps in vertebrate evolution. *Science,* 1967, **158**, 1629–1637.

462*Ibid.*, 1637.

463Washburn, S. L. & Harding, R. S. Evolution of primate behavior. In F. O. Schmitt (Ed.). *The neurosciences.* New York: Rockefeller Univ. Press, 1970, 39.

464Lorenz, K. Z. The comparative method in studying innate behavior patterns. In Symposia of the Society for Experimental Biology. Vol. 4. *Physiological mechanisms in animal behavior.* New York: Academic Press, 1950, 221–268.

465Zuckerkandl, E. The evolution of hemoglobin. *Sci. Amer.,* 1965, **212**(5), 110–118.

466Romer, A. S. *Op. cit.*, 1633–1634. Copyright 1967 by the American Association for the Advancement of Science. Reprinted by permission.

467Paillard, J. *Op. cit.*, 1679–1680.

468Hubel, D. H. & Wiesel, T. N. Receptive fields, binocular interaction and functional architecture in the cat's visual cortex. *J. Physiol.*, 1962, **160**, 106–154.

469Washburn, S. L. & Avis, V. Evolution of human behavior. In A. Roe & G. G. Simpson (Eds.). *Behavior and evolution.* New Haven: Yale Univ. Press, 1958, 421–436.

470Holloway, R. L., Jr. Cranial capacity, neural reorganization, and hominid evolution: a search for more suitable parameters. *Amer. Anthropol.*, 1966, **68**, 103–121.

471*Ibid.*, 109.

472*Ibid.*, 114–115. Reproduced by permission of The American Anthropological Association from *American Anthropologist,* **68**(1), 1966.

473Dobzhansky, T. Changing man. *Science,* 1967, **155**, 409–415.

474Darwin, C. *Expression of emotion in man and animals.* New York: Appleton, 1873.

475Watson, D. M. S. & Richards, A. Embryology. *Encyclopaedia Britannica.* Vol. 8. Chicago: Encyclopaedia Britannica, 1958, 388–399.
Cf. also Balinsky, B. I. Development, animal. *Encyclopaedia Britannica,* Vol. 5. Chicago: Encyclopaedia Britannica, 1974, 625–631.

476Butler, J. A. V. *Inside the living cell.* New York: Basic Books, 1959, 77.

477Rose, S. M. Feedback in the differentiation of cells. *Sci. Amer.*, 1963, **199**(6), 36–41.

478*Ibid.*, 38–39.

479Weiss, P. Neural development in biological perspective. In F. O. Schmitt (Ed.). *The neurosciences.* New York: Rockefeller Univ. Press, 1970, 59.

480Sperry, R. W. Developmental patterning of neural circuits. *Chicago Medical School Quart.*, 1951, **12**(2), 41.

[481]Weiss, P. A. Chairman's synthesis. In P. A. Weiss (Ed.). Specificity in the neurosciences. *Neurosci. Res. Prog. Bull.*, 1965, **3**(5), 5–35.

[482]Medawar, P. B. *Op. cit.*, 120.

[483]von Bertalanffy, L. Quantitative laws in metabolism and growth. *Quart. Rev. Biol.*, 1957, **32**, 217–231.

[484]Holt, L. E. & Howland, J., Jr. Revised by Holt, L. E., Jr. & McIntosh, R. *Diseases of infancy and childhood.* (11th ed.) New York: D. Appleton-Century, 1940, 9–10.

[485]Loevinger, J. Models and measures of developmental variation. *Ann. N.Y. Acad. Sci.*, 1966, **134**, 585–590.

[486]van Overbeek, J. The control of plant growth. *Sci. Amer.*, 1968, **219**(1), 77.

[487]Schneiderman, H. A. & Gilbert, L. I. Control of growth and development in insects. *Science*, 1964, **143**, 325.

[488]*Ibid.*, 326.

[489]*Ibid.*, 327.

[490]Weininger, O. The effects of early experience on behavior and growth characteristics. *J. comp. physiol. Psychol.*, 1956, **49**, 1–9.

[491]Rueyamer, W. R. & Bernstein, L. Growth, food utilization and thyroid activity in the albino rat as a function of extra handling. *Science*, 1954, **120**, 184–185.

[492]Fuller, J. L. Experiential deprivation and later behavior. *Science*, 1967, **158**, 1645–1652.

[493]Levine, S. & Mullins, R. F., Jr. Hormonal influences on brain organization in infant rats. *Science*, 1966, **152**, 1585–1592.

[494]Bovard, E. W. The effects of early handling on viability of the albino rat. *Psychol. Rev.*, 1958, **65**, 257–271.

[495]Sperry, R. W. Developmental basis of behavior. In A. Roe & G. G. Simpson (Eds.). *Behavior and evolution.* New Haven: Yale Univ. Press, 1958, 128–139.
Cf. also Neuringer A. & Neuringer, M. Learning by following a food source. *Science*, 1974, **184**, 1005–1008.

[496]Sackett, G. P. Monkeys reared in isolation with pictures as visual input: evidence for an innate releasing mechanism. *Science*, 1966, **154**, 1468–1473.

[497]Lenneberg, E. H. On explaining language. *Science*, 1969, **164**, 635. Copyright 1969 by the American Association for the Advancement of Science. Reprinted by permission.

[498]Piaget, J. *The language and thought of the child.* New York: Harcourt-Brace, 1926, 205.

[499]Burt, C. The genetic determination of differences in intelligence: a study of monozygotic twins reared together and apart. *Brit. J. Psychol.*, 1966, **57**, 137–153.

[500]Cattell, R. B., Stice, G. F., & Norton, F. K. A first approximation to nature–nurture ratios for eleven primary personality factors in objective tests. *J. abnorm. soc. Psychol.*, 1957, **54**, 143–159.

[501]Nichols, R. C. *The inheritance of general and specific ability.* Evanston, Ill.: National Merit Scholarship Corp. National Merit Scholarship Res. Rep. 1965, **1**, No. 1.

[502]Bayley, N. & Oden, M. H. The maintenance of intellectual ability in gifted adults. *J. Gerontol.*, 1955, **10**, Section B, 91–107.

[503]Bayley, N. On the growth of intelligence. *Amer. Psychol.*, 1955, **10**, 805–818.

[504]Freud, S. Introductory lectures on psycho-analysis. (Part III). In J. Strachey (Tr.). *The complete psychological works of Sigmund Freud*, Vol. 16. London: Hogarth Press, 1963, 27.

[505]Cattell, R. B., Stice, G. F., & Norton, F. K. *Op. cit.*

[506]Vandenberg, S. G. Hereditary factors in psychological variables in man, with a special emphasis on cognition. (Presented at *Wenner-Gren Symp. Behav. Consequences Genet. Differences Man.*) Burg Wartenstein, Austria, 1964.

Cf. also Cattell, R. B. Statistical methods and logical considerations in investigating inheritance. *Proc. Second Internat. Congr. Hum. Genet. (Rome, 1961)*, **3**, 1963, 1712–1717.

[507]Collins, H. H., Jr. *Complete field guide to American wildlife: East, Central and North.* New York: Harper & Row, 1959, 365.

[508]Galtsoff, P. S. Sponges. *Encyclopaedia Britannica.* Vol. 21. Chicago: Encyclopaedia Britannica, 1958, 253–260.

[509]Scrimshaw, N. S. Infant malnutrition and adult learning. *Sat. Rev.*, 16 March 1968, **51**, 64–66, 84.

[510]Beach, F. A. & Jaynes, J. Effects of early experience upon the behavior of animals. *Psychol. Bull.*, 1954, **51**, 239–263.

[511]Rosenzweig, M. R. & Leiman, A. L. Brain functions. *Ann. Rev. Psychol.*, 1968, **19**, 55–98.

[512]Witt, P. N., Reed, C. F., & Peakall, D. B. *A spider's web.* New York: Springer-Verlag, 1968, 55–73.

[513]Ritter, C. *A woman in the polar night.* New York: Century, 1900, 132–133.

[514]Muir, D. W. & Mitchell, D. E. Visual resolution and experience: acuity deficits in cats following early selective visual deprivation. *Science*, 1973, **180**, 420–422.

[515]Cross, H. A. & Harlow, H. F. Prolonged and progressive effects of partial isolation on the behavior of macaque monkeys. *J. exper. Res. Pers.*, 1965, **1**, 39–49.

[516]McCarthy, D. Language development in children. In L. Carmichael (Ed.). *Manual of child psychology.* (2d ed.) New York: Wiley, 1954, 492–630.

[517]Jersild, A. Emotional development. In L. Carmichael (Ed.). *Manual of child psychology.* (2d ed.) New York: Wiley, 1954, 833–917.

[518]McCarthy, D. *Op. cit.*, 586–587.

[519]Skeels, H. M. Adult status of children with contrasting early life experiences. *Monogr. Soc. Res. Child Develop.*, 1966, **31**, 1–65.

[520]Hubel, D. H. Effects of distortion of sensory input on the visual system of kittens. *The Physiologist*, 1967, **10**, 17–45.

[521]*Ibid.*, 43. Reprinted by permission.

[522]Grinker, R. R. & Sahs, A. L. *Op. cit.*, 291.

[523]McClearn, G. E. & Meredith, W. Behavioral genetics. *Ann. Rev. Psychol.*, 1966, **17**, 515–550.

[524]*Ibid.*, 518.

[525]*Ibid.*, 520.

[526]Bearn, A. G. Inborn errors of metabolism. Introduction: genetic principles. In P. B. Beeson & W. McDermott (Eds.). *Cecil-Loeb textbook of medicine.* (11th ed.) Philadelphia: W. B. Saunders, 1963, 1232–1277.

[527]Jacobs, P. A. Chromosome studies in the general population. In R. J. C. Harris (Ed.). *Cytogenetics of cells in culture.* New York: Academic Press, 1964, 111–121.

[528]Sergovich, F., Valentine, G. H., Chen, A. T. L., Kinch, R. A. H., & Smout, M. S. Chromosome aberrations in 2159 consecutive newborn babies. *New. Eng. J. Med.*, 1969, **280**, 851–855.

[529]Gutman, A. B. Galactosemia. In P. B. Beeson & W. McDermott (Eds.). *Cecil-Loeb textbook of medicine.* Philadelphia: W. B. Saunders, 1963, 1241–1242.

[530]Rimoin, D. L., Merimee, T. J., & McKusick, V. A. Growth-hormone deficiency in man: an isolated, recessively inherited defect. *Science*, 1966, **152**, 1635–1637.

[531]McClearn, G. E. & Meredith, W. *Op. cit.*, 528–529.

[532]Mandell, A. J. & Spooner, C. E. Psychochemical research studies in man. *Science*, 1968, **162**, 1448–1449.

[533]*Ibid.*

[534]Costa, E. & Brodie, B. B. The nature of sympathetic nerve endings. In M. Rinkel (Ed.). *Biological treatment of mental illness.* New York: Page, 1968, 262–277.

535Himwich, H. E. & Brune, G. G. Relationship between indole metabolism and schizophrenic behavior. In M. Rinkel (Ed.). *Biological treatment of mental illness.* New York: Page, 1968, 284–302.

536Gottlieb, J. S., Frohman, C. E., & Beckett, P. G. S. The characteristics of a serum factor in schizophrenia. In M. Rinkel (Ed.). *Biological treatment of mental illness.* New York: Page, 1968, 334–354.

537*Ibid.,* 334–354.

Also Ehrensvard, G. Some observations on serum constituents in relation to schizophrenia. In M. Rinkel (Ed.). *Biological treatment of mental illness.* New York: Page, 1968, 355–371.

Also Heath, R. G., Leach, B. E., Verster, F. DeB., & Byers, L. W. Serum fractions in schizophrenia. In M. Rinkel (Ed.). *Biological treatment of mental illness.* New York: Page, 1968, 372–389.

Also Bogoch, S. Nervous system glycoproteins in mental disorders. In M. Rinkel (Ed.). *Biological treatment of mental illness.* New York: Page, 1968, 406–423.

538Mandell, A. J. & Spooner, C. E. *Op. cit.,* 1450–1451.

539Gottlieb, J. S., Frohman, C. E., & Beckett, P. G. S. *Op. cit.,* 338–346.

540*Ibid.,* 347–349.

541Mirsky, A. F. Neuropsychological bases of schizophrenia. *Ann. Rev. Psychol.,* 1969, **20,** 321–348.

542Menninger, K. *Op. cit.,* 125–152.

543*Ibid.,* 153–270.

544Selye, H. *The stress of life. Op. cit.,* 128–209.

545*Ibid.,* 151–156.

546Sawrey, W. L. Conditioned responses of fear in relationship to ulceration. *J. comp. physiol. Psychol.,* 1961, **54,** 347–348.

547Mason, J. W., Mangan, G., Jr., Brady, J. V., Conrad, D., & Rioch, D. McK. Concurrent plasma epinephrine, norepinephrine and 17-hydroxycorticosteroid levels during conditioned emotional disturbances in monkeys. *Psychosom. Med.,* 1961, **23,** 344–353.

548Weiner, M. F. Private communication.

549Flavell, J. H., Draguns, J., Feinberg, L. D., & Budin, W. A microgenetic approach to word association. *J. abnorm. soc. Psychol.,* 1958, **57,** 1–7.

550Usdansky, G. & Chapman, L. J. Schizophrenic-like responses in normal subjects under time pressure. *J. abnorm. soc. Psychol.,* 1960, **60,** 143–146.

551Miller, J. G. Psychological aspects of communication overloads. *Internat. Psychiat. Clinics,* 1964, **1,** 201–223.

552Silverman, J. The problem of attention in research and theory in schizophrenia. *Psychol. Rev.,* 1964, **71,** 352–379.

553Yates, A. J. Psychological deficit. *Ann. Rev. Psychol.,* 1966, **17,** 111–144.

554*Ibid.,* 124–130.

555*Ibid.*

556*Ibid.,* 129.

557Hayflick, L. Human cells and aging. *Sci. Amer.,* 1968, **218**(3), 32–37.

558Butler, J. A. V. *Op. cit.,* 152.

559Comfort, A. The life span of animals. *Sci. Amer.,* 1961, **205**(2), 108–119.

560Butler, J. A. V. *Op. cit.,* 152.

561Medawar, P. B. *Op. cit.,* 62–70.

562Hayflick, L. *Op. cit.,* 32.

563Klopfer, W. G. Clinical patterns of aging. In B. B. Wolman (Ed.). *Handbook of clinical psychology.* New York: McGraw-Hill, 1965, 826–837.

564Hayflick, L. *Op. cit.,* 32.

565*Ibid.,* 37.

566Selye, H. *The stress of life. Op. cit.,* 66.

567Shock, N. W. The physiology of aging. *Sci. Amer.,* 1962, **206**(1), 100–110.

568*Ibid.*

569Grinker, R. R. & Sahs, A. L. *Op. cit.,* 1116.

570*Ibid.*

571*Ibid.*

572Shock, N. W. *Op. cit.,* 100.

573*Ibid.,* 101–102.

574Chown, S. & Heron, A. Psychological aspects of aging in man. *Ann. Rev. Psychol.,* 1965, **16,** 417–450.

575Owens, W. A. Age and mental abilities: a second adult follow-up. *J. educ. Psychol.,* 1966, **57,** 311–325.

576Glanzer, M., Glaser, R., & Richlin, M. *Development of a test battery for study of age-related changes in intellectual and perceptual abilities.* Air University, School of Aviation Medicine, USAF, Randolph AFB, Texas, March, 1958.

577Crook, M. N., Devoe, D. B., Hageman, K. C., Hanson, J. A., Krulee, G. K., & Ronio, P. G. *Age and the judgment of collision courses.* Air University, School of Aviation Medicine, USAF, Randolph AFB, Texas, September, 1957.

578Chown, S. & Heron, A. *Op. cit.,* 419–423.

579Klopfer, W. G. *Op. cit.,* 835–836.

580Ecclesiastes 12: 6–7.

581Bloch, C. *The golem.* Vienna, Austria: John N. Vernay, 1925.

582Rostand, J. *Can man be modified?* (Trans. J. Griffin.) New York: Basic Books, 1959, 55–56. © 1956 by Librairie Gallimard, © 1959 by Martin Secker and Warburg Ltd., Basic Books, Inc. Publishers. Reprinted by permission.

583Cf. Asimov, I. Reason, April, 1941; Liar, May, 1941; Runaround, March, 1942; Catch that rabbit, February, 1944; Paradoxical escape, August, 1945; Evidence, September, 1946; Little lost robot, March, 1947; Evitable conflict, June, 1950. In John W. Campbell (Ed.). *Astounding Science Fiction.* New York: Street & Smith.

584Walter, W. G. *The living brain.* New York: Norton, 1953, 125–135.

585Johnsen, E. G. & Corliss, W. R. *Teleoperators and human augmentation.* Washington, D.C.: NASA Report SP-5047, 1967, 4.

586*Ibid.,* 1–49.

587Corliss, W. R. & Johnsen, E. G. *Teleoperator controls.* Washington, D.C.: NASA Report SP-5070, 1968, 31.

588*Ibid.,* 31.

589*Ibid.,* 30.

590Barrows, H. S. Simulated patients in medical teaching. *Canad. Med. Assn. J.,* 1968, **98,** 674–676.

591Rochester, N., Holland, J., Haibt, L., & Duda, W. Test on a cell assembly theory of the action of the brain using a large digital computer. *I.R.A. Trans. Inform. Theory,* 1956, I.T.-2, 80–93.

592Feigenbaum, E. A. & Feldman, J. (Eds.). *Computers and thought.* New York: McGraw-Hill, 1963, 3.

593Kleene, S. C. Representation of events in nerve nets and finite automata. In C. E. Shannon & J. McCarthy (Eds.). *Automata studies.* Princeton: Princeton Univ. Press, 1956, 3–41.

594Armer, P. Attitudes toward intelligent machines. In E. A. Feigenbaum & J. Feldman (Eds.). *Computers and thought.* New York: McGraw-Hill, 1963, **3,** 389–405.

595MacKay, D. M. Mindlike behavior in artifacts. *Brit. J. Philos. Sci.,* 1951, **2,** 105–121. Reprinted by permission of Cambridge University Press, New York.

[596]McCulloch, W. S. & Pitts, W. H. A logical calculus of the ideas immanent in nervous activity. *Bull. math. Biophys.,* 1943, **5,** 115–133.

[597]Rapoport, A. Net theory as a tool in the study of gross properties of nervous systems. *Perspectives in Biol. and Med.,* 1965, **9,** 142–164.

[598]McCulloch, W. S., Arbib, M. A., & Cowan, J. D. Neurological models and integrative processes. In M. C. Yovits, G. T. Jacobi, and G. D. Goldstein (Eds.). *Self-organizing systems.* New York: Spartan Books, 1962, 49–59.

[599]Beurle, R. L. *Op. cit.,* 55–94.

[600]Farley, B. G. Some similarities between the behavior of a neural network model and electrophysiological experiments. In M. C. Yovits, G. T. Jacobi, & G. D. Goldstein (Eds.). *Self-organizing systems.* New York: Spartan Books, 1962, 535–550.

[601]Rapoport, A. *Mathematics of organization and the nervous system.* Preprint No. 18. Ann Arbor: Mental Health Research Inst., Univ. of Mich., 1958, 23.

[602]Wiener, N. *Cybernetics.* New York: Wiley, 1948, 1–56.

[603]Ashby, W. R. Adaptiveness and equilibrium. *J. ment. Sci.,* 1940, **86,** 478–483.

[604]Rosenblueth, A., Wiener, N., & Bigelow, J. Behavior, purpose and teleology. *Philos. Sci.,* 1943, **10,** 18–24.

[605]Cf. Wiener. *Op. cit.,* 19.

[606]*Ibid.*

[607]Ashby, W. R. *Design for a brain.* New York: Wiley, 1954, 47.

[608]*Ibid.,* 35.

[609]*Ibid.,* 190–199.

[610]*Ibid.,* 93–99.

[611]Deland, E. C. & Bradham, G. B. Fluid balance and electrolyte distribution in the human body. *Ann. N.Y. Acad. Sci.,* 1966, **128,** 795–809.

[612]Stark, L. Classical and statistical mathematical models for a neurological feedback system. In L. Stark & J. F. Dickson, III. (Eds.). *Mathematical concepts of central nervous system function. Neurosci. Res. Prog. Bull.,* 1965, **3**(2), 55–60.

[613]Stark, L. Stability, oscillations, and noise in the human pupil servomechanism. *Proc. I.R.E.,* 1959, **47,** 1925–1939.

[614]Sandberg, A. & Stark, L. Wiener G-function analysis as an approach to non-linear characteristics of human pupil light reflex. *Brain Res.,* 1968, **11,** 194–211.

[615]Selfridge, O. G. Pattern recognition and modern computers. *Proc. Western Joint Computer Conference.* Los Angeles, 1955, 91–93.

[616]Uhr, L. *Pattern recognition.* New York: Wiley, 1966, 291. Also Uhr, L. "Pattern recognition" computers as models for form perception. *Psychol. Bull.,* 1963, **60,** 40–73.

[617]Hartline, M. K., Ratliff, F., & Miller, W. H. Inhibitory interaction in the retina and its significance in vision. *Proc. internat. symp. "nervous inhibition."* New York: Pergamon, 1961, 241–284.

[618]Beddoes, M. P., Connor, D. J., & Melzak, Z. A. Simulation of a visual receptor network. *IEEE Trans. bio-med. Engin.,* 1965, BME-12(3,4), 136–138. Also Connor, D. J. *Lateral inhibition and the area operator in visual pattern processing.* Vancouver: Department of Electrical Engineering, Univ. of British Columbia, June, 1969. (Unpublished doctoral thesis.)

[619]Selfridge, O. G. & Neisser, U. Pattern recognition by machine. In E. A. Feigenbaum & J. Feldman (Eds.). *Computers and thought.* New York: McGraw-Hill, 1963, 237–268. Cf. also Uhr, L. & Vossler, C. A pattern-recognition program that generates, evaluates and adjusts its own operators. In E. A. Feigenbaum & J. Feldman (Eds.). *Computers and thought.* New York: McGraw-Hill, 1963, 251–252.

[620]Rosenblatt, F. A comparison of several perceptron models. In M. C. Yovits, G. T. Jacobi, & G. D. Goldstein (Eds.). *Self-organizing systems.* New York: Spartan Books, 1962, 463–484.

[621]*Ibid.,* 468–474.

[622]*Ibid.,* 476.

[623]*Ibid.,* 477.

[624]*Ibid.,* 482–483.

[625]Selfridge, O. G. Pandemonium: a paradigm for learning. In *Mechanisation of thought processes.* Vol. 1. *National Physical Laboratory Symposium No. 10.* London: Her Majesty's Stationery Office, 1959, 513–526.

[626]Uhr, L. & Vossler, C. *Op. cit.,* 251–268.

[627]*Ibid.,* 253–261.

[628]*Ibid.,* 267.

[629]Elder, H. A. On the feasibility of voice input to an on-line computer processing system. *Communications of the ACM,* 1970, **13,** 339–346.

[630]Simmons, R. F. *Answering English questions by computer: a survey.* Santa Monica, Calif.: System Development Corporation, SP-1556, 2 April 1964.

[631]*Ibid.,* 56.

[632]Rashevsky, N. *Mathematical biophysics.* (rev. ed.) Chicago: Univ. of Chicago Press, 1948, 430–433.

[633]McCulloch, W. S. & Pitts, W. H. *Op. cit.,* 124–129.

[634]Shimbel, A. Contributions to the mathematical biophysics of the central nervous system with special reference to learning. *Bull. math. Biophys.,* 1950, **12,** 241–275.

[635]Estes, W. K. The statistical approach to learning theory. In S. Koch (Ed.). *Psychology: a study of a science.* Vol. 2. New York: McGraw-Hill, 1959, 380–491.

[636]*Ibid.*

[637]Estes, W. K. Toward a statistical theory of learning. *Psychol. Rev.,* 1950, **57,** 94–107.

[638]Estes, W. K. & Burke, C. J. A theory of stimulus variability in learning. *Psychol. Rev.,* 1953, **60,** 276–286.

[639]Bush, R. R. & Mosteller, F. A mathematical model for simple learning. *Psychol. Rev.,* 1951, **58,** 313–323.

[640]Flood, M. M. Stochastic learning theory applied to choice experiments with rats, dogs, and men. *Behav. Sci.,* 1962, **7,** 289–314.

[641]Flood, M. M. Stochastic learning in rats with hypothalamic implants. *Ann. N.Y. Acad. Sci.,* 1961, **89,** 795–822.

[642]Marzocco, F. N. & Bartram, P. R. Statistical learning models for behavior of an artificial organism. In E. E. Bernard & M. R. Kare (Eds.). *Biological prototypes and synthetic systems.* Vol. 1. New York: Plenum, 1962, 88–96.

[643]Feigenbaum, E. A. The simulation of verbal learning behavior. In E. A. Feigenbaum & J. Feldman (Eds.). *Computers and thought.* New York: McGraw-Hill, 1963, 301. Reprinted by permission.

[644]Deutsch, J. A. A new type of behaviour theory. *Brit. J. Psychol.,* 1953, **44,** 304–317.

[645]Atkinson, R. C. & Shiffrin, R. M. *Mathematical models for memory and learning.* Tech. Rep. 79. Stanford: Inst. for Math. Studies in Soc. Sci., Stanford Univ., Sept. 20, 1965.

[646]*Ibid.,* 83.

[647]Atkinson, R. C., Brelsford, J. W., & Shiffrin, R. M. *Multi-process models for memory with applications to a continuous presentation task.* Tech. Rep. 96. Stanford: Inst. for Math. Studies in Soc. Sci., Stanford Univ., April 13, 1966.

[648]Feigenbaum, E. A. *Op. cit.,* 306. Cf. also Feigenbaum, E. A. & Simon, H. A. Elementary perceiver and memorizer: review of experiments. In A. C. Hoggatt & F. E. Balderston (Eds.). *Symposium on simulation models.* Chicago: Southwestern Publishing Co., 1963, 105.

[649]Feigenbaum, E. A. & Simon, H. A. *Op. cit.,* 105–110.

[650]Danziger, L. & Elmgreen, G. L. Mathematical theory of periodic relapsing catatonia. *Bull. math. Biophys.* 1954, **16,** 15–21.

[651]von Neumann, J. & Morgenstern, O. *Theory of games and economic behavior.* Princeton: Princeton Univ. Press, 1953, 8–16.

[652]*Ibid.,* 31.

[653]Rapoport, A. & Chammah, A. M. *Prisoner's dilemma.* Ann Arbor: Univ. of Michigan Press, 1965.

[654]Luce, R. D. *Op. cit.,* 5–7.

[655]Newell, A., Shaw, J. C., & Simon, H. A. Empirical explorations with the logic theory machine: a case study in heuristics. In E. A. Feigenbaum & J. Feldman (Eds.). *Computers and thought.* New York: McGraw-Hill, 1963, 109–133.

[656]Wang, H. Toward mechanical mathematics. *IBM J. Res. & Develop.,* 1960, **4,** 2–22.

[657]Newell, A., Shaw, J. C., & Simon, H. A. *Op. cit.,* 117–133.

[658]*Ibid.,* 129–130.

[659]Newell, A. & Simon, H. A. GPS, a program that simulates human thought. In E. A. Feigenbaum & J. Feldman (Eds.). *Computers and thought.* New York: McGraw-Hill, 1963, 279–293.

[660]Samuel, A. L. Some studies in machine learning using the game of checkers. In E. A. Feigenbaum & J. Feldman (Eds.). *Computers and thought.* New York: McGraw-Hill, 1963, 71–105.

[661]Cf. Zobrist, A. L. & Carlson, F. R., Jr. An advice-taking chess computer. *Sci. Amer.,* 1973, **228**(6), 93–105.

[662]Loehlin, J. C. A computer program that simulates personality. In S. S. Tomkins & S. Messick (Eds.). *Computer simulation of personality.* New York: Wiley, 1963, 189–211.

The Group

A group is a set of single organisms, commonly called *members*, which, over a period of time or multiple interrupted periods, relate to one another face-to-face, processing matter-energy and information. The components of groups are animals—human and subhuman. Monerans, protistans, fungi, and plants do not form groups. Often human groups have artifacts as inclusions. An experiment deals with groups rather than organisms if the outputs studied result from interactions among group members and are not simply outputs of individual organisms that are near one another in space-time.

Groups differ from organizations, the next higher level of living systems, in three ways: (*a*) The members, though ordinarily mobile, are usually near enough together to see and hear one another; (*b*) each one potentially can communicate directly with every other one over two-way channels, although some of these may not be open at all times; and (*c*) there are no echelons (see pages 29, 595, and 596), since by definition an organization is a system with echelons composed chiefly of groups (and perhaps some single individual organisms).

The group level includes natural groups—like families and friendship groups, work groups, clubs, committees, juries, and therapy or social-change groups—and artificial laboratory groups. Included also are groups of social insects. These are often called *societies*. In my conceptual system this terminology is inaccurate because the components of these groups are organisms, while the components of societies are chiefly organizations. This level also includes groups of higher animals, of which each type or species has

its own special characteristics. These differ so markedly from species to species that the English language is enriched with scores of collective nouns which are correctly used for only one type of animal—a herd of cattle, a pride of lions, a gaggle of geese, a skulk of foxes, a school of fish, a flock of sheep, a pack of wolves, a murder of crows, a litter of pups, a covey of partridges, a maculation of leopards, an exaltation of larks.[1]

Any of these groups may endure over time or be evanescent.

The view that a group is a concrete reality has weakened in recent years, according to Back.[2] Some general theories of social psychology and of group dynamics are neutral on the reality of groups. Certain social psychologists consider a group to be no more than a collection of individual organisms. I do not agree, but hold that groups are concrete entities, a distinct level of living systems.

The components of many types of human groups are not specialized. Their members are capable of carrying out any one of the critical group processes. Thus they frequently may transfer some process they have been carrying out to another component and undertake a new one. This is not so likely to occur in groups like families or work units, where age, sex, status, or special training determines allocations of processes among the components.

Often the number of a group's components is smaller than the number of critical subsystems on my list (see pages 52 to 54). For example, a dyad of hunters in the wilderness together must constitute the components of all the critical matter-energy and information processing subsystems if they are to survive as a two-person group. The fact that groups can have fewer components than they have subsystems is one reason for the prominence in group theory of the concept of "role," a term for the processes typically carried out by a subsystem or component (see page 30).

Responsibility for group processes is assigned to components on many bases, including those mentioned above. A special ability such as strength or keen eyesight may determine which member will be a warrior or a scout, a cook or a weaver. A person's sex usually decides what his or her relation to child rearing will be. The status of a group member in the suprasystem, his social or institutional prestige, his title, his position by birth, or other accepted criteria for group adjustment may determine his role or what subsystem processes he will carry out. These considerations are of special importance in groups which interact so briefly or superficially that the members cannot evaluate one another's abilities. In some groups the fact that many or all members are capable of carrying out all subsystem processes makes assignment of functions essential in order to prevent neglect or duplication of important processes, *e.g.*, everyone or no one cooking food, everyone talking at once, or no one keeping minutes to store information about a meeting.

When a committee convenes for a day and then disbands, it may be apparent which participants were components of the information processing subsystems—*e.g.*, of the input transducer, internal transducer, memory, decider, or output transducer. But who were the matter-energy processing subsystems? In our civilized politeness or effeteness we often neglect to mention or consider critical matter-energy processing functions which support life and which have become habitual second nature—providing clothes, heating rooms, preparing food or refreshments, maintaining washrooms. Anyone who has organized a conference, however, knows the importance of these matters. Many groups in modern life lack matter-energy transmission subsystems and hence are parasitic upon, or symbiotic with, other systems. These processes may be upwardly dispersed to the organization or society of which the group is a component or outwardly dispersed to other groups in its environment.

Though matter-energy processing is as essential to a group as it is to a system at any other level, the subsystems that do this have not been investigated so thoroughly as the group information processsing subsystems. This is partly because researchers have not been interested in them and partly because most labo-

ratory groups have not carried out all their life-support processes but have been parasitic upon, or symbiotic with, other systems for most of their matter-energy processing (see page 32). We therefore currently know much more about the information processing subsystems at this level.

Members of a group must interact over time to develop the full complement of systems characteristics of which the group is capable. In those groups in which a charter or tradition (which is an implicit charter) prescribes the formal structural characteristics and designates the person or persons who will be responsible for the various processes, the allocations of the processes to the structures that actually carry them out over the long range take time to occur. Ultimately, however, two groups with identical charters (such as two artillery batteries in the same regiment) may in fact have quite disparate allocation of processes to their component structures. The structure and interactions of a family or of a tourist group that has been traveling together for a month are clearly not the same as those of most experimental groups or of a committee that meets once a year. One set of research findings supports this view.[3] Even at the first meeting of a group, the free fatty acid content of the blood of its members (perhaps related to how responsive they are to threats) is significantly higher if they were previously friends than if they are strangers.

1. Structure

1.1   System size   Group psychologists and sociologists use the word "size" to mean the number of members in a group. I use the term in this chapter, as in all the others, to refer to spatial extent (see page 560), employing the phrase "number of members" when mentioning how many persons are in a group.

Perhaps the smallest group is a mating dyad of the smallest animal species (probably some member of the microscopic *Aschelminthes, Arthropoda, Ectoprocta,* or *Chordata*). The diameter of such a minute group is perhaps about 10^{-4} meter (m).

At the other extreme, the largest group may be a herd of blue whales (which individually grow to 34 m or more, or 3.4×10^1 m). Such a herd frolicking in the ocean would perhaps cover several miles (an area with a diameter of about 10^3 m). The largest human group might be astronauts in a space vehicle who, linked through space by radio, form a group with their ground communicator. (This would be so unless the communicator had command authority over the astronauts, under which circumstance the system would be an organization rather than a group because of its echelon structure.) If the distance from the moon to the earth separated members of such a group, its diameter would be of the order of 10^8 m, and if more distant space travel occurs in the future, it could be much larger.

As at the level of the organism, the median size of groups would necessarily be small because the median size of animals is so small. Also, there are more groups numbering only a few members than groups with many. No estimate of median group diameter exists, but possibly a diameter of the order of a few centimeters, or 10^{-1} m is about right. The median human group probably has a diameter of about 5 m, or 5×10^1 m.

1.2   Structural taxonomy of types of systems   Structural classifications exist for various types of groups, both those occurring naturally and those formed artificially for experimental purposes.

Because in almost all types of groups the subsystems are not identical with the components, the structure of subsystems may be difficult to determine (see page 31). To discover what group member or members form a given subsystem at a given time may require close study of the group.

Form of dwelling artifact is an important structural variable in subhuman and some human groups. The type of hive or nest constructed by social insects or birds or mammals is important since infrahuman groups are more dependent on environmental variables than human groups because they can do less to modify them. The dwelling can determine group processes. This is true also of human beings—an Eskimo family's igloo requires more restricted behavior than the dwelling of a Balinese family.

Number of members has been an important variable in laboratory research on groups. Dyads and three-person, four-person, and larger groups necessarily have different structures. Number of members also is significant in "natural" groups: the childless family, the "broken" family with children but only one parent, the one-child-and-two-parent family, and families with other numbers of adults and young. Each such group must assign functions in a particular way appropriate to its membership.

Number of members in critical subsystems is another structural variable which has received attention and becomes the basis for classifications. There may be one member in the decider—a captain, a boss, an autocrat, or a chairman. Other groups may have the decider dispersed so that all members are parts of that subsystem. Psychologists have differentiated "autocratic," "democratic," and "laissez-faire" groups according to the structures of their deciders, since their processes differ (see page 568).

Number of members in the channel and net subsystem, along with the *pattern* of open and closed channels

linking them, is a structural characteristic which has led to such classifications as "five-man star" (see pages 533 and 534 and Fig. 9-2). Other arrangements have also been named. Some apply to a variety of numbers of members, *e.g.,* "circle." Others apply only to certain specific numbers, *e.g.,* "slash," which can have only four members (see page 534 and Fig. 9-3). Communication flows in groups differ as these network patterns and numbers of members differ.

Another sort of classification by structure is used in anthropology. Critical processes in family groups are differently assigned when primary affiliation is to the maternal line (a *matrilineal* family) and when it is to the paternal line (a *patrilineal* family). In a matrilineal society the mother's brother, instead of the father, may be the decider. The distinction between immediate (or nuclear) and extended families (in which the married children and their offspring continue to interact intimately with their parents) is also a structural classification.[4]

2. Process

In most groups the relative position in space of the subsystems or components is subject to continual change over time. The similarity of groups to lower levels of living systems is somewhat masked by the fact that their components do not always maintain such close spatial contact as do components of those systems which are bounded by skins, exoskeletons, capsules, or membrances.

2.1   System and subsystem indicators   Few generally accepted indicators exist that measure group variables. This is because there is little agreement on what are group characteristics, as distinct from characteristics of the group's individual organism components. The few generally agreed-upon group variables, such as cohesiveness, lack accepted measures, and no normal limits or extreme ranges for them have been established. In many group researches certain variables have been measured and found to covary, but such studies have rarely been repeated often enough to give those measures general acceptance. In certain studies reported in this chapter the scientists have tried to develop precise indicators for particular variables and to relate them to other measures of group processes. *Centrality* is one such variable (see page 536). Cattell's concept of *syntality* is another (see page 543).

2.2   Process taxonomy of types of systems   Most groups, whether they exist primarily to process matter-energy or to process information, possess all the information transmission subsystems themselves and do not depend on other systems to carry out these processes for them. This is true in general even of those groups which are parasitic upon, or symbiotic

Fig. 9-1   Communications team of a modern ocean liner. Subsystem components of this group are identified.

Subsystem which processes both matter-energy and information: Boundary (Bo), wall of radio room (artifact).

Subsystems which process matter-energy: Ingestor (IN), stewardess who brings food into radio room from ship's galley; Distributor (DI), stewardess who hands out food to members of communications team; Converter (CO), stewardess who cuts bread, meat, and cheese for sandwiches; Producer (PR), stewardess who makes sandwiches and coffee; Matter-Energy Storage (MS), stewardess who stores various sorts of artifacts, including food in refrigerator, coats and hats of team members in closet, blankets and pillows in closet, and tools and equipment in chest of drawers; Extruder (EX), stewardess who removes used dishes, wastepaper, and other wastes from radio room; Supporter (SU), floor, walls, ceiling, furniture of radio room (artifacts).

Subsystems which process information: Input Transducer (it), radio operator who receives radio messages; Internal Transducer (in), day-shift foreman who reports to chief signal officer on efficiency and morale of team members on his shift; Channel and Net (cn), all members of group who intercommunicate by speech which travels through the air of the radio room; Decoder (dc), radio operator who transcribes into English messages received in Morse code; Memory (me), secretary who keeps records of all messages received and transmitted; Decider (de), chief signal officer, who commands communications team; Encoder (en), radio operator who encodes English messages into Morse code; Output Transducer (ot), radio operator who transmits radio messages.

with, other systems for matter-energy processing. An isolated mountain family cannot depend to any degree upon a suprasystem organization such as a town or city. It must carry out more critical subsystem processes than, say, a Girl Scout troop in Chicago. Hypothesis 2-3 (see page 92) applies here. It states that the more isolated a system is, the more totipotential it must be. Modern human family groups are rarely totipotential, but a high degree of independence can occur even in the twentieth century, especially in primitive societies and isolated regions. This is dramatically true of astronaut groups in space satellites and aquanaut groups at the bottom of the sea. An important taxonomic distinction based on process, therefore, is the one between groups which carry out their own life-support matter-energy processes and those which are dependent upon other systems for them.

Groups are frequently classified according to the processes they carry out in their suprasystems. A few of these designations are work group, play group, psychotherapy group, experimental group, club, team, family, and committee. Groups studied in experiments may be classified as "task-oriented" if they are instructed to cooperate on a mission.[5] Otherwise, they are "nontask-oriented" groups interacting socially or to entertain themselves.

3. Subsystems

In groups of social insects, higher animals, and human beings, division of labor allocates the different subsystem processes to various individuals or subgroups. The subsystems of groups are described below. Examples considered are all human groups unless otherwise indicated. Figure 9-1 pictures a human group, showing its subsystems. In this particular case the group is the communications team of a modern ocean liner, which carries out various information processing activities of the liner. Figure 8-1 pictured the central woman in this group and her subsystems, without her clothing artifacts. Table 9-1 identifies the components which make up the critical subsystems of a group.

3.1   Subsystems which process both matter-energy and information

3.1.1   Reproducer, the subsystem which is capable of giving rise to other groups similar to the one it is in.

3.1.1.1   Structure   The new organisms required to continue groups and higher-level social systems over longer times than the lifetime of one generation result from the reproduction of organisms. The unit for this reproduction in most species is a group—a male and female mating dyad, such as a husband and wife or a queen bee and a male of the reproductive caste. At the group level the reproducer also includes

persons or subgroups that produce an implicit or explicit charter, a template for a new group.

3.1.1.2   Process   The reproductive behavior of animal species may be categorized into four classes in terms of how sociable an interbreeding, genetically related group is.[6] First, there are the extremely nonsocial animals which meet only to fight or to mate. Second, there are the species in which the parents remain together with the offspring, for a brief or long period. Third, there are the species in which aggregations of the same sex stay together throughout the year, meeting the opposite sex only for mating. And fourth, there are the gregarious or social species in which individuals of both sexes and all ages remain together in groups of various sizes throughout the year. Each species has its own characteristic variant of these general patterns.

Groups or colonies of the social insects, which fall in the fourth class, have been called *supraorganisms* by some scholars who have studied them.[7] Such insects reproduce their colonies when the population of the founding colony reaches a certain number. A new queen is developed from an organism of the reproductive caste of the insects. She then leaves the founding colony, taking with her some of its members. A queen of such a species is analogous to a sex cell of an organism, according to Emerson. He says:

> The reproductive castes function for the maintenance of the species and for the founding of new colonies. In becoming specialized for reproduction, enlargement of the gonads in the queens is accompanied by specialized sexual behavior and regression of feeding and protective adaptations. The reproductive castes may thus be analogized with the gametes of the organism, which have also become specialized for maintenance of the species and do not develop the functions of the somatic cells.[8]

Human groups do not reproduce in the sense that organisms do. New groups arise as a result of processes within the organizations which are their suprasystems. Individual organisms within the suprasystem of some organizations or within the suprasuprasystem of the society may voluntarily band together in social clubs or task-oriented groups, allocating critical processes among the components on their own initiative. Or the organization of which they are subcomponents may assign them to groups, as when a company sets up a new section or when a denomination establishes a church. These new groups do not create new members, however. These either move in from other locations or are generated by the sexual interactions of organisms, usually as mating dyads, commonly in families.

Different types or species of sexual plants or animals have evolved various means of assuring the formation

TABLE 9-1   Components of the 19 Critical Subsystems of a Group

3.1 SUBSYSTEMS WHICH PROCESS BOTH MATTER-ENERGY AND INFORMATION

3.1.1 *Reproducer*

Mating dyad, male and female; persons or groups that produce an implicit or explicit charter for a new group

3.1.2 *Boundary*

Such subgroups or individuals as soldier insect, membership chairman or committee, sergeant-at-arms, teacher, group therapy leader, corresponding secretary; may be laterally dispersed to some or all group members; or upwardly dispersed to suprasystem organization such as the police or fire departments of a city that protect a family in that city or the court officials who guard a jury; artifacts such as a room, building, fence, wall

3.2 SUBSYSTEMS WHICH PROCESS MATTER-ENERGY

3.2.1 *Ingestor*

Such subgroups or individual persons as refreshment chairman or committee, gatherer of firewood, person who brings supplies to a group, person who acquires and brings food to a group; may be laterally dispersed to some or all group members; or upwardly dispersed to suprasystem organizations such as a corporation which operates a cafeteria

3.2.2 *Distributor*

Such subgroups or individuals as worker insect, mother who passes out food to family, man who passes out tools to work group, nurse who feeds patients, monitor who issues pencils and examination books; may be laterally dispersed to some or all group members, like workers on an assembly line; or upwardly dispersed to a higher-level system such as a company delivery service or the national mails; artifacts such as delivery truck

3.2.3 *Converter*

Such subgroups or individuals as worker insect, chopper of wood, grinder of corn, butcher; may be laterally dispersed to some or all members of group; or upwardly dispersed to a higher level; artifacts such as hand tools and manufacturing machinery

3.2.4 *Producer*

Such subgroups or individuals as worker insect, cook, tailor; maker, repairer, or maintainer of furniture, shelters, tools, machines, books, toys, games, objects of art; may be laterally dispersed to some or all members of group; or upwardly dispersed to a higher level

3.2.5 *Matter-energy storage*

Such subgroups or individuals as honey ant replete, stock clerk, spare-parts man, family member who stores food or other useful energy or material; may be laterally dispersed to some or all members of group; or upwardly dispersed to a higher level like a factory or city that stores matter-energy for its component work groups or families

3.3 SUBSYSTEMS WHICH PROCESS INFORMATION

3.3.1 *Input transducer*

Such subgroups or individual persons as lookout, scout, group member who changes written words to spoken words; may be dispersed upwardly to an informant from a higher-level system; laterally to some or all group members who report to group; or downwardly if each group member transduces input for himself; artifacts such as television receiver

3.3.2 *Internal transducer*

A subgroup or individual person who receives from others in the group and conveys to the group decider information about the group tasks, about group interactions, or about internal states of group members as they interact, including their feelings about group processes

3.3.3 *Channel and net*

Each group member who communicates to one or more other group members; may be upwardly dispersed to a higher level; artifacts such as paper with written or printed messages, telephone, telegraph, walkie-talkie

3.3.4 *Decoder*

Such subgroups or individual persons as guide, interpreter, radar man, radio man, adult responsible for children, scientific or technical expert, companion of blind persons; may be laterally dispersed to some or all members of group; or upwardly dispersed to a higher level

3.3.5 *Associator*

Laterally dispersed to some or all members of the group who associate bits of information or skills for use by the group; artifacts such as computer may be able to do some associating for group

3.3.6 *Memory*

Elderly animals in herds; such subgroups or individual persons as parents or grandparents in families, secretaries or treasurers of committees; may be laterally dispersed to some or all members of groups or upwardly dispersed to components of higher-level systems like county or church offices that keep records; banks; artifacts such as notes, written minutes, photograph, financial record, book, tape recording, filing system, computer, money

3.3.7 *Decider*

Such subgroups or individual persons as father, mother's brother, oldest male in family, mother, foreman, president, chairman, selected specialists or other members, depending on type of decision to be made; leader; whichever group member has a certain position in the group communication net; may be laterally dispersed to all group members

3.3.8 *Encoder*
Such subgroups or individual persons as compose a letter, speech, or statement presenting the common views of the group, or translate a group statement into some foreign language; may be laterally dispersed to all group members

3.2.6 *Extruder*
Such subgroups or individual persons as cleaning woman, soldier policing up his barracks, janitor, "bouncer"; may be laterally dispersed to some or all members of group; or upwardly dispersed to higher-level systems; artifacts such as wastebasket, garbage disposal

3.3.9 *Output transducer*
Such subgroups or individual persons as write a letter or make a report or statement for a group; typist; printer; spokesman; publicity agent; official; chairman; department head; bookkeeper; union steward; inspector; operations analyst; artifacts such as telephone, telegraph, radio, television

3.2.7 *Motor*
None known at this level except artifacts such as bus, truck, plane, boat; may be laterally dispersed to some or all members of group who plan or carry out move jointly; or upwardly dispersed to transportation operated by higher-level systems; artifacts such as bus, truck, or plane

3.2.8 *Supporter*
One or more persons supporting others in group; artifacts such as nest, cave, building, room, car, train, plane, furniture

---

of mating dyads and securing the necessary amount of protection for the young. Ordinarily, the reproductive processes allocated to the male component are different from those allocated to the female component. Plant parents never unite directly; rather, the wind, gravity, insects or other animals, or human hands are their agents. Hermaphroditic worms have both sexes in one animal; the male genitalia of one mate with the female organs of the other, while the male genitalia of the second are returning the compliment to the female organs of the first. Parthenogenetic female potato lice, which may not mate for generations since they convey stored sperm from mother to daughter, are in this sense dyads—rather lonely dyads. Fish parents may never meet. Female deer herd together, and males stay apart until rutting time, when one male asserts his rights over a harem of females. Some birds form lifetime monogamous pairs.

In the human species it is usual for a male from one family and a female from another to unite to form a new group. This group may separate entirely from the two parental families—the usual pattern in Western cultures—or may remain with one of them. Variants of this structure include polygamy and the raising of children by others than their parents, but some sort of group structure is enforced by the reproductive requirements of human beings everywhere, particularly because the infant is altricial, that is, obliged to be parasitic upon adults.

In order to mate, animal organisms must respond to signals which enable them to find and recognize other organisms of the opposite sex of their own type or species who are ready to mate (see page 439). Animals which normally live in social aggregates have little difficulty locating mates, but they require signs to distinguish the sex and state of readiness of other animals. Two little insects in a large forest have a major tracking problem locating each other. If they are to get together, powerful signals must be emitted by one or both. Then goal-seeking behavior occurs, using negative feedback. The almost unbelievably low threshold of males of many types of insects to odors of females increases the probability that mating will occur.

Courtship rituals, mating plumage, special calls, and odors not only attract the animals to each other but also act as "releasers" for mating behavior and "suppressors" for other sorts of behavior, such as food-gathering and aggression (see page 366). Among spiders this suppression is so brief that the male is often eaten immediately after copulation, before he can get away. Among cats, aggressive behavior is so integral to mating that onlookers cannot always tell whether they are witnessing a tender scene or a battle.

The participation of the two sexes in care of the young varies widely even among closely related species. With all their skill at construction, for instance, male bower birds do not help in nest building. They terminate their reproductive activity when they have built the ornamental bowers they construct during courtship and have exercised enough skill to be permitted to fertilize the female. In human beings the parents often—but not always—stay together longer, nourishing, training, and acculturating their offspring jointly.

Another sort of reproduction of groups occurs when individual organisms already in existence band together to form a new group—as the bride and groom do at a wedding or as neighbors do when they form a country club. They create an explicit or implicit charter, almost always copied from similar charters of groups formed earlier—a template which specifies the structure of the system, who shall be the various subsystems, what their subsystem processes or roles shall be, and how they shall carry out these processes.

Representative *variables* of the process of reproducing are: *Sorts of matter-energy used in reproducing.* Example: When there was only one bull in a large herd of cattle, he would mate with only the younger cows. *Meaning of information used in reproducing.* Example: The social club's charter specified its structure and general principles of functioning, which could be altered by majority vote. *Sorts of information used in reproducing.* Example: The bylaws committee of the new Boy Scout troop visited several of the established troops in the city and finally selected the bylaws of Troop 16 as a model. *Changes in reproducing over time.* Example: As the temple's congregation grew older, it began to form new temples in the suburbs. *Changes in reproducing with different circumstances.* Example: After their freshman year the class formed fewer new friendship groups. *Rate of reproducing.* Example: Between 10 and 40 new troops of Girl Scouts were organized in the state each year. *Frequency of reproducing.* Example: The state Republican organization chartered new local groups only once a year except in years of national elections. *Lag in reproducing.* Example: The Town Council established the Police Review Board the week after the election, but the Fair Housing Commission was not set up until 3 weeks later. *Costs of reproducing.* Example: The Greek father gave a third of his property as a dowry for his only daughter.

3.1.2 Boundary, the subsystem at the perimeter of a group that holds together the components which make up the group, protects them from environmental stresses, and excludes or permits entry to various sorts of matter-energy and information.

3.1.2.1 Structure   The problems of locating the boundaries of living systems at the levels of the group, organization, society, and supranational system have been discussed previously (see pages 52, 56, and 57). Such boundaries often have very complex shapes in the four dimensions of space-time, their channel and net and other subsystems often sharing space with other groups. Boundaries at the level of the group and above have special structural characteristics which derive from the physical separateness and independent

mobility of their component organisms (see pages 609, 610, 770, 771, and 913). Ordinarily lacking physical continuity, the living boundary subsystem is composed of individual organisms or subgroups. The territory occupied by groups may change rapidly in both size and shape. The living boundary subsystems at the level of the group and above are frequently supplemented by artifacts such as rooms, buildings, fences, walls, or other structures. In certain groups, like extended families whose members live in different parts of the same city or even in different cities, some components may be physically far removed from others. Consequently, their territory is discontinuous.

As in other living systems, the areas of the group boundary permeable to matter-energy may differ from those permeable to information.

Matter-energy boundary.   An individual organism or subgroup—such as the soldiers of social insects that defend the nest, adult males of higher animals that protect the herd, a membership chairman or committee, or a guard or sergeant at arms—may constitute this subsystem. The soldiers of the social insects, as Emerson describes them, are particularly interesting examples of a subsystem differentiated for the role of maintaining and guarding their group's matter-energy boundary:

Soldiers are primarily the protective caste. The soldier is the primitive sterile caste among the termites, may be either a male or female, and in the final ontogenetic state functions wholly for the protection of the colony against predaceous enemies. Soldiers are absent from the bee and wasp societies, in which the worker defends the colony in addition to its other functions. Among the ants, the soldier is always a sterile female, and shows many intergradations of structure and behavior with the worker caste. The army ant *(Eciton)* "soldier" is the largest form of a polymorphic series of workers. It captures and transports the prey, as well as defends the colony with its sting and large mandibles. The smaller army ant workers also defend the colony with their stings and smaller mandibles. In the leaf-cutting ants *(Atta),* the soldiers (also the largest form of a polymorphic series) remain in the ground nests unless disturbed; they then emerge in great numbers for the defense of the colony. Their function seems to be wholly protective. In some ants with a sharp morphological difference between the soldier and worker (i.e., *Pheidole),* experimental colonies composed of reproductives, larvae, and soldiers, without workers, are maintained in a healthy state by the soldiers.[9]

Sometimes the matter-energy boundary is laterally dispersed to all members of a group, as when an infantry squad spreads out to protect the perimeter of the territory it is holding. Under some circumstances it is upwardly dispersed to an organization. This is true in cities where the police and fire departments protect the territories of families, *i.e.,* their homes and property.

Information boundary.   A single organism (such as a teacher, a group-therapy leader, or a corresponding secretary) or a subgroup (such as a committee) may filter and otherwise regulate information flow to and from a group and so constitute this subsystem. This boundary, like the one for matter-energy, may be laterally dispersed to all group members. The information boundaries of some sorts of groups—juries are an example—are, at least in part, upwardly dispersed to the organization that is their suprasystem. A trial court is an organization including judge, jury, bailiff, other court officers, lawyers, witnesses, and others, since it has two echelons—the judge being able to overrule the jury, and the jury at times meeting as a group not face-to-face with the others in the court. This organization follows established procedures in regulating the inputs of information to its group component, the jury.

3.1.2.2 Process   At the levels of the group and above, the periphery of the system's territory ordinarily is the outer limit of the region of most intensive exchange of both matter-energy and information within the system, as well as being the region through which both matter-energy and information may possibly flow less easily and in less quantity than on either side, as is suggested by Hypotheses 3.1.2.2-1, 3.1.2.2-2, and 3.1.2.2-3 (see page 93). Groups are not always assembled, and yet by my definition they remain groups (see page 515). Even when they are assembled, not all members are always present. Not every cousin gets to every family reunion. Among groups which are spatially scattered or those in which some members are acting as joint subsystems or components of other groups and are not physically present, special boundary processes are necessary to ensure that they remain members of the group.

Matter-energy boundary.   In order for the boundary to filter out matter-energy in the form of nonmembers or intruders, a guard or guards may be posted at the entrance to, or around the periphery of, the group's territory. A remarkable example of this in an insect society is described by Emerson:

The soldiers of the ant genera *Colobopsis* and *Cryptocerus* have phragmatic heads that have convergently evolved as plugs for the entrance holes of the nests. Each colony of *Cryptocerus* occupying an enlarged hollow twig contains only one or two soldiers, whose only function seems to be that of being "doorman" for the colony, preventing the entrance of predators and trespassers, and allowing the workers easy entrance and exit. The soldiers of certain genera of termites . . . have evolved phragmatic heads . . . that plug the internal burrows and thus protect the colony from invasion. The mandibles of these soldiers are somewhat reduced, compared with those of their relatives whose soldiers have no phragmatic adaptation.[10]

Much like the Dutch boy who saved his town by placing his thumb in the dike, these insects protect their colonies with their heads.

Some sorts of groups are able to enforce a certain degree of boundary protection even around members who are not within the same area. As the Cosa Nostra well knows, a sufficiently menacing attitude on the part of members of a gang can ensure that no one will attack or inconvenience any member wherever the gang is known and respected or feared.

Matter-energy in the form of new members is admitted across boundaries in a variety of ways by different sorts of groups. New members of families enter by birth, adoption, or marriage. New members of clubs enter by election of membership committees. Orders from the suprasystem assign new members to military squads.

Social groups' boundaries differ in their permeability to new members. It takes years to be admitted to some London clubs even if you are of the "right sort." On the other hand, anyone with the necessary pounds sterling can immediately become a member of the "private clubs" which are London's peculiar form of bistro.

Information boundary.   Transmissions of information among members of spatially separated groups maintain them as systems. Consequently, information exchanges often must depend upon transmission of markers over channels and nets in the suprasystem, such as runners conveying oral messages or communications accomplished by artifacts like pen and parchment, telephones, or closed-circuit television. Protecting these channels is a boundary process of the group which uses them. Decisions controlling these channels and nets are often made not by the group but by its suprasystem. This may lead to conflict of the group with other groups in the suprasystem or with the suprasystem itself. Components separated from the others usually exchange matter-energy and information with the group or suprasystem in which they are currently located, but they remain coordinated with other groups by information transmissions (or memory, stored information) and often join the other members when an appointed time arrives. In this way organisms can simultaneously be members of many groups.

Money and its equivalents are forms of information which flow into and out of some sorts of groups, *e.g.,* families.

The living boundary subsystems maintain the integrity of the group's information boundary (*e.g.,* telephone installers or switchboard operators). Technicians who are members of the group or who are supplied by a suprasystem organization (an upwardly dispersed process) may keep the channels of higher-level systems operating across the boundary.

Groups which are assembled regulate inputs and outputs of information at their boundaries in various ways. The borders of the territory may be closed by shutting doors so that information from outside cannot enter and so that information from inside cannot escape. Censorship can be exercised on some sorts of groups, like mental patients or prisoners, by limiting their mail privileges and restricting their reading materials. An executive committee laterally disperses to all its members the keeping of its proceedings secret after the meeting is over. This boundary process often is poorly accomplished because one or more members "leak" the secrets. Information flows are restricted in both directions across the boundaries of juries by processes dispersed laterally among the members and upwardly to the court.

Methods have been worked out to determine objectively which components of crowds or organizations belong within the boundary of a given group. Information, at least of certain sorts, flows more easily and in larger amounts outside and inside a group than it does across its boundary, as Hypotheses 3.1.2.2-2 and 3.1.2.2-3 suggest (see page 93).[11] Group and clique or subgroup members communicate more with one another than with persons outside the group.[12]

Representative *variables* of boundary process include: *Sorts of matter-energy crossing the boundary.* Example: During the winter, the family received regular deliveries of oil. *Meaning of information crossing the boundary.* Example: The Forsyte family talked freely with their associates, but out of a sense of loyalty they never discussed family matters publicly. *Sorts of information crossing the boundary.* Example: The Jones family got the bad news by telegram. *Degree of permeability of the boundary to matter-energy.* Example: After the storm the Smiths' roof leaked. *Degree of permeability of the boundary to information.* Example: The conditions of the experiment required that the chairman prevent the group from receiving more than 3 bits of new information per minute (min). *Percentage of matter-energy arriving at the boundary which enters the system.* Example: Only eight of the ten trampolines delivered were accepted by the gymnastic team as undamaged. The rest were sent back. *Percentage of information arriving at the boundary which enters the system.* Example: Ten percent of the new books were found to be unsuitable for the first-grade group. The teacher would not accept these for the bookshelves. *Changes in matter-energy processing at the boundary over time.* Example: As the children grew older, the family no longer kept the neighborhood children out of the yard. *Changes in information processing at the boundary over time.* Example: The committee decided to receive no telephone calls during meetings and so instructed the secretary. *Changes in matter-energy processing at the boundary with different circumstances.* Example: While the children had measles, no visitors were allowed in

the house. *Changes in information processing at the boundary with different circumstances.* Example: After their country had won an important battle, the group of prisoners of war was not allowed to receive mail. *Rate of matter-energy processing at the boundary.* Example: The rummage-sale committee could sort and decide upon about three boxes of used clothing an hour. *Rate of information processing at the boundary.* Example: Each year the membership chairman passed upon about 20 written applications for club membership. *Frequency of matter-energy processing at the boundary.* Example: Candidates for membership in the fraternity were invited to a rushing party once a year. Most of them were found unacceptable. *Frequency of information processing at the boundary.* Example: The secretary checked the mail weekly to decide what should be presented to the members of the club. *Lag in matter-energy processing at the boundary.* Example: The work group was so busy that it did not log in the new tools for more than a month. *Lag in information processing at the boundary.* Example: The seminar group argued for an hour before deciding not to allow a guest speaker to discuss a political subject. *Costs of matter-energy processing at the boundary.* Example: An ordnance expert was added to the underground sabotage team to inspect and decide upon the suitability of captured explosives for their work. He was paid at the union hourly rate. *Costs of information processing at the boundary.* Example: The Boy Scouts in the Beaver Patrol spent the first hour of their time choosing which of a list of scientific displays to construct. That left them only a half hour to build it, and so the Wolf Patrol won the prize because it produced a better display.

3.2   Subsystems which process matter-energy

3.2.1   Ingestor, the subsystem which brings matter-energy across the group boundary from the environment.

3.2.1.1   Structure   This subsystem may be trivial or lacking in some sorts of groups, mainly those which are together for short periods or which do not carry out their own life-support matter-energy processes. This is true of some experimental and social groups. A single member of a group may compose this subsystem, or it may also be laterally dispersed to more, even to the entire group. The subsystem may also be upwardly dispersed to the organization that is the suprasystem, as when a corporation operates a cafeteria for all its employees in the offices of its central headquarters building. A refreshment chairman or refreshment committee; a gatherer of firewood; a work-group member in charge of supplies, such as raw materials or paper and pencils; women and children gathering fruits or harvesting potatoes; men planting corn or hunting deer; a housewife bringing home a station wagon full of groceries; or combinations of these are components of the ingestor in one sort of group or another. A recruiter who brings new members to a club or new employees to a store is also part of the ingestor.

3.2.1.2 Process Honey ant workers gather honeydew, an extrusion of sap-sucking aphids, and transport it in their crops back to the nest. Honeybees fly out and bring back pollen. *Polyergus* ants make slaves of *Formica* ants, who build nests and feed them. Deprived of their slaves, on whom they are parasitic, *Polyergus* worker ants will starve even in the presence of abundant food.[13] Clearly, the social insects assign ingesting to specialists.

Chimpanzees often hunt and capture their prey in coordinated groups.[14] They operate as an integrated unit until the kill and then share the food they have ingested.

The rate of ingestion and the quantities of matter-energy ingested by human groups differ not only with current needs for the items ingested but in some cases with projected future needs. More fruits and vegetables are ingested by a farm family during the summer, when they are available cheaply from the fields, than in the winter, when they must be bought at stores. Excess is processed and stored (see pages 527 and 528).

The percentage of its time that a group assigns to ingesting is also variable. A primitive family spends most of its time providing for its matter-energy requirements. It must go out into the fields and forests to harvest or gather much of the input. A modern urban family spends a great deal less time on the process. A new Boy Scout troop may in the first months of its existence devote more than half of its total effort to recruiting. Several people brought together to constitute an experimental group usually lack the subsystem and spend no time at all on the ingesting process.

Matter-energy is ingested into groups at the cost of expenditure of energy. Totipotential groups of all sorts, and work groups which gather materials for their processes, pay for it with the sweat of their brows, with energy provided by their artifacts, or with a combination of both. Modern urban families expend money instead of their own energy for much of the ingesting process, themselves having perhaps only to bring delivered materials in from the back porch, carry bundles home from a store, or go to a restaurant.

Representative *variables* of the process of ingesting include: *Sorts of matter-energy ingested.* Example: Sometimes mother bought meat, and other times fish, for the family dinner. *Degree of openness of the inges-*

tor. Example: The ladies' social group had not admitted a new member since 1973. *Changes in ingesting over time.* Example: As the members grew older, it was decided to buy only low-calorie drinks for the refreshment period. *Changes in ingesting with different circumstances.* Example: The family bought a new furnace, and after that they bought coal instead of wood for fuel. *Rate of ingesting.* Example: The Indian family gathered about a bushel of corn a day. *Frequency of ingesting.* Example: The boat went back to port once every month to take on supplies and fuel. *Lag in ingesting.* Example: Everyone was nearly starved by the time the pizza was delivered. *Costs of ingesting.* Example: Most of the farm family's energy and time went into securing food.

3.2.2 Distributor, the subsystem which carries inputs from outside the group or outputs from its subsystems around the group to each component.

3.2.2.1 Structure Specific members or subgroups are components of the distributor in some groups of lower animals. The worker caste among social insects, for example, belongs to this as well as to other matter-energy processing subsystems such as the converter, the producer, matter-energy storage, and the extruder. In most human families the mother passes out food to the children. In other human groups, the distributor subsystem is laterally dispersed to all members. Routes of flow may be prescribed, as in work groups, or they may be informal and variable, as in social groups. The member of the family who serves the plates or waits on the table, the man who hands out tools or materials to a work group, the nurse who feeds patients on a ward, and the monitor who issues pencils and examination books are all distributor components. In some work groups materials are passed in an orderly fashion to each separate member in turn. This is true whenever assembly-line methods are used. In such a group all members are distributor components. In groups in which each member helps himself to materials, the subsystem is laterally dispersed to more than one organism.

Matter-energy flows among group members who are widely separated in space or interacting in other systems may be distributed by a group member or may flow through the distribution subsystem of the organization that is the suprasystem or the society that is the suprasuprasystem (*e.g.*, a company delivery service, an express company, or the national mails), under which circumstances the subsystem is upwardly dispersed. Artifacts may be used, such as a delivery truck, express van, or railroad mail car.

3.2.2.2 Process Among the social insects, members of the worker caste distribute food to adults of the other castes and to the young, or they may eat the food and supply nutritive secretions and excretions instead of food. Emerson describes the workers' behavior in distributing, converting, producing, and storing food for their group:

In the more primitive social Hymenoptera (wasps, bees, and ponerine ants), the worker caste is the only sterile caste and is always female. In the termites, the worker is found only among the more specialized families and may be either a sterile male or female. Among the primitive termites, nymphs of the other castes perform the functions of the workers, which are primarily nutritive and collect food from the habitat (trophoporic field). In a few instances the worker termites and ants cultivate gardens of fungi or, among certain ants, tend animals such as aphids or coccids that may be guarded and enclosed within shelters. Food may be stored by the workers, either in portions of the nest or in their own bodies ("repletes" of honey ants). The workers feed the other castes and young, either with the gathered food or with digested foods or secretions. Shelters ranging from simple burrows to elaborate constructions are built by the workers.[15]

How matter-energy flows after being ingested by a human group is usually determined by allocations made by the decider of the group itself, by the decider of its distributor subsystem, or by the decider of the suprasystem. Men in primitive families receive more meat than women, to make them strong and brave. Children are given milk, while adults drink coffee.

Even when a group is not local, matter-energy often flows among members. Clothing is sent to a child in college, or Christmas gifts are mailed to an absent member. When group members are separated, however, they are usually components of other local groups, receiving the major part of their matter-energy from the distributors of those groups. For example, the college student eats his meals at his fraternity house.

Rates of matter-energy flow through group distributors become important in work groups, where output may be limited by inefficient distribution of materials.

Representative *variables* of the distributing process are: *Sorts of matter-energy distributed to various parts of the system.* Example: Each garment worker in the shop received the materials for his own part in the process: bolts of cloth went to the cutters, and sequins and lace to the stitchers. *Changes in distributing over time.* Example: The children were given no coffee until they were in their teens. *Changes in distributing with different circumstances.* Example: The explorers decided to allow each man only one meal a day while game was scarce. *Rate of distributing.* Example: The conveyor belt carried 500 units an hour to the group of inspectors. *Frequency of distributing.* Example: Books were given out to the class at the beginning of each new period.

Lag in distributing. Example: The soup plates were so hot that mother could not pass them for several minutes. *Costs of distributing.* Example: The chain saw was so heavy that it took the efforts of two men to carry it around to the other loggers.

3.2.3   Converter, the subsystem which changes certain inputs to the group into forms more useful for the special processes of that particular group.

3.2.3.1   Structure   I have noted in the previous section that the worker caste of social insects carries out converting processes. In most animal species this function is laterally dispersed to each individual, and it may be in human groups also. If a work group has members who prepare input raw materials for the processes of the group or if all participate in this, the members involved are parts of the converter. Many sorts of groups, including matter-energy processing groups which receive their input already prepared for processing, office groups which process chiefly information, and some sorts of social and experimental groups, do not have converter subsystems. In some of these, like shops which manufacture from ready-prepared materials, the subsystem is dispersed upwardly to the suprasystem.

Normally there is a converter subsystem in families. It is more frequently present, and represented in more components, in the nearly totipotential rural or primitive family groups which do most or all of their own life-support matter-energy processing than in partipotential modern urban groups. (This is true of other matter-energy subsystems as well.) Choppers of wood, grinders of corn, and those who butcher animals for food and other uses are examples of group converter components.

All members of the family except small children can be part of this structure, but some of the processes are assigned according to sex. In most primitive cultures, men chop wood and women grind corn. Work groups processing matter-energy often assign specific members or subgroups to this subsystem. Artifacts, ranging from stone axes to complicated manufacturing machinery, commonly assist the human components.

3.2.3.2   Process   Modern urban families receive their matter-energy in more immediately usable form than most rural families do. Wood need not be chopped by the urban family. If it is used at all, it arrives already cut to fit a fireplace. Other fuels are piped or carried in by organizations which distribute it in a form that requires no converting. Even many kinds of food are prepared in advance by manufacturing organizations. In contrast, rural families start with intact trees, corn in the shock, large dead animals complete with fur or feathers, and sometimes pieces of cloth to be cut up for clothing. Before these can be used, they must be converted to suitable forms, the waste being separated from the useful materials.

Representative *variables* of the converting process are: *Sorts of matter-energy converted.* Example: Indian women ground corn into meal for baking bread and butchered animals for meat. *Percentage of matter-energy converted.* Example: Half the wood the family was able to gather was chopped up by the hired man to fit the stove. The rest was stacked. *Changes in converting over time.* Example: As the winter went on, the apples could not be used whole, but could be cut up by the cook for salad or applesauce. *Changes in converting with different circumstances.* Example: The assembly-line supervisor found that the new machine required that the metal be cut much smaller. *Rate of converting.* Example: At each meeting the Red Cross committee could cut up cloth for 100 bandages. *Frequency of converting.* Example: All the wheat needed for a year's supply of flour could be harvested in a few hours by the farmer and his sons. *Lag in converting.* Example: It took the host a quarter of an hour to cut up the roast, and so the meat was cold by the time he served it to his guests. *Costs of converting.* Example: The cost of the threshing machine was greater each year, constituting a major expense to the eight farmers who operated the collective farm.

3.2.4 Producer, the subsystem which forms stable associations that endure for significant periods among matter-energy inputs to the group or outputs from its converter, the materials synthesized being for growth, damage repair, or replacement of components of the group or for providing energy for moving or constituting the group's outputs of products or information markers to its suprasystem.

3.2.4.1 Structure   I have noted above that the worker caste of social insects produces the food for the other castes and the young. Most human families, many sorts of work groups, and some social groups have a producer. It makes one or more of the wide range of products and artifacts that human beings construct for use within the group or by other systems. This includes food, clothing, furniture, shelters, tools, machines, books, toys, games, and objects of art. Whoever looks after the growth of members of the group and the healing of their illnesses is a component of this subsystem. Persons who use input matter-energy to repair and maintain such artifacts that belong to the group are also components.

This subsystem is lacking in many groups whose chief functions concern information processing. These systems are parasitic upon, or symbiotic with, suprasystem organizations or suprasuprasystem societies

for the products and artifacts they need to survive. In a totipotential family all members except infants commonly are a part of this subsystem—"He who will not work cannot eat."

3.2.4.2 Process   A totipotential rural or primitive family processes all its raw matter-energy inputs. It makes from them whatever it needs for its members to live, grow, and remain healthy. Some urban families, on the other hand, do little more for themselves than make coffee. Producing functions may be assigned to various group members on the basis of sex—men build fences, and women make clothing. Or the assignment may be made by the decider on the basis of what skills each member has.

The amount of time and the proportion of the group's resources devoted to this process depend upon the type of group, the availability and cost of ready-produced materials, and the magnitude of the strains (*i.e.,* the needs or demands within the group or its suprasystem) which can be reduced by the resultant product. (For instance, an exploring party threatened with a blizzard employs all its members full time to construct a shelter.) The type of product, the quantities made, and the rates of producing depend upon these and many other factors, such as the season of the year and the perishability of the materials.

Among the *variables* in the producing process are: *Sorts of matter-energy produced.* Example: The Swiss family made music boxes and carved animals. *Quality of matter-energy produced.* Example: The bride's first biscuits were as heavy as lead. *Percentage of matter-energy used in producing.* Example: The New England housewife put all the vegetables, meat trimmings, and bones into a soup, using every edible scrap. *Changes in producing over time.* Example: The occupational therapy group became more skillful and began to make simple furniture instead of wooden trays. *Changes in producing with different circumstances.* Example: When the armistice was signed, the women's group stopped knitting socks and began to sew layettes. *Rate of producing.* Example: The work group increased daily production after its grievances were settled. *Frequency of producing.* Example: The boys' group made Christmas tree ornaments only once a year. *Lag in producing.* Example: It took 2 hours (h) of work by the whole party to build an ice shelter. By the time they were finished, the blizzard was upon them. *Costs of producing.* Example: Gold was so expensive that the art class decided to use silver for their jewelry instead.

3.2.5 Matter-energy storage, the subsystem which retains in the group, for different periods of time, deposits of various sorts of matter-energy.

3.2.5.1 **Structure**   In groups of lower animals materials may be cooperatively stored in nests. Food is stored only by certain species—the thrifty habits of the honeybee, as opposed to the shiftlessness of the grasshopper, are legendary. Those species which carry out such storage usually disperse it downwardly to fat deposits on the bodies of each individual animal, although honey ant "repletes" are specialized for group storage, and squirrels store nuts underground.

Components of this subsystem in human families are the members responsible for placing foods and other useful items in storage areas in the family's territory. Some groups may store certain materials or forms of energy required for their activities. For instance, repairmen often keep their tools, fuel for blowtorches and welding equipment, and spare parts in trucks which they drive to the scenes of their jobs. But often work groups upwardly disperse the storage process to the suprasystem, the organization of which the group is a component, like assemblers in an automobile factory or road maintenance men in a city. In work groups, social clubs, and athletic and military teams, a single member—a stock clerk or spare-parts man—commonly is responsible for maintaining materials in storage and withdrawing them as needed, making him a component of this subsystem.

3.2.5.2 **Process**   Honey ants demonstrate a remarkable form of group matter-energy storage.[16] Among these creatures, workers return to the nest with their crops full of honeydew. There they transfer it to repletes, which are ants specialized to be storage receptacles. These organisms have hugely distended crops. When other ants solicit it, the replete disgorges droplets. In one species, repletes constitute 80 percent of the workers in the fall through the spring, but this proportion decreases to 67 percent when food is readily available.

Human groups which are relatively totipotential, many of which are isolated from other suprasystem components, often store large amounts of matter-energy to guard against lack stresses. Primitive families living in tropical areas may find their matter-energy strains easily reduced from day to day by a bountiful nature, but if there are seasonal variations in availability of necessary matter-energy, man must store or starve. Many farm wives devote large amounts of their time to canning food and hoarding other necessities against the winter, while male members of the family pile up wood for fuel and store crops in barns and cellars. Expeditions away from organized communities may have to be totipotential and carry all their supplies with them. A South Polar exploring party must do this since little to support life is available near the pole. So, of course, must a lunar exploration team.

Much matter-energy storage for modern groups is upwardly dispersed to organizations. Commercial stores, utility companies, and other such organizations keep large supplies available, to be withdrawn by group ingestor components.

How long something has been stored is a significant consideration in the storage process when the matter-energy is perishable. By lowering the temperature of a refrigerator in which food is kept, the rate of spoiling can be slowed. This prolongs the time the food can be stored. The amount of a group's territory which can be devoted to storage is also important. Rates of putting in, and removing from, storage quantities of any form of matter-energy stored vary with the type of group, the availability of the items at a given time, and a large number of other factors such as threats of future lack stresses or of cost increases.

Among the *variables* in the process of storing matter-energy are: *Sorts of matter-energy stored.* Example: The clubhouse cupboard held a box of crackers, some candy, and a bottle of wine. *Total storage capacity.* Example: Four women shared a cabin with two small closets and a single chest. *Percentage of matter-energy stored.* Example: The family kept a basket of apples for immediate use and stored the rest in the cellar. *Place of storage.* Example: The carpenters piled their wood in a large heap near the front door of the new house. *Changes in storing over time.* Example: With increasing experience, the owner of the jewelry store gradually increased the percentage of platinum rings in stock. *Changes in storing with different circumstances.* Example: When the supermarket was built across the street, the family no longer bought canned goods in quantity. *Rate of storing.* Example: The Boy Scouts stacked a cord of wood every half-hour for 2 hours. *Lag in storing.* Example: It was December before the last of the corn was in the silo. *Costs of storing.* Example: The family paid 100 francs monthly on a new refrigerator. *Rate of breakdown of organization of matter-energy in storage.* Example: About a liter of wine had evaporated when the monks opened the cask. *Sorts of matter-energy retrieved.* Example: When the priest had the tomb in the chapel opened, only gold and silver ornaments remained. *Percentage of matter-energy retrieved.* Example: Ninety percent of the loot was still in the cave when the robbers returned. *Order of retrieval.* Example: The play group used all the red crayons first and then changed to blue. *Rate of retrieval.* Example: The family used flour from the barrel at the rate of 5 kilograms (kg) per week. *Lag in retrieval.* Example: The research group was delayed for a week until the spectroscope was found. *Costs of retrieval.* Example:

The mechanics used up 2 h of their working day removing their equipment from the garage.

3.2.6 Extruder, the subsystem which transmits matter-energy out of the group in the form of products or wastes.

3.2.6.1 Structure   Components of this subsystem are those group members who are responsible for removing products and wastes or unwanted inclusions, such as living intruders, from the area of the group. The strongest adults, often the males, are usually the members of groups of lower animals that chase intruders out of their territory. Most animal species do not remove wastes from where they live, but social insects assign this task to some of their members. In some ant species the worker caste extrudes the wastes.[17] A cleaning woman, a soldier who polices up his barracks, a janitor, and a nightclub "bouncer" are all parts of extruders in human groups. In families all members often are parts of this subsystem at one time or another. Work groups commonly assign members to this subsystem or, like family groups, share in its processes. Some parts of a group's territory and certain types of artifacts, like wastepaper baskets and garbage disposals, are often used to facilitate waste removal.

Those persons, like salesmen or delivery boys, who arrange for products of the group to be sent out to the environment are also parts of this subsystem. If these products are markers bearing signals, this may be an output transducing process (see page 555). Often a part of the subsystem is upwardly dispersed to higher-level systems.

3.2.6.2 Process   Most species of animals do not remove wastes that accumulate in their living space. The social insects are exceptions, since their workers or other adults remove wastes from their small nests or hives at a rate which prevents them from filling up with wastes, which would soon happen if they were not extruded.

Persons and animals within the territory of human groups are input–output systems constantly outputting products or wastes in their individual matter-energy processing activities, including their work. The organized group activities also result in products or wastes. The total rate of these activities determines how rapidly materials pile up in the group's territory, which creates strains that must be reduced by extruding. Thus the rate and effort required for extruding are determined. Except for totipotential groups, it is usual for groups to be partially parasitic upon organizations for their extruding. Members of work groups put waste in containers and products on distributor artifacts such as moving belts or carts or delivery trucks. These are carried out of the group's area by compo-

nents of the organization who are often not members of the group, such as customers who buy products of the group or workers with trucks who enter the yard and carry away the wastes. Waste pipes from the house run into sewers maintained by the city. Human and animal intruders may be forcibly removed, sometimes by components of the suprasystem organization, like city or company police. Many species of animals also force intruders out of their territory, by physical attack if necessary.

Some groups have no matter-energy product but extrude matter-energy markers bearing information of various sorts. A family member carries the mail to the city box or post office, a secretary puts letters from her office into a mail chute, and a messenger from a company comes for the tape recording of its executive committee's minutes. This sort of extruding is really output transducing, since groups often use part of their extruder for such processes.

The *variables* of the process of extruding include: *Sorts of products and wastes extruded.* Example: The women made apple pies and threw away peelings and cores. *Percentage of products and wastes extruded.* Example: The work group turned 60 percent of the wood into toys, and the rest was thrown away as shavings. *Changes in extruding over time.* Example: At first, most of the wicker baskets were woven badly and had to be discarded. When the group became more skillful, this rarely happened. *Changes in extruding with different circumstances.* Example: When the miners got into the main lode, they discarded much less waste. *Rate of extruding.* Example: The shop delivered more than 40 pizzas an hour. *Frequency of extruding.* Example: Jacky put the trash out on the same day every week. *Lag in extruding.* Example: Orders for the sewing group's aprons were a week ahead of delivery. *Costs of extruding.* Example: It took the whole group of fishermen to drag the whale off the beach and into the water.

3.2.7 Motor, the subsystem which moves the group or parts of it in relation to part or all of its environment or moves components of its environment in relation to each other.

3.2.7.1 Structure   Systems at this level and above, composed as they are of relatively autonomous separate organisms, lack the sort of motor that is found in systems whose components are held together within skins or membranes. Either moving is dispersed to the organism level, or artifacts are used, powered by the physical energy of animals, engines, or subgroups like the porters on a safari. A group member driving a bus or truck or piloting a plane in which the group rides is an example of a component of a group motor subsystem, as are group members row-ing a boat. Another possible sort of component is a member or the subgroup responsible for organizing and carrying out a move.

The motor subsystem is dispersed upward if the transportation used, including a driver or other personnel, is part of a city or state organization (a taxi or bus company) or a component of a society distributor (such as a company for moving household goods, a railway, a steamship line, or an airline).

3.2.7.2 Process　Groups move to work or play or to change their territories. Members, of course, move about within the group territory or enter and leave it as separate organisms, but groups also move in coordination. Dancers in a ballet, football players on a field, marching bands, and some sorts of work groups, such as a railroad yard gang or builders of prefabricated houses, all call upon the physical energy and muscular components of their members to carry out complex interrelated group movements. Groups also move from one location in space to another. This can be highly coordinated, as in the case of a rope of mountain climbers on the face of the Eiger, or quite uncoordinated, as when the members of a group gather their belongings together and each one proceeds separately to an agreed-upon destination. In all these cases, the actual movement is laterally dispersed. The coordination is ordinarily achieved by exchange of information, although in some cases physical compulsion is used upon a refractory member, like a small child or a chain-gang prisoner who wants to go in the wrong direction.

Birds, fish, insects, and mammalian species that live in social aggregations of various sorts sometimes move about together with wonderful patterning and precision, like flocks of starlings.[18]

Some species have characteristic spatial arrangements of members as they eat their way across fields or swing through trees. Groups of baboons move along with dominant males, females, and young at their center and with front and rear guards of subordinate males.[19]

Schooling in fishes has been extensively studied. As Shaw describes it:

A school of fish is something more . . . than a crowd of fish; it is a social organization to which the fish are bound by rigorously stereotyped behavior and even by anatomical specialization. Schooling fishes do not merely live in close proximity to their kind, as many other fishes do; they maintain, during most of their activities, a remarkably constant geometric orientation to their fellows heading in the same direction, their bodies parallel and with virtually equal spacing from fish to fish. Swimming together, approaching, turning and fleeing together, all doing the same thing at the same time, they create the illusion of a huge single animal moving in a sinuous path through the water.[20]

These schools can have as many as a million members who are arranged in three-dimensional array in the water. Typical species shapes of the school are maintained. The primary form of information involved in coordinating daylight schooling is visual information received by each individual fish from an aggregation of individuals of the same species.[21] Catfish, which have poor vision, push one another, evidently adding tactile cues to the existing visual ones. Blinded catfish, however, do not school. Species which school at night make use of olfactory cues. Mechanical information from the lateral-line transducers (special sorts of input transducers in fish—see page 378) is also believed to be important in maintaining these spatial relationships.

Human groups sometimes use artifacts, such as walkie-talkie radios, to transmit coordinating auditory information. With their symbolic skills, human groups often remain coordinated over time by use of stored information, following written plans or maps or relying upon memory storage of one or more members.

The rate of movement of a group is set by task demands and many other factors, both internal and external, like the threat of darkness, the weakness of a sick member, heavy material to be carried along, or the musical score to which the group dances. The amount of energy which a group expends upon movement depends upon the physical strength of its members or the mechanical or other energy available to them.

Sometimes movements of a group may convey information, as when a marching band spells out words or when a group presents a play or operates a television station. In such cases a part of the motor is used for output transducing (see page 555).

Representative *variables* of the moving process are: *Sorts of movements made.* Example: Almost the entire team ran out of bounds on the play. *Changes in moving over time.* Example: The mountain-climbing party went more slowly as the day wore on. *Changes in moving with different circumstances.* Example: When the infantry company reached a bridge, it broke its marching cadence, its soldiers no longer keeping in step with one another. *Rate of moving.* Example: The patrol crossed the desert at a steady 2 kilometers (km) per h. *Rate of output of work.* Example: The work group operated a press that punched out 400 metal frames per h. *Frequency of moving.* Example: The band of apes moved only by day. *Duration of moving.* Example: The shipwrecked sailors had been drifting in their boat for 13 days before the airplane located them. *Lag in moving.* Example: The robbers stood dazzled in the glare of lights and then made a dash for it. *Costs of moving.*

Example: The family rented the motorboat for $5 per h plus the cost of gasoline.

3.2.8 Supporter, the subsystem which maintains the proper spatial relationships among components of the group, so that they can interact without weighting each other down or crowding each other.

3.2.8.1 Structure Systems at the level of the group and higher lack skeletons or other internal supporters. Except for rather trivial examples, like the strong man with a human pyramid balanced on his shoulders, dispersing the group supporter laterally to the organism level, groups use artifacts as supporters. Social insects live in hives or nests, often elaborately constructed according to a characteristic design for that species. The building which houses a family and the room which is the meeting place of a group not only act as boundary artifacts (see page 522) but also support the group and maintain relationships among the members in space. Vehicles such as cars, trains, and airplanes have supporting as well as moving functions. The chairs and conference table supplement the organism supporters of the members of a committee, often with specified positions for each member. We are so accustomed to the pieces of furniture which surround us that we must stop to think a moment before we realize that they are in fact prostheses for a group system which lacks a living supporter subsystem. Very primitive human groups and almost all animals make do with natural objects like logs, caves, and trees for the same purpose. A troop of chimpanzees nesting in a forest has the advantage of being cozily supported high above the ground, like a family in an apartment house, but with better cross ventilation.

3.2.8.2 Process This subsystem provides rigid support, and so it has little action to describe. If a family's house or some of its pieces of furniture collapse, the components in the family system are disorganized and perhaps damaged, and so strength of the supporter is important. Its cost and its efficiency in performing its functions are also major concerns.

Representative *variables* in the supporting process include: *Strength of the supporter.* Example: It was necessary for the trapeze to hold all four performers at once. *Costs of supporting.* Example: The new lookout tower for the ranger team cost $10,000.

3.3 Subsystems which process information

3.3.1 Input transducer, the sensory subsystem which brings markers bearing information into the group, changing them to other matter-energy forms suitable for transmission within it.

3.3.1.1 Structure Components of this subsystem are animals or persons who bring information into a group from the environment or suprasystem, trans-

ducing it from one form of matter-energy marker to another. These same components are frequently, but not always, also components of the group decoder (see page 540).

Living components of the input transducer are found at least some of the time in almost all sorts of groups. Animal groups post lookouts which give warning of approaching enemies. Military patrols also send their scouts into the environment to gather visual information concerning enemy activities and report it verbally. Committees delegate a member or a subcommittee to get facts from the library on a subject of interest. They transduce written words into spoken words. These components commonly decode as they report. The input transducer and decoder are in separate components when one member receives and reports the message to the group and another explains or translates it.

The input transducer of groups can be dispersed in various ways. A messenger who is a component of the suprasystem (organization) or of the suprasuprasystem (society) sometimes enters a group to give information. This is an example of a part of the input transducer subsystem upwardly dispersed. Dispersion laterally to all members occurs if each concentrates upon a part of the input, reporting his part to the group, as when each member of the crew of a military aircraft acts as lookout for a part of the sky. It can also be downwardly dispersed, if each member transduces (and decodes) input for himself. This occurs when a sound from outside—such as a recess bell in school—constitutes a signal for the group to change its activities.

In modern times artifacts often serve as input transducers to groups. A television receiver, for example, brings into a home news of the world, music and entertainment, and information about the latest washday miracles, transducing the broadcast signals into visual and sound patterns.

3.3.1.2 Process

(a) *Input–output transfer functions.* Like input transducers at other levels of living systems, those of groups can affect inputs to the system in various ways. Omissions of information occur when part of the signal is too weak for the transducer to receive, when there is noise in the channel, when the channel capacity of the input transducer is overloaded, when part of the information is filtered out as unimportant, or when the transducer is imperfect, suffering from poor memory or inattention or sleepiness. Distortions of input can also occur. Just as a radio sometimes emits static instead of patterns of sounds, so a human component can be too young to verbalize or have a speech defect which produces a similar effect, that of a message which cannot be decoded. Distortion also occurs when material is added which was not present in the signal. A maid receiving a telephone message and passing it on, for example, sometimes draws upon her imagination for lively details missing from the original message.

(*b*) *Mode of adaptation.* I know of no evidence on this aspect of input transducing processes at the level of the group.

(*c*) *Channel capacity.* A group's input transducer channel capacity can be raised by selecting the best observers for it or by increasing their number. If the input transducer has more than one component, it can use them and the multiple channels to which they lead to correct for omissions by comparing the separate messages or by assigning portions of the total input to different components.

(*d*) *Threshold.* There appear to be no researches on the thresholds of group input transducers.

(*e*) *Lag.* If the information to be transduced is complex or if the channel is overloaded (see pages 156 and 157), delays in processing it through a single human organism can be important, particularly when the group is under stress. An input transducer with more components can reduce lags, but sometimes it may increase them, depending largely upon how efficiently its components are coordinated. If an agreement among several components is necessary before a report is produced, delay frequently results.

(*f*) *Accessory functions.* Various living components and nonliving artifacts protect, conduct, concentrate, analyze, amplify, diminish, filter, distort, or add noise to input signals to groups. These include scouts who shield their eyes with their hands, visors, or sunglasses in order to see better in bright sun; operators of sonar or radar who report their findings to other members of a boat's crew; sergeants at arms who maintain quiet in committee meetings at which persons are reporting or testifying about events that have occurred outside the group; and an operator of a projector that brings a live television broadcast to an audience.

Included among representative *variables* of the input transducing process are: *Meaning of information input which is transduced.* Example: When the blue light appeared on the boat approaching the beach, the spies waiting there knew they were about to be rescued. *Sorts of information input which are transduced.* Example: Joe had left the cave to see whether the sun had set, when suddenly he gave the low whistle that meant strangers were entering the gang's territory. *Percentage of the information input which is transduced.* Example: The scout reported only half the enemy soldiers. He mistook the rest for rocks. *Threshold of the input transducer.* Example: The twins were chosen to watch for rabbits because they had sharp eyes. *Changes in input transducing over time.* Example: As his eyes became tired, the iceberg lookout began to skip reporting some of the ice floes. *Changes in input transducing with different circumstances.* Example: Since the doorbell was broken, the family posted a child near the door to tell when the visitors were approaching. *Channel capacity of the input transducer.* Example: So many people tried to phone the group that two telephones were installed, and two members were chosen to answer them. *Number of channels in use in the input transducer.* Example: Of the two lookouts, one was sound asleep, and the other was inattentive. *Distortion of the input transducer.* Example: Old Mrs. Jones never could remember anything right, and so the sewing circle heard a garbled version of the rumor. *Signal-to-noise ratio of the input transducer.* Example: It was necessary for the committee to use the public address system because the sound of traffic in the street drowned out their voices. *Rate of input transducing.* Example: Bobby could not speak rapidly, and so the group did not learn his news for 5 minutes. *Lag in input transducing.* Example: Mr. Taylor went out to lunch before telling the others in his office that the armored car had arrived, and by the time he returned, it had left without collecting the bankroll. *Costs of input transducing.* Example: The new television set cost the family more than $500.

3.3.2 Internal transducer, the sensory subsystem which receives, from subsystems or components within the group, markers bearing information about significant alterations in those subsystems or components, changing them to other matter-energy forms of a sort which can be transmitted within it.

3.3.2.1 Structure   Any group member or subgroup is a component of the internal transducer that receives from other members and conveys to the group decider information about the group task, about group interactions, or about their internal states as they interact, including their feelings about group processes.

3.3.2.2 Process   A sensitive mother knows every day how her husband and each of their children feel by the time they get to the breakfast table, sometimes by subtle signs. She transduces these and may make comments about the family members' emotional states, which can lead to decisions or interactions based on those feelings. Members of a work group must communicate about their task activities in order to get the job done. Many good committee chairmen systematically poll each committee member on his opinions on every major policy matter. The direct, face-to-face contacts of groups provide a much better opportunity for easy internal transducing than occurs in systems at higher levels, but the function is crucial at all levels.

The internal transducer subsystem transmits information to the group over a number of different bands of the various sensory modalities (see pages 406 and 536).

It is generally agreed that the channels connecting group members carry two sorts of information: (a) information about the group task and (b) information about housekeeping or organizing matters, the socioemotional management of the group, and its members' attitudes and feelings. Information of the first sort is transduced either from outside the group by the input transducer (see page 531) or— if the task concerns the group itself rather than something external to it—from inside the group by the internal transducer. Information of the second sort comes only through the internal transducer. These two types of communication Thelen categorizes as "work" and "emotionality."[22] The group's "external system," in the terms of Homans, processes information concerning those aspects of group behavior which enable the group to survive in its environment or, in other words, to perform its task.[23] The "internal system" handles messages about the sentiments which the group members develop toward one another as they interact. The same dichotomy is employed by Bales, who divides the categories by which he analyzes group processes into task-related and socioemotional acts.[24] His widely used technique, interaction process analysis, is carried out by raters who observe a group or listen to sound recordings of its conversation and classify each comment by the participants according to Bales' 12 categories:

A. Positive socioemotional acts
    1. Shows solidarity
    2. Shows tension release
    3. Agrees
B. Task-related attempted answers
    4. Gives suggestion
    5. Gives opinion
    6. Gives information
C. Task-related questions
    7. Asks for information
    8. Asks for opinion
    9. Asks for suggestion
D. Negative socioemotional acts
    10. Disagrees
    11. Shows tension
    12. Shows antagonism

Often two or more independent raters are used in order to get accuracy of categorization. Experience has shown that trained raters can achieve high agreement. This procedure, of course, is a sort of content analysis and has the shortcomings of most current efforts to categorize or quantify meaning (see page 1030). There is, however, at present no more rigorous way of handling this problem. Once the rating is done, within the limits of its reliability, patterns and rates of group interactions can be related to other variables.

In the course of group interactions some members often disagree with majority decisions or are unable to gain attention for their viewpoints. They become emotionally disturbed. Group solidarity may be threatened. Internal transducing in groups has been studied by using an artifact, an apparatus which is an intragroup signaling network—lights that are visible to all the members and are secretly activated by switches, each one of which is controlled by a group member.[25] A green light means that a member is content with the proceedings; a red light means that he is not. Any member who is not comfortable about the group process secretly changes his light from green to red. When an agreed-upon number of lights turn red, the group stops working on its task and discusses its feelings. This apparatus is an artifact which aids internal transducing in a group. However, sophisticated chairmen have been doing a similar thing the best way they can for a long time.

Organizing or socioemotional information, on the one hand, and task information, on the other, have been experimentally separated in group network studies (see pages 536 to 539) by imposing constraints against exchanging the former sort of information and allowing processing only of the latter. In these experiments the subjects usually do not know what sort of network they are in and cannot see the other subjects. Part of the time they try to understand the structure of their system, sending organizing messages like: "I get messages from four people" or "To whom can you send?"[26] The effects of communication restriction on task performance, according to Bavelas and Leavitt, were different from its effects on organizing behavior.[27] These effects have been separated in experiments.[28] In these experiments the task at hand was discussed by the group only at certain times. Between these times the group was permitted 2-min intervals which they could use as they wished for asking questions about the equipment, making comments on speed of performance, and organizing messages like attempts to clarify and understand the structure of the net or plans to improve the system structure or process. The experimenters studied 56 groups, each in one of three sorts of five-person group nets: circle (O), star, and totally connected. These three, along with eight other five-person nets used in group research, are shown in Fig. 9-2. In the star and circle (O), which greatly restricted communication, the subjects devoted much higher percentages of their total messages during the intertrial intervals to understanding the group structure than the subjects in the totally connected net did. For the star group it was 86 percent, and for the circle (O) it was 70 percent, while for the totally connected group it was only 35 percent.

The morale of group members—their "socioemotional" satisfactions or dissatisfactions—is discovered by internal transducing. This function is essential for good group performance. Such information is harder to obtain in some group structures than in others. The subjects in the above experiments devoted 37 percent of all their messages to questions, answers, and other comments about socioemotional matters in the totally connected group, 30 percent in the star, and 41 percent in the circle (O). All groups spend some time processing such information from the internal transducer subsystem; otherwise, they could not maintain their cohesion and continue to perform their tasks.

Tests have been made of the effects upon an experimental group of having information needed for problem solutions unevenly divided among group members.[29] This information was obtained in written form from the experimenter and was memorized by individual members of the group before any group interaction began. While together in the group, these members reported the information they had stored before the interaction began. This was, therefore, an internal transducer function on their part. These tests were done on 15 groups in 3 four-person artificially constrained networks: the wheel, the slash, and the circle. These three nets and a fourth, a four-person totally connected net (which has been used in some other studies and which I shall describe later), are shown in Fig. 9-3. In some of these groups information was equally divided among all members, and in others it was not. It was found that if one member gets access to more information, his morale increases, and

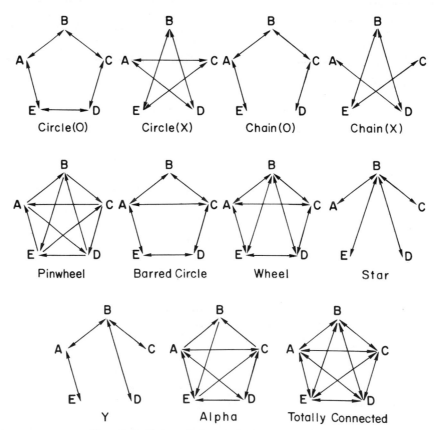

Fig. 9-2 Five-person group nets. (From L. S. Christie, R. D. Luce, & J. Macy, Jr. *Communications and learning in task-oriented groups.* Cambridge, Mass.: M.I.T., Research Laboratory of Electronics, Technical Report No. 231, May 13, 1952, 20. *Reprinted by permission.*)

so do the speed with which he transmits items of information and the probability that he will become a leader in the group. Increasing or decreasing the amount of information available to a member has

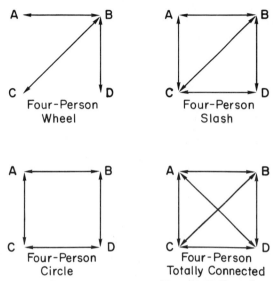

Four-Person
Wheel

Four-Person
Slash

Four-Person
Circle

Four-Person
Totally Connected

Fig. 9-3 Four-person group nets. (From M. E. Shaw. Some effects of unequal distribution of information upon group performance in various communication nets. *J. abnorm. soc. Psychol.*, 1954, **49**, 548, and M. E. Shaw & G. H. Rothschild. Some effects of prolonged experience in communication nets. *J. appl. Psychol.*, 1956, **40**, 281. Copyright 1954 and 1956 by the American Psychological Association. *Reprinted by permission.*)

effects like those of increasing or decreasing his "relative centrality" or ease of access for purposes of communication to the other members (see pages 536 and 549). In several experiments various sorts of suggestions or information given to one member in different trials determined the probability of a correct answer in that trial if accepted by the group.[30] The information held by that member might, for example, apply to all decisions, but lead to correct group decisions only 75 percent of the time; or it might apply 66⅔ percent of the time, but lead to correct decisions, if accepted, 31¼ percent of the time. These groups did not merely accept or reject such suggestions or information, but accepted them in proportion to their correctness. The effects of introducing irrelevant information into 24 four-person groups have also been investigated.[31] Of these groups, 12 were arranged in the wheel network, and 12 in the totally connected net. In half the groups in each net each member was given only facts relevant

to the solution of the problem. In the other half each member was given both relevant and irrelevant facts. It was found that the greater complexity of the latter task increased the inefficiency of the more centralized communication net (the wheel). The time required to reach a solution increased significantly with the irrelevant facts and always was greater for the wheel than for the totally connected net. The number of messages sent before reaching a solution was greater for the wheel when irrelevant facts were included. The subjects were less satisfied with the group operation in the wheel than in the other net.

Representative *variables* of the internal transducing process include: *Meaning of internal information which is transduced.* Example: The tone of her voice revealed to her mother that Sue was angry. *Sorts of internal information which are transduced.* Example: Georgie expressed resentment about his mother's attention to the new baby. *Percentage of the internal information which is transduced.* Example: Each member was limited to a brief factual discussion. No emotional reactions of the members were hinted at. *Threshold of the internal transducer.* Example: The former chairman was insensitive to the feelings of the committee members, but the present one is responsive to every whim in the group, and so they feel more secure with him. *Changes in internal transducing over time.* Example: After the first year the couple understood each other so well that speech was frequently unnecessary. *Changes in internal transducing with different circumstances.* Example: The new employee in the group elicited an essential review of its proceedings over the past several months. *Channel capacity of the internal transducer.* Example: When the women members began to describe their feelings, the jury could not continue its deliberations, but had to stop and listen. *Number of channels in use in the internal transducer.* Example: The chairman made the rule that only one member could have the floor at any time; the others had to wait their turn. *Distortion of the internal transducer.* Example: Everyone had to make allowance for the coach's well-known prejudices as he described the team's morale. *Signal-to-noise ratio of the internal transducer.* Example: The patients were so disturbed that their feelings about group therapy could not be learned. *Rate of internal transducing.* Example: Reports on subcommittee activities ordinarily took 5 minutes so that there would be more time for games. *Lag in internal transducing.* Example: Father waited a whole month to tell the family how he felt about the need for more family discussions. *Costs of internal transducing.* Example: The partners spent so much time talking about their mutual hostilities that their company's business suffered.

3.3.3   Channel and net, the subsystem composed of a single route in physical space, or multiple interconnected routes, by which markers bearing information are transmitted to all parts of the group.

3.3.3.1   Structure   Each group member is a part of the group channel and net subsystem, although when the group is not meeting, when a member is absent, or when the group process or the research design requires it, some or all of the channels may not be in use. If the direction of information flow or the number of channels in use is limited by the research design in relation to a group being studied experimentally or by a change in group relationships, this alters the structure of the channel and net subsystem of the group. This is the case, for example, when a new pattern of information processing is imposed upon a work group. If the change in channels produces a decider structured with two or more hierarchically arranged echelons, so that the decisions of part of the group are transmitted to another part by one or more persons, the group segregates, at least temporarily, into an organization of at least two echelons (see page 595). This is true even when the change in channel or net pattern was not planned by the investigators to have this practical effect. I consider below an experiment in which group structure converted to organization structure when the channel and net subsystem changed (see page 539).

Various sorts of physical channels can connect group members. More than one of these are often in use simultaneously. The most usual form of communication is speech, carried over the auditory band through the surrounding air. Expressive sounds and music are also carried on the auditory band. Gestures, facial expressions, and postural changes are viewed on the visual band. Bodily contact is another available channel. Among animals, odor is a commonly used communication medium. Written messages, including money, checks, and other financial papers, are distributed on markers which can be viewed on the visual band. Electronic artifacts, such as walkie-talkies, today can provide communication among group members who must work with high surrounding noise levels or who are separated in space. The distance may be great, as when three astronauts in orbit interact as a group with their mission controller on earth. Groups in which some or all of the members are interacting in other groups, sometimes at great distances, may use a channel or net upwardly dispersed to the suprasystem or suprasuprasystem. The internal telephone lines or delivery services of an organization or the telephone, telegraph, banking services, or mail services which are a part of the channel and net subsystem of the society may connect them.

Group communication nets have been studied experimentally more than any other group subsystem, usually in the laboratory. The number of channels used can be artificially constrained by restricting messages to written notes and specifying who may send them and who may receive them or by using only an experimenter-controlled electronic network among members who are separated from one another by partitions.

The original experiments on group communication nets used five-person groups similar to those shown in Fig. 9-2.[32] Others have used four-person groups (see Fig. 9-3) or three-person groups (see Fig. 9-4).[33] As the number of members becomes larger, the number of possible arrangements and the complexity of net patterning increase. In a five-man group there are about 60 possible arrangements, but many of these are isomorphic with others. In at least one experiment groups were included with each of the 11 arrangements of five-man groups which are shown in Fig. 9-2.[34] These five-person groups differ markedly in the number of channels available. For instance, the circle (O) and the circle (X) have 10, the wheel has 8, and the totally connected group has 20. This last has five symmetrical positions, as against four for the wheel and five for both forms of the circle. The circles require at least two relays by intermediary members for any one member to get a message to all the others, but one person in the wheel can reach all the others directly, and in the totally connected group everyone can reach everyone else.

A measure has been constructed by Bavelas which represents the ease of access, for purposes of communication, of a member in any position to the other members of any group.[35] In the chain (O), for example, one can sum the minimum number of communication channels necessary for each member to communicate with each of the others. This sum for each end member is 10: for the member in the middle, 6; and for each of the other two, 7. The sum of all these distances for each of the individual positions in the group net divided by the total sum of distances for any one position is the latter position's "relative centrality." In the five-member chain (O) this value is 4.0 for each end member, 6.7 for the middle member, and 5.7 for each of the other two. Relative centrality of group members correlates with many functional differences among them, such as their problem-solving speed and effectiveness, their proneness to leadership (see pages 548 and 549), and individual morale (see page 535). The total of the relative centralities in any net is the "net centrality." In the five-member chain (O) group, for instance, this is 26.1.

An alternative "peripherality index" has been proposed by Leavitt.[36] It measures the difference between the centrality of a given position and the centrality of the most central position. For the two end members in the five-member chain (O) the peripherality index is 2.7. The use of this measure makes comparison of groups with the same structure but different numbers of members possible, as Bavelas's centrality index does not. Most research with these nets has used the measure of relative centrality, however, rather than that of peripherality.

3.3.3.2   Process   The functioning of the channel and net subsystem of groups has been extensively investigated. These researches have provided insights into such aspects of this functioning as what sorts of channels are used, what factors restrict and facilitate the use of channels, the rates of message transmission through the network, and the effects of differences in number of group members and structure of the network on information processing in the network. I shall now discuss a few of these researches.

Each active participant has his place in the group communication net, with at least one sense-modality channel open for information input and one for output. In a dyad there must be one two-way channel which is open at least part of the time in each direction, but in a larger group the channels may be only one-way, as long as each has input from someone and output to someone. In some real-life groups (like artillery batteries) one or more members (like the target spotters) may be connected by telephone or other private communication channels, sending and receiving messages only through a single other member who forwards information to and from the others in the group. Helen Keller was a member of groups largely through communication with her companion over the channel of her primary sensory modality, touch.

Money is a form of information which flows through channels in groups. In some groups no money flows at all. In some there are trivial flows of money. In others—families, for example—flows of money are important. One or both parents receive payments for their participation in the suprasystem. This is divided—channeled—to the other members. Mother is given grocery money. The children receive allowances, payments for chores, or money for schoolbooks. Father keeps what is left, if anything. Many work groups upwardly disperse this channel and net process to the organization which is the suprasystem, but others receive payments for their products or services and share these rewards.

As at other levels, information often does not travel completely or accurately through the nets of even the smallest groups. In a triad two members frequently form a coalition which at least partly excludes the other, and thus they do not communicate all information to him. This has the effect of closing the channel part of the time. Years ago experiments demonstrated the distortion of stories which pass through a group from one member to another, much as in the parlor game of "telephone."[37] These findings clearly support Hypothesis 3.3.3.2-2, page 96, which states that all channels have systematic distortion, and Hypothesis 3.3.3.2-4, page 96, which states that a system never completely compensates for such distortion. A channel can be made inefficient or be effectively closed by noise at this level as at others. The functional state of an individual or subgroup at a given moment also determines access to information, since a member who has dozed off during a dull committee meeting or a pair of members who are gossiping will miss some available information. Patterns of information spread in groups are also affected by the locations of subgroup boundaries, the spatial distances among members, and the contents of the messages. Early in their existence groups establish their channel and net structures. Much of their later task performance (and other interactions) is influenced by whether this is, accidentally or by design, an effective structure.

Who communicates with whom in a group, and how, has been analyzed by several different methods. Everything said at a meeting may be electrically recorded and later analyzed by raters in a number of ways.[38] The amount of time or number of words used by each speaker can be determined. The number of times each one addresses every other one can be counted. The emotional tones used by each speaker can be interpreted. The content of the statements can be rated according to Bales' categories (see page 533) or other rubrics. The interaction chronograph has been used to measure the amount of time each person is speaking or silent, who interrupts whom, and which people talk at the same time.[39] Matrix algebra has been employed to analyze group nets, much as electrical nets with open or closed switches are analyzed.[40]

Flows of information through a group are determined partly by personal liking, since friends are probably more likely to transmit information to one another than to those with whom they are not friends. In one study of this phenomenon, friendship preferences in a junior high school in Ann Arbor, Michigan, were determined.[41] Each child was asked to state his best friend, his second best friend, and so on, until he had listed eight or had run out of friends to name, whichever occurred sooner. These replies provided the basis for constructing a large sociogram describing one aspect of communication among 861 students in the school. The findings demonstrated that one cannot properly assume that each pair of children in a junior high school is equally likely to intercommunicate—an assumption like that of equiprobability of contact made in some studies of the spread of contagious diseases. There are biases in the social networks through which information actually flows. Some of these biases depend on characteristics of one individual in the group, such as her or his popularity; others depend on various relationships among individuals, such as whether they are in the same "clique." A particular mathematical model (the compound Poisson distribution of Greenwood and Yule, which is like the Polya contagion process) described the distribution of popularity of children in the school. These data could be explained if each child were assumed to have the same degree of popularity on all ballots on which his name appeared. A fairly good fit of the empirical sociogram could be made by a mathematical model which included two free parameters, one representing a "cliquishness" bias and the other a "popularity" bias. This study is directly relevant to Hypothesis 3.3.3.1-1 (see page 95), which proposes that communication nets are similar enough at various levels of living systems to be described by similar mathematical models.

Message diffusion has been studied in a boys' camp.[42] Three of the forty-two boys enrolled were given large yellow buttons bearing the name of the camp and a question mark in black lettering. These "starters" circulated during the noon rest period and, when asked about the buttons, said that they had been told a few more of them were obtainable at the lodge where they had received theirs. The exact time at which each boy came in to ask for a similar button was recorded. The rate of increase in number of hearers per teller was high at first, but gradually waned over the next 2 h. Altogether, 39 boys came to the lodge to ask for a button.

The effects of variations of net structure upon group process have been studied largely by means of artificially constrained network studies like those I have discussed in the section on the internal transducer of the group (see pages 533 to 535). The value of such experiments has been questioned. In the opinion of Glanzer and Glaser, the groups involved are so different from natural groups that the findings are not applicable to the latter.[43] They consider that the findings are more applicable to the level of the organization, where constraints on communication are the rule, many relationships are not face-to-face, inadequate information may be available about components which are not nearby, and all components are forced to participate.

That such applications are possible is recognized by the experimenters with such nets.[44] On the other hand, while it is true that in most groups all members may communicate with all others, making the group similar to a totally connected net (see Fig. 9-2), it has been shown that the actual working structure of totally connected groups in net studies often involves only certain channels, making the group similar to one of the other, more limited nets (see page 539). As I have noted above, the number of channels open and the direction of flow are constrained by various influences. This may well be the case also with natural groups. In a club business meeting, established parliamentary procedure is commonly followed to determine who may speak and in what order. Certainly in some families, also, communication flows among members are far from even. The mother, for instance, sometimes receives messages from the children which they will communicate only to her, and she passes them on to the father later. The net in use in such a group could be studied experimentally.

The effects of surrounding noise upon processes in nets of different structures have been studied.[45] Three-person groups tried to solve three different kinds of problems. Communication among group members was by microphones and earphones, with white noise introduced in all the channels. The noise served to mask outside sounds. In addition, the speech-to-noise ratio was systematically altered. The groups were arranged in the five different networks shown in Fig. 9-4. The first kind of problem involved reconstituting a list of words from three sublists, one of which was given to each member. Group efficiency was measured by time or number of spoken words needed to complete the task. The group with the one-

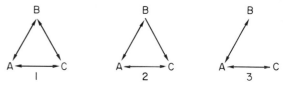

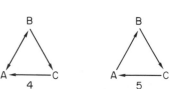

Fig. 9-4   Three-person group nets. (From G. A. Heise & G. A. Miller. Problem solving by small groups using various communication nets. *J. abnorm. soc. Psychol.*, 1951. **46**, 328. Copyright 1951 by the American Psychological Association. *Reprinted by permission.*)

way closed chain (Fig. 9-4, number 5) was least efficient; the open chain, which permitted two-way communication among any two adjacent persons (Fig. 9-4, number 3), was intermediate; and the closed chain, where everyone could talk to everyone else (Fig. 9-4, number 1), was most efficient. Decreasing the signal-to-noise ratio exaggerated the differences among the three networks. The second kind of problem involved building sentences from three partial sentences, one of which was given to each member. Results with this less rigidly structured type of problem were generally similar to those with the first type. It put a greater premium on group coordination, however, and probably for this reason the two-way open chain with a central coordinator (Fig. 9-4, number 3) was more efficient than network number 1 of Fig. 9-4. The third sort of problem, forming anagrams, required no communication, and this was done equally well by groups arranged in all the five networks. In another group experiment (see page 542) the subjects increased the redundancy of their communications to combat channel noise or error.[46]

Modes of information processing have been investigated in five-person groups which collect information dispersed among the members, make a decision (solve a problem) with it, and then send the answer through a circle (O), star, or totally connected net (see Fig. 9-2).[47] The flows of messages through different channels were counted in order to determine which groups were stable, reliably using the same channels to transmit information. (See Hypothesis 3.3.3.2-17, page 97, which states that when a channel has conveyed a message, its later use to convey others is more probable.) The groups with totally connected nets, which provided many alternatives, were significantly less stable than those with more restricted nets. The star was more stable than the circle (O). The circle (O) groups had difficulty structuring their information networks. In such groups it was imperative to relay messages, since no member could communicate directly with all the others. By the end of the twentieth trial, 10 of the 21 circle (O) groups had developed three-echelon networks for sending answers, but only three of these used an identical network design to gather information. Some occasionally used semistable "round robins." Most of the circle (O) groups and some of the totally connected groups did not develop structured network hierarchies, all their channels remaining open. In these, each group member broadcast his information, including answers when he got them, to all other members to whom he could send messages. Such groups performed their tasks more slowly than those with restricted structures.

All star groups, after three to four trials, segregated

(see page 39) into two-echelon hierarchies, in which each of the four end men (A, C, D, and E) sent their information to the key man (B), who decided on the correct solution and sent the answer back.

All but three of the totally connected groups also developed a two-echelon hierarchical network arrangement for their initial information exchange. (In the three exceptions each member sent messages to all the others.) But only 11 of the 17 groups used the same hierarchical network for transmitting the answers to the other group members. A three-echelon hierarchy for transmitting answers was developed by 6 of the 17 groups; in this hierarchy the key member returned answers to two other members, who relayed the answers to the remaining two. The totally connected groups had the additional problem of developing their own restrictions on information transmissions in their networks, since 20 one-way channels provided too many opportunities for communication.

A similar research studied four-man groups in four-person wheel, four-person slash, and four-person totally connected patterns (see Fig. 9-3).[48] All these groups used either no network flow pattern or one of two network flow patterns: Either (a) all facts were sent to one person, who solved the problem and sent the answer out to the others, or (b) all facts were sent to all group members, and then each one solved the problem independently. The totally connected groups got the most satisfaction from the experiment, the slash groups got the next most, and the wheel groups got the least. The totally connected groups were fastest, but used more messages than the wheel groups; the wheel and slash groups were slow, and the latter used the most messages. Leaders appeared most frequently in the wheel groups. In the totally connected groups each member characteristically communicated with all the others; the wheel groups usually developed a procedure for transmitting all the facts to one person; the slash groups were usually disorganized.

Many *variables* of channel and net processing can be measured. Some representative ones are: *Meaning of information channeled to various parts of the system.* Example: The firing of the cannon on the foredeck of the racing committee's boat signaled the start of the yacht race. *Sorts of information channeled to various parts of the system.* Example: Only auditory and visual signals were channeled through the group. *Percentage of information arriving at the appropriate receiver in the channel and net.* Example: The cards got mixed up, and only one of the five members received the correct instructions for his job. *Threshold of the channel and net.* Example: Emma whispered an answer to the lawyer's question, but no one in court heard her. *Changes in channel and net processing over time.* Example: Late in the day, more mistakes were made in passing stock quotations from one clerk to the other. *Changes in channel and net processing with different circumstances.* Example: After dark, the oil-well drillers signaled with colored lights instead of gestures. *Information capacity of the channel and net.* Example: The experimental group could process 5 bits per min through their net. *Distortion of the channel and net.* Example: Ed, the club secretary, was slightly deaf, and consequently the club minutes did not summarize the group discussion correctly. *Signal-to-noise ratio in the channel and net.* Example: Everyone had to shout when the cocktail party was in full swing. *Rate of processing of information over the channel and net.* Example: The news of Marge's divorce reached all members of the club within the first hour. *Lag in channel and net processing.* Example: The intercom broke down, and a messenger had to carry all messages to the members of the work group. Communication was then much slower than usual. *Costs of channel and net processing.* Example: Walkie-talkies were bought to give the surveyors better communication. They were expensive, but they were worth it.

3.3.4   Decoder, the subsystem which alters the code of information input to it through the input transducer or the internal transducer into a "private" code that can be used internally by the group.

3.3.4.1   Structure   Usually when a group forms, its members immediately begin to use a common language, spoken by all. If all members do not ordinarily speak the same language, their first discussion involves the selection of the language they will use. If some members do not know that language, others must translate for them until they learn it. When a group has interacted over time, its members' common interests and experiences lead it to develop a private language, a special technical jargon, a system of abbreviations, or another convenient way to express ideas used frequently in that particular system. The group members employ codes that are efficient for their purposes, using simple signals for the messages which are most frequently transmitted in their group, which is consistent with Hypothesis 3.3.4.2-1(*a*) (see page 98). A group employs its decoder subsystem when it receives information from outside the group coded in such a way that it is not in the private language of the group or a language understood by all group members. If it is in such a language, the decoder is not needed.

A group of tourists traveling in a foreign country often depends upon one or a few members who understand the language. A bomber crew has a radar man who decodes his instrument's blips. A ship has a radio man who sends and receives Morse code. A mother explains to her children how people in their society talk and act. A seminar often has a member who can interpret an input that others in the group cannot understand, such as a description of group behavior written in the mathematical code of set theory. A member of a family, trying to describe an acquaintance, may use a sentence such as "He walks like Joe." This conveys a wealth of meaning that would take several sentences to explain to a stranger, if it could be done at all. All these group members are decoder components.

A group's decoder may be local, limited to one component, or it may be laterally dispersed to several members or to all. The decoding of nonlinguistic information inputs, a process known as *perception* (see pages 402 to 404), is often laterally dispersed to all the individual organism components of the group. Exceptions occur, for example, when a parent answers the repeated question "What's that?" asked by a young child who is seeing new things for the first time in a fascinating new world; when a blind group member depends upon verbal decoding of visual input by an associate; and when a guide in a planetarium, a scientific laboratory, or a strange country explains to a group things they have never seen before. Decoding is upwardly dispersed when a component of a suprasystem organization or suprasystem society who is not a member of the group does the needed explaining or translating. A company employee who guides a group of visitors through an automobile factory is an example.

3.3.4.2   Process   Groups, both animal and human, coordinate their processes by exchange of coded signals. The encoding and decoding of alpha-, beta-, and gamma-coded signals by organisms are discussed above (see pages 404 to 406 and 439 to 442). Alpha codes are inherited by group members in their genetic templates. Beta codes may be genetically determined, as the fright signals of starlings are, or they may be learned. While no human society has ever been found that did not use language, the specific codes used in gamma-coded communication must be learned, and (with some possible exceptions) codes used in nonverbal communication in human groups are also learned.

Recent research has concentrated on the importance of eye-to-eye contact in human communication, *i.e.,* when two people look directly into each other's eyes. This helps the receiver of the message conveyed by gesture or facial expression to decode it. One such experiment used discussion groups composed of two naive subjects and one confederate of the experimenter.[49] All were female undergraduates. When the confederate's arguments were good, it was found that she received more eye contact and more leadership votes from the naïve group members.

Young children in families and neophytes or apprentices in any group must learn that group's codes before they can decode for the group. As Hypothesis 3.3.4.2-8 (see page 98) states, over time systems cut down the amount of decoding required by developing common codes used on a systemwide basis. This includes not only symbolic languages like Spanish, Chinese, or Morse code but also skills like flying a jet plane in close formation with three others, waiting on a table, or singing in a choir. Gradually this process of associative learning makes the decoder able to process accurately, and with less delay, a higher and higher percentage of its inputs (see Hypothesis 3.3.4.2-3, page 98). Also, the threshold of the decoder is lowered, and so there is a greater probability that this subsystem can distinguish signals from noise or see patterns in ambiguous structures, as in the "noisy marble" experiment, which I describe below. Redundancy—multiple components of the decoder simultaneously processing the input or a single one repeating it—may decrease omissions and identify and correct errors. This is the principle referred to in Hypothesis 3.3.4.2-6 (see page 98). For conviction of the serious crime of treason, the American Constitution requires two witnesses to an overt act. When his children are having a quarrel, a fair father hears all versions of the situation before deciding how to settle it. Extra redundancy in any system, of course, has its costs.

The personal biases of an individual member who is decoding for a group can distort his output. As Hypothesis 3.3.4.2-10 (see page 99) states, as the strength of a strain increases, information inputs will more and more be interpreted (or decoded) as required to reduce that strain within the system. A translator for a United Nations committee is aware of this and consequently tries—usually successfully—to be a dispassionate technician so that any nationalistic or political bias he may have will not affect his translation.

If information inputs or social perceptions are ambiguous or have meaning not readily apparent to all members, the information may be discussed and then decoded at the level of the group. How group members exert pressures which distort even relatively simple perceptual judgments of an individual component of the decoder, to bring them into conformity with judgments of the other components, was discussed in the last chapter (see page 437). I made the point there that this change is rarely a true recoding at the organism level. That is, the person's perception

probably remains the same, but he changes his judgment—a decider process.

Certain communication networks in groups improve their decoding. A so-called "noisy marble" experiment demonstrated this.[50] This research studied 4 five-person groups of college students in each of three networks—circle (O), chain (O), and star—and 4 five-person groups of enlisted military personnel in each of three networks—circle (O), pinwheel, and star—with feedback. The experimenter, at the end of each trial, provided feedback to the group on the errors they made (see page 573). There were 24 groups altogether. These networks are reproduced in Fig. 9-5. Each of these groups sat at a table partitioned into five compartments, with slots arranged so that members could send message cards to other members and receive cards from them according to the network diagram of their type of group. Each subject had a rubber tube which ran downhill to the experimenter. The subjects were told before the experiment that each one would receive five marbles of different colors. Each of the five subjects would be given one marble that was of the same color as one received by each of the other four subjects. None of the other subjects would have marbles the same color as his other four. The group's task was to determine which color was

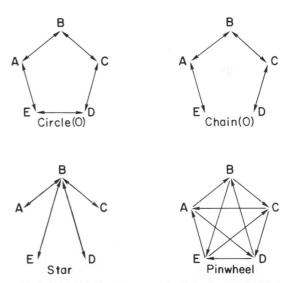

Fig. 9-5 Five-person group nets used in "noisy marble" experiment. (From L. S. Christie, R. D. Luce, & J. Macy, Jr. *Communications and learning in task-oriented groups.* Cambridge, Mass.: M.I.T., Research Laboratory of Electronics, Technical Report No. 231, May 13, 1952, 20. *Reprinted by permission.*)

shared by them all. This can be considered a decoding situation in which the group members were trying to arrive at a common symbol to be applied to a nonsymbolic input, in this case a color. They were to do this by sending written messages to one another. Also, each subject was to drop his marble of that color down his tube to the experimenter. He could correct an error by dropping another. A trial ended when every subject had dropped at least one. Each group had 30 trials—the first 15 with marbles of plain, ordinary colors and the remaining trials with marbles of cloudy, indistinct, mottled colors. It was not possible to control for individual variations in color perception in this experiment.[51]

It was found that there was little difference among the networks on the trials with the ordinary colors. Differences became evident, however, on the trials when the group had difficulty naming the mottled colors because of coding ambiguity or "semantic noise." Under these conditions, both circle groups were significantly more accurate than all other groups in the last six trials, an evidence of error reduction through learning. The pinwheel was more subject to error in the first few trials than all other groups. The star with additional feedback was more accurate than the original star or chain groups in the last few trials.

In order to measure the coding noise of the subjects, the experimenters computed a numerical measure of ambiguity which fundamentally concerned how many different marbles were called by one name. After making some assumptions which they call "questionable," they concluded that this ambiguity is a function and therefore a possible measure of the coding noise.[52] They predicted, correctly, that the errors of group members in selecting the common-color marble would increase as the coding ambiguity or "semantic noise" increased. Also, they found that redundant coding (multiple names for colors of marbles) was used to decrease error.

Several of the hypotheses related to the decoder stated in Chap. 4 seem likely to be confirmed at the group level. The noisy marble experiment appears to give some support to Hypothesis 3.3.4.2-1(b) (see page 98), which states that as groups mature (or learn), they use increasingly more efficient codes and, particularly, that the symbols are selected to minimize confusion among them. The findings also support the view that as groups mature, they increasingly use codes that make the transmission as free from error as possible (see Hypothesis 3.3.4.2-4, page 98), combating increasing noise in a channel with increasing redundancy in the message (see Hypothesis 3.3.4.2-6, page 98). Groups need more such redundancy to correct errors than merely to detect them (see Hypoth-

esis 3.3.4.2-7, page 98). Another way to achieve redundancy is for two or more group members to decode simultaneously (see Hypothesis 3.3.3.2-9, page 99).

Though not demonstrated in this experiment, it seems likely that the codes used affect the speed of decoding (see Hypotheses 3.3.4.2-2, 3.3.4.2-3, and 3.3.4.2-6, page 98). It also seems probable that over time, groups decrease the amount of recoding necessary among members, since all members have developed the same associations and learned the same codes. For example, a football team has repeated drills until all the players perfectly associate signals with plays (see Hypothesis 3.3.4.2-8, page 98). Distortions in group coding also seem most likely to occur when there is a small amount of information input (*i.e.*, it is ambiguous). An example is group agreement about psychic phenomena at a séance in a darkened room. Such ambiguous information input is commonly interpreted by the decoder in a way that reduces the strains of its components, as Hypothesis 3.3.4.2-9 (see page 99) states. For instance, a boy who has seen a baseball game tells his family of disputed umpire's decisions with a bias favorable to the home team—"We were robbed!" As Hypothesis 3.3.4.2-10 (see page 99) indicates, it may well be that as the strength of such a strain increases, information inputs will more and more be interpreted (or decoded) as required to reduce the strain.

Included among the *variables* of the process of decoding are: *Meaning of information which is decoded.* Example: The Intourist guide rapidly translated a wide range of written signs as the visitors rode along in their bus—from billboards to the names of subway stations. *Sorts of information which are decoded.* Example: The radar team observed two large shapes, one of which turned out to be a thunderstorm, and the other a blimp. *Percentage of the information input which is decoded.* Example: Three words of the 10-word message were illegible to all the players. *Threshold of the decoder.* Example: Neither the fore nor the aft sonar operator in the ship could distinguish a submarine from a whale at a range greater than a mile. *Changes in decoding over time.* Example: The whole squad became so fluent in Swahili that it no longer had to depend upon its translator. *Changes in decoding with different circumstances.* Example: As daylight waned, errors in transmission of messages between the two scout patrols increased because the boys found it difficult to distinguish the signal flags. *Channel capacity of the decoder.* Example: So many mathematical papers were relevant that a new member was added to the seminar to explain them. *Distortion of the decoder.* Example: The interpreter obviously allowed his political views to bias his translations of what was said to the team of foreign engineers. *Signal-to-noise ratio of the decoder.* Example: The cloudier the marbles were, the more errors the group made in agreeing on names for them. *Rate of decoding.* Example: All the groups with circle networks finished sooner than any of the others. *Percentage of omissions in decoding.* Example: About 10 percent of the notes written to the class from abroad could not be deciphered by the teacher. *Percentage of errors in decoding.* Example: An error rate of about 2 percent was considered normal for foreign-service employees translating Cambodian for their embassy delegations. *Code employed.* Example: When the gang wanted to discuss secret business, it used pig Latin. *Redundancy of the code employed.* Example: The telephone operator spelled the name of the exchange as follows: "Trafalgar, T-Thomas, R-Richard, A-Andrew." *Lag in decoding.* Example: It took the class 2 h to figure out the meaning of the symbolic logic in which the paper was written. *Costs of decoding.* Example: The Japanese tourist party hired—at $15 an hour—a full-time interpreter in order to get around in New York.

3.3.5 Associator, the subsystem which carries out the first stage of the learning process, forming enduring associations among items of information in the group.

3.3.5.1 Structure   At levels of group and above, the association of items of information must be done by one or more organism components. In a group it is always a laterally dispersed process. It is *not* necessary for the association to have taken place in every organism component, although that is often the case. It is conceivable, in a group with a single decider component, that one person alone might have made the association. If the group carried out his orders on the basis of that association, their actions would indicate that the association had been made.

Other possible arrangements are for a single organism or a subgroup to master a particular skill or for the group to divide a task requiring association so that each member takes responsibility for a part. Although different assignments of tasks in the associator are observed in the same group under different conditions, the subsystem usually includes all group members at some time, perhaps aided by computer.

3.3.5.2 Process   Successful groups, as they interact over time, associate in ways that are reinforced by feedbacks from past group actions that reduce strains. A family finds that solutions arise more rapidly and with less bickering if problems of importance are not discussed until after dinner. A work group associates increased pay with a particularly efficient way of organizing its task. A social group has more fun if its members refrain from arguments. A group of boys finds that mischief leads to trouble with the police. With such feedbacks the group's internal processes, and its responses in the environment and suprasystem, change. Groups in situations in which adaptation is required alter their total system behavior in much the same way as organisms do.

In discussing group learning, Cattell called this process a change in "syntality" (his term for the group equivalent of "personality" in an individual).[53] This change is brought about by rewards and punishments from the suprasystem which reduce and increase strains, as they do at the organism level, but more slowly since they are secondary to acquiring new responses by individual members. Rewards and punishments in groups vary in their impacts from one member to another. Feedbacks are sometimes delayed and indirect and therefore difficult for the group to associate with the event which elicits them.[54]

Another sort of feedback often involved in associating by groups is checking among the members to obtain confirmation that they share the same associations. This is what the cast of a play does in rehearsal.

Some details of group associating have been investigated experimentally with attention to such questions as: What form do curves of acquisition of group responses take? What sorts of rewards are effective? How do feedbacks on performance influence the associating process? How do groups compare with organisms in speed and efficiency of associating? Is the multiperson system better than any single member? If the group is better, why is it better? How do variations in group organization affect associating?

Research has been done on all these questions, as reported below, but the conclusions from it are not yet definitive. Experimental designs vary greatly, and results depend upon the sorts of constraints imposed. On the whole it appears that as groups carry out tasks, they improve in two general classes of actions: (*a*) dealing with the inputs from the environment which represent their task and (*b*) organizing their members to work together.

Some of these experiments have investigated two-person groups as they carry out "social tracking" tasks.[55] These are laboratory situations in which movements by one member of the group produce input signals to the other member to which he can respond, and vice versa. In one study two subjects sat side by side, each provided with his own hand control which he could move back and forth laterally for a distance of about 8 centimeters (cm). When either of these was moved, it influenced the signals on an oscilloscope in front of the subjects. The subjects' task was to move in coordination to compensate for, or negate, variations that occurred in computer-generated signals on the oscilloscope. Any error in such tracking made by either subject was indicated on the display. Over the first fifteen of twenty 1-min trials, separated by rest periods of 30 seconds (s), the average group showed progressive learning, particularly in the first eight trials. This improvement in group performance is particularly interesting because individual subjects in similar tracking tasks show little or no learning.

Groups' curves of acquisition of nonsense words were found in one study to be similar to those of persons carrying out the same sort of task, except that they rose faster.[56] Nineteen 2-syllable words were read to each group, and the group was asked to repeat the list immediately afterward. Any member was free to contribute, but the total group had to accept, change, or reject each word suggested. The final response was a group product, written down by a recorder or group output transducer. Discussion and correction were encouraged. Groups were forbidden to apportion the task explicitly so that each member was responsible for, say, six words. Whenever the group was silent for more than 30 s, the experimenter reread the list. Altogether it was repeated five times. At the end of the fifth reading, each member tried to write down the list independently. The members were then individually given another such list for five repetitions. Twenty groups were used, half of which had the experience as independent subjects before the group experience, and half afterward.

This situation provided a comparison of groups and single organisms on the same sort of problems under the same conditions. Single subjects who worked first in the group situation had significantly higher total scores and repeated lists more rapidly than those who first worked alone, and so the group experience was practice for independent performance of the same sort of task later. The accelerated group curves were matched by those of the best single subjects who had had prior practice with groups. Groups required more time than single subjects during early trials, but later group trials were about as long as those of single subjects, and in that time groups repeated more correct words. These findings suggest that a comparison of the organism and group levels at least partly disconfirms, for those levels, Hypothesis 3.3.5.2-6 (see page 99), which states that in general the higher the level of the system, the slower association is. Groups were more efficient at sifting out incorrect words, but also they invented more words, apparently in making efforts to reach agreement.

Although groups were forbidden to apportion their tasks explicitly among members, this was done implicitly. The same member often contributed the same words on successive trials, and other members left them to him and concentrated on others. Groups found the task less fatiguing than the single subjects did, perhaps because shared effort cost each participant less.

The findings indicated that groups are superior to organisms in this situation, not just because groups have more organisms with nervous systems, each processing less information, or because different members have different past experiences to call upon, but because multiple members can correct one another's errors and profit more from error feedback. Also, inputs may be more likely to be attended to and observed if there are multiple input transducers in operation.

In an experiment on learning numbers, five-person groups were arranged in different communication networks.[57] For each trial each subject received from the experimenter specific input information—a number from 0 to 99. Then each member was asked to learn what number had been given to each of the other members. The nine group networks in this study were circle (O), circle (X), chain (O), chain (X), pinwheel, barred circle, wheel, totally connected, and alpha (see Fig. 9-6). Five to twenty groups were run in each network. The subjects in each group were seated at a round table, separated by five radial wooden partitions. They were limited to written communication and could not exchange information related to the organization of the group or other matters unrelated to the problem. At the center of the table a slotted block of wood enabled each subject to transmit message cards over the channels permitted in the particular network to which his group was restricted. He could write messages only of the form: "From Subject Red, Subject Blue has the number 43." When he was ready to send a message, he would push a button, and after all five were ready, they would hear a bell signaling them to transmit their messages simultaneously. Thus all five would act at once, which constituted a single group action. This would be repeated until the end of the trial, which occurred when each subject knew what number every other one had received as input information. Each group had 25 trials in one network. They were told in advance the minimum number of acts in which a trial could be completed. Each message sent, the time required for each action, and the number of actions were recorded.

Even in the earliest trials group performance was better than random. As the number of trials increased, the number of actions and time required in trials decreased, the amount varying from network to network. Circle (X), barred circle, and chain (X) improved the most, and totally connected and pinwheel improved the least. The apparently local rational behavior of individual members plus the topological properties of the nets seemed to account for these differences. The curves of group improvement were often, but not always, smooth and slow. On occasion one or two successive minimum solutions altered performance from few such perfect solutions to almost all perfect solutions. In the noisy marble experiment described above, in which groups determined which color marbles all members shared (see pages 541 and 542), two characteristics were necessary for effective error reduction: (a) There must be enough interconnection among members to allow each one to receive, a fairly high percentage of the time, what purports to be the same information by two or more routes. This provides error feedback, which, as Hypothesis 3.3.5.2-3(a) (see page 99) states, is essential for associating. This is the same principle as von Neumann's concept of how reliable circuits can be made from unreliable components (see Hypothesis 3.3.4.2-7, page 98). (b) There must be a sufficient number of two-way communication channels for the members to correct the errors after they identify them. In principle it would seem that having each person connected to every other in the network would accomplish this, but in practice error correction becomes difficult if A must always talk to B through C.

The circle (O) has both error feedback and two-way channels, and in it errors were reduced well. The pinwheel has only error feedback, and in it there was some initial improvement and little further error reduction. The chain (O) and star showed no improvement as their respective members interacted. Some star groups were given feedback by the experimenter on the number of errors they had made and the number of marbles they had dropped erroneously. This is at least as much feedback about error as the circle would get, and yet the stars with this error feedback improved only slowly. It seems likely that the relatively poor performances of the star (with or without error feedback) and of the chain (O) result from the fact that each has one member in a control position through whom much of the information must pass, and he becomes relatively overloaded. The other members are unable to participate as actively in reducing error as they do in the circle (O) or pinwheel.

An investigation of group integration as members worked together in artificially constrained nets indicated that an individual member apparently was rewarded when he received responses from a given direction in the group network.[58] His transmission of messages in that direction was reinforced, and he continued to transmit them that way. Groupwide insightful planning also took place. Severe restrictions on

communication opportunities permitted only improvement of individual performances, but in freer situations the entire group also planned insightfully.

The effects of group task and communication net structure on associative learning as indicated by error reduction and improved performance in three-person groups have also been investigated in a research which I mentioned in an earlier chapter (see pages 152 and 153).[59] Groups were presented with a simulated aircraft control problem in which the members adjusted switches as instrument dial readings periodically changed. Members sat in separate booths and communicated by interphone. Information necessary for adjusting the controls in one booth was either entirely unavailable at first to the member who must operate those controls (Low-Autonomy condition) or available except for only one fact (High-Autonomy condition). The missing information was in another booth and had to be obtained from there. The rate of

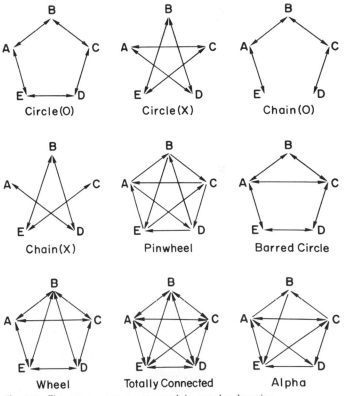

Fig. 9-6 Five-person group nets used in number-learning experiment. (From L. S. Christie, R. D. Luce, & J. Macy, Jr. *Communications and learning in task-oriented groups.* Cambridge, Mass.: M.I.T., Research Laboratory of Electronics, Technical Report No. 231, May 13, 1952, 20. *Reprinted by permission.*)

information input from changing dial readings was varied. As groups learned, they reduced their errors and improved their performances (*e.g.,* more and briefer messages were transmitted, and more of the trial time was used for communication). Learning was better at slow than at fast rates of information input to the group. Performance was better for the High-Autonomy condition than for the Low-Autonomy condition, which required more interpersonal interaction of the group.

Groups of three were studied in another sort of information-acquisition task using the Delta apparatus diagramed in Fig. 9-7.[60] Each of the three members sat at one side of the triangular apparatus. They were free to communicate as they wished and to assign subtasks among themselves. Each faced two lights and between them a switch, which could be moved either right or left. At the beginning of each trial all six lights would be on. The task was to extinguish them by using the switches. By moving their switches simultaneously toward each other, two subjects could cooperatively put out the two lights (connected by dotted lines in Fig. 9-7) between them. For instance, if Subject A pushed his switch to the left and B pushed his to the right, lights 5 and 4 would go out. The order in which the three switches were moved therefore determined the order in which the six lights were extinguished. There are six possible orders in which this can be done—*a, b, c, d, e,* and *f.* In each problem, the digits 1, 2, 3, 4, 5, and 6 were assigned, in a different permutation, to these six orders. The task of the group was to learn to associate digits with the orders to which they were assigned. In every trial each digit

was called out three times by the experimenter. After each time, the group extinguished the lights in some order. Then the experimenter gave them the feedback, saying whether they were right or wrong. All groups went through six to ten repeated cycles of eight such problems each. A decrease in error rate was observed as the experiment continued.

Calculating the number of bits of information in a problem, Rapoport, the experimenter, assumed that the rate of gain of information per error in such a task is constant. He also assumed that the residual uncertainty was distributed equally among the various digits representing different orders of extinguishing the lights. Adjusting two parameters—k, representing the extent to which the group used feedback, and E, representing the efficiency with which the group communicated to assign the total task among its members—he calculated theoretical curves of acquisition of the information: group learning curves. They fitted well the curves drawn from the data, suggesting that the assumptions on which they were calculated were correct. In such experimental games it has been demonstrated that group associative learning can enable the members to increase their cooperation, advance the common good, and discover the advantages of resisting temptations to substitute personal gain. They are much more likely to develop the mutual trust necessary to do this if they can intercommunicate than if they cannot.

Representative *variables* of the process of associating include: *Meaning of information which is associated.* Example: When the group changed its learning task from nonsense syllables to portions of a play, their rate of associative learning rose 300 percent. *Sorts of information which are associated.* Example: The group found that they earned more if they were less careful about quality and turned out more units. *Percentage of the information input which is associated to other information.* Example: The three crack detectives quickly made every clue they could find fit into the theory. *Changes in associating over time.* Example: The curve of acquisition of the nonsense syllables accelerated as the group improved. *Changes in associating with different circumstances.* Example: After the boss began to point out their errors, the work group gradually improved the wiring of the fuse boxes. *Channel capacity of the associator.* Example: The students were able to complete the work only by adding two others to their group and dividing up the task among them, each acquiring part of the list and ignoring the rest. *Rate of associating.* Example: It took about a minute for the group to acquire each new word in the list of 50. *Lag in associating.* Example: The children were uninterested and took months to comprehend the relationship between cleanliness and godliness. *Costs of associat-*

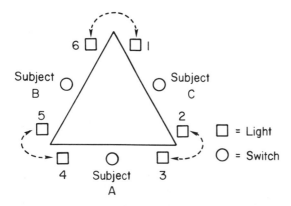

Fig. 9-7 The Delta apparatus. [From A. Rapoport. Some self-organizing parameters in three-person groups. In H. Von Foerster & G. W. Zopf, Jr. (Eds.). *Principles of self-organization.* New York: Pergamon, 1962, 2. Copyright © 1962 Pergamon Press, Ltd. *Reprinted by permission.*]

ing. Example: The group paid their instructor for three lessons before they became able to fit the motions of the dance to the odd rhythm of the music.

3.3.6 Memory, the subsystem which carries out the second stage of the learning process, storing various sorts of information in the group for different periods of time.

3.3.6.1 Structure This subsystem usually is laterally dispersed to all group members, each of whom stores information in his own nervous system (see page 32). In most groups, therefore, there is no group memory as such. In some cases, however, particular members, like secretaries or treasurers or parents of families, have special responsibility for keeping records or storing particular sorts of information such as facts about the managing of money belonging to the group. Parents and grandparents are often reservoirs of information for their children and grandchildren. The third generation taps the wisdom of the second and the first.

Notes, written minutes, photographs, financial records, books, tape recordings, filing systems, computers, and various other artifacts augment this subsystem in different sorts of groups.

Subhuman groups also sometimes depend on specialized components for memory. Altmann, who for years has observed elk herds in their natural habitat, has learned that memory of paths to food is stored in the elder females, who outlive the males.[61] Even in deep snow that spoils the scent, these old cows can use their lifesaving memories to lead the herd to food.

Groups may upwardly disperse some of their memory processes. Records of family events like births, deaths, and marriages are kept in organization memories like county or church offices. Money is kept in banks.

3.3.6.2 Process (*a*) *Reading into storage.* Groups have an advantage over single organisms in storing information. They have available as many central nervous systems as there are group members. Thus they are potentially able to store that many times as much information as the average member. Actually they never do, for everyone in any true group stores some common information.

(*b*) *Maintaining information in storage.* The limits of long-term storage capacity of a single human brain have not been demonstrated (see page 420). There is, however, a known limitation upon immediate memory. Most people cannot remember and recall at a single moment more than six or seven digits or nonsense words or repeat an extended prose passage after hearing it once or a few times. Groups can extend this capacity if each member shares the task. Also, if each participant brings to the group a different background of experience, as in juries and interdis-

ciplinary panels, the total system can store much more information than any individual could hope to.

(*c*) *Loss and alteration during storage.* Multiple storage in a group can adjust for individual differences in permanency and accuracy of memory (see Hypothesis 3.3.6.2-1, page 99) or in the probability of loss and increase in errors of memory over time. One member may not have learned a fact or may forget it, but another will remember it. Husbands and wives often help each other this way. A member may be wounded or may age and lose his memory and need to depend on others, or he may become ill and be unable to function—the reason that most theatrical casts train understudies.

Insofar as the memories of groups are dispersed to each of the group members, the fundamental problems of group storage and retrieval of information must be studied at the level of the organism. Many problems in this area remain to be solved. Because some groups also use artifacts for storage, the operating characteristics of these artifacts are relevant too. A research group, for instance, can depend, if it is lucky, on a computer with a core memory capacity of 1 million words or more, 36 bits per word, and tens of billions of bits of slower access memory. Retrieval is in microseconds or milliseconds.

(*d*) *Retrieval from storage.* It is possible to study retrieval of information stored in the nervous systems of groups under controlled laboratory conditions. The research on group learning of nonsense syllables described above (see page 544) is pertinent not only to the formation of associations but to their storage as well.

A group appears, under some circumstances, to need fewer trials than single subjects to solve problems[62]—although the process may be slower than individual problem solving[63]—because usually each move is verbalized and stored in the memories of group members; thus when a move is proposed, one member, several members, or all members will recall that it has been tried before and what the result was. The research on the group working with the Delta apparatus which is described above (see page 546) suggests that a freely communicating group can improve its problem-solving performance by parceling out memory storage functions efficiently among its members. If there are six problems in a task before a three-person group, each one can ordinarily remember the facts required to solve one or two of them. Communication among group members then can locate the solutions to all of them. One function of a chairman or decider in some groups is to organize an efficient and smoothly operating information retrieval process.

Representative *variables* of the process of remembering include: *Meaning of information stored in memory.* Example: The football team stored memories of dozens of plays, any one of which could be retrieved when the quarterback called the appropriate number. *Sorts of information stored in memory.* Example: The family remembered times when they had run out of money, and so they put a few lire in a mattress every week. *Total memory capacity.* Example: The ensemble could play together for more than 24 hours without using music and never repeat a composition. *Percentage of information input stored.* Example: During Sunday dinner the family could recall only three of the five points in the pastor's sermon. *Changes in remembering over time.* Example: The students gradually developed a system for sharing the task of remembering the lectures. *Changes in remembering with different circumstances.* Example: The study group at first kept no minutes, but they began to develop such good ideas that they decided to write them down. *Rate of reading into memory.* Example: The group was able to memorize about 100 nonsense syllables during each experimental hour. *Lag in reading into memory.* Example: More than an hour passed before the cast learned the scene's new lines. *Costs of reading into memory.* Example: The conference group paid a secretary $25 for tape-recording their discussion. *Rate of distortion of information during storage.* Example: The surviving occupants of the Presidential car were certain that their memories of what happened during the moments of the assassination of President Kennedy were in no way distorted after 3 years. *Time information is in storage before being forgotten.* Example: After about a year, the group could no longer remember what they had objected to about the new meeting room. *Sorts of information retrieved.* Example: All three authors searched their childhood memories for examples of rope-jumping rhymes to put into the play they were jointly writing. *Percentage of stored information retrieved from memory.* Example: After much hard work, current versions of the first three verses of the old song were put together by the club, but the fourth verse eluded them. *Order of retrieval from memory.* Example: The team remembered all the words concerned with colors first, and then the more abstract ones. *Rate of retrieval from memory.* Example: The cheering section spelled out a new letter with its cards every 5 s. *Lag in retrieval from memory.* Example: After the explosion and the prison break, everyone's mind went blank for a few seconds; then many details began to be recalled, some by one guard only and some by several. *Costs of retrieval from memory.* Example: The whole story of the accident was finally recalled, but getting the three witnesses to remember it took several hours, during which time each lawyer was paid $50 an hour.

3.3.7 Decider, the executive subsystem which receives information inputs from all other subsystems and transmits to them information outputs that control the entire group.

3.3.7.1 Structure   The decider of a group may be in a single component organism, which is often the case in work groups or authoritarian family groups; it may include certain members for one type of decision and other members for another type; or it may include the whole group in a democratic process. A single group often uses different decider structures in different circumstances. For instance, an American family will sometimes delegate two members to choose materials for a group project, committing the group to their decision. When choice of entertainment is offered, a vote by the whole group is taken. But when they are on a hiking trip, on a dangerous trail everyone follows the path chosen by the father.

Decider structures of groups are often prescribed by the suprasystem. Different cultures designate the father, the mother's brother, or the oldest male as head of the family. The scope of issues over which he decides may also be culturally prescribed. The particular areas concerning which a husband makes decisions and those which are the province of his wife may also be specified. Usually the wife makes decisions in matters concerning the household and young children. A cross-cultural study of domestic problem-solving situations found that the spouse whose prestige was bolstered by the society's kinship system tended to dominate the deciding.[64] Among Navahos, who inherit through the mother's line, family decisions were made in the wife's favor 46 times to the husband's 34. Among the Mormons, the paternal line is dominant, and the ratio was reversed: husbands, 42; wives, 29.

Work groups are frequently headed by foremen designated by management. Juries also have foremen who sometimes dominate decision making, but in the United States all the jurors are expected to be components of the decider, since in many cases unanimity is required and any member can "hang" the jury. On the other hand, when an American President and his Cabinet vote on a policy issue, there may be twelve negative votes and one affirmative. But if the affirmative is the President's, that represents the final decision because his role as the sole ultimate decider is prescribed by the nation's charter, the Constitution.

In many sorts of groups in which the structure of the decider subsystem is not prescribed by its suprasystem, it is determined as a by-product of other structural characteristics of the group. Position in the group's communication network, for example, is an important determinant of the decider in artificially constrained networks. In some net structures there may be more than one decision maker.[65] In the group networks used in one experiment on group decision making (see Fig. 9-8), the central member, B, was always the decision maker in the star. This was true also in the Y. But in the chain (O), the process was different. Usually information was channeled to the

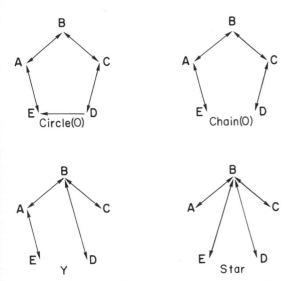

Fig. 9-8 Five-person group nets used in decision-making experiment. (From H. J. Leavitt. Some effects of certain communication patterns on group performance. *J. abnorm. soc. Psychol.*, 1951, **46**, 39, 42. Copyright 1951 by the American Psychological Association. *Reprinted by permission.*)

center from both ends, and the central member, B, decided what was the proper answer. Sometimes one of B's two flankers, A or C, decided on the answer and passed it on to B. In the circle (O), information was simply sent in both directions until any member got the answer. It was found that a group's network structure significantly affected the probability that it would select a leader at all. Only 13 out of 25 people who worked in the circle (O) identified any leader, and those named were scattered among all the positions in the circle. In the chain (O), Y, and star the frequency of naming a leader, and the unanimity of agreement as to who it was, increased in that order. In the star, all members who recognized a leader said it was the member in position B.

Other experiments have confirmed that the communication network structure in a group is a determinant not only of who transmits and receives information but also of who does the deciding.[66] In the five-person star, for instance (see Fig. 9-2), the central member (B) was almost forced by the net structure to become the decider. In the circle (O) and totally connected groups, each person had equal potential for carrying out this

function, and so if the group did not plan who should do the deciding, it remained undifferentiated, with the deciding dispersed to more than one member, and perhaps all members.

3.3.7.2 Process   The structure of a group's information processing network affects its deciding processes. One experiment showed that structure can determine how fast decisions are made.[67] The experimenters asked four-person groups using the four-person wheel, four-person slash, and four-person totally connected networks (see Fig 9-9) to decide on the best solutions to various human relations problems. Average decision times were markedly different, that of the wheel being 16.62 min, that of the slash being 14.00 min, and that of the totally connected net being 9.71 min. The number of message units required for solution did not differ significantly, but the average number of units transmitted per minute were significantly different—3.60, 4.95, and 7.19, respectively. The percentages of decisions of members who disagreed with the majority of their particular group were 18.75 for the wheel, 16.07 for the slash, and 9.38 for the totally connected net. Unanimity, therefore, was greater in the totally connected group, although the first two types spent more time trying to come to agreement. The individual decisions of the central members of such networks rarely deviated from group decisions, either because they used their centrality to get their opinions accepted or because they were in a position to be quickly pressured into conformity. By either explanation they appeared to be important in the decision-making process.

The individual information processing characteristics of the group member with the highest centrality have been found to alter significantly the functioning of the above-mentioned four-man group networks during the process of deciding.[68] Structures which have one member with high centrality are more vulnerable to disturbance in decision making because this person is especially likely to suffer from information input overload (see page 153) in carrying out his group functions. A central member may act as a

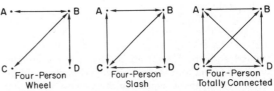

Fig. 9-9 Four-person group nets used in decision-making experiment. (From M. E. Shaw, G. H. Rothschild, & J. F. Strickland. Decision processes in communication nets. *J. abnorm. soc. Psychol.*, 1957, **54**, 324. Copyright 1957 by the American Psychological Association. *Reprinted by permission.*)

relayer or as an integrator. If he is a relayer, he passes on all information. If he is an integrator, he may handle his overload by using the adjustment process of filtering (see page 123), not sending on to other members each separate item of information as he receives it, but waiting until he decides on the solution and transmitting only this. This centralizes the decision process in him. Since the above-mentioned four-man groups were newly formed and performed on only three or four tasks, Mulder contends that the central members had no opportunity to develop such adjustments, and so their decision processes had not become centralized.[69] He constructed an index to measure the centralization of deciding on the "leader" position. Applying this index to groups, he found that whether decision making was centralized was, to a considerable degree, independent of the information network structure. Centralized group deciders, he found, are vulnerable to information input overload, particularly at the beginning of tasks. At such times information input and output demands on the leader are sometimes more than he can meet. This quickly disturbs the functioning of the entire group. Later development of a centralized decision structure, however, can be so efficient that this negative effect is canceled out.

On first thought, one is likely to say that deciding in groups is a function of the leader.[70] And, indeed, it often is. For example, in one analysis of leadership in the United States Army, decision making was found to be one of seven primary activities of group leaders.[71] Most groups appear to have leaders, and the commonsense concept that the leader is the primary decider has received much attention in group research. But there is no consensus as to what a leader is. In fact, he almost always seems to be all things to all investigators in this area. No clear-cut operational definition of the leader's function exists. He is a specialist in generality.[72] Nearly always he is said to carry out multiple functions. This blurs the concept of leadership so much that it has little scientific value. A different categorization of group subsystem processes or roles, like that in my conceptual system, should supersede the earliest one, made centuries ago, of leader and follower.

Group deciding seems commonly to follow the same four stages that are found at lower levels (see page 68 to 100 and also Hypothesis 3.3.7.2-1, page 100). Experimental and other empirical studies are not equally available for all four stages, but experiments could be conducted on those aspects of the process which are not yet thoroughly investigated.

(a) *Establishing purposes or goals.* Since few groups are totipotential, their relations to the suprasystem place limitations upon their decider processes. Setting of goals is an aspect of deciding that is often at least in part upwardly dispersed. The organization, either by charter or in the course of its ongoing processes, frequently determines that a given group exists for the purpose of carrying out certain activities. Often it also sets rates, quantities, and limits of variation of quality which will be acceptable. Even in such a situation, however, groups may carry out goal-setting activities. In their classical study of work groups at the Western Electric Hawthorne plant, Roethlisberger and Dickson found that there was a group code of values concerning the appropriate rate for a worker to put out work or turn out products.[73] This code served to apply negative feedbacks to regulate the output rate of the group, keeping it in a steady-state range. The code was enforced by approval and acceptance of those who conformed. In brief, it was this: "You should not turn out too much work; otherwise, you are being a ratebuster. You should not turn out too little work; otherwise, you are a chiseler." The group attempted by these rules to keep its output rate constant so that management would not demand faster production and yet would accept them as honest workers. The group would satisfice, making sufficiently good approximation to accomplishment in order to survive in that particular environment (see Hypothesis 3.3.7.2-16, pages 101 and 436). The output goals set by such groups cannot, of course, be too much at variance with the requirements of the organization's goal-setting activities.

There is a large literature on the activities of group leaders. These activities relate to many subsystem processes. Some that have been found to be characteristic of leaders are related to the part they play in this first stage of deciding. These are as follows:[74] deciding on the group's goals (D); making policies (G); controlling the group, even while embodying its norms and being controlled by it (F); and dominating it (C). [The letters in parentheses indicate which of the authors in Note 74 mentioned each particular activity.] Some of these are equally applicable to other stages of deciding.

A group of seven subjects in one experiment was asked to decide which one of several valuable objects the group as a whole would most like to have; then the group was asked to agree on a procedure to select which member of the group could keep it.[75] The various group members were known to have different orders of preference for the objects. The first of the two group activities is a goal-setting function. According to game theory, the way to accomplish the task set for the group would be for all members to form a "grand coalition" to agree upon which object had the greatest absolute utility to any one of them, although game theory cannot prescribe the ultimate settlement.[76] As it actually turned out, the experimental group eliminated all but three objects by discussion and then made their final joint choice by lot. There are a number of alternative procedures for making the choice, but none satisfies all conceivable requirements of equity. This has been demonstrated by a formal mathematical proof.[77]

(b) *Analysis.* In this stage of decision making the group sums up the situation, evaluates what sort of adjustment processes are needed to change it to conform to the group's goals, and discovers what alternatives are available. These range from a binary choice between two simple actions to a selection, involving the weighing of many variables, from among a complicated set of possible strategies, the probable outcomes of which are not always known. This process of analysis in groups is similar to that at all levels of systems, but particularly in organisms, and much of what I have said about analysis in mammalian organisms is applicable here (see pages 432 and 433). The presence of several nervous systems in a group makes the discovery of a number of alternatives more likely if the interactions of the members allow each one to participate in the discovery process.

The Justices of the United States Supreme Court, when meeting in private conference to discuss their views on a case, traditionally speak in order from the most junior to the most senior, the Chief Justice giving his opinion last. Experience through the years has led them to a procedure of group decision making which permits a wide range of alternatives to be reviewed and which diminishes the chances that the Court's internal status or prestige structure will result in the consideration of a restricted and homogeneous range of alternatives. One study indicated the wisdom of this procedure.[78] Thirty-six aircrews, numbering between 9 and 15 men each, participated. Each crew was shown, for 15 s, a large white card containing 3,155 irregularly arranged black dots. Then they were asked to come to a crew decision as to how many dots there were, following various set discussion procedures. The findings yielded suggestive, but statistically inconclusive, evidence that when a public survey of individual opinions is made at the outset of a discussion, more alternatives are considered by the group and the resultant decision is more accurate. Also, when the survey of opinions is made from the top to the bottom of the group's power hierarchy, fewer alternatives are considered than when the survey is in the opposite order because the first order tends to make juniors transform their views to match those expressed by their seniors.

Among the activities which have been found to characterize leaders, one seems particularly related to the analysis stage of decision making—thinking of the "best ideas" (A). [See Note 74.]

(c) *Synthesis.* This stage involves the actual determination of a strategy for action, an allocation of matter-energy or information among the group's components, or an agreement upon a judgment. Or the order in which competing plans will be tried may be selected. The number of alternative strategies which have been proposed is decreased in various ways, some of them logical. In the research described on page 550 and above, in which the group had to decide which one of several valuable objects it would like to have, this choice was carried out first. Then the group arrived at an "agreement" as to which member was to receive the prize. How this happened was amazing. One member simply took it and offered to sell it to the others at amounts less than they had declared it to be worth. No one bought it, and so he kept it, apparently not minding the obvious disapproval of the others. This "strategy" is not one which game theory even considers, and yet it resulted in a rapid selection of one out of seven alternatives.

Some conceivable plans of action will not even be considered. They will be laughed at or scorned and rejected. Like individual organisms, groups seem to rank alternatives in terms of their own value structure, their level of aspiration, and the probabilities they attach to the expected outcomes (see pages 435 and 436).

There is little empirical work available on the actual process of problem solving by groups. Many studies have been done on the effect of a group upon judgments made individually by its members (see pages 436 and 437). There are also a number of studies which compare the accuracy and effectiveness of group judgments and decisions with the accuracy and effectiveness of those of organisms. Hypothesis 3.3.7.2-21 (see page 102) suggests that groups should do better.

A large literature exists concerning the influence processes within groups which affect group decisions. In any group, some members are much more able to exert influence than others. This is one important skill of those who are considered leaders. Certain individuals tend to become leaders of whatever group they are in.[79] Bell and French consider characteristic behaviors of such people to be more determinant of leadership than the specific nature of a given group situation. Some of the characteristics of leaders which give them this sort of relation to the other group members are the following: being a "father figure" in Freudian terms (G); making plans (G); being an executive (G) or an arbitrator (F, G); assuming responsibility for decisions which belongs to other group members, thus helping them to "escape from freedom" (B, G); exerting control or influence on the group and its internal relationships (B, C, G, H); being a node in the group net, receiving many messages, and therefore being well informed (A, F); purveying rewards and punishments (B, H); dealing with those who disobey (F); and having the ability to satisfy the needs of members (H). [The letters in parentheses indicate which of the authors in Note 74 mentioned each particular activity.]

A number of characteristics of individual members have been found to be important in determining their places in the group decision making. Among these are sexual characteristics and skills in social interactions. Social status in the suprasystem organization or the society also influences who in a group makes the decisions. The different subsystem processes carried out or the roles played by men and women in jury deliberations are, in part, determined by the juror's sex.[80] In one investigation jurors were asked to indicate the four fellow jurors who most helped their group arrive at its decision. A total of 127 jurors were studied. They were classed as (a) either male or female, (b) either active or inactive in the jury, and (c) either important or unimportant in deciding. The authors sum up their findings to conclude that male jurors initiate relatively long sequences of acts directed at the solution of the problem, while women tend to react more to the contributions of others. The men are concerned more with task performance, and the women more with socioemotional issues. In another study it was shown that while women produced as many creative problem solutions as men, they did less well as leaders when they were forbidden to delegate decisions to the total group.[81] It may be that men's and women's functions in family life influence to an extent how they act in nonfamily groups.

Because juries are chosen from various strata of society, one can study in them the effects of status in the suprasuprasystem society upon group relationships.[82] A research on the impact of social status on group decision making employed simulated jury situations by using tape recordings of negligence trials and choosing experimental subjects from regular jury panels in Chicago, St. Louis, and Minneapolis.[83] The panels acted like real juries, under the supervision of actual court bailiffs. They deliberated in a jury room, selected a foreman, and reported their verdict to the "court." Their discussions were fully recorded and transcribed. In some experiments questionnaires were used as well. These juries were—and all real juries are—similar to most groups used in laboratory experiments, in that members are strangers who are brought together solely to work on a specific problem and are paid for their performances.

Each member of 28 such "juries" was asked who he thought contributed most to his jury's decision making. He was also asked whether he would prefer to have property owners, clerical workers, skilled personnel, or laboring people on a jury which tried a member of his family. Each of these categories was chosen by some jurors, but property owners were chosen 3½ times as often as laborers. Only one-fifth as many women were chosen as would be expected by chance. In the jury deliberations males of all four occupational categories talked more than females. Proprietors and clerical workers participated more than the average, and the skilled and unskilled laborers participated less than the average. Jurors were asked after the "trial" and before the deliberation what, if anything, they would award the plaintiff. When this judgment was compared with the final jury verdict, it was found that the most active jurors, usually proprietors, did not change their views after discussion as much as the less active ones. There was a significant correlation between the prior judgments of the jurors who spoke most and the final jury decisions.

In some sorts of situations the group decision is wrong, or the judgment is mistaken. Group errors have been found to arise when the group immediately and unanimously agrees to a wrong answer or when conflicts among members are resolved by an inaccurate compromise or surrender by socially less aggressive but correct members.[84] Whatever foreshortens group discussion before decisions are reached increases the likelihood of error, since such discussion stimulates concentration on the issues, careful thinking, consideration of a wide range of alternative solutions, and objective, critical testing of conclusions.

Two sets of four jury panels each were studied in one research.[85] Each jury sat on the same case in a moot court, in which the plaintiff was seriously injured as a passenger in the defendant's car. The experimenters arranged for stooges to be made the foremen of the juries. These stooges had either high or low prestige with the jury, and they used either autocratic or democratic procedures. Each foreman tried to get his panel to agree that the defendant was negligent and that the plaintiff should be awarded $40,000 damages, which was a higher award than the average juror considered appropriate. All juries found that there had been negligence. And all but one, after deliberation, increased the amount that they considered to be adequate compensatory damages, changing the average of their independent individual decisions made before such discussion in the direction of $40,000. The prestige of the leader and his mode of leadership did not significantly affect the results. The group decisions appeared to be arrived at by explicitly making rough averages of individual estimates of the members. The juries all seemed to discuss similar topics and go about deciding in similar ways, emphasizing the giving of orienting information and of personal opinions. Deciding involved a complex interplay of cognitive and affective processes, influenced by the particular situation and by the personal impact of the foreman, as well as other members. Individual members did not always agree with the group decision, but they supported it because the jury had to be unanimous if its decision was to be implemented—if the case was not to end with a hung jury.

In determining equitable damage awards, juries appear to be less likely to analyze each component of the damage systematically than to strive for a single sum which all the jurors can accept.[86] Cultural background and social and economic status affect a juror's attitudes toward damages. The judge's charge can carry great weight. Also, the jury can ease the strict necessity of determining a defendant to be either liable or not liable by flexibly modifying the amounts of damages. Claims of pain and injury do not influence juries as much as many people think they do. If the defendant is known to the jury to be insured, the jury is more likely to make him pay the full amount of damages.

The United States Supreme Court meets as a face-to-face group to arrive at decisions after formal presentation of arguments, individual study, and discussion among individual justices. Since decisions need not be unanimous and since dissenters as well as the majority record their legal reasoning, there is material upon which study of their deciding processes can be based. A factor-analytic study was made of the decisions of Supreme Court justices during 1943–1944 and 1944–1945.[87] The decisions of individuals clustered in such a way that three factors explained most of their votes, but the authors could not associate these factors with any obvious variables. Lawyers with whom they discussed the results related them chiefly to the personalities of the judges rather than to legal points of view upon which Supreme Court members might be expected to differ.

The Rules Committee of the United States House of Representatives is another powerful group of 12 congressmen.[88] This committee schedules the agenda of the House and determines what parliamentary procedure is to be followed. The influence brought to bear upon House members is usually informal. The leadership of the House never testifies before the committee, but an informal communication net exists through which its opinions are made known. Members meet at lunch and in other such situations and exert influence upon one another. The prestige of the influencer affects how successful he is. The objectives of his

party, his previous life experiences and social background, his church, his social class, his profession, the strength of competing demands, and the claims of his constituency—all are important. His colleagues do not expect him, in deciding how to vote, to jeopardize his political future unnecessarily.

Utility theory, first applied to decisions made by single persons, has been extended to group decisions in a growing literature.[89] Cardinal as well as ordinal scales can, under certain conditions, be employed to measure the relevant utilities, and if preferences of individual members of a group can be scaled, it is frequently possible to calculate the optimal group compromise decision which will most nearly satisfy the preferences of each member. This is a rational approach to the synthesis stage of the decision-making process.

(d) *Implementing.* In this stage, if action is to be taken, the group members agree upon one or more components to carry out the processes decided upon and determine how they are to perform them. They might agree, for instance, that the whole group will slow down its production rate, that one member will write a letter to the king, or that several will undertake a mission while the others wait. Group processes or the special characteristics of the chosen members or suprasystem requirements determine which components act upon the decider's commands. There is little useful research on the way groups typically implement their decisions.

The effectiveness of group decision-making processes was examined in conferences of 72 business, governmental, and industrial groups.[90] The activities covered were goal setting, problem proposing, and solution proposing. These appear to coincide with the first three stages of decision making as I have analyzed them. "Group productivity" was taken as the measure of the effectiveness of decision making. Demands for productivity, it was found, increased urgency, since if the suprasystem required that a decision be made, some sort of action ordinarily was taken. Productivity also increased when the group believed that it had sufficient power to assure that its decisions would be implemented to handle the problem under consideration. Adequate communication, in terms of audibility, understandability, and freedom of all group members to participate, favored productivity. Productive groups were orderly in procedure, penetrated deeply into problems, were rarely repetitious, and did not often discuss more than one topic simultaneously.

Group productivity diminished as the group members expressed more self-oriented needs. Greater group integration did not increase productivity. Groups with formal procedural structuring and emphasis on the differentiation between leaders and members were no more or less productive than less organized groups, although the members liked them more. Group members did not like the sharing of leadership by multiple participants, but they did not decrease productivity.

Groups in which all members agreed with the final group decision were neither more nor less productive than those in which there was minority disagreement. They did not report more satisfaction with the decision immediately after the meeting, but after a lapse of time their satisfaction was greater. Members of groups in which everyone felt accepted and supported and in which everyone believed that jointly they had the power to deal with the problem, after the meeting, agreed more with the decision. Groups with high agreement among the members proceeded in a more orderly and efficient manner, had better communication, paid more attention to group processes, and were more sensitive to what was happening in the group. Groups with more disagreement during the meeting also showed more disagreement afterward. Productivity, satisfaction, and residual disagreement were relatively uncorrelated, positively or negatively.

Representative *variables* of the process of deciding include: *Meaning of information employed in deciding.* Example: When the PTA learned that some of the members' own children had been hurt in the riot, their decision to intervene was made instantly. *Sorts of information employed in deciding.* Example: A search of the records revealed that there was a precedent, which the council decided to follow. *Amount of information employed in deciding.* Example: The matter was quickly decided by the jury after review of only two of the several verdicts which the judge had said would be acceptable. *Changes in deciding over time.* Example: As the board of trustees learned to work together, the several areas in which decisions had to be made were divided among the members. *Changes in deciding with different circumstances.* Example: When the deadline was reached, suddenly the collective bargainers were able to compromise on one of the alternatives that was wholly pleasing to no one. *Number of alternatives in input before decision and in output afterward.* Example: Out of three legal plays, the team chose one and lost. *Rewards and punishments attached to alternatives reviewed in deciding.* Example: The choice made by the company board was risky because the probability of striking oil was low and the chance of losing their stake was high. *Rate of deciding.* Example: The county commissioners considered and decided upon about three applications for street curbs and gutters at each meeting. *Lag in deciding.* Example: The family argued for 6 weeks about whether to plant onions or petunias. *Costs of deciding.* Example: The Boy Scout troop spent so much time deciding whether to go camping that they finally arrived at the site a day late.

3.3.8 Encoder, the subsystem which alters the code of information input to it from other information processing subsystems, from a "private" code used internally by the group into a "public" code which can be interpreted by other groups in its environment.

3.3.8.1 Structure   A single-component organism, a subgroup, or all members together may constitute this subsystem. A mother composes a letter in the name of the family. A publicity agent takes responsibility for preparing a press release for the soccer team. The group works together on a statement of their grievances. Sometimes translation into a language foreign to group members or into some sort of code is done by the encoder.

3.3.8.2 Process   Little research has been carried out on group encoding. One study, however, was done on African shrikes, birds which sing two or more parts simultaneously.[91] When they are apart, they cannot produce complex songs, and their vocalization regresses. Together they work out orderly and precise song patterns—even quartets and quintets. Another research showed that persons who interact for long periods come to use words with increasingly similar connotations.[92] The final wording of a group report or statement frequently conceals the private language used and the private group interactions which led to its issuance. The comment that the camel "looks like an animal that was put together by a committee" reflects some of the problems of report writing or encoding at this level.

Some of the most important *variables* of the encoding process are: *Meaning of information which is encoded.* Example: The press secretary prepared a press release to announce the decision of the president's cabinet, the first time any press release had dealt with the military invasion. *Sorts of information which are encoded.* Example: The entire office group contributed ideas to the memo requesting an air conditioner. *Percentage of the information input which is encoded.* Example: Less than a quarter of the laboratory's findings were written up for the public report. *Threshold of the encoder.* Example: The translator could not translate the address when the speaker's voice fell to a whisper. *Changes in encoding over time.* Example: The editorial staff became more and more skillful in getting out their annual reports, each adding a few paragraphs from personal experience. *Changes in encoding with different circumstances.* Example: The secretary of the local L'Alliance Française translated the poetry into French to send to a correspondent in Paris. *Channel capacity of the encoder.* Example: Three signal officers working on encoding the message together could process no more than 150 words an hour. *Dis-*

tortion of the encoder. Example: Somehow the wording of the announcement did not make the intention of the club clear. *Signal-to-noise ratio of the encoder.* Example: The Arab spoke so softly that the translator misinterpreted what he said to the Israeli ambassador. *Rate of encoding.* Example: The family wrote about 25 messages each day on their Christmas cards. *Percentage of omissions in encoding.* Example: What the crew put in their report about the mutiny was about half of what really happened. *Percentage of errors in encoding.* Example: None of the grocers in the store remembered the prices well, and one out of five was incorrect. *Code employed.* Example: The research team wrote their computer program in FORTRAN IV. *Redundancy of the code employed.* Example: The report of the operations research team first expressed the relationships in equations and then explained them in English. *Lag in encoding.* Example: It took several hours for the family to write a letter of condolence that satisfied them all. *Costs of encoding.* Example: All members of the group spent half a workday composing a poem for the boss's birthday.

3.3.9 Output transducer, the subsystem which puts out markers bearing information from the group, changing markers within the group into other matter-energy forms which can be transmitted over channels in the group's environment.

3.3.9.1 Structure   It is not unusual for encoder and output transducer components of groups to be the same or for a part of the encoder to perform output transducing as well. Mother not only composes a letter from the family to a sick friend but also transduces the words into written form, or one of the political party workers who helped to devise a press release also types it. Such is not necessarily the case, however. An officer in a military command may dictate a report to a sergeant who will type and transmit it to a higher headquarters, or a spokesman may represent his fraternity chapter at a national meeting and voice policy opinions prepared by several of his fraternity brothers at home. A publicity agent, official, or chairman may similarly speak for his group using the words of others.

The output transducers of groups include department heads, each of whom reports on activities of his own unit; bookkeepers who report on expenditures by departments; those in each unit who gather data on absences and hours worked which are needed to make up payrolls; representatives of working groups who report to echelons above them on employee satisfaction or demands, including union stewards or grievance committees; inspectors; operations analysts; and many others. Political groups or groups of citizens are parts of this subsystem when they sign petitions, speak for or against policies, or vote on issues.

Components of the group's extruder may also be components of its output transducer if the products of the groups are markers bearing information—*e.g.,* delivery boys from printshops or press agents who produce and hand out press releases. Also, components of the motor may be parts of the output transducer—*e.g.,* the council of ministers who go in a body to Queen Elizabeth to give her an official document, the athletic team that brings a petition to the college faculty, or the marching band that spells out words.

This subsystem may also be laterally dispersed to the organism level. Formal arrangements such as suggestion boxes or rewards for new ideas may exist to permit any individual employee to transduce information about the group directly to the group's environment or to the organization which is its suprasystem. Informal transducers are not uncommon. The president's secretary may gather information during her coffee breaks about the morale in the office of the vice president for planning and take it directly to the top. Artifacts are commonly used in the processes of this subsystem—telephones, teletypewriters, radio, and closed-circuit television, for example.

3.3.9.2 Process   Output transducing in groups appears not to have received scientific study. Publicity agents, officials, and spokesmen in various walks of life, however, have stored up much commonsense wisdom about what they should report about their groups and what they should keep private. In many organizations an important proportion of the time and energy of department heads is taken up with output transducing. Interoffice memos, slips to be signed and sent to other departments about various aspects of department activity, reports on the efficiency of employees and on the status of work in progress, reports of excesses or lacks of matter-energy and requests for correction of them, budget data, and necessary "housekeeping" information constantly flow out from many units and departments.

Distortions of information frequently occur in such transducing. A particularly vociferous minority in a town may make noises like a large majority, at least until the votes are counted. The personality characteristics of a committee chairman or the head of a department may make him withhold information about lack of harmony among those under him. Lags and omissions also occur as a result of the transducing process. Pressure of work can account for lags. Human error can bring about omissions.

Representative *variables* of the output transducing process are: *Meaning of information output which is transduced.* Example: The report of icebergs from the crow's nest meant that the ocean liner was in dire danger of collision. *Sorts of information output which are transduced.* Example: The older daughter typed the letter to the mail-order company. *Threshold of the output transducer*. Example: The auctioneer announced every one of the bids, no matter how quietly it was made. *Changes in output transducing over time*. Example: In recent years it had become the practice for the family to call Grandmother long-distance instead of writing. *Changes in output transducing with different circumstances*. Example: When the boy went overseas, his neighbors resorted to the mails to keep him abreast of community happenings. *Channel capacity of the output transducer*. Example: The library staff borrowed a second typewriter so that their report could be put in final form more rapidly. *Number of channels in use in the output transducer*. Example: Three of the department members prepared separate reports to the company president. *Distortion of the output transducer*. Example: The girl who typed the departmental report left out every reference in it to her own efficiency. *Rate of output transducing*. Example: The grievance committee passed on about five requests for reconsideration of a firing each month. *Lag in output transducing*. Example: The secretary could not stenotype as fast as the members could deliver their reports, and so she fell behind. *Intensity of information output*. Example: The group in the lifeboat screamed for help so loudly that the sound was heard through the darkness by a destroyer a half mile away. *Costs of output transducing*. Example: The jazz combo all contributed to pay rent for the flügelhorn.

4.   Relationships among subsystems or components

The subsystems and components of the group level may be associated by a much greater number and variety of relationships than those of any of the lower levels. Particularly the relationships which involve meaning, conveyed by interorganismic communication, are fundamental at this level. They are the essence of much group process, and in human groups they are often complex and subtle. Some of the relationships in human groups have been investigated in depth, as I shall indicate below. Often the group is studied in terms of a single kind of relationship selected by the observer from all the others for a particular analysis.

4.1   Structural relationships

4.1.1   Containment   Example: The women's garden club refreshment chairman (the club's ingestor) always sat as a voting member of the executive committee (the club's decider).

4.1.2   Number   Example: Five of the members of the twelve-man board of directors spoke little during the monthly meetings.

The relations between number of members interacting through the group network and other group variables have been studied extensively. Years ago Simmel made the point that the number of members determines the "forms and organs" which a group will develop.[93] Some forms of system structure are impossible if a group has too few or too many members, and others are imposed by changes in number. Triads are unlike dyads, for instance, because, among other reasons, each member of a three-person group intervenes between the other two. Besides the dyadic relationships between each member and each of the others, there is an indirect relationship between each dyad and the third member.

A study was made of 81 meetings of 36 groups numbering between 6 and 12 members each.[94] There was no differentiation of function among the members, and there was no control over how much they participated. Their members differed over a significant range in their amount of participation. A simple exponential model described reasonably well the relative participation of the various members, from most talkative to least. The larger the number of members in a group, the greater was the participation of the leader. A group numbering five, according to Slater, is optimal for information processing tasks.[95] Members of groups with more than five members say that their colleagues are too aggressive, impulsive, competitive, and inconsiderate and that the group is too hierarchical, centralized, and disorganized. Members of groups with fewer than five members are too tense, passive, tactful, and restrained to work together efficiently and happily. A five-person group appears to be large enough to permit members to express their feelings freely, make active efforts to solve problems even at the risk of antagonizing one another, and tolerate the loss of a member, and yet it is small enough so that there is regard for the feelings and needs of each person and a sense of loss if anyone should not be present or should leave.

After long years of experience, according to Thrasher, college fraternities have learned that they cannot exceed a maximum size of 35 to 40 members if intimate relationships and communal integration with unity of purpose are to be maintained.[96] If membership exceeds that number, the fraternity becomes so impersonal that the custom is to refer to the house as a "hotel." Thrasher also studied the organization of gangs; he found that 806 out of 895 gangs had memberships of 50 or under, with the largest number having between 6 and 10 members and the next largest number having between 11 and 15 members, most of these being loosely and informally organized and not solidly integrated among themselves or overtly incorporated into the community as recognized components. The latter was usually the situation of the gangs with more members. Only 89 had memberships from 51 to 2,000, and only 13 had more than 200. In larger gangs there were usually three more or less well-defined classes of members—the inner circle, members in good standing, and hangers-on. In general, as more members joined, the original gang became the inner circle or active nucleus, and new members did not have such intimate associations. The gangs had a division of labor in which each boy acted characteristically in relation to others and had a definite status.

Rating groups by interaction process analysis (see page 533), Bales and Borgatta did a research on how the number of members in a group is related to its types of social interaction.[97] Their groups varied from two to seven members. Four groups of each size were studied as they discussed a problem in human relations. The interactions of dyads were quite different from those of larger groups. For those larger than two, as the numbers of members rose, there was a marked increase in showing tension release (Bales's Category 2—see page 533) and in giving suggestions (Category 4); showing solidarity (Category 1) increased somewhat. Giving information (Category 6) increased, and giving opinion (Category 5) lessened. Showing tension or strain (Category 11) decreased, as did showing agreement (Category 3) and asking for opinion (Category 8).

The authors explained their findings as follows: As the number of members in a group rises, each member can be permitted less time to talk, and yet he has more relationships to maintain. There is consequently less time to build an argument; thus suggestions increase, and opinions, both asked and offered, decrease. Suggestions are more direct approaches to the group task than opinions, and with time at a premium, suggestions are given without taking time for a full review of opinions. Time pressure also diminishes the amount of agreement shown in larger groups. A large group is more likely to level sanctions than a small one, and the fact that opinions are more liable to sanctions than mere information is may explain why in larger groups there are fewer opinions and more information. Showing solidarity increases with number in the group, probably because the number of relationships which must be maintained increases faster than the number of members. Strain decrease is shown chiefly through laughter, which can occur simultaneously with other actions and does not compete for time with them. Infrequent participants in the group may show a high proportion of their behavior in this category under time pressure, and so strain decreases in the larger groups. Less strain is shown in them, possibly because there are more members among whom to distribute the necessary group functions, so that no

one is under great stress. Also, in large groups persons under strain do not need to become deeply involved, and so they do not show their strain.

Groups with more members in this study showed more variability in the behavior of individual members (possibly because of the greater number of subsystem functions or roles available to them), greater variability among sessions, and greater variability among groups. There was some evidence that each of these groups, even though short-lived, developed and maintained its own individualistic structural features.

Groups of 5 and of 12 Boy Scouts have been contrasted.[98] In those with 12 members, less consensus arose in discussion sessions, and more dissatisfaction was expressed. Scouts who were followers rather than leaders participated less frequently in such groups, feeling that their opinions were not important. The leaders had less influence in changing opinions in the larger groups.

Many-membered groups are characterized by more frequent contributors, less opportunity for any individual to become a leader, less influence of leaders on group consensus, less consensus, greater speed in solving abstract problems, and less speed on concrete problems.[99] One study divided 210 air crewmen into groups of from two to six. Also, some individual subjects were used. Each group or person had (a) to decide on the number of dots on a card which contained over 3,000 randomly scattered dots and (b) to solve some problems requiring judgment. Each was asked also to express the degree of satisfaction he experienced in the process. Errors in decision decreased as the number in the group increased, while satisfaction increased as the number went up from a single individual to four members. Five-man groups, however, were the least satisfied.

There are conflicting findings about the relationship of the number of members to the amount of influence they wield over their associates and to the efficiency of decision making. Comparison of results is difficult because the types of problems and conditions of decision making in the groups differed. In one such research, the ability of 15 individuals to solve problems in the game of Twenty Questions was compared by Taylor and Faust with the ability of 15 two-person groups and that of 15 four-person groups.[100] The individual subjects, two-person groups, and four-person groups all rapidly improved their performances over 4 days. In solving the problems, the groups averaged fewer questions, fewer failures, and less time per problem than individuals. Groups of four, however, were not superior to groups of two except that they failed less often to solve problems. Individuals averaged fewer man-minutes to solution than two-person groups, who averaged fewer than four-person groups. The authors speculated that perhaps their broader range of relevant information and their greater flexibility in approach accounted for what superiority groups showed over single persons in these tasks. It is not, they demonstrated, simply that a group is as good as its best member and that larger groups are more likely to have an outstanding member.

The emergence of a single-component decider or leader in two-, four-, six-, eight-, and twelve-member groups has been investigated.[101] The six-member groups were found to be most likely to develop a leader. A questionnaire concerning the behavior of superior leaders of groups with more than 30 and with less than 30 members was administered in another study.[102] It revealed that as the number of members of groups increases, demands upon the leader are greater and more frequent, and tolerance increases for leader-centered direction. Leadership becomes more impersonal and firm, emphasizing impartial enforcement of rules.

There also seem to be important differences between odd- and even-numbered groups.[103] Even-numbered groups are able to reach a deadlock with opinions equally divided, are more likely to show disagreement and antagonism, and are less likely to ask for suggestions. This odd–even difference may, of course, contribute to conflicting findings in studies on the number of members in groups where it is not controlled.

In an evaluative review of the literature (31 empirical articles) on the effects of numbers of members in a group on its function, Thomas and Fink concluded that the present research indicates that as the number of members in a group increases, the following things take place:[104] (a) Under some conditions both quality of group performance and group productivity tend to increase; less numerous groups are never superior in these aspects. (b) Expressions of disagreements and dissatisfactions occur more frequently. (c) Individual members can interact less. (d) Individual members have less opportunity to lead. (e) The average amount of participation per member decreases. (f) Group cohesion, measured chiefly by sociometric choices, decreases. (g) The least active member contributes less. (h) Members vary more among themselves in interaction. (i) A wider range of ways to solve problems is suggested and adopted by the group. (j) Each member suggests a wider range of ways to solve problems. (k) More votes are required to reach decisions. (l) More suggestions are passed on to others by those who did not originate them. (m) There is more specialization in ways to solve problems. (n) There is more organization and division of labor in the group. (o)

There are more cliques in the group. (p) Member satisfaction in discussion groups trying to solve problems decreases. Research also indicates that classes with many students are either better for instructional purposes than those with few students or at least not worse. Thomas and Fink also point out that many of these findings arise from the fact that both matter-energy and information inputs to groups increase with the number of members and that the total number of demands for attention, affection, and interaction by group members also increases. Also, the group (a) becomes more representative of the population from which it comes, (b) becomes more heterogeneous, and (c) increases geometrically in the number of possible relations which can exist among members.

All the foregoing findings indicate how extensively the structural relationship of number of group members has been investigated and how fundamentally this number affects group processes.

4.1.3   Order   Example: Women and children stood in front of men in the line waiting to enter the lifeboats when the yacht was sinking.

4.1.4   Position   Example: In the group of young Victorian aristocrats, the men accompanying women along the sidewalk walked between them and the street.

Spatial position of a member is clearly important in groups whose channel and net structure and process are experimentally constrained, for it affects his access to information, depending on which sort of net he is in. Spatial position is a determiner of the likelihood that he will exert leadership and influence and of the amount of his contribution to problem solutions (see pages 548 and 549). This is true also in public conveyances like buses or planes, where the operator or pilot is at the front, or at banquets or lectures, where the speakers are at head tables or on platforms before the audience.

Behavioral scientists often refer to positional relationships in groups. Adolescent gangs have been observed to gather around their leaders in a bowling alley and a cafeteria.[105] Cultural differences in such positions have been noted.[106] Latin Americans stand closer to each other than North Americans, Lebanese converse across long distances sitting at opposite sides of a room, and French leaders prefer to remain in the middle of their subordinates. Groups seem implicitly to recognize an "ideal sphere" of physical space which each member is entitled to have around him.[107]

In a nine-person group with a leader and in a ten-person leaderless group it was found that position in the circle in discussion groups affected the probability that one member would directly follow another in speaking.[108] Those seated opposite to the last speaker were significantly more likely to speak next. This effect has also been observed in other groups, members interacting more with persons sitting at a greater distance from them than with some others, if the former were within their line of vision.[109] Under another condition of leadership, members of six-person groups meeting regularly for 8 weeks interacted most with people sitting next to them. Apparently the type of leadership in a group influences position effects.

Each group member was rated on leadership in experiments by Bass and Klubeck on 20 six-person, 29 seven-person, and 12 eight-person leaderless discussion groups arranged as in Fig. 9-10.[110] They decided that their data did not demonstrate any effect of the seating position a person occupied upon his leadership rating. When Strodtbeck and Hook reanalyzed the data separately for groups of six, seven, and eight (which Bass and Klubeck had not done), they came to a different conclusion.[111] Leadership was most likely to be shown by those in the first and sixth positions in six-person groups, they decided, and by those in the first, third, sixth, and eighth positions in eight-person groups. The pattern of leadership was different in seven-person groups. The member at the point of the "V" (number 4—see Fig. 9-10b) shifted participation away from the end members (1 and 7) to himself and to his two closest associates (3 and 5), so that the three at the point showed the most leadership, and those at the end showed the least. Strodtbeck and Hook believe these data indicate that participation in groups is determined more by visual accessibility than by distance. In a circle, they point out, a person is most affected by the one he can see most easily, the person opposite him (who happens also to be the most distant), so that here the effects of distance and accessibility cannot be distinguished.

When three- to six-person groups sat down at a

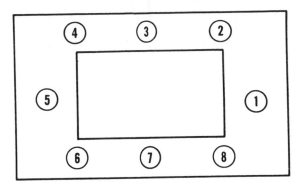

Fig. 9-11 Arrangement of Sommer's groups. (From R. Sommer. Leadership and group geography. *Sociometry.* 1961, **24**, 101. *Reprinted by permission.*)

rectangular cafeteria table with chairs arranged as indicated in Fig. 9-11, Sommer found that the designated leaders in three-person groups showed no position preference but that in the larger groups they usually sat at an end position (*i.e.*, 1 or 5).[112] When the leader sat there, the others preferred the chairs nearest her or him (2 and 8 if the leader was at 1; 4 and 6 if the leader was at 5). When the leader was in a corner chair (2, 4, 6, or 8), the others tended to sit opposite her or him or at the end next to her or him (at 8 or 1 if the leader was at 2). When the leader was in a side-center position (3 or 7), the others showed no seating preference. Members would rather take a position facing a leader than put her or him in a central position. Leaderless groups took places symmetrically around one end of the table, though this was less true of the larger groups that filled most of the seats. In such groups the central positions (3 and 7) are nearest to all the others. In another situation using couches but no tables, when the couches were less than 1 m apart, dyads chose to sit opposite each other (so putting their faces 1.6 m apart), but if the couches were separated by 1 m or more, they preferred to sit side by side.

Sixty-nine experimental jury deliberations were studied by Strodtbeck and Hook.[113] The jurors were drawn by lot, listened to a recorded trial, went into a jury room, seated themselves at a jury table with five jurors on each side and one at each end (as indicated in Fig. 9-12), deliberated, and returned a verdict. Each juror was then asked to select the four other jurors he preferred in his group by means of a sociometric test in which he was asked to check each of four seating positions on a diagram of the jury table. Preferences of jurors were found to be determined to some extent by physical distances, but also by other considerations. Table length, visual accessibility, and table width appeared to be three primary determinants of the

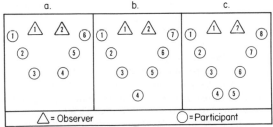

a.	b.	c.

Six-Person Group   Seven-Person Group   Eight-Person Group

△ = Observer   ○ = Participant

Fig. 9-10 Arrangements of Bass and Klubeck's groups. (Adapted from B. M. Bass & S. Klubeck. Effects of seating arrangement on leaderless group discussions. *J. abnorm. soc. Psychol.*, 1952, **47**, 725. Copyright 1952 by the American Psychological Association. *Reprinted by permission.*)

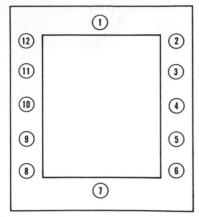

Fig. 9-12   Arrangement of Strodtbeck and Hook's juries. (From F. L. Strodtbeck & L. H. Hook. The social dimensions of a twelve-man jury table. *Sociometry*, 1961, **24**, 400. *Reprinted by permission.*)

sociometric choices. Jurors seated at the ends of the table were selected most frequently, followed by those in the middle of the sides and then by those flanking the middle; those at a corner were selected least of all. If the number of sociometric choices can be considered a measure of abstract "social distance" of the jurors at one position as compared with the social distance of those at the others, then while physical distance influenced social distance in these juries, other factors were also important.

The distance between the spatial positions of group members is significant in another way also. Dyads which continue their relationship when distance is increased do so at a higher cost in transportation time and effort.[114] Therefore, if the "principle of least effort" (see page 35, Note 101 on page 50, and page 436) applies to them, they must get greater rewards from more distant relationships. One study of a housing development indicated that residents formed friends partly on the basis of proximity (see page 9).[115] They had far more agreement on attitudes toward educational policies, use of leisure time, politics, religion, and such matters with friends living outside their development than with friends who were neighbors. This suggested a willingness to expend more energy to associate with persons having similar values, although other uncontrolled factors may also have influenced these findings.

The above studies are selected from an extensive literature on the position relationships in physical space of group members, a literature which makes it clear that such position affects group processes in important ways.

4.1.5   Direction   Example: The teacher and her class faced each other.

4.1.6   Size   Example: The pioneer women and children huddled together, while the men spread out in a wide circle around them.

In group research "size," which I use to signify the amount of area of the physical space which is included within the boundary of a group, is frequently used to mean the number of members because spatial coordinates are often neglected in group research. Size is, however, a relevant variable quite aside from number. It is true that ordinary speech reinforces this confusion: When we say that a man has a large family, we do not ordinarily mean that he lives on more than an acre of land. At the levels of organization and society also, the two concepts are confused regularly. Australia is a "large" country with a "small" population, for example, and Italy is the reverse. The size of the area within the group's boundaries affects many of its subsystem processes. The type of physical channel that can be used depends upon this, since a voice or gesture can be transmitted over only a limited distance without electronic aid, particularly when the noise level of other conditions is not optimal. In very spread-out groups, a multicomponent decider, or memorized or written instructions, may be necessary to keep the group coordinated. Matter-energy processing is also affected. Separate storage areas for supplies become necessary if matter-energy exchange is made difficult by distance.

4.1.7   Pattern   Example: The Michigan State football team started to play in "split T" formation.

4.1.8   Density   Example: When the fifth child was born, the house became so crowded that it was necessary to install bunk beds.

Density, the ratio of the number of members in a group to the size of the area occupied, has important effects upon group process. A family of five forced to live in one room has different processes from those of a family of the same size living in a mansion. The overcrowded classroom increases the difficulties for both students and teacher. A group of secretaries whose desks are so crowded together that they touch is often less efficient than a group in which all members have their own private areas.

4.2   Process relationships

4.2.1   Temporal relationships

4.2.1.1   Containment in time   Example: A clean-up committee was formed to work during the night after the annual party; then it disbanded.

4.2.1.2   Number in time   Example: During the experiment, the most peripheral member of the group sent 12 messages to the central member.

4.2.1.3   Order in time   Example: Each associate justice of the Supreme Court in the private discussions of cases spoke in inverse order of seniority, and last of all the Chief Justice gave his views.

4.2.1.4 Position in time   Example: In the first play of the fourth quarter, the quarterback carried the ball.

4.2.1.5 Direction in time   Example: The bowler bowled, and then the batsman swung.

4.2.1.6 Duration   Example: The Chairman and the Ways and Means Committee conferred for an hour.

4.2.1.7 Pattern in time   Example: Little interaction occurred during the early part of the meeting, but conversation later became heated, and a fight broke out.

4.2.2 Spatiotemporal relationships

4.2.2.1 Action   Example: Jack shoved, and Joe fell off his chair.

4.2.2.2 Communication   Example: The officer commanded his men to report the events of their mission, and they did.

4.2.2.3 Direction of action   Example: The successful candidate moved through the group to the front of the room.

4.2.2.4 Pattern of action   Example: The dance group followed an intricate pattern of whirling, leaping motions.

4.2.2.5 Entering or leaving containment   Example: The oldest member stalked out of the subcommittee meeting in a huff.

4.3 Relationships among subsystems or components which involve meaning   Example: The researcher discovered that the following interpersonal relationships were basic to the interactions of the scouts in the Eagle Patrol—liking or not liking others in the patrol, evaluating them, exerting control on them or submitting to their control, sharing or disagreeing about attitudes, adhering to mutual values or debating them, working on the same task or on different ones or on none, being similar or not, possessing or not possessing, causing or not causing, and belonging or not belonging.

5. System processes

5.1 Process relationships between inputs and outputs   The internal processes of groups, unlike those of living systems at lower levels, are so readily observable that studies of interlevel hypotheses about how component member organisms carry out adjustment processes within them are more common than researches on intralevel hypotheses that deal with groups as "black boxes." Under various circumstances, regularities in relationships between inputs and outputs of groups are of practical interest, however. One such situation occurs when a suprasystem organization is concerned primarily with whether the group is producing a satisfactory output, considering its inputs. Another example is a situation in which the privacy of the group is so nearly inviolable, as in the case of juries, that an outsider has great difficulty making objective observations of its internal activities.

(a) *Matter-energy inputs related to matter-energy outputs.*   Certain general relationships between matter-energy inputs and outputs at this level appear obvious. The quality of the material inputs to a work group, for instance, affects the quality of the outputs, the quantity or number of units output per unit input, and the rate at which units are output. The amount of material available for use in a unit of output also affects the quality and other aspects of a product under some circumstances. An instance is when cloth is cut by a group of ladies' garment makers into dresses with overly narrow seam allowances or not enough material in the pleats for good fit.

Rates and precision of processing by manufacturing groups in industrial organizations are determined both by the technology involved in particular jobs and by the skill and effectiveness of the groups employed. Often the former is the dominant factor, and the actual input–output rates are not affected importantly by how the work group interacts. Tasks in modern factories are usually shredded out, and each aspect is then suballocated to a specific group. Both upper and lower limits are set for speed and quality of the product in order to maintain a steady rate of output and to minimize variations in quality.[116] Materials or units move along at speeds determined on the basis of a large number of variables of the production process, including rates of processes immediately before and after the one under consideration and production goals of the organization as a whole. Rates for any group of workers are often agreed upon in union–management negotiations.

(b) *Matter-energy inputs related to information outputs.*   Matter-energy for markers must be input in quantities and at rates sufficient to bear all the information to be output from a group. This includes the paper for pamphlets, newsletters, reports, or other written outputs of a committee or the radio equipment by which groups of explorers or scouts keep in touch with a base camp. Also, the group must obtain the machinery needed for inscribing the message on the marker, for example, a linotype in a printshop or the engraving tools and press without which a gang of counterfeiters is forced into unwilling rectitude. The materials needed for maintenance and repair of such equipment are also matter-energy inputs required for information outputs. Rates of inputting these determine the output rate when they are scarce, but usually not otherwise. Information, not including that output by counterfeiters, can ordinarily be conveyed by different sorts of markers. Therefore, the format of a message output by a group is determined by what kind of materials capable of being markers have been input. When their radio breaks down, for instance, a band of explorers may appeal for help by lighting flares or by writing in the snow.

(c) *Information inputs related to matter-energy outputs.* Orders or requests for a group's product, instructions as to rates or quantities to be manufactured, and money or other inducements to a group to continue producing its output or to produce it at a high rate are all important information inputs related to matter-energy outputs. Money for purchasing materials needed for a group's product is another important information input. The amount of money input places limits on the quality, rate, and quantity of the output.

A group of kindergarten children will cheerfully make as many paper snowflakes as the teacher wants to paste on the windows. This willingness to produce in response to demand does not characterize work groups in industrial organizations. The question of how best to induce them to keep on putting out their product at an acceptable rate over long periods has occupied the attention of factory managers and industrial psychologists. Each member of a work group is paid for his or her participation in the group and organization outputs. Further money inputs in the form of increases in individual pay for the best performers in a group or special rewards to high-producing groups are commonly used. There is some evidence that these incentives work better when they are directed to individuals rather than to groups.[117] In many industrial situations, however, the individual contribution to a group output cannot be easily determined. Efforts to do so may be seen as attempts to "sweat" the workers or to exploit or divide their work group. They can result in poorer rather than improved performance.[118] "System rewards," which include higher pay for longer service, retirement pay, and fringe benefits of various sorts, are frequently offered to workers in groups in the hope that these will motivate them to work hard and well. Advancement to more desirable work groups and higher-paying or more powerful or prestigious positions may also be offered to individuals. Punishments are the opposite of such rewards. These also may be used as motivations (see page 409). An organization can refuse advancement to a whole group or to members in it. It can also admonish employees to work harder or threaten to fire them for poor work.

Changing job descriptions or making performance evaluations can cause work groups to refuse to do work that they have willingly done before. This may be the effect, even though the intent of providing new job descriptions is simply to make explicit to each group of workers exactly what is currently included in

its work. The following example, given by Dubin, indicates how the information input of a job description affected the work output of a group of welders:

On production welding, finish welders were refusing to do tack welding and fitting work. Before making the finish welds requiring high uniformity and accuracy, large parts were put in a fixture holding the pieces in place. Then temporary "tack" welds were made at regular intervals to hold the pieces together rigidly for the finish weld. Fitting and tack welding were lower skilled and lower rated jobs, but the finish welders were ordered by management to do them in the interests of maintaining continuity of production. Management guaranteed the finish welding rate even while tack welding and fitting were being done. The finish welders refused, claiming tack welding and fitting did not come within their job descriptions. The finish welders had been segregated by their job descriptions as a high class work group. They refused to perform lower level work even though it involved no financial sacrifice, and had they done it, would have increased overall output. Job descriptions made work assignments rigid and actually impaired output efficiency in this case.[119]

(d) *Information inputs related to information outputs.* The relationship of information inputs to information outputs is similar in many ways to their relationship to matter-energy outputs as far as rewards and punishments are concerned. Effective incentives increase the rate and quality of output from a group processing information, just as they do in the case of a matter-energy processing group. A group's information output may also be directly affected by instructions from its organization suprasystem. The judge's instructions to a jury as to the legal principles affecting their decision and his directives that they ignore certain aspects of a person's behavior and testimony during the trial have a compelling influence on their deliberations and findings. When in doubt, they may request further clarification of difficult points. A sales manager influences the performance of the group of salesmen under him by describing to them the sales pitch they are expected to use in promoting their product. Indoctrination in an organization's goals may also be reflected in increased proselytizing for the organization by groups within it, such as a membership committee or pairs of missionaries that go from door to door preaching to housewives.

5.2   Adjustment processes among subsystem or components, used in maintaining variables in steady states

5.2.1.   Matter-energy input processes Adjustments to lack stresses of matter-energy input include (a) adding group members to the ingestor, as when the chief of a nomad band of Bedouins sends out most of his men to forage for food when it is scarce; (b) enlarging the territory through which a search is made, for instance, extending the hunt for chickens to the neighbor's yard; (c) facilitating exchanges across the boundary with other groups so that plentiful items may be easily traded for those in short supply; (d) replacing a less efficient ingestor with a more efficient one, as when the son goes out to earn the family's living, rather than the aging father; (e) praying or carrying out some ritual to propitiate supernatural powers so that they will provide the needed inputs, as in Zuni rain dances; (f) building artifacts, like dams or wells or mills, to collect, store, or process scarce forms of matter-energy; and (g) substituting a more readily available form of matter-energy for the preferred one, as when a poor family buys bread instead of lamb. Threats of impending matter-energy input lack stresses are often met by group action such as storing the input while it is still available. For example, a family may harvest and garner grain as soon as the winds of autumn begin to blow, so avoiding the legendary plight of La Fountaine's hungry cricket. All these adjustments have costs in human or animal or machine work expended, various sorts of matter-energy used, or money spent.

Excess stresses of matter-energy inputs can be either gluts of otherwise desirable matter-energy or damaging onslaughts of such things as floods, storms, fires, or hostile organisms. Gluts of imperishable substances can sometimes be handled by the group's matter-energy storage subsystem. Increased use by group members of the abundant product instead of some other less plentiful one may be the solution, as many a delighted American infantry squad in Patton's army found when, as they advanced in the region of Épernay, they made champagne sauce for their field rations. Or it may be distributed more widely within the group so that more members share it, as when an agency has so many rugs that every office can have one. The extruder may put excess materials outside the group's boundary, or the group may select out only the most desirable constituents of the input and reject the rest, which is how royalty copes with the many gifts they receive. Allocation of an abundance is less likely to provoke strains among components of a group than allocation of a dearth. Also, the costs of the adjustments may be less, although in their accomplishment they all use up at least a little human effort.

When a group receives a threat warning of some impending excess stress, it usually prepares to cope with it. The boundary may be strengthened; guards or lookouts may be posted, ready to shoot an invader or to give the alarm. Defense of a group occurs in the lower animals. For example, if a stranger rat enters a pack of rats which have lived together, it does not smell "right" to the others, and so they attack it violently, with their eyes bulging and their hair standing on end, and tear it to pieces.[120] If, however, it is placed in a small pen where it is protected by wire netting until it has had time to acquire the pack's odor, the other rats will accept it. If a rat born in the pack leaves it long enough to lose its characteristic odor of the pack, that rat is treated like a stranger when it returns.

Animal groups of some social species adjust aggressively to the entrance of a predator into their environment. Flocks of small birds will mob an owl which they discover by day, when it is sleepy and cannot see well. They drive it far out of their territory. A herd of zebras will jointly molest a leopard if they find it in an area where cover, from which it could attack them, is scarce and when they can surround it.[121] When animals defend their territory, the cost may be the wounding or even the death of an invader or a defender, or both.

When he sees the threat of a funnel cloud, a farmer may collect his family and run to the cyclone cellar that was dug in advance. All members of the family except the aged, the infants, and the sick may work desperately to dig a firebreak around their home or shore up the levee. This behavior is consistent with Hypothesis 5.2-2 (see page 106), which states that the greater a threat or stress upon a system, the more components of it are involved in adjusting to it. Previous internal strains among components of the group are temporarily neglected, and the group integration increases under such threat or stress. This is exactly what Hypothesis 5.2-13 (see page 107) proposes as a cross-level proposition. The group ordinarily will comply willingly with the orders from its chosen or natural decider—perhaps only to begin squabbling again when the threat has passed. Another adjustment is to solicit help from other groups—a ham radio operator, as the output transducer for a stranded troop of campers, may call for emergency aid. Or if the group finds it difficult to cope alone with the environment, it may add new members—as Robinson Crusoe and Friday so much wished to do. All these adjustments have costs in human energy expended.

On the other hand, it may be inconsistent with the values or purposes of a group to admit too many members, and so the boundary subsystem decreases its permeability. For instance, the admissions committee of an exclusive social club, by being highly selective, keeps the members from becoming so numerous that they do not know one another. At times such a group may become so exclusive that no one enters, and the ultimate cost is that it dies out.

5.2.2 Information input processes Information input underload, a lack stress, can be combated in various ways by different sorts of groups. A group of soldiers in the field sends out scouts to bring back vital information about their environment—terrain, enemies, food sources, and so forth. A firm's board of directors names a member to arrange for research on the marketing activities of its competitors.

Isolated groups have more defenses against underload of information than individual organisms do because they can draw on their own information transmission and storage processes, talking, telling stories, or playing games. Yet groups in isolation are subject to internal strains which can be disruptive. This fact supports at the group level Hypothesis 5.1-42 (see page 105), which states that a minimum rate of information input to a system must be maintained for it to function normally. When two men are shut up together in the cabin of a spaceship, information input lack can lead to boredom. Hours may pass while they carry out monotonous tasks, monitoring their instruments. In one experiment teams of two men each remained in a space-cabin simulator for as long as 30 days, performing appropriate tasks assigned by the experimenters, Cramer and Flinn.[122] Many problems arose, including strains between the two men, but there were fewer signs of sensory deprivation (see pages 452 to 454) than occurred in an earlier one-man space-simulator experiment. Perceptual distortions occurred at least once, however, in nearly half the subjects. These were transient and not associated with a true loss of contact with reality or disruption of performance. An example given is this: "It seems strange that at times in the far-off distance it sounds like I can hear music playing or at times sleeping in the bunk a noise was heard that sounds like an F-100 taking off. This probably comes from big blowers that circulate the air. Sometimes you think the noise is coming from the outside but that is hardly possible. B *had the same experience so I don't feel that I am off my rocker.*"[123] The presence of someone else makes it possible for a person to check his or her own experiences to see whether they are illusions. Whatever a group does to adjust to information input underload entails costs in energy expenditure by the members.

Group adjustments to the excess stress of information input overload have already been described (see pages 182 to 187). All the adjustments against overload available to all living systems can be used by groups. But groups and higher-level systems are more able than organisms to employ the *multiple channels* adjustment or division of labor (see pages 159 to 161).

5.2.3 Matter-energy internal processes Animals have a number of adjustment processes which enable groups of different types or species to share the same environment. What has been called an "ecological niche" may make this possible (see pages 77, 465, and 469). If one species lives and feeds high in the trees, while another species—even a closely related one—lives on the ground, they are in different niches and need not compete. Both can survive.

Animals of the same type or species live together in a variety of groupings which range from extremely nonsocial to extremely gregarious. In each species the individual organisms maintain typical distances from one another and arrange themselves in typical spatial patterns. These patternings represent adjustments among a number of variables, including how aggressive the species is, how social it is, and how food in its area is distributed.

Aggression among members of the same species is adaptive in several ways:[124] (*a*) To avoid attack, individuals spread over the available environment and so are in less competition for the same food; (*b*) aggression selects the strongest animals for breeding and prevents the weaker ones from participating; and (*c*) aggression by parents against potential molesters of the young preserves the young.

Among nonsocial animals, individuals defend particular hunting or nesting territories, which often vary in size with the strength of the animal. In some unaggressive species individuals space themselves for reasons unrelated to protection from attack. Some tree frogs, for example, live alone except at mating time and space themselves to avoid the quacking sound made by others in the species. Other species cannot bear the smell of their own kind and consequently keep away from one another.[125]

Even among social animals which flock together, aggressiveness may play a part in spacing. Lorenz says:

The important effect of intraspecific aggression, dispersing and spacing out the animals of a species, is essentially opposed to that of herd attraction. Strong aggression and very close herding exclude one another, but less extreme expressions of the two behavior mechanisms are not incompatible. In many species which form large flocks, the individuals never come nearer to each other than a certain minimum distance; there is always a constant space between every two animals. Starlings, sitting like a string of pearls at exactly regular intervals along a telegraph wire, are a good example of this spacing. The distance between the individuals corresponds exactly to the distance at which two starlings can reach each other with their beaks. Immediately after landing, they sit irregularly distributed, but soon those that are too close together begin to peck at each other and continue to do so until the "prescribed" *individual distance*, as Hediger appropriately called it, is established. We may conceive the space, whose radius is represented by the individual distance, as a very small, movable territory, since the behavior mechanisms ensuring its maintenance are fundamentally the same as those which effect the demarcation of territory. There are also genuine territories, for example in the colony-nesting gannets, arising in the same way as the perching distribution of starlings: the tiny territory of a gannet pair is just big enough to prevent two neighboring birds, in the center of their territories—that is, when they are sitting on their nests—from reaching each other with the tips of their beaks if they stretch out their necks as far as they can.[126]

Chickens behave similarly.[127] Neighboring birds more than 75 centimeters (cm) apart pay little attention to one another except, perhaps, to turn to avoid one another's faces. Between 40 and 75 cm this avoidance becomes more marked. At less than 40 cm, they turn beak-to-beak in an offensive or defensive position.

If animals are to live in social groupings, aggression among them must be controlled. One common adjustment in flocks or herds is based upon recognition of individuals by one another. A hen in a flock knows about 50 other hens and can remember them for about 2 weeks if she is removed from the flock and then returned. Recognition is by sight in fowls, but sound or smell is used in other species.[128] Recognition is important in the internal adjustment of animal groups because it is essential in determining the standing of an individual in the dominance hierarchy of its flock or herd. Interactions of many species are importantly influenced by such dominance hierarchies. The peck order of chickens, for instance, has been investigated thoroughly. In any barnyard group of them there is a clear and abiding order of dominance. Typically this is a steady state, a sort of group inertia or stability. According to Guhl who has experimented on the peck order in chickens, this stability is an example at the group level of the principle of general living systems theory (see page 36) that all living systems tend to maintain steady states of many variables by means of negative feedback processes controlling subsystems which distribute energy or matter to keep an orderly balance.[129] The group adjusts to the changing physiology of one of its members, resulting from that individual's growth, illness, or aging, by altering this order of dominance. This order is evidenced by which animals attack which others, which go first to food, and which decide in what direction the flock will move. One animal is always queen—or if roosters are present, king—of the roost. Individual characteristics such as sex, bodily ornamentation, average rate of energy output, strength, size, bearing, and age seem to determine this sort of dominance.[130] Injections of the male hormone, testosterone propionate, elevate the status of a hen in the peck order.[131] Mathematical models have been developed which analyze the transitivity or intransitivity of such peck orders.[132] Similar dominance structures have been demonstrated among children and adolescent gangs.[133]

A number of other sorts of behavior relax aggression and make social aggregation possible.[134] Play and grooming activities are among these. Interactions in which a weaker animal behaves submissively toward a stronger or more dominant one also prevent aggression. A wolf may expose its neck to another wolf, for example. This act of submission leads the dominant wolf to stop threatening it. If individuals keep far enough apart in space so that they are not threats to one another, aggression is also decreased. All the internal group adjustment processes involving aggression have costs, including huge amounts of energy expended unconstructively in attack or threatened attack, as well as the discomfort of subjugation by an associate and sometimes actual pain or even death in extreme cases.

Ordinarily there are rules in a group concerning how to distribute supplies of matter-energy. Perhaps they determine order—e.g., dessert is not served until the spinach is eaten. A group of thieves may divide their boodle in accordance with the power structure of the group or the amount of responsibility taken by each in acquiring it. Food or medicine may be distributed to those who need it most; for example, milk is fed to infants to help them grow, and meat is given to tribal hunters so that they will remain strong and be able to hunt. Or the strong or powerful—Pharisee or publican—may simply rob the weak. These are the same sorts of processes that were discussed in connection with matter-energy input adjustments; for instance, division of labor in performing the group task is also relevant here. The division may be egalitarian; it may be based on sex—men hunting and women keeping house; or it may be between the master, who does little matter-energy processing, and his household slaves, who do almost all of it. Matter-energy rewards and deprivations may be used by the decider or imposed by the suprasystem to secure group conformity and cooperation. There are always costs in terms of matter employed, energy used, or money expended in these various adjustment processes.

Spatial matter-energy adjustments take place when members leave or enter a group. When a boy goes to college, his brothers may get separate rooms. Room must be made for a new member. A new baby shares its sister's room, cutting into her space and limiting her privacy. The older child may have to play in the family living quarters. Spatial crowding has been proved to be a stress for rats (see page 166) and almost certainly is stressful for humans also (see page 560).

5.2.4 **Information internal processes** Groups are coordinated internally almost entirely by transmissions of information. Durkheim said of group regulation:

For organic solidarity to exist, it is not enough that there be a system of organs necessary to one another, which in a general way feel solidary, but it is also necessary that the way in which they should come together, if not in every kind of meeting, at least in circumstances which most frequently occur, be predetermined. Otherwise, at every moment new conflicts would have to be equilibrated, for the conditions of equilibrium can be discovered only through gropings in the course of which one part treats the other as an adversary as much as an auxiliary. These conflicts would incessantly crop out anew, and, consequently, solidarity would be scarcely more than potential, if mutual obligations had to be fought over entirely anew in each particular instance. . . . In other words, there is a certain sorting of rights and duties which is established by usage and becomes obligatory.[135]

This passage is close in meaning to Hypothesis 5.2-26, page 108: "If a system has multiple purposes and goals, and they are not placed in clear priority and commonly known by all components or subsystems, conflict among them will ensue." If Durkheim's observations are accurate, Hypothesis 5.2-26 applies at the group level.

There are a number of different analyses of the roles or subsystem processes which individuals may carry out in groups. These are all logical classifications based on observation of group behavior, and of course they differ from one theorist to another. According to Bales, the roles of group members vary along four fundamental dimensions: (a) degree of access to resources, (b) degree of control over persons, (c) degree of status in a stratified scale of importance or prestige, and (d) degree of solidarity or identification with the group as against other systems in the suprasystem.[136]

Functional roles of group members may be classed under three rubrics: group task roles, group building and maintenance roles, and individual roles (functions to satisfy needs of a given member, unrelated to group tasks or group building and maintenance). A list of task roles prepared by Benne and Sheats neglects matter-energy processing and is concerned only with information processing: information seeker and opinion seeker (both of whom search memories of group members); initiator-contributor, information giver, and opinion giver (all of whom do input transducing); elaborator, coordinator, orienter, evaluator-critic, energizer, and procedural technician (who do various forms of deciding); and recorder (who remembers).[137] The group maintenance roles in general do not concern matter-energy processing. They deal with information exclusively. They are encourager, harmonizer, compromiser, and standard setter (who do various sorts of deciding); group observer and commentator (who does internal transducing); expediter (who attempts to keep communication channels open or proposes regulation of communication and so is con-cerned with channel and net activity); and follower (who has no function except to respond when other group members do and who thus is a component of the motor or output transducer).

Rates of information flows in groups. How much each member speaks is one aspect of group process which is maintained in a steady state by rule, custom, or tacit agreement. A change in membership alters this steady state. According to Chapple and Coon, each participant in a group interacts at a characteristic rate.[138] One is talkative, another silent. Anything which disturbs a personal steady state of one member will affect all the others. If a member leaves the group, some or all of the others adjust their rates of interaction to allow for this lack. It seems probable that if the member who leaves the group has participated in its interactions more than the average, more other members' interaction rates will have to change to adjust. This fits with the proposition in Hypothesis 5.2-2 (see page 106) that the greater a stress upon a system, the more components of it are involved in adjusting to the stress. If one person in a family of five dies and another family member has been interacting with him at a given rate for an hour a day, that member must find some way of making up for what he has lost. He will probably increase his interaction with one or more other persons either within the group or outside it; if this is impossible, he will try some other adjustment—reading or looking at television more, for instance.

A new member entering a group will probably not have the same rate of interaction as the one he replaces, and so adjustments to this new person will be necessary. If a new member is added without loss of an old one, the rates of interaction of each of the members will be distributed differently, perhaps causing a decrease in the individual interactions among some of them in order to provide a place for the new person. Probably to minimize this disturbance and so decrease resentment against him for limiting the interaction opportunities of old-timers, a new-comer commonly says little until he has been in the group long enough to be thoroughly incorporated into it. Thus a new member of the United States Senate is usually silent on the floor and may not give his maiden speech until many months after he has been elected. In *The Late George Apley* the father advised his son not to speak in the meetings of their exclusive club for several years after he was admitted.[139] The longer a steady state is maintained, the more fixed and automatic it becomes, so that although a group which has been interacting for a long time may be more stable, its range of stability is smaller. Such a group can withstand great input stresses, but it will find adjustments to an internal change, like loss of a member, most difficult. Chapple and Coon suggest that one can determine that a group is in a steady state of interaction if the rates of origination of interactions, of response to them, and of synchronized behavior are constant. Another test is to observe whether the rates return to their previous values after a disturbance. The previous former state cannot be exactly restored after a change of membership unless the new member has precisely the same interaction rate as the person he replaces, and this is unlikely.

The rates of spoken information processing of jurors aligned in factions (or opposing components) decrease as the size of the faction increases.[140] This can be explained partly on the basis of personality differences among the jurors. The more active talkers may also be more resistant to persuasion, so that minority factions are made up of high participators. Some evidence suggests that group pressure increases the participation rate.[141] On the basis of observations of jury interactions, Hawkins says:

In the juries group pressure comes from the number of people lined up with or against you. Apparently jurors in minority factions not only get more opportunity to talk but are actually forced to talk even if they don't want to. A holdout juror who can keep from having his rate of speech forced way up seems to have a better chance of hanging a jury. Therefore, both explanations may be partly true: factional splits operate to select persons with characteristically high rates of speech and also produce an increase in rates among minority faction jurors which is inversely proportional to their number.[142]

As the size of a faction in a jury increases, the total time used by the faction in argument increases, but the talking time per juror decreases.

A possible alternative explanation for Hawkins's findings is that the amount of argument for the point of view of any one faction depends upon three factors: (a) Since each faction is implicitly entitled to an equal amount of time, however many may belong to it, the fewer members there are to make the argument, the more time each participant may have; (b) every additional member of a faction adds to the total time by adding either a new argument or a new version of previously stated arguments; and (c) the amount of argument depends on the relative number of jurors in the faction. The greater the disproportion in numbers between the majority and minority factions, the greater the pressure on those who defend the minority position. As the amount of such pressure increases, so does the amount of argument.[143]

Differences in habitual rate of interaction were a source of difficulty in the space-cabin simulator which I described above (see page 564). When a talkative person becomes anxious because his taciturn partner seems unresponsive, he talks more, trying to get a response. Since silent people typically become more silent when annoyed, the talkative person's behavior has the opposite of its intended effect, and irritation mounts in both members of the crew. The interactions have the characteristics of positive feedback destroying a steady state rather than negative feedbacks maintaining it.

Satisfaction and productivity in groups. Members participate in groups because the resulting rewards to them are greater than the costs. A sort of "taxation" is one of the most consistent characteristics of groups.[144] Members of a group accept such a requirement to help pay the costs of group activity in matter, energy or effort, money, time, or some other utile in proportion to the strength of their interest in the group. The system gives some sort of rewards to members for their functions—money, status, prerogatives, social contacts, specialized information, or other satisfactions valued by the members—and members pay by their functions the costs of what they obtain. This economic interchange is the essence of either symbiosis or parasitism, as the case may be. A "reward-cost matrix" of group function has been proposed by Thibaut and Kelley.[145] By it a balance of any individual member's satisfactions from, and contributions to, each aspect of group process can be calculated, making possible a determination of whether that person will be satisfied with a relationship or situation.

Rewards and contributions figure also in some equations by which Riecken and Homans described group processes.[146] They held that three sets of relationships are interdependent, so that change in one will produce change in the others. These three are effectiveness, social structure, and individual satisfaction or efficiency. This third depends upon the external and internal rewards available to a given member. External rewards, such as pay or public recognition, come from achievement of the group purpose, while internal rewards derive from association and interaction with others. For instance, if the group structure were changed in order to improve its efficiency by raising one member to chief and subordinating all the others to him, this dropping of the rank of most members might lower their motivation and so cancel out any increase in efficiency that might be achieved. If the increased effectiveness resulted in much larger external rewards, however, and if those were liberally distributed among members, motivation might remain high despite the lessening of the internal rewards. In one study the procedures of a group of salesmen in a men's clothing store were altered so that greater external rewards—pay—resulted from increased competition to make sales within the group.[147] Salesmen began to steal customers from one another. No salesman wanted to work on stock or displays. Bickering and conflict among the employees appeared. Production increased, but there was a decrease in the internal rewards since discontent and dissatisfaction were rife. Finally an agreement was made by which each salesman took a turn at stock and display work. This equalized time with customers and thus tended to equalize pay. High production continued, however, because although some salesmen lost pay, the increased internal rewards from friendly interactions kept the group producing.

The sort of direction which a group is given affects the satisfactions of its members.[148] Boys in clubs under autocratic leadership were found in one study to display hostility, aggression, and discontent, limiting their conversation to the immediate task. They directed some of their aggression against scapegoats, and even though they did not rebel overtly, some boys left the group. Two other sorts of leadership conditions, democratic and laissez-faire, were contrasted with this sort. The laissez-faire leadership produced less work on the club tasks, and it was not of good quality. Play often replaced work. Democratic leadership produced somewhat less work than autocratic leadership, but it was more original. The boys in democratic groups liked their leader, were friendly, praised others more than the boys in the other groups, and were more playful and willing to share.

In groups with artificially constrained group networks, position in the net affects morale and satisfaction. The more access a member has to task-relevant information, the greater are his satisfactions.[149] A group with the circle (O) net (see Fig. 9-2) tends to transmit numerous messages and to be leaderless, unorganized, and erratic, but pleasing to its members. A star group, on the other hand, sends many messages, has a leader, and is organized, but gives low average satisfaction.[150] In the network patterns with one or more members having positions of high centrality, group structure develops more quickly and remains more stable. Such groups, as compared with those with less centrality, carry out their tasks with fewer errors, but morale drops gradually, so that in the long run performance worsens.[151] The more autonomy a member has in the group network (usually in a position of high centrality), the higher is his morale.[152]

It may seem that some of the variables of group process referred to in this chapter, such as group satisfaction, morale, or productivity, are really statistical averages of variables in the individual members making up the group rather than group variables. This is the case when one speaks of the "tall basketball team" whose members average 2 m (6 ft, 7 in) in height. But it is not true of variables like group satisfaction, morale, or productivity, even though these may be measured by first scoring each member on an appropriate scale (or a sample of members using some survey technique) and then averaging the scores. Even when the scores are derived in this way, they measure group variables because the state of each member at any moment is ordinarily a result of the previous interactions among everyone in the group.

A group which participates in planning a task is more likely to have high morale and productivity than one which has not been involved in such planning.[153] Performance is better, and attitudes (see pages 459 and 460) involve associated effects that are more favorable to the system, when a group carries out plans that the members developed themselves than when they work from plans prepared entirely by others.

Group "balance." Interpersonal relations in a group have been described in the last chapter (see pages 460 and 461) as perceived by one of the group members. I have described how a person's decider attempts to minimize tensions or strains by achieving or maintaining a steady state or balance, reducing imbalance or dissonance among sentiments or attitudes and interpersonal relationships. At the level of the group the decider also tries to reduce tensions or strains, achieving and maintaining a steady state by a process which appears to be formally identical to the process at the organism level. Because responsibility for subsystem processes is often decentralized and can be easily and frequently redistributed among human group members, because the members may often belong to multiple groups, and because mobility of members constantly changes group processes, much group energy is expended in information processing designed to assure that relationships among members remain in steady states. In order to maintain such steady states, members of human groups constantly communicate in order to determine what information and attitudes other members have. They carry out whatever actions and conversations are necessary to keep dissonance or imbalance below the point which will decrease the efficiency of the group. If it becomes too great, the group loses its integration and cannot continue as a system. As Hypothesis 5.4.3-1 states (see page 109), segregated systems require more information transmission for their coordination than integrated systems do.

The concept of "strain toward symmetry" is applied by Newcomb to explain why such communicative acts occur in groups, as when Person A gives to Person B information about X or about Person B's or some other member's attitude toward X.[154] People tend to have friends with attitudes like their own. One's attempts to influence another person vary with one's attractiveness to that person. When asymmetry exists in groups, A can try to achieve symmetry by influencing B to change B's attitudes about X; by changing his (A's) own attitudes about X to be more like B's attitudes; by developing a false or distorted concept of B's attitudes about X; by changing other aspects of the situation, *e.g.*, acting to make himself (A) less or more attractive to B; or simply by tolerating some degree of asymmetry, without changing the situation in any way.

This sort of theory does not appear to deal adequately with the fact that relationships such as liking can be asymmetric in the sense that A might like B, but B might not return the sentiment.[155] Such theories also do not distinguish between the opposite of a relationship and its complement, for instance, between disliking and not liking. They are concerned, ordinarily, with only a limited range of meaning relationships among group members. A definition of "balance" has been stated by Cartwright and Harary which is intended to overcome these shortcomings and to apply more widely—to communication in networks, to the distribution of power, and to other relationships like those revealed by sociometric procedures. They relate their steady-state concept to cognitive units, to groups, and to higher levels of systems. They approach this problem through the mathematical theory of linear graphs using signed, directed graphs. For them, group members are represented by points, relations become directed lines, and the positive or negative signs of relations become the signs of

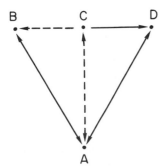

Fig. 9-13 A signed graph having four points and five lines. Solid lines represent a positive sign and dashed lines a negative sign. If each point stands for a group member, the lines indicate the existence of a liking relationship, and the arrows the direction of the relationship. This signed graph shows that A and B have a relationship of liking; so do A and D; A and C have one of disliking; B and D have one of indifference (neither liking nor disliking). (Based on D. Cartwright & F. Harary. Structural balance: a generalization of Heider's theory. *Psychol. Rev.*, 1956, **63**, 283. Copyright 1956 by the American Psychological Association. *Reprinted by permission.*)

directed lines. A configuration like AB, BC, CA in Fig. 9-13 is called a "cycle." Cycles are referred to as "positive" if they contain an even number of negative lines or if the lines are all positive; otherwise, the cycles are negative. A graph is "balanced" if every one of its cycles is positive. The "degree of balance" is the ratio of the number of positive cycles to the total number of cycles. With these concepts Cartwright and Harary state a number of theorems which can be applied to groups. Some of these relate group tendencies toward balance to the number of lines which must be changed in some way to bring about balance. This can be done either be deleting the line or by changing its sign.[156] A group may alter the relationships among its members, or it may expel a member to achieve such a steady state.

A probing search by two friends for a comfortable steady state by which they could continue to live in harmony is insightfully portrayed in a scene from Bolt's profound dramatic study of Sir Thomas More, *A Man for All Seasons.*[157]* More, the Lord Chancellor, cannot in conscience approve of Henry VIII's desire for a divorce. Norfolk, the most powerful peer of the realm and More's lifelong friend, supports the King:

NORFOLK: . . . You're behaving like a fool. You're behaving like a crank. You're not behaving like a gentleman—All right, that means nothing to you; but what about your friends?
MORE: What about them?
NORFOLK: Goddammit, you're dangerous to know!
MORE: Then don't know me.
NORFOLK: There's something further . . . You must have realized by now there's a . . . policy, with regards to you. (MORE *nods*) The King is using me in it.
MORE: That's clever. That's Cromwell . . . You're between the upper and the nether millstones then.
NORFOLK: I am!
MORE: Howard, you must cease to know me.
NORFOLK: I do know you! I wish I didn't but I do!
MORE: I mean as a friend.
NORFOLK: You *are* my friend!
MORE: I can't relieve you of your obedience to the King, Howard. You must relieve yourself of our friendship. No one's safe now, and you have a son.
NORFOLK: You might as well advise a man to change the color of his hair! I'm fond of you, and there it is! You're fond of me, and there it is!
MORE: What's to be done then?
NORFOLK: (*With deep appeal*) Give in.
MORE: (*Gently*) I can't give in, Howard— (*A smile*) You might as well advise a man to change the color of his eyes. I can't. Our friendship's more mutable than *that*.
NORFOLK: Oh, that's immutable, is it? The one fixed point in a world of changing friendships is that Thomas More will not give in!
MORE: (*Urgent to explain*) To me it *has* to be, for that's myself!

*From *A man for all seasons,* by Robert Bolt. Copyright © 1960, 1962 by Robert Bolt. Reprinted by permission of Random House, Inc.

Affection goes as deep in me as you think, but only God is love right through, Howard; and *that's* my *self.*

NORFOLK: And who are you? Goddammit, man, it's disproportionate! *We're* supposed to be the arrogant ones, the proud, splenetic ones—and we've all given in! Why must you stand out? *(Quietly and quickly)* You'll break my heart.

MORE: *(Moved)* We'll do it now, Howard: part, as friends, and meets as strangers.

(He attempts to take NORFOLK'S *hand)*

NORFOLK: *(Throwing it off)* Daft, Thomas! Why d'you want to take your friendship from me? For friendship's sake! You say we'll meet as strangers and every word you've said confirms our friendship!

MORE: *(Takes a last affectionate look at him)* Oh, that can be remedied. *(Walks away, turns; in a tone of deliberate insult)* Norfolk, you're a fool.

NORFOLK: *(Starts; then smiles and folds his arms)* You can't place a quarrel; you haven't the style.

MORE: Hear me out. You and your class have "given in"—as you rightly call it—because the religion of this country means nothing to you one way or the other.

NORFOLK: Well, that's a foolish saying for a start; the nobility of England has always been—

MORE: The nobility of England, my lord, would have snored through the Sermon on the Mount. But you'll labor like Thomas Aquinas over a rat-dog's pedigree. Now what's the name of those distorted creatures you're all breeding at the moment?

NORFOLK: *(Steadily, but roused towards anger by* MORE'S *tone)* An artificial quarrel's not a quarrel.

MORE: Don't deceive yourself, my lord, we've had a quarrel since the day we met, our friendship was but sloth.

NORFOLK: You can be cruel when you've a mind to be; but I've always known that.

Influence and conformity in groups.   People frequently desire to influence the behavior and decisions of the groups they are in. They also usually want to "belong" and agree with other group members. Members often resign, are forced out, or withdraw from regular contact with groups because they do not agree with other members or do not feel accepted by them. When members deviate from the opinions, decisions, or customs of the group, strains are created, and the group undertakes adjustment processes to establish a steady state by bringing them into line. If that is not possible, it may give them unimportant functions, ignore their comments, or entirely exclude them from communication or from membership. There has been a great deal of study of group influence on individual judgments and decisions. People differ in their readiness to change their opinions under pressure. If a test of opinion against reality is possible, the incorrect views are often easy to change. (Some aspects of reality, however, may reinforce a view which other aspects of reality reveal as being in error.) If such a test is not possible, the more members there are who support any view, the more likely the point of view is to be accepted by the entire group. One expression of disagreement usually creates less dissonance than many. The subject of the disagreement and the identity of the

person who disagrees are important. An expert or a personable member creates more disturbance by his contrary stand than others do. On a very important subject, only a little disagreement can be tolerated.[158]

Position in a group's communication net can influence conformity and deviation. In one study of a sizable number of four-man groups, the person in the most central position in the star configuration never disagreed with the majority, or the majority never differed with him.[159] The more central positions in the slash network showed markedly few disagreements, as compared with peripheral members. Central members were in a position either to get their opinions accepted or to be pressured quickly into agreement. More messages were directed toward deviant members than toward those who were in agreement. If a group member is quite confident, he will direct his communications toward those who disagree with him most, but if he needs support, he will communicate with those who already agree with him. Influence processes work better when they decrease rather than increase dissonance. Feedback from hearing one's own self openly state an attitude appears to reinforce that attitude. When a subject in a group told another member something which was contrary to his private opinion (that a boring task which he had just completed was interesting and fun), his private opinion changed to correspond more closely with his statement.[160] If he was rewarded with $1 for making the statement, interestingly enough, his opinion was changed more than if he was rewarded with $20.

I have already reviewed what is known about how groups can influence the judgments of an individual and the many variables that affect this (see pages 436 and 437). When a group disagrees with him, a subject often changes even a fairly obvious judgment, such as one concerning the lengths of two lines which are almost equal, one of which, however, is noticeably longer than the other. This will occur, even though the individual still sees the lines the same as he always has.

Influencing another person means affecting his or her behavior and ideas. It means exerting power over this person (see page 38). The power of Person A over Person B has been defined by Lewin and by Cartwright as the maximum psychological force (not precisely defined) which A can bring to bear on B divided by the maximum resistance B can exert against this force.[161] Sometimes such power may be exerted only by one agent upon another. Or it may be reflexive—that is, each of two interacting agents may have power over the other. The relationship also may or may not be transitive—that is, if A has power over B and B has power over C, it still is not necessary that A have power over C. Cartwright generalizes his formulation to more than one level, since his agents can be individual organisms, groups, organizations, or higher-level social systems.

The theory of directed graphs is used by French to analyze power relationships in groups. French deals with field forces like those conceptualized by Lewin in which group members exert attractions and repulsions on one another in an abstracted system in a psychological life space rather than in physical space.[162] Such forces are not directly measurable. I believe it better to replace such concepts with concepts of information signals among members which elicit more or less compliance from the receiver (see page 38). Three postulates have been stated by French about the wielding of power in groups. They concern interpersonal forces and their strengths. He supports the hypotheses with experimental findings from the literature. They are:[163]

Postulate 1. For any given discrepancy of opinion between [two group members] A and B, the strength of the resultant force which an inducer A can exert on an inducee B, in the direction of agreeing with A's opinion, is proportional to the strength of the bases of power of A over B.

Postulate 2. The strength of the force which an inducer A exerts on an inducee B, in the direction of agreeing with A's opinion, is proportional to the size of the discrepancy between their opinions. [This postulate is in some ways similar to my Hypothesis 5.2-3 (see page 105).]

Postulate 3. In one unit, each person who is being influenced will change his opinion until he reaches the equilibrium point where the resultant force (of the forces induced by other members at the beginning of the unit and the resisting force corresponding to his own resistance to change) is equal to zero.

Two theorems which French applies to the adjustment processes within groups are:

Theorem 1. For all possible patterns of initial opinion, in a completely connected power structure the opinions of all members will reach a common equilibrium level equal to the arithmetic mean of the initial opinions of all the members, and this final common opinion will be reached in one unit [of time].

Theorem 2. The amount of change of the deviate toward the opinions of the majority is proportional to the sum of the deviations of all other members from the deviate.

If the amount of influence attempted is held constant, the amount of change in the deviate increases as the degree of discrepancy of opinion increases.[164] This is true unless the deviate rejects the authority of the inducer, after which the influence becomes an inverse function of degree of discrepancy. The more discrepant a member is, the more other group members attempt to influence him to change his behavior or views.[165] This holds only until the deviate is rejected by the group. Such rejection alters the power of the group to influence that individual, as is implied by Postulate 1 above.

Cohesiveness has been defined by Festinger as "the resultant of all the forces acting on the members to remain in the group."[166] This is more like my definition of "integration" (see pages 80 and 81) than my definition of "cohesiveness" (see pages 79 and 80). By means of several hypotheses he analyzed the forces in groups which tend toward uniformity and counteract deviance. These hypotheses involve the following five variables and one parameter: (a) the perceived *discrepancy* of opinion on a topic, "item x," among members of the group at a given time; (b) the *pressure* upon members to communicate with one another at a given time; (c) the amount of *listening* of members to influence by communications from other members at a given time; (d) the *cohesiveness* of members in the group at a given time; (e) the perceived pressure to achieve *uniformity* of opinions at a given time; and (f) the *relevance* of the topic, "item x," to the group, which is taken to be a parameter, constant over time.

Five of these hypotheses deal with the group as a total system:[167]

Hypothesis 1: "The pressure on members to communicate to others in the group concerning 'item x' increases monotonically with increase in the perceived discrepancy in opinion concerning 'item x' among members of the group."

This hypothesis is in certain ways similar to my Hypothesis 5.2-3 (see page 106).

Hypothesis 2: "The pressure on a member to communicate to others in the group concerning 'item x' increases monotonically with increase in the degree of relevance of 'item x' to the functioning of the group."

Hypothesis 3: "The pressure on members to communicate to others in the group concerning 'item x' increases monotonically with increase in the cohesiveness of the group."

Hypothesis 4: "The amount of change in opinion resulting from receiving a communication will increase as the pressure towards uniformity in the group increases."

Hypothesis 5: "The amount of change in opinion resulting from receiving a communication will increase as the strength of the resultant force to remain in the group increases for the recipient."

And five of the hypotheses deal with a particular deviant member of the group:

Hypothesis 6: "The pressure to communicate about 'item x' to a particular member of the group will increase as the discrepancy in opinion between that member and the communicator increases."

Hypothesis 7: "The force to communicate about 'item x' to a particular person will decrease to the extent that he is perceived as not a member of the group or to the extent that he is not wanted as a member of the group."

Hypothesis 8: "The force to communicate 'item x' to a particular member will increase the more it is perceived that the communication will change that member's opinion in the desired direction."

Hypothesis 9: "The tendency to change the composition of the psychological group (pushing members out of the group) increases as the perceived discrepancy in opinion increases."

Hypothesis 10: "When non-conformity exists, the tendency to change the composition of the psychological group increases as the cohesiveness of the group increases and as the relevance of the issue to the group increases."

A detailed and precise analysis of these hypotheses has been made by Simon and Guetzkow.[168] They used a number of equations which together represent a mathematical model according to which the variables listed above covary in specific stated ways and produce steady or unsteady states. From this model they derived several deductions which they showed to have been confirmed from various group experiments. For instance, in one research on dyads, each member of two-person groups was given some pictures to be looked at alone, then discussed with the other person, and then looked at again alone.[169] Then the individual wrote an interpretation of the picture. Each subject thought his pictures were identical to those seen by the other group member, but actually they were somewhat different. Content analysis of the similarities and differences in the interpretations written by the two group members provided the measure of opinion change. The experimenter used various ways to increase the cohesiveness of some of his groups and decrease the cohesiveness of others. The model of Simon and Guetzkow predicted that the decrease in discrepancy of opinion would be less than the increase of cohesiveness and also less than the increase of relevance. The experimental findings supported these predictions, but they did not support all the aspects of the Simon-Guetzkow model. They did not strongly contradict any of them. The model also fitted findings of certain other researches moderately well, and at the same time it clarified certain of their shortcomings.[170]

These last internal informational adjustment processes of groups relate closely, as I have indicated, to cohesiveness. I shall review this topic further below (see pages 575 and 576), and there I shall mention other related internal informational adjustments.

The adjustment processes of coalition formation within groups are discussed below (see pages 578 and 579).

Adjustments to distortions in communications. An experiment has thrown light on how members of small groups adjust to information distortions.[171] Group members were assigned the task of solving problems which required them to exchange information about ambiguous line drawings which certain members of the group could not see. It was found that in order to avoid distorted concepts, the speakers gave longer descriptions, talked slower, and used more redundant speech.

5.2.5 Matter-energy output processes   Groups can maintain internal steady states sometimes by con-trolling outputs from the group. A farm family, for example, may sell only that part of its produce which it cannot eat, getting rid of the excess profitably and at the same time avoiding overload within the system. The costs, of course, are the loss of the product and the expenditure of work, materials, and funds for the marketing.

5.2.6 Information output processes   The space-cabin simulator project described above (see pages 564 and 567) provided an example of an information output adjustment process. When irritation between members of the crew became great, it was rarely expressed by overt hostility, although there were covert expressions. Instead, this anger was directed toward the monitor, who was known to be listening. Astronaut Walter Shirra behaved similarly, refusing to comply with some directives from the ground, under the stresses of a respiratory infection and perhaps of information input underload, while he was in orbit in Apollo 7 in 1968. This was displacement of aggression to another innocent system, as referred to in Hypothesis 5.2-7(b) (see page 106). By adjusting information output in this way, strains were lessened within the group. The cost could perhaps have been anger aroused in the monitor.

Sometimes a group will decide that certain things which happened to it or which were done by a member should be known only to the group. Parents, out of loyalty, may not tell anyone outside the family of their children's naughtinesses. Football teams do not reveal to their opponents what their next play will be. Such secrecy, or limitation of information output, may protect the feeling of security of the group, protect its status in the suprasystem, improve its performance, or adjust strains within it.

5.2.7 Feedbacks   A remarkable sort of negative feedback controls the rates of reproduction and population of various castes of social insects.[172] Queens, kings, and soldiers give off inhibitor substances which prevent an undifferentiated nymph from developing into a member of their castes as long as they are around, so keeping the proportional representation of each caste in the population in steady state. These inhibiting chemicals are interestingly like the repressor substances in cells that stop production of substances which are in adequate supply. Indeed, the social insects' inhibiting hormones probably block enzymatic processes in cells of nymphs in some comparable way.

A comical lesson about feedback in a two-person group has been learned by more than one married couple who accidentally reversed the respective bedside controls of their dual-control electric blanket. If both spouses have the correct control for their half of the blanket, they use negative feedback to keep a stable temperature. Either one can turn the heat up or down, as desired. When the controls are accidentally reversed, however, if the husband is cold, he turns up his wife's heat. This makes her too warm, and so she turns down the heat on her husband's side. This makes him even colder, and so he turns hers up more. And she, then being warmer yet, turns his down. And so forth. Positive feedback results from the unplanned crossing of controls which puts two negative feedback loops in series. Each of the two members of the group makes decisions about the state of the other without any knowledge of that state. Without such feedback, she or he is likely to make a change in a direction which causes an unsteady state. The other one gets feedback from this change, but takes action which will alter the first one's steady state rather than her or his own, and in the direction which makes it worse rather than better. As Hypothesis 5.2-6 (see page 106) states, positive feedbacks give rise to "spiral effects" that destroy one or more steady states of a system.

Feedback to the two-person groups has been experimentally modified.[173] Each member, in one study, carried out a task in which he turned knobs; then a dial showed an error signal. With feedback about his own performance a member's accuracy improved. Associative learning occurred. Confounded feedback, made up of a mixture of results from the team members, helped somewhat. In the equivalent of the electric blanket situation, when the subject received feedback only about this teammate's response, accuracy was as bad as, or worse than, it was when there was no feedback at all.

The effects of feedbacks in controlling an individual member so that he conforms to group norms has also been studied.[174] After several other group members acting as stooges had agreed on an incorrect response about a perceptual task, the subject was asked for his response. The experimenter thereupon said the rigged response of the majority was correct, regardless of what the subject had said. Such external feedback from the suprasystem (represented by the experimenter) elicited a rapid increase by the subjects in responses conforming to controlling internal feedbacks concerning inaccurate group consensus. Feedback from the experimenter objectively confirming the correct alternative inhibits conformity to inaccurate group consensus more than feedback supporting an incorrect consensus promotes such conformity.[175]

In groups with artificially constrained nets, feedback is a necessary but not sufficient condition for good performance, which requires a capacity to correct errors.[176] The type of net affects a group's error-corrective power.[177] In one experiment fewer errors were corrected in the four-person wheel than in the four-person slash or circle. A likely reason for this is the fact that, in the wheel, an error can be detected in only three ways: A member can (a) detect his own mistake, (b) pass on to another group member a set of computations containing an error, or (c) pass on two conflicting statements to the same receiver. In the four-person slash and circle there is an additional way to correct errors: A member can receive information about the same topic from two or more different sources. More errors are corrected when the net makes such feedback possible.

Four degrees of feedback in groups were investigated in another study.[178] From least to most, these were as follows: (a) Zero feedback. (An instructor, the sender, sat behind a movable blackboard and described a series of geometric patterns, which his students, the receivers, tried to draw. They could not ask questions or make sounds.) (b) Visible audience. (The instructor and students could see one another, but no speaking by students was allowed.) (c) Yes-no. (The audience could say only "yes" or "no" in answer to questions from the instructor.) (d) Free feedback. (Any participant could speak at will.) As the degree of feedback increased, the accuracy with which the students drew the patterns, and also the confidence of the sender and the receivers in their performance, increased. Feedback takes time, which is a cost, but with practice the time required to complete the pattern-drawing task with free feedback decreased to little more than the time required to complete the task with zero feedback. Sender and receivers gradually develop a common, private language that diminishes the number of words required in the feedback. Performance of both sender and receivers can improve with zero feedback, perhaps because some unrecognized feedback occurs, perhaps because they both learn to attend more carefully to their tasks, or perhaps because the sender learns how to describe better. Zero feedback engenders doubt and consequent hostility in both the sender and the receivers.

The importance of feedback as an adjustment process in maintaining steady states in families was emphasized by Jackson.[179] His clinical observations led him to see family interaction as information flow with corrective feedback. For example, in one family a boy won a popularity contest, but he found that this displeased his mother. The son then used various adjustment processes in order to restore her favor, including efforts to keep from being so popular after that. Psychotherapy received by one member of a family can change her or his interactions with the others, so altering the whole family interpersonal steady state. The subtle functions of feedbacks in coordinating groups are revealed with particular beauty and precision in örchestras, ballet troupes, athletic teams, and gymnastic groups. A blind man, lacking visual feedback, probably could never learn to be a member of an acrobatic team on the high wire.

5.3 Evolution   The first dyad of organisms that mated sexually was probably the first group. This sort of system may have appeared first about 500 million years ago, but this date is highly speculative.

As I have noted above (see page 564) groups of different animal species can be ordered according to the amount of socialization they exhibit. At the bottom of the scale are the species of isolates, whose individuals meet briefly to mate or to fight, but otherwise keep apart at distances characteristic of the species. Other species show temporary or permanent parental behavior in family groups. Among others, larger aggregations of animals of the same sex occur, usually with seasonal aggregation of both sexes. Finally, there are extremely gregarious species in which groups of mixed sex remain together through the year.[180] These sorts of groups have evolved along with the physical evolution of component organisms.

Discussing the evolutionary development of animal groupings, Lorenz wrote:

Some sociologists are of the opinion that the family is the most primitive form of social aggregation, and that the different forms of communities in the higher animals have arisen from it phylogenetically. This theory may be true of several social insects, such as bees, ants, and termites, and possibly of some mammals too, including the primates to which man belongs, but it cannot be applied generally. The most primitive form of a "society" in the broadest sense of the term is the anonymous flock, of which the shoal of ocean fishes is the most typical example. Inside the shoal, there is no structure of any kind, there is no leader and there are no led, but just a huge collection of like elements. Of course these influence each other mutually, and there are certain very simple forms of "communication" between the individuals of the shoal. When one of them senses danger and flees, it infects with its mood all the others which have perceived its fear. How far the panic in a big shoal spreads, and whether it is able to make the whole shoal turn and flee, is purely a quantitative question, the answer to which depends on how many individuals become frightened and flee and how intensively they do so.[181]

Aggressiveness within species and spacing behavior (see pages 564 and 565) are the basis of evolution of groups, according to McBride.[182] He says: "It is probable that evolutionary change has been predominantly in the direction of increased organizational complexity with consequent increased range of social behavior. This increase in organization, which occurs at the aggregated group end of the spectrum, represents the behavioral adaptation to intraspecfic aggressiveness."[183] Such groupings are valuable to the survival of a species in a number of ways. They resemble somewhat the circular encampments of the pioneers'

wagon trains in hostile Indian country in the early American West. They protect weaker members of the group, creating a boundary of protecting fighters around females with young. And they cut down the amount of individual fighting and so increase the average available feeding time of young and adults alike. Here is a shred-out of the critical subsystem processes of organisms (see pages 1 and 4), the beginning at the group level of social organization with delegation of functions or division of labor among organisms.

Complexity of social organization does not increase in any clearly continuous way from lower to higher animal phyla. Complex social structures seem to have evolved independently in different phyla. There is direct evidence that groupings of social insects existed in the Cretaceous period, 100 million years ago, and circumstantial indication that they might have existed 200 million years ago.[184] The very large swarms or nests of insects with hundreds, thousands, or tens of thousands of individual organisms must have been preceded by smaller, family-like groups. One can find evolutionary sequences from solitary life to simple groupings to complexly organized groups in closely related insect species.

Man has apparently always lived in some form of group, like his closest animal relatives, the large apes. Human groups arise probably because human beings reproduce by mating dyads, because both human sexes are almost always capable of sexual response and so can derive repeated gratification by remaining together, because human infants are altricial and need prolonged parental care, and because members of groups can adjust better to environmental stresses by employing division of labor. Even *Zinjanthropus bóisei*, an ancestor of man that lived 1.5 million years ago, might have had some crude form of structured groupings, possibly allowing for cooperative hunting of animals.[185]

5.3.1 Emergents   At least superficially there appears to be more difference between the group and the organism than between any other level of living systems and the next lower level of living systems. (The difference between the cell and the next lower level, made up of nonliving systems, may be as great or greater.) Certain emergents not found at lower levels account for much of the cross-level difference between organisms and the more complex groups made up of organisms. Group emergents include: (a) *Longer duration of survival.* Just as, on the average, an organism can endure longer than one of its cells, so a group's greater complexity provides it with adjustment processes against stresses which a single organism does not have. Many groups, therefore, have survived longer than any organism can. Termite nests can exist much longer than any individual termite. Human families may continue for centuries, as the British royal family and many peasant families in Europe have. (*b*) *The ability to extend over a much larger spatial region than a single organism can.* A sort of cooperative activity, impossible at lower levels, enables a group, among other things, to control a larger living territory, hunt for food over a wider area, and obtain information about potential enemies and other threats sooner. (*c*) *The possibility of shifting a subsystem process from one component to another.* This can occur in various sorts of groups—chiefly human. In some groups most or all members are capable of carrying out most or all subsystem processes. This adaptability makes groups flexible. If one member tires or becomes bored or dies, another can take up where he left off. This is rarely, if ever, possible in lower-level systems. Certainly, components which can interchangeably carry out the processes of several subsystems are rarely found. (*d*) *The ability to perform motor activities and to make artifacts that would be beyond the capacity of a single organism.* It takes a swarm of bees to build a hive and a group of people to haul the stones to build a castle. (*e*) *Markedly increased physical separateness and more autonomous mobility of components in physical space.* Red blood corpuscles, leukocytes, and macrophages in organs of organisms are quite mobile, but even taking size differences into account, the components of groups are significantly more mobile. A family with children of college age may be dispersed all over the country and yet interact continuously as a group. A party of coal miners may carry out integrated mining activities even though they are separated by miles of tunnels and shafts. Astronauts may rendezvous in space from points thousands of miles apart. The ability of members to communicate, often with the aid of artifacts, makes it possible for a group to be a cohesive and coordinated system even when its members are dispersed and in constant motion. (*f*) *The sharing of a single component by multiple groups.* A mother may in rapid alternation engage in conversation with guests and participate in games with her young children. A man may be a Catholic, a Rotarian, a Knight of Columbus, and a father, participating at different times in various physical meetings of the groups of which he is a member. (*g*) *The ability of components to be integrated and to coordinate and control one another by symbolic languages.* While language skills are emergents at the organism level (see page 468), it takes a group of two or more organisms, at least one sender and one receiver, to have a conversation or interact in writing. (*h*) *The capability of creating and implementing an implicit or explicit charter for a new group or higher-level system.* The charter establishes the relationships among the components of the new system, which are made by biological reproduction of systems at a lower level (see page 55). This sort of reproduction is dependent on interactions among two or more people, using symbolic language.

5.4   Growth, cohesiveness, and integration

5.4.1   Growth   Groups grow by adding to their numbers, but some groups may not grow at all after the moment they come into being. Two friends may simply remain a dyad until one of them dies. A court may be composed of five judges over its entire history. A family group grows as children are born and then may return to a dyad as the children leave to form their own families. In some cultures married sons or daughters do not leave the parental family, so that the group grows by the addition of marriage partners and their children.

5.4.2   Cohesiveness   I shall apply the term "cohesiveness" in this chapter to the maintenance of close proximity in space-time of group members either to one another or to physical channels that convey information among them (see pages 79 and 80). This usage is consistent with my use of the concept at the levels of the cell, organ, and organism, where it applies to the strength of the physical forces holding a system together (see pages 298, 299, 352, and 472).

My use of the term is different from the ordinary practice among students of groups, who usually apply it to the attractiveness a group has for its members, based upon prestige of group membership, liking of members for one another, and prestige of the task. Although in many cases the tendency of members to remain spatially near one another is based upon their mutual liking and their desire to remain in the group, the two would not always vary together in all types of groups. The relationships usually considered in discussions of group cohesiveness are included in my conceptual system under *integration*, discussed in the next section.

Groups are not held together by physical forces such as valence bonds between atoms or the adherence of tissues, as lower-level systems are, although some sorts of groups are bound together by artifacts, like the man at the head and the man at the tail of a carnival horse or mountain climbers on a rope. Rather, they depend primarily upon messages, information flows over the group channel and net, to increase or decrease their cohesiveness. The meaning of these messages, *i.e.*, their impact on the receivers, determines how close to one another in space-time the group members remain. A signal from a quarterback may cause his team either to huddle or to spread out over the field in defense against a passing attack. A mother may call her children together for dinner, or the leader of a patrol of Boy Scouts may direct them to disperse in order to search over a wider area for a lost child. Whether the group remains close in space depends on what is required to accomplish its purposes and goals. A work group composed of three astronauts in space and their associates at the ground-control center on earth is about as noncohesive in my sense of the term as a system can be. They, of course, remain coordinated partly because of the radio and television transmission between them and the telemetry that automatically reports aspects of the space mission and partly because of their previous programming and that of their intricate artifact, the spaceship.

The spatial relationships maintained among group members are important in understanding their processes. Special adjustment processes may be required in groups that are widely separated in order to maintain their group relationships. Such an adjustment would be a family's use of conference telephone calls to resolve emotional problems or make important group decisions. Over time, if the distance is maintained, emotional ties may become weaker and relationships may become more formal than they would be if all lived close together and could interact more often on a face-to-face basis.

5.4.3 Integration   Integration of the various castes of social insects so that they act in coordination is accomplished by trophallaxis, exchange of pheromones among the insects (see page 81). The secretions which are the markers bearing signals to act or to stop acting are transferred from one individual to the next. In spatially discontinuous groups other modes of information processing are essential. One such technique is the "dance" of the bees (see page 440). Human gesture and speech are others.

Phases of group integration.   When a human group is newly formed, the members progressively establish relationships to one another. These relationships, of course, go on changing as long as the group continues. A number of group theorists relate the behavior of group members to their early life experiences. Some say that any group is symbolically a reflection of the important emotional relationships of early family life.[186] This view is derived from Freud's doctrines, being based on his concept of transference in the dyadic relationship between an analyst and analysand. The behavior of an adult in a group, according to Schutz, depends upon whether he perceives his position to be like that of a child with his parents or sees himself to be like a parent.[187] Schutz studied group behavior through a series of questionnaires to members about their early reactions and their parents'

behavior and through ratings of the behavior of the person in experimental groups and in other situations. He defined three aspects of an individual's participation in a group: (a) *Inclusion*, the amount of participation in, or withdrawal from, group activity. He assumed that a child who received a great deal of attention from his parents would participate freely in groups in later life, and his data confirmed this. (b) *Control*, which involves discipline. He found that a person who had been strictly disciplined developed authoritarian attitudes and in later life attempted to influence decisions in an authoritarian manner. (c) *Affection* from parents in early life. He found that emotional warmth from parents in childhood increased the desire for personal closeness in later life. The opposite also was true.

Group processes over time were analyzed by Schutz in terms of these three variables: (a) His groups' first interactions concerned inclusion, all members finding where they belonged and deciding how much of their time to devote to the group. Schutz says that during this period, the group boundary is being established. (b) During the second phase, control is at issue. Power relations, selection of a leader, and formulation of decision-making procedures take up the time of the group. Functions and responsibilities of group members are worked out. (c) In the third phase, affection—positive and negative feelings—finds expression, coalitions of group members are formed, and jealousies become evident. These phases are not distinct, but usually overlap.

According to Bales (see page 533), there ordinarily are six phases in the course of a 1-h meeting of several experimental groups which have been dealing with a single major problem:[188] (a) The first activity involves getting the problem clear. (b) Then a goal is decided upon which takes account of values, needs, and desires of group members. (c) After this, the ways of reaching the goal are considered. (d) The actual decision follows. (e) The members are then relaxed and can joke and dissipate their tensions. (f) A final period of reward, praise, and encouragement often knits the group together as the meeting ends.

As groups get older and have more members, Bales finds, they also become more heterogeneous, since some members are new and some are old. As the groups become more variegated, their complexity increases, their adaptability becomes less, and there is greater differentiation of property rights and status, greater specificity of functions of members, greater formality of authority, and lesser overall solidarity. These findings seem to support Hypothesis 5.4.1-2(a) to (e) (see page 108). A group which holds its membership constant over time, however, tends to have increased rather than lessened solidarity.

An imaginative yet well-controlled study of group integration was made in a boys' camp for 20 normal 12-year-old boys.[189] Before going to the camp, the boys did not know one another, but they had similar religious, social, and educational backgrounds. The experimenters observed the interactions among these boys, first when they were in two groups which were entirely unaware of each other's existence, then during a period when tension was allowed to grow up between the two groups, and finally during a period when they were brought together while cooperating in a common task. These groups developed their structures during the ordinary functions of choosing bunks, playing games, and carrying on other activities. The staff rarely interfered, so that this development could proceed freely. Each group established its own norms. One was "tough" and disapproved of a member's crying when he was hurt; the other was not, but disapproved of homesickness. Definite status hierarchies developed, and recognized leaders emerged and kept their positions. During decision making, most of the communications were addressed to the leader, and few directly to anyone else, although some were meant for the group as a whole.

After these relationships had become stabilized, the two groups, which had been several miles apart, went for a hike and were allowed to discover each other. Competitive games were suggested. Captains were chosen. A great deal of intergroup hostility developed. Sociometric studies showed that performance of members of the ingroup was judged as significantly higher than that of members of the outgroup, when it was in fact the same. This appears to be an indication of group integration.

In the final phase of the study, pipes supplying the camp's water supply were secretly blocked by the experimenters. When the boys became thirsty, both groups cooperatively tried to restore it. Under a common stress, centralized decision making occurred, behavior compatible with Hypothesis 5.4.3-7 (page 109). This broke down some of their intergroup hostility. Another problem, raising money for a movie to be shown in camp, further broke down the lines between the two groups, and at the end everyone was friendly. The conclusion was that groups which have friction between them will cooperate if one group alone cannot solve a common problem and must work with another. Having a common goal reduces strains.

Integrating effect of the attraction of a group for its members. Groups whose members like one another, enjoy being together, are interested in the group's pro-

cesses, and feel that the group has prestige are more likely to remain together and to cooperate in working together toward the group purposes and goals than groups who lack these attributes.

Group members expend energy in the group's processes, part of which is used in the work of achieving the goals of the system and part of which is used in integrating the group. The energy available to a group Cattell calls its "synergy."[190] His factor-analytic studies have shown that a factor he calls "morale" includes both the amount of energy the group puts into its activities and its resistance to dispersion. The average disinclination of members to leave the group, the number of friends they have in the group, and the hostility they show toward other groups which threaten their group's purposes and goals are all related to this factor. He considers these to be manifestations of the group's synergy.

The attractiveness of a newly formed group to its members was found, in another factor-analytic study, to depend mainly upon the personalities of the members. Individuals with paranoid characteristics reduced the available synergy of the group. Group members with more outgoing personalities produced high verbal interaction, common group emotion, and more synergy. Threat of loss of status by the group and severe frustration increase adherence of members to the group. Reduction in frustration does not.

If group members like one another and are compatible or if they previously have been in groups together, the group is more attractive to them.[191] Selective mutual attractiveness among a pair of members or a subgroup, however, can reduce the integration of the group as a whole.[192] When members like one another enough so that they make most of their positive sociometric choices within the group rather than outside it, one would ordinarily assume that the group would be strongly attractive to them, but this is true only when the satisfactions which underlie the choices can be obtained only within the group and not from alternative relationships. The centripetal influences must be stronger than the centrifugal ones.

Acceptance of common values by group members reduces conflict among them, decreases the cost of communication, and improves group task performance. Commonly held values also make the group less susceptible to disruption by external forces. An experiment with a group of children showed that once a tradition (i.e., an implicit charter) had become established among them, a new child coming into the group had to act within its constraints, even though he was a more active leader than the original members.[193] Groups are more likely to continue to hold their members if they have cooperative rather than competitive internal processes.[194] If two or more group members share leadership, that is, if the decider has multiple components, the group is less mutually attractive unless the tasks to be performed are urgent.[195]

Pressures toward uniformity are strong in groups with strong mutual attractiveness among members (see pages 570 to 572). A deviate is rejected more. Initially, communications are directed toward him with high frequency, but even if his deviation continues, their rate declines.[196] More efforts to reach agreement, more attempts to influence, more argument, and fewer instances of withdrawal occur. The members like one another more, and there is less difference among individuals in the amounts of their participation.[197]

How groups achieve conformity is illustrated by the following experiment of March and Feigenbaum.[198] They asked male students independently to rank in order of beauty five pictures of girls, one of which was more overtly sexy than the others. They all chose the sexy picture as the most beautiful. After discussion, in which groups decided that it was not right to equate sexiness and beauty, the groups as units and later the individual members privately selected other pictures. Thus the establishment of group-defined evaluation criteria influenced group decisions as well as postdiscussion individual decisions in the direction of conformity to the established standards.

A phenomenon called "deindividuation" by Festinger, Pepitone, and Newcomb contributes to group integration.[199] Individual members tend to exert fewer controls than usual on information outputs at their own organismic boundaries when they are together. In a sense, their information boundary maintenance functions are turned over to group control on the assumption that the group will exert appropriate restraints on information flow at its boundary. Festinger, Pepitone, and Newcomb studied this process. They used as a measure of such reduction of control by individuals the willingness of college students in groups to discuss their personal feelings toward their parents and reveal negative attitudes. As a measure of deindividuation they used the errors made in recalling which group member had said what. The more errors, the more deindividuation. They found that groups which induce this phenomenon are highly attractive to their members.

Cliques and coalitions. Some groups are stable, but in most groups the forms of integration—the relationships among the members—change over time. Some may leave the group, and others may enter. Different individuals or subgroups may carry out certain sub-system processes. Some members may form cliques. Groups sometimes split completely, so that the two parts are no longer coordinated by direct flows of information. Sometimes they are coordinated by their relationship to a larger organization, and sometimes they remain entirely distinct groups. Separate groups may also merge, usually with an expectation of mutual benefit.

Cliques, which can be defined as subgroups with greater-than-average communication among their components, form as a result of a large number of different factors. These represent some commonality that holds the individuals in relationships. Some of these are similar backgrounds of members,[200] previous group memberships,[201] kinship and marriage relationships,[202] previous relationships,[203] similar religious backgrounds,[204] similar ethnic or racial derivations,[205] age, sex, common interests or opinions, and ability to do a particular job. In a study of clique formation among fellow workers, Roethlisberger and Dickson found that the following factors contributed to the determination of the clique membership: closeness of work stations in the workroom, a feeling of similar status (one group felt superior to the other), similar occupations, comparability of output rates (neither too much nor too little was allowed), and a sort of conformity that would keep a member from maintaining social distance or from "squealing" to the supervisor about an associate.[206] Workers were kept out of cliques—even when they worked right in the midst of the members—if they broke rules of accepted procedure or did other things to make themselves disliked. A man with a speech defect was left out of both cliques which formed in one room. One worker who produced at a high rate did not report all his output. Consequently, he was thought to be conforming to the workers' norms and so was in a clique. On the other hand, another one who did more work than the usual standard and reported it was not in a clique.

Four sorts of groups, which differ in the degree of covariation they exhibit, have been distinguished by Marschak.[207] From least unified to most unified, these are (a) games, in which two or more components (organisms or subgroups) interact, each trying to maximize its own gain; (b) coalitions, in which two or more band together to act in unison, cooperating against one or more other group components with the intention of mutually maximizing their own gains, if necessary at the cost of the others; (c) foundations, in which each component works for an overall goal but in which each also has a subordinate goal to which it devotes more effort than it does to the subordinate goals of others; and (d) teams, in which each component subordinates its own goals to the overall purpose of the group, receiving its share of rewards only as a component of that system.

An early observer of social processes, Simmel noted that a three-person group is unstable and tends to break into a coalition of two plus a third party, who may be a mediator, a holder of balance of power, or a constant disturber of solidarity between the pair in coalition.[208] One study found such a two-and-one dissociation, confirming Simmel's main point by experiments on 48 three-person groups.[209] Another study examined the behavior of naïve subjects put into groups with two role-playing assistants to the experimenters.[210] These acted out four different kinds of intragroup relationships: (*a*) The two role players cooperated with the subject to create an integrated group; (*b*) the subject was part of a coalition with one role player against the other; (*c*) the group was disorganized, with the subject and the two role players all acting independently; and (*d*) the two role players formed a coalition which rejected the subject. After a period of interaction among the three, a fourth man entered the picture. How he was accepted depended upon the previous interaction. When the group was strongly integrated (*a*), the newcomer was accepted into the fellowship. In a two-way split (*b*) and (*d*), he joined the major group, so creating a three-to-one split instead of making two pairs. When the group was disorganized (*c*), he joined nobody. There was, in other words, a tendency to continue the essentials of the interaction structure which existed at the time the new member was added.

Coalitions may form when a number of opposed interests are involved in a bargaining or gaming situation. An investigation was made of the development of coalitions with three-person groups in a bargaining situation in which no one member could by his own effort obtain the total sum for which they bargained.[211] A coalition of two could, however, and the two could divide what they got as they chose. Stable coalitions in general were found to organize against any member of the group who gained a clear advantage, and if he then wanted a coalition, he had to offer more. More stable coalitions formed as the importance of the task increased.

Game theory applied to groups. Experiments based on game theory can provide insights into how groups may be integrated or kept from integrating. I have already outlined how game theory applies to the interactions of two players whose interests are completely opposed (see page 496). There are games, however, in which the interests of players coincide, so that collusion in coalitions can be a valuable strategy. Games also may be conducted between opposed groups instead of individuals. The mathematical strategy of such games is the same, whether the parties are persons or groups. The strategies derived from the mathematical theory of games do not predict the actual behavior of actual subjects, except in certain forms of the zero-sum two-person game in which "rational behavior" is predictable. Experimental studies on some of them are therefore essential if one is to predict actual human behavior in such situations.

Depending upon the way the payoffs are arranged, cooperation or competition may develop between players, as Hypothesis 5.4.3-8 (see page 109) implies. In general, group members cooperate when cooperation is rewarded and compete when it is punished. Various sorts of two-person Prisoner's Dilemma games have been analyzed to determine, for each sort, how much control each player has over his own gains and those of his opponent. In Prisoner's Dilemma games cooperative action provides a moderate payoff for each player, but if both defect, acting in their own self-interest alone, both lose. If one is trustworthy and the other defects, the defector gains the whole payoff. With communication, deals can be made, but ordinarily players do not cooperate.[212] The following variations have been studied:[213] (*a*) In the first sort of game, choices of one player have no effect on the gains of the other. Little communication or negotiation is needed. This provides absolute control over personal gains. (*b*) There is also conditional control, in which the first player can maximize his own gain only if he knows what the second player will do. In this sort of game, the first player can make much larger gains if he knows what his opponent's subsequent choice will be, but the second cannot alter his chances by any action, since his outcomes are the same in any case. In such games deals can be made in which the second player trades advance information about his choice in return for part of the consequent greater gains of the first player. (*c*) It is also possible for each player to have absolute control over the other's gain without his affecting his own gains. This leads to negotiations and agreements upon plays. (*d*) Then each player may have conditional control over the other's gain, which makes negotiation advantageous but tempts players to become undependable and increase personal payoffs after negotiation is concluded. (*e*) There are various combinations of the above sorts of games. The actual amounts of cooperation or competition which develop depend upon the sort of game. The authors point out that, besides the sort of game, the values of the participants are important. There is complex interaction between the game itself and extragame relations. If the future gains can be made from cooperation, for instance, a player often will not reduce his opponent's gain in a given instance in which he has the power to do so. The importance of personal gain to the participant, the response of the player to the exercise of power, his reactions to influencing the other's gains and having his own influenced, and the conceptual system by which he interprets the other's behavior and justifies his own are all probably important, but there is little experimental evidence on these.

Manipulations of payoffs in three-person groups can alter players' goals and consequently produce different strategies of play: *egotistic,* when the player is *competitive,* working for his own satisfactions alone; *altruistic,* when each is *symbiotic,* benefiting chiefly from the efforts of others; *egalitarian,* when all are *cooperative,* sharing alike; and *despotic,* when all players work chiefly for the benefit of a single one, who is *parasitic.*[214] If a person gets little reward for his efforts, he will usually not continue to exert himself fully.

One experiment was carried out using an apparatus called "sympar" (symbiosis-parasitism), which made it possible to change the payoff rules and consequently the relationships among players in three-person groups. By considering the payoff schedule, the experimenters could in general predict whether all three in the group would be working at the end of the game or whether one or two would be parasitic. A social optimum, in which all players maximized their payoffs, was reached only when some form of communication was possible among the players. Information flow among the members over some sort of channel or net was essential to the internal adjustment of the group. Which conditions elicit cooperation and which elicit competition in two-person games have been studied under a number of variations of payoff, communication, and instructions to the subjects.

Variations of the Prisoner's Dilemma game were used to investigate the extent to which tacit collusions arose. Sometimes explicit collusions were permitted to develop.[215] Without communication, only 2 out of 22 pairs of subjects collaborated, and even with collusion, noncooperative choices were still more frequent than cooperative ones, although the number of cooperative choices increased. Cooperative choices tended to decrease as the game progressed. In another investigation similar variations of the Prisoner's Dilemma were used, designed to increase collaboration by making the payoffs higher.[216] It was found that even when the subjects have nothing to gain and something to lose by playing the noncooperative strategy, they still use that strategy. Even when the game was rigged so that the payoff matrix was irrelevant and the subject was always paid for a cooperative choice, 64 percent of the choices were noncooperative. The Prisoner's Dilemma situation elicits puzzling behavior tending to destroy group integration. Individual members often act against their own interests.

The amount of communication among the players was varied in one study. It was found that there were more cooperative choices when there was communication than when it was prevented.[217]

Group cooperation requires some mutual trust among members. This was studied with subjects who rated high and others who rated low on a test of trustworthiness.[218] They played a game against an opponent who did not really exist, although they had been led to think that he did. The experimenter announced to the subject in each case that this "opponent" had made the trusting or cooperative choice. Each subject played the game twice, once playing first, before the fictitious opponent, and playing second the other time. The results showed that persons who were trusting when they made the first choice in a game were trustworthy when they made the second choice. And they expected the same behavior of the other player. The suspicious and untrustworthy subjects expected to be exploited by the other player and responded to a trusting choice by taking advantage of it.

Another experimenter attempted to predict when cooperative behavior would occur in Prisoner's Dilemma games.[219] He chose subjects who had received extreme scores on a test of internationalist attitudes, which indicated that they were strong supporters of either internationalism or isolationism. Pairs of internationalists acted cooperatively significantly more often than pairs of isolationists. There was no greater cooperation than normal in the internationalist groups, but the isolationist groups were more uncooperative.

Three-person groups playing long series of non-zero-sum nonnegotiable games were investigated in another research.[220] Personality factors were found to be important determinants of the subjects' behavior in these games. The subjects fell into three classes of personality types: (*a*) One type constantly tried to communicate to the other group members that he was willing to cooperate by playing a long series of cooperative moves, consistently losing money in the process. (*b*) One type settled on a noncooperative move and was not willing to change, despite cooperative moves by the other two members. He did not perceive or did not care that these cooperative moves were aimed at him. (*c*) A third type fell in between the above two. He was willing to cooperate if a second player took the initiative, but would revert to noncooperation if, after a few moves, the social optimum maximizing each player's gain was not achieved. In the three-person and *n*-person games in general, the outcomes depend upon personality, social, and other factors as well as the mathematical game strategy.[221]

5.5   Pathology   There are several major categories of pathology in groups, a topic considered more in relation to families than any other type of groups.[222]

(a) *Lacks of matter-energy inputs.*   A group's orderly processes can deteriorate rapidly when oxygen input to it is inadequate. The usual command control of the captain, the decider, may disappear in a damaged submarine under the sea as its oxygen is consumed. Firemen report that human beings will claw at each other's throats and trample on children when a fire burns up their oxygen and stifles them. In his satirical, fictional, but lifelike poem *Don Juan*, Byron relates how starving civilized men, adrift in a lifeboat, drew lots to determine which one of them should be killed and cannibalized by the others.[223] On land, lacks of water, food, or means of keeping warm may destroy the organization of a family, each member wandering off by himself and searching for what he needs. Every member of an explorer's group in the Arctic or of a Chinese family during a famine may meet a similar solitary end. Group control and division of labor decrease or disappear, as Hypothesis 5.6-1 states (see page 110). If the stress is relieved before the system ceases to survive, it may return to normal.

(b) *Excesses of matter-energy inputs.*   Severe trauma such as fire, tornado, typhoon, the ravages of war, or an automobile or plane accident may kill or injure one or more members of a military squad, an athletic team, a working group, a social club, or a family. It may damage artifacts which are critical to them. Such destruction can alter the range of stability of certain group variables to new steady states. The group as a consequence may suffer cold, become malnourished, or have to work harder. A bus accident may kill one-third of the members of a basketball team, the resultant damage to its interactions being revealed by the score of the next game played by the surviving teammates. The entire mode of life and the standard of living of a family can be changed when a tornado destroys their home or fire razes their uninsured business. When a mother of eight suddenly has triplets or a father with ten children finds himself responsible for an additional six offspring of his brother and his wife after the latter are killed by bombs, the excess of inputs may put such stress on the family that it cannot survive as a system.

(c) *Inputs of inappropriate forms of matter-energy.*   Tear gas or mace shot into any group or committee can disrupt its processes. Poison gas can destroy it. An epidemic of tuberculosis in a class or of influenza in an office group can bring all but the most essential of its activities to a halt. A hail of bullets can disperse an infantry squad so that even an experienced sergeant is hard pressed to keep them together, operating effectively under his command and defending their assigned territory. A defective child born into a family or a wounded colleague added to a band of spies trying to escape from the enemy can rapidly terminate the group's survival.

(d) *Lacks of information inputs.*   As I have noted above (see pages 564 and 572), groups suffering from information input underload or sensory deprivation may refuse to comply with command signals from their leaders or may quarrel among themselves. Boredom at isolated military posts or in ships on long voyages may break down the group into cliques and coalitions or inactivate standard decision-making procedures. In extreme cases this disintegration may terminate the system's control processes. The group may decompose into multiple components (see Hypothesis 5.6-1, page 110), and the final outcome may be murder or mutiny. Lack stresses of inputs of monetary information, *i.e.*, poverty; lack stresses of general or technical information, *i.e.*, poor education; or lack stresses of information which represents recognition and acceptance by peers can contribute to pathological processes in families. In the United States the rate of breakdown of family structure is higher among people suffering from such lack stresses of information than it is among people not subjected to these stresses.

(e) *Excesses of information inputs.*   In Chap. 5 (see pages 185 to 187) I have analyzed the normal group adjustments to information input overload. On busy days office staffs or the crews of operators at telephone switchboards everywhere develop internal strains which occasionally result in pathology such as severe arguments, resignations, chronic insubordination, or neglect of essential procedures. In general, the higher the echelon of an executive, the faster the information flows into his office. If the office is the headquarters of the general commanding the air defense of a nation, the White House, or the Kremlin, the stress may at times mount so high that the group has great difficulty maintaining the integration required for effective functioning. Inappropriate information inputs may also disturb group processes, *e.g.*, irrelevant testimony introduced into court proceedings or jokes and facetious remarks made at a committee meeting.

(f) *Inputs of maladaptive genetic information in the template.*   If a mayor distributes his staff functions so that he does not have assistants to help him in all aspects of his work, there can be severe functional pathology in his office. Some subsystem processes will not be carried out. This will be true also if he makes overlapping role assignments. And if an industrial executive decentralizes decision making to his subordinates without describing their authority or gives functions to subordinates which they are not equipped to carry out, pathology results. Stable family emotional and role relationships, particularly during early life, are vital to normal development of the children. Adding an adopted child after the other children have become accustomed to their family's relationships can threaten or destroy the established structure.

(g) *Abnormalities in internal matter-energy processes.* Unfair food or water distribution in a herd of animals, which results in the strongest getting the most and the weakest the least, often destroys the organized structure so that the weaklings walk off alone to die or gang up to attack the strong. The subsystems that process the many kinds of matter and energy which a group requires may act abnormally or stop entirely. This results in group pathology. A Cinderella may sit in the ashes wearing the cast-off clothes of her sisters and eating the leavings from their meals. The pioneer father who goes to hunt may drink instead and not bring home the nourishment his family expects of him in his capacity as family ingestor. The sailor who, as the distributor, has the key to the tank of water in the lifeboat may drink most of the water himself and pass out inadequate amounts to his shipwrecked companions. Parents may be profligate and not store food in the summer, with the result that their children starve in the winter. A nursing-home staff may not take the trouble to wash some of its senile patients who cannot bathe themselves. A maid may not remove accumulated rubbish and garbage from the house, though it is her assignment to do so, acting as the group extruder.

Family groups, of course, often lose a parent through death, separation, or divorce. When a group member is lost, from whatever cause, particularly a mother, father, leader, or other component of the decider, the group's matter-energy processing immediately becomes pathological.[224] I have already discussed the normal adjustments which groups make following the loss of a member (see page 566). Many groups cannot accomplish such adjustments. The new steady state which is achieved, by redistribution of critical functions, after an important component of the group dies or leaves the group, often is less satisfactory than the old one to all remaining members. An infantry squad whose sergeant is shot in battle, for example, is more likely to have casualties under the less experienced command of a corporal. Or a mother may have to go out and earn the living after the father deserts his family, but she may not have been trained in any skill and so cannot make much money. Furthermore, the children must be left to care for themselves during the daytime.

(h) *Abnormalities in internal information processes.* Failure of informational adjustment processes within a group can reduce or destroy its cohesiveness. If the chairman does not carry out his responsibilities, a committee accomplishes nothing and may dissolve. Poor morale is another form of group pathology. If a team of laborers feels it has no purposes or cannot define them well, it will have trouble deciding how to act, and the members will be dissatisfied with their relationships. Inadequate use of adjustments can affect not only decision making and satisfaction but also group productive capacity. Discontented work groups slow down their outputs (see pages 578 and 674 to 677). If they strike, the outputs stop.

Unresolved conflicts can produce enduring pathological group relationships. More than one couple have remained married and have lived in the same house for years without exchanging a word. Conflicts may ultimately split a group into smaller, less effective groups, or they may destroy it entirely. Splitting a group, however, is not always pathological. It can be a stage in the healthy growth of a group into an organization.

Highly cohesive groups can also process information pathologically. For example, in some families a mother controls her grown children so completely that she prevents them from carrying out the normal actions of marrying and initiating new families. The longer some families or professional partnerships stay together, the more the members work at cross-purposes. Their efficiency of interaction may decrease greatly, but they remain together because they derive some rewards from their relationship.

Either chronic illness or a defect in one member of a family elicits adjustment processes by the entire group. I have considered the effects of cancer, a disease of cells, at the level of the cell (see pages 301 and 302), the organ (see page 354), and the organism (see page 475). This and other serious illnesses may disturb the steady states of many family-group variables, including the economic ones that concern the flow of money. They may result in death of a member, which requires major adjustments by the survivors. Other stresses which many families adjust to abnormally include departure of a child to go to school or college; adolescence of a child, including the revolt against parental authority which comes from his efforts to make decisions independently; sexual aging of the husband or wife; and retirement of one or both parents from regular employment.

A normal family, according to Jackson (see page 573), is in homeostatic balance or a steady state.[225] He emphasized the need to study the entire family during psychiatric treatment of a child. He held that certain patterns of family interactions lead to particular sets of symptoms in the child, who is the primary focus of attention. Other members of the family often should receive treatment at the same time. He gave the following example:

In a family where the parents' hostility toward each other is handled in part by *covertly* disagreeing over the child, but *overtly* appearing firm and united, special ways of integrating will be developed by the child. For example, if the mother is markedly fearful of any aggression, including her own, and the father, despite a stern front, allows her to exploit him with phobic symptoms (masking his hostility by assuming a protective role toward his wife and child), then the child caught in the middle of such a situation may manifest phobias, and particularly if a girl, may have a marked fear of "losing control"—a fear pertaining to sexual and aggressive expressions.[226]

Sometimes only one member of the family group appears to have problems until he is cured, and then others develop symptoms. Jackson gave the example of a husband who urged that his wife be treated because of her frigidity, only to become impotent himself when she began to show improvement.

Not only family groups show pathological behavior. Office groups often develop such internal conflicts that some of the employees are fired or leave voluntarily. Congressional hearings have been known to break up with committee members in a fist fight. Juries often are hung, unable to reach a decision. When one or more members leave a group, its internal channel and net functions may worsen. If it loses its translator or its spokesman, its decoding or encoding may suffer. If it loses its leader, its decision making may become less expert. If it loses its secretary, much of its memory may go with him. Though subsystem processes may be reassigned after such losses, group information processing may be permanently harmed by them.

Another form of pathology of internal information processing in groups arises from incorrect or distorted signal transmission among members. If the maid cannot speak her employer's language, the household runs poorly. If the parents always alter their conversation with their children to conceal their arguments, ultimately family solidarity may suffer from this deceit.

5.6 Decay and termination   Groups differ in how long their members expect them to last. An experimental group lasts for an hour or a few hours. On the other hand, some groupings, like clubs, fraternities, or business partnerships, which replace their members if they leave or die, last longer than the lifetime of any member. Complete failure of any subsystem to carry out any of the critical subsystem processes of course results in the termination of the group, unless some other system carries them out. In any group a favorable ratio of inputs and outputs, of rewards and

costs, must be maintained if it is to survive. As components of groups get older, the system processes may become feebler. The finesse of collaboration of a string quartet will eventually falter as the players age. A group which does not replace members as they leave or die, of course, finally disappears. Families, for instance, may be destroyed by separation, divorce, or death of their members.

The failure of some groups to survive may be explained by lack of feedback and reinforcement, since reinforced reactions in human interpersonal behavior become stabilized and those which receive no reward disappear.[227] Groups that do not support other groups with which they are symbiotic also terminate. Groups which tolerate more parasitic subgroups than they can support fail. And so may those which establish value hierarchies that do not enable them to adjust effectively in the suprasystem. A family whose values are antisocial and which lives by crime may disintegrate as its members are arrested.

6. Models and simulations

Of the four classes of models and simulations (see page 85), two are not represented: (*b*) *living, usually human, representations* and (*d*) *living system–computer interactions*. I present a special case of class (*a*) and several examples of class (*c*) below:

(*a*) *Nonliving artifacts.*   The artifact in one simulation was a tape recording which represented group members with whom a single living subject interacted.[228] A judgment situation was used in which a decision was made as to how far a light moved. This is the autokinetic phenomenon, an illusion in which a stationary light in complete darkness is seen by the subject to move. The effect has been shown to be sensitive to social-influence processes.[229] Each subject was seated in a dark room and was told that he was connected by headphones to other subjects in adjoining rooms. The judgments which preceded the subject's own judgment were tape-recorded. Three ranges of judgments were used. A control group of subjects working alone was also used.

The social pressures usually felt in a group were effectively simulated by this technique, and the subject's judgments were influenced by the recorded ranges. This technique eliminates the need for paid stooges, reduces the problems of scheduling groups, and makes the situation exactly standard from one subject to another.

(*c*) *Models in words, numbers, or other symbols, including computer programs.*   A model suitable for Monte Carlo simulation (see page 486), which takes into account several important aspects of group functions, was developed by Rainio.[230] The focus of the theory underlying this work is upon the learning of an individual as he is rewarded by similar acts or punished by dissimilar acts of group members whom he contacts. The "two-operator" model of Bush and Mosteller, whose stochastic mathematical theory of organismic learning I have discussed earlier (see page 492), is the basis for Rainio's model. He says his chief idea is that reinforcement of organismic learning may depend on the interactions of the whole group of which a person is a member. That is, a person is rewarded or punished if others associated with him behave in a particular way. Communication facilitates such learning, and this is why language use grows in social situations.

He conceives of a group as an "organism," in my terms a concrete system with interrelated components. As a result of this interrelatedness, the probability that an initiation of behavior by one person toward another at a given time will succeed is conditional, depending on the fact that at the same moment another person or a number of other people are also making initiations toward other group members. Thus group learning occurs. In order to use the Monte Carlo method to predict the behavior of a given group member, not only the probability of his independent behavior must be considered, but also the probabilities of behavior of all others in the group and their interactions—the total configuration of group processes. The computer is then programmed to generate, in any given run of the simulation, a sequence of random data corresponding to those probabilities.

Rainio's simplest interaction model is composed of six members. All interact at the same rate. Social contacts take place in pairs. Each member of the pair knows whether the other behaves as he himself does. If the other, because of a tendency to imitate, acts in the same way, this constitutes a reinforcement which increases the likelihood of more behavior of this sort. The probability of further contacts with the same person is increased or decreased, depending upon whether the two behave the same or differently. Uniform cliques can emerge from such interactions.

This model is then extended to allow some group members to be more active than others, to allow for differences in success of contacts, to permit individual members to contact subgroups as well as other single persons, to allow for multiple modes of contacts, to replace the concept of imitation by the more general formulation that one member is rewarded when another one behaves in the manner the first one expects, and to include contacts with outsiders not in the group.

An "organism" model (that is, one which views the group as a concrete system) is also presented. It also is stated first in simplified form and then extended. In its first form, the success or failure of the initiations of three people in a group depends on the configuration of all of them at the time in question. Later the possibility is introduced that social interaction in advance may change the probabilities of their acts. Task performances in which persons may see each other but not speak are considered first, and then tasks involving verbal communication. "Ideational responses" which intervene between overt responses are also introduced. These are based on individuals' assumptions about one another's behavior, on information about others' intentions, and on others' suggestions. Actions may be rewarding or punishing, depending upon the actor's own conception of a successful configuration. The possibility that this model can have cross-level application to inanimate systems, primitive animate organisms, and single human beings is mentioned by Rainio.

He initiated laboratory experiments designed to test the hypothesis that a person contacts people who share his opinions more often than people who do not. Six-man groups were used. Members were in separate booths, and the actual communications that they sent to one another by electric signals were not transmitted, but were replaced by controlled messages in which the first person a member contacted appeared always to agree with his views, the second always disagreed, the third always agreed, and the fourth and fifth, if they were contacted, always appeared to disagree. Thus two persons contacted were always rewarding, and the others were always punishing, according to Rainio's terminology. The results tended to confirm his hypothesis.

Another simulation, which makes use of the concepts of social theory, learning theory, and classical economics, is the computer model of social behavior, HOMUNCULUS (poorly named since it represents *two* interacting persons), developed by Gullahorn and Gullahorn.[231] Their simulation has interesting similarities to Rainio's model. The theoretical base of their work is Homans's treatment of face-to-face contact among individuals in which a person's future actions depend on the payoffs—the psychological, social, or economic rewards or punishments—which his past interactions with other persons have elicited. These payoffs are relatively direct and immediate. Homans views interpersonal interaction as a sort of mutual psychoeconomic exchange. The Gullahorns translate into computer routines the following five hypotheses of Homans:

[1] *If in the past the occurrence of a particular stimulus-situation has been the occasion on which a man's activity has been rewarded, then the more similar the present stimulus-situation is to*

the past one, the more likely he is to emit the activity, or some similiar activity, now.

[2] *The more often within a given period of time a man's activity rewards the activity of another, the more often the other will emit the activity.*

[3] *The more valuable to a man a unit of the activity another gives him, the more often he will emit activity rewarded by the activity of the other.*

[4] *The more often a man has in the recent past received a rewarding activity from another, the less valuable any further unit of that activity becomes to him.*

[5] *The more to a man's disadvantage the rule of distributive justice fails of realization, the more likely he is to display the emotional behavior we call anger.* [232]

This simulation creates a dyad, Ted and George, in a situation in which one asks the other for help in his work. The social economics of such consultations have been analyzed. [233] Both participants benefit, and both pay a price. The one asking help is rewarded by being able to do a better job, but pays by admitting his inferiority, while the consultant gains prestige and loses time from his own work.

The computer simulation program is written in Information Processing Language, Version 5 (IPL-5). [234] Flowcharts are included. Data routines are written in the form of hierarchies of lists which may be complex and which associate with any symbol its attributes and their values. A person is represented by a list structure containing numerous lists describing his identity, his abilities, his relative and absolute positions in social groups, his images of reference groups, and his images of other group members. An example of the operation of these lists is the memory list which George consults to determine whether the input he has just received is among the inputs which have previously been reinforced. He selects his activities from a list which has been rewarded in the past by the other member of the dyad.

The authors consider this language flexible and efficient for representing complex, symbolic social behavior. They say that their model is deterministic rather than probabilistic, emphasizing nonnumerical processes. The decision-making process is assumed to be serial. They say:

Furthermore, our model conceives of a person as a hypothesis-testing, information-processing organism capable of receiving, analyzing, reconstructing, and storing information. HOMUNCULUS is an attempt to explicate in a way not possible with verbal theory the ability of a person engaged in normal social interaction to evaluate the context of behavior, retrieve information necessary to project alternative plans of action, and—before actually committing himself overtly—to select the conditions under which he will emit one activity rather than another. [235]

A computer simulation of some of the small-group artificially constrained communication network experiments was undertaken by McWhinney. [236] It is a combination of one program representing each group member and one program representing the research design of the particular experiment simulated. According to the program, each member acts under two constraints which make him act in a reasonable fashion: (*a*) He sends to other group members only information he does not know them to possess, and (*b*) he includes all such information available to him in each message. Each member is given a repertoire of behaviors which real subjects showed in previous such group experiments, particularly those by Guetzkow and Simon and by Guetzkow and Dill (see pages 533, 534, 539, 545, and 549). The program also can give probabilistic reinforcement, increasing the likelihood of future use of behaviors which, when first adopted, reduced group solution time and decreasing the likelihood of use of those which lengthened solution time. The subjects can be placed in any desired network. The runs can consist of any desired number of trials, in each of which each member receives an item of information from every other member.

The reinforcement feature was included in some runs of the simulation but not in others. The runs which were carried out made it possible to compare the performances of the simulated-group members with those of the subjects of Christie, Luce, and Macy (see pages 544 and 545). The study showed that of groups working in five different networks, the members of totally connected nets made the best performances. The simulated behavior, according to McWhinney, bore:

. . . good resemblance to the behavior of the many real groups which themselves failed to settle on a particular scheme for performing the task effectively. This conclusion comes from comparing the best simulation run with empirical data obtained from the files of the Guetzkow experiments. The comparison was established by two measures, one of effort and one of time, for two archetype networks: the circle, which is a simple closed loop, and the all-connected network. The effort measure compared the number of messages required to complete the task at each trial. In the circle network the match was extremely good. There was no significant difference after the first few trials in which the real and simulated groups took different paths to their nonlearning performance level. For the all-channel runs the comparison was less accurate. The simulation required about 21 messages versus a mean of about 19 per trial for the actual groups. The potential range is from about 30 messages down to a minimum of eight.

The second measure compared the mean duration of trials with a quantitized measure of time-to-solution. The circle simulation was again relatively accurate. It showed more concentration of times about the mean time than did the actual but the means of distributions differed by only 0.4 periods in a range of about 10 periods (4σ). The all-channel runs produced the same double-peaked distribution as did the actual runs, but it was a more concentrated distribution and shifted 1.4 periods above the actual—an error in the same direction as in the message count. Serial correlations of the trial-to-trial durations of the actual and simulated trials did not differ significantly for runs in either network. [237]

This simulation makes it possible to increase the number of group members beyond five—the largest number of subjects ever used in real-group communication network experiments. Seven- and eight-member simulated groups behaved quite differently from smaller ones, not being able to complete the task in the allotted number of trials. This program may be particularly useful in simulating complex systems with numerous members and many organizational arrangements, which could not be studied with live subjects because of prohibitive costs in money and subject time.

A graph-theory model has been constructed by Harary and Schwenk to analyze a related problem about the most efficient ways to disseminate information in one-way and two-way artificially constrained group communication networks.[238] It provides solutions under a number of different conditions.

7. Conclusions

It is historically interesting, and a bit puzzling, that a period of extensive experimentation and theory construction which produced valuable data and a number of important hypotheses concerning group structure and processes ended in the early 1960s. It has been succeeded by a period in which little that is new and important has been introduced to the field and in which confirmation of hypotheses has lagged. Indeed, some former group-observation laboratories are at present being used for other sorts of psychological experimentation because group research is languishing.[239] All this is true even though articles on groups continue to pour out at a brisk rate—3,400 between 1967 and 1972.[240]

Over the last three decades, however, a wealth of theoretical and experimental work on group processes has accumulated. Much of this is traditional, and much shows little concern for external validity or possible applications.[241] The ratio of theory to experiment unfortunately is still too high, and group dynamics has never had a unifying theoretical position. Systems concepts appear in some authors' writings about groups, but usually such formulations have been about the roles played—like leader, mother, or subordinate—rather than about the specific members who interact in functional relationships. In other words, the theories have ordinarily concerned abstracted rather than concrete systems. Also, they have been deeply influenced by Lewin's attempts to apply topology and field theory to an abstracted system of "life space" or some intrapsychic "space," rather than to physical space-time. This is partly because much group interaction concerns meaning variables like hostility, status, and affect, for which good objective quantification is not yet possible.

A great deal of the rigorous research has been carried out on groups artificially brought together in laboratories for experimental purposes. These investigations have yielded much significant understanding of this level of living system. But such laboratory groups differ significantly from natural groups which assemble by the usual processes of interaction in a society, just as cells cultured in glass differ greatly from those which grow in a multicellular organism. Furthermore, such experimental groups usually are partipotential, commonly lacking their own matter-energy processing subsystems and sometimes some information processing subsystems as well. They depend for their matter-energy processing on the society which provides the experimental subjects who compose them (see page 516). Extrapolation to all systems at the group level from experiments with laboratory groups consequently gives the false impression that groups in general are more exclusively concerned with information processing than they really are. Studies of matter-energy processing in groups are few, and consequently the sections in this chapter on those activities are brief. Many experimental groups are ephemeral. They do not have time to become integrated and develop significant and influential interpersonal relationships. The members may never have met before the experiment began, may interact little during the study, and usually do not have to live together after it is over. The atmosphere is often like that surrounding a consultant who is requested to visit a laboratory to give his opinion on its research. All can be honeymoon while he is there, and he can go away feeling complimented at the attention paid to his ideas. But he is not going to be there tomorrow, he is not involved in the local power processes, and the laboratory staff can ignore his recommendations entirely if it wishes. We need many more controlled experiments with natural groups which are important in their members' lives and which endure for significant periods, like those which have been conducted on college students' dormitory groups, juries, boys' camping groups, families, or long-term psychotherapeutic groups. In such systems some of the division of functions typical of real life can appear. Interactions in many experimental groups are casual in some of the ways that they are in a national committee which meets only once a year. The members are almost strangers. Because ordinarily everyone is totipotential, capable of carrying out most or all functions of the group, each member must make the courteous assumption that all present can do everything equally well. Real trade-offs of rewards and punishments or costs rarely occur. What rewards and punishments are involved are those of the general society rather than the particular group. Consequently, the group may reflect the systems processes of the society but only dimly those of the group itself. It is therefore hard under such circumstances to demonstrate the complex interactions which occur in natural groups.

Frequently a group has fewer members than critical subsystem processes, so that a member may carry out more than one of these processes. Indeed, in very small groups, one member may perform nearly all of them. On the other hand, a single subsystem process, like input transducing, may be carried out by all members of the group. For such reasons it is often harder in groups to determine what component or components constitute a given subsystem than it is in cells, organs, organisms, or the larger social systems which I shall discuss in succeeding chapters.

The commonsense concept of the leader of the group is of decreasing importance in sophisticated theory of group process, but still the notion is used without adequate definition. At times it is assumed that the leader is the decider, responsible exclusively for decision making, but carrying out no other functions. Actually, however, decision making is often dispersed among members, and on the other hand, the leader frequently carries out several other processes, such as decoding, internal transducing, or even ingesting. The commonsense distinction of leader and follower therefore has in the past produced a conceptualization of the components of groups which makes it difficult to match structure to process. This has resulted in conceptual confusion.

Decision making in groups often is explicitly or implicitly accomplished by voting, each member getting one vote, but sometimes other procedures are used, such as giving extra weight to the leader's vote. Because groups rarely, if ever, have clear one-to-one relationships between members and subsystem processes, at times no member may feel responsible for certain subsystems. Consequently, those subsystems may at those times have no influence upon group decisions. This form of decision making is consequently quite different from that seen at lower levels of living systems.

Group research concentrates particularly on such processes as segregation and integration, which have not received so much emphasis at some other levels. Conversely, it neglects most matter-energy processing almost entirely and pays much less attention to such information processes as learning and memory, which are intensively studied at, say, the organism level. These traditional differences in research emphasis make groups appear to be more unlike organisms and other levels of systems than they really are.

Groups composed of higher organisms interact and cohere largely through information processing. This is also important in bringing about interaction and cohe-sion of components of cells, organs, and organisms. At these lower levels, however, physical propinquity of components retained within the system's boundary and attached to the supporter is also instrumental in a way which is not true of groups. This makes members of groups seem very different from the components of lower-level systems. They often shift rapidly from functioning in one group to functioning in another, and sometimes they may function in several groups almost simultaneously. While this shifting is real and important, it sometimes masks the similarities between groups and systems at lower levels, formal identities which I have emphasized throughout this chapter.

This chapter indicates that there are still many challenging questions yet unanswered about the nature of groups and how they are similar to, or different from, systems at the other levels. I shall list a few of these:

Is it regularly true that information flows more easily and in larger amounts inside a group and in its suprasystem than it does across its boundary (see page 56), as may well be true at other levels of systems (see Hypotheses 3.1.2.2-2 and 3.1.2.2-3, page 93)?

Since various types of groups store quite different kinds and amounts of matter-energy (see pages 527 and 528), what are the variables which determine what and how much the group stores?

What are the quantitative characteristics of the feedbacks which enable schools of fish, clouds of starlings, and human *corps de ballet* to move with their fine coordination and precision (see pages 529 and 530)?

Under what circumstances is it most efficient for a group to centralize input transducing in a single individual, and when is it better to disperse it laterally to all the members or downwardly so that each member transduces inputs for himself (see page 531)? Are the principles which determine this in groups similar to those which apply at other levels?

Totally connected experimental groups sometimes have higher morale and are more efficient than groups with other communication networks (see pages 538, 539, 542, 544, 545, and 585). What determines when this is true and when it is not?

A central member in a group's decision network is especially likely to be its decider or to participate in its decision making (see pages 549 and 550). He is also probably most subject to information input overload (see page 545). Do these joint facts have as much implication for how decisions are made at organization, society, and supranational system levels as they do at the group level? If so, they may have great social significance.

Groups seem to comply more willingly with orders from the decider when they are under stress or threat than they do before or after the stress or threat (see page 563 and Hypotheses 5.2-13 and 5.4.3-7, pages 107 and 109). Does this principle concerning integration under stress also apply at other levels?

Message diffusion in the channel and net subsystem has been studied in groups (see pages 537 and 538). It has some characteristics like those of such diffusion at the organization, society, and supranational system levels, supporting Hypothesis 3.3.3.1-1 (see page 95). Is this true also at other levels?

We know little about how organizations arise from groups, but in one study of totally connected groups working at a task (see page 539), two- and three-echelon hierarchical networks developed. Is this how organizations arise from groups? What determines such development?

In the noisy marble experiment (see page 542), as the groups matured (or learned), they used increasingly more efficient codes. The principles of improving codes in groups seem to be like those which apply to systems at other levels (see pages 396, 404, and 636 and Hypotheses 3.3.4.2-1, 3.3.4.2-4, 3.3.4.2-6, and 3.3.4.2-7, page 98). Why?

The differences between the associative learning of human organisms and groups suggest why, at least in some situations, groups learn better (see page 544). Groups have more than one organism with a nervous system, and so when a group learns something, each nervous system needs to process less information. Also, the totality of the members usually has had more relevant past experiences which may aid in learning. Moreover, since multiple members can correct one another's errors, groups profit from more error feedback. Also, perhaps simultaneous operation of multiple input transducers provides better observation. Relatively how important is each of these cross-level differences?

Do group productivity and efficiency increase (see pages 553, 554, 568, and 577) as group members achieve integration, agreement, and liking for one another, and as they participate more in group planning?

The processes of groups with few members are quite different from those of groups with many (see pages 556 to 558). Groups with many members are unlike those with few in being more representative of the population from which they come, being more heterogeneous, and having many more possible relations among their members. Are there similar differences depending on the number of subsystems and components in systems at lower and higher levels?

The amount of physical space among the members of animal groups like chickens appears to determine how they interact. If they are quite a distance apart, they neglect one another, but if they are close, they interact offensively or defensively (see pages 564 and

565). Is this true of components of organizations, societies, or supranational systems?

Current theory suggests that there are group tendencies toward balance or "strains toward symmetry" which appear to lead to resolution of conflicts among components (see pages 568 to 570). Acceptance of common values by group members reduces conflict among them, decreases the costs of communication, improves task performance, and makes them more cooperative and integrative (see pages 577 and 578). Integrative groups have strong pressures toward uniformity and toward rejection of deviates. Is this true at other levels as well?

The above paragraphs indicate that we can ask similar questions about groups as about other levels of living systems. The analysis of groups as concrete systems, it appears from this presentation, can help us conceptualize and understand them. It shows us major emphases about groups which have been neglected and gaps in our present knowledge, e.g., about matter-energy processing in groups. It suggests shortcomings in our previous experimental methods, e.g., neglecting to study parallels between groups and systems at other levels or neglecting to investigate group processes when their members' motivation is determined more by the group than by the levels above or the organism level below. The continual changing of roles by members of some groups has drawn attention away from the fact that groups have subsystem structures and processes like those of other levels of living systems. As these become manifest, new vistas of potential group research appear.

NOTES AND REFERENCES

[1] Cf. Lipton, J. *An exaltation of larks: the venereal game.* New York: Grossman, 1968.

[2] Back, K. W. Intervention techniques: small groups. *Ann. Rev. Psychol.*, 1974, **25**, 374–375.

[3] Back, K. W. Influence through social communication. *J. abnorm. soc. Psychol.*, 1951, **46**, 9–23.

[4] Chapple, E. D. & Coon, C. S. *Principles of anthropology.* New York: Holt, 1942.

[5] Anderson, R. E. & Carter, I. E. *Human behavior in the social environment.* Chicago: Aldine, 1974, 75–78.

[6] McBride, G. A general theory of social organization and behaviour. *University of Queensland Papers. Faculty of Veterinary Science*, **1**(2). St. Lucia: Univ. of Queensland Press, 1964.

[7] E.g., Emerson, A. E. The supraorganismic aspects of the society. *Colloques internationaux du Centre de la Recherche Scientifique*, **34**. Paris: Centre National de la Recherche Scientifique, 1952, 333–353.

[8] Emerson, A. E. The organization of insect societies. In W. C. Allee, A. E. Emerson, O. Park, T. Park, & K. P. Schmidt. *Principles of animal ecology.* Philadelphia: Saunders, 1949, 420. Reprinted by permission.
NOTE: Cf. for Emerson's view on cross-level analogies Emerson, A. E. The supraorganismic aspects of the society. *Op. cit.*

[9]*Ibid.* Reprinted by permission.

[10]*Ibid.*, 425. Reprinted by permission.

[11]Homans, G. C. *The human group.* New York: Harcourt, Brace, 1950.
Cf. also Deutsch, K. W. *Nationalism and social communication.* Cambridge, Mass.: M.I.T. Press, 1953.

[12]Newcomb, T. M. An approach to the study of communicative acts. *Psychol. Rev.*, 1953, **60**, 393–404.

[13]Emerson, A. E. The organization of insect societies. *Op. cit.*, 424–425.

[14]Teleki, G. The omnivorous chimpanzee. *Sci. Amer.*, 1973, **228**(1), 33–42.

[15]Emerson, A. E. The organization of insect societies. *Op cit.*, 420–421. Reprinted by permission.

[16]*Ibid.*, 424.

[17]*Ibid.*, 423.

[18]Wynne-Edwards, V. C. *Animal dispersion in relation to social behaviour.* New York: Hafner, 1962, 284–288.

[19]Washburn, S. L. & DeVore, I. The social life of baboons. *Sci. Amer.*, 1961, **204**(6), 62–71.

[20]Shaw, E. The schooling of fishes. *Sci. Amer.*, June 1962, **206**(6), 128. Reprinted by permission of *Scientific American.*

[21]Thines, G. & Vandenbussche, E. The effects of alarm substance on the schooling behaviour of *Rasbora heteromorpha Duncker* in day and night conditions. *Anim. Behav.*, 1966, **14**, 296–302.

[22]Thelen, H. A. *Methods for studying work and emotionality in group operation.* Chicago: Human Dynamics Laboratory, Univ. of Chicago, 1954.

[23]Homans, G. C. *Op. cit.*, 90–94.

[24]Bales, R. F. *Interaction process analysis: a method for the study of small groups.* Cambridge, Mass.: Addison-Wesley, 1950.

[25]Thelen, H. A. & Whithall, J. Three frames of reference: the description of climate. *Human Relat.*, 1949, **2**, 159–176.

[26]Guetzkow, H. & Dill, W. R. Factors in the organizational development of task-oriented groups. *Sociometry*, 1957, **20**, 186.

[27]Bavelas, A. Communication patterns in task-oriented groups. *J. Acoust. Soc.*, 1950, **22**, 725–730.
Cf. also Leavitt, H. J. Some effects of certain communication patterns on group performance. *J. abnorm. soc. Psychol.*, 1951, **46**, 38–50.

[28]Guetzkow, H. & Simon, H. A. The impact of certain communication nets upon organization and performance in task-oriented groups. *Mgmt. Sci.*, 1955, **1**, 233–250.

[29]Shaw, M. E. Some effects of unequal distribution of information upon group performance in various communication nets. *J. abnorm. soc. Psychol.*, 1954, **49**, 547–553.

[30]Shaw, M. E. Some factors influencing the use of information in small groups. *Psychol. Rep.*, 1961, **8**, 187–198.

[31]*Ibid.*

[32]Bavelas, A. *Op cit.*
Cf. also Leavitt, H. J. Some effects of certain communication patterns on group performance. *J. abnorm. soc. Psychol.*, 1951, **46**, 38–50.

[33]Shaw, M. E. Some factors influencing the use of information in small groups. *Op. cit.*
Cf. also Heise, G. A. & Miller, G. A. Problem solving by small groups using various communication nets. *J. abnorm. soc. Psychol.*, 1951, **46**, 327–335.

[34]Christie, L. S., Luce, R. D., & Macy, J., Jr. *Communication and learning in task-oriented groups.* Cambridge, Mass.: M.I.T., Research Laboratory of Electronics, Technical Report No. 231, May 13, 1952.

[35]Bavelas, A. A mathematical model for group structures. *Appl. Anthropol.*, 1948, **7**(3), 16–30.

NOTE: Bavelas developed his mathematical model in the above article from a background of Lewin's efforts to borrow concepts from topology to develop a sort of geometry useful in psychological analysis, which he called "hodology." Bavelas did not insist on dealing only with communication among persons or among groups over channels in physical space, but he also contended that his earliest formulation could apply to communication among ideas and attitudes. This intermingling of physical spaces with other spaces, which occurs in other studies of social structure and process (see pages 9 to 11), can lead to conceptual confusion. Bavelas's later article (see Reference 27) appears to be limited to information processing in nets in physical space.

[36]Leavitt, H. J. Some effects of certain communication patterns on group performance. *J. abnorm. soc. Psychol.*, 1951, **46**, 38–50.

[37]Bartlett, F. C. *Remembering: a study in experimental and social psychology.* New York: Cambridge Univ. Press, 1932 & 1961, 63–94.

[38]Thelen, H. A. *Op cit.*

[39]Chapple, E. D. The standard experimental (stress) interview as used in interaction chronograph investigations. *Human Organization*, 1953, **12**(2), 23–32.

[40]Cherry, C. *On human communication.* Cambridge, Mass. & New York: M.I.T. Press & Wiley, 1957, 27.

[41]Rapoport, A. & Horvath, W. J. A study of a large sociogram. *Behav. Sci.*, 1961, **6**, 279–291.

[42]Dodd, S. C. Testing message diffusion in harmonic logistic curves. *Psychometrika*, 1956, **21**, 203–205.

[43]Glanzer, M. & Glaser, R. *Techniques for the study of team structure and behavior. II. Empirical studies of the effects of structure.* Pittsburgh: American Institute for Research, Contract N7ONR-37008, NR-154-079, June, 1957.

[44]*E.g.*, Bavelas, A. Communication patterns in task-oriented groups. *Op. cit.*
Cf. also Luce, R. D., Macy, J., Jr., Christie, L. S., & Hay, D. H. *Information flow in task-oriented groups.* Cambridge, Mass.: M.I.T., Research Laboratory of Electronics, Technical Report No. 264, Aug. 31, 1953.

[45]Heise, G. A. & Miller, G. A. *Op. cit.*

[46]Christie, L. S., Luce, R. D., & Macy, J., Jr. *Op. cit.*, 148–152.

[47]Guetzkow, H. & Simon, H. A. *Op. cit.*
Cf. also Guetzkow, H. & Dill, W. R. *Op. cit.*

[48]Shaw, M. E. & Rothschild, G. H. Some effects of prolonged experience in communication nets. *J. appl. Psychol.*, 1956, **40**, 281–286.

[49]Burroughs, W., Schultz, W., & Autrey, S. Quality of argument, leadership votes, and eye contact in three-person leaderless groups. *J. soc. Psychol.*, 1973, **90**, 89–93.

[50]Christie, L. S., Luce, R. D., & Macy, J., Jr. *Op. cit.*, 136–152.

[51]*Ibid.*, 138.

[52]*Ibid.*, 143–146.

[53]Cattell, R. B. On the theory of group learning. *J. soc. Psychol.*, 1953, **37**, 27–52.

[54]Cattell, R. B. Concepts and methods in the measurement of group syntality. *Psychol. Rev.*, 1948, **55**, 58–59.

[55]Smith, K. U. & Kao, H. Social feedback: determination of social learning. *J. nerv. & ment. Dis.*, 1971, **152**, 289–297.

[56]Perlmutter, H. V. & DeMontmollin, G. Group learning of nonsense syllables. *J. abnorm. soc. Psychol.*, 1952, **47**, 762–769.

[57]Christie, L. S., Luce, R. D., & Macy, J., Jr. *Op. cit.*, 102, 188–198.

[58]Guetzkow, H. & Dill, W. R. *Op. cit.*, 202–203.

[59]Lanzetta, J. T. & Roby, T. B. Group learning and communication as a function of task and structure "demands." *J. abnorm. soc. Psychol.*, 1957, **55**, 121–131.

[60]Rapoport, A. Some self-organization parameters in three-person groups. In H. Von Foerster & G. W. Zopf, Jr. (Eds.). *Principles of self-organization.* New York: Pergamon Press, 1962, 1–24.
Cf. also Deutsch, M. Trust and suspicion. *J. Conflict Resolution*, 1958, **2**, 265–279.

[61]Altmann, M. Social behavior of elk, *Cervus canadensis nelsoni*, in the Jackson Hole area of Wyoming. *Behaviour*, 1952, **4**, 116–143.

[62]Lorge, I., Fox, D., Davitz, J., & Brenner, M. A survey of studies contrasting the quality of group performance and individual performance. *Psychol. Bull.*, 1958, **15**, 337–372.
Cf. also Van de Geer, J. P. & Jaspars, J. M. F. Cognitive functions. *Ann. Rev. Psychol.*, 1966, **17**, 160–162.
Rapoport, A. *Group performance on a logical task under various experimental conditions.* Ann Arbor: Univ. of Michigan, Mental Health Research Institute, Report No. 8, June, 1959.

[63]Kelley, H. H. & Thibaut, J. W. Experimental studies of group problem solving and process. In G. Lindzey (Ed.). *Handbook of social psychology.* Cambridge, Mass.: Addison-Wesley, 1954, 735–785.

[64]Strodtbeck, F. L. Husband-wife interaction over revealed differences. *Amer. sociol. Rev.*, 1951, **16**, 468–473.

[65]Leavitt, H. J. *Op cit.*

[66]Guetzkow, H. & Simon, H. A. *Op. cit.*
Cf. also Guetzkow, H. & Dill, W. R. *Op. cit.*

[67]Shaw, M. E., Rothschild, G. H., & Strickland, J. F. Decision processes in communication nets. *J. abnorm. soc. Psychol.*, 1957, **54**, 323–330.

[68]Mulder, M. Group-structure and group-performance. *Acta psychol. Amst.*, 1959, **16**, 356–402.

[69]*Ibid.*

[70]White, R. & Lippitt, R. Leader behavior and member reaction in three "social climates." In D. Cartwright & A. Zander (Eds.). *Group dynamics.* Evanston, Ill.: Row, Peterson, 1953, 536.

[71]Carter, J. H. Military leadership. *Military Rev.*, 1952, **32**, 14–18.

[72]Cf. Hare, A. P., Borgatta, E. F., & Bales, R. F. (Eds.). *Small groups.* New York: Knopf, 1955, 347.

[73]Roethlisberger, F. J. & Dickson, W. J. *Management and the worker.* Cambridge, Mass.: Harvard Univ. Press, 1956, 522.

[74]A. Bales, R. F. In T. Parsons, R. F. Bales, & E. A. Shils (Eds.). *Working papers in the theory of action.* Glencoe, Ill.: Free Press, 1953, 111–161.
B. Carter, J. H. *Op. cit.*
C. Cartwright, D. & Zander, A. (Eds.). *Group dynamics.* Evanston, Ill.: Row, Peterson, 1953, 25–26, 537–544.
D. Cattell, R. B. New concepts for measuring leadership, in terms of group syntality. *Human Relat.*, 1951, **4**, 161–184.
E. Hare, A. P., Borgatta, E. F., & Bales, R. F. *Op. cit.*
F. Homans, G. C. *Op. cit.*, 188–189, 422.
G. Krech, D. & Crutchfield, R. S. *Theories and problems of social psychology.* New York: McGraw-Hill, 1948, 417–422.
H. Wolman, B. Leadership and group dynamics. *J. soc. Psychol.*, 1953, **43**, 11–25.

[75]Flood, M. M. *A group preference experiment. Mathematical models of human behavior: proceedings of a symposium.* Stamford, Conn.: Dunlap & Assoc., 1955, 1–21.

[76]Rapoport, A. & Orwant, C. Experimental games: a review. *Behav. Sci.*, 1962, **7**, 22.

[77]Arrow, K. J. *Social choice and individual values.* New York: Wiley, 1951.

[78]Ziller, R. C. Scales of judgment: a determinant of the accuracy of group decisions. *Human Relat.*, 1955, **8**, 153–164.

[79]Bell, G. B. & French, R. L. Consistency of individual leadership position in small groups of varying membership. *J. abnorm. soc. Psychol.*, 1950, **45**, 764–767.

[80]Strodtbeck, F. L. & Mann, R. D. Sex role differentiation in jury deliberations. *Sociometry*, 1956, **19**, 3–11.

[81]Shaskin, M. & Meier, N. Sex effects in delegations. *Personnel Psychol.*, 1971, **24**, 471–476.

[82]NOTE: The choice of veniremen for jury panels is more or less random except for the fact that minors, aliens, and certain professionals such as doctors, clergymen, lawyers, and teachers are often excluded, along with the sick, civil servants, and criminals.

[83]Strodtbeck, F. L., James, R. M., & Hawkins, C. Social status in jury deliberations. *Amer. sociol. Rev.*, 1957, **22**, 713–719.

[84]Barnlund, D. C. A comparative study of individual, majority, and group judgment. *J. abnorm. soc. Psychol.*, 1959, **58**, 55–60.

[85]Bevan, W., Albert, R. S., Loiseaux, P. R., Mayfield, P. N., & Wright, G. Jury behavior as a function of the prestige of the foreman and the nature of his leadership. *J. public Law*, 1958, **7**, 419–449.

[86]Kalven, H., Jr. Report on the jury project. In A. F. Conard (Ed.). *Conference on aims and methods of legal research.* Ann Arbor: Univ. of Michigan Law School, 1957, 155–174.

[87]Thurstone, L. L. & Degan, J. W. A factorial study of the Supreme Court. *Proc. Nat. Acad. Sci.*, 1951, **37**, 628–635.

[88]Robinson, J. A. Decision making in the House Rules Committee. *Admin. Sci. Quart.*, 1958, **3**, 73–86.

[89]Arrow, K. J. *Op. cit.*
Cf. also Harsanyi, J. C. Cardinal welfare, individualistic ethics, and interpersonal comparisons of utility. *J. polit. Economy*, 1955, **63**, 309–321.

[90]Marquis, D. G., Guetzkow, H., & Heyns, R. W. A social psychological study of the decision-making conference. In H. Guetzkow (Ed.). *Groups, leadership and men: research in human relations.* Pittsburgh: Carnegie Press, 1951, 55–67.

[91]Thorpe, W. H. Duet-singing birds. *Sci. Amer.*, 1973, **229**(2), 70–79.

[92]Ofshe, R. Cognitive consistency and language behavior. In R. J. Ofshe (Ed.). *Interpersonal behavior in small groups.* Englewood Cliffs, N.J.: Prentice-Hall, 1973, 96–107.

[93]Simmel, G. *The sociology of Georg Simmel.* (Trans. by K. H. Wolff.) Glencoe, Ill.: Free Press, 1950.

[94]Stephan, F. F. & Mishler, E. G. The distribution of participation in small groups: an exponential approximation. *Amer. sociol. Rev.*, 1952, **17**, 598–608.

[95]Slater, P. E. Contrasting correlates of group size. *Sociometry*, 1958, **21**, 129–139.

[96]Thrasher, F. M. *The gang.* Chicago: Univ. of Chicago Press, 1927.

[97]Bales, R. F. & Borgatta, E. F. Size of group as a factor in the interaction profile. In A. P. Hare, E. F. Borgatta, & R. F. Bales (Eds.). *Small groups.* New York: Knopf, 1955, 396–413.

[98]Hare, A. P. A study of interaction and consensus in different sized groups. *Amer. sociol. Rev.*, 1952, **17**, 261–267.

[99]Ziller, R. C. Group size: a determinant of the quality and stability of group decisions. *Sociometry*, 1957, **20**, 165–173.

[100]Taylor, D. W. & Faust, W. L. Twenty questions: efficiency in problem solving as a function of size of group. *J. exper. Psychol.*, 1952, **44**, 360–368.

[101]Bass, B. M. & Morton, F. M. Group size and leaderless discussion. *J. appl. Psychol.*, 1951, **35**, 397–400.

[102]Hemphill, J. K. Relations between the size of the group and the behavior of "superior" leaders. *J. soc. Psychol.*, 1950, **32**, 11–22.

[103]Bales, R. F. & Borgatta, E. F. *Op. cit.*

[104]Thomas, E. J. & Fink, C. F. Effects of group size. *Psychol. Bull.*, 1963, **60**, 371–384.

[105]Whyte, W. F. *Street corner society.* Chicago: Univ. of Chicago Press, 1943.

[106]Hall, E. T. *The silent language.* Garden City, N.Y.: Double-

day, 1959.

[107]Simmel, G. *Op. cit.*, 321.

[108]Steinzor, B. The spatial factor in face to face discussion groups. *J. abnorm. soc. Psychol.*, 1950, **45**, 552–555.

[109]Hearn, G. Leadership and the spatial factor in small groups. *J. abnorm. soc. Psychol.*, 1957, **54**, 269–272.

[110]Bass, B. M. & Klubeck, S. Effects of seating arrangement on leaderless group discussions. *J. abnorm. soc. Psychol.*, 1952, **47**, 724–727.

[111]Strodtbeck, F. L. & Hook, L. H. The social dimensions of a twelve-man jury table. *Sociometry*, 1961, **24**, 397–415.

[112]Sommer, R. Leadership and group geography. *Sociometry*, 1961, **24**, 99–110.

[113]Strodtbeck, F. L. & Hook, L. H. *Op. cit.*, 414.

[114]Thibaut, J. W. & Kelley, H. H. *The social psychology of groups*. New York: Wiley, 1959, 41.

[115]Williams, R. M. *The reduction of intergroup tensions*. New York: Social Science Research Council, Bulletin 57, 1947.

[116]Dubin, R. *The world of work*. Englewood Cliffs, N.J.: Prentice-Hall, 1958, 187.

[117]March, J. G. & Simon, H. A. *Organizations*. New York: Wiley, 1958, 62.

[118]Katz, D. & Kahn, R. L. *The social psychology of organizations*. New York: Wiley, 1966, 353–357.

[119]Dubin, R. *Op. cit.*, 235. Reprinted by permission.

[120]Lorenz, K. *On aggression*. (Trans. by M. K. Wilson.) New York: Harcourt, Brace & World, 1963, 161–163.

[121]*Ibid.*, 27.

[122]Cramer, E. H. & Flinn, D. E. *Psychiatric aspects of the SAM two-man space cabin simulator*. USAF School of Aerospace Medicine, Aerospace Medical Division (ASFC), Report SAM-TDR-63-27, Brooks Air Force Base, Tex., 1963.

[123]*Ibid.*, 7, Reprinted by permission.

[124]Lorenz, K. *Op. cit.*, 38–39.

[125]*Ibid.*, 38.

[126]*Ibid.*, 146–147. Reprinted by permission.

[127]McBride, G., *Op. cit.*, 81.

[128]*Ibid.*, 86.

[129]Guhl, A. M. The social order of chickens. *Sci. Amer.*, 1956, **194**(2), 42–46.
Also Guhl, A. M. Social inertia and social stability in chickens. *Anim. Behav.*, 1968, **16**, 219.

[130]Masure, R. H. & Allee, W. C. The social order in flocks of the common chicken and the pigeon. *Auk*, 1934, **51**, 306–327.

[131]Allee, W. C., Collias, N. E., & Lutherman, C. Z. Modification of the social order in flocks of hens by the injection of testosterone propionate. *Physiol. Zool.*, 1939, **12**, 412–440.

[132]Rapoport, A. Outline of a probabilistic approach to animal sociology. I. *Bull. math. Biophys.*, 1948, **11**, 183–196.
Cf. also Rapoport, A. Outline of a probabilistic approach to animal sociology. II. *Bull. math. Biophys.*, 1949, **11**, 273–281.
Rapoport, A. Outline of a probabilistic approach to animal sociology. III. *Bull. math. Biophys.*, 1950, **12**, 7–17.
Landau, H. G. On dominance relations and the structure of animal societies. I. Effect of inherent characteristics. *Bull. math. Biophys.*, 1951, **13**, 1–19.
Landau, H. G. On dominance relations and the structure of animal societies. II. Some effects of possible social factors. *Bull. math. Biophys.*, 1951, **13**, 245–262.

[133]Hanfmann, E. Social structure of a group of kindergarten children. *Amer. J. Orthopsychiat.*, 1935, **5**, 407–410.
Cf. also Deutschberger, P. The structure of dominance. *Amer. J. Orthopsychiat.*, 1947, **17**, 343–351.

[134]McBride, G. *Op. cit.*, 83.

[135]Durkheim, E. *Division of labor in society*. (Trans. from the French by George Simpson, Ph.D.) Glencoe, Ill.: Free Press, 1947, 365–366. Copyright 1933 by the Macmillan Company.

Copyright 1947 The Free Press. Reprinted by permission.

[136]Bales, R. F. *Op. cit.*, 73.

[137]Benne, K. D. & Sheats, P. Functional roles of group members. *J. soc. Issues*, 1948, **4**(2), 41–49.

[138]Chapple, E. D. & Coon, C. S. *Op. cit.*, 47.

[139]Marquand, J. P. *The late George Apley*. Boston: Little, Brown, 1937.

[140]Hawkins, C. H. Interaction rates of jurors aligned in factions. *Amer. sociol. Rev.*, 1962, **27**, 689–691.

[141]Schachter, S. Deviation, rejection, and communication. *J. abnorm. soc. Psychol.*, 1951, **46**, 190–207.

[142]Hawkins, C. H. *Op. cit.*, 691. Reprinted by permission.

[143]Zeisel, H. What determines the amount of argument per juror? *Amer. sociol. Rev.*, 1963, **28**, 279.

[144]Cattell, R. B. Concepts and methods in the measurement of group syntality. *Op. cit.*, 48–63.

[145]Thibaut, J. W. & Kelley, H. H. *Op. cit.*, 10.

[146]Riecken, H. W. & Homans, G. C. Psychological aspects of social structure. In G. Lindzey (Ed.). *Handbook of social psychology*. Cambridge, Mass.: Addison-Wesley, 1954, 786–833.

[147]Cf. Babchuk, N. & Goode, W. J. Work incentives in a self-determined group. *Amer. sociol. Rev.*, 1951, **16**, 679–687.

[148]White, R. K. & Lippitt, R. *Autocracy and democracy*. New York: Harper, 1960.

[149]Bavelas, A. A mathematical model for group structure. *Op. cit.*
Cf. also Bavelas, A. Communication patterns in task-oriented groups. *Op. cit.*
Leavitt, H. J. *Op. cit.*
Shaw, M. E. Some effects of unequal distribution of information upon group performance in various communication nets. *Op. cit.*, 547–553.

[150]Leavitt, H. J. *Op. cit.*

[151]Bavelas, A. Communication patterns in task-oriented groups. *Op. cit.*

[152]Leavitt, H. J. *Op. cit.*

[153]Bass, B. M. & Leavitt, H. J. Some experiments in planning and operating. *Mgmt. Sci.*, 1962–1963, **9**, 574–585.

[154]Newcomb, T. M. An approach to the study of communicative acts. *Psychol. Rev.*, 1953, **60**, 393–404.

[155]Cartwright, D. & Harary, F. Structural balance: a generalization of Heider's theory. *Psychol. Rev.*, 1956, **63**, 277–293.

[156]Harary, F. On the measurement of structural balance. *Behav. Sci.*, 1959, **4**, 316–323.
Cf. also Harary, F. Structural duality. *Behav. Sci.*, 1957, **2**, 255–265.

[157]Bolt, R. *A man for all seasons*. New York: Random House, 1960, 120–123.

[158]Festinger, L. *A theory of cognitive dissonance*. Stanford, Calif.: Stanford Univ. Press, 1957, 188–196.

[159]Shaw, M. E., Rothschild, G. H., & Strickland, J. F. *Op. cit.*

[160]Festinger, L. & Carlsmith, J. M. Cognitive consequences of forced compliance. *J. abnorm. soc. Psychol.*, 1959, **58**, 203–210.

[161]Lewin, K. *Field theory in social science*. New York: Harper, 1951, 336.
Cf. also Cartwright, D. A field theoretical conception of power. In D. Cartwright (Ed.). *Studies in social power*. Ann Arbor: Univ. of Michigan, Institute for Social Research, 1959, 188.

[162]French, J. R. P., Jr. A formal theory of social power. *Psychol. Rev.*, 1956, **63**, 181–194.
Cf. also Lewin, K. The conceptual representation and the measurement of psychological forces. *Contributions to Psychological Theory*, 1938, **1**(4), 1–247.

[163]French, J. R. P., Jr. *Op. cit.*, 184–190. Reprinted by permission. [I have italicized the text of the postulates and theo

rems because they are like my hypotheses, which are italicized in Chap. 4. I renumbered the theorems to fit my exposition.]

[164]Goldberg, S. C. Three situational determinants of conformity to social norms. *J. abnorm. soc. Psychol.*, 1954, **49,** 325–329.

[165]Festinger, L. & Thibaut, J. Interpersonal communication in small groups. *J. abnorm. soc. Psychol.*, 1951, **46,** 92–99.
Cf. also Festinger, L., Gerard, H. B., Hymovitch, B., Kelley, H. H., & Raven, B. The influence process in the presence of extreme deviates. *Human Relat.*, 1952, **5,** 327–346.

[166]Festinger, L. Informal social communication. *Psychol. Rev.,* 1950, **57,** 274.

[167]*Ibid.,* 271–282. Reprinted by permission.
NOTE: These hypotheses are quoted from Festinger, but renumbered and rearranged. The rearrangement follows that in H. A. Simon & H. Guetzkow. Mechanisms involved in pressures toward uniformity in groups, and Mechanisms involved in group pressures on deviate-members. In H. A. Simon. *Models of man.* New York: Wiley, 1957, 115–130, 131–144.

[168]Simon, H. A. & Guetzkow, H. *Ibid.*

[169]Back, K. W. Influence through social communication. *Op. cit.*

[170]*E.g.,* Festinger, L. & Thibaut, J. *Op. cit.*
Cf. also Festinger, L., Schachter, S., & Back, K. W. *Social pressures in informal groups.* Stanford, Calif.: Stanford Univ. Press, 1963.
Schachter, S. *Op. cit.,* 190–207.

[171]Longhurst, T. M. & Siegel, G. M. Effects of communication failure on speaker and listener behavior. *J. Speech Res. & Hearing Res.*, 1973, **16,** 128–140.

[172]Emerson, A. E. Populations of social insects. *Ecological Mgmt.*, 1939, **9,** 291.

[173]Rosenberg, S. & Hall, R. L. The effects of different social feedback conditions upon performance in dyadic teams. *J. abnorm. soc. Psychol.,* 1958, **57,** 271–277.

[174]Crutchfield, R. S. Conformity and character. *Amer. Psychol.*, 1955, **10,** 191–198.

[175]Jones, E. E., Wells, H. H., & Torrey, R. Some effects of feedback from the experimenter on conformity of behavior. *J. abnorm. soc. Psychol.,* 1958, **57,** 207–213.

[176]Christie, L. S., Luce, R. D., & Macy, J., Jr. *Op. cit.*

[177]Shaw, M. E. Some effects of unequal distribution of information upon group performance in various communication nets. *Op. cit.*

[178]Leavitt, H. J. & Mueller, R. A. H. Some effects of feedback on communication. *Human Relat.*, 1951, **4,** 401–410.

[179]Jackson, D. D. The question of family homeostasis. *Psychiat. Quart. Suppl.*, 1957, **31,** 79–90.

[180]McBride, G. *Op. cit.*

[181]Lorenz, K. *Op. cit.,* 144–145. Reprinted by permission.

[182]McBride, G. *Op. cit.,* 86.

[183]*Ibid.,* 103. Reprinted by permission.

[184]Emerson, A. E. Human cultural evolution and its relation to organic evolution of insect societies. In H. R. Barringer, G. I. Blanksten, & R. W. Mack (Eds.). *Social change in developing areas.* Cambridge, Mass.: Schenkman, 1965, 50–67.

[185]*Ibid.*

[186]Scheidlinger, S. *Psychoanalysis and group behavior.* New York: Norton, 1952.

[187]Schutz, W. C. *FIRO.* New York: Holt, 1960.
Also Rogers, C. R. *Carl Rogers on encounter groups.* New York: Harper & Row, 1970.
Anderson, R. E. & Carter, I. E. *Op. cit.,* 82–89.

[188]Bales, R. F. *Op. cit.*

[189]Sherif, M., Harvey, O. J., White, B. J., Hood, W. R., & Sherif, C. W. *Intergroup conflict and cooperation. Robbers Cave experiment.* Norman, Okla.: Univ. Book Exchange, 1961.

[190]Cattell, R. B. New concepts for measuring leadership in terms of group syntality. *Op. cit.*

[191]French, J. R. P., Jr. The disruption and cohesion of groups. *J. abnorm. soc. Psychol.*, 1941, **36,** 361–377.
Cf. also Thibaut, J. W. & Kelley, H. H. *Op. cit.,* 193–195, 258–259.

[192]Thibaut, J. W. & Kelley, H. H. *Op. cit.,* 193–195.

[193]Merei, F. Group leadership and institutionalization. *Human Relat.*, 1949, **2,** 23–29.

[194]Rosenthal, D. & Cofer, C. N. The effect on group performance of an indifferent and neglectful attitude showed by one group member. *J. exper. Psychol.*, 1948, **38,** 568–577.

[195]Berkowitz, L. Sharing leadership in small, decision-making groups. *J. abnorm. soc. Psychol.*, 1953, **48,** 231–238.

[196]Schachter, S. *Op. cit.*

[197]Back, K. W. Influence through social communication. *Op. cit.*

[198]March, J. G. & Feigenbaum, E. A. Latent motives, group discussion, and the "quality" of group decisions in a non-objective decision problem. *Sociometry*, 1960, **23,** 50–56.

[199]Festinger, L., Pepitone, A., & Newcomb, T. Some consequences of deindividuation in a group. *J. abnorm. soc. Psychol.*, 1952, **47,** 382–389.

[200]Lundberg, G. A., Hertzler, V. B., & Dickson, L. Attraction patterns in a university. *Sociometry*, 1949, **12,** 158–169.

[201]Loomis, C. P. & Davidson, D. M., Jr. Measurement of the dissolution of in-groups in the integration of a rural settlement project. *Sociometry*, 1939, **2,** 84–94.

[202]Loomis, C. P. & Beegle, J. A. *Rural social systems.* New York: Prentice-Hall, 1950.

[203]Hunt, J. McV. & Solomon, R. L. The stability and some correlates of group-status in a summer-camp group of young boys. *Amer. J. Psychol.*, 1942, **55,** 33–45.

[204]Goodnow, R. E. & Tagiuri, R. Religious ethnocentrism and its recognition among adolescent boys. *J. abnorm. soc. Psychol.*, 1952, **47,** 316–320.
Cf. also Festinger, L. The role of group belongingness in a voting situation. *Human Relat.*, 1947–1948, **1,** 154–180.

[205]Hughes, E. C. The knitting of racial groups in industry. *Amer. sociol. Rev.*, 1946, **11,** 512–519.

[206]Roethlisberger, F. J. & Dickson, W. J. *Op. cit.*

[207]Marschak, J. *Towards an economic theory of organization and information.* Chicago: Univ. of Chicago, Cowles Commission for Research in Economics, Cowles Commission Papers, New Series, No. 95, 1954.

[208]Simmel, G. *Op. cit.*

[209]Mills, T. M. Power relations in three-person groups. *Amer. sociol. Rev.*, 1953, **18,** 351–357.

[210]Mills, T. M., Gauslaa, A., Løchen, Y., Mathiesen, T., Nørstebø, G., Ramsoy, O., Skirbekk, S., Skårdal, O., Torgersen, L., Tysnes, B., & Øyen, Ø. *Group structure and the newcomer: an experimental study of group expansion.* Oslo: Oslo Univ. Press, 1957.

[211]Hoffman, P. J., Festinger, L., & Lawrence, D. H. Tendencies toward group comparability in competitive bargaining. In R. M. Thrall, C. H. Coombs, & R. L. Davis (Eds.). *Decision processes.* New York: Wiley, 1954, 231–253.

[212]Rapoport, A. *Fights, games, and debates.* Ann Arbor: Univ. of Michigan Press, 1960, 173.

[213]Wilson, K. V. & Bixenstine, V. E. Forms of social control in two-person, two-choice games. *Behav. Sci.*, 1962, **7,** 92–102.

[214]Rapoport, A. Some game-theoretical aspects of parasitism and symbiosis. *Bull. math. Biophys.*, 1956, **18,** 15–30.

Cf. also Foster, C. & Rapoport, A. Parasitism and symbiosis in an N-person non-constant-sum continuous game. *Bull. math. Biophys.*, 1956, **18**, 219–231.

[215]Scodel, A., Minas, J. S., Ratoosh, P., & Lipetz, M. Some descriptive aspects of two-person non-zero-sum games. *J. conflict Resolution*, 1959, **3**, 114–119.

[216]Minas, J. S., Scodel, A., Marlowe, D., & Rawson, H. Some descriptive aspects of two-person non-zero-sum games. II. *J. conflict Resolution*, 1960, **4**, 193–197.

[217]Deutsch, M. The effect of motivational orientation upon threat and suspicion. *Human Relat.*, 1960, **13**, 123–139.

[218]Deutsch, M. Trust, trustworthiness and the F scale. *J. abnorm. soc. Psychol.*, 1960, **61**, 138–140.

[219]Lutzker, D. R. Internationalism as a predictor of cooperative behavior. *J. conflict Resolution*, 1960, **4**, 426–430.

[220]Rapoport, A., Chammah, A., Dwyer, J., & Gyr, J. Three-person non-zero-sum nonnegotiable games. *Behav. Sci.*, 1962, **7**, 38–58.

[221]Cf. Shapley, L. S. Simple games: an outline of the descriptive theory. *Behav. Sci.*, 1962, **7**, 59–66.

[222]NOTE: Cf. Hill, R. Generic features of families under stress. In H. J. Parad (Ed.). *Crisis intervention: selected readings.* New York: Family Service Association of America, 1965, 32–52. His concepts have been applied, in an approach based on Gerald Caplan's work in public health and my general living systems theory, in W. M. Bolman (Ed.). Preventive psychiatry for the family: theory, approaches, and programs. *Amer. J. Psychiat.*, 1968, **125**, 458–471.

[223]Byron, Lord G. G. *Don Juan.* Canto 2, LVI-LXXXII. In Lord Byron. *Don Juan and other satirical poems.* (Ed. by L. I. Bredvold.) New York: Odyssey Press, 1935, 241–248.

[224]Bronfenbrenner, U. The origins of alienation. *Sci. Amer.*, 1974, **231**(2), 53–61.

[225]Jackson, D. D. *Op. cit.*

[226]*Ibid.*, 85.

[227]Cattell, R. B. Concepts and methods in the measurement of group syntality. *Op. cit.*

[228]Blake, R. R. & Brehm, J. W. The use of tape recording to simulate a group atmosphere. *J. abnorm. soc. Psychol.*, 1954, **49**, 311–313.

[229]Sherif, M. A study of some social factors in perception. *Arch. Psychol.*, 1935, No. 187.

[230]Rainio, K. A stochastic model of social interaction. *Transactions of the Westermarck Society.* Copenhagen: Munksgaard, 1961, 7, 15.

[231]Gullahorn, J. T. & Gullahorn, J. E. A computer model of elementary social behavior. *Behav. Sci.*, 1963, **8**, 354–362.
Cf. also Gullahorn, J. T. & Gullahorn, J. E. Computer simulation of role conflict resolution. In J. M. Dutton & W. H. Starbuck (Eds.). *Computer simulation of human behavior.* New York: Wiley, 1971, 350–363.

[232]Homans, G. C. *Social behavior: its elementary forms.* New York: Harcourt, Brace & World, 1961, 53–55, 75. Reprinted by permission. [Quoted material in the original was capitalized throughout, but is italicized here to fit the form of other hypotheses in this book.]

[233]Blau, P. M. *The dynamics of bureaucracy.* (Rev. ed.) Chicago: Univ. of Chicago Press, 1963.

[234]Newell, A. *Information processing language-V manual.* Englewood Cliffs, N.J.: Prentice-Hall, 1961.

[235]Gullahorn, J. T. & Gullahorn, J. E. *Op. cit.*, 362. Reprinted by permission.

[236]McWhinney, W. H. Simulating the communication network experiments. *Behav. Sci.*, 1964, **9**, 80–84.

[237]*Ibid.*, 83. Reprinted by permission.

[238]Harary, F. & Schwenk, A. J. Efficiency of dissemination of information in one-way and two-way communication networks. *Behav. Sci.*, 1974, **19**, 133–135.

[239]Back, K. W. Intervention techniques: small groups. *Op. cit.*, 379.

[240]Helmreich, R., Bakeman, R., & Scherwitz, L. The study of small groups. *Ann. Rev. Psychol.*, 1973, **24**, 337.

[241]*Ibid.*

The Organization

Organizations are systems with multiechelon deciders whose components and subsystems may be subsidiary organizations, groups, and (uncommonly) single persons. In my conceptual system they are concrete living systems with components that are also concrete living systems rather than abstracted systems whose units are actions or roles (see page 19). Organizations are subsystems, components, or subcomponents of societies, sometimes of more than one society (see page 910). Some societies have single organisms or groups, as well as organizations, as principal components (see page 765). International and supranational systems, such as General Motors and Interpol, have organizational components which exist in more than one society. These are often separately chartered or incorporated under the laws of each society. Organizational components can also be inclusions (see page 33) in societies other than the one to whose subsystem structure they belong, *e.g.*, Japanese marketing organizations in Australia and Canada. The critical difference between organizations and groups is in the structure of the decider. Organizations always have at least two echelons in their deciders, even when they are so small that each person can interact in a face-to-face relationship with all the others (see pages 642 to 644). Group deciders have no formally designated echelons.

It has been suggested that local communities—like cities, metropolitan areas, or rural districts—are not organizations but a higher level of living systems, between organizations and societies.[1] After all, many components of such communities are themselves organizations—banks, stores, schools, hospitals, and so on. Even though this is a reasonable view, commu-

nities do not seem enough unlike other organizations to be classed as a different level.

Hypothesis 1-1 (see page 92), which states that the more components a system has, in general the more echelons it has, is true of organizations. According to Weber, administration by persons occupying a hierarchy of offices and deriving their authority from legal sources is characteristic of one type of organized social system. Examples of this type are bureaucratic governments and the sort of business organizations that developed after the industrial revolution and are characteristic of the twentieth century.[2] The definition, in general systems theory terms, of an organization as a "goal-seeking system which has interacting goal-seeking subsystems with different goals arranged in a hierarchy" given by Mesarović, Sanders, and Sprague is like mine in using the echelon, or hierarchical structure, as the primary characteristic differentiating an organization from lower-level systems.[3] An organization, in their conceptual system, is a "multilevel-multigoal system" in which the "goal-seeking subsystem" can be either a single human decision maker or a group or committee. Here they use the word "level" as I use "echelon."

Deciders of modern societies also have a number of echelons. Societies are generally more nearly totipotential than organizations. Deciders of organizations are limited by the past and present decisions of their society. Organizations, in fact, are much like organs in their parasitism upon, or symbiosis with, the suprasystem of which they are a part. There are no free-living organs as there are free-living cells (see page 315). If an organization is to exist independently, as happens rarely in the case of a plundering, invading army or a migrant gypsy tribe, for example, it must atypically develop all the critical subsystems, or it will disappear.

Many different sorts of aggregations of organisms and groups fall within the definition of "organization" given above. Among these are the personnel of factories, industrial complexes, professional firms, businesses, schools, universities, churches, prisons, fraternities, railroads, steamship companies and airlines, charitable societies, foundations, ships and planes, police and fire departments, cities, towns, villages, counties, states, provinces, executive departments of government such as foreign ministries or postal services, subordinate government agencies like the Federal Bureau of Investigation or Scotland Yard, armies, army bases and camps, local and national legislative bodies, courts, and labor unions.

The distinction may not always be clear-cut between certain organizations, on the one hand, and certain groups or societies that may be closely similar, on the other. Some small businesses, such as some family enterprises or partnerships, are groups according to my definition because their decisions are made by means of face-to-face discussion and common agreement and their deciders have no echelons. States, provinces, and colonies may be so nearly totipotential as to be essentially separate societies rather than organizations within a larger society. This is true of parts of the British Commonwealth of Nations and was true also of some American territories. In the course of growth and differentiation or of decline, systems of these sorts change from one level to another as they become more or less totipotential (see page 799).

Certain other units have some system characteristics but not all that are required to meet the definition of an organization. Metropolitan areas, for example, often have little or nothing corresponding to a central decider subsystem. Consequently, they are collections of separate organizations interacting in a suprasystem rather than a single system. They may be in transition to a new structure.

A minimum system at this level could be a business with a single person, the owner-operator, at the higher echelon and a few employees at the lower. The largest and structurally most complex organizations, like the Soviet Union's republics or America's states, huge corporations, or even large cities, have subsidiary governmental bodies or corporations as components and many echelons. New York City, for instance, has five borough governments under the central city government. Each of these is in itself an organization which includes organizations as components.

Organizations, even some of those with many components and complex echelon structures, often either completely lack some subsystems or have them in trivial form. Usually matter-energy processing rather than information processing subsystems are missing. Organizations that perform the same function in the suprasystem often differ from one another in their structures. One may manufacture its product from components output in completed form by other organizations, while a second begins with raw materials and converts them before producing the parts it needs. The first may have no significant development of converter structure. The second must have, since raw materials are rarely, if ever, usable without preparation. Whether the organization will make, or perhaps mine or harvest, rather than buy certain items or will acquire as a component an organization already producing the necessary precursors is an important organizational decision.

Some types of organizations, such as hospitals, schools, universities, prisons, hotels, ships, and stores, have inclusions within their boundaries made up of persons from the suprasystem. These inclusions may be organizations or groups which interact with the encompassing system in various ways, or they may constitute unorganized aggregations.

The clients of most organizations do not unite together into systems of their own, but this does happen in many cases. The guests of a hotel, the patients in hospitals for short-term illnesses, and the passengers on most planes, trains, and buses do not form systems. Patients in hospitals that treat chronic diseases and passengers on long voyages, however, interact over extended periods and do organize into groups. Organized student groups are the rule in most schools and colleges. Prisoners usually develop systematic interactions. This sort of structure is described by Blau and Scott as that in which the "public-in-contact" is part of the organization.[4]

Artifacts, such as buildings, machinery, and equipment, are prominent aspects of many organizations. Artifacts may replace human organisms in the structure of subsystems and components. In automated factories such as oil refineries, for instance, the ratio of human beings to mechanical components may be 1:1,000 or more.

The organizations discussed in this chapter are all parts of human societies. Animals other than man do not appear to form systems at levels higher than the group (see page 515).

1. Structure

No commonly accepted view of what the basic units of organizational structure are and how they are arranged exists as yet to serve organization theorists as the concepts of the cell and the organism serve biologists.[5] In the absence of such a unifying concept, the many variables and relationships with which organization theory is concerned lack integration. Consequently, it is difficult to test new ideas and findings for relevance. Theoretical or factual gaps are often not evident. Differentiae for classifying organizations into types cannot be logically derived.

Many organizations have a formal table of organization. It defines the various jobs or positions, specifies the responsibility and authority of each, and outlines their interrelationships. But there is no agreement about what such a chart should contain. The range of variation in the organization tables of a large sample of industrial corporations is described by Woodward as follows:

Some were very elaborate. In one firm the general manager had a chart 20 feet long on his office wall; in another, detailed departmental charts were bound together in a book the size and weight of a family Bible. In a third firm, a manager produced two charts; one displayed on his office wall showed the existing organization, the other, kept in a drawer in his desk, showed how it would be if he could ignore the personal idiosyncrasies and weaknesses of his present managers.[6]

Those organizations which had no charts often had definite, clearly understood structures. But some did not, and in such a company it was frequently difficult for an outsider to discover what the structure was.

General living systems theory can provide a unifying conceptual system for organization theory, including a definition which differentiates organizations from living systems at other levels, and identification of the chief subsystems of all organizations with their analogs at other levels. It can also provide a basis for understanding how organizations differ and for applying quantitative techniques and formal models to the study of organizations. Probably no organization has yet been explicitly subdivided into departments and other units, however, which correspond exactly to my set of subsystems.

1.1 System size The physical size of organizations ranges from a minimum diameter of perhaps 10 meters (m) for a very small department store or factory to the diameters of the states or other major components of nations. The largest unit of a sovereign nation is the Russian Socialist Federated Soviet Republic of the Soviet Union, whose east-west diameter is only about 600 kilometers (km) less than the diameter of the whole Soviet Union, since it extends from the Finnish frontier on the west to the eastern tip of Siberia at the Bering Strait. As at lower levels, there are more of the smaller systems than the larger, and so the median organization diameter is probably that of a moderately large manufacturing organization, or about 100 m.

1.2 Structural taxonomy of types of systems Most classifications of organizations are based predominantly upon process rather than structure, although a given taxonomy may include some structural differentiae. Examples of such differentiae are:

(a) *Number of persons included in, or related to, the system.* This is one of the distinctions between two fundamental sorts of human communities that have been described in somewhat different terms in several sociological theories (see page 601). It is also a basis for distinguishing among political units such as villages, towns, cities, or states. For instance, the American Constitution provides that, for admission to the Union as a state, a territory must have a minimum population of 60,000.

(b) *Number of echelons.* The more components there are in an organization, in general the more echelons there are in its decider, as Hypothesis 1-1 (see page 92) states. A relatively small organization with only two echelons—such as a small town—is a vastly different sort of system from one like the state of New York or California, with many echelons.

(c) *Structure of the decider.* The difference between democratic and authoritarian systems is fundamental at this level as well as at others (see page 568). Not only does a greater proportion of the system's components participate in decision making in the democratic system, but also the arrangement of the network through which decisions are channeled in the two sorts of systems is different (see page 790). The number of echelons in the decider, the number of components at each echelon, and the number of echelons through which an appeal of a decision must be channeled are some of the rubrics in a classification of industrial organizations developed by Evan (see pages 600 and 601).

(d) *Other aspects of subsystem structures.* The ratio of administrative to production personnel (essentially the ratio of information processing to matter-energy processing personnel) is one such distinction.[7]

A criterion which apparently has not so far been used, but which would differentiate types of organizations, is the presence or absence of particular subsystems and the proportion of the system's components in each subsystem. For instance, an organization manufacturing a product from raw materials necessarily has well-developed matter-energy processing subsystems. An insurance company emphasizes the information processing subsystems and may lack some which process matter-energy, being parasitic on, or symbiotic with, the society for such processes.

2. Process

Any organization, no matter what its function in the society, must maintain itself as a system. It must perform its specialized activities, such as production and output of a given sort of matter-energy or information product or service. And it must coordinate its activities with those of other components of the suprasystem. The essential activities of organizations are not categorized identically by all organization theorists, but there is some agreement.

An analysis by Katz and Kahn, based upon abstracted system concepts (see page 19), lists five basic sorts of subsystems: (a) *production* subsystems concerned with the work of the organization; (b) *supportive* subsystems for procurement, disposal, and institutional relations; (c) *maintenance* subsystems for tying people into their functional roles, *i.e.,* personnel administration; (d) *adaptive* subsystems concerned with organizational change; and (e) *managerial* subsystems for the direction, adjudication, and control of the many subsystems and activities of the organization.[8] As in many other analyses in terms of roles or abstracted system concepts, this classification has a rather disembodied character. Which structures carry out each subsystem process is not made explicit. (This categorization differs significantly from mine. The production subsystems in it would include various of my *subsystems which process matter-energy* and *subsystems which process information*. My *decider* would carry out several of its maintenance, adaptive, and managerial activities.)

Another analysis, that of Bakke, does not distinguish between matter-energy and information processing, but it can be related to my subsystem classification.[9] His list of organizational activities follows, with my equivalent subsystem processes indicated in parentheses after each of his activities.

"1. Activities to define, make clear, legitimize, and symbolize the image of the unique wholeness of the organization including its function and the main features which distinguish it from other organizations." These processes, which Bakke calls *identification* activities, involve the image of the organization both as it is held by the components of the subsystem and as it appears to persons outside the system and to other organizations.

(The view of the organization as held by a human component of it is obtained through the *internal transducer*. The conception held by those outside the system is derived from the outputs of the *extruder, motor, encoder,* and *output transducer* subsystems. All these information flows concern the function of the organization as a system in its suprasystem.)

"2. Activities to acquire, maintain, transform, develop, and renew the basic resources utilized by agents of the organization in the performance of their work for the organization." Under this Bakke includes *personnel* activities to assure that the organization has

enough people with appropriate abilities; *service* activities to assure that there are sufficient materials, equipment, and plants; *finance* activities to guarantee that there is adequate capital; *thoughtways* activities to provide necessary ideas about future organizational processes; and *conservation* activities to guarantee that essential natural resources exist, that the organization has access to them, and that they are adapted to the requirements of all the organization's activities.

(Personnel recruitment activities I would categorize as processes of the *ingestor* subsystem, in accordance with my decision to consider people as matter-energy inputs [see page 1027]; personnel training would be done by the *associator,* and personnel management by the *decider.* Service activities include processes of the *ingestor,* like obtaining supplies, and of the *distributor,* like transporting them to subsystems that need them. Finance activities are information transmission processes [see page 1027], the handling of money or credit. They involve most or all *subsystems which process information.* Thoughtways activities seem almost the equivalent of the total of what I call *information processing* activities, and conservation activities seem to be like the total of what I call *matter-energy processing* activities.)

"3. Activities to create or produce an output, *i.e.,* the product or service satisfying the human need which it is the organization's function to supply, and to distribute the output advantageously to the continued operation of the organization." These Bakke calls *workflow* activities.

(They include all the matter-energy processing activities carried out on raw materials by the *converter* as well as the processes of the *distributor, matter-energy storage, extruder,* and *motor.* If the organization's chief work is information processing, they include the comparable *information processing* functions.)

"4. Activities that assure and control the performance, coordination, and focusing on the organizational function of all activities carried out by agents and equipment of the organization."

(These include *internal transducer* and *decider* processes primarily.)

"5. Activities which serve to stabilize and vitalize the organization as a whole in an evolving state of dynamic equilibrium."

(These are processes of all the subsystems which maintain organizational variables in steady states.)

There is some agreement in the two analyses by Katz and Kahn and by Bakke, but also there are fundamental differences. An alternative is to employ a general systems conceptual framework, as I do, with cross-level formal identities in subsystem taxonomies based on the view that subsystems of systems at higher levels are shredded out from those at lower levels (see pages 1 and 4). Such an approach reduces idiosyncratic variation among theorists at different levels. It may also elicit wider scientific support than previous taxonomies of organizations, all of which have been limited to one level.

2.1 System and subsystem indicators Particular organizations may be analyzed or diagnosed for basic research purposes or to achieve practical ends such as aiding management decisions, deciding whether an organization should be accredited or certified as providing acceptable services, or guiding prospective stockholders or investors in the organization.

Various sets of organizational indicators have been devised. One is designed to analyze effectiveness of organizational performance. Its developers, Seashore and his associates, state that it is conceptually consistent with systems theory.[10] They selected 76 indicators and, after measuring 75 insurance companies with them, did a factor analysis of their data, which produced the following 10 performance factors: business volume, production cost, new-member productivity, youthfulness of members, mix of kinds of business, manpower growth, management emphasis, maintenance cost, man-hour productivity, and market penetration. Most of these factors were measured by two or more indicators.

In related work, an outline for making organizational analyses has been prepared by Levinson.[11] His conceptual framework is like mine in viewing organizations as open, living systems comparable to organisms in having multiple subsystems.[12] His analysis is in terms of their histories, structures, and processes (functions), such as genetic development, energy flows, communication or information flows, and decision making.

Some of the organizational indicators in the following list were suggested by Seashore's and Levinson's studies. Certain indicators are specific to particular types of organizations and to no others. Others apply to a variety of different types. Some are precisely quantifiable. Others depend upon more subjective evaluations, like responses to questionnaires.

A list of some possible organizational indicators follows.

Personnel indicators. Number of people employed. Manpower growth rate. Number of different types of personnel, such as laborers or professionals. Average employee age. Rates of remuneration. Management reputation. History and present state of labor relations as shown by number and duration of strikes, turnover rates, and absentee rates. Accident rate. Average service in different sorts of jobs. Seasonal fluctuations. Types of training offered. Number of trainees.

Employee satisfaction as shown by questionnaires or other measures. Ratio of incomes of managers and workers.

Product or service indicators. Total inventory. Total output or processing capacity per unit of time. Rate of sales or number of services provided. Average demand for products or services. Competitiveness of products or services. Diversification of outputs. Product-waste ratio. Worker-hours per unit of products or services. Production time per unit. Money cost per unit. Overhead cost per unit. Amount of product or service innovation—new ones added or old ones improved. Amount of unfilled demand. Customer, patient, or client satisfaction. Ratio of old customers to new. Percentage penetration of total market.

Financial indicators concerned with monetary information flows. Value of capital investments. Planned additions to physical assets. Profit or loss over a given fiscal period. Selling price of common stock. Price-earnings ratio of stock. Performance of common stock over a stated period. Dividends to stockholders in a given period. Demand for bonds or other fixed-yield evidence of indebtedness. Current cash position. Total bank loans. Total indebtedness. Interest and capital repayment costs. Total annual sales. Growth potential. Dividends to stockholders in a given period.

Other indicators. Of the innumerable other possible indicators, a few important ones are: Lag between demand for services and response. Geographic distribution of components (*e.g.,* locations of offices throughout the world, arrangement of housing units in a city, or positions of police stations in a community). Number of human inclusions or clients (*e.g.,* census of patients in a hospital or enrollment of students in a university). Amount of information processed per unit of time. Content categories of information processed.

Many of these indicators are clearly measures of the subsystem variables mentioned throughout this chapter.

2.2 Process taxonomy of types of systems The traditional differentiation among types of organizations is in terms of the primary processes they carry out in the suprasystem. There are, for instance, *economic, political, educational, religious, charitable, recreational, social, artistic,* and *scientific* organizations. Each of these categories includes different subtypes, much as a genus of organisms includes different species. Manufacturing, farming, transportation, banking, mining, communications, and merchandizing organizations belong to the *economic* classification. Political parties, legislatures, and courts are *political* organizations.

Some students have attempted systematic process

taxonomies of organizations, although no single such conceptual system is generally accepted. One of these is a comprehensive classification by Katz and Kahn.[13] They divide organizations into four classes according to the kinds of processes they carry out in their suprasystem, the society: (a) *Productive* or *economic* organizations, which are concerned with providing goods and services. These include farms, mining and manufacturing corporations, and communications companies. (b) *Managerial-political* organizations, which adjudicate conflicts or coordinate and control people and resources. This class includes governments, agencies of government, pressure groups, labor unions, and various special-interest organizations. (c) *Maintenance* organizations, which socialize and train people for roles in other organizations and in the society. These include schools, universities, and churches. (d) *Adaptive* organizations, which create new knowledge and innovative solutions to problems. Colleges and universities with research programs as well as other research organizations are included here. (Evidently, the categories are not mutually exclusive, since a university can belong to two of them.)

Second-order characteristics by which Katz and Kahn create subclassifications under the above four major classes include (a) the nature of the organizational products—whether they are goods or services; (b) the nature of the processes whereby they recruit and keep their personnel—whether they attract and hold them by intrinsic or extraneous rewards; (c) the nature of their boundary processes—whether it is easy to enter or leave the organization; (d) the amount of specialization—whether many different organizational roles exist; (e) the number of echelons; and (f) the type of equilibrium—whether the organization simply maintains the status quo or attempts to grow or expand. [Katz and Kahn include (c), (d), and (e) in a single category.]

In another classification of organizations, based on the persons who constitute their prime beneficiaries, Blau and Scott differentiate four major types: (a) *mutual-benefit associations,* whose members are the prime beneficiaries; (b) *business concerns,* whose owners are the prime beneficiaries; (c) *service organizations,* whose clients receive the benefits; and (d) *commonweal organizations,* whose prime beneficiaries are members of the public at large.[14] They apply other criteria within each category to differentiate each of these classes further. Examples of mutual-benefit associations are unions, fraternal organizations, professional organizations, and religious sects. Business concerns include industrial firms, stores, banks, insurance companies, and other such profit-making enterprises. Service organizations include hospitals,

social work agencies, schools, legal aid societies, and mental health clinics. Among the commonweal organizations are the police, armies, fire departments, and some administrative units within governments, such as the Internal Revenue Service or the Foreign Office. Some organizations are borderline cases. Philanthropic agencies are often both mutual-benefit and service organizations, since they serve their members' interests while also serving the interests of others. Universities in their teaching functions are service organizations, but in their research functions they belong to the commonweal group.

A different sort of process classification is proposed by Sells.[15] It should, he believes, conform to the general systems approach, but he differs from my conceptualization in employing rubrics based not on concrete systems but on abstracted systems of roles.

This taxonomic system is concerned with a large number of variables, of three primary classes: (a) *Characteristics of individuals participating, e.g.,* abilities, motivational and stylistic personality traits, background, past experience and training, and ethnic factors. These are variables at the level of the organism. (b) *Organizational characteristics, e.g.,* goals, tasks, group structure, facilities, and procedures. These are variables at the level of the organization. (c) *Characteristics of the physical and social environment.* These are variables at the level of the society and above. The total range of organizational behavior, Sell assumes, can be accounted for by combinations of these three classes of variables. He neglects the level of the group. A factor analysis of such variables, he expects, would indicate various patterns of variables or organizational behavior. In turn these patterns would become the basis for a taxonomic scheme. Such a classification so far is only a proposal. If implemented, it would certainly be different from the others mentioned above, and it is difficult to predict what the factors might be. The factor-analytic approach has been used similarly in classifying the personalities of individual human beings (see page 472).

In addition to classification schemes for organizations generally, some taxonomies have been created for particular types of organizations. The classification of industrial organizations developed by Evan involves a number of structural differentiae, as I mentioned above (see page 597). It also includes several process differentiae, such as the total amount of training in the organization for the tasks performed and the spread through the staff of special skills; the ratio of maximum to minimum earnings; the ratios of the earnings of personnel in adjacent statuses, such as foremen and workers or supervisors and foremen; aspects of the decision structure, such as a staff member's authority to commit resources or the degree of centralization of decision making; and the amount of limitation on management's decision making resulting from appeals to higher powers.[16] A Standard Industrial Classification developed by the Executive Office of the President of the United States classifies "establishments" according to their major activities.[17] An establishment is defined as an economic unit producing goods and services. It is not necessarily identical with a firm or company, since a single company may include a number of separate establishments carrying out different processes. The divisions and major groups of this classification system are shown in Table 10-1. Each sort of establishment is given a code number. Its first two digits are those of the major group to which it belongs, as indicated in Table 10-1. Third and fourth digits may be added when further breakdowns are desired. For example, Major Group 25, Furniture and fixtures, includes 251, Household furniture; 252, Office furniture; and so forth. In my conceptual system the most logical taxonomy of organizations is in terms of the subsystems of the suprasystem—the society—to which they belong. The divisions and major groups in Table 10-1 fit rather well into such categories. Consequently, I have indicated in brackets after each group the societal subsystem or subsystems under which the major processes of that group should be categorized (see page 763).

Several sociologists have classified social systems, including organizations. Some have identified two basic types of human communities, different in both structure and process.[18] One is a small, somewhat isolated, and usually primitive community. The other is exemplified by large, modern cities. Such a dichotomous taxonomy focuses upon certain differences among human communities and permits intermediate forms to be placed along a continuum between the two extremes. It can apply to whole societies, but both types of communities may coexist in the same society—e.g., Turkey, South Africa, or Australia.

A small, isolated community is ordinarily more nearly totipotential than a large community. A farm town in Burgundy may be able to survive for long periods cut off from the rest of France. Paris, on the other hand, is dependent upon other communities—some far off—for food, water, manufactured goods, and essential information. A total siege of Paris would cause great internal stresses in only a few days. Hypothesis 2-3 (see page 92) is relevant to this dichotomy since it states that the more isolated a system is, the more totipotential it must be. A small, primitive community, according to Durkheim, has "mechanical solidarity" based upon the relative homogeneity of the processes carried out by persons and

groups in it.[19] A large, modern community, on the other hand, has what he calls "organic solidarity." This term refers to increased division of labor, meaning that persons and groups in the community are dependent upon others outside the community for many processes they would have carried out themselves under an earlier form of community organization. In my terms, there is increased differentiation of subsystems. Hypothesis 1-2 (see page 92) asserts a similar principle. It states that the more structurally different types of members or components a system has, the more segregation of functions there is. The primitive social grouping was characterized by Tönnies as *Gemeinschaft* (translated "community"), in which mutual participation and common interests produce cooperation among people. The advanced one is ordinarily called *Gesellschaft* (translated "association"), in which voluntary affiliations and more formalized relationships, involving division of labor, produce cooperation.[20]

The rhythm, tempo, and timing of the different types of communities are also said to be different.[21] Independent and dependent communities are distinguished by Hawley. The independent community is regulated more by natural rhythms such as changes of season and the sleeping-waking patterns of its inhabitants. It divides time into units no smaller than parts of a day. The dependent community divides time into minutes and sometimes seconds. The dependent community is more responsive in its rhythm to other communities than to its local environment. For instance, people in all cities in a time zone have dinner at about the same time regardless of when the sun sets. The dependent community has a faster tempo, which accelerates as the number or complexity of components increases. The amount of change in processes between day and night is more marked in smaller communities. In metropolises the events of the day are much like those which take place at night. New York is lighted, busy, and noisy all night, although less so than during the day. Many small towns are completely closed and darkened at night, without even a gas station lighted or a policeman on guard.

Even the best of the current taxonomies does not provide a workable scheme by which all organizations, regardless of their structures and particular suprasystem functions, can be related to one another and upon which generalizations and models can be based. The taxonomies at best indicate the range of structures and processes included at this level, pointing to some of the relevant variables. General living systems theory may provide a more satisfactory classification of concrete organizational systems. This would be a taxonomy classifying each system in terms

TABLE 10-1   Categories of Organizations in the *Standard Industrial Classification Manual*

Division A. Agriculture, forestry, and fishing
  Major Group 01. Agricultural production—crops [*ingestor*]
  Major Group 02. Agricultural production—livestock [*ingestor*]
  Major Group 07. Agricultural services [*ingestor*]
  Major Group 08. Forestry [*ingestor*]
  Major Group 09. Fishing, hunting, and trapping [*ingestor*]

Division B. Mining
  Major Group 10. Metal mining [*ingestor*]
  Major Group 11. Anthracite mining [*ingestor*]
  Major Group 12. Bituminous coal and lignite mining [*ingestor*]
  Major Group 13. Oil and gas extraction [*ingestor*]
  Major Group 14. Mining and quarrying of nonmetallic minerals, except fuels [*ingestor*]

Division C. Construction
  Major Group 15. Building construction—general contractors, operative builders [*producer*]
  Major Group 16. Construction other than building construction—general contractors [*producer*]
  Major Group 17. Construction—special trade contractors [*producer*]

Division D. Manufacturing
  Major Group 20. Food and kindred products [*converter, producer*]
  Major Group 21. Tobacco manufactures [*converter, producer*]
  Major Group 22. Textile mill products [*converter, producer*]
  Major Group 23. Apparel and other finished products made from fabrics and similar materials [*producer*]
  Major Group 24. Lumber and wood products, except furniture [*producer*]
  Major Group 25. Furniture and fixtures [*producer*]
  Major Group 26. Paper and allied products [*converter, producer*]
  Major Group 27. Printing, publishing, and allied industries [*internal transducer, channel and net, encoder, output transducer*]
  Major Group 28. Chemicals and allied products [*converter, producer*]
  Major Group 29. Petroleum refining and related industries [*converter, producer*]
  Major Group 30. Rubber and miscellaneous plastics products [*converter, producer*]
  Major Group 31. Leather and leather products [*converter, producer*]
  Major Group 32. Stone, clay, glass, and concrete products [*converter, producer*]
  Major Group 33. Primary metal industries [*converter*]
  Major Group 34. Fabricated metal products, except machinery and transportation equipment [*producer*]
  Major Group 35. Machinery, except electrical [*producer*]
  Major Group 36. Electrical and electronic machinery, equipment, and supplies [*producer*]
  Major Group 37. Transportation equipment [*producer*]
  Major Group 38. Measuring, analyzing, and controlling instruments; photographic, medical and optical goods; watches and clocks [*producer*]
  Major Group 39. Miscellaneous manufacturing industries [*producer*]

Division E. Transportation, communications, electric, gas, and sanitary services
  Major Group 40. Railroad transportation [*distributor*]
  Major Group 41. Local and suburban transit and interurban highway passenger transportation [*distributor*]
  Major Group 42. Motor freight transportation and warehousing [*distributor, matter-energy storage*]
  Major Group 43. U.S. Postal Service [*channel and net*]
  Major Group 44. Water transportation [*distributor*]
  Major Group 45. Transportation by air [*distributor*]
  Major Group 46. Pipe lines, except natural gas [*distributor*]
  Major Group 47. Transportation services [*distributor*]
  Major Group 48. Communication [*input transducer, internal transducer, channel and net, decoder, encoder, output transducer*]
  Major Group 49. Electric, gas, and sanitary services [*distributor, extruder*]

Division F. Wholesale trade
  Major Group 50. Wholesale trade—durable goods [*distributor*]
  Major Group 51. Wholesale trade—nondurable goods [*distributor*]

TABLE 10-1   Categories of Organizations in the *Standard Industrial Classification Manual* (Cont.)

Division G. Retail trade
  Major Group 52. Building materials, hardware, garden supply, and mobile home dealers [*distributor*]
  Major Group 53. General merchandise stores [*distributor*]
  Major Group 54. Food stores [*distributor*]
  Major Group 55. Automotive dealers and gasoline service stations [*distributor*]
  Major Group 56. Apparel and accessory stores [*distributor*]
  Major Group 57. Furniture, home furnishings, and equipment stores [*distributor*]
  Major Group 58. Eating and drinking places [*distributor*]
  Major Group 59. Miscellaneous retail [*distributor*]

Division H. Finance, insurance, and real estate [*The information processed by all the major groups in this division is money, credit, and title to property.*]
  Major Group 60. Banking [*channel and net, memory*]
  Major Group 61. Credit agencies other than banks [*channel and net, memory*]
  Major Group 62. Security and commodity brokers, dealers, exchanges, and services [*channel and net*]
  Major Group 63. Insurance [*channel and net, memory*]
  Major Group 64. Insurance agents, brokers, and services [*channel and net*]
  Major Group 65. Real estate [*supporter, channel and net*]
  Major Group 66. Combinations of real estate, insurance, loans, law offices [*channel and net, memory*]
  Major Group 67. Holding and other investment offices [*channel and net, memory*]

Division I. Services
  Major Group 70. Hotels, rooming houses, camps, and other lodging places [*matter-energy storage*]
  Major Group 72. Personal services [*several subsystems*]
  Major Group 73. Business services [*several subsystems*]
  Major Group 75. Automotive repair, services, and garages [*producer, matter-energy storage*]
  Major Group 76. Miscellaneous repair services [*producer*]
  Major Group 78. Motion pictures [*internal transducer, channel and net, encoder, output transducer*]
  Major Group 79. Amusement and recreation services, except motion pictures [*several subsystems*]
  Major Group 80. Health services [*reproducer, producer*]
  Major Group 81. Legal services [*decider*]
  Major Group 82. Educational services [*associator*]
  Major Group 83. Social services [*several subsystems*]
  Major Group 84. Museums, art galleries, botanical and zoological gardens [*matter-energy storage, memory, output transducer*]
  Major Group 86. Membership organizations [*several subsystems*]
  Major Group 88. Private households [*these are groups—not organizations*]
  Major Group 89. Miscellaneous services [*several subsystems*]

Division J. Public administration
  Major Group 91. Executive, legislative, and general government, except finance [*internal transducer, decider*]
  Major Group 92. Justice, public order, and safety [*decider*]
  Major Group 93. Public finance, taxation, and monetary policy [*decider*]
  Major Group 94. Administration of human resources programs [*decider*]
  Major Group 95. Administration of environmental quality and housing programs [*decider*]
  Major Group 96. Administration of economic programs [*decider*]
  Major Group 97. National security and international affairs [*boundary, decider, decider of supranational system*]

Division K. Nonclassifiable establishments
  Major Group 99. Nonclassifiable establishments [*several subsystems*]

SOURCE: Executive Office of the President, Office of Management and Budget. *Standard industrial classification manual.* Washington: GPO, 1972, 5–7.

of the subsystems which are most extensively developed or most specialized in it. Ordinarily these particular subsystems are the ones which carry out the organization's primary processes in the suprasystem. To a large extent, therefore, the same organizations would be grouped together under such a taxonomy that would be grouped under a categorization by the processes carried out in the suprasystem, as in Table

10-1. This classification has the advantage of using as categories the same subsystems I employ at other levels of living systems and so preserves the possibility of cross-level analysis. In it the major division of organizations is into three chief classes: (*a*) those in which subsystems which process matter-energy have the greatest development, (*b*) those in which subsystems which process information have the greatest develop-

Fig. 10-1 A modern ocean liner. Subsystems of this organization are identified.

Subsystems which process both matter-energy and information: Reproducer (Re), representatives of the owning corporation; Boundary (Bo), ship's hull and personnel who guard and maintain it.

Subsystems which process matter-energy: Ingestor (IN), hatchway into ship's hold and personnel who load passengers, baggage, and freight into the ship; Distributor (DI), gangways, decks, staircases, and stewards, waiters, and porters who carry food, beverages, baggage, and various other sorts of matter-energy on them, as well as passengers who move about the ship on them; Converter (CO), galley personnel peeling vegetables and preparing other food for cooking; Producer (PR), chefs cooking food and bakers baking in ship's galley; Matter-Energy Storage (MS), ship's hold and fuel tanks and personnel in charge of them; Extruder (EX), smokestack for gaseous wastes, garbage and sewage outlets for liquid and solid wastes, and operating personnel responsible for seeing that wastes are properly removed; Motor (MO), ship's engines, drive shaft, propellers, and the entire hull of the ship, which moves passengers, crew, and freight in the sea, as well as engineers responsible for managing this movement; Supporter (SU), hull, sides, walls, and decks of ship and personnel who maintain them.

Subsystems which process information: Input Transducer (it), radio operator and other members of communications team who receive messages to ship; Internal Transducer (in), officer who reports to senior officer of the watch on states of various components that make up the ship; Channel and Net (cn), air between watch officers on the bridge of the ship over which they transmit and receive messages; Decoder (dc), radio operator in communications team who decodes Morse code messages into English after they are received; Memory (me), logbooks of past trips, charts of the seas, and those personnel who consult them in the ship's chart room; Decider (de), captain and other ship's officers; Encoder (en), radio operator in communications team who encodes English messages into Morse code in order to transmit them; Output Transducer (ot), radio operator and other members of communications team who transmit messages from ship.

ment, and (c) those in which the two sorts of subsystems, or subsystems which process both matter-energy and information, like the reproducer or boundary, are comparably developed. This is like my classification of subsystems in Table 10-2.

(a) Farms, mines, factories, airlines, railroads, hospitals, and the organizations that store and distribute their outputs to consumers are examples of the first class. All these organizations have information processing subsystems, but their chief purposes concern matter-energy processing. Most of the worker hours of the organization's employees are devoted to these activities. The information processing carried out is subsidiary, directed toward furthering the primary purposes of the organization.

(b) Libraries, banks, stock exchanges, real estate agencies (since money, credit, and titles to property are information), news services, universities, churches, advertising agencies, courts, and legislatures belong to the second class. Some of these have little or no indigenous development of matter-energy processing subsystems, depending on other organizations of the society for these processes. But information processing is emphasized in all of them.

(c) The third class includes cities, towns, and other organized communities, since their citizens process both matter-energy and information; prisons, which have boundaries that filter in or out certain sorts of both matter-energy and information, other subsystems for the physical care of their inmates and employees, and often subsystems for education and rehabilitation as well; armies and navies; and department stores that sell clothing, furniture, and appliances as well as books, tapes, and phonograph records.

Within the above three primary divisions finer and finer distinctions can be made on such bases as (a) the subsystem that carries out the organization's major specialized activities, (b) the particular sorts of matter-energy or information it processes, and (c) its characteristic input-output relationships. As in the classification of organisms (see page 362), the ultimate fine distinctions can differentiate each individual organization from all others of its type. Just as an organism can be classed by its kingdom, class, order, family, genus, and species, so can an organization. For instance, the Orly International Airport outside Paris is a *matter-energy processing organization* involved chiefly in activities of its *distributor subsystem, i.e.,* processing such forms of matter-energy as *passengers* through its buildings, *planes* on its runways as they take off and land, *supplies* from points of input to the planes or other areas where they will be used, and

baggage and *freight* onto and off of planes. Though this organization has a larger development of its distributor than of any other subsystem, another important activity is processing over its *channel and net subsystem* of information related to *aviation* and *mail.* Its most important input-output relationships, which distinguish Orly from other airports, include such variables as the rate of movement of planes in and out during a given period, the number of those planes which cross national boundaries in their flights, the average amount of time a plane stays on the ground for servicing and taking on passengers and freight, and the number of passengers provided service daily.

3. Subsystems

The subsystems of organizations are described below. Figure 10-1 pictures a particular organization, showing its subsystems. In this case it is the crew of a modern ocean liner, along with various artifacts including the ship herself. This type of organization ordinarily has inclusions consisting of organisms and groups, the passengers, as well as freight and baggage. The communications team of this particular ship, located in a compartment somewhat aft of the bridge on the starboard side, is the group pictured in Fig. 9-1. Table 10-2 identifies the components which make up the critical subsystems of an organization.

3.1 Subsystems which process both matter-energy and information

3.1.1 Reproducer, the subsystem which is capable of giving rise to other organizations similar to the one it is in.

3.1.1.1 Structure Any organization or group that produces a formal or informal, explicit or implicit charter for a new organization is a component of this subsystem. These components may themselves separate from the parent organization to become components of the newly formed system, or they may recruit others as components of the new structure.

Members of an industrial organization delegated to set up a subsidiary are examples of such components, as are groups of citizens of a community who separate off to form a new political unit. The organization or group that charters a new organization may not be acting as a component of the reproducer of any existing organization. Such organizations or groups are components of the society that bring together human beings, other matter-energy resources, and information, including the necessary money to start the organization. The template or charter is usually copied from those of other organizations of the type to which the new one will belong.

TABLE 10-2 Components of the 19 Critical Subsystems of an Organization

3.1 SUBSYSTEMS WHICH PROCESS BOTH MATTER-ENERGY AND INFORMATION

3.1.1 *Reproducer.* Any organization or group that produces an explicit or implicit charter for a new organization; may be downwardly dispersed to a single person

3.1.2 *Boundary.* Such subsidiary organizations or groups as guards, doorkeepers, police, personnel offices, admitting officers, admissions committees, membership committees, purchasing departments, personnel at receiving and loading docks, inspectors, receptionists, tour guides, ticket sellers and takers, maintenance staffs, janitorial staffs, military censors, security officers, library committees, loan committees, credit departments, organization officers, and mail-room employees; may be upwardly dispersed to other organizations which serve the entire society; downwardly dispersed to one or all persons in the organization; artifacts such as building, fence, city wall, dike

3.2 SUBSYSTEMS WHICH PROCESS MATTER-ENERGY

3.2.1 *Ingestor.* Such subsidiary organizations or groups as receiving departments, loading-dock workers, purchasing departments, buyers, selection committees, receptionists, admitting officers, admissions committees, orientation groups, missionaries, guides, porters, recruiters, and doormen; may be downwardly dispersed to particular persons

3.2.2 *Distributor.* Such subsidiary organizations or groups as operate organizational transportation facilities such as traffic bureau and police; supply officers; drivers; helicopter or airplane pilots; train engineers in mine; elevator operators; waiters, busboys, ushers; car, truck, and bus drivers; quartermaster department of army; may be upwardly dispersed to the society, as when national railroad carries freight between company plants or when a supranational pipeline, railroad, steamship, or airline does so; or downwardly, as when people walk or drive their own cars; animals such as donkeys and horses; artifacts such as road, trail, passageway; bus, subway, train, truck; moving sidewalk, escalator, stair, fire escape, elevator, conveyor belt, chute, pipeline, pneumatic tube, dumbwaiter; traffic control system, service facility, check-out counter, and toll booth; tray, plate, bucket, cup

3.3 SUBSYSTEMS WHICH PROCESS INFORMATION

3.3.1 *Input transducer.* Such subsidiary organizations or groups as military intelligence agency or unit; guards, lookouts, fire watchers, meteorologists, astronomers, and others who observe and report upon environmental conditions or changes; market research department, persons that report on product or service acceptance or on economic and social trends which may affect the organization; sales department and others that take orders for the organization's products or services; intake department of social service or other organizations; medical personnel who take histories and examine patients on admission to clinics or hospitals; complaint department; legal department that obtains patents or licenses; radar, radio, and telephone operators; library acquisition staff; solicitors of money or credit for an organization; ticket sellers; dues collectors; tax collectors; and bank tellers; may be outwardly dispersed to consultants or researchers from another organization or downwardly dispersed to individual persons who transduce information inputs; artifacts include such communication and detection devices as telescope, field glasses, radar, radio, telephones, television

3.3.2 *Internal transducer.* Such subsidiary organizations or groups as make reports within an organization or ascertain needs, attitudes, or efficiency of components or subcomponents; spokesmen for components, like committee chairmen, department heads, union stewards and other officials, public opinion pollers, inspectors; bookkeepers, comptroller's office, payroll department, accountants; operations analysts; citizens' groups or organizations; may be outwardly dispersed to union stewards who speak for the union, another organization, or consultants from another organization; or downwardly to individuals who report opinions or activities or start rumors; artifacts such as computer, other business machines, microphone, telephone, closed-circuit television, typewriter, other writing materials, time clock, suggestion box

3.3.3 *Channel and net.* Such subsidiary organizations or groups as private telephone exchange with switchboard operators, communications maintenance men; messengers, executives, liaison officers, department heads, supervisors, officers of citizens' groups, heads of households, secretaries; may be upwardly dispersed to communications personnel of the society, including employees of telephone and telegraph companies, the postal service, messenger services, broadcasting services, newspapers and other publications; or downwardly to individual employees, voters, or other persons; artifacts such as letter paper, electronic channel and related equipment, vehicle that distributes publications, armored car that carries money and securities, computer

3.2.3 *Converter.* Such subsidiary organizations or groups as operate electric generating plants, oil refineries, steel mills, glass factories, packing plants, canneries, flour mills, dairies, many chemical plants, textile mills; may be upwardly dispersed to the society, as when an aluminum factory converts ore to metal for an entire nation; artifacts such as knife, axe, hammer, refining equipment, ore-conversion machinery, cotton gin, threshing machine, grinder, chopper, melter, crusher

3.2.4 *Producer.* Such subsidiary organizations or groups as production workers in factories, cooks, bakers, binders; maintenance workers, health personnel; artifacts such as manufacturing machine, tool, assembly line, maintenance equipment, medical instruments, and drugs

3.2.5 *Matter-energy storage.* Such subsidiary organizations or groups as factory personnel in charge of supplies; personnel in charge of warehouse, garage, parking area, reservoir, stockroom, cattle pen, storage tank, grain elevator, coatroom, waiting room, dock, holding area, airport airway; supply clerks; may be laterally dispersed to departments of an organization; or downwardly to individual persons in it; artifacts like parking lot, barn, silo, warehouse, storage room, closet, file, container

3.2.6 *Extruder.* Such subsidiary organizations or groups as city department of sanitation, street cleaning, and sewers; personnel that operate garbage, trash, express, and delivery trucks; bus, train, boat, and plane crews; packing or shipping department; police or others empowered to expel intruders from organization or its territory; discipline committee that discharges or expels employees or members; personnel officers; janitors, custodians, maids, cleaning staff; doctors and nurses who participate in discharge of patients from hospitals; college officials who graduate students; may be outwardly dispersed to city sanitation department that removes wastes from organization territory; laterally to families in a community where each family disposes of its own wastes; or downwardly when each person disposes of his own wastes; artifacts such as dump truck, other vehicle, barge, sewer pipe, smokestack, waste can, mop, broom, street-cleaning equipment, dolly, chute, conveyor belt, firearm

3.2.7 *Motor.* Such subsidiary organizations or groups as domesticated animals; crew, pilots, drivers, operators, or maintenance personnel of man-animal or man-machine systems; may be downwardly dispersed to individual persons in an organization, as when an army marches; or upwardly dispersed to transportation operated for the entire society, such as airline, steamship line, railroad, bus line, trucking line; artifacts such as ship, aircraft, spacecraft, truck, bus; tool or machine such as earthmover, tractor, saw, shovel

3.2.8 *Supporter.* No living supporter known at this level, but organizations must make use of parcels of land or artifacts such as building, platform, ship, road, vehicle

3.3.4 *Decoder.* Such subsidiary organizations or groups as foreign-language translators, cryptographers, signal officers, telegraphers, radar and sonar operators, experts in reporting technical and scientific findings; persons who use confidential business codes; religious leaders and mystics; meteorologists and other interpreters of signs; may be upwardly dispersed to society, like diplomats who translate documents for companies in their countries; or downwardly to individual members and employees; artifacts such as teletypewriter, print reader, computer; other data processing machines, pattern-recognition machines like check readers and punched-card readers

3.3.5 *Associator.* No system at this level has an associator subsystem; this subsystem is downwardly dispersed to individual persons or, occasionally, outwardly dispersed to operations researchers or management consultants from another organization; an artifact such as a computer may do some associating for an organization

3.3.6 *Memory.* Such subsidiary organizations or groups as filing department, bookkeeping department, secretaries, computer experts, bibliographers, librarians, curators; may be upwardly dispersed to banks, stockbrokers, libraries; or downwardly dispersed to individual secretaries and specialists; artifacts such as paper, book, film, microform, magnetic tape, computer memory, filing cabinet, container, teaching machine

3.3.7 *Decider.* Such subsidiary organizations or groups as board of directors, executives, judges, rabbis, bishops, commanders, captains, stockholders, members, voters; may be upwardly dispersed to court-appointed officials; outwardly dispersed to management firms; laterally dispersed to component groups; downwardly dispersed to a single ruler or executive; artifacts such as computer

3.3.8 *Encoder.* Such subsidiary organizations or groups as write and edit speeches, publications, other communications; code communications; translate languages; design trademarks, buildings, other artifacts; act as lawyers, labor relations experts, lobbyists; advertising or public relations department; may be joint with decider, output transducer subsystems; outwardly dispersed to organizations like advertising, public relations firms, or trade association; downwardly to individual persons acting in above capacities, salesperson, recruiter, solicitor; artifacts such as writing materials, paints, computer

3.3.9 *Output transducer.* Such subsidiary organizations or groups as public relations department; spokesmen; labor negotiators; salespeople; missionaries; lobbyists and pressure groups; secretaries; publication, mailing, or circulation department; printers; actors and other performers; media department; broadcasters; maintenance staff for electronic equipment; may be joint with decider or encoder components; outwardly dispersed to other organizations like advertising agency or television station; downwardly dispersed to decentralized groups or individual persons; artifacts such as electronic answering device, public address system, television, radio; printing, duplicating, and mailing equipment; computer

This subsystem may be downwardly dispersed to a single person. Many famous companies have been founded by a single person, such as Maxim's Restaurant and the Ford Motor Company.

3.1.1.2 Process What is required for an organization to be created? A viable new organization is usually formed in response to a present or predicted demand for certain products or services. Sometimes the organization's establishers must create the demand by making potential users in the society aware of what such outputs can do for them. This often is necessary when an invention is introduced into a society. Matter-energy, including human participants and materials, is required. Also, the template or charter as well as other information, including capital, technology, skill, and professional competence, are indispensable.

Several modes of creation of new organizations can be distinguished. Some are established by their originators entirely *de novo* and are not derived from any preexisting organizations. Washington, D.C.; Canberra, Australia; and Brasilia, Brazil are capital cities which have had such histories. So have the new total communities being built in the countryside as answers to the problem of urban blight, such as Cumbernault, Scotland; Tapiola, Finland; and Columbia, Maryland.[22] Other organizations come into being as a result of changes in precursor systems, as when an antitrust suit or other considerations leads a company to dissolve the relationships that hold its subsidiary organizations in the system. These subsidiaries then become independent. One example of the formation of an independent organization from an industrial subsidiary was the "spin-off" of cable television and syndication units from the Columbia Broadcasting Company.[23] An independent board of directors and executives was chosen. Ownership remained initially in the hands of Columbia Broadcasting System stockholders, but independent listing of the stock assured that the ownership would not stay identical with that of the parent company.

Some organizations are formed when a group grows in number of personnel and develops echelons. Almost every national college sorority or fraternity began as a small group on one campus and spread to others. Similarly, the Salvation Army and other welfare organizations began as single groups and spread nationally or internationally. Henry Ford began his business in a shed behind his home and induced several associates to join him; ultimately this group grew into a huge, worldwide corporation. An organization such as a state, province, or canton can begin when a society voluntarily or under military duress surrenders its totipotentiality and subordinates its

decider to that of a larger political unit such as a nation, confederation, or empire (see page 768).

Legal actions commonly are required to include organizations as officially recognized components of their suprasystem. Some organizations become legal entities by being incorporated under the laws of their particular state or nation. In the United States many are set up in Delaware, which requires that business corporations be incorporated by filing a certificate of incorporation (usually referred to as a "charter") giving the corporate name; the place in the state where it will have an agent; the nature of the business; the number of shares of stock to be authorized; the amount of capital, which must be at least $1,000; the names and residences of the incorporators (three or more); the limit of duration of the corporation, if any; and the liability of the shareholders for corporate debts, if any. Rights of shareholders must be stated if there are different classes of shares unless the directors are given the power to determine these from time to time. Other information may be included, such as the powers of the directors. Companies limited by shares in Great Britain and other parts of the British Empire and *sociétés anonymes* in France are established legally in comparable ways.

The laws concerning incorporation of other types of organizations, such as cities, religious organizations, and other nonbusiness corporations, are separate but somewhat similar. When a political group is incorporated in a nation, confederation, or empire, ordinarily its constitution must be rewritten.

The template or charter of an organization "programs" the system. It indicates its purposes and goals and specifies what subsystems it will have initially and which relationships will exist among them. A charter usually states the organization's name; its functions, goals, and major policies; the rights and obligations of its human components; and some of the relationships it will have to other components of the suprasystem.[24] It may also specify symbols or insignia. Certain fundamental decision rules for the components may be given. A charter may also make it possible to distinguish which of an organization's outputs are products and which are wastes. General Motors exists to put out cars, not metal scraps, although it extrudes both. Universities exist to produce educated persons and scholars, not retired professors or academic failures.

Many organizations, of course, have implicit rather than explicit, written charters. Others have developed far beyond the scope and complexity originally envisioned in their charters.

Representative *variables* of the process of reproducing are: *Sorts of matter-energy used in reproducing.*

Example: The Senate committee recommended confirmation of the appointment of a woman to administer the new agency. *Meaning of information used in reproducing.* Example: Article 4 of the charter specified who should be the chief officers in the company's table of organization. *Sorts of information used in reproducing.* Example: A bank loan of several thousand dollars provided the initial capital for the small factory. *Changes in reproducing over time.* Example: Before 1844 a British company could be incorporated only by a royal charter through a special act of Parliament, but after that any company could be incorporated simply by making application. *Changes in reproducing with different circumstances.* Example: During the Depression new sorts of relief agencies were created by the government. *Rate of reproducing.* Example: As social unrest increased, the militant underground formed radical political parties in the different states at a rate of about one a month. *Frequency of reproducing.* Example: The queen chartered new corporations only once a year. *Lag in reproducing.* Example: It took the directors more than a month to get the company organized after it was chartered. *Costs of reproducing.* Example: A bond issue for $13 million was authorized for building the new campus.

3.1.2 Boundary, the subsystem at the perimeter of an organization that holds together the components which make up the organization, protects them from environmental stresses, and excludes or permits entry to various sorts of matter-energy and information.

3.1.2.1 Structure   The boundaries of organizations, like those of groups (see page 522), often have complex shapes. Their unusual spatial configurations derive from the physical separateness of their component subsidiary organizations and groups and from the independent mobility of persons who are subcomponents. As for groups, so for organizations the various parts of the boundary do not necessarily have immediate physical continuity.

Artifacts, such as buildings and fences, are also important components of boundaries of many types of organizations. For centuries cities were often walled to keep out invaders. In a number of Dutch cities there are dikes to hold out excess water.

An organization usually has territory as well as one or more buildings, offices, and meeting rooms, although some highly mobile organizations, like clandestine armies, carry out their processes in the territories of other organizations and societies, having none of their own. The spatial size of an organization at a given time may not be coextensive with its territory.

The portions of the organizational boundaries that are permeable to matter-energy are often different from those which are permeable to information, as is true in living systems at other levels.

Matter-energy boundary.   Many disparate sorts of human components can be parts of the matter-energy boundaries of organizations, including groups of guards, doorkeepers, city or special police like plant or university security officers, personnel or labor relations departments, admissions counselors of colleges or admitting officers of hospitals, membership committees, purchasing departments, employees at receiving and loading docks, inspectors, receptionists, maintenance and janitorial staffs, and persons responsible for receiving and interacting with visitors—for instance, those who arrange tours of a factory and those who sell and take tickets to enter a museum or theater. Some of these are components of other subsystems as well.

The boundary may also be upwardly dispersed to other organizations which serve the whole society, as when a nation's army protects a corporation's components.

Information boundary.   Military censors, security officers, library committees, loan committees, credit departments, and officers with access to closed files or an organization's secrets are components of the information boundary. In some types of organizations such as fraternities, each member is a component of this subsystem, although groups may also carry out specialized boundary functions. Mail-room employees who screen out unwanted incoming mail, such as advertisements, are parts of the information boundary as well as of other subsystems.

The boundary may also be upwardly dispersed to other organizations which serve the entire society, as when a nation's army protects the capital city.

The subsystem is in some cases downwardly dispersed to all persons in the organization, but usually there is at least a partially differentiated boundary subsystem. When the living subsystem consists of a single person, the boundary subsystem is downwardly dispersed to the level of the organism. The one-man police force of a small town is such a component.

Some components which others include in the boundary subsystem I assign to different subsystems. Marketing and research departments or other groups that gather information from outside the organizational boundaries are included in the boundary subsystem by Katz and Kahn, but I consider them to be input transducer components (see page 623).[25]

3.1.2.1 Process   Like a group (see page 523), an organization remains a system even though its human subcomponents move daily from home to office or are scattered throughout the suprasystem, often participating in subsystem processes of other organizations. Channels maintained by the channel and net subsystem of the community or society connect such components and permit the flow of information among them. The widely separated components of some organizations, which may be parts of the subsystem structure of different states or even of different countries (see page 910), are also coordinated by use of such channels.

Matter-energy boundary. Selective filtering is performed at the boundaries of organizations upon several classes of matter-energy, including (a) raw materials for the system's producer processes, if any; (b) artifacts required for subsystem processes, such as pencils, business machines, paper, and furniture; (c) materials for repair and maintenance of the system's property; (d) matter-energy, like food and drink, needed for subsystem processes of the organization's subcomponents; (e) harmful or unwanted matter-energy such as pollutants; (f) persons arriving at, and sometimes departing from, the organization's territory, including persons bent upon mischief; (g) prospective members or employees wishing to join the organization; (h) sales representatives from other organizations, passengers, clients, and others who are potential inclusions in the system; and (i) the system's matter-energy outputs—products and wastes. Each of these sorts of matter-energy is subjected to inspection and sometimes to testing. Those which lack the requirements for being ingested or extruded, as the case may be, are prevented from crossing the boundary. As Hypothesis 3.1.2.2-1 maintains (see page 93), more work is expended in crossing most organizations' boundaries, except at ingestor or extruder points, than in moving through the regions on either side.

The boundary must be permeable so that differentials between the system and its environment can be maintained within a steady-state range. For example, a telephone company may attempt to have 1 operator for each 1,000 subscribers, no matter how much the latter number fluctuates. The optimal degree of permeability, however, differs among types of organizations. Some, such as American political parties, are eager to gain as many members as they can, while others, including professional and business organizations, set up strict membership requirements. Bar associations, for example, have educational requirements, impose examinations, and prescribe high ethical and moral standards.

The discontinuous parts of some organizations' boundaries may exchange matter-energy independently with the local environment, as armies often do, or use suprasystem distributor channels to exchange it among the separated parts, as factories of an automobile manufacturer do. Some organizations maintain distributor channels of their own such as pipelines or private railroads that link their separate installations.

Information boundary. Filtering of information at the boundary includes confirming that checks deposited in a bank account have cleared before payments are made from it, countersigning checks by more than one person to ensure their correctness, approving credit risks before loans are made by special committees or departments, and taking similar precautions against inappropriate outflow of funds. Prisoners' incoming and outgoing mail is often filtered by censors.

It is not uncommon for organizations to control flow of confidential information across their boundaries. A company's secret recipe for piccalilli, for instance, may be known only to top management and those directly involved in its production. The design of new models of automobiles is kept secret for unveiling shortly before they are marketed, precautions being taken against spies from competitor organizations who might penetrate the boundaries. Governments have special departments which attempt to enforce strict security. Certain sorts of organizations impart secrets to all members and pledge them to secrecy. They may require proof that a stranger is entitled to pass inside the organization's boundary by asking him to show an identity card or give a password. Each member is responsible for keeping people outside the organization from learning its secrets.

The components of organizations are joined in a network which permits ready transmission of information over its channels (see pages 627 and 629). Hypothesis 3.1.2.2-3 (see page 93) states that the amount of information transmitted between points within a system is significantly larger than the amount transmitted across its boundary. It seems possible that this may be true for at least some sorts of organizations. Are more interoffice memos than external letters written and received? Are more internal than external telephone calls made and received? Data to answer these questions apparently do not exist, but it would be feasible to collect them for some organizations.

Representative *variables* of boundary process include: *Sorts of matter-energy crossing the boundary.* Example: Steel of inferior quality was refused by the inspectors at the aerospace factory, and only that which met high quality standards was accepted. *Meaning of information crossing the boundary.* Example: Citizens of the city ignored the national weather bureau's heavy thunderstorm warning, but reacted to the tornado alert. *Sorts of information crossing the boundary.* Example: Applications in writing for jobs at the school had to be mailed to the principal. *Degree of permeability of the boundary to matter-energy.* Example: The wildlife conservation organization accepted as a member anyone who paid the nominal fee. *Degree of permeability of the boundary to information.* Example: The board of directors refused entirely to listen to a report advocating computerized management methods. *Percentage of matter-energy arriving at the boundary which enters the system.* Example: Only 2 percent of the shipment of batteries was rejected by the factory. *Percentage of information arriving at the boundary which enters the system.* Example: About 0.5 percent of the orders which arrived at the store had no return addresses and were discarded. *Changes in matter-energy processing at the boundary over time.* Example: Lulled into a sense of security, the guards allowed peasants to enter and leave the castle freely instead of checking their identifications at the drawbridge. *Changes in information processing at the boundary over time.* Example: The city's board of censors gradually relaxed their standards so that more "adult movies" were shown. *Changes in matter-energy processing at the boundary with different circumstances.* Example: No nonunion workers were hired at the mine after settlement of the strike. *Changes in information processing at the boundary with different circumstances.* Example: Briefcases were checked by the student working at the university library exit only during the months when classes were in session and never during vacations. *Rate of matter-energy processing at the boundary.* Example: All day Sunday automobiles were processed by the officials at the turnpike's entrance toll gates at a rate averaging more than 20 a minute. *Rate of information processing at the boundary.* Example: At each meeting the national officers could consider only three or four applications to establish new chapters. *Frequency of matter-energy processing at the boundary.* Example: The admissions committee of the college passed upon applications once a year in the spring. *Frequency of information processing at the boundary.* Example: Incoming letters were censored by the regimental security officer only in the morning. *Lag in matter-energy processing at the boundary.* Example: An absent employee in the department store's inspection unit caused a 3-week delay in the acceptance of supplies. *Lag in information processing at the boundary.* Example: It took the library committee a month to decide whether to accept the gift of the journals. *Costs of matter-energy processing at the boundary.* Example: The new electronic machine, which measured the iron content of ore shipments to the steel mill so that delivery could be refused if they did not meet specifi-

cations, cost \$3,500. *Costs of information processing at the boundary.* Example: The mail-room staff of four men devoted the first hour of every working day to sorting the mail for the entire office building.

3.2 Subsystems which process matter-energy

3.2.1 Ingestor, the subsystem which brings matter-energy across the organization boundary from the environment.

3.2.1.1 Structure Subsidiary organizations and groups which are ingestor components include receiving departments, loading dock workers, purchasing departments, buyers, public utilities, commercial vendors, selection committees, receptionists, admitting officers, admissions committees, orientation groups, missionaries, guides, porters, recruiters, and doormen. The subsystem may be downwardly dispersed to individual persons who are subcomponents of the organization. The ingestor and boundary often have some or all components in common.

3.2.1.2 Process Organizations ingest various sorts of nonliving and living matter-energy, including human beings who become components of the organization and others who cross the boundary from the suprasystem and become inclusions (see page 596), commonly receiving services of some sort from the organization. Since ingestion of these diverse categories of matter-energy is usually carried out by different components, I treat the processes separately below.

(a) Ingestion of nonhuman matter-energy. The sorts and quantities of nonliving matter-energy, plants, and animals needed for system processes and maintenance and the components that ingest them vary from one type of organization to another. An organization like a library whose chief tasks are to process information has different matter-energy requirements from those of an organization which processes chiefly matter-energy, like a meat-packing plant. Consequently, these organizations have different sorts of components in their ingestors.

A city of 1 million population requires as much as 625,000 tons of water, 2,000 tons of food, and 9,500 tons of fuel every day.[26] This is ingested by system components such as the public electric, water, and gas utilities; commercial organizations or groups that bring food or fuel into the city and offer it for sale; or individual citizens who grow their own vegetables, have their own wells, or bring their own property and purchases into the city. Ingestor components of a city may include groups that arrange for regional distributors to transport the matter-energy to the city.

The input–output relationships of a particular organization are important also since two factories producing similar units for output do not necessarily ingest similar matter-energy. One may begin with raw materials, while the other assembles its product from partially completed components. The rate of input of each sort of matter-energy needed by the organization must be sufficient to meet its demands when they arise. If flows are continuous and demands known to vary within certain limits, as is the case with the natural gas input to a city, the material can be ingested at a predetermined rate, which is changed when conditions are altered. Flows of merchandise into a department store or of manufactured parts into a factory, on the other hand, are discontinuous. Since a large amount of an organization's money may be tied up in inventories of supplies on hand for production and goods offered for sale and because deterioration of materials during storage, seasonal variations in demands, costs of storage of oversupplies, and inability to fill orders all affect profits, adjustment of the ingesting process is vital to many sorts of organizations.

Mathematical calculations and simulations using a variety of models have been applied to the processes of ordering in business organizations.[27] These produce recommendations as to the quantity of an item to order and the time to reorder. They take into account the cost of the ordering process, the cost of holding the item in stock, the expected depletion of the stock by use or sale over a given period, the cost in lost sales if the item is allowed to run out, and the amount of time before the item ordered will reach the organization. Reordering may be done when the supply reaches a particular level, the reorder point, or at fixed ordering times. If the latter system is used, a review of the stock on hand determines the quantity to order. An example of the effect of a faulty computer program is given by Ackoff.[28] The program was intended to control the stock of parts needed for production, and the computer kept track of stock, ordered items when required, and generated reports to management. Unfortunately, it confused the maximum stock level with the reorder point, and so reordering was premature, and stock levels remained at their maximums. The organization behaved like an organism that always feels hungry even though its stomach is full. The faulty computer program, as a result of excess inventories, cost the company $150,000 more each month than the hand system it had replaced.

If available matter-energy varies greatly in quality or price or if there is a shortage in the suprasystem, ingesting may involve a search for an alternative that will meet the needs of the system at a price the system can afford. A premanufactured part from a foreign country may replace one made within the organiza-

tion's own suprasystem society, or a part made from plastic may be used instead of one made from metal. Some organizations have centralized departments which specialize in purchasing materials and supplies, gaining advantages from larger purchases. Others decentralize the process, so that subsidiary organizations, departments, or other units are responsible for buying needed materials. Balanced against the savings to be gained by centralized buying are the costs of the purchasing department itself, which, in some cases, can be greater than the savings from centralization. The United States government, which centralizes purchasing, is said to pay 20 percent more for a pencil than an ordinary citizen who goes to the five-and-ten-cent store.[29]

(b) *Ingestion of human components and inclusions.* A person who crosses an organization's boundary or receives services from it must be processed in some way. If he is to be a patient in a hospital, he is admitted, weighed, examined, and put to bed. If he is to be a passenger on a ship, he is sold a ticket, directed up the gangway, and escorted to the part of the ship he is to occupy. If he is a salesman wishing to talk to the director of purchasing, he is asked to wait by the latter's secretary. If he is an important visitor, he is given treatment appropriate to his position and the importance of the organization he represents. Perhaps his plane is met at the airport, and he is driven in an organization car and ushered into the building by a member of top management. In any event, all such persons continue to be outsiders, not members of the organization, even when they remain for extended periods within the boundaries of the organization and interact with its components. Since a consultant or person doing research on organizations ordinarily enters as an inclusion, his outsider position increases the difficulties of his work.[30]

A person who crosses the boundary to become a member or component of an organization is usually processed differently from the way an inclusion is and by different components. Ingestion of new members or employees may be an active recruiting process. If union labor is hired, a special labor relations officer or department may deal with union officers to secure the necessary number of workers in the relevant unions. If a new president is needed for a firm or for a university, a committee set up by the board of directors often carries out the boundary process of screening and selection as well as the ingesting process of admitting the newly hired executive to the system, giving him the appropriate information and access to records and introducing him to the people with whom he will interact. Employees of other sorts may present themselves for screening and possible selection by the personnel office or by the department member responsible for hiring.

Processing of new members of churches or fraternal organizations may involve special rites such as baptism or an initiation ceremony in which the secrets of the organization are revealed. Some other types of organizations merely put the new member on their mailing list, send him a bill for dues, and share with him information not sent to the general public.

Representative *variables* of the process of ingesting include: *Sorts of matter-energy ingested.* Example: Rather than producing its own transistors, the Japanese manufacturing firm imported them from India, where cheap labor was available. *Degree of openness of the ingestor.* Example: No new employees were hired during the company's financial crisis. *Changes in ingesting over time.* Example: Since the jobs were all filled, the agency hired no new workers after the first week. *Changes in ingesting with different circumstances.* Example: Orders for bulk ice cream went up 50 percent in a month, making it necessary for the manufacturer to increase orders for the eggs, dairy products, flavorings, and sugar used in making it. *Rate of ingesting.* Example: Five new members a year were chosen and inducted into the lodge. *Frequency of ingesting.* Example: New members were received into the church at the monthly communion service. *Lag in ingesting.* Example: The recruits arrived at the army base at 8 A.M., but were not inducted until midafternoon. *Costs of ingesting.* Example: The new purchasing officer commanded a much higher salary and insisted upon two assistants and two secretaries.

3.2.2 Distributor, the subsystem which carries inputs from outside the organization or outputs from its subsystems around the organization to each component.

3.2.2.1 Structure Among human components are traffic bureaus and police; supply officers; drivers; helicopter or airplane pilots; elevator operators; waiters, busboys, and ushers; car, truck, and bus drivers; and the quartermaster department of an army. Animals such as donkeys and horses are also included. Artifacts are indispensable components of this subsystem, including roads, trails, and passageways; vehicles such as buses, subway trains, and trucks belonging to the organization; moving sidewalks, escalators, stairs, fire escapes, elevators, conveyor belts, chutes, pipelines, pneumatic tubes, and dumbwaiters; traffic control systems; and trays, plates, buckets, and cups.

Some organizations upwardly disperse some of the distributing process to the society, as when a national railroad carries parts manufactured in one plant to another for assembly. In some cases more than one society supplies distributor processes for an organization, as when a pipeline, railroad, steamship, or airline crosses international borders. Part of the subsystem is downwardly dispersed in cities where people walk or drive their own cars over sidewalks and streets provided and maintained by the city.

3.2.2.2 Process The distributor process requires conversion into work of the energy of some power source, such as animal or human muscular activity, wind, water, gravity, gasoline, or electricity, so that matter-energy of various forms can be transported within organizations. Processes of this subsystem are particularly important in organizations in which either numerous human components or large quantities of other sorts of matter-energy must move to places and at times specified by the system's decider with a minimum of confusion and expense. The logistics functions of an army or navy, with units in many parts of the world and tens of thousands of different items to be transported to and from them is one example. The flow of wastes through the sewers or of traffic through the streets of a city, the movement of materials and products in various stages of completion through the assembly lines of a factory (see Fig. 10-2), and the routing of thousands of patients daily through the examination and treatment facilities of hospitals like Cook County in Chicago or Wayne County General near Detroit are others.

The components of a single industrial installation are usually arranged spatially, often in close propinquity, to facilitate efficient flow of materials. When parts of an organization must be widely separated, however, special distributor artifacts such as pipelines can be used to carry crude oil from a company's inland wells to its seaside storage tanks. Such pipelines can be very long and large. The Foothills Group and Northwest Pipeline Corp., for instance, plan a 3,300-km, 1.2-m diameter gas pipeline running from Prudhoe Bay, Alaska, to a point in Alberta where it will connect to an existing 4,500-km pipeline network serving parts of the United States and Canada.[31] The initial capacity of the planned pipeline will be 45.3 million cubic meters of gas daily.

Cities usually have public transportation like bus lines and subways available to carry people from place to place within the city. Most cities have grown with little or no plan and usually do not lend themselves to efficient flows of matter-energy through their streets. The result of this, as Doxiadis indicates, is that no existing megalopolis (see pages 688 and 689) has solved its problems of transportation.[32] In the central areas of cities the average driving speed is 8 to 16 km per hour (h), which is less than the top speed of horse-drawn vehicles at the beginning of the twentieth century.

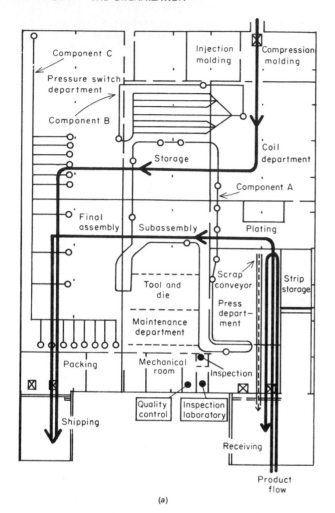

Component C

Pressure switch department

Component B

Injection molding

Compression molding

Storage

Coil department

Component A

Final assembly

Subassembly

Plating

Scrap conveyor

Tool and die

Press department

Strip storage

Maintenance department

Packing

Mechanical room

Inspection

Quality control

Inspection laboratory

Shipping

Receiving

Product flow

(a)

(c)

(d)

(b)

(e)

Furthermore, it is significantly more dangerous for people to walk about in today's traffic.

In one city an automatic traffic control system which adjusted traffic lights to changing conditions shortened the rush hour by 30 minutes (min) and lessened its maximal intensity.[33] The lights were timed progressively so that a driver could maintain the proper speed and meet only green lights. This is difficult to arrange in both directions at once, and so one direction must be favored. The automatic controls received inputs from pressure transducers which measured traffic flows by transmitting a signal each time a wheel passed over them. Capacitors received and stored the signals for 6 min at a time, after which they sent a signal graded according to the traffic load. When there was little traffic, the lights were adjusted to permit a rapid flow of traffic on the main streets without long delays in crosstown traffic. When traffic was heavy, inbound or outbound traffic was favored, depending on the time of day.

A comparable control system for the sewers of Minneapolis-St. Paul is in operation.[34] Remote input transducers report rainfall, pumping-station operation, and waste-water levels in the sewers. On the basis of this input information a control computer makes decisions and sends command signals to control devices which regulate overflow and pumping stations. This sort of system can control the distribution of wastes so well that 90 percent of overflows are prevented.

Matter-energy flows can be analyzed mathematically as aids in the design and adjustment of complex systems. Queuing theory is applicable to many situations in the distributors of complex organizations.[35]

The routes of these distributors include such components as service facilities, check-out counters, toll booths, and traffic lights. The inputs include machines to be serviced, people or cars to pass through the channels, and airplanes to be cleared for landing. Queuing theory can answer questions about the number of routes needed to bring waiting time to a mini-

mum. If there are multiple routes and varied holding times, the problem may be too difficult for analytic solution. This is true, for instance, of the London airport. It can be viewed as a system of interlinked queues. As soon as a plane crosses one junction point or route, it becomes a "customer" for another queue whose customers arrived by different routes. At one time in this airport there were about 25 junctions serving aircraft following 30 different paths. As many as four streams of traffic could pass through the same junction.

The principles of Hypothesis 3.2.2.2-1 (see page 94) apply to flows of fuels and foods as inputs over the distributor of an organization like a city or apartment house. On the input side, the farther the flows travel, the lower the concentration of fuels or foods. On the output side, the farther they travel, the higher the concentration of products or wastes. Hypothesis 3.2.2.2-2 (see page 94) certainly applies to flows of sewage in apartments and cities, total entropy per unit cubic contents increasing progressively the farther they go.

Representative *variables* of the distributing process are: *Sorts of matter-energy distributed to various parts of the system.* Example: All finished units went to shipping except those rejected by the armory's inspectors. These were returned to the appropriate department for correction. *Changes in distributing over time.* Example: Late in the day the bank's cash supplies ran low, and so only half the requisitioned amount of money was sent to each branch. *Changes in distributing with different circumstances.* Example: During the bus strike, people walked or drove their cars to work. *Rate of distributing.* Example: The factory's conveyor belt carried 200 units a day through the automated assembly line. *Frequency of distributing.* Example: Rations were issued to army units twice a day. *Lag in distributing.* Example: The breakdown of a truck caused an hour's delay in moving the doors from the stamping plant to the organization's finishing plant. *Costs of distributing.* Example: The costs of the automated fac-

◀ **Fig. 10-2** Artifacts in distributor subsystem of a factory: three overlapping, integrated conveyor subsystem components that provide a programmable flow of small parts through fabricating, processing, and assembly departments of Controls Company of America Pressure Switch plant in Fremont, Ohio. (*a*) Schematic diagram of U-shaped flow pattern in factory, arranged to minimize ton-miles over which heavy steel must travel. Other materials are small or lightweight. Three conveyor subsystem components all carry materials in tote pans of standard dimensions to mechanize handling. Component A is an interdepartmental conveyor loop that connects receiving, punch press, plating, coil winding, storage, pressure switch subassembly, and final assembly units. Component B stores molded parts being processed in dead space above stock room. Parts are segregated into seven sorts, each sort being switched onto its particular overhead conveyor spur. Later, tote pans containing any of the seven sorts of parts can be retrieved by remote control. Component C carries tote pans containing finished products from the pressure switch and final assembly departments to eight packing lines. (*b*) Worker places magnetized reflector on side of tote pan to program its destination on conveyor. (*c*) Tote pans travel overhead on Component A. (*d*) Roller conveyors used to stack tote pans at various stations. (*e*) Trolley drops to convenient height for loading and unloading tote pans at one station. (From Anon. The 1968 wheel awards for excellence in materials handling. *Modern Manufacturing.* 1969, 2 January, 61, 65–66. *Reprinted by permission* from *Factory*, a Morgan-Grampion publication.)

tory were less for employee wages but much more for electric power to run the equipment.

3.2.3 Converter, the subsystem which changes certain inputs to the organization into forms more useful for the special processes of that particular organization.

3.2.3.1 Structure The number of converter components and the amount of space and resources devoted to them vary greatly from one type of organization to another. If the organization's prime purpose is information processing, this subsystem is often trivial or lacking because some other system carries out converting processes for the organization. In matter-energy processing organizations, on the other hand, it is ordinarily developed significantly, being represented by either subsidiary organizations or groups.

Human components of the converter include subsidiary organizations or groups which operate electric generating plants, oil refineries, steel mills, glass factories, packing plants, canneries, flour mills, dairies, many chemical plants, and textile mills.

The converter is upwardly dispersed to the society if an organization depends, as many do, upon other organizations in its suprasystem for preliminary preparation of part or all of the matter-energy required for its production processes. An aluminum factory may convert ore to metal for an entire country.

Artifacts are prominent in this subsystem. In primitive societies knives, axes, or hammers were used. Modern organizations use machinery such as petroleum refining equipment, the various machines that convert ore to usable form, cotton gins, threshing machines, and innumerable other machines that grind, chop, melt, crush, and otherwise prepare materials for producing processes.

3.2.3.2 Process Matter-energy rarely occurs naturally in the form best suited for use by organizations in their production processes. Even air and water frequently require cleaning, heating, or cooling. Other forms of matter-energy, such as ore, crude oil, wheat, or wool, require much more elaborate conversion before they can be manufactured into products consumers can use.

Conversion of some materials requires a series of processes. For example, iron ore, distributed by a pipeline in the form of slurry (mixed with water), is first converted to marble-sized pellets of iron oxide in a pelletizing machine, and then reduced in a metallizing furnace to chunks of 95 percent pure iron, a form which can be used in the production of steel.[36] Many sorts of conversions of matter-energy permit variation of output from the subsystem to meet needs of the total system. This is true, for example, in the refining of crude oil since the proportions of different hydrocarbons in a refinery's outputs can be adjusted to the demand.

Representative *variables* of the converting process are: *Sorts of matter-energy converted.* Example: The air reduction company got the rare gases xenon and argon, as well as helium, from the air. *Percentage of matter-energy converted.* Example: Half the wheat was delivered to the mill after the harvest was ground into flour, and the rest was stored. *Changes in converting over time.* Example: The percentage yield of octane in the petroleum refinery was increased or decreased from time to time in accordance with demand. *Changes in converting with different circumstances.* Example: The Australian subsidiary converted 11 million kilograms of nickel concentrate from ore each year during the war, but afterward the output decreased markedly. *Rate of converting.* Example: The mill's electric-arc furnace melted 150 tons of scrap steel in about 3 h. *Frequency of converting.* Example: Lamb was prepared at the packing house only once a year, in the spring. *Lag in converting.* Example: Lumber was piled in the lumberyard to season for several months before it was cut into boards. *Costs of converting.* Example: The workers in the refinery cut down the gold ingot so that when finished it weighed only 99.9 percent of what it had when it came out of the mold.

3.2.4 Producer, the subsystem which forms stable associations that endure for significant periods among matter-energy inputs to the organization or outputs from its converter, the materials synthesized being for growth, damage repair, or replacement of components of the organization or for providing energy for moving or constituting the organization's outputs of products or information markers to its suprasystem.

3.2.4.1 Structure To this subsystem belong not only the subsidiary organizations and groups of production workers in factories and other matter-energy processing organizations but also components like the cooks and bakers in a hospital kitchen and the binders in an information processing organization like a publishing firm or library.

Personnel who carry out repair and maintenance on buildings, grounds, and machinery, as well as personnel responsible for the health care provided by the organization to its human subsubcomponents, are included.

Artifacts employed by this subsystem include manufacturing machines and tools. Some companies use massive and complex production equipment such as automatic assembly lines. Examples are Goodyear Tire and Rubber Company's press that makes big rubber belting and Bendix Corporation's "transfer machine," which performs 28 machining operations without human intervention.[37] Included also is equipment used in the maintenance of buildings, grounds, machinery, and furniture, as well as medical instruments and drugs used in the health care of personnel.

3.2.4.2 Process All producing processes of organizations are carried out by the application of some form of energy. This is derived from a conversion process performed within the organization (if, for example, it uses water power to operate its machinery or generates its own electricity) or by other organizations in the society, such as power companies.[38] Besides the materials used in the product, each specific process requires a source of energy (such as a laborer, a chemical solution, or an electric battery) and a piece of equipment (such as a hammer and nails, a welding torch, or an electroplating vat) by means of which the energy is applied. Various combinations of these result in different "production functions," a term economists use for an equation describing the relationships among terms representing capital, labor, materials, and energy. The term "function" is used here in the mathematical sense (see pages 16 and 17). Such functions make possible comparison of the effectiveness of various combinations of the basic variables in accomplishing a given production. These functions can be related to costs of production processes. Also, one can calculate the production functions of whole plants, by combining the functions for their various processes, and thus compare organizations using different technologies to achieve the same purpose, such as a television set manufacturer that uses hand assembly of vacuum tubes and other components and one that uses machine assembly of printed circuits and solid-state components.

Most investigators who study organizations emphasize their administrative or decider processes. Only a few have focused attention on interorganizational differences in producer processes. Among these is Dubin, who has explicitly recognized the pervasive influence of the kinds of technological processes and equipment employed in an organization upon the functions of its workers and upon its authority and status structures (see page 650).[39]

Another investigator who recognizes the importance of producer processes is Woodward. In one of a relatively few researches which have collected data on a large population of organizations, she analyzed 100 industrial organizations in South Essex, England.[40] These firms varied in number of workers from 100 to over 8,000 and produced a wide variety of outputs. Preliminary to determining the effects upon organiza-

tions of the sort of technology used, she made a study of "production systems"—in my terms, producer subsystems (see Table 10-3). Each firm studied was to some extent unique. Eight could not be placed in any category and are not included in the classification. Within the commonly used categories of "jobbing," "batch," and "mass" production, Woodward made further divisions to yield 11 types of producer subsystems. "Integral products" refers to products that are manufactured in units—singly, in batches, or by mass production. "Dimensional products" are measured by weight or volume, as chemicals, liquids, and gases are.

Types I to IX form a scale of increasing technological complexity, the more complex types being of more recent historical development. Each, however, has its place in a modern society, since some products do not lend themselves to standardization or to continuous-flow production because they are large or complex, because they are prototypes, or because the units are manufactured to the customer's order and each differs from the others.

Comparing the various types in Table 10-3, Woodward says:

> Moving along the scale from Systems I to IX, it becomes increasingly possible to exercise control over manufacturing operations, the physical limitations of production becoming better known and understood. Targets can be set and reached more effectively in continuous-flow production plants than they can in the most up-to-date and efficient batch production firms, and the factors likely to limit performance can be allowed for. However well-developed production control procedures may be in batch production firms, there will be a degree of uncertainty in the prediction of results. Production proceeds by drives and a continuous attempt is made to push back physical limitations by setting ever higher targets. The difficulties of exercising effective control, particularly of prototype manufacture, are greatest in unit production. It is almost impossible to predict the results of development work either in terms of time or money.
>
> In general it is also true to say that prediction and control are easier in the manufacture of dimensional products than in the manufacture of integral products.[41]

The characteristics of the producer subsystem determine the sort of employees in the organization, the nature of the work they do, and their relationships to one another, to their supervisors, and within the suprasystem society.[42] Woodward's study revealed some direct relationships between the degree of technological complexity and organizational characteristics as well as some similarities between organizations at the extreme ends of her scale.[43] As technological complexity increased, so did some structural characteristics of the organization's decider (see page 644) and other subsystems. The most complex had a larger

TABLE 10-3   Frequency of Occurrence of Various Types of Producer Subsystems in 92 South Essex Industries

	No. of Firms	Type of Producer Subsystem	No. of Firms	Production Engineering Classification
(A) INTEGRAL PRODUCTS	5	I Production of units to customers' requirements		
Unit and Small Batch Production	10	II Production of prototypes	17	Jobbing
	2	III Fabrication of large equipments in stages		
	7	IV Production of small batches to customers' orders		
Large Batch and Mass Production	14	V Production of large batches	32	Batch
	11	VI Production of large batches on assembly lines		
	6	VII Mass production	6	Mass
(B) DIMENSIONAL PRODUCTS	13	VIII Intermittent production of chemicals in multipurpose plant	13	Batch
Process Production	12	IX Continuous flow production of liquids, gases, and crystalline substances	12	Mass
(C) COMBINED SYSTEMS	3	X Production of standardized components in large batches subsequently assembled diversely		
	9	XI Process production of crystalline substances, subsequently prepared for sale by standardized production methods.		
Total Firms	92			

SOURCE: J. Woodward. *Industrial organization: theory and practice.* London: Oxford Univ. Press, 1965, 39. Reprinted by permission of The Clarendon Press, Oxford.

ratio of workers who maintained plant and machinery to those who actually carried out production processes, a higher proportion of supervisors to operators, more highly qualified supervisors who were graduates of a technical college, and a lower percentage of the total costs of the organization devoted to labor.

The extremes of the scale, unit production (Types I, II, and III) and process production (Types X and XI), on the other hand, were more similar to each other than to Types IV through IX in having a more intimate relationship between the work group and its immediate supervisor, a larger number of skilled workers, and a more flexible organization with less distinction between line and staff employees. Supervisors in unit production firms of Types I, II, and III tended to be older men with technical competence acquired by long

practical experience. In firms of Types VIII and IX, on the other hand, the supervisors also were technically competent men, but were younger and formally educated for their responsibilities.

Skilled workers performed different functions in the various types of companies. In unit production firms they were concerned directly with production, semiskilled workers doing the more mechanical parts of the job and unskilled workers servicing them. In the large batch and mass production firms the skilled workers were largely responsible for maintaining the tools and plant, while semiskilled labor was actually responsible for the production. In these plants, unskilled workers did much the same work as in unit production firms except that they were more concerned with servicing sections or departments than with individuals. Standardization had eliminated from the main production tasks the need for perceptual and conceptual skills, although motor skill and manual dexterity were still required in much of the work. While skilled workers in the unit production firms were well paid and enjoyed high status, in the large batch and mass production systems their earnings were not much more than those of the semiskilled, and they did not determine patterns of behavior within the production subsystem.

Among the firms within each type of producer subsystem the range of costs of production was wide, determined to a large extent by costs of raw materials.

How assembly lines are designed exerts a major influence on the producer processes of manufacturing firms. Three major problems arise in the design of assembly lines, both those which are fully automated and those which use human labor:[44] (a) breaking the job into a suitable number of stages (line balancing), (b) locating the storage spaces for materials in process, and (c) determining the size or capacity of such storage. These problems are often solved by practical, intuitive means as experience with the assembly line increases over time. Mathematical solutions can also be sought, and in some cases they have been successfully applied.

One linear programming approach (see pages 722 and 723) to a line-balancing problem resulted in large savings at the General Electric Company.[45] It provided a schedule for a production which satisfied a number of conditions, including: (a) The time established for each separate task by agreement between unions and management and by time and motion studies was observed; (b) the time available for each man to do his job and return to his station for the next operation was determined by this time, by the speed of the continuously moving belt, and by the space he could cover; (c) some operations had to follow others (nuts, for instance, must be put on after bolts) although others were interchangeable; and (d) the sum of the idle times had to be held to a minimum.

Accumulation of materials or units in storage spaces for them at the various stages of a production line assures that no stage will be delayed by absence of inputs from the stage before and that no machines will stand idle because there is no room for their outputs. The amount of such space needed in a particular situation can be mathematically determined.[46] This buffer storage (see page 620) within the producer subsystem regulates the flow of production. In-process storage problems can be approached by considering the production line as a series of single queues, the output of one serving as the input for the next.[47] The problems and solutions differ as varying restrictions are applied to the queues.

The timing of producer processes is determined by various factors. Production is necessarily seasonal, for example, in organizations which depend upon a seasonal crop, as some food processing companies do. The manufacture of passenger cars is seasonal by custom in the United States, where a yearly model makes obsolete the output of the year before. This is not necessarily true in other countries. A company's production schedule also depends upon actual or expected demand from its market and upon its ability to compete successfully with other organizations producing similar outputs. The availability of matter (e.g., steel or plastic), energy (e.g., gas or electricity), and employees with the necessary skills and desire to work in the organization also affects production schedules.

Repair processes—maintenance and health care. Most organizations must repair and maintain their buildings and grounds, equipment, and furniture. Most employ personnel who are assigned the special functions. Clinics and health services are found in many organizations, maintaining the physical capability of personnel in the organization. This is a repair process also—keeping the organization's component personnel healthy and capable of functioning.

Among the *variables* in the producing process are: *Sorts of matter-energy produced.* Example: The automobile company produced passenger cars, buses, and trucks. *Quality of matter-energy produced.* Example: Dresses mass-produced for the lowest-priced market were cut from cheaper cloth and with less seam allowance. *Percentage of matter-energy used in producing.* Example: All parts of the pigs except their squeals were put to use by the meat-packing company. *Changes in producing over time.* Example: Late in the model year few cars were produced by any automobile manufacturer. *Changes in producing with different circumstances.* Example: During the war the airplane manufacturers made more bombers and fewer private planes. *Rate of producing.* Example: The daily output of bathtubs of the large corporation was 20 times that of the small factory. *Frequency of producing.* Example: All restaurants in the chain made fish chowder every Friday. *Lag in producing.* Example: The summer dresses had to be designed by Christmas in order to be ready in time. *Costs of producing.* Example: The costs of raw materials were high in the silversmith's production of sterling plates.

3.2.5 Matter-energy storage, the subsystem which retains in the organization, for different periods of time, deposits of various sorts of matter-energy.

3.2.5.1 Structure Almost every organization processes some artifacts such as supplies, furniture, equipment, or machinery. These are usually stored by a matter-energy storage subsystem somewhere on the organization's territory. This subsystem includes subsidiary organizations and groups responsible for warehouses, garages, parking areas, reservoirs, stock rooms, cattle pens, storage tanks, grain elevators, coatrooms, waiting rooms, docks, and other holding areas for matter-energy. Supply clerks are also included. Air traffic controllers who regulate the "stacking" of planes in the airways near an airport are components of this subsystem during peak load periods.

When articles of special value are placed in a bank vault for safekeeping or when the organization draws upon city or regional storage for water or electricity, this part of the subsystem is upwardly dispersed to the society level. Usually a large organization laterally disperses some part of its storage processes to its departments, each of which keeps a certain quantity of matter-energy for immediate use in its processes. Certain components of a system may be downwardly dispersed to individual persons in it, as in the case of the Swiss soldiers who store army guns and ammunition in their homes.

The subsystem's artifacts include parking lots; buildings like barns, silos, and warehouses; rooms; and shelves, closets, files, and containers of all sorts used for storage.

3.2.5.2 Process   Matter-energy storage by organizations can be divided according to the expected holding time into long-term, short-term, and buffer storage, the last of these being the storage of people or other matter-energy in queues. Times for each of these types of storage vary greatly. What is long-term storage for a shipment of fresh strawberries or an emergency-ward patient with an acute coronary obstruction may be short-term storage for a locomotive part or a bottle of vintage wine. The storage process will be discussed in the following sections under (a) storing and maintaining in storage, (b) loss from storage, and (c) retrieval from storage.

(a) *Storing and maintaining in storage.*   The matter-energy to be stored and the length of time it is to be held are not usually decided within the storage subsystem. What level of inventory should be maintained, for instance, is an important management decision that may involve adjustment of many system variables (see pages 731 and 732). Organizations store not only matter-energy for the system's processes and maintenance but also people waiting to become inclusions or members of the system, people who are inclusions in the system, and matter-energy waiting to be extruded from the system as either products or wastes. Suitable space must be provided for all of these. I have

already considered storage of in-process matter-energy within the producer subsystem (see page 619).

How materials are stored varies with the sort of matter-energy to be stored, which ranges all the way from batteries for electricity; to piles of boards stacked in a lumberyard; to tanks for oil; to hospital beds for patients; to theater lobbies for customers waiting for the next show; to elaborate equipment to maintain high pressure, a vacuum, low temperature, or some other condition required by perishable things.

Techniques have been developed to improve placement of items in storage so that, for example, the most recently acquired foods are placed behind older ones or the books in greatest demand are placed nearest to the library's charging desk.

Organizations that expect queues of people, of automobiles, or of other sorts of matter-energy awaiting service must provide space sufficient to hold the maximum number or amount expected. The suprasystem may regulate the number of people permitted to occupy a given space, such as a theater lobby. Such buffer storage has special characteristics that make it unlike other forms of storage in organizations. It is frequently short-term, the time being determined often at the level of the organisms in the queue rather than by the organization. Queuing theory usually assumes that input rate and holding times are not affected by queue length, but this is rarely true. People will not usually join a queue of excessive length. Personal preferences are important in this. People will sit in a line all night to buy a ticket for the World Series, but not to see a sandlot game. They will leave their television sets for repair indefinitely in a repair shop, having little choice because all other local television repair shops have similar lengthy queues.

A warehouse can be conceptualized as a buffer storage whose inputs are products from a factory and whose outputs occur when sales are made. Storage times can be considered to be more or less randomly distributed.[48] With these assumptions, queuing theory mathematics can be applied to some warehousing problems.

(b) *Loss from storage.*   This results from physical deterioration of stored matter-energy, from its removal by unauthorized persons—not an unusual event—or from the decline in usefulness of stored items as a result of obsolescence or change in demand. This last may occur when a seasonal item is left in stock after the season ends.[49]

(c) *Retrieval from storage.*   The problems of finding an item in a storage area when it is needed are met by rational storage systems, including storage codes, inventory lists, and catalogs.

Queuing theory often assumes that each customer retains his proper position in the line and is therefore retrieved from this buffer storage in the order in which he entered the queue.[50] This is not true if priorities are assigned. An air traffic controller, for instance, must give priority in landing to those planes near their limit of fuel in the stack in the skies near the airport. Other organizations grant priorities for other reasons, such as obvious hardship in the servicing of relief clients or a physical handicap in the seating of airline passengers. In the queue to leave a sinking ship, women and children go first.

Costs. Matter-energy storage costs include the rent or purchase price of the space and storage equipment, the expenses of its maintenance, the pay of the personnel required, and expenditures for insurance, taxes, and reimbursement of clients for any losses.

Among the *variables* in the process of storing matter-energy are: *Sorts of matter-energy stored.* Example: The assembly plant kept several months' supply of tractor parts. *Total storage capacity.* Example: The express company's storage shed had an area of 30 by 30 m. *Percentage of matter-energy stored.* Example: Whenever bags of flour were delivered, they were put immediately into the bakery's bins. *Place of storage.* Example: The city had a reservoir on the east side and one in the mountains. *Changes in storing over time.* Example: It became too expensive to guard the gold, and so no advance supply was kept. *Changes in storing with different circumstances.* Example: When the city limits were extended beyond the organization's territory, it was no longer necessary to maintain a water storage tank. *Rate of storing.* Example: Two thousand passenger cars were placed in the assembly plant's shipping area each working day. *Lag in storing.* Example: Some of the fish spoiled because space was not available in the freezer for several hours after they were delivered to the cannery. *Costs of storing.* Example: The city constructed a new building for storing schoolbooks at a cost of $50,000. *Rate of breakdown of organization of matter-energy in storage.* Example: The disinfectant in the hospital's spraying pipes evaporated at the rate of about a liter (l) every 24 h. *Sorts of matter-energy retrieved.* Example: By the end of June, the salespersons had sold 50 percent of the ice that had been put into the icehouse in January. *Percentage of matter-energy retrieved.* Example: The fruit weighed about 3 percent less after 5 months of storage in the producer's warehouse. *Order of retrieval.* Example: Stock was taken from the supermarket shelves according to the date of storage, the oldest material being taken first. *Rate of retrieval.* Example: The pumping station removed 400,000 l of water an hour from the reservoir. *Lag in retrieval.* Example: For 20 min the stock-room clerk could not find the pads of forms needed by the municipal court's judges. *Costs of retrieval.* Example: The parking garage paid the attendants union scale.

3.2.6 Extruder, the subsystem which transmits matter-energy out of the organization in the form of products or wastes.

3.2.6.1 Structure   Among the many and diverse components of the organization extruder are such subsidiary organizations and groups as city departments of sanitation, street cleaning, and sewers; personnel that operate garbage, trash, express, and delivery trucks; bus, train, boat, and plane crews; packing and shipping departments; police or others empowered to expel intruders from an organization or its territory; discipline committees that discharge or expel employees or members; personnel officers; janitors, custodians, maids, and cleaning women; doctors who discharge patients from hospitals; and college officials who preside at the graduation of students.

The subsystem is outwardly dispersed when a city sanitation department sends its employees to enter another organization's territory and carry out garbage and waste. It is laterally dispersed when each family in a community must burn or bury its own garbage and maintain a septic tank. It is downwardly dispersed to the organism level when each person in an organization takes his own trash to a city receptacle or dump.

Artifacts employed by this subsystem include dump trucks and vehicles of many other kinds, barges, sewer pipes, smokestacks, waste cans, mops, brooms, street-cleaning equipment, dollies, chutes, and conveyor belts. Firearms may be required on occasions when forceful expulsion of persons from an organization is necessary.

3.2.6.2 Process   Organizations extrude human components, wastes, and products or items for sale.

(a) Extruding human components.   People who are inclusions in an organization often are extruded when they leave its territory through openings in its boundary such as airports, docks, or factory gates. Organization members and some human inclusions like visiting consultants or patients who go home for a visit, however, pass through extruder components without extrusion from the organization because of the nature of the information boundary of organizations (see page 56). These members or inclusions retain their rights to reenter at appropriate times and continue to share in the information flows of the organization. Members and employees are removed from access to the channel and net and from their relationship to the organization's decider by some formal process like

being discharged or dropped from membership, resigning, or being graduated. Occasionally an entire department or subsidiary organization is extruded from the system. In some cases certain components of such units are retained and made parts of other departments or subsidiaries.

(b) *Extruding the wastes of organizations.* Disposal of wastes from some types of organizations constitutes a major problem not only for the organization itself but also for its environment. This is true of large cities, whose smokestacks and chimneys belch forth gases and particulate matter and whose buildings extrude solid wastes and sewage in great quantities. Each day New York City produces about 19,000 metric tons of solid wastes.[51] Discarded newsprint alone adds up to 318,000 metric tons each year. More than 63,000 metric tons of dust and soot particles are emitted into its atmosphere each year, mostly from oil burners and incinerators in its 30,000 apartment houses. Both carbon dioxide and sulfur dioxide accumulate to undesirable concentrations in its atmosphere. It generates 4.9 billion liters of sewage each day, some of which enters environmental waters in untreated condition. These awesome rates are increasing and already constitute a crisis for the city and a burden for other components of the society. A single comprehensive city agency, the Environmental Protection Administration, was created in New York in 1968 to be responsible for street sanitation, water supply, water and air pollution control, and noise abatement. Some new laws have been passed against polluting, and a $200-million capital program has been begun for constructing incinerators which burn cleanly.

Since environmental pollution is a societywide problem, requiring for its solution technological developments and cultural changes, it is discussed in the next chapter (see pages 781, 782, and 835 to 840).

(c) *Extruding products or items for sale.* Products are extruded at the point where they leave the organization's territory or its artifacts. A delivery truck, which is an artifact of the extruder subsystem, is the part of the system where the final act of extruding takes place. The driver and his or her helper, as well as those who wrap and package the product or load the truck, are the human components involved in this extruder process.

The *variables* of the process of extruding include: *Sorts of products and wastes extruded.* Example: The cabinetmaking company sent out furniture on order and burned shavings, discharging the smoke into the atmosphere and the ashes into trash cans. *Percentage of products and wastes extruded.* Example: All but a small fraction of 1 percent of the gold was used by the firm to make jewelry; the remainder was lost in the

form of dust. *Changes in extruding over time.* Example: As the economy improved, there were fewer dropouts and more graduates from the high school. *Changes in extruding with different circumstances.* Example: The new smokestacks reduced the factory's visible air pollution to an amount acceptable to the society of which it was a component. *Rate of extruding.* Example: Twenty boxcar loads a day were shipped from the factory to Boston. *Frequency of extruding.* Example: The automobile parts company sent shipments to the West Coast only twice a month. *Lag in extruding.* Example: Some of the steel girders rusted while transportation from the mill was being arranged. *Costs of extruding.* Example: The toy manufacturer's shipping department employed 10 workers full time.

3.2.7   Motor, the subsystem which moves the organization or parts of it in relation to part or all of its environment or moves components of its environment in relation to each other.

3.2.7.1   Structure   The motors of organizations are usually man–animal or man–machine systems, the human components of which are such subsidiary organizations and groups as crews, pilots, drivers, operators, or maintenance personnel. Organizations like cities, corporations, armies, and navies supply their needs for motor components by using either domesticated animals or vehicles such as ships, aircraft, spacecraft, trucks, and buses for moving, through space-time in the suprasystem, the whole living system, component groups, artifacts, and any living inclusions. For acting upon nonliving components of the environment, they can call on any of a great variety of specialized tools and machines, including earthmovers, tractors, saws, and shovels.

Also, the motor subsystem may be downwardly dispersed to the motor subsystems of the individual persons who make it up. An army, for example, may have airplanes, trains, trucks, buses, tanks, ships, spacecraft, and other vehicles for carrying groups of soldiers; it may have horses or elephants for the cavalry; or the soldiers may march on foot. If the motor artifacts are components of organizations which serve the entire society, like airlines, steamship lines, railroads, bus lines, or trucking lines, the subsystem is upwardly dispersed to the level of the society.

3.2.7.2   Process   Some organizational components, including crews of boats and trains and their conveyances, units of armed forces, salesmen, and advance men of theatrical organizations, travel about in the performance of their functions. Whole villages in some cultures move regularly whenever their slash-and-burn agriculture makes a region unsuitable for continued use or when movement of game or depletion of forage for herds limits the food supply. The people gather together their belongings and pack up or abandon their shelters, moving to find a new temporary location, usually within a definite territory to which they have rights. Religious sects like the Mormons or Pilgrims at times have moved to escape persecution. If a modern city or large organization must relocate, the cost in money, energy, and disruption of functions is enormous. Such moves are undertaken only for compelling reasons, as when the society needs their territory for some other use.

Builders of roads and buildings, lumber companies, operators of quarries and mines, housewreckers, and movers are a few of many types of organizations whose processes in the society require movements that act upon components of the environment. Some of their work that has traditionally been done by laborers with pick, shovel, or ax now frequently is carried out with specialized machinery. The human operators sit in the cabs and control cranes or earthmovers or use such equipment as pneumatic drills, automatic lifts, or a hydraulic shear that can cut a tree down at a single clip. These machines greatly increase the amount of work an organization can do in a given time.

Representative *variables* of the moving process are: *Sorts of movements made.* Example: The cannery was relocated on an adjacent mountainside so as to make room for a dam. *Changes in moving over time.* Example: The second move the company made was much more difficult than the first because of the larger amount of heavy machinery it owned. *Changes in moving with different circumstances.* Example: The entire army was deployed to the seacoast when enemy ships were sighted. *Rate of moving.* Example: The express train crossed Austria at 100 km per h. *Rate of output of work.* Example: The contractor's earthmover displaced 50 tons of dirt a day. *Frequency of moving.* Example: The religious sect moved its various camps twice in 10 years to avoid persecution. *Duration of moving.* Example: The lumber company's hydraulic shear cut down a tree in one quick snip. *Lag in moving.* Example: The Fifth Army was delayed by a blown-up bridge and failed to contact the enemy on schedule. *Costs of moving.* Example: The conglomerate corporation paid $400,000 for its executive jet.

3.2.8 Supporter, the subsystem which maintains the proper spatial relationships among components of the organization so that they can interact without weighting one another down or crowding each other.

3.2.8.1 Structure Organizations, like almost all human groups (see page 531), have no living supporters. They must make use of parcels of land or artifacts for this aspect of their structure. Such artifacts include buildings, platforms, ships, roads, and vehicles.

3.2.8.2 Process Some types of organizations require a particular sort of artifact or physical arrangement in order to carry out their processes with efficient flows of matter-energy and information. A factory is often arranged to minimize the distances that materials used in its processes must be moved. The rooms of museums are often planned so that the visitor is led easily from room to room without missing any part of the collection.

The arrangement of the components within buildings often reflects their relationships within the organization. Members of "top management" may literally be on the top floors of an office building, where they are relatively inaccessible, while members of the sales staff occupy lower floors, where they can more easily meet the public. The bridge of a ship is built to place the captain and other officers high in the bow, where they can get a good view of the sea and the ship.

Representative *variables* in the supporting process include: *Strength of the supporter.* Example: The factory floor was reinforced to hold heavy machinery. *Costs of supporting.* Example: The new building cost the real estate company $2 million.

3.3 Subsystems which process information

3.3.1 Input transducer, the sensory subsystem which brings markers bearing information into the organization, changing them to other matter-energy forms suitable for transmission within it.

3.3.1.1 Structure Living components of organizational input transducers include military intelligence agencies and units; guards, lookouts, fire watchers, meteorologists, astronomers, and others who observe and report upon environmental conditions or changes; market research departments, which report on product or service acceptance or on economic and social trends that may affect the organization; sales departments and others that take orders for the organization's products or services; intake departments of social service agencies that record applicants' requests for service and similar sections in other sorts of organizations; medical staffs that take histories when patients are admitted to clinics or hospitals and examine them, recording their findings in the patients' medical records; complaint departments; research and development departments; legal departments of companies that arrange to purchase or obtain licenses to use patents; operators of detection or communications devices, such as radar, radio, or telephone; library acquisitions staffs that order books or information on other sorts of markers; organization members who solicit contributions to religious and charitable organizations or secure government or foundation grants for research or experimental projects in universities or other organizations; officers or board members who obtain inputs of money and credit for an organization; ticket sellers; treasurers of organizations who collect dues; tax collectors of cities or states; and bank tellers.

The input transducer subsystem is outwardly dispersed when outside consultants or research teams from other organizations carry out surveys for the organization or conduct teaching or training sessions among employees. It is downwardly dispersed to the level of the organism when individual members of the organization rather than groups transduce the input.

Artifacts used in input transducing include communication and detection devices, telescopes, field glasses, radar, radio, telephone, television, research instruments, and automatic coin-collecting machines.

3.3.1.2 Process   Many different sorts of information are transduced into organization channels and nets. Transduction may be carried out by human components who observe an environmental event and activate a warning system like an air-raid signal or who watch and report upon the readings of an instrument, such as a radarscope. The transduction is sometimes entirely electronic, as when news of a national emergency is transmitted throughout a city over a national television channel. In some situations, information may cross the boundary of an organization in a form suitable for transmission, and no transduction is required. Out-of-town newspapers or magazines entering a city are examples.

Organizations of all sorts need money or credit. Some acquire this by collecting dues or contributions from members or by soliciting the public. Others are supported by taxes. Publicly owned corporations issue new shares of stock or bonds when they need funds for building or expanding. Many types of organizations charge for their services or products, an input–output relationship discussed below (see page 669). The organizational components that receive the money, checks, credit-card information, or other evidences of payment record the amounts and other relevant facts in writing, on cash-register tapes, or in computer memory. In this form the information enters the channels of the organization. The actual money rarely flows in these channels.

Innovations in products or processes bring information into the channels of organizations. These come from two sources: either (a) through the input transducer subsystem from other organizations that have pioneered an idea or from inventors who sell or license a patent to the organization or (b) through the internal transducer subsystem from component groups or subcomponent persons in the organization's own research and development department or

other organization members. A study of organizations in the plastics industry showed that they competed most over the development of new and revised products and processes.[52] Without constant innovative inputs, any firm was doomed to decline. By contrast, organizations producing containers had essentially no interest in innovation since products of different organizations were required to be interchangeable.[53]

The large producers within an industry are rarely the sources of major inventions.[54] Of seven major innovations in the aluminum industry, one, dip brazing, was originated by a large producer of aluminum in cooperation with an aircraft company. Three were the work of independent inventors. In the petroleum industry, all seven basic major inventions underlying the refining process were the work of independent inventors. Of the 25 major innovations of the Du Pont company between 1920 and 1950, 10 originated in research conducted by the firm; the other 15 originated outside and were developed by Du Pont laboratories. In a related study by Myers and Marquis of 567 technical innovations named as "most important" by 121 firms in 5 manufacturing industries, 23 percent were found to be adopted from other companies.[55]

Input transducer functions.   Operating characteristics cannot be given accurately for the input transducers of organizations, except for some functions for certain components that act as channels for queues of input signals, such as buy or sell orders to a stock market. For these, the *channel capacity* can be figured, as can the *lag*. Of course, the functions of electronic components can be precisely given.

Included among representative *variables* of the input transducing process are: *Meaning of information input which is transduced.* Example: The air force lookouts reported to headquarters that they saw vapor trails high in the sky, indicating that jet planes had flown over recently. *Sorts of information input which are transduced.* Example: The department store's sales force received and processed more than 500 telephone orders in one day. *Percentage of the information input which is transduced.* Example: The ship's new radar equipment enabled the officers of the watch to see every iceberg within 5 miles, never missing even small ones. *Threshold of the input transducer.* Example: The company's stock-market analysts reported only price swings of more than 10 points. *Changes in input transducing over time.* Example: Since all its pictures made money, the motion-picture company began to pay less attention to public clamor about its subject matter. *Changes in input transducing with different circumstances.* Example: When the fighting increased on the western border, the army shifted much of its intelligence activity to that area. *Channel capacity of the input transducer.* Example: The advertising firm's consumer testing department had three members and so could transmit no more than 100 pages of reports a day. *Number of channels in use in the input transducer.* Example: One of the chemical company's six research staff members was out sick for a week, and so the five remaining members had to do all the work. *Distortion of the input transducer.* Example: The head market analyst provided biased reports to his company because he usually discounted the findings of computer studies. *Signal-to-noise ratio of the input transducer.* Example: Drilling in the street interfered with the television station's switchboard operator's ability to handle incoming calls quickly. *Rate of input transducing.* Example: The five telegraphers at the division headquarters each received messages at a rate of about 30 words a minute. *Lag in input transducing.* Example: The stock-market ticker tape ran a half hour late at the end of the trading day. *Costs of input transducing.* Example: The supermarket chain in 1 year paid $40,-000 in salaries to public opinion pollers.

3.3.2 Internal transducer, the sensory subsystem which receives, from subsystems or components within the organization, markers bearing information about significant alterations in those subsystems or components, changing them to other matter-energy forms of a sort which can be transmitted within it.

3.3.2.1 Structure Components of the internal transducer include all departments or divisions responsible for making internal reports of various sorts within an organization, as well as those which ascertain needs and attitudes of components and subcomponents, as an ombudsman's office does, or report upon attitudes or efficiency of operations in the organization. Some unions include "internal communications specialists" as advisory staff members.[56] Spokesmen for components are also included, such as committee chairmen, department heads, and other officials who represent one echelon to a higher one. Other such components are opinion polling groups in communities or large organizations; inspectors, like the staff of an army's inspector general; bookkeepers, comptroller's offices, payroll departments that keep records of hours worked by employees, and accountants who make and report upon cost-effectiveness analyses; operations analysts; and citizens' groups or organizations in communities.

The subsystem may have outwardly dispersed components. For instance, employees who are union stewards speaking for the union, another organization, may report grievances of fellow employees. Or consultants from a management advisory firm may enter an organization to study and report to its administration about its internal operations and morale. The subsystem often has downwardly dispersed components. Individual members or employees may transduce their own opinions about organizational matters or innovative ideas (see page 656) into such channels of the organization as house publications or a suggestion box. Rumors may be transduced into an organization's channels by a single person. Or individual members or subgroups of committees or groups in the organization may make statements about their group's activities to others in the organization.

Artifacts often used by this subsystem include computers and other business machines, microphones, telephones, closed-circuit television, typewriters and other writing materials, time clocks, and suggestion boxes.

3.3.2.2 Process The sorts of messages which are input by the internal transducer into the channels of organizations are statements about the current statuses of, and recent changes in, the variables of organization subsystems and components. They also contain information about the feelings, attitudes, and ideas, including innovations, of the persons who make them up. As at lower levels, a single such communication sometimes involves transducing each of several categories of information onto its appropriate channel or band (see page 406). Feelings and attitudes are often carried in nonlinguistic, beta-coded form (see pages 439 and 440), accompanying the verbal message. When a group of disgruntled citizens, for instance, presents a written petition to their mayor, they transduce its content into the formal and official channels of their community. At the same time, they may by their gestures and bodily attitudes give obvious evidences of their hostile and aggressive feelings about the situation from which the complaints arise. Their spokesman, by his tone of voice and emphasis as well as by his words, expresses contempt for the persons considered responsible for these conditions.

Many organizations set fixed times for their components to express their opinions and attitudes. Such times include deadlines for submission of periodic reports, set hours for public hearings, and dates for elections, when candidates are chosen from among those representing particular points of view or political parties. There are also deadlines for circulation of petitions to get an issue on the ballot. Elections, of course, have decider as well as internal transducer functions (see page 643). Dissatisfaction with working conditions or personal or financial rewards in industrial organizations is ordinarily indicated at regular intervals when unions hold meetings to prepare or state their contract demands. Other sorts of organizations have annual meetings at which elections are held and policy is decided and at which members' points of view can be transduced into the organizational channels.

Information can be transduced at other times than during regular elections or meetings. Concerned citizens in most communities have the right to meet whenever they wish. Often they can express their views by referendum or initiative votes or by recall petitions against their officials. Grievances that arise in the course of a job can be transduced at any time into the channels leading to the organization's decider. Also, members of the management, components of the decider, want to know the opinions and attitudes of other members or employees. They can administer questionnaires or opinion polls to elicit reactions from them, or the questioning can be outwardly dispersed to other organizations that specialize in polling.

Computerized management information systems are designed to collect, store, perform operations upon, and retrieve information relevant to operations of organizations. Such procedures aid the processes of other subsystems besides the internal transducer (see page 656), but when they assemble information from the various units that make up the organization, they are carrying out internal transducer processes. The mass of information that is transduced into channels leading to the decider of a large organization can become so great as to constitute overload (see pages 157 to 164 and 169). Management information systems filter and abstract these data, so helping to prevent such overload.

Like transducers at other levels of living systems, the internal transducers of organizations introduce distortions, omissions, errors, and redundancy into messages. Possibly they also amplify, if overemphasis of certain attitudes or feelings of members of the organization can be called amplification.

Biases of components whose evaluations of information are in terms of local rather than systemwide values produce distortions. On occasion, information may be filtered out because it is conceived to be against the interests of the processing group, department, or transducer. In authoritarian organizations, particularly, it is common for people to distort messages they transmit to higher echelons, reporting what they think their superiors want to hear or what they want them to hear.[57] They may not report objectively and fully for fear of reprisals from superiors, peers, or subordinates. All these forms of distortion illustrate Hypothesis 3.3.3.2-6 (see page 96), which states that a system tends to distort information in a direction to make it more likely to elicit rewards or less likely to elicit punishments to itself.

Certain field studies in industrial organizations appear to support this principle.[58] In one it was found that the aspiration of an executive to move to a higher position in an organization correlated $-.41$ with the accuracy of his communications about major problems with superiors. That is, a subordinate who wished to advance in status was more likely to withhold from his superiors information that was potentially threatening to his status than a subordinate who did not want such advancement. Among those who did not trust their superiors' motives and intentions toward their career aspirations, the correlation was $-.66$, compared with $-.16$ for those who did trust their superiors. That is, persons who distrusted their superiors withheld more potentially threatening information than persons who trusted them.

Representative *variables* of the internal transducing process include: *Meaning of internal information which is transduced.* Example: Sabotage on the factory assembly line alerted management to the workers' negative attitudes. *Sorts of internal information which are transduced.* Example: The ship's chief engineer reported that members of the engine-room watch were confined to their bunks by flu. *Percentage of the internal information which is transduced.* Example: The treasurer's financial summary took so long at the corporation's annual meeting that only about half the department heads were able to give their reports in the time that was left. *Threshold of the internal transducer.* Example: The union steward was replaced because he paid no attention to employee grievances. *Changes in internal transducing over time.* Example: The college's computerized management information system replaced a large number of separate reports. *Changes in internal transducing with different circumstances.* Example: During the postal strike the laborers' grievances were stated by union negotiators rather than by the workers themselves. *Channel capacity of the internal transducer.* Example: A new administrative procedure doubled the number of reports submitted each month to the college president. *Number of channels in use in the internal transducer.* Example: Forty department heads in the city government wrote annual statements on employee morale. *Distortion of the internal transducer.* Example: The head of the purchasing department tried in his talk with the vice president to make it appear that the lag in obtaining steel was shorter than it really was. *Signal-to-noise ratio of the internal transducer.* Example: The mob yelled so loudly that the mayor could not hear the complaints of the rioters. *Rate of internal transducing.* Example: Each month the grievance committee of the pharmaceutical firm passed on about five requests for reconsideration of discharges. *Lag in internal transducing.* Example: The department chairmen usually submitted reports on their faculty members' current schedules about 6 weeks after each new semester began. *Costs of internal transducing.* Example: The poll of precinct workers cost the political party's national office $40,000.

3.3.3   Channel and net, the subsystem composed of a single route in physical space, or multiple interconnected routes, by which markers bearing information are transmitted to all parts of the organization.

3.3.3.1   Structure   The channels and nets of an organization connect all its subsidiary organizations, groups, departments, and other components. They include two-way connections "up" and "down" among the decider and components of other subsystems and among echelons, and also laterally among subsidiary organizations, groups, or organisms at the same echelon.

The communications structure of organizations is complicated by the large number of differently constituted component systems, each of which has its own channel and net subsystem, linked in various ways to the net of the organization as a whole. The channel and net subsystem of each organization has unique structural characteristics. Some of these result from such aspects of the structure of the producer of the organization as the spatial arrangements of its components. Some derive from aspects of the structure of the decider such as the number of echelons it has and the number of components at each echelon (see pages 642 and 643). Some arise from such other structural aspects as the size in physical space of the territory of the organization, the number of components it has, and whether these components are geographically close together or separated. These structural variations affect the number, physical nature, and length of channels; the shape and interconnectedness of the net; the components connected; and the sorts of markers employed. Some subsidiary companies in large corporations, for example, are connected into the total network only at the top echelons.

The human components of the channel and net include those employees or members who operate and maintain the artifacts upon which much of the communication within the organization depends, like a private telephone exchange with switchboard operators and communications maintenance men who are employees of the organization. Messengers, like the students who deliver campus mail in universities or the girls on roller skates who speed messages and packages around one large aircraft factory, are also components of this subsystem. So are those members of the organization who act either as nodes or as decision points. These are often at the boundaries of groups or other components. They include executives, liaison officers, heads of departments, unit supervisors, heads of departments in an organized community, presidents or corresponding secretaries of citizens' groups like a branch of the League of Women Voters, and heads of households. Secretaries in offices are sometimes nodes in the channel, but on many issues they are also deciders more often than most bosses realize. Likert has described a type of total organizational structure in which groups have overlapping memberships that provide channels for communication among them (see page 644).[59]

Applying graph theory to the study of organizational networks, Cartwright pointed out that the traditional organization chart is a tree.[60] Every point of a tree which is not an end point is what he called an "articulation point" and what I call either a "node" or a "decider," depending on how it functions. He emphasizes the importance of articulation points in the graphs of organizations. The removal of one of these, such as a liaison officer or representative of a department to a higher echelon, can divide the structure into two unconnected subgraphs. Besides these formally recognized nodes or deciders, other organization members may be either nodes or deciders from time to time, particularly for certain sorts of information flows, like rumors.

Upwardly dispersed components of the channel and net subsystem include communications workers of organizations that serve the entire society, such as telephone maintenance personnel, who are not components of the organization but who enter its territory to maintain the internal channels and nets. When organizations have geographically separated parts, channel and net components of the society may be employed as upwardly dispersed components of organizational channels and nets. These include telephone and telegraph companies, the postal service, messenger services, and broadcasting companies. Parts of this subsystem are downwardly dispersed to the organism level, as when individual persons pass factual communications and rumors from one departmental component to another.

Physical channels include the air between loudspeakers and persons in the organization; the air which conveys microwaves or radio waves, like shortwave police radio that connects the dispersed components riding in patrol cars or motorcycles; telephone wires and switching centers (see Fig. 10-3); and roads, conveyors, or passages over which markers like letters or books are transported. Artifacts used in this subsystem are paper markers like letter paper, electronic channels and related equipment, vehicles like the

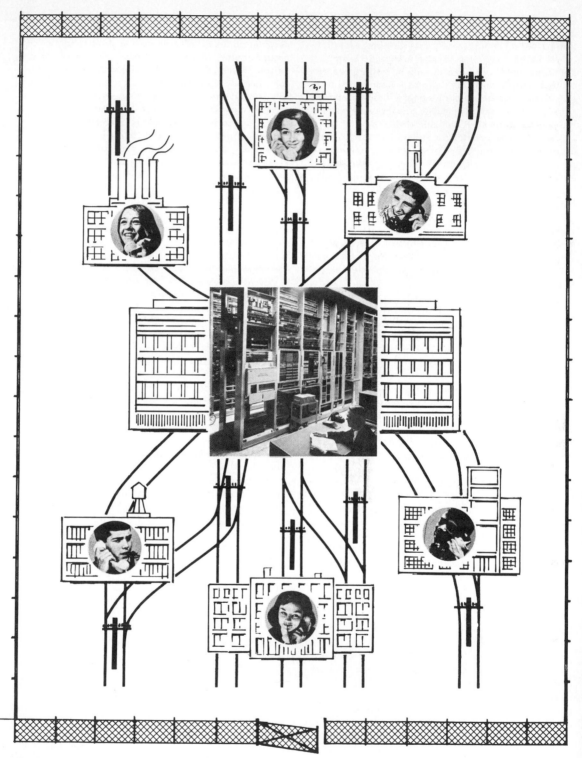

Fig. 10-3 Channel and net and switching center in an industrial organization. *(Photographs reprinted by permission of Bell System and Western Electric Company.)*

trucks that distribute newspapers and other publications through a city or other organizations, and the armored cars that carry money and securities between the central office and the branches of a bank. A computer may be used in this subsystem. An example is the computer which controls display terminals that give instant information to the headquarters of the New York City police about the availability of patrol cars or other emergency equipment, speeding the department's response time.[61]

3.3.3.2 Process   In this section I shall discuss the different kinds of messages carried on organizational channels and nets, as well as the factors that determine what routing is used through the net and what sorts of markers are used.

Each message transmitted on organizational channels is explicitly or implicitly addressed to the component or components that are to receive it. The communication may be one-to-one, as in a discussion between a supervisor and an employee; one-to-many, as when the company president addresses a meeting of department heads; one-to-all, as when a general announcement is made to all members by memorandum or over a public address system; many-to-one, as when several groups join to petition the president; many-to-many, as when workers for certain unions ask that other workers in their company support their demands; or "to-whom-it-may-concern," like signs on bulletin boards.

Types of messages.   The different sorts of messages that enter the net by transduction of input or internal information can be classified according to their content as concerning (*a*) command and governance of subsystems, (*b*) task performance, (*c*) social or professional relationships among groups or representatives of groups in the organization, and (*d*) maintenance and control of the network. Socioemotional interactions among all the superiors and subordinates in the echelon structure are included in this last category. Each of these types of messages is discussed below. Any given transmission of information can include elements of more than one of these categories.

The relative proportion of each kind of information flow in a given organization differs from one type of organization to another. Informal organizations which provide a social life for their members have few authority relationships within them and a correspondingly small number of command and governance messages. The channels of a highly authoritarian organization, such as an army, carry many orders. In the immensely complicated networks of organized communities, particularly large ones, there is an abundance of all the types of messages.

(*a*) *Messages concerning command and governance* include statements of general policy, *i.e.*, information

about the range of alternatives within which decisions can be made, and directives about specific actions to be taken or procedures to be followed. Command and governance messages flow downward in the two-way channels that connect components of the decider with components over which they exercise authority. These two-way channels closely follow the echelon structure of an organization. Channels carrying commands in some organizations are long, running directly from the highest echelons of the decider down to the components at the lowest echelon. This is the pattern in deciders of systems described as "mechanistic" (see page 649), in which a top echelon sends command signals directly to the lowest echelons. In "organic" systems, on the other hand (see page 649), the channels tend to be shorter, with more command information entering the net at lower echelons.

The length of a channel from a high echelon over which information on systemwide procedures passes is generally greater than the length of one over which specific job instructions are transmitted, since they are usually communicated from a lower-echelon supervisor to an organization member.[62] In such channels Hypothesis 3.3.3.2-11 (see page 97) quite likely can be confirmed. It states that the probability of error in a channel increases as the number of components in it goes up. Also, as Hypothesis 3.3.4.2-7 (see page 98) suggests, such errors can be detected by redundancy in signals, including double transmission of messages and use of multiple channels. An example of the latter is the common requirement in courts, legislatures, stock markets, and many corporations that spoken messages transmitted by telephone or in face-to-face conversation be confirmed by written messages (*e.g.*, the court record). Or written endorsement may be required of the decider at each successive echelon, a common military rule.

Effective operation of channels which convey commands is vital to many organizations. This has been demonstrated in the modern, extremely large airplanes. A 360-passenger Boeing 747 airplane once had to make an emergency landing when its public-address system was inoperative.[63] Great confusion resulted because the pilot could not issue orders to the passengers. In another case a DC-9 jet ditched in the ocean near the Virgin Islands, and 23 passengers were killed. The public-address system was broken, and the pilot could not warn the passengers of the need to make a landing. Some of them were standing or had their seat belts unfastened at the time of impact.

(*b*) *Messages concerning task performance* may be propagated upward, downward, and laterally. Downward transmissions from decider components may include feedbacks about such performance or results of actions taken, explanations of decisions, requests for more or better information, and messages about rewards or punishments like pay increases or loss of weekend privileges. Information designed to aid in understanding a particular task in relation to other organizational tasks is also channeled downward.[64]

Upward transmissions include the various sorts of job-related internal transductions I have discussed above (see page 625) as well as task-related inputs from outside the organization such as orders for the organization's products or services and feedbacks on the quality or effectiveness of the organization's performance. These are channeled to the appropriate component or components. In accordance with Hypothesis 3.3.3.2-18 (see page 97), they may elicit actions by lower echelons of the organization without flowing up to higher echelons. For instance, a foreman may act to decrease absenteeism among employees reporting to him without notifying the plant manager about the problem.

Lateral transmissions convey task-related information over two-way channels among persons or groups at the same echelon. They commonly promote coordination and carry requests for opinions or advice and responses to such requests among local groups, work teams, committees, departments, or other organizational components.

Rumors, defined by Guetzkow as "dissemination of unofficial information with high interest value by informal, person-to-person communication," are often transduced into the organization's net.[65] Ordinarily the transducer of such messages is difficult to trace. Some scientists who study rumors believe that they enter the net because official information is incomplete or not considered trustworthy.[66] But rumors are not generated only to meet a lack stress of information, since even if there is effective formal communication in an organization, there is usually also an active grapevine.

Task-related information in a community includes messages concerning not only the activities of civil employees but also political acts of citizens such as voting or paying taxes. The local news media are channels for such information, the broadcasters, writers, and editors acting as nodes and decision points in the network. The local mails and telephone lines are also channels, operated on an upwardly dispersed basis by organizations which are components of the society.

(c) *Messages concerning social or professional relationships* among persons or groups in the organization include notices and reports about union meetings, educational sessions, and meetings or parties of social groups or teams. Many of these flows are lateral at a single echelon, but more than one echelon may be involved. Professional meetings include, for instance,

conferences attended by all members of a certain specialty—like lawyers, engineers, or psychologists—who are members of the organization.

(d) *Messages concerning maintenance and control of the network* include instructions about the use of electronic or other equipment necessary to the net, such as rules about who may use telephones for what sorts of messages. Included also are rules about priorities for messages with certain sorts of content or from certain sources. The chief executive officer of an organization may ask that some sorts of phone calls be put through to him directly or that he be informed immediately if a particular event occurs. Rules or agreements concerning net biases (see page 538) are also included.

Socioemotional information accompanies the other categories of meaningful transmissions in the channel and net. Often these flows are on different markers being coded for nonverbal communication bands (see pages 406, 439, 449, and 625). Command and governance communications, for instance, in addition to their content, carry the expectation of compliance. The legitimacy of the power relationship is usually recognized by both sender and receiver. Recognition of varying status and influence relationships among occupants of positions at different echelons, or of positions at the same echelon which differ in prestige, and sentiments such as trust, liking, approval, and confidence or their opposites are also propagated among organization members. Rumors concerning others' feelings of this sort may also circulate, as when the head of a department is said to have a favorite among his assistants.

Interconnections of channels.   An organization's complex net is often described as a number of separate superimposed nets.[67] The nodes and deciders involved in processing one category of information are often different from those which process another. Although operating characteristics, such as rates, distortions, and lags, may vary from one such set of channels to another, I prefer to emphasize the interconnections that are possible in most or all parts of the net. In my view, its functions indicate that it is composed of multiple interconnected channels but not separate nets.

A totally connected network (see pages 533 to 535) could function only in organizations so informal and small that their processes are more like those of groups than those of organizations. In fact, like groups, even such informal organizations have biased nets (see Hypothesis 3.3.3.1-1, page 95 and also pages 633, 634, and 734), some channels being used much more frequently than others. Some may never be used.

A number of factors determine what channels will be used, whether their use will be routine or unusual, and the types of markers that will be employed:

(*a*) *Formal and informal nets.* In many organizations certain formal channels are prescribed by charter, regulation, or custom. These carry the two-way flow of messages necessary for decision making and control of subsystems. Official channels are rigidly enforced in military and bureaucratic organizations. These and other authoritarian organizations tend to restrict lateral communications except among components involved in staff work or those with a "need to know." Such restrictions may be used as a form of social control, since communication among peers can act as a check on the power of leaders at higher echelons.[68] Other types of organizations have few such restrictions, those which exist applying only during formal business meetings or rituals or applying to the information processing procedures of officers. As Katz and Kahn emphasize, unrestricted communication is a source of noise and inefficiency.[69]

The patterns of channel usage in organizations often vary considerably from those envisioned in the charts or tables of organizations that outline the formal network structure because that structure is supplemented by informal communication channels.[70] Informal lateral channels develop, for example, if no official provision is made for them. When these are set up in violation of formal regulations, their effectiveness may be diminished.[71] Channels and nets change and develop as an organization's processes require, regardless of whether the formal network is altered to match this development. Organizations with few formally prescribed channels nevertheless form working nets which limit and direct their information flows. Experimental studies of the development of networks in task-oriented groups (see pages 539 and 712 to 716) most likely are relevant to the development of working nets in these larger systems as well.

(*b*) *Network patterns.* The pattern of communication channels has important effects on decision making.[72] A research and development unit which has frequent communications with sales engineers and infrequent communications with persons engaged in fundamental research has a different attitude toward developing new products from that of a unit with the opposite pattern. The time available for study and consideration is crucial here because if time for the analysis stage of deciding is short (see pages 655 and 656), only rapidly available information is likely to be brought to bear. This is consistent with Hypothesis 3.3.7.2-6 (see page 100), which postulates that the shorter the decision period, the less thorough in general is the search within the information processing network for relevant facts and alternative solutions. With sufficient time, relevant information anywhere in the organization or its environment may be used.

Hypothesis 3.3.3.2-8 (see page 96), which states that the rate of information flow among components is less the farther they are from one another and the longer the channels between them, may also be relevant here. For instance, an analysis of Project Fifty, a university research organization, indicated that poor coordination, which existed when the components were separated by several miles, disappeared when they were all moved to a single site.[73] Not only the physical length of the channels of a network but also its configuration in space may influence which channels are used.

Those components which act as nodes or deciders of a communication network (see page 63) are also crucial to organizational processes because parts of the organization cannot communicate with one another except through these units. They may be overloaded and become bottlenecks, or if they systematically filter out certain types of information, parts of the organization will be poorly informed about important matters.

(*c*) *Restrictions on channels.* Regulations which limit the channels over which information may flow have the disadvantage of impeding problem solving. Unrestricted flow of ideas, criticism, and advice usually contributes to problem solutions. If there are restrictions, one part of the organization may possess information relevant to a decision, unbeknown to those in other parts who need it. This often happens in organizations which deal with secret intelligence. Restrictions may also prevent a higher echelon of the decider from obtaining information from lower echelons to apply in a particular situation. All these observations support Hypothesis 3.3.3.2-5 (see page 96), which states that strains, errors, and distortions increase in a system as the number of channels over which information transmission is blocked increases. The conflict between the requirement to limit network flows in order to achieve central control and coordination and the requirement to permit unrestricted flows in order to facilitate problem solving has been said to present organizations with an insoluble dilemma.[74]

(*d*) *Directness of channels.* Transmissions over channels with many nodes and deciders between the echelon which sends a message and the component which receives it are often unsatisfactory. Since each node and each decider introduces a lag, such transmissions are often slow. Also, the successive filtering of information that occurs at several echelons results in blocked or distorted messages. The upward flow of messages is subject to distortion and delay in all organizations. A classic example is the blocking of the information that Pearl Harbor was about to be attacked. Gross describes the situation:

Even when special units are set up to gather information and serve as message centers, major blockages may undermine their operations. Two days before the Japanese attack on Pearl Harbor three intelligence officers interpreted intercepted Japanese codes as indicating "attack on an American installation in the Pacific by one P.M. on December 7, 1941. But their efforts were unsuccessful because of the poor repute associated with Intelligence, inferior rank, and the province of the specialist or longhair. General Gerow, head of the Army's War Plans Division, for example, felt that 'enemy information of such grave moment would be brought to my attention . . . by the Assistant Chief of Staff, G-2, and not by a Signal Corps Officer.' "[75]

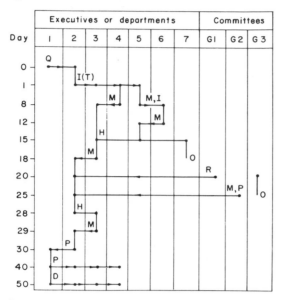

Fig. 10-4 Communication flows in an organization. The executives and departments that participated in the exchange of messages are listed at the top, along with the participant committees. Executive 1 sends a query to Executive 2, who then makes inquiries by telephone [I(T)] of Executives 3, 4, and 5. Executive 4 writes a memorandum (M) to Executive 3. At about the same time Executive 5 sends a memorandum and an inquiry to Executive 6, who responds with a memorandum. A meeting of Executives 3, 5, and 7 (H) then takes place, resulting in a memorandum sent by Executive 3 (who convened the meeting) to Executive 2, who, after receiving a routine report (R) from Committee G1 and a memorandum and proposals (M, P) from Committee G2, meets Executive 3 and gets a memorandum from him. (Committee G3 also discussed the issue, but contributed nothing.) Executive 2 then sends in his proposals (P) to Executive 1, who then formulates his decision (D). First, however, he tests Executives 2, 3, and 4 by sending them his draft proposals. Then, in the absence of any comments from them, he issues his instructions. Twice in the example, messages were expected from Executive 7 (row 5) and from Committee G3 (row 7), but none arrived (O). (From S. Eilon. Taxonomy of communications. *Admin. Sci. Quart.*, 1968, **13**, 279–280. *Reprinted by permission.*)

Because such blockages of channels are not uncommon—though few are so momentous—organizations often officially approve use of bypasses or direct chan-

nels for messages of certain sorts or from particular senders. Standard procedures, formulated for use in emergencies, provide direct upward channels from input or internal transducers to the decider component responsible for dealing with the situation. Warnings by special signals are then transmitted over direct downward channels like a public address system to all affected components, sometimes to every individual member or employee. Information transduced into a suggestion box usually bypasses intervening echelons to take a direct route upward to decider components. Ombudsmen and union grievance committees also transduce their information concerning the state of organizational components into upward channels with special access to administrators. Organization newspapers or newsletters can act as markers conveying information downward, direct from the decider to all personnel in the system.

(e) *Sort of task carried out.* A method of studying and charting communication flows in an organization during the carrying out of a particular job has been outlined by Eilon.[76] Such a chart (see Fig. 10-4) identifies the executives, departments, and committees involved; the direction of communications (shown by arrows); and the type of marker used, whether written memorandum, verbal discussion in meetings, or telephone conversation. Lines drawn vertically show the connections between consecutive messages. In getting a job done, those responsible for it seek the advice and cooperation of others in the organization whose contribution is expected to be relevant. In the example given here, some of the components consulted failed to respond with any contributions. This sort of chart not only records the sequence of communications in a particular instance but also can be used to study interrelationships and control in the organization and the functions of individuals in the communication network.

The type of producer subsystem an industrial organization has affects its communication patterns and the markers employed in it. In Woodward's study (see pages 617 to 619), as production technology advanced, oral communications were replaced by written ones up to the complexity of assembly-line production firms.[77] As the technology increased even further in complexity, oral communications became predominant again. Also, interdepartmental communication varied with the sort of production.[78] In unit production firms close and continuous cooperation was required between managers and supervisors responsible for development and those responsible for marketing. Channels of communication between these departments were direct and speedy, which was important because a crisis at any stage of the manufacturing process could quickly involve all departments. The large batch and mass production firms in this study all had a high degree of functional separation between product development, production, and marketing. Maintenance of the necessary communications between these functionally independent departments became a problem. The process firms studied were still different, since even greater separation was found among task functions. Research departments, for example, were occupied with pure research and were entirely separate from product development and from production. There was little exchange of information between research and other factory activities. In some cases such communication was discouraged in order to keep secret discoveries from reaching competitors. This lack of communication caused no problem, however, since the processes of the departments were almost wholly unrelated.

(f) *Previous channel usage.*   Hypothesis 3.3.3.2-17 (see page 97) states that when a channel has conveyed one signal or message, its use to convey others is more probable. This is what March and Simon refer to as the "self-reinforcing" character of channel usage.[79] They find that a channel which is frequently used for one purpose tends also to be used for other, unrelated purposes. Formal hierarchical channels tend to become general-purpose channels to be used when no special-purpose channel is available. If individuals are brought into face-to-face contact, the self-reinforcement is particularly strong.

(g) *Interpersonal relationships.*   Within any organization special friendship groups and social relationships form as people interact. These relationships create channels which are often used in carrying out an organization's tasks (see page 660). People at decision points tend to channel their communications to those with whom they are most friendly if no other, more compelling influence is operating. This may affect the choice of persons to whom requests are directed for consultation on task problems or for support in decisions. Employing a channel for task-related communication, March and Simon point out, also tends to reinforce its use for informal social communication.[80]   Conversely, channels which have proved unsatisfactory tend to be used no more than necessary. It is not uncommon for organizations to bypass incompetent or intransigent decision makers.

Other interpersonal characteristics facilitate communication. One is possession of a common language by two persons or two organizational units.[81] Links between members of a common profession or people of similar ethnic background, education, age, and experience may also increase information flows between them. This behavior accords with Hypothesis 3.3.3.2-16 (see page 97), which suggests that the less decoding and encoding a channel requires, the more it is used. Personal status within an organization also affects the information flow in its channels, but different studies do not agree on the nature of this influence.[82] Experiments on small groups suggest that persons of low status communicate more with those of high status than vice versa, but a field study carried on in one organization indicated that more communication flowed downward or laterally than upward.

Studies on the spread of rumors over informal channels indicate that they represent only a small percentage of all communications in an organization and that they are propagated in much the same way as other task-related flows.[83]

Functions of the channel and net.   Little is known about the operating characteristics of organizational channels and nets. We lack the sort of accurate measurements that are available for components of cells and organisms, although these could be collected for organizations. Some observations have been carried out, however, on input–output functions.

Input–output transfer functions.   Studies have been made of the spread of messages from input to output through the channel and net subsystem of a community.[84] These spreads are ordinarily by face-to-face contact, although in passing on oral material, the telephone is also used. One study was done in a town of 905 inhabitants. On a Monday morning the doorbells of a randomly selected 20 percent of the homes were rung. The housewives there were told the slogan for a new brand of coffee and also were told that every woman in town who knew the slogan by Wednesday would receive a free pound of the coffee. They were invited to tell their neighbors about this. On Tuesday an airplane dropped 30,000 leaflets on the town saying that one housewife in five knew the slogan and that everyone who knew it by the next day would get a pound of coffee. On Wednesday households were checked to find who knew the slogan, the time and place at which they learned it, and whom they had contacted. It was possible to map 184 pairs of matched receivers and senders of the message. The distribution of distances between their homes was recorded. The spread of the information was found to decrease as the distance between the homes increased. Obviously, interpersonal relations among the housewives also affected the information diffusion.

Another study tested the variation in rates and amount of diffusion in six towns of different sizes by dropping leaflets which were to be returned in order to help spread a message that could help save lives in case of a military bombing during a war.[85] It was found that the interaction, as measured by the return of leaflets which people had either picked up or received from someone else, varied inversely with town size. The amount of contact and diffusion was greater in smaller towns.

A method using "chain tags" was developed to determine the rate at which various sorts of information passed through a social network.[86] A chain tag is a cellophane-wrapped pack of identical postcards given to each of several persons who input the information into the channel and net subsystem of each of several communities. Each such person received a pack of 10 postcards, a subpack, and a "tracer" card, which gave instructions and asked a few questions. He was to pass the remaining subpack of nine identical cards in a single cellophane wrapping on to anyone else. The second person in the chain responded to his tracer card and passed on a subpack of eight. In this way each recipient gave away his subpack and mailed in one filled-out card. The tracer cards recorded the names and addresses of the senders (or givers) and receivers, as well as the times and places of transfer and certain background data.

The persons who first received the packs in each of four communities represented various occupations, such as newspaper editor, teacher, grocer, minister, or bartender. A different message was used in each town. Records of the time of giving and getting the chain tags, as noted on the tracer cards, showed that the median time taken to pass on the subpacks to someone else was 14 min. For one theme, connected with civil defense, this time was only 10 min. The speed of transmission shows that most persons allowed message diffusion to take precedence over whatever they were doing when the card reached them.

Rates of transmission in organizational channels have not been precisely determined. They probably vary with the meaning of information being processed, the number and nature of the components through which information must be processed in any channel, and the markers which carry the messages. Information transmissions in organizations in general probably are slower than in systems at lower levels (see Hypothesis 5.1-28, page 104), though some evidence does not support this generalization (see page 193).

A certain amount of distortion appears to be inevitable in organizational channels. This is in accordance with Hypothesis 3.3.3.2-2 (see page 96), which says that there is always a constant systematic distortion between input and output of information in a channel. The type of marker is important in this, since the distortion in a written or tape-recorded communication often approaches zero. Errors in transcription of notes or of tapes account for most of the distortion that occurs. Long channels in which information is passed

in spoken form from one person who acts as a decider to another are subject to greater distortion. This accounts for the great distortions which commonly occur in rumors and gossip. Hypothesis 3.3.3.2-11 (see page 97), which states that probability of error in messages increases with the number of components in the channel over which they flow, may be true of organizations.

Hypothesis 3.3.3.2-3 (see page 96), suggesting that noise or entropy increases in a channel and that the output information per unit time is therefore always less than it was at the input, appears to be confirmable in some organizational situations, especially when the deciders filter and recode information (see page 631). The assertion of Hypothesis 3.3.3.2-4 (see page 96), which states that a system never completely compensates for this distortion, also seems confirmable. Lag in any organizational channel seems to be related to the number of decision points through which it must pass, the input rate to the channel, the amount of filtering or other processing that must take place, the marker used, and the amount of priority given the message. Hypothesis 3.3.3.2-20 (see page 97) says that information which will relieve a strain (*i.e.*, which the organization "needs") receives priority processing. This hypothesis is probably confirmable for organizations if the information is transduced into a channel leading to the appropriate components. The remainder of the hypothesis, that neutral information is neglected and that information which will increase a strain is rejected, may be confirmable for some sorts of information flows but certainly not for others. Notices to a corporation to appear before a government regulatory board, for instance, increase strains in that company, but they are not rejected.

Many *variables* of channel and net processing can be measured. Some representative ones are: *Meaning of information channeled to various parts of the system.* Example: The factory foreman's request for clarification of a directive went up three echelons, being reacted to by a decider in each. *Sorts of information channeled to various parts of the system.* Example: Complaints about the product were sent to the firm's home office and from there to the manager of production. *Percentage of information arriving at the appropriate receiver in the channel and net.* Example: All mail arriving at the university went to the right rooms that unusual Monday morning. *Threshold of the channel and net.* Example: Just before the merger, even the most preposterous rumors were accepted and circulated through the bank. *Changes in channel and net processing over time.* Example: By 1910 the heads of departments in the insurance company had begun to use the telephone to speak to each other instead of using office boys to carry the memos. *Changes in channel and net processing with different circumstances.* Example: During the holidays the department store switchboard was swamped, and its executives had to visit each other's offices to confer because they could not get an inside telephone line. *Information capacity of the channel and net.* Example: The organization had only 20 inside lines to carry all telephone communication among the executives. *Distortion of the channel and net.* Example: The academic vice president misunderstood the president's decision and told the dean that no further faculty could be hired in the College of Liberal Arts. *Signal-to-noise ratio in the channel and net.* Example: During the gale the lookout could barely hear the commands shouted by the captain from the bridge. *Rate of processing of information over the channel and net.* Example: With the new public address system, announcements could reach all workers in the refinery within a few seconds after they were sent to the announcer. *Lag in channel and net processing.* Example: Old Mr. Jones always kept memoranda on his desk in the anteroom for several hours before sending them on to other offices in the company. *Costs of channel and net processing.* Example: A communications specialist was paid $20,000 annually to expedite the flow of information in the palace.

3.3.4 Decoder, the subsystem which alters the code of information input to it through the input transducer or internal transducer into a "private" code that can be used internally by the organization.

3.3.4.1 Structure Among the living components of the decoder at this level are departments or other units consisting of, or including, translators of foreign languages; cryptographers; signal officers; telegraphers; radar and sonar operators; experts in reporting upon mathematical, statistical, economic, technical, or scientific findings; employees who code orders or requests for merchandise or services into suitable form for processing in a firm; and religious leaders, prophets, astrologers, soothsayers, experts on weather or other natural phenomena, and other such interpreters of signs.

Much decoding in organizations is downwardly dispersed to individual members or employees. Some is upwardly dispersed to the society, as when a nation's diplomats translate and interpret reports about foreign business activities for that nation's corporations.

Artifacts used for decoding by organizations include teletypewriters, print readers, programmed computers, some other data processing machines, and pattern-recognition machines. Automatic bank-check readers that respond to special characters coded in magnetic ink and card-sorting machines that separate cards by decoding the patterns of holes in them are examples of special-purpose machines of this sort in use in organizations. Computer programs capable of decoding verbal or symbolic inputs of varying forms, somewhat as people do, are described in Chap. 8 (see pages 488 to 491).

3.3.4.2 Process Only rarely are messages decoded by organizations *alpha-coded* into signals conveyed by chemical molecules, as they are so frequently in cells, organs, and organisms. The burning of incense and the administration of special foods, wines, or drugs in religious services are the primary examples of such communication.

Beta-coded, or nonlinguistic, signals are also decoded by organizational components. Music is employed to convey a wide variety of messages in a multitude of diverse ceremonies. Belligerent or uncooperative behavior of disgruntled employees can also act as a beta-coded signal to management before any formal complaints are brought by representatives of the dissatisfied groups. The silent carpet on the floor of an executive's office, as clearly as the gamma-coded title written in words on his door, bespeaks his position. Ritualized behaviors, like prostrating oneself or genuflecting and the wearing of certain costumes and uniforms by members of the organization to proclaim their status in it, are also beta-coded signals.

The "private language" of an organization reflects the categories of meaning or sets of concepts by which information from the environment or from within the organization is classified by its components. Messages in such an internal code of an organization are *gamma-coded* information. The codes of organizations of the same type are usually similar, reflecting comparable aspects of their structure and processes. They differ between divergent types, like churches and factories. A specific cross-level comparison between perceptual coding in human organisms and the coding of groups and organizations has been made by Katz and Kahn:

Individuals, groups, and organizations share a general characteristic which must be recognized as a major determinant of communication: the coding process. Any system which is the recipient of information, whether it be an individual or an organization, has a characteristic coding process, a limited set of coding categories to which it assimilates the information received. The nature of the system imposes omission, selection, refinement, elaboration, distortion, and transformation upon the incoming communications. Just as the human eye selects and transforms light waves to which it is attuned to give perceptions of color and objects, so too does any system convert stimulation according to its own properties.[87]

Coded inputs from the environment may be in a foreign language or unfamiliar set of symbols, requiring translation or explanation by decoder components. Except in the case of some religious organizations whose priests and initiates communicate in archaic languages and in the case of ethnic and foreign-language associations, the language in which members communicate among themselves is almost always that of the society of which the organization is a component. This language is supplemented and suited peculiarly to the organization by the use of technical, professional, or ritualistic terms; idiosyncratic expressions, slang, or jargon; and numerical or other symbolic codes. These codes may identify, date, or indicate secretly the purchase price of products, or they may identify and classify records or legal documents. When a new member or employee enters an organization, he must learn to decode these signals, understand their special significances, and think in terms of the organization's accepted conceptual system. These thoughtways often are so completely accepted that the members view them as attributes of the world rather than mere conventions.[88]

Use of internal classification systems and codes increases efficiency of communication, permitting detailed exchange of precise information with the use of fewer symbols than would otherwise be necessary.[89] It also contributes to the ability of an organization to coordinate its activities. Because they have a common set of concepts, members can communicate easily about organizational problems. Anything that does not fit these concepts is more difficult to communicate.[90]

If an organization is large, with a number of departments and a wide range of variously trained and educated personnel doing different kinds of work, the internal code will not be in all ways homogeneous. The production department, for instance, usually differs from the research and development department in the special terms they use, their informal names for processes or machines, and even in the way they employ words in their common language. Within each component, members can usually communicate readily, but those from different components—say, a Ph.D. from the research laboratory and a line executive from the factory—may need a certain amount of translation and explanation when they discuss a project. This is partly a result of selective channeling of information, since separate selections of information are sent to different departments. Hypothesis 3.3.3.2-13 (see page 97), which relates differences in decoding among components of a system to limitations on access to information, can probably be confirmed for organizations. Hypothesis 3.3.3.2-15 (see page 97), stating that these differences are greater the more segregation of information there is, appears also to be confirmable at this level. It can also be predicted that decoding will be more alike among components located close together in space or having similar units or functions, as Hypothesis 3.3.3.2-14 (see page 97) maintains. Hypothesis 3.3.4.2-8 (see page 98) may also be true of some types of organizations. As it suggests, less recoding probably is necessary as more common systemwide codes are developed over time.

When an organization does not have concepts or codes for communication of specialized information originating in some part of it, it requires decoder components capable of preparing reports based upon that information. For instance, if a corporation has a scientific research unit, it may also need a group of science writers who explain and interpret to all the company's employees the significance of their discoveries and inventions.

In any situation like this in which inferences are drawn from evidence and the inferences rather than the evidence are communicated, "uncertainty absorption" (*e.g.,* information absorption) takes place, according to March and Simon.[91] This is likely to be accomplished in terms of the categories of the organization's conventionally accepted conceptual scheme. The information absorption takes place closer to the source of the information, and the more complex the data are and the less adequate the organization's language is to deal with them, the greater the amount of summarizing. A component's need for raw rather than summarized data, the distribution in the organization of people competent to interpret and summarize such data, and the need to compare facts from two or more sources in order to interpret them also determine where in the organization information absorption takes place.

Distortions often occur in the decoding process. The human components of this subsystem are subject to error and bias. They may change the emphasis of a communication or omit part of it. An example of a decoding error of serious proportions occurred in the Pearl Harbor information center a little more than half an hour before the attack on Pearl Harbor.[92] The incoming Japanese planes were seen as blips on a radar screen while still 220 km away, but were decoded as friendly aircraft. As a result, no warning was sent to the American fleet, troops, or air force. The consequences were historic.

Included among the *variables* of the process of decoding are: *Meaning of information which is decoded.* Example: When the stock market continued to go down, the bank interpreted the action as a sign to liquidate many of its trusts. *Sorts of information which are decoded.* Example: The army succeeded in "cracking" the enemy code. *Percentage of the information input which is decoded.* Example: Out of the 120 communications that arrived that day, 3 were not translated because they were in Hindi, which no one in the intelligence service could read. *Threshold of the decoder.* Example: The bank's handwriting experts could read any sort of script, no matter how badly written it was. *Changes in decoding over time.* Example: As the waitresses and cooks worked together longer at the grill, they developed short expressions for the most common orders. *Changes in decoding with different circumstances.* Example: In the archdiocese mass was ordinarily said in English, but Latin was used in the pontifical high mass. *Channel capacity of the decoder.* Example: During the international crisis the army base added several new cryptographers, more than tripling their capacity to decode messages. *Distortion of the decoder.* Example: The bias of the marketing division was evident in the statistics they presented to the staff meeting. *Signal-to-noise ratio of the decoder.* Example: The high waves caused confusing signals on the ship's radarscope. *Rate of decoding.* Example: The agency's computer could read addresses in a special type about 500 times as fast as the group of employees had done previously. *Percentage of omissions in decoding.* Example: About 3 out of 300 letters could not be delivered because their addresses could not be read at the post office. *Percentage of errors in decoding.* Example: Only about half the blinker signals were read correctly while the ship was pitching. *Code employed.* Example: Blueprints were prepared for the shop. *Redundancy of the code employed.* Example: The code was deliberately made more repetitive by the army in order to ensure its accurate reception. *Lag in decoding.* Example: It took several hours for the accounting firm to determine the trends shown in the financial reports. *Costs of decoding.* Example: An expert was hired by the glass company at a high salary to explain the advances in the field of ceramics.

3.3.5 Associator, the subsystem which carries out the first stage of the learning process, forming enduring associations among items of information in the organization.

3.3.5.1 Structure The associator at this level, like associators at all levels above the organism, is downwardly dispersed to organism components in whose nervous systems the connections among items of information are made. These organisms are in the parts of the organization that can discover relationships among items of information or can change the organization's responses to information flows. When, occasionally, operations researchers or management consultants from another organization work with a given organization to help it improve its efficiency or learn how to carry out certain of its processes better, at least part of this subsystem is outwardly dispersed.

An artifact like a computer with a learning program may do some associating for an organization in sophisticated data analysis or in the operation of a management information system.

3.3.5.2 Process An organization has formed a new association to one item of information when its response to a subsequent transmission of that item or a similar one, from the environment or from within the organization, is altered. This is the usual criterion of associative learning at the level of the organism (see pages 407 to 409), and it seems applicable at this level also. The association, according to Deutsch, results from " . . . those inner changes in an organization that occur in response to some repeated outside stimulus and that change the system's subsequent response to it."[93] These changes and similar ones that occur in response to internal events may affect any organizational process. Because the human subcomponents of organizations are independently mobile and because the group and organizational components can readily be rearranged, reversible or irreversible changes in structure as well as alterations in process can result from such associations.

Evidences that an organization has associated items of information appear in changes of processes and standard operating procedures, categories for decoding, decision rules, matter-energy and information outputs, steady-state ranges, and ways of interacting with other systems in the environment. Examples are seen in such policy revisions or "institutional innovations" as the following: A manufacturer of dog food that has always advertised only in national magazines decides, after a market survey, to advertise only on television in the future. A hospital that has always admitted patients individually to their beds before carrying out any diagnostic procedures institutes new procedures to carry out preliminary diagnostic screening in the emergency ward, admitting only those patients in need of immediate care. A university attempts to increase its summer classroom utilization by instituting two 6-week sessions instead of one 12-week session. An automobile manufacturer replaces 48 employees with a new, completely automated chassis assembly line. A library puts a small piece of metal in the binding of each of its books and sets up metal detectors at all its exits to prevent book thefts. A church begins taking up the offering early in the service rather than at the end so that worshipers cannot leave before the collection. A college decides to monitor examinations rather than administer them on an honor basis. A department store shifts its annual furniture sale from spring to summer in the hope of bolstering sales during a slow time of the year. An aircraft carrier alters its fire-drill procedures to disembark all personnel on the lee side. The national council of the Boy Scouts decides that, as a routine, matches rather than fire by friction will be used to light campfires.

Within the organization, systems at the levels of organism, group, and subsidiary organizations make associations relevant to organizational activities. A new production employee, for instance, associates feedback information from motions of his hand with successful performance of an unfamiliar operation; a work group associates more rapid processing of orders with a new division of labor; and a factory associates failure to meet quotas with excessive absenteeism. Nevertheless, regardless of how many subsidiary units have learned a given association, no association at the organization level has occurred unless it influences components of the organization's decider subsystem to change its future structure or process in some way.

Organizations which depend for their outputs upon coordinated behavior of the individual persons and groups that make them up have a different pattern of learning. Members of a fire department become so proficient in their work as a result of practicing together that the performance of the department as a whole, as measured by the speed of reaching the site and effective action against fires, receives an award for outstanding achievement.

Hypothesis 3.3.5.2-3 (see page 99), which states that associations are not formed without feedback as to the effect of a new output and reinforcement or strain reduction by the output, probably applies to organizational associative learning. Feedbacks to organizations include facts as to increased or decreased profits or efficiency, better or worse quality of output products or services, more or fewer satisfied members, recognition or blame from the suprasystem, an increase or decrease in the number of members or other components, and other indications of success or failure attributable to particular acts of the organization. Feedbacks can also be neutral, indicating no relationship between a particular act or decision and the dependent variable. A change in routing cases through a clinic may, for instance, have no discernible effect upon the rate of processing or the expressed satisfaction of the patients. Feedback loops in organizations are often long, in some cases passing through many components. Consequently, they often process feedback signals much more slowly than lower-level systems, which is consistent with Hypothesis 5.1-28 (see pages 104, 669, and 685).

The strains within an organization vary from one type of organization to another. Pressures from the environment in the form of demands for products or services create some of the strains. Others arise from a social organization's desire for new members or a commercial firm's desire for a large volume of sales, from pressure on a court or clinic to process a long queue of waiting cases, from an unsatisfactory profit balance in a commercial organization, or from problems in securing raw materials for an industrial process. Others are caused by imbalances within the system such as breakdowns of machinery, need for new equipment, or problems of cooperation and coordination among the human components. Strains exist also if the decider cannot elicit compliance, as sometimes happens, for example, in universities; if management is not trusted by employees; or if representatives of various local units bicker among themselves and cannot resolve their conflicts.

Actions that reduce such strains are positively reinforcing. Unless the strains are reduced only after a long delay, similar situations in the future can be expected to elicit comparable responses. If feedback indicates that the action either did not reduce the strain or aggravated it, it is less likely to occur again. Over time feedback can also eliminate errors and inefficiencies in the initial action.

Some organizations carry out associative learning more effectively than others. Among the reasons listed by Servan-Schreiber why American businesses have taken away large portions of the European markets from European firms are that the American corporations were more adaptable, corrected their errors more readily, and demonstrated more innovative behavior.[94] In other words, they have greater capacity for associative learning. They have had previous experience with highly demanding environments and have survived, a natural-selection process which has screened them for their creativity and flexibility, among other characteristics.

There has never been a measurement of the rate of associating of an organization. Hypothesis 3.3.5.2-6 (see page 99) predicts that associating will be found to be slower for higher levels of living systems. This was at least partly disconfirmed at the group level (see page 544). Organizations have multiple individual nervous systems in which associations can be made. Consequently, a given association is more likely to be made within a given period of time in an organization than by a single person. This should speed organizational associating. Also, many persons working together are more likely than a single person to correct errors (see page 544). On the other hand, segregation of organization members within component boundaries may prevent them from communicating easily.

Such segregation works against the making of an association between items of information which exist in different parts of the organization. It often takes time to learn what information is available in an organization. Furthermore, long feedback loops, which often pass through many components, also slow associations. An organization associates less well if the time between an act or decision and its consequences is long. Sometimes years pass and human subcomponents change, perhaps several times, before the results of an action appear. The connection may be difficult to discover or be lost entirely. In general it seems probable that the more components there are in an organization and the more diverse they are, the more slowly it associates.

Organizations of different types appear to undergo change at quite different rates. One reason for this may be that they vary significantly in their rates of associating. Religious organizations, for instance, are slow to alter their established responses to inputs, as compared with business organizations. The latter cannot survive unless they provide new products or services to meet rapidly changing environmental demands, but, at least until this century, few such requirements have been made of religious bodies. An organization associates at a rate that makes it possible for it to adapt to environmental variables. This rate may well be determined by the optimal ratio of correct learning trials to error trials—a ratio which depends upon the probability that specific signals will coincide in an organization's environment, as Hypothesis 3.3.5.2-5 (see page 99) suggests.

Representative *variables* of the process of associating include: *Meaning of information which is associated.* Example: Sabotage on the automobile factory's assembly line showed the workers' dissatisfaction and boredom. *Sorts of information which are associated.* Example: The computer manufacturer's annual report made it clear that the advertising campaign had led to a sharp rise in the sales curve. *Percentage of the information input which is associated to other information.* Example: Only about 1 percent of the suggestions made by customers to the airline president appeared sufficiently relevant to ongoing activities to be given serious consideration. *Changes in associating over time.* Example: The grocery chain found that the locations in shopping centers had become more profitable than those on neighborhood corners, which had previously proved the best. *Changes in associating with different circumstances.* Example: When the denomination began to lose members, the bishops began to relate their unpopularity to the intolerance of their dogmas. *Channel capacity of the associator.* Example: The

orchestra could learn no more than 200 pages of new music a week. *Rate of associating.* Example: The leading manufacturer of plastic tubing revised its process and altered its product within 2 months to keep abreast of the changing demand. *Lag in associating.* Example: When the effects of the legislature's action became apparent several weeks later, it turned out to have been a mistake. *Costs of associating.* Example: The cereal manufacturer wasted a lot of time and lost a lot of profits before the management made the connection between the dull yellow color of the new breakfast food box and the decline in sales.

3.3.6 Memory, the subsystem which carries out the second stage of the learning process, storing various sorts of information in the organization for different periods of time.

3.3.6.1 Structure The subsidiary organizations, groups, and departments responsible for storage and retrieval of the voluminous records that most organizations must keep are living components of this subsystem. These include filing departments, bookkeeping departments, cashiers, secretaries, and computer programmers and operators. In addition, groups and departments of bibliographers, librarians, and curators responsible for storage and retrieval of information of other sorts, like library books, financial and correspondence files, blueprints, fingerprints, magnetic tapes, phonograph records, and collections of paintings and photographs, are included in this subsystem.

Upwardly dispersed components of the memory subsystem include banks, stockbrokers, libraries, and other agencies which serve all components of the suprasystem (see page 796). There are also always downwardly dispersed components in this subsystem. Downwardly dispersed to the level of the group are departmental or private official files kept within a department or work group or by an individual secretary. Also, each member of an organization—teachers and professors, researchers, skilled workmen, experienced executives, and long-term employees—must store the part of the organization's information relating to her or his own role. Consequently, each member is a downwardly dispersed component of the organization's memory at the level of the organism.

Memory subsystem artifacts include the markers, such as paper, books, film, microform, magnetic tape, and computer memory components, as well as filing cabinets and other containers for stored markers. Teaching machines are also included.

3.3.6.2 Process Storage of information by organizations is carried out in the same four phases as in other levels of living systems: (*a*) reading into storage, (*b*) maintaining information in storage, (*c*) loss and alteration during storage, and (*d*) retrieval from storage. These will be considered in turn.

(*a*) *Reading into storage.* An organization's charter and its accumulated store of decoding categories and standard procedures are kept in memory, which helps to preserve the identity and continuity of the system. Organizations also store information concerning their past decisions and actions, interactions among components, interactions with other systems in the environment, and money and credit information.

The form of storage of a particular item of information depends upon characteristics of the organization itself and upon the nature of the information. Organizations in primitive societies and informal organizations, usually small, whose essential processes are similar to those of groups, depend largely or completely upon the memories of their human subcomponents. The larger, more formally structured systems record a greater proportion of their information flows in written, printed, taped, or microfilmed form or read it into computer memories. How certain sorts of producer subsystems tend to use written memoranda, while others rely chiefly on oral communications, I have noted above (see pages 632 and 633).

Certain sorts of information must be stored in the memories of organisms. The matter-energy and information processes necessary for a job usually can be learned only by those people and groups who do it. This sort of storage includes the motor skills required for performance of production tasks and the special skills and knowledges of executive, clerical, sales, professional, and other specialized personnel. In some organizations details of services rendered to the public or to members of the organization are recorded only or largely at the organism level. Ministers, guidance counselors, social workers, parole officers of courts, and such professional persons typically keep either no written record or personal files about their contacts with the people they serve. Some sorts of organizations select organism subcomponents for the special stores of information they have. History departments of universities aim to have specialists on various areas of the world and periods of time represented on their staffs in order to offer a variety of courses. Hospital staffs include physicians certified by various specialty boards so that their stored knowledge can be available for treatment of patients and for teaching.

Few modern organizations rely entirely upon downwardly dispersed memory components, however. Instead they provide for storage by the organization of information inscribed on suitable markers. The capacity in bits of the information storage of organizations is very large, since it includes some of the capacity of

the groups and organisms within it in addition to the information stored on markers by its own storage subsystem. The Harvard University libraries contain more than 8 million volumes. Taking a hypothetical but reasonable average of 500 pages in each book and an estimated 350 words on each page and assuming that each letter or number on a page represents about 8 bits of information, one can calculate that there are something more than 10^{13} bits in the library part of Harvard's memory alone. Of course some of this is redundant because every library owns multiple copies of some works. If the material of all sorts in the files and the relevant storage by human components could be estimated and added, the figure for the total information stored at Harvard would be large indeed.

Use of computers for storage of large amounts of information is increasing rapidly. These machines can replace many of the files ordinarily maintained in organizations, with the advantages of central location, avoidance of duplication, speedy updating, and rapid access to the stored information from remote terminals. A data communication system capable of collecting information from components in more than a thousand places is in use in one industrial organization.[95] The capacities of the memories of many modern computers are very large. A single computer memory at Livermore Laboratories of the University of California, for instance, has a memory capacity of 10^{12} bits.

Microfilm is a very compact form of storage applicable to libraries and many other components of organizations in which documents or other written materials are kept. With this form of storage, the entire Bible can be put on a piece of microfilm the size of a 35-millimeter (mm) transparency. The contents of a library so stored would occupy only a few filing cases. This form of storage is useful, too, to protect rare and valuable documents that would be damaged by circulation.

The cost to organizations of keeping masses of information in storage is high. It includes not only the wages of the living components of the memory subsystem but also the costs of building and maintaining space where markers can be kept and of buying or leasing artifacts needed in the subsystem. Universities usually cannot afford to spend more than about 5 percent of their budgets on their libraries, but this, in a large university, can amount to several million dollars annually.

(*b*) *Maintaining information in storage.* Maintenance in storage involves arranging markers in the storage space and caring for them. Ordinarily in any collection of information some is consulted much more frequently than the rest. Adjustment to this varying demand can be made by putting the most frequently used information in the most accessible locations. Removing records not used for a year, or 5 years, from the active file to one less accessible increases availability of current records.

(c) *Loss and alteration during storage.* Information stored in downwardly dispersed organism components may be lost or unavailable as a result of forgetting, or it may be altered in the various ways that organisms' memories commonly change over time (see page 421). In addition, people die or move away, and information stored in their nervous systems is thus lost to the organization.

Each of the other kinds of markers has its own rate and sort of loss or deterioration. Computer memories can be accidentally erased by electrical or magnetic forces in the immediate environment or by human error. Such loss is permanent. Paper slowly deteriorates and is subject to destruction by fire, water, and hard use. Books can be stolen or lost by their readers. Worms and mold attack old books and documents. Dirt and sunlight deteriorate paintings. And so forth. Also, some planned loss from storage, systematically weeding out little-used materials, is usually desirable in organizations' memory subsystems.

(d) *Retrieval from storage.* Some sorts of information stored in the organization's subcomponent organisms are retrieved whenever the person performs the part of his job requiring it. Other sorts are retrieved, sometimes after long periods, when a need arises and the person who has stored the information is available.

Retrieval from organism memory also takes place in problem solving, as March and Simon recognize:

Where an organization becomes aware of a problem, and a proposed solution does not accompany the communication of the problem awareness, repertories of problem solutions "stored" in the memories of organization members will be the principal source of solution proposals. As awareness of the problem is communicated through the organization, solutions will be evoked from these repertories and will become attached to it. The broader the problem, the more will the solution be affected by the numbers and diversity in the people among whom it is circulated. With the increase in the number of persons who become aware of the problem (without a corresponding increase in diversity) the number of solutions will increase, but at a negatively accelerated rate. . . . We see that a good deal of the internal communication in an organization concerning new programs is aimed at a search of the organization's (collective) memory for relevant considerations—whether in the nature of program proposals or feasibility tests.[96]

With this dispersed form of organization memory it is difficult in a large organization to be sure that all items relevant to a solution or decision are retrieved. Information may be in somebody's memory or in some department's files, undiscovered by those who need it.

A study of a large university library, by Meier, disclosed that the normal time required for seeking a title was 6 to 7 min but that during times of peak demand, this increased by 20 percent.[97] Meier also calculated the time cost to faculty members of withdrawing books from storage.[98] The central library comprised about 1 million volumes, of which 440 items were withdrawn in a typical week in 1958. The total time spent by all faculty members in obtaining those books, assuming each one takes the shortest route from his office, laboratory, or clinic, was calculated as 679 h, or slightly more than 1.5 h per book. At the average rate of faculty pay, therefore, $9 worth of the faculty member's time was spent before he had an opportunity to read a book or to gain by-product advantages from library visits. The cost was much less for departmental libraries in the same institution. The money cost to the library for providing the book (circulation cost) was 60 to 80 cents.

The enormous mass of information stored in books, periodicals, reports, doctoral dissertations, and other forms in libraries can cause a physical crisis.[99] Costs in time and money of processing these by the library staff produce an operational crisis, and the difficulties of retrieving particular pieces of information from the accumulation bring about an intellectual crisis. Similar overloads are found also in other sorts of information storage. A number of automated and electronic devices are being developed to cope with these problems. Of these, storage of information in computers has already been mentioned. Access times in these machines are in fractions of milliseconds for each item. Automated search and retrieval apparatus, such as the Randtriever, can locate and deliver books from a random storage by storing all the addresses. Card-sort machines select the titles listed under particular headings for bibliographical work, locate fingerprint cards for the FBI, select tax records according to name or geographic location, and carry out similar retrieval processes. In the development stage are automated encyclopedias, actually question-answering machines, which will store input statements and reproduce them on demand.[100] Time-sharing computers with large memories and great computing capacities can be used by several organizations simultaneously. I discuss them in the next chapter (see page 796). Numerous organizations with many components also use such computers.

Representative *variables* of the process of remembering include: *Meaning of information stored in memory.* Example: All the plans for the merger were in the corporation president's files. *Sorts of information stored in memory.* Example: The clerk searched the files for the first annual report of the city. *Total memory capac-*

ity. Example: The new law firm had three secretaries and ten filing cases in addition to a professional staff of four people. *Percentage of information input stored.* Example: The college library kept all but about a third of the material it received. *Changes in remembering over time.* Example: As the business grew older, it was necessary to keep written records of all agreements instead of having the boss remember them himself. *Changes in remembering with different circumstances.* Example: Though profits were low, the railroad installed a new microfilm process for record keeping. *Rate of reading into memory.* Example: Each girl in the newspaper's filing department filed about 20 letters an hour. *Lag in reading into memory.* Example: The insurance company's typing pool was 3 weeks behind in typing the minutes of the sales meeting. *Costs of reading into memory.* Example: Each hospital record clerk was paid about $5,000 yearly. *Rate of distortion of information during storage.* Example: Some of the museum's carbon copies had faded and were almost illegible after about 50 years. *Time information is in storage before being forgotten.* Example: In the 20 years after the team won the world championship, the city had forgotten the members' names. *Sorts of information retrieved.* Example: Eighty-two percent of patients returned for further treatment at the clinic, and their records were retrieved from the files. *Percentage of stored information retrieved from memory.* Example: The department-store computer failed to retrieve less than 0.001 percent of the payment records. *Order of retrieval from memory.* Example: The research team at the social service agency withdrew clients' records from the old files, beginning with the oldest and working on up through the 10 years. *Rate of retrieval from memory.* Example: The airline company's worldwide time-sharing reservation system retrieved more than 10,000 reservations per hour. *Lag in retrieval from memory.* Example: It regularly took the hospital record room about a half-hour to find a patient's record. *Costs of retrieval from memory.* Example: The worldwide reservation system cost the hotel chain $60,000 monthly.

3.3.7 Decider, the executive subsystem which receives information inputs from all other subsystems and transmits to them information outputs that control the entire organization.

3.3.7.1 Structure   The central decider of an organization is the group—or, in some organizations, the person—that determines chief purposes, sets primary goals, and controls subsystems of the organization as a whole. The human components of the decider often have titles like "chief," "chairman of the board," "director," "trustee," "president," "mayor," "councilman," "judge," "bishop," "rabbi," "commander," or "captain." Additional decider components are usually found at each lower echelon, where the deci-

ders of component groups and organizations control their own subsystems and components more or less in accordance with the overall goals of the organization, under some degree of control by the highest echelon of the organization's decider. A decider structured into echelons is one of the characteristics of modern capitalistic bureaucracies, according to Weber (see page 595). This view has led many to identify an echelon structure with an authoritarian decider, but, in fact, echelons are characteristic of all types of organizations including those of primitive societies (see page 799). Organizations differ greatly in the structures of their deciders, considerable variation being found even within the same type. Religious organizations, for example, vary in this subsystem from highly formalized structures with many echelons to informal structures with few. I have already said that Hypothesis 1-1 (see page 92) appears in general to apply to organizations (see page 595). It states that in general, the more components a system has, the more echelons it has.

Some types of organizations include separate executive, legislative, and judicial components in their decider structures. This is true of organized communities and many higher political jurisdictions, as well as professional associations like the American Bar Association, the American Psychological Association, and the American Medical Association.

One analysis of the echelon structure of industrial organizations, that of Blake and Mouton, includes the following eight levels:

Level 1: Chairman of the Board, persons with supraorganization responsibilities.

Level 2: President and vice presidents to whom more than one major organization segment report.

Level 3: Vice presidents and department managers responsible for the operation of a single major function with multiple units.

Level 4: General manager responsible for a region or for a large operating unit, *i.e.,* a factory, a sales division, overall responsibility for an R&D [research and development] facility, and those reporting directly to the general manager or regional executive. Typical supervisory titles included might be Regional Sales Manager, General Manager, Assistant General Manager, Products Manager, Coordination Manager, Administrative Manager, Technical Manager.

Level 5: Department and assistant department heads in headquarters locations (staff or line) and department and assistant heads in field locations (staff or line) generally fall into Level 5. Typical supervisory titles are Area Sales Manager, Operating Superintendent, M&C [mechanical and construction] Superintendent, Technical Superintendent, Department Head—Technical, Service Laboratory Head, Division Engineer, Chief Accountant, Head of Business Services, Employee Relations Manager, Purchasing Agent, Department Head R&D. Typical professional titles are Engineering Associate, Research Associate, Assistant to Administrative Manager.

Level 6: Section and unit heads and other senior supervisory personnel reporting to department level in either headquarters or field. Typical supervisory titles include Head of Section, General Foreman, Assistant Chief Accountant, Section Head—Employee relations, Section Head—Purchasing, Zone Supervisor—M&C, Section Head—Technical, Section Head—R&D, Senior Supervisor Engineer; typical professional titles include Senior Staff Engineer, Senior Research Specialist, Physician.

Level 7: Second line supervisors, those to whom more than one direct work supervisor reports and who, in turn, report to a section head or his equivalent in either headquarters or field installations. Typical supervisory titles include Foreman or Assistant Foreman—Operations, Section Head—Accounting, Head of Plant Services, Craft Foreman—M&C, Assistant Zone Supervisor—M&C, Foreman—M&C, Technical [supervisor]—R&D. Typical professional titles include Senior Professional, Senior Engineer, Assistant Cost Engineer, Coordination Specialist, Senior Research Chemist.

Level 8: Those responsible for the direct supervision of work. Typical supervisory titles include Group Head—Accounting, (Group) (Section) Supervisor, Area Supervisor—M&C, Supervisor—Technical. Typical professional titles include Engineer, Assistant Engineer, Senior P/R Assistant.[101]

Deciders of organizations are commonly described as being pyramidal in shape, with many components at the lowest echelon and fewer at each higher one. This is not always the case, however, as Gross has pointed out. He describes octagonal and even pentagonal shapes in which the middle levels of the system—a bombing squadron is an example—have proliferated, while the lower levels have declined in number of components.[102] It is also usual, he says, to find an inverted pyramid above the traditional pyramid. In this sort of structure, the "top executives" occupy a position at the point where the two pyramids come together. Above them Gross places three echelons, the highest of which he calls the "holders of ultimate authority." This echelon includes stockholders of corporations, members of associations, and voters. Organizations like trade associations, whose components are other organizations, have these as their ultimate authority. In organizations where ultimate authority is held by members or workers, as in a workers' cooperative or a democratically governed city, members of lower echelons are found also at the highest echelon. In a city, the garbage collector is also a voter and as such has a voice in selecting the mayor.

Below this highest echelon are representatives of the ultimately responsible group, such as boards of directors and city councils. Below these is a level Gross calls "directorates," which includes executive committees. Of decider structures Gross says:

There are interesting size variations. In some organizations—particularly the smallest—there may be no upper pyramid at all. In others all three levels may be concentrated into a small directorate. In a family-owned corporation the holders of ultimate authority may indeed be fewer in number than the members of the directorate—in which case we once again have a pyramid-type structure resting on its base rather than its apex. With universities and hospitals, likewise, there may be but two levels: a large board of governors, which holds the ultimate authority, and a smaller directorate. With many associations, the inverted pyramid at the top of the structure may be gigantic in comparison with the relatively small pyramidal structure of employed staff.[103]

The pyramidal structure has the advantage of bringing many components under the control of the top echelon of the decider. An eight-echelon structure can suffice for huge organizations. Gross has found few with as many as 10 and none with more than 12.[104] Pyramids differ also in number of components at each echelon. Some are "fat," with few echelons and relatively more components at each, while others are "thin."

A formal table of organization showing the echelon structure of any system at this level is rarely, if ever, an accurate picture of the working decider structure. Like the communications network, the decider ordinarily has informal as well as formal components, and as a result of adjustment processes to internal information flows, the distribution of power, authority, and responsibility among the formally recognized components may be different from that envisioned in the organization chart (see page 646). The length of the lines of control between a decider component and those over whom he exercises authority may differ also in organizations with similar echelon structures. In some organizations, the central decider is connected to components all the way down in the echelon structure. In others, lines are shorter, perhaps reaching down only two or three echelons.

Structure, by my definition (see page 22), is the spatial arrangement of components. Organizational components, lacking as they are in physical cohesiveness, do not maintain spatial arrangements in the same way as systems at the level of the organism and below. They are connected by formal organizational channels, represented by the lines in tables of organization and also informal channels, but their actual arrangement in space is only slightly, if at all, similar to the design of the table of organization. An effort is usually made to minimize the actual physical distance between components directly related in the authority structure. Often their offices are adjacent. Physical separation of parts of an organization ordinarily increases as systems grow, and this separation commonly is associated with greater segregation of the decider, although this is not invariably the case (see pages 699 and 700 and Hypothesis 5.4.3-2, page 109).

Three types of organization of the decider were found by Woodward in her sample of industrial firms.[105] These are reflected in the arrangement of components, as shown in the organization chart. The three types are (*a*) line organization, (*b*) functional organization, and (*c*) line-staff organization.

"Line" personnel are those directly responsible for end results. In a factory these are the people who are accountable for the quality and other aspects of the product. In an army, they command men in the field. "Staff" positions provide support and service to the line. (*a*) Line organization (see Fig. 10-5) exists in a

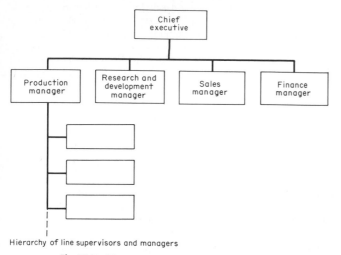

Hierarchy of line supervisors and managers

Fig. 10-5   Line organization. (From J. Woodward. *Industrial organization: theory and practice.* London: Oxford Univ. Press, 1965, 101. *Reprinted by permission of The Clarendon Press, Oxford.*)

decider in which the channels of control lead directly from the chief executive or executives at the top echelon of the organization to the immediate subordinates and from them to lower echelons and workers. There is little or no specialization in such a system. A modified form provides departments organized on a task basis. Thirty-five firms in Woodward's sample were of this kind. (*b*) Functional organization (see Fig. 10-6) divides the task of the organization into separate skills and places one component in control of each. In this type of system the classic rule that each man have only one supervisor does not apply, so that the lines of authority connect several specialized supervisors with a single worker. Only two of Woodward's firms had this type. In one, the departmental managers received direct executive instructions from five divisional managers, each a specialist in one particular part of the organization's task. (*c*) Line-staff organization (see Fig. 10-7) developed as a compromise which provides for use of special skills and at the same time maintains the hierarchy of authority linking each individual subcomponent with one superior. Functionalized staff departments work through a line supervisor. Fifty-nine of Woodward's firms had this type of decider structure.

A multiple overlapping group form of decider structure is recommended by Likert to provide for effective use of his "System 4" management system.[106] Figure 10-8 is a chart illustrating this structure for a highly functionalized industrial organization manufacturing consumer products. The work groups are made up of people from different departments who could be expected to deal effectively with the particular problems of some aspect of the organization's task.

Upwardly dispersed components of the decider subsystem are rare. When a firm is in receivership, the top echelon of the decider may be replaced for a time by components appointed by a court, which constitutes upward dispersal of the subsystem to the level of the society. In some organizations the decider components that select the board or chief executive are components of the suprasystem decider, like a president or king. This is an upwardly dispersed part of the decider.

Management firms sometimes administer small organizations like apartment houses for a fee, hiring and firing the people who work there and managing the money for the owners. They are components of an outwardly dispersed decider subsystem.

Laterally dispersed decider subsystems are very common, since it is rare for a single person or group to control all aspects of an organization's process. As I have just indicated, laterally dispersed decision making carried out by groups is recommended by Likert.

Downwardly dispersed components are sometimes found in organizations when a single human subcomponent rather than a group represents the subsystem. This is the case when a hereditary duke controls all aspects of the decider of a city or region or when a single man dominates a corporation and makes all its decisions.

Computers are increasingly used artifacts in the analytic and synthetic processes of decider subsystems of organizations.

3.3.7.2 Process   The decider processes of organizations include the development of purposes, goals, and procedures as well as the direction of subsystem processes to implement the system's purposes and goals. In carrying out these processes, decider components adjust organizational inputs and outputs; allocate resources, including money, artifacts, and human subsystem components; set standards for task performance; evaluate the performance of human and other components; determine and administer rewards and punishments; develop plans; solve problems related to all organizational processes; resolve intraorganizational conflicts; and direct the organization's relationships with other systems, including human inclusions

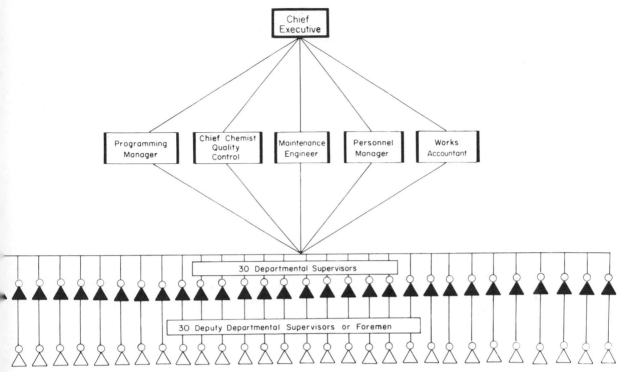

Fig. 10-6   Functional organization. (From J. Woodward. *Industrial organization: theory and practice.* London: Oxford Univ. Press, 1965, 119. *Reprinted by permission of The Clarendon Press, Oxford.*)

like students, patients, or hotel guests. Because systems at this level are man-made, changes in subsystem structure are among the possible activities of decider components.

The decider exercises power over all components (see page 38), being responsible and held accountable for events throughout the system. I shall discuss in turn the various sorts of power relationships in organizations; the distribution of power, authority, and influence among organizational components; and the four stages of the deciding process (see Hypothesis 3.3.7.2-1, page 100) as they are carried out in organizations.

Power, authority, and influence.   I have defined *power* as the ability of a system to elicit compliance from other systems (see page 38). Power is exercised both within organizations and by organizations over other systems in the environment such as groups, organisms, and other organizations. Use of power is fundamental to the processes of police departments, armies, courts, and other regulatory agencies in their activities as subsystem components of societies. Foundations, banks, and loan companies also exert power through their command of assets. Foundations, for example,

participate in decisions about which researches will be carried out in universities by funding some projects rather than others.

One analysis of different types of organizations in terms of the rewards and punishments they use to control their members or employees divides the power exercised into coercive, utilitarian, and identitive.[107] Coercive power involves the use of physical means to achieve compliance. Utilitarian power is gained by the use of payments that can be exchanged for goods and services or by the use of the goods and services themselves. Identitive power is achieved by granting symbolic rewards such as symbols of prestige, esteem, love, and acceptance. Such power is exercised when those higher in rank use an individual's identification with his peer group to control him, as a teacher may do in a classroom.

Within a given type of organization, individual organizations differ in how they wield power to elicit compliance from their components.[108] Labor unions, for example, sometimes use coercive power and sometimes base their power upon their ability to get wage increases and material benefits for their members. Still others use identitive power, such as identification

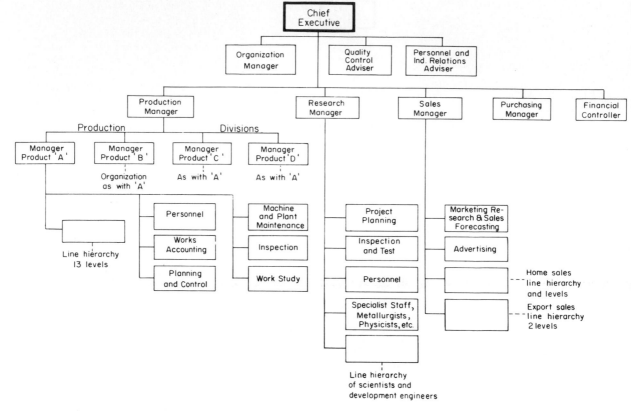

Fig. 10-7 Line-staff organization. (From J. Woodward. *Industrial organization: theory and practice.* London: Oxford Univ. Press, 1965, 108. *Reprinted by permission of The Clarendon Press, Oxford.*)

with a socialist ideology or informal pressure by a community of workers.

Coercive power exercised over organization members or employees is rare in today's world, but some organizations, such as some prisons and mental hospitals, use such power over the human beings included within their boundaries.

Utilitarian power is predominant in factories, insurance companies, banks, the civil service, and peacetime military organizations. Identitive power is predominant in religious organizations, ideological-political organizations, colleges and universities, voluntary associations, schools, and therapeutic mental hospitals.

Exercise of power is not confined to official decider components. "Lower participants," in Mechanic's terms, achieve power not associated with their formal positions by obtaining, maintaining, and controlling "access to persons, information, and instrumentali-

ties."[109] By establishing and manipulating dependency of high-ranking participants upon them, such people gain power over organizational processes. An example of such a relationship is the dependency of an overloaded ward physician upon ward attendants who receive increased power in making decisions concerning the patients in exchange for taking over part of the physician's duties. Some other sources of such dependency are expert knowledge and willingness to exert effort in an area in which higher participants are uninterested. Some of the power of secretaries to make decisions comes from the delegation to them of responsibility for such things as ordering and allocating supplies and handling complaints. A person's attractiveness, central location in physical space, and position in the communication channels are also important in establishing access and dependency. Mechanic suggests four hypotheses (H6 through H9) concerning these sorts of power relationships:

H6: Other factors remaining constant, there is a direct relationship between the amount of effort a person is willing to exert in an area and the power he can command.

H7: Other factors remaining constant, the less effort and interest higher-ranking participants are willing to devote to a task, the more likely are lower participants to obtain power relevant to the task.

H8: Other factors remaining constant, the more attractive a person, the more likely he is to obtain access to persons and control over these persons.

H9: Other factors remaining constant, the more central a person is in an organization, the greater is his access to persons, information, and instrumentalities.[110]

Authority. When power is accepted as legitimate by both the transmitter and the receiver of command information, the transmitter or wielder of power exercises authority (see page 38). The authority held by components of some organizations, typically those which are parts of modern industrialized societies, is generally considered, following Weber's analyses, an attribute of a particular position in the subsystem structure of the organization occupied by the component.[111] In armies the salute is given to the uniform and insignia, not to the man wearing them. When a group or individual holding a position is replaced, the right to exercise authority is transferred to the new in-

cumbents or incumbent, along with the other rights and duties of the position. Authority in some other types of organizations is at least partly an attribute of a particular group or individual, derived from hereditary succession, personal magnetism, or supposed supernatural election. When such a component is deposed or replaced, some of his right to exercise authority remains with him. A defrocked priest may be a priest still, although forbidden by the church organization to use his power. A nobleman still commands obedience from loyalists among his countrymen after the republicans have exiled him.

Organizational components who are professionally trained lawyers, doctors, holders of Ph.D. degrees, or other such specialists differ from nonprofessional employees in the source and exercise of their authority.[112] Because of their training, professional persons are expected to have a body of knowledge not held by people untrained in their specialty and to adhere to a code of ethics governing their conduct. Other members of the same profession can make professional judgments about them but no one else is considered to have this capability. When professionals are employed in nonprofessional organizations, the con-

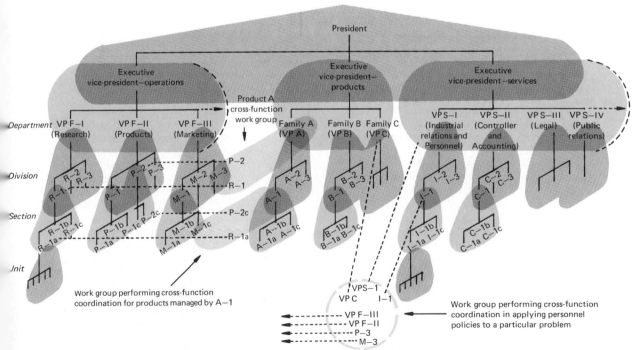

Fig. 10-8 Multiple overlapping group structure. (From R. Likert. *The human organization.* New York: McGraw-Hill, 1967, 168–169. *Reprinted by permission.*)

flict between bureaucratic and professional orientation is a fundamental issue.[113] It may be that a professional orientation motivates one to do a better quality of work, but it also can give one a reason for ignoring administrative constraints and so lead one to act in ways that decrease overall organizational efficiency. Since more and more professionals are working in bureaucratic organizations, the conflicts as to how authority shall be exercised in such agencies are mounting.

Influence is a more pervasively exercised power relationship. It exists whenever one system is able to bring about significant alterations in the actions of another system over which it may or may not have the right to exercise authority. Influence flows laterally as well as up and down in the echelon structure of an organization. Peers commonly influence one another, often reciprocally. Influence may be exercised in subtle and unrecognized ways. This sort of power of people over each other appears to be a part of all interpersonal relationships (see pages 570 to 572). When it is exerted to affect organizational decisions, the component exerting the influence is, formally or informally, a part of the organization's decider process. Influence is the only kind of power held by any component in some organizations, such as small social or recreational institutions whose officers have no real authority.

The different sorts of power relationships are not mutually exclusive. A position of authority increases its holder's influence and may make it possible for him to elicit compliance in some circumstances from components over which he has no direct authority. Some trade-off is usually assumed to be a part of any power relationship. That is, the relationship is symbiotic. In return for a salary and fringe benefits, status, privileges of various sorts, or other rewards appropriate to a particular organization, a person accepts the authority of the organization's decider and agrees to participate in the system's processes in a manner appropriate to the position he or she will occupy. Influence relationships also include rewards, usually less tangible, like approval, friendship, and a feeling of importance or the opportunity for advancement in the organization.

Power usually also involves sanctions for failure to comply. Threats of possible physical punishment, arrest and detention, loss of approval or status, diminished pay, fines, expulsion from the organization, and other penalties are used in different kinds of organizations to enforce the power of the decider (see pages 645 to 647). Sanctions can also be imposed by people upon whom decider components become dependent. For example, in one case when a physician failed to

honor an agreement he had made with ward attendants, their refusal to cooperate deprived him of necessary information and help with paperwork and slowed down his ward activities.[114] The amount of power held by organizations over their employees or members varies. Some political or religious organizations demand absolute control over even intimate aspects of the lives of their adherents, and military organizations require that a man be willing to risk his life for the organization's purposes. On the other hand, some charitable organizations ask only an annual voluntary contribution.

Distribution of power in organizations. Two organizations with similar officially designated positions often have greatly differing distributions of power. This is true, for example, when a president is weak or a figurehead and the processes appropriate to his office are carried out at the echelon below. At any time the effective decider subsystem includes the components that actually do the deciding regardless of their official titles.

Particular sorts of decisions are characteristic of the different echelons of organizations. Decisions concerning the purposes, goals, and fundamental procedures of the system, that is policy decisions, are ordinarily made by the highest echelons, as Hypothesis 3.3.7.2-13 (see page 101) suggests. The highest levels deal with problems in the greatest generality, often with long-range plans far into the future. Stockholders or voting members of organizations have a voice in broad general policies by their choice of executive personnel. Boards of directors and top executives ordinarily form specific policies. Their decisions are general and affect the behavior of many components. They are expected to consider long-range effects. They commit the organization over long periods and are not subject to immediate or detailed review.

Lower echelons make decisions designed to implement policy and achieve organizational goals and purposes. Usually much of what they do is preprogrammed and the scope ordinarily is limited to a specific aspect of organizational process. Their concerns are much more specific and more immediate in time and locale than those of the higher echelons. The power of lower echelons is ordinarily considered to be delegated. Responsibility for outcomes remains with the delegating component. This is true also of the overlapping group form of organization, in which group members make decisions about the aspects of the system's work that are delegated to them (see page 644 and Fig. 10-8).

The basic responsibility and accountability which accompany decision making in organizations do not rest with all group members but are almost universally held to reside at the highest echelon. As Likert says: "The superior is accountable for all decisions, for their execution, and for the results."[115] This principle represents fundamental and explicit doctrine of all military organizations and most civilian ones. Nevertheless, because each echelon has its role in the decision process, it is in practice difficult to pin down accountability. A basic reason for this is that at each echelon distortions often occur both in command messages flowing downward and in reports flowing upward. An historic example of such distortion apparently was responsible for the My Lai massacre of innocent Vietnamese civilians by American troops in 1968. Reporters said that in the American army at that time orders tended to be more and more broadly interpreted as they were passed from echelon to echelon down the chain of command. On the basis of firsthand knowledge Faas and Arnett have written:

A reporter was present at a hamlet burned down by the U.S. Army's 1st Air Cavalry Division in 1967. Investigation showed that the order from the division headquarters to the brigade was: "On no occasion must hamlets be burned down."
The brigade radioed the battalion: "Do not burn down any hamlets unless you are absolutely convinced that the Viet Cong are in them."
The battalion radioed the infantry company at the scene: "If you think there are any Viet Cong in the hamlet, burn it down."
The company commander ordered his troops: "Burn down that hamlet."[116]

General Motors is the second largest company in the United States (see page 692). In 1952 its top policy was made by the board of directors, especially two committees of the board having to do with operations policy and financial policy.[117] Ten policy groups, each headed by an executive in the central office staff whose function was related to the interests of the group, discussed policy questions and made recommendations concerning policy in their special areas, sending them to the operations policy committee. The president was chairman of this committee. The structural relationships of the policy-forming components of General Motors are shown in Fig. 10-9.

Management theory, developed originally to increase the productivity and efficiency of industrial and business organizations, has been concerned with finding the decider structure and processes most likely to ensure the success of organizations, particularly industrial corporations. An early period of search for principles that would provide general rules for administration resulted in such prescriptions as "one man, one supervisor," unity of command, matched authority and responsibility, the necessity of delegation of authority, and an optimal span of control of five or six subordinates to one supervisor.[118] These prescriptions were not entirely satisfactory in practice.[119] At the Hawthorne plant of Western Electric (see page 675), making changes to conform to such administrative principles did less to raise productivity than improving interpersonal relationships did.

Study of functioning organizations has indicated that no single management system is best for all industrial firms. Two quite different sorts of management were identified by Burns and Stalker in their study of a number of British and Scottish firms.[120] "Mechanistic" organizations shred out their tasks into distinct subtasks to be carried out by persons or groups as though they were subcontracting for that part of the work. "Somebody at the top" sees to the relevance of each job. Technical methods, duties, and powers are defined, and operations and working behavior are governed by the decisions and instructions of superiors. Within management, interaction is vertical, between superior and subordinate, with the top echelon, perhaps only one person, having knowledge of all parts of the system. In such a structure, familiar in organization charts (see page 643), information flows upward through a succession of filters and decider echelons, and instructions flow downward. In this series of studies such decision making appeared to be appropriate for an enterprise operating under relatively stable conditions.

"Organic" systems, on the other hand, lack formal definition of methods, duties, and powers. These are continually reevaluated in the course of interactions. In such a system, workers must see their jobs in the light of the operation of the firm as a whole, and top management cannot be regarded as omniscient. Such decision making is well adapted to unstable conditions, when problems arise which cannot be assigned among the specialists in a clearly defined hierarchy.

In her study of South Essex industrial firms, Woodward made similar findings.[121] Success and failure in the large batch production firms she studied (see pages 617 to 619) depended on mechanistic management methods in which the duties of components were clearly defined on paper. This was the procedure in all the successful firms and none of the unsuccessful ones. Those large batch production firms which followed such management prescriptions as unity of command, separation (at least on paper) of advisory from executive responsibilities, and control by an executive of no more than five or six direct subordinates survived and flourished. In the companies at the extremes of Woodward's scale of technological complexity, i.e., those using unit and process production, management was organic.[122]

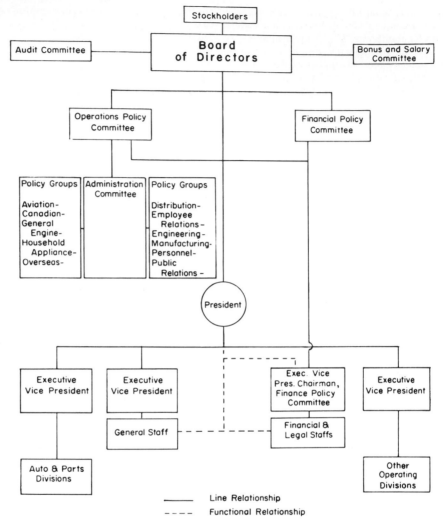

Fig. 10-9   Structure of policy-forming components of General Motors Corporation. (From E. Dale. *Planning and developing the company organization structure.* New York: American Management Associations, 1952, 141. *Reprinted by permission.*)

Requirements of the production process appeared to explain these observed differences. In unit production, difficulties of control and prediction made necessary a wider area of discretion for individuals at every echelon. Detailed organization of the work, including considerable planning and control, was left to foremen.[123] Process plants were highly automated.[124] Much of the planning and implementing was incorporated in the design of the plants. The job of production personnel was to keep them running as near to full capacity as possible. Process control, performance evaluation, and initiation of corrective actions were also facilitated by the design of these plants.

A number of theorists recommend particular methods or styles of management. One such style Likert calls "System 4." This management method is the one he prefers, being related to his overlapping-group type of structure (see page 644). But the two are not inseparable. Likert analyzes management methods into four types, which range from extremely authoritarian (System 1) to one that gives a large share of deciding to work groups (System 4).[125] Management styles are conceptualized by Blake and Mouton as being arranged on a grid covering a gamut from authoritarian (9,1) to sympathetic (9,9).[126] Theory Y of McGregor is similar to System 4 and management style 9,9 (see page 678). These are prescriptions for conduct of human relations within an organization. As such, they are relevant to the adjustment processes of organizations.

Stages of deciding process. As at other levels of living systems, the deciding process appears to go through the four stages mentioned in Hypothesis 3.3.7.2-1 (see page 100):

(a) *Establishing purposes or goals.* An organization comes into being to carry out specific subsystem processes in the society of which it is a component. Its original *purposes,* defined as preferences for particular internal steady states (see pages 34 to 37), are given in its charter or in laws of the society that apply to it. They differ among organizational types. Industrial organizations usually prefer steady states that result in output of the best possible product or services at the highest possible profit to the system. They consider other variables also, like the welfare and satisfaction of their employees and their contribution to the well-being of the society as a whole. Mutual-benefit associations (see page 600) have decision rules that primarily maximize steady states in which the satisfaction of members is as high as possible.

These purposes can change over time as a result of rewards or punishments from the suprasystem. Changing attitudes and hairstyles of black Americans, for example, reduced the profits of a company manufacturing a hair straightener. Consequently, it adjusted its subsystem processes to making and outputting conditioners for the newly popular natural hairstyles, which feature the very curl that had previously been considered undesirable.[127] It is difficult to change purposes in charitable or educational systems with endowment funds restricted by deed or gift to narrow uses. A Society for Improving the Condition of Decayed Gentlewomen has little relevance to current social needs, but it may have difficulty in changing its purposes legally.

As living systems, organizations seek to maintain steady states of their variables in changing environments. This implies a purpose of survival. Ordinarily a decision that would cause the organization to terminate, at least before the time specified in its template, will be avoided. In some sorts of organizations, preservation of structure and process without significant change becomes a purpose that is sometimes disastrous for the system.[128] In such organizations, bureaucratic survival is often put ahead of the major goals of the system, and the top executives lose their flexibility. Hypothesis 3.3.7.2-11 (see page 101), which suggests that the longer a decider exists, the more likely it is to resist change, may be relevant here.

Subsidiary purposes exist which require adjustment of internal subsystem relationships by decider components of the organization. For instance, conflicts among components at times threaten the overall goals of the organization, as when the production manager fails to cooperate with the sales manager and output is impaired. Such a conflict can be resolved by reference to a comparison signal involving the preferred state and by cooperative setting of subsystem goals.

Organizations have hierarchies of values which generate hierarchies of purposes, subpurposes, and subsubpurposes. Preferred states of internal variables may be different with reference to long and short time spans, with the result that there are long- and short-term purposes, as there are long- and short-term goals.

The external *goals* (see page 39) of organizations in relation to their environments are as various as the functions of the many types of systems at this level. An organization usually has many goals simultaneously. They include general goals, like putting a man on the moon, representing the majority of workers in an industry, or building a ward heeler into a nationally recognized politician, and specific goals, like developing an effective heat shield for a spacecraft, organizing the workers in a particular plant, or getting a client elected to the state assembly. The long-term goals of organizations may conflict with their short-term goals. This can occur if a profit goal for a single year depends upon taking actions that diminish the probability of attainment of a long-term goal of stability. Hypothesis 3.3.7.2-16 (see page 101) states that the deciders of a system's subsystems and components satisfice shorter-term goals than the decider of the total system does. Decisions about goal conflicts of either this or other sorts must be made at high echelons, in accordance with Hypothesis 3.3.7.2-13 (see page 101), which says that decisions overtly altering major values of a system are made only at the highest echelon.

The separate components of complex organizations have distinct purposes and goals, which are ordinarily intended to further the goals of the total system. In segregated systems such components may be in competition with one another, and their goals may be mutually antagonistic. Several breakfast cereals made by the same industrial giant, each with its own advertising campaigns and salesmen, may compete to capture the largest share of the market. These goals further a goal of the total organization to sell more cereal of all kinds than its competitors.

Observations of organizations, say Cyert and March, do not support the view that an organization ordinarily has a single, consistent set of goals.[129] More commonly it has a number of different goals, some of which may be in conflict.

One of the means of dealing with the conflict engendered by the multiple goals is to use aspiration-level goals (see page 681), rather than maximizing or minimizing goals. For example, a company might state that in the next year, "profits must exceed $27 million," rather than set the policy that "profits should be maximized." An aspiration-level goal does not demand such consistent striving as a maximization goal. It does not demand that executives and workers exploit the environment remorselessly, and it permits the organization to conserve some resources to make up for small failures, errors, and inconsistencies.

When the highest echelon of an organization selects a goal, a path toward it must be specified, according to Buck.[130] This path becomes the goal of the next lower echelon, and the path to that goal is the goal of the echelon below. Buck uses the example of a company which hopes to earn a profit for its stockholders by the manufacture and sale of chrome-plated widgets. Figure 10-10 shows the goals and paths in this process.

Questions on goal orientation were included in the study of six plastics firms mentioned above (see page 624).[131] The investigators predicted that managers of each of the four functional departments—sales, production, applied research, and fundamental research—would differ in their goals. These managers were asked about their concern with nine different decision-making criteria: three about the market, three technoeconomic, and three scientific. Examples of the criteria are the probable response of competitors to the decision, the plant facilities required by the decision, and the effect of the decision on contributions to scientific knowledge. The expected difference was found. Sales personnel were concerned primarily with customer problems, competitive activities, and other events in the marketplace. Manufacturing personnel were interested primarily in cost reduction, process efficiency, and similar matters. Research personnel were not so wholeheartedly concerned with science as had been predicted, and they showed more concern with technoeconomic factors, like improvements for cost reduction and quality control. These factors, however, were directly related to their task of product improvement.

Goals of organizations change over time. A particular goal may be achieved, or it may become evident that the organization cannot meet it. Managers of industries and factories often set annual or semiannual goals for sales of a product and gear their production to them. Changes in economic variables of the society can cause these to be revised. In her study of industrial organizations, Woodward found that there was a tendency in the batch and intermittent production firms for objectives to change in an unplanned, purposeless way.[132] Over a period of time subsidiary objectives became primary objectives, and the purposes of the firm changed, with no specific policy decisions being made at the board level. This appeared to result from the "fragmentation" of planning that occurred when the responsible chief executive delegated much of the deciding on production matters to specialist departments. Decisions about quality, quantity, time, and cost were made by various people at different times, presumably in accordance with a master plan and supposedly integrated by the chief executive. The plan was usually more myth than reality. In these firms, however, the specialist departments operated independently or even in isolation. General policy directives emanating from

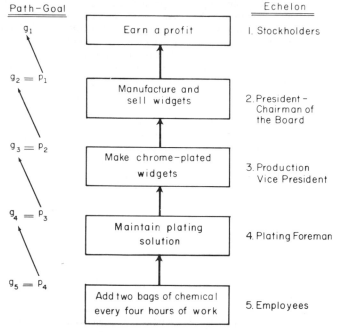

Fig. 10-10 Examples of paths becoming goals. Key: g = goal; p = path. [From V. E. Buck. A model for viewing an organization as a system of constraints. In J. D. Thompson (Ed.). *Approaches to organizational design*. Pittsburgh: Univ. of Pittsburgh Press, 1966, 116. *Reprinted by permission of the University of Pittsburgh Press.* © 1966 by the University of Pittsburgh Press.]

the board were interpreted separately by each. What is more, in this type of production there were no fixed periods at which appraisal and redefinition of objectives took place, as there were in special-order and continuous-flow production. In special-order production the periods were relatively short. In process production they were much longer. In batch and intermittent production even planned changes came about chiefly in response to internal strains. The primary objective became the survival of the firm rather than production of specific goods or provision of services. Decisions about production were part of the strategy of keeping the firm going. Fragmentation of the planning also resulted in subsidiary objectives that were in conflict with one another. When line supervisors could not meet schedules and maintain quality at the same time or keep within the standard costs, they were the ones who determined which was more important.

Seven kinds of performance objectives (purposes and goals) for organizations are listed by Gross: " . . . activities to (1) satisfy the varying interests of people and groups by (2) producing outputs of services or goods, (3) making efficient use of inputs relative to outputs, (4) investing in the system, (5) acquiring resources, and (6) doing all these things in a manner that conforms with various codes of behavior and (7) varying conceptions of technical and administrative rationality."[133] Each of these includes a number of subobjectives. Satisfying interests, for example, breaks down into three groups whose interests an organization might want to serve: members, clients, and others. Producing output includes providing a satisfactory output mix, as well as quantity, quality, and rate of output flow.

Examination of specific types of organizations can provide insights into organizational goals and purposes. Take a university, for example. What can be its goals and purposes?

One class of goals concerns meeting the demands of the community and society of which it is a part, its suprasystem. A university graduates educated ladies and gentlemen. Or perhaps it produces married, socialized ladies and gentlemen, which is a different thing. Perhaps it graduates useful citizens or contributing workers. Perhaps it produces leaders who, instead of conforming to the society, irritate it and its establishment. It may graduate all these types.

Maybe a goal of a university is to achieve a proper conformity–innovation ratio between itself and the society, and perhaps universities are therefore always out of phase with society. The hope of somehow getting a university to conform to its environment may be mistaken, since any organization that leads cannot, by definition, so conform. Perhaps the main goal of a university is to produce ideas. Or it may be to meet the special demands of the trustees or regents, the alumni, the students, the government, or the church.

A university may strive to meet internal purposes. These may be intellectual—to improve the accuracy, speed, or completeness of its information flows; to maximize the cost-effectiveness ratio of its information flows; to speed the rate of learning of the average student, the best student, or the minimal student; to increase the generality of students' learning or the depth of their specializations; to expand the number of scholarships or the amount of research; or to increase the amount of faculty time devoted to teaching. Or the purposes may be social—to increase the time students spend with people in the university who are known personally to them, the number of student-faculty contacts, or the number of student-student contacts. Perhaps one purpose of a university is to advance the careers and improve the perquisites of the faculty, since the institution that neglects such matters entirely cannot keep a qualified faculty.

Obviously, these goals and purposes conflict in many ways. Any one of them can be maximized or minimized, and each of them has its costs. Until they are made specific, however, performance criteria cannot be rationally established, and decisions as to allocation of personnel, effort, and time will be largely arbitrary. Any organization's goals and purposes, of course, must constantly be reevaluated.

Goals of business and industrial organizations have interested economists and management scientists. The classical economic model describes such firms as maximizing profit in a perfectly competitive market (see pages 657 and 876). The organization is viewed as a single decision maker with the single goal of maximizing profit. As Feldman and Kanter explain, this statement is either imprecise and correct as a predictor of firm behavior or precise and wrong.[134] More accurate alternative models (see pages 657 and 658) recognize that more than one purpose or goal affects the decision making of firms, or they substitute other goals, such as the maximization of gross sales.

A study of the purposes and goals of business managements, as expressed by chief executives or deputy chiefs of 145 business establishments, revealed that the goals most frequently mentioned are profits, public service in the form of good products, employee welfare, and growth.[135] Some managers included other goals such as meeting or staying ahead of competitors and contributing to the community. Several responded with more than one goal.

In a confidential interview executives were asked, "What are the aims of top management in your company?'' Profit was mentioned by slightly more than one-half of the executives. This fraction might well have been larger if other goals were not considered to be more socially acceptable. A significant relationship was found between the number of employees in the business and mention of the goal ''public service in the form of good products.'' The number of managers who included this goal was larger in the organizations with a greater number of employees. Possibly the larger firms were better established and more in the public eye and so felt the need to be public-spirited. Executives of large businesses in which the employees were organized were more likely to mention employee welfare than managers of smaller ones, even if they were unionized. More professional managers than owner-managers of unionized companies mentioned this goal. The nature of the labor force influenced some goals. Fewer managers of white-collar than of blue-collar establishments mentioned profits as a goal, and managers of white-collar firms mentioned growth.

(b) Analysis

Free flow of information. If there is to be effective governance of subsystems, complete and undistorted information relevant to the decisions that are to be made must reach the decider. If the channels from input or internal transducers are blocked or if deciders in the net filter or distort information, analysis cannot reflect all dimensions of the situation. Free flow of ideas, criticisms, and advice contributes to problem solving in other ways as well.[136] Consultation with other components of the organization's decider can provide support and mitigate anxiety that could block associations leading to solutions. When several people cooperate, the mistakes and blind spots of one person can be detected by the others. Competition for respect occurs during discussions and provides incentives for making good suggestions and criticizing those which seem poor. Since network studies with groups indicate that restrictions on communication are necessary for efficient coordination (see page 539), the opposing requirements of coordination and problem solving create a dilemma with which the organization must constantly live.

Organizational components responsible for a particular decider function such as allocation of funds or solution of a specific problem are likely to be most effective if they include those who have specialized knowledge or experience related to the general class of decisions of which this is an example. Decentralization of the deciding process often provides such specialization. The overlapping-group form of decider structure (see page 644) explicitly provides for consti-

tuting problem-oriented groups of organizational components that can be expected to contribute toward solutions, gathering them from different parts of the organization. Hypothesis 3.3.7.2-5 (see page 100) concerns the effect of experience upon deciding. It suggests that, up to a limit, the longer a system has been making decisions of a certain sort, the less time each decision takes. This seems likely to be confirmable for organizational deciders.

Evaluation. Study of feedbacks about the system's current state of attainment of purposes and goals is a necessary first stage of analysis: ''Where are we now?'' and ''Where do we want to go?'' For the broader, more general goals, like ''raising the standards of professional care in the community'' or ''providing a quality education for disadvantaged young people,'' the criteria for judging the system's present state may not be immediately evident. For more specific goals, like ''increasing the membership by 20 percent in this calendar year,'' the criteria are often obvious. In the more general case, the goals must be made sufficiently specific to be measured and compared with the goals of other, similar systems. Usually some external standard is available as a comparison signal (see page 36) against which feedback from the system's achievements can be evaluated. Hospitals undertake studies of treatment outcomes, including autopsy studies to check the accuracy of diagnoses, comparing their statistics with those derived from similar studies of other institutions. Mental hospitals calculate the percentage of patients able to return to the community and the percentage that later relapse. The educational and professional success of graduates indicates to a school or college how well it is achieving its educational goals. Commercial and industrial organizations assemble reports at regular intervals to keep management informed of the success of their pursuit of the goals of profit, sales, and market share. All organizations have feedbacks from the suprasystem in the form of increased or decreased sales and acceptance of products or services, rising or falling numbers of applicants for membership, praise or complaints, evidence of improved or worsened status, or other indicators.

In order to evaluate how well any system is attaining its specific purposes and goals, it is essential to obtain operational measures of performance. Suppose that a grade school principal was considering whether the physical education program of his school was accomplishing its fundamental purposes and immediate goals or whether it should be altered in some way. He might proceed to restate the purposes and goals as follows:

Purpose A: To develop physical skills and fitness to the extent of each pupil's ability. *Specific Goal A:* To achieve a mean score for the students in the top 25 percent on the physical-fitness screening test of New York State.

Purpose B: To provide wide experience in sports to students, both as players and as leaders. *Specific Goal B:* To have each student develop skill in three team sports and five individual sports or activities.

Purpose C: To develop the leadership attributes of courage, self-control, sportsmanship, aggressiveness, poise, and perseverance. *Specific Goal C:* To have each student advance, from the beginning of the school year to the end, 10 points on a leadership rating scale filled out by his fellow students.

Purpose D: To provide outlets for physical activity. *Specific Goal D:* To have each student exercise for a minimun of a half hour a day outside of school hours.

When goals are operationalized in this way, measures which analyze achievement can be developed.

If information reaching the decider from inside or outside the system signals a significant deviation of a process from the comparison signals representing particular purposes or goals or if a threat is signaled from the environment, control signals must be output from the decider to correct the deviation or meet the threat. The analysis stage of deciding includes gathering information relevant to an actual or imminent disturbance in steady state and discovering available adjustment processes. This stage is necessary for solving problems and meeting crises for which no readily applicable rule or standard procedure is available. It is also essential to routine decisions like those which continually allocate among competing components such resources of the system as time, space, energy, money, materials, artifacts, and human beings.

Each decision requires specific information about particular organizational structures and processes. To make decisions about subsystem adjustments, one must evaluate the effectiveness of components in contributing to the solution of the task of the system as a whole. Superiors are commonly held responsible for knowing how well each person under them is doing his work. In service organizations an important part of the evaluation comes from the public that is served in addition to that from members of the organization. Such evaluation reaches deciders by feedbacks such as spoken and written comments by clients or patrons as well as the amount of their patronage (see page 685). Voters of organized communities evaluate the public behavior of a mayor, legislator, or department head— his speeches, responses to their requests, financial statements, and decisions—according to their some-

times eccentric value systems. Their feedback is at the ballot box.

Evaluation of professional components of organizations can be a thorny problem. Colleges and universities, for example, must evaluate faculty and academic staff members for purposes of making promotions or determining salary and other rewards, but the commonly used indices—status in the field of competence and number of publications—provide no measure of teaching skill or ability to interact constructively with students. Some educational systems use ratings by students, a method that has its own built-in pitfalls. Others make no attempt at objective evaluation. Professionals employed in organizations, people like factory doctors and nurses, pose a dilemma because only colleagues trained in their specialty are really qualified to rate their performance, and so they can escape from the usual bureaucratic discipline.[137] Unless they are grossly unethical or incompetent, they are almost exempt from evaluation.

Cost-effectiveness accounting, by which the contributions of components are balanced against their costs, provides information useful in evaluation. This is straightforward enough for production or marketing divisions of an industrial organization. It is much more difficult for units that contribute indirectly to the total effort by, for example, increasing the satisfaction of human subcomponents. Cost-effectiveness calculations, Likert points out, should properly include "human asset accounting," assigning a reasonable value to variables like the number of experienced, long-term employees included in the department or division being evaluated.[138]

Search for alternative solutions. Given a precisely specified goal and a suitable objective measure for determining the extent to which it is being attained, the decider must attempt to discover whatever alternative paths to it exist. This involves search. Many organizational decisions require little prior search, only routine activation of previously learned programs or procedures that appear to apply. Other situations can be met by recombining or adapting existing programs. Unable to analyze easily the complexity of interrelated subsystem processes, the top echelon of the decider of large organizations often confines its activities almost wholly to selection from among stereotyped responses.[139] The decider of complex organizations cannot realistically deal with all relevant details and instead gives overall directions, employing general or holistic concepts, using or adapting existing programs, and expecting lower echelons to work out the applications to their own areas of responsibility. Top management may, for example, budget a dollar amount to component divisions or departments and allow specific suballocations to programs and persons to be made by the decider components at each echelon.

Only a relatively small proportion of decisions in established organizations (but more in new ones) require innovation. Organizations have a potential advantage over individual persons and groups in solving problems that require development of new programs or products because they have many people who can contribute creative, innovative ideas. It is probably unlikely that all such sources are ever tapped in large systems. I have already considered some sources of inputs of this kind (see page 624). One way of discovering alternatives of this sort is through the technique of "brainstorming." This is carried out in a group session in which free flows of ideas are encouraged. Whatever ideas are put forth are at first uncritically accepted, no matter how impractical or even foolish they may be. Among them may be some valuable suggestions. Later, at another session, they may be evaluated for practicality. Of course, organizations that have a constant need for innovations to keep abreast of the market in which they operate have specialized departments charged with research and development of new ideas, products, and procedures. Hypothesis 3.3.7.2-6 (see page 100) suggests that when the time for decision is short, search through the information network for relevant facts and alternatives is not thorough. This is probably true of organizations generally, particularly in times of crisis.

Organizational choice is exercised within a simplified "definition of the situation," according to the theory of rational choice of March and Simon.[140] This definition includes knowledge or assumptions about the future, about alternatives and their consequences, and about the preferences of the organization, as embodied in its value system or standard operating procedures.

Given the definition of the situation, the rules for search may reflect simple concepts of causality.[141] Initially, search may be guided by two rules: The first is to look for solutions closely related to the problem symptom. The second is to seek a new solution which is quite similar to the current alternative. These rules reflect the basic notions about causality that a cause is closely related to its effect and that a new solution will be found near in space-time to an old one. In accordance with the first rule, when some indication is gained that a goal is not being met or may not be met, the first search will be in the department identified with the goal. If sales are not reaching their goal, the search begins with the sales program. If no cause can

be found there, the search may be extended to price, product quality, and finally production costs. The second rule limits the consideration of radically new alternatives except when there is great urgency for a solution.

If these rules do not produce a solution, the organization may use more complex search, further from the problem, following a third rule: Search in organizationally vulnerable areas. If there is organizational slack, investigate the slack parts.

Organizations cannot, as a rule, pursue all their purposes and goals simultaneously because resources are limited. Determination of priorities is therefore an essential process of the highest echelons of the decider. An organization which wants to reach new customers by means of a special $100,000 advertising campaign over and above its regular publicity program but which must undertake a product change that will cost $100,000 for the campaign to be effective has to set up priorities if the total amount available for both goals is $100,000.[142] Such constraints are usual in organizations, since unlimited resources are essentially never available. Analysis of the above situation may show that the organization can either mass-produce a less excellent product and spend the money on the advertising campaign or use the money to redesign the product at a high standard of excellence and forgo the increased advertising. Another alternative may be to borrow the needed capital and do both.

(c) *Synthesis.* The way organizational deciders choose from among alternatives, decreasing the degrees of freedom of action, is similar to human deciding at the levels of the organism and the group (see pages 433 to 437 and 551 to 553). That is, the process conforms to some criterion of rationality, taking into account known or probable outcomes when information on them is available, as well as preferences, utilities, and values of the system. Logical or computational processes are performed upon the alternatives arrived at during the analytic phase of deciding. Increasingly computerized management information systems are being employed by governmental agencies, large corporations, and educational systems to collect and organize the data required to make such calculations (see page 626). By these means various alternatives are eliminated, and the subsequent course of decider activity is determined—either to enter the stage of implementation at once or to initiate further steps in a problem-solving sequence. Organizations do not necessarily reduce the number of alternatives to be adopted in a particular decision situation to a single one, since it is often practicable to undertake several different courses of action that contribute to a problem solution simultaneously, or even to authorize competitive attempts at solution by different components.

Plans and strategies (see pages 433 to 435) committing resources of the organization over time may be developed during the synthesis stage of deciding. Top-echelon deciders not infrequently divide problems into subproblems and assign these to different lower-echelon components, which must then undertake the analysis and subsequent solution of the part for which they are responsible.[143]

No decision is entirely rational or satisfactory, a fact which can give administrators some solace. There is no perfectly rational solution to most administrative problems. The higher the echelon, the truer this is of the issues which confront it. The dimensions along which many decisions must be made are incommensurable. Human lives are incommensurable with money. Money is incommensurable with time. Time is incommensurable with professional excellence. Yet all these are in scarce supply to a given organization, and trade-offs among them must be decided upon.

Furthermore, the needs and goals of the various components of an organization are different, and one can never satisfy them all. Ordinarily, one does not attempt a theoretical optimal solution; rather, one satisfices (see Hypothesis 3.3.7.2-16, page 101). The administrator is deluded if he thinks he optimizes, for he almost never does. He does well if the organization merely survives. That is all nature requires of organisms, and that is often all an administrator's reputation requires.

Theories about the stage of synthesis. Although economists and organization theorists are concerned with how deciding is carried out in organizations, little empirical evidence is available on this crucial stage of the process for most types of organizations, possibly because managing large organizations is still practiced as an art by administrators, who rarely subject their deliberations to scientific scrutiny.

Theoretical treatments of organizational deciding exist. They deal primarily with business or industrial corporations, but are often adaptable to some other types of organizations as well.

According to classical economic theory, the market of a society consists of "households" and "production units" or firms. The model assumes an ideal competitive economy in which each production unit is capable of producing alternative sets of goods or services.[144] It buys inputs and sells outputs. Prices are assumed to be perfectly known by all participants in the market.

In such an economy, production units choose to produce particular sets of goods or services for which

profit is not less than it would be for any other set. That is, they maximize profit in order to survive. The interactions of industrial corporations and households establish price equilibria (see pages 876 to 878). This model can be adapted to fit deciding within organizations viewed as miniature economies (see page 734). With variations for monopoly or oligopoly conditions (that is, if there is only one or at most a few sellers of a product) or for situations in which prices are not given, the model predicts quite well the profit-maximizing behavior of industrial organizations in different kinds of economic systems.

Whatever its value as economic theory, however, this is generally conceded to be an inadequate theory of organizational activity.[145] It does not, as indeed it was not intended to, model the internal decision making of a system with multiple goals and numerous decider components. Prices are ordinarily not set by the suprasystem of the organization in the way the theory envisions. Instead, the organization itself may set its prices. This may be done competitively, so that different organizations produce identical products differing only in price. Or agreements among them may reduce the competitiveness of the market in which they operate. Demands may be determined by outputs rather than the reverse (see pages 668 and 669). Maximization of profit as a rule governing choice among alternatives is unsatisfactory unless it is made so general that it amounts to a preference for more rather than less profit.[146] Firms must ordinarily be operated at a profit, except when they are subsidized by their suprasystem, but profits may be long- or short-term. Unprofitable components are often tolerated, particularly during periods of growth and development reducing the overall profit of the system, sometimes for several years. There is no basis for the theory's assumption that the organizational decider has perfect knowledge of alternatives and of payoffs. And, as I have indicated above, organizations do not optimize or maximize; rather, they satisfice.

Current theories attempt to provide more realistic descriptions of organizational decision making. One such description is provided by Cyert and March:

To all appearances, at least, uncertainty is a feature of organizational decision making with which organizations must live. In the case of the business firm, there are uncertainties with respect to the behavior of the market, the deliveries of suppliers, the attitudes of shareholders, the behavior of competitors, the future actions of governmental agencies, and so on. As a result, much of modern decision theory has been concerned with the problems of decision making under risk and under certainty. The solutions involved have been largely procedures for finding certainty equivalents (*e.g.*, expected value) or introducing rules for "living" with uncertainties (*e.g.*, game theory).

Our studies indicate quite a different strategy on the part of organizations. Organizations avoid uncertainty. They avoid uncertainty in two major ways. First, they avoid the requirement that they correctly anticipate events in the distant future by using decision rules emphasizing short-run reaction to short-run feedback rather than anticipation of long-run uncertain events. They solve pressing problems rather than develop long-run strategies. [Financial concerns that make long-term investments, like insurance and savings and loan companies, may be exceptions.] Second, they avoid the requirement that they anticipate future reactions of other parts of their environment by arranging a negotiated environment. They impose plans, standard operating procedures, industry tradition, and uncertainty-absorbing contracts on that environment. In short, they achieve a reasonably manageable decision situation by avoiding planning where plans depend on predictions of uncertain future events and by emphasizing planning where the plans can be made self-confirming through some control device.[147]

An analysis by Thompson of organizational deciding in terms of differing degrees of uncertainty (see Table 10-4) points out that the uncertainty can concern either what are relevant cause-and-effect relationships or what are the organization's preferences.[148] In the first case, the decider is uncertain about which alternative will yield the most of whatever outcome it is seeking. In the second, it is not sure what outcome it wants. This results in four types of decision issues, each of them with a different strategy appropriate to it. When both preferences and causation are certain and simple, the solution appears as common sense. When there are many variables, a prolonged analytic period, perhaps using a computer, must precede the choice of alternatives. This is decision by *computation*.

TABLE 10-4   Organizational Deciding with Different Degrees of Certainty

		Preferences about possible outcomes	
		Certain	Uncertain
Beliefs about causation	Certain	Computation	Compromise
	Uncertain	Judgment	Inspiration

SOURCE: J. D. Thompson. Decision-making, the firm, and the market. In W. W. Cooper, H. J. Leavitt, & M. W. Shelly II (Eds.). *New perspectives in organization research.* New York: Wiley, 1964, 336. Copyright © 1964 by John Wiley & Sons, Inc. Reprinted by permission.

When causation is uncertain or disputed but preferences are clear, as often occurs in the choice of a candidate for office, likelihood and probability estimates become necessary. The decision requires *judgment*.

If causation is clear but preferences are uncertain, as in organizational situations when attainment of one goal will be at the expense of another, some form of compromise to accommodate competing preferences is appropriate.

When both causation and preference are uncertain, as when the organization is in a serious crisis, a new vision, image, or belief may be brought forward to pull it together. This is decision by *inspiration*.

In most organizations the highest echelon of the decider devotes much time to the fusion function. When most other influences in the organization are centrifugal, the top administration must be centripetal. It must attempt to weld together a system out of disparate components, each of which has its own homeostasis, each hard at work keeping its own variables in steady state. This unifying function demands much energy and effort. It is crucial for the success of any organization. At times management must concern itself with the subsubcomponents, the individual human beings that make up the organization. They have personal goals. They have individual strains or drives which are different from those of their organizations. They often have a depressing sense of impersonal anonymity which increases as the organization grows. A basic task of leadership is to fashion an effective system out of a collection of very different people. This fusion function McDonald describes as follows:

For want of a better word, call it *melding*, which dictionaries say is a blend of melting and welding. Seeking a satisfactory solution of the interests of all parties, the chief executive internalizes what would otherwise be bargaining among the parties. This works if the payoffs satisfy the interested parties. If they don't, the result nowadays may be the outbreak of a corporate game in which the stake is control. . . .

On each occasion when he makes a major decision, the chief executive tries to join the interests of the different parties in the corporation in terms of the true payoffs to each of them—that is, in accordance with how each of them evaluates what he receives from the corporation. Ideally, this process would lead to formation of a new single line of value out of the composite set of values in the chief executive's head. Such an abstract creation would provide a numerical scale of cardinal numbers—not just an ordering of preferences, but a weighting of them. A preference for any alternative in a problem of decision then would come down simply to choosing a higher number on this scale over a lower one—always choosing to make more money, for example, if money were the scale. Libraries of theoretical books and papers have been written on this subject, mainly on how an individual might assemble his own diverse values. Both the theorists and chief executives are in the same boat in wanting such numbers as the basis for choosing one alternative over another. Neither group, however, has got very far in actually producing a numerical scale for situations where values appear in many combinations and dimensions. . . .

In real-life games, such as games of business, knowledge of the rules is rarely if ever complete. And among the rules, the most obscure is the payoff to the players, a payoff that is determined by how they personally value the outcome of the game. Before he can choose strategies in the various games of business in the outside world, the chief executive has to get his information straight on how various outcomes will be valued by the people who own his corporation or work for it.

The chief executive makes judgments in these matters not in general—except for some rules of thumb—but in connection with specific decisions. Through them he steers the corporation in continuous movement over time. The decisions—on a new product, a merger, a large investment—may have no perceptible effect on current profits, but only on the movement of the corporation into the future. Chief executives know that what they deal in is expectations. "We invest in the future with charges against the present," said one president, "but the future payoff is viewed now."[149]

Which interests should the highest echelons of an organization's decider take into consideration as it carries out its fusion function? Since the beginning of this century, the accepted views on this have changed markedly. For example, at the turn of the century, the officers of most large business corporations took few interests into consideration except those of the stockholders. Their chief task was to make a profit for the owners. With the advent to power of labor unions, managements began to give greater consideration to the interests of their employees. Even more recently there has been an increased concern for the true interests of the customers, as opposed simply to what must be done to make them buy products or services.

Beginning in the 1930s, certain executives of major corporations in the United States, like Fowler McCormick, Owen D. Young, Gerard Swope, and John D. Rockefeller, Jr., began to proclaim the responsibility of a profit-making corporation to the entire society of which it is a component.[150] Explicitly recognizing the similarity of a company to other levels of living systems, McCormick asserted that a healthy corporation attempts to maximize the benefits and fulfill the reasonable expectations of its employees and customers as well as its owners. He and other business leaders took practical actions in their companies to carry out their philosophy. The fusion function, as they practiced it, dealt with components outside the system—the customers—as well as the human beings within it. And it attempted to resolve conflicts not only at the organism level—between individual officers, employees, and customers—but also between groups in the organization, between the corporation and other organizations like unions and competitors, and between the corporation and its suprasystem society, represented by the government.

Constraints on decision making. Certain alternative solutions are eliminated for an organization's decider by constraints on it, either from inside the system or from outside. The internal constraints include:

(i) *Constraints imposed by the system's own purposes and goals.*   Any alternative that tends to disrupt internal steady states or prevent the development of a steady state considered desirable by the decider will be quickly eliminated. An employee considered a troublemaker, for instance, would be discharged for the greater benefit of many components were it not that his seniority and special influence with a number of other employees make it appear likely that a disturbance will result in the currently satisfactory relationship with organized labor. Instead, perhaps, he will be promoted to a position in which his access to the channels through which he has performed his mischief is diminished.

(ii) *Constraints imposed by the values, utilities, and preferences of the system.*   The values of an organization are usually not completely congruent with those of any group or organism component. They may also not be congruent with statements of policy made by founders or decider components. The system's values can be determined by observing its actions. No matter how sincerely the president speaks at meetings about the tremendous value the organization places on maintaining a healthy and beautiful environment, if it dumps its wastes into the adjacent river under cover of darkness, it is clear that the relief of the strain of excess matter-energy by extruding it takes priority over preservation of a normal environment.

(iii) *Constraints imposed by limited resources.*   An organization frequently has more goals that appear desirable than it has money, manpower, and other resources to implement them. After a goal has been selected, the alternative ways of achieving it differ in their requirements for these scarce resources. Often a preferred alternative is abandoned because it is too costly in scarce resources. If, for instance, the preferred one requires too much time of experienced, highly paid personnel for the benefits expected to accrue from it or if a less expensive alternative is almost as good, it will be eliminated. This situation militates against adoption of new programs or innovations since at the beginning they involve extra costs.[151]

(iv) *Constraints imposed by the organization's past experience.*   Courses of action that have been successful as solutions to previous problems tend to be adopted in solving a new one. Prior experience of organizational components may therefore result in the choice of an alternative that does not lead to the hoped-for outcome.

This has been subjected to experimental test by Allen and Marquis.[152] The amount and kind of relevant prior experience of firms which had submitted proposals on two contracts for the Air Force Electronic Systems Division were ascertained, and interviews were held with people responsible for proposal preparation in eight of them, five on one problem and three on the other. Both problems involved design of pieces of equipment—one was a meteorological set that could be dropped from an airplane by parachute, and the other was an apparatus to measure radio signals in the ionosphere. It was found that prior experience with similar problems in itself did not lead to satisfactory solutions, since both successful and unsuccessful firms produced satisfactory solutions. The prior experience helped only when it had involved a solution applicable to the present problem. Otherwise it could be a handicap. Problem solutions could be biased either positively or negatively by previous problem solutions.

(*v*) *Constraints imposed by the procedures and programs of the system.*   Certain alternatives may be eliminated because choosing them would involve changing established procedures and programs that have been satisfactory in the past.

(*vi*) *Constraints deriving from the steady states in existence in the organization at the time the decision is to be made.*   Certain alternatives are eliminated because they would disturb a subsystem relationship which may be in precarious balance. Assigning a group of workers to a different project, for example, so that increased effort could be expended in achieving a given goal might involve taking them away from a department that, for one reason or another, would create conflict in the organization in response to such a change.

(*vii*) *Constraints imposed by interactions of groups or individuals in the system.*   Alternatives involving interaction of components known to be incompatible may be avoided, while people who have worked together smoothly in the past are more likely to be selected to do so again. As Hypothesis 3.3.3.2-17 (see page 97) suggests, a channel that has conveyed one message is more likely to be used to transmit others.

When a decision is to be made by a group in which different echelons are represented, persons at higher echelons tend to exert greater influence in getting the alternatives they suggest accepted, even when these are not clearly better than others.

(*viii*) *Constraints imposed by consideration of risk.* Some alternatives with large payoffs carry risk of financial loss or of physical danger to components. The hypothesis that deciders composed of several human components tend to be conservative and cautious in their approach to risky situations has been put to experimental test (see page 102). Executives in experimentally created groups were more willing to make risky choices than they were when they dealt with the same sort of problems individually.

Hypothesis 3.3.7.2-9 (see page 101) suggests that a system which decides to take novel action soon after the state of its environment reaches the point at which such action is possible does so on a smaller scale than one which decides later. If this is true, it may be because the organization's decider believes there is greater risk in trying something new.

Hypothesis 3.3.7.2-10 (see page 101) states that initial decisions are more likely than later ones to favor a course of action that does not rule out subsequent alternatives. This hypothesis may well apply to organizations, and such behavior, too, could be a result of attitudes toward risk.

There are also external constraints on organizational decision making, including:

(*i*) *Constraints arising from purposes and goals of the suprasystem society.*   When it is the purpose of a society to control inflation, for instance, organizations may not increase prices, as they would otherwise have done. They may refrain from such actions even without a specific directive from the national government. Or schools may voluntarily adjust their curricula to teach black history when the society's purpose is to promote integration of blacks.

(*ii*) *Constraints imposed by the values of the suprasystem.*   In a society which protects the rights of all minorities to voice their opinions, organizations hesitate to violate such rights, even though no specific law exists requiring organizations to subscribe to such values. At annual meetings of American corporations, for example, individual dissenters from company policy are often given more freedom of speech than parliamentary procedure requires.

(*iii*) *Constraints arising from customs, laws, and regulations of the suprasystem.*   Customs, laws, and regulations limit organizations of all sorts in innumerable ways. During the centuries when women were expected to remain home rather than take jobs, organizations did not hire female secretaries. One example of the impact of law on decisions is that in the United States, labor unions cannot strike but must return to work during the cooling-off period after the President invokes the Taft-Hartley labor relations act.

(*iv*) *Constraints imposed by activities of other organizations in the suprasystem.*   Organizations interact in the society in many ways. If one chain of stores decides to remain open on Friday evenings, it is often necessary for others to do so too, in order to compete for customers. If one bank raises or lowers its interest rates, others commonly follow. The fact that a large, successful firm is manufacturing a certain item often keeps others from trying to compete, particularly when the item cannot be made different and more attractive.

(*v*) *Constraints arising from relationships with groups and persons in the suprasystem.*   A hospital cannot decide to forbid all visitors, as some would probably like to do, because of the unpopularity of such a decision with the public served. A political party is effectively prevented from choosing as a candidate a man, no matter how able, who has a history of sexual deviation.

Organizations interact with other organizations in the suprasystem either competitively or cooperatively, according to Thompson.[153] They may compete for resources as well as clients, customers, or members. Cooperation can involve bargaining (or compromise), cooptation, or coalition. In bargaining, agreements are made with other organizations to exchange goods and services with each other, a form of symbiosis. Cooptation permits representatives of another organization to participate in the decision process, there thus being a joint decider subsystem. Coalition means that two or more organizations combine certain processes for a given purpose, so having one or more joint subsystems, *e.g.*, converter or producer subsystems. Each of these arrangements constrains the organization's decisions—bargaining because the other organization may veto the final choice of alternatives, cooptation by keeping the organization from choosing unilaterally from among alternatives, and coalition by requiring that all decisions about certain processes be made jointly.

Computers are being employed increasingly in the synthesis stage of organizational decision making. Management games (see pages 713 to 716) are being used to simulate situations in which industrial corporations find themselves and to aid executives in arriving at optimal decision strategies. In a number of large corporations the president and chairman of the board are continually advised in their decision making by experts in operations research. These specialists develop and keep current computer models of their organization, simulating various alternative strategies and reporting the outcomes to the chief executives before major corporate decisions are made. The same is true in an increasing number of public agencies. As Keeney and Raiffa state: ". . .the theory of such disciplines as operations research, systems analysis, and in particular the methodology of decision analysis are now developed to the degree where they can be a significant aid to the public decision maker. It is important to accumulate critical experience with the use of those techniques on societal problems."[154]

The management of small businesses such as some supermarkets is also being aided in decision making by computers. In a market in Baldwin Hills, California, for example, a special remote computer terminal is used by the checker at each check-out counter to record the code number of each item purchased by each buyer.[155] The computer, which stores in its memory the prices of all items as well as other relevant information, calculates the total cost, tax, number of trading stamps due, proper change, and other data, providing the buyer with a tape on which is printed out a detailed record of the transaction. The computer thus carries out various functions of several organizational subsystems, including the input and output transducers, channel and net, and decider.

It also aids in the store manager's overall management decision making. As every item is checked out, the computer updates the store inventory, accumulating data for reordering and for market research. The manager at any moment can learn how much of any item he has in stock, how rapidly it is being sold, how much any clerk or department has sold in a given day, or how much any checker has handled. Moreover, the computer automatically reorders each item whenever the amount in stock falls below a specified level. It also provides weekly statements on income, costs of merchandise, amount of taxes paid, amount of merchandise lost or stolen, and similar matters relevant to long-range management planning.

(d) Implementing.   The messages transmitted from the decider into organizational channels at this last stage of deciding have certain specific characteristics: (*i*) They are intended to initiate implementation of a decision or the part of it relevant to a particular component, (*ii*) they are addressed to some specific receiver or receivers, (*iii*) they have a signature identifying the source and showing its legitimacy, and (*iv*) they carry the expectation of compliance (see page 38). Hypothesis 3.3.7.2-4 (see page 100) says that the signature is an important determinant of the probability of compliance. At this level this appears obvious.

Command, control, and coordinating communications tend to be general directives at higher echelons but detailed and specific instructions at lower ones, except when a familiar program is to be followed.

What makes implementation interesting at the level of the organization—and is a major reason why management of organizations is a challenge—is that compliance of components is far from automatic. The initial agreement by which they undertake to participate in the organization's processes in exchange for its benefits does not always produce entirely satisfactory compliance (see Hypothesis 5.4.3-8, page 109). There are many reasons for this, the major one being the relative totipotentiality of components. Even the most committed members of the most demanding organizations subordinate only a part of their processes to the organization. In this they differ greatly from cells and organs of organisms, which are much less independent in their decision making. It is necessary to secure the cooperation of the organization's personnel in furthering its purposes and goals. Management theory is concerned to a large extent with the system structure and the techniques of administration that are effective in securing such cooperation.

Representative *variables* of the process of deciding include: *Meaning of information employed in deciding.* Example: The candidate's references were all strongly positive, and so the bank hired him as a vice president. *Sorts of information employed in deciding.* Example: The president asked for all records of the grocery-store chain's sales over the past 5 years in order to help decide which advertising approach was most successful. *Amount of information employed in deciding.* Example: The executive committee reviewed 24 pages of computer printouts before deciding on the factory's annual budget. *Changes in deciding over time.* Example: Over the first 5 years the new insurance company gradually developed operating procedures that covered most routine situations. *Changes in deciding with different circumstances.* Example: After the computerized regulators were installed, it was no longer necessary to rely on the foreman's judgment for controlling flows of fluids through the refinery. *Number of alternatives in input before decision and in output afterward.* Example: A single course was chosen by the ocean liner's captain only after the officers had analyzed six possible routes. *Rewards and punishments attached to alternatives reviewed in deciding.* Example: It appeared to the management of the real estate company that a small but sure profit would derive from the purchase of a dozen houses throughout the city but that either great profit or great loss would result from the construction of a new high-rise condominium. *Rate of deciding.* Example: Several top-management jobs were filled each month until, after a year, the new federal agency was completely staffed. *Lag in deciding.* Example: It took the boss of the amusement park a month to make up his mind to fire the Ferris wheel operator. *Costs of deciding.* Example: The bicycle manufacturer's engineer spent $50,000 developing a hand brake to replace the one which had proved unsatisfactory.

3.3.8 Encoder, the subsystem which alters the code of information input to it from other information processing subsystems, changing it from a "private" code used internally by the organization into a "public" code which can be interpreted by other organizations in its environment.

3.3.8.1 Structure   Included are subsidiary organizations and groups that write and edit speeches, publications, letters, contracts, reports, estimates, or proposals; code secret communications; translate from one language to another; design trademarks or other symbolic representations of organizations; design

buildings or other artifacts for organizations; and act as lawyers, labor relations experts, or lobbyists. Also included are advertising and public relations departments.

It is not unusual for encoder components to be joint components of the decider or the output transducer subsystems, or both. This occurs, for instance, when the head of an organization writes and delivers his own speeches. Some components of the encoder are outwardly dispersed to other organizations in the suprasystem. Advertising and public relations firms, for example, sell their services to organizations of many types, some of which maintain no such component of their own. This arrangement is recommended by Townsend as the most effective one for advertising a business organization such as a chain of car rental agencies.[156] Trade associations and other organizations representing collections of organizations, like the Council of Churches or the Federation of Women's Clubs, encode information for their members. Downwardly dispersed components include individual members and employees who encode information when they serve in capacities like those mentioned above in this section or as salesmen, recruiters, or solicitors.

Artifacts such as pencils, typewriters, paper, brushes, and paints are useful tools for human beings in this subsystem, but they are not components of it, as various sorts of machines, including computers, in the producer and decider subsystems are. Machines so far cannot replace human encoders very effectively, although some steps have been taken in this direction (see pages 404 to 406).

3.3.8.2 Process   Organizations do not use *alpha-coded* messages in communicating with other living systems.

Beta-coded messages include the pictorial and musical elements of television commercials. The paint and feathers that make primitive war parties look fierce also are beta-coded communications that convey warning and elicit fear in their beholders. Uniforms and insignia generally transmit organizational information, identifying the organization to which the wearer belongs and informing the viewer of the role the wearer plays in its processes. Napoleon was disturbed at the unfortunate effects upon his armies when on occasion their various uniforms became confused. He wrote to one of his commanders:

My lord Duc of Feltre, in your general inventory report, you list the Méditerannée, Walcheren, Belle-Ile and Isle de Ré Regiments after the front line infantry. Consequently it is impossible for me to see if these regiments are either part of front line infantry, or of light infantry. One must list after LIGHT INFANTRY those regiments who wear the light infantry uniform, and after FRONT LINE INFANTRY those regiments wearing front line uniforms. So I pray God that you were in His holy hand, Chartres June 3rd 1811.

Napoleon[157]

The gestures and facial expressions of the group or person that acts as output transducer for an organization also transmit beta-coded signals.

Organizations of many types are eager to establish an identity—an "image"—as a unitary system with a set of distinguishing characteristics similar to those of an individual human personality. To do this, some of them adopt distinctive architectural designs for their places of business, like the Howard Johnson chain of restaurants, or readily recognizable signs, like the Holiday Inns. Many organizations make use of trademarks or similar emblems, like the sleeping kitten which so long represented the Chesapeake and Ohio Railroad or the red feathers used by associations of charitable agencies in many cities. In recent decades there has been an increasing tendency toward the use of stylized or abstract graphic symbols rather than more representational ones.[158]

Such symbols are beta-coded when they do not carry a written message and gamma-coded when they consist of initials or words. They also can employ mixed beta and gamma coding.

These symbols include the organization's name or appear in association with it on advertising material, letterheads, buildings, freight cars, and products. They remain constant over many years, sometimes over several generations. Some of them become familiar and meaningful to the users of the products, thus achieving their intended aim. They provide continuity and survive many changes in organizational structure and processes. In some cases they help to counteract the feeling of many customers that they are dealing with a huge, impersonal system. When the organization alters its name or is merged into another, its symbol is usually changed or modified. Such symbols are often updated, usually in such a way as to continue elements of the older forms in the new. The Greek temple, symbol of the Squibb company since 1905, has recently been changed. The old and the new forms appear in Fig. 10-11. The symbol is now stylized in

accordance with modern taste. Elimination of the words on the temple, which represented ideals of the company, makes it more suitable for use internationally in different language areas. The Bell System bell has undergone a series of such changes (see Fig. 10-12).

Fig. 10-11 Old and new forms of symbol of E. R. Squibb & Sons, Inc. *(Registered trademark reprinted by permission of E. R. Squibb & Sons, Inc.)*

Most information encoded for output by organizations is in *gamma-coded* messages. These include the letters, bills, conversations between representatives of different organizations, speeches made by representatives of the organization, sales talks, advertising, and other verbal messages by which the organization transacts its business with the suprasystem. Encoding of organizational messages is usually controlled as

Fig. 10-12 Several forms of symbol of the Bell System. *(Reprinted by permission of American Telephone & Telegraph Co.)*

closely as possible by decider components of both military and civilian organizations. Much of it is done by them. They often insist on approving all encoded messages before they are transduced out of the organization. It is common to limit the number and type of components empowered to encode for the organization to a small number that can be expected to do so in a trustworthy manner.

Codes chosen by organizations for transmission of a particular message depend upon the nature of the message, the channel over which it must pass, and the receiver to whom it is addressed. Large organizations often make use of encoder components skilled in employing various languages, codes, or special terminologies for the different kinds of messages. In nations where one language is spoken, translators are often employed to recode a message into the language of another country. Lawyers, physicians, scientists, engineers, and other specialists are usually the only ones who can accurately decode or encode their technical communications, since their terminologies are so specialized as to be unintelligible to many laymen. Technical writing, like directions to television repairmen, uses one sort of terminology; instructions to laymen use another. The formal language of business letters or government memoranda is something else again.

Editors of newspapers, magazines, and some books try to recode the writing input by authors into a style and form which their readers can understand and enjoy.

Some of the most important *variables* of the encoding process are: *Meaning of information which is encoded.* Example: The third-quarter financial report of the scientific instrument company showed profits of about $1 million. *Sorts of information which are encoded.* Example: The child welfare organization's fund raisers wrote letters asking for funds and distributed a pamphlet giving some case histories. *Percentage of the information input which is encoded.* Example: The press releases from the Academy of Sciences consisted of brief, popularized summaries of scientific papers, not the entire papers. *Threshold of the encoder.* Example: The corporation president's speech writers could not hear the president's recorded directions until they raised the volume of their cassette player. *Changes in encoding over time.* Example: As the university grew, more attention was given to improving its public image by means of press releases from the public relations department. *Changes in encoding with different circumstances.* Example: A competitor threatened to pass the manufacturer in volume of sales, and so the firm prepared advertisements calling attention to a new ingredient added to its toothpaste. *Channel capacity of the*

encoder. Example: The advertising company's art staff included five artists, who could paint a total of about 10 pictures or designs a week. *Distortion of the encoder.* Example: The pharmaceutical firm's report to the press neglected to mention the side effects of the new drug. *Signal-to-noise ratio of the encoder.* Example: The oil company's Arabic translator made at least one grammatical error in every paragraph. *Rate of encoding.* Example: Several letters a day were drafted by the oil company's lobbyists to be sent to congressmen. *Percentage of omissions in encoding.* Example: The electric utility company did not inform the public about the five accidents that occurred during the 100 trials of the new machine, but only about the 95 successes. *Percentage of errors in encoding.* Example: The airline's public relations department got three out of five birth dates wrong in the press release. *Code employed.* Example: All letters from the Foreign Office to other countries were sent in the language of the country in which the receiver lived. *Redundancy of the code employed.* Example: In telegrams for orders of new parts, all important words and numbers were repeated by the automobile manufacturing company. *Lag in encoding.* Example: The department-store artists argued for several hours about how to depict the benefits of the new soap. *Costs of encoding.* Example: The new woman in the advertising department received $12,000 per year, raising the total annual budget of the department to $87,000.

3.3.9   Output transducer, the subsystem which puts out markers bearing information from the organization, changing markers within the organization into other matter-energy forms which can be transmitted over channels in the organization's environment.

3.3.9.1   Structure   Subsidiary organizations and groups such as public relations departments; spokesmen; labor negotiators; salesmen; missionaries; lobbyists and pressure groups; secretaries; publication, mailing, and circulation departments; printers; actors and other performers; media departments; and broadcasters, as well as those who operate and maintain electronic devices used in the subsystem, are components of the output transducer subsystem of organizations.

In certain systems some output transducer components are joint with the decider or encoder subsystem.

Parts of this subsystem are often outwardly dispersed to other organizations in the suprasystem. This is the situation when an advertising agency employs the singers and actors who perform in a commercial for an organization, while still another organization, the television company, broadcasts it.

The output transducer of some types of organizations is downwardly dispersed to group components, particularly when these are geographically separated from the central office. Political parties and many religious bodies, as well as some other types of organizations, expect all members to participate in processes of the output transducer—in proselytizing new members, for example. These functions are downwardly dispersed to organism subcomponents.

Artifacts like electronic answering devices; public address systems; television; radio; and printing, duplicating, and mailing equipment are important adjuncts to this subsystem and may, as in the case of computers programmed to send out bills, act as components of it.

3.3.9.2 Process   An organization's relationships with other organizations in the suprasystem are carried on by designated members who are empowered to speak for the system on a particular subject or all subjects and in a particular situation or all situations. Organizations, even many of those with decentralized deciders, exercise a good deal of control over this process. Often only top management can issue official communications. This is partly to avoid uncontrolled commitment of the organization's resources and partly to make certain that the organization appears as a unified system. Publicity and advertising, which are aimed at whole societies or large segments of them, are also carefully controlled.

The organization's interactions with systems at lower levels are less strictly controlled. Much of this is decentralized to departments responsible for such processes as answering complaints and inquiries, sending out bills, and performing similar routine jobs.

The markers on which organizations output messages into the suprasystem include written or printed materials, radio and television signals, and sound waves.

Some output transducer components act under directives to devote a large part of their activities to communicating outside the system.[159] Labor relations departments, for example, deal with other organizations, the unions, in fixing pay and conditions of employment for union members. These components are often perceived by others in their company as being especially sympathetic to the organizations with which they deal, and they are often considered marginal members of the organization that employs them.[160] The unions, on the other hand, frequently regard them with suspicion.

Occasional use may be made of components that are actually but not officially parts of this subsystem to "leak" information. They understand that if the feedback from the society is unfavorable, the organization's decider will deny any responsibility for the information leaked.

Representative *variables* of the output transducing process are: *Meaning of information output which is transduced.* Example: The candy company's singing commercial was designed to convince the public that their products were not fattening. *Sorts of information output which are transduced.* Example: The alumni association published a newsletter giving news of graduates. *Threshold of the output transducer.* Example: The anchor man who was announcer for the television network did not hear the instructions to remain on the air and signed off the network. *Changes in output transducing over time.* Example: The steel manufacturer's annual report went out with colored illustrations after 1945. *Changes in output transducing with different circumstances.* Example: A crisis developed when the largest freezer broke down, and so the head of the ice cream company called long-distance instead of writing to its manufacturer. *Channel capacity of the output transducer.* Example: The university's typing pool numbered 52 girls, each of whom could type an average of about 6 pages an hour, for a total of about 312 pages per hour. *Number of channels in use in the output transducer.* Example: During the coffee break, only one telegrapher was on duty at the railroad station. *Distortion of the output transducer.* Example: The artist who painted the billboard for the department store made the bicycle appear much bigger and stronger than it actually was. *Rate of output transducing.* Example: One press release a day was issued regularly at noon by the army in the field. *Lag in output transducing.* Example: The secretarial service's duplicating machine operator was several days behind. *Intensity of information output.* Example: When he shouted, the captain of the ocean liner could not be heard on the dock, and so he spoke through an electric amplifier. *Costs of output transducing.* Example: The public relations department, with a budget that doubled in 8 years, was expensive to the city.

4. Relationships among subsystems or components

The relationship which the subsystems or components of organizations bear to one another are more varied than those at any lower level of system. There are many obvious relationships in physical space-time, including those between persons and the territory, buildings, or other artifacts used by the organization. But the relationships that involve meaning are the chief concern of the scientists who study organizations. Beginning with the charter of every new organization, this sort of relationship is specified by written and other interpersonal communications. They are the glue which unites the parts of organizations and higher levels of human systems. Without them, these levels could never have come into existence.

Examples of the various kinds of relationships in organizations which are related to structure, process, or meaning are given below.

4.1 Structural relationships

4.1.1 Containment   Example: The executive committee of the bank was made up entirely of members of the board of directors.

4.1.2 Number   Example: The yacht manufacturing company had eight branch sales offices.

4.1.3 Order   Example: The assembly line in the plant near the stockyard was arranged with the packers last.

4.1.4 Position   Example: The executive offices were on the fourth floor, and the sales office was on the first.

4.1.5 Direction   Example: The city was laid out with the city hall just north of the courthouse.

4.1.6 Size   Example: The assembled employees filled a large auditorium.

4.1.7 Pattern   Example: All the tents were arranged in a circle at the Boy Scout jamboree.

4.1.8 Density   Example: In the old building, all five departments of the board of elections were crowded into a single huge room.

4.2 Process relationships

4.2.1 Temporal relationships

4.2.1.1 Containment in time   Example: Between 1900 and 1925 all the weaving at the textile factory was done by hand.

4.2.1.2 Number in time   Example: The production department in the refrigerator factory sent 5,000 units to shipping during the first month of the fiscal year.

4.2.1.3 Order in time   Example: On the assembly line the axle was connected to the chassis first and then to the wheels; finally the body was put in place.

4.2.1.4 Position in time   Example: The government agency's top council met each Monday at noon.

4.2.1.5 Direction in time   Example: At the brewery it turned out to be more efficient to have the full bottles boxed first and then capped, rather than the reverse.

4.2.1.6 Duration   Example: The real estate firm's training team met with the new salesmen for an hour each morning.

4.2.1.7 Pattern in time   Example: The generating plant's records showed that there were two peak load periods every 24 hours.

4.2.2 Spatiotemporal relationships

4.2.2.1 Action   Example: A ton of new copper plates was sent to the mill's cutting department, which had to work overtime to process them.

4.2.2.2 Communication   Example: An order was transmitted from the president's office requesting all department chairmen to submit reports.

4.2.2.3 Direction of action   Example: One tank division advanced toward the city.

4.2.2.4 Pattern of action   Example: Joshua's army marched around and around the city of Jericho until the walls fell down.

4.2.2.5 Entering or leaving containment   Example: The representatives of the steelworkers voted to leave the convention hall.

4.3 Relationships among subsystems or components which involve meaning   Example: The students demonstrated because they had no voice in administering the university.

5. System processes

5.1 Process relationships between inputs and outputs   The marked diversity in the input–output relationships of systems at this level results from the fact that they are frequently partipotential. They exist to perform certain processes in societies and are adapted in structure and process for those purposes. The inputs to an organization, the internal processing which these inputs receive, and the nature of the outputs depend upon this specialization. In this, organizations resemble the organ components of organisms, which ordinarily are also highly specialized partipotential systems.

The relative totipotentiality of the organism subcomponents of organizations, particularly their ability to participate easily in the subsystem processes of several organizations almost simultaneously, receiving the benefits of system membership from each, makes it possible for some organizations to do without certain processes, depending upon other organizations symbiotically or parasitically to provide them for their joint components. This is particularly true of the matter-energy processes. Organizations vary markedly in their patterns of dependency on other systems, and so, even among organizations of the same type, marked individual differences in input–output relationships are the rule.

In this section I make an intralevel analysis of organizational input–output relationships. I view the organization as a "black box," observing the flow of inputs and outputs over the system boundary and studying their relationships. This differs from the usual input–output studies of organizations, which are ordinarily interlevel analyses of the making of a product of the organization and the fluctuations of internal variables, like the number of hours of work per unit, which occur during this process. Input–output relationships exist among flows both of matter-energy and of information, including money, as they pass in and out across an organization's boundary.

What is more, I do not limit my definition of outputs to "goods and services," as Gross does, for example;

he defines output as "the goods or services that an organization, unit or individual makes or helps make available for use by clients."[161] Gross's definition is in accord with the common usage in economics, which defines "national product" in terms of goods and services (see page 845). He specifically states that outputs do not include people extruded from an organization and extruded wastes, except to compare products and wastes in measures of efficiency and productivity. I include both people and wastes. Attention to waste outputs leads one to focus upon their nature and quantity, facilitating consideration of recycling or other productive use of them as well as other sorts of disposition of them in the suprasystem. Gross considers services to be products of organizations, whereas I consider them to be process outputs, reserving the term "product" for material outputs that are neither wastes nor people. I do not consider an educated man to be the "product" of his university. He received a service from it while he was a student (an inclusion) in it.

By "services" I mean both certain types of communications to clients, like advice, instruction, and counseling, and certain sorts of matter-energy processing activities, like cleaning carpets, towing cars, moving furniture, transporting people, and painting buildings.

My conceptual system requires specification of whether organizational inputs and outputs are matter-energy, or information. This distinction makes for more precise analysis of input–output relationships at this level, just as it is an improvement over the non-specific stimulus–response terminology at the organism level (see page 410). The distinction also makes it simpler to study all types of organizations together, both those which process primarily matter-energy and those which process chiefly information. Also, it facilitates cross-level comparisons.

Any given organization has its own unique combination of inputs and outputs. It may include proportions of matter-energy and information unlike those of even very similar organizations.

(a) *Matter-energy inputs related to matter-energy outputs.* Like other living systems, organizations must keep their matter-energy inputs and outputs within a steady-state range. That is, if the outputs are not used for growth, storage, maintenance, and repair or extruded as products or wastes, they accumulate in the system to the detriment of various processes. Of the thousands of possible matter-energy input–output relationships, one of particular practical significance is the problem of cities in disposing of wastes. The sorts of detergents that wholesalers bring into a city, which later go into its sewers; the sorts of bottles and cans that are brought in, sold, used, and thrown away; and

the grades of coal that are transported into the city and burned in its furnaces—all affect the types of potentially polluting matter-energy extruded into the environment (see page 622).

The sorts of human employees who are input to an organization whose primary purpose is matter-energy processing, such as a factory, obviously affect the quality and quantity of outputs, the proportion of products to wastes, and other characteristics of the matter-energy products and services output as a result of their labor and management activities. The sorts of nonliving materials input and the rates at which such inputs are made also have major influences on the characteristics of the outputs. Shortages of necessary inputs, if no substitutes can be found, will sooner or later reduce the rate and possibly also the quality of the outputs.[162] They may also alter the proportions of products to wastes.

The costs of organizational processes are measured by the inputs they require, and their productivity is measured by their outputs. The ratio of their inputs to their outputs measures the efficiency or effectiveness of the system (see page 41). The quantification of costs is relatively simple. It is done in terms of amounts or rates of matter-energy or persons input, worker-hours or time required for a process, or dollars needed to pay for essential inputs. Such standard measures of costs are widely used and well understood.

Measures of productivity and efficiency or effectiveness, on the other hand, are employed much less frequently and are as yet not well conceptualized or generally comprehended and accepted. The widespread use of many economic indicators related to costs—dollar values, budgets, stock-market averages, prime interest rates, cost-of-living indices, and so forth—focuses our attention constantly on costs of organizational operations. The lack of satisfactory standard measures of productivity and efficiency means that we usually underestimate these aspects of organizational evaluation. Indeed, in many profit and nonprofit organizations, the attention of management is directed exclusively to the costs of operations because their measures are so obvious. This currently pervasive and unfortunate emphasis on the costs, and neglect of the productivity and accomplishments of organizations along with the social and psychological satisfactions they bring those they serve, Toffler refers to as the "econcentric view."[163]

Some advances, however, have been made in the complicated problem of quantifying organizational effectiveness. One input–output computation measures "value added."[164] This is determined by subtracting the cost of the goods input and services provided in producing the outputs from the total dollar value of those outputs. This measure is far from perfect, however. The monetary value of an input or output is only a "distant and distorted fiscal echo," having no commensurability or linear relationship with the amount or sort of matter-energy or information in it.[165] The value added by a factory that merely assembles components made elsewhere is less than the value added by one that also produces the parts from raw materials. Value added can be calculated as the total for a given period of time or as the incremental change or rate of change between one time and another.[166] The effects of such changes on satisfactions of the clientele served by the organization can be calculated.

The concept of organizational effectiveness has been analyzed by Katz and Kahn in a sophisticated systems theoretical approach.[167] They point out that in addition to the input–ouput ratio efficiency measure discussed above, there are other measures, like the rate of growth of the organization (see pages 692, 693, and 702), the length of time it maintains the negentropy it needs in order to survive, and the percentage of its personnel who carry out its basic processes as compared with the percentage who carry out support activities.

An important measure of efficiency in a profit-making company is the rate at which it makes profit. As the organization's efficiency improves, the rate improves, if the prices paid in the environment, set by demand, do not change. In such an organization there is rapid and clear feedback from the environment as to whether the society is using its goods and services. The returns from sales, dollar payments input to the system, make this clear. If they do not occur, the system falters and may not even survive.

Measuring the efficiency of a nonprofit organization is harder. There is no sales feedback from the society. The feedback comes, instead, in various forms of public support for the functions the organization carries out: Tuition is paid to a college or university, gifts are presented to it, or a subsidy is voted by a state legislature. Appropriations are voted by the Congress to provide inputs of tax dollars to the Navy, or a draft is enacted to guarantee inputs of soldiers to the Army. Charitable contributions support a city's community fund if the citizens believe it is performing needed services and if they are unselfish enough. Dues are input to support social clubs that give their members satisfactory services. In all these cases feedbacks from the environment decide whether the organization shall survive. In most cases, though costs are carefully weighed, efficiency is only dimly evaluated, if at all. Usually it is assumed without evidence that the organization is efficient. Sometimes spurious or irrelevant pseudoproofs of efficiency are accepted (see page 686).

An organization can be efficient and yet not accomplish its purposes effectively. This is because internal input–output efficiency is insufficient unless the interaction with the environment is also good. (a) Unless the organization is strategically located in space close to inputs it needs and clients it serves, it may not do well, no matter how efficient it is. (b) Unless it has free and undistorted inputs of information about the environment, it will not do well. (c) Unless it gets special considerations in the suprasystem—favors from friends, subsidies, a partial or complete monopoly, restraints on the trade of its competitors, or cheap labor or slaves—it may not do well.

The above discussion of organizational efficiency or effectiveness is at the organization level of discourse. It could have been at the organism level, under which circumstances one would ask how much product or service the organization gave its clients or consumers for a given cost or how much satisfaction it provided its members or employees for a given payment or energy expenditure by them. Or the discussion could have been at the society level. Then the question would concern how effectively the organization carries out its established purposes and makes its contributions to society. If it has a partial or complete monopoly or constrains its competitors, that may be justified if the organization is making a crucial contribution to the society. If its outputs are unusually costly, they may still be justified by social need. If, for instance, a "war on cancer" or a crash "war on urban poverty" is important enough that a society is willing to subsidize it, then cost-effectiveness may not be the prime consideration. It all depends on the view from the level of the living system at which the evaluation is made.

(b) *Matter-energy inputs related to information outputs.*   Inputs of appropriate human components are as important for information outputs as for matter-energy outputs. So, too, are certain artifacts and materials for markers, without which the information cannot be sent into the suprasystem. Newspapers and magazines require paper and ink; radio and television stations require electronic equipment and electricity. Restriction on the accessibility of these required forms of matter and energy can limit the rates at which markers are output.

Organizations which must provide for the physical needs of their human and animal components cannot continue to output information for long without receiving inputs of food and other necessities for their organism components. The quality and quantity of such inputs have little direct effect upon the information output except when they are poor enough to cause disease in, or diminish the activity of, the organisms in the organization.

(c) *Information inputs related to matter-energy outputs.*   The rates at which products or services are output are often determined by the demand present in the suprasystem as evidenced by orders or requests for service, previous sales, and other feedbacks (see page 685). Planning for production in industrial organizations is based upon projections of expected demands derived from records of the immediate past and information inputs about the state of the economy and probable new markets. Information from the society concerning regulations about the construction of an item or the manner in which service may be given also affects the planning for future outputs. Such information may also determine the proportion of one sort of output to others produced by an industrial organization. If sales are high in one division and low in a second and if this is determined to be caused by poor acceptance of the product of the second, changes will be made in the amount produced, in its quality, or in other aspects.

Orders or requests elicit outputs of specific quantities of the product or service requested. Processing times required for these information inputs to elicit matter-energy outputs can be determined and are important in the functioning of the system. Average processing times vary from one type of organization to another and, within types, for different products, qualities, or other variations. They also differ from busy seasons to slack seasons. Customers of a department store are required to wait up to 6 months for pieces of furniture, which are often finished to order, but they expect telephone orders for standard items of clothing to be delivered within a week. The time between request for television service and actual repair of the set may be days or even weeks, but emergency-room care in a hospital is usually begun within minutes.

Inputs of distress signals from the environment activate emergency organizations like police and fire departments, rescue services, defense forces, and disaster units, eliciting expenditures of energy intended to cope with the reported stresses or strains.

Average processing time for such services tend to be short. An efficient city fire department responds to a call within seconds by an outpouring of trucks, men, and equipment. At the sound of a fire alarm in a small town, volunteers from several places rush to the trucks and are off within minutes to the fire. Disaster units pride themselves upon alerting their staffs and being in the field within an hour after the impact of a flood, tornado, or major explosion. Some of these responses are like lower-echelon reflexes of organisms (see page 425) since they are mediated through short pathways and do not require processing by the top echelon of the organization's decider.

(d) *Information inputs related to information outputs.* Business and industrial firms or other systems that exchange their services for money or credit cannot exist indefinitely in society unless their inputs and outputs of money or credit are in balance. This ordinarily means that the enterprise must make a profit, but subsidized systems do exist. Governments, for example, contribute to the support of unprofitable services in the public interest. Also, foundations, charitable contributions, or endowments cover part of the costs of endeavors such as privately supported educational institutions and hospitals.

The inward and outward flows of information over the boundaries of organizations include messages initiated by other systems and addressed to components of the organization and messages originating in the organization and addressed to systems outside. Some of these messages of both kinds elicit no response, but many such communications are reacted to by receiving systems, forming complete communication loops between the system and parts of the environment. The amount of such information flowing into and out of large, busy systems is enormous.

An organization cannot ordinarily react as fast as a person or a group. It normally responds in days or weeks rather than seconds or minutes. Moreover, like matter-energy responses to information inputs, the processing times of information input–output sequences are variable among organizations. A city government may respond within an hour to a criticism from an adjacent suburb and never respond to a criticism from one of its welfare recipients. Responses of organizations to increasing rates of information inputs to the point of information input overload are discussed above (see pages 157 to 164).

A number of hypotheses of Chap. 4 deal with processing time and appear applicable to organizations. Hypothesis 5.1-28 (see page 104), which says that higher-level systems have longer information processing times, could probably be confirmed in general for organizations, as compared with single organisms, simply because more than one person is usually involved in any organizational information transmission. Hypothesis 5.1-29 (see page 104) states that the higher the level of a system, the more variation in general there is in its processing times. This is because there are more components which are possible sources for this variation. In organizations with many components, human errors, differences in personality, variations in efficiency among departments, and complexity of the channels involved can all alter processing times.

The variations in organizational processing times are determined by the number and types of channels through which the signals must pass, the number of nodes and deciders in them, and the complexity of the information processing that is required. A communication that must be taken by a corporation president to the board of directors cannot ordinarily be rapidly processed unless it is so urgent that a special meeting must be called. Difficult issues that require much examination before a decision is made, as at other levels, take longer.

5.2 Adjustment processes among subsystems or components, used in maintaining variables in steady states

5.2.1 Matter-energy input processes

Adjustments to lacks of matter-energy inputs. Organizations often have programs for adjusting to lacks of matter-energy inputs. Many generalizations apply to adjustment processes that cope with such lacks. For example, a strain that develops rapidly is usually more dangerous to the system than one that develops slowly, and unexpected lack stresses for which no preparation has been made are more disruptive than those which have been predicted and consequently prepared for. These generalizations probably also apply to excess stresses. Normal adjustment processes to matter-energy lacks in industrial organizations include retrieval of previously stored matter-energy; widened search for what is needed; layoffs of personnel, for example, eliminating a shift in a factory; or closing down part or all of an organization during the slack season.

If the possibility of a lack stress has been anticipated and matter-energy inputs have been stored in anticipation of it, Hypothesis 5.2-4 (see page 106) may apply. That is, the range of stability of the system for the particular variable may be a monotonically increasing function of the amount of storage of the input. A city that stores enough food and water for several months can withstand siege much longer than one that is unprepared when surrounded by an enemy.

When severe lack stresses occur, rationing of scarce inputs may be undertaken by communities. When transportation workers strike, for instance, only infants and patients get milk. Another adjustment is for organizations to do their own converting or producing in the event of failure of these functions, which are under ordinary circumstances upwardly dispersed to the society. Hospitals, for instance, usually have electric generators or batteries for use during times when electrical inputs from public power companies are cut off.

Frequently the sorts of matter-energy inputs of which there is a lack are people—employees, members, clients, or other human inclusions. Adjustments for such shortages can be made by altering boundary filtering processes to admit previously unacceptable people or by changing internal processes to accommo-

date them. A social organization that wants more members lowers its admission requirements; a university needing more teachers decides to recruit some young people who have not yet won their doctorates; a corporation that needs additional employees hires untrained workmen and trains them on the job.

Costs of adjustment processes tend to be greater for more severe excess and lack strains. If the winter is hard, snow-removal equipment may break down before its normal time, creating repair and replacement costs. A devastating flood may deplete a city's treasury. Long-term projects to avert floods are expensive, but probably less so than the cumulative costs of annual flooding.

Like systems at lower levels, organizations ordinarily prefer to adapt or extend existing programs rather than seek creative solutions or undertake innovations (see page 624). In general they also choose the least expensive adjustment process first, moving to more costly ones when it proves inadequate (see Hypothesis 3.3.7.2-14, page 101).

Adjustments to excess matter-energy inputs. Organizations commonly also have programmed adjustments to overloads in matter-energy inputs. Such excess flows over the boundaries of organizations are of two sorts: (a) increases that can be anticipated because of rhythms of nature (like harvest time for particular crops) or regular changes in society (like peak patronage of downtown restaurants at midday), and (b) increases that result from emergencies or unexpected changes in the environment or the society. Organizations ordinarily have preprogrammed adjustments for both sorts of excess stresses, particularly the first. The first class of adjustments includes provisions in organized communities for snow removal or flood control; arrangements by businesses for hiring extra personnel, shifting personnel from processes that are not undergoing stress to those which are, or opening temporary departments or facilities; and provision of extra seating and public address facilities for overflow crowds.

The second class includes plans for action in case of unpredictable matter-energy input excess stresses beyond the corrective power of the system's usual adjustment processes. Fire drills, air-raid drills, and the use of public shelters against bombs or tornadoes are among these. A city by a large river often has levees high enough to contain the usual spring flood-waters. As the water rises above flood stage, however, extra workers may be employed to build up the levees, strengthen weak places, and report parts which are likely to collapse. As the danger increases, citizen volunteers help at the levees, and aid from the supra-system, such as units of the National Guard, may be sent in. Residents are evacuated from endangered homes and taken to safer areas. When the waters have receded, they return to clean and repair their damaged property.

Hypothesis 5.2-3 (see page 106) states that when variables in a system return to a steady state after stress, the rate of return and the strength of the restorative forces are functions—with increasing first derivatives greater than 1—of the amount of displacement from the range of stability. This proposition appears to be testable for matter-energy input stresses on organizations and is likely to be confirmed. For example, as enemy bombardment on an army becomes heavier, the army's efforts to defend itself increase even more. It appears also that an input constitutes a greater strain if no program has been developed to meet it. A relatively small increase can seriously disturb steady states if no preparation for it has been made. Hypothesis 5.2-4 (see page 106), which states that the range of stability of a system for a specific variable under excess strain is a monotonically increasing function of the rate of output, also appears to receive some confirmation from observations of organizations. For example, an overcrowded county fair at which people are arriving in large numbers through all the entrances is able to deal increasingly well with its crowding as the rates of the flow of persons passing through the exits go up. Hypothesis 5.2-5 (see page 106) suggests that there is an inertia to matter-energy processing variables and that change in their ranges of stability is therefore less disruptive of system controls if it is undertaken gradually. This also seems to be true of organizations in general. A moderate rise in the water level of the Great Lakes, which has occurred over a period of several years, creates some problems but does not constitute a serious strain for surrounding communities. If a similar rise occurred suddenly, communities on the shores of the lakes would suffer much more property damage, and their citizens might be in some danger. A sudden influx of people into a community can strain its resources, particularly if there are many of them and if they arrive in a short period. Refugees can constitute such an input. So can hordes of hippies coming to a rock festival like Woodstock. So can large numbers of migrants flowing in from other parts of the nation, as has happened in some Northern industrial cities of the United States. To adjust to such influxes, a community often solicits contributions from its citizens or organizations and provides emergency care. Increases in welfare budgets and expansion of class sizes in schools are other possible adjustments.

5.2.2 Information input processes Information flows into organizations vary in rate and meaning.

Extremes of the first produce either information input overload or information input underload. Variations in meaning elicit adjustment processes appropriate to the content of the messages. Most organizations have routines for processing the expected amount of input information such as the normal flow of orders. Standard procedures for processing different categories of meaningful input and for handling inputs of money are also developed in most systems. Adjustments to ordinary changes in all these flows are commonly planned in advance.

Lacks of necessary information inputs create strains which elicit adjustments in organizations. Cities adjust to loss of information inputs during emergencies by using informal channels, such as ham radio operators, to replace inactivated communications components. When a community fund fails to meet its goal for monetary information inputs, all organizations depending upon it must cut services, eliminate staff, and economize in other ways. When city bond issues fail, schools may be closed entirely, or parts of their programs may be eliminated.

Changing information inputs from the environment may indicate that the demand for an organization's services, its share of the market, or its return on investments has fallen below satisfactory values. Or information inputs may show other organizations to be more successful because they use different methods or materials. Such inputs (see page 624) may give rise to innovations, novel solutions to problems, or use of new methods or materials as alternatives to accustomed procedures. Strains created by internal or output matter-energy or information processing may also elicit such innovations.

Since the costs of such changes are often greater than the costs of existing programs, the changes will usually not be undertaken unless the present programs are clearly less advantageous. Costs include those of discovering and developing the new course of action and of obtaining whatever new artifacts, buildings, departments, or employees are required.[168] Some of the resistance to change observed in organizations can be explained by the need to justify the greatly increased costs which initiation of new programs or innovation of any sort will incur. Many of these costs commit the organization over long periods and significantly reduce the profit margins or, in nonprofit organizations, capital or operating funds.

Other resistance to change comes from members of the organization who believe they may be disadvantaged or inconvenienced by it or who fear that the untried program may be worse than present ones. After a change is decided upon, further resistance ordinarily continues among components of the organization. Although the firms which Woodward studied that were changing their production methods in South Essex (see pages 680 and 681) had progressive management and their employees seemed ready to accept change, introduction of change did not move smoothly.[169] Two problems appeared in every firm studied: The initiation and implementation of change were extremely slow, and no matter how carefully the idea was introduced, opposition was the immediate and almost automatic response of lower supervisors and operators. Four years passed while intentions materialized into plans and decisions were made. In two of the seven firms a substantial part of this time was used to build a plant and install machinery. Most of the time was spent on meetings designed to arrange compromises among individuals and departments with conflicting interests. Although the human effort expended over this protracted period was expensive, those involved appeared to be unaware of this cost.

The resistance to change found in this study was greatest among the most successful individuals and groups and the most secure workers, the elite of the labor force who would have had no trouble getting other jobs if they had chosen to do so. They used the change as an occasion to bargain for either a reduction of effort or an increase in wages. Resistance finally evaporated when terms were agreed upon. A similar bargaining process took place over the distribution of power at middle-management and supervisory levels. These decider components were determined to get something out of the change, and, like the workers, these managers and supervisors also insisted upon gaining either by increasing their relative power positions or by making top management conscious of the critical role they played in the change. All this resulted in their receiving better performance ratings and higher salaries.

Excess rates of information inputs elicit the adjustments to information input overloads (see pages 157 to 164 and 187 to 192). Organizations also meet such overloads by reassigning people to the components affected by the overload, such as the input transducer or the producer, or by recruiting human components temporarily or permanently. Costs of these must be balanced against benefits they are expected to produce. Overloads of monetary inputs are not usually a problem at this level. Profits are used for growth, investment, dividends to stockholders, and other such purposes, as well as for paying excess profits taxes.

Orders or requests for service are information inputs which transmit a demand that the system output particular products or services to specific addresses. Sudden increases in such inputs, such as occur in welfare agencies during a big local strike or in industrial organizations when some environmental change makes more people demand their products, affect components throughout the organization, particularly when the products requested have not been, or cannot be, stored in sufficient quantities to meet the demand or when the capacity of the organization is already reached. Speedup of converting and producing, elimination of less urgent services, and other such adjustments are undertaken to counter these stresses.

5.2.3 Matter-energy internal processes These processes include those which avoid or adjust for strains arising from delays or other problems in the flow of matter-energy from input to output in the organization's activities and also those arising from movement or distribution of human components by the organization.

Among these are a large number of adjustments designed to eliminate or prevent bottlenecks, waste, deterioration, or delay. These involve production scheduling, materials handling, and other such practical aspects of operations appropriate to the sort of product or service being output by the organization.

Such adjustments also are concerned with coordination of activities of different subsystems. For instance, an efficient flow of patients to appropriate areas of a clinic, which is a distributor process, requires that the channels carrying information operate at a rate that permits patient records, x-rays, and findings to arrive with or before the patient. A goal of systems analysis of organizational processes carried out by industrial engineers, management consultants, or operations research experts is to determine the causes of internal matter-energy strains. These can then be reduced by changes in standard procedures, rearrangement of components in space, use of automation, alterations in products, or adjustments of associated internal information processing variables.

If internal matter-energy processes are to be carried out efficiently in large organizations, many variables must be kept in steady states. To assist in this, their complex interrelationships can be studied by computer simulations. One example, developed by Abe for Exxon Corporation, includes information about its fleet of tankers, its refineries, and the sources of its crude oil.[170] Some of its variables are throughput rates at refineries, which change when oil is depleted and must be replenished, when the crude runs out and another grade is substituted, or when breakdown occurs; seasonal changes in inventory; storage capacities; queues of tankers awaiting unloading; sizes of tankers; permanent or supplemental status of a particular tanker; travel times of each tanker, adjusted for season and for storms; and grade of oil needed by each refinery. The simulation schedules tankers and chooses their destinations to minimize delays and costs and to avoid shortages of crude oil at any refinery. This is an efficient approach to a highly complex problem in internal matter-energy adjustments of a worldwide organization.

Adjustments to movement or distribution of human and group components are important in many sorts of organizations. Communities have numerous such adjustment processes. The independent mobility of each human component and the biological and social rhythms governing the times at which people are active have profound effects upon communities. Regular flows into industrial areas and the business centers of cities occur at specified times each day, and return flows take place at night. These rhythms are somewhat different for factory districts and for business sections, since shifts change at different hours and in some cases there is such activity several times during a 24-h period. The usual pattern in all cities is for activity to diminish at night. Further mass movements take place at lunchtime and at hours when entertainment, sports activities, or special events attract people.

The movement and assembling of large numbers of people place strains upon many components of communities. Streets are usually crowded at periods of peak flow, and so traffic is often routed in one direction at such times. Public vehicles are ordinarily crowded at rush hours, and thus additional mass-transportation equipment is employed during these periods. Automobile accidents occur, requiring the presence of police, ambulances, and wrecker services; crowd control by police may be required. Very large crowds may require that police work overtime, increasing the cost of their services, which the community must pay. On the other hand, at night many organizations close, and the demand for community services diminishes. As the number of people in a community increases, other sorts of adjustments must be made. Not only must more transportation and parking facilities be provided, but also more public servants must be employed. Also, significant alterations of velocities, acceleration patterns, and latencies of traffic flows, both pedestrian and automotive, are required to avoid collisions.

Family-group components within cities move frequently. About 20 percent of the population of the United States changes homes each year, frequently within the same community.[171] The reasons for these moves are various, many of them having to do with group variables like increase in size of family, change in income, and independence of grown children. In any given area, however, removal of some families is

adjusted to by other, similar families, moving in, so that over long periods of time the distribution of families within a city remains quite stable, maintaining the steady state of the system. Typically, the grouping of people in communities is strongly affected by income and ethnic group or race. Over longer periods, however, patterns of settlement change as the community grows and develops and as changes in steady states occur. Often these are quite sudden; for example, within a few months a primarily Jewish section may become chiefly black, or a primarily black section may become chiefly Puerto Rican. Some of these changes are clearly pathological (see pages 703, 704, 710, and 711).

5.2.4 Information internal processes This class of adjustment processes includes many social interactions among components of organizations as well as some system processes initiated for the purpose of avoiding or compensating for strains resulting from disturbances of steady states of internal information processing variables. Not all interpersonal relationships among members of an organization are relevant to the organization. Whether, for example, typist Susie prefers file clerk Elsie to secretary Jane or whether one of the accountants is dating a computer programmer usually has little effect on organizational processes. These are system interactions at the group level. They become important organizationally only when they determine the choice of channels for transmission of organizational information (see pages 633 and 660) or when they outweigh other considerations in increasing a person's influence on organizational decisions or helping him obtain rewards, such as promotion, which he might not otherwise receive.

In her survey, Woodward found the fact of differential status among divisions and departments of the firms (see pages 617 to 619) to be an important aspect of their internal steady states. Each of these firms had what she analyzed as a "critical function"—production, marketing, or development. It was a characteristic of all firms above average in success that their status systems gave adequate recognition to the importance of the critical function.[172] In unit production firms (see page 618), for instance, which depended upon research and development for success and survival, the research and development department had high status, and its scientists were an elite.[173] In process firms (see page 618) marketing was critical, and that department had high status, but the people were not an elite since they were not well known to the rest of the organization.[174] In one process firm studied a "social system within a social system" had developed among the personnel involved in the operation of the plant. A network of relationships with its own status system, system of communication, and authority included only those people and excluded everyone in other departments, such as marketing or technology. Status in the firms studied was also ascribed to the department from which the current chief executive had originally come.[175] Strains resulted when this was a department other than the one performing the critical function.

Organizational information internal adjustment processes include those concerned with (a) *motivation* of members or employees to join and remain in the organization and to accept its authority and further its goals, (b) *productivity* of the system and of components within it, (c) *satisfaction* of components, (d) *coordination* of the system, and (e) *resolution of conflict* among components.

(a) *Motivation.* One of the earliest entrants into the field of management theory was Taylor. He had observed industrial systems from inside, as a worker and later as a foreman in a steel company. He viewed workers as naturally lazy and resistant to work.[176] When brought together in groups, as they are in a factory, he considered them even more effective at resisting work. He considered that the way to get the most work out of them was to subject them to discipline, use incentive pay to motivate them, and instruct them in the detailed performance of their tasks. He studied each operation of workmen by breaking it down into its smallest components in order to eliminate slow, false, and useless movements and to develop new ways of doing the same work more efficiently. He further recommended a functional management system (see page 644) in which each worker received orders and help from eight bosses, each a specialist uniquely qualified to transmit information about a particular aspect of the job.

Four sorts of management are distinguished by Likert in terms of their use of motivations (see page 650).[177] System 1 motivates subordinates by fear, threats, punishments, and occasional rewards. System 2 motivates subordinates by rewards and some actual or potential punishments. System 3 uses rewards, occasional punishments, and some involvement of subordinates in decision making. System 4 provides subordinates with economic rewards based on a compensation system developed through their participation, as well as group participation and involvement in setting goals, improving methods, and appraising progress toward goals.

Large corporations, faced with absenteeism, tardiness, and poor performance, find it necessary to develop ways to motivate their employees.[178] This is particularly true in the automobile industry, which is committed to the monotonous work of the assembly line. Training foremen to increase their skill as leaders and their understanding of new workers who may have special tensions because of their backgrounds is one approach. Increasing rewards, including fringe benefits and retirement, after a stated number of years of service is another. Use of bonuses and incentive pay is another (see page 675).

The probability that a person will leave an organization is viewed by March and Simon in terms of an inducement-contribution balance.[179] If inducement utilities are greater than contribution utilities, a person is not likely to leave an organization. A balance in favor of contribution utilities has the opposite effect. This balance is a function of the perceived desirability of leaving the organization and the perceived ease of movement from it. The first is influenced by a number of factors, including conformity of the job to the person's estimate of his own independence, worth, specialized competences, and interests. The second is influenced by the state of the economy. People do not usually quit when alternatives are not available. Other factors such as sex, age, individual personality, social status, length of service, and prestige of the organization are also important. Organizational adjustments designed to increase the satisfaction of employees affect this balance as well (see pages 676 to 679). Employees who find their jobs unpleasant or their rewards unsatisfactory often leave the organization. A turnover rate of 25.2 percent in an automobile plant in 1 year, for example, clearly indicated widespread worker dissatisfaction.[180]

(b) *Productivity.* The decisions of employees to join or to remain in an organization and participate in its process in accordance with their agreement when they joined it (see page 645) do not prevent them from performing halfheartedly, pursuing goals of components rather than overall organizational goals when these are not compatible, and even deliberately sabotaging activities which have been undertaken on directives by the decider. Such responses by components that do not accept the established organizational goals obviously reduce the efficiency and productivity of the total system.

Evidence that organizational goals are more acceptable to those components which have participated in forming them than to those which have not is found in an experimental study that used as subjects managers and supervisors in a training laboratory.[181] The tasks used were word and number games. They required coordinated efforts among the three subjects in each group. Some groups devised their own plans, some received plans created by planning groups, and some were given no planning periods before beginning the task. When the subjects were carrying out plans they had developed for themselves, their performance was somewhat better and their attitudes were more positive than when they were acting out plans made by others. The results were moderately significant statistically.

When cost-effectiveness analyses or other measures show one division or department of a corporation to be performing in an unsatisfactory manner, that component may be punished in various ways, such as having promotions or other rewards withheld from it by its decider components. The manager or head of the unit may be given further training, counseled, exhorted, or discharged. The unit may be reorganized in an effort to improve its output. Other personnel changes designed to strengthen what appear to be weak points in its structure may be undertaken. Budget allocations are sometimes increased to permit staff expansion, new machinery, more automation, enlarged space, or other improvements.

Productivity of the whole organization or of divisions and departments is hard to measure (see pages 667 and 668). Productivity of individual workers is frequently even more difficult or impossible to evaluate. This is true, for instance, on an assembly line, which produces a group output and on which the demands of the standard procedure keep variations in workers' productivity to a minimum. Personal incentives for improved productivity are a part of the Scanlon plan, a union-management cooperative arrangement which features money bonuses to all members in proportion to their base rates of pay for all improvements in company efficiency during a stated period. Work-improvement committees are set up that include multiple echelons in the organization.[182] This plan has been successfully implemented in a number of corporations.

It seems reasonable to expect that the sort of management methods used should affect organizational productivity. Research, however, has not demonstrated any clear and consistent relationship between them. Leadership style and output have appeared to be unrelated in some studies but significantly correlated in others.[183] In one study, management methods were experimentally varied by increasing the control by the lowest echelon, or rank and file, in two divisions and increasing the control by the higher echelons in the other two divisions of one department of a nonunion industrial organization.[184] These four parallel divisions engaged in similar, relatively routine clerical work. Most of the employees were women. In the first pair of divisions the people who made up the higher echelons were persuaded to delegate some of their authority downward. This experimental procedure was known as the "autonomy program." The other two divisions of the department received the opposite treatment; that is, they were moved toward tighter hierarchical control and were designated the "hierarchically controlled program." The satisfactions of individual workers increased significantly under the autonomy program and decreased significantly under the hierarchically controlled program. The effects on productivity were not comparable, however. Productivity as quantified by one measure increased under both programs, but more under the hierarchically controlled program. There was evidence, however, that personnel turnover was higher under this latter program.

It is interesting to compare the above results with the findings of one part of the Hawthorne studies.[185] In the latter, productivity was improved by employing informal instead of strict supervision, granting workers permission to talk freely in the work group, discussing projected changes with the people affected, and generally relaxing the old rules intended to promote efficiency. The employees who were subjects received special attention from top management and others. They were proud to be in the study. They became a cooperative, close-knit group; they derived satisfaction from their work; and they had a feeling of loyalty to their associates and enjoyed personal relationships with them. To industrial psychologists and engineers, the publication of these findings came as a "great illumination." The study gave pioneering evidence that attention to human relations can increase organizational productivity. Later analyses have shown that the attention paid to workers by experimenters in the course of their studies may to some extent improve the workers' productivity. Also, it is now clear that careful concern for good interpersonal relations is not by itself enough to guarantee good organizational effectiveness.

Under some circumstances, close and detailed supervision appears to be necessary. This is true, for example, if the requirements of the job tax the capacities of the worker.[186] Under these circumstances he cannot be permitted to make important decisions. If a supervisor has information that his subordinates need for their work, constant close supervision is essential for efficiency. Some research findings lend support to this principle. While general supervision was the best for a group of clerical workers, in a railroad maintenance gang the opposite proved true, possibly because their boss had much technical knowledge that was useful in their work.

In another research designed to investigate how management style affects productivity, the mode of supervision was changed in a service company with 250 employees, part of a national organization.[187]

Strong hierarchical control was replaced by supervision of groups rather than single workers and by group decision making, processes to which the supervisors gave sympathetic support. An important finding of this study, confirmed also by the previously cited one, is that it takes time for productivity to be increased by such changes. At the end of the 6-month period of the study, improvement of some intervening variables, such as motivation and attitudes of employees, was apparent. It took 1½ years, however, for significant changes in productivity to occur. When they did, they were substantial and enduring.

According to Likert's analysis, when a firm attempts to reduce its costs and improve its productivity by tightening hierarchical controls, increasing pressure for productivity, cutting budgets, limiting the numbers of personnel, and tightening work standards, the immediate effect is often improvement in productivity and cost reduction, which is at its maximum in about a year. But after this, hostility builds up among lower echelons of decider components and among nonsupervisory personnel. Then adverse effects such as faster turnover of personnel, increased absenteeism, deteriorating labor relations, greater waste, higher costs, reduced service to customers, and lower quality of products or services occur. Furthermore, the clients in the suprasystem often become dissatisfied with the products or services being provided and begin to complain or to turn to competing organizations to meet their needs. All this usually happens slowly and may be difficult to relate to the changes in management methods.[188]

In recent years the managements of many organizations, particularly in business and industry, have made extensive efforts to bring about planned change in order to improve organizational effectiveness and productivity.[189] Some of the adjustment processes used to facilitate such organizational change operate at the organism and group levels rather than at the organization level.[190] The assumption, not always recognized, is that adjustments at the lower levels favorably modify the organization. Included are adjustments in skills, knowledge, personalities, and attitudes of single persons; in interpersonal relationships among members of peer groups; in the norms of peer groups; and in interpersonal relationships between a supervisor and those reporting directly to him. Psychotherapy of members of management and employees has been used extensively to try to accomplish such adjustments. Concerning the use of either individual or group therapy to produce improvements in organizational processes, Katz and Kahn say:

. . . to approach institutional change solely in individual terms involves an impressive and discouraging series of assumptions—assumptions which are too often left implicit. They include, at the very least: the assumption that the individual can be provided with new insight and knowledge; that these will produce some significant alteration in his motivational pattern; that these insights and motivations will be retained even when the individual leaves the protected situation in which they were learned and returns to his accustomed role in the organization; that he will be able to adapt his new knowledge to that real-life situation; that he will be able to persuade his coworkers to accept the changes in his behavior which he now desires; and that he will also be able to persuade them to make complementary changes in their own expectations and behavior.[191]

Even when the changed person is the head of an organization or of a major unit, there is no guarantee of organizational change as a result of therapy or of sensitivity training, a group experience designed to increase awareness of group processes and the person's reactions to them. When such leaders are involved, however, the probability of important impact is increased.[192] Psychotherapy with peer groups drawn from the organization, such as groups of foremen or of executives at the same echelon, may significantly affect their attitudes. There is, however, no assurance that the changes produced in these people will be in directions desired by the organization's management.[193] Indeed, as their group identification is strengthened, resistance to organizational needs may also increase. Moreover, if the group is made up of people at a low echelon, changes in them may have little direct effect upon organizational processes. Group therapy undertaken for the purpose of producing change at every echelon of a factory has in at least one case produced changed attitudes and clarification of relationships among components, which is an organizational change.[194]

(c) *Satisfaction.* An effective organization adjusts its processes so that its components are sufficiently satisfied with the system to continue to carry out their functions in it. The satisfactions derived from system participation differ from one type of organization to another and, within any organization, among the components which perform the various functions. Working in a social agency obviously offers different rewards from those offered by working in a bank. Within each agency officers, professional staff, and clerks each derive somewhat different satisfactions.

The owners or stockholders, management, and other employees of a business or industrial organization must all receive some return for their participation in the system. It is the exchange of rewards for services which creates the symbiosis that keeps components of the organization interacting (see page 32). If resources were unlimited, the interests of these components would not be opposed. Since this is never the case, however, benefits to one can be seen as limiting rewards to others. High wages in profit-making corporations, for instance, are often interpreted by stockholders as decreasing profit margins and threatening dividends. Large profits and high returns to investors may be taken by employees as evidence that they are not receiving a fair proportion of the fruits of their labors. Management must continuously monitor adjustment processes to assure that rewards to all components are being satisficed, to ensure that the satisfactions of all are enough to keep them co-operating.

Levels of aspiration of all components tend to be revised upward as the components' rewards increase, and this leads to reduced satisfactions.[195] Recognizing this, business firms often do not raise dividends in good years, but instead pay supplementary dividends. Thus they avoid heightening expectations for future years.[196] Stockholders must be kept satisfied because when they are not, they sell their stock. If enough of them do this, its value declines. This adjustment process decreases public confidence and limits the firm's ability to raise further capital by issuing stock or other securities. Also, dissatisfied stockholders, acting as an organized component of the decider subsystem, can demand reorganization of the company or replacement of top management.

Organizations must also use adjustment processes to increase the satisfactions of their employees, since doing so is known to diminish employee absenteeism and turnover.[197] Job satisfaction is a complicated variable, made up of a number of factors such as the following:

(i) *Fulfillment and pride in the work.*   These prove to be highest in professions, in service careers, and in occupations that demand skill and present a challenge.[198] They are lowest in unskilled, highly automatic jobs. Unit production is the manufacturing of single products to customers' orders in which a skilled employee works in a small group and is aware of the entire process from start to finish (see page 618). It appeared to be the most satisfying form of production of those studied by Woodward in South Essex because the workers felt responsible for what they made and took pride in it.[199]

Changing the nature of jobs to make them more gratifying to workers would seem to be a good way to increase organizational productivity. Unfortunately, this is expensive and difficult for the very jobs that appear to need it most. For instance, making automobiles in some way other than on the assembly line would require a revolution in methods and machinery with corresponding need for capital. In the end, any other method of production would be likely to prove more costly.

One opportunity to observe how the changing of work procedures alters job satisfactions arose when new technology necessitated modifications in traditional methods of mining coal in Great Britain.[200] Before the change, each miner had been able to perform all the tasks involved in mining. Work had been carried on in self-selected groups, usually composed of men with about the same degree of skill and experience. They had a feeling of autonomy. Since pay was based upon how much coal each group mined, earnings were directly related to performance. Feedback on productivity was rapid and direct. The workers found such work satisfying.

Then newly invented machinery made it possible for much larger groups simultaneously to mine a much greater surface (the longwall method). This new procedure led to the abandonment of the old work groups. Work assignments were made differently, on the model of a mass-production industry. Miners on each shift were limited to one part of the total task. Within shifts, further specialization was required.

This adjustment to the new technology eliminated aspects of the work that the miners previously had found satisfying. No longer was each worker associated with a small group of men whose skills and support he knew he could rely on. These associations had been comforting in the dangerous, unpredictable underground work. Status and pay differences based upon skills required for the specialized tasks under the new procedure created resentment among the men, particularly the experienced ones who could do any of the jobs but were assigned to lower-paying work. Absenteeism increased among these men. Also, the relationship of productivity to pay was lost.

Other mines did not make such major changes in procedure, but retained many older ways of doing things while adapting to the new machinery. They used a "composite longwall method." The miners were rotated through a variety of jobs in response to current demands of the task. They worked in large groups which chose their own members, so preserving an important aspect of the old procedure. As formerly, the group took responsibility for getting the task done. Pay was tied to productivity, the base pay for effective groups being raised. Absenteeism under the composite procedure was less than half what it had been under the conventional longwall method. Productivity was also better under the composite procedure.

It would be most difficult and expensive to make the sort of fundamental changes in procedures that would make assembly-line jobs more satisfying. Therefore, some industrial organizations have tried to increase the meaningfulness of such circumscribed jobs by using training films to acquaint the workers with their role in the whole production process. They have also encouraged supervisors and inspectors to show approval rather than passive acceptance of finished work.[201] Using more pervasive automation to eliminate such jobs is another organizational adjustment process, one which has costs in creating strains at the level of the society.

(ii) *Remuneration and perquisites.* Pay, retirement annuities, insurance plans, and other fringe benefits are a second source of job satisfaction. Working conditions, such as adequate space, clean surroundings, and absence of petty regulations, are related sources of work satisfaction. Bargaining is the major adjustment process by which employees and components of the decider come to agreement on these matters. Union officials often represent employees in this process. A union is an organization, part of which is an inclusion in each of the organizations that employ its members. Since its membership is usually drawn from many organizations, it is a component of the society, carrying out societywide adjustment processes (see page 700). Bargaining by unions representing employees of an organization is therefore an outwardly dispersed adjustment process at the organization level. Bargaining between management and employees who are not union members is usually an individual matter. In such cases, however, upper and lower limits of possible pay and a general standard for other benefits at a particular grade or rank are often set by the current practices in the society at large.

After the initial bargain is made, advancement through grades may be more or less automatic, review may be at stated intervals as a part of the supervision process, or either party may initiate reconsideration of the agreement. Downward adjustments of pay occur only under special circumstances. When the organization is in trouble, particularly when the whole economy is depressed, employees may accept decreased pay, usually regarded as temporary, until times improve. "Cost-of-living" clauses in union contracts provide for protection against inflation by adjusting pay automatically as the cost-of-living index changes. Such clauses are not generally favored by management and are not yet common.[202]

(iii) *Status.* Recognized status and the prerogatives that go with it are significant sources of satisfaction for most people whose positions rate it. The amount of recognition of a position or its holder is determined by the attitudes of other organizational components. The status ascribed to a position not only belongs to the person holding it but also extends to include others associated with him. The president's secretary has high status not only among secretaries but also among others in the organization, deriving from her access to him. A common adjustment process to increase the status of a position, often as added

inducement to make a lower-level job attractive or to save the self-esteem of an employee who cannot perform adequately and cannot be fired because of seniority or other reasons, is to give him or her a title that implies more real importance in the decider structure than the holder of the position really has. Others in the organization usually become aware of just how much this means, but the adjustment probably succeeds to some extent in spite of this, particularly since the title is reinforced by other prerogatives.

(iv) *Prospect for advancement.* Awareness that the job is not a "dead end" increases satisfaction from tasks that a person might, if he regarded them as permanent, be unwilling to continue doing. It is not uncommon for management to encourage several people at the same echelon to hope for promotion to a higher level, although only one will attain their common goal. This can cause interpersonal conflict within organizations (see page 680). It can also motivate a person to produce.

(v) *The feeling of exercising control.* Within the decider subsystem the experience of being in charge has been shown experimentally to produce satisfaction. A survey of a number of different types of organizations revealed that high performance and member loyalty resulted when a substantial amount of control was exercised and when both rank-and-file members and management had important voices in it.[203] Some studies show that under certain circumstances, vigorous control is considered more important than who wields it. Many union members, for instance, prefer strong control by their leaders to other sorts of organizational decision making because they believe it is the most efficient way to achieve the goals of the organization.[204]

Participation in job assignment, an aspect of job control, has been shown in researches of army and industrial units to make employees more willing to remain in the organization.[205] Lack of independence and control in the work situation has also been shown to increase dissatisfaction with the job.[206]

It has been suggested that actual control is less important than the feeling of control.[207] An attempt to verify this hypothesis, using data from a study of League of Women Voters organizations, indicated that actual control and perceived control are possibly both important to persons in organizations.[208]

Changes in decider processes to permit greater control by components at lower echelons of organizations are features of a number of current organization theories. These include some I have already discussed and that of McGregor, who contrasted Theory Y, which involves participation by all components in decision making, with Theory X, an authoritarian management theory.[209] All these antiauthoritarian theories Leavitt classes as "power equalization" theories.[210] Ordinarily they are not implemented in organizations by profound changes in the decider subsystem structure. Rather, they are tied into a human relations approach which relies upon change of individual personality variables in a significant proportion of an organization's decider personnel to produce changes in the desired direction (see page 676). Results of such efforts so far are equivocal, but really thorough, large-scale trials of them have been few. Their proponents firmly believe that organizational decision making will evolve in this direction (see page 690).

An adjustment process designed to increase the feeling of control by participants without actually doing so is used, deliberately or not, by some executives who consult everybody interested in a given problem and then do what they intended to do all along. These tactics may lead at least some of those consulted to believe that they have influenced the decision.

(vi) *Pleasant working relationships.* Most people are happier and more productive in an organization of any type when their work can be carried out through harmonious interactions with peers, superiors, and subordinates (see page 675).

Theory Y, System 4, and the 9,9 management style, among other current organization theories (see pages 650 and 651), all stress the use of supportive, ego-building relationships by supervisors. They maintain, on the basis of various studies, that such behavior improves the effectiveness of organizations. There seems little doubt that people prefer being treated in ways that enhance their personal dignity.

(vii) *Gratification of social needs.* Organizations frequently provide facilities for relaxation, recreations, and sports not directly connected with the work of the system. These are particularly needed in systems that are remote from such resources in the suprasystem, like military bases in foreign countries or mining communities remote from cities. Workers in larger communities ordinarily are components of many other groups and organizations and commonly prefer to satisfy many of their social needs outside the work setting.[211] Social relationships differ from one type of organization to another. Members of religious organizations often live quite separately from the community at large, in some cases segregated by sex. For other reasons, inmates in prisons and patients in mental and general hospitals lead restricted social lives. University faculties tend to satisfy their social needs within the system, often within their own departments or specialty groups, possibly as a result of the traditional separation of town and gown.

The satisfaction derived from a job is usually the result of several of the above factors in varying proportions. Monotonous work is bearable if remuneration prospects for the future, and working conditions are good. An executive may prefer to be the president of a small organization, exercising a large amount of control, rather than accept an offer to head a large division of a great corporation at higher pay but with little autonomy.

(d) *Coordination.* All components of organizations that interact in carrying out system processes must be coordinated. Some interact infrequently or only indirectly and so need little coordination, and that perhaps only by the top echelon of the decider. For instance, branches of a large organization that carry on similar processes in separate geographic areas require few adjustments to achieve coordination. When they are needed, they are carried out under direction of the home office.

Typical coordination problems arise when accurate timing is important for processes of several subsystems or components or when a novel situation affecting multiple subsystems requires cooperative problem solving among them. Strains requiring adjustments of coordination can be met either by structural changes in the organization or by adjustments of process, depending upon the circumstances.

The pyramidal form of the decider structure (see page 643) provides not only control but also coordination, although much of the coordinating information in organizations does not flow up or down through hierarchical channels.[212] A great deal of coordination is carried out over lateral channels, by means of conversations, memoranda, or meetings of decider components responsible for different processes at the same echelon. Department managers with mutual problems may discuss them over lunch. Social workers at different branches of the same agency may discuss cases by telephone, using an informal lateral channel that makes it unnecessary for them to request written record materials.

Organizational structure can be arranged so that certain departments, groups, or persons act as coordinators or liaison officers among other components. In the overlapping group structure (see page 644), for instance, a person who is a member of both groups meets with each of them separately and provides coordination between them. Departments or groups, which Lawrence and Lorsch call "integrators," whose purpose is coordination among the other departments, existed in all the plastics firms they studied (see page 624).[213] They were required because the fundamental orientations and attitudes of the basic departments were different enough to cause communication problems. The four basic departments in all these firms were sales, promotion, applied research, and fundamental research.[214] They varied in formality of structure; kinds of interpersonal relationships among members; orientation toward time, related to the rapidity with which they received feedback (see pages 685 and 686); and objectives and goals, which were determined by their differing assignments. The integrator units were the production control, budget planning, and cost control departments.[215] Because of the differences among the basic departments, these integrators were most successful when they were intermediate in their orientations and when they were seen by others in the organization as having influence in decision making.[216] Top managers provided integration on broad policies and strategies.[217] Departmental managers were responsible for integration of their departments with others. To accomplish another sort of coordination, adjusting for strains that arose during technological change, special engineering departments were established in two industrial organizations in Woodward's sample.[218] Their purposes were to bridge the gap between development and production and to solve the design problems that appeared when new products were being transferred from development to the production lines. In one firm the new department became the channel of communication it was intended to be; in the other it did not. Other internal states of the two organizations differed, such as amount of education of the people in the affected departments. In the company in which the personnel were well educated, communication was relatively easy, and the bridging effort succeeded. In the other firm the communication was difficult, and the new department did not achieve its goal. Also, in the latter firm the new department was given little power. The results suggest that when the communication gap is small, as in the successful case, a bridging department can succeed but that it is not likely to establish good communication between hostile departments.

The structure of highly automated organizations or departments represents preplanned coordination of their processes. For instance, if assembly-line machinery is well designed, it takes into account all the information flows required to coordinate production activities. A distinction is made by March and Simon between coordination by plan and coordination by feedback.[219] The first includes programs for behavior in standardized situations. When these are developed, they include coordinating information. Schedules for jobs are also examples of this sort of coordination. If the situation does not conform exactly to the original plan, however, further coordination by feedback is needed. Advance plans rarely are complete enough to obviate the need for feedback coordination. Of course, they are not always intended to include operating procedures for all conceivable situations.

Some are developed for a single anticipated situation, and they may specify coordination, often in great detail. The top echelon of the Allied high command, for example, developed detailed programs for all units that were to be involved in the 1944 D-day invasion of Normandy, transmitted as much as was necessary to decider components at lower echelons, and directed that drills and practices of the intended exercises be undertaken. The high command attempted to reduce the need for localized deciding and coordinating adjustments by foreseeing all contingencies. By contrast, more informal organizations that deal with less crucial problems may use feedback coordination almost entirely.

(*e*) *Resolution of conflict.* Given the complicated nature of organizational goals; the fact that optimal solutions for one component may not be equally satisfactory for others; the competitiveness that may develop among individual, group, departmental, or divisional components; the uncertainty of the environment; the scarceness of resources; and the orneriness of human nature, some degree of conflict is probably inevitable in most systems at this level.

The issues around which conflicts typically center and the components most likely to be involved differ from one type of organization to another. Any stage of decision making (see Hypothesis 3.3.7.2-1, pages 100 and 651 to 662), including establishing purposes or goals, analysis, synthesis, and implementing, can become the subject of conflict when components must decide jointly or must coordinate their activities. Conflict can rage around the scope of the deciding power at different echelons or of various components at the same echelon. Components which must compete for scarce resources of any sort can also come into conflict.

Possibly organizations in which detailed specifications of duties and responsibilities of all components exist have less conflict than those in which components interact more freely. As a result, conflict is more likely to arise in new organizations that are still working out their internal processes than in older ones in which interrelationships have been more or less settled.

Change tends to precipitate conflict by producing unprecedented situations.[220] The resulting uncertainty as to how to proceed may provoke power struggles, as some components move to control the decisions needing to be made and as others join or oppose them.

Conflict was associated with change in some firms in Woodward's South Essex study (see pages 617 to 619). This took place when one firm changed from unit to batch production.[221] Labor disputes, including several stoppages of a few hours and a 3-day strike, appeared to be caused by resentment because the production superintendent no longer was as available to deal with the workers' grievances as he had been previously and because the foremen were not equipped to fill the gap but were, like the workers, anxious and insecure as a result of loss of the production superintendent's attention.

In several other companies that changed to batch from unit production, the status structure was upset. This brought about bitter, disruptive, and long-lasting conflicts. Development engineers, who had been an elite group, were threatened by the increased importance of production activities. Within the production department, power, status, and the scope of discretion of line supervisors and middle managers were reduced. The status struggle produced deterioration of personal relationships. Friction grew between development engineers and the production planning and control staffs. More design changes were made, probably because of the development engineers' desire to assert themselves, and these were attended with waste and delays. Other departments, which felt they had lost out as a result of the new methods, enjoyed the confusion and sided with the development engineers. All this resulted from a management decision to make a basic change in the processes of the organization's producer subsystem.

When a manager is judged by the results he achieves and is given freedom to exercise initiative, he usually seeks to promote the interests and increase the jurisdiction of his department, thus coming into conflict with other managers.[222] If these conflicts are settled, further issues arise later as changing conditions present new challenges. Both union and management also try to improve their economic positions, and consequently they come into conflict. Success of one in attaining a goal may upset the status relationships, motivating the one displaced to try to recover its advantage. Labor wants higher wages and better working conditions and uses collective bargaining or strikes to fight for them. Management wants lower costs and increased productivity. To attain these ends, it may purchase new machinery. This may lessen work satisfaction, and labor may start grievance procedures as a result. And so it goes.

Not all conflicts are resolved. Many organizations live with a good deal of conflict. Cyert and March say:

Specialization and delegation are used to reduce the complex conflict situation facing the systems as a whole into a series of simpler, less conflicting situations. [This supports Hypothesis 5.2-16, page 107, which states that a system tends to reduce multiple component conflicts to conflicts among a lesser number of blocs of components.] The organization divides its decision problems into subproblems, but it does so under circumstances in which there is no guarantee that the conflict will be thereby resolved. There is no guarantee that local decisions satisfying local demands will necessarily provide a joint decision satisfying all demands on the system. Thus, an organization requires mechanisms for facilitating over-all consistency.

We can cite here two such mechanisms. First, the use of aspiration-level goals. . . . the demands of the organization participants (and, therefore, the goals of the organization) are stated in terms of acceptable levels of reward, performance, etc. Thus, we assume a profit goal of the form, "Profits must exceed $X" rather than of the form, "Maximize profits." Aspiration level goals impose relatively weak consistency demands on the system. Ordinarily, we will expect a "solution" to such a system to be nonunique in the sense that more than one allocation of resources will meet the joint demands. At the same time, aspiration level goals tend to under-exploit the environment and thereby leave excess potential resources to absorb potential inconsistencies in local decisions [see page 652].

Second, the sequential attention to goals. Ordinarily when we talk of "consistency" of goals or decisions we refer to some way of assessing their internal logic at a point of time. As a result, in many theories of organizational choice, we are inclined to insist on consistency within a cross section of goals. Such an insistence seems to us inaccurate as a representation of organizational behavior. Organizations resolve conflict among goals, in part, by attending to different goals at different times. The business firm is likely to resolve pressures for two conflicting behaviors by first doing one and then doing the other. The resulting time buffer between goals permits the organization to solve one problem at a time, attending to one goal at a time.[223]

Ways in which organizational conflicts may be handled include:

(i) Use of physical power. When conflict erupts into violence, as it does in cities and universities from time to time, the decider may call upon the police or other component to exert force, or it may request similar help from the suprasystem.

(ii) Use of threat of sanctions. Among such penalties may be expulsion from the system or loss of remuneration, perquisites, or status.

(iii) Use of authority. Under some circumstances a decider component decides to favor one course of action or point of view or competing component over others. Components may take conflicts to top management and force a high-level decision that is satisfactory to one side only. This way of resolving conflicts, Lawrence and Lorsch found, was resorted to by successful plastics companies when other methods did not succeed.[224]

(iv) Use of influence. This includes several processes designed either to form a group consensus or to fashion a solution to which others will agree without necessarily accepting the point of view.

Consensus may be reached as a result of *confrontation* among people who speak for different points of view. Townsend says that conflict within an organization is:

. . . a sign of a healthy organization—up to a point. A good manager doesn't try to eliminate conflict; he tries to keep it from wasting the energies of his people . . .

Conviction is a flame that must burn itself out—in trying an idea or fighting for a chance to try it. If bottled up inside, it will eat a man's heart away.

If you're the boss and your people fight you openly when they think you're wrong—that's healthy. If your men fight each other openly in your presence for what they believe in—that's healthy. But keep all the conflict eyeball to eyeball.[225]

Confrontation was the most used means of conflict resolution in Lawrence and Lorsch's successful plastics firms.[226] The integrators' intermediate position in the structure was important in effective conflict resolution. They were more useful if they were competent in the area of the problem and if they felt that they were rewarded for success in mediation, which was only one aspect of their jobs. Other participants in the problem-solving group, the managers of concerned departments, resolved conflicts better if they were confident that they had influence and that their points of view were considered. Such confidence made them less hostile, even when the decision did not seem ideal to them. It was also important that the components that represented departmental points of view come from a managerial echelon where knowledge to make the decisions was available. These echelons differed from department to department. Given proper composition of the group that had the responsibility for decision, confrontation or "thrashing out" of the problem was highly effective in the plastic companies.

In systems in which votes determine decisions, *political activity* directed toward achieving a particular outcome is common. Coalitions are formed among persons who receive or expect to receive benefits of some sort in exchange for their support. Groups of members of some organizations form more or less stable coalitions which hold together under most stresses or strains. They band together for various reasons; for example, they may come from similar racial, ethnic, religious, educational, or professional backgrounds; they may have comparable economic or social status; they may share similar interests; or they may simply be friends. Coalition formation and behavior have been analyzed in terms of game theoretical concepts (see pages 579 and 580). Coalitions may be formed by bargaining, in which payoffs to members are made explicit. A congressman may get a position on a powerful congressional committee or support on an issue of importance to his constituency in exchange for his vote on a particular bill.

An analysis by Lazar of the decision-making processes of the United States National Railroad Adjustment Board has shown that the Board is affected by more than the content of the arguments made before it.[227] The influence or power of certain special-interest groups or coalitions also have impact. The Board includes three groups of components: representatives of "regular" unions, representatives of the railroad companies, and neutral referees. A large majority of the cases heard by the Board, Lazar found, involved employees who were members of the regular unions represented on the Board, but a few cases concerned employees who were members of "outside" unions or who were not union members. Before analyzing his data, he hypothesized that it would be strain-reducing both to regular labor and to management to reject the claims of outside unions and nonunion employees. The regular labor representatives would want to reject them because sustaining these claims would bypass regular channels and weaken their labor organizations. Management would want to reject them because paying the claims would be costly. Neutral referees would try to reduce strains by agreeing with the other two. After reviewing approximately 8,700 cases heard by the Board involving train and yard service employees, Lazar found that all aspects of his hypotheses were clearly confirmed. Only 1 case of an outside union out of 53 and only 1 case of a nonunion employee out of 127 were sustained without going to the neutral referees. Of cases heard by referees, only 6 percent of those concerning outside unions and 5 percent of those concerning nonunion employees were sustained, although neutral referees sustained 24 percent of regular cases.

Persuasion may influence members of organizations to join a coalition or back a point of view. A good presentation, perhaps employing impressive charts, effective arguments, and appeals to sentiments such as loyalty to a particular decider component, is useful in convincing others of the superiority of a point of view or in obtaining their acceptance of it for other reasons.

A person increases his power in organizational conflict resolution if his chance of being critical to the success of a winning coalition is great. As Hypothesis 3.3.7.2-2, page 100, states, this chance increases if the person has relevant information. As Hypothesis 3.3.7.2-3, page 100, states, this chance also increases as the number of persons transmitting information to the decider decreases. A scale for measuring the power of a particular person in a given situation has been devised. It extends from one extreme of complete control through no power to the other extreme of power to cause others to react negatively.[228] This scale was used in developing a way to measure the power of a specific person in a given situation. Thus the comparative power of members of a board of directors to influence a specific decision of the board can be expressed quantitatively.[229] The power of an individual member of such a board differs with structural and procedural factors. For instance, a chairman of a board who casts only tie-breaking votes, if all the other members vote on every issue, has more power if there is an odd number of members than if there is an even number. In the first case he will never vote, but in the latter his vote will be as likely to affect passage as the vote of any other member. A board chairman who has veto power, of course, has complete control. This is true of every member of a board that requires a unanimous vote for passage of any measure.

Compromise solutions to a conflict may be reached, either in a group decision or when a single executive must make the final decision, if no component can marshal enough support or exert sufficient persuasive power to get exactly what it desires.

Organizations function better if conflicts are resolved when they arise, rather than being merely smoothed over.[230] In the study of the plastics industry, a *smoothing over* of conflict was an adjustment process found to be used by one low-performing and one medium-performing company but by no high-performing companies. The managers of one low-performing organization made efforts to maintain friendly relations and smooth over conflict to the extent that this seriously impaired their ability to resolve interdepartmental differences. The authors of this study concluded that such smoothing over handicapped effective conflict resolution. Confrontation between opponents, together with pressure applied to speed a resolution, seemed the best procedure in these companies.

Dealing with a dissident group in an organization by accepting it as a legitimate component has been called *protest absorption.*[231] The history of the Roman Catholic Church provides one example of this adjustment process. In sixteenth-century Spain, St. Teresa and St. John of the Cross tried to revive asceticism in a period of laxity in the church. Initial attempts to suppress their followers did not succeed, and eventually the church permitted them to exist as a separate order engaged in missionary work.

The adjustment of protest absorption is most likely to be used in military, religious, academic, and other organizations in which the decider exerts power by distributing symbolic rewards (see page 645). In these systems the important offices or positions have, besides status, charisma. The persons performing the functions of these offices are viewed as having special powers and are set off from others in the organization by distinctive costumes, uniforms, badges of office, or courtesies showed to them. Such practices help to support the authority of the organization over its members. Strains arise, however, if a particular person, rather than his or her office, is attributed charisma. If in an organization that has a centralized decider, charisma is distributed throughout the echelon structure, a nonconforming enclave may form around a particular leader. Unlike a deviant, such a leader proclaims his dissent and challenges the existing situation, hoping to reform it without destroying the organization. His followers usually adopt distinctive symbols, dress, or behavior.

Circumstances within the organization may favor the development of such an enclave. If acceptance of the legitimacy of the power of the decider decreases; if the decider is insensitive to the developing nonconformity because information inputs about the revolt which come to it from the internal transducer are incomplete, erroneous, or distorted; if authority is weakened by corruption of officers; or if the organization is engaged in adjusting to an environmental stress, it may not discover the enclave in time to check its growth. The organization then must eliminate it by condemning or expelling its ringleaders, avoid it, or absorb it.

If the dissenting group becomes a legitimate unit of the organization, its leaders accept the authority of the top echelon of the decider and comply with its directives. They bring their finances under organizational control, and their scope of action is defined and limited. The leader or his successor again becomes an officer of the organization without special personal charisma. Thus the nonconforming enclave is tamed. Its concern with innovation usually diminishes. It remains distinctive, however, because of its history of nonconformity. Any persons it recruits may be required to undergo an exceptionally arduous indoctrination emphasizing the authority of the organization's decider because such enclaves are particularly susceptible to new cycles of protest and protest absorption.

5.2.5. Matter-energy output processes   Human subcomponents, human or other inclusions, wastes, or products may be output in excess amounts from organizations. The adjustments used depend upon what form of matter-energy is being output in excess.

An organization that is insensitive to the demands of its components may have to face an excessive number of resignations. Such personnel turnover produces strains, since too many new employees are inexperienced and too few are skilled in the system's processes. Loss of top decider components may be particularly serious in disrupting system processes. Experienced personnel may leave because the organization's management presses them strongly for increased productivity, makes decisions in an authoritarian manner, or pays little attention to employees' job satisfaction. Attempts by management to cut costs by refusing to increase wages or salaries to meet those of similar organizations can mean that skilled people leave, to be replaced by persons with less ability and fewer opportunities to join other organizations. A continuous accounting of an organization's human assets, in addition to the traditional accounting of its assets of money and property, can reveal whether there are excess personnel outputs.[232] A correction of the balance of inducements and contributions can adjust for this.

Loss of component organizations, groups, and individual residents is a major problem of large, modern cities. Such outward movement, often a flight from urban blight to the more attractive suburbs, aggravates the pathology of cities (see pages 702 to 704).

When the rate of extrusion shows a step-function increase, as when a panic in a theater or the Friday afternoon rush to leave the city overloads the usual output routes, immediate and effective adjustments are required. Emergency exits may be used to get the crowd out of the theater rapidly. Extra traffic lanes may be used to accommodate the rush-hour traffic. An attempted prison break is another example of an output excess strain to which vigorous adjustments—armed guards to reinforce the boundary—may be required. Excess outputs of wastes from an organization into its environment can occur when poor raw materials are input, methods of production are inefficient, storage facilities are inadequate, no equipment exists capable of recycling harmful wastes into more acceptable outputs, or boundaries are excessively permeable. Adjustments of the relevant structures or processes of the subsystem or subsystems involved can correct for such strains.

One measure of an industrial organization's efficiency is the ratio of its products to its wastes. When this ratio is too low, adjustments in converter, producer, or decider processes; replacements of components of these subsystems; changes in input materials; or combinations of all these may be necessary to compensate for the resulting strains.

Up to a point, strains from lacks of matter-energy outputs can be reduced simply by speeding the processes of the extruder subsystem. Sometimes just this, and no organization-level adjustment processes, may be required. On the other hand, in the case of a manufacturing firm with an excess of its products in its warehouses, an advertising campaign or a price cut may be required to accelerate this extrusion process. When a sudden major change in market demand occurs so that the normal flow of outputs to the suprasystem is stopped or drastically reduced, matter-energy storage may be arranged in space belonging to other subsystems. Or it may be necessary to disperse the storage process outwardly into rented quarters belonging to another organization. If the strain continues for long, input, converting, and producing rates must also be limited. Overtime may be eliminated, a shift may be dropped, and layoffs may occur. Ultimately, entire manufacturing plants may have to shut down.

Similar adjustments must take place when human components or inclusions do not leave the system at the expected rate. If, for example, an unusually large number of patrons stay to see a movie over again instead of going home, input of new customers may have to be curtailed. Legend reports that P. T. Barnum used various stratagems to keep the sideshow of his circus from being overcrowded. The most imaginative was posting a sign reading "To the Egress" over an exit door. Patrons eagerly expecting to see some exotic beast went through the door and found themselves outside the sideshow.

5.2.6.   Information output processes   Strains from excess information outputs may occur in systems when information "leaks" into the suprasystem through improperly maintained boundary filtering processes. A dramatic example is the publication of the "Pentagon Papers," arranged by Daniel Ellsberg. Decider components may be embarrassed by such events, and persons responsible may be punished. As adjustments, denials or attempts at explanation are addressed to the suprasystem. Often system controls on internal information flows are increased to improve security.

Internal strains resulting from lacks of information outputs from an organization can occur when censorship is enforced. Relaxation or elimination of the censorship, or storage of censored messages until they can be safely released into the environment, may reduce such strains at least partially. If the output transducer of an organization is closed, as when the workers at a post office are on strike, strains can build up rapidly. Possible adjustments include settling the strike, hiring new workers, or not accepting input mail. Strains occur also when there are insufficient supplies of the matter-energy used for markers and consequently outputs of information are halted. One possible adjustment is to change the channel or form of marker employed. For instance, when a newspaper cannot obtain newsprint, one adjustment that has been used is for newspaper reporters or editors to broadcast the main news items, death notices, and information about public meetings over a radio or television station.

5.2.7.   Feedbacks   Positive and negative internal and external feedbacks influence the steady-state ranges of both matter-energy and information processing variables in organizations. A single process may be influenced by multiple information flows involving more than one class of feedbacks.

External feedbacks. Among the external loops used by profit-making corporations are those by which information concerning public reaction to the quality of products or services and to the content of public relations outputs, including advertising, is fed back and used to guide future system adjustment processes. If a laundry receives many complaints, it may buy new equipment. If an advertising campaign produces no great increase in sales, a different publicity effort may be devised.

An organization need not wait until its products are returned, its sales diminish, or a reader threatens to horsewhip the editor. Frequently, circuits are purposely arranged to obtain faster and more complete feedbacks. Many hotels and motels place questionnaires in every room asking about specific aspects of their services and leaving space for the customer's complaints. A survey organization may be hired to query consumers as to what they think about a product. Students are sometimes asked to give ratings of, or comment upon, how their course syllabuses are written and how their professors teach.

The possible complexities of organizational processes which respond to fluctuating demands of consumers for products are described by Forrester in feedback terms.[233] He has developed a complicated computer simulation of a corporation involved in production and distribution in which both internal and environmental variables can be altered (see pages 719 and 720). Among these variables he includes three principal sorts of orders requesting changes in rates of inputs of supplies from the environment to the system: (a) orders to replace goods sold, (b) orders to adjust inventories of stored matter-energy upward or downward as the rate of business activity changes, and (c) orders to fill the organization's distributor with products being manufactured and ready for shipment. How any sort of feedback functions, he says, depends upon the particular structure of the system, the lags which always occur in communications and actions, and the degree of amplification of actions. Amplification, in Forrester's terms, means that an action is more forceful than might at first seem to be implied by the information inputs to the decider.

For profit-making corporations, lag times of external feedbacks are long, compared with such lags in the organisms affected by them. Because organizational feedbacks are slower, they are characteristically looser, permitting wider ranges of fluctuation of steady-state variables. Corrective action following a feedback signal is also slower, and signals are often amplified so

that extreme fluctuations of internal processes result from a relatively small feedback signal that leads to an appropriately small correction. A sudden 10 percent increase in retail sales, for instance, produces very large fluctuations in the rates at which inputs are ordered to arrive, in the rates of factory outputs, in the size of factory warehouse inventories, and in unfilled orders (see Fig. 10-21). Delays in accounting, purchasing, and mailing cause the increase in distributors' orders from retailers to lag about a month in reaching the 10 percent level. The rise, however, continues to a peak of 18 percent at the eleventh week, which increases inventories and raises factory orders from distributors until this increased demand is met, after which the rate of such orders falls. Factory warehouse unfilled orders also fluctuate. At the fourteenth week they reach 34 percent above the month before. As factory warehouse unfilled orders increase and inventory drops 15 percent, manufacturing orders rise 51 percent at the fifteenth week, and factory output, 45 percent above the previous month, reaches a peak in the twenty-first week. At this point, retail sales are still at 10 percent above the month before, but the increase in production is over four times that great. These changes are reversible, and as the rate of inputs ordered decreases, when retailers fill their inventories, by the thirty-second week inputs are ordered to arrive at a rate slower than retail sales—below the month before and 13 percent below current retail sales. It takes more than a year for all ordering and manufacturing rates to stabilize at their proper levels for the 10 percent retail sales increase.

Actually, these organizational processes are seen to be even more complicated when consideration is given to the effects of random variations of retail sales, limited factory capacity, advertising, and economic fluctuations in the suprasystem.

A further characteristic of organizations of this sort is that they are unstable; that is, they tend not to return to the predisturbance steady state, but rather experience amplification of an initial disturbance which leads to growth (see page 692) or to oscillations of increasing amplitude.[234] These continue until they are restrained by nonlinear influences such as labor shortages, limitations on production capacity, and declining availability of materials. Feedbacks that lead to such increases which diminish steady states are, of course, positive feedbacks, opposite to the negative feedbacks that produce stability.

Departmental components of organizations have been shown to differ in the time span of feedback.[235] This was found to be more pronounced in the plastics industry, which depends heavily upon innovation and in which departments differ greatly from one another, than in the food industry. It was least marked in the container industry. Sales and production departments received rapid feedback from the suprasystem about results of their work. They dealt with matters that affected profits as soon as 1 month in the future, receiving their feedback from the market and the technoeconomic portions of the environment. By contrast, feedback reached administrators and scientists in fundamental research laboratories as late as several years after they had completed their development of new products or processes. They had to wait until a project was ended. The applied research departments had a medium to long feedback lag.

Though feedbacks in organizations, as I have noted, have longer lags than those in organisms, at least in profit-making corporations they are often accurate and rapid enough to be effective. Within a few days or weeks after an automobile manufacturer puts out a new model, for instance, the rate of sales indicates how popular it is with the public. If it is a Volkswagen, that is soon apparent. If it is an Edsel, that is soon clear also. Plans can be made accordingly.

So far in the discussion of external feedbacks I have dealt only with profit-making organizations. The situation is quite different in many nonprofit organizations. This is because the monetary inputs to profit-making corporations, in addition to being cash income, also represent signals about the acceptance of the system's products or services by its environment. Regardless of whether the purchasers know what is good quality or what is best for them, they know what they are willing to pay for. Thus the amount of income (or number of units purchased) represents feedback about the organization's effectiveness in satisfying the user.

Many nonprofit organizations operate without any such clear indication of effectiveness. A university, for example, may annually receive a certain income from endowment regardless of whether it performs any services. Or it may receive a lump-sum annual appropriation from the state or one based on the number of students enrolled or the number of student credit hours taught—regardless of how well the instruction is carried out. Similarly, there is little or no connection between the income and effectiveness of many schools, hospitals, mental hospitals, or other social agencies or governmental units. Before deciding what income these organizations shall receive, donors, boards of trustees, or legislators may try to find out how well they are achieving their goals. Often, however, these efforts are feeble, if they are made at all. Commonly the donors have little idea what the goals of such organizations should be or how to evaluate their effectiveness. Favorable or unfavorable publicity

about the agency—often distorted—frequently affects decisions about their funding. All this means that feedbacks about effectiveness usually flow to nonprofit organizations over tortuous channels. The signals are often limited in usefulness, distorted, and very slow, if they arrive at all. As a result, measures of costs—which usually are quite apparent and often accurate—are much more important than considerations of effectiveness in determining the level of support of many nonprofit organizations.

Internal feedbacks. Much of the information flow in organizational channels can be classed as coordinating feedback (see page 680). Planning for such feedback is an important aspect of organizational design. Control of processes is achieved by comparing the output of a component with a signal that represents some standard or desired output and feeding back information concerning the discrepancy, if any, to correct for it in future operations (see page 36).[236] The feedback can take different forms, increasing in sophistication. The simplest is *amplitude control; i.e.,* if production is five units per hour less than the comparison quantity, orders are given to increase the rate by five units per hour. This is a case of extremum adaptation (see page 37). Internal variables tend to fluctuate greatly with this sort of control. In the next hour, production may overshoot the desired level if the order is given at a time when the process is already being accelerated to correct for the discrepancy. *Rate control,* which compares the present rate of production with the desired one, is better because it tends to dampen the oscillations. This is a system-variable adaptation (see page 37). It is inadequate, however, if demand fluctuates, as it does in most such systems. *Acceleration control,* which compares the present acceleration of production with the desired one, is also a system-variable adaptation, but a more sophisticated one. It dampens out oscillations around the changing desired production rate more efficiently. In general, the more complex the system, the more sophisticated the sort of control required. Large multiman–machine systems, with their lengthy lag times, require very complex forms of feedback control.

Feedback is necessary also to maintain good human relations in organizations. Unless employees are kept informed of their superiors' evaluation of their activities, their performance cannot be expected to improve. There is no learning without feedback of results (see pages 409 and 638 and Hypothesis 3.3.5.2-3, page 99). Management should obtain feedbacks about how its decisions are implemented, receiving them quickly enough to institute corrections if they are needed. Management information systems can be designed to provide such information about relevant aspects of subsystem processes to the echelons that need it (see pages 626, 656, and 701).

Often administrators receive information about the human side of an organization only when conflict surfaces or a grievance is reported. In order to improve feedback of this sort, organizations sometimes make surveys of employee morale and attitudes.[237] All too often such surveys result in reports which are filed and which have no effective feedback function. Employees ordinarily like to be asked their opinions, but they often feel quite frustrated if their comments have no impact. Feedback is useless unless it leads to corrective action when that is indicated.

5.3 Evolution   Just as the evolution of organs depends upon changes in information content of the genetic material of organisms, so the evolution of organizations depends upon changes in associated or learned information transmitted through successive generations of the societies of which they are components. The structures and processes of a society's organizations express its culture. They reflect its beliefs, laws, and values; its scientific, technological, and artistic attainments; and its caste or class distinctions. The number and density of population of a society are also important in determining what types of organizations develop in it. Both ancient and modern societies with large populations have shredded out their processes, employing division of labor among different sorts of organizations. Also, according to Durkheim, when communities alter their processes from mechanical to organic solidarity (see page 601), the change results primarily from increased population density.

The history of each of the many types of organizational components of present-day large industrial societies can be studied, and their relationships to earlier organizational forms determined. Some types have tended to modify their structures and processes slowly, adapting reluctantly to changes in other aspects of societies. This is true, for instance, of religious institutions in most societies. Others have changed more rapidly in response to social pressures. Organizations concerned with production have, in general, tended to alter quickly following major shifts in markets and demands.

I shall now consider the evolution of two types of organizations: (*a*) cities and (*b*) factories.

(*a*) *Evolution of cities.* Homo sapiens reached his present form and intellectual capacity, eliminating competing types of early man, by the end of the Pleistocene era (see page 465). For most of the period since then, until about 9,000 years ago, he was dependent upon hunting and gathering for his food and so did not build permanent communities. At about that time, in Southwest Asia, people learned to cultivate wheat and legumes and began to live in villages or cities like Jericho, which they built near year-round water sources.[238]

In the succeeding 1,000 to 2,000 years—a brief time as compared with the preceding 100,000 years, when new techniques were acquired very slowly—pigs and cattle were tamed; new crops such as olives, flax, dates, and barley were cultivated; and pottery was invented. Division of labor accompanied these changes, the first specializations probably being agriculture and herding. Trading apparently took place among settlements of this period. Shell beads dug up by archaeologists in sites far from the sea have been interpreted as evidence that they were brought there by traders. Irrigation appeared for the first time about 6,500 years ago in the plain of the Tigris and Euphrates Rivers.

Throughout this period many communities increased in size, and towns developed. They had temples and marketplaces as well as houses. Their inhabitants were politically and socially stratified. Written languages and number systems were devised, which made it possible for records to be kept. Some of these towns grew into city-states which controlled the area surrounding them, including other communities. Codified laws and other cultural characteristics made each of these systems distinctive. A similar progression from hunting and gathering to city dwelling appears to have been followed in other parts of the world, including China and South America, at different times and with local variations.

By about 3500 B.C. cities were in existence in lower Mesopotamia and the Nile Valley.[239] Sumer, Akkad-Eridu, Erech, Lagash, Kish, and Ur were among these. Each included 5,000 to 10,000 people. By 3100 B.C. cities had developed in the Nile Delta, and others appeared soon after in the valley of the Indus in Pakistan and along the Yellow River in China. In the first millennium A.D. the Mayan city of Teotihuacan may have grown to a population of 100,000.

Each type of human settlement so far described was largely totipotential, constituting an evolutionary precursor of both modern organized communities and modern societies.

In creating his settlements, according to Doxiadis, man has obeyed general principles and laws which derive from his biological nature.[240] Recognizing a cross-level identity, Doxiadis referred to these as a "biology of larger systems." He called this science of human settlements "ekistics." The term is derived from the Greek words οἶκος ("home") and οἰκῶ ("settle down"). Basic to his analysis of cities is the concept of the kinetic field, which is a circle or sphere representing the distance a person can move within a certain period by walking or by riding on animals or in vehicles. Before the era of cities, the kinetic fields of families or small groups did not overlap with those of other groups. Later they touched and overlapped. This contact initially probably produced conflict. But eventually people recognized the advantages to them of interaction. They moved close together, so that instead of living in separate fields, many people shared a common region—a city. Then they had to determine how to organize the space so that it could be used jointly (see page 694).

A succession of types of cities, based on kinetic fields, was identified by Doxiadis.[241]

The first type, *A-level organization* of cities, was characterized by compact urban settlements which occupied an area of no more than 2 by 2 km and usually had no more than 50,000 inhabitants. In these cities a man did not have to walk for more than 10 min to reach the center from the periphery. The region of influence of the city-state covered an area not more than 50 km in diameter, since a person could not walk farther than that between sunrise and sunset. Many of these settlements were smaller, and people could go across the city and return in a day.

B-level organization of cities characterized capital cities of empires, such as Rome, Constantinople, and Peking. These had populations of more than 50,000 because more than that number of people were needed to administer the empire. They were as large as 6 by 6 km. The walking time from periphery to center was more than 30 min. Horse-drawn carts and paved roads were used to move people more rapidly, but such large cities were difficult to govern, developed slums, and were often controlled by mobs. When an empire collapsed, such a city reverted to A-level organization.

In about the middle of the seventeenth century, as the scientific revolution got under way, many cities began to grow to a size too great for A-level organization. Capitals of nation-states and cities of commercial and industrial importance changed as railways and highway networks developed in the societies. By the mid-nineteenth century some of them had become metropolises. Because their total size was so large, they were organized as loose alliances of villages. In Paris and some other cities an attempt to superimpose B-level organization was made by constructing wide avenues for horse-drawn vehicles. These were laid out in diagonals across the existing grid of streets. This construction was expensive and did not solve the problem of size since the time required to travel between remote points in the cities was not sufficiently reduced.

C-level organization, which depended upon the building of subways or elevated lines in big cities like London, Paris, and New York, was more satisfactory but only for a short time. When automobiles became popular, the transportation processes of cities became more confused. A- and B-level organization, the earlier forms, were still present in the C-level cities. The automobile impeded A-level transportation and improved B-level transportation. That is, it interfered with human walking space, but moved people more rapidly over roads.

New freeways cutting through the cities were built in an effort to provide greater speed. Cities changed to a fourth form, *D-level organization.* These freeways did not increase the speed enough, and they added many problems. More and more cars were fed into the A- and B-level streets. Parking spaces were insufficient.

Now, before D-level organization has really been achieved, a fifth form, *E-level organization,* is made necessary as the metropolis grows into a megalopolis. Pathology in many cities results from failure to solve problems of D-level organization (see pages 702 to 704). How cities must evolve in the future was clear to Doxiadis:

We must set ourselves clear goals and work toward their realization. We must first be realistic about the frame within which man must move: it cannot be anything less than the world, as man's ultimate city has the surface of the earth as its realistic limit. To overlook this basic fact is unrealistic, as man already moves about the ancient city-state in less time than it took him to cross the ancient city-state. Though at this stage we need not concern ourselves with extraterrestrial flights for the average man, we must be aware that the frame of his city is extrahuman, and our goal is to create, in spite of the inevitable extrahuman frame, a city with human content. . . .

We must start by defining the city we envision in terms of its kinetic fields and its transportation needs. We must then write specifications for the transportation systems and guide the technology that will develop them. We start with the same transportation times that determined the size of the ancient city-state—that is, an average of 10 minutes of walking time for the radius of the built-up area and of 8 hours for the radius of the city-state as a whole. With today's technology we can still have a city within whose built-up area man can move from point to point, by foot or vehicle, in 10 minutes and from which he can reach the most distant point in the city's area of influence in 8 hours, but now this area of influence will have become the whole world.

What would be the distance from the heart to the outskirts of such a city—that is, the radius of the central area? At what speed would an inhabitant have to move in order to reach the outskirts from the heart of the central area in 10 minutes? Here we can learn from nature's most developed organisms and try an assumption based on their physiology. In mammals, the ratio of the speed at which blood moves in the capillaries and the speed at which it moves in the aorta is about 1:400. If we borrow this ratio we find that if man moves by foot in the "capillaries" of the city at 5 kilometers per hour, the maximum vehicular speed within the central or urban area of his modern "city-state" should be 2000 kilometers per hour. At such a speed man can cover in 10 minutes about 330 kilometers, or, when allowance is made for lower starting and stopping speeds, about 150 kilometers.[242]

The universal city or "ecumenopolis" is the ultimate. In it the distance between any two points can be covered within 10 min by any of several means of transportation. The first phase in building such an organization, which can be begun at once, is to construct distributors for moving gases, liquids, and solids underground, employing high-speed transportation through tubes. This will separate the kinetic fields based on man's normal rate of walking from those based on machine transportation. The second phase will be to arrange to transport people underground. This should be no real hardship, since no journey will last more than 10 min. Areas of high population density and high income will pioneer in such technologies, at first with systems that carry people at less than the most desirable speed.

Cities of the future could be delightful places whose residents could be surrounded with beauty, comfort, and convenience if the dreams of modern city planners are translated into reality. These combine already available artistic and technical elements to direct the evolution of cities in ways that would provide more satisfaction to their human occupants, rather than permitting cities to develop with inadequate planning, as they have usually done in the past.

A concept of "collective form," discussed by Maki and Ohtaka, expands the present method of designing groups of buildings into an overall plan for a "megastructure," which includes all the functions of an entire city, or large part of a city, in a total design.[243] This would, if ideally carried out, provide visual consistency and continuing order and still allow for the changes that take place over time in all cities. Beautiful old communities, such as the medieval Italian towns still in existence, used consistent basic materials and construction methods and have always fitted agreeably into their topography with buildings convenient to human scale. These towns, of course, developed over long periods as houses, walls, gates, and towers were added.

Contemporary designers must work over a time span much shorter than that during which these lovely relics developed. In considering the planning of Tokyo, now the biggest city in the world and still growing rapidly, Maki and Ohtaka suggest that a proper master program should be developed and that pilot projects should form the cells and cores for future developments. Designs for redevelopment of one of the large subcenters in Tokyo illustrate their ideas (see Fig. 10-13).

(b) *Evolution of factories.* When, and under what circumstances, the first organization for producing goods arose is lost in prehistory. Some jobs are too big for one person to perform alone. At some time the advantages of cooperation in securing a greater output for the same amount of individual effort must have become evident, and so collective effort was undertaken. Perhaps the first such organizations were temporary, similar to the antelope-hunting organizations of the Navahos, in which a good hunter is explicitly chosen as leader, a member of the group is elected to supervise division of the game among participants, and specific job assignments are made on the basis of ability.[244]

There is archaeological evidence that organized flint mines with associated factories produced ax heads in Neolithic Europe.[245] Mine shafts, cut through solid chalk to a depth of as much as 6 m, by the use of antler picks and bone shovels, sometimes had not only a simple pit but also regular galleries branching from them. The necessity of leaving pillars to support the roof was understood, but then, as now, workers were sometimes killed by falls. In the British Isles and Denmark, at least, it appears that these factories were in regular production, although the operators and distributors probably were not full-time specialists.

Tubal Cain is reputed to have been, in the words of the book of Genesis, "an instructor of every artificer in brass and iron," a specialist in the early period of metalworking in Mesopotamia.[246] Mining and refining metal in quantity must always have required some form of organization of human participation. Records have been found of copper mines operated on the Sinai Peninsula by King Seneferu about 3800 B.C.[247] Large amounts of copper were produced also on the island of Cyprus, for which the metal was named, about 3000 B.C.

Organizations engaged in manufacturing are found in modern nonindustrial societies. A study of "administrative rationality" in 426 organizations in 150 primitive, peasant, and traditional societies was conducted by Udy.[248] Among these organizations, 34 that had three or more echelons were chosen for special attention, each from a different society. An organization was considered by Udy to have administrative rationality if its processes were directed to limited, specific objectives and if it explicitly defined the roles of its personnel by mutual contractual agreement. Commonly it also emphasized rewards dependent on the amount or quality of work performed, specialization or division of labor, payments in money or goods made by higher echelons of the organization to persons in lower echelons, and centralized management.

Fig. 10-13   Maki and Ohtaka's model of Shinjuku Redevelopment Project (Photo Watanabe). [From G. Kepes (Ed.). *Structure in art and in science.* New York: George Braziller, Inc., 1965, 123. *Reprinted by permission.*]

The companies in the sample from the nonindustrial societies extended over the entire scale from high administrative rationality to low. When highly rational organizations were compared with the others, it was found that rational administration was somewhat harder to achieve in societies in which status and political succession are hereditary or in which slavery is practiced.[249] No highly rational organization was found in a society with a complex stratification system. Although no clear-cut evolutionary sequence could be discovered in these results, organizations in current industrial societies generally showed high administrative rationality. This may be because such societies are less stratified than many of their historical predecessors.

Various theorists have speculated as to how organizations will evolve in the future. They have often expressed hope that this evolution will be influenced by application of research findings, particularly in the area of human relations, to the design and control of these large systems. Such applications would very likely change organizations' decider structures from the presently typical authoritarian hierarchy to some

less centralized, more democratic form. Likert's overlapping group structure, which I have already described (see page 644), is one example. It retains superior–subordinate relationships, but decentralizes much decision making to groups. A more radical alteration of traditional structure has been suggested by Forrester. It would eliminate the superior–subordinate relationship entirely, replacing it with "individual self-discipline arising from the self-interest created by a competitive market mechanism."[250] Each person would freely negotiate with others in the organization with whom he exchanged goods and services. Policy making and accounting would be adjusted so that self-interest and the objectives of the total system would coincide. There would be competition among individuals or small partnerships, each a profit center (see page 701), as to who could make the most profit. Accounting would measure the profit made by each small profit center in a way to induce it to maximize the difference between its costs and the value of its outputs. Compensation would depend upon such profit. This, Forrester contends, would eliminate the conflicts which now commonly exist between departments that want as large budgets as possible (a result of the fact that the salary and status of administrators increase as they are able to hire larger and larger numbers of employees and spend more and more money) and the comptroller's office, which is responsible for imposing restraint.

Other characteristics of this projected form of organization would include (*a*) separating policy making from operational decision making in such a way that coordination and determination of objectives would occur without hampering freedom to innovate; (*b*) replacing the usual meshlike information net with one using electronic data processing in which information storage and computing occur at a hub, with channels extending to each input and each output location; (*c*) increasing general access to information and eliminating information monopolies within the system; and (*d*) doing away with monopolies on particular services and specific sorts of activities.

In such an organization, an individual would grow as an administrator going from managing her or his own time to managing small projects to becoming "an entrepreneur who matches customer needs to the ability of the organization."[251] It would be harder to enter such an organization than it is to join most organizations today. More care would be taken in reaching the initial agreement to participate. But the organization would permit its members more freedom. It would be easier to leave voluntarily because rights or deferred compensation would not be lost when a member resigned. Individual rights of members would be guaranteed by a "constitution," and judicial review of grievances or conflicts would be available.

The focus was also on the individual human being in a look into the future of organizations that Bennis permitted himself in 1966.[252] He thought that bureaucracy would not long continue as either the ideal or even a practical structure for an organization, largely because such a system cannot adapt rapidly to changes in its environment. Many species of organisms, over the course of evolution, were eliminated by natural selection for the same reason. Alterations in organizational components of societies result, Bennis maintained, from social changes. Among these he identified the exponential growth of scientific research and development and the rise of intellectual technology. An organization's environment is more full of turbulent stresses today than in the past, with increasing interactions and interdependencies among components of the suprasystem such as trade unions, competitors, suppliers of raw materials and power, sources of managerial personnel, and governmental agencies. Since bureaucracy thrives best in stable and predictable environments, today's rapid change must imply the ultimate end of such organizational forms.

Education and mobility have increased in the population. At the same time tasks of the firm, Bennis observed, are becoming more technical, complicated, and unprogrammed, relying more on intellectual power and the higher cognitive processes. They are likely to be too complicated for one person to comprehend and control, and they will call for collaboration of professionals.

Bennis recommended what he called an "organic-adaptive structure" for organizations of the future consisting of temporary units of diverse specialists solving problems. Liaison personnel who linked such units would be important. People would be differentiated according to skills and training, not ranks or roles. The jobs would be intrinsically satisfying, and therefore the goals of the individual and the organization would coincide. In such a structure there would be reduced commitment to work groups, although the importance of skills in human interaction would increase. "Learning how to live with ambiguity and to be self-directing will be the task of education and the goal of maturity."[253]

Four years later, in 1970, Bennis noted that "a funny thing [had] happened" on the way to the future he had foreseen.[254] The expected changes toward more democratic organizational forms had not taken place. Instead, widespread questioning of the legitimacy of power and of the adequacy of the democratic process itself had occurred, particularly in the universities. While some conditions favorable to democratic developments were evident, threats to the democratic process were also present, and he saw no justification for optimism.

Bennis's new forecast still considered the organization's response to the environment to be crucial. He wrote:

. . . I anticipate an erratic environment where various organizations coexist at different stages of evolution. Rather than neat, linear, and uniform evolutionary developments, I expect that we will see both more centralization (in large-scale instrumental bureaucracies) and more decentralization (in delivery of health, education, and welfare services); both the increase of bureaucratic-pragmatic and/or revolutionary-charismatic leaderships; both the increase in size and centralization of many municipal and governmental units and the proliferation of self-contained minisocieties. . . . [255]

Bennis looked for the rise of legislative and judicial as well as executive components in organizations. He also thought that in the future, more people will divide their time among more than one organization.

As in the past, evolution of organizations will continue to be directly affected by the evolution of the societies of which they are components. Present trends appear to be toward greater centralization of top-echelon deciders. Within the past few years, for instance, the world has seen the emergence of a new form of corporate structure, the conglomerate. These systems combine organizations of diverse function in the society under central control, concentrating huge amounts of capital in the hands of a few decider components.

5.3.1 Emergents The echelon structure that differentiates organizations from groups is not emergent at this level since echelons are found in systems at several lower levels. The appearance of echelons when increased numbers of people began to live together and to satisfy their needs collectively, however, resulted in emergent forms of human interaction and emergent technologies.

Among the new sorts of interactions were qualitatively different relationships among people derived from their positions in an organization rather than from their family relationships, including a different base for both authority and status. New sorts of human loyalties arose. These were to an organization—the city-state of Sparta, the Catholic Church, the Marine Corps, or General Motors—rather than to specific people or members of a particular family. Perhaps concern for people outside the kinship group is also an emergent at this level, the sort of concern that leads to broad humanitarian feelings and philanthropic actions, for example.

Technological methods that depended upon cooperative action of many people to build great structures, dig deeply into the earth, or move and lift heavy stones were made possible by organizations and emerged at this level. Without organizations, neither the Egyptians nor the Mayans could have built pyramids.

5.4 Growth, cohesiveness, and integration

5.4.1 Growth As growing organizations increase the number of their individual organism, group, or subsidiary organizational components, they often, but not always, expand their spatial extent by acquiring more land or more space in buildings. The number of their nonliving subsystem components may also rise. Not infrequently, changes in complexity of subsystem structure accompany growth, such as a rise in the number of echelons in the decider or the number of components at some of these echelons. Changes in spatial relationships among components also occur when, for example, a department or division becomes geographically separate from other components of the organization.

Different units are used to measure growth in various situations: (a) The number of human components is the commonest index of growth in some types of organizations, such as cities, religious denominations, and political parties. (b) The number of actual or potential inclusions is sometimes used. A hospital is said to grow larger when it adds more beds and therefore is able to serve more patients, even if the staff remains the same size and simply works harder. (c) The annual monetary value of the organization's output is the usual measure of growth and the usual basis for comparative ranking of business and industrial systems. This is the value of sales and/or services which they render over a stated period. It may or may not correlate directly with the number of employees. *Fortune* magazine annually lists in order the 500 largest industrial corporations. The largest industrial corporation in 1975, as in 1974, was Exxon, with over $44 billion in sales. This was an increase of more than $2 billion over the year before.[256] General Motors, however, had the largest number of employees, averaging 681,000 for the year. Exxon was twelfth in number of employees, reflecting important differences in technology between these two industries.

No genetic template ordinarily specifies explicitly the course and limits of an organization's growth, although the size of some is controlled by charter. A decision to grow may be made by a system's own deciders, as when a city bank builds a suburban branch, a conglomerate buys a new company, or an apartment house opens a new wing and advertises for more tenants. A decision by the suprasystem sometimes instigates growth, as when a government decides to give financial support to a vital industry, such as its airlines or its railroads. Growth in some systems is unplanned, an outcome of efficient management or the result of fortuitous circumstances, like the location of a city near undiscovered natural resources that later attract mines or factories.

Growth appears to be closely related to survival in many types of organizations, being associated with the adjustments by which they adapt to their environments.[257] Failure to grow may mean either actual contraction or relative loss of rank among competitors, neither of which is a good omen for long-term survival. It is true, nevertheless, that many small businesses are profitable over extended periods and elect to remain small.

Not all parts of a growing organization grow at the same rate. This variation in growth rates Boulding has called the "principle of nonproportional change," and Gross the "law of disproportionality."[258] One or more parts of a growing organization may experience a growth spurt while others remain about the same size or even decline. There is a general impression that as organizations grow, the number of staff components increases faster than the number of line components.[259] Parkinson's law, a witty analysis of bureaucratic organizations, explains this in terms of the desire of each staff member to have subordinates and the fact that workers in organizations make work for one another, regardless of the total amount of work to be done.[260] Research, however, does not support this "law" of organizational growth. Not only is the rate of increase in the number of administrative personnel not directly related to the rate of growth of an organization, but it may even be inversely related to it.[261] In many companies the production work force is the first component to grow.[262] A majority of firms in one study did not add to their managerial or clerical personnel until their annual sales went over $100,000. There is evidence that the number of decider components rises as the number of different kinds of departments, divisions, and units increases.

In what he explicitly describes as a study of cross-level formal identities between two levels of living systems, Noell studied, for all 50 states of the United States, the relationships between several variables.[263] These were increases in population number, number of people in the state government component of the decider subsystem, complexity of the state government, complexity of the social structure of the state, wealth of the state, and land area of the state. Several other scholars had maintained that these variables are correlated in various types of organizations and in societies. The data Noell collected on the 50 states supported all the following hypotheses:

I. (*a*) The relative size of the governmental bureaucracies of the 50 states will decrease as the population of the state increases; (*b*) the complexity of the state government bureaucracies will increase as the population of the state increases.
II. (*a*) The relative size of the governmental bureaus will increase as the complexity of the social structures of the state increases; (*b*) the complexity of the governmental bureaucracies will increase as the complexity of the social structures of the state increases.
III. (*a*) The relative size of the governmental bureaucracies will increase as the wealth of the population of the state increases; (*b*) the complexity of the bureaus will increase as the wealth of the population increases.
IV. (*a*) The relative size of the governmental bureaucracies of the states will decrease as the land area of the state increases; and (*b*) the complexity of the bureaucracies will decrease as the land area of the state increases.[264]

In his research Noell compared findings by others on hospitals and similar organizations with his data on states of the United States. He held the latter to be at a higher level than organizations, and so to him the comparison was cross-level. In my terminology these states are also organizations, not societies; thus his empirical comparison, while most interesting, is in my view a cross-type study among various sorts of organizations rather than a cross-level study.

Efforts have been made to detect a fundamental law of growth which would explain the observed growth sequences of organizations and relate them to other levels of living systems. Boulding applies the square–cube law (see page 79) to living systems at all levels. This law states that a uniform increase in the linear dimensions of a structure will increase all its areas as the square, and its volumes as the cube, of the increase in the linear dimension. But he does not give details of its application to organizations.[265]

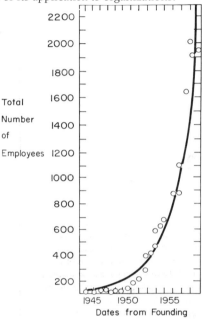

Fig. 10-14 Growth curve—Haire's Company A. [From M. Haire. Biological models and empirical histories of the growth of organizations. In M. Haire (Ed.). *Modern organization theory.* New York: Wiley, 1959, 280. *Reprinted by permission.*]

The square–cube law is also used in Haire's analysis of the growth of a number of organizations (see Fig. 10-14).[266] He defines as "internal" functions such processes as personnel activities and as "external" functions those which contact the organization's environment, like labor negotiating. The number of internal employees he considered as the volume. The number of external employees was the surface. When the square root of external employees was plotted against the cube root of inside employees, the data closely fitted a straight line (see Fig. 10-15). This was taken as confirming the square–cube law. These "laws" are not yet sufficiently understood, however, to be of use in predicting organizational growth patterns.

Growth of cities. Increase in the number of people living in cities is related to the exponential growth of populations and to the changes in settlement patterns of societies in the direction of more urbanization (see pages 842 and 843). In general, as the populations of two adjacent communities increase, the larger of the two absorbs the smaller. Almost universally, com-

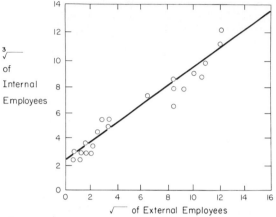

Fig. 10-15 External–internal ratio of Haire's Company A. [From M. Haire. Biological models and empirical histories of the growth of organizations. In M. Haire (Ed.). *Modern organization theory.* New York: Wiley, 1959, 286. *Reprinted by permission.*]

munities are patterned in concentric zones.[267] The growth of Paris, from a small walled community on the Seine to its present extent, illustrates this (see Fig. 10-16). As the city expanded, walls were built farther and farther from the center. The last, the wall of Thiers, was finally razed in 1919.[268]

This concentric pattern is modified when some natural limit, such as a mountain or ocean, presents a barrier to expansion in one direction. In Arizona and New Mexico such a barrier is formed by the Santa Fe railroad and Route 66, which follows its course. Flagstaff, Arizona and Gallup, New Mexico are large cities that have a long, narrow shape, confined almost wholly to one side of the railroad. This barrier is now reinforced by the automobile freeway that parallels the railroad to the south.

Within the circle of the city limits, to a large extent its components are clustered according to function. Typically, American cities have a "downtown" area with banks, large stores, hotels, government buildings, and such centralized services. Factories cluster in other areas, until recently staying near the center but now, in many cities, moving to the outskirts, where land is less costly and taxes are lower. Dwellings are concentrated in neighborhoods of varying ethnic and economic composition, the more costly ones often

being farther from the center of the city. These various sorts of components increase or decrease their population at different rates. The central areas of present-day American cities commonly lose population or remain about the same, while outer areas gain.[269]

Four principles have operated to shape growing human settlements, according to Doxiadis.[270] These are maximization of man's potential contacts with the elements of nature, other people, and the works of man, like buildings and roads; minimization of the effort required to achieve such contacts, a principle of least effort (see page 436); optimization of man's protective space, so that he can keep his contacts with other persons, animals, and objects without sensory or psychological discomfort; and optimization of the quality of man's relationship with his environment, a principle that leads to physiological and aesthetic order and influences architecture and art. Doxiadis also stated as a fifth principle that man attempts to achieve an optimum synthesis of the first four principles. When this last is satisfied, the human settlement is successful.

Limits to growth of organizations. The lower limit to the number of component individuals in any organization is set by the definition of this level of system. It must have enough people for two echelons; that is, conceivably there could be a minimum of two people, but it is much more likely that there would be several more. Lower limits to the number of components in some types of production organizations are set by the minimum number of people required to do the work. The nature of the work also sets lower limits for the required amounts of other sorts of matter-energy and for the amount of information, including money. If the organization is a steel mill, its lower limit is high compared with the lower limit of, for instance, a real estate firm. As automation increases, the number of human components, as compared with the mass of artifact components, decreases.

Upper limits may be set by charter, particularly in social organizations, some of which keep a prospective member waiting until he can take the place of a member who dies or resigns. Upper limits may also be set by decision of the suprasystem. Antitrust actions in the United States, for example, prevent any company from monopolizing any market, although limits are not ordinarily set upon overall organizational growth.

Can an organization become so large that internal factors such as decreased efficiency or administrative difficulties keep it from growing? Some economists consider that the lower unit costs and greater returns commonly found in large companies—the "advantages of scale"—disappear in the largest organizations. A "law of diminishing returns to scale" is

Wall of Thiers 1845

Wall of the Fermiers Généraux 1791

Wall of Philippe-Auguste 1210

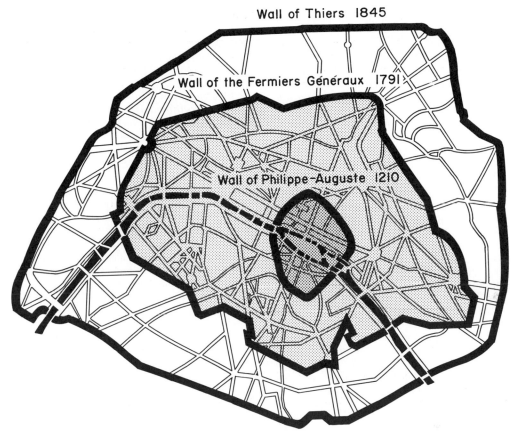

Fig. 10-16 Growth of Paris.

believed to begin to operate at some point, differing among types of organizations. If they grow beyond that size, the returns are less.[271] The size at which this turnaround occurs appears to be optimum for that particular system. The idea that long-run unit costs rise as a firm grows is rejected by Penrose, however. She sees no theoretical reason why firms cannot expand indefinitely, as long as they have satisfactory decision making and management.[272] There is an optimum size for a firm, therefore, only if its management cannot adapt to the increased requirements imposed by growth.

Expansion in the number of components ultimately requires changes in decider structure (see page 697). If such changes do not take place, it seems possible that a system could become so unsatisfying to its members and to those it serves that it might become essentially ungovernable. Such a situation creates strains that could prevent further growth and even survival (see pages 703 and 704).

Another factor that can certainly limit growth of an organization is the amount of demand for its product or services. Search for new markets is an important management function. Many large firms have continued to grow by becoming international, setting up foreign subsidiaries in places where new demands have occurred. Diversification of output, to manufacture products for which there is known demand or for which a demand can be created, also removes limitations to growth of the single-product firm. Conglomerates combine organizations of widely different functions under a single top-echelon decider. Such diversification protects against loss of profits through drop in demand or loss of markets for the products or services of one or more components. When International Telephone and Telegraph Corporation began to lose its business because of expropriations in many countries, it diversified and became a conglomerate. Other types of organizations increase the number and kind of services they offer. A golf club may, for instance, install tennis courts and a swimming pool to attract more members.

The theoretical limits to city growth are no smaller than the surface of the planet (see page 688). A particular city, however, may be limited in its territorial expansion when it reaches the limits of surrounding cities with which it cannot merge or when it reaches natural barriers, like a surrounding ocean. Within this limited region, the density of population can increase if higher buildings are constructed, if buildings are built closer together, or if more people are crowded into buildings than they were intended to accommodate. Such increased density, however, may in the long run limit growth because persons occupying the area do not like it and move out.

I have already discussed the limit imposed on the growth of communities by the rate at which a person can walk or move through the streets using some form of conveyance (see page 688). Urban growth depends also upon adequate communication among the people of a community. Before the development of modern communication technology, the flow of information through cities was constrained by the rate at which a messenger could move on foot or with the aid of animals or machines. Coordination of components became increasingly difficult as the extent of a settlement increased.[273]

Development of organizations. No single sort of growth curve or succession of stages appears to characterize all organizations or even all of a single type. Ordinarily organizations start with a few members and increase their numbers over time, but the rate of this increase can be quite different when two organizations of the same type are compared. Similarly, there appears to be no typical curve of decline as organizations age. As long as they adapt their processes to the changing suprasystem and continue to satisfy needs and demands of components and of the people they serve, they enjoy a kind of immortality. The Catholic Church, for instance, has continued without interruption as an organization since the first century. Among American industrial corporations, Merck & Company claims to be the oldest, since it was set up as the American branch of a German firm of the same name that was founded in 1668.[274] Of 1969's 500 largest American industrial corporations, 80 can claim more than a century of corporate existence. Most of these are youthful as compared with the oldest European firms.

A voluntary organization, which attracts members because of their interest in the organization's objectives, often has an initial burst of membership expansion, after which the rate of growth slows.[275] If the organization's objectives are achieved or if its particular goals lose popularity or become outmoded, its survival may be threatened. Some voluntary organizations like the still existing Townsend movement, begun during the Depression of the 1930s to achieve stable income for the elderly, continue for a long time with changed goals and reduced vitality. Others do not survive for long.

The growth of business and industrial organizations has been studied more thoroughly than that of other types. These systems often start small, some of them as one-man businesses, and meet a demand successfully enough to increase in profits and in number of employees. This is not the only possible corporate growth pattern, since some business organizations begin their existence by combining two or more older firms or by splintering off from a large corporation (see pages 605 and 608).

The patterns of growth and development of organizations vary widely, depending upon a large number of variables. One mathematical model of growth, which can be applied to either the growth of sales of a product made by a company or the growth of a small company dependent upon a single product, includes 160 variables.[276] Some of these are length of time required for product development from a research idea to a design ready for production, man-hours required for this development, length of time needed to establish production facilities, and time required for customers to become familiar with the product and for demand to develop. These variables alone can determine two different patterns of growth. In the first, the development time and the market learning time are very long, but the product preparation time is short. No long period can be anticipated during which the originator has a monopoly, since his designs and samples are available for competitors to study and they can set up production faster than the market grows. The early developers may therefore not become the major producers.

A second pattern occurs when market learning time is very short, production facilities are expensive, technology is complicated, and a long period of development is required. With such a product, the market develops almost simultaneously with the production output and well before competitors can get into production. This ensures a period of good profit margins and rapid recovery of development and capital equipment costs.

As Forrester points out, some companies are "conspicuously and continuously" successful because they select projects that can succeed, have the foresight to start early enough even if they must risk their own internal funds before they can interest sponsors, and have the courage to be realistic about estimates and to lose contracts if the source of funds cannot appreciate when a plan is realistic even though high-priced.[277] Such organizations establish a reputation for success, and a cycle of success breeding success results. Other companies which make bids on the basis of funds available rather than the amount needed, and according to a timetable that is not realistic, end up with projects that have passed the crisis point and are completed too late to succeed. These firms develop a reputation that leads to their getting jobs that are refused by the successful organizations. Failure is rewarded by tasks for which the probability of success is not great.

A number of theorists have identified stages in the development of a new organization, in each of which the structure of the decider becomes more complex as new echelons are added and as the sort of decisions made at the top echelon changes. In the first stage of a new small restaurant business, for example, there is rarely much division of labor among the owner-manager and his helpers.[278] Relationships are usually informal. In the second stage, as more employees are added, specialization becomes necessary, and the manager gradually begins to be primarily a supervisor over his employees. The third and fourth stages involve the creation of one and then a second new echelon as new staff is added. Relationships become more formal. Feedback to and from management becomes faulty, and procedures must be developed if these faults are to be corrected. Controls on costs, quantity, and quality of food served become necessary. Management skills increase in importance. The fifth stage arrives if and when the restaurant becomes a chain and recipes and service procedures must be standardized, since customers of such businesses want to know what to expect, no matter which unit they patronize. In such a sequence the owner can fail at many points, his skills proving inadequate or his decisions turning out to be wrong.

Another study, by Dale, found that new sorts of management problems arise at different stages in the growth of businesses.[279] This study compared corporations with differing numbers of employees rather than studying changes which occur slowly over years in a single organization. This procedure was used to enable the research to be carried out within a period of months rather than years and because organizations do not keep the sort of records that make historical study of these variables possible. Table 10-5 summarizes the seven major stages of company growth found in this study, their associated problems, and the possible consequences of these.

A research by Wickesberg investigating 106 small manufacturing firms in Minnesota used interviews with executives to discover what organizational units were present in their firms and how committees and outside consulting firms were used to supplement these.[280] Of these firms, 13 had fewer than 10 employees, 42 had from 10 to 49, 20 had from 50 to 99, and 31 had from 100 to 499. Annual sales ranged from $35,000 to $18 million. Almost one-third of the firms in the sample were started following World War II. About half were less than 30 years old. Of the 106 firms, 90 indicated at least some interest in growth.

TABLE 10-5   Seven Major Stages of Company Growth

Stage of growth	Size (number of employees)*	Organizational problem and its possible consequences
I	3–7 (Any size)	Formulation of objectives: *division of work*
II	25 (10)	Delegation of responsibility: *the accommodation of personalities*
III	125 (50–100)	Delegation of more management functions: *span of control*
IV	500 (50–300)	Reducing the executive's burden: *the staff assistant*
V	1,500 (100–400)	Establishing a new function (functionalization): *the staff specialist*
VI	5,000 (100–500)	Coordination of management functions: *group decision making*
VII	465,000 (Over 500)	Determining the degree of delegation: *decentralization*

*The first figure indicates the actual size of the company studied. The second figure in parentheses indicates very broadly the size of the company when the particular organizational problem may arise for the first time. The rise of the organizational problem is, of course, not necessarily tied to the size indicated, but merely reflects very roughly the findings of the limited sample.

SOURCE: E. Dale. *Planning and developing the company organization.* New York: American Management Associations, 1952, 26–27. Reprinted by permission.

How soon after the founding of a firm its specialized functional units were formed is shown in Table 10-6. According to Hypothesis 5.4.3-3 (see page 109), as a system's components become more numerous, they become more specialized and consequently more interdependent. The rise of specialized functional units as numbers of employees increase supports this hypothesis. Production and sales departments are generally the first to be formed.[281] In one study over one-third of these were part of the initial structure of the organization. Purchasing, quality control, product research and development, and credits and collections units were much less frequently formed when the business began. Personnel, production planning and control, industrial engineering, and market research departments were generally found only in older firms, having been formed a number of years after the founding of the company.

TABLE 10-6   Time of Formation of Various Sorts of Specialized Functional Units in 106 Firms

	Number of firms forming formal unit for									
	Production	Sales	Purchasing	Quality control	Product research and development	Credits and collections	Personnel	Production planning and control	Industrial engineering	Market research
In founding year	17	13	2	3	2	1	—	—	—	—
From 1 to 15 years after founding	12	10	7	8	6	2	1	1	—	1
During second 15 years after founding	11	2	6	2	4	3	2	4	2	—
Over 30 years after founding	7	9	9	7	3	3	4	—	2	2
Data not available	23	14	7	2	1	4	1	=	=	=
Total formal units	70	48	31	22	16	13	8	5	4	3

SOURCE: A. K. Wickesberg. *Organizational relationships in the growing small manufacturing firm.* Minneapolis: Univ. of Minnesota Press, 1961, 28. Reprinted by permission.

The appearance of various sorts of formal units in a corporation's structure correlated both with the number of employees the firm had at the time and with its current annual dollar sales. Production departments were found in companies of all sizes, but only 2 out of a total of 13 with fewer than 10 employees had such units, and none with annual sales under $100,000 had them. When a firm reached annual sales of $400,000, it was very likely to have such a unit, and all firms with annual sales over $7 million did. If a company had no formal units responsible for production and sales, the president or other chief executive was usually responsible for them. The least common specialized functional unit was market research, which occurred in no firm with less than $3 million in annual sales. The smallest firm to have such a unit had 70 employees, and the next smallest had over 200. All three firms which had market research units were over 25 years old; one of them was 78. The sales vice president was the usual person to assume this responsibility. Nine of the smallest firms used outside market research services.

Besides these components within the system, 12 different sorts of consultants were used. Auditors and lawyers were almost universally retained, and 50 percent of the companies used advertising and personnel consultants. Over half used four or more outside consulting services. Only 2 percent used none. The infor-

mality of these firms is indicated by the fact that at the time of the study, only eight of them—all among the larger, older ones—had any sort of organization chart.

Although the relationship of the structural developments to the increasing number of employees and annual volume of sales in these firms seems clear, Woodward discovered that in her sample, it was almost impossible to find out why a given department had been established at the particular time it appeared.[282] A minority of the departments had been formed because of dissatisfaction with the existing organizational structure. In some cases a change in top management occurred at about the same time. In some the chief executive had paid more attention to organizational structure after he had brought in consultants, had attended a high-level management course, or had become an officer of a management association. Some structural changes came about spontaneously as the result of a crisis, some to accommodate given individual persons, and some in response to management fashion. All firms seemed to have been modified to accommodate individuals. New posts were created for bright young people or for misfits who, for one reason or another, could not be fired. The new departments persisted long after the reason for establishing them had disappeared. Hypothesis 5.4.1-3 (see page 108) says that increase in the total number of components in a system requires a disproportionately larger percentage rise in the number of components specialized for information processing and deciding. This proposition may be confirmable in some organizations, since each new unit that is established requires management subcomponents and information processing services as well as the operating personnel.

Organizations do not have a life cycle analogous to the life cycles of organisms or even to those of some types of groups, like nuclear families, which do not outlast the lives of the original members. The probability of termination is not a function of time for organizations, as it is for organisms. In fact, since organizations learn and adapt to changing circumstances and replace their organism components, there is a definite correlation between advancing age and the probability of continued success. Proportionally more young than old corporations show annual deficits.[283] Old organizations, or at least old deciders in organizations, are frequently believed to resist change, as Hypothesis 3.3.7.2-11 (see page 101) maintains, but research results on this issue are not conclusive.[284]

5.4.2   Cohesiveness   Organizations differ in how close their components remain to one another in physical space. The group and organizational components of highly coherent organizations transmit information among their members over short physical channels, but longer channels are necessary in less coherent systems. Having all components under one roof or within a continuous matter-energy boundary ordinarily makes it possible for the subsystem processes of an organization to be controlled and coordinated with less difficulty and expense than when they are geographically decentralized.

Very large organizations find it impractical or impossible to aggregate all the human components of their subsystems at any place and time. Many organizations cannot have a cohesive arrangement in physical space if they are to achieve their goals. Religious services of all denominations, for example, are held in geographically dispersed congregations so that the faithful can attend them. Businesses that retail commodities like gasoline usually solve their distribution problems by a net of storage facilities, distributors, and outlets located where customers can reach them.

The reason people agglomerate into cities and remain in close physical proximity to one another rather than spreading out over the territory of a society in a more even pattern is given, by Meier, as attraction brought about as a result of communication among them.[285] Although I do not question the importance of communication in forging and maintaining the cohesiveness of cities, it seems to me that the communication is not the primary attractant, as Meier conceptualizes it, but rather that people communicate to achieve the goals they have as organisms as well as the goals of the larger systems they are in. In other words, following the principle of least effort, people stay in cities because in them, movements over relatively short distances can reduce multiple strains. More alternative social interactions are also possible where many people and groups are readily available. More work is required in rural areas, where one must travel longer distances to obtain needed products or services. Also, the advantages of division of labor are harder to achieve in rural areas.

Decentralization. When the number of members or components in an organization increases to a certain size, the top echelon of the decider has too many subordinates. It begins to be stressed by overloads of its information processing capacity, and decisions are not well made or are not made at all. It therefore becomes essential to create a new echelon and decentralize some of the decision making.

Organizations can be decentralized in at least three different ways, the first of which is relevant to cohesiveness and the others to integration (see pages 700 to 702). In a cross-level analysis of decentralization, Kochen and Deutsch distinguished these three distinct meanings in current use by organization theo-

rists.[286] The first, *pluralization,* exists when an organization creates a number of essentially identical but spatially separate units, such as repair facilities for each of its several production departments. The second meaning of "decentralization" is *decentralization by function.* The third is *decentralization of decision making* in the echelon structure of a system's decider. These overlap in practical situations, and numbers of units, kinds of functions, and loci of authority may all be altered when a system's structure is changed. Kochen and Deutsch's analysis of pluralization makes the fundamental distinction between matter-energy and information.[287] For their purposes, pluralization of decider components can be treated in the same set of models as pluralization of repair facilities, considering decisions as a form of service to be supplied to components of a system (see pages 736 and 737).

5.4.3 Integration Organizations vary greatly in how much their processes are integrated under the control of a central decider and in the developmental sequence by which their integration is achieved. Very small organizations, such as a small business with an owner-manager who makes all important decisions and has a few people working with him in a face-to-face relationship, are highly integrated. If such systems grow, however, developing more echelons and more differentiated functions or departments, they also at the same time become less integrated as part of the responsibility for decisions is delegated to decider components at lower echelons.

Organizations that begin by merging two or more independent companies under a single management usually increase their integration progressively, some to the point where component boundaries completely disappear and a highly centralized organization is formed. They may, however, remain decentralized in many of their functions, as General Motors has done.

Modern conglomerate corporations are made up of several component companies, often with entirely dissimilar processes. These have little or no need for interdependence or interaction. Conglomerates are therefore extremely decentralized and unintegrated, more so even than General Motors. Litton Industries, Inc., for instance, at one time controlled or owned all the capital stock of numerous companies which manufactured scientific instruments, transformers, electronic equipment, mechanical control systems, data-processing systems, x-ray equipment, typewriters, copying machines, conveyors, tools, calculating and adding machines, precision machines, paper, metal and wood office furniture, navigation systems, patient monitoring systems, refrigerated showcases, radio communications systems, nuclear submarines, computer components, and many other products.[288] It also owned a chain of restaurants, retail stores, publishers of textbooks and trade publications, and printing companies. Its 219 major manufacturing plants and laboratories and 1,508 other facilities, not counting regional sales offices and other small installations, were geographically distributed in 35 countries and all over the United States.

As labor unions have grown, their decider processes have become more and more centralized.[289] One evidence of this is the fact that their members meet in conventions less frequently as their numbers increase. Union organizations tend to grow by addition of new locals, which implies a smaller decision-making role for any single local. They are separated geographically, which militates against coalition formation among locals. Instead, their national integration is accomplished through information exchanges with the national office. This makes for the centralization of control. Such centralization is facilitated also by the greater financial resources and power that accumulate as the system grows. More and more full-time officials and experts are added to the staff, and as a result, large numbers of convention delegates come from this group of people, who are not likely to challenge central control. National officers negotiate on an industry-wide basis, while local leaders are more likely to be administrators than organizers and directors of union activity. Union locals also have lost the bargaining power with their national organizations that the presence of competing national unions made possible in the past. Agreements among national labor organizations concerning their jurisdictions have eliminated alternative national affiliations which once were available to dissatisfied locals, although jurisdictional disputes still sometimes arise, as when the United Farm Workers Organizing Committee, led by César Chavez, clashed with the Teamsters' Union over organizing farm laborers in California.

This centralization of decision making is counteracted in some unions by large locals that are able to challenge the national office. Such challenges may be associated with regional wildcat strikes and include demands that the right to bargain on local issues, as well as the right to call strikes, be granted locals. The United Automobile Workers (UAW) was obliged to decentralize bargaining on local issues for another reason—because the number of issues was too great for national bargaining.[290] In 1970 General Motors received 39,131 demands from its 155 UAW locals, many of which were negotiated locally. Such negotiations clearly threaten centralized power.

Universities have traditionally been decentralized in their control of academic affairs. Chairmen and tenured faculty of each department have exercised primary control over courses, the hiring of nontenured research and teaching members, standards for teachers and students, and choice of graduate students. As professionals, they are more willing to be judged by peers in their particular professions, especially their national professional organizations, than by their administrative superiors within the university. Regional or national accrediting bodies, representing the society as a whole, reinforce this decentralization by rating the excellence of each department in terms of national standards for its discipline. Their power arises from their ability to withhold accreditation; as a result, academic credits earned by students of a department or a whole university are not acceptable for transfer to other colleges and universities, and this may handicap graduates in getting jobs in their specialized fields.

Although control of university funds is centralized, many departments or individual professors obtain fiscal power by receiving grants or contracts from governmental agencies, private foundations, or other sources. With minimal constraints from the university administration they are often able to decide how this money shall be spent. Not only have population growth and increasing demands for higher education produced rises in the numbers of students and faculty in individual universities, but also, as state university campuses have grown, many states have decentralized the educational process to new campuses, geographically separated from the older institutions, with their own administrators and often with their own trustees. In many states boards of regents, an echelon higher than the top echelon of the separate campuses, increasingly exercise centralized control over many aspects of these systems. At the same time students, the primary clients served by universities, have demanded a voice in hiring professors, deciding about curriculum and grading standards, and determining policies about teaching and student social life. The efforts of various components of universities to wield power have produced strains and conflict within these systems.

Managerial decentralization in such organizations as large industrial corporations and governmental agencies involves delegation of responsibility and authority from higher to lower echelons. This is distinct from geographic decentralization (see page 699). A firm may have a number of separate plants, each with its own manager, but if the managers are not permitted to deviate from established procedures, the management remains centralized.[291] In a study by Meyer of 254 city, county, and state departments of finance the data showed that decision-making authority was more highly centralized as the number of subordinate organizations or groups in an organization grew.[292] This finding appears to negate other observations (see pages 697 and 698) and Hypothesis 5.4.3-2 (page 109), which states the exact opposite. On the other hand, as the number of echelons in the decider grew, decentralization increased, and rules promulgated by the top echelons to guide decisions throughout the entire organization proliferated.

If the decision making of an organization is decentralized, provision must be made for integrating the processes of its separate parts. Some means of assuring coordination are discussed above (see pages 679 and 680), including the use of special integrating components, coordination by feedback, coordination by planning, and computerized management information systems (see pages 626 and 656) which provide top echelons with data that enable them to make decisions, or monitor those made by others, more easily and effectively. Another method, described by March and Simon, involves the establishment in an organization of profit centers.[293] These operate on a competitive basis, and each is held responsible for its own profit and loss.[294] They either have separate staffs or pay for services at the market rate. In theory, as each such component manages its affairs and sets prices for its products and services in order to maximize its own profit, the profit of the whole system will be maximized. This sort of coordination is possible only in a large organization in which strong policies are developed by top management. I shall discuss a mathematical model of such decision making below (see page 734).

Decentralization of decisions is essential in large organizations, but it always has both advantages and disadvantages. Particular aspects of organizations, such as the length of the distances which separate the components, the kinds of products made, or the types of services provided, determine which decision-making structures and processes are optimal.

Among the advantages which may arise from decentralization are: (a) Decisions are made closer to the problem. Hypothesis 5.4.3-4 (see page 109) states that decentralization of decision making in general increases the speed and accuracy of decisions which reduce local strains. (b) There is usually less noise in shorter channels, as Hypothesis 3.3.3.2-3 (see page 96) suggests, and this is probably true also of distortion (see Hypotheses 3.3.3.2-2 and 3.3.3.2-4, page 96). (c) Local executives take more responsibility and do not go to headquarters with every problem, which may speed decisions and improve efficiency, as Hypothesis 5.4.3-4 (see page 109) states. (d) Consequently, there is less overload on the top echelons of the decider, which are thus free to concentrate on

major issues. (e) Cost savings may be made because paperwork and other communications are reduced, as Hypothesis 5.4.3-2 (see page 109) suggests. (f) Better training is provided for young executives since they are given experience in bearing responsibility. (g) Organizational morale is improved since participation in decisions makes work more satisfying for many people (see page 678). (h) As long as a sufficient amount of coordination is carried out, decentralization may provide for better interaction among components, in accordance with Hypothesis 5.4.3-9 (see page 109).

Decentralization also has its disadvantages, including: (a) The impermeability of component boundaries, which tend to block flows of information from one part of the organization to another, is increased. Hypothesis 5.4.3-5 (see page 109) says that as decentralization increases, decisions are increasingly made by components without the benefit of relevant information existing elsewhere in the system. This can include failure to use the advice of central components. (b) Decisions in various parts of the system may lack uniformity. Hypothesis 5.4.3-6 (see page 109) suggests that when the decider is decentralized, there is more likely to be discordant information in different parts of the system, and consequently there are internal strains and poor coordination. (c) A larger number of people must be employed who are capable of making reasonable decisions.

His study of deciding in companies of different sizes led Dale to conclude:

Despite all the talk we hear about decentralization and the delegation of decision making, an examination of the actual activities of chief executives discloses that they continue to make most or all major decisions either directly or through a formal framework of strict rules, checks and balances, informal instructions, and through mental compulsion to act as the boss would act. Chief executives also make final decisions on matters which are relatively or absolutely unimportant. An amusing commentary on the centralization of minutiae appeared on the wall of the janitor's broom closet in a small station of one of our railroads, where a frustrated employee posted this inscription: "Before emptying trash cans, wire Omaha for approval."[295]

Difficulties in integration can be expected to occur if the lack of cohesiveness, or geographic separation among components of an organization, is great, particularly if national boundaries intervene between an organizational component in one country and the faraway home office in another. Such separated components of many sorts of organizations often develop their own independent ways of doing things and may deviate considerably from policy set by the central decider. Organizations appear to be especially likely to lose at some time components which are far removed or separated into multiple systems by national boundaries. The branches of various American corporations in Latin America, for example, are vulnerable to being expropriated. Highly segregated organizations like conglomerates can be readily separated into component organizations.

A bizarre case of segregation of parts of an organization concerns the Butterfield Division of UTD Corporation, which makes precision cutting instruments.[296] This factory straddles the international border between Vermont and Quebec, with its front door in Canada and its back door in the United States. As a result of a treaty made in 1842, the Canadian-American border was fixed through a number of existing communities, sometimes even dividing buildings. One of these was this precision instrument factory. Both matter-energy and information processes are affected by this split. An imaginary line, which only top executives cross, is drawn through the plant. On the American side the plant buys raw steel from producers in the United States, maintains a separate stock room and machine shop, and hires citizens of the United States, who are paid in United States dollars. On the Canadian side the plant buys from Canadian producers, also maintains a separate stock room and machine shop, and hires workers from Canada, who are paid in the currency of that country. Since moving steel from one side of the shop to the other would constitute smuggling, steel on one side of the factory is "exported," driven across the international border, and "imported" through customs, where forms are filled out and duty is paid. At regular intervals taxes are paid to each government based upon the profit made on that part of the operation which is inside its borders.

5.5 Pathology   Diagnosis of pathology in organizations is difficult because there are neither generally accepted indicators of organizational health and disease nor any established ranges of stability for organizational variables. It is hard for us, with our present primitive understanding of the structure and process of organizations, to know when they are in trouble. In a few cases this may be clear, as when a corporation fails to make a profit, when an overt conflict breaks out among an organization's components, when there is great destruction or loss of its property, or when a significant number of people in it leave or die. When a political party can no longer attract adherents or win sufficient support to be represented in legislatures and public offices, when a college is deprived of accreditation, when a city faces disintegration, or when a business goes into receivership, obviously the organization's adjustment processes which ordinarily maintain its vital steady states have failed. In any single system

it is then usually possible to discover disturbances in internal steady states which probably have been responsible for the outcome. A wide normal range of variations in management policies and internal steady states of organizations of the same type, however, can be found. How these variations affect the continued survival of the system can rarely be ascertained. In only a few studies have variables such as management structure (see page 649) or subsystem differentiation and system integration (see page 701) been found to correlate with organizational success or failure.

The generally accepted signs of pathology differ from one type of organization to another. Profit-making business organizations in the United States, for instance, are commonly expected not only to make a profit but also to increase annually their dollar volume of sales and earnings by an amount at least as great as the average or median of other, similar firms (see page 692). In 1975, for example, a year marked by worldwide inflation and recession, industry medians in sales increases ranged from 1.7 percent for motor vehicles to 12.3 percent for mining and crude-oil production.[297] A company is often considered to be suffering from some pathology if it cannot perform as well as most of its competitors. Performance poorer than that of other organizations in its industry or failure to make a profit over an extended period affects the value of a company's stock and, if it continues, limits its access to capital. Signs of poor industrial health which may appear as consequences of this financial limitation include forced reduction in the number of an organization's members or components, inability to compete for top administrators to fill management positions or failure to hold the best employees, deterioration of buildings and equipment, and often limitation of output and decrease in quality of products, brought about by the necessity of cutting costs in every possible way.

In nonprofit organizations pathology is less immediately apparent, as I have indicated (see pages 668 and 686), since the monetary inputs to them do not necessarily provide clear and immediate feedbacks about how effective they are in meeting public needs.

The signs of pathology in cities are all too evident today in urban communities around the world. They include a sorry list of miseries for their citizens such as polluted air, inadequate municipal services of many sorts, disgruntled public employees, poorly maintained and overcrowded streets, economically and socially disadvantaged people in decaying housing, and high rates of crime and violence. Although there is no unanimity as to what constitutes a healthy and desirable city, there is general agreement that these characteristics are pathological.

Because the structures and processes of many types

of organizations are to a large extent under the control of the system's own decider, the greatest variety of forms of organizational pathology concern internal information processing. Even if the immediate stress to a system comes from its environment in the form of a natural disaster or from the suprasystem in the form of an economic recession, acts of the decider in failing to foresee the crisis or to prepare adequate adjustments are ultimately responsible for the pathology.

(*a*) *Lacks of matter-energy inputs.* Lack stresses of the matter-energy inputs required for subsystem processes and maintenance of organism components, if they are sufficiently severe and last long enough, exhaust available adjustments and severely disturb an organization's steady states. The matter-energy which is lacking may be organisms, both in the form of new members or employees and in the form of inclusions such as customers of a store or a theater. Or it may be any other sort of matter-energy the system needs.

Organizations that undergo such a severe lack stress over an extended period of time ultimately fail to survive unless they can find a substitute base of support and a new steady state. As a region becomes a "dust bowl," for example, its towns lose population. Young people go elsewhere to find work and do not return. Houses stand empty and businesses fail. Eventually the formerly thriving community becomes a ghost town. Sometimes, as when mines are worked out, the pathological process can be stopped and perhaps reversed by finding other resources, like gambling casinos or ski resorts, to support the town. The new steady state is quite unlike the old one in this case. Many people prefer it. Some do not.

Failure to obtain inputs of sufficient new members to take the places of those lost through normal processes of attrition can damage or destroy an organization. A religious denomination which no longer appears relevant to some of its members diminishes in numbers. More and more, the congregations consist of old people. Lacking the contributions of time and money that a large and vigorous membership would provide, the sect is unable to maintain its buildings and finds it increasingly hard to attract men to its ministry. Such systems sometimes dwindle away until they are no longer viable.

(*b*) *Excesses of matter-energy inputs.* Some types of organizations can be overwhelmed by inputs of kinds of matter-energy that, in smaller quantities, are necessary for their processes. A city requires regular inputs of newborn citizens produced by the reproductive activity of its inhabitants and also regular inputs of newcomers who move into it. Since the population of most societies is increasing, cities typically show regular growth. When the population grows too rapidly for the system to provide the new arrivals with the jobs, the housing, and the services they need, poverty and overcrowding result. Increased demands are made upon schools and other educational facilities. Stories appear in the newspapers and on television about hospitals that do not have enough rooms for patients and must keep some in the corridors or refuse to accept them at the emergency ward. There are cases of mental hospitals with twice as many patients as they are designed for. The "reaction time" of organizations is greatly prolonged. Some welfare agencies can inteview some of their clients only once a year. Health care is inadequate. Police departments may respond to only the most urgent calls for assistance, neglecting the others. Fire departments frequently dispatch their equipment after intolerable delays. Telephone companies also show a number of measurable indications of information overloads resulting from the increased numbers of telephone users.[298] It takes longer for a new phone to be installed; the average time before repairs are made after a set develops operating problems increases; more customers have to make repeated calls for service before receiving it; the users have to wait a few seconds longer for a dial tone when making a call; and more long-distance calls have to be placed over again because of equipment problems.

Population increases, among other causes, contributed to the breakdown of the processes of criminal justice in New York City in 1970.[299] The accused often had to wait many months for trial. In the 3 years preceding, the average daily census in all jails jumped from 9,534 to 13,170 inmates. More than 70,000 people accused of crimes ignored criminal court appearances, becoming fugitives from justice, but they were largely unhunted. Each day in the Manhattan Criminal Court judges heard almost 300 cases, and so the average defendant's "day in court" lasted about 100 s. The pathologies which arose from this overload included a striking rise in the number of crimes committed, riots and suicides among prisoners who were being held for long periods under intolerable conditions, and, undoubtedly, miscarriages of justice.

Once the system has been stressed beyond the point of being able to adjust adequately and provide necessary services to its population, those people who are able to do so leave the area. Subtle shifts indicate that it has begun to turn into a slum or ghetto. The development of this pathology is described by Gleisser:

It takes more than just poor people to start a slum.

Often it is something you can't see or touch. It is a feeling. Even before the poor appear, there is a restive feeling among the people who live or work in the area where the gnawing has started.

Litter lies on the sidewalk a little longer than usual. There is more turnover in neighborhood stores. Police take a little longer answering calls. Insurance companies become cool. Mortgage lenders are slower to approve loans.

You don't see the subtle shiftings by driving past. You have to get out and walk in the streets and talk with the people who have been there a long time. Sometimes the anger in their answers says more than the words they use.

The infection of an area is a crucial time. It is the time when a street . . . a neighborhood . . . a city can still be saved. It is the beginning of a movement away, the gathering of forces that end in smashed windows and burned-out houses.

When abandonment becomes visible, the slum sickness has long ago eaten away the heart of the community.

It is important to know the symptoms of the slide. Knowing can help rally forces needed to fight the death of inner cities. The knowing is needed to save new housing and shops surrounded by the desperation of the old. . . .

There are certain key things for which to watch: A slow-down in police reaction that encourages petty vandalism and shoplifting; large homes that can be subdivided by speculators and congested as building codes are winked aside; lenders declining conventional loans and leaning more on government-protected programs.

In one area, many gasoline stations could be seen where drug stores, restaurants, and shops used to be. One section of the main street showed good stability, but a few blocks away shop owners felt the area was going down and would be bad in five years. . . .

In another neighborhood, already in a steeper decline, store owners felt the old businesses were moving out and nothing moving in. This left empty store fronts.[300]

Violent inputs of matter and energy into communities or other organizations also produce pathology. A disaster has been defined as:

. . . the impinging upon a structured community, or one of its sections, of an external force capable of destroying human life or its resources for survival, on a scale wide enough to excite public alarm, to disrupt normal patterns of behavior, and to impair or overload any of the central services necessary to the conduct of normal affairs or to the prevention or alleviation of suffering and loss. Usually, the term disaster refers to an episode with tragic consequences to a substantial portion of the population . . . it is . . . stress on people, and on their group and community patterns.[301]

While not all disasters result from excess matter-energy inputs, some which have this as their chief characteristic are tornadoes, earthquakes, explosions, fires, and floods. Such violent inputs of matter-energy are usually concentrated within a relatively short time—a few minutes for tornadoes, a few days for floods—and their effects are usually limited geographically. Secondary effects, such as epidemics from polluted water supplies, starvation of people isolated by disaster, and fires following earthquakes, continue beyond the period of impact, prolonging and magnifying the effects of the original catastrophic inputs.

The spatial extent of a disaster has been conceptualized, by Wallace, as a "disaster-space" in which the area of *total impact* is at the center (see Fig. 10-17) and

surrounding areas are less seriously affected (see Hypothesis 5.5-1, page 110).[302] In the area of total impact the destruction, while rarely total, is the most severe. Surrounding this is the area of *fringe impact*, in which destruction is less serious. The *filter area*,

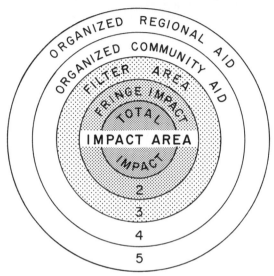

Fig. 10-17 Disaster regions. (From A. F. C. Wallace. *Tornado in Worcester*. Washington: National Academy of Sciences–National Research Council, Committee on Disaster Studies. Publication 392. 1956, 3. *Reprinted by permission.*)

immediately adjacent, is the region through which matter-energy and information must flow to reach the areas of impact. Its capacity is limited, and so filtering must take place here. Some help comes from here also. The area of *organized community aid* is outside this. This is the part of the community in which impact had little or no damaging effect and from which services and supplies can be brought. *Organized regional aid* comes from farther away. The boundaries of these last two may be difficult to fix. Some aid may come from the total society. These distinctions are often administrative rather than geographic, however, depending upon the administrative echelon from which the aid is directed.

These regions bring to mind Ashby's description of an ultrastable system which responds to stress upon one component by means of adjustment processes in surrounding components, the nearer ones being more involved than those farther away, and a greater area being involved if the stress is great than if it is small (see pages 36 and 487). The repair of traumatized tissues proceeds in a comparable fashion (see page 329).

A community passes through several stages

between the predisaster steady state and the steady state that is attained after the disaster. One analysis, that of Powell, Finesinger, and Greenhill, identified these as warning, threat, inventory, rescue, remedy, and recovery.[303] Wallace has a somewhat different list and adds a final stage, irreversible change.[304] In the first two, information about the possible or probable stress reaches the system. In the period of impact, *disaster* strikes. These violent inputs enter the system more rapidly than it can adjust to them. Hypothesis 5.2-5 (see page 106) mentions the inertia of steady-state system variables and predicts that a system is less disrupted if the input is gradual. This may be true in the case of floods, since the rate of rise of the waters is important in the amount of destruction of human life and property that takes place. A slow rate permits evacuation of people and valuables. Hypothesis 5.2-4 (see page 106), which suggests that under excess strain the range of stability of a system for a specific variable is a monotonically increasing function of the rate of output, appears to be confirmable for floods but certainly not for tornadoes.

At impact, the boundary of the system is breached. Communications with other systems in the environment are disrupted. Internal communications break down, and with them the system controls and coordination. The structure of the system is fragmented. If planning for disaster, such as provision of public shelters or fire drills in factories, has taken place, it is rarely adequate, although it may lessen the damage and reduce the number of casualties. Human components meet impact alone or in small groups, taking what protective action they can. Hypothesis 5.2-10 (see page 107) states that, under equal stress, functions developed later in the phylogenetic history of a given type of system break down before more primitive functions do. Under disaster conditions, there is confirmation of this in the cohesion of families and some other sorts of groups, while others break down to "every man for himself."[305] A mother gathers her children together to seek cover. A teacher leads her class to the school basement. Organism and group adjustment processes, rather than organization and society level adjustments, occur during and immediately after impact.

People differ in the appropriateness of their behavior. Some seem to require a period of reorientation, to take in what is happening.[306] This was surely the case when a girl climbed calmly into a music store through a broken display window, purchased a record while a tornado was blowing objects around inside the store, and walked out again.

A reporter with the army during World War II described the variations of behavior among soldiers during an attack, a situation involving extreme matter-energy excess inputs comparable to those which produce natural disasters:

The following figures aren't literal for any certain camp or particular bombing, but just my own generalizations, which I believe a real survey would have authenticated. Let's say there was a camp of five thousand men, and they went through dive-bombing and machinegun strafing. One man out of that five thousand would break completely and go berserk. He might never recover. Perhaps twenty-five would momentarily lose their heads and start dashing around foolishly. A couple of hundred would decide to change trenches when the bombs seemed too close, forgetting that the safest place was the hole where they were. The four thousand seven hundred and seventy-four others would stay right in their trenches, thoroughly scared, but in full possession of themselves. They would do exactly the right thing.[307]

Panic can lead to maladaptive behavior during stress. Mohammed of Nessa, a contemporary chronicler, described the capture in A.D. 1221 of the city of Nessa, a major city of the Khwarezmian empire, close to the present frontier between Iran and Asiatic Russia, by the Mongols.[308] Everyone in the city was so terrified that there was no thought of resisting. The Mongols gathered them together and ordered them to tie one another's hands behind their backs. "They obeyed meekly. If they had scattered and fled to the nearby mountains, most might have been saved. When they were bound, however, the Mongols surrounded them and shot all the men, women, and children down with arrows."

After the fury of the energic input has abated, the period of *inventory* follows. The dazed survivors look about them and see that destruction has occurred. Dead and wounded may be lying about. Cries for help are heard. A Udall, Kansas, housewife described the immediate aftermath of a tornado, saying: " . . . after it was over, my husband and I just got up and jumped out the window and ran. I don't know where we were running to but . . . I didn't care. I just wanted to run. We heard people hollering and everything."[309]

Even the components of the community responsible for relief of suffering may undergo a temporary paralysis before they get into action. This period of confusion is similar to the lag seen in other feedback adjustment processes, before correction toward equilibrium occurs. One author writes that in Hiroshima, destroyed in 1945 by an American atomic bomb, the lag before organized relief activity occurred was 36 h.[310] In less severe situations it may be very brief.

The period of *rescue* begins when people begin to help themselves and one another. The people in the impact zone when Texas City, Texas was rocked by an explosion remained basically social creatures.[311] The survivors not only performed individual acts of heroism but also began to form organized groups almost immediately and to cooperate in helping one another. The organization was new and spontaneous, informal and on a small scale. One survivor said:

Just as I got outside the building, Foster fell right in front of me. I was crawling. I said "Come on Foster, let's get out of here." He said, "I can't walk, I'm dying!" I said, "Come on, you can crawl, I'll guide you." Then Johnny and Clyde came along. I said "Johnny help us—we can't walk." His arms were broken and he said, "I can't help you, but I'll stay with you. If you can crawl, I'll guide you." Talk about cheer—that helped me more than anything, just when he said, "I'll stay with you." Johnny guided us out. Clyde was blinded, but he held on to Johnny's arm. Foster and I crawled behind them. We didn't pay any attention to anybody that didn't look like he was alive. I just thought, "He's dead."[312]

During this period, old community patterns of personal interaction may be altered by the necessity for cooperation. When a derailed tank car released a huge cloud of chlorine gas in 1961 between New Roads and Morganza, Louisiana, men and animals alike were in danger of poisoning.[313] Racial distinctions between black and white people, usually strongly enforced, were completely disregarded, only to reappear afterward.

Many of the people who are first to begin rescue operations are those with special training or experience. Doctors, ministers, nurses, firemen, and others used to performing similar functions in the community overcome their bewilderment first. After the city of Worcester, Massachusetts, was struck by a tornado, few people assumed leadership during the first 15 min after impact who had not had formal responsibility in the community before impact.[314] Officials are first to reassume their part in organization processes.

During the rescue period, the area of impact is isolated, receiving no help from outside. The length of this period depends upon the availability of aid from the filter area. It will vary even within one disaster region since some places are more accessible than others. With roads impassable and telephones inoperative, the survivors of some kinds of disasters cannot easily get word of their plight out of the impact area. After the Udall, Kansas, tornado, a boy who had been in four previous tornadoes hitchhiked to another town to inform police and ask for help.[315] His previous experience with such disasters made him capable of caring for his mother and the other children while many adults were still unable to function. In the city of Zeirikzee, Holland, inundated by the great floods of February 1953, in which more than 1,700 people lost their lives and one-fifth of the country was under water, only one ham radio operator was able to transmit a call for help.[316] Some victims waited as long as 36 h for assistance.

Help from outside, when it arrives, brings the dam-

aged regions to the stage of *remedy*. During this time efficient filtering of the people and supplies that converge toward the area of impact is necessary.[317] This matter-energy flow creates traffic control problems and retards organized relief. Among the converging mass are needed supplies, experts, and helpers, but there often are also sightseers, thrill seekers, and perhaps potential vandals and looters. Roadblocks are often set up to permit the inward flow of needed goods and services, while keeping out people who have no business in the area. One example of improper filtering occurred when the policeman at one roadblock refused to allow ambulances in until he was argued into understanding the need for them. He had been told to exclude vehicles, and he did.

In this stage, too, the area's communication network is disrupted. Rumors spread by informal communications channels, replacing accurate information. One community, struck by a tornado during the night, was in total darkness.[318] Nobody in authority undertook a real survey of the damage. Officials acted upon word-of-mouth information brought by citizens. Consequently, the most seriously damaged area was not identified immediately or reached rapidly by official assistance. Also, because of misinformation, important state police equipment was dispatched in the wrong direction. It spent 2 h trying to get back. In the absence of reliable communication, a rumor sprang up that a drive-in theater known to be crowded with people had been hit. Equipment was sent there because of this false report, only to become snarled in traffic and confusion outside the real impact area of the disaster.

Breakdown of function of distributor components such as roads also hampers relief. In Holland, with roads under water, rescue and relief work required helicopters and amphibious transport. Seaplanes could not land on the shallow water, and even most small boats had too much draft to get through.

As the stage of remedy continues, however, help does get through, first from nearby and then from farther away as the suprasystem becomes informed of the need.

During this stage, when system controls are lost in the impact area, Hypothesis 5.6-1 (see page 110) appears to apply. This states that if a system's negative feedback discontinues and is not restored by that system or by another with which it becomes parasitic or symbiotic, it decomposes into multiple components and its suprasystem assumes control of them. For the period of remedy, the impact area is parasitic upon other units of the society for inputs of matter-energy and information and for maintenance of many of its internal subsystem processes.

In our modern world of instantaneous communication and rapid transportaion, help may come from great distances. After the Worcester tornado, equipment and supplies poured in from all over the Northeast, and 425 trailers were hauled all the way from Missouri.[319] Wallace likens such an outpouring of aid to a cornucopia from which flow material and personnel. Such excess inputs have been common after modern disasters in the United States and some other parts of the world where needs are usually met promptly and reasonably well.[320]

As this stage progresses, the community begins to reorganize. The system restores its internal controls and relationships—quickly if the disaster was limited and not serious, and much more slowly if the destruction and disruption were great. Specialists take charge in their specific spheres of competence. Police immediately act in the field, but do not assume community-wide authority. This they leave to the highest political officials—the mayor or perhaps the governor, depending upon the extent of the disaster. The suprasystem continues to perform functions that the community cannot perform for itself. State police, the National Guard, or the Red Cross continue to give assistance. The normal organizational superior–subordinate relationships usually prevail, even when subordinates are more competent.

People tend to work with others like them. Local police work with state police, doctors look to hospitals for orientation, and hospitals rely on one another before looking to nonmedical groups. Fire chiefs communicate with other fire chiefs. This of course leads to failures of communication, to conflicts, and to decisions being made without consulting qualified experts. In the floods in Holland, conflict among Dutch agencies, too much control from top governmental officials, and the need to use long, circuitous lines of communication hampered effective work in the field.[321]

As the system begins to function again, survivors have sometimes been observed to become almost cheerful, a phenomenon that has been called "fiesta at the disaster":

The second day was different. The bright sun seemed to break the gloom of despair and all concerned seemed to look at the situation with a different eye. Even the midmorning coffee seemed to taste better: the sandwiches appeared a little fresher. Across the street from the Red Cross a large area suddenly appeared to be very clean.

At noon, as the crowds began to move in, people began to stand around in small groups talking. Old friends would greet each other. The whole atmosphere was one of festivity. . . .

The "coke" was running low, so a thoughtful "volunteer" went over to the ruins of the grocery store and carried cases of soft drinks to the cooler. They were dispensed almost before he could place them in the box.[322]

The final state of the system develops in the period of *recovery*. All that can be done is done, but the system does not return to its predisaster state, for some of the changes are irreversible. The dead are buried. The decisions as to whether and how to rebuild are made and carried out. Udall, for instance, was completely blown away by a tornado, and it was necessary to reconstruct every house in town.[323] These were rebuilt as modern, ranch-style homes, with the view of creating a commuter's suburb for Wichita workers to replace the sleepy village that had been there before. In place of red brick false-front stores, the businesses reopened in modern buildings with new fronts, new fixtures, and new goods. Since most of the people who inhabited Udall immediately after the restoration had lived there before, it was in one way still the "same town." But there was an entirely new steady state. Udall was an extreme case of irreversible, historical process, since it suffered a more nearly complete disaster than any other community ever provided relief by the American Red Cross. A comparably damaged city—Warsaw, Poland, in its postwar reconstruction after 85 percent destruction—elected to establish an entirely new city. The only exception was the restoration of one section, the historic ghetto, whose decorated medieval buildings were restored exactly as they had been before the war.

The postdisaster states of these cities, like the recovery states of some patients after severe illnesses, were superior in some ways to the original steady states of the systems. A survey made after a tornado in Lake View, Texas, and repeated after a second heavy storm had hit the area, revealed this to be true also of that community. More than half the people questioned believed their city and their neighborhood were better off than before.[324] A severe hurricane, Celia, hit Corpus Christi, Texas, in August 1970.[325] Nearly 9,000 homes were destroyed, and 90 percent of the business section was damaged. Five months later more than $1 billion in federal aid had been poured into reconstruction, and the damage from the storm was hard to find. A local economic recession was staved off by these funds. New or refurbished tourist facilities were appearing throughout the city.

In Flagler, Colorado, where an airplane dived into a crowd, killing 20 persons—over 2 percent of the population—and injuring 30 others, a change in community attitudes followed the disaster.[326] The heroic behavior of the Catholic priest who happened to be there, and the fact that some Catholic families suffered severely and became the focus of sympathy, led to improvement in the status of Catholic families and a diminution of anti-Catholic feeling in this predominately Protestant town. It was also agreed that air shows would never again be part of local celebrations, and after an investigation the Civil Aeronautics Board banned aerobatics in air shows throughout the United States.

Disasters often produce long-term effects upon individual organism components who have suffered loss, mutilation, or extreme terror. For instance, the number of families who equipped their homes with storm cellars in Lake View increased greatly. This was one indication of the strength of their emotional reactions to the tornado.[327] Psychological disturbances were so widespread, particularly among children, after severe earthquakes in California that emergency treatment facilities were organized in some communities.

(c) *Inputs of inappropriate forms of matter-energy.* Among the inappropriate inputs of matter and energy that can elicit pathology in organizations are wastes extruded into the environment by other organizations or by systems at other levels. Communities are vulnerable to air, water, and food pollution from various sources. Such pollution damages their appearance, weakens or sickens their citizens, causes residents to move away from them, and increases the expense of operating and maintaining them. Commercial and nonprofit organizations alike are susceptible to injury by such inappropriate inputs if, for example, their source of pure water is fouled.

Inputs of employees who do not function acceptably in subsystem processes or who disrupt them frequently damage many types of organizations.

(d) *Lacks of information inputs.* Inadequate rates of input of money, either capital for growth and development or funds for operating expenses, can give rise to organizational pathology. An industrial firm which cannot secure loans can lose a chance to expand, while competitors in a better position to borrow capital seize control of new markets. A small business can fail to show a profit because of uncollectible accounts.

Lack of information about the suprasystem can also damage organizations. Without an adequate market survey, a company's place of business or other facility may be located in the wrong place, with the result that the demand for its products or services is less than it would have been if a more enlightened decision about its location had been made.

If they do not receive adequate information feedbacks from the suprasystem, organizations will continue to use their resources and deploy their personnel in ways that are not best for achieving their goals (see pages 685 and 686). If commercial competition puts a premium on small differences in the appearance of products or the nature of services, failure to take account of public preferences in such matters may drastically reduce sales.

(e) *Excesses of information inputs.* I have dealt with the effects of information input overload on organizations in Chap. 5 (see pages 157 to 164). If an organiza-

tion cannot process a flood of orders or requests for service, it will probably lose public goodwill. Also, its customers, members, patients, or clients seeking products or services will go to other systems that are better prepared to meet their demands.

(f) *Inputs of maladaptive genetic information in the template.* A fundamental fault in many organizations, analogous to genetic or congenital abnormalities in organisms, is a defective charter. An example of such a defect in a charter is a provision limiting the functions of the organization in such a way that it cannot adapt to changing environmental conditions. A college is handicapped in this way if it cannot racially desegregate its student body without risking loss of its endowment funds, given to it under a charter that excluded black students.

(g) *Abnormalities in internal matter-energy processes.* Abnormalities of this sort include inefficient or inappropriate handling of energy, materials, or human components and inclusions. If the rates of distribution of materials and work in progress to their destinations in a factory are too fast, materials stacked in work areas can interfere with workers who are trying to do their jobs. If distribution rates are too slow, workers are obliged to be idle during part of their working day. If a restaurant is laid out so that food becomes cold as it travels from the kitchen to the table, customers are dissatisfied. A storage system that loses or makes inaccessible items that are necessary for any process causes delays, waste, and inefficiency. Patients in a clinic who are made to wait unduly long for care may even die. Workers who must spend their days in dreary and uncomfortable surroundings can be expected to be dissatisfied. If a factory building is structurally weak and heavy machinery breaks through a floor, repairs and delays are expensive. An imaginative and irritating sort of pathology of internal matter-energy processing was planned by the students of Miami University in Ohio as a protest against the administration.[328] In 1970 they held a "flush-in." They operated all plumbing equipment continuously and drained the university and city of nearly all their water supply—5 million gallons.

All such abnormalities unduly increase costs in human and other energy and in money and decrease the quality and quantity of output goods or services. Demand for the organization's output will usually diminish if other systems offer alternative outputs. Profits or other returns to the system will usually decrease also, and survival of the system may be threatened. Many of these abnormalities are secondary to pathologies of internal information processing, often in the decider.

(h) *Abnormalities in internal information processes.* Organization theorists have given considerable attention to disorders in internal information flows, particularly in business and industrial organizations. The most common form of decider structure in such systems, successful and unsuccessful alike, centralizes a "mechanistic" management (see page 649) authority in a hierarchy. The sorts of pathology that can develop in systems with that sort of decider are well documented. As I noted earlier (see page 651), Blake and Mouton describe decision making in such an organization as the authoritarian, or 9,1, management style.[329] They do not question that it can elicit high productivity and that the requirements of mass production and competition promote its use. But they maintain that it has produced fierce struggles between unions and management in many organizations. These battles arise from the fact that educated employees, especially, resent this sort of management, and on the whole employees are better educated than they were at the time this style was first developed. They dislike the fact that such management does not permit them to realize their potential. Also, administrators below the top echelon are not fully used, and many of them adapt to the lack of challenge by exerting themselves in their work as little as possible and seeking their satisfaction in outside activities.

This sort of pathological passivity in reaction to tightly centralized authoritarian control is seen in other organizations besides businesses. In a 1970 report on American schools, Silberman contended that in most of them the administrators were preoccupied with maintaining control over the students, enforcing order and routine for their own sake.[330] He observed that by systematically repressing the students and teaching them all in a uniform manner, school principals and teachers create many of their chief disciplinary problems. They promote passivity, docility, and conformity in their students rather than initiative, curiosity, and imaginativeness.

Another sort of organizational pathology, seen especially in authoritarian and "mechanistic" systems, has been called "canceling out."[331] This is a term for efforts of individual members and groups to control, counteract, or exploit one another which might more usefully be devoted to furthering the organization's overall goals. Such activities necessitate further canceling-out processes to make sure that members are cooperating toward such systemwide goals. Such policing includes checking, reporting, evaluating, accounting, control, supervision, and discipline. It appears to be necessary when there is much canceling-out activity. Policing of this kind is more destructive in some organizations and in some sorts of situations than in others.

Other sorts of decider structures and management practices besides the authoritarian also have typical pathologies. Paternalism is a management style which attempts to increase the happiness of workers by doing things for them, while maintaining the other characteristics of the authoritarian style.[332] Despite its altruistic intents, it can give rise to violent reactions from members of the organization. As Blake and Mouton state: " . . . the formula for concocting hate consists of arousing frustrations under conditions of dependence."[333] As a result, manpower is wasted, the operation's efficiency is reduced, costs are high, inspections and repairs are needed more often, and warranty claims that products are defective are made more frequently.

Another pathological form of organizational administration—the permissive, or 1,9, management style—has the primary goal of making the employees happy. It is feasible only if a company is operating on a cost-plus basis, if demand is so high that profits are inevitable, in a monopoly, or a nonprofit organization. The following remarkable example of this style is provided by Blake and Mouton:

A large manufacturing establishment, up to several years ago, maintained a practice, built up over years, of employing an extra group of temporary laborers during summer months. This was done to compensate for the absence of regular work force members on vacation. Vacations for permanent organizational members were *not* scheduled with production objectives in mind. Instead, the organization "picked up the bill" through employing substitutes. The result was that each member of the wage force was able to have his vacation exactly when he wanted. A dramatic conclusion from this 1,9 way of life occurred, however. Because its product became hopelessly noncompetitive, the plant shut down. *With this luxury style of management—not facing the problem of involving people in solving the real issues of production*—everyone then had 52 weeks of vacation per year![334]

The apathetic, or 1,1, management style described by the same authors is so pathological that organizations cannot survive when it is used except in specialized situations.[335] It is often seen if task simplification and division of labor have been carried to the extreme and if employees' personal goals and expectations are not known or considered by management. It is a common adjustment if management is extremely authoritarian or if the assigned tasks, like assembly-line jobs, are monotonous, repetitive, and unchallenging. Then the employees become bored, uninvolved in the job, and uninterested. This constitutes a personal defeat for the individual employee and a failure for the organization, since potential productive contributions of its components are lost. Interestingly, apathy and anomie (see pages 872 and 873) occur not only when there is too much administrative control but also when there is too little. During the last months that John W. McCormack served as Speaker of the United States House of Representatives, he was in his late seventies and had become relatively ineffective as a leader.[336] One important congressman of the Speaker's party expressed a commonly held view when he said: "The trouble is that nobody is running the railroad around here anymore." And another congressman stated a natural reaction to this situation: "A man is crazy to want to work here anymore."

Pathology in organizations can be traced to disorders of information flow in other information processing subsystems besides the decider. I have already described a decoder failure of historic significance at Pearl Harbor (see page 636).

Blockages or distortions in information flows and inadequate two-way feedbacks, especially across boundaries between subsystems or components, are further sources of pathology. These were among the causes of the difficulties encountered by a rapidly growing conglomerate, Automatic Sprinkler.[337] The management of this corporation acquired many new companies in a short time. Some of these had poor earnings, obsolete facilities, or labor problems. The intention was, of course, to correct these deficiencies by means of sound management practices. This conglomerate, like others, had only a few executives in the main office. About 30 men were expected to oversee the multidivisional company with sales in the hundreds of millions of dollars. To succeed, they needed a foolproof reporting system to alert top management to anything unusual occurring in the divisions. Even if such a system could be designed, common accounting and reporting methods compatible with those of the parent company would still be required. Further, competent controllers would be needed in the divisions. Most small companies do not have such men. These necessities were all lacking at Automatic Sprinkler. As a result, earnings per share dropped sharply, for the highest echelon of the decider was, until too late, unaware of serious problems in various components, and a massive sell-off of the company's stock by major investors took place. In 1967 the earnings were $1.43 a share, up from the year before but below projected earnings. In 1968 they were only 10 cents a share.

Breakdowns in communication also helped to cause the violence and disruption that occurred in colleges and universities during the 1960s and 1970s. These, of course, reflected pathologies in the suprasystem as well as in the system. Students often complained that no channel to their organization's decider was available to them to enable them to express their ideas and to provide feedback about the educational process as it applied to them. They also wanted some measure of control over the planning of courses, teaching, and policy making. Fundamentally, they protested and

disrupted system processes as tactics to become components of the system's decider, rather than clients or living inclusions who merely received services from the system without being a part of it.

A frequent fault of military organizations is that they process essential information poorly or not at all across boundaries between components or units under separate commands. The extreme identification with components which military discipline commonly engenders often creates competitiveness among them. An example was seen during World War II at Fersfield, an air base in England which was the base of Operation Aphrodite. The goal of this mission was to fly a drone plane filled with explosives across the English Channel to blow up bunkers where the Germans were preparing to launch missiles against the British Isles. Both army and navy units at the base were involved in the mission, and as soon as they got together, they began competitive feuding. The army unit had been unsuccessful in its first efforts, and the navy unit, which came later, offended the army men by suggesting that they, the navy men, had been called in to bail them out. The navy men brought with them a drone plane full of electronic control equipment. The army unit wanted to inspect it to see what the navy had that was superior to the army equipment. The navy men, however, guarded the drone with a sentry who lowered his gun on any army man who tried to board her. The navy unit concluded that the army men were trying to steal their ideas from them. As Olsen tells the story:

"They'll steal us blind," one of the young lieutenants told his guard detail. "Keep 'em off our gear!" So the two projects, nearly identical in theory and using similar techniques and equipment, chugged along at their separate paces, and cross-fertilization and impartial criticism were thereby denied to both. Only the commanding officer, Lieutenant Colonel Roy Forrest, had been permitted a peek at the Navy equipment, and this because he had become a fast friend of Commander Smith and because he was not a technician. Word had leaked back that Forrest was critical of the Navy arming panel, but no one paid attention. Forrest was an amateur.[338]

In the end it turned out that the arming panel was indeed defective. If constructive criticism had flowed unhampered and undistorted across the boundary between the army and the navy components, the defect might have been corrected. And Joseph Kennedy, the "jump pilot" of the drone and the eldest brother of John, Robert, and Edward Kennedy, might not have been killed in a later explosion possibly caused by the defect.

The desperate states of many American cities may also arise from abnormalities of information flows within them. These pathologies are aspects of nationwide processes, including attitudes toward race, economic processes, and social values (see pages 802 to 804). The separation of the white and black populations of many American cities results from such pathological information flows. Isolation of blacks to ugly and dilapidated ghettos results from prejudice that sets boundaries limiting the blacks access to education, good jobs, and better neighborhoods; from legal barriers enforcing or supporting segregation which are slowly being removed; and from certain attitudes of the black people themselves, many of whom prefer black neighborhoods to possibly unfriendly white ones. Earlier white immigrants to the United States of various ethnic backgrounds were faced with similar boundaries among components of the community, which resulted from language differences and poverty. These boundaries were more readily permeable to these white newcomers when they became acculturated and made a good living than such boundaries have been to the blacks. I discuss a simulation of ghetto expansion below (see pages 735 and 736).

5.6 Decay and termination   As organizations age, they may also decay in various ways. Their members or components may establish claims to various prerogatives which become endorsed by tradition and are extremely hard to change. This makes the entire organization more rigid and less able to adjust to stresses and strains. Regulations of the organization, like the rules of many legislatures, may specify that the most important officers are selected on the basis of seniority. This assures that these officers will be older men, often not current with modern ideas and limited in their intellectual abilities by advancing age. Also, some organizations which started with idealistic values and lofty goals may, as they age, gradually lose their sense of mission and their support. For instance, the Peace Corps of the United States began with fervid enthusiasm in the early months of the Kennedy administration in 1961. By 1970 it had lost much of its popular appeal, and consideration was being given to merging it with other governmental programs.[339] Applications to join the Peace Corps fell from a peak of 42,246 in the 1966 fiscal year to 19,022 in 1970. Overseas volunteers fell from 12,886 in 1967 to 7,889 in 1970. Nearly one in every three volunteers in 1970 failed to finish his or her 2-year enrollment period. To many younger Americans the Peace Corps had become "just another bureaucratic federal agency."

Complete change of all human components is inevitable in every organization that endures over several generations, and this process does not necessarily disturb its continuity. Loss of all human components at one time, however, does of course terminate an organization as a living system.

Organizations do not decline and terminate as a result of age alone (see page 696). As long as they fulfill a function as a component of a suprasystem, they can continue, sometimes for centuries. Many cities—Rome, Athens, and Istanbul, for instance—have repeatedly survived the collapse of their suprasystem societies.

Termination of an organization is not always a clear-cut event, like the death of an organism, although most organizations eventually do cease to exist. They terminate when the purpose for which they were founded is accomplished or abandoned, unless a new purpose can be found (see page 696). They may terminate because their membership falls below some critical number. Suprasystem decisions also can force them to discontinue operations. For instance, many liquor stores went out of business when prohibition began in the United States. A large organization may be broken down into a number of separate organizations as a result of a court decision in an antitrust case. This terminates its existence, but not that of its components. Business organizations are subject to dissolution by bankruptcy, particularly in their early years, the first 5 years being the most dangerous.[340] As they become older, their life expectancy improves. Bankruptcy is far more likely to overcome small systems than large ones in the present-day American economy, although major failures do sometimes occur. This happened to the Penn Central Railroad in 1970, when it had $4.6 billion of paper assets. Reorganization with a change of decider components and a supply of new capital are commonly arranged for faltering large systems, and in some cases collapse is prevented by a decision of the suprasystem to subsidize them, as in the case of the Lockheed Corporation in 1971. An industrial organization that is operating at a loss but is producing a product or service for which there is a demand may be considered a desirable acquisition by a merger-oriented organization with sufficient capital to gain control of a majority or all of its stock. Its losses initially give a tax advantage to the system that acquires it, and an infusion of new capital and new management can make it profitable again.

Termination by merger may involve loss of individual identity of both systems or some other degree of unification, including merely a new ownership with other aspects of the system left essentially unchanged.

Hypothesis 5.6-1 (see page 110) states that loss of negative feedback control causes a system to decompose into multiple components over which the suprasystem assumes control. This hypothesis is applicable at this level since when an organization terminates, in bankruptcy or otherwise, the component groups or subcomponent persons are free to continue as independent individuals, but, under the law, the state or society takes over control of any residual property or continuing processes.

6. Models and simulations

Of the four classes of models and simulations (see page 85), three are represented at this level. No class (a) models, in which nonliving artifacts simulate a living organizational system, are available, although scale models and working models of machinery and equipment are common. But class (b) *living, usually human, representations,* class (c) *models in words, numbers, or other symbols, including computer programs,* and class (d) *living system–computer interactions* are all used at this level in research, operations, or training. They will be discussed in turn.

(b) *Living, usually human, representations.* Groups are commonly used to represent organizations in laboratory experiments and in games designed for research or training. Some of the artificially constrained group network studies discussed above (see page 539) were designed to have relevance to organizations. The appropriateness of extrapolating results of these group-level experiments to the organization level has been questioned, but the practice has been defended on the ground that these nets in some ways more closely resemble the communication structure of organizations, in which channels are prescribed and much interaction is indirect, than those of face-to-face groups.[341]

Other organization simulations using groups attempt to create realistic organizations in the laboratory and study their processes. For these to have relevance to actual organizations, subjects must become involved so that the consequences of task performance become important to them.[342] This has proved to be difficult. Under at least some conditions involvement has been furthered by making the subjects familiar with the setting and the task, by paying the subjects, by arranging interactions among group members to promote involvement rather than detachment, by giving feedback concerning errors or productivity, or by selecting tasks that are inherently interesting to the subjects. In many of these experiments subjects are drawn from the personnel of organizations, and their experimental tasks are similar to their real-life jobs. This was true of the research, which I reported above, on the acceptability of organizational goals, in which managers and supervisors were used in a training laboratory as subjects (see pages 674 and 675).

Except in the network studies, simulated organizations have ordinarily had about 15 to 20 members, often divided into subgroups and typically representing three echelons, which often corresponded to president, supervisor, and worker.[343] In one experiment the subjects received their job assignments on the basis of a bogus "managerial abilities test." Positions differed in amount of responsibility, salary, and "closeness to the source of decision making." An organization chart was provided on which subjects could find their places. This served to establish a credible hierarchy.

Problems of using groups to simulate organizations and some solutions to them have been summed up by Weick.[344] He concluded that laboratory groups differ from natural organizations or their components in being small, in having brief rather than prolonged contacts, in having unimportant outcomes, in receiving clear rather than ambiguous feedback, and in having independent rather than dependent actions. In these ways such simulations are unrealistic. Modifications of features of the experimental setting, like the frequency of progress reports and the rules given the subjects, can increase the resemblance to real organizations and permit the experimenter to test hypotheses without losing control of the situation.

A set of simulation experiments reported by Bass succeeded in giving the subjects a sense of involvement.[345] The purpose of the simulation was experimental comparison of different organizational structures. Two forms of the experiment were run, each using two competing "companies." The subjects were participants in a management training laboratory and were all employees of the same plant.

The design of the first experiment specified that each company would have a general manager, six members of management in line or staff positions, and six production workers. They were permitted to organize in any way they chose. Both set up line-staff structures (see page 644); one was simple, and the other—a copy of the decider of the home plant—was more complicated. The companies were directed to manufacture a product, the experimenter whimsically decreeing that it should be triangular portholes constructed out of business machine punch cards, paper clips and Scotch tape. Labor costs, management salaries, costs of materials, costs of storage of raw materials and unsold products, and equipment rental charges were given. Representatives of the two companies developed uniform accounting methods to ensure that their reports would be comparable. Market demand was variable, stated by the experimenter in "hourly market advisories." In order to simulate the fact that any two persons in a large organization are likely to interact infrequently, only four men were permitted to work together in one room after production began. The subjects' sense of involvement came partly from the fact that participants were simulating their own real-life performances or those of their bosses. The simulation was carried out in the presence of real-life associates, and so a good or bad job was apparent to them. This fact increased the intensity of the involvement.

The second experiment was conducted with two different groups of executives, supervisors, and technicians from the same plant as the subjects in the first simulation. These simulated companies had fifteen men each: seven management personnel—A, B, C, D, E, F, and G—and eight wage earners. The experimenters required one company to have all decisions made independently by single persons. The other company was instructed to operate only in committees of three or more men. Four overlapping management committees were set up (see Fig. 10-18). Each committee member could belong to more than one committee. Also, the eight wage earners were divided into two work groups: Work Group I, made up of H, I, J, and K, and Work Group II, made up of L, M, N, and O.

Results of the first experiment, in which a simple and a more complex line-staff organization were compared, indicated that the simpler structure was in general superior.[346] It produced more products for sale

at a lower operating cost, its overall profits were higher, its inventory control was more adequate, it adapted better to market conditions, and the satisfaction of its members increased steadily, while there was a regular decrease in satisfaction with company operation in the complex organization. Goals became clearer as the work progressed in the simple organization, while the opposite occurred in the complex one. In both types of structure there was a positive relationship between overall satisfaction and higher status.[347] As in real life, layoffs and strike threats began to appear, engineering modifications were introduced without concern for their human impact, and important trade secrets were lost because people failed to recognize their value as secrets.

In the second experiment, the company which had been instructed to make decisions in committees worked out a structure very similar to Likert's overlapping-group structure (see pages 644 and 654). That is, they set up temporary committees on functional lines: on planning and economics, on accounting, on production, and on developing the organizational structure.[348] This turned into the final structure described above.

The company which had been instructed that all its decisions were to be made by individuals elected a general manager and gave him responsibility for developing the entire organization by appointing subordinates. He selected one man to head administrative functions and another to be in charge of operations, and these men chose division heads to serve under them. Eight men were left in the labor force. These immediately organized a union and elected a president. They then began bargaining at a series of union-management meetings marked for their conflict and disagreement.

The overlapping-group form of organization turned out to be greatly superior, outproducing and outperforming the more traditional line-staff organization.[349] Profits were almost five times as great, sales volume was 157 percent higher, and operating and inventory costs were lower. The administrative structure was more flexible and more satisfying to the persons involved. It provided better communication than the line-staff organization. One reason for some of these differences was the union-management trouble in the first company, with the line-staff organization. Planning, however, was inadequate in the overlapping-committee company. With better planning it could have captured even more of the market than it did.

Simulation games have been designed for training management personnel. They deal with variables believed by their inventors to relate to management success and failure in the sort of organization being

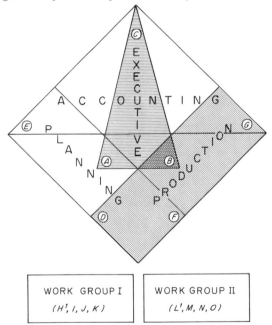

WORK GROUP I
(H¹, I, J, K)

WORK GROUP II
(L¹, M, N, O)

Fig. 10-18 Organization chart of company with overlapping management committees. (A), (B), (C), (D), (E), (F), and (G) are seven persons, each of whom is a member of one or more management committees. For instance (A) is a member of the Planning as well as the Executive Committee; (H¹) and (L¹) are contact men for the two work groups. (From B. M. Bass. *Experimenting with simulated manufacturing organizations. Technical Report 27.* Washington: ONR, Group Psychology Branch, March 1961, 131.1)

Fig. 10-19   Panoramic view of the Miniature Armor Battlefield. (From R. A. Baker, J. G. Cook, W. L. Warnick, & J. P. Robinson. *Development and evaluation of systems for the conduct of tactical training at the tank platoon level. Technical Report 88.* Washington: HumRRO, George Washington University, 1964, 8.)

simulated. An example of such a game is one developed for training Chrysler dealers.[350] A large proportion of these men were believed by the Chrysler management to be inadequately trained in business techniques. Their skills were thought to be deficient, hurting their own businesses as well as the entire company. The dealers themselves, however, did not think they needed training and felt that the training sessions were not worth their time and money. They were oriented toward action and felt their time would be better spent working on sales.

The industry simulation was developed for the purpose of motivating the dealers to attend, to learn and apply advanced analytic techniques, to ask for additional training for their colleagues, and to act decisively in their managerial activities. The game was a simulation of a realistic situation in which a team of dealers managed a dealership in competition with three other teams. Each team made decisions on 40 factors in each decision period, which represented 1 month. The goal was to maximize profits in new cars,

used cars, service and parts, and finance and insurance. Decisions included such things as the number of new cars to order, the amount and sorts of sales promotion to use, and the desirability of expansion of service facilities. Both total market potential and individual market share depended upon the decisions of the competitors. A successful team had to determine the nature of the market, plan a consistent strategy, and adjust to the actions of its competitors.

The game stimulated the dealers to consider alternative approaches to the problems of automobile dealerships and to learn to know their own strengths and weaknesses as managers. Rapid feedback enabled them to profit from mistakes. Evaluation of the game indicated that the team members were motivated as the game planners intended and that many of them made beneficial changes in their business methods in the period following the training sessions.

Some business games make use of artifacts that model equipment used in the actual system. One such was developed by Grayson to simulate decision making in the petroleum industry.[351] Participants "drill" for oil or gas by plunging rods into holes in simulated drilling sites. They buy and sell leases and decide whether to drill wells, considering operational costs and geological reports. The simulated field then either rewards or disappoints their efforts. According to Grayson, this game, known as Gusher, successfully duplicates actual decisions. Among the considerations are how much to bid for various sorts of locations, either "wildcat" or proved areas; whether to deepen wells; how to allocate funds; and whether to renew leases. The game illustrates the penalties for putting money into expensive properties which do not produce soon, the danger of ruin to an operator with limited funds, and the behavior of competitors.

Military games are an established part of training procedures in armed forces. These include field exercises in which opposing "armies" deploy and engage in combat, using noisy charges rather than live ammunition. Another sort of training game employs model tanks on a simulated field of battle (see Fig. 10-19).[352] Two forms of this simulation were developed and

used; one was the Miniature Armor Battlefield, which employed from 1 to 25 battery-operated radio-controlled scale-model tanks on a terrain measuring 23 by 6 m. Five "friendly" and five "aggressor" crews opposed each other in combat. Tank fire was simulated by use of thin beams of light which disabled enemy machines by hitting electronic cells on their sides and turning them off. Harmless explosive pellets from specially adapted air rifles represented artillery fire; implanted charges of flash and magnesium powder simulated atomic weapons; and small firecrackers, activated by the instructor, took the place of enemy mines. Planted charges of smoke grenade powder provided both friendly and enemy rounds of smoke, and assistant instructors could fire tank-killing rounds from a surrounding balcony. Theater curtains divided the terrain into three equal segments in order to limit visibility for personnel in friendly tanks and hide aggressors' activities. The curtains were operated by the instructor.

The second system, the Armor Combat Decisions Games, made use of a terrain board measuring 2.4 by

Fig. 10-20 Overview of terrain board and Armor Combat Decisions Games players. (From R. A. Baker, J. G. Cook, W. L. Warnick, & J. P. Robinson. *Development and evaluation of systems for the conduct of tactical training at the tank platoon level. Technical Report 88.* Washington: HumRRO, George Washington University, 1964, 8.)

4.9 m (see Fig. 10-20). Commercially available plastic models of trees, bridges, railroads, and other terrain features could be grouped in any arrangements the tactical exercises required. These games were used in conjunction with a series of written tests designed to evaluate the proficiency of officers and enlisted personnel and their knowledge of their jobs.

Experiments with these battlefield games showed that they were effective for training tank platoon leaders in essential combat skills but that they did not increase knowledge of armor. It was concluded that while the simulations could not replace field training with real equipment, they could reduce the amount of such training required.

(c) *Models in words, numbers, or other symbols, including computer programs.* Use of organizational simulations has burgeoned, particularly in industrial corporations, since 1966.[353] Most of these developments have depended upon the increasing capacity and sophistication of digital computers, which are used to solve the multivariate mathematical problems characteristic of such simulations. At the level of the organization the line between a model and a simulation is fine. As Meier, Newell, and Pazer define it, ". . . simulation refers to the operation of a numerical model that represents the structure of a dynamic process. Given the values of initial conditions, parameters, and exogenous variables, a simulation is run to represent the behavior of the process over time. This simulation run may be considered to be an experiment on the model."[354] This is consistent with my definitions stated previously (see pages 83 to 85).

The variables frequently employed in organizational simulations include amounts of materials used; square feet of space specified; funds involved in such budgetary items as costs, profits, tuition fees, grants, debts, wages, salaries, and depreciation; numbers of students, customers, or patients who received services; man-hours worked; and estimated values of suprasystem economic indices. If these values are properly chosen and the model places them in their correct relationships, their interactions over time can be accurately depicted and even forecast.

Except for theoretical models, usually in words, like this chapter and many of the books to which it refers, few models of organizations deal with the behavior of living components of the system, except indirectly. Variables of human satisfaction, feelings, motivations, effectiveness, and interpersonal reactions have little place in current mathematical models and computerized simulations of organizations, although some attempts to incorporate them have been made (see pages 720 to 722). The chief reason may be that these variables are difficult to quantify. When such varia-bles are neglected, management decisions are based on incomplete analyses. Thinking of people in computer terms—as numbers, percentages, norms, and mass alone—according to Levinson, eliminates consideration of other aspects of human beings, like their feelings, that cannot yet be accurately measured.[355] Such aspects do not disappear just because they are ignored.

A philosophical analysis, by Churchman, of the idea that rational models can be expanded until they eventually embrace "the entire world" concludes that it is wrong because the information that is needed is not "out there" in a reality that can be examined and modeled.[356] The nature of reality, he thinks, is not such that it can be observed, and the facts "plugged in" to models which will therefore be realistic. Models, he says, mean nothing unless they use the correct information, but in order to determine that the information is correct, it is necessary to understand the whole system: we need the information to get the model, and the model to get the information. One solution to this is to "do what is feasible," which comes down to doing something people will accept. Another solution, one that is sometimes chosen by intuitive deciders, is to make no use of system models at all. Churchman says:

There is less and less excuse for an ignorance about modern analytical technology on the part of today's top managers in industry and government. They are irresponsible if they pretend that the use of models and computers in their planning is "beyond them," or that they don't need to know about these newer developments because they've gotten so far without them. They are equally irresponsible if they expect to see positive results from planning models in one or two years at a minimum expenditure of time and effort. By this late date, intuitive managers should be realizing that an understanding of how their organizations really work is at least as difficult as an understanding of how a high-class rocket works. We live in an age of model building for decision making, and we can make this age the most significant of all time if we all work on the problems together. . . .

A large planning model is a story—it is one idea of what reality is like and what it could be like. It is a marvelously told story in its way—not dramatic perhaps, but as a mosaic of details it is unsurpassed. One can wander endlessly in the ramifications of the fabric of the tale, touching on this or that episode and the way it will affect our lives.[357]

What is necessary, he concludes, is to build different models of the same reality and choose from among them.

Models and simulations at this level represent aspects of the behavior either of a total system or of some limited part of it, such as a single subsystem or component or a particular process. No clear line separates these various sorts, since models are always abstractions and never represent the totality of the subsystem processes in an organization. I shall discuss some representative systemwide models first and then a number that apply to subsystems, components, or limited processes of organizations.

(i) *Whole system models and simulations.*   Models of a number of different types of systems at this level exist, but most of them apply to business and industrial systems, usually large ones, which have their own operations research staffs or employ consultants and have computers. System simulations are costly in time and money. Costs include computer time, salaries of programmers and operations experts, and expenses of collecting the necessary data. An average of 3.5 man-years is required to develop the first working version of a corporate model.[358] Small companies and nonprofit organizations usually conclude that they cannot afford them. Several large universities, however, which have computers and trained research people are currently developing system simulations (see pages 723 to 725).

A problem for researchers studying organizations from the outside is that adequate data, based upon actual systems, are not available. The facts and figures used in the working simulations of business and industrial organizations are commonly kept very confidential by their managements because these organizations operate in a highly competitive environment. Simulation may take the place of experimentation upon a concrete organization. Such experimentation, if possible at all, is usually much more costly and disturbing to the system than a computer simulation. A model can be manipulated in ways a concrete system cannot be. The time required for the effects of an experimental change of an organizational variable to become evident may be intolerably long. The effects of such changes are sometimes not readily reversed, and usually a decision to try one sort of experiment eliminates others that might also have been undertaken. Some variables cannot be directly experimented upon. For many reasons it is essentially impossible and unfeasible, for example, to make an experimental analysis of the effects upon an automobile factory of operating it at the South Pole. Experimental programs using the concrete system, therefore, are limited in scope and are designed to commit as little as possible of the organization's resources. Simulation experiments can rapidly reveal the probable effects of a particular change in variables and can compare the effects of other changes—all at a cost to which that organization can adjust.

Use of a simulation model to represent a real system is of practical value only if it includes information from an adequate data base which accurately reflects the past and present states of the variables. Collection of such information is a major undertaking in a large organization. It is expensive in man-hours and dollars, but if it can be part of day-to-day operations, it can improve efficiency of the system and make up for its costs. This is not a one-time requirement. The data used in a working simulation must be kept up-to-date. The organization must be on line with the simulation.

Validation of models of organizations is difficult.[359] If a model is not isomorphic with the system it is supposed to represent, its functions cannot explain the system's actions. The following section presents a review of several representative examples of the many business simulations which have been designed; this is followed by a discussion of some university simulations and a single simulation of an urban area.

Business and industrial simulations.   Corporate simulation can be approached either from "the top down," taking the point of view of the top echelon of the decider, or from "the bottom up," developing detailed models of components which can be integrated into a whole-system model.[360] The first sort of model initially includes the whole system, but in little detail. Detail is added as the model is refined. Such models use aggregated figures and a high degree of mathematical abstraction. They can be designed and put to use in a shorter time than bottom-up models, but they are more difficult to validate.

Beginning with detailed models of components requires a longer period of data collection, but has the advantage of providing the basis for a management information system as well as a planning model. Such a model is particularly useful if the decider structure of the organization is decentralized because the model is developed to reflect policies and practices of components. The data for the model are the statistics that lower-echelon deciders put into their reports to their superiors. This assures that the superiors can understand the part of the program that applies to their part of the organization. Results of simulation runs can be useful to them with little interpretation by the builders of the model.

A study by Gershefski, based on 323 replies to a questionnaire, showed that by the end of 1969, 102 of the companies surveyed expected to have corporate models in use or under development.[361] These represented large and small companies in a wide variety of industries. The models were used in long-range planning, setting corporate goals at least 3 years in the future, and forming programs for achieving them. The models in this survey and in a later, smaller study emphasize financial inputs and outputs.[362] They project reports, such as income statements, balance sheets, and statements of the sources and uses of funds. Most of them are deterministic, with only 12 percent of the first study and none of the second permitting probabilistic distributions for variables. These deterministic simulations "employ the computer as a large, fast adding machine to examine various effects and interactions of the input values upon the output values such as sales, costs, and earnings."[363] For the most part these models are used as aids to high-echelon decision makers. They enable an analyst to predict the probable effects upon given output variables of a set of decision rules or decision variables.[364]

In Gershefski's study, responding companies listed 11 ways in which their models were used to help management.[365] They were reported to evaluate alternative operating or investment strategies, provide revised financial projections rapidly, assist in determining feasible corporate goals, analyze the effects of interactions among variables, determine sensitivity of earnings to external factors, develop a documented projection of financial position, allow management to consider more variables when planning, determine the need for long-term debt, validate manually prepared projections and existing procedures, develop a corporate data base or information system, and assist in the evaluation of capital investment proposals.

Other corporate models are used to simulate operations, like the Crude Supply Simulation for Exxon Corporation described above (see page 672), and the same company's General Marine Terminal Simulation, which includes such variables as ship arrivals, the time a ship must wait for a berth after arrival, the waiting time for unloading facilities, and other operating characteristics of terminals.[366]

Industrial dynamics.   Industrial dynamics, developed by Forrester, is an approach to analysis of large systems at the level of the organization and above. It views them as series of interconnected feedback loops consisting of decisions, resulting actions, and feedbacks reporting on the actions, that is, as information feedback control systems (see page 686).[367] Simulation is an essential technique of this analysis. Industrial dynamics looks at an organization from the position of top management—not close enough, Forrester says, to see each separate decision, but not so far away as to be unaware of the decision point and its place in the system.[368] Industrial dynamics is formulated in all three sorts of conceptual systems I have discussed above (see page 16), in prose statements, in mathematical models, and in computer simulations of the models. In addition, flow diagrams describe system processes.

Although industrial dynamics was developed originally to study business firms, it is applicable to other systems that change through time and have positive or negative feedbacks.[369] Forrester believes it to be particularly useful for modeling "complex systems," which he defines as having hierarchical controls made up of many nonlinear feedback loops. All social systems, he thinks, belong to this class of systems, including the management structure of a corporation, an urban area, a national government, and national or international economies. So do complex biological systems. Even a limited-purpose model can be as great as the hundredth order. The urban system which I describe below (see pages 726 to 731) is of the twentieth order. Complex systems differ from simple ones in being "counterintuitive," *i.e.*, in not behaving as one might expect them to.[370] They are remarkably insensitive to changes in many system parameters; *i.e.*, they are ultrastable (see page 36). They stubbornly resist policy changes. They contain influential pressure points, often in unexpected places, which can alter system steady states dramatically. They are able to compensate for externally applied efforts to correct them by reducing internal activity that corresponds to that applied. They often react to a policy change in the long run in a way opposite to their reaction in the short run. And they tend toward low performance. This seems to imply that the adjustment processes that keep such systems in steady state, even if that steady state is neither healthy nor desirable, are powerful and difficult to counteract.

The counterintuitive behavior of these systems is described by Forrester as follows:

Intuition and judgment, generated by a lifetime of experience with the simple systems that surround one's every action, create a network of expectations and perceptions that could hardly be better designed to mislead the unwary when he moves into the realm of complex systems.

. . . the complex system is far more devious and diabolical than merely being different from the simple systems with which we have experience. Although it is truly different, it appears to be the same. The complex system presents an apparent cause that is close in time and space to the observed symptoms. But the relationship is usually not one of cause and effect. Instead both are coincident symptoms arising from the dynamics of the system structure. Almost all variables in a complex system are highly correlated, but time correlation means little in distinguishing cause from effect. Much statistical and correlation analysis is futilely pursuing this will-o'-the-wisp.

In a situation where coincident symptoms appear to be causes, a person acts to dispel the symptoms. But the underlying causes remain. The treatment is either ineffective or actually detrimental. With a high degree of confidence we can say that the intuitive solutions to the problems of complex social systems will be wrong most of the time. Here lies much of the explanation for the problems of faltering companies, disappointments in developing nations, foreign-exchange crises, and troubles of urban areas.[371]

Essential features of Forrester's dynamic models

are:[372] (a) *Accumulations* in "reservoirs" within the system of resources such as inventories, bank balances, and factory space in an industrial corporation and people, houses, and buildings in a city. The value of an accumulation at a given time Forrester calls its "level." [When I use his term "level," I shall put it in quotation marks to avoid confusion with the particular meaning of the same word in my conceptual system—see page 25.] (b) *Flows* that transport the contents of one accumulation to another. Flows occur at *rates* which vary from time to time. A rate measures an activity, while a "level" measures a state resulting from an activity. Decisions as to what the rates will be are determined by information about "levels" of the system, never by information about other rates. (c) *Decision functions* (also called *rate equations*). These are statements of policy that determine how the available information about current levels leads to decisions as to what the rates will be in the next time period.

Flow rates transport contents from one accumulation to another in an industrial organization through six interrelated networks, each of which deals with only one kind of stored item. These are a materials network, an orders network, a money or cash network, a personnel network, a capital equipment network, and an information network, which has a subordinate role in relation to the others because it interconnects them all. Process in each of the networks is described by an alternating sequence of rates and "levels." For example, information about the current rate of incoming orders is averaged to produce the "level" of average incoming orders. This "level" will usually be an input to a decision about the rate of ordering in the next time period on the order network. Delays, amplification, and distortion occur in all networks.

Industrial dynamics models treat flows within systems as continuous rather than discreet events, although the latter can be added as the models are refined. They deal with variables in aggregated form—a result of the top-echelon viewpoint, which is "above the separate individual transactions."[373] They consist of two fundamental sorts of equations corresponding to the system's "levels" and rates.[374] These control the changing interactions of the variables as time advances. They are continually recomputed after small time intervals of equal duration to yield successive new states of the system. The intervals are short enough to approximate continuous variation. "Levels" are determined first, and the results used in rate equations.

"Level" equations are the means of calculating the varying contents of the reservoirs, *e.g.*, inventories or cash balances. There are "levels" for information as well as matter-energy. All memory of past states which provides continuity of the system from past to present is represented in the "levels." The units in which they are calculated are those of the real system being modeled. They are not all transformed into monetary units, as in some economic models. "Level" equations include flow rates in units of time, such as items per week. Since they represent averages—integrations over a period of time—the concept of "levels" retains meaning even if the activity which generates the accumulation they measure comes to a halt. Average sales for the last year remain unchanged, for example, even though all present selling activity is stopped.

Rate equations are the means of calculating the rates of flow among accumulations. They are the decision functions of the system that determine what is to happen next. Rates are evaluated from present "levels," often including the accumulations from which the flow comes and to which it goes. The rates cause changes in the "levels" which can later influence other rates. Changes in "levels" and rates of the model make it possible to simulate stable organizations, organizations that grow, and effects of decisions or alterations of variables or parameters in organizations.

The equations of these models are supplemented by detailed flow diagrams that show the interrelationships among equations. These diagrams use a set of standard symbols for "levels," flows over the different networks, decision functions, variables, parameters, delays, and other aspects of the models. Results from a computer run of the model can be displayed graphically, as in Fig. 10-21, which represents the response of a production-distribution firm to a sudden 10 percent increase and later decrease in retail sales, a situation which I have discussed above (see page 685).

A special computer program, DYNAMO, has been developed for simulating industrial dynamics models. It accepts the equations of the models as inputs, checks them for logical and structural errors and inconsistencies, creates a running code, evaluates the equations once for each simulated time period, records values of the variables, and prints out coded descriptions of the flow diagrams with values for the different variables at different times.[375]

Such an industrial dynamics model was applied to an actual company that manufactured an electronic component used in military and industrial equipment.[376] The company's production and employment in the particular product line had been fluctuating more widely than actual product usage. The research was undertaken to determine whether the instabilities arose from the internal policies and structure of the system and, if so, how they might be corrected. After study of the company to determine its structure and

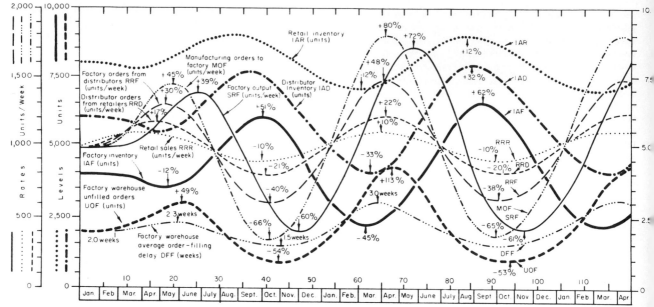

Fig. 10-21   Response of a production-distribution firm to a 10 percent unexpected rise and fall in retail sales over a 1-year period. (Reprinted from *Industrial Dynamics* by J. W. Forrester, 1961, 26–27, by permission of The M.I.T. Press, Cambridge, Massachusetts. Copyright © 1961 by the Massachusetts Institute of Technology.)

the interrelationships of its parts, a mathematical model was developed which included about 90 active variables, 40 initial-condition equations, and 40 constants that defined the system. A sudden 10 percent increase in customer ordering rate was then simulated. This produced fluctuations similar to those observed in the actual system. Disturbances were found to be amplified over a period of 2 years. When the model was refined sufficiently to become an acceptable representation of the concrete system, its response to changes of parameters and management policies was explored. It appeared that changing the policies for controlling the "level" of the number of men in the labor force (which in the concrete organization was adjusted as demand changed) and revising the information flows controlling inventory might correct the undesirable fluctuations. The sources from which certain information came, the policies for controlling labor level, and the equations and parameters controlling inventory all were changed to make inventory variations assist in providing employment stability instead of contributing to its instability. These alterations produced a system which made only a small response to a 1-year fluctuation of 10 percent in the customer ordering rate. Its ratio of employment change to change in incoming orders was only 38 percent, compared with 185 percent under the original conditions.

Models that include behavioral variables. Although human motivations and feelings are usually not explicitly a part of simulations of industrial organizations, some attempts have been made to incorporate these important variables in whole-organization models. One industrial dynamics model of the response of an organization to the introduction of a new policy incorporates feedback loops that include variables of human effort and satisfaction.[377] Like other models of this sort, this one uses aggregated variables, *e.g.*, amounts of effort that must be allocated to implement a new policy.

"Levels" like *degree of new-policy effort allocation* and *internalization of the new policy* are connected by flows, just as the more quantitative "levels" of the system are. No standard unit measures amounts or rates of flow of these variables. Numerical values are assigned by scaling. Numbers representing percentage amounts of each are used in the equations of the system.

A system model of a firm, by Bonini, includes in its decision rules such variables as the amount of psychological pressure felt by each employee as a result of the expectations of his supervisors about his performance, the amount of organizational slack, and the level of aspiration.[378] This model was developed as a research tool on which to test propositions drawn from a synthesis of findings from the many disciplines concerned with organizations. It is designed to show the systemwide effects of specific decisions.

The particular firm investigated in this study, which manufactures and sells a product, is modeled as having a four-echelon decider subsystem. The structure of the echelons and the processes carried out at each are shown in Fig. 10-22. The decision rules in this model are subroutines that specify completely how each decision is made. Besides behavioral decision rules, they include rules of market behavior drawn from economic theory and rules-of-thumb that represent how published articles describe businessmen as operating. These include rules by which budgets, production schedules, and cost standards are set.

Behavioral variables influence information flows in the model in various ways. The amount of psychological pressure exerted upon an individual at any echelon is expressed, for example, as an "index of felt pressure" which is made up of a number of weighted factors. For a salesman, these are an index of psychological pressure exerted by the district sales manager, his boss; his own quota relative to his past month's sales; sales of the average salesman in his district compared with his own; an index based on the percentage of his products which are less than 75 percent of his quota; and his total quota for the past quarter relative to his total sales for the same period.[379] Individual salesmen, four types of which are considered, react to pressure in different ways: by calling only on sure customers, by increasing their effort and making more sales, by decreasing their effort, or by convincing buyers to overstock, a sort of borrowing from the future.[380] In the model the index affects the measure of each salesman's performance during the month by altering the mean and standard deviation of his probable sales distribution.

Experiments with the model involved changing information flows, decision rules, or environment. The changes were based on hypotheses relevant to real firms. Each presented a pair of alternatives. A hypothesis concerning external world variability, for example, was stated so as to have stable costs and sales opposed to fluctuating costs and sales.

Results of the simulation experiments raised some

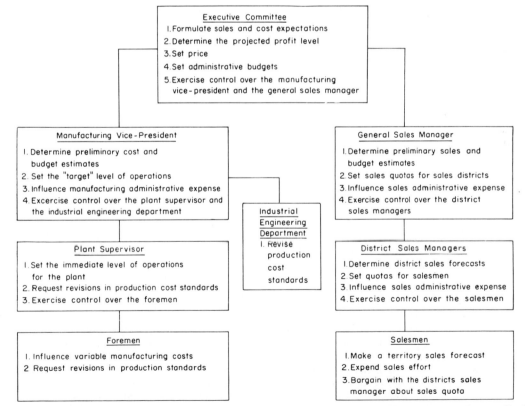

Fig. 10-22 Four-echelon decider structure of a firm indicating the decisions made at each echelon. (From C. P. Bonini. *Simulation of information and decision systems in the firm.* Chicago: Markham, 1967, 31. *Reprinted by permission.*)

interesting questions about common assumptions in organization theory, which in some cases were not borne out. One of these was the effect of high variation in the external environment. It might be expected that a firm would be able to predict more accurately and plan more efficiently in a stable than in a variable environment. In fact, in a highly variable environment the firm had lower costs, higher sales, and greater profits than in a relatively stable environment. Rather than conclude that the model was wrong, Bonini suggested that perhaps organization theorists have overlooked some important psychological factors in organizations. It is possible that occasional downward fluctuations, which created crises, kept the firm "on its toes." Pressure increased within the firm under these conditions, and apparently deciders were more likely to take advantage of opportunities when they arose. During the occasional crisis periods, costs were cut, sales were increased, and slack was removed from the company with beneficial results.

Bottom-up models.   The models discussed so far have viewed the whole organization from the position of top management. Some working corporate models, on the other hand, are built by developing detailed functional models that can be put together to form a total system simulation. Examples are Corning Glass Company's group of models.[381] This large corporation has a number of separate divisions making different products. Several years ago the company rejected the plan to develop a total corporate simulation because the necessary estimates concerning new products, upon which the company depends for growth, could not be made with sufficient accuracy to justify it. It was felt also that managers would not understand what was then a new method well enough to use it in making decisions and that experience with more limited models would be a useful training experience. Limited models of four types, however, have been developed. These deal with financial planning, multinational investment, econometric simulation, and new-product planning. More than one model may be included under a type. Information from each of these can be used as inputs for others. A corporate planning model is being created to integrate them.

A series of "instant models," developed to be marketed and adapted to the requirements of different firms at a cost much lower than that of individual total systems simulations, also takes the bottom-up approach.[382] This series consists of a number of linked modules, which can be adjusted and put together into an aggregated model. A firm can begin with a simple budget model for the total corporation and then add a number of plant models which are capable of being aggregated into divisional, group, and finally corporate models. These can be further adapted and elabo-

rated. These simulations are based upon a program applicable to organizations in general which is stored centrally in a time-shared computer with remote terminals in the offices of the firms. Unique logic and data for each firm are also stored, as well as a general data base and logic for macromodels. Such "instant models" have been applied to a variety of uses in a number of different organizations. For example, they have simulated steel production operations for a steel company to determine raw-material requirements to meet sales forecasts and estimate unit costs. For a builder of health-care facilities they have been used to monitor cash flows in over 40 different construction sites.

Linear programming models.   Linear programming is applicable to problems of allocation of resources or scheduling of operations or services in organizations.[383] This technique provides optimal solutions to the set of data provided. That is, it indicates the best possible use of the resources, locating the point at which a given variable such as cost or time is maximized or minimized within a given set of constraints upon the values variables can take. Constraints include time limits, cost limits, limitations of materials, and legal restrictions. Solutions often require extensive computation, and this fact has set limits on the size of problems that can be handled. Application of linear programming models to organizations has been confined until recently to representation of subsystem processes. As computers increase in capacity, however, the size of problems undertaken has risen to the point where linear programming is now possible in large system models of organizations.

One such model allocates resources as a part of operations planning for a large bank.[384] It is designed to aid the decisions involved in making investments and loans. It maximizes the net earnings from these variables over a planning period of 1 month. The simulation can be extended over time by using output from one period as input to the next.

Information inputs to the model include forecasts of environmental variables such as amounts in deposit accounts and loan demands. These are made in two ways: (a) by statistics, applying, to a number of separate categories of deposits and loans, an exponential smoothing model that takes account of seasonal variations and (b) with forecasts, by managers, of some variables that depend upon subtle factors and for which the stable historical patterns required for statistical treatment are lacking. These include interest rate structure and trust department deposits, among other things.

In addition, policy decisions made by a steering committee, which identifies constraints such as form of liquidity, capital adequacy, and loan and investment maturity schedules, are used in the model. The committee sets the parameter values for many of these, for example, the maximum loan-to-deposit ratio or the upper limit on total bank borrowing. This is a continuing part of the simulation because changes, usually of parametric values but sometimes of the constraints, frequently become necessary.

The model includes 101 variables, of which 46 are exogenous inputs, supplied from outside the model, and 55 are endogenous decision variables, values of which are determined by the optimizing linear programming algorithm. For example, investment activity is defined by 30 variables, of which 28 are endogenous and 2, the bank's Federal Reserve Bank stock and European investments, are exogenous. Constraints on investments include the resources held in bonds with varying times to maturity and the required investment in Federal Reserve Bank stock and other required allocations.

Output from the resource-allocation model is a set of reports to be used as guidelines to the bank investment committee, which considers them in relation to other factors, not included in the model, in making its decisions. The model can be used to analyze the consequences of possible environmental changes and to experiment with alternative forms of constraints. Many more alternative decision strategies can be evaluated with the model than without it.

University simulations. University administrators are increasingly turning to systems analysis as an approach to planning, managing, and budgeting. The number of components of universities and the complexity of their interactions make intuitive approaches to their administration inadequate. In many states the "state university" is composed of several separate campuses. The largest of these is the State University of New York, which in the academic year 1970–1971 had 320,206 students on 68 campuses.[385] The City University of New York had, in the same year, 18 separate units, including seven community colleges, eight colleges, a graduate division, a medical school, and a college of criminal justice. A full- and part-time teaching staff of 12,350 taught 185,969 students. The University of California, on nine campuses, had 105,831 students and a teaching staff of 13,582. The largest annual budget for such a system, that of the University of California in 1969–1970, was $739,667,152. Including the three laboratories of the Atomic Energy Commission administered by the university, the budget totaled $1,031,754,881.[386] In the same fiscal year the budget of the State University of New York was $488,944,666, and that of the City University of New York was $333,550,000. The large private universities, often with many separate schools and colleges, can have 15,000 to 20,000 students. In 1969–1970 Harvard, the

wealthiest private university, spent $188,446,774. All these institutions are big business.

University deciders, like those of business organizations, must allocate resources such as space, money, equipment, and personnel among competing components such as graduate and undergraduate teaching in many departments and other units, student housing, research, maintenance, athletic programs, counseling, business functions, and recreational facilities. In recent years their problems have been more severe because demand for service has, in most universities, increased more rapidly than annual income. A further incentive to efficient use of resources in a public institution is the fact that universities and colleges compete for tax revenues with many other useful public services like urban development, agriculture assistance, public welfare, and law enforcement.[387] Savings of funds in one field make possible increased expenditures in another.

A survey of models developed for computer-assisted planning in North American universities disclosed that there are over 40 of them.[388] These include comprehensive system models and specialized programs limited to particular processes. Not all were operational at the time of the survey. Among the universities represented were the University of California, Michigan State University, the University of Toronto, and the University of Rochester, all of which had comprehensive models in operation or under development, and the University of Washington, Tulane University, the University of Wisconsin, and a number of others which had specialized operational programs.

Development of a comprehensive university model which can be used to simulate the total system requires the accumulation of an accurate and extensive data base. This is an expensive and time-consuming process. The ordinary data collection of the university is often carried out separately for the many different components. Often, not all the data required for a model of this sort are collected routinely. To make these models fully operational, it is necessary to create a management information system including a formalized reporting system. The data must be in a form that suits the computerized model, and they must be kept up-to-date.

A comprehensive model of Michigan State University subdivides the system into several interacting sectors or components, each representing specific operations or functions.[389] Each of these is modeled separately in a set of equations which describe the relationships between the activities of the sector and the resources required to carry them out. These are brought together into a total model by describing the constraints or restrictions that the different sectors impose on one another. Resources include personnel, space, and equipment. Products are developed manpower, research, and public or technical services. This model and others of the same sort do not include qualitative measures of educational variables or goals of the university. These are outside the scope of the model, which can, however, aid the decision maker in arriving at such judgments. Variables are measurable quantities like hours of lecture, numbers of students, and square feet of building space. Only features of the educational process that can be characterized in terms of flow rates and associated unit values in dollars are considered.

The model deals with six sectors: student, academic production, nonacademic production, personnel resources, physical facilities, and administrative control, the source of policy decisions. The equations which concern the student sector—to examine one in detail—describe the dependence of the enrollment distribution on the previous year's distribution; on the enrollment choices of new students; on available graduate assistantships, fellowships, scholarships, and other financial aids; and on other factors. Also, they describe the number and educational status of the students who leave the university—their fields of study and matriculation levels and the average cost of education per student. Finally, they make it possible to calculate from the enrollment distribution the number of student credits and hours of research or teaching that must be produced to satisfy the student demand.

The coefficients in the equations for this sector depend on the behavioral patterns of the students in shifting from one classification to another, in selecting courses, and in using financial aid.

The equations for the other sectors in the total model include relationships relevant to their activities. The administrative control sector differs from the others in not outputting units of a particular sort, but rather allocations of resources. It alters the input–output relationships of each other sector by setting policies as to how resources are allocated to meet requirements. A decision to change policies of resource allocation alters the production equations of other sectors.

When the independent descriptions of the sectors are combined, constraints are imposed on the values that the related variables may assume. For instance, the credit hours produced by the academic production sector are those demanded by the student sector. Some such variables both represent a demand on the system and are also used as a resource to meet other demands. Such variables represent feedback loops. An increase in the variable as a resource feeds an additional demand back into the system. These con- straints play an important part in the stability and control of the system.

Mathematically this model is stochastic rather than deterministic.[390] It is also an optimizing model. Associated with it is a computer simulation program, MSUSIM, which permits experiments using the model to be constructed. The data base necessary for simulation of an entire university with this model has not yet been developed, but tests have been run on the simulation, and limited applications have been made. It is sufficiently general in form to be used with data from any university. It can also be used to describe a total educational system of several campuses and as a component in a model of the manpower sector of a national economy.

CAMPUS (Comprehensive Analytical Method for Planning in the University Sphere) simulates the University of Toronto.[391] It is one of three components in a larger system. The other two are a program planning and budgeting activity and an integrated information system that provides the necessary data base. CAMPUS is a set of computer programs simulating undergraduate academic activities, graduate programs, and combination undergraduate and graduate programs. For each of these, the model includes five sectors: (a) objectives of the activity; (b) the resources needed, the use to which they will be put, and the decision rules by which use is determined; (c) the specific amounts of money, personnel, and facilities needed; (d) preparation of budgets and reports that reflect the first three steps; and (e) experimentation and analysis to modify the variables and estimate the results of alternative courses of action.

The University Cost Simulation Model, designed by Weathersby at the University of California, is a working computer simulation of the major campuses of that university.[392] The program can be run with data from any or all of the campuses. It is designed to assist university decision makers in achieving what they judge to be a good allocation of resources. It provides a description of the behavior of the system, with values reflecting either the present condition of the system or some alternative condition.

The program for the simulation consists of a set of mathematical expressions of relationships among parameters and a set of values for the parameters. The two can be varied independently. The university resources dealt with consist of personnel, physical space, and equipment. Costs are divided into five categories: instruction; instructional support, including support personnel, supplies, equipment, and facilities needed to serve faculty in teaching and research; organized research and organized activities, including separate research institutes, bureaus, studies, and centers; campuswide administration service functions, such as general administration, libraries, student aid, and housing; and physical space and maintenance and operation of the above. The academic disciplines are divided into 12 subject fields which correspond to the divisions used in the University of California's existing data base.

The simulation assumes that all five cost categories, while generally interdependent, exert their effects independently upon total university systems costs in dollars, personnel, equipment, and physical facilities. No feedback loops from one to another exist in the model.

A brief discussion of the category of *instruction*, which is phase 1 of a two-stage model that also includes *instructional support*, indicates how the model works. Student enrollment is the main exogenous variable in the model. Since the number and type of faculty and the amounts of their salaries, as well as the nature and costs of nonacademic support personnel and equipment needed by departments, depend largely upon the student enrollment, the initial phase of the simulation concerns this. The number of students in each undergraduate year and in various stages of advanced degree programs and their major subject fields or fields of specialization are arranged in an enrollment matrix. Students' course preferences by subject fields are displayed in a set of 13 additional matrices. Then, by multiplying the appropriate preference matrix by the corresponding enrollment vector, it is possible to determine the total student credit hours desired by students at any level of instruction in any of the 12 subject fields. After products for all 13 preference matrices have been obtained, the total number of student credit hours taken by all students at each level of instruction of each subject field can be determined by summing. From these it is possible to determine the number of weekly hours that faculty and students are together. This varies with the field, advancement of the student, and manner of instruction, since independent study, classroom lectures, and laboratories require different amounts of faculty time. Each of these weekly student hours must be allocated to one of seven ranks of faculty. The sorts of courses and other teaching contacts provided, and the way in which teaching is carried out, have important effects upon the number of faculty required at each rank and in each subject field. The average salary and other benefits for each rank and information about other aspects of instruction and instructional support are also included in the simulation.

With this part of the simulation alone, university administrators can test the effects of certain policies. The enrollment matrix, for example, reflects the independent choices of thousands of students to go to the University of California, to stay there, or to go on to graduate work. It also reflects choices of a particular campus over others and choices of a subject field. Changes in university policies about how much in tuition or fees a student must pay, as well as about course offerings or educational methods, also influence the simulation. Planning about the composition of the faculty can be aided by the simulation since it clarifies the needs of the system for each rank of faculty in each subject field.

Tests of the whole model have shown it to be a useful representation of the real system. Its output is reports of varying sorts and degrees of detail. Reports can be made on student credit hours likely to be requested as well as those expected to be provided, listed by origin of student, level of course, and academic discipline. Reports can also be prepared on costs to the university of each discipline in a particular year.

The model can be used to judge the immediate and long-term consequences of a proposed program by inserting appropriate values into it. The expected costs of specific curriculum plans, the policy goals, the space requirements, and the salary scales can be determined. Changes of various sorts in operation of the university can also be evaluated in this way.

Urban simulations. Growing concern about the steady deterioration of cities, a deterioration that has managed to keep pace with renewal programs, has led to attempts at system analysis of these complex and baffling organizations. So far, however, even models developed for a particular urban area have not been put to their intended uses.[393] They do, however, shed some light on system processes.

Some of these models apply to one or a few subsystems (see pages 733 and 734, 735 and 736). Two large simulations, one using computer simulation techniques and the other using an application of industrial dynamics techniques, include multiple subsystems.

One initial difficulty in modeling a city is fixing the boundaries of the system to be simulated. The first example I shall discuss, developed by Wolfe and Ernst as a part of San Francisco's urban renewal program, models the whole city, not including its suburbs.[394] The second example, Forrester's urban dynamics simulation (see pages 726 to 731), confines itself to a central part of a hypothetical city. Critics of such limitations have pointed to the importance of metropolitan, suburban, and even national variables to urban processes. They are most relevant to Forrester's dynamic model (see pages 730 and 731). While it is obvious that any detailed model has to stop somewhere, size is not the only reason for the choice of boundaries in the San Francisco simulation.[395] It would have been preferable to include the entire metropolitan area, rather than the city alone, since the whole area is involved in vital issues like transportation, housing, schooling, and health care. But there is no political unit corresponding to the metropolitan area, and therefore it was unrealistic to expect that it would be practical to implement any plans for it. Consequently, the simulation was limited to the city proper.

This model centers on the activities of the private market in real estate, since the stock of housing in American cities is almost wholly controlled by individual property owners.[396] Elements of the model are housing stocks and space transitions.

The housing stocks include the dwelling units, on 4,980 land units known as "fracts," in 106 neighborhoods. Dwelling units are considered to be homogeneous, and no mixed land use occurs in a fract. Changes in building condition or in use of space take place a fract at a time. Neighborhoods, the smallest identifiable geographic areas in the simulation, were chosen to represent areas with similar amenities and housing. Four categories representing the condition or state of repair of the buildings are included in the model: sound, needs minor repair, deteriorating, and dilapidated.

Space transitions include changes in normal yield from property brought about by public actions (like zoning, assessment, capital improvements, code enforcement, or externally caused changes in rental values) and private actions (like new construction, conversion, rehabilitation, or merger). Normal yield is a ratio between rental and market value and includes net return on investment and normal expenses like interest, insurance, taxes, upkeep, and management costs. Space pressure is the ratio between the demand for a housing type and the supply. As this pressure increases, rents go up, to a maximum rate of 4 percent a year. As pressure decreases, so do rents.

People who can afford to pay high rents will look first for sound houses and will accept those needing minor repairs only if the best is not available. Those who cannot afford the better conditions will rent the deteriorating and dilapidated housing. The population of the city is divided into 114 household types with similar housing needs, locational preferences, and housing budgets. Variables that determine the types include number of children, age of head of household, race, income, rent-paying ability, and preference.

This model takes account of the changes that occur as housing ages. Rehabilitation, poor maintenance, and normal aging are the three possible fates of dwelling units. In the latter case, the rate of deterioration depends upon the degree of use, the kind of structure, and the neighborhood.

Current housing data, yield data, household preferences, and other information are first input to the computer, and then a simulation run is made. A complete run consists of nine periods, each representing 2 years. For each time period, the steps shown in Fig. 10-23 are carried out.

This model has not been used in urban renewal planning for San Francisco. It is operational, however, and has been used to verify the wisdom of some of the plans that were made. It can answer such questions as: "If this population group was increased in size by a factor of ten, how would this influence the supply and characteristics of housing available in the City of San Francisco and the degree to which housing demand was filled?"[397] Its output shows housing characteristics and availability such as an experienced city planner would expect. It has been an educational experience for city planners who have worked with it. Like other organizational models, urban models depend on a large data base. But this requirement need not be prohibitive. The authors say:

We recognize that the United States, with its large and careful census data, is probably quite wealthy in this regard. However, one of the main lessons we have relearned in developing the San Francisco model is the high degree of aggregation which is practical in studying many urban problems, provided a careful and appropriate model structure is available. Even in countries where the data base is far less developed than in the United States, we believe these models can receive useful application if they are properly designed, and can be supported by a limited amount of sampling of relevant population and housing characteristics.[398]

A dynamic simulation of the life cycle of an urban area, by Forrester, is a generalized model that describes no actual area.[399] The system modeled could be either a part of a large city, such as the central area, or a suburban area, but not both. Starting with a nearly empty land area, it represents growth of the system to maturity and a final stagnant equilibrium, similar to that observed in many modern cities. The model is then used to examine possible urban revitalization programs of four common kinds.

This urban-dynamics model depends upon the assumption that the causes of aging and stagnation in cities lie within the city itself, not in the surrounding society. The boundary of the conceptual system is set to include the interactions that give the system its characteristic behavior. In this sense it is a closed boundary. It is not, however, a closed system because the surrounding environment is a source of inputs and a destination of outputs. The model includes no external feedback loops. The environment is conceived of as limitless. The system communicates with it without influencing it. This is, in effect, a system without a suprasystem. By becoming more or less attractive than other areas, the urban region causes people and industry to move in or out over its boundaries.

The basic framework of the model includes nine

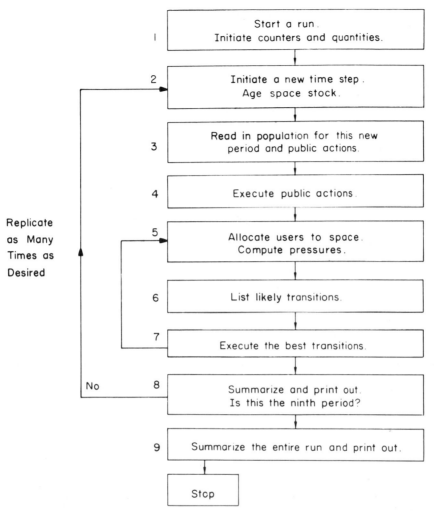

Fig. 10-23 Abbreviated flow chart of San Francisco housing simulation. [Reprinted from H. B. Wolfe & M. L. Ernst. Simulation models and urban planning. In P. M. Morse (Ed.). *Operations research for public systems*. Cambridge: M.I.T. Press, 1967, 74, by permission of The M.I.T. Press, Cambridge, Massachusetts. Copyright © 1967 by the Massachusetts Institute of Technology.]

"levels" (see page 719), including three categories each of business (new enterprise, mature business, and declining industry), housing (premium housing, worker housing, and underemployed housing), and population (management–professional, worker, and underemployed).

Flow rates in this model are stated in terms of a "normal" rate that is modified by a *multiplier* that represents the deviation of the actual area from this rate. Each rate is affected by a number of influences. Table 10-7 summarizes the influences that determine the attractiveness-for-migration multiplier, which in turn determines the rate of arrival of underemployed in the area. Figure 10-24 shows how these influences

combine to generate the flow of underemployed people into the area. An example of an equation of the model is the one below, which combines the terms summarized in Fig. 10-24 into a product representing the attractiveness of the area to the underemployed population:[400]

$$AMM.K = (UAMM.K)\ (UHM.K)\ (PEM.K)\ (UJM.K)$$
$$(UHPM.K)\ (AMF)$$

$$AMF = 1$$

AMM: Attractiveness-for-migration multiplier (dimensionless)

UAMM: Underemployed-arrivals-mobility multiplier (dimensionless)

TABLE 10-7   Influences on Underemployed-Arrival Rate

Graphic symbol	Name of multiplier	Situation evaluated by multiplier	Response to evaluation
UAMM UAMMT* 4	Underemployed-arrivals-mobility multiplier	How readily are the underemployed moving into the skilled-labor class?	The larger the percentage that moves from the underemployed to the labor class per year, the more attractive is the city to outsiders.
UHM UHMT* 5	Underemployed/housing multiplier	Are there underemployed-housing vacancies in the city?	The more underemployed-housing vacancies in the city, the greater the attractiveness of the city.
PEM PEMT* 7	Public-expenditure multiplier	How much tax money is being spent per capita in the city?	The more spent per capita, the greater is the public service offered by the city and the greater its attractiveness to outsiders.
UJM UJMT* 10	Underemployed/job multiplier	How many jobs are available for underemployed people?	The more jobs there are available, the more attractive is the city to outsiders.
UHPM UHPMT* 11	Underemployed-housing-program multiplier	Is there a construction program for low-cost housing in operation?	The more houses constructed per year in the program, the greater the attractiveness of the city.

*T *represents a table function to be looked up in the appropriate table, there being one for each of the five inferences on the underemployed-arrival rate.*

SOURCE: Reprinted from *Urban dynamics* by J. W. Forrester, page 22, by permission of The M.I.T. Press, Cambridge, Massachusetts. Copyright © 1969 by The Massachusetts Institute of Technology.

UHM: Underemployed/housing multiplier (dimensionless)

PEM: Public-expenditure multiplier (dimensionless)

UJM: Underemployed/job multiplier (dimensionless)

UHPM: Underemployed-housing-program multiplier (dimensionless)

AMF: Attractiveness-for-migration factor (dimensionless)

Each of the five multiplier inputs is a table function that permits the program to represent any choice of interdependence between two variables. These variations produce different rates of flow between "levels." As the ratio of underemployed to available housing falls, for example, attractiveness increases, although excess housing produces little added effect. As that ratio increases, crowding occurs and attractiveness declines. A ratio of 1 provides no incentive for people to move in or out of the system. Other influences on attractiveness are upward mobility of the underemployed to the labor class, per capita tax expenditure, available jobs, and presence of a low-cost-housing program. Parameters and initial values of the variables

are assigned as a part of the simulation. The system is not highly sensitive to variations in these, and its typical final steady state covers a wide range of values.

A simulation of an urban life cycle during 250 years begins with the land area 3 percent occupied and a normal balance among its activities.[401] During the first 100 years, positive feedback loops generate exponential growth of the system. These do not continue to be positive indefinitely. As the population increases, conditions change and the positive feedback is suppressed. As the land area becomes full, construction-land multipliers decline toward zero, and so new construction declines. Changes in economic and housing conditions cause reduced arrival rates and increased departure rates of people into and out of the area until the population stabilizes. Each of the "levels" reaches its highest point at a different time. For example, the peak in new enterprises occurs just before the year 100. As time passes, businesses shift into the mature category, which peaks at year 112. These businesses age and deteriorate so that declining industry peaks at year 140. Patterns in the other "level" variables are similar, but for different reasons.

By the year 100 the land area of the system is filled. New construction can take place only if old buildings

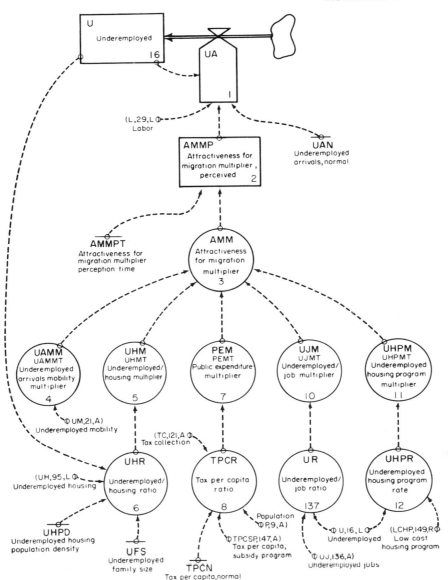

Fig. 10-24 Relationships among some concepts in urban dynamics simulation indicating how various influences combine to generate a flow of underemployed arrivals (UA) into the area. Rectangle [   ] represents state variable or "level" that can be measured directly; valve [   ]⊠ represents rate that can influence state variable or "level"; circle ◯ represents auxiliary variable that can influence the rate equation, including those in Table 10-7; cloud ⬭ represents a source of input flow of people; ——→ represents real flow of people; – – – → represents causal relationship. (From J. W. Forrester. *Urban dynamics*. Cambridge: M.I.T. Press, 1969, 24. Reprinted from *Urban dynamics* by J. W. Forrester by permission of The M.I.T. Press, Cambridge, Massachusetts. Copyright © 1969 by the Massachusetts Institute of Technology.)

are demolished. Industry matures and begins to decline. Premium and worker houses become old and bring about a rising level of underemployed housing. Depression and despondency between the years 100 and 140 suppress building below normal values. A stable steady state is reached at 200 years. In an actual economic system, suprasystem events would cause a fluctuation around the steady-state values rather than the static equilibrium that occurs in the model.

Starting with the steady-state conditions at year 250, simulations of various programs designed to counteract stagnation in cities were undertaken.[402] These included, successively, a job program for 10 percent of the underemployed, a training program to upgrade the skills of the underemployed, financial aid from outside, and low-cost housing construction. The changes were made in single "levels," with no initial alterations in other system variables. Jobs, for example, were created not by changing commercial and industrial conditions in the area but by undertaking some artificial process that is not part of the model, like transporting people to jobs elsewhere. Since the new jobs were added to the already existing jobs, the effect was to decrease the underemployed/job ratio— an improvement. It also increased the underemployed/job multiplier, which is one of the attractiveness multipliers that determine flows into and out of the system. This increase prevented the program from achieving its ends. Underemployed already in the area stayed, and others, attracted by the possibility of jobs, came in. Effects of these changes on other variables included declines in new enterprise and mature business, declines in numbers of managerial–professional people and workers, and declines in premium and workers' housing. Increases occurred in levels of underemployed people, underemployed housing, declining industry, and the tax ratio.

The other program simulations also illustrate the counterintuitive nature of urban systems, since they appear to be doing something that should help the city but instead increase the attractiveness-for-migration multiplier without increasing the capacity of the area to care for the people. Low-cost housing construction was much more detrimental than the others.

Experimental changes of other sorts were made to discover what might reduce urban decay. The system responded favorably to a program which demolished slum housing in favor of new business enterprise.[403] With new industry generated at a rate of 1.2 percent of total productive units in the area per year, all population classes and all business categories rose. This program also increased attractiveness, and a small improvement in the underemployed/job ratio resulted. The favorable result achieved in this way

was not sufficient, however, to correct the economic imbalance in the city. Furthermore, such a program is not one that a city government by itself can carry out or impose on the city.

A series of further experimental simulation runs included worker-housing construction, premium-housing construction, new-enterprise construction, declining-industry demolition, slum-housing demolition, discouraging construction of housing, and encouraging industry. In general, those programs which favored industry rather than emphasizing housing had the more beneficial results.

Forrester concludes that jobs and housing are the two most important influences on both attractiveness of the city and upward mobility within it. Aging cities usually have too much housing and too few jobs for the underemployed population. This model suggests that it is this situation that must be corrected if urban decay is to be reversed. Three streams of change are involved:

1. Slum demolition for gradually consolidating land into parcels large enough for the needed industrial centers (and any associated landscaping, parks, etc.).
2. Voluntary relocation from underemployed housing to worker housing as upward economic mobility makes such improvements in living conditions possible.
3. Economic relocation arising from revival activity as older housing is replaced by new housing and declining industry by new enterprise.[404]

Such changes do not come about quickly in an already decayed city, but since the equilibrium is not dependent on history, the policies that revive decayed areas should, if continuously applied, act to prevent decay before it occurs. Programs favoring industry are not easy to put into effect because they appear to be carried out at the expense of the underemployed. Yet, Forrester points out, short-run efforts to ameliorate undesirable conditions only hurt the people they are trying to help. Although Forrester makes it clear that he does not intend the results of this model to be applied to cities unless it is found to be an accurate model of them, he draws many conclusions and makes recommendations for urban planners.

Critics of this model have pointed to the isolation of the partial system that is simulated, saying that the prescriptions for planning in urban areas are not justified because the neglected effects of the suburbs are great enough to invalidate the model.[405]

Although the developer of a conceptual model has a right to draw his conceptual boundaries where he pleases and although the test of a model's applicability lies in its degree of isomorphism to the real system or partial system which it represents rather than in its success or failure in satisfying standards of social right or wrong, some skepticism seems justified in this case. This is because the central city is interdependent in so many ways with its suburbs or surrounding population areas. It would be interesting to find out whether an enlargement of the model—for example, one that allowed for unified planning for an entire metropolitan area—would result in the same prescriptions as this more limited one. If low-income housing were distributed throughout a large area instead of being concentrated in the central city and if the taxing power were given to an overall metropolitan government rather than being divided into a large number of competing small governments, the outcome might well be different. In recent years the cities of Indianapolis, Indiana, and Jacksonville, Florida, have expanded to the point where they essentially constitute such metropolitan forms of government.

This model does simulate the situation in most urban areas, the city planners exercising control over no system other than their own and having little power to influence decisions in suburban systems. Power to decentralize low-income housing may even be limited within their own system because of the influence of middle-class voters who do not accept change readily. If the central city is indeed bounded in such a way that practical planning for it can include no other area, this model may be isomorphic to the real system. If more tax money were available, if deteriorated and other low-income housing were reduced, and if new businesses were attracted, Forrester's recommendations would be substantially carried out without consigning the poor to perpetual limbo, particularly if societywide adjustments were made at the same time (see pages 842 to 844).

(ii) Partial models. Models of more limited matter-energy and information flows are common at this level because of their use in operations research. Most of these apply to business and industrial systems, but some represent other types of systems, among which are hospitals and universities.

Matter-energy processing models. Mathematical and computer models of matter-energy flows at this level are developed as aids to organizational deciders. When values of variables are set to describe the state of a process at the beginning of a time period and the results are used as values in a succeeding period, and so on for any desired number of periods, the behavior of the process over time can be simulated.[406]

Mathematical models and simulations have proved to be particularly applicable to some processes, which may be activities of one or a number of subsystems. A partial list of matter-energy processes for which models and simulations have been developed includes inventory control, transportation of people and materials, distribution, scheduling of jobs or use of machines or services, warehousing, maintenance, assembly-line balancing, flows of people or things through service facilities such as hospitals and airline terminals, traffic control, road network design, logistics, quality control, diffusion of people in cities, and decentralization of organizational components. I shall discuss examples of some of these, identifying in each case the principal subsystems that are modeled.

Matter-energy storage. Inventory models are among those which apply to matter-energy storage. They are concerned primarily with amounts of matter-energy kept in the system, such as stock offered for sale by a department store, finished products available for distribution from a factory, or the purchased parts and raw materials required for a production process. Depending upon the purpose of the inventory, models may indicate interactions of this subsystem with ingesting (purchasing or procurement), producing (manufacturing or finishing items), or extruding (shipment). They may also depend upon forecasts of sales or demands, which are information transactions. Many organizations computerize inventory control. The decisions to which these models apply are:[407] When do we buy or make something? And how much do we buy or make? Models may also be used to determine the number of spare parts that should be kept on hand for a fleet of aircraft or a bank of machines, how much water should be released daily or weekly from a dam used for electric power generation and irrigation, how much coal should be prepared for loading in a strip mine, how many storage tanks should be installed in a chemical plant, or how long a conveyor system in a plant should be.

Inventory models express decision rules for the process to be modeled. At least 15 alternative approaches have been developed, some suitable for one sort of system and some for another. Many of these are variants of four basic types. If P represents *when* and Q represents *how much*, the four types are (a) Q fixed, P fixed (fixed order quantity policy); (b) Q fixed, P variable (regular replenishment of a fixed quantity); (c) Q variable, P fixed (optional replenishment policy); and (d) Q variable, P variable (replenishment policy). Others included models based upon different mathematical techniques like linear programming or queuing theory.

An example of a computer simulation of an inventory problem includes production, inventory, and distribution.[408] This program can include as many products, branches, and plants as the memory of the computer can handle. One version of this concerns a system that consists of branch warehouses that receive orders for products from customers and obtain their supplies from a single plant.[409] The model assumes that all demand that cannot be filled immediately from branch inventory is lost. Branches review their stocks and issue replenishment orders at periodic intervals.

This model was written in SIMSCRIPT, a programming language that prepared a set of computer instructions from a system description and operating programs and supplied a timing routine and some other simulation details. The system description consisted of entities (system variables which could be either "permanent," lasting throughout the simulation, or "temporary," changing during it), attributes of the entities, attributes of the system, and sets in which entities could be filed or classified. Each set was conceived of as "belonging" to some entity. The occurrence of exogenous and endogenous events changed the state of the system. The sort and time of the former were specified before the simulation began. The latter were scheduled during the run. After one event had occurred, the program advanced time to the next scheduled event.

The inventory simulation included branches and products as permanent entities. These were given initial values that specified the number of each during each run. Other variables were branch stock level, order point, order quantity, and stock on order from the factory. Each of these was defined for each branch and product combination. Shipping time was a random variable, identified as to the branch to which a replenishment order was being shipped. Transit times were also selected at random from a shipping-time distribution for the particular branch. Production rate was also identified in terms of a product. Total demand and lost demand were used to collect summary statistics for each branch and product combination. The review period was the number of simulated time periods between reviews of branch inventories. Temporary system variables included branch orders, which listed the branch, the product ordered, the quantity, the scheduled completion time, and the arrival time at the branch.

The list of branch orders at the plant was set, the only one in this simulation. Branch orders were placed in the set ranked according to completion date. Scheduled endogenous events were branch review and order arrival. Exogenous events included customer demands and the beginnings and ends of runs. When a demand occurred, information concerning the event number and time, branch, product, and quantity was read from stored memory, after which the routine updated the total demand accumulating variable and subtracted the demand from the proper branch stock. If the result was not negative, the timing routine moved the simulation to the next scheduled event. If it became negative, unfilled demand was lost, and the lost demand accumulating variable was updated. The

branch stock then was set at zero. The final exogenous-event routine was the end of simulation, which elicited a report routine, a printout of a summary of statistics collected during the run. These results affected values of variables in the next simulated period. The inventory status for all branch and product combinations was determined, and if inventories were below order points, a replenishment order was placed in the schedule file. It calculated production time, found the earliest starting time for production if other orders preceded it, and calculated arrival time of the completed order at the branch. When it arrived, the branch stock was updated.

A problem similar to that of maintaining an inventory in an industrial organization is that of keeping the bed-occupancy rate in a hospital as high and as constant as possible in the face of varying need.[410] A computer simulation has been written in SIMSCRIPT to analyze the use of beds in a maternity hospital.[411] Data for the simulation were collected at a community hospital and included observed distributions of times in labor, delivery, postpartum recovery, and the bedroom. Hospital admissions have been shown to conform to a Poisson distribution.[412] Scheduled patients, including those who will undergo Caesareans and/or elective inductions and regular patients, move through the system in accordance with rules that may, for instance, exclude elective patients on particular days or limit their number on any day.[413] Separate routines determine availability of each of the different types of facilities needed, such as a bedroom or a delivery room. If a facility is not available, the patient is assigned to a queue. As each patient leaves one sort of facility to move to the next or to leave the hospital, the facility is made available for another. Reports were output at the end of each run. Minimum required sample size was found to be 3,000 patients. Stable estimates of critical parameters required 5,000 patients.

Experiments with this model permitted examination of a variety of alternative policies. When admissions were increased from 1,130 patients per year to 1,320 and then to 1,660, a critical load was placed on the 25 beds provided, and the service given decreased sharply, although the labor and delivery facilities could handle even the larger increase. When a policy change was simulated which allowed admission twice a day of a maximum of seven patients for elective induction, about the same number of beds was required to give the same service, but the use of the labor facilities increased. When the input rate was smoothed out, the same service could be provided with one less bed. A decrease in the length of stay of normal patients had little effect on bed occupancy, largely because many patients had to stay longer than the normal time because of complications, and this time was not affected by the policy change.

Distributor.   Control of traffic in cities is a distributor process for which a number of models and simulations have been developed. One of these is a computer simulation program which Sakai and Nagao applied to the busiest part of the city of Kyoto, Japan.[414] The aims of this simulation were (a) to discover the effects of such simulation parameters as signal settings and rates of input, in a search for an optimum signal system for a complicated road network, especially one with numerous loops and a variety of traffic problems, and (b) to test the effects of various traffic conditions on such a road network.

The simulation was divided into discrete intervals of 4 s. Roads were segmented into blocks 50 m long, the mean distance a car travels during this interval. No car was made to move farther than to the next block during such an interval. This rule was adopted in order to keep simple an algorithm used in the simulation. The number of cars transferred from one block to the next was calculated by a formula that took into account the length of a block, the maximum number of cars the block could hold, the maximum speed allowed, and the average speed of cars. Average speed was determined by the relative density of cars in the block and the effects of buses and streetcars in slowing down traffic. This formula conformed well to observed traffic conditions under ordinary distributions of the variable that represented the number of cars in the block at a certain moment. The ratio of cars turning left or right at the intersections, as well as the time interval in which the cars could turn or go straight ahead, including delays caused by pedestrian traffic and cars going in the opposite direction, was also calculated by a formula that depended upon the number of cars traveling in each direction and the number of pedestrians crossing at the light. The number of cars going into the road network at entrances was assumed to conform to a Poisson distribution. The actual number entering was calculated from a random-number table. No attention was paid to the capacity of the outlet. It did not in any way hamper cars leaving the network. At each block, the increase and decrease of cars were simulated, some entering, some leaving, and others circulating within the network.

The road network was represented in the computer memory in a list structure which was bidirectional. This made it possible to trace a pathway through the network in either direction beginning at any point. The simulation contained information about the traffic within each block and information needed for running the program, such as addresses in the memory in which data were stored about adjacent blocks or intersections. Information stored about blocks between intersections dealt with the maximum capacity, the number of cars actually in the block, the number of cars that appeared or disappeared during a simulation interval, the change in the number of cars in the block during an interval, and the length of the block. Information stored about the blocks directly connected to intersections concerned traffic-signal settings; the ratio and number of cars that went straight, turned left, or turned right; the number of cars in the block; and the change in the number of cars in the block when cars went straight, turned left, or turned right from the block during an interval. An intersection was viewed as a link only, and its representation in the simulation carried only information about the number of branches it had and the addresses in the memory of the blocks directly connected with it.

As the simulation ran, in each period cars entered and left the network, moved from block to block when the signal was green, stood still when it was red, and turned or went straight at intersections. The simulation calculated the number of cars forced to stop by lights or by traffic jams, and it printed out the distribution of the cars in the simulation area as well as the parameter values.

Measurements of the actual flows in the simulation area were made by driving a test car. Simulation experiments were done with different signal settings and numbers of cars. Results showed that improvement in traffic flows could be achieved by making certain changes in signal settings. These were improvements in average travel time from one point to another and avoidance of waiting lines at lights. Optimal settings were different when the traffic load increased. Progress of the simulation could be observed on a display board on which small lamps represented lengths of road corresponding to the length of a car. This was on line with the computer and showed the state of the area at 4-s intervals and the moving pattern from one state to the next. The lighted lamps made the motion appear as smooth as that of an actual car. The chief advantages of this display were that changes could be made in parameters as indicated by the simulation and that their effects could be observed immediately.

Mathematical models of various sorts have been developed for allocation of emergency units, such as police cars, fire engines, and ambulances in cities.[415] These deal with variables like the number of calls at various times of day and night, the waiting time between receipt of a call and response by an appropriate unit, the number of units needed to meet emergencies satisfactorily, and the optional positioning of units. Two distinctive aspects of these systems which affect the construction and analysis of mathematical models are (a) the probability over time of demands for service and (*b*) the probabilities of distributions of demands and response units over the territory of the city. Queuing theory mathematics is an appropriate analytic tool for (*a*), and (*b*) can be approached by a number of queuing, geometric, and other mathematical models.

A study employing such a model was used to improve the effectiveness of New York City's emergency services.[416]

Information processing subsystem models and simulations. Models of this sort represent the decider processes of organizations or are developed as aids to central deciders or subsystem deciders in making decisions relating to specific subsystem activities, such as marketing or money management. I have referred to certain information processing models above. The experiments with spreads of information through the channels and nets of a town, for example, were based upon the mathematical theory of biased networks which I have discussed above (see pages 633 and 634).

Although writers on the "economic theory of the firm" such as Marschak do not model individual organizations in detail, adaptations of economic theory can be applied to an organization by regarding it as a miniature economy.[417] These scientists assume that an organization makes its choices from a specified set of actions in an environment over which it has no control. The environment changes, but these changes are always from a specified set of possible alternatives. A further usual assumption in such models is that a complete ordering of preferences is possible and that payoff functions can be determined. Organizations with such complete preference ordering of pairs of alternatives are known as "teams," since the members all have the same goals. In this model, decisions of a number of managers within a firm result in a situation similar to the ideal competitive economy (see page 657). Each manager is in charge of a set of production possibilities, and each chooses a bundle to be produced that falls within this set. Each bundle can be defined by the quantities per time unit of tools that are used or produced. The payoff function is profit per time unit earned on the chosen bundle at the current market prices. Such models can be used also to compare different decision rules, particularly to establish the organizational superiority of decentralized decision processes for teams over possible alternatives. Such theories often are highly technical, expressed in the sort of mathematical equations that is characteristic of present-day economic theory.

There exist two simulations of how investments are managed, one for a university and the other for a business organization. Yale University's simulation of endowment funds management is used as an aid in estimating the amount of annual income from endowment that will be available for the operating budget for the following year.[418] This model consists of 12 simultaneous differential equations which simulate variations in university policy and in the business cycle. The simulation includes a 20-year period. A study of market variations over the past 10 years supplied values, which were used in turn as starting values for the simulation. From the results it was possible to construct probability distributions that gave some idea of what the future earnings from the endowment might be. On the basis of the simulation, it appeared that separation of the single pool of securities into several subsidiary funds using different investment strategies was desirable.

The management of American Telephone and Telegraph Company's liquid assets fund has also been simulated, although the simulation has not been used as an aid to investment decisions.[419] This fund was an accumulation of cash, bank deposits, and short-term investments. It included money to pay company taxes and money from employees' social security tax payments. It was used by operating units of the company as a bank from which they borrowed on a daily basis for their cash needs and to pay interest on their loans. This money earned substantially less used in this way than it would have if it had been invested in the telephone company's plant. Thus a cost of maintaining the fund was the loss from not putting the money in such higher-yielding investments. On the other hand, there would be costs if the company ran short of liquid assets. Among these would be the penalties of having to borrow at unfavorable rates, of having to cut back on plant or equipment construction, or of losing prestige in the business community or credit rating. It would have been desirable to find an optimum amount of money for such a pool. The difficulties in determining quantitatively the costs of running short of funds and the fluctuations of the pool itself made real optimization using the model impossible. It was possible, however, to categorize the reasons for the daily changes into calendar items, disasters, financing, and random fluctuations. The simulation, starting with the initial amount of the pool and values of other parameters, calculated the amount of the pool each simulated day. The daily change was the sum of the above four categories of daily changes, each of which was calculated. The simulation made it possible to experiment with fund management policies that could not be tried in real life. This simulation was also used as a predictive game (see page 737).

Marketing models aid in making decisions about sales and advertising by testing effects upon sales of different decision rules concerning such matters as sales, prices, and advertising.[420] An example of such a simulation emphasized advertising budget decisions, using as variables the amount of advertising, the marketing situation for a product class, and the share of the market secured by a particular brand. It assumed that if advertising were eliminated, the brand's share would fall to a certain minimum in a given time period. If advertising were increased a great deal, the share would rise to a maximum in one time period. Some advertising rate was assumed to exist that would maintain the initial share of the market, and it was possible to estimate the effect of a 50 percent increase in advertising. An equation that represented these relationships could be applied to specific situations to give reasonable answers.

Further equations included effects of time delays, media efficiency, and copy effectiveness as well as a product-class index that varied as a result of seasonal changes and trends. The effects of nonadvertising variables like product change and price change were included as an index based upon estimates made by the product manager using the model. The simulation included also a standard set of values against which changes could be measured.

This model has been used to assist in the quarterly review of a marketing plan for a particular brand of product. It is usual for such a plan to be developed for a year in advance and then to be reviewed and, if necessary, changed from time to time. The model was initially set up to reproduce the original plan for the brand. At the end of the first quarter, sales were off from the forecast value, and less had been spent than had been originally planned. Only part of the decrease in sales could be attributed to the decreased spending, and so the index of nonadvertising effects in the model was adjusted. At this point, when the simulation of the brand plan was rerun with the new parameters, it resulted in a pessimistic forecast. The model was then used to evaluate some proposed new strategies, which suggested that certain changes in advertising spending allocations and budgets might lead to substantial improvement.

Matter energy internal adjustment process simulations. The distribution of people among city neighborhoods is dependent upon income, ethnic and racial factors, and personal factors like friendships or access to jobs, schools, and churches. To the black citizen, race is of overwhelming importance because of white resistance to his free mobility. A simulation study of the expansion of black areas of Northern cities conceptualized the spread of black neighborhoods as a slow diffusion process.[421] Presumably, it occurs through the distributor subsystem of a city. Starting from a point of origin, the ghetto gradually spreads in a block-by-block penetration of the surrounding white areas. Resistance takes the form of rebuffs of attempts to buy

and diminishing willingness to sell. These attitudes strengthen with increasing distance from areas already settled by blacks. Once a block has black residents, however, such resistance decreases. Usually blacks have to try more than once to buy in a neighborhood before a sale is made.

A probabilistic simulation model was chosen to simulate this process because the simulation was based on a small sample, including only a few people in a small area and covering only a short period, and because not enough was known concerning the individual motivations involved in specific house-to-house moves. The probability of a typical family's moving was determined, and the location of its new housing was decided by using a random-number table. This produced a model of a spatial pattern of moves that spread the settlement of black people into new blocks and increased it in old ones. This diffusion model is similar to network models used in biology, sociology, and communication science. The spread of the ghetto is like the spread of signals in a neural net, gossip in a school, or rumor in a town (see Hypothesis 3.3.3.1-1, pages 95 and 96, and pages 355, 356, 537, 538, and 630).

Data from the city of Seattle, Washington, were used to evaluate the simulation. Starting with the residential pattern observed in 1940, ten 2-year periods from 1940 to 1960 were simulated. In Seattle, the increase of the black population by excess of births over deaths was observed to be 5 percent every 2 years, and blacks moved in from outside the area at a rate of 10 percent every 2 years. This population increase was included in the simulation. New arrivals from outside were assigned to neighborhoods by use of random numbers, the probability of their entering any particular neighborhood being determined by its proportion of black residents, as it apparently is in actual cities. After an initial period of residence they commonly made further moves within the city. In the simulation, 20 percent of all black households changed their housing each period. The probabilities of a family's moving any particular distance and in any direction were derived from empirical observation of the moves of actual families. The probabilities were modeled as declining as distance increased. This was done because observation showed that black families were much more likely to move to an adjacent block than to more distant ones. The specific destination for each move was chosen by random numbers. If the number indicated a block in which black people already resided, the move was made immediately because there would be little or no resistance. If, however, the indicated block was all white, contact was registered, but no move was made. If this same block was again contacted during the same or the next 2-year period, the move was made. Thus penetration of new areas was gradual. If an original contact was not followed soon enough by another, no migration into that area took place. One geographical direction demonstrated so much resistance that the simulation permitted a move that way only after three contacts. When the number of people on a block reached the upper limit, as a result of an excess of births over deaths, the simulation required that the surplus families be moved. Neither they nor persons coming newly into the city could be moved into full blocks.

The actual and the simulated expansions of the Seattle ghetto for the simulated periods turned out to correspond closely. The model was found not to have taken sufficient account of the quality and values of homes or of topographical features that made lots with views much more desirable than others. A predictive simulation of the periods 1960 to 1962 and 1962 to 1964 also turned out to be approximately correct.

The mathematical models which Kochen and Deutsch use to develop their theory of decentralization (see page 699) are relevant to both matter-energy and information processes. They are also cross-level, since they can apply to societies and supranational systems as well as to organizations.[422] The theory addresses itself to problems of cost-effectiveness of centralization or decentralization of facilities, the conditions under which decentralization is favored, and the optimal amount of decentralization for a given set of conditions. The initial models are relatively simple. Their complexity grows as new variables are added to increase realism. With such changes analytic solutions become more difficult, and the authors have suggested that further explorations of these problems should be written as computer simulations. Their first model is concerned with balancing marginal and transport or communication costs.[423] Its variables are:

- n: The desirable number of dispersed facilities providing a particular service. This is to be calculated from the variables which follow.
- D: The length of the line from any point at which a request for the service can originate and be processed, and the response returned.
- L: The total load of demand for the service, in requests per month from this line.
- v: The speed in miles per hour at which a request gets from one point on the line to another.
- c: The variable cost, in dollars per hour, of transport or communication of requests or responses from one point on the line to another.
- C: The fixed operating cost, including capital, amortization, and maintenance in dollars per month, of one service facility capable of handling the entire load.

Facilities are assumed to be dispersed uniformly with respect to the distribution of the demand. This dispersion is considered optimal.

Theorems concerned with the effect of the variables of demand, distance, speed, and costs upon the number of facilities are stated and proved. The resulting formula for n leads to the conclusion that decentralization is favored by increases in total demand or in distance, increases in the ratio per unit of time of variable transport or communication cost to fixed cost per facility, and increases in the time it takes for transport or communication to cover a mile. Further realistic variables alter the results, including the number of times a request has to be forwarded before a response is returned, the cost of forwarding a bulky package, the capacity of the transport or communication channel, and the effects of a transport or communication channel which picks up requests in batches. Nevertheless, the balance is still in favor of decentralization.

Another model of Kochen and Deutsch concerns issues of marginal utility related to information transmissions in channels and nets. It deals with a number of communication channels, each with a capacity (B) in bits per hour and a length (x) in miles. The number of bits per request (b) is considered to be the same for all requests. The equations concern the effects of costs and distances, as well as the load, on requests per month. The formula for n that results from this model is similar to that derived from the first. Conditions that favor decentralization are increasing demand—thought to be a likely trend, considering current developments in communications technology; large length of line; long messages; low fixed operating cost; and low channel capacity, which is considered to occur less and less frequently since new technologies that expand channel capacities are constantly being developed. More rapid growth of demand than of the capacity of the channel favors decentralization.

Another series of models concerns both the decentralization of facilities which differ in function and the effects of functional decentralization without spatial dispersion, *i.e.,* location of differently specialized facilities at one place.[424] The conclusions derived from this model are: (*a*) As the utility of time increases, so does the optimal degree of decentralization[425]; (*b*) decentralization produces side benefits in reduced mean time loss as a result of failure[426]; (*c*) parameters like service load, extent of the territory to be serviced, and likelihood of equipment breakdown are crucial in determing the optimal amount of decentralization; (*d*) the introduction of functional specialization in addition to geographic dispersion favors decentralization[427]; (*e*) availability of a great deal of capital favors centralization[428]; and (*f*) increasing the number of functional specialties favors decentralization.[429]

(*d*) *Living system–computer interactions.* Examples of simulations in this class include some management games and a simulated man-machine system. In these games the human participants act as deciders either at a sequence of choice points in a computer simulation run or before the run begins.[430] Such games may be closely related to organizational simulations developed for other purposes. Some of the latter are readily converted into games by permitting players to determine decision rules or make other decisions which determine values of variables or parameters for the program. One such game was developed from the "pool of funds" model of the American Telephone and Telegraph Company (see page 734).[431] This was done by stopping the computer at fixed intervals, such as every 10 simulation days, or at a sequence of times specified in advance by the player, to allow him to take actions like selling stocks, borrowing from a bank, or changing the construction budget.

PERT-SIM is a computerized game in which participants place competitive bids on a construction project and then supervise construction in a simulated environment.[432] The project is to build a road under conditions of uncertainty about the terrain, the nature of the underlying soil, and the cost. Participants may purchase more exact information than that originally supplied, but this adds to their total cost. After studying the information they obtain, they must submit a bid for the work, including a dollar amount and a project completion date. From these the computer calculates the probability that the bidder would win the contract, on the basis of the rank of the bid and the dollar differences between his bid and those of the other participants. The objective is to maximize profit within the competitive situation. In supervising the project, a participant schedules the various activities, receives a report on the time they take and their dollar costs, and then, if he wishes, changes his schedule. This cycle is repeated several times during the project. A participant may purchase additional information throughout the game. At the end, total cost of the project, plus the information purchased, is computed for each participant, subtracted from his bid, and multiplied by the probability of his having obtained the bid, to compute his total project profit or loss.

An air defense center is an organization designed to assist in protecting the society against enemy air attacks by maintaining radar surveillance over an area, identifying aircraft as friendly or hostile, and directing interceptor aircraft against hostile planes. A simulation of such a center, a suborganization of the United States Air Force, was carried out at Rand Corporation to study its operations, particularly under high load conditions.[433] The study was intended not only to find ways of improving air defense but also to provide insights that could be generalized to other organizations, both military and industrial.

In the 1950s, when this simulation was done, an actual center of this sort included about 40 officers, noncommissioned officers, and airmen. Its task was to watch radarscopes, identify friendly planes, and direct interceptors toward unknown planes. If the aircraft proved to be hostile, the senior officer had the authority to order the interceptors to fire upon it. He also could put the entire air defense system and the whole country on emergency alert. Information inputs to the center came not only from the radar but also from the communication net of radios and telephones connected to subsidiary early-warning stations, from higher echelons of the Air Force, and from the Civil Aeronautics Authority, which transmitted flight plans of planes intending to enter the area.

The physical equipment of the simulated center duplicated that of a real center, but input information was supplied by the experimenters. Radar inputs were simulated by computer programs whose outputs were input to the radarscopes. Reviews of operations provided feedback after each simulated session.

This simulation was successful in involving organization members deeply. Their excitement during simulated enemy attacks was obvious, and individual members reported bad dreams and restless nights. They once ignored the broken leg of one man during such an attack, just as they might have during a real emergency. The organization learned as interdependencies and coordinating skills among the members developed. Some positions were reassigned. Members improved their individual performances. During periods of stress some members questioned the organization's goal and gave evidence of poor morale. Such behavior occurred in both successful and unsuccessful crews. Adjustment processes to the information input overload appeared (see page 157).

7. Conclusions

It is not new to conceptualize organizations as living systems. Socrates, in Plato's *Republic,* repeatedly pointed out explicit cross-level analogies between a person and a city-state.[434] Today several different system theories about organizations are current. For the most part they view organizations as abstracted systems of relationships among roles. This theoretical position often leads to confusion between structure and process (see pages 22 to 24). Also, its adherents, like many students of groups, often pay little attention to matter-energy processes. Many more studies like those of Dubin and of Woodward on processes of the producer subsystem (see pages 617 to 619) are needed.

Confusion of levels is common in organization theory. This, too, seems to be promoted by emphasis on role theory, for the primary focus of such concepts is upon the psychological problems of the persons in those roles and their interpersonal interactions in group components. Variables of the organization level receive less attention. Such attempts to analyze organizational processes by concentrating upon components, important as they are, seem unlikely to be completely successful, in the light of Forrester's assertion that organizations, with their numerous hierarchical feedbacks, often function in ways that cannot be intuitively predicted (see page 718).

Much research on organizations concentrates upon processes of the decider subsystem, accentuating the neglect of matter-energy processes. Top deciders, however, are usually busy and inaccessible to scholars. Their deliberations on important questions rarely can be investigated. Thus the empirical data on deciding processes are not extensive. Few studies are done on such processes as encoding and output transducing at this level, except in the applied fields of advertising and marketing.

Value judgments underlie many conclusions of many theoretical papers on organizations. Discussions of how power is wielded in organizations are tinged by an attitude which is widely held by organization theorists. This attitude reflects a primary value of our culture, that authoritarian exercise of power is inherently bad and that a democratic approach is good.[435]

Organization theory is a field without a large body of empirically established fact. Like medicine before 1930, management science is based largely upon case studies. Theoretical conclusions and practical actions depend upon the intuitions and observations of experienced managers. As March and Simon have pointed out, it is often hard to determine the size of the sample on which such conclusions are based.[436] The available large-sample studies, like those of Myers and Marquis (see page 624) and of Woodward (see pages 617 and 618), do not always confirm these insights. Much of the research on organizations is done on small groups, and the validity of the cross-level application of results has not been firmly established. More studies of organizational variables are needed. Also, we need to know normal and pathological values of various organizational input–output relationships, steady-state variables, and cost-effectiveness measures (see pages 654, 655, 667, 668, and 675).

Scholars in this area also would profit from an agreement, which they have not yet been able to achieve, as

to what are the basic subsystems common to all organizations. I suggest that comparisons with the other levels of living systems can provide this. A generally accepted taxonomy of types of organizations is also desirable, and general living systems theory may be able to provide it (see pages 597, 599 to 603, and 605). It would classify each system by those of its subsystems which are most extensively developed or specialized. These are the subsystems that ordinarily carry out the organization's processes which are of most importance in its suprasystem.

The science of organizations also would benefit from many more careful quantitative studies observing and measuring matter-energy and information flows from one component to another. There have been some such researches on traffic flows in cities (see pages 615 and 733), and there has been a study on information flows in a library (see page 641), but the potential of such investigations has not yet been exploited sufficiently.

In addition, the field needs researches designed to answer many challenging questions which have been raised but not resolved. Among these are:

Do organizations really learn by the optimal ratios of correct learning trials to error trials which suit their environments, as suggested by Hypothesis 3.3.5.2-5? (See pages 99 and 639).

What are the most effective ways to wield power in order to keep an organization integrated? (See pages 681 and 682.)

Are old organizational deciders more likely to resist change than young ones, as Hypothesis 3.3.7.2-11 maintains? (See pages 101, 651, and 698.)

How can one accurately describe the purposes and goals of an organization? (See pages 651 to 654.)

Is effective governance of organizations possible with completely free flow of information? If not, what restrictions on communication are necessary? (See page 631.)

How can feedbacks from the environment serve optimally to improve organizational performance? (See pages 685 and 686.)

What are normal and abnormal reaction times or processing times of organizations? (See pages 669, 670, and 685 and Hypothesis 5.1-28, page 104.)

What can be done to alter resistance to desirable change in organizations? (See pages 680 and 681.)

What are the interactions of employee motivation, satisfaction, and productivity? How do these interactions influence the selection of strategies for organizational coordination and control? (See pages 674 to 679.)

Which methods of conflict resolution work best in organizations? (See pages 681 to 683.)

What can be done to keep growth from creating

such large organizations that they get out of management control? (See pages 694, 695, 703, 704, and 710.)

How can urban and other organizational decay be reversed? (See pages 703, 704, and 721 to 731.)

Some problems in the science of organizations arise from the fact that industrial systems have received disproportionate attention because their managers have been able to afford to hire consultants or to maintain their own operations research staffs. These men, however, often have little confidence in the suggestions they receive from these sources. Many top deciders in major business firms and other sorts of large organizations practice what they recognize to be an art—an art they believe to be further advanced than the science of management. This attitude was repeatedly attested to in reports by management scientists, in a symposium on corporate simulation models, who found that convincing their employers of the value of their ideas and models was one of their major problems.[437] What is more, the results of studies made by consultants or employees of an organization are its property. They can usually be published only in general terms, since the data are frequently regarded as confidential. Comparison of organizations or aggregation of statistics over a population of such companies is therefore difficult or impossible. Until a significant body of facts about organizations is collected, however, the view that organizations, even those which operate at a substantial profit, could be much better managed than they are can be neither established nor refuted.

On the whole, as Katz and Kahn have recognized, the field pays little attention to the external relationships of organizations with their suprasystems, and this is unfortunate.[438]

Most of all, the science of organizations needs a rational theory of their processes, their "physiology." If it is true, as Forrester has asserted, that large numbers of feedbacks arranged in hierarchies make some organizational behavior counterintuitive, it may be that today's confident practitioners of the art of managing organizations are wrong to rely on a "seat of the-pants" approach. In a competitive world, art may not prove out against managers whose styles mix control with good human relations (see pages 650, 651, 675, 676, and 679) and who consult management information systems and simulations before they make decisions. Many managers of this generation may resist such methods, and with reason, for they are certainly not yet proved. Systems research must advance further than it has so far before these techniques can become entirely reliable.

Organization theory and operations research have developed astonishingly in the last two decades. Both are grounded on systems theory. Today both are vig-

orous fields. They have far to go, but they are beginning to enable us to comprehend the structures and processes, the physiology and pathology, of organizations. And for modern men and women, who must live in organizations as surely as they exist as organisms, this is important.

NOTES AND REFERENCES

[1]Anderson, R. E. & Carter, I. E. *Human behavior in the social environment.* Chicago: Aldine, 1974, 45–57.

[2]Weber, M. *The theory of social and economic organization.* (Ed. by T. Parsons. Trans. by A. M. Henderson & T. Parsons.) New York: Oxford Univ. Press, 1947, 328–341.

[3]Mesarović, M. D., Sanders, J. L., & Sprague, C. F. An axiomatic approach to organizations from a general systems viewpoint. In W. W. Cooper, H. J. Leavitt, & M. W. Shelly II (Eds.). *New perspectives in organization research.* New York: Wiley, 1964, 493–504.

[4]Blau, P. M. & Scott, W. R. *Formal organizations.* San Francisco: Chandler, 1962, 42.

[5]Cf. Bakke, E. W. Concept of the social organization. In M. Haire (Ed.). *Modern organization theory.* New York: Wiley, 1959, 16–75.

[6]Woodward, J. *Industrial organization: theory and practice.* London: Oxford Univ. Press, 1965, 12. Reprinted by permission of the Clarendon Press, Oxford.

[7]Evan, W. M. Indices of the hierarchical structure of industrial organizations. *Mgmt. Sci.,* 1963, **9**, 468–477.

[8]Katz, D. & Kahn, R. L. *The social psychology of organizations.* New York: Wiley, 1966, 39–47.

[9]Bakke, E. W. *Op. cit.,* 51–58. Copyright © 1959 by John Wiley & Sons, Inc. Reprinted by permission of John Wiley & Sons, Inc.

[10]Seashore, S. E. & Yuchtman, E. Factorial analysis of organizational performance. *Admin. Sci. Quart.,* 1967, **12**, 377–395.
Also Seashore, S. E. & Bowers, D. G. Durability of organizational change. *Amer. Psychol.,* 1970, **25**, 227–233.

[11]Levinson, H. *Organizational diagnosis.* Cambridge, Mass.: Harvard Univ. Press, 1972.

[12]*Ibid.,* 3–9.

[13]Katz, D. & Kahn, R. L. *Op. cit.,* 110–117.

[14]Blau, P. M. & Scott, W. R. *Op. cit.,* 45–58.

[15]Sells, S. B. Toward a taxonomy of organizations. In W. W. Cooper, H. J. Leavitt, & M. W. Shelly II (Eds.). *New perspectives in organization research.* New York: Wiley, 1964, 515–532.

[16]Evan, W. M. *Op. cit.*

[17]Executive Office of the President, Office of Management and Budget. *Standard industrial classification manual.* Washington: GPO, 1972.

[18]Sorokin, P. A. *Sociological theories of today.* New York: Harper & Row, 1966, 503–506.

[19]Durkheim, E. *The division of labor in society.* Glencoe, Ill.: Free Press, 1933.

[20]Tönnies, F. *Community and society (Gemeinschaft und Gesellschaft).* (Trans. by C. P. Loomis.) East Lansing: Mich. State Univ. Press, 1957.

[21]Hawley, A. H. *Human ecology.* New York: Ronald Press, 1950, 222–233.

[22]Cf. Lieberman, M. (Ed.). New business on the urban frontier communities. *Saturday Review,* 1971, **54**, 20–31, 55–57.

[23]*Wall Street Journal,* June 30, 1970, **50**(182), 8.

[24]Bakke, E. W. *Op. cit.,* 37–39.

[25]Katz, D. & Kahn, R. L. *Op. cit.,* 89.

[26]Wolman, A. The metabolism of cities. *Sci. Amer.,* 1965, **213**(3), 180.

[27]Buchan, J. & Koenigsberg, E. *Scientific inventory management.* Englewood Cliffs, N.J.: Prentice-Hall, 1963, 2–75.

[28]Ackoff, R. L. Management misinformation systems. *Mgmt. Sci.,* 1967, **14,** B-152–B-153.

[29]Townsend, R. *Up the organization.* New York: Knopf, 1970, 159.

[30]Blau, P. M. & Scott, W. R. *Op. cit.,* 21–22.

[31]Foothills Pipe Lines (Yukon) Ltd. *48" Alaska Highway pipeline project.* Calgory, Alberta: Foothills Pipe Lines (Yukon) Ltd., April 1977.

[32]Doxiadis, C. A. Man's movement and his city. *Science,* 18 October 1968, **162,** 326–334.

[33]Goode, H. H. & Machol, R. E. *System engineering.* New York: McGraw-Hill, 1957, 15–16.

[34]*Cleveland Plain Dealer,* July 27, 1970, **208,** 4A.

[35]Goode, H. H. & Machol, R. E. *Op. cit.,* 328–356.

[36]Anon. The lonely efficiency of new machines. *Fortune,* 1970, **81**(5), 162.

[37]*Ibid.,* 166.

[38]Leontief, W., Chenery, H. B., Clark, P. G., Duesenberry, J. S., Ferguson, A. R., Grosse, A. P., Grosse, R. N., Holzman, M., Isard, W., & Kistin, H. *Studies in the structure of the American economy.* New York: Oxford Univ. Press, 1953, 297–311.

[39]Dubin, R. *The world of work.* Englewood Cliffs, N.J.: Prentice-Hall, 1958, 174–179.

[40]Woodward, J. *Op. cit.*

[41]*Ibid.,* 40, 42. Reprinted by permission.

[42]Dubin, R. *Op. cit.,* 176–179.

[43]Woodward, J. *Op. cit.,* 53–67.

[44]Buchan, J. & Koenigsberg, E. *Op. cit.,* 418–433.

[45]Goode, H. H. & Machol, R. E. *Op. cit.,* 387–388.

[46]Buchan, J. & Koenigsberg, E. *Op. cit.,* 419–426.

[47]*Ibid.,* 419–420.

[48]Goode, H. H. & Machol, R. E. *Op. cit.,* 333–334.

[49]Cf. Hertz, D. B. & Shaffir, K. H. A forecasting method for management of seasonal style-goods inventories. *Operations Res.,* 1960, **8,** 45–52.

[50]Goode, H. H. & Machol, R. E. *Op. cit.,* 332.

[51]Eisenbud, M. Environmental protection in the city of New York. *Science,* 1970, **170,** 706–712.

[52]Lawrence, P. R. & Lorsch, J. W. *Organization and environment.* Boston: Harvard Graduate School of Business Administration, Division of Research, 1967, 25–26.

[53]*Ibid.,* 89–90.

[54]Myers, S. & Marquis, D. G. *Successful industrial innovations.* Washington: National Science Foundation, Report NSF 69-17, 1969, 2.

[55]*Ibid.,* 3.

[56]Tannenbaum, A. S. Unions. In J. G. March (Ed.). *Handbook of organizations.* Chicago: Rand McNally, 1965, 745.

[57]Katz, D. & Kahn, R. L. *Op. cit.,* 246.

[58]Guetzkow, H. Communications in organizations. In J. G. March (Ed.). *Handbook of organizations.* Chicago: Rand McNally, 1965, 555.

[59]Likert, R. *The human organization.* New York: McGraw-Hill, 1967, 160–180.

[60]Cartwright, D. Graph theory and organization. In M. Haire (Ed.). *Modern organization theory.* New York: Wiley, 1958, 261.

[61]International Business Machines Corporation. *Annual Report.* Armonk, N.Y.: IBM Corp., 1970, 56–57.

[62]Katz, D. & Kahn, R. L. *Op. cit.,* 239.

[63]Haugland, V. Airliner PA system may be a must. *Cleveland Plain Dealer,* Aug. 19, 1970, 6F.

[64]Katz, D. & Kahn, R. L. *Op. cit.,* 241.

[65]Guetzkow, H. *Op. cit.,* 562.

[66]*Ibid.,* 564.

[67]*Ibid.,* 542.

[68]Katz, D. & Kahn, R. L. *Op. cit.,* 244.

[69]*Ibid.,* 225–226.

[70]Gross, B. M. *The managing of organizations.* Vol. 1. Glencoe, Ill.: Free Press, 1964, 390.

[71]Likert, R. *Op. cit.,* 170.

[72]March, J. G. & Simon, H. A. *Organizations.* New York: Wiley, 1958, 168.

[73]Shepard, H. A. The value system of a university research group. *Amer. Sociol. Rev.,* 1954, **19,** 456–462.

[74]Blau, P. M. & Scott, W. R. *Op. cit.,* 242, 244.

[75]Gross, B. M. *The managing of organizations.* Vol. 2. *Op. cit.,* 771. Copyright © 1964 by The Free Press of Glencoe, a Division of the Macmillan Company. Reprinted by permission.

[76]Eilon, S. Taxonomy of communications. *Admin. Sci. Quart.,* 1968, **13,** 278–281.

[77]Woodward, J. *Op. cit.,* 66–67.

[78]*Ibid.,* 134.

[79]March, J. G. & Simon, H. A. *Op. cit.,* 167–168.

[80]*Ibid.*

[81]*Ibid.,* 167.

[82]Guetzkow, H. *Op. cit.,* 548.

[83]*Ibid.,* 561–565.

[84]Dodd, S. C. The counteractance model. *Amer. J. Sociol.,* 1957, **63,** 273–284.

[85]Dodd, S. C. A power of town size predicts an internal interacting. *Social Forces,* 1957, **36,** 132–137.

[86]Dodd, S. C. A test of message diffusion by chain tags. *Amer. J. Sociol.,* 1956, **61,** 425–432.

[87]Katz, D. & Kahn, R. L. *Op. cit.,* 227. Reprinted by permission.

[88]March, J. G. & Simon, H. A. *Op. cit.,* 164–166.

[89]*Ibid.,* 162.

[90]*Ibid.,* 164–166.

[91]*Ibid.*

[92]Lord, W. *Day of infamy.* New York: Holt, 1957, 46–49.

[93]Deutsch, K. W. On communication models in the social sciences. *Publ. Opin. Quart.,* 1952, **16,** 372.

[94]Servan-Schreiber, J.-J. *The American challenge.* New York: Atheneum, 1968, 3–30.

[95]International Business Machines Corporation. *Op. cit.,* 7.

[96]March, J. G. & Simon, H. A. *Op. cit.,* 189–190. Reprinted by permission.

[97]Meier, R. L. Information input overload: features of growth in communications-oriented institutions. In F. Massarik & P. Ratoosh (Eds.). *Mathematical explorations in behavioral science.* Homewood, Ill.: Dorsey-Irwin, 1965, 240–273.

[98]*Ibid.,* 260–266.

[99]Overhage, C. F. J. & Harman, R. J. (Eds.). *INTREX: report of a planning conference on information transfer experiments.* Cambridge, Mass.: M.I.T. Press, 1965, 1.

[100]Kochen, M. *Principles of information retrieval.* New York: Wiley, 1974, 125–131.

[101]Blake, R. R. & Mouton, J. S. *The managerial grid.* Houston: Gulf Publishing Company, 1964, 244–245. Reprinted by permission.

[102]Gross, B. M. *The managing of organizations.* Vol. 1. *Op. cit.,* 373–377.

[103]*Ibid.*, 374. Copyright © 1964 by The Free Press of Glencoe, a Division of the Macmillan Company. Reprinted by permission.

[104]*Ibid.*, 375.

[105]Woodward, J. *Op. cit.*, 17–21.

[106]Likert, R. *Op. cit.*, 163–178.

[107]Etzioni, A. Organizational control structure. In J. G. March (Ed.). *Handbook of organizations*. Chicago: Rand McNally, 1965, 650–652.

[108]*Ibid.*

[109]Mechanic, D. Sources of power of lower participants in complex organizations. In W. W. Cooper, H. J. Leavitt, & M. S. Shelly II (Eds.). *New perspectives in organization research*. New York: Wiley, 1964, 142–143.

[110]*Ibid.*, 143–147. Copyright © 1964 by John Wiley & Sons, Inc. Reprinted by permission.

[111]Weber, M. *Op. cit.*

[112]Blau, P. M. & Scott, W. R. *Op. cit.*, 60–74.

[113]*Ibid.*, 246.

[114]Mechanic, D. *Op. cit.*, 142.

[115]Likert, R. *Op. cit.*, 51.

[116]Faas, H. & Arnett, P. Civilians fear My Lai is U.S. "Achilles heel." *Cleveland Plain Dealer*, Dec. 8, 1969, 6. Reprinted by permission of the Associated Press.

[117]Dale, E. *Planning and developing the company organization structure*. New York: American Mgmt. Association, 1952, 100–102.
Cf. also Woodward, J. *Op. cit.*, 242–243.

[118]Gross, B. M. *The managing of organizations*. Vol. 1. *Op. cit.*, 128–148.

[119]*Ibid.*, 149–171.

[120]Burns, T. & Stalker, G. M. *The management of innovation*. London: Tavistock Publications, 1961, 5–6.

[121]Woodward, J. *Op. cit.*, 71.

[122]*Ibid.*, 64.

[123]*Ibid.*, 165–170.

[124]*Ibid.*, 162.

[125]Likert, R. *Op. cit.*, 165.

[126]Blake, R. R. & Mouton, J. S. *Op. cit.*, 170.

[127]*Wall Street Journal*, Sept. 22, 1970, **50**(241), 1.

[128]Katz, D. & Kahn, R. L. *Op. cit.*, 265–266.

[129]Cyert, R. M. & March, J. G. The behavioral theory of the firm: a behavioral science–economics amalgam. In W. W. Cooper, H. J. Leavitt, & M. W. Shelly II (Eds.). *New perspectives in organization research*. New York: Wiley, 1964, 291–292.

[130]Buck, V. E. A model for viewing an organization as a system of constraints. In J. D. Thompson (Ed.). *Approaches to organizational design*. Pittsburgh, Pa.: Univ. of Pittsburgh Press, 1966, 115–119.

[131]Lawrence, P. R. & Lorsch, J. W. *Op. cit.*, 37–38.

[132]Woodward, J. *Op. cit.*, 170.

[133]Gross, B. M. What are your organization's objectives? *Human Relat.*, 1965, **18**, 198. Reprinted by permission of Plenum Publishing Company.

[134]Feldman, J. & Kanter, H. E. Organizational decision making. In J. G. March (Ed.). *Handbook of organizations*. Chicago: Rand McNally, 1965, 629.

[135]Dent, J. K. Organizational correlates of the goals of business managements. *J. Personnel Psychol.*, 1959, **12**, 365–393.

[136]Blau, P. M. & Scott, W. R. *Op. cit.*, 243–244.

[137]*Ibid.*, 244–246.

[138]Likert, R. *Op. cit.*, 146–155.

[139]March, J. G. & Simon, H. A. *Op. cit.*, 150.

[140]*Ibid.*, 139.

[141]Cyert, R. M. & March, J. G. Organizational design and theory. In W. W. Cooper, H. J. Leavitt, & M. W. Shelly II (Eds.). *New perspectives in organization research*. New York: Wiley, 1964, 565.

[142]Buck, V. E. *Op. cit.*, 108–109.

[143]March, J. G. & Simon, H. A. *Op. cit.*, 151.

[144]Marschak, T. A. Economic theories of organization. In J. G. March (Ed.). *Handbook of organizations*. Chicago: Rand McNally, 1965, 424–426.

[145]*Ibid.*, 447.
Cf. also Feldman, J. & Kanter, H. E. *Op. cit.*, 629.
Also March, J. G. & Simon, H. A. *Op. cit.*, 138.

[146]Marschak, T. A. *Op. cit.*, 425.

[147]Cyert, R. M. & March, J. G. The behavioral theory of the firm: a behavioral science–economics amalgam. *Op. cit.*, 293. Copyright © 1964 by John Wiley & Sons, Inc. Reprinted by permission.

[148]Thompson, J. D. Decision-making, the firm, and the market. In W. W. Cooper, H. J. Leavitt, & M. W. Shelly II (Eds.). *New perspectives in organization research*. New York: Wiley, 1964, 335.

[149]McDonald, J. How the man at the top avoids crises. *Fortune*, 1970, **81**(1), 121–122. Reprinted by permission.

[150]McCormick, F. *Harvester foremanship*. Chicago: International Harvester Co., 1937.

[151]March, J. G. & Simon, H. A. *Op. cit.*, 173.

[152]Allen, T. J., Jr. & Marquis, D. G. *Positive and negative biasing sets: the effects of prior experience on research performance*. Cambridge, Mass.: M.I.T., School of Industrial Management, Working Paper No. 21-63, July 1963.

[153]Thompson, J. D. *Op. cit.*, 337–338.

[154]Keeney, R. L. & Raiffa, H. A critique of formal analysis in public decision making. In A. W. Drake, R. L. Keeney, & P. M. Morse (Eds.). *Analysis of public systems*. Cambridge, Mass.: M.I.T. Press, 1972, 64–74. Reprinted by permission.

[155]Hansen, B. Computer working in supermart. *Los Angeles Times*, Dec. 29, 1969, V-1.

[156]Townsend, R. *Op. cit.*, 19–20.

[157]Napoleon I. Manuscript letter to the Duc de Feltre, June 3, 1811. (My translation.)

[158]McQuade, W. The search for corporate identity. *Fortune*, 1970, **82**(6), 140–141.

[159]Katz, D. & Kahn, R. L. *Op. cit.*, 81–83.

[160]Blau, P. M. & Scott, W. R. *Op. cit.*, 197–198.

[161]Gross, B. M. *The managing of organizations*. Vol. 2. Op. cit., 542.

[162]*Ibid.*, 578.

[163]Toffler, A. *Future shock*. New York: Random House, 1970, 396–405.

[164]Gross, B. M. *The managing of organizations*. Vol. 2. *Op. cit.*, 544–546.

[165]Katz, D. & Kahn, R. L. *Op. cit.*, 152.

[166]Gross, B. M. *The managing of organizations*. Vol. 2. *Op. cit.*, 546–547.

[167]Katz, D. & Kahn, R. L. *Op. cit.*, 149–170.

[168]March, J. G. & Simon, H. A. *Op. cit.*, 173.

[169]Woodward, J. *Op. cit.*, 192–195.

[170]Abe, D. K. Corporate model system. In A. N. Schrieber (Ed.). *Corporate simulation models*. Providence, R.I.: College on Simulation and Gaming, The Institute of Management Science; & Seattle, Wash.: Univ. of Washington, Graduate School of Business Administration, 1970, 86–88.

[171]Simmons, J. W. Changing residence in the city. *Geograph. Rev.*, 1968, **58**, 622.

[172]Woodward, J. *Op. cit.*, 126–127.

[173]*Ibid.*, 140.

[174]*Ibid.*, 150.

[175]*Ibid.*, 127.

[176]Cf. Gross, B. M. *The managing of organizations.* Vol. 1. *Op. cit.*, 121–125, 135.

[177]Likert, R. *Op. cit.*, 199.

[178]Gooding, J. Blue-collar blues on the assembly line. *Fortune,* 1970, **82**(1), 69–71, 112–117.

[179]March, J. G. & Simon, H. A. *Op. cit.*, 93.

[180]Gooding, J. *Op. cit.*, 70.

[181]Bass, B. M. & Leavitt, H. J. Some experiments in planning and operating. *Mgmt. Sci.*, 1963, **9**, 574–585.

[182]Leavitt, H. J. Applied organization change in industry. In J. G. March (Ed.). *Handbook of organizations.* Chicago: Rand McNally, 1965, 1153–1167.

[183]Likert, R. *Op. cit.*, 78.

[184]Morse, N. & Reimer, E. The experimental change of a major organizational variable. *J. abnorm. soc. Psychol.*, 1956, **52**, 120–129.

[185]Roethlisberger, F. J. & Dickson, W. J. *Management and the worker.* Cambridge, Mass.: Harvard Univ. Press, 1941, 3–186.
Cf. also Gross, B. M. *The managing of organizations.* Vol. 1. *Op. cit.*, 160–163.

[186]March, J. G. & Simon, H. A. *Op. cit.*, 53–55.

[187]Cf. Likert, R. *Op. cit.*, 80.

[188]*Ibid.*, 86.

[189]Friedlander, F. & Brown, L. D. Organizational development. *Ann. Rev. Psychol.*, 1974, **25**, 314.
Cf. also Levinson, H. *Op. cit.*,

[190]Katz, D. & Kahn, R. L. *Op. cit.*, 390.

[191]*Ibid.*, 391. Reprinted by permission.

[192]*Ibid.*, 407.

[193]*Ibid.*, 395–396.

[194]*Ibid.*, 413–414.

[195]March, J. G. & Simon, H. A. *Op. cit.*, 48.

[196]*Ibid.*, 108.

[197]*Ibid.*, 94.
Cf. also Katz, D. & Kahn, R. L. *Op. cit.*, 375–377.

[198]Katz, D. & Kahn, R. L. *Op. cit.*, 368–370.

[199]Woodward, J. *Op. cit.*, 160.

[200]Trist, E. L., Higgin, G. W., Murray, H., & Pollock, A. B. *Organizational choice.* London: Tavistock Publications, 1963, 289–295.

[201]Gooding, J. *Op. cit.*, 117.

[202]Armstrong, R. Labor 1970: angry, aggressive, acquisitive. *Fortune,* 1969, **80**(5), 96.

[203]Smith, C. G. & Tannenbaum, A. S. Organizational control structure. *Human Relat.*, 1963, **16**, 299–316.

[204]Tannenbaum, A. S. *Op. cit.*, 750.

[205]March, J. G. & Simon, H. A. *Op. cit.*, 96.

[206]*Ibid.*, 371–372.

[207]*Ibid.*, 54.

[208]Tannenbaum, A. S. & Smith, C. G. Effects of member influence in an organization. *J. abnorm. soc. Psychol.*, 1964, **69**, 401–410.

[209]McGregor, D. The human side of enterprise. In W. G. Bennis, K. D. Benne, & R. Chin (Eds.). *The planning of change.* New York: Holt, 1961, 422–431.

[210]Leavitt, H. J. *Op. cit.*, 1159.

[211]Etzioni, A. *Op. cit.*, 672.

[212]March, J. G. & Simon, H. A. *Op. cit.*, 161.

[213]Lawrence, P. R. & Lorsch, J. W. *Op. cit.*, 46.

[214]*Ibid.*, 30–53.

[215]*Ibid.*, 223–224.

[216]*Ibid.*, 58–67.

[217]*Ibid.*, 56.

[218]Woodward, J. *Op. cit.*, 196–198.

[219]March, J. G. & Simon, H. A. *Op. cit.*, 160.

[220]Blau, P. M. & Scott, W. R. *Op. cit.*, 240–241.

[221]Woodward, J. *Op. cit.*, 219.

[222]Blau, P. M. & Scott, W. R. *Op. cit.*, 251.

[223]Cyert, R. M. & March, J. G. The behavioral theory of the firm: a behavioral science–economics amalgam. *Op. cit.*, 292. Copyright © 1964 by John Wiley & Sons. Reprinted by permission.

[224]Lawrence, P. R. & Lorsch, J. W. *Op. cit.*, 77–78.

[225]Townsend, R. *Op. cit.*, 39. Copyright © 1970 by Robert Townsend. Reprinted by permission of Alfred A. Knopf, Inc.

[226]Lawrence, P. R. & Lorsch, J. W. *Op. cit.*, 58–78.

[227]Lazar J. Economics: a behavioral-science view of the National Railroad Adjustment Board system. *Duke Law J.,* 1961, **2**, 262–273.

[228]Dahl, R. A. The concept of power. *Behav. Sci.*, 1957, **2**, 201–215.

[229]Sherrard, W. R. & Steade, R. D. Power comparability: its contribution to a theory of firm behavior. *Mgmt. Sci.*, 1966, **13**, B-186–B-193.

[230]Lawrence, P. R. & Lorsch, J. W. *Op. cit.*, 76–78.

[231]Leeds, R. The absorption of protest. In W. W. Cooper, H. J. Leavitt, & M. W. Shelly II (Eds.). *New perspectives in organization research.* New York: Wiley, 1964, 115–135.

[232]Likert, R. *Op. cit.*, 104.

[233]Forrester, J. W. *Industrial dynamics.* Cambridge, Mass.: M.I.T. Press, 1961, 13–42.

[234]*Ibid.*, 51.

[235]Lawrence, P. R. & Lorsch, J. W. *Op. cit.*, 94–95.

[236]Briggs, G. E. Engineering systems approaches to organizations. In W. W. Cooper, H. J. Leavitt, & M. W. Shelly II (Eds.). *New perspectives in organization research.* New York: Wiley, 1964, 485.

[237]Katz, D. & Kahn, R. L. *Op. cit.*, 417.

[238]Meier, R. L. *A communications theory of urban growth.* Cambridge, Mass.: M.I.T. Press, 1962, 29–32.

[239]Sjoberg, G. The origin and evolution of cities. *Sci. Amer.,* 1965, **213**(3), 56.

[240]Doxiadis, C. A. Ekistics, the science of human settlements. *Science,* 1970, **170**, 393–396.

[241]Doxiadis, C. A. Man's movement and his city. *Op. cit.*

[242]*Ibid.*, 333–334. Copyright 1968 by the American Association for the Advancement of Science. Reprinted by permission.

[243]Maki, F. & Ohtaka, M. Some thoughts on collective form. In G. Kepes (Ed.). *Structure in art and in science.* New York: Braziller, 1965, 116–127.

[244]Udy, S. H., Jr. Administrative rationality and social setting. In W. W. Cooper, H. J. Leavitt, & M. W. Shelly II (Eds.). *New perspectives in organization research.* New York: Wiley, 1964, 181.

[245]Childe, V. G. Archaeology. *Encyclopaedia Britannica.* Vol. 2. Chicago: Encyclopaedia Britannica, 1958, 254.

[246]Genesis 4:22.

[247]Spielman, J. P. Copper. *Encyclopaedia Britannica.* Vol. 6. Chicago: Encyclopaedia Britannica, 1958, 414.

[248]Udy, S. R., Jr. *Op. cit.*, 177.

[249]*Ibid.*, 187.

[250]Forrester, J. W. A new corporate design. *Indust. Mgmt. Rev.*, 1965, **7**, 6.

[251]*Ibid.*, 12.

[252]Bennis, W. G. Organizational developments and the fate of bureaucracy. *Indust. Mgmt. Rev.*, 1966, **7**, 41–55.

[253]*Ibid.*, 53.

[254]Bennis, W. G. A funny thing happened on the way to the future. *Amer. Psychol.*, 1970, **25**, 605.

[255]*Ibid.* Reprinted by permission.

[256]Nazem, S. G. The Fortune directory of the 500 largest U.S. industrial corporations. *Fortune*, 1976, **93**(5), 318–319.

[257]Gross, B. M. *The managing of organizations.* Vol. 2. *Op. cit.,* 672.

[258]Boulding, K. E. Towards a general theory of growth. *Canad. J. econ. pol. Sci.,* 1953, **19**, 335.
Also Gross, B. M. *The managing of organizations.* Vol. 2. *Op. cit.,* 672–674.

[259]Blau, P. M. & Scott, W. R. *Op. cit.,* 225.

[260]Parkinson, C. N. *Parkinson's Law.* Boston: Houghton Mifflin, 1957, 2–13.

[261]Blau, P. M. & Scott, W. R. *Op. cit.,* 227.
Also Anderson, T. R. & Warkov, S. Organizational size and functional complexity. *Amer. sociol. Rev.,* 1961, **26**, 23–28.
Also Blau, P. M. Interdependence and hierarchy in organizations. *Soc. Sci. Res.,* 1972, **1** (April), 1–24.

[262]Starbuck, W. H. Organizational growth and development. In J. G. March (Ed.). *Handbook of organizations.* Chicago: Rand McNally, 1965, 477.

[263]Noell, J. J. On the administrative sector of social systems: an analysis of the size and complexity of government bureaucracies in the American states. *Social Forces,* 1974, **52**, 549–558.

[264]*Ibid.,* 553. Reprinted from *Social Forces* 52, June, 1974. On the administrative sector of social systems: an analysis of the size and complexity of government bureaucracies in the American states. Copyright © The University of North Carolina Press. Reprinted by permission.

[265]Boulding, K. E. *Op. cit.,* 335.

[266]Haire, M. Biological models and empirical histories of the growth of organizations. In M. Haire (Ed.). *Modern organization theory.* New York: Wiley, 1959, 274–275.

[267]Hawley, A. H. *Op. cit.,* 234–287.

[268]Laffont, R. (Ed.). *The illustrated history of Paris and the Parisians.* (Trans. by I. Quigly & B. Bray.) Garden City, N.Y.: Doubleday & Co., 1958, 143.

[269]Blumenfeld, H. The modern metropolis. *Sci. Amer.,* 1965, **213**(3), 68.

[270]Doxiadis, C. A. Ekistics, the science of human settlements. *Op. cit.,* 393–394.

[271]Gross, B. M. *The managing of organizations.* Vol. 2. *Op. cit.,* 677–681.

[272]Penrose, E. T. *The theory of the growth of the firm.* New York: Wiley, 1959, 43–64, 88–99.

[273]Blumenfeld, H. *Op. cit.,* 64–74.

[274]Anon. The oldest companies. *Fortune,* 1970, **81**(5), 316.

[275]Starbuck, W. H. *Op. cit.,* 477.

[276]Forrester, J. W. *Industrial dynamics. Op. cit.,* 320.

[277]*Ibid.,* 328–329.

[278]Whyte, W. F. *Human relations in the restaurant industry.* New York: McGraw-Hill, 1948, 21–30.

[279]Dale, E. *Op. cit.,* 22.

[280]Wickesberg, A. K. *Organizational relationships in the growing small manufacturing firm.* Minneapolis: Univ. of Minnesota Press, 1961, 5–6.

[281]*Ibid.,* 9–52.

[282]Woodward, J. *Op. cit.,* 21–23.

[283]Starbuck, W. H. *Op. cit.,* 464.

[284]*Ibid.,* 473.

[285]Meier, R. L. *A communications theory of urban growth. Op. cit.,* 26, 28.

[286]Kochen, M. & Deutsch, K. W. *Decentralization: a mathematical model.* Ann Arbor: Univ. of Michigan, Mental Health Research Institute, Communication No. 266, March 1970, 1–6.

[287]Kochen, M. & Deutsch, K. W. Toward a rational theory of decentralization: some implications of a mathematical approach. *Amer. pol. Sci. Rev.,* 1969, **63,** 734.

[288]*Moody's industrial manual,* 1970, 2647–2648.

[289]Tannenbaum, A. S. *Op. cit.,* 751–756.

[290]Pearlstine, N. How local strikes curb G.M. production and could hurt Ford and Chrysler output. *Wall Street Journal,* Midwest Edition, Nov. 24, 1970, **50,** 34.

[291]Dale, E. *Op. cit.,* 106.

[292]Meyer, M. W. The two authority structures of bureaucratic organizations. *Admin. Sci. Quart.,* 1968, **13,** 211–228.

[293]March, J. G. & Simon, H. A. *Op. cit.,* 201.

[294]Massie, J. L. Management theory. In J. G. March (Ed.). *Handbook of organizations.* Chicago: Rand McNally, 1965, 401–402.

[295]Dale, E. *Op. cit.,* 118. Reprinted by permission.

[296]*Wall Street Journal,* Midwest Edition, June 22, 1970, **50,** 1, 9.

[297]Nazem, S. G. *Op. cit.,* 339.

[298]Cf. Bloomfield, D. Telephone system here impaired, FCC survey says. *Cleveland Plain Dealer,* May 22, 1971, 34C.

[299]Goldman, J. J. New York criminal justice machinery on verge of breakdown. *Cleveland Plain Dealer,* Dec. 9, 1970, 3E.

[300]Gleisser, M. Subtle shifts show the start of nice area's slide into slum. *Cleveland Plain Dealer,* Nov. 28, 1971, 15D. Reprinted by permission.

[301]Powell, J. W., Finesinger, J. E., & Greenhill, M. H. *An introduction to the natural history of disaster.* College Park: Univ. of Maryland, Psychiatric Institute, Disaster Research Project, final contract report, 1954, 2, 1. Reprinted by permission.

[302]Wallace, A. F. C. *Tornado in Worcester.* Washington: National Academy of Sciences–National Research Council, Committee on Disaster Studies, Publication 392, 1956, 7.

[303]Powell, J. W., Finesinger, J. E., & Greenhill, M. H. *Op. cit.,* 13.

[304]Wallace, A. F. C. *Op. cit.,* 7–15.

[305]Quarantelli, E. R. & Dynes, R. R. When disaster strikes (it isn't much like what you've heard and read about). *Psychology Today,* 1972, **5**(9), 68.

[306]Moore, H. E. *Tornadoes over Texas.* Austin: Univ. of Texas Press, 1958, 311–312.

[307]Pyle, E. *Here is your war.* Cleveland: World, 1943, 132. Copyright 1943 by Lester Cowan. Copyright © 1971 by Holt, Rinehart and Winston. Reprinted by permission of Holt, Rinehart and Winston, Inc., publishers.

[308]Devereux, G. Catastrophic reactions in normals: a note on the dynamics of the psychic unity of mankind. *Amer. Image,* 1950, **7,** 345.

[309]Hamilton, R. V., Taylor, R. M., & Rice, G. E., Jr. *A social psychological interpretation of the Udall, Kansas tornado.* Washington: National Academy of Sciences–National Research Council, Committee on Disaster Studies, 1955, 56–57. Reproduced with permission of the National Academy of Sciences.

[310]Siemes, Fr. J. A. *Eyewitness account, Hiroshima, August 6, 1945.* Unpublished paper.
Cf. also Hershey, J. *Hiroshima.* New York: Knopf, 1946.

[311]Logan, L., Killian, L. M., & Marrs, W. *A study of the effect of catastrophe on social disorganization.* Chevy Chase, Md.: Operations Research Office, 1952.

[312]*Ibid.,* 31. Reprinted by permission.

[313]Segaloff, L. *TASK SIROCCO, community reaction to an accidental chlorine exposure.* Philadelphia: Univ. of Pennsylvania, Institute for Cooperative Research, 1961, 31.

[314]Wallace, A. F. C. *Op. cit.,* 66–67.

[315]Hamilton, R. V., Taylor, R. M., & Rice, G. E., Jr. *Op. cit.*, 28.

[316]Ludwig, H. C. *Sanitary engineering in "Operation Tulip."* Washington: U.S. Public Health Reports, 1954, **69**, 533–537.

[317]Fritz, C. E. & Mathewson, J. H. *Convergence behavior in disasters.* Washington: National Academy of Sciences–National Research Council, Committee on Disaster Studies, Publication 476, 1957.

[318]Rosow, I. L. *Public authorities in two tornadoes.* Washington: National Academy of Sciences–National Research Council, Committee on Disaster Studies, 1954, 449.

[319]Wallace, A. F. C. *Op. cit.*, 155–156.

[320]*Ibid.*

[321]Ludwig, H. C. *Op. cit.*

[322]Hamilton, R. V., Taylor, R. M., & Rice, G. E., Jr. *Op. cit.*, 56–57. Reproduced with permission of the National Academy of Sciences.

[323]*Ibid.*

[324]Moore, H. E. *Op. cit.*

[325]Joseph, R. Ill wind blew city much good. *Cleveland Plain Dealer*, Dec. 6, 1970, 7H.

[326]*Conference on Field Studies of Reactions to Disasters.* Chicago: Univ. of Chicago, National Opinion Research Center, Report No. 47, 1953, 164–182.

[327]Moore, H. E. *Op. cit.*, 226–227.

[328]Anon. Strike ends at Miami U. after flush-in. *Cleveland Plain Dealer*, Apr. 23, 1970, D1.

[329]Blake, R. R. & Mouton, J. S. *Op. cit.*, 45–48.

[330]Silberman, C. E. *Crisis in the classroom.* New York: Random House, 1970.

[331]Shepard, H. A. Changing interpersonal and intergroup relationships in organizations. In J. G. March (Ed.). *Handbook of organizations.* Chicago: Rand McNally, 1965, 1122–1123.

[332]Blake, R. R. & Mouton, J. S. *Op. cit.*, 212–216.

[333]*Ibid.*, 215.

[334]*Ibid.*, 78. Reprinted by permission.

[335]*Ibid.*, 103.

[336]Finney, J. W. The Speaker: his position has been damaged. *New York Times*, Nov. 2, 1969, (4)4.

[337]Rukeyser, W. S. Why rain fell on "Automatic" Sprinkler. *Fortune*, 1969, **79**(5), 88–91, 126–129.

[338]Olsen, J. *Aphrodite: desperate mission.* New York: Putnam, 1970, 185–186. Reprinted by permission.

[339]Steif, W. Peace Corps heads for a merger. *Cleveland Press*, Dec. 2, 1970, A6.

[340]Gross, B. M. *The managing of organizations.* Vol. 2. *Op. cit.*, 662.

[341]Weick, K. E. Laboratory experimentation with organizations. In J. G. March (Ed.). *Handbook of organizations.* Chicago: Rand McNally, 1965, 202, 211–214.

[342]*Ibid.*, 244–254.

[343]*Ibid.*, 210–214.

[344]*Ibid.*, 225–226.

[345]Bass, B. M. *Experimenting with simulated manufacturing organizations.* ONR, Group Psychology Branch, Technical Cf. also Bass, B. M. Some experimental approaches to the study of organizational psychology. *Mgmt. Internat.*, 1963, **3**, 96–97.

[346]Bass, B. M. *Experimenting with simulated manufacturing organizations. Op. cit.*, 28–37.

[347]*Ibid.*, 95–96.

[348]*Ibid.*, 49–52.

[349]*Ibid.*, 97.

[350]Modesitt, C. L. Simulation: the nucleus of decision-making training for dealers. In A. N. Schrieber (Ed.). *Corporate simulation models.* Providence, R.I.: College on Simulation and Gaming, The Institute of Management Science; & Seattle: Univ. of Washington, Graduate School of Business Administration, 1970, 510–529.

[351]Grayson, C. J., Jr. *Decisions under uncertainty: drilling decisions by oil and gas operators.* Boston: Harvard Graduate School of Business Administration, Division of Research, 1960.

[352]Baker, R. A., Cook, J. G., Warnick, W. L., & Robinson, J. P. *Development and evaluation of systems for the conduct of tactical training at the tank platoon level.* Washington: George Washington Univ., HumRRO, Technical Report No. 88, 1964.

[353]Gershefski, G. W. Corporate models: the state of the art. In A. N. Schrieber (Ed.). *Corporate simulation models.* Providence, R.I.: College on Simulation and Gaming, The Institute of Management Science; & Seattle: Univ. of Washington, Graduate School of Business Administration, 1970, 29.

[354]Meier, R. C., Newell, W. T., & Pazer, H. L. *Simulation in business and economics.* Englewood Cliffs, N.J.: Prentice-Hall, 1969, 1. Reprinted by permission.

[355]Levinson, H. *The exceptional executive.* Cambridge, Mass.: Harvard Univ. Press, 1968, 96–97.

[356]Churchman, C. W. *Challenge to reason.* New York: McGraw-Hill, 1968, 159–160.

[357]*Ibid.*, 160. Reprinted by permission.

[358]Gershefski, G. W. *Op. cit.*, 26–42.

[359]Meier, R. C., Newell, W. T., & Pazer, H. L. *Op. cit.*, 294–296.

[360]Dickson, G. W., Jauriel, J. J., & Anderson, J. C. Computer assisted planning models: a functional analysis. In A. N. Schrieber (Ed.). *Corporate simulation models.* Providence, R.I.: College on Simulation and Gaming, The Institute of Management Science; & Seattle: Univ. of Washington, Graduate School of Business Administration, 1970, 61.

[361]Gershefski, G. W. *Op. cit.*, 29.

[362]Dickson, G. W., Jauriel, J. J., & Anderson, J. C. *Op. cit.*, 31.

[363]*Ibid.*, 53.

[364]Naylor, T. H. Corporate simulation models and the economic theory of the firm. In A. N. Schrieber (Ed.). *Corporate simulation models.* Providence, R.I.: College on Simulation and Gaming, The Institute of Management Science; & Seattle: Univ. of Washington, Graduate School of Business Administration, 1970, 7–8.

[365]Gershefski, G. W. *Op. cit.*, 37.

[366]Abe, D. K. Corporate model system. In A. N. Schrieber (Ed.). *Corporate simulation models.* Providence, R.I.: College on Simulation and Gaming, The Institute of Management Science; & Seattle: Univ. of Washington, Graduate School of Business Administration, 1970, 89–91.

[367]Forrester, J. W. *Industrial dynamics. Op. cit.*, 61–63.

[368]*Ibid.*, 96.

[369]Forrester, J. W. *Urban dynamics.* Cambridge, Mass.: M.I.T. Press, 1969, 1–11, 107.

[370]*Ibid.*, 107–114.

[371]*Ibid.*, 109–110. Reprinted by permission.

[372]Forrester, J. W. *Industrial dynamics. Op. cit.*, 67–72.

[373]*Ibid.*, 64–66.

[374]*Ibid.*, 73–80.

[375]Forrester, J. W. *Industrial dynamics. Op. cit.*, 369. Cf. also Meier, R. C., Newell, W. T., & Pazer, H. L., *Op. cit.*, 226.

[376]Forrester, J. W. *Industrial dynamics. Op. cit.*, 208–308.

[377]McPherson, L. F. Organizational change. *Indust. Mgmt. Rev.*, 1965, **6**, 51–64.

[378]Bonini, C. P. *Simulation of information and decision systems in the firm.* Chicago: Markham, 1967.

[379]*Ibid.*, 20, 54–59.

[380]*Ibid.*, 64–68.

[381]Chambers, J. C., Mullick, S. K., & Smith, D. D. The use of simulation models at Corning Glass Works. In A. N. Schrieber (Ed.). *Corporate simulation models.* Providence, R.I.: College on Simulation and Gaming, The Institute of Management Science; & Seattle: Univ. of Washington, Graduate School of Business Administration, 1970, 138–162.

[382]Boulden. J. B. Instant modeling. In A. N. Schrieber (Ed.). *Corporate simulation models.* Providence, R.I.: College on Simulation and Gaming, The Institute of Management Science; & Seattle: Univ. of Washington, Graduate School of Business Administration, 1970, 578–599.

[383]Buchan, J. & Koenigsberg, E. *Op. cit.*, 461–489.

[384]Chervany, N. L., Strom, J. S., & Boehlke, R. F. An operations planning model for the Northwestern National Bank of Minneapolis. In A. N. Schrieber (Ed.). *Corporate simulation models.* Providence, R.I.: College on Simulation and Gaming, The Institute of Management Science; & Seattle: Univ. of Washington, Graduate School of Business Administration, 1970, 208–245.

[385]Parker, G. G. Statistics of attendance in American universities and colleges. *School & Society*, 1971, **99**, 23–31, 107–108.

[386]University budgets obtained from personal communications of their financial officers.

[387]Weathersby, G. *The development and applications of a university cost simulation model.* Berkeley, Calif.: Univ. of Calif., Graduate School of Business Administration and Office of Analytical Studies, 1967.

[388]Casasco, J. A. *Planning techniques for university management.* Washington: American Council on Education, 1970, 9–73.

[389]Koenig, H. E., Keeney, M. G., & Zemach, R. *A systems model for management, planning, and resource allocation in institutions of higher education.* East Lansing: Michigan State Univ., Division of Engineering Research, 1968, 7–14.

[390]*Ibid.*, 17.

[391]SRG Systems Research Group. *Introduction to planning with a CAMPUS model.* (Rev. ed.) New York: Systems Research Group, 1971. Unpublished paper.

[392]Weathersby, G. *Op. cit.*

[393]Wolfe, H. B. & Ernst, M. L. Simulation models and urban planning. In P. M. Morse (Ed.). *Operations research for public systems.* Cambridge, Mass.: M.I.T. Press, 1967, 51.

[394]*Ibid.*, 53.

[395]*Ibid.*, 53–54.

[396]*Ibid.*, 54.

[397]*Ibid.*, 78.

[398]*Ibid.*, 80. Reprinted by permission.

[399]Forrester, J. W. *Urban dynamics. Op. cit.*

[400]*Ibid.*, 26.

[401]*Ibid.*, 38–50.

[402]*Ibid.*, 51–70.

[403]*Ibid.*, 71–106.

[404]*Ibid.*, 128–129. Reprinted by permission.

[405]Kain, J. F. A computer version of how a city works. *Fortune*, 1969, **80**(6), 241–242.

[406]Meier, R. C., Newell, W. T., & Pazer, H. L. *Op. cit.*, 1–2.

[407]Buchan, J. & Koenigsberg, E. *Op. cit.*, 285–289.

[408]Meier, R. C., Newell, W. T., & Pazer, H. L. *Op. cit.*, 31–32.

[409]*Ibid.*, 233–241.

[410]Horvath, W. J. Operations research in medical and hospital practice. In P. M. Morse (Ed.). *Operations research for public systems.* Cambridge, Mass.: M.I.T. Press, 1967, 127–144.

[411]Fetter, R. B. & Thompson, J. D. The simulation of hospital systems. *Operations Res.*, 1965, **13**, 690–699.

[412]Horvath, W. J. *Op. cit.*, 128.

[413]Fetter, R. B. & Thompson, J. D. *Op. cit.*, 690–691.

[414]Sakai, T. & Nagao, M. Simulation of traffic flows in a network. *Communications of the ACM*, 1969, **12**, 311–318.

[415]Chaiken, J. M. & Larson, R. C. Methods for allocating urban emergency units. In A. W. Drake, R. L. Keeney, & P. M. Morse (Eds.). *Analysis of public systems.* Cambridge, Mass.: M.I.T. Press, 1972, 181–215.

[416]Larson, R. C. Improving the effectiveness of New York City's 911. In A. W. Drake, R. L. Keeney, & P. M. Morse (Eds.). *Analysis of public systems.* Cambridge, Mass.: M.I.T. Press, 1972, 151–180.

[417]Marschak, T. A. *Op. cit.*, 433–445.

[418]Bowman, E. H. A budget model of a university. *Socio-econ. Plan. Sci.*, 1969, **2**, 175–178.

[419]Linhart, P. A pool of funds model. In A. N. Schrieber (Ed.). *Corporate simulation models.* Providence, R.I.: College on Simulation and Gaming, The Institute of Management Science; & Seattle: Univ. of Washington, Graduate School of Business Administration, 1970, 449–465.

[420]Little, J. D. C. Models and managers: the concept of a decision calculus. *Mgmt. Sci.*, 1970, **16**, B-471–B-482.

[421]Morrill, R. L. The Negro ghetto: problems and alternatives. *Geog. Rev.*, 1965, **40**, 348–361.

[422]Kochen, M. & Deutsch, K. W. Toward a rational theory of decentralization: some implications of a mathematical approach. *Op. cit.*, 734–749.

[423]Kochen, M. & Deutsch, K. W. *Decentralization: a mathematical model. Op. cit.*

[424]Kochen, M. & Deutsch, K. W. *Decentralization by function and location.* Ann Arbor: Univ. of Michigan, Mental Health Research Institute, Communication No. 267, 1970.

[425]Kochen, M. & Deutsch, K. W. *Decentralization: a mathematical model. Op. cit.*, 16.

[426]*Ibid.*, 21.

[427]Kochen, M. & Deutsch, K. W. *Decentralization by function and location. Op. cit.*, 20.

[428]*Ibid.*, 23.

[429]*Ibid.*, 28.

[430]Meier, R. C., Newell, W. T., & Pazer, H. L. *Op. cit.*, 199–203.

[431]Linhart, P. *Op. cit.*, 459–460.

[432]Meier, R. C., Newell, W. T., & Pazer, H. L. *Op. cit.*, 198–199.

[433]Chapman, R. L., Kennedy, J. L., Newell, A., & Biel, W. C. *The system research laboratory's air defense experiments. Report P 1202.* Santa Monica, Calif.: RAND Corp., 1957.

[434]Jowett, B. (Trans.) *The dialogues of Plato.* Chicago: Encyclopaedia Britannica, 1952, 404–416.

[435]Katz, D. & Kahn, R. L. *Op. cit.*, 460–463.

[436]March, J. G. & Simon, H. A. *Op. cit.*, 46.

[437]Dickens, J. H. Linear programming in corporate simulations. In A. N. Schrieber (Ed.). *Corporate simulation models.* Providence, R.I.: College on Simulation and Gaming, The Institute of Management Science; & Seattle: Univ. of Washington, Graduate School of Business Administration, 1970, 311.

[438]Katz, D. & Kahn, R. L. *Op. cit.*, 96–97. Cf. also Parsons, T. *Structure and process in modern societies.* New York: Free Press, 1960, 60–65.

The Society

A society is a large, living, concrete system with organizations and lower levels of living systems as subsystems and components. Ancient city-states and kingdoms were societies, as are modern nation-states and empires that are not supranational systems. Small, primitive, totipotential communities are also societies if they are not components of another society. Some scholars define the word "society" differently from the way I do. Toynbee, for example, wrote:

What then is the right way of describing the relation between human societies and individuals? The truth seems to be that a human society is, in itself, a system of relationships between human beings who are not only individuals but are also social animals in the sense that they could not exist at all without being in this relationship to one another. A society, we may say, is a product of the relations between individuals, and these relations of theirs arise from the coincidence of their individual fields of action. This coincidence combines the individual fields into a common ground, and this common ground is what we call a society.

If this definition is accepted, an important though obvious corollary emerges from it. Society is a "field of action" but the *source* of all action is in the individuals composing it.[1]

Though some of his wording suggests that Toynbee saw societies as concrete systems, his paramount view seems to have been that they are abstracted systems (see pages 19 to 22) whose peoples share similar cultures regardless of which particular government rules them.[2] What I call *societies* he called *universal states* (empires like the Persian Empire) or *national states* (when he referred to modern countries). He dealt with abstracted systems, which he considered useful units for historical study, and not with concrete nation-states having independent decider subsystems. In all history he identified 21 of his societies, which were also *civilizations,* and a much larger number of primitive societies. The following civilizations in his list persist today: Western Christendom; the Orthodox Christian culture of Southeastern Europe and Russia, which may be divided into Orthodox Byzantine and Orthodox Russian; Islam; the subtropical Indian area dominated by the Hindu religion; and a Far Eastern area in the subtropical and temperate regions between the arid zone and the Pacific, which may be divided into Chinese and Korean-Japanese areas.

Parsons, Shils, and their associates have defined a "social system" as "Any system of interactive relationships of a plurality of individual actors. . . ." and a "society" as " . . . the type of social system which contains within itself all the essential prerequisites for its maintenance as a self-subsistent system. Among the more essential of these prerequisites are (1) organization around the foci of territorial location and kinship, (2) a system for determining functions and allocating facilities and rewards, and (3) integrative structures controlling these allocations and regulating conflicts and competitive processes."[3] As I noted in Chap. 2 (see pages 19 to 22), this concept of society is an abstracted system while mine is a concrete system. Also Parsons and his associates make no clear distinction, as I do, among levels of systems.

1. Structure

Unlike most organizations, all societies, as Parsons and his associates noted, are totipotential. They have a complete set of matter-energy and information processing subsystems. They are, however, sometimes dependent on other societies for assistance in carrying out the processes of one or more of these subsystems.

747

For instance, Austria and Bangladesh cannot produce all the food they need, and at present the United States cannot produce all the oil it needs. The subsystems of a society ordinarily are organizations or complexes of organizations, but in some societies one or more subsystem processes are carried out by groups or even occasionally by individual persons, like queens, emperors, or presidents.

In being totipotential, societies differ also from supranational systems, which commonly lack some subsystems. In fact, most associations among societies do not have the most essential critical subsystem, a decider. Consequently, so far in the history of the world there have been few truly supranational systems. Enduring supranational systems may develop in the future, but currently societies are, for all practical purposes, the highest level of totipotential living systems.

As at other levels, transitional forms occur between systems which are clearly societies and those which are unequivocally at the next lower level (organizations) or the next higher level (supranational systems). These transitional systems include isolated, remote villages that depend so little upon their suprasystem societies that they may be regarded almost as separate societies—inclusions within the territory of a larger society with which they more or less rarely exchange matter-energy and information. They illustrate Hypothesis 2-3 (see page 92), which states that the more isolated a system is, the more totipotential it must be.

It may be hard to distinguish between a community that is a component of a society and one that is an inclusion in a society. About one of the first sort, Redfield wrote: "The Maya village I knew is not fully self-contained. To describe it completely we must reckon with parts of outside communities, or influences from communities that have their centers and their principal being elsewhere than in the village."[4] The Siriano Indian tribes that live deep within the Bolivian forest, at least until recent years, were truly totipotential small societies, which were really inclusions in Bolivia.[5] These tribes not only rejected the culture of the society in whose territory they lived but also avoided contact as much as possible.

Federations of states in which components have few shared subsystem processes, and either no central decider or a weak one, are something between societies and supranational systems, though more like the latter. Examples are the British Commonwealth of Nations and the Arab League.

1.1   System size   The more than 130 sovereign nations in the world vary greatly in size. The smallest, Vatican City, is only about 0.66 kilometer (km) in diameter and has an area of 0.44 km²; Nauru, a Commonwealth republic in the West Pacific, is about 5 km in diameter and has an area of 21 km². The largest of them all, the Soviet Union, has an east-west diameter of about 11,000 km and an area of 22,272,190 km². The median modern nation has a diameter of about 1,010 km and an area of about 1,020,100 km².

1.2   Structural taxonomy of types of systems   Classifications of societies make some use of differences in structure, even though most are based primarily upon differences in process. Among the structural differentiae in use are size of territory; number of persons (subsubcomponents) in the population; density of persons in the population; arrangement of components within the system's territory, *e.g.,* number of cities over 20,000 persons each, per million persons in the total societal population; and sorts of artifacts, including buildings, used by subsystems. The dichotomous classifications that contrast two types of organizations (see page 601) are sometimes applied to whole societies, although real societies do not conform perfectly to either ideal type. Agrarian societies, for example, differ widely in their percentages of farmers. The commonest dichotomy of societal types is the following:

One extreme is variously called *agraria,* the *independent society, Gemeinschaft,* or the *folk society.* Its population is relatively small, low in density, and spread out in small villages or farms. It uses artifacts appropriate to agriculture and small-scale production, and its human subsystem components are selected on hereditary or familial bases.

The other extreme is called *industria,* the *dependent society, Gesellschaft,* or the *urban society.* It has a large population, densely concentrated in cities. It uses artifacts like factories, steel mills, and heavy machinery, and it selects personnel on the basis of impersonal criteria of organizational status or effectiveness, producing a bureaucratic subsystem structure.

The structure of a society's decider subsystem, that is, its type of government, is another basis for classifying societal systems. A particular nation, for instance, is considered a democracy (single-party or multiparty), an autocracy, a constitutional monarchy, an oligarchy, a theocracy, or a dictatorship.

2. Process

The primary emphasis of my presentation at all levels of living systems has been on process rather than structure, for process is the essence of life (see pages 23 and 24). The vastly complex and vigorous processes in living cells have been described, but they are apparent only under the microscope and after laboratory studies in cellular biology. Motile cells are obviously active, but sessile cells, to the unaided eye of the human observer, seem inert. Most organs, though they may be carrying out many processes simultaneously, appear similarly inactive, and when they move, the limitations of their actions are obvious. Organisms—especially higher animals and human beings—are constantly active and often innovative. Except when they cut their hair or nails, undergo plastic surgery, or receive organ transplants or prostheses, they are unable to change their structures. An emergent characteristic of living systems at the level of the group is an apparent new freedom to change the spatial arrangement of system components. Groups and systems at higher levels can extend over a much larger spatial region than cells, organs, or organisms. Also, their components are not held together by physical forces, and so they may be much more separate in space and more independently mobile. The larger organizations, societies, and supranational systems become, however, the less mobility they have. The largest rarely or never move. Also, systems at the group level and above reorganize their internal structures much more than systems at lower levels. Frequently they shift a particular subsystem process from one component to another. [This is not unknown at lower levels, however—individual myxamoeba cells can cluster together and "delegate" certain processes to specialized cells in the cluster (see page 203); the spleen and liver in human adults can produce red blood corpuscles if for any reason the usual component that does this, bone marrow, cannot (see page 317); and the medulla can send signals to other organs to decrease an internal strain of high blood acidity if for any reason increasing the breathing rate does not adjust adequately to it (see pages 113 and 424).]

Many students of social systems are particularly impressed with societies' obvious great activity, ability to learn from experience even if only slowly, and facility in making rapid and significant changes in their own structures and processes. Some of these scholars have concluded that general living systems theory does not adequately explain such active changes.[6] It is difficult for me to understand how a careful study of my theory of living systems, with its explicit and continuous emphasis on process, can result in such an interpretation.

Perhaps one reason is that some look on my concept of a social system as "quasiorganic" or rooted in biology—and indeed I do maintain that the level of the society evolved from the lower levels. But perhaps the multiplex activity of the lower levels has not been studied in enough detail to be appreciated. Certainly, on the other hand, I do not deny that at its most complicated, it is more restricted than the activity of the higher levels. A prime tenet of my conceptual system is that emergent new processes arise at each higher level.

Another reason may be that it is a basic principle of my approach, whenever possible, to identify precisely the structure that carries out every process—the actor for every action. This is not always done in the functional social sciences. To some it may seem to restrict actions unnecessarily to tie them down to specific structures.

A further reason possibly is my view that every action arises from multiple antecedent actions—the primitive assumption of causality common to all sorts of deterministic science. Actions of a person or other system do not arise "voluntarily" in the sense that they are uncaused by preceding events. And few social scientists today would argue that they do, though some seem uncertain about their views on this issue. Even seemingly novel actions of all systems are elicited by changes in inputs (or resultant changes in internal states) of matter-energy or information. If there are few degrees of freedom in the information input, the action may seem routine and clearly a response to immediately prior events. If many alternative actions are possible because there are many degrees of freedom, the action may appear highly original. At a lower level, the signals which elicit contractions of "involuntary" muscles flow over channels which permit few alternative responses. The signals which elicit contractions of "voluntary" muscles pass over complex cortical and other channels which make possible a great number of alternative immediate and delayed responses. That is the difference—in societies as well as at lower levels.

My approach to societies emphasizes processes in every subsystem, a large repertory of complex system-wide adjustment processes, evolution, emergent processes, growth, and integration. All these constitute a vast activity—lively, continuous change.

A concept of major importance in social science is that of culture. It refers to process rather than structure. The people of each society store in their memories a particular complex set of symbols which they all learn. This is the content of their culture, and it determines their characteristic modes of information processing; the patterns of information which appear in their speech, actions, and rituals; their artifacts of all sorts; and their social structure. In this sense the culture of a society is an abstraction like the personality of a human organism (see pages 457 to 460) and the syntality of a group (see page 543).

The boundaries within which live the people who share a culture often are not the same as the borders of

TABLE 11-1   Classification of Cyclical Economic Indicators

Economic process	Leading indicators	Roughly coincident indicators	Lagging indicators	Unclassified
		Relation to business cycle		
Employment and unemployment	Average workweek Average weekly overtime Hiring rate Layoff rate New unemployment insurance claims	Job vacancies Total employment Total unemployment	Long-duration unemployment	
Production, income, consumption, and trade		Total production, income, and sales		
Fixed capital investment	Formation of business enterprises New investment commitments	Backlog of investment commitments	Investment expenditures	
Inventories and inventory investment	Inventory investment and purchasing		Inventories	
Prices, costs, and profits	Sensitive commodity prices Stock prices Profits and profit margins Cash flows	Wholesale price index	Labor costs per unit of output	Consumer price index
Money and credit	Flows of money and credit Business failures and credit delinquencies	Bank reserves Money-market interest rates	Outstanding debt Bank-loan and mortgage interest rates	
Foreign trade and balance of payments				Imports, exports, and export orders Payments balances
Federal government activities				Receipts and expenditures Defense purchases, contracts, and orders

NOTE: These indicators are classified by major economic process, such as employment and unemployment, and by their relation to changes in the business cycle. Those shown here are only a few of the many indicators that may be classified in this way.
SOURCE: U.S. Department of Commerce. *Business conditions digest.* Washington: GPO, June, 1974, 74–91.

a society. Multiple cultures or subcultures can be included within a society. Also, more than one society can share essentially the same culture, with modifications peculiar to each system. Societal borders can differ from one period to another, but at any time they have definite delimited locations in space. Transitions among cultures often are more gradual. In one area of India where a plain slopes from the Indian Ocean up to a high plateau, for instance, the languages of plain and plateau are mutually unintelligible, and yet at no one point do neighbors fail to understand one another.[7] Societies in which diverse cultures coexist—

those nations, for example, where a number of languages are spoken or whose citizens adhere to different religions—are more difficult to integrate than culturally homogeneous societies.

2.1   System and subsystem indicators   For several decades modern governments have monitored the state of economic variables by analyzing *economic indicators*.[8] These are statistical indices calculated at regular intervals to generate time series that permit comparisons over an extended period and reveal long-term trends and short-term variations that change systematically in the economy. These statistics can be disaggregated geographically, by attributes of the persons involved, or in other useful ways. The selected indicators may lead, be coincident with, or lag behind changes in the processes they reflect. Average work-week and overtime, hiring and layoff rates, and new unemployment insurance, for example, are leading indicators of the changes in employment and unemployment related to changes in the business cycle. Job vacancies and total employment and unemployment are roughly coincident with such changes, and long-duration unemployment is a lagging indicator. Relationships among indicators may also be important. Indices of stock-market activity, for example, tend to lead changes in business activity. Such indices appear to relate to interactions of movements in profits, interest, and other factors.

Indicators may be used to predict fluctuations in the business cycle or to determine the conditions of the economy at a given time. Table 11-1 shows some selected cyclical economic indicators.

These indicators are reliable enough so that decision makers often use them in determining economic policy. Adjustment of variables, *e.g.*, money supply, under the control of central banks like the Federal Reserve Bank of the United States, may be made when indicators point either to slowing down or to "heating up" of the economy. Although political and other considerations are also important in determining the policy of the President or Congress, both may be guided by indicators, particularly when they change markedly.

The abundant statistics collected by governments and other organizations on economic variables provide data for indicator analysis and other mathematical and statistical methods used in monitoring the economy and forecasting its future activity (see pages 875 to 885).

Measures that can be used as indicators for non-economic societal processes are less available. In 1960 members of the United States President's Commission on National Goals agreed upon 81 specific statements of domestic goals.[9] These were classified under 11 categories (see Table 11-2). For only 59 percent of the statements were any statistical data available which could be considered relevant, even applying loose criteria of relevance.[10] Health and welfare, education, and economic growth were the only categories for which indicators relevant to all the goals could be found in the *Statistical Abstract of the United States, 1962*, or the *Historical Statistics of the United States, Colonial Times to 1957*.

The greater availability of economic indicators reflects not only the value placed upon financial variables by modern societies but also the greater advancement

TABLE 11-2 Availability of Indicators Relevant to United States National Goals Formulated by President's Commission on National Goals in 1960

Goal area	Number of specific goals	Number of goals to which some indicator is relevant	Number of goals to which no indicator is relevant
The individual	6	3	3
Equality	3	2	1
Democratic process	11	5	6
Education	5	5	0
Arts and sciences	8	2	6
Democratic economy	9	4	5
Economic growth	9	9	0
Technological change	5	1	4
Agriculture	5	4	1
Living conditions	10	2	8
Health and welfare	10	9	1
Total	81	46	35

NOTE: The numbers of indicators found in the *Statistical Abstract of the United States, 1962* or *Historical Statistics of the United States, Colonial Times to 1957* are indicated above.

SOURCE: (Data from President's Commission on National Goals. *Goals for Americans*. Englewood Cliffs, N.J.: Prentice-Hall, 1960, and President's Research Committee on Social Trends. *Recent social trends in the United States*. New York: McGraw-Hill, 1933.) A. D. Biderman. Social indicators and goals. In R. A. Bauer (Ed.). *Social indicators*. Cambridge, Mass.: M.I.T. Press, 1966, 88. Reprinted by permission.

of economics in observing and measuring variables of concern in that field.[11] Gross, a social scientist who approaches such issues with a general systems orientation, says:

. . . the highly quantitative economic data in today's economic survey documents tend to distract attention from ideas that cannot be so readily expressed in quantitative terms. When a statistical indicator has been established—whether it is for gross national product or a cost of living index—it tends to take on a lifelong character of its own. Attention is inevitably directed to the small changes that take place from time to time in the selected indicator while other important and relevant aspects of the situation are neglected. Economic statistics, as a whole, emphasize the monetary value of goods and services. By so doing, they tend to discriminate against non-monetary values and against public services for which costs invariably serve as surrogates of output value.[12]

The proved usefulness of economic indicators and the dearth of indicators for these other processes have led to a vigorous movement favoring development of a similar set of *social indicators*. Their use has been referred to as the *keeping of social accounts, social bookkeeping,* or *monitoring social change*.[13]

Support by the United States government for use of social indicators began in the mid-1960s when Secretary of Health, Education, and Welfare John Gardner appointed a panel of social scientists to study the matter. His successor, Wilbur Cohen, continued to promote this approach. He suggested that a social

report be made annually. It would be useful in measuring various aspects of social change, establishing
societal goals, and evaluating the accomplishments of
public programs.[14]

Moore and Sheldon published an early paper on
monitoring social change in 1965, and Bauer, Biderman, and Gross published on social indicators in 1966.
In 1973, the Office of Management and Budget of the
United States issued the first of a planned series of
biannual publications, *Social Indicators 1973*. This is a
book of statistics selected to describe social conditions
and trends in that year in that society.[15] These indicators are organized under headings of health, public
safety, education, employment, income, housing, leisure and recreation, and population. One or more
indicators for each of the social concerns included
have been identified. Under health, the three major
social concerns are (1) long life, the major indicator of
which is the average life expectancy at birth; (2) quality of health or life free from disability, which is
measured by the average number of days of disability
per person per year; and (3) access to medical care, of
which two indirect measures are indicators—(*a*) personal confidence in the ability to obtain good health
care and (*b*) percent of the population covered by
health insurance.

Social indicators are of interest in other societies as
well. Great Britain, France, the four Scandinavian
countries, and Japan have recently issued reports on
social trends that use indicators based upon statistical
studies and surveys.[16] Thus it is now possible to make
regular quantitative comparisons among individual
nations and across types of societies.

The development and use of social indicators is
attended by a number of problems, as its proponents
are well aware. Sheldon and Freeman, who consider
that there is critical need for a continuing body of
social data, identify the most serious problems as
deciding what to measure and what valid operational
measures of critical phenomena are available. They
say:

> With more knowledge on what to measure and better opera-
> tional measures, work on understanding the past and predict-
> ing the future would be made more effective. There are no
> simple solutions, for no agreement exists either on the out-
> lines of the major institutions and social systems in the society
> or on what constitutes the major social problems, deviant
> behaviors, and conditions of social disorganization. We have
> yet to determine what degrees of regularity exist so that
> appropriate time intervals between measures can be deter-
> mined in order to establish critical changes in rates and
> direction.[17]

These authors also emphasize that until the necessary
data are available, social indicators cannot be adequate for formulating policy and planning action.

Etzioni and Lehman discuss the "dysfunctions" that
social measurement may have for social planning.[18]
Among these are problems of *internal validity*. There
may be disparity between a particular theoretical concept and the particular indicator selected to measure
it. Another problem is that of *fractional measurement*,
that is, measuring only part and leaving out important
aspects of the thing being measured. For instance, the
average number of television sets per household may
be determined, but other artifactual inputs to each
home, like food, bathtubs, furniture, washers, and
sporting equipment, may be ignored. Indicators
based on a single class of such objects reveal only part
of the picture. A number of such measures can be
combined in a joint index, but this too has pitfalls,
since internal variation among the dimensions may
not be reflected.

A further problem occurs when measurement of
means is substituted for measurement of goals. It is
easier to measure church attendance than to measure
authentic religious commitment, although the latter is
usually the ultimate goal of religious organizations.
Inherent problems are increased when the measurements used are indirect. Further dysfunctions are
elaborate statistical procedures applied to essentially
unreliable data, treating abstracted social units such as
census districts as if they were concrete systems, and
aggregating attributes of members of a system rather
than devising measures for the system itself apart
from its members.

A continuing problem for social scientists is that the
information that would best indicate the state of a
particular social variable is not collected. For instance,
Cohen found that many more quantitative and qualitative data are needed on which to base indicators in
the area of education.[19] Developing them would
require further fundamental research into human
behavior and learning. It would also be necessary to
collect detailed information on aspects of educational
activities and achievements, such as quality of teaching, effects of racial segregation of students on learning, distribution of student dropouts in the population as a whole, failure rates in different sorts of
schools, the efficiency and economy of the operation
of educational institutions, the relationship of education to personal satisfaction, and the relationship of
education to political participation.

Social Indicators 1973 lists two major socially
accepted educational goals:[20]

1. *The achievement of a basic education.* The relevant indicators measure the amount of schooling
attained by individuals, determined from the percentage of people who graduate from high school and from
their knowledge, skills, and attitudes as shown by

their performance on tests of the National Assessment of Educational Progress, a program to evaluate educational achievement in the United States.

2. *The opportunity for higher and continuing education.* An indicator of this is the percentage of the adult population that participates in formal education. This is broken down into the percentage of people enrolled in 2-year and 4-year college programs, the percentage of the adult population that attains a college degree, and the percentage that participates in continuing education. These indicators deal with some of the issues raised by Cohen, but leave others unanswered.

An encompassing problem for those who would develop a comprehensive system of social indicators is that of inadequate conceptualization of the society itself. Sheldon and Freeman say:

Despite its weakness and limited rigor, economic theory provides a definition and the specifications of an economic system, and the linkages are at least hypothesized, if not empirically demonstrated, between many variables in the system. From such a point of departure, an administrator or a set of administrators can design policies that make possible the manipulation of one or more of the variables in that system. Because the changes are of a relatively short-term nature, feedback is rather prompt, say six months to a year, and policies and programs are vulnerable to further modification, alteration, and manipulation. At least to some extent, this model has worked and economic indicators and accounts are useful policy tools.

Although some social scientists have promised similar usefulness for social indicators and social accounts, this is not even a reasonable anticipation. There is no social theory, even of a tentative nature, which defines the variables of a social system and the relationships between them.[21]

Also, Land points out the need for models that specify the inputs, transformations, and outputs of social institutions.[22] Social indicators, in his view, should be parameters or variables in a model of a social system or part of one. He says that more time should be devoted to specification of the equation systems governing the transformations of the inputs of social institutions into outputs and estimating parameters of such systems.

In my opinion, the wait will be long for a usable set of social indicators that are based upon a mathematical model of a society sufficiently isomorphic to the real system to be used to prove theorems about it, although such a model is a desirable goal. There is, however, a more quickly achievable alternative. From the beginning of the social-indicators movement, Gross has used a general systems model of society.[23] He suggested that it is necessary to provide a conceptual model of a concrete society—a set of general categories covering all aspects of the society, as well as a useful and reasonable ordering of the categories. Land

considers this sort of model of a society too general to be of value, preferring a more detailed and precise mathematical specification.[24]

The conceptualization of a society which I provide in this chapter does not include mathematical models of the subsystems or of their interactions, feedbacks, or other adjustment processes. Nor does it or any other model provide a common unit, the equivalent of money in the economic models, that would make the development of social indicators easier. It does, however, list a specific, and possibly exhaustive, set of critical subsystems present in every society as well as in living systems at other levels. It identifies the structures that carry out the subsystem processes and provides a selected list of variables for each subsystem at every level. These are not exhaustive, but they cover many important processes. Also, it identifies some variables of total systems. It also makes clear what level of system the variable refers to: organism, group, organization, or society. Further, it analyzes the interactions of these variables in societal adjustment processes, describes some of the feedbacks among them, and hypothesizes some other relationships among them. It thus provides a basis for creating a set of indicators that can measure processes common to every society.

Social Indicators 1973 selects only six aspects of society and gives current data from the United States for a few indicators for each. Obviously, many more indicators are required for evaluating the states of all the subsystems of any society or for identifying the important trends within it. A chairman of the United States Council on Environmental Quality, for example, called for development of a number of environmental indices to illustrate major trends, to demonstrate the existence of significant environmental conditions, and to measure the success of federal, state, local, and private programs.[25] This task alone would require more indicators than are considered in the above publication. The indicators it lists, however, are measures of certain important aspects of the society. Each of these, it turns out, is related to variables of my conceptual system. As examples, I shall discuss one indicator from each of the six aspects of society included in *Social Indicators 1973* and identify its relationship to my conceptual system:

1. *Health.* The indicator *average life expectancy* is related to a general desire of societal members to live long—the "life" of "life, liberty, and the pursuit of happiness." Average life expectancy is an aggregation of data collected on individual human beings, at the organism level. It projects the probable number of years a newborn infant can, on the average, expect to live. The average lifetime of individual persons in a

society is a useful measure of the health of the total society considering its age composition (see page 865). This indicator can be disaggregated by sex, race, or age.

2. *Public safety.* The indicator *combined annual rate of murder and nonnegligent manslaughter, forcible rape, aggravated assault, and robbery* is a measure of pathology at the society level in my conceptual system. It measures rates of pathological interpersonal matter-energy and information transactions within the society, given as the number of instances of particular crimes per 100,000 population. Statistics are taken from *Uniform Crime Reports,* published by the Federal Bureau of Investigation. It reports separately official crime statistics and responses to a national survey that asks respondents whether they had been victims of crimes. It is disaggregated by the four separate categories into which crimes are classified, as well as by race, sex, age, and income of victim; sex of victim and of offender; and race of victim and of offender.

3. *Education.* The indicator *amount of schooling attained by individuals* is measured by the percentage of the population graduating from high school. In my conceptual system, this is the combined output of one set of components of the nation's associator subsystem—its combined high schools. The systems from which the data come are organizations, aggregated for the whole society. Unlike the indicators discussed above, this is an annual percentage rather than a rate, although it could have been expressed as a rate.

4. *Employment.* The indicator *overall unemployment rate* is a measure of the extent to which people who are capable of working can find employment. This is a total system variable in my conceptual system, since it is concerned with the number of people engaged (or, in this case, not engaged) in performing societal subsystem processes. The measure is at the organism level, since each potential worker is listed separately as employed or unemployed. The aggregated indicator measures an important variable of the society. This measure, like the education indicator, is a percentage rather than a rate. It can be disaggregated by age, sex, race, educational attainment, and occupation, as well as some other categories.

5. *Income.* The indicator *median family income* measures a fundamental societal variable—the amount of money each family unit has to live on. This is related to an information processing variable of my conceptual system, at the level of the group, the input transducer for monetary information input. It is also related to the societal channel and net for monetary information, since it measures flow of this sort of information to various parts of the society. This indicator can be disaggregated by race, age, sex, and edu-

cation of family head and by number of earners that contribute to the total income.

6. *Housing.* The indicator *percentage of households living in units classified as substandard* reflects a goal of the society—that every family have a decent home. It reflects a norm held by the society, since housing considered substandard in one society can be acceptable in another. This is a variable of the supporter subsystem at the level of the group (the family), aggregated for the total society. An excess of substandard dwellings in a society is one sort of matter-energy internal pathology at the level of the society. It may indicate that there is a lack strain of monetary information in the society. This is a dichotomous measure, dividing all housing into two categories—standard and substandard. It can be disaggregated by size of household, race, whether the house is occupied by owner or renter, location of the unit, income of the occupant, and age of the dwelling.

2.2 Process taxonomy of types of systems   Types of societies are classified much more often in terms of their processes than in terms of their structures. There have been many such taxonomies. There is little agreement among them, which is understandable because they have been derived from studies of different sets of societies and different time periods. Also, these researches have employed data from a wide variety of sources about those societies. They have investigated a large number of variables and indices, and their analytic methods have been quite divergent. Nevertheless, some agreement exists among them (see Table 11-6, pages 762 and 763).

Out of the many process taxonomies, I shall discuss only eight. They are based on conclusions about the evolution of societal types derived from archaeological, historical, and anthropological observations. They classify the societies by the stages through which they appear to have passed in going from primitive to fully developed systems. These schemes are all concerned with observable differences in ways of obtaining food and other necessities, types of community and governmental organizations, and other cultural variables, such as characteristic institutions, religious practices, art forms, and the manner of division of labor among the people.

1. To begin with, there is the classical dichotomy discussed above (see pages 601 and 748) of *agraria, Gemeinschaft,* the independent society, or the folk society, on the one hand, and *industria, Gesellschaft,* the dependent society, or the urban society, on the other. This classification is based to some extent on structural characteristics of societies but chiefly on process criteria such as the sort of technologies used by their subsystem processes, their religious practices,

the sorts of family relationships they recognize, their educational activities, aspects of the culture and behavior of their populations, and the degree of toti-potentiality of components like communities in the system as a whole. A third category of societies, "post-industrial," has been identified by Gross.[26] Such societies have fewer people who make products than people who provide services. This is the current situation in the United States and is a recent development.

2. As I have already noted (see page 747), Toyn-bee's two basic classes of societies are civilizations, of which there have been about 21, and primitive societies, of which there have been many more.[27] The latter have smaller populations, lesser geographic extent, and shorter durations of existence. In seeking the essential difference between these two types, Toynbee focused on process characteristics. Mature primitive societies, he found, are "static." The people in them imitate older generations and dead ancestors. But mature civilizations continue to change and grow.[28]

3. Steward identifies a nine-stage developmental sequence.[29] From least to most developed, these are hunting and gathering, incipient agriculture, formative, regional florescence (the early period of civilized city-building societies), initial conquest, the Dark Ages, cyclical conquests, Iron Age culture, and the industrial revolution.

4. An index of development devised by Naroll was calculated from weighted scores for three variables: the number of inhabitants of the largest community, which represents the degree of urbanization of the society; the number of occupational specialties; and the number of types of component groups or organizations, which he called "teams."[30] The population of the settlement was an independent variable; the other two were dependent variables. A major change in any of these variables is likely to be accompanied by a change in each of the others. Increased population of a settlement, for example, makes it more necessary to regulate community life and makes specialism practical (see pages 865 and 866).

As Naroll uses the term, a "team" may be a group or organization made up of three or more people clearly recognized as members. It must have formal leadership, and the leader must interact with the other members at least once a year. A team may have parts which are themselves teams. An extended-family household is an example. Naroll applied his index to 30 tribes for which relevant information was available, finding that their index numbers ranged from 12 to 58. The tribes included ancient societies like the Aztecs and Incas and others that were observed during the period between 1830 and 1940. On the basis of their index numbers he divided them into seven stages (or "lev-

els") of social development. Since he included no industrialized societies, all seven of his stages are earlier phases of societal development.

5. Working on the hypothesis that determining whether a given society was on one or the other pole of several such dichotomies really served to locate its position along a single dimension—social complexity—Freeman and Winch made a factor analysis of 48 preindustrial societies.[31] They employed six commonly discussed social variables, all of which could be scored with a minimum of interpretation. Each variable was considered to have two possible values, the first representing greater complexity and the second representing less complexity. They were (a) economy—use of money vs. barter; (b) formal legal punishment—crimes punished by government officials vs. crimes punished by the victim, his kin, or the gods; (c) religion—full-time specialized real priests (i.e., not a diviner or healer) vs. no such priest; (d) education—formal, with full-time specialized teachers, vs. informal, without full-time specialized teachers; (e) government—full-time bureaucrats unrelated to the head of government vs. part-time bureaucrats, bureaucrats related to the head of government, or none; and (f) written language—written language vs. no written language.

"Complexity" in this study is a measure of how complicated the processes of the society are, not its structures. Greater differentiation of subsystem components, a structural characteristic, is found when full-time specialists perform subsystem processes, but ordinarily information processing is also more complex. Information processing also increases in complexity when money is used and when language is written as well as spoken.

The societies in this study were selected to maximize cultural variation. The 48 societies chosen were all well enough known that adequate data were available in the Cross-Cultural Survey and the Human Relations Area Files on all six variables. The six variables formed a unidimensional array. These dichotomous measures, Freeman and Winch concluded, describe a single dimension, which they called "societal complexity."

Freeman and Winch believed that their analysis established a series of types along a scale which can be used to describe and arrange societies, permit comparison among them, and generate hypotheses for testing. They stated one such hypothesis: " . . . as a society of the least complex type became more complex, it would first adopt a money economy, then a formal legal system, full-time priests, educators, and government bureaucrats in that order, and, finally, a written language."[32]

TABLE 11-3   Scalogram Showing a Perfect Scale

SOCIETAL CHARACTERISTICS	SOCIETIES											
	Tasmanians	Semang	Yahgan	Vedda	Mundurucú	Ao Naga	Bontoc	Iroquois	Tanala	Marquesans	Dahomey	Incas
Paved streets	−	−	−	−	−	−	−	−	−	−	−	+
Sumptuary laws	−	−	−	−	−	−	−	−	−	−	+	+
Full-time service specialists	−	−	−	−	−	−	−	−	−	+	+	+
Ruler grants audiences	−	−	−	−	−	−	−	−	+	+	+	+
Political leader has considerable authority	−	−	−	−	−	−	−	+	+	+	+	+
Surplus of food regularly produced	−	−	−	−	−	−	+	+	+	+	+	+
Agriculture provides 75%+ of subsistence	−	−	−	−	−	+	+	+	+	+	+	+
Settlements of 100+ persons	−	−	−	−	+	+	+	+	+	+	+	+
Headman, chief, or king	−	−	−	+	+	+	+	+	+	+	+	+
Trade between communities	−	−	+	+	+	+	+	+	+	+	+	+
Special religious practitioners	−	+	+	+	+	+	+	+	+	+	+	+

NOTE: This represents a selected set of societies from Table 11-4 and a selected set of societal characteristics.

SOURCE: R. L. Carneiro. Scale analysis, evolutionary sequences, and the rating of cultures. In R. Naroll & R. Cohen (Eds.). *A handbook of method in cultural anthropology*. Garden City, N.Y.: Doubleday, 1970, 836. Copyright © 1970 by Raoul Naroll & Ronald Cohen. Reprinted by permission of Doubleday and Company, Inc.

6. A six-stage taxonomy of societies was developed by Coon based on "levels of complexity" as measured by three variables: the number of specialists, the amount of trade, and the number and complexity of institutions.[33] A Stage 1 society has no full-time specialists, although there are some shamans or witch doctors. There is little trade, and there is only one institution or group, the family, which is simply organized. In a Stage 6 society specialization is the rule—nearly everyone is a specialist in something. There is an almost complete exchange of products, and there are hundreds of institutions, arranged in complex and interlocking hierarchies, many with component departments.

7. One can construct a matrix by listing societies along the abscissa of a graph and societal characteristics along the ordinate. Then one can put a plus in the appropriate square for each characteristic possessed by each society. The rows of the matrix can then be arranged so that the characteristic with the most pluses is at the bottom and the one with the fewest is at the top. Also, the columns, one for each society, can be arranged with the one having the fewest pluses at the left end and the one having the most at the right. The resultant new matrix is a *scalogram*.[34] If the traits selected form a scale, the matrix has a regular stair-step profile (see Table 11-3). If the relationships among the traits and societies are not regular in this way, no scale will result. Not all societal traits scale. In order to

scale, a characteristic must in general be retained once it is adopted.

The orderliness evident in such scalograms has an evolutionary explanation:*

. . . the order in which the traits are arranged, from bottom to top, is the order in which the societies have evolved them. Those traits toward the bottom of the scalogram are earlier and simpler, and consequently more societies have them. Those near the top are later and more complex, and therefore are possessed by fewer societies. By the same token, the order on the scalogram of the societies themselves represents their relative degrees of evolution. Those toward the left have fewer traits and are thus simpler and less evolved, while those on the right have more traits and are therefore more complex and more evolved.[35]

Increase in complexity appears to be fundamental in societal evolution.

A study by Carneiro of 100 preindustrial societies rated on 354 characteristics disclosed that 90 characteristics produced a regular scale.[36] These characteristics he considered to be a main sequence of cultural evolution. It is a developmental series through which societies have usually passed. Instead of saying that societies tend to pass through the same stages, Carneiro prefers to say that they tend to evolve certain charac-

*From *A handbook of method in cultural anthropology*. Copyright © 1970 by Raoul Naroll and Ronald Cohen. Reprinted by permission of Doubleday & Company, Inc.

TABLE 11-4   Rank Order of 100 Societies from Most to Least Complex, According to the Number out of 354 Characteristics They Possess

Rank order	Number of characteristics	Rank order	Number of characteristics
1. New Kingdom Egypt (1350 B.C.)	329	51. Flathead	38
2. Roman Empire (A.D. 100)	323	52. Kiwai	37
3. Assyrian Empire (650 B.C.)	311	53. Gururumba	36
4. Aztecs	303	53. Todas	36
5. China (Han Dynasty)	299	55. Klallam	34
6. Incas	288	55. Mala	34
7. Kingdom of León	271	57. Reindeer Lapps	33
8. Vikings	225	58. Guaraní	31
9. Dahomey	202	59. Yukaghir	30
10. Ashanti	198	60. Nuer	28
11. Baganda	181	61. Tanaina	27
12. Marquesans	142	62. Tukuna	25
13. Tahitians	140	62. Comanche	25
14. Hawaiians	127	64. Tenino	24
15. Mano	126	65. Blackfoot	23
16. Bavenda	124	65. Havasupai	23
17. Batak	119	65. Canela	23
18. Fijians	114	65. Warao	23
19. Bemba	100	69. Yupa	22
20. Suku	99	69. Koryak	22
21. Tanala	94	69. Jívaro	22
22. Maori	92	72. Kamar	21
23. Pokot	86	73. Kuikuru	19
24. Acoma	82	74. Tehuelche	18
25. Rwala	79	74. Mundurucú	18
26. Creek	77	74. Gros Ventres	18
27. Tuareg	76	74. Barama River Carib	18
28. Kayan	72	78. Campa	17
29. Futunans	71	79. Yaruro	16
30. Kofyar	70	80. Cubeo	14
31. Thonga	68	81. Northern Maidu	13
32. Iroquois	64	82. Amahuaca	11
33. Bontoc	60	83. Copper Eskimo	10
33. Boloki	60	83. Chippewa	10
35. Kwakiutl	57	83. Andamanese	10
36. Molima	56	83. Ammassalik	10
37. Elgeyo	55	87. Lengua	9
38. Chiga	52	88. Sirionó	7
39. Karen	51	88. Vedda	7
40. Lango	50	88. Kaska	7
41. Ao Naga	49	91. Naskapi	6
42. Mandan	47	92. Bushmen	5
43. Omaha	45	92. Yahgan	5
43. Ifaluk	45	92. Walbiri	5
45. Nama Hottentot	44	92. Murngin	5
46. Menomini	43	96. Washo	4
47. Manobo	41	97. Semang	3
48. Tupinambá	40	97. Kurnai	3
49. Siuai	39	97. Bambuti Pygmies	3
49. Cheyenne	39	100. Tasmanians	0

SOURCE: R. L. Carneiro. Scale analysis, evolutionary sequences, and the rating of cultures. In R. Naroll & R. Cohen (Eds.). *A handbook of method in cultural anthropology*. Garden City, N.Y.: Doubleday, 1970, 846. Copyright © 1970 by Raoul Naroll & Ronald Cohen. Reprinted by permission of Doubleday and Company, Inc.

teristics in the same order. The greater the number of these characteristics in a society, the higher its degree of evolution. When the sample of 100 societies was rank-ordered on the 354 characteristics, the total number a society possessed was considered its *index of*

cultural accumulation. Table 11-4 ranks the 100 societies according to their totals. This listing agrees well with Kroeber's intuitive grading of the aboriginal cultures of North America on their "levels of cultural intensity" and with Naroll's index of cultural development, although there were variations in rank-orderings.

8. An anthropological investigation paying particular attention to cultural differences in musical communication has been conducted by Lomax and Berkowitz.[37] They used factor analysis to derive an evolutionary classification of 148 societies (called "cultures" in this study). Like Naroll, they did not include industrialized societies. A first factor-analytic computation

grouped these societies into 13 distinct clusters that were geographically continuous, historically continuous, or both (see Fig. 11-1).

An associated factor-analytic computation used 71 measures of these societies, including not only social and economic variables but also musical-communication variables relating to song styles, such as whether the society had unison or multipart singing; the nature of its rhythms, vocalizing, musical ornamenta-

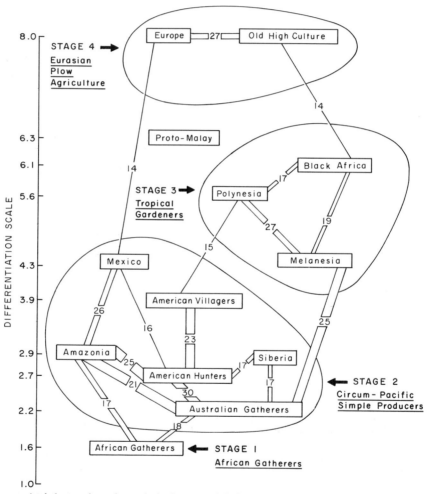

Fig. 11-1 Thirteen societal clusters from the study by Lomax and Berkowitz, arranged according to their scores on a scale of differentiation or evolutionary development, and grouped into four major types or developmental stages. The number in, and the different widths of, the connections among the 13 factored clusters from a factor analysis of 148 preindustrial societies, organized according to the measures displayed in Table 11-5, represent the degrees of their similarity as indicated by their two strongest residual bonds. No bond lower than 13 is shown. (From A. Lomax & N. Berkowitz. The evolutionary taxonomy of culture. *Science*, 21 July, 1972, **177**, 230. Copyright 1972 by the American Association for the Advancement of Science. *Reprinted by permission.*)

TABLE 11-5   Summary of Second Factor Analysis by Lomax and Berkowitz of 71 Social, Economic, and Musical Communication Measures Applied to 148 Preindustrial Societies

1. *Differentiation*
   Productive range
   Intensity of agriculture
   Percent of animal husbandry
   Size of settlement
   Number of extralocal
      hierarchies
   Inheritance of land
   Degree of stratification
   Presence of metalworking
   Task differentiation by sex
   Percent of repeated text
   Percent of precise
      enunciation
   Interval size
      Degree of melodic variation
      Severity of premarital sex
         sanctions
      Games of skill *vs.* games of
         strategy
      Rules for leadership
         succession (unique)
      Difficulty of wiving (unique)
2. *Caloric value of produce*
   Size of domestic animals
   Root *vs.* grain agriculture
   Percent of fishing
      Importance of
         milking
      Presence and
         activity of gods
      Games of skill *vs.* games of
         strategy
      Kinship system
3. *Sexual division of labor*
   In main productive activity
   In overall productive acts
   Percent collecting *vs.* percent
      hunting, fishing

4. *Organization of groups*
   Importance of leaders *vs.*
      group
   Unison *vs.* multipart
      choruses
5. *Level of cohesiveness*
   In rhythm of vocal group
   In vocal blend
   In orchestral tonal blend
   In rhythm of orchestra
   Organization of vocal
      group rhythm orchestral
      rhythmic type
6. *Noise and tension*
   Raspy vocalizing
   Nasal vocalizing
   Tight and narrow
      vocalizing
   Severity of premarital sex
      sanctions
7. *Ornamentation*
   Melisma
   Glissando
   Embellishment
   Glottal shake
   Tremolo
   Degree of melodic
      variation
8. *Community type*
   Solidarity-index
   Unilineal-bilateral
   Solidary kin organizations
      Kinship system
9. *Matri-patri*
   Female-male inheritance
      of real property
   Female-male inheritance
      of movable property
   Marital residence rules
      (F-M)
   Matrilineal-patrilineal

10. *Size and type of statement*
    Number of phrases
    Litany, strophe,
       through-composed
    Symmetry of form
    Melodic range
    Presence and activity of
       gods
11. *Orchestral model*
    Social organization of the
       orchestra
    Unison *vs.* multipart in
       the orchestra
    Organization of
       orchestral group rhythm
    Relations of orchestra to
       vocal part orchestral
       rhythmic type
12. *Vocal rhythm*
    Vocal rhythmic type
       (regular to irregular)
    Tempo
    Phrase length
13. *Dynamics*
    Soft-loud vocalizing
    Lax-forceful vocal accents
    Low-high register
       Importance of milking
14. *Part organization*
    Type of polyphony
    Social organization of
       chorus
15. *Type of family*
16. *Size of family*
17. *Segregation of boys*
18. *Female dominance in
       pottery, weaving,
       leatherwork*
19. *Position of final note in
       songs*

NOTE: The analysis yielded 14 cluster factors and 5 single factors. Each cluster consists of two or more measures. With a few exceptions, all measures in these clusters represent a single basic attribute. Indented measures either are attached with equal strength to two factors or also occur as a single factor.
   SOURCE: A. Lomax & N. Berkowitz. The evolutionary taxonomy of culture. *Science,* 21 July, 1972, **177,** 233. Copyright 1972 by the American Association for the Advancement of Science. Reprinted by permission.

tion, and melody ranges; and the social organization of its orchestras. Concerning these musical measures they found that there were:

. . . strong statistical relations between song style and social norms—for instance, that the explicitness, or information load, of song varies with the level of economic productivity, that cohesiveness of performance is an indicator of the level of community solidarity, that multipart singing occurs in societies where the sexes have a complementary relationship, and that degree of ornamentation increases with increased social stratification. Thus song appears to function as a reinforcement of a culture's social structure, and profiles of song performance can be used as indicators of culture pattern.[38]

The second factor-analytic computation produced 14 cluster factors and 5 single factors (see Table 11-5). Factor 1—differentiation—was interpreted by the investigators to provide a measure of how much evolutionary development a society shows. In Fig. 11-1 the 13 societal clusters derived in the first computation are arranged along a vertical scale according to their scores on this differentiation factor. Bonds linking these clusters were also calculated from measures of similarity among the clusters. From all these data, four types of societies representing four major stages of evolutionary development were identified. They are:

Stage 1. African gatherers. This societal type is made up of leaderless, egalitarian, nomadic bands in which the sexes have a complementary relationship. They include present-day Bushmen and Pygmies of Africa, as well as trace societies in refuge areas on every continent.

Stage 2. Circum-Pacific simple producers. This societal type probably spread from Siberia around the Pacific shores and into the Americas. The people are seminomadic, living by hunting, fishing, or slash-and-burn agriculture without animal husbandry.

Stage 3. Tropical gardeners. This societal type practices full agriculture with animal husbandry. They live in settled villages, among which there are confederacies, and they have a two-class system. There is evidence for an early continuous distribution of this type from Melanesia through Southeast and Southern Asia to East Africa and the Sudan. Later such societies spread into sub-Saharan Africa, east into Polynesia, and west into the New World.

Stage 4. Eurasian plow agriculture. This societal type has large towns, centralized government, and complex social stratification. Citizens of such societies practiced agriculture and dairying in Europe in preindustrial times and are still found in rural areas of otherwise industrialized societies where peasants follow an ancient life-style.

The eight societal taxonomies which I have just discussed all assume that many primitive societies evolve into more complex and sophisticated civilizations. Table 11-6 compares the developmental sequences of these eight taxonomies. My comparison set out in it is very tentative because the descriptions of the societal types in the various publications about them are often unclear, and I may have misunderstood some of them. The comparative timing of the various stages is uncertain. Also, the data and methods employed in creating the taxonomies differ greatly. Certain general conclusions may be made from them, however: Matter-energy processing—particularly the ingesting and producing of food by the societal ingestor, converter, and producer subsystems—is a predominant concern of primitive societies. The techniques for carrying out these processes become increasingly sophisticated as societies develop. Other sorts of matter-energy and information processing really get under way in a major fashion only after regular food surpluses dependably give leisure for them. As the number of persons in a settlement grows, the amount of specialization of labor increases, as Hypothesis 5.4.1-2 (see page 108) suggests, making possible more advanced types of society. As such development occurs, the power wielded by the decider subsystem grows, and the government becomes increasingly centralized from dispersed individual persons and groups to larger and more inclusive societal components. Also, other forms of information processing—spoken and written language and education, which are functions of the channel and net, decoder, associator, memory, and encoder subsystems of the society—become more and more important.

A factor-analytic study not based on evolutionary concepts was carried out by Cattell on 69 modern nations using 80 variables.[39] These were commonly measured social indicators on which statistics were available for these countries for the years 1837 to 1937 in various standard reference works. They included gross population, density of population, territorial area, change in territorial area from 1837 to 1937, warmth of climate, degree of governmental censorship, percentages of population of various religions, number of telephones per 1,000 population, percentage of national budget devoted to arms and defense, ratio of export to import values, expenditures on education per capita, number of language groups in the country, percentages of deaths from various causes, measures of creativity, birthrates and death rates, number of cities over 20,000 population per 1 million population, and many more. Some of these variables are similar to the variables listed at the end of each description of a subsystem in Sec. 3 of this chapter (see, for instance, pages 773 and 774) and those listed in Sec. 4, on relationships between subsystems and components (see page 828).

This research by Cattell uses methods comparable to those employed in his factor-analytic studies of persons and of groups, which I have discussed in earlier chapters (see pages 472 and 577).

Cattell's mathematical treatment of his data yielded 12 factors or dimensions along which the 69 nations differed; these can be briefly described as follows: (1) size—small *vs.* large; (2) cultural control *vs.* freedom; (3) affluence *vs.* poverty; (4) conservatism *vs.* desire for change; (5) slow *vs.* rapid pace of life; (6) science and work *vs.* emotion and relaxation; (7) ordered activity *vs.* unadapted rigidity; (8) bourgeois carefulness *vs.* bohemianism; (9) peaceful progressiveness *vs.* militaristic conservatism; (10) fastidiousness *vs.* forcefulness; (11) presence *vs.* absence of Buddhism-Mongolism; and (12) poor *vs.* good morale and morality.

How the various social indicators used by Cattell correlated with these factors can be understood by examining a few of them. Factor 1, for example, concerning the size of the system, was positively correlated with such structural variables or indicators as large geographic area, large population, and large cities, as well as such process variables as many political assassinations, many riots and local rebellions, and many different language groups. Factor 3, concerning affluence *vs.* poverty, was positively correlated with a high average real income of a society's people, a high standard of living, high expenditures on education and tourism, a large area, and a low death rate from tuberculosis. Factor 4, concerning conservatism *vs.* desire for change, was positively correlated with variables that indicated predominance of masculine values, restrictive religious customs, and few telephones.

Each country had a characteristic profile when it was scored on the 12 factors. On the basis of similarities of their profiles the 69 nations were found to group into 13 nuclear clusters or sets of countries whose profiles overlapped significantly. One of these, for instance, had a nuclear group that included Bolivia, Brazil, Costa Rica, Cuba, Honduras, Lithuania, Paraguay, Romania, and 14 fringe members, among which were Mexico and a number of other Latin American countries, Finland, Greece, and Spain.

When these clusters were examined for sets of nations with high average intercorrelations, 12 "families" of nations closely similar in their culture patterns were distinguished. Approximately 12 nations, including some which are important as world leaders, had such low correlations with other countries that they had to be considered isolates. These included France, Germany, Japan, the United States, the United Kingdom, the Soviet Union, and Mexico, as well as some small countries.

Examples of the culture-pattern families identified are Eastern European, older Catholic colonial, Mohammedan, East Baltic, and Scandinavian. The Scandinavian family included Denmark, Sweden, Norway, and Switzerland in its nucleus and the Netherlands, Iceland, and Newfoundland as fringe members. These nations had in common the characteristics of having small populations but being high in scientific industriousness, order, pace of life, and affluence. This cultural pattern contrasts with the Mohammedan pattern shared by Afghanistan, Iraq, Turkey, Arabia, and Egypt in its nucleus and Iran as a fringe member. This family was low in affluence, slow in pace of life, and low in fastidiousness and peaceful progressiveness.

When these groupings are compared with Toynbee's historically derived societies (see page 747), the correspondence is far from exact. His Islamic society is the same as Cattell's Mohammedan pattern, but Toynbee's Western society is split into several families and four or five isolates in Cattell's research.[40] Of course Toynbee's view extended over all history, while Cattell's statistics covered only the period 1837 to 1937.

In modern times, one frequently used taxonomy of societies is based on economic variables, particularly how wages and earnings are distributed and whether capital is controlled by the state (socialism or communism) or by lower levels (organizations, groups, or individual persons—capitalism or free enterprise).

From the above discussion it is apparent that many process taxonomies of societies have been proposed, but no single classification has received general acceptance. They are, of course, not mutually exclusive.

3. Subsystems

Analyses of societies, whatever the theoretical position of the analyst, agree in general as to what the essential processes are that a society must carry out. National planners often approach their task by sector analysis, which divides the total process of a society into a limited number of categories or sectors. One list of such sectors appears below.[41] It is taken from the *Standard Industrial Classification Manual* of the Executive Office of the President of the United States. Every sector is composed of a set of types of organizations or "establishments" which I listed in the last chapter (see pages 602 and 603). Each sector is followed (in italics in parentheses) by the comparable subsystem or subsystems in my conceptual system.

  1. Agriculture, forestry, and fishing sector (*ingestor*)
  2. Mining sector (*ingestor*)
  3. Construction sector (*producer*)
  4. Manufacturing sector (primarily *converter, producer*)
  5. Transportation, communications, electric, gas, and sanitary services sector (primarily *distributor, matter-energy storage, extruder, channel and net*)
  6. Wholesale trade sector (*distributor*)
  7. Retail trade sector (*distributor*)
  8. Finance, insurance, and real estate sector (primarily *supporter, input transducer, internal transducer, channel and net, decoder, memory, encoder,* and *output transducer* of information—money, credit, and title to property)
  9. Services sector (*all subsystems*)
  10. Public administration sector (*boundary, internal transducer, decider*)

This particular list of societal sectors has only a moderate similarity to my list of subsystems.

Another, quite different list of the requisite activities of societies, that of Levy, includes the following processes.[42] (Subsystems from my conceptual system that carry out comparable processes appear in italics in parentheses.)

  1. Providing for sexual recruitment and the other biological needs of members of the society (*reproducer* and all the *matter-energy processing subsystems*)

TABLE 11-6 Tentative Comparison of Eight Taxonomies of Societal Types

(1) Tönnies	(2) Toynbee	(3) Steward	(4) Naroll
Agraria or *Gemeinschaft*	Primitive society	Hunting and gathering	"Level I" (Index numbers 12–18)
		Incipient agriculture	
	Civilization	Formative	"Level II" (Index numbers 19–25)
			"Level III" (Index numbers 26–32)
		Regional florescence	
			"Level IV" (Index numbers 33–39)
			"Level V" (Index numbers 40–46)
			"Level VI" (Index numbers 47–52)
		Initial conquest	
		Dark Ages	
		Cyclical conquests	"Level VII" (Index numbers 53–60)
		Iron Age	
Industria or *Gesellschaft*		Industrial revolution	[No statement made]
Postindustrial	[No statement made]	[No statement made]	[No statement made]

NOTE: Approximate temporal order of appearance of societal types is indicated by their positions in each column, the earliest at the top and the latest at the bottom. Types opposite each other in various columns are roughly contemporaneous.

(5) Freeman and Winch	(6) Coon	(7) Carneiro	(8) Lomax and Berkowitz
Money economy	Part-time shamans are the only specialists; little trade; family only institution	Special religious practitioners	Gatherers
Formal legal system			Simple producers
Full-time priests			Tropical gardeners
Educators			
Governmental bureaucrats			
Written language		Trade between communities	Plow agriculture
[No statement made]			
	Shamans, usually part-time, are specialists, and also perhaps part-time work specialists; moderate trade; two institutions—family, and band or village	Headman, chief, or king	
		Settlements of 100 + persons	
		Agriculture provides 75% + of subsistence	
	Full-time shamans and some other specialists; increased trade, including some tools and food; 2 to 12 institutions, including ritual groups and shamans' and traders' clienteles	Surplus of food regularly produced	
		Political leader has considerable authority	
		Ruler grants audiences	
	Relatively numerous specialists; half of consumer goods except food traded; up to 24 institutions, some with stable hierarchies	Full-time service specialists	
		Sumptuary laws	
	Half of population are non-food-producing specialists; more than half of consumer goods and some food traded; up to 100 institu-tions, some hierarchical and some with component departments	Paved streets	
	Nearly everyone is a specialist; widespread trade; many institutions, with hierarchies and departments		
[No statement made]		[No statement made]	[No statement made]
[No statement made]	[No statement made]	[No statement made]	[No statement made]

Fig. 11-2 The Netherlands. Components of most subsystems of this society are identified.

Subsystems which process both matter-energy and information: Boundary , organizations defending, gua policing the national border.

Subsystems which process matter-energy: Ingestor , organizations, such as airlines, railroads, trucking co or steamship lines, which import various forms of matter-energy into the country; Distributor , national orga tions which transport various forms of matter-energy by water, road, railroad, or airline; Converter , organiz which convert raw forms of matter-energy into other forms useful to the society; Producer , manufacturing organizations which make products for the society or for export; Matter-Energy Storage , organizations like v houses, reservoirs, and electric power plants which store various forms of matter-energy; Extruder , organiz which export products of the Netherlands to other nations or eject wastes into the sea and agencies which deport unwanted persons; Motor , units of transportation or construction industry, armed forces, or space agency; Supporter , public buildings and land.

Subsystems which process information: Input Transducer , organizations that receive telegraph, cable telephone, or radar signals or foreign news from outside borders of the Netherlands; Internal Transducer  representative legislature, political party officials, or public opinion polling organization that receives communicatic and reports from all parts of the Netherlands; Channel and Net , national communications facility; Decoder , foreign office that decodes secret dispatches received from Netherlands embassies throughout the world; Associator , Dutch teaching institutions; Memory , libraries; Decider , the Queen and her government in The Hague; Encoder , governmental press secretary or speech writers; Output Transducer persons who speak officially for The Netherlands.

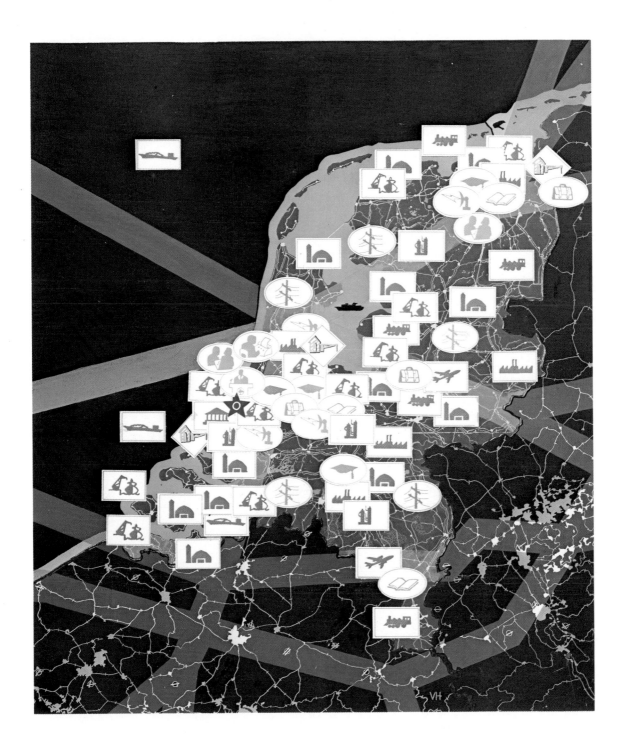

2. Differentiating and assigning roles (one process of the *decider*)

3. Communicating (*input transducer, internal transducer, channel and net, decoder, encoder,* and *output transducer*)

4. Sharing cognitive orientations (*internal transducer, channel and net, associator,* and *memory*)

5. Sharing an articulated set of goals (*internal transducer, channel and net, associator, memory,* and *decider*)

6. Regulating the choice of means (*decider*)

7. Regulating affective expression (*decider*)

8. Adequate socializing (*internal transducer, channel and net,* and *decider;* also *subsystems that carry out adjustment processes*)

9. Controlling disruptive behavior (*decider*)

10. Adequate institutionalizing (*decider*)

About half of my subsystems are embraced in Levy's first item. His last five items include various aspects of what I call "decider processes." Though there probably is general consensus between us as to what the primary societal processes are, we certainly classify them very differently, since his concern centers on decider processes.

The general theory of action of Parsons and his associates has received recognition for the trenchancy of its analyses of social processes. It is in some ways like the approaches of Levy and myself, but its categorization of the processes is profoundly different. All social systems, including societies, must solve four "independent functional imperatives" or problems, according to Parsons and Smelser.[43] To solve them, societies tend to differentiate into four "subsystems," by which term these authors refer to processes. They make it clear they are *not* discussing concrete structural subsystems, which they call "collectivities."[44] The four subsystems and the problems or "imperatives" which they respectively address are:

1. The latent pattern-maintenance and tension-management subsystem: maintaining the stability of the system and its institutionalized value system against pressures to change that arise either from outside the system or from within it.

2. The goal attainment subsystem (polity): attaining goals, *i.e.*, seeking the "situational objects" that maximize the stability of the system by controlling elements of the situation. These goal states may either maximize positive inputs or minimize negative ones. (This concept of "polity" does not refer to government in the usual sense.)

3. The adaptive subsystem (economy): carrying out economic activity, providing facilities to accomplish a variety of system and subsystem goals, and producing wealth or utility.

4. The integrative subsystem: maintaining solidarity in the relations between units of the system in the interest of effective functioning.

Each of these subsystems, in turn, differentiates into comparable subsubsystem processes.

Other classifications of social processes have been advanced, but none is widely accepted. Common agreement among societal scientists on such a fundamental issue is clearly desirable. I propose my analysis of subsystem processes for consideration by others concerned with the investigation of social systems.

The subsystems of societies are usually organizations or sets of organizations, but occasionally their processes are downwardly dispersed to groups or individual persons. In primitive societies the organizations may not be large, but in modern developed nations they are often very large and complex.

Figure 11-2 maps a society (the Netherlands) and shows its subsystems. In the harbor of Amsterdam is a symbol representing the ocean liner which was pictured in Fig. 10-1. It is one component of the ingestor subsystem of the Netherlands.

Table 11-7 identifies the components that make up the critical subsystems of a society. Inspection of this table makes it apparent that downward dispersal of subsystem processes is common in modern societies. In countries with market economies most processes are carried out by independent, competitive organizations. In nonmarket economies they may be carried out by relatively autonomous governmental organizations. In either case the deciders of such organizations are subject to more or less control by the decider of the society, which regulates various aspects of their activities (see page 861). They are controlled to some degree also by deciders of states, which wield downwardly dispersed power. Societies differ in the extent to which subsystem processes are downwardly dispersed. The central decider of most nations has the authority and power under certain conditions to assume greater control over any of these processes—by declaring martial law or by "nationalizing" or expropriating facilities like railroads or mines, for example. This is true regardless of whether these facilities are publicly or privately owned.

3.1 Subsystems which process both matter-energy and information

3.1.1 Reproducer, the subsystem which is capable of giving rise to other societies similar to the one it is in.

3.1.1.1 Structure   The organizations that establish a new society, creating and implementing the written or unwritten charter that determines the forms of its government and institutions, are reproducer

TABLE 11-7   Components of the 19 Critical Subsystems of a Society

---

3.1 SUBSYSTEMS WHICH PROCESS BOTH MATTER-ENERGY AND INFORMATION

3.1.1 *Reproducer*

Organization which creates and implements a charter for a new society, including tribal members who leave their tribe and occupy new territory, leaders who achieve national independence, constitutional convention, representatives of federating governments, successful revolutionaries; empire builder, ruler who sets up national government when empire breaks down; international peace conference, committee, and commission; may be downwardly dispersed to group; artifacts such as ship, fortification, gun, sword, pen, parchment

---

3.1.2 *Boundary*

Organization located on or near national borders; or which defends, guards, or polices national borders, such as army, navy, air force, coast guard, customs service, immigration service, public health service; diplomatic mission; unit of military bases on foreign soil; organization which processes information at national borders, such as censorship agency, security organization, national police, radio or television regulatory agency; bank or currency exchange; may be downwardly dispersed to group or individual person such as farmer, hunter, fisherman; worker that is on or near national borders or that guards embassy, extraterritorial property, ship, or plane at sea; astronauts or cosmonauts in space; artifacts such as missile base, fortification, weapon, ship, airplane, dike, gate, wall, fence, barrier, border station, radar installation

3.2 SUBSYSTEMS WHICH PROCESS MATTER-ENERGY

3.2.1 *Ingestor*

Organization which imports matter-energy, including airline, railroad, trucking company, steamship line; porters' or dock workers' union; customs and immigration service; importing firm; truck farm; agricultural, fishing, mining, or lumbering company; fishing boats; may be downwardly dispersed to group or individual person that carries out similar processes; artifacts such as port, airport, terminal, building; plane, train, truck, ship, dock machinery, agricultural machinery, fishing boat, mining and lumbering equipment

3.3. SUBSYSTEMS WHICH PROCESS INFORMATION

3.3.1 *Input transducer*

Such organization as gateway exchange for telegraph, cable, or telephone communications; ground station for satellite; foreign news service; diplomatic or consular service; military observation post at the society's border; weather bureau; exploring expedition; foreign intelligence agency; international or central bank; may be downwardly dispersed to organizational units stationed abroad, to groups such as businessmen, missionaries, research workers like anthropologists, or to individual organism or person such as traveler who visits other countries, immigrant, ham radio operator, listener to foreign broadcasts; may be outwardly dispersed to visitors to the society such as foreign diplomat, businessman, traveler, missionary, teacher; may be upwardly dispersed to supranational or international teaching mission or cultural exchange; artifacts used in receiving foreign messages such as book, publication, electronic or other device, telegraph, cable, telephone, radio, television, radar, satellite

3.3.2 *Internal transducer*

Such organization as representative legislature, political party, board of election, survey or public opinion polling organization, secret police, governmental statistical organization; advertising and public relations businesses, social-change organization, ethnic organization, labor union, grange, legislative lobby, chamber of commerce, church, service organization, news medium; bank or financial institution; may be downwardly dispersed to group or to individual person such as cartoon artist; writer of book, article, tract; "presidential listening post"; may be upwardly dispersed to organizer of a plebiscite or election under international or supranational auspices; may be outwardly dispersed to component of another society "penetrating" or strongly influencing the society in question; artifacts such as various sorts of marker, computer, voting machine, other machine used in transducing

3.2.2 *Distributor*

Organization which makes decisions about, regulates, constructs, or operates national or regional transportation facility within a country, such as governmental regulatory agency controlling transportation; highway construction company; road maintenance organization, airline, airport, bus or truck company; moving or express company; railroad; domestic shipping, power, or pipeline company; may be downwardly dispersed to group or to individual person that carries out such functions; artifacts such as road, airplane, train bus, truck, steamboat; pipeline; electric wire; tool

3.3.3 *Channel and net*

Organization which operates regional or national communications facility such as mail service, telephone, telegraph, radio, or television network; publisher of printed news medium, magazines; disseminators of book, film, phonograph record, tape recording; display advertising company; lecture bureau; organization of actors, musicians, performers; art gallery, museum, or sales company; public meeting, rally, demonstration; conference, convention, meeting; censor that decides what information may flow in the net; bank, financial institution, stock market through which money flows; often

TABLE 11-7 Components of the 19 Critical Subsystems of a Society *(Continued)*

downwardly dispersed to group or to individual person in person-to-person communication, including, in primitive society, sender of smoke signals, jungle drum communicator, runner; messenger; spokesman, fashion leader, business leader, religious leader; artifacts such as telephone, telegraph, television, or radio network; responder television, communications satellite, computer network, picture phone; mail truck, airplane, mail railroad car

3.2.3 *Converter*
Organization that converts raw materials, such as smelting plant, chemical company, sawmill, mill, slaughterhouse, meat-packing plant, oil refinery, power company; may be downwardly dispersed to group or to individual person who carries out such functions; artifacts such as building, smelter, laboratory, sawmill, mill, conveyor belt, truck, refinery, generator, tool

3.3.4 *Decoder*
Organization such as foreign office, department of state, news medium, observatory, weather bureau, financial institution, religious organization, scientific community, teaching institution; may be downwardly dispersed to group or to individual person such as presidential adviser, language translator, interpreter, cryptographer, news or market analyst; artifacts such as computer, sensing and recording device like seismograph, barometer, and radiation-detection device

3.2.4 *Producer*
Organization which makes any of a wide range of products in factory, food processing company; road or building construction company; organization which carries out building or product repair and maintenance; organization which is involved in the reproduction of the people in the society or aids them by providing health and welfare services, such as tribal moiety, certain legal, governmental, or religious organizations; organization that operates park, theater, motel, hotel, computer dating bureau, hospital, clinic, other medical facility, welfare organization, health insurance organization; many of these processes may be downwardly dispersed to group, including mating dyad, or to individual person; or outwardly dispersed to other societies; artifacts such as machine tool, diverse kinds of machines, assembly line, truck, bus, airplane, medical equipment

3.3.5 *Associator*
Organization such as school, college, university, other teaching institution, research organization, foundation, scientific or professional organization; may be downwardly dispersed to group such as student group, exploring group, research and development department; also downwardly dispersed primarily to each individual person, who does most of any society's associating; artifacts such as computer and other data-processing equipment, space vehicle, laboratory equipment

3.2.5 *Matter-energy storage*
Organization which determines storage regulations or actually stores matter-energy such as the Treasury Department, the armed services, the Energy Research and Development Administration, the Environmental Protection Agency, the Interior Department, the National Park Service; organization that operates such storage facilities as grain elevator, stockyard, water reservoir, petroleum storage depot, coal mine, oil field, rock quarry, timber tract, shipyard, food store, warehouse, waste dump, cemetery; laterally dispersed throughout a society, as well as downwardly to lower levels; sometimes outwardly dispersed to other countries and upwardly to supranational system; artifacts such as storage building, shipyard, cattle pen, reservoir, freight car, ore boat, tank, and machinery such as crane, lift, truck, mining machinery

3.3.6 *Memory*
Organization such as religious body; teaching institution; cultural, craft, or professional organization; national archive; centralized data bank, document storage and retrieval organization, national information network, scientific information service, library, museum, historical place, national monument, art gallery, bank, treasury; may be downwardly dispersed to group such as family that carries on moral and other traditions of ancestors; or to individual person such as priest, singer, storyteller, dancer, medicine man, teacher, artist, potter; artifacts such as library building and equipment, computer

3.3.7 *Decider*
Society's voters; organization such as office of emperor, king, queen, president, chancellor, prime minister, regent, first secretary, chairman of the council of ministers, premier; executive agency; legislative body, parliament; judicial body; religious organization, group such as council of state, cabinet; quasijudicial organization such as Securities and Exchange Commission, Federal Reserve Board, Interstate Commerce Commission, Federal Trade Commission; private corporation; state or local goverment, political party, research organization; may be downwardly dispersed to group or to individual person; may be outwardly dispersed to component of another society "penetrating" the society in question; artifacts such as building, computer

TABLE 11-7   Components of the 19 Critical Subsystems of a Society (*Continued*)

3.2.6 *Extruder*

Organization that sets government policy on or promotes national export trade or extrusion of wastes; organization that extrudes products (such as export company, land, sea, or air transport company, pipeline company, general trading company); organization that deports persons not wanted in the country, such as immigration service, armed services, penal authority, or national police; organization that makes decisions concerning national waste disposal policies; oil company that exports its products; waste disposal organization that extrudes wastes of regions, states, or cities beyond national borders, as into the sea; may be outwardly dispersed to another nation or to an organization in it, like a steamship company that exports products from the first nation; artifacts such as ship, barge, railroad, car, truck, airplane, dock facility, loading machinery, airport facility, pipeline

3.2.7 *Motor*

Organization in transportation or construction industry, armed forces, space agency; may be downwardly dispersed to group such as family, work group, or to individual person or domesticated animal; artifacts such as windmill, mill wheel, wagon, sailboat, truck, locomotive, ship, military tank, plane, missile, earthmoving machine

3.2.8 *Supporter*

Land and waters of the society; artifacts such as public building, public housing

3.3.8 *Encoder*

Governmental organization including chief of state and his or her office; department of state, foreign office, other executive agency; Congress, legislature, parliament; judiciary; organization that writes, creates, or produces radio or television presentation for official international broadcast; cultural mission; may be downwardly dispersed to group or to individual person such as national spokesperson like diplomat, chief of state, official who represents the society in international or supranational contacts; military leader; speech writer, propaganda writer; coding expert; translator; press secretary; teacher; technical expert; representative of news media; artist and designer of societal symbols; artifacts such as writing materials, encoding equipment, coding machine

3.3.9 *Output transducer*

Governmental organization that sends messages to another society, or international or supranational body, including chief of state and his or her office, department of state, foreign office, other executive agency; Congress, legislature, parliament; judiciary; organization that operates radio or television stations or publishes newspapers or magazines that convey messages over society's borders; organization that transmits telephone or telegraph messages over society's border; some components may be joint between the output transducer and the encoder; may be downwardly dispersed to group or to individual person including person who speaks officially for nation such as delegate to international or supranational body; governmental press secretary, public relations officer, radio operator, pilot who drops propaganda leaflets; radio technician, publisher, actor, speaker, teacher, singer, dancer, missionary, traveler; artifacts such as press release, book, art object, manufactured product, broadcasting equipment, teletype machine, telephone equipment, cable

---

components at this level. Historically, many different sorts of units have carried out such activities. Among them are tribal members who move into a new territory separated from their society by distance or natural barriers; national leaders who achieve independence of the people and their territory from rule by another society and who establish a government; constitutional conventions; representatives of governments in process of federation; members of successful revolutionary movements that impose new governmental forms upon established societies; empire builders who bring previously separate societies under a centralized government; and rulers who form governments in the vacuum created by the breakdown of empires which can no longer supply the services or mobilize the governmental power to hold their components together.

International bodies such as peace conferences that create new societies by revising national boundaries

are also reproducer components. The Congress of Vienna and the diplomats who wrote and signed the Treaty of Versailles and other treaties following World War I are examples of such bodies. Committees or commissions or an international body like the League of Nations or the United Nations may guide the formation of a new nation and act as parts of the reproducer for that society.

These processes may be downwardly dispersed to groups.

In these processes military activities may require artifacts like ships, fortifications, guns, and swords, or the task may be accomplished peacefully with pens and parchment.

[Components of a society that provide for system continuity over time by furthering and regulating the reproduction of its members are parts of the producer rather than the reproducer subsystem (see pages 778 and 779).]

3.1.1.2 Process   A new society comes into being when decider components are organized in accordance with a written or unwritten charter. Organization or reorganization of other subsystems follows as the system takes form and begins to function. New societies are always composed of elements of preexisting societies. The people are not usually brought together for the purpose of forming a society, although in modern Israel something of the sort has occurred. More usually the population has occupied the land on which it lives for a period of time before the new society is formed, either as an indigenous population or as colonists from another society. They have genetic continuity with previous occupants of the same territory and may have distinctive genetically determined characteristics. Their culture, including their language or languages, has a similar continuity over time. They and their ancestors may have been parts of successive societies in the same region extending far into the past. Many modern inhabitants of the Italian peninsula, for example, are descendants of persons who lived in the same region in Roman times, from whom they derive their culture, which has been continuously modified over the centuries.

Among primitive societies, when one clan becomes so numerous that it spreads beyond natural barriers like mountains, it may become economically as well as geographically independent.[45] It then inevitably forms a separate system which traces its ancestry back to the pioneers who led the clan members into their new country. Among the Tungus of Eastern Siberia this occurred when the population increased so that tribesmen spread out over a hunting territory too large to permit regular interaction. They then split up into separate systems or local groups, the leaders of each being the reproducers of a new system.

New societies also arise when changes take place in the relative power of components of an earlier society. Supporters of an alternative type of system organization then assume control. Empires form when a powerful society conquers several others. Federations are formed because their members perceive themselves as weak in relation to possible enemies or as lacking resources.

All societies are potentially susceptible to revolution. They always include at least a few groups which, under appropriate circumstances, could provide support for a revolutionary movement that could create a new society. Of these Etzioni says:*

Once a deviant enclave has been founded, its future development and the chances that it will become a major societal force, a transforming alternative, or perhaps even the basis of a new societal conformity, depend not only on the numbers of unsucccessfully socialized people or the extent to which the society's "education" efforts are encompassing and intensive but also on the distribution of the means between the societal units mobilized in support of the prevailing patterns and those which are deviating. Revolutions occur not so much because the deviant asset base [*e.g.*, money or political power] in itself has been greatly extended but because the asset base of the supporters of the conforming patterns is collapsing. The weakness of the governments of Russia in 1917, China in 1949, and France in 1789 was a "final" cause of the transformations of these societies.[46]

In discussing "transformation" of societies, Etzioni makes it clear that this can occur not only by revolution and sudden change in decider structure and process but also by an accumulation of small changes, although he believes that " . . . no society so far has significantly levelled its power base and stratification structure without a revolution."[47] Revolutions, however, may be carried out peacefully. Chile instituted a Marxist government under Allende without violence, although it was ended by violence. Etzioni admits that the transition in both Britain and the United States from argricultural to industrial societies constituted major peaceful transformations. †

The transition in Britain and the United States from agricultural to industrial societies entailed the transformation of all the major institutions of these two societies, including peaceful change of the state and its control and a shift of the concentration of political power from the aristocracy (in Britain) and rural collectivities (in the United States) to capitalist, urban collectivities. Now, a second transformation is in process—an expanding welfare state, government guidance of the economy and other societal processes, and mobilization of weaker collectivities. Labor governments in the United Kingdom and the participation of labor in the political processes in the United States have already transformed an "early" capitalism into "mature" (or "welfare") capitalism, and the process is still unfolding.[48]

This being the case, it is not always clear when a change in the decider represents a "new society" and at what point in the transition the society has become a new society. When a revolution sweeps away the existing order and institutes a new one with a new charter, radically changed relationships among the components, and acceptance of a different hierarchy of values—as in the French and Russian revolutions—the new system is reasonably considered a new society. On the other hand, revolutions which replace one "strong man" with another but which effect no fundamental change in the system do not represent the beginning of a new society.

In gradual transformations, new charters may or may not be written. The United States manages to fit social change into its Constitution with a minimum of amendments and a great deal of interpretation. The United States Constitution is a very general document. The constitution of the Soviet Union covers many of the same topics, being more specific on some of them. Great Britain, with no written constitution, makes laws to conform to social change and thus is continually revising its charter.

Representative *variables* of the process of reproducing are: *Sorts of matter-energy used in reproducing.* Example: The dissident minority which founded the new nation included about 5,000 men and women. *Meaning of information used in reproducing.* Example: The Declaration of Independence signaled the decision of the 13 Colonies to free themselves from British rule. *Sorts of information used in reproducing.* Example: The constitution of the newly formed nation specified a democracy with a president and council of elders. *Changes in reproducing over time.* Example: New societies in the twentieth century were formed from what had been colonies of major powers rather than by the actions of dissident groups claiming land in newly discovered areas. *Changes in reproducing with different circumstances.* Example: Breakdowns in the effectiveness of government led to the splitting up of some old, established monarchies. *Rate of reproducing.* Example: Two colonies were given independence in a single year. *Frequency of reproducing.* Example: During the sixteenth century Spain and England founded several colonies in the New World. *Lag in reproducing.* Example: The colony won its independence by a plebiscite after 50 years of political activity. *Costs of reproducing.* Example: The war of independence claimed 1,000 lives.

3.1.2 Boundary, the subsystem at the perimeter of a society that holds together the components which make up the society, protects them from environmental stresses, and excludes or permits entry to various sorts of matter-energy and information.

3.1.2.1 Structure

Matter-energy boundary. It is important in considering boundaries of societies to distinguish between the boundary of the living system and the border of the system's territory, a distinction that is particularly important at this level. The boundary, like corresponding structures at the levels of the group and the organization, varies in shape with the changing distribution in the three spatial dimensions—on the ground, in the air or in space, and in the sea—of the system's living components. Gypsy tribes live as inclusions in the territories of other societies. Since they have no territories of their own, they have no borders, only living boundary subsystems.

The land borders of a society's territory may be determined by natural features like mountains, rivers, lakes, or seas, or they may be set by surveyors carrying out international agreements or the directives of a conquering government. The borders of most modern countries are precisely delimited, although disputes about them between adjacent nations are common. Territories of neighboring primitive societies, the range in which they hunt and gather food or establish villages, may grade into each other.

All three-dimensional borders of a society's territory are boundaries of nonliving systems. They may not be distinct, as the boundaries of all living systems are. The land and water borders at shorelines and the land and air borders at the ground level are clear-cut. But all nations with a coast on an international body of water extend their official borders into it. Distances of claimed borders are from 4.8 km to 322 km. There is no agreement concerning how far into the ground borders go, or how high into space. If the claim were to the center of the earth, it would overlap other countries' claims unless the borders were perpendicular to the earth's crust. This would produce an irregular conical or pyramidal solid figure whose edges would have the shape of the boundary of the earth but would constantly diminish to a point at the center of the earth. In the sky the reverse would be true; the space within the extended perpendicular to the ground would gradually increase in area with distance above the earth. Some have suggested that each country owns the space above the earth up to the theoretical limit of the earth's atmosphere, but practically no countries have complained about the flight of missiles or satellites above them (usually thousands of kilometers), although they have often shot down planes flying above them (usually thousands of meters). The fact is that most national territorial borders are abstracted system boundaries and are set arbitrarily. They are continuous up, down, across land, and into the sea. Various rationales for setting territorial limits can be made. Differing rationales can lead to disagreement among nations and often have produced legal disputes and wars.

A society's territory is ordinarily continuous, but sometimes it is divided by the territory of other societies or by international air and water. The United States provides an example of this because Alaska, Hawaii, Puerto Rico, and its Pacific island dependencies are not continuous with its mainland.

The concept of extraterritoriality in international law defines a country's embassies and certain military posts located within the borders of other nations as its territory. Their staffs and the visitors to such areas are considered to be within the borders of that country. Conversely, extraterritorial "islands" exist in that country which belong to other nations. Ships at sea and space vehicles bearing the flag of a particular country are also considered to be its territory. At the group and organization levels, components that travel or work outside their boundaries are still considered to be members. Thus nationals of one country who are outside its territory nevertheless remain its citizens.

Organizations that occupy the perimeter of the living system, such as cities on an international border; organizations that defend, guard, or police national borders, such as armies, navies, air forces, coast guards, customs services, immigration services, and public health services; diplomatic missions; and units of military bases on foreign soil are components of this subsystem.

The subsystem may be downwardly dispersed to groups or individual persons such as farmers, hunters, fishermen, or workers living or ranging near the edge of a country; guards of embassies and other extraterritorial lands or buildings; guards of ships or planes at sea; and astronauts or cosmonauts in space.

Artifacts like missile bases, fortifications, weapons, ships, airplanes, dikes, gates, walls, fences, barriers, border stations, and radar installations of various sorts are nonliving boundary components.

Information boundary. The information boundary of a society is complex in shape, since it encompasses far-flung components like nationals traveling abroad, diplomatic missions, personnel at military posts on foreign soil, and astronauts in space who are connected to the society by information channels (see page 52). Subsystem components include some that also process matter-energy—customs organizations, for example, which may impose duty on, refuse entry to, or impound certain money, books, pictures, films, or secret documents. Censorship agencies, security organizations, national police, and radio and television regulatory agencies that monitor broadcasts at national borders are other examples. Banks or currency exchanges may be components of the information boundary, as well as of the input transducer, decoder, and encoder.

The information boundary usually has groups or individual persons as downwardly dispersed components.

3.1.2.2 Process

Mattery-energy boundary. The matter-energy boundary of a society performs the three boundary processes of (a) acting as a barrier to flows of matter-energy in and out of the system, (b) filtering matter-energy, and (c) maintaining steady-state differentials of various sorts of matter-energy between the inside and the outside of the system (see page 56).

Components of this subsystem repel citizens of other countries who are unwanted or who arrive to invade the society's territory; turn back immigrants seeking to cross the territorial boundary illegally at some point other than a legal port of entry; destroy or capture unauthorized planes that fly over the territory or ships that enter territorial waters without permission; and, in some societies, refuse tourists and other aliens permission to enter. Some nations restrict exports and ban foreign travel or emigration by certain of their citizens.

Societies may attempt to prevent entrance of harmful forms of matter-energy such as pathogenic bacteria and viruses, radioactive emissions, missiles, floodwaters, predatory insects, and the voraciously destructive piranha fish. They may refuse to permit removal of various sorts of things, like antiquities, gold, Siamese cats, or petroleum. Both inputs and outputs of unauthorized drugs may be prevented.

The boundary filtering process is exemplified by customs inspections, selective immigration policies, citizenship examinations, and quarantine regulations. Some nations allow only citizens with valid exit permits to leave the country. They may withhold passports required for reentry from those they want to keep in.

Steady-state rates of flow across a nation's boundary of particular forms of matter-energy may be achieved by setting monthly or annual quotas. Immigration into the United States is subject to such quotas. So is export of diamonds from South Africa. International agreements set import and export rates for many sorts of manufactured goods and raw materials so that markets will not be flooded with excessive amounts. Tariffs are another means of accomplishing this purpose.

Information boundary. Information arrives at the borders of a society in many forms, including letters, foreign publications, and other written materials; radio and television broadcasts from other nations; the designs of artifacts imported or brought back by travelers; ideas carried by missionaries, teachers, or others; and cultural patterns of information diffused from one area to another.

Regulation of information flows across the boundaries of societies is accomplished by two different processes, often used simultaneously. The first is censorship or some other process that filters out markers bearing certain sorts of information. The second is a more subtle process involving education or attitude training of citizens to disregard certain sorts of information already present in the society.

People believed to be carrying dangerous ideas are often turned away by border officials. In the first two decades of this century Abyssinia refused admission to missionaries and most other white men. Japan was closed to the West for centuries until the middle of the nineteenth century. Radio and television programs may be jammed; books and other printed matter may be confiscated or censored.

Societies differ in the penetrability of their boundaries to incoming information. Currency may be rigorously controlled by banks and customs officers so that, as in the Soviet Union, foreign money does not circulate within the society. On the other hand, as in Panama and parts of Canada, foreign money, *i.e.,* the United States dollar, may be quite generally accepted.

Similar subsystem processes may keep information from crossing a nation's boundary outwardly to other countries. The secrets of producing certain sorts of admired indigenous artifacts are often jealously guarded within a country. Export of currency is also restricted by many societies.

Step-function changes in cultural communications occur at some society boundaries. These may be marked where Christian and Moslem or Moslem and Hindu cultures meet, as between Greece and Turkey. The languages of contiguous societies are frequently different, although usually some individuals are bilingual in an area on both sides of the border. The need to translate or recode language restricts information flow in such areas. As Lévi-Strauss has pointed out, since communication easily crosses the boundaries of most societies, such borders " . . . constitute thresholds where the rate and forms of communication, without waning altogether, reach a much lower level. This condition is usually meaningful enough for the population, both inside and outside the borders, to become aware of it."[49]

Information reaching a society may be filtered out because all members have been educated to believe that it is wrong and dangerous. In general, if as good or as acceptable a cultural equivalent is already established in a society, a new, imported one will have little acceptance.

Studies by Deutsch show an effect of national boundaries upon flow of information.[50] Of the various possible measures of communication flows like speed, fidelity, source, or response, he selected volume, by which he means frequency of communication, for an initial study. He found that the ratio of within-boundary to cross-boundary flows in societies, as indicated by a larger number of letters written per capita, was higher with greater geographic area, larger population, and more economic, social, and cultural activity.

Domestic mail, however, always exceeds foreign. If a country's ratio is much larger or smaller than its size, number of members, and amount of letter writing would indicate, a cause can very probably be found. Mozambique, a colony, and Israel, with many relationships outside its boundary, have below-average ratios, while communist dictatorships like Bulgaria and large, less developed countries have above-average ratios.

The effect of national boundaries is the same as that of a large increase in distance between the communicators, according to Stewart, who calculates that the probability that any two people will interact decreases as the square of the physical distance between them.[51]

Hypothesis 3.1.2.2-3 (see page 93), which asserts that more information is transmitted within a system than across its boundary, and 3.1.2.2-4 (see page 93), which says that the ratio of information transmitted within the system to that crossing the boundary will be higher in a large system, both receive confirmation from these studies. Hypothesis 3.1.2.2-2 (see page 93), which suggests that more work is required to move a marker across a boundary at the input transducer than to move it the same distance on either side of the boundary, is also relevant here, although data concerning it have not yet been collected.

Representative *variables* of boundary process include: *Sorts of matter-energy crossing the boundary.* Example: The Indian government imported a herd of purebred cattle. *Meaning of information crossing the boundary.* Example: The quotation from Villon which was broadcast by Radio London indicated to the French when the 1944 invasion would begin. *Sorts of information crossing the boundary.* Example: Missionaries for a new religion received permission to teach their doctrines to members of the society. *Degree of permeability of the boundary to matter-energy.* Example: Switzerland rarely accepts a citizen for naturalization. *Degree of permeability of the boundary to information.* Example: All foreign radio and television broadcasts were jammed during the riots. *Percentage of matter-energy arriving at the boundary which enters the system.* Example: Less than 80 percent of immigrants were accepted for naturalization during a 10-year period. *Percentage of information arriving at the boundary which enters the system.* Example: Over half the foreign newspapers were censored. *Changes in matter-energy processing at the boundary over time.* Example: During the twentieth century it was necessary for all plants and animals to pass an inspection before being imported. *Changes in information processing at the boundary over time.* Example: As the government became more stable, it began to encourage the performance of music of other societies. *Changes in matter-energy processing at the boundary with different circumstances.* Example: During the epidemic of hoof-and-mouth disease, no cattle were admitted into the country. *Changes in information processing at the boundary with different circumstances.* Example: The population explosion forced the government to import new methods of agriculture. *Rate of matter-energy processing at the boundary.* Example: An average of more than 40,000 American tourists enter France each month. *Rate of information processing at the boundary.* Example: On the average, a dozen rumors a day carried by refugees were checked against the other information available. *Frequency of matter-energy processing at the boundary.* Example: The customs office was open every day during business hours. *Frequency of information processing at the boundary.* Example: News from the rest of the world reached the little society only when the fishing boats put in for water. *Lag in matter-energy processing at the boundary.* Example: On a busy day it took several hours to get the cargo cleared for entrance. *Lag in information processing at the boundary.* Example: The news of the revolution in the neighboring society was not released for a week. *Costs of matter-energy processing at the boundary.* Example: A group of four soldiers was placed at each road entering the society to look for the wanted criminal, and each man spent 4 days on this job. *Costs of information processing at the boundary.* Example: The government maintained a large staff of experts to censor personal letters of citizens before allowing them to go outside the society.

3.2 Subsystems which process matter-energy

3.2.1   Ingestor, the subsystem which brings matter-energy across the society boundary from the environment.

3.2.1.1 Structure   Inputs of matter-energy enter a society from the environment either inside or outside the territorial boundary. Ingested matter-energy includes new citizens, temporary human inclusions like tourists and official representatives of other societies, and all the living and nonliving forms of matter-energy the society imports, harvests, mines, or secures in other ways. Components include all those organizations which are engaged in bringing matter-energy that has passed the boundary filtering process through entries in the boundary. Imports arrive by air, land, and water, carried by airlines, railroads, trucking companies, and steamship lines. Porters' and dockworkers' unions; customs and immigration services (which are also boundary components); and truck farms and other agricultural, fishing, mining, and lumber companies are other ingestor components A society's ingestor usually includes downwardly dispersed components—groups and individual persons that independently carry out processes like those of

the above organizations. A society like the Soviet Union, which permits no private ownership of land, the major part of its agriculture being organized under the central decider, has few downwardly dispersed components. Others may disperse the entire process of ingesting materials from the environment to group and organization components.

Ingestor components like airlines, railroads, trucking companies, and steamship lines; porters' or dockworkers' unions; immigration services; and importing firms station appropriate units at or near openings in the territorial boundary. Others, like truck farms and agricultural, fishing, mining, or lumbering companies, are placed within the society's territory where the particular matter-energy forms with which they deal are available. Still others place ingestor components like fishing boats outside the society's territory in international waters.

The subsystem may also be downwardly dispersed to groups or individual persons that carry out similar processes.

Artifacts in this subsystem include ports, airports, terminals, various sorts of buildings, planes, trains, trucks, ships, dock machinery, agricultural machinery, fishing boats, and mining and lumbering equipment.

3.2.1.2 Process   The forms of matter-energy a society ingests depend upon its available natural resources and upon environmental variables like climate. Important also are its customs, technology, religion, wealth, and pattern of distribution of wealth. If everyone can afford caviar, as much as possible will be imported. If pork is forbidden, none will be provided. Clearly a society's matter-energy processing depends to a degree upon its information processing. Technologically advanced societies know how to exploit types of resources that primitive societies cannot use. A society must ingest, in suitable forms, sufficient amounts of matter-energy to meet the metabolic and other physical needs of its components. To this extent it is similar to living systems at the levels of cell, organ, and organism. Since human metabolism requires minerals, proteins, fats, and carbohydrates, maintenance of the society as a system requires that it ingest all these. Beyond these and other basic requirements, ingestion by societies is subject to learned preferences and prejudices of the persons in them.

Representative *variables* of the process of ingesting include: *Sorts of matter-energy ingested.* Example: Beans and rice were the staple foods of the people because they were easily grown on the land. *Degree of openness of the ingestor.* Example: No duty was placed upon imports. *Changes in ingesting over time.* Example: After tomatoes were proved to be nonpoisonous, many tons a year were grown. *Changes in ingesting with different circumstances.* Example: During the famine it was necessary to import rice for the first time. *Rate of ingesting.* Example: Thousands of tons of steel a month were imported from the industrial society by the developing nation. *Frequency of ingesting.* Example: Shipments of manufactured articles from abroad reached the island society only twice a year. *Lag in ingesting.* Example: The harvest was delayed because of scarcity of farm labor. *Costs of ingesting.* Example: Most of the physical energy of the agrarian society was spent in securing food.

3.2.2 Distributor, the subsystem which carries inputs from outside the society or outputs from its subsystems around the society to each component.

3.2.2.1 Structure   The components that make up the distributor subsystem in the United States include some governmental organizations that make centralized decisions. Among these are such regulatory agencies as the Department of Transportation, the Interstate Commerce Commission, the Federal Aviation Administration, and the Federal Highway Administration. In 1970 a new agency of the government, the Environmental Protection Agency, was formed to have authority over states, industries, and municipalities in controlling pollution. To the extent that this agency regulates transportation of wastes through the society for extrusion, it is a component of the decider of the distributor of the society. Major components of the societal distributor also include national or more restricted regional transportation facilities such as highway construction companies, road maintenance organizations, airlines, airports, bus and truck companies, moving and express companies, railroads and domestic shipping companies, power companies, and companies that build and operate pipelines for gas, oil, and other substances.

The distributor at this level does not include delivery, transportation, or road-building operations whose activities are carried on entirely within an organization such as a city or state, since these are components of the distributor of the organization.

The distributors of all modern nations have similar components, although the relative proportions of the different sorts of units vary. The United States and Brazil, for instance, prefer automotive and airline components over railroads, while some other societies have emphasized the latter. In the United States, by August 1975, 59,524 km of major interstate roads out of a projected 68,397 km had been completed.[52] This was in addition to a vast network of other federal highways. These link state and county roads and city streets throughout the society.

Geographic or other factors that hamper a society's distributor may affect other system processes: " . . . the fairly continuous line of mountains between the coastal plains and the higher, cooler interior has been a great hindrance to the growth of Brazil. The ranges form a barrier that for more than 400 years has helped keep most of the population encamped along the eastern edge of the country as if before a fortress."[53]

Societies differ as to what parts of this subsystem are controlled nationally and what parts are controlled regionally or locally. The pattern in the United States is a complex interrelationship of national, state, and local components, the former ordinarily in the decider. Other societies have state ownership of railroads, shipping, or airlines—in some cases, of all these.

Functions of this subsystem may be downwardly dispersed to groups or individual persons.

Artifacts in this subsystem are roads; vehicles like airplanes, trains, buses, trucks, and steamboats; pipelines; electric wires; and tools.

3.2.2.2 Process   Enormous quantities of matter-energy are distributed in present-day societies. The Soviet Union's more than 63,000 km of natural-gas pipelines carried more than 495 million cubic meters (m^3) of gas daily in the first quarter of 1970.[54] In the same year, 1.39 trillion metric ton-kilometers of intercity freight was hauled in the United States—40 percent by rail, 21 percent by truck, and the remainder by boats and pipelines.[55]

An efficient distributor makes foods available to Americans far from the places where the crops grow:*

Buying vegetables for a restaurant is an art which might well awe the average housewife. Lüchow's buyer must know how to choose among the wholesale arrays of farm produce displayed daily to restaurateurs, a task immensely complicated by the fact that a great many grades and qualities of every vegetable are available from day to day. Naturally, Lüchow's man selects only the top quality in any vegetable.

Asparagus must come from California or Pennsylvania, because that vegetable grows most tender and flavorful in these two garden spots. String beans must be flat and green. Carrots must come from the West Coast, because they are sweeter. This is also true of iceberg lettuce.

Large onions destined for salads, marinades, and ragouts in Lüchow's kitchen come from New Mexico and Texas. Spinach from southern Virginia is greener and has a better flavor. Idaho potatoes are best for baking, but the season qualifies potatoes and sweet potatoes from several other sections of the country for our table.

Sweet corn, bought from nearby farms, must be very young and as fresh as possible. Dried vegetables like lentils, beans, and peas used in soups are as carefully chosen for quality as their fresh brothers in the green department.[56]

*Extract from *Lüchow's German cookbook*, by Jan Mitchell. Copyright 1952 by Leonard Jan Mitchell. Reprinted by permission of Doubleday & Company, Inc.

Technological improvements and innovations have decreased the rates of movement of matter-energy through a society's distributor. Powerful truck engines and high-speed limited-access highways now make it possible for trucks to speed across the United States in 72 hours (h), although limited supplies of fuel have recently slowed traffic. Some passenger trains can travel at more than 250 km per h.

In the United States, at least, the efficiency of the distributor subsystem is not high because of uneconomic allocation of freight traffic and unused transport capacity.[57]

Hypothesis 3.2.2.2-2 (see page 94) asserts that total entropy of contents increases progressively between input and output points of a distributor. This is obviously true of many sorts of perishable freight. And certainly long-distance travelers tire. Increased rates of transport reduce entropy in perishable things like fresh foods and flowers. Refrigerated railroad cars and trucks have a similar purpose.

Entropy is an important factor in transmission of electric power over long distances. Scientists have carried out successful demonstrations of transmission of power with virtually no loss over superconductive lines.[58] Such demonstrations take advantage of the fact that some metals, one of which is niobium, become perfect conductors, i.e., lose all resistance to an electrical current, at temperatures near absolute zero. Underground transmission over refrigerated niobium on copper lines may become common by the last part of this century. If this occurs, a 345-kilovolt (kV) superconducting line 50 centimeters (cm) in diameter could carry as many as 22 conventional cables each 25 cm in diameter, more than enough to meet the present needs of New York City.

Hypothesis 3.2.2.2-1 (see page 94) says that the farther a specific matter-energy transmission passes along a distributor from the point of input toward the final point of output, the more the concentration is altered by lowering useful materials as they are taken up by subsystems and increasing the concentration of products or wastes as they are output by those subsystems. This is true of the human vascular distributor, which carries products and wastes together. It is not true of the distributor of a society, since wastes are ordinarily carried separately from useful materials.

Costs of this subsystem in the United States in 1970 amounted to almost $200 billion, nearly a fifth of the gross national product.[59]

Representative *variables* of the distributing process are: *Sorts of matter-energy distributed to various parts of the system.* Example: Oranges were carried from California to Boston, and fresh fish from Boston to the Middle West. *Changes in distributing over time.* Example: More and more goods were shipped by truck than by railroads during the 1930s and after. *Changes in distributing with different circumstances.* Example: Failure of the crop made it necessary to import onions to the West Coast. *Rate of distributing.* Example: Parts could be sent anywhere in the country in less than a month. *Frequency of distributing.* Example: The government distributed surplus food only during emergencies. *Lag in distributing.* Example: Army units could not reach the border from the capital in less than 2 days. *Costs of distributing.* Example: The roads were built with federal matching funds.

3.2.3 Converter, the subsystem which changes certain inputs to the society into forms more useful for the special processes of that particular society.

3.2.3.1 Structure The organizations which are components of this subsystem include smelting plants, chemical companies, sawmills, mills, slaughterhouses, meat-packing plants, oil refineries, power companies, and many others that convert raw materials into other matter-energy forms useful in the society.

The subsystem has many downwardly dispersed components since groups or individual persons often convert matter-energy for their own needs.

Artifacts include appropriate buildings, smelters, laboratories, sawmills, mills, conveyor belts, trucks, refineries, generators, and tools. These latter vary with the technological state of the society, from primitive axes and knives to elaborate automated equipment.

3.2.3.2 Process Societal converting processes include conversion of matter to energy, as when fuel is burned to produce heat; matter to matter, as when iron ore is changed to pig iron; and energy to energy, as when turbines convert the waterpower dammed up behind a hydroelectric plant into electricity.

All matter-energy and information processes at this and all other levels of living systems require expenditure of energy.

The most primitive societies have available only human physical energy for use in their processes. Such energy conversion is downwardly dispersed, since it is carried out in the muscular tissue of organisms. These societies have available only about one-twentieth of one horsepower (hp) per capita, assuming 0.1 hp for a man and a fraction of this for women and children. This poverty of energy limits their cultural development.[60] Progress in exploiting natural energy resources is an important determining factor in cultural evolution (see page 859). Consumption of energy by societies has risen steadily as man has become more technologically sophisticated.

As long as man's energy consumption depended on the food he could eat, the rate of consumption was some 2,000 kilocalories per day; the domestication of fire may have raised it to 4,000 kilocalories. In a primitive agricultural society with some domestic animals the rate rose to perhaps 12,000 kilocalories; more advanced farming societies may have doubled that consumption. At the height of the low-technology industrial revolution, say between 1850 and 1870, per capita daily consumption reached 70,000 kilocalories in England, Germany and the U.S. The succeeding high-technology revolution was brought about by the central electric-power station and the automobile, which enable the average person to apply power in his home and on the road. Beginning shortly before 1900, per capita energy consumption in the U.S. rose at an increasing rate to the 1970 figure: about 230,000 kilocalories per day, or about 65×10^{15} British thermal units (BTU) per year for the country as a whole. Today the industrial regions, with 30 percent of the world's people, consume 80 percent of the world's energy. The U.S., with 6 percent of the people, consumes 35 percent of the energy.[61]

The importance of energy to the matter-energy processing of societies is recognized by Leontief, who says:

To an economist "production" means anything that happens to an object or set of objects which increases its value. This action is most often a change in form, but it may be merely a change in space or in time. The basic physical condition necessary to effect any of these changes (except the last) is that energy must be applied to the material in some form. As a result change in the energy configuration of the system takes place. The application of energy is one element common to both the economist's and the engineer's concept of production. . . .

The concept of production as the application of energy to materials leads to a division of economic inputs according to their technological function. The basic distinction is between inputs which form part of the final product (materials) and those which do not (services). This distinction corresponds in general to the relation of the input to the energy transformation; the material inputs "receive" energy while the service inputs supply it. The latter will be called "processing factors." (In the case of chemical change, the material being processed may either gain or lose energy. The distinction can still be made between inputs which physically enter the final product and those which do not.)[62]

The three functions of the processing factors, he says, are to supply energy, to transform the energy which has been supplied into another form, and to control the process. The first belongs, in my conceptual system, to the ingestor. Converting processes are included in the second, along with producing. The third I would consider a process of an organization or society decider.

Besides using human work, societies supply their energy needs from the work of animals, from windpower and waterpower, and from fuels like coal, gas, and petroleum. Nuclear fuels can substitute for conventional fuels in heating water as a part of the process of generating electricity. A possible future development is direct conversion of nuclear-fusion energy to electrical power, although the technical problems could prove insoluble.[63]

The maximum efficiency of energy conversion in human muscle is 40 percent; this falls to 20 percent when the heat of recovery is considered.[64]

Comparative efficiencies of some other sorts of energy conversions are 30 percent for steam engines, 32 percent for present nuclear power plants, 41 percent for fossil-fuel plants, 50 percent for gasoline engines, 90 percent for electric motors, and a theoretical near 100 percent for the as yet unachieved direct heat to electric energy conversion.[65]

Total gross energy consumption in the United States rises more than 4 percent each year.[66] In 1969 the total consumption of anthracite and bituminous coal, lignite, natural gas, petroleum, hydropower, and nuclear power was 65,773 trillion British thermal units (Btu). [A Btu represents about 0.00029 kilowatt (kW).] This includes imports as well as inputs from the society's own resources.[67] At that time the capacity of the United States for all types of energy amounted to 10 kW for each of its citizens, as compared with a worldwide average of about 1.5 kW.[68]

The costs to societies of converting include depletion of natural resources, costs in energy required for the conversion of energy, and charges to components, like industries and households. Real costs of energy have been rising throughout the world. There have been inflationary increases, but also demands have accelerated rapidly, and supplies of fossil fuels have dwindled, creating an energy crisis. In 1968 the value of the United States output of crude oil was $9.78 billion, and the total value of bituminous coal and lignite was more than $2.57 billion. Both reflected price increases.[69] Since 1968 prices have risen dramatically.

Representative *variables* of the converting process are: *Sorts of matter-energy converted.* Example: The primitive society used tools shaped from stone. *Percentage of matter-energy converted.* Example: By 1975 the society had burned over half its known petroleum resources. *Changes in converting over time.* Example: Nuclear fuel gradually replaced fossil fuels during the last quarter of the twentieth century. *Changes in converting with different circumstances.* Example: The society smelted iron for tools to replace stone axes after contact with a more advanced culture. *Rate of converting.* Example: The total output of flour from the society's mills was a million tons a year. *Frequency of converting.* Example: The sacred trees could be cut down only once a year. *Lag in converting.* Example: A nationwide strike shut down all blast furnaces for a month. *Costs of converting.* Example: Electric energy generated by a nuclear-fusion reaction is expected to cost less than energy generated by a nuclear-fission system when development is complete.

3.2.4 Producer, the subsystem which forms stable associations that endure for significant periods among matter-energy inputs to the society or outputs from its converter, the materials synthesized being for growth, damage repair, or replacement of components of the society or for providing energy for moving or constituting the society's outputs of products or information markers to its suprasystem.

3.2.4.1 Structure Organizations which are components of a society's producer include those concerned (a) with manufacture and repair of artifacts and (b) with promotion of growth, replacement of parts, and continuity over time of the society's subsystems, as well as with the health and well-being of human subcomponents—the maintenance and repair, or health care, of human beings that make up the living system.

(a) Components of the first sort in modern industrialized societies are combiners of matter-energy like factories of innumerable kinds, producing a vast range of products from automobiles to zippers; food processing companies; road and building construction companies; and repair and maintenance organizations like the ones that fill chuckholes in pavements, modernize buildings, fix appliances, and keep machinery in working order. Components of this sort in less developed societies are, of course, less complex. The producer subsystems of primitive societies usually have specialists in crafts like basket weaving, pottery-making, and fabrication of weapons. Often they disperse these activities downwardly to groups or individual persons.

(b) Inclusion of components of the second sort in this subsystem requires explanation. Growth of the society and continuity from generation to generation depend upon reproduction of the people that participate in its subsystems. For this reason, those components concerned with assuring such growth and continuity might reasonably seem to belong to the reproducer of the society. I have placed them in the producer, however, because the reproducer at this level reproduces societies, not organisms. Just as production of materials for growth and replacement of parts of an organism is downwardly dispersed to the cells, which carry out fundamental organic syntheses and, by dividing, produce growth and replacement parts (see page 239), so replacement of human units of societies is downwardly dispersed to mating dyads. The processes at both organism and society levels are under the control of components of the higher-level system. In the case of organisms, the genetic material and neural and endocrine components of the organism control the flows of matter-energy involved in production. In the case of societies, reproduction of members is carried out subject to laws and customs of the society, under the control of specific institutions and organizations.

Societies differ greatly in the kind of components they have in their producers which relate to reproduction of human beings and to their health and welfare. Tribal moities, that is, divisions of the society from which mates may be chosen, are commonly components of primitive societies. Certain legal, governmental, and religious organizations function as components of the producer of industrialized societies, exerting controls upon societal growth and continuity from generation to generation. Organizations that operate parks, theaters, motels, and hotels, and even computer dating bureaus, facilitate not only recreation, which relates to health and welfare, but also courtship and the sexual activity essential to the production of new generations. Components concerned with the health and welfare of people in the society include hospitals, clinics, and other medical facilities; welfare organizations such as a social security agency, aid to dependent children, and public health services; private social agencies; and public and private health insurance organizations.

Downwardly dispersed components are common in this subsystem. Organizations sometimes produce the parts necessary for their products and often have repair facilities for many of their artifacts as a part of their own producer subsystems. Besides the downward dispersal of organism reproduction, some societies disperse the health and welfare services downward to individual physicians or to religious groups which take care of their own.

Most societies disperse part of this subsystem outwardly to other societies from which they purchase manufactured goods. This is true of agrarian societies which must depend upon industrialized societies with which they are symbiotic for production of artifacts.

Many sorts of artifacts are used by the producer subsystems of societies, including machine tools, diverse kinds of machines, assembly lines, trucks, buses, airplanes, and medical equipment.

3.2.4.2 Process I shall discuss the two sorts of producer processes separately.

(a) *Production of artifacts.* Societies produce goods for use within the system and for export to other societies. Among the factors that interact to determine the amounts, rates, and character of the output from a society's producer are the nature and availability of raw materials and energy sources, the availability of importable matter-energy, foreign and domestic demand for its products, the availability of means of transport of products to the source of demand, costs of producing and other relevant processes, and cultural determinants, like the artistic skills of members and the available technology.

The extent of development of a society's technology determines not only what sorts of things it is capable of converting or producing but also how efficiently it can carry out such processes. Input of technical information to a society can quickly bring about a step-function change in all aspects of matter-energy processing including producing. Technological progress in the American economy is a case in point. With increased use of machinery and improvement of the efficiency of machines, the economy has achieved a steady decrease in the number of man-hours and the amount of plant and equipment required for each unit of output since 1880. Leontief says:

Looking back, one can see that 1910 marked the real turning point in this country's economic and social development. That was the year when the last wave of immigration reached its crest; the year, also, when our rural population began to decline in absolute terms. Between 1890 and 1910 our national input of human labor had shot up from 28.3 million standard man-years to 42.5 million. Then in 1909 the model-T Ford began to roll off the first continuous production line. This great shift to mass production by machine was immediately reflected in shorter hours. In the next decade our manpower input increased by only one million man-years, and after 1920 it leveled off and remained almost constant until the early 1940's. Even at the peak of the recent war effort our total labor input, with an enormously larger population, was only 10 percent greater than in 1910. Automatization will accelerate the operation of forces which have already shaped the development of this country.[70]

(One may add that two distinguished physicians, Roger Lee and L. J. Henderson, agreed that 1910 was the first year in which a visit to an internist was more likely to effect a medical cure than not.[71]) The year 1910 was therefore important for two disparate producer processes.

(b) *Maintenance and repair of the living system of the society.* Modern societies, in general, recognize that a healthy, vigorous society depends upon healthy human components. Traditionally, kings were expected to have concern for even their lowliest subjects and to dispense largesse and their healing touch on ceremonial occasions. The concern of current societies is ordinarily expressed in programs to combat poverty and disease and to assure children of necessary care. Societies with socialist or communist ideologies, like the Soviet Union, provide more or less well for their nationals throughout their entire lives. Some other countries—England, for example—also undertake "cradle-to-grave" social security and tax-supported, government-administered health care.

Health and welfare processes are less centralized in many other societies. In the United States these processes are carried out by agencies of cities, counties, states, and the federal government as well as by private social agencies, hospitals, religious organizations, insurance companies, and individual practitioners of medicine and other specialties. This widely dispersed responsibility does not always accomplish all its purposes because persons in the society cannot agree upon fundamentals like the causes of poverty and the obligation of the central government to concern itself with such problems. It is a problem of value conflict (see page 804).

Societies invariably regulate mating among members in some way. The transmission of genetic information is specialized to certain age groups and to certain sorts of pairs of parents.[72] Even though it is a widely dispersed process (which has the effect that only widespread trauma to a society can seriously impair it), law and custom prescribe along what channels genetic information may flow, contributing importantly to the structure of society by determining who become mates. Societies have varying patterns of permissions, prohibitions, and obligations based upon marital status, kinship, social status, race, and various special circumstances. Societies commonly frown upon children begotten out of marriage. Kinship regulations, which appear in all societies, take the form of incest taboos and requirements to choose mates from particular parts of the society or outside the society. The closeness of genetic relatedness is not the only factor considered, for nearly all societies forbid marriage between adopted brothers and sisters.

Most societies, however, also have restrictions upon marriage to outsiders or to others who are too different. Approved marriages seem to be those which will least upset the equilibria of the parents.[73] This usually means a mate whose class and institutional affiliations are similar. For instance, in the Italian section of Boston, a young man's preferred mate was found to be a virgin related to one of his friends or, distantly, to him.[74] In many societies, a widow marries her former husband's brother, or a widower marries his dead wife's sister. And a father may send his daughter to an expensive college chiefly so that she will marry a boy from "the right people." Often societies prescribe special behaviors among members of a reproducing subsystem. These vary widely, and many feature obligatory joking and extreme license. Class differences were found by an American survey to determine both sexual behavior and the way mates are selected.[75] In the American and British upper classes, who one's ancestors were is more important than one's own achievement.[76] This is not so in the middle and lower classes. This has made the upper class a highly stable intermarrying group, at least until recent years, when the opprobrium associated with marrying "out of one's station" has lessened. This class consciousness determines mate selection in all classes. A survey of Elmstown, a small city in the United States, found that members of five distinguishable social classes there chose their mates with marked consideration of class.[77] Class differences in fertility were also found, related to such factors as age at marriage, percentage of the class who ever marry, and extent of use of contraception.[78] Persons who live near one another have a marked tendency to intermarry. This is true in mountain valleys, but there are also communities closely united by kinship of 1,000 to 2,800 individuals in urban areas like Lyon, Bordeaux, and Paris in France.[79] These are about the size of intermarrying communities in primitive societies. Surprisingly, their size is not greatly affected by the increasing complexity of modern society.

Among the *variables* in the producing process are: *Sorts of matter-energy produced.* Example: The economy depended greatly upon the production of heavy machinery for export. *Quality of matter-energy produced.* Example: The country specialized in cheap copies of better-made European goods. *Percentage of matter-energy used in producing.* Example: Over 50 percent of all cranberries grown in the United States are used in canned or frozen products. *Changes in producing over time.* Example: As contact with a more advanced culture continued, the little society's production functions reflected a more efficient technology. *Changes in producing with different circumstances.* Example: As much energy as could be mobilized by the society was put to work rebuilding after the devasting earthquake. *Rate of producing.* Example: All the factories worked round the clock to turn out twice as many fighter planes per day as had been produced before. *Frequency of producing.* Example: All the catsup made in the society was bottled by the canneries in August and September each year. *Lag in producing.* Example: During the annual model change the entire American automobile industry suspended production. *Costs of producing.* Example: The underdeveloped nation could not produce its own machinery at a cost low enough to compete with imported machines.

3.2.5 Matter-energy storage, the subsystem which retains in the society, for different periods of time, deposits of various sorts of matter-energy.

3.2.5.1 Structure   Organizational components of the matter-energy storage subsystem of the United States include some governmental agencies which determine storage regulations or store matter-energy. Parts of the Treasury Department, which stores gold and paper for markers for monetary information; the armed services; the Energy Research and Develop-

ment Administration, which stores uranium and other atomic fuels; the Environmental Protection Agency, which controls waste storage; the Interior Department, including the National Park Service; and many others are examples. Other components are organizations that operate grain elevators or stockyards, water departments with reservoirs, petroleum storage depots, coal mines, oil fields, rock quarries, timber tracts, shipyards, food stores, warehouses, waste dumps, and cemetaries. Components of this subsystem in other large, modern societies are comparable.

Matter-energy storage is laterally dispersed extensively to be readily available through the society, as well as downwardly through the society, since the society and systems within it at each lower level store for their own needs. It is outwardly dispersed to another society when a nation uses surplus foods, drugs, or medical supplies stored by another nation during disasters and wars. When supranational systems stockpile goods for use by member nations, as when UNICEF provides clothing and medicine for suffering children, storage and retrieval of the materials for each nation are upwardly dispersed.

Artifacts in the subsystem are buildings housing all sorts of stores, facilities like shipyards, cattle pens, reservoirs, freight cars, ore boats, tanks and machinery of various sorts used in storage and retrieval processes, like cranes, lifts, trucks, and mining machinery.

3.2.5.2 Process   By storing matter-energy of innumerable kinds, societies assure adequate supplies for distribution to components equalizing matter-energy flows within the system over changing seasons, changing demands, and alterations in ingesting caused by variations in crop yields, strikes, or failure of an import to arrive from another society. Storage of equipment like aircraft, ships, and defensive weapons improves a nation's strategic position in bargaining with other societies and reduces lag time for adjustment processes in response to threat from outside the system (see page 834). Storage of strategic metals and fissionable materials increases a country's power and independence in negotiations with other nations. The United States, for example, holds enough copper to control international markets for this important metal. Storage of gold by societies continues to be important even though the international monetary system is no longer on the gold standard. Under various circumstances societies may "store" different classes of people in federal prisons, refugee camps, sanatoria, nursing homes, or other specialized facilities.

(a) Storing and maintaining in storage.   What quantities of matter-energy are stored in organization components of the society level storage subsystem is determined by societal deciders in consideration of

projected needs for the stored materials. Matter-energy storage is an aspect of some societal adjustment processes, as when a government purchases farm crop surpluses to help farmers keep up the price of their produce. Uses are later found for the stored materials, or they are occasionally merely allowed to deteriorate in storage.

The location of storage is often near the place of its intended use. In the United States ships and aircraft may be stored in decentralized areas on the two coasts. Very valuable or strategically important things are often placed a long distance away from territorial boundaries, in the center of the country, for greater protection. Switzerland, for instance, keeps stores of military hardware deep in its mountains where they cannot easily be reached by invaders. Missiles are stored underground in many places in the United States and the Soviet Union.

Long-term and short-term stores may be carried out separately, with greater protection and less immediate availability for the long-term stores. "Mothball" fleets are examples of long-term stores. They are composed of ships not ready for service.

Societies store very large quantities, often over long time spans. The exact mathematical programming of storage sometimes found in organizations is not usual in societies. The total storage of important items in a country includes not only what is held in societal facilities but also what is stored by component organizations as well as groups and individual persons. In the case of failure of a necessary input, the length of time a society can go without experiencing strain depends upon the sizes and availabilities of all these storage sources.

A country's natural resources represent storage upon which each succeeding generation draws. Societies have been slow to recognize that forests, mineral resources, oil and coal deposits, and fresh water are not limitless. The United States has available a dependable natural supply of fresh water estimated at 2,450 billion (2.45×10^{12}) liters (l) per day. This cannot be appreciably expanded.[80] By the year 2000 projections indicate that demand will reach 3,800 billion (3.8×10^{12}) l per day. The excess will have to be met by finding new sources of water or by reusing water. As a means of preserving the natural water supply, the United States passed a Water Quality Act in 1965 and a Clean Water Restoration Act in 1966 which set water quality standards and limited extruding by organizations into the water supply (see pages 839 and 840).

Supplies of coal and petroleum cannot increase, although not all have been discovered. At present rates of use, these can be exhausted in time. Forests, however, can be cared for and protected so that trees are harvested without destroying the forest as a natu-ral resource. Planting new forests to replace those which are cut down is a form of storing this resource for the future.

(b) *Loss from storage.*   Each of the great number of different sorts of matter-energy stored by societies has its own rate of loss. Entropy affects gold reserves too slowly to be important. But grains and other foods deteriorate, and within a definite number of years, different for each type and for various storage conditions, the food is no longer usable.

(c) *Retrieval from storage*   Governments may limit the use of natural resources in order to prevent too rapid use. Protection of wild animals from excessive hunting or careless exploitation and protection of forests from fire are examples of this.

In using natural resources, societies ordinarily first use up those which are relatively easy to get and those which give a high yield. High-grade ore lying near the surface is mined before deeper lodes. As supplies dwindle, low-grade ore is mined that yields less metal and requires greater energy to extract.

Costs of storage at this level include the costs of maintaining storage areas; of putting matter-energy into storage, protecting it, and withdrawing it; and of loss and obsolescence.

Among the *variables* in the process of storing matter-energy are: *Sorts of matter-energy stored.* Example: The remaining bison were kept in a national park. *Total storage capacity.* Example: All the elevators in the country could hold barely enough grain for the winter. *Percentage of matter-energy stored.* Example: More than half the titanium mined in the year was bought and held by the government. *Place of storage.* Example: The gold was stored in Fort Knox. *Changes in storing over time.* Example: After several years the surplus butter deteriorated until it could no longer be used. *Changes in storing with different circumstances.* Example: Storage of scrap metal increased during the actual shortage. *Rate of storing.* Example: Hundreds of thousands of trees a year were planted in national forests. *Lag in storing.* Example: Because of the national holiday, the machines were not moved into the government storage areas for 24 hours after they were delivered. *Costs of storing.* Example: The government built an underground storage facility for atomic bombs at a cost of $100 million. *Rate of breakdown of organization of matter-energy in storage.* Example: Mold destroyed 100 metric tons of grain a year in government elevators. *Sorts of matter-energy retrieved.* Example: During the famine the supply of stored rice was passed out to the people. *Percentage of matter-energy retrieved.* Example: It became too expensive to work the mines under the labor conditions in that society after 59 percent of the coal was removed. *Order of retrieval.* Example: The most recently stored food was used first, but as the emergency continued, some which was old and partly deteriorated had to be used. *Rate of retrieval.* Examples: Forests in the national parks were cut at the same rate that reforestation was carried on. *Lag in retrieval.* Example: Suffering was widespread in the society by the time relief supplies were taken from the depots and distributed. *Costs of retrieval.* Example: A new government agency was created, and funds were voted by the legislature to mine fissionable materials on the society's territory.

3.2.6 Extruder, the subsystem which transmits matter-energy out of the society in the forms of products or wastes.

3.2.6.1 Structure   Societies   ordinarily   have structurally distinct components for extruding products, wastes, and human subsubcomponents and inclusions (*e.g.,* illegal immigrants). Those concerned with product extrusion include such organizations as export companies; land, sea, and air transport companies; and pipeline companies. Societies with highly centralized deciders, like modern communistic nations, have components responsible for product extrusion in the central decider. Japan centralizes export policy under a Supreme Trade Council headed by the Prime Minister. In addition, the Ministry of International Trade and Industry, a government-owned export promotion company, and a unique form of organization known as a *soogoo shoosha,* or general trading company, belong to the extruder as well as to the other subsystems.[81]

Immigration services, units of the armed services, penal authorities, and national police are components which extrude or deport aliens from the territory of the system.

Nations have only recently begun to add to their structure components concerned with extrusion of wastes. So far these have to do almost wholly with the extruder subsystem's decider processes concerning policies about waste disposal. The Environmental Protection Agency of the United States, formed in 1970 by amalgamating 15 separate components concerned with water quality, atomic radiation standards, licensing of pesticides, building sewage collection and treatment facilities, and other extruder processes, is an example.

Some organizations transport their own products out of the society as well as out of the organization, as an oil company does when it carries its oil to other societies. Also, a large number of regional, state, or city environmental agencies, boards, councils, or departments for environmental protection extrude wastes from the society as well as the region, state, or city, perhaps by dumping them at sea.

A process is outwardly dispersed when, for example, the tankers of another society, or some organiza-

tion in it, enter a nation's territory to carry away oil.

Artifacts in the subsystem include ships, barges, international railroads, cars, trucks, airplanes, dock facilities and loading machinery, airport facilities, and pipelines.

3.2.6.2 Process   Extrusion of products by a society affects various adjustment processes within the society (see pages 835 to 840) and among components of the suprasystem (see page 926). Because of the political and economic importance of exporting, societies ordinarily exercise control upon the type, quantity, and destination of exports. Export of some sorts of products, such as strategic metals, may be restricted. Export licenses are often required.

Referring to unwanted people as "wastes" is repugnant, but the process of getting rid of political dissidents or criminals by deportation or execution or of eliminating unwanted infants and unfit or aged people, as some societies have done, is comparable at this level to waste-extrusion processes at lower levels. So is extrusion of undesirable aliens or illegal immigrants. Disposition of dead human beings is more obviously an extruder process. All societies accompany burial or other disposal of their dead with ceremonies.

Although concern with environmental pollution has been expressed for a century, the attempt by societies to cope with the problem of wastes extruded by their component organizations is largely a phenomenon of the second half of the twentieth century. Most societies have not had any semblance of an organized extruder subsystem. Recently a few are beginning to, although in general most extruding is still dispersed downward. Increases in the amounts of matter-energy extruded by such components, as a result of population growth and industrial expansion, are forcing the development of society-level extruder structures. The underlying problem at this level, as Deutsch makes clear, is one of scale.[82] In a natural ecosystem, wastes are recycled through a chain of organisms. An animal's excretions, extruded into the environment, are converted for use in the metabolism of bacteria and plants, as are dead organisms. Since natural controls on population growth and spacing of individual organisms exist, waste which the environment cannot recycle does not accumulate. A balanced-life aquarium is a miniature example of such a natural system. To a large extent this balance existed for groups, organizations, and even small societies as long as the environmental capacity for waste disposal remained large in proportion to the quantity of extruded matter-energy. Even a good-sized city had no serious problem as long as it was surrounded by rural areas. Present-day industrialized societies, however, are very large in relation to a region's resources for recycling wastes.

They include within their boundaries much of the environment into which wastes are extruded. As the number of components of the living subsystems and the number of artifacts increase, this environment becomes more and more nearly saturated with wastes. While some discarded matter-energy—like particulate matter in the air, radiation, sewage extruded into streams, or garbage dumped at sea—does go outside the society's territory, much of it remains inside the system where it can poison human, animal, and plant organisms. Increased extrusion by societies into the environment outside the system's territory results in deterioration of the quality of all the earth and its atmosphere (see page 926).

Costs of extruding include not only the money costs of machinery and other components of the subsystem but also the costs to the society of extruding by its lower-level components. Societies are increasingly undertaking more responsibilty for matter-energy internal adjustment processes intended to neutralize or render less noxious wastes that cannot be extruded, and they are seeking new technologies which diminish pollution (see pages 837 to 840).

The *variables* of the process of extruding include: *Sorts of products and wastes extruded.* Example: Japan exports cameras, automobiles, color television sets, and thousands of other sorts of manufactured items, including whole factories. *Percentage of products and wastes extruded.* Example: Fewer than 1 percent of the immigrants were eventually deported. *Changes in extruding over time.* Example: Later in the revolution, dissident members of the society were not permitted to go into exile. *Changes in extruding with different circumstances.* Example: Because of a drought, the United States exported less wheat in the summer of 1974. *Rate of extruding.* Example: Hundreds of tons of cattle a day were sent from Argentina to Europe. *Frequency of extruding.* Example: The country deported undesirable aliens daily. *Lag in extruding.* Example: After the deportation order was signed, the man had 30 days to appeal. *Costs of extruding.* Example: The government appropriated $200 million for new sewer construction.

3.2.7   Motor, the subsystem which moves the society or parts of it in relation to part or all of its environment or moves components of its environment in relation to each other.

3.2.7.1   Structure   The organizations in the transportation industry are components of this subsystem. Construction companies are joint components of motor and producer subsystems since they move earth and other parts of the environment. The armed forces are primarily motor components since they implement some sorts of societal decisions by the use of physical force. They are joint components with the matter-energy boundary. Space agencies may also move parts of the society beyond its borders.

Primitive societies disperse the motor downward to families, work groups, other groups, or individual persons. The motive power in such societies is human muscular work. Somewhat more developed societies use domesticated animals, wind, or water to supply energy for their motors.

Artifacts of the motor subsystems of less developed societies include windmills, mill wheels, wagons, and sailboats. Industrialized societies use powered machines such as trucks, locomotives, ships, military tanks, planes, missiles, and earthmoving machines.

3.2.7.2   Process   History records some great movements of people over long distances that can be considered movements of whole societies. The book of Exodus tells the story of one such migration.

Societies more commonly move human or other components with relation to the environment, either inside or outside their territories, using the motive power of human or animal muscles or machines. Primitive societies that practice slash-and-burn agriculture regularly move their villages within their home territories. Nomadic peoples, like the Lapps, who follow their reindeer herds to seasonal pastures, also move their settlements within a large home area. The American West was settled by expansion of the living system within its territory as people made their way on horseback, by covered wagon, or on foot to claim homesteads.

Components move outside the territory when armies are sent to invade other societies or explorers penetrate unknown regions, like the American continent or the moon.

Large societies move various parts of the environment in relation to one another. Such feats as systems of dikes to hold back the sea or irrigation canals to bring water from mountains to the desert are by no means confined to modern societies. Advanced technologies for converting and applying energy have, however, extended the power of societies to move environmental components and have greatly increased the rate at which such engineering can be done. Mountains are literally moved out of the path of distributor components, such as roads, by organizations specialized for this work. Only developed technological societies like the Soviet Union and the United States can mobilize sufficient energy and equipment to send components into space.

Costs of moving are the costs of the energy supply, machines, and human labor.

Representative *variables* of the moving process are: *Sorts of movements made.* Example: The society diverted a river to provide water to a desert settlement. *Changes in moving over time.* Example: The rush westward slowed toward the end of the century. *Changes in moving with different circumstances.* Example: The invention of new solid rocket fuels made it possible to send components of the society into space. *Rate of moving.* Example: The interstate road was cut through the mountain at the rate of about a quarter of a mile a day. *Rate of output of work.* Example: The rocket engines developed enough thrust to lift the spacecraft beyond the pull of gravity at 4,200 km per hour. *Frequency of moving.* Example: The Lapps moved their reindeer herds in the spring and fall. *Duration of moving.* Example: Moses grew old and died before the Israelites reached the promised land. *Lag in moving.* Example: Two more disastrous floods occurred before landfill raised the level of the shore above the danger level. *Costs of moving.* Example: The cost of subjugating a neighboring small nation amounted to about 5 percent of the budget of the invading country for that year.

3.2.8 Supporter, the subsystem which maintains the proper spatial relationships among components of the society, so that they can interact without weighting each other down or crowding each other.

3.2.8.1 Structure   The land upon which a society is built and its waters constitute its primary supporter.

Artifacts include public buildings and other structures such as bridges, docks, and storage facilities like tanks and grain elevators in the society.

3.2.8.2 Process   The nature of the land that supports a society is an important determiner of the spatial relationships among the components. A society's climate and size and the arrangement of its hills, plains, valleys, and bodies of water all affect the distances between societal components, the pattern of their distribution, and the sorts of houses and other buildings that are erected. The supporter can be changed significantly—bodies of water can be altered by dams and locks, swamps can be drained, and new land can be claimed from the sea.

Societies ordinarily either own all national lands, as in communist countries, or can claim a right of eminent domain over private land, as many capitalist nations do. Many countries have extensive public lands and agencies, like national parks services, to protect and maintain them.

Societies also maintain public buildings, including imposing edifices to house legislative bodies, palaces for heads of state, and many others. In the United States, the General Services Administration maintains these.

Most buildings in capitalist societies are under the control of various sorts of local components such as industrial organizations, businesses, states, or cities. Real estate boards, zoning boards, and institutions that provide money for mortgages determine to a large extent where housing will be built, what sorts of structures (such as single-family dwellings or apartments) are constructed, and who will own them. Governments undertake to build public housing, usually for low-income families, or to provide funds to encourage and subsidize private construction of homes when the housing provided by the downwardly dispersed components is unsatisfactory.

Representative *variables* in the supporting process include: *Strength of the supporter.* Example: A large part of the country was located on desert land, on which skyscrapers could never be built. *Cost of supporting.* Example: Congress voted funds for a public housing program.

3.3 Subsystems which process information

3.3.1 Input transducer, the sensory subsystem which brings markers bearing information into the society, changing them to other matter-energy forms suitable for transmission within it.

3.3.1.1 Structure   The input transducer of a modern society has numerous component organizations. These include gateway exchanges for telegraph, cable, and telephone communications, through which messages from foreign lands flow into the country; ground stations for satellites; foreign news services; the foreign office or department of state, including the foreign minister or secretary and diplomatic and consular services; parts of the armed services that man observation posts at the society's border; the national weather bureau; official exploring expeditions like the Soviet and American moon missions; foreign intelligence organizations such as the Central Intelligence Agency of the United States; and international or central banks.

Components downwardly dispersed to the level of the group are organizational units stationed abroad such as executives or sales personnel of business or industrial corporations, missionaries representing religious organizations of the society, and research workers like teams of anthropologists representing universities, museums, or institutes.

Some components are downwardly dispersed to the level of the organism, such as travelers who visit other societies, as Marco Polo did; immigrants into a society; and ham radio operators or others who listen to foreign broadcasts.

Components of other societies, like foreign diplomats, sales representatives of foreign businesses, travelers, missionaries, and teachers employed or visiting in a society, may be outwardly dispersed components.

Teaching missions or cultural exchanges from supranational or international organizations are upwardly dispersed components.

Artifacts are the electronic or other devices used in receiving foreign messages, including books, publications, telegraph, cable, telephone, radio, television, radar, and satellite.

3.3.1.2 Process

Information enters societies from outside their boundaries in the form of communications from components of other societies; communications from members of the society who are or have been outside the society; natural signs of states of the environment like the threat of a thundershower or a red sky in the morning; behavioral signs of other societies, like evidences of nuclear testing in the atmosphere; cultural elements gained from contacts with other societies that differ in the forms of their artifacts, amount of mechanization, religion, political ideas, or social behavior; and money and credit.

The various components of the input transducer are located in widely separate places but are so arranged that each receives messages from a specific kind of source or sources and transduces them into the channel and net of the society at appropriate nodes. Diplomatic missions, for example, receive messages from formally designated components of output transducers of other societies or by observing the behavior and the information flows of the system in which they are stationed. They transduce information into channels that lead directly to high-echelon decider components, such as a foreign minister or secretary of state. Reports are usually written and transmitted through official diplomatic channels. In delicate or tense situations, however, the ambassador may return to his home capital to report in person to the chief of state or other high official. Components of this sort are enjoined from using other than prescribed channels. When they "leak" foreign information to news media of their home country or talk to the wrong people about official business, they are acting as downwardly dispersed organismic components of the input transducer.

News agencies transduce information directly into a nation's channel and net subsystem through radio, television, or newspapers.

Downwardly dispersed components at the organization level transduce information in their reports to the deciders of their own organizations, from which it enters societal channels in the form of published reports, speeches, or private communications, sometimes to societal decider components.

Group and organism level components transduce information to communications media or person-to-person. Some of these communications may be propagated through the society's net as rumors. Communications need not be explicit: By adopting a particular style of dress, a new way of cooking, or a distinctive form of artistic expression, people transmit cultural information to their society.

Transductions from these different sorts of components vary in amount of distortion and other characteristics of transducer function (see below). They differ also in the probability that a communication originating from them will be propagated through the net or will reach deciders to affect behavior of the system. A single organism at a low echelon in the society does not usually send a strong signal. When a large group bands together, the probability of propagation increases, particularly if the group can attract radio or television coverage of some sort.

Information inputs affect all processes of societies, including matter-energy processes, differently from the way they affect processes in systems at lower levels. Cells, organs, and organisms have relatively fixed metabolism and provision for energy production and use. Groups and organizations depend largely upon societies for the information, particularly the technology, that determines their matter-energy and information processes. Societies may make step-function changes in their staple foods, their sources of energy and manner of conversion, and other aspects of their processes as a result of information inputs (see page 834). Information gained from contact with other cultures is crucial as the characteristics of societal processes develop from primitive levels to more advanced ones (see page 860).

Information in the form of money and credit enters societies from outside in the form of payments for goods, loans, and sometimes subsidies. Most of these exchanges are in the form of credit, which is transduced in the same way as other symbols on paper.

Little has yet been said quantitatively about the functional characteristics of the input transducer as a transducer. The input–output transfer functions of component organizations of the subsystem depend upon many variables, such as the number of nodes and deciders in the network over which information flows through the component, the nature of the information and its urgency, and the amount of information to be processed on a given day. The amount of distortion, for example, in a transduction made through an ambassador to a chief of state may be expected to be less than in a transduction made through a news service, partly because there are steps from informant to reporter to rewrite man to editor and finally through the production process, each organism component introducing a possibility of distortion through error or filtering. Many societies are provided with sufficient redundancy in the flow of news into the society through the news media as a whole so that their nationals can compare the accounts of different reporters and eliminate errors and distortions. Societies in which the press is controlled by the government ordinarily have only one official version of an input, and this can be distorted in many ways, including by deliberate intention of the nation's deciders.

The channel capacity of a societal input transducer is large indeed, considering all the transducer components at the organization and other levels. No accurate estimate is available.

Costs of input transducing include the large costs to the society of maintaining the many components of this subsystem.

Included among representative *variables* of the input transducing process are: *Meaning of information input which is transduced.* Example: The concentration of military equipment near the border of a neighboring society was reported by spies and appeared to mean that the society was planning to defend itself. *Sorts of information input which are transduced.* Example: A weather satellite transmitted information about a storm several hundred miles off the coast. *Percentage of the information input which is transduced.* Example: On the average of once a week, censors refused to allow certain foreign publications into the country, but on other days they were permitted to circulate. *Threshold of the input transducer.* Example: The foreign branch of the secret service was instructed to transmit even the most unlikely rumors that came to its attention. *Changes in input transducing over time.* Example: Only during the preceding few years had it become possible to detect approaching missiles with great accuracy. *Changes in input transducing with different circumstances.* Example: The early-warning system of the society was put on alert after the breakdown of international negotiations. *Channel capacity of the input transducer.* Example: Receiving stations in operation were capable of receiving a total of six foreign television programs. *Number of channels in use in the input transducer.* Example: Only a single government-sponsored news bureau was allowed to send reports into the country. *Distortion of the input transducer.* Example: All United Nations reports were deprecated in local radio news. *Signal-to-noise ratio of the input transducer.* Example: Among all the confused rumors and allegations, an important clue about the plans of a hostile neighboring country was completely missed. *Rate of input transducing.* Example: More foreign news was circulated as the population of Ethiopia became more interested in the outside world. *Lag in input transducing.* Example: The President had known about the peace overtures for a week before he informed either Congress or the public. *Costs of input transducing.* Example: A large but undisclosed amount of the national budget was used in maintaining an espionage network throughout the world.

3.3.2 Internal transducer, the sensory subsystem which receives, from subsystems or components within the society, markers bearing information about significant alterations in those subsystems or components, changing them to other matter-energy forms of a sort which can be transmitted within it.

3.3.2.1 Structure The organizations that together form the internal transducer of a large, modern society include parliaments and other representative legislative bodies (joint components with the society's decider subsystem); political parties; the complex machinery of election of public officials, including boards of election; survey or public opinion polling organizations; secret police; governmental statistical organizations such as, in the United States, the Bureau of the Census, the Bureau of Labor Statistics, and the National Center of Health Statistics of the Department of Health, Education, and Welfare. Comparable organizations are components in other nations. Further organized components are the advertising business; the public relations business; organizations which attempt to gain public support to correct aspects of the society which they believe need change, like the Sierra Club, the National Association of Manufacturers, the Students for a Democratic Society, the Wildlife Federation, women's liberation organizations, and the Urban League; ethnic organizations; and labor unions, granges, legislative lobbies, chambers of commerce, churches, service organizations, and countless others. Domestic news media of all sorts belong to this subsystem. Banks and other financial institutions also transduce internal information.

This subsystem may be downwardly dispersed to the group or organism level. Public attitudes are expressed by cartoon artists and writers of books, articles, and tracts. "Presidential listening posts," an innovation of President Nixon, were formed to provide a channel for transduction from members of the society to him.[83] This subsystem may be upwardly dispersed to organizers of plebiscites or elections conducted under the auspices of the United Nations or other supranational or international agency. Components of other societies may act as outwardly dispersed components of this subsystem in a *penetrated society* (see page 800).

Computers, voting machines or their substitutes, and the electronic or other machinery required for transduction of the information into the society's channels are artifacts used by this subsystem.

3.3.2.2 Process Without accurate information about the current states of societal subsystems and components, optimal guidance and control of a society are not possible. Most internal transducing at this level is done by output transducers of subordinate governmental organizations, such as cities or states, or by the special-purpose organizations listed above. An occasional eloquent or determined group or person can create a signal strong enough to enter the society's channels, but causes usually require organizations to transduce them if they are to gain the attention of the system in general. The same is usually true of technical innovations. Inventors and originators need organizations to exploit their ideas, which may then be accepted widely in the society.

Internal transducing processes at this level are of three sorts: (a) constitutional or legally sanctioned provisions for exercise of choice or expression of opinion by components, (b) other processes by which decider components find out about the states of the system, and (c) other processes initiated by components to discover or publish information concerning their own or others' needs, wishes, and opinions. I shall discuss each in turn.

(a) Voting for or against people or legislation, using processes of initiative or referendum to introduce or change legislation, and, in many countries, amending the constitution are examples of the first sort of internal transducing processes. Legislators selected by vote represent their constituencies in the societal decider and are expected to transduce into decider subsystem channels and into the societal net opinions acceptable to their constituencies (see page 816).

Political parties in the United States and certain other countries are not part of the constitutional election machinery, but they are formally recognized. The candidates they select are persons whose attitudes are shared and approved by significant numbers of the population. The election of a preponderance of representatives of one party to the national legislature may provide a signal about the prevailing attitudes in the society, such as conservatism or a trend toward greater centralized control of societal processes.

National decision makers at times make use of special referendum elections to determine the will of the people. This is more true in democracies than in totalitarian systems, since public opinion is usually given more regard by democratic leaders. Imperfect internal transduction is a weakness of totalitarian states.[84]

(b) In the category of other internal transducing processes initiated by the decider are public opinion surveys, statistical studies, fact-finding hearings or investigations, internal intelligence activities of various sorts, and content analyses of executive or legislative mail.

Sophisticated estimates of the range of opinion on, and distribution of attitudes toward, critical questions in a population can be obtained by survey organizations which employ carefully designed techniques for sample selection, framing questions, and interviewing. In forming policy and in planning, deciders place increasing reliance upon the results of such polls. These studies have demonstrated that the views and behavior of people and organizations are consistent over time. The rate and directions of changes can be reported, and the outcome of social processes like elections can usually be predicted with reasonable accuracy.

Content analysis is another means of studying the climate of opinion in a society. The most highly developed techniques of this procedure are not ordinarily used in the day-to-day analysis of political attitudes by decider components. Analysis of executive or legislative mail in terms of the majority feeling expressed by writers does not, for instance, resort to detailed word counts. Content analysis of sample interviews is, however, used in framing questions for public opinion polls.

Societies in which free expression of opinion is not permitted cannot make full use of either of these methods. During the Nazi regime in Germany, for example, the public had good reason not to express its true beliefs and attitudes, and yet the government needed such information for its control and guidance activities. The chief device used was regular reports from leaders of local groups and regional organizations on even minute aspects of public opinion, particularly in the area of morale.[85] Such societies must also, perforce, rely upon the reports of secret police and informers for estimates of how public sentiment is running and the location of dissident factions. Such components are used also in less rigidly controlled societies, usually when opinions are in sharp conflict. Techniques of such components, which may include electronic monitoring of private conversations, transduce into societal channels information relevant to the levels of organism and group.[86]

(c) Processes in this category are originated by components outside the decider that are interested in the outcome of societal decisions. They may wish to gain the support of organizations, groups, or individual persons for some cause or undertaking or, by lobbying, to influence the votes of legislative bodies, either by persuasion or by giving favors. Special-interest organizations often support lobbies and may also use educational programs, publications, demonstrations, speeches, or group meetings to transduce information into societal channels. An organization of "welfare mothers," for example, may inform the public and the societal decider of the problems of disadvantaged mothers.

Internal transducer processes convey "demands" to the decider subsystem. A demand is defined by Easton as "an expression of opinion that an authoritative allocation with regard to a particular subject matter should or should not be made by those responsible for doing so."[87] Demands may be specific, like the demand for a dam in a flood area or for improved control over some aspect of subsystem processes, or they may be general, like a plea for better government or for greater attention to the underprivileged. Internal transducers also provide support for decider components, for processes of which they approve, or for alternatives available to the system.

In an analysis of foreign-policy leadership in the United States, Rosenau identifies as "opinion-makers" "members of the society who occupy positions which enable them to transmit, with some regularity, opinions about foreign policy."[88] These are societywide rather than local leaders. They include governmental officials as well as people who are prominent in respected local or national organizations or who have had personal success in some field:

On the basis of these definitions, then, the ranks of national leadership are wide and diverse. Roughly speaking, they include top elected and appointed officials of the federal government; directors of large corporations; chiefs of international unions; publishers, reporters, and other contributors to communications media with widely dispersed audiences; administrators and scholars of large or prestigeful colleges and universities; high-ranking military officers; spokesmen for the various religious faiths; prominent scientists, entertainers, and writers; politicians affiliated with the Democratic and Republican National Committees; and elected and administrative heads of large trade associations, veterans organizations, women's clubs, farm groups, world affairs councils, and innumerable other types of nationally organized voluntary associations. An estimate of the total number of leaders in all these groups is not easy to make. Empirical data have not been assembled on the basis of the foregoing definition, and, in addition, the ranks of the national opinion-making public will vary as different issues activate different segments of it. On a common sense basis, however, one might reasonably assume that the full range of foreign policy issues encompasses no more than several hundred thousand national opinion-makers and no fewer than fifty thousand.[89]

Leaders of this sort bring issues to the attention of the decider, act as advisers during the analytic stage of deciding, and affect the selection of alternatives (see pages 849 and 850). Because of the importance of consensus among such leaders, federal officials, including presidents, seek their understanding and approval by discussing issues with them. Other countries have similar procedures for obtaining opinions from many components of the society.

Such opinion-makers are not the only source of internal transductions of this sort. Segments of the public supported by no large organizations and with no nationally recognized opinion-maker's help may organize for a cause. For instance, the pressure of Southern blacks for desegregation began with a small organization, the Southern Christian Leadership Conference, led by Martin Luther King, who was then unknown outside his own religious denomination. It gathered support as it gained public attention. The powerful demand for change in the Southeast Asian policy of the United States during the Vietnam war was initially expressed by university student organizations.

In a study of "top leaders" in the United States, Hunter found agreement on the steps necessary to influence national deciders to make a given policy decision. These were:

1. Establish the policy purpose and secure a dedication to this purpose by interested individuals.
2. Seek an unselfish working together of individuals and groups to achieve what they believe to be a policy direction for the good of the country.
3. Recruit successful men to help in furthering the idea.
4. Widen but restrict the circle of informed men.
5. Enlist the services of an established national organization in the cause, or set up a new organization if the existing organizations cannot embrace the new policy in their framework of action.
6. Utilize research to develop a factual base of operations.
7. Use a small but technically qualified group to give objective consideration and criticism to the facts.
8. Have facts and strategic problems analyzed by competent citizen groups.
9. Enlist public opinion through publicity of general news and special media.
10. Urge and re-urge vigorous support of all men who have knowledge of the program.
11. Use personal contact methods on other national leaders, the national administration, and Congress.
12. Appear publicly before committees of Congress or request hearings before administrative tribunals.
13. Be resolved to get action from the national administration.
14. Be resolved to get action from the houses of Congress.
15. Be prepared to use varying combinations of the above steps, and to begin over if not successful the first time.[90]

These steps appear designed to amplify the signal output from a particular component of the internal transducer into the societal net and to improve the probability of its transmission to its intended address in a number of ways: (a) increasing the number of transducer components that transmit it; (b) increasing the efficiency of the transduction by using components capable of sending a strong signal with a high probability of propagation, i.e., influential men; (c) increasing the redundancy of the signal by sending it separately through different nodes in the net and by using different sorts of channels; (d) increasing the signal-to-noise ratio by increasing the "determination" of senders, that is, the strength and persistence of the signal they transmit; (e) sending the signal from nodes close to the components to which it is addressed, by means of public appearances and hearings, thus increasing the probability that it will not be attenuated by channel noise; (*f*) decreasing errors in the transmission by use of experts and research; and (*g*) decreasing noise by assuring that different senders will agree upon the signal to be sent (unselfishly working together).

Functional characteristics of the internal transducer, like those of the input transducer, have not been determined (see pages 784 and 785). Costs of internal transducing to the society are the costs of maintaining the organizations through which most of the transducing is done and of conducting surveys or other relevant research.

Representative *variables* of the internal transducing process include: *Meaning of internal information which is transduced.* Example: The poll showed that 67 percent of the population favored the government's economic program. *Sorts of internal information which are transduced.* Example: The research organization studied the attitude of the population toward family planning. *Percentage of the internal information which is transduced.* Example: The minority group, which made up 30 percent of the population, was not permitted to vote. *Threshold of the internal transducer.* Example: The strength of public attitudes was not realized until riots broke out. *Changes in internal transducing over time.* Example: Election results in the United States were more accurately forecast in 1972 than ever before. *Changes in internal transducing with different circumstances.* Example: When a dictator governed, the opinions of the population were ignored. *Channel capacity of the internal transducer.* Example: Three survey organizations in the society could accept no more assignments because of overload during the last weeks before the presidential election. *Number of channels in use in the internal transducer.* Example: All but one newspaper were suppressed when civil violence broke out. *Distortion of the internal transducer.* Example: A biased sample gave the premier an inaccurate picture of public sentiment on an important issue, and so he was defeated in the election. *Signal-to-noise ratio of the internal transducer.* Example: The potentially valuable invention was ignored in the flood of innovations in the rapidly developing society. *Rate of internal transducing.* Example: Pollsters in each province interviewed about 10 respondents a day. *Lag in internal transducing.* Example: The editor received the results of the informal poll, but he did not publish them until other evidence was presented. *Costs of internal transducing.* Example: The Statistical Policy Division of the Office of Management and Budget was given more

than $1 million to compile a set of national social indicators.

3.3.3   Channel and net, the subsystem composed of a single route in physical space, or multiple interconnected routes, by which markers bearing information are transmitted to all parts of the society.

3.3.3.1   Structure   The channels and nets of modern societies are made up of many organizations whose encoders and output transducers, acting as internal transducers for the society, are nodes or deciders in the nets or maintain and operate artifacts used in transmission. These channel and net components link together the internal nets of the many organizations that compose the society.

Among these components are the society's mail service; national telephone, telegraph, radio, and television networks; publishers and circulators of printed news media and of magazines, including scientific and technical journals other than those restricted to a single organization; disseminators of books, films, phonograph records, and tape recordings; display advertising companies; lecture bureaus and those who give public lectures; organizations of actors, musicians, and other performers; art galleries, museums, or sales companies; public meetings, rallies, and demonstrations; and private conferences, conventions, and meetings that include representatives of a number of organizations. Censors are deciders in the net. A country's banks and other financial institutions, including its stock markets, are also components that exchange monetary information.

The basic structure of the channel and net subsystem of all societies is a downwardly dispersed, person-to-person, often face-to-face network that connects each person in the living system with at least one other person, at least occasionally. This network penetrates boundaries of component groups and organizations, since their members have multiple organizational and group memberships and communicate with members of groups and organizations to which they do not belong. Very small, primitive societies have only this component. At a somewhat more advanced stage, societies may have senders of smoke signals, beaters of jungle drums, or runners who transmit messages from one region to another. Preindustrial societies depended upon messengers carrying written communications. An important survival of this sort of communication is the diplomatic pouch in which messages are exchanged between a society's deciders and some of its representatives stationed abroad.

Other downwardly dispersed components are "key people" who are spokesmen for large, sometimes very large, unorganized segments of the population. These may be arbiters of fashion whose word is law among teen-agers, wealthy and influential businessmen who publicly favor reduced taxes for industries in general, or religious leaders who advocate the cause of the poor and downtrodden.

Artifacts are of overwhelming importance in the channels and nets of modern societies. In 1972 the highly urbanized, industrialized United States had 132 million telephones—628 per 1,000 population.[91] These were connected into a network in which 16,056 telephone central offices were linked by 1,121 billion km of wire, 495 million km of coaxial tube, and 2,073 km of broadband, one-way channel microwave radio relay. Telegraph, television, and radio networks are also important. Some sophisticated new artifacts in this subsystem are responder television, communications satellites, computer networks, and picture phones. Other sorts of networks use mail trucks, airplanes, or railroad mail cars.

3.3.3.2 Process   Like nets at lower levels of living systems, nets at the society level are biased; that is, transmissions are not equiprobable between any node and any other. Distance is one biasing factor. People tend to communicate more with people near them— friends, relatives, and others with whom they come into daily contact. Americans made 513 million local telephone calls on an average day in 1972, about two for every man, woman, and child. The number of long-distance calls was only 33 million. This is balanced to some extent by the greater number of first-class letters sent out of the local area than within it. In Louisville, Kentucky, only about 27 percent of the daily average of 650,000 first-class letters are communications between local people. (Many of those sent outside the locality were bills sent by Louisville companies, rather than personal communications.[92])

Common interests are another biasing factor. Special networks throughout the society connect people of the same professions, political complexions, avocations, or organizational memberships. These contacts are made not only through person-to-person communications but also through interactions at conventions and other meetings and through organization newsletters.

Among scientists, men and women within a research specialty communicate frequently among themselves. The informal communication within such specialties has been termed "invisible colleges" and is considered to be critical to the functioning of these research areas within a large, diffuse, national and international discipline.[93] A study of communication behavior of scientists revealed that the number of significant contacts among scientists within research

specialties was no greater than would be expected among active members of an entire discipline.[94] It was a Poisson distribution. When the very productive people were studied separately, however, their rate of interaction was about eight times higher than the mean. These people formed a separate distribution and had a considerably higher number of contacts within their specialties.

Patterns of communication among technologists, whose activities include applied research, exploratory development, and engineering development, differ from those among scientists.[95] The technologists publish less and devote less time to reading. Their mode of transmission is primarily oral, and communication is most usually with other members of their own organization, which is typically either a part of government or a business. These organizations enforce boundaries to information output. Under these circumstances, invisible colleges cannot form. Technologists make greater use of unpublished technical reports as vehicles for their communications and less use of published journal articles. Dissemination of such reports can be limited by the organization to internal channels and to selected external receivers. Organizations often transmit their reports to other organizations, but these are protected from further dissemination, to a third organization, by informal understandings.

Information takes a long time to travel through the channels between scientists and technologists, for results of scientific research reach technologists only after they are included in textbooks.[96] Long delays are introduced by the periods before original publication in scientific journals, the period between that and publication in textbooks, and the variable period between a person's education and his or her use of the information.

Within recent years, since 1966, serious planning for the development of electronic networks to interconnect colleges and universities throughout the United States has been under way.[97] Such a network, EDU-NET, ultimately may include multiple media such as radio, television, computer data, teletype, photofacsimile transmission, and telephone. Progress toward implementation of such an idea has now occurred. A computer-to-computer network, ARPANET, was operational by 1969 among a group of Western universities. It was later expanded across the country. Roberts describes the advantages of such a network: " . . . leased lines can provide very effective computer-to-computer interaction. With them, your own computer can have access to the resources of any of the other computers in the net, no matter where they are in the country. Those resources will be available as reliably and as responsively as though you were at the other site, and with no degradation of service. . . ."[98] A network of this sort would of course bias the total societal net because it would give participant colleges and universities ready access to sources of information not so available to others.

Bias is also introduced into societal networks by the fact that societies place constraints upon information flows and enforce them by law or custom. A component which desires to transduce a new idea may meet with a restriction against its transmission over the societal net. An unpopular creed may meet the same fate. This internal censorship is particularly important in autocratically governed societies. Other sorts of information dissemination are forbidden as threats to public morality.

Demographic gravitation. This concept has been employed by Stewart in an effort to explain the directions of human information flows.[99] He has fitted a number of relations in social systems to equations dealing with attractions of masses, behaviors of gases, and other strictly physical phenomena. Large masses of people, according to this controversial theory, attract each other and exert a drawing power upon those in intervening areas. *Demographic energy,* in this conceptual system, is associated with the mutual gravitation of two populations spaced a known distance apart. This is relevant to social channels and nets since it can be shown that rates of a number of types of information flows are functions of this quantity, or of another, *potential of population,* which is associated with it. These are long-distance telephone calls, interregional flows of bank checks and postal money orders, newspaper circulations at a distance, news items by city datelines, and newspaper obituaries by city datelines. Stewart says that correlation coefficients calculated between such variables have never been below .5. This is, of course, another way of saying that information flows to and from cities in proportion to their size. No references to any sort of gravity are necessary to explain these interesting findings, which are quite probably accurate. It is enough to assume that the larger and the nearer two populations are, the more reasons there are for them to exchange information.

The effects of regional boundaries upon spread of information were studied by Rice in 1928.[100] He had intended to contrast the difference in "progressive" political attitudes between farmers and workingmen in Minnesota. He found, however, that while these occupational cleavages did exist, the more outstanding differences occurred among regions into which the state appeared to be divided. As one passed through the state, attitudes, as indicated by the vote, changed gradually. There was an urban–rural difference, but there was also a difference between farmers who lived in the south of the state and grew corn and the wheat-growing farmers of the northwest. These differences held in other states as well and were great enough to cancel out occupational differences within the regions. In the valley of the Red River, which runs through the heart of the wheat belt, separating Minnesota and North Dakota, the counties on opposite sides of the river are opposite politically. The counties which lie on the east bank of the river are the most radical in Minnesota. Those on the west bank are the most conservative in North Dakota. Rice concludes that (*a*) state boundaries are real barriers to spread of political views over the societal net in contiguous areas, (*b*) the influence of state boundaries is reduced in areas which share common trading centers, (*c*) it is possible that information diffusion may be accelerated by regular lines of rail or mail communication, and (*d*) analysis in one state indicates lessening intensity of particular political views as the distance from a center of those views increases.

Tuchman describes a situation in which component boundaries acted to block information flows during an important period of history in Great Britain, August 1914, at the beginning of World War I: "Within the army, field officers despised Staff officers as 'having the brains of canaries and the manners of Potsdam' but both groups were as one in their distaste for interference by civilian ministers who were known as 'the frocks.' The civil arm in its turn referred to the military as 'the boneheads.' As a consequence each group told the other as little as possible."[101]

Findings from the above studies by Rice and Tuchman appear to support Hypothesis 3.1.2.2-2 (see page 93) at the society level. It suggests that more work is expended in moving a marker bearing information over a boundary at the input transducer than in moving it the same distance immediately outside or inside the boundary.

Anthropologists, particularly, have been interested in cultural diffusion, by which innovations in ideas, practices, and artifacts spread through populations, after being input from some other culture or originated within the society. Experimental studies have been made of spread of information in groups and organizations, but experimental testing of spread through a whole society is obviously difficult because of the complexity of such a system. Studies have been made which are applicable at this level if the assumption is made that what is true of a sample of communities is true in general of the whole society. It is clear that rates of diffusion will differ in various parts of the society, depending upon the state of the communications net and the conservatism of the population. In order to study channel and net processes in a society, it is necessary to separate the knowledge of the new cultural item (spread of information about it over the net) from its acceptance, which is different—an aspect of societal adjustment processes (see page 834). Strictly speaking, as Barnett points out, diffusion, as viewed by anthropologists, is acceptance.[102] A cultural item has not diffused until it is accepted.

Two studies have been made in the United States which separate the knowledge of an innovation from its acceptance. These are discussed and compared by Katz.[103] The first was a study of the spread of knowledge of hybrid sweet corn among farmers; the second was a study of the adoption of a new drug by physicians. Both were done in the American Middle West in more than one community. Two farming communities were used in the first, and four cities in the second.

Hybrid sweet corn seed emerged from the experimental stage in 1927. This study disclosed that it took about 13 years for news of the innovation to travel over the societal net and reach every single farmer. Over 90 percent had heard about the corn by 1934. The spread of knowledge about it occurred chiefly during a 3-year period, when 60 percent learned about it.

The process of disseminating information about the new drug was much more rapid. About two-thirds of the doctors dated their first knowledge of the drug to within 4 months of its earliest availability. The rate of processing of information over the component of the societal net interconnecting physicians was distinctly faster than the rate of information processing over the component interconnecting farmers.

The source from which each doctor or farmer received the information was discovered in both studies. Almost one-half of the farmers indicated that a salesman brought them their first information. The next most important sources were farmer-friends, relatives, and neighbors. Other sources, in order of importance, were farm journals, radio advertising, and an agricultural extension service.

Drug salesmen were as important for the doctors as seed company salesmen were for the farmers. Fifty-seven percent first heard about the innovation from "detail men" sent out by the drug companies. The only other source of any importance for first news in this study was direct mail from the drug company. Some doctors mentioned other physicians or a professional journal, but altogether these represented only 14 percent of the informants.

Coins and bills, markers for a society's currency, are transported among component organizations of the society over distributor routes, often in armored trucks. Such transmissions, while important, take a second place to flows of a great variety of checks, bills, stocks, bonds, credit-card receipts, loan records, and so forth. These travel by mail, teletype, or special messengers. Cash changes hands to balance accounts at the end of a day or other stated period. I shall discuss these flows of money and credit information further below (see pages 844 to 849).

The operating characteristics of the several parts of the societal channel and net subsystems are somewhat different. Rates, lags, distortions, and channel capacities of each sort of channel can be determined.

Distortions in transmissions of information through societal channels can occur for many reasons. One of them is the same at this level as at group and organization levels, namely, the effect of being passed through a number of nodes. People who receive a message not directly from a mass-communication source but after it has been passed from person to person usually get a shorter version—one that is selectively edited and is distorted to conform with prevailing stereotypes, cultural themes, and verbal habits.[104]

One effort has been made to estimate the channel capacity of a society.[105] Some believe the limit of human ability to receive information to be about 10^9 bits per capita per annum. This obviously varies with the percentage of illiteracy in the population. Estimating the amount of time allocated to reading, television, lecture and discussion, observation of the environment, radio, films, and miscellaneous sources, Meier calculated that in a metropolitan area like San Francisco, people at present receive about 10^8 bits per capita per year. In a place like Addis Ababa, with a large number of illiterate citizens, the amount is about 10^6 bits per capita per year.

Many *variables* of channel and net processing can be measured. Some representative ones are: *Meaning of information channeled to various parts of the system.* Example: In his televised speech, the leader of the liberal party advocated a tax-the-rich policy. *Sorts of information channeled to various parts of the system.* Example: The government sent all physicians notices about a new drug. *Percentage of information arriving at the appropriate receiver in the channel and net.* Example: Half the country's farmers who received notice of the new seed never planted that crop. *Threshold of the channel and net.* Example: The students found that a peaceful protest got little national television coverage. *Changes in channel and net processing over time.* Example: The laws against demonstrating in public places were gradually relaxed. *Changes in channel and net processing with different circumstances.* Example: Emergency television announcements preempted regular programs during the revolution. *Information capacity of the channel and net.* Example: The reported arrival of extraterrestrial ambassadors swamped long-distance lines to Washington. *Distortion of the channel and net.* Example: The rumor circulated that the king was dying, although he merely had the flu. *Signal-to-noise ratio in the channel and net.* Example: The news of the internationally famous writer's death was almost completely suppressed by the clamor over the assassination of the young president. *Rate of processing of information over the channel and net.* Example: Hundreds of cities each week learned of the new technical advances in water treatment. *Lag in channel and net processing.* Example: It took several weeks for news of John Adams's election to reach all parts of the United States. *Costs of channel and net processing.* Example: The cost of transmission in the nationwide computer network was 30 to 40 cents per megabit of information.

3.3.4   Decoder, the subsystem which alters the code of information input to it through the input transducer or internal transducer into a "private" code that can be used internally by the society.

3.3.4.1   Structure   Organizations that make up the decoder of a complex modern society include foreign offices, departments of state, news media, observatories, weather bureaus, financial institutions, religious organizations, the scientific community, and teaching institutions of all kinds. Some of these are also components of the input or internal transducer or of the channel and net.

All societies have components of this subsystem downwardly dispersed to the group and organism levels. Decoding for the society may be done by such groups as presidential advisers, who interpret governmental intelligence or news developments. Most decoding is first carried out in the nervous systems of organism components. Other groups or individual persons in this subsystem are language translators, interpreters, cryptographers, and news or market analysts.

Artifacts include computers and sensing devices that record amounts or rates of inputs as they are transducing them. These include apparatuses like seismographs, barometers, and radiation-detection devices that indicate levels by markings on their dials or in other ways.

3.3.4.2   Process   The decoder subsystem at the society level is concerned largely with interpretations, since sensory perception is almost wholly dispersed downwardly to the organism level, and translation of languages to the organization level or below.

A society can receive alpha- and beta-coded signals from outside its boundaries through its input transducer, from its natural environment, or from other systems in the environment. Alpha- and beta-coded signals may also be internally transduced from living or nonliving components of the system or from the natural environment within the system's territorial boundaries.

Components of the societal decoder interpret signs of alterations in states of the natural environment, such as changes in the weather, which may have significance for components like farmers or seaside communities; movements of heavenly bodies; or changes in the steady states of polar ice caps or seas that are of scientific interest. Decoder components also monitor radiation levels in the atmosphere that can potentially give indications of nuclear testing by other societies. In some societies astrologers, soothsayers, or prophets interpret natural phenomena to reveal implications they see in them for the society.

Changes in the steady states of nonhuman living systems in the environment, such as a great increase in certain species or the disappearance of others, are also decoded, either straightforwardly or as indications of attitudes of supernatural beings toward the society. A plague of locusts can be viewed as a problem of natural ecological balance, but at one time it was interpreted as an indication that the Egyptians should let the Israelites leave their territory.

Decoder components also interpret actions of other societies and of components of the society itself. Although many of the signals from these sources are gamma-coded, occurrences like internal troop movements, unusual channel and net activity, sudden news blackouts, and arrival of refugees in unusual numbers may give indications of events inside a country that controls its information outputs. For instance, "China-watching" is avidly carried out by other nations in order to find out about events that are not even hinted at in written or spoken outputs transduced through that country's effectively controlled information boundary. In the same way, unusual activity among dissident factions of a population, or among known criminals, can alert internal decider components to probable trouble. This happened when reports of a gathering of gang members in the Adirondack Mountains of New York State indicated an opportunity for police to capture some wanted men.

Societies usually have one or more common languages, used internally and understood by significant numbers of their populations. The Soviet Union, for example, whose more than 240 million people speak more than 60 indigenous languages, provides that all citizens learn Russian, the native tongue of only 60 percent of them.[106] Tiny Switzerland, with fewer than 7 million people, has four official languages into which information is decoded, the languages of four ethnic groups—German, French, Italian, and Rhaeto-

Romanic.[107] In countries with many languages, much decoding of internal information flows is necessary, but even in countries with a single language understood by the vast majority of people, like the United States, "translation" of technical or specialized communications for the benefit of the general public is common. When the President of the United States finishes a speech on national radio and television, news analysts immediately tell the country what he said and what he probably meant by it. In the following days other news media carry further interpretations of the content of the speech.

Each newborn member of a society must acquire, in the first years of life, not only the sounds and grammatical forms of the language necessary for communication with others of his society but also the mutually agreed-upon coding categories under which experience is classified in the culture and subculture to which he belongs. Much of the learning of the growing child involves acquiring the codings of his own society so that he can send and receive the gestures, tones, words, expressed feelings, attitudes, and values used in communication within his society. It is characteristic of societies that their citizens share a common culture of learning and past experiences and that they interpret, perceive, or decode various sorts of incoming information in a relatively standard way because of this common background. Even in societies with varying subcultures there is usually a dominant pattern that is understood to some extent by those persons who do not share it. People in a society agree upon connotations of gestures, tones, accents, symbols, words, customs, art forms, and artifacts, as well as particular traditions and norms.[108] Events and incoming information tend to be classified and evaluated similarly by a large percentage of the population. As a result, plays which succeed in New York may fail in London, and the reverse is also true. Most members of a society in a given area laugh at the same sorts of things and often find the jokes and humor of another country unintelligible. Though the language is the same, English and American humor differ greatly—as do Oriental and Occidental music.

The shared common coding of a language, while undergoing modification generation after generation, is still highly stable. This shared code alters or distorts information flows in sensory perception or thought so that peoples using different languages actually live in different "worlds of reality."[109] The idea that language reflects and also influences the world view of the society was suggested by Sapir and others and vigorously advanced by Whorf.[110] The evidence adduced is at times confusing. Sometimes it appears merely to show that languages differ among societies, as do world views. At other times it seems to show that the language differences are responsible for some of the deviations in world views. One procedure that has been used to show the effect of different societies' codes has been to translate some concept literally from one language, like English, into a different tongue and then back again to the first language. Thus we find "dripping spring" being translated into Apache and then translated back as "water, whiteness moves downward."

The way a society codes experience is held by some to determine sensory perception to a certain extent. Hoijer says: "The Eskimo, who distinguishes in speech several varieties of snow surface (and who lacks a general term corresponding to our 'snow'), is responding to a whole complex of cultural patterns which require that he make these distinctions, so vital to his physical welfare and that of the group. It is as if the culture as a whole (including the language) selected from the landscape certain features more important than others and so gave to the landscape an organization or structure peculiar to the group."[111] The variability in human coding is limited, however. The Navajo people, who use the same word for "blue" and "green," are still able to distinguish between them. Jung contended that certain primitive symbols are inherited by all human beings, the archetypes of what he called the "racial unconscious," and that these have common meanings across cultural boundaries.[112] Cultural relativism also does not extend to basic logical relationships, which appear to be the same in all known human languages. The thought of human beings everywhere appears to be consistent with the propositions of Western symbolic logic, as Wallace points out.[113] It is the content, not the form of the relations, of propositions which is culture-specific. Wallace uses the example of Handsome Lake, an illiterate Seneca Indian, who preached temperance to his people. His speech to them contrasted the values and effects of apples and corn to those of hard cider and whiskey. As Wallace points out, this is a logically valid argument, not "prelogical" thinking, in spite of the cultural difference and the illiteracy of the speaker.

Representative *variables* of the decoding process include: *Meaning of information which is decoded.* Example: The rapid increase in radiation in the upper atmosphere was interpreted to indicate that another country had tested a powerful new atomic weapon. *Sorts of information which are decoded.* Example: A State Department official explained the reaction of North Vietnam to a peace overture. *Percentage of the information input which is decoded.* Example: The king explained only three of the enemy's ten demands to the people. *Threshold of the decoder.* Example: The only foreign-service officer who had any knowledge of the African language in which the peace offer was written could read only the simplest sentences. *Changes in decoding over time.* Example: The language in which diplomats from the two countries communicated changed from French to English in the middle of the twentieth century. *Changes in decoding with different circumstances.* Example: The government carried on a campaign of public education to explain the uses of imported farm machinery when it finally became available. *Channel capacity of the decoder.* Example: It was necessary to add several experts on Asian affairs as contacts with distant countries increased. *Distortion of the decoder.* Example: The expert on primitive peoples misunderstood the reaction of the islanders to the new policies and overemphasized the importance of their taboo. *Signal-to-noise ratio of the decoder.* Example: The Latin American government changed hands so frequently that contradictory messages were received and it was hard to arrive at the truth of what was going on. *Rate of decoding.* Example: The translators could manage only about a page an hour. *Percentage of omissions in decoding.* Example: All three peace overtures were kept secret by the government and were not reported or explained to the people. *Percentage of errors in decoding.* Example: Of the three treaties, one was erroneously interpreted. *Code employed.* Example: It was necessary to explain the communication in Flemish for the benefit of part of the Dutch population. *Redundancy of the code employed.* Example: The Swiss government sent out information about the communication from Italy in four languages. *Lag in decoding.* Example: The government had the diplomatic note for several days before explaining it to the public. *Costs of decoding.* Example: The president's budget listed a large sum for experts on foreign affairs.

3.3.5 Associator, the subsystem which carries out the first stage of the learning process, forming enduring associations among items of information in the society.

3.3.5.1 Structure   The associator of a modern society includes component schools, colleges, universities, and other teaching institutions; research organizations; foundations; and scientific and professional organizations. It is also downwardly dispersed to groups of students or explorers and components of organizations, like research and development departments, whose innovations eventually enter the society's channel and net. The associator subsystem of all societies, however, like the associator of other systems in which human organisms or units made up of them are components, is primarily downwardly dispersed to the individual persons in whose nervous systems associations among items of information must be made.

Artifacts in the associator include computers and other data processing equipment and also devices like space vehicles and laboratory equipment used in research and discovery.

3.3.5.2 Process   Societies, like other systems that learn, modify their behavior in response to repeated inputs of the same sort, and they increase their accumulation of knowledge as a consequence of making and storing associations among items of information. The source of the items may be events that affect the system; the stored wisdom of the past; information about innovations in conceptual systems, art, technology, or the conduct of affairs, transduced into the societal net through input or internal transducers; or feedback concerning effects of previous actions of the system itself.

Not all social change is the result of learning by the society. Some results from adjustment processes to such things as increased population, worldwide depression, or climatic change (see pages 840 to 844 and 847 to 849). Evidence that learning has taken place in a society may be found in alterations in its subsystem structure, its characteristic ways of carrying out its processes, its typical decoding categories, its reactions to particular sorts of events, the motifs of its art, or the state of advancement of its science and technology.

The fact that a single societal citizen or a small group has made an association does not mean that the association has been made by the society as a system. An innovation of potential value to a system can be present within it for a long time without being propagated to those parts of the system necessary for its system-wide adoption. The same is true of recognition of the effects of an action. Lone voices cry in many wildernesses.

The conditions under which a society can be expected to learn and the details of the learning processes at this level—the rates, lags, and channel capacity—are difficult to establish because of the long time that intervenes between an action by the system and its consequences and because of the practical impossibility of setting up crucial experiments on systems of such complexity. Hypothesis 3.3.5.2-6 (see page 99) states that the higher the level of the system, the slower association is. The suggested reason for this, that feedback channels are longer and more subject to error, seems intuitively true of societies, particularly for the sorts of changes that necessarily involve large numbers of units in the subcomponents and below. Belated recognition of the disadvantages of a deeply rooted child-rearing practice like swaddling and subsequent elimination of it may be an example of this (see page 797). What has been called the "counterintuitive" nature of complex systems (see page 718) also retards the rate of learning, since what appear to be the consequences of a policy change or action of the system may, in fact, be attributable to other causes and since the true effects may be difficult to determine. This also makes it difficult for a society to do what Hypothesis 3.3.5.2-2 (see page 99) states that systems do, *i.e.,* associate the strain with the acts that relieve it.

What Forrester calls the "drift to low performance" applies to societies. He says:

Complex social systems tend toward a condition of poor performance. Their counterintuitive nature causes detrimental design changes. Also, the opposite direction of short-term and long-term responses leads to policies that produce a less satisfactory system. For example, a particular change in policy may improve matters for a period of a year or two while setting the stage for changes that lower performance and desirability further in the future. But the natural interpretation is to observe that good resulted from the change and when matters become worse the original efforts are redoubled. The intensified action produces another short-term improvement and still deeper long-term difficulty. Again the complex system is cunning in its ability to mislead.[114]

In spite of these difficulties, social change as a result of a learning process does seem to occur in societies. Rewards and punishments appear to reinforce or extinguish system response to classes of input. Repeated experiences with the same or similar patterns of relationships among items of information cause societies (like organisms, groups, and organizations) to acquire habitual ways of responding. They set up programmed activities which can be followed more or less automatically without the attention of the decider to each separate event. The ordinarily smooth course of elections in established democracies, in which thousands of citizens carry out official responsibilities of various sorts and millions visit the proper polling places during the right hours, results from establishment of laws, procedures, customs, and norms at all echelons of the society, as a result of experience with repeated instances of the same activities.

Specific examples of social learning can be identified. The United States in the 1930s made the associations that led to the abandonment of isolationism. In the 1970s different experiences in the course of international relationships may be leading to reversal of the pattern. During the economic depression of the 1930s, the relationship between some of the ways in which the economy had been managed and a disastrous outcome appeared so abundantly evident that policies and platforms of both major political parties

reflected these associations, and changes were made in relevant laws and organizational structures.

Katona has shown that the attitudes and information of the citizens of a country, as tested by opinion polls, change over time as a result of experience. He lists a number of such opinions which have been held by middle-income and upper-middle-income citizens in recent years, many of which, whether objectively correct or not, have influenced national policy formation:

Depressions are no longer inevitable.
The government has the power to overcome depressions, to reduce unemployment, and to insure good times.
Rearmament does not have a beneficial effect on the economy.
Inflation is bad; when price increases are general, economic conditions are not good. Stable prices and even slightly declining prices are good for the economy.
Banks are safe; putting money in savings accounts is a good way to save. Common stocks are risky; one must have "information" to select the "right" stocks.[115]

Some associations which appear equally obvious have not been made, according to Katona, who says:

The years of substantial armament expenditures were good years; yet most people have not drawn any consequences from these experiences. Most years of inflation in the recent past were very good years for most people; nevertheless, the notion that inflation is bad has not been shaken. Recording the events that have taken place does not enable us to predict their impact on people's thinking.[116]

Societies differ in their rates of establishing new patterns as a result of associations. Societies classified as "primitive" by Toynbee are relatively static (see page 755).[117] In them custom rules. Civilizations, on the other hand, imitate creative, pioneering people instead of their elders and their dead ancestors. They change and grow. Association of information into novel patterns certainly proceeds at a more rapid rate in civilizations.

Two of Cattell's factors (see pages 760 and 761) reflect societal characteristics of this sort. Factor 4, *conservative patriarchal solidarity vs. ferment of release,* and Factor 5, *pace of life and emancipation vs. unsophisticated stability* clearly do.[118] Factor 6, *scientific industriousness vs. relaxed and emotional life,* and Factor 3, *enlightened affluence vs. narrow poverty,* probably also reflect a higher rate of associating. Cluster patterns are reasonably consistent in these differences.[119] The Scandinavian family of nations, for example, is high in Factors 6, 5, and 3, while the Mohammedan pattern is low in Factors 3 and 5. There appear to be real differences among these cultures.

Along with possibly being slower in associating than lower levels of living systems, it may be that societies are more variable in their associating processes. Do recency, frequency, and the other variables of inputs that influence the rate of organism learning influence these larger systems also? Probably so. Toynbee found "challenge and response" to be crucial to development of civilizations.[120] Societies make use of research, exploration, and investigation, not only for the input of new ideas (see page 624), but also to discover relationships among them. The development of statistical methods, which reveal the degree of significance of correlations among items of information, aids societal associating. The development of rapid computerized methods of making computations with social indicators vastly extends the associating power of societies that use them. Also, it increases the probability that the correct associations will be made among confusing or overabundant data.

Representative *variables* of the process of associating include: *Meaning of information which is associated.* Example: The discovery that increased atmospheric pollution and a rising cancer death rate were correlated meant, to one society, that controls must be imposed on the design of automobile exhaust systems. *Sorts of information which are associated.* Example: The defeat of the army in battle was attributed to the anger of the gods. *Percentage of the information input which is associated to other information.* Example: When the third tidal wave devastated the coast, the government finally saw the need for measures to protect the coastal population. *Changes in associating over time.* Example: The society gradually became aware of the relationship between the use of pesticides and the death of ocean fish. *Changes in associating with different circumstances.* Example: As a result of the stock-market crash, the society realized that it must regulate stock exchanges. *Channel capacity of the associator.* Example: While its neighbor was concerned with an internal revolutionary uprising, the hostile society moved its troops close to the border. *Rate of associating.* Example: Only a few technological discoveries of real importance were adopted by the society each year. *Lag in associating.* Example: It took 10 years for the government to realize the effects of its shortsighted farm policy. *Costs of associating.* Example: The government footed the bill for research that showed the connection between the farming methods commonly used and erosion of the soil.

3.3.6 Memory, the subsystem which carries out the second stage of the learning process, storing various sorts of information in the society for different periods of time.

3.3.6.1 Structure   The memory of a modern society is composed of a variety of specialized component organizations, including its religious bodies, teaching institutions, cultural organizations, craft organizations, professional organizations, national archives, centralized data banks or document storage and retrieval organizations, national information networks, scientific information services, libraries, museums, historical places and national monuments, art galleries, banks, and the national treasury.

Specialized components of governmental units store information not only for the agency of which they are a part but also for various other components or subcomponents of the society. Some, among many, examples of such components in the United States are the Office of Technology Utilization of NASA, the Office of Scientific Information Service of the National Science Foundation, the National Agricultural Library within the Department of Agriculture, the Office of Public Affairs in the Energy Research and Development Administration, the Defense Documentation Center, and the Systems Research and Development Service within the Federal Aviation Agency.[121]

Proposals exist in the United States for a coordinated national network of information systems under the Committee of Scientific and Technical Information. This would have two parts: a complex of library systems and a complex of information evaluation and retrieval systems.[122] The Library of Congress is expected to become a central part of an automated national system of libraries and information centers.

A number of other network organizations—some governmental and others not—link separate component organizations in the United States. Among these is MEDLINE, formerly MEDLARS (*Medical Literature Analysis and Retrieval System*), which has over a million abstracts of biomedical literature classified according to subject headings. Teletypes anywhere in the United States can send requests to the central computer to search under specific subject categories and print out on a terminal the abstract so retrieved. Time-sharing computers, linked by telephone lines to organizations distant from one another, store information originating in many organizations.

All societies downwardly disperse cultural information to the levels of group and organism. Families carry on moral and other traditions from generation to generation. Priests, singers, storytellers, dancers, medicine men, teachers, artists, potters, and many others are specialized components of this subsystem. In preliterate societies almost all the subsystem is downwardly dispersed to organisms.

Artifacts in this subsystem include the buildings and equipment of libraries and other storage organizations as well as computers.

3.3.6.2 Process   The memory processes of (a) reading into storage, (b) maintaining information in storage, (c) loss and alteration during storage, and (d) retrieval from storage at this level depend upon the durability of artifacts, the learning processes of organisms, and the information storage techniques of organizations. The multiplicity of components of this sort in a society and the long time over which storage continues present these large systems with problems not encountered at lower levels of living systems.

(a) *Reading into storage.*   Information to be stored only in the memories of organisms is communicated by members of each generation, who act as storage components for particular sorts of cultural items, to members of succeeding generations. In this way the memories of a preliterate society are perpetuated beyond the lifetimes of the persons to whom the storage is downwardly dispersed.

Societies assure their cultural continuity by passing from each generation to the next the unique set of commonly held meanings and behavioral patterns that taken together are frequently described as culture or "national character." Some societies include more than one set of cultural patterns. The child-rearing practices of a people are designed to assure that each generation stores information considered important by their parents. The Russian custom of tightly swaddling infants illustrates one way in which this occurs. Mead says:

... when Russians (who themselves embody their whole culture) handle their own children (who are in the process of learning to be Russians) in a particular way that this way of handling becomes a form of communication between parent and child in which the child learns something the adult has already learned, not necessarily by the same means. . . . Such a view of culture assumes, furthermore, that each member of a society is systematically representative of the cultural pattern of that society, so that the treatment accorded infant or immigrant, pupils or employees or rulers, is indicative of the culturally regular character-forming methods of that society.[123]

In addition to this fundamental form of storage, modern societies store vast amounts of information in written or otherwise recorded form. The Library of Congress of the United States, which has copies of all United States publications and many from foreign countries, as well as other documents and historical materials, in 1966 had more than 44 million items. Each year new acquisitions total a million.[124] This is only a small part of the information stored in the society, since floods of data, mountains of unpublished historical materials, all the filed records of transactions, all the punched cards, and all the electronically stored information certainly more than

equal it. Artifacts, such as monuments and historical documents, like the original Constitution of the United States or the Declaration of Independence, preserve memories of a nation's past.

A modern society's memory for many sorts of items does not necessarily depend upon human nervous systems. Internally transduced information, such as income tax forms and census data, can be read into storage automatically.

(b) *Maintaining in storage.*   To assure that a society's traditional crafts, artistic motifs, conceptual systems, and other distinguishing features remain in memory, conservative groups and organizations within it collect relevant information and record it in writing, in pictures, or in other ways. Some teach dances or ancient crafts; some work to keep alive traditional religious practices. Deeply held values, like patriotism, reverence for institutions, and reverence for symbols like a flag, are maintained partly by acts of public allegiance or by commemorative celebrations. Americans pledge allegiance to their flag; British subjects toast their Queen. Births of famous men, dates of battles, declarations of peace, and the society's founding are remembered by special joyous or solemn days and ritualized forms of celebration.

Information stored on markers is protected from damage in appropriate ways, and it may be deliberately stored redundantly so that even if some copies are lost, the information will still be retained.

Little of a specific nature can be said about the duration of a society's memories. In general they fade from common currency over decades or centuries—though recorded history preserves them for students and scholars. Very vivid events which affect many individuals at the time they happen and which become embodied in myths, literature, or artistic expressions of other sorts may, often in distorted form, outlast the society. Durable markers, like the Rosetta stone, may do the same. Relevance of an occurrence to the lives of succeeding generations must favor retention of memories concerning it. On the other hand, it is often said that societies forget quickly. Men often outlive the popular memories of their deeds.

(c) *Loss and alteration during storage.*   Information held in human memory over long periods is subject to distortion while it is stored, as research at other levels has shown (see page 421). Details are simplified, memorable aspects of events are accented, and similar facts are merged. Such distortion, some of it deliberate, occurs also in written materials as they are edited, repeated, and interpreted over time, particularly if no reliable original source material has survived or if the society's deeply held values are concerned. Heroes become braver; villains, more dastardly. Bad men, like Billy the Kid and the James brothers, become popular heroes.

(*d*) *Retrieval from storage.* Retrieval is a major problem in large, modern societies with their enormous volume of stored information, dispersed to many organizations, groups, and persons spread widely in space. Information needed to solve a crucial problem may be available in the nervous system of a particular person, in the files of a single organization, or in the stacks of a specific library, but it is of no value to the society if it remains in an inaccessible location. An example of successful retrieval of valuable information is given by Busch:

It is estimated that only one-fourth of the country's available scientific literature is catalogued. Just one fourth! There is no way to tell what might be of value in the rest. And who can prophesy what may seem relatively unimportant today, may not turn out to be vital tomorrow?

Of course, we all know about the Manhattan Project in World War II, which led to the first successfully controlled nuclear fission. Some of you may recall that in 1942 scientists in this project had trouble getting good castings of high-purity uranium needed for the critical experiments Fermi was conducting.

The powdered form of uranium that was first used was causing difficulty. The scientists began to consider the possibility of producing uranium metal initially in massive form. Had it ever been done before? It had.

Sixteen years before, four New Hampshire University research workers had charged a steel container with uranium tetrachloride and calcium, heated it electrically in a vacuum chamber, let it cool, and recovered a 3-pound fused lump of metallic uranium.

In 1926, the process was of potential interest only to the ceramic industry which was using small amounts of uranium as a pottery coloring agent—and for lack of high quality materials needed, the process was abandoned.

But the researchers published their findings—and fortunately, the American Chemical Society's Chemical Abstract Service gave their report an 8-line summary among some 29,000 other abstracts published that year. In 1942, atomic research teams found the abstract, repeated the experiment. It was a significant assist.

But trying to find such possible assists today—searching our mounting "paper haystack" for a few pertinent pages—has become an overwhelming task.

Five years ago the publication, MACHINE DESIGN, headed a report on the problem thus: "As one observer notes: We are in danger of redesigning the wheel three times a week."[125]

As a result of these retrieval problems, many components of this subsystem at the society level are concerned with retrieval only, leaving the storage in dispersed form. Scientific associations, like the American Psychological Association, publish annual abstracts that give a brief summary of the contents of thousands of books, papers, and other scientific reports relevant to the field. Hundreds of abstracting and indexing services provide coverage of published materials for industry.[126] The National Referral Center for Science and Technology at the Library of Congress refers people seeking material on specific topics in science or technology to an information source in government, industry, a university, or a professional organization.

Computerized union catalogs, available to remote terminals, link libraries that are often geographically far apart. Access to materials is accomplished by sending originals or facsimiles of articles or complete books through the mail.

Access to information stored in downwardly dispersed components presents societies with ethical decisions (see page 803). Torture of prisoners of war, tapping of telephone lines by police or other governmental units, and use of the power of subpoena by courts are all methods employed by some governments to retrieve information from organism and group components against their will. When methods like these are used by other than official units, they are punishable under law. Governments of societies also ask, and often receive, voluntary cooperation in supplying information from groups and persons, although in complying, they may reveal things their associates do not want made public. Surveys and research projects that interview people who remember historic events or culturally interesting songs or stories are less authoritarian ways of retrieving downwardly dispersed information.

Representative *variables* of the process of remembering include: *Meaning of information stored in the memory.* Example: The new constitution included a bill of rights that expressed the founders' concern for individual citizens. *Sorts of information stored in the memory.* Example: The Swiss have kept complete records of births and deaths for more than 200 years. *Total memory capacity.* Example: More than 10^{16} bits of information were stored by the persons and artifacts in the United States. *Percentage of information input stored.* Example: Every word spoken in the United States Congress is preserved in the *Congressional Record. Changes in remembering over time.* Example: When the people had become literate, the society began to keep written records. *Changes in remembering with different circumstances.* Example: The information load became so heavy that several hundred computers were used to keep records of the government. *Rate of reading into memory.* Example: The Library of Congress acquires a million new titles each year. *Lag in reading into memory.* Example: The Indian folk songs and stories were almost forgotten because no one had written them down. *Costs of reading into memory.* Example:

Putting the card catalogs of the Library of Congress on tapes could cost as much as $70 million. *Rate of distortion of information during storage.* Example: After 500 years the story of Rome's founding was sheer myth. *Time information is in storage before being forgotten.* Example: The society had used a red glaze on its pottery for hundreds of years, but no one in the last generation knew how to produce it. *Sorts of information retrieved.* Example: The assistant attorney general subpoenaed all the recent transactions among leaders of the plumbing supply industry during an antitrust investigation. *Percentage of stored information retrieved from memory.* Example: One of six federally indicted firms had lost its files, making them unavailable. *Order of retrieval from memory.* Example: Recently published books were more in demand than older ones at the national library. *Rate of retrieval from memory.* Example: Scholars from a number of different universities asked for permission to see the national museum's collection of rare coins each day. *Lag in retrieval from memory.* Example: After several weeks of searching among citizens of the country, a man was found who could read the inscriptions on the latest archaeological discovery. *Cost of retrieval from memory.* Example: The nationwide record search cost several thousand dollars but resulted in substantial savings for the space program.

3.3.7 Decider, the executive subsystem which receives information inputs from all other subsystems and transmits to them information outputs that control the entire society.

3.3.7.1 Structure A society's decider consists of its central governing components. They select the major goals and purposes which are to be pursued by the system at a given time and which legitimately commit the system's components and resources toward their attainment.

In democracies the organized structure of all voters is the highest echelon. The degree to which individual citizens of a country act as components of the societal decider varies from one nation to another. The deciders of societies, like those of corporations (see page 643), have at least two governmental echelons below the voters (or stockholders), if these exercise any power. A societal decider of minimum complexity is that of Muscat and Oman, a country which in 1970 had 565,000 people, who were headed by an absolute monarch with a personal adviser and a minister of interior in its lower echelon.[127] Saudi Arabia, with 8.4 million people, has a 13-man council as a second echelon under an absolute monarch.[128] Deciders of larger societies have a complex structure composed of many organizations arranged in several echelons. Hypothesis 1-1 (see page 92) seems to apply to societies, since

in general the more components there are, the more echelons a society's decider seems to have.

The highest echelon of a society's decider is commonly occupied by a man or woman with the title "emperor," "king," "queen," "president," "chancellor," "prime minister," "regent," or other such designation, but a dyad, like a ruling king and queen, or a small group, like a military junta, may occupy the top position. While many societies combine the positions of chief of state and head of government, as Mexico, Paraguay, and the United States do, others, like West Germany and England, have separate components for the two positions. The government of the Soviet Union is officially headed by the President of the Presidium, but the executive and administrative responsibility is shared by the First Secretary of the Central Committee of the Communist party and the Chairman of the Council of Ministers. Switzerland's chief executive is a Federal Council composed of seven councilors and the President and Vice President of the Council.

Although the title may be held by a single person or group, the office of the chief decider in large societies is nonetheless an organization. The Presidency of the United States, for example, is an organization of over 2,000 people, headed by the President and including Cabinet secretaries, assistants to the President, and many others.[129]

Below the top echelons, the structure of societal deciders varies greatly from system to system, since each society develops and modifies its individual governing subsystem in the course of its unique history. Many present-day societies reflect their origins as amalgamations of two or more separate societies by having federal decider structures. This is true of Cameroon, which has a single president as head of state and head of the federal government, and two prime ministers, one for East Cameroon, formerly the Republic of Cameroon, and one for West Cameroon, formerly a part of the British Empire. The Soviet Union, Czechoslovakia, the United States, Switzerland, Italy, and Brazil are other federations. The republics, states, or other component units are represented in central deciders of countries of this sort. They may, as in elections of presidents of the United States, be the units which select the chief decider.

The traditional tribal social organization of both Western Samoa and Botswana is continued in their present-day deciders. A House of Chiefs, representing the principal tribes, advises the President of Botswana. Western Samoa has a complicated combination of parliamentary and tribal governmental forms.

The overwhelming majority of present-day societies have numerous executive agencies. Also, they have legislatures, parliaments, or similar bodies as parts of their decider structures, often as a second echelon under the governmental head. The requirements of modern life make unworkable a democracy in which all voters participate in all decisions, and so legislators are selected to represent them. Only two absolute monarchs and the Pope head decider subsystems with no provision for legislative bodies (but see page 801).

Judicial and religious organizations may also be decider components.

In addition to the executive, legislative, and judicial branches of the United States government, a large number of quasijudicial organizations, like the Securities and Exchange Commission, the Federal Reserve Board, the Interstate Commerce Commission, and the Federal Trade Commission, are decider components that are not part of the structure of any of the three branches, although the President appoints their heads and Congress allocates necessary funds.

The table of organization of a decider like the United States government is complex indeed. If a chart were drawn of it, the orderly "chain of central command" found in charts of large corporations would not be in evidence. It is clear that a system of this sort must develop appropriate adjustment processes for internal information flows and coordination if it is to work (see pages 849 and 850).

The structure of nations with more centralized deciders, like the Soviet Union and China, reflects their greater amount of central control in their "monolithic" form and more clearly drawn lines of command reaching from the highest governmental echelon to all component organizations of the system. China, like the Soviet Union, has a decider with a dual structure, the party chairman and the premier constituting the top echelon. An elected legislature is a second echelon (see page 799). Directly under the central authority are three administrative echelons: provinces, autonomous regions, and municipalities. Peoples's congresses and people's councils are local decider components.

The range of societal functions which the central decider can directly control differs from one society to another (see page 867). Except during war emergencies and periods of economic instability, private corporations in capitalist societies typically make many sorts of decisions related to business and commerce. Components at the top echelon of the society may consist largely of regulatory or advisory boards or mediators between labor and management. Decisions to merge large business and industrial organizations in the United States, for example, are subject to review by the Interstate Commerce Commission, which may forbid them if there is a possibility that a monopoly will develop, but ordinary business decisions are made without governmental participation. The situation is radically different in China and the Soviet Union, where the top echelon of the decider subsystem can control all aspects of the economy.

Deciders of states of the United States are the highest echelon for many sorts of decisions, certain of which, like some that affect the environment, are crucial to neighboring states or to the entire society. Air pollution, for example, cannot be stopped from crossing state boundaries. Revenue sharing in the United States permits decision making about allocations of federal funds by states and local governments. In societies whose political parties are not part of the official decider structure, private organizations choose candidates to run for public office. Candidates for President of the United States are selected by vote among members of such parties.

Research organizations are components of the decider when lump-sum payments for which no detailed research proposal is required are allocated to the organization.

Decisions to adopt a style or an innovation are usually downwardly dispersed to group and organism levels, although official components of some societies do this. Turkey, in the early part of the twentieth century, enforced laws against veiling of women. The Soviet Union makes centralized decisions about what styles of clothing are to be manufactured and sold and about whether private cars will be built.

When, as a result of war or other disruption, components of another society act as an echelon above the society's own decider, the components are outwardly dispersed, and the society is *externally penetrated*.[130] The United States penetrated Japan in this way for several years immediately following Japan's surrender at the end of World War II. An expansion of the concept of external penetration includes also indirect involvement of another country in selecting goals, allocating values and costs, mobilizing resources and capabilities, and integrating the society.[131] Such hegemony is implemented when outsiders exert influence on various echelons of a society's decider. These outsiders may include officials who provide foreign aid, teachers, multinational business and industrial organizations, religious workers, Peace Corps workers, and governmental and military advisers.

Artifacts in this subsystem are the buildings that shelter component organizations and machines such as computers, which are increasingly used in the analytic stage of the decider process.

3.3.7.2 Process   A society's rights over people, physical resources, land, money, and credit supersede the rights of lower-level systems. In *The Common Law*, Oliver Wendell Holmes, Jr., said:

No society has ever admitted that it could not sacrifice individual welfare to its own existence. If conscripts are necessary for its army, it seizes them, and marches them, with bayonets in their rear, to death. It runs highways and railroads through old family places in spite of the owner's protest, paying in this instance the market value, to be sure, because no civilized government sacrifices the citizen more than it can help, but still sacrificing his will and his welfare to that of the rest.[132]

Citizens of a society often acknowledge these rights as legitimate. They may regard their source as supernatural. European kings ruled by "divine right." Egyptian pharaohs and Japanese emperors were themselves considered gods. On the other hand, the United States, in the words of the Declaration of Independence, derives its just powers from "the consent of the governed," and the Soviet Union has its mandate from "the people."

This societal prerogative is usually limited by constitutional restrictions (like the Bill of Rights of the United States), by law, or by custom, although some absolute monarchies and dictatorships have held essentially unlimited power over components of the system. Even in these societies exercise of such power is restricted by the limits of components' acquiescence. Central decider components of some federations, like Switzerland, have only specific, limited power under the society's constitution. In these, states or other units decide on all other matters. Limitations on decider power may also be imposed by other societies or by supranational systems that can intervene between a society's decider and its other subsystems or components.

In any society, therefore, some particular set of processes is subject to control by the central decider, while others are not. Many economic variables of a society with a mixed economy, for example, are controlled by adjustment processes among components with a minimum of governmental regulations (see pages 845 and 846). These are centrally controlled in some other types of societies. Societal deciders, whatever their constitutional powers, differ in their ability to elicit compliance from their own components or other systems in the environment. A society exercises its power by use of its assets, such as the gold in its treasury; the wealth of nongovernmental components that can be mobilized when necessary; its supply of people, natural resources, and artifacts; the strength of its armies and police; and, less tangible but no less real, the amount of support it receives from components, sometimes from other systems in its environment (see page 808).[133] Either a "weak" government has fewer assets that can be converted to power than a "strong" one, or it does not convert the assets it has. Power may be either potential or actual.[134]

The power of a societal decider is subject to variation with fluctuations of support, changes in financial variables, changes in laws or procedures, or changes in the number and importance of processes under central control. During the twentieth century, many governments have extended their scope so that processes previously left to groups or organizations have been brought under central regulation. Health and welfare services in the United States are examples.

The power of a large, modern society is divided among the complex of organizations, groups, and persons that forms the decider. Each of these is charged constitutionally or by executive or legislative decision with responsibility for particular sorts of decisions. Each of these organizations governs its own subsystem processes.

The deciders of lower-echelon organizations, however, are subject to constraints imposed by organizations higher in the echelon structure. Agencies of the United States government, for example, are constrained by congressional control over funding.

A society's power, whatever its extent, is dispersed among the echelons of the decider in ways that cannot be determined from examination of decider structure. Like organizations (see page 648), societies with closely similar decider structures may carry out their decider processes quite differently. Although legislative bodies are part of almost all present-day societal deciders (see page 800), they may exercise little power. In China, the National People's Congress met for the first time in more than a decade in 1975. Poland's Sejm meets to endorse party programs. Some South American societies concentrate power in the president. In 1970, the top echelon of at least 15 societies was occupied by a dictatorship. In such societies the constitution and the legislative bodies may be suspended.

An *a priori* calculation, using game theory, of the power distribution between the two branches of the United States legislature and the Presidency determined that the ratio of power of a single representative to the Presidency was, at the time of the study, 2:250.[135] A single senator's power, compared with the President's, was 9:350. The House of Representatives and the Senate as units have equal power, and the Presidency is two-fifths as powerful. However, if the Constitution were amended so that the President's veto could not be overridden, the House would be slightly less powerful than the Senate, and the Presidency would be twice as powerful as either.

Depending upon the extent of the franchise, a wide or narrow segment of the population participates in choice of legislators or executives. If there is a popular referendum, the voters may decide directly upon issues.

Societal decisions require consensus among components at some or all stages of the decision process. This is true because, like the organization-level decider and unlike that at the organism level, the decider at this level does not exercise automatic control over the components under its jurisdiction. They must accept its right to govern them and acquiesce to its decisions.

A dictionary definition of "consensus" is "agreement" or "majority opinion." The extent and nature of the necessary consensus vary in societies of different governmental forms, but any effective government must be accepted as legitimate. A society could be imagined in which this basic form of consensus was the only one necessary because all components would passively acquiesce in all acts of their legitimate government. Practically, much of the business of government is, in fact, carried out on such a basis. Decisions that are routine, noncontroversial, or specialized may attract little attention and present no difficulty in implementation. These rest upon a basic consensus as to the legitimacy of the decider and its right to control the system and upon previously formed consensus concerning specific policies.

In specific situations, components may form a consensus to demand adjustment of value orientations, choice of a particular purpose or goal, selection of alternative pathways to a purpose or goal, or control of the means of implementation of a decision. That is, consensus can develop at any of the four stages of deciding (see below). Although consensus is not necessary at all phases of all decisions, as when unpopular decisions are made by decider components, lack of consensus, when it results in conflict, may delay or block the making of a decision or complicate its implementation (see page 823). Adjustment processes designed to achieve consensus among societal components are discussed on pages 849 and 850.

Consensus forms when demands made by disparate units of the society are sufficiently alike that these can make common cause together. In the United States, alliances among a majority of societal units have tended to be long-lasting. One party or the other combines enough units to command a majority which typically exists through several administrations. Eventually, however, they weaken as the interests of members become less congruent. After the Civil War the Republican party commanded such a majority. From the election of Grant in 1869 to the end of Hoover's Presidency in 1933, only two Democratic Presidents were elected, Cleveland and Wilson, for two terms each.[136] From then until the end of President Johnson's administration in 1969, only one Republican, Dwight D. Eisenhower, served as President. The New Deal coalition, put together by Franklin D. Roosevelt

during the Depression of the early 1930s, included organized labor, black and ethnic components that together formed a voting bloc in large cities, many intellectual liberals such as university faculty members, the traditionally Democratic white voters of the South, and an unorganized mass of disadvantaged people who hoped for improvement in their condition through political action. Such coalitions are uneasy, since, together with the common demands of their elements, they also have opposed interests. Nevertheless, they permit continued guidance of the society in consistent directions for periods of time longer than the 4 or 8 years of one President's administration.

Echelons of societies differ in the sorts of decisions they make, just as echelons of organizations do. Policy decisions, those which concern the basic purposes, goals, and procedures of the society, are ordinarily made at high echelons, as Hypothesis 3.3.7.2-13 (see page 101) suggests. Such decisions provide a context within which other decisions are made.[137] They are more generalized and more abstract than decisions made lower in the echelon structure, which are more concerned with implementation of specific directives and established programs.

Societal deciding involves political activity, defined as " . . . those interactions through which values are authoritatively allocated for a society."[138]

Present-day societies, on the whole, are not particularly well governed. Human components arrive at their positions in most deciders by virtue of political acumen and learn their difficult craft "on the job." Their task is complicated by the fact that the connection between specific acts of guidance and their outcomes is difficult to establish. Etzioni notes that:* "Most societies, most of the time, are unable to achieve the goals they pursue or to solve the problems they seek to solve. The generally low capacity to guide societal processes, especially societal change, can be traced analytically to two major kinds of limitations—to deficiencies in control processes and to the lack of consensus."[139]

Decision processes of societies take place in four stages, as Hypothesis 3.3.7.2-1 suggests (see page 100): establishing purposes or goals, analysis, synthesis, and implementing.

(a) *Establishing purposes or goals.* Each society has its unique set of values which condition the behavior of members, influence its purposes, and are important in determining its purposes and the goals it will pursue (see page 39). These, like the values of living systems at other levels, do not all have equal importance, so that a hierarchy of values characterizes any society. Values are expressed in attitudes toward human or other life, human behavior, social relationships, money and property, nature, and the supernatural. It is possible that some are universal in human societies. Kluckhohn's analysis of societal values identified a number of fundamental questions that underlie the values of all societies.[140] The value hierarchy of a society is established by typical people in the culture making choices on the following 13 dichotomies, grouped into three clusters.[141]

Man and nature

1. *Determinate–indeterminate.* The contrast between belief in an orderly, lawful universe and one in which chance or caprice makes prediction and control impossible *in principle.* The first is expressed in Western science, in attempts at supernatural control of events, and in fatalistic acceptance, depending upon the culture. A resigned attitude or extreme voluntarism may stem from the second.

2. *Unitary–pluralistic.* Is the world conceived to be a single manifold, or is it ruled by two or more principles, each with different laws? Yang and Yin, mind and body, and the powers of light and the powers of darkness are examples of pluralistic divisions.

3. *Evil–good.* This is concerned with whether nature and human nature are seen as basically good or evil.

Man and man

4. *Individual–group.* Is the individual person or a higher level of living system, such as a family, tribe, or nation, given priority?

5. *Self–other.* The relative emphasis on egoism or altruism. Whether the needs of the self are placed high or low as compared with the needs of others such as members of a family.

6. *Autonomy–dependence.* The contrast between individualism and dependence upon others.

7. *Active–acceptant.* This contrasts trying to intervene, either actively or passively, in determining one's fate with acceptance of the order of events as unchangeable.

8. *Discipline–fulfillment.* This is the Apollonian-Dionysian contrast. Safety, control, and adjustment to the culture are opposed to adventure, expansion, and internal harmony.

9. *Physical–mental.* Either sensual or intellectual activities and reactions are placed higher in the value hierarchy.

10. *Tense–relaxed.* This is exhibited in the degree to which tension of any kind is pervasive or is balanced by a sense of humor and a calm easygoingness.

11. *Now–then.* The placing of emphasis on the here and now, as opposed to either the past or the future. The emphasis upon this life or a hereafter is a special case.

Both nature and man

12. *Quality–quantity.* Can the natural world and human experience be atomized? The extent to which measurement or other standardization, rather than qualitative considerations, is found in a culture.

13. *Unique–general.* The contrast between concrete literalness in which abstraction from experience is looked upon with suspicion (exemplified in Oriental cultures) and an attitude which abstracts and seeks for similarities in experience (typical of Western culture.)

These categories interact in various ways. Whether a culture which makes the "indeterminate" choice on the first dichotomy expresses this attitude in resignation or extreme rationalism depends upon other choices such as the active–acceptant dimension. If it is in principle not possible to control or predict events, either pessimistic acceptance or "free will" may result. Some combinations are mutually exclusive. Determinate–acceptant, autonomy–acceptant, and now–quality are among these. Societies differ in the ability of their members to verbalize these ideas and beliefs and in whether they are expressed primarily as positive "dos" or negative "don'ts." Each of five subcultures in the American Southwest—Mormon, homesteader, Spanish-American, Zuni, and Navaho—had a different profile when they were compared on these dichotomies.[142]

Values related to social interactions are completely specified, in the Parsonian conceptual system (see pages 19, 20, and 765), by the choices "actors" make on five dichotomous categories, the "pattern variables" of the system.[143] No action is possible until these choices are made, since situations otherwise lack meaning. They are: (*a*) affectivity–affective neutrality, the choice between immediate gratification and restraint pending evaluation of social consequences; (*b*) self-orientation–collectivity-orientation, the choice between personal and collective moral standards, interests, or goals; (*c*) universalism–particularism, the choice between applying cognitive or appreciative standards to situations, that is, whether general standards or aspects of the particular situation will receive priority in evaluation; (*d*) ascription–achievement, the choice between making evaluations in terms of the general attributes or the actual or potential performance of the system being evaluated; and (*e*) specificity–diffuseness, the choice between acting on the basis of any potential significance of a "social object"—such as prior obligation—or according to particular defined relevances. The typical choices of units of the society on these pattern variables reveal the society's value orientation.

These analyses are clearly relevant to the different types of societies discussed above (see pages 754 to 761). They are not exhaustive. Gross suggests that "modes of communication" should be added as a category on which values are based, since societies differ in the balance between verbal and nonverbal communication, the pace of communication, the balance between honesty and deviousness, and the degree of directness and indirectness of communication.[144]

In fact, it seems that almost any aspect of culture can become the basis for values. What these are for a given society is revealed in the things its members consider right or wrong, take for granted, and believe to be decreed by God; the things they treasure or consider beautiful; the personal attributes they reward; the things they will fight for; the provisions of the society's charter; and the society's religion, taboos, laws, etiquette, and child-rearing practices. The society's hierarchy of values is revealed in the choices it makes when values conflict and in its readiness to change a value-based cultural characteristic. "We hold these truths to be self-evident" says the Constitution of the United States of its basic value statements, but in practice, some are more self-evident than others to the country's citizens.

The values of a society are not to be regarded as fixed and immutable, although some basic values are essentially so. The general abhorrence of murder, as opposed to legal killing of people, is an example. It is based upon high valuation of fellow citizens' lives. Few societies, even in the modern world, place as high a value on aliens' lives. Beyond the most basic values on which few would disagree, societal components are not necessarily either certain about, or in agreement on, values. Etzioni says:*

Society decision-making centers frequently do not have an agreed-upon set of values and goals; there may be dissensus within the decision-making centers themselves or in a higher-ranking unit that instructs the decision-makers, and/or the values and goals may be too vague to provide the necessary criteria. Values often become more specific only as decisions are implemented, as the actual consequences of a decision become visible. Moreover, member-units continually change their perspectives because of changes in their internal composition or in the environment. *Values are not given but are fluid*

*Reprinted with permission of Macmillan Publishing Co., Inc. from *The active society* by Amitai Etzioni. Copyright © 1968 by The Free Press, a Division of The Macmillan Company.

and affected by the decisions made as well as affecting them. The assumption that values and facts, means and ends, can be neatly (or even less neatly) separated by decision-makers seems to be invalid.[145]

Subcultures of a society usually diverge from the dominant cultures to some extent, and sometimes greatly, in specific values and in their value hierarchies. The unwillingness of the Amish people to accept machinery, for example, which reflects a religious value placed upon a particular way of life, goes contrary to the high esteem in which most other citizens of the United States hold science and progress. In addition, each system within the society at the levels of organization, group, and organism has its individual value emphases, which may vary more or less from societal norms.

Societies are able to live with values that are not fully compatible, although not without a certain amount of conflict. Modern values concerning equality, for instance, conflict with a high valuation of achievement. The conflict complicates attitudes toward welfare, guaranteed income, and other programs that take from the rich and give to the poor.[146] A society in which conflicts of values are severe must undertake internal information adjustment processes to resolve conflict (see pages 849 and 850) since otherwise its integration can be threatened.

It is important, in considering the purposes and goals of societies, to point out that my definitions of these terms (see page 39) result in a restricted use of "goal." The purposes of a society are its preferences for certain sorts of steady states rather than others. These provide comparison signals that enable the system to determine whether variables are within acceptable steady-state ranges. Some general purposes appear to be common to all societies. They all prefer steady states which permit people to live together in an orderly manner. They expect component goals and purposes to be subordinated, at least to some extent, to those of the system as a whole. They prefer to meet at least the minimum needs of components rather than to ignore them. All these purposes are related to an even more general purpose of survival of the system.

Goals are the specific external things or states toward which the system directs itself at any given time, like improving the next year's harvest or sending men to the moon. While goals are ordinarily set with the intention of fulfilling the society's purposes, conflicts between purposes and specific goals can arise. Goals of components can also come into conflict with purposes and goals of the total system.

Decisions must be made by a society when variables are forced out of steady-state range by internal or external changes, when steady states that have prevailed become unsatisfactory, and when components with access to channels demand change. They are not ordinarily made in the absence of internal or external strains, although some, like annual allocation of budgets, are programmed to anticipate needs. Laws are made when changed conditions result in disputes or inequities. Programs are developed to meet needs. Threats and emergencies elicit activity to avoid or correct them. National planning is said to occur only in response to "the perception of imminent crisis."[147]

Societies that live in balance with their environments and in which the needs of components are met by the existing conditions have to make few decisions. Usually they change slowly.

A purpose or goal is adopted by the society when a controlling set of decider components accept it as appropriate. A chief of state may determine that a problem should be solved in the private sector of the economy rather than by the government. A proposed bill may be allowed to die in a legislative committee, never coming to consideration of the body as a whole. The Supreme Court has the option to issue a writ of certiorari, agreeing to hear a case. But it may refuse to do so. When officials make decisions not to act, societal steady states are essentially unchanged. The issue remains a purpose or goal of a subsystem or component, which must then abandon it, renew its demands, try to broaden its base of support, or seek another route to a central decision, such as demanding executive action if the legislature refuses to enact a bill or developing a "test case" for the Supreme Court if other routes to its goal are closed. When support for the purpose or goal is strong in the society, proponents sometimes resort to adjustment processes like civil disobedience or changes in decider structure that exert coercive force upon the decider.

Acceptance and pursuit of a goal or purpose require some measure of consensus among components of the society. Leadership by decider components includes enunciating purposes, to make components aware of the need for action or change, and marshaling support. The New Deal, the New Frontier, and the Great Society were all programs of social change toward new purposes for which Presidents of the United States have sought support in recent decades.

Large societies can realize many purposes and goals simultaneously, but their resources are never unlimited. It becomes necessary to determine priorities and select goals and purposes for which support exists or can be mobilized or which will reduce serious strains in the society that must be dealt with immediately.

(b) *Analysis.* This second stage of the decision process includes both evaluation of the problem and identification of alternatives. Since societies, like systems at lower levels, develop plans and programs that commit the society over time and involve a number of steps, the analytic process of evaluation occurs at intervals in ongoing programs to determine to what extent a purpose or goal is being achieved. A secondary set of alternatives, designed to improve performance, may be reviewed if performance is not satisfactory.

Societies face a severe and continuing problem in analysis because, for many goals and purposes, relevant social indicators and other information for use in analysis and in determination of alternatives are often extraordinarily hard to come by. Sometimes the question of what information would be useful or even relevant cannot be answered. There is far more agreement on goals and purposes in American society, for example, than on the means to attain them.[148]

(c) *Synthesis.* Societies, like living systems at other levels, select one or more alternatives for implementation in a particular decision situation, subject to constraints resulting from characteristics of the system itself, of other living systems in its environment, and of its physical environment. Some constraints upon societal deciding fall under the following classifications, certain ones of which are similar to those identified at the level of the organization:

(i) *Constraints imposed by the physical environment.* The extent of a society's territory, its natural resources, and its spatial relations to other societies and to mountains, bodies of water, and other geographic features constrain its decisions in many ways. Some options are irreversibly closed. Others, like expanding agriculture in polar regions or building a tunnel under the English Channel, are difficult and expensive.

(ii) *Constraints imposed by the system's own purposes and goals.* Societies can pursue many purposes and goals at the same time. Complete harmony among them is neither possible nor necessary. Choice of some alternatives, however, would directly threaten important steady states in the system itself or in the environment. These are rejected if the decision makers are aware of the conflict. If, for example, a society is deeply committed to making free education available to all capable children, it will not try to solve pressing financial or social problems by eliminating public schools.

(iii) *Constraints imposed by the values of the system.* Some alternatives are so unacceptable that they may never even be considered. A Moslem country would not bring into its search for economical sources of animal protein the suggestion that more hogs be raised for food.

Values affect priorities in deciding which among possible programs are to be implemented and the amount of resources to be allocated to each. The effect of values upon decisions concerning electric power production in the United States has changed over time:

Earlier in our history, when the prevailing value system assigned an overriding priority to the first-order effects of technology, our society would have resolved the conflict in favor of increased production almost as a matter of course. The side effects, such as pollution, would have been taken in stride. In recent years the values of the society seem to have shifted from an automatic acceptance of new technology for its own sake toward a deepening concern for environmental and other social consequences. The shift in values has begun to permeate the political process and is reflected in the President's statement of the national objectives relating to power as "both a high-energy civilization and a beautiful and healthy environment." It will remain necessary for the decision-makers to resolve the conflicts between the enterprise and the societal outlooks and the criteria that they respectively emphasize, but the old, routine and almost unconscious assumption that environmental protection must give way to production has become altogether untenable.[149]

(iv) Constraints imposed by limited resources. Alternative solutions to social problems or means to social ends vary in their cost in money, human and nonhuman resources, and time, which, for many decisions, can be regarded as a scarce resource. Large societies can, in addition to maintaining essential services of many kinds, undertake broad social welfare programs, implement extensive building projects, and even send explorers into space, all at the same time, but competing uses for available resources limit the amount that can be spent in implementing any one decision, and annual budgets are not infinitely elastic (see page 844). Limitation of time constrains choice of certain alternatives because of a pressing need for immediate results. A payoff in 50 years, even in the absence of an emergency, has less appeal than a more immediate result, if alternatives are otherwise comparable.

Societies face a problem in measuring comparative costs of alternatives, since a decision to commit funds or resources to a course of action must depend upon the benefits expected to result from it. Unfortunately, social indicators to measure the benefits and effectiveness of most social programs are not yet well developed (see pages 750 to 754). A cost-benefit analysis (see page 839) of a comprehensive program, like one to aid education in the United States, is not yet possible. Money costs, in terms of the number of tax dollars allocated to the Department of Health, Educa-

tion, and Welfare and other components responsible for implementing the decision, appear in congressional appropriations for each year and in the financial reports of each of the agencies. The benefits, however, are measured most importantly in human terms, and will not be entirely clear until young children affected by the program grow up to fill their adult social roles. Such outlays of dollars can be regarded as "hidden investments" in people and in expansion of knowledge.[150] What is more, most of the money governments channel to societal components does not leave the system, but remains to help sustain economic activity and stimulate flow of tax dollars to the national treasury.

(v) Constraints imposed by the society's past experience. A situation in which selection of an alternative has been constrained by past experience is seen in the effect of prohibition in the United States. The nation has come to associate the legal prohibition of the manufacture and sale of alcoholic beverages in the 1920s not only with its manifest difficulties in enforcement but also with increased crime and relaxation of social restraints. As a result, the view is now widely accepted that "you can't legislate morals."

(vi) Constraints imposed by the procedures and programs of the system. Societies operate within a set of written or unwritten laws. An alternative that goes contrary to established law or one that cannot be implemented unless the Constitution is amended will be avoided when possible.

Established social customs, morals, and etiquette may be harder to change than laws and can be expected to figure importantly in choice of alternatives.

Ongoing programs and standard operating procedures also constrain choice. Usually these will not be easy to change because of habit and the interests of the components involved.

(vii) Constraints deriving from the steady states in existence in the society at the time the decision is to be made. If the national economy is thriving, the government will hesitate to make major changes in its monetary or tax policies. Also, the political philosophy of the particular decider components that happen to be in power strongly affects their choice of alternatives. When the Labour party is in power, alternatives involving nationalization of railroads and coal mines are quite in order in England. They are not so much so when Conservatives are running the government.

(viii) Constraints imposed by need of consensus within the decider itself or among other components of the society. Deciders usually try to avoid any action that seriously threatens the consensus upon which contin-

uation of a party or administration in power depends, since remaining in power is an important personal or organizational goal for incumbent officials and political parties.

Since values, purposes, and goals of the organizations that make up a decider subsystem may differ, alternatives that are known to have substantial opposition within the government may be avoided. In the United States, for example, this sometimes keeps the legislative branch from passing a bill that is certain of presidential veto. The Attorney General's opinion that the Supreme Court would find an alternative unconstitutional or contrary to the known attitudes of the Court majority may also weigh against its choice.

The need for acceptance of a program or policy by components of the system outside the decider may also constrain choice. Deciders do adopt unpopular measures, like wage and price controls, rationing, and higher taxes, particularly in er ergencies, but usually public opposition, with its threat of loss of support for officials in power, leads deciders to avoid such actions.

(*ix*) *Constraints imposed by consideration of risk.*   Do the deciders of societies make more risky decisions than those of organizations, just as groups appear willing to make more risky decisions than their members when they act individually? It seems possible that they do. History celebrates bold leaders who win against the odds. Glory has not traditionally been gained by running a peaceful regime. In *The Prince*, Machiavelli extols one leader:

Nothing makes a prince so much esteemed as great enterprises and setting a fine example. We have in our time Ferdinand of Aragon, the present King of Spain. He can almost be called a new prince, because he has risen by fame and glory, from being an insignificant king to be the foremost king in Christendom; and if you will consider his deeds you will find them all great and some of them extraordinary. In the beginning of his reign he attacked Granada, and this enterprise was the foundation of his dominions. He did this quietly at first and without any fear of hindrance, for he held the minds of the barons of Castile occupied in thinking of the war and not anticipating any innovations; thus they did not perceive that by these means he was acquiring power and authority over them. He was able with the money of the Church and of the people to sustain his armies, and by that long war to lay the foundation for the military skill which has since distinguished him. Further, always using religion as a plea, so as to undertake greater schemes, he devoted himself with a pious cruelty to driving out and clearing his kingdom of the Moors; nor could there be a more admirable example, nor one more rare. Under this same cloak he assailed Africa, he came down on Italy, he has finally attacked France; and thus his achievements and designs have always been great, and have kept the minds of his people in suspense and admiration and occupied with the issue of them. And his actions have arisen in such a way, one out of the other, that men have never been given time to work steadily against him.[151]

Visits to the Nelson monument in Trafalgar Square, the many memorials to the Duke of Wellington, Napoleon's tomb, the statues of Winston Churchill, or any of a number of memorials to national wartime leaders in numerous other societies make it obvious that the paths to glory have not changed greatly between the fifteenth century and today.

In spite of the rewards accorded to risk takers, especially the successful ones, considerations of risk must enter the choice of alternatives, not only in war making, but also in carrying out the more productive processes of the society. Machiavelli says: "Never let any Government imagine that it can choose perfectly safe courses; rather let it expect to have to take very doubtful ones, because it is found in ordinary affairs, that one never seeks to avoid one trouble without running into another; but prudence consists in knowing how to distinguish the character of troubles, and for choice to take the lesser evil."[152]

The "lesser evil" was surely what was selected by President Kennedy when, during the Cuban missile crisis of 1962, he and a group of about 15 advisers determined that he had six alternatives, not all mutually exclusive. They were:[153] (*a*) Do nothing; (*b*) use warnings, diplomatic pressure, and bargaining, in this case offering to close our missile bases in Turkey in exchange for removal of Soviet missiles from Cuba; (*c*) try to split Castro from the Soviets by warning that an alliance with them would be his country's downfall and that the Soviets would sell him out; (*d*) set up a blockade of some sort; (*e*) order an air strike against the missiles only or against other military targets as well; and (*f*) undertake an invasion. Each alternative involved risk and danger in different degrees.

The risks connected with banning the missiles in Cuba, as the President saw them, were not only those posed by atomic warheads aimed at the heartland of the United States, since that threat exists in any case. He was also concerned with the major alterations in the global political balance that would occur as a result of their presence. Any course leading to their removal risked nuclear war with the Soviet Union, but it was intolerable to have them there. The first alternative was therefore immediately rejected. Soon the list was reduced to two, the air strike and the blockade. Of this, Sorensen writes:

The air strike advocates did not shrink from the fact that a Soviet military riposte was likely. "What will the Soviets do in response?" one consultant favoring this course was asked.
    "I know the Soviets pretty well," he replied. "I think they'll knock out our missile bases in Turkey."
    "What do we do then?"
    "Under our NATO treaty we'd be obligated to knock out a base inside the Soviet Union."

"What will they do then?"

"Why, then we hope everyone will cool down and want to talk." It seemed rather cool in the conference room as he spoke.[154]

The risks of a blockade, the alternative eventually selected, were great. It could become necessary, if the Soviet ships ignored it, to fire upon them and provoke retaliation elsewhere. It required a two-thirds vote in the OAS, or it would not be a legal blockade, which was important for a number of reasons. And it took time, during which the missiles could become operational, an outcome unacceptable to the deciders. It also had advantages that the others did not. It permitted the Soviets to avoid a clash by keeping their ships away. It could be initiated without firing a shot. It was more limited and less strident than an air strike. And if there was to be military action, a naval engagement in the Caribbean between the stronger fleet of the United States close to home and the weaker Russian fleet far from its bases was the best sort for the United States. It would appeal more to other nations. It allowed the Soviet Union some options. And the United States could still attack the bases by air if necessary. In the end, the blockade appeared to be the least objectionable alternative, and it was adopted, with the result that the missile bases were removed. Later, President Kennedy said that he had regarded the odds that the Soviet Union would go all the way to war to be "somewhere between one out of three and even."[155]

Both Hypothesis 3.3.7.2-9 (see page 101) and Hypothesis 3.3.7.2-10 (see page 101) receive some support from this historic episode. The first states that a system which decides to take novel action soon after the state of its environment reaches the point at which such action is possible, does so on a smaller scale than does one which decides later. This action was, indeed, taken as soon as possible, with a feeling of emergency. The action was on a smaller scale than other alternatives that could have been expected to produce the desired result. The second hypothesis states that initial decisions are more likely than later ones to favor a course of action that does not rule out subsequent alternatives. This, of course, also characterized the alternative chosen in this case.

(x) Constraints arising from the purposes and goals of the supranational system of which the society is a member. Supranational systems in the present-day world are, on the whole, less integrated and more partipotential than their component societies. Societies do, however, cooperate within them in some ways, subordinating their own immediate interests to those of the larger community. The United Nations, for example, adopted a resolution in 1961 that outer space and celestial bodies would be free for exploration by all nations under international law and that none could expropriate any part of extraterrestrial space. So far only two nations, the Soviet Union and the United States, have space programs and the capability of space exploration. They were both among the signers. Decisions to occupy the moon as a strategic base are constrained by this agreement.

(xi) Constraints imposed by the values of the supranational system. It is conceivable that a member nation of the United Nations might be deterred from genocide or from exploitation of the natural resources of another society because these have been stated as contrary to the values of the United Nations.

(xii) Constraints imposed by other societies. These are common in the international community. A society may be dissuaded from putting high tariffs on the goods of another society because reciprocal trade agreements would be upset. When smaller nations are disposed to go to war, sometimes their larger allies refuse the support that would make this possible. Blocs of smaller societies form to meet competition from larger ones, as the countries of the European Economic Community have done, limiting the power of the larger society to control and manipulate markets. The knowledge that one or more other societies would employ coercive force in the event of certain actions by a societal decider also acts as a constraint in many situations, such as the Cuban missile crisis, described above.

Decision processes of a nation extensively penetrated and influenced by another society are constrained by the values, goals, and purposes of the penetrating society. The extent of the constraint is determined by the degree of penetration and the number of societal processes affected.

Rationality in societies. In any form of societal decider, the arguments against the applicability of a strictly rational decision model that requires perfect knowledge of the complete set of alternatives in a decision situation, as well as of the outcomes to be expected from each, are no less compelling at the society level than they are at the organism, group, and organization levels (see pages 496, 579, 656, and 657). The possibility of satisfying these requirements may, in fact, be even more remote at this level.

The constraints arising from time limits make anything like a complete review of alternatives unfeasible, although some societal deciders have excellent information-gathering facilities. Hypothesis 3.3.7.2-6 (see page 100) suggests that the shorter the decision period, the less thorough in general is the search for relevant facts and alternative solutions. Of the alternatives that are identified, only a limited number can be thoroughly explored. The difficulty of connecting past decisions with their outcomes, which complicates the learning process for societies (see pages 794 to 796), also affects deciding, since consequences may be remote in time and far removed in the system from the events that brought them about. It is difficult to attach probabilities to possible outcomes. Estimation of the comparative costs of the different alternatives is a formidable job also because of the variety of units in which they are assessed, including long-term loss of confidence in decider components by components of the system, erosion of minority rights, diversion of funds and energy from other important goals and purposes of the system, and depletion of, or damage to, valuable natural resources. Comparative money costs over the long run may also be difficult to estimate. Like deciders of other levels of living systems, those of societies must satisfice rather than optimize, using what information they can gain as effectively as they can to guide the complex systems for which they are responsible.

Societal deciders, using an alternative strategy, may avoid any broad scan of alternatives, but instead confine their attention to those which will make little change in policies or procedures.[156] They try a limited change, discover the consequences, and, if necessary, correct it in further steps of an incremental process, developing evaluative criteria along the way.

A theory that seems to describe the process as it actually occurs in reasonably well-managed systems more realistically than either of the foregoing is that of Etzioni, who rejects both a classically rationalistic and an incrementalist description of societal deciding and develops a "mixed-scanning model."[157] This assumes that two fundamental forms of decisions are made in societies: contextuating (or fundamental) decisions and bit decisions. Contextuating decisions follow an exploration of alternatives, but do not require the complete scan or perfect knowledge of a rational approach. Bit decisions are made incrementally. In mixed scanning, fundamental decisions set the contexts for the more numerous bit decisions which follow and which tend in the same general direction. Bit decisions may prepare for fundamental ones. Rather than choosing between the two sorts of decision making, societal deciders use both. Etzioni says further that the decisions of decider components of high and low echelons differ in kind. Deciders at low echelons have a more instrumental orientation, making their decisions in the service of one goal, while the higher, and especially the highest, echelons are concerned with balancing several goals. Lower-echelon deciders make more bit decisions, while contextuating decisions characterize high echelons.

The mixed-scanning strategy, written as an "imaginary set of instructions for an unimaginative decision-maker" who is assumed to be committed to no strategy and to face a crisis that indicates fundamental review of earlier policy, is presented as a program:*

(*a*) *On strategic occasions* (for definition see *d* below) (*i*) list all relevant alternatives that come to mind, that the staff raises, and that advisers advocate (including alternatives not usually considered feasible).

(*ii*) Examine briefly the alternatives under (*i*) (for definition of "briefly" see *d* below), and reject those that reveal a "crippling objection." These include: (*a*) utilitarian objections to alternatives which require means that are not available, (*b*) normative objections to alternatives which violate the basic values of the decision-makers, and (*c*) political objections to alternatives which violate the basic values or interests of other actors whose support seems essential for making the decision and/or implementing it.

(*iii*) For all alternatives not rejected under (*ii*), repeat (*ii*) in greater though not in full detail (for definition of scale see *d*).

(*iv*) For those alternatives remaining after (*iii*), repeat (*ii*) in still fuller detail (see *d*). Continue until only one alternative is left, or randomize the choice among those remaining (and ask the staff in the future to collect enough information to differentiate among all the alternatives to be reviewed).

(*b*) *Before implementation.* (*i*) when possible, fragment the implementation into several sequential steps (an administrative rule).

(*ii*) When possible, divide the commitment to implement into several serial steps (a political rule).

(*iii*) When possible, divide the commitment of assets into several serial steps and maintain a strategic reserve (a utilitarian rule).

(*iv*) Arrange implementation in such a way that, if possible, costly and less reversible decisions will appear later in the process than those which are more reversible and less costly.

(*v*) Provide a time schedule for the additional collection and processing of information so that information will become available at the key turning points of the subsequent decisions, but assume "unanticipated" delays in the availability of these inputs. Return to more encompassing scanning when such information becomes available and before such turning points.

(*c*) *Review while implementing.* (*i*) Scan on a semi-encompassing level after the first sub-set of increments is implemented. If they "work," continue to scan on a semi-encompassing level after longer intervals and in full, over-all review, still less frequently.

(*ii*) Scan more encompassingly whenever a series of increments, although each one seems a step in the right direction, results in deeper difficulties.

(*iii*) Be sure to scan at set intervals in full, over-all review even if everything seems all right, because: (*a*) a major danger that was not visible during earlier scanning but becomes observable now that it is closer might loom a few steps (or increments) ahead; (*b*) a better strategy might now be possible although it was ruled out in earlier rounds (see if one or more of the crippling objections was removed, but also look for new alternatives not previously examined); and (*c*) the goal may have been realized and, therefore, need no further incremen-

tation. If this occurs, ask for new goal(s), and consider terminating the project.

(*d*) *Formulate a rule for the allocation of assets and time among
the various levels of scanning.* The rule is to assign "slices" of
the available pie to (*i*) "normal" routines (when incrementing
"works"); (*ii*) semi-encompassing reviews; (*iii*) over-all
reviews; (*iv*) initial reviews when a whole new problem or
strategy is considered; (*v*) a time "trigger" at set intervals, to
initiate more encompassing reviews without waiting for a
crisis to develop; and (*vi*) an occasional review of the allocation rule in the over-all review, and the establishment of the
patterns of allocation in the original strategic review.[158]

While such a "program" would not be applied in
exactly the same way by different sorts of decider
units and at different echelons of the societal decider,
it is applicable to the processes of the Presidency, a
legislature, a quasijudicial agency of government, or
other high-echelon decider. A similar sequence of
decisions can occur also in the development of law by
courts, when a "landmark" case before the Supreme
Court is decided on the basis of a body of opinion that
has been accumulating in lower state and federal
courts. These may, in turn, reflect a changing climate
of opinion in the society. The final result may be a
reversal of a previous trend in decisions or the enunci-
ation of a new principle. The landmark decision then
sets the context for other court decisions throughout
the society until it is reversed or otherwise changed by
later court actions (see pages 820 to 822).

The following analysis of deciding in different sorts
of societal decider components is confined to the
United States. Individual differences in the decider
structures and processes of other societies are sufficiently great to make it unsafe to generalize without
restraint from this decider to others, even those of
similar form. This is, therefore, a case study of one
societal decider.

Presidential deciding. The United States Constitution says: "The executive power shall be vested in a
President of the United States of America." It further
specifies that the President will be Commander in
Chief of the armed forces and will have the power to
grant reprieves and pardons for offenses against the
United States and to make treaties "by and with the
advice and consent of the Senate." He also has the
power, again with the advice and consent of the Senate, to appoint ambassadors, judges of the Supreme
Court, and all other officers "whose appointments are
not herein otherwise provided for," as well as any
others Congress may think proper. The Constitution
gives the President veto power over legislation passed
by Congress and provides for congressional passage of
legislation over his veto. His further major powers, as
detailed in Article II, Section 3, are:

He shall from time to time give to the Congress information of
the state of the Union, and recommend to their consideration

such measures as he shall judge necessary and expedient; he
may, on extraordinary occasions, convene both Houses, or
either of them, and in case of disagreement between them
with respect to the time of adjournment, he may adjourn them
to such time as he shall think proper; he shall receive ambassadors and other public ministers; he shall take care that the
laws be faithfully executed, and shall commission all the officers of the United States.

These powers are considerably less than those exercised by the British monarchs in 1788, when the Constitution was adopted. The royal powers that were
retained when the Colonies became independent were
partialed among the three branches of the United
States government.[159] Nevertheless, they add up to an
impressive concentration of decision-making power
in a single person. Aside from having to act with the
"advice and consent" of the Senate on specific sorts of
questions, the President is unconstrained by any constitutional obligation to include any man or group in
his deliberations or decisions. Not the Vice President,
since his only constitutional role is to preside over the
Senate. Not the Cabinet, although many Presidents
have consulted with it on policy matters.[160] The heads
of executive departments, who together form the President's Cabinet, have met in a group with the President since Washington's administration, but this has
been a matter of custom, not law.[161] Not until 1907 did
a law recognize the Cabinet. The recognition came
when department heads who were also Cabinet members received an increase in salary.

Presidents have permitted no attrition of their powers over the years. The importance of the executive
relative to the other branches has, in fact, increased as
Presidents have jealously guarded their prerogatives
and claimed inherent powers on the strength of the
wording of the Constitution that "vests" the executive
power in them. Of President Kennedy, Sorenson says:

Any affront to his office—whether it came from Congress on
the B-70, Khruschev on Cuba, Big Steel on prices, or his own
church on education—was resisted. What he could not accomplish through legislation—to fight recession, inflation, race
discrimination and other problems—he sought to accomplish
through Executive Orders, proclamations, contingency funds,
inherent powers, unused statutes, transfers of appropriations,
reorganization plans, patronage, procurement, pardons, Presidential memos, public speeches, and private pressures.

Example: In the summer of 1963, unable to obtain passage of
his education bill and concerned about growing youth unemployment, he used his Presidential "emergency fund" to distribute $250,000 for guidance counselors in a drive against
school dropouts.

Example: His first Executive Order, improving surplus food
distribution to the needy, had been previously held up by his
predecessor for lack of clear statutory authority. Kennedy
issued it immediately, drawing upon his constitutional powers and on revenues available from custom fees.[162]

In his memoirs President Lyndon Johnson describes
a struggle with Congress over an amendment to a

foreign-aid bill which would have made loans to finance trade with communist countries illegal, an amendment he did not want. He called the House of Representatives back from their Christmas holidays, and after he finally won he said: "At that moment the power of the federal government began flowing back to the White House. . . . I had just completed one of the most trying and most intensive, sustained efforts of my life. While I knew there would be hard days ahead—and bitterly fought battles—I knew at least that the reins of government were firmly in my hands for a while. And I believe the nation knew it too."[163]*

A President of the United States is expected to be a leader of his people and to give international leadership as well. He is expected to initiate programs; maintain reasonably harmonious relationships among components of the system, such as labor and management; act as executive over government departments; be a communicator to his own society and to the world; take an active role in directing the armed forces in war or peace; take steps to correct deviations of economic variables from steady state; know and meet the needs of special groups in the population, while being the single representative of all the people; take responsibility for upholding obedience to the laws; head the political party that elected him; take an active role in forming foreign policy; direct and participate in interactions with other governments; make foreign policy; and much more.

Legitimate demands are made upon the President from five sources: citizens at large, his partisans, the Congress, his own executive branch, and countries other than his own.[164] With most of these he must deal in the public view. All his acts are taken in the knowledge of their widespread and sometimes incalculable effects. He knows also that all acts of his administration are considered to be *his* acts, decisions made during his tenure to be *his* decisions, and the responsibility for the state of the system during his Presidency to be *his*. This is true whether or not he personally has been involved. In most of the matters that he must deal with, he is the highest authority.

A President also has the responsibility, and the support, that go with being an object of intense emotional attachment, even veneration, from many citizens, who may have little conception of government aside from the President. President Eisenhower recalls that, at the moment his close friend General Omar Bradley addressed him not as "Ike" but as "Mr. President," " . . . from then onward, for as long as I held the office, I would, except for my family, to a very

definite degree be separated from all others, including my oldest and best friends. I would be far more alone now than when commanding the Allied forces in Europe in World War II."[165]

Each of the men who have filled the office of President has dealt with these facts of the office in his own distinctive way. Each has had his own style of deciding, administering, and interacting with people, groups, and organizations. In an attempt to explain the striking divergence among Presidents in style, character, and world view, Barber looks to their life histories, on the common psychological assumption that a man forms his personality as he interacts in his environment.[166] Character, he believes, develops largely in childhood, world view in adolescence, and style in early adulthood as a man moves into responsible action. The special culture which surrounds him, as well as the accidents of history that furnish opportunities for action and present a platform and an audience for his views at crucial times, are also important in making a President.

Barber maintains that Presidents divide into four types on the basis of two relatively unsophisticated dimensions of personality: *activity–passivity*, which describes the amount of energy a man invests in his Presidency, and *positive–negative affect*, the feelings of satisfaction he seems to derive from it.[167] Some Presidents have enjoyed the job. Others have seemed to suffer in it. Since each is a unique personality, none fits a category exactly, and success in the Presidency is not confined to any single type.

The four types are:

(i) *Active-positive.* Such a man enjoys being President, has relatively high self-esteem, relates successfully to his environment, sees productiveness as an important value, is most interested in achieving results, has well-defined personal goals, and tends to try to act rationally. If he gets into trouble, it may be because he fails to take account of irrationality in politics and finds it difficult to understand why others do not see things his way. Of the first four Presidents, Thomas Jefferson exemplifies this type. "A man of catholic interests and delightful humor, Jefferson combined a clear and open vision of what the country could be with a profound political sense, expressed in his famous phrase, 'Every difference of opinion is not a difference of principle.'"[168]* Franklin D. Roosevelt, Harry Truman, and John Kennedy, Barber says, are modern examples of this type.[169]

(ii) *Active-negative.* These Presidents work hard for little emotional reward. Their activity has a com-

---

pulsive character, as if it were an escape from something. They struggle to achieve power and to hold it. In this, they are hampered by conscience. They may have trouble managing aggressive feelings. John Adams was such a man.[170] He brought the country close to war with France, and under him the first political repression was legislated, the Alien and Sedition Acts. Modern Presidents of this type were Woodrow Wilson, Herbert Hoover, Lyndon Johnson, and Richard Nixon, according to Barber.[171]

(*iii*) *Passive-positive.* These are compliant, dependent, unassertive men whose lives are engaged in a search for affection as a reward for being agreeable. James Madison, an irresolute man, a compromiser, and an overly compliant person, fits the passive-positive description quite well.[172] He gave in to those who demanded war with Britain, and when he left the Presidency, the United States was on the edge of bankruptcy and secession. William Howard Taft, described by Will Rogers as "three hundred pounds of solid charity to everybody, and love and affection for all his fellow men," was another.[173] For him the Presidency was an unhappy experience. Although no dire effects resulted for the country, his political party was torn apart and lost power. He found his true vocation as a Supreme Court Justice. Warren Harding, said by some to have been the nation's "worst" President, was also passive-positive.

(*iv*) *Passive-negative.* Presidents of this type do not enjoy politics and tend to do little in office. They are in politics because they think they ought to be. They tend to withdraw from conflict and to emphasize principles and procedures. They are above sordid politicking. George Washington, who was persuaded against his wishes to accept the Presidency, was such a man.[174] He remained aloof and was no innovator, but he inspired confidence, giving the nation time to develop and organize. Dwight Eisenhower, who also accepted the Presidency reluctantly, fits best into this category. Calvin Coolidge was another man of this sort.

In Barber's opinion, the above four-way categorization provides an instrument for predicting the sort of President any particular candidate will become. In any event, a highly personalized approach to office is probably inevitable in a system which focuses so sharply upon a single man. When a man becomes President, he acts in accordance with his character and in response to the forces that impinge upon him in office. The result is highly individual performance.

President Franklin Roosevelt, for example, was said to have enjoyed making decisions. He organized and administered his personal staff and executive offices in such a way that no important decisions were made by anyone else.[175] In the course of a decision, he sought information from every possible source. Almost 100 people could phone him directly without first stating their business to a secretary.[176] He was willing to listen to arguments and even to allow direct disagreement from those around him. But when he changed from "I think" or "in my judgment" to "the President thinks," the discussion was over.[177]

A President's deciding on any question—the alternatives he considers; the values, risks, and payoffs he attaches to them; and the political and personal factors that enter the equation—can probably never be fully known. Presidents and those close to them have, however, tried to describe the decision process as it took place in some important acts. Presidents Truman, Eisenhower, and Johnson published accounts of their Presidencies soon after they left office. President Kennedy's short term in office has been described in detail by others. Excerpts from one such account appear above (see pages 807, 808, and 810).

Among the most fateful decisions made for the United States by any recent President were those of President Lyndon Johnson concerning the conflict in Southeast Asia. It was during the Johnson Presidency that United States involvement in the affairs of Vietnam grew from the 16,000 "military advisers" sent there by President Kennedy in 1963 to the more than 500,000 men engaged in air and ground warfare in 1968.[178] President Johnson has provided an account of a series of decisions that led toward this result. His first decision, made in 1963, soon after he succeeded to the Presidency after President Kennedy's assassination, was to continue the policies of the previous government.[179] His second, in August 1964, the one that changed the character of participation from advice and training to commitment of American men to battle, was to engage in air strikes against North Vietnamese PT boats and a single oil depot in reprisal for attacks upon destroyers of the United States in the Tonkin Gulf and to ask for a congressional resolution in support of his Southeast Asian policy.[180] The third, in February 1965, was to attack military targets in North Vietnam below the 19th parallel with air power.[181] The fourth, on May 10, 1965, was to undertake a limited bomb pause in the hope that the government of North Vietnam would engage in peace talks.[182] When they did not, bombing was resumed. The fifth, which the President considered the hardest, took place in July 1965.[183] It committed the United States to major combat in Vietnam. During this whole period the number of men in Vietnam had been increasing and had reached 75,000, including four Marine divisions and one Marine air squadron. Their role had changed gradually from that of "advisers" to that of independent ground soldiers. Congress had increased its funding of the operation, including a supplemental appropriation of $700 million. This was done in a number of decisions that arose out of specific situations.[184]

The decisions that followed these throughout President Johnson's term concerned the conduct of the war and the continuing attempts to arrange a negotiated settlement that would permit withdrawal of United States forces from Vietnam.[185]

In each of these decision situations the President and his advisers perceived that they had alternatives. Although the final decision was the President's, his advisers, both military and civilian, were involved throughout the decision process. These men submitted reports and recommendations and met to discuss possible courses of action. One such report, written by Undersecretary of State George Ball, was submitted in October 1964 to Dean Rusk, Secretary of State, and to two of the President's closest advisers, Robert McNamara, Secretary of Defense, and McGeorge Bundy, the President's Special Assistant for National Security Affairs. In 1972 the press obtained a copy, which was published.[186] The President received this report in January 1965, at about the time his third decision—to attack North Vietnam with air power—was being synthesized. Pressure to take this course had been exerted for some time by the Joint Chiefs of Staff and Ambassador Taylor, who represented the United States in Vietnam, because American bases were being attacked, planes destroyed, and men killed.[187] The President had yielded to the extent of permitting United States jets to be used against the Viet Cong if General Westmoreland, the United States field commander, considered it absolutely necessary.

As Ball analyzed the situation, four alternatives were discernible:[188] (a) To continue the course of action that was being followed at the time, that is, an effort to support and strengthen the South Vietnamese. Since the situation was deteriorating rapidly and a neutralist South Vietnamese government appeared likely to come into power, this course would certainly lead either to withdrawal from Saigon or to being forced into one of the other alternatives. (b) To take over the war by sending United States ground forces to Vietnam under United States military command. (c) To undertake an air offensive against the North, either to persuade the government in Hanoi that its support of the Viet Cong in the South was not worth the consequences or to improve the bargaining position with the South to make possible an acceptable political solution through negotiation. (d) To adopt a course of action that would allow a negotiated political solution without direct United States military involvement. Goals of such a solution would be to check or delay the extension of Communist power in Vietnam; protect Thailand, Malaysia, and South Asia; and minimize

damage to the prestige of the United States throughout the world. After analyzing each of these possibilities in detail Ball wrote:

The analysis contained in Part One suggests the following:

1. Unless the political base in Saigon can be made secure, the mounting of military pressure against the North would involve unacceptable risks.

2. To persuade the North Vietnamese Government to leave South Viet-Nam alone, military pressure against Hanoi would have to be substantial and sustained.

3. Even with substantial and sustained military pressure it is improbable that Hanoi would permanently abandon its aggressive tendencies against South Viet-Nam so long as the governmental structure in South Viet-Nam remained weak and incapable of rallying the full support of the South Vietnamese people.

4. The United States cannot substitute its own presence for an effective South Vietnamese Government and maintain a free South Viet-Nam over a sustained period of time.

5. We must be clear as to the profound consequences of a United States move to apply sustained and substantial military pressure against North Viet-Nam. The response to that move—or even the deployments required by prudence in anticipation of a response—would radically change the character of the war and the United States' relation to the war. The war would become a direct conflict between the United States and the Asian Communists (North Viet-Nam cum Red China.)

6. Once the United States had actively committed itself to direct conflict with the North Vietnamese and Hanoi had responded, we could not be certain of controlling the scope and extent of escalation. We cannot ignore the danger—slight though some believe it to be—that we might set in train a series of events leading, at the end of the road, to the direct intervention of China and nuclear war.

7. Finally, it remains to be proved that in terms of U.S. prestige and our world position, we would risk less or gain more through enlarging the war than through searching for an immediate political solution that would avoid deeper U.S. involvement.[189]

Ball continued his analysis by discussing a political solution in terms of cost-effectiveness. He made the point that in his opinion, an air offensive would not improve the negotiating position of the United States and would be done at risks and costs incommensurate with the possible benefits. He contended that negotiation arrived at after such pressure would not necessarily be any better than negotiation carried out without such pressure.

He considered the goals of negotiation to be agreement of the North Vietnamese to stop the insurgency in the South; establishment of an independent government in Saigon, free to call on the United States or other friendly power for help if necessary; and enforcible guarantees of the independence of the Saigon government.

The paper concluded:

What I am urging is that our Southeast Asian policy be looked at in all of its aspects and in the light of our total world situation. It is essential that this be done before we commit military forces to a line of action that could put events in the saddle and destroy our freedom to choose the policies that are at once the most effective and the most prudent.[190]

President Johnson's account does not indicate that he considered this set of four alternatives. One set that he did consider was formulated by Bundy and McNamara—to use military power in the Far East in order to force a change in communist policy and to negotiate from the present position.[191] The President said: " . . . the consequences of both escalation and withdrawal are so bad that we simply must find a way of making our present policy work."[192]

President Johnson made it clear that his own analysis of the situation included his belief that in the years before Pearl Harbor isolationism had not been in the national interest of the United States. Examples of ill-conceived isolationist policies were: refusing to strengthen Guam for fear of the Japanese; trying to defeat extension of the draft, an attempt frustrated by a majority of only one vote in the House of Representatives; and in 1947, opposing aid for Greece and Turkey in their struggle against Communist take-over.[193] He blamed isolationists for the failure of the League of Nations; he believed that the United States had dismantled its military forces following World War II too soon and had risked Russian domination of all Europe. And he applauded Truman's 1950 decision to resist aggression in Korea. In all of these situations the military solution, in his opinion, was the best solution. Moreover, the United States had signed the Southeast Asia Collective Defense Treaty in the 1950s during Eisenhower's Presidency, and Johnson believed that this treaty committed the United States to the course it eventually followed. In addition, the opinions he received from the military and intelligence officers he consulted were strongly in favor of a military solution.

At this point, major attacks on the United States Army's advisers' barracks at Pleiku killed eight Americans, wounded more than a hundred, and destroyed and damaged a number of aircraft. Everyone consulted, except Senator Mike Mansfield, is said to have agreed with the decision to undertake an air strike against Hanoi. George Ball was specifically included.[194]

At the time the last of the series of decisions that brought the United States into full-scale war was being forged, President Johnson presented five alternatives to the National Security Council:

We can bring the enemy to his knees by using our Strategic Air Command," I said, describing our first option. "Another group thinks we ought to pack up and go home.

"Third, we could stay there as we are—and suffer the consequences, continue to lose territory and take casualties.

You wouldn't want your own boy to be out there crying for help and not get it.

"Then, we could go to Congress and ask for great sums of money; we could call up the reserves and increase the draft; go on a war footing; declare a state of emergency. There is a good deal of feeling that ought to be done. We have considered this. But if we go into that kind of land war, then North Vietnam would go to its friends, China and Russia, and ask them to give help. They would be forced into increasing aid. For that reason I don't want to be overly dramatic and cause tensions. I think we can get our people to support us without having to be too provocative and warlike.

"Finally, we can give our commanders in the field the men and supplies they say they need."[195]*

He summarized his own synthesis of the situation by saying: " . . . in my opinion the real choice lay between alternatives four and five . . . 'to go the full congressional route now' or 'to give the congressional leadership the story now and the bill later.'" The arguments against declaring a state of emergency were that it could provoke China and Russia into increasing their assistance to North Vietnam. At the same time, efforts toward negotiations would continue. Again, only Senator Mansfield failed to agree. He spoke of the discontent of the people at this time. But he, too, agreed to support the President.

In his "lonely vigils" President Johnson thought of the possible outcomes of alternatives that let South Vietnam fall to Hanoi. As he saw them, they were the following:[196] All of Southeast Asia would pass under Communist control. This was the "domino theory," and Presidents Kennedy and Eisenhower had also accepted it. The debate within the United States would be "divisive and destructive" about "who lost Vietnam." Our allies would conclude that our word was worth little or nothing. Moscow and Peking would move to "exploit the disarray in the United States and in the alliances of the Free World. . . . Finally, as we faced the implications of what we had done as a nation, I was sure the United States would not then passively submit to the consequences. With Moscow and Peking and perhaps others moving forward, we would return to a world role to prevent their full takeover of Europe, Asia, and the Middle East— *after* they had committed themselves." He thought, also, of young Americans going into combat and dying and of how their families would grieve. And he found this decision to be his " . . . most agonizing and most painful duty. . . ." No decision faced by a President carries greater risks and costs and has more incalculable outcomes than one which takes his people into war.

*This and paraphrases and quotations in this column are from *The vantage point* by Lyndon Baines Johnson. Copyright © 1971 by HEC Public Affairs Foundation. Reprinted by permission of Holt, Rinehart and Winston, publishers.

The memoirs of President Johnson and other Presidents repeatedly confirm that the synthetic phase in the making of major national decisions is a comparison of the cost-effectiveness of various alternative strategies, often in a very complex situation, culminating in the final selection of one particular strategy for resolving the problem.

From the President's office must flow a continual stream of decisions on topics related to all the many facets of his complex role. No man could carry out all the presidential responsibilities without expert help and a lot of it, and no President attempts to. As the society itself increased in size, population, and complexity and as its demands upon, and expectations of, the Presidency became more numerous, the task of the Chief Executive would have become impossible without an increase in the numbers of presidential aides. Assistants—multiple channels—were required if the President was to cope with his information input overload. During the administration of Franklin Roosevelt, a period when a step-function increase in the number and kind of processes under centralized control took place, the possibility of the Presidency being a "one-man show" ended.[197] Under that administration, the Executive Office of the President was given the organizational form which succeeding administrations have followed. It now includes a variegated assortment of organizations, groups, and people among which are the Office of Management and Budget (formerly the Bureau of the Budget), the National Security Council, and the Council of Economic Advisers. This has been referred to as "the institutionalized Presidency."[198] A President has also a personal staff, people who aid him directly, such as speech writers.

Recent Presidents have embodied their policy goals in comprehensive legislative programs. Beginning with President Truman, it has become customary for the President to present a legislative program at the opening of Congress. One such was President Johnson's "war on poverty," presented to Congress in 1965.[199]

Case studies of presidential decision making indicate that many components of the decider play a part in some decisions, not only by providing staff support and information processing services, but also by influencing the choice of alternatives. When an issue is important to several executive agencies, affects the personal power of high-echelon executives, and is crucial to the President's programs, decisions concerning it become the center of intense political activity. The processes that culminate in decisions are often complex and sometimes devious, as when President Eisenhower's staff, particularly Attorney General Brownell, without the President's support, "boot-legged" a civil rights measure to Congress.[200] It did not become law (see pages 818 to 820).

Congressional deciding. An essential difference between congressional and presidential deciding is that in Congress, the vote of each legislator on measures that reach the floor has equal importance. In the Presidency, the individual values, purposes, and goals of persons other than the President are often influential in the decision process, as are the separate values, purposes, and goals of component groups and subsidiary organizations. In the end, however, it is the President who settles disputes, and it is the values, purposes, and goals that he deems important that are represented in decisions. Abraham Lincoln was one of the Presidents who had little use for the Cabinet as a body. He is said to have remarked with reference to meetings in which all the Cabinet members disagreed with him: "Ayes one, noes seven. The ayes have it."[201]

In representative bodies like the United States Senate and House of Representatives, and in the similar bodies of other societies in which decision is by majority vote, the effort of the separate interests to marshal the critical number of votes on one side of an issue or another is a crucial political process. In this the members are by no means equal in their effect upon the outcome, since the power of individual members varies greatly.

A second important difference between presidential and congressional deciding in the United States is in the distribution of responsibility for decisions among components of the two branches. The high degree of centralization of deciding in the Presidency is not matched in the House of Representatives and the Senate. In these bodies, largely autonomous committees, each with jurisdiction over a particular sort of legislation, have the crucial responsibility of determining whether, when, and in what form measures come to the floor for a vote by the whole body. Ordinarily the full chamber accepts the position of the relevant committee on a measure when it is put to the vote.[202] These committees, in turn, are permitted to allow subcommittees the real responsibility for specialized decisions. As a result, subcommittee decisions may be voted upon by the House or Senate and become the law of the land without revision by the committee or by Congress.[203] Joint committees of the two houses coordinate their activities.

Members of the United States Congress perform three separate functions: lawmaking, overseeing the agencies of the executive branch, and representing their constituencies.[204]

Except for some sorts of decisions made by the President alone, all policy actions of the government require authorization by Congress, congressional appropriation of funds, or both. Each of the standing committees into which the House and Senate are divided oversees those executive agencies whose functions fall within its scope. The agencies involved in distribution of surplus foods, for instance, are overseen by the Agriculture Committee of the House of Representatives. This committee is also responsible for legislation concerned with surplus-food distribution. The surveillance is exercised through informal discussions by committee members with agency heads; by formal hearings, particularly budget hearings when the whole conduct of the agency's business comes under scrutiny; and by the requirement of consent to appointments of executives. The third function of Congress, that of representation, is the business of each legislator, who takes the views of his constituents into account in deciding upon the stands he will take on legislative issues (see page 786).

An important aspect of the autonomy of congressional committees is their freedom to organize and conduct their business as they see fit. As a result, some committee chairmen exercise dictatorial powers, while others manage their committees more democratically. In recent years the House of Representatives has begun to require chairmen of committees to be more responsive to the will of the majority of members of the House than they have hitherto been.

Voting in both the House of Representatives and the Senate has been extensively studied, since it is a part of the societal decision process that takes place in public. Every note and debate that is not secret is published in the *Congressional Record.* Some votes require that each member of the legislative body answer to a roll call, and so individual decisions become a matter of record as well.

Senators and representatives are targets of demands transduced from their constituencies, particularly members of the party upon which each depends for continuance in office. A legislator receives demands also from organizations in the society at large or from individuals outside his constituency who hope to gain his attention. His party leadership within the legislative body of which he is a member, within the government and outside the government (the state party organization, for example), may also result in pressure being exerted upon him. And last, but not least, people who serve in executive agencies, sit with him on committees, or interact with him in legislative business exert their varying sorts of influence upon his decisions.

A study of the activities of organizations attempting to influence the votes of congressmen in a decision involving tariffs showed that although the popular impression of well-financed lobbies "buying, bully-

ing, or cajoling" congressmen, gained largely from an occasional public scandal, was inaccurate, pressure groups did exert important influence by organizing and channeling communications.[205] That is, if a congressman needed facts or a witness for a hearing, he turned to the organization that was the recognized spokesman for a particular point of view. Also, communications from individual constituents and from organizations bombard congressmen and are usually taken seriously.

A factor analysis of 111 Senate roll-call votes in the Eighty-fifth Congress, which ended its session on August 30, 1957, found six significant factors:[206] a farm-program attitude, a liberal-humanist attitude, two separate economy attitudes, an internationalist attitude, and a domestic-progressive attitude.

Cluster analysis of these data revealed 11 clusters. Cluster A represented the Republican as contrasted with the Democratic attitude. Cluster B could be called domestic-liberal humanism, and included the antitrust attitude. Cluster C was a loose cluster which generally favored civil rights and a progressive attitude. Cluster D involved generosity; its negative would be an economy cluster. Cluster E was anti-Communist in a form extreme enough to abridge individual liberties if necessary. Cluster F was another, separate economy cluster. Cluster G was a housing-program cluster. Cluster H involved pay increases for federal employees. Cluster I was opposed to public power. Cluster J represented an attitude favoring adequate federal support for the government of the District of Columbia. And Cluster K was an internationalism cluster. Some variables occurred in no cluster.

Another factor analysis studied Senate voting coalitions using a three-mode technique which permitted extracting factors related to individual senators and factors related to issues and which also permitted examination of changes in voting behavior over time.[207] Data for the study were senators' decisions on a total of 419 roll calls on votes related to eight essentially nonoverlapping major issues during the years 1964 to 1969. The eight categories and the kinds of legislation they include are:[208]

1. *Social justice.* All civil rights legislation and other related bills originating in the Judiciary Committee

2. *Constituency patronage.* Public works bills and others originating in the Public Works and Appropriations Committees

3. *Regulatory agencies.* Bills originating in the Commerce Committee

4. *Foreign affairs.* Ideological issues concerning foreign affairs originating in the Foreign Relations Committee

5. *Economic policy.* Issues of taxation, currency, and national debt originating in the Banking and Currency Committee

6. *Education and welfare.* Educational and labor bills originating in the Labor and Public Welfare Committee and the Post Office and Civil Service Committee

7. *Natural resources.* Bills relating to environmental issues and those originating in the Agricultural and Forestry Committee and the Interior and Insular Affairs Committee

8. *Military.* Bills originating in the Armed Services Committee and the Astronautical and Space Committee

Roll calls on these issues represented about 26 percent of all roll calls in the 6 years studied and about 90 percent of all roll calls originating from the committees mentioned above.

A senator's strength of feeling on each issue was inferred from the correlation between his votes and the "popularity" of the roll call, determined by dividing the number of "yea" votes by the total number of votes. Justification for this is found in the tendency of senators not to vote at all when they know they are in the minority, except when they feel strongly about an issue.

Mathematical analysis resulted in three sets of factors: (*i*) three time factors, one peaking in 1961, one in 1966, and one in 1968, the time periods during which senators' voting behaviors were correlated; (*ii*) four issue factors, indicating that certain sets of issues evoked similar voting patterns; and (*iii*) five senator factors, representing various persistent coalitions that affected the voting behavior of senators in the years 1964 to 1969.

The time factors were not, as might be anticipated, related to the fact that one-third of the Senate is up for election every 2 years, although they peaked in election years—1964, 1966, and 1968. They were, however, related to the fact that during presidential election years, general national issues are in question, while during off years, issues related to regional interests predominate. Thus in 1964 and 1968, the issues of foreign affairs, military policy, and economic policy were important, while the time factor which peaked in 1966 was loaded by issues of patronage and social justice.

The issue factors included one that was dominated by the issues of military and foreign affairs; a second dominated by social justice with education and welfare a distant second; a third dominated by patronage with education, welfare, and economic policy also included; and a fourth dominated by regulatory agencies with education and welfare second. The issue of

natural resources had not by then become very important.

The five senator factors were:

1. *Ideological.* Liberals scored high, and conservatives low. Economic policy appeared to be a major discriminator between these two groups.

2. *Partisan coalitions.* Most Republicans clustered together at one pole of the scale, and most Democrats at the other. Predominant issues were social justice, foreign affairs, and military and economic policy, the last being weaker than the others.

3. *A monopolar factor that separates out the states'-rights advocates,* i.e., *those who oppose expansion of the federal role.* States'-rights senators differ from the majority chiefly on issues that represent intrusion of the federal government into the domain of the state, such as patronage, regulatory agencies, education and welfare, and natural resources.

4. *A maverick factor.* Senators who consistently voted against the majority were represented here. On the negative end of the distribution were some senators who refused to "play the Senate game correctly." The positive end was dominated by Southern conservatives. The conservatives were mavericks on the issue of patronage, while the others were mavericks on just about everything else. There was a wide range of deviation on the scores of individual senators on this total factor, from Senator Morse, with a score of -0.7583, to Senators Hayden and Hill, with scores of about $+0.4$.

5. *A factor differentiating two kinds of conservatives, with conservative senators from all parts of the nation except the South getting positive scores, and Southerners getting negative scores.* On at least some kinds of issues, conservatives vote in opposite directions. These issues concern social justice, education and welfare, natural resources, and regulatory agencies. They agree most on foreign affairs and military matters.

Interrelationships among factors were found. Ideology and party were correlated, indicating that Democrats were more liberal than Republicans. Ideology and states' rights were also correlated, so that increased liberalism implied a decrease in the tendency toward a states'-rights position. Ideology correlated negatively with the maverick factor, indicating that liberals were more likely to be mavericks. There was a negative correlation between mavericks and states'-righters.

These factors were used in a decision-theory model in which prediction of an individual senator's vote on an upcoming roll call was attempted.[209] The hypothesis tested was that several stable sets of voting coalitions exist in the Senate and that the result of any particular roll call can be expressed as a weighted, nonlinear combination of these. One of these was the vote on confirmation of Judge G. Harrold Carswell, whose nomination to the Supreme Court by President Nixon was defeated 45 to 51 in April 1970, although confirmation had been expected.

An attempt to predict the votes of individual senators on the Carswell nomination, using all five of the above senator factors, resulted in about 91 percent correct predictions. Essentially the same result could be obtained by using only Factors 1 (ideology) and 4 (maverickness). Among those senators incorrectly predicted were some who had been under great constituency pressure. One of these was Senator Fong of Hawaii, whose state legislature had passed a resolution condemning Carswell as racist. Senator Fong had originally leaned toward Carswell but decided to vote against him. These influences were represented in an index of lobbying pressure, constructed for this roll call alone. When this additional information was included, the estimated vote predicted 94 percent of the senators' votes correctly, with only six misclassified.

A legislator's political party membership is an important determiner of his voting behavior, although the two parties differ in their tendency to vote as integrated units.[210] Party leaders within the legislative body exert influence to secure united action from members of their party, but members frequently defect. If this were not so, it would be unnecessary to vote, since the number of each party in any session is known. It is the job of party leaders to try to keep party members together on votes. Six factors appear to determine their success:[211] leadership commitment, knowledge, and activity; the nature of the issues (procedural *vs.* substantive, with the greatest unity on strictly procedural issues); low visibility of the issue; high visibility of the action; constituency pressures; and the activities of state delegations. In evaluating the polls taken by party "whips" to determine the probable outcome of votes, it was found that after waverers were identified by polling, leaders undertook to persuade them to change their votes.

An affirmative vote by a member obviously does not always reflect his personal preferences. Personal conviction is indeed one important motivation for voting, but if this is not in accord with what a legislator believes to be the attitudes of his constituents, the latter may be the controlling factor. Analysis of survey results in 116 districts of the House of Representatives showed that, on the question of civil rights, a congressman's perception of his district's views accounted for more than twice as much variance in his roll-call behavior as the representative's own atti-

tude.[212] When the issue was social welfare, however, the congressman's own attitude was more important.

A further significant determinant of individual voting behavior of legislators is agreements among members.[213] Reciprocity among members, also known as "logrolling," "back scratching," or "trading off," permits members to succeed on projects of particular interest to their own districts and thus to keep election promises by gaining the support of others who have no stake in the matter at hand, in exchange for similar aid to be returned when needed.

A legislative case study. A detailed account of a society's decision-making process on a major policy issue was provided by Anderson in a case study of the fate of a set of proposals for new civil rights legislation that were brought before Congress in 1956.[214] The bill that was voted upon that year was doomed to failure, but the debate over the issue in Congress and throughout the society led to passage, in 1957, of the first civil rights legislation to be enacted into law since 1875.[215] The House of Representatives had passed civil rights bills eight times since 1937, all of which had been either prevented from reaching the Senate floor or filibustered.[216] The principle at issue was the extension of civil rights enforcement *vs.* the tradition of congressional inactivity in civil rights matters.[217]

Principals from the executive branch concerned in the decision were President Eisenhower, Attorney General Herbert Brownell, members of the Civil Rights Section of the Justice Department, and other members of the Cabinet, which under Eisenhower acted as an advisory body on policy matters. Legislative components included the entire House of Representatives, which divided on this issue along sectional as well as the usual party lines. Within the House a group of Southern Democrats and some conservative Republicans opposed a bipartisan liberal group, many of whose members represented constituencies in large Northern cities. Also involved were Speaker Sam Rayburn, the full Judiciary Committee, Subcommittee Number Two of the Judiciary Committee, and the Rules Committee. In the Senate, the components most involved were the Judiciary Committee under the chairmanship of Senator Eastland, a Southern Democrat opposed to civil rights legislation in any form; a group of three senators deeply committed to the cause of civil rights; the Majority Leader of the Senate, who at that time was Lyndon Johnson; and some other senators who advocated or opposed civil rights legislation.

The third major decider component of the United States government, the Supreme Court, did not participate directly in this legislative effort, but its rulings on civil rights cases before and during the period when the legislation was being discussed were a part of the background of any new legislation.

No clear demand for correction of the inequities suffered by the black minority reached the society decider until the 1940s, when large sections of the American public began to shift from an attitude of apathy toward minority rights to active concern. These supported an increasingly well-educated, urbanized, and angry black population in gaining access to channels that carried awareness of the problem to the whole society. The blacks also became more effective in bringing their grievances to court.

In response to this growing concern, President Truman, in 1946–1947, had established a commission which made recommendations that included practically every major civil rights proposal that would be brought before Congress in the next decade, including all those embodied in the legislation that was finally passed in 1957.[218]

The issue of states' rights was central to the civil rights debate (see page 817) since, as the Supreme Court began to make decisions in favor of the minority, the new federal law came into direct conflict with a body of law that Southern states had passed to reinforce segregation. As matters stood in 1956, one who obeyed the federal ruling on school desegregation could incur state sanctions.

A number of instances of civil strife occurred, and the governors of Virginia and Texas openly sided with mobs against federal orders to desegregate schools.

The Justice Department, charged with implementing the President's constitutional duty to enforce the laws (see page 810), could not meet the increasingly serious situation effectively without legislation giving it broader enforcement powers. The process of achieving this legislation took place in several distinct phases, the first of which featured interactions within the executive branch.

It is not difficult to understand that President Eisenhower had no great enthusiasm for initiating legislation that seemed so clearly destined to cause dissension and go down to defeat, although he was personally sympathetic with the cause of the black minority.[219]

The legislation on civil rights was initiated by Attorney General Brownell while the President was recovering from a heart attack. He obtained the consent of the Cabinet, which was running the Presidency in the President's absence, and later received the consent of President Eisenhower to the drafting of the legislation. However, the President refused to permit bills containing the enforcement provisions needed by the Justice Department to be sent to Congress.[220]

The Attorney General then exceeded his authority and "bootlegged the bills to the Hill." In his discussions with the House Judiciary Committee he described "four matters," making no distinction between two bills the President had cleared and two "suggestions," which included the material in the bills he had refused to clear. When he was asked whether the suggestions could be put in the form of legislation, he quickly supplied the enforcement bills, which were introduced the next day by the Republican leadership of the House of Representatives.

While the bills were before the House, no one thought they had much chance, but civil rights advocates wanted the House to pass the legislation in spite of the general assumption that it would not get through the Senate. They thought such action would help liberals in their election campaigns. While neither party could risk open opposition, the senators who opposed it decided to prevent action by preventing voting until the end of the session. A tactical struggle followed, with each attempt to delay blocked by those who favored the legislation.

When the bill reached the House committee, delaying tactics were evident:*

The full Committee met while the House was in session, and soon discovered itself the target of new harassment. The House convened at noon, and eleven minutes later a quorum call was demanded. The bells rang, and the Committee members ran for the elevators. In time they returned to the committee room. Then at 1:28 P.M. there was another quorum call. The third came at 2:05 P.M., and upon the fourth, at 2:55 P.M., (Chairman Emanuel) Celler adjourned the Committee with nothing accomplished. The House adjourned shortly after. "A filibuster by quorum calls."[221]

The next usual legislative step—the writing of minority and majority reports on the bill—was delayed until May 21. Since, in the past, six of the eight civil rights bills previously passed by the House had been brought to the floor only by discharging the Rules Committee, by petition of a majority of the House, proponents of the bill prepared and circulated a discharge petition. In spite of the petition, however, the bill went to the Rules Committee, which, after more deliberate delay, granted a rule opening the way for its consideration on the floor of the House. Further postponements followed, but by July 16 no further dilatory tactics were possible, and the House finally resolved itself into the Committee of the Whole to consider the civil rights bill, H.R. 627.

Debates over bills are concerned with the substance of the legislation to be passed and, as in this case,

*J. W. Anderson. *Eisenhower, Brownell and the Congress.* Copyright 1964, Inter-University Case Program, Box 229, Syracuse, N.Y. 13210. This and the subsequent quotation from this work reproduced with permission of the ICP.

other considerations. Four accusations were leveled against this one: (*a*) that the Attorney General would be given the authority to initiate school desegregation suits, (*b*) that its procedures would eliminate trial by jury for defendants accused of violating the rights of blacks, (*c*) that the President did not really support it, and (*d*) that its scope was unduly broad and vague.

A final delaying tactic was a flood of amendments— some useful, and others designed to take up time and to confuse the issue. The bill finally passed the House.

Although the Senate had received the original bills at the same time as the House and although the Senate Judiciary Committee had held perfunctory hearings, no action was intended. When the House bill arrived, however, a small group of men decided to try to force a vote.

Again strong opposition organized to block it. Anderson says:

> House procedure is simplicity itself in comparison with the Senate's. It is correct to say that the Senate is able to accomplish its annual labors only by a system of unanimous agreements to disregard its rules. Liberals have repeatedly complained that the Senate's rules are designed specifically to impede liberal legislation, and in particular, civil rights bills. That exaggeration ignores the history of the Senate. Like any system of law, the rules enforce tradition, they provide leaders with more power than followers, and they give a decided advantage in every combat to those who take the trouble to familiarize themselves with the system. The Senate liberals had almost a tradition of disdain for the rules.
>
> When the Senate convened Tuesday morning, it rapidly became apparent that the civil rights issue had been very deftly shut up in a tight box. Bills and motions can be freely introduced only in the morning hour that opens the Senate's day. But by merely recessing the previous night rather than adjourning, the Senate was technically continuing the previous day's business where it had left off. Even the simplest words are terms of art in the Senate, and a day runs precisely as long as the Senate means it to. Each new day begins with a morning hour that occupies two hours of the early afternoon. But a new day begins only after an adjournment has ended the old day; if there is no new day, then the rules provide no morning hour. Although the calendar showed the date as July 24, the Senate was in fact still in the legislative day of July 16. And, as the Senate's President Pro Tempore, Walter George, explained it from the chair to Bennings, "In view of the fact that the Senate recessed yesterday, morning business is not in order except by unanimous consent."[222]

In the end, the Senate adjourned at 12 midnight, July 29, allowing H.R. 627 to "die" in committee.

Up to this point it appears that a small group of skillful politicians had succeeded in preventing social change desired by the majority of the society. The fact that this was an election year, however, permitted the powerful channels for internal transductions provided by nominating conventions, campaigns, and the election itself to make all societal components aware of the issue also.

Both parties included civil rights planks in their platforms. Both were compromises between the extreme positions.

With a clear mandate from the citizenry in parts of the society outside the South, and with some support in the South, Congress could no longer remain aloof from civil rights issues, and bills were quickly passed in the succeeding session.

Judicial deciding. The judicial power of the United States is vested in "one Supreme Court and such other lesser courts as Congress may establish." It is given original jurisdiction in cases in which both parties to the action are states, as when states in the West argue over water rights, and in certain other types of cases, like trials of ambassadors. It is the court of final appeal in the system of federal courts, which includes the federal district courts and the circuit courts. In this capacity it heard the final appeal in the Rosenberg trial for treason. It is the appellate court also, after all other remedies are exhausted, in cases which involve points of constitutional interpretation. Such a case was the one in which the death penalty was held to be "cruel and unusual" punishment, contrary to constitutional guarantees. It is the "guardian of the Constitution," deciding about the constitutionality of legislation that has been passed by the Congress and signed into law by the President. Such decisions are made only with reference to particular cases that challenge a law, and so a law can be in effect for a long time before it is overthrown. The Court also hears appeals in which decisions of state courts are tested for constitutionality.

A majority of the Justices sitting on a case is needed for decisions, but not all nine Justices necessarily consider all cases. Lawyers for the opposing parties submit briefs and may be questioned. Except where it holds original jurisdiction, the Court does not hear new evidence or question witnesses. Each Justice has a staff of legal assistants who search legal reports for applicable cases and review state and federal laws and precedents. Each Justice makes up his own mind. The Justices communicate with one another in private. The final decision is made in closed session, each Justice stating his opinion in order of seniority, beginning with the most junior and ending with the Chief Justice. Published majority and minority opinions support the decisions with detailed analyses of relevant law and of the precedents established by previous decisions of federal and state courts in similar cases. They also interpret applicable constitutional provisions.

The Court has great freedom in coming to its decisions since it may reverse decisions of lower courts or even previous decisions of the Supreme Court itself.

This latitude extends to constitutional interpretation. The Court may reverse a previous opinion or extend a constitutional provision beyond any former application. The Court is expected to be learned and impartial, above the sorts of direct influence exerted on other decider components.

The latitude allowed the Court in deciding what is, in fact, the law of the society has been referred to as the Court's "legislative function." In discussing the contributions of Justice Oliver Wendell Holmes, Frank says:

Ever and again he has reverted to his early position that "in substance the growth of the law is legislative," that "the secret root from which the law draws all the juices of life" are considerations of what is expedient for the community concerned, more or less definitely understood views of public policy. These are considerations "which judges most rarely mention and always with an apology." They are "most generally . . . the unconscious result of instinctive preferences and inarticulate syllogisms. The process of judicial law-making has been largely unconscious." It is important to insist on a "more conscious recognition of the legislative function of courts."[223]

Inevitably the Court determines policy for the society, since it must often make explicit choices among conflicting societal values. These choices cannot always be made automatically by referring to the preponderance of law and precedent or to the wording of the Constitution, which is a very general document. As Dahl says:

Very often, then, the cases before the Court involve alternatives about which there is severe disagreement in the society, as in the case of segregation or economic regulation; that is, the setting of the case is "political." Moreover, they are usually cases where competent students of constitutional law, including the learned justices of the Supreme Court themselves, disagree; where the words of the Constitution are general, vague, ambiguous, or not clearly applicable; where precedent may be found on both sides; and where experts differ in predicting the consequences of the various alternatives or the degree of probability that the possible consequences will actually ensue. Typically, in other words, although there may be considerable agreement as to the alternatives thought to be open . . . there is very serious disagreement as to questions of fact bearing on consequences and probabilities . . . and as to questions of value, of the way in which different alternatives are to be ordered according to criteria establishing relative preferability.[224]

Changes in interpretation and reversals of previous decisions by a Court reflect differences in legal reasoning, attitudes, and personal characteristics of the men who are Justices at the time, as well as changes in values of the society. One variable that continually affects judgments is the Justices' positions on the broad issue of states' rights. The issue, which is as old as the nation, is whether to assume that the intent of the Constitution was to limit the powers of the federal government, the decider of the system, to those specifically listed in the document and to leave the final jurisdiction in all others to the several states (system components) or to assume that the very broad, general powers given to the central government were not intended to be limited by later wording.[225]

In upholding the constitutionality of the parts of the Social Security Act of August 14, 1935, that impose taxes on employers and employees to provide federal old-age benefits, the Supreme Court reversed a circuit court decision that such a tax was not within the power of Congress but was within the powers reserved for the states by the Constitution. In its opinion, written by Justice Benjamin Cardozo, a specific statement of national policy is made:

Whether wisdom or unwisdom resides in the scheme of benefits set forth in Title II is not for us to say. The answer to such inquiries must come from Congress, not the courts. Our concern here, as often, is with power, not with wisdom. Counsel for respondent has recalled to us the virtues of self-reliance and frugality. There is a possibility, he says, that aid from a paternal government may sap those sturdy virtues and breed a race of weaklings. If Massachusetts so believes and shapes her laws in that conviction, must her breed of sons be changed, he asks, because some other philosophy of government finds favor in the halls of Congress? But the answer is not doubtful. One might ask with equal reason whether the system of protective tariffs is to be set aside at will in one state or another whenever local policy prefers the rule of *laissez faire*. The issue is a closed one. It was fought out long ago. When money is spent to promote the general welfare, the concept of welfare or the opposite is shaped by Congress, not the states. So the concept be not arbitrary, the locality must yield.[226]

The Justices, as men of their own times, living in a contemporary climate of opinion and receiving internal transductions from other societal components, reflect, in their opinions, value judgments prevailing in the society in which they live. If it were otherwise—for instance, had the Court been so insulated from the rest of the society that its judgments and interpretations remained rigidly that of a past time—legislated social change would become difficult. This is why President Franklin D. Roosevelt, who wished to change the nation, became so frustrated at the Justices of the Court, whom he labeled the "nine old men," that he tried to "pack" the Court by increasing the number of Justices. The men who are appointed to the Court are usually of known attitudes, opinions, and legal philosophies. They are identified as "liberal" or "conservative" by their past public advocacy of one side or another of causes. Some have developed in unexpected ways in their performance of the functions of the Court, but a President can usually, by his appointments, influence the sort of decisions the Court will make.

A study of 86 instances in which the Supreme Court declared federal legislation unconstitutional, however, shows that the Court is rarely at odds for very long with the views of the "lawmaking majority," which includes the majorities in the House and Senate and the President. This lawmaking majority can be expected to reflect the opinions of the coalitions of minorities on which elected officials depend for support and continuance in office (see page 850).[227] Since these coalitions often last for years or decades, national decision making tends to be consistent over time.

Over the whole history of the Court, about half the decisions that have held federal legislation unconstitutional were handed down more than 4 years after the legislation was passed, that is, after the lawmaking majority could have changed.[228] Exceptions occurred in the early years of the New Deal, when the Court and President Roosevelt were in conflict. Some other exceptions were not very important to the lawmakers in power. In those cases in which the Court opposed the other decider components, the policy results of the decisions were ultimately reversed, even if the decision itself was not. In a few cases the reversal occurred quickly; in others, only after a struggle.

Since the Court does respond to the information flows in the society and is aware of the demands upon the decider from other components of the system, it has, on occasion, led the rest of the decider in establishing policy. The Court evidently does not function nonpolitically, above the remainder of the decider and the society as a whole, to act as a sort of "Galahad" in protecting the liberties of minorities against the tyrannies of majorities, a role that would, in fact, be inconsistent with democracy.[229] Rather:

Considered as a political system, democracy is a set of basic procedures for arriving at decisions. The operation of these procedures presupposes the existence of certain rights, obligations, liberties, and restraints; in short, certain patterns of behavior. The existence of these patterns of behavior in turn presupposes widespread agreement (particularly among the politically active and influential segments of the population) on the validity and propriety of the behavior. Although its record is by no means lacking in serious blemishes, at its best the Court operates to confer legitimacy, not simply on the particular and parochial policies of the dominant political alliance, but upon the basic patterns of behavior required for the operation of a democracy.[230]

Deciding by regulatory bodies. Numerous boards, commissions, authorities, and other bodies make up the "fourth branch" of the United States government. They are charged with making decisions, including policy decisions of great importance, for the society, each dealing with specific societal components. In general, each of these consists of a group of men, appointed by the President and confirmed by the Senate, who are responsible for carrying out the agency's functions. They do not report to the President (see page 800), and he cannot reverse their decisions. As a result, conflict often arises between them and the executive branch. As in other organizations, routine or technical decisions may be made at lower echelons, but policy decisions or decisions of importance to the society are the responsibility of the top echelon.

The Securities and Exchange Commission, for example, has the responsibility of overseeing and regulating securities markets and brokerage houses. It determines such questions as how a customer pays his broker for stock—what percentage of the total price he must pay in cash and what percentage he may, if he chooses, charge to his margin account; what brokerage fees should be paid for stock and bond purchases; the amount of readily available assets a broker must have to allow for fluctuations in demand; and how securities are placed on the market, bought, and sold. Experts and investigative staff of the Securities and Exchange Commission observe and analyze the transactions under its jurisdiction, with a view to protecting the public and the financial community in general from the consequences of poor procedures, greed, incompetence, or dishonesty. The Commission has the right to demand compliance with its rulings. Like many other bodies of this kind, it has a quasijudicial function. It has the power to hold hearings to investigate any operations in the nation's securities markets and may, in cases of violations, call organizations to account for their conduct. The commissioners take testimony, consider evidence, and hear arguments. They may levy fines, order suspension of operations, or disqualify individuals from dealing in securities, if their findings justify such action. Ordinarily their decisions on the facts of a case may not be appealed to a court, unless questions of jurisdiction, procedure, or law are raised. Evidence of criminal activity is reported to appropriate state and federal officers.

The interactions among board members or commissioners in bodies of this sort, by which they reach their decisions, are like those of the Supreme Court Justices; their activities are not open to public scrutiny, but written opinions support their decisions.

(d) *Implementing.* Effective implementation of societal decisions depends upon a continuing relationship between the society's decider and the other subsystems. Decisions of the former are usually, but not always, complied with by the latter. If compliance falls below a critical point, the decider is impotent to guide the system toward achievement of its purposes and goals.

Societal components comply with the decider's directives either voluntarily because they recognize that the directives are legitimate and in the best interests of the total system or involuntarily because they are forced to, or perhaps for a combination of these reasons.

Societal deciders achieve implementation of their decisions by coercive, utilitarian, or identitive power (see page 645). They ordinarily use a mixture of the three. All use coercion against criminal or revolutionary components. Most prefer to use the milder forms of power if possible. The decider's ability to implement its decisions and the means by which it does so depend upon interaction of a number of variables. Some of these are (i) the decider's assets, (ii) the degree to which components accept the decider as legitimate, (iii) the nature of the consensus upon which the decider depends, and (iv) the extent to which the decider satisfies the reasonable demands of its components.

(i) The deciders of some systems have sharply limited powers. In a loose confederation in which unit governments come near to being totipotential, the central decider may be able to implement its decisions only because of agreements of components to cooperate. On the other hand, strongly centralized governments which own all the land, means of production, and money assets are in a position to implement decisions through the use of utilitarian rewards.

(ii) The legitimacy accorded governments by societal components and its citizens ranges all the way from belief in the divinity of a ruler who holds his position by supernatural power to the doubtful credentials of the latest revolutionary junta or government imposed upon a society by some stronger nation outside. High legitimacy carries with it an assumption on the part of components that the government has a right to decide and that other parts of the society have an obligation to comply with decisions. In democracies the fact that members have participated in the elective process supports the legitimacy of the decider, even for those members in the minority whose candidates were defeated. A legitimate decider has access to the symbols toward which patriotic emotion is directed and can use them in implementation of even unpopular decisions. A man dies for the flag or pays taxes to support "Uncle Sam." The persuasive power of the decider is enhanced by this.

(iii) No decider holds its position without consensus either of a minority of powerful units or of a majority of all components. Complete agreement is rare because the interests of all components can rarely be simultaneously satisfied by a decision and the unsatisfied components are inclined to disagree with it. The nature of the consensus determines the need for the use of power.

(iv) Societal members who feel that their needs and demands are ignored by the system over time tend to become less cooperative in complying with decisions.

A system that confers few benefits or rewards on many of its members loses some of its persuasive power over them. Many societies have resorted to the use of force to control alienated minorities. On the other hand, those who benefit from the system are often law-abiding and eager to support its acts.

Even in a society in which the conditions favor successful implementation, generally a message or directive concerning every individual decision must be sent to the deciders of affected components. These must then decide whether to comply with the message and must direct components under their control to implement the decision.

Implementation of a decision includes assigning responsibility for carrying it out, which is not usually a serious problem; securing the cooperation of those who must do the work; and assuring the compliance of affected organizations, groups, and individual people throughout the society.

Implementation of some decisions meets with resistance. Others are implemented routinely. Resistance can appear within the decider, at high echelons, or anywhere else in the system. It can take the form of opposition in the courts or of unorganized and generalized failure to comply. The Eighteenth Amendment to the United States Constitution prohibited the manufacture, transport, sale, import, and export of intoxicating liquors. But refusal to comply with it by many American citizens, groups, and organizations overwhelmed the enforcement powers of the system.

In the United States, implementation of societal decisions is among the President's constitutional duties: "He shall take care that the laws be faithfully executed. . . ." The structure of the executive branch of the government includes components responsible for management of the various parts of the society, and much of the task of implementation involves supervision of the functions of these units. The President can also act in various ways to establish new structures required to implement a decision. The executive branch includes also a number of components concerned with forcing compliance from reluctant, rebellious, or criminal units. These are under the Departments of Justice; Treasury; Health, Education, and Welfare; and Defense. They include federal marshals; Secret Service, Treasury, and FBI agents; enforcement officers of the Bureau of Narcotics and Dangerous Drugs; customs, immigration, and public health officers; units of the Army, the Coast Guard, and the National Guard when it is nationalized; and others.

Persuasion is the tactic most employed by Presidents in implementing their decisions.[231] The President must persuade the independent branches of the government, political and business leaders, and the people in general that his policies and his chosen means of implementation are right for them and for the system.

Representative *variables* of the process of deciding include: *Meaning of information employed in deciding.* Example: Statistics for a 6-month period showed both the cost of living and the rate of unemployment to be increasing, and so the prime minister decided to impose economic controls. *Sorts of information employed in deciding.* Example: Congress based its new legislation on findings of an investigative committee. *Amount of information employed in deciding.* Example: It was necessary for the king to decide immediately, with the advice only of his foreign minister and without taking time for a public opinion poll or research study. *Changes in deciding over time.* Example: As the ministers worked together with the young regent, they began to trust his judgment and accept his decisions. *Changes in deciding with different circumstances.* Example: After the Republican President appointed two conservative Justices to the Supreme Court, its decisions involved fewer liberal constructions of the Constitution. *Number of alternatives in input before decision and in output afterward.* Example: The National Security Council presented seven alternative strategies for advancing *détente,* and the President selected one. *Rewards and punishments attached to alternatives reviewed in deciding.* Example: A majority of members of the Knesset would have preferred not to reduce taxes, but they were afraid they would lose their seats if they did not. *Rate of deciding.* Example: The governor made several important decisions every hour during the first few days after his colony was invaded. *Lag in deciding.* Example: The king was a vacillating person who often took months to make up his mind. *Costs of deciding.* Example: The salary and expense allowance of the premier totaled less than 50,000 rubles yearly.

3.3.8   Encoder, the subsystem which alters the code of information input to it from other information processing subsystems, from a "private" code used internally by the society into a "public" code which can be interpreted by other societies in its environment.

3.3.8.1   Structure   The encoder of societies is made up of many component organizations. The government of the United States, for instance, has encoder components in all three of its branches. The Presidency, the Department of State, and other executive agencies have encoding as a primary function. Chiefs of state and their offices, foreign offices, and other executive agencies in other countries have comparable encoding functions. Congress, which must consent to treaties and executive agreements with other societies and which has the power to declare war, also encodes for communication over international channels. So do other legislatures and parliaments. Members of the judiciary write opinions.

Encoder components also include various organizations that write, create, or produce radio or television presentations for official international broadcasts, as well as cultural missions.

This subsystem often is downwardly dispersed to groups or individual persons such as diplomats, chiefs of state, or other officials when they talk to representatives of other societies and prepare or make speeches directed toward others outside their own boundaries, including supranational organizations; military leaders when they communicate with enemy leaders; speech writers; coding experts; translators; press secretaries; teachers; technical experts; and propaganda writers. Some of these are joint components with other subsystems, as are chiefs of state who are also part of the decider. The person or group that encodes a message may be a component of the output transducer as well as of the encoder.

Also in this subsystem may be representatives of broadcasting companies or other news media who may prepare statements of the ideas or intentions of societal deciders to a world audience. Artists who design symbols representing the society for display outside its boundaries, and the people who design flags, uniforms, and insignia of the society, are also in it.

Artifacts in this subsystem include writing materials, equipment used in the various sorts of encoding processes, and coding machines.

3.3.8.2   Process   Not all transmissions of information across the boundaries of societies are encoded by or for official societal spokesmen. Others besides them carry out the output transducing for which encoding is essential. These others who communicate with persons or components in other societies, over channels that cross the societal boundary, include international associations of legislators, judges, professional men, scientists, businessmen, labor unions, journalists, and many traveling groups and individual persons. These are information transmissions at the level at which they occur, not downwardly dispersed components of the society's encoder.

Societies do not use *alpha-coded* messages in communicating with other living systems. *Beta-coded* messages are transmitted by works of art, flags, uniforms, and insignia used by a society's armed forces; they are also transmitted by symbols such as those painted on containers of exports to other nations. All these transmit information about the society or identify the people and materials as coming from the society. *Gamma-coded* messages are by far the most usual. A society selects from among available international and supranational channels one that is appropriate for an intended message and encodes for that channel, in a text prepared for a speech, written material for publication, or an agenda for a meeting or a conference. Encoding at this level is frequently a two-stage process: The information is first encoded in the language of the society itself and then is recoded into another language. At the United Nations, some listeners receive the message in the code employed by the speaker; others receive it in the languages into which it is simultaneously recoded. Recoding may be into the dots and dashes of the telegraph code, into a cryptic code used between allies, or into the formal language of diplomacy. (For example, a prime minister says, using the private language of his system, "Tell him to drop dead." This is not the form, however, in which the ambassador who delivers the message encodes it. As the prime minister intended, the ambassador says: "My government has instructed me to say that it finds your proposals entirely unacceptable. . . .")

Communication among societies has traditionally been through formal channels, through notes sent to a society's embassies, or through face-to-face transmissions by an ambassador. Increasingly, however, top-echelon deciders bypass these formal components and communicate directly with their opposite numbers. Recently, Presidents of the United States have substituted envoys representing them personally for the State Department representatives who would be expected to represent the nation. Henry Kissinger performed such service for two Presidents in delicate negotiations in the Middle East. Presidents seem to hope that such envoys will encode the intentions of the government more accurately than ambassadors would. Increasingly, also, chiefs of state themselves fly about the world holding private conversations with the highest-echelon components of other governments. Visits of kings and premiers to the White House are now common occurrences. By encoding (and output transducing) the information himself, the leader knows exactly what is said and has an immediate response. Communication error is reduced by having fewer components in the channel. (See Hypothesis 3.3.3.2-11, page 97, which states that the probability of error in or overload of an information channel is a monotonic increasing function of the number of components in it.) The slowness of transportation prior to the twentieth century made personal communications among chiefs of state unusual during the years before World War I. This remained true even during the crisis period that preceded the outbreak of that war, as shown in a study of all communications exchanged between European governments during that period.[232] Direct communications between top leaders, however, increased significantly during the last 7 days before the declaration of war. Between June 27 and July 28, 1914, a little over 4 weeks, only 74 of 1,530 messages between European nations were direct communications between heads of state. In the subsequent week, July 29 through August 4, the last 7 days before war began, 116 of 1,134 messages were direct communications of this sort.

During the Cuban missile crisis, when the danger of war between the United States and the Soviet Union seemed great, personal communications between Chairman Khrushchev and President Kennedy played an important part in finally resolving the confrontation. Before this, President Kennedy had taken advantage of the international channel provided by his press conferences to include a carefully encoded warning that if a Communist buildup in Cuba ever endangered the United States, or if Cuba should become an offensive base for the Soviet Union, the United States would "do whatever must be done to protect its own security and that of its allies."[233] The Soviet Union had warned that any attack on Cuba would bring nuclear retaliation. In the early days of the crisis, the Soviets had inaccurately insisted that no missiles had been placed in Cuba. Even after United States intelligence flights on October 9, 1962 had proved the presence of the missiles in Cuba, Soviet Foreign Minister Gromyko, in a meeting with President Kennedy, continued to state the Soviet position. Chairman Khrushchev, in conversation with the United States Ambassador to Moscow, had also maintained the same posture. After a blockade had been agreed upon by the United States government, the intentions of the United States were encoded in a speech written by members of President Kennedy's staff and edited by the President himself. This speech was used to brief all United States diplomatic representatives throughout the world, an internal communication of the United States government. It served also as the basis of a message given to Soviet Ambassador Dobrynin in Secretary of State Rusk's office and by United States Ambassador Kohler in Moscow. This speech was then broadcast on October 22 by the President to the people of the United States—and simultaneously to the world.

Soviet response came in a Soviet government statement and in two private letters from Chairman Khrushchev to President Kennedy. These did not admit that there were missiles in Cuba.[234] Members of the United States executive branch, working with the President, immediately answered these communications. As the blockade continued, it became clear that the Soviet government did not intend to carry the situation to open warfare. A new letter was sent by Khrushchev to Kennedy on October 26. It included threats, polemics, and denunciations, but it indicated also that a settlement was possible. As the Executive Committee of the United States National Security Council was working on a draft of a reply, a second, public, letter was received in which terms unpleasing to the United States were mentioned. The work on the missile sites in Cuba continued. A United States U-2 plane was shot down, and the pilot killed. Both sides were poised for war, and the largest invasion force since World War II was assembled in Florida.

Since the first letter was personal and the second public, President Kennedy decided to treat the public letter as propaganda and concentrate on the private one. A White House statement was issued in which the second letter was said to contain inconsistent and conflicting proposals. At the same time, a private letter to the Secretary General of the United Nations asked him to find out whether the Soviet Union was willing to stop work on the bases and permit United Nations verification that the weapons had been made inoperable.

The Executive Committee of the National Security Council then set to work to answer the private letter. When agreement was difficult, two members were chosen to encode a final version. Adlai Stevenson, then Ambassador to the United Nations, who had been conducting talks at the United Nations, approved the version. The President made amendments and also approved it. It stated the position of the United States that work on the missiles must stop and that they must be made inoperable, under effective international guarantees. A copy was delivered to the Soviet Ambassador by Robert Kennedy, then Attorney General, and a verbal message given at the same time: the point of escalation was at hand. The choice was either peace and disarmament or strong retaliation.

As implementation of this tough stance was under consideration, the crisis was resolved by yet another letter from Chairman Khrushchev, broadcast publicly in the interest of speed, in which President Kennedy's terms were accepted. These negotiations had involved numerous examples of encoding and decoding of various sorts. Following this dangerous confrontation, the "hot-line" teletype link between Moscow and Washington was set up to make possible quick, accurate, private communication between the top leaders of these two societies in emergencies.[235] Each exchange between Kennedy and Khrushchev during the missile crisis had taken 4 h, including time for translation, decoding, encoding, and diplomatic presentation.

Representative *variables* of the encoding process include: *Meaning of information which is encoded.* Example: Acting the opposite of some ladies, if the diplomat said "yes," he meant "maybe"; if he said "maybe," he meant "no"; and if he had ever said "no," he would have been no diplomat. *Sorts of information which are encoded.* Example: The president's speech carefully evaded the question of the society's neutrality while emphasizing its friendly intentions toward its neighbor. *Percentage of information input which is encoded.* Example: The message center at the White House put into code only about 10 percent of the messages it transmitted. *Threshold of the encoder.* Example: The emperor had never written a speech for an international audience until the invasion of his country forced him to appeal for help to the League of Nations. *Changes in encoding over time.* Example: The premier's statements became more and more aggressive as violations of the society's territorial waters continued. *Changes in encoding with different circumstances.* Example: After war was declared, the allies used a secret code in all their communications. *Channel capacity of the encoder.* Example: No one but the dictator could speak for the society in international communications. *Distortion of the encoder.* Example: The premier proclaimed his peaceful intentions while greatly increasing the size of the army and its capability. *Signal-to-noise ratio of the encoder.* Example: The country's translators in the United Nations could not be heard because they usually spoke very softly. *Rate of encoding.* Example: Millions of words of propaganda were written each month for dissemination over the border to other countries. *Percentage of omissions in encoding.* Example: The propaganda leaflets deliberately avoided mentioning three of the four incidents that had taken place at the border. *Percentage of errors in encoding.* Example: The translator got only about 90 percent of the ultimatum message correct. *Code employed.* Example: The foreign office code was a common one, substituting numbers for letters. *Redundancy of the code employed.* Example: The diplomat gave his message verbally and also handed the written text of it to the premier. *Lag in encoding.* Example: The speech writers took 2 weeks to prepare the queen's Christmas message to her people. *Costs of encoding.* Example: Money for the Voice of America was raised by a public appeal to all United States citizens.

3.3.9   Output transducer, the subsystem which puts out markers bearing information from the society, changing markers within the society into other matter-energy forms which can be transmitted over channels in the society's environment.

3.3.9.1   Structure   The chief of state and his office constitute a component of this subsystem. So do a department of state, a foreign office, and officials of another executive agency; the Congress, another legislature or parliament; a judicial body that sends messages to another society; and an international or supranational body. Such organizations employ press secretaries, public relations officers, radio operators, and others involved in output transducing. Included in this subsystem also are organizations that transmit messages over the society's borders to other nations or supranational systems by operating radio or television stations and publishing newspapers or magazines. In the United States, telephone and telegraph companies with international connections are also in it. In the United Kingdom, the Soviet Union, and many other countries some or all of these are under centralized governmental control, even though geographically dispersed.

Some of these may be joint components between the output transducer and the encoder. The chief of state and his office are, when they both write a speech and read or send it out internationally over a television satellite network, radio, or other medium. So are a department of state, a foreign office, and officials of another executive agency; the Congress, another legislature or parliament; and a judicial body that not only encodes communications but also transduces them into the international or supranational channel and net.

The output transducer of societies may be downwardly dispersed to a group or an individual person, including many different specialists, depending upon what marker is to be used to carry the information. These may be official national spokesmen such as delegates to international or supranational bodies, governmental press secretaries, public relations officers, radio operators, pilots who drop propaganda leaflets, radio technicians, publishers, actors, speakers, teachers, singers, dancers, missionaries, or travelers.

The output transducer makes use of a variety of artifacts, such as press releases, books, art objects, manufactured products, broadcasting equipment, teletype machines, telephone equipment, and cables.

3.3.9.2 Process Official communications among societies generally comply with strict formalities developed over centuries of uneasy interactions. The appropriate channels through which these messages are transduced are determined by such protocol. Only certain components may transduce official messages.

Components at the highest echelon—kings, emperors, prime ministers, premiers, chairmen, and presidents—ordinarily use diplomats to transduce their verbal messages or to deliver written notes. They also release information to news media to be transduced by announcers or printers, and they may do the trans-

ducing personally by international television and radio or at international conferences. When they communicate directly in face-to-face meetings with leaders of other societies, months of negotiations by diplomats and staff members often precede the conversations. Such direct conversations are probably worth the trouble since messages of this sort may be effective where more routine approaches are not. President Nixon himself traveled to China to discuss with Chairman Mao, Premier Chou En-lai, and others at the top echelon of the Chinese republic the change in relationships between the two countries that followed.

Below the top echelon, representatives of governmental or other organizations are empowered to speak on certain topics. International agreements are made on everything from fishing grounds to deep space, in each case following conferences by representatives of the society knowledgeable on the particular subjects to be discussed.

A good deal of information is transduced over societal boundaries against the wishes of deciders of the receiving society. Whenever that society censors or jams information inputs across its boundaries, those transmissions must be strong enough to get the signals inside the receiving society's territory. To this end, radio transmitters, often very powerful, are placed as near the borders of the receiving society as possible. They may be on ships in international waters beyond the territorial waters of that society.

Representative variables of output transducing include: *Meaning of information output which is transduced.* Example: The national ballet performed a special dance expressing the warm friendship of its country for the small African nation in which it performed. *Sorts of information which are transduced.* Example: The king broadcast his speech on the oil crisis to the world by communications satellite. *Threshold of the output transducer.* Example: The President had to issue an order before the television networks would broadcast his speech to a world audience. *Changes in output transducing over time.* Example: Nations only gradually began to make use of electronic transduction of messages between governments. *Changes in output transducing with different circumstances.* Example: Since speed was imperative, the President used the "hot line" to inform officials in Moscow that the leak into the atmosphere from the explosion in the Mojave Desert was an error by the United States. *Channel capacity of the output transducer.* Example: A second powerful radio transmitter was placed where it could be beamed into distant societies, doubling the communications capacity. *Number of channels in use in the output transducer.* Example: Only the premier voted at the United Nations. *Distortion of the output transducer.* Example: The religious intolerance of the two countries toward each other was so great that most official statements of their negotiators were colored by it. *Rate of output transducing.* Example: Several diplomatic messages a day passed from one country to the other as they prepared for a summit conference. *Lag in output transducing.* Example: The king's acceptance of the cease-fire was delayed 24 hours because the broadcasting station had been damaged by gunfire. *Intensity of information output.* Example: The radio station near the border sent a signal so strong that it made the signal from the neighboring nation's own station inaudible. *Costs of output transducing.* Example: The high-powered transmitter needed to send a strong signal deep into a distant society was an important item in the budget of the Foreign Office.

4. Relationships among subsystems or components

The following examples illustrate the sorts of relationships that exist in a society between one subsystem and one or more others, between a subsystem and one or more components, or between a component and one or more others.

4.1 Structural relationships

4.1.1 Containment   Example: All states except Alaska and Hawaii lie within continuous boundaries of the United States.

4.1.2 Number   Example: There are 15 republics in the Soviet Union.

Both large population (number in my terms) and large area (size in my terms) in a given country have been shown by factor analysis to be positively correlated with a high frequency of political assassinations in that country, a high frequency of riots and local rebellions (between 1837 and 1937), the presence of many different language groups, a comparatively recent rise in industrial production, a high ratio of divorces to marriages, frequency of secret treaties (between 1837 and 1937), comparatively more cities over 20,000 per 1 million population of the country, and a high percentage of governmental expenditure devoted to education.[236]

4.1.3 Order   Example: Traveling south on the Pan American Highway, one passes through Mexico, Guatemala, and then El Salvador.

4.1.4 Position   Example: Austria is on the Danube River.

4.1.5 Direction   Example: Scotland is north of England in Great Britain.

4.1.6 Size   Example: The area of the Republic of San Marino is only about 61 km².

It has been shown that both the area of a country and the number of persons in it correlate significantly

and similarly with several other societal variables (see Sec. 4.1.2 above).

4.1.7 Pattern   Example: The Israelites camped in the wilderness with the Levites nearest to the tabernacle and 12 other tribes farther away, three on each side.

4.1.8 Density   Example: Cities are closer together on the Atlantic seaboard of the United States than on the plains.

4.2 Process relationships

4.2.1 Temporal relationships

4.2.1.1 Containment in time   Examples: During the first century B.C., the Roman Empire was twice ruled by triumvirates.

4.2.1.2 Number in time   Example: In 1791, after Vermont was admitted to the Union, there were 14 states in the United States.

4.2.1.3 Order in time   Example: Agriculture developed before manufacturing in the history of societies.

4.2.1.4 Position in time   Example: France had a democratic form of government between the fall of the Bourbon dynasty and the rise of Napoleon.

4.2.1.5 Direction in time   Example: British rule came before independence in India.

4.2.1.6 Duration   Example: The "1,000-year Reich" lasted only 12 years.

4.2.1.7 Pattern in time   Example: National political conventions in the United States occur once every 4 years.

4.2.2 Spatiotemporal relationships

4.2.2.1 Action   Example: The President sent army units to force the state of Arkansas to desegregate its schools racially.

4.2.2.2 Communication   Example: The Japanese government initiated conversations with the Chinese government.

4.2.2.3 Direction of action   Example: The population of the United States moved steadily westward during the nineteenth century.

4.2.2.4 Pattern of action   Example: In less than 20 years the interstate highway program connected all state capitals with Washington, D.C.

4.2.2.5 Entering or leaving containment   Example: The Sudan acted to remove itself from within the boundaries of the British Commonwealth of Nations.

4.3 Relationships among subsystems or components which involve meaning   Example: The southern states voted together partly because of their common attitudes toward racial issues.

5. System processes

5.1 Process relationships between inputs and outputs   Many internal processes of societies are open

to observation, and what goes on inside these large systems is usually of greater interest than an external, or "black-box," view of the system. Some societies limited foreign observers to an external view by making their boundaries so nearly impermeable that neither people nor markers were allowed to cross them, and they did not engage in foreign trade. Under these circumstances, the little information about them that came to the world was an unsatisfactory mixture of rumor and fancy. Japan before 1860 was such a closed society.

The relationships between a society's inputs and its outputs also are often of interest and scientific importance. As is true of living systems at all levels, the input and output mix of a particular society is unique. Studies of changes in inputs and outputs of a single society or of differences among societies can be useful.

(a) *Matter-energy inputs related to matter-energy outputs.* Societies export some of their matter-energy inputs as unprocessed materials, energy (electricity), or manufactured goods to other societies. A significant percentage of matter-energy inputs is extruded into the environment within the system's territory or outside its boundary.

The particular materials and manufactured items that any society exports are usually importantly related to the natural resources within the system. Societies with much fertile land often export a part of their abundant harvests. Also, raw materials, manufactured parts, and machinery may be imported and used in producing finished goods for export. In 1967 the United States led the world in production of aluminum, copper, crude oil, steel, and sulfur.[237] In 1968 it led the world in motor-vehicle production (10,820,-410 units) and listed motor vehicles and parts as its largest export item, sending $3.126 billion worth over the system borders to other societies.[238] In spite of this huge production, however, motor vehicles and parts were also its largest *import* item. Both iron and steel mill products, exported in quantity by the United States, also were among its principal imports.

Societies differ in the efficiency of their converting and producing processes and in their recovery of by-products for use. The product–waste ratio can therefore differ greatly from nation to nation. Sweden, for example, recovers valuable minerals from the same sort of industrial processes that, in the United States, extrude them as poisons into the environment and into the bodies of human, animal, and plant components. Primitive smelting methods recover much less metal from ores than advanced technological processes, and they are therefore less efficient overall than some of those employed in highly developed industrial societies.

The overall efficiency of the energy-conversion processes in the United States is calculated as about 51 percent. In Cook's words:

All energy conversions are more or less inefficient, of course. . . . In the case of electricity there are losses at the power plant, in transmission and at the point of application of power; in the case of fuels consumed in end uses the loss comes at the point of use. The 1970 U.S. gross consumption of 64.6×10^{15} BTU of energy (or 16.3×10^{15} kilocalories, or 19×10^{12} kilowatt-hours) ends up as 32.8×10^{15} BTU of useful work and 31.8×10^{15} BTU of waste heat amounting to an overall efficiency of about 51 percent.[239]

The major flows of energy through the United States system in 1970 are shown in Fig. 11-3. The economic efficiency of the system is less than the efficiency of conversions because work is involved in the passage of the fuel through the matter-energy processing subsystems from its source in a mine or well to the point of its use, the production and operation of power plants and equipment, the distribution of electricity by power networks, the handling of waste and protection of the environment, and the information processing required to coordinate and manage all these activities.[240] Economic efficiency has decreased in the United States as the society has consumed more energy for each dollar of goods and services. One reason for this is the increased use of electricity, which has an efficiency in producing heat of about 32 percent, in place of alternate fuels, which range from 60 to 90 percent. Much of this increase is required for air conditioning, a use which produces little increase in the gross national product (GNP).

The number of people who leave one society to join another or to become inclusions there may also be related to amounts of matter-energy inputs. A poor country with insufficient matter-energy inputs for its essential processes tends to lose people to more prosperous systems. A rich country tends to gain them.

(b) *Matter-energy inputs related to information outputs.* The rate of outputs of communication information from societies and the forms in which they are transmitted depend upon the sort of matter or energy inputs available for use as markers. Before the Egyptians learned to use inputs of papyrus for markers for written communications, societies chiseled important information on rocks.

A society that inputs matter-energy from other societies must output monetary information to pay for it. The United States, in the year 1968, imported goods for which it paid $33.252 billion, according to official governmental statistics.[241]

(c) *Information inputs related to matter-energy outputs.* The relation of information inputs representing demands for products or services to outputs on inter-

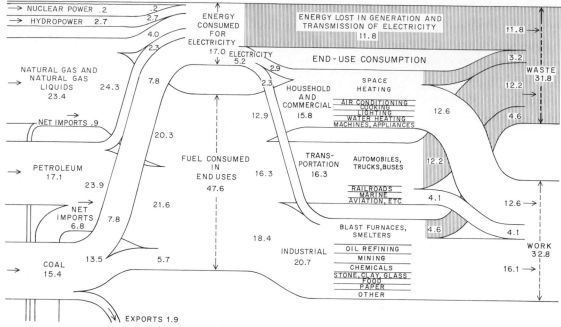

Fig. 11-3   Flow of energy through the United States in 1970. This is traced from production of energy commodities (left) to the ultimate conversion of energy into work for various industrial end products and waste heat (right). (Units for all numbers are 10^{15} Btu.) Total consumption of energy in 1970 was 64.6×10^{15} Btu. (Adding nonenergy uses of fossil fuels, primarily for petrochemicals, would raise the total to 68.8×10^{15} Btu.) The overall efficiency of the system was about 51 percent. Some of the fossil-fuel energy is consumed directly and some is converted to generate electricity. The efficiency of electrical generation and transmission is taken to be about 31 percent, based on the ratio of utility electricity purchased in 1970 to the gross energy input for generation in that year. Efficiency of direct fuel use in transportation is taken as 25 percent; efficiency of fuel use in other applications, as 75 percent. [From E. Cook. The flow of energy in an industrial society. *Sci. Amer.,* 1971, Sept. **224**(3), 138–139. Copyright © 1971 by Scientific American, Inc. All rights reserved. *Reprinted by permission.*]

national markets is the same as on markets within the society (see pages 876 and 877). Because demand—to take two examples out of many—for foot-powered sewing machines and hand-operated clothes wringers has been input to industrial societies from parts of the world where electric energy is not readily available, they were produced for export after housewives in more advanced societies had begun to use electrically powered machines.

Inputs of information about new technology—"know-how"—to a society can change the nature and quantity of exported products or the product-waste ratio of the society with respect to certain materials.

Increased inflow of monetary information to a society, either from stepped-up demand or orders for its exports or as loans or subsidies from other societies, can affect both the quantity and the quality of output products. The society can then pay for more and better materials, improved machinery, and more skilled people in its producer processes.

(*d*) *Information inputs related to information outputs.*   Because communication is two-way and many messages are answered, the quantities of information inputs to and outputs from a society tend to be similar. A society's components communicate much more with some parts of the world than with others, so that the flows of input and output information are both biased in certain directions.

Balance of trade in monetary terms is an information input-output relationship. Societies endeavor to avoid negative balances over any extended period.

5.2   Adjustment processes among subsystems or components, used in maintaining variables in steady states   The number of adjustment processes used by societies to keep variables in steady-state range is very large. This is in accordance with the assertion of Hypothesis 5.1-4 (see page 103) that in general, higher-level living systems have the emergent characteristics of more kinds and more complex combinations of adjustment processes than living systems at lower levels. As a result of this intricacy of structure and process, we do not yet know enough to write an exhaustive account of the various classes of adjustment processes at this level. Instead, I discuss in each section a limited number of processes.

Several hypotheses suggest some of the factors that might influence choice of adjustment processes in specific matter-energy and information stress situations. Subject to the constraints discussed above (see pages 805 to 808), it is possible that in normal societies the least costly adjustment process perceived to be possible will ordinarily be undertaken first, with increasingly more costly processes selected only when the original processes have failed to meet the need (see Hypothesis 3.3.7.2-14, page 101). If two adjustment processes are equal in cost, it may be that societies select the one which is expected to do the job most rapidly or efficiently, in accordance with Hypothesis 3.3.7.2-19 (see page 101). When, as is ordinarily the case, more than one variable is displaced from steady state and not all can be corrected simultaneously, and yet the costs are identical, the system, if it confirms Hypothesis 3.3.7.2-20 (see page 102), will correct the most displaced variable first. It appears intuitively reasonable that societal deciders would behave as much as possible in this way.

Societies typically have wide ranges of stability for many sorts of matter-energy variables. Regularly recurring events, like seasonal fluctuations in the amounts of essential food substances, variations in climate, and inequalities of rainfall throughout the year, usually do not constitute stresses because societies have learned to adjust to them. Only extreme variations are stresses. In addition to adjusting to predictable variations of flows of matter-energy inputs, societies must develop adjustment processes for unexpected, often disastrous excesses or lacks of matter-energy, the timing and extent of which cannot be dependably forecast. The sudden loss of a major part of a grain crop as a result of blight or an attack by insects is one example. Withholding of fuel inputs by oil-producing countries, natural disasters, and wars are others.

A society's culture is shaped in important and distinctive ways by the adjustment processes it develops.

5.2.1 Matter-energy input processes

Adjustments to excess matter-energy inputs. Societies regularly deal with seasonal excesses of inputs of certain foods by recruiting components from other parts of the system to help with the harvest. Farm women and children regularly help the men in the fields at that time. In many farming communities, schools remain closed during the period when major crops are brought in. Migrant laborers, some from outside the society, stay in one area until its crop is harvested and then move to another.

The annual inundation of the land bordering the Nile is an excess matter-energy input that is predictable in its timing but not in its extent. Adjustment processes to the flooding produced the unique culture of ancient Egypt and continue to influence the modern nation. The water it brings is an absolutely necessary input, since Egypt is nearly rainless, but it could also be an annual disaster were it not for the adaptation of the society.

The earliest dwellers in the narrow fertile areas bordering the river probably retreated before the rising waters, abandoning their shelters. The more permanent towns that came later depended upon technological developments such as dams and canals. Engineering developed early. An accurate calendar, a precursor of the one we use today, divided the year into inundation, emergence of the fields from the water, and drought.[242] During each of these periods the people engaged in different activities. Nilometers, to measure the depth of the water, were developed and placed at various points on the Nile to provide prediction of the amount of rise to be expected downstream. The periodicity of the flooding was reflected in the Egyptian religion. Osiris, an earth god, was believed to die each year in the drought season, only to be miraculously reborn in the period of inundation.[243]

Modern societies also reflect in their cultures their adjustments to seasonal, predictable matter-energy excess. The steeply sloped roofs of buildings in societies with rainy climates and the many adaptations to extreme heat, like the siesta and air conditioning, are examples. Hypothesis 3.2-1 (see page 93), which states that an optimal mean temperature at which process is most efficient is maintained by a living system, may well be true of societies.

Most large, modern societies make some effort to predict and guard against matter-energy input disasters. Since these rarely affect more than a small part of the society at any one time, the primary responsibility for adjustment may be left to components. Only when local and regional adjustment processes are insufficient do adjustment processes of the entire society come into use. This is in accordance with Hypothesis 5.2-2 (see page 106), which says that the greater a threat to, or stress upon, a system, the more components are involved in adjusting to it.

For those matter-energy input stresses which require the efforts of the total system for correction, many countries have national organizations, such as the Red Cross, which gather money and supplies from throughout the society and send disaster teams where they are needed. Federal funds for relief and reconstruction are made available when the President of the United States declares a region to be a disaster area. Units of the armed forces may also be sent to supplement state and local units.

In addition to the formal arrangements for meeting matter-energy input stresses, components throughout the system, including individual persons, groups, and organizations, may converge upon the affected part of a nation, acting without direction from societal deciders, to bring aid of various sorts. Volunteers supplement the formal components to increase the strength of the force applied against the stress.

An increase in the rate of input of people to a society, whether it is the result of the natural increase of the population or of immigration of people from other societies, can cause strains upon the steady states of many societal variables. This is particularly true if the increase is sudden. Hypothesis 5.2-5 (see page 106) suggests that there is inertia to the matter-energy and information processing variables which a system maintains in steady state, so that change in their ranges of stability is much less disruptive of system controls if it happens gradually. Such a sudden increase in input rate of people occurred in India when war in Pakistan caused refugees to pour across the border. Normal boundary processes that would have prevented their entrance were not invoked for humanitarian reasons.

If the usual rate of reproduction for each mating dyad is above the replacement number that would keep a population stable, little strain is felt initially, but eventually a "population explosion" strains the resources and facilities of the system. Animal groups and primitive human societies have internal matter-energy adjustment processes that avoid the development of strains from input of too many organisms (see page 841). As long as the population problem affected only a few societies and as long as unexploited land was available in the world, people could readily migrate. As overpopulation has become a world problem, the situation has changed markedly.

Adjustments to lacks of matter-energy inputs. Societies adjust to lacks of a particular sort of matter-energy by allowing prices to rise, forcing demand down as supply diminishes, restricting use, employing rationing, using substitutes which may be of lower quality, and seeking new substitutes. If a shortage is foreseen and the society plans for it, its impact can be lessened. Population increases and industrialization have already put pressure upon energy sources in many of the world's societies. The initial supply of coal in the United States is estimated to have been 1.5×10^{12} metric tons.[244] Although no real shortage is likely to occur for a long time, the use of high-sulfur coal, which produces potentially harmful air pollution, may soon become necessary. The total amount of oil in the 48 contiguous states and the continental shelves is thought to be about 165 billion barrels (bbl), of which 82 percent had been discovered by 1965.[245] Drilling for the readily available middle 80 percent was begun in 1934, and that supply will be depleted by 1999. Natural gas, too, will begin to decline in quantity after 1980. Although imported oil is available, the price is high. Planning for the anticipated shortages has become a current high priority of the United States, as well as many other modern nations.

The long-term prospect for development of new energy sources is good. The necessary research and installations to provide the necessary energy, however, usually require societal participation in funding, since the costs of development and construction are enormous.

Five kinds of energy that do not require fossil fuels are solar energy used directly, solar energy used indirectly, tidal energy, geothermal energy, and nuclear energy.[246] The energy of winds within 80 meters (m) of the ground and that of the temperature differences in the sea are other possible sources.[247] It is more practical to harness some of these sources than others.

Radiant energy from the sun can be converted to electric energy, using either a conventional steam power plant or a magnetohydrodynamic conversion that employs the magnetic field surrounding a high-velocity stream of hot gases to generate current.[248] Three proposed schemes depend upon extensive collecting areas in deserts within 35 degrees north or south of the equator. These parts of the world receive from 3,000 to 4,000 h of sunshine each year, which provides 300 to 650 calories (cal) per square centimeter (cm²) per day. The areas required for a 1,000-megawatt (MW) power plant range from 23 to 70 km. Storage of the heat must be provided. Efficiencies of these systems range from 10 to 30 percent. With the least of the three efficiencies, the area needed to provide as much power as the power plants of the United States generated in 1970 would be 24,500 km², somewhat less than a tenth the area of Arizona. Solar energy for heating and cooling buildings is in the experimental stage, and preliminary efforts to develop solar power plants are under way. The technical problems of collection, concentration, and storage of the energy are not yet satisfactorily solved, particularly if it is to serve areas other than deserts.[249] A fourth scheme, a spin-off from the space program of the United States, would place an

8-km-square array of solar cells in orbit 35,900 km above the equator to convey power by a superconducting cable to a satellite.[250] There it would be converted to microwave energy, which would be beamed to a receiving antenna on earth for reconversion to usable power. A wire mesh antenna 10 km in diameter which received energy from such an array of solar cells could provide heat sufficient to generate enough power to supply New York City. The receiving station would not block sunlight from the earth beneath it, and this sunlight could therefore be used. This technique would require further development of the capacity to fabricate large structures in space and probably could not be carried out on an experimental basis before sometime between 1985 and 1990. Indirect use of solar power is less promising, since it relies upon either wind power or waterpower.[251]

Both tidal power, which uses the energy generated by filling and emptying a bay that can be closed by a dam, and geothermal power, which uses the earth's heat, are in use at present. The total potential tidal power is only about 2 percent of the world's potential waterpower. Geothermal energy is producing electricity in at least seven countries.[252] It could become a major energy source with a by-product of desalted water for arid regions if the considerable technical problems are solved.

Present nuclear power plants depend upon fission of uranium 235. If nuclear energy depended entirely upon this process, it would provide power for only a short time. Uranium is not plentiful.[253] Breeder reactors exist which create more nuclear fuel than they consume. They transform uranium 238 into fissionable plutonium 239, or thorium 232 into fissionable uranium 233, by absorbing surplus neutrons from the fission process in the reactor. Such reactors provide one solution to the problems presented by the limited supply of uranium 235. These have not yet been developed on a large scale. In 1971, the United States was funding a fast breeder program at a rate of $200 million a year.[254] The process is, however, dangerous. If a sudden burst of energy, to which breeder reactions are subject, should break the containment vessel, it could release catastrophic amounts of radioactive isotopes into the society. Increased safety costs a great deal of money.

Controlled nuclear fusion, used in hydrogen bombs, is an as yet unrealized process for producing unlimited useful power. Several fusion reactions that could theoretically be used in a controlled reaction are known.[255] The reaction of deuterium and tritium, both isotopes of hydrogen, is promising, since deuterium can be extracted from ordinary water without difficulty. Tritium, which does not occur in nature, could be regenerated as a part of the process. When deuterium and tritium are brought together at speeds great enough to overcome their natural repulsion, which occurs when they are completely ionized in a plasma at temperatures exceeding 10^8 K, the nuclei fuse. They produce helium and free neutrons and liberate a huge amount of energy, since the energy required to hold the original nuclei together is greater than that required to keep the helium molecule together. The problems involved in controlling a reaction of this sort are awesome. The great heat under which the reaction takes place and the pressure it generates make confinement of the plasma the principal difficulty. Regeneration of the tritium is another problem. If and when practical fusion reactors are developed, they are expected to be less hazardous than fission reactors. Also, costs would probably be lower.

Nuclear reactors are used in producing electricity, just as fossil-fuel plants are. They heat large boilers to produce steam, which runs turbines to make power. It is theoretically possible, however, to convert electricity directly from the charged particles that leak from the plasma chamber of a fusion reactor. Theoretically, such a direct conversion would be more efficient than other means of producing electricity.

It is not certain that fusion power will ever be economically feasible, but as Rose points out, some pleasant surprises occur in the course of technological development. He says:

In 1680 Christiaan Huygens decided to control gunpowder for peaceful purposes, as a perpetual boon to mankind, and set his assistant Denys Papin to invent a controlled gunpowder engine. After 10 years of difficulty, Papin had a different idea, wrote in his diary, "Since it is a property of water that a small quantity of it turned into vapour by heat has an elastic force like that of air, but upon cold supervening is again resolved into water, so that no trace of the said elastic force remains, I concluded that machines could be constructed wherein water, by the help of no very intense heat, and at little cost, could produce that perfect vacuum which could by no means be obtained by gunpowder." then invented the expanding and condensing steam cycle, which made possible the industrial revolution.[256]

5.2.2 Information input processes   Societies make their most important adjustments to the meaning rather than to the rate, either too fast (excess stress) or too slow (lack stress), of information input. An exception is monetary information. A society has many input channels, each a part of one of its subsystem components. And much of the processing of input information is downwardly dispersed. Consequently, only in extreme situations does alteration of the rate of flow of information into a society constitute either underload or overload. When such situations occur, they are pathological and indicate that the system is breaking down.

It is, of course, possible to overload one or more societal input transducer components or the channels from them. Such components react to the excess stress in ways characteristic of their level, which is usually the level of the organization. In crisis situations, too, the decider and other information processing subsystems may be overloaded.

Mobilization in response to information input containing a threat of war changes the processes of all subsystems of a society in a matter of days or weeks, sometimes before any matter-energy inputs resulting from hostile action impinge upon the system.

Profound changes are brought about in societies by information inputs from cultural contacts with other societies. Historically, invading armies have carried elements of their culture with them and have exposed the societies they entered to these elements. They have also taken home with them cultural elements from the societies they invaded. Trading among societies of different cultures has also provided contact that permitted exchange of cultural elements. Cultural spread has occurred particularly in places where trade routes have converged. Toynbee said:

When we look into the characteristics of the Oxus-Jaxartes Basin and of Syria and compare them with each other, we find that each of them had been endowed by Nature with the capacity for serving as a "roundabout," where traffic coming in from any point of the compass could be switched to any other point of the compass in any number of alternative combinations. On the Syrian roundabout, routes converged from the Nile Basin, from the Mediterranean, from Anatolia with its South-East European hinterland, from the Tigris-Euphrates Basin and from the Arabian Steppe. On the Central Asian roundabout, similarly, routes converged from the Tigris-Euphrates Basin via the Iranian Plateau, from India through the passes over the Hindu Kush, from the Far East via the Tarim Basin, and from an adjacent Eurasian Steppe that had taken the place, and inherited the conductivity, of a now desiccated "Second Mediterranean," whose former presence there was attested by its fragmentary survival in the Caspian Sea, the Sea of Aral, and Lake Balkash.

The role for which Nature had thus designed these two potential traffic centres had actually been played by each of them again and again during the five or six thousand years since the emergence of the earliest civilizations. Syria had been the scene of encounters, in successive periods, between the Sumeric and Egyptiac civilizations; between the Egyptiac, Hittite and Minoan civilizations; between the Syriac, Babylonic, Egyptiac, and Hellenic civilizations; between the Syriac, Orthodox Christian, and Western Christian civilizations; and, in a final bout of contacts, between the Arabic, Iranic, and Western civilizations. The Oxus-Jaxartes Basin had similarly been the scene of encounters in successive periods between the Syriac and Indic civilizations; between the Syr-

iac, Indic, Hellenic, and Sinic civilizations; and between the Syriac and Far Eastern civilizations. As a result of these encounters, each of these two peculiarly "numeniferous" (religion-bearing) regions had been included in the universal states of a number of different civilizations, and the exceptionally active intercourse between civilizations in these two areas explains the extraordinary concentration, within their limits, of the birth places of higher religions.[257]

Effects of contacts between societies of different cultures may be as temporary and superficial in a society as fads, such as the sudden interests in acupuncture by Americans following renewal of diplomatic and trade relations with China. More fundamental changes occur when a technologically developed society contacts a less developed one. Such influence by the British Empire upon India resulted in profound changes in steady states of many variables in the Indian society.[258] These included, among many others, a weakening of the deciders of villages, changes in concepts of property, the establishment of democratic governmental forms, changes in village social structure, the creation of new occupations, and the emergence of new values, such as recognition of education and achievement in determining social status. Crane says:

Whichever aspect of the change of recent decades we study, our examination would seem to expose certain important characteristics of the *process* of change. The most striking are that those actions which reduced the power of the traditional decision-makers to enforce their controls were of genuine significance in creating or facilitating change. Similarly, those actions which reduced the dependency of one group on another or of an individual upon his group facilitated change. Another factor for change was the establishment of "attractive" alternatives to the traditional order, though it should be noted that an alternative which might be attractive to some groups in Indian society might not be attractive to other groups. We may also mention the change-facilitating effect of steps which weakened the traditional system and/or the rewards obtainable therefrom and thus drove people out of the traditional system and into the new and alien system. The loss, for instance, of a "service" position in the village due to influx of factory goods could push people out of the traditional system of values and controls. Finally, we may observe that, for the most westernized sector of the population there was a denigration of indigenous values and their replacement by an alien set of values.[259]

Many of these changes persisted after the British withdrew.

Adjustment processes occur also in response to changes in flows of monetary information. Loans and subsidies from developed societies, for example, aid less developed systems in many ways (see pages 949 and 950). Profound social changes may follow sudden increase in wealth such as oil-producing countries experienced in the 1970s.

5.2.3 Matter-energy internal processes I shall now discuss three of the many sorts of internal matter-energy adjustments of societies: (a) adjustments to the environmental effects of the society's use of matter and energy, (b) adjustments to population increases, and (c) adjustments of spatial distribution of population. These are, of course, interrelated.

(a) *Adjustments to the environmental effects of the society's use of matter and energy.* Successful hunting and gathering societies, like successful plant communities and animal groups, live in steady states with their environments. The number and distribution of organisms are appropriate to the amount of matter-energy available for input and to the capacity of the environment to recycle waste. Balanced life aquaria and terraria provide small-scale ecological models of such steady states. In them the life processes of the plant and animal organisms do not destroy the crystal clarity of the medium in which they live. The whole world was like this when man appeared upon the scene. Explorers from Europe discovered such a balanced ecosystem in the New World. How beautiful it must have been!

Large societies, particularly industrial societies, strain the environment in many ways. Intensive agriculture substitutes for the natural complex plant community a simplified system of one or a few crops.[260] The first can ingest its needed matter-energy inputs from sun and soil and establish a balanced relationship with the local insect population. The second must have supplementary inputs of fertilizers to supply energy for growth, as well as insecticides to hold down the unbalanced increase of the insects that are specialized to feed upon it. DDT, until recently a freely used insecticide, has been found to be hazardous to animal and human life because it gets into streams and oceans and becomes concentrated in marine life, starting with plankton and going through the chain of life to large fishes, birds, and man.[261] The movement of DDT from its use through the chain of life to man is shown in Fig. 11-4.

Satisfaction of the energic demands of large industrial societies depletes and scars the environment, disrupts watersheds, befouls water, and further destroys the natural ecological balance. Use of the products of industry by societies results in mountains of waste—everything from old beer cans to abandoned hulks of automobiles. The industrial processes and machinery of large societies release heat and chemicals into the air and water and onto the land. The results are a polluted environment and lowered quality of life.

The underlying problem of large societies in dealing with matter-energy flows is the fundamental physical fact of the conservation of mass.[262] According to Ayres and Kneese, environmental pollution and its control can be usefully considered a materials-balance problem for societies. They say:

The inputs to the system are fuels, foods and raw materials which are partly converted into final goods and partly become waste residuals. Except for increases in inventory, final goods also ultimately enter the waste stream. Thus goods which are "consumed" really only render certain services. Their material substance remains in existence and must either be reused or discharged to the ambient environment.

In an economy which is closed (no imports or exports) and where there is no net accumulation of stocks (plant, equipment, inventories, consumer durables, or residential buildings), the amount of residuals inserted into the natural environment must be approximately equal to the weight of basic fuels, food, and raw materials entering the processing and production system, plus oxygen taken from the atmosphere.

APPLICATION

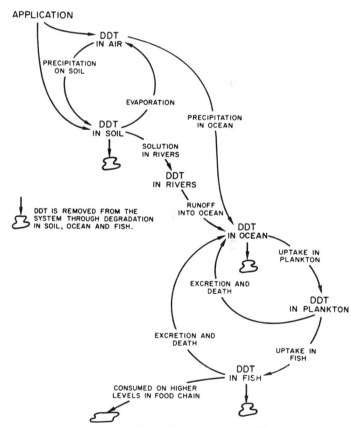

Fig. 11-4 Movement of DDT through the environment. [From J. Randers. DDT movement in the global environment. In D. L. Meadows & D. H. Meadows (Eds.). *Toward global equilibrium: collected papers.* Cambridge, Mass.: Wright-Allen Press, 1973, 55. Copyright © 1973 Wright-Allen Press, Inc., Cambridge, MA 02142 USA. *Reprinted by permission.*]

This result, while obvious upon reflection, leads to the, at first rather surprising, corollary that residuals disposal involves a greater tonnage of materials than basic materials processing, although many of the residuals, being gaseous, require no physical "handling."[263]

Figure 11-5 depicts a system of this sort.

The three available media into which wastes can be extruded—air, water, and soil—are not identical in their capacity to return to an unpolluted state, although all three can purify themselves in time.[264] The capacity of soil, however, is much greater than that of air and water.

One of the most serious aspects of the disposal problem is that the organism or other system respon-

sible for pollution of the environment is commonly not the most immediate sufferer from its effects. Belching smoke from a factory chimney affects everyone downwind. A city that discharges its waste into a flowing stream destroys the water supply of downstream systems, but its own water supply may not be threatened. A paper factory that keeps its costs low by discharging untreated organic wastes into a river may force up the costs of operating a fishery downstream to the point where demand for fish goes down. Society then gets paper but not enough fish.[265]

It is now increasingly clear that air and water are not only valuable common resources for all components of society but also scarce resources. Societies have barely

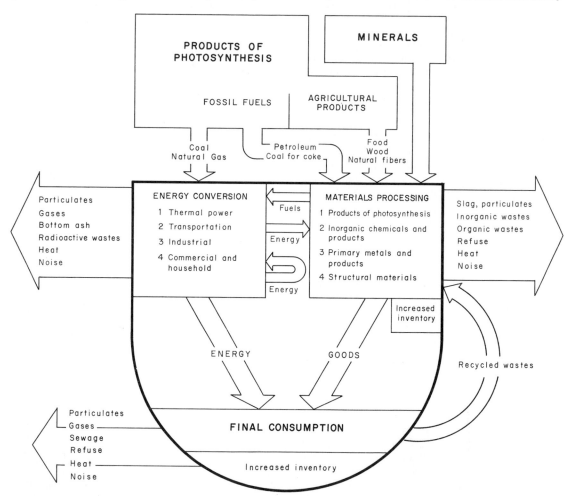

Fig. 11-5 Flows of matter-energy in the industrial society. [From S. Rose. The economics of environmental quality. *Fortune.* 1970, **81**(2), 121. Adapted from R. U. Ayres & A. V. Kneese. Production, consumption, and externalities. *Amer. econ. Rev.*, 1969, **59**,3, 285. Drawing by Tom Cardamone for *Fortune* magazine. *Reprinted by permission of* Fortune *magazine.*]

yet begun to hold polluters responsible for these "external effects" of their activities. Solow says:

We are used to these consequences of "external effects." I mean that we are accustomed to them as citizens; and we understand them as economists. But economists realize, as citizens sometimes do not, that the implication of external effects must be traced further. They have secondary effects on the system of resource allocation. If electric power is "too cheap" to the customer because he is not charged with its full social cost, then other things will happen. Other commodities that are produced with the help of large amounts of electric power will also be cheap, and they will be overproduced. Other industries will be tempted to adopt techniques of production that use more electric power than they would if the price of electric power were higher. The rest of the society will find itself subsidizing those people—if they are an identifiable group—who consume a lot of electricity or a lot of goods made with a lot of electricity.[266]

Economists have suggested various ways of dealing with this inequity. One possibility is to require all sources of pollution to keep their extrusion below a set rate.[267] This is a reasonable way to deal with poisons. Many nations use this approach to the disposal of lead, mercury, and DDT, among other dangerous substances. Use of lead-free gasoline can lower the rate at which automobiles emit some sorts of atmospheric pollutants, for example. Or a factory may diminish the rate at which it emits particulate smoke by "scrubbing" the gases in its smokestacks. In so doing, it may produce a liquid waste which must be discharged somewhere. The air pollution standards may do more harm than good if the liquid wastes are dumped into a river.

Organizations may find that the costs of meeting societal standards differ greatly from one situation to another, since some sources are easier to correct than others. A fair resolution of such a disparity might be to require less of a factory with high costs and more of one with low costs. Or it might be possible to levy effluent charges or tax all pollution sources proportionally to their rates of emission of pollutants. Industrial corporations under such circumstances could probably be relied on to cut costs by minimizing pollution, since their profits would depend upon it. If automobile owners paid the true indirect costs of pollution resulting from the operating of their vehicles, the number of cars on the streets and highways would probably be reduced. The money collected could be used to improve the environment.

Another approach might be for the government to collect a materials-use fee on matter-energy removed from the environment. The producer or importer would be charged an amount equal to the true social cost if that particular matter-energy was eventually returned to the environment in the most harmful form. Refunds would then be made to anyone demon-

strating that the matter-energy had been disposed of in a less harmful way. Recycled materials would be charged no materials-use fee. If choice were possible among alternative sorts of matter-energy, the selection under such conditions might well be closer to the social optimum. Containers or detergents that were biodegradable would be selected over those which were not because their total cost including the materials-use fee, would be less. Such regulation of environmental pollution, of course, would penalize owners of deposits of certain materials, such as high-sulfur coal. Whether a given society does this depends on how committed it is to maintaining a desirable environment.

A demonstration of what can be done when a firm environmental policy is backed up by determination of components and subcomponents of the system has been provided by the state of Oregon. It succeeded in reducing pollution of the Willamette River by 90 percent in 5 years.[268] The Willamette rises in the Cascade Mountains and runs south 411 km through the state to empty into the Columbia River. Along its banks are the largest cities in the state. Before antipollution policies were instituted, its waters received wastes from 21 municipalities, some 600 industrial facilities (including paper mills, lumber mills, canneries, and metallurgical plants), and animal feeding lots.

Oregon created a Department of Environmental Quality, which issued annual permits to municipalities and industries granting them their "pollution ration" for the year. If more organizations requested permits to extrude wastes into the river, less pollution was allowed per permit. This served to maintain the river's quality. Fines of up to $500 a day were levied on violators that extruded wastes at a higher rate than they were allowed. When a large paper mill installed a defective control system that leaked waste into the river, the plant was closed until the leaks were stopped. Sewage treatment standards were also set, requiring not only primary treatment, which removes solids and suspended matter, but also secondary treatment, by which organic matter in the water is decomposed.

The result of all this has been greatly improved water quality. In a river that was essentially dead, fish are again plentiful, and salmon again spawn. Millions of boaters have used the river, which formerly was unsuited for such activity, and sport fishermen regularly catch salmon in it.

The wastes recovered from the river are used in many ways. Animal wastes from lots where they feed are mixed with water in lagoons and used to irrigate and fertilize farmlands. Heated waste water is used to fight spring frosts in nearby orchards. Some dried wastes are bagged and used as fertilizers or as high-protein fish food.

This was not done without cost. Many municipalities had to construct sewage treatment plants at a cost of $150 million or more, and some industries have spent as much as $50 million. The state paid 30 percent of the cost to municipalities, and the industries received tax breaks. Legislation enables the federal government to participate in such large projects.

Fundamentally, what such projects do is develop alternative distributor components for a society so that its rivers can be used for activities like fishing and boating, which can best be carried out there. If they are used as distributors for large societal systems, they inevitably become polluted with high-entropy wastes. This supports Hypothesis 3.2.2.2-1 (see page 94), which states that the farther a specific matter-energy transmission passes along a distributor from the point of its input to it and toward the final point of its output from it, the more it is altered by lowering the concentration of the kinds of matter-energy it contains which are used by the system's subsystems and by increasing the concentration of the products or wastes produced by it and output by those subsystems. The pollution of rivers used as distributors also supports Hypothesis 3.2.2.2-2 (see page 94), which says that in general, total entropy per unit cubic contents increases progressively along a distributor between the points of input and output.

Since conversion of energy is one of the most environmentally damaging processes in industrial societies, the exponential rise in energy consumption is a threat not only to the continued supply of energy but also to the environment. Nations will not be able to go on doubling their use of energy every few years unless some clean, relatively inexhaustible source is discovered. It should have a high efficiency so that it does not pour more heat than necessary into the environment. Power from nuclear fusion (see page 776) may be just such a source if it proves usable.

Hydrogen is a sort of fuel which does not pollute. When it burns, water vapor is formed.[269] The hydrogen could be produced by electrolysis of sea water, using electricity generated by nuclear power plants several miles off shore and piped to distribution stations on land. The water vapor generated when it burned would increase the humidity, but it would in time return to the sea to become again a source of hydrogen. The deuterium needed for nuclear-fusion reactions would be a by-product of the electrolysis of water. The concept of a society in which hydrogen is the sole fuel has been called a "hydrogen economy." None yet exists.

Much of the technology needed for such an economy has been developed for use in spaceships. Liquid hydrogen fuels rockets, and hydrogen-oxygen fuel cells supply spaceships with electric power. Hydrogen could be distributed through the present network of gas lines. The idea is far from new. In 1874 Jules Verne, in *The Mysterious Island,* had an engineer answer the question of what men would burn when coal and other fuels were exhausted by saying: "Water. . . . Yes, my friends, I believe that water will one day be employed as fuel, that hydrogen and oxygen which constitute it, used singly or together will furnish an inexhaustible source of heat and light. . . ."[270]

A mixed bag of suggestions, from many sources, for alleviating the problems of energy use includes using the heat from power plants to heat whole cities; making greater use of new technologies for deriving gas, a cleaner fuel, from residual oil and coal; developing pollution-free motors for cars; substituting public transportation for much private use of automobiles; allocating appropriate fuels for different uses; making imaginative use of solid wastes, such as putting them into sanitary landfills to improve low-value real estate; using subterranean hydrogen bombs to atomize solid wastes and saving the resulting accumulation of hydrogen for use as a fuel; and shooting solid wastes out into space with rockets.

These obviously vary in practicality. It is also clear that for many reasons, societies do not have the option to return to primeval modes of life. One of these is the fact that such life-styles would prevent them from supporting their large populations.

Because the soil can abate pollution, Bohn and Cauthorn make an argument for greater and more imaginative use of it for this purpose. They say:

Our handling of wastes has been unimaginative and expensive. We have been wrong in considering wastes useless, rather than as matter and energy in a less useful form and place. Man's role has been to shift matter and energy from the lithosphere to the hydrosphere and atmosphere. His insistence upon removing wastes in the shortest possible time has also played a part in this mismanagement: the fluid media rapidly flush away waste material but do not eliminate it, thereby making one man's pollution another man's problem. Those pollutants which in water and air give rise to serious and costly problems are disposed of quickly in the soil and converted into plant nutrients with little or no intervention by man. Eutrophication of the soil rather than water enhances the production of food and the type of environment which we cherish. In summary, compared to air and water, the soil has a vastly greater potential for waste disposal and transformation. It has been absorbing and recycling nature's wastes for some three and one-half billion years on earth without impairment of its functions, and it still has the capacity to absorb far more material than it can produce or than is added to it.[271]

The many suggestions for cleaning up and protecting the environment carry varying price tags, but the annual bill will certainly be high for as long as the present sort of societal processes continue. That bill will most likely be paid in tax money and in added costs to industrial organizations and cities. A cost-benefit analysis must balance these monetary outlays against many costs that are hard to establish, like costs in lost wages to the household sector of the economy resulting from illness brought about by air and water pollution; costs to organizations of absenteeism resulting from the same cause; costs in lowered real estate values, particularly in central cities or in neighborhoods downwind from large industrial areas; and costs in lost beauty like the sight of a clear blue sky, the fresh smell of clean wind, the unspoiled wilderness, and the wonderful natural variety of birds, fish, insects, and other animals.

Estimates of the actual amounts of money lost by pollution damage vary widely. It is possible, for example, to establish damage to cities by knowing their median property values, the number of their owner-occupied residential properties, and indices of local sulfur trioxide.[272] Annual damage is calculated by multiplying the lost value by the current interest rate to account for what the lost value would have earned if pollution had not wiped it out. When this was done for 85 American cities for the year 1965, the combined property-value losses worked out to $621 million.

The benefits to be gained by cleaning up a city to an acceptable degree must be compared with the costs to determine whether such action should be taken. Such a calculation was made for the Delaware River.[273] On the benefit side was possible increased recreational use of the river for boating and fishing over the period 1965 to 1990. On the other side were costs of improving water quality. According to this study, if one day's boating were worth as much as $2.55 to a boater, it would have paid to clean up the Delaware considerably in 1965 just to improve boating conditions. Such calculations would be necessary on many other variables as well.

Societies sooner or later are forced to make value judgments about their matter-energy processing. Should the awesome Grand Canyon be flooded to provide more power, as some propose? If the Alaska pipeline will, in fact, melt the permafrost and disturb the ecology of the whole area, does the society still want it? How unhealthy, dirty, crowded, and unaesthetic are our cities willing to become in order to use energy at an ever-expanding rate? Societies need facts upon which to base economic and value choices. Is the situation indeed as gloomy as it appears to be?

Or is it better? Or far worse? There is need for research, some of which is now in progress. Environmental indicators (see page 753) urgently need to be developed so that relationships between changes in societal variables and environmental variables can be reliably established.

Today many steps are being taken toward environmental improvement. Legislation in the United Kingdom, which some years ago restricted the use of coal that had not been treated to reduce pollutants and which established smoke-free zones where no coal could be used, significantly reduced smoke and sulfur dioxide in the atmosphere. This occurred in spite of a 10 percent increase in population and a 17 percent rise in energy consumption.[274] An added benefit has been a 50 percent increase in the amount of winter sunshine in London.

The United States has had legislation to protect the environment since the Refuse Act of 1899 was enacted to prevent the dumping of refuse into navigable waters. In places where no injury to navigation would result, under this law permission could be given to mines or stamp works to deposit debris into water.[275] Basic environmental policy for the United States is stated in the National Environmental Policy Act of 1969, which also set up the Council on Environmental Quality.[276] The Council prepares an annual environmental quality report for the President in which it describes environmental conditions and the adequacy of resources, reviews programs, and makes recommendations for improvements, new policy, and legislation. Additional legislation, the Environmental Quality Improvement Act, established the Office of Environmental Quality in the Executive Office of the President. Among other things, it assists in relevant studies and reviews, aids in coordination of environmental programs among the various federal departments and agencies, and collects and interprets data and information on environmental quality, ecological research, and evaluation.

Also, the United States has passed a Federal Water Pollution Control Act, a Solid Wastes Disposal Act, a Clean Air Act, a Noise Control Act, and a National Emission Standards Act, which controls pollution by motor vehicles. These recognize the primary responsibility of states for the processes they concern. Central boards and agencies set standards, carry out research and data collection, and decide upon grants to states, interstate agencies, and public or private agencies or institutions for such things as reservoirs, sewage disposal plants, and training programs. Environmental measures are included that provide for inspections, fines, and court actions by the government or by citizens who are injured by violations. Federal funding of such environmental activities is massive.

(*b*) *Adjustments to population increases.* The number of people in a society is of critical importance. If its population falls below the minimum needed to perform the society's essential subsystem processes, particularly the producer processes that provide the successive new generations upon which the system's continuity depends, its future is threatened. Sharp population decreases have terminated some small, primitive societies (see page 873).

Societies can augment their numbers by recruitment from outside. Brazil, for instance, encourages immigration in spite of its high birthrate because of the challenge of its extensive undeveloped and unpopulated land. Societies also have encouraged procreation by means of propaganda or by rewarding fecundity in various ways, including tax benefits and public praise. France, Italy, and the Soviet Union, among other countries, have had governmental policies favoring childbearing. The effectiveness of such policies remains to be proved, at least partly because reproduction is downwardly dispersed to the level of the group or mating dyad. It is therefore more directly susceptible to lower-level strains, such as those caused by increased employment among women, rising expectations for living conditions, or limitations of housing. The usual adjustment processes to such strains involve producing fewer rather than more children.

Strains arising from excess population are being experienced by many contemporary societies, and the belief is widespread that at the present rate of human increase, even those societies best able to provide for their members will eventually develop such strains, possibly within a few generations. In the United States an average of only three children to a family in 100 years would produce nearly 1 billion people.[277] It is unlikely that the standard of living enjoyed by today's 200 million Americans could be provided to such a multitude.

A child born in the United States in 1971 will, in her or his lifetime, require about 69 million liters (l) of water, 25.5 metric tons of iron and steel, 143,089 l of petroleum, 5,897 kilograms (kg) of paper, and 45.5 metric tons of food. He or she will receive about $10,000 of public services.[278] According to another set of figures:

. . . every child born into the American economy—taking the 1968 figures—contrives by the time he grows up to consume every year over a million calories and 13 metric tons of coal equivalent (or 2,700 gallons [10,200 l] of gasoline) in energy. He has probably nearly 10 metric tons of steel attached

to him for various uses, particularly in the motorcar which is on the way to being owned by one of two of all citizens. He probably has another 150 kilograms of both copper and lead and 100 kilograms of aluminum and of zinc in use in his various appliances and artifacts. To keep him supplied with all these needs, the country's roads, railways, and freight planes transport 15,000 tons of materials per kilometer and to his door they bring the TV sets, the washing machines, the refrigerator owned by over 70 percent of the population. They also deliver the second car and color TV to 30 percent of the people and—a booming, expanding market—air conditioners to 20 percent.[279]

Each person in a society also increases, by some fraction, the strains upon information processing subsystems.

At present, population strains are greatest in less developed nations like Bangladesh, which cannot provide an acceptable standard of living for many of its people. In less developed societies it is not entirely the large population that brings about the strain, but the large population combined with inadequate matter-energy processing. Primitive agricultural methods and a small share of world markets result in inadequate inputs from both inside and outside the societal boundaries. In contrast, the prosperous Netherlands, though it is the most heavily populated country in the world, manages to enjoy a high standard of living. Its more than 12 million people are comfortably accommodated on only 36,000 km² of land, some of which was dredged from the sea and must be maintained by dikes. Like many less developed countries, The Netherlands cannot produce all the matter-energy needed by its large population from within its own borders, but unlike them it can buy a large part of what it needs on international markets in exchange for its industrial output. It is among the leading trading partners of the United States. *Fortune* magazine's listing of the 300 largest industrial corporations outside the United States for 1974 contains nine, including three of the first five, that are wholly or partly owned by The Netherlands.[280] By contrast, India appears in the list only twice, with Indian Oil ranked 157th and the Steel Authority of India ranked 263d. Total sales of the nine Dutch corporations were in excess of $69 billion. The two Indian corporations totaled about $2 billion in sales.

Obviously, an adjustment process that would help less developed countries would be to change their matter-energy processing subsystems to improve agriculture and industry and gain a competitive position in world markets. The process of development is proceeding in many societies throughout the world, but in many of these the population grows so rapidly that increased demand quickly nullifies even substantial gains, leaving the people still poverty-stricken. Along with development, a slower rate of population growth is necessary if a desirable steady state is to be attained.

Self-regulation of number is an adjustment process in populations of nonhuman organisms and in primitive societies as well. Observation of animals in their natural habitats lends support to an alternative to the Darwinian hypothesis that all populations strive to increase in numbers and that controls are imposed by environmental means, such as limited food supply, rigorous climate, and disease.[281] Intrinsic factors appear to produce a nice adjustment of population to food supply. Population growth is limited, but starvation is the exceptional rather than the normal means of control. This adjustment, however, cannot occur in unstable or transitory environments, like agricultural lands, where plowing, seeding, spraying, harvesting, and rotation of crops create environmental turmoil. In such areas, violent fluctuations of populations of insect pests are among the many undesirable conditions that may develop.

Experimental results with laboratory animals of species as varied as flies, water fleas, guppies, mice, and rats have shown that in the absence of food restriction, disease, or interference by the experimenter, population densities become stable in time.

Animal groups regulate their sizes by controlling access to food and the number of organisms allowed to breed. They do this by such means as adjusting sizes of feeding territories (see pages 564 and 565), limiting access to breeding sites (see page 521), preventing animals low in the pecking order (see page 565) from feeding when the supply is low, and preventing breeding by some of the animals.

Wolf packs, for instance, keep their populations in balance with the available food supply by means of a number of behavioral devices.[282] Each wolf pack respects the territorial boundaries between packs, and so hunting grounds are kept from overcrowding. Within packs, mating is almost always the prerogative of the top-ranking male and female, who police the lower-ranking members of their sexes to curb mating tendencies. Care of the young, however, is shared with other members of the pack. If the number of prey animals fluctuates beyond certain limits, the wolves adjust to this by permitting their population to grow or by showing less concern than usual for the weaker members of the group so that in bad winters they are allowed to die. If the pack is below the number the environment can support, their concern for the weaker members increases, improving their chances of survival.

Primitive human societies appear also to have adjusted their numbers in various ways like those used by these animal groups to protect their steady states. Studies on existing South American Indian societies, which appear more similar in their breeding behavior to primitive hunting and gathering societies than to modern societies, shed some light on how primitive man may have controlled population size.[283] The Yanomama Indians achieve an average effective live birthrate of approximately one child every 4 to 5 years during the childbearing period. One way this is done is by infanticide, primarily of infants whose older siblings are not ready for weaning, deformed infants, infants thought to have resulted from extramarital relationships, and some females.[284] The total number of infants killed at birth probably amounts to 15 to 20 percent of all live births. Other means are abortion and intercourse taboos that protect a woman from conception during the first 3 years of her infant's life before it is weaned. Prolonged lactation in itself is a deterrent to conception.

A historical study of Europe between 1750 and 1850, a period during which the population of Europe nearly doubled, indicates that the population explosion took place in spite of controls on population growth.[285] Malthus, in his essay of the period, said that war, famine, and disease kept the human population from outstripping the food supply. At that time war was almost continuous, diseases like smallpox and the plague ravaged Europe, and famines occurred whenever crops failed. It was probably the importation from America of potatoes and maize that, by increasing the food supply, allowed the observed population increase. The people of Europe supplemented such drastic controls with other population checks. These included frequent postponement of marriage to the middle twenties for women and the late twenties for men; celibacy enforced upon the clergy; inability of younger sons of nobles to marry because only the first son inherited property; legal restriction of marriage among the poor; a large number of unmarried women—as many as 30 to 40 percent in France; restrictions by guilds on marriage of apprentices and even journeymen; and a large number of men in armies, of whom many were killed and many others never married. The practice of Swiss soldiers acting as mercenaries in the armies of other European countries is estimated to have prevented 35 to 40 percent of the natural increase of that country.

In addition to these social controls, an appalling number of infants were either killed directly or abandoned, which was a slower but just as sure means of achieving the same end. These practices persisted in spite of denunciations by the church until a change in attitude toward children, particularly the newborn, took place in the middle of the nineteenth century.

Modern societies under stress of population pressure have adopted governmental policies designed to stabilize their numbers. Japan, China, and India have done so, and Japan has succeeded in reducing its annual population increase to 1 percent.[286] Like governmental campaigns to increase birthrates, however, these probably can succeed only if they are in accord with the wishes of family groups. That the current sentiment in the United States favors limitation of population growth is suggested by a study which disclosed that in 1965, American women really wanted an average of only 2.5 children.[287] An estimated one-fifth of all births were unwanted. If this is so, the population stability rate of 2.1 children per family would not be impossible to attain. The long-term trend in birthrate has been downward in the United States, with some interruptions at the time of World War II.

Discussing governmental policies, Ward and Dubos say:

. . . two factors of equal importance are involved in the critical issue of slowing down the world's present untenable speed of population growth. The first is a new factor—strong governmental policy in favor of smaller families. The second is the older, more complex but already fairly successful solution—the change of the whole context of people's lives into the more modern habits of high education, female emancipation, rapid industrialization, productive, modernized agriculture, and city life. On ecological principles, we may guess that the second solution is likely to be more effective, since fully sustainable changes tend to result from interacting, complementary, and mutually reinforcing developments.[288]

What would be the effect of population stability upon other societal variables? One analysis, by a *Fortune* magazine staff writer, suggests that although prosperity probably does not depend upon continued population growth, the size of the GNP would be smaller with a stabilized than with a growing population.[289] More women would probably go to work, but when their employment reached a ceiling, the labor force would be stable in number and the economy could grow only as fast as the growth of the average output per worker. The average standard of living would probably be higher, since resources freed from providing consumer goods, services, and social overhead would be used for both private and public investment. Each member of the labor force would be working with a larger or more advanced stock of capital, which would result in more output and more income per worker. With smaller families, income per person would also rise. The number of people of each age up to about 50 would be roughly the same, and

with zero growth, all age groups except the very old would be the same size. Adjustments in markets would follow. There would be more money spent on recreation and adult clothing, but businesses catering to infants and those providing food and drink would not grow. Production costs would probably not go up. Social security taxes and pension costs would rise, however. There would be fewer poor families and more education per child, which would imply a more skilled labor force and perhaps enhanced ability to innovate or cope with advanced technology. There would be less need for governmental regulation or intervention of many kinds. Fewer governmental expenditures for education, health, recreation, and water supply would be needed. Presumably, with fewer juveniles there would be less juvenile delinquency.

Disadvantages might include an increase in the average age of the people in authority and control of politics, as well as slower advancement in business, politics, and other organized activities.

(*c*) *Adjustments of spatial distribution of population.* An outstanding feature of population distribution in societies throughout the world during recent history has been the increase in urbanization. Between 1950 and 1970 the proportion of the world's people living in cities grew from 28 to 37 percent.[290] While the process went further in developed countries, which showed an increase in urban population from 51 to 88 percent, the less developed countries showed the same trend, changing from 16 to 25 percent. United Nations projections for the 15-year period following 1970 forecast a continuation of this trend throughout the world. No nation is expected to increase the percentage of its rural population.

The trend toward urbanization has been a long-term one in Europe and the United States. In 1790, 95 percent of Americans lived in rural environments.[291] By the end of the nineteenth century, the move toward the cities was well under way. One peak urbanization rate of 56.5 percent was reached during the census period 1880–1890. By 1900 only 6 in every 10 Americans were classified as rural, and by 1920 the country was more than half urbanized. In 1970, 73.5 percent of Americans lived in cities and towns of 2,500 or more. Half the counties lost population; half the remainder gained little.[292]

It is obvious that the environmental impact of great concentrations of people and their artifacts is different from that of the same population living in more spread-out patterns. The ills of the cities (see pages 703 and 704) exacerbate with increasing size of the urbanized area under present conditions, so that the quality of life in the central regions of great cities becomes poor. In fact the "population problem" in the United States is almost wholly one of distribution, since the actual average density of the population in relation to the extent of the land is only 8.5 people per square kilometer (10.1 per square kilometer if Alaska is excluded).[293] Density in central cities averages about 2,700 per square kilometer.[294] It is more than 10 times as high in some European countries.

A further aspect of urbanization in the United States is the enormous increase in the population of metropolitan areas, at the expense of both rural regions and central cities.[295] Of the 25 largest cities, 12 lost population during the decade 1960–1970. Four lost more than 10 percent. But of the 50 leading metropolitan areas, all but one showed substantial gains in number. In fact the Standard Metropolitan Statistical Areas, that is, cities of over 50,000 people and the counties they dominate, absorbed 84 percent of the total national population expansion during the decade.

Citizens of the United States move about a great deal, probably more than nationals of most other societies. Much of this is for economic reasons—a search for better jobs. More and better job opportunities and health and welfare services account for some of the attractiveness of urban life. Many rural Southerners, black and white, have abandoned efforts to make a living on the land and have moved to other parts of the country. But the South has not lost population. After the West, which for a long time has been attracting more new residents than any other part of the country, it showed the greatest gain of any region, concentrated in the states of Florida, Texas, Maryland, and Virginia. Many older citizens choose sunny Florida for their retirement home. Maryland and Virginia are a part of the great East Coast concentration. Texas has the lure of the West and the attraction of a mild climate. Hauser discusses this:

In the U.S. as elsewhere the main attractions for migratory movement are greater economic opportunity and a less rigorous climate. The strong streams of migration to California and Florida represent a combination of these factors. Usually the free movement of people toward areas of better economic opportunity serves to improve the balance between the population and the nation's economic resources. Thus over the long run the shifts of population in the U.S. can be expected to smooth out regional differences in the standard of living.[296]

A number of adjustment processes have been considered or tried in societies to counteract the problems of urbanization. The trend itself is hard to reverse. Attempts to stop the growth of London, Paris, Tokyo, and Moscow have all failed.

Comprehensive social planning, to guide growth and control land use, has been adopted in several societies. The Netherlands has a National Physical Planning Act, passed in 1965, which permits elected authorities to develop overall standards within which localities can plan.[297] This makes it possible to treat as a single unit the almost continuous urban region that includes Rotterdam, Amsterdam, The Hague, and several other cities. In this conurbation, a third of the national population lives on one-twentieth of the land. Without planning, industry and slums could cover the entire territory, obscuring all natural beauty as well as the charm of the cities.

Romania has also approached the problem of land use in an integrated way.[298] The whole territory of the society, in which 20 million people live on about 237,000 km² of land, has been mapped, and its assets inventoried. The centralized control in this society enabled the Romanians to channel their rapid industrialization into a dispersed pattern, so that although urban population has doubled, Bucharest has increased only moderately in number of inhabitants. This country also had the advantage of starting its comprehensive plan when 40 percent of its people were still engaged in agriculture.

Another adjustment that many societies have undertaken is to build new cities, either starting with a small town and expanding it or beginning entirely new, as Brazil did in creating Brasilia. This new capital is planned with six satellite cities to absorb expected future population increases.[299] Britain has started 27 new cities since 1946, but this has not improved the conditions in London.[300] The Soviet Union has constructed 900 new cities to help allay its monumental housing shortage.[301]

Comprehensive land-use plans in many societies are concerned with concentrations of populations, preservation of farmlands, and protection of unspoiled natural beauty. The national park services in the United States, Canada, some African societies, and other countries seek to keep wilderness areas and their animal populations as resources for the future. England, Wales, and Scotland have Countryside Commissions, which can designate Areas of Outstanding Natural Beauty and can give local authorities up to 75 percent of the cost of maintaining them.[302] The French government has preserved some rural areas as national parks so that the work of a thousand years of farming can be kept intact.

As a part of a total plan for its society, the Soviet Union has arranged its internal boundaries so that each republic will be, insofar as possible, self-sufficient. It has also charted all its mountains, rivers, and coastal areas to plan for increased recreational needs as the average workweek gets shorter.[303]

Such plans are not confined to industrialized societies with high average density of inhabitants. Kenya is now planning for its expected development by studying its towns and evaluating their suitability for intensive development.[304] Tanzania is planning specific "poles of growth" to draw economic activity away from Dar es Salaam.

The societies given here as examples vary in the degree to which they view their entire nation as a single system and exercise central control over land use and development. Worldwide experience so far does not lead to the conclusion that downwardly dispersed control produces maximal benefits for an entire society. If thousands of independent organizations each maximize their own utilities in the housing and land markets, no mysterious hand protects the system as a whole. It frequently is very much to the benefit of a development corporation to build densely packed high-rises of mediocre quality in the expensive central areas of cities. The people who are affected by the consequent urban blight are often not the builders themselves or their stockholders. The latter frequently make their profits and sell their interests before the area completely deteriorates. Also, it often is highly profitable for corporations to despoil irreplaceable natural resources with strip mining and lumbering.

What, then, can a society committed to free markets and individual initiative do to protect the interests of the total system, while preserving its basic economic principles? Concern of the citizens of a society for preservation of its resources and environment in general has some observable effect. This can be supplemented with stricter governmental regulation of organizational activities and use of government funds in restoration. Voluntary cooperation alone usually cannot be counted upon to do the job. Also, businesses can be required to pay the full costs of the pollution, waste disposal, and traffic congestion which they give rise to and also pay for the benefits they derive from public facilities such as airports and highways.[305]

5.2.4 Information internal processes   Of the many sorts of systemwide information internal adjustment processes found in societies, I shall discuss in the following section examples from only two broad categories: (a) adjustments to changes in transmissions of monetary information and (b) adjustments to strains in internal information flows brought about by the need for support and consensus in the society.

(a) *Adjustments to changes in transmissions of monetary information.*   Much has been learned by economists working with quantitative data and models about the adjustment processes of societies as they react to alterations in the flows of money.

Since few of the products or services necessary for life or valued by societies are so abundant as to be freely available to anyone in any desired quantity,

societies must make fundamental economic decisions as to which and how much of the many possible alternative goods and services they will make available, how and by whom these will be provided, and to what components of the system or environment they will be distributed. How adjustments among economic variables are made varies widely among societies. They may be determined by tradition. Or the government of a society with a highly centralized economic system may make these decisions, or they may be downwardly dispersed to the levels of the organization, the group, or the individual person, each separate component or subcomponent seeking its own best interests, as in classical free-enterprise capitalism. Or some pattern of mixed central responsibility and independent adjustment processes may prevail, as in modern "mixed economies."[306]

Monetary information conveys a special set of meanings through the societal channel and net which differs in some ways from other communications. People in the United States have constitutional guarantees about ordinary communications—guarantees of free speech. They are generally free to transmit or not transmit, and to receive or not receive, such messages. Sometimes the society compels a citizen to transmit or receive certain such communications, as when a witness is subpoenaed and required to testify in a hearing or when a draftee is required by a federal marshal to accept service of a document ordering him to report for induction. But these are unusual situations. By far the greatest part of human communication is voluntary.

Monetary information transmissions are in large measure voluntary also. Most people are free to decide what products or services they wish to buy or sell. But some sorts of sales or purchases are illegal. Many countries require everyone within their borders to use a single currency, while others permit the currencies of all nations to be exchanged. Some allow import and export of their own and other currencies, while others limit such transmissions or ban them altogether. In most modern nations the local money has been declared legal tender. This means that banks and many other public and private organizations are required to accept it, at least up to certain specified total amounts. The credit of the government is behind such money, and consequently it is usually acceptable to all citizens. It is a medium of general exchange, so that earnings from one sale can be spent to purchase any product or service. Monetary information is more likely to cause a person to provide a product or service than ordinary communication. Money talks. Legal tender therefore makes economic exchanges, employing monetary information, much more convenient and flexible than transactions in more primitive barter economies of the past or present, which have employed chiefly matter-energy exchanges.

Flows of monetary information in a society are important not only because money is used in exchanges of products and services but also because societies keep accounts of both matter-energy and information flows within them in terms of money. Using money as a standard, transactions in all the diverse products and services become comparable. A society's annual national income, its GNP, is the total monetary value of all the flows of products and services that have taken place in the economy during the year. Corrected for changing prices, computation of the GNP makes it possible to compare the performance of the economy from year to year and, with adjustments for different currencies, allows comparison of the economic performance of different societies. I discuss below a computerized model of the information flows that make up the national income (see pages 878 to 881).

Each present-day industrialized society organizes its production and exchange of goods and services by a distinctive combination of free enterprise adjustment processes and governmental control. The "mix" varies from society to society. The highly centralized systems have to some degree accepted monetary incentives, interest rates (known as *capital charges*), and some other characteristics of free markets. Capitalist societies in recent decades have moved toward greater control of economic variables.

The economies of modern capitalist societies are modifications of capitalistic free enterprise systems in which the basic production and consumption adjustments establish equilibria among variables in a free competitive market. Detailed models have been developed for the pure form of such systems and for variants of different sorts in which perfect competition, a requirement of the classical model, is modified or in which products offered in a market are differentiated rather than identical, as the theory requires (see page 878).[307]

In such an economy, according to Leontief, " . . . the overall economic goal is determined by a kind of universal suffrage in which everyone has a multiple vote proportional to his dollar income."[308] Leontief looks on the workings of the economy as functions of a societal system, comparing the economic system with a computer:*

. . . the economic system can be viewed as a gigantic computing machine which tirelessly grinds out the solutions of an unending stream of quantitative problems: the problems of the optimal allocation of labor, capital, and natural resources, the proper balance between the rates of production and consumption of thousands of individual goods, the problems of a proper division of the stream of current output between consumption and investment, and many others.

Each of these problems can—in principle at least—be thought of as being represented by a system of equations. Under conditions of perfect competition an impersonal automatic computer—to which we usually refer as the economic system—has been solving these equations year after year, day after day, before the mathematical economists even thought of constructing their systems. . . .[309]

This "computer" solves its equations by iterative methods, that is, by the method of successive approximations. Elegant and effective as these automatic adjustment processes are, however, the governments of nations with modern mixed economies do not put complete reliance upon them. At times they act to limit and direct their effects. Sometimes such intervention is not wholly corrective, and large fluctuations in production and consumption of products and services are experienced, referred to as *business cycles*. Leontief says:†

When a machine does not perform as expected, one naturally is tempted to interfere. Such interference may consist simply of oiling a bearing or tightening a screw; occasionally we find it necessary to take the computation out of the machine and perform at least some part of it by hand.

Any kind of active economic policy or economic planning represents a purposeful interference with the operation of the competitive machine. If in the pursuit of their particular aims the policymakers rely on such instruments as tariffs, subsidies, or taxes, most of the economic computations still continue to be performed by the market mechanism, the corrective action adds new components to the computer, but does not really interfere with its automatic operation. In designing counter-cyclical fiscal policies, one might introduce, for instance, compensatory taxes which rise automatically during prosperity and fall when depression tends to set in.

Like any other complicated apparatus, a competitive economy tends to malfunction under stress and such stress appears whenever it is confronted with problems which differ greatly from those it has been solving before. It is not surprising, for example, that in transition from peace to war or from war to peace, in transition from long stagnation to rapid growth, or in facing the problems of fast and discontinuous technological change, a certain amount of guiding assistance, that is of planning, might facilitate the solution of general equilibrium problems facing the economic computing machine.[310]

In a free enterprise economy, changes in flows of monetary information are important determinants of adjustment processes in the flows of matter-energy and other sorts of information through the society.

---

*From *Essays in economics: theories and theorizing* by Wassily Leontief. Copyright © 1966 by Oxford University Press, Inc. Reprinted by permission.

†From *Essays in economics: theories and theorizing* by Wassily Leontief. Copyright © 1966 by Oxford University Press, Inc. Reprinted by permission.

What will be produced, and how much? Usually whatever is recognized to be in demand, and in whatever quantities are demanded. The products will be provided by sellers who can compete successfully in the market. They will end up in the hands of people with money to pay the current prices and a desire to exchange it for the goods they want.

Such an outcome conflicts with the values of most modern societies. Therefore, in order to adjust to societal strains and protect the welfare of the population, government intervention is usual. No present-day economist would permit himself to say, as Ricardo did in 1817, in a discussion of the market price of labor: "It is only after privations have reduced their number, or the demand for labor has increased, that the market price of labor will rise to its natural price."[311]

All modern societies redistribute wealth among their members, although their programs vary in effectiveness. Social security programs, public health and welfare programs, subsidized public housing, and old-age and retirement programs are among the adjustments they use. Money to fund such programs comes from taxes.

In the United States the work of welfare recipients has been restricted. Usually any money earned is deducted from welfare payments, and some families are actually worse off having some earned income than being wholly on welfare. This provides a disincentive toward work.

An alternative solution has been suggested—a "negative income tax."[312] The graduated tax now in effect is paid by all individuals and families with incomes above an amount that varies with family size. The negative tax would provide for payments to those whose income is below a minimum amount. The supplement would be reduced as other income rose, but by an amount lower than the rise in income. Above a set amount payments would stop. If the guaranteed minimum was $3,000 and the rate of reduction was 50 percent, a family of four could earn up to $5,000 and still receive a $500 supplement. Above $5,500 no supplement would be given. A family with other income of $4,000 would be guaranteed a total of $5,000.

The proponents of this plan believe that it would be economically more efficient than the programs it would replace because it would be administered by the relatively efficient Internal Revenue Service instead of a complex of agencies of local and state governments and the national government. They feel it would be less demeaning to the poor. It would eliminate the great regional differences in assistance that result from the present welfare system. It would

not be expected to destroy incentive to work. Opponents point out that it would be costly and that costs would be likely to increase as time went on, as often happens with such programs. They say that it would not replace welfare. Regional disparities would still exist, since what is only adequate in New York would be lavish in the rural South. It also offends against the high value the majority of citizens place on working for a living.

A study in which a negative income tax program was tested showed that it did not cause a significant decline in weekly earnings of those receiving it, as some had predicted.[313] Presumably, introduction of such a program would not incite many to voluntary idleness.

Another alternative is for the government to guarantee a job to anyone who cannot find one on the open labor market. This plan would be more difficult to administer and would present the government with the problem of placing people who could not be usefully employed. Many would still require welfare. Job training or retraining, to increase the employability of young people or of those whose skills are no longer needed because of changing technology or demand, is a promising alternative.

Money paid to members of the community as wages or other payments goes into immediate purchases of necessities and luxuries or into savings for the future in bank accounts, insurances, or other savings. Money received by businesses, above that required for operation and for dividends to stockholders, may be invested in equipment, buildings, inventories, and increased numbers of employees, making the organization grow and increasing the stock of capital in the society, unless management decides to defer expansion. These uses of money by components interact to determine the national income (NNP, or net national product), which comes into equilibrium at a point at which the desired saving of families and the desired investment of business match. Figure 11-6 illustrates the intersection of the curves representing saving and investment. In the illustration, the intersection is well below the shaded area, which indicates full employment in the society. A similar curve can be drawn for the equilibrium between consumption and investment. It determines the national income in the same way.[314] A change in the amount of saving or consumption alters the amount business has to spend and moves the equilibrium point. If people throughout the society decide to save their money, inventories increase as goods are not sold. The businessman has less money and cannot invest in the expansion of his enterprise. More goods will sell at lower prices, but a

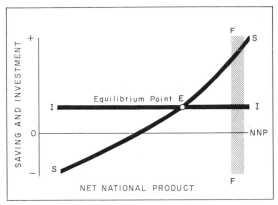

Fig. 11-6 How saving and investment determine income. E marks the point where investment (I—I) and saving (S—S) curves intersect. Equilibrium is at the intersection of the S—S and I—I curves because at no other level of the net national product (NNP) could the desired saving of families continually match the desired investment of business. The shaded area F–F depicts the full-employment NNP. [Adapted from P. A. Samuelson. *Economics.* (8th ed.) New York: McGraw-Hill, 1970, 210. *Reprinted by permission.*]

business cannot sell below the amount it needs for very long. The system moves to a new equilibrium, in this case one that is even further from full employment. The NNP drops. To a person accustomed to thinking in terms of family financial planning, it is surprising that thrift, which is recommended for systems at organism and family-group levels, may not be the best thing for the society as a whole if too many people engage in it during a deflation. Samuelson says:

An increased desire to consume—which is another way of looking at a decreased desire to save—is likely to boost business sales and increase investment. On the other hand, a decreased desire to consume—i.e., an increase in thriftiness—is likely to reduce inflationary pressure in times of booming incomes; but in time of depression, it could make the depression worse and reduce the amount of actual net capital formation in the community. *High consumption and high investment are then hand in hand rather than opposed to each other.*[315]

For one who usually does not think in systems theory terms, the fact that the good of lower-level systems may not be identical with that of the higher level may provide an example of what Forrester calls "counterintuitive" behavior of large systems (see page 718). They do not necessarily act in the way that intuition would lead one to expect.

The relationships among economic variables are not linear. Increase in the amount of investment increases the NNP by a multiplied amount.[316] This is because a chain of spending is started with each receiver of part

of the money using it on consumption goods. If the capital investment is in a new building, the laborers on the job and the suppliers of materials all receive part of the money invested. If the amount of investment is $1,000 and each person in the chain spends two-thirds of the part of it he receives, the original $1,000 provides $3,000 worth of consumption.

This is an automatic adjustment process by which actions of millions of private organisms, groups, and organizations together produce effects upon the total society. These effects can, in their extreme cases, produce runaway inflation. Consumption rises so much that at full employment and with factories running at capacity, producers cannot meet the demand. Price increases are inevitable. The multiplier works in the other direction too. Then it brings about deflation in the economy.

Cycles of economic activity have characterized industrialized societies for at least 150 years.[317] A period of inflation has been followed by a period of deflation, the whole pattern repeating in major cycles of 8 to 10 years. Figure 11-7 shows the cycles in the economy of the United States since the year 1899.

Economists believe that the relation between consumption and investment is such that sales to consumers must grow to keep investment where it is and that if they grow too slowly or level off, investment is stopped and prosperity declines. This nonlinearity in the effects of sales upon investment is known as the *acceleration principle*. This interacts with multiplier effects on spending. If, for example, investment in new machinery is curtailed, less income from those industries will be spent on food and clothing, and the multiplier effects on spending will follow. Cutback on sales of clothing will further reduce investment. The deflationary spiral results. When, at last, firms work their capital stock down far enough to match the low level of income, they will again need to invest, and the spiral starts back up.

These automatic adjustments, like supply and demand adjustments, are not ordinarily permitted by governments to run unchecked. Not only is the disposition that people and organizations make of their money important to societal adjustment processes, but also the quantity of money in circulation and the velocity with which it circulates are significant factors. Governments can influence these latter variables.

All modern societies have banking systems which can influence monetary flows. In the United States the central bank is the Federal Reserve Bank, which consists of a Federal Reserve Board in Washington and 12 regional banks. Commercial banks in the society may be members of the system.

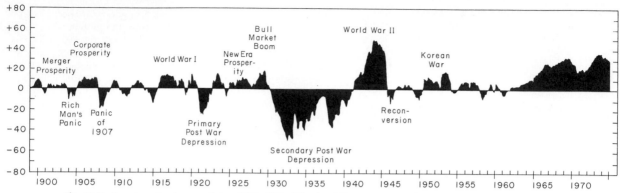

Fig. 11-7   American business activity, 1899–1975. (Cleveland Trust. *American business activity from 1790 to today.* Cleveland: Cleveland Trust, 1975. *Reprinted by permission.*)

Commercial banks receive deposits from components of the society. Part of this they must either keep on hand to satisfy demand or else deposit in the Federal Reserve bank in their district. Usually this is about one-sixth of demand deposits. The remainder they use as loans, interest from which provides income for the bank and permits it to pay interest on various sorts of time deposits. As a result of this activity, the amount of money in circulation increases or decreases according to the amount of money put out in loans by banks. This happens because a multiplier effect occurs as the money lent is paid for goods and services and finds its way into a second bank, a third bank, and more banks, each of which keeps part of it and lends the rest. An original $1,000 in deposits can create $5,000 in demand deposits in this way.[318] When money is circulating rapidly in and out of banks and they have money available for loans, interest rates are favorable and prices rise. The effect is inflationary. When the economy "heats up" in this way, the Federal Reserve intervenes to "cool it down." Because it can produce the opposite effect as well, the Federal Reserve is a stabilizer of the economy. It does this by buying or selling government bonds on the open market, which alters the amount of bank reserves; by increasing or decreasing the discount rate for loans to banks, so altering their reserves; or—a drastic method—by changing the amount of reserves that the banks are required to hold.

In addition to making central bank adjustments, governments can affect the economy by increasing or decreasing their own expenditures. Public works programs and expanded federal programs of all sorts act as stimulants to the economy.

Governmental control of economic variables lacks fine adjustments. Lags in response to its actions are long, and so effects may continue to increase after the original intent is achieved. Complex feedback relationships result in unexpected effects. This is what happened during the 1960s, when the United States adopted inflationary measures because the economy appeared to be stagnating. These included an investment tax credit, reduced personal and corporate income taxes, and increased public expenditures on defense and space. These measures succeeded in bringing the country to essentially full employment and produced economic growth. They also produced an undesirable amount of inflation. To counteract this, voluntary wage and price guideposts were enforced by Presidential intervention.

The Vietnam war, with its pyramiding costs, however, brought about further inflation. Tax increases, which could have been used as a controlling adjustment were not employed. By early 1971 the inflationary spiral had begun.[319] Faced with this situation, the President turned to "tight money" and decreased federal spending, which produced some slowing of inflation but resulted also in increased unemployment. He then turned to limited wage and price controls. These were intended to hold the line on those prices affected by them until the tendency toward inflation had reduced. After a period the controls were removed. Decreases in federal spending, increases by the Federal Reserve in interest rates, decreases in expansion of the money supply by tightening credits, and similar controls were put into effect in an attempt to dampen inflation without increasing unemployment.

Throughout this period, real growth in the GNP was far above the 4 or 5 percent considered to be an acceptable long-term rate.[320] During 1974 the rate rose above 12 percent.

Subsequently, international as well as national economic variables interacted to exert stress on the economies of many societies, including that of the United

States. The accepted adjustment processes appeared inadequate to control paradoxical movements of economic variables as increased prices signaled inflation and as other indicators, such as housing starts, employment, and the GNP, moved in directions that indicated deflation.

Brazil, a society with centralized control of its economy, has adopted systemwide adjustment processes to permit it to live with a rate of inflation that ordinarily would be considered unacceptable.[321] This society has adjusted to an annual 20 percent inflation by accepting it as an inevitable part of the rapid growth to which it is committed. It makes use of "monetary correction" to reduce the more painful aspects of inflation, a sort of universal cost-of-living adjustment. Wages, rents, corporate assets, taxes, government bonds, savings accounts, and foreign exchange rates are adjusted in value to the government estimate of inflation. This has the effect of keeping relative values constant while the value of money is reduced. Interest rates also are adjusted periodically so that neither the borrower nor the lender is injured. This reduces the risks in mortgages and other secured loans. The international value of the cruziero is periodically adjusted to keep it in line with the difference between Brazil's domestic rate of inflation and those of the societies with which it trades on international markets.

(b) *Adjustments to strains in internal information flows brought about by the need for support and consensus in the society.* The concept of "support" as Easton uses it and the concept of "consensus" as Etzioni employs it apply to the same general class of societal phenomena. The first is concerned with actions of decider and other components to uphold or reject the decider subsystem and its actions. The second focuses upon the relationships among components in advocating or rejecting courses of action, candidates, or policies.

The populations of societies are never homogeneous, although some are far more so than others. Instead, their citizens can be classified into abstract groupings according to income, class, race, occupation, status, religion, ethnic origin, language, or other differentiating characteristics. Interests of persons in these various classifications are different and may be opposed. In no society are the attitudes, opinions, and actions of all classifications equally influential. Some are more "politically relevant" than others.[322] Societies must have effective internal information adjustment processes to assure the continuation of support for the system and to produce sufficient consensus concerning policies and means of implementation to permit effective performance of system processes. The lack of such adjustment processes makes system continuity, effective administration, and positive programs

of social change impossible. This class of adjustment processes may be initiated by the decider or by other components of the system and may be directed toward specific classifications of the population, toward specific organizations, or toward the society as a whole.

The specific adjustment processes used by a given society depend upon the form of its government. A totalitarian system and a democracy do not carry out their essential processes in the same way, nor do they have the same sort of relationships among components. In each of these, however, and in societies of other sorts, the opinions and attitudes of some components are more important than those of others. In a military dictatorship the number of components needed for support of a government or its decisions may be small indeed, with the great mass of the people indifferent or, in some cases, terrorized into acquiescence. In most modern societies, however, the number is greater. It includes people in positions of power, like labor and ethnic leaders, who can enlist the support and influence the opinions of people in various classifications of the population. In both the Soviet Union and the United States, according to Deutsch, politicians must pay careful attention to the attitudes of between 30 and 40 percent of the total population.[323]

Deciders of all types of societies use internal transducers to gauge the amount of support they can count upon, and they act to maintain or increase such support, both generally and for particular policies or programs. These tasks are particularly hard in a society with deep divisions among opposed interests. They are difficult also if the structure of the decider subsystem is newly formed following a revolution or in a country newly emerged from colonial status. Such societies do not have a backlog of support gained over the years, and they lack the habitual compliance of a large part of the population. Some ways in which deciders attempt to build or maintain support make use of the established legitimacy of the structure and processes of the system and of the rightfully elected holders of offices. This is particularly effective in nations with histories of stability and prosperity. Appeals to loyalty and patriotism, reference to the country's symbols, and evocation of past national glories all have their place in this process. They can be counted upon to rouse important organizations in the society and gain their support in many situations, particularly if their own interests are not directly threatened. Deciders also have the power to satisfy some demands of dissidents, although few political systems are able to offer *quid pro quo*.[324] A President of the United States can offer to introduce legislation, for example. Also, he can give it important support because of his command of the societal channel and net as well as internal transducers, including his political party, and his influence over legislative and judicial components of the decider. He can give funds and political power to components whose support he needs, and he can keep them from those who oppose him. Deciders also can include members of dissident or disaffected segments of the population in order to induce them to increase their support of decider policies.

The activity of forging a consensus within the society can be initiated and carried out either "from the top" by decider components or "from the bottom" by components of other subsystems. Such a consensus rarely, if ever, includes everyone in the society. A representative legislature is an important part of the consensus-forming process of democracies since the interests of regions, or of classifications of the population, are debated before action is decided upon.

A president or other top decider who wishes to initiate significant social change may move to build a consensus among societal components. In any society, conservative elements resist change. Others are indifferent or fail to see how such change will improve their condition. Important classifications of the population, like labor and management, may disagree on the need for change and the means of producing it. By mediating among organizational representatives of these opposed points of view, the decider may reduce the differences among them and achieve a consensus to support the projected changes. Consensus is by no means necessary in every situation. Within limits, deciders are granted a good deal of leeway.

The units that are involved in consensus formation are ordinarily organizations that represent interests. These are formed to advance a cause, or they are enlisted in its favor. Recognition of a need for social change may begin with a few people, often not those expected to benefit directly from the proposed change. For instance, an advocate of prison reforms is ordinarily not a prisoner or ex prisoner, but a concerned member of a community. Processes of recruitment and mobilization may take many years, even beyond the lifetime of the first supporters. Eventually, if the movement is successful, however, the number and relevance of the organizations in favor of it become great enough to gain the attention of leaders of the political process, who may succeed in obtaining the backing of a political party for their ideas. Interest groups voice a demand, and political parties are able to transform this demand into action.[325]

In ordinary political situations, in which backing for a policy or candidate is being sought, leaders of a local party often call upon persons and organizations that owe them favors. Or, like legislators, they may exchange agreement to join in a consensus on one issue for similar action on another.

It is not unheard of for organizations that have been opposed on almost every issue to make common cause on one that serves the interests of both. The consensus may arise not from identical interests but from overlapping ones. Different aspects of a policy may appeal to the organizations, which will continue their opposition on other issues. Strange bedfellows are not unusual in political maneuvering.

The patterns of consensus in a large society change from issue to issue, although some alignments are usually predictable. Also, the intensity of feeling varies with issues. Heads of organizations do not ordinarily deliver the votes of everyone in their organization. If the organization is an ethnic society, its appeal may reach far beyond the membership, and thus a popular issue can mobilize more votes than the organization can usually command. Consensus formation is further complicated by the fact that on really involved issues, not two, but many, opposed interests must be accommodated. Totalitarian societies have been said to be more likely than democracies to take action first and then seek consensus, although some effort may be made to marshal public acceptance in advance.[326] As Etzioni says:*

Mature totalitarian societies . . . are not without consensus-formation structures, but they seem quite different from those of capitalist-democratic societies. . . . Totalitarian guidance mechanisms are like jeeps built to drive on rough roads; they are constructed to carry heavier loads with less support. The system relies more on a mixture of normative and coercive power and less on utilitarian power than the capitalist-democratic one. It is basically less reponsive to the needs of its members but probably more responsive to those of the system, at least under adverse social and non-social environmental conditions. The decision-making processes involve only a very limited segment of the membership and have only a very limited capacity to determine the needs and performances of the membership at large, even if—or when—the determination of such indications are [sic] the prevailing norm. In that sense, the member collectivities' participation in the political processes is much more limited than in the democratic model, and the capacity of the system to respond to the members is much smaller.[327]

5.2.5 Matter-energy output processes

In recent years excessive emigration of people, especially those in particular categories, like able young men or intellectuals, has caused some societies to make it difficult for individual persons to leave. Permission to emigrate may be hard to gain, and export of possessions may be forbidden. Physical obstructions, like walls and fences, may reinforce the usual boundary structures.

Outflow of certain commodities or artifacts has frequently been sufficient to cause strains. Both Greece and Egypt lost many valuable antiquities to the collecting zeal of anthropologists, archaeologists, exporters, and tourists. Boundary processes were invoked not only to keep such things from being carried away but also to prevent digging by unauthorized persons. Expeditions were screened, and their numbers were limited. International negotiations also succeeded in getting some things back.

The "gold drain" from the United States has constituted a matter-energy (as well as a monetary information) output strain against which a variety of economic adjustment processes have been used.

5.2.6 Information output processes Adjustments in the boundary subsystem that control outflows of monetary and other information from societies are discussed above. In addition to enforcement of boundary controls on export of money and state secrets, there are some multisubsystem control processes. Boundary processes to restrain leakage of classified information to other societies may be coupled with internal transductions and broadcasting of messages over the system's channel and net to warn and educate the public. During World War II such a campaign was carried out in the United States to keep people from talking about even innocent aspects of defense work or any details of troop movements.

Excessive outflows of the society's money in foreign trade may decrease the value of its currency in international transactions. When this occurs, a boundary protection process—the imposition of tariffs—may be invoked. This results in higher prices for foreign goods within the country, decreased demand for them, and an indirect limitation on the rate of outflow from the society of money to pay for them. I discuss this adjustment further in the following chapter (see pages 956 to 958).

5.2.7 Feedbacks Societal processes are guided by innumerable and complex internal and external feedbacks, positive and negative. These do not necessarily include the central components of the system's decider. They may adjust relations among other subsystems. For instance, in the United States representatives of labor unions and management settle wage disputes without governmental intervention unless they cannot agree or unless they inconvenience the whole system by too severe or prolonged a strike or labor disturbance. Interstate affairs are usually controlled by interactions among representatives of the states unless federal courts or regulatory bodies become involved and resolve disputes. In mixed economies, many economic variables are controlled by central components of the societal decider only when deviation becomes extreme. Otherwise, the economic

adjustment processes described above (see page 845), which are feedback processes, keep the economy in steady state. Prices respond to the fluctuations of supply and demand, for example, as a result of feedbacks from buyers to sellers in the market. Central banks and centralized economic planners receive information concerning fluctuations in economic variables and intervene only when societal economic indicators signal excessive deviation.

Positive feedbacks. Inflationary spirals are examples of positive feedbacks. In these, one variable—such as wages—feeds back to affect prices of goods or services produced by the wage earners. The prices rise and lead the workers to demand increased wages, and so on. If a government prints more money to meet price increases, another positive feedback can be set up, and "runaway inflation" results. Rashevsky spoke of paying 10,000 rubles for a plate of borscht in Russia, and over 190,000 marks for a dinner in Germany, during times of extreme inflation.[328] Another positive feedback exists in a population of whites with prejudices against blacks and racially segregated schools. The stronger the prejudice or the more strictly segregated the schools, the greater is the prejudice inculcated in the younger generation. Discussing school segregation in the United States as a positive feedback process, Rashevsky said:

We may ask ourselves what parameters in the situation should be varied and how, in order to "open" the feedback circuit. One interesting conclusion concerns the effect of legislative prohibition of segregation. If such legislation is strictly enforced, but if the enforcement lasts less than a certain critical time, then after the reinforcement ends, the original situation will be re-established. If, however, the reinforcement lasts longer than the critical period of time, then even if the legislative ban on segregation is lifted, society will move towards a stable point of no segregation.[329]

A mathematical model of this circuit is discussed below (see page 892).

Escalation of violence in social confrontations is also a positive feedback process.[330] In the Watts district of Los Angeles in 1966, for example, resentment over racial discrimination and social inequities was expressed in violence which was met by police action and the killing of 34 people by the National Guard. Anger flared higher among the ghetto dwellers, who increased their arson and rioting and violence against the police. In response to this, more armored trucks and more repressive controls led to escalating violence on both sides. Similar positive feedback processes have operated in the seemingly endless hostilities during the 1960s and 1970s between the Catholics and Protestants in Northern Ireland.

The above are examples of unfortunate positive feedback effects, but such positive feedbacks do not necessarily lead to disaster. Improvement of the education of a depressed minority could raise their economic position and social acceptance, which in turn could give them even better educational opportunities—a positive feedback process. "Bandwagon" effects in elections also illustrate societal positive feedback.[331] Results of public opinion polls are published in the course of election campaigns in many countries. These feed information back to voters, who often make subsequent choices in favor of a more popular candidate or issue over the less popular alternatives. This increase of support is reflected in later polls, enticing more voters onto the developing bandwagon. In the end, a "landslide" may appear. The bandwagon effect may be balanced to some extent by voters who use the feedback to back the "underdog," a negative feedback adjustment. Critics of computerized election coverage, which enables television stations to predict winners early on election evening, fear that this reporting might create a bandwagon effect because results in the East are being broadcast while the polls are still open in the West.

Positive feedbacks in societies do not necessarily run unchecked. If the relationship between variables is not linear, the curve of their upward rise flattens out, and a ceiling is placed on the rise. If, for example, for each rise in prices, a smaller rise in wages takes place, the process does not run out of control.

Negative feedback relationships of the central decider. Societal guidance and control in most societies are influenced by information flowing through feedback loops between the decider and other components of the system. In some countries individuals may write letters to editors or governmental officials and receive attention to their opinions or needs. But elsewhere feedback, like consensus, is ordinarily mediated and distorted by special-interest organizations. And in some nations feedback loops have little or no effect on national policy formation. Governmental deciders act without knowledge of the results of policies previously followed. This was true in the France of Louis XVI, and the French Revolution resulted. Conditions were similar in Nazi Germany during the last days of the Hitler regime. The structure of the country was disintegrating at the time. National goals were set unrealistically and could not be modified to suit changing conditions.

Soviet planning under Stalin has been criticized for failure to make use of feedback.[332] Plans were made for several years ahead, with the assumption that they could best be carried out if the effects on other components of the society (second-order effects) were ignored. Therefore, when undesirable outcomes appeared in various parts of the system, feedback concerning them was discouraged until the problems

were of sufficient seriousness to require corrective action. More recently, Soviet planning has attempted to anticipate consequences. This is contrasted with the British system of "muddling through," which is low on long-range planning but high on sensitivity to feedback. Which approach is more adaptive is an interesting question for research.

The breakup of the United Arab Republic, created in 1958, into its constituent societies, Egypt and Syria, in 1961 is said to have resulted at least partly from the failure of Egypt's President Nasser to take account of incoming information:*

Initially, there was a fairly sizeable Syrian representation in the joint government and in two regional ones, and elections in Syria affected the composition of these representative bodies. They served to bring to Nasser's attention the changing perspectives and power relations *in* Syria. But, gradually, Nasser replaced the Syrians with Egyptians, and the parties as well as elections with the National Union, a downward organization set up by Cairo. Regional governments were abolished. Consequently, the Cairo government increasingly lost contact with Syrian representatives. At the same time, dissatisfaction with the union mounted in Syria following a drought, unemployment, flight of capital, and the introduction of a nationalization scheme. Nasser relied increasingly on a secret police machine (the *Deuxième Bureau*) for his information about Syria. When reports reached him that Syria was about to rebel, the President of the United Arab Republic is said to have ignored them. Had there been free elections in Syria, Nasser would have been aware of the gradual loss of support for the union and the inadequacy of the measures he introduced in reaction to incoming signals. If his legislation for Syria had had to be approved by Syrian representatives, many of the acts introduced would not have been approved. Had he himself been subject to re-election, he would have found it more difficult to ignore signs of mounting dissatisfaction; and, if he had continued to ignore these signs, the result might have been his replacement by a more flexible leader rather than dissolution of the Union.[333]

It is quite possible for a nondemocratic decider to take account of feedbacks from all parts of the system and to respond appropriately. There is also no guarantee that a society with democratic governmental forms will attend to the feedback from more than a limited, powerful part of the society.

Easton has diagramed the multiple feedback loops of a "political system," which includes what I have referred to as decider and internal transducer components (see Fig. 11-8).

Feedback is regulated somewhat differently in democratic and totalitarian regimes. Formal channels for reporting may be similar, as they are in organizations of similar size and complexity, but handling of positive and negative expressions of support from components is dissimilar. In a democratic system it is ordi-

*Reprinted with permission of Macmillan Publishing Co., Inc. from *The active society* by Amitai Etzioni. Copyright © 1968 by The Free Press, a Division of The Macmillan Company.

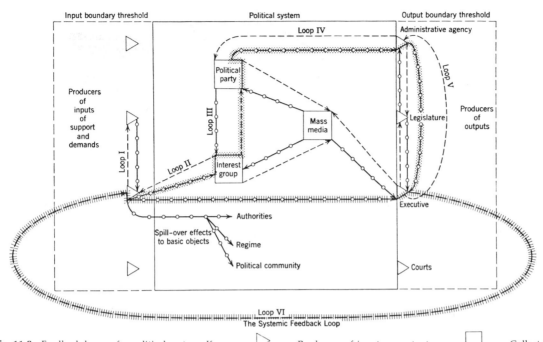

Fig. 11-8 Feedback loops of a political system. Key: ▷ Producers of inputs or outputs; ☐ Collectors and transmitters of support and demands; ---- Outputs and outcomes; ‑o‑o‑ Flow of support; ⊢⊢⊢⊢ Pathway of systemic feedback loop; ⚹⚹⚹ Alternate pathway of systemic loop. (From D. Easton. *A systems analysis of political life.* New York: Wiley, 1965, 374. *Reprinted by permission.*)

narily acceptable for private citizens, groups, or organizations to speak, write, demonstrate, or otherwise make clear their positions on matters of importance to them. A veritable feedback in every sense of the term was provided to President Nixon by a woman who sent 400 peanut-butter sandwiches to the White House to protest high meat prices. The freedom to express opinion may be withheld from particular organizations and may be restricted during national emergencies, but in general such societies have many open channels through which feedbacks can flow. Totalitarian regimes are equally dependent upon feedback, but more opposed to expressions of hostility or disapproval. One way in which they regulate the collection and reporting of feedback from societal components is by use of the many organizations to which citizens of such systems are expected to belong. Easton writes:

Group life may at times take on even greater importance than under other systems, so much so indeed that members of the dictatorial system are either encouraged or compelled to join a variety of different and overlapping groups. If we consider the USSR as an illustration, members are expected to belong to a whole series of groups as they mature and take their place in the economic, political, and social life of the system. Children and youth groups, party, sports and social groups, vocational and directly governmental organizations provide a meeting ground in many different and overlapping settings for the members of the system. Far from isolating the individual so that he confronts the authorities or latent power structure as a lone atom, the individual is deliberately pressed into complex sets of relationships with others in society.

As in democratic systems, the authorities in dictatorial systems, under conditions of mass society at least, need information about feedback response. The sustenance of a group structure provides the necessary basis for it. As in democratic systems, such groups act as points for collecting and regulating the discharge of support or oppositional sentiments. They enable the authorities in dictatorial systems to inform themselves in a manageable way of the state of mind of the membership about support for all political objects.[334]

Members of representative legislatures act as internal transducer subcomponents, collectors of feedback information for the part of the population they represent. They are expected to use this information in deciding on policies and to make it known to other deciders. Public opinion organizations also provide feedback, as do the statistics of the various social and economic indicators.

Societies are capable of tight feedbacks where crucial processes are concerned. Information coming by communication satellite or cable that a society's currency is in trouble on international markets can within a day bring about emergency sessions of its top national deciders and central bankers to take corrective steps. Some of the automatic feedback adjustment processes are quite tight. For example, stock markets rise and fall within minutes after the reporting of major national and international news. Feedbacks are more characteristically loose at this level, however. That is, indicators are often reported slowly and then allowed to vary markedly before national deciders take corrective action, if they ever do. This slowness of response often is adaptive, since interactions of components can correct some deviations without decider intervention.

Analogies to mechanical systems such as thermostats and the governors on motors do not fully and adequately describe feedback processes at the level of society, as they also do not at other levels of living systems. Such mechanical systems do not ordinarily set or change their own goals or "reference signals," as higher-level living systems do.[335]

Information channels that carry feedback have the same characteristics as channels that convey other sorts of information. At the level of the society they tend to be complex, passing through a number of deciders in the net before they reach the decider component to which the information is relevant. Each of these deciders can introduce lags or distortions. The net is biased in several ways, one of which is determined by the varying power relationships of the organizations that mediate most feedbacks.

Lags may be deliberately introduced into the flow of feedbacks by organizations which collect these responses and wait until they have enough material to be convincing and until the time is right for bringing it to the attention of deciders. Unfortunately, quantitative studies using feedback analysis developed by other disciplines (see pages 36 and 37) have not been used by scientists on societal data to determine exactly what classes of feedbacks societies have and their specific characteristics.

5.3 Evolution   The idea that societies evolved much as organisms did was a direct outcome of nineteenth-century scientists' acceptance of the doctrine of organic evolution, although societal development from primitive to more modern forms had interested philosophers long before that.[336] Herbert Spencer had extended his theory of gradual modification of species to include mental as well as physical traits even before the publication of Darwin's theory.[337] By 1855 he had developed the idea of "superorganic" evolution: "If there has been evolution, that form of it here distinguished as super-organic must have come by insensible steps out of the organic. But we may conveniently mark it off as including all those processes and products that imply the coordinated actions of many individuals."[338]

Evolutionary theories of such men as Spencer, Tylor, Morgan, Bergson, and Marx dominated social theory until the 1920s. Each theory differed from the others in important ways, but some ideas characterize the thought of the period. Belief in progress was one. Men and societies were conceived as having progressed from lower to higher forms. Marx's theory of history held that society progresses toward an ideal state through a sequence of forms (see page 967). Spencer's theory was Lamarckian and considered social development to accompany organic development, both in response to the environment.[339]

These early scientists created hypothetical accounts of the origins of specific elements of society and then looked for supporting evidence in accounts of aboriginal and tribal societies. In these accounts, people in such societies were described as physically and mentally inferior to those in more developed societies. At least some of these theorists believed that the course of development of social institutions was similar everywhere.[340] The theoretical reconstructions were used in explanation of existing social phenomena. As anthropology became more scientific, the whole idea of evolution of society fell into disfavor. More recent theories again make use of it, emphasizing the factors responsible for evolutionary changes in societies, the adaptive value of change, and the effects of societies upon one another in the diffusion of ideas.

Societal evolution, in my view, is a part of the evolution of all living systems that began with the emergence of life from nonliving matter. The biological evolutionary changes that gave man his unique hands and manipulative ability; high general intelligence; socially cooperative nature; ability to vocalize, communicate, and imitate; and capability of using symbols were what made human society possible.[341] Although genetic evolutionary changes in man continue, these human attributes have remained stable over time and are in all important respects alike throughout the human species. Evolution of society does not depend to any important extent upon genetic variations but primarily upon the accumulation and transmission of learned information from one generation to another. Evolutionary changes occur in the charters, written or unwritten, of societies and in their cultural aspects rather than in human genetic templates.

A feedback relationship between the two sorts of evolution appears, however, to have been of mutual benefit, since the probability of human survival was increased by cooperative living. A reverse effect of the continuing feedback relationship could occur as a result of the practice, in present-day developed societies, of preserving detrimental mutations in the human genetic pool instead of pursuing a policy of limiting breeding by people with pathological genes.

In the process of shred-out (see pages 1 and 4) between every level of living systems and the next higher level, undoubtedly there were transitional forms of systems, as there were between the early organizations and the societies. Some primitive tribal "societies" had groups as components rather than organizations. They were not societies in my sense, since the preponderance of their components were not organizations. Since organizations did not arise until about 9000 B.C., societies composed of a preponderance of organizations probably did not appear until about 5000 B.C. Much of their evolution occurred in prehistoric times. Although the characteristics of the earliest human societies are unknown, Lomax and Berkowitz suggest that they were similar to those of their Stage I societies (see page 760). The societies of present-day Bushmen and Pygmies of Africa and the Australian aborigines are probably much like these earliest societies. Archeological evidence and the fact that small remnants of such societies are found on all continents suggest that originally they were widely distributed. Some conclusions about the first humans can be drawn from observing their ways of life. It is probably correct not to view early man as ". . . a bloodthirsty caveman, whose adaptive success was due to his interest in weaponry combined with a calculated ferocity. Like our nearest relatives, the great apes, and like present-day gatherers, early human societies were probably nonaggressive, highly intrasupportive teams of foraging amateur botanists, quarterbacked by women and guarded by males."[342]

The worldwide distribution of hunting and gathering societies suggests that this original type of society radiated with little change from the parts of the earth in which it first occurred, adapting to widely varying environmental conditions but retaining its primitive form.

A fundamental aspect of societal evolution is increasing ability of the system to adjust effectively to environmental stresses, minimizing the resulting strains. A factor-analytic study, which grouped societies into 13 cultural clusters or types (see pages 758 to 760), found that position in the evolutionary scale is correlated with a factor that includes variables related to productivity as well as increase in complexity of social structure, including development of multiechelon deciders.[343] Many archaeologists believe that there was no single area in which the development of more complex forms of societies began, no "cradle of civilization," but that evolutionary changes began independently in various parts of the world and at different times. Although several general types of societies

can be identified (see pages 748 and 755 to 761), each particular society has its own way of processing information for every meaningful aspect of life. Cultural elements of any society form an interrelated whole with recognizable themes.[344] Within the general tendency toward increased complexity and the overall similarity in development of cultural traits by societies, much individual variation has occurred. Understandably, a society may rank differently on various aspects of culture, as Carneiro discovered (see pages 756 to 758). He found that the Incas, for example, ranked third in political organization but only tenth in economics among the societies he studied.

Some cultural patterns recur in widely separated societies.[345] Those which build circular houses, for example, prefer straight-line figures in their art styles, and those with rectangular houses prefer curved figures. Societies with rectangular houses are also more readily deceived by the Müller-Lyer visual illusion, in which lines of equal length appear unequal.

Biological and societal evolution.   Societal evolution is analogous to biological evolution in some ways and different in others. In both, as the system becomes more complex and passes through a variety of forms, each viable, the separate parts also become modified in various ways. Some components regress or disappear as their survival value decreases. Others change in the direction of becoming more complex and adaptive. Rapoport considers that the underlying principles of both are the same:

Principles of evolution through natural selection are another example of universal principles operating in complex systems. Even artifacts made by human beings evolve according to principles of natural selection. Observe the evolution of the automobile from the carriage, a classical example of technological evolution. The example is remarkable in that even such features as vestigial parts are observed in the early models of the automobile. Those early versions still had sockets in which whips were inserted on carriages. The gradual change of shape of the automobile, the elimination of superfluous parts, such as the running board, the adaptation of the engine to the changes in fuel, etc., all of these are manifestations of true evolution.

There is little doubt that the principles operating in the evolution of societies are very much like the principles of organic evolution. It is not necessary to invoke any mystical or metaphysical notions to subscribe to this view, such as were invoked by Goethe, Lamarck, and Bergson, the "romantic" exponents of evolution. Natural selection is a simple, extremely "prosaic" principle, and it acts without distinction on biological, technological, and social phenomena. Even topographical features can be often explained in terms of "natural selection," for example, the arrangement of pebbles according to their sizes along the water line of a beach. The regular gradation from fine to coarse is a result of differential rates at which the pebbles are dropped by the wave that carries them.[346]

This is true even in the evolution of artifacts like telephones, as Fig. 11-9 illustrates.

1876   LIQUID TELEPHONE

"Mr. Watson, come here; I want you!" It was the night of March 10. These first historic words, uttered by Alexander Graham Bell when he spilled some sulphuric acid he had been using in his tests, climaxed two years of extensive experimentation.

1877   FIRST COMMERCIAL TELEPHONE

The camera-like opening served as both transmitter and receiver, making mouth-to-ear shifts necessary. Developed by Bell in 1876, it went into service in 1877 when a banker leased two instruments and a line to connect his Boston office and his home in Somerville.

1878   WALL SET

Switching the same instrument from mouth to ear proved confusing for some people, so a second wooden transmitter-receiver was added. Either could be used for talking or listening. Turning the crank generated power to signal the operator.

1880   BLAKE

United States population was now 50 million, and the improved voice clarity of the Blake carbon transmitter greatly aided the fledgling telephone service. It was invented by Francis Blake, Jr., based on work by Thomas Edison. Here, it is used in a primitive desk set.

1886   LONG DISTANCE TRANSMITTER

In the year that the Statue of Liberty was dedicated in New York harbor, the search for improved long distance transmission took a major step forward with this model, whose platinum diaphragm improved clarity. The instrument shown was actually used by Bell.

1897   DESK SET

America was on the verge of its great transformation from a rural to an urban nation, and the telephone was beginning to take the shape that would be familiar during that change. This early desk set, made of cast brass, was a refinement of previous models.

1900   COMMON BATTERY

Improving telephone service is a constant goal. The earliest sets were voice-powered. Next came the wet battery, which occasionally leaked on the rug; then the dry battery. This model, a major advance, received its power from the telephone exchange, hence its name.

1919   DIAL TELEPHONE

Coast-to-coast phone service had begun in 1915, and the United States had topped 100 million in population. Dial service was coming in strongly. Invented in 1892, it was many years before the complex equipment had been sufficiently developed for use in larger cities.

Fig. 11-9 Stages in the evolution of the telephone. ® Registered Trademark of AT&T Co. *(Reprinted with permission of Western Electric Company.)*

Some of the similarities between biological and societal evolution are:

(*a*) Units (genes which convey alpha-, beta-, or gamma-coded items of cultural information) are passed from one generation to another.[347]

(*b*) Units may persist unchanged through many generations.

(*c*) Variation may take place in a single unit and be transmitted in changed form to alter its somatic or social expressions in the succeeding generation.

(*d*) Units combine and recombine and form new systems with characteristics different from those of the systems which gave rise to them.

(*e*) Partial or complete isolation of populations results, after a period of time, in development of distinctive cultural as well as physical characteristics.

(*f*) Selection processes operate in both to eliminate maladaptive units from the genetic pool or from the culture.

(*g*) Changes often take place in or affect many units and therefore many parts of the system. Modification of one part of the system may require alterations in others in order to maintain steady states of critical variables.

(*h*) Periods of stability of form and process may be succeeded by brief periods in which profound changes result in new system organization and capacities.[348] Platt refers to such changes as "hierarchical restructuring" and generalizes them to both nonliving and living systems at all levels.[349] He suggests that evolution in general may take place not so much by steady change as by a number of sudden reorganizations of one subsystem and then another.

(*i*) Each succeeding level of organization has emergent characteristics.

(*j*) Adaptive radiation (see page 77) is rapid after a period of change. An organism better equipped for survival than its ancestors rapidly takes over new territories and spreads beyond the range previously occupied by its species. In these territories it undergoes adaptive change. An innovation in technology or religion similarly spreads through, and often far beyond, the society in which it originated, undergoing cultural adaptations to the societies it is in.

1937   "300" TYPE DESK SET

A major innovation that offered added convenience to telephone subscribers placed the bell in the base, previously housed in a separate box. The "300" served throughout World War II while the energies of most telephone people were devoted to defense work.

1958   SPEAKERPHONE SET

Hands-free telephoning arrived with the introduction of the Speakerphone, which also permits conference calls between groups at different locations. Above is the "4A" model, introduced in 1974, which has improved sound qualities and an omnidirectional microphone.

1958   CALL DIRECTOR® TELEPHONE

Keeping pace with the increasingly complex communications needs of its business customers, the Bell System introduced this set designed to handle several incoming, outgoing, and inter-office calls simultaneously. It is available in both 18 and 30-button models.

1959   PRINCESS® TELEPHONE

The desk set received a smart, new look. Compactness, attractive styling and illuminated dial (it lights up when you lift the handset or you can keep it on as a night light) contribute to the all-round usefulness of the Princess set. It also comes with a Touch-Tone dial.

1964   TOUCH-TONE® TELEPHONE

As America neared the 200 million mark in population, the Bell System heralded a new era in telephoning services with push-button calling. Combined with electronic central offices, Touch-Tone service will expand the uses of the telephone many-fold.

1969   PICTUREPHONE® SET

Men walked on the moon and a new model of telephone that made it possible to see the person to whom you're talking was market-tested. The Mod II set has a feature for individual or group viewing. Major use is for visual conferencing between different cities.

1973   TOUCH-A-MATIC® TELEPHONE

The Touch-A-Matic set is the first telephone with a solid state memory. At the touch of a single button, it can automatically dial any of 31 pre-recorded numbers. It is one of many communications advances that derive from the invention of the transistor by Bell Labs.

1976   TRANSACTION® TELEPHONE

As the telephone marks its 100th birthday, the Bell System offers a phone to make shopping more convenient. The Transaction telephone links with a bank's or credit bureau's computer to verify balances or transfer funds. It can also perform inventory control jobs.

(k) Selection is determined by an internal hierarchy of drives or strains—see (g) on page 856—elicited by external stresses.

(l) Evolutionary shred-out progresses through a series of stable or unstable intermediate forms (see pages 1, 4, and 78). System types that persist retain the same matter-energy and information subsystems they had when they evolved because these subsystems are necessary to their survival.

(m) Earlier system forms continue in later ones. Cells and multicellular organ systems retain system characteristics in organisms. The evolution of nervous systems with new components superimposed on old ones (see pages 466 to 468) is pertinent. Societies impose echelons of control above existing groups and organizations, which nonetheless remain parts of the higher-level system.

(n) Not all types of systems of each sort evolve at the same rate. Some organisms and societies persist for long time periods in relatively unchanged form.

(o) Similar characteristics may develop independently in different phyla (like color vision in insects and some vertebrates) and in widely separated cultures (e.g., agriculture developed independently in several places).

The correspondences between biological and cultural evolution recognized by Gerard, Kluckhohn, and Rapoport are summarized in Table 11-8.

Differences between the two sorts of evolution are:

(a) The underlying specific processes by which the comparable results are achieved are not the same. It is therefore not possible to predict cultural phenomena from the behavior of the much better understood genetic systems.[350] There is no parallel to sexual selection and the sexual combination and recombination of genes. The similarities are, in the biological sense, analogies rather than homologies.

(b) Because of this difference in process, aspects of culture such as ideas, techniques, and institutions can be combined and hybridized regardless of the dissimilarities of the cultures that produced them.[351]

(c) Cultural and social evolution progress more rapidly than biological evolution. The rates have accelerated as time has passed. Culture adapts human beings to their environment, and the environment to them, allowing them to spread into hostile environments without awaiting organic adaptation. (If human beings, like other animals, had to wait until they developed fur and the ability to hibernate before they could live in cold parts of the world, they would still be confined to a small part of the earth's surface.)

TABLE 11-8   Correspondences between Biological and Cultural Evolution

Biological evolution	Cultural evolution
Distinct species and varieties	Distinct cultures and subcultures
Morphology, structural organization	Directly observable artifacts and customs distinctive of cultures
Physiology, functional attributes	Functional properties attributable to directly observable cultural characteristics
Genetic complex determining structures and functions	"Implicit culture," i.e., the inferred cultural structure of "cultural genotype"
Preservation of species but replacement of individuals	Preservation of cultures but replacement of individuals and artifacts
Hereditary transmission of genetic complex, generating particular species	"Hereditary" transmission of idea-custom-artifact complexes, generating particular cultures
Modification of genetic complex by mutations, selection, migration, and "genetic drift"	Culture change through invention and discovery; adaptation; diffusion and other forms of culture contact; "cultural drift"
Natural selection of genetic complexes generally leading to adaptation to environment	Adaptive and "accidental" (i.e., historically determined) selection of ideas, customs, and artifacts
Extinction of maladapted and maladjusted species	Extinction of maladapted and maladjusted cultures

SOURCE: R. W. Gerard, C. Kluckhohn, & A. Rapoport. Biological and cultural evolution: some analogies and explorations. *Behav. Sci.*, 1956, **1**, 10. Reprinted by permission.

(d) Biological evolution can be pictured as a branching tree with diverging lines of descent. Lines of cultural descent have no such clarity. A society gains cultural elements in many different ways and modifies them in a highly individual manner. It acquires information not only by transmission from the preceding generation—which is the only way biological information can be transmitted—but also by communication with other societies from which it adopts and adapts cultural information.

(e) Cultural evolution, depending as it does upon learning by each generation of the stored information from the past, is more susceptible to loss. A group of modern men living in isolation could transmit only a small part of their cultural inheritance to their descendants, and much of it would be irrelevant to the lives of the isolated generation. Under these circumstances, the centuries of evolution of culture that had produced the societies from which the parents came would be lost to their children, who, if they survived, would return to primitive ways of life. It would take a worldwide disaster to wipe out the accumulation of knowledge and technical know-how in the present-day world, but it is conceivable that survivors of a nuclear war might return to the Stone Age.

(f) To some extent biological evolution can be deliberately directed by selective breeding. Societies can plan to change from one type to another, as developing nations all over the world are now doing.

Some directional tendencies in societal evolution were identified by Naroll from a review of cross-cultural studies.[352] These are: (a) *Weak to strong*. A society becomes strong as it increases its ability to adjust to the environment. Development of sources of power is one aspect of this increasing strength. (b) *Generalists to specialists*. This change has resulted in an enormous accumulation of information in societies. No single person could hope to encompass all the specialized knowledge in his society, even in a relatively primitive society. (c) *Simple organization to complex organization*. (d) *Rural to urban*. (e) *Wealth sharing to wealth hoarding*. Money economies rather than reciprocal exchange systems characterize the more highly evolved societies (see page 755). Capitalism, socialism, and mixed economies are alike in tending toward concentration of wealth. (f) *Consensual leadership to authoritative leadership*. This involves a steady tendency to increase the proportion and importance of authoritative officials. Formal legal systems and emphasis on responsibility and obedience in training children seem to go along with this. (g) *Responsible elite to exploitative elite*. Naroll says: "An elite does seem to be indispensable in highly civilized societies; such elites invariably occur, even in revolutionary societies expressly designed to abolish them. The steady growth in importance of elites seems clear; but their presumed tendency to usurp the lion's share of societal wealth awaits formal documentation for all but a few modern nations."[353] (h) *Vengeance war to political war*. Warfare is common among primitive tribes, but they do not ordinarily expect to gain wealth, prestige, or political authority from it. They exact vengeance or protect their boundaries in this way. What is more, while war was unknown in primitive societies, civilized societies all have warlike histories, and warlike societies have expanded at the expense of peace-loving ones.

Factors in evolutionary change. The course of societal evolution from prehistoric times to the present has proceeded in a series of step-function changes separated by periods of relatively slow development. Several analyses of this process identify factors important in evolutionary development of some parts of the world and some societies.

Toynbee concluded that the change from static to dynamic that caused primitive societies to develop into civilizations was brought about by "the challenge of the environment."[354] Some of these challenges were threats or stresses; others were opportunities. Difficult physical conditions; a new previously unexploited territory; a sudden crushing defeat; the pressure of living under threat of constant attack; and the penalization of slavery all constituted challenges that stimulated one or another society to progress into civilization. Societies faced with too great a challenge did not develop beyond their primitive states and remained static throughout their histories. Some began their development in a successful response to one challenge, only to become arrested when a later challenge was too great. There is a golden mean that favors development.[355]

Sheer increase in numbers of people, by creating disequilibria of several variables, can produce an important strain that elicits development activities as a societal adjustment. When the number of people in a society increases, this greater number and other factors interact to increase the complexity of societal structure and process (see pages 865 and 866).

Several theories identify changes that have acted like genetic mutations. After each of these, both the number of people in a society and its complexity increased. According to Linton, three basic mutations have produced new cultural processes:[356] (1) the use of tools, fire, and language; (2) the discovery of how to raise food, which was associated with the development of the wheel, plow, loom, and other machines and which led to the establishment of the fundamental patterns of civilization; and (3) the discovery of how to get power from heat and other sources, combined with the discovery of the scientific method, which was begun in the late 1700s and continues until the present. Each of these arose with a sudden step function, as a mutation does, preceded by small cumulative changes. Each added significant new information to society, becoming a "hereditary," fixed element of the culture. Following each, a given amount of land could support more people.

A similar analysis refers to the periods of sudden change as "revolutions." These followed periods of slow accumulation of information.[357] They were (1) the discovery of how to produce food, about 7000 B.C.; (2) the discovery of writing, metallurgy, urbanization, and more complex political organizations, about 3000 B.C.; (3) a sudden spurt in religion about 600 B.C., when both doctrine and institutional organization developed rapidly; and (4) the rapid development of science, technology, invention, industry, and wealth, still in its period of adaptive radiation.

White sees culture as "an elaborate thermodynamic mechanical system" designed to carry on the life processes of man by harnessing and controlling energy.[358] Culture, according to this analysis, evolves as the amount of energy harnessed per capita per year increases.[359] All other aspects of culture are adjuncts to, and expressions of, this technological process. Only two stages have followed the original, primitive organization of society. Each permitted great increase in population.

The first stage followed a revolution in agriculture that put an end to hundreds of thousands of years of Stone Age culture. Man learned to make use of plants and the physical strength of domesticated animals.[360] This revolution occurred independently in the Old and New Worlds, separated by some thousands of years. It stimulated profound change in all aspects of the societies involved.[361] Political organization became more complex, and cities, nations, and empires replaced primitive villages, tribes, and confederacies. Writing was invented. The fine arts, architecture, astronomy, medicine, and the use of metals developed rapidly. By about 1000 B.C. the cultural impetus had run its course, and progress leveled off.

The second stage was the fuel or power revolution, when man learned to increase the amount of power available to him. First coal was used, and later oil and gas. Again more complex political units were organized, and the arts and sciences moved forward. As the momentum from this revolution began to slow, atomic energy, space science, and other technical innovations occurred, extending the period of rapid social change.

These revolutions fit Platt's concept of hierarchical restructuring. Several of the characteristics of these sudden "jumps" in systems' steady states are described by Platt, who makes use of the concept of cognitive dissonance (or strains) in analyzing them (see page 461). He writes:

. . . Kuhn describes in considerable detail the scientific dissonance that precedes his scientific revolutions. First, there are accumulating bits of data that do not fit the old predictions; or rules of thumb in certain areas that seem to be justified only by odd assumptions. In the beginning, these difficulties are dismissed as trivial or as errors of measurement or crackpot arguments, but they do not go away, and they get more numerous. After a time, the confrontation with the old system comes to be recognized as fundamental, and various proposals for a reconciliation are brought forward. Then suddenly a simplification from some entirely different point of view makes big parts of the problem snap into new and clearer relationships. There is a collective sense of relief and achievement, even though a long period of working-out may lie ahead.[362]

Other aspects of societies also evidence such dissonance or strains. Transformations of economic systems follow a general realization that there is dissonance between the existing situation and the values and goals of the society. A second feature of these hierarchical jumps is their overall character, illustrated by the foregoing discussion of the effects of changes in energy available to the society.

A third feature is the suddenness of these jumps. In a few months the French Revolution overthrew the royalty, the aristocracy, the church, and the army. The new societal structure, of course, did not emerge that suddenly.[363] Three time frames are involved: One period—ordinarily from a few weeks to several years—covers the time required to accomplish ordinary adjustments by means of the feedback loops of the entire society. A second period—ordinarily from a few decades to centuries—covers the time over which the basic steady state of the society endures. And a third period—often a brief span of a few weeks or months—covers the transition time for the change from an old, basic societal steady state to a new one. This time may be short because the old feedback loops that determine adjustment time may be bypassed. The transition therefore does not have to wait for them to function in their usual way. The Russian Revolution took 10 days, and the United States Constitution was created in a few weeks.

A fourth characteristic of the hierarchical jumps is "simplification." Science is moving toward simpler and more general theories. Simplification represents a permanent step forward because it is easy to hold and hard to go back from. Money makes exchange easier. Democracy is simpler than "complex ranks and obligations."

According to Platt, Karl Deutsch has emphasized the fifth and final characteristic, that these jumps involve actions across system levels between old subsystems and the new system in the process of formation.[364] Dissonance or strains at the level of the system cannot be changed by restructuring the subsystems of that system because their relationships are stable and self-maintaining. Any restructuring fits the largest well-functioning subsystems into the structure of the newly forming system in order to make it serve better the larger integration of the suprasystem. A junta of powerful generals, for instance, one day decides to disobey the minister of defense of a developing country, combines with the naval commanders, and compels the president to enforce economic measures to protect the nation's currency and balance of trade in the world economy.

Recent social change. It was not possible for tiny *Eohippus* to accelerate the processes of biological evolution which transformed its body into that of a horse. Societies, however, may control their evolution from one type to another and accelerate it if the mat-

ter-energy and information necessary for the transformation are available and if consensus favoring change is present. Many less developed societies are changing and developing rapidly at present. These include not only societies that have existed for decades or centuries but also some that have been formed recently as colonial empires dissolved and as tribal or cultural entities organized national governments. At the same time, industrialized societies are changing toward postindustrial (or postmodern) structures (see page 755).

Societies in the process of development may receive monetary aid from other nations or supranational systems and may increase their wealth by exploitation of their natural resources. Technologists and teachers from other countries and their own foreign-educated students bring in knowledge. Exposure to communication media increases their peoples' awareness of better living conditions elsewhere and helps to build support for leaders who promise change.

Nations undergoing development now do not pass through all the evolutionary stages by which more advanced societies reached their present stages of development. Instead, they telescope the processes that originally took centuries into a few years of profound alteration of structure and process. Few members of the society escape more or less drastic changes in life-style. Their homes, occupations, social settings, institutions, actions, group relationships, experiences, expectations, and needs may all be altered. This process has been called *social mobilization*.[365] Many people greatly increase their political participation. They may take part in demonstrations or strikes. Governments may change as internal political strains increase in severity. Such changes not only are consequences of the process of modernization but also influence its further course in a feedback relationship. An unfortunate aspect of such development in many places is rejection of worthwhile values and cultural elements of the past.

As development progresses, certain social and economic indicators (such as percentage of the population that has experienced exposure to significant aspects of modern life, size of the mass-media audience, percentage of people who have changed their places of residence, percentage living in towns or cities, percentage in nonagricultural occupations, GNP per capita, and percentage of literates) rise, although not at the same rate. These are some of the measures of variables generally agreed to be important in the development process, such as social mobilization, urbanization, economic development, literacy, minority representation in societal decision making, presence of organizations that represent interests of parts of the population (interest articulation), economic and political participation by members, competition among political parties, and exposure of the people to communications media.[366] The highest correlations among these variables in one study of 19 developing countries were urbanization with economic development, urbanization with interest articulation, and urbanization with minority representation.

Numerous stresses create serious strains in developing societies.[367] They arise when increasing expectations of the people are not met. The resulting dissatisfaction causes the people to make demands of governments which they are unable to meet. Such a sequence of events guarantees political trouble. A society that raises the level of literacy and increases access to mass media cannot help but raise expectations throughout the society faster than developing opportunities can satisfy them. A society that educates large numbers of people who have no immediate prospects for jobs similarly disrupts a steady state.

Nations are changing in type from "industrial" to "postindustrial" (or from "modern" to "postmodern"), but the new type that is evolving has not yet developed enough so that a complete description is possible. Many of its distinctive characteristics are extensions of trends that began during the society's industrial period. Among the changes which have already occurred in some societies and which appear to be related to the emergence of a new type are:

(*a*) Fewer members of the society producing goods than providing services. This is Gross's definition of the postindustrial society (see page 755). Etzioni relates this characteristic to an increasing importance of symbols over objects. He cites the increased expenditures on research and development and the increasing importance of education.

(*b*) Extension of the control exercised by the central decider over other subsystems. Etzioni identifies two "revolutions" which were stages in societal development.[368] The first came with the rise of modern types of organizations such as corporations; it occurred when the society was transformed by the industrial revolution, which provided societies with more effective ways of getting things done. These organizations were not tightly controlled by the societal decider. The second revolution added an echelon of control and guidance above the organizations that do the work. Both the United States and the Soviet Union appear to be in transition into the postmodern period, and both have extended the control of their decider subsystems or governments over other subsystems.

(*c*) Mixed economies. Both the United States and the Soviet Union have mixed economies (see page 844).

(*d*) Emphasis on the satisfaction of the needs of individual persons and on their interests and values. Increased life expectancy, a higher educational level of the population, and large-scale conservation of natural resources are some elements of the change.

(*e*) A step-function increase in information processing capacity. Etzioni writes:*

The advent of the post-modern period has been marked by the rapid rise of a new technology of knowledge, which serves data collection and analysis, simulation, and systems analysis. It has been said that the computer is to the production of knowledge what the steam engine was to production of materials. This is a fair, only slightly exaggerated, comparison, even if one relies on more conservative estimates of computer capacities. . . . In the first two decades of the post-modern period, investment in research and development has grown much more rapidly than GNP, especially in modernized countries. The rapid construction of organizations specializing in the production and processing of knowledge is a post-modern parallel to economic development which characterized modernization. As a result, society has much more information about itself, a development which generates a whole new set of options for societal control, new decisions to be made, and a new range of processes to be guided.

Also growing is an awareness of the ability to restructure society and of how to go about it at a smaller societal cost.[369]

(*f*) Increased interdependence among societies and increased interest in international and supranational decision making (see pages 967 and 968).

Alternative futures. It is obviously impossible by any method we now have to predict the future evolution of societies. Many possible futures have been suggested, their characteristics depending upon the present trends the forecaster extrapolates and upon his optimism or pessimism. Gloomy scenarios predict mankind's failure to survive beyond the next few years, when some combination of nuclear war, overpopulation, exhausted resources, and ruined environment brings the evolution of living systems on earth to a sudden or gradual end. More optimistic forecasts, like those of Doxiadis, foresee solution of the pressing problems now facing societies and development of an ideal setting for human life (see pages 688 and 689).

Etzioni considers it possible that societies of the present will become "transformed" slowly and that latent energy and assets will be made available for furthering system goals and purposes.[370] While central control would increase, it would rest upon an authentic consensus among components that would make alienating forms of control unnecessary.

5.3.1 Emergents Among the emergents at the level of society are cultural characteristics that make it possible to carry out subsystem processes of increasingly large and complex systems with ever-greater populations. These are concerned with either matter-energy or information processing.

The fundamental process in societal evolution is said by Lomax and Berkowitz to be "man's concern with differential control of his environment."[371] Differentiative capacity, according to this theory, increases with evolutionary development. Their factor-analytic study (see pages 758 to 760) groups traits of 10 types of societies under three factors: *differentiation, integration,* and *communication.* No industrialized societies were included in this study.

Differentiation includes variables related to the growth in complexity of social structure and in productivity. Integration refers to the closeness with which members of societies live and work together, that is, to what I call "cohesiveness." Communication, in this study, includes only variables related to how singing is done in the society.

The traits in integration and communication do not change in an orderly fashion as the evolutionary stage advances, although they arise from, and are consistent with, the total culture of any society in which they appear.

Traits included under differentiation do, however, increase as evolution progresses. At each evolutionary stage, emergent traits become statistically distinctive. For Australian aboriginal societies, for example, the emergent is a government by older males. Among aboriginal North Americans, who were corn farmers, larger communities developed, and tribal confederacies and clan-based community organizations appeared.

As societies evolved beyond the stages of peasant agriculture and of irrigation empire, the most advanced in this study, further cultural traits emerged. Among these were technological inventions that made it possible to process matter-energy more efficiently; shred-out of processes to more specialized types of organizations; a vast increase in the complexity of organizations (an emergent at the level of the organization, but dependent upon the resources of the society); new types of decider and internal transducer subsystems that increased simultaneously in centralization of control and in participation in the deciding process by components at many echelons; and the discovery of new forms of energy to power the society's processes.

As a part of a revolution in information processing, emergents were the many channel and net components of modern societies that make rapid communication possible and increase the capability of controlling big areas and many people. Computer technology permits the processing of large amounts of informa-

tion, increasing the coordination and many other aspects of these large systems. Modern science is a further emergent that has undergone enormous expansion in industrial and postindustrial societies. Concerning the emergent characteristics of industrial societies, Lomax and Berkowitz say:

. . . the differentiative factors continue their ascent as science and machinery multiply man's economic range. An expanding economy and growing population are accompanied by the rise of a monstrous administrative bureaucracy, along with an increase in the range, capacity, speed, and precision of communications media. . . .

Less noticed is the fact that the coming of industry involves organizational changes that are reflected in an upward swing of the integration factor. In the stage of plow agriculture, women stayed largely in the harem, the home, or the garden, going out only in the company of chaperoning relatives or neighbors. Modern city life tends to break these ties or loosen their restraints. Factories and offices bring women back into public productive function, not at first as equals, but in an ever more complementary relation to men. . . .

This recent trend in human evolution thus seems to indicate that culture is moving into a stage where a peak for integration will match an unparalleled high in differentiation. A somewhat similar situation prevailed once before in man's cultural evolution—in one of its earliest stages. The Mbuti Pygmies have apparently lived for many millennia in remarkable balance with their environment. . . . After twenty millennia of blood, sweat, and tears, we have a technology that can reduce environmental pressures to a minimum, if it is administered properly. Man might again, like his remote African ancestors, live in balance with his environment, with all his needs provided for in a genuinely egalitarian, sharing society.[372]

5.4   Growth, cohesiveness, and integration

5.4.1   Growth   Societies increase the numbers of their citizens when their birthrates exceed their death rates. They grow also from immigration and from annexation of populated territories. Expansion of the society's territory may or may not accompany growth of population.

Hale, in 1677, observed the gradual increase in the numbers of mankind and stated the exponential nature of population growth:

And upon this account we may justly suppose these things: 1. That these two Children may be coexisting with their Parents for nearly 30 years; for if the eldest be born at 27 Years of age of the Father, and the other at 30 Years of his age, and live till the Father be 60 Years old, the youngest is 30 years old at the extremity of his Father's age, which we suppose 60 Years; and 2, these two Children by Intermarriage may have likewise two, three, or more Children by that time the Father attains 60 Years; So that in the compass of about 34 Years the number of two, namely the Father and Mother, is increased to the number of eight, namely the Father and Mother, their two Children, and four Grand-children; so that in 34 Years they become increased in a quadruple proportion, and all coexisting; and although by that time, we suppose the Father and Mother die, yet in the like Period of thirty four by a Geometrical Proportion their Increase is multiplied proportionable to the excess of their number above Two.[373]

Hypothesis 5.4.1-1 (see page 108) states the exponential nature of the rate of increase in number of components of a young system, and it says also that the rate of growth may be altered by environmental or other factors. This is confirmable at the level of society. The doctrine of Malthus, first published in 1798, postulated a universal tendency for population to grow at a geometric progression.[374] In the American colonies, in fact, Benjamin Franklin observed that population doubled every 25 years. That it did not do so in parts of the world where the amount of land was fixed was considered by Malthus to be because of the operation of checks to growth. The law of diminishing returns operated inexorably, so that as population doubled and redoubled, it was exactly as if the earth were shrinking. The food supply could not, then, keep up with the rate of population growth. Other positive checks were pestilence and war. In his later formulation Malthus added "moral restraint" as a possible preventive check.

Economics became known as the "dismal science" because the equilibrium point derived in Malthusian theory is at the minimum subsistence level, the "dismal theorem."[375] The prospect is even more dismal because the result of any improvement such as extension of available land area is an increase in population until the subsistence point is again reached.

Present-day economists recognize the Malthusian doctrine as an oversimplification, although a fundamental relationship certainly exists between the number of people a society can support, the standard of living they can maintain, and the society's available resources. The expansion of populations that occurred after each of the evolutionary "revolutions" I have considered above (see page 859) demonstrates this. It can also be seen in its more dismal form in present-day Bangladesh and other societies in which population numbers and food supply are in precarious balance.

The growth in numbers of the population of societies all over the world has resulted in a tripling of world population since 1800.[376] This increase has resulted from improvement of living standards, reduction of death rates (particularly among infants), and a great increase in life expectancy. Within this overall increase, however, rates of growth have varied from one society to another and within a given society at different times. Growth of the United States population between 1790 and 1970 is shown in Fig. 11-10. The pronounced slowing of the rate during and after the Depression of the 1930s can be seen clearly. This growth rate includes substantial numbers of immigrants as well as an excess of births over deaths in the population. Rates of growth have varied from the low

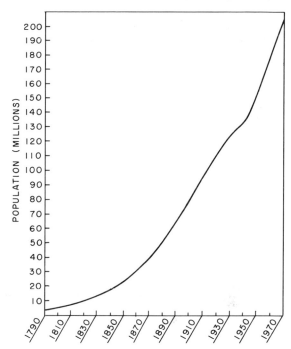

Fig. 11-10 Growth of the population of the United States. The population of the United States has grown from 3.9 million at the first census in 1790 to 203.2 million at the census of 1970. [From U.S. Bureau of Census. *Statistical abstract of the United States.* (94th ed.) Washington: GPO, 1973, 5.]

7.2 percent in the decade of the 1930s to high points of 21 percent during the first decade of the twentieth century and 18.5 percent during the 1950s, when the postwar "baby boom" had its effect and when the economy was growing rapidly. During this period large families became the style. People married earlier. The growth rate slowed again to 13.3 percent during the 1960s, a return to a long-term downward trend.[377] Immigration had not fallen off. In fact, it was higher than during the 1950s. Two million fewer babies were born, and, possibly because of the larger number of older people in the population, the number of deaths increased. The excess of births over deaths dropped to 4.5 million in that decade. The downward trend has continued into the 1970s.

A population grows when each pair of parents not only replaces itself by producing two children but also more than makes up for members of the population who do not become parents. Zero population growth is considered to occur when an average of 2.1 children is born to each woman. *Net reproduction rate* (NRR) is defined as the average number of girl babies that will

TABLE 11-9   Net Reproduction Rates for Various Countries

Australia	0.98	1935–1939
	1.40	1965
Belgium	0.90	1939
	1.28	1965
France	0.86	1935–1937
	1.32	1966
German Federal Republic	0.94	1950–1954
	1.17	1965
Israel	1.90	1955–1959
	1.57	1963
Japan	1.49	1935–1939
	1.01	1965
Netherlands	1.15	1935–1939
	1.43	1965
Sweden	0.78	1935–1939
	1.13	1966
United Kingdom	0.79	1935–1939
	1.29	1966
United States—total	1.42	1946–1949
	1.38	1965
White	1.32	1965
Nonwhite	1.76	1965

NOTE: A net reproduction rate (NRR) permanently greater than 1 means ultimate population growth. An NRR less than 1 means ultimate population decline. The NRR for the United States is still above 1, but has been declining in the 1970s. The NRR is corrected for changing age distribution.

SOURCE: *Population Index*, 1968, **34**, 249–255. Reprinted by permission.

be born to a newly born girl in her lifetime.[378] If 1,000 girls born in 1970 produce 1,600 girl babies by 2020, the NRR is 1.6. Maintained indefinitely, this would produce a 60 percent growth of the population in every 25-year generation. An NRR of 1.0 represents zero growth. Table 11-9 compares the NRRs of several societies.

In 1969 women in the United States were bearing children at a rate that, if sustained, would result in an average of 2.5 children for each woman during her lifetime. An average of three children for each family would bring the population to 300 million by 1989, 400 million by 2014, and nearly 1,000 million by 2070.[379] If, on the other hand, the average were to drop to two children, which is below the zero population growth point, the population would still increase until near the end of the twenty-first century, when it would stabilize at 370 to 400 million people.

Estimates of future populations for some other countries, based upon their percentage of annual growth, are:

United Kingdom, annual growth 0.7 percent—1980, 60.6 million

France, annual growth 1.1 percent—1980, 57 million

Soviet Union, annual growth 1.2 percent—1980, 275 million

Japan, annual growth 1.0 percent—1980, 114 million[380]

Because of the exponential growth of populations, with each generation of women giving birth to a greater number of potential mothers, populations grow more and more rapidly.[381] It took nearly 150 years for the United States to reach its first 100 million people, a figure that includes both natural increase and an average of 1 million immigrants a year during the early twentieth century. The next 100 million arrived in only about 50 years. If these were to have three children in each family, the next 100 million would be added in 25 years, and the next in 10.

Developed countries like the United States, the Soviet Union, and European countries grow less rapidly than many of the less developed countries. Table 11-10 lists a number of countries in order of population increase between mid-1974 and mid-1975. Mainland China and India have such enormous populations that together they contributed nearly 38 percent of the world's total increase.

Growth of societies, like that of living systems at lower levels, does not increase all parts of the system at equal rates. The age composition of a society varies with the rate at which it grows. A high rate of increase produces many infants and young children. Zero pop-

TABLE 11-10   National Sources of World Population Increase between Mid-1974 and Mid-1975

Country	1974–1975 population increase in millions of people
India	14.5
People's Republic of China	13.4
Indonesia	3.4
Brazil	3.0
Pakistan	2.2
Soviet Union	2.0
United States	2.0
Mexico	1.9
Nigeria	1.6
Philippines	1.4
Japan	1.4
Thailand	1.3
Turkey	1.0
Egypt	0.8
Iran	0.9
Colombia	0.8
Republic of Korea	0.6
Burma	0.7
Ethiopia	0.7
Republic of South Africa	0.7
All other countries	19.7
Total	74.0

SOURCE: *1975 world population data sheet* and *world population estimates mid-1974 (millions) for 160 countries.* Washington: Population Reference Bureau, 1975.

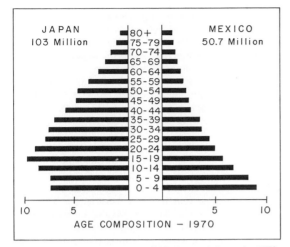

Fig. 11-11 Age composition of Mexico and Japan in 1970. (From *Seminars in population dynamics.* Washington: The Office of Population, U.S. Agency for International Development, 8.)

ulation growth gives rise to a population with similar numbers in each age group up to about 50.[382] Figure 11-11 displays the age composition of Japan and Mexico, the first with a decrease in birthrate brought about by the use of family planning (see page 842), and the second with a high birthrate. Figure 11-12 contrasts the projected age composition of Mexico in 1990 with no change in fertility or mortality rates and with reduced fertility rates. Since the people above age 20 have already been born, the variation is all below that age. Reduction in number of children from 0 to 4 years old is from 17 to 9 million. I discuss above some consequences of changing the age distribution of a population (see page 842).

Rates of growth can differ from one part of a living system to another. This is true at several levels of such systems. At the level of the organism bodily components grow at different rates (see page 470). At the level of the organization the *principle of nonproportional change* and the *law of disproportionality* describe the variations in growth rates of different parts of organizations (see pages 692 to 694). The *allometric growth* formula expresses a constant ratio between the specific growth rate of an element and the specific growth rate of another element or of the total system.[383] This formula was used by Pareto to relate the magnitude of a variable, such as the population of a city, to the rank of the same variable. Zipf's law in linguistics expresses similar relationships. In biology the allometric formula has been applied to state the relationship between brain size and body size, and between

heart size and body size, in mammals and birds.

The index of social development discussed above (see page 755) is based upon allometric relationships among societal variables.[384] The population of the largest settlement of a society (an urbanization measure) and the total number of occupational specialties have been found to be related in this way.[385] So have the population of the largest settlement and the total number of organizational types in a society. Both these allometric functions suggest that increase in the number of people in a society is related to complexity of structure and process within it.

Hypothesis 5.4.1-2 (see page 108) presents as a cross-level generalization the proposition that systems grow in the direction of (*a*) more differentiation of subsystems, (*b*) more decentralization of decision making, (*c*) more interdependence of subsystems, (*d*) more elaborate adjustment processes, (*e*) sharper subsystem boundaries, (*f*) increased differential sensitivity to inputs, and (*g*) more elaborate and patterned outputs. Can each part of this hypothesis be confirmed for societies?

(*a*) Evidence that increase in the amount of work specialization accompanies evolutionary advance in societies appears above (see pages 754 to 760). Comparison of societies at early stages of development with modern industrialized societies on amount of specialization revealed a fundamental change in developmental dynamics.[386] With a population of a million or more in the largest settlement, a proliferation of spe-

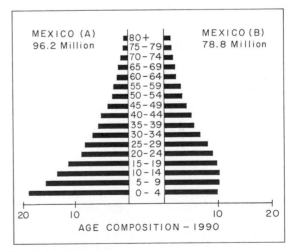

Fig. 11-12 Projected age composition of Mexico, 1990: (A) With no change in fertility or mortality rates, and (B) with reduced fertility rates. (From *Seminars in population dynamics.* Washington: The Office of Population, U.S. Agency for International Development, 12.)

cialists occurred. The data on urbanization in both developed and less developed countries also support this assumption.

(b) As societies grow, they do not appear to make their most important decisions in a more decentralized way, although the total number of decentralized decisions may increase. In fact, modern nations seem to make more centralized decisions than societies of previous centuries did.

(c) Evidence is lacking that interdependence of subsystems is greater or less in one society than in another. *Components* of societies do, however, appear to become more interdependent as societies become larger and as the components become less totipotential.

(d) The adjustment processes of large societies are indeed more elaborate, since they must adjust a much greater number of variables in the more complex society.

(e) The shred-out of subsystem processes to more components and more specialized components that is a part of evolution at all levels of living systems has the predicted effect at the society level. Each of the processes that may be carried out by a single human organism or a small group in very undeveloped societies is carried out by specialized organizations in more developed societies. Organizations, on the other hand, are often made up of components that are parts of many different subsystems. Firm organizational boundaries segregate such components from others of the same sort in other organizations.

(f) The elaboration and refinement of input transducers in more developed, but not necessarily numerically larger, systems assure that increased differential sensitivity to input will be present.

(g) Although certain artifacts, like language or Persian rugs or Chinese temples, may be more elaborate and patterned in less developed societies than their modern equivalents in highly developed ones, the developed societies have many more kinds of both matter-energy and information outputs, making their total output more elaborate and patterned. Some of their outputs, like the circuitry of electronic devices and space vehicle guidance and support systems, are more elaborate and patterned than anything seen before in the world.

Hypothesis 5.4.1-3 (see page 108) states that increase in the number of components in a system requires a disproportionately larger increase in the number of information processing and deciding components. The statistical studies that would confirm or disconfirm this statement at this level have not been done. It seems intuitively probable, however, that

societies are similar to organizations in having the relationships specified in the hypothesis. Research on this matter would be worthwhile.

Limits to growth. The extreme upper limits to growth in population of a society are set by limits of available resources and other physical factors. The upper limit of the number of components that can be effectively governed by a centralized decider appears to depend upon the design of the particular societal system.

A study of political integration suggests that the growth of states by annexation of territory may be self-limiting because the larger a state becomes, the less attention its political leaders can give to units that were tempted to join it: " . . . very large states . . . might find it impossible to absorb any more people or territory, or even to retain the loyalties of all the smaller groups and political units that had become joined to them in the past. This means that greater political responsiveness . . . cannot be expected to emerge automatically as a by-product of historical evolution."[387]

Life cycles of societies. Societies are formed, maintain steady states for varying lengths of time, and are replaced by others, but no typical pattern of growth can be discerned. New and old societies may, however, differ in their characteristics. When a society is first formed, by separating from a larger unit of which it was a part, by revolution, or by treaty (as Israel was), the enthusiasm of its members is high. If a popular revolution has upset a previous unpopular system and has replaced it, the proportion of members willing to commit energy and resources to its goals may be higher than in an established society.[388]

Hypothesis 3.3.7.2-11 (see page 101) says that the longer a decider exists, the more likely it is to resist change. This could be true. Some long-lived systems have behaved in this way. Long-lasting deciders also appear to achieve considerable stability in many cases and to have fewer challenges to their legitimacy.

Long-lived societies may become more efficient if Hypothesis 3.3.7.2-5 (see page 100) is confirmable at this level, as seems possible. It says that the longer a system has made decisions of a certain sort, the less time each decision takes, up to a limit.

5.4.2 Cohesiveness   Patterns of dispersal of components within a society's territory are determined by the natural features of the environment, the proportion of industry to agriculture in the society's economy, and other such considerations. Although some societies exist in which the people do not live in villages, but spread out more evenly over the territory, by far the most common situation is for components to be concentrated in particular areas—in villages, towns, cities, or great conurbations.

Some sorts of organizational components are more effective if they are divided into separate facilities and placed in various parts of the system's territory. This is particularly important in large societies, where there are many centers of population. Mathematical models of the decentralization process are relevant to both organizations and societies (see pages 736 and 737).

Societies whose territories are divided by natural barriers, like oceans, or by the territory of other societies cannot be as cohesive as those with continuous territories. They have special problems integrating their separated components into the larger society. Pakistan and East Pakistan, now Bangladesh, were for years separated by part of India. In addition, there were cultural differences between the parts. These two separated components did not continue as a single nation. The United States, with two states separated from the others, has been able to integrate them more successfully. Both information and matter-energy flow freely between the mainland of the nation and Alaska and Hawaii. In addition, the states agree in perceiving advantages in continuing the relationship.

5.4.3 Integration Integration under the control of a central decider varies among societies of different structures. Hypothesis 5.4.3-1 (see page 109) states that more transmission of information is necessary to coordinate segregated systems (like federations) than integrated ones (like totalitarian states). This may well be true at the society level. Segregated systems, in which deciders of components such as states are relatively powerful as compared with the federal government, appear, on the whole, to be less well coordinated. The lack of uniformity of laws among the states of the United States is one indication of this. Life imprisonment may be the punishment exacted in one state for an offense that carries only a small fine in another. The amount of information flow necessary to write and enact uniform legal codes would be enormous.

One advantage of a highly integrated society is the greater coordination possible in such a system. For this reason, among others, societies do tend, in accordance with Hypothesis 5.4.3-7 (see page 109), to centralize their decider processes under stress. In times of war, natural disaster, or other emergency, central governments are often granted powers greater than their ordinary powers.

Highly integrated societies may also have greater access to the assets available within the system which can be used to further system goals. Ordinarily, most of the assets of a segregated society are controlled by components at organization, group, and organism levels. During crisis, segregated systems mobilize much more energy and resources in the service of the system than they do during normal times.[389]

Segregated forms of societal deciders provide greater opportunities for variation and for autonomy of their parts. A federation that reserves some power to the culturally diverse units that compose it gives each more opportunity to manage its affairs in its own way and to follow its individual life-style.

Federal governments frequently manifest a lack of integration by disharmony among the central governments and those of the components. Political parties tend to magnify this disharmony rather than minimize it. A study of relationships within the federal government of the United States used an index of power derived from game theory.[390] A power index of each political party was calculated by summing the separately derived individual power indices of the federal officials, such as President, senators, and representatives. Indices for each of the 50 states were similarly derived by summing indices of all the state legislators and governors belonging to the party and by multiplying by 1/50. If any party or coalition of parties has majority control of the national legislative process (a federal party-power index over 0.5), then the index of partisan disharmony is 1 minus the party-power index in the states. (If the power index in the states is 0.54, the disharmony index is $1 - 0.54 = 0.46$.) That is, the larger the power index in the states of the national majority party, the less the partisan disharmony. This index revealed that during approximately half the time between 1937 and 1955, American federalism had what was in this study considered a serious amount of disharmony. Similar calculations for Canada and for Australia showed more fluctuation of their indices and greater system-component conflict than for the United States. They also demonstrated that controversies between states and the federal government which were carried up to the United States Supreme Court increased in number when the disharmony index increased. There was a significant correlation of .79 between them, empirical evidence that the disharmony index measures meaningful fluctuations in the amount of system–subsystem integration.

Federations have some advantages that serve to balance these disharmonies. In federations the functions of the systems as a whole are separate from those of the component states or cantons. A voter may often consistently support the policies and candidates of one party at the national level and the policies and candidates of another at the state level. Party policies differ from state to state. In unitary governments the voter has to accept one party's rule in all matters, and consequently many voters are frustrated. This sort of frustration is usually less in federations because voters can express themselves separately on federal and state issues.

Immigrants to an established society tend to live near others who share their cultural background and, often, their language. If the new arrivals are peasants or come from primitive societies and if the society they enter is industrialized, with a higher standard of living and a more educated citizenry, the newcomers almost inevitably become objects of discrimination. Job opportunities and neighborhoods are restricted, and they and even their native-born children cannot easily become absorbed into their adopted system. Deutsch describes the assimilation process as depending upon six aspects of system functioning:[391]

(a) *Similarity of communication habits.* The greater the similarity and compatibility of the language and culture, the easier assimilation is.

(b) *Learning–teaching balance.* Assimilation proceeds more rapidly when the newcomers' learning capacity is high and when good teachers and facilities are available to teach them the new language, if necessary, as well as the accepted way of behavior.

(c) *Contact balance.* This is a balance between the frequency and range of the average person's communication across linguistic and cultural barriers as compared with the frequency and range of his communication with members of his own group.

(d) *Balance of material rewards.* If employment, promotion, higher income, freedom of choice, security, and prestige are to be gained by assimilating, the rate of assimilation is higher than when the newcomer has been used to a higher standard of living. Representatives of the same culture may have very different rates of assimilation, depending upon where they go.

(e) *Balance of values and desires.* Under some circumstances, adherence to values of their home culture may be more important to immigrants than the material rewards to be gained by abandoning them. People of some cultural patterns simply are not interested in power and cultural survival and do not seek them when they come into contact with alien values.

(f) *Balance of national symbols and barriers.* Specific prejudices may prevent a differentiated group from being accepted by the dominant culture, even if the national values favor their acceptance. Blacks in the United States have faced this problem. Jews in Germany who thought of themselves as Germans were unacceptable to the majority. The opposite may also be the case. Adherence to symbols of the minority culture may bar people from assimilation. Religious

minorities often do not really join another culture because of their obligations to their religious customs.

When a society includes all or part of the territory and people that formerly belonged to another society, differentiation of these people may be extreme. These components have elements of system organization carried over from participation in the previous system. Even if they joined the system voluntarily, they may have no wish to integrate to the extent that they adopt another language, accept another religion, or change their ways of life. Primitive societies that find themselves unwillingly a part of a modern society within whose boundaries their territory lies often have little wish, at least initially, to become acculturated to an alien way of life.

In many societies people of low income and social status or inferior caste cannot participate fully in the culture because they lack the assets. Such poor people may form an important unintegrated segment of the population.

The presence in a society of significant numbers of people who are unable to gain their fair share of the good things a country has to offer or who feel that the government under which they are obliged to live is not legitimately entitled to rule them is a threat to the integration of the society in a number of ways: (a) Since they have little vested interest in the preservation of the society as it is and are in an excellent position to observe the discrepancy between the society's expressed values and its performance, they are often available for mobilization on the side of an alternative form of government, ready to join a revolutionary leader who promises to redress the injustices they feel they have suffered and give them a greater measure of control over their fate. (b) If there are numerous people in a single culture and they live in a delimited territory within a society, they may demand division of the country either to form their own totipotential system or to join another society. (c) They may, through lack of the resources to live in accordance with the values of the society, become the source of deviants who disrupt societal steady states in various ways, including criminal behavior. Significant numbers of disadvantaged people within a country always erode the quality of the national life.

Societies may react in a number of ways to the presence of differentiated minorities among them. It has not been uncommon for some of these people to be confined to specific places such as reservations or ghettos. They have often been persecuted or driven out. Sometimes they have been made slaves.

Such differentiated segments can be integrated into societies in a number of ways:

(*a*) Fusion of differing peoples may occur over time, as it has in Mexico, where invaders from Spain and the indigenous Indians produced a distinctive people and culture.[392] Fusion may also occur by dividing the territory and permitting a large degree of autonomy to the separate parts under a federated form of government, as was true over some years for the Turks and Greeks in Cyprus.

(*b*) The differentiated group may become assimilated. Many, and eventually all, of the distinctive characteristics of the newcomers are lost as these people become acculturated and accept the language and norms of the new society. This assimilation is never entirely one-sided, of course. The many ingredients that went into the "melting pot" of the United States were not without effect upon innumerable aspects of the society. However, the English language and other aspects of the values and behaviors of the controlling society remained dominant.

Some societies have been more tolerant of cultural and physical differences among people than others. The immigrants and the society may share the opinion that assimilation is good. By taking steps to throw the weight toward the favorable side of the balances listed above—that is, by providing teaching suitable to the newcomers, providing for contact across linguistic and cultural barriers, and increasing rewards—the process can be furthered. Brazil has such national policies.

Many blacks entered the United States involuntarily while it was still colonial and for a number of years thereafter. Only in recent years or decades have laws been enacted, and pressures been placed on white citizens, to permit blacks to have equal rights. At the same time, a strong countermovement against integration began among blacks. Societies may also try to force integration of minorities by making language learning mandatory, forbidding certain religious practices, or using other means. Where this has occurred, it has usually required coercive methods.

Early in the history of Israel the society contained such a diversity of languages, cultural backgrounds, and education that an attempt was made to force integration by breaking up traditional groups and mixing the immigrants in modern units like classrooms, new settlements, and the army.[393] The effect was to increase the adherence of the immigrants to their old languages, customs, and groups. They were successfully integrated when traditional groups were maintained and their leaders supported the change.

A case study of two primitive societies that came into contact with advanced societies reveals some of the processes of acculturation.[394] These were the Northeastern Algonkians (Montagnais) of Canada and the Mundurucú of Brazil, both of which occupied territories within the boundaries of modern societies. The Algonkian bands originally lived by hunting and fishing. The Mundurucú lived in villages and practiced hunting and tropical gardening. Four factors were important in bringing them into the dominant society. The first was involvement in a credit-barter economy in which a trader exchanged manufactured goods—such as axes, pots, traps, and firearms—for furs in Canada and for manioc and, later, rubber in Brazil. The native people were ordinarily in debt to the trader. The second involved a growing dependency on the trader and a weakening of the bonds within the societies. Most importantly, the influence of the chiefs declined. They became intermediaries and were even appointed by the trader. Third, since both furs and rubber were more efficiently exploited by a single man on a particular territory, individual claims to the use of land were initiated. And fourth, it was necessary in both cases for each family group to live some distance from others.

The process of assimilation is not yet complete in either of these societies. Neither has lost its identity in the regional subculture of the society. As they learn the national language, marry outside their own society, and acquire values and behavior patterns of the dominant culture, their cultural distinctiveness is likely to be lost.

Societies differ in their acceptance of differences among their components. An optimal steady state would seem to be one in which all differentiated peoples could be free to live and work where they pleased and receive respect for their differences along with access to education, jobs, and the other rewards the society has to offer. In this way some of the interesting variety among people and cultures might be preserved from homogenization.

5.5 Pathology The idea that a society may be "sick" is not new. Much of the world agrees that Germany under Adolf Hitler functioned pathologically. Historians take this view, not only because Germany's expansionist policies from 1933 to 1945 were unpopular with neighboring nations, but also because the country as a whole adopted a value system deviant from that of other contemporary societies. This value system reflected the personal psychopathy of Hitler in the attempts to eliminate "non-Aryan" people from the regions under the control of Germany and in other actions considered unacceptable by other societies. The eventual termination of the Nazi government was brought about not only by the stresses its enemies inflicted upon it from outside but also by the disordered functioning of the system itself, particularly its loss of feedbacks from system components.

No clear criteria for normality and pathology, or for ranges of stability for many critical variables, have been determined for societies. Only gross manifestations, like inability of the system to maintain order among its components, runaway inflation, loss of faith in money issued by the government, widespread famine, lack of control or stability of the central decider, or civil war, are generally recognized as signs of pathology. Uncorrected, they can bring about collapse of the system. Although many social indicators have been developed and are in use, general agreement upon implications of changes in them is often lacking. And, of course, societies differ greatly in structure and process and in their hierarchies of values, so that what is normal for one may not be for another.

These large and complex systems are able to make adjustments that reduce many sorts of strains. Only when adjustment processes are inadequate or exhausted can aspects of the system be considered pathological. Hypothesis 5.2-10 (see page 107) states that processes developed later in the phylogenetic history of a given type of system break down under stress before more primitive processes do. Historical studies of societies undergoing dissolution could confirm or disconfirm this hypothesis at the societal level.

Just as accurate diagnosis of system pathology is difficult at this level, so also is "treatment." Ordinarily the remedies recommended for social ills reflect ideology or economic theory, varying with the preferences of the person, group, or organization doing the prescribing. Frequently the effects of actions are not those which were intended or anticipated. Changes in economic variables intended to correct deflation, for example, may lead to an unacceptable rate of inflation.

Pathologies in the categories found in living systems at other levels occur also at the level of society. I discuss these pathologies below.

(a) *Lacks of matter-energy inputs.* When sufficient quantities of any of the forms of matter-energy required for critical subsystem processes cannot be supplied and suitable substitutes cannot be found, those processes are impaired or destroyed. Because critical subsystem processes are coupled together and are interdependent, effects of these shortages spread throughout the ultrastable system (see page 36), affecting first those most closely related to the impaired processes and later the more distant processes. This occurred when supplies of petroleum in several countries were interrupted during the "energy crisis" of 1974. An immediate effect was shortage of gasoline. Lines formed at gasoline pumps, and stations closed on weekends. People experienced minor inconveniences or more serious disruptions of their lives, particularly if they had to drive to work. Almost immediately, other effects became apparent. The industries that depended upon petroleum derivatives were unable to produce their usual quantities of products. Shortages of all sorts of things, from steel to plastics, resulted. The effect on the economy was inflationary. Prices of food and almost everything else rose as the price of petroleum products increased.

Lack stresses of foods, which occur in some of the less developed societies, also affect the entire system in many ways. Widespread malnutrition results in high infant death rates and increased disease. People who are hungry and sick lack energy. They may appear lazy. Artifacts are poorly maintained. Revolutionary movements gain support, particularly among the better-fed and better-educated members of the society who supply leadership for social change. The country's decider may be weakened. The nation loses vigorous and educated younger people to other countries where opportunities are better, leaving a disproportionate number of old, weak, or very young people to carry on the processes of the society.

When lack of food is severe and continues over a long period, small societies may be totally destroyed. Some peoples of the drought area of Africa, for instance, now face such a possible calamity.

(b) *Excesses of matter-energy inputs.* Inputs of this sort may be people, animals, raw materials, products, or natural forces like hurricane winds, tidal waves, or earthquakes that devastate parts of the society.

Excess inputs of people result from unrestrained human reproduction, excessive immigration from other societies, or the invasion of armies. When reproduction outruns the ability of a society to provide adequately for a significant proportion of its people and when the available adjustment processes have not proved effective, a low standard of living is inevitable for all but the fortunate minority. Such a country may cast a hungry eye on the territories of its neighbors to relieve its population pressure. It may decide to adjust to the inequity by sending out its army to devastate or destroy neighboring societies. Excessive inputs of people from other societies, such as imported low-wage laborers or domestic workers, often have strained the job market of countries, adding to the number of unemployed to be cared for by the state and to the deterioration of the cities to which they migrate.

Animals like locusts and hamsters, which are inoffensive, useful, or attractive in small numbers, sometimes multiply so greatly that they destroy food crops or forests, thus creating lack stresses in the society or in parts of it. Such excess animals include the spruce budworms that for several years have been destroying the spruce forests of New England and Canada. No effective way has yet been discovered to eliminate them in the vast acreages where they are devastating trees, and the economy and natural beauty of the areas are seriously impaired.

Excessive imports from other societies of raw materials such as foods, crude oil, and ores, as well as products like automobiles and electronic equipment and appliances, may flood a country and, by reducing demand for the society's own goods, produce serious unemployment in its agricultural, mining, and manufacturing industries.

Some archaeologists believe that the ancient society of Crete was totally destroyed by an earthquake which made rubble of its buildings and killed or displaced its population. Natural disasters do not impinge upon the total territory of large societies, but their secondary effects upon economic variables may damage a society severely if the area affected provides essential crops.

(c) *Inputs of inappropriate forms of matter-energy.* Matter-energy entering societies is inappropriate if it does not have uses in the system's subsystem processes. At best, such inputs are excreted at some cost but without damage to the system. At worst, they are harmful and produce system pathology. In several instances, animals inappropriate to the ecology of a country have been deliberately imported in the expectation they could serve some useful purpose. Lacking natural enemies to control their population, they have sometimes destroyed valuable plants or displaced useful native animals. This occurred in Australia when rabbits were imported and more recently when large bullfrogs were introduced.

Viruses or bacteria to which populations have not developed immunity have threatened the existence of some small societies by sickening or killing a large proportion of the population. Children's diseases like chicken pox and measles are deadly to nonimmune populations. The plague, introduced from Asia in the sixth century, spread devastating epidemics through European countries.

Pollutants like radioactive fallout from nuclear explosions and other poisons carried by air and water are also inappropriate forms of matter-energy inputs that can severely harm a receiving society, which usually can do little to protect itself. Illegal importation of narcotics is another example of a potentially damaging input.

(d) *Lacks of information inputs.* Societies, like systems at all other levels, probably cannot maintain steady states without inputs of information from other societies and from the rest of their environments. Flows of information from other societies are ordinarily maintained at rates high enough to provide the signals a country needs to maintain steady states.

Since no practical way is now known to reduce significantly the rate of flow of inputs from the environment, information input underload is an unlikely source of societal breakdown.

Lacks of specific sorts of information can, however, damage societies. A shortage of technological information may result from deliberate filtering out of such information at the boundary by a country, such as Tibet, Nepal, or Afghanistan, which at a certain time believes such information will threaten its desirable way of life. Lack of such information may not harm a small, isolated, highly totipotential society living in balance with its physical environment. But in a system with a population too large to be nourished by primitive farming methods, absence of information about modern agricultural technologies can result in severe lack strains of food and consequently grave societal pathology. Such a society may have valuable resources which it cannot exploit to the full. Or it may be harvesting far less food per acre than it could with modern methods. Without technical knowledge it can neither increase the quantities of goods available for use within the system nor produce exports that could obtain foreign exchange.

(e) *Excesses of information inputs.* Societies as wholes probably do not experience this class of stresses because they have many channels to process inputs and many adjustment processes for diminishing information flows over their numerous input channels. An excess of certain sorts of information inputs can overload their decider components, however. A possible result can be that meeting short-term goals and coping with immediate emergencies leave no time for long-term planning. Warnings of obvious impending shortages of energy in many parts of the world, for instance, did not receive sufficient attention from deciders of these societies until a crisis occurred. Development of alternative energy sources has generally lagged behind what would have been possible. Deciders have dealt with more urgent emergency situations or more compelling political issues. For years little money was allocated, or efforts devoted, to research and development on solutions to the energy shortage.

(f) *Inputs of maladaptive genetic information in the template.* Societal pathology often arises from a defective constitution or implicit charter. Dictatorships by single leaders or juntas in Europe and Latin America have shown over and over again that failure to provide for orderly transfer of power from one set of decider components to their successors usually leads to damaging power struggles among rival factions. Revolutionary regimes which suspend a society's constitution when they come to power and do not replace it operate on defective charters. When such a government no longer commands even the low consensus generally needed to govern in such systems, or when a leader dies and no clearly designated successor is present, turmoil disrupts the society's domestic tranquillity or steady states.

A societal charter is defective if it fails to provide protection of the rights of lower-level systems that compose it. The Constitution of the Soviet Union provides for all the legal safeguards to civil rights embodied in the Bill of Rights of the Constitution of the United States or the unwritten British constitution. In each country these rights can be suspended under emergency conditions. The nature of such emergencies differs among these three countries. The charters of absolute monarchies have not always guaranteed such civil rights. Individual persons, groups, and organizations cannot carry out their essential processes optimally in a society in which their assets can be seized without due process, their homes can be searched, or they can be imprisoned at the whim of rulers. Such circumstances generally prevail in totalitarian regimes.

A constitution which cannot be amended or which can be changed with ease is defective. An immutable charter results in a society that cannot adapt to a changing world. One that can be readily amended reduces a nation's stability.

(g) *Abnormalities in internal matter-energy processes.* Any matter-energy processing subsystem of a society can function inadequately, leading to disruption of processes, inconvenience or serious deprivation to people in the society, or national inability to compete successfully with other countries in world trade. Deficiencies in producer processes, for example, may lead to poor maintenance of roads and other artifacts, dirty and inadequate public transportation, squalid and run-down housing, or poorly designed and badly made products.

Violence in a society—crime, civil war, rebellion, or excessive—coercive power wielded by decider components—involves major matter-energy internal pathology. Few societies, if any, have been able to avoid serious damage from such violence at some time. Some, like Ireland, have suffered from it constantly for centuries.

Pathologies of this sort often result from abnormalities in information processing. The society may suffer from a chronic strain due to inadequate monetary information, or it may have allowed its technology to become outmoded. Deciders may allocate resources unwisely, with the result that not enough money goes into research and development. Taxes may be levied so heavily that components cannot improve their

functions. Education may be neglected. Technology may be weak.

Environmental pollution may be a severe internal matter-energy pathology, diminishing the efficiency of processes throughout the system. This, too, is often secondary to defects in information processing. It may reflect a value hierarchy that permits components to maximize their profits at the expense of the system as a whole. Or it may result from lack of technological information that would enable producer and extruder processes to give rise to less pollution.

(h) *Abnormalities in internal information processes.* Most ills of modern societies fall into this category. They include economic inflation or depression revealed by fluctuations of economic indicators; inequitable decisions allocating goods and services unjustly among components; repression of internal transductions or channel and net defects, which distort or block feedbacks that control societal steady states; unchecked damaging positive feedbacks; unresponsiveness of deciders to needs and desires of segments of the population; dishonesty of decider components; failure of the decider to implement laws equitably; passage of laws that are perceived by many citizens to be unjust; and class hatreds and prejudices.

Anomie, as described by Durkheim, is a disorder of internal information processing that is characteristic of industrialized societies.[395] Although he wrote during the Industrial Revolution, when changes in the organization of production had affected almost all aspects of newly industrialized societies, many of the problems he observed have not yet been solved. Most importantly, the old rules by which collective life had been regulated had broken down, and no generally accepted rules had emerged for competition, labor-management relationships, or protection of consumers. In the anomic society, the various "organs," or functional parts, did not interact sufficiently to establish the rules of equilibrium among them. Economic life was characterized by conflicts in which the strong demolished the weak. Workers in the factories were degraded to the condition of machines, performing monotonous motions which they did not necessarily understand. With the disappearance of their old craft organizations, they lost the protection, the associations, and the control these organizations had afforded. A profound disturbance of individual human beings resulted.

In the anomic society, also, the automatic economic adjustment processes are likely to fail. With society-wide or worldwide markets, producers do not readily adjust their outputs to the needs of consumers. Periodic economic crises occur. As a result of such disruption, citizens often feel that their basic needs and wants are disregarded. Frequently, therefore, they do not give willing compliance to directives from societal deciders. The civil rights movement in the United States and the civil disobedience movement in India were attempts to bring about social change that people felt could not be achieved by legal means.

Citizens who become convinced that a society's values are being ignored or distorted may reject the values and goals of the system as they perceive it and "drop out" to join countercultures. Such behavior is by no means a modern novelty in the United States. The hippies and their communes had their predecessors in the utopian communities of the nineteenth century, the Shakers, the Mormons—and even the Pilgrims. A society, Etzioni observes, can itself be deviant if it fails to conform to some fundamental human essentials.[396] He identifies *alienation* as a pervading pathology of modern societies, causing severe strains among societal components and subcomponents at the levels of the organization, the group, and the organism. If a society is highly alienating, it cannot form an authentic consensus.[397] Postmodern societies, whatever their form of government, according to Etzioni, exhibit this pathology to a significant extent:*

Our central propositions are: (a) that post-modern society is inauthentic to a significant degree, though the scope and depth of its inauthenticity have not yet been established; (b) that this condition of post-modern society seems to be more the result of the inauthenticity of political processes than of the disintegration of cohesive units or technological-economic factors; and (c) that inauthenticity in one institution nourishes it in others, and, hence, while research may have to study one sector at a time, analysis—if it is not to be inauthentic itself—must explore the macroscopic context.

Inauthentic institutions seem to have (a) comparatively high investment in manipulative activities (e.g., post-modern societies seem to spend more on public relations than did the modern ones); (b) inter-rank (or status) strains resulting from the split between the appearance of community and the underlying bureaucratic reality (*above and beyond* the strains resulting from alienation itself); and (c) the incapacity to mobilize adequately the energy of their members. Energy is either "bottled-up," generating various personal distortions, or it leads to uninstitutionalized ("mass") societal expressions.[398]

5.6 Decay and termination   Ordinarily, a society terminates when its structure and processes are transformed by revolution, peaceful or otherwise, to produce a new society composed of some or all of its components or when it merges, peacefully or otherwise, with another society under new governmental forms and with a newly structured decider. Small, isolated societies are susceptible to termination by an

*Reprinted with permission of Macmillan Publishing Co., Inc. from *The active society* by Amitai Etzioni. Copyright © 1968 by The Free Press, a Division of The Macmillan Company.

overwhelming catastrophe which kills so many of their members that those who are left cannot maintain the system; larger societies, however, rarely encounter such forces. Small societies sometimes disappear when their populations die out because they are not replaced by birth or immigration.

Situations that tend to confirm Hypothesis 5.6-1 (see page 110) can occur at the societal level. The hypothesis states that, if a system's negative feedback discontinues and is not restored by that system or by another on which it becomes parasitic or symbiotic, it decomposes into multiple components and its suprasystem assumes control of them. An example of a decider that stopped receiving negative feedbacks is Nazi Germany in its last days, when central decider components isolated themselves and received no feedback. In accordance with Hypothesis 5.6-1, the system broke down, and the suprasystem—in this case, an international military government—assumed control.

6. Models and simulations

Models and simulations are useful to scholars who study the society and to planners and policy makers because of the large number of variables that affect even apparently straightforward processes at this level and because of the problems of experimenting on these large systems. Such experimentation is difficult because there is no large population of strictly comparable societies; because the time span of experiments would have to be long, since effects of societal actions and decisions extend far into the future; and because it is hard to relate cause and effect if it is not obvious which variables interact.

An accurate simulation can avoid at least some of these problems. Computer time is only a minute fraction of real time; a multitude of variables can be manipulated at will without harmful effects upon real living systems; and potentially damaging effects can be foreseen.

Since prose cannot effectively describe complex economic phenomena, economics has been a mathematical science for about a century. Theoretical economics, statistical economics, and a wealth of economic data collected by banks, corporations, and governments have made mathematical economic models and simulations practical.

Simulation is also used for designing such large-scale projects as highway systems, health delivery systems, educational systems, and military defense systems. It is employed in the formation of policies for environmental protection, in planning for future power needs, in economic planning, in predicting legislative and judicial decision processes, and in other situations in which a look at the future is desired. For instance, in Nigeria, a developing nation, a simulation model for planning is in use that includes separate submodels for the northern agricultural region, which specializes in cattle production; the southern agricultural region; a nonagricultural input– output model of the economy; a population model; and a market and interregional trade submodel of the national food market.[399]

Models at this level are necessarily complex. If a whole society is to be modeled, variables must be grouped into rough categories, and the number of relationships among them must be limited. Even then, a simulation can be unmanageably large. A statistical description of the household sector of an economy that uses only two types of household, nine age categories for adults, sex, and five categories of marital status of heads of households, as well as number, sex, and nine categories of ages of children, presents the experimenter with several million cross-classifications.[400] A mathematical model of these households could include $10^{50,000}$ possible states of a household at a given time. Nevertheless, complex, multivariate simulations of societies or aspects of societies are being constructed. Some of them are important contributions of system science which can advance our basic understanding of societal structure and process, as well as provide more rigorous ways to analyze social problems.

This section includes only three of the four classes of models and simulations (see page 85). There are none of class (*a*) *nonliving artifacts*. There are examples of classes (*b*) *living, usually human, representations* and (*d*) *living system–computer interactions*. But the models and simulations of the greatest interest at this level are in class (*c*) *models in words, numbers, or other symbols, including computer programs*.

(*b*) *Living, usually human, representations*. Most of the simulation games in which participants represent societal deciders fall into one of two categories. Either they are essentially studies of human cognitive processes that are more relevant to the level of the organism than to that of the society, or they are concerned with interactions among societies and are included with supranational simulations (see pages 974 to 980). One game that simulates processes at the level of the society is discussed here.

National policy formation simulation. Two pilot studies with this simulation depicted the internal transduction processes by which significant components of a society reach consensus on public policies.[401] Each participant represented an "interest group" in the United States in negotiations on public policies concerned with the long-range impact of disarmament on the American economy. Following each period of negotiations, participants made a series of decisions

regarding the policies under discussion. Among these were:

Individual tax exemptions should be raised from $600 to $800 per year.

The work week should be reduced from 40 hours to 35 hours without any reduction in wages.

Federal aid to education should be increased by $3 billion (100 percent).

The Federal government should spend $11 billion to eliminate extreme poverty through direct subsidies to the poor.

The United States should negotiate with the Soviets an agreement for complete disarmament.[402]

In the first study, subjects were professional people and administrators. In the second, they were graduate students in political science. They represented business, labor, civil rights, the military, internationalists, and nationalists.

A socioeconomic model defined the relationships among the policies under consideration and national statistical indicators like the GNP and unemployment rates. The policies adopted in one period of the exercise changed the values of indicators in the next period.

The goals of each interest group were specified by the experimenters, and each participant was provided with policy statements, convention resolutions, constitutions, bylaws, in-house publications, and external propaganda of real organizations that held views similar to those he was to support. Participants were also given descriptions of the national and international conditions assumed to be current at the time of the experiment, like the status of the ongoing cold war, the state of disarmament negotiations, comparative military strengths, defense budgets, the status of space projects, the amounts of foreign aid, the state of the United Nations, civil rights conditions, unemployment problems, the GNP, the total federal budget, the high school dropout rate, the number of dwellers in substandard housing, and trends of economic and social indicators.

Participants supported or opposed policies by allocating "resource units," which they received in January of each simulated year. Adoption of a policy required 200 units. At the end of each 6-month period, subjects made allocation decisions and received feedback in the form of new data.

In the second experiment, two different conditions were imposed. The first assumed an armed world in which the arms race then in progress continued. The second assumed an agreement for arms control.

As the experimenters recognized, this research had questionable validity (see page 85) because only one person represented an entire segment of the public opinion of a large society. The processes of this small simulation group could not represent a real system in any but the most general way. An interesting observation which may have its parallel in actual societal processes, however, was the phenomenon of *issue crystallization*. When deviations in indicators exceeded certain limits, participants began to search for corrective policies and for allies to lend support to them. The contrasting armed and less armed worlds produced crystallization around different policies. In the armed-world phase, for instance, a policy of negotiation with the Soviet Union on an agreement for complete disarmament received support only from the internationalists. During the less armed phase a strong coalition of civil rights supporters and representatives of labor and business emerged to counteract a military-nationalist coalition that had forced abrogation of the disarmament treaty.

(c) *Models in words, numbers, or other symbols, including computer programs.* The models in this section represent a range of subsystem processes and adjustment processes of societies. They include models intended for practical use by deciders of the societies they represent, as well as some developed for research on societal processes. Among them are economic models, models of the legislative process, a demographic model, models concerned with planning for the future energy needs of specific societies, and a model of a positive feedback process.

Economic models. Economics is the study of the ways in which societies decide to use their scarce resources to produce various commodities and distribute them for present or future use throughout the society.[403] Economic models ordinarily represent flows of goods and services in terms of their money value and are therefore primarily models of flows of monetary information through the society (channel and net process) and of the information internal adjustment processes related to such flows. This is not always the case, however, since physical units are sometimes used. Flows of goods through a society take place as a result of inputs to, and outputs from, all the matter-energy processing subsystems. Services may be either matter-energy or information subsystem processes. Societal processes that cannot be represented in monetary terms or other quantifiable units are not directly included in economic models, but central decider processes by which governmental components set or otherwise influence values of economic variables may be represented by the values of variables and parameters used in these models. Millions of decisions by individual persons, groups, and organizations determine the values of economic variables, like supply and demand, and are represented in this way, as are the value hierarchies of components and of the system as a whole.

Current economic theory is the most recent development in a theoretical tradition that began with Adam Smith, the first modern economist, whose *Wealth of Nations* appeared in 1776. It is a complex of interrelated deductive models which, to the extent that the premises of any model fit the conditions of an actual society, can be usefully applied to predict or explain the behavior of the real system. In fact, modern economic theory fits present-day economies well enough so that its policy prescriptions permit a large degree of control of societal variables and of the cyclical activity that plagues societies.[404]

Macroeconomic models are concerned with the "big picture" of the variables that determine the national income. They deal with aggregates of incomes, employment, and prices; with money and banking; and with fiscal and monetary policy.[405] *Microeconomic* models study parts of the aggregate, such as the interaction of supply and demand, to determine the price of particular goods and the variables that affect wages and employment. Microeconomics, therefore, is concerned with the allocation of resources in a private enterprise economy.[406]

Levels of living systems from organisms to supranational systems are modeled by economists. The way in which individual organisms and family groups make their economic choices, and the production and marketing decisions of firms, are discussed above (see pages 435, 436, 657, 734, 735, 846, and 847). Models in this section depict units that include more than a single organization.

The concept of *economic equilibrium* is basic to economic theory. Such an equilibrium occurs when opposing economic forces move variables to a point at which they are exactly balanced and at which they will remain until the relative strengths of the forces alter.

The interaction of saving and investment to determine the NNP is described above (see pages 846 and 847). Economic equilibria do not necessarily represent optimal conditions for societies. If, for example, investment opportunities happen to match full-employment saving, establishing an equilibrium with full employment, the equilibrium can be considered optimal. If, however, a deficiency of investment to full-employment saving occurs, a deflationary gap exists, and employment must fall. If the discrepancy is in the opposite direction, the equilibrium point cannot move far because both production and employment are already at capacity. The result is increase in prices and inflation.

In these cases, government fiscal policy can change the equilibrium point. Changes in taxes and governmental expenditures bring the equilibrium point into a more satisfactory range. Figure 11-13 illustrates the effects on the equilibrium point of national income of fiscal policies of (a) increase in governmental expenditures and (b) tax reduction.

EFFECT OF MORE GOVERNMENTAL EXPENDITURES

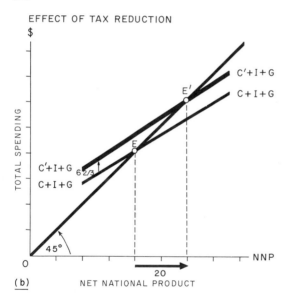

(a)

EFFECT OF TAX REDUCTION

(b)

Fig. 11-13 Effect of more governmental expenditures and of tax reductions on national income determination. In this figure, NNP represents net national product; C represents consumption spending; I represents investment spending; G represents governmental spending; E represents equilibrium point of national income. In (a), an increase in governmental expenditures on goods and services will shift C + I + G up to C + I + G', raising national income from E to E'. In (b), tax reduction has similar expansionary effects on national income. Lower tax collections leave more disposable income out of NNP and hence shift consumption upward, somewhat less, however, than a matching increase in governmental expenditures. [Adapted from P. A. Samuelson. *Economics.* (8th ed.) New York: McGraw-Hill, 1970, 317. *Reprinted by permission.*]

Three classes of economic models are discussed here: (*i*) microeconomic models, (*ii*) input–output macroeconomic models, and (*iii*) econometric macroeconomic models. These three sorts of models are related. The first constitute the basic theory by which economists describe and explain the interactions of economic variables. They are general models, not intended to describe the particularities of specific societies. The second two apply economic theory to specific situations of particular societies. In their equations they use empirically determined values of societal variables, such as the actual price units of a commodity at a given time.

(*i*) *Microeconomic models.* The economy of societies in basic economic models is pure laissez-faire capitalism. Prices serve to allocate scarce resources among components. Each person or household has particular preferences and utilities that determine choices among economic goods as well as the quantity of any goods that will be acquired at a given price. Each person or household is assumed to maximize utility (see pages 435 and 436). At the same time, each firm selects from among its production possibilities a particular set of goods or services for which the profit is not less than it would be for any other set. That is, it maximizes profit (see page 657). These firms and households interact in a strictly defined *perfectly competitive market.*[407]

Five basic assumptions underlie the concept: (*a*) *The product is homogeneous.* Since selling price must be the only factor that determines choice, no lack of uniformity of product must enter into the decision. (*b*) *Each participant in the market has perfect knowledge of current opportunities.* He will not, then, take a lower price or pay a higher one than others in the market at the same time. This requirement applies to finished goods, factors of production (labor, rent, and capital goods), wages paid to labor, and terms of borrowing capital. (*c*) *Individuals maximize utility, and firms maximize profit* (see previous paragraph). (*d*) *Competition is atomistic.* No single buyer or seller has sufficient power to affect price. There must be many buyers and sellers, each of whom is so small a factor that no matter how much he buys or sells, he cannot affect the market. Neither sellers nor buyers can get together to affect prices. (*e*) *Entry and exit of resources must be free.* Productive resources, including land, labor, capital, and entrepreneurship, are assumed to be unspecialized and can enter or leave any industry whenever the owners wish. If profits are better in another industry, resources are quickly moved to it.

In such a market, a price for any economic good is determined by the forces of supply and demand. An equilibrium price for each sort of good is established at the point at which the amount supplied exactly matches the amount demanded. Figure 11-14 and

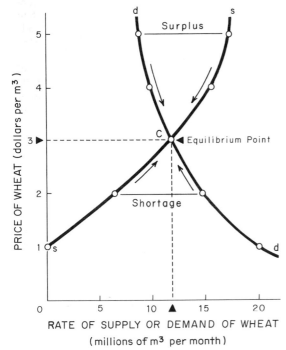

Fig. 11-14 Supply, demand, and price of wheat. In this figure, C represents the third situation in Table 11-11, the equilibrium price; s—s represents supply curve; d—d represents demand curve. At the equilibrium intersection, C, the price is such that the rate of supply of wheat just matches the rate of demand of wheat. At any lower price, the excess amount demanded will force the price back up. At any higher price, the amount supplied will be excessive and the price will be forced back down. [Adapted from P. A. Samuelson. *Economics.* (8th ed.) New York: McGraw-Hill, 1970, 61. *Reprinted by permission.*]

Table 11-11 illustrate the way in which an equilibrium price is set by supply and demand. Just as changes in saving and investment can alter the equilibrium point of national income, so shifts in demand or supply can change the equilibrium price for an economic good. The price of a good or service, however, depends also upon the prices of alternative goods and services. What is more, a change in the demand for one commodity affects not only its price and the quantity sold but also the prices and quantities sold of other commodities that compete with it or are required in its production.

Analysis of this sort of situation cannot be satisfactorily accomplished verbally. *General equilibrium analysis* is therefore best approached by use of a mathematical model. Cohen and Cyert present a highly simplified model that includes only a consumer sector and a business sector of an economy.[408]

The equations in this model are (*a*) an equation showing the amounts of commodities that households consume and the quantities of services provided, that is, demand equations for commodities and supply equations for productive services; (*b*) an equation showing that the demand by a firm for productive service in manufacturing its commodity is dependent upon the prices of all factors of production, the quantity manufactured, and the production function of the firm; (*c*) an equation indicating that a firm's total revenues from sale of its commodity equal its total costs of production (no profits are included in this model); (*d*) an equation expressing the equilibrium in which total demand of households for a product equals firms' total supply of that product; and (*e*) a similar "clearing" equation for the factor market which shows that the total demand by firms for the factor must equal the total supply by households of that factor.

Solution of the model is possible only if a "feasible and consistent" set of values can be assigned to the variables so that the six equations of the model are simultaneously satisfied. In this case, the system is *underdetermined,* since the set of supply and demand forces represented in the basic equations are insufficient to determine unique values for all commodity and factor prices and flows. The number of variables to be determined exceeds the number of equations by 1. This system can become *determined* if any one commodity or factor is used as a standard for measuring all the others. The price of that commodity (the numeraire) will be 1. Prices of the others are multiples of this price. The solution of the general equilibrium model uniquely determines price ratios but not the absolute level of prices. This is true because the model lacks relations pertaining to the market for money. It is a *real* model, since prices are stated in terms of a

TABLE 11-11   Supply and Demand Schedules for Wheat

SITUATION	POSSIBLE PRICES ($ per m³)	RATE OF DEMAND (million m³ per month)	RATE OF SUPPLY (million m³ per month)	PRESSURE ON PRICE
A	$5	9	8	↓ Downward
B	4	10	16	▼ Downward
C	3	12	12	Neutral
D	2	15	7	▲ Upward
E	1	20	0	↑ Upward

NOTE: Only in Situation C, at the equilibrium price of $3, will the rate of demand of wheat by consumers equal the rate of supply of wheat by producers. At any lower price, demand would exceed supply; at any higher price, supply would exceed demand.

SOURCE: Adapted from P. A. Samuelson. *Economics* (8th ed.) New York: McGraw-Hill, 1970, 61. Reprinted by permission.

commodity which is consumed (the one chosen as numeraire) rather than in numbers of dollars. In order to assure that the solution to the model is unique and economically meaningful (that is, to assure that all prices and flows are positive), further constraints and conditions are necessary.

If such a system is to be made empirically applicable, it must be restructured to eliminate references to individual firms and households, since there are too many of each in a real economy for inclusion in a model.[409] Market supply and demand equations for commodities and factors replace the equations relating to individual households and firms. The clearing equations are rewritten in terms of the market variables. This aggregate form of a general equilibrium system has the same characteristic as the earlier one. That is, it has one more variable than equation. The solution to that problem is the same—select a numeraire and solve for all prices in terms of that commodity or factor.

A general equilibrium model of the economy of a modern society would, of course, be enormously more complex than these examples.

Models have been developed also for a monopoly market, in which there is only one seller of a product; a situation of monopolistic competition in which the requirement for homogeneity of product is relaxed to permit product differentiation; duopoly, in which there are two sellers; and oligopoly, in which there is a relatively small number of sellers.[410] In addition, *welfare economics* creates models that seek social optima in distribution, employment, and competition or other aspects of the economy by appropriate alterations of variables in the basic model of perfect competition

(ii) *Input–output macroeconomic models.* In the words of its originator, Leontief, "The input–output method is an adaptation of the neo-classical theory of general equilibrium to the empirical study of the quantitative interdependence between interrelated economic activities."[411] This method deals with flows of inputs and outputs of various sorts of matter-energy and information through a set of sectors in the economy which are in some ways similar to subsystems of the society. The conceptual systems underlying input–output models and general living systems theory have important similarities.

These and other sorts of quantitative economic models make use of the wealth of statistical data continuously collected in modern societies. Input–output models present, in mathematical and tabular form, a detailed account of the intermediate flows of goods and services that are included in national accounts. They break down such terms as "gross national product," "total output," "value added by manufacture,"

"federal government expenditures," "personal consumption expenditures," and "exports" so that their elements are evident.[412] The look "under the hood" they provide relates the state of the total system to the supply and demand relationships within it.

In such a model, it is possible to trace the flow of any specific good or service from its output by its original producer to each of the industries that use it and finally to households, the government, and exports. In addition, the input from other producers and from labor that is required to produce the particular good or service is evident.

Models of this class have many uses. The United States government and many other governments throughout the world maintain and regularly update computerized input–output models as a part of their national economic accounts. Detailed information about interrelationships among a society's industries is made available in this way. In addition, the effects upon other sectors of the economy of anticipated or hypothetical changes in demand or availability of a good or service can be discovered by appropriate changes in quantities in the model. The implications of economic programs can also be shown, as well as the effects of changes in technology, wages, profits, or taxes.

On the basis of such models, industries can estimate future requirements for labor, plant, and equipment. As of 1970, some 50 major United States corporations were using computerized input–output models of the national economy to get immediate answers to such questions as: "Assuming a gross national product of $1.17 trillion in 1980, what will sales of the electronics industry to the aircraft industry be?" or "Assuming that imports cut demand for United States automobiles in 1975 to $40 billion from a projected $44 billion, how will steel output be affected?"[413]

Input–output models can be used experimentally to simulate the effects of major changes in an economy, such as would result from an arms cut.[414] A model can include the separate contributions of regions or political divisions of an economy and the effects of policies or changes upon their internal economies. This is done for the separate Soviet republics as a part of the Soviet Union's national accounts.[415]

These models can also be used as forecasting instruments, for example, to analyze the effects of continuing inflation on the separate industries within the United States economy.[416]

Comparison of the economies of different societies for which the necessary statistics are available can be done using input–output models designed for the purpose.[417]

Input–output models are systems of equations similar to the other economic models discussed in this

TABLE 11-12   Input–Output Relationships in a Three-Sector Economy

FROM \ INTO	Sector 1: Agriculture	Sector 2: Manufacture	Sector 3: Households	Total output
Sector 1: Agriculture	25	20	55	100 m³ of wheat
Sector 2: Manufacture	14	6	30	50 m of cloth
Sector 3: Households	80	180	40	300 worker-years of labor

SOURCE: Adapted from W. Leontief. *Input–output economics.* New York: Oxford Univ. Press, 1966, 135. Copyright © 1966 by Wassily Leontief. Reprinted by permission of Oxford University Press.

section. They may be *static* or *dynamic.* A simulation is dynamic if values of variables in a given period depend upon values of variables determined in a prior period. The equations of the system describe the overall input–output balance of the economy.

The economy to be modeled is divided into a number of sectors representing producers, *i.e.,* industries or groups of industries (components of the converter, producer, and several other matter-energy or information processing subsystems) and a final demand sector that includes the various consumers of goods and services—households, the government, foreign nations that buy exports, and others. The quantity of the output of a given sector (*i*) absorbed by another sector (*j*) per unit of its total output is called the *input coefficient* of sector *i* into sector *j*. These coefficients must be derived from empirical data. When the sets of coefficients for all producing sectors of the economy are arranged in the form of a rectangular table, they constitute the *structural matrix* of the economy.

A very simplified example of the derivation of such a matrix begins with an input–output table that describes the flows in a three-sector economy (see Table 11-12). In this table, outputs are given in the last column in appropriate physical units (*e.g.,* cubic meters of wheat, meters of cloth, or worker-years of labor). Agriculture is shown in that table to absorb 25 m³ of its own product, wheat; 20 m of cloth from the manufacturing sector; and 55 worker-years of labor output by the household sector in producing its 100 m³ of total output. The structural matrix for the simplified economy is derived by dividing the quantity of each input absorbed by the total output of the sector, with the result shown in Table 11-13. For example, "Sector 1: Agriculture" absorbed 25 m³ of wheat out of a total output of 100, for a value of 0.25 in the structural matrix; 20 m of cloth out of a total output of 50, for a value of 0.40; and 55 worker-years of labor out of a total output of 300, for a value of 0.183.

The overall input–output balance of the whole national economy is described in a set of as many linear equations as there are sectors in the economy,

These express the general equilibrium relationships between the total outputs of all producing sectors and the final bill of goods absorbed by the final demand sector. If these final demands are assumed to be given, the system can be solved for the unknown total output of each of the sectors. An increase or decrease in the output of any industry can result from a change in the final demand, a change in the structure of the system, or a combination of both.

Dynamic input–output models incorporate lags or rates of change over time.[418] In addition to the coefficients of the static model, the dynamic models require a corresponding table of capital coefficients. These show the number of units of input of a good that would have to be added to the capital stocks held by an industry if the productive capacity of that sector were raised to the point where it could increase its annual production by one unit. The equations of the system describe the dependence of the total output of the products of each sector in each model year on the levels of final deliveries in each year. This procedure can also be used to incorporate structural change by adding time subscripts to the input and capital coefficients. The numerical value of these coefficients could then change from year to year.

A special-purpose dynamic model was designed by Leontief for use by forecasters or planners in determining the limitations on the possible growth of an

TABLE 11-13   Structural Matrix of a Simplified Economy

FROM \ INTO	Sector 1: Agriculture	Sector 2: Manufacture	Sector 3: Households
Sector 1: Agriculture	0.25	0.40	0.183
Sector 2: Manufacture	0.14	0.12	0.100
Sector 3: Households	0.80	3.60	0.133

SOURCE: W. Leontief. *Input–output economics.* New York: Oxford Univ. Press, 1966, 138. Copyright © 1966 by Wassily Leontief. Reprinted by permission of Oxford University Press.

economy imposed by given sorts of input–output coefficients.[419] This can be employed in long-run projections for less developed countries, in which population trends have a critical effect on developmental prospects, by including equations that describe demographic relationships. These include not only variables that determine the size and composition of the population in successive years but also variables concerned with such matters as the general level of consumption and the distribution of labor between agricultural and manufacturing employment.

The coefficients of the matrix described above were derived from a table that used physical units of measurement—worker-years of labor, cubic meters of wheat, and meters of cloth. In practice, the matrices would usually be computed from input–output tables constructed in monetary units. From the matrix of input coefficients, however derived, a table showing monetary flows in the economy can be constructed. Table 11-14 is a highly simplified example of such a dollar-flow input–output table.

Not only does such a table detail the sales of each sector to each of the others, but also, by summing across the rows horizontally, the total output of the sector can be determined. The value added rows at the bottom of the table include the wage bill, deprecia-

tion, profit, and other "prime-factor" charges that make up the industry's own contribution to the GNP over and above the value of its inputs from other sectors. The sum of all the entries in the value-added rows is equal to the sum of all the entries in the total final demand. This figure is the GNP.

New input–output tables for the United States were issued for 1947, 1958, and 1963. Updating is done between major revisions. An enormous amount of work is obviously involved in compiling such a table. In preparing the tables for 1963, estimates were prepared for about 370 separate industries.[420]

Analysis of these tables reveals interesting information about the economy. Industries varied widely in the amount of their output sold to final demand, as one would expect. Footwear and household furniture both sold over three-fourths of their output to final markets and are directly affected by change in these markets. Agricultural services and iron and ferroalloy mining, on the other hand, sold almost exclusively to intermediate consumers and had a connection to final markets traceable only through their customers. The heavy interdependence among industries, typical of the economy of the United States, is also shown: "Almost all industries required inputs from at least 30 others. As many as 57 industries required inputs from

TABLE 11-14   Format of an Input-Output Table

		PRODUCERS								FINAL MARKETS			
		Agri-culture	Mining	Construc-tion	Manufac-turing	Trade	Transpor-tation	Services	Other	Persons	Investors	Foreign-ers	Govern-ment
PRODUCERS	Agriculture									Personal consumption expenditures	Gross private domestic investment	Net exports of goods and services	Government purchases of goods and services
	Mining												
	Construction												
	Manufacturing												
	Trade												
	Transportation												
	Services												
	Other												
VALUE ADDED	Employees	Employee compensation								GROSS NATIONAL PRODUCT			
	Owners of Business and Capital	Profit-type income and capital consumption allowances											
	Government	Indirect business taxes and current surplus of govt. enterprises, etc.											

NOTE: In each box in the shaded area may be put the dollar value of sale of raw materials, semifinished products, and intermediate service, from the producer industry in the row to the producer industry in the column.
SOURCE: National Economics Division of the Office of Business Economics, U.S. Department of Commerce. Input–output structure of the United States economy: 1963. *Survey of current Business*, 1969, **49**(11), 19.

over 50 industries. The chemicals industry . . . for example, required inputs from 73 industries, only eight of which are producers of basic raw materials."[421]

(*iii*) *Econometric macroeconomic models.* An econometric model is a set of simultaneous equations that represent quantitative relationships among economic variables. If values and relationships in a model are set to correspond to values and relationships in a society, the model can be used to simulate that society's economic processes. Like input–output models, econometric models can be either static or dynamic (see page 879). They may represent an entire economy or emphasize particular aspects of it, such as monetary policy.

Developed by researchers in universities and governmental agencies, econometric models are designed to be of use in (*a*) analyzing the behavior of an overall economy; (*b*) testing hypotheses about economic phenomena like, for example, business cycles; (*c*) predicting the changes in the society that could result from continuation of present trends into the future; (*d*) determining the probable outcomes of alternative pol-

icies; (*e*) indicating the effects over time of changes in key variables such as population or technology; and (*f*) defining a desirable future state of an economy.

Econometric models include three sorts of variables.[422] *Endogenous* variables are unknowns for which the system of equations is to be solved. Values of *exogenous* variables are determined outside the system. They may represent governmental policies, known as *instruments;* variables over which the real system has no control, like foreign demand for exports; or any other variables the experimenters elect to use as "given" either to limit the size of the model or because the model cannot predict them adequately. Endogenous variables for which values have been determined in one time period may be used in the same way as exogenous variables in a succeeding time period. These are *lagged endogenous* variables. Equations expressing *identities* are definitional statements needed to complete the model.

A quarterly econometric model of the United States, developed by the U.S. Office of Business Economics (OBE), consists of 48 equations, including identi-

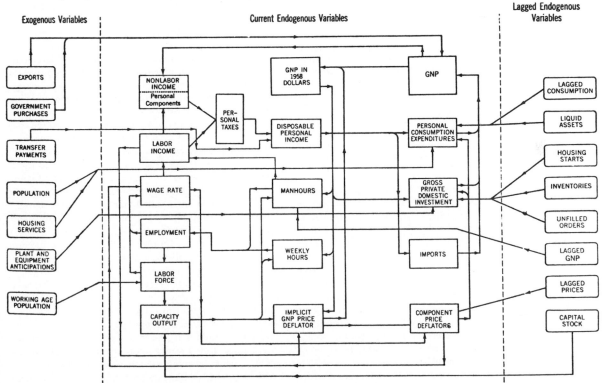

Fig. 11-15 Condensed flow diagram of the OBE model. [SOURCE: Office of Business Economics, U.S. Department of Commerce. From M. Liebenberg, A. A. Hirsch, & J. Popkin. A quarterly econometric model of the United States: a progress report. *Survey current Business*, 1966, **46**(5), 19.]

ties, divided into six groups.[423] These are (*a*) components of the GNP, (*b*) prices and wage rates, (*c*) labor-force and employment-related magnitudes, (*d*) income components, (*e*) monetary variables, and (*f*) miscellaneous variables. Values of the predetermined variables, including lagged endogenous variables and exogenous variables, are set at the beginning of a period, and the entire set of equations is solved simultaneously by a computer to determine values of the endogenous variables. Values determined for the exogenous variables depend not only upon their original magnitudes but also upon the magnitudes of the coefficients that represent the parameters.

In the working model, complex interdependencies exist among the equations. Figure 11-15 is a condensed diagram of the OBE model. Among the interrelationships made evident by the arrows in that diagram is the linkage between product and income. In order to adjust for changes in buying power of the dollar subsequent to the base-line year of 1958, *deflator* equations are necessary. Of this model, Liebenberg, Hirsch, and Popkin say:

> The boxes representing the GNP components at the right of the endogenous portion of the chart plus government purchases and exports make up total GNP. By deflating the latter (see the line connecting the implicit GNP deflator with the line emanating from GNP), GNP in 1958 dollars is obtained. The main linkage to the income side of the accounts is shown by the line leading from GNP in 1958 dollars to the box for man-hours and the box for weekly hours. One important link thus occurs via employment variables. The nest of boxes concerned with employment and with the wage rate determines labor income. . . .
> The feedback from income to product can also be delineated. As expected, the main linkage is revealed via the chain ''income–taxes–disposable income–consumer expenditures.'' This chain can easily be followed in the chart.[424]

If a model is to be used for forecasting, it is necessary to secure reasonable projections of the exogenous variables based on expert opinion by informed sources, such as the United States Departments of Commerce and of Labor.[425] Extrapolations of governmental policies can be made on the basis of budgets, pending economic legislation, and the current directions of monetary policy. These might lead to such assumptions as that the tax rate will not change, that government purchases and transfer payments will be at the levels set in the budget, and that growth in supplies of money and credit will continue at its recent rate. The solution will indicate a possible outcome of continuation of these policies.

If a model is to be used to test the effects of alternative policies, values of the predetermined variables can be set appropriately, and alternative futures can be described by the solution.

If a model is to be used to define a desirable future state of the economy, such as full-employment peace-time economy, relevant exogenous variables can be extrapolated, and the model can be solved to determine the path to these solutions.

The OBE model was tested for a sample period in the United States. This was done by postdicting (*i.e.*, ''forecasting'' backward in time) each of the 13 years from 1953 through 1965.[426] In each year the model was run for the four quarters, using the last quarter of the previous year as the starting point. Known values of exogenous variables were used in each case, but the lagged endogenous variables arising within the year were those yielded by the model rather than the actual values. The simulation performed well at predicting the GNP, with a slight tendency to overestimation. Its performance in predicting turning points in the cyclical behavior of the economy was most precise when the starting quarter was close to the actual turning point. The year 1965 was outside the test period for which the model had been fitted. This was a difficult year to predict, since a dock strike, accelerated production following auto strikes, and the threat of a steel strike, which caused producers and consumers to accumulate inventories, complicated the picture. In addition, excise taxes on a number of consumer goods were removed. The model did predict the degree and pattern of economic expansion during the year, but its performance on wages and prices was not satisfactory. This was improved by making prices exogenous. This model is still under development.

The Federal Reserve-M.I.T. econometric model has been created specifically to quantify monetary policy and its effects on the economy of the United States.[427] An initial report describes the performance of three large blocks of equations as part of a projected complete model: (*a*) supply and demand equations for financial claims and their dynamics; (*b*) fixed investments, including housing, plant and equipment, and the behavior of state and local governments; and (*c*) the consumption-inventory block, including income shares, imports, and federal personal taxes as well as consumption and inventory investment.

The first block describes the behavior of financial markets, particularly the supply and demand for demand deposits, time deposits, and free reserves. The demand for these depends upon interest rates, which rise and fall in the short run to bring quantities demanded into balance with the supply of unborrowed bank reserves, which is set exogenously by federal policy. GNP is another important determinant of demand. In tests on this block, GNP and its components were also treated as exogenous. Dynamic predictions of this block, tested separately, successfully forecast unusually large increases and declines in interest rates in 1966 and early 1967. They also forecast an economic slowdown, but not the actual large decline in demand deposit holdings, in 1966. This block and the others of the model were much more accurate when actual values of lagged variables were used for a single-period simulation instead of the values generated in the previous period. This model, however, is intended for evaluations of alternative policies over several quarters. Therefore, tests using the dynamic model—which proceeds from one quarter to the next, employing values generated in previous period—are more relevant to the purposes for which the model is being developed.

Simulation results are given for two possible Federal Reserve policies: one showing the effects over time of a step increase in unborrowed reserves, and the other tracing the effects of a step increase in GNP. Figure 11-16 shows the effects on a number of economic variables in the financial block of an increase of $1 billion in unborrowed reserves. Simulations were also made of policy changes relevant to the other blocks of equations.

The three groups were then combined into a single set of simultaneous equations, and dynamic predictions and simulations were made with the entire system. Predictions for the combined system, starting in the second quarter of 1965 and continuing into 1966, were not so good as those for the single sectors. Nevertheless, the model successfully predicted a slowdown in growth that began in the second quarter of 1966, although it failed to predict the short-lived recovery in the fourth quarter. Results on other variables were mixed.

Three policy changes were simulated with the combined model: (a) a $1-billion step increase in unborrowed reserves; (b) an increase in personal tax rate, which in 1963–1964 was about 0.20, by 2 percentage points (approximately 10 percent); and (c) a $5-billion step increase in defense spending. The first simulation indicated little effect of the $1-billion step increase on GNP in the first few quarters. The effects accelerated, however, with the multiplier influence of an increase in fixed investment and decelerated again as the peak in fixed investment was reached. At the end of 3 years, GNP had increased by more than $11 billion. This

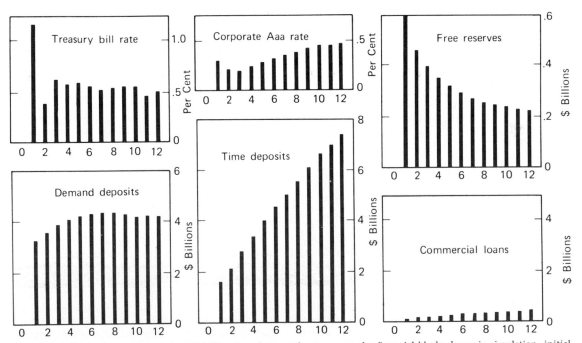

Fig. 11-16 Effects of a step increase of $1 billion in unborrowed reserves on the financial block; dynamic simulation, initial conditions of 1963, Quarter I. The figure illustrates the differences between solution values for the simulation situation and solution values for the model beginning in 1963, Quarter I, with actual unborrowed reserves. All variables exogenous to the financial block are held at actual values for both solutions. Lagged values of endogenous variables are generated by the model in both solutions. (From F. DeLeeuw & E. Gramlich. Staff economic study: the Federal Reserve-MIT econometric model. *Fed. Reserve Bull.*, 1968, **54**, 15.)

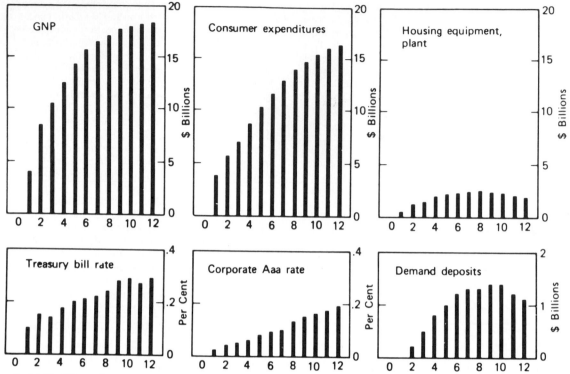

Fig. 11-17 Effects of a step increase of two percentage points (about 10 percent) in the personal tax rate, three blocks combined; dynamic simulation, initial conditions of 1963, Quarter 1. The figure indicates the difference between a solution showing the policy changes and one that does not. (From F. DeLeeuw & E. Gramlich. Staff economic study: the Federal Reserve-MIT econometric model. *Fed. Reserve Bull.*, 1968, **54**, 28.)

showed a higher multiplier than other models of the same process.

The implication of this finding for policy is that monetary policy is powerful but that lags are long, making it difficult to use as an economic stabilizer. The impact of a policy change of this sort will not be felt until a year later, when it is more difficult to predict what policies will be needed.

The other two simulations were in the area of fiscal policy. The effects of these were evident less than half a year after the policy change. Lags in this process occurred between recognition of the need for action and changes in tax rates or expenditures rather than in the response of the economy to fiscal policy changes. Figures 11-17 and 11-18 depict this situation clearly.

Current econometric models cannot be used to predict more than 2 or 3 years into the future for several reasons. In the first place, noneconomic variables of subsystems that process other kinds of flows besides money have unknown effects upon the equations of the system. Some of these are technological:

One example is the extent to which emerging communications technology will affect the demand for all types of transportation. Communications is a partial substitute for transportation and how the widespread use of the large-screen videophone, for instance, will affect the demand for new cars and commercial airline travel is unknown. At the response threshold, the decline in demand for airline travel may be quite dramatic, or alternatively, there may be no effect at all. Thus, the equations lack important variables entering from other parts of the society.[428]

A further reason for limitations on the predictive power of these models is that nonlinearities which do not appear during the period when the model is being tested may become very important during the forecast period. What is more, if the economy of the future were to be more perfectly controlled, or if growth and employment goals were reached, some models would no longer be adequate. Consequently, a policy maker who relied upon them could make an error that would lead, perhaps, to a recession. The assumption that economies of the future will be essentially like those of the present is unwarranted.

Compared with other means of forecasting the future paths of economic variables, however, such simulations have certain advantages:

The econometric approach is comparable in validity to alternative approaches—for instance, the "judgmental" method, which may also use econometric methods but which does not rely on an explicit set of simultaneous equations, or the "economic indicators" approach originally developed by the National Bureau of Economic Research. The particular promise of the econometric method stems from the fact that it provides explicit formulations of the cause-effect relationships in the economy which can be communicated and which are open to inspection and testing. In addition, compared with methods confined to predicting only directional change, the method has the clear advantage of quantification.[429]

Models of the legislative process. The models in this section represent parts of the decider processes of a particular society, the United States. The effects of internal transducer variables, such as constituency pressures or preferences, and the influences of legislators upon one another are modeled in most of these. In addition, decider processes at the level of the organism are specifically included in each model.

These models are experimental and have not reached a state of development that permits their use for definitive testing of hypotheses, nor are they of much use for predicting behavior of even the specific systems for which they have been developed. They do, however, provide insights into important societal processes, indicate directions for further research, and suggest refinements for future models of legislative systems.

I shall now discuss decision-making models of both houses of the United States Congress. While much of the decision-making activity of individual members of these bodies cannot be open to public scrutiny, factors significant in determining their decisions can be analyzed quantitatively.

Model of United States Senate voting. A statistical study of the individual voting behavior of United States senators tested two hypotheses: (a) that sena-

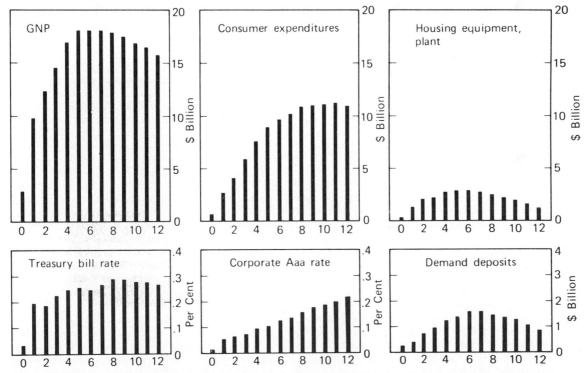

Fig. 11-18 Effects of a step increase in defense expenditures of $5 billion, three blocks combined; dynamic simulation, initial conditions of 1963, Quarter I. The figure indicates the difference between a solution showing the policy changes and one that does not. (From F. DeLeeuw & E. Gramlich. Staff economic study. The Federal Reserve-MIT econometric mode. *Fed. Reserve Bull.*, 1968, **54**, 29.)

tors develop standard routines for obtaining information and deciding how to vote on a majority of bills and (*b*) that the important influences in this process are the senator's constituency, his party leaders, knowledgeable committee members, the President, and informal leaders.[430]

The study assumed that the decision processes of each senator could be described as repetitive problem-solving behavior (see page 433). That is, when a vote is required, a senator will behave as she or he has behaved before in such situations and will follow a "program" specifying a limited information search and a process for selecting from among alternatives.

Voting behavior becomes routine because not every senator can become familiar with all the complicated and diverse issues that come before the Senate. In addition, decisions must often be made rapidly on a number of issues simultaneously, and voting is only a part of the work of a senator.

Individual statistical models were set up for each member of the Senate in the Eighty-seventh Congress (1961–1962), which served during the Kennedy administration.

The equations of the model, based upon research in the field, specified different voting behavior for Democrats, whose party was in power, and for Republicans. Democratic votes were assumed to be influenced by the senator's constituency, the majority leader, the majority whip, the President, and the chairman of the committee that reported the bill. Republican votes were assumed to be influenced by the senator's constituency, the minority leader, the minority whip, the ranking minority committee member, the policy committee chairman, and the President.

The equations were altered for some senators. If both senators from a state were of the same party, the senior one was assumed to influence the junior one, but not vice versa. Some senators were assumed to be influenced also by notable liberals or conservatives with whom they were known to agree. The majority leader's vote was assumed to be a function of influences from his constituency, the President, the relevant committee chairman, and a median senator of his party.

Guttman scale analysis was used to measure the voting behavior of each senator on individual bills. Votes on Senate bills are complicated since senators must decide not only to pass or reject a bill but also whether or not to accept a number of proposed amendments. Thirty-six separate scales were constructed for bills that came before the Eighty-seventh Congress. Most of these were for multiple votes on single bills, but four included votes on more than one bill. The 5-point scale ranged from 0 to 4. The most

conservative position a senator could take was represented by 0. The votes used to construct the scales represented 46 percent of all the votes taken in 1961 and 36 percent of the 1962 votes.

Scales were also constructed for the President on the basis of analysis by the *Congressional Quarterly* of his speeches, messages, conferences, and other public statements. On the basis of this evidence the position of the President was rated on one scale for each bill. On a second scale a rating of 1 was given for each bill if the President had taken a public position on it, and a rating of 0 was given if he had not.

Constituency preferences for the separate states were estimated on the basis of demographic and regional characteristics. If a senator's votes corresponded to his constituency's preferences, constituency influence was assumed. Influences of party leaders, the President, regional and informal leaders, senior senators, and median senators were estimated from the coefficients of correlation between their voting behavior and that of individual senators.

A voting model for each senator could then be estimated, using his score on each of the 36 bills, his state's constituency variable, the two Presidential variables, scores of other senators, and scores of the committee members who influenced him.

Results for individual senators were statistically significant and accounted for a high percentage of the variance. Only two senators' models were not significant at the 0.5 level. Important regional differences were found, however. In general, the models predicted better for Southern Democrats than for Western Democrats, possibly because the Westerners are more inclined to trade their votes.

The most regularly significant variable for these senators was constituency, but it was less important for Democrats not from the South than for Southern Democrats and Republicans. In contrast, the influence of party leaders upon Democrats not from the South was greater than that upon Republicans and Southern Democrats. Some of this difference probably results from organizational differences between the two parties. At that time, also, Southern Democrats were out of sympathy with their party leadership. The influence of chairmen or leading members of the reporting committee was also significant. This reflects not only the political influence of committee chairmen but also the role of committee members as experts. The hypothesized influence of senior senators upon the junior senators from their state was confirmed. Variables that did not receive satisfactory confirmation were Presidential influence, influence of regional and informal leaders, a hypothesized monolithic Southern vote, and the hypothesized relationship between the majority leader's voting and that of the median senator.

The experimenters concluded that the results supported the hypothesis that senators develop standard routines for deciding how to vote on roll-call votes. The routine was found to be largely invariant with the type of legislation. The models generally work as well for foreign-aid and trade legislation as for civil rights and farm subsidies. It is also apparent that senators develop quite divergent individual models. They were responsive to different influences and weighted them differently. The findings did not, however, discriminate among several alternative theories that are offered to explain legislative voting.

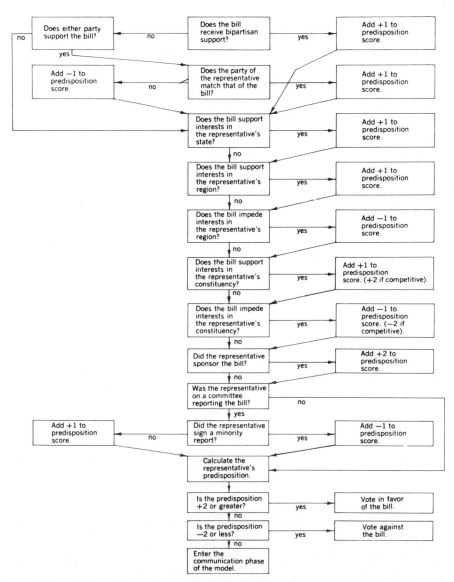

Fig. 11-19 The predisposition phase of the roll-call voting model. (From C. H. Cherryholmes & M. J. Shapiro. *Representatives and roll calls.* New York: Bobbs-Merrill, 1969, 60–61. Copyright © 1969, The Bobbs-Merrill Company, Inc. *Reprinted by permission of the publisher.*)

A simulation of voting in the United States House of Representatives. A computer simulation of roll-call voting in the House of Representatives determined votes of individual representatives by a two-stage process.[431] The first stage, the predisposition phase of the simulation, developed a predisposition score for each representative on each bill. The second phase simulated the communications that influence a representative to vote affirmatively or negatively on a given bill. Variables were selected on the basis of previous studies of legislative voting behavior.

The predisposition phase modeled the cognitive processes of each representative as he developed a predisposition to vote "yea" or "nay" on a bill. A representative considering a bill is assumed to take into account his own past voting behavior on bills of that type, the positive or negative position of individuals and groups in the House toward it, and its benefits and disadvantages for his own constituency and region.

The model represents members of the House, defined by status variables that include party, state delegation, region, constituency, personal ideology, committee assignment, leadership position, and seniority.

Inputs to the simulation were legislative bills or motions, defined by the following variables: party introducing the roll call, states favorably affected by it, regions favoring or opposing it, types of constituencies supporting or opposing it, the committee reporting the measure, members of the committee signing a minority report, whether a high support score would favor or oppose the vote, and the party, region, and state of the President.

Predisposition scores represented the sum of positive and negative influences on the congressman. If there was a match between the dimension of a variable on the bill and the corresponding characteristic of the congressman, either plus 1 or plus 2 was added, depending upon the variable. A mismatch resulted in minus 1 or minus 2. Figure 11-19 shows the predisposition phase of the model, with the scoring of the variables.

On the basis of the net predisposition score, representatives were divided between those who had made up their minds and those who were undecided. Those with scores of plus 2 or above entered the second, or communication, phase of the model as influencers. The greater the score, the greater their influence. Those who scored below plus 2 were targets of influence. Figure 11-20 shows the relationship between the two phases of the model.

The first stage of the model was deterministic. The second involved a stochastic process.[432] Since chance at least partly determines to whom a representative talks, conversation partners were chosen on a probabilistic basis.

Components of the second phase were again individual representatives. Input variables were the predispositions generated in the predisposition phase. Status variables of each representative were the same. The relationships included communication with the President, interaction with leaders of the House, interaction with party whips, rank-and-file interactions, and interactions with seniority leaders. Probabilities for conversation with the President and with all 434 of his colleagues were calculated for each man.

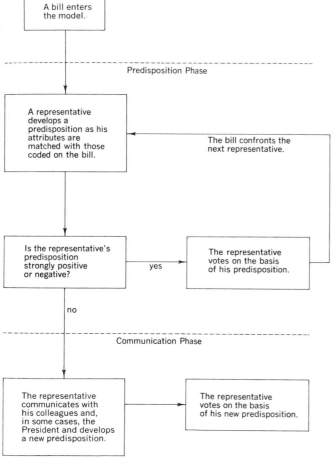

Fig. 11-20 Relationship between predisposition and communication phases of the roll-call voting model. (From C. H. Cherryholmes & M. J. Shapiro. *Representatives and roll calls.* New York: Bobbs-Merrill, 1969, 47. Copyright © 1969, The Bobbs-Merrill Company, Inc. *Reprinted by permission of the publisher.*)

The President, on the basis of previous findings, was given more contacts with members of his own party and from his own state and region than with others. He was assumed to interact with representatives to the same extent as leaders of the majority party, an assumption that may be reasonable if interactions with the President's staff are included. Interactions of a rank-and-file member of the House are shown in Fig. 11-21.

Figure 11-22 shows the communication phase of the model. The process concluded when all voting decisions were made.

The model was tested by simulating voting on two sorts of bills, 21 roll calls in which the role of the federal government was an issue and 27 foreign-affairs roll calls.[433] The role of the federal government was an issue in votes on aid to education, agriculture, urban affairs, due process, mental health, and regulation of communications—all issues in which states traditionally assert their rights. The final vote was determined by aggregating individual votes. The average percentage of individuals correctly simulated on the 21 roll calls on the role of the federal government was 84. On the 4 bills that had bipartisan sponsorship, 89 percent of votes were correctly simulated. For the 11 sponsored by the Democratic party, the percentage was 82, and for 6 Republican bills it was 85. Averages for all bills yielded 86 and 79 percent for Democratic and Republican sponsored bills, respectively.

The model performed most poorly on Southern representatives, only 78 percent of whose votes were correctly simulated for the 21 bills. This is readily explained by the fact that these congressmen form a coalition with Republicans on some bills, although they are coded like other Democrats. Eastern Republicans often join Democrats on liberal legislation. They were correctly simulated on only 83 percent of the roll calls. The Midwest, Far West, and West had, respectively, 88, 86, and 86 percent correctly simulated votes.

The simulated voting outcome was correct for all bills. The average difference between "yeas" and "nays"—the split in the vote—was 141 in the simulation and 109 in the actual situation. The coefficient of correlation between simulated and actual outcomes was .97.

The simulation performed best for the 5 bipartisan roll calls, with an accuracy of 98 percent. Accuracy was 82 percent for 13 bills sponsored by Democrats and 86 percent for 9 Republican-sponsored recommittal motions. The overall agreement between simulated and actual votes was 84 percent. Simulated yea–nay splits correlated .89 with the actual splits. The model performed better for the majority than for the minority party, for low-seniority than for high-seniority con-

gressmen, and, as in votes on the role of the federal government, for representatives not from the South than for Southern representatives.

A microanalytic demographic model. As the initial step in developing a complete model of the United States economy, Orcutt, Greenberger, Korbel, and Rivlin present a model of the household sector.[434] The households of a society are subcomponents at the level of the group; taken together, they form an important segment of the society. Their aggregated economic choices form one of the determinants of the economic variables of demand for goods and services through-

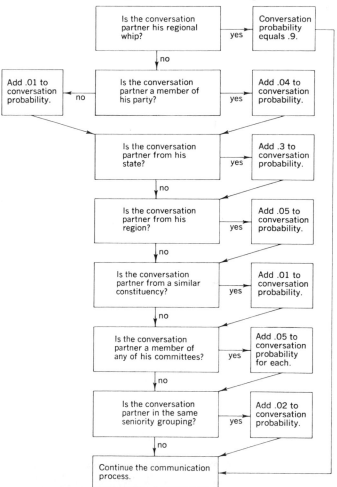

Fig. 11-21 Interactions of a rank-and-file member of the House of Representatives in the roll-call voting model. (From C. H. Cherryholmes & M. J. Shapiro. *Representatives and roll calls.* New York: Bobbs-Merrill, 1969, 47. Copyright © 1969, The Bobbs-Merrill Company, Inc. *Reprinted by permission of the publisher.*)

out the society. Their marital and reproductive choices determine the number and composition of the population.

The model described here is a population-projection model that shows the population in each period to be dependent upon the marriages, divorces, births, and deaths in the preceding period.

Composition of the initial population of the model conformed to the United States population as of April 1950, as reported in the United States census.[435] It consisted of 4,580 family units containing 10,358 individuals. Family units in this simulation are not the same as the households in the census, but consist of married couples and single people over 18. Each individual is modeled separately. Births, marriages, divorces, and deaths occur in proportion to those in the simulated society. They are also jointly distributed to represent members of the society according to color, age, marital status, and, for females, the number of children they have borne.

Information for coding individuals was drawn from the United States census figures and from survey materials.

The model is stochastic. For each of the coded characteristics, a function is developed that indicates the probability of that characteristic's applying to the person being modeled in a particular time period. The probability of death, for instance, is estimated by fitting a trend to mortality rates in each race-sex-age group from 1933 to 1954 and extrapolating the curve.[436] From this the experiments derived an estimate that a person of a particular age will die in a given month. With 2 races, 2 sexes, and 11 ages, this produced 44 equations for each month of the year.

Probability functions for the other characteristics were estimated in comparable ways. Marriage was calculated for both males and females. Mates were chosen from the sample, and marriage probabilities for each sex were divided by 2 to avoid doubling the number of marriages. Marriage probabilities were related to an economic indicator. This was done by taking the year 1950 as unity and calculating the ratio of marriages in each year to those in 1950.[437] This was considered analogous to a price index computed with constant weights.

It was assumed that only married couples had babies. Variables were age, number of children the woman had borne, length of time married, and time since the last child. The birth was assigned by a random drawing, and the sex of the child was selected according to known probabilities.

The simulation begins with the initial population stored on tape for computer processing. It has dimensions of population and time, both of which consist of a finite number of discrete intervals. Population intervals are adjacent but independent households; time intervals are sequential 1-month time periods. For each possible action of the household, such as marriage of an eligible daughter, the probability of alternative actions is computed from the function stored in the computer. This probability is compared with a random drawing, carried out by a subroutine. The action takes place if the drawing is less than the computed probability. This routine is repeated for every possible action of the household. All households are processed for each time period and are entered on an

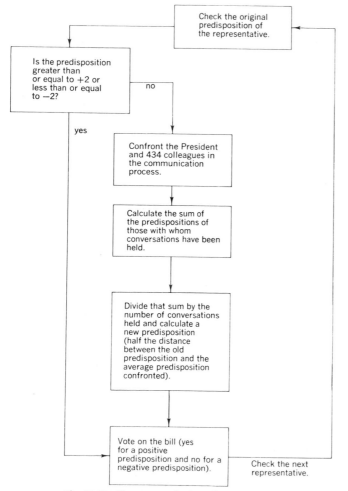

Fig. 11-22 The communication phase of the roll-call voting model. (From C. H. Cherryholmes & M. J. Shapiro. *Representatives and roll calls.* New York: Bobbs-Merrill, 1969, 83. Copyright © 1969, The Bobbs-Merrill Company, Inc. *Reprinted by permission of the publisher.*)

output tape, which becomes the input tape for the next "pass."

This simulation may be used in either of two modes.[438] Mode I adjusts the probabilities of events proportionally on each pass to make the simulated number of each kind of event track expected numbers based on summed predictions for members of the sample. In Mode II the probabilities used in the simulation are adjusted to numbers fed in to, rather than generated by, the program. It can therefore be made to track the economy being simulated.

An example of the results of simulations in Mode I is:

From the results obtained we see that a 1 percent increase in death probabilities starting with month 1 would result in deaths being about 1 percent higher during month 1–3 but only 0.91 higher by the month 10–12. The drop-off is presumably due to the higher death rate reducing over time the proportion of individuals remaining in the high-risk categories.

The effect on deaths of a 1 percent increase in birth probabilities starting with month 1 is initially zero, but by months 34–36 is shown as increasing deaths by 0.16 percent. The increase of deaths over time is presumably due to the gradual build-up of the proportion of very young children with their higher mortality. The effect of the 1 percent increase in birth probabilities is seen to result in nearly a 1 percent increase in births for all months 1–36. This was to be expected, because interval since previous birth did not enter into the model used for these sensitivity experiments.[439]

Models of energy use by societies. Great Britain and the German Democratic Republic, among other societies, use mathematical models to aid in making policy decisions concerned with provision of energy for the many societal processes that require it. This is a major concern of modern societies, particularly in the light of the possibility of shortages in sources of energy.

To represent the whole process of providing energy, a model must include processes of ingestor, converter, distributor, and matter-energy storage subsystems. Each of the several different sources from which energy is derived has different problems of input, handling, and distribution.

Like other models that deal with multivariate societal processes, energy models can be constructed with varying amounts of aggregation. For maximal usefulness, however, considerable detail is required. The power industry of the German Democratic Republic is developing a highly aggregated central model and separate, less aggregated models for coal, electric energy, gas, and crude oil.[440]

A set of coordinated models being developed for use in making energy-policy decisions in Great Britain has been reported in some detail.[441] Thirteen percent of the total domestic expenditure and 8 percent of the gross domestic fixed capital formation of that society are devoted to provision of power. Eight full divisions of the Ministry of Power have responsibility for advising the Minister for Industry on power problems. In addition to aiding these ministries, the model is expected to help the separate industries concerned with power production in planning their activities.

Objectives of the group developing the model are to produce a computable model of the energy economy of the United Kingdom that accounts for supplies and demands in several separate markets for each of the types of energy. The model must resolve the system for the current year, a single year ahead, the medium term (5 to 10 years) and the long term (up to 30 years ahead).[442]

Many power problems lend themselves to linear programming because they can be conceptualized as optimization problems (see pages 722 and 723). This is the type of mathematics used in the German model mentioned above. The British set of models includes a submodel that represents demand and four supply models for gas, electricity, coal, and petroleum. These are organized in such a way that they can eventually be integrated. Each of the four main industries of the supply models takes primary energy—coal, oil, natural gas, nuclear fuel, hydropower, or other—and sells it to final consumers in the form of various fuel products.

The technique used in the demand submodel is multiple linear regression. It is a stochastic model. Demand is projected separately for nine types of final users, in each case using the method found most appropriate for the data and the historic behavior of the market. The nine types of final users are domestic, iron and steel, other industry, public administration, miscellaneous and agriculture, transport (rail), transport (road), transport (water), and transport (air). Demands for primary fuel for conversion to secondary forms of energy are not a part of the model.

The second phase of the model represents the ideal choice of fuel for each sort of consumer in order to obtain a given total rate of energy input. It is assumed that the consumer can adjust his buying of fuels immediately and has no need to buy or install alternative equipment to use a different fuel. In this case the quantity of any fuel purchased would be determined by its price.

The third phase of the model represents actual market shares and shows that actual purchasing behavior is adjusted toward the ideal but that only a certain proportion of consumers change their fuel-using equipment in any year.

The electric power model represents the principal investment decisions of the industry concerning the types of plants to be built to meet the ever-growing demand for electricity. For each new generating station, variables of the model represent its capacity, uses to be made of it over its lifetime, and what fuel it will use. The total cost of adding any new capacity to the system is evaluated from data about the capital cost, running cost, and fuel cost of a particular type of station. From among the possible combinations of plants that could be used, the model makes a choice that minimizes the total cost of meeting the demands made on the system. In order to do this, one must know the future load and pattern of demand, existing capacity, physical characteristics of plants such as the sort of fuel they burn, their thermal efficiency, and any predetermined order in which plants must be built. In addition, detailed costs and other financial data, such as discount rates and depreciation pattern, as well as minimum or maximum constraints on quantities of fuel, must also be determined.

The program operates under a number of constraints, including the requirements that demand for electricity always be met and that sufficient excess be available to avoid the risk of lack of electricity resulting from plant failure. If plutonium is the fuel, it must be kept in positive balance. Fast reactors cannot be introduced unless there is sufficient plutonium available to them from thermal reactors.

The program analyzes data for selected years and briefer temporal units. States of variables between these years can be determined from the model by interpolation. The model can output the following information for a system that can operate at minimal cost: number of new plants built in each year studied, amount of electricity generated by each plant type in each year, quantities of fuel used in each year, capital and operating costs in each year, production and consumption of plutonium between selected years, estimates of the marginal costs of different patterns of load increment, and availability of the system in each year.

A feedback model. Another model analyzes segregation of blacks and whites in school systems of the United States as controlled by a positive feedback circuit, described by a set of differential equations.[443] Populations of persons exist in which tendencies toward two mutually exclusive activities are continuously distributed. The tendency may be represented by a value Φ. If a person prefers activity A to activity B, Φ is greater than 0. If he prefers B to A, Φ is less than 0. And if he is indifferent, Φ equals 0.

As Rashevsky applied this model to racial segregation in schools, a positive value of Φ denotes antiblack feeling, and a negative value denotes antiwhite feeling. Since the latter attitude is unlikely in a white

population, only values equal to, or greater than, 0 are considered in the model.

On the assumption that segregation of schools indoctrinates young white children in antiblack feelings, an index of segregation is developed. It shows segregation to be equivalent to the ratio of the number of segregated schools in a region to the number of unsegregated ones. The set of differential equations shows the reaction of such a system to a court ruling abolishing segregation and to educational effects upon the entire population. Both of these bring the system to an equilibrium point at which $\Phi = 0$. In the case of legislated or administratively decreed social change, however, it is necessary for the enforcement to last longer than a certain time, or the system will return to its segregated state.

(d) *Living system–computer interactions.* Few models of this class exist which simulate societal systems. The several interesting game simulations in which individual people or small groups enact the roles of societal deciders are concerned with interactions among societies and are therefore simulations of supranational systems.

A game simulation in which teams make decisions concerned with societal resources in a region of the United States was developed for the Environmental Protection Agency to give practice to regional decision makers.[444] Participants in the game are assigned responsibility for allocating the major economic, social, governmental, and water resources for a system that simulates a particular region of a society.

A computer program represents the characteristics of the real system. At the start of each game the initial configuration of relevant variables is specified by the director. He may include outside influences such as state or federal aid or regulations of state or federal governments. The computer responds to decisions made by participating teams with detailed information on their effects on such variables as pollution, housing selection, employment, shopping, and leisure activities. Each cycle of the simulation represents the passage of a year, and the simulation may be run for as many cycles as the users wish.

This simulation is not intended to be predictive. Its correspondence with the real system is not close. It permits the users to apply their own sets of objective and subjective criteria on the basis of a set of indicators and measures produced during the game.

7. Conclusions

Societies are readily conceptualized as systems. Parsons, Levy, and Etzioni in sociology; Easton, Deutsch, and Singer in political science; Leontief in economics;

and Chapple, Coon, and White in anthropology, among many others, have used system concepts or developed theories of societies as systems.

At this level, theories usually give little explicit recognition to matter-energy processing subsystems. Among the information processing subsystems, the decider receives by far the greatest emphasis. In the light of the neglect of other subsystems, it is probably undue emphasis. Internal transducing and channel and net processes have also received a good deal of attention.

For a decade or two the study of societies as systems has been dominated in several disciplines by the abstracted system concepts of Parsons and others, with results at this level similar to those identified at the level of the organization (see pages 19, 20, 598, and 765). That is, variables of the system under consideration have been neglected in favor of variables relating to persons occupying roles in it. Matter-energy processing by societies has been underemphasized. Quantification has been infrequent. In recent years, however, the theoretical emphasis seems to be changing.

Analysis of societies in terms of my conceptual system shows them to have all the critical subsystems or to be clearly parasitic upon, or symbiotic with, other living systems for any subsystem processes they lack. Hypothesis 2-3 (see page 92) states that the more isolated a system is, the more totipotential it must be. A correlate of this may be that as the population of a society increases and as the distances between it and other societies decrease, its totipotentiality also decreases because it has increasingly less of the resources necessary for totipotentiality. As such processes go on throughout the world, all societies have more and more trouble meeting their needs without developing interdependencies with other countries for both matter-energy and information. Consequently, the decider processes of some societies are penetrated by components of other societies (see page 800).

Modern societies have difficulty with control and guidance of subsystem processes. Some societies, like dictatorships, may be overcontrolled. Others, like Bangladesh, lack coordination of their processes. Still others, like Northern Ireland and the United States, have high rates of crime or antisocial behavior. The governments of modern societies are expected to provide many more services than they have given previously. Health care, welfare, education, and social security have been centralized at the society level only in the twentieth century. Demands are also made upon national central deciders to regulate economic and financial affairs that were previously left to an unregulated market. The efficiency of such operations is usually less than it could be, particularly in large and complex societies, and, as Hypothesis 3.3.7.2-17 (see page 101) states, a system cannot survive unless it makes decisions that maintain the functions of all its subsystems at a sufficiently high efficiency and their costs at a sufficiently low level that there are more than enough resources to keep it operating satisfactorily.

A number of cross-level hypotheses suggest research which might lead to increased effectiveness and lowered costs in meeting such demands. Hypothesis 3.3-1 (see page 94), which relates survival of a system to its committing a high percentage of its resources to information flows controlling system processes, may be confirmable at this level. Coordination of the complex processes of modern societies may well require more channel and net processing, particularly the operation of feedback loops, which, as Hypothesis 3.3.3.2-12 (see page 97) says, facilitate processes that reduce error. Hypothesis 5.2-14 (see page 107) states that conflict among subsystems or components may be increased by their segregation from one another. Hypothesis 5.2-17 (see page 107) states that conflict may be increased by mutual dependence of two or more subsystems or components on a single limited input or store of matter-energy or information. Hypothesis 5.2-18 (see page 107) states that conflict may be increased by necessary interdependence in timing of processes of two or more subsystems or components. And Hypothesis 5.2-26 (see page 108) states that conflict may be increased if the priorities of a system's multiple purposes and goals are not clearly known by all components or subsystems. All these hypotheses may be confirmed at this level, shedding light on some sources of internal strains in societies.

Hypothesis 5.2-9 (see page 106) says that heterogeneous components in a system adjust to one another best if they group together into two or more partially autonomous components on the basis of similarities. Hypothesis 5.4.3-2 (see page 109) says that as systems grow, the components become increasingly independent in decision making. And Hypothesis 5.4.3-9 (see page 109) says that if all relevant information flows to all components of the decider, the more decentralized a system's decider is, the better will be the interactions in the system. All three of these hypotheses deal with effects of integration or decentralization of decider processes on system functions. They are worth evaluating at this level in order to determine whether they state principles of optimal organization of the decider subsystem—the government of a society.

Societies as presently organized seem to be enormously vulnerable to disruption. Many recent examples can be found of *coups d' état* in which the government of a nation has been taken over by surprisingly small numbers of determined people. The Russian Revolution is a striking example. The repeated changes of regime in several Latin American countries are other examples. Apparently, control by others of only a few key components of a nation can render the government helpless. This fact may partially disconfirm for societies Hypothesis 5.2-12 (see page 107), which states that more complex systems, which contain more different components, each of which can adjust against one or more specific environmental stresses and maintain in steady state one or more specific variables not maintained by any other component, if they adequately coordinate the processes in their components, survive longer on the average than less complex systems.

Many other important questions suggest themselves for research at this level. Among them are the following: Are the materials learned by a society those which have primacy, recency, and frequency of presentation, as at the organism level? How is learning by societies like learning by individual persons, and how does it differ? Are there practical ways to apply learning theory to educate or "propagandize" total nations? Do deciders of societies make riskier decisions than individual persons? If so, does this help to confirm Hypothesis 3.3.7.2-21 (see page 102), which states that the higher the level of a system, the more correct or adaptive its decisions are?

Better estimates of normal values of many variables are needed at this level. Lack of norms makes it difficult to determine whether a given system is operating normally. Pathology of societies can now be diagnosed only when it is extreme.

A major essential for the advancement of system science at the societal level is that social scientists develop a consensus on what subsystems are essential in every society. There is agreement among scientists on the essential subsystems at the levels of the cell, the organ, and the organism. Similar agreement is needed at levels above the organism. Such consensus must also be sought on the major variables of each of these subsystems, and many multivariant studies of the relations among such variables must be carried out. Examples of such studies in this chapter are those of Cattell, which I discuss on pages 760 and 761. When we develop consensus on the subsystems of the society and the major variables, we should then press forward to similar consensus on social indicators that measure these societal variables.

More quantitative studies are required concerning all aspects of social systems. Far too few such researches have been reported in this chapter because far too few exist. There is much wisdom about how parts of societies interact. There are many useful essays on policy. There are many naturalistic observations, case histories, and important qualitative analyses. Examples of these are seen in the sections in this chapter on decider processes and on matter-energy and information internal adjustment processes. Much of this scholarly work is fascinating and insightful. But it is not quantitative.

This is not to say that this field lacks important quantitative materials. In addition to Cattell's multivariate analyses and Deutsch's work comparing rates of information transmissions across societal boundaries and inside them (see page 772), there are many public opinion polls with quantitative sophistication. There are societal models and simulations and also econometric analyses. Social indicators are constantly being developed and applied to measure social variables quantitatively.

The governments of most nations now collect statistics which can serve as societal indicators on their economy and on the health and education of their people, as well as on demographic variables like population growth and population distribution within their territory. The volume of governmental statistics of all sorts of numerous countries is great. These statistics show present states of the system and, when plotted over time, may reveal trends that can be used to forecast future system behavior. They constitute valuable sources of data for quantitative researches on societies. Certain important societal processes, however, still are not measured by satisfactory indicators (see page 751).

Except for economics, present-day social sciences lack the solid theoretical base and precise methodology necessary for understanding and conceptualizing the system so that these indicators can be useful in producing desirable social change. Perhaps general living systems theory can contribute to this.

Models and simulations are put to practical use in quantitative studies at this level, probably more than at any other. Governments all over the world employ economic models and models of specific processes for which planning is necessary. The simulations are generally based on a systems approach. Systems science consequently has a major opportunity now to contribute to better social planning in all nations. If more social scientists had the motivation and discipline to do the hard work necessary to identify important variables, construct indicators to measure them, and collect data in large quantities, as has been done at other levels, we would know vastly more about society than we do today. Such advances are needed because their potential is great for helping modern nations solve their vast and urgent problems.

NOTES AND REFERENCES

[1]Toynbee, A. J. *A study of history*. Vol. 1. (Abridg. by D. C. Somervell.) New York: Oxford Univ. Press, 1946, 211. Reprinted by permission.

[2]*Ibid.*, 8–34.

[3]Parsons, T., Shils, E. A., Allport, G. W., Kluckhohn, C., Murray, H. A., Sears, R. R., Sheldon, R. C., Stouffer, S. A., & Tolman, E. C. Some fundamental categories of the theory of action: a general statement. In T. Parsons & E. A. Shils (Eds.). *Toward a general theory of action*. Cambridge, Mass.: Harvard Univ. Press, 1951, 26. Reprinted by permission.

[4]Redfield, R. *The little community*. Chicago: Univ. of Chicago Press, 1955, 114.

[5]*Ibid.*, 117.

[6]Etzioni, A. *The active society*. New York: The Free Press, 1968, 65–73. Copyright © 1968 by The Free Press, a Division of the Macmillan Company.

[7]Crane, R. Personal communication.

[8]Moore, G. H. The analysis of economic indicators. *Sci. Amer.*, 1975, **232**(1), 17–23.

[9]Biderman, A. D. Social indicators and goals. In R. A. Bauer (Ed.). *Social indicators*. Cambridge, Mass.: M.I.T. Press, 1966, 87.

[10]*Ibid.*

[11]*Ibid.*, 98.

[12]Gross, B. M. The state of the nation: social systems accounting. In R. A. Bauer (Ed.). *Social indicators*. Cambridge, Mass.: M.I.T. Press, 1966, 167–168. Reprinted by permission.

[13]Sheldon, E. B. & Freeman, H. E. Notes on social indicators: promises and potential. *Policy Sciences*, 1970, **1**, 97–98.

[14]U.S. Department of Health, Education, and Welfare. *Toward a social report*. Washington: GPO, 1969.

[15]Office of Management and Budget, Executive Office of the President. *Social Indicators 1973*. Washington: GPO, 1973.

[16]Social Science Research Council. *Social indicators newsletter*. Washington: Social Science Research Council, Center for Coordination of Research on Social Indicators, 1974, 4.

[17]Sheldon, E. B. & Freeman, H. E. *Op. cit.*, 104. Reprinted from *Policy Sciences* (1970) vol. 1, no. 1, pp. 97–112, with permission of Elsevier Scientific Publishing Company, Amsterdam.

[18]Etzioni, A. & Lehman, E. Some dangers in "valid" social measurements. In B. W. Gross (Ed.). *The annals of social and political sciences*. September 1967, **373**, 1–15.

[19]Cohen, W. J. Education and learning. *Policy Sciences*, 1970, **1**, 79–101.

[20]Office of Management and Budget, Executive Office of the President. *Op. cit.*, 75–110.

[21]Sheldon, E. B. & Freeman, H. E. *Op. cit.*, 102–103. Reprinted from *Policy Sciences*, 1970, vol. 1, no. 1, pp. 97–112, with permission of Elsevier Scientific Publishing Company, Amsterdam.

[22]Land, K. C. *Social indicators*. Unpublished paper.

[23]Gross, B. M. *Op cit.*, 182.

[24]Land, K. C. *Op. cit.*

[25]Train, R. E. The quest for environmental indices. *Science*, 1972, **178**, 121.

[26]Gross, B. M. The coming general systems models of social systems. *Human Relat.*, 1967, **20**, 358–359. Cf. also Gross, B. M. The state of the nation: social systems accounting. *Op. cit.*, 211–213. Also Etzioni, A. *Op. cit.*, viii.

[27]Toynbee, A. J. *Op. cit.*, 35.

[28]*Ibid.*, 48–51.

[29]Steward, J. H. Cultural causality and law: a trial formulation of the development of early civilizations. *Amer. Anthropol.*, 1949, **51**, 1–27.

[30]Naroll, R. A preliminary index of social development. *Amer. Anthropol.*, 1956, **58**, 687–715. Cf. also Tatje, T. J. & Naroll, R. Two measures of societal complexity: an empirical cross-cultural comparison. In R. Naroll & R. Cohen (Eds.). *A handbook of method in cultural anthropology*. Garden City, N.Y.: Doubleday, 1970, 766–833.

[31]Freeman, L. C. & Winch, R. F. Societal complexity: an empirical test of a typology of societies. *Amer. J. Sociol.*, 1957, **62**, 461–466.

[32]*Ibid.*, 464.

[33]Coon, C. S. *A reader in general anthropology*. New York: Henry Holt, 1948, 611–614.

[34]Carneiro, R. L. Scale analysis, evolutionary sequences, and the rating of cultures. In R. Naroll & R. Cohen (Eds.). *A handbook of method in cultural anthropology*. Garden City, N.Y.: Doubleday, 1970, 836.

[35]*Ibid.*, 837.

[36]*Ibid.*, 838–848.

[37]Lomax, A. & Berkowitz, N. The evolutionary taxonomy of culture. *Science*, 1972, **177**, 228–239.

[38]*Ibid.*, 229.

[39]Cattell, R. B. The principal culture patterns discoverable in the syntal dimensions of existing nations. *J. soc. Psychol.*, 1950, **32**, 215–253. Cf. also Cattell, R. B. The dimensions of culture patterns by factorization of national characters. *J. abnorm. soc. Psychol.*, 1949, **44**, 443–469. Also Cattell, R. B., Breul, H., & Hartman, H. P. An attempt at more refined definition of the cultural dimensions of syntality in modern nations. *Amer. sociol. Rev.*, 1952, **17**, 408–421.

[40]Cattell, R. B. The principal culture patterns discoverable in the syntal dimensions of existing nations. *Op. cit.*, 243–249.

[41]Office of Management and Budget, Executive Office of the President. *Standard industrial classification manual*. Washington: GPO, 1972, 5–7.

[42]Levy, M. J., Jr. *The structure of society*. Princeton, N.J.: Princeton Univ. Press, 1952, 197.

[43]Parsons, T. & Smelser, N. J. *Economy and society*. Glencoe, Ill.: Free Press, 1946, 6–53.

[44]*Ibid.*, 14–16, 54.

[45]Chapple, E. D. & Coon C. S. *Principles of anthropology*. New York: Henry Holt, 1942, 1322. Also Neel, J. V. Lessons from a "primitive" people. *Science*, 1970, **170**, 816.

[46]Etzioni, A. *Op. cit.*, 328.

[47]*Ibid.*, 530.

[48]*Ibid.*

[49]Lévi-Strauss, C. Social structure. In A. L. Kroeber (Ed.). *Anthropology today: an encyclopedic inventory*. Chicago: Univ. of Chicago Press, 1953, 536.

[50]Deutsch, K. W. Shifts in the balance of communication flows: a problem of measurement in international relations. *Publ. Opin. Quart.*, 1956, **20**, 145–152.

[51]Stewart, J. Q. Demographic gravitation: evidence and applications. *Sociometry*, 1948, **11**, 31–58.

[52]Federal Highway Administration, Department of Transportation. *Department of Transportation News FHWA 78-75*. Washington: Aug. 27, 1975, 1–2.

[53]Bishop, E. & the Editors of *Life*. *Brazil*. New York: Time, Inc., 1962, 29. Reprinted by permission of Time-Life Books.

[54]Davies, E. A. J. Pipelines. *Britannica Book of the Year, 1971*. Chicago: Encyclopaedia Britannica, 1971, 737.

[55]Burck, G. Transportation's troubled abundance. *Fortune*, 1971, **84**(1), 61.

[56]Mitchell, J. *Lüchow's German Cookbook*. Garden City, N.Y.: Doubleday, 1952, 157.

[57]Burck, G. *Op. cit.*, 59–60.

[58]Lessing, L. New ways to more power with less pollution. *Fortune*, 1970, **82**(5), 80–81.

[59]Burck, G. *Op. cit.*, 59.

[60]White, L. A. *The science of culture*. New York: Grove Press, 1949, 369.

[61]Cook, E. The flow of energy in an industrial society. *Sci. Amer.*, September 1971, **224**(3), 135. Reprinted by permission of *Scientific American* and W. H. Freeman and Company Publisher.

[62]Leontief, W. *Studies in the structure of the American economy*. New York: Oxford Univ. Press, 1953, 299–300. Reprinted by permission.

[63]Rose, D. J. Controlled nuclear fusion: status and outlook. *Science*, 21 May 1971, **172**, 803.

[64]Williams, R. G. Metabolism in muscular activity. In C. H. Best & N. B. Taylor (Eds.). *The physiological basis of medical practice*. (7th ed.) Baltimore: Williams & Wilkins, 1961, 878.

[65]Wilson, M. and the Editors of *Life*. *Energy*. New York: Time, Inc., 1963, 124.
Cf. also Rose, D. J. *Op. cit.*, 807.
Also Alexander, T. The hot new promise of thermonuclear power. *Fortune*, 1970, **81**(6), 130.

[66]Mayer, L. A. Why the U.S. is in an "energy crisis." *Fortune*, 1970, **82**(5), 75.

[67]U.S. Bureau of Mines. *Minerals yearbook, 1969*. Vol. 1. Washington: GPO, 25.

[68]Alexander, T. *Op. cit.*, 132.

[69]Kurtz, S. (Ed.). *New York Times encyclopedic almanac, 1970*. New York: New York Times Book & Educational Division, 1969, 654.

[70]Leontief, W. *Essays in economics: theories and theorizing*. New York: Oxford Univ. Press, 1966, 197–198. Reprinted by permission.

[71]Lee, R. & Henderson, L. J. Personal communication.

[72]Murdock, G. P. *Social structure*. New York: Macmillan, 1949.

[73]Chapple, E. D. & Coon, C. S. *Op. cit.*, 328.

[74]Whyte, W. F. A slum sex code. In R. Bendix & S. M. Lipset (Eds.). *Class, status and power*. Glencoe, Ill.: Free Press, 1953, 308–316.

[75]Kinsey, A. C., Pomeroy, W. B., & Martin, C. E. Social level and sexual outlet. In R. Bendix & S. M. Lipset (Eds.). *Class, status and power*. Glencoe, Ill.: Free Press, 1953, 300–308.

[76]Hollingshead, A. B. Class difference in family stability. In R. Bendix & S. M. Lipset (Eds.). *Class, status and power*. Glencoe, Ill.: Free Press, 1953, 284–292.

[77]Hollingshead, A. B. Selected characteristics of classes in a Middle Western community. In R. Bendix & S. M. Lipset (Eds.). *Class, status and power*. Glencoe, Ill.: Free Press, 1953, 213–224.

[78]Notestein, F. W. Class differences in fertility. In R. Bendix & S. M. Lipset (Eds.). *Class, status and power*. Glencoe, Ill.: Free Press, 1953, 271–281.

[79]Lévi-Strauss, C. *Op. Cit.*, 535.

[80]Bylinsky. G. The limited war on water pollution. *Fortune*, 1970, **81**(2), 103.

[81]Kraar, L. How the Japanese mount that export blitz. *Fortune*, 1970, **82**(3), 130.

[82]Deutsch, K. W. Personal communication.

[83]Calame, B. E. Nixon effort to elicit citizens' complaints falters at both ends. *Wall Street Journal*, Apr. 28, 1970, 1.

[84]Nielson, W. A. Attitude research and government. *J. soc. Issues*, 1946, **2**(2), 1–12.

[85]Unger, A. L. The public opinion reports of the Nazi party. *Publ. Opin. Quart.*, 1965, **29**, 565–582.

[86]Deutsch, K. W. Personal communication.

[87]Easton, D. *A systems analysis of political life*. New York: Wiley, 1965, 37–56.

[88]Rosenau, J. N. *National leadership and foreign policy: a case study in the mobilization of public support*. Princeton, N.J.: Princeton Univ. Press, 1963, 6.

[89]*Ibid.*, 7–8. Copyright © 1963 by Princeton University Press published for the Center of International Studies, Princeton University. Reprinted by permission of Princeton University Press.

[90]Hunter, F. *Top leadership, U.S.A.* Chapel Hill: Univ. of North Carolina Press, 1959, 189–191. Reprinted by permission.

[91]Bureau of the Census. *Statistical Abstract of the United States*. (94th ed.) Washington: U.S. Department of Commerce, Social and Economic Statistics Administration, 1973, 494–495.

[92]De Vito, S. N. (Postmaster, Louisville, Ky.) Personal communication.

[93]Griffith, B. C., John, M. J., & Miller, A. J. Informal contacts in science: a probabilistic model for communication process. *Science*, 1971, **173**, 164–165.

[94]*Ibid.*

[95]Marquis, D. G. & Allen, T. J. Communication patterns in applied technology. *Amer. Psychol.*, 1966, **21**, 1052–1060.

[96]*Ibid.*, 1057.

[97]Brown, G. W., Miller, J. G., & Keenan, T. A. *EDUNET*. New York: Wiley, 1967, 54–61.

[98]Roberts, L. G. National networks. In J. LeGates. Networks in higher education: proceedings of the EDUCOM Council Meeting Seminar. *Behav. Sci.*, 1971, **16**, 500.

[99]Stewart, J. Q. The development of social physics. *Amer. J. Physics*, 1950, **18**, 239–253.

[100]Rice, S. A. *Quantitative methods in politics*. New York: Knopf, 1928.

[101]Tuchman, B. W. *The guns of August*. New York: Macmillan, 1962, 195. © Barbara W. Tuchman 1962. Reprinted by permission of the Macmillan Company and Russell & Volkening, Inc.

[102]Barnett, H. G. *Innovation: the basis of cultural change*. New York: McGraw-Hill, 1953, 291–292.

[103]Katz, E. The social itinerary of technical change. *Human Organization*, **20**, 1961, 70–82.

[104]De Fleur, M. L. Mass communication and the study of rumor. *Sociol. Inquiry*, 1962, **32**, 51–70.

[105]Meier, R. L. *The measurement of social change*. Ann Arbor: Univ. of Michigan, Mental Health Research Institute, Preprint 24, January 1959.

[106]Kurtz, S. (Ed.). *Op. cit.*, 870.

[107]*Ibid.*, 875.

[108]Deutsch, K. W. *Nationalism and social communication*. New York: Wiley, 1953, 70.

[109]Hoijer, H. The relation of language to culture. In A. L. Kroeber (Ed.). *Anthropology today: an encyclopedic inventory*. Chicago: Univ. of Chicago Press, 1953, 558.

[110]Sapir, E. The status of linguistics as a science. In D. G. Mandlebaum (Ed.). *Selected writings of Edward Sapir in language, culture and personality*. Los Angeles: Univ. of California Press, 1951, 160–166.
Also Whorf, B. L. (Ed. by J. B. Carroll.) *Language, thought, and reality: selected writings of Benjamin Lee Whorf*. Cambridge, Mass.: M.I.T. Press, 1956.

[111]Hoijer, H. *Op. cit.*, 560. Copyright 1953 by the University of Chicago. Reprinted by permission from University of Chicago Press.

[112]Jung, C. G. *The collected works of C. G. Jung: the archetypes and the collective unconscious*. Vol. 9. New York: Pantheon, 1959.

[113]Wallace, A. F. C. Culture and cognition. *Science*, 1962, **135**, 356.

[114]Forrester, J. W. *Urban dynamics*. Cambridge, Mass.: M.I.T. Press, 1969, 112. Reprinted by permission.

[115]Katona, G. *The role of ideas in social change*. (Paper read at Conference on Social Change, May 1959.) Ann Arbor: Univ. of Michigan, Survey Research Center, 1959, 2.
Cf. also Katona, G. *Psychological economics*. New York: Elsevier, 1975.

[116]*Ibid.*, 3.

[117]Toynbee, A. J. *Op cit.*, 49.

[118]Cattell, R. B. The principal culture patterns discoverable in the syntal dimensions of existing nations. *Op cit.*, 222–223.

[119]*Ibid.*, 241–242.

[120]Toynbee, A. J. *Op. cit.*, 140.

[121]Busch, A. E. *Equating information with currency*. (Keynote address at 1966 International Visual Communications Congress, Nov. 5, 1966.) Los Angeles: Keuffel & Esser Co., 1966, 6–7.

[122]*Ibid.*, 9.

[123]Mead, M. National character. In A. L. Kroeber (Ed.). *Anthropology today: an encyclopedic inventory*. Chicago: Univ. of Chicago Press, 1953, 644, 645. Copyright 1953 by the University of Chicago. Reprinted by permission from University of Chicago Press.

[124]Busch, A. E. *Op. cit.*, 6.

[125]*Ibid.*, 3–4. Reprinted by permission.

[126]*Ibid.*, 8.

[127]Kurtz, S. (Ed.). *Op. cit.*, 839.

[128]*Ibid.*, 861.

[129]Neustadt, R. E. *Presidential power*. New York: Wiley, 1960, 15.

[130]Rosenau, J. Pre-theories and theories of foreign policy. In R. B. Farrell (Ed.). *Approaches to comparative and international politics*. Evanston, Ill.: Northwestern Univ. Press, 1966, 27–92.

[131]Blong, C. K. *Political systems, external penetration and foreign policy behavior*. (Paper prepared for delivery to the Panel on Systems Theory: Applications in International Relations at the meeting of the Society for General Systems Research, Mid-Atlantic States Division, American University, Washington, Apr. 14, 1973.)

[132]Holmes, O. W., Jr. *The common law*. Boston: Little, Brown, 1881, 43. Reprinted by permission.

[133]Etzioni, A. *Op. cit.*, 314–317, 357–359.

[134]*Ibid.*, 315.

[135]Shapley, L. S. & Shubik, M. A method of evaluating the distribution of power in a committee system. *Amer. pol. Sci. Rev.*, 1954, **48**, 787–792.

[136]Dahl, R. A. The supreme court as national policy-maker. In L. N. Rieselbach (Ed.). *The congressional system: notes and readings*. Belmont, Calif.: Wadsworth, 1970, 322.

[137]Etzioni, A. *Op. cit.*, 283–286.

[138]Easton, D. *Op. cit.*, 21.

[139]Etzioni, A. *Op. cit.*, 124.

[140]Kluckhohn, C. M. Toward a comparison of value-emphases in different cultures. In L. D. White (Ed.). *The state of the social sciences*. Chicago: Univ. of Chicago Press, 1956, 118.

[141]*Ibid.*, 120–126.

[142]*Ibid.*, 126.

[143]Parsons, T. & Shils, E. A., with the assistance of Olds, J. Values, motives, and systems of action. Part 2. In T. Parsons & E. A. Shils (Eds.). *Toward a general theory of action*. Cambridge, Mass.: Harvard Univ. Press, 1951, 76–91.

[144]Gross, B. M. The state of the nation: social systems accounting. *Op. cit.*, 207.

[145]Etzioni, A. *Op. cit.*, 265.

[146]Lipset, S. M. *The first new nation: the United States in historical and comparative perspective*. New York: Basic Books, 1963, 2.

[147]Gross, B. M. National planning: findings and fallacies. *Publ. Admin. Rev.*, 1965, **25**, 265.

[148]Biderman, A. D. *Op. cit.*, 86.

[149]Katz, M. Decision-making in the production of power. *Sci. Amer.*, September 1971, **224**(3), 192. Reprinted by permission of *Scientific American* and W. H. Freeman and Company Publishers.

[150]Gross, B. M. The state of the nation: social systems accounting. *Op. cit.*, 169.

[151]Machiavelli. *The prince*. (Trans. by W. K. Marriott.) In R. M. Hutchins (Ed.). *Great books of the Western world*. Vol. 23. Chicago Encyclopaedia Britannica, 1952, 31–32. Reprinted by permission.

[152]*Ibid.*, 32. Reprinted by permission.

[153]Sorensen, T. C. *Kennedy*. New York: Harper & Row, 1965, 682.

[154]*Ibid.*, 685. Reprinted by permission.

[155]*Ibid.*, 705.

[156]Etzioni, A. *Op. cit.*, 270–273.

[157]*Ibid.*, 282–284.

[158]*Ibid.*, 286–288.

[159]Crosskey. A. A. *Politics and the Constitution in the history of the United States*. Chicago: Univ. of Chicago Press, 1953, 428–437.

[160]Eisenhower, D. D. *Mandate for change*. Garden City, N.Y.: Doubleday & Company Inc., 1963, 133.

[161]Cochran, T. C. & Andrews, W. (Eds.). *Concise dictionary of American history*. New York: Scribner, 1962, 127.

[162]Sorensen, T. C. *Op. cit.*, 389–390. Reprinted by permission.

[163]Johnson, L. B. *The vantage point*. New York: Holt, 1971, 40.

[164]Neustadt, R. E. *Op. cit.*, 20.

[165]Eisenhower, D. D. *Op. cit.*, 113. Copyright © 1963 by Dwight D. Eisenhower. Reprinted by permission from Doubleday & Company, Inc.

[166]Barber, J. D. *The presidential character*. Englewood Cliffs, N.J.: Prentice-Hall, 1972, 9–10.

[167]*Ibid.*, 12–13.

[168]*Ibid.*, 14.

[169]*Ibid.*, 209–343.

[170]*Ibid.*, 14.

[171]*Ibid.*, 58–98.

[172]*Ibid.*, 14.

[173]*Ibid.*, 174.

[174]*Ibid.*, 145–173.

[175]Schlesinger, A. M., Jr. *The coming of the New Deal*. Boston: Houghton Mifflin, 1959, 527–528.

[176]*Ibid.*, 523.

[177]*Ibid.*, 530–531.

[178]Johnson, L. B. *Op. cit.*, 370.

[179]*Ibid.*, 116.

[180]*Ibid.*

[181]*Ibid.,* 132.

[182]*Ibid.,* 137.

[183]*Ibid.,* 153.

[184]*Ibid.,* 112–153.

[185]*Ibid.,* 365–424.

[186]Manning, R. A light that failed. *Atlantic,* 1972, **230**(1), 33–34.

[187]Johnson, L. B. *Op. cit.,* 120–122.

[188]Ball, G. W. Top secret: the prophecy the president rejected. *Atlantic,* 1972, **230**(1), 36.

[189]*Ibid.,* 44–45. Copyright © 1972, by The Atlantic Monthly Company, Boston, Mass. Reprinted by permission.

[190]*Ibid.,* 49. Copyright © 1972, by The Atlantic Monthly Company, Boston, Mass. Reprinted by permission.

[191]Johnson, L. B. *Op. cit.,* 122.

[192]*Ibid.,* 123.

[193]*Ibid.,* 46–47.

[194]*Ibid.,* 124–125.

[195]*Ibid.,* 149.

[196]*Ibid.,* 151–153.

[197]Hobbs, E. H. The president and administration. In C. E. Lindblom (Ed.). *The policy-making process.* Englewood Cliffs, N.J.: Prentice-Hall, 1968, 74.

[198]Neustadt, R. E. *Op. cit.,* 146.

[199]Johnson, L. B. *Op. cit.,* 69–87.

[200]Anderson, J. W. *Eisenhower, Brownell, and the Congress.* University: Univ. of Alabama Press, 1964, 41.

[201]Schlesinger, A. M., Jr. *Op. cit.,* 518.

[202]Rieselbach, L. N. The nature of the congressional system. In L. N. Rieselbach (Ed.). *The congressional system: notes and readings.* Belmont, Calif.: Wadsworth, 1970, 38.

[203]*Ibid.*
Also Goodwin, G., Jr. Subcommittees: the miniature legislatures of Congress. In L. N. Rieselbach (Ed.). *The congressional system: notes and readings.* Belmont, Calif.: Wadsworth, 1970, 98.

[204]Rieselbach, L. N. Introduction: Congress as a political system. In L. N. Rieselbach (Ed.). *The congressional system: notes and readings.* Belmont, Calif.: Wadsworth, 1970, 21–24.

[205]Bauer, R. A., Pool, I. de S., & Dexter, L. A. The pressure groups. In L. N. Rieselbach (Ed.). *The congressional system: notes and readings.* Belmont, Calif.: Wadsworth, 1970, 286.

[206]Cureton, E. E. *Excursion into politics.* Unpublished paper.

[207]Wainer, H., Gruvaeus, G., & Zill, N., II. Senatorial decision making: I. The determination of structure. *Behav. Sci.,* 1973, **18**, 7–19.

[208]*Ibid.,* 7–8.

[209]Wainer, H., Zill, N., II, & Gruvaeus, G. Senatorial decision making: II. Prediction. *Behav. Sci.,* 1973, **18**, 20–26.

[210]Froman, L. A. & Ripley, R. B. Conditions for party leadership. In L. N. Rieselbach (Ed.). *The congressional system: notes and readings.* Belmont, Calif.: Wadsworth, 1970, 128–148, 135–136, 138.
Also Miller, W. E. & Stokes, D. E. Constituency influence in Congress. In L. N. Rieselbach (Ed.). *The congressional system: notes and readings.* Belmont, Calif.: Wadsworth, 1970, 442–446.

[211]Matthews, D. R. The folkways of the United States Senate. In L. N. Rieselbach (Ed.). *The congressional system: notes and readings.* Belmont, Calif.: Wadsworth, 1970, 157–159.

[212]Miller, W. E. & Stokes, D. E. *Op. cit.,* 445–446.

[213]Matthews, D. R. *Op. cit.,* 157–159.

[214]Anderson, J. W. *Op. cit.*

[215]*Ibid.,* 14, 48.

[216]*Ibid.,* 47–48.

[217]*Ibid.,* 96.

[218]*Ibid.,* 12.

[219]*Ibid.,* 29.

[220]*Ibid.,* 39.

[221]*Ibid.,* 59.

[222]*Ibid.,* 101–102.

[223]Frank, J. *Law and the modern mind.* New York: Tudor, 1936, 255. Reprinted by permission.

[224]Dahl, R. A. *Op. cit.,* 308. Reprinted by permission.

[225]Crosskey, A. A. *Op. cit.,* 493–508.

[226]Levy, B. H. *Cardozo.* Cleveland: Case Western Reserve Press, 1969, 307–309. Reprinted by permission.

[227]Dahl, R. A. *Op. cit.,* 312.

[228]*Ibid.,* 314–329.

[229]*Ibid.,* 313.

[230]*Ibid.,* 324. Reprinted by permission.

[231]Neustadt, R. E. *Op. cit.,* 43.

[232]Holsti, O. R. *Perceptions of time, perceptions of alternatives, and patterns of communication as factors in crisis decision-making.* Stanford, Calif.: Stanford Univ., Studies in International Conflict and Integration, 1964, 63.

[233]Sorensen, T. C. *Op. cit.,* 671.

[234]*Ibid.,* 709.

[235]*Ibid.,* 727.

[236]Cattell, R. B. The principal culture patterns discoverable in the syntal dimensions of existing nations. *Op. cit.,* 220.

[237]Kurtz, S. (Ed.). *Op. cit.,* 657.

[238]*Ibid.,* 651.

[239]Cook, E. *Op. cit.,* 139.

[240]*Ibid.,* 138.

[241]Kurtz, S. (Ed.). *Op. cit.,* 658.

[242]Casson, L. & the Editors of *Life. Ancient Egypt.* New York: Time, Inc., 1965, 31.

[243]*Ibid.,* 184.

[244]Hubbert, M. K. The energy resources of the earth. *Sci. Amer.,* 1971, **224**(3), 64, 68.

[245]*Ibid.,* 65.

[246]Hubbert, M. K. *Op. cit.,* 66–67.

[247]Hammond, A. L. Energy options: challenge for the future. *Science,* 1972, **177**, 876.

[248]Hubbert, M. K. *Op. cit.,* 67.

[249]Hammond, A. L. Solar energy: the largest resource. *Science,* 1972, **177**, 1088–1090.

[250]Lessing, L. *Op. cit.,* 132.

[251]Hubbert, M. K. *Op. cit.,* 67.

[252]Hammond, A. L. Geothermal energy: an emerging major resource. *Science,* 1972, **177**, 978–980.

[253]Hubbert, M. K. *Op. cit.,* 67–68.

[254]Meadows, D. H. Testimony before the Education Committee of the Massachusetts Great and General Court on behalf of House Bill 3787, Mar. 31, 1971.

[255]Rose, D. J. *Op. cit.,* 797–808.
Also Metz, W. D. Magnetic containment fusion: what are the prospects? *Science,* 1972, **178**, 291–293.

[256]Rose, D. J. *Op. cit.,* 808. Copyright 1971 by the American Association for the Advancement of Science. Reprinted by permission.

[257]Toynbee, A. J. *A study of history.* Vol. 2 *Op. cit.,* 145.

[258]Crane, R. I. Aspects of social change in modern India. Unpublished paper, page 51.

[259]*Ibid.,* 54–55.

[260]Rappaport, R. A. The flow of energy in an agricultural society. *Sci. Amer.,* 1971, **224**(3), 129–132.

[261]Ward, B. & Dubos, R. *Only one earth.* New York: Norton, 1972, 60–63.

[262]Solow, R. M. The economist's approach to pollution and its control. *Science*, 1971, **173**, 500.

[263]Ayres, R. U. & Kneese, A. V. Production, consumption, and externalities. *Amer. econ. Rev.*, 1969, **59**(3), 284–285. Reprinted by permission.

[264]Bohn, H. L. & Cauthorn, R. C. Pollution: the problem of misplaced wastes. *Amer. Sci.*, 1972, **60**, 561–565.

[265]Solow, R. M. *Op. cit.*, 499.

[266]*Ibid.*, 499–503. Copyright 1971 by the American Association for the Advancement of Science. Reprinted by permission.

[267]Bylinsky, G. Metallic menaces in the environment. *Fortune*, 1971, **83**(1), 110–113.

[268]Bylin, J. E. Oregon's tough policy revives the Willamette: pollution drops by 90%. *Wall Street Journal*, 1972, **180**(80), 1, 31.

[269]Bockris, J. O'M. A hydrogen economy. *Science*, 1972, **176**, 1323.
Cf. also Lessing, L. The coming hydrogen economy. *Fortune*, 1972, **86**(5), 138–146.

[270]Verne, J. *L'île mystérieuse. L'abandonné. Deuxième partie.* Paris: Collection Hetzel, n.d., 162–163. (Trans. as: *The mysterious island.* New York: Scribner, 1920, 252.)

[271]Bohn, H. L. & Cauthorn, R. C. *Op cit.*, 565. Reprinted by permission, *American Scientist*, journal of Sigma Xi, The Scientific Research Society of North America, Inc.

[272]Rose, S. The economics of environmental quality. *Fortune*, 1970, **81**(2), 123.

[273]*Ibid.*

[274]Ward, B. & Dubos, R. *Op. cit.*, 58.

[275]Refuse Act of 1899. 33 U.S.C. 1899, Secs. 407, 407a, 411.

[276]National Environmental Policy Act of 1969. 42 U.S.C. 1970, Secs. 4321, 4331–4335, 4341–4347.

[277]Ward, B. & Dubos, R. *Op. cit.*, 117.

[278]Meadows, D. H. *Op. cit.*

[279]Ward, B. & Dubos, R. *Op. cit.*, 118. Reprinted by permission.

[280]Anon. The *Fortune* directory of the 300 largest industrial corporations outside the U.S. *Fortune*, 1975, **92**(2), 155–161.

[281]Wynne-Edwards, V. C. Self-regulating systems in populations of animals. *Science*, 1965, **147**, 1543–1548.

[282]Brown, D. & the Editors of *Life. Wild Alaska.* New York: Time, Inc., 1972, 134–135.

[283]Neel, J. V. *Op. cit.*

[284]*Ibid.*, 816–817.

[285]Langer, W. L. Checks on population growth: 1750–1850. *Sci. Amer.*, 1972, **226**(2), 92–99.

[286]Harcourt, D. G. & Leroux, E. J. Population regulation in insects and man. *Amer. Sci.*, 1967, **55**, 412.

[287]Mayer, L. A. U.S. population growth: would slower be better? *Fortune*, 1970, **81**(6), 82.

[288]Ward, B. & Dubos, R. *Op. cit.*, 152. Reprinted by permission.

[289]Mayer, L. A. U.S. population growth: would slower be better? *Op. cit.*, 166–168.

[290]Anon. As cidades: um dia será preciso dizer "lotadas"? *Realidade*, 1972, **7**(74), 210.

[291]Lampard, E. *Urban-rural conflict in the United States, 1870–1920.* 1959. Unpublished paper.

[292]Hauser, P. M. The census of 1970. *Sci. Amer.*, July 1971, **225**(1), 19.

[293]Mayer, L. A. U.S. population growth: would slower be better? *Op. cit.*, 83.

[294]Hauser, P. M. *Op. cit.*, 19.

[295]*Ibid.*, 18. Reprinted by permission of *Scientific American*.

[296]*Ibid.*

[297]Ward. B., & Dubos, R. *Op. cit.*, 90.

[298]*Ibid.*, 104–105.

[299]Anon. Brasilia. *Realidade*, 1972, **7**(74), 243–245.

[300]Mayer, L. A. U.S. population growth: would slower be better? *Op. cit.*, 83.

[301]Ward, B. & Dubos, R. *Op. cit.*, 94.

[302]*Ibid.*, 111.

[303]*Ibid.*, 90.

[304]*Ibid.*, 185.

[305]Mayer, L. A. U.S. population growth: would slower be better? *Op. cit.*, 83.

[306]Samuelson, P. A. *Economics.* (8th ed.) New York: McGraw-Hill, 1970, 37.

[307]*Ibid.*, 463–466.

[308]Leontief, W. *Essays in economics: theories and theorizing. Op. cit.*, 229.

[309]*Ibid.*, 238.

[310]*Ibid.*, 239.

[311]Ricardo, D. *Principles of political economy and taxation.* London: George Bill & Sons, 1903, 72.

[312]Samuelson, P. A. *Op. cit.*, 773–775.

[313]Kershaw, D. N. A negative-income-tax experiment. *Sci. Amer.*, 1972, **227**(4), 23.

[314]Samuelson, P. A. *Op. cit.*, 224.

[315]*Ibid.* Reprinted by permission.

[316]*Ibid.*, 215–217.

[317]*Ibid.*, 234–240.

[318]*Ibid.*, 281–301.

[319]Lekachman, R. Training a pleasant demon. *Saturday Review*, Mar. 6, 1971, 15–18.

[320]Anon. The new permissiveness calls for prudence. *Fortune*, 1973, **87**(2), 9.

[321]Beman, L. How the Brazilians manage their boom. *Fortune*, 1972, **86**(6), 110–114, 176, 178.

[322]Deutsch, K. W. *Politics and government.* Boston: Houghton Mifflin, 1970, 45–48.

[323]*Ibid.*, 48.

[324]Easton, D. *Op. cit.*, 275.

[325]Deutsch, K. W. *Politics and government. Op. cit.*, 56.

[326]Etzioni, A. *Op. cit.*, 484.

[327]*Ibid.*, 523–524.

[328]Rashevsky, N. Feedbacks in social systems. In M. C. Yovits, D. M. Gilford, R. H. Wilcox, E. Staveley, & H. D. Lerner (Eds.). *Research program effectiveness.* New York: Gordon and Breach, 1966, 389.

[329]*Ibid.*, 395–396. Reprinted by permission.

[330]Deutsch, K. W. *Politics and government. Op. cit.*, 146–147.

[331]Simon, H. A. *Models of man.* New York: Wiley, 1957, 79–80.

[332]Bauer, R. A. The nature of the task. In R. A. Bauer (Ed.). *Social indicators.* Cambridge, Mass.: M.I.T. Press, 1966, 6–7.

[333]Etzioni, A. *Op. cit.*, 509.

[334]Easton, D. *Op. cit.*, 427. Reprinted by permission.

[335]*Ibid.*, 371.

[336]Huxley, T. H. *Collected essays.* Vol. 9. *Evolution and ethics and other essays.* New York: Appleton, 1902, 1–116.

[337]Darwin, C. *The origin of species.* In R. M. Hutchins (Ed.). *Great books of the Western world.* Vol. 49. Chicago: Encyclopaedia Britannica, 1952, 4.

[338]Spencer, H. *Principles of sociology.* Vol. 1. New York: Appleton, 1896, 3–4.

[339]*Ibid.*, 56.

[340]Ginsberg, M. *Essays in sociology and social philosophy.* Vol. 1. *On the diversity of morals.* New York: Macmillan, 1957, 181–183.

[341]Cf. Kluckhohn, C. & Kroeber, A. L. Social and cultural evolution. In S. Tax (Ed.). *Evolution after Darwin.* Vol. 3.

Issues in evolution. Chicago: Univ. of Chicago Press, 1960, 214.

[342]Lomax, A. & Berkowitz, N. *Op. cit.*, 234. Copyright 1972 by the American Association for the Advancement of Science. Reprinted by permission.

[343]*Ibid.*, 232.

[344]Naroll, R. What have we learned from cross-cultural surveys? *Amer. Anthropol.*, 1970, **72**, 1247.

[345]*Ibid.*

[346]Rapoport, A. *Approaches to the study of total societies.* (Unpublished paper prepared for "Camelot" Program Conference on Theory and Methodology in the Study of Total Societies. Bureau of Social Science Research, July 28–29, 1965, Washington, D.C. page 9.)

[347]Emerson, A. E. Human cultural evolution and its relation to organic evolution of insect societies. In H. R. Barringer, G. I. Blanksten, & R. W. Mack (Eds.). *Social change in developing areas.* Cambridge, Mass.: Schenkman, 1965, 56.

[348]Kluckhohn, C. & Kroeber, A. L. *Op. cit.*, 209.

[349]Platt, J. Hierarchical growth. *Bull. atom. Sci.*, 1970, **26**, 2–4, 46–48.

[350]Emerson, A. E. *Op. cit.*, 56.

[351]Kluckhohn, C. & Kroeber, A. L. *Op. cit.*, 209.

[352]Naroll, R. What have we learned from cross-cultural surveys? *Op. cit.*, 1243–1247.

[353]*Ibid.*, 1246. Reproduced by permission of the American Anthropological Association from the *American Anthropologist*, 72: 1246, 1970.

[354]Toynbee, A. J. *A study of history.* Vol. 1. *Op. cit.*, 88.

[355]Toynbee, A. J. *A study of history.* Vol. 2. *Op. cit.*, 360–361.

[356]Linton, R. Present world conditions in cultural perspective. In R. Linton (Ed.). *The science of man in the world crisis.* New York: Columbia Univ. Press, 1945, 201–221.

[357]Kluckhohn, C. & Kroeber, A. L. *Op. cit.*, 209.

[358]White, L. A. *Op. cit.*, 361.

[359]*Ibid.*, 368.

[360]*Ibid.*
Cf. Kluckhohn, C. & Kroeber, A. L. *Op. cit.*, 229.

[361]White, L. A. *Op. cit.*, 4.

[362]Platt, J. *Op. cit.*, 4. Reprinted by permission of the *Bulletin of the Atomic Scientists.* Copyright © 1970 by the Educational Foundation for Nuclear Science.

[363]*Ibid.*

[364]*Ibid.*, 46.

[365]Deutsch, K. W. Social mobilization and political development. *Amer. pol. Sci. Rev.*, 1961, **55**, 493–514.

[366]Tanter, R. Toward a theory of political development. In R. Naroll & R. Cohen (Eds.). *A handbook of method in cultural anthropology.* Garden City, N.Y.: Doubleday, 1970, 116.

[367]Deutsch, K. W. Social mobilization and political development. *Op. cit.*, 503.

[368]Etzioni, A. *Op. cit.*, 7.

[369]*Ibid.*. 9–10.

[370]*Ibid.*, 7, 405–406, 503–540.

[371]Lomax, A. & Berkowitz, N. *Op. cit.*, 234.

[372]Copyright 1972 by the American Association for the Advancement of Science. Reprinted by permission.

[373]Hale, M. *The primitive origination of mankind. Ms. 14.* London: William Godbid, for William Shrowsbery at the Sign of the Bible in Duke-Lane, 1677, 205.

[374]Malthus, T. R. *An essay on the principle of population.* London: T. Bensley, 1803.
Cf. also Samuelson, P. A. *Op. cit.*, 28.

[375]Boulding, K. E. The Malthusian model as a general system. *Soc. and economic Studies*, 1955, **4**, 197.

[376]Samuelson, P. A. *Op. cit.*, 29.

[377]Hauser, P. M. *Op. cit.*, 17.

[378]Samuelson, P. A. *Op. cit.*, 31.

[379]Ward, B. & Dubos, R. *Op. cit.*, 117.

[380]Samuelson, P. A. *Op. cit.*, 33.

[381]Ward, B. & Dubos, R. *Op. cit.*, 116.

[382]Mayer, L. A. U.S. population growth: would slower be better? *Op. cit.*, 82.

[383]Naroll, R. S. & von Bertalanffy, L. The principle of allometry in biology and the social sciences. *Gen. Systems*, 1956, **1**, 76.

[384]Naroll, R. A preliminary index of social development. *Op. cit.*, 689.

[385]*Ibid.*, 695.

[386]Tatje, T. A. & Naroll, R. Two measures of societal complexity: an empirical cross-cultural comparison. In R. Naroll & R. Cohen (Eds.). *A handbook of method in cultural anthropology.* Garden City, N.Y.: Doubleday, 1970, 777.

[387]Deutsch, K. W., Burrell, S. A., Kann, R. A., Lee, M. Jr., Lichterman, M., Lindgren, R. E., Loewenheim, F. L., & Van Wagenen, R. W. *Political community and the North Atlantic area: international organization in the light of historical experience.* Princeton, N.J.: Princeton Univ. Press, 1957, 119. Copyright © 1957 by Princeton University Press. A publication of the Center for Research on World Political Institutions, Princeton University. Reprinted by permission of Princeton University Press.

[388]Etzioni, A. *Op. cit.*, 397–417.

[389]*Ibid.*, 397–399.

[390]Riker, W. H. & Schaps, R. Disharmony in federal government. *Behav. Sci.*, 1957, **2**, 276–290.

[391]Deutsch, K. W. *Nationalism and social communication. Op. cit.*, 156–162.

[392]Barnett, H. G., Broom, L., Siegel, B. J., Vogt, E. Z. Watson, J. B. Acculturation: an exploratory formulation. *Amer. Anthropol.*, 1954, **56**, 987–988.

[393]Etzioni, A. *Op. cit.*, 420.

[394]Murphy, R. F. & Steward, J. H. Tappers and trappers: parallel process in acculturation. *Econ. Develop. and cul. Change*, 1956, **4**, 335–353.

[395]Durkheim, E. Division of labor in society. (Trans. by G. Simpson.) Glencoe, Ill.: Free Press, 1947, 1–18, 353–373.

[396]Etzioni, A. *Op. cit.*, 618.

[397]*Ibid.*, 621.

[398]*Ibid.*, 635.

[399]Abkin, M. H. System simulation and policy-making for economic development. *Simulation Today,* no date, 7, 25.

[400]Orcutt, G. H., Greenberger, M., Korbel, J., & Rivlin, A. M. *Microanalysis of socioeconomic systems: a simulation study.* New York: Harper & Row, 1961, 287–289.

[401]Boguslaw, R. & Davis, R. H. Simulating national policy formation. *SDC Magazine*, 1965, **8**(4), 5–16.

[402]*Ibid.*, 7. Reprinted by permission.

[403]Samuelson, P. A. *Op. cit.*, 4.

[404]*Ibid.*, 249–250.

[405]*Ibid.*, 193, 357.

[406]Cohen, K. J. & Cyert, R. M. *Theory of the firm.* Englewood Cliffs, N.J.: Prentice-Hall, 1965, 45.

[407]*Ibid.*, 50–51.

[408]*Ibid.*, 166–174.

[409]*Ibid.*, 174–175.

[410]*Ibid.*, 187–281.

[411]Leontief, W. *Input–output economics.* New York: Oxford Univ. Press, 1966, 134.

[412]*Ibid.*, 156.

[413]Ulman, N. Divining the future. Firms rely increasingly on a computer model of economy in planning. *Wall Street Journal*, 1970, **60**, Feb. 17, 1. Reprinted by permission.

[414]Leontief, W. *Input–output economics. Op. cit.*, 184–206.

[415]Treml, V. C. A note on Soviet input–output tables. *Soviet Studies*, 1969, **21**, 21–34.

[416]Fisher, W. H. The anatomy of inflation: 1953–1975. *Sci. Amer.*, 1971, **225**(5), 15–21.

[417]Leontief, W. *Input–output economics. Op. cit.*, 41–67.

[418]*Ibid.*, 145–151.

[419]Leontief, W. An open dynamic system for long range projection of economic growth. *Artha Vyjnana*, 1967, **9**, 370–390.

[420]National Economics Division of the Office of Business Economics, U.S. Department of Commerce. Input–output structure of the U.S. economy. *Survey current Bus.*, 1969, **11**, 16.

[421]*Ibid.*, 24.

[422]Bennett, J. P. Simulating alternative economic futures. In D. D. Swarder (Ed.). *Systems and simulations in the service of society.* Simulation Councils Proc. Series, 1971, **1**(2), 15.

[423]Liebenberg, M., Hirsch, A. A., & Popkin, J. A quarterly econometric model of the United States: a progress report. *Survey current Bus.*, 1966, **46**(5) 13–39.

[424]*Ibid.*, 20.

[425]Bennett, J. P. *Op. cit.*, 16–17.

[426]Liebenberg, M., Hirsch, A. A., & Popkin, J. *Op. cit.*, 21–29.

[427]De Leeuw, F. & Gramlich, E. Staff economic study: the Federal Reserve-MIT econometric model. *Fed. Reserve Bull.*, 1968, **54**, 11–40.

[428]Bennett, J. P. *Op. cit.*, 17. Reprinted by permission.

[429]Liebenberg, M., Hirsch, A. A., & Popkin, J. *Op. cit.*, 16.

[430]Jackson, J. E. Statistical models of senator roll call voting. *Amer. pol. Sci. Rev.*, 1971, **65**, 467.

[431]Cherryholmes, C. H. & Shapiro, M. J. *Representatives and roll calls.* New York: Bobbs-Merrill, 1969.

[432]*Ibid.*, 63.

[433]*Ibid.*, 85–104, 121–139.

[434]Orcutt, G. H., Greenberger, M., Korbel, J., & Rivlin, A. M. *Op. cit.*, 45–284.

[435]*Ibid.*, 131–132.

[436]*Ibid.*, 66–71.

[437]*Ibid.*, 77–78.

[438]*Ibid.*, 373–375.

[439]*Ibid.*, 397. Reprinted by permission.

[440]Knop, H. Application of economic-mathematical methods for optimization of power industry of the GDR. *Proc. IIASA planning conf. on energy systems.* Laxenburg, Austria: International Institute for Applied Systems Analysis (IIASA), 1973, 223–237.

[441]Hutber, F. W. Modelling of energy supply and demand. *Proc. IIASA planning conf. on energy systems.* Laxenburg, Austria: International Institute for Applied Systems Analysis (IIASA), 1973, 126–175.

[442]*Ibid.*, 128.

[443]Rashevsky, N. Some cybernetic aspects of sociology: cybernetics of segregation. In N. Weiner & J. P. Schade (Eds.). *Progress in biocybernetics.* Vol. 2. Amsterdam: Elsevier, 1965, 186–199.

[444]Anon. The river basin model. Computer output. U.S. Environmental Protection Agency, Water Pollution Control Series 16110 FRU 12/71-12. Washington: Enviro. Metrics, December 1971.

The Supranational System

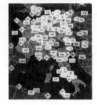

A supranational system is composed of two or more societies, some or all of whose processes are under the control of a decider that is superordinate to their highest echelons. "Suprasocietal" would be a more descriptive designation for this level since it would not imply that components were nations, a modern form of society. The term "supranational," however, has become accepted in political science. It will be used here to describe any type of system with societies as components.

The extent and duration of control of supranational deciders vary. No supranational system with a complete set of differentiated subsystem structures under control of its decider exists today. There is some question as to whether any of the empires of the past met such a criterion. The deciders of modern supranational systems ordinarily can make decisions which control only a limited set of processes.

Societies may interact without being parts of supranational systems. Mutual dependency, exchange of matter-energy and information, and joint deciding may confer many system characteristics upon international relationships, but if a superordinate decider is not in control, there is no concrete supranational system. In many systems a superordinate decider exists, but has little power. Nevertheless, I shall call such systems "supranational." This is a distinction like Kaplan's. He divides *international actors* into two sets: *national actors,* which are nations like France and Italy, and *universal actors,* which are blocs of nations (see pages 906 and 907).[1]

Such classifications differ from Etzioni's. He distinguishes between "international" and "supranational" on the basis of the power of the decider to control component deciders.[2] Even when a system has the form of a supranational system, if its decider subsystem is so weak that the decider of a society can get the upper hand when there is a conflict between them, it is not supranational in Etzioni's view. He therefore considers the United Nations to be "almost exclusively" international rather than supranational while I, in accordance with my basic definition, will treat it (and others like it in structure) as a supranational system, realizing that its decider has little capability of implementing many of its decisions.

In the absence of a supranational decider, decisions that affect several nations of the modern world must be made by international agreements or by adjustment processes among nations. This chapter is concerned with such international accommodations as well as with interactions of nations in supranational systems.

Differentiation of supranational systems from the mixed living and nonliving systems at levels above them presents no problem. The borderline between societies and supranational systems, on the other hand, is sometimes less obvious. For instance, federations (see page 908) may be societies or supranational systems, depending upon how their components interact with the suprasystem decider. If organizations, groups, and individual persons in the component societies have direct channels of communication with the highest echelon of the system's decider and if it, in turn, exerts significant direct control over them, the system is a society. If, on the other hand, the supranational echelon receives communications from, and outputs its control and guidance signals to, upper-echelon societal deciders only and if they control the components below them in the echelon structure, the system is supranational. Historically, the internal boundaries between echelons of successful supranational systems have tended to weaken, so that they have become more and more like societies, losing their supranational characteristics. The United States, for example, was initially a supranational system whose central decider had only specified powers, all residual powers belonging to the component states. But in the course of history the federal government has acquired more and more direct relationships with national nongovernmental organizations, groups, and individual citizens, and the system can now properly be called a "society."

As the world is now constituted, nations (often called "nation-states" by political scientists) are the dominant type of society. Most modern nations are highly totipotential, ordinarily possess the power to implement their decisions, and can prevent their components from seceding. Currently existing supranational systems, with nations as their components, are much less totipotential. They all lack one or more critical subsystems, usually those which process matter-energy, and they disperse those subsystem processes downward to the level of the society or below. Unlike societies, most of them have little power to enforce decisions or to restrain components that wish to separate from them.

An argument could be made that there is no supranational level of living systems, but that a supranational system is a transitional form in the history of those societies which grow by integration of a number of smaller societies into a new whole. A successful supranational system, in this view, is likely to become a society. Several present-day societies, including East and West Germany, Italy, Great Britain, Switzerland, the United States, and the Soviet Union, are unions of several previously independent societies. All retain some supranational characteristics.

I take the position that supranational systems, limited as they are today, and newer than systems at any other level, do constitute a level of living systems above that of the society.

All human societies exist in the total system of the earth and are subject to natural law. In recent years the need for cooperation among all societies in protecting this world suprasystem and using its resources prudently has become evident. Ward and Dubos write:

All these concerns with global air pollution lie beyond the effective protection of individual governments. It is no use one nation checking its energy use to keep the ice caps in place if no other government joins in. It is no use the devel-oped nations suggesting lower energy use just at the moment when the developing nations see increased use as their only exit from the trap of poverty. The global interdependence of man's airs and climates is such that local decisions are simply inadequate. Even the sum of all local separate decisions, wisely made, may not be a sufficient safeguard and it would take a bold optimist to assume such general wisdom. Man's global interdependence begins to require, in these fields, a new capacity for global decision-making and global care. It requires coordinating powers for monitoring and research. It means new conventions to draw up ground rules to control emissions from aircraft and to assess supersonic experiments. It requires a new commitment to global responsibilities. Equally, it needs effective action among the nations to make responsibility a fact. And all these necessities—for more research, better monitoring, stricter control, and more global action—are simply reinforced when we turn to man's other universal environment—the world of the seas and oceans.[3]

In this chapter I shall discuss this global suprasystem of our common worldwide environment as well as the structures and processes of supranational systems and other associations among societies.

1. Structure

The subsystems of supranational systems have as components member societies, represented by delegates who communicate the policies of their societies and act in accordance with instructions, or command signals, from them. Each societal component of a supranational system may be a part of many or all subsystems of the system. Or a single society, through its representatives, may constitute most or all of one subsystem. Rome, for example, was the decider for the entire Roman Empire.

Representatives of societies come together in groups, such as conferences, or in organizations, like the United Nations or the International Atomic Energy Agency (IAEA). These groups or organizations constitute the organizational structure of the supranational system.

Similar groups and organizations that lack the supranational echelon also include representatives of two or more societies. Official representatives of societies, therefore, meet in a number of different sorts of systems: supranational systems, international organizations, and conference groups, all of which are systems at one level or another. In addition, components that do not represent the society decider directly interact in nongovernmental organizations of various sorts (see page 910).

1.1 System size The earliest large empires—the Chinese, the Persian, the Greek, and the Roman—at their greatest size each extended about 4,800 kilometers (km) from east to west, covering about 23 million km². The British, Spanish, French, and other colonial empires covered half the earth or more, but covered it spottily. The "sun never set" on the British Empire at its height.

The European Economic Community (EEC) extends about 1,600 km north and south and the same distance east and west, with a total area of 1,525,000 km². The North Atlantic Treaty Organization (NATO) has the same member nations (except Ireland) plus the United States, Canada, Iceland, Norway, Portugal, Greece, and Turkey. For NATO the total east-west diameter, from the eastern border of Turkey across the Atlantic Ocean and on to the Aleutian Islands of the United States, is nearly 16,000 km, and the total area is 22,-230,000 km². The communist Council for Mutual Economic Assistance (COMECON or CMEA) in Europe has a north-south diameter of about 1,900 km, and in parts of Asia nearly 4,800 km. With the giant Soviet Union as a member, it is about 12,900 km in east-west diameter, from the eastern coast of Siberia to the western border of East Germany. The total area covered is 24,940,000 km². The median diameter of a supranational system is probably about 5,150 km, and the median land area is probably of the order of 2×10^7 km². But there has been great variation over history. On the whole, however they may vary, the chief supranational systems of history have covered much more geographic area than the average society.

1.2 Structural taxonomy of types of systems   A variety of recognizably different types of supranational systems exist now or have existed at some previous time. They are classified primarily on the basis of their processes, although some structural differentiae are also important in distinguishing one type from another. Regional associations, for instance, which are a subtype of multipurpose intergovernmental organizations (see page 908), are classified as such primarily because their component societies are contiguous or near one another in the same area of the globe, a structural characteristic.

Possible structural differentiae include size and shape of the geographic area occupied, geographic contiguity or lack of it, number of societal components, number of organizational subcomponents, echelon structure, number of echelons, number of subsystems, and structural aspects of particular subsystems like the boundary or the channel and net.

2. Process

2.1 System and subsystem indicators   Quantitative study of supranational systemwide, as well as subsystem, processes can be advanced by developing supranational indicators to measure system and subsystem variables. These can be derived from factual and statistical data collected throughout the world.

Some of these indicators may be aggregated data assembled by separate societal governments or by such international or supranational organizations as the Statistical Commission of the Economic and Social Council (ECOSOC) of the United Nations.[4]

Indicators for the entire world or specific regions of it, like *total population, total energy consumption, birthrates and death rates, total disease rates, total food production, total industrial output,* or *total literacy rates,* can be secured by aggregating the statistical data of all the societies in the world or the region, if the data are collected in uniform fashion. Other indicators, like measures of flows of *matter-energy* or *information* from one part of the world to another, can be determined from import-export data. At present, much potentially useful information is not collected at all, is not made available, or is not compatible from one nation to another.

Developers of World II and World III, which are computer simulations of worldwide processes, have used as indicators available statistical data, supplementing them if necessary with informed estimates (see pages 980 to 987). The state variables of these models, *e.g., population, natural resources, capital investment, capital investment in agriculture,* and *pollution,* are indicators of the state of the world. Changes in these indicators over time and with different policies could be used as bases for policy decisions in the real world. Another variable, *quality of life,* measures the "output" or "performance" of the world system. It is calculated from *food ratios, material standard of living, crowding,* and *pollution.* Such a calculation, if made from sound data, might constitute a reliable indicator for conditions in the total world or in regions of it.

Other world models and simulations use similar indicators (see pages 987 and 988, and 1012 to 1016). At this level, as at the society level, information on the less easily measurable aspects of systems is harder to collect and less reliable. Many appropriate supranational indicators are similar to, or identical with, societal indicators (see pages 750 to 754). At the higher level, however, differences between societal systems in government, values, customs, and national action patterns complicate the problem of aggregation.

Some students of international relations have developed indicators relevant to particular processes they wish to study. For instance, Deutsch employed the T/Y ratio to measure in each of a number of countries the relationship between total foreign-commodity trade (T) and total national income (Y).[5] He used this ratio as an indicator of how international the country was— the higher the ratio, the more closely it was linked to the other countries it traded with.

In their studies of the correlates of war, Small and Singer used some supranational indicators, developed from data on modern wars and alliances.[6] They used two measures as alliance indicators: *alliance aggregation,* the percentage of states of a given type which belong to one or more alliances of any given class in each successive year of the period studied, and *alliance commitment,* the number of dominant alliance commitments for each nation in the study in each year.

2.2 Process taxonomy of types of systems   Most classifications of systems at this level are based on the sorts of processes they carry out. Among process differentiae are the particular subsystem processes the system includes; the relative amount of effort devoted to one sort of process compared with the amount devoted to others, *e.g.,* to decider or to channel and net processes; the relationship of societal components to the central decider, including the ability of component deciders to refuse unilaterally to comply with its decisions without incurring sanctions; the duration of survival of the system; the kinds of relationships that exist among the societal components of the system; and the frequency of its meetings.

Although, as I have said, no worldwide supranational system exists at present, the United Nations is supranational in structure and includes a majority of the world's societies in its membership. But it is incapable of obtaining compliance with many of its decisions (see pages 941 and 942). Lacking a central decider, the nations of today's world maintain uneasy steady states based largely upon international power relationships.

In his systems analysis of international politics, Kaplan identifies several types of "international systems—or . . . states of equilibrium of one ultrastable international system. . . ."[7] These are ideal types and do not necessarily have their counterparts in any historical international situation. The list is not exhaustive, since it relates only to the modern world. Kaplan specifies the interrelationships among nations that characterize each of his equilibria and the rules by which each operates. Only two of these conform fully to the definition of a supranational system. The several kinds of steady states he identifies are discussed below.

(*a*) *Balance-of-power equilibrium.*   The relationships among the major European powers in the long period of stability that preceded World War I were of this sort. Five or more powers, *essential actors,* are necessary for this type of steady state. It is not a supranational system because it has no supranational echelon. Its operating rules are that a nation should treat all essential nations as acceptable partners; act to increase

its own capabilities, but negotiate rather than fight; fight rather than lose an opportunity to increase its capabilities; stop fighting rather than eliminate one of the essential actors; act to oppose any nation or coalition that tries to become dominant over the others; constrain nations that subscribe to supranational organizing principles; and permit defeated or constrained essential nations to reenter the system or, alternatively, give essential status to some previously inessential nation.

(*b*) *Loose bipolar equilibrium.*   This sort of steady state arose after the breakdown of the pre-World War I balance of power. Not only nations but also organizations of nations such as the League of Nations and the United Nations are included as participants. Nations are combined into two strong blocs such as the NATO and communist blocs. One or more weak blocs may also form. Each bloc has a leading nation but is not a true supranational system. Nations of the world are differentiated according to the parts they play as bloc leaders, bloc members, or unaligned nations.

The characteristics of this sort of equilibrium depend upon the relationships that exist among bloc members. They may be organized hierarchically, so that it is difficult for member states which are not bloc leaders to withdraw or to form viable entities if they do withdraw. Or they may be organized loosely, so that nations can enter or leave blocs at will. Different sorts of equilibria result if both strong blocs are hierarchical, both are relatively loose, or the two differ.

In a loose bipolar equilibrium the rules differ for the two blocs, for the nations which are not members of a bloc, and for "universal actors" which are international organizations. The rules of this sort of equilibrium oblige all member nations of either bloc to join together in major wars to prevent the rival bloc from gaining preponderance. In each bloc all nations will negotiate rather than fight or will fight minor rather than major wars to increase capabilities. Countries in a hierarchical bloc will engage in major war to eliminate a rival if the cost and risk permit, but members of nonhierarchical blocs will not.

All bloc members will subordinate the objectives of the international organization to those of their own bloc, but they will subordinate the objectives of the rival bloc to those of the international organization. They will attempt to extend the membership of their bloc, but they will tolerate independence from any bloc by a nation if acting to recruit that nation would force it into joining or supporting the other bloc.

Nations that are not in any bloc coordinate their own objectives with those of the international organization and subordinate those of the bloc members to the larger system. When possible, they act to reduce the danger of war among the blocs. They refuse to support one bloc against another except when they act as members of international organizations.

International organizations mobilize nations that are not in any bloc against bloc activities, like use of military force, that deviate grossly from accepted international actions. Any international organization that acts in this way is a supranational system in my sense.

(c) *Tight bipolar equilibrium*. A structure of this sort is defined as consisting of two blocs of nations, both of which are hierarchically organized. Up to the present no such structure has ever existed. In such an equilibrium, organizations like the United Nations would no longer be important in world affairs, if they existed at all. There are no uncommitted nations. The leading nations of each bloc control policy and pay less attention to the demands and objectives of the other countries in their bloc than in the loose bipolar equilibrium. Only the rules instituted by the bloc prevail. Each bloc comes close to being a supranational system.

(d) *Universal international equilibrium*. Proponents of a world society have something like this in mind. It is a supranational system since it has a central decider subsystem. Of it, Kaplan says:

At least with respect to some functions, it will determine the jurisdictional boundaries of its members. On the other hand, the universal system is unlikely to do this for all decision-making functions, some of which will still be regulated by the national subsystems of the international system. It may be even further removed from being a political system if it operates on other political systems rather than on individual human beings. The universal system will then fall within the class of confederated systems.

The universal international system will be an integrated and solidary system. It will possess integrating mechanisms performing judicial, economic, political, and administrative functions. National actors will attempt to obtain their objectives only within the normal confines of the system, although they may combine informally within the organizational structure of the universal system. Various territorially based coalitions to achieve political objectives may be formed, for instance, rich versus poor national actors. Or, it may prove advisable for some of the rich national actors to offer rewards to poor national actors to enter into coalitions with them. Some coalitions may be *ad hoc* or for purposes of logrolling. However, the distinguishing feature of such maneuvering will be its constraint by the formal political rules of the system.[8]

The rules of this system require that nations attempt to increase their own rewards and access to facilities and to increase the resources and productive base of the universal system. Conflict between the two is expected to be resolved in favor of the universal system. No nation is to increase its own rewards at the expense of minimal standards for another. Only peaceful means of attaining objectives are to be used. Officials of the universal system are to make decisions according to its requirements and not according to the interests of their own nations.

(e) *Hierarchical international system*. This type of system, if it were to develop, would begin as a supranational system, either a directive system imposed by force or a nondirective democratic system, evolved from a universal system. Since component nations would lose their totipotentiality and become regional components of the larger system and since the decider would operate directly upon individuals through unions, industries, and other organizations the system would have characteristics of a society. Societies would become integrated over a wider range of functions than in the universal system.

(f) *Unit veto international equilibrium*. This is far from being a supranational system, and nothing like it has ever existed. In this unpleasant sort of world, which could consist either of nations acting separately or of blocs, each would have weapons that would enable it to destroy any other, even if it could not prevent its own destruction. This would result in a standoff. A surprise knockout blow would have to be technologically impossible; otherwise, one nation could eliminate all the others and organize a hierarchical worldwide system out of whatever was left.

The real systems in which societies interact are of several types. In the following list, some types are supranational systems, and some are not. All but one type have societies as components; that is, the representatives of the society to the international or supranational organization represent the central decider of the society. Interactions among representatives of components of the society other than the decider are included in nongovernmental organizations, which are also described below. The *Yearbook of International Organizations* of 1974 lists 4,310.[9] These include both governmental and nongovernmental organizations.

The types of intersocietal systems are:

(a) *Empires*. The breakup, in this century, of the empires controlled by European nations left this form of system with no existing representatives. But in past centuries the Babylonian, Egyptian, Persian, Roman, Chinese, Spanish, French, and British empires were immensely large and powerful. In an empire, the decider of one society constituted an echelon above those of a number of other societies. Each of the component societies retained its separate decider structure, but usually components of the dominant society occupied the highest echelons, that society being represented in each country by consuls, viceroys, or governors general. The distributor, channel and net, and decider subsystems of each society were connected into the comparable subsystems of the total system. Most societal boundary processes were retained.

(b) *Federations and unions.* These systems also have separate deciders in each of the component societies, republics, states, provinces, or other units. They have one or more echelons above the top national deciders, usually consisting of some form of executive, legislative, and judicial branches, making them supranational systems. The Federation of Arab Republics, established in 1971, is an example of such a system. It is intended to maintain a unified Arab socialist society. It is supranational in structure, headed by a Council made up of Presidents of the republics, a National Assembly formed of representatives of People's Councils of the republics, Ministers, and a Court. Republics control their own armed forces, may make separate treaties and agreements with foreign countries, and exchange diplomatic and consular representation with other countries. They are permitted to deal with all matters not assigned to the federation government.

Some unions and federations are classified as societies rather than supranational systems (see page 903). Societies that join in unions or federations are usually geographically contiguous and surrounded by a common boundary, although this is not invariably true.

Both matter-energy and information internal boundaries persist in the unified supranational system, although they have fewer components than boundaries in more totipotential societies. Customs and immigration components are usually eliminated between the member societies. Also, the distributor and channel and net components of the separate societies are more closely interconnected than in contiguous nonfederated societies.

(c) *Intergovernmental organizations.* These organizations, in which representatives of societies interact, are of two sorts: multipurpose and single-purpose. They may be the executive components of supranational systems, or they may be international in character. The number of presently existing intergovernmental organizations is large. In 1964 there were 192 intergovernmental organizations established by formal agreement, convention, or treaty between national governments and composed of at least two nations, having permanent headquarters, secretariats, annually recurring budgets, and at least two general conferences each decade.[10] The number of such organizations has risen continuously from 1816 on. Most have been formed in recent years. There is no reason

to think the number has declined since 1964. Those which are supranational are empowered to make binding decisions on one or more processes of the systems which compose them.

A list of selected multilateral international associations in which the United States participated in 1974, as provided in treaties, other international agreements, congressional legislation, or executive arrangements, included 15 associations of the United Nations and specialized agencies, 10 inter-American associations, and 59 others.[11] In addition, the United States was included in seven bilateral organizations (four involving aspects of Canadian–United States relationships, two involving the United States and Mexico, and one involving the United States and Brazil). Other modern countries have comparable relationships with other governments.

(d) *Multipurpose intergovernmental organizations.* Such organizations combine several societies in a structure less integrated than that of a federation. They do not carry out all the processes that a complete system does. Their component societies engage in joint deciding in certain specified areas. These systems differ among themselves in the processes under the control of the central decider and in the degree to which they relinquish power to the central decider.

The United Nations, with 136 member nations as of 1974, is supranational in structure and has processes related to all the critical subsystems, although these may be limited in their scope, usually to information processing aspects of the subsystems.

In several parts of the world, small nations have combined their economic processes to achieve greater power than their individual GNPs and population sizes would give them. Benelux, which combines the economies of Belgium, the Netherlands, and Luxembourg, enables these countries to act as a unit economically. These societies are components of the European Communities. This term includes the EEC and also the European Coal and Steel Community, and the European Atomic Energy Community (EURATOM). Other members are France, the Federal Republic of Germany, Ireland, Italy, Denmark, and the United Kingdom. This system is supranational in structure and has political union as its ultimate aim.[12] The report of the activities of this system for the year 1972 says: "If a European identity is to emerge, Europe's place in the world must first be defined. Then Europe must be given a form of organization, a structure, which, through the interplay of economic, monetary, social, industrial, regional and other policies, would put it on the road toward irreversible union."[13] A number of projected steps toward such unification are given (see page 916).

A discussion of the Court of Justice of the European Communities expresses a similar idea:

These two spheres of law—Municipal Law [*i.e.*, national law], because of the exiguous nature of its domain—International Law, because of its lack of direct adaptation to the needs of individuals—were both inadequate to meet the challenge of the evolving new European order. This order requires a direct response to the conflicting demands which are no longer demands of states themselves but of the subjects, individual or corporate, of which they are comprised. These demands are created by the progressive abolition of economic frontiers as these become increasingly meaningless through the extending range of human needs and interests.

In place of such rules [International Law], thus created, has come a new concept of law, in the form of an institutionalized "supranational" Power, sanctioned ultimately by the consent of those subject to its authority, and by their confidence in its being appropriately exercised in accordance with requirements of the shrinking world of today—a Power possessing full legal competence within the scope assigned to it for making binding rules, of its own motion, unassisted by other lawmaking powers established singly in the member States.[14]

The formation of the Central American Common Market followed more than a century of unsuccessful efforts of countries in that part of the world to unite. The Market preserves the sovereignty of the component societies, while integrating their economies. McClelland says: "Having taken the bold decision in the early 1960's to create its Common Market, Central America has moved, within a few years, from five economies of roughly 2–5 million people each to what, in many respects, is a single economy of nearly 15 million. Almost overnight, as it were, it is having an opportunity to realize the economic advantages of a medium-sized country."[15] The effectiveness of the economic integration was greater in the period between 1962 and 1969 than later because armed conflict took place betweeen El Salvador and Honduras in 1969.

Other organizations of this sort are the Regional Co-Operation for Development, which includes Iran, Pakistan, and Turkey; the East African Community, including Kenya, Tanzania, and Uganda, with Zambia, Ethiopia, Somalia, and Burundi having made application to join; a projected West African Economic Community; and the Conseil de l'Entente, which includes Dahomey, Ivory Coast, Niger, Togo, and Upper Volta.

Some multipurpose intergovernmental organizations are intended to promote cooperation or advance common goals without integrating the components economically. The British Commonwealth of Nations is one such. Other examples are COMECON, which was formed to assist the economic development of the member communist nations; the Arab League; the Latin American Free Trade Association, which aims at establishing a Common Market among Latin American countries; the Nordic Council; and the Organization of American States (OAS). The OAS includes 23 nations of the Western Hemisphere and was founded to "foster mutual understanding and cooperation among the nations of the Western Hemisphere."[16] It has a General Assembly that meets annually; meetings of foreign ministers of the members; a permanent council; the Inter-American Economic and Social Council; the Inter-American Council for Education, Science, and Culture; the Inter-American Juridical Committee; the Inter-American Commission on Human Rights; six specialized organizations concerned with such things as agricultural sciences, health, children, and Indians; special agencies and commissions concerned with defense, statistics, nuclear energy, and security; and an executive body, the General Secretariat. In addition, it holds specialized conferences to deal with technical matters and inter-American cooperation.

(*e*) *Single-purpose intergovernmental organizations.* These organizations are of two subtypes. The first type includes a variety of organizations created by two or more nations to cooperate in achieving some particular nonmilitary purpose. Several are concerned with the use and development of rivers—the Indus, the Mekong, the Rhine, and others. Some deal with monetary matters, like the Franc Zone, whose members all hold their reserves in the form of French francs and exchange on the French market. The Organization of Petroleum Exporting Countries (OPEC) coordinates member nations' petroleum policies. The Intergovernmental Committee for European Migration is concerned with resettlement of refugees.

Some autonomous intergovernmental organizations are related to the United Nations by special arrangements and are coordinated by ECOSOC. These are the IAEA; the International Labour Organisation (ILO); the Food and Agriculture Organization of the United Nations (FAO); the United Nations Educational, Scientific, and Cultural Organization (UNESCO); the World Health Organization (WHO); the International Bank for Reconstruction and Development (World Bank or IBRD); the International Finance Corporation (IFC); the International Development Association (IDA); the International Monetary Fund (IMF); the International Civil Aviation Organization (ICAO); the Universal Postal Union (UPU); the International Telecommunication Union (ITU); the World Meteorological Organization (WMO); and the Inter-Governmental Maritime Consultative Organization (IMCO).

A second type of single-purpose intergovernmental organization is the military alliance, the most ancient form of international organization.[17] Organizations of this type are usually concerned with fewer societies and a smaller geographic area than those of the first type. Their processes relate to a single military purpose. Their decision processes usually require unanimity, every member nation having a veto. They ordinarily survive for a shorter time than other intergovernmental organizations. Typically they do not have supranational structure or power. With certain exceptions, like the Warsaw Pact, NATO, and the Southeast Asia Treaty Organization (SEATO), representatives of the member nations do not meet in permanent organizations. While they are usually created by written treaties, they may arise from informal agreements among high-echelon deciders. There are three subtypes: defense pacts, which require military intervention on the side of a treaty partner if attacked; neutrality or nonaggression pacts, by which partner countries agree to remain neutral if a cosignatory is attacked; and ententes, which call for consultation and/or cooperation in times of specific political or military crises.[18]

(f) *Coalitions and blocs.* These are associations among nations that ordinarily do not have organizational structure and are not formally set up under any treaty or document, although the member societies are usually linked by bilateral or more inclusive treaties. Societies that are members of the same bloc may have military alliances among them. They are often linked also by trade agreements and other economic ties, like foreign aid given by a highly developed nation to a less developed one.

Blocs are important in present-day international interactions. They consist of a strong nation, one or more secondary powers, and perhaps a set of smaller and less powerful nations.[19] At any time in modern history there have been several blocs of nations, as well as some unaligned nations, which have received economic assistance and/or arms from, and have carried on trade relations with, one or more of the blocs. Some nations shift in and out of blocs, although the leading nation and its closest associates usually remain in the bloc for an extended period.

(g) *Security communities.* This is a process classification based upon the quality of relationships among societies. A security community exists when a *sense of community* among component societies has developed to the point where they agree that common social problems must and can be resolved by peaceful change.[20] If the whole world were integrated in a security community, war would be eliminated. Security communities may be either supranational or international.

(h) *Nongovernmental organizations.* These are organizations in which representatives of components of societies outside the central decider carry out processes in more than one society. They are of two subtypes. The first includes professional, religious, and cultural organizations with member units in more than one society and with international organizational structure. The International Red Cross, which performs essential humane services in most parts of the world, is such an organization. The second includes multinational corporations (see page 968).

Nongovernmental organizations are not supranational, since they do not have societies as components, but they carry out important international processes. Some of the first type are used as consultants for United Nations organizations. In 1968, no less than 19 were consultants for the IAEA.[21]

Multinational corporations are not a new phenomenon, but their importance has increased greatly since 1950.[22] While many are American, other major industrial countries such as Britain, France, West Germany, Canada, and Japan have taken advantage of opportunities created by, for example, the emergence of the EEC to extend their business interests outside their own boundaries. The United States' capital investment in European manufacturing increased more than 10 times between 1950 and 1967 to $9 billion. A 1969 count revealed, in 14 European countries and the United States, 7,045 parent companies with affiliates in one or more countries. This figure does not include Japan, Canada, or the communist countries.

The largest and most powerful of these multinational corporations may have sufficient influence over some governments to affect their policies. They have been known to penetrate the internal political processes of societies in order to influence the fates of governments, as by providing financial support to a particular political party in a national election.

A rank ordering, in one single list, of nations (by gross national product) and multinational corporations (by gross annual sales) shows that in the period around 1969 and 1970, General Motors, the largest multinational corporation, was twenty-third on the list, next below the country of Argentina (see Table 12-1). The productivity of this single corporation was greater than that of Switzerland and 36 other countries that produced less than Argentina! Multinational corporations often have extensive resources in many countries.[23] Such a system may do its research in Germany, its engineering design in Japan, and its manufacturing in still another country, for sales in a hundred national markets. To do this, it may transfer technology, capital, managers and other technical personnel, and products from country to country.

3. Subsystems

The subsystems of supranational systems are described below. Some of the subsystem components

TABLE 12-1   Joint List of Nations Rank-ordered by Gross National Product and
MULTINATIONAL CORPORATIONS Rank-ordered by Gross Annual Sales
(In Billions of Dollars)

1. United States	$974.10	51. Egypt	6.58
2. Soviet Union	504.70	52. Thailand	6.51
3. Japan	197.18	53. ITT	6.36
4. West Germany	186.35	54. TEXACO	6.35
5. France	147.53	55. Portugal	6.22
6. Britain	121.02	56. New Zealand	6.08
7. Italy	93.19	57. Peru	5.92
8. China	82.50	58. WESTERN ELECTRIC	5.86
9. Canada	80.38	59. Nigeria	5.80
10. India	52.92	60. Taiwan	5.46
11. Poland	42.32	61. GULF OIL	5.40
12. East Germany	37.61	62. U.S. STEEL	4.81
13. Australia	36.10	63. Cuba	4.80
14. Brazil	34.60	64. Israel	4.39
15. Mexico	33.18	65. VOLKSWAGENWERK	4.31
16. Sweden	32.58	66. WESTINGHOUSE ELECTRIC	4.31
17. Spain	32.26	67. STANDARD OIL (Calif.)	4.19
18. Netherlands	31.25	68. Algeria	4.18
19. Czechoslovakia	28.84	69. PHILIPS ELECTRIC	4.16
20. Romania	28.01	70. Ireland	4.10
21. Belgium	25.70	71. BRITISH PETROLEUM	4.06
22. Argentina	25.42	72. Malaysia	3.84
23. GENERAL MOTORS	24.30	73. LING-TEMCO-VOUGHT	3.77
24. Switzerland	20.48	74. STANDARD OIL (Ind.)	3.73
25. Pakistan	17.50	75. BOEING	3.68
26. South Africa	16.69	76. DUPONT	3.62
27. STANDARD OIL (N.J.) *	16.55	77. Hong Kong	3.62
28. Denmark	15.57	78. SHELL OIL	3.59
29. FORD MOTOR	14.98	79. IMPERIAL CHEMICAL	3.51
30. Austria	14.31	80. BRITISH STEEL	3.50
31. Yugoslavia	14.02	81. North Korea	3.50
32. Indonesia	12.60	82. GENERAL TELEPHONE	3.44
33. Bulgaria	11.82	83. NIPPON STEEL	3.40
34. Norway	11.39	84. Morocco	3.34
35. Hungary	11.33	85. HITACHI	3.33
36. ROYAL DUTCH/SHELL	10.80	86. RCA	3.30
37. Philippines	10.23	87. GOODYEAR TIRE	3.20
38. Finland	10.20	88. SIEMENS	3.20
39. Iran	10.18	89. South Vietnam	3.20
40. Venezuela	9.58	90. Libya	3.14
41. Greece	9.54	91. Saudi Arabia	3.14
42. Turkey	9.04	92. SWIFT	3.08
43. GENERAL ELECTRIC	8.73	93. FARBWERKE HOECHST	3.03
44. South Korea	8.21	94. UNION CARBIDE	3.03
45. IBM	7.50	95. DAIMLER-BENZ	3.02
46. Chile	7.39	96. PROCTOR & GAMBLE	2.98
47. MOBIL OIL	7.26	97. AUGUST THYSSEN-HUTTE	2.96
48. CHRYSLER	7.00	98. BETHLEHEM STEEL	2.94
49. UNILEVER	6.88	99. BASF	2.87
50. Colombia	6.61		

NOTE: Data for 1970 are used for all the above corporations and nations including China, but 1969 data are used for the other nations with centrally planned economies and for General Motors.

SOURCE: *The Washington Post*, Nov. 12, 1972, **95**, B4. Reprinted by permission.

*Current corporate name is EXXON.

included are intergovernmental organizations which are not under the control of a supranational decider but which are concerned with international processes. If a world system were to arise, the organizations responsible for specific subsystem processes might well be similar to these. Figure 12-1 pictures a particular supranational system, the EEC (as of 1971). Subsystems and component countries are shown. One of the latter is the Netherlands, a society which was pictured in Fig. 11-2. Table 12-2 identifies the components that make up the critical subsystems of a supranational system.

Fig. 12-1 The European Economic Community (as of 1971). Components of most subsystems of this supranational system are identified.

Subsystems which process both matter-energy and information: Boundary , supranational border guards.

Subsystems which process matter-energy: Ingestor , officials of the EEC who operate international ports; Distributor , EEC-licensed cross-frontier transport company; Converter , example: EURATOM SENA pressurized water nuclear reactor operated by France and Belgium; Producer , steel mill financed by European Coal and Steel Community; Matter-Energy Storage , EURATOM stored supply of fissionable materials; Extruder , EEC Commission on Industrial Pollution; Motor , NATO armed forces composed of EEC members; Supporter , EEC buildings and land.

Subsystems which process information: Input Transducer , example: EURATOM Joint Research Centre at Ispra, Italy; Internal Transducer , EEC Economic and Social Committee; Channel and Net , European inter-governmental communications network; Decoder , EEC translators of official documents into the EEC official languages; Associator , example: Università Europea of European Communities in Florence, Italy; Memory , EEC library; Decider , Council of Ministers of EEC and Commission of the European Communities; Encoder , EEC public information office; Output Transducer , official EEC spokesmen.

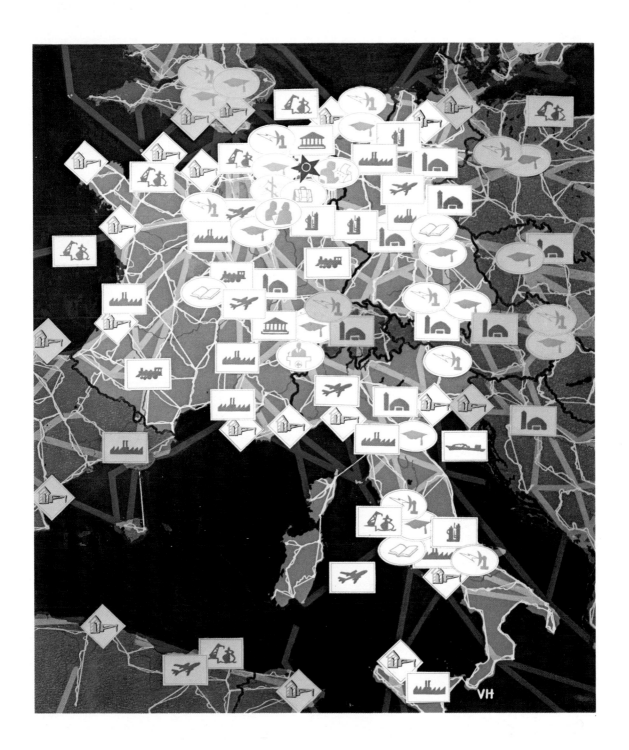

3.1 Subsystems which process both matter-energy and information

3.1.1 Reproducer, the subsystem which is capable of giving rise to other supranational systems similar to the one it is in.

3.1.1.1 Structure This subsystem structure varies for the different sorts of systems at this level. Except for the situation in which a multipurpose supranational system (*e.g.,* the European Communities) creates a single-purpose intergovernmental organization with supranational decider components (*e.g.,* EURATOM), the process is downwardly dispersed to the society level.

In the case of some empires and blocs, a single society acts as reproducer (*e.g.,* Rome in the time of Julius Caesar or France in the time of Napoleon). Or two or more societies may be components making up the reproducer subsystem (*e.g.,* the original nations in the EEC).

The components responsible for reproduction of the new system are organizations whose members represent societies. Such organizations ordinarily include several echelons—chief of state, ministers, diplomats, military officers, other officials, and secretaries—and legislatures that act on their proposals. These may be treaty conferences, special commissions, or other such constitutional organizations.

In the process of establishing empires and blocs, such artifacts as ships, fortifications, tanks, guns, and swords may be used; the actual chartering of supranational systems may require pens and parchment.

3.1.1.2 Process A powerful society may use coercion to form an empire or other type of multisociety system. The conquering armies of Cyrus, Genghis Kahn, Tamerlane, and Hitler gave the societies they invaded no choice. The mere threat of an unequal war or other sanction may be sufficient without an invasion to bring an unwilling society into the system.

When two or more societies agree upon the formation of a supranational system, they determine its scope, prepare its charter or founding agreement, and assign or permit their components to act in its subsystems. They also provide necessary matter-energy and money for the new system.

Representative *variables* of the process of reproducing are: *Sorts of matter-energy used in reproducing.* Example: The Warsaw Pact included eight countries. *Sorts of information used in reproducing.* Example: The nations signed a treaty creating a supranational atomic energy commission. *Meaning of information used in reproducing.* Example: The veto power given the five permanent member nations of the Security Council meant that any of those nations could block any definitive action of the Council. *Changes in reproducing over time.* Example: More and more countries formed regional associations during the latter part of the nineteenth century. *Changes in reproducing with different circumstances.* Example: At the close of wars, the number of new intergovernmental organizations rises.[24] *Rate of reproducing.* Example: Between 1950 and 1964 an average of 31 new intergovernmental organizations were formed in each 5-year period.[25] *Frequency of reproducing.* Example: About the same number of intergovernmental organizations were formed between 1900 and 1904 as between 1960 and 1964. *Lag in reproducing.* Example: The alliance was formed so slowly that its joint command had not been organized when the attack came. *Costs of reproducing.* Example: Each country was asked to contribute to the organizing costs of the federation.

3.1.2 Boundary, the subsystem at the perimeter of a supranational system that holds together the components which make up the supranational system, protects them from environmental stresses, and excludes or permits entry to various sorts of matter-energy and information.

3.1.2.1 Structure

Matter-energy boundary. The physical boundaries of supranational systems are like those of societies. When the territory of the system is a single land mass or is not interrupted by international waters, this boundary is continuous around the perimeter of the combined territories of the component societies. If the territory of the supranational system is separated by other systems (as was true of the French Empire in Africa) or by international waters (as was true of the British Empire), the borders are discontinuous, as societal borders may be. Supranational systems may also have a special territory or territories within the borders of one or more host countries where headquarters buildings or other artifacts are located, as the United Nations has in New York and Geneva. These, like foreign embassies on a nation's territory, are regarded as extraterritorial inclusions within the host territory.

Living matter-energy boundary subsystems include forces located on or near supranational borders which defend, guard, or police them, such as armies, navies, air forces, and police like those maintained by NATO, the Warsaw Treaty Organization, or the Canadian–United States North American Air Defense Command, as well as the missile bases, weapons, ships, airplanes, radar installations, and other artifacts used in such functions. If joint customs or immigration services replace the individual customs services of the component societies, these also are parts of the matter-energy boundary.

TABLE 12-2 Components of the 19 Critical Subsystems of a Supranational System

---

3.1 SUBSYSTEMS WHICH PROCESS BOTH MATTER-ENERGY AND INFORMATION

3.1.1 *Reproducer*

Any multipurpose supranational system which creates a single-purpose supranational organization; may be downwardly dispersed to one or more societies which form organizations to write and implement the charter or other document for a new supranational system; artifacts such as ship, fortification, tank, gun, sword, pen, and parchment

---

3.1.2 *Boundary*

Supranational forces, usually located on or near supranational borders, which defend, guard, or police them, such as army, navy, air force, police; supranational customs and immigration service; supranational security force, military police, intelligence officers, and censors; ordinarily downwardly dispersed to component societies for such processes as control of monetary flows over boundaries; artifacts such as missile base, fortification, weapon, ship, airplane, dike, gate, wall, fence, barrier, border station, radar installation

---

3.2 SUBSYSTEMS WHICH PROCESS MATTER-ENERGY

3.2.1 *Ingestor*

Component of supranational system, intergovernmental organization, or regional association that admits new member nations; unit of intergovernmental organization made up of multiple nations that are concerned with operating international port, argiculture, mining, use of natural resources; may be downwardly dispersed to unilateral foreign-aid programs of various nations or multinational organizations that operate oil well or mine metal; artifacts such as building, port facilities, oil well, mine

3.2.2 *Distributor*

Supranational or international agency, such as many components of the United Nations and intergovernmental organizations and conferences, which is concerned with distribution of matter-energy of various sorts; may be downwardly dispersed to national or private transport or philanthropic agency; supranational or international electric power network; artifacts such as electric power network, pipeline, road, railroad, vehicle, ship, plane, that cross national borders

3.3 SUBSYSTEMS WHICH PROCESS INFORMATION

3.3.1 *Input transducer*

Society or other component that monitors or receives communications from outside the supranational system and transmits them into system channels; may be downwardly dispersed to organizations, groups, or individual persons such as ambassador, observer, traveling representative, secret agents; worker in news media that brings information into the system, and the readers, listeners, or viewers; research worker who studies phenomena outside the system; central bank or other organization that receives money or monetary equivalents from outside the system; artifacts such as radio, television, radar, observation satellite, other electronic equipment, newspaper, magazine, money, check, other money equivalent

3.3.2 *Internal transducer*

Representatives of societies to supranational bodies or intergovernmental organizations; may be downwardly dispersed to research team, statistician, or others who prepare or deliver reports to such organizations; supranational inspection team; representative sent by supranational officials to trouble spots; lawyer representing nation before supranational court; artifacts such as information marker, scientific instrument

3.3.3 *Channel and net*

Formal or informal channels in supranational and intergovernmental agency; channel among comparable echelons of the deciders of two or more nations; formal diplomatic channel; intergovernmental organization like UPU or ITU specifically concerned with processes of this subsystem; may be downwardly dispersed to nation that operates satellites, radio, television, or information agency for communication with other member states; organizations like multinational corporation, especially one concerned with international communications by computer, telephone, telegraph, radio, television, or news services; multinational nongovernmental cultural or professional organization; group or individual person that communicates across national borders within the supranational system; supranational or international organization which transmits money and money equivalents; may be downwardly dispersed to society or organization which has security or money market, international bank, multinational corporation, foundation, religious and philanthropic organization; artifacts such as information marker, money, check, other money equivalent; cable, satellite

3.2.3 *Converter*
Supranational or international agency related to the conversion of energy, particularly nuclear energy; usually downwardly dispersed to nation or organization which converts matter-energy; artifacts such as nuclear research reactor or accelerator

3.2.4 *Producer*
When two nations join together to manufacture something, there is a supranational producer, but such situations are rare; some supranational agencies are concerned with worldwide health problems; may be downwardly dispersed to society, to organization, or to multinational enterprise organization; artifacts such as machine, tool, truck, medical equipment

3.2.5 *Matter-energy storage*
Component of supranational system, such as supranational military forces; agency for providing ecological control by storing water, providing health care, relief, or food; may be downwardly dispersed to society or organization; artifacts such as storehouse, dam, arsenal, garage

3.2.6 *Extruder*
One supranational body, the IAEA, has a component concerned with the extrusion of atomic wastes; otherwise, downwardly dispersed to society or organization; artifacts for containing atomic waste

3.2.7 *Motor*
Transport component of forces of the UN or military forces of some supranational alliance; may be downwardly dispersed by other intergovernmental agency to society or organization with capability of transportation across its own boundaries; artifacts such as airplane, ship, railroad, truck, car, supply facility

3.2.8 *Supporter*
Component of supranational system that maintains its territories, land, or buildings; may be downwardly dispersed to society; artifacts such as building

3.3.4 *Decoder*
Usually downwardly dispersed to organization, group, or individual person that translates languages; decodes secret messages; reports on scientific or professional matters; explains the local culture and interprets those of other nations; interprets radar, telegraph, or radio signals; analyzes outputs of scientific instruments; artifacts such as radar, telegraph, coding equipment, scientific instrument

3.3.5 *Associator*
Supranational universities; downwardly dispersed to supranational system leader or other official who leads her or his society, organization, or group in carrying out associative learning, which alters the structure, policy, or procedure of a supranational system; also specialist or teacher who associates scientific, technological, or cultural information that modifies supranational processes; artifacts such as book, other publication, file, chart, other audiovisual aid

3.3.6 *Memory*
Supranational or intergovernmental unit or nongovernmental organization or society which maintains for supranational use archives, library, filing service; international or supranational bank; may be downwardly dispersed to organization, group, or individual person that stores and retrieves information; artifacts such as archives, library, or bank building; book, other publication; file, financial record, bookshelf, microform, audio or video tape, disc, computer, information network

3.3.7 *Decider*
Policy-making council or assembly; may be downwardly dispersed to a variety of organizations, groups, or individual persons, including emperor, top executive, court, secretariat, official, or staff of supranational systems; artifacts such as palace, capitol, headquarters, administrative or court building; meeting room

3.3.8 *Encoder*
Specialized organization of supranational system or intergovernmental organization, such as public information agency, publishing agency; may be downwardly dispersed to organization, group, or individual person such as drafting committee which prepares policy paper, staff group, professional writer, translator, expert in audiovisual materials who prepares or translates statements for chief executive or other official who speaks for system or organization; artifacts such as typewriter, other writing material, audiovisual material

3.3.9 *Output transducer*
Subordinate organization or group in supranational or intergovernmental organization such as publishing agency, radio or television broadcast organization; group or individual person in it such as official who speaks for system or organization, press liaison officer, typist, artist, actor, demonstrator, mail service personnel; may be downwardly dispersed to societal component; artifacts such as radio, television, printing press, loudspeaker, typewriter

Information boundary. Military alliances with combined commands, like the Warsaw Treaty Organization and NATO forces, have security arrangements comparable to those of national armies, with such components as military police, intelligence officers, and censors. Intergovernmental organizations also have their security officers and procedures. Few other components of this subsystem exist at this level. Boundary processes are largely downwardly dispersed. Boundaries to flows of money are ordinarily downwardly dispersed to component societies, which, in current supranational systems, have retained their own currency.

Artifacts used include missile bases, fortifications, weapons, ships, airplanes, dikes, gates, walls, fences, barriers, border stations, and radar installations.

3.1.2.2 Process

Matter-energy boundary. When a number of societies join to form a supranational federation or union, national boundaries to matter-energy flows inside the system are weakened or removed, but supranational boundaries around the periphery of the federation are maintained and often strengthened (see Hypothesis 3.1.2.2-1, page 93). When Belgium, France, Luxembourg, Germany, Italy, and the Netherlands signed the Rome Treaty of 1957 to form the EEC, they eliminated all trade restrictions inside the community, and they planned to eliminate all internal tariffs and institute uniform external tariffs. These steps have been taken gradually according to plan, but were not yet fully in effect by 1972. Similar agreements on tariff equalization have been made by Central American Common Market countries.[26] Tariffs increase the monetary cost of importing matter-energy across supranational or national boundaries and consequently make the process more difficult. When they are eliminated between member countries of a supranational system, the distribution of matter-energy within that system is facilitated (see page 919). Between 1953 and 1958 in the European Common Market trade between member countries rose from 28.4 to 30.5 percent. Between 1958 and 1963 it rose to 42.4 percent. In 1965 it was 43.4 percent.[27] Belgium, Luxembourg, and the Netherlands sent more than half their exports to other nations of the EEC and received more than half their imports from within the EEC in 1963 and 1965.

The boundaries of the supranational territories included within societies have the same status as international boundaries for many purposes. Political refugees may seek asylum inside them, for instance, and the surrounding society's forces may not enter to seize them.

Information boundary. Although the components that restrict information flows at the boundaries of supranational systems usually are officials of the separate societies, sometimes supranational officials carry out such processes. Societies that are military allies, as well as those in some other sorts of supranational systems, share with one another information (*e.g.,* strategic plans or weapon designs) which they attempt to keep from societies outside the system. This is one reason why at the supranational level it may be possible to confirm Hypothesis 3.1.2.2-3 (see page 93), which states that the amount of information transmitted between points within a system is significantly larger than the amount transmitted across its boundary.

Representative *variables* of boundary processes include: *Sorts of matter-energy crossing boundary.* Example: The Organization for African Unity must import industrial products. *Meaning of information crossing the boundary.* Example: The allied powers fighting Napoleon learned that his forces were preparing to invade Russia. *Sorts of information crossing the boundary.* Example: The United Nations received a request from Angola to become a member. *Degree of permeability of the boundary to matter-energy.* Example: Only products not manufactured within the EEC were permitted to enter without high tariffs. *Degree of permeability of the boundary to information.* Example: Classified information leaked from the secret conferences of the entente with disquieting regularity. *Percentage of matter-energy arriving at the boundary which enters the system.* Example: The supranational defensive organization destroyed 98 percent of its own practice missiles before it crossed its boundary from the sea. *Percentage of information arriving at the boundary which enters the system.* Example: The new federation accepted all the foreign-aid funds it could get. *Changes in matter-energy processing at the boundary over time.* Example: As the production capacity of the Central American Common Market countries grew stronger, they raised tariffs on imports of many industrial products. *Changes in information processing at the boundary over time.* Example: As the colonial empires were dissolved, the United Nations received more requests from new nations for membership status. *Changes in matter-energy processing at the boundary with different circumstances.* Example: Crop failure caused the EEC to remove restrictions against imports of foreign grain. *Changes in information processing at the boundary with different circumstances.* Example: The formation of the Central American Common Market increased foreign financial assistance to that part of the world, since some other governments approved the integration. *Rate of matter-energy processing at the boundary.* Example: The customs service of the EEC confiscated several kilos of narcotic drugs a month at the supranational border. *Rate of information processing at the boundary.* Example: The NATO powers exchanged several communications a month over the hot line to Moscow. *Frequency of matter-energy processing at the boundary.* Example: In the month of July an average of three Panamanian ships a day discharged cargoes in Rotterdam harbor. *Frequency of information processing at the boundary.* Example: NORAD received only a few reports each year of unknown planes approaching its borders. *Lag in matter-energy processing at the boundary.* Example: The customs service in Paris was unable to keep up with the influx of transatlantic tourists and the long lines formed at Orly airport. *Lag in information processing at the boundary.* Example: Ordinarily, several months elapsed between submission of an application for membership in the United Nations and action by the Assembly. *Costs of matter-energy processing at the boundary.* Example: Each nation of the alliance paid its share in maintaining the joint security force. *Costs of information processing at the boundary.* Example: Export of large amounts of the system's currency was prevented, but the cost of maintaining the inspection force at the borders was extremely high.

3.2 Subsystems which process matter-energy

3.2.1   Ingestor, the subsystem which brings matter-energy across the supranational system boundary from the environment.

3.2.1.1   Structure   Components of supranational systems that admit new member nations are parts of this subsystem. So are the units which act on countries' applications for admission to each intergovernmental organization. In addition, units which carry out such ingestive processes as the operation of international ports are included. Agriculture, mining, and the use of natural resources are concerns of the United Nations Development Program (UNDP), the Economic Commissions for Africa and for Latin America, and several intergovernmental organizations of the United Nations, including FAO, IAEA, IBRD, and IDA.

Regional associations like the EEC and the Organization of American States (OAS) also have such components.

Downwardly dispersed components to the level of the society include unilateral foreign-aid programs. The Soviet Union, China, West Germany, Japan, and the United States have such programs. Organizations like multinational oil companies are downwardly dispersed subcomponents, along with multinational cartels like those which mine copper, tin, and other metals.

Artifacts include buildings of intergovernmental organizations, port facilities, oil wells, and mines.

3.2.1.2   Process   Various official bodies are responsible for accepting applications from nations that want to become members of the different supranational systems or intergovernmental organizations. Therefore, they bring living matter-energy into that system. Similar components in regional associations carry out the same processes.

The multinational agencies listed above are concerned with agriculture or with the discovery, mining, or preparation for use of natural resources, such as water, minerals, oil, and other forms of energy. All these are ingesting activities. Some of the above agencies carry out research and surveys; hold training seminars, meetings, and conferences; carry on field demonstration projects; and give technical assistance. These organizations do not usually engage directly in farming, mining, or other ingestor activities, except in demonstration projects. At the request of governments they are prepared to supply experts to give technical assistance or train members of the society. They also supply equipment and provide maintenance for it. Loans from the international banks and single nations or foundations finance development programs.

The UNDP, funded by voluntary contributions of member states, supports development activities carried out by various intergovernmental organizations, some of which are concerned with agriculture and use of marine resources, minerals, water resources, and power. The FAO continually reviews the world food and agriculture situation and is concerned with practical activities such as agricultural planning, testing varieties of grains, carrying on a seed-exchange service, reducing livestock diseases, and developing water resources. The IAEA works with the FAO to improve food crops through use of nuclear techniques. Their programs deal with soil fertility, crop production, pest control, and use of induced mutations to develop superior varieties of rice.[28]

The societal foreign-aid agencies are downwardly dispersed components, with similar activities. For example, members of the Peace Corps of various nations live in less developed areas and, among other things, teach modern methods of agriculture and animal husbandry to native peoples.

Organizational subcomponents are multinational corporations that prospect and drill for oil, mine, produce agricultural machinery, and do farming, as well as private foundations and other nongovernmental organizations that carry out processes related to this subsystem, including consulting with intergovernmental organizations and governments. Rockefeller

Foundation funds, for example, promoted the "green revolution" in agriculture, which developed and disseminated new varieties of rice that increased the yield of rice in many societies. Various intergovernmental organizations were also involved in this.

Representative *variables* of the process of ingesting include: *Sorts of matter-energy ingested.* Example: Triticale, a new cereal hybrid of wheat and rye, is now being grown in 52 countries. *Degree of openness of the ingestor.* Example: The severe protein deficiency in a large part of the world caused the federation of less developed countries to consider using marine algae as human food. *Changes in ingesting over time.* Example: As the worldwide costs of petroleum products rose, the UNDP began to search for sources of geothermal power throughout the world. *Changes in ingesting with different circumstances.* Example: A supranational program to introduce new varieties of disease-resistant corn was instituted when the corn crop failed in a number of countries. *Rate of ingesting.* Example: Hydrocarbons (coal, oil, and gas) equivalent to about 5.4 billion metric tons of coal were extracted and burned each year throughout the world. *Frequency of ingesting.* Example: About one new nation a year was added to the multinational organization. *Lag in ingesting.* Example: The multinational oil company did not begin to take oil from its wells until several months after they were drilled. *Costs of ingesting.* Example: United Nations technical programs were budgeted $6,908,000 in 1970, a large proportion of this being for supranational activities related to ingesting.

3.2.2 Distributor, the subsystem which carries inputs from outside the supranational system or outputs from its subsystems around the supranational system to each component.

3.2.2.1 Structure Compared with other matter-energy processing subsystems at this level, the distributor is well developed. Because they are concerned with the transmission of forms of matter-energy through supranational systems, many nations and components of the United Nations and intergovernmental organizations are parts of it, as well as of other subsystems. Directly concerned with transportation are the European Organization for the Safety of Air Navigation (EUROCONTROL), with three members; the European Conference of Ministers of Transport; the Central Commission for Navigation of the Rhine; the ICAO; and many other governmental and nongovernmental organizations. Also among the components are UNESCO; ILO; FAO; WHO; UNICEF; the Economic Commissions for Asia and the Far East, Europe, Africa, and Latin America; UNDP; the Office of the High Commissioner for Refugees; the Confer-

ence on Trade and Development; the Relief and Works Agency for Palestine Refugees in the Near East (UNRWA); the Inter-Governmental Maritime Consultative Organization; and the World Food Program. In addition, intergovernmental conferences like the one that led to the General Agreement on Tariffs and Trade (GATT), also known as the "Kennedy round," are units of this subsystem.

Parts of this subsystem are downwardly dispersed to nationally owned or private international airline, shipping, and other transportation agencies and also to national philanthropic organizations which distribute food, equipment, and other essentials to needy countries.

Parts are also downwardly dispersed to private organizations like the International Committee of the Red Cross, many nongovernmental relief organizations, the International Air Transport Association (composed of representatives of the world's airlines), and business organizations that operate international carriers of all sorts.

Electric energy distribution over power networks in parts of Europe is supranational. The networks of Canada and the United States connect at Niagara Falls and elsewhere. The St. Lawrence Power and Seaway Project, one aim of which was to develop 1.6 million kilowatts (kW) of electricity, was a joint undertaking of the Power Authority of the State of New York and the Hydro-Electric Power Commission of Ontario, Canada. Electrical brownouts and blackouts on the East Coast of the United States have been alleviated by Canadian current provided over the connected networks of the two societies.

Artifacts in this subsystem are the electric power networks, pipelines, roads, railroads, vehicles, ships, and planes that cross national borders.

3.2.2.2 Process A massive, intricate worldwide transportation network today connects conveniently by land, sea, or air almost all the world's societies, with less easy connections to very remote societies. Some of the routes over which one commodity—oil—is transported from its origins to its users are shown in Fig. 12-2.

Throughout the world are nations and organizations prepared to distribute food, medicines, and other relief to unfortunate people everywhere on earth and to repatriate or relocate refugees. These are international or supranational distributor processes.

From the time the ancient trade routes were built, like the famous silk road from China through the Himalayas and past Samarkand to Europe, people and goods have moved from society to society. Usually they have been protected by international treaties or agreements that permitted them to pass through foreign territories. Rules for international use of the seas also developed early in the history of transportation, although war and piracy have always threatened the safety of maritime travel. International or supranational agreements today regulate many aspects of travel, such as road signs, road traffic, traffic on waterways and in the air, and many aspects of railway transport, including such details as design of automatic couplers for rolling stock and of containerized shipping. All means of transport of dangerous goods are also so regulated. The Economic Commission for Europe has turned its attention to all these matters. The Economic Commission for Asia and the Far East has a project to develop an Asian highway, and the Economic Commission for Africa has been concerned with establishing transportation links among African nations.

Evidently, the distributor subsystem is among the first to receive attention when societies combine economically. The EEC has improved its distributing by working to establish uniform road-safety and traffic rules, remove tariffs and trade restrictions within the Community, eliminate national differences in transport costs, assure unrestricted mobility of labor, and facilitate free entrepreneurship among states.[29] The Central American Common Market secured the completion of the Central American portion of the Inter-American Highway, which is planned one day to run from Alaska to Argentina.[30] The World Banks have provided loans for transportation networks.

Displacement of refugees is among the gravest societal pathologies created by wars. Beginning with the aftermath of World War II, the United Nations has had agencies that are responsible, among other things, for repatriating or relocating refugees. A High Commissioner for Refugees heads an organization (UNHCR) with offices in many parts of the world. By the end of 1970 this agency was concerned with an estimated 2.5 million refugees.[31] Most of these had been socially and economically integrated into the countries to which they had gone and required no material aid, but they remained under international protection until they returned to their old homes or became naturalized in their new ones. One million of these were in Africa, 160,000 in Asia, 750,000 in Europe, and 665,000 in other places. The problem has been further complicated in Africa by interchanges of refugees between neighboring countries. In 1970 Gabon, the Ivory Coast, and Nigeria invited the UNHCR to assist in an airlift to return some 5,000 Nigerian children who had been evacuated during the civil war.

People migrate from one society to another in search of work. The ILO is concerned with them. The FAO has a land-settlement program. The problem of hunger and want in the world has been faced by a number of organizations. The United Nations has a World Food Program. An important aspect of FAO's work is feeding the hungry. In addition, a great many other public and private organizations participate in the distribution of relief supplies. In many such relief operations in which food and supplies are transported long distances under the auspices of supranational agencies, there is a good deal of loss and waste, resulting from vandalism, inefficiency, and unavoidable damage. This is consistent with Hypothesis 3.2.2.2-1 (see page 94), which states that the farther matter-energy is transported along a distributor, the more is lost or contaminated by products or wastes that enter the distributor.

Another supranational distribution problem is the spread of epidemics and of animals and plants which are vectors carrying disease. This is a concern of WHO.

Components of unilateral societal aid organizations perform many of the same activities as the multilateral organizations. Components at the organization level may be concerned with transport, like the International Air Transport Association, or they may be concerned with relief, like the International Committee of the Red Cross.

Representative *variables* of the distributing process are: *Sorts of matter-energy distributed to various parts of the system.* Example: Industrial equipment made in West Germany was shipped throughout the EEC. *Changes in distributing over time.* Example: The EEC set a 12-year period over which tariffs would be equalized. *Changes in distributing with different circumstances.* Example: At the end of the hostilities, Nigerian children were airlifted home by the United Nations. *Rate of distributing.* Example: Thousands of migrant workers each year move from Mexico to the United States and back. *Frequency of distributing.* Example: The Red Cross distributed food daily to the people in Bangladesh. *Lag in distributing.* Example: Before the new economic community removed all internal tariff barriers, goods were delayed at its borders. *Costs of distributing.* Example: In 1970 the UNHCR was budgeted $4,722,000, much of which went for administrative costs of repatriating or resettling refugees.

3.2.3   Converter, the subsystem which changes certain inputs to the supranational system into forms more useful for the special processes of that particular supranational system.

3.2.3.1   Structure   Few components of this subsystem are found at this level. Those which exist are

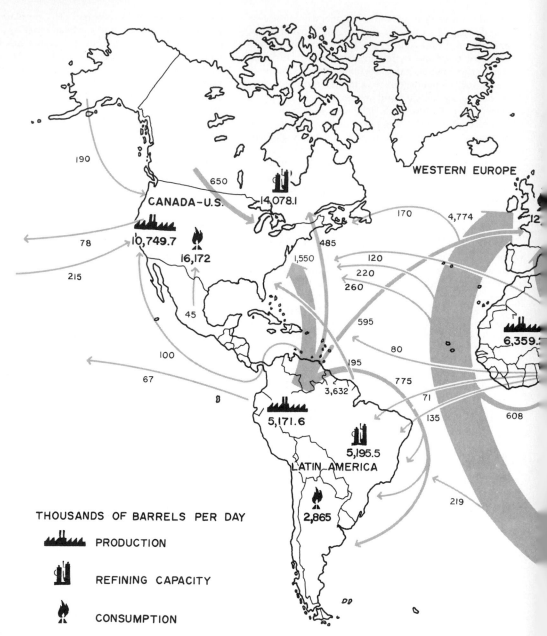

Fig. 12-2 Worldwide oil production, refining, shipping, and consumption in 1970. All quantities are in thousands of barrels per day. Export figures for China, USSR, and eastern Europe refer only to exports from those countries to other parts of the world and not to exchanges among them. Arrows indicate general directions of oil movements, not precise routes. [SOURCE: Adapted from D. B. Luten. The economic geography of energy. *Sci. Amer.*, 1971, September **224**(3), 166–167. Copyright © 1971 by Scientific American Inc. All rights reserved. *Reprinted by permission.*]

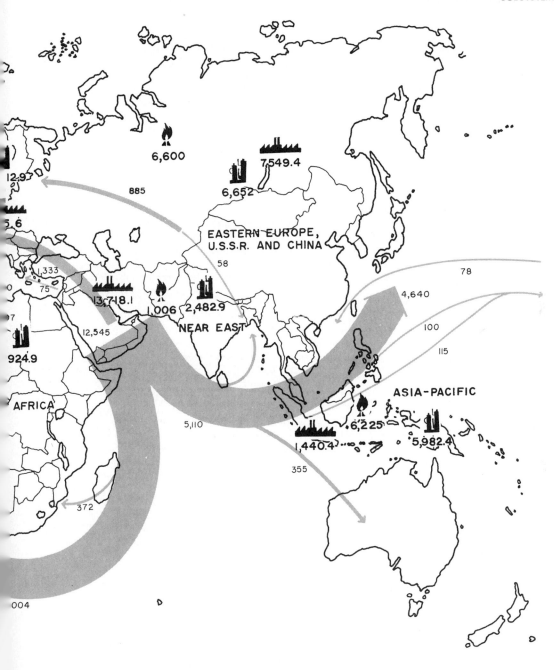

6,600

7,549.4

6,652

885

EASTERN EUROPE,
U.S.S.R. AND CHINA

58

78

4,640

100

115

1,333

75

13,718.1

1,006 2,482.9

NEAR EAST

12,545

924.9

AFRICA

5,110

ASIA-PACIFIC

6,225

1,440.4

5,982.4

355

372

004

related to the conversion of energy, particularly nuclear energy. Components at this level include IAEA; EURATOM, which operates a research nuclear reactor; the European Organization for Nuclear Research (CERN), which operates particle accelerators; and the Inter-American Nuclear Energy Commission.[32] CERN has as member states Austria, Belgium, Denmark, the Federal Republic of Germany, France, Greece, Italy, the Netherlands, Norway, Sweden, Switzerland, and the United Kingdom, with Poland, Turkey, and Yugoslavia as observers. It has its headquarters at Geneva. Its two laboratories, adjacent to each other, extend across the international boundary into France.

This is an almost entirely downwardly dispersed subsystem—to the society level in nations in which power plants and industries that convert matter-energy are state-owned and state-managed and to the organization level, where private ownership of such facilities is the rule.

Artifacts used by this subsystem at this level are nuclear research reactors and accelerators.

3.2.3.2 Process   Almost all energy for processes of all living systems on earth comes ultimately from the sun. Each second, our planet receives 4×10^{13} kilocalories (kcal), 40 percent of which reaches the earth's surface.[33] Ananichev says:

Part of the solar energy reaching the earth is reflected and escapes into space in the form of short-wave radiation. A further part is absorbed by the earth's atmosphere, hydrosphere, lithosphere and biosphere. The absorption of energy by the atmosphere and the hydrosphere gives rise to evaporation, atmospheric precipitation, winds, waves, and—to some extent—ocean currents and other phenomena. Through photosynthesis, the energy absorbed by the biosphere becomes incorporated in the biomass of plants and animals on land and in the sea. The energy absorbed by the lithosphere re-emerges as thermal, chemical and nuclear energy—including hydrocarbon fuels, which result from the decomposition of living matter.

As a result of evaporation, atmospheric precipitation, the movement of ocean waters, the respiration of plants and animals, and the combustion of hydrocarbon fuels, part of the solar energy accumulated by the earth is also returned to space in the form of long-wave radiation. . . .

There are also power sources, however, which are not directly linked with solar radiation—they include the earth's internal heat and tidal movements. These forms of accumulated energy result from gravitational forces, the earth's rotation, electromagnetism and various other phenomena.

Man has four forms of energy at his disposal: solar energy; the kinetic and potential energy of the earth's gravitational forces; the earth's internal heat; the energy resulting from the earth's rotation, and the circulation of the earth's atmosphere.[34]

Clearly, there is no real energy shortage on earth. The problem is conversion of energy. At present,

hydrocarbon fuels are the most used, but these are nonrenewable resources which will become scarcer over the next few years, at the same time that the demand throughout the world is expected to increase as populations increase and as world standards of living rise. A change to new power sources is essential. Recognition of this fact has led to international and supranational research and planning for new sources of energy, as well as independent activities by and within societies.

Much of the international and supranational activity is related to planning, research, and policy formation rather than the actual conversion of matter and energy. Among these activities are a number of programs related to the conversion of atomic energy. From the first, atomic energy has been almost wholly under the control of governments, for military reasons and because of the awesome dangers involved. Governments cooperate in programs like those of IAEA. Some of these assist developing countries in planning and implementing nuclear power projects. They give advice, teach, and do research on nuclear matters. Some assist member states in developing fast breeder reactors, including operating prototype and demonstration plants in France, the Federal Republic of Germany, Japan, and the Soviet Union.[35] IAEA has projects on nuclear power plant operation and on coordinating international efforts in reactor engineering and components. It has supplied special nuclear materials to 33 member states of the United Nations.

Representative *variables* of the converting process are: *Sorts of matter-energy converted.* Example: The nuclear reactor owned by the EEC converted uranium by fission into electricity. *Percentage of matter-energy converted.* Example: Only about 35 percent of the power from the EEC reactor is converted for use in the forms of heat, mechanical power, and electricity. *Changes in converting over time.* Example: Projections for 1985 show an increase of over several hundred percent in world use of nuclear fuel as a power source over 1975. *Changes in converting with different circumstances.* Example: As the earth's supply of readily available high-grade coal became exhausted, nations of the world began to use lower-grade ores for heat and power. *Rate of converting.* Example: Worldwide, about 42×10^{15} kcal of energy are converted from 6×10^9 tons of coal equivalent in hydrocarbon fuels each year.[36] *Frequency of converting.* Example: IAEA's research nuclear reactor was continually in use for one project or another. *Lag in converting.* Example: Resistance to the presence of large nuclear reactors throughout the world led to slow adoption of nuclear power. *Costs of converting.* Example: It is only a question of time until the descending cost curve of hydrogen fuel produced by nuclear reactors crosses the rising cost curves of coke, natural gas, oil, and coal.[37]

3.2.4 Producer, the subsystem which forms stable associations that endure for significant periods among matter-energy inputs to the supranational system or outputs from its converter, the materials synthesized being for growth, damage repair, or replacement of components of the supranational system or for providing energy for moving or constituting the supranational system's outputs of products or information markers to its suprasystem.

3.2.4.1 Structure   When France and Great Britain joined to design and build the Concorde supersonic jet aircraft, a supranational producer component was formed. Such cooperation among nations is unusual. Some supranational organizations, like WHO, that are concerned with such worldwide health problems as epidemics, malnutrition, and drug abuse, are also components of a supranational producer. Otherwise, this subsystem is downwardly dispersed to societies or to multinational enterprise organizations.

Artifacts such as machines, tools, trucks, and medical equipment are used in this system.

3.2.4.2 Process   With the important exception of such joint enterprises as that by Great Britain and France, supranational systems do not often carry out production or own factories, although various patterns of cooperation among societies in manufacturing can be found. One society in a bloc may produce arms, planes, or other artifacts for sale on favorable terms to others because it has the necessary components for heavy industry, while the others do not. Among the communist bloc of nations, only the Soviet Union in the early 1950s could make commercial planes, missiles, and some types of heavy machinery, and among the NATO nations, only the United States could manufacture atomic missiles. Members of a supranational system may work under agreements that one country will produce certain goods, while other nations will specialize in other products—a sort of division of labor.

Recently, some examples of cooperation have arisen among some multinational private corporations and the producer components of centralized societies. Some members of the communist bloc of nations, for instance, have made agreements with such companies as Fiat and Ford to produce automobiles within their territories, using local labor.

A large number of multinational enterprises manufacture artifacts in different countries, where they can get materials at favorable prices or labor at favorable wages or where they are near markets for their prod-

ucts. In 1969 there were 7,045 parent companies in 14 European countries and the United States with affiliates located in one or more other countries.[38]

Medical care for supranational system employees and certain categories of persons under the care of supranational systems is dealt with by this subsystem. So also are major epidemics, drug abuse, and drug traffic. All these health issues are concerns of WHO.

Among the *variables* of the producing process are: *Sorts of matter-energy produced.* Example: Motors for the multinational corporation's automobiles were constructed in Germany, some of the instruments were produced in France, and the bodies were made in Italy. *Quality of matter-energy produced.* Example: The communist nations invited a multinational firm with an excellent reputation to produce low-cost automobiles within their borders. *Percentage of matter-energy used in producing.* Example: All the iron mined in the country was used to produce high-grade steel for use within the supranational community of which it was a part. *Changes in producing over time.* Example: When the supply of copper ran out, the nations of the world had to find substitutes to use in their producing processes. *Changes in producing with different circumstances.* Example: Removal of tariff barriers between member nations made it feasible for each country of the supranational system to produce, for distribution throughout the system, the products that it could make most advantageously. *Rate of producing.* Example: The multinational automobile company produced 50,000 cars a month for the international market. *Frequency of producing.* Example: The fish catch was canned during the late fall each year for distribution throughout the world. *Lag in producing.* Example: As the international situation became more grave, the chief nation in the bloc fell more and more behind in keeping up with its allies' demands for arms production. *Costs of producing.* Example: Costs of producing meat were so high in Japan that it made a trade agreement with Argentina to import beef.

3.2.5 Matter-energy storage, the subsystem which retains in the supranational system, for different periods of time, deposits of various sorts of matter-energy.

3.2.5.1 Structure   Water, atmosphere, minerals, and energy-rich fuels are stored in, on, or above the earth, available to living systems. So are plants and animals that are useful to men as food and in many other ways, including maintenance of the ecological balance. An international treaty involving storage has been signed by Canada and the United States. It deals with the building of storage dams on the Columbia River. These are intended to correct seasonal variations that used to cause power shortages in autumn and winter when the river was low. Joint bodies that implement this treaty are the Permanent Engineering Board and the International Joint Commission.

Components of supranational systems charged with providing health care, relief, or food, or supranational military forces, may be responsible for storing medicine, temporary housing facilities, food, or weapons.

Downwardly dispersed components at the levels of the society and the organization also may carry out the processes of this subsystem.

Artifacts used by this subsystem include storehouses, dams, arsenals, and garages.

3.2.5.2 Process   Only recently has the finiteness of nonliving and living natural resources been comprehended by large numbers of people and by governments. These are coming to be regarded by many as being in storage for future generations as well as the present one. This view makes it incumbent on governments to cooperate in maintaining their quality, replacing them if possible, using them at a reasonable rate, and seeking alternatives for those which are scarce. According to one estimate, there is only enough mercury in the world to last 10 to 14 years at the present rate of use, and somewhat less if the tendency to increase this rate each year continues (see Table 12-3).[39] Other metals crucial to present-day

industrial processes face total depletion in from 15 to 110 years at the projected 2.5 percent rate of increase of use per year. A somewhat less pessimistic view suggests that new techniques of recovery of metals from low-grade ores will greatly increase available supplies. In the absence of richer supplies, mining poorer sources will become economically feasible at the higher prices the metals would then command.[40] Complete exhaustion of the supplies of most metals is therefore unlikely. Iron, for example, makes up 6 percent of the earth's crust and is unlikely ever to be used up. Even if the present situation is viewed optimistically, it is serious, since limits could be placed upon even abundant metals by the great amount of energy needed to recover them from poor sources. Limits could be set also by the environmental destructiveness of mining operations in which metals are taken from poor sources. Mountains of waste rock and great scars in the earth remain after the ore is removed.

The long-term prospect is also grave for adequate supplies of the materials used by industrialized societies for energy sources. Oil, coal, gas, and uranium supply 96 percent of the energy used in the world at present.[41] Of these, the supply of coal is projected to last 200 years at an annual 2.5 percent rate of increase in use. The initial world supply of minable coal is estimated to have been 7.6×10^{12} metric tons.[42] If the

TABLE 12-3   Number of Years Present Supplies of Scarce Matter-Energy Resources Will Last at Present Rate of Use and at an Annual 2.5 Percent Increase

Resource	Years' supply at present use rate	Years' supply at 2.5 percent annual increase in use rate	Current annual percentage of increase in use rate
Material resources			
Chromium	560	110	4.0
Iron	400	98	
Manganese	160	65	
Cobalt	160	65	
Aluminum	160	65	7.0–8.0
Nickel	130	59	
Molybdenum	100	51	5.0
Tungsten	45	31	5.0
Copper	40	28	
Tin	25	19	6.0
Silver	23	18	6.0
Zinc	20	17	
Gold	19	16	
Platinum	19	16	
Lead	18	15	2.0
Mercury	14	13	3.0
Energy resources			
Oil	33	25	6.9
Coal	800	200	3.6
Natural gas	20	17	6.6
Uranium 235	66	60	6.0

SOURCE: Adapted from D. H. Meadows. *Testimony before the Education Committee at the Massachusetts Great and General Court on behalf of House Bill 3787, Mar. 31, 1971.*

present rate of mining does not double more than three times, the peak rate will be reached between the years 2100 and 2150. The length of time required to mine the middle 80 percent of the world's coal will be the three centuries from about 2000 to 2300. Both the initial and the final amounts of such natural resources are recovered at much slower rates.

Estimated supplies of the other scarce energy sources may be depleted much sooner (see Table 12-3).

The United States, according to its Energy Research and Development Administration (ERDA), between 1970 and 1980 will require 187,000 metric tons of uranium oxide (see page 833). The European Nuclear Energy Agency and IAEA project a need of 390,000 metric tons for noncommunist European nations during the same period. Present United States reserves can produce only 220,000 metric tons at $17.60 per kilogram (kg), and world reserves are estimated in the European report as 760,000 metric tons at $22 per kg. Using present atomic energy reactors, more than 900,000 metric tons will have to be discovered and developed by 1985.

Obviously, discovery of large supplies of any or all of these matter-energy forms would postpone a crisis. Except for uranium, which has been less thoroughly exploited, such discoveries are becoming increasingly unlikely. Studies, for instance, have been made of all coal-bearing areas of the world.[43]

At present, supranational activities to maintain resources in storage and withdraw them wisely are lagging behind the awakening recognition that they can be exhausted, which would precipitate a serious plight for mankind. Proposals for firm international agreements on catching whales, fish, or shrimp and on harvesting other resources in international waters have not been met with enthusiasm.

Recently, multinational attention to water resources has grown. Most great rivers of the world run through more than one nation. Europe gets the major part of its water supply from a few rivers. The Rhine and the Rhone, for example, arise within a short distance of each other in the Alps and flow through Western Europe, into the North Sea and the Mediterranean, respectively. At long last the countries that share the Rhine have become concerned about the increasing pollution of its water and have begun a program of cooperation to correct it. So have the nations along the banks of the Tisza River, as well as numerous others.

Storage by supranational organizations takes place in supranational military organizations which maintain bases and storage areas for troops and military equipment. Those which distribute food or other relief supplies may have special areas in which "buffer inventories" of those materials are collected under supranational control to ensure rapid and reliable distribution during famines, after disasters, or in other crises. As Hypothesis 3.2.5.2-1 (see page 94) indicates, such buffer inventories can make the rate of distribution of relief supplies more reliable in future crises. This storage process is often downwardly dispersed to the societies that supply the materials.

Among the *variables* in the process of storing matter-energy are: *Sorts of matter-energy stored.* Example: A United Nations observation unit was kept in the area between Israel and Egypt. *Total storage capacity.* Example: It is estimated that there are about 315 million metric tons of fish in the sea.[44] *Percentage of matter-energy stored.* Example: About 66 percent of the world's known reserves of oil are located in the Middle East. *Place of storage.* Example: NATO kept its planes in Europe. *Changes in storing over time.* Example: The number of whales in the world decreased greatly during the twentieth century. *Changes in storing with different circumstances.* Example: The United Nations withdrew some of its observers from the Suez to place them in the Golan Heights. *Rate of storing.* Example: The supranational relief organization stored 10^4 metric tons of food each year. *Lag in storing.* Example: It took years after the great increase in concentration of mercury in the seas occurred before its toxic effects on deep-sea fish became apparent. *Costs of storing.* Example: Costs of storing fissionable material for research were borne by the countries belonging to the supranational research organization. *Rate of breakdown of organization of matter-energy in storage.* Example: The half-life of the uranium 235 was found to be 7.13×10^8 years. *Sorts of matter-energy retrieved.* Example: The nations of the world used all the vanadium they could get for making steel. *Percentage of matter-energy retrieved.* Example: About one-tenth of the fish in the sea were harvested each year. *Order of retrieval.* Example: Worldwide, the high-quality, easily retrieved minerals were used first, and then the less desirable minerals. *Rate of retrieval.* Example: The mining of tin increased exponentially as world demand increased. *Lag in retrieval.* Example: Geothermal power was known about decades before it was exploited commercially in various parts of the world. *Costs of retrieval.* Example: At first, since hydrocarbon fuel was readily available, the cost of nuclear fuel, with the early reactor technology, was too high for it to be competitive commercially.

3.2.6 Extruder, the subsystem which transmits matter-energy out of the supranational system in the forms of products or wastes.

3.2.6.1 Structure IAEA has a component related to extrusion of atomic wastes. No component for extrusion of products exists at this level since the extruder for products is downwardly dispersed to the levels of the society and the organization. Also, the extruder for persons and for most wastes is downwardly dispersed to the level of the society or below.

Artifacts include containers for atomic wastes.

3.2.6.2 Process   Only in recent years has there been worldwide recognition that extrusion of wastes by human societies is a global problem for which global solutions must be sought. The assumption that the seas are endless and that unwanted matter-energy can be harmlessly disposed of in them is difficult to eradicate. The industrial activities of societies pollute not only the atmosphere above them but also the atmosphere of the entire earth. Fresh water lakes and streams in developed countries are often heavily polluted. International studies of the streams that flow through Hungary and into neighboring societies have shown, for example, that while the main body of the Tisza River is of acceptable quality, the Duna (Danube) is unacceptable both when it enters and when it leaves Hungary. Its oxygen (O_2) content is inadequate, and its acidity; total iron; ammonium, nitrate, and manganese ions; phenols; detergents; cyanide ions; and oil are at pollution levels.[45]

A problem of increasing importance to all living systems on earth is the disposal of atomic wastes, which remain radioactive and dangerous for thousands of years. Because of the critical worldwide importance of this disposal, supranational systems concern themselves with it. An IAEA program reviews the management of wastes derived from atomic energy activities and makes sure that policies and practices of all countries conform to a set of principles that protect the world public. Establishment of supranational storage and disposal sites has been under consideration.[46] Of all the kinds of pollution, only that caused by radioactive wastes has as yet received supranational attention. Certain substances, like radioactive tritium, krypton, and iodine, are likely to pollute the environment beyond national boundaries, even if they are disposed of by a society within its own territory. Also, as present-day nuclear facilities become outmoded and are decommissioned, their components must be disposed of safely. The various forms of waste disposal include burying it in the ground and putting it into the sea or into fresh water. These all can endanger human and other life. Containers used to package wastes for disposal must remain unbroken for the period during which their contents are dangerous. This is difficult to ensure, since these periods often are very long and there are many ways in which containers can be damaged.

A related problem is the discharge of heat or hot water from nuclear plants, which can have adverse effects upon the environment.

Wastes disposed of by the living systems of the world have always gone into the planetary environment. They have not been extruded outside the total global system. Suggestions have been made in recent years that earthly pollution be avoided by putting dangerous wastes into orbit, sending them far into space, or rocketing them into the sun. To most scientists and laymen today these ideas seem fanciful. While the danger of cluttering deep space would appear to be slight, it is possible to visualize a time when an orbiting junkyard could become a menace to space vehicles and experimental rockets.

The *variables* of the process of extruding include: *Sorts of products and wastes extruded.* Example: All nations with access to the sea dumped their garbage into it, thus contaminating international waters. *Percentage of products and wastes extruded.* Example: Perhaps one-third of all industrial chemical wastes eventually end up in international seas. *Changes in extruding over time.* Example: As nuclear energy replaced energy derived from hydrocarbons, the problem of concentration of sulfur dioxide in the world's atmosphere lessened and radioactive wastes became more important. *Changes in extruding with different circumstances.* Example: An international agreement put an end to use of some international waters for waste disposal. *Rate of extruding.* Example: Mercury was extruded into the oceans of the world at the rate of approximately 7,200 metric tons per year. *Frequency of extruding.* Example: The yearly rate of putting satellites into orbit from the earth has increased since Sputnik I, from two a year in 1957 to more than one a month at present. *Lag in extruding.* Example: Particles in the earth's atmosphere slowed the escape of infrared rays into space. *Costs of extruding.* Example: Pollution of the world's environment by radioactive wastes resulting from the nuclear production of the electric power estimated to be required by the entire world for the year 2000 would increase the incidence of genetic mutations and malignancy slightly—about as much as 1 extra day per year of the present natural world radioactivity.[47]

3.2.7 Motor, the subsystem which moves the supranational system or part of it in relation to part or all of its environment or which moves components of its environment in relation to each other.

3.2.7.1 Structure   Motors of supranational systems are like those of organizations and societies; *i.e.,* they are usually man-machine systems. For example, forces of the United Nations, as well as of supranational alliances like NATO and the Warsaw Treaty Organization, have many transport components with a complex variety of vehicles and supply facilities. Other intergovernmental agencies ordinarily disperse their motor processes downward to societies or organizations that have personnel capable of transportation across their own boundaries.

Artifacts such as airplanes, ships, railroads, trucks, cars, or other means of transportation which can cross national borders, as well as supply facilities, are used by this subsystem.

3.2.7.2 Process   While whole supranational systems do not move about, their armed forces, peacekeeping missions, and other components certainly do, carrying out the processes of their systems in various parts of the world. They also arrange for the movement of large numbers of refugees returning to their homelands and for the movement of huge amounts of food, medical supplies, clothing, and materials of other sorts to places in the world where they are needed. They undertake international construction projects. Research organizations send single experts and missions to various parts of the world to study health, farming, engineering, and many other sorts of problems.

Representative *variables* of the moving process are: *Sorts of movements made.* Example: A United Nations force patrolled the demilitarized zone to prevent violations of the cease-fire. *Changes in moving over time.* Example: NATO gradually shifted from ground to air transport of men and materials. *Changes in moving with different circumstances.* Example: Relief supplies were sent by the Red Cross to victims of each new war, wherever in the world it was. *Rate of moving.* Example: About 500 tons of food a day were sent to India and distributed by FAO personnel. *Rate of output of work.* Example: The international brigade moved 90 metric tons of equipment about 40 km each day. *Frequency of moving.* Example: After months of negotiation, a single truckload of released prisoners of war was repatriated by the United Nations mission from Egypt to Israel. *Duration of moving.* Example: It took 6 years of international cooperation to complete the dam. *Lag in moving.* Example: Within a few days, food and other necessities from many countries began to move toward the flood area in Bangladesh. *Costs of moving.* Example: Contributions from members of the intergovernmental organization were supplemented by donations from private sources.

3.2.8 Supporter, the subsystem which maintains the proper spatial relationships among components of the supranational system, so that they can interact without weighing each other down or crowding each other.

3.2.8.1 Structure   The United Nations has its own land and buildings in New York and Geneva. Like foreign embassies, the United Nations has the right of extraterritoriality in these areas, over which

the United Nations flag is flown. The land, buildings, and people that maintain them are supporter components at this level. Other intergovernmental organizations have buildings and land.

Supranational systems or components that do not have their own territories disperse this subsystem downward to the societies that are their hosts.

The chief artifacts are buildings.

3.2.8.2 Process   The activities of this subsystem are like those of similar subsystems of societies or organizations. The components adapt and maintain all parts of the supporter.

Representative *variables* in the supporting process include: *Strength of the supporter.* Example: The island federation had to build seawalls to combat erosion of their lands. *Costs of supporting.* Example: The United Nations budget provided funds for maintenance of its buildings, posts, and landholdings all over the world.

3.3 Subsystems which process information
Hypothesis 3.3-1 (see page 94) states that up to a maximum higher than yet obtained in any living system but less than 100 percent, the larger the percentage of all matter-energy input that it consumes in information processing controlling its various system processes, as opposed to matter-energy processing, the more likely the system is to survive. If this is correct, supranational systems have a good prognosis because information processing constitutes a high percentage of their activities. Of course one reason for this, as I repeatedly indicated in the last section, is that much matter-energy processing is downwardly dispersed to lower levels of systems.

3.3.1 Input transducer, the sensory subsystem which brings markers bearing information into the supranational system, changing them to other matter-energy forms suitable for transmission within it.

3.3.1.1 Structure   This subsystem is to be found in all supranational systems and intergovernmental organizations. It is made up of those societies or other components responsible for monitoring or receiving communications from outside the system and for transmitting them into system channels. It may be downwardly dispersed to organizations, groups, or individual persons such as ambassadors, observers, traveling representatives, or secret agents sent into nonmember societies; workers in all the news media that bring information to the system as well as their readers, listeners, or viewers; and research workers who investigate environmental variables or study conditions in nonmember societies.

Central banks and other organizations that receive money or money equivalents from outside the supranational system are components involved in bringing financial inputs into the system.

Artifacts used by this subsystem may include radio, television, radar, observation satellites, and other electronic equipment, as well as markers that bear the incoming information, such as newspapers and magazines, money, and checks, as well as other money equivalents.

3.3.1.2 Process   Many of these systems, including the United Nations and its allied intergovernmental organizations, have provisions for adding new members who meet their qualifications. A prospective member of the United Nations may submit an application to the Security Council, which, if it approves the application, transmits it to the General Assembly for acceptance or rejection.

The Security Council deals with complaints about aggression or other violations by one nation of another's rights. The United Nations Charter provides that any nonmember state may be invited to participate in discussions of disputes to which it is a party. The representative of such a state transduces information about its position in the matter to the Security Council. A nonmember state may also bring a dispute to the attention of the Security Council if it accepts in advance the obligation to pacific settlement provided for in the Charter.

Member nations may transduce information about complaints of a nonmember. This occurred in 1966, for example, when the United Kingdom requested a meeting of the Security Council to consider an air attack said to have been made on a town of the Federation of South Arabia by planes of the United Arab Republic. At that time the United Kingdom was responsible for protection of this society.

The International Court of Justice also may hear cases brought by nonmember states if they agree to accept its jurisdiction. The input transducing component which receives such requests is the Registrar of the Court.

Information is brought into supranational systems and intergovernmental organizations by staff members and consultants, who report on matters on which they are experts to committees of the system. A primary process of many of these agencies is research. This may be research on problems within the system (internal transducing) or on the environment or parts of the world outside the system (input transducing).

In 1966 the United Nations General Assembly passed a resolution intended to make the use of marine resources more effective. The General Assembly requested UNESCO and its Intergovernmental Oceanographic Commission, FAO, and WMO to study many aspects of the oceans, including their physics, chemistry, geology, dynamics, and interactions with the atmosphere. These organizations, together with the Inter-Governmental Maritime Consultative Organization, coordinated their work and created a Joint Working Party to set up a long-term program. This includes research on ocean circulation and ocean-atmosphere interaction, life in the ocean, marine pollution, and dynamics of the ocean floor.[48] Research ships, submarines, and various other sorts of research instruments were to be employed in these studies. These organizations have planned to monitor pollution worldwide. Monitoring would be carried on in the air, sea, rivers, and marine biota of the world. When one considers that the Joint Working Party is just one of many intergovernmental organizations that carry out researches that belong to this subsystem, the importance of this sort of input transducing to supranational systems becomes clear.

Other important forms of supranational input transducing include overt and secret gathering of intelligence about nonmember nations by alliances and federations, receiving news from media that cross supranational borders, and accepting money and money equivalents from nonmember nations.

Included among representative *variables* of the input transducing process are: *Meaning of information input which is transduced.* Example: A large amount of mercury was found in tissues of deep-sea fish in every ocean, indicating that such pollution was worldwide. *Sorts of information input which are transduced.* Example: The antimissile radar on the DEW line picked up some unexplained blips, which were reported to North American Defense (NORAD) headquarters. *Percentage of the information input which is transduced.* Example: Perhaps 20 percent of the official secrets of supranational blocs are found out by other blocs. *Threshold of the input transducer.* Example: At its greatest range the NATO defense radar could not distinguish two objects from one if they were closer than a half mile apart, but this became possible when the power of the radar was increased. *Changes in input transducing over time.* Example: Requests from countries for membership were received less frequently as nearly all the nations of the world entered the United Nations. *Changes in input transducing with different circumstances.* Example: Several years of international peace caused the joint security organization to reduce its intelligence staff. *Channel capacity of the input transducer.* Example: The General Assembly directed that facilities and personnel be increased and that several new areas of research be undertaken by the intergovernmental organizations. *Number of channels in use in the input transducer.* Example: Eight nations requested that the plight of a small nonmember country be considered. *Distortion of the input transducer.* Example: Claims of genocide made to the United

Nations by the small nation were not supported by the facts. *Signal-to-noise ratio of the input transducer.* Example: Eventually one bloc of nations stopped jamming the other's radio broadcasts so that their people could hear them. *Rate of input transducing.* Example: Only about one complaint a year was received by the Security Council from a nonmember nation. *Lag in input transducing.* Example: The newspapers from the Axis powers took 3 days to reach Allied headquarters in London through neutral Switzerland. *Costs of input transducing.* Example: IAEA estimated that $760,000 would be needed for one of its research projects in 1974.

3.3.2 Internal transducer, the sensory subsystem which receives, from all subsystems or components within the supranational system, markers bearing information about significant alterations in those subsystems or components, changing them to other matter-energy forms of a sort which can be transmitted within it.

3.3.2.1 Structure   This subsystem is made up of the representatives of societies at various echelons who speak to, bring complaints to, or vote in supranational bodies or intergovernmental organizations, including chiefs of state, prime ministers, foreign ministers, ambassadors, delegates, their staffs, and others. It may be downwardly dispersed to research teams, statisticians, and others who prepare or deliver reports, like the annual reports of components of the United Nations, to such organizations; supranational inspection teams; representatives who are sent from time to time by the Secretary General of the United Nations or other officials to trouble spots within the system; and lawyers who plead cases brought by member governments before supranational courts.

Artifacts employed are markers of various sorts bearing reports on other communications and any scientific instrument necessary for gathering the information.

3.3.2.2 Process   Most, if not all, supranational systems or intergovernmental organizations receive or gather information about the state of their components. Each principal body of the United Nations, for example, has internal transducing functions as well as others. Member nations bring disputes or questions to each of them. The General Assembly discusses matters relating to maintenance of internal peace and security that are brought to it by member nations. It initiates studies that require reports from component nations. These studies are designed to promote international cooperation in international law and in political, economic, social, cultural, educational, and health fields. The Security Council may investigate the facts about complaints, disputes, or situations that are brought

before it by member states to determine whether a threat to peace exists. ECOSOC conducts investigations, makes studies, and prepares reports on international economic, social, cultural, educational, health, and related matters. Also it makes recommendations concerning them to the General Assembly, member states of the United Nations, and specialized agencies concerned.[49] The International Court of Justice may request public international organizations to supply information relevant to a particular case, or it may receive information presented by such an organization through its lawyers or other spokesmen. The Trusteeship Council arranges periodic visits to trust territories. It is charged with formulating a questionnaire on the political, economic, social, and educational advancement of the inhabitants of these territories, which must be answered annually by the authorities of each territory. In addition, the Secretary General may send special representatives to parts of the world where there are disputes among member nations to find out what is going on there and what the people of the region want. In 1966, for instance, such a representative was sent to the frontier between Cambodia and Thailand, each of which had complained to the Secretary General and to the president of the Security Council that the other was firing across the border. Each nation denied the charges of the other.

The United Nations Statistical Office cooperates with secretariats of regional economic commissions and specialized agencies which collect data relevant to their own interests. It works to improve national data collection and to standardize statistical reporting on economic activities, international trade, industry, and population. It collects and publishes supranational and societal indicators (see pages 905 and 906 and 750 to 754), *i.e.*, statistics on the main economic and social characteristics of the world as a whole and of its national components.

Specialized intergovernmental organizations also carry out much research involving internal transducing on their own fields of interest. FAO, for example, collects information on nutrition, agriculture, forestry, and fisheries; processing, marketing, and distributing of food; conservation; agricultural credit; and resource development. ILO collects facts about such matters as wages, hours, working conditions, migratory labor, the status of women workers, the rights of labor to collective bargaining, and the protection of colonial workers from exploitation.

In 1947 UNESCO authorized a study of strains ("tensions") affecting understanding among nations, including inquiries into opinions which the people of one nation hold of their own and other nations.[50] Polls were taken in Australia, Britain, France, Germany, Italy, the Netherlands, Norway, Mexico, and the United States (all members of the United Nations), using the same questions in all countries at approximately the same time. Questions dealt with the respondent's estimate of his own class position and the relation of his class position to his concepts of others in his own and other lands; how secure he felt and his satisfaction with life in his own country; the foreign people toward whom he had the most and the least friendly attitudes; the stereotypes he had developed of his own people and of certain foreign peoples; and his opinions on whether it is possible or easy to change human behavior, how national characteristics are determined, whether world peace is possible and likely to be obtained, and whether a world government is desirable.

This pilot study involved intensive, frank internal transducing. It produced significant findings about relations among nations. It revealed that the views of the respondents were constricted by narrowly limited horizons. They had clear-cut views about those people most likely to affect them directly, but vague ones about the rest of the world. The study indicated that if a person's own status improves, he identifies more with his own country as well as with members of his own class abroad. As their conditions in life become better, nationals of certain other countries (not including the Soviet Union) tend to like the United States more, dislike Russia more, and become more satisfied with life in their own countries.

Friendliness of the people of one country toward those of another seems to be influenced by (a) geographic proximity, which permits easier flow of information and matter-energy; (b) common language or coding; (c) the policies of their own government concerning neutrality; and (d) military or ideological alliances, which imply previous coaction. The authors say: "These aspects determine how much attention a nation attracts abroad and whether it stimulates confidence or apprehension. It appears that the individual, after deciding whether a nation threatens or reassures him, then fills in with a description of the people of that nation, coloring them in predominantly attractive or predominantly unattractive characteristics to suit his purposes."[51]

Stereotyped views about the people of certain countries tended to be fairly similar in all the other nations that were studied. Favorable stereotypes about the individual's own nationality were usual. There was evidence that people react to those stereotypes even though they contain only a kernel of truth or represent conditions that do not exist currently. It also appeared that people often attribute unfavorable stereotypes to other nations after becoming hostile to them. People who believed that human behavior could be changed also tended to hold that all nations could live at peace with one another and that there should be a world government.

A research by Holsti on decision making during international crisis includes findings relevant to supranational internal transducing.[52] The supranational systems involved were the great alliances which opposed each other and finally went to war in the period between June 27 and August 4, 1914. One hypothesis this study confirmed was that communication within coalitions increases as the stress of international crisis grows, while intercoalition communications decrease. This is consistent with Hypothesis 3.1.2.2-3 (see page 93), which states that the amount of information transmitted between points within a system is significantly larger than the amount transmitted across its boundary. Even though the subject matter of the communications was not reported, it appears reasonable that some of them were between member nations of coalitions, for the purpose of finding out the attitudes of their allies toward events and how they intended to act under various conceivable circumstances. This is internal transduction. During the first month after the assassination of Archduke Francis Ferdinand of Austria-Hungary at Sarajevo, 54.3 percent of international communications were between members of opposing alliances. During the last week before war was declared, the percentage was only 46.6.

Representative *variables* of the internal transducing process include: *Meaning of internal information which is transduced*. Example: Though the reports to the Trusteeship Council were diplomatically worded, they clearly indicated that the people in certain territories were so unhappy that they were near to revolt. *Sorts of internal information which are transduced*. Example: UNESCO conducted polls in member nations of attitudes and opinions related to understanding among nations. *Percentage of the internal information which is transduced*. Example: Only those aspects of national attitudes relevant to working conditions were reported to the ILO, a small percentage of all the topics on which national attitudes can be determined. *Threshold of the internal transducer*. Example: The research branch of the supranational system was inadequate to detect and report to the main body any but major attitude changes in member nations. *Changes in internal transducing over time*. Example: As the impact of the United Nations Statistical Office increased, worldwide reporting of societal and supranational indicators improved. *Changes in internal transducing with different circumstances*. Example: During the crisis the allies consulted each other daily, instead of monthly, as before. *Channel capacity of the internal transducer.* Example: Canada, Denmark, France, Paraguay, the United Kingdom, and the United States requested a Security Council meeting. *Number of channels in use in the internal transducer.* Example: The Secretary General sent a single special representative to Bahrain to discover the will of the majority of the people. *Distortion of the internal transducer.* Example: The delegate secretly favored apartheid, with the result that all his reports were biased in favor of that policy. *Signal-to-noise ratio of the internal transducer.* Example: Small countries had little chance to express their grievances during the great debate among the big powers. *Rate of internal transducing.* Example: Each delegate was permitted to express his nation's views only once at each meeting, taking no more than 10 minutes. *Lag in internal transducing.* Example: The grave food shortage in Mali did not come to the attention of the United Nations for 7 weeks. *Costs of internal transducing.* Example: Delegates on the international inspection commission were paid $100 a day plus expenses.

3.3.3 Channel and net, the subsystem composed of a single route in physical space, or multiple interconnected routes, by which markers bearing information are transmitted to all parts of the supranational system.

3.3.3.1 Structure   Both formal, prescribed channels and informal ones are found at the supranational system level, as at the levels of the group, organization, and society. The supranational or intergovernmental bodies of which societies are components provide formal channels for communication among representatives of societies, face-to-face, in writing, or in other ways. The General Assembly of the United Nations, its Security Council, and alliances among nations are examples. These bodies also enable delegates to form important informal channels. Formal supranational and international channels connect comparable echelons of the decider subsystems of different nations, such as chiefs of state, foreign ministers, other ministers, ambassadors, representatives, and staffs. In the European Communities, for example, the European Parliament is made up of the presidents and vice presidents of each component nation, while the Council includes the foreign ministers of each member state. "Summit conferences," the increasingly frequent meetings among chiefs of state, and formal diplomatic channels are other formal network components.

Among the many intergovernmental organizations, the UPU and the ITU are specifically concerned with the processes of this subsystem.

The subsystem has many downwardly dispersed components, including member nations that operate satellites, radio and television linkages, and information agencies to provide direct channels between persons in different member states.

At the level of the organization, many multinational corporations are specifically concerned with communications. These include international computer, telephone, telegraph, radio, and television companies and international news services. All types of multinational corporations and nongovernmental cultural and professional organizations maintain international channels among their far-flung components.

At the levels of the group and organism are groups or individual persons who cross supranational borders as tourists or who form other communication linkages with groups or persons in other member nations.

Certain supranational and international components are parts of the net over which monetary information flows. This, like channels for other sorts of information, connects all but the most remote societies of the world. Under the United Nations, for example, are the World Bank or IBRD, IFC, and IDA. Downwardly dispersed, usually to the society level, are the international security and money markets like the Bourse in France. At the organization levels are banks that carry on international business and have branches in other countries or maintain special relationships with certain foreign banks. Of course, multinational corporations are also important channels through which money flows among societies. Some foundations and religious and philanthropic organizations that provide financial help rather than help in kind for members of other societies are also components.

Artifacts in this subsystem are markers that convey information, like letter paper, newsprint, and money, checks, and other money equivalents, as well as communications artifacts, like cables and satellites.

3.3.3.2 Process   Especially in recent years, a network has developed that is potentially capable of connecting almost every member of each separate society with every other living person. It is a worldwide multimedium network of great complexity. At present this net is ordinarily constrained at national boundaries, and so the number of channels into and out of a society is much smaller than the number within. The waiting time to complete a telephone call to another country is consequently usually longer than the time required to complete a domestic call. But channels cross the boundaries of even the most remote and isolated societies, and in the modern world many different sorts of channels increasingly connect each society with the others.

The different sorts of components of this subsystem are unlike in process and contribute differently to the total interactions among world societies. Some channels, usually downwardly dispersed, employ artifacts like telegraph, Telex, telephone, radio, television, cable, and satellite that are designed to facilitate—but sometimes frustrate—intersocietal communications. Multinational corporations ordinarily install and maintain these services. Some multinational organizations like UPU and ITU are supranational decider components for this subsystem, with regulatory powers over the special communications modalities of the international postal service and telecommunications. Other organizations exist to provide face-to-face communication among societal representatives. Still others are concerned with transfer of funds. An example of this is the IMF, which assists in establishing a multilateral system of payments for current transactions between member governments. Member nations may exchange their own currency for that of other members. The Fund's function decreases the degree and duration of strains in international monetary exchanges resulting from members' positive or negative balances of payments, *e.g.*, excess monetary input or output stresses.

The worldwide network among societies, like nets at lower levels, is biased. That is, not all channels are used with equal probability. Although the existence of a channel does not guarantee that it will be used, Hypothesis 3.3.3.2-17 (see page 97) is probably verifiable at this level. That is, when a channel has conveyed one signal or message, its use to convey others is more probable. When an international body or supranational system like the Security Council has been used once as a forum for settling differences between nations, these nations are probably more likely to use it again in future attempts to settle differences. This has been true of the Security Council, but interestingly the World Court, conceived of as a major instrument for conflict resolution, has rarely been called upon to adjudicate differences.

One of the chief factors biasing networks at this level is the existence of laws and customs concerning who may communicate to whom, and on what subjects. Only a few people, such as the chiefs of state and the chief foreign officers of the United States and the Soviet Union, may use the hot line between Washington and Moscow. Aside from them, the technicians who keep the system working may communicate over it to determine whether it is functioning properly. They exchange poetry and other neutral-content materials. Only official delegates may act as nodes and deciders in the formal nets of supranational committees and deliberative bodies. Parliamentary rules are

also contributors to network bias, since at any time access to the net interconnecting the delegates is limited to a single person who is recognized by the chair. Further biases come from the existence of blocs and alliances among nations. Communications flow more freely within blocs than among members of rival blocs (see page 916). Some societies have boundaries that are less permeable to information flows than others. This also is a biasing factor. It affects all sorts of communications, both at the highest echelons and at the echelon of the common man.

Nations also vary in how freely they allow money to cross their boundaries. Any restriction on such monetary flows biases the world networks through which they are transmitted.

Hypothesis 3.3.3.2-8 (see page 96) says that in general the farther components of a system are from one another and the longer the channels between them are, the less is the rate of information flow among them. In these modern times of instantaneous world communications and rapid transportation, this would seem to be unimportant for high-echelon communications at this level. National and corporate leaders have the capability of contacting almost anyone anywhere, at any time. Distance at present seems to lessen the probability of communication by less well financed organizations, groups, and persons, however. It is interesting that communications satellites may change this before long, since it costs no more to communicate by them over a long distance on the earth than a short distance. Ground distances are shorter than the 36,000 km up to the satellite and the 36,000 km back.

Specialized intergovernmental organizations provide channels for particular sorts of information. Some of these are face-to-face meetings, seminars, symposia, or congresses. Others are international data networks, which are proliferating rapidly. The WMO, to select one particular example, has a weather-reporting worldwide network in which about 8,000 ground stations, 3,000 transport and reconnaisance aircraft, and 4,000 ships transmit simultaneous weather observations at regular intervals, day and night, over such channels as radiotelephone, radiotelegraph, and teletype.[53] These reports are supplemented by information relayed by weather satellites. Other international data exchanges are planned by WMO.[54] Cooperating with the World Weather Watch, this organization intends to have continuously updated data on the surface properties of the ocean instantly available. Variables such as water-surface temperature and the state of the sea will be reported.

In addition, IAEA has a joint program with the International Nuclear Data Center for worldwide exchange of data on nuclear physics.[55] This involves a number of neutron data centers, including the Nuclear Data Center of the Soviet Union, the Technical Information Center of the Office of Public Affairs of the United States Energy Research and Development Administration, the United States National Neutron Cross-Section Center, the Neutron Data Compilation Center of the Organization for Economic Cooperation and Development (OECD), the European-American Nuclear Data Committee, the EURATOM Central Bureau for Nuclear Measurements, and the Committee on Data for Science and Technology of the International Council of Scientific Unions (ICSU). A computer-based system for the worldwide exchange of experimental neutron data has been in operation since July 1970. In a single year 300 data sets with 50,000 data lines were supplied upon request to 16 countries outside OECD.

A world science information system (UNISIST) is planned by UNESCO in cooperation with ICSU. This is expected to involve a world network of interconnected referral services in which the major nodes would be presently existing large services.[56] Eventually, an international coordinating unit might be added.

At present MEDLINE, formerly MEDLARS, a computerized information network in the biomedical sciences of the United States National Library of Medicine, extends to some other nations. Excerpta Medica Foundation of Amsterdam, in addition to making information available on significant basic biomedical research and clinical findings reported in any language anywhere in the world, provides data concerning all drugs or chemical compounds in the biomedical literature. In addition, the All-Union Research Institute for Medical and Medico-Technical Information of the Soviet Union provides a similar service for its own country. The UNISIST report points out: "The co-existence of this powerful system in parallel with Excerpta Medica and MEDLARS is a good illustration of the progress that still has to be made before anyone can reasonably speak of a worldwide medical information network, made up of cooperative, nationally supported components."[57]

The international professional associations channel information on specialized subjects to many parts of the world. And the multinational corporations, by importing technologies to various parts of the world, act as channels for this type of information. International banks and other financial organizations channel money, checks, and other money equivalents.

Messages are often distorted in international and supranational channels. Hypothesis 3.3.3.2-2 (see page 96) states that there is always a constant systematic distortion between input and output of informa-

tion in a channel. Hypothesis 3.3.3.2-4 (see page 96) says that a system never completely compensates for the distortion in information flow in its channels. Both these hypotheses seem confirmable at this level. As innumerable misunderstandings in supranational systems attest, the emotional effects of disparate cultures and national interests also bring about distortion in communications. In addition, the common problems of distortion by media in the interests of brevity and newsworthiness can be important. Channels in supranational systems probably have more components than those at any other level. Transmission through a number of nodes and deciders almost invariably distorts messages, as Hypothesis 3.3.3.2-7 (see page 96) suggests. It states that the farther away along channels a component is from a process, or the more components there are between the component and the process, the more error there is in the component's information about that process. The increasing number of visits of chiefs of state with each other may reflect their desire to communicate privately and directly in order to avoid such error or distortion.

Representative *variables* of channel and net processing include: *Meaning of information channeled to various parts of the system.* Example: The Secretary General's proposed budget for the next year showed that the United Nations had fewer funds than it needed to carry out the many tasks the Assembly had directed it to perform. *Sorts of information channeled to various parts of the system.* Example: The Secretary General of the United Nations discussed a border dispute with representatives of two African states. *Percentage of information arriving at the appropriate receiver in the channel and net.* Example: Only two-thirds of the nations had representatives present when the resolution was read in ECOSOC. *Threshold of the channel and net.* Example: It was easy to start rumors at the supranational meeting during such troubled times. *Changes in channel and net processing over time.* Example: As communications techniques improved, more and more telephone calls between nations were dialed directly. *Changes in channel and net processing with different circumstances.* Example: When the two member states of the United Nations established diplomatic relations, they began to communicate directly rather than through neutral countries. *Information capacity of the channel and net.* Example: The Security Council could not handle any other business while it was dealing with a serious dispute between two member nations that was brought to it. *Distortion of the channel and net.* Example: The opposing delegates gave highly disparate accounts of the attitudes of citizens of Cyprus at the peace conference. *Signal-to-noise ratio in the channel and net.* Example: Protesters entered the committee chambers at the United Nations and shouted down the speaker. *Rate of processing of information over the channel and net.* Example: The two chiefs of state bypassed official diplomatic channels in order to communicate speedily in a crisis. *Lag in channel and net processing.* Example: It took several days for the delegate to contact all the other nations of his bloc in order to make sure of their votes on his resolution. *Costs of channel and net processing.* Example: The budgetary expenses of the IMF are met on a quota basis.

3.3.4   Decoder, the subsystem which alters the code of information input to it through the input transducer or the internal transducer into a "private" code that can be used internally by the supranational system.

3.3.4.1   Structure   Within supranational systems and international agencies the decoder is usually downwardly dispersed to organizations, groups, or persons who translate languages; decode secret messages; report on scientific or professional matters; explain their own cultures to members of other societies in the system; interpret cultural aspects of other nations to their own peoples; interpret radar, telegraph, or radio signals; or analyze the outputs of scientific instruments.

Artifacts include radar, telegraph, coding equipment, and various scientific instruments.

3.3.4.2   Process   International and supranational bodies, particularly those with many societies as members, must deal with a large number of languages. There is no real agreement about the number of languages in the world, since it depends upon what is considered a language and what is considered a dialect. But there are enough to create a problem in mutual understanding if many nations are included in any supranational system. In the nine countries of the EEC, for example, at least eight languages are spoken.

The United Nations attempts to solve its problem by using five official languages—Chinese, English, French, Russian, and Spanish—and simultaneous translations to accommodate those who do not understand the language in use at the moment. If a speaker knows none of the official languages, what he says is translated into all of them.

The problems of language decoding are not minor for supranational systems or international interactions, as the following quotation from the report of a feasibility study for a world science information system (UNISIST) indicates:

. . . rough surveys are sufficient to indicate that a number of countries are having a hard time overcoming language barriers, in two complementary senses: providing specialists

with means to understand the findings of world science, and ensuring that their own work is understandable to the rest of the world. The problem is not restricted to the so-called minority languages in science, i.e. languages other than English, Russian, French and German: on the average, both English and Russian speaking scientists are unable to read more than half or one third of the whole literature in their field, unless they know the other language as well. The position is far worse for French and German speaking specialists, who simply cannot do much serious research without a thorough knowledge of English and/or Russian; and the difference with speakers of other languages in the Romance, German or Slavic group—or Japanese and Chinese, for this matter—is now just a matter of degree. The greatest drawback, however, is in developing countries, where the many years spent in learning a mother-tongue are practically wasted as far as science information is concerned: Arabic, African or Indo-Malayan languages provide absolutely no channels of exchange—either way—with the scientific community of the northern hemisphere.[58]

In addition to the language problem itself, the differences in the more subtle aspects of communication, such as gesture, intonation, and rhetoric, present a decoding problem to people of very different cultures. Although simultaneous translation of such communications is not practicable, cultural interpretation among components can increase understanding. Because of the fierce patriotic loyalties generated by competing ideologies of nations and blocs, omissions, errors, and distortions are common in supranational decoding, particularly in times of stress. No quantitative comparison has been made of changes in decoding during crises. The United Nations, however, makes efforts to assure that personal attitudes of its translators do not decrease the accuracy of their translations. Great care is taken in translating documents so that their meaning is identical in all the languages used.

Hypothesis 3.3.3.2-16 (see page 97) says that the less decoding and encoding a channel requires, the more it is used. Although successful political unions among people of different languages are commonplace, those nations and persons who can communicate freely probably interact more than those who cannot. Many persons in large supranational systems may never encounter anyone belonging to most of the other nations. Consequently, they need not speak a common language or have a common code for communication. All that is necessary is that they share the basic values of the system. There has been a trend, however, for one language to become common throughout large parts of the world. Direct communication thus becomes easier. In the past, French was the most common second language in much of the world. English now is. Russian, Chinese, and Japanese may in the future be used more widely than at present.

Representative *variables* of the decoding process include: *Meaning of information which is decoded.* Example: The Secretary General of the United Nations talked through a translator with a diplomatic representative of a nonmember nation in an attempt to mediate in a dispute between that nation and a group of members. *Sorts of information which are decoded.* Example: The entire debate of the General Assembly was translated into all the official languages. *Percentage of the information input which is decoded.* Example: The high command of the alliance decided to publish, in the native languages of their component nations, only one of the four communications received from the enemy. *Threshold of the decoder.* Example: The SEATO translator missed the subtleties of the delegate's argument because his English was not as good as his Thai. *Changes in decoding over time.* Example: Over the years more and more scientific speeches at UNESCO were given in English, and since nearly all the scientists understood that language, simultaneous translation often was not required. *Changes in decoding with different circumstances.* Example: The political fugitive from Burundi spoke only Swahili, a language unknown to most delegates to the Security Council, so his testimony was translated into five languages. *Channel capacity of the decoder.* Example: A third working language was added to the simultaneous translations, and thus new equipment with another channel had to be installed at each seat in the United Nations committee room. *Distortion of the decoder.* Example: The African expert did not understand the tribal organization of the developing country and overemphasized the power of the matriarchy in his report to UNESCO. *Signal-to-noise ratio of the decoder.* Example: The delegates to the General Assembly applauded so loudly that the translator could barely hear the next passage and made errors. *Rate of decoding.* Example: The simultaneous translation into the official United Nations languages was carried on at the rate of normal speech, about 200 words per minute. *Percentage of omissions in decoding.* Example: The SEATO interpreter left out an occasional phrase when the prime minister spoke too rapidly. *Percentage of errors in decoding.* Example: Translators were hired by ILO only if their rate of errors in their preselection tests was less than 1 percent. *Code employed.* Example: French, German, and English were the official languages of the alliance. *Redundancy of the code employed.* Example: Articles and prepositions were often omitted in telegraphic messages among NATO nations in order to decrease redundancy and cut transmission costs. *Lag in decoding.* Example: It took the security officers 3 hours to decode the message from the alliance's military code. *Costs of decoding.* Example: Each member nation of the world

organization contributed to the salaries and expenses of its staff translators.

3.3.5   Associator, the subsystem which carries out the first stage of the learning process, forming enduring associations among items of information in the supranational system.

3.3.5.1   Structure   As at other levels above the organism, most of this process is downwardly dispersed, though there are some supranational universities where associating is done. Some persons who are in this subsystem are so placed in the structure of supranational or international organizations that their associations contribute to changes in structure, policy, or procedure of their component societies, organizations, or groups. Supranational system leaders and other officials often carry out such functions. Those who associate items of information drawn from science, technology, or culture and who thereby contribute to systemwide or worldwide changes in values or behavior are also parts of this subsystem, as are those who instruct others in knowledge or skills that contribute to such changes. Included among such instructors are teachers, leaders of conferences and symposia, and those who conduct demonstration projects in many supranational intergovernmental organizations.

Artifacts used include books, other publications, files, charts, and other audiovisual aids.

3.3.5.2   Process   In an analysis of the development of international law, Gould and Barkun provide some insights into the associating or learning processes of supranational systems.[59] International law is not a codified system, like the Code Napoléon, nor is it a system of case law, like the English common law, in which previous court decisions in similar matters are usually followed, although it is closer to the latter. Instead, it is a set of recognized customs which have the force of rules but ordinarily are not enforceable as laws. They are certainly not always obeyed. They have, however, survived and are applied, along with treaties, in adjudications made in supranational and international courts and other judicial bodies. Since such rules are neither enacted into law by legislative bodies nor changed by the decisions of a supranational "supreme court," the gradual adaptation of such customary law to changes in international realities constitutes a supranational learning process.

Underlying customary law are the values and norms of the system in which the laws are applied. As these change, so do the customs. Gould and Barkun discuss this situation:*

*Selections from Wesley L. Gould and Michael Barkun, *International law and the social sciences* (copyright © 1970 by Princeton University Press) pp. 187, 186–187 and 200–201. Reprinted by permission of Princeton University Press.

Among the norm-generating forces or stimuli to which attention may be given are the following: (1) environmental influences, (2) situational influences, (3) conflict, (4) claims and demands, (5) actions of deviants, (6) activities of private persons, (7) past acts or precedents. How these factors are interrelated is a problem to be approached through systems analysis with particular attention to communications, information processing, and decision-making as affected by such things as perceptions and attitude structures.[60]

According to these authors, customary rule changes incrementally as the cumulative effect of unilateral acts:

Few guides exist in the literature of international law concerning the cumulative effect of unilateral acts, even though the rapid development of a legal regime of the continental shelf has recently traveled the course from successive unilateral acts past custom to the status of treaty law. Discussions of unilateral acts have largely concerned the binding effects of unilateral declarations. Redundancy patterns have been ignored, particularly the redundancy patterns in unilateral actions not brought to the attention of the courts. One method of tracing such patterns, while also attempting to ascertain legal quality, would be to tabulate the reactions of states to specified acts by other states. To do so requires the assumption that reactive behavior can be a norm-generating force and is also at some point of time evidence of the consensus said to underlie all law—an obverse manifestation of the consensus declared positively for particular legal norms. This consensus may be regarded as a convergence of expectations, while the tabulation of reactions would be evidence of the rise and spread of expectations that states shall act in certain ways and that, if they do not, certain responses are proper.[61]

This is supranational learning. World habits are built from repetition of particular acts which have been rewarded. Gould and Barkun make it clear that alternatives are selected for repetition not only because they have been chosen in the past but also because past situations in which they have been used were successfully resolved.[62]

These customs do not all arise from the common responses of nations. They may develop from behavior of systems at lower levels (see page 964).[63] Associative changes in the behavior of levels of systems below the level of the supranational system—all the way down to the individual worker, farmer, scientist, or other citizen of any society in the world—may lead to worldwide associative processes and changes in approaches to problems. Intergovernmental organizations concerned with particular subsystem activities of societies throughout the world disseminate information through teaching programs, seminars, scholarships, and meetings of specialists. These may have an important impact. IAEA, for instance, holds conferences and panel sessions on various aspects of nuclear physics and technology.[64] Multinational corporations also spread learning about technology. Their employees, in

every country where they set up business, must acquire new knowledge and skills.[65]

There appears to be no useful information on rates or other variables of the associating process at this level. Hypothesis 3.3.5.2-6 (see page 99), which states that, in general, the higher the level of the system, the slower association is, may be verifiable at this level. But data to support it are not available. Gould and Barkun point out that lags are characteristic of changes in international customary law.[66] These lags may be years long. This is not necessarily undesirable, but change can come too slowly. The world has adapted ponderously to much technological innovation. International whale and fish conservation agreements, for instance, have lagged far behind modern changes in deep-sea fishing techniques.[67]

Representative *variables* of the associating process at the supranational level include: *Meaning of information which is associated.* Example: New modes of agriculture adopted by all the SEATO nations significantly improved their crop yields. *Sorts of information which are associated.* Example: As a result of teaching by the IAEA, a uniform set of rules for disposing of atomic wastes began to emerge among countries of the United Nations. *Percentage of the information input which is associated to other information.* Example: Although reports of the sinking of thousands of ships over the centuries seemed to have no impact, the news of the sinking of one more ship, the *Titanic*, though constituting a minute percentage of such reports, so startled the international community that it finally learned the need for major changes in maritime safety procedures. *Changes in associating over time.* Example: Member countries of the United Nations began bringing their disputes to the Security Council rather than resorting to immediate war as they observed that in some cases, that body successfully resolved international problems. *Changes in associating with different circumstances.* Example: Registration of treaties with the United Nations increased as member nations learned that the United Nations would not assist in enforcing unregistered treaties. *Channel capacity of the associator.* Example: The total population of farmers making up the agricultural components of the nations of the world considered a huge amount of technological information as they became convinced that modern farming methods increased the food supply. *Rate of associating.* Example: Every 5 years COMECON reviewed its previous performance and made new plans on the basis of the findings. *Lag in associating.* Example: Thirty years after Hiroshima, the world was still building atomic bombs. *Costs of associating.* Example: IAEA spent a large part of its budget on teaching representatives of participant nations about the technology which provides atomic energy.

3.3.6 Memory, the subsystem which carries out the second stage of the learning process, storing various sorts of information in the supranational system for different periods of time.

3.3.6.1 Structure The memory subsystem of supranational systems is structurally similar to memory subsystems at all levels above the organism. That is, storage in human memories is supplemented by such things as files, financial records, libraries, and computerized data banks, each operated by appropriate personnel. Many supranational or other intergovernmental units maintain stores of specialized information. An example is the Dag Hammarskjöld Library, concentrating chiefly in international law and political, economic, and social affairs. It serves primarily the delegations and the Secretariat of the United Nations. Also, ILO acts as a world information center on labor problems. WHO collects and disseminates epidemiological information. UNESCO maintains a library in Paris, where its headquarters are, and is sponsoring the publication of a world history, which is intended to be written without nationalistic biases.[68] The archives of the Pan American Union, the central organization of the OAS, constitute another supranational memory component. The archives store instruments of ratification of inter-American agreements and act as custodian of documents and records of conferences. Its Columbus Memorial Library contains more than 200,000 volumes and many maps relating to the member nations.

The Inter-University Consortium for Political Research, a nongovernmental organization with headquarters at the Survey Research Center of The University of Michigan, is concerned with storage and retrieval of information on social science. It includes components from universities in Canada, Great Britain, Europe, and the United States. The actual storage of its information is downwardly dispersed to certain groups and individuals but is retrievable by all members.

A report by UNESCO and ICSU, which I have already referred to (see page 933), describes the present world situation in science information storage.[69] It examines the feasibility of establishing a worldwide science information system (UNISIST) to integrate science information services all over the world into a network of cooperating libraries, data banks, and similar components. This report describes a complex of literally hundreds of separate institutions and information networks already in existence. These include many that are parts of international networks, including some operated by governmental components and others that are separate organizations. Examples of the first are NASA's worldwide exchange of aerospace information, which serves more than 300 organizations in some 50 countries, and the scientific and technical network set up by the Council for Mutual Economic Assistance of the Eastern European communist countries, with its international institute in Moscow.

A nongovernmental organization of this sort is Excerpta Medica Foundation, which maintains a set of 33 English-language abstract journals; 33 monthly computerized publications, "Classified Titles"; computerized subject indexes, references, and abstracts for information searches; magnetic tapes, bearing such information as data on drugs and other chemical compounds from the biomedical literature, which are distributed to subscribers at weekly, monthly, or other intervals; and programs for storage and retrieval available to the subscriber's data-processing center. In addition to these stores of scientific information, national libraries and other information collections of one country are often available for use by citizens of other nations.

International and supranational banks are storage components for monetary information.

Artifacts used include archives, libraries, and bank buildings; books and other publications; files, financial records, bookshelves, microforms, and audio or video tapes and disks; computers; and information networks.

3.3.6.2 Process The memory processes at this level, as at others, include reading into storage, maintaining in storage, loss and alteration during storage, and retrieval from storage. The total of all the information in the world's memory stores is obviously very great, perhaps of the order of 10^{16} bits.

(a) *Reading into storage.* The information stored in supranational memories is most commonly in writing, on paper. Some is in other symbols, such as musical or mathematical notation, and some is in the form of pictures or charts. Various more recently developed storage forms are in increasing use: microform reproductions of pages; recorded tapes, cassettes, and disks; and computer memories are all used by components at this level. Tape recordings of meetings contain a complete audio record of what occurred, without the reporting error that commonly appears in secretaries' notes or reports written later.

The funds stored in the group of World Banks are subscribed by United Nations member nations. Only 10 percent of the amount subscribed is actually transferred to them, however.

(*b*) *Maintaining information in storage.* This process is not different in character at the supranational level from the comparable processes at the levels of the organization and the society. The use of the mails and electronic networks to interconnect information storage facilities makes it unnecessary for each separate component of the memory subsystem to have a copy of all the information stored.

(*c*) *Loss and alteration during storage.* Hypothesis 3.3.6.2-2 (see page 99) states that information stored in the memory of a living system increasingly over time undergoes regular changes, and this is true at the level of supranational systems. All the markers on which information is stored are changed, at different rates, by entropy over time, and natural disasters or violence may destroy records or collections.

(*d*) *Retrieval from storage.* Access to information stored in components of the memory of a supranational system may be limited in a number of ways. Records of meetings and other transactions of systems at this level may be classified as confidential, secret, or top secret and made available only to certain officials. The coding of the storage is a limiting factor for many of the world's people who cannot read or understand the languages of the stored materials. The UNISIST report recommends that a world science network reformulate the content of documents into various other natural and artificial languages in order to facilitate access to scientific literature by people who cannot read the language in which the documents are written.[70] If machine translation, which is at present inadequate, should be improved, computers could assist in this.

Another limitation upon access to world science literature is financial. The costs are much higher in some parts of the world than in others. Translation costs may be high for those who do not read one of the primary languages in which science literature is recorded. In the present state of the world, also, the arrangements for procuring materials from a distance are unsatisfactory in many places. No efficient supranational scientific information system exists today. The UNISIST report says:

. . . the concept of an organized transfer of information only makes sense [to scientists] if it is thought out in terms of a world service, that pools pieces of knowledge from all sources and re-distributes them over the whole scientific community, irrespective of national, economic or linguistic barriers.

By and large, such a service exists to-day: if any individual were rich and mobile enough to travel over the earth, visiting the major information centres, collecting papers and references from all of them on any subject matter of interest to him, there is indeed a good chance that he might secure all the available information on this subject. In other words, by moving from one place to another, our errant scholar would himself provide the switch from one local information system or network to another, viz. the integrating device which is at present missing. But there is no other way of materializing the fiction of a world pool of knowledge: no single access point, no single *system* exists, through which individual scholars might obtain the whole *collectanea* available at a given time on any research subject or area, in a form understandable and convenient to him.[71]

Funds held in the World Banks may be borrowed by member governments, government agencies, and private enterprises under governmental guarantee. This is retrieval of monetary information. Most of this money is in national currencies and may be lent by the banks only with the consent of the member nation that provides the funds.[72]

Representative *variables* of the memory process at the supranational level include: *Meaning of information stored in memory.* Example: The Dag Hammarskjöld Library of the United Nations contains an excellent collection of books on international law. *Sorts of information stored in memory.* Example: Experimental neutron data are stored in the EXFOR computer.[73] *Total memory capacity.* Example: The *Index Medicus* has a bibliographical data base of more than 1 million articles.[74] *Percentage of information input stored.* Example: Only 10 percent of the money subscribed by member nations to the World Bank is actually deposited, the rest being held in the member countries. *Changes in remembering over time.* Example: Storage in microfiche gradually replaced storage of complete documents in the United Nations libraries. *Changes in remembering with different circumstances.* Example: Worldwide concern about pollution caused IAEA to collect information on the effects of radionuclides on the marine environment. *Rate of reading into memory.* Example: A monthly statistical bulletin by the Statistical Council of ECOSOC reports current values of various economic and social indices for the world as a whole and for component nations. *Lag in reading into memory.* Example: The team of experts took several months to write their reports for the COMECON files. *Costs of reading into memory.* Example: The WMO estimates that costs of collecting and compiling oceanographic planning information and preliminary results would be offset by savings in research costs.[75] *Rate of distortion of information during storage.* Example: The historians of today's alliances, when permitted to publish freely, prevent the rapid alteration of the records about past events which was common when Thucydides and Herodotus chronicled the history of the Grecian Empire. *Time information is in storage before being forgotten.* Example: Ten years after the transactions, records of all purchases were routinely eliminated from computer storage by the supranational system's purchasing office. *Sorts of information retrieved.* Example:

New computer equipment will make it possible for member nations to obtain charts of any combination of oceanographic data from the main archives by one brief long-distance telephone call. *Percentage of stored information retrieved from memory*. Example: The scientist, who read only Russian and English, could search only one-third of the current world literature in his field. *Order of retrieval from memory*. Example: Delegates from each nation gave their reports in order of the date of entrance of their country into the supranational system. *Rate of retrieval from memory*. Example: In one year the IAEA collection of evaluated neutron data supplied 800 data sets with 700,000 data lines to scientists in 13 countries outside the OECD.[76] *Lag in retrieval from memory*. Example: The United Nations library usually responded to a request for a document within 24 hours. *Costs of retrieval from memory*. Example: The average cost to IAEA of responding to a request for information retrieval was $10.

3.3.7 Decider, the executive subsystem which receives information inputs from all other subsystems and transmits to them information outputs that control the entire supranational system.

3.3.7.1 Structure   The deciders of empires from ancient to modern times have had a variety of structures. Generally they have been downwardly dispersed to an emperor or empress and subordinate kings, nobles, priests, courtiers, ambassadors, consuls, soldiers, and other officials structured into various organizational or group relationships.

Deciders of contemporary supranational systems have at their top echelon a council or assembly, of which the components are representatives of societies. The largest of these systems, the United Nations, has the General Assembly at its top echelon. Nations are represented in meetings by permanent representatives, each of whom heads a permanent mission from his society. Nonmember states maintain offices of permanent observers. Other decider components are downwardly dispersed. The internal organization of the Assembly includes a President and Vice Presidents, elected for each annual session by the Assembly. Seven main committees, on which all member states have a right to be represented, divide the agenda for the session among them.

Five other principal organs of the United Nations are the Security Council, ECOSOC, the Trusteeship Council, the International Court of Justice, and the Secretariat. Varying numbers of member nations of the United Nations are components of the first three. With the exception of the five permanent members of the Security Council—China, France, the Soviet Union, the United Kingdom, and the United States—members of these bodies are elected by the General Assembly.

The 15 independent judges of the International Court of Justice are elected separately by the General Assembly and the Security Council and must have a majority in each. These judges are nominated, after consultation with national and international law bodies, by government-appointed national groups of international law experts. They do not represent their societies, but rather the main forms of civilization and the principal legal systems of the world. Terms are 9 years, and judges may be reelected. Terms of 5 of the 15 expire at the end of every 3 years.

The Secretary General of the United Nations heads the Secretariat. He is appointed by the General Assembly upon recommendation of the Security Council.

The structure of the European Communities similarly represents the component societies. A European Parliament, composed of the presidents and vice presidents of each of the member states; a Council, composed of the foreign ministers of each; a Commission, composed of representatives of governments of the member states; and a Court of Justice are its primary components. There are three component communities—the European Coal and Steel Community, EEC, and EURATOM.

The intergovernmental organizations related to the United Nations are similarly headed by representative bodies. The IAEA, for example, has a General Conference composed of all its member nations, a Board of Governors with 25 member nations designated or elected on a technological and regional basis, and a Secretariat. The supreme body of the ILO is the International Labor Conference, whose more than 1,000 members meet annually to elect the governing body of the ILO, adopt the budget, set international labor standards, and provide a world forum for discussing social and labor questions. Each member state has two governmental delegates, one employers' delegate, and one workers' delegate. Other multipurpose intergovernmental organizations have similar structures.

The decider structures of federations are described above (see page 908).

The decider structures of blocs and alliances are ordinarily conferences held among decider components of the member societies. In a hierarchically organized bloc, however, the dominant nation or that nation and its strongest and closest allies may be, in effect, the decider for the entire system.

Those alliances, like NATO and SEATO, which have permanent organizational structures, have decider components. For NATO this is the North Atlantic Council, made up of ministers or permanent representatives of member states. The Military Committee is made up of one of the chiefs of staff (or his representative) from each member country except France, which has withdrawn from this committee.

Artifacts employed by this subsystem include palaces, capitols, and headquarters; administrative and court buildings; and meeting rooms.

3.3.7.2 Process Deciding in many of the systems described above is by vote, some form of a majority ordinarily being needed for decision. In alliances, unanimity among component societies is ordinarily required (see page 910).[77] If such decisions in fact guided and controlled the actions of the total systems and their components, the systems would have supranational deciding. Since nations do not lightly surrender their sovereignty, however, the deciders of these systems are limited in various ways. Some of these limitations become clear when the four stages of the deciding process at this level are examined. As at other levels, in accordance with Hypothesis 3.3.7.2-1 (see page 100), the four stages appear to be (a) establishing the purpose or goal whose achievement is to be advanced by the decision, (b) analyzing the information relevant to the decision, (c) synthesizing a solution selecting the alternative action or actions most likely to accomplish the purpose or goal, and (d) implementing the decision by issuing a command signal to carry out the action or actions.

(a) *Establishing purposes or goals.* The primary goals of systems at this level are ordinarily those for which the system was created. These are specified in the charter. Hypothesis 3.3.6.2-4 (see page 100) states that the higher the level of a system, the less its decider's activities are determined by the information of the system's template, and the more by the information of experience stored in its memory. This appears to be true of goal setting at this level, since the generally vague charters of supranational systems are constantly, in effect, modified by the experience of the systems, which creates precedents and traditions and alters structures and procedures.

Subsidiary goals may be determined within the system. The goals of the United Nations, for example, as stated in its Charter, are: "1. to maintain international peace and security; 2. to develop friendly relations among nations based on respect for the principle of equal rights and self-determination of people; 3. to cooperate in solving international problems of an economic, social, cultural or humanitarian character, and in promoting respect for human rights and fundamental freedoms for all; and 4. to be a centre for harmonizing the actions of nations in attaining these common ends."[78] Under these general goals, the program of the United Nations has expanded into the enormous complex of subprograms it is today, each of these directed toward a subsidiary goal.

Member nations of the United Nations may bring situations to the attention of the General Assembly. The Secretary General may also bring to the attention of the Security Council any matter which he thinks may threaten maintenance of international peace and security. In 1953, for example, the President of the United States suggested to the General Assembly that a world organization be created that would be devoted exclusively to the peaceful uses of atomic energy. This led to creation of IAEA, which has as its goal accelerating and enlarging the contribution of atomic energy to peace, health, and prosperity throughout the world, without furthering any military purpose. From this general goal developed all the programs, carried out by cooperation with other agencies, in which that organization is now engaged.

Goals of the blocs into which the world is now divided usually do not develop so formally. The nations of a bloc have some common values, and complex alliance relationships usually exist among them. A *suprapower* exercises, in Etzioni's words, "contextuating control" over other members of the bloc.[79] That is, the suprapower sets limits of foreign and domestic policies that it will tolerate, and it exerts pressure to follow the policies it favors. Essentially it sets the goals which the bloc will pursue, attempting not to deviate from the values of the other member nations so greatly that they will leave the bloc.

(b) *Analysis.* This process appears to be the same at this level and at the levels of the organization and the society. The autonomy of some of their nearly totipotential component nations may limit the access of supranational systems and intergovernmental organizations to some information that would be useful in identifying alternatives. Various supranational or intergovernmental organizations carry out various sorts of studies to determine the extent to which certain of their supranational system variables vary from desirable steady states. They may use consultants to define problems and recommend possible courses of action. For many variables at this level, however, there is little agreement upon what constitutes an acceptable steady state. One study by a military commission, for instance, may recommend that the safety of an alliance requires that it double its troop strength, but the member nations may be unwilling to make the necessary commitments.

(c) *Synthesis.* Selection of alternatives at this level, as at others, is influenced by the value hierarchy of the system. An aspect of the contextuating activity of the nations that head blocs is that selections from among alternative courses of action are carried out by member countries on the basis of policies determined largely by the head nation. The rules of the different sorts of international equilibria identified by Kaplan (see pages 906 and 907) include some of the constraints on choice from among alternatives, like making war.

Selection from among alternatives by blocs is constrained in the present-day world by the presence of opposing powerful blocs which can effectively oppose action with action.

(*d*) *Implementing.* In this stage of deciding the partipotentiality and the weakness of decider control of all present-day supranational systems are most evident. Some limitations on the deciders derive from the systems' operating rules. NATO, for example, is predominantly international rather than supranational. Its decisions, like those of most other alliances, must be accepted unanimously by member governments. NATO has broad powers to review and criticize national efforts. It can set goals for production of military supplies, recruitment of troops, and organization of national armies. But it cannot compel member nations to meet these goals, and often they do not. Each member decides how much effort of what sorts to devote to its defense. NATO is responsible for planning realistic defense of the alliance within its available resources.

The General Assembly of the United Nations has little power to control actions of member nations. It issues recommendations rather than directives. Decisions made by majority vote that concern activities of United Nations organizations are, of course, binding upon those components.

The Security Council is given important responsibilities by the United Nations Charter. It may investigate disputes among member or nonmember states, who accept the obligation of pacific settlement. It may determine the existence of a threat to peace, a breach of peace, or an act of aggression. It may make recommendations or decide to take enforcement measures, if necessary, to restore peace and security. Enforcement measures may include both economic sanctions and military action, and a member country against which such action has been taken may be suspended from exercising the rights and privileges of membership. A member state that persists in violating principles of the Charter may be expelled from the United Nations on recommendation of the Security Council, and the Charter does not say whether it may later reenter. The Security Council recommends to the General Assembly the admission of new members, after which the General Assembly may admit them by a two-thirds majority. It elects the judges of the International Court of Justice, along with the General Assembly, which also acts independently. And it recommends the Secretary General for appointment by the General Assembly.

The power of this body is limited by the requirement that the majority of nine required for any decision include all five of the permanent members. This constitutes the "veto" that permits any one of the five to prevent action by the Security Council. In each of the situations in which it has set up peace-keeping missions or military forces, such unanimity among five permanent members has existed. Whenever the interests of one of these members or an ally are at stake, however, the Security Council is unable to act. According to Morgenthau, such stalemates have increased the effective power of the General Assembly and have led to a tendency for its recommendations to be treated under some circumstances as legally binding decisions.[80]

International courts have a considerable amount of power to decide cases that are brought before them since the parties to the action agree in advance to accept the court's jurisdiction. In the International Court of Justice these decisions are binding only on the parties concerned and in respect of the particular case. Previous decisions may be considered, but such precedents do not have the force that they have in English common law. Though it is the court with the broadest potential jurisdiction in the world, what moderate impact it has arises from its stability, the prestige of its members, and the excellence of its decisions rather than from any great authority given it by the United Nations Charter. The numerous other international courts of limited scope need not comply with its precedents, and their decisions cannot be appealed to it. The international judicial system is highly decentralized.[81] While judgments of the International Court of Justice are final and without appeal, they are not always obeyed. If a nation which comes before the Court fails to perform its obligations under a judgment, the other country which is a party may take the case to the Security Council.

The scope of the Court of Justice of the European Communities is greater than that of the International Court of Justice. Its authority is described as follows:

In place of such rules [international law] thus created, has come a new concept of law, in the form of an institutionalized "supranational" Power, sanctioned ultimately by the consent of those subject to its authority, and by their confidence in its being appropriately exercised in accordance with requirements of the shrinking world of today—a Power possessing full legal competence within the scope assigned to it for making binding rules, of its own motion, unassisted by other lawmaking powers established singly in the Member States.[82]

This court can give instructions and orders not only to member states but also directly to industrial undertakings within member states. It can require that the High Authority of the European Communities obey its treaty obligations. It hears disputes between member states, cases of administrative law when the High Authority is defendant, and disputes between the European Communities and its employees.

Representative *variables* of the decider process include: *Meaning of information employed in deciding.* Example: The International Court of Justice advisory opinion, stating that the resolution adopted by the Security Council that the presence of South African authorities in Namibia was illegal, meant that members of the United Nations were obliged to recognize the illegality of this presence and refrain from any acts that would imply recognition of its legality.[83] *Sorts of information employed in deciding.* Example: Delegates from several nations made speeches favoring or opposing the admission of the new member state. *Amount of information employed in deciding.* Example: The International Court of Justice heard 6 weeks of testimony, consulted relevant legal references, and asked an intergovernmental agency for pertinent information before handing down a decision. *Changes in deciding over time.* Example: The emergence of a "third world" gradually changed the actions of the dominant blocs toward a number of smaller countries. *Changes in deciding with different circumstances.* Example: The threat to life in the sea caused a number of nations to demand a supranational control over fishing rights. *Number of alternatives in input before decision and in output afterward.* Example: Four different versions of the treaty were analyzed before the nations of the OAS selected one. *Rewards and punishments attached to alternatives reviewed in deciding.* Example: It was certain that China would veto a move in the Security Council to impose sanctions on North Korea. *Rate of deciding.* Example: Faced with crisis, the Security Council made several important decisions every day it met. *Lag in deciding.* Example: Objections by several small states delayed more than a month, but ultimately did not prevent, economic sanctions against the aggressor. *Costs of deciding.* Example: In 1970 the United Nations budgeted $4,704,900 for sessions of the General Assembly, councils, commissions, committees, special meetings, and conferences.

3.3.8 Encoder, the subsystem which alters the code of information input to it from other information processing subsystems, changing it from a "private" code used internally by the supranational system into a "public" code which can be interpreted by other supranational systems in its environment.

3.3.8.1 Structure   The structure of the encoder of supranational systems is similar to that of societies and organizations, since the encoding processes of supranational systems are carried out through specialized organizations of supranational or intergovernmental organizations, such as public information

agencies and publishing agencies. It may be downwardly dispersed to subsidiary organizations, groups, or individual people who prepare or translate statements for chief executives or other spokesmen, including drafting committees, staff groups, professional writers, translators, and experts in audiovisual materials.

Artifacts which are used include typewriters, other writing materials, and audiovisual materials.

3.3.8.2 Process   Information is output from supranational systems in spoken or written natural languages; in various telegraph, teletype, and computer codes; in graphic form; and sometimes in the form of artistic performances, such as those sponsored by UNESCO and UNICEF. Each such transmission must be encoded in a language or other code appropriate for the intended receiver, which, at this level, may be another supranational system or a system at the level of the society or below.

Meetings between representatives of opposing alliances and "summit meetings" between leaders of different blocs are examples of situations in which encoding is for output to another supranational system. Ordinarily a series of recodings, rather than one encoding, takes place before the communication attains the final form in which it is output from the system. Diplomatic language is a special subcode, requiring expert consultation. Information is coded to carry the intended meaning, often by the speaker himself, and then, perhaps, is translated into a natural language other than the speaker's own, appropriate for transmission to the receiving system or systems. Diplomatic language is a special usage of natural language employed by professionals in official international communications.

Preparing information outputs is a major task of many intergovernmental organizations. The information may be atomic data, weather or sea-surface reports, nutritional guidance, or other specialized material. Data may be recovered from a computer memory, automatically transmitted, and printed out at the receiving end. Teaching materials may be in beta-coded graphic or demonstration form or translated into numerous gamma-coded symbolic languages for dissemination throughout the world. Supranational systems have public relations offices which prepare and issue written and graphic materials to explain the work of the system. UNICEF appeals for funds in many languages to nations all over the world.

Information is output from supranational courts in the form of legal opinions. These are drafted by legal experts and are often translated into multiple languages of the receivers. The International Court of Justice has two official languages, English and French. Parties to an action must decide which will be used. The opinion is always given in the language in which the trial was conducted.

Representative *variables* of the encoding process include: *Meaning of information which is encoded.* Example: When the diplomat representing the alliance said that the terms offered were unsatisfactory, he was indicating that hostilities might be resumed. *Sorts of information which are encoded.* Example: A committee of ILO worked out the wording of a new labor convention. *Percentage of the information input which is encoded.* Example: The office of the Council of the European Communities translated about 30 percent of its messages into the several languages spoken in its member countries. *Threshold of the encoder.* Example: The Secretary General of the United Nations called in his legal advisors to draft his statement only after the international situation became a crisis. *Changes in encoding over time.* Example: As new literacy programs were undertaken, UNESCO began to prepare instructional materials in new languages. *Changes in encoding with different circumstances.* Example: The exponential increase in world population caused the International Planned Parenthood Federation (IPPF) to prepare a new set of brochures giving information on family planning. *Channel capacity of the encoder.* Example: The Chinese translator of the United Nations could not translate the press release at a rate faster than 100 words a minute. *Distortion of the encoder.* Example: Speaking in French, the United Nations diplomat said *nous demandons,* which sounded peremptory to his English-speaking listeners. *Signal-to-noise ratio of the encoder.* Example: In the crowd the emperor often could not hear the soft voice of his translator telling him what to say. *Rate of encoding.* Example: The IAEA computer printed out nuclear data at a rate of 1,800 lines a minute. *Percentage of omissions in encoding.* Example: The ambassador from Afghanistan spoke to the Security Council so rapidly that the translation bureau missed more than 20 percent of his words in its simultaneous translation into Russian. *Percentage of errors in encoding.* Example: The Secretary General's speech writer made twice as many errors when he wrote in Russian as when he wrote in French. *Code employed.* Example: The letter to the nation applying for membership in the intergovernmental organization was written in its native African dialect. *Redundancy of the code employed.* Example: The meeting between the alliances was conducted in French, which is less redundant than Russian. *Lag in encoding.* Example: The final report of the Conference on the Law of the Sea came out 8 months after the meeting. *Costs of encoding.* Example: Because the United Nations translators were highly skilled, they were paid $200 a day.

3.3.9 Output transducer, the subsystem which puts out markers bearing information from the suprana-tional system, changing markers within the supranational system into other matter-energy forms which can be transmitted over channels in the supranational system's environment.

3.3.9.1 Structure   This subsystem has components much like those found in the output transducers of societies and organizations. They include subordinate organizations in supranational or intergovernmental organizations such as publishing agencies and radio and television broadcast stations, as well as groups or individual persons in them such as spokesmen, press liaison officers, typists, artists, actors, demonstrators, and mail-service personnel.

The subsystem may be downwardly dispersed to societal components that perform the output transducing for the supranational system.

Artifacts in the output transducer include printing presses, radio, television, loudspeakers, and typewriters.

3.3.9.2 Process   Because of the many languages and codes in which these systems output information, this can be a complex process. Even a speech delivered at a meeting of world leaders by a single spokesman can require the services of many people, who assist him and transmit his words in various languages within the meeting hall and by various media outside—perhaps around the world.

Payment departments of supranational banks output monetary information in payments to other financial organizations.

Representative *variables* of the output transducing process are: *Meaning of information output which is transduced.* Example: Information output from the weather satellite of the WMO showed that a hurricane was forming in the Caribbean. *Sorts of information output which are transduced.* Example: The UNESCO printing office published a report on information networks and a statistical study of world literacy. *Threshold of the output transducer.* Example: Only the voices of the delegates who spoke loudly at the General Assembly were heard on the radio. *Changes in output transducing over time.* Example: The new satellite made it unnecessary to use telephone lines for transmitting information from the IAEA computer. *Changes in output transducing with different circumstances.* Example: All official representatives in both alliances understood English, and so it was unnecessary to use translators at their meeting. *Channel capacity of the output transducer.* Example: Simultaneous translations into four languages could be sent out to the world by the EEC. *Number of channels in use in the output transducer.* Example: The Secretary General's address to the world was simultaneously translated into five languages and broadcast over radio and television. *Distortion of the output transducer.* Example:

The Swahili version of the United Nations report was so full of proofreading errors that it was almost unintelligible. *Rate of output transducing.* Example: Thousands of letters a day were sent out through the United Nations post office. *Lag in output transducing.* Example: The printed version of the speech of the President of the General Assembly was issued to the press as soon as the speaker finished. *Costs of output transducing.* Example: It cost less to maintain the IAEA typing pool in Vienna than in New York.

4. Relationships among subsystems or components

4.1 Structural relationships

4.1.1 Containment   Example: Belgium contains the capital of the EEC.

4.1.2 Number   Example: There are 23 countries in the OAS.

4.1.3 Order   Example: Southward from the Netherlands, the EEC nations lie in the following order: first Belgium, then France, and then Italy.

4.1.4 Position   Example: Guatemala City is located between 14° and 15° North, 90° and 91° West, in the Central American Common Market area.

4.1.5 Direction   Example: The United States lies to the west, south, and north of one NATO city—Windsor, Canada.

4.1.6 Size Example: The Soviet Union occupies the largest land mass of the COMECON nations.

4.1.7 Pattern   Example: The central position of France in the European continent gives it a crucial role in both the EEC and NATO.

4.1.8 Density   Example: The densest concentration of nations in the OAS is in Central America.

4.2 Process relationships

4.2.1 Temporal relationships

4.2.1.1 Containment in time   Example: Between November 19, 1946, and January 1, 1976, more than 80 nations were added to the original 51 members of the United Nations, bringing the total membership to more than 130.

4.2.1.2 Number in time   Example: The World Bank group made 73 loans to 42 countries during the year that ended June 30, 1973.

4.2.1.3 Order in time   Example: Trygve Lie was the first Secretary General of the United Nations, followed by Dag Hammarskjöld, U Thant, and Kurt Waldheim, in that order.

4.2.1.4 Position in time   Example: In 1965 Indonesia became the first nation to withdraw from the United Nations.

4.2.1.5 Direction in time   Example: The United Nations membership has grown steadily from its founding to the present.

4.2.1.6 Duration   Example: The European Common Market lasted from 1951 until 1969, when it became the EEC.

4.2.1.7 Pattern in time   Example: During the period 1970 to 1975, a worldwide economic inflation increased at about twice the rate of the preceding 5 years.

4.2.2 Spatiotemporal relationships

4.2.2.1 Action   Example: The United Nations moved great quantities of food into the famine areas of India.

4.2.2.2 Communication   Example: In 1974 multilateral discussions were held among all the concerned nations, which then agreed to a cease-fire in the Middle Eastern war.

4.2.2.3 Direction of action   Example: The headquarters of the Secretariat of the United Nations moved from Geneva to New York in 1951.

4.2.2.4 Pattern of action   Example: Each time one of the blocs increased its atomic capability, so did the other.

4.2.2.5 Entering or leaving containment   Example: Goa was made a colony of Portugal in 1510, taken over by Indian forces in 1961, and annexed by India in 1962.

4.3 Relationships among subsystems or components which involve meaning   Example: Most of the members of COMECON speak related Slavic languages.

5. System processes

5.1 Process relationships between inputs and outputs   Supranational systems function through organizations which have input–output relationships similar to those of other organizations whose primary purpose is to process information. Most present-day supranational systems are incomplete and poorly integrated. Their deciders have little power. Even those which are concerned chiefly with control of matter-energy flows actually process little matter-energy. Instead, they disperse the handling of materials downward to component societies. Although a certain amount of both matter-energy and information exchange takes place over their boundaries, between supranational systems and either nonmember societies or other supranational systems, most of their important transactions take place within the system.

(*a*) *Matter-energy inputs related to matter-energy outputs.* Throughout this chapter, I have emphasized the dependence of all living systems on earth upon steady states of the nonliving environment. Some of the models and simulations in Sec. 6 (see pages 988 to 994) are concerned with the total system of our planet—with all its living and nonliving components.

The input–output relationships of this large system are important to all supranational systems.

The earth as a whole receives from the sun each second 4×10^{13} kcal of radiant energy.[84] Part of this is reflected and escapes into space in the form of short-wave radiation. Part is absorbed by components of the earth: the atmosphere, the surface water, the roads, and the soil. As a result of photosynthesis by plants, radiant energy is captured and ultimately used by all living things. Some of the energy which impinges on the earth is returned to space in the form of long-wave radiation (heat) from evaporation, burning, respiration of plants and animals, and other processes. These energy inputs and outputs are continuous.

Concerning (b) *Matter-energy inputs related to information outputs*, (c) *Information inputs related to matter-energy outputs*, and (d) *Information inputs related to information outputs* I have found no studies of importance.

5.2 Adjustment processes among subsystems or components, used in maintaining variables in steady states Many, if not all, of the supranational and international bodies now on the world scene were created to provide processes for adjusting to strains arising in the course of interactions among societies. I discuss below adjustment processes not only of supranational systems but also of societies engaged in joint activities without formation of a supranational system. The interdependence among present-day societies is so great, and their processes are limited and determined by so many feedback links among them, that their interactions have many characteristics of a worldwide system, even though no such supranational system now exists.

5.2.1 Matter-energy input processes In a world in which most of the matter-energy processing is downwardly dispersed to the level of the society or below, the adjustment processes to lacks or excesses of matter-energy input are likewise ordinarily carried out at the level of the society or below. Some problems are massive enough to affect in one way or another all the world's societies—so big that unilateral responses are inadequate. Cooperation among societies is often nonexistent or feeble, but some is evident in a number of areas. I shall consider three examples in this section: (a) cooperation in use of water resources, (b) cooperation in providing adequate food for the peoples of the world, and (c) collaboration in preventing excessive world population growth.

(a) *Water resources.* As the world has become aware of a global scarcity of water, nations have undertaken cooperative efforts to develop water resources. The Mekong, one of the great rivers, arises in Tibet, flows along the border of Burma, and, in its lower basin, runs through Laos, Thailand, Cambodia, and Vietnam into the South China Sea. The Regional Conference on Water Resources Development of the Economic Commission for Asia and the Far East (ECAFE) is developing the resources of the lower basin, both mainstream and tributaries, in cooperation with Cambodia, Laos, Thailand, and Vietnam. It is concerned with water supply, hydroelectric power, irrigation, and flood control, all matter-energy input processes. Similar international cooperation is taking place with regard to other rivers, one of which is the Indus. Canada and the United States are collaborating in building dams to produce electricity on the Columbia River. In addition, the United Nations is promoting the development of desalination plants to provide drinkable water for water-short regions.

(b) *Food.* Nations also cooperate in preventing widespread starvation. Strains arising from chronic low input of food from the agricultural activities of certain less developed countries were exacerbated by a series of bad crop years in more developed parts of the world during the early 1970s. In 1974 world grain reserves fell to a level equal to about 27 days' supply as a result of increased demand arising from population growth in poor countries and use of beef in rich countries.[85] At the same time, high petroleum prices created a shortage of nitrogen fertilizers and lessened the ability of farmers to pump irrigation water.

Distribution of food as foreign aid and efforts now under way to improve agricultural yield might not prove adequate to prevent massive starvation in a period of worldwide shortages. No satisfactory adjustment process has been initiated as yet, but matter-energy storing in world food reserves would serve to even out flows of food into the system, in good years and bad. Such a "food bank" should have stores of wheat and other cereals; legumes, including soybeans; fertilizers; reserve land; technological and other relevant information; and stores of crop genes so that seeds of new varieties could be quickly multiplied if the old varieties fell victim to pests or disease. To be adequate, a world food bank would have to store at least 5 percent of the world's average yearly production.[86] There is nothing new about this kind of adjustment process, which has been used within societies regularly since biblical times. No such process has yet been undertaken on a worldwide scale.

The seas have been an important source of human food and, within recent years, of oil as well. Unrestrained harvesting of fish and other marine life, as well as the rush to lay claim to as much as 320 km of continental shelf adjacent to national territories, has created strains in international relations. Some forms of marine life are threatened with extinction, and disturbance of the vital food chain of the sea is a real possibility.

The United Nations has held a series of conferences on the law of the sea to examine not only legal but also technical, biological, economic, and political aspects of problems related to the seas and their resources. Such a conference was held in 1974 in Caracas. Problems it considered which related to matter-energy input processes included the use of fish and whales and the control of the seas' oil resources. That conference did not produce a workable international agreement. There is some demand for the creation of supranational components with power to make and implement decisions controlling the seas, but, like the world food bank, this is still a suggested, rather than an actual, supranational adjustment process.

(c) *Population growth.* Inputs of excessive numbers of newly born human beings create strains in many parts of the world, and nations are joining together to cope with this problem. Not all societies are affected directly, since some, such as Brazil, could accommodate larger populations, but the increasing demand for food supplies is a worldwide problem. The existence of numbers of poor and disadvantaged people in the world also creates severe health problems and political instability.

Supranational efforts to find adjustment processes to meet the excessive rise in world population are being made. In 1974 the rate of increase of the human population as a whole was the highest it had ever been in human history. The total world population rose by nearly 80 million in that year, a number as large as the population of Bangladesh, the eighth largest country.[87] Coale vividly describes the results of such growth if it continues at this rate:

The present rate of world population increase—20 per 1,000—is almost certainly without precedent, and it is hundreds of times greater than the rate that has been the norm for most of man's history. Without doubt this period of growth will be a transitory episode in the history of the population. If the present rate were to be maintained, the population would double approximately every 35 years, it would be multiplied by 1,000 every 350 years and by a million every 700 years. The consequences of sustained growth at this pace are clearly impossible: in less than 700 years there would be one person for every square foot on the surface of the earth; in less than 1,200 years the human population would outweigh the earth; in less than 6,000 years the mass of humanity would form a sphere expanding at the speed of light. Considering more realistic limits for the future, if the present population is not multiplied by a factor greater than 500 and thus does not exceed two trillion, and if it does not fall below the estimated population of preagricultural society, then the rate of increase or decrease during the next 10,000 years must fall as close to zero as it was during the past 10,000 years.[88]

No information is available upon the size of the human population when man first evolved, but probably a few thousand people contributed to the original gene pool.[89] An estimated 8 million people lived on the earth at the end of the hunting and gathering period, which preceded the development of agriculture. An annual rate of increase of 0.36 per 1,000 resulted in a human population of about 300 million in A.D. 1. From then until 1750 the number increased to about 800 million, representing a rate of 0.56 per 1,000.

After 1750 the rate of growth accelerated greatly. By 1850 there were 1.3 billion people, and by 1900 there were 1.7 billion, the respective growth rates being 5.2 and 5.4 per 1,000. The world population is about 3.9 billion at present and is expected to reach 6.4 billion by 2000, at an annual growth rate during the next 25 years of 19 per 1,000. Some consequences of unrestrained population growth are examined in simulations which I discuss below (see pages 980 to 987 and 1012 to 1016).

Obviously, at some point in the expansion of world population, the harsh realities predicted by Malthus (see page 863) must act to limit further increase. Long before the earth is so crowded with human beings that there is no room for them to sit down, the food supply and other limiting factors like pollution and crowding will produce an equilibrium unattractive to contemplate. The maximum number of people that our planet could support in reasonable health and comfort is difficult to determine since it is impossible to predict the effects of future, unguessed advances in technology. One estimate is 40 to 50 billion people.[90]

A population increases when the rate of births exceeds the rate of deaths. Population growth, decline, or equilibrium can come about as a result of various patterns of fertility and mortality. In the present-day world, developed and less developed regions exhibit different rates of growth and patterns of birth and death.[91] Among developed societies, infant deaths number fewer than 25 per 1,000 births, and the expectation of life at birth is 71 years. The fertility rates in such countries are low (see pages 863 to 865). Less developed societies have high infant mortality, from 50 to 250 per 1,000 births. The overall mortality in these societies is higher than in the developed ones, but it has been rapidly reduced in recent years. Their fertility rates are high. As a result of these different patterns, populations of developed societies are increasing so slowly that if they continue unchanged for two generations, zero population growth will be reached. Less developed societies account for most of the rapid increase, with a growth rate of about 2.4 percent per year.

The potential for human misery represented in the statistics of population growth has led the United

Nations to concern itself with the problem. One of the major subsidiary organizations of ECOSOC is the Population Commission This body recommended in 1969 that United Nations programs of research and technical work concern themselves with five priority areas: fertility and family planning, mortality, urbanization and migration, demographic aspects of social development, and demographic aspects of economic development.[92]

The World Bank and IDA have also entered into the process of population planning in recent years. The objectives of their program are "to help develop viable family planning organizations and programs, strengthen information and communication activities, and promote a deeper understanding of the socio-economic factors that influence fertility."[93] They make loans for population planning and technical assistance. In 1973 they contributed a total of $65 million for seven projects in India, Indonesia, Iran, Jamaica, Malaysia, Trinidad and Tobago, and Tunisia. In the following 5-year period they planned to increase the number of projects to about 30, in some cases cooperating with other agencies, such as the United Nations Fund for Population Activities. Funds have been used for the construction of clinics, maternity centers, maternity hospitals, and training schools and for the purchase of equipment and vehicles. The World Bank and IDA also provide advice on program planning, organization, administration, and evaluation; training of personnel; and communications.

The United Nations sponsored a series of World Population Conferences in 1954, 1965, and 1974. The first two were gatherings of scientists. The last included policy makers.[94]

The necessity of population control has sometimes been challenged by religious organizations, by communist nations, and by some noncommunist nations, like Brazil, which are not under population pressure. The religious organizations and societies oppose birth control and abortion on moral grounds. Communist nations have held that, with proper development of resources and equitable distribution of wealth, population growth will not get out of control. This position gains some support from the observed course of population change in developed countries. But there is no scientific evidence that societies are able to influence the decisions of their members to bear or not to bear children (see pages 841 and 842). Westoff says:

The pervasiveness of the decline of fertility throughout the developed world should caution us against invoking currently fashionable causal explanations such as the women's rights movement, the "pill," "zero population growth" or the recent concern for the environment, although these factors have undoubtedly played a role in some countries, such as the U.S. and Canada. One can think of particular factors relevant to fertility that have operated in certain countries, such as abortion in Japan and a chronic housing shortage coupled with easy abortion and a demand for women in the labor force in Eastern Europe. A more persuasive case can be made, however, by taking the long-term historical view that links the demographic transition with the development of an industrial society, with secularization, with education and with the emergence of the demands of the individual over and above those of the family and the community. This transition has been proceeding in the U.S. and France since about 1800 and in the rest of Europe for about a century.[95]

For the most part, the governments of these societies have adopted policies to increase their birthrates.[96] Several have given financial rewards in the form of income tax deductions (e.g., the United States), direct money payments to mothers (e.g., England), and other maternity benefits, all of which increase the probability that more children will be born. Some governments did such things while at the same time providing fertility control services in public health programs.

Governmental policies in many less developed societies have favored limitation of population growth, and many of them have family planning programs. Some have introduced incentives to family limitation. In some of these, birthrates have fallen as the use of birth control has increased. But the reduction might have occurred without government intervention.[97] If the desires of the government and the inclinations of the nation's citizens are in agreement, educational and incentive programs may speed change.

One fundamental adjustment process does not involve any governmental or intergovernmental decision. People in developed societies no longer have to have many babies in order to be sure that some will live to grow up. Also, children have diminished economic value as workers and as a form of old-age insurance. Consequently, fertility has less practical value, and birthrates decline. In a given region it is hard to predict when this decline in fertility will occur.[98] Patterns that led to the present low rates in developed countries were variable. In some places fertility did not decline until after education was almost universal, the population mostly urban, and the economy primarily nonagricultural.

The United Nations declared 1974 to be World Population Year.[99] Throughout the year symposia were held, fertility surveys were made, and regional conferences were conducted. A World Population Conference was held in Bucharest, where delegates signed a World Plan of Action. Of this, Margaret Mead, a delegate, wrote:

At Bucharest it was affirmed that continuing, unrestricted worldwide population growth can negate any socioeconomic gains and fatally imperil the environment. The Conference recognized that constructive changes in the consumption patterns of affluent countries are vitally necessary to cope with the limited resources of the planet; that mere access to contraceptives and safe abortion will not reduce growth among those without hope of an improved life, although they are essential in realizing such hopes.

The earlier extreme views—that social and economic justice alone can somehow offset population increase and that the mere provision of contraception can sufficiently reduce population—were defeated. A new view emerges: to the sovereign right of states to determine domestic policies is now added responsibility for the quality of international life; to the human right of individuals and couples to decide on the number and spacing of their children, there is now the responsibility for the well-being of future children and the community. Those governments, for which excessive population growth is detrimental to their national purpose, are given a target date of 1985 to provide information and methods for implementing these goals.

The specter of the possible death by famine of as many as 30 million people in the next few years stood before us all. The Conference approved the negotiated plan by voice vote, followed by formal expressions of dissent.[100]

5.2.2 Information input processes No studies are available on responses to changes in quantity of communicative information flows into supranational systems, either overloads or underloads. The organizations through which they act, of course, have adjustment processes to overloads like those of other organizations (see pages 157 to 164 and 187 to 192), and they react like other organizations to stresses elicited by meaningful inputs.

The multinational aggregates that carry out international adjustment processes in the modern world react more to varying meanings in information inputs than to quantitative changes in the amounts of these inputs. World leaders are in almost continual communication with each other, either directly or through the public press which reports their statements and activities to the world. Even those blocs which enforce strong controls against outputs of information across their boundaries are penetrated by observers who monitor their communications channels, observe unusual internal movements of people or materials, gather intelligence within their borders, and communicate their findings to other systems. The latter then initiate adjustment processes if the information they receive indicates that international or supranational steady states are out of their normal ranges or could move in such directions. The adjustments they employ may include appeals to world opinion and demands for sanctions in the United Nations, efforts at conflict resolution, counterthreats, mobilization of troops, increased expenditures by component societies for aircraft and weapons, attempts to secure the support or at least the neutrality of unaligned nations,

or changes in economic policies. The international and supranational adjustment processes related to war are discussed below (see page 955 and 956).

In today's polarized world, propaganda is directed to members of opposing blocs as well as to unaligned nations. Such information inputs may alter adjustments in the power relationships among nations.

Nonaligned nations and small blocs also affect the policies of major blocs through information inputs to them. Intimation from a nonaligned nation that it might cast its lot with an opposing bloc can modify behavior of a powerful bloc. The importance of flows of information, rather than matter-energy, in maintaining the balance of world affairs following World War II is brought out in the following statement by Etzioni. Each of the *superpowers* in the world situation he describes led a bloc of nations that ordinarily endorsed its policies and could be expected to support it in any confrontation:*

The year 1945 began a period of bipolarity: The European Great Powers of the past were overshadowed by two continent-sized superpowers, the United States and the Soviet Union. A true balance-of-power system was precluded by a bipolar division of power. There were no third, fourth, and fifth powers who could be relied upon to prevent either superpower from gaining dominance. Despite this new development, the old idea of balance-of-power continued to guide the statesmen and strategists who molded the relationships between the two superpowers and their camps: The two superpowers were to "balance" each other.

But in the early 1950s there was added to the already bipolar pattern the element of *nuclear* bipolarity. Armed with nuclear weapons that were made increasingly invulnerable to attack by shielding and concealing devices, neither side could rationally launch a war against the other, since massive nuclear retaliation was likely to follow. The initiation of nuclear war, it was argued, meant national suicide. In this sense, the two nuclear giants "balanced" each other. As the balance achieved was based not on the actual use of strategic weapons but on threats of their use, the system was described as one of *deterrence.*[101]

Deterrence can be regarded as an adjustment process in which comparable threats, particular sorts of information inputs (see page 963), are perceived by both sides of a potential conflict. The policy of *détente* that has been pursued by both camps during the period of the late 1960s and early 1970s involves further adjustments to threat—attempts to create a climate in which the mutual threat is minimized and interdependance and cooperation are increased.

Joint policy-making adjustments among nations may have the goal of increasing the inputs of information to the cooperating countries. Examples of such adjustments are the coordinated actions of such organizations as OPEC and the Organization of Arab Petroleum Exporting Countries.

5.2.3 Matter-energy internal processes Supranational systems are stressed by several different sorts of disturbances of steady states of internal matter-energy. Among their ways of coping are (a) adjustments to stresses arising from inequitable distribution of matter-energy, (b) adjustments to stresses caused by harmful or potentially harmful matter-energy in the system, and (c) adjustments to stresses caused by war.

(a) *Adjustments to stresses arising from inequitable distribution of matter-energy.* From his earliest days, man has migrated from one place to another when his territory became overcrowded, when resources for life or comfort failed, when he encountered political and cultural opposition (information stresses), and when war or natural forces devastated his homeland and threatened his life. This was an adjustment process at the levels of the organism, the family group, the organization, and sometimes the whole society. In the present-day world there exist some supranational and international adjustments concerned with movements of people. The Intergovernmental Committee of European Migration, which is composed of 31 member nations and 8 observer nations, helps with resettlement of refugees in countries of permanent asylum, sponsors immigration into the less developed countries, and helps Europeans to immigrate who could not do so without assistance.[102] Since many of the people it deals with are refugees, this organization cooperates with the United Nations refugee programs. It selects people to fill the needs of receiving countries, like Australia, Brazil, South Africa, and the United States. It provides counseling, orientation, language training, vocational training, and other services, and will arrange transport and, if necessary, finance the movement. Its selective migration program sends experienced and professional people to less developed countries as a form of aid to speed up economic and social development.

So many parts of the United Nations are concerned with migration problems that a special Technical Working Group on Migration has been set up to coordinate their activities. The agencies concerned include ILO, ECOSOC, FAO, WHO, UNESCO, and the Office of the High Commissioner for Refugees.

Migrant workers ordinarily intend to return to their homes after a period of employment in another country. They may be men who have left their families behind to find industrial employment, or they may be whole families, all but the infants doing agricultural work. Each year thousands of Mexican laborers cross the border to the United States to work in places as far away as the Michigan bean and sugar beet fields. About 8 million foreign workers are employed in Western Europe. Many are temporary residents.[103] They come from Algeria, Greece, Morocco, Spain, Turkey, Yugoslavia, and other nations where the rate of unemployment is high.

Annually, particularly in summer, another sort of migration takes place in many parts of the world. Tourists travel to other countries to see what they are like. Since their visits are important economically, the World Bank and the IFC both help less developed countries expand tourism. The IFC invested in five hotels in Indonesia, Kenya, Turkey, and Tunisia, increasing its total commitment to such activities to over $40 million.[104] In addition, at least 19 nongovernmental organizations are concerned with promoting tourism in various regions and representing the interests of travel agents, hotel owners, and travelers.

Natural resources, agricultural land and skills, and industrial development are not evenly divided among nations. To adjust for the unevenness of distribution, societies establish trading relationships which permit them to exchange what they have in abundance for things they need. These economic relationships are discussed below (see pages 956 to 958).

International trade in primary commodities like tin, copper, zinc, sugar, olive oil, coffee, and cocoa is regulated by international agreements. These may set export quotas, establish buffer stocks, determine the disposition of surpluses, divide the world market among producing societies, and establish prices in order to produce favorable balance between supply and demand and to promote development of less developed societies. The United Nations Conference on Trade and Development (UNCTAD) is a permanent part of the Assembly. The various regional economic commissions also are concerned with trade.

Disastrous shortages in matter-energy in any part of the world are ordinarily met with multinational relief efforts involving many agencies devoted to alleviation of human suffering. The chronic poverty and need that afflict many less developed societies have stimulated organizations, societies, and supranational systems to work toward speeding up the development process and increasing the GNP of those societies. The World Bank Group (see page 909), which includes IBRD, IDA, and IFC, borrows money from central banks, governments, and governmental agencies and lends it to less developed countries. Loans from the World Bank and credits from IDA are given for agriculture; development finance companies (state enterprises, pollution control, research and development); education; electric power; industry; population (family planning); nonproject uses (imports of raw materials and components); telecommunications; tourism; and transportation. These two agencies have similar functions, but IDA makes its loans (credits) to poorer countries on easier terms. IFC promotes growth of private enterprise in such societies.

In accordance with their policy of providing more assistance to the poorest countries, 38 percent of total Bank and IDA, and 84 percent of IDA loans and credits, were made to such societies in 1975.[105] Loans and credits in that year totaled $5,895.8 million. The cumulative total as of June 30 was $36,308.8 million to 123 countries. The annual report of the World Bank/IDA for 1973 describes the effect of their agricultural aid:

No precise estimate is possible of the number of farmers or people living in the rural areas that have benefited from Bank-supported projects. Some programs, such as research on seed multiplication, can benefit many millions. Others, such as capital-intensive irrigation works or large-scale ranching, might provide direct benefits for relatively few. In addition, projects have secondary and tertiary effects which can benefit many producers as well as consumers, by influencing both prices and incomes. However, on the basis of rough estimates, it appears that anywhere from 3 to 5 million farm families, representing 15 to 25 million people, may have benefited directly from projects assisted by the Bank. Many millions more have benefited indirectly, increasing numbers of them having benefited within the past few years.[106]

The IFC, in the 17 years following 1956, invested $848.1 million in 203 enterprises in 51 developing countries.[107] Ordinarily, the IFC cooperates with other investors, business firms, and financial institutions. American firms, like Cabot Corporation and Intercontinental Hotels, and corporations from Mexico, the United Kingdom, France, Kenya, Japan, Iran, Nigeria, Switzerland, Turkey, Italy, and the Philippines were associated with IFC, as were financial institutions (banks and investment companies) in many countries. During 1973 IFC invested in most of the important industries in the developing world. New industries were supported in the Philippines, Iran, Nigeria, and Zambia. Mining was the most heavily supported industry. IFC also gave technical assistance in development planning.

To apportion the earth's surface and the resources upon and under it, during much of human history societies have taken and held what they could, fighting other societies if they have had to. Territories often passed from control by one country to control by another as a consequence of war or the settlements following wars, although sales and exchanges have also occurred. The United States bought Louisiana from France in 1804 and Alaska from Russia in 1867. At times international boundaries have been determined by plebiscites, as in the case of the Saar plebiscites of 1935 and 1947.

Under the United Nations, the International Court of Justice decides territorial arguments brought to it by governments that agree to accept its jurisdiction. One such dispute, between France and the United Kingdom, concerned the ownership of the Miniquiers and Ecrehos, two groups of islets in the English Channel between the British island of Jersey and the coast of France.[108] Both nations based their claims on the same treaty, concluded in 1204 between France and Normandy, which at that time held both England and the islands in the Channel. Since France did not occupy the islands at that time, the United Kingdom considered them to be a part of its lands. France contended that the islands had passed to its control along with Normandy. The Court held that actual exercise of sovereignty over the disputed territory, rather than indirect presumptions based on events in the Middle Ages, was decisive and made a ruling favoring the United Kingdom.

The territories of societies extend some distance into the sea. The 1974 Caracas conference on the law of the sea (see page 946) was held to determine, among other things, how great that distance would be.[109] Some societies claimed as much as 320 km, and others as little as 5. How far a society's territory extends into the sea has increased importance in the light of the shortage of natural resources and the need for societies to increase their food supplies. The continental shelves are known to hold resources of oil and other minerals, and fishing grounds adjacent to a society are important sources of protein food.

The conference on the law of the sea also discussed use of the resources of the seabed and ocean floor and the subsoil beyond the limits of national jurisdiction. If these are regarded as open territory, any society with sufficient resources to exploit it could seize that wealth of minerals and could threaten the existence of important marine species by failing to practice conservation. In fact, whales and some other species today are in danger of extinction.

In summing up the results of the conference, its President, H. Shirley Amerasinghe, of Sri Lanka, said: "There has so far been no agreement on any final text on any single subject or issue, despite the lengthy deliberations in the Sea-Bed Committee that formed the prelude to our discussions in the Conference itself. We can, however, derive some legitimate satisfaction from the thought that most of the issues or most of the key issues have been identified and exhaustively discussed and the extent and depth of divergence and disagreement on them have become manifest."[110]

(b) *Adjustments to stresses caused by harmful or potentially harmful matter-energy in the system.* Among such sorts of matter-energy for which international adjustments are undertaken are narcotics and other drugs; bacteria or viruses which cause serious disease; chemical, bacteriological, and atomic weapons; and pollutants.

Illicit use of narcotics and other dangerous drugs is a worldwide public health menace and causes international tensions. Some frequently abused substances are produced for legitimate medicinal use, but others, including *cannabis* and LSD, have no generally recognized therapeutic effects and are produced and used illegally for their effects on subjective experience.

World trade in narcotics is regulated by international treaties, agreements, and conventions. The first international conference on narcotics met in Shanghai in 1909.[111] When the League of Nations was formed, it was given responsibility for narcotics control. The United Nations now has that responsibility, which it exercises through the Commission on Narcotic Drugs, its Secretariat, the Division on Narcotic Drugs, and the International Narcotics Control Board (INCB).[112] These various bodies supervise the implementation by governments of the various multilateral treaties; review drug requirements of nations, which submit annual estimates of their needs; review statistics of both legal and illicit drug trades; ensure that the international control system operates as efficiently as possible; issue reports on legal and illegal trade in drugs; and collect and publish relevant statistics from governments, the International Criminal Police Organization (Interpol), and observers in countries where illicit traffic exists. The Division of Narcotic Drugs has a laboratory at Geneva which carries out research on opiates. INCB also has a semijudicial role which permits it to require governments found to be violating treaties to take remedial measures. It can bring treaty violations to the attention of ECOSOC and the world public. It also can recommend an embargo on drug traffic to and from any country that fails in its treaty obligations. Technical assistance and training for enforcement officers and rehabilitation workers are given by ECOSOC.

Societies that are parties to the Convention on Narcotic Drugs agree to prohibit nonmedicinal use of narcotics and to control their manufacture, use, and trade. They do not permit import or export of such substances without authorization from both sending and receiving governments. They exchange information on the laws they pass dealing with narcotics, agreeing to make intentional violations of the rules of the Convention punishable offenses and to take account of foreign convictions in considering drug cases. They are asked to put an end to cultivation of *cannabis* in their countries. Extradition is recommended for offenders against narcotics laws. If that cannot be arranged, foreign violators are to be prosecuted either in the country in which the offense was committed or in the country in which they are apprehended.

In the past few years there has been widespread abuse of certain drugs that had not previously been abused. These include depressants, central nervous system stimulants, and hallucinogens. A new treaty, the Convention on Psychotropic Substances, adopted in 1971, sets up a system of control even more severe than the control of narcotics. This treaty also imposes lesser controls for some substances like sleeping pills and tranquilizers.

Drug control is a difficult problem, however. *Cannabis* grows wild in many parts of the world and is readily cultivated, often in regions far enough from urban centers to make policing difficult. Growers of opium poppies for the legal trade also provide them at greater profit to themselves for the illicit trade, and their governments may be unwilling or unable to prevent them. The probability of being detected in international drug smuggling is low enough, and the rewards for success high enough, that a well-organized trade continues in spite of efforts to stop it. And the demand is growing.

Recognition that protection of the environment is a proper concern of international and supranational bodies has been increasing over the past two decades. The sea is not a limitless repository for societies' wastes. The fact that harm can come to the basic food chain upon which man depends for much protein food has been demonstrated by findings of contaminants in waters far from any large society and by demonstration of chemical poisons in marine life and sea birds. The possibility of damage to the atmosphere of the entire earth by various pollutants is now recognized. No single government acting alone can eliminate such contamination. The report of the United Nations Conference on the Human Environment, held in Stockholm in 1972, stated:

Man has constantly to sum up experience and go on discovering, inventing, creating and advancing. In our time, man's capability to transform his surroundings, if used wisely, can bring to all peoples the benefits of development and the opportunity to enhance the quality of life. Wrongly or heedlessly applied, the same power can do incalculable harm to human beings and the human environment. We see around us growing evidence of man-made harm in many regions of the earth: dangerous levels of pollution in water, air, earth and living beings; major and undesirable disturbances to the ecological balance of the biosphere; destruction and depletion of irreplaceable resources; and gross deficiencies harmful to the physical, mental and social health of man, in the man-made environment, particularly in the living and working environment.[113]

One of the first serious pollution problems to be dealt with internationally was that of oil spills in the seas. In 1962 the *Torrey Canyon,* an oil tanker, was wrecked in the Atlantic off the coast of England, creating disastrous pollution along the coast. IMCO appointed a legal committee which drafted two new conventions, the International Convention relating to Intervention on the High Seas in Cases of Oil Pollution Casualties and the International Convention on Civil Liability for Oil Pollution Damage, both adopted in 1969.[114] IMCO also adopted some technical measures designed to minimize ship collisions and avoid accidental spills. These included more stringent requirements for equipment like radar, echo sounders, and radiotelegraphy. Discharge of oil into the sea was prohibited. IMCO has also been concerned with the design, construction, and equipment of ships that carry potentially harmful cargoes.

The United Nations Conference on the Human Environment of 1972 included representatives of 113 states. It resulted in more than 100 recommendations and an "action plan."[115] The emphasis was on research, data gathering, training, and information dissemination on a wide range of environmental problems—not only pollution, but also care of wildlife, forest management, human population control, and protection of genetic resources. Such activities of all concerned agencies were to be coordinated by a Governing Council for Environmental Programmes appointed by the General Assembly.

Earlier, WHO had undertaken work relating to environmental protection. It has established reference systems for studying data on community water supplies, waste disposal, air and water pollution, and radiation protection.[116] The six most common air pollutants are being studied also to establish criteria and guides for air quality. An international network has been set up for monitoring and studying levels of sulfur dioxide and dust particles in the air as a basis for an early-warning system.

Pollution of the seas was a concern also of the 1974 conference on the law of the sea (see page 946 and 950). It discussed a new agency to deal with the many problems of the sea, seabed, and continental shelves beyond national borders.[117] Brown has emphasized the necessity of such an agency and described its possible activities:

A world environmental agency would have several functions. First, it would have a monitoring function, gathering a vast amount of data on environmental variables on a worldwide basis. Using the information accumulated over time, it would need to assess the impact of man's various interventions in the environment, whether they be turning a river around, speeding up the nitrogen cycle, or emptying mercuric wastes into rivers which feed into the ocean. This in itself is a massive undertaking requiring an enormous amount of manpower and financial resources, considering that man is now discharging some 500,000 compounds into the biosphere. But the next step, determining the precise effect on the ecosystem of these interventions, is a far more complex, time-consuming process of research and analysis. The knowledge gap must be filled, however, if the earth's ecosystem is to be preserved. Once the necessary information and analysis is complete, tolerance levels can be established and translated into the necessary regulations of human economic activity. No doubt ensuring compliance with these regulations will be exceedingly difficult. Nowhere does the gap between advancing technology and the institutions to cope with it so imperil the human condition as in the relationship between man and the environment.[118]

I describe below some simulations that deal with environmental variables (see pages 988 to 994).

Without question, the sorts of matter-energy accumulated in societies that present the most immediate international threat are chemical, bacterial, viral, and atomic weapons. These are capable of destroying civilization even more rapidly than environmental deterioration. Atomic testing also contributes to environmental pollution.

All modern nations are aware of the danger of such weapons to their own people as well as their enemies, but the international situation has made them unwilling to eliminate these weapons completely. In 1970 global military expenditures totaled $204 billion; this represented a large share of the total resources of the world that could otherwise have been used more constructively.[119] Both the United States and the Soviet Union had far more than enough weapons to wipe each other out, and other nations were increasing their armaments.

Mutual agreement to disarm, if it could be attained and if controls were accepted by all nations concerned, is an obvious and valuable adjustment process to correct the strains brought about by the continuing arms race. As of mid-1977, however, although some limited agreements had been reached, negotiations had not been successful. From 1945, when nuclear bombs were developed, to 1975, the United States increased its stock of nuclear warheads to almost 10,000.[120] A novel development is the MIRV (*M*ultiple *I*ndependently targeted *R*eentry *V*ehicle), which permits one rocket to launch warheads at several targets simultaneously or at the same target on several different trajectories. With obvious first-strike capability, these threaten the delicate "balance of terror."

Multilateral arms-limitation pacts, as well as bilateral ones, have been made between the United States and the Soviet Union. Since 1959 pacts have been signed by varying numbers of nations, from 17 to 106. Tables 12-4 and 12-5 list multilateral and bilateral agreements subsequent to 1959.

An analysis, by Singer, of the possible policies nations might adopt with regard to arms identifies six: (*i*) preventive war, (*ii*) crude preponderance, (*iii*) sophisticated deterrence, (*iv*) arms control, (*v*) multilateral disarmament, and (*vi*) unilateral disarmament.[121] They are listed in order from the most to the least bellicose. (*i*) In preventive war, national deciders would be so certain that war is inevitable that they would strike first. Although no experts openly advocate such action at present, it has been suggested by extremists in the past. (*ii*) Crude preponderance is a policy that would set up an arms race intended to assure an advantage to one nation, usually on the theory that war is inevitable. (*iii*) Sophisticated deterrence is a strategic doctrine held by people who would accept limitations to reduce the probability of war. (*iv*) Arms control is advocated by those who would mini-

mize the probability of surprise attack, or accidental or unintended war, by slowing and stabilizing the armaments race. Under this doctrine, total armament of the nations involved would neither increase nor decrease. Armament in each country would be determined by multilateral agreements. (*v*) Multilateral disarmament would go much further, although ordinarily its proponents do not advocate total elimination of all weapons of war. A minimum position would be to retain just enough armaments to ensure domestic tranquillity. Others would eliminate nuclear but not conventional weapons, or they would include chemical, bacterial, and viral weapons among those eliminated. (*vi*) Finally, there are the extreme pacifists, who would disarm unilaterally.

The SALT agreements between the United States and the Soviet Union clearly adopt a limited disarmament position (see Table 12-5). A correlate of limitation is agreed to be some form of verification and control that would protect each nation that is a party to

TABLE 12-4   Multilateral Arms Agreements

Year signed	Year in force	Agreement	Provisions of agreement	Number of parties
1959	1961	Antarctic Treaty	Prohibits all military activity in antarctic area	17
1963	1963	Partial-Nuclear-Test-Ban Treaty	Prohibits nuclear explosions in the atmosphere, in outer space, and under water	106
1967	1967	Outer-Space Treaty	Prohibits all military activity in outer space, including the moon and other celestial bodies	71
1967	1967	Treaty of Tlatelolco	Prohibits nuclear weapons in Latin America	18
1968	1970	Nonproliferation Treaty	Prohibits acquisition of nuclear weapons by nonnuclear nations	82
1971	1972	Sea-Bed Treaty	Prohibits emplacement of nuclear weapons and other weapons of mass destruction on ocean floor or subsoil thereof	52
1972	1975	Biological-Weapons Convention	Prohibits development, production, and stockpiling of bacterial, viral, or toxinic weapons and requires destruction of existing biological weapons	31

NOTE: Multilateral arms pacts negotiated in recent years are listed here in chronological order, together with short statements of their major provisions. The column at the extreme right gives the total number of nations that were parties to each treaty as of Dec. 31, 1973. The convention on biological weapons had been ratified by 31 nations by that date. Since then, it has been ratified by the United States, the United Kingdom, and the Soviet Union.

SOURCE: Adapted from A. Myrdal. The international control of disarmament. *Sci. Amer.*, 1974, Oct. **231**(4), 24. Copyright © 1974 by Scientific American, Inc. All rights reserved. Reprinted by permission.

TABLE 12-5   Bilateral Arms Agreements

Year signed	Year in force	Agreement	Provisions of agreement
1963	1963	"Hot-line" agreement	Establishes direct radio and telegraph communications between United States and Soviet Union for use in emergency
1971	1971	"Hot-line" modernization agreement	Increases reliability of original "hot-line" system by adding two satellite-communications circuits
1971	1971	Nuclear-accidents agreement	Institutes various measures to reduce risk of accidental nuclear war between United States and Soviet Union
1972	1972	High-seas agreement	Provides for measures to help prevent dangerous incidents on or over the high seas involving ships and aircraft of both parties
1972	1972	SALT I ABM treaty	Limits deployment of antiballistic-missile systems to two sites in each country
1972	1972	SALT I interim offensive-arms agreement	Provides for 5-year freeze on aggregate number of fixed land-based intercontinental ballistic missiles (ICBMs) and submarine-launched ballistic missiles (SLBMs) on each side
1973	1973	Protocol to high-seas agreement	Prohibits simulated attacks by ships and aircraft of each party aimed at nonmilitary ships of other party
1973	1973	Nuclear-war-prevention agreement	Institutes various measures to help avert outbreak of nuclear war in crisis situations
1974	1974	SALT II ABM treaty	Limits deployment of antiballistic-missile systems to one site in each country
1974		SALT II threshold nuclear-test-ban treaty	Prohibits underground tests of nuclear weapons with explosive yields greater than 150 kilotons
1974		SALT II interim offensive-arms agreement	Commits both parties to negotiate extension of SALT I interim offensive-arms agreement through 1985

NOTE: Arms agreements between the United States and the Soviet Union cover mostly peripheral matters of immediate concern only to the two superpowers. Critics of the agreements reached in the strategic-arms-limitation talks (SALT I and II) contend that the bilateral approach has succeeded only in outlawing weapons systems that neither side wanted anyway. The net result was that the arms race has merely been redirected. By August 1976, only one of the SALT II treaties, which were signed in Moscow on July 3, 1974, had been ratified by the United States Congress and was in force.

SOURCE: Adapted from A. Myrdal. The international control of disarmament. *Sci. Amer.*, 1974, Oct., **231**(4), 26. Copyright © 1974 by Scientific American, Inc. All rights reserved. Reprinted by permission.

an agreement from noncompliance on the part of others. Such controls and inspections for verification can be imposed upon the testing, production, possession, or deployment of missiles or on combinations of these. A simulation of arms inspections is discussed below (see pages 996 to 998).

Each type of control has its own problems.[122] Common to all is the reluctance of sovereign nations to be inspected by foreigners. Myrdal says:

It is of prime importance to resort as little as possible to intrusive methods of investigation, be they conducted by spies or through on-site inspections. Modern technology is very helpful in this regard, since it provides ever more efficient means for unobtrusively checking events from a distance. Radar and sonar, the analysis of radioactive emissions and the monitoring of telecommunication frequency patterns are just a few of the less intrusive methods of surveillance made available by modern technology. One such method has had special prominence in the recently concluded agreements, namely observations from satellites. The satellite surveillance of launchers for land-based strategic missiles, for example, made it unnecessary for the parties in the SALT I agreement to seek the right of direct observation of the missiles.

The use of sensors on satellites for making observations raises in the most acute form problems of ethics that are inherent in all attempts at control and verification. Control by whom? Because satellite observations are now virtually the monopoly of the superpowers, there must be an international demand that the observations of military satellites be made openly available, at least to the countries being observed. Only a certain sharing of data of relevance to environmental matters is in the offing so far. At a recent meeting of the UN Working Group on Remote Sensing of the Earth by Satellites the representative of the U.S. promised that data from his country's satellites would be released regularly for international use. The same demand for the internationalization of knowledge must be made in regard to observations of relevance to armaments and disarmament. The most desirable development would be direct international management of a satellite system.[123]

The importance of free flow of information in control of arms is emphasized by Myrdal. She envisions an International Disarmament Control Organization, which would function as an open clearinghouse to relay information on disarmament to all nations. The organization should, in her opinion, also be given responsibilities for coordinating, referring, and verifying. The organization she proposes would have four levels—one societal and three international. On the societal level each nation would have not only a parliamentary committee to oversee military activities and expenditures, as all current democratic societies have, but also committees representing governmental and public organizations to assure that the country's weapons complied with international humanitarian rules of war. Citizens should also have access to facts on arms and arms limitations to enable them to act as watchdogs and thus ensure that disarmament agreements are respected within their nation's borders.

Two international levels would be responsible for collection of information, mandatory verification, and investigation of challenges by parties to treaties. The highest international level would be the United Nations Security Council, which would have judicial powers in cases of disputes.

(c) *Adjustments to stresses caused by war.* International and supranational adjustments to the internal matter-energy disruptions brought about by war among nations include limitations on the use of certain sorts of weapons, rules designed to protect civilians and care for refugees or displaced persons, and agreements concerned with the well-being of prisoners of war. Punishment of "crimes against humanity" has also been carried out by international bodies.

Rules for the conduct of warfare are not new. Exchanges of prisoners, care of wounded under flags of truce, and recognition of noncombatant status have been practiced for centuries. Humanitarian rules were agreed upon internationally in the Hague Conventions of 1899 and 1907, the Geneva Protocol of 1925, and the Geneva Conventions of 1949. The United Nations has concerned itself with many war-related humanitarian problems throughout the world.

After World War I, the use of poison gas was outlawed by international agreement. An agreement on bacterial, viral, and toxinic weapons is mentioned in Table 12-4.

The United Nations Assembly at its twenty-fifth session in 1970 adopted five resolutions relating to human rights in armed conflicts. One of these included eight principles:

1. Fundamental human rights, as accepted in international law and laid down in international instruments, continue to apply fully in situations of armed conflicts.
2. In the conduct of military operations during armed conflicts, a distinction must be made at all times between persons actively taking part in the hostilities and civilian populations.
3. In the conduct of military operations, every effort should be made to spare civilian populations from the ravages of war, and all necessary precautions should be taken to avoid injury, loss or damage to civilian populations.
4. Civilian populations as such should not be the object of military operations.
5. Dwellings and other installations that are used only by civilian populations should not be the object of military operations.
6. Places or areas designated for the sole protection of civilians, such as hospital zones or similar refuges, should not be the object of military operations.
7. Civilian populations, or individual members thereof, should not be the object of reprisals, forcible transfers or other assaults on their integrity.
8. The provision of international relief to civilian populations is in conformity with the humanitarian principles of the United Nations Charter, the Universal Declaration of Human Rights and other international instruments in the field of human rights. The Declaration of Principles for International Humanitarian Relief to the Civil Population in Disaster Situations, as laid down by the 21st International Conference of the Red Cross, shall apply in situations of armed conflict, and all parties to a conflict should make every effort to facilitate this application.[124]

The 1949 Geneva Convention on Treatment of Prisoners of War provides for repatriation of seriously sick or wounded prisoners, repatriation or internment in a neutral country of able-bodied prisoners, and regular inspections by a protecting power or humanitarian organization of the places in which they are kept. The record of compliance with these and other humanitarian principles and agreements is a sorry one. Some nations have never subscribed to any of these rules or conventions, and many others have violated them.

5.2.4 Information internal processes   Among the adjustment processes of this class are those having to do with supranational and international control of financial transactions among nations and those used in efforts of supranational and international bodies to resolve conflicts among nations. I shall discuss two sorts of such adjustments: (*a*) financial adjustment processes and (*b*) conflict resolution.

(*a*) *Financial adjustment processes.*   A network of financial organizations links virtually all the world's societies. Over this network flow markers representing money or money equivalents—payments for goods and services exchanged by public agencies and private companies, public and private loans and investments, repayments on principal, interest payments, foreign-aid loans and grants, money orders or checks sent by immigrants to friends or relatives in their native countries, and gold or other reserve assets transferred from one nation to another to make up deficits in the balance between financial imports and exports. Each society keeps an account of international transactions in which credits and debits must balance. Table 12-6 summarizes international transactions of the United States for 1974.

In international financial exchanges, each country must ultimately be paid in its own currency, since that is the only sort of money that can be used within its borders.[125] These currencies differ in their basic units and in their buying power. Payments from one country to another depend upon foreign-exchange rates, calculations of the value of each currency relative to that of each of the others. These rates can be set in various ways, and, in fact, the basis for foreign exchange has changed and developed during this century. Two of many possible modes of international exchange are (*i*) the gold (or bimetallic gold and silver) standard and (*ii*) free supply and demand. The first corresponds closely to the accepted mode in the period before 1914. The second has been approximated more recently. Neither has ever existed in pure form.

(*i*) *The gold standard.*   In this mode of exchange monetary values depended upon the weight of gold represented by each unit of currency. As the stock of gold increased or decreased, internal prices fluctuated. An automatic adjustment process maintained a steady state of international imports and exports since a country that was losing gold would attempt to decrease its purchase of relatively costly imports and

to increase its export of relatively cheap home-produced goods. If one country imported from another more than it exported to it, gold could be shipped to balance the account. A change in the rate at which a country bought or sold gold altered the value of the country's money relative to those countries which did not devalue their currency.

One major difficulty with a worldwide gold standard is that gold is a scarce commodity. Samuelson says:

Even in its brief heyday, several crises caused the gold standard to break down periodically (as, for example, when our [United States] Civil War forced us off gold for more than a decade). Moreover, the price level was at the mercy of the happenstance of gold discoveries. If world physical production was increasing in the years 1875 to 1895 at the rate of 5 per cent per year, the gold supply would—according to the Quantity Theory of Money—have to increase by 5 per cent per year to keep prices stable. But mines, because of the ending of the Californian and Australian gold rushes, were not producing this much gold then; and as a result price levels were sagging all over the world in the last third of the nineteenth century.

This gave rise to much social unrest. In an ideal world of perfect price and wage flexibility, where the Quantity Theory worked smoothly both down and up, falling prices should not have mattered much. But . . . prices and wages tend to be sticky downward; and falling price levels tend to lead to labor unrest, strikes, unemployment, and radical movements generally. Precisely that happened in the United States and other countries during the 1875–1895 era of populism. . . . Since gold seemed to be squeezing prices downward, there was a clamor on the part of farmers and workers for use of silver to supplement gold. This culminated in the historic speech by William Jennings Bryan in favor of "bimetallism" at the 1896 Democratic Convention, where the "Boy Orator of the Platte" warned against crucifying mankind on a cross of gold.[126]

(*ii*) *Supply and demand.*   A second mode of foreign exchange is an adjustment process whereby rates are set by supply and demand. That is, if one nation purchases the outputs of another which cost more than it can obtain by selling to that nation, the rate of exchange between the two currencies fluctuates enough to bring demand into balance with supply, unless some other currency is exchanged between the two nations. As a country's money becomes more valuable, the price of its goods to the country to which they are imported rises, decreasing the demand for them. At the same time the price of exports of the country with the cheaper currency falls in foreign markets, increasing the demand. Domestic price levels do not necessarily change when the value of a society's money fluctuates in international trade.

The free operation of such automatic international adjustments of purchase and sale of goods and of prices has been limited by governmentally imposed tariffs or import quotas. These prevent the most advantageous worldwide production patterns by increasing the price of imported goods relative to that

TABLE 12-6.   United States Balance of International Payments Account for 1974
(In Millions of Dollars)

No.	Items	Credits	Debits	Net credits (+) or debits (−)	
I	Current account				
1	(Private) merchandise trade balance	$98,268	$103,796	−$ 5,528	
	Invisibles:				
2	Travel and transportation			− 2,692	
3	Investment income	26,068	15,946	+ 10,122	
4	Other services net			+ 3,830	
5	Balance on private goods and services				+$ 5,732
6	Military transactions			− 2,158	
7	Remittances, pensions, and other transfers net			− 1,721	
8	U.S. government grants (excluding military)			− 5,461	
9	Government current balance				−$ 9,340
10	Balance on current account				−$ 3,608
II	Capital account				
	Long-term loans (−) or borrowing (+)				
11	Private			− 8,437	
12	Government			+ 1,119	
13	Net long-term foreign investment				−$ 7,318
14	Basic balance on current account and long-term capital				−$10,927
15	Nonliquid short-term private capital flows, net			− 12,949	
16	Allocations of new SDRs to U.S. by IMF			+ —	
17	Errors and omissions, net			+ 4,834	
18	Short-term capital movements				−$ 8,115
19	Net liquidity balance				−$19,043
20	Liquid private capital flows (from foreigners to their central banks)				+$10,669
21	Official reserves transactions balance				−$ 8,374
III	Net reserve-and-gold asset movements				
22	Liabilities to foreign official agencies incurred			+ 8,481	
23	U.S. official-reserve assets net outflow			− 107	
24	Total				+$ 8,374
25	Formal over-all net total				0

SOURCE: Adapted from P. A. Samuelson. *Economics.* New York: McGraw-Hill, 1976, 658. (Data from U.S. Department of Commerce.) Reprinted by permission.

of domestic goods.[127] Although many economists deplore tariffs except under special circumstances, industries that could not operate competitively in a free-trade world continue to demand such protection.

The various customs unions and common markets throughout the world have been formed to achieve the advantages of free trade and free movement of capital within the system, while often maintaining them in external transactions.

The present-day monetary exchange system contains features of both the gold standard and supply and demand, as well as some other adjustment processes imposed by agreements among governments.

The development of modern banking, in which a particular bank actually holds only a fraction of its

reserves, has reduced the amount of gold required to support price levels. Decades ago countries also began to keep less than 100 percent of the gold necessary to back their currencies. Some small ones held little or no gold, but instead kept the money in some large country that was on the gold standard. Following World War II the world was on a gold and dollar standard. The Bretton Woods Conference of 1944 defined parities in terms of gold and of the dollar, which was worth as much as $\frac{1}{35}$ ounce of gold.[128] Most of the gold in the world had accumulated in Fort Knox, Kentucky. Products of the United States were in great demand. Without special adjustment processes, the soaring price of the dollar might have forced depreciation of foreign currencies. This was postponed by exchange and import controls in the countries with overvalued currencies and by United States aid and loan programs.[129] Since citizens of the United States hesitated to take the risks of lending capital for development and reconstruction throughout the world, the Bretton Woods Conference set up the IBRD, to which nations with money to lend subscribe funds for sound long-term loans. This bank can also float bonds backed by the credit of member nations. The IMF was set up at the same conference in the hope of securing the advantages of the gold standard without its disadvantages. International cooperation was to replace the previous automatic adjustment processes. It was thought that it might help keep countries from deflating themselves into drastic unemployment and that the need for import controls might decrease. Samuelson says:

Ordinarily, a country pays for its imports by means of its exports or long-term borrowing. Suppose a country, say, England, is in need of short-term credit from the Fund. How does the Fund enable such a debtor country to get hold of dollars, for instance? It does this by extending "purchasing rights." It simply permits the British to buy with British currency some of the Fund's own holdings of dollars. After the British balance of payments has improved, Britain is expected to buy back with gold (or with dollars or . . . with . . . "paper gold") the pounds it has sold to the Fund.

The Fund tries to set up rules and procedures to keep a country from going too deeply into debt, year after year. After a country has been piling up debts for a considerable period, certain financial penalties are applied. More important, the Fund's directors consult with the country and make recommendations for remedying the disequilibrium. However, they do not advise a country to create a depression in order to cut its national income down to such a low level that its imports will finally fall within its means. Instead, the country itself is permitted first to depreciate (or appreciate in opposite situations) its currency by 10 per cent. This tends to restore equilibrium in its trade by expanding its exports and contracting imports.

If this is still not enough to correct the so-called "overvaluation" of the debtor country's currency, the Fund authorities may, after proper consultation, permit still further depreciation of the debtor country's exchange rate. But note this: All changes in rates are to take place in an orderly way. Most of the time, there is to be international stability. There is also provision for flexibility when needed, which is better by far than waiting for a great smash.

By the 1960s the IMF realized that it must also shift onto the surplus countries an obligation to help restore basic equilibrium. Thus, Germany may be encouraged to appreciate the mark (as she did in 1961 and finally in 1969.) She may be encouraged to lower import barriers and export subsidies; to lend abroad and enlarge her foreign aid; to reflate her economy if she is stagnating.[130]

Although this set of adjustment processes appeared to work well through the 1950s, weaknesses began to appear early in the 1960s, and by the early 1970s the procedures faced possible breakdown. The relatively inflexible exchange rates which had been determined at Bretton Woods proved to be a weakness. Although this conference provided for adjustment in parities, these were so planned that they could not be instituted until after disequilibrium became obvious. The lag of the adjustment processes was too great. During the period of steady-state disturbance, speculators sold weak currencies short without risk and with a good chance that any change would be in their favor. When speculators acted together, they could precipitate crises profitable for them. During the same period, the increased volume of international trade far outstripped the supply of new gold. The supply could not keep up with the liquidity needs of the system. Also, the dollar, which had been the standard at the time the system was set up, weakened and was no longer universally acceptable as a substitute for gold.

Crop shortages, which increased grain prices, and extremely high prices set for oil by the countries which produced it contributed to inflation. This threatened weak economies like that of Italy. Those countries which experienced famine found that high fertilizer prices, which fluctuate with oil prices, barred increased food production.

Some adjustment processes have been undertaken to correct deviations from world economic steady states. In 1968 a conference held by 10 major nations set up a two-tier gold system which provided that transactions in gold would not flow from those governments to the free market.[131] The 10 nations, which included, besides the United States, Great Britain and several other European countries, would keep all their official gold reserves. Intergovernmental payments would still be made in gold at set prices. Outside the IMF, gold prices were to be set by supply and demand. Since the supply of gold is not great enough to provide international liquidity, the IMF set up Special Drawing Rights called "paper gold."[132] Allocations are made among member nations by quota. This is a form of reserve assets set up by a vote of IMF members, subject to veto by 15 percent of the voting quotas.

These adjustments have not solved many international financial problems of the 1970s. It is increasingly apparent that fundamental changes will be needed. In 1977, the international economic steady states of the past were changing in major ways, with little indication of the nature of the new steady states that might eventually result.

(b) *Conflict resolution.* Throughout the greater part of history, war has been considered both an inevitable and a glorious way to make international decisions and to resolve conflicts and achieve ultimate peaceful adjustments among nations. If they were victorious in arms, men attained wealth and power, and their societies prospered. Only in the twentieth century has a world without war been widely regarded as a valid goal. Ironically, throughout this century, large and small wars have been continuous. Practical (as opposed to idealistic) pacifism has been generally unpopular. At the same time the search for a way to peaceful world steady states has continued.

Among the components of the United States most concerned with attainment of world peace are many persons in the academic community, particularly the social scientists. Their concern has manifested itself in both theoretical studies and empirical research into the causes of war and the means of preventing it. A similar concern on the part of some societal deciders has led to international and supranational adjustment processes designed to resolve disputes among nations by peaceful means rather than by war. Some simulation studies of actions of nations in crisis are discussed below (see pages 1000 to 1009, 1011, and 1012). Some empirical studies of war-related behavior obtain data from historical records of past conflicts:

Modern social science methods coupled with the use of computers may transform history into something approaching a laboratory of international behavior. With machines and appropriate techniques, the scholar can now reduce documentary materials from various national archives into replicable, countable units and analyze quantities of data which would have required a battalion of research assistants by traditional standards. With these methods, moreover, it is now feasible to order new concepts, test new kinds of hypotheses, and derive new types of findings from the usual documents of history. . . .

What can these new historical approaches offer to the social scientist who is interested primarily in contemporary phenomena, or to the policy-maker whose focus is on the present and on the future? What relevance, for example, does an historical crisis have for crises of today—crises in a nuclear age? Clearly the circumstances are different, the nations and leaders are different, and the weapons are different. Why dig into the half-forgotten past? What can we learn that will be useful in meeting problems of the future?

Social science approaches to historical situations are based upon the fundamental assumption that there are patterns, repetitions, and close analogies throughout the history of human affairs. The circumstances and paraphernalia will differ between the Peloponnesian War and the War of the Roses or between World War I and World War II, but the patterns of human fears and anxieties and perceptions of threat and injury may not be dissimilar. A fundamental part of the problem lies in identifying the levels of abstraction where likenesses can be found between problems or events that are widely separated in time and also in space.[133]

Information processing during international crises. North and his colleagues have made use of the abundant historical material that is available about most of the participant nations in World War I to study various aspects of the international information processing which went on during that crisis period. I have discussed studies of communication patterns among and within nations above (see pages 824 to 826).

Using the method of content analysis, Holsti and North tested the hypothesis that knowledge of the fact that its capabilities are inferior may not deter a nation from going to war if it perceives strongly enough that it has been injured.[134] This research was based on the assumption that perception of threat by leaders of one society leads to hostile defensive activity. This evokes defensive hostility from another country, from which the threat was perceived (correctly or incorrectly) to come. This response serves to verify the original perception of the first nation. From that point on, responses of both countries become more emotional and less reasoned, as hostile perceptions and threats lead to exchange of lethal strikes. To confirm the hypothesis, three requirements had to be met: (i) Superior forces failed to deter, (ii) one of the nations perceived that its forces were inferior, and (iii) a nation's leaders believed that they were victims of injury during the crisis that led to war. These three conditions were shown to exist in 1914, as follows:

(i) The fact that the crisis culminated in a general European war clearly showed that superior forces failed to deter hostilities.

(ii) A study of the 1914 crisis showed that the chief German leaders knew that Germany did not then have the capability to wage a general European war.[135]

(iii) The perception of injury was measured by two indices. The first, an *index of persecution*, measured the extent to which decision makers saw their own nation to be primarily the target rather than the agent of hostility. This was expressed as:

$$\frac{\text{Units of hostility as target}}{\text{Units of hostility as agent}}$$

The second, an *index of rejection*, measured the degree to which decision makers considered that their friendly policies toward other nations were unreciprocated:

$$\frac{\text{Units of hostility as agent}}{\text{Units of hostility as target}}$$

From these, an *index of injury* was calculated by the formula:

$$\frac{\text{Units of hostility as target} + \text{Units of friendship as agent}}{\text{Units of hostility as agent} + \text{Units of friendship as target}}$$

Table 12-7 shows the index of injury of each participant nation in World War I. When the index of injury of each of the five major powers in World War I is plotted against the historical course of events, two

TABLE 12-7   Index of Injury of Each Participant Nation in World War I

Perceiver	Perceived	(1) Agent of hostility	(2) Target of hostility	(3) Agent of friendship	(4) Target of friendship	$\frac{(2)+(3)}{(1)+(4)}$ Index of injury
Germany	Austria-Hungary	320.27	409.98	76.00	243.00	0.86
Triple Entente*	Austria-Hungary	700.33	232.34	12.50	117.00	0.30
Austria-Hungary	Germany	22.66	9.37	97.50	57.50	1.33
Triple Entente	Germany	548.89	165.01	127.50	111.50	0.49
France and Russia	Great Britain	17.33	3.33	58.00	135.00	0.44
Dual Alliance†	Great Britain	75.66	19.00	79.00	25.00	0.98
Great Britain and Russia	France	3.33	46.34	60.50	57.00	1.77
Dual Alliance	France	538.29	117.01	40.50	50.00	0.27
Great Britain and France	Russia	109.64	89.67	187.00	195.50	0.91
Dual Alliance	Russia	583.97	244.63	90.00	158.00	0.45

*France, Russia, and Great Britain.
†Austria-Hungary and Germany.
SOURCE: O. R. Holsti & R. C. North. The history of human conflict. In E. B. McNeil (Ed.). *The nature of human conflict.* Englewood Cliffs, N.J.: Prentice-Hall, 1965, 166. © 1965. Reprinted by permission of Prentice-Hall, Inc. Englewood Cliffs, N.J.

major peaks in the intensity of indices for all five are found to correspond to the two phases of the crisis—the local war between Austria and Serbia and the later general war that involved all five. Moreover, each nation felt very strongly that it was the victim of injury at the precise time when its leaders were making the most crucial policy decisions. Holsti and North sum up the events in Europe in the summer of 1914 as follows:

World War I was not originally a conflict between two monolithic and mutually antagonistic blocs. . . . Rather, the initial spiralling of tensions, of perceived threats and counterthreats, occurred within a series of lower-level relationships. Serbia and Austria-Hungary had been linked in such a situation well before the assassination of Francis Ferdinand. That act of violence was only one of a series of events which led to the outbreak of local war between them. Russia and Germany, which had made binding commitments to Serbia and Austria-Hungary respectively, were similarly linked. For a variety of reasons Russia was unable to make clear to Germany its intention to aid Serbia without attacking Germany. The Kaiser's reaction not only brought Russia into conflict on a larger scale by triggering off the "unalterable" Schlieffen Plan, but Wilhelm also extended the war to Western Europe. Thus France and Great Britain, hardly more than bystanders in the early phases of the crisis, and neither of which had made clear its position, were drawn in.[136]

The findings of the research demonstrated that: "Perceptions of inferior capability, if perceptions of anxiety, fear, threat, or injury are great enough, will fail to deter a nation from going to war."[137]

A set of computer programs that perform content analyses on written records in order to study political behavior, with particular attention to measurement of perceptions, has been prepared by Holsti.[138] This Stanford General Inquirer consists of a political dictionary, a dictionary of proper names, a procedure for data preparation, and a series of programs for retrieval and analysis of data. The basic unit of analysis is the *perception*, which is defined in terms of a *perceiver*, a *perceived*, an *attitude* or *action*, and a *target*. Sentences take the form: "The United States perceives that the Soviet Union is establishing missile bases in Cuba" or "The United States perceives that the United States will blockade Cuba." Attitude, action, and modifiers are scaled for intensity. The political dictionary is used to measure frequency and intensity changes in verbalized perceptions. Measurement is made along the three dimensions which Osgood and his associates have found useful in measuring meaning in a variety of cultures (see pages 10, 406, and 1030): strength–weakness, activity–passivity, and positive affect–

negative affect. This procedure can measure complex relationships and subtle differences. In a simple analysis of a perception of one country by another with three dimensions and three intensity levels, the program may register any of 343 different combinations to describe one nation's perception of another. With more participants and more complex relationships, the number of possibilities becomes much larger.

Each nation perceives itself as being either strong or weak, active or passive, and positive or negative in affect in its relationship with another country. It also has perceptions on the same dimensions of the other country in their relationship. At the same time the other nation has a comparable set of perceptions. It is important whether the two countries perceive the relationship as symmetrical or asymmetrical. If one country perceives itself as strong, active, and positive and another country as weak, passive, and negative, while the other country perceives both itself and the first country as strong, active, and positive, there is asymmetry.

Expectations of the future may also be included in the analysis. A highly unstable situation, in which each nation sees itself as able to dominate the other, but expects that its position will weaken with time, may lead one or the other to decide that preemptive attack is the only solution. This is what happened in 1914 when Austro-Hungarian leaders attacked Serbia. Table 12-8 summarizes that situation.

Correlates of war. A continuing statistical research on war is the "correlates of war" project of Singer, Small, and their associates.[139] This study is designed to compare conflicts that terminate in war with those which are resolved without violence. Analysis of data on the frequency, magnitude, severity, and intensity of wars that occurred between 1815 and 1965 is expected to provide insights into such unanswered questions about war as: What patterns of international interactions are associated with fluctuations in the incidence of war? What types of nations have been most and least prone to war? During what periods in the histories of various nations were they most and least prone to war? What diplomatic, military, political, economic, and cultural links have existed between pairs, and among clusters, of nations over time? And what modes of behavior lead to war, on the one hand, or to more peaceful international adjustments, on the other?[140]

The study is concerned with five "levels" of hierarchically arranged living systems. (I put their term "level" in quotation marks to avoid confusion with the particular meaning of the same word in my conceptual system.) Singer and Small define "system" as "any aggregation of individuals or groups who manifest a modest . . . degree of interdependence, similarity or common destiny, and whose treatment as a single unit is scientifically useful to the researcher."[141] Their "levels" constitute different abstracted systems, sets of what I call "supranational systems" or of interacting societies. The five "levels" are (i) the *global* system, which includes all mankind and any worldwide groupings of people that may exist and be of interest; (ii) the *international* system, which is composed of all the national political units in existence at a given time and all their people and subsystems; (iii) the *interstate* system, which includes all independent national entities with populations above 500,000 and governments accepted as legitimate by other nations or governments in exile with an independent fighting force of 100,000 or more; (iv) the *central* system, limited to certain states which are particularly interdependent and which play vigorous parts in interstate

TABLE 12-8   Perceptions of Austria-Hungary and Serbia about Their Relationship in 1914

In its relationship with Serbia, Austria-Hungary perceives the *present* as:		In its relationship with Austria-Hungary, Serbia perceives the *present* as:	
Self	*Serbia*	*Austria-Hungary*	*Self*
Positive ⟷ Negative		Negative ⟷ Positive	
Strong ⟷ Weak		Weak ⟷ Strong	
Active ⟷ Passive		Passive ⟷ Active	

But,

In its relationship with Serbia, Austria-Hungary perceives the *future* as:		In its relationship with Austria-Hungary, Serbia perceives the *future* as:	
Self	*Serbia*	*Austria-Hungary*	*Self*
Negative ⟷ Negative		Negative ⟷ Negative	
Weak ⟷ Strong		Strong ⟷ Weak	
Active ⟷ Active		Active ⟷ Active	

SOURCE: Adapted from R. C. North. The behavior of nation-states: problems of conflict and integration. In M. A. Kaplan (Ed.). *New approaches to international relations.* New York: St. Martin's Press, 1968, 346. Reprinted by permission.

politics; and (*v*) the *major power* system, limited to a few states which are generally agreed to deserve this designation. The last four "levels" are considered to be subsystems of the global system.

After defining different sorts of wars and specifying criteria for a state to be considered a member of the interstate system, as well as for a state to be considered a participant in a war, Singer and Small selected three sets of indicators: one of the *magnitude,* another of the *severity,* and a third of the *intensity* of a given war. Magnitude includes both spatial and temporal extent and is measured in "nation months." Severity is measured by the number of battle-connected deaths. And intensity reflects the ratio between battle deaths and nation months, as well as the total size of prewar armed forces of all participants, and the total prewar populations of all participants.

With these measures one can describe any particular war, compare many wars, and determine the *amount* of war in the world at any given time. Nations and regions can be compared as to their war-related behavior at different times. The outcomes of such behavior can also be compared.

On the basis of their data analyses, Singer and Small say of the period from 1815 to 1965:

. . . we find that, according to our particular measures, there were 50 interstate wars and 43 imperial and colonial wars, leading directly to the death of over 29 million military personnel, exclusive of civilians. There was some sort of international war underway in all but 24 of the 150 years covered, consuming over 4500 nation months of active combat; with 144 nations having been in the system at one time or another, and its size ranging from 23 to 124, this is 5.2 percent of the total nation months available. On the average, an interstate war began every three years and an extra-systemic one began every three and a half years. In terms of possible nation months, 1917 and 1943 were the most warlike years in the century and a half, with 169.8 and 178.5 nation months of war underway, respectively, or 32.2 and 28.6 percent of the maximum possible. And while we could not compute the number of battle deaths sustained on an annual basis, 1939 and 1914 were the bloodiest in terms of military personnel killed during the wars that began in those years, with over 15 million and over 8 million, respectively; with civilian casualties included, these figures would be appreciably greater.

Looking at the entire period, there is no solid evidence that war has been on the increase. The number of wars, the battle deaths, and the nation months have fluctuated considerably over time, with the "average" decade seeing 6.2 wars, over 300 nation months of war, and almost 2 million battle deaths. Nor have later wars generally been any more intense, in terms of deaths per capita or per nation month. On the other hand, there is some tentative evidence for the general belief in war cycles. Wars do not seem to *begin* according to any cyclical pattern, but there is some suggestion of a 20-year periodicity between peaks in the amount of war underway at any given time. Shifting from annual to seasonal observations, we discovered that more wars begin in spring and autumn than in winter and summer, with April and October the preferred months. On the other hand, advances in the technology of war, agriculture, and industry seem to have had only a modest impact on these seasonal propensities.[142]

The nations of Europe were found most prone to war, with England and France, each with 19 wars, at the top of the list. The same nations led in battle deaths. Consistent preferences in enemies were surprisingly absent. Lines of hostility and alliance have been fluid, with some exceptions like the continuing enmity between France and Germany. No threshold number of battle deaths was found to bring about the end of wars. The victors were found to lose as many men as the vanquished, or even more, in nearly one-third of the wars. Initiators of wars, however, came out on top in 70 percent of the interstate wars and sustained fewer battle deaths in nearly 80 percent of the cases.

Multivariate analyses of international conflict. A research program by Haas used multivariate analysis, including factor analysis and cluster analysis, to study international conflict.[143] He recognized that such complex processes result from cross-level interactions among individual national leaders, who make decisions about international relations in conjunction with participating groups and organizations, as well as societal and supranational systems. He employed indicators to measure variables of systems of three orders of complexity, which he called "levels": (*i*) *interpersonal* (my organism, group, and organization levels combined); (*ii*) *societal* (my society level); and (*iii*) *international* (my supranational system level). With such measures he determined which factors are most important in eliciting international conflicts. The dependent variable throughout the study was *decision to resort to violence or warfare to settle disputes.*[144]

(*i*) *Interpersonal level.* Data for the interpersonal analysis were derived from a study of records about 32 historical decisions made between 1887 and 1962.[145] About two-thirds of these, involving at least 20 nations, were concerned with international affairs. Several decisions on domestic matters of the United States were included for comparison, to determine whether foreign and domestic politics are similar, and for methodological reasons. Half of both foreign and domestic decisions involved violence, and half did not. Half of both sorts of decisions were institutional, and half were not.

Agreeing with several other students of international relations whom he mentions, Haas maintains that such decisions occur in four stages.[146] He names them *prestimulus, stimulus, information-processing,* and *outcome.* Each of these has *structural, cognitive, affec-*

tive, and *evaluative* aspects. The evaluative aspect of Haas's prestimulus stage includes my first stage of decision making, establishing purposes or goals (see page 940 and Hypothesis 3.3.7.2-1, page 100). His last three stages are similar to my last three stages of decision making.

In relevant researches by various students of international conflict, Haas located 61 independent variables.[147] Each of these he classified into a 16-cell matrix with his four stages in four columns and their four aspects in four rows. Then he coded or scored the records of each of the 32 historical decisions he had selected for each of the 61 independent variables and for four dependent variables related to violence— *ongoing violence* (during the prestimulus stage), *threat of violence* (during the stimulus stage), *violence considered* (during the information-processing stage), and *decision for violence* (during the outcome stage). Three variables were added for quality control. He then intercorrelated all the scores on the independent, dependent, and quality control variables. After that, he carried out factor- and cluster-analytic studies on the data.[148]

Haas found the following conditions to be most strongly related to decisions to resort to violence: (1) The decision involves substantive rather than procedural consequences; (2) the decision maker strongly wants power; (3) the decision maker is not allied or aligned with the nation or bloc against which violence is directed; (4) the decision appears crucial to the decision maker; (5) the decision upsets a status quo; (6) the decision maker expresses many perceptions of hostility; and (7) the decision maker takes excessive risks.[149]

It appeared that violence can often be avoided if decision makers "keep their cool" and avoid words characteristic of crises and showdowns.

(ii) Societal level. Haas described societies along six dimensions: *spatial, temporal, kinetic* (active-passive or dynamic-static), *entropic* (order, efficiency, and organization, or the lack of them), *allocational* (distribution of values), and *transactional* (interaction with the environment).[150] He also dealt with six fundamental attributes of societies, including *resources* (nonliving matter-energy or information of use to the society), *demo-types* (makeup of the human population), *attitudes, behavior, functions,* and *structures.*[151] Each attribute may vary across all six dimensions. Societies differ from one another in their patterns of attributes.[152] Patterns may vary in several ways. Among others, they may have *asymmetry* or *symmetry.* Asymmetry exists when two or more elements are so related that the converse relationship is logically impossible;

symmetry exists if it is possible. Haas believes that measures of pattern symmetry or asymmetry are useful in studying societal violence. Such measures differ from one dimension to another. Annual change rates of attributes are measures of temporal asymmetry, for example, while entropic asymmetry may be measured by the amount of deviation from a 50–50 distribution of any sort of system component. Six attributes, each varying along six dimensions and each of which may be symmetrical or asymmetrical, produce a matrix of 36 continua. Each of these ranges from a symmetrical to an asymmetrical pattern, and so altogether there are 72 patterns, each of which can be given a reasonable label.

For each of 85 countries Haas correlated a total of 179 indicators for these 72 patterns (many had multiple indicators) with four indicators of international conflict: *number of wars, number of smaller foreign clashes, number of population killed in wars and foreign clashes,* and *ratio of number killed in wars and foreign clashes to population.*[153] While some patterns were correlated with foreign conflict, an asymmetrical pattern was as likely to be associated with military resolutions or foreign-policy disputes as a symmetrical pattern. The variables which correlated most highly with indicators of foreign violence were (1) prominence in its bloc of nations, (2) military mobilizations, (3) public perceptions of hostility toward people of other countries, (4) a high proportion of gross national product devoted to military and public administration, (5) a large amount of foreign aid sent or received, (6) a high percentage of the population serving in the armed forces, and (7) equality in income levels.[154]

Haas then did factor and cluster analyses on correlations of the 183 variables determined for the 85 countries. In summarizing the complicated results for the societal level, he says:

Foreign violence is associated with task-oriented trends in societies undergoing directive but faltering modernization. More specifically, Foreign Conflict and Discontented Laxity form a pair of factors that are labelled Aggressive on the second-order factor analysis, while foreign conflict is nested together with the development of a military-industrial complex and the pursuit of power politics, and is found within large countries that have several ethnic and religious groups living side by side. Our scenario of the peaceful country concurs with capitalist theorists of the early nineteenth century, for development and democracy together direct countries toward both internal and external cooperation. There is no direct connection between foreign and domestic conflict, but both are concomitants of an underlying process of disintegration in the extent of democratic consent, which in turn results when there is unsteady economic growth. . . .

By dividing countries into the categories of developed, developing, and undeveloped, three different routes toward war are evident. In all three cases an increase in military expenditures precedes war, but motivations to step up arms production come from different sources. The least developed countries find themselves at war if they are administratively stagnant. Developing countries are tempted to embark upon wars when their population is heterogeneous and are thus prone toward domestic conflicts. Advanced countries enter wars most often during periods of economic downswings.[155]

(iii) International level. The definition of *international system* used by Haas is an aggregation of societies. Subsystems are subsets of these. In addition, he defines an *international conflict subsystem* as a set of *actors* (which need not be sovereign states but which may include units like the Viet Cong) that carry out their military plan-making implementation and other relevant activities together.[156] Twenty-one international subsystems were defined in terms of their geographic boundaries and the dates of their beginning and end. Typical power distribution ("loose bipolarity," "tight multipolarity," "tight tripolarity," etc.) was also determined.

A set of functions was defined and classified into three categories, following Easton, of input, withinput, and output.[157] Variables were collected from two separate sets of data, one from Richardson and the other from Wright, both of whom published statistical studies of war. The two samples were analyzed separately. After intercorrelation of 183 variables and factor and cluster analyses, the variables most closely related to multipolarity in an "international subsystem" were found to be: (1) Many wars occur between physically similar peoples; (2) most wars involving major powers are fought to destabilize a balance of power; (3) disturbance of stability increases over time; (4) there is a procedural, rather than substantive, emphasis in adapting norms of international conduct to new situations; (5) treaties are seldom written to conclude wars; (6) wars including major power participants are lengthy; and (7) each major power wins several victories on the battlefield.[158]

Tight power stratification is most closely associated with the following: (1) There is little cooperation among the poles; (2) levels of technological development are high; (3) outside the core subsystem, major powers are seldom victorious; (4) there are few years in which postwar treaties are concluded; (5) diplomatic representation by major and middle powers is extensive; (6) major powers enter few of the wars fought; and (7) if a war is started by a major power, it will not be ended by a treaty. Haas says:

These two sets of findings depict a scene in which the best guarantee of international peace is to have as few power blocs as possible within the conflict subsystem, keeping the number of major powers to a minimum. A tight stratification of power is more common in recent eras of history, and major powers tend to avoid direct confrontations as much as possible in view of the all-or-nothing implications of a single thermonuclear encounter.[159]

These findings appear to give some support, as far as the level of supranational systems is concerned, to Hypothesis 5.2-14 (see page 107), which states that segregation increases conflict among subsystems or components of a system, and to Hypothesis 5.2-16 (see page 107), which states that systems tend to reduce multiple-component conflicts to conflicts among a lesser number of blocs of components.

International law, international and supranational organizations, and conflict resolution. The peaceful settlement of disputes through negotiation and bargaining among nations and the development of a recognized body of international law long predate the existence of international courts of law. Diplomatic and consular officials, treaty councils and conferences, and meetings among national deciders often served to keep the peace, just as they sometimes regulated war and determined peace terms.

The body of international law currently in use to maintain steady states among nations has been derived less from decisions handed down by formal bodies than from customs established as a result of interactions among citizens of different countries as they engaged in travel or commerce on sea and land:

It should be obvious that the simple effort of sailors to avoid collisions generated rules of the sea, that the undertakings of merchants to do business in far-off lands led to rules concerning the treatment of aliens, and that the enterprise of riverboat owners led to rules concerning freedom of navigation and even to the internationalization of some rivers. . . . It is customary for treaties on international law to make reference to Grotius' argument for the freedom of the seas and to the mythical "battle of the books" between Grotius and Selden. Much more important to the development of freedom of the seas, to the establishment of a customary regime of territorial waters, and to the contention for the rule "free ships, free goods" were the activities of Dutch fishermen in the herring fishery, the enterprise of Netherlands shipbuilders in producing the then largest fishing and merchant fleets, and the defiance by Dutch shipping interests of the restrictive laws and policies concerning trading emanating from their own public authorities.[160]

Some international law is written in the form of treaties. A certain amount is codified. The International Law Commission of the United Nations has responsibility for developing and codifying law on particular topics suggested by the General Assembly or submitted by the Commission to the General Assembly.[161] This body of 25 legal experts, elected by the General Assembly, meets annually to discuss and adopt the draft articles written by members selected as special rapporteurs for particular topics. These are then submitted to the governments of member states for comments and, after revision, are submitted to the General Assembly, which may convoke an international conference to conclude a convention on the subject. The Conventions on Law of the Sea and the Convention on Diplomatic Intercourse and Immunities are examples. Many items relating to peace and security have not resulted in conventions but have been circulated among nations in the form of draft declarations. One of these is the Declaration on Principles of International Law concerning Friendly Relations and Cooperation among States in accordance with the Charter of the United Nations. It consists of seven principles, which assert that states should refrain from the use of force, settle their disputes by peaceful means, and avoid intervening in domestic affairs of other states. It also supports the principle of equal rights and self-determination of peoples, the principle of sovereign equality of states, and the duty of states to cooperate and fulfill their obligations under the United Nations Charter.

Other relevant draft declarations and codes concern international criminal jurisdiction, the desirability of establishing an international judicial organ for trial of persons accused of genocide and certain other crimes, and offenses against the peace and security of mankind, as well as the question of defining aggression.

The formation of supranational and international bodies specifically intended to carry out adjustment processes for maintaining peace and security began with the formation of the League of Nations after World War I. All the complex activities of the United Nations and its associated organizations are justified primarily on the basis of their contributions to peaceful relations among nations.

The question of whether international organizations in themselves promote peaceful resolution of international conflicts has been studied by Singer and Wallace. They say:

In the three centuries or so since the modern international system began to take on its present shape, its component members have come together in a wide variety of organizations, for a wide variety of purposes. Those who act on behalf of the nations have turned to international organizations to oversee peace settlements, to strengthen their collective defense capacity, to mediate conflicts between themselves, to discourage interference from the outside, to harmonize their trade relations, to supervise international waterways, to accelerate the production of food, to codify diplomatic practice, and to formalize legal proceedings. Some organizations are established primarily for the neutral purpose of making coexistence possible, others for the more affirmative purposes of positive cooperation. Some have been directed toward the modification of the system, others toward the preservation of its status quo.

Whether the orientation is positive, neutral, or even negative, the preservation of peace is generally one of the prime considerations of the organization's architects. . . .

There are, admittedly, some occasions on which nations organize for rather less benign purposes. But even when the organization appears aggressive on its surface, those who created it often seek only to deter a potential enemy, to intimidate an adversary into capitulation without war, to postpone a struggle that might otherwise be imminent, or, at worst, to so organize that a potentially long and bloody stalemate might be replaced with a quick and relatively inexpensive victory. Furthermore, most of these military oriented activities are carried on via temporary arrangements, and rarely do they lead to the creation of international organizations as traditionally defined. That is, seldom do they see the establishment of a permanent headquarters, a multinational secretariat, and regularized budgetary provisions.[162]

Using the definitions of "interstate system" and the specifications of wars described above, as well as an indicator for the amount of intergovernmental organization present in each year from 1816 to 1964, Singer and Wallace determined the correlation between intergovernmental organization and war. They also looked for evidence that statesmen believe intergovernmental organization to be an important means of reducing war and, if they do, for historical justification of such a belief.

An increase in the amount of intergovernmental organization among nations following their participation in war was taken as an indicator of belief by statesmen in the efficacy of such organization in reducing war. Results showed that statesmen did act as if they held that belief, although alternative explanations for the observed surges in intergovernmental organization could not be ruled out. There was, however, almost no correlation between the amount of intergovernmental organization existing in any period and the amount of war that began in the following period. Therefore, any belief in intergovernmental organization as dependably preventing war appears to be unjustified. The authors concluded that as long as nations are competing for scarce resources, increase in the number of intergovernmental organizations cannot decrease the amount of war. Indeed, such organizations perpetuate the power of some countries: " . . . our view is that war is basically inherent in the continued coexistence of the nation-state and the international system as we know it."[163]

A related study found that alliance aggregation and bipolarity (see pages 906 and 907) had strong positive correlation with the amount of war that followed within 3 years during the twentieth century but an inverse correlation to almost the same degree during the nineteenth century.[164]

In Etzioni's view, prevention of war requires that a world community become able to "encapsulate" international conflict, that is, modify it by rules that prevent all, or at least some, use of arms.[165] This state would be less demanding than complete pacification, since basic differences and even aggressive attitudes among nations could continue, but nations would agree to arms limitations and would set up organizations to enforce that agreement. Pacification, Etzioni contends, would be less lasting if the powers remained independent. Without supranational or international controls, they could again become involved in conflicts that could lead to war. If nations, however, sacrificed some of their autonomy and became parts of an intergovernmental organization that would provide a foundation for consensus, the probability of armed conflict would be reduced. He says:*

If there is to be movement toward a world community, it must be self-propelling. Once an authority superior to the contending superpowers—a world government or a powerful United Nations police force—is viewed as a prerequisite, an authority is posited that can impose rules on the contending parties and, thus, keep their conflicts limited to those channels allowed by the world community. But such an authority is not presently available. The search for possible patterns to achieve a world community must, therefore, focus on those conflicts in which, through the very process of conflict, the participants initate self-imposed limitations on the means and modes of strife, leading toward further encapsulation and community-building.[166]

5.2.5 Matter-energy output processes   With the exception of highly integrated supranational systems that closely resemble societies, such as the European Communities, systems at this level have few adjustments to increased or decreased flows of matter-energy outward to the environment. Extruding is ordinarily downwardly dispersed to the level of the society or below, and so are the adjustment processes related to it.

5.2.6 Information output processes   Adjustment processes related to information output from supranational systems are ordinarily downwardly dispersed to societies. Such processes include adjustments which reduce strains brought about by changes in rate or in other information output variables. When, however, secret or sensitive intelligence is improperly output from a military alliance, both internal surveillance and boundary precautions may be increased by the supranational system itself.

5.2.7 Feedbacks   Both positive and negative feedbacks adjust processes at this level. An arms race is a classic example of positive feedback (see pages 979 and 980). Information that a potential aggressor is increasing its arms may lead a bloc or alliance not only to match the increase but also to better it. When the

other retaliates in kind, the upward spiral begins. Because agreements among the competing systems can set limits, such races do not necessarily run out of control, but without such agreements, greater and greater proportions of the GNPs of the two systems are diverted from other subsystem processes to production and deployment of weapons. Limits are then set by economic capacity or by the refusal of voters or other decider components of the society to support further military expansion.

Population numbers of global or lesser systems are set by both positive and negative feedback adjustments. The relationship between food supply and population constitutes a positive feedback which is ultimately limited by Malthusian negative feedbacks if not otherwise controlled (see page 946). The composition and numbers of populations also respond to negative feedbacks between the birthrate and the death rate (see pages 980 to 987).

The automatic adjustments that maintain the steady states of global environmental processes like weather, climate, and the composition of the atmosphere are negative feedbacks. Changes in any one of a large number of variables produce alterations in all the others. I shall consider the possible effects of human actions upon such variables in the discussion of simulation models of supranational systems below (see pages 991 to 994). Other simulation models depict the complexity of feedbacks among variables of a total global system (see pages 1012 to 1016).

The automatic economic and monetary information adjustment processes that determine supply, demand, and prices in international trading relationships are accomplished by feedbacks. These are normally negative feedbacks, but positive spirals may occur when, for example, values of a society's money are driven downward on international money markets by speculative trading. Unless these are limited by international action, they can ruin the economies of societies with weak currencies.

The established communication channels from component societies to central decider subsystems of supranational systems go through designated output transducer components of the societies. With increase in world communication, however, the attitudes and opinions of subcomponents of societies, or subordinate units, down to individual citizens, may also become parts of feedback loops in such systems.

Many world societies do not ingest from their own lands sufficient food to maintain their populations. For some this shortage can be met by a simple societal adjustment process, since they can exchange their manufactured goods for the food products of other societies. Poor nations throughout the world have a

*Reprinted with permission of Macmillan Publishing Co., Inc. from *The active society* by Amitai Etzioni. Copyright © 1968 by The Free Press, a Division of The Macmillan Company.

more serious problem which can be met only by supranational feedbacks. Within recent years various supranational bodies have undertaken adjustment processes aimed at increasing the efficiency of agricultural processes in less developed societies.

5.3 Evolution   Interactions among primitive societies in war or trade did not require a supranational subsystem structure. Alliances which involved cooperation of societies toward a common goal, however, did need meetings, councils, or conferences to make decisions. This minimal decider structure appears to have been the first type of multinational structure to develop. Its origin—the date when the deciders of two societies first made common cause together—is lost in prehistory. Alliances clearly had survival value for many of their component societies, for they provided the advantages of greater defensive or striking force against enemies.

Federations and empires were also ancient forms of social organization that brought two or more societies under control by a common decider for at least some of their processes. The ancient city of Ur of the Chaldees was probably the capital of the first empire, the Sumerian Empire, in the twenty-fifth century B.C. It exercised control over a part of the world that included numerous cities and other units, including tribes and states, which were certainly not complex societies like modern nations. Empires were often formed forcibly by a conqueror like Cyrus or Alexander, and yet several large systems that were built by conquest were relatively stable over long time spans.

The evolutionary history of living systems, from the initial combination of nonliving macromolecules into living cells to the forms of social organization now in existence, has exhibited shred-out and overall increase in complexity. Such change has not proceeded evenly. Supranational systems, for instance, have been set up over and over, only to disintegrate in a few years, decades, or centuries into their component societies. The present organization of the world follows the dissolution of the European colonial empires into many nations, some perhaps too small to continue in their present form. At the same time, the amount of intergovernmental organization is at a high point, the interdependence of societies for exchanges of matter-energy and information is increasing, and both governments and their citizens view formation of supranational regulatory agencies as a means of conflict resolution. While the types of intergovernmental organizations now in existence have far less power than their component societies, they can implement some sorts of decisions, particularly those which do not threaten the sovereignty of components. The probability that such organizations will gain broad

supranational powers appears low, according to Singer and Wallace:

. . . even though international organizations are becoming more numerous, and larger in membership and resources over time, they are invariably based not only on territorial national states as their major component but on the continuing and virtually untrammelled sovereignty of these states. One might even argue that, whether national states are becoming more powerful or not, international governmental organization is doing little to diminish, and quite a bit to perpetuate that power. Thus, if the present pattern and basis is continued, there is little reason for believing that they—or more particularly, their secretariats—will acquire sufficient power to exercise any effective control over the behavior and interaction of their member states.[167]

The interesting current evolutionary question is whether some more advanced type of supranational system, which may provide unprecedented peace and stability in the world, is in the process of formation and, if it is, what characteristics it may have and how soon it may be expected to appear. Many theorists consider that some form of worldwide suprasystem decider will prove to be necessary to prevent wars among nations competing for the ever-scarcer natural resources and to provide equitable distribution of goods and opportunities among people in all parts of the world. But nationalism is a powerful force opposing such development.

Some evolutionary theories of history have speculated upon the way in which a world government of some sort could come about. In Marxian theory, a worldwide communist society is the inevitable result of economic and social forces that include increased industrialization, certain inherent weaknesses of capitalism, development of international activities at the expense of nationalism, and the class struggle that will result in workers everywhere seizing the means of production and destroying the capitalist class. Present-day communist societies have not abandoned the Marxian goal of a world communist community, but they see it as developing through a period in which separate societies experience revolution and build communism separately.[168] Nationalism is to them, therefore, a developmental stage through which societies pass on the way to establishment of a supranational system.

Another theory of the way in which supranational unification could come about is held by functionalist political theorists who think that participation by nations in intergovernmental organizations will gradually lead to more and more unification, as more and more processes are brought under supranational control.[169] Etzioni questions the effectiveness of this path to supranational control because shared activities like postal unions, public health programs, and labor organizations are limited to only a small part of the processes of the subsystem to which they belong and because what supranational activities are involved do not diminish the power of the national decider. Unified military and economic activities, considered by more recent functionalists to lead to unification, have more effect because the specific activities involved are more closely linked to other processes of each component society. Etzioni considers that a slow accumulation of extranational elements could increase and strengthen the bonds among the already interdependent nations, which could lead to formation of "a layer of action, control, and consensus" above deciders of nations.[170] He believes that the following three-stage evolutionary process might produce a world community:[171] The first stage is a *fused* society, with little differentiation of activities and little development of decider structure. A small, illiterate primitive society is an example. The second stage is a *differentiated* society with developed subsystems and with a central decider. Coordination and control in this sort of system are weak. Industrial societies in laissez-faire periods are of this sort. These first two stages fit the descriptions of *Gemeinschaft* and *Gesellschaft*, respectively, in their structures, organization, and value emphases (see page 601). The third stage has elements of each of the others. It is *reintegrated*. Political, economic, and ideological bonds create a complex, unified whole. Both control and consensus are planned, and systemwide goals are primary. If it developed, such a system could bind together elements of several internally differentiated societies. Such a multiechelon structure could develop with various small groups of nations uniting, these associations later combining into a larger union in which they could continue as units for consensus formation.[172]

The above discussions have focused on the decider subsystems of societies and supranational systems, since the one must become less powerful, and the other more so, in the process of supranational system evolution. The possible role of components outside the decider must, however, also be considered. Multinational corporations and international professional associations create a network of relationships that cross national boundaries. Evan suggests that their importance has been overlooked by political scientists:

The field of international relations has . . . not done justice to these types of organizations. Many scholars in this field evidently assume that these types of organizations, though operating in the interstices of nation-states, have little consequence for the future development of the international system. In subscribing to this view they may be overlooking the potential of these organizations for cumulatively and unanticipatedly transforming the international system. . . .[173]

Even though the broad direction of the evolution of living systems has been toward greater complexity and more levels, it is obviously impossible to predict the future course of development of supranational systems. Etzioni says:*

Whether or not a world community will eventually be built and the alienation of differentiation overcome are questions which, we believe, cannot in principle be answered, as they are concerned with the ways in which future actors will exercise their options. All we may be able to establish is the nature of these options and the directions in which alternative sequences of choices point. Societal actors can exercise the option of community-building, we argue, because we see, at present and in the future, the necessary developments in the techniques of the guidance of societal processes, just as, in the modern age, techniques of the control of work and machines evolved.[174]

5.3.1 Emergents   The most important emergent at this level is the international or supranational agency. The many systems of this sort set up in recent years have vastly increased international cooperation. Such agencies have been created to carry out adjustment processes among nations for a large number of special purposes, such as communication and transportation, and for the general purpose of supranational decision making and peaceful resolution of conflicts. Supranational regulation of flows of monetary information modifies the automatic economic adjustment processes and can be used to protect the financial position of societies that could otherwise experience financial collapse. International banks promote development of less developed societies. International assistance is possible on a scale not previously possible in relief, education, medical care, and many other activities. International cooperation in science replaces the sometimes uncoordinated efforts of members of separate societies to advance knowledge, as in development of peaceful uses of atomic energy and in geophysics, meteorology, space technology, and systems science.

5.4 Growth, cohesiveness, and integration

5.4.1 Growth   After their initial formation, which may be by voluntary association among societies or by forcible seizure of one or more weaker societies by a powerful one, supranational systems grow by addition of new societies or parts of societies as further conquests or voluntary associations occur. Such additions increase the size of the system and the number of lower-level living systems under its control. Without addition of further societal components, supranational systems may increase the numbers of their human subcomponents by excess of births over deaths or by immigration into the territories of the system. They may also increase in complexity by expansion and differentiation of their subsystem structure as they grow. No typical life cycle, however, has as yet been identified for all systems at this level. The small number of supranational systems that have existed, the variety of types that have developed, and the length of time—decades or centuries—over which they must be observed make it hard to generalize about their life cycles.

Some characteristics of the growth of "security communities" have been analyzed by Deutsch, Burrell, Kann, Lee, Lichterman, Lindgren, Lowenheim, and Van Wagenen from case studies of about 3 dozen relevant historical situations.[175] Two types of security communities were identified in this research: (a) *pluralistic,* a loosely organized relationship among independent societies in which a "sense of community" is present, and (b) *amalgamated,* in which formerly independent societies merge under some form of common government. The latter is clearly a supranational system in my sense, but the former is not.

Before amalgamating, the research showed, societies first develop close relationships in trade and communication, and usually some common cultural bonds.[176] Some of the security communities studied were amalgamated by force. In the voluntary cases, war between member nations was viewed as unacceptable even before they concluded a formal union. Party divisions which reinforced the boundaries between the political units declined, and instead party divisions cut across boundaries. In some cases the amalgamation occurred in stages, some functions becoming amalgamated first, and others following. Pluralistic security communities often preceded full amalgamation. They are easier to achieve and they succeed under less favorable conditions.

A nation joins an amalgamated community because it expects to attain from it economic advantages, greater freedom, or other benefits. The decision to amalgamate follows a political process in which leaders of various nations who favor it exert their persuasive power to gain popular support of, and participation in, the movement. This did not happen in any case of unsuccessful effort to form such communities included in the study.

Political amalgamation, this research concluded, is a nuclear process which occurs around a single core or one that amalgamated previously.[177] But once states have formed, the authors of the study report, they:

> . . . do not seem to grow by a "snowballing process." We found that successful amalgamation of smaller units into larger ones tended to increase both the resources and the skills necessary for integration on the part of the larger unit. But we found that this also might increase the preoccupation of these units with domestic affairs, reducing their ability to respond promptly and effectively to the needs and interests of people outside the national borders. This ability of governments to respond to the interests of "outsiders" has always been important, but has become even more important in our own time. To the extent that very large states may tend to imprison the minds of their rulers in a web of domestic complexities, pressures, and preoccupations, the growth of states might turn out to be a self-limiting process. The larger a state, the less attention and understanding might its political leaders be able to give to any additional small territory or population that might be tempted to join it, or whose loyalties after amalgamation might have to be secured and maintained. At the end of such a development, very large states, empires, or federations might find it impossible to absorb any more people or territory, or even to retain the loyalties of all the smaller groups and political units that had become joined to them in the past. This means that greater political responsiveness—which, we shall see later, is of great importance to integration—cannot be expected to emerge automatically as a by-product of historical evolution. Instead, governments and leaders who wish to promote integration may have to strive for greater responsiveness as a distinct aim.[178]

My discussion above applies largely to the amalgamated type of security community, clearly a supranational system, although many of the points apply equally to pluralistic communities. Growth in other sorts of supranational systems is subject to some of the same influences. The limited-purpose, intergovernmental organizations also grow by adding societal members, but they grow also, as other organizations do, by expanding their processes and increasing the number of components in their organizational structures. Societies expect to achieve certain goals by joining such a system as the United Nations, which grew from 51 societies in 1945 to 138 in 1974. Mutual trust and shared culture are less essential to such a system since it controls none of the territory or political processes of its components. However limited its success may be in preserving world peace, it does provide a forum for expression of world opinion as well as a means of exerting some power in international decision, and so nations do not wish to be excluded from it.

5.4.2 Cohesiveness While not all types of supranational systems have components that are close together in space, lasting associations like federations appear most likely to develop among adjacent societies. Cohesiveness evidently favors integration. Also blocs frequently form among geographically close societies. Aggressive societies may seize weaker neighbors with which they have common borders and, after amalgamating with them, proceed to annex *their* neighbors. The European colonial empires were, of course, exceptions to this since they had components scattered all over the world, wherever they could occupy, seize, or recruit them.

The United Nations Charter provides that regional associations will be respected. Such associations unite societies which have common interests besides their geographic location. Cultures of neighboring countries are likely to be similar. Supranational or international transportation and communication are facilitated by cohesiveness.

5.4.3 Integration   The analysis of amalgamated security communities discussed above found a number of essential requirements for successful integration of the component societies.[179] Some of these were already present when the amalgamation took place, having developed before. They are (*a*) compatibility of important values; (*b*) a distinctive way of life; (*c*) expectations of economic gains; (*d*) marked increase in the political and administrative capabilities of some participating units; (*e*) superior economic growth of at least some units; (*f*) open channels of communication among geographic areas and social strata; (*g*) broadening of the political elite; (*h*) mobility of persons, at least those who are politically relevant; and (*i*) many different sorts of communication and transactions among components. Others that may be essential are (*a*) balance of rewards, initiatives, and respect among participants; (*b*) frequent changes of roles in system processes so that no divisions between majority and minority become permanent; and (*c*) a good deal of mutual predictability of behavior.

Requirements for successful integration of pluralistic security communities were less stringent.[180] They were able to withstand disintegrative processes that would have destroyed an amalgamated system.

Many of these factors must operate in other types of international and supranational relationships. The importance of ideology in the integration of the communist bloc of nations is clear. The influence and power of the Soviet Union also support integration among these societies. Its capability of protecting others against potential aggressors is important also, as in the case of Cuba.

The amount of integration in the United Nations is low, but a common goal to prevent major war does operate to secure some measure of compliance with decisions of its governing bodies.

Although successful integration of a supranational system implies that totipotentiality of component societies will be reduced to partipotentiality, weakness of component governments apparently does not favor such integration. The recent history of the EEC suggests that the effect of weak components is to reduce the integration of the suprasystem, at least in the early stages of development. During 1974, severe internal political difficulties beset seven of the nine members as worldwide inflation and monetary instability threatened their steady states. New leaders of coalition governments did not support the EEC as strongly as their predecessors had, but tended rather to seek nationalistic solutions to their problems. Italy, the most sorely pressed of the nine, imposed import controls contrary to the agreements of the Treaty of Rome, on which the EEC was based. The United Kingdom, which had joined the EEC only the year before, reopened the question of its membership. As the history of every supranational system has shown, integration of every such large system has been hard to achieve and maintain.

5.5 Pathology

(*a*) *Lacks of matter-energy inputs.*   Ordinarily, matter-energy lacks result in pathologies at the level of the society rather than the supranational system. Some are, however, of global concern because their potential effects are worldwide. Belated realization that the earth's supplies of available natural resources like metals and hydrocarbons are finite and can be exhausted has in recent years produced forecasts of serious lack stresses of many sorts of matter-energy. I have already discussed possible adjustment processes for such stresses (see page 945), but the long-range outlook remains uncertain at best. Simulations of this increasing lack stress and its possible interaction with other variables like population and pollution are described below (see pages 980 to 988). Most current forecasts are gloomy over the long range, but they differ considerably in the amount of time thought to be available for systemwide adjustments.

Unless adequate adjustment processes to mounting lack stresses are developed, worldwide political and economic variables will inevitably be forced out of their steady-state ranges as nationalistic societies compete for ever-scarcer resources. A war over oil, for example, is not impossible as industrial nations find their processes slowed down and their economies deteriorating. The effect upon supranational systems may well be bad if the behavior of the EEC during the oil crisis of 1974 is any indication. Member nations of that system tended to forsake centralized planning and to deal separately with the petroleum producers, thus weakening the system.[181]

(b) *Excesses of matter-energy inputs.* The world-wide population explosion provides an excess of new human beings who must be provided with the necessities of life. At present these excess inputs adversely affect some societies and not others. I have already considered above some international and supranational adjustment processes to these localized stresses (see pages 946 to 948). If the natural increase of human populations cannot be slowed so that the numbers of mankind come into steady state with the supply of food and other resources, disaster is forecast (see page 981). In the present state of the world, even increased agricultural outputs and good climatic conditions have not prevented hunger and malnutrition in some societies. In years in which harvests were poor, famine has occurred. The relatively recently developed sense of responsibility of more fortunate nations for suffering in distant parts of the world could conceivably be eroded quickly if alleviation of that suffering would have to occur at a cost of a markedly diminished standard of living at home. In a nationalistic world the tendency to forsake supranational planning is obviously present. It is a question of whether the belief of many in the superior ability of supranational adjustment processes, under the control of supranational agencies, to achieve acceptable steady states will prevail in the face of crisis.

(c) *Inputs of inappropriate forms of matter-energy.* Inappropriate forms of matter-energy include pathogens, pollutants, nuclear rockets, and other missiles of war. Pathologies of societies caused by the first two rarely, except in cases of international epidemics or heavy industrial pollution of air or waters, have specific pathological effects upon the supranational systems of which they are members. A losing war, however, may be a direct cause for destruction of alliances and other supranational systems. Governments of member societies may be overthrown, boundary lines may be redrawn, and new alignments of allies may result.

(d) *Lacks of information inputs.* No studies have been made on responses of supranational systems to low rates of input communications, and no pathology resulting from this cause has been identified.

Lacks of inputs of monetary information into supranational systems have results like those of such lacks in organizations and societies. The programs of the organizations that carry out international and supranational processes must be curtailed when money is withheld from them. The budget of the United Nations, for instance, severely restricts its scope. The more totipotential systems like federations, which are responsible for a relatively complete set of subsystem processes, may be curtailed in providing essential public services. All aspects of system functioning can be adversely affected.

(e) *Excesses of information inputs.* Information input overload is a known stress in organizations that leads to breakdown of functions during the period of overload if it is sufficiently severe and long-continued. The organizations that carry out the processes of supranational systems are subject to the same sorts of stresses that plague other organizations.

No pathology has been discovered that is caused by excesses of monetary inputs into supranational systems.

(f) *Inputs of maladaptive genetic information in the template.* Some of the obvious failings of multipurpose and single-purpose intergovernmental organizations arise from charters which do not permit the deciders to implement their decisions and which make them weak in relation to component societies. The veto powers of five countries in the United Nations Security Council have prevented action on important issues. This was a necessary provision of the Charter in order to secure the participation of these societies in the system; however, in the light of the stated goals of the system, it must be regarded as a defect in the Charter.

(g) *Abnormalities in internal matter-energy processes.* Among the disordered internal matter-energy processes that threaten the earth's steady states, both physical and political, are pollution, exponential increase in population, and uneven distribution of matter-energy among societies. The last results from the nature of the planet itself as well as from the system of allocation that prevails. All these problems have been discussed above (see pages 946 to 952). Although adjustment processes are available to supranational and lower-level systems, their adequacy is unproved, and in the absence of adequate adjustments, the comfort and even the continued existence of living systems are threatened.

(h) *Abnormalities in internal information processes.* Pathologies of internal information processing that disturb systems at this level derive to an important extent from the relative impermeability of information boundaries of many of the world's nations and the nationalistic goals that motivate societal deciders. Although communication channels link virtually all societies and although people throughout the world are becoming more and more aware of the ways of life of distant societies, the flows within societal boundaries are of overwhelming importance in determining attitudes of their members. The ancient tribal feeling that misfortunes and deaths of members of other societies are relatively unimportant is still very much present everywhere. The belief that some foreign societies are inferior and undeserving is common. Suspicion and hostility, often deliberately fostered within societies by national leaders, evoke positive feedbacks that justify war and make it possible. All these and other information flows of similar sorts reduce the effectiveness of the types of supranational systems that are created to carry out adjustment processes among nations and to promote peace. Conceivably such information flows could create internal strains that would destroy these supranational systems.

I have discussed above disturbed steady states of economic variables that produce international inflation and monetary instability. As with other pathological conditions, failure of adjustment processes may bring about disastrous outcomes.

5.6 Decay and termination Supranational systems, depending upon their type, terminate when they have achieved their purposes (*e.g.*, treaty conferences); when their component societies change their alignments (*e.g.*, blocs and alliances); when they are absorbed by new systems with somewhat different structures and processes (*e.g.*, limited-purpose intergovernmental organizations such as the permanent Central Narcotics Board and the Drug Supervisory Body, which were superseded by the International Narcotics Control Board); or as a result of inability to maintain steady states of their crucial variables (*e.g.*, empires, federations, and security communities).

The various types of supranational systems have differed markedly in the duration of their existence. Both ancient and modern empires have typically spanned centuries, during which they grew in size and number of components. They declined as their deciders became unable to maintain control over the systems or unable to withstand enemy attack or other stresses in their environments. Final breakdown followed.

Durations of some other supranational or intergovernmental systems are 19 years for the League of Nations and 30, as of 1976, for the United Nations and most of its specialized agencies.[182] Some specialized agencies are older. In 1976 ILO was 56 years old; UPU, 101; and ITU, 110. Shorter-lived were 112 formal alliances entered into between 1815 and 1939, which lasted an average of only 7.7 years. Defense pacts endured for an average of 9.8 years, neutrality pacts for 6.6 years, and ententes for just 6 years.

Life-spans for federations and unions of separate societies under a common government have often been long, although in such systems the supranational characteristics have tended to become attenuated, and the systems to become more and more like societies, with boundaries between component states becoming weaker and (as in France) even being redrawn for administrative purposes, so that the originally federated societies no longer have separate existence except as regions. Some attempts at such a union, on the other hand, have been short-lived, like that between Norway and Sweden, which broke down in 1905 after a brief existence.

Although empires, both ancient and recent, have had long durations, they eventually have become unable to control their many component societies. Etzioni considers that this was the result of "premature and unbalanced reductions of tribalism":*

The premature nature of empires has been demonstrated by showing that they did not have the cybernetic capacity and power, the communication and transportation means, and the consensus-formation structures necessary to keep a large or extending polity integrated and guided. (The Roman Empire at its zenith encompassed 50 to 60 million people and several million land acres, more than most contemporary nation-states.) Most pre-modern empires seem to have "faded" as the distance from the capital grew, in that the capital of the empire often had little information about and even less control of many of the provinces. The imperial policy was superimposed on feudal or tribal local systems, without effectively committing many of their politically active citizens. If one were to construct an index of controlling capacities which took into account the number of people included, the scope of the activities controlled, and the intensiveness of the control, much if not all the "anomaly" of pre-modern empires would disappear: Their capacities were *lower* than those of the modern nation-states; these capacities only seemed larger because they were spread (more thinly) over a larger area. Historically, the capacity to control did grow, but not the extent of the territories which the empires attempted to encompass. Modern empires had more control capacities than earlier ones, but they still were not sufficient for effectively controlling a territory which spans many parts of the world. Above all, modern, like earlier, empires were unbalanced; they relied more on coercion than on the utilitarian reallocation of assets among the controlled units, and they were unable to commit many of the active citizens of their member units; their low levels of responsiveness and their deficient consensus-building capacities undermined them. In short, these empires had controlling overlayers, but not guidance mechanisms. Hence, when nationalism, a movement with mass appeal, appeared, it could mobilize the members and disintegrate the empires.[183]

Some of the conditions which led to disintegration of amalgamated political communities have been discovered by historical study of such communities.[184] Some pathological conditions were present in all cases of disintegration (although they were present also in some systems that survived, having been outweighed by factors that favored continuation of the system). Even in the presence of all nine of the essential conditions for integration (see page 970), these pathological conditions could prevent formation of an amalgamated security community. Also, they could endanger or destroy it once it was formed. They were of two sorts: (a) conditions that increased the burdens upon amalgamated governments and (b) conditions that reduced the capability of such governments to cope with their responsibilities. Among these were heavy military burdens; substantial increase in political participation by populations, regions, or organizations which had previously been politically passive, like the peasant party in Norway; increase in ethnic or linguistic differentiation; prolonged economic decline or stagnation; relative closure of the ranks of the political elite, which resulted in the rise of opposed elites among ethnic or other groups not included; excessive delays in making political, social, or economic reforms; and major failures on the part of formerly strong or privileged components to adjust to loss of dominance resulting from the amalgamation. For this latter reason, among others, the Northern Irish Protestants have opposed amalgamation with the rest of Ireland. Indeed, considering the massive problems of control inherent in governing the vast empires which have dominated the history of mankind, it is amazing that they did not decay and terminate much sooner than they did. It is highly questionable whether the modern forms of supranational systems can survive as long.

6. Models and simulations

This section concerns models and simulations of supranational systems and international interactions, including some of global processes that involve variables like climate, natural resources, and human population.

Simulation is a promising way to study the complex phenomena at this level, but building models of supranational systems is hampered by lack of a body of generally accepted theory on which conceptualizations can be based.[185]

Reliable data, moreover, are indispensable for identifying variables and relationships and for assigning values to parameters and variables of models. But uniform collection of statistical data from the world's societies is in its early stages. Some nations keep certain facts confidential, such as those concerning census figures, military activities, budgets, or public health. Much valuable historical material is unavailable to scholars because it is classified in governmental files.

Political scientists and historians studying international relations have traditionally reported present events or re-created past ones carefully and accurately. But they have usually not analyzed these facts so as to produce the quantitative data which are essential for testing scientific theories. As Singer has observed about the methods of international studies:

. . . we have gone along for decades, in both the empirical and the theoretical vineyards, under the illusion that our digging in the former was contributing to a fine vintage in the latter. That this is largely an illusion is best indicated by an examination of our theoretical writings. More often than not, the most compelling evidence an author can marshall on behalf of his generalization is an illustration or two that *he* considers relevant. A couple of such anecdotes not only represent a pitifully small sample of the universe of events or conditions about which he is generalizing, but his critics have little difficulty in arguing that the sample is either terribly biased or irrelevant. The past decade has, happily, seen a gradually increasing awareness that the inductive road to theory must be paved with data and that the deductive road must eventually—if it is to lead beyond speculation and into scientific knowledge—be appraised by an empirical yardstick. On the other hand, we all recognize that the difficulty of converting facts into data varies markedly from field to field, and in no social science field is it any more difficult than in international relations. Even the original gathering of reliable facts is surrounded with the impediments of governmentally imposed secrecy and distortion as well as the diffuseness of such facts in time and space. Before we ever get to the problem of systematic data-making we are confronted with awkward problems of information-gathering.[186]

The major problem with simulations at this level is that the simulated world may not be sufficiently like the real world for anyone to be able to predict outcomes from them or to verify hypotheses validly.[187] Until data are available from the living system being analyzed, the researcher will not know how valid his simulations are. Validity (see page 85) is certainly a central problem, therefore, in supranational and international simulations. Some simulations discussed below have been evaluated as to their validity (see pages 1007 to 1010). Simulations of classes (b) and (d), in which people represent components of international relationships or supranational systems, have special validity problems. Can students, for example, represent policy makers of societies validly enough to test theories of international relations? In Hermann's words: "How can college students behave like experienced political leaders? How can participants represent the cultural values of other societies? How can players reflect the considerations involved in a national decision to go to war, when their wars cause no death or destruction?"[188]

No effort has been made to include every model and simulation that applies to this level of living systems. Instead, examples have been selected which illustrate the operation of classes of models such as those based on game theory, the numerous variants of Guetzkow's Inter-Nation Simulation, and the computerized "world" models. When they exist, simulations which have been subjected to experimental test are emphasized. Included below are one "world model," which has been experimented upon for some time, as well as other world or "global" models now being developed and tested. In addition, I discuss several models that concentrate on a limited number of subsystems or adjustment processes. Many models are concerned only with the decider subsystem.

Of the four classes of models and simulations (see page 85), examples can be found of all but class (*a*), in which *nonliving artifacts* simulate a supranational system. Models of classes (*b*) *living, usually human, representations,* and (*c*) *models in words, numbers, or other symbols, including computer programs,* are well represented at this level. Class (*d*) models, *living system—computer interactions,* include models similar to those of class (*b*), with the added feature that a computer program is used to store data on variables and determine outcomes of decisions.

(*b*) *Living, usually human, representations.* Many simulations of this class are games, and all represent the interactions of decider subsystems of two or more societies. In these simulations individual persons or small groups serve as deciders of simulated societies or supranational systems interacting in international situations. Mock United Nations General Assemblies and Security Councils, a form of simulation sometimes used for teaching, copy the structures of the supranational organizations they represent. They use a local group or organization to simulate a supranational organization. This sort of exercise evidently has considerable face validity. Students often become much involved. Interactions among the "delegates" take place under the real United Nations rules. The Inter-Nation Simulation (INS) (see pages 1000 to 1009), which has both a class (*b*) (without computer) and a class (*d*) (with computer) form, is unusual among experimental game-type simulations in also specifically simulating societal deciders as organizations rather than as groups. This is achieved by arranging the participants in echelons.

The Political-Military Exercise (PME). The PME is a family of games that derive from prototypes developed for Rand Corporation beginning about 1954.[189] They were variants of more traditional "war games" and were intended to be used as aids in political-military analysis and policy making, to help participants evaluate foreign-policy alternatives and anticipate the consequences of decisions. In keeping with this purpose, participants in many of the exercises have been political, military, or academic professionals. The initial experiments used senior Foreign Service officers and specialists in social science, economics, and physics. Variants of the PME have been employed in undergraduate and graduate instruction,

with students as participants. A number of agencies of the United States government, including the Department of Defense, have used such exercises for training and policy research.[190]

In the PME, teams of participants, usually consisting of three to five members, play the roles of top deciders of each of several nations or groups of nations, like the Afro-Asian bloc. Participants do not attempt to portray specific people, but instead try to select strategies typical of the living systems they represent. Some experiments have also included a United Nations team. Military advisers and other specialist consultants are also available. A control team manages the game. This group represents "nature" by introducing unexpected events; acts as umpires, ruling on the plausibility of moves and deciding outcomes; monitors communications; and provides inputs from nations not represented by teams. If United Nations Assembly or Security Council action is required, the control group counts votes and specifies the action to be taken. It decides the number and length of the discontinuous move periods, provides input based upon events of previous periods to the simulated governments at the beginning of each period, and determines the relationship of game time to real time in each period. Periods have simulated from 8 to 195 days, depending upon such things as the intensity of the crisis, the complexity of the diplomatic negotiations undertaken, and the speed of escalation during the play. Typical exercises continue for several days.

Each exercise is based upon a scenario that specifies the prior history, capabilities, and military dispositions of the nations being simulated and describes a developing crisis situation with which play must begin. Scenarios for some published games have featured crises precipitated by involvement of various countries in the affairs of other nations in Southeast Asia, a civil war in an African nation, a war in the Near East, the death of the head of the Polish government, and the international interactions around Berlin in 1959.[191] A series of several games carried out for a United States Naval Ordnance Test Station explored the role of sea-based strategic deterrence weapons systems in international crisis situations. Aside from the scenarios, no program is provided, and no moves or consequences of moves are prescribed. Within limits set by the control group, interaction among participants is free.

With the exception of some face-to-face negotiations or discussions, which are monitored by the control team and summarized in writing, all moves, including diplomatic messages, public speeches, movements of troops, and secret strategic plans, are recorded in writing on standard message forms. Messages are channeled by a message center to or from the control group or through it to other powers.

Decision responsibilities within teams may be assigned by the team itself or by the control group before play begins. The initial part of each move period is used by teams to define basic strategies, analyze moves of other teams, consider possible alternative events and actions to be taken, and decide upon their next move. During play, "hot-line" messages may be delivered at any time.

Data from the simulation include the message forms submitted by teams, summaries prepared by a game historian, accounts of the decision-making process within teams by team reporters, a verbatim record of a postgame critique session, and questionnaires filled out by participants after the exercise is terminated.

In the opinion of some experimenters, PME games are better than other methods of policy research for disclosing some possibilities that have not previously been examined in depth. They have been called "organized brainstorming." They are said to yield useful information about policy alternatives, such as the choices that confront the decider who uses a particular strategy, and to permit relevant policy inferences.

A series of four games—CONEX I, II, III, and IV, each a version of the PME—was carried out in 1968 and 1969 to analyze issues involved in decision making about policies of the United States toward conflicts, real or potential, among the nations in Latin America, Asia, Africa, and the Middle East.[192] Arms, arms control, and problems of dealing with instability and of minimizing violence and possible escalation were central issues.

Earlier studies had produced a number of propositions about United States policy toward possible local conflicts. These were made the basis of game design and data gathering for CONEX. Hypothetical situations were planned in which the deciders representing the United States had to choose whether to try to arrange things so that the United States controlled ideological outcomes or to follow a policy of either minimizing violence, regardless of outcome, or abstaining from involvement.

Games were designed in two parts: The first was placed early enough in time so that the United States still had a range of open options. The second was placed at a later time, when the crisis was acute. Competing policy pressures became more apparent in the latter—an immediate resolution needed to be made.

Subjects for these exercises were American scholars and experts in regional affairs, United States foreign policy, military strategy, and public opinion. For CONEX I, III, and IV, these were divided into two

United States teams (Blue and Green) and one to represent the leadership of whatever less developed country was to be simulated. For CONEX II, which simulated arms-transfer problems between the parties to a local conflict, the principal teams represented the two societies in conflict. A third represented the United States. The two United States teams in CONEX I, III, and IV played entirely separately, reacting to the moves of the other society independently. This innovation in PME technique was instituted as a scientific control to provide a check as to whether the play of a single team was idiosyncratic. Such a situation might well have posed a problem for control in framing responses from the other society. Since both United States teams reacted in fundamentally similar ways, this difficulty did not develop.

The CONEX games differed somewhat from earlier versions of the PME. The experimenters wished to increase experimental control without abandoning the "free-play" aspects of the games. In order to do this, explicit hypotheses were formulated in advance of play, and the game was designed to elicit relevant behavior. Control used these as a guide also in planning and formulating responses to team messages. These games differed also in allowing less interaction among teams and in having more preprogramming of the general trend of events. This preprogramming reduced the free activities of the control team. A further innovation in CONEX IV was use of computer-aided storing, retrieving, and analyzing of data on local conflicts. This system was available to only one of the two United States teams, and a special hypothesis was developed to examine the comparative responses of the teams. In this game also a computer-based network for communications among teams was used. These and other innovations increased the rigor of experimental techniques and data gathering.

Data from the games were analyzed for their bearing upon 25 hypotheses related to United States policy toward local conflict, arms transfers, and arms controls. As an example, data on all the United States teams in CONEX I, III, and IV were relevant to a hypothesis concerning the tendency of the United States to avoid conflict, a tendency that was particularly evident at the time these experiments were conducted. The hypothesis was: "If the Soviets or Chinese take sides and their gain becomes manifest, the U.S. concern with a favorable political outcome will overtake its violence-avoidance objective and the U.S. will directly oppose, if necessary through unilateral military intervention, unless fear of nuclear escalation supervenes."[193]

The outcomes of the various simulation runs did not support this hypothesis. In CONEX III and IV it seemed that not even significant Soviet or Chinese gains could overcome the basic policy of the United States to avoid conflict. In CONEX III it appeared that fear of escalation was not the reason for such behavior. Rather, it was that a Soviet gain in a situation of potential conflict between African states was not regarded by either United States team as necessarily an American loss. This was even clearer in CONEX IV. In it the United States preferred significant Soviet gains in South Asia to involvement of its country in conflict. The primary goals of United States teams were peaceful. Even in the third period of the experiment, when threat of Soviet gains increased significantly, this avoidance of conflict persisted. Only in CONEX IV, when Chinese military intervention in India became a possibility, did this attitude weaken. Then the United States teams positioned military units in the vicinity of India as a show of force.

Although a substantial number of policy inferences and conclusions were drawn from these exercises, the experimenters were careful to disclaim the value of the PME for testing substantive propositions about foreign policy. They cautiously said it was useful for testing "propositions about the predicted behavior of individuals or groups who simulate official decision makers."[194]

Early users of the PME were little concerned with validation of their simulations. Systematic analysis of results, replication, and comparison of real-world and simulated-world behavior, all of which could contribute to validation, have been slow to develop. Each experiment with the PME was essentially unique, like a case history. The increased rigor of the CONEX series is a move toward more scientific experimental design, data collection, and analysis. A formidable obstacle to replication is the difficulty of securing the services of qualified high-ranking participants for the necessary amount of time. All the PME simulations had good face validity; *i.e.*, they appeared to an ordinary observer to be reasonably designed for their stated purpose. The participants became highly involved in the task, whether they were specialists or students. Also, the experimenters believed that the results were realistic and of practical value. It is reasonable to ask, however, whether even persons expert in international affairs are able to simulate decision processes of people of another nation. Could Russians staff a team assigned to simulate Japanese decision making, or could Americans carry out the task of French decision makers?

A few replications of games have been conducted. One such experiment compared behaviors on the same games of officials in different types of positions and at various echelons in the federal government of

the United States. The experimenters tentatively concluded that responses of teams from the United States had "amazing uniformity."[195] It would be useful also to repeat games with different control teams. Such replication using the same scenario would test the hypothesis that outcomes of simulation runs are related to explicit or implicit assumptions of control-team members.

Discussing the validity of the PME, Smoker says:

Until empirical analyses of performance are undertaken with output from the PME, it is difficult, if not impossible, to evaluate its validity. It can be that the nature of the control team and the nature of the crisis problems tackled are such that PME acts as a reinforcer of basically incorrect perceptions of reality and incorrect theory. . . . Certainly there is no compelling empirical evidence to suggest that the results from PME be taken seriously, and there is some apprehension that the exercise has been used by United States government agencies with, apparently, no particular concern as to its real world validity as a policy device other than subjective untestable propositions about output from the simulations.[196]

The Tactical and Negotiations Game (TNG).   This simulation game has been used by Streufert to study psychological variables of individual persons and groups.[197] In much of the work the international character of the subject matter was incidental to the purposes of the experiment. The game results proved, however, to have relevance to international strategic decision making, since they contribute to understanding of variables that might affect the course of international negotiations and conflicts.

In the TNG, human decision makers interact not with opposing teams but with a program. The simulated environment and the progress of the game are determined almost entirely by the program, which is written to create situations that can throw light on hypotheses that interest the experimenters. Such programming provides less realistic situations and includes fewer variables than simulations, like the PME, which include much unprogrammed activity. On the other hand, it avoids the lack of comparability of runs and generates more data suitable for statistical analysis. Unlike the PME, the TNG also distinguishes the variables involved in alternative decisions, making possible study of the effects of specific variables on psychological and political behavior.

The TNG simulates a small-scale conflict, such as the war in Korea or Vietnam. It is played from both sides of the conflict. The teams on each side are composed of subteams; one makes decisions about economic matters, one about intelligence matters, and one about military matters, while another subteam attempts to negotiate a settlement in accordance with terms suggested by its government. A simulated country, "Shamba," is presented to the participants on a relief map and is described in historical, economic, and military terms. Shamba is a less developed country with variegated terrain and climate, somewhat smaller than South Vietnam. It has an authoritarian government, with frequent changes of regime. Decision makers on both sides receive the same factual information, but it is worded in propaganda terminology so that each side begins the simulation feeling hostile to its opponents.

Those subteams which make economic decisions may invest funds in various projects, those which deal with intelligence can ask for information, and those which deal with military affairs can order up military forces of fixed strength or request use of atomic weapons. The latter are invariably denied to them. Counterinsurgency operations are also possible. It is important to note that participants interact only with the program and that any decisions made by them in any area have no effect upon the progress of the game. The program determines the outcome no matter what they do.

Negotiation decision makers on one side deal with the negotiation decision makers of the other side in a simulated environment. They never interact face-to-face, however. These negotiators may communicate with the tactical-economic teams, but in fact messages are preprogrammed. The information they receive about the progress of the military-economic team has no relationship to the actual progress of the game, which is programmed.

While credibility and face validity would seem to be problems in such a highly artificial situation, participants, in fact, enjoyed the game and became involved in it, attributed outcomes to their own and their opponents' decisions, and rarely blamed experimenters, even in situations in which failure was the programmed outcome.

Four variables of the "environmental inputs" to the participants from the experimenters were studied: (*i*) information input rate; (*ii*) success—the proportion of information that communicated success of operations; (*iii*) failure—the proportion of information that communicated failure; and (*iv*) complexity, a summative function of the other three. Individual participants were found to differ in their abilities to discriminate, differentiate, and integrate environmental inputs.[198] Participants' personalities were classified as "structurally complex" or "structurally simple."

There is evidence that elevated information input rate, more success, and more failure all should first increase and then decrease strategic decision making.[199] (This decision making takes into consideration likely events beyond the next action.) If two of these

motivations increase or decrease simultaneously, the effect would be expected to be cumulative.

To study the effects of information input rates, decision-making teams were exposed in random order to 2, 5, 8, 10, 12, 15, or 25 independent statements of relevant information per half-hour period. All teams were exposed to all input rates at some time during a single afternoon and night. Decision making was measured in terms of the strategy employed. Results were that optimal strategic decision making occurred at an input rate of 10 items per half hour. Few strategic decisions were made at very low input rates (load 2) and very high input rates (load 25). Under low input rates the decision makers made trial-and-error decisions to explore their effects. Under high load the subjects were not able to sort out relevant information and base strategic decisions on an optimal amount of such information. At or above an input rate of 7, some statements were disregarded. At 12 to 15 items, processing broke down. What is more, decisions at high input rates tended to be retaliatory and usually aggressive. Under both underload and overload random behavior occurs. The experimenters saw no examples of unplanned or unstrategic aggressiveness at optimal or near-optimal conditions.

These findings are obviously relevant to the studies of information input overload reported in Chap. 5, particularly the other work of Streufert and his associates on the TNG (see pages 155 and 156).

The data from the TNG were also relevant to the effects of load on the participant's perception of the strategy of the opponent and its interaction with his own nation. It was found that the same input rates that produced optimal strategic decison-making behavior also produced optimal perceptual capacity.

Information input rate also affected the sort of information search that a decision maker would undertake. If the information search was self-initiated, as the information input rate increased beyond the critical optimal point, search decreased. This finding supports Hypothesis 3.3.7.2-6 (see page 100), which states that the shorter the decision period, the less thorough in general is the search within the information processing network for relevant facts and alternative solutions. This was not true of delegated information search in which the subjects requested more information. They continued to request more information no matter how high the information input rate, but subjects were not able to use this new information strategically.

To measure the effects of success and failure, the information input rate was kept somewhat slower than the rate at which optimal messages indicating success or failure were introduced. Out of seven messages, the number of success or failure messages rose from one out of seven to seven out of seven, including all proportions in between.

Results in the case of failure were similar to those found for information load. As failure increased, rational strategic decision making increased, and at proportions of two out of seven or three out of seven it was optimal. Above those ratios it decreased. Retaliatory decision making increased with increase of failure conditions. Analysis of the success condition had not been completed when the report was published.

Both increasing success and increasing failure increased military risk taking. At odds of 5 to 7, however, the trend reversed.

Subjects for these experiments were selected after they were tested as to their "structural complexity." The strategic capacity of the complex subjects under optimal input rates proved to be far greater than the capacity of the structurally simple subjects. They also rated higher in tolerance of uncertainty, in consideration, and in predictive accuracy. Simple leaders rated higher in initiation of structure, in production emphasis, and in demanding reconciliation.

This simulation was not intended to represent any specific conflict, although the Vietnam War was a model for it. Experimenters noted, however, that subjects in the TNG frequently anticipated by 4 to 6 months methods of political, military, and economic warfare that the United States used in Vietnam.

Implications for conduct of international relations were drawn from the simulation, particularly from the effects of information input overload. Streufert suggested that leaders who experience overload might well make use of information-integration staffs who themselves have limited information loads.

The ABC game. This research-oriented paper game was named ABC because it concerns choices to *a*ccommodate, *b*oycott, or *c*onfront opponents.[200] It was designed to compare the behavior of American players with that of Japanese players in a negotiation situation in order to provide a test of cultural differences in patterns of strategic choice in negotiations. The published version was regarded by its author as a preliminary study, to be followed by further studies increasing the number of countries compared and testing a more refined set of hypotheses.

The negotiation situations to which the ABC game is supposed to apply are limited to those in which participants have fundamentally opposed goals in a highly uncertain situation and in which successive decisions are necessary.

Participants in the study were instructed that they represented the nation of Algo in peace talks with Bingo. Bingo was represented not by other participants but by a standardized opponent whose responses were available in tabular form. Negotiators, who are not described in the report, discussed various issues, also not specified. After each discussion, both Algo and Bingo stated their positions.

By their choices of strategies, players affect the movement of a negotiation point on a board from its central position toward their target. The Algo target is a point at the upper left-hand corner of the board. The Bingo target is at the lower right-hand corner. The relative success of the strategies is indicated by the position of the point relative to the targets. A chance factor, introduced to represent the uncertainty in the negotiation situation, also affects the position of the point.

Three types of negotiation strategies were available to the participants: (*a*) *accommodation,* a minimax strategy, attempting to minimize the possible loss, measured by the distance from the target; (*b*) *boycott,* a relative-gain maximizing strategy, taking a loss in order to inflict a greater loss on the opponent; and (*c*) *confrontation,* a possible-gain maximizing strategy. The third is risky and depends upon luck, but it brings the greatest gain. The second is not justified in a single decision but is justifiable when future choices may permit recovery of the previous loss. The three deal differently with uncertainty. The first accepts uncertainty; the second is pessimistic; and the third is optimistic. According to the author, the second is characteristic of the Japanese emphasis on "letting the enemy cut your flesh in order to cut his bones" and of guerilla strategy in other lands.

According to the rules of the game, if both sides choose a possible-gain strategy (strategy *c*), chance determines which one maximizes his gain. If one chooses to maximize possible gain (strategy *c*) and the other chooses to minimize possible loss (strategy *a*), a moderate gain is given to the side favored by chance. If both choose possible-loss minimization (strategy *a*), the point moves without advantage to either. When one chooses possible-gain maximizing and the other chooses relative-gain maximizing, both lose, but the possible-gain maximizer loses more. The minimax strategy loses moderately to the relative-gain maximizing strategy, and if both select the relative-gain strategy, the point moves without advantage to either.

Both Algo and Bingo are given influence units which represent military potential, diplomatic efforts, or propaganda campaign cost. The game ends when one side has spent all its influence units or when the negotiation point goes off the board. Accommodation costs the player 2 influence units; boycott and confrontation each 1 unit. The reported experiment included 45 Japanese and 36 American participants.

Approximately half the players of each nationality received 10 influence units, and the other half received 20 influence units. Those with 10 were under greater time pressure, while the others had more time to bring the points closer to their targets.

The game tested six hypotheses, all of which were concerned with cultural differences between the decider processes of the two types of participants. On the basis of these, several predictions were made as to choice of strategies by the participants.

Analysis of results showed differences between the decision making of participants from the two cultures, mainly in the predicted directions, but more tests seemed to be needed. The Japanese were found to be more likely to choose a relative-gain strategy. If a subject chose a possible-loss minimizing strategy, it was safe to predict he was American. When combinations of strategies were investigated, the Japanese most often responded to an apparent relative-gain maximizing strategy of the opponents with choice of the same strategy and rarely responded to the minimax choice with possible-gain maximizing. The Americans most commonly responded to the relative-gain strategy with possible-gain maximizing and to the minimax choice of their opponents with the same strategy.

Prisoner's Dilemma. Mathematical game theory, which is concerned with rational choice in situations where opposed interests exist, has been used in simulating or modeling certain sorts of international interactions that involve negotiation or conflict. In an example of such experiments, the game known as "Prisoner's Dilemma" (see pages 579 and 580) was used to simulate an arms race, with pairs of players deciding to convert missiles to factories producing nonmilitary goods, or vice versa.[201] In the simple form of this nonzero-sum game, two choices are possible to each of two players. Payoffs to each player depend not only upon his own choice but also upon that of the other player. In this case the choices are identified as *to arm* or *to disarm*. If both disarmed, the payoff to each would be the same; if both armed, neither would receive a payoff; and if one disarmed and the other armed, the one that disarmed would receive the total payoff, and the other would receive nothing. Choices in this basic game are made without communication between the two sides.

In the form of Prisoner's Dilemma used in this experiment, players could choose any degree of disarmament from 0 to 20. The game was played on a board divided into 20 squares. On each square was a poker chip with a white side with a missile on it and a blue side with a factory. At the beginning of the game, disarmament was 0—all missiles were showing. Each

move allowed a player to convert one, two, or none of his chips from missile to factory or from factory back to missile. A trial consisted of 20 moves performed simultaneously by each of the two players. Payoffs reflected their relative statuses at the end of the twentieth move. Twenty-five games were played by each set of players. Players were aware of the stakes involved for every possible combination of moves. The matrix in Fig. 12-3 is a reduced form, with fewer squares, of one which was given to each player before play began. On any given trial, an individual player would fare better if he remained fully armed no matter what the other player did, but mutual cooperation would result in greater combined rewards to both. Following each of the 25 games, each player was told how many missiles were retained by the other side. Neither visual nor verbal contact between players was permitted.

Four groups of sixteen pairs of players participated. The first, the control group, received the information concerning the game outcome given at the end of each game as the sole source of feedback throughout the experiments. In each of the other three sets of games, "inspections" were made by the experimenter in charge of the game. He told each player what the actual situation on his opponent's board was. The inspection took place after the fifth move for one set of players, after the tenth move for a second, and after the fifteenth move for a third. In the moves remaining

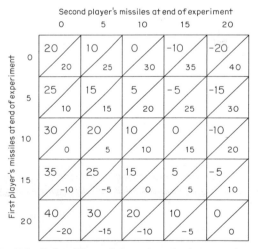

Fig. 12-3 Reduced form of players' matrix shown to players. The upper, larger figure in each box represents the first player's payoff. The lower, smaller figure is the payoff for the second player. (From M. Pilisuk, J. A. Winter, R. Chapman, & N. Haas. Honesty, deceit, and timing in the display of intentions. *Behav. Sci.*, 1967, **12**, 208. *Reprinted by permission.*)

after the inspection, each player could, of course, change his armed state. Inspection after the tenth move allowed a fully disarmed player to become fully armed in the 10 remaining moves before the game's end. Inspection after the fifth move would not allow more than 50 percent disarmament by the inspection time, and that percentage could easily be returned to 100 percent by the game's end. Three types of behaviors can be displayed in this game: *deceiving* (when a player displays more missiles at the payoff move than at the inspection move), *telling the truth* (when the number of missiles reported is identical at inspection and at payoff), and *disarmament gesturing* (when the number of missiles is fewer at payoff than at inspection). The inspection procedure permitted players to communicate regarding their intentions, but it also permitted deception, and so players could not necessarily trust an appearance of cooperation by the other side.

(c) *Models in words, numbers, or other symbols, including computer programs.*

LINK. The LINK system is an econometric world macromodel that combines existing econometric models of societies.[202] It is so constructed that as more governments begin to use econometric models, they can be linked into it. One experiment on this model simulated the worldwide impact of the 1971 new economic policy of the United States. The simulation was conducted shortly after the policy went into effect. It accurately predicted decreases in the real value of world trade—slight in 1971 and more significant in 1972.

Dynamic world models

World II and World III. The world model created by Forrester for the Club of Rome Project on the Predicament of Mankind has received much attention and criticism, partly because of the disturbing predictions that resulted from it.[203] This model is similar in form to the corporate and urban models developed by the same research group (see pages 718 to 722 and 726 to 731). It is written in the DYNAMO language used for the others. Like them, it deals with changes in highly aggregated variables. The first published form of this model (World II) was followed by a revised, somewhat less aggregated form (World III) developed by Meadows and others. The two are similar in important respects, and predictions made using the later model do not contradict those made using the earlier one.

Both World II and World III have five basic variables describing states of the system, or "levels." (I put their term "levels" in quotation marks to avoid confusion with the particular meaning of the same word in my conceptual system.) Those of World II are population,

natural resources, capital investment, capital investment in agriculture, and pollution.[204] The state variables of World III are population, capital, food, nonrenewable resources, and pollution.[205] In both, population reflects the average population of a world without national boundaries. World II uses real data for population in 1900 and 1970, but relies on guesses for the remainder of its figures. World III is based to a much greater extent on data, but does not make use of sophisticated statistical techniques for selecting the best figures. The extension of the model over a long time span also is said to lead to errors in extrapolation. Only the long-lived, globally distributed pollutants like lead, mercury, asbestos, stable pesticides, and radioisotopes are included. Natural resources are represented by a generalized concept of the combined reserves of all nonrenewable resources. The other state variables are similarly inclusive.

The state variables represent physical quantities that can be measured directly. They are increased or decreased by rates of input, throughput, and output such as birthrates and death rates and rates of resource consumption. These, in turn, are determined by the state variables, in a feedback relationship. The basic diagram of World III appears in Fig. 12-4. This diagram and the quite similar one for the World II model contain multiple interlocking feedback loops shown as closed paths through the diagram. Feedbacks from birthrate and death rate, for instance, determine population, which ordinarily shows an annual exponential increase. Birthrates and death rates are "normal" when a standard set of world conditions, including food, material standard of living, crowding, and pollution, are at their normal rates. When these change, reflecting the favorableness or unfavorableness of the environment, they increase and decrease the normal rates of population variables. These and other influences on the state variables are represented by "multipliers."[206] Feedback loops can have positive effects, like the one that generates population growth, or negative effects, like the one by which deaths decrease the population. Taken together, they interact to determine whether the population will increase exponentially, decline toward zero, or find an equilibrium. A total system in equilibrium would maintain a constant population through opposing adjustments in birthrates and death rates. Similar feedbacks control the rates of the other state variables.

The computer programs for these models express the assumptions upon which the models are based in a set of difference equations which together constitute a theory of the world system. Examples given below are from World II, for which the entire program is published. It assumes, for example, that the death rate depends on food, crowding, material standard of living, and pollution.

The program specifies and defines the factors that determine the values of each of the state variables and the actions of each of the multipliers and auxiliary variables, like quality of life (QL), and ratios, like the effective capital investment rate (ECIR).

ECIR is defined as:

> . . . the capital-investment ratio CIR, multiplied by the natural-resource-extraction multiplier NREM, multiplied by the variable fraction (1 − CIAF) of capital not used in agriculture, divided by the constant (1 − CIAFN) which is the "normal" fraction of capital not used in agriculture under 1970 conditions. The resulting ratio ECIR is, at any point in time, the ratio of effective capital units per person to the 1970 capital units per person.
> ECIR.K = (CIR.K) (1 − CIAF.K) (NREM.K) / (1 − CIAFN)
> ECIR—Effective-Capital-Investment Ratio (Capital units /person)
> CIR—Capital-Investment-Ratio (Capital units/person)
> CIAF—Capital-Investment-In-Agriculture Fraction (Dimensionless)
> NREM—Natural-Resource-Extraction-Multiplier (Dimensionless)
> CIAFN—Capital-Investment-In-Agriculture Fraction Normal (Dimensionless).[207]

K following a decimal point in this system is a time-step indicator referring to the time at which the equation is being evaluated.

Quality of life is a measure of performance of the world system. It is computed from the standard QLS, the value of the quality of life for 1970, multiplied by multipliers derived from values assigned to material standard of living, crowding, food, and pollution. Forrester says:

> The four component inputs to quality of life must be derived and combined in such a way that they properly reflect the urgency of the different components of quality of life. For example, a low food ratio is of more immediate and pressing concern than a low material standard of living or a high pollution ratio. Also, the adequacy levels of quality-of-life components are recognized. Above a sufficient amount of food, further increments of food rapidly lose capability to raise the quality of life. Likewise, below some acceptable level of pollution, further pollution reduction carries a low priority.
> It is from the nonlinear character of quality-of-life factors that shifting emphasis comes. Throughout history, man has struggled first for food and second for material standard of living. Crowding has had a third-priority significance because crowding could often be relieved by invading thinly settled areas of the earth. Pollution was of the least concern.
> But priorities can reverse quickly. Pollution and crowding can rise to where they compete for attention even with the need for food. Furthermore, they both can reach a severity where they impinge on the primary needs for air, water, and food. These shifting priorities should be reflected in the composite quality of life QL which is generated from its components. . . .[208]

The Quality of Life measures are:
QL—Quality of Life (Satisfaction units)
QLS—Quality of Life Standard (Satisfaction units)
QLM—Quality of Life From Material Standard of Living (Dimensionless)
QLC—Quality of Life From Crowding (Dimensionless)
QLF—Quality of Life From Food (Dimensionless)
QLP—Quality of Life From Pollution (Dimensionless).[208]

In order to set the program in operation, it is necessary only to assign values to the state variables, since the other elements of the system can be computed from them.[209] Values for the year 1970 are taken as "normal" in the published models. Multipliers have the value of 1 when the levels are set for that year. In operation, the model can be "stepped" through time to simulate the changing world. Used in this way, both models can show what happens when exponential growth collides with a fixed environment. Results, displayed on a series of computer graphs, show the interactions that limit the exponential growth of population and industrialization, which without such limiting factors would double at fixed intervals indefinitely. The basic performance of the model over the years 1900 to 2100 is shown in Fig. 12-5. It includes effects of four of the state variables on quality of life. As natural resources become exhausted, quality of life by 1940 falls below its earlier slope of rise, although for a time it continues its upward direction. Population and capital investment reach their peaks and begin to decline, and pollution also reaches its peak and begins to decline. The similar graph for World III from 1900 to 2100 is given in Fig. 12-6. In this all variables follow historical values from 1910 to 1970. Food, industrial output, and population grow until they are limited by the diminishing resource base. Natural delays, however, permit "overshoot." And population continues to grow after the peak in industrialization until a rising death rate halts its growth. What is more, it appears that if controls are placed on one of the factors, such as pollution, growth continues until another, perhaps food shortages or resource depletion, brings it to an end. Even if a number of policies are introduced simultaneously, seeking to control other factors as well, improvement is only temporary. A situation of this sort is shown in Fig. 12-7. According to Forrester, this happens as a result of the nature of complex systems of the sort being depicted here. He says:

> The intuitively obvious "solutions" to social problems are apt to fall into one of several traps set by the character of complex systems. First, an attempt to relieve one set of symptoms may

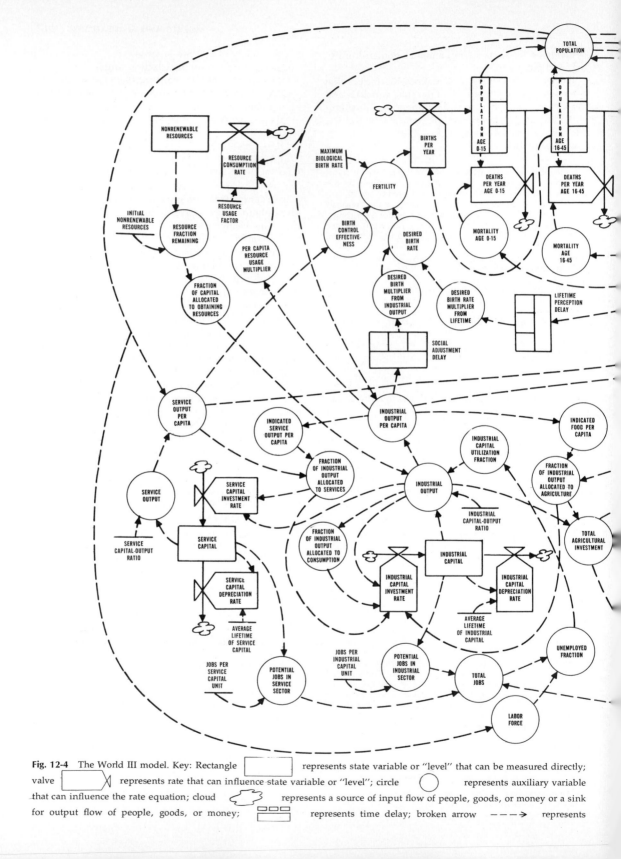

Fig. 12-4 The World III model. Key: Rectangle [   ] represents state variable or "level" that can be measured directly; valve [▷] represents rate that can influence state variable or "level"; circle ( ) represents auxiliary variable that can influence the rate equation; cloud ⟨☁⟩ represents a source of input flow of people, goods, or money or a sink for output flow of people, goods, or money; ▭▭▭ represents time delay; broken arrow – – – → represents

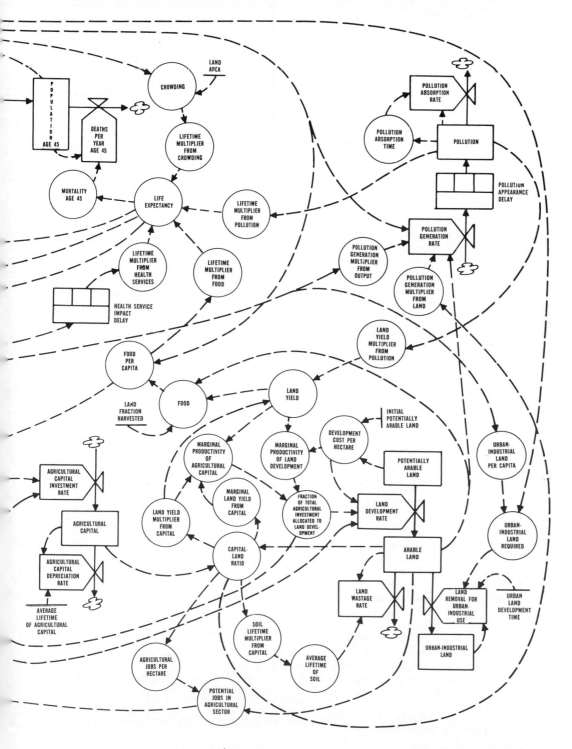

causal relationship; solid arrow ————————> represents real flow of people, goods, or money. (From *The limits to growth: a report for The Club of Rome's project on the predicament of mankind,* by Donella H. Meadows, Dennis L. Meadows, Jørgen Randers, & William W. Behrens, III. A Potomac Associates book published by Universe Books, New York, 1972, pages 102–103. Graphics by Potomac Associates. *Reprinted by permission.*)

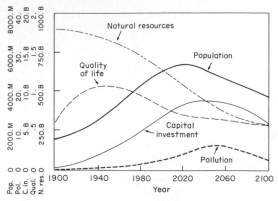

Fig. 12-5   Basic behavior of World II model, showing the mode in which industrialization and population are suppressed by falling natural resources. The meanings of the symbols along the vertical scale are as follows: B represents billions; M represents millions; Pop. represents population; Pol. represents pollution; C.in. represents capital investment; Qual. represents quality of life; N.res. represents natural resources. The units of measurement are: population—numbers of people; pollution—the ratio of the amount of pollution to the amount in 1970; capital investment—the ratio of the amount of capital investment per person to the amount per person in 1970; quality of life—the ratio of the quality of life measure to that measure in 1970; natural resources—the amount of non-replaceable natural resources consumed annually per person × 250 years (average time before exhaustion) × world population. [SOURCE: Adapted and reprinted, with permission, from *World Dynamics* by Jay W. Forrester (2d ed.). Copyright © 1973, Wright-Allen Press, Inc. Cambridge, MA 02142, USA, page 70.]

only create a new mode of system behavior that also has unpleasant consequences. Second, the attempt to produce short-term improvement often sets the stage for a long-term degradation. Third, the local goals of a part of a system often conflict with the objectives of the larger system. Fourth, people are often led to intervene at points in a system where little leverage exists and where effort and money have but slight effect.[210]

A suggested way to prevent population overshoot is to interrupt the positive feedback loops that generate population growth. This could be done by deliberate control of the birthrate so that the number of babies born each year would equal the number of deaths. The more usual approach, weakening the negative feedbacks, like pollution, famine, and depletion of nonrenewable resources, produces only further growth.[211] Interrupting the positive feedback loops that generate population growth would not prevent population overshoot unless the other of the two positive feedbacks now dominant in the world, industrial growth, was also controlled by similar means.

The best outcome that could be achieved, if this world model is an accurate predictor, is a world in

which a global equilibrium is induced by deliberate constraints. The stabilized world model shown in Fig. 12-8 was produced by Strategy I, a combination of the following policies:[212]

1. The birthrate was set equal to the death rate as of 1975. Natural increase in industrial capital continues until 1990, when it is stabilized by setting the investment rate equal to the depreciation rate.

2. To avoid a nonrenewable-resource shortage, resource consumption per unit of industrial output is reduced, in 1975, to one-fourth of its 1970 value.

3. To reduce resource depletion and pollution, the economic preferences of society are changed so that services like education and health facilities are preferred to factory-produced material goods, as of 1975.

4. Pollution generation per unit of industrial and agricultural output is reduced, after 1975, to one-fourth of its 1970 value.

5. Capital is diverted to food production, even if this would be considered uneconomic, in order to avoid the inequalities of distribution that would result from the low amount of food per capita.

6. The use of agricultural capital has been altered to make soil enrichment and preservation a high prior-

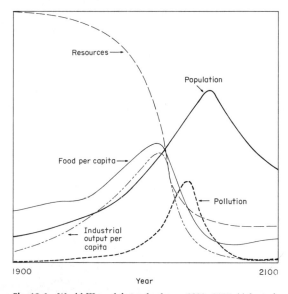

Fig. 12-6   World III model standard run, 1900–2100. (Adapted from *The limits to growth: a report for The Club of Rome's project on the predicament of mankind,* by Donella H. Meadows, Dennis L. Meadows, Jørgen Randers, & William W. Behrens, III. A Potomac book published by Universe Books, New York, 1972, page 124. Graphics by Potomac Associates. *Reprinted by permission.*)

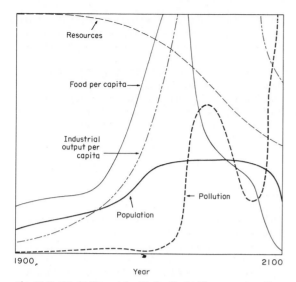

Fig. 12-7 World III model with "unlimited" resources, pollution controls, increased agricultural productivity, and "perfect" birth control. (Adapted from *The limits to growth: a report for The Club of Rome's project on the predicament of mankind,* by Donella H. Meadows, Dennis L. Meadows, Jørgen Randers, & William W. Behrens, III. A Potomac book published by Universe Books, New York, 1972, page 140. Graphics by Potomac Associates. *Reprinted by permission.*)

ity. This would, for example, require that capital be used to compost urban organic wastes and return them to the land, reducing pollution as well as correcting for the rapid soil erosion and depletion of fertility that would follow diversion of capital to food production.

7. The drains on industrial capital for increased food production and resource cycling would result in less industrial capital for other purposes. To counteract this, the average lifetime of industrial capital goods is increased. This is accomplished by better design for durability and repair and less discarding as a result of obsolescence. This would also reduce resource depletion and pollution.

The equilibrium produced by these measures, Strategy I, could be sustained far into the future. Resource depletion would, of course, continue, but time would be gained for discovery of alternative technologies. The equilibrium value of industrial output per capita in the stabilized model is three times the 1970 world average. Population is only slightly larger than at present. There is more than twice as much food per person as in 1970, and the average life expectancy throughout the world is nearly 70 years. Services per capita have

tripled. Average income per capita is approximately $1,800, which is about half the United States average at present but equal to the average European income and three times the average world income.

With other strategies, stable systems of other sorts could be achieved within the capacity of our earth to sustain them. According to Strategy II, for example, the unrealistic assumptions that population and capital could suddenly be stabilized would be dropped. Effective birth control, an average desired family of two children, and maintenance of average industrial output per capita at the 1975 level would be substituted for Strategy I. Then world population would grow much larger, and material goods, food, and services per capita would stabilize at lower values than with Strategy I, but they would still be higher than the present world average. If the same policies were not to be instituted until the year 2000, however, the resulting equilibrium state could not be sustained. Population and industrial capital would reach levels high enough to bring about food and resource shortages before the year 2100.

The dramatic conclusion to be drawn from this world model is that unless deliberate measures are

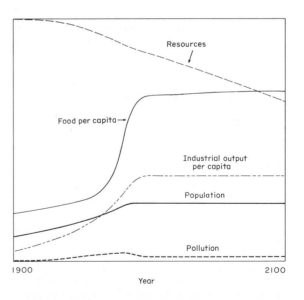

Fig. 12-8 World III model, stabilized world submodel I. (Adapted from *The limits to growth: a report for The Club of Rome's project on the predicament of mankind,* by Donella H. Meadows, Dennis L. Meadows, Jørgen Randers, & William W. Behrens, III. A Potomac book published by Universe Books, New York, 1972, page 165. Graphics by Potomac Associates. *Reprinted by permission.*)

taken to control growth, the limits to growth will be reached within less than 100 years, with the consequent collapse of society as we know it. With a goal of a steady-state society and commitment to its achievement, the authors see hope for a new form of world society.

Publication of the above world dynamic models has attracted increased attention to the serious world problems with which they are concerned and to simulation as an aid in policy making for a total world system. Critics were not slow, however, to point out what they considered to be the faults of these models. Some of the major criticisms are:

1. Although both Forrester and Meadows state repeatedly that their models are preliminary and unfinished, the conclusions they draw from them seem to be offered as prescriptions for policy changes that would profoundly affect the future of human society. Critics questioned whether models as simple as these, with only five state variables and with parameter and variable values based on admittedly inadequate data, can reasonably be made bases for such decisions. The M.I.T. group that developed the models thinks that they can because: " . . . the model described here is already sufficiently developed to be of some use to decision-makers. Furthermore, the basic behavior modes we have already observed in this model appear to be so fundamental and general that we do not expect our broad conclusions to be substantially altered by further revisions."[213]

Some of their critics disagree. The conclusion of an extensive analysis of both World II and World III by a group of scientists at the University of Sussex explicitly says: "What, then, remains of Forrester's and Meadows' efforts? Nothing, it seems to us, that can be immediately used for policy formation by decision makers; a technique, one among several—systems dynamics—of promise which needs improvement; but above all a challenge to all concerned with man's future to do better."[214]

2. The models are said to be oversimplified, limited to physical properties of the world and ignoring such important variables as politics, human values, the impacts of changes in technology, the effects of social structure, and the ability of people to change their behavior adaptively. Some assert that inclusion of these variables and the important feedbacks from them to the remainder of the system would significantly alter the results and that consequently their omission invalidates the models.[215]

Another scientist objects to the absence in the models of important adjustment processes that have served to avert catastrophe in the past.[216] The economic factor of price, for example, which is important

in determining demand and in stimulating search for new goods, is omitted. The models include no government which could exert control and no sort of social learning.

Also, the large amount of data aggregation in calculations with these models is said to result in neglect of important adjustment processes. No substitution of one product or service for another is possible since all are included in the same state variable. No difference in output mix can adjust for shortages, no difference in specific resources used can affect the depletion of resources, and no provision is made for research, development, or exploration. In response to similar criticisms, the Meadows team says that prices do not appear as a variable but that they do influence some of the relationships in the model.[217] Instead of stating that a decrease in supply causes a rise in price which brings about a social response, the model condenses this causal chain to a decrease in supply which leads to a social response. What is more, Meadows and his associates argue that since price rises are delayed signals of scarcity, the world dynamic models, which do not include the delay, are moderate in underestimating the tendency for demand in real economic systems to overshoot supply.

As to technological innovations, Meadows and his associates believe that it is better to search for understanding and better policies based on the constraints of the system as it actually exists rather than as it would be in some unimaginable future form. Human values are, they say, included in the system, but unknown future changes in values cannot be predicted. The model can, however, be used to test the effects of specific value changes. Tests have been made of the effects of some changes in values, including desired family size, fraction of the output consumed, and the relative demand for food and services.

3. World II and World III are presented as improvements for policy making over "mental models." One criticism holds that this contention could be valid only if the simulation were sensitive to different sets of plausible assumptions. Otherwise, all that occurs is that one set of computerized models is substituted for a set of conflicting "mental models."[218] Computer output, it is contended, depends upon computer input:

. . . "Malthus in, Malthus out" does bring out the essential point that what is on the computer print-out depends on the assumptions which are made about real-world relationships, and these assumptions in turn are heavily influenced by those contemporary social theories and values to which the computer modelers are exposed. . . . the critique of a computer model is not just a question of looking at the structure, or conducting mathematical tests. Far more important is the examination of the underlying assumptions.[219]

A common criticism of the models' assumptions is that they are too pessimistic.[220] If the vastly more encouraging figures that are available on technological progress, future reserves of nonrenewable resources, and the ability of the world to absorb and control pollution are adopted, the limits to growth would not occur until several centuries later, and in the meantime, all sorts of adjustments which can be expected to occur without any general recognition that limits are being approached would slow down the decline.

In a study designed to test the sensitivity of World II to changes in assumptions, Boyd altered the model to conform to the views of a "technological optimist."[221] A rate equation for technology, for example, supposes that as quality of life declines, society will find the technology necessary to improve it. He introduced three multipliers to represent the effect of technology on the rest of the model. These assumed that a sixfold increase in technology over the 1970 level would increase the food ratio by a factor of 8, that a fourfold increase in technology over the 1970 level would decrease pollution output per unit of material standard of living to zero, and that when technological effort quadruples, the natural resources input per unit of material standard of living would be reduced to zero. In addition, birthrate multipliers for material and food were altered in more optimistic directions.

With these changes the model indicated that technological advances increased productivity, which increased the standard of living, which reduced birthrates to the point where a "utopian" equilibrium was reached. When birth control was added to the above assumptions, the results were opposite to those which emerged when birth control was added to Forrester's assumptions. Instead of worsening the equilibrium, as Forrester found, birth control in this case resulted in a smaller population level and produced an even better equilibrium state. Boyd concluded that Forrester's model fails the test. It is unable to resolve the technological optimist–Malthusian controversy. In fact, the output of the model under each of the different sets of assumptions is the same as was reached without the use of a computer. Thus Forrester's simulation is not useful as a tool for policy makers, and even within his own framework, Forrester was unjustified in making such strong policy recommendations. Boyd wrote: "The great strength of Forrester's methodology is its ability to assimilate expert opinion easily. A model with a larger number of more disaggregated state variables would allow experts in various fields to involve their knowledge more usefully. Such a model might be a practical policy tool. And in a way, such a model would be the good science that Forrester's reviewers were looking for."[222]

Another set of experiments with changes in the dynamic world models also found them sensitive to parameter changes.[223] The results indicate that removal of a pessimistic bias in World III causes a change in results such that continued growth is possible, provided that the total costs of resource extraction and pollution do not exceed about one-quarter of the total industrial investment. These costs could be balanced by realistic improvements in industrial technology. These experiments show that even on the basis of World III and with a high population figure, no physical limits to growth will be reached in the next two centuries. Another criticism of the world dynamics models contends that available statistical techniques for fitting data and estimating parameters were not used.

In a statistical study which applied optimization techniques to World II to determine parameter settings, the computer selected an optimal value for normal birthrate that was lower than the one selected by Forrester and was therefore harder to achieve.[224] But the restraints on natural-resource usage it found to be optimal were less severe. The computer-determined policy recommends allowing pollution generation to increase. The resultant plot did not show excessive pollution. The values chosen for agricultural production and capital investment generations were less restrictive and easier to achieve.

Further statistical operations (open-loop optimal control) indicated, as previous work has also, that different value systems, here associated with different weightings of the performance measures associated with quality of life, produced varying results.

GLOBE6. This dynamic world model was developed by the Battelle Institute DEMATEL (*DE*cision-*MA*king *T*rial and *E*valuation *L*aboratory) program. Its ultimate purpose is to assist in defining priorities and developing improved decision-making techniques for meeting world problems.[225] A predecessor, GLOBE5, was based upon the flowchart of Forrester's World II. Relationships among elements of the world system contained in the flowchart were expressed in a set of about 40 algebraic and differential equations. Both World II and GLOBE5 aggregated variables on a worldwide basis, with no consideration of national distribution. GLOBE6 was developed to take account of such distribution.

The five primary elements of GLOBE6 are population, agriculture, industry, resources, and pollution. These are also represented in the state variables of World II, although they are calculated differently and their interrelationships are not in every case the same.

The major way this model's description of the world differs from that of World II is in its division of nations

into two classes distinguished by their economic statuses—the developed and the less developed nations.
These classes were modeled separately and coupled by
equations representing flows of population, resources, agricultural products, industrial products,

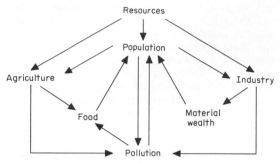

Fig. 12-9 Major elements and feedback paths in GLOBE6.
(From R. A. Burnett & P. J. Dionne. GLOBE6: a multiregion
interactive world simulation. *Simulation*, June 1973, 194. *Reprinted by permission.*)

and pollution. Figure 12-9 shows the major elements
and feedback paths in GLOBE6.

A second major difference between GLOBE6 and
World II is found in the structure of the population
submodel. The Forrester model includes the total
world population as a single variable with its rate of
change determined by one average birthrate and one
average death rate. Each class of nations in GLOBE6
has a submodel that divides the population into five
subgroups, each with age-specific birthrates and
death rates computed for each group. Figure 12-10
represents the population-dynamics submodel in
GLOBE6.

GLOBE6 and World II also treat the environmental
effects of pollution differently. In Forrester's model the
rate at which the environment can absorb or dissipate
pollution depends upon the pollution level itself, since
increase in pollution diminishes the ability of the
environment to absorb it. The resulting feedback loop
is very strong, which explains the dominant behavior
of the pollution variable in the model. In GLOBE6 the
time constant for absorption of pollution is a true
constant that yields a first-order exponential relationship, which is often found in nature.

Trade flows in GLOBE6 are controlled by the propensity of each class of nations to import or export
given categories of products. The propensities are
determined by per capita production rate of the class
as compared with a desired minimum or maximum.
The desired rates are input by the experimenter. Fig-

ure 12-11 describes the propensities to import or
export food.

Matter-energy processing models

Concern with the availability of resources and the
effects of man's activities upon the global environment has led to development of many models of distributor, producer, matter-energy storage, and extruder processes. These are intended as aids to research
and policy formation for natural-resource planning
and pollution control.

Several submodels for World III represent such processes. They present selected aspects of the large
model in less aggregated form. Among them are simulations of mercury and DDT flows in the global environment, natural-resource utilization, and solid-waste
generation.[226]

World III represents all forms of persistent pollutants by one variable. Obviously, each particular pollutant acts somewhat differently from all the others in
such characteristics as the total system it affects, its
distribution in living and nonliving components, its
rates of flow, its persistence in the sites where it
remains, and the nature of its effects upon individual
components and upon the total system.

World III mercury submodel.   Like World II and World
III, this is a dynamic model, written in the DYNAMO
computer language. It traces the path of mercury from
its natural sources to its natural sinks and examines
the contaminating effects of mercury production and
of its use by industry and agriculture.[227] The model
separately represents flows of two different chemical
forms of mercury, metal-inorganic and organomercurials. Of the two, organomercurials are the more toxic.

The submodel was first used to simulate the natural
flow of mercury, unaffected by man's activities. In the
world uninfluenced by man's technology, mercury is
released into the atmosphere by weathering of rocks,
by volcanic activity, and possibly by degasification of
the earth's crust. It enters sediments in streams as a
result of erosion of mercury-bearing rocks, such as
cinnabar. Mercury is carried from the air to the soil or
upper layer of the ocean by rainfall. It is washed from
the soil to streams and finally to the ocean. In the
ocean some of it enters the natural food chain when it
is ingested by marine microorganisms and reaches
man from the fish he eats. The remainder is deposited
on the ocean floor. A major assumption of the model is
that a simulation of natural sources and sinks should
demonstrate constant amounts of mercury in the various environmental sectors of the model—the air, the
soil, fresh water and its sediments, the oceans, and
fish (the food chain). Local differences among these

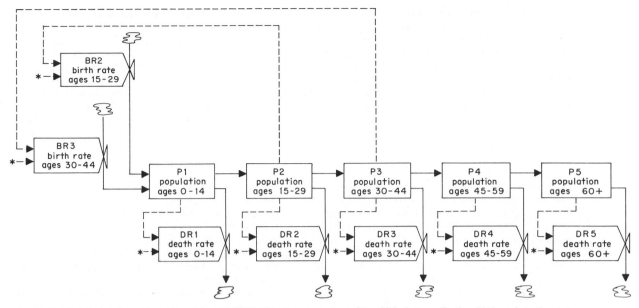

Fig. 12-10   Population-dynamics submodel in GLOBE6. Key: * represents quality of life factors affecting birth and death rates; rectangle [rectangle] represents state variable or "level" that can be measured directly; valve [valve] represents rate that can influence state variable or "level"; cloud [cloud] represents a source of input flow of people or a sink for output flow of people; broken arrow – – – – → represents information flow; solid arrow ———→ represents flow of people.

Total population (PTOT) = P1 + P2 + P3 + P4 + P5

(From R. A. Burnett & P. J. Dionne. GLOBE6: a multiregion interactive world simulation. *Simulation,* June 1973, 194. *Reprinted by permission.*)

sectors in mercury concentrations are considered less important than the global mercury levels that build up over the time span of 150 years represented in the model—from 1900 to 2050. A further assumption is that all input of mercury from natural sources is balanced by an equal output to the natural sink, the ocean floor.

State variables, or "levels," of this model are the concentrations of mercury in air, soil, stream sediments, ocean, and fish. Rates of flow represented are mercury entering the system from volcanos and weathering, precipitation on soil, evaporation from soil, precipitation on oceans, runoff from soil to streams, erosion, runoff from streams to oceans, sedimentation, uptake by fish, excretion by fish to upper layers of oceans, excretion to ocean bottoms, and loss on death of fish. In addition, rates of conversion of metal-inorganic mercury to organomercurials in streams and sediments by bacterial conversion and fish conversion are included. A number of auxiliary variables representing concentrations of mercury determine rates.

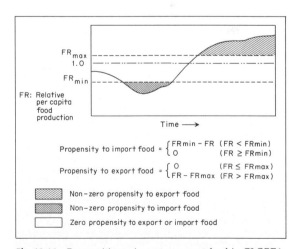

$$\text{Propensity to import food} = \begin{cases} FR_{min} - FR & (FR < FR_{min}) \\ 0 & (FR \geq FR_{min}) \end{cases}$$

$$\text{Propensity to export food} = \begin{cases} 0 & (FR \leq FR_{max}) \\ FR - FR_{max} & (FR > FR_{max}) \end{cases}$$

▨ Non-zero propensity to export food

▦ Non-zero propensity to import food

▢ Zero propensity to export or import food

Fig. 12-11   Propensities to import or export food in GLOBE6. (From R. A. Burnett & P. J. Dionne. GLOBE6: a multiregion interactive world simulation. *Simulation.* June 1973, 195. *Reprinted by permission.*)

To begin the simulation of the natural flow of mercury, initial values of mercury were assigned for each state variable. These represented estimates of the amounts of mercury present in 1900 and were expected to remain unchanged in the absence of man-made inputs until 2050. At this point the need for research into the background amounts of mercury present in the various environmental sectors of the model became apparent. Accurate data were not available. A throughput of about 500 tons per year was assumed, on the basis of calculations from available data. Rate parameters for translocation of mercury were set to be consistent with this quantity.

A run of this model over a simulated 150 years yielded a nearly steady-state distribution of mercury through the sectors modeled. Figure 12-12 represents the simulation of the natural flow of mercury through the global system from 1900 to 2050.

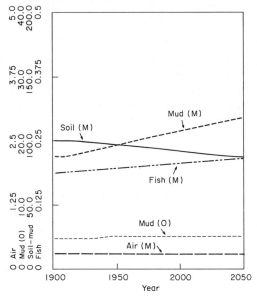

Fig. 12-12 Simulation of the natural flow of mercury through the global system from 1900 to 2050. Key: (M) represents metal-inorganic mercury; (O) represents organomercurials; Air represents concentrations of metal-inorganic mercury in air (measured in nanograms per cubic meter); Mud represents concentrations of metal-inorganic mercury or organomercurials in mud (measured in parts per billion); Soil represents concentrations of metal-inorganic mercury in soil (measured in parts per billion); Fish represents concentrations of metal-inorganic mercury in fish (measured in parts per million). [Adapted and reprinted from Alison A. Anderson & Jay Martin Anderson. System simulation to identify environmental research needs: mercury contamination. In D. L. Meadows & D. H. Meadows (Eds.). *Toward global equilibrium: collected papers.* Copyright © Wright-Allen Press, Inc., Cambridge, MA 02142, USA, 1973, page 97. *Reprinted by permission.*]

The second phase of the simulation was an examination of the consequences of man's introduction of mercury into the environment.[228] For the purposes of this simulation, a "pollutant" is defined as "a material that persists in remaining out of its natural place in the environment and depresses the normal functions of living species." To carry out this simulation, it was necessary to add to the model man-made sources of metal-inorganic mercury and organomercurials. Mercury enters the air, soil, streams and sediments in streams, rivers, and oceans from production of mercury in the course of mining and smelting, since 3 percent of the gross production is lost to the air. Of the total production in 1968, 82 percent was dissipated into the air, soil, and streams as inorganic or organic mercury compounds. With present technology, about 18 percent of mercury is recycled. Another major source of mercury is the burning of coal and oil.

To the model also were added rates of release of mercurials from these sources to various modeled sectors of the environment. Added auxiliary variables are the rates of consumption of mercury, coal, and oil, which affect the rates of release of mercurials. Values for all these rates and variables were determined by known past use of mercury, coal, and oil and by projections for future use. The simulation assumed that production will remain constant from 2000 to 2050. It may result in projected values which are too high, since mercury is expected to become more and more scarce during that period.

A simulation of the mercury flow model, with projection of mercury added by man to the natural flow, indicates that mercury in the air rises steadily over the simulated period, leveling off in the year 2000, when production is assumed to stop increasing. Metal-inorganic mercury in the soil changes little, and organomercurials in the soil, used in agriculture, rise. Mercury in streams was shown to be a local, not a global, problem. Its concentration is highest where man has dumped industrial effluents. Mercury discharge into the soil and stream sectors does not have a major impact because the concentration of mercury in those sectors is high already and because flows through them are slow. Mercury in the ocean comes primarily from the air because the route to the oceans through streams, stream sediments, and soil is very slow. The amount of mercury in fish alters as the amount in the ocean does, lagging slightly behind.

When parameters for soil and stream translocation were decreased, this model proved to be sensitive to such changes, indicating the need for more precise data for analysis of the problem of mercury pollution. On the other hand, change in the fraction of mercury recycled by man, from 18 to 50 percent, had only a slight effect on global pollution. In one simulation run, all human consumption of mercury ceased in 1980. After that, organomercury in the streams did not return to its 1950 level for 70 years, and the metal-inorganic mercury in streams and sediments remained high over the entire 150-year span.

A simulation with mercury from fuel consumption added to the natural flow and the production of mercury by man indicated that for the air and ocean sectors of the model, this source was even more important than mercury consumption itself. Results showed that by the end of the twentieth century, the average amount of mercury in fish could rise well above present United States Food and Drug Administration standards for safety. Since the model is sensitive to parameter changes, if coal and oil contain more mercury than the amount assumed in the simulation, which was conservatively estimated, this will occur even sooner. The conclusion drawn from the simulation is that control of mercury pollution, to be effective, must anticipate transmissions of mercury up to 60 years in the future.

Figure 12-13 shows the flow diagram for the full mercury model.

Models of the earth-atmosphere system. Today scientists are asking whether man can change such a major aspect of his world as its climate, intentionally or inadvertently. There is fear that irreparable damage may be done by pollution or hope that meteorological engineering could improve local climatic conditions in some parts of the world. These issues are of major concern for living systems up to the supranational level, for they must keep their ambient temperature (as well as other climatic features) within a steady-state range so that they can maintain an optimal mean temperature at which process is most efficient, as Hypothesis 3.2-1 (see page 93) says living systems do.

Models of the earth-atmosphere system have explored the effects of removing the arctic ice sheet, which would, for example, warm the climate of the Soviet Union, lowering the reflectivity (or *albedo*) of the earth's surface, decreasing the amount of sunlight that reaches the earth, and increasing the amount of heat generated by energy conversions in human societies.

One such *global-climatic* model relates all parts of the earth to all others in such a way that modification of climate of a small section of the world can affect the whole globe and result in a new steady state.[229] It incorporates a set of equations in which the average annual sea-level temperature in each 10-degree latitude belt is the dependent variable. The independent variables are the amount of incoming solar energy, the transparency of the atmosphere to terrestrial radiation, the planetary albedo, the ability of the atmosphere to carry heat and water vapor from source to sink, and the heat storage potential of the oceans and land. The model is based upon an equation for the energy balance of the earth-atmosphere system that expresses the radiation balance of a given latitude belt as equal to the latent heat of condensation times the net fluxes from the belt of water vapor by atmospheric currents, sensible heat by atmospheric currents, and sensible heat by ocean currents. The temperature in each latitude belt is related to that in each of the others by an iterative process.

The relationships and values of variables in the model are based upon a considerable body of empirical research in atmospheric physics. Not unexpectedly, the relationships are complex, and the available data are not yet sufficient to provide all the detail that would be desirable. Using these data, the model successfully computed relationships that described present reality well. Experiments on the model were offered with reservations, however, because of (i) the need for extension and improvement of the model, (ii) the possible extremely long lags of the order of 1,000 years resulting from the heat storage capacity of the oceans that might occur in the formation of a new global steady state, and (iii) the possible alterations of calculations by neglected higher-order or nonlinear effects.

Because of the advantages that might accrue to the Soviet Union if the part of their land within the Arctic Circle were to become available for agriculture, some of their scientists have been interested in the effects to be anticipated if the polar ice sheet were either melted or covered with a black powder. The planetary albedo varies predominately with changes in the surface snow cover, and so either of these changes would be expected to make a significant difference in the temperatures of those regions. Changing the parameter that represents the planetary albedo at high latitudes was the only modification in the model necessary for experiments on the effects of these changes. Results indicated that if the North Polar ice were removed, the temperature of the area north of 70 degrees north would be changed by 7°C at most. The change in the tropics would be about 1°C, and that near the South Pole would be 1 to 3°C. If the same thing were done in the antarctic, which has a higher albedo, the temperature there would increase 12 to 15°C, and the temperature in the arctic would rise about 4°C. If both were treated, the temperature in the arctic would rise 7 to 10°C, and that in the antarctic would rise 13 to 15°C. The tropics would never change more than 2°C. This shows that albedo manipulations at either pole would

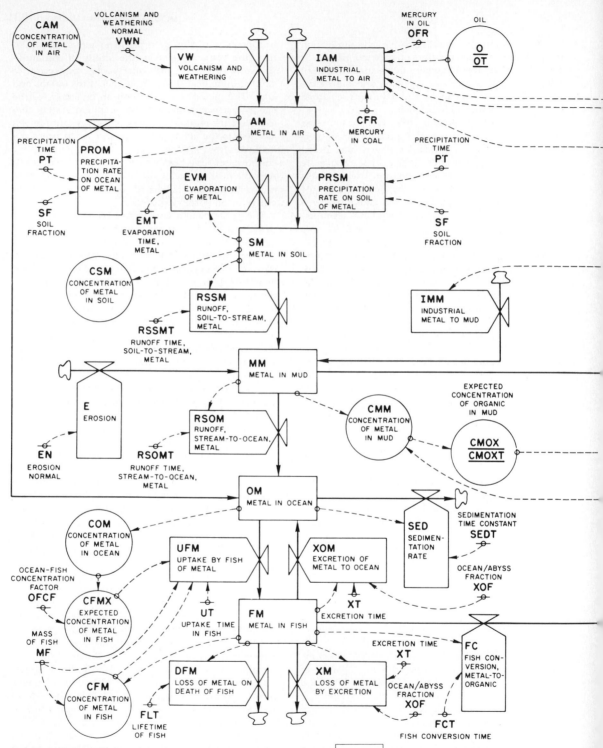

Fig. 12-13 DYNAMO flow diagram for mercury model. Key: Rectangle ☐ represents state variable or "level" that can be measured directly; valve ⧓ represents rate that can influence state variable or "level"; circle ◯ represents concentration of metal-inorganic mercury or organomercurials; cloud ☁ represents a source of input flow of metal-inorganic mercury or organomercurials or a sink for output flow of metal-inorganic mercury or organomercurials; solid

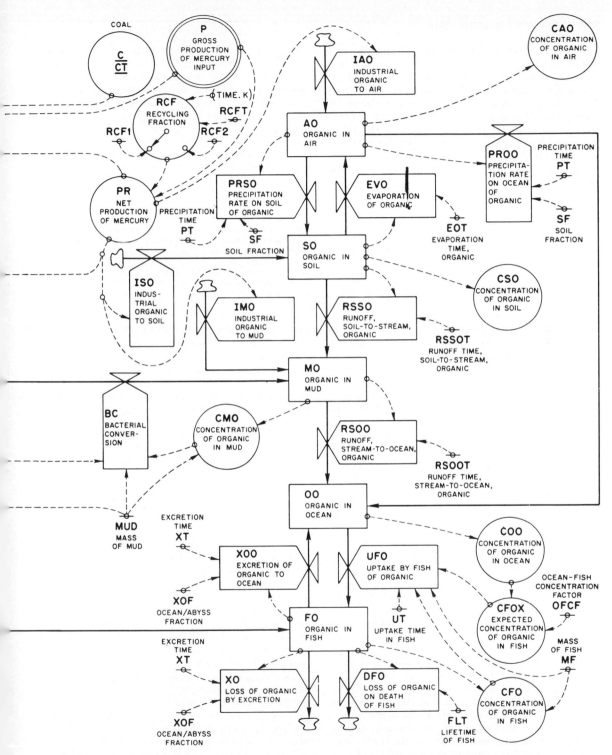

arrow ——————▶ represents flow of metal-inorganic mercury or organomercurials; broken arrow ————▶ represents causal relationship. [Source: Adapted and reprinted from Alison A. Anderson & Jay Martin Anderson. System simulation to identify environmental research needs: mercury contamination. In D. L. Meadows & D. H. Meadows (Eds.), *Toward global equilibrium: collected papers.* Copyright © Wright-Allen Press, Inc., Cambridge, MA 02142, USA, 1973, pages 108–109. *Reprinted with permission.*]

have worldwide effects. The effects are less, however, than those calculated by earlier studies.

The same model was used to study the effect of changing the intensity of solar radiation on earth. This could occur as a result of increased dust in the upper atmosphere. One theory of the recurrent ice ages of the last million years is that changes in the solar constant, brought about by dust of cosmic or volcanic origin, resulted in warming and cooling of the earth. Experiments were run with the albedos held constant and, more realistically, with the albedos allowed to vary with temperature. With a 10 percent increase in the solar constant and the albedos held constant, this simulation indicated that the global mean temperature should rise about 12°C. If they are allowed to vary, only a 2 percent decrease in the solar constant produced another ice age with ice caps extending to 50 degrees latitude and mountain glaciers and heavy winter snow extending to 30 degrees latitude. Any further reduction resulted in an ice-covered earth with an equilibrium temperature of −100°C.

Another study suggested that explosive development of the ice caps might take place as soon as the ice coverage extended below 50 degrees of latitude. On the other hand, an increase in the solar constant of about 3 percent would probably be sufficient to melt the ice sheets, and an increase of more than 10 percent would completely eliminate snowfall on earth. A relatively small change in the ability of the atmosphere and oceans to transfer heat toward the poles could, as this simulation shows, offset these effects. This last finding calls attention to the risk of changing one variable without accounting for possible changes in the others.

If the variable that represents the ability of the atmosphere to transmit infrared radiation is decreased by 3 percent, the effect is much the same as that of similar changes in the solar constant. The world would again be on the brink of an ice age. Since this variable is dependent upon the amount of carbon dioxide in the atmosphere, which is increasing, the real-world effect should be a rise rather than a decline in the global mean temperature.

Man's use of stored energy is increasing exponentially, and if this continues, the model indicates that in less than 200 years, the climate of the earth could be greatly affected. Cities are the main sources of such heat. By assuming (*i*) that the distribution of cities will not change significantly during the next 200 years and (*ii*) that the heat is spread among the various latitude belts, the simulation results show that a temperature rise of about 15°C on the average, ranging from 11°C near the equator to 27°C at the North Pole, would be enough to eliminate all permanent ice fields,

leaving only a few mountain glaciers on Antarctica and perhaps Greenland. These results do not take account of a possible decrease in the intensity of solar radiation brought about by air pollution, but the predicted effects of projected amounts of pollution make a difference of only a few degrees. The author concludes:

Thus, man's activity, if it continues unabated should eventually lead to the elimination of the ice caps and to a climate much warmer than today. Annual mean temperatures of 26 C, now characteristic of the tropics, would exist as far poleward as 40 degrees. Considering the thermal inertia of the world's oceans, it is impossible to state how long it will take for this warming to occur—possibly as little as 100 years or as long as 1,000 years. During this time it is not inconceivable that the solar constant will change. A decrease of slightly more than 7 percent in its value would yield a global mean temperature equal to that existing today. Since such a large drop in the solar constant over any extended period is on the fringe of being highly unlikely. . . . man may inadvertently generate his own climate.[230]

Econometric models.   I have discussed some national econometric models, which now exist in a significant number of countries, in Chap. 11 (see pages 881 to 885). Similar models have been conceived and are under development at the supranational level as well. Their creation is facilitated by increasing interrelations among nations in trade; in economics and economic record keeping; in production, storage, and transmission of matter-energy; and in communication. National econometric models, according to Zvetanov, should be integrated internationally.[231] This can be done by defining and quantifying factors which determine imports (inputs) to, and exports (outputs) from, all countries. National decisions (possibly based on national models) can have combined effects that can decide the character of worldwide, supranational processes. To build a worldwide model, the first step might be to group countries in geographic regions according to combinations of such criteria as similar economies, similar resources, comparable industrial development, similar trade, comparable climate, and compatible economic records. Such a model should deal with supply and demand in various countries and with worldwide distribution of various types of matter, energy, and information, including monetary information. Efforts to work toward this ambitious goal are now under way.

Tin supranational econometric model.   One econometric world model dealing with a particular sort of matter, tin, is being developed.[232] It is intended to study policies for stabilization of the price of tin in the face of cyclical changes in demand, linking major variables of input (ore from the tin mines), output (consumption of tin), and price with macroeconomic variables related to business cycles. Consumption of tin is confined mainly to industrially developed countries. The tin originally comes from less developed countries. It is always used in alloy form, usually as tinplate, a sheet of steel with a thin coating of tin. The amount of tin in this tinplate has been declining, but the primary importance of tinplate is not threatened. Other alloys of tin include solder, bronze, and brass, all of which have a variety of uses. For the purposes of the model, there are two classes of tin—that used for tinplate and that not used for tinplate.

The United States is the largest single consumer of tin. The model represents the United States separately, puts Canada and the countries of the Organization for European Economic Cooperation (OEEC) together, and lumps together tin consumption by the rest of the world.

The ownership of tin mines comes close to being a cartel except that mines in Bolivia and Indonesia have been nationalized. Few smelters exist, and ownership and holding interests are knit together by interlocking directorates. Not suprisingly, price stabilization has been heavily biased toward producers. Control is exercised through international agreements on prices, output restrictions, and maintenance of buffer stocks. The model includes price stabilizing by producers to prevent low prices—by restricting output and by storing buffer stocks. It also allows for sales from stocks of consumer countries, especially the stockpile of the United States, in order to assure that prices do not rise above the ceiling.

The 18 simultaneous equations of the model include 18 *endogenous variables,* or unknowns whose values can be determined by solving the system of equations for the time period under consideration. Of these, 15 pertain to consumption, 1 to output, 1 to stocks, and 1 to prices. The 17 externally determined variables, or *exogenous variables,* include some *lagged endogenous variables* of output and stocks, whose values were determined by solving the equations for a previous time period. Also included are exogenous variables representing the economic effects of the Korean war and of the steel strike in the United States, output of food, consumer expenditures for food, defense purchases, and other economically relevant factors.

Simulation runs on the model tested the effectiveness of alternative stabilization policies. The simulation was run over a 25-year period with three alternative assumptions: (*i*) the system of equations described above with no modifying assumptions; (*ii*) the system with no downward trend in the use of tinplate and tin other than tinplate in the United States (consistent with recent history) but with downward trends in OEEC and Canada; and (*iii*) the system

with a downward trend in the United States, OEEC, and Canada.

The simulation employing assumption (*i*), which did not include the downward trends in OEEC and Canada, resulted in an upward trend in demand in those places and the rest of the world which led to complete exhaustion of tin in the eighth year. When the tin stockpile of the United States was added, tin lasted until the nineteenth year. Prices moved continuously upward. This simulation was not realistic because in the past, demand had been decreased by reducing the tin content in tinplate, but this could not continue because the lowest feasible tin content had been reached.

Other simulation runs were made using assumption (*ii*). It was presumed that in the United States, there would be no further substitution of other materials for tin beyond the 1961 values but that there would be such substitution in Canada and OEEC until the end of the seventh year.

Simulation runs using assumption (*iii*) resulted in overly pessimistic price solutions and were not continued. When the stock of tin was kept at the 1961 level of 73,077,000 metric tons, price stability and high average gross revenue were achieved at high cost. Price fluctuations resulted only from fluctuations in demand. All extra output was bought at the flow price of £657 a metric ton and was placed in a buffer stock. It was sold at the going price if output fell short of demand.

Restriction of output combined with purchase and sale of buffer stock constituted a more successful strategy. From the model it was concluded that noninterference with the price of tin and the output of tin gave the worst results, while a combination of crude-output control and a large-sized buffer stock can assure virtual stability of prices and high revenue.

Models of international conflict and conflict resolution. Throughout history, wars, although lethal and destructive, have constituted one chief form of international decision making and have been a primary sort of adjustment process among nations. Concern with avoidance of war has stimulated a body of research on war, conflict resolution, and related subjects which includes several mathematical and computer models. Richardson was the pioneer in this field. He devoted 30 years to developing mathematical and statistical models of arms races and "deadly quarrels." The latter included not only wars but also murders, riots, civil disturbances, and revolutions, all of which are aggressions that result in one or more deaths.[233] His models were deterministic, like classical models in the physical sciences. They were based upon voluminous data. While they do not constitute an adequate theory of war, they tend to disprove theories which ascribe religious or economic causation to wars or which claim that some nations are especially warlike.[234] Richardson's models and others in the same tradition apply scientific method to complex social events. Subsequent works use different sorts of mathematics or include different variables. One study of war alliances that conceptualizes each of them as the outcome of a stochastic process, for example, concludes that Richardson was correct in conjecturing that there is a difference between peaceful groups and those which can be described as an "aggregation for aggression."[235] The difference, these authors say, lies in the rules for formation and dissolution of the groups. No member leaves an aggressive group until the whole group is dissolved. Exit from peaceful groups is easier.

Model of United States wars. According to Voevodsky, war is an "orderly, mathematically lawful, behavioral event."[236] He compares statistics from the four major wars in which the United States has engaged in the past 100 years—the Civil War, World War I, World War II, and the Korean War—with those available for the Vietnam War as of June 1969. All but the Civil War involved international or supranational coalitions. Quantitative data on battle strength, battle casualties, and battle deaths of army personnel are analyzed to identify the significant relationships among them. These are presented in four equations.

The first equation relates battle deaths and battle casualties. This is described mathematically by a power function:

$$D = \gamma C^\delta$$

where D is battle deaths at a given time, C is battle casualties at the same time, and γ and δ are constants which define a family of curves relating battle deaths and battle casualties for each war. In the model, γ and δ also define the net effectiveness of the enemy's weapons systems over the effectiveness of the measures that are taken to protect troops. At the upper boundary of this equation battle casualties equal battle deaths. The Vietnam War divides into two periods in which the effectiveness of enemy weapons systems differs considerably. In the year 1965, weapons available to the North Vietnamese suddenly improved.

The second equation, relating battle strength and battle casualties, is a similar power function:

$$S = \alpha C^\beta$$

where S is the total military strength at a given time, C is battle casualties at the same time, and α and β are constants which, combined, define the battle intensity. Figure 12-14 shows this relationship. The upper boundary is the limit on the degree of mobilization that a nation's citizens will accept as they prepare for, and participate in, a major war. The lower boundary is the limit in strength buildup and casualties that a nation will sustain before it accepts defeat, changes its leadership, or acquires new allies. In 1965, as Fig. 12-14 shows, the United States abruptly escalated its military activities.

The third equation relates the battle strength, battle casualties, and battle deaths of each side to those of the other. Again, the relationship is a power function. It indicates that if one side changes its war variables, a similar change occurs also on the other side.

The fourth equation relates army battle strength and time. From it the relationship of the other variables to time can also be determined. Calculations were made using this equation concerning the Vietnam War, which was in progress at the time. They indicated that 63 percent of the troops that were to be committed to the battle zone would have been committed in the first 1.56 years. In the next 1.56 years, 86 percent of the troops would have been committed, and in the next 1.56 years, 95 percent of the ultimate forces would have been committed. The enemy's strength in the battle zone would have increased by the same percentages. The other wars in the study behaved similarly; thus if battle strength is expressed in terms of the percentage of forces to be engaged and is plotted against the time constant for that war, all wars studied are described by a single mathematical relationship. Each war forms a pattern over time, and history repeats this pattern in other wars. Figure 12-15 compares the Vietnam War with the other wars analyzed and indicates that by June 30, 1965, 90 percent of the troops to be used by both sides had been committed. The rate of change, according to this theory, should be minimal after that. At the time this model was published, the Vietnam War had reached that point. The theory predicts that this is the point at which either a settlement is possible or another major escalation takes place.

Disarmament-inspection simulation. A continuing problem of disarmament negotiations between the United States and the Soviet Union has been inspecting for weapons production. Both nations accepted the idea that some form of inspection was necessary to provide assurance that weapons were not being produced contrary to an international agreement. A computer simulation of the process of inspection compares the relative effectiveness of three different inspection methods in discovering any evasions of the rules

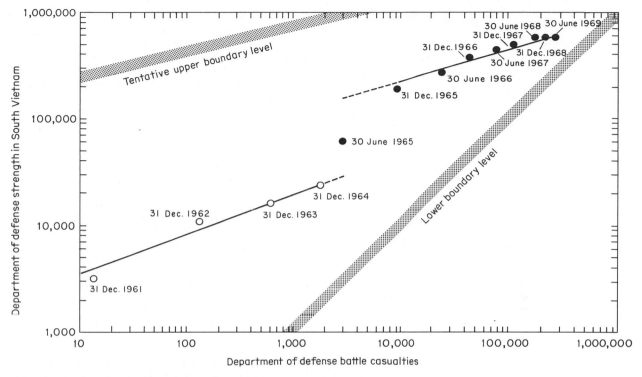

Fig. 12-14 United States battle strength in South Vietnam plotted against battle casualties. Key: ○———○ Vietnam War I, 1961–1964; ●———● Vietnam War II, 1965–1969. Lower boundary level represents the points where battle casualties equal battle strengths, to the right of which a nation apparently cannot pass and still sustain its war effort; upper boundary level represents limit of mobilization that a nation's citizens will accept. [From J. Voevodsky. Modeling the dynamics of warfare. In D. E. Knight, H. W. Curtis, & L. J. Fogel (Eds.). *Cybernetics, simulation, and conflict resolution*. New York: Spartan Books, 1971, 155.]

under varying production methods and evasion schemes.[237]

The three sets of variables in the simulation represent alternative production procedures, possible evasion schemes, and various inspection methods. Production-procedure variables are (*i*) the number of production areas that are operating in each of four production stages—raw-material production, parts production, subassembly, and final assembly—with major focus on final assembly, and (*ii*) the number of production points of the 20 in each of the production areas that are operating.

Evasion-scheme variables are (*i*) the number and identities of production areas evading in each stage, (*ii*) the number and identities of evading production points in each area, and (*iii*) the starting and finishing days of evasion in each production stage.

Inspection-method variables are (*i*) the average probability of correct detection assumed for each run in every stage, (*ii*) the average probability of false detection assumed for each run in every stage, and (*iii*) the frequency and time pattern of on-site inspections for each production area. The above probabilities were determined from established performance ranges for operations under normal conditions and were modified by random numbers to reflect short-run fluctuations in the inspection process. Values for the other variables were calculated or assigned in various ways. Cost variables were also included.

At the beginning of each run, information was put into the computer as to which production procedure is in use, where and when evasions are actually occurring in that production system, and which inspection techniques to employ. Inputs were modified for each of the 400 iterations. Thus a large number of combinations of conditions were studied. During the runs, a

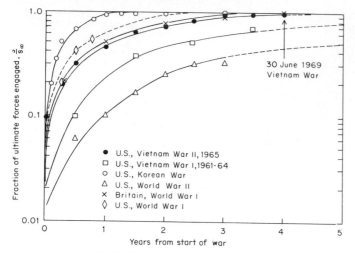

Fig. 12-15 Battle strength in the major United States wars, expressed as the fraction of ultimate United States or British forces engaged, plotted against years from the start of the war. [From J. Voevodsky. Modeling the dynamics of warfare. In D. E. Knight, H. W. Curtis, & L. J. Fogel (Eds.). *Cybernetics, simulation, and conflict resolution.* New York: Spartan Books, 1971, 163.]

random number was generated by the computer for each evading production point, and that was compared with the modification of the probability of correct detection that applied to the particular inspection method used. If the probability of correct detection was greater than, or equal to, the random number, the evasion was considered to be correctly detected. For each nonevading production point another random number was generated and compared with the modified probability of false detection applicable to the inspection method used. If the random number exceeded the probability, the run was said to have observed correctly that no evasion was occurring, but if it was equal to, or less than, the probability, a false detection was recorded. The computer reported, as an inspector would, which areas and points in each of the first three stages of production were believed to be engaging in illegal production or assembly and the point of progress between start and finish at which evasion was alleged to have occurred. This information was then checked against the internal information concerning which areas and points had been engaged in illegal activity. It printed out the distribution of correct detections and false detections. It was then possible to appraise the performance of each detection method. The cost-effectiveness of an inspection

method was determined from the number of evasions that were correctly detected, the number of false detections that were reported, and cost factors.

TEMPER (T*echnological,* **E***conomic,* **M***ilitary, and* **P***oliti-* **c***al* **E***valuation* **R***outine*)**. This is a computer simulation of global "cold war" conflict. It represents the confrontation of the superpowers—the Soviet Union and the United States—and their allies as a bipolar system.[238] It was developed for the United States Department of Defense. While it was not planned to be used as a predictive device, it was intended to represent the real world closely enough to be suitable for analysis of probable international interactions. It was thought that it might in the future be improved to the point where it could be used for prediction. A man-computer version of TEMPER has also been developed for use in training military officers.

The world described by the computer version of TEMPER consists of 39 nation groups, divided into three blocs—East, West, and neutral. The neutral group is not conceived to have power and does not negotiate in the interactions depicted by the program. The superpowers compete for neutral support. The world is divided into 20 conflict regions, 13 on land and 7 on the seas. An important assumption of the model is that coalitions of nations act with a common purpose, without internal dissension or subversion. Nations of a given kind (East, West, or neutral) are assumed to act similarly, although differences in emphasis are also assumed. No internal processes of the coalitions are included in the model, and no international or supranational organizations or multinational businesses are included.

TEMPER uses data for 117 nations, aggregated to suit the classifications of the model. A computer program intended to represent global interactions realistically must be extensive, requiring large computer power. TEMPER consists of 4 submodels, each of which has from 4 to 12 subroutines. Each subroutine includes the effects of several variables.

The fundamental assumptions of TEMPER are that the nations of the world constitute a global system. Each nation is a decision-making unit that tries to minimize the discrepancy between its state at a given time and its ideal state by allocating political, military, and economic resources within acceptable costs.

A summary of TEMPER variables (the Mark II version) gives some insights into the simulation's complexity, theoretical assumptions, and methods of calculation.[239] Figure 12-16 shows the sequencing of the subroutines and indicates the relationships in time between them. The submodels and variables of TEMPER are as follows:

The TEMPER Program

PSYCHOLOGICAL SUBMODEL

Proposition: Information transmitted through communications channels is affected by such variables as bias, ambiguity, distortion, and the time intervals at which they are received. (See Hypothesis 3.3.3.2-2, page 96, which states that there is always a constant systematic distortion between input and output of information in a channel.)

Subroutines	Description
THREAT (threat)	Threat perceived as coming from another nation is assumed to arouse hostility and builds upon existing bias. It is simulated by aggregating five kinds of military and political threats. Military threats receive the greatest weights.
PERCEP (perception)	The tactical hostility between nations is computed from the desire for land, military capacity, and tactical threat. It is used to determine the perceived values for counterforce utility, desired land, level of military operations, and verbal (deterrent) threat. It is assumed that as threat increases, all nations will tend, at differing rates, toward strong internal controls. (See Hypothesis 5.2-13, page 107, which states that under threat or stress, a system that survives, in the common good of total system survival, temporarily subordinates conflicts among subsystems or components until the threat or stress is relieved, when internal conflicts recur.)
XPERCE (experience)	This introduces distortions assumed to arise in transmission of information through diplomatic intelligence and communications channels from one nation to another.
KULTUR (culture)	National culture is defined in terms of six cultural-ideological factors called *motives:* the propensity to use force to settle disputes, vigor in pursuing international goals (external dynamism), habits in GNP reinvestment, defense-spending habits, tax rates and their limits, and desired military power ratios.

ECONOMIC SUBMODEL

PDCNTL (production control)	This simulates the economy of each of the coalitions of nations and computes inventories and production for each of six major sectors that make up the total economy.
ALOKT (demand allocation)	This determines governmental and private demand for each of six economic sectors. It assumes that all economies have the same growth properties and that distribution will vary with taxes and pay.
CONTRA (control trade)	Nations will first use opportunities to export to regain declining friendship and then will import to satisfy internal demand.
TRADER (trading)	As in CONTRA, trade is used as an instrument of foreign policy.
WINECO (win over economically)	This represents the adjustments in TRADER needed to win the support of the other nations.
FORMAP (force maintenance and procurement)	This assumes that military-force maintenance and procurement are limited by budgetary considerations.

WAR SUBMODEL

Proposition: Land exchange (advance–retreat) is a function of the difference in military-force levels.

LIWAR (limited war control)
FIGHT (fight the land battle)
STAGER (staging)
NAVFYT (naval fight)
SHIFT (shift in military forces)
REMOVE (force removal)
NAVLOG (naval logistics)

DECISION-MAKER SUBMODEL

DMFILE (decision-maker file)	Friendship between states does not remain constant, but increases or decreases as a function of trade (WINECO) or military aid (WINOVR).
STRDM (strategic decision maker)	This assumes that in a nuclear exchange, a first strike by either the Soviet Union or the United States will be a counterforce blow aimed against the weapons of the other side. If a country strikes first, it wants to limit civilian destruction. Population losses will be from fallout rather than direct strikes.

PROREC (problem recognition)	This assumes that governments make rational choices in the process of recognizing and dealing with internal and external problems.
WEBARG (bargaining control) BARGY (bargaining) ACBARG (bargain acceptance)	Nations calculate their problems in dollar utility units and attempt to reduce them through negotiations on a *quid pro quo* basis. The offer and request are weighed in terms of the bargainers' values and accepted or rejected.
BUDGET (budget makeup)	
CDALC (command allocation)	The war terminates when both sides find that losses exceed both gains and enthusiasm for war.
WINIT (war initiation)	States decide whether to escalate, deescalate, or maintain the status quo on the basis of six quantifiable variables: potential gain or loss of territory by escalating, probability of winning a conventional war, potential loss from a nuclear initiation in retaliation, probability that a conventional war will occur, threshold of minimum calculated utility which must be obtained to escalate military operations, and a random number between 0 and 1. Quantities are established for these probabilities and values, and they are summed to obtain a function that represents utility of gain.
LIANCE (alliance control) XLIANC (alliance-control extension) WINOVR (win over through military aid)	Friendship between nations depends on their willingness to give military or economic aid. If the recipient nation offers military aid to the donor nation, if it satisfies the latter's consumer demands, or if it buys its surplus inventories, the value will increase. If none of these occurs, the value will gradually decrease.

The assumptions embodied in TEMPER obviously vary in plausibility. The fundamental assumptions of the system accord well with general living systems theory. The view of nations and systems of nations as decision-making units that attempt to find acceptable steady states by checking their state at a given time with a comparison signal—the ideal state to which they aspire—is also compatible with my theory.

No objective evaluation of the TEMPER simulation in terms of empirical comparisons with action in the real world is possible, according to Smoker, because its performance characteristics are essentially unknown, since no empirical validity studies have been undertaken on the model.[240] From the output that is available, Smoker finds that some impression can be gained of its representation of world trade. This is defined in an unorthodox fashion, and, in fact, if the trade tables of the simulation are inspected, most trade relations between nations are zero. The simulation permits no trade between coalitions of nations, an unrealistic restriction. Where trade is modeled, it does not represent the real world with even minimal accuracy.

In a critique of the international relations theory expressed and implied in TEMPER, Clemens gives it full credit for providing a coherent system which identifies and connects processes that simulate the many dimensions of world politics—which political science in general has not done.[241] He believes other advantages of it are the explicit sequence of subroutines and the provision for simulation of the system operating over time, as well as the fact that the simulated world is modified week by week on the basis of the responses of the coalitions of nations.

(*d*) *Living system–computer interactions.* Use of a computer program in conjunction with the activity of human participants in game-type simulations not only can add to the speed and convenience with which necessary calculations are made but also may permit more rigorous specification of a greater number of variables and relationships than can be achieved with noncomputerized forms of the same games. The mix of man and computer varies in games of this sort. An almost wholly computerized exercise is Benson's Simple Diplomatic Game, in which human participants instruct the program to perform operations selected from a predetermined set of options, but do not interact in unprogrammed activity.[242] By contrast, the computer may be an incidental convenience.

Inter-Nation Simulation (INS). Although a relatively simple all-human interaction form of INS exists (see page 974), the form in which human participants freely interact with a computer program is of greater interest. INS has been developed and refined over a period of years by Guetzkow and many associates for use in teaching international relations courses and in developing theory, testing hypotheses, and comparing alternative theoretical models in political science. It has also undergone modification and expansion by his group and others to adapt it for specific experimental uses.

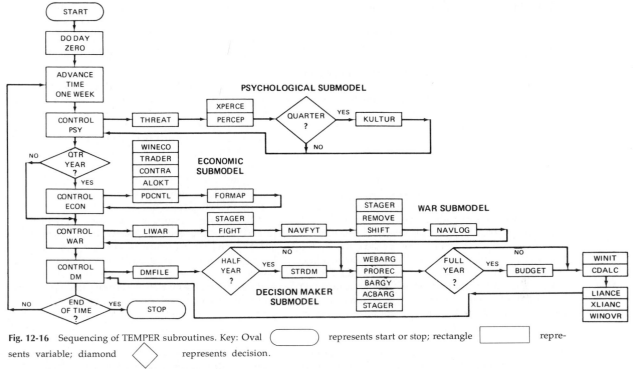

Fig. 12-16 Sequencing of TEMPER subroutines. Key: Oval ( ) represents start or stop; rectangle [ ] represents variable; diamond ◇ represents decision.

[From Paul Smoker. International relations simulations. In H. Guetzkow, P. Kotler, & R. L. Schultz (Eds.). *Simulation in social and administrative science*. Englewood Cliffs, N.J.: Prentice-Hall, 1972, 305. Adapted from S. T. De La Mater, J. V. Dunham, R. W. Granston, H. H. Schulke, C. R. Smith, & F. R. Westfall. *ICAF analysis of TEMPER MARK II*. Washington: Industrial College for the Armed Forces, 1966, 3-1. *Reprinted by permission of Prentice-Hall, Inc.*]

In this simulation, "nations," each made up of two or more participants, interact with one another.[243] The nations are identified by names (such as Omne and Utro) that suggest no actual society or by letters, in order to minimize the possibility of participants' associating them with specific societies. Each nation has a central decision maker, the chief of state or executive who is responsible for final policy decisions concerning both internal and external affairs. Also, there are one or more other decision makers, who are responsible for foreign affairs, defense, or economic affairs. In some experiments an aspiring decision maker is added. This participant is not a member of the government, but seeks to gain office and may replace the central decision maker under specified conditions. He submits policy views and writes papers advocating alternatives to the government's policies. The multi-echelon hierarchical structures of the simulated national deciders are more like real societies than the face-to-face groups usually used in simulations at the levels of the society and the supranational system. Indirect, mediated relationships among societal components with programmed time lags are also realistic.

Prior to the beginning of the game, goals for each nation are determined in different experimental situations either by the researchers or by the participants themselves. They are reformulated as the game proceeds. Participants ordinarily receive background information about the internal affairs of the nation they are to simulate.[244] This may consist of a fabricated history of past decisions and their outcomes. No history of past international relationships is included.

During the simulation, decision makers arrange for conferences, make treaties, form alliances, engage in trade, give or receive foreign aid, wage war, and carry out other international interactions. At the same time, they attempt to conduct the internal affairs of their nations in a way designed to guarantee that they will be retained in office. A central decision maker's continuance in office depends upon validators, that is, upon the voters, elites, or other components of their societies capable of keeping a decision maker in office. Validators are not human participants. Rather, satisfaction of validators is computed from the record of decisions made by participants in the course of play. Both orderly and revolutionary transfers of power are possible. The latter occur when validator satisfaction drops below a specified threshold.

During the simulation each nation periodically receives from the experimenters resources which can be allocated to internal or external uses. Internal allocations can be for immediate satisfaction of demands arising within the system or for building up capabilities. Resources can be committed externally, as aid to other nations or to build strategic strength. Nations increase or decrease the amounts of their resources over time by the allocations they make.

Deciders receive communications during the simulation, not only in conferences or through diplomatic channels, but also in a "world newspaper" which carries news about changes in officeholders, treaties and alliances, and foreign-aid arrangements. Also, press releases may be sent to the newspaper.

The basic INS model is capable of many sorts of variation. Procedural rules may be adapted to the needs of a particular research. The durations of simulation runs can be varied from 10 to 40 hours (h) or longer. The number of nations has ranged in different experiments from five to nine. Subjects differ in number, educational background, cultural background, and professional experience.

Nations are varied by providing them with different initial histories, by changing parameter values of programmed variables to alter the decision latitude of deciders (which simulates differences among types of governments and alters the impact of validator satisfaction), by changing "generation rates" that reflect differences in basic resources and productivity (which can simulate the differences between developed and less developed nations), by altering validator satisfaction, and by changing force capability, the amount of coercion the nation can exert in internal and external affairs. Force capability can be conventional only or can include nuclear capability as well. Basic assumptions concerning relationships among variables can also be altered, resulting in variation of the unprogrammed activity of human deciders and hence of the interaction of nations in the world of the simulation.

The following quotation describes a typical situation of the simulation:

The national profiles at the beginning of the run may be summarized as follows: Nation G was underdeveloped and had a past history of internal revolution. At the time of the new regime's accession to power, however, its decision latitude was quite high. Nations K and M, although also underdeveloped, had managed to preserve political stability in the recent past in the face of their economic problems—this in spite of fairly moderate decision latitude in M. Nations P and S, although neither rich nor fully developed, were the wealthiest and strongest nations in the world. They each enjoyed a favorable productivity rate for force capability. The new government about to take over in P was the first such change in some time, whereas S had a history of more frequent, but normal, transitions in its officeholders. Unless changed, the political structure in both P and S was such that the office tenure of the decision-makers would be quite dependent upon their ability to satisfy their validators.[245]

The simulation is divided into time periods. At the beginning of a time period, each decision maker receives decision forms which give the results for his nation of the previous period's decisions or, in the case of the first period, data provided by the experimenters. Decisions for the current period are entered on this form. These are collected by the experimenters during the simulation period and are used in calculating such things as validator satisfaction and outcomes of wars.

INS ordinarily simulates international interactions rather than supranational systems, but in some runs supranational structure has developed spontaneously. Examples are an international bank controlled by a board made up of representatives of participating nations and an international grant-in-aid corporation. Some modifications of the simulation, such as one intended to test hypotheses about nuclear proliferation, have included international organizations in the initial design.

Data from INS consist of the decision forms, messages, written plans, treaties, recorded conferences, press releases, and other materials generated by the operation of the simulation. In some simulation runs, pencil-and-paper tests have been given at intervals to discover the attitudes and perceptions of decision makers concerning other nations. These, too, became data for the simulation.[246]

The foregoing is the essential form of INS. If a noncomputerized version is used, researchers perform calculations to determine outcomes of decisions made by human participants. The living system–computer version provides a program to do this. Equations of the program state relationships among approximately 30 basic variables of the system, selected because experts in the field agree upon their importance as determiners of foreign policy.[247] Almost all are concerned with internal processes of nations.

Each of the variables of INS represents an aggregate of real-world phenomena. Each is specified by an equation that relates it to other variables. *Validator satisfaction* (VS_m), for example, is made up of two parts which together relate economic and military factors to the operation of political pressures.[248] The equation is given as:

$$VS_m = eVS_{cs} + gVS_{ns}$$

The subscripts *cs* and *ns* refer to validator satisfaction with consumption standards and with national security. The coefficients e and g are parameters that are used to alter the relative importance of the two in determining mean satisfaction.

The VS_{cs} component of that equation depends upon the actual consumption standard of the nation at a particular time, which is determined by the human decision maker's commitment of his country's basic resources to consumption. He can allocate any amount up to the entire national income for this purpose. He may not, however, fall below a given minimum since if he did, the nation could not function. The equation that expresses the composition of VS_{cs} is:

$$VS_{cs} = 1 + r \left(\frac{CS}{CS_{min}} - 1 \right) - v \left(\frac{CS_{max}}{CS_{min}} - 1 \right)$$

This embodies the assumption of a "saturation effect" such that the increase in VS_{cs} for a given increment of expenditure decreases as the minimum increases in the second term of the equation. Further, citizens of wealthier nations are expected to be harder to please because they expect larger expenditures for consumption. Parameters r and v weight the terms. Table 12-9 lists the main programmed variables of INS and their typical ranges, together with some comments on each.

The behavior of decision makers in the simulation is motivated by the need to continue in office. The probability of officeholding (pOH) is therefore a central variable of the system. This depends upon the mean validator satisfaction (VS_m) and upon the variable of decision latitude (DL). High DL characterizes an authoritarian government in which the decision makers are powerful and the validators are correspondingly less so. A lower DL describes a government in which many powerful individuals and groups reduce the individual power of the central decider. The first equation involving DL is:[249]

$$pOH = a(b - DL)VS_m + c(DL - d)$$

In it, a, c, and d represent parameters.

As the simulation proceeds, when the probability of a regime's remaining in office falls below a specified value, stochastic processes determine whether a change in regime will take place. If it does, the person acting as central decision maker must leave the simulation, to be replaced by another person. At a lower value a revolution may take place. Subprograms determine whether revolution is attempted and whether, if attempted, it succeeds.

The deciders of each simulated nation receive a number of basic capability units at the beginning of the simulation.[250] These may be used to purchase force-capability units, usually with a one-period delay. They may also be used to purchase consumption-standard units in a quantity determined by the generation rate for such units and within the minimum and maximum consumption standards specified for the nation.

Deciders may, by their allocations, improve both the basic capability and the force capability of their nations. They have several other policy alternatives. If, for example, revolution appears probable, a part of the nation's force capability may be committed to reducing the probability of its success by increasing internal control. Deciders may, at a cost, force changes in their decision latitude. They may selectively increase resource commitments to consumption or to national-security components of VS_m. Finally, they may make alliances with other nations and so increase national security or undertake trading relationships in the hope of increasing basic capabilities and consumption standards. Equations of the program state the detailed relationships among variables involved in these alternatives and determine their consequences. Figure 12-17 illustrates some of these program relationships.

Relations among nations in the simulation are unprogrammed, with the exception of rules for communication and war.[251] A programmed assumption relating to communication sets the rate of leakage of restricted information to the mass media at 20 percent. Every fifth message is leaked.

Wars may involve single nations or groups of allied nations. When a nation makes war, a temporary increase in validator satisfaction is programmed. Wars are divided into phases.[252] In each phase, the chance of winning is determined by a ratio of the relative power possessed by each side, defined in terms of externally available force capability (FC_{ex}) and productive capability (BC level):

$$pOW = 1 - \frac{\sum_{\text{adversaries}} (FC_{ex} + a'BC)}{\sum_{\text{all combatants}} (FC_{ex} + a'BC)}$$

(usually $a' = \frac{1}{2}$)

This ratio is repeatedly calculated until one or both sides are destroyed or an armistice is arranged. The costs of war to a nation are levied against both force capability and basic capability. They are computed as proportional to the force capabilities applied by its adversary.

When INS is used as a teaching device, the fact that it does not simulate interactions among real societies is valuable in focusing student attention upon the general factors that affect national policies rather than upon policies and problems of specific societies. The behavior of the simulated nations is not expected to

TABLE 12-9   Alphabetic List of the Main Programmed Variables in INS

Variable	Definition	Typical range	Comments
BC	Basic capability	From below zero to in the 100,000s	Key allocation unit (like GNP)
BC growth, etc.	BCs invested in sector growth	0–10 % of a nation's BC level	BCs designated for improving FC or CS generation rates could be similarly labeled
CS	Consumption standard	Not allowed below CS_{min}	Bought with BCs each period
CS_{min} CS_{max}	"Minimum" or "maximum" CS level	CSs available from converting a considerable fraction of one's BCs	Important in determining VS_{cs}
Δ	Change (intended or not)	Varies with variable; ΔFC and ΔBC are sometimes 10 or 20 %	Used to indicate forced DL changes, consequences of war, revolution, etc.
DL	Decision latitude	From 1 (low latitude) to 10 (complete latitude)	Corresponds roughly to "unresponsiveness" or "insensitivity" to validators (thus "democracies" have low DLs)
ΔDL_v ΔDL_{cdm}	DL changes by validators or central decision makers	0, ±1, 0, +1, respectively	"Forced" or "validator-induced" changes in DL
FC	Force capability	Some small fraction of BCs after conversion to FCs	Equals $FC_{ic} + FC_{ex}$
FC_{ic}	FCs devoted to internal controls	0–30% of one's FCs	Useful for decreasing pSR and pR
FC_{ex}	FCs available for external use	0–100 % of one's FCs	Used in calculations of VS_{ns}
OH	Officeholding	Yes or no	Gives authoritative decision-making capability
pOH	Probability of officeholding	From 0 (certainty of losing office) to 10 (certainty of keeping office)	Used periodically stochastically to calculate whether orderly transfer of power (*e.g.*, electoral defeat) occurs
pOH_m	Cumulated pOH	0–10	
pOW	Probability of winning a war	$0 < pOW < 1$	Depends on ratio of adversaries' $(FC_{ex} + a'BC)$ to the $(FC_{ex} + a'BC)$ of all combatants
pR	Probability of revolution	$0.2 \leq pR \leq 1$	Depends on DL and pSR
pSR	Probability of a successful revolution	$0.4 \leq pSR \leq 1$	Depends inversely on FC_{ic}/FC
VS_m	Overall validator satisfaction	0–10	Depends on VS_{ns} and VS_{cs}; $VS_m = 3$ is a crucial revolutionary threshold
VS_{cs}	VS derived from consumer satisfaction	0–10	Depends on BCs spent on CSs, CS_{max}, CS_{min}
VS_{ns}	VS derived from national security validators	0–10	Depends on ratio of allies' $FC_{ex} + a'BC$ to others' $FC_{ex} + a'BC$

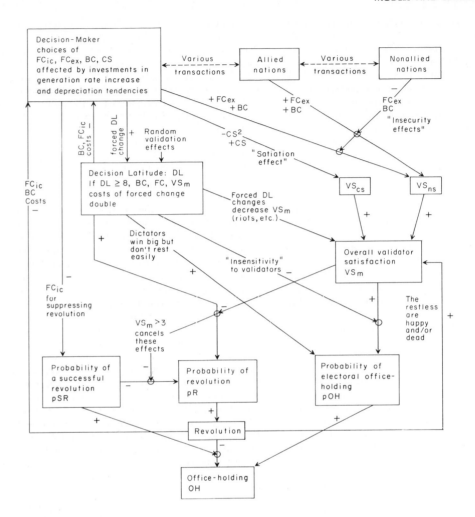

Fig. 12-17 Programmed relationships among variables of the INS. The possibilities of war and of certain longer-range effect have been excluded. The abbreviations are defined in Table 12-9. Key: Rectangle ⬜ represents variable; ⟶⁺ represents positive effect; ⟶⁻ represents negative effect; ⁺↓⁻ represents a negative throttling of a positive effect; ⟶ represents ignore interaction; ----→ represents multiple transactions. [From H. R. Alker, Jr. *Decision-makers' environments in the inter-nation simulation.* In W. D. Coplin (Ed.). *Simulation in the study of politics.* Chicago: Markham, 1968, 40. © 1968 by Markham Publishing Company. *Reprinted by permission of Rand McNally College Publishing Company.*]

SOURCE for Table 12-9 and Fig. 12-17: H. R. Alker, Jr. *Decision-makers' environments in the inter-nation simulation.* In W. D. Coplin (Ed.). *Simulation in the study of politics.* Chicago: Markham, 1968, 38–39. © 1968 by Markham Publishing Company. Reprinted by permission of Rand McNally College Publishing Company.

conform to any particular international or supranational situation. Some adaptations of the basic simulation, however, have been made to test hypotheses about real-world behavior or to model interactions among existing societies. These are of interest only when they correspond closely to the behavior of the societies they are designed to represent.

One such adaptation was made to analyze the effects of the spread of nuclear weapons from two to n nations.[253] In the years following World War II, only the Soviet Union and the United States had nuclear capability. Development programs in other nations, however, made it obvious that a world in which many powers had nuclear capability was inevitable. The "nth-country problem," which required prediction of the nature of the interactions among $2 + n$, rather than 2, nuclear powers interested some social scientists. A list of propositions garnered from the literature of the period included some that were essentially general statements of the seriousness of the problems:[254*] "The spread of nuclear weapons will create problems of which our current ones are pale shadows" and " . . . a further increase [in the number of nuclear powers] would make the international situation and the achievement of a general disarmament more difficult." Others were concerned with the motives for a nation's developing nuclear capacity: "A nation may be attracted toward a nuclear development of its own . . . not only because nuclear weapons mean power, honor, and a fuller sovereignty in general in our time, but also because in particular a nation so equipped can now itself make the key decisions, to defend itself with these weapons and pull its allies into the fight." Several propositions, however, embodied more specific predictions and could be made the basis of testable hypotheses concerning changes in the relations among societies that might follow wider distribution of nuclear power. These were not all equally plausible, and in some cases they contradicted each other. For example, both increased and decreased cohesiveness of existing alliances were predicted by different social scientists.

Adaptation of INS for analyzing the nth-country problem involved increasing the number of nations from five to seven, a number considered to be more representative of the real world, and including an international organization with universal membership and regular sessions of permanent representa-

tives in the initial structure. In addition, force capability was differentiated into "nuclear" and "conventional"; nations were permitted to allocate both nuclear force capability and basic capability to "passive defense against attack," and procedures for conducting "research and development" were introduced.[255] The abstract nature of the simulation was retained. Simulated nations were not identified with real ones.

At the start, the simulated nations were divided into two coalitions, each dominated by a large and powerful nuclear power. These blocs were essentially equal in strength and were trade alliances as well as military alliances. Nonnuclear members of each bloc could acquire nuclear capability by allocating resources to it, but because it was significantly more expensive to produce than conventional armament, the basic capability of the nation had to exceed a certain size before such allocation could be made. In fact, the prearranged program of the game provided that this threshold was high enough to prevent any nation except the two original nuclear powers from achieving nuclear status before all are informed they have it.

The initial world of the simulation conformed to a "tight bipolar system" and resembled the real world of the period after World War II. In such a world, it was hypothesized (*i*) that nations would regard those other nations not included in the same coalition with them as hostile and would perceive greater threat to come from them than from members of their own bloc; (*ii*) that nations would interact and communicate more within their own bloc than with nations outside it; (*iii*) that blocs would be hierarchically organized, the nonnuclear nations being dependent on their nuclear bloc leaders; and (*iv*) that the amount of interaction would be negatively related to perception of threat.[256]

In the nth-country situation after the spread of nuclear weapons, it was hypothesized (*i*) that perception of interbloc threat would be markedly reduced and that intrabloc tension and perception of threat would increase, (*ii*) that the tendency to interact within the bloc rather than between the blocs would decrease, (*iii*) that the hierarchical structure of the blocs would break down, and (*iv*) that the former nonnuclear nations would communicate as readily with leaders outside their bloc as with those inside.

After 17 runs of the simulation, each of which included 12 simulation periods and occupied 4 half days of real time, analysis of data confirmed all but one of the above two sets of hypotheses. The hierarchical structure of the blocs did not break down as expected after the spread of nuclear weapons. Surprisingly, national leaders communicated as much with leaders outside their bloc as with those inside. The

*These excerpts from "Some systemic effects of the spread of nuclear weapons technology: a study through simulation of a multi-nuclear future," by Richard A. Brody are reprinted from *Journal of Conflict Resolution* Vol. VII, No. 4 (Dec. 1963) pp 689-691 by permission of the Publisher, Sage Publications, Inc.

experimenters explained this by pointing out that the dependency which existed in the earlier period was both military and economic and that the economic dependency continued into the nth-country situation even after the military dependency diminished.

The abstract nature of INS was abandoned in a modification that simulated the Vietnam war.[257] Simulated nations were called by the name of the real nation they represented. Their decision makers were selected because they sympathized with the political point of view of the nation whose deciders they simulated. In one run held at a British university, for example, the "President of the United States" was an American student, the Chinese deciders were students in the department of Chinese, recruits from the university Communist party manned the Russian and North Vietnamese nations, and the Foreign Minister of South Vietnam was a Thai who sympathized with American involvement in Vietnam and with the Vietnamese government then in power.

The primary decisions to be made during the simulation were military. South Vietnam was divided into 12 zones—3 in the north and 9 in the south. Forces could be allocated to zones by means of a strategy form. Deciders of the United States and South Vietnam could use air, land, or sea forces and could adopt a strategy of either attack or defense. The Soviet Union and China were not involved in the beginning, but could become involved directly, after which they would have the same options as the United States and South Vietnam. The National Liberation Front and North Vietnam had different options. They had no air or sea forces initially and could opt only for open warfare or guerrilla warfare. Like the others, they could either attack or defend.

The simulation also included other aspects of international interaction such as trade, aid, and a variety of domestic constraints like public opinion and consumers' satisfaction with the standard of living. As in the standard INS, the central decision maker's continuation in office depended upon overall validator satisfaction.

The computer model for the Vietnam simulation included 1,800 variables and used 550 data inputs from the free activity of participants.[258] The program was designed to be used either as a whole, with decision makers receiving complete feedback once in each period, or in sections, with relevant parts of the data being fed in and with partial outputs being obtained periodically. For this purpose the program was written in 12 parts, each of which dealt with a different aspect of the simulation. These included military losses; conventional forces, decision latitude, and nuclear forces; polarization weightings; national security; international opinion; consumer satisfaction; probability of a revolution and probability of a successful revolution; basic resources; antimissile missiles and "hardened" missiles with launching sites designed for decreased vulnerability; public opinion and probability of a cabinet reshuffle; overall validator satisfaction and probability of holding office; and consumer requirements for the next period. Feedback on particular items was available at any time in the simulation.

Participants in the simulation became highly involved, to the extent that in one run the President of the United States and the Secretary General of the United Nations had to be separated to avoid a fistfight. Events during the runs differed greatly. During the first four development runs of the Vietnam simulation a massive nuclear war broke out once, North Vietnam was destroyed in a limited nuclear war once, Russia and China intervened in South Vietnam with troops once, and an uneasy truce was set up in South Vietnam under a Buddhist neutralist government once.[259]

INS validation.   Those who have worked with INS have been deeply concerned with problems of validity in their own and other game-type simulations. INS can be evaluated in terms of the five sorts of simulation validity (see page 85): (*i*) Face validity is achieved to a considerable extent by INS, as shown by the degree of personal involvement of participants and the (perhaps biased) opinions expressed by experimenters. (*ii*) Internal validity or reliability, which is indicated by little variation among replications of the simulation, is obviously low. It may well be that considerable between-run variance is inevitable when, as in INS, a number of events are equally likely. (*iii*) Variable-parameter validity, determined by comparison of the variables and parameters of INS with their assumed counterparts in the observable universe, appears to be poor. (*iv*) Event validity is poor, probably because the experimenters, along with all other social scientists, did not have adequate means to conceptualize the system they were simulating. (*v*) Hypothesis validity is poor, probably for the same reason. Discussing such issues of simulation validity, Guetzkow says:

Work is beginning on efforts to validate aspects of the functioning of the INS model—*the* key question, whether one is interested in the use of man-computer simulation for teaching *or* for research. . . .

Although the lack of empirical underpinnings of international relations precludes at present the creation of a fact-based INS, recent developments in "data making" will be of considerable aid. This new thrust in research in international politics is particularly important when we face such problems as trying to make simulate nations in the INS isomorphic to particular nations in the real world. . . . At least three recent efforts have been devoted to creating "banks" of data. Further, these data have been analyzed with multivariate procedures to get at the underlying *dimensions* of nations, i.e., those major factors which describe a nation. These two kinds of research may yield central variables useful to describe nations, as well as provide the values of the variables for particular nations, so that initial conditions may be established in the INS with more adequacy when we are simulating the nations of the international system.

Validity work based on such data may offer insights about the ways in which the INS might be restructured so as to give the simulate a closer correspondence with the world. . . . It seems clear that much work needs to be done, so that the use of man-computer simulation for both teaching *and* research may be placed upon firmer ground.[260]

The data banks to which Guetzkow referred contained survey materials and political and social indicators. One of the studies designed to investigate the validity of INS used a historical situation, the outbreak of World War I, for which detailed data are available. Hermann and Hermann say:

Model validity is always a matter of degree and is affected by (1) the purpose for which the model is used, (2) whether or not human participants are involved, and (3) the types of criteria employed. The World War I simulation explores the third area—criteria for estimating validity. It focuses on possible standards or criteria for establishing the goodness of fit between the simulation and the system represented. To what extent do features of a political system or its processes correspond to their simplified representation in a model? One means of investigating this question is to ascertain if a simulation produces events similar to those reported in a historical situation. Another approach is to determine whether the simulation supports more general hypotheses about political phenomena which previously have been confirmed by independent methods. Both events and hypotheses are used as validity criteria in the simulation of the 1914 crisis.[261]

A further purpose of the Hermann and Hermann INS simulation was to study the effects of personality characteristics on outcomes of simulated political events. Participants were selected to represent two policy makers in each of the five European nations that were represented in the simulation. The names used for these countries, as usual in INS runs, were not similar to those of any real country. The persons chosen to be represented in the simulation were those who (*i*) dominated foreign policy at the time of the crisis (whether or not they were officially invested with authority to make such decisions), (*ii*) received and dispatched diplomatic cables and related foreign-policy documents, and (*iii*) were described in available biographical or autobiographical materials. Personality characteristics relevant to the political behavior of these persons were determined by content analysis of their personal letters, autobiographies, and biographies. This yielded a distinctive profile for every leader.

The participants were high school students who were experienced in INS experiments and whose personality profiles, as revealed by psychological tests, matched as closely as possible those of the leaders to be simulated. (The ages and backgrounds of the students of modern America and the leaders of early-twentieth-century Europe were so different that such matching could not be very close.) They were not told that the simulated nations, whose deciders they were, were based upon any actual nations or that the crisis with which they were confronted was a historical one. They were, however, in a departure from usual INS procedures, given a history of selected international affairs that preceded the crisis, statements of current domestic and foreign policies of their nations and the reason they were being followed, a sketch of the personality traits of the policy makers they were to simulate, and a set of relevant historical diplomatic messages, conversations, and newspaper articles from the time between the assassination of the Austro-Hungarian Archduke Ferdinand in Sarajevo on June 28, 1914 and the Serbian reply to the ultimatum on July 25. The programmed parameters and variables of the simulation were made to fit the national profiles of the countries involved.

One reason it was possible to use the 1914 crisis in this way is that the countries represented—Austria-Hungary, England, France, Germany, and Russia—have been thoroughly studied by historians. Documents, diplomatic communications, and statistical data on these countries at this time are available.

Because the usual INS run occupies simulated years, while this one represented only a few simulated days, participants were led to expect that the simulation would continue into periods representing years. This was done so that they would consider long-term consequences in their decision making.

Two hypotheses which have been studied for the 1914 crisis were explored with simulation data. The first was: "If a state's perception of injury (or frustration, dissatisfaction, hostility, or threat) to itself [a particular nation] is 'sufficiently' great, this perception will offset perceptions of insufficient capability, making the perception of capability much less important a factor in a decision to go to war."[262]

The second hypothesis asserted that when opposing alliances emerge in international politics, the communication between the blocs will be much less than that among alliance partners.

The first hypothesis was confirmed for the 1914 data and for both runs of the simulation. Thus the behavior of the participants in this INS simulation confirmed the findings of Holsti and North in their content analysis study of the same hypothesis (see pages 959 to 961). The second hypothesis was confirmed for the 1914 data and for one run of the simulation but not the other. The two runs were dissimilar. The one that more closely approximated the World War I crisis used participants whose personalities more closely matched those of the historical figures they represented.

The simulation had a number of problems. In the first place, modification of INS to run over only a few simulated weeks did not provide an opportunity for investigating the programmed relationships of INS, which are revealed in annual statistics. Such programmed variables are constants in such brief periods. Moreover, the programmed portion of the simulation used variables which were broad representations of properties of nations, while the microanalysis yielded more specific events. It was not clear that these specific events were produced by the aggregate variables that composed the model. Several participants, also, recognized the similarity between the game and the historical events that were simulated.

The experimenters concluded that short-term crises are not appropriate for determining the validity of INS.[263] The problems that were identified, however, did not present insurmountable obstacles to the use of historical situations as validity tests for simulations since careful attention to selection of participants and historical occurrences to be simulated could minimize them.

In an attempt to learn more about the validity of international simulations, especially the many variations of INS, Guetzkow reviewed congruences between simulations of international relations and empirical findings from political, economic, and military studies of international affairs and from other relevant scientific researches.[264] Examining personality variables of decision makers, he found that those with simpler conceptual structures, as determined by psychological testing, involved their simulated nations in more aggressive behavior.[265] This finding accorded well with data in other sorts of research that relate cognitive simplicity to aggression. Other test results indicated that simulation participants scoring high in cognitive rigidity tended to perceive conflicts in moral rather than instrumental terms. This finding accorded to some degree with studies made of Woodrow Wilson and John Foster Dulles, both of whom were said to exemplify these two characteristics.

Another study compared the behavior in INS simulations of diplomats in 26 foreign embassies in Washington, D.C., and in the United States Department of State with that of high school and college students. No important differences were observed between the actions of these two apparently diverse groups. This suggests that international simulations with students may have greater validity than skeptics might think. Another comparison disclosed some effect of cultural background on the behavior of participants in INS, but other variables were not controlled. It is possible, therefore, that with careful selection of participants from within a single culture, at least some important cross-cultural differences might be demonstrated in a simulation. Other efforts by Guetzkow to compare group decision making and communications in international simulations and among real nations were inconclusive.

In discussing the broad implications of such results, Guetzkow makes an interesting cross-level suggestion regarding simulations at various levels of living systems, a number of which appear in this book. He says:

In moving onward with the reconstruction and elaboration of simulations for the study of international relations, it would seem possible to borrow components from simulations constructed by others. Such soon may be possible within each segment of the Inter-Nation Simulation, as the following examples illustrate. To simulate "Decision-Makers and Their Nations," perhaps humans might be replaced to an extent by computer programs, such as the General Problem Solver developed by Alan Newell and Simon. Eventually, even aspects of personality might be incorporated into such surrogates for the "decision-makers," as Kenneth Colby and others have demonstrated. Aspects of computer models both of artificial intelligence and of affect have been incorporated, for example, in the Crisiscom simulation. The "nations" might be operated by programmed bureaucracies, as presaged in the work of the Gullahorns and of Beatrice and Sydney Rome, including even budgetary processes. The economists have made important advances in simulating the entire economy of a national entity, as embodied in *The Brookings Quarterly* economic model of the United States and as projected in "A Programme for Growth" by members of Cambridge University's Department of Applied Economics. Does Noel's pioneer work toward enrichment of the economic part of the Inter-Nation Simulation provide guidelines for incorporation of features of these efforts? Perhaps some of the models built for intrasocietal processes could be extrapolated to the inter-nation area, so that the "Relations Among Nations" might be simulated with more adequacy. The work of Abelson and Bernstein on community referenda controversies included a communication process, as did the computer simulations of William N. McPhee and Ithiel de Sola Pool, of Shapiro, and Cherryholmes. Hans Thorelli's international business game ("INTOP") might be used wholesale in adding companies operating overseas to a simulation of the international system, as Smoker has suggested.[266]

Intersimulation validation. For validation purposes, the performance of TEMPER (see pages 998 to 1000) has been compared with that of one PME experimental scenario (see pages 974 to 976) (DETEX II) and with that of INS (see pages 1000 to 1009). The same DETEX II scenario was used in comparing them.[267] It concerns the crisis brought about by the discovery of an experimental nuclear test. The control team notified both the United States and the Soviet teams that an explosion of a 1-megaton-range nuclear device had just been detected. The United States team was also told that the United States Strategic Air Command had immediately gone on yellow alert. The Soviet team was told that when the Soviet High Command received the notification, they had automatically gone on air-raid alert.

The general description of international relations as unchanged since 1964 was sufficient for PME, but it had to be made explicit in the programs of INS and TEMPER. National military and political resources also had to be made explicit for INS and TEMPER. For these two simulations the crisis had to be put into terms to suit their particular versions of the world. For TEMPER it was necessary also to specify quantities for a number of variables.

In all three simulations, the international situation constituted a "loose bipolar system" in which leaders of two coalitions of nations dominate their blocs and compete for the favor of a "third world," sometimes in the forum of an international organization. Only in INS, however, could significant changes in the system occur without the outbreak of a major war. In TEMPER, the coalitions of nations act in unified and symmetrical fashion because they use the same set of information-processing and decision-making equations, differing only in data and parameters. Coordination and communication are perfect in TEMPER. Bloc members, also, do not directly affect the goal definitions or actions taken by national actors. Connections between nations in a conflict region are very loose, and so they are not really affected by one another's problems. TEMPER cannot represent internal political events, as the other two can, and this was a disadvantage. The assumption that all political elites act upon cost-effective economic considerations seemed to the experimenters to be wishful thinking. In spite of its fixed bloc structure, the TEMPER simulation produced some system changes at the supranational level.

In the three simulations, the decision sequences that affected the likelihood of war were different, brought about by differences in their rules. Only in DETEX II did the probability of war become high, nuclear conflict being on the verge of breaking out as the simulation run ended. In TEMPER, alternatives were progressively defined and eliminated, as they were also in the PME; in INS, they were not. Variations among these simulations were, in part, results of the differences in their intended uses. Also, their designers held diverging theoretical views.

International processes simulation (IPS). This is an expansion of INS which retains many of the features of the original but which is modified to include more international and supranational structures and processes.[268] Two forms of IPS represent alternative worlds, one of which, the Nation State Model, has less development of international components than the other, the International Model. The familiar abstract nations, such as Algo and Bingo, prototypes of different sorts of real societies, interact in the simulated worlds of IPS. They differ in decision latitude, as they do in INS. As in INS, human decision makers interact with a computer program. Some of the programmed assumptions of INS are retained. Others appear in revised form. To these are added programmed assumptions not found in INS.

No account of experiments with the model is given. It is of interest, however, because it explicitly differentiates public and private—governmental and nongovernmental—components of the global system. International governmental and nongovernmental organizations and international corporations are included. A similar differentiation is found within nations. Public and private national economic components are distinguished. More human participants are required for IPS than for INS. Each simulated nation has participants representing the chief of state, a domestic adviser, a foreign-affairs diplomat, an international organization delegate, a citizen, and the executive director of a corporation. An IPS simulation run involving six nations, five corporations, and one international organization requires more than 40 participants. Citizens hold conferences, strike, demonstrate, riot, and undertake subversion.

A Parsonian system theory as interpreted by Deutsch is the theoretical basis of the IPS models.[269] In this theory the four basic requirements of a social system—(i) pattern maintenance, (ii) goal attainment, (iii) adaptation, and (iv) integration—are represented by components at the societal level (see pages 19 to 22, 747, and 765). Smoker discusses its extension to the international level: "A nation-state system is for our purposes defined as a system where interaction between nations is primarily an interaction between goal attainment subsystems; a classical interpretation of this is power politics. . . . There is, by definition, no integrative subsystem between nations in such a situation. The situation resembles a zero-sum game where might is right."[270] International components in such a model are (i) pattern-maintenance components— individuals and their families who are "international persons," traveling frequently and living transculturally, for example, civil servants of an international governmental organization like the United Nations, executives of international corporations, and entertainers with an international following; (ii) goal-attainment components—international governmental activities; (*iii*) adaptive components—an international economic system which includes international corporations; and (*iv*) integrative components—cultural activities of nongovernmental organizations, international conferences, the worldwide press, press associations, and communications media.

Programs of the IPS model are:

(1) *Program load.* This program places starting data in 19 files of the computer's memory.

(2) *Program facts.* This reads data into each of the 19 data files and provides a description of the state of the simulation environment at any time.

(3) *Research and development program.* This set of programmed assumptions relates to corporations. It includes capital investment and investment in research and development. Both nations and corporations can invest in corporations, and corporations can invest in nations, which improves the nation's trading position. Research and development by nations and corporations lower production costs. The program converts research and development and capital investment appropriations into research and development payoffs, increases basic capabilities for industries, and creates a changing distribution of industrial plants. It is assumed that, up to a saturation point, as investment in research and development increases, unit costs are reduced.

(4) *Economic program.* This program also represents a set of assumptions about economic processes. Trade among nations is not government-controlled except under special circumstances. Import and export patterns depend on the distribution of industrial plants in the nations, the needs of governments and of citizens, and available markets. This program calculates an import–export matrix, taking into account geographic distribution of industry and company sales. Balance sheets for each corporation in each country show profit and loss on each product imported from, or exported to, each other nation. A mass-production effect is included.

(5) *Political program.* This is adapted from the INS program. It calculates the probability of the chief of state's holding office, of a revolution, and of orderly and disorderly transfers of power, as well as various national attributes and capabilities such as national security and consumer satisfaction. It also estimates national economic variables like the level of basic resources, and it takes world opinion on various actions of nations into account.

(6) *War program.* This program calculates outcomes in the event of war.

(7) and (8) *Trade-agreement and trade-termination programs.* These are bookkeeping programs which check trade agreements to be sure that particular

transactions are possible, to implement trade terminations, to adjust the data base for the next period, and to print out existing agreements for the start of the next period.

Crisiscom. This simulation of national deciders processing information during an international crisis bases its scenarios upon historical crises in order to discover how closely the decisions of simulated national leaders resemble those of their historical counterparts.[271] The emphasis is upon psychological processes of national deciders. Other admittedly important influences upon outcomes of crises are not considered.

Crisiscom is designed to be used in living system–computer games to represent teams not staffed by humans and aspects of the environment not played out by the human players. Comparable processes are performed by the control team in PME, the preprogrammed messages in TNG, and the computer program in INS (see pages 974, 976, and 1002 to 1005).

A published instance of this simulation deals with interactions between the German Kaiser and the Tsar of Russia during the week before the outbreak of World War I—July 25 through July 31, 1914. In this version, human participants make decisions, and the computer processes information and introduces biases and distortions. The program can be expanded to include more than two national leaders. The interactions of the Kaiser, the Tsar, and their aides during this period have been studied in great detail by historians. The records of these researches, together with the relevant newspaper accounts, were made the basis for the scenario of this game. A man–computer game concerned with the same period is described above (see pages 1008 and 1009).

The simulation is based on the following psychological hypotheses, all of which would be considered valid generalizations about human behavior by many psychologists:*

1. People pay more attention to news that deals with them. [This may well be an example of the principle stated in Hypothesis 3.3.3.2-20 (see page 97) that a system gives priority processing to information which will relieve a strain (*i.e.*, which it "needs"), neglecting neutral information.]
2. People pay less attention to facts that contradict their previous views.
3. People pay more attention to news from trusted, liked sources.
4. People pay more attention to facts that they will have to act upon or discuss because of attention by others.

---

*This excerpt from "The Kaiser, the Tsar, and the computer: information processing in a crisis," by I. de Sola Poole and A. Kessler is reprinted from the *American Behavioral Scientist*, vol. 8, no. 9 (May 1965) p. 33 by permission of the Publishers, Sage Publications, Inc.

5. People pay more attention to facts bearing on actions they are already involved in, i.e., action creates commitment.[272]

The computer program represents the information to which each of the two leaders attends. Each receives information about himself and the other leader in the form of messages, which make up the scenario of the simulation. Each message is in the form A_j, R_a, A_k. The As represent the two simulated decision makers (J and K), and the R stands for relationships between them (see pages 568 to 570). In the present simulation only two relationships are included, although expansion could include more. They are (i) *affect*, the attitudes or feelings of one toward the other, and (ii) *salience*, the importance of one to the other or the importance of one's interpersonal relationship with the other.

In accordance with the hypotheses listed above, the decision maker selects from among the input messages those which win his attention and ignores the others. These not only are recorded as having received his attention but also serve to change the basic image of the world with which he started the simulation. This is represented by an affect matrix which tells how each leader feels about the other. It is assumed that important events reduce the number of things to which a person can pay attention. Ordinarily, players attend to fewer than the maximum number of messages to which they are limited, which is nine. Events on which no message is received for 2 days are considered to be no longer attended to and are stored in memory. The flowchart of the simulation, Fig. 12-18, describes the way information is processed by this program.

In a test of this simulation, almost the same set of messages was sent to the Kaiser and to the Tsar. The messages selected by the computer for attention by the two rulers differed, however. On the first day, the primary message to which each gave attention was the Austrian ultimatum to Serbia. The Kaiser was also concerned with the fact that mobs in Germany rallied for war, which was almost as important to him. The Tsar gave second significance to the reaction to the ultimatum in Serbia. The reaction of Germans to this news was also important to him, being third in rank. Russia's own reaction came fourth. As the 7 simulated days went on, between July 25 and July 31, each of the two simulated decision makers concerned himself with different news. By the end of the period, they were attending to two very different worlds.

Three events were attended to by both men: Germany's mobilization, Russia's mobilization, and the secret treaties of the period immediately before World War I.

The Kaiser, however, also attended to the collapse of Europe's stock markets and German's military precautions. The Tsar selected the reactions of Serbia's Balkan allies and the Russian press. Even when the same event was in both men's minds, their pictures of it were not the same because each player had his own associations to the event.

The experimenters considered that the selections of events for attention by the computer simulation were reasonable in the light of what is known about the two historical figures and the events with which they were confronted. They concluded that the model handles information in ways that conform to the complexity of human thought processes.

Multilevel World Model. This model, intended as a tool for decision makers and policy analysts, is based upon the cybernetic systems theory of Mesarović and Pestel, its developers. They conceive of the world as a multilevel, multigoal system.[273] They emphasize the use, by human decision makers in the system's decider subsystem, of strategies to advance its goals in a changeable environment rather than the use of input–output analysis. Instead of viewing the future as determined solely by past and present conditions, as in the World II and World III simulations, this model includes the activities of men and sociopolitical institutions in shaping the future.[274] This is achieved by having a living decision maker interact with a computer program. The human being in this system contributes more to the decision process than he does in the fully computerized world models included under class (c) above. The experimenter merely sets the parameters and values of class (c) models to simulate a given world situation, and the computer then reads out the results of its calculations (see page 981). But the human participant in the Multilevel World Model simulation does less deciding than the participants, who carry out their unprogrammed activities in the game-type simulations like INS. The former simulations are dialogues between a person and a computer in which the person "decides on values, priorities, costs and the level of risks to be taken; the computer indicates the breadth of choices and likely consequences."[275] The use of this interactive mode permits evaluation of the possible effects of such variables as technical innovations, discoveries, substitute materials, degree of cultural diversity, and especially social, political, and psychological changes.

The analysis of the global system upon which the model is based differentiates several hierarchical strata. In the model, these are aggregated into three:

(i) The *causal stratum* contains processes which, left to operate undisturbed, will continue historic trends.[276] Included are physical and ecological pro-

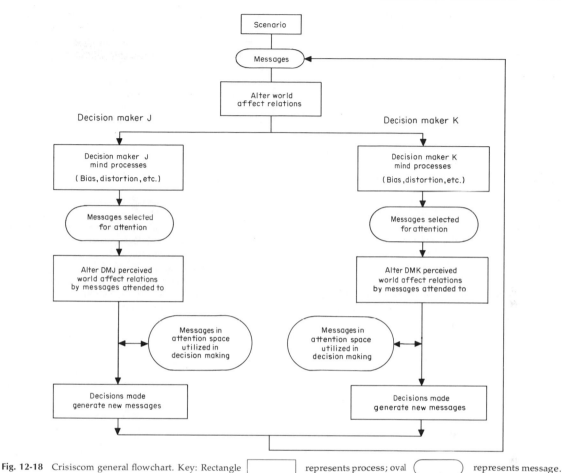

Fig. 12-18 Crisiscom general flowchart. Key: Rectangle ⬚ represents process; oval ⬭ represents message.

[This figure, adapted from The Kaiser, the Tsar, and the computer: information processing in a crisis, by I. de Sola Pool & A. Kessler, is reprinted from *Amer. Behav. Sci.* May 1965, **8**(9), 33 by permission of the Publishers, Sage Publications, Inc.]

cesses and short-term economic operations which are controlled by feedbacks from immediate economic events and conditions. In one application of the model, concerning policies about the world's oil resources (see pages 1015 and 1016), the causal stratum represents the economy of a region and the basic energy relationships of concern to the policy maker.[277] It contains information about the past functioning of the economy relevant to oil that led to its present state, including production, export, import, and consumption of oil; capital formation; and other data. The functioning of the economy is described by a large set of economic indicators. The causal stratum contains also a population growth model designed to inform the decision maker of the number of people living in the region at any time.

(*ii*) The *organizational* (or *decisional*) *stratum* represents the collective actions of all decision makers who influence, mold, and change the causal stratum.[278] This includes activities not only of governments but also of other organizations such as businesses and unions.

(*iii*) The *norms stratum* represents the activities of groups and organizations which transform the desires of many individual persons into social forces and which determine the goals, objectives, and values that govern the organizational stratum at any particular time.

In this hierarchical model, the primary decision making is done by the organizational stratum. Its decisions result in actions that guide and control the causal stratum and influence the norms stratum.

Since the world community cannot be viewed as a single entity insofar as its goals and aspirations are concerned, it was divided in the initial work with the model into three regions on the basis of economic differences. These were (*i*) market economy, (*ii*) planned economy, and (*iii*) underdeveloped economy. A minimal form of the model is diagramed in Fig. 12-19.

The process of the organizational (or decisional) stratum is analyzed as having four subprocesses (or *layers*). These four have interesting similarities to the four stages of processes of the decider subsystem as stated in my conceptual system (see pages 940 to 942). The layers of Mesarović and Pestel's models are:

(*i*) The *planning and forecasting layer* is responsible for anticipating future needs and possibilities, indicating the set of alternatives that could affect future development. It sets the stage for the policy considerations. In a model concerning world energy processing, it indicates the possible increase in energy-production cost over the time period in consideration.

(*ii*) The *policy layer* is responsible for decisions that concern political and social expectations and possibili-ties. In an energy crisis, a choice of policies might include emphasizing restoration of energy abundance over all other considerations, limiting consumption and preserving energy resources, or making necessary adjustments to limit dependence on imports.

(*iii*) The *strategy layer* is responsible for finding the strategy to carry out the selected policy. If the overall policy is to make as much energy as possible available, the appropriate strategy could be to shift the investment from the industrial sector or to transfer the investment from both the industrial and the service sectors.

(*iv*) The *implementation layer* is responsible for determining the exact magnitude of changes needed to implement the decision. If the decision is to shift 40 percent and 60 percent of the investment from the industrial and service sectors, respectively, the implementation layer must determine the exact value of investment needed, its effects on other investments, and its effects on other parts of the economy. A final decision is the result of the processes of all four layers. These layers are categorized somewhat differently in later applications of the model. One uses the terms

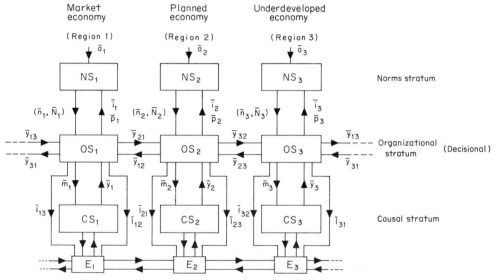

Fig. 12-19 Minimal structure of the world model. Key: NS represents norms stratum; OS represents organizational stratum; CS represents causal stratum; E represents environment; $\bar{a}$ represents inputs to the norms stratum; $\bar{n}$ represents the set of norm values with k_n components; $\bar{N}$ represents the satisfaction range within which any set $\bar{y}$ must lie in order to be deemed acceptable; $\bar{I}$ represents the set of k_I information units, about both the causal stratum and exchange with other regions, input from the organizational stratum to the norms stratum; $\bar{p}$ represents the set of k_p actions of persuasion and inducement for obtaining more "advantageous" societal norms; $\bar{y}$ represents the set of k_y process-information outputs of the regions to the organizational stratum; $\bar{m}$ represents the set of k_m actions available to the organizational stratum of influence the causal stratum; $\bar{I}$ represents the set of k_I actions by which the organizational stratum attempts to influence exchanges between the regions. (From M. D. Mesarović & E. C. Pestel. A goal-seeking and regionalized model for analysis of critical world relationships—the conceptual foundation. *Kybernetes*, 1972, **1**, 80. *Reprinted by permission.*)

"goal" layer, "policy" layer, "action" layer, and "implementation" layer.[279] Another has five layers: "goal," "policy," "strategic," "tactical," and "implementation."

For a simulation of the energy crisis in the developed world, some potential problems which may arise about world energy processing are stored in the computer memory. These include limited availability of imports, effects on costs of resource scarcities, effects on costs of measures for environmental protection, increasing demand for energy, and the overly slow development of energy technology.[280] The program also includes the policies available to human decision makers, among which are to increase imports, elevate energy production by increasing or shifting investment, or follow a mixed policy of adjustments of imports and investments. The program also represents processes and relationships with which the simulation is concerned, including a simplified model, provided in a subroutine, of the basic economic relationships that involve energy variables. All necessary data and starting values are also stored in computer memory.

In the simulation, the human decision maker communicates to the machine by the use of coded words that are strings of uppercase letters from the English alphabet and numbers. For example, *PD1* means *Policy Decision number 1,* and *EGH* means *Economy Graphs* of information on *Historical* values. The decision maker may request information or instruct the machine as to his decisions on policies, strategies, parameters, or implementations. He may also tell the computer to return to a previous stage of the model for additional consideration. The computer responds by making statements in English or by giving the desired data, mathematical relationships, or graphs. As the simulation runs and changes over time, the human decider watches a set of indicators. When, in his judgment, corrective action is required, he may intervene to change variables and observe the effects of the changes.

In a typical sequence, the computer, programmed by the *planning and forecasting layer,* indicates a trend beginning in a given year that can lead to serious difficulties at some later date.

The decision maker asks for and receives from the *policy layer* more information on relevant indicators. He also asks for and receives from it the relevant set of policy alternatives, and he may need additional explanation of some of them. He may ask what the economic, political, or environmental implications of a particular policy are. A sequence of this sort leads to choice of a policy.

The decider then proceeds to the *strategy layer* of the decision process, selection of a strategy. In this way

the entire decision process is carried out, and a final decision is made.

Then the *implementation layer* indicates how to carry it out.

Several submodels are being developed for a 10-region world. These 10, unlike the economic divisions of the initial model, are specific geographic regions: (1) North America, (2) Western Europe, (3) Japan, (4) the other noncommunist developed countries, (5) Eastern Europe, (6) Latin America, (7) the Middle East, (8) Africa, (9) Southeast Asia, and (10) China. For some purposes, other sorts of aggregation can be used, *e.g.,* the total world or a two-region world that combines regions 1 to 5 and 6 to 10. Economic, population, food, energy, and water-resource submodels are planned, as well as some others. In the complete model these will be interconnected.[281]

The economic submodel will be a dynamic simulation of economic growth in which various microeconomic models for each of the 10 regions are aggregated into macroeconomic models (see page 876). The economic submodels—not meant for forecasting, but making projections 25 to 50 years or more into the future—are so complex that they can include only the most basic economic trends. The economic submodel differentiates three types of economies: developed market economies (regions 1, 2, 3, and 4), centrally planned economies (regions 5 and 10), and less developed economies (regions 6, 7, 8, and 9). Equations that specify production, employment, and trade differ among the three.[282] It is planned to divide each regional economy into nine sectors, including agriculture, mining, energy, food, manufacturing, construction, dwellings, and two classes of services. Several versions of the macroeconomic model have been designed, implemented, and validated.[283] All are said by the developers to agree with historical data in a satisfactory way.

The population submodel is well developed.[284] It is intended to study population growth in the 10 regions under different population policies and as influenced by interaction with other submodels such as the food submodel. It is also to be used to study the influence of population increase on economic, ecological, food, energy, and other submodels.

A set of separate energy submodels for different regions study outcomes of alternative scenarios, including developments of alternative technologies.[285] A world oil submodel uses the economic submodel as a basis for projection of economic growth in each of the 10 regions.[286] It uses data on supply and demand for oil, from such sources as the United Nations statistical series, to predict outcomes of several possible scenarios. The standard run of the model assumes general international cooperation in all regions, whether they have a surplus of oil or a deficit.[287] Regions with surpluses do not limit production or exports, nor do they adopt extreme pricing policies. Regions with deficits do not use retaliatory pricing policies or make special efforts to become independent of the suppliers. Major variables of interest are the price of oil, the size of the capital flows, and the proportions of capital which oil-selling nations commit to long-term investments in other regions as well as to immediate consumption.[288] The model suggests that while the sudden, great increases in the price of Middle Eastern oil in 1974 had disruptive economic effects on developed nations, and nearly catastrophic effects on underdeveloped countries, a price of oil higher than the former $1.35 a barrel will produce more economic stability and greater economic growth in most regions.[289] Furthermore, the effects of higher oil prices on the world monetary system are not so large as some experts estimated.[290] This scenario of international cooperation predicted a fairly comfortable world future, but conflict scenarios did not.[291]

Global input–output model.   Similar economic and environmental issues are addressed in a global input–output model created by Leontief *et al.*[292] As a basis for international development policies, it compares the world economy of 1970 (divided into 15 regions, each with 45 sectors), with hypothetical economies in 1990 and 2000.

Altogether I have discussed in this section 19 supranational or international models or simulations, some of which have several variations. Seven of the simulations are clearly supranational. They deal with systems made up of two or more nations which have a supranational decider subsystem. The other simulations are either international or, in some cases, perhaps supranational.

The simulations all include decider subsystems— supranational, societal, or both. In all but three of them the decider subsystem processes are clearly the main concern. But generally the simulations neglect most of the 19 subsystems which I consider critical for living systems (see Table 12-2). No simulation includes more than 10 of these 19 critical subsystems. Some have as few as two. Four of the critical subsystems never appear in any simulation. My experience is like that of Sokolow, who reviewed 10 different urban dynamics models.[293] Most of what he considered major properties of systems did not appear in most of the models. Even though obviously the developers of the simulations planned them for various purposes, it is still clear that they include different subsystems. It is apparent that they have no common agreement about what the subsystems are that compose a supra-national system or a society. Agreement on the 19 subsystems I propose, or on a reasonable alternative, would make it much easier to integrate such simulations or otherwise relate them to one another.

There appears not to be any common agreement, either, about the variables or indicators (see pages 905 and 906) of each of the subsystems which should be included in supranational models. As Mar found in another detailed assessment of a number of systems models: "The survey . . . revealed that persons responsible for model formulation had no basic theory that could be used to justify the method by which a variable is introduced into a model."[294] A few, but not many, of the subsystem variables which I list in this chapter were employed in the simulations.

Some of the supranational variables or indicators used in the above simulations, classified under the appropriate critical subsystems of my conceptual scheme, are:

Boundary. Planetary albedo (reflectivity of the earth); transparency of the atmosphere to terrestrial radiation

Ingestor. Rate of absorption of mercury in air, soil, stream sediments, ocean waters, and fish; solar energy input rates; rates of use of various natural resources; import rates

Distributor. Rates of international trade; temperature distribution in various latitude belts

Producer. Birthrates; disease rates; weapon-production rates

Matter-energy storage. Quantities of tin or of oil stored; rates of storage of tin or of oil

Extruder. Export rates; rates of pollution of the atmosphere or the seas

Motor. Weapon strength; armed-forces strength; battle casualties; battle deaths

Input transducer. Types of intelligence information received; amounts of intelligence information received

Internal transducer. Favorable or unfavorable world opinions about supranational actions; validator satisfaction (see pages 1001 and 1002) about decider subsystem actions; reports of supranational arms inspections teams

Channel and net. Rates of flow of money; differences in communications media, *e.g.,* private messages, conferences, official statements, and press releases

Memory. Cultural attitudes; amounts of capital invested

Decider. Decision strategies, *e.g.,* competitive *vs.* cooperative; decision latitudes of leaders

Output transducer. Truthfulness of communications about armament or disarmament; rates of giving foreign financial aid

I have been able to classify under the 19 critical

subsystems every one of the dozens of variables in the models and simulations reviewed in this chapter.

Many of the simulation models discussed in this chapter have striking formal identities to those considered in previous chapters dealing with lower levels of living systems. They have multiple differential equations dealing with inputs, throughputs, and outputs of various sorts of matter-energy and information interacting over time in a set of interrelated subsystems. This striking similarity of simulations of systems at this level and lower ones strongly supports my view that there are cross-level formal identities.

7. Conclusions

The decades since the end of World War I have seen the breakup of an earlier form of suprasocietal system, the colonial empires that had dominated the world scene, and the emergence of new forms of systems with modern nation-states as components.

The number of nations in the world has increased rapidly, as one society after another has demanded its independence and organized a national government. Each of these governments has promptly joined the United Nations. Most of them belong also to regional organizations and special-purpose intergovernmental organizations. Most align themselves, more or less consistently, with one of the blocs of nations into which the world is divided.

As a result of these developments, nationalism and internationalism are in strong opposition in the world today. Both old, established nations and newly independent ones are jealous of their national sovereignty and unwilling to become integrated under a powerful supranational decider. On the other hand, the mutual interdependence among nations has increased. This is partially a result of the reduced isolation of societies in the modern world. In accordance with Hypothesis 2-3 (see page 92), the more isolated a system is, the more totipotential it must be. The presence of virtually worldwide distributor and channel and net components leaves no nation unable to exchange matter-energy and information with others. Only a few small, primitive societies, usually inclusions in the territory of more modern systems, like some Amazon Indian tribes, are outside the range of these components. Increasing industrialization also reduces totipotentiality since industrialization increases specialization. Exponential increase in population in many of the world's societies also makes self-sufficiency impossible, even for the most basic human needs.

Of the two forces, nationalism and internationalism, the former appears to be the stronger at present. Systems with formal supranational decider structures and processes are limited by charter or in practice so that they have limited power to implement their deci-

sions. If conflict arises between the decider of a component and the supranational decider, the component generally prevails.

The supranational decider processes with real impact tend to be limited to specific processes that do not seriously threaten, and indeed may support, the societal deciders. The regulation of international carriers and communications and the regulation of certain flows of money and credit are examples. These processes, however, meet important needs of the modern world. The number of such supranational activities increases steadily. The number of nations participating in them grows constantly. Not only political scientists but also many governments see them as means of conflict resolution among nations and as alternatives to war when disputes arise. At the same time, societies continue to seek physical and financial security by means of older forms of international and supranational organizations, alliances, blocs, and federations.

Science has never yet been able, after examining a type of living system at a given period in its evolution, to predict accurately the later stages through which it would pass and the point at which it would reach its highest development, regress, or fail to survive. The future of supranational systems cannot be predicted. Will present international relationships and supranational bodies develop until they eventually bind all societies in a single worldwide supranational system? Are they basically incompatible with nations, so that countries must change their character if supranational systems are to evolve further? Can societies remain separate under a supranational decider, or must boundaries essentially disappear and the system become a larger society, as many federations have done? Will the present forms of supranational structure prove to be nonviable, and will some new form, as yet unimagined, appear? These questions cannot be answered now.

Scientific measurement and collection of quantitative data on international and supranational variables have begun only in the last decade or two. Nevertheless, some studies cited in this chapter make it clear that the scientific method is applicable at this level of living systems as well as at other levels. Research at this level has frequently made explicit use of systems concepts and has applied techniques of mathematical modeling and simulation much earlier in the scientific development of the field than has been the case at any other level. This approach emphasizes the relationships among variables and the nature of the complex feedbacks in very large systems.

The simulations so far developed deal with problems of conflict among nations, exponential increase in population, resource shortages, global changes in climate and ecology, pollution, monetary flows, and matter-energy flows among nations. Some "world" or "global" models include many of these variables in such a way that the effects of changes in one can be traced throughout the system. A variety of efforts at prediction have been made on the basis of these studies.

Although the use of such conceptual tools has undoubtedly advanced the understanding of the systems they represent, their use before data relevant to the variables they employ have been collected has reduced their precision, their credibility, and their practical value. There has been almost no effort to use comparable subsystems, components, variables, and indicators in different simulations. Agreement on such matters among scholars in this field would greatly increase the usefulness and compatibility of their simulations and would advance the integration of scientific effort at this level. As it is, one aspect of world or supranational process is isolated out, and those who study it make arbitrary selections of subsystems, components, variables, and indicators. Values for parameters and variables are estimated, often impressionistically, in the absence of reliable data.

One goal of this chapter has been to provide a conceptual framework within which studies of the many relevant variables could be integrated and related to the scientific findings at other levels. Another has been to identify some of the areas in which research can usefully be done and to discover some of the questions that can be asked about systems at this level. It is critical that many unanswered problems about world population be investigated within a relatively short period. For example: What is the optimal population for the earth? How can population control best be achieved?

Questions about the causes and prevention of war are occupying many researchers at present. For example: Can supranational deciding reduce the amount of conflict in the world? Some data that may suggest answers to such questions are available. Others are being collected.

Among the cross-level hypotheses in Chap. 4, some are of greater interest than others at this level. Some suggestions for cross-level research that could apply to the supranational level appear on pages 110 to 112.

Several of the hypotheses state that values of particular variables are greater at higher levels of living systems than at lower levels. If so, it is reasonable that they would be greatest at this highest level. Hypotheses 3.3.6.2-4 and 3.3.6.2-5 (see page 100) assert that the higher the level of a system, or the higher the echelon of a multiechelon system, the less its activities are determined by the information of the

system's template and the more they are determined by the information of experience stored in its memory. Hypothesis 3.3.6.2-6 (see page 100) states that higher-level systems in general have more complex memory storage and search rules and are more efficient in terms of energy costs per bit of information. Higher-level systems, according to Hypothesis 5.1-4 (see page 103), in general have more kinds and more complex combinations of adjustment processes than living systems at lower levels. Also, Hypothesis 3.3.7.2-21 (see page 102) asserts that they are more correct or adaptive in their decisions than systems at lower levels. Collection of data relevant to these hypotheses would advance understanding of supranational systems as well as systems at other levels.

Hypotheses 5.1-29 and 5.1-30 (see page 104) state that higher-level systems have more variation in general in their information processing times and a greater cost per correct information unit processed. Hypothesis 5.2-12 (see page 107) says that more complex systems, which contain more different components, each of which can adjust against one or more specific environmental stresses and maintain in steady state one or more specific variables not maintained by any other component, if they adequately coordinate the processes in their components, survive longer on the average than less complex systems. Since many supranational systems are highly complex, this hypothesis is particularly relevant to this level.

Hypothesis 3.3.3.2-5 (see page 96) asserts that strains, errors, and distortions increase in a system as the number of channels over which information transmission is blocked rises. Since international channels between nations are often blocked, confirmation of this hypothesis would add to an understanding of supranational systems. Hypothesis 3.3.7.2-16 (see page 101) states that deciders of a system's subsystems and components satisfice shorter-term goals than the decider of the total system. It would be interesting to determine whether a set of decisions made by selected component societies of the United Nations satisfied shorter-term goals than a comparable set of decisions of the General Assembly or Security Council. One could also determine whether Hypothesis 5.2-13 (see page 107) could be confirmed for supranational systems. It states that a system which survives temporarily subordinates conflicts among subsystems or components to the good of the total system when a threat or stress arises.

Many of the conflict-resolution hypotheses are testable at this level, including Hypothesis 5.2-14 (see page 107), which asserts that segregation increases conflict among subsystems or components of a system, requiring the system to devote more adjustment processes to resolving such conflicts. There appears to be support at this level for Hypothesis 5.2-16 (see page 107), which states that systems tend to reduce multiple-component conflicts to conflicts among a lesser number of blocs of components (see pages 962 to 964).

Hypothesis 5.2-17 (see page 107) is applicable to the present-day world and also to the expected future state of the world. It states that the greater the mutual dependence of two or more subsystems or components on a single limited input or store of matter-energy or information, the more probable conflict among them is. This hypothesis would be easy and interesting to evaluate at this level.

Compared with work at other levels of living systems, the current research at the supranational level is more primitive and certainly is neither very precise nor very quantitative. The scientific method is being applied to systems at this level by quite a number of investigators, and the reliability of their results is slowly improving. The issues at this level are so important to all human beings and so urgently demanding of solutions that they cannot be neglected. Perhaps cross-level comparisons from lower levels of living systems, where studies have been carried out using more sophisticated methods than those generally employed at this level, will help us to advance our understanding of our world, now shared by more than 3 billion people

A note preceding the first scene of Thomas Hardy's epic drama of the Napoleonic Wars reads:

The nether sky opens, and Europe is disclosed as a prone and emaciated figure, the Alps shaping like a backbone, and the branching mountain-chains like ribs, the peninsular plateau of Spain forming a head. Broad and lengthy lowlands stretch from the north of France across Russia like a grey-green garment hemmed by the Ural mountains and the glistening Arctic Ocean.

The point of view then sinks downwards through space, and draws near to the surface of the perturbed countries, where the peoples, distressed by events which they did not cause, are seen writhing, crawling, heaving, and vibrating in their various cities and nationalities.[295]

Mankind's suffering is not less today—it is vaster and more in need of understanding and relief.

When general living systems theory dissects Europe or the EEC, the world or the United Nations, into subsystems and uses computer simulations to analyze the perturbed nations with their vibrating cities and distressed peoples, it may seem to be aloof and dispassionate. But the earth's crises are too real for that. If we examine formal identities between supranational systems and other, better-understood levels of life, it must be with the fervent hope that such analyses can help to relieve some of this planet's ominous pathologies.

NOTES AND REFERENCES

[1]Kaplan, M. A. *System and process in international politics.* New York: Wiley, 1957, 20, 113.

[2]Etzioni, A. *The active society.* New York: Free Press, 1968, 564–565.

[3]Ward, B. & Dubos, R. *Only one earth.* New York: Norton, 1972, 195. Reprinted by permission.

[4]United Nations Office of Public Information. *Everyman's United Nations: a complete handbook of the activities and evolution of the United Nations during its first twenty years, 1945–1965.* (8th ed.) New York: United Nations, 1968, 267–270.

[5]Deutsch, K. W. & Eckstein, A. National industrialization and the declining share of the international economic sector, 1890–1950. *World Politics,* 1961, **13**, 289.

[6]Small, M. & Singer, J. D. *Formal alliances 1816–1965: an extension of the basic data.* Ann Arbor: Univ. of Michigan, Mental Health Research Institute, Communication No. 249, April 1969.

[7]Kaplan, M. A. *Op. cit.,* 21–53.

[8]*Ibid.,* 45–46. Reprinted by permission.

[9]Hall, R. A. (Ed.). *Yearbook of international organizations.* (13th ed.) Brussels: Union of International Associations, 1974, 746.

[10]Singer, J. D. & Wallace, M. Intergovernmental organization and the preservation of peace, 1816–1964: some bivariate relationships. *Int. Organization,* 1970, **24**, 532.

[11]*U.S. government manual, 1973–74.* Washington: GPO, 1974, 607–608.

[12]*The Europa year book, 1973, a world survey.* Vol. 1. London: Europa Publications Limited, 214.

[13]Commission of the European Communities. *Sixth general report on the activities of the communities, 1972.* Brussels: Commission of the European Communities, 1972, xiii.

[14]Wall, E. H., Hammes, C. L., & Wilberforce, Lord. *The Court of Justice of the European Communities.* London: Butterworth, 1966, xi, xii. Reprinted by permission.

[15]McClelland, D. H. *The Central American Common Market.* New York: Praeger, 1972, 3. Reprinted by permission.

[16]*The Europa year book, 1973, a world survey. Op. cit.,* 358–372.

[17]Singer, J. D. The global system and its sub-systems. In J. N. Rosenau (Ed.). *Linkage politics.* New York: Free Press, 1969, 27.

[18]*Ibid.*

[19]Etzioni, A. *Op. cit.,* 583.

[20]Deutsch, K. W., Burrell, S. A., Kann, R. A., Lee, M., Jr., Lichterman, M., Lindgren, R. E., Loewenheim, F. L., & Van Wagenen, R. W. *Political community and the North Atlantic area: international organization in the light of historical experience.* Princeton, N.J.: Princeton Univ. Press, 1957, 5–9.

[21]United Nations Office of Public Information. *Everyman's United Nations: a complete handbook of the activities and evolution of the United Nations during its first twenty years, 1945–1965.* (8th ed.) *Op. cit.,* 490.

[22]Evan, W. M. MNC's and IPA's: an international organization research frontier. *Int. Associations,* 1972, **24**, 92.

[23]*Ibid.*

[24]Singer, J. D. & Wallace, M. *Op. cit.,* 19.

[25]*Ibid.,* 17.

[26]McClelland, D. H. *Op. cit.,* 191.

[27]Walter, I. *The European Common Market.* New York: Praeger, 1967, 155.

[28]International Atomic Energy Agency. *The agency's program for 1973–78 and budget for 1973.* Austria: IAEA, 1972, 43.

[29]Commission of the European Communities. *Op. cit.,* xix–xxix.

[30]McClelland, D. H. *Op. cit.,* 97.

[31]United Nations Office of Public Information. *Everyman's United Nations: a summary of the activities of the United Nations during the five-year period 1966–1970.* New York: United Nations, 1971, 126.

[32]CERN Public Information Office. *CERN and its laboratories. CERN PIO 71-7.* Geneva: CERN, June 1972, 3.

[33]Ananichev, K. V. Energy problems and the utilization of power sources. *Proc. IIASA planning conf. on energy systems.* Laxenburg, Austria: International Institute for Applied Systems Analysis (IIASA), 1973, 238.

[34]*Ibid.,* 238–239. Reprinted by permission.

[35]International Atomic Energy Agency. *Op. cit.,* 115.

[36]Ananichev, K. V. *Op. cit.,* 240.

[37]Marchetti, C. Hydrogen and energy. *Chem. Economy & Engineering Rev.,* 1973, **5**(1), 7–25.

[38]Evan, W. M. *Op. cit.,* 92.

[39]Meadows, D. H. *Testimony before the Education Committee of the Massachusetts Great and General Court on behalf of House Bill 3787,* Mar. 31, 1971.
Note: Later estimates differ somewhat from the above as shown in D. L. Meadows, W. W. Behrens, III., D. H. Meadows, R. F. Naill, J. Randers, & E. K. Zahn. *Dynamics of growth in a finite world.* Cambridge, Mass.: Wright-Allen Press, 1974, 372–373.

[40]Faltermayer, E. Metals: the warning signals are up. *Fortune,* 1972, **86**(4), 109–111.

[41]Meadows, D. H. *Op. cit.,* 5.

[42]Hubbert, M. K. The energy resources of the earth. *Sci. Amer.,* 1971, **224**(3), 64, 68.

[43]*Ibid.,* 64.

[44]Ward, B. & Dubos, R. *Op. cit.,* 196.

[45]Water Resources Department. *Quality of surface waters in Hungary (map).* Budapest: NWA Water Resources Center, 1972.

[46]International Atomic Energy Agency. *Op. cit.,* 129.

[47]Daw, H. T. The impact of radiological burden on health. *Proc. IIASA planning conf. on medical systems.* Laxenburg, Austria: International Institute for Applied Systems Analysis (IIASA), 1973, 111.

[48]Joint Working Party. *Global ocean research. Reports on marine science affairs.* Geneva: World Meteorological Organization, Report No. 1, 1970.

[49]United Nations Office of Public Information. *Everyman's United Nations: a complete handbook of the activities and evolution of the United Nations during its first twenty years, 1945–1965.* (8th ed.) *Op. cit.,* 18.

[50]Buchanan, W. & Cantril, H. *How nations see each other.* Urbana: Univ. of Illinois Press, 1953.
Cf. also Klineberg, O. *Tensions affecting international understanding.* New York: Social Science Research Council, 1950.

[51]Buchanan, W. & Cantril, H. *Op. cit.,* 93. Reprinted by permission.

[52]Holsti, O. R. *Perceptions of time, perceptions of alternatives, and patterns of communication as factors in crisis decision-making.* Stanford, Calif.: Stanford Univ., Studies in International Conflict and Integration, 1964.

[53]United Nations Office of Public Information. *Everyman's United Nations: a complete handbook of the activities and evolution of the United Nations during its first twenty years, 1945–1965.* (8th ed.) *Op. cit.,* 539.

[54]Joint Working Party. *Op. cit.,* 3.

[55]International Atomic Energy Agency. *Op. cit.,* 83.

[56]UNESCO and International Council of Scientific Unions. *UNISIST. Study report on the feasibility of a world science information system.* Paris: UNESCO, 1971, 79–82, 91.

[57]*Ibid.,* 56. © Unesco 1971. Reprinted by permission.

[58]*Ibid.,* 72. © Unesco 1971. Reprinted by permission.

[59]Gould, W. L. & Barkun, M. *International law and the social sciences.* Princeton, N.J.: Princeton Univ. Press, 1970, 176–247.

[60]*Ibid.,* 187.

[61]*Ibid.,* 186–187.

[62]*Ibid.,* 206–207.

[63]*Ibid.,* 200.

[64]International Atomic Energy Agency. *Op. cit.*

[65]Evan, W. M. *Op. cit.,* 92.

[66]Gould, W. L. & Barkun, M. *Op. cit.,* 183.

[67]*Ibid.,* 190.

[68]Hawkes, J. & Wooley, L. *Prehistory and the beginnings of civilization.* New York: Harper & Row, 1963.
Also Pareti, L. *The ancient world.* New York: Harper & Row, 1965.

[69]UNESCO and International Council of Scientific Unions. *Op. cit.,* 85.

[70]*Ibid.,* 102.

[71]*Ibid.,* 34. © Unesco 1971. Reprinted by permission.

[72]United Nations Office of Public Information. *Everyman's United Nations: a complete handbook of the activities and evolution of the United Nations during its first twenty years, 1945–1965.* (8th ed.) *Op. cit.,* 515.

[73]International Atomic Energy Agency. *Op. cit.,* 83.

[74]UNESCO and International Council of Scientific Unions. *Op. cit.,* 54.

[75]Joint Working Party. *Op. cit.,* 43.

[76]International Atomic Energy Agency. *Op. cit.,* 84.

[77]Singer, J. D. *Op. cit.,* 28.

[78]United Nations Office of Public Information. *Everyman's United Nations: a complete handbook of the activities and evolution of the United Nations during its first twenty years, 1945–1965.* (8th ed.) *Op. cit.,* 4.

[79]Etzioni, A. *Op. cit.,* 583–586.

[80]Morgenthau, H. J. *Politics among nations.* (3d ed.) New York: Knopf, 1960.

[81]*Ibid.,* 531.

[82]Wall, E. H., Hammes, C. L., & Wilberforce, Lord. *Op. cit.,* xii. Reprinted by permission.

[83]United Nations Office of Public Information. *Everyman's United Nations: a summary of the activities of the United Nations during the five year period 1966–1970. Op. cit.,* 198.

[84]Ananichev, K. V. *Op. cit.,* 238–239.

[85]Revelle, R. Will there be enough food? *Science,* 1974, **184,** 1135.

[86]Revelle, R. Food and population. *Sci. Amer.,* 1974, **231**(3), 166.

[87]Freedman, R. & Berelson, B. The human population. *Sci. Amer.,* 1974, **231**(3), 31.

[88]Coale, A. J. The history of the human population. *Sci. Amer.,* Sept. 1974, **231**(3), 51. Reprinted by permission of *Scientific American.*

[89]*Ibid.,* 41–42.

[90]Revelle, R. Food and population. *Op. cit.,* 161.

[91]Demeny, P. The populations of the underdeveloped countries. *Sci. Amer.,* 1974, **231**(3), 149–152.

[92]United Nations Office of Public Information. *Everyman's United Nations: a summary of the activities of the United Nations during the five-year period 1966–1970. Op. cit.,* 75.

[93]McNamara, R. S. *World Bank/IDA annual report, 1973.* Washington: International Bank for Reconstruction and Development and International Development Association, 1973, 18.

[94]Holden, C. World population: U.N. on the move but grounds for optimism are scant. *Science,* 1974, **183**, 833–836.

[95]Westoff, C. F. The populations of the developed countries. *Sci. Amer.,* Sept. 1974, **231**(3), 113–114. Reprinted by permission of *Scientific American.*

[96]*Ibid.,* 117–118.

[97]Freedman, R. & Berelson, B. *Op. cit.,* 35.

[98]Coale, A. J. *Op. cit.,* 51.

[99]Holden, C. *Op. cit.,* 833.

[100]Mead, M. World population: world responsibility. *Science,* 27 Sept. 1974, **185,** 1113. Copyright 1974 by the American Association for the Advancement of Science. Reprinted by permission.

[101]Etzioni, A. *Op. cit.,* 570.

[102]*The Europa year book, 1973, a world survey.* Vol. 1. *Op. cit.,* 275–276.

[103]McNamara, R. S. *Op. cit.,* 35–36.

[104]McNamara, R. S. *International Finance Corporation 1973 annual report.* Washington, D.C.: International Finance Corporation, 1973, 17–21.

[105]McNamara, R. S. *World Bank/IDA annual report, 1975.* Washington, D.C.: International Bank for Reconstruction and Development and International Development Association, 1975, 5, 136–139.

[106]McNamara, R. S. *World Bank/IDA annual report, 1973. Op. cit.,* 15–16.

[107]McNamara, R. S. *International Finance Corporation 1973 annual report. Op. cit.,* 6.

[108]United Nations Office of Public Information. *Everyman's United Nations: a complete handbook of the activities and evolution of the United Nations during its first twenty years, 1945–1965.* (8th ed.) *Op. cit.,* 431–432.

[109]Knauss, J. A. Marine science and the 1974 law of the sea conference. *Science,* 1974, **184,** 1335.

[110]United Nations Office of Public Information. *Caracas session of Third United Nations conference on law of the sea,* June 20–Aug. 29, 1974. Unpublished paper.

[111]United Nations Office of Public Information. *Everyman's United Nations: a complete handbook of the activities and evolution of the United Nations during its first twenty years, 1945–1965.* (8th ed.) *Op. cit.,* 325.

[112]United Nations Office of Public Information. *Everyman's United Nations: a summary of the activities of the United Nations during the five-year period 1966–1970. Op. cit.,* 128–130.

[113]United Nations Office of Public Information. *Report of the United Nations conference on the human environment, Stockholm, 5–16 June, 1972.* (A/Conf. 48/14/Rev 1.) New York: United Nations, 1973, 3.

[114]United Nations Office of Public Information. *Everyman's United Nations: a summary of the activities of the United Nations during the five-year period 1966–1970. Op. cit.,* 232.

[115]United Nations Office of Public Information. *Report of the United Nations conference on the human environment, Stockholm, 5–16 June, 1972.* (A/Conf. 48/14/Rev 1.) *Op. cit.,* 43.

[116]United Nations Office of Public Information. *Everyman's United Nations: a summary of the activities of the United Nations during the five-year period 1966–1970. Op. cit.,* 224–225.

[117]Rattray, K. O. *United Nations third conference on the law of the sea. Statement of activities of the conference during its first and second sessions.* (A/Conf. 62/L.8/Rev. 1, 17 October 1974.) New York: United Nations, 1974.

[118]Brown, L. R. *World without borders.* New York: Random House, Inc. 1972, 308. Copyright © 1972 by Lester R. Brown. Reprinted by permission of Random House.

[119]*Ibid.*

[120]York, H. F. Multiple warhead missiles. *Sci. Amer.,* 1973, **229**(5), 18–27.

[121]Singer, J. D. *Deterrence, arms control, and disarmament.* Columbus: Ohio State Univ. Press, 1962, 12–15.

[122]*Ibid.,* 192–237.

[123]Myrdal, A. The international control of disarmament. *Sci. Amer.,* October 1974, **231**(4), 27. Reprinted by permission of *Scientific American.*

[124]United Nations Office of Public Information. *Everyman's United Nations: a summary of the activities of the United Nations during the five-year period 1966–1970. Op. cit.,* 152–153.

[125]Samuelson, P. A. *Economics.* (8th ed.) New York: McGraw-Hill, 1970, 622–625.

[126]*Ibid.,* 628–629.

[127]*Ibid.,* 645–667.

[128]*Ibid.,* 630.

[129]*Ibid.,* 684.

[130]*Ibid.,* 687–688.

[131]*Ibid.,* 698–699.

[132]*Ibid.,* 703.

[133]Holsti, O. R. & North, R. C. The history of human conflict. In E. B. McNeil (Ed.). *The nature of human conflict.* Englewood Cliffs, N.J.: Prentice-Hall, 1965, 155–156. Reprinted by permission.

[134]*Ibid.,* 158–171.

[135]*Ibid.,* 161.

[136]*Ibid.,* 169–170. Reprinted by permission.

[137]*Ibid.,* 169.

[138]North, R. C. The behavior of nation-states: problems of conflict and integration. In M. A. Kaplan (Ed.). *New approaches to international relations.* New York: St. Martin's Press, 1968, 343–346.

[139]Singer, J. D. & Small, M. *The wages of war: 1816–1965.* New York: Wiley, 1972.

[140]*Ibid.,* 376–378.

[141]*Ibid.,* 16.

[142]*Ibid.,* 374–375. Reprinted by permission.

[143]Haas, M. *International conflict.* Indianapolis: Bobbs-Merrill, 1974.

[144]*Ibid.,* 357.

[145]*Ibid.,* 91–96.

[146]*Ibid.,* 101–106.

[147]*Ibid.,* 105–125.

[148]*Ibid.,* 126–157.

[149]*Ibid.,* 456–460.

[150]*Ibid.,* 174–179.

[151]*Ibid.,* 172–174.

[152]*Ibid.,* 179–184.

[153]*Ibid.,* 185–240.

[154]*Ibid.,* 461.

[155]*Ibid.,* 465–466. Reprinted by permission.

[156]*Ibid.,* 328–329.

[157]*Ibid.,* 359–453.

[158]*Ibid.,* 467.

[159]*Ibid.,* 467–468. Reprinted by permission.

[160]Gould, W. L. & Barkun, M. *Op. cit.,* 200–201.

[161]United Nations Office of Public Information. *Everyman's United Nations: a complete handbook of the activities and evolution of the United Nations during its first twenty years, 1945–1965.* (8th ed.) *Op. cit.,* 450–463.

[162]Singer, J. D. & Wallace, M. *Op. cit.*, 520–521. © World Peace Foundation. Reprinted by permission of University of Wisconsin Press.

[163]*Ibid.*, 545.

[164]Singer, J. D. & Small, M. Alliance aggregation and the onset of war, 1815–1945. In J. D. Singer (Ed.). *Quantitative international politics.* New York: Free Press, 1968, 247–286.

[165]Etzioni, A. *Op. cit.*, 587.

[166]*Ibid.*, 588.

[167]Singer, J. D. & Wallace, M. *Inter-governmental organization and the preservation of peace, 1816–1965: a preliminary examination.* Ann Arbor: Univ. of Michigan, Mental Health Research Institute, Communication No. 235, December 1968, 31–32. Reprinted by permission.

[168]Shoup, P. Communism, nationalism and the growth of the communist community of nations after World War II. *Amer. pol. Sci. Rev.*, 1962, **56,** 886–898.

[169]Etzioni, A. *Op. cit.*, 561–563.

[170]*Ibid.*, 575–576.

[171]*Ibid.*, 573–574.

[172]Etzioni, A. The dialectics of supranational unification. *Amer. pol. Sci. Rev.*, 1962, **56,** 929–935.

[173]Evan, W. M. *Op. cit.*, 97. Reprinted by permission.

[174]Etzioni, A. *The active society. Op. cit.*, 575.

[175]Deutsch, K. W., Burrell, S. A., Kann, R. A., Lee, M., Jr., Lichterman, M., Lindgren, R. E., Loewenheim, F. L., & Van Wagenen, R. W. *Op. cit.*

[176]*Ibid.*, 70–79.

[177]*Ibid.*, 38.

[178]*Ibid.*, 119–120. Copyright © 1957 by Princeton University Press. A publication of the Center for World Political Institutions, Princeton University. Reprinted by permission of Princeton University Press.

[179]*Ibid.*, 46–58.

[180]*Ibid.*, 65.

[181]Anon. European community: pragmatic is the word for the new "Europeans." *Science,* 1974, **184,** 961–962.

[182]Singer, J. D. The global system and its sub-systems. *Op. cit.*, 28.

[183]Etzioni, A. The active society. *Op. cit.*, 580-581.

[184]Deutsch, K. W., Burrell, S. A., Kann, R. A., Lee, M., Jr., Lichterman, M., Lindgren, R. E., Loewenheim, F. L., & Van Wagenen, R. W. *Op. cit.*, 59–65.

[185]Guetzkow, H. Simulations in international relations. In W. D. Coplin (Ed.). *Simulation in the study of politics.* Chicago: Markham, 1968, 9–10.

[186]Singer, J. D. Data-making in international relations. *Behav. Sci.*, 1965, **10,** 69. Reprinted by permission.

[187]*Ibid.*, 77.

[188]Hermann, C. F. Validation problems in games and simulations with special reference to models of international politics. *Behav. Sci.*, 1967, **12,** 226. Reprinted by permission.

[189]Goldhamer, H. & Speier, H. Some observations on political gaming. *World Politics,* 1959, **1,** 71–83.

[190]Bloomfield, L. P. & Whaley, B. The political-military exercise: a progress report. *ORBIS,* 1965, **8,** 854–870.

[191]*Ibid.*, 856.
Cf. also Bloomfield, L. P. & Padleford, N. J. Three experiments in political gaming. *Amer. pol. Sci. Rev.*, 1959, **53,** 1105.

[192]Bloomfield, L. P., Gearin, C. J., & Foster, J. L. *Arms control and local conflict. Vol 2. Anticipating conflict-control policies.* Arms Control Project, Center for International Studies. Cambridge, Mass.: M.I.T. Press, February 1970, C/70–10.

[193]*Ibid.*, 81. Reprinted by permission.

[194]*Ibid.*, 210.

[195]Bloomfield, L. P. & Whaley, B. *Op. cit.*, 869.

[196]Smoker, P. International relations simulations. In H. Guetzkow, P. Kotler, & R. L. Schultz (Eds.). *Simulation in social and administrative science.* Englewood Cliffs, N.J.: Prentice-Hall, 1972, 315. © 1972 by Prentice-Hall, Inc., Englewood Cliffs, New Jersey. Reprinted by permission of Prentice-Hall, Inc., Englewood Cliffs, New Jersey.

[197]Streufert, S. *The tactical and negotiations game: a simulation of local conflict. An analysis of some psychopolitical and applied implications of TNG simulation research.* Washington: Office of Naval Research, Contract N000014-67-A-0115-0002, NR 177-911, Technical Report No. 8, January 1958.

[198]*Ibid.*, 5–6.

[199]*Ibid.*, 6.

[200]Mushakoji, K. The strategies of negotiation: an American-Japanese comparison. In J. A. Laponce & P. Smoker (Eds.). *Experimentation and simulation in political science.* Toronto: Univ. of Toronto Press, 1972, 109–131.

[201]Pilisuk, M., Winter, A., Chapman, R., & Haas, N. Honesty, deceit, and timing in the display of intentions. *Behav. Sci.*, 1967, **12,** 205–215.

[202]McLeod, J. LINK. *Sim. Service Society,* 1972, 2,2:4:3.

[203]Forrester, J. W. *World dynamics.* (2d ed.) Cambridge, Mass.: Wright-Allen, 1973.

[204]*Ibid.*, 19.

[205]Meadows, D. H., Meadows, D. L., Randers, J., & Behrens, W. W., III. *The limits to growth.* New York: Universe Books, 1972, 89.

[206]Forrester, J. W. *Op. cit.*, 22.

[207]*Ibid.*, 36–37. Reprinted, with permission, from *World Dynamics* (2d ed.) by Jay W. Forrester. Copyright © 1973, Wright-Allen Press, Inc., Cambridge, Mass. 02142 USA.

[208]*Ibid.*, 60. Reprinted, with permission, from *World Dynamics* (2d ed.) by Jay W. Forrester. Copyright © 1973, Wright-Allen Press, Inc., Cambridge, Mass. 02142 USA.

[209]*Ibid.*, 67.

[210]*Ibid.*, 94. Reprinted, with permission, from *World Dynamics* (2d ed.) by Jay W. Forrester. Copyright © 1973, Wright-Allen Press, Inc., Cambridge, Mass. 02142 USA.

[211]Meadows, D. H., Meadows, D. L., Randers, J., & Behrens, W. W., III. *Op. cit.*, 157–161.

[212]*Ibid.*, 163–164.

[213]*Ibid.*, 22. *The limits to growth: a report for The Club of Rome's project on the predicament of mankind,* by Donella H. Meadows, Dennis L. Meadows, Jorgen Randers, William W. Behrens, III. A Potomac Associates book published by Universe Books, New York, 1972. Graphics by Potomac Associates. Reprinted with permission.

[214]Jahoda, M. Postscript on social change. In H. S. D. Cole, C. Freeman, M. Jahoda, & K. L. R. Pavitt (Eds.). *Models of doom.* New York: Universe Books, 1973, 215. Reprinted by permission.

[215]Cole, H. S. D. The structure of the world models. In H. S. D. Cole, C. Freeman, M. Jahoda, & K. L. R. Pavitt (Eds.). *Models of doom.* New York: Universe Books, 1973, 27–32. Cf. also Jahoda, M. Postscript on social change. *Op. cit.*, 210–215.

[216]Ridker, R. G. To grow or not to grow: that's not the relevant question. *Science,* 1973, **182,** 1315.

[217]Meadows, D. H., Meadows, D. L., Randers, J., & Behrens, W. W., III. A response to Sussex. In H. S. D. Cole, C. Freeman, M. Jahoda, & K. L. R. Pavitt (Eds.). *Models of doom.* New York: Universe Books, 1973, 232.

[218]Boyd, R. World dynamics: a note. *Science,* 11 Aug. 1972, **177,** 516.

[219]Freeman, C. Malthus with a computer. In H. S. D. Cole, C. Freeman, M. Jahoda, & K. L. R. Pavitt (Eds.). *Models of doom*. New York: Universe Books, 1973, 8–9. Reprinted by permission.

[220]Ridker, R. G. *Op. cit.*, 1315–1316.

[221]Boyd, R. *Op. cit.*, 517–518.

[222]*Ibid.*, 518-519. Copyright 1972 by the American Association for the Advancement of Science. Reprinted by permission.

[223]Cole, H. S. D. & Curnow, R. C. An evaluation of the world models. In H. S. D. Cole, C. Freeman, M. Jahoda, & K. L. R. Pavitt (Eds.). *Models of doom*. New York: Universe Books, 1973, 110–131.

[224]Burns, J. R. & Malone, D. W. Optimization techniques applied to the Forrester model of the world. *IEEE Trans. on Systems, Man, & Cybernetics,* 1974, SMC-4, 164–171.

[225]Burnett, R. A. & Dionne, P. J. GLOBE6: a multiregion interactive world simulation. *Simulation,* June 1973, 192–197.

[226]Randers, J. DDT movement in the global environment. In D. L. Meadows & D. H. Meadows (Eds.). *Toward global equilibrium: collected papers*. Cambridge, Mass.: Wright-Allen Press, 1973, 49–83.

Also Anderson, A. A. & Anderson, J. M. System simulation to identify environmental research needs: mercury contamination. In D. L. Meadows & D. H. Meadows (Eds.). *Toward global equilibrium: collected papers*. Cambridge, Mass.: Wright-Allen Press, 1973, 85–115.

Also Behrens, W. W., III. The dynamics of natural resource utilization. In D. L. Meadows & D. H. Meadows (Eds.). *Toward global equilibrium: collected papers*. Cambridge, Mass.: Wright-Allen Press, 1973, 141–164.

Also Randers, J. & Meadows, D. L. The dynamics of solid waste generation. In D. L. Meadows & D. H. Meadows (Eds.). *Toward global equilibrium: collected papers*. Cambridge, Mass.: Wright-Allen Press, 1973, 165–211.

[227]Anderson, A. A. & Anderson, J. M. *Op. cit.*

[228]*Ibid.*, 98–115.

[229]Sellers, W. D. A global climatic model based on the energy balance of the earth-atmosphere system. *J. appl. Meteorol.,* 1969, **8,** 392–400.

[230]*Ibid.*, 399. Reprinted by permission.

[231]Zvetanov, P. Energy system: econometric modeling demand and supply. *Proc. IIASA planning conf. on energy systems*. Laxenburg, Austria: International Institute for Applied Systems Analysis (IIASA), 1973, 216–222.

[232]Desai, M. An econometric model of the world tin economy, 1948–1961. In J. M. Dutton & W. H. Starbuck (Eds.). *Computer simulation of human behavior*. New York: Wiley, 1971, 490–511.

[233]Richardson, L. F. (Ed. by Q. Wright & C. C. Lienau.) *Statistics of deadly quarrels*. Pittsburgh: Boxwood Press, 1960.

[234]Kecskemeti, P. Arms and insecurity: statistics of deadly quarrels. *Science,* 1960, **132,** 1931–1932.

Cf. also Rapoport, A. Lewis F. Richardson's mathematical theory of war. *Gen. Systems,* 1957, **2,** 55–91.

[235]Horvath, W. J. & Foster, C. C. Stochastic models of war alliances. *J. conflict Resolut.,* 1963, **7,** 110–116.

[236]Voevodsky, J. Modeling the dynamics of warfare. In D. E. Knight, H. W. Curtis, & L. J. Fogel (Eds.). *Cybernetics, simulation, and conflict resolution*. New York: Spartan Books, 1971, 145–167.

[237]Singer, J. D. & Hinomoto, H. Inspecting for weapons production. *J. Peace Res.,* 1965, **1,** 18–38.

[238]Clemens, W. C., Jr. A propositional analysis of the international relations theory in TEMPER: a computer simulation

of cold war conflict. In W. D. Coplin (Ed.). *Simulation in the study of politics*. Chicago: Markham, 1968, 59–104.

[239]*Ibid.*, 78–94.

[240]Smoker, P. *Op. cit.*, 310.

[241]Clemens, W. C., Jr. *Op. cit.*, 64–65.

[242]Benson, O. A simple diplomatic game. In J. N. Rosenau (Ed.). *International politics and foreign policy*. New York: Free Press, 1961.

[243]Noel, R. C. Inter-nation simulation participants' manual. In H. Guetzkow, C. F. Alger, R. A. Brody, R. C. Noel, & R. C. Snyder (Eds.). *Simulation in international relations*. Englewood Cliffs, N.J.: Prentice-Hall, 1963, 43–68.

Also Noel, R. C. Evolution of the inter-nation simulation. In H. Guetzkow, C. F. Alger, R. A. Brody, R. C. Noel, & R. C. Snyder (Eds.). *Simulation in international relations*. Englewood Cliffs, N.J.: Prentice-Hall, 1963, 69–102.

[244]Guetzkow, H. A use of simulation in the study of inter-nation relations. In H. Guetzkow, C. F. Alger, R. A. Brody, R. C. Noel, & R. C. Snyder (Eds.).*Simulation in international relations*. Englewood Cliffs, N.J.: Prentice-Hall, 1963, 29.

[245]Noel, R. C. Evolution of the inter-nation simulation. *Op. cit.*, 77. Reprinted by permission.

[246]Brody, R. A. Some systemic effects of the spread of nuclear weapons technology. *J. conflict Resolut.,* 1963, **7,** 663–753.

[247]Guetzkow, H. Structural programs and their relations to free activities within the inter-nation simulation. In H. Guetzkow, C. F. Alger, R. A. Brody, R. C. Noel, & R. C. Snyder (Eds.). *Simulation in international relations*. Englewood Cliffs, N.J.: Prentice-Hall, 1963, 147.

[248]Guetzkow, H. Simulations in international relations. *Op. cit.*, 15.

[249]*Ibid.*, 14.

[250]Alker, H. R., Jr. Decision-makers' environments in the inter-nation simulation. In W. D. Coplin (Ed.). *Simulation in the study of politics*. Chicago: Markham, 1968, 41.

[251]Guetzkow, H. Structural programs and their relations to free activities within the inter-nation simulation. *Op. cit.*, 135.

[252]Alker, H. R., Jr. *Op. cit.*, 50–51.

[253]Brody, R. A. *Op. cit.*, 663–753.

[254]*Ibid.*, 689–691.

[255]*Ibid.*, 702.

[256]*Ibid.*, 732–742.

[257]Macrae, J. & Smoker, P. A Vietnam simulation. *J. Peace Res.,* 1967, **1,** 1–24.

[258]*Ibid.*, 12.

[259]*Ibid.*, 5.

[260]Guetzkow, H. Simulations in international relations. *Op. cit.*, 20. Reprinted by permission.

[261]Hermann, C. F. & Hermann, M. G. An attempt to simulate the outbreak of World War I. In H. Guetzkow, P. Kotler, & R. L. Schultz (Eds.). *Simulation in social and administrative science*. Englewood Cliffs, N.J.: Prentice-Hall, 1972, 341. © 1972 by Prentice-Hall, Inc., Englewood Cliffs, New Jersey. Reprinted by permission of Prentice-Hall, Inc., Englewood Cliffs, New Jersey.

[262]*Ibid.*, 355–356. © 1972 by Prentice-Hall, Inc., Englewood Cliffs, New Jersey. Reprinted by permission of Prentice-Hall, Inc., Englewood Cliffs, New Jersey.

[263]*Ibid.*, 361.

[264]Guetzkow, H. Some correspondences between simulations and "realities" in international relations. In H. Guetzkow, P. Kotler, & R. L. Schultz (Eds.). *Simulation in social and administrative science*. Englewood Cliffs, N.J.: Prentice-Hall, 1972, 697.

[265]*Ibid.*, 699–710.

266*Ibid.*, 740–741. Reprinted by permission.

267Alker, H. R., Jr. & Brunner, R. D. Simulating international conflict: a comparison of three approaches. *Internat. Studies Quart.*, 1969, **13**, 70–110.

268Smoker, P. International processes simulation: a description. In J. A. Laponce & P. Smoker (Eds.). *Experimentation and simulation in political science.* Toronto: Univ. of Toronto Press, 1972, 315–365.

269*Ibid.*, 316.

270*Ibid.* Reprinted by permission.

271Pool, I. de S. & Kessler, A. The Kaiser, the Tsar, and the computer: information processing in a crisis. *Amer. behav. Sci.*, 1965, **8**(9), 31–38.

272*Ibid.*, 31.

273Mesarović, M. D. & Pestel, E. C. A goal-seeking and regionalized model for analysis of critical world relationships: the conceptual foundation. *Kybernetes*, 1972, **1**, 79–85.

274Mesarović, M., Pestel, E., Hughes, B., Shook, T., Pestel, R., Gille, P., & Yoshii, S. *An interactive decision stratum for the multilevel world model.* Hanover, Germany: Tech. Univ. of Hanover, Multilevel World Model Project, Report No. 3, January 1973.

275*Ibid.*, 2.

276*Ibid.*, 3.

277Rechenmann, F. *Conversational use of multi-layer decision models.* Hanover, Germany: Tech. Univ. of Hanover, Multilevel Regionalized World Modeling Project, 1974.

278Mesarović, M., Pestel, E., Hughes, B., Shook, T., Pestel, R., Gille, P., & Yoshii, S. *Op. cit.*

279Klabbers, J. H. G. *Human computer decision-making: notes concerning the interactive model.* Hanover, Germany: Tech. Univ. of Hanover, Multilevel Regionalized World Modeling Project, 1974.

280Mesarović, M., Pestel, E., Hughes, B., Shook, T., Pestel, R., Gille, P., & Yoshii, S. *Op. cit.*

281Blankenship, G., Gille, P., Hickman, B., Klein, L., Kominek, K., McCarthy, M., Mesarović, E., Pestel, R., Shook, T., & Shuttic, G. *Construction of regionalized world economic model.* Hanover, Germany: Tech. Univ. of Hanover, Multilevel Regionalized World Modeling Project, 1974.

282*Ibid.*, 20–34.

283*Ibid.*, 57.

284Oehmen, K. H. & Paul, W. *Population model.* Hanover, Germany: Tech. Univ. of Hanover, Multilevel World Model Project, 1974.

285Bauerschmidt, R., Bossil, H., Chu, N., Denton, R., Hughes, B. B., & Maier, H. H. *Energy models.* Hanover, Germany: Tech. Univ. of Hanover, Multilevel Regionalized World Modeling Project, 1974.

286Hughes, B., Mesarović, M., & Pestel, E. *World oil: model description and scenario assessment.* Hanover, Germany: Tech. Univ. of Hanover, Multilevel Regionalized World Modeling Project, 1974.

287*Ibid.*, II-1.

288*Ibid.*, I-4.

289*Ibid.*, II-7.

290*Ibid.*, II-21–II-22.

291*Ibid.*, II-48.

292Leontief, W. *et al. The future of the world economy.* New York: Oxford Univ. Press, 1977.

293Sokolow, V. *On some major systems' properties.* Laxenburg, Austria: International Institute for Applied Systems Analysis (IIASA), 1974, 13.

294Mar, B. W. Where resources and environmental simulation models are going wrong. *Proc. IIASA planning conf. on ecol. sys.* Laxenburg, Austria: International Institute for Applied Systems Analysis (IIASA), 1973, 57.

295Hardy, T. *The dynasts.* New York: Macmillan Publishing Co., 1944, 9. Copyright, 1904, by the Macmillan Company. Copyright, 1931, by Florence E. Hardy. Reprinted by permission of the Trustees of the Hardy Estate and Macmillan London and Basingstoke.

Conclusions

In this book I have tried to do a number of things: show that a general theory of living systems can be constructed; bring together enough of the important relevant research to make it clear that the facts at each level conform to a pattern which also fits the other levels; point to gaps of knowledge that need to be filled; and emphasize methods which make possible comparisons across the levels and investigations of interrelationships among them. In doing this, I attempt to clarify the need for a unification of science. Also, I hope to demonstrate the potential practical value of such general theory.

All nature is a continuum. The endless complexity of life is organized into patterns which repeat themselves—theme and variations—at each level of system. These similarities and differences are proper concerns for science. From the ceaseless streaming of protoplasm to the many-vectored activities of supranational systems, there are continuous flows through living systems as they maintain their highly organized steady states.

A mutuality exists among the components of a system. Each makes its contribution toward the processes of the whole and receives in return a portion of the benefits derived from those activities. This mutual interrelationship extends across the levels. Cells and organs of the body receive nourishment from the food which the organism obtains from its suprasystem; the employees of a firm do work and are paid from that company's profits; and the member countries of a supranational system receive the benefits which flow from the communal activities to which each one con-

tributes. The larger, higher-level systems have emergent capabilities which enable them to accomplish things that systems at lower levels cannot achieve. All the components and subcomponents of these systems, however, may profit from these accomplishments. Often, but not always, the benefits of higher levels of systems organization are distributed to all the component systems at lower levels. Sometimes the benefits are not equitably distributed. If the inequity is gross enough and if the pathology continues long enough, the total system will decay and finally terminate.

The general theory of living systems presented in this book is eclectic. It ties together past discoveries from many disciplines and provides an outline into which new findings can be fitted. It is to be expected, and indeed hoped, that my formulation will be supplanted by more advanced theories as systems science progresses, using more adequate methods of observation, measurement, and theory construction. In this book I have described and evaluated relevant past theories. In like manner, if a cumulative science of systems is to develop, my theory should be critically taken into account by those who attempt in the future to improve on it.

The fit between the conceptual system and the empirical findings reported in this book appears poorest at the highest two or three levels. Essays and naturalistic observations abound at these levels, but good controls and sophisticated quantification are rare. Fortunately, however, more and more careful, quantitative researches are appearing. As more reliable methods are employed to investigate organizations, societies, and supranational systems, the findings may possibly give better support to my conceptual system.

In its most embracing form, general systems theory is a conceptual metatheory. It uses abstract mathematics, logic, and methodological analysis to determine how to construct any sort of theory about any sort of system—conceptual, abstracted, or concrete.[1] It deals with units and relationships, in conceptual systems, abstracted systems, or concrete systems (see pages 16 to 22). The general living systems theory presented in this book is a scientific theory and is therefore less general than a metatheory. It is not about how to form theories. Rather, it is a specific conceptualization which can be confirmed or disconfirmed by empirical observations. In preceding chapters I have discussed many such observations. Some can be interpreted as supporting certain hypotheses of my theory.

The conceptual system outlined in this book concerns concrete systems that exist in physical space-time and have the constraints that go with such existence. It does not, however, relate to all possible such concrete systems. Rather, it deals with a subset of such concrete systems—a very limited, but a very fascinating, subset—the living systems. Also, it concerns various artifacts or prostheses which have been created by living systems but which are themselves nonliving systems.

1. Some basic concepts of general living systems theory in retrospect

In the light of the detailed review of facts about the various levels of living systems in the preceding chapters, let us reevaluate the basic concepts of my theory:

1.1 Concrete systems The sciences of living systems will develop most effectively if all such systems are conceptualized as concrete rather than abstracted systems. Their structures exist in specific locations in three-dimensional physical space. Processes of their subsystems produce changes over time. Life is process, continual change. Throughout this book I have said much more about process than structure. Nevertheless, all process occurs in a structure, and science has now advanced to the point where we can identify, with only 7 exceptions out of 133, the components which carry out the 19 subsystem processes at all 7 levels of living systems (see Table 13-1). In this book I have shown that one can deal with the subject matter of both biological and social science in terms of concrete systems. It has not been necessary to conceptualize the higher levels of living systems as abstracted systems, even though many social scientists do so. A unified view of all the levels has been achieved.

In all general scientific theories the same dimensionality must be used across all the cases studied, or the necessary transformations of all units of measurement employed to this basic dimensionality must be known. If this were not true, the theory would be only a set of special theories without precisely known interrelationships among all the concepts. It has been possible in most cases to measure the phenomena I have dealt with in the dimensions of physical space-time using the centimeter-gram-second metric system, or dimensions of spaces which have known relationships or transformations to these dimensions. The chief exception is the *meaning* of communications, a very important dimension which cannot yet be quantified in such units (see pages 11 and 12). Most of the other data discussed in this book can be measured in units of the metric system as applied to specific locations in physical space-time. Such procedure unifies the data from all levels and types of living systems.

Many modern social scientists are helping to perpetuate an unfortunate and pervasive confusion between structure and function. This leads to a series of misunderstandings and ambiguities. The fact that a certain pattern of function occurs repeatedly over time does not justify calling it a "structure." Functionalists sometimes resist the use of space-time coordinates because they seem static. This is a misapprehension. One must first establish such coordinates before observing or measuring any form of motion, flux, or process.

Subjectivists may resist space-time coordinates because their private experience is not usually presented to them on such coordinates. This is not a sufficient reason for neglecting the useful exercise of pinpointing phenomena in such coordinates whenever possible. Some psychologists and social scientists feel that there is much more motion or activity in individual social and psychological relationships, groups, and social systems than in biological organisms. They conclude, therefore, that space-time coordinates are less important in social science than in biology, since components can be almost anywhere at any time. A thorough understanding of biological organisms confutes this. Cells seethe with activity. White cells in the bloodstream, for example, are migrant nomads.

When structure and function are confused, frequently boundaries seem to be only arbitrary choices of the scientist involved. They are imposed by the observer, like the dotted construction lines in some geometric proofs. If analyses are not made with boundaries of systems, subsystems, or components conceptually located at the place where they are empirically found to be in natural systems, the boundaries may well cut across important processes of the systems. It can be difficult or impossible to keep in mind the many interrelationships within the system which arbitrarily placed boundaries can interrupt. At no point in this book has it been necessary to confuse structure in three-dimensional space with process over time to describe or analyze phenomena.

1.2 Living systems   The living systems discussed in this book are all viewed as concrete systems having the following characteristics (see page 18):

(*a*) They are open systems, with significant inputs, throughputs, and outputs of various sorts of matter-energy and information. Processing these is all they do—a deceptively simple fact not widely recognized by the scientists who study them.

(*b*) They maintain a steady state of negentropy even though entropic changes occur in them, as they do everywhere else. This they do by taking in inputs of foods or fuels, matter-energy higher in complexity or organization or negentropy, *i.e.*, lower in entropy, than their outputs. The difference permits them to restore their own energy and repair breakdowns in their own organized structure. In living systems many substances are produced as well as broken down; gradients are set up as well as destroyed; learning as well as forgetting occurs. To go uphill against entropy in this manner, such systems must be open and have continuous inputs of matter-energy and information. Walling off living systems to prevent exchanges across their boundaries results in death. Since the second law of thermodynamics is an arrow pointing along the one-way road of the inevitable forward movement which we call time, entropy will always increase in walled-off living systems. The consequent disorganization will ultimately result in the termination of the system.

(*c*) They have more than a certain minimum degree of complexity.

(*d*) They either contain genetic material composed of deoxyribonucleic acid (DNA), presumably descended from some primordial DNA common to all life, or have a charter. One of these is the template—the original "blueprint" or "program"—of their structure and process from the moment of their origin.

(*e*) They are composed largely of an aqueous suspension of macromolecules, proteins constructed from about 20 amino acids and other characteristic organic compounds.

(*f*) They have a decider—the essential, critical subsystem which controls the entire system, causing its subsystems and components to interact. Without such interaction under decider control there is no system.

(*g*) They also have certain other specific critical subsystems, or they have symbiotic or parasitic relationships with other living or nonliving systems which carry out the processes of any such subsystem they lack.

(*h*) Their subsystems are integrated together to form actively self-regulating, developing, unitary systems with purposes and goals.

(*i*) They can exist only in a certain environment. Any change in their environment of such variables as temperature, air pressure, hydration, oxygen content of the atmosphere, or intensity of radiation, outside a relatively narrow range which occurs on the surface of the earth, produces stresses to which they cannot adjust. Under such stresses they cannot survive.

1.3 Matter-energy flows   A useful basic strategy for observing and investigating living systems is to trace their inputs, throughputs, and outputs through the various subsystems and components in which they flow in sequence, measuring various variables of those transmissions as they occur.

A wide range of sorts of matter and several sorts of energy are essential in varying amounts for various living systems. Within these systems both matter and energy are transformed constantly into new forms useful within them. How these processes are carried out is the study of the energetics of living systems, a classical subject for scientific investigation.

One special class of matter-energy transmissions of great importance to human living systems at the levels of the group and above consists of human beings, a species of organisms that bring not only matter-energy but also stored information or experience into any system they enter. Though I recognize that they process both matter-energy and information, in this book I have, for simplicity, followed the convention of referring to flows of human beings in higher-level systems as a special sort of matter-energy transmission.

1.4 Information flows   All information flows are sequences of patterns that pass over a channel in space-time, from a transmitter to a receiver. Each pattern is conveyed on a marker, a bundle of matter-energy. The pattern cannot be transmitted unless it is borne on a marker.

The most general form of information flow, seen in all living systems, is communication. At the higher levels of human systems—the level of the group and above—there is a special form, the flow of money, which is one sort of information. It is found only in advanced human societies.

1.5 Negative feedbacks   By multiple examples at each level of living systems I have shown that varia-

TABLE 13-1   Selected Major Components of Each of the 19 Critical Subsystems at Each of the Seven Levels of Living Systems

SUBSYSTEM \ LEVEL	Cell	Organ	Organism	Group	Organization	Society	Supranational System
Reproducer 3.1.1	Chromosome	*None; downwardly dispersed to cell level*	Genitalia	Mating dyad	Group that produces a charter for an organization	Constitutional convention	Supranational system which creates another supranational system
Boundary 3.1.2	Cell membrane	Capsule of viscus	Skin	Sergeant at arms	Guard of an organization's property	Organization of border guards	Supranational organization of border guards
Ingestor 3.2.1	Gap in cell membrane	Input artery of organ	Mouth	Refreshment chairman	Receiving department	Import company	Supranational system officials who operate international ports
Distributor 3.2.2	Endoplasmic reticulum	Blood vessels of organ	Vascular system	Mother who passes out food to family	Driver	Transportation company	United Nations Childrens Fund (UNICEF), which distributes food to needy children
Converter 3.2.3	Enzyme in mitochondrion	Parenchymal cell	Upper gastrointestinal tract	Butcher	Oil refinery operating group	Oil refinery	European Atomic Energy Community (EURATOM), concerned with conversion of atomic energy
Producer 3.2.4	Enzyme in mitochondrion	Parenchymal cell	*Unknown**	Cook	Factory production unit	Factory	World Health Organization (WHO)
Matter-energy storage 3.2.5	Adenosine triphosphate (ATP)	Intercellular fluid	Fatty tissues	Family member who stores food	Stock-room operating group	Warehouse company	International Red Cross, which stores materials for disaster relief
Extruder 3.2.6	Gap in cell membrane	Output vein of organ	Urethra	Cleaning woman	Delivery department	Export company	Component of the International Atomic Energy Agency (IAEA) concerned with waste extrusion
Motor 3.2.7	Microtubule	Muscle tissue of organ	Muscle of legs	*None; laterally dispersed to all members of group who move jointly*	Crew of machine that moves organization personnel	Trucking company	Transport component of the North Atlantic Treaty Organization (NATO)
Supporter 3.2.8	Microtubule	Stroma	Skeleton	Person who physically supports others in group	Group that operates organization's building	National officials who operate public buildings and land	Supranational officials who operate United Nations buildings and land

TABLE 13-1 Selected Major Components of Each of the 19 Critical Subsystems at Each of the Seven Levels of Living Systems (Cont.)

SUBSYSTEM \ LEVEL	Cell	Organ	Organism	Group	Organization	Society	Supranational System
Input transducer 3.3.1	Specialized receptor site of cell membrane	Receptor cell of sense organ	Exteroceptive sense organ	Lookout	Telephone operator group	Foreign news service	News service that brings information into supranational system
Internal transducer 3.3.2	Repressor molecule	Specialized cell of sinoatrial node of heart	Receptor cell that responds to changes in blood states	Group member who reports group states to decider	Inspection unit	Public opinion polling agency	Supranational inspection organization
Channel and net 3.3.3	Cell membrane	Nerve net of organ	Components of neural network	Group member who communicates by signals through the air to other members	Private telephone exchange	National telephone network	Universal Postal Union (UPU)
Decoder 3.3.4	Molecular binding site	Receptor or second-echelon cell of sense organ	Cells in sensory nuclei	Interpreter	Foreign-language translation group	Language-translation unit	Supranational language translation unit
Associator 3.3.5	*Unknown**	*Unknown**	*Unknown**	*None:* laterally dispersed to members who associate for group	*None:* downwardly dispersed to individual persons, organism level	Teaching institution	Supranational university
Memory 3.3.6	*Unknown**	*Unknown**	*Unknown**	Adult in a family	Filing department	Library	United Nations library
Decider 3.3.7	Regulator gene	Sympathetic fiber of sinoatrial node of heart	Part of cerebral cortex	Head of a family	Executive office	Government	Council of Ministers of the European Communities
Encoder 3.3.8	Component producing hormone	Presynaptic region of output neuron of organ	Temporoparietal area of dominant hemisphere of human brain	Person who composes a group statement	Speech-writing department	Press secretary	United Nations Office of Public Information
Output transducer 3.3.9	Presynaptic membrane	Presynaptic region of output neuron of organ	Larynx	Spokesman	Public relations department	Office of national spokesman	Official spokesman of the Warsaw Treaty Organization

NOTE: The components of seven subsystems, identified by an asterisk (*), are as yet unknown.

Animal components are selected in preference to plants, although many components of plants are comparable. If possible, human components are mentioned in preference to components of other types of living systems, although comparable components exist for many other types. When a choice must be made at the level of the group, the family is selected in preference to committees or other sorts of groups because the mating dyad and then the family were the original groups and are still of prime importance. When a selection must be made at the level of the group and above, examples from the United States are given, although there are usually comparable examples in other societies. At the level of the group and above, communication information flows are selected in preference to monetary information flows, since the former sort of flow is found in all types of living systems including human systems; while the latter are limited to only some higher-level systems of human beings.

1029

bles are maintained in steady-state ranges by negative feedbacks. The governance or control of living systems, as matter-energy and information processes go on, with flows from input to output, maintains related variables within steady-state ranges, Negative feedbacks damp down either increases or decreases in a particular variable to maintain its stability. The exact channel through which such a feedback is maintained has in many cases been identified by research which I have discussed in this book. So have the normal value of the variable and the steady-state ranges which the feedback maintains. The energetics of the flow of markers is the same as that of any other matter-energy flow. That is one reason why matter-energy and information flows have similarities, although there are some differences, as the arrangement of Table 1-1 suggests. For instance, there are no matter-energy processes that correspond to encoding and decoding of information. Information flows also convey meaning, which matter-energy flows do not.

1.6 Matter-energy, information, and meaning
Information is the patterning of matter-energy in systems. To the observer of any particular system, the more complex it is, the more information is required to describe it. One can measure precisely not only the matter-energy characteristics of a system but also, using the Shannon information statistic, its complexity, patterning, or organization (see pages 11 to 13 and Note 20, page 43). Thus both matter and form can be measured. The Shannon statistic, $H = \Sigma p_i \log_2 p_i$, is the negative of the measure for entropy. Thus a precise relationship is known of entropy to negentropy to information. We know that $E = mc^2$ states the relation of energy to mass. And energy is one of the five basic state variables of thermodynamics—pressure, temperature, volume, energy, and entropy. (If the values of any three of these variables are known, those of the other two can be calculated.) Consequently, a precise relationship is now known between the measures of matter, energy, and information.

The mass, the amount of energy, and the amount of entropy can all be measured in units of the metric system. The amount of information can be measured by the Shannon statistic (H), which is the negative of entropy. But for a complete measurement of the processes of living systems, another sort of unit, not yet discovered, is essential. This is a unit to quantify the meaning of an information transmission to the system that receives it. Such a measure would identify specific patterns out of all the alternatives in an ensemble. Any one of these specific patterns can be sent in a message from a transmitter over a channel to a receiver. The meaning of that pattern is the change the

information brings about in the actions of that particular receiver, either immediately or later.

At present we must use human beings as meters to measure variables relating to meaning, rather than more objective instruments. People often make distorted observations, and so they are less than satisfactory measuring instruments. A quantification of meaning would have to establish the basic categories or dimensions of meaning. As yet we do not have any reliable way of determining *a posteriori* the categories of meaning and then measuring them objectively.

Whenever possible, the categories of meaning should be determined objectively or empirically *a posteriori* after collection of a sample of all possible messages, rather than *a priori* by the observer. Perhaps computer pattern-recognition programs can analyze phenomena or patterns according to objective criteria and so determine into which categories the total ensemble of possible meanings can be cast. To measure the meaning of information, we must progress from idiosyncratic imposition of observations upon the phenomena to public operations for determining the categories of meaning. When we are able to quantify meaning reliably by such objective methods, systems science will have a new capability of dealing with important variables that it cannot yet measure with precision.

1.7 Levels   The previous chapters are integrated presentations of the current state of our scientific knowledge about seven levels of living systems—cell, organ, organism, group, organization, society, and supranational system. The systems at each of the levels are controlled by a single decider subsystem, which is the most essential of the critical subsystems. The supranational level is the newest—perhaps still in a stage of formation. It is hard to identify a supranational system in existence today with a single unitary decider capable of controlling all the processes and components of the system.

There may be more than seven levels of living systems—for instance, the tissue may exist as a level between the cell and the organ, although there are probably no tissues all of whose cells are controlled by a single decider. Also, some scientists consider the community to be a level between the organization and the society. If there is a level of decision and control higher than that of the organizations in the community—the schools, the banks, the factories, the stores, and so forth—but lower than the level of the society, it may reasonably be considered a separate level. Others will call it simply a higher-echelon organization.

1.8 Subsystems   The 19 critical subsystems essential for life and common to all living systems (see

Table 1-1) are listed in the 19 rows of Table 13-1. The seven levels of living systems appear in its seven columns. This table is derived from the charts of the critical subsystems at the beginning of each chapter from Chap. 6, on cells, through Chap. 12, on supranational systems. In each of the chapters multiple examples of components of most of the subsystems are given. Table 13-1 shows a single example in each square of the chart, *i.e.*, for each subsystem at each level. The chart is less than perfect because a single example often cannot be representative of all existing cases. Some of the principles followed in making the selection are stated in the note below the table.

There are 133 cells in this table. Only three of them indicate that there is no component for that subsystem at that level, its processes probably being dispersed to another level. Seven cells indicate that the component is as yet unknown, but there is still evidence that the subsystem processes are carried out. The fact that such a high percentage of the components which carry out the subsystem processes at all the levels can be identified strongly suggests that every process is carried out by a component or components. The few cases in which the component that performs observed processes is unknown constitute challenges for further basic research. This is particularly true of the associator and memory subsystems. At the levels of the cell, organ, and organism it is not yet known exactly what components do the learning or associating of information and the storing and retrieving of information, although clearly these processes go on. Experimental psychology has emphasized the processes (rather than the structures) of these subsystems more than those of the other subsystems because they are central to human behavior and because research has not yet succeeded in identifying their structural correlates.

If Table 13-1 had concentrated on species other than man, there would be other gaps in this table. It seems likely that some free-living cells and plants do not have all the information processing subsystems (*e.g.,* memory, associator, encoder, and decoder). Many plants and some sessile animals low in the evolutionary scale do not have motor subsystems. Plants need for inputs only the carbon dioxide that surrounds them in the atmosphere and the salts that are in solution in the medium around them.[2] Consequently, they can remain stationary and do not need the information processing subsystems and motors required to forage in the environment or remember where food is located. Only a limited number of plant species make motor ouputs such as reflex responses to information inputs. Animals above the lowest species require food

derived from other organisms and so much have the subsystems needed to find and eat it.

General living systems theory has not achieved its ultimate goal with the simple proof that all living systems have boundaries or ingestor subsystems. We must know more. What different sorts of boundaries and ingestors are there? What is structurally common, and what is different, about all the sorts of boundaries or ingestors? How are their processes the same and different? Which sorts minimize costs or function faster or more efficiently? When such precise facts are known, dependable and important generalizations about subsystems will be possible.

1.9 Cross-level formal identities Chapter 4 lists 173 hypotheses or propositions applicable to two or more levels of living systems, and a good many others could be added without much effort. In that chapter, I also suggest experimental designs for evaluating several of these hypotheses, and in Chap. 5 I report in detail on a study we carried out to evaluate one set of such hypotheses concerned with information input overload.

Some of these hypotheses appear to apply across all levels, and others to only a lesser number. Why this is true is as yet unresolved. Perhaps those which are relevant only to certain levels concern emergent structures or processes which exist at those levels alone and are not found at the others below them. Conceivably, some may apply only to structures or processes characteristic of lower-level systems which do not exist at higher levels.

These hypothesized cross-level formal identities are central to my theory. Their importance derives from the evolutionary conclusion that all living systems arise from a single primordial source by the shred-out process. They are more than poetic analogies, for example, like the ancient metaphor that refers to the captain of a ship or military unit as its head ("captain" being derived from *caput*, the Latin word for "head"). They propose possible rigorous, scientifically testable analogies between different levels of living systems.

Scientists have learned the value of generalizing from one system of a certain type (*e.g.,* a cell or a person) to another. They have advanced beyond that to generalizing from one species or type to another (*e.g.,* from lower mammals to human beings), recognizing of course that types have differences as well as similarities. The further methodological advance to generalizing from one level of living system to another is not yet a general scientific practice. As a result, discoveries made today about the nature of living systems at one level are rarely extended to others. We find comparable subsystems, variables, indicators, pathologies, and even artifacts at all levels. And I have repeatedly demonstrated in this book that experimental or other empirical data collected independently at two or more levels may support a given cross-level hypothesis. Despite this, possible cross-level formal identities are generally ignored by scientists. For example, discoveries in biological science are not being applied to higher-level systems, where much more understanding is needed to solve problems of great human urgency.

Many more years and lifetimes of scientific effort should be devoted to searching for cross-level formal identities and testing them quantitatively. The hope of important payoffs at multiple levels of living systems may provide broadly trained individual scientists and interdisciplinary groups with the incentive to carry out such investigations. Those scientists must first, of course, become convinced that such generalization is feasible, meaningful, and potentially applicable to important problems in the biological and social sciences. Perhaps the comparisons of systems across levels in this book will influence some to carry out such research.

Doing basic studies of cross-level hypotheses may seem like a slow approach to the pressing human problems scientists face today. Yet basic research has been the key to the greatest advances in all the natural sciences. It may well form a more solid grounding for the solution of such problems than the anecdotal individual studies, the naturalistic observations, and the case studies which are so common in the behavioral sciences today. It will be objective research rather than normative evaluation. It will attempt to use comparable dimensions for making measurements at different levels, which is essential if cross-level formal identities are to be confirmed or disconfirmed. It is certainly a tedious, long way around, but it may be the shortest way home to a unified science of complex, large-scale living systems.

1.10   Cross-level similarities in models and simulations   In each chapter which deals with a level of living systems, I have identified three general classes of models—verbal models, mathematical or logical models, and computer simulations. Computers have already proved themselves to be instruments of major importance to systems science because they can be used to simulate systems of great complexity. To simulate a system effectively, one must be able to state precisely, in a form a computer can handle, a number of facts about its input–output characteristics: what kinds of matter-energy and information flow through it, the relationships in space and time of its flows and other processes, and what feedbacks there are. The

next few years are likely to produce great extensions of this technique for studying living systems.

It is interesting to observe the formal similarities of the models and simulations described in the preceding chapters on the various levels of systems. They were developed by independent investigators who rarely referred to, or even knew the details of, similar models and simulations created by specialists at other levels. Nevertheless, several of these simulations have been designed to employ similar mathematical instruments, specifically systems of differential equations with multiple interacting variables including inputs, throughputs, and outputs. Frequently these transmissions are clearly recognizable as either matter-energy or information flows. Like the arguments for general living systems theory derived from cross-level formal identities, the use by independent investigators of similar formal structures in their simulations is another strong argument for the usefulness of general theory that deals with similarities across levels.

If it is possible to use the same simulation at more than one level, there is a cross-level formal identity. Forrester, for example, has employed the same general model for two levels—the organization and the supranational system.[3] He did this to study problems at each of the levels and not to prove that there were cross-level formal identities.

In a 1974 literature survey of models applied to large-scale living systems, Mar concluded that constructors of such models do not have theories which can determine how to apply a given model to a specific real situation or how to select variables to include in a model.[4] The following principles, based on my conceptual approach, suggest which sorts of models are relevant to which subsystems of living systems and so provide a rationale for employing them to describe living systems: For input–output flows of both matter-energy and information, linear programming is applicable. In addition, statistics that measure the amount of information in a message can be applied to flows of information. Such statistics can also measure the capacity of any channel. Processing rates can be measured in all subsystems except the supporter. Cost-effectiveness measures are relevant to all subsystems. Queuing theory measures are applicable to any subsystem that processes units of matter-energy or information by one means or another sequentially past a certain point. Most subsystems of living systems do this.

Measures of the amount of filtering, or the degree of distortion, and of the level of the threshold are applicable to the ingestor, the input transducer, and the internal transducer. Measures of accuracy of pattern recognition are applicable to both the input transducer and the internal transducer. Measures derived from net theory and the theory of buffer storage are applicable to both the distributor and the channel and net. Buffer storage measures may also be useful in analyzing the processes of some converter and producer subsystems. Coding theorems of information theory are applicable to the decoder and encoder. Stochastic learning-theory models can be used to analyze associator processes. Measures derived from inventory theory and buffer storage theory can be applied to matter-energy storage and information storage (or memory) subsystems. Game theory and statistical decision theory apply to the decider. Various measures of stress, strain, and the strength of materials which engineers commonly use can be applied to the supporter.

In future simulations of living systems the above suggestions may well be adopted as common practice in analyzing or simulating the interactions of system or subsystem variables.

1.11   Shred-out   General living systems theory is an evolutionary theory. In each chapter of this book that deals with a level, from cell to supranational system, Section 5.3 discusses how that level evolved. I maintain that this occurred by a process of shred-out—as if each strand of a many-stranded rope had unraveled progressively into more and more pieces. This is a process of progressive division of labor, differentiation, or specialization of function of each subsystem, from the least to the most advanced level of living systems (see pages 1, 4, 26, 27, and 29). Every one of the 19 critical subsystems was essential for the continuation of life of every living system at every point in this evolution. If any one of these subsystems had ceased to carry out its processes even briefly, the system it was in would have ceased to exist. For that reason, evolution did not eliminate any critical subsystems. Therefore, all 19 subsystems are represented at each level of living system (see Fig. 13-1). This figure is basically the same as Fig. 1-2. It appears here again to emphasize the evolutionary nature of the rise of the seven levels of living systems. Also, it summarizes two sorts of data from Chaps. 6 through 12: data on (a) the approximate number of years since the period of origin of each level, from Sec. 5.3 in each chapter, and (b) the approximate median diameter size (in meters) of each level, from Sec. 1.1 of each chapter.

Since the general direction of evolution is toward greater complexity (see page 76), systems are, in general, larger and more complicated at higher levels. They are capable of using more adjustment processes, which enables them to resist more environmental stresses. Consequently, they can survive longer.

For decades biologists and social scientists have made analogies between various levels of living systems. Bonner wrote about comparable aspects of cells and societies.[5] Spencer, Huxley, White, Darlington, and others have discussed similarities in the evolution of biological and social systems (see page 854).[6] Wheeler, Emerson, and Gerard have referred to the social insects as "supraorganisms" or have made other comparisons between biological and social systems.[7] These writers have been subjected to skeptical questions by other scientists as to whether cross-level analogies are anything but metaphors. The concept of shred-out provides one way to settle such controversy. It formulates the issue in a way which is not mere analogy. It states the proposition that the same 19 critical subsystems are present at each of the levels and gives the evolutionary reason why. This proposition, that all levels of living systems must have these 19 critical subsystems, is subject to scientific proof or disproof. Some exceptions have been mentioned above (see pages 33, 54, and 55).

Scientific disciplines, on the basis of observations and theories made by specialists in the field, traditionally have developed a consensus about what subsystems compose the systems with which they are concerned. Ordinarily, they have not looked at similar classifications of subsystems, by specialists in other sciences, that might be related. Yet one discipline might well profit from such work done in another field. I suggest that, instead of making a new classification of subsystems at each level of living system, without regard to the structures and functions classically recognized at lower and higher levels, we rely on the principle of shred-out to justify a serious search to determine whether comparable subsystems do exist at the different levels of living systems. There may even be similarities to some nonliving systems. Though this seems to be a reasonable approach for any scientist who believes in the continuity of life, it has not been a popular scientific strategy. One reason for this, unfortunately, has been that many specialists at one level have been unaware of, and often uninterested in, scientific findings at other levels.

1.11.1   Progressive shred-out of an illustrative subsystem   One can trace out along a single row of Table 13-1 the shred-out of each subsystem. I have chosen the channel and net as an example:

Cell.   The cell membranes of certain types of cells, such as neurons, are channels for beta-coded information conveyed over them by bioelectric pulses. Also, inside the membrane of every cell the cytoplasmic

LEVEL	APPROXIMATE NUMBER OF YEARS SINCE PERIOD OF ORIGIN	APPROXIMATE MEDIAN DIAMETER SIZE (IN METERS)
Cell	3×10^9	10^{-6}
Organ	$5 \times 10^{8}+?$	10^{-3}
Organism	5×10^8	10^{-2}
Group	5×10^8 ?	10^{-1}
Organization	1.1×10^4	10^2
Society	7×10^3	10^6
Supranational System	4.5×10^3	5×10^6

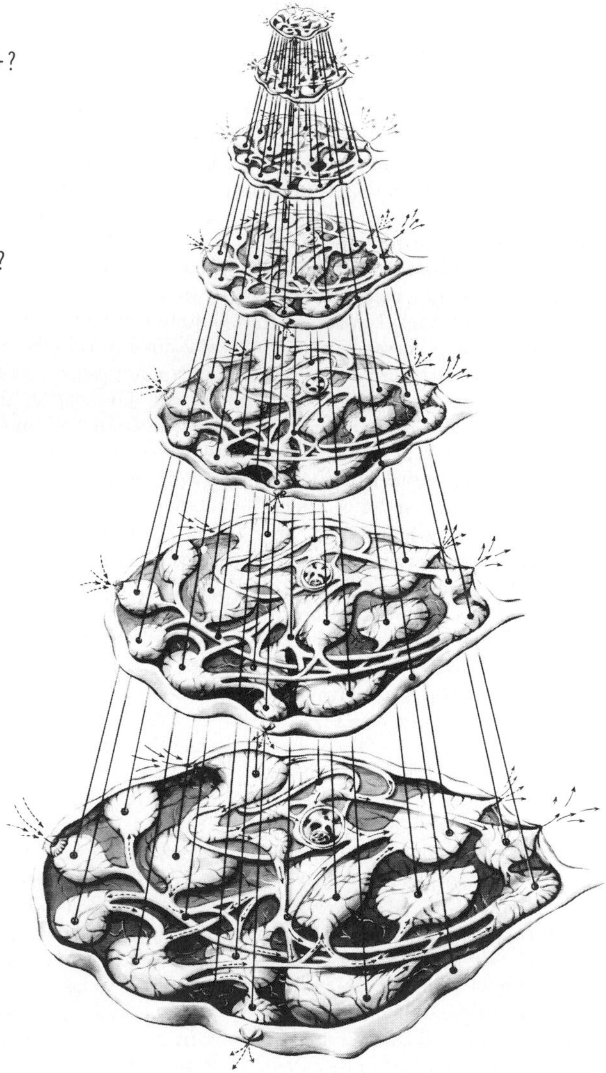

Fig. 13-1 Shred-out.

reticulum, a network of tubules and vesicles, extends to all parts of the cytoplasm. Over it and throughout the cytoplasm molecules flow. These include messenger RNA molecules passing from the nucleus to various organelles, inducer and energizer molecules, hormones, enzymes, and transmitter substances. The molecular shapes of these markers convey alpha-coded information.

Organ. In many organs intrinsic nerve nets are formed by junction of separate neurons. Bioelectric pulses passing over them convey beta-coded information. Also, hormones which flow out of cells that synthesize them convey alpha-coded information into the intercellular fluids of organs and through their blood and lymph vascular channels. These intercellular fluids merge with the blood and lymph to form both distributors for matter-energy and channels for information.

Organism. At this level many subordinate networks of neurons join to create the complex and specialized neural net of the autonomic and central nervous systems. Advanced forms of neural transmission of beta-coded information evolve. Myelin insulates neural fibers, making possible more rapid transmissions, which are essential for coordination of large organisms. Despite the advances of neural information processing at this level, alpha-coded information transmission does not disappear in any species of organism. Hormones travel in intracellular fluids and over vascular networks from the transmitter organ which produces these alpha-coded messages to the target tissues which receive them. These media through which hormones flow have evolved into a single interconnected net that supplies the entire organism.

Group. In a major evolutionary transition, the air between free-moving organisms becomes the most important channel at this level. Through it alpha-, beta-, and gamma-coded messages travel. Chemical transmissions of alpha-coded molecules such as pheromones are conveyed by direct contact among insects or through the air. Beta-coded signals such as vocal inflections, bodily positions, and facial gestures move on airborne waves. And gamma-coded spoken or written language communicated between group members also passes through the air.

Organization. Organizations have informal and formal interpersonal and intergroup channels. In informal communications, much more complex channels than those of groups ordinarily convey spoken languages and gestures through the air or speech over electronic channels such as private telephone exchanges. In addition, messages are transmitted in formal channels by messengers, memoranda, letters, telegraph, and other electronic media.

Society. Spoken and written language is the chief mode of transmission of information in societies, through all the channels employed by organizations, as well as through postal services and national telephone, telegraph, radio, television, and other electronic networks.

Supranational systems. Language is almost always the means of communication at this level. All forms of networks known at the societal level in modern times have been extended across international borders. One of the first organized supranational networks was the worldwide postal system, coordinated now by the Universal Postal Union (UPU). The other sorts of supranational networks developed later.

Overall, the evolutionary shred-out of the channel and net subsystem is from slow, inefficient, alpha-coded chemical transmission by diffusion at the cell level up to increasingly rapid and cost-effective gamma-coded symbolic linguistic transmissions over complicated networks at the higher levels of living systems. For each system at every level the basic process of transmitting information bearing markers over one sort of physical channel or another is basically the same. It is essential if the system is to survive.

2. Differences among the seven levels of living systems

2.1   Periods of origin of the levels   Although much speculation is involved in dating the approximate periods of evolution of each of the seven levels, as shown in Fig. 13-1, there still is some relevant scientific and historical evidence which I have outlined in previous chapters. I shall summarize here what is known about all the levels, as stated in Sec. 5.3 of each relevant chapter above.

Cell.   Chemical evolution probably produced the first cells at least 3 billion (3×10^9) years ago.

Organ.   The closest sort of system to an independent, totipotential organ appeared when *Mesozoa* evolved. They are parasites made up of only a few cells and are not specialized like organs in organisms. They seem to be links between cells and organisms.[8] One can speculate that they evolved in a period not long before organisms composed of organ subsystems appeared, perhaps somewhat more than 500 million $(5 \times 10^8 + ?)$ years ago. There is no evidence from paleontology that, except for *Mesozoa*, organs ever existed independently of organisms.

Organism.   Organisms, as I have said, appeared perhaps 500 million (5×10^8) years ago.

Group. The first dyad of organisms that mated sexually was probably the first group. This sort of system may have appeared shortly after the first organism, or approximately 500 million (5×10^8?) years ago. This date is highly speculative.

Organization. The first organization was probably formed about 9000 B.C., or 11,000 (1.1×10^4) years ago. It may well have been a village or city like Jericho or some other human activity involving groups arranged in two or more echelons.

Society. The first society was probably formed somewhat later, perhaps around 5000 B.C., or 7,000 (7×10^3) years ago, at about the beginning of history. In all likelihood there were primitive tribal "societies" before that, whose components were groups. But if organizations, in my sense, did not arise until about 9000 B.C., living systems with a preponderance of organizations as components (which is my definition of a society) did not appear until later, perhaps around 5000 B.C., or, 7,000 years ago. Much of this evolution is shrouded in prehistory. As at every level, there were probably transitional forms of systems between the early organizations and societies as I define them.

Supranational system. Finally the supranational system evolved. Probably the first empire of which there is historical and archaeological evidence was the Sumerian Empire of the Southern Mesopotamian valley. Its first dynasty ruled in the twenty-fifth century B.C., or 4,500 (4.5×10^3) years ago. It controlled a region of the world that had several cities and numerous tribes or states, which were not societies at all comparable in complexity to modern nations. In recent decades the character of supranational systems has altered markedly, and none of the present ones has the sort of absolute power and integrated decider processes of some of the early empires.

2.2 Sizes of the levels The sizes to which living systems have evolved are discussed in Sec. 1.1 of each chapter dealing with one of the seven levels. The approximate median diameters of each level appear in Fig. 13-1. The following paragraphs summarize what is known about system size at each level.

Cell. The smallest cells are 200 nanometers (nm), or 2×10^{-7} meters (m), in diameter. The largest cell of any surviving species is the ostrich egg, about 0.2 m long, 1 million times the length of the smallest cells. Almost its entire mass is food included in the cell. The germinal materials are minute by comparison. The median cell diameter is probably about 10^{-6} m.

Organ. The smallest organs are only a few cells in size, about 10^{-5} m in diameter. The largest organs are probably the boundaries of the largest sequoia trees (at times more than 83 m in height and 9 m in trunk diameter). The largest animal organs are either the boundaries of whales (at times more than 32 m long) or the intestinal components of the converter of some animals like elephants, which can be more than 60 m long. The median organ diameter, considering that there are more small species than large ones and that the former have many more members, is perhaps 10^{-3} m.

Organism. Organisms range in size from microscopic plants and animals to trees that attain heights of more than 83 m and trunk diameters of more than 9 m. Considering that animal species with large members tend to be more populous, the median organism diameter is probably about 10^{-2} m.

Group. Probably the smallest group is a mating dyad of microscopic animal species. The diameter of such a group is perhaps about 10^{-4} m. The largest group may be a herd of blue whales. Such a herd frolicking in the ocean would cover perhaps several miles, an area with a diameter of about 10^3 m. The median group diameter is small because the median size of animals is small. Also, there are more groups with only a few members than groups with many. No estimate of median group diameter exists, but perhaps 10^{-1} m is a good estimate. The median human-group diameter is about 5×10^1 m.

Organization. The diameters of organizations range from about 10 m for a very small department store or factory to the diameter of a state or other major component of a nation. The largest of these is the Russian Socialist Federated Soviet Republic of the Soviet Union, with an east-west diameter only about 600 kilometers (km) less than that of the whole Soviet Union. The median organization diameter is probably that of a moderately large manufacturing organization, or about 10^2 m.

Society. The smallest sovereign nation, Vatican City, is only about 1 km in diameter, and the largest, the Soviet Union, has an east-west diameter of about 11,000 km. The median modern nation has a diameter of about 10^3 km, or 10^6 m.

Supranational system. The smallest supranational system was perhaps the Austrian-Hungarian Empire, which was about 300 km in diameter. The largest is perhaps the North Atlantic Treaty Organization, which is nearly 16,000 km in diameter. The median diameter of a supranational system is probably about 5×10^3 km, or 5×10^6 m.

The above data comparing the sizes of systems at the seven levels indicate that the progressive shredding-out of each subsystem required larger systems at each higher level to accommodate its increasing complexity.

2.3 Emergents General living systems theory has been criticized as being reductionist because it finds formal identities across levels from cells to supranational systems. This criticism assumes that the existence of such formal identities implies that behavior of higher levels can be completely explained by analyzing processes at lower levels—that there are no disidentities or characteristics of higher-level systems not found at lower levels. An emphasis upon similar processes in systems at all levels displeases some who prize human superiority.

The theory described in this book is not reductionist as defined above. It holds that systems at higher levels have emergent characteristics. These enable them to cope with excess and lack stresses that would be beyond the adjustment capabilities of lower-level systems, and these characteristics also result in greater structural complexity than exists at lower levels. A parallel may be found in the difference between two nonliving systems—a radio set and a television set. The first can receive audio programs. The second can be described as a radio set with added components, such as a picture tube, that together can receive both audio and video signals. This is an emergent capability.

In each preceding chapter which discusses a particular system level, Sec. 5.3.1 describes the emergents at that level. A brief consideration of all these follows.

Cell. At the level of the cell, the emergent, of course, is life itself—a new sort of organization of matter and energy that can maintain an island of negative entropy and stability in an environment with less stability and a greater overall rate of entropy.

Organ. The ability of an organized mass of cells to replace its constituent cells as they die is emergent at the level of the organ. As a consequence, many types of organs live longer than the individual cells that compose them. Other emergent characteristics come from the pooled resources of different kinds of component cells in organs—the ability to withstand localized stresses that kill cells upon which they impinge but that do not extend over a large enough region of physical space to destroy the entire organ; the ability to produce larger amounts of matter-energy or information outputs than cells can; the increased efficiency which is derived from processes that are shredded out to more complex structures; and the greater genetic variety present in organs of multicellular organisms than in free-living cells.

Organism. Associative learning may well be emergent at this level. Organs do not become conditioned independently of organisms. The evidence for conditioning in free-living cells is not conclusive. If this is an emergent at the level of the organism, it first appears in a relatively simple animal phylum. Some investigators have obtained statistically significant evidence of associating by flatworms. Emotions may also be emergent at the level of the animal organism, although no operation is known which could prove or disprove subjective states in cells, organs, or plants. Higher animals at times act in ways that resemble human emotional behavior.

Gamma-coded, symbolic language is a major emergent in organisms. It has not been observed below the primates and is well developed only in human beings.

Group. Cooperative activity, impossible at lower levels, emerges at the level of the group. A group of animals or persons can control a much larger living and hunting territory than a single organism of the same species can. It can devise cooperative strategies for gathering information and gaining food. Human groups can carry out more intricate motor activity and make more complicated artifacts than a single person.

Since many sorts of groups can endure beyond the lifetimes of their components, their matter-energy and information processes can continue over more than a single generation.

The physical separateness and autonomy of organism components make it possible for different groups to share some of the same organisms. In many sorts of groups, subsystem functions can be shifted from one member or subgroup to others. There can be fewer components than the number of subsystems. Although the capacity for gamma-coded language was an emergent at the level of the organism, based upon evolutionary changes in human bodies, communication is emergent in groups.

Groups also can create higher-level systems by specifying their written or unwritten charters.

Organization. Emergent at this level are new forms of social organization that bring about novel sorts of human interactions, such as the changed basis for personal status and the impersonal relationships characteristic of bureaucratic organizations. Technological achievements in both matter-energy and information processing can be much greater in organizations than in the most competent groups.

Society. At each stage of societal evolution, from primitive to postmodern, previously unknown structures and processes have appeared. Each embodied greater stores of cultural information and made it possible for larger numbers of people to organize their social lives. These social emergents have included elaborate kinship systems, new types of governments, and various artistic and technological advances. The modern period has produced, among other things, the awesome achievements of modern science and technology devised by brilliant, educated individual human beings. Implementing them required the capabilities of organizations, which are societal components, as well as access to resources that is possible only in highly developed nations. Among these resources are rapid and inexpensive dissemination of information, ready retrieval of information stored almost anywhere in the world, and adequate financing and management of great projects that require cooperation of many organizations.

Supranational system.   A recent emergent at this level is the international or supranational agency, created for a single purpose or as a multipurpose system, with a primary goal of resolving conflicts among nations.

2.4   Variables   Each of the 19 critical subsystems keeps a set of variables in steady-state ranges. The system as a whole maintains the steady states of other variables by adjusting relationships among subsystems or changing its relationship to aspects of its environment. Variables of an illustrative subsystem, the channel and net of human organisms, are shown in Fig. 13-2.

The variables which I list for each subsystem apply to all seven levels. My lists are certainly not exhaustive—there may be many such variables. Also, each of the levels has variables not present at the others. Even where the variable is present at all levels, the process to which it relates may be far more developed at one level than at another.

Some variables exist in all subsystems, since a number of characteristics of both matter-energy and information flows are similar no matter where they occur. Rate of processing, for example, is a variable of all subsystems. Costs can be assessed for all subsystem processes. Meaning variables are common to all information processing systems. Lags and distortions characterize all information flows. Many of the cross-level hypotheses discussed in this book are predictions that specific quantitative relationships can be discovered between two subsystem or system variables.

2.5   Indicators   At every level of living system, changing values of certain objectively determinable indicators have proved to be reliable measures of specific states of variables. They are instruments which can be observed to change in real space-time as variables, which we conceptualize, alter in a particular concrete system. They can be used to evaluate the current condition of a system, to measure the amount of departure of variables from established norms, or by extrapolation to forecast changes in system states in the immediate or more distant future.

Indicator values are ordinarily determined repeatedly, either for the same system at different times or for each of a set of systems of comparable types. Indicators are preferably in centimeter-gram-second units, in monetary units, or in some other units that can be quantified. Indicators may, however, concern qualitative aspects of systems as well as quantitative ones. It is important that an indicator validly measure the variable with which it is supposed to vary. If the indicator is a sample of some population of data, the sample must be representative.

The following are examples of indicators at each level, which are discussed in Sec. 2.1 of each chapter dealing with one of the seven levels.

Cell.   Microscopic examinations of the nuclei of cells in organisms may reveal the presence of mitotic figures, indicators of abnormal proliferation that may be cancerous. This is an indicator both of abnormality at the level of the cell and of pathology, or incipient pathology, at the level of the organism. Sickle-shaped red blood corpuscles are indicators of a cellular pathology which makes such corpuscles fragile and so causes anemia in the organism.

Organ.   Tissues, fluids, or cellular material, extracted from an organ by needle biopsy or some other technique, can be analyzed chemically or microscopically. The findings can then be compared with previously established norms for that particular type of organ. Identification of specific pathological states by such means can lead to corrective action.

Organism.   Norms have been established for hundreds, if not thousands, of matter-energy and information processing variables at this level. Tests have been devised to measure them. Figure 13-2 includes a list of indicators for an illustrative subsystem, the channel and net of the human organism.

The measurement of blood pressure by use of a sphygmomanometer is one indicator of the condition of the cardiovascular components of the distributor subsystem. A psychological examiner may administer an intelligence test and from the results calculate a child's IQ. This is a ratio between the child's scores on certain standardized information processing tasks and his or her age. Such an indicator can predict with some validity the child's probable success in school. This success is dependent on, among other things, the efficiency of functioning of the associator and memory subsystems.

Group.   A measure of central tendency, like the mean, median, and mode, or a measure of dispersion, applied to social and economic variables of family groups, can be used to determine the position of a particular family in its community. Data on the housing, occupations, educational attainments, and income of a family can be combined to produce an indicator of its socioeconomic status. A family income can be determined, for example, to be in the top 20 percent of the society, and its housing to be substandard as compared with others in a deteriorating neighborhood.

Organization. The ratio indicator of dollar cost per unit product or per unit service is one measure of the cost-effectiveness of organization processes. Changes over time in this indicator may alert deciders to the need to correct technological or managerial procedures in the organization. Results of a survey among workers that show an unacceptably high level of dissatisfaction with working conditions may be an indicator that can predict an outbreak of labor troubles unless corrective action is taken.

Society. Economic indicators like the rate of unemployment, the number of housing starts, the various indices of stock-market activity, and the GNP are used to evaluate the current state of the national economy, forecast cyclic changes in business activity, and perhaps reveal the need for actions by the Federal Reserve Board (in the United States), the President, or the legislature. Some social indicators measure less quantifiable aspects of the society. Now in the process of development, such indicators are not yet as widely used as economic indicators. They may be based upon aggregated statistics for the society of objective measures, like the number of people who have health insurance or who have graduated from high school, or upon measures of more subjective aspects of life, like trust in public officials, as determined by public opinion surveys. These data can be disaggregated by region of the country; by age, sex, race, or educational status; or by other categories.

Supranational system. As yet there are relatively few standard supranational indicators, although states of supranational systems can be determined by the use of aggregated statistics about component societies on such variables as total populations or quantities of natural resources. Global measures of rates of use of scarce resources or of growth of the population of the entire world may indicate probable dates when the total world system must inevitably deteriorate unless adjustment processes slow or reverse present trends.

2.6 Artifacts   All levels of living systems make use of man-made, nonliving artifacts as prostheses to improve their cost-effectiveness. They differ greatly from one level to another. One reason for this is that these artifacts must be adapted to the size and structure of the system to whose processes they contribute.

Cell. Drugs are manufactured and are administered to cells in order to alter cellular processes, frequently channel and net or decider processes. Here are some examples: (1) Thyroxine hormone administered as a drug affects enzyme processes in a cell and accelerates its use of oxygen; (2) some chemotherapeutic agents can injure or kill cancer cells, while altering normal

cells to a lesser degree; and (3) the drug puromycin affects the producer processes of individual cells, blocking the synthesis of protein.

Organ. As everyone knows, organ components— *e.g.,* hearts, kidneys, and corneas—can be transplanted from one organism into another. Transplants are not strictly man-made artifacts. However, one can also replace a diseased artery, like an aorta with an aneurysm, by a plastic aorta, and a diseased kidney can be replaced by a renal dialysis machine. Also, there are information processing prostheses, like an electrical pacemaker, which maintains a normal rhythm in a heart that has developed pathological irregular rhythms.

Organism. Artifacts for human organisms include hats and coats for the boundary subsystem, wheelchairs and carts for the motor subsystem, chairs and beds for the supporter subsystem, calculators and computers for the decider subsystem, and typewriters and microphones for the output transducer.

Group. Artifacts used by groups include rooms with furniture; houses for family groups; automobiles, buses, airplanes, and sailboats; and public address systems to process information.

Organization. Factories are essential artifacts for manufacturing companies. Universities have campuses. Cities require mass-transportation systems for matter-energy processing, and they need telephone systems, radio transmitters, and television stations as information processing systems.

Society. Most countries have artifacts like railroads, buses, trucks, roads, and airplanes for transporting matter-energy, including people. National postal networks, which use the above artifacts, as well as national telephone and television networks, are essential to modern societies.

Supranational system. At this level systems employ artifacts like supranational border defenses and fortifications, as well as all the prostheses mentioned in the paragraph above. Also, they may make use of supranational communication satellites which process information across international borders.

2.7 State of scientific knowledge about each level
Each of the previous chapters that concentrated upon a particular level concluded with some observations about the characteristics of systems at that level and the state of the disciplines that study them. A comparison of these conclusions discloses some of the ways in which systems, and the study of systems, are alike and different.

Cell. Recent scientific advances are probably more impressive at this level than at any other. The two last decades have produced rapid theoretical and technical development in cellular biology. Exciting new meth-

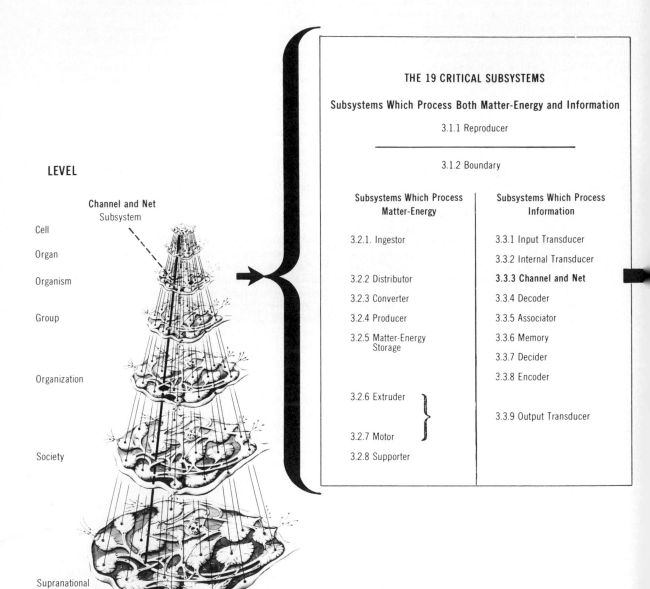

LEVEL

Cell

Organ

Organism

Group

Organization

Society

Supranational
System

Channel and Net
Subsystem

THE 19 CRITICAL SUBSYSTEMS

Subsystems Which Process Both Matter-Energy and Information

3.1.1 Reproducer

3.1.2 Boundary

Subsystems Which Process Matter-Energy	Subsystems Which Process Information
3.2.1. Ingestor	3.3.1 Input Transducer
	3.3.2 Internal Transducer
3.2.2 Distributor	**3.3.3 Channel and Net**
3.2.3 Converter	3.3.4 Decoder
3.2.4 Producer	3.3.5 Associator
3.2.5 Matter-Energy Storage	3.3.6 Memory
	3.3.7 Decider
	3.3.8 Encoder
3.2.6 Extruder	
3.2.7 Motor	3.3.9 Output Transducer
3.2.8 Supporter	

Fig. 13-2   An illustrative critical subsystem: the channel and net subsystem at the level of the organism—its variables and indicators.

VARIABLES
All Levels
(Channel and Net Subsystem)

Meaning of information channeled to various parts of the system

Sorts of information channeled to various parts of the system

Percentage of information arriving at the appropriate receiver in the channel and net

Threshold of the channel and net

Changes in channel and net processing over time

Changes in channel and net processing with different circumstances

Information capacity of the channel and net

Distortion of the channel and net

Signal-to-noise ratio in the channel and net

Rate of processing of information over the channel and net

Lag in channel and net processing

Costs of channel and net processing

INDICATORS
Organism Level
(Channel and Net Subsystem, Neural Components)

Measure of the change of the signals transmitted over a neural tract on the processes of the organism

Frequency range or source of information of transducer which inputs signal into a neural tract

Percentage of total number of bits input to a neural tract that are output from it in a specific period

Intensity of output from another information processing subsystem required to input a signal over a neural tract

Differences in meaning, sort, rate, distortion, or other aspects of signal transmitted over a neural tract between one time and another

Differences in meaning, sort, rate, distortion, or other aspects of signal transmitted over a neural tract between one time when one or more independent variables have one value or set of values and another time when that value or set of values is different

Maximum number of bits per second that can be transmitted over a neural tract

Amount of alteration in the wave-form or relationships between various frequency components of a signal transmitted over a neural tract.

The ratio in decibels between the amplitude of the signal and the background noise in a neural tract

Number of bits of information transmitted over a neural tract in a specific second

Number of seconds between input and output of a signal over a neural tract

Amount of matter-energy expended in a specific transmission of information over a particular neural tract ods, such as the microtechniques that permit study of molecular events within cells, have made it possible to discover how the genetic code specifies proteins; what the roles of DNA, the various species of RNA, and enzymes in cellular control processes are; and how hormones and other substances initiate or repress cellular activities. Scientists have also gained understanding of the major functions of the various organelles of cells.

Many cellular physiologists believe that organismic learning and memory will ultimately be explained by molecular cellular events. How information is coded, stored, and retrieved by neurons and other cells is a major unsolved problem of this level. It is comparably important to the recently solved question of how the genetic message is coded.

Organ. The structures of organs have been studied for centuries. Organ processes have been accorded increasing attention in recent decades, as techniques for studying them have improved. Organs cannot survive separately from organisms. Perhaps, at some early evolutionary stage, separate organlike systems existed that were made up of cellular components, like organs, rather than being constructed from organ components, like organisms.

The fact that organs cannot live independently of organisms may lead some to question whether the organ is really a distinct level of living system. However, organs are clearly different in structure from either cells or organisms, and some organs do have local decision-making processes. These facts are the reasons for maintaining that organs are, indeed, a separate level.

The nervous systems of animal organisms include several organs, since they provide the structure for all the information processing subsystems. Although research has disclosed much that is important about the channels for specific sorts of information transmissions and the coding of information by sense organs and some higher centers, some of the most fundamental questions about information processing organs are still to be answered.

Organism. Organisms are obviously real, concrete living systems with the capacity for totipotentiality. Vast amounts of data have been collected on all aspects of matter-energy and information processing at this level. Some of the most interesting current problems deal with how information is processed through organism nervous systems—problems similar to those which are important at the levels of the cell and the organ. The issue of how and where input information elicits learning and then is stored in memory and retrieved still is unresolved.

A problem with science, at this level, is that the traditional biological disciplines such as anatomy,

biochemistry, and physiology do not communicate very effectively or relate well conceptually with psychology. Much psychology is not quantitative, but even psychological researchers that do employ measurement often do not make use of units that can be converted to the centimeter-gram-second system in which measurements are made in the biological sciences. The differences in reliability of objective and subjective data are still debated among these disciplines. The mind-matter dilemma is still at issue. Systems theory offers an approach which can resolve some of these classical questions (see page 500).

Group. Many groups lack one or more subsystems and consequently must depend on organisms, organizations, or societies to carry out the processes they cannot perform. All the critical subsystems exist at this level, and some groups are totipotential. This is clearly a separate level of living system.

Vigorous research on groups in the 1930s and 1940s provided insights into such processes as the functioning of the group channel and net and the influence of group members upon one another. Some processes, like segregation and integration, have been given more attention at this level than at others. Interest in basic research on groups began to diminish in the 1950s and 1960s. Currently, most investigations on groups either repeat earlier studies with minor variations or use groups to study organism variables of individual members. Much current work is on groups formed for therapy or attitude change of the members. Many current studies on "groups" have only a single subject, the remainder of the group consisting of either confederates of the experimenter or standardized tape recordings which simulate living members.

Much research at this level has used artificial groups, put together in the laboratory for experimental purposes. The members of such groups are deliberately selected to have no continuing relationships among them. This sort of design helps to eliminate variables other than those to be studied, but generalizing from such groups to more permanent groups is dangerous.

The concept of the leader has been important in group research. It has not, however, been clearly defined. Obviously, it is not coextensive with the decider subsystem as I define it, since group leaders perform functions related to other subsystems and may have no more decision power than other members.

A return to basic research on group processes, rather than organism processes of members, could help to clarify how group subsystem processes are carried out. More study of natural groups, such as families, friendship groups, or work groups, would also be desirable.

Organization. Organizations are readily conceptualized as systems. Research on organization processes has continued for more than half a century. A chief emphasis over much of this period has been placed upon increasing production or improving labor-management relations in industrial organizations. Management science has become a profession whose members attend upon ailing organizations of all kinds to prescribe remedies for their pathologies. The people who actually control organizations, however, often reject a science-based orientation toward management in favor of insights gained through experience and intuition.

Organization theory has suffered from a confusion of levels, stemming from emphasis upon role theory, which focuses upon psychological problems of occupants of positions in organizational structures, and it may neglect organization level variables.

Recent research has concentrated upon decider and the channel and net processes rather than upon other information processing activities and upon distributor processes among the matter-energy activities. Among system processes, information internal adjustment processes have received the most attention. Studies of other subsystem processes would be desirable. Relatively few studies have collected data from populations of organizations to support generalizations about systems at this level. The case-study method is still the most common approach to the study of organizations. Simulations are increasingly used by researchers and the decision makers of some organizations, particularly large organizations, to test the effects of policy alternatives.

Society. A number of theories in sociology, political science, anthropology, and economics conceptualize societies as systems. Present societies are less totipotential than earlier ones because larger populations and industrialization have increased interdependency and because the need for protection from attack by hostile societies leads to penetration of many societies by components of other societies, which influence their deciders and reduce their autonomy. Modern societies tend to be defective in control and guidance of subsystem processes and are often highly vulnerable to disruption. At the same time, they are expected to provide more services and control more variables than earlier societies were.

Theories at this level have been dominated by abstracted systems concepts, with results similar to those at the level of the organization. Except for the science of economics, which has a strong theoretical base and a tradition of quantitative analysis of variables, research at this level is only beginning to be quantitative and to develop models that can be tested and applied. Because of the complexity of the feedbacks in these large systems and the long time spans involved, cause-and-effect relationships in them are difficult to determine. Governments are increasingly using models not only of economics but also of such things as ecological systems, natural resources, and energy distribution to guide policy formation. Quantitative research on other matter-energy and information processing subsystem variables is needed to advance understanding of system processes and to develop models and indicators to support or disconfirm theories and guide deciders at this level. Although the results of such researches are slow to affect deciders, the wide acceptance of economic findings and models makes it apparent that reliable research findings can be put to use in these systems.

Supranational system. Modern forms of supranational systems are of such recent development, having emerged in only the past 50 years or so, that none has a complete set of subsystems. Moreover, the subsystems which have developed tend to consist of few components besides the decider. These systems do little matter-energy processing. None approaches totipotentiality. The power of component societies today is almost always greater than the power of supranational deciders.

In spite of the weakness of existing systems, there is a general trend, slow though it often seems, toward greater reliance on international decision making and increasing demands for supranational control of certain global variables. Such international and supranational controls can reduce conflict among nations over scarce resources and protect weaker nations from exploitation by stronger ones. They arise partly because of general awareness of the importance of global environmental variables which evidently cannot be adjusted by unilateral actions of societies. Many adjustment processes of worldwide scope are carried on, not through formal supranational organizations, but through international decision making, expansion of international law, the development of international cartels, voluntary acceptance by societies of international monetary agreements, and use of international agencies to improve distribution of scarce resources like food and technological information. Such global endeavors are made feasible by new communications technologies and rapid transportation.

Traditionally, theory at this level has been based upon intuition and study of history rather than data collections. Some quantitative research is now being done, and construction of global-system models and simulations is currently burgeoning.

Summary. The analysis of living systems presented here has given an overall picture of the current status of the sciences of living systems. Following the same outline in my consideration of theory and research at each level has revealed differences in structure and process among the systems themselves, as well as differences in approach and emphasis of the scientific disciplines that investigate them. Overemphasis by scientists at one level on one particular issue, and neglect of the same issue by scientists at another level, may mask similarities between the levels.

Scientific studies at each level have focused on particular structures and processes because these are especially intriguing at that level. (Information storage, for instance, is now of special interest to cellular biologists.) Or attention at one level may be drawn to a given issue as a result of the work of brilliant or influential scientists. (At the level of the organism, learning research, for example, has expanded greatly following the theoretical and experimental work of people like Hull and Tolman.)

Phenomena at each level are measured by characteristic units of measurement, which may or may not be commensurate with the units used at other levels. Standards of reliability for data differ markedly from one level to another.

Despite this difference in emphasis, the 19 subsystems and other basic notions of general living systems theory appear to apply generally to all seven levels of living systems. This is not surprising in systems of common evolutionary origin. Some subsystems, like the channel and net, and some system processes, like the information internal adjustment processes, have been investigated in reliable scientific experiments at all levels. Mathematical network models have been applied at all levels from cell through organization, and would almost certainly fit the larger systems as well. The information input overload phenomenon and adjustment processes to it have been demonstrated at the same levels.

Comparison of experimental data collected at different levels can suggest areas in which studies are needed. Our review of the current status of the sciences of living systems has revealed numerous gaps in knowledge at each level—possibly one of the major contributions of an integrative conceptual scheme.

3. Some questions and answers about general living systems theory

A number of questions will inevitably be asked about the general living systems theory presented in this book. Some likely questions, and answers to them, are as follows:

1. *How do you know that only matter-energy and information flow in living systems?* A review of the literature indicates that no scientist has seriously suggested that anything else is transmitted or processed in living systems. And, indeed, what else is there to be processed?

2. *How do you know there are exactly seven levels?* It is possible that the tissue is a level between the cell and the organ or that the community is a level between the organization and the society, in some systems at least. Probably, however, there are no tissues all of whose cells are controlled by a common decider, and communities ordinarily have little development of any subsystem *except* the decider between the organization and society levels.

Each of the seven levels of systems which I have identified is distinctive in having its subsystems composed primarily of components of the level below and in being components of the system above. There are step-function changes in the magnitudes of variables like median diameter and median duration of existence from one level to another. These seven levels are those traditionally recognized by the various specialties which study living systems. They have comparable subsystems and are obvious and convenient units with which to work, just as particles, atoms, and molecules are obvious and convenient units for physical science.

3. *How do you know there are exactly 19 subsystems?* This is a question for scientific discussion associated with theory making and data collection. Because matter-energy and information are transmitted continuously in living systems from input through various subsystems to output, it is important to specify the operations by which subsystem boundaries are located. A boundary between subsystems can be identified by clear changes in processes or step functions in values of variables between one subsystem and the next. The distinctions made here between two subsystems and the assignment of processes to one or the other may appear arbitrary, particularly when only one level is considered. At the level of the organism, for example, the associator and memory processes might be regarded as being carried out by a single learning subsystem. At other levels they are, however, much more obviously separated. There are variables which change by step functions as information passes from one subsystem to the next.

The channel and net and decoder subsystems could also be considered a single subsystem in many types of living systems in which information is repeatedly recorded as it is transmitted from one part of the channel and net to another. The transmission of unaltered information in channels and nets appears, however, to be sufficiently different from the processes of decoder components, which are dispersed throughout the nets, to maintain the distinction. It is clear that some variables change by step functions as information flows from a channel and net component to a decoder component.

Specialists subdivide subsystems and concentrate on certain component structures and their processes. The input transducer, for example, is ordinarily subdivided by sensory modalities. These can be further subdivided for detailed study.

At some levels of living systems, or in certain species or individuals, additional subsystems have perhaps emerged. For example, in systems at the level of the organism and above, purely recreational activities are carried out. These seem not to be directly related to any process of the 19 critical subsystems, and special structures are formed for these activities. They do not appear to be essential for continued life of these systems. I classify them as adjustment processes of various sorts, but others may prefer to add a new "recreational" subsystem to my 19.

4. *How do you select variables?*   (See page 16.)

5. *How do you select indicators?*   (See page 51.)

6. *How does general systems research on living systems differ from research that does not have this orientation?* The major difference lies in the selection of hypotheses to be tested rather than in the techniques used for gathering or analyzing data. Various degrees of generalization are possible in research on living systems: (*a*) Variables, or interactions among variables, can be measured for a population of systems of the same type and level to determine, for example, the rate of associating in three-toed sloths or the effect on verbal output transducing in human subjects of varying lags in auditory feedback. (*b*) The same variables can be measured in systems of various types at the same level, for instance, to compare the rates of spread of information through the channel and net of a democracy and of a totalitarian society. (*c*) The same variables can be measured for systems at different levels, for example, to compare the lags in encoding information in systems at the four levels from organism to society. While all three degrees of generalization are relevant to living systems theory, the third is very rarely used except by general living systems theorists.

Characteristically, general systems research on living systems is concerned with confirming or disconfirming a hypothesis relevant to a given critical subsystem or to an adjustment process or other aspect of a total system. This is tested on one type of system at one level. The question may then be asked whether the same proposition has been or could be tested on other types of systems at the same level or on systems at other levels, using comparable dimensions. If functions of variables or similar mathematical models are applicable at more tha   e level, this cross-level for-

mal identity interests the general systems scientist. Differences among levels are also interesting. Identities and disidentities must both be considered to obtain full understanding of the phenomena of life.

At each of the levels of living systems, the variables and indicators are derived from more than one academic discipline. The general systems approach is necessarily interdisciplinary, even antidisciplinary. No traditional academic discipline prepares a scientist to deal with all the relevant variables of a living system.

General living systems theory takes an evolutionary approach to the study of the complexity of higher levels. This is not, of course, a unique aspect of this conceptual approach. The analysis of levels, however, makes it possible to trace the variables of one subsystem and the components that make it up to its comparable subsystem at a lower or higher level and see how the structures and processes are shredded out from one level to another.

7. *Isn't systems terminology just new jargon replacing traditional terms?*   My answer is no. It is an attempt to find the most neutral and acceptable words to fit all types and levels of systems and reveal whatever cross-level identities may exist.

8. *Is this whole conceptual system more than a programmatic approach; that is, is it really a general theory?*   Many theoretical statements are made that are capable of being confirmed or disconfirmed by research. Each cross-level hypothesis is one such confirmable or disconfirmable statement, and there are many others.

9. *Does an elaborate intellectual exercise of this sort have any practical uses?*   Yes, several. Some of them are the following:

(*a*) It outlines a reasonably parsimonious framework of basic concepts which is capable of organizing the complex facts of the various sciences of life in a rational and unified way.

(*b*) This conceptual mosaic can identify variables that have not been studied, as well as gaps in knowledge of systems at any given level. It can also reveal underemphasis or overemphasis on certain topics.

(*c*) If research at one level establishes reliable relationships among variables or derives a useful indicator, similar measurements can be made at other levels in order to see whether they can advance understanding of that level.

(*d*) Once the steady-state range of a certain variable has been determined at one level, its range may be estimated for a higher or a lower level. There may be some basis for deciding whether the same variable has a higher or lower range at each higher level. Consider as an example our information input overload research (see pages 169 to 195). Once it is known that a cell's capacity is around 4,000 bits per second (s) and that an organ's channel capacity is around 55 bits per s, one has reason to hypothesize that at each higher level, the channel capacity will be less. Furthermore, suppose that a certain model applies at one level—say, a curve indicating that as input rate to a channel rises, output rises to the channel capacity and then gradually falls. Knowing this, one has a sound basis for hypothesizing that this model also may fit the same subsystem variable at other levels.

Such extrapolation across levels is vaguely comparable to the way chemists use Mendeleyev's periodic table of the elements. He arranged the chemical elements in a particular order of columns and rows which made it possible to predict the specific characteristics of undiscovered elements. His work stimulated further research.

(e) This approach to living systems has other scientific value. It can aid a scientist in recognizing previously unseen relationships between a set of his or her own findings and those of others who work on comparable problems at the same or a different level. It suggests relationships between the variables and indicators in one study and those in others. Scientists can learn the degree of generalizability of their findings for living systems of all sorts. The data may not be relevant beyond the individual, type, or level studied, or they may be widely generalizable.

The work of Skinner on operant conditioning (see page 408), for instance, was first done on such animals as pigeons and rats. It has been confirmed with many other species, including human beings. It has proved to have applications in therapy and education. In his book *Walden II*, Skinner has also suggested that it might be extended to societies. In this novel he wrote as a humanist rather than a scientist. My conceptual system indicates a possible scientific rationale for such extension.

(f) This conceptual system puts emphasis on establishing normal values for variables and indicators as well as their usual steady-state ranges. Doing this facilitates determining when there is pathology in a system at any level, and what its characteristics are. If a relationship can be found among deviations from normal steady-state ranges in various parts of a system, this relationship can be identified as a syndrome, and its underlying cause or causes can be sought. Efforts can be made to remedy pathological structures or processes. The means of doing this will, of course, vary from level to level and among system types. It may be possible to change the structure of a system or its subsystems, for example, to alter the reporting relationships within an organization. An artifact, such

as a computer or a hearing aid, may be obtained to act as a prosthesis. Or some form of symbiosis or parasitism may be set up between the system under study and another system, at the same or a different level, that can carry out the necessary processes. One society, for example, may agree to provide aid to another in order to speed its development. Or trading partners may be found to exchange necessary matter-energy plentiful in one and lacking in another. Such remedies can aid a system with pathology to survive and to carry out its processes in a more cost-effective way.

(g) Finally, such an intellectual endeavor as this can have practical payoffs in applications. I shall discuss some of these below.

4. Present impact of general living systems theory

As general living systems theory has developed, it has been presented to the scientific and general public in a number of articles, the first of which was published in 1953.[9] The general paradigm of my theory has been referred to by quite a number of other writers: living systems with subsystems and suprasystems whose boundaries are open to transmissions of matter-energy and information, and with hierarchical organization. These principles are, of course, basic to the views of a number of other general systems theorists.

My identification of the seven levels of living systems which have cross-level formal identities has also been mentioned by various scientific writers. For instance, Glassman has used these seven levels in his analysis of the evidence concerning loose coupling in living systems.[10] In her analysis of the various forms of hierarchy, Wilson found these concepts to be useful tools in synthesizing scientific knowledge.[11] These concepts have also been used by Scheflen in his systems approach to psychosomatic medicine.[12] And my work has been mentioned by Brody in an article on the implications for medicine, science, and ethics of the systems view of man.[13]

Working in the framework of general systems theory Sahal has studied the concept of complexity of systems and possible ways of measuring complexity.[14] She has incorporated in her thinking two aspects of my viewpoint: (a) that negentropy is a possible measure of complexity, and (b) that structures of less than a certain degree of complexity cannot have all the characteristics of living systems. Becht has developed a holistic theory about biological systems such as cells, organs, organisms, and species.[15] In this work he refers to my basic principle that such systems are made up of living subsystems or components which are produced, repaired, and maintained by the living systems of which they are a part.

Writing primarily about organs in an analysis of cognitive processes and the effects of brain damage and recovery from such pathology, Glassman made use of general living systems theory, recognizing that what he said about organ systems could apply to other levels.[16]

At the level of the organism, a textbook of psychology was written by Coleman explicitly based on general living systems theory.[17] Also, Gordon Allport, in an article on personality theory published in 1960, discussed my particular concept of open systems, but did not accept my entire viewpoint.[18] It was, however, adopted by Kolouch as a model for diagnosing a patient's physical and psychological states in an approach he called a "living systems autopsy."[19] In this he dealt with levels which I have outlined—the organism and its pathological cell and organ subcomponents and components—and the therapeutic relationship used to treat the patient's illness. A somewhat similar approach to the diagnosis and treatment of asthma has been suggested by Kluger.[20] General systems theory was stated by Beckett to have important relevance to clinical psychiatry and psychotherapy.[21] Bolman has analyzed one particular psychoneurosis, school phobia, in general systems terms.[22] Pinderhughes and Peterfreund have both tried to show how it is compatible with psychoanalysis.[23] Meir maintains, and Gray and Rizzo agree, that it can be used to unify the study of man in medicine and psychiatry.[24] In formulating his systems philosophy of human values, Laszlo has expressed his agreement with my framework of basic concepts, emphasizing particularly the views that stresses can produce internal strains within a system and that the relative urgency of reducing these strains represents a system's hierarchy of values.[25]

In developing a comprehensive approach to group psychotherapy, Durkin has found general living systems theory useful, as has Piehuta.[26] Warren Miller has analyzed psychiatric consultation practice in terms of this conceptual system.[27] Work groups have been conceptualized by Susman as open systems.[28]

General living systems theory has also been applied at the levels of the organism, the group, and the organization or community by Hearn and his students in the field of social service.[29] Newbrough found aspects of it to be helpful in his study of community psychology.[30] He was particularly interested in cross-level formal identities between the levels of the organism and of the organization or community. Deutsch has also used this approach in his work on community psychology.[31] Bolman has proposed using my theory to model community mental health activities.[32] And Baker has analyzed how it applies to community mental health

centers and other health delivery systems.[33] A similar approach to the evaluation of mental health service systems, with special emphasis on the channel and net subsystem, has been worked out by Burgess, Nelson, and Wallhaus.[34] Smith has made some use of my conceptual system in developing a model for a community psychiatric system.[35] A model for hospital nursing and patient care, using the same framework, has been described by Pierce.[36] An entire book discussing a wide range of applications of general living systems theory and related approaches to health research has been edited by Werley, Zuzich, Zajkowski, and Zagornik.[37] Also, Weiss and Rein have advocated my theory as a framework for evaluating the effectiveness of various broad-aim programs designed to improve community life.[38] Broskowski has conceptualized schools as open systems.[39] College classes have been analyzed by Robey and entire universities by Buss in terms of general living systems theory.[40] Duncan has made a detailed application of my approach to the study of large-scale industrial organizations.[41] According to Lichtman and Hunt, Berrien, and Alderfer the general study of organizations can benefit from the application of this approach.[42] Rogers and Rogers consider systems theories, including mine, to be the most useful of three approaches to organizations, which they identify as the scientific management school, the human relations school, and the systems school.[43] They have also listed a series of propositions, similar to my hypotheses, which apply to systems at the organization level. Reese believes it can be helpful to psychiatric and other administrators.[44] Working in terms of my approach, Noell has analyzed comparatively the size and the complexity of the decider subsystems, or "administrative sector," of hospitals and also of the states of the United States.[45]

In an important book edited by Bauer, which has had a significant influence on social science, Gross referred to my theoretical work on systems in his orientation to the problem of collecting social indicators.[46] Others who have dealt with this general approach at the society level include Bostock, who accepts some aspects, while rejecting others.[47] In a detailed critique of general systems theory, Peery noted that its popularity has grown over the last 25 years. He then commented as follows: "Its adoption as a central framework by social scientists who have long been trying to develop an integrated theoretical approach has become commonplace."[48] From the point of view of a geographer, Golant has developed a model of large-scale movements such as migration, based on my conceptual system.[49] The presentations in two textbooks, one on sociological theory by Klapp and one on several levels of social systems by Anderson and Carter, are strongly influenced by my approach.[50] Its relevance to political science has been examined in detail by Nettl.[51] Its applicability to specific issues of anthropological and archeological research have been discussed in four articles by Judge, Schiffer, Plog, and Hage.[52] My conceptual system has also been used by Paquet and Wallot in an article on the history of lower Canada.[53]

At the supranational level, Singer studies all the nations of the world, which he calls the "global system." Basically he accepts general living systems theory, and particularly its emphasis on concrete rather than abstracted systems.[54] Stephens has also written, a good deal more negatively, about general systems theory in relation to the study of international systems.[55] He is skeptical as to whether formal identities across levels of systems can be of real value in such research. On the other hand, Skjelsbaek, in an article on the structure of the network of international organizations, gave some support to my work. He stated his impression, based on his observations, that my cross-level Hypothesis 1.1 (see page 92), which states that in general, the more components a system has, the more echelons it has, can be confirmed for international organizations.[56] Systems simulation, as we have repeatedly indicated, is relevant to all levels of living systems. McLeod has included several of my basic concept definitions in his lexicon, which he suggests for general use by simulators.[57]

In *Science* magazine Karl Deutsch, John Platt, and Dieter Senghaas, who have been associated with the development of general systems research, listed 62 basic innovations in social science made between 1900 and 1965.[58] One of these was the general systems analysis made by our group. One must recognize the inevitable bias of two of these writers because of their own personal involvement in these activities.

The research on information input overload which our group did and which is described in Chap. 5 has attracted some attention in the scientific community. It was the first effort to conduct an experimental evaluation of a cross-level hypothesis. Five levels of living systems—cell, organ, organism, group, and organization—were studied. In a very few cases the published comments on this work have referred to its cross-level aspects, which are its primary emphasis. A majority, however, do not. Most have emphasized only its implications for the level of the organism. Of course, the findings presumably are valid at that level, but unfortunately the main purpose of the study has not so far been generally recognized. For example, it was a central theme of Toffler's *Future Shock*.[59] However, his references to this work deal only with the organism level. Of course, seeing significance in this research

even at one level implies some acceptance of the systems approach. Our work is viewed similarly by Lipowski.[60] He sees that information input overload may cause psychopathology, and he is interested in what adjustment processes may be employed to cope with it. Coleman has similar concerns.[61] Investigating problems which arise when a person is required to perform multiple tasks simultaneously, Rolfe referred to the adjustment processes which we found to be used to cope with information input overload (see page 123).[62] Huntley carried out an experiment on individual male subjects somewhat similar to our information input overload research at the organism level, and obtained results compatible with ours.[63] The difference between his study and ours is that his subjects were asked to respond to increasing input rates during a single trial, while we used several separate trials, each with a different input rate. The effects of redundancy on the performance of individual human subjects under information overload has been investigated by Hurst and McKendry.[64] They found that changes in the redundancies in the input could increase or decrease the performance decrement in the output. Support for our view that schizophrenics in some ways perform like normal persons under information input overload (see pages 167 to 169) is found in the work of Hawks and Marshall.[65]

Cummings and DeCotiis used our work to explain pathology which arises in organizations when certain persons suffer from "role overload."[66] This occurs when their various responsibilities require them to process information inputs at rates beyond their capacity. Policy makers, commonly, but particularly in crises, suffer from an unmanageable overload of information input, as Holsti points out.[67] He indicates that in international crises governmental leaders resort to adjustment processes we have identified, including filtering out of unpleasant inputs and of the results of detailed searches for alternative solutions, as well as use of multiple channels to handle the overload. A theory of administrative decentralization in modern, large, complex organizations has been developed by James, who explained such decentralization as a response to information input overload.[68] He pointed out that decentralization, which is use of the multiple-channels adjustment process, gives greater latitude to specialists and consequently blurs overall organizational goals. An input–output analysis of the Federal Trade Commission was made by Nystrom.[69] He found that a great increase in the number of cases coming before the FTC had occurred over a 10-year period, creating information input overload on that organization. He discovered that it used some of the adjustment processes we had identified, such as omission, filtering, and abstracting, to cope with this overload. In an investigation of the role of the legislative staff in the state of New York, Balutis found that the legislators were overloaded with messages, reports, memoranda, and other communications.[70] They commonly turned the processing of such information over to staff assistants, a use of the multiple-channels adjustment process. This could produce organizational pathology because the assistants sometimes filtered the information which they passed on to the legislators, forwarding that which supported their personal preferences and culling out that which opposed those preferences.

In an ecological analysis of the changes in energy costs resulting from growth of such organizations as cities or power plants, Odum concluded that the growth might increase cost-effectiveness for a time, but that beyond a certain optimum the output curve decreased.[71] He likened this organizational effect to our findings on the effects of information input overload on living systems.

The fluctuating opening and closing of societal boundaries to information inputs have been analyzed by Klapp in terms of our concepts of information overload.[72] He recognized that communication imbalances can arise which create pathologies in societies, including not only information excess and lack stresses but also other abnormalities, as in the ratios of face-to-face communication to communication by impersonal media, or of nonverbal to verbal communication.

And finally, in an article on information distortion, Ehrle interprets our research on information input overload as it was intended—as a study of a possible formal identity in the information processing characteristics of channels at five levels of living systems.[73] Further, he refers to some of the critical subsystems which I have listed, including the boundary and the input transducer, analyzing their roles in producing distortion in communication.

General living systems theory is supposed to apply to all aspects of biological and social systems, and the publications which have referred to our work have certainly extended over a wide range of disciplines. This is as it should be. At least the general paradigm of the theory appears relevant to specialists in many areas. Nevertheless, many of its basic ideas have not yet had important impact. There have been a few references to cross-level formal identities, but so far no one has published research explicitly designed to evaluate one of my cross-level hypotheses or some cross-level hypothesis of his or her own at two or more levels. Also, though there have been incidental references to my 19 critical subsystems, no one else has applied this analysis to even one level of living systems. There seems to be little explicit acceptance of my

claim that we need consensus as to what are the subsystems or component parts of living systems at all levels, as to the variables of those subsystems, and as to indicators to measure those variables.

There is some agreement that various forms of matter-energy and information flow through living systems. But there is no general recognition of the methodological importance of tracing these flows from inputs through the various components to their outputs. The evolutionary notion of shred-out as a way to explain the similarities across the seven levels of living systems—and therefore to give a rationale for cross-level formal identities—has not yet influenced science significantly. We must wait for the future to see whether these concepts will be generally accepted or rejected.

5. Applications of general living systems theory

Basic research on general living systems theory is possible at all levels. It should also have applications to all those levels. So far, only a few of the possible applications have been realized. Professionals in a number of applied specialties are working in limited areas in terms of implicit or explicit mutually accepted conceptual systems without recognizing that they can gain from fitting their restricted conceptual systems into more general ones. Often they do not see, or care to see, how to generalize applications from one field to another.

Basic living systems theory and research do not, at first glance, seem to have much relevance to such important human problems as war, economic cycles, racial differences, civil rights legislation, cancer, improved education, the population explosion, or the energy crisis. As a result, many people try to solve these problems directly, without reference to a basic conceptual system. Just as doctors use a conceptual framework based on anatomy, physiology, and biochemistry in understanding a patient's recovery from cancer, so general living systems theory provides a conceptual framework which can enhance decision making and improve cost-effectiveness in a wide range of applications.

The analyses at the levels of the organ and organism can improve applications in fields like pharmacology, medicine, veterinary medicine, applied botany, agriculture, psychiatry, and the various forms of applied psychology.

My integration of group research can provide a basis for better applications of group dynamics and group psychotherapy, as well as for improved design of artifacts which groups can use as prostheses, like cars and houses.

The work at organizational levels can facilitate operations research on governmental agencies, transportation systems, communication services, corporations, farms, factories, other means of production and provision of services, educational delivery systems, health delivery systems, justice delivery systems, waste disposal systems, and urban systems. It can improve administration and the development of management information systems for administration of many types of organizations.

Increasingly, internationally and nationally, systems approaches are being used in the following areas of major human relevance: population increase and family planning, energy resources (including all the modalities), water resources, pollution of various sorts, health delivery systems, municipal systems, large-scale industrial systems and other large-scale organizations, education delivery systems, public health, and so forth. The work done at society and supranational system levels can apply to this.

Also, systems research at the societal level can aid military operations, environmental planning, social and economic planning, national government, and law enforcement.

The work on supranational systems can improve international relations, international education, international law, world government, integration of worldwide functions, international monetary systems, and international communication by cable, radio, satellite, television, and other methods, as well as making contributions to space travel and life in space.

The conceptual system can also provide a framework for the design of artifacts at all the levels.

6. The continuity of science

It is impossible that man should not be a part of nature, or that he should not follow her general order.

—Spinoza

I have noticed that a biologist's interests and understanding, and also, in a curious way, his loyalties, tend to spread horizontally, along strata, rather than up and down. Our instinct is to try to master what belongs to our chosen plane of analysis and to leave to others the research that belongs above that level or below.

—Medawar

The cooperative contributions of all the biological and social sciences, as well as some physical science, engineering, mathematics, logic, and statistics, are needed for understanding life at all levels. Each area of science has its own biases, which often distort interdisciplinary communication. A field may have a self-consistent view of its role that neglects the relationships between it and other disciplines. Such insularity arbitrarily interrupts the continuity of the study of living systems. As a result important matters may fall between two fields and receive no attention.

Just as there is a continuity in the universe as a whole, so there is a special continuity in that particular aspect of the universe known as life. Thus there should be a continuity in the sciences of life. As the number of facts in these various fields has increased, however, many scholars have attempted to protect themselves against information overload by specializing in a given area. They generally accept the traditions, terminology, and modes of thought of that area. They get their recognition, rewards, and esteem from their colleagues with similar interests. Unable to judge the competence of colleagues in other areas, they collaborate in a courteous pact of uninformed mutual acceptance. The result is that they do not perceive continuity among the life sciences. They are laymen to all scientists but a few fellow specialists.

Scientists differ in style and vary in taste. Their interests in subject matters range from sex to gall wasps, from polymers to polyandry. Some are "clinicians" concerned with individual organisms, groups, organizations, or societies. Others are general theorists. Some enjoy collecting data, and others enjoy analyzing them. Some are quantitatively minded, and others are not. Some care more for elegance of method than for a new finding. Others prefer the reverse. In science they all have a valuable role.

Specialists qualify as such by learning the details of their fields—as they should. They concentrate on them rather than on the similarities between their own area and others which they do not know so well. To many specialists the differences between the subject matter of their own and another scientific field are so obvious that it is hard for them to believe that commonalities could exist which would make findings at other levels relevant to what they do. If anyone makes the implausible suggestion that they investigate a seemingly unrelated area, they may become impatient and be unwilling to invest much time in such an undertaking because they calculate that the payoff will be low. Nevertheless, if there is a continuity of science resulting from a continuity of nature, important relationships of this sort must exist. Someone should study them.

The scientific endeavor is a large-scale living system—a worldwide enterprise. Specialists, discoverers, methodologists, experimentalists, theorists, applied scientists, practitioners—all are essential. But so also are synthesizers, reviewers, critics, and bibliographers. All the necessary system components, from discoverers to practitioners—from input to output—should be welcomed, supported, and rewarded if science is to serve humanity.

All scientists have a right to select their own parameters and variables, to limit their thought as they deem best. But limits exclude the rest of the world. The chosen parameters and variables and the hardened categories may have no known relationships to other conceptual spaces. There are conceptual gaps. Science, as a responsible social activity—as a total system—connects and integrates all this. Collective science must submit to the imperative to fill in the gaps for integration. Individual scientists need not heed this demand if they do not have the talent or taste for it, but each one must recognize how all science benefits if others integrate his or her work into the cumulative body of knowledge.

A future task for academics, as Clark Kerr sees it, is to unify the world of the intellect. He says:

We need to make contact between the two, the three, the many cultures; to open channels of intelligent conversation across the disciplines and divisions; to close the gap between C. P. Snow's "Luddites" and scientists; to answer fragmentation with general theories and sensitivities. Even philosophy, which once was the hub of the intellectual universe, is now itself fragmented into such diverse specialties as mathematics and semantics. However, the physical sciences are drawing together as new discoveries create more basic general theories; the biological sciences may be pulled together in the process now going on; the social sciences might be unified around the study of organizations and the relations of individuals to and within them. Chemistry and social psychology may come to be central focalizing fields. As knowledge is drawn together, if in fact it is, a faculty may again become a community of masters; but "a sense of the unity . . . of all knowledge" is still a very long way off.[74]

Sullivan suggests that our present view of the physical universe may change profoundly:

This change will come about through the development of biology. If biology finds it absolutely necessary, for the description of living things, to develop new concepts of its own, then the present outlook on "inorganic nature" will also be profoundly affected. For science will not lightly sacrifice the principle of continuity. The richer insight into the nature of living matter will throw the properties of dead matter into a new perspective. In fact, the distinction between the two, as far as may be, will be abolished.

This effort is already being made, of course, but from the other end. The present tendency is to reduce living organisms to mechanical systems. In view of what is now happening in physics itself, it does not seem likely that this effort will be successful. "Particle" physics, with simple location in space and time, has definitely proved itself inadequate. It is very probable, as Whitehead maintains, that the notion of particle

will have to be replaced by the notion of organism. In order to avoid a break of continuity the notions of physics will have to be enriched, and this enrichment will come from biology. We can look forward to further synthesis. The science of mind, at present in such a rudimentary state, will one day take control. In the service of the principle of continuity its concepts will be extended throughout the whole of nature. Only so will science reach the unity towards which it is aiming, and the differences between the sciences of mind, life, and matter, in their present form, will be seen to be unreal.[75]

Among the widely dispersed, irregularly arranged particles, stars, and galaxies of the universe exist the living systems, in constant flux and yet maintaining the most intricate patterns of stability we know. They occur in particular profusion—it may be exclusively—on this earth. Scavengers of the world's stores of energy and information, they have developed unique forms of complexity, particular critical subsystems, which, working together, enable them to postpone for varying periods the destruction of their patterns by the disorganizing decay of entropy. Much of their behavior is explained by this striving for survival, but the higher levels of systems also can afford the luxury of other emergent processes directed toward goals that the lower systems do not have the resources to achieve. And the higher levels are associated with a subtle and sensitive subjectivity.

The relations among the components of living systems are not put there by the imagination of the observer, as shepherds idly trace out a crab in the stars or as patients find bats in inkblots. The relations are inherent in the totality of the system and are empirically discovered by the scientist because they are there, patterning the coacting reality. We must pass beyond metaphysics, beyond raw empiricism, beyond the provincialism of the disciplines, and learn from quantitative experiments designed to evaluate general theory. Thus we can discover, in all its impressive generality and its fascinating particularity, how life makes form from flux. *Plus ça change, plus c'est la même chose.*

Or, as Whitehead wrote, process is reality: " . . . each actual entity is itself only describable as an organic process. It repeats in microcosm what the universe is in macrocosm. It is a process proceeding from phase to phase, each phase being the real basis from which its successor proceeds. . . ."[76]

A short time after completing War and Peace, *an unconfirmed story says, Tolstoy suddenly exclaimed to a friend: "I forgot to put in the yacht race!" That can never be said of this book. (See page 539, column 2, line 45.)*

NOTES AND REFERENCES

[1]Sadovsky, V. N. General systems theory: its task and methods of construction. *General Systems,* 1972, **17**, 171–179.

[2]deBeer, Sir G. Evolution. *Encyclopedia Britannica.* Vol. 7. Chicago: Encyclopaedia Britannica, 1974, 18.

[3]Forrester, J. W. *Urban dynamics.* Cambridge, Mass.: M.I.T. Press, 1969.

Also Forrester, J. W. *World dynamics.* Cambridge, Mass.: Wright-Allen Press, 1971.

[4]Mar, B. W. Where resources and environmental simulation models are going wrong. *Proc. IIASA planning conf. on ecol. sys.* Laxenburg, Austria: International Institute for Applied Systems Analysis (IIAS), 1973, **2**, 52–67.

[5]Bonner, J. T. *Cells and societies.* Princeton, N.J.: Princeton Univ. Press, 1955.

[6]Spencer, H. *The study of sociology.* New York: Appleton, 1896.

Also Huxley, T. H. *Collected essays. Evolution and ethics and other essays.* New York: Appleton, 1902. (Reprinted New York: Greenwood Press, 1968, 1–116.)

Also White, L. A. *The science of culture.* New York: Grove Press, 1949, 55–117.

Also Darlington, C. D. *Evolution of genetic systems.* (2d ed. rev.) Edinburgh: Oliver & Boyd, 1958.

[7]Wheeler, W. M. The ant-colony as an organism. *J. Morphol.,* 1911, **22**, 307–325.

Also Emerson, A. E. The supraorganismic aspects of the society. *Colloques internationaux du Centre de la Recherche Scientifique, 34.* Paris: Centre National de la Recherche Scientifique, 1952, 333–353.

Also Gerard, R. W. Organism, society and science. *Sci. Monthly,* 1940, **50**, 340–350, 403–412, 530–535.

[8]McConnaughey, B. H. Mesozoa. *Encyclopaedia Britannica.* Vol. 11. Chicago: Encyclopaedia Brittanica, 1974, 1013.

[9]NOTE: The following articles deal with various aspects of general living systems theory:

Miller, J. G. & Members of the Committee on the Behavioral Sciences. *Symposium: profits and problems of homeostatic models in the behavioral sciences.* Chicago: Univ. of Chicago, Committee on the Behavioral Sciences, 1953.

Also Miller, J. G. Toward a general theory for the behavioral sciences. *Amer. Psychol.,* 1955, **10**, 513–531.

Also Miller, J. G. The organization of life. *Perspectives in Biol. & Med.,* 1965, **9**, 107–125.

Also Miller, J. G. Living systems: basic concepts. *Behav. Sci.,* 1965, **10**, 193–237.

Also Miller, J. G. Living systems: structure and process. *Behav. Sci.,* 1965, **10**, 337–379.

Also Miller, J. G. Living systems: cross-level hypotheses. *Behav. Sci.,* 1965, **10**, 380–411.

Also Miller, J. G. Living systems: the cell. *Currents in modern Biol.,* 1971, **4**, 78–206.

Also Miller, J. G. Living systems: the organ. *Currents in modern Biol.,* 1971, **4**, 207–256.

Also Miller, J. G. Living systems: the organism. *Quart. Rev. Biol.,* 1973, **48**(2), 92–276.

Also Miller, J. G. Living systems: the group. *Behav. Sci.,* 1971, **16**, 302–398.

Also Miller, J. G. Living systems: the organization. *Behav. Sci.,* 1972, **17**, 1–182.

Also Miller, J. G. Living systems: the society. *Behav. Sci.,* 1975, **20**, 366–535.

Also Miller, J. G. Living systems: the supranational system. *Behav. Sci.,* 1976, **21**, 320–468.

The following articles relate to research on information input overload:

Miller, J. G. Information input overload and psychopathology. *Amer. J. Psychiat.,* 1960, **116**, 695–704.

Also Miller, J. G. Sensory overloading. In B. E. Flaherty (Ed.). *Psychophysiological aspects of space flight.* New York: Columbia Univ. Press, 1961, 215–224.

Also Miller, J. G. Information input overload. In M. C. Yovits, G. T. Jacobi, & G. D. Goldstein (Eds.). *Self-organizing systems.* Washington: Spartan Books, 1962, 61–78.

Also Miller, J. G. The individual as an information processing system. In W. S. Fields & W. Abbott (Eds.). *Information storage and neural control.* Springfield, Ill.: Charles C Thomas, 1963, 1–28.

Also Horvath, W. J., Halick, P., Peretz, B., & Miller, J. G. Precision measurements of latency and the variability of latency in single nerve fibers. *Proc. 4th internat. conf. on medical electronics.* New York: IRE, 1961, 79. Also Ann Arbor: Univ. of Michigan, Mental Health Research Institute, Preprint 115, August 1963.

Also Miller, J. G. Adjusting to overloads of information. In D. McK. Rioch & E. A. Weinstein (Eds.). *Disorders of communication.* Baltimore: Williams & Wilkins, 1964, 87–100.

Also Miller, J. G. Psychological aspects of communication overloads. In R. W. Waggoner & D. J. Carek (Eds.). *International psychiatry clinics: communication in clinical practice.* Boston: Little, Brown, 1964, 201–224.

Also Miller, J. G. Coping with administrators' information overload. *J. med. Ed.,* 1964, **29** (11, Part 2), 47–54, 182–189.

Also Miller, J. G. The dynamics of informational adjustment processes. In J. Masserman (Ed.). *Science and psychoanalysis.* Vol. 8. *Communication and community.* New York: Grune & Stratton, 1965, 38–48.

The following articles deal with applications of general living systems theory and research:

Miller, J. G. Programmed instruction and information theory: significance for medical education. In J. P. Lysaught, C. D. Sherman, Jr., & H. Jason (Eds.). Programmed instruction in medical education. *Proc. 1st Rochester conf.* Rochester, N.Y.: The Rochester Clearinghouse for Information on Self-Instruction in Medical Education, 1965, 127–135.

Also Miller, J. G. Role of communication. *Proc. White House conf. on health.* Washington: GPO, 1965, 253–275.

Also Miller, J. G. Administration: top level information flow. In R. W. Gerard (Ed.). *Computers and education.* New York: McGraw-Hill, 1967, 229–273.

Also Miller, J. G. Potentialities of a multi-media, interuniversity educational network. In A. deReuck & J. Knight (Eds.). *Ciba Foundation symposium on communication in science: documentation and automation.* London: J. & A. Churchill, 1967, 235–252.

Also Miller, J. G. The university as a living, information processing system. In Anon. *Architecture and the college.* Urbana: Univ. of Illinois Press, 1968, 9–24.

Also Miller, J. G. *Research and development priorities in instructional technologies for the less developed countries.* Washington: Academy for Educational Development, 1973.

Also Miller, J. G. *Alternative communication systems for education in the less developed countries.* Washington: Academy for Educational Development, 1973.

The following were papers written for the Presidential Commission on Instructional Technology and are included in *To improve learning: a report to the President and the Congress of the United States, March, 1970.* Washington: GPO, 1970.

Miller, J. G. The nature of living systems. In S. G. Tickton (Ed.). *To improve learning: an evaluation of instructional technology.* Vol. 2. New York: Bowker, 1971, 241–260.

Also Miller, J. G. The living systems involved in the educational process. In S. G. Tickton (Ed.). *To improve learning: an evaluation of instructional technology*. Vol. 2. New York: Bowker, 1971, 261–270.

Also Miller, J. G. A ten-year program for developing, evaluating, and implementing instructional technologies. In S. G. Tickton (Ed.). *To improve learning: an evaluation of instructional technology*. Vol. 2. New York: Bowker, 1971, 271–279.

Also Miller, J. G. Deciding whether and how to use educational technology in the light of cost-effectiveness evaluation. In S. G. Tickton (Ed.). *To improve learning: an evaluation of instructional technology*. Vol. 2. New York: Bowker, 1971, 1007–1027.

Also Miller, J. G. & Rath, G. J. Planning-programming-budgeting and cost-effectiveness analysis in educational systems. In S. G. Tickton (Ed.). *To improve learning: an evaluation of instructional technology*. Vol. 2. New York: Bowker, 1971, 1029–1059.

[10]Glassman, R. B. Persistence and loose coupling in living systems. *Behav. Sci.*, 1973, **18**, 87, 90.

[11]Wilson, D. Forms of hierarchy: a selected bibliography. *General Systems.*, 1969, **14**, 8.

[12]Scheflen, A. E. Systems and psychosomatics: an introduction to psychosomatic manifestations of rapport in psychotherapy. *Psychosom. Med.*, 1966, **28**, 298–299.

[13]Brody, H. The systems view of man: implications for medicine, science, and ethics. *Perspectives in Biol. & Med.*, 1973, **17**, 74–75.

[14]Sahal, D. Elements of an emerging theory of complexity per se. *Cybernetica*, 1976, **19**(1), 5–38.

[15]Becht, G. Systems theory, the key to holism and reductionism. *BioSci.*, 1974, **24**(10), 569–579.

[16]Glassman, R. B. Selection processes in living systems: role in cognitive construction and recovery from brain damage. *Behav. Sci.*, 1974, **19**, 150.

[17]Coleman, J. C. *Personality dynamics and effective behavior.* Chicago: Scott, Foresman, 1960.
Cf. also Coleman, J. C. & Hammen, C. L. *Contemporary psychology and effective behavior.* Glenview, Ill.: Scott, Foresman, 1974.

[18]Allport, G. W. The open system in personality theory. *J. abnorm. soc. Psychol.*, 1960, **61**, 3, 307.

[19]Kolouch, F. T. Hypnosis in living systems theory: a living systems autopsy in a polysurgical, polymedical, polypsychiatric patient addicted to Talwin. *Amer. J. clin. Hypnosis*, 1970, **13**, 1, 22–34.

[20]Kluger, J. M. Childhood asthma and the social milieu. *J. Amer. Acad. Child Psychiat.*, 1969, **8**, 353–366.

[21]Beckett, J. A. General systems theory, psychiatry and psychotherapy. *Int. J. Group Practice*, 1973, **23**, 292–305.

[22]Bolman, W. M. Systems theory, psychiatry, and school phobia. *Amer. J. Psychiat.*, 1970, **127**, 65–72.

[23]Pinderhughes, C. A. Ego development and cultural development. *Amer. J. Psychiat.*, 1974, **131**, 171–175.
Also Peterfreund, E. Information, systems, and psychoanalysis. *Psychol. Issues*, 1971, **7** (Monograph 25/26), 141–142.

[24]Meir, A. Z. General system theory developments and perspectives for medicine and psychiatry. *Arch. gen. Psychiat.*, 1969, 21, 304–307.
Also Gray, W. & Rizzo, N. D. History and development of general systems theory. In W. Gray, F. J. Duhl, & N. D. Rizzo (Eds.). *General systems theory and psychiatry.* Boston: Little, Brown, 1969, 16.

[25]Laszlo, E. A systems philosophy of human values. *Behav. Sci.*, 1973, **18**, 255.

[26]Durkin, H. E. General systems theory and group therapy: an introduction. *Int. J. Group Practice*, 1972, **22**, 159–166.
Also Piehuta, J. P. Systems concepts and family therapy. (Unpublished paper)

[27]Miller, W. B. Psychiatric consultation. Part I. A general systems approach. *Psychiat. in Med.*, 1973, **4**, 135–145.

[28]Susman, G. I. The impact of automation on work group autonomy and task specialization. *Human Relat.*, 1970, **23**, 568.

[29]Hearn, G. *Theory building in social work.* Toronto: Univ. of Toronto Press, 1958.

[30]Newbrough, J. R. Community psychology. *Amer. Psychol.*, 1972, **27**, 770.

[31]Deutsch, S. H. A parallel process systems theory of the community organization process, and its application to some historical issues as illustrative of its use. (Unpublished paper)

[32]Bolman, W. M. Theoretical and community bases of community mental health. *Amer. J. Psychiat.*, 1967, **124**, 7–21.

[33]Baker, F. General systems theory, research, and medical care. In A. Sheldon, F. Baker, & C. P. McLaughlin (Eds.). *Systems and medical care.* Cambridge, Mass.: MIT Press, 1970, 1–26.
Also Baker, F. & O'Brien, G. Intersystems relations and coordination of human service organizations. *Amer. J. pub. Health*, 1971, **61**, 130–137.

[34]Burgess, J., Nelson, R. H., & Wallhaus, R. Network analysis as a method for the evaluation of service delivery systems. *Comm. Men. Health J.*, 1974, **10**(3), 337–345.

[35]Smith, C. M. Crisis and aftermath: community psychiatry in Saskatchewan, 1963–69. *Canad. Psychiat. Assoc. J.*, 1971, **16**, 71.

[36]Pierce, L. M. Usefulness of a systems approach for problem conceptualization and investigation. *Nurs. Res.*, 1972, **21**, 509–517.

[37]Werley, H. H., Zuzich, A., Zajkowski, M., & Zagornik, A. D. (Eds.). *Health research: the systems approach.* New York: Springer, 1976.

[38]Weiss, R. S. & Rein, M. The evaluation of broad-aim programs: experimental design, its difficulties, and an alternative. *Admin. Sci. Quart.*, 1970, **15**(1), 97–109.

[39]Broskowski, A. Concepts of teacher-centered consultation. *Professional Psychol.*, 1973, **4**, 50–51.

[40]Robey, D. Classroom cybernetics. *Peabody J. Ed.*, 1975, **52**, 135.
Also Buss, A. R. Systems theory, generation theory, and the university: some predictions. *Higher Ed.*, 1975, **4**, 429–445.

[41]Duncan, D. M. James G. Miller's living systems theory: issues for management thought and practice. *Acad. Mgmt. J.*, 1972, **15**, 513–523.

[42]Lichtman, C. M. & Hunt, R. G. Personality and organization theory: a review of some conceptual literature. *Psychol. Bull.*, 1971, **76**, 285–287.
Also Berrien, F. K. A general systems approach to organizations. In M. D. Dunnette (Ed.). *Handbook of industrial and organizational psychology.* Chicago: Rand McNally, 1976, 42–43.
Also Alderfer, C. P. Change processes in organizations. In M. D. Dunnette (Ed.). *Handbook of industrial and organizational psychology.* Chicago: Rand McNally, 1976, 1592–1594.

[43]Rogers, E. M. & Rogers, R. A. *Communication in organizations.* New York: Free Press, 1976, 29–58.

[44]Reese, W. G. An essay on administration. *Amer. J. Psychiat.*, 1972, **128**, 69–72.

[45]Noell, J. J. On the administrative sector of social systems: an analysis of the size and complexity of government bureaucracies in the American states. *Social Forces*, 1974, **52**, 549–558.

[46]Gross, B. M. The state of the nation: social systems account-

ing. In R. A. Bauer (Ed.). *Social indicators.* Cambridge, Mass.: MIT Press, 1966, 158, 179–180.

[47]Bostock, W. The cultural explanation of politics. *Pol. Sci.,* 1973, **25,** 41–42.

[48]Peery, N. S., Jr. General systems theory: an inquiry into its social philosophy. *Acad. Mgmt. J.,* 1972, **15,** 496.

[49]Golant, S. M. Adjustment process in a system. *Geographical anal.,* 1971, **3,** 203–220.

[50]Klapp, O. E. *Models of social order: an introduction to socio-logical theory.* Palo Alto, Calif.: National Press Books, 1973. Also Anderson, R. E. & Carter, I. E. *Human behavior in the social environment.* Chicago: Aldine Publishing Co., 1974.

[51]Nettl, P. The concept of system in political science. *Pol. Studies,* 1966, **14,** 305–338.

[52]Judge, W. J. Systems analysis and the Folsom-Midlan question. *Southwest. J. Anthropol.,* 1970, **26,** 41. Also Schiffer, M. B. Archaeological context and systemic context. *Amer. Antiq.,* 1972, **37,** 157. Also Plog, F. T. Systems theory in archeological research. *Ann. Rev. Anthropol.,* 1975, **4,** 218–219. Also Hage, P. Structural balance and clustering in bushmen kinship relations. *Behav. Sci.,* 1976, **21,** 36–47.

[53]Paquet, G. & Wallot, J.-P. International circumstances of Lower Canada, 1786–1810: prolegomenon. *Canad. hist. Rev.,* 1972, **53,** 375.

[54]Singer, J. D. The global system and its sub-systems. In J. N. Rosenau (Ed.). *Linkage politics.* New York: Free Press, 1969, 35.

[55]Stephens, J. An appraisal of some system approaches in the study of international systems. *Internat. Stud. Quart.,* 1972, **16,** 321–349. Skjelsbaek, K. Peace and the structure of the international organization network. *J. Peace Res.,* 1972, **9,** 321.

[57]McLeod, J. Behavioral science, system theory—and simulation. *Behav. Sci.,* 1974, **19,** 58.

[58]Deutsch, K. W., Platt, J., & Senghaas, D. Conditions favoring major advances in social science. *Science,* 1971, **191,** 453.

[59]Toffler, A. *Future shock.* New York: Random House, 1970, 139–141.

[60]Lipowski, Z. J. Surfeit of attractive information inputs: a hallmark of our environment. *Behav. Sci.,* 1971, **61,** 468. Also Lipowski, Z. J. Psychosomatic medicine in a changing society: some current trends in theory and research. *Com-*

prehensive Psychiat., 1973, **14,** 207, 209. Also Lipowski, Z. J. Sensory overloads, information over-loads and behavior. *Psychother. Psychosom.,* 1974, **23,** 265.

[61]Coleman, J. C. Life stress and maladaptive behavior. *Amer. J. occupat. Therapy,* 1973, **27,** 170.

[62]Rolfe, J. M. Multiple task performance: operator overload. *Occupational Psychol.,* 1971, **45,** 126–127.

[63]Huntley, M. S., Jr. Task complexity and serial performance under steadily increasing input rates. *Human Factors,* 1972, **14**(1), 65, 74–75.

[64]Hurst, P. M. & McKendry, J. M. Effects of redundancy on performance under overload stress. *Percept. & motor Skills,* 1971, **32,** 907–915.

[65]Hawks, D. V. & Marshall, W. L. A parsimonious theory of overinclusive thinking and retardation in schizophrenia. *Br. J. med. Psychol.,* 1971, **44,** 75–83.

[66]Cummings, L. L. & DeCotiis, T. A. Organizational correlates of perceived stress in a professional organization. *Publ. Personnel Management.,* 1973, **2,** 277.

[67]Holsti, O. R. Crisis, stress and decision-making. *Internat. soc. sci. J.,* 1971, **23,** 63–66.

[68]James, B. J. Functions of half-conscious administration: a theory of decentralization. (Unpublished paper read at the American Society for Public Administration Annual Meeting, April 22, 1976, Washington, D.C.)

[69]Nystrom, P. C. Input-output processes of the Federal Trade Commission. *Admin. Sci. Quart.,* 1975, **20,** 104–113.

[70]Balutis, A. P. The role of the staff in the legislature: the case of New York. *Public Admin. Rev.,* 1975, **35,** 357.

[71]Odum, E. P. Energy, ecosystem development and environmental risk. *J. Risk & Insur.,* 1976, **43,** 9–10.

[72]Klapp, O. E. Opening and closing in open systems. *Behav. Sci.,* 1975, **20,** 251–257.

[73]Ehrle, R. A. Information distortion. *ETC.,* 1973, **30,** 147–149.

[74]Kerr, C. *The uses of the university.* Cambridge, Mass.: Harvard Univ. Press, 1963, 119–120. Reprinted by permission.

[75]Sullivan, J. W. N. *The limitations of science.* New York: Viking Press, 1933, 302–303. Copyright 1933, by The Viking Press, Inc. Reprinted by permission. Whitehead, A. N. *Process and reality.* New York: Macmillan, 1930, 327. Copyright, 1929, by The Macmillan Company. Reprinted by permission of The Macmillan Company and Cambridge University Press.

Bibliographic Index

The following is an alphabetical listing of the names of authors or editors in the notes and references in each chapter of this book. Anonymous references are listed under the publisher or publication in which they appear. The chapter numbers are in **boldface**; the note and reference numbers are in lightface.

Abbott, W. (Ed.), **5**:181; **8**:196; **13**:9
Abe, D. K., **10**:170, 366
Abelson, R. P., **8**:437, 440, 441, 443, 447
Abkin, M. H., **11**:399
Abramson, N. M., **4**:53
Ackoff, R. L., **3**:1, 2; **4**:63, 108; **10**:28
Adams, J. A., **5**:92
Adey, W. R., **8**:58, 59, 65, 70, 280, 332, 333, 391, 416
Adler, J., **6**:308
Adrian, E. D. (Ed.), **8**:243
Agranoff, B. W., **8**:199, 218, 219, 233–235, 239
Air, G. M., **6**:39
Albert, R. S., **9**:85
Alderfer, C. P., **13**:42
Alexander, T., **11**:65, 68
Alger, C. F. (Ed.), **12**:243, 244, 247
Alker, H. R., Jr., **12**:250, 252, 267
Allee, W. C., **2**:86; **9**:8, 130, 131
Allen, G., **8**:310
Allen, R. D., **6**:106, 161, 172, 180, 449
Allen, R. D. (Ed.), **6**:178
Allen, T. J., **10**:152; **11**:95, 96
Allin, P., **6**:448
Allport, F. H., **8**:146, 317, 370
Allport, G. W., **4**:32, 162; **11**:3; **13**:18
Alluisi, E. A., **5**:34, 35, 83, 84, 122; **8**:367

Alsop, S., **5**:155
Altman, J., **8**:191, 210, 211
Altmann, M., **9**:61
Amassian, V. E., **5**:15, 66
American Telephone and Telegraph Company, **5**:113
Ananichev, K. V., **12**:33, 34, 36, 84
Ancevich, S. S., **5**:175
Anderson, A. A., **12**:226–228
Anderson, E. G., **7**:12
Anderson, J. C., **10**:360, 362, 363
Anderson, J. M., **12**:226–228
Anderson, J. W., **11**:200, 214–222
Anderson, R. E., **2**:76; **9**:5, 187; **10**:1; **13**:50
Anderson, T. R., **10**:261
Andrew, A. M., **4**:53
Andrews, W. (Ed.), **11**:161
Apgar, J., **6**:38
Appley, M. H. (Ed.), **5**:89
Arbib, M. A., **8**:598
Ardrey, R., **2**:88
Arieti, S. (Ed.), **7**:86–88
Armer, P., **8**:594
Armstrong, R., **10**:202
Arnett, P., **10**:116
Arnoff, E. L., **4**:108
Aronson, E., **8**:443

Aronson, E. (Ed.), **8**:437, 440, 441, 447
Arrow, K. J., **9**:77, 89
Arvy, L., **6**:149
Asch, S. E., **8**:327
Aschoff, J., **8**:405–407
Ashby, W. R., **2**:43, 45, 98, 102, 104, 105, 111, 113; **3**:4, 12; **4**:5, 54, 116; **8**:603, 607–610
Asimov, I., **8**:583
Atkinson, D. E., **6**:328, 403, 404, 406–408, 426
Atkinson, J. W., **4**:67
Atkinson, R. C., **8**:645–647
Auerbach, F., **5**:34
Augenstine, L., **2**:26
Autrey, S., **9**:49
Autrum, H., **6**:201, 202; **8**:28
Avers, C. J., **6**:113, 114
Avis, H. H., **8**:223
Avis, V., **8**:469
Ayres, R. U., **11**:263

Babchuk, N., **9**:147
Back, K. W., **9**:2, 3, 169, 170, 197, 239
Baer, R. M., **2**:26
Bahrick, H. P., **5**:98; **8**:453
Baier, R., **7**:19

Bakeman, R., **9**:240, 241
Baker, D., **7**:95
Baker, E. J., **5**:35
Baker, F., **13**:33
Baker, R. A., **10**:352
Baker, W. O., **1**:2; **3**:18
Bakke, E. W., **10**:5, 9, 24
Balderston, F. E. (Ed.), **8**:648, 649
Bales, R. F., **9**:24, 74, 97, 103, 136, 188
Bales, R. F. (Ed.), **9**:72, 74
Balinsky, B. I., **8**:475
Ball, G. W., **11**:188–190
Balutis, A. P., **13**:70
Barber, J. D., **11**:166–174
Barch, A. M., **8**:325
Bardin, C. W., **7**:37, 39, 53
Barghoorn, E. X., **6**:410
Barker, R. G., **4**:142
Barkun, M., **12**:59–63, 66, 67, 160
Barlow, H. B., **8**:34, 42, 56
Barnard, G. A., **4**:53
Barnett, H. G., **11**:102, 392
Barnlund, D. C., **4**:95, 99–102; **9**:84
Barondes, S. H., **8**:222, 224
Barrell, B. G., **6**:39
Barringer, H. R. (Ed.), **9**:184, 185; **11**:347
Barrows, H. S., **8**:590
Barth, R. H., Jr., **8**:340
Bartlett, F. C., **8**:246; **9**:37
Bartley, S. H., **5**:17; **8**:37, 39, 119
Bartram, P. R., **8**:642
Basowitz, H., **8**:448
Bass, B. M., **9**:101, 110, 153; **10**:181, 345–349
Bauer, R. A., **11**:205, 332
Bauer, R. A. (Ed.), **11**:9–12; **13**:46
Bauerschmidt, R., **12**:285
Baumgartner, G., **5**:16
Bavelas, A., **9**:27, 32, 35, 44, 149, 151
Bayley, N., **8**:502, 503
Beach, F. A., **2**:37; **8**:510
Beach, F. A. (Ed.), **8**:162
Beadle, G., **6**:40
Beament, J. W. L. (Ed.), **8**:41, 104, 105
Bearn, A. G., **8**:526
Becht, G., **13**:15
Beckett, J. A., **13**:21
Beckett, P. G. S., **8**:536, 537, 539, 540
Beddoes, M. P., **8**:618
Beebe-Center, J. G., **5**:52, 59
Beecher, H. K., **8**:287
Beegle, J. A., **9**:202
Beeson, P. B. (Ed.), **8**:526, 529
Behrens, W. W., III, **3**:46; **4**:150; **12**:39, 205, 211–213, 217, 226
Beidler, L. M., **8**:66–68, 71, 73, 75, 80, 82
Bell, G. B., **9**:79
Bell, G. H., **7**:17, 21
Belmont, I., **5**:169

Beman, L., **11**:321
Bendix, R. (Ed.), **11**:74–78
Benne, K. D., **9**:137
Benne, K. D. (Ed.), **10**:209
Bennett, J. P., **11**:422, 425, 428
Bennis, W. G., **5**:142; **10**:252–255
Bennis, W. G. (Ed.), **10**:209
Benson, O., **12**:242
Benton, R., **7**:92
Benzer, S., **6**:33
Berelson, B., **4**:4, 7–11, 16, 31, 33, 34, 36, 38, 47–50, 52, 65, 66, 68, 71, 72, 78, 79, 87, 116, 118–120, 122, 123, 137–141, 153, 157, 158, 160, 177; **8**:256, 276; **12**:87, 97
Berkowitz, L., **9**:195
Berkowitz, N., **11**:37, 38, 342, 343, 371, 372
Berkun, M. M., **8**:417
Berlyne, D. E., **4**:113; **8**:444
Berman, A. L., **5**:20
Bernal, J. D., **6**:419
Bernard, E. E. (Ed.), **8**:642
Bernhard, W., **6**:469
Bernhardt, W., **6**:148
Bernstein, J., **3**:8
Bernstein, L., **8**:491
Berrien, F. K., **13**:42
Bertalanffy, L. v., **2**:42, 44, 71, 73, 120; **8**:483; **11**:383
Bertelson, P., **5**:46
Best, C. H. (Ed.), **6**:364; **7**:4, 50, 51; **8**:18, 114, 291, 292, 412; **11**:64
Beswick, F. B., **6**:277
Beurle, R. L., **8**:163, 599
Bevan, W., **9**:85
Bialek, H. M., **8**:417
Biderman, A. D., **11**:9–11, 148
Biederman-Thorson, M., **6**:216, 223, 224
Biehl, J., **6**:447
Biel, W. C., **10**:433
Bigelow, J., **2**:103, 114; **8**:604
Billodeau, E. A., **8**:320, 460
Billodeau, I. McD., **8**:460
Bingley, M. S., **6**:181
Birch, H. G., **5**:169
Bird, C., **5**:115
Bird, H. H., **4**:171
Birdwhistell, R. L., **8**:159
Birk, L. (Ed.), **8**:166, 168
Bishop, E., **11**:53
Bishop, G. H., **6**:251
Bixenstine, V. E., **9**:213
Blackler, A. W., **7**:67
Blair, D. H., Jr., **6**:2
Blake, R. R., **9**:228; **10**:101, 126, 329, 332–335
Blank, G., **5**:30
Blankenship, G., **12**:281–283

Blanksten, G. I. (Ed.), **9**:184, 185; **11**:347
Blau, P. M., **9**:233; **10**:4, 14, 30, 74, 112, 113, 136, 137, 160, 220, 222, 259, 261
Bledsoe, W. W., **3**:29
Bliss, C. I., **4**:15
Bliss, E. L., **5**:28
Bloch, C., **8**:581
Blong, C. K., **11**:131
Bloom, W., **7**:8, 23, 24
Bloomfield, D., **10**:298
Bloomfield, L. P., **12**:190–195
Bluemle, L. W., Jr., **7**:77
Blumenfeld, H., **10**:269, 273
Bockris, J. O'M., **11**:269
Boehlke, R. F., **10**:384
Bogoch, S., **8**:537
Boguslaw, R., **11**:401, 402
Bohdanecky, M., **8**:225
Bohdanecky, Z., **8**:225
Bohn, H. L., **11**:264, 271
Bolman, W. M., **13**:22, 32
Bolman, W. M., (Ed.), **9**:222
Bolt, R., **9**:157
Boltzmann, L., **2**:16
Bonini, C. P., **10**:378–380
Bonner, J. T., **3**:47; **6**:2; **8**:25, 108; **13**:5
Borgatta, E. F., **9**:97, 103
Borgatta, E. F. (Ed.), **9**:72, 74
Borst, J. M., **8**:152
Bossil, H., **12**:285
Bostock, W., **13**:47
Boulden, J. B., **10**:382
Boulding, K. E., **3**:44; **10**:258, 265; **11**:375
Bourne, L. E., Jr., **8**:458, 459
Bovard, E. W., **8**:494
Bowers, D. G., **10**:10
Bowman, E. H., **10**:418
Bowman, R. L., **7**:76
Boyd, R., **12**:218, 221, 222
Brabb, B., **5**:37, 75
Brachet, J., **6**:28, 30, 46, 48, 76, 107, 109, 112, 141, 150, 162, 164
Brachet, J. (Ed.), **6**:50–53, 55, 65, 149, 320, 437–439, 449, 456, 462, 465, 469, 471, 477, 480; **7**:5, 6
Brackett, H. R., **8**:248
Braden, I., **8**:281, 392
Bradham, G. B., **8**:611
Brady, J. V., **8**:166, 547
Braham, M., **1**:1
Branson, H. R., **2**:26; **6**:10
Braun, A. C., **6**:476
Braun, W., **6**:36, 126, 128, 237, 302, 311, 327
Braynes, S. N., **2**:83
Brazier, M. A. B. (Ed.), **6**:24, 268; **7**:7, 41; **8**:206, 212
Bredvold, L. I. (Ed.), **9**:223
Brehm, J. W., **8**:444; **9**:228

Breiman, L., **4**:53
Brelsford, J. W., **8**:647
Bremer, F. (Ed.), **8**:243
Bremer, J. L., **7**:2, 64
Bremermann, H. J., **2**:11; **3**:22
Brenner, M., **9**:62
Brenner, S., **6**:241, 307, 312, 313
Bretscher, M. S., **6**:67
Breuer, H., **5**:124
Breul, H., **11**:39
Bricker, P. D., **5**:33
Briggs, G. E., **10**:236
Brillouin, L., **2**:25, 26, 34, 50
Britten, R. J., **6**:306, 323
Broadbent, D. E., **5**:91, 93–96, 99–101;
    8:227, 229, 371, 372
Brobeck, J. R., **7**:42; **8**:111, 350, 451
Brobeck, J. R. (Ed.), **4**:148; **7**:9, 10, 15,
    18, 20, 25, 33–35, 37, 39, 43–47,
    52–54, 57–60; **8**:111, 115, 350, 451
Brock, L. J., **5**:3
Brock, T. D., **6**:49
Brodbeck, A. A., Jr., **8**:160
Brodie, B. B., **8**:534
Brody, H., **13**:13
Brody, R. A., **4**:128; **12**:246, 253–256
Brody, R. A. (Ed.), **12**:243, 244, 247
Brogden, W. J., **5**:97
Bronfenbrenner, U., **9**:224
Broom, L., **11**:392
Broskowski, A., **13**:39
Brown, D., **11**:282
Brown, G. W., **5**:111; **8**:302, 311; **11**:97
Brown, J., **8**:241
Brown, J. S., **4**:142; **8**:444
Brown, L. D., **10**:189
Brown, L. R., **12**:118, 119
Brown, N. L., **6**:39
Brown, R. A., **4**:171
Brozek, J., **8**:361
Bruck, H. W., **4**:6, 86
Brues, A. M. (Ed.), **7**:75
Brüike, F. (Ed.), **4**:170
Brune, G. G., **8**:535
Bruner, J. S., **8**:370
Brunner, R. D., **12**:267
Buchan, J., **10**:27, 44, 46, 47, 383, 407
Buchanan, W., **12**:50, 51
Buck, R. C., **2**:58, 91, 98
Buck, V. E., **10**:130, 142
Bucy, P. C., **8**:292
Budin, W., **5**:176; **8**:549
Bullock, T. H., **6**:264, 330, 332, 334, 335,
    347–349, 351, 359
Burck, G., **11**:55, 57, 59
Burgers, J. M., **2**:40
Burgess, J., **5**:48; **13**:34
Burke, C. J., **8**:638
Burnell, D., **6**:495

Burnett, R. A., **12**:225
Burns, A. L., **4**:132
Burns, J. R., **12**:224
Burns, T., **10**:120
Burrell, S. A., **11**:387; **12**:20, 175–180, 184
Burroughs, W., **9**:49
Burt, C., **8**:499
Busch, A. E., **11**:121, 122, 124–126
Buschke, H., **8**:247
Bush, R. R., **8**:639
Bush, R. R. (Ed.), **5**:45, 186
Bush, V., **5**:109, 110
Busnel, R. G., **8**:342
Buss, A., **4**:88; **13**:40
Butler, J. A. V., **2**:85; **6**:3; **8**:476, 558, 560
Byers, L. W., **8**:537
Bylin, J. E., **11**:268
Bylinsky, G., **11**:80, 267
Byron, Lord G. G., **9**:223

Cahn, M. B., **6**:444
Cahn, R. D., **6**:444
Calame, B. E., **11**:83
Calhoun, J. B., **5**:155
Calvin, M., **6**:54, 415, 419
Campbell, D. T., **2**:48
Campbell, J. W. (Ed.), **8**:583
Cannon, W. B., **2**:98; **3**:51; **4**:93; **8**:410
Cantril, H., **12**:50, 51
Capaldi, R. A., **6**:71
Carek, D. J. (Ed.), **5**:179, 181; **13**:9
Carlsmith, J. M., **9**:160
Carlson, A. J., **7**:11
Carlson, F. D. (Ed.), **8**:199
Carlson, F. R., Jr., **8**:661
Carlton, P. L., **8**:223
Carmichael, L., **1**:2
Carmichael, L. (Ed.), **8**:516, 517
Carneiro, R. L., **11**:34–36
Carroll, J. B. (Ed.), **11**:110
Carter, I. E., **2**:76; **9**:5, 187; **10**:1; **13**:50
Carter, J. H., **9**:71, 74
Cartwright, D., **1**:2; **9**:155, 161; **10**:60
Cartwright, D. (Ed.), **9**:70, 74
Casaco, J. A., **10**:388
Casola, L., **8**:218, 219
Casson, L., **11**:242, 243
Cattell, R. B., **1**:2; **8**:420–422, 500, 505,
    506; **9**:53, 54, 74, 144, 190, 227;
    11:39, 40, 118, 119, 236
Cauthorn, R. C., **11**:264, 271
Cavert, H. M., **7**:11
Cervinka, V., **2**:51
Chaiken, J. M., **10**:415
Chamberlain, T. J., **7**:42
Chambers, J. C., **10**:381
Chambers, R. W., **5**:92
Chammah, A. M., **8**:653; **9**:220

Chance, B., **6**:488
Chang, H.-T., **6**:365, 366
Changeux, J.-P., **6**:239, 309, 405, 427
Chapanis, A., **5**:61
Chapman, D. W., **5**:70
Chapman, J., **5**:170–172; **8**:550
Chapman, R., **12**:201
Chapman, R. L., **5**:135, 138; **10**:433
Chapple, E. D., **9**:4, 39, 138; **11**:45, 73
Charley, R. J. (Ed.), **3**:13
Chase, R. A., **8**:454, 456, 457
Chemical and Engineering News, **6**:474
Chen, A. T. L., **8**:528
Chenery, H. B., **10**:38
Cherry, C., **9**:40
Cherry, C. (Ed.), **4**:53, 57; **5**:9, 24, 37, 76
Cherryholmes, C. H., **11**:431–433
Chervany, N. L., **10**:384
Childe, V. G., **10**:245
Chin, R. (Ed.), **10**:209
Chisholm, M. (Ed.), **3**:13; **4**:19
Chorley, R. J. (Ed.), **4**:19
Chown, S., **8**:574, 578
Christie, L. S., **2**:9; **5**:44; **9**:34, 44, 46,
    50–52, 57, 176
Chu, N., **12**:285
Churchman, C. W., **4**:108; **8**:322;
    10:356, 357
Cieciura, S. J., **7**:69
Claiborne, R. (Ed.), **6**:67
Clark, P. G., **10**:38
Clemens, W. C., Jr., **12**:238, 239, 241
Cleveland Plain Dealer, **10**:34, 328
Coale, A. J., **12**:88, 89, 98
Cochran, T. C. (Ed.), **11**:161
Cofer, C. N., **9**:194
Coffin, R. W., **6**:487
Cohen, A. R., **8**:444
Cohen, B. D., **5**:164
Cohen, H. D., **8**:222, 224
Cohen, J. E., **2**:8, 93
Cohen, K. J., **11**:406–410
Cohen, R. (Ed.), **11**:30, 34–36, 366, 386
Cohen, W. J., **11**:19
Cohn, V. H., Jr., **8**:413
Cole, H. S. D., **12**:215, 223
Cole, H. S. D. (Ed.), **12**:214, 217, 219
Coleman, J. C., **2**:73; **13**:17, 61
Collias, N. E., **9**:131
Collins, H. H., Jr., **8**:507
Colter, J. S., **4**:171
Comfort, A., **8**:559
Commission of the European
    Communities, **12**:13, 29
Conard, A. F. (Ed.), **9**:86
Cone, R. A., **8**:43
Congdon, J. D., **8**:17
Connor, D. J., **8**:618
Conrad, D., **8**:547

Conroy, R. T. W. L., 6:277
Cook, E., 11:61, 239, 240
Cook, J. G., 10:352
Cook, S. W., 4:35
Coombs, C. H., 8:323
Coombs, C. H. (Ed.), 8:319; 9:211
Coombs, J. S., 5:3
Coon, C. S., 9:4, 138; 11:33, 45, 73
Coon, H., 6:444
Coonan, T. J., 5:54
Cooper, F. S., 8:118, 152, 344, 354
Cooper, I., 7:91
Cooper, W. W. (Ed.), 10:3, 15, 109, 110, 114, 129, 141, 147, 148, 153, 223, 231, 236, 244
Coplin, W. D. (Ed.), 12:185, 238, 239, 248–250
Corliss, W. R., 8:585–589
Corning, W. C., 4:172
Cornsweet, J. C., 8:40
Cornsweet, T. N., 8:40
Costa, E., 8:534
Coulson, A. R., 6:39
Cowan, J. D., 8:598
Cramer, E. H., 9:122, 123
Crandall, M. A., 6:49
Crane, R. I., 11:7, 258, 259
Creutzfeldt, O., 5:10; 8:127
Crick, F. H. C., 6:31, 42
Crook, M. N., 8:577
Crosby, E. C., 6:144, 482; 7:30; 8:23, 117, 137, 142, 293, 297–299, 337, 351, 356, 419
Cross, H. A., 8:515
Crosskey, A. A., 11:159, 225
Crossman, E. R. F. W., 5:32
Crutchfield, R. S., 9:74, 174
Cullen, J. K., Jr., 8:454
Cummings, L. L., 13:66
Cureton, E. E., 11:206
Curnow, R. C., 12:223
Curtis, A. S. G., 7:71
Curtis, H. W. (Ed.), 12:236
Cutler, C. C., 2:32
Cuzin, F., 6:241, 307, 312, 313
Cyert, R. M., 10:129, 141, 147, 223; 11:406–410

Dahl, R. A., 10:228; 11:136, 224, 227–230
Dale, E., 10:117, 279, 291, 295
Dancoff, S. M., 6:7
Danev, S. G., 5:178
Danielli, J. F., 6:67, 142
Danowski, T. S., 2:106, 108
Danziger, L., 8:650
Dardik, H., 7:19
Dardik, I. I., 7:19

Darlington, C. D., 13:6
Darnell, J. E., 6:130, 310
Darwin, C., 8:474; 11:337
Davidson, D. M., Jr., 9:201
Davidson, E. H., 6:306, 323
Davidson, J. N., 7:17, 21
Davidson, N., 6:450; 7:27
Davies, E. A. J., 11:54
Davies, P. W., 5:20
Davis, B. D., 6:319, 425
Davis, H., 5:18; 6:371, 379; 8:49, 50, 53–55, 131–132
Davis, R. E., 8:199, 218, 219, 233–235, 239
Davis, R. H., 11:401
Davis, R. L. (Ed.), 8:319, 9:211
Davitz, J., 9:62
Davson, H., 7:16
Daw, H. T., 12:47
Dean, R. D., 8:364
de Beauregard, O. C., 2:6
de Beer, Sir G., 13:2
DeCotiis, T. A., 13:66
De Fleur, M. L., 11:104
Degan, J. W., 9:87
De Groot, S. R., 2:30
De Haven, J. C., 7:91
Delafresnaye, J. F. (Ed.), 4:170; 8:243
Deland, E. C., 7:91; 8:611
De Leeuw, F., 11:427
Demeny, P., 12:91
De Montmollin, G., 9:56
Denny-Brown, D., 8:252
Dent, J. K., 10:135
Denton, R., 12:285
de Reuck, A. (Ed.), 13:9
de Robertis, E. D. P., 6:67
de Robertis, E. M. F., Jr., 6:67
Desai, M., 12:232
de Terra, N., 6:70
Dethier, V. G., 8:341
Detweiler, D. K., 7:9, 10, 15, 18–20, 33–35, 44, 57–60; 8:115
Deutsch, J. A., 8:644
Deutsch, K. W., 2:1, 112; 4:14, 15, 45, 46, 129; 9:11; 10:93, 286, 287, 422–429; 11:50, 108, 322, 323, 325, 330, 365, 367, 387, 391; 12:5, 20, 175–180, 184; 13:58
Deutsch, M., 9:60, 217, 218
Deutsch, S. H., 13:31
De Valois, R., 5:17
Devereux, G., 10:308
De Vito, S. N., 11:92
Devoe, D. B., 8:577
De Vore, I., 9:19
De Vries, H., 8:69
Dewinter, C. R., 5:178
Dexter, L. A., 11:205

Di Cara, L., 8:166
Dickens, J. H., 10:437
Dickson, G. W., 10:360, 362, 363
Dickson, J. F., III, 6:487
Dickson, J. F., III (Ed.), 8:612
Dickson, L., 9:200
Dickson, W. J., 9:73, 206; 10:185
Diehn, B., 6:188, 493
Dill, W. R., 9:26, 47, 58, 66
Dionne, P. J., 12:225
Ditchburn, R. W., 8:40
Doane, B. K., 8:395
Dobzhansky, T., 8:473
Dodd, S. C., 4:29; 9:42; 10:84–86
Domino, E. F., 5:164
Donovan, B. T., 6:364; 8:291, 412
Dorland, W. A. N., 7:1
Dowling, J. E., 6:377
Doxiadis, C. A., 10:32, 240–242, 270
Draguns, J., 5:176; 8:549
Drake, A. W. (Ed.), 10:154, 415, 416
Draker, J. (Ed.), 5:32
Driesch, H. A., 2:118
Driml, M., 4:53
Driver, M. J., 5:130–132, 134
Dubin, R., 5:143; 9:116, 119; 10:39, 42
Dubin, R. (Ed.), 4:126
Dubos, R., 11:261, 274, 277, 279, 288, 297, 298, 301–304, 379, 381; 12:3, 44
Duda, W., 8:591
Duesenberry, J. S., 10:38
Duhl, F. J., 13:24
Duncan, D. M., 13:41
Duncan, O. D., 4:105
Dunnette, M. D. (Ed.), 13:42
Durkheim, E., 9:135; 10:19; 11:395
Durkin, H. E., 13:26
Dutton, J. M. (Ed.), 9:231; 12:232
Dwyer, J., 9:220
Dykman, R. A., 8:179
Dynes, R. R., 10:305

Easton, D., 1:2; 2:98; 11:87, 138, 324, 334, 335
Ebbinghaus, H., 8:244
Eberhart, S. S., 2:117
Ebert, J. D., 6:301, 317, 433, 443, 445, 446, 464, 472, 473, 475, 479
Eccles, J. C., 5:3, 11, 12; 6:189, 191, 194, 195, 199, 203, 205–207, 209, 219, 222, 226, 229, 230, 254, 256, 259–262, 287–290, 332, 342, 344, 346, 353, 355, 358, 362, 381, 382, 384, 385, 401; 7:40; 8:209
Eccles, J. C. (Ed.), 4:22, 24, 25; 5:13; 6:263; 8:127
Ecclesiastes, 8:580
Eckstein, A., 4:15; 12:5
Edds, M. V., Jr., 6:409

Edelman, G. M., **6**:272
Edey, M. A. (Ed.), **6**:1
Edgar, R. S., **6**:318, 420
Edwards, E. O., **4**:89
Edwards, W., **8**:318
Ehrensvard, G., **8**:537
Ehrle, R. A., **13**:73
Eigen, M., **6**:234, 300, 424
Eilon, S., **10**:76
Eisenbud, M., **10**:51
Eisenhower, D. D., **11**:160, 165
Ekel, J., **5**:36
Elder, H. A., **8**:629
Elias, P., **3**:6; **4**:53
Elkind, J. I., **4**:109; **5**:129
Elkinton, J. R., **2**:106, 108
Ellis, R. M., **7**:95
Elmgreen, G. L., **8**:650
Elsasser, W. M., **3**:8
Emerson, A. E., **2**:86; **9**:7–10, 13, 15, 172, 184, 185; **11**:347, 350; **13**:7
Emery, F. E., **3**:1, 2; **4**:63
Emlen, J. M., **2**:74
Emslie-Smith, D., **7**:17, 21
Engel, B. T., **8**:166
Erickson, R. P., **8**:136
Eriksen, C. W., **5**:55, 56, 64
Erlanger, J., **6**:258
Ernst, M. L., **10**:393–398
Ervin, J. R., **4**:173
Estabrook, R. W., **6**:486
Estes, W. K., **8**:635–638
Etzioni, A., **2**:60; **3**:50; **10**:107, 108, 211; **11**:6, 18, 26, 46–48, 133, 134, 137, 139, 145, 156–158, 326, 327, 333, 368–370, 388, 389, 393, 396–398; **12**:2, 19, 79, 101, 165, 166, 169–172, 174, 183
The Europa year book, 1973, a world survey, **12**:12, 16, 102
European Organization for Nuclear Research (CERN) Public Information Office, **12**:32
Evan, W. M., **10**:7, 16; **12**:22, 23, 38, 65, 173
Evans, J. N., **8**:362, 378, 390
Everett, G. A., **6**:38
Executive Office of the President, Office of Management and Budget, **10**:17; **11**:15, 20, 41
Eyzaguirre, C., **5**:4–6

Faas, H., **10**:116
Fagan, R. E., **2**:47; **3**:49
Fain, G. L., **6**:377
Faltermayer, E., **12**:40
Fano, R. M., **4**:56
Farber, S. M. (Ed.), **8**:373
Farkashidy, J., **8**:274

Farley, B. G., **8**:600
Farrell, R. B. (Ed.), **11**:130
Faust, W. L., **4**:103; **9**:100
Fawcett, D. W., **7**:29
Feder, N., **6**:441
Feierabend, I. K., **4**:121
Feigenbaum, E. A., **8**:643, 648, 649; **9**:198
Feigenbaum, E. A. (Ed.), **8**:592, 594, 619, 626–628, 655, 659
Feigl, H. (Ed.), **2**:58, 91, 98
Feinberg, L. D., **5**:176; **8**:549
Feindel, W., **8**:195
Feinstein, A., **3**:6
Feldman, J., **10**:134, 145
Feldman, J. (Ed.), **8**:592, 594, 619, 626–628, 643, 655, 659
Ferguson, A. R., **10**:38
Ferguson, J. K. W., **8**:18
Fernandez, L., **8**:380
Fernández-Morán, H., **2**:10; **6**:324
Festinger, L., **8**:444, 445; **9**:158, 160, 165–167, 170, 199, 204, 211
Fetter, R. B., **10**:411, 413
Ficks, L., **5**:63
Fiddes, J. C., **6**:39
Field, J. (Ed.), **6**:201, 202, 211, 332, 340, 365, 366, 379, 454; **7**:13, 22, 26, 28, 31, 36, 49, 56, 63; **8**:11, 22, 27–30, 36, 37, 45, 49, 58, 59, 73, 76, 84–86, 110, 111, 144, 145, 180, 252, 261, 266, 283, 332, 333, 349, 353, 452
Fields, W. S. (Ed.), **5**:181; **8**:196; **13**:9
Findley, J. D., **8**:166
Finesinger, J. E., **10**:301, 303
Finger, I., **6**:338
Fink, C. F., **9**:104
Finney, J. W., **10**:336
Fischberg, M., **7**:67
Fisher, A. H., **8**:413
Fisher, W. H., **11**:416
Fiske, D. W., **5**:89
Fitts, P. M., **5**:81, 83, 98, 122; **8**:367
Flaherty, B. E. (Ed.), **5**:88, 181; **13**:9
Flavell, J. H., **5**:176; **8**:549
Fleming, G. W. T. H. (Ed.), **2**:104
Flexner, J. B., **6**:299; **8**:204, 220, 221, 226, 232
Flexner, L. B., **6**:299; **8**:204, 220, 221, 226, 232
Flinn, D. E., **5**:161; **9**:122, 123
Flood, M. M., **4**:169; **8**:640, 641; **9**:75
Flores, J., **6**:411
Fogel, L. J. (Ed.), **4**:121; **12**:236
Fontaine, A. B., **4**:53
Foothills Pipe Lines (Yukon) Ltd., **10**:31
Forrester, J. W., **10**:233, 234, 250, 251, 276, 277, 367–376, 399–404; **11**:114; **12**:203, 204, 206–210; **13**:3
Fortune, **10**:36, 37, 274; **11**:280, 320

Foster, C. C., **2**:28; **4**:27, 28; **9**:214; **12**:235
Foster, J. L., **12**:192–194
Foulke, E., **8**:160
Fox, D., **9**:62
Fox, H. M., **8**:411
Fox, S. S., **4**:112; **8**:168, 280, 391
Fox, S. W., **6**:414, 417
Fox, S. W. (Ed.), **3**:7; **6**:411, 412, 416, 418, 419, 422, 423, 428, 429
Frank, J., **11**:223
Franklin, D. L., **7**:95
Franklin, W. S., **2**:2
Franzini-Armstrong, C., **6**:90, 94, 119, 151, 158, 159, 166, 176
Fraser, A., **6**:495
Freedman, R., **12**:87, 97
Freeman, C., **12**:219
Freeman, C. (Ed.), **12**:214, 215, 217, 223
Freeman, H. E., **11**:13, 17, 21
Freeman, J. L., **4**:143
Freeman, L. C., **11**:31, 32
French, J. R. P., Jr., **5**:160; **9**:162, 163, 191
French, R. L., **9**:79
Freud, A., **3**:34; **8**:427, 431
Freud, S., **8**:284, 418, 427, 504
Frey, A. (Ed.), **3**:13; **4**:19
Frick, F. C., **5**:58
Friedlander, F., **10**:189
Frings, H., **8**:342
Frings, M., **8**:342
Fritz, C. E., **10**:317
Fritz, E. L., **5**:137
Frohman, C. E., **8**:536, 537, 539, 540
Froman, L. A., **11**:210
Frommer, G. P., **8**:136
Fry, G. A., **8**:36
Fukuda, N., **6**:485
Fuller, J. L., **8**:492
Fuster, J. M., **8**:127

Gabe, M., **6**:149
Gabor, D., **2**:5
Gaffron, H., **6**:423
Galambos, R., **6**:371; **8**:180, 182
Galant, J. S., **5**:162
Galanter, E., **8**:313, 315
Galanter, E. (Ed.), **5**:45, 186
Gallager, R. G., **3**:15
Galtsoff, P. S., **7**:74; **8**:508
Gantt, W. H. (Ed.), **3**:24
Gapp, A., **5**:105
Gardiner, R. W., **8**:369
Gardner, B. T., **8**:346, 347
Gardner, R. A., **8**:346, 347
Gardner, W. H., **7**:78
Garfinkel, D., **6**:490
Garfinkel, H., **4**:156

Garner, W. R., **2**:39, 65; **5**:51, 53
Gasser, H. S., **6**:258
Gauslaa, A., **9**:210
Gay, H., **6**:248
Gearin, C. J., **12**:192–194
Gelber, B., **6**:266, 269, 270
Geldard, F. A., **5**:62; **8**:97
Gelehrter, T. D., **6**:240, 306, 321, 322, 336
Genesis, **10**:246
Gerard, H. B., **9**:165
Gerard, R. W., **2**:66; **3**:14, 27; **4**:170, 175, 176; **7**:42; **8**:26, 116, 207, 230, 238; **13**:7
Gerard, R. W. (Ed.), **2**:64; **13**:9
Gernandt, B. E., **8**:45–48
Gershefski, G. W., **10**:353, 358, 361, 365
Geschwind, N., **6**:25
Gibbs, J. W., **2**:18
Gibian, J., **8**:342
Giese, A. C., **6**:8, 9, 11, 20, 23, 75, 77, 79, 80, 82–87, 108, 110, 111, 116–118, 121–125, 127, 132, 133, 138, 143, 152–154, 157, 165, 175, 177, 184, 186, 245, 363, 386, 393, 451, 453, 457, 460, 463
Gifford, J. V., **2**:98
Gifford, S., **8**:411
Gilbert, L., **6**:316; **8**:487–489
Gilbert, W., **6**:233
Gilchrist, J. C., **4**:76
Gilden, L., **8**:457
Gilford, D. M. (Ed.), **11**:328
Gille, P., **12**:274–276, 278, 280–283
Gilliam, W. J., **8**:166
Ginsberg, M., **11**:340
Ginsborg, B. L., **8**:40
Gist, N. P., **4**:106
Glanzer, M., **8**:576; **9**:43
Glaser, R., **8**:576; **9**:43
Glassman, R. B., **1**:1; **13**:10, 16
Glazer, N., **1**:12
Gleisser, M., **10**:300
Glezer, V. D., **5**:73
Goblick, T. J., Jr., **4**:53
Goheen, H. E., **6**:487
Golant, S. M., **8**:277; **13**:49
Goldberg, S. C., **9**:164
Goldberger, L., **8**:403
Goldberger, R. F., **6**:326
Goldhamer, H., **12**:189
Goldman, J. J., **10**:299
Goldstein, G. D. (Ed.), **2**:11; **3**:22; **5**:181; **8**:598, 600, 620–624; **13**:9
Goldstein, L., **6**:140, 250, 314, 432, 434, 455
Goldstein, L. (Ed.), **6**:135, 237, 246, 247, 249, 303, 325, 338
Goode, H. H., **2**:79; **10**:33, 35, 45, 48, 50
Goode, W. J., **9**:147

Gooding, J., **10**:178, 180, 201
Goodman, C. C., **8**:370
Goodnow, R. E., **9**:204
Goodwin, G., Jr., **11**:203
Gordon, K. H., **4**:94
Gorini, L., **6**:396
Goss, C. M. (Ed.), **8**:21
Gottlieb, J. S., **5**:164; **8**:536, 537, 539, 540
Gottlieb, J. S. (Ed.), **8**:411
Gould, W. L., **12**:59–63, 66, 67, 160
Gramlich, E., **11**:427
Granit, R., **5**:7, 8; **7**:36; **8**:27, 38, 44
Granner, D., **6**:240, 306, 321, 322, 336
Gray, H., **8**:21
Gray, J. A. B., **6**:211, 368, 369, 372, 375, 380; **8**:104, 121, 122
Gray, W., **13**:24
Grayson, C. J., Jr., **10**:351
Great Britain, National Physical Laboratory, **8**:241
Green, D. E., **6**:115
Green, D. M., **8**:309
Greenberger, M., **11**:400, 434–439
Greenhill, M. H., **10**:301, 303
Greer, P., **5**:154
Gregg, D. E., **8**:114
Gregg, L. W., **5**:97
Grier, G. W., Jr., **5**:137
Griffith, B. C., **11**:93, 94
Griffiths, W. J., **8**:415
Grimes, C., **5**:177
Grinker, R. R., **8**:336, 348, 356, 419, 522, 569–571
Grinker, R. R. (Ed.), **2**:54, 56
Gromet, P., **8**:342
Gross, B. M., **10**:70, 75, 102–104, 118, 119, 133, 161, 162, 164, 166, 176, 185, 257, 258, 271, 340; **11**:12, 23, 26, 144, 147, 150; **13**:46
Gross, B. W. (Ed.), **11**:18
Gross, L. (Ed.), **3**:54
Gross, N. B., **8**:413
Grosse, A. P., **10**:38
Grosse, R. N., **10**:38
Gruenberg, G., **8**:161
Grundfest, H., **6**:331, 360
Grüsser, O. J., **5**:1, 10
Gruvaeus, G., **11**:207–209
Guetzkow, H., **4**:9; **9**:26, 28, 47, 58, 66, 90, 167, 168; **10**:58, 65–67, 82, 83; **12**:185, 244, 247–249, 251, 260, 264–266
Guetzkow, H. (Ed.), **9**:90; **12**:196, 243, 261–263
Guhl, A. M., **9**:129
Guilfoyle, G., **8**:457
Gullahorn, J. E., **9**:231, 235
Gullahorn, J. T., **9**:231, 235
Gurnee, H., **4**:94, 97, 98
Gutman, A. B., **8**:529

Guyton, A. C., **7**:61, 92
Gyr, J. W., **8**:310; **9**:220

Haas, M., **12**:143–159
Haas, N., **12**:201
Hage, P., **13**:52
Hageman, K. C., **8**:577
Haggett, P. (Ed.), **3**:13; **4**:19
Haibt, L., **8**:591
Haire, M., **4**:152; **10**:266
Haire, M. (Ed.), **10**:5, 9, 24, 60
Haist, R. E., **7**:51
Hake, H. W., **5**:53, 55
Hakerem, G., **5**:22, 23
Halbert, L. A., **4**:106
Hale, M., **11**:373
Halick, P., **5**:183; **7**:42; **13**:9
Hall, A. D., **2**:47; **3**:49
Hall, E. T., **9**:106
Hall, R. A. (Ed.), **12**:9
Hall, R. L., **9**:173
Halperin, M. H., **8**:362, 378, 390
Halpern, B. P., **8**:136
Halsey, R. M., **5**:61
Hamburger, V. (Ed.), **6**:409
Hamilton, R. V., **10**:309, 315, 322, 323
Hammen, C. L., **2**:73; **13**:17
Hammes, C. L., **12**:14, 82
Hamming, R. W., **4**:53
Hammond, A. L., **11**:247, 249, 252
Hammond, J., **8**:7, 376
Handy, R., **3**:33
Hanfmann, E., **9**:133
Hansen, B., **10**:155
Hanson, J. A., **8**:577
Harada, K., **6**:414
Harary, F., **9**:155, 156, 238
Harcourt, D. G., **11**:286
Harding, R. S., **8**:463
Hardy, T., **1**:11; **12**:295
Hare, A. P., **9**:98
Hare, A. P. (Ed.), **9**:72, 74, 97, 103
Harington, C. R., **3**:53
Harlow, H. F., **2**:38; **4**:114; **8**:169, 177, 178, 279, 515
Harlow, M. K., **2**:38
Harman, R. J. (Ed.), **5**:111; **10**:99
Harmon, L. D., **6**:484; **7**:82, 84
Harper, F. A., **1**:16
Harris, A. H., **8**:166
Harris, D. D., **4**:105
Harris, G. W., **6**:364; **8**:110, 111, 291, 412
Harris, H. E., **7**:78
Harris, R., **6**:448
Harris, R. J. C. (Ed.), **8**:527
Harsanyi, J. C., **9**:89
Hartley, R. V. L., **2**:3
Hartline, H. K., **8**:130, 617

Hartman, B. O., **5**:88
Hartman, H. P., **11**:39
Hartmanis, J., **2**:44
Haruna, I., **6**:45
Harvey, O. J., **9**:189
Harvey, S., **8**:456
Harwood, E., **5**:174
Hassler, R., **8**:452
Haugland, V., **10**:63
Hauser, P. M., **11**:292, 294–296, 377
Hawkes, J., **12**:68
Hawkins, C., **9**:83, 140, 142
Hawks, D. V., **13**:65
Hawley, A. H., **10**:21, 267
Hayashi, T., **6**:179, 183
Hayes, J. R. M., **5**:67
Hayflick, L., **8**:557, 562, 564, 565
Hearn, G., **2**:72; **3**:5; **9**:109; **13**:29
Heath, R. G., **8**:295, 537
Hebb, D. O., **4**:111; **8**:164, 174
Hebb, D. O. (Ed.), **8**:162
Heider, F., **8**:438, 439
Heinmets, F., **7**:97
Heise, G. A., **9**:33, 45
Helmholtz, II. L. F. v., **2**:17
Helmreich, R., **9**:240, 241
Hemphill, J. K., **9**:102
Henderson, L. J., **Preface**:4; **2**:80; **11**:71
Hendricks, S. B., **8**:386, 387
Henmon, V. A. C., **5**:34
Henry, N., **5**:106
Herbst, P. G., **2**:78
Hermann, C. F., **3**:55, 56; **12**:188, 261–263
Hermann, M. G., **12**:261–263
Hernández-Peón, R., **8**:267–271
Heron, A., **8**:574, 578
Heron, W., **4**:111; **8**:395
Herrick, C. F., **3**:38
Herrington, R. N., **8**:151
Herschman, A., **7**:97
Hershey, J., **10**:310
Hertz, D. B., **10**:49
Hertzler, V. B., **9**:200
Herz, A., **8**:127
Hess, B., **6**:242, 244, 337, 394, 397, 489
Hess, E. H., **4**:51
Heyns, R. W., **9**:90
Hick, E. E., **5**:32
Hick, W. E., **5**:123
Hickman, B., **12**:281–283
Higashino, S., **7**:27
Higgin, G. W., **10**:200
Higgins, J. J., **6**:490
Hightower, N. C., **7**:25
Hill, R., **9**:222
Hillarp, N. A., **7**:26, 28, 31, 56
Hillyard, S. A., **8**:258
Himwich, H. E., **8**:535
Hink, R. F., **8**:258

Hinomoto, H., **12**:237
Hirsch, A. A., **11**:423, 424, 426, 429
Hobbs, E. H., **11**:197
Hoehling, A. A., **5**:149
Hoffman, H.-P., **6**:113, 114
Hoffman, P. J., **9**:211
Hoggatt, A. C. (Ed.), **8**:648, 649
Hoijer, H., **11**:109, 111
Hokin, M. R., **7**:14
Holden, C., **12**:94, 99
Holland, J., **8**:591
Holley, R. W., **6**:38
Hollingshead, A. B., **11**:76, 77
Holloway, R. L., Jr., **8**:470–472
Holmes, E., **8**:161
Holmes, O. W., Jr., **11**:132
Holsti, O. R., **11**:232; **12**:52, 133–137; **13**:67
Holt, L. E., **8**:484
Holter, H., **6**:72, 73, 78, 81, 155
Holtzer, H., **6**:447, 448
Holzer, H., **6**:148
Holzman, M., **10**:38
Holzmann, P. S., **8**:368, 369
Homans, G. C., **4**:3; **9**:11, 23, 74, 146, 232
Hood, W. R., **9**:189
Hook, L. H., **2**:61; **9**:111, 113
Horne, R. W., **6**:19
Horridge, G. A., **6**:264
Horstein, M., **4**:53
Horvath, W. J., **4**:28; **5**:2, 21, 152, 183; **9**:41; **10**:410, 412; **12**:235; **13**:9
Houser, P. M. (Ed.), **4**:105
Howland, J., Jr., **8**:484
Hubbard, W. N., Jr., **2**:73
Hubbert, M. K., **11**:244–246, 248, 251, 253; **12**:42, 43
Hubel, D. H., **8**:124, 126, 468, 520, 521
Huey, R. B., **8**:374
Huffman, D. A., **4**:57
Hughes, B., **12**:274–276, 278, 280, 285–291
Hughes, C. C., **2**:70
Hughes, E. C., **9**:205
Humphrey, T., **6**:144, 482; **7**:30; **8**:23, 117, 137, 142, 293, 297–299, 337, 351, 356, 419
Humphreys, T., **7**:72, 73
Hund, J. M., **4**:154, 155
Hunt, C. C., **6**:373
Hunt, H. F., **8**:167
Hunt, J. McV., **8**:278; **9**:203
Hunt, J. McV. (Ed.), **4**:142; **8**:444
Hunt, R. G., **13**:42
Hunter, F., **11**:90
Huntington, E., **4**:17
Huntley, M. S., Jr., **13**:63
Hurley, W. V., **2**:121
Hurst, P. M., **13**:64

Hutber, F. W., **11**:441, 442
Hutchins, R. M. (Ed.), **11**:151, 152, 337
Hutchison, C. A., III, **6**:39
Huxley, A., **3**:10
Huxley, H. E., **6**:167–170, 175, 329
Huxley, T. H., **11**:336; **13**:6
Hydén, H., **4**:170; **6**:295, 297, 298, 400, 480; **7**:5, 6; **8**:212, 236, 237
Hyman, R., **5**:32
Hymovitch, B., **9**:165

Ibrahim, I. M., **7**:19
International Atomic Energy Agency, **12**:28, 35, 46, 55, 64, 73, 76
International Business Machines Corporation, **10**:61, 95
Ireland, P. E., **8**:274
Isaac, D. J., **5**:186
Isard, W., **2**:1; **10**:38

Jackson, D. D., **9**:179, 225, 226
Jackson, J. E., **11**:430
Jackson, K. F., **5**:86
Jackson, W. (Ed.), **2**:5
Jacob, F., **6**:235, 236, 238, 239, 241, 243, 271, 307, 309, 312, 313, 427
Jacobi, G. T. (Ed.), **2**:11; **3**:22; **5**:181; **8**:598, 600, 620–624; **13**:9
Jacobs, P. A., **8**:527
Jacobson, H., **3**:41, 43
Jaffe, J., **5**:166
Jahoda, M., **12**:214
Jahoda, M. (Ed.), **12**:215, 217, 219, 223
Jakob, H., **6**:325
James, B. J., **13**:68
James, R. M., **9**:83
Janowitz, H. D., **7**:25
Jarvik, M. E., **8**:225
Jason, H. (Ed.), **13**:9
Jaspars, J. M. F., **9**:62
Jaspers, H. H. (Ed.), **8**:243
Jauriel, J. J., **10**:360, 362, 363
Jay, E. S., **5**:202
Jaynes, J., **2**:37; **8**:510
Jeantheau, G., **5**:85
Jeffress, L. A. (Ed.), **2**:95; **3**:8
Jelinek, F., **4**:53
Jelinek, W. R., **6**:130, 310
Jensen, D. D., **6**:267
Jeon, K. W., **6**:142
Jersild, A., **8**:517
John, E. R., **4**:172, 174; **8**:151, 183, 185, 203, 310
John, M. J., **11**:93, 94
Johnsen, E. G., **8**:585–589
Johnson, E. M., **5**:32

Johnson, L. B., **11**:163, 178–185, 187, 191–196, 199
Johnson, R. B., **8**:248
Johnson, S. M., **7**:91
Johnson, V., **7**:11
Johnson, W. H., **6**:64, 156
Jones, A., **8**:281, 392
Jones, E., **8**:428–430
Jones, E. E., **9**:175
Jordan, N., **8**:440
Joseph, R., **10**:325
Josephson, R. K., **7**:90
Jouvet, M., **8**:268
Jowett, B., **10**:434
Judge, W. J., **13**:52
Judges, **3**:11
Jukes, T. H., **6**:428–429
Jumber, J., **8**:342
Jung, C. G., **11**:112
Jung, R., **5**:16; **8**:117, 128, 452

Kaada, B. R., **8**:261
Kafotos, F. C., **6**:441
Kahn, R. L., **5**:145, 160; **9**:118; **10**:8, 13, 25, 57, 62, 64, 68, 69, 87, 128, 159, 165, 167, 190–194, 197, 198, 237, 435, 438
Kain, J. F., **10**:405
Kalven, H., Jr., **9**:86
Kamiya, J., **8**:168
Kamiya, N. (Ed.), **6**:178
Kandel, E. R., **6**:276, 278–281, 285, 286, 291–293
Kann, R. A., **11**:387; **12**:20, 175–180, 184
Kanno, Y., **7**:27
Kanter, H. E., **7**:91; **10**:134, 145
Kao, H., **9**:55
Kaplan, I. R., **6**:411
Kaplan, M. A., **2**:63, 73, 98; **12**:1, 7, 8
Kaplan, M. A. (Ed.), **12**:138
Kare, M. R. (Ed.), **8**:642
Katona, G., **11**:115, 116
Katz, B., **6**:257, 367
Katz, D., **5**:145; **9**:118; **10**:8, 13, 25, 57, 62, 64, 68, 69, 87, 128, 159, 165, 167, 190–194, 197, 198, 237, 435, 438
Katz, E., **11**:103
Katz, M., **11**:149
Kauffman, P. E., **8**:157
Kaufman, E. L., **5**:71
Kazda, L. F., **2**:110
Kecskemeti, P., **12**:234
Keenan, T. A., **5**:111; **11**:97
Keeney, M. G., **10**:389, 390
Keeney, R. L., **10**:154
Keeney, R. L. (Ed.), **10**:415, 416
Kelley, H. H., **9**:63, 114, 145, 165, 191, 192
Kempf, E. J., **2**:98

Kendler, H. H., **8**:172
Kennedy, J. L., **5**:135, 136, 138; **10**:433
Kepes, G. (Ed.), **10**:243
Kern, R. P., **8**:417
Kerr, C., **4**:126; **13**:74
Kershaw, D. N., **11**:313
Kessler, A., **12**:271, 272
Kety, S. S., **7**:48
Khinchin, A. I., **4**:53
Kilburn, K. H., **6**:182
Killam, K. F., **4**:174; **8**:183
Killian, J. R., **1**:6
Killian, L. M., **10**:311, 312
Kimble, D. P. (Ed.), **6**:191, 287, 289, 290; **8**:197, 209
Kinch, R. A. H., **8**:528
King, W. W., **8**:17
Kinscella, H. G., **5**:26
Kinsey, A. C., **11**:75
Kistin, H., **10**:38
Klabbers, J. H. G., **12**:279
Klapp, O. E., **13**:50, 72
Kleene, S. C., **8**:593
Klein, D. F., **5**:169
Klein, G. S., **8**:368
Klein, L., **12**:281–283
Klemmer, E. T., **5**:54, 58, 82, 104
Klineberg, O., **12**:50
Klinger, P. D., **8**:218
Klopfer, W. G., **8**:563, 579
Klubeck, S., **9**:110
Kluckhohn, C., **2**:59; **3**:27; **11**:3, 140–142, 341, 348, 351, 357, 360
Kluger, J. M., **13**:20
Knauss, J. A., **12**:109
Kneese, A. V., **11**:263
Knight, D. E. (Ed.), **4**:121; **12**:236
Knight, J. (Ed.), **13**:9
Knop, H., **11**:440
Koch, S. (Ed.), **2**:64, 66; **4**:69; **8**:169, 282, 359, 423–426, 635
Kochen, M., **10**:100, 286, 287, 422–429
Kochen, M. (Ed.), **5**:107
Koenig, H. E., **10**:389, 390
Koenigsberg, E., **10**:27, 44, 47, 383, 407
Köhler, W., **2**:44, 84; **8**:314
Kolff, W. J., **7**:79
Kolobow, T., **7**:76
Kolouch, F. T., **13**:19
Kominek, K., **12**:281–283
Konigsberg, I. R., **7**:68
Kopin, I. J., **6**:343, 402
Korbel, J., **11**:400, 434–439
Korchin, S. J., **8**:448, 449
Korn, E. D., **6**:67, 70
Kornberg, A., **3**:9; **6**:44, 146
Kornberg, R. D., **6**:47
Kornblum, S., **5**:37, 47, 48
Kornhauser, A. W. (Ed.), **4**:126
Kotler, P. (Ed.), **12**:196, 261–266

Kozesnik, J. (Ed.), **4**:53
Kozloff, E. N., **7**:3
Kraar, L., **11**:81
Kramer, B. M., **4**:32
Kramer, F. R., **6**:411
Kravitz, E. A., **6**:345, 461
Krech, D., **8**:191; **9**:74
Krieg, W. J. S., **7**:43
Kries, J. v., **5**:34
Krissoff, M., **7**:38
Krnjević, K., **5**:14
Kroeber, A. L., **2**:59; **11**:341, 348, 351, 357, 360
Kroeber, A. L. (Ed.), **11**:49, 109, 123
Krulee, G. K., **5**:105; **8**:577
Kubie, L. S., **8**:430
Kubzansky, P. E. (Ed.), **4**:111; **8**:396
Kudarauskas, E. N., **8**:411
Kuffler, S. W., **5**:4–6
Kurland, A. A., **8**:288
Kurtz, P., **3**:33
Kurtz, S. (Ed.), **11**:69, 106, 107, 127, 128, 237, 238, 241
Kvenvolden, K., **6**:411

Lacey, J. I., **5**:89
Laemmel, A. E., **4**:53
Laffont, R. (Ed.), **10**:268
Lamarck, J. B., **3**:39
Lampard, E., **11**:291
Land, K. C., **11**:22, 24
Landau, H. G., **9**:132
Landgren, S., **8**:135
Landi, D. M., **5**:105
Lang, A. (Ed.), **5**:25
Langer, W. L., **11**:285
Langston, J. B., **7**:61
Lanzetta, J. T., **4**:37; **5**:125–128; **9**:59
Laponce, J. A. (Ed.), **12**:200, 268–270
Larson, R. C., **10**:415, 416
Lasek, R. J., **6**:99
Lashley, K. S., **8**:162
Laszlo, C. A., **1**:1
Laszlo, E., **13**:25
Lauer, E. W., **6**:144, 482; **7**:30; **8**:23, 117, 137, 142, 293, 297–299, 337, 351, 356, 419
Laverty, S. G., **5**:175
Lawless, J., **6**:411
Lawrence, D. H., **9**:211
Lawrence, J. II. (Ed.), **6**:212–215, 225, 227, 356, 357
Lawrence, P. R., **10**:52, 53, 131, 213–217, 224, 226, 230, 235
Lawson, J. S., **5**:170, 172
Lazar, J., **10**:227
Lazarsfeld, P. F., **1**:9
Lazarsfeld, P. F. (Ed.), **1**:10
Leach, B. E., **8**:537

Leake, C. D., **2**:73
Leavitt, H. J., **9**:27, 32, 36, 65, 149, 150, 152, 153, 178; **10**:181, 182, 210
Leavitt, H. J. (Ed.), **10**:3, 15, 109, 110, 114, 129, 141, 147, 148, 153, 223, 231, 236, 244
Leblond, C. P., **6**:12, 139
LeBreton, E., **6**:471
Le Châtelier, H., **2**:97
Lee, A. M., **5**:141
Lee, M., Jr., **11**:387; **12**:20, 175–180, 184
Lee, R., **11**:71
Leeds, R., **10**:231
LeGates, J., **11**:98
Lehman, E., **11**:18
Lehninger, A. L., **3**:9; **6**:55, 56, 61, 62, 115, 120, 134, 391, 395, 421, 450, 452
Leiderman, P. H., **8**:396, 397, 399
Leighton, A. H., **2**:67, 68, 70
Leiman, A. L., **8**:511
Lekachman, R., **11**:319
Lenneberg, E. H., **8**:497
Leontief, W., **10**:38; **11**:62, 70, 308–310, 411, 412, 414, 417–419; **12**:292
Lerner, D. (Ed.), **1**:12
Lerner, H. D. (Ed.), **11**:328
Lerner, W. (Ed.), **5**:114
Leroux, E. J., **11**:286
Lessing, L., **11**:58, 250, 269
Lett, J. T., **6**:481
Lettvin, J. Y., **5**:9, 24; **8**:123
Levine, M. D., **1**:1
Levine, S., **8**:449, 493
Levinson, D. J., **2**:89
Levinson, H., **3**:52; **10**:11, 12, 189, 355
Levinson, J., **7**:84
Lévi-Strauss, C., **11**:49, 79
Levy, B. H., **11**:226
Levy, M., **7**:19
Levy, M. J., Jr., **2**:57; **4**:13; **11**:42
Lewin, K., **1**:2; **8**:317; **9**:161, 162
Ley, W., **8**:450
Liberman, A. M., **8**:118, 152, 344, 354
Liberman, E. A., **8**:129
Lichterman, M., **11**:387; **12**:20, 175–180, 184
Lichtman, C. M., **13**:42
Licklider, J. C. R., **5**:111; **8**:49, 51, 57
Lidsky, A., **5**:22, 23
Liebenberg, M., **11**:423, 424, 426, 429
Lieberman, M. (Ed.), **10**:22
Liebowitz, H. W., **5**:173
Liederman, P. H. (Ed.), **4**:111
Lienau, C. C. (Ed.), **12**:233
Likert, R., **10**:59, 71, 106, 115, 125, 138, 177, 183, 187, 188, 232
Lilly, J., **8**:397
Lim, R., **8**:218, 219

Lindblom, C. E. (Ed.), **11**:197
Lindgren, R. E., **11**:387; **12**:20, 175–180, 184
Lindman, H. R., **4**:107
Lindsley, D. B., **8**:266, 292
Lindsley, D. F., **8**:280, 391
Lindzey, G. (Ed.), **9**:63, 146
Linhart, P., **10**:419, 431
Linschitz, H., **2**:26; **6**:7
Linton, R., **11**:356
Lipetz, L. E., **6**:212–215, 225, 227, 356, 357
Lipetz, M., **9**:215
Lipmann, F., **6**:422
Lipowski, Z. J., **5**:157, 158; **13**:60
Lippitt, R., **9**:70, 148
Lipset, S. M., **11**:146
Lipset, S. M. (Ed.), **11**:74–78
Lipton, J., **9**:1
Little, J. D. C., **10**:420
Livanov, M. N., **4**:174
Lloyd, D. P. C., **8**:22, 251
Løchen, Y., **9**:210
Loehlin, J. C., **9**:662
Loevinger, J., **8**:485
Loewenheim, F. L., **11**:387; **12**:20, 175–180, 184
Loewenstein, W. R., **7**:27
Logan, L., **10**:311, 312
Loiseaux, P. R., **9**:85
Lomax, A., **11**:37, 38, 342, 343, 371, 372
Longhurst, T. M., **9**:171
Loomis, C. P., **9**:201, 202
Loomis, S., **4**:91
Lorch, I. J., **6**:142
Lord, A. B., **3**:28
Lord, M. W., **5**:71
Lord, W., **10**:92
Lorenz, K., **8**:464; **9**:120, 121, 124–126, 181
Lorge, I., **9**:62
Lorsch, J. W., **10**:52, 53, 131, 213–217, 224, 226, 230, 235
Los Angeles Times, **5**:147
Lowry, H. F. (Ed.), **8**:446
Lozano, R., **8**:381
Luby, E. D., **5**:164
Luce, R. D., **2**:9; **5**:44; **8**:305, 654; **9**:34, 44, 46, 50–52, 57, 176
Luce, R. D. (Ed.), **5**:45, 186
Luco, J. V., **7**:41
Ludwig, H. C., **10**:316, 321
Luft, U. C., **8**:360
Lundberg, G. A., **9**:200
Lundstet, S., **5**:111
Lutherman, C. Z., **9**:131
Lutzker, D. R., **9**:219
Lyons, R. H., **8**:375, 377
Lysaught, J. P. (Ed.), **13**:9

Maas, W. K., **6**:396
McAlister, A. J., **6**:483
McBride, G., **9**:6, 127, 128, 134, 180, 182, 183
McCarthy, D., **8**:516, 518
McCarthy, J. (Ed.), **4**:166, 167; **8**:593
McCarthy, M., **12**:281–283
McClearn, G. E., **8**:523–525, 531
McClelland, D. C., **4**:18, 67
McClelland, D. H., **12**:15, 26, 30
McConnaughey, B. H., **7**:3; **13**:8
McConnell, J. V., **4**:47; **6**:265; **8**:165, 170, 176, 213–217
McCormick, F., **10**:150
McCornack, R. L., **5**:202
McCulloch, W. S., **4**:168; **5**:1, 9, 24; **7**:85; **8**:123, 147, 596, 598, 633
McCurdy, D. K., **7**:77
McDermott, W. (Ed.), **8**:526, 529
McDonald, J., **10**:149
McFarland, R. A., **8**:362, 363, 378, 379, 383, 390
McGhie, A., **5**:170–172, 177
McGill, W., **5**:45, 185
McGlothlen, C. L., **8**:364
McGregor, D., **10**:209
McGuire, W. J., **8**:435, 436, 447
McGuire, W. J. (Ed.), **8**:437, 440, 441, 443
McHale, J., **5**:106
Machiavelli, N., **11**:151, 152
Machol, R. E., **10**:33, 35, 45, 48, 50
Machol, R. E. (Ed.), **8**:302
Mack, R., **6**:416
Mack, R. W., **4**:127, 131, 135
Mack, R. W. (Ed.), **9**:184, 185; **11**:347
MacKay, D. M., **5**:1; **8**:595
McKendry, J. M., **13**:64
McKenzie, R. E., **5**:88
Macko, D., **2**:73, 77
McKusick, V. A., **8**:530
Mackworth, J. F., **8**:198, 227
Mackworth, J. S., **5**:87
Mackworth, N. H., **5**:87
McLachlan, D., Jr., **3**:19
McLaughlin, C. P. (Ed.), **13**:33
McLennan, H., **6**:190, 192, 193, 196, 200, 204, 206–208, 218, 221, 228, 231, 232, 252, 253, 334, 341, 354, 361, 383
McLeod, J., **Preface**:7; **12**:202; **13**:57
McMahon, T., **8**:4, 5
McNamara, R. S., **12**:93, 103–107
McNeil, E. B. (Ed.), **12**:133
McNemar, Q. (Ed.), **4**:142
McPherson, L. F., **10**:377
McQuade, W., **10**:158
Macrae, J., **12**:257–259
McWhinney, W. H., **9**:236, 237
Macy, J., Jr., **2**:9; **9**:34, 44, 46, 50–52, 57, 176

Maddi, S. R., **5**:89
Madison, J. T., **6**:38
Madow, W. G., **5**:186
Magee, D. F., **7**:12
Magoun, H. W., **6**:268; **7**:62; **8**:12, 193, 202, 254, 257, 259, 262–264, 266, 294, 296, 300, 301
Maier, H. H., **12**:285
Maier, N. R. F., **8**:314
Main, E. C., **8**:326
Maki, F., **10**:243
Malcolm, D. G., **2**:79
Malone, D. W., **12**:224
Malthus, T. R., **4**:148; **11**:374
Mandell, A. J., **8**:532, 533, 538
Mandlebaum, D. G. (Ed.), **11**:110
Mandler, G., **8**:143, 175
Manelski, D. M., **5**:105
Mangan, G., Jr., **8**:547
Mann, R. D., **9**:80
Manning, R., **11**:186
Manry, C. H., **8**:375, 377
Mar, B. W., **12**:294; **13**:4
March, J. G., **3**:19–21; **4**:20, 39–44, 73, 74, 117, 125, 133, 134, 136, 145–147; **9**:117, 198; **10**:72, 79–81, 88–91, 96, 129, 139–141, 143, 145, 147, 151, 168, 179, 186, 195–197, 205–207, 212, 219, 223, 293, 436
March, J. G. (Ed.), **10**:56, 58, 65–67, 82, 83, 107, 108, 134, 144, 146, 182, 262, 275, 283, 284, 294, 331, 341–344
Marchetti, C., **12**:37
Marcus, P. I., **7**:69
Marlowe, D., **9**:216
Marquand, J. P., **9**:139
Marquis, D. G., **4**:104; **8**:365, 366; **9**:90; **10**:54, 55, 152; **11**:95, 96
Marquisee, M., **6**:38
Marrs, W., **10**:311, 312
Marschak, J., **9**:207
Marschak, T. A., **10**:144–146, 417
Marshall, N. B., **6**:339
Marshall, W. L., **13**:65
Martin, C. E., **11**:75
Martin, D., Jr., **6**:240, 306, 321, 322, 336
Martin, H. B., **8**:367
Marx, J. L., **6**:67, 71, 466, 470
Marzocco, F. N., **8**:642
Mason, J. W., **8**:547
Massarik, F. (Ed.), **5**:150; **10**:97, 98
Masserman, J. H., **8**:431
Masserman, J. H. (Ed.), **5**:181; **13**:9
Massie, J. L., **10**:294
Masure, R. H., **9**:130
Mathewson, J. H., **10**:317
Mathiesen, T., **9**:210
Matthews, D. R., **11**:211, 213
Maturana, H. R., **8**:123
Maugh, T. H., **6**:318, 467

Maximow, A. A., **7**:8, 23, 24
Maxwell, J. C., **2**:14, 24
Mayer, L. A., **11**:66, 287, 289, 293, 300, 305, 382
Mayfield, P. N., **9**:85
Mayhew, E., **6**:69, 468, 470
Mazia, D., **6**:43, 50–53, 55, 59, 315, 320, 437–439, 456, 465, 477
Mead, M., **11**:123; **12**:100
Meadows, D. H., **3**:46; **4**:150; **11**:254, 278; **12**:39, 41, 205, 211–213, 217
Meadows, D. H. (Ed.), **12**:226, 227
Meadows, D. L., **3**:46; **4**:150; **12**:39, 205, 211–213, 217
Meadows, D. L. (Ed.), **12**:226, 227
Meadows, P., **Preface**:6
Means, A. R., **6**:388
Mechanic, D., **10**:109, 110, 114
Medawar, P. B., **8**:2, 6, 482, 561
Meier, N., **9**:81
Meier, R. C., **10**:354, 359, 375, 406, 408, 409, 430, 432
Meier, R. L., **5**:144, 150, 151, 153; **10**:97, 98, 238, 285; **11**:105
Meir, A. Z., **13**:24
Meldman, M. J., **5**:90
Melnechuk, T., **8**:335, 346
Melnechuk, T. (Ed.), **6**:54–56, 61, 62, 145, 234, 272–276, 278–286, 291–293, 295–298, 319, 324, 331–334, 340, 343, 345–352, 359, 360, 370, 374, 376, 389–391, 395, 398–400, 406, 409, 415, 419, 421, 424–426, 443, 445, 450, 452, 461, 472, 475; **8**:187, 191, 203, 208, 210, 211, 236, 237, 253
Melton, A. W., **8**:231
Melzak, Z. A., **8**:618
Mendelson, J., **8**:396, 397, 399
Mendelson, J. H. (Ed.), **4**:111
Menninger, K., **5**:163; **8**:432–434, 542, 543
Meredith, W., **8**:523–525, 531
Merei, F., **9**:193
Merimee, T. J., **8**:530
Merkel, J., **5**:29
Merrill, H., **6**:38
Merrill, M. A. (Ed.), **4**:142
Merton, R. K., **1**:8; **2**:66
Merton, R. K. (Ed.), **1**:10
Mesarović, M., **2**:73, 77; **10**:3; **12**:273–276, 278, 280–283, 286–291
Mesarović, M. (Ed.), **6**:242, 244, 337, 392, 394, 397, 489
Messel, K. (Ed.), **2**:40
Messick, S. (Ed.), **8**:662
Metz, W. D., **11**:255
Meyer, L. B., **2**:93
Meyer, M. W., **10**:292
Mierke, K., **5**:103

Milborn, H. T., Jr., **7**:92
Miledi, R., **5**:14
Milgram, S., **5**:119–121
Mill, J. S., **4**:2
Miller, A. J., **8**:228; **11**:93, 94
Miller, G. A., **1**:3; **3**:17; **4**:26; **5**:31, 49, 57, 60, 65, 68, 69, 186; **8**:245, 313, 315; **9**:33, 45
Miller, J. G., **Preface**:2, 9; **4**:47, 115; **5**:111, 179, 181, 183; **8**:310, 321, 373, 551; **11**:97; **13**:9
Miller, N. E., **4**:142; **8**:166, 282, 444
Miller, S. L., **6**:413
Miller, W. B., **13**:27
Miller, W. E., **11**:210, 212
Miller, W. H., **8**:617
Mills, D. R., **6**:411
Mills, T. M., **9**:209, 210
Milner, P., **8**:295
Milsum, J. H., **1**:1
Minas, J. S., **9**:215, 216
Minsky, M., **2**:12
Mirsky, A. E. (Ed.), **6**:50–53, 55, 65, 149, 320, 437–439, 449, 456, 462, 465, 469, 471, 477, 480; **7**:5, 6
Mirsky, A. F., **8**:541
Mishler, E. G., **4**:12, 159; **9**:94
Mitchell, D. E., **8**:514
Mitchell, J., **11**:56
Modesitt, C. L., **10**:350
Molloy, G. R., **6**:130, 310
Monod, J., **6**:235, 236, 238, 239, 243, 271, 309, 427
Monroy, A. (Ed.), **6**:447
Moody's industrial manual, **10**:288
Moore, C., **6**:411
Moore, G. H., **11**:8
Moore, H. E., **10**:306, 324, 327
Moore, R., **8**:8
Morgan, C. T., **8**:180, 182
Morgan, C. T. (Ed.), **8**:162
Morgan, H. E., **4**:148
Morgenstern, O., **8**:651, 652
Morgenthau, H. J., **12**:80, 81
Morowitz, H. J., **2**:26; **6**:13, 18, 21, 22
Morrell, F., **6**:282–284, 352, 374, 376; **8**:196, 206, 253, 255, 260
Morrill, R. L., **10**:421
Morse, N., **10**:184
Morse, P. M. (Ed.), **10**:154, 393–398, 410, 412, 415, 416
Mortimore, G. E., **7**:52
Morton, F. M., **9**:101
Moscona, A. A., **7**:65, 70
Mosteller, F., **8**:639
Moulé, Y., **6**:471
Mounolou, J. C., **6**:325
Mountcastle, V. B., **4**:9, 22, 24, 25; **5**:13, 19, 20; **6**:263, 350, 370; **8**:29, 83, 88, 94, 99, 138, 139, 141

Mouton, J. S., **10**:101, 126, 329, 332–335
Mowbray, G. H., **5**:38–43
Mowrer, O. H., **5**:28
Moyer, A. W., **4**:171
Mrosovsky, N., **8**:384, 385
Mueller, R. A. H., **9**:178
Muhlethaler, K., **6**:65
Muir, D. W., **8**:514
Mulder, M., **9**:68, 69
Muller, P. F., Jr., **5**:82–84, 122; **8**:367
Müller-Hill, B., **6**:233
Mullick, S. K., **10**:381
Mulligan, G. A., **3**:53
Mullins, R. F., Jr., **8**:493
Murawski, B. J., **8**:411
Murdock, G. P., **11**:72
Murphy, R. F., **11**:394
Murray, H., **10**:200
Murray, H. A., **2**:64, 66; **8**:423–426; **11**:3
Muses, C. A., **2**:24
Mushakoji, K., **12**:200
Myers, S., **10**:54, 55
Myrdal, A., **12**:123

Nabl, J., **2**:16
Nagao, M., **10**:414
Naill, R. F., **12**:39
Nakai, J., **6**:178
Nangle, J., **8**:325
Nanney, D. L., **6**:57
Napalkov, A. V., **2**:83
Napoleon, I., **10**:157
Naroll, R., **11**:30, 344, 345, 352, 353, 384–386
Naroll, R. (Ed.), **11**:34–36, 366
Nass, M. M. K., **6**:60, 63
National Academy of Sciences, National Research Council of, **4**:124
Navar, G., **7**:61
Naylor, G. F. K., **5**:174
Naylor, T. H., **10**:364
Nazem, S. G., **10**:256, 297
Nedoma, J., **4**:53
Neel, J. V., **11**:45, 283, 284
Neff, W. D., **8**:133
Neisser, U., **8**:619
Nelson, P. G., **8**:208
Nelson, R. H., **13**:34
Nettl, P., **13**:51
Neumann, J. v., **2**:9, 95; **3**:8; **4**:166, 167; **8**:651, 652
Neurath, H., **6**:430
Neuringer, A., **8**:495
Neuringer, M., **8**:495
Neustadt, R. E., **11**:129, 164, 198, 231
Neutra, M., **6**:12, 139
Newbrough, J. R., **13**:30
Newcomb, T. M., **8**:441; **9**:12, 154, 199

Newcomb, T. M. (Ed.), **8**:437, 440, 443, 447
Newell, A., **8**:655, 657–659; **9**:234; **10**:433
Newell, W. T., **10**:354, 359, 375, 406, 408, 409, 430, 432
Neyman, J., **2**:75
Neyman, J. (Ed.), **4**:53, 55
Nichols, R. C., **8**:501
Nicolson, G. L., **6**:67, 71
Nidorf, L. J., **5**:172
Nielson, W. A., **11**:84
Nierlich, D. P., **6**:440
Nikoomanesh, P., **8**:166
Nirenberg, M. W., **6**:31, 32, 34, 35, 37
Nissen, H. W. (Ed.), **8**:162
Noble, M., **5**:81, 98
Noel, R. C., **12**:243, 245
Noel, R. C. (Ed.), **12**:244, 247
Noell, J. J., **10**:263, 264; **13**:45
Noell, W. K., **8**:360
Nomura, M., **6**:130
Nørstebø, G., **9**:210
North, R. C., **12**:133–138
Norton, F. K., **8**:500, 505
Nossal, G. J. V., **6**:131, 273
Notestein, F. W., **11**:78
NWA Water Resources Center, **12**:45
Nystrom, P. C., **13**:69

Oberling, C., **6**:469
O'Brien, G., **13**:33
Ochs, S., **6**:99
O'Connell, D. N., **5**:52, 59
O'Connor, B. M., **5**:186
Oden, M. H., **8**:502
Odum, E. P., **13**:71
Odum, H. T., **4**:9, 92
Oehmen, K.-H., **12**:284
Ofshe, R., **9**:92
Ohtaka, M., **10**:243
Ojemann, R. G., **8**:188–190, 192, 194, 200, 201
Olds, J., **8**:295
Olsen, J., **10**:338
O'Malley, B. W., **6**:388
Omura, K., **8**:60
Oparin, A. I., **6**:411, 418
Openshaw, J. W., **8**:454
Oppenheimer, J. R., **1**:17
Orcutt, G. H., **11**:400, 434–439
Ordway, F. I., III (Ed.), **2**:32
Ortega y Gasset, J., **5**:108
Ortmann, R., **6**:340
Orwant, C., **4**:27, 28; **9**:76
Orwell, G., **1**:15
Osborne, J. W., **5**:72
Osgood, C. E., **8**:155

Osgood, C. E. (Ed.), **8**:156, 159, 240, 343, 345
Overhage, C. F. J. (Ed.), **5**:111; **10**:99
Owens, W. A., **8**:575
Øyen, O., **9**:210

Padleford, N. J., **12**:191
Paige, G. D., **4**:77, 81, 85
Paillard, J., **8**:353, 467
Palade, G. E., **6**:89, 129
Palay, S. L., **6**:24, 340; **7**:7
Panten, K., **6**:148
Paquet, G., **13**:53
Parad, H. J. (Ed.), **9**:222
Pardee, A. B., **6**:408
Pareti, L., **12**:68
Pareto, V., **2**:98
Park, O., **2**:86; **9**:8, 13
Park, T., **2**:86; **9**:8, 13
Parker, G. G., **10**:385
Parkinson, C. N., **2**:82; **10**:260
Parsons, T., **10**:438; **11**:3, 43, 44, 143
Parsons, T. (Ed.), **2**:53; **9**:74; **10**:2
Pascal, B., **2**:123
Pask, G., **2**:39, 45, 46
Passer, H. C., **4**:89, 151
Pattee, H. H., **3**:7
Paul, W., **12**:284
Pauling, L., **3**:23
Pavitt, K. L. R. (Ed.), **12**:214, 215, 217, 219, 223
Pavlov, I. P., **3**:24
Payne, R. W., **5**:175
Pazer, H. L., **10**:354, 359, 375, 406, 408, 409, 430, 432
Peakall, D. B., **8**:512
Pearl, R., **3**:45
Pearlstine, N., **10**:290
Peery, N. S., Jr., **13**:48
Pendleton, R. B., **8**:459
Penfield, W., **8**:195, 205, 242, 243, 328
Penrose, E. T., **10**:272
Penswick, J. R., **6**:38
Pepinsky, H. B. (Ed.), **5**:102
Pepitone, A., **9**:199
Peretz, B., **5**:183; **13**:9
Perez, A., **3**:32
Pering, K., **6**:411
Perlmutter, H. V., **9**:56
Perot, P., **8**:205, 242
Pert, C. B., **8**:106, 107
Pestel, E., **12**:273–276, 278, 280, 286–291
Pestel, R., **12**:274–276, 278, 280–283
Peterfreund, E., **13**:23
Peterson, E., **6**:411
Peterson, W. W., **4**:53
Pfaffman, C., **8**:73, 76–79, 136
Phillips, C. G., **5**:7, 8
Piaget, J., **8**:498

Picton, T. W., 8:258
Piehuta, J. P., 13:26
Pierce, J. R., 2:32; 3:15; 4:30, 58, 60–62, 64; 5:112
Pierce, L. M., 13:36
Pilisuk, M., 12:201
Pinderhughes, C. A., 13:23
Pinkerton, R. C., 4:9, 92
Pishkin, V., 5:173
Pittendrigh, C. S. (Ed.), 2:10
Pitts, R. F., 8:375, 377
Pitts, W., 5:9, 24; 7:85; 8:123, 147, 596, 633
Planck, M., 2:15
Platt, J. R., 3:31; 6:136, 137; 11:349, 362–364; 13:58
Plog, F. T., 13:52
Ploog, D., 8:335, 346
Plutchik, R., 8:286
Pollack, I., 5:50, 60, 63, 67
Pollack, M., 5:169
Pollock, A. B., 10:200
Polt, J. M., 4:51
Polyakov, K. L., 4:174
Pomeroy, W. B., 11:75
Ponnamperuma, C., 6:411, 416
Pool, I. de S., 11:205; 12:271, 272
Pope, A., 8:446
Popkin, J., 11:423, 424, 426, 429
Porsild, A. E., 3:53
Porter, K. R., 6:27, 89–94, 101, 105, 119, 129, 151, 158, 159, 163, 166, 173, 174, 176, 187, 255
Porter, K. R. (Ed.), 8:20
Postman, L., 4:162; 8:249
Powell, J. W., 10:301, 303
Powell, R. M., 2:62
Prato, Y., 8:380
Prescott, D. M., 6:27, 140, 250, 314, 432, 434, 455
Pribram, K. H., 8:14, 148, 149, 306, 307, 313, 315, 329–331, 334
Price, D. J. de S., 1:7, 17
Prigogine, I., 2:29, 31, 99, 100
Pringle, J. W. S., 3:40
Psykunova, T. M., 5:73
Puck, T. T., 6:459; 7:69
Purpura, D. P., 6:333, 334
Pyle, E., 10:307

Quarantelli, E. R., 10:305
Quarton, G. C. (Ed.), 6:54–56, 61, 62, 145, 234, 272–276, 278–286, 291–293, 295–298, 319, 324, 331–334, 340, 343, 345–352, 359, 360, 370, 374, 376, 389–391, 395, 398–400, 406, 409, 415, 419, 421, 424–426, 443, 445, 450, 452, 461, 472, 475; 8:187, 191, 203, 208, 210, 211, 236, 237, 253

Quastler, H., 2:13, 39; 5:37, 72, 74–79, 185; 6:7
Quastler, H. (Ed.), 2:26; 5:33; 6:10

Rabe, A., 4:176
Rabinovich, M. Y., 4:174
Raiffa, H., 10:154
Rainio, K., 9:230
Ramsøy, O., 9:210
Randers, J., 3:46; 4:150; 12:39, 205, 211–213, 217, 226
Ransmeier, R. E., 4:175
Rapin, I., 8:456, 457
Rapoport, A., 1:2; 2:22, 28; 3:27, 54; 4:27, 28; 5:2; 7:86–89; 8:597, 601, 653; 9:41, 60, 62, 76, 132, 212, 214, 220; 11:346; 12:234
Rappaport, R. A., 11:260
Rashevsky, N., 2:81; 3:5; 8:632; 11:328, 329, 443
Rasmussen, G. L., 8:273
Rasmussen, H., 7:32
Rasmussen, T., 8:328
Rath, G. J., 13:9
Ratliff, F., 8:40, 130, 617
Ratoosh, P., 5:150; 9:215
Ratoosh, P. (Ed.), 8:322; 10:97, 98
Rattray, K. O., 12:117
Raven, B., 9:165
Rawson, H., 9:216
Rayman, N. N., 5:28
Razran, G., 8:166, 184
Realidade, 11:290, 299
Rechenmann, F., 12:277
Redfield, R., 11:4, 5
Reed, C. F., 8:512
Reed, L. J., 3:45; 6:389, 390
Reedy, M., 6:171, 174
Reese, T. W., 5:71
Reese, W. G., 13:44
Reid, L. S., 8:248
Reiffen, B., 4:53
Reimer, E., 10:184
Rein, M., 13:38
Reiss, R. F., 7:90
Restle, F., 8:316
Revelle, R., 12:85, 86, 90
Reynafarje, C., 8:381
Rhoades, M. V., 5:38, 41–43
Rhodes, J. M., 8:401
Ricardo, D., 11:311
Rice, G. E., Jr., 10:309, 315, 322, 323
Rice, S. A., 11:100
Richards, A., 8:475
Richardson, L. F., 12:233
Richlin, M., 8:576
Richter, C. P., 8:414
Ridker, R. G., 12:216, 220
Riecken, H. W., 9:146
Rieselbach, L. N., 11:202–204

Rieselbach, L. N. (Ed.), 11:136, 205, 210, 211
Riggs, L., 8:40
Rignano, E., 2:119
Riker, W. H., 11:390
Rimoin, D. L., 8:530
Rinkel, M. (Ed.), 8:193, 534–537
Rioch, D. McK., 8:547
Rioch, D. McK. (Ed.), 5:181; 13:9
Ripley, R. B., 11:210
Ritter, C., 8:513
Rivlin, A. M., 11:400, 434–439
Rizzo, N. D., 8:411; 13:24
Roberts, E., 8:197
Roberts, L. G., 11:98
Roberts, R. B., 6:299; 8:220, 221, 232
Robertson, J. D., 6:66, 68, 88
Robertson, J. P. S., 5:169
Robey, D., 13:40
Robinson, J. A., 9:88
Robinson, J. P., 10:352
Roby, T. B., 4:37; 5:125–128; 9:59
Rochester, N., 8:591
Roe, A. (Ed.), 7:66; 8:469, 495
Roethlisberger, F. J., 9:73, 206; 10:185
Rogers, C. R., 9:187
Rogers, E. M., 4:82–84; 13:43
Rogers, M. S., 5:52, 59
Rogers, R. A., 13:43
Rolfe, J. M., 13:62
Romer, A. S., 8:461, 462, 466
Ronio, P. G., 8:577
Rose, D. J., 11:63, 65, 255, 256
Rose, J. E., 5:19; 8:29, 83, 88, 94, 99, 138
Rose, S., 11:272, 273
Rose, S. M., 8:477, 478
Rosenau, J. N., 11:88, 89, 130
Rosenau, J. N. (Ed.), 12:17, 18, 242; 13:54
Rosenbaum, G., 5:164
Rosenberg, M. J. (Ed.), 8:437, 440–443, 447
Rosenberg, S., 9:173
Rosenblatt, F., 8:620–624
Rosenblith, W. A. (Ed.), 4:23; 8:31, 32, 66–69, 89, 97, 117, 123, 133, 135, 136, 139, 267
Rosenblueth, A., 2:103, 114; 8:604
Rosenfeld, J. P., 8:168
Rosenthal, D., 5:169; 9:194
Rosenzweig, M. R., 8:511
Rosner, B. S., 8:89
Rosow, I. L., 10:318
Ross, A. M. (Ed.), 4:126
Ross, R., 7:92
Rostand, J., 8:582
Roston, S., 4:149
Rothschild, G. H., 9:48, 67, 159
Rothstein, J., 2:24, 43, 115
Roy, O. Z., 7:80
Royce, J. R., 1:4; 4:88

Rubin, H., **6**:473
Rudell, A. P., **8**:168
Rudman, R., **4**:148
Ruesch, J., **2**:55
Rueyamer, W. R., **8**:491
Rukeyser, W. S., **10**:337
Rushmer, R. F., **7**:95
Rushton, W. A. H., **8**:41
Rusinov, V. S., **4**:174
Russell, W. R., **4**:173
Rustad, R. C., **6**:74
Rutledge, H. D., **6**:490
Rutter, W. J., **6**:442

Sacher, G. A. (Ed.), **7**:75
Sackett, G. P., **8**:496
Sadler, J. R., **6**:237, 303
Sadovsky, V. N., **2**:41, 122; **13**:1
Saez, F. A., **6**:67
Sagan, C., **6**:412
Sager, R., **6**:60
Sahal, D., **13**:14
Sahs, A. L., **8**:336, 348, 356, 419, 522, 569–571
Sakai, T., **10**:414
Salter, J. M., **7**:50
Salzano, J. V., **6**:182
Sams, C. F., **7**:91
Samson, F. E., Jr., **6**:185, 198, 217, 378
Samuel, A. L., **8**:660
Samuels, H. H., **6**:240, 306, 321, 322, 336
Samuelson, P. A., **11**:306, 307, 312, 314–318, 374, 376, 378, 380, 403–405; **12**:125–132
Sandberg, A., **8**:614
Sanders, J. L., **10**:3
Sanger, F., **6**:39
San Martin, M., **8**:380
Sapin, B., **4**:6
Sapir, E., **11**:110
Sawrey, W. L., **8**:546
Sawyer, C. H., **8**:11, 13, 15
Sayles, L. R., **4**:80
Schachter, S., **8**:289, 290; **9**:141, 170, 196
Schade, J. P. (Ed.), **11**:443
Schafroth, M. R., **2**:40
Schanck, R. L., **Preface**:5
Schaps, R., **11**:390
Scheflen, A. E., **13**:12
Scheibel, A. B., **6**:399
Scheibel, M. E., **6**:399
Scheidlinger, S., **9**:186
Scheier, I. H., **8**:420, 421
Scher, J. M. (Ed.), **8**:185
Scherrer, H., **8**:268
Scherwitz, L., **9**:240, 241
Schiffer, M. B., **13**:52
Schlesinger, A. M., Jr., **11**:175–177, 201
Schmidt, C. F., **7**:48
Schmidt, K. P., **2**:86; **9**:8, 13

Schmitt, F. O., **4**:170; **6**:25, 103, 160, 185, 198, 217, 296, 378
Schmitt, F. O. (Ed.), **6**:54–56, 61, 62, 145, 234, 272–276, 278–286, 291–293, 295–298, 319, 324, 331–334, 340, 343, 345–352, 359, 360, 370, 374, 376, 389–391, 395, 398–400, 406, 409, 415, 419, 421, 424–426, 443, 445, 450, 452, 461, 472, 475; **8**:109, 187, 191, 203, 208, 210, 211, 236, 237, 253, 463, 479
Schneiderman, H. A., **6**:316; **8**:487–489
Schopf, J. W., **6**:410
Schramm, G., **6**:416
Schreuder, O. B., **8**:404
Schrieber, A. N. (Ed.), **10**:170, 350, 353, 358, 360–366, 381, 382, 384, 419, 437
Schroder, H. M., **5**:130–132
Schrödinger, E., **2**:21, 49
Schroeder, H. E., **8**:326
Schultz, R. L. (Ed.), **12**:196, 261–266
Schultz, W., **9**:49
Schumpeter, J. A., **2**:98
Schumsky, D. A., **8**:460
Schuster, M. M., **8**:166
Schutz, W. C., **9**:187
Schwenck, A. J., **9**:238
Schwent, V. L., **8**:258
Science, **12**:181
Scodel, A., **9**:215, 216
Scott, E. L., **2**:75
Scott, T. H., **8**:395
Scott, W. R., **10**:4, 14, 30, 74, 112, 113, 136, 137, 160, 220, 222, 259, 261
Scrimshaw, N. S., **8**:509
Scriven, M. (Ed.), **2**:58, 91, 98
Seaborg, G. T., **2**:73
Sears, R. R., **11**:3
Seashore, S. E., **10**:10
Sebeok, T. A., **3**:16; **8**:153, 154, 159, 338, 343, 345
Sebeok, T. A. (Ed.), **8**:156, 240
Segaloff, L., **10**:313
Selby, C. C., **7**:29
Selfridge, O. G., **8**:615, 619, 625
Sellers, W. D., **12**:229, 230
Sells, S. B., **10**:15
Selye, H., **2**:96; **8**:388, 389, 544, 545, 566
Senghaas, D., **13**:58
Sergovich, F., **8**:528
Servan-Schreiber, J.-J., **10**:94
Shaffir, K. H., **10**:49
Shakespeare, W., **8**:24
Shane, C. D., **2**:75
Shankweiler, D. P., **8**:118, 152, 344, 354
Shannon, C. E., **2**:4, 20, 35, 36; **3**:6, 15, 25, 26; **4**:30, 53, 55, 59, 60; **5**:151
Shannon, C. E. (Ed.), **4**:166, 167; **8**:593
Shapiro, M. J., **11**:431–433
Shapley, L. S., **9**:221; **11**:135
Shaskin, M., **9**:81

Shaw, E., **9**:20
Shaw, J. C., **8**:655, 657, 658
Shaw, M. E., **4**:76, 161; **9**:29–31, 33, 48, 67, 149, 159, 177
Shay, J., **6**:27
Sheats, P., **9**:137
Sheldon, A. (Ed.), **13**:33
Sheldon, E. B., **11**:13, 17, 21
Sheldon, R. C., **11**:3
Shelly, M. W., II (Ed.), **10**:3, 15, 109, 110, 114, 129, 141, 147, 148, 153, 223, 231, 236, 244
Shepard, H. A., **10**:73, 331
Sherif, C. W., **9**:189
Sherif, M., **9**:189, 229
Sherman, C. D., Jr. (Ed.), **13**:9
Sherrard, W. R., **10**:229
Sherrington, C. S., **6**:294; **8**:308
Shetler, S. G., **8**:16
Shibuya, T., **8**:61–63, 134
Shiffrin, R. M., **8**:645–647
Shils, E. A., **9**:74; **11**:3, 143
Shils, E. A. (Ed.), **2**:53
Shimbel, A., **8**:634
Shock, N. W., **8**:567, 568, 572, 573
Shook, T., **12**:274–276, 278, 280–283
Shoup, P., **12**:168
Shubik, M., **11**:135
Shurrager, P. S., **8**:179
Shuttic, G., **12**:281–283
Sidorsky, R. C., **5**:122
Siegel, A., **4**:126
Siegel, B. J., **11**:392
Siegel, G. M., **9**:171
Siegel, J. A., **8**:171
Siegel, R. S., **8**:369
Siegel, S., **8**:285
Siegel, W., **8**:171
Siemes, Fr. J. A., **10**:310
Siguel, E., **5**:48
Silberman, C. E., **10**:330
Silverman, J., **5**:89; **8**:552
Simmel, G., **9**:93, 107, 208
Simmons, J. W., **10**:171
Simmons, R. F., **8**:630, 631
Simms, H., **7**:75
Simon, H. A., **2**:7, 52, 73; **3**:19–21, 30, 42; **4**:1, 20, 39–44, 73, 74, 90, 110, 117, 125, 133, 134, 136, 145–147; **8**:303, 304, 312, 648, 649, 655, 657–659; **9**:28, 47, 66, 117, 167, 168; **10**:72, 79–81, 88–91, 96, 143, 145, 151, 168, 179, 186, 195–197, 205–207, 212, 219, 293, 436; **11**:331
Simon, P. A., **8**:303, 312
Simpson, G. G. (Ed.), **7**:66; **8**:469, 495
Singer, J. D., **4**:129, 130; **12**:6, 10, 17, 18, 24, 25, 77, 121, 122, 139–142, 162–164, 167, 182, 186, 187, 237; **13**:54
Singer, J. E., **8**:289
Singer, M., **6**:26, 45
Sjoberg, G., **10**:239

Skårdal, O., **9**:210
Skeels, H. M., **8**:519
Skinner, B. F., **4**:69, 163–165; **8**:359
Skirbekk, S., **9**:210
Skjelsbaek, K., **13**:56
Slater, P. E., **9**:95
Slivinske, A. J., **5**:122
Slocombe, P. M., **6**:39
Slonimski, P. P., **6**:325
Small, M., **4**:130; **12**:6, 139–142, 164
Smelser, N. J., **11**:43, 44
Smith, C. G., **10**:203, 208
Smith, C. M., **13**:35
Smith, D. D., **10**:381
Smith, D. S., **8**:20
Smith, K. U., **9**:55
Smith, M., **6**:39
Smith, S., **5**:69
Smith, T. E., **5**:173
Smoker, P., **12**:196, 240, 257–259, 268–270
Smoker, P. (Ed.), **12**:200
Smout, M. S., **8**:528
Snyder, R. C., **4**:6, 77, 81, 85, 127, 131, 135
Snyder, R. C. (Ed.), **12**:243, 244, 247
Snyder, S., **5**:169
Snyder, S. H., **8**:106, 107
Social Science Research Council, **11**:16
Socolar, S. J., **7**:27
Sokoloff, L., **7**:13, 22, 49, 63
Sokolow, V., **12**:293
Soll, D., **6**:26
Solomon, P., **8**:396, 397, 399
Solomon, P. (Ed.), **4**:111
Solomon, R. L., **9**:203
Solow, R. M., **11**:262, 265, 266
Somjen, G., **6**:210, 215, 216; **7**:55; **8**:72, 125, 265
Sommer, R., **9**:112
Sommerhoff, G., **2**:116; **3**:36, 37, 48
Sonneborn, T. M., **6**:33, 38, 58
Sorensen, T. C., **11**:153–155, 162, 233–235
Sorokin, P. A., **10**:18
Soskin, W. F., **8**:157
Speier, H., **12**:189
Spencer, H., **11**:338, 339; **13**:6
Spencer, W. A., **6**:277
Sperry, R. W., **7**:66; **8**:181, 187, 480, 495
Spiegelman, S., **6**:45, 411
Spielman, J. P., **10**:247
Spitz, R. A., **5**:156
Spooner, C. E., **8**:532, 533, 538
Sprague, C. F., **10**:3
Sprague, J. M. (Ed.), **8**:272
Sprayregen, S., **7**:19
SRG (Systems Research Group), **10**:391
Stahl, W. R., **6**:487
Stalker, G. M., **10**:120

Stämpfli, R., **5**:184
Standfast, S., **8**:456
Stanley, W. M., **6**:4–6, 14–17, 29, 147
Starbuck, W. H., **10**:262, 275, 283, 284
Starbuck, W. H. (Ed.), **9**:231; **12**:232
Stark, L., **6**:487; **8**:455, 612–614
Starkweather, J. A., **8**:158
Starr, C., **4**:148
Staveley, E. (Ed.), **11**:328
Steade, R. D., **10**:229
Steif, W., **10**:339
Steiner, G. A., **4**:4, 7–11, 16, 31, 33, 34, 36, 38, 47–50, 52, 65, 66, 68, 71, 72, 78, 79, 87, 116, 118–120, 122, 123, 137–141, 153, 157, 158, 160, 177; **8**:256, 276
Steinzor, B., **9**:108
Stellar, E., **8**:204, 283
Stellar, E. (Ed.), **8**:272
Stephan, F. F., **9**:94
Stephens, J., **13**:55
Stephens, R. E., **6**:104
Stephenson, T. A., **8**:19
Stevens, A. R., **6**:246, 247, 249
Stevens, J. D., **5**:165
Stevens, S. S., **4**:23; **8**:31, 32, 35, 52, 64, 74, 100, 101, 322
Stevens, S. S. (Ed.), **8**:49, 51, 292
Steward, J. H., **11**:29, 394
Stewart, J. Q., **11**:51, 99
Stice, G. F., **8**:500, 505
Stokes, D. E., **11**:210, 212
Stone, S. A., **5**:92
Størmer, L., **8**:3
Stouffer, S. A., **1**:10; **11**:3
Straschill, M., **8**:127
Stratton, R. A., **7**:45–47
Streufert, S., **5**:130–134; **12**:197–199
Strickland, J. F., **9**:67, 159
Strodtbeck, F. L., **2**:61; **9**:64, 80, 83, 111, 113
Strom, J. S., **10**:384
Stroop, J. R., **4**:94
Strumwasser, F., **6**:274, 275, 398
Studdert-Kennedy, M., **8**:118, 152, 344, 354
Stuiver, M., **8**:69
Suci, G. J., **8**:155
Suedfeld, P., **5**:134
Sugita, M., **6**:485
Sullivan, J. W. N., **13**:75
Sullivan, S. A., **8**:454
Susman, G. I., **13**:28
Sutton, S., **8**:150, 151, 456 457
Svechinskiy, V. B., **2**:83
Swarder, D. D. (Ed.), **11**:422
Swedish Working Party, **5**:106
Sweet, W. H., **4**:173; **8**:86, 87, 93, 98, 102, 103, 140
Swets, J. A., **8**:309

Swift, H., **6**:47, 317
Szekely, M., **6**:39
Sziklai, G. C., **5**:73
Szilard, L., **2**:23, 33; **8**:250

Tagiuri, R., **9**:204
Takagi, S. F., **8**:60–63, 134
Takahara, Y., **2**:73, 77
Talland, G. A., **4**:173
Tandl, L., **3**:32
Tannenbaum, A. S., **10**:56, 203, 204, 208, 289
Tannenbaum, P. H., **8**:155
Tannenbaum, P. H. (Ed.), **8**:437, 440–443, 447
Tanter, R., **11**:366
Tart, C. T. (Ed.), **8**:168
Tasaki, I., **5**:18
Tatje, T. J., **11**:30, 386
Tax, S. (Ed.), **2**:66; **11**:341
Taylor, D. W., **4**:103; **9**:100
Taylor, E. W., **6**:160
Taylor, I. A., **5**:169
Taylor, N. B. (Ed.), **6**:364; **7**:4, 50, 51; **8**:18, 114, 291, 292, 412; **11**:64
Taylor, R. M., **10**:309, 315, 322, 323
Teleki, G., **9**:14
Telford, C. W., **5**:27
Terzuolo, C. A., **8**:332, 333, 416
Teuber, H.-L., **8**:144, 145
Thatcher, J., **8**:310
Thelen, H. A., **9**:22, 25, 38
Thibaut, J. W., **9**:63, 114, 145, 165, 170, 191, 192
Thines, G., **9**:21
Thom, R., **1**:1, 17
Thomas, C. A., Jr., **6**:145
Thomas, E. J., **9**:104
Thomas, J. E., **7**:4
Thomasian, A. J., **4**:53
Thompson, C. M., **6**:181
Thompson, D'A. W., **3**:47
Thompson, E. B., **6**:240, 306, 321, 322, 336
Thompson, J. D., **10**:148, 153, 411, 413
Thompson, J. D. (Ed.), **10**:130, 142
Thorndike, R. L., **4**:97
Thorp, W. (Ed.), **8**:446
Thorpe, W. H., **9**:91
Thorson, J., **6**:216, 223, 224
Thrall, R. M. (Ed.), **8**:319; **9**:211
Thrasher, F. M., **9**:96
Thurmond, J. B., **5**:34
Thurstone, L. L., **9**:87
Tickton, S. G. (Ed.), **13**:9
Tinbergen, N., **8**:409
Tobias, C. A. (Ed.), **6**:212–215, 225, 227, 356, 357
Toffler, A., **5**:116–118; **10**:163; **13**:59

Tolman, E. C., **2**:87; **11**:3
Tomkins, G. N., **6**:240, 306, 321, 322, 336
Tomkins, S. S. (Ed.), **8**:662
Tönnies, F., **10**:20
Torgersen, L., **9**:210
Torrey, R., **9**:175
Tourtellotte, M. E., **6**:13, 18, 21, 22
Townsend, R., **10**:29, 156, 225
Toynbee, A. J., **11**:1, 2, 27, 28, 117, 120, 257, 354, 355
Trager, W., **6**:462
Train, R. E., **11**:25
Treml, V. C., **11**:415
Trist, E. L., **10**:200
Trucco, E., **2**:28
Trumbo, D., **8**:325
Trumbull, R., **8**:396
Trumbull, R. (Ed.), **4**:111; **5**:89
Truxal, J. G., **2**:107
Tsanev, R. (Ed.), **6**:447
Tschirgi, R. D., **7**:16
Tso, W.-W., **6**:308
Tsukkerman, I. I., **5**:73
Tubbs, W. E., **8**:331
Tuchman, B. W., **11**:101
Tueting, P., **8**:150
Turner, G. B., **4**:75, 144
Turner, R., **2**:69
Tweedell, K. S., **5**:72
Tysnes, B., **9**:210

Udy, S. H., Jr., **10**:244, 248, 249
Uhr, L., **8**:616, 619, 626–628
Ullman, E. L., **4**:105
Ullmann, C. A., **5**:159
Ulman, N., **11**:413
Unger, A. L., **11**:85
United Nations Educational, Scientific and Cultural Organization (UNESCO) and International Council of Scientific Unions, **12**:56–58, 69–71, 74
United Nations Office of Public Information, **12**:4, 21, 31, 49, 53, 72, 78, 83, 92, 108, 110–116, 124, 161
United States Bureau of the Census, **11**:91
United States Bureau of Mines, **11**:67
United States Department of Commerce, Office of Business Economics, National Economics Division of, **11**:420, 421
United States Department of Health, Education, and Welfare, **11**:14
United States Department of Transportation, Federal Highway Administration, **11**:52

United States Environmental Protection Agency, **11**:444
United States government manual, 1973–74, **12**:11
United States Library of Congress, Reference Department, Scientific Division, **1**:5
United States National Environmental Policy Act of 1969, **11**:276
United States National Library of Medicine, **5**:111
United States Refuse Act of 1899, **11**:275
University of Chicago, National Opinion Research Center, **10**:326
University of Chicago, National Opinion Research Center, **10**:326
University of Illinois, Control Systems Laboratory, Staff Bio-Systems Group of, **5**:73
Usdansky, G., **8**:550
Uttal, W. R., **7**:38; **8**:33, 120

Vail, S., **8**:319
Valdivia, E., **8**:382
Valens, E. G., **6**:4–6, 14–17, 29, 147
Valentine, G. H., **8**:528
Valentinuzzi, M., **2**:27
Valentinuzzi, M. E., **2**:27
van Bergeijk, W. A., **7**:83
Van de Geer, J. P., **9**:62
Vandenberg, S. G., **8**:506
Vandenbussche, E., **9**:21
van Overbeek, J., **8**:486
Van Wagenen, R. W., **11**:387; **12**:20, 175–180, 184
Veltistov, Y. E., **2**:105
Venables, P. H., **5**:169
Veomett, G., **6**:27
Verne, J., **11**:270
Versace, J., **5**:139, 140
Verster, F. De B., **8**:537
Vickers, G., **2**:109
Vince, M. A., **5**:80
Virchow, R., **2**:73
Vitt, L. J., **8**:17
Viza, D., **6**:448
Voevodsky, J., **12**:236
Vogt, E. Z., **11**:392
Volkman, J., **5**:71
Von Foerster, H., **2**:44
Von Foerster, H. (Ed.), **2**:43, 113; **9**:60
Vossler, C., **8**:619, 626–628

Waggoner, R. W. (Ed.), **5**:179, 181; **13**:9
Wagner, H. G., **8**:130
Wagner, R. C., **5**:81
Wainer, H., **11**:207–209
Wald, G., **6**:454; **8**:30, 36

Waldenberg, M. J., **3**:13; **4**:19
Walk, A. (Ed.), **2**:104
Walker, L. C., **4**:76
Walker, T. G., **8**:326
Walkley, R. P., **4**:35
Wall, E. H., **12**:14, 82
Wall, P. D., **5**:9, 24
Wall Street Journal, **10**:23, 127, 296
Wallace, A. F. C., **10**:302, 304, 314, 319, 320; **11**:113
Wallace, M., **12**:10, 24, 25, 162, 163, 167
Wallhaus, R., **13**:34
Wallot, J.-P., **13**:53
Walsh, K. A., **6**:430
Walter, I., **12**:27
Walter, W. G., **8**:584
Wang, H., **8**:656
Ward, B., **11**:261, 274, 277, 279, 288, 297, 298, 301–304, 379, 381; **12**:3, 44
Ware, G. C., **6**:494
Warkov, S., **10**:261
Warner, H. R., **7**:93, 94
Warner, J. R., **6**:135
Warnick, W. L., **10**:352
Wartna, G. F., **5**:178
Washburn, S. L., **8**:463, 469; **9**:19
Washington Post, **5**:148
Watson, A. J., **8**:173
Watson, D. M. S., **8**:475
Watson, G. B., **4**:94, 96
Watson, J. B., **11**:392
Watson, J. D., **6**:31
Watt, J. M., **7**:96
Watt, K. E., **2**:74
Weathersby, G., **10**:387, 392
Weaver, W., **4**:30, 59, 60
Weber, M., **2**:90; **10**:2, 111
Wecker, E., **4**:171
Weckowicz, T. E., **5**:169
Weick, K. E., **5**:102; **10**:341–344
Weiner, M. F., **5**:167; **8**:548
Weiner, N. (Ed.), **11**:443
Weininger, O., **8**:490
Weinstein, E. A. (Ed.), **5**:181; **13**:9
Weintraub, H., **6**:447
Weiss, E., **7**:81
Weiss, L., **6**:69, 468, 470
Weiss, P., **2**:44, 64, 98; **6**:95–98, 100, 409; **8**:479, 481
Weiss, R. S., **13**:38
Weissmann, G. W. (Ed.), **6**:67
Welford, N. T., **5**:92
Wells, H. G., **5**:107
Wells, H. H., **9**:175
Wendt, R. H., **8**:280, 391
Werley, H. H. (Ed.), **13**:37
Wessells, N. K., **6**:442
Westoff, C. F., **12**:95, 96
Wexler, D., **8**:396, 397, 399
Wexler, D. (Ed.), **4**:111

Whaley, B., **12**:190, 191, 195
Wharton, T., **2**:92
Wheaton, J. L., **8**:393, 394, 398, 400
Wheeler, K. T., **6**:481
Wheeler, L., **8**:290
Wheeler, W. M., **13**:7
White, B. J., **9**:189
White, L. A., **11**:60, 358–361; **13**:6
White, L. D. (Ed.), **11**:140–142
White, R., **9**:70, 148
Whitehead, A. N., **Preface**:1, 3; **1**:13; **13**:76
Whitfield, C. F., **7**:54
Whithall, J., **9**:25
Whittaker, R. H., **8**:9, 10
Whorf, B. L., **2**:94; **11**:110
Whyte, J., **9**:105; **10**:278; **11**:74
Whyte, W. H., Jr., **1**:14
Wick, G. L., **6**:304, 305
Wickesberg, A. K., **10**:280, 281
Wiener, N., **2**:19, 103, 105, 114; **5**:146; **8**:602, 604–606
Wiesel, T. N., **8**:468
Wigdor, R., **6**:277
Wiggins, I. L., **8**:1
Wiggins, W. S., **8**:375, 377
Wigner, E. P., **3**:8
Wilberforce, Lord R., **12**:14, 82
Wilcox, R. H., **5**:99; **11**:328
Wilkinson, H. J., **8**:281, 392
Williams, C. M., **6**:478
Williams, R. G., **11**:64
Williams, R. M., **9**:115
Willier, B. H. (Ed.), **6**:409
Willmer, E. N., **3**:35
Wilner, D. M., **4**:35
Wilson, D., **13**:11
Wilson, E. O., **8**:339
Wilson, K. C., **5**:72
Wilson, K. V., **9**:213
Wilson, M., **11**:65
Wilson, R. H. L. (Ed.), **8**:373

Winch, R. F., **11**:31, 32
Windle, W. F. (Ed.), **8**:273
Winkelbauer, K., **4**:53
Winter, A., **12**:201
Winter, W. P., **6**:430
Wiseman, D. R., **6**:41
Witt, P. N., **8**:512
Wolfe, H. B., **10**:393–398
Wolfle, D. (Ed.), **1**:2; **3**:18
Wolfowitz, J., **4**:53
Wollmans, S. J., **4**:70
Wolman, A., **10**:26
Wolman, B., **9**:74
Wolman, B. B. (Ed.), **8**:563
Wood, W. B., **6**:318, 420
Woodruff, L. L., **6**:102, 387
Woodward, J., **10**:6, 40, 41, 43, 77, 78, 105, 117, 121–124, 132, 169, 172–175, 199, 218, 221, 282
Woodworth, R. S., **5**:29; **8**:365, 366
Wooley, L., **12**:68
Worden, F. G., **8**:272, 275
World Meteorological Organization, **12**:48, 54, 75
Worthy, R. M., **7**:90
Wortis, J. (Ed.), **8**:186
Wouk, H., **3**:3
Wozencraft, J. M., **4**:53
Wright, B. E., **6**:392, 491, 492
Wright, G., **9**:85
Wright, Q. (Ed.), **12**:233
Wulff, V. J., **5**:74, 77, 79
Wurtman, R. J., **6**:197, 220; **8**:109, 112
Wyers, E. J., **8**:401
Wynne-Edwards, V. C., **9**:18; **11**:281

Yagi, K., **8**:417
Yamamoto, W. S., **8**:113
Yanagimachi, R., **6**:67, 71
Yates, A. J., **5**:164, 168, 180; **8**:553–556

York, H. F., **12**:120
Yoshii, S., **12**:274–276, 278, 280
Yost, H. T., **6**:431, 435, 436
Young, A., **7**:96
Young, J. Z., **8**:186
Young, L. R., **8**:455
Yovits, M. C. (Ed.), **2**:11; **3**:22; **5**:181; **8**:598, 600, 620–624; **11**:328; **13**:9
Yuchtman, E., **10**:10

Zagornik, A. D. (Ed.), **13**:37
Zahn, E. K., **12**:39
Zajkowski, M. (Ed.), **13**:37
Zamir, A., **6**:38
Zander, A. (Ed.), **9**:70, 74
Zangwill, O. L., **8**:349, 352, 355, 357, 358
Zarrow, M. X. (Ed.), **6**:42, 43, 59, 408, 458, 459, 476, 478; **7**:65, 70; **8**:7, 108, 376
Zeisel, H., **9**:143
Zemach, R., **10**:389, 390
Zeman, J., **2**:6
Zetterberg, L., **4**:53
Zeuthen, E., **6**:458
Zieleniewski, J., **Preface**:8; **2**:73
Zill, N., II, **11**:207–209
Ziller, R. C., **9**:78, 99
Zimmerman, R. R., **4**:114
Zinkin, S., **8**:228
Zipf, G. K., **2**:101; **8**:324
Ziv, J., **4**:53
Zobrist, A. L., **8**:661
Zopf, G. W. (Ed.), **2**:43, 113; **9**:60
Zotterman, Y., **8**:84, 85, 90–92, 95, 96, 105
Zubek, J. P. (Ed.), **8**:403
Zubin, J., **8**:150
Zuckerkandl, E., **8**:465
Zuzich, A. (Ed.), **13**:37
Zvetanov, P., **12**:231

Subject Index

Many entries in this index are keyed to the Outline on pages *xxiii–xxix* and the List of Hypotheses on pages *xxxi–xli* in the front of this book. These two charts list all places where the outline points or hypotheses appear in the book.

For example, Associator (*see also* 3.3.5 Outline, *xxvi*) leads the reader to every mention of the associator subsystem in all chapters, and Associator, hypotheses (*see* 2-1, 3.3.5.2-1 to 3.3.5.2-6 List of Hypotheses, *xxxi, xxxv*) guides the reader to relevant hypotheses across levels.

An entry such as 43:*n*26 refers to note 26 on page 43.

Proper names in the text not cited in the Bibliographic Index are indexed here.

ABC game, 978–979
Abstracted system [*see* System(s), abstracted]
Abstracting adjustment process [*see* Adjustment process(es), to information input overload, abstracting]
Abyssinia, 772
Acceleration control, feedback, 686
Accessory function(s), 257, 264, 380, 382–384, 386, 389
Accessory structure(s), 248, 257, 377
Acetylcholine [*see* Transmitter substance(s), acetylcholine]
Acrasin, 203, 276, 277, 284, 305, 352
Action (*see also* 4.2.2.1 Outline, *xxvii*), 11, 15
Action current [*see* Neuron(s), action currents in]
Action potential [*see* Neuron(s), action potentials in]
Activator RNA, 272
Active transport (*see* Transport, active)
Actomyosin, 244–246, 273

Adams, John, 812
Adaptation, mode of (*see* Mode of adaptation)
Adaptive radiation (*see* Evolution, adaptive radiation)
Addis Ababa, 791
Address of message, 38, 64, 661
Adenosine diphosphate (ADP), 237, 285, 291
Adenosine monophosphate (AMP), 288, 289, 291
Adenosine triphosphate (ATP), 236, 237, 240, 241, 243–245
Adjustment process(es) (*see also* 5.2 Outline, *xxviii*), 35–36
  bargaining as, 678
  to barrier, 106
  to central nervous system damage, 456
  in conflict resolution (*see* Conflict, resolution)
  in coordination of system, 636, 674, 679–680
  coping device(s), 459

Adjustment process(es) (*Cont.*):
  cost of [*see* Cost(s), of adjustment processes]
  cross-level differences in, 124
  cross-level formal identities in, 123–124
  dietary, 449–450
  economic, 844–849, 956, 968
    and anomie, 872
  emergency, 392, 430–431, 448, 455
  encystment as, 285
  and enzyme-catalyzed processes, 285–287
  financial (*see* economic, *above*)
  to food, 945
  Freudian defense mechanisms as, 458–459
  in glycolosis and respiration, 287
  of heart, 347
  hypotheses (*see* 5.2-1 to 5.2-29 List of Hypotheses, *xxxix–xl*
  to inflation, 849
  information (*see* 5.2.2, 5.2.4, 5.2.6, and 5.2.7 Outline, *xxviii*)

Adjustment process(es) (*Cont.*):
to information input overload (*see also* Information, input: excess; overload), 72, 123, 127, 131, 143–147, 152, 156, 164, 171, 173, 178–183, 185–187, 189–190, 193–195, 1048–1049
  abstracting, 61, 64, 72, 123, 134, 137, 148, 152, 153, 160, 161, 164, 168, 175–177, 179, 181–184, 186, 187, 190, 191, 193–195, 452, 1048
  chunking, 61, 72, 123, 146–148, 151, 152, 452
  error, 61, 64, 72, 123, 127, 131, 143, 144, 146–148, 152, 153, 156, 158, 159, 162, 164, 169, 171, 173, 178–180, 182, 185–187, 189–195
  escape, 61, 72, 123, 146, 148, 150, 152, 161, 164, 189, 452
  filtering, 61, 64, 72, 123, 131, 144–146, 148, 156, 157, 161, 162, 164, 168, 179, 181, 182, 186, 189, 191, 193, 194, 452, 1048, 1049
  error, 179, 181, 182, 186, 187, 189, 193, 195
  omission, 64, 178, 179, 181, 182, 186, 187, 189, 191, 193, 195
  multiple channels, 61, 72, 123, 137, 144, 146, 148, 152, 159–161, 164, 173, 191, 195, 452, 1048, 1049
  hypothesis (*see* 3.3.3.2-9 List of Hypotheses, *xxxiii*)
  omission, 64, 178, 179, 181, 182, 186, 143, 144, 146, 148, 152, 160, 161, 164, 169, 171, 173, 177–180, 182, 185–187, 189–195, 452, 1048
  queuing, 61, 72, 123, 131, 137, 143–146, 148, 152, 158–161, 164, 177, 178, 180, 182, 185–187, 189, 191–195, 452
innovation as, 671
matter-energy (*see also* Matter-energy), to meaning, 74, 454–456
in mitochondria, 286
for motivation, 674
for productivity, 674–677
purposes of, 71
and rates of chemical reaction, 286–287
in reticular formation, 347
for satisfaction of components, 567–568, 674, 676–677
seasonal, 450–451
spatial, 451–452, 565
to stress, 451–452
and structural relationships, 285–286
temporal, in cell, 287
in water balance, 36–37, 455
ADP (*see* Adenosine diphosphate)

Adrenal gland [*see also* Hormone(s), adrenal], 349, 391, 392, 423, 424, 430, 455, 456, 463
and GAS, 451
Afghanistan, 761, 871
Africa, 855, 870
Aging:
  of cell, 302
  of city, 726–731
  of group, 576–577
  human, 302, 481–482
  hypotheses (*see* 3.3.7.2-11 List of Hypotheses, *xxxvi*)
  of organ, 354
  of organism, 302, 480–482
  of organization, 698, 711
Aggregated cells [*see* Cell(s), aggregated]
Aggression:
  control of, in animal groups, 565
  group, 564–565, 568, 572, 574
  and spacing, 564–565
Agraria, 748, 754
Agriculture in Globe6 model, 987
Air defense direction center, simulation of, 737
  and information input overload, 157
Air traffic control system, 157–159, 164
Alaska, 770, 867
Aldous simulation, 498–499
Algonkian society, 869
Alienation, 861, 873
Allende (Gossens), Salvador, 769
Alliance(s), 909–910, 928, 931, 940, 965
  boundary of, as net bias, 932
  decider in, 939
  duration of, 972
Allometric formula for growth, 865
Allosteric molecule(s), 258, 259, 272–273, 275, 294, 295, 299
All-Union Research Institute for Medical and Medico-Technical Information (U.S.S.R.), 933
Alpha coding [*see* Code(s), alpha; Coding: decoding, alpha; encoding, alpha]
Alternative futures, 861
Alternatives, choice among (*see* Choice)
American Bar Association, 642
American Chemical Society, 798
American Medical Association, 642
American Psychological Association, 642, 798
American Stock Exchange, information input overload in, 161–163
American Telephone and Telegraph Company, 855–857
  Bell System, symbol of, 663
  simulations, 734, 737

Amoeba:
  chromosomes in, 305
  DNA replication in, 274
  life cycle of, 296
  reassembly of, 240
  temperature and, 299
Amoeboid movement, 210, 244, 246
  of organism cells, 210, 247
AMP (*see* Adenosine monophosphate)
Amplitude control, feedback, 686
Amygdala (*see* Brain, amygdala)
Anaerobic decomposition of glucose [*see also* Muscle(s)], 237, 246
Analogy:
  and formal identity, 83
  among levels of living systems, 1033
  models and simulations as, 84
Analysis (*see* Deciding, stages of, analysis)
Animal kingdom, 362
Anomie, 872
Anoxia, 372, 446, 450, 474
Anxiety, 456–457, 479, 500
Aphasia, 406, 441–442
Aplysia, parietovisceral abdominal ganglion of, 269–270, 287
  and circadian rhythms, 269, 287
  conditioning analog in, 270
  endogenous rhythm in, 270
  habituation in, 269
Arab League, 909
Arabia, 761
Argentina, 919
Armor Combat Decision game, 715–716
Arms limitation pacts, 953–954
Arms policy, 953
Arms race, 952, 966
Arousal state, 427–428, 431
ARPANET (computer-to-computer network), 789
Artifact(s) (*see also* Nonliving artifacts in models and simulations; Prosthesis), 33–34, 78, 219, 527, 563, 575, 1026, 1039
  subsystem: associator, 66, 520, 543, 607, 637, 767, 794, 915, 935
  boundary, 56, 365, 367, 520, 522, 606, 609, 766, 771, 914, 916
  channel and net, 63, 520, 536, 606, 627–628, 766, 789, 914, 931
  converter, 58, 520, 526, 607, 616, 767, 775, 915, 922
  decider, 323, 341, 365, 424, 607, 644, 767, 800, 915, 940
  decoder, 64, 365, 395, 607, 635, 767, 792, 915, 934
  distributor, 57, 323, 327, 520, 525, 606, 613, 615, 766, 774, 914, 918
  encoder, 607, 662, 768, 824, 915, 942

Artifact(s), subsystem (*Cont.*):
extruder, 59, 323, 331, 365, 373, 521, 529, 607, 621, 768, 781, 915, 926
ingestor, 57, 323, 326, 365, 368, 766, 773, 914, 917
input transducer, 62, 323, 335, 365, 379, 520, 531, 606, 624, 766, 784, 914, 928
internal transducer, 606, 625, 766, 785, 914, 929
matter-energy storage, 58, 607, 612–621, 767, 779, 915, 924
memory, 66, 520, 547, 607, 639, 767, 796, 915, 937
motor, 59, 323, 332, 365, 375, 521, 529, 607, 622, 768, 782, 915, 927
output transducer, 69, 365, 443, 521, 555, 607, 665, 768, 827, 915, 943
producer, 58, 607, 616–617, 767, 777, 915, 923
reproducer, 363, 365, 766, 768, 913, 914
supporter, 60, 323, 333, 365, 377, 521, 531, 607, 623, 768, 783, 915, 927
Artificial intelligence, 84, 485, 488, 490
Artificial neuron [*see* Models and simulations, list of, neuron(s)]
Asia, 813, 871
Assembly line:
and coordination, 680
design of, 614, 615
and worker satisfaction, 674, 677–678
Assimilation process, 868–869
Associating:
by cells, 266, 267, 269–270
conditions of, 409–410
feedback in, 409, 464, 638
motivation and, 409
neural locus of, 441–443
physiology of, 413
rate of, 638
and system level, 795–796
reinforcement and (*see* Learning, reinforcement in)
in spinal cord, 407, 411–412
Associator (*see also* 3.3.5 Outline, *xxvi*)
bond formation by, 65
hypotheses (*see* 2-1, 3.3.5.2-1 to 3.3.5.2-6 List of Hypotheses, *xxxi, xxxv*)
simulations (*see also* Models and simulations), 491–495
Atmosphere, 290, 926
simulation of, 991–994
Atomic waste, 926
ATP (*see* Adenosine triphosphate)
Attention, 137, 426–429, 463
Attitudes, 448, 459–460, 707, 786

Attractiveness of group, 575, 577–578
Australia, 595, 601, 855, 867, 871
Austria, 828
Austria-Hungary, 960–961, 1036
Authentic institutions, 873
Authority (*see also* Power), 643, 645, 647–648, 765
and conflict resolution, 681
Automata:
animals as, 487
theory of, 45:*n*44, 112, 485, 486
Automatic Sprinkler Company, 710
Autonomic nervous system [*see* Nervous system(s), autonomic]
Autonomic neuron [*see* Neuron(s), autonomic]
Autonomic plexus, 324, 337, 340
Autoregulation (*see also* Self-regulation), 341, 346, 347, 358
Auxin, 375, 470
Axon(s) [*see* Neuron(s), axons of]
Axoplasm, 214, 234–235, 260

Bacteria, 204, 207, 208
boundary of, 228
DNA repair in, 241
drug resistance in, 294
enzyme synthesis in, 258
growth of culture, simulation of, 303–304
ingesting in, 233
mutation of, 294
reproduction of, 223–224
Bacteriophage (*see also* Virus), 240–242, 274
ΦX174, 222
T₄, 274, 293
Balance:
group, 568–570
of international transactions, 956
of power, 906
international equilibrium, 907
of trade, 830
Bales' categories, 533, 537
Ball, George W., 813–814
Bandwagon effect, 852
Bandwidth, 61
hypothesis (*see* 3.3.3.2-1 List of Hypotheses, *xxxiii*)
Bangladesh, 840, 863, 867, 893, 946
Bank(s) 847–848, 927, 931, 937, 943, 957, 968
Bargaining, 579
as adjustment process, 678
among organizations, 661
Barnum, P. T., 684
Batch production [*see* Production system(s), batch]
Battelle Institute, 987

Behavior, voluntary (*see* Voluntary behavior)
Behavioral science, origin of modern usage, *xv*
Belgium, 908
Bell System, symbol of, 663
Bendix Corporation, 617
Beneficiaries of organizations, 600
Benelux, 908
Bergson, Henri, 29
Beta-coding (*see* Coding: decoding, beta; encoding, beta)
Bible on microfilm, 640
Bill of Rights, 801, 872
Binding site(s) [*see also* Receptor site(s)], 233, 258, 259, 265, 385
Biological clock [*see also* Circadian rhythm(s); Hibernation], 366
Bipolar cell, 378, 398, 399
Birthrate, 946–947
in World II and World III models, 980, 984
Bit, 11
Black box, 446, 486, 499, 561, 666
Bladder, urinary, 334, 338, 342, 347, 499
Bloc, 906–907, 910, 913, 923, 940, 972
Blood, 210, 317
Blood-brain barrier, 325
Blood circulation:
simulation of control of, 356–357
time of, 393
Bolivia, 761
Bond(s):
in cell cohesion, 247, 291, 298, 352
hydrogen, 223
peptide, 204, 237, 240, 291
phosphate, 237
Border(s), national [*see* Boundary(ies), national]
Botswana, 799
Boundary(ies) (*see also* 3.1.2 Outline, *xxiv*), 1026–1027, 1049
of concrete system, 17–18
continuity in space, 52–53, 913
congruence of subsystem and component, 31
and disaster, 705
filtering by, 230, 324–325, 367, 523
hypotheses (*see* 3.1.2.2-1 to 3.1.2.2-4 List of Hypotheses, *xxxii*)
international, and plebiscites, 950
national, 770–771, 916
and communication, 772
and system segregation, 701–702
permeability of [*see also* Cell(s), membrane, permeability of], 522, 772, 829
postganglionic synapses and, 324
regional, and information spread, 790
Bradley, Omar, 811

Brain [*see also* Nervous system(s)]:
  amygdala, 414, 415, 431, 432, 467
  basal ganglia, 424, 425, 428, 438, 481
  blood-brain barrier, 325
  brainstem, 392
  Broca's area, 395, 439, 442–444
  cerebellum, 402, 423–425, 438, 463
  cerebral cortex, 128, 130, 351, 366,
      392, 401, 402, 407, 412, 413, 424–
      432, 441, 467
    auditory, 412
    frontal, 407, 414, 417, 431, 437, 442,
      467
    motor, 412, 426, 430, 437, 439, 443,
      463
    neocortex, 366, 417, 425
    prefrontal, 402, 431, 438
    visual, 395, 398–400, 412
  colliculi, 401, 412, 429, 432
  conditioning and, 412
  corpus collosum, 412, 414
  cortical projection areas, 395, 398,
      402, 403, 406, 414
  decider components in, 425–426, 438,
      463
  diencephalon, 425, 431, 432, 438, 444
  and drive, 431–432
  electrical activity of (*see also*
      Reverberating circuit), 403–404,
      416–420, 427–429, 479, 482
  and emotion, 430–431
  evolution of (*see* Evolution, neural)
  extrinsic sector, 403
  feeding components in, 432, 451
  filtering in, 145, 325
  forebrain, 431, 432
  fornix, 414, 467
  geniculate bodies, 397–401, 412, 429
  growth of, 417
  gyri of, 395, 414, 415, 426, 439
  hippocampus: and associating, 407,
      412
    electrical rhythms in, 416, 418, 426
    and memory, 414–417, 419
  hypothalamus, 391, 424
    and body water balance, 36–37
    and drinking, 390, 432
    and eating, 390, 432, 451
    and emotion, 430–432
    and memory, 414, 415
    and motor control, 425
    and pituitary control, 392
    and sexual behavior, 366
    in temperature control, 451
  and language, 395, 471
  limbic areas, 423, 424, 428, 439
  medulla, 402, 424, 425
  and memory, 414–418, 437
  meninges of, 324

Brain (*Cont.*):
  midbrain, 415, 424, 425, 431, 432, 438
  nonspecific areas, 414, 423, 428, 438
  of octopod, 414
  as organ, 315–316
  oxygen use by, 344–346, 450
  pons, 424, 425
  posterior intrinsic sector, 403, 433,
      437
  reticular formation of, 73, 288, 347,
      402, 417, 425, 428, 429
  rhinencephalon, 366, 424
  and senility, 481
  size of human, 467
  skin representation in, 351
  speech components in (*see* Speech,
      brain areas in)
  split, 412, 414
  striatum, 366, 395, 399
  telencephalon, 412, 425, 431
  temporal lobe, 407, 414, 416, 417, 441
  temporoparietal lobe, 251, 395, 406,
      407, 439–441
  thalamus, 130, 366, 402, 403, 407, 414,
      415, 424, 428, 430, 431
  vascularity of, 327
  ventricles of, 414, 417
Brain hormone of insects, 470
Brainstorming, 656
Brasilia, 608, 843
Brazil, 761, 774, 799, 840, 843, 849, 869, 947
  Mundurucú society in, 869
Bretton Woods Conference, 958
British Commonwealth of Nations (*see*
    United Kingdom)
British Empire (*see* United Kingdom)
Broca's area (*see* Brain, Broca's area)
Brownell, Herbert, Jr., 815, 818, 819
Bucharest, World Population
    Conference, 947
Buffer storage (*see* Matter-energy
    storage, buffer)
Bulgaria, 772
Bundy, McGeorge, 813–814
Bureaucracy, 595, 642, 691
Burns, J. T., 169
Business concern(s), 595, 600
Business cycle(s), 751, 845
Butterfield Division of UTD
    Corporation, 702

Cabot, R. A., 169
Caine (fictional ship), 52
Cairo, 852
California, 597, 700, 708
Cambodia, 929
Cameroon, 799
Camp, integration in, 577

CAMPUS simulation, 724–725
Canada, 772, 908, 910, 918
  acculturation in, 869
  system-component conflict in, 867
Canberra, Australia, 608
Cancer, 299, 301–302, 354, 475, 582
Cancer cell, 299, 301–302
Capital investment, in World II model,
    980
  in agriculture, 980
Carbohydrate synthesis, 239, 240
Cardozo, Benjamin, 821
Carrier molecule(s), 233, 235, 243
Carswell, G. Harrold, 818
Catholic Church, 683, 696
Cattell, R. B., 894
Cell(s) [*see also* Muscle(s): cells of;
    fibers; Neuron(s)], 203–214
  aggregated, 207, 210–216, 300, 305
    differentiation of, 294, 296–298,
      319, 351
    division of, 294–295
    evolution of, 294–295
  aging in, 302
  anaerobic, 237, 239, 291, 293
  assemblies, 403, 411, 413, 484, 485
  cancer, 299, 301–302
  complexity of, 204, 293–294, 304
    minimum for reproduction, 207
  components of, 205–207, 219, 293
  conditioning of, 267, 269–270
  culture, rate of growth, 352
  differentiated, 296–298
    cancerous changes in, 301–302,
      306
  dissociated, reaggregation of, 351–
      353
  division of, 224–227, 295, 296
    in cancer, 301
    and growth, 296
    signals for, 227, 296
    synchronous, 299
  DNA replication in, 273–274
  epithelial, 210, 337
  free-living (*see also* Amoeba;
      Euglenophytes; Paramecia), 83,
      203, 207, 208, 210, 232, 240, 248,
      254, 266, 285, 287, 300, 302, 305
    adjustment processes of, 284
    information processing
      subsystems of, 248, 276–277,
      1033
    as organism, 203
  information input overload in, 124–
      127, 170–173
  life cycle of, 295–296
  as living system, 203–204, 304–305
  membrane, 171, 205–206, 228–233,
      242–243, 247, 265, 273

Cell(s), membrane (*Cont.*):
  and cohesion, 298
  of excitable cell, 260
  of muscle cell, 263
  of neuron [*see* Neuron(s),
    membrane of]
  permeability of (*see also* Transport:
    active; passive), 230, 233, 243,
    254–256, 263, 385
  pores in, 233, 248
  potential difference in, 229–230
  transport across (*see also* Transport:
    active; passive), 230, 233, 243
molecular constituents of, 204–205
molecular recognition in, 258, 259,
    265, 271, 296
movement of parts of, 246–247, 304
nucleus, 207, 210, 211, 213, 214
  in deciding, 272–275
  membrane of [*see also* Neuron(s),
    membrane of], 207, 224, 227,
    235, 260–262
    pores in, 224, 260, 262
  and memory, 268, 269
  polynucleotides of, 217–223
  in reproduction, 223–227
  transportation of, 274, 297
"off," 381, 383–384, 397, 399, 400
"on," 381, 383–384, 397, 399, 400
"on-off," 381, 383–384, 400
organelles of, 205–207, 217
of organism: codes in, 265
  in memory, 269–271
  memory-like processes in, 268–269
  RNA transcription in, 275
parasites of, 300
phasic, 125, 256, 264, 266, 282, 397
  of eye, 380, 381
  touch and pressure, 388
  of vestibule, 382
primitive, 294, 305
radiation and, 299
receptor, 249–256, 263, 280, 333, 377–
    387, 389, 396–397
  auditory, 377, 378
  of central nervous system, 250–251,
    290
  chemoreceptor, 377, 383
  cnidoblast, 249
  cold, 386–389
  electric energy, 377
  free nerve endings, 251, 375, 378,
    386
  Golgi organ, 375
  Kraus end bulb, 379
  magnetic, 377
  mechanoreceptor, 251, 256, 376,
    378, 382, 387, 388
  Meissner corpuscle, 379

Cell(s), receptor (*Cont.*):
  Merkel disk, 379
  mormyromast, 249, 265
  muscle spindle, 255, 375, 376, 463
  olfactory, 254, 256, 378, 383
  as organ input transducer, 333, 335
  Pacinian corpuscle, 249–251, 255,
    375, 379, 386, 388, 389, 397
  pain, 375, 386–389
  photoreceptor, 249, 255, 377–378
  pressure, 254, 367, 387
  Ruffini ending, 379
  taste bud, 378, 385
  touch, 367, 386–388
  vestibular, 377, 382
  warmth, 386–389
repair of, 240, 241, 318
retinal, 378
retinal ganglion, 378, 397–398, 400
Schwann, 214, 216, 240, 318
scientific knowledge of, 1039, 1042
simulation of metabolism of, 303
size, 207–208, 304
stages of development of, 295–296
systems theory and, 305
techniques of study of, 304
temperature and, 230, 263, 296, 299,
    353
tonic, 125, 256, 264, 266, 282, 380–
    383, 385, 388, 397
Central American Common Market,
    909, 916, 919
Centrality, 517, 535–537, 549–550, 568,
    570, 587
Centralized system (*see* Decider,
    centralized)
CERN (European Organization for
    Nuclear Research), 922
Change:
  organizational, 639, 671–672, 676,
    680–681, 691
  social (*see also* Transformation,
    societal), 794–795, 804, 849, 860–
    861
  and organization, 691
Channel(s) (*see also* Channel and net):
  binaural input on, 144–146
  capacity, 61, 73, 121, 452, 791, 794,
    1046
    of bloodstream, 393
    of cell, 127, 283
    central decision process and, 151
    of channel and net, 264, 393, 791
    and choice reaction time, 132
    coding and, 141–143, 151
    cross-level differences in, 124
    of ear, 383
    of eye, 381
    in flash display, 137

Channel(s), capacity (*Cont.*):
  of group, 153, 156
  of higher-level systems, 192
  of human input transducer, 380
  hypothesis (*see* 3.3.3.2-1 List of
    Hypotheses, *xxxii*)
  and information input overload,
    122
  and information processing, 132,
    139, 151
  and input information, 134, 137
  of input transducer, 257, 531, 624,
    784
  of internal transducer, 259, 390
  measurement of, 122–123, 1032
  of neural membranes, 264
  of neural units, 130–131
  of neuron, 122–123, 127
  olfactory, 384
  of organ, 173, 343
  of organism, 151, 156, 447
    for sequential input, 138–139
  of organization, 164, 191
  of skin, 388
  of society, 791
  for taste, 385
  of vestibule, 382
  competing, 448
  direct, 631–632
  formal, 631, 633, 931
  informal, 631, 633, 700, 931, 1035
  and net (*see* Channel and net)
  noise, 14, 64, 531, 538–539, 634, 787,
    788
    cross-level research design, 110–
      111
    hypotheses (*see* 3.3.3.2-3, 3.3.4.2-2,
      3.3.4.2-4 to 3.3.4.2-6 List of
      Hypotheses, *xxxiii*, *xxxiv*)
  of organ, 336–337
  organism as, 63, 447
  restricted, 631, 932
  system as, 63, 447
Channel and net (*see also* 3.3.3 Outline,
    xxv)
  channel capacity of, 393, 788–789,
    791, 1032
  of community, 633–634
  complexity of, 500, 501
  decider in (*see* Decider, in channel
    and net)
  hypotheses (*see* 3.3.3.1-1 to 3.3.3.2-21
    List of Hypotheses, *xxxii–xxxiv*)
  input–output transfer function of,
    393, 633
  lag in, 393, 791
  neural membranes of, channel
    capacity of, 264
  shred-out in, 1033–1035

Channel and net (*Cont.*):
　as taxonomic variable, 517, 905
　threshold of, 393
Charter (*see also* Template), 34, 55, 516,
　519, 522, 575, 605, 608, 640, 651,
　708, 765–769, 871–872, 913, 1017
　defective, 871–872, 971
　of United Nations, 941, 965
Chavez, César, 700
Checker-playing computer program,
　497, 498
Chemical evolution (*see* Evolution,
　chemical)
Chemoreceptor, 377, 383
Chesapeake and Ohio Railroad, 663
Chess, 12, 433–434, 497, 498
Chile, 769
Chimpanzees, language in, 404, 439, 441
China, 769, 792, 800, 801, 813–814, 827,
　834, 842
　population growth in, 864
Chloroplast, 207, 236, 238
Choice, 656
　axiom, 497
　behavior, 435–437
　binary, 433
　economic, 432
　reaction time, 132–136, 447
　and risk, 102, 435, 660, 807–808, 812,
　978
Chromatin, 207, 224, 301
Chromosome(s), 207, 221, 224, 274
　in cancer cells, 301
　disease and, 301, 476–478
　in interphase, 224
　in meiosis, 225–226
　in mitosis, 224–225
　in normal population, 477
　puffing of, 274, 470
Chrysler management game, 714
Chunking [*see also* Adjustment
　process(es), to information input
　overload, chunking]:
　and cerebral cortex, 437
　hypotheses (*see* 3.3.4.2-1 and 5.1-35
　List of Hypotheses, *xxxiv, xxxix*)
　in memory, 137, 415
Cilia, 205, 227, 233, 244, 251, 285, 375
　movement of, 246–247
Circadian rhythm(s) (*see also* Biological
　clock), 269, 287, 454
Circuits, reliable, from unreliable
　components, 98, 112, 545
Cistron, 221, 239
City(ies):
　evolution of, 688–689
　growth of, 693–694
　new, 608, 843
　organization levels, 687–689
　pathology, 702, 703, 725–730, 842–843

Civil rights legislation, 819–820
Civilization(s), 747, 755, 762, 795, 834
Cleveland, Grover, 802
Clique, 578
CMEA (Council for Mutual Economic
　Assistance) (U.S.S.R.), 905, 909, 937
Coalition(s), 537, 578–580, 661, 910, 931
　in conflict resolution, 682
　in games, 496
　in United States Senate, 816–818
Code(s) (*see also* Coding), 942
　alpha, 64–65, 265, 277–280, 338, 1035
　　genetic determination of, 540
　　output of, 442, 443
　analog, 278
　beta, 64–65, 265, 278–280, 625, 1035
　　genetic determination of, 540
　　and learning, 540
　　output of, 442, 443
　　symbols of, 663
　binary, 122
　digital, 278
　DNA (*see* Deoxyribonucleic acid)
　efficient, 447
　gamma, 64–65, 663–664
　　as emergent, 404, 468, 575, 1035
　　and feedback, 573
　　output of, 442–444
　genetic, 217–222, 305
　hypothesis (*see* 3.3.4.2-1 List of
　　Hypotheses, *xxxiv*)
　neural [*see also* Intensity–frequency
　　relationship; Neuron(s), codes
　　in], 395–396, 400
　private or internal, 64, 69, 265, 276,
　　343, 540, 554, 635, 636
　public, 64, 69, 265, 276
　types of, 64–65
Coding [*see also* Language(s); Pattern
　recognition; Speech]:
　in allosteric molecules, 294
　and channel capacity, 141–143
　decoding: alpha, 265, 404, 540, 792
　　pheromones and, 404
　　auditory, 338–339
　　beta, 265, 635, 792
　　of binocular information, 400
　　color and, 400
　　cross-level comparison, 635
　　distortion in, 636, 934
　　at echelons of organism, 64, 399
　　error, probability of, 14, 65
　　feedback in, 442
　　gamma, 394, 404–406, 635–636,
　　792–793, 934
　　by animals, 404, 439, 441
　　hypotheses (*see* 3.3.3.2-13 to
　　3.3.3.2-16, 3.3.4.2-9, and 3.3.4.2-
　　10 List of Hypotheses, *xxxiv,
　　xxxv*)

Coding, decoding (*Cont.*):
　learning and, 440, 541, 542
　meaning and, 403, 454–455, 541,
　　635, 792–793
　multichannel, 396
　multiechelon, 396
　multiparameter, 395
　multiple modalities, 402
　multivariable, 395
　of optimal codes, 14
　perception as, 64, 402–404, 406, 793
　rate of, 542
　　in spinal cord, 402
　　visual, 338
　encoding: alpha, 277–278, 438, 439,
　　824
　　in nonneural cells, 662
　　beta, 278, 438–440, 824
　　in neuron, 662–663
　　feedback in, 442
　　gamma, 438–442, 663–664, 824–825
　　by animals, 441
　　neural locus of, 441–442
　hypotheses (*see* 3.3.3.2-16, 3.3.4.2-1,
　　and 3.3.4.2-5 to 3.3.4.2-7 List of
　　Hypotheses, *xxxiv–xxxv*)
　in nervous system [*see* Code(s),
　　neural]
　and organizational coordination, 636
　recoding, 134, 265, 398, 401
　　hypothesis (*see* 3.3.4.2-8 List of
　　Hypotheses, *xxxv*)
　and sensory perception, 793
　of speech, 404–406
　theorems, 1033
Coelenterate(s), 316, 356, 361, 368, 369,
　374–375, 390, 393, 409, 465, 466, 473
Coercive power, 645, 646, 823, 915
Cognitive balance theory, 460–461
Cognitive consistency theory, 460–461
Cognitive dissonance, 434, 461, 570,
　859
Cognitive map, 67, 411
Cohen, Wilbur, 751
Cohesion, cell [*see* Bond(s), in cell
　cohesion]
Cohesive system, 38–39
　sensation of, 386, 387
Cohesiveness (*see* 5.4.2 Outline, *xxviii*)
Cold, sensation of, 386, 387
Cold receptors, 386–389
Colonial organisms, 361
Columbia, Maryland, 608
Columbia Broadcasting Company, 608
Columbia River, 837
　dam project, 923–924, 945
Columbus Memorial Library (OAS), 937
COMECON (Council for Mutual
　Economic Assistance) (U.S.S.R.),
　905, 909, 937

Command signals:
 compliance with (*see* Compliance)
 hypotheses (*see* 5.2-21 to 5.2-23 List
  of Hypotheses, *xli*)
Commission on Narcotic Drugs (UN),
 951
Committee on the Behavioral Sciences,
 xv
Common Law, The, 800
Common market:
 Central American, 909
 European, 916
 Latin American, 909
Commonweal organization, 600
Communication (*see also* 4.2.2.2
 Outline, *xxvii*), 12–13, 861
 acrasin in, 277
 bands of, 406, 448, 536, 625
 of birds, 406, 440
 efficiency of, 636
 functions of, 406
 insect, 439
 musical, 758–760
 net(s) [*see also* Channel and net;
  Net(s)]: artificial, 533–536, 538–
  539, 541–542, 544–545, 548–550,
  568, 570, 573, 586, 654, 712
  simulation of, 585–586
 in disaster, 706
 in paramecia, 227
 patterns of: of scientists, 789–
  790
  of technologists, 789–790
 by satellite, 932
Community(ies) [*see also* Security
 community; Society(ies)], 25,
 601
 as level, 595, 1030, 1044
 types of, 597, 601
Comparison signal, 36, 68, 432, 654,
 655, 686, 804
Comparison value, 39
Competition, 661
Complexion, 44:*n*43
Complexity, 18, 1027
 increase in, 293–294, 692, 1033
 social, 755–756
 technological, 617–618, 650
Compliance (*see also* Power), 38, 630,
 645, 661, 801, 822–824
 hypotheses (*see* 3.3.7.2-2, 3.3.7.2-4,
  and 5.4.3-8 List of Hypotheses,
  xxxvi, *xli*)
Component(s), 17, 22, 23, 29–31, 33, 52,
 112, 473, 515, 587, 866, 1025, 1026,
 1028–1029
 joint, 824, 827
 subsystem: associator, 66, 266, 365,
  407–413, 520, 543, 607, 637–639,
  767, 794, 915, 935

Component(s), subsystem (*Cont.*):
 boundary, 56, 219, 228–229, 321,
  323–324, 365, 367, 520, 522–523,
  606, 609, 766, 770–771, 913, 914,
  916
 channel and net, 63–64, 219, 260,
  323, 336–337, 365, 390–392, 520,
  536–537, 606, 627–629, 766–767,
  788, 914, 931–933
 converter, 57–58, 219, 236, 323, 328,
  365, 370, 520, 526, 607, 616, 766,
  775, 915, 919, 922
 decider, 67–68, 219, 272–273, 323,
  340–341, 365, 422–424, 520, 548,
  607, 642–644, 767, 799–800, 915,
  939–941
 decoder, 64, 219, 265, 323, 338, 365,
  394–406, 520, 540, 607, 635–636,
  767, 792, 915, 934
 distributor, 57, 219, 234, 322, 323,
  326–327, 365, 369, 520, 525, 606,
  613, 766, 774, 914, 918–919
 encoder, 69, 219, 276–277, 323,
  342–343, 365, 438–439, 521,
  554, 607, 662, 768, 824, 915,
  942
 extruder, 59, 219, 242, 323, 331, 365,
  373, 521, 529, 607, 621–622, 768,
  781, 915, 925–926
 ingestor, 57, 219, 231–232, 323, 326,
  365, 368, 520, 524–525, 606, 611–
  612, 766, 773, 914, 917
 input transducer, 62, 219, 248–254,
  323, 333–335, 365, 377–379, 520,
  531, 606, 623–624, 766, 783–784,
  914, 927–928
 internal transducer, 62–63, 219,
  257–258, 323, 335–336, 365, 389–
  390, 520, 532–533, 606, 625–626,
  766, 785, 914, 929
 matter-energy storage, 58, 219, 241,
  323, 330–331, 365, 371, 520, 528,
  607, 619–620, 767, 779, 915, 923–
  924
 memory, 66, 268, 365, 413–414, 520,
  547, 607, 639–641, 767, 796, 915,
  937
 motor, 59, 219, 244, 323, 332, 365,
  374–375, 521, 529, 607, 622–623,
  768, 782, 915, 926–927
 output transducer, 69, 219, 279,
  323, 343, 365, 442–444, 521, 555,
  607, 664–665, 768, 826–827, 915,
  943
 producer, 58, 219, 238, 323, 328–
  329, 365, 370, 520, 527, 607, 766,
  777, 915, 923
 reproducer, 219, 223–224, 363, 365,
  519–521, 605, 606, 766, 768, 913,
  914

Component(s), subsystem (*Cont.*):
 supporter, 60, 219, 247, 323, 333,
  365, 376–377, 521, 531, 607, 623,
  768, 783, 915, 927
Compressor, 380, 381, 383, 385
Compromise, 658, 661, 672, 683
Computer(s) [*see also* 6(*c*) and 6(*d*)
 Outline, *xxix*], 28, 303
 economy as, 845
 in deciding, 644, 656, 661
 in information storage, 640
 program as formal identity,
  84
 in systems science, 1032
Conceptual system, 16, 17, 22
Conclusions (*see also* 7. Outline, *xxix*),
 1025–1054
Concrete system [*see* System(s),
 concrete]
Conditioning, 408, 416, 491, 1046
 autonomic, 408
 brain electrical activity and, 412–
  413
 of brain waves, 408–409
 of cells, 267, 269–270
 in decorticate animals, 412
 memory and cortical, 99
 models of, 491–493
 in paramecia, 267, 269–270
 in planarians, 411
 in spinal cord, 411–412
CONEX games, 975–976
Conflict, 39, 1017
 among goals, 651–653
 model of, 995–996
 multivariate analysis, 962–964
 as pathology, 582
 resolution, 674, 680–683, 932, 956,
  958–966, 1017, 1018
 hypotheses (*see* 3.3.7.2-14, 5.2-13
  to 5.2-29 List of Hypotheses,
  xxxvi, *xl*)
 models of, 995–1000
 among values, 804
Conformity, 570, 573, 578
Confrontation, 681–682
Confusional state (*see* Information,
 input, overload)
Conglomerate organization, 692, 699–
 700, 702
Congress of Vienna, 768
Connective tissue (*see* Tissue,
 connective)
Conseil de l'Entente, 909
Consensus, 387, 802, 804, 822, 823,
 849–850, 861
Constancy principle, 458
Constraints on deciding, 659–660, 790,
 801, 805–808, 941
Contact inhibition, 351

Containment (*see* 4.1.1 Outline, *xxvi*)
Containment in time (*see* 4.2.1.1 Outline, *xxvii*)
Content analysis, 572, 786, 959–960
Contraction of muscle cells, 246
Control:
  by decider (*see* Decider, power of)
  fate, 38
  and satisfaction, 678–679
Convention on Narcotic Drugs, 951
Convention on Psychotropic Substances, 951
Converter (*see also* 3.2.3 Outline, *xxiv*), oxidation in, 236–237
Cook County Hospital (Illinois), 613
Coolidge, Calvin, 812
Cooperation, 580, 661
Coordinate repression, 289
Coordination, 636, 674, 679–680
Coping device(s), 459
Corning Glass Company, 722
Corpus Christi, Texas, 707
Cortex:
  adrenal (*see* Adrenal gland)
  cerebral (*see* Brain, cerebral cortex)
Cost(s), 41, 79, 525, 1049
  of adjustment processes, 75, 285, 347, 448, 452, 455, 456, 459, 461, 462, 671, 672, 676, 775, 776, 782, 785, 788, 809, 839, 893
  of coping device(s), 459
  and economic behavior, 435–436
  and efficiency, 41
  of environmental protection, 839
  of feedback, 573
  of Freudian defense mechanisms, 459
  of general adaptation syndrome (GAS), 452
  hypotheses (*see* 3.3.7.2-14, 3.3.7.2-17, 3.3.7.2-19, 3.3.7.2-20, 5.1-18 to 5.1-24 List of Hypotheses, *xxxvi–xxxviii*)
  and inflation, 848
  measurement of, 806
  and organizational growth, 695
  and principle of least effort, 560
  in value-added measure, 667
Cost-benefit analysis, 806, 839
Cost-effectiveness, 41, 655, 668, 675, 738, 1032, 1049
Costa Rica, 761
Council for Mutual Economic Assistance (CMEA or COMECON) (U.S.S.R.), 905, 909, 937
Counterintuitive behavior, 718, 738, 739, 795, 847, 981–984
Creativity, 432, 434, 435, 458
Crete, 871
Crisis research, 930
Crisiscom, 1011–1012
Cross-Cultural Survey, 755

Cross-level comparison(s), 102, 123, 603–605, 635
Cross-level experiments, 169–195, 1048–1049
Cross-level formal identity (*see* Formal identity, cross-level)
Cross-level research designs, 110–114, 584, 1031–1032
Cross-level similarities, 1027–1035
Cuba, 761, 807
Cuban missile crisis, 807, 825–826
Cultural diffusion (*see also* Innovation, diffusion of), 790–791, 834
Cultural evolution (*see* Evolution, cultural)
Cultural spread (*see* Cultural diffusion)
Culture, 687, 749–750, 784, 796–797, 933
  as abstracted system, 21
  boundaries of, 749–750
  language in, 793
  pattern(s) of, 761, 855
Cumbernauld, Scotland, 608
Cybernetic models, 486–487, 494
Cybernetics, 36, 486–487
  and systems theory, *xv*, 487
Cyprus, 869
Cytochromes, 239, 295
Cytoplasm, 205, 214, 234, 238, 260, 275, 298, 302
Cytoskeleton, 247
Czechoslovakia, 799

Dag Hammarskjöld Library (UN), 937
Dahomey, 909
Danube River, 926
Dar es Salaam, 844
Darwin, Charles, 854
Data centers, 932–933
DDT in environment, 835
Death (*see* 5.6 Outline, *xxix*)
Death rates, 946
  in World II and World III models, 980, 984
Decay and termination (*see* 5.6 Outline, *xxix*)
  hypothesis (*see* 5.6-1 List of Hypotheses, *xlii*)
Decentralization (*see* Decider, decentralized)
Decentralized system (*see* Decider, decentralized)
Decider (*see also* 3.3.7 Outline, *xxvi*; Deciding)
  assets of, 801, 823
  authoritarian, 597, 626, 642, 678, 690
  of cancer cell, 301
  cell nucleus in, 272–275
  centrality and, 587

Decider (*Cont.*):
  centralized (*see also* Integration), 39, 81, 550, 690, 692, 699, 700, 823, 844, 854, 866, 867
  in channel and net, 64, 67, 186, 193, 394, 501, 627, 630, 631, 633, 635, 639, 654, 669, 784, 932, 933
  compliance to (*see* Compliance; Power)
  decentralized (*see also* Segregation), 73, 79, 81, 109, 654, 699–702, 736–737, 866, 867, 941
  hypotheses (*see* 5.2-14, 5.4.3-4 to 5.4.3-7, and 5.4.3-9 List of Hypotheses, *xl, xli*)
  democratic, 597, 690
  in denervated organ, 341–342
  echelons of (*see* Echelon)
  as essential subsystem, 18, 32, 67, 293, 315, 333
  foreign policy leadership, 787
  of heart, 340
  hypotheses (*see* 3.3.7.2-1 to 3.3.7.2-21, 5.4.1-2, 5.4.1-3, 5.4.3-2, 5.4.3-4 to 5.4.3-7, and 5.4.3-9 List of Hypotheses, *xxxvi, xxxvii, xli*)
  informal components, 643
  legitimacy of (*see* Legitimacy, of decider)
  models of, 495–499
  plant, 423
  power of, 800–801, 834, 849–850, 861, 903, 940–942
  process (*see* Deciding)
  structure: and classification of systems, 597, 748
    federal, 799, 823, 867
    functional, 644–645
    line, 643, 644
    line-staff, 644
    organic adaptive, 691
    overlapping group, 627, 644, 648, 650, 654, 679, 690, 713
    profit centers, 690, 701
    pyramidal, 643, 679
    and technological complexity, 617
    types of organization of, 642–644
    of United States (*see* United States)
Deciding (*see also* Decider):
  brain in, 423–433, 437–438
  brainstorming in, 656
  central process as bottleneck, 151
  on civil rights legislation, 818–820
  computers in, 615, 644, 656, 661
  constraints on (*see* Constraints on deciding)
  determination of priorities, 656
  effectiveness of, 553
  errors in, 552

Deciding (*Cont.*):
  evaluation in, 654–655
  executive, 701
  mixed-scanning model, 809–810
  in NATO, 941
  and prior experience, 659–660
  rationality in, 656–657, 689–690
  under risk, 102, 435, 660, 807–808,
    812, 978
  and social status, 552
  stages of: analysis, 68, 273, 342, 432–
      433, 551, 654–656, 805, 904
    establishing purposes or goals, 68,
      273, 342, 429–432, 550–551, 651–
      654, 802–805, 904
    of M. Haas, 962–963
    hypothesis (*see* 3.3.7.2-1 List of
      Hypotheses, *xxxvi*)
    implementing, 68, 273, 342, 437–
      438, 553–554, 661–662, 822–824,
      941–942
    synthesis, 68, 273, 342, 433–437,
      551–553, 656–661, 805–822, 940–
      941
  in United States Congress, 815–820
  in United States House of
    Representatives, 553
  by United States President, 810–815
  by United States regulatory bodies,
    822–824
  in United States Supreme Court, 551,
    553, 820–822
Decision(s):
  binary, 132, 432
  landmark, 810
  making (*see* Deciding)
  point (*see* Decider, in channel and
    net)
  policy, 802
  sequential, 134
  under uncertainty, 432, 657–658
Decision theory, statistical, 496–497
Decision tree, 493, 497
Decoder (*see also* 3.3.4 Outline, *xxvi*;
    Coding, decoding):
  hypotheses (*see* 3.3.4.2-1 to 3.3.4.2-10
    List of Hypotheses, *xxxiv–xxxv*)
  models of, 488–491
Defense mechanism(s), 458–459
Definition of the situation, 656
Deindividuation, 578
Deiters' neuron(s), 271, 418
Delaware, 608
Delaware River, cost of cleaning, 839
Delta apparatus, 546
Demand(s), 787, 829
  and consensus, 802
  on United States senators and
    representatives, 816
  on United States President, 811
DEMATEL program, 987–988

Democracy, 799, 850, 852
  and Supreme Court, 820–822
Demographic gravitation, 790
Dendrite [*see* Neuron(s), dendrites of]
Denko, J., 169
Denmark, 761, 908
Density (*see also* 4.1.8 Outline, *xxvii*),
    748
  effect of, on rats, 166
  hypothesis (*see* 4.1.8-1 List of
    Hypotheses, *xxxvii*)
  of United States population, 843
Deoxyribonucleic acid (DNA), 217–223,
    1027
  bacterial, 272
  of cancer cells, 301
  code of, 217, 265
  cytoplasmic, 217, 224, 227, 228, 272,
    275, 293, 299
    bacterial origin of, 293
  information storage in, 217–222, 268
  laboratory synthesis of components
    of, 291–292
  mitochondrial, 228, 275
  in organelle replication, 227–228
  in protein synthesis, 222–223, 239
  recoding of, 265
  repair of, 239, 241
  replication of, 223, 227, 273–274
  and repressor, 258
  synthesis of, 273, 295–297, 301
  transcription of, 223, 265, 273, 274–
    275, 293
  viral, 274, 293
Dependent society, 748, 754
Development (*see also* 5.4 Outline,
    xxviii; Differentiation; Growth):
  economic, 950
  embryonic: of nervous system, 350
    of organism cells, 296–298
    of organs, 350–351
  index of, 755
  and information input underload, 16,
    82, 475–476
  psychosexual, 472
  stages of, 295–298, 468, 696–698, 754–
    764
Deviation, 570–572, 578
Differentiating response, 403, 411
Differentiation (*see also* 5.4 Outline,
    xxxviii; Development; Growth), 28
  cell, 296–298, 303
  organ, 350–351
  in social structure, 862
  of tissues, 468–469
Diffusion:
  cultural, 790–791
  of messages, 633–634
Direction (*see* 4.1.5 Outline, *xxvii*)
Direction of action (*see* 4.2.2.3 Outline,
    xxvii)

Direction in time (*see* 4.2.1.5 Outline,
    xxvii)
Disarmament inspection, 996–998
Disaster, 831
  cornucopia effect, 707
Dispersed subsystem(s) [*see*
  Subsystem(s), dispersed]
Dissonance (*see* Cognitive dissonance)
Distortion, 61, 583
  adjustments to, 572
  in channel, 393, 394, 537, 541, 631,
    634, 649, 654, 791, 854, 933
  and deciding, 654
  in decoding, 397, 542, 636
  hypotheses (*see* 3.3.3.2-2, 3.3.3.2-4 to
    3.3.3.2-6, 3.3.6.2-1, and 3.3.6.2-2
    List of Hypotheses, *xxxiii*, *xxxv*)
  in input transducing, 379, 381, 383,
    384, 531, 784, 1032
  in internal transducing, 626, 1032
  in memory, 99, 421, 797
  in output transducing, 555
Distributor (*see also* 3.2.2 Outline, *xxiv*):
  automatic control of, 615
  as channel and net, 63, 390
  hypotheses (*see* 3.2.2.1-1, 3.2.2.2-1, and
    3.2.2.2-2 List of Hypotheses, *xxxii*)
Diurnal rhythm [*see* Biological clock;
  Circadian rhythm(s)]
Division of labor [*see also* Adjustment
  process(es), to information input
  overload, multiple channels;
  Shred-out, as division of labor], 1,
  26, 81, 357, 519, 601, 1033
DNA (*see* Deoxyribonucleic acid)
Down's syndrome, 476
Downwardly dispersed subsystem [*see*
  Subsystem(s), dispersed,
  downwardly]
Doxiadis, C. A., 861
Drive(s), 429, 431–432, 457, 459
Drug(s):
  and behavior, 447, 448
  control of, 951
  and memory, 415, 418–419, 422
  and spider webs, 474
Dubin, R., 738
Duna River (*see* Danube River)
Duration (*see* 4.2.1.6 Outline, *xxvii*)
Dwarfism, 477
Dyad, 457, 515, 516, 519, 521, 537, 556,
    574, 575, 585, 777, 799
DYNAMO computer language, 719, 988

Earth, 904, 922
Earth-atmosphere system, 991–994
East Africa Community, 909
ECAFE (Economic Commission for
    Asia and the Far East) (UN), 918,
    919, 945

Ecdysone, 470
Echelon, 29, 64, 67, 68, 272, 273, 275, 289, 424–426, 595, 597, 643, 648, 649, 655, 689, 799–803, 907, 939–940
  coding and, 64, 394–395
  and communication, 629, 630
  development of, 857
    by group, 536, 539
  and goals, 652
  and growth, 79, 692
  and heart beat, 347
  hypotheses (*see* 1-1, 3.3.6.2-5, and 3.3.7.2-13 List of Hypotheses, *xxxi, xxxvi*)
  in organism integration, 473
  and sexual behavior, 366
  in United Nations, 939
  of visual channels, 397–401
Ecological niche, 77, 465, 469, 564
Economic and Social Council (ECOSOC) (*see* United Nations, Economic and Social Council)
Economic behavior, 435–436, 496
Economic Commission for Africa (UN), 917–919
Economic Commission for Asia and the Far East (ECAFE) (UN), 918, 919, 945
Economic Commission for Europe (UN), 918, 919
Economic Commission for Latin America (UN), 917, 918
Economic crisis, 872
Economic equilibrium, 875
Economic forecasting, 878–880, 882, 884–885
Economic indicators, 750–751, 885, 894
Economic models (*see* Models and simulations, economic)
Economic theory, 432, 435–436, 496, 579, 657–658, 734, 753, 808, 845, 875–888
Economy, 778
  business cycles in, 751, 845, 847
  ideal competitive, 657
  mixed, 801, 844, 845, 861
Ectoderm, 316–318, 350, 392, 468, 469
Ecumenopolis, 689
EDUNET (educational network), 789
EEC (*see* European Communities, European Economic Community)
EEG (electroencephalogram) (*see* Brain, electrical activity of)
Effective Capital Investment Rate (ECIR), 981
Effectiveness (*see also* Efficiency), 567, 617, 654, 667–668, 676, 679, 867
  and feedback, 686
  of group deciding, 102, 553
  and planned change, 676

Effector, 272, 288–289, 297
Efficiency (*see also* Effectiveness), 41, 79, 305, 346, 567, 650, 667–668, 672, 684, 775, 776, 778, 787, 829, 866
  of communication, 636
  of energy conversion, 237, 776, 829, 832
  hypotheses (*see* 3.3.7.2-17 and 3.3.7.2-18 List of Hypotheses, *xxxvi*)
Ego, 430, 458, 459
Egypt, 761, 801, 831
  and United Arab Republic, 852
Eisenhower, Dwight D., 802, 811, 812, 815
  and civil rights legislation, 819–820
Ekistics, 687
Electric fish, 242, 260, 263
Electrical transmission of information (*see* Synapse, electrical)
Electroencephalogram (EEG) (*see* Brain, electrical activity of)
Electronic conduction [*see* Neuron(s)]
Electroplaque, 242, 260, 262, 263, 266, 277, 280
Electroretinography, 380–381
Electrotonic conduction [*see* Neuron(s), electrotonic conduction in]
El Salvador, 828, 909
Embryonic development (*see* Development, embryonic)
Emergents (*see also* 5.3.1 Outline, *xxviii*), 28–29, 856, 1025, 1036–1038, 1043
  hypotheses (*see* 5.1-4 List of Hypotheses, *xxxvii*)
Emotion, 68, 430–431, 468
Emotionality, 533
Empire(s), 747, 769, 904, 907–908, 913, 939, 967, 972, 1017, 1036
Encoder (*see* 3.3.8 Outline, *xxvi*; Coding, encoding)
Encystment, 230, 285
Endocrine net, 391–393
Endocrine-neural interconnections, 392
Endoderm, 316–318, 350, 468
Endogenous rhythm [*see also* Circadian rhythm(s)], 287
Endoplasmic reticulum, 207, 214, 219, 234, 238, 260, 261
End-product repression, 258, 275, 286, 288
Energy, 11, 617, 776, 829, 923, 1016–1017, 1049
  atomic, 922
  consumption in United States, 776, 829, 830
  conversion of, 237, 775–776, 832, 838, 859, 922
  and cultural evolution, 775–776
  electric, 832, 891–892

Energy (*Cont.*):
  geothermal, 832, 833
  hypotheses (*see* 3.3.7.2-18 List of Hypotheses, *xxxvi*)
  and information transmission, 13–16
  nuclear, 832–833
    IAEA nuclear power project, 922
  oil submodel of multilevel world model, 1013
  radiant, 832–833, 944
  solar, 832–833
  sources of, 832–833, 922
  supranational network, 918
  tidal, 832, 833
  use and climate of, 834
Energy crisis, 870, 871, 925
  simulation of, 1015
England (*see* United Kingdom)
Ensemble, 11, 64, 65, 144
  implicit and explicit, 129, 133, 134, 136–139
  input and output, 60, 61, 65
Enteric plexus (*see* Autonomic plexus)
Entering or leaving containment (*see* 4.2.2.5 Outline, *xxvii*)
Entropy, 13–16, 42:*n*6, 83
  in channels, 394, 634
  in closed systems, 18, 35
  cross-level research on, 110–111
  in distributor, 369, 775
  hypotheses (*see* 3.2.2.2-2, 3.3.3.2-3, and 3.3.6.2-2 List of Hypotheses, *xxxii, xxxiii, xxxv*)
  information and, 13–16
  measurement of, 1030
  negative, 13–16, 18, 43:*n*26, 295, 394, 1027
  in open system(s), 35, 1027
  and steady state(s), 35
Environment, 29–30
  energy and, 835–840
  laws affecting, 839
  and nuclear plants, 926
  pollution of, 622, 781, 836–837, 871–872, 926, 971, 987
    in world models, 980–988, 991, 994
    world monitoring, 928
  protection of, 951–952
Environment–heredity controversy, 77
Enzyme(s):
  in adjustment processes, 285–287
  allosteric, 258, 259, 272–273, 275, 294, 299
  in DNA repair, 241
  evolution of, 295
  inducible, 258, 304
  induction of, 259, 268–269, 275, 302
  and metabolic error, 477
  regulatory, 294
  repressible, 258, 304

Enzyme(s) (*Cont.*):
repression of, 258–259, 275
end-product, 275, 286–289
spatial arrangement of, 236, 286, 287
EPAM (Elementary Perceiver and
Memorizer), 493–495
Ephapse (*see* Synapse, electrical)
Epinephrine [*see also* Transmitter
substance(s)], 428, 431, 451, 455, 480
in adjustment processes, 451
Episome, 272
Epithelial tissue (*see* Tissue, epithelial)
Equifinality, 41
Equilibrium(ia) (*see also* Homeostasis;
Steady state):
balance of power, 906
bipolar, 906
simulations of, 998, 1006, 1010
economic, 845, 847, 875
global, in World III model, 984–985
international, 907
price, 657
striving for, 458
Equivocation, 61
Error [*see also* Adjustment process(es),
to information input overload,
error]:
checking, 146
filtering [*see* Adjustment process(es),
to information input overload,
filtering]
hypotheses (*see* 3.3.3.2-5, 3.3.3.2-7,
3.3.3.2-11, 3.3.3.2-12, 3.3.4.2-4,
3.3.4.2-6, 3.3.4.2-7, 3.3.5.2-5,
and 3.3.6.2-2 List of Hypotheses,
xxxiii–xxxv)
information processing, 152–153,
555, 626, 784, 788
and noise, 65
probability of, 14, 36, 65
Escape [*see* Adjustment process(es), to
information input overload,
escape]
Escherichia coli:
bacteriophage and, 272–274, 293
enzyme synthesis in, 258, 259, 287
Establishing purposes or goals (*see*
Deciding, stages of)
Euglenophytes, 210, 303
EURATOM (European Atomic Energy
Community), 922, 933, 939
European-American Nuclear Data
Committee, 933
European Atomic Energy Community
(EURATOM), 922, 933, 939
European Coal and Steel Community,
908, 939
European Communities, 908, 910, 913,
939
Commission of, 939

European Communities (*Cont.*):
Council of, 939
Court of Justice, 909, 939, 941
European Atomic Energy
Community (EURATOM), 922,
939
Central Bureau for Nuclear
Measurement, 933
European Coal and Steel
Community, 908, 939
European Common Market, 916
European Economic Community
(EEC), 808, 905, 911, 916, 919,
939, 970
European Parliament, 939
European Conference of Ministers of
Transport, 918
European Economic Community (*see*
European Communities, European
Economic Community)
European Nuclear Energy Agency, 925
European Organization for Nuclear
Research (CERN), 922
European Organization for the Safety of
Air Navigation (EUROCONTROL),
918
European Parliament, 939
Evaluation, 654–655, 805
Evans, R. V., 169
Evolution (*see also* 5.3 Outline, *xxviii*;
Shred-out), 26–27, 1033–1038
adaptive radiation, 77, 465, 855
and adjustment processes, 448–449
of aggregated cells, 294–295
chemical, 289–293, 1035
of cities, 687–689
criteria of progress in, 76
cultural, 756–760, 855, 857–860
and energy, 775–776, 859
and death, 480–481
direction of, 76
encephalization, 425, 467
environmental adaptation, 465–466
of extruder, 465
of factories, 689–691
feedback in, 467, 854
and general living systems theory,
749, 1033
genetic basis, 465
genetic drift, random, 77, 294
genetic recombination, 225–226, 465
of heart, 347–348
of hemoglobin, 294–295, 466
and history, 851, 967–968
and increase in complexity, 293–294,
347–348, 574, 692, 855, 859, 967,
968
isolation in, 77, 294, 465, 856
Lamarckian, 854
and learning, 77

Evolution (*Cont.*):
of man, probability of, 78
of multicellular organizations, 76
mutation in, 1, 76–77, 294, 465, 476,
859
natural selection, 1, 77, 294, 349, 380,
429, 465, 476, 481, 856
neural, 466–468
oxygen-carrier molecule(s), 294–295,
466
revolution and, 859–861
sexual selection in, 77, 465
Evolutionary theory of history, 851,
967–968
Excerpta Medica Foundation, 933, 937
Executive decisions, 699, 701
Expander, 380, 387
Experience, early: and behavior, 409
and growth, 470–471
and pathology, 475–476, 479
Exponent in sensation, 95, 282–283,
379–381, 383–385, 387
External effects, 837
External feedback, 37, 463–464, 685–686
Extinction (*see* Memory, extinction)
Extraterritoriality, 770, 913
Extruder (*see also* 3.2.6 Outline, *xxv*):
components in output transducer, 59,
69, 279, 373, 442, 555
and organizational adjustment
processes, 684
Exxon Corporation, 672, 692, 718

Factory, evolution of, 689–691
Family, 517, 548
pathology in, 582–583
settlement patterns in city, 673
FAO (*see* United Nations, Food and
Agriculture Organization of the
United Nations)
Federal Republic of Germany, 904, 910
Federal Reserve-M.I.T. model of United
States economy, 882–885
Federation, 748, 903, 908, 967, 971, 972
duration of, 972
formation of, 748
Federation of Arab Republics, 908
Feedback(s) (*see also* 5.2.7 Outline,
xxviii, 36–37)
acceleration control, 686
in aging, 481
amplitude control, 686
and associating, 409, 464, 638, 794–
795
in attention, 429, 463
in autoregulation of kidney, 346, 347
and cognitive dissonance, 570
comparison signal in (*see*
Comparison signal)

Feedback(s) (*Cont.*):
in control of matter-energy processes, 462–463
coordination by, 686, 687
cross-level research design, 111
in deciding, 654
delayed, 543
disturbance of, 464
effector activation as, 288–289
error in, 36
in evolution, 77, 467, 854
experimental modification, 573
external, 37, 463–464, 685–686
extremum adaptation, 37, 686
in families, 573
gain in, 36, 77
and group termination, 583
hypotheses (*see* 3.3.3.2-12, 3.3.5.2-3, 5.2-6, and 5.6-1 List of Hypotheses, *xxxiii, xxxv, xl, xli*)
input signal adaptation, 37, 289, 463
internal, 37, 288, 462–463, 686–687
and knowledge of results, 464
lag in, 36, 131, 685, 686, 854
and learning, 409, 464, 544–546, 588, 638, 686
loose, 37, 471, 685, 854
and mass action, 289
model of, 892
negative, 36, 37, 305, 462–464, 499, 684, 685, 852–854, 873, 1027–1030
in aging, 481
in body temperature control, 461
in cell control processes, 288–289
in cybernetics, 486
in economic adjustment processes, 966
end-product repression as, 275, 288
in global environmental processes, 966
in personality theory, 457
in pupil of eye, 130–131, 488
and purpose, 39
of society decider, 852–854
and steady state, 499, 565
switching, 289
in teleoperator, 483–484
opinion survey as, 687
and organizational goals, 654, 708
passive adaptation, 37
positive, 36, 77, 573, 684, 685, 851–852, 892, 972
in arms race, 966
in international money market, 966
population and food supply, 966
in population growth, 980, 984
in pupil of eye, 130–131, 488
rate control, 686
and reinforcement, 409, 464, 570, 583

Feedback(s) (*Cont.*):
and semantic noise, 111
in speech, 442, 464
system characteristic adaptation, 37, 686
and system termination, 302, 354, 481, 583, 711–712, 873, 972–973
system variable adaptation, 37, 463
tight, 37, 289, 463, 853–854
time span, 685–686
in tracking, 463–464
in World II and World III models, 980, 982–984
Feeding, brain components for, 432, 451
Fensch, F., 169
Field, bioelectric, brain as, 403
Field theory (*see also* Gestalt theory), 44: *n*44, 403, 411, 434
Filtering, 531, 626, 634, 654, 771, 784
in brain, 145, 325, 428
in environment, 77
measure of, in subsystem process, 1032
in organization channels, 631
Filtering adjustment process [*see* Adjustment process(es), to information input overload, filtering]
Finland, 761
Flagella, 205, 244, 246–247, 285
Flagler, Colorado, 707
Flicker frequency, 128, 381
Flicker fusion (*see* Flicker frequency)
Fluid balance (*see* Water balance)
"Flush-in," 708
Folk society, 748, 754
Food:
adjustment processes related to, 945
in World III model, 980
Food and Agriculture Organization of the United Nations (FAO), 909, 917–919, 928, 929, 949
Food bank, world, 945
Food chain, basic, 951
Foothills Group, 613
Ford, Henry, 608
Ford Motor Company, 608, 609
Forecasting, economic (*see* Economic forecasting)
Foreign policy leadership, 787
Forgetting (*see also* Memory, stages of, loss and alteration during storage), curve of, 421
Formal identity (*see also* Isomorphism), 17, 27, 28, 31, 50: *n*105, 54, 91, 305, 1031–1032, 1049
and analogy, 83, 85
cross-individual, 26

Formal identity (*Cont.*):
cross-level, 4, 26–28, 85, 123–124, 305, 687, 693, 1048–1049
general living systems theory and, 28
and scientists, 1031
in simulations, 1017, 1019, 1032
cross-type, 26–28, 693
and disidentity, 17, 27, 28
models and simulations as, 83
square–cube law of growth as, 693
Formal similarity, cross-level, 1032, 1033
Fortune, largest industrial corporations listed in, 692, 840
Foster, C. C., 169
Franc zone, 909
France, 608, 752, 761, 769, 840, 903, 908, 910, 950
national parks in, 843
French Revolution, 852, 860
Function:
mathematical, 16
and structure, 22–23
in social science, 22–23, 1026–1027
of system, 23, 633
of transducer, 60, 61, 95, 122, 125, 256, 257, 259, 263, 264, 282, 283, 379–386, 388–390, 531, 555, 624, 626
Weber (*see* Weber function)
Functional organization of decider (*see* Decider)
Fungi, 18, 210, 362, 363, 368, 407, 413, 438, 448
Fusion function, 658–659
Future Shock (Toffler), 1048
Future shock, concept of, 149–150

GABA (gamma-aminobutyric acid), 277, 278
Gabon, 919
Gain, 36, 77
Game(s) [*see also* Models and simulations, game(s)]:
management, 661, 713–715, 737
military, 715–716
national policy formation, 874–875
Prisoner's Dilemma, 579, 580, 979–980
war, 974–976
Game simulation, 892, 974–980
Game theory, 579–580, 801, 979–980
Gamma-aminobutyric acid (GABA), 277, 278
Gamma-decoding (*see* Coding, decoding, gamma)
Gardner, John, 751
GAS (*see* General adaptation syndrome)

Gemeinschaft, 601, 748, 754, 968
Gene(s), 221, 224
  architectural, 228, 272
  as decider, 221
  regulator, 221, 224, 257, 272, 478
  in schizophrenia, 477–479
  simulation of, 303
  structural, 221, 272, 274, 478
  temporal, 272
  viral, 274
General adaptation syndrome (GAS),
  451–452, 455, 456, 471, 479–480
General Agreement on Tariffs and
  Trade (GATT) (UN), 918
General Assembly (*see* United Nations,
  General Assembly)
General Electric Company, 619
General living systems theory (*see also*
  General systems theory; Systems
  theory), 1, 4–7, 9, 90, 430, 749,
  1019, 1025–1035, 1044–1050
  applications of, 1049–1050
  basic concepts of, 9–50, 1026–1035
  and evolution, 1033
  as innovation, 1048
  and organism, 499
  and organization, 597
  practical uses of, 1045–1046
  present impact of, 1046–1049
General Motors Corporation, 595, 608,
  649, 650, 910, 911
General Problem Solver (GPS), 498
General systems research, 1045, 1048
  cross-level experiments on, 169–195,
  1048–1049
General systems theory (*see also*
  General living systems theory;
  Systems theory), 1–7, 9, 15, 36, 41–
  42, 46:*n*73, 90, 753
General theory of action (*see* Parsonian
  conceptual system)
Generalization, intersystem, 25–28,
  1031–1032
Generating current in neurons, 254–
  256
Generating potential, 254–256
Genetic code, 217–222
  efficiency of, 305
Genetic drift, random, 77, 294
Genetic information (*see also* 5.5 (*f*)
  Outline, *xxix*), 228, 275, 351
Genetic material, 224, 227, 272, 295
Genetic message, 221–223, 274
Geneva Convention on Treatment of
  Prisoners of War (1949), 955–956
Genome, 222, 272, 274, 275, 294, 295,
  297
  promotor region, 274
Geopolitical factors, 21
George, Walter, 820

German Democratic Republic, energy
  model of, 891
Germany, 761, 851, 852, 868, 908
  and negative feedback, 873
  pathology in, 869
Gesellschaft, 601, 748, 754, 968
Gestalt theory, 44:*n*44, 403, 411, 434
Glia, 214, 216, 318, 333, 415, 417,
  467
Globe6, 987–988
Glycolysis, 237, 287
  in cancer cells, 301
Goal(s) (*see also* Deciding, stages of),
  18, 39–41
  acceptability of, 654
  aspiration-level, 652, 681
  of business and industry, 652–654
  conflict among, 651–653, 680, 681
    hypotheses (*see* 5.2-25 and 5.2-26
    List of Hypotheses, *xli*)
  educational, 752
  external, 39, 651
  hierarchy of, 651
  and level of aspiration, 430
  measurement of, 752
  operationalization of, 654–655
  path toward, 652
  and segregated systems, 651
  of United Nations, 940
  of university, 653
Goethe, J. W. von, 855
Gold:
  "paper gold," 958
  supply and demand of, 956–958
  two-tier system and, 958
Gold drain from the United States, 851
Gold standard, 779, 956, 958
Golgi apparatus (*see* Golgi body)
Golgi body, 207, 210, 211, 240
Golgi organ, 375
Goodyear Tire and Rubber Company,
  616–617
Grand Canyon, 839
Grant, Ulysses S., 802
Graph theory, 569, 571, 586, 627
Great Britain (*see* United Kingdom)
Greece, 761, 772
Green revolution, 918
Grid, management, 651
Gromyko, Andrei A., 825
Gross national product (*see also*
  National product; Net national
  product), 829, 845, 849, 860
Ground substance (*see also* Cytoplasm),
  205, 247, 260
Group, 515–593
  centrality (*see* Centrality)
  coordination of, 530, 565–566, 587
  dyadic (*see* Dyad)
  effectiveness of, 102, 437, 567

Group (*Cont.*):
  efficiency of, 535, 567
  experimental, extrapolation from, 586
  family (*see* Family)
  influence processes in, 551
  as living system, 515
  net [*see* Communication, net(s),
    artificial]
  in organization simulations, 712
  overlapping (*see* Decider, structure,
    overlapping group)
  position in, 558–560
  scientific knowledge of, 1042
  size of, 516–517, 597
  spacing behavior of (*see* Spacing
    behavior)
  types of, 515–517, 578
Group discussion, spatial effects in,
  558–560
Group leader, 535, 550–552, 587, 1042
  and group attractiveness, 578
  and group number, 558
Group leadership, 558–560
Group morale, 568
Group number (*see also* 4.1.2 Outline,
  xxvi), 515, 517, 556–558, 579, 587,
  588
Group pressure and individual
  judgment, 570–571
Group productivity (*see* Productivity)
Group satisfaction, 567–568
Growth (*see also* 5.4.1 Outline, *xxviii*;
  Development; Differentiation):
  and aging, 480
  allometric formula for, 865
  of brain, 417
  cognitive, 472
  costs and 694–695, 1049
  early experience and, 470–471
  embryonic (*see* Development,
    embryonic)
  hormones in, 274
  hypotheses (*see* 5.4.1-1 to 5.4.1-4 List
    of Hypotheses, *xli*)
  and information input underload (*see
    also* Development, and
    information input underload;
    Information, input, underload),
    300, 470–471
  insect metamorphosis, 296–297, 469,
    470
  language acquisition, 471
  laws of, 79, 692, 694–695, 865, 986
    square–cube, 693
  limits to, 694–696, 866
  as measurement of organization,
    692
  neural, 469
  new echelons in, 79, 81
  of new levels, 79

Growth (*Cont.*):
  of number of components, 79, 693–695
  of Paris, 694–695
  pheromones and, 439
  of population, 864–865
  principle of nonproportional change in, 865
  relationships among parts in, 79, 864
  reorganization in, 79
  and reproduction, 777
Growth curves, 78, 469–470
Growth patterns, 469, 470, 696
Growth rate, 78, 296, 350, 352, 469–470, 692–693, 696, 865
Guam, 814
Guatamala, 828
Gusher, 714–715

Habit family hierarchies, verbal associations as, 420
Habituation, 340, 409
Hanoi, 814
Harding, Warren G., 812
Harvard University, 640
  Society of Fellows, *xiv, xx*
Hawaii, 770, 867
Hawthorne studies, 578, 675
Health care, 777
  delivery systems, 732–733, 777, 1047
Hearing, 382–383, 401
Heart:
  adjustment process of, 347
  autonomous activity in, 340
  evolution of, 347–348
Heart-lung machine, 355
Hemoglobin, 294–295, 466
Henderson, L. J., 778
Hibernation, 450–451
Hierarchy(ies):
  of events or processes, 45:*n*66
  of goals, 651
  habit family, verbal associations as, 420
  of purposes, 651
  of values [*see* Value(s), hierarchy]
High Commissioner for Refugees, United Nations (UNHCR), 918, 919, 949
History:
  evolutionary theory of, 967–968
  of systems, 23
Holland (*see* Netherlands)
Holmes, Oliver Wendell, 821
Homeostasis [*see also* Equilibrium(ia); Steady state]:
  Cannon's theory of, 49:*n*98, 458
  family, 582–583

Homeostasis (*Cont.*):
  in Freudian theory, 458
  in Menninger theory, 459
  in organization, 658
Homology, 83
HOMUNCULUS, 584–585
Honduras, 761, 909
Hoover, Herbert C., 802, 812
Hormone(s) (*see also* Adrenal gland; Pituitary gland)
  adrenal, 349, 431, 450, 451, 455, 463, 471, 477, 479–480
  alpha code in, 277, 390
  antidiuretic, 456
  and autonomic transmitters, 256, 455
  auxin, 375, 470
  in coordination, 343
  in endocrine net, 391–392
  in feedback(s), 463
  in growth, 274
  in human pathology, 477
  insect, 274, 302, 451, 470
  insulin, 345
  in organ input–output relationships, 391–393
  ovarian, 345, 391
  parathyroid, 345
  pituitary, 345, 349, 366, 391–393, 479
  plant, 390
  and stress, 471
  in system coordination, 343
  thyroid, 282, 300, 345, 463
Hormonostat, 471
Horowitz, A. E., 169
Horvath, W. J., 169
Hospital, simulation of, 732–733
Hot line, 932
House, R. F., 169
House shape and Müller-Lyer visual illusion, 855
Human relations approach, 690
Human Relations Area Files, 755
Hungary, 926
Huygens, Christiaan, 833
Hydrogen as fuel, 838
Hydrogen bonds, 298
Hydrogen economy, 838
Hydrophobic interactions, 298
Hypothalamus (*see* Brain, hypothalamus)
Hypotheses (*see also* List of Hypotheses, *xxxi–xli*):
  cross-level, 89–92, 1031–1032
    applications of, 1031–1032
    interlevel, 561
    intralevel, 561
    research designs on, 110–114
  of L. Festinger, 571–572
  of G. C. Homans, 584–585
  of D. Mechanic, 646–647

IAEA (*see* United Nations, autonomous intergovernmental agencies, International Atomic Energy Agency)
IBRD (*see* United Nations, autonomous intergovernmental agencies, International Bank for Reconstruction and Development)
ICAO (International Civil Aviation Organization) (UN), 909, 910, 918
Iceland, 761
Id, 430, 458
IDA (International Development Association) (UN), 909, 917, 931, 947, 949
IFC (International Finance Corporation) (UN), 909, 931, 949–950
ILO (International Labor Organization) (UN), 909, 918, 919, 929, 937, 939, 949, 972
Implementing (*see* Deciding, stages of, implementing)
Imprinting, 409
Incentive(s) (*see also* Reward), 562, 674, 675, 845
Inclusion, 33, 207, 210, 595, 596, 610, 612, 621, 667, 671, 678, 683, 684, 710, 748, 770, 781, 829
Independent society, 748, 754
Index:
  of cultural accumulation, 757
  of development, 755, 757
  of injury, 959–960
  of power, 867
India, 834, 947
  population growth in, 864
Indicators (*see also* 2.1 Outline, *xxiii*), 51, 892, 905–906, 965, 1038–1041
  economic, 750, 751, 860
    classification of, 751
  environmental, 753, 893
  of international conflict, 963–964
  social, 751–754, 760, 805, 860, 894
  in supranational simulations, 1016
  of war, 962
Indonesia, 947
Inducement-contribution balance, 674
Inducer, 260
Inducible enzymes, 258, 304
Induction [*see* Enzyme(s), induction of]
Indus River, 909
Industria, 748, 754
Industrial organization(s), 600–601, 617–619, 692, 840
Industry in Globe6 model, 987–988
Infantile experience (*see* Experience, early)
Inflation, 848–849
  as positive feedback, 851

Influence, 436–437, 551, 570–572, 645–648
  and conflict resolution, 681
  on Congressmen, 816
  on policy decision, 787
Information (*H*) (*see also* Coding: decoding; encoding), 1, 11–16
  adjustment processes (*see* 5.2.2, 5.2.4, 5.2.6, and 5.2.7 Outline, *xxviii*)
  capacity per signal, 130
  diffusion of, 537–538, 633–634
  and entropy, 13–16
  flow(s) [*see* transmission(s), *below*]
  flow rate(s) of, 566–567, 629–630, 1032
  genetic, 268
    and organ growth, 351
    social regulation of, 778
  group task, 533
  hormonal [*see* Hormone(s)]
  hypotheses (*see* 3.3-1 and 3.3.6.2-3 List of Hypotheses, *xxxii, xxxv*)
  input (*see also* Input transducer): and arousal, 427–428
    on competing channels, 448
    excess [*see also* 5.2.2 and 5.5(*e*) Outline, *xxviii, xxix*], 72, 284, 346, 564, 671, 771
    hypothesis (*see* 3.3.1.2-2 List of Hypotheses, *xxxii*)
    in infancy (*see* Development; Growth)
    lack of [*see also* 5.2.2 and 5.5(*d*) Outline, *xxviii, xxix*], 72, 284, 346, 563–564, 671, 771, 971
    overlap, 61, 72, 144, 152, 158
    overload [*see also* 5.2.2 and 5.5(*e*) Outline, *xxvii, xxix*], 121–202, 971, 1048–1049
      adjustment processes to [*see* Adjustment process(es), to information input overload]
      in air defense direction center, 157
      in air traffic control, 157, 164
      in cell, 124–127, 165, 170–173
      in cities, 150
      in communications systems, 160
      confusional state in, 61, 122, 140, 144–145, 151–153, 164
      cross-level comparisons, 192–195, 1049
      cross-level experiments on, 169–195, 1048–1049
      curve of, 123, 164, 173, 174, 179–180, 183, 184, 186, 188, 192–193
      on executives, 149, 159–160, 167, 581, 1048–1049

Information (*H*), input, overload (*Cont.*):
      in governmental system(s), 160, 1048–1049
      in group, 152–157, 169, 182–187, 549
      hypotheses (*see* 5.1-1 to 5.1-3, 5.1-10, 5.1-24, 5.1-32 to 5.1-35 List of Hypotheses, *xxxvii–xxxix*)
      in library, 161
      modern forms of, 147–150, 1048–1049
      and neural activity, 144
      in nonliving systems, 123
      in organ, 127–131, 173
      in organism, 131–152, 165–169, 173–182, 1048
      in organization, 157–164, 169, 187–195, 1048–1049
      pathological effects of, 164–169, 1048
      role overload as, 167, 1048–1049
      and schizophrenia, 167–169, 1048
      in society, 834, 948, 1048–1049
      in stock exchange(s), 161–163
    pulse-interval coded, 170–173, 182, 187, 194
    rate of: and deciding, 977–978
      hypothesis (*see* 5.1-42 List of Hypotheses, *xxxix*)
    sequential [*see* Channel(s), capacity]
    underload (*see also* lack of, *above*; Sensory deprivation), 35, 452–454, 475
      hypotheses (*see* 5.1-42 and 5.4.1-4 List of Hypotheses, *xxxix, xli*)
  measurement of, 12, 43:*n*20, 1030, 1032
  medical, 933
  metabolism of, 53, 60
  monetary (*see* Monetary information)
  money as (*see* Monetary information)
  and negentropy, 42:*n*6
  nuclear, 932–933
  organizing, 532–533
  output (*see* Output transducer)
  processing: and brain-evoked potentials, 403–404, 428–429
    and channel capacity, 139
    and error, 152–153
    hypotheses (*see* 3.1.2.2-2 to 3.1.2.2-4 List of Hypotheses, *xxxii*)
    in international crisis, 959–971
    multichannel, 448
    and range, 61, 138–140, 142–144, 151
    rate of, 794
    and stress, 450, 453
    time, 61, 638, 669, 685
    socioemotional, 533–535, 629–630

Information (*H*) (*Cont.*):
  storage (*see also* Memory), 43:*n*26
    computer, 640
    genetic, 268, 420
    macromolecular, 271, 418–420
  task, 533, 630
  theory, 11–13, 131, 499
  transmission(s), 15, 1027
    coordination by, 56, 60, 343, 565–566
    hypotheses (*see* 3.1.2.2-3, 3.3.3.2-8, 3.3.3.2-9, 3.3.3.2-11, 3.3.3.2-12, 3.3.4.2-1 to 3.3.4.2-7 List of Hypotheses, *xxxii–xxxv*)
    limit, 64
    molecular, 260–262
  and uncertainty, 43:*n*39
Information processing subsystems (*see* 3.1 and 3.3 Outline, *xxiv, xxv*)
Ingestor (*see* 3.2.1 Outline, *xxiv*)
Initiator, 224, 257, 259, 272, 385
Innovation (*see also* Cultural diffusion), 624, 656
  as adjustment process, 671–672
  costs of, 671
  diffusion of, 791
  general living systems theory as, 1048
  institutional, 637
  in organizations, 624, 671–672
Input(s) (*see* Information, input; Matter-energy input)
Input ensemble, 60, 61, 65
Input–output compatibility, 60, 141, 151, 447
Input–output economic models, 878–881, 1016
Input–output relationship(s) (*see also* 5.1 Outline, *xxviii*; Information, input, overload), 252
  cell, 95, 124–128, 170–173
  epithelium in, 319
  individual variations in, 448, 455
  information, socioemotional, 629–630, 533–535
  intralevel analysis of, 666
  linear programming in, 1032
  of organ, 320, 344
  in organizational ingesting, 611–612
  of society, 829
  and states of awareness, 426
  of touch transducers, 94–95
Input–output transfer function(s) (*see also* Distortion), 60, 95, 122, 125, 256, 259, 263, 282, 379–387, 390, 393, 633, 634, 784
Input Overload Testing Aid (*see* IOTA apparatus)
Input priority, 61
Input signal adaptation (feedback), 37, 289, 463

Input transducer (*see also* 3.3.1 Outline, *xxv*), 1049
 accessory functions of, 257, 380, 382–384, 386, 389, 532
 accessory structures of, 377
 amplification in, 379, 381, 388
 autonomic postganglionic neurons as, 333–335
 channel capacity of, 257, 380, 381, 383, 388, 532, 624, 785
 distortion in (*see* Distortion, in input transducing)
 of gland cells, 254
 hypotheses (*see* 3.3.1.2-1 and 3.3.1.2-2 List of Hypotheses, *xxxii–xxxiii*)
 input–output transfer function of, 256, 379–387, 531, 784
 lag in, 257, 380, 382–384, 386, 389, 624
 mode of adaptation of, 256–257, 380–385, 387–388, 532
 of organism: auditory component, 378, 382–383
  central processes in, 385, 386
  cutaneous components of, 378–379, 386–389
  olfactory component of, 378, 383–384
  other components of, 379
  taste component of, 378, 384–386
  vestibular component of, 378, 382
  visual component of, 377, 380–382, 488
 threshold of, 257, 380–385, 388, 390, 393, 532
INS (*see* Inter-Nation Simulation)
Insect(s):
 hormone(s), 274, 302, 451, 470
 metamorphosis, 296–297
 social, 439, 440, 519, 522–523. 525–528, 572
  pheromones of [*see* Pheromone(s)]
Insulin, 345
Integrated system, 39
Integration (*see also* 5.4.3 Outline, *xxix*; Decider, centralized), 39, 80–81, 545, 576–577, 862, 866, 1027
 and cohesiveness, 571, 862, 866
 hypotheses (*see* 5.4.3-1 to 5.4.3-9 List of Hypotheses, *xli*)
 requirements for supranational, 970
Integrators, 679–680
Intelligence, 471–472, 482, 485, 490
 artificial, 84, 484, 488
 and cranial capacity, 467
Intensity–frequency relationship (*see also* Weber function), 127, 266, 282, 283, 381
Interaction:
 chronograph, 537
 process analysis, 533, 557
 rate of group, 566–567

Inter-American Commission on Human Beings (*see* Organization of American States)
Inter-American Council for Education, Science, and Culture (*see* Organization of American States)
Inter-American Economic and Social Council (*see* Organization of American States)
Inter-American Highway, 919
Inter-American Juridical Committee (*see* Organization of American States)
Inter-American Nuclear Energy Commission, 922
Intercellular fluid, 327, 337
Intergovernmental agencies (*see* United Nations, autonomous intergovernmental agencies)
Intergovernmental Committee for European Migration, 909, 949
Inter-governmental Maritime Consultative Organization (IMCO) (UN), 909, 918, 928
Intergovernmental Oceanographic Commission (UN), 928
Intergovernmental organization, 908–909, 911, 940
 as channel, 932
 and international conflict, 965–966
 multipurpose, 905, 908–909
 single-purpose, 909–910
Internal feedback [*see* Feedback(s), internal]
Internal transducer (*see also* 3.3.2 Outline, *xxv*):
 channel capacity, 259
 input–output transfer function, 259
 lag, 259
 legislator as, 853
 mode of adaptation of, 259
 in societal adjustment processes, 849
 threshold of, 259
Inter-Nation Simulation (INS) (*see also* Models and simulations), 973
 computerized form, 1000–1009
  and intersimulation validation, 1009–1010
  "*n*th country problem" and, 1006
  revolution in, 1003
  simulation of 1914 crisis, 1008–1009
  validation of, 1007–1010
  variables of, 1002–1005
  Vietnamese War simulation, 1007
  war in, 1003
 noncomputerized form, 974
International Air Transport Association (IATA), 918, 919
International Atomic Energy Agency (IAEA) (UN), 904, 909, 910, 917, 922, 925, 926, 932–933, 936, 939, 940

International Bank for Reconstruction and Development (*see* United Nations, autonomous intergovernmental agencies, International Bank for Reconstruction and Development)
International Civil Aviation Organization (ICAO) (UN), 909, 910, 918
International Convention on Civil Liability for Oil Pollution Damage, 952
International Convention Relating to Intervention on the High Seas in Cases of Oil Pollution Casualties, 952
International Council of Scientific Unions (ICSU), 933, 937
International Court of Justice (UN), 928, 929, 932, 939, 941
International Criminal Police Organization (Interpol), 595, 951
International crisis, 959–961
International Development Association (IDA) (UN), 909, 917, 931, 947, 949
International Finance Corporation (IFC) (UN), 909, 931, 949–950
International Institute for Applied Systems Analysis (IIASA), *xix*
International Joint Commission, 924
International Labor Organization (ILO) (UN), 909, 918, 919, 929, 937, 939, 949, 972
International law, 909
International Law Commission (UN), 964
International Monetary Fund (IMF) (UN), 909, 932, 958
International Narcotics Control Board (UN), 951, 972
International Nuclear Data Center (U.S.S.R.), 933
International Processes Simulation (IPS), 1010–1011
International Red Cross (*see* Red Cross)
International Telecommunications Union (ITU) (UN), 909, 931, 932, 972
International Telephone and Telegraph Corporation (ITT), 695
International trade, 949
 balance of, 956–958
Interpol (International Criminal Police Organization), 595, 951
Interstate Commerce Commission, 774, 800
Inter-University Consortium for Political Research, 937
Invention (*see* Innovation)
Inventory models, 731–732
Inventory theory, 1033

Invisible colleges, 789
Ionic bond(s), 298
Ionic pump, 230, 243, 252, 263, 288
IOTA (Input Overload Testing Aid) apparatus, 173–195
Iran, 761, 909, 947
Iraq, 761
Ireland, 908
   Northern, 851, 893
Isolation (*see* Evolution, isolation in)
Isolation syndrome, 453
Isomorphism (*see also* Formal identity), 17, 83, 84
Israel, integration in, 869
Italy, 840, 903, 904, 908
ITU (International Telecommunications Union) (UN), 909, 931, 932, 972
Ivory Coast, 909, 919

Jackson, H. M., 169
Jamaica, 947
Japan, 752, 761, 772, 781, 801, 814, 829, 842
   marketing organizations in, 595, 781
   as penetrated society, 800
   population growth in, 865
   simulation of Kyoto, 733
Jay, E. S., 169
Jefferson, Thomas, 811
Johnson, Lyndon B., 810, 812–815, 818
Joint subsystem, 32, 79
Joint Working Party, 928
Juchartz, C., 169
Judgment, individual: and group decoding, 541
   and group pressure, 436–437, 570
   in organizational deciding, 658–659
   span of absolute, 136–137
Jury, 523, 548, 552–553, 559–560, 562, 567
Juvenile hormone [*see also* Hormone(s), insect], 470

Kaiser in computer simulation, 1011–1012
Kelly, L., 169
Kennedy, Edward M., 710
Kennedy, John F., 710, 807, 810–812, 825–826, 886
Kennedy, Joseph P., Jr., 710
Kennedy, Robert F., 710, 826
Kenya, 843, 844, 909
Khrushchev, Nikita S., 825–826
Kinetic field, 687–689
Kinetosome(s), 207, 228, 244
King, Martin Luther, 787

Kingdoms, taxonomic, 208–210, 362
Kissinger, Henry, 825
Kohler, Foy D., 814
Korea, 814
Krause end bulb(s), 379
Krebs cycle, 237, 240, 246, 289
Kyoto, simulation of, 733

Labor:
   division of (*see* Division of labor)
   migratory, 919
Labor union(s), 625, 632, 645–646, 678, 700, 851
Lag, 61, 257, 259, 264, 283, 380, 382–384, 386, 389, 390, 393, 532, 555, 685, 779, 789, 794–795, 936
   in feedback, 36, 77, 464, 685, 686, 854
   in law, 936
   in stock exchange, 162
Lake View, Texas, tornado in, 707
Lamarck, J.-B. de M., 855
Language(s) [*see also* Code(s); Coding: encoding; of speech], 792–793, 825
   as artifact, 34
   of bees, 406, 440
   in chimpanzees, 404, 439, 441
   computer programs for, 490–491, 494–495
   as emergent, 404, 468
   of United Nations, 934, 942
Large batch production [*see* Production system(s), batch]
Latin American Free Trade Association, 909
Law, O. T., 169
Law(s), 806
   of conservation of mass and environment, 835
   customary, 935–936
   of diminishing returns to scale, 694–695
   of disproportionality, 692, 865
   environmental, 839
   of growth (*see* Growth, laws of)
   international, 909, 935–936, 941, 964
     and conflict resolution, 964–966
     extraterritoriality in, 770
     lags in, 936
     as net bias, 932
   of mass action, 273
   Parkinson's, 693
   of thermodynamics (*see* Thermodynamics, laws of)
Law of the sea:
   conference on, 945–946, 950–952
   conventions on, 965
Law-making majority, 822
Leader (*see* Group leader)

League of Nations, 768
   duration of, 972
   and narcotics control, 951
League of Women Voters, 627, 678
Learning (*see also* Associator; Memory):
   cell assembly(ies) in, 413, 484, 485
   conditioning, 267–269, 408, 412
     brain activity in, 412
   and evolution, 77
   and feedback, 409, 464, 495, 638, 686
   group–organism comparison, 544, 588
   to learn, 409
   machine, 489, 493–495
   models of, 491–495
   motor, 408
   motor components in, 410, 412
   perceptual, 408
   reinforcement in (*see also* Reward), 409, 464, 491, 493
   reverberating circuits in, 411, 413, 484, 491
   social, 749, 795, 809, 936
   trial and error, 408
   verbal, 408, 412, 413
Learning curve(s), 544
Learning theory, 410–411
   mathematical, 491–493
     simulation of, 583–584
   stochastic, 1033
Least effort, principle of, 50:n101, 246, 268, 436, 560, 694, 699
Le Châtelier principle, 35
Lee, Roger, 778
Legislative process, models of, 885–891
Legitimacy:
   of decider, 38, 40, 160, 163, 661, 801, 802, 822, 823, 849
   of power, 38, 40, 630, 647
Level(s), 1, 25, 46:n73, 47:n79
   of aspiration [*see also* Goal(s)], 430, 677
   in J. W. Forrester system, 719
   of living systems, 1, 25, 749, 753, 904, 1025, 1030, 1031, 1044
     analogies among, 1033
     difference among, 1035–1044
     distinguishing criteria, 25, 1030, 1044
     evolution and, 78
     and growth, 79
     hypotheses (*see* 3.3.3.1-1, 3.3.5.2-6, 3.3.6.2-4, 3.3.6.2-6, 3.3.7.2-21, 5.1-4, 5.1-25 to 5.1-32 List of Hypotheses, *xxxiii*, *xxxv–xxxviii*)
     number of, 1030
     period(s) of origin, 1034–1036
     scientific knowledge of, 1039–1044
     size(s) of, 1034, 1036
   in system design, 47:n79

Lewin, Kurt, 10
Library:
    capacity of Harvard University, 640
    study of, 161, 641
Library of Congress, 796–799
Life cycle(s):
    of cell, 227, 295–296, 299
    of city, simulation of, 726–731
    of organism, 302
    of society, 866
    of supranational system, 969
Life expectancy, 946
Life span:
    of organism, 481
    of supranational system, 972
Light-sensitive pigment, 248, 251, 254, 255
Limbic system (see Brain, limbic areas)
Limulus eye, 255–256, 401, 488
Lincoln, Abraham, 815
Line balancing, 619
Line organizaton, 643–644
Line-staff organization, 644, 646
    simulation of, 712–713
Linear programming, 619, 722–723, 1032
LINK world model, 980
Lipochondria, 207, 241
List-processing program(s), 303
Lithuania, 761
Litton Industries, 699
Liver:
    embryonic development of, 350–351
    regeneration of, 329
Living, usually human, representations in models and simulations [see 6(b) Outline, *xxix*]
Living system [see System(s), living]
Living system–computer interactions in models and simulations [see 6(d) Outline, *xxix*]
Lobbying, 786
Local subsystem, 31, 79
Lockheed Corporation, 711
Logic and thought, 793
Logic Theory Machine (LT), 497–499
London, 843
    and environmental pollution, 839
Loose feedback, 37, 471, 685, 854
Los Angeles, Watts riots, 851
Louisville, Kentucky, first class mail in, 789
Lüchow's restaurant in New York City, 774
Luxembourg, 908
Lysosome(s), 207, 236

McCormack, John W., 709–710
McCormick, Fowler, 659

McCornack, R. L., 169
McNamara, Robert, 813, 814
Macroeconomic models, 875, 878–885, 1016
Madison, James, 812
Mahs, T., 169
Mail:
    in Louisville, Kentucky, 789
    ratio of domestic to foreign, 93, 772
Malaysia, 947
Malthusian doctrine, 841, 863, 946, 966
    in world dynamic models, 986
Man for All Seasons, A, 569
Man-machine system, 686
Management (see also Decider; Deciding):
    authoritarian, 642, 651, 678, 709
    of university, 700, 723
Management game, 661, 674–675, 713–715, 737
Management grid, 651
Management information system, 626, 656, 686, 701
Management methods and productivity, 675–676, 709
Management style, 651, 679, 709
Management system (see also Decider, structure), 650
    functional, 643, 644, 674
    mechanistic, 629, 649, 709
    organic, 649
    paternalistic, 709
    System 1, 2, 3, and 4, 650, 674
    Theory X, 678–679
    Theory Y, 651, 678–679
Management theory, 649–650, 662
Mansfield, Mike, 814
Mapping, biotopological, 47–49:*n*81
Marker, 12–13, 66–67, 555, 563, 634, 639, 641, 665, 1027
    for alpha code, 64–65
    for beta code, 260
    chemical, 64, 254, 260, 279
    coding of, 122
    food as, 439
    matter-energy and, 12–13
    in memory storage, 54
    molecular, 64, 254, 260, 279
    monetary, 791
    transmitter substances as, 242, 260
Market:
    competitive, 653, 647, 829–830, 845, 876
    international, 829–830
Marketing models, 734–735
Marquis, D. G., 169, 738
Marquis, K. H., 169
Marriage, 778
Marschak, J., 94

Marx, Karl, 854
Marxian theory, 967
Mass action, 273, 289
Mass production [see Production system(s), mass]
Matter, 11
Matter-energy, 11
    adjustment processes (see 5.2.1, 5.2.3, 5.2.5, and 5.2.7 Outline, *xxviii*)
    and information flows, 15, 1027, 1044
    metabolism of, 53, 60
    people as, 525, 598, 611, 633, 917, 1027
Matter-energy input (see also Ingestor, 3.2.1 Outline, *xxiv*):
    epithelium and, 319
    excess [see also 5.5(b) Outline, *xxix*], 284, 346, 449, 670–671, 831–832, 834, 870–871, 946–948
    lack [see also 5.5(a) Outline, *xxix*], 284, 346, 449–450, 670–671, 832–834, 870, 945–946
Matter-energy output (see also Extruder), 683, 684
    epithelium and, 319
Matter-energy processing subsystems (see 3.1 and 3.2 Outline, *xxiv*)
Matter-energy storage (see also 3.2.5 Outline, *xxv*)
    buffer (see also Inventory models), 241, 330, 619–621, 1033
    hypothesis (see 3.2.5.2-1 List of Hypotheses, *xxxii*)
    as mirror of environment, 58
    simulation of, 731–733
Maxim's restaurant in Paris, 608
Maximization, 652, 653, 657, 876
    and goals, 652
    of profit, 657, 876
    of utility, 435, 876
Maxwell's demon, 13
Maynard, D. M., 169
Meaning (see also 4.3 Outline, *xxvii*), 11, 153, 154, 410, 491, 797, 1026
    adjustment processes to, 72, 454–455, 671, 833
    and evoked potential, 403
    and matter-energy and information, 1030
    measurement of, 12, 1026, 1030
    quantification of, 70, 500, 501, 1030
Mechanical solidarity, 601, 687
Mechanoreceptor(s) [see Cell(s), receptor: mechanoreceptor; Pacinian corpuscle]
Medawar, Sir P. B., 1050
MEDLARS (see MEDLINE)
MEDLINE, 796
Megalopolis, 613, 688–689

Meier, R. L., 169
Meiosis, 225–226, 476
Meissner corpuscle(s), 379
Mekong River, 909, 945
Memory (*see also* 3.3.6 Outline, *xxvi*; Learning):
    antibody formation as, 268
    brain electrical activity and, 416
    cellular basis of organism, 270–272
    chunking in, 137, 415
    computer, 640, 796
    cross-level research design, 112–113
    DNA in, 420
    drugs and, 415, 418–419, 422
    extinction, 268, 407, 421, 492, 795
    forgetting, 407, 421
    genome and, 420
    goldfish, 416, 418–420
    hypotheses (*see* 3.3.6.2-1 to 3.3.6.2-6 List of Hypotheses, *xxxv–xxxvi*)
    of language, 420–421
    long-term, 419–420, 495
    macromolecular storage, 271, 418–419
    marker in, 54
    as mirror of environment, 67
    model of, 494–495
    nerve net in, 417–418
    neural locus, 413–417
    noise and, 419
    output transducer and, 422
    in planarian(s), 413, 418
    posttetanic potentiation and, 269, 339–340
    protein synthesis inhibitors and, 416–417, 419
    rate of reading into, 415
    retrieval, automated, 641
    retroactive inhibition, 495
    reverberation in, 419, 484, 491
    ribonucleic acid and (*see* Ribonucleic acid, and memory)
    short-term, 271, 401, 419–420, 444, 448
    span of human, 137
    in spinal cord, 340
    stages of, 66
        loss and alteration during storage, 421, 547, 641, 797
        maintaining in storage, 67, 416–421, 547, 640, 797
        reading into storage, 67, 414–416, 547, 640, 797
        retrieval from storage, 67, 422, 547, 641, 798
    thoracic ganglion of cockroach and, 340
    time limit for, 67
    trace, 416, 421–422, 501
Memory-like processes, 268–269, 409
Mendeleyev table of elements, 5, 1046

Mental Health Research Institute, *xvi–xvii*
Merck & Company, 696
Merkel disk(s), 379
Mesoderm, 316–318, 350, 468
Mesozoan(s), 315, 316, 347, 1035
Message(s):
    address of, 629
    types of, 629–630
Metabolism:
    of information, 53, 54, 305
    of matter-energy, 53, 54, 260, 305
Metamorphosis, 296–297
Metaphor of science, *xiv*
Mexico, 761, 799, 828, 869, 908
    population growth in, 864–865
Miami University, "flush-in," 708
Micelles, 205
Michigan State University simulation (MSUSIM), 723–724
Microeconomic models, 875–878
Microfilament(s), 205, 234, 235, 244, 246, 247
    in cell movement, 244–246
    in cytoskeleton, 247
    in pseudopodia, 245
Microfilm, 640
Microtubules(s), 205, 234, 235, 244, 246, 247
    in cell movement, 244–246
    in cytoskeleton, 247
    in input transducer, 254, 256
    in pseudopodia, 245
Migration, 949
    of labor, 919
    of United States population, 843
Mind-matter dilemma, 500, 1042
Miniature armor battlefield, 715
Miniquiers and Ecrehos Islands, 950
Minneapolis, Minnesota, 615
Minnesota, 790
Mirror of environment:
    living system as, 30, 35
    matter-energy storage as, 58
    memory as, 67
MIRV (Multiple Independently targeted Reentry Vehicle), 952
Mitochondrion(a), 207, 210, 214, 215, 224, 234, 236, 246, 260, 294
    ATP adjustment processes of, 286
    bacterial origin of, 293
    DNA in, 228, 275, 293
    movement of, 234, 235
    protein synthesis in, 228, 293
    in respiration, 237, 286
Mitosis, 224–225, 235, 295
    in organ repair, 329
Mode of adaptation, 256–257, 259, 264, 282–283, 380–385, 387–388, 390, 397

Model(s) (*see also* Models and simulations):
    mixed scanning, 809
    simulations as, 83
Models and simulations (*see also* 6. Outline, *xxix*)
    as analogy, 83
    bottom-up, 722
    classification of, 85
    cross-level similarities in, 1032–1033
    cybernetic, 494
    deductive, 84
    distinction between, 83
    dynamic: industrial, 718–722
        urban, 726–731
        world, 980–987
            of mercury flows in environment, 988–991
    economic, 734, 875–885, 1015–1016
        macroeconomic, 875, 878–885, 1016
            econometric, 722, 881–885, 994–995, 1016
            input–output, 878–881, 1016
        microeconomic, 875–878
    and formal identity, 83
    game(s), 713, 737, 874–875, 892, 974–980, 1000–1011
    game theory, 496, 979–980
    inductive, 84
    information processing, 302–303, 355–356, 488–499, 734–737
    intersimulation validation, 1009–1010
    list of: advertising budget decisions, 735
        air defense center, 737
        air-raid warning system, 191
        air traffic control, 157–159
        arms race, 979–980
        automobile dealerships, 714
        bank, 722–723
        Bromsulphalein transfer, 357
        business and industry: bank, 722–723
            Corning Glass Company, 722
            manufacturing firm, 718–722
        cell assemblies, 484
        cell biochemical processes, 303
        cell culture growth, 303–304
        cell membrane, 303
        checker playing, 497, 498
        chess playing, 483, 497, 498
        choice among alternatives, 496
        circulatory control, 356–357
        city: life cycle, 726–731
            residential pattern, 735–736
        cochlea, 355
        coelenterate nerve net, 356
        communication nets, 585
        company structures, 712–713

Models and simulations, list of (*Cont.*):
  conflict: TEMPER, 998–1000
    United States wars, 996–998
  Corning Glass Company, 722
  crisis, international (Crisiscom), 1011–1012
  crude oil distribution, 672, 718
  decentralization, 736–737
  deciding: international, 974–980
    ABC Game, 978–979
    Political-Military Exercise (PME), 974–976
    Tactical and Negotiations Game (TNG), 976–978
  disarmament inspection, 996–998
  dyadic interaction, 584–585
  earth-atmosphere system, 991–994
  energy use, 891–892, 1015–1016
  Euglena, 303
  fluid balance, 487
  House of Representatives voting, 888–891
  household sector, United States, 874, 889–891
  human organism: automata and robots, 482–483
    teleoperators, 483–484
  international relations (INS) (*see also* Inter-Nation Simulation), 973, 1000–1009
  investment management, 734
  learning process, 491–494, 1033
    two-operator model, 584
  legislative process, 885–889
  manufacturing firm, 732–733
  maternity hospital, 732–733
  memory, 494–495
  military operations, 715–716
  monetary policy, United States, 882–884
  national policy formation, 874–875
  natural resource management, 892
  nervous systems, 485–487
  neural nets, 355–356, 488–490
  neuron(s), 302–303, 355, 486
  New York emergency services, 733
  patients, 484
  pattern recognition, 488–491
    Limulus eye, 356, 488–489
    Pandemonium, 490
    Perceptrons, 489–490
  personality (Aldous), 498–499
  petroleum industry decisions (Gusher), 714–715
  pituitary-thyroid relationships, 496
  problem-solving, 497–498
  pupillary response to light, 488
  racial segregation, 892
  renal autoregulation, 346–347, 357
  resource allocation, 891–892

Models and simulations, list of (*Cont.*):
  respiratory control, 356
  respiratory system, 356
  retina, 355, 489
    of *Limulus*, 356, 488–489
  road construction (PERT-SIM), 737
  Senate voting, 885–888
  slime mold differentiation, 303
  social behavior, 584–585
  social pressure and judgment, 583
  social system, 753
  speech perception, 490–491
  traffic control, 733
  turtles, 483
  United States economy (OBE model), 881–882
  universities, 723–725, 734
    Michigan State University (MSUSIM), 723–724
    University of California, 723–725
    University of Toronto (CAMPUS), 724
    Yale University, 734
  urban areas: life cycle of, 718–722
    San Francisco, 725–726
    Seattle ghetto expansions, 735–736
  vascular control, 356
  of warehouse operation, 731–732
  world: Global input–output model, 1016
    Globe6, 987–988
    LINK, 980
    Multilevel World Model, 1012–1016
    World II and III, 905, 980–987
      mercury submodel, 988–991
  world climate, 991–994
  world tin economy, 994–995
  marketing, 734–735
  mathematical, 84, 489, 491–493, 696, 731, 733, 736–737
  matter-energy processing, 303–304, 356–357, 487–488, 496, 731–737, 891–892, 988–994
  Monte Carlo method in, 486, 583, 584
  partial: inventory, 731–732
    of organizations, 731–734
  prostheses, 355
  top-down, 717–722
  types of: living, usually human, representations [*see* 6(*b*) Outline, *xxix*]
    living system–computer interactions [*see* 6(*d*) Outline, *xxix*]
    models in words, numbers, or other symbols, including computer programs [*see* 6(*c*) Outline, *xxix*]

Models and simulations, types of (*Cont.*):
    nonliving artifacts [*see* 6(*a*) Outline, *xxix*]
  uses of, 4, 83, 354–355, 483, 717, 718, 731, 873–874, 894
  validation of, 976, 1009–1010
  validity of, 85, 808, 973, 976, 977
Modulator (*see* Effector)
Mohammed of Nessa, 705
Monerans, 208, 239, 244, 362
Monetary information, 41, 523, 537, 581, 598, 624, 784, 791, 829, 830, 833, 834, 844–849, 872, 931, 937, 938, 943, 966, 968, 1027
Money, 523, 537, 624, 844–845, 851, 956
  as information (*see* Monetary information)
Monte Carlo method, 486, 583, 584
Morgan, T. H., 854
Mormyroid fish, 249, 265
Moscow, 814, 843
Moss, S. M., 169
Motivation, 68, 409, 429–430, 468, 562, 674
  variables in, 430
Motive, 429
Motor [*see also* 3.2.7 Outline, *xxv*; Movement; Muscle(s); Voluntary behavior]:
  components in learning, 410, 412
  control of, 425–426, 433, 462–463
  cortex (*see* Brain, cerebral cortex)
  and extrapyramidal system, 425
  neuron [*see* Neuron(s), motor]
  and output transducer, 59, 69, 374, 375, 442, 530, 555
  and pyramidal tract, 425, 426, 437, 443, 463
Motor unit, 374, 377
Movement [*see also* Amoeboid movement; Motor; Muscle(s); Voluntary behavior], 375, 376, 438
Moving:
  coordination of group, 530
  organization of, 530
Mozambique, 772
MSUSIM (Michigan State University simulation), 723–724
Müller-Lyer visual illusion:
  and house shape, 855
  and primitive society, 855
Multilevel World Model, 1012–1016
Multinational corporation, 595, 910–911, 917, 923, 931–933, 936, 968
Multiple channels adjustment process [*see* Adjustment process(es), to information input overload, multiple channels]
Mundurucú society in Brazil, 869
Muscat and Oman, 799

Muscle(s) [*see also* Motor; Movement; Neuron(s), motor; Tissue, muscular], 317–318, 326–328, 332, 333, 346, 374–377
cardiac, 330, 337, 347, 371, 374
cells of, 213, 214, 234, 249, 256, 263, 469
coordination of, 433
fibers, 128, 213–214, 244, 249, 375
contraction of, 245, 246
end plate of, 128, 249, 256
potentials of, 256, 263
and subsystem components, 374
limb-grafting and, 469
metabolism of, 239, 246, 326, 372, 462
receptors in [*see* Cell(s), receptor]
repair of, 330
smooth or visceral, 317, 330, 332, 337, 338, 347, 372, 374
striated or skeletal, 337, 374
Muscle spindle, 255, 375, 376, 463
Muscular tissue (*see* Tissue, muscular)
Musical communication, 758–759
Mutation (*see* Evolution, mutation in)
Mutual benefit associations, 600, 651
Myenteric plexus (*see also* Autonomic plexus), 336, 340, 341
Myenteric reflex, 325, 336, 337, 341
Myers, S., 738
My Lai massacre, 649–650
Myofibril, 244, 245, 247
Myogenicity, 298, 319, 336, 338, 346
Myoglobin, 294, 466
Myotatic reflex, 376
Myxamoeba (*see* Slime mold)

Napoleon Bonaparte, 662–663
Narcotic drugs [*see also* Drug(s)], 951
NASA (National Aeronautics and Space Administration), 796
Nasser, Gamal, 852
Nation, 747, 904
National Association of Manufacturers, 785
National Center for Health Statistics, 785
National product (*see also* Gross national product; Net national product), 667
National Referral Center for Science and Technology, 798
NATO (*see* North Atlantic Treaty Organization)
Natural resources:
depletion of, 924–925
lack stresses of, 970
marine, 928
as storage for future, 780, 924–925
water, 925, 945
in World II model, 980–987

Natural selection (*see* Evolution, natural selection)
Nature-nurture controversy, 77
Navaho society, 793
Needs, 431–432, 457, 634
Negative entropy (*see* Entropy, negative)
Negative feedback [*see* Feedback(s), negative]
Negative income tax, 846
Negentropy (*see* Entropy, negative)
Nepal, 871
Nervous system(s) [*see also* Communication, net(s); Net(s), nerve; Neuron(s); Tissue, nervous], 63, 318, 394, 424–426, 433
adaptation for gamma-coded outputs, 443
and aging, 481
autonomic, 318, 324, 333, 336, 337, 341, 342, 346, 424, 426, 430, 455, 1035
ganglia, 324, 336, 337, 342, 394
nerves, 392
parasympathetic division, 324, 334, 337, 432, 433
plexus, 324, 337
sympathetic division, 278, 324, 333, 334, 339–340, 433, 455
blood-brain barrier in, 325
central, 318, 325, 390, 392, 394, 413, 426, 1035
codes in [*see* Code(s)]
decider components in, 423–424
drugs and, 447, 474
embryonic development of (*see* Development, embryonic)
evolution of (*see* Evolution)
glia of, 216, 318, 333
human complexity of, 392, 500
and information storage, 416–418
and learning, 407, 413
and motor control, 426, 430, 432,

as organ, 315–316
parasympathetic (*see* autonomic, *above*)
and perception, 403–404
peripheral, 318, 390
cerebrospinal division, 318
pheromones and, 439
regeneration in, 469
simulations of (*see* Models and simulations)
specificity of connections, 469
and stress, 475–476
sympathetic [*see* Nervous system(s), autonomic]
transmitter substances in [*see* Transmitter substance(s)]
Nessa, Mohammed of, 705

Net(s) (*see also* Decider, in channel and net; Node, of net):
artificial [*see* Communication, net(s); Models and simulations, list of, neuron(s)]
biased, 95–96, 355–356, 537–538, 630, 734, 789, 790, 854, 932
communication [*see* Communication, net(s)]
decider in (*see* Decider)
and deciding, 631
electronic, 789–790
endocrine, 391–393
financial, 956
formal, 631
informal, 631, 700
mathematics, 95–96, 355–356, 403, 485–486
nerve (*see also* mathematics, *above*), 336–337, 390, 392–394, 403
power, 918
theory, 54, 355, 1033
applicability of, 54, 485–486
hypothesis (*see* 3.3.3.1-1 List of Hypotheses, *xxxiii*)
in organ simulation, 355–356
totally connected, 533, 536, 538, 539, 544, 587, 630
transportation, 918
Net national product (NNP) (*see also* Gross national product; National product), 846–847, 875–876
Net reproduction rate (NRR), 862
Netherlands, 707, 761, 840, 908, 911
National Physical Planning Act, 843
Network [*see* Net(s)]
Neurofibril(s), 214
Neurofilament(s), 214, 260
Neuromime [*see* Models and simulations, list of, neuron(s)]
Neuromyal junction, 249, 284, 300, 318, 339
Neuron(s) (*see also* Synapse):
A, B, C fibers of, 264, 387
action currents in, 259, 262, 263, 276
action potentials in, 124–126, 171, 257, 262–263, 276
aging and, 302
analog activity in, 485
antidromic currents in, 125, 126, 262–263, 393
autonomic: parasympathetic, 333
postganglionic, 324, 333, 335–337
preganglionic, 333–337
sympathetic, 324, 333
axons of, 214–215, 263–264
as decider components, 423, 424
channel capacity of, 122–123, 127

Neuron(s) (*Cont.*):
circadian rhythm in, 269
codes in, 122, 125, 129–130, 170, 265, 278, 397, 400
as decider components, 424
dendrites of, 125, 214, 248, 249, 262, 270–271, 276, 302, 342, 417, 485–487
diameters of, 214
digital activity in, 485
effects of experience on, 467
as electric cable, 262
electrotonic conduction in, 257, 259, 262, 265, 269, 276, 339
and embryonic growth, 351
endings of, 124, 214, 215, 249, 255, 280, 342, 378, 379
excitatory postsynaptic potential in, 126, 262, 263, 265, 276
generating current in, 254–256
information input overload in (*see* Information, input, overload)
inhibitory postsynaptic potential of, 262
input–output relationships of (*see* Information, input, overload; Input–output relationship; Input–output transfer function)
input transducer of (*see also* 3.3.1 Outline, *xxv*), 248–249
interneuron(s), 418
of *Limulus* eye, 488
membrane of: electrical activity of, 260, 262–263, 270–271, 275–276
postsynaptic, 262, 269
presynaptic, 229
subsynaptic, 229, 248, 255–256, 262, 269, 288, 339
in memory processes, 269–271
microneurons, 415, 417
motor, 125, 249, 255, 262, 264, 375, 376, 425, 463
alpha, 425, 463, 469
gamma, 463
input–output transfer function of, 125
neuromyal junction, 249, 339
phasic [*see also* Cell(s), phasic], 125, 266
postganglionic, 324, 333–336, 338
postsynaptic, 248, 257, 265, 339
preganglionic, 335–337
presynaptic, 342, 343
refractory period of, 122, 125, 126, 129, 171, 263
repair of, 330
retinal ganglion, 397–400
sheath of (*see* Sheath of Schwann)
spatial summation in, 276
spike in, 125, 262–263, 270
temporal summation in, 276

Neuron(s) (*Cont.*):
tonic [*see also* Cell(s), tonic], 124, 264, 265
transmission rates of, 127, 263–264
transmitter substance(s) in (*see also* Transmitter substance), 254–257
Neurotubules, 214, 260
New York City:
criminal justice system, 703
emergency services in, 629
Environmental Protection Agency, 622
waste in, 622
New York state, 597
New York Stock Exchange, 161–163
Newfoundland, 761
Newton, Sir Isaac, 5, 89
Niagara Falls, 918
Niche, ecological, 77, 465, 469, 564
Niger, 908
Nigeria, 919
simulation in, 874
Nixon, Richard M., 785, 812, 827, 853
NNP (*see* Net national product)
Node:
of net, 63, 67, 186, 193, 394, 501, 627, 630, 631, 669, 784, 787–789, 791, 932, 933
of Ranvier, 215, 216, 273
Noise, 14–16
channel [*see* Channel(s), noise]
and channel capacity, 64
and coding, 14–15
and entropy, 14
and error, 65
hypotheses (*see* 3.3.3.2-3, 3.3.4.2-2 to 3.3.4.2-6 and 3.3.6.2-2 List of Hypotheses, *xxxiii, xxxiv*)
in net, 538–539, 634, 787, 788
semantic, 111
signal-to-noise ratio, 538, 539
as stress, 35
thermal or white, 14
Noisy marble experiment, 541–542
Nongovernmental organization(s), 910
Nonliving artifacts in models and simulations [*see* 6(*a*) Outline, *xxix*]
Nordic Council, 909
Norepinephrine (*see* Transmitter substance)
Normandy invasion, 680
North Atlantic Treaty Organization (NATO), 905, 906, 910, 923, 926, 939, 941, 1036
North Dakota, 790
Northwest Pipeline Corporation, 613
Norway, 761, 972
*n*th-country problem, 1006–1007
Nuclear fission, 833
Nuclear fusion, 833, 838

Nuclear membrane [*see* Cell(s): nucleus, membrane of,]
Nuclear physics, international channels for, 932
Nuclear power, 833
Nuclear reactors, 833
Nuclear weapons in INS, 1003
Nuclear weapons inspection in simulations, 996–998
Nucleus [*see* Cell(s), nucleus]
Number (*see* 4.1.2 Outline, *xxvi*)
Number of group members (*see* Group number)
Number in time (*see* 4.2.1.2 Outline, *xxvi*)

OAS (*see* Organization of American States)
Octopod, 403, 411, 414
OECD (Organization for Economic Cooperation and Development), 933
"Off" cell [*see* Cell(s), "off"]
Oil spills, 952
Olfaction, 378, 383–384, 401
Ombudsman, 625, 632
Omission, 555, 626
Omission adjustment process [*see* Adjustment process(es), to information input overload, omission]
Omission filtering [*see* Adjustment process(es), to information input overload, filtering]
"On" cell [*see* Cell(s), "on"]
"On-off" cell [*see* Cell(s), "on-off"]
OPEC (Organization of Petroleum Exporting Countries), 909
Operation Aphrodite, 710
Operations research, 161, 661, 739
Operator, 221, 258, 272
Opinion maker, 787
Opinion polls (*see* Public opinion survey)
Optimizing, 435–436, 657, 723
Order (*see also* 4.1.3 Outline, *xxvii*), 43–44:*n*40
Order in time (*see* 4.2.1.3 Outline, *xxvii*)
Order-analytic method, 446
Oregon, Department of Environmental Quality, 837
Organ, 315–360
differentiation of, 316, 350–351
formation of, 316, 350
free-living, 315, 316, 347
information input overload in, 127–131, 173
as level of living system, 315, 357, 1042
partipotentiality of, 357
repair of, 329–330

Organ (*Cont.*):
scientific knowledge of, 1042
size of, 319, 349–350
tissues of (*see also* Tissue), 316–319
totipotential, 465
Organelle(s), 205–208, 210, 217, 260
origin of, 293
replication of, 227–228
self-assembly of, 227, 293
Organic management system, 649
Organic solidarity, 601, 629, 650, 687
Organism(s), 361–514
increase in complexity of, 47–49:*n*81,
465, 466
information input overload in, 131–
152, 173–182
as living system, 501
scientific knowledge of, 1042
as signal channel, 63, 447
tissues of, 210–216, 316–319, 329–
330, 350–351, 371
Organization(s), 595–745
activities of, 598–599
characterization of, 44:*n*43
as component of society, 765
conglomerate, 692, 699–700
development of, 696–698
by group, 536, 539
industrial: classification of, 601
Fortune 300 largest, 840
Fortune 500 largest, 692
life cycle of, 698
multinational (*see* Multinational
corporation)
nonprofit: and feedback, 686
pathology in, 668, 702
reaction time of, 703, 699
scientific knowledge of, 1043
as subsystem of society, 765
success of, 696
supranational, and conflict resolution,
964–966
theory of, 738
types of subsystems of, 598–599
Organization of American States
(OAS), 808, 909, 917
Columbus Memorial Library, 937
Organization for Economic
Cooperation and Development
(OECD), 933
Organization of Petroleum Exporting
Countries (OPEC), 909
Organization theory, 738
Orly International Airport, 605
Osgood, C. E., 10, 960
Osmosis, 233
Output (*see also* 5.1 Outline, *xxviii*)
ensemble (*see* Ensemble, input and
output)
epithelium in, 319
people as, 683

Output transducer (*see also* 3.3.9
Outline, *xxvi*)
extruder components in, 279, 373,
442, 555
and motor, 374, 375, 531, 555
Overlapping group (*see* Decider,
structure, overlapping group)
Overload, information input (*see*
Information input, overload)
Oxus-Jaxartes basin as traffic center,
834
Oxygen:
adjustment processes to, 346, 350
debt, 462
input to lung, 326
in muscle, 239, 246
and nervous system, 325, 326, 328, 331,
345, 346, 474
and organ distributor, 327

Pacinian corpuscle [*see* Cell(s),
receptor, Pacinian corpuscle]
Pain [*see also* Cell(s), receptor, pain],
386, 388, 402
Pakistan, 909
Panama, 772
Pan American Highway, 828
Pan American Union (*see also*
Organization of American States),
937
Pancreas, 297, 316, 345
Pandemonium, 490
Papin, Denys, 833
Paraguay, 761, 799
Paramecia, 210, 232, 233, 243, 254, 267
conditioning in, 267, 269–270
memory in, 268
Parasitism, 18–20, 32, 67, 79, 90, 204, 217,
315, 363, 481, 516, 517, 527, 529,
567, 580, 583, 595, 597, 666, 873,
893, 1027
Parathyroid hormone, 345
Paris:
growth of, 694, 695, 843
Orly International Airport, 605
Parkinson's law, 693
Parsonian conceptual system, 19–20,
747, 765, 803, 893, 1010
Partipotentiality, 18–19, 203, 304, 333,
357, 375, 586, 666, 808, 970
Passive adaptation, 37
Passive transport, 233, 279
Pathology (*see also* 5.5 Outline, *xxix*),
1047
cancer [*see* Cell(s) cancer]
diseases of adaptation, 479
hypotheses (*see* 5.5-1 and 5.5-2 List of
Hypotheses, *xli*)
light deprivation and, 474
metabolic diseases and, 477

Pathology (*Cont.*):
schizophrenia, 167–169, 477–480, 500
and toxins, 300
Pattern (*see* 4.1.7 Outline, *xxvii*)
Pattern of action (*see* 4.2.2.4 Outline,
xxvii)
hypothesis (*see* 4.2.2.4-1 List of
Hypotheses, *xxxvii*)
Pattern in time (*see* 4.2.1.7 Outline,
xxvii)
Pattern recognition:
as decoding, 64
devices for, 395
simulations of, 488–491
Peace Corps, 711, 917
Pearl Harbor, 631, 636, 814
Peck order, 565
Peking, 688, 814
Penn Central Railroad, 711
People as matter-energy, 525, 598, 611,
683, 917, 1027
Perception (*see also* Coding, decoding;
Pattern recognition), 64, 402–404,
793
Perceptron, 489–491
Perceptual defense, 99
Peretz, B. E., 169
Peripherality index, 536–537
Permanent Engineering Board, 924
Personality, 21, 434, 457–461, 498–499,
543
presidential, 811–812
Persuasive power (*see also* Power, types
of), 682–683, 823–824
PERT-SIM, 737
Phagocytosis, 232–233
Pheromone(s), 370, 404, 438, 439, 442,
443, 521
Phosphate(s), synthesis of, 240
Phosphate bonds, 237
Photosynthesis, 239–240, 290, 293, 362,
368, 450
Pigeons in a Pelican, 111–112
Pinocytosis, 233
Pituitary gland [*see also* Hormone(s),
pituitary], 345, 391, 392, 424, 432,
451, 456, 463, 470, 471, 479
Planarian(s), 371, 407, 411, 413, 418
Plants, 33, 72, 208, 239, 362, 363, 367–
372, 374–377, 390, 407, 413, 422, 438
information processing subsystems
of, 33, 1031
tumors of, 301–302
Plato's *Republic,* 737
Pleasure center, 432, 492
Pleiku, 814
Pluralization, 699
Poland, 801
Political-Military Exercise (PME), 974–
976, 1009–1010
Political parties, 802, 867

Polls (*see* Public opinion survey)
Pollution (*see* Environment, pollution of)
Pope, the, 800
Population:
  adjustments to excess, 832, 840–842, 946–948
  control of, 781, 841–842
    insect, 572
    wolf, 841
  effect of stable, 842–844
  growth of, 862–866, 946–948
    zero, 863–864
  models of, 1015
    Globe6, 987–988
    World II and World III, 980–987
  spatial distribution of, 842–844
    in the United States, 842
Population explosion, 832, 840, 841, 971
Position (*see* 4.1.4 Outline, *xxvii*)
Position in time (*see* 4.2.1.4 Outline, *xxvii*)
Positive feedback [*see* Feedback(s), positive]
Posttetanic potentiation, 269, 339–340
Potassium ion(s), 230, 243, 254, 256
Potential(s) [*see also* Neuron(s)]:
  action [*see* Neuron(s)]
  evoked (*see* Brain, electrical activity of)
  generating, 254–256
  generator, 255
  gradient, 233
  pacemaker, 276
  postsynaptic [*see* Neuron(s), postsynaptic]
  receptor, 255
  resting, 229, 256
Potential difference, 229–230, 233, 256
Power (*see also* Energy), 37–39, 643, 645–651
  command signal, 38, 629, 649, 661, 765, 768
    hypotheses (*see* 5.2-21 to 5.2-23 List of Hypotheses, *xl*)
  of federal decider, 645–646, 661–662, 823
    hypothesis (*see* 3.3.7.2-2 List of Hypotheses, *xxxvi*)
  index of, 867
  legitimacy of, 38, 40, 630, 647
  measures of, 39
  of the President, 799, 810–815
  relationship, 645–648
  scale of, 682–683
  types of, 645–648, 808, 823–824
Power function(s) (*see also* Weber function), 94–95, 256, 282–283, 380, 381, 383–385, 387
  hypothesis (*see* 3.3.1.2-1 List of Hypotheses, *xxxii*)
  in subjective values and utilities, 436

Prejudice, 96
Presidency, United States (*see* United States, the Presidency)
President, United States (*see* United States, the President)
Presidential deciding, 810–815
Presidential listening posts, 785
Press, 457
Pressure transducers [*see* Cell(s), receptor]
Primitive society [*see* Society(ies), primitive]
Prince, The, 807
Principia Mathematica, 497
Principle of least effort (*see* Least effort, principle of)
Principle of nonproportional change, 694, 865
Prisoner's Dilemma game, 579, 580, 979–980
Probability, 433, 435
  of evolution of man, 78
Problem-solving, 433–434, 655–657
Process(es) (*see also* 2. Outline, *xxiii*), 23–24, 30–31, 51
  adjustment [*see* Adjustment process(es)]
  irreversible, 23
  production [*see* Production system(s), process]
  reversible, 23
  and structure, 1, 23–24, 30–31, 46:*n*69, 51, 1031
Process relationships (*see* 4.2 Outline, *xxvii*), between inputs and outputs (*see* 5.1 Outline, *xxviii*)
Producer (*see also* 3.2.4 Outline, *xxiv*), 632
  and energy, 617
  and health care, 777, 778
  and human reproduction, 777
Production function, 617
Production system(s), 617–619, 632, 653
  batch, 617–619, 633, 650, 653, 680–681
  and communication patterns, 632–633
  and conflict, 681
  mass, 617–619, 633, 709
  process, 618, 633, 650, 673–674
  unit, 618, 619, 632, 650, 673, 680–681
  and worker satisfaction, 677
Productivity, 553–554, 567–568, 650, 667, 674–677, 709, 829
Professional association(s), 968
Profit center(s), 690, 701
Program budgeting, 41
Progressive integration, 81
Progressive segregation, 81
Promotor region, 272, 274
Prosthesis [*see also* Artifact(s)], 33, 331, 332, 335, 341, 355, 531, 1026, 1039
  as simulations, 84

Protein, 204–205
  allosteric [*see* Allosteric molecule(s)]
  antigenic, 268, 276
  in cell membrane, 229
  in communication, 276, 277
  information content of molecule, 205
  in information transducing, 258
  in reconstitution of cell components, 293
  regulatory, 294
  synthesis of, 221, 223, 239–240, 274–275, 291
    and aging, 481
    induction in, 275
    and memory, 271, 418–420
    in mitochondria, 228, 293
    and pathology, 477
    repression in, 275
  transport of, 235
Proteinoid(s), 291
Protest absorption, 683
Protistan(s), 208–210, 239, 244, 362, 448
Protozoa(n) [*see* Cell(s), free-living]
  graph of, 47–49:*n*81
Pseudopodia, 232, 244–246
Psychosexual development, 472
Psychosis, 167–169, 477–480, 500
Psychosomatic symptom(s), 458, 479
Public-in-contact, 596
Public opinion survey, 685, 852, 929–930
  in internal transducer, 626, 786
Puerto Rico, 770
Pulse-interval coded inputs (*see* Information, input, pulse-interval coded)
Pump, ionic, 230, 243, 252, 263
Purpose(s) (*see also* Deciding, stages of), 18, 39–41
  and charter, 651
  and goals, 654–655, 1027
  as constraints, 659
  of university, 653
  and values, 39

Quality of life in World II and World III models, 981
Quantification of meaning, 500, 501, 1030
Quasijudicial organization(s), 800
Queue, 615, 619–621, 624
Queuing adjustment process [*see* Adjustment process(es), to information input overload, queuing]
Queuing theory, 54, 94, 104, 615, 620, 621, 734, 1032
  hypotheses (*see* 5.1-36 and 5.1-37 List of Hypotheses, *xxxix*)

Racial unconscious, 793
Radiation effects on cell, 299–300
Rand Corporation, 737, 974
Range, 61, 138–140, 142–144, 151
Rate of interaction, 566–567
Rate control feedback, 686
Rational behavior, 435, 496, 545
Rationality, 496, 553, 579, 656–657, 689–690, 808–810
Rats, effects of crowding on, 166
Rayburn, Sam, 818
Reaction time, 140, 388, 393, 447, 669, 703
  choice, 132–136, 144, 151, 447
Reaggregation of dissociated cells, 351–353
Recall (see Memory, retrieval)
Receptor cell(s) [see Cell(s), receptor]
Receptor potential, 255
Receptor site(s), 248, 256, 257, 262, 265, 379
Recoding (see Coding, recoding)
Recognition, molecular [see Cell(s), molecular recognition in]
Red Cross, 707, 831–832
  International Committee, 910, 918, 919
Reducing atmosphere, 290
Redundancy [see also Adjustment process(es), to information input overload, multiple channels], 61, 112, 541, 542, 626, 629, 784, 787
  and coding, 98, 541–542
    hypotheses (see 3.3.4.2-1, 3.3.4.2-6, and 3.3.4.2-7 List of Hypotheses, xxxiv–xxxv)
  cross-level research design, 111–112
Referendum, 786, 801
Reflex:
  arc, 336, 410
  axon, 424
  myenteric, 325, 336, 337, 341
  myotatic, 376
  spinal, 376, 394, 425
  stretch, 376
Refractory period [see Neuron(s), refractory period of]
Refugees, United Nations High Commissioner for (UNHCR), 918, 919, 949
Regeneration [see Repair process(es)]
Regional association(s), 905, 970
Regional Co-operation for Development, 909
Reinforcement, 409, 411, 464, 491, 492, 545, 638, 795
  and feedback, 409, 464, 570, 583
  and group termination, 583
  simulation, 584
Relationship(s), 16, 19, 22
  overemphasis upon, 45:n63

Relationship(s) (Cont.):
  among subsystems or components (see 4. Outline, xxvi)
  among systems, 17
Releaser, 366, 409, 521
Relief and Works Agency for Palestine Refugees in the Near East (UNRWA), 918
Repair process(es), 241, 329, 330, 371, 456
Repertoire, 11, 60
Replication:
  of genetic material, 223, 224, 257, 273–274, 295
  of organelles, 227–228
Replicator, 221, 224, 257, 265, 272, 274
Replicon, 244, 272
Representatives, United States (see United States, House of Representatives)
Repression:
  end-product, 258, 275, 286, 288
  psychoanalytic, 422, 458
Repressor(s), 257–259, 265
Reproducer (see also 3.1.1 Outline, xxiv), 1
  signal to, 521
Republic, Plato's, 737
Resources in Globe6 model, 987–988
Respiration, 237, 285–287, 291, 301, 450
Reticular formation (see Brain, reticular formation of)
Retina, 377, 378, 380–382, 397–399
  cells in, 378, 397–398, 400
  simulation of, 355, 489
Retrieval (see Matter-energy storage; Memory)
Reverberating circuit, 66, 411, 413, 417, 419, 484, 491
Revolution, 769–770, 872
  and evolution, 859–861
  in Inter-Nation Simulation (INS), 1003
Reward, 545, 562, 936
  and punishment, 407–409, 483, 562, 586, 645, 795
    hypotheses (see 3.3.3.2-6, 5.4.3-8, and 5.5-2 List of Hypotheses, xxxiii, xli)
Reward-cost matrix, 567
Rhine River, 909, 925
Rhone River, 925
Rhythm(s) [see Biological clock; Circadian rhythm(s)]
Ribonucleic acid (RNA), 217–223, 294
  activator, 272
  and circadian rhythm, 269
  and information storage, 268
  in information transmission, 260
  and memory, 268, 270, 271, 418–420
  messenger, 239, 240
  molecular weights of, 238

Ribonucleic acid (RNA) (Cont.):
  in protein synthesis, 239–240
  and repressor(s), 258
  ribosomal, 239
  synthesis of, 295
    of components, 291
  transcription, 223, 269, 273–275
  transfer, 239, 240, 305–306
  translation, 223, 269
  of virus, 207, 293
Ribosome(s), 207, 238–240, 294
Risk (see also Choice, and risk), deciding under, 102, 435, 660, 807, 812, 894
RNA (see Ribonucleic acid)
Rockefeller, John D., Jr., 659
Rockefeller Foundation and green revolution, 917–918
Rogers, Will, 812
Role, 19, 30, 566, 737–738
  overload, 167, 1049
Roll call votes, 816–817
  model of, 885–889
Roman empire, 688, 904
Romania, 761, 843
Rome, 904
Roosevelt, Franklin D., 802, 811, 812, 815
Ruffini endings, 379
Rumor, 630, 634, 706, 784
Rusk, Dean, 813, 825
Russia (see also Union of Soviet Socialist Republics), 769, 814, 851
  infant swaddling in, 797
  number of scientists in, 5
  revolution in, 860, 894
Russian Socialist Federated Soviet Republic, size of, 1036

Saigon, 813
St. John of the Cross, 683
St. Lawrence Power and Seaway Project, 918
St. Paul, Minnesota, 615
St. Teresa, 683
SALT agreement, 953–955
San Francisco, California:
  information input in, 791
  simulation of urban renewal program, 725–726
Sarcolemma, 244, 246
Sarcomere, 245
Sarcoplasmic reticulum, 207, 242–244, 246, 260
Satisfaction of components, adjustment processes for, 567–568, 674, 676–677
Satisficing, 436, 550, 657
  hypothesis (see 3.3.7.2-16 List of Hypotheses, xxxvi)
Saudi Arabia, 799

Scalogram, 756
Scandinavian countries, 752
Scanlon plan, 675
Schemata, 411, 434
Schizophrenia (*see* Pathology,
    schizophrenia)
Science:
    continuity of, 1025, 1050–1051
    as living system, 1050–1051
Science, 1048
Scientific and technical periodicals,
    number of, 5
Scotland, 828
Search, 656
    hypothesis (*see* 3.3.7.2-6 List of
        Hypotheses, *xxxvi*)
SEATO (*see* South East Asia Treaty
    Organization)
Seattle, Washington, 735–736
Secretory granule, 207, 241
Sector analysis, 761, 765
Securities and Exchange Commission
    (SEC), 800, 822
Security community, 910, 969, 970, 972–
    973
Security Council (UN) (*see* United
    Nations, Security Council)
Segregated system (*see* Segregation)
Segregation, 39, 536, 867
    coordination and, 867
    and goals, 651
    hypotheses (*see* 3.3.3.2-15 and 5.4.3-1
        List of Hypotheses, *xxxiv, xli*)
    racial, 851, 892
    rate of associating, 638–639
Self-organization, 81, 293, 486
Self-regulation (*see also*
        Autoregulation), 18, 81
    of body water balance, 36–37
    of primitive society, 841
Senate, United States (*see* United
    States, Senate)
Senators, United States (*see* United
    States, Senate)
Sensitization, 409
Sensory deprivation (*see also*
        Information, input, underload),
        452–454, 475
Services, 666, 667
Settlement pattern, urban, 673
Shannon information statistic, 11–13,
    43:*n*20, 178, 1030
Sheath of Schwann, 214, 216, 229, 240,
    318
Shred-out (*see also* Division of Labor;
        Evolution), 1–4, 26, 27, 29, 65, 91,
        294, 305, 348–349, 465, 467, 855,
        857, 866, 967, 1031, 1033–1035, 1049
    as division of labor, 26, 687
    and emergent(s), 1, 29

in evolution of ingestor, 348–349
Sierra Club, 785
Signal termination:
    fast [*see* Cell(s), phasic; Neuron(s),
        phasic]
    slow [*see* Cell(s), tonic; Neuron(s),
        tonic]
Signature of message, 38, 661
    hypothesis (*see* 3.3.7.2-4 List of
        Hypotheses, *xxxvi*)
Simulation(s) (*see also* 6. Outline, *xxix;*
        Models and simulations):
    in corporations, 661, 717–718, 878
    in deciding, 661
    as model(s), 83
    prostheses and, 84
    in social planning, 873–874
Size (*see also* 1.1 and 4.1.6 Outline,
        xxiii, xxvii; Growth), 1036–1038
    hypothesis (*see* 3.1.2.2-4 List of
        Hypotheses, *xxxii*)
Skin:
    boundary of, 321
    in communication, 406
    healing of, 329
    receptors in [*see* Cell(s), receptor]
    representation in brain, 351
Skinner, B. F., 1046
Sleep, 428, 454
Slime mold, 203, 210, 276, 277, 284, 303,
    305, 352, 374
Small batch production [*see* Production
    system(s), batch]
Smell (*see* Olfaction)
Smith, Adam, 875
Snow, Lord C. P., 1051
Social accounts, 751, 753
Social change (*see* Change, social)
Social class and marriage, 779
Social complexity, 755
Social indicators (*see* Indicators, social)
Social mobilization, 860
Social planning, 752
Social security, 778, 846
Social system, 747
Society(ies), 747–901
    dependent, 748, 754
    independent, 748, 754
    industrial, 781
    insect [*see also* Insect(s), social], 523
    less developed, 861, 866
    penetrated, 785, 800, 808
    postindustrial, 755, 760, 860–861,
        873
    postmodern (*see* postindustrial,
        above)
    preindustrial, 755, 756, 788
    primitive, 94, 747, 755, 769, 777, 779,
        782, 788, 795, 855
        acculturation of, 868–869

Society(ies), primitive (*Cont.*):
    energy in, 775–776
    Müller-Lyer visual illusion and, 855
    population control in, 841
    self-regulation in, 841
scientific knowledge of, 893, 1043
as system, 892
territorial borders, 770–771
totalitarian, 850, 852, 853
transformation of, 769–770
types of, 754–761
urban, 748, 754
Socioemotional information, 533–535,
    629–630
Sociogram, 537–538
Sociometric choice, 559–560
Socius, 45:*n*51
Socrates, 737
Sodium ions:
    in active transport, 243
    in motor end plate, 256
    in synapse, 254
Somesthetic senses, 378–379, 386–389,
    402
Soogoo shoosha, 781
South Africa, 601
South East Asia Treaty Organization
    (SEATO), 910, 939
South Essex, 617, 680
Southeast Asia Collective Defense
    Treaty, 814
Southern Christian Leadership
    Conference, 787
Space, 9–11
    psychological, 434
Space cabin simulator, 564, 567, 572
Space program(s), 808
Spacing behavior, 564–565, 588
    and evolution, 574
Spain, 761
Span of absolute judgment, 136–137
Spatiotemporal relationships (*see* 4.2.2
    Outline, *xxxvii*)
Species, 362
    as system, 24
Spectrogram, 404–405
Speech [*see also* Code(s); coding:
        decoding, gamma; encoding,
        gamma; of speech; Language]:
    brain areas in, 395, 406, 412, 439–444
    coding in, 404–406, 440–442
    control of, 443, 444
    as emergent, 404
    feedback in, 442, 464
    output of, 442–445
Spencer, Herbert, 854
Spiders, drugs and, 474
Spinal cord:
    alpha motor neuron(s), 425
    associating in, 407

Spinal cord (*Cont.*):
  conditioning in, 411–412
  effects of transection, 425
  in endocrine-neural connections, 392
  information storage in, 340, 416
  motor nuclei of, 432–433
  organization of, 425
  and sexual behavior, 366
Spinoza, B. de, 1050
Split brain, 412, 414
Sponge, 316, 362, 368, 369, 373, 375, 473
Square–cube law, 693
Squibb, E. R., & Sons, Inc., symbol of, 663
Standard Industrial Classification, 601
Standard Oil of New Jersey (*see* Exxon Corporation)
Stat rats (statistical rats), 492–493
State University of New York, 723
Statistical decision theory, 661, 1033
Status, 552, 626, 633, 673, 674, 678, 681
Steady state [*see also* 5.2 Outline, *xxviii*; Equilibrium(ia); Homeostasis], 18, 22, 34–41, 49–50:*n*98, 52, 71, 73, 81, 83, 285, 429, 433, 449, 568–570, 572, 582–583, 650, 672, 771, 793, 804, 940, 1027, 1030, 1038
  of brain oxygen, 345–346
  and disaster, 705, 707
  and homeostasis, 499, 658
  maintenance of spatial, 382
  and parasympathetic nervous system, 455
  and peck order, 565
  in personality theory, 457
  and rate of interaction, 566–567
  and sympathetic-adrenal control, 455
Stevenson, Adlai, 826
Stimulus–response, 407, 408, 410, 411, 491–493, 499
Stock exchange(s), information input overload in, 161–163
Strain, 34–35, 39, 72, 73, 459, 462, 479, 564, 634, 670, 671, 684, 699, 795, 870
  and behavior, 429
  and economic behavior, 436
  and goal setting, 429
  and growth, 78
  hypotheses (*see* 3.3.3.2-20, 3.3.3.2-21, 3.3.4.2-10, 3.3.5.2-2, 3.3.5.2-3, 5.2-4, and 5.2-7 List of Hypotheses, *xxiv, xxxv, xl*)
  motivating, 409, 429
  reduction, 408, 409, 421, 464, 496, 527, 528, 542, 638, 1047
Strategy, 433, 551, 657, 661, 809
Stress, 34–36, 93, 284, 349, 449–453, 455, 456, 459, 474–476, 479, 481, 867
  and adjustment processes (*see also* 5.2 Outline, *xxviii*), 831–833, 1047

Stress (*Cont.*):
  effect of combined, 447
  and general adaptation syndrome (GAS) (*see* General adaptation syndrome)
  and group compliance, 587–588
  and growth, 471
  hypotheses (*see* 3.3.3.2-12, 3.3.7.2-14, 3.3.7.2-15, 5.2-1 to 5.2-3, 5.2-10 to 5.2-13, and 5.4.3-7 List of Hypotheses, *xxxiv, xxxvi, xxxix–xli*)
  information: excess (*see* Information, input: excess; overload)
    lack (*see also* Information, input: lack; underload; Sensory deprivation), 563–564, 671
    monetary, 581
  matter-energy: excess (*see also* Matter-energy input, excess), 831–832, 870
    lack (*see also* Matter-energy input, lack), 832, 870, 970
Stretch reflex, 376
Structural change, 697
Structural relationships (*see* 4.1 Outline, *xxvi*)
Structure (*see also* 1. Outline, *xxiii*), 22
  and function in social science, 22–24, 1026–1027
  hypothesis (*see* 1-1 List of Hypotheses, *xxxi*)
  and process, 23–24, 30–31, 46:*n*69, 1031
Students for a Democratic Society, 785
Subcomponent, 204
Subsubsystem, 25
Subsynaptic membrane [*see* Neuron(s), membrane of, subsynaptic]
Subsystem(s) (*see also* 3., 3.1, 3.2, and 3.3 Outline, *xxiv–xxvi*), 18, 22, 25, 30–33, 1028–1030
  combined, 31
  coordination of, 672
  critical, 1–4, 32–33, 753, 1028–1031, 1044–1045
    lacking, 33, 204, 210, 596, 944, 1027, 1031, 1043
    in supranational simulations, 1016
  dispersed, 31–32, 53, 333
    associator, 66
    decider, 67
    decoder, 265
    encoder, 69
    memory, 66, 547
  dispersed downwardly, 32, 333, 357, 587, 765
    associator, 607, 637, 767, 794, 915, 935
    boundary, 606, 609, 766, 771, 914, 916

Subsystem(s), dispersed downwardly (*Cont.*):
    channel and net, 606, 627, 767, 788–789, 914, 931, 932
    converter, 328, 370, 767, 775, 914, 922
    decider, 342, 358, 607, 644, 767, 800, 915, 939
    decoder, 64, 607, 635, 767, 792, 915, 934
    distributor, 606, 613, 766, 774, 914, 918
    encoder, 342, 768, 824, 915, 942
    extruder, 375, 607, 621, 915, 925–926
    ingestor, 57, 606, 611, 766, 773, 914, 917
    input transducer, 62, 377, 520, 531, 606, 624, 766, 783–784, 914, 927
    internal transducer, 335–336, 606, 625, 766, 785, 914, 929
    matter-energy storage, 330, 528, 607, 620, 767, 779, 915, 924, 925
    memory, 607, 639, 767, 796–798, 915, 937
    motor, 59, 607, 622, 768, 782, 915, 926–927
    output transducer, 69, 768, 827, 915, 943
    producer, 370, 767, 777, 915, 923
    reproducer, 55, 606, 608, 766, 768, 913, 914
    supporter, 783, 915, 927
  dispersed laterally, 32, 316, 357, 587
    associator, 66, 520, 543
    boundary, 520, 522–524
    converter, 520, 526
    decider, 520, 548, 607, 644
    decoder, 520, 540
    distributor, 520, 525
    encoder, 69, 521, 554
    extruder, 521, 529, 607, 621
    ingestor, 520, 524
    input transducer, 520, 531
    matter-energy storage, 520, 528, 607, 620, 767, 779
    memory, 66, 520, 547
    motor, 521, 529–530
    output transducer, 343, 521, 555
    producer, 520, 527
    supporter, 521, 531
  dispersed outwardly, 32, 516
    associator, 607, 637
    decider, 67, 607, 644, 767, 800
    extruder, 607, 621, 768, 781
  input transducer, 606, 624, 766, 783
  internal transducer, 606, 625, 766, 785

Subsystem(s), dispersed outwardly (*Cont.*):
  matter-energy storage, 767, 779
  producer, 767, 777
dispersed upwardly, 333
  associator, 339, 357
  boundary, 520, 522, 523
  channel and net, 520, 536, 537, 606, 627
  converter, 520, 526, 607, 616
  decider, 340, 358, 607, 644
  decoder, 520, 540, 606, 635
  distributor, 520, 525, 606, 613
  extruder, 521, 529
  ingestor, 520, 524
  input transducer, 520, 531, 766, 784
  internal transducer, 335–336, 766, 785
  matter-energy storage, 520, 528, 620, 767, 779
  memory, 339, 357, 520, 607, 639
  motor, 332, 521, 530, 607, 622
  producer, 520, 527
  reproducer, 321
hypotheses (*see* 3.1.2.2-1 to 3.3.7.2-21 List of Hypotheses, *xxxii–xxxvii*)
information processing (*see also* 3.3 Outline, *xxv–xxvi*)
  in free-living cells, 1031
  hypotheses (*see* 3.3-1 to 3.3.7.2-18 List of Hypotheses, *xxxii–xxxvii*)
  models and simulations of, 302–303, 355–356, 488–499, 734–737
  and nervous tissue, 324
  in plants, 1031
joint, 32, 79
local, 31, 79
matter-energy and information processing (*see* 3.1 Outline, *xxiv*)
  hypotheses (*see* 3.1.2.2-1 to 3.1.2.2-4 List of Hypotheses, *xxxii*)
matter-energy processing (*see* 3.2 Outline, *xxiv–xxv*)
  hypotheses (*see* 3.2-1 to 3.2.5.2-1 List of Hypotheses, *xxxii*)
  models and simulations of, 303–304, 356–357, 487–488, 496, 731–737, 891–892, 988–994
noncritical, 55, 1045
nonessential, 55, 1045
scientific consensus on, 1033
types of organization, 598–599
variables of [*see* Variable(s), of subsystems]
Subsystems which process both matter-energy and information (*see* 3.1 Outline, *xxiv*)
Subsystems which process information (*see* 3.3 Outline, *xxv–xxvi*)

Subsystem which process matter-energy (*see* 3.2 Outline, *xxiv–xxv*)
Summit conference, 931, 942
Superconductive power lines, 775
Superego, 430, 458
Support (*see* Consensus)
Supporter (*see* 3.2.8 Outline, *xxv*)
Suppressor(s), 521
Supranational system(s), 595, 903–1024
  duration of, 972
  as level of living system, 904
  scientific knowledge of, 1043
Supraorganism, 519
Suprasuprasystem, 25, 519, 525, 536
  hypothesis (*see* 2-4 List of Hypotheses, *xxxvi*)
Suprasystem, 25, 29–30, 52, 519, 525, 536, 562, 644, 654, 657, 660, 665
  hypothesis (*see* 2-4 List of Hypotheses, *xxxi*)
Supreme Court, United States (*see* United States, Supreme Court)
Survey (*see* Public opinion survey)
Survival, 651, 692, 804
  cross-level research design, 113–114
  hypotheses (*see* 3.3-1, 3.3.7.2-2, 3.3.7.2-14, 3.3.7.2-17, and 5.2-13 List of Hypotheses, *xxxii, xxxvi, xl*)
Sweden, 761, 972
Switching feedback, 289
Switzerland, 761, 904
  government in, 799
  language in, 792
Swope, Gerard, 659
Symbiosis, 18–32, 67, 79, 293, 363, 481, 516, 517, 527, 567, 580, 583, 595, 597, 661, 666, 676, 873, 893, 1027
Symbol:
  of organizations, 663
  of society(ies), 823
Symmetry, group, 568–569
Sympar apparatus, 580
Synapse, 215, 248, 249, 257, 263, 279, 318, 335, 392, 469
  adrenergic, 278
  in brain, 270
  chemical, 249, 254, 277–280, 337
  electrical, 249, 254, 262–263, 265, 278–280, 318, 337
  excitatory, 254, 256, 335
  inhibitory, 254, 255, 270, 335
  and memory, 270
  in organ walls, 337
  retinal, 257
Synaptic transmission, 254–255, 277–278, 280, 335
  minimum rate of, 122
Synaptic vesicle(s), 215, 234, 243, 256, 279, 280
Synchronous division, 299

Synergy, 577
Syntality, 517, 543
Synthesis (*see* Deciding, stages of, synthesis)
Syria, 852
  as traffic center, 834
System(s), 1, 9, 16–22, 52
  abstracted, 19–22, 598, 737, 893, 1026–1027, 1043
    society as, 747
  analysis, 661, 723
  bipolar [*see* Equilibrium(ia), bipolar]
  centralized (*see* Decider, centralized)
  closed, 17–18
    Le Châtelier principle in, 35
  cohesive, 38
  complex: counterintuitive behavior in (*see* Counterintuitive behavior)
    simulation and, 718
  component conflict, 867
  conceptual, 1, 16–17, 803
  concrete, 1, 17–19, 747
    in theory of living systems, 1026–1027
  decentralized (*see* Decider, decentralized)
    hypotheses (*see* 5.2-14, 5.4.3-4 to 5.4.3-7 and 5.4.3-9 List of Hypotheses, *xl–xli*)
  economic, 753
  external, of group, 533
  as Gestalt, 44:*n*44
  global, 904, 945
  integrated (*see* Integration)
  internal, of group, 533
  living, 1, 18–19, 34, 36, 37, 967, 1027, 1051
    as mirror of environment, 30, 35
  man-machine, 686, 926
  management (*see* Management system)
  nervous [*see* Nervous system(s)]
  noncohesive, 38
  nonliving, 18
  open, 1, 17, 1027
    Le Châtelier principle in, 35
  political, feedback in, 853
  process (*see* 2. Outline, *xxiii*)
  reliable, from unreliable components, 98, 112, 545
  segregated (*see* Segregation)
  self-organizing, 486
  self-regulating (*see also* Auto-regulation), 18, 36, 37, 81, 841
  survival of (*see* Survival)
  terminology of, 1045
  theory of (*see* General living systems theory; General systems theory; Systems theory)

System(s) (*Cont.*):
  type of, 24–26, 28
  ultrastable, 36, 487, 704, 718
  variable adaptation, 37, 463
System characteristic feedback, 37, 686
System Development Corporation, 169
Systems theory (*see also* General living
    systems theory; General systems
    theory), 305, 739, 1045
  advantages of concrete, 21–22

T/Y ratio, 905
Table of organization, 643, 800
Tactical and Negotiations Game (TNG),
    155, 976–978
Tactical War Game, 154–156
Taft, William, 812
Tanzania, 909
  poles of growth, 844
Tapiola, Finland, 608
Taste, 378, 385–386, 401–402
Tautology, 90
Taxonomy:
  process, of types of systems (*see* 2.2
    Outline, *xxiv*)
  structural, of types of systems (*see* 1.2
    Outline, *xxiii*)
Taylor, F., 674
Taylor, Maxwell D., 813
Team, 755
Teamsters Union, 700
Technological complexity, 617–618,
    650
Technology, 775, 830, 856
  and American economy, 778
  and integration, 701–702
  and worker satisfaction, 677
Teleoperators, 483–484
Telephone:
  evolution of, 855–857
  game, 537
TEMPER, 998–1000, 1009–1010
Temperature [*see also* Cell(s),
    temperature and]
  hypothesis (*see* 3.2-1 List of
    Hypotheses, *xxxii*)
  optimal, 93–94
  sensation, 378, 387–389, 402
Template (*see also* Charter), 18, 34, 55,
    224, 240, 299, 321, 351, 366, 519,
    605, 608, 692, 1027
  gene as, 221
  and goals, 940
  hypotheses (*see* 3.3.6.2-3 to 3.3.6.2-5
    and 5.2-8 List of Hypotheses,
    xxxv, xxxvi, xxxix)
  matching, 488
  and pathology, 971
Tempo of communities, 601

Temporal relationships (*see* 4.2.1
    Outline, *xxvii*)
Termination, decay and (*see* 5.6
    Outline, *xxix*)
Territory, 30, 522–524, 564–565, 609, 627,
    770–771, 913, 916, 950
Texas City, Louisiana, explosion in, 705
Thailand, 929
Thema, 457
Theory X (management), 678–679
Theory Y (management), 651, 678–679
Thermodynamics:
  laws of, 11, 13, 14, 18, 43:*n*24, 110,
    295, 1027
  of open systems, 14
Thoracic ganglion and memory, 340
Threat, 34–35, 705
Threshold (*see also* Channel and net;
    Input transducer; Internal
    transducer), 61
Thyroid gland [*see also* Hormone(s)],
    463
  seventeenth-century conception of,
    31
  simulation of, 303
Tibet, 871, 945
Tight feedback [*see* Feedback(s), tight]
Time, 11
  limit in memory, 67
  minimum discriminable, 122
Tin economy, model of, 994–995
Tissue, 315–319
  aging of, 354, 481–482
  connective, 210–213, 316–318, 472
    repair of, 329–330, 371
  differentiation of, 316, 350–351
  embryonic, 316
    ectoderm, 316–318, 350, 392, 468, 469
    endoderm, 316–318, 350, 468
    mesoderm, 316–318, 350, 468
  epithelial, 210, 316, 319
    repair of, 329
  as level of living system, 315
  muscular [*see also* Motor; Muscle(s)],
    213–214, 316
    repair of, 330, 371
  nervous [*see also* Nervous system(s)],
    214–216, 316, 318
    and information processing
      subsystems, 315–316
    repair of, 330, 371
  primary, 316
  regeneration of, 329–331, 349
  repair of, 329–331, 349
  reticular, 317
  scar, 329
  of stomach, 318–319
Tobago, 947
Togo, 909
Tokyo, planning for, 689–690
Tolstoy, Leo, 1051

Torrey Canyon, 952
Totipotentiality, 18, 25, 203, 302, 304,
    357, 362, 465, 501, 519, 528, 529,
    595, 596, 601, 608, 661, 666, 687,
    747, 904, 908, 940, 970, 971
  hypotheses (*see* 2-2 and 2-3 List of
    Hypotheses, *xxxi*)
Touch, 94, 386, 388, 389, 402
Tourism, 949
Townsend Movement, 696
Trace (*see* Memory, trace)
Tracking, 446, 463
Trade routes, 918–919
Traffic control simulation, 733
Transcription in protein synthesis, 223,
    269, 273–275, 296
Transducer(s) (*see* Input
    transducer; Internal transducer;
    Output transducer)
Transformation, societal, 769, 859
Translation in protein synthesis, 223,
    269
Transmitter substance(s), 124, 126, 235,
    243, 254, 256, 257, 262, 265, 277–
    278, 335, 338, 392, 455
  acetylcholine, 128, 254, 257, 278, 479
    in information input overload, 128
  autonomic, 338
  gamma-aminobutyric acid (GABA),
    277, 278
  glutamate, 235
  norepinephrine, 254, 277, 278, 431,
    451, 455, 480
  of sympathetic nervous system, 256,
    278, 338
  synaptic, 254–257, 335, 338, 392, 443
Transport:
  active, 230, 231, 233, 235, 256, 279, 327
  passive, 233, 279
Transportation, 613–615, 687–689
Treaty as international law, 964
Treaty of Versailles, 768
Trinidad, 947
Trophallaxis, 81, 576
Truman, Harry S., 67, 811, 812, 815, 819
Trusteeship Council (UN), 929, 939
Tsar in computer simulation, 1011–1012
Tulane University, 723
Tunisia, 947
Turkey, 601, 761, 772, 800, 807, 909
Twenty Questions, 102
Tylor, E. B., 854
Type of system, 24–26, 28

Udall, Kansas, tornado in, 705
Uhr, L. M., 169
Ultrastability [*see also* System(s),
    ultrastable], 487
Uncertainty absorption, 636, 658

Union of Soviet Socialist Republics (U.S.S.R., Soviet Union), 597, 748, 761, 772, 778, 780, 799, 800, 807, 808, 825–828, 840, 849, 872, 904
All-Union Research Institute for Medical and Medico-Technical Information, 933
constitution of, 770
Council for Mutual Economic Assistance (CMEA or COMECON), 905, 909, 937
decider of, 800
economy of, 861
feedback in, 852
government of, 799
input–output economics in, 878
internal boundaries of, 843
International Nuclear Data Center, 933
languages of, 792
natural gas pipe lines, 774
new cities in, 843
population growth of, 864
size of, 748
UNISIST (United Nations world science information system), 933, 934, 937, 938
Unit(s):
of measurement in scientific theory, 1026
production [see Production system(s), unit]
of systems, 16, 17, 19, 20, 22, 31
United Arab Republic, 852
and negative feedback, 852
United Farm Workers Organizing Committee, 700
United Kingdom (British Empire, British Commonwealth of Nations, England, and Great Britain), 596, 608, 752, 761, 769, 778, 779, 828, 843, 891, 904, 908–910
coal mining in, 677
Countryside Commissions, 843
new cities in, 843
United Nations, 768, 785, 808, 903, 906, 908, 928, 931, 934, 939, 948, 970, 972, 1017
autonomous intergovernmental agencies, 909
Food and Agriculture Organization of the United Nations (FAO), 909, 917–919, 928, 929, 949
Inter-Governmental Maritime Consultative Organization (IMCO), 909, 918, 928
International Atomic Energy Agency (IAEA), 904, 909, 910, 917, 922, 925, 926, 932–933, 936, 939, 940

United Nations, autonomous inter-governmental agencies (Cont.):
International Bank for Reconstruction and Development (IBRD or World Bank), 909, 917, 919, 931, 937, 949–950
Bretton Woods Conference, 957–958
and population planning, 947
International Civil Aviation Organization (ICAO), 909, 910, 918
International Development Association (IDA), 909, 917, 931, 947, 949
International Finance Corporation (IFC), 909, 931, 949–950
International Labor Organization (ILO), 909, 918, 919, 929, 937, 939, 949, 972
International Monetary Fund (IMF), 909, 932, 958
International Telecommunications Union (ITU), 909, 931, 932, 972
United Nations Educational and Scientific Organization (UNESCO), 909, 918, 928–930, 933, 937, 942, 949
Intergovernmental Oceanographic Commission, 928
world science information system (UNISIST), 933, 934, 937, 938
Universal Postal Union (UPU), 909, 931, 932, 972
World Food Program, 918, 919
World Health Organization (WHO), 909, 918, 919, 923, 937, 949, 952
World Meteorological Organization (WMO), 909, 928, 932
Charter of, 941, 965, 970, 971
Children's Fund (UNICEF), 779, 918, 942
Commission on Narcotic Drugs, 951
Conference on the Human Environment, 951–952
Conference on the Law of the Sea, 945, 950, 965
Conference on Narcotic Drugs, 951
Conference on Trade and Development (UNCTAD), 918, 949
Convention on Law of the Sea, 965
Convention on Narcotic Drugs, 951
Development Program (UNDP), 917, 918

United Nations (Cont.):
Economic and Social Council (ECOSOC), 905, 909, 929, 949
and autonomous intergovernmental agencies, 939
Commission on Narcotic Drugs, 951
Population Commission, 946
Economic Commission for Africa, 917–919
Economic Commission for Asia and the Far East (ECAFE), 918, 919, 945
Economic Commission for Europe, 918, 919
Economic Commission for Latin America, 917, 918
General Agreement on Tariffs and Trade (GATT), 918
General Assembly, 928, 929, 931, 939–941, 964–965
resolutions on human rights in armed conflicts, 955
goals of, 940
High Commissioner for Refugees (UNHCR), 918, 919, 949
integration in, 970
International Court of Justice, 928, 929, 932, 939, 941
International Law Commission, 964
International Narcotics Control Board (INCB), 951, 972
languages of, 934, 942
Relief and Works Agency for Palestine Refugees in the Near East (UNRWA), 918
Secretariat, 826, 929, 937, 939, 951
Security Council, 928, 929, 931, 932, 939–941, 971
in simulations, 974–975
Statistical Office, 929
Technical Working Group on Migration, 949
Trusteeship Council, 929, 939
World Food Program, 918, 919
World Population Conferences, 947
World Population Year, 947
United States, 761, 770, 774, 778, 795, 799–802, 807–808, 810–815, 825–829, 832–833, 839, 840, 843, 851, 864, 867–869, 904, 908, 910, 918
Army, 823
War Plans Division, 632
Atomic Energy Commission, 723
Bill of Rights, 801, 872
Bureau of the Budget, 815
Bureau of the Census, 785
Bureau of Labor Statistics, 785
Bureau of Narcotics and Dangerous Drugs, 823

United States (*Cont.*):
  Central Intelligence Agency, 783
  Civil Aeronautics Board, 707–708
  Clean Water Restoration Act, 780
  Coast Guard, 823
  Committee on Scientific and
    Technical Information
    (COSATI), 796
  Congress, 815, 824
    deciding in, 815–820
  Constitution of, 770, 797, 804, 810,
    823, 872
  Council of Economic Advisors, 815
  Council on Environmental Quality,
    753, 839
  crime in, 893
  Declaration of Independence, 797,
    801
  Department of Agriculture, National
    Agricultural Library, 796
  Department of Defense, 823
  Department of Health, Education,
    and Welfare, 785, 823
  Department of the Interior, 779
  Department of Justice, 819, 823
  Department of State, 824
  Department of Transportation, 774
  Department of the Treasury, 823
  economy of, 861
    simulation of, 882–885
  Energy Research and Development
    Administration, 779, 796, 925,
    933
  environmental legislation, 839
  Environmental Protection Agency,
    774, 779, 781, 892
  executive branch, 823
  Executive Office of the President,
    815, 839
    Office of Management and Budget,
    752, 815
  Federal Aviation Administration, 774
  Federal Aviation Agency, 796
  Federal Bureau of Investigation, 754,
    823
  Federal Highway Administration,
    774
  Federal Reserve Bank, 847–848
  Federal Reserve Board, 800, 847
  Federal Trade Commission, 800
  General Services Administration, 783
  House of Representatives, 801, 815–
    820
    Judiciary Committee, 818
    model of voting in, 885–889
    Rules Committee, 553, 818, 819
    source of demands on
      representatives, 816
  Internal Revenue Commission, 846

United States (*Cont.*):
  Interstate Commerce Commission,
    774, 800
  labor relations in, 851
  Library of Congress, 796–799
  National Aeronautics and Space
    Administration (NASA), 796
  National Center of Health Statistics,
    785
  National Library of Medicine, 933
  National Neutron Cross-Section Data
    Center, 933
  National Parks Service, 779
  in national policy simulation, 874–
    875
  National Railroad Adjustment Board,
    682
  National Science Foundation, 796
  National Security Council, 814–815,
    826
  Office of Business Economics (OBE)
    model, 881–882
  Office of Management and Budget,
    752, 815
  Peace Corps, 711, 800
  political parties, 786
  population: distribution of, 842–843
    growth of, 694
  the Presidency, 799, 801, 810, 811,
    815, 819
  the President, 751, 799, 800, 805, 812,
    815, 819, 822, 823
    Cabinet of, 815
    deciding by, 810–815, 823
    and inflation, 848
    and legislation, 849–850
    personality types of, 811–812
    power of, 810, 823
    simulation of, 888, 1007
  President's Commission on National
    Goals, 751
  quasijudicial organizations, 800, 810
  regulatory bodies, 822
  Secret Service, 823
  Securities and Exchange Commission
    (SEC), 800, 822
  Senate, 801, 815–820
    models of, 816–817, 885–889
  Strategic Air Command, 814
  Supreme Court, 805, 819, 822
    deciding in, 551, 553
  system-component conflict in, 867
  telephones in, 789
  Vice President of the United States,
    810
  Water Quality Act, 780
  welfare services in, 801
United States regulatory bodies, 822
Universal state, 747

University of California, 723
University of Chicago, Committee on
  the Behavioral Sciences, *xv*
University of Michigan, Mental Health
  Research Institute, *xvi–xvii*
University of Rochester, 723
University of Toronto, CAMPUS
  simulation, 723, 724
University of Washington, 723
Upper Volta, 909
Urban dynamics, 726–731
Urban League, 785
Urban society, 748, 754
Urbanization, 694, 703–704, 842–843,
  866
U.S.S.R. (*see* Union of Soviet Socialist
  Republics)
Utility, 659, 674, 736
  economic, 435–436
  in game theory, 496
  maximization of, 435, 496, 876
  scaling of, 438
  theory of, 553

Vacuole, 207, 233, 235, 243
Validation of simulations, 976, 1009–
  1010
Validity of simulations, 85, 808, 973,
  976, 977
Value(s), 39, 436, 651, 802–804, 806, 935
  added, 667–668
  in choice behavior, 436
  common, 436
    in group integration, 577
  conflicts among, 804
  in congressional deciding, 815
  as constraints, 659, 660, 804–808
  dichotomies, 803–804
  hierarchy, 39, 73, 751, 803–804, 872,
    940, 1047
  hypothesis (*see* 3.3.7.2-13 List of
    Hypotheses, *xxxvi*)
  in Nazi Germany, 869
  and Supreme Court decisions, 821
Van der Waals interactions, 298, 352
Variable(s), 4, 16, 17, 40, 940, 1038–1041
  classes of, 71
  economic, 751, 761, 801, 845
  endogenous, 881
  exogenous, 881
  group, as statistical averages, 568
  and indicators, 1038–1040
  range of stability of, 831
  in simulations, 716, 720–722
    state, of World II and World III
      models, 905
  of subsystems: associator, 66, 267,
    413, 546–547, 639, 796, 936–937

Variable(s), of subsystems (*Cont.*):
boundary, 57, 231, 325–326, 367–368, 524, 610–611, 772–773, 916–917
channel and net, 64, 264–265, 338, 394, 539–540, 634–635, 791–792, 933–934
converter, 58, 237–238, 328, 370, 527, 616, 776–777, 922–923
decider, 68, 276, 342, 438, 554, 662, 824, 942
decoder, 65, 266, 339, 406–407, 542–543, 636–637, 793–794, 935
distributor, 57, 235–236, 328, 369–370, 526, 615–616, 775, 919
encoder, 69, 278–279, 442, 554–555, 664, 826, 943
extruder, 59, 243–244, 332, 373–374, 529, 622, 782, 926
ingestor, 57, 233–234, 326, 369, 525, 613, 773–774, 918
input transducer, 62, 257, 335, 389, 532, 624–625, 785, 928–929
internal transducer, 63, 259–260, 336, 390, 535, 626–627, 788, 930–931
matter-energy storage, 58, 242, 331, 372–373, 528, 621, 780–781, 925
memory, 67, 272, 422, 547–548, 641–642, 798–799, 938–939
motor, 59–60, 247, 332–333, 376, 530, 623, 782–783, 927
output transducer, 69–70, 280, 445, 555–556, 665, 827–828, 943
producer, 58, 241, 330, 371, 527, 619, 779, 923
reproducer, 55, 228, 366–367, 522, 609, 770, 913
supporter, 60, 247, 333, 377, 531, 623, 783, 927
Vatican City, 1036
Versailles, Treaty of, 768
Veto in United Nations Security Council, 941

Vibration sense, 386
Vice President of the United States, 810
Viet Cong, 813
Vietnam, 812–814, 848
North, 812–814
simulation of war in, 996
Virgin Islands, 629
Virus (*see also* Bacteriophage), 203–204, 207–208, 221, 222, 274, 293, 871
Voluntary behavior, 410, 424, 426, 433, 437–439
Voting as internal transducing, 786
Voting behavior, 749

Walden II, 1046
War, 955–956
correlates of, 961–962
in Inter-Nation Simulation (INS), 1003
model of, 996
War and Peace, 1051
Warmth, 386, 387
receptors, 386–389
Warner, W. L., 10
Warsaw Pact, 910
Warsaw Treaty Organization, 910, 926
Washington, George, 812
Washington, D.C., 608
Washoe (chimpanzee), 441
Waste(s), 926
organization, 622, 667
recycling of, 781
Water balance, 36–37, 455–456
simulation of, 487
Water resources, 925, 945
Wayne County General Hospital (Michigan), 613
Wealth of Nations, The, 875
Weber function [*see also* Power function(s)] 94–95, 255, 282, 283, 335
hypothesis (*see* 3.3.1.2-1 List of Hypotheses, *xxxii*)
Welfare economics, 846, 878

West African Economic Community, 909
West Germany, 904, 910
Western Electric Company Hawthorne plant, 650
WHO (World Health Organization), 909, 918, 919, 923, 937, 949, 952
Wildlife Federation, 785
Willamette River, 837
Wilson, Woodrow, 31
Wolf population, 841
Woodstock Festival (New York State), 671
Woodward, Joan, 738
Worcester, Massachusetts, 706
World II and World III models, 905, 980–987
mercury submodel, 988–991
World Bank (*see* United Nations, autonomous intergovernmental agencies, International Bank for Reconstruction and Development)
World Court (United Nations, International Court of Justice), 928, 929, 932, 939, 941
World government, 968
World Meteorological Organization (WMO), 909, 928, 932
World Population Conferences (UN), 947
World Population Year, 947
World science information system (UNISIST), 933, 934, 937, 938
World tin economy, model of, 994–995
World War I, simulation of, 1008, 1011
World Weather Watch, 933

Yacht race, 539, 1051
Yale University investment model, 734
Young, Owen D., 659

Zero population growth, 863–864
Zeirikzee, Holland, 706